D1153988

PEARSON TEXAS

WORLD HISTORY

Elisabeth Gaynor Ellis
Anthony Esler

PEARSON

Boston, Massachusetts Chandler, Arizona Glenview, Illinois Hoboken, New Jersey

TEACHER'S EDITION

Cover Image: Sphinx in front of pyramids, Giza, Cairo, Egypt. Glow Images/Alamy. Acknowledgments appear at the end of the book, which constitutes an extension of this copyright page.

PEARSON

ISBN-13: 978-0-13-332313-9
ISBN-10: 0-13-332313-7

1 2 3 4 5 6 7 8 9 10 V0UD 18 17 16 15 14

Authors/Program Consultants/Partners

[Authors]

Elisabeth Gaynor Ellis

Elisabeth Gaynor Ellis holds a BS from Smith College and an MA and MS from Columbia University. Before she began writing textbooks, Ms. Ellis taught World Cultures, European History, and Russian Studies in Ardsley, New York. Ms. Ellis coauthored Prentice Hall's *World History: Connections to Today* with Dr. Anthony Esler. Ms. Ellis has also written other social studies materials, including *America's Holidays*, individual state histories, and a variety of Teacher's Edition materials.

Anthony Esler

Anthony Esler is an Emeritus Professor of History at the College of William and Mary in Williamsburg, Virginia. His books include several studies of the conflict of generations in world history, half a dozen historical novels, and two other surveys of world and Western history besides this one. He is a member of the American Historical Association, the World History Association, and the Authors Guild. He has received Fulbright, Social Science Research Council, and other research grants, and is listed in the *Directory of American Scholars*, the *Directory of Poets and Fiction Writers*, and *Who's Who in America*. Books by Dr. Esler include *Bombs, Beards, and Barricades, Forbidden City,* and *The Human Venture*.

[Program Consultants]

Kathy Swan is an Associate Professor of Curriculum and Instruction at the University of Kentucky. Her research focuses on standards-based technology integration, authentic intellectual work, and documentary-making in the social studies classroom. Swan has been a four-time recipient of the National Technology Leadership Award in Social Studies Education. She is also the advisor for the Social Studies Assessment, Curriculum, and Instruction Collaborative (SSACI) at CCSSO.

Mary Lynn Johnson is the Social Studies Specialist for the Harris County Department of Education. She was named the 2012 "Supervisor of the Year" by the Texas Social Studies Supervisors Association. Mary Lynn held both teacher and supervisor positions at Spring and Spring Branch. She earned a Master's in Educatic from Sam Houston State University.

[Program Partners]

NBC Learn, the educational arm of NBC News, develops original stories for use in the classroom and makes archival NBC News stories, images, and primary source documents available on demand to teachers, students, and parents. NBC Learn partnered with Pearson to produce the myStory videos that support this program.

Constitutional Rights Foundatior is a nonprofit, nonpartisan organizatior ised on educating students about the impo e of civic participation in a democratic society. Constitution hts Foundation is the lead contributor to the development c Civic Discussion Topic Inquiries for this program. Constitutic ghts Foundation is also the provider of the Civic Action Pro AP) for the *Economics* and *Magruder's American Governmen* ams. CAP is a project-based learning model for civics, gov t, and economics courses.

Reviewers & Academic Consultants

Pearson Texas World History was developed especially for Texas and covers 100% of the Texas Essential Knowledge and Skills for Social Studies. The story of its creation began with a three-day Innovation Lab in which teachers, historians, students, and authors came together to imagine our ideal Social Studies teaching and learning experiences. We refined the plan with a series of teacher roundtables in cities across the state of Texas that shaped this new approach to ensure TEKS mastery. A dedicated team, made up of Pearson authors, content experts, and social studies teachers from Texas as well as educators from all over the country, worked to bring our collective vision into reality. Mary Lynn Johnson, Social Studies Specialist for the Harris County Department of Education, served as our expert advisor on Texas curriculum.

Pearson would like to extend a special thank you to all of the teachers from across the state of Texas who helped guide the development of this program. We gratefully acknowledge your efforts to realize Next Generation Social Studies teaching and learning that will prepare Texas students for college, careers, and active citizenship.

[Program Advisors]

Campaign for the Civic Mission of Schools is a coalition of over 70 national civic learning, education, civic engagement, and business groups committed to improving the quality and quantity of civic learning in American schools. The Campaign served as an advisor on this program.

Buck Institute for Education is a nonprofit organization dedicated to helping teachers implement the effective use of Project-Based Learning in their classrooms. Buck Institute staff consulted on the Project-Based Learning Topic Inquiries for this program.

[Program Academic Consultants]

Barba Brown
Directof Outreach
College Arts and Sciences
African udies Center
Boston versity
Boston ssachusetts

Willia hilds
Profess History Emeritus
The Oh te University
Columb hio

Jennif lielmo
Associa essor of History
Smith C
Northha Massachusetts

Joanne r Green
Professo tment Chair
Political
Texas C University
Fort Wor

Ramdas h.D.
Associat r of Religion
Universit ii at Manoa
Honolulu

Huping Ling
Changjiang Scholar Chair Professor
Professor of History
Truman State University
Kirksville, Missouri

Jeffery Long, Ph.D.
Professor of Religion and Asian Studies
Elizabethtown College
Elizabethtown, Pennsylvania

Gordon Newby
Professor of Islamic, Jewish and Comparative Studies
Department of Middle Eastern and South Asian Studies
Emory University
Atlanta, Georgia

Mark Peterson
Associate Professor
Department of Asian and Near Eastern Languages
Brigham Young University
Provo, Utah

William Pitts
Professor, Department of Religion
Baylor University
Waco, Texas

Benjamin Ravid
Professor Emeritus of Jewish History
Department of Near Eastern and Judaic Studies
Brandeis University
Waltham, Massachusetts

Harpreet Singh
College Fellow
Department of South Asian Studies
Harvard University
Cambridge, Massachusetts

Christopher E. Smith, J.D., Ph.D.
Professor
Michigan State University
MSU School of Criminal Justice
East Lansing, Michigan

John Voll
Professor of Islamic History
Georgetown University
Washington, D.C.

Michael R. Wolf
Associate Professor
Department of Political Science
Indiana University-Purdue University Fort Wayne
Fort Wayne, Indiana

Reimagine Learning

Realize Results. Social studies is more than dots on a map or dates on a timeline. It's where we've been and where we're going. It's stories from the past and our stories today. And in today's fast-paced, interconnected world, it's essential.

Instruction Your Way!

Comprehensive teaching support is available in three different formats:

- **Teacher's Edition for Digital Course:** Designed like a "T.V. Guide," teaching suggestions are paired with preview images of digital resources.
- **Teaching Support Online:** Teaching suggestions, answer keys, blackline masters, and other resources are provided at point-of-use online in Realize.
- **Teacher's Edition for Textbook:** This time-tested, familiar option can be used in tandem with the Student Edition for page-by-page teaching support.

TEKS Mastery System

This complete system for teaching and learning the **TEKS** uses best practices, technology, and a four-part framework—Connect, Investigate, Synthesize, and Demonstrate—to prepare students to be college-and-career ready.

- **100% coverage of the Texas Essential Knowledge and Skills for Social Studies**
- Higher-level content that gives students support to access complex text, acquire skills, and tackle rigorous questions.
- Inquiry-focused Projects, Civic Discussions, and Document-Based Questions that prepare students for real-world challenges.
- Digital content on Pearson Realize that is dynamic, is flexible, and uses the power of technology to bring social studies to life.

Connect
Make meaning personal

Demonstrate
Show understanding

TEKS
Mastery

Investigate
Acquire knowledge and skills

Synthesize
Practice knowledge and skills

Table of Contents for Today's Learners

Today's learners research new information by using a search engine and browsing by topic. Breaking out of a book metaphor of "chapters," this TEKS-focused table of contents is organized by:

- **Topic:** As you decide what you want to teach, you search first for the topic.
- **Lesson:** Within each topic are several lessons where you will find a variety of diverse resources to support teaching and learning.
- **Text:** Each lesson contains chunked information called Texts. This is the same informational text that appears in the print Student Edition.

This organization saves time, improves pacing, and makes it easy to rearrange content.

» Go online to learn more and see the program overview video.

PEARSON realize™

CONNECT! **Texas students will begin the Pearson TEKS Mastery System by engaging in the topic story and connecting it to their own lives.**

TEKS Preview—Each Topic opens with TEKS, allowing students to preview expected learning outcomes. Students will also find TEKS at the beginning, throughout, and at the end of every lesson. TEKS process skills are closely integrated with the content.

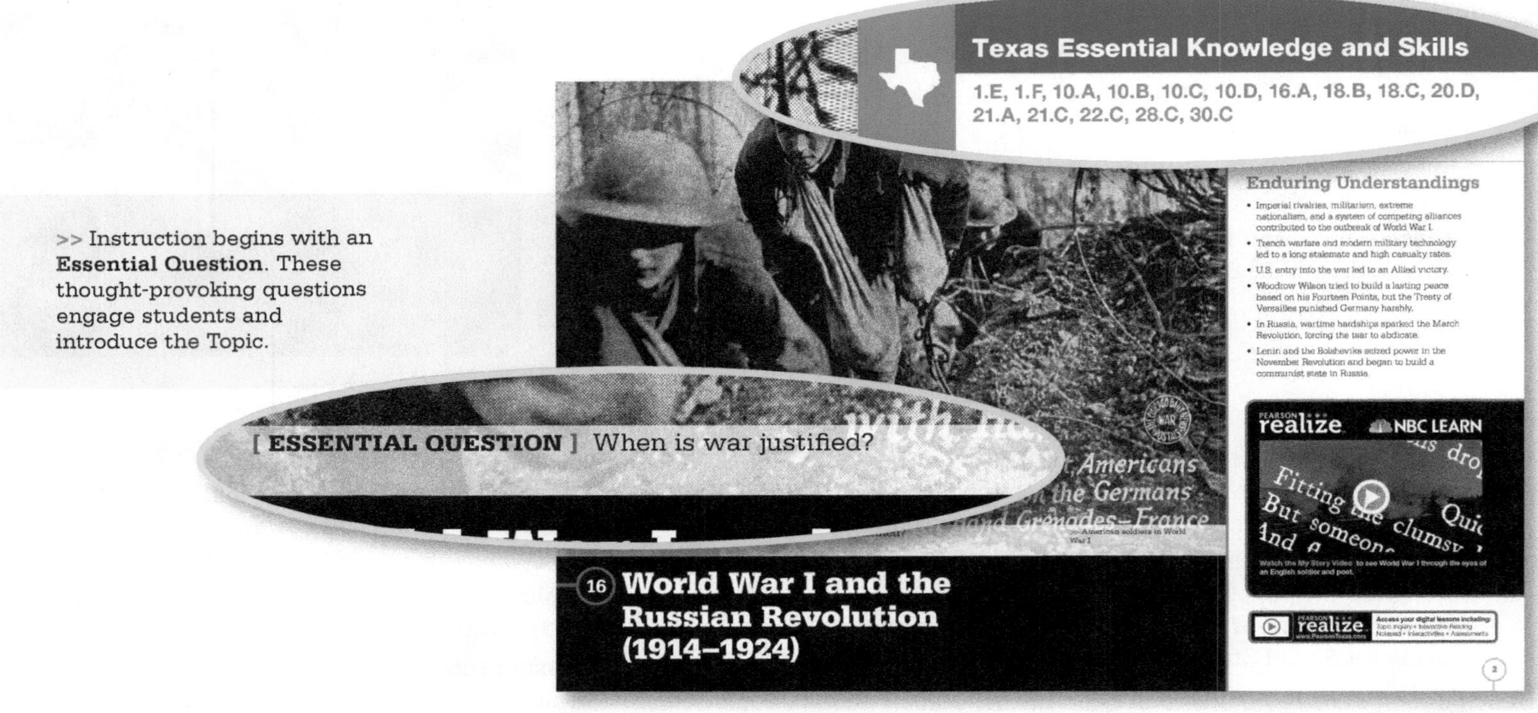

Texas Essential Knowledge and Skills
1.E, 1.F, 10.A, 10.B, 10.C, 10.D, 16.A, 18.B, 18.C, 20.D, 21.A, 21.C, 22.C, 28.C, 30.C
Enduring Understandings
Imperial rivalries, militarism, extreme nationalism, and a system of competing alliances contributed to the outbreak of World War I.
Trench warfare and modern military technology led to a long stalemate and high casualty rates.
U.S. entry into the war led to an Allied victory.
Woodrow Wilson tried to build a lasting peace based on his Fourteen Points, but the Treaty of Versailles punished Germany harshly.
In Russia, wartime hardships sparked the March Revolution, forcing the tsar to abdicate.
Lenin and the Bolsheviks seized power in the November Revolution and began to build a communist state in Russia.
[ESSENTIAL QUESTION] When is war justified?
realize
NBC LEARN
16 World War I and the Russian Revolution (1914–1924)

>> Instruction begins with an **Essential Question**. These thought-provoking questions engage students and introduce the Topic.

Developed in partnership with NBC Learn, the **My Story Videos** help students connect to the Topic content by hearing the personal story of an individual whose life is related to the content students are about to learn.

Investigate: Acquire Knowledge and Skills

INVESTIGATE! Step two of the TEKS Mastery System allows Texas students to investigate the topic story through a number of engaging features as they learn the content.

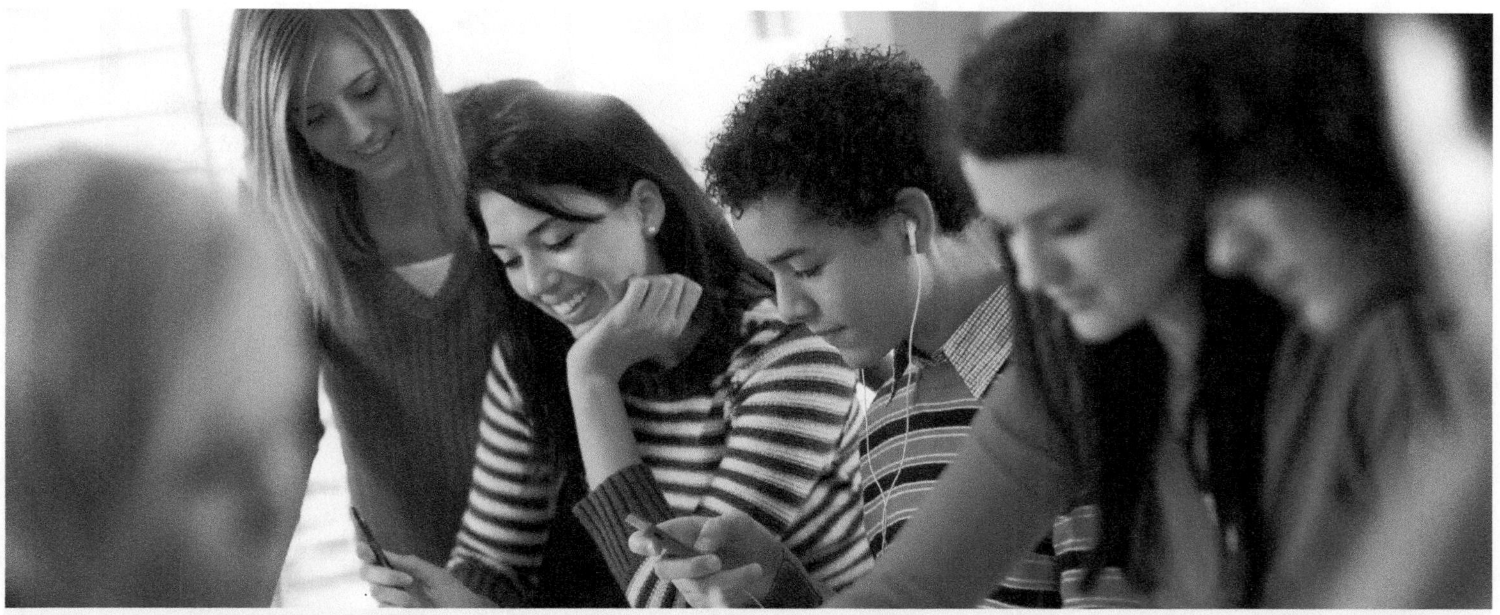

>> **Active Classroom Strategies** integrated in the daily lesson plans help to increase in-class participation and raise student energy levels and attentiveness, all while engaging students in the story. Use these 5–15-minute activities to have students use what they have learned to draw, write, speak, and decide.

>> **Interactive Primary Source Galleries:** Students can use primary source image galleries throughout the lesson to see, analyze, and interact with images that tie to the Topic story content.

Investigate

>> Students will feel like they are a part of the story as they use **interactive 3-D models**.

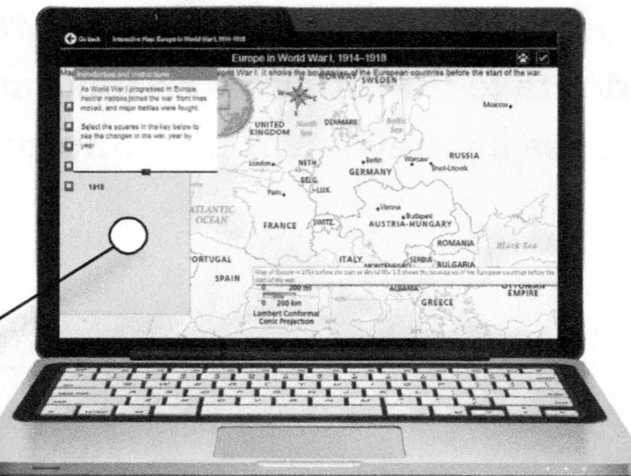

>> Students will continue to investigate the topic story through **dynamic interactive maps**. Students build rigorous analytical skills while covering the TEKS.

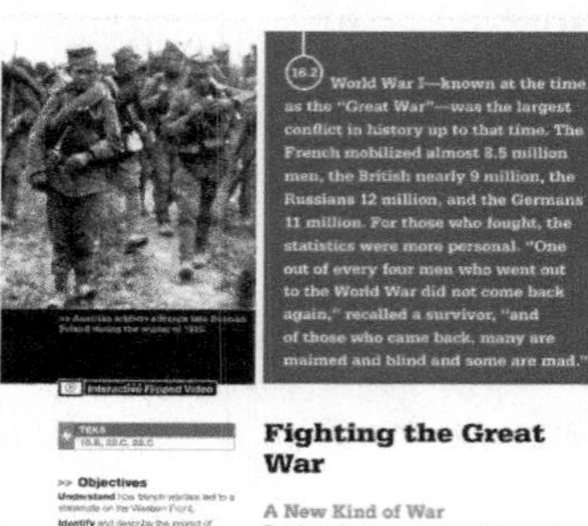

>> Students can learn content by reading narrative text online or in a printed Student Edition.

Synthesize: Practice Knowledge and Skills

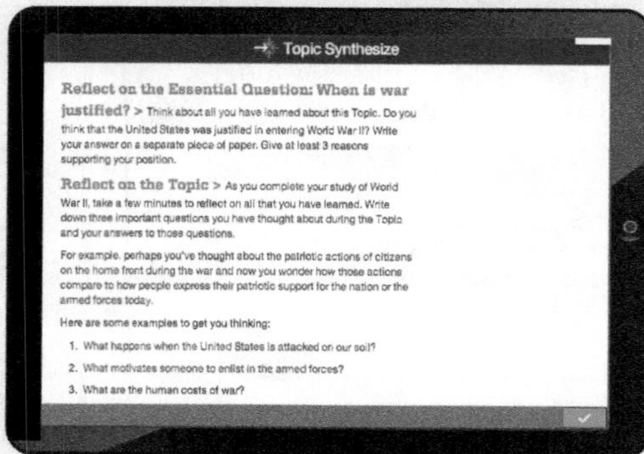

SYNTHESIZE!

In step three of the TEKS Mastery System, students pause to reflect on their learning and revisit an Essential Question.

Demonstrate: Show Understanding

DEMONSTRATE! The final step of the TEKS Mastery System is for each student to demonstrate understanding of the TEKS.

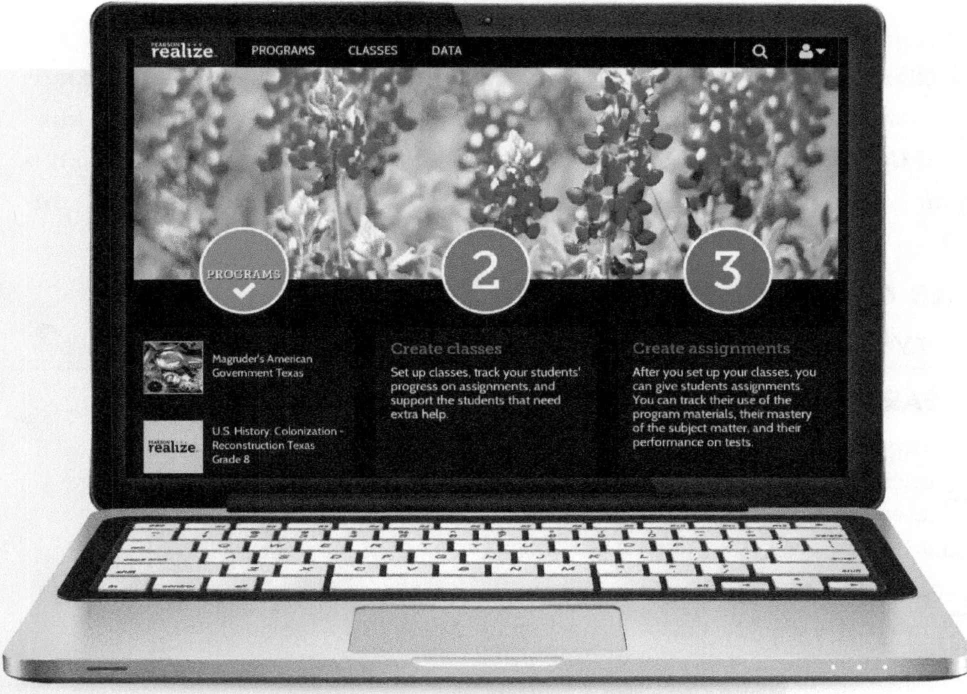

PEARSON realize™

>> **The digital course on Realize!** The program's digital course on Realize puts engaging TEKS-aligned content, embedded assessments, instant data, and flexible tools at your fingertips.

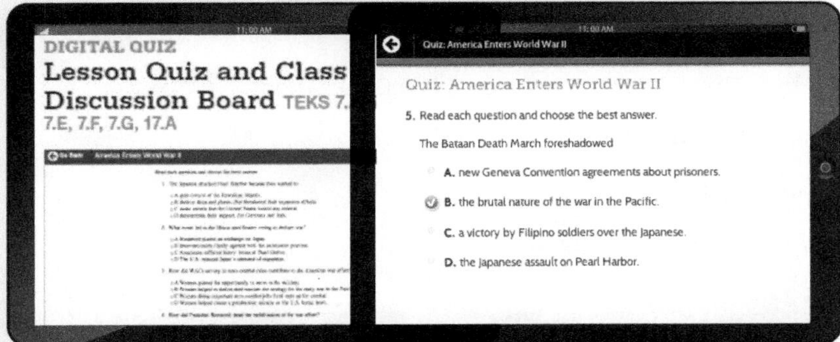

>> **TEKS Assessment.** At the end of each lesson and topic, students demonstrate understanding through Lesson Quizzes, Topic Tests, and Topic Inquiry performance assessments. The system provides each student with remediation and enrichment recommendations based on their individual performance toward TEKS mastery.

>> **Class and Data** features on Realize make it easy to use students' TEKS mastery data to show if time is needed to reteach or to move ahead.

Table of Contents

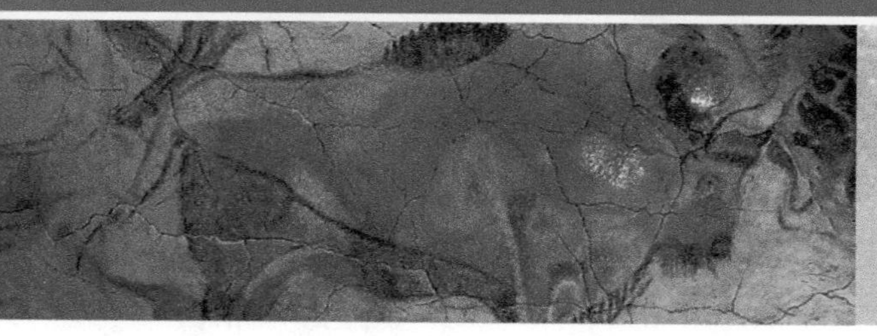

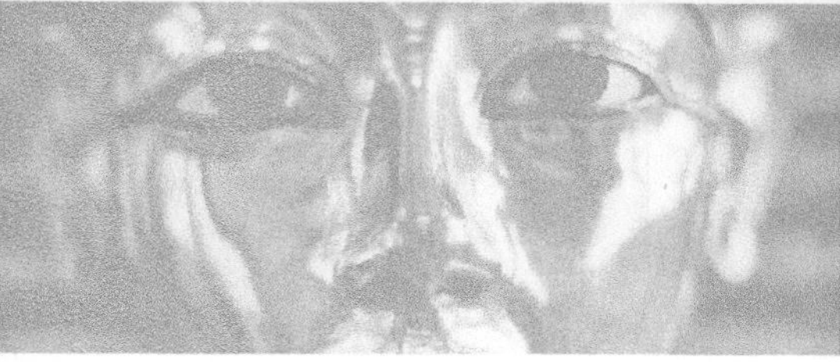

TOPIC 2 The Ancient Middle East and Egypt (3200 B.C.–500 B.C.) 28

Table of Contents

TOPIC 3 Ancient India and China

(2600 B.C.–A.D. 550) 66

TOPIC 4 The Americas (Prehistory–A.D. 1570) 108

TEKS
1.A, 6.A, 15.A, 16.A, 16.C, 26.B, 27.B, 29.F, 30.D

Table of Contents

TOPIC 5 Ancient Greece (1750 B.C.–133 B.C.) 136

TEKS
1.B, 3.A, 16.A, 19.A, 19.B, 20.A, 21.B, 22.A, 22.B, 24.A, 25.B, 26.B, 26.C, 27.A, 27.E, 29.F, 30.C

TOPIC 6 Ancient Rome and the Origins of Christianity (509 B.C.–A.D. 476) 170

TEKS
1.B, 1.C, 3.A, 3.B, 3.C, 19.B, 20.A, 21.B, 22.A, 22.B, 23.A, 24.A, 25.B, 26.B, 27.A, 29.F, 29.H, 30.C, 30.D

Table of Contents

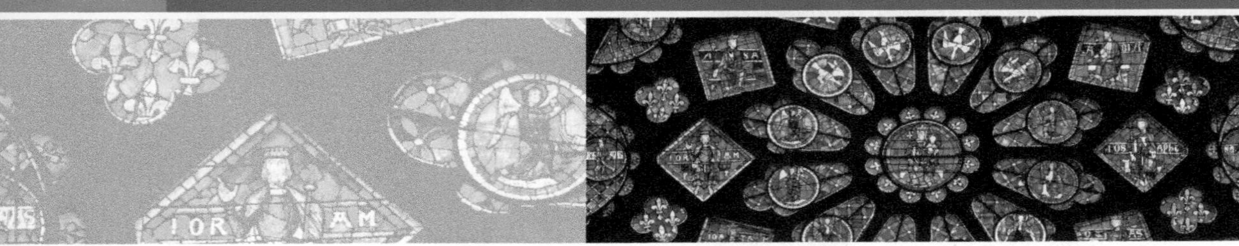

TOPIC 7 Medieval Christian Europe (330–1450) 206

TEKS

1.C, 3.B, 4.A, 4.B, 4.C, 4.D, 4.E, 4.G, 4.K, 15.A, 16.A, 16.C, 19.B, 20.A, 20.B, 20.C, 23.A, 23.B, 24.A, 26.B, 29.F, 29.H, 30.C, 30.D

PEARSON realize
www.PearsonTexas.com
Access your Digital Lesson

Table of Contents

TOPIC 10 The Renaissance and Reformation (1300–1650)

Table of Contents

TOPIC 11 New Global Connections (1415–1796) 416

TEKS
1.D, 4.F, 4.I, 6.B, 7.A, 7.B, 7.C, 7.E, 7.F, 16.A, 16.B, 18.F

TOPIC 12 Absolutism and Revolution (1550–1850) 462

TEKS
1.E, 9.A, 9.B, 9.D, 15.A, 16.A, 18.A, 19.B, 20.A, 20.B, 20.C, 21.B, 21.C, 22.F, 23.B, 24.B, 25.C, 26.B, 26.C, 29.C, 29.E, 29.F, 29.G, 30.B, 30.C

Table of Contents

TOPIC 14 Nationalism and the Spread of Democracy (1790–1914) 584

TEKS
8.B, 9.B, 9.C, 9.D, 18.A, 18.C, 21.A, 21.B, 21.C, 24.A, 24.B

Table of Contents

TOPIC 15 The Age of Imperialism (1800–1914) 644

TEKS
1.E, 8.C, 8.D, 9.D, 16.B, 22.C, 28.B, 29.D, 29.E, 29.F, 29.G

www.PearsonTexas.com
Access your Digital Lesson

TOPIC 16 World War I and the Russian Revolution (1914–1924) 696

TEKS
1.E, 1.F, 10.A, 10.B, 10.C, 10.D, 16.A, 18.B, 18.C, 20.D, 21.A, 21.C, 22.C, 28.C, 30.C

Table of Contents

TOPIC 17 The World Between the Wars (1910–1939) 732

TOPIC 18 World War II (1930–1945) 796

TEKS
1.F, 12.B, 12.C, 16.A, 20.D, 21.A, 22.D, 28.C

Table of Contents

TOPIC 20 New Nations Emerge (1945–Present) 878

TEKS
1.F, 10.C, 13.E, 13.F, 14.A, 15.A, 16.A, 16.C, 22.D, 24.B, 25.D, 31.B

Table of Contents

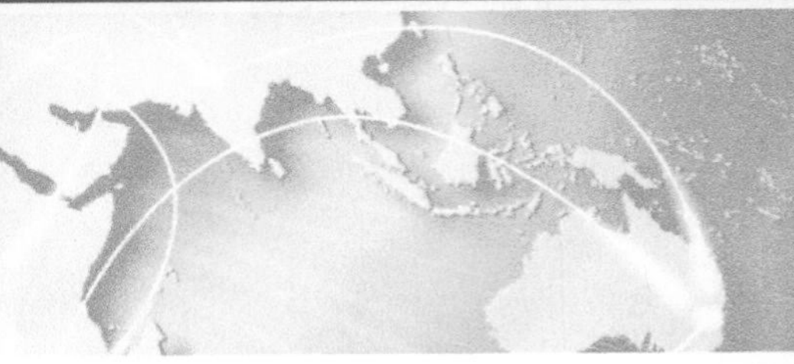

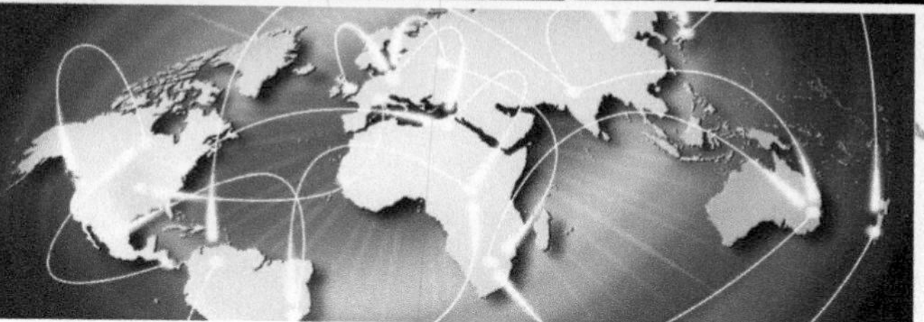

PEARSON realize

www.PearsonTexas.com
Access your Digital Lesson

Digital Resources

Many types of digital resources help you investigate the topics in this course. You'll find biographies, primary sources, maps, and more. These resources will bring the topics to life and help you master the TEKS.

Core Concepts

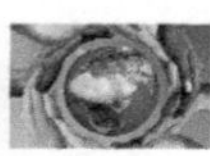

Culture

- What Is Culture?
- Families and Societies
- Language
- Religion
- The Arts
- Cultural Diffusion and Change
- Science and Technology

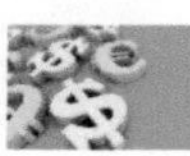

Economics

- Economics Basics
- Economic Process
- Economic Systems
- Economic Development
- Trade
- Money Management

Geography

- The Study of Earth
- Geography's Five Themes
- Ways to Show Earth's Surface
- Understanding Maps
- Earth in Space
- Time and Earth's Rotation
- Forces on Earth's Surface
- Forces Inside Earth
- Climate and Weather
- Temperature
- Water and Climate
- Air Circulation and Precipitation
- Types of Climate
- Ecosystems
- Environment and Resources
- Land Use
- People's Impact on the Environment
- Population
- Migration
- Urbanization

Government and Civics

- Foundations of Government
- Political Systems
- Political Structures
- Conflict and Cooperation
- Citizenship

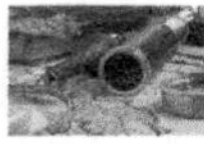

History

- How Do Historians Study History?
- Measuring Time
- Historical Sources
- Archaeology and Other Sources
- Historical Maps

Personal Finance

- Your Fiscal Fitness: An Introduction
- Budgeting
- Checking
- Investments
- Savings and Retirement
- Credit and Debt
- Risk Management
- Consumer Smarts
- After High School
- Taxes and Income

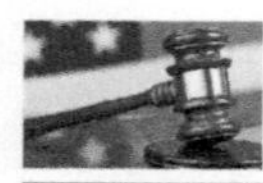

Landmark Supreme Court Cases

- *Korematsu* v. *United States*
- *Marbury* v. *Madison*
- *McCulloch* v. *Maryland*
- *Gibbons* v. *Ogden*
- *Worcester* v. *Georgia*
- *Dred Scott* v. *Sandford*
- *Plessy* v. *Ferguson*
- *Schenck* v. *United States*
- *Brown* v. *Board of Education*
- *Engel* v. *Vitale*
- *Sweatt* v. *Painter*
- *Mapp* v. *Ohio*
- *Hernandez* v. *Texas*
- *Gideon* v. *Wainwright*
- *Wisconsin* v. *Yoder*
- *Miranda* v. *Arizona*
- *White* v. *Regester*
- *Tinker* v. *Des Moines School District*
- *Roe* v. *Wade*
- *Baker* v. *Carr*
- *Grutter* v. *Bollinger*
- *Edgewood* v. *Kirby*
- *Texas* v. *Johnson*
- *National Federation of Independent Businesses et al.* v. *Sebelius et al.*
- *Mendez* v. *Westminster* and *Delgado* v. *Bastrop*

Interactive Primary Sources

- Code of Hammurabi
- Psalm 23
- The Republic, Plato
- Politics, Aristotle
- Edicts, Asoka
- Analects, Confucius
- First Letter to the Corinthians, Paul
- The Quran
- The Magna Carta
- Travels, Ibn Battuta
- The Destruction of the Indies, Bartolomé de Las Casas
- Mayflower Compact
- English Petition of Right
- English Bill of Rights
- Two Treatises of Government, John Locke
- The Spirit of the Laws, Baron de Montesquieu
- The Social Contract, Jean-Jacques Rousseau
- The Interesting Narrative of the Life of Olaudah Equiano
- "Give Me Liberty or Give Me Death," Patrick Henry
- "Remember the Ladies," Abigail Adams
- Common Sense, Thomas Paine
- Declaration of Independence
- Virginia Declaration of Rights
- Virginia Statute for Religious Freedom, Thomas Jefferson
- "To His Excellency, General Washington," Phillis Wheatley
- Articles of Confederation
- Anti-Federalist Papers
- The Federalist No. 10, James Madison
- The Federalist No. 39, James Madison
- The Federalist No. 51
- The Federalist No. 78, Alexander Hamilton
- Northwest Ordinance
- Iroquois Constitution
- Declaration of the Rights of Man and the Citizen
- Farewell Address, George Washington
- Mexican Federal Constitution of 1824
- State Colonization Law of 1825
- Law of April 6, 1830
- Debate Over Nullification, Webster and Calhoun
- Turtle Bayou Resolutions
- Democracy in America, Alexis de Tocqueville
- 1836 Victory or Death Letter from the Alamo, Travis
- Texas Declaration of Independence
- Declaration of Sentiments and Resolutions
- "Ain't I a Woman?," Sojourner Truth
- Uncle Tom's Cabin, Harriet Beecher Stowe
- "A House Divided," Abraham Lincoln
- First Inaugural Address, Abraham Lincoln
- Declaration of Causes: February 2, 1861
- Emancipation Proclamation, Abraham Lincoln
- Gettysburg Address, Abraham Lincoln
- Second Inaugural Address, Abraham Lincoln
- "I Will Fight No More Forever," Chief Joseph
- How the Other Half Lives, Jacob Riis
- The Pledge of Allegiance
- Preamble to the Platform of the Populist Party
- Atlanta Exposition Address, Booker T. Washington
- The Jungle, Upton Sinclair
- Hind Swaraj, Mohandas Gandhi
- The Fourteen Points, Woodrow Wilson
- Two Poems, Langston Hughes
- Four Freedoms, Franklin D. Roosevelt
- Anne Frank: The Diary of a Young Girl, Anne Frank
- Charter of the United Nations
- Universal Declaration of Human Rights
- Autobiography, Kwame Nkrumah
- Inaugural Address, John F. Kennedy
- Silent Spring, Rachel Carson
- "I Have a Dream," Martin Luther King, Jr.
- "Letter From Birmingham Jail," Martin Luther King, Jr.
- "Tear Down This Wall," Ronald Reagan
- "Freedom From Fear," Aung San Suu Kyi
- "Glory and Hope," Nelson Mandela

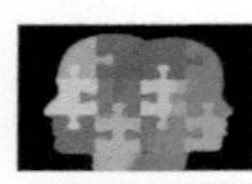

Biographies

- Abigail Adams
- John Adams
- John Quincy Adams
- Samuel Adams
- James Armistead
- Crispus Attucks
- Moses Austin
- Stephen F. Austin
- James A. Baker III
- William Blackstone
- Simón Bolívar
- Napoleon Bonaparte
- Chief Bowles
- Omar Bradley
- John C. Calhoun
- César Chávez
- Wentworth Cheswell
- George Childress
- Winston Churchill
- Henry Clay
- Bill Clinton
- Jefferson Davis
- Martin De León
- Green DeWitt
- Dwight Eisenhower
- James Fannin
- James L. Farmer, Jr.
- Benjamin Franklin
- Milton Friedman
- Betty Friedan
- Bernardo de Gálvez
- Hector P. Garcia
- John Nance Garner
- King George III
- Henry B. González
- Raul A. Gonzalez, Jr.
- Mikhail Gorbachev
- William Goyens
- Ulysses S. Grant
- José Gutiérrez de Lara
- Alexander Hamilton
- Hammurabi
- Warren Harding
- Friedrich Hayek
- Jack Coffee Hays
- Patrick Henry
- Adolf Hitler
- Oveta Culp Hobby
- James Hogg
- Sam Houston
- Kay Bailey Hutchison
- Andrew Jackson
- John Jay
- Thomas Jefferson
- Lyndon B. Johnson
- Anson Jones
- Barbara Jordan
- Justinian
- John F. Kennedy
- John Maynard Keynes
- Martin Luther King, Jr.
- Marquis de Lafayette
- Mirabeau B. Lamar
- Robert E. Lee
- Abraham Lincoln
- John Locke
- James Madison
- John Marshall
- George Marshall
- Karl Marx
- George Mason
- Mary Maverick
- Jane McCallum
- Joseph McCarthy
- James Monroe
- Charles de Montesquieu
- Edwin W. Moore
- Moses
- Benito Mussolini
- José Antonio Navarro
- Chester A. Nimitz
- Richard M. Nixon
- Barack Obama
- Sandra Day O'Connor
- Thomas Paine
- Quanah Parker
- Rosa Parks
- George Patton
- John J. Pershing
- John Paul II
- Sam Rayburn
- Ronald Reagan
- Hiram Rhodes Revels
- Franklin D. Roosevelt
- Theodore Roosevelt
- Lawrence Sullivan Ross
- Haym Soloman
- Antonio Lopez de Santa Anna
- Phyllis Schlafly
- Erasmo Seguín
- Juan N. Seguín
- Roger Sherman
- Adam Smith
- Joseph Stalin
- Raymond L. Telles
- Alexis de Tocqueville
- Hideki Tojo
- William B. Travis
- Harry Truman
- Lech Walesa
- Mercy Otis Warren
- George Washington
- Daniel Webster
- Lulu Belle Madison White
- William Wilberforce
- James Wilson
- Woodrow Wilson
- Lorenzo de Zavala
- Mao Zedong

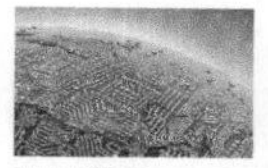

21st Century Skills

- Identify Main Ideas and Details
- Set a Purpose for Reading
- Use Context Clues
- Analyze Cause and Effect
- Categorize
- Compare and Contrast
- Draw Conclusions
- Draw Inferences
- Generalize
- Make Decisions
- Make Predictions
- Sequence
- Solve Problems
- Summarize
- Analyze Media Content
- Analyze Primary and Secondary Sources
- Compare Viewpoints
- Distinguish Between Fact and Opinion
- Identify Bias
- Analyze Data and Models
- Analyze Images
- Analyze Political Cartoons
- Create Charts and Maps
- Create Databases
- Read Charts, Graphs, and Tables
- Read Physical Maps
- Read Political Maps
- Read Special-Purpose Maps
- Use Parts of a Map
- Ask Questions
- Avoid Plagiarism
- Create a Research Hypothesis
- Evaluate Web Sites
- Identify Evidence
- Identify Trends
- Interpret Sources
- Search for Information on the Internet
- Synthesize
- Take Effective Notes
- Develop a Clear Thesis
- Organize Your Ideas
- Support Ideas With Evidence
- Evaluate Existing Arguments
- Consider & Counter Opposing Arguments
- Give an Effective Presentation
- Participate in a Discussion or Debate
- Publish Your Work
- Write a Journal Entry
- Write an Essay
- Share Responsibility
- Compromise
- Develop Cultural Awareness
- Generate New Ideas
- Innovate
- Make a Difference
- Work in Teams
- Being an Informed Citizen
- Paying Taxes
- Political Participation
- Serving on a Jury
- Voting

Atlas

- United States: Political
- United States: Physical
- World Political
- World Physical
- World Climate
- World Ecosystems
- World Population Density
- World Land Use
- North Africa and Southwest Asia: Political
- North Africa and Southwest Asia: Physical
- Sub-Saharan Africa: Political
- Sub-Saharan Africa: Physical
- South Asia: Political
- South Asia: Physical
- East Asia: Political
- East Asia: Physical
- Southeast Asia: Political
- Southeast Asia: Physical
- Europe: Political
- Europe: Physical
- Russia, Central Asia, and the Caucasus: Political
- Russia, Central Asia, and the Caucasus: Physical
- North America: Political
- North America: Physical
- Central America and the Caribbean: Political
- Central America and the Caribbean: Physical
- South America: Political
- South America: Physical
- Australia and the Pacific: Political
- Australia and the Pacific: Physical

TEKS at a Glance

	WHERE YOU WILL FIND IT
1 **History.** The student understands traditional historical points of reference in world history. The student is expected to:	
1.A identify major causes and describe the major effects of the following events from 8000 BC to 500 BC: the development of agriculture and the development of the river valley civilizations;	**1.2, 1.3, 2.1, 2.4, 3.1, 3.2, 3.4, 4.3, 8.5**
1.B identify major causes and describe the major effects of the following events from 500 BC to AD 600: the development of the classical civilizations of Greece, Rome, Persia, India (Maurya and Gupta), China (Zhou, Qin, and Han), and the development of major world religions;	**2.2, 2.3, 3.2, 3.3, 3.4, 3.5, 5.1, 5.2, 5.3, 5.4, 6.1, 6.2, 6.3, 6.4**
1.C identify major causes and describe the major effects of the following important turning points in world history from 600 to 1450: the spread of Christianity, the decline of Rome and the formation of medieval Europe; the development of Islamic caliphates and their impact on Asia, Africa, and Europe; the Mongol invasions and their impact on Europe, China, India, and Southwest Asia;	**6.2, 7.1, 7.3, 7.4, 7.5, 7.8, 8.2, 8.5, 8.7, 9.1, 9.2, 9.3**
1.D identify major causes and describe the major effects of the following important turning points in world history from 1450 to 1750: the rise of the Ottoman Empire, the influence of the Ming dynasty on world trade, European exploration and the Columbian Exchange, European expansion, and the Renaissance and the Reformation;	**4.3, 8.4, 9.3, 10.1, 10.2, 10.3, 10.4, 11.1, 11.2, 11.3, 11.4, 11.5, 11.6**
1.E identify major causes and describe the major effects of the following important turning points in world history from 1750 to 1914: the Scientific Revolution, the Industrial Revolution and its impact on the development of modern economic systems, European imperialism, and the Enlightenment's impact on political revolutions; and	**10.5, 12.4, 12.5, 12.6, 13.1, 13.2, 13.3, 13.4, 15.1, 15.2, 15.3, 15.4, 15.5, 15.6, 15.7, 15.8, 16.1, 16.2, 21.6**
1.F identify major causes and describe the major effects of the following important turning points in world history from 1914 to the present: the world wars and their impact on political, economic, and social systems; communist revolutions and their impact on the Cold War; independence movements; and globalization.	**16.1, 16.2, 16.3, 16.4, 17.2, 17.3, 17.4, 17.5, 17.6, 17.7, 17.8, 18.4, 18.5, 19.1, 19.2, 19.3, 19.4, 20.1, 20.2, 20.3, 21.6**
2 **History.** The student understands how early civilizations developed from 8000 BC to 500 BC. The student is expected to:	
2.A summarize the impact of the development of farming (Neolithic Revolution) on the creation of river valley civilizations;	**1.2, 1.3**
2.B identify the characteristics of civilization; and	**1.3**
2.C explain how major river valley civilizations influenced the development of the classical civilizations.	**2.1, 2.2, 2.3, 2.4, 3.1, 3.4**
3 **History.** The student understands the contributions and influence of classical civilizations from 500 BC to AD 600 on subsequent civilizations. The student is expected to:	
3.A describe the major political, religious/philosophical, and cultural influences of Persia, India, China, Israel, Greece, and Rome, including the development of monotheism, Judaism, and Christianity;	**2.2, 2.3, 3.1, 3.2, 3.3, 3.4, 3.5, 5.1, 5.2, 5.3, 5.4, 6.1, 6.2, 6.3, 6.4, 8.4**
3.B explain the impact of the fall of Rome on Western Europe; and	**6.2, 7.1**
3.C compare the factors that led to the collapse of Rome and Han China.	**Topic 6 Topic Review and Assessment**
4 **History.** The student understands how, after the collapse of classical empires, new political, economic, and social systems evolved and expanded from 600 to 1450. The student is expected to:	
4.A explain the development of Christianity as a unifying social and political factor in medieval Europe and the Byzantine Empire;	**7.1, 7.3, 7.5, 7.6**

	WHERE YOU WILL FIND IT
4.B explain the characteristics of Roman Catholicism and Eastern Orthodoxy;	**7.3, 7.8**
4.C describe the major characteristics of and the factors contributing to the development of the political/social system of feudalism and the economic system of manorialism;	**7.2**
4.D explain the political, economic, and social impact of Islam on Europe, Asia, and Africa;	**7.4, 8.1, 8.2, 8.3, 8.4, 8.6, 8.7, 9.1**
4.E describe the interactions among Muslim, Christian, and Jewish societies in Europe, Asia, and North Africa;	**7.1, 7.3, 7.4, 8.2, 8.5, 8.7, 8.8**
4.F describe the interactions between Muslim and Hindu societies in South Asia;	**9.1, 11.2**
4.G explain how the Crusades, the Black Death, the Hundred Years' War, and the Great Schism contributed to the end of medieval Europe;	**7.4, 7.7**
4.H summarize the major political, economic, and cultural developments in Tang and Song China and their impact on Eastern Asia;	**9.2, 9.4, 9.5**
4.I explain the development of the slave trade;	**11.5**
4.J analyze how the Silk Road and the African gold-salt trade facilitated the spread of ideas and trade; and	**3.5, 8.6, 9.2**
4.K summarize the changes resulting from the Mongol invasions of Russia, China, and the Islamic world.	**7.8, 8.2, 9.3**
5 **History.** The student understands the causes, characteristics, and impact of the European Renaissance and the Reformation from 1450 to 1750. The student is expected to:	
5.A explain the political, intellectual, artistic, economic, and religious impact of the Renaissance; and	**10.1, 10.2, 10.3**
5.B explain the political, intellectual, artistic, economic, and religious impact of the Reformation.	**10.3, 10.4**
6 **History.** The student understands the characteristics and impact of the Maya, Inca, and Aztec civilizations. The student is expected to:	
6.A compare the major political, economic, social, and cultural developments of the Maya, Inca, and Aztec civilizations and explain how prior civilizations influenced their development; and	**4.1, 4.2**
6.B explain how the Inca and Aztec empires were impacted by European exploration/colonization.	**11.3**
7 **History.** The student understands the causes and impact of European expansion from 1450 to 1750. The student is expected to:	
7.A analyze the causes of European expansion from 1450 to 1750;	**11.1, 11.2, 11.3, 11.4, 11.5, 11.6**
7.B explain the impact of the Columbian Exchange on the Americas and Europe;	**11.6**
7.C explain the impact of the Atlantic slave trade on West Africa and the Americas;	**11.5**
7.D explain the impact of the Ottoman Empire on Eastern Europe and global trade;	**8.4**
7.E explain Ming China's impact on global trade; and	**9.3, 11.2**
7.F explain new economic factors and principles that contributed to the success of Europe's Commercial Revolution.	**11.6**
8 **History.** The student understands the causes and the global impact of the Industrial Revolution and European imperialism from 1750 to 1914. The student is expected to:	
8.A explain how 17th and 18th century European scientific advancements led to the Industrial Revolution;	**13.1**

		WHERE YOU WILL FIND IT
	8.B explain how the Industrial Revolution led to political, economic, and social changes in Europe;	**13.1, 13.2, 13.3, 13.4, 14.3, 14.5**
	8.C identify the major political, economic, and social motivations that influenced European imperialism;	**15.1, 15.2, 15.3, 15.4, 15.5, 15.7, 15.8**
	8.D explain the major characteristics and impact of European imperialism; and	**15.1, 15.2, 15.3, 15.4, 15.5, 15.6, 15.7, 15.8**
	8.E explain the effects of free enterprise in the Industrial Revolution.	**13.2, 13.3**
9	**History.** The student understands the causes and effects of major political revolutions between 1750 and 1914. The student is expected to:	
	9.A compare the causes, characteristics, and consequences of the American and French revolutions, emphasizing the role of the Enlightenment, the Glorious Revolution, and religion;	**12.6, 12.7**
	9.B explain the impact of Napoleon Bonaparte and the Napoleonic Wars on Europe and Latin America;	**12.8, 14.2, 14.3**
	9.C trace the influence of the American and French revolutions on Latin America, including the role of Simón Bolivar; and	**14.2**
	9.D identify the influence of ideas such as separation of powers, checks and balances, liberty, equality, democracy, popular sovereignty, human rights, constitutionalism, and nationalism on political revolutions.	**12.5, 12.6, 12.7, 14.1, 14.2, 14.3, 14.4, 14.8, 15.3, 15.4, 15.5, 17.1**
10	**History.** The student understands the causes and impact of World War I. The student is expected to:	
	10.A identify the importance of imperialism, nationalism, militarism, and the alliance system in causing World War I;	**16.1**
	10.B identify major characteristics of World War I, including total war, trench warfare, modern military technology, and high casualty rates;	**16.2, 16.3, 16.4**
	10.C explain the political impact of Woodrow Wilson's Fourteen Points and the political and economic impact of the Treaty of Versailles, including changes in boundaries and the mandate system; and	**16.3, 17.2, 20.3**
	10.D identify the causes of the February (March) and October revolutions of 1917 in Russia, their effects on the outcome of World War I, and the Bolshevik establishment of the Union of Soviet Socialist Republics.	**16.3, 16.4**
11	**History.** The student understands the causes and impact of the global economic depression immediately following World War I. The student is expected to:	
	11.A summarize the international, political, and economic causes of the global depression; and	**17.1, 17.5**
	11.B explain the responses of governments in the United States, Germany, and the Soviet Union to the global depression.	**17.5, 17.7, 17.8**
12	**History.** The student understands the causes and impact of World War II. The student is expected to:	
	12.A describe the emergence and characteristics of totalitarianism;	**17.6, 17.7, 17.8**
	12.B explain the roles of various world leaders, including Benito Mussolini, Adolf Hitler, Hideki Tojo, Joseph Stalin, Franklin D. Roosevelt, and Winston Churchill, prior to and during World War II; and	**17.5, 17.6, 17.7, 17.8, 18.1, 18.2, 18.3, 18.4, 18.5**
	12.C explain the major causes and events of World War II, including the German invasions of Poland and the Soviet Union, the Holocaust, Japanese imperialism, the attack on Pearl Harbor, the Normandy landings, and the dropping of the atomic bombs.	**17.4, 18.1, 18.2, 18.3, 18.4, 18.5**

		WHERE YOU WILL FIND IT
13	**History.** The student understands the impact of major events associated with the Cold War and independence movements. The student is expected to:	
	13.A summarize how the outcome of World War II contributed to the development of the Cold War;	**19.1, 19.2, 19.3, 19.4**
	13.B summarize the factors that contributed to communism in China, including Mao Zedong's role in its rise, and how it differed from Soviet communism;	**17.4, 19.3**
	13.C identify the following major events of the Cold War, including the Korean War, the Vietnam War, and the arms race;	**19.1, 19.3, 19.4**
	13.D explain the roles of modern world leaders, including Ronald Reagan, Mikhail Gorbachev, Lech Walesa, and Pope John Paul II, in the collapse of communism in Eastern Europe and the Soviet Union;	**19.5**
	13.E summarize the rise of independence movements in Africa, the Middle East, and South Asia and reasons for ongoing conflicts; and	**20.1, 20.2, 20.3, 20.4, 21.2, 21.8**
	13.F explain how Arab rejection of the State of Israel has led to ongoing conflict.	**20.3, 20.4, 21.8**
14	**History.** The student understands the development of radical Islamic fundamentalism and the subsequent use of terrorism by some of its adherents. The student is expected to:	
	14.A summarize the development and impact of radical Islamic fundamentalism on events in the second half of the 20th century, including Palestinian terrorism and the growth of al Qaeda; and	**20.3, 20.4, 21.8**
	14.B explain the U.S. response to terrorism from September 11, 2001, to the present.	**21.5, 21.8**
15	**Geography.** The student uses geographic skills and tools to collect, analyze, and interpret data. The student is expected to:	
	15.A create and interpret thematic maps, graphs, and charts to demonstrate the relationship between geography and the historical development of a region or nation; and	**7.8, 13.1, 17.2, 20.1, 20.3, 20.4, 21.1**
	15.B analyze and compare geographic distributions and patterns in world history shown on maps, graphs, charts, and models.	**13.1, 21.1, 21.6**
16	**Geography.** The student understands the impact of geographic factors on major historic events and processes. The student is expected to:	
	16.A locate places and regions of historical significance directly related to major eras and turning points in world history;	**1.3, 4.2, 4.3, 5.1, 5.2, 7.3, 7.4, 8.2, 11.3, 12.1, 12.2, 12.8, 13.1, 15.8, 16.1, 16.2, 16.3, 18.1, 18.2, 20.1, 20.2, 20.3, 20.4**
	16.B analyze the influence of human and physical geographic factors on major events in world history, including the development of river valley civilizations, trade in the Indian Ocean, and the opening of the Panama and Suez canals; and	**1.3, 2.1, 2.4, 3.1, 3.4, 8.5, 8.7, 9.6, 11.1, 11.2, 15.3, 15.4, 15.7, 15.8**
	16.C interpret maps, charts, and graphs to explain how geography has influenced people and events in the past.	**1.3, 7.8, 8.5, 13.1, 17.2, 19.5, 20.3**
17	**Economics.** The student understands the impact of the Neolithic and Industrial revolutions and globalization on humanity. The student is expected to:	
	17.A identify important changes in human life caused by the Neolithic Revolution and the Industrial Revolution;	**1.2, 1.3, 13.2, 13.3, 13.4**

		WHERE YOU WILL FIND IT
	17.B summarize the role of economics in driving political changes as related to the Neolithic Revolution and the Industrial Revolution; and	**1.2, 1.3, 13.2, 13.3, 13.4**
	17.C summarize the economic and social impact of 20th century globalization.	**21.3, 21.5, 21.6, 21.7**
18	**Economics.** The student understands the historical origins of contemporary economic systems and the benefits of free enterprise in world history. The student is expected to:	
	18.A identify the historical origins and characteristics of the free enterprise system, including the contributions of Adam Smith, especially the influence of his ideas found in *The Wealth of Nations*;	**12.4, 13.2, 14.1, 14.5, 14.7, 19.1, 19.2**
	18.B identify the historical origins and characteristics of communism, including the influences of Karl Marx;	**13.2, 16.4, 19.2, 19.3**
	18.C identify the historical origins and characteristics of socialism;	**13.2, 14.3, 16.4, 21.2**
	18.D identify the historical origins and characteristics of fascism;	**17.6**
	18.E explain why communist command economies collapsed in competition with free market economies at the end of the 20th century; and	**19.5, 21.1, 21.2, 21.5**
	18.F formulate generalizations on how economic freedom improved the human condition, based on students' knowledge of the benefits of free enterprise in Europe's Commercial Revolution, the Industrial Revolution, and 20th-century free market economies, compared to communist command communities.	**11.6, 13.2, 13.4, 19.1, 19.2, 19.5, 21.3, 21.5**
19	**Government.** The student understands the characteristics of major political systems throughout history. The student is expected to:	
	19.A identify the characteristics of monarchies and theocracies as forms of government in early civilizations; and	**1.3, 2.1, 2.2, 2.4, 3.4, 3.5, 5.2**
	19.B identify the characteristics of the following political systems: theocracy, absolute monarchy, democracy, republic, oligarchy, limited monarchy, and totalitarianism.	**1.3, 5.2, 6.1, 6.2, 7.5, 10.3, 12.1, 12.2, 12.3, 12.5, 17.6, 17.7**
20	**Government.** The student understands how contemporary political systems have developed from earlier systems of government. The student is expected to:	
	20.A explain the development of democratic-republican government from its beginnings in the Judeo-Christian legal tradition and classical Greece and Rome through the English Civil War and the Enlightenment;	**2.3, 5.2, 5.4, 6.1, 6.2, 6.4, 12.3, 12.4**
	20.B identify the impact of political and legal ideas contained in the following documents: Hammurabi's Code, the Jewish Ten Commandments, Justinian's Code of Laws, Magna Carta, the English Bill of Rights, the Declaration of Independence, the U.S. Constitution, and the Declaration of the Rights of Man and of the Citizen;	**2.2, 2.3, 7.1, 7.5, 12.3, 12.5, 12.6**
	20.C explain the political philosophies of individuals such as John Locke, Thomas Hobbes, Voltaire, Charles de Montesquieu, Jean-Jacques Rousseau, Thomas Aquinas, John Calvin, Thomas Jefferson, and William Blackstone; and	**7.6, 10.3, 12.4, 12.5**
	20.D explain the significance of the League of Nations and the United Nations.	**16.3, 17.5, 18.1, 18.5, 21.6, 21.7**
21	**Citizenship.** The student understands the significance of political choices and decisions made by individuals, groups, and nations throughout history. The student is expected to:	
	21.A describe how people have participated in supporting or changing their governments;	**14.1, 14.2, 14.3, 14.5, 14.6, 14.7, 14.8, 16.3, 16.4, 17.1, 17.2, 17.3, 17.6, 18.4, 19.2, 19.5, 20.3**

	WHERE YOU WILL FIND IT
21.B describe the rights and responsibilities of citizens and noncitizens in civic participation throughout history; and	**5.2, 6.1, 6.2, 12.5, 14.5**
21.C identify examples of key persons who were successful in shifting political thought, including William Wilberforce.	**12.4, 12.5, 13.2, 14.2, 14.5, 16.3, 16.4, 17.3, 17.6, 17.8, 21.2**
22 Citizenship. The student understands the historical development of significant legal and political concepts related to the rights and responsibilities of citizenship. The student is expected to:	
22.A summarize the development of the rule of law from ancient to modern times;	**5.2, 6.3**
22.B identify the influence of ideas regarding the right to a "trial by a jury of your peers" and the concepts of "innocent until proven guilty" and "equality before the law" that originated from the Judeo-Christian legal tradition and in Greece and Rome;	**2.3, 5.2, 6.3**
22.C identify examples of politically motivated mass murders in Cambodia, China, Latin America, the Soviet Union, and Armenia;	**15.3, 16.2, 17.7, 19.3, 19.4, 21.4**
22.D identify examples of genocide, including the Holocaust and genocide in the Balkans, Rwanda, and Darfur;	**18.3, 20.2, 21.5**
22.E identify examples of individuals who led resistance to political oppression such as Nelson Mandela, Mohandas Gandhi, Oscar Romero, Natan Sharansky, Las Madres de la Plaza de Mayo, and Chinese student protestors in Tiananmen Square; and	**17.3, 19.1, 19.5, 21.2, 21.3, 21.4**
22.F assess the degree to which American ideals have advanced human rights and democratic ideas throughout the world.	**12.5**
23 Culture. The student understands the history and relevance of major religious and philosophical traditions. The student is expected to:	
23.A describe the historical origins, central ideas, and spread of major religious and philosophical traditions, including Buddhism, Christianity, Confucianism, Hinduism, Islam, Judaism, Sikhism, and the development of monotheism; and	**2.3, 3.2, 3.4, 6.4, 7.3, 8.1, 8.2, 8.3, 8.4, 9.1, 9.4, 9.5, 9.6, 17.2**
23.B identify examples of religious influence on various events referenced in the major eras of world history.	**2.3, 3.2, 7.4, 7.8, 8.2, 8.7, 10.3, 10.4, 12.4**
24 Culture. The student understands the roles of women, children, and families in different historical cultures. The student is expected to:	
24.A describe the changing roles of women, children, and families during major eras of world history; and	**2.4, 5.2, 5.4, 6.1, 7.4, 7.6, 8.1, 8.8, 9.5, 13.2, 13.4, 14.5, 14.7, 21.1, 21.3, 21.7**
24.B describe the major influences of women such as Elizabeth I, Queen Victoria, Mother Teresa, Indira Gandhi, Margaret Thatcher, and Golda Meir during major eras of world history.	**10.4, 12.1, 12.2, 14.5, 19.2, 20.1, 20.3, 20.4, 21.3**
25 Culture. The student understands how the development of ideas has influenced institutions and societies. The student is expected to:	
25.A summarize the fundamental ideas and institutions of Eastern civilizations that originated in China and India;	**3.1, 3.2, 3.3, 3.4, 9.1, 9.2, 9.3, 9.4, 9.5, 9.6**
25.B summarize the fundamental ideas and institutions of Western civilizations that originated in Greece and Rome;	**5.1, 5.2, 5.3, 6.2, 6.3**

		WHERE YOU WILL FIND IT
	25.C explain the relationship among Christianity, individualism, and growing secularism that began with the Renaissance and how the relationship influenced subsequent political developments; and	**10.1, 10.3, 10.4, 10.5, 12.4**
	25.D explain how Islam influences law and government in the Muslim world.	**8.1, 20.3, 20.4, 21.8**
26	**Culture.** The student understands the relationship between the arts and the times during which they were created. The student is expected to:	
	26.A identify significant examples of art and architecture that demonstrate an artistic ideal or visual principle from selected cultures;	**9.1, 9.4, 10.1**
	26.B analyze examples of how art, architecture, literature, music, and drama reflect the history of the cultures in which they are produced; and	**2.4, 3.1, 4.1, 4.3, 5.1, 5.3, 5.4, 6.3, 7.6, 8.2, 8.3, 8.4, 8.5, 8.6, 8.7, 8.8, 9.1, 9.2, 9.3, 9.5, 10.1, 10.2, 12.1, 12.4, 13.4, 17.1, 17.2, 17.5, 17.7, 17.8**
	26.C identify examples of art, music, and literature that transcend the cultures in which they were created and convey universal themes.	**5.3, 10.1, 10.2, 12.4, 13.4, 17.2, 17.5**
27	**Science, technology, and society.** The student understands how major scientific and mathematical discoveries and technological innovations affected societies prior to 1750. The student is expected to:	
	27.A identify the origin and diffusion of major ideas in mathematics, science, and technology that occurred in river valley civilizations, classical Greece and Rome, classical India, and the Islamic caliphates between 700 and 1200 and in China from the Tang to Ming dynasties;	**2.1, 2.2, 2.4, 3.1, 3.3, 3.4, 3.5, 5.4, 6.3, 8.3, 9.2, 9.3, 9.4, 9.6**
	27.B summarize the major ideas in astronomy, mathematics, and architectural engineering that developed in the Maya, Inca, and Aztec civilizations;	**4.1, 4.2**
	27.C explain the impact of the printing press on the Renaissance and the Reformation in Europe;	**10.2, 10.3**
	27.D describe the origins of the Scientific Revolution in 16th century Europe and explain its impact on scientific thinking worldwide; and	**10.5**
	27.E identify the contributions of significant scientists such as Archimedes, Copernicus, Eratosthenes, Galileo, Pythagoras, Isaac Newton, and Robert Boyle.	**5.4, 10.5**
28	**Science, technology, and society.** The student understands how major scientific and mathematical discoveries and technological innovations have affected societies from 1750 to the present. The student is expected to:	
	28.A explain the role of textile manufacturing and steam technology in initiating the Industrial Revolution and the role of the factory system and transportation technology in advancing the Industrial Revolution;	**13.1, 13.2, 13.3**
	28.B explain the roles of military technology, transportation technology, communication technology, and medical advancements in initiating and advancing 19th century imperialism;	**15.1, 15.2, 15.4, 15.5, 15.6, 15.7, 15.8**
	28.C explain the effects of major new military technologies on World War I, World War II, and the Cold War;	**16.2, 18.2, 18.4, 18.5, 19.1, 19.4**
	28.D explain the role of telecommunication technology, computer technology, transportation technology, and medical advancements in developing the modern global economy and society; and	**21.6, 21.9**
	28.E identify the contributions of significant scientists and inventors such as Marie Curie, Thomas Edison, Albert Einstein, Louis Pasteur, and James Watt.	**13.1, 13.3, 17.5**

	WHERE YOU WILL FIND IT
29 **Social studies skills.** The student applies critical-thinking skills to organize and use information acquired from a variety of valid sources, including electronic technology. The student is expected to:	
29.A identify methods used by archaeologists, anthropologists, historians, and geographers to analyze evidence;	**1.1, 1.2**
29.B explain how historians, when examining sources, analyze frame of reference, historical context, and point of view to interpret historical events;	**1.1**
29.C explain the differences between primary and secondary sources and examine those sources to analyze frame of reference, historical context, and point of view;	**1.1**
29.D evaluate the validity of a source based on language, corroboration with other sources, and information about the author;	**1.1**
29.E identify bias in written, oral, and visual material;	**1.1**
29.F analyze information by sequencing, categorizing, identifying cause-and-effect relationships, comparing, contrasting, finding the main idea, summarizing, making generalizations and predictions, drawing inferences and conclusions, and developing connections between historical events over time;	**1.2, 1.3, 3.2, 4.1, 7.7, 8.2, 17.8**
29.G construct a thesis on a social studies issue or event supported by evidence; and	**12.1, 12.2**
29.H use appropriate reading and mathematical skills to interpret social studies information such as maps and graphs.	**1.2, 1.3, 6.1, 7.1, 7.4, 9.6**
30 **Social studies skills.** The student communicates in written, oral, and visual forms. The student is expected to:	
30.A use social studies terminology correctly;	**Topic 2 Topic Review and Assessment**
30.B use standard grammar, spelling, sentence structure, and punctuation;	**Topic 2 Topic Review and Assessment, Topic 12 Topic Review and Assessment**
30.C interpret and create written, oral, and visual presentations of social studies information; and	**2.1, 2.3**
30.D transfer information from one medium to another.	**7.1**
31 **Social studies skills.** The student uses problem-solving and decision-making skills, working independently and with others, in a variety of settings. The student is expected to:	
31.A use a problem-solving process to identify a problem, gather information, list and consider options, consider advantages and disadvantages, choose and implement a solution, and evaluate the effectiveness of the solution; and	**Topic 21 Topic Review and Assessment**
31.B use a decision-making process to identify a situation that requires a decision, gather information, identify options, predict consequences, and take action to implement a decision.	**17.8**

ELPS at a Glance

	WHERE YOU WILL FIND IT
1 **Cross-curricular second language acquisition/learning strategies.** The ELL uses language learning strategies to develop an awareness of his or her own learning processes in all content areas. In order for the ELL to meet grade-level learning expectations across the foundation and enrichment curriculum, all instruction delivered in English must be linguistically accommodated (communicated, sequenced, and scaffolded) commensurate with the student's level of English language proficiency. The student is expected to:	
(A) use prior knowledge and experiences to understand meanings in English	**1.1, 18.5, 19.1, 21.3, 21.4**
(B) monitor oral and written language production and employ self-corrective techniques or other resources	**1.3, 19.2, 21.5**
(C) use strategic learning techniques such as concept mapping, drawing, memorizing, comparing, contrasting, and reviewing to acquire basic and grade-level vocabulary	**2.2, 19.4, 21.7**
(D) speak using learning strategies such as requesting assistance, employing non-verbal cues, and using synonyms and circumlocution (conveying ideas by defining or describing when exact English words are not known)	**2.3, 19.5, 21.8**
(F) use accessible language and learn new and essential language in the process	**2.1, 3.4, 21.1**
2 **Cross-curricular second language acquisition/listening.** The ELL listens to a variety of speakers including teachers, peers, and electronic media to gain an increasing level of comprehension of newly acquired language in all content areas. ELLs may be at the beginning, intermediate, advanced, or advanced high stage of English language acquisition in listening. In order for the ELL to meet grade-level learning expectations across the foundation and enrichment curriculum, all instruction delivered in English must be linguistically accommodated (communicated, sequenced, and scaffolded) commensurate with the student's level of English language proficiency. The student is expected to:	
(C) learn new language structures, expressions, and basic and academic vocabulary heard during classroom instruction and interactions	**3.1, 3.2, 3.4, 3.5, 5.3, 5.4, 6.1, 6.2, 21.8, 21.9**
(D) monitor understanding of spoken language during classroom instruction and interactions and seek clarification as needed	**3.3, 3.4, 6.3, 6.4**
(E) use visual, contextual, and linguistic support to enhance and confirm understanding of increasingly complex and elaborated spoken language	**4.2, 7.2**
(I) demonstrate listening comprehension of increasingly complex spoken English by following directions, retelling or summarizing spoken messages, responding to questions and requests, collaborating with peers, and taking notes commensurate with content and grade-level needs	**7.5, 7.6, 7.7, 7.8, 9.2, 9.3, 9.4, 9.5**
3 **Cross-curricular second language acquisition/speaking.** The ELL speaks in a variety of modes for a variety of purposes with an awareness of different language registers (formal/informal) using vocabulary with increasing fluency and accuracy in language arts and all content areas. ELLs may be at the beginning, intermediate, advanced, or advanced high stage of English language acquisition in speaking. In order for the ELL to meet grade-level learning expectations across the foundation and enrichment curriculum, all instruction delivered in English must be linguistically accommodated (communicated, sequenced, and scaffolded) commensurate with the student's level of English language proficiency. The student is expected to:	
(B) expand and internalize initial English vocabulary by learning and using high-frequency English words necessary for identifying and describing people, places, and objects, by retelling simple stories and basic information represented or supported by pictures, and by learning and using routine language needed for classroom communication	**8.3, 8.4, 10.2, 10.3**
(C) speak using a variety of grammatical structures, sentence lengths, sentence types, and connecting words with increasing accuracy and ease as more English is acquired	**8.7, 9.1, 11.1, 11.2**

	WHERE YOU WILL FIND IT
(D) speak using grade-level content area vocabulary in context to internalize new English words and build academic language proficiency	**9.2, 9.3, 11.3, 11.4**
(E) share information in cooperative learning interactions	**9.4, 11.5**
(F) ask and give information ranging from using a very limited bank of high-frequency, high-need, concrete vocabulary, including key words and expressions needed for basic communication in academic and social contexts, to using abstract and content-based vocabulary during extended speaking assignments	**9.5, 9.6, 11.6, 17.8**
(G) express opinions, ideas, and feelings ranging from communicating single words and short phrases to participating in extended discussions on a variety of social and grade-appropriate academic topics	**10.1, 10.2, 12.1, 12.2**
(H) narrate, describe, and explain with increasing specificity and detail as more English is acquired	**11.1, 12.6**
4 **Cross-curricular second language acquisition/reading.** The ELL reads a variety of texts for a variety of purposes with an increasing level of comprehension in all content areas. ELLs may be at the beginning, intermediate, advanced, or advanced high stage of English language acquisition in reading. In order for the ELL to meet grade-level learning expectations across the foundation and enrichment curriculum, all instruction delivered in English must be linguistically accommodated (communicated, sequenced, and scaffolded) commensurate with the student's level of English language proficiency. For kindergarten and grade 1, certain of these student expectations apply to text read aloud for students not yet at the stage of decoding written text. The student is expected to:	
(C) develop basic sight vocabulary, derive meaning of environmental print, and comprehend English vocabulary and language structures used routinely in written classroom materials	**12.2, 12.3, 12.4, 12.5, 14.2, 14.3, 14.5**
(D) use prereading supports such as graphic organizers, illustrations, and pretaught topic-related vocabulary and other prereading activities to enhance comprehension of written text	**12.6, 14.6**
(E) read linguistically accommodated content area material with a decreasing need for linguistic accommodations as more English is learned	**12.7, 14.7**
(F) use visual and contextual support and support from peers and teachers to read grade-appropriate content area text, enhance and confirm understanding, and develop vocabulary, grasp of language structures, and background knowledge needed to comprehend increasingly challenging language	**12.8, 13.1, 13.2, 13.4, 14.1, 14.2, 14.3, 14.4, 14.5, 14.8, 15.1, 15.2, 15.4, 15.5, 15.6, 15.7, 15.8, 16.1**
(G) demonstrate comprehension of increasingly complex English by participating in shared reading, retelling or summarizing material, responding to questions, and taking notes commensurate with content area and grade level needs	**14.7, 14.8, 15.1, 16.3, 16.4, 17.1**

College and Career Readiness Standards

This program fully addresses the Texas College and Career Readiness Standards. Each of the concepts and skills is introduced in the Core Concepts lessons, Topic Inquiries, and 21st Century Skills Tutorials as shown in the chart below. These concepts and skills are then reinforced within the topics and lessons of the course as they play out in the course content. For example, students are introduced to the concept of migration in the Geography Core Concepts: Migration lesson but then encounter real examples of human migration in their study of history, contemporary cultures, or economic or political disruption.

CCR Standards	Core Concept Lessons and Topic Inquiries	21st Century Skills Tutorials
I. Interrelated Disciplines and Skills		
A. Spatial analysis of physical and cultural processes that shape the human experience		
I.A.1. Use the tools and concepts of geography appropriately and accurately.	· Geography Core Concepts: The Study of Earth · Geography Core Concepts: Ways to Show Earth's Surface	· Analyze Data and Models · Read Political Maps · Read Special-Purpose Maps · Use Parts of a Map
I.A.2. Analyze the interaction between human communities and the environment.	· Geography Core Concepts: Land Use · Geography Core Concepts: People's Impact on the Environment	· Analyze Data and Models · Read Political Maps · Read Special-Purpose Maps · Use Parts of a Map
I.A.3. Analyze how physical and cultural processes have shaped human communities over time.	· Culture Core Concepts: Cultural Diffusion and Change · Geography Core Concepts: Land Use	· Analyze Data and Models · Read Political Maps · Read Special-Purpose Maps · Use Parts of a Map
I.A.4. Evaluate the causes and effects of human migration patterns over time.	· Geography Core Concepts: Migration	· Analyze Cause and Effect
I.A.5. Analyze how various cultural regions have changed over time.	· Culture Core Concepts: Cultural Diffusion and Change	· Read Special-Purpose Maps
I.A.6. Analyze the relationship between geography and the development of human communities.	· Geography Core Concepts: Land Use	· Draw Conclusions · Draw Inferences
B. Periodization and chronological reasoning		
I.B.1. Examine how and why historians divide the past into eras.	· History Core Concepts: Measuring Time	· Categorize Sequence · Identify Trends
I.B.2. Identify and evaluate sources and patterns of change and continuity across time and place.	· Culture Core Concepts: Cultural Diffusion and Change · Culture Core Concepts: Science and Technology · History Core Concepts: How Do Historians Study History?	· Interpret Sources · Analyze Primary and Secondary Sources · Identify Trends
I.B.3. Analyze causes and effects of major political, economic, and social changes in U.S. and world history.	· History Core Concepts: How Do Historians Study History?	· Analyze Cause and Effect
C. Change and continuity of political ideologies, constitutions, and political behavior		
I.C.1. Evaluate different governmental systems and functions.	· Government and Civics Core Concepts: Foundations of Government · Government and Civics Core Concepts: Political Systems · Government and Civics Core Concepts: Political Structures	· Compare and Contrast · Draw Conclusions

CCR Standards	Core Concept Lessons and Topic Inquiries	21st Century Skills Tutorials
I. Interrelated Disciplines and Skills		
I.C.2. Evaluate changes in the functions and structures of government across time.	· Government and Civics Core Concepts: Foundations of Government · Government and Civics Core Concepts: Political Systems · Government and Civics Core Concepts: Political Structures	· Compare and Contrast · Draw Conclusions
I.C.3. Explain and analyze the importance of civic engagement.	· Government and Civics Core Concepts: Citizenship	· Being an Informed Citizen · Political Participation · Voting
D. Change and continuity of economic systems and processes		
I.D.1. Identify and evaluate the strengths and weaknesses of different economic systems.	· Economics Core Concepts: Economic Systems	· Identify Evidence · Compare and Contrast · Draw Conclusions
I.D.2. Analyze the basic functions and structures of international economics.	· Economics Core Concepts: Trade	· Analyze Data and Models · Read Charts, Graphs, and Tables
E. Change and continuity of social groups, civic organizations, institutions, and their interaction		
I.E.1. Identify different social groups (e.g., clubs, religious organizations) and examine how they form and how and why they sustain themselves.	· Culture Core Concepts: Families and Societies	· Develop Cultural Awareness · Develop a Clear Thesis
I.E.2. Define the concept of socialization and analyze the role socialization plays in human development and behavior.	· Culture Core Concepts: Families and Societies	· Develop Cultural Awareness · Develop a Clear Thesis
I.E.3. Analyze how social institutions (e.g., marriage, family, churches, schools) function and meet the needs of society.	· Culture Core Concepts: Families and Societies	· Develop Cultural Awareness · Develop a Clear Thesis
I.E.4. Identify and evaluate the sources and consequences of social conflict.	· Culture Core Concepts: Families and Societies	· Develop Cultural Awareness · Analyze Cause and Effect
F. Problem-solving and decision-making skills		
I.F.1. Use a variety of research and analytical tools to explore questions or issues thoroughly and fairly.	· History Core Concepts: How Do Historians Study History?	· Ask Questions · Analyze Media Content · Analyze Primary and Secondary Sources · Compare Viewpoints · Dinstinguish Between Fact and Opinion · Identify Bias · Search for Information on the Internet
I.F.2. Analyze ethical issues in historical, cultural, and social contexts.	· Culture Core Concepts: Families and Societies · Culture Core Concepts: Science and Technology	· Develop Cultural Awareness · Support Ideas With Evidence

College and Career Readiness Standards

CCR Standards	Core Concept Lessons and Topic Inquiries	21st Century Skills Tutorials
II. Diverse Human Perspectives and Experiences		
A. Multicultural societies		
II.A.1. Define a "multicultural society" and consider both the positive and negative qualities of multiculturalism.	· Culture Core Concepts: Families and Societies	· Consider and Counter Opposing Arguments · Compare and Contrast
II.A.2. Evaluate the experiences and contributions of diverse groups to multicultural societies.	· Culture Core Concepts: Families and Societies	· Draw Conclusions · Identify Evidence
B. Factors that influence personal and group identities (e.g., race, ethnicity, gender, nationality, institutional affiliations, socioeconomic status)		
II.B.1. Explain and evaluate the concepts of race, ethnicity, and nationalism.	· Culture Core Concepts: What Is Culture?	· Develop Cultural Awareness · Organize Your Ideas · Support Ideas with Evidence
II.B.2. Explain and evaluate the concept of gender.	· Culture Core Concepts: Families and Societies	· Develop Cultural Awareness · Organize Your Ideas · Support Ideas with Evidence
II.B.3. Analyze diverse religious concepts, structures, and institutions around the world.	· Culture Core Concepts: Religion	· Develop Cultural Awareness · Organize Your Ideas · Support Ideas with Evidence
II.B.4. Evaluate how major philosophical and intellectual concepts influence human behavior or identity.	· Culture Core Concepts: Religion	· Develop Cultural Awareness · Organize Your Ideas · Support Ideas with Evidence
II.B.5. Explain the concepts of socioeconomic status and stratification.	· Culture Core Concepts: Families and Societies	· Develop Cultural Awareness · Organize Your Ideas · Support Ideas with Evidence
II.B.6. Analyze how individual and group identities are established and change over time.	· Culture Core Concepts: Families and Societies	· Develop Cultural Awareness · Organize Your Ideas · Support Ideas with Evidence
III. Interdependence of Global Communities		
A. Spatial understanding of global, regional, national, and local communities		
III.A.1. Distinguish spatial patterns of human communities that exist between or within contemporary political boundaries.	· Geography Core Concepts: Understanding Maps · Geography Core Concepts: Population · Geography Core Concepts: Urbanization	· Analyze Data and Models · Read Political Maps · Read Special-Purpose Maps · Use Parts of a Map
III.A.2. Connect regional or local developments to global ones.	· Culture Core Concepts: Science and Technology · Geography Core Concepts: Migration · Geography Core Concepts: Population	· Analyze Data and Models · Read Political Maps · Read Special-Purpose Maps · Draw Conclusions
III.A.3. Analyze how and why diverse communities interact and become dependent on each other.	· Culture Core Concepts: Families and Societies · Economics Core Concepts: Trade · Geography Core Concepts: Migration	· Analyze Data and Models · Draw Conclusions

CCR Standards	Core Concept Lessons and Topic Inquiries	21st Century Skills Tutorials
III. Interdependence of Global Communities		
III.B.1. Apply social studies methodologies to compare societies and cultures.	· Culture Core Concepts: Families and Societies	· Create a Research Hypothesis · Evaluate Web Sites · Ask Questions · Compare and Contrast · Interpret Sources · Support Ideas With Evidence
IV. Analysis, Synthesis, and Evaluation of Information		
A. Critical examination of texts, images, and other sources of information		
IV.A.1. Identify and analyze the main idea(s) and point(s)-of-view in sources.	· History Core Concepts: How Do Historians Study History? · History Core Concepts: Historical Sources · History Core Concepts: Archaeology and Other Sources · Topic Inquiry: Document-Based Question · Topic Inquiry: Civic Discussion	· Identify Main Ideas and Details · Compare Viewpoints · Distinguish Between Fact and Opinion · Identify Bias
IV.A.2. Situate an informational source in its appropriate contexts (contemporary, historical, cultural).	· History Core Concepts: How Do Historians Study History? · History Core Concepts: Historical Sources · History Core Concepts: Archaeology and Other Sources	· Analyze Media Content · Analyze Primary and Secondary Sources · Analyze Data and Models · Analyze Images · Analyze Political Cartoons · Evaluate Web Sites
IV.A.3. Evaluate sources from multiple perspectives.	· History Core Concepts: How Do Historians Study History? · History Core Concepts: Historical Sources · History Core Concepts: Archaeology and Other Sources	· Compare Viewpoints · Consider and Counter Opposing Arguments
IV.A.4. Understand the differences between a primary and secondary source and use each appropriately to conduct research and construct arguments.	· History Core Concepts: How Do Historians Study History? · History Core Concepts: Historical Sources · History Core Concepts: Archaeology and Other Sources	· Analyze Primary and Secondary Sources · Identify Evidence · Develop a Clear Thesis · Organize Your Ideas · Support Ideas With Evidence
IV.A.5. Read narrative texts critically.	· History Core Concepts: How Do Historians Study History? · History Core Concepts: Historical Sources	· Ask Questions · Identify Main Ideas and Details · Set a Purpose for Reading · Use Context Clues · Summarize
IV.A.6. Read research data critically.	· History Core Concepts: How Do Historians Study History? · History Core Concepts: Historical Sources · History Core Concepts: Archaeology and Other Sources	· Analyze Data and Models

College and Career Readiness Standards

CCR Standards	Core Concept Lessons and Topic Inquiries	21st Century Skills Tutorials
IV. Analysis, Synthesis, and Evaluation of Information		
B. Research and methods		
IV.B.1. Use established research methodologies.	· History Core Concepts: How Do Historians Study History? · History Core Concepts: Historical Sources · History Core Concepts: Archaeology and Other Sources	· Create a Research Hypothesis · Evaluate Web Sites · Ask Questions · Compare and Contrast · Interpret Sources · Identify Evidence · Support Ideas With Evidence · Develop a Clear Thesis · Organize Your Ideas
IV.B.2. Explain how historians and other social scientists develop new and competing views of past phenomena.	· History Core Concepts: How Do Historians Study History? · History Core Concepts: Historical Sources · History Core Concepts: Archaeology and Other Sources	· Evaluate Existing Arguments · Interpret Sources · Create a Research Hypothesis · Work in Teams · Innovate · Publish Your Work
IV.B.3. Gather, organize, and display the results of data and research.	· History Core Concepts: How Do Historians Study History? · History Core Concepts: Historical Sources · History Core Concepts: Archaeology and Other Sources · Topic Inquiry: Project-Based Learning	· Give an Effective Presentation · Create Charts and Maps · Create Databases
IV.B.4. Identify and collect sources.	· History Core Concepts: How Do Historians Study History? · History Core Concepts: Historical Sources · History Core Concepts: Archaeology and Other Sources · Topic Inquiry: Project-Based Learning	· Identify Evidence · Search for Information on the Internet · Take Effective Notes
C. Critical listening		
IV.C.1. Understand and interpret presentations (e.g., speeches, lectures, informal presentations) critically.	· Topic Inquiry: Civic Discussion	· Participate in a Discussion or Debate · Take Effective Notes · Analyze Media Content
D. Reaching conclusions		
IV.D.1. Construct a thesis that is supported by evidence.	· History Core Concepts: How Do Historians Study History? · History Core Concepts: Historical Sources · Topic Inquiry: Document-Based Question · Topic Inquiry: Civic Discussion	· Develop a Clear Thesis · Support Ideas With Evidence

CCR Standards	Core Concept Lessons and Topic Inquiries	21st Century Skills Tutorials
IV. Analysis, Synthesis, and Evaluation of Information		
IV.D.2. Recognize and evaluate counter-arguments.	· History Core Concepts: How Do Historians Study History? · History Core Concepts: Historical Sources · Topic Inquiry: Civic Discussion	· Consider and Counter Opposing Arguments · Evaluate Existing Arguments
V. Effective Communication		
A. Clear and coherent oral and written communication		
V.A.1. Use appropriate oral communication techniques depending on the context or nature of the interaction.	· History Core Concepts: How Do Historians Study History? · History Core Concepts: Historical Sources · Topic Inquiry: Civic Discussion	· Give an Effective Presentation · Participate in a Discussion or Debate
V.A.2. Use conventions of standard written English.	· History Core Concepts: How Do Historians Study History? · History Core Concepts: Historical Sources · Topic Inquiry: Document-Based Question	· Give an Effective Presentation · Publish Your Work · Write an Essay
B. Academic integrity		
V.B.1. Attribute ideas and information to source materials and authors.	· History Core Concepts: How Do Historians Study History? · History Core Concepts: Historical Sources · Topic Inquiry: Document-Based Question	· Avoid Plagiarism

Creating an Active Classroom

This Texas Social Studies program places a strong emphasis on **Inquiry** in the form of

- Document-Based Questions
- Project-Based Learning
- Civic Discussions

Each inquiry strand requires students to formulate their own arguments based on evidence. To support this learning approach, the program integrates **Active Classroom strategies** throughout each lesson. These strategies encourage students to begin building their own arguments and collecting evidence about the past and present at even the earliest stages of a lesson.

You can use these strategies to help students participate in their own learning as you call upon them to

- draw
- write
- speak
- decide

You'll find a rich variety of these strategy suggestions throughout both the Teacher's Edition and online **Teacher Support** for each lesson.

ACTIVE CLASSROOM STRATEGIES	
ACTIVITY NAME	**HOW TO ACTIVATE**
Quickdraw	· Pair students and give them 30 seconds to share what they know about a concept or Key Term by creating a symbol or drawing.
Graffiti Concepts	· Ask students to reflect on the meaning of a concept or idea and create a visual image and/or written phrase that represents that concept. Allow approximately 3–5 minutes. · Next ask students to post their "graffiti" on the board or on chart paper and ask students to look at all the various responses. · Next discuss similarities and differences in the responses as a group.
Word Wall	· Ask students to chose one of the Key Terms for the lesson and create a visual image with a text definition. Allow approximately 3–5 minutes. · Ask students to post their words on the board or on chart paper and ask students to look at all the various responses. · Discuss similarities and differences in the responses as a group. · Pick a few favorites and post them on the class "Word Wall" for the year.
Cartoon It	· Ask students to make a quick drawing of one compelling image from this lesson on a piece of paper. · Next ask students to turn their drawing into a political cartoon that illustrates a key concept or main idea from the lesson by adding a text caption or text "bubbles." · Ask students to share their cartoons with a partner or within small groups.
Wallpaper	· Ask students to review information they have learned in a topic and design a piece of "wallpaper" that encapsulates key learnings. · Then have students post their wallpaper and take a "gallery" walk noting what others have written and illustrated in their samples.
Quick Write	· Ask students to write what they know about a key idea or term in 30 seconds.
Make Headlines	· Have students write a headline that captures the key idea in a map, photo, timeline, or reading. · Ask students to share their headline with a partner.
Circle Write	· Break into groups and provide a writing prompt or key question. · Have students write as much as they can in response to the question or prompt for 1 minute. · Next have students give their response to the person on their right. That person should improve or elaborate on the response where the other person left off. · Continue to pass each response to the right until the original response comes back to the first person. · Each group then reviews all the responses and decides which is the best composition and shares that with the larger group.

Creating an Active Classroom

ACTIVE CLASSROOM STRATEGIES

ACTIVITY NAME	HOW TO ACTIVATE
Write 1-Get 3 (or Write 5-Get 4)	· Ask a question with multiple answers, such as: What are 4 key characteristics of ______ (a dictator)? What are the 5 key causes of _____? · Have students write down 1 response and then go around the room asking for 3 other responses. If they think a response is correct, ask them to write it down. · Have students keep asking and writing until they have 3 more responses on their page. · Have students share and discuss responses with the class.
Sticky Notes	· Ask students to spend three minutes jotting down their response to a critical thinking question on a sticky note. · Ask students to work in pairs and share their responses. · Next ask students to post their sticky notes on the board or on chart paper and read all the notes. · Discuss similarities and differences in the responses as a group.
Connect Two	· Select 10 to 12 words or phrases you think are important for students to know prior to reading a selection. · List the words on the board. · Ask students to "Connect Two" or choose two words they think might belong together, and state the reason. "I would connect ______ and ______ because ______." Consider posting their Connect Two statements on the board. · As students read the text they should look for evidence to support or refute their Connect Two statements.
Conversation With History	· Ask students to choose one of the people mentioned or pictured in the text and write down a question they would like to ask that person if they could. · Next ask students to write what they think that person would say in response and then what they would say in response to that.
Walking Tour	· Post passages from a reading around the room. · Ask small groups to tour the room and discuss each passage. · Summarize each passage as a class. · Alternatively, assign each small group to a passage and have them summarize that passage for the rest of the class.
Audio Tour	· Ask students to work in pairs. Have the first student give the second a verbal "tour" of a map or graph or infographic. · Have the second student give the first an explanation of what the graphic shows.

ACTIVE CLASSROOM STRATEGIES

ACTIVITY NAME	HOW TO ACTIVATE
My Metaphor	· Post the following metaphor on the board: This (map, timeline, image, primary source) shows that _____ is like _________ because __________________. · Ask students to fill in the metaphor prompt based on their understanding of the source.
Act It Out	· Choose an image in the lesson and ask students to think about one of the following questions as appropriate to the image: · What may have happened next in this image? · What may have happened just before this image? · What do you think the people in this image are thinking? · What do you think the people in this image are saying to each other?
If Photos/Images/Art Could Talk	· Ask the following questions about an image in the course: What do you think the person in this photo would say if they could talk? What's your evidence?
See-Think-Wonder	· Ask students to work in pairs. · Ask them to look at an image, map, or graph and answer these questions: · What do you see? · What does that make you think? · What are you wondering about now that you've seen this? · Have students share their answers with the class.
A Closer Look	· Project a map or image on the board and divide it into four numbered quadrants. · Have students count off from 1 to 4 into four small groups. Have each group look closely at the part of the image in their quadrant. · Have each small group report on what they observed and learned as a result of their focus on this part of the image.

ACTIVE CLASSROOM STRATEGIES	
ACTIVITY NAME	**HOW TO ACTIVATE**
Take a Stand	· Ask students to take a stand on a yes-or-no or agree/disagree critical thinking question. · Ask students to divide into two groups based on their answer and move to separate areas of the classroom. · Ask students to talk with each other to compare their reasons for answering yes or no. · Ask a representative from each side to present and defend the group's point of view. · Note: you can adapt this activity to have students take their place on a continuum line from 1 to 10 depending on how strongly they agree or disagree.
Rank It	· List a group of items/concepts/steps/causes/events on the board. · Ask students to rank the items/steps . . . according to X criteria (which is most important, which had the greatest impact . . . most influential, essential, changed, affected). · Ask students to provide a justification for the ranking decisions they made. · Then ask students to work in pairs to share their rankings and justifications. · Poll the class to see if there is agreement on the ranking. OR · Place stickies on the board with key events from the lesson or topic. · Break students into small groups and ask each group to go up and choose the sticky with what they think is the most significant event. · Ask the group to discuss among themselves why they think it is most significant. · Ask one person from each group to explain why the group chose that event.
Sequence It	· Place key events from a lesson or topic on sticky notes on the board. · Ask students to place the events in chronological order. · You could do this activity with multiple groups in different parts of the classroom.
PMI Plus/Minus/Interesting	· Place students in groups and give each group a 3-column organizer with headings Plus/Minus/Interesting for recording responses. · Ask students to analyze a text or examine an issue and then answer these three questions in their organizer: 1. What was positive about this text/issue? 2. What was negative about this text/issue? 3. What was interesting about this text/issue?

Celebrate Freedom

PRINT STUDENT EDITION

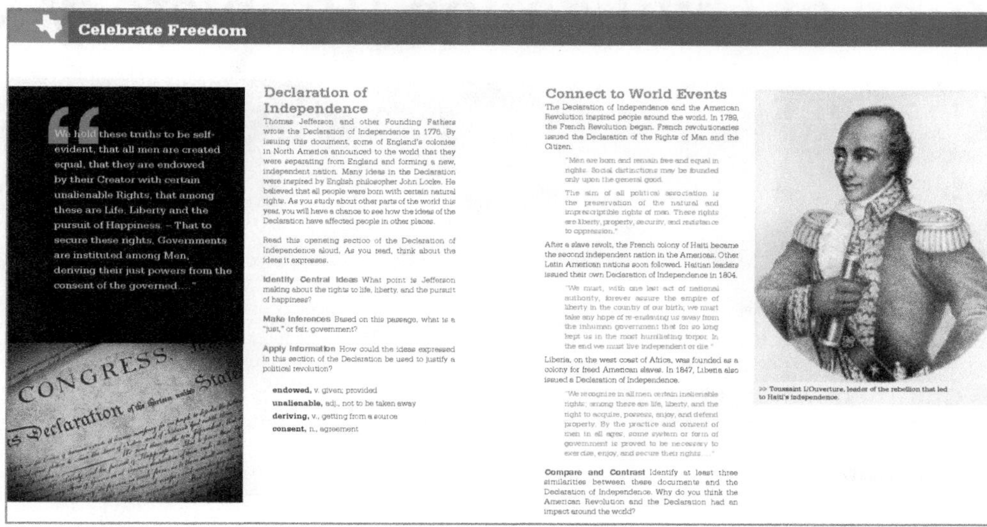

Celebrate Freedom

"We hold these truths to be self-evident, that all men are created equal, that they are endowed by their Creator with certain unalienable Rights, that among these are Life, Liberty and the pursuit of Happiness. – That to secure these rights, Governments are instituted among Men, deriving their just powers from the consent of the governed. . . ."

Declaration of Independence

Thomas Jefferson and other Founding Fathers wrote the Declaration of Independence in 1776. By issuing this document, some of England's colonies in North America announced to the world that they were separating from England and forming a new, independent nation. Many ideas in the Declaration were inspired by English philosopher John Locke. He believed that all people were born with certain natural rights. As you study about other parts of the world this year, you will have a chance to see how the ideas of the Declaration have affected people in other places.

Read this opening section of the Declaration of Independence aloud. As you read, think about the ideas it expresses.

Identify Central Ideas What point is Jefferson making about the rights to life, liberty, and the pursuit of happiness?

Make Inferences Based on this passage, what is a "just," or fair, government?

Apply Information How could the ideas expressed in this section of the Declaration be used to justify a political revolution?

endowed, v. given; provided
unalienable, adj., not to be taken away
deriving, v., getting from a source
consent, n., agreement

Connect to World Events

The Declaration of Independence and the American Revolution inspired people around the world. In 1789, the French Revolution began. French revolutionaries issued the Declaration of the Rights of Man and the Citizen.

"Men are born and remain free and equal in rights. Social distinctions may be founded only upon the general good.

The aim of all political association is the preservation of the natural and imprescriptible rights of man. These rights are liberty, property, security, and resistance to oppression."

After a slave revolt, the French colony of Haiti became the second independent nation in the Americas. Other Latin American nations soon followed. Haitian leaders issued their own Declaration of Independence in 1804.

"We must, with one last act of national authority, forever assure the empire of liberty in the country of our birth; we must take any hope of re-enslaving us away from the inhuman government that for so long kept us in the most humiliating torpor. In the end we must live independent or die."

Liberia, on the west coast of Africa, was founded as a colony for freed American slaves. In 1847, Liberia also issued a Declaration of Independence.

"We recognize in all men certain inalienable rights; among these are life, liberty, and the right to acquire, possess, enjoy, and defend property. By the practice and consent of men in all ages, some system or form of government is proved to be necessary to exercise, enjoy, and secure their rights. . . ."

Compare and Contrast Identify at least three similarities between these documents and the Declaration of Independence. Why do you think the American Revolution and the Declaration had an impact around the world?

>> Toussaint L'Ouverture, leader of the rebellion that led to Haiti's independence.

Objective 1: Understand the intent, meaning, and importance of the Declaration of Independence; 2: Recite the opening text from the Declaration of Independence.

Quick Instruction

Using these materials, students can prepare for Celebrate Freedom Week by thinking about the importance of the Declaration of Independence. The materials will help you make links between the Declaration and your course of study.

Aa Vocabulary Development: Before students recite the words from the Declaration, review key terms such as "endowed," "unalienable," "deriving," and "consent." Ask students to compose a sentence using each word. Then have students paraphrase the excerpt from the Declaration, putting the ideas into their own words.

Have students recite the key section from the Declaration of Independence, "We hold these truths . . ." to each other or as a whole class.

Identify Central Ideas *that everyone is entitled to these rights*

Make Inferences *a government that is based on the will of the people*

Apply Information *Government gets its power from the people, so if it does not follow the wishes of the people, the people have the right to change the government, even if it means by revolution.*

Further Instruction

Connect to World Events

Plan Have students read the documents from France, Haiti, and Liberia. Ask them to look for phrases and terms that are similar in each of these documents, including the Declaration of Independence.

Explore Organize students into three groups and assign one historical document to each group. Have students paraphrase their document to be sure they understand it. Then have the groups share their understandings with the class.

Communicate Ask students to think about the rights mentioned in these documents. What does each right mentioned refer to? For example, what does the "right to security" mean? the "right to property?" Why do they think each of these is so important that it is specifically called out in these documents?

Compare and Contrast *Similarities include: government is based on mutual consent of the people and is charged with preserving their rights; people are free and equal, and are entitled to certain rights such as life, liberty, and property; people have the right to resist oppression.*

Possible answer: The Declaration inspired other people to recognize their rights, and the idea that Americans could be successful in their revolution encouraged people around the world to gain these rights for themselves.

ADDITIONAL LESSON RESOURCES

- Print student text
- Declaration of Independence
- United States Constitution
- Pledge of Allegiance to the U.S. Flag
- Pledge of Allegiance to the Texas Flag
- Celebrate Freedom Resources

Origins of Civilization (Prehistory–300 B.C.)

TOPIC 1 ORGANIZER	PACING: APPROX. 1 PERIOD, .5 BLOCKS		
	PACING	TEKS	ELPS
Connect	1 period		
MY STORY VIDEO **Uncovering the Past**	10 min.		
DIGITAL ESSENTIAL QUESTION ACTIVITY **Why is Culture Important?**	10 min.	2.B	
DIGITAL TIMELINE ACTIVITY **Early Civilizations**	10 min.	1.A	
TOPIC INQUIRY: PROJECT-BASED LEARNING **Create an Early Civilizations Video Game**	20 min.		
Investigate	1–3 periods		
TOPIC INQUIRY: PROJECT-BASED LEARNING **Create an Early Civilizations Video Game**	Ongoing		
LESSON 1 **Learning About Our Past**	30–40 min.	29.A	1.A.1, 1.E.2
LESSON 2 **The Neolithic Revolution**	30–40 min.	1.A, 2.A, 17.A, 17.B	1.E.3
LESSON 3 **Civilization Begins**	30–40 min.	1.A, 2.A, 2.B, 16.A, 16.B, 17.A, 17.B, 19.A, 19.B	1.E.4, 1.B.1
Synthesize	1 period		
DIGITAL ESSENTIAL QUESTION ACTIVITY **Reflect on the Essential Question and Topic**	10 min.	2.B	
TOPIC INQUIRY: PROJECT-BASED LEARNING **Create an Early Civilizations Video Game**	20 min.		
Demonstrate	1–2 periods		
DIGITAL TOPIC TEST **Origins of Civilization**	10 min.		
TOPIC INQUIRY: PROJECT-BASED LEARNING **Create an Early Civilizations Video Game**	20 min.		

AUTHOR'S NOTE

The Discovery of Agriculture

Agriculture most likely began with the simple practice of harvesting edible grains found growing wild, part of the normal food-gathering procedures of Old Stone Age people. Alert gatherers might sometimes encourage the ripening of the crop by extra care—for instance, by watering plants at the end of a dry summer. But the great break-through came when the bands of *Homo sapiens sapiens* learned to plant some of the grain in order to guarantee a harvest the following year. Wherever this occurred—with wheat and barely in the Near East, millet in North China, corn in Central America—the wandering days of the hunting band were numbered and a new way of life was set in train. . . .

Life thus grew in complexity as the Neolithic centuries rolled on. The settled agricultural peoples of the Near East, like their fellows in many parts of the globe, learned to cultivate their stock to fertilize their croplands. They discovered how to breed stock for meat or for strength, how to use milk, milk products, and other animal and vegetable products seldom utilized by their hunting-and-gathering predecessors. First in the rain-watered hills, then in the river valleys that provide the most fertile land, these prehistoric farmers reaped a greater bounty than nature had normally provided for their Paleolithic ancestors.

Above all, they grew in numbers. Farming was hard work, probably more demanding than hunting and gathering had been. But agriculture had the great advantage of feeding many more people from the same tract of land than could be fed by hunting and gathering. One estimate suggests that whereas the foraging economy could support one person per square kilometer, even primitive farming could feed fifty persons from a single square kilometer. From this population growth came the Neolithic agricultural village and—in time—the city, the political state, and all their history.

—Anthony Esler, *The Human Venture: From Prehistory to the Present,* (Upper Saddle River, New Jersey: Pearson Education, 2004), pp. 21–23

TOPIC INQUIRY: PROJECT-BASED LEARNING

Create an Early Civilizations Video Game

TEKS 1.A, 2.A, 2.B, 16.B, 17.A, 29.F, 29.H, 30.B, 30.C, 30.D, 31.B

In this Topic Inquiry, students will work in teams to create a video game that illustrates how culture impacted early peoples' progression through the stages of civilization. Learning about culture and its impact on each stage of development of early civilizations will deepen students' understanding of how the cultures of hunter-gatherers and Neolithic civilizations led to the establishment of complex river valley civilizations. It will also contribute to their understanding of the Topic Essential Question: Why is culture important?

STEP 1: CONNECT

Develop Questions and Plan the Investigation

Launch the Project and Generate Questions

Display the Entry Event, which is a fictional letter from an archaeological society. Direct students to critical points in the letter. Tell students that for this project, they will learn why culture is important, based on how early people shifted from simple nomadic bands to complex river valley civilizations.

Divide the class into teams of four to six students. Explain that each team will research, plan, and create a video game about the development of early cultures/civilizations. Tell students that their video games should include goals and a way for players to advance through each of the three stages. It must allow every player to perform as the leader of people at each of three stages, from hunter-gatherer bands to Neolithic villages to people of river valley civilizations. The choices will allow players and their team to either advance to the next stage or decline.

Then project and review with students the bullet-point list of key features of the three stages of culture and civilizations that students will study. Point out that they can use the key features of each stage to design "worlds" or game environments for their video games.

Finally, provide time for teams to discuss the bullet-point list. Have them brainstorm ideas about features of Stone Age hunter-gatherer clans, Neolithic villages, and river valley civilizations that led them to advance or establish the next stage.

Resources

- Project Tracker
- Entry Event
- Rubric for an Early Civilizations Video Game
- Need-to-Know Questions
- Work in Teams Tutorial
- Student Instructions

STEP 2: INVESTIGATE

Apply Disciplinary Concepts and Tools

Collect Source Material

Prepare for Project Work Have students complete the 21st Century Skills Tutorial *Search for Information on the Internet* to review tips for finding information online. Then, guide a discussion of tips from the tutorial, emphasising key ideas. Project the list of possible sources and invite students to suggest why they might be useful. You may want to project one of the sites such as the Smithsonian: National Museum of Natural History, Early Stone Age Tools, as an example of a site with information targeted to a particular stage, and features of that stage of human development.

If time allows, have students begin researching early civilizations. Remind students to complete assigned tasks and fill in the Project Tracker as tasks are completed. Remind students that when searching online or in other sources, they should choose sources that are related to the features of the culture or civilizations that lead toward its development to the next level of civilization. Tell them to use the *Need-to-Know Questions* to help focus their research and notes. Encourage students to consult the readings and activities for this Topic, along with conducting research to try to answer all of the questions, or as many as possible with the information available.

Create and Edit Flowcharts and Content Charts

Project the first page of the *Information Organizer: Early Civilizations Video Game*. Explain that this flowchart will help them organize and design the structure, story, and mechanics of their video game. Tell students to add, delete, and rename shapes in the flowchart to fit their ideas.

Resources

- 21st Century Skills Tutorial *Search for Information on the Internet*
- Information Organizer

STEP 3: SYNTHESIZE

Evaluate Sources and Use Evidence to Formulate Conclusions

Build Your Video Game

Build Your Video Game Project the second page of the *Information Organizer: Early Civilization Video Game*. Explain that this chart will help guide their team to describe each part of their game. Have students complete one chart for each aspect of their video game, including its player goals and options, stories, mechanics, rules, and the media elements they will use. Then have them return to the flowchart(s) to begin building their game. Stress that their game should have options with rewards that lead to advancement through stages or levels to win the game and that there can be multiple ways to win. Remind them to focus on the relationship between culture and the progression of early peoples, through stages, to the establishment of river valley civilizations.

Once students have finished researching, creating, and editing narratives and have planned how to design their video game using the chart, have them work as a team to build their video game with a free software program such as *Unity 3d* [https://unity3d.com/unity/download]. Remind students that they are not required to use Unity 3d and may use any video game building tool you approve to create their video game.

Write a Conclusion

Tell students they should write a thorough conclusion that clearly describes some of the important things they learned from creating a video game about the three stages of culture/civilization. Remind students that their conclusions should demonstrate an understanding of why culture is important. Project and discuss questions to help students focus their conclusions. Think about how the information you used in your game showed what made each culture distinctive, and helped the culture progress.

STEP 4: DEMONSTRATE

Communicate Conclusions and Take Informed Action

Present Your Early Civilizations Video Game

Before students present their video game, suggest that they review the 21st Century Skills Tutorial: Give an Effective Presentation. Have students project their video game and invite their audience to observe as they demonstrate their video game and explain their findings and conclusions. Remind students to ask their audience to share their reactions to their video game work. Allow time for questions and answers, and if time allows, for teams to play each other's games.

Reflect on the Project

After students have finished creating and presenting their video games, provide your assessment, and help them identify what worked well and where improvements could be beneficial, so they can incorporate feedback to use for future projects. When all teams have completed their video games and presentations, schedule time for meetings to allow teams to reflect on what they have learned and how their group worked together as a team. Then, have all team members complete the **Self Assessment.**

Resources

- 21st Century Skills Tutorial: Give an Effective Presentation
- Self Assessment

PROFESSIONAL DEVELOPMENT

Project-Based Learning

Be sure to view the Project-Based Learning Professional Development resources in the online course.

Learning About Our Past

Objectives

Objective 1: Learn how scholars study the historical past.

Objective 2: Find out how anthropologists investigate the period of prehistory.

Objective 3: Understand how discoveries in Africa and beyond have influenced anthropologists' views about early humans and their ancestors.

LESSON 1 ORGANIZER	PACING: APPROX. 1 PERIOD, .5 BLOCKS					
			RESOURCES			
	OBJECTIVES	PACING	Print	Online	TEKS	ELPS
Connect						
DIGITAL START UP ACTIVITY **Learning About Our Past**		5 min.		●	29.A	
Investigate						
READ **Studying Prehistory**	Objective 1	10 min.	●	●	29.A, 29.B	1.A.1
INTERACTIVE GALLERY **Piecing the Past Together**		10 min.		●	29.A, 29.B	
READ **Investigating Prehistory**	Objective 2	10 min.	●	●	29.A, 29.B	
READ **Discoveries in Africa and Beyond**	Objective 3	10 min.	●	●	29.B	1.E.2
INTERACTIVE MAP **Migrations of *Homo sapiens***		10 min.		●		
Synthesize						
DIGITAL ACTIVITY **Archaeologists at Work**		5 min.		●	29.A	
Demonstrate						
DIGITAL QUIZ **Lesson Quiz and Class Discussion Board**		10 min.		●	29.A, 29.B	

www.PearsonTexas.com
Access your Digital Lesson

Focus on Texas Standards

Texas Essential Knowledge and Skills

29.A identify methods used by archaeologists, anthropologists, historians, and geographers to analyze evidence

NOTES

The Neolithic Revolution

Objectives

Objective 1: Describe the skills and beliefs that early modern humans developed during the Old Stone Age.

Objective 2: Analyze why the development of agriculture is considered the start of the New Stone Age and the Neolithic Revolution.

Objective 3: Explain how the Neolithic Revolution dramatically changed the way people lived.

LESSON 2 ORGANIZER	PACING: APPROX. 1 PERIOD, .5 BLOCKS					
			RESOURCES			
	OBJECTIVES	PACING	Print	Online	TEKS	ELPS
Connect						
DIGITAL START UP ACTIVITY **The Neolithic Revolution**		5 min.		●	1.A, 17A	
Investigate						
READ **Old Stone Age Skills and Beliefs**	Objective 1	10 min.	●	●	17.A	
INTERACTIVE GALLERY **Neolithic Cave Art**		10 min.		●	2.A, 17.A, 29.A, 29.B	
READ **Farming Begins a New Stone Age**	Objective 2	10 min.	●	●	1.A, 2.A	1.E.3
READ **Dramatic Change With the Neolithic Revolution**	Objective 3	10 min.	●	●	17.A, 17.B	
INTERACTIVE GALLERY **Otzi—the Neolithic Ice Man**		10 min.		●	1.A, 17.A	
Synthesize						
DIGITAL ACTIVITY **Paleolithic Versus Neolithic**		5 min.		●	1.A, 17.A, 17.B	
Demonstrate						
DIGITAL QUIZ **Lesson Quiz and Class Discussion Board**		10 min.		●	1.A, 17.A, 17B	

PEARSON realize™ www.PearsonTexas.com Access your Digital Lesson

Focus on Texas Standards

Texas Essential Knowledge and Skills

1.A identify major causes and describe the major effects of the following events from 8000 BC to 500 BC: the development of agriculture and the development of the river valley civilizations

2.A summarize the impact of the development of farming (Neolithic Revolution) on the creation of river valley civilizations

17.A identify important changes in human life caused by the Neolithic Revolution and the Industrial Revolution

17.B summarize the role of economics in driving political changes as related to the Neolithic Revolution and the Industrial Revolution

NOTES

Civilization Begins

Objectives

Objective 1: Analyze the conditions under which the first cities and civilizations arose.

Objective 2: Outline the basic features that define civilization.

Objective 3: Understand the ways in which civilizations have changed over time.

LESSON 3 ORGANIZER	PACING: APPROX. 1 PERIOD, .5 BLOCKS					
			RESOURCES			
	OBJECTIVES	PACING	Print	Online	TEKS	ELPS
Connect						
DIGITAL START UP ACTIVITY **Civilization Begins**		5 min.		●	2.B	
Investigate						
READ **The First Cities and Civilizations**	Objective 1	10 min.		●	1.A, 16.B	1.E.4
INTERACTIVE MAP **River Valley Civilizations**	Objective 1	10 min.		●	1.A, 16.A, 16.B, 16.C	
READ **Features That Define Civilization**	Objective 2	10 min.		●	1.A, 2.A, 16.B, 17.A, 19.A, 19.B	1.B.1
INTERACTIVE CHART **The Rise of River Valley Civilizations**	Objective 2	10 min.		●	16.B	
READ **Civilizations Change**	Objective 3	10 min.		●	16.B	
Synthesize						
DIGITAL ACTIVITY **Cities and Civilizations Arise: Cause and Effect**		5 min.		●	1.A, 2.A	
Demonstrate						
DIGITAL QUIZ **Lesson Quiz and Class Discussion Board**		10 min.		●	1.A, 2.B, 16.A, 16.C	

Focus on Texas Standards

Texas Essential Knowledge and Skills

1.A identify major causes and describe the major effects of the following events from 8000 BC to 500 BC: the development of agriculture and the development of the river valley civilizations

2.A summarize the impact of the development of farming (Neolithic Revolution) on the creation of river valley civilizations

2.B identify the characteristics of civilization

16.A locate places and regions of historical significance directly related to major eras and turning points in world history

16.B analyze the influence of human and physical geographic factors on major events in world history, including the development of river valley civilizations, trade in the Indian Ocean, and the opening of the Panama and Suez canals

17.A identify important changes in human life caused by the Neolithic Revolution and the Industrial Revolution

17.B summarize the role of economics in driving political changes as related to the Neolithic Revolution and the Industrial Revolution

19.A identify the characteristics of monarchies and theocracies as forms of government in early civilizations

19.B identify the characteristics of the following political systems: theocracy, absolute monarchy, democracy, republic, oligarchy, limited monarchy, and totalitarianism

NOTES

Origins of Civilization (Prehistory–300 B.C.)

In this Topic, you will learn about the origins of human civilization. You know the TEKS are very important, and this course will make it fun to learn about the things that will help you master them. Keep reading to see how.

LESSON OUTLINE

Your study will help you master these TEKS:

TEKS

1.A, 2.A, 2.B, 15.A, 16.A, 16.B, 16.C, 17.A, 17.B, 19.A, 19.B, 29.A, 29.B, 29.C, 29.D, 29.F, 30.B, 30.C, 31.A, 31.B

Connect

My Story Video and Topic Essential Question—see how they connect to your past experience or to what you have already learned. The Essential Question for this Topic is: Why is culture important?

Begin your study by trying the following:

NBC LEARN Watch My Story Video:

Uncovering the Past

Launch your Project:

Create an Early Civilization Video Game

Investigate

Then you will investigate the Topic through a group of lessons. The story of the origins of civilization will come to life as you read and interact with key content. You will get a chance to read about what happened and why. And you'll be able to interact with a lot of fascinating online materials.

You'll also keep working on your Project as you build further mastery of the Topic TEKS.

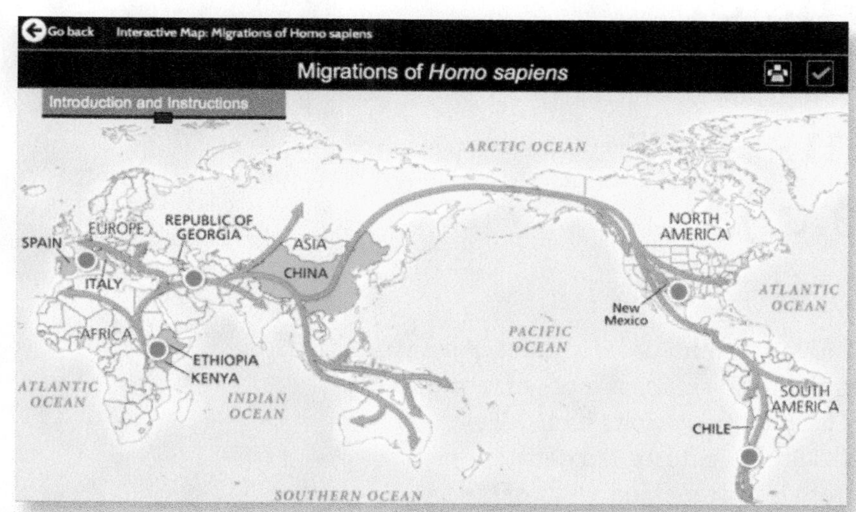

>> Digital interactivity from the online course

Synthesize

Next you will pull it all together by reflecting on the Essential Question. This will give you a chance to be the storyteller, to show how you would answer this big question.

Demonstrate

Finally, you can show what you know. You can write an essay, hold a discussion, or make a presentation. You can answer questions about every TEKS on the Topic Review and Assessment pages. Or you can finish your Project for this Topic and share it with the class.

TEKS in Topic 1	Topic Review and Assessment Questions
1.A	1, 3, 4, 7, 8, 12
2.A	9, 11
2.B	2
15.A	10
16.A	6
16.B	14
16.C	13
17.A	5
19.A	15
19.B	16
29.A	3, 5, 10, 16
29.B	2, 12
29.C	1, 7
29.D	4
29.F.	9, 11
31.B	8

Topic 1

Origins of Civilization (Prehistory–300 B.C.)

Introduction

The cultural advances and development of early peoples led first to the establishment of farming villages, and later to prosperous river valley civilizations. Cultural features led early peoples to progress from less organized ways of life to prosper in complex civilizations. Eventually, advances in agriculture, technology, and other areas led to changes in culture, which led to the establishment of river valley civilizations. How did the cultures of river valley civilizations impact the world?

ESSENTIAL QUESTION

Ask students to think about the Essential Question for this Topic: Why is culture important? Project the Essential Question activity from the course. Have students work with a partner to complete the activity. Then have students share their ideas with the class.

Evaluate Impact How does this cave painting reflect the importance of culture? *(Possible answer: It shows that people took time to make art, felt a desire to communicate ideas, had religious beliefs, and developed tools not only to support basic needs, but also to make paintings.)*

Predict Consequences How might farming change the lives and culture of hunter-gatherers? *(Possible answer: Farming might eliminate the need to roam to find food and result in permanent settlements. This might lead to more complex societies and culture as a result of new tools; technologies; and economic, political, and religious structures.)*

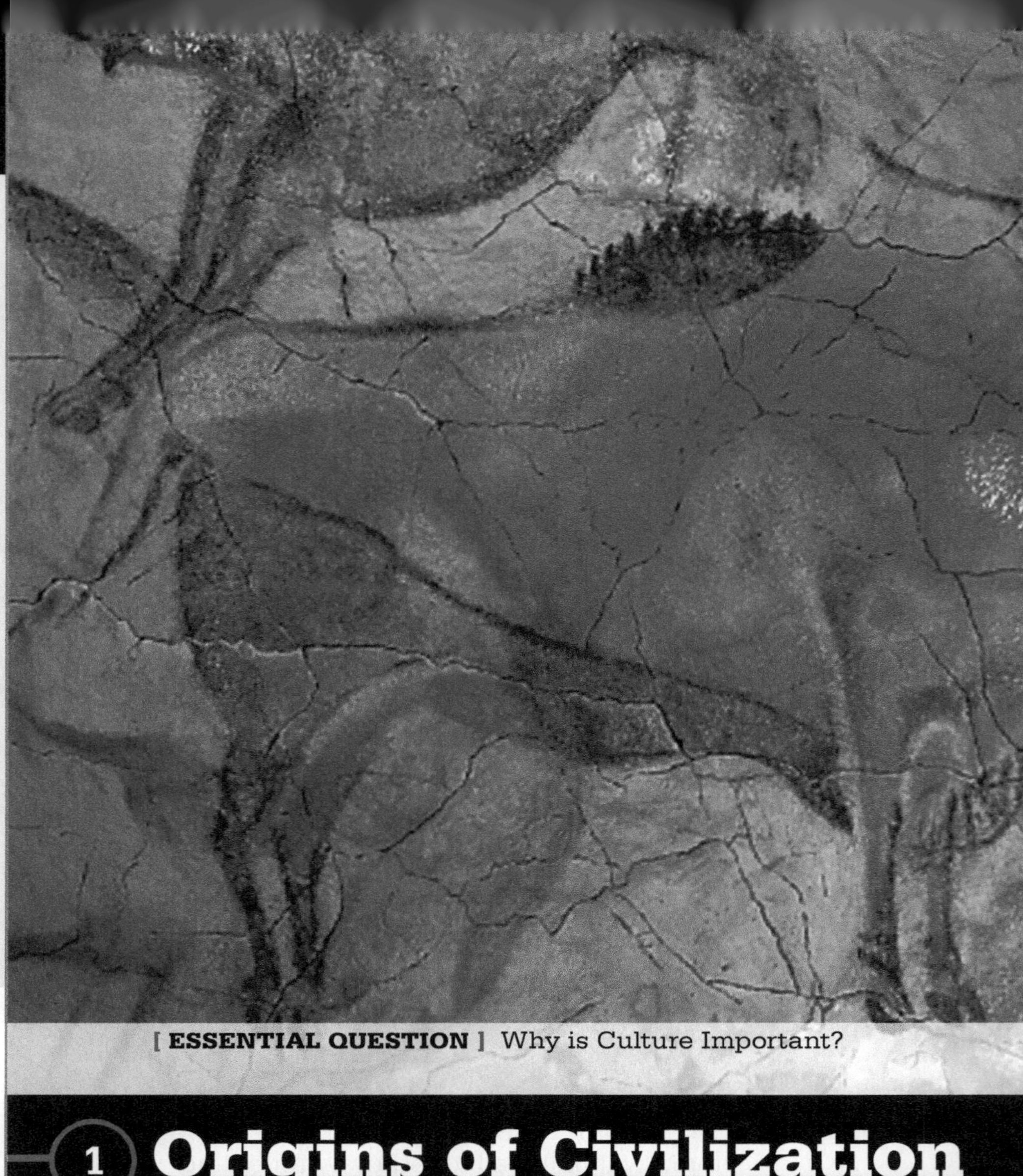

[**ESSENTIAL QUESTION**] Why is Culture Important?

1 Origins of Civilization (Prehistory–300 B.C.)

Analyze Images

Ask students to examine the image shown in this photograph. Explain that this painting of a steppe bison (an extinct relative of the American buffalo) is found in the Cave of Altamira, along with images of other animals. Ask students to predict what this image tells us about the lives of the people who lived in northern Spain at that time and what was important to them.

>> A prehistoric cave painting in northern Spain

Enduring Understandings

- Scholars study artifacts and other evidence to learn more about the lives of our ancestors.
- Human life changed dramatically after the Neolithic Revolution, when people learned to farm and to domesticate animals, allowing them to settle in permanent villages.
- The earliest civilizations developed in fertile river valleys and the rise of cities was their main feature.
- Early civilizations all had certain basic features in common, including organized governments, complex religions, job specialization, and social classes.

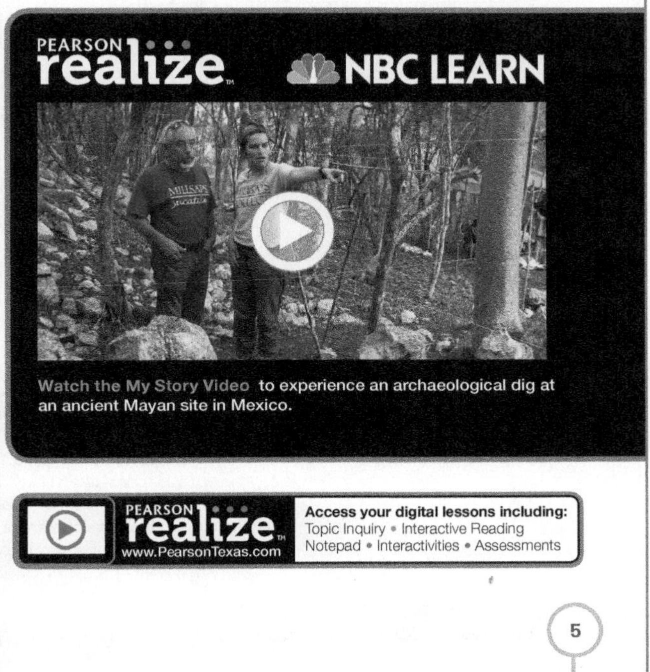

Watch the My Story Video to experience an archaeological dig at an ancient Mayan site in Mexico.

PEARSON realize www.PearsonTexas.com | Access your digital lessons including: Topic Inquiry • Interactive Reading Notepad • Interactivities • Assessments

5

NBC LEARN MY STORY VIDEO

Project the My Story Video that introduces students to an archaeological dig at an ancient Mayan site in Mexico.

Online My Story Video: **Uncovering the Past**.

OVERVIEW ACTIVITY

Online Project the **Timeline: Origin of Civilizations** showing the key periods of early human development. Students studying this Topic will learn about these periods and more, but this timeline will provide a framework in which they can compare early cultures and understand features that caused effects on other cultures.

Check Understanding What event on the timeline provides evidence that art has been important to humans since early times? *(Possible answer: The cave paintings found as early as 30,000 B.C.)*

Topic Inquiry

If you choose to assign the Topic Inquiry, launch the project after introducing the Topic.

D **Differentiate Extra Support** How many years are there between when *Homo sapiens* began to spread throughout the world and when people learned to grow their own crops? *(91,000 years;* Homo sapiens *began to spread throughout the world around 100,000 B.C., and people learned to grow their own crops around 9,000 B.C.)*

Learning About Our Past

CONNECT

Preview Have students preview the **Lesson Objectives** and the list of **Key Terms**.

Students can also preview all the **Key Terms** and **Academic Vocabulary** using the **Interactive Reading Notepad** on the digital course or preview a summary of the lesson in the **Reading and Note Taking Study Guide**.

Online Use the **Editable Presentation** found on the digital course to present the main ideas for this lesson.

Start Up Activity

Tell students that anthropologist Mary Leakey discovered a set of ancient footprints in Laetoli, Tanzania, in 1978 and wrote, "The traveler stops, pauses, turns to the left to glance at some possible threat or irregularity," and "experienced a moment of doubt." Ask students to answer the following question and then have them share their ideas with another student.

Discuss Ask students how they think Leakey could identify "a moment of doubt" from a set of ancient footprints. *(Possible answer: The physical evidence allows her to reconstruct the mind-set of an early human based on his or her actions.)*

Online You can also project the **Start Up Activity** from the course.

INVESTIGATE

Have students read the section using the **Reading and Note Taking Study Guide** to help them take notes and understand the text as they read.

Studying Prehistory

Explain to students that scientists rely on various methods to learn about our past. One method is to study the bones of early humans, such as the skeleton of Turkana Boy, a nearly complete 1.6 million-year-old fossil, buried for centuries. The historian's goal is to evaluate how early humans developed. To do this, historians examine sources and analyze their frame of reference, historical context, and point of view. This process helps them to interpret historical events. Such information also helps us to understand what might happen in the future.

>> Studying ancient footprints is one way scientists can learn about the past. These footprints, preserved in volcanic ash, were made in Tanzania some 3.5 million years ago.

Interactive Flipped Video

1.1 By about 5,000 years ago, groups of people in different parts of the world had begun to keep written records. The invention and use of writing marked the beginning of recorded history. However, humans and their ancestors had lived on Earth for thousands upon thousands of years before the recording of history began. We call the long period of time before people invented writing prehistory.

TEKS 29.A

>> **Objectives**

Learn how scholars study the historical past.

Find out how anthropologists investigate the period of prehistory.

Understand how discoveries in Africa and beyond have influenced anthropologists' views about early humans and their ancestors.

>> **Key Terms**

prehistory
historian
artifact
anthropology
culture
archaeology
Mary Leakey
Louis Leakey
Olduvai Gorge
technology
Donald Johanson

Learning About Our Past

Studying Prehistory

Understanding Our Past **Historians** are scholars who study and write about the historical past. Historians often learn details of the past from **artifacts,** or objects made by humans. Clothing, coins, artwork, and tombstones are all types of artifacts. However, historians rely even more on written evidence, such as letters or tax records.

Although it is often hard to find thorough written records from early times, those that exist offer us a narrative of events, as well as names and dates. Historians of the recent past also study such evidence as photographs or films.

Like a detective, a historian must evaluate all evidence to determine if it is reliable. Do records of a meeting between two officials tell us exactly what was said? Who was taking notes? Was a letter writer really giving an eyewitness report or just passing on rumors? Could the letter be a forgery? Historians try to find the answers to questions like these. They then interpret the evidence, or explain what it means. Often, a historian's goal is to determine the causes of a certain development or event, such as a war or an economic collapse. By explaining why things occurred in the past, historians can help us

www.PearsonTexas.com Access your Digital Lesson.

6

Aa Vocabulary Builder

1. Have students pronounce the following academic vocabulary terms in this lesson and clarify the part of speech. For difficult or polysyllabic words, break them into syllables and pronounce them with the students.
2. Explain what the word means in common "student-friendly" language using synonyms and antonyms when possible. Provide concrete examples to clarify the meaning, and rephrase the definition.

narrative: written or spoken account of events that are connected

technique: procedure, skill, or art used in a particular task understand what happens today and what may happen in the future.

Generally, historians try to give a straightforward account of events. However, sometimes their personal experiences, cultural backgrounds, or political opinions bias their interpretations. Other times, historians disagree with one another about what the evidence proves. Such differences can lead to lively debates.

SUMMARIZE What kinds of evidence do historians use to study the past?

ELPS **ELPS 1.A.1** Practice using prior knowledge to understand key terms in *Studying Prehistory*.

Investigating Prehistory

About 150 years ago, scholars began studying the period of prehistory. They hoped to learn about the origins and development of people and their societies. Today, we call this field of study **anthropology.**

The Field of Anthropology Modern anthropologists specialize in certain areas of their field. For example, some study the bones of our ancestors to understand how human physical traits have changed over time. Other anthropologists focus on the characteristics of human cultures from both the past and present. In anthropology, **culture** refers to the way of life of a society, which includes its beliefs, values, and practices. Culture is handed down from one generation to the next through learning and experience.

The Field of Archaeology Within the field of anthropology, a specialized branch exists called archaeology (ahr kee AHL uh jee). **Archaeology** is the study of past people and cultures through their material remains. These remains include buildings, and artifacts such as tools, weapons, pottery, clothing, and jewelry. Archaeologists find and analyze artifacts to learn about life during prehistory as well as during historical times. This helps them draw conclusions about the beliefs, values, and activities of our ancestors. However, most archaeologists agree that the story of the past is never fully known. Since archaeologists make new discoveries frequently, at times they must revise their theories in light of the new evidence.

Archaeologists at Work Finding ancient artifacts can be difficult, but archaeologists have devised many useful means of doing so. In the 1800s and early 1900s, archaeologists would pick a likely place, called a site, and begin digging. The farther down they dug, the older the artifacts they found.

Some of the objects, which had been buried for very long periods of time, crumbled as soon as they were removed from the ground. Today, archaeologists and

Dating Material Remains

RELATIVE DATING METHODS	
WHAT IS IT?	Determining whether material remains are older or newer than one another.
WHEN IS IT USED?	To study artifacts that charge in style over time.
HOW DO SCIENTISTS USE IT?	To create a chronology based on the general fact that older artifacts are found in lower levels of an archaeological site than newer ones.
ABSOLUTE DATING METHODS	
WHAT IS IT?	Determining exact ages of organic objects such as bones, by measuring carbon-14, a radioactive element.
WHEN IS IT USED?	To determine whether bones found near each other were buried at the same time.
HOW DO SCIENTISTS USE IT?	All living things contain carbon-14, which decays at a set rate. As a result, archaeologists can use carbon-14 levels to date the remains of once-living items such as bones, wood, and ash.

>> **Analyze Charts** Which dating method would you use to determine the age of a fossilized tooth fragment?

Topic 1 Lesson 1

Investigating Prehistory

Project or point out the graphic **Dating Material Remains**. Explain to students that accurately dating artifacts, relics, and bones is an important part of investigating prehistory. There are two ways that archaeologists and anthropologists can date bones and artifacts: relative dating and absolute dating. Relative dating allows scientists to create a chronology of artifacts based on the general fact that older artifacts are found deeper in the ground than newer artifacts. Absolute dating allows scientists to determine the age of a bone or some other organic material by measuring the decay of carbon-14, a radioactive element that decays at a set rate.

Guided Reading and Discussion

Ask students the following questions:

Draw Inferences What impact has carbon-dating had on archaeology and our understanding of prehistoric times? *(Students might say that carbon dating gives scientists an accurate way to determine the age of once-living, organic materials, including bones.)*

Discuss Why is studying prehistory the responsibility not just of archaeologists, but of many other scientists, including geologists, botanists, biologists, anthropologists, and others? *(Possible answer: These other scientists provide vital, necessary information from their fields to help archaeologists better understand how our ancient ancestors lived, worked, fought, farmed, and generally adapted to their environment.)*

Answers

Summarize *A variety of artifacts including clothing, coins, artwork, tombstones, and photographs, as well as written evidence such as letters, tax records, and other documents.*

Analyze Charts *You would use absolute dating.*

English Language Proficiency Standards

Learning Strategies 1.A.1 Write and display the word *prehistory* for students and ask them to brainstorm what they know about *prehistory*. Then guide students through one of the following activities to use prior knowledge to understand a new word according to their English proficiency level.

Beginning Ask students how *pre-* and *history* form *prehistory* and invite them to share their thoughts with partners. Read the first paragraph of "Studying Prehistory" aloud. Ask students what they know about *prehistory*. Review the definition.

Intermediate Repeat the first steps of the Beginning activity. Ask students to keep the definition of *prehistory* in mind as you read "Studying Prehistory" aloud.

Advanced Have students brainstorm what they know about *prehistory*. Ask what part of history each word part refers to and how it relates to the study of history. Have the class develop a definition based on the brainstorm. Display the definition so students can see it as they read "Studying Prehistory" silently.

Advanced High Have students repeat the Advanced activity working with a partner rather than as a whole class. Ask partners to share their definitions with another pair. Have students read "Studying Prehistory" silently.

Topic 1 Lesson 1

Online Project the **Interactive Gallery: Piecing the Past Together** and click through the images with students. Explain that scientists rely on various methods to learn about our past. One method is to study the bones of early humans. Explain to students that the historian's goal is to evaluate how early humans developed. To do this, historians examine sources and analyze their frame of reference, historical context, and point of view. This process helps them to interpret historical events. Such information also helps us to understand what might happen in the future.

ACTIVE CLASSROOM

Ask students to choose one of these vocabulary words: *prehistory, anthropology, archaeology, artifact, culture,* or *historian,* and tell them to create a visual image with a definition. Ask students to post their words and images on the board. Next, have students look at the various responses and allow them time as a group to discuss similarities and differences.

Guided Reading and Discussion

Ask students to list, evaluate, and explain the different types of evidence historians use to study the past. Students should show they understand that historians study written records, artifacts, clothing, coins, artwork, and other relics. Students should also show an understanding that some types of evidence yield more information than others.

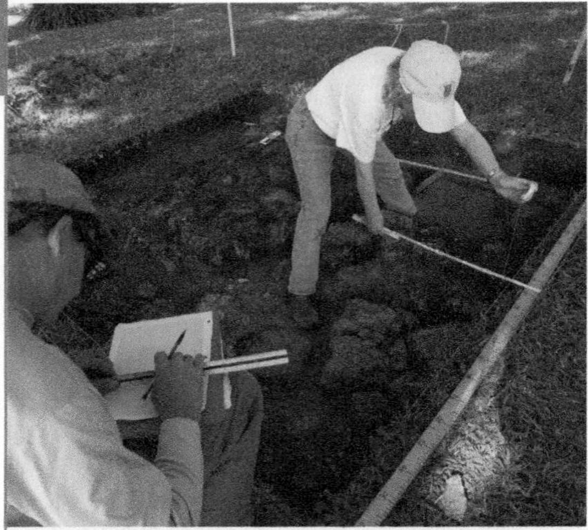

>> **Analyze Information** When researching an archaeological site, scientists use exact measurements. Why do you think archaeologists have to be so precise?

Interactive Gallery

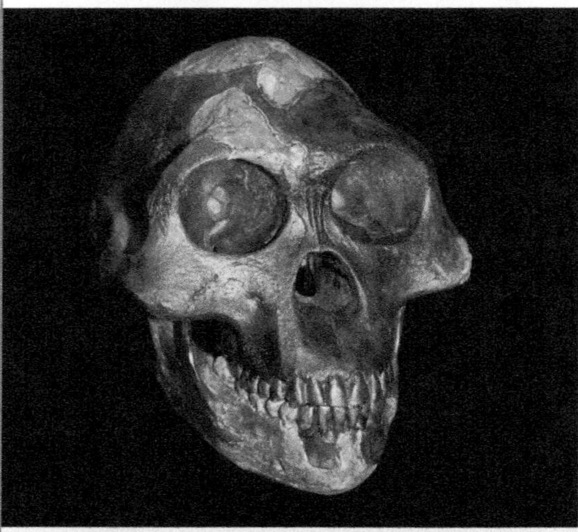

>> "Lucy" was discovered in Ethiopia in 1974. Scientists date the skeleton to at least 3 million years ago. It was the first time archaeologists had enough of one skeleton to reconstruct and view an actual hominid.

others who work with them take great care to preserve such fragile artifacts.

Once archaeologists have found artifacts, they analyze them. One technique is to mark the location of each type of artifact found on a map of the site. After studying the map, an archaeologist may be able to tell what activities people took part in at different locations within the site. An area full of rabbit bones, for example, might suggest the workplace of a cook. Archaeologists also need to find out how old the artifacts are.

Geologists, or experts on earth science, can help with this task by determining the age of rocks located near archaeological sites. In addition, botanists and zoologists—experts on plants and on animals—examine seeds and animal bones to learn about the diets of our ancestors. Experts on climate determine what conditions our ancestors faced on the plains of Africa or in ice-covered parts of Europe.

Biologists analyze human bones as well as bloodstains found on old stone tools and weapons. Geographers provide three-dimensional maps of the terrain at archaeological sites.

In addition to working with experts in various fields, archaeologists today use many modern innovations to study their findings. Computers help them store and sort data or develop accurate maps of archaeological sites. Aerial photographs help archaeologists to better see the layout of land and structures once lived in by past people. Techniques for measuring radioactivity aid scientists in determining the age of objects.

DESCRIBE Why is it that the farther down an archaeologist digs, the more he or she can find out about the past?

Discoveries in Africa and Beyond

Before the 1950s, anthropologists knew little about early humans and their ancestors. Prehistoric groups did not have cities, countries, organized central governments, or complex inventions, so clues about them were hard to find. However, archaeologists in East Africa started uncovering ancient footprints, bones, and tools. With these first key discoveries, scholars began to form a picture of life during prehistory.

East Africa In the 1930s, anthropologists **Mary Leakey** and **Louis Leakey** started searching for clues to the human past in a deep canyon in Tanzania called **Olduvai Gorge**(OHL duh vy). Geologists have dated the bottom layers of Olduvai Gorge to an age of 1.7 to 2.1 million years. As the Leakeys searched the sides of

English Language Proficiency Standards

Learning Strategies 1.E.2 Read "Discoveries in Africa and Beyond" aloud. Write and display the words *humans, cities, countries, footprints, bones,* and *tools,* and have students copy them into their notebooks. Have them complete one activity according to their level of English proficiency.

Beginning Provide a basic definition for each word. Use each in a simple phrase. Write each phrase and ask students to copy them into their notebooks. Assign a phrase to each student and have students practice saying their phrase aloud.

Intermediate Instruct students to use bilingual dictionaries to find definitions. Have students develop meaningful phrases for each word. Write each phrase and ask students to copy them into their notebooks. Have students take turns practicing saying the phrases aloud. Assist with pronunciation.

Advanced Instruct pairs of students to use English dictionaries to find a definition for each word. Have partners write sentences using each word in their notebooks and take turns speaking the sentences aloud. Assist with pronunciation.

Answers

Analyze Information *Students might say that in order for scientists to detail the past accurately, they need to identify the exact locations of where they find bones and relics.*

Describe *Older artifacts are generally found deep in the ground where they have been covered over time by layers of rock and sediment.*

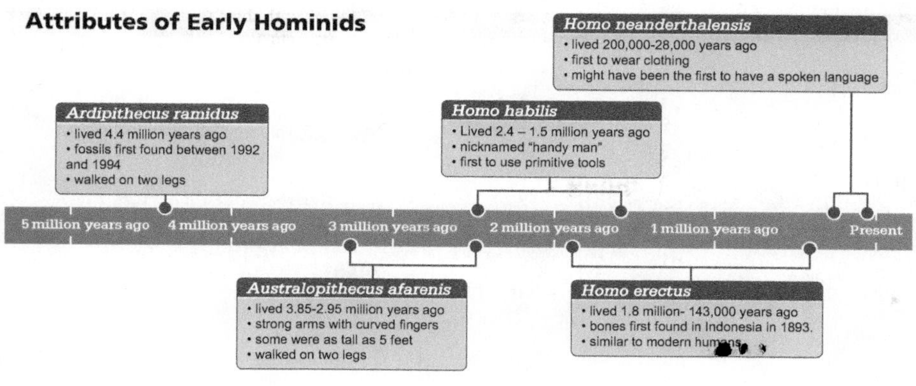

Attributes of Early Hominids
Homo neanderthalensis
• lived 200,000-28,000 years ago
• first to wear clothing
• might have been the first to have a spoken language
Ardipithecus ramidus
• lived 4.4 million years ago
• fossils first found between 1992 and 1994
• walked on two legs
Homo habilis
• Lived 2.4 – 1.5 million years ago
• nickname "handy man"
• first to use primitive tools
5 million years ago
4 million years ago
3 million years ago
2 million years ago
1 million years ago
Present
Australopithecus afarensis
• lived 3.85-2.95 million years ago
• strong arms with curved fingers
• some were as tall as 5 feet
• walked on two legs
Homo erectus
• lived 1.8 million- 143,000 years ago
• bones first found in Indonesia in 1893.
• similar to modern humans

Source: Smithsonian Institution

>> As the centuries passed, hominid groups developed physically and gained new skills.

the gorge, they found very ancient tools chipped from stone. Although these tools looked simple, with jagged edges and rough surfaces, they showed that whoever had made them had learned to develop technologies to help them survive.

Technology refers to the skills and tools people use to meet their basic needs and wants. More recent stone tools proved more sophisticated—both smooth and polished—but the older ones were exciting to the Leakeys. They felt there must be evidence of the makers of those tools in Olduvai Gorge as well.

In 1959, after more than two decades of searching, Mary Leakey found a skull embedded in ancient rock at Olduvai Gorge. After careful testing, the Leakeys concluded that the skull belonged to an early hominid. Hominids, a group that includes humans and their closest relatives, all walk upright on two feet. Humans are the only hominids that live today.

Additional evidence of early hominids was found in 1974 by anthropologist **Donald Johanson.** In Ethiopia, Johanson found many pieces of a single hominid skeleton, which was dated to at least 3 million years ago. For the first time, archaeologists had enough of one skeleton to piece together and really look at an early hominid. Johanson named his historic find "Lucy" after a Beatles' song. Studying Lucy's skeleton, Johanson could see that she was an upright walker who was about 4 feet (1.2 meters) tall.

Early Hominid Groups As of today, scientists and anthropologists have discovered and studied numerous remains and artifacts of hominids.

From this work, they have established that a number of different groups of hominids lived over the course of several million years. They call the earliest group of hominids australopithecines (aw stray loh PITH uh synz).

Lucy and the hominids who left their footprints in Laetoli were australopithecines. All the australopithecines lived in Africa. Anthropologists think that they may have lived there as early as 7 million years ago.

About 2 million years ago, a group of hominids emerged that anthropologists call *Homo habilis*. Scholars gave the group this name, which means "handy man," because they thought these were the first hominids to make stone tools. Since the discovery of *Homo habilis*, anthropologists have uncovered even older stone tools—2.6 million years in age—but they have not determined which hominids created them. By studying many stone tools, anthropologists have concluded that *Homo habilis* used their tools for purposes such as cutting, scraping, chopping, or sawing plants, animals, and wood.

Another group of hominids, called *Homo erectus*, also appeared around 2 million years ago. They were given their name, which means "upright man," because their skeletons show that they were fully upright walkers. *Homo erectus* were notable for having

Topic 1 Lesson 1

Discoveries in Africa and Beyond

Online Project and discuss the **Interactive Map: Migrations of *Homo sapiens***.

Explain that early humans migrated out of Africa and populated the world. Scientists and anthropologists have discovered evidence of many early human groups on each continent. The earliest group, Australopithecus, left their footprints in Africa some 7 million years ago. Scientists believe modern humans emerged between 250,000 and 100,000 years ago.

Analyze Maps Have students study the "Migrations of *Homo sapiens*" map. Ask why early humans migrated as they did. *(Students may say early humans were following large herds of animals for food. They might also cite changing climate and other environmental conditions.)*

ACTIVE CLASSROOM

Have students use the images and text associated with the interactive map to write a headline for each image that captures the most important aspects of that image. Each student can pass his or her headline to a partner to review.

Key Terms

Ask students to find the key term **technology** (in bold) in the text. Explain that while common usage of the word today typically refers to electronic devices such as phones and computers, it can also apply to any skills or tools used to meet basic needs.

Guided Reading and Discussion

Pose these questions for students:

Draw Inferences What else did animals provide early humans with beside a source of food? *(Animals provided bones for tools and hides for clothing.)*

Identify Cause and Effect How might climate change have impacted the migration routes of early humans? *(Possible answer: People migrated toward climates that were more suitable for survival.)*

Advanced High Have students work individually to find definitions in an English dictionary and write sentences using each word in their notebooks. Then have students read the sentences aloud to a partner. Assist with pronunciation.

D Differentiate Extra Support To better understand how historians work, ask students to write down the day-to-day details of what has happened to them in the past week. Next, ask students to think about why certain events took place, or why things happened as they did. Finally, ask students what lessons they learned that they can apply in the future.

SYNTHESIZE

Online Project the **Digital Activity: Ancient Civilizations of the Indian Subcontinent**. Ask students to reread the quote from Howard Carter. Ask this key question:

What methods does Carter, as an archaeologist, use to analyze the past? Using the Circle Write strategy, have students write as much as they can for one minute on the key question, then switch with the person on their right. That person should improve or elaborate the response. Have students continue to switch until they receive their original work. Have students share what they have written with the rest of the class.

DEMONSTRATE

Online Assign the **Digital Lesson Quiz** for this lesson if you haven't already done so. Students will be offered automatic remediation or enrichment based on their score.

Point out to students that they have learned how scientists and scholars study the historical past. They have also learned about some of the techniques anthropologists use to investigate prehistory, and how archaeological discoveries in Africa and elsewhere have influenced views about early humans and their ancestors. Pose this question on the Discussion Board:

Evaluate Why might someone devote his or her life to studying early humans? *(Students might say that those who devote their lives to studying early humans are curious as to how people in the past lived and are interested in the process of discovery. Students might also say that by studying our ancestors and how they adapted to changes, we can learn something about our world.)*

Topic Inquiry

Have students continue their investigations for the Topic Inquiry.

Migrations of *Homo sapiens*

>> **Analyze Maps** *Homo sapiens* migrated along the routes shown on the map. Why would early *Homo sapiens* follow large herds of animals?

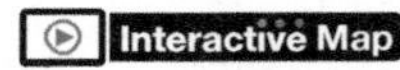

larger brains and bones and smaller teeth than other hominids.

They also showed a greater range of capabilities. For example, *Homo erectus* are thought to be the first hominids to learn how to use fire. They also pioneered a new form of stone tool, called a hand ax, that could be used as the earlier tools were but also worked for digging, shattering stone or bone, and boring holes into hard surfaces. *Homo erectus* remains have been found in Asia and Europe, making scholars think they were the first hominids to migrate out of Africa.

Evidence of *Homo Sapiens* Scientists think that between 250,000 and 100,000 years ago, *Homo erectus* disappeared and a new group of hominids emerged.

This new group, called *Homo sapiens*, is the group to which modern humans belong. There is some dispute over where *Homo sapiens* first lived. Many scholars think the archaeological and scientific evidence supports the "Out of Africa" theory, which says that *Homo sapiens* first lived in Africa and then migrated into other areas of the world. Other scientists think that *Homo erectus* developed into *Homo sapiens* around the same time in different parts of the world.

Either way, scholars think that two groups of *Homo sapiens* soon arose—Neanderthals and the earliest modern humans. Early modern humans eventually spread all over the world, while Neanderthals lived mostly in Europe and western Asia. Sometime between 50,000 and 30,000 years ago, the Neanderthals disappeared, leaving early modern humans as the only hominids on Earth.

CONNECT How did *Homo habilis* use the tools they fashioned?

ASSESSMENT

1. **Apply Concepts** What types of obstacles do historians have to overcome to give a straight-forward account of past events?
2. **Describe** Describe the "Out of Africa" theory.
3. **Connect** How have anthropologists learned about the ancestors of modern humans?
4. **Classify** What is the significance of the Olduvai Gorge in East Africa?
5. **Explain** Why did scholars give *Homo habilis* the nickname "handy man?"

Assessment

1. Historians have to be careful of letting their own biased viewpoints cloud their work.
2. The "Out of Africa" theory suggests that *Homo sapiens* first lived in Africa and then migrated to other areas around the globe.
3. By studying bone and artifact evidence, anthropologists have pieced together what life was like for the earliest humans.
4. The geology of the gorge is made up of numerous layers of ash and lava that have been deposited over millions of years. Scientists can date each distinct layer, which allowed them to date artifacts near the bottom to an age of 1.7 to 2.1 million years.
5. Scientists discovered that *Homo habilis* were the first hominids to make and use tools.

Answers

Connect Homo habilis *used tools for cutting, scraping, chopping, or sawing plants, meat, and wood.*

1.2 Based on the evidence gathered by anthropologists over many years, scholars have divided prehistory into different eras. They call the long period from at least 2 million B.C. to about 10,000 B.C. the Old Stone Age, or Paleolithic Period. They refer to the period from about 10,000 B.C. until the end of prehistory as the New Stone Age, or Neolithic Period. During both eras, people created and used various types of stone tools. However, during the New Stone Age, people began to develop new skills and technologies that led to dramatic changes in their everyday lives.

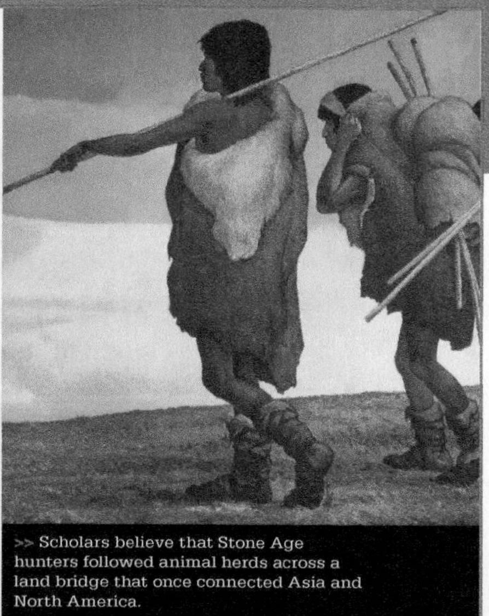

>> Scholars believe that Stone Age hunters followed animal herds across a land bridge that once connected Asia and North America.

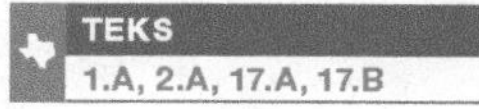

Interactive Flipped Video

Topic 1 Lesson 2

The Neolithic Revolution

The Neolithic Revolution

TEKS
1.A, 2.A, 17.A, 17.B

>> **Objectives**

Describe the skills and beliefs that early modern humans developed during the Old Stone Age.

Analyze why the development of agriculture is considered the start of the New Stone Age and the Neolithic Revolution.

Explain how the Neolithic Revolution dramatically changed the way people lived.

>> **Key Terms**

Old Stone Age
Paleolithic Period
New Stone Age
Neolithic Period
nomad
animism
Neolithic Revolution
domesticate
Çatalhüyük
Jericho

Old Stone Age Skills and Beliefs

Early modern humans lived toward the end of the Old Stone Age. Researchers have pieced together evidence left by early modern humans to paint a picture of what daily life was like for them.

Early modern people were **nomads,** or people who move from place to place to find food. Typically, about 20 or 30 people lived together in small bands, or groups. They survived by hunting and by gathering food.

In general, men hunted or fished. Women and children gathered berries, fruits, nuts, grains, roots, or shellfish. This food kept the band alive when game animals were scarce.

Strategies for Survival Early people depended heavily on their environment for food and shelter. They also found ways to adapt their surroundings to their needs. As hominids had throughout the Stone Age, early humans made tools and weapons out of the materials at hand—stone, bone, or wood. They built fires for cooking and used animal skins for clothing. At some point, early modern humans developed spoken language, which allowed them to cooperate during the hunt and perhaps discuss plans for the future.

11

PEARSON realize. www.PearsonTexas.com Access your Digital Lesson.

CONNECT

Have students preview the **Lesson Objectives** and the list of **Key Terms**.

Students can also preview all the **Key Terms** and **Academic Vocabulary** using the **Interactive Reading Notepad** on the digital course or preview a summary of the lesson in the **Reading and Note Taking Study Guide**.

Online Use the **Editable Presentation** found on the digital course to present the main ideas for this lesson.

Start Up Activity

Read aloud the following statement by archaeologist Kathleen Kenyon about the discoveries that led to the world's first revolution.

> For hundreds of thousands of years, [man] had lived on wild foods, as a hunter and gatherer. . . . The revolutionary step forward was the discovery that wild grains could be cultivated and made more productive, and wild animals herded and their products made constantly available. With this discovery, the growth of fixed settlements became possible. . . . From this, all civilization is derived.

Have students discuss the following question: How was the introduction of farming a turning point in prehistory? *(Answers will vary. Students should show an understanding that farming led to the development of permanent villages from which civilizations grew and flourished.)*

Online You can also project the **Start Up Activity** from the course.

INVESTIGATE

Have students read the section using the **Reading and Note Taking Study Guide** to help them take notes and understand the text as they read.

Old Stone Age Skills and Beliefs

Early peoples were nomads who depended on their environment for food, clothing, and shelter. They made tools from the materials available and developed spoken language, which broadened their ability to communicate and plan.

Aa Vocabulary Builder

1. Have students pronounce the following academic vocabulary term in this lesson and clarify the part of speech. Break the word into syllables and pronounce them with the students.
2. Explain what the word means in common "student-friendly" language using synonyms and antonyms when possible. Provide concrete examples to clarify the meaning, and rephrase the definition.

transition: process of undergoing change from one stage to another.

Topic 1 Lesson 2

Online Project the **Interactive Gallery: Neolithic Art** and click through the images with students. Introduce the activity by telling students that at the end of the Old Stone Age, people began leaving evidence of their beliefs in a spiritual world. They buried their dead with tools and weapons, indicating a belief in an afterlife. The Neolithic cave art found in Lascaux, France, depicts some of their religious beliefs.

ACTIVE CLASSROOM

Ask students to study the images of the art carefully. Using the See-Think-Wonder strategy, have students pair with a partner. Ask them: What do you see? What does that make you think? What are you wondering about now that you've seen this? Have students share insights with the class.

Guided Reading and Discussion

Ask students the following question:

Discuss Ask students to describe how scientists might go about analyzing, evaluating, and putting into historical context evidence of Neolithic religious beliefs. *(Students might say that by comparing evidence of religious activity [such as cave art and evidence of ceremonial rites] scientists can piece together how early religions developed and spread.)*

Farming Begins a New Stone Age

Explain to students that about 12,000 years ago, early humans scrapped their nomadic lifestyle and began to farm. Instead of searching for animals as a source of food, farming allowed people to settle in one area. As a result, permanent villages began to form, as did new technologies and skills. People also began to domesticate animals and plants that were better suited for human use.

>> **Draw Conclusions** Based on this illustration, what evidence would archaeologists use to learn about the interior of Neolithic houses?

>> Scientists study Neolithic cave art to understand early religious beliefs known as animism.

Interactive Gallery

Some Old Stone Age people also learned to travel across water, which helped them spread into new places. For example, people boated from Southeast Asia to Australia at least 40,000 years ago, most likely using rafts or canoes. They may have stopped for years at islands along the way, but in between they would have had to boat across as much as 40 miles (64 kilometers) of open ocean.

Early Religious Beliefs Toward the end of the Old Stone Age, people began to leave evidence of their belief in a spiritual world. About 100,000 years ago, some people began burying their dead with great care. Some anthropologists think that this practice suggests a belief in life after death. Old Stone Age people may have believed the afterlife would be similar to life in this world and thus provided the dead with tools, weapons, and other needed goods to take with them.

Many scholars think that our ancestors believed the world was full of spirits and forces that might reside in animals, objects, or dreams. Such beliefs are known as **animism.** In Europe, Australia, and Africa, cave or rock paintings vividly portray animals such as deer, horses, and buffaloes. Some cave paintings show people, too. The paintings often lie deep in caves, far from a band's living quarters. Some scholars think cave paintings were created as part of animist religious rituals.

DESCRIBE What skills did Old Stone Age people develop to adapt and meet their needs?

Farming Begins a New Stone Age

The New Stone Age began about 12,000 years ago (or about 10,000 B.C.), when nomadic people made a breakthrough that had far-reaching effects—they learned to farm.

The Neolithic Revolution By producing their own food, people no longer needed to roam in search of animals, fish, or plants. For the first time, they could remain in one place throughout the year. As a result, early farmers settled the first permanent villages. They also developed entirely new skills and technologies. This transition from nomadic life to settled farming brought about such dramatic changes in way of life that it is often called the **Neolithic Revolution.**

The Domestication of Plants and Animals These early farmers were the first humans to **domesticate** plants and animals—that is, to raise them in a controlled way that makes them best suited to human

English Language Proficiency Standards

Listening Strategies 1.E.3 Read the selection "Farming Begins a New Stone Age" aloud. Have students copy the academic vocabulary words *Neolithic Revolution* and *domesticate* into their notebooks and then complete one activity according to their English proficiency.

Beginning Provide a definition for each word. Restate the content of the selection. Ask students questions using the vocabulary words.

Intermediate Help students find definitions in bilingual dictionaries. Restate the content of the selection. Ask questions using vocabulary words. Help students work together to answer.

Advanced Have students work in small groups to look up words in dictionaries and then discuss the selection by asking and answering questions about the vocabulary words.

Advanced High Have individual students use context clues to find the meaning of each word. Have them discuss the selection by asking and answering questions about the vocabulary words with a partner.

Answers

Describe *Old Stone Age people learned to make tools and weapons out of stone or other materials; they built fires for cooking, used animal skins for clothing, developed a spoken language, and learned to travel across water.*

Draw Conclusions *Archaeologists would use the remaining artifacts, including pots, tools, weapons, and clothing, as well as the materials from the ruins of the structure.*

use. Plant domestication may have begun with food gatherers realizing that seeds scattered on the ground would produce new plants the next year. Animal domestication may have begun with people deciding to round up the animals they usually hunted. They could then use the animals as they always had—for food and skins—as well as to provide other benefits, such as milk or eggs.

Evidence shows that people began to farm in different parts of the world at different times, and that they did not domesticate all the same plants or animals in each place.

The dog was probably the first animal to be domesticated, at least 15,000 years ago. People brought domesticated dogs wherever they migrated. From about 8000 B.C. to 6000 B.C., people in western Asia and northern Africa domesticated goats, sheep, pigs, and cattle; and people in South America domesticated llamas and alpacas.

Around the same time—from about 10,000 B.C. to 6000 B.C.—people in West Africa and Southeast Asia domesticated yams, in China millet and rice, in Central America and Mexico squash, and in the Middle East barley, chickpeas, peas, lentils, and wheat.

IDENTIFY MAIN IDEAS How did farming change the lives of Neolithic people?

Dramatic Change with the Neolithic Revolution

Once the Neolithic Revolution had begun, no greater change in the way people lived took place until the Industrial Revolution of the late 1700s. Settled farming led to the establishment of the first villages and to significant advances in technology and culture. As you will read in the next section, these advances eventually led to a new stage of development—the emergence of cities and civilizations.

Establishing the Earliest Villages Archaeologists have unearthed the remains of some of the first Neolithic villages, including **Çatalhüyük**(chah TAHL hyoo YOOK) in modern-day Turkey and **Jericho**(JEHR ih koh), which still exists today as an Israeli-controlled city. Jericho was built between 10,000 and 9000 B.C. Although the village was tiny—about the size of a few soccer fields—a few thousand people lived in it.

The village was surrounded by a huge wall, which suggests that it had a government or leader who was able to organize a large construction project. Çatalhüyük seems to have developed around 7000 B.C. and may have had a population as large as 6,500 people.

>> Visitors can still see the ruins of ancient Jericho, located on Israel's West Bank.

>> During the Neolithic Period, people used tools and weapons, built boats, cooked over fires, and domesticated dogs.

Interactive Gallery

Guided Reading and Discussion

Ask students the following questions:

Identify Central Issues How did agriculture and the domestication of plants and animals develop in different parts of the world? *(Students might say that evidence shows that the domestication of different plants and animals occurred at different times and in different places.)*

Apply Concepts How did the development of farming contribute to permanent villages? *(Students might say that farming led to a more settled way of life, since humans could grow their own food and did not need to roam to feed themselves.)*

Discuss Explain the concept of revolution as it relates to farming and the Neolithic Revolution. *(Students should show an understanding that change is revolutionary when it is dramatic, is all-encompassing, and requires great effort. The shift from a nomadic to a more settled way of life gave early humans greater control of their environment, creating a revolutionary change.)*

Dramatic Change with the Neolithic Revolution

Great changes came about during the Neolithic Revolution. Settled people changed their way of life by inventing new technologies that, among other things, helped them farm and measure time.

Key Terms

Ask students to find the key term **animism** (in bold) in the text. Explain that *anima-* means "life or soul" and *-ism* refers to a belief.

D Differentiate Extra Support After you discuss the cave art, ask students to think about where they have seen pictures that communicate specific information, such as a handicapped sign in a parking lot, no smoking signs, and school bus stop signs. Ask students to think about why these pictures work well. Next, have them draw a picture that communicates something important without using words. Have the class try to guess what information the picture is trying to convey.

Answers

Identify Main Ideas *Farming allowed people to build and settle permanent villages, and develop new skills such as the domestication of plants and animals.*

Topic 1 Lesson 2

Online Project the **Interactive Gallery: Otzi—the Neolithic Ice Man** and click through the images. Introduce the activity by telling students that great changes came about during the Neolithic Revolution. People invented new technologies that, among other things, helped them farm and measure time. Archaeologists know about this period from finds such as Otzi, a Neolithic "Ice Man" found preserved in the European Alps alongside various tools and other belongings.

ACTIVE CLASSROOM

Ask students to study the images of the "Ice Man." Have students visualize that they are having a conversation with the Iceman as if he were alive. Have students write down a series of questions they would like the Iceman to answer, and what he would say to them.

Guided Reading and Discussion

Discuss with students how farming, especially in the river valleys, brought social, political, and economic change as urban civilizations and governments developed. For example, Neolithic peoples worked together and formed governments to direct projects such as the building of dikes and dams. When farming created surpluses of food, some farmers gained wealth, and in times of scarcity, hunters and warriors gained prestige. This marked the beginning of a social class system.

Draw Inferences How did farming encourage the development of new technologies? *(Students might say that early farmers had to develop new methods and tools to till the soil, protect their crops, make sure that they measured the right amount of seed, and know when to plant.)*

Discuss How did the development of farming contribute to the growth of civilizations? *(Students might say that farming led to he establishment of villages, which led to the creation of governments and significant advances in technology and culture.)*

The village covered about three times more land than Jericho and included hundreds of rectangular mud-brick houses, all connected and all about the same size.

Settled People Change Their Ways of Life Like their Paleolithic ancestors, early farmers probably divided up the work by gender and age. Still, important differences began to emerge. In settled farming communities, men came to dominate family, economic, and political life. Heads of families, probably older men, formed a council of elders and made decisions about when to plant and harvest. When food was scarce, warfare increased, and some men gained prestige as warriors. These elite warriors asserted power over others in society.

Settled people had more personal property than nomadic people. In addition, some settled people accumulated more possessions than their neighbors, so differences in wealth began to appear.

New Technologies To farm successfully, people had to develop new technologies. Like farmers today, they had to find ways to protect their crops and measure out enough seed for the next year's harvest. They also needed to measure time accurately to know when to plant and harvest. Eventually, people would use such measurements to create the first calendars.

Many farmers learned to use animals such as oxen or water buffalo to plow the fields.

Archaeological evidence shows that some villages had separate workshops where villagers made tools, including smooth, polished ax heads and chipped arrowheads. In some parts of the world, Neolithic people learned to weave cloth from animal hair or vegetable fibers. Many Neolithic people began using clay to create pottery for cooking and storage. Archaeologists have learned about life during this period from finds such as "the Iceman"—the body of a Neolithic man found preserved in snow in the European Alps alongside various tools and belongings.

Technologies were not invented everywhere at the same time. Knowledge of some traveled slowly from one area to another, perhaps taking thousands of years to spread across continents. Other technologies were invented separately in different parts of the world and showed varying degrees of similarity.

The Neolithic Impact The Neolithic Revolution had a tremendous impact. Farming, especially in the river valleys, would form the social and economic cornerstones of urban civilization and government. For example, floods could often wipe out entire villages if they were not be contained. As a result, Neolithic peoples worked together and formed governments to

Before and After the Neolithic Revolution

Thousand of years after it began, the Neolithic Revolution still affects our lives.

BEFORE	AFTER
STRATEGIES FOR SURVIVAL	**STRATEGIES FOR SURVIVAL**
• Nomadic hunters and gatherers • Depended on environment for food and shelter	• Domesticated plants and animals • Settled in farming villages • Surpluses of food
GOVERNMENT	**GOVERNMENT**
• Family ruled by the male	• Village government with chief and council • Cities had organized government • Built public works construction projects
ECONOMY	**ECONOMY**
• No real economy	• Traditional economy—the barter system
TECHNOLOGY	**TECHNOLOGIES**
• Technology • Language developed	• Plowing • Weaving • Pottery • Calendars

>> **Analyze Charts** Based on this chart, which statement would be correct? Paleolithic people were more advanced than Neolithic people; or Neolithic people were more advanced than Paleolithic people.

History Background

The Walled City of Jericho: The earliest settlers of Jericho were probably Mesolithic, and date to about 9000 B.C. Jericho gradually developed into a farming society whose people built walls around their city. These inhabitants were displaced around 7000 B.C., possibly by invaders from northern Syria. For the next 3,000 years, occupation of Jericho was sparse. By 2300 B.C., however, Jericho was walled again, and nomadic settlers, the Amorites, occupied the city. The Amorites were succeeded by the Canaanites, the Canaanites by the Romans, and the Romans by the Muslims. After Jericho was incorporated into Jordan in 1949, large groups of Arab refugees populated the area. Today Jericho falls within the boundaries of the Israeli-occupied West Bank.

Answers

Analyze Charts *Neolithic people were more advanced than Paleolithic people.*

Identify *Farmers divided the workload between the genders, which allowed men to dominate a village's social, economic, and political life.*

direct projects such as the building of dikes and dams. Farming also resulted in surpluses of food, which allowed some farmers to gain wealth. That wealth, often passed to succeeding generations, was the basis of a social class system.

? IDENTIFY What role did gender play in early Neolithic villages?

ASSESSMENT

1. **Predict Consequences** How might the development of spoken language have influenced the religious beliefs of Neolithic people?
2. **Determine Relevance** Why is the beginning of farming considered the beginning of the Neolithic Revolution?
3. **Draw Conclusions** How did the social status of males change in villages during the Neolithic Revolution?
4. **Hypothesize** What would modern society look like today had the Neolithic Revolution not taken place?
5. **Cite Evidence** What change marked the beginning of the New Stone Age and how did that change impact people's ways of life?

SYNTHESIZE

Online Project the graphic organizer on the whiteboard. Ask students to discuss Paleolithic versus Neolithic. Using the PMI strategy, create three columns on the blackboard titled Plus/Minus/Interesting. Discuss each point in the graphic organizer. Ask students to answer these three questions for each point: What are the positive aspects of this point? What are the negative aspects of this point? What is interesting about this point?

DEMONSTRATE

Online Assign the **Digital Lesson Quiz** for this lesson if you haven't already done so. Students will be offered automatic remediation or enrichment based on their score.

Point out to students that they have learned how early modern humans lived toward the end of the Old Stone Age. They also learned how Neolithic peoples stopped being nomads and settled down in farming communities, how they developed their early religious beliefs and technologies, and how they domesticated plants and animals. Pose this question on the Discussion Board:

Determine Relevance How did the Neolithic Revolution impact the modern world? *(Students might say the world's modern civilizations might not have developed had it not been for the changes brought by the Neolithic Revolution.)*

Topic Inquiry

Have students continue their investigations for the Topic Inquiry.

Assessment

1. Language allowed people to communicate with one another, which allowed religious beliefs to spread quickly.
2. Farming allowed societies to move away from the nomadic lifestyle of hunting and gathering to a more settled lifestyle that would ultimately form the foundations of civilization.
3. Men began dominating the social, political, and economic life of villages.
4. The development of cities and many civilizations might not have occurred if not for the Neolithic Revolution.
5. The establishment of farming allowed people to settle permanently in villages, form governments, amass wealth, and create social classes.

Topic 1 Lesson 3

Civilization Begins

CONNECT

Preview Have students preview the **Lesson Objectives** and the list of **Key Terms**.

Students can also preview all the **Key Terms** and **Academic Vocabulary** using the **Interactive Reading Notepad** on the digital course or preview a summary of the lesson in the **Reading and Note Taking Study Guide**.

Online Use the **Editable Presentation** found on the digital course to present the main ideas for this lesson.

Start Up Activity

Ask students to answer this question as they enter and get settled: How did job specialization shape early civilizations? *(Students should show an understanding that as a variety of new tasks emerged in early civilizations, no one person could master all the skills needed to make tools, weapons, or other goods. Some became artisans, weavers, metalworkers, merchants, or carpenters.)*

Discuss Once students answer the question, have them share their ideas with another student, either in class or through a chat room or blog.

Online You can also project the **Start Up Activity** from the course.

INVESTIGATE

Have students read the section using the **Reading and Note Taking Study Guide** to help them take notes and understand the text as they read.

The First Cities and Civilizations

Explain that the world's first civilizations emerged near major rivers. Rivers provided ample food, as animals flocked to drink. Rivers were also travel routes. Perhaps the most important aspect of river valleys was the fertile soil that allowed farming to thrive. As agriculture grew, farmers produced surpluses of food that fed growing populations. Food surpluses meant some people could do work other than gathering food or meeting basic survival needs. As a result, urban populations grew.

D Differentiate Challenge Have students research one of the areas where river valley civilizations thrived. Have them research and select an article from a current newspaper, Internet news site, or magazine, and use the content to analyze how geography continues to affect events and developments in their particular region.

>> **Apply Concepts** Why was farming so crucial to the development of river valley civilizations, including those that flourished in Egypt?

Interactive Flipped Video

1.3 During the Neolithic Revolution, the establishment of villages such as Çatalhüyük and Jericho symbolized a huge step in human development. Societies were becoming more organized, and people's technological innovations were becoming increasingly complex. Soon would follow a momentous change in human existence—the development of civilizations.

TEKS
1.A, 2.A, 2.B, 16.A, 16.B, 17.A, 17.B, 19.A, 19.B

>> Objectives

Analyze the conditions under which the first cities and civilizations arose.

Outline the basic features that define civilization.

Understand the ways in which civilizations have changed over time.

>> Key Terms

surpluses
traditional economy
civilization
steppe
polytheistic
artisan
pictograph
scribe
cultural diffusion
city-state
empire
theocracy,

Civilization Begins

The First Cities and Civilizations

The earliest civilizations to develop were situated near major rivers. These rivers provided a regular water supply and a means of transportation. The animals that flocked to the rivers to drink were a source of food. Perhaps most important, conditions in the river valleys favored farming. Floodwaters spread silt—tiny bits of rock and dirt from the river bottom—across the valleys, renewing the soil and keeping it fertile.

In such rich conditions, farmers were able to produce a **surplus** of food, or more than was necessary. These surpluses allowed them to feed growing populations and to store food for the future. Thus they were able to produce enough food to support increasingly large populations.

As populations expanded, some villages swelled into the world's first cities. In these cities, some of the people were able to work at jobs other than farming. This was a radical departure from the traditional economies of the Stone Age. A **traditional economy** relies on habit, custom, or ritual and tends not to change over time.

Villagers had to work cooperatively to build bridges, dams, and other projects that benefited the community. In large cities, governments were formed to organize these projects. Projects that facilitated production and trade brought economic benefits. Early

PEARSON realize. www.PearsonTexas.com Access your Digital Lesson.

16

Aa Vocabulary Builder

1. Have students pronounce the following academic vocabulary terms and clarify the part of speech. Break difficult or polysyllabic words into syllables and pronounce them with students.
2. Explain what the word means in "student-friendly" language using synonyms and antonyms when possible. Provide concrete examples to clarify the meaning, and rephrase the definition.

complex: made up of many interrelated parts
significant: relatively large in amount

Neolithic governments extended their political power to create new economic opportunities as trade began to flourish.

River Valley Civilizations The rise of cities was the main feature of civilization. A **civilization** is a complex, highly organized social order. The world's first civilizations arose independently in a number of river valleys. These River Valley Civilizations include Sumer, between the Tigris and Euphrates rivers in the Middle East; Egypt, along the Nile River; the Indus civilization, along the Indus River in India; and the Shang civilization, along the Huang (hwahng) River, or Yellow River, in China. You will read in depth about each of these River Valley Civilizations in later topics.

Civilizations in the Americas Unlike the first civilizations in Asia and Africa, the first civilizations in the Americas arose away from river valleys. Major civilizations emerged in the highlands of Peru, Mexico, and Central America, where people learned to farm on the sides of mountains or to fill in swamps with land for farming.

Life Away From Cities Away from the first cities, many people continued to hunt, gather food, or live in farming villages. On some less fertile lands or on sparse, dry grasslands called **steppes,** nomadic herders tended cattle, sheep, goats, or other animals. Because the lands did not have abundant water or grass, these nomads had to keep moving to find new pasture.

DESCRIBE Describe how river valleys were ideal locations for the development of civilization.

Features That Define Civilization

What did the early civilizations that arose in different parts of the world have in common? While cities are the main feature of civilization, historians distinguish several other basic features of most early civilizations. Seven of the major features are (1) organized governments, (2) complex religions, (3) job specialization, (4) social classes, (5) arts and architecture, (6) public works, and (7) writing.

Organized Governments Councils of elders or chiefs ruled many of the world's farming villages. However, in cities, more powerful organized governments arose to oversee large-scale efforts that benefited the people. For example, as cities grew, their residents required a steady supply of food. A central government could coordinate the production of large amounts of food.

In addition, farmers near rivers needed to control flooding and channel waters to the fields. A well-organized government could bring people together for

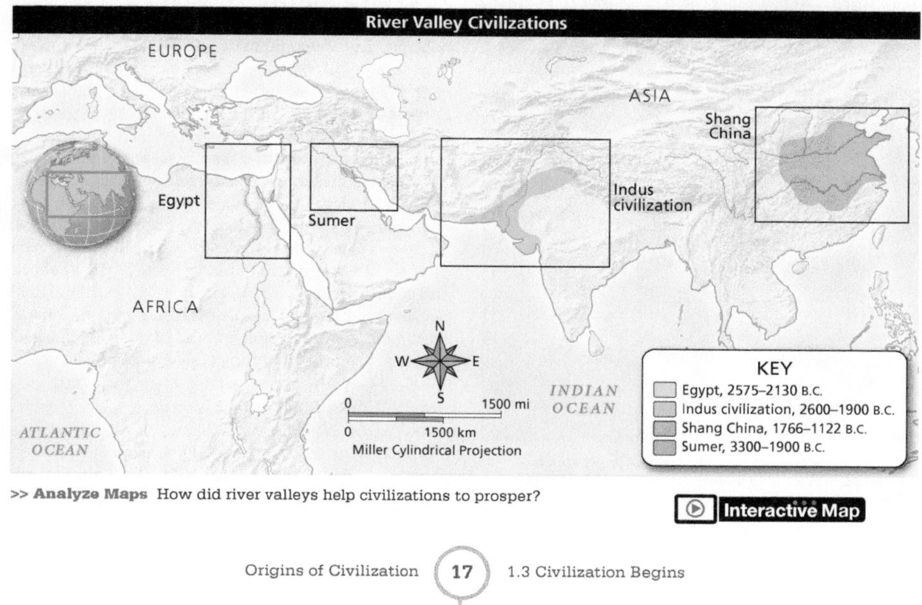

>> **Analyze Maps** How did river valleys help civilizations to prosper?

Interactive Map

Topic 1 Lesson 3

Online Project the **Interactive Map: River Valley Civilizations** and click through each of the hotspot maps with students.

ACTIVE CLASSROOM

Divide the class by having students count off 1 to 4. Each number should correspond to one of the four civilizations shown on the map. Next, have students look closely at the rectangle containing their civilization and have them describe how geography played a role in the development of the civilization that flourished in that region.

Guided Reading and Discussion

Use the Editable Presentation to present the main ideas for this Core Reading. Ask students to explain why the first civilizations grew up around rivers.

Discuss Why were early civilizations in the Americas able to thrive away from river valleys? *(Students might say that people adapted to their environment by learning to farm on the sides of mountains or fill in swampy areas to farm.)*

Evaluate Impact How did civilizations that developed away from river valleys satisfy their need for water? *(Students might say that other civilizations developed by lakes or in climates where rain was plentiful. Others found ways to divert water to their farming settlements.)*

English Language Proficiency Standards

ELPS Learning Strategies 1.E.4 Read "First Cities and Civilizations" aloud. Have students complete one activity according to their English proficiency.

Beginning With students, find, write, and display the bolded words. Say words aloud and have students repeat. Provide definitions and write out a sentence for each word. Ask students to copy sentences into their notebooks.

Intermediate Use the Beginning activity, and then assist students in writing another simple sentence for each word in their notebooks.

Advanced Have pairs of students review the text to find bolded words. Instruct pairs to write the words and use context clues to define each word in their notebooks. Ask pairs to write a sentence for each word. Pairs may share their work with the class.

Advanced High Have individual students review the text to find bolded words, write them in their notebooks, and develop definitions using context clues. Ask students to write a sentence for each word and share their work with a partner.

Answers

Apply Concepts *Under the fertile growing conditions provided by certain river valleys, farmers were able to produce a surplus of food, which allowed them to store food and feed a growing population.*

Describe *River valleys provided fresh water and routes of transportation. Animals that drank at rivers were a source of food, and floods provided fertile soil for farming.*

Analyze Maps *River valleys provided favorable conditions for creating permanent settlements with enough food for a large population, to support jobs other than farming, and to engage in trade and organize large building projects.*

Topic 1 Lesson 3

Features That Define Civilization

Explain to students that while early civilizations arose in different parts of the world, they had many things in common. They all formed organized governments, complex religions, job specialization, social classes, arts and architecture, public works, and systems of writing.

Key Terms

Ask students to find the key term **theocracy** (in bold) in the text. Explain that the term means a form of government in which religious leaders are rulers. Compare the words **democracy** and **theocracy**, pointing out the word part *-cracy*, and explain that this word part is from a Greek word meaning "form of government."

projects such as building dikes, digging canals, and carving out irrigation ditches.

Many rulers relied on royal officials to help them govern. They issued laws, collected taxes, and organized defense systems. Over time, governments became more complex, and separate departments evolved to oversee different functions of government. In many early governments, priests probably had the greatest power. In a **theocracy,** the government was run by religious leaders. In other governments, warrior kings emerged as the main political leaders. Often, they claimed their right to rule came from the gods, and power was passed from father to son. Thus, many political rulers gained religious power as well.

Complex Religions Most ancient people were **polytheistic,** which means they believed in many gods.

People appealed to sun gods, river goddesses, and other gods that they believed controlled natural forces or human activities such as birth or war.

In early religions, priests and worshipers sought to gain the favor of the gods through complex rituals such as ceremonies, dances, prayers, and hymns. To ensure divine help, people built temples and sacrificed animals, crops, or sometimes other humans to the gods. Sacrifices and other ceremonies required the full-time attention of priests, who had special training and knowledge.

>> These daggers are from the tomb of an Egyptian pharaoh, or ruler. The dagger on top has a blade of gold. The bottom dagger has a blade of iron.

Job Specialization The lives of city dwellers differed from those of nomads. Urban people developed so many new crafts that a single individual could not master all the skills needed to make tools, weapons, or other goods. For the first time, individuals began to specialize in certain jobs. Some became **artisans,** or skilled craftspeople, and made pottery or finely carved or woven goods. Among the crafts developed in cities, metalworking was particularly important.

People learned to make tools and weapons, first out of copper and later out of bronze, a more durable mixture of copper and tin.

Cities had other specialists, too. Bricklayers built city walls. Soldiers defended these walls. Merchants sold goods in the marketplace. Singers, dancers, and storytellers entertained on public occasions. Such specialization made people dependent on others for their various needs.

Social Classes In cities, social organization became more complex. People were ranked according to their jobs. Such ranking led to the growth of social classes. Priests and nobles usually occupied the top level of an ancient society. Next came a small class of wealthy merchants, followed by artisans. Below them came the vast majority of people—peasant farmers who lived in the surrounding villages and produced food for the city.

In many civilizations, slaves occupied the lowest social level. Poor families sometimes sold family members into slavery to pay their debts. Others became slaves as punishment for crimes or were prisoners captured in war. Because male captives were often killed, women and children made up the largest number of slaves in some societies.

Arts and Architecture The arts and architecture of ancient civilizations expressed the talents, beliefs, and values of the people who created them. Temples and palaces often dominated the city landscape. Many rulers may have ordered such buildings to be constructed in order to remind people of the strength and power of their government and religion. The skilled workers who built these massive buildings decorated them with wall paintings, statues of gods, goddesses, or rulers, and other stunning pieces of design work.

Public Works Strong rulers also ordered vast public works to be built. Such projects included irrigation systems, roads, bridges, and defensive walls.

These public works projects were meant to benefit the city by protecting it from attack, ensuring its food

Origins of Civilization 18 1.3 Civilization Begins

History Background

Allowing Ancient Art to Last: In September 1940, four French teenagers stumbled upon the entrance to the Lascaux cave in France, which contains some of the finest examples of Paleolithic art yet discovered. After World War II, the cave became a major tourist attraction, with as many as 1,200 visitors a day. By 1955 the carbon dioxide in the visitors' breath had begun to affect the paintings. To prevent further deterioration, the French government closed the cave to the public in 1963. Tests later showed that this action reversed the damage the visitors' breath had caused. The French government has kept the site closed, but has built a reproduction of the cave paintings nearby for tourists.

Basic Features of Civilizations

FEATURE	DESCRIPTION
Cities	• Larger and more organized than villages • Cities support the other features of civilization
Governments	• Coordinate public works projects such as bridge and dam construction • Establish laws and organize defense
Complex Religions	• Belief in one or more gods or goddesses • Institution of rituals
Job Specialization	• Different types of jobs that leads workers to specialize on one task
Social Classes	• Ranked groups are based on job or economic standing
Arts and Architecture	• Artwork that expresses a society's talents, beliefs, and values
Public Works	• Large-scale projects for the mutual benefit of a city and its people
Writing	• Structured writing system initially used by governments and religious leaders to record important information

>> **Analyze Charts** Which features do you think most affected the daily lives of average people?

supply, or enhancing the reputation of its ruler. The projects were often quite costly, requiring a great deal of human labor and sometimes resulting in the loss of lives during construction.

Writing Of the earliest civilizations, some but not all developed a critical skill—writing. The first writing systems were established in different places and at different times, in many cases with no contact among the different groups who created them. Thus the earliest writing systems varied in appearance, structure, and purpose.

Some were first used in temples, where priests needed to record amounts of grain collected, accurate information about the seasons, and precise rituals and prayers. Other writing systems were first used on public monuments, where rulers spelled out their greatest achievements as a means of advertising their power to the people. Archaeologists have found masses of ancient writings, some on clay tablets or vases, others on stone statues, and yet others on the walls of buildings.

The first step people made toward developing writing was to use **pictographs** (also called pictograms), or simple drawings that look like the objects they represent.

Later, they developed complex writing systems including symbols that represent words, syllables, or letters. As writing grew more complex, only specially trained people called **scribes** could read and write. Scribes kept records for priests, rulers, and merchants. Only a few societies permitted women to become scribes, an occupation that could lead to political power.

Nomadic Life and Civilizations Nomadic cultures differed from civilizations in their social organization—that is, they did not exhibit many of the characteristics of civilization. The people did not build cities, and their governments were simpler than those of civilizations. However, nomadic peoples often excelled in arts and sciences. For example, many groups developed sophisticated traditions in oral poetry, music, weaving, jewelry making, and animal raising.

IDENTIFY CENTRAL IDEAS What role did religion play in early civilizations?

ELPS 1.B.1 Discuss *Features That Define Civilization* with your classmates. Identify and correct any speaking errors that you make.

Online Project the **Interactive Chart: The Rise of River Valley Civilizations** and have students complete the activity individually, as a class, or in small groups.

ACTIVE CLASSROOM

Using the Rank It strategy, ask students to rank the features that define a civilization, from those that had the greatest impact to those that had the least impact. Ask students to provide a justification for the ranking decisions they made. Then ask students to work in pairs to share their rankings and justifications. Poll the class to see if there is agreement on the ranking.

Guided Reading and Discussion

Ask students to describe what the most important aspects of a civilization are.

Tell students that governments became more complex, and separate departments evolved to oversee different functions of government. In many early governments, priests probably had the greatest power. In a theocracy, the government was run by religious leaders. In other governments, warrior kings emerged as the main political leaders. Often, they claimed their right to rule came from the gods, and power was passed from father to son. Thus, many political rulers gained religious power as well.

Define What is the definition of a complex religion? *(Students might say that complex religions are religions that worship many gods or goddesses.)*

Evaluate Impact How did the development of a writing system aid in the development of civilization? *(Students should show an understanding that the development of ancient writing systems was the dividing line between prehistory and history. Writing allowed records to be kept and histories to be written. As a result, civilizations thrived as their citizens became literate.)*

English Language Proficiency Standards

Learning Strategies 1.B.1 Read "Features That Define Civilization." Identify one feature as the subject of a class discussion.

Beginning Use images, drawings, charts, maps, or the glossary to help students understand the content. Ask questions about one of the features. Give students specific feedback on their responses and provide opportunities to correct errors.

Intermediate Follow the instructions in the Beginning activity. Give students feedback on pronunciation, vocabulary, and fluency. Provide opportunities to correct any speaking errors.

Advanced Provide student groups with discussion questions about the content and one of the features. Instruct each student to contribute to the group discussion. Provide feedback on pronunciation, vocabulary, and fluency and opportunities to correct any speaking errors.

Advanced High Follow the instructions in the Advanced activity, but encourage students to share feedback on classmates' pronunciation, vocabulary, and fluency. Provide opportunities to correct errors.

Answers

Analyze Charts *Answers may vary, but they should be supported by a clear and logical explanation.*

Identify Central Ideas *People believed that a god, or gods, influenced human activities such as farming, birth, and war. As a result, early civilizations sought to gain the favor of these deities through a series of complex rituals and ceremonies, dances, and the building of temples.*

Civilizations Change

Explain to students that as the centuries passed, ancient civilizations changed in many ways. People interacted with each other differently; their physical environment changed; and cities expanded into large empires. Note that it was not only natural disasters, such as volcanic eruptions or earthquakes, that affected cities and human migration patterns, but also factors created by humans, such as soil depletion and loss of timber sources. Migration, along with trade, contributed to cultural diffusion.

Guided Reading and Discussion

Ask students to explain the reasons why civilizations evolved.

Identify Cause and Effect How did cultural diffusion impact civilizations over time? *(Students should show an understanding that cultural diffusion, which occurred as people traded, migrated, and fought one another, allowed ideas, customs, religions, and technologies to spread.)*

Identify Cause and Effect How did Earth's ever-changing environment facilitate the spread of ideas? *(Students should show an understanding that environmental disasters forced many people to migrate to other areas where they interacted with others from different cultures. As a result, people shared and adapted ideas and other aspects of life.)*

Evaluate Impact What was the impact of warfare on early civilizations? *(Students should say that as rival leaders battled for power, some were able to conquer many cities and villages, creating the first empires. Moreover, warfare sometimes brought benefits to the conquered, ending hostilities between neighboring communities and creating common bonds between people.)*

Civilizations Change

Ancient civilizations changed in many ways over the centuries. Among the chief causes of change were shifts in the physical environment and interactions among people. Among the major results was the expansion of cities into larger political entities.

The Effect of the Environment Like their Stone Age ancestors, people living in early civilizations depended heavily on the physical environment. They needed ample rain and fertile soil to be able to produce crops. Resources such as stone, timber, or metals were also essential. Significant changes in the environment could have an immediate impact on people's lives.

At times, a sudden, drastic event would devastate a community. An earthquake or the eruption of a volcano could wipe out an entire civilization. Farming the same land too much could destroy soil fertility, and rivers could become too salty. Cities would then suffer famine, and survivors would be forced to move away.

If people used up nearby timber or ran out of other building resources, they would have to find ways to adapt to this scarcity. They might, for example, trade with people in areas where such resources were readily available. Or they might use alternate building materials such as reeds.

>> This store room in Pompeii shows various bowls and the remains of one person who was buried alive after a volcano rained hot ash down on the ancient city.

Cultural Diffusion Another major source of change for people living in ancient times was **cultural diffusion,** the spread of ideas, customs, and technologies from one people to another. Cultural diffusion occurred through migration, trade, and warfare.

As famine, drought, or other disasters led people to migrate, they interacted with others whose lives differed from their own. As a result, people often shared and adapted the customs of others. Trade, too, introduced people to new goods or better methods of producing them.

In ancient times, skills such as working with bronze and writing, as well as religious beliefs, passed from one society to another.

Warfare also brought change. Often, victorious armies forced their way of life upon the people they defeated. On other occasions, the victors incorporated the ways of a conquered people into their society.

Cities Become City-States As ancient rulers gained more power, they conquered territories beyond the boundaries of their cities. This expansion led to the rise of the **city-state,** a political unit that included a city and its surrounding lands and villages. Rulers, nobles, and priests often controlled the land outside the city and forced peasants to give them some of the crops they grew on it. In some places, a significant portion of each harvest went to support the government and temples.

The First Empires Rival leaders often battled for power. Sometimes, ambitious rulers conquered many cities and villages, creating the first empires. An **empire** is a group of states or territories controlled by one ruler. For the conquered people, defeat was painful and often cruel.

At the same time, empire building also brought benefits. It helped end war between neighboring communities and created common bonds among people. As you will soon read, many impressive civilizations and powerful empires developed all over the world and left a lasting legacy behind them.

? CONNECT How did warfare influence cultural diffusion?

D Differentiate Extra Support Organize students into groups of three or four. Give each group a card with a key term from the digital reading. Allow time for each group to brainstorm the meaning of the term and prepare a short presentation in which they will act out the term's meaning in front of the class. At the end of the skit, the rest of the class should be able to answer: "What did the term mean?"

Answers

Connect *Victorious armies forced their way of life upon conquered people.*

ASSESSMENT

1. **Compare** How did the development of early Asian and African civilizations compare to the development of early American civilizations?
2. **Cite Evidence** How did religion influence government?
3. **Identify** Name the seven basic features of civilization.
4. **Summarize** How did the establishment of a writing system change civilization?
5. **Draw Conclusions** How did warfare further empire building?

SYNTHESIZE

Online Project the graphic organizer on the whiteboard. Using a version of the Rank It strategy, put sticky notes on the whiteboard for each "cause" listed on the graphic organizer. Next, have students work in groups and write down on separate sticky notes the "effect" for each "cause" they see on the board. Ask each group to go up to the board and pair the causes and the effects. When they are finished, have the students evaluate and discuss which group was more accurate.

DEMONSTRATE

Online **Digital Quiz** Assign the online Lesson Quiz for this lesson if you haven't already done so. Students will be offered automatic remediation or enrichment based on their score.

In "Civilization Begins," you learned how early civilizations developed over time. You learned how the first civilizations grew and prospered along river valleys, while other groups flourished in other geographic regions. You also learned what the main features of civilization are. Pose the following questions on the Discussion Board.

Identify Cause and Effect How did religion influence the establishment of governments and social classes in early civilizations? *(Students might say that in many early civilizations, priests held great power in government, while religion created a social class system in which priests, along with nobles, were at the top of an increasingly hierarchical society. Also, many rulers claimed that their right to rule came from the gods, and they passed their power to their sons, creating a government hierarchy.)*

Draw Conclusions Why would nomadic life not be classified as a civilization? *(Students might say that nomads did not exhibit any of the basic features that define civilization. They did not form governments, have job specialization or social classes, or excel in the arts and sciences.)*

Topic Inquiry

Have students continue their investigations for the Topic Inquiry.

Assessment

1. In Asia and Africa, civilizations developed along rivers, while in the Americas, civilizations developed in swamps and in mountainous regions.
2. Priests often held great power in government and were at the top of society. Political rulers gained religious power by claiming their right to rule came from the gods.
3. organized government; complex religions; job specialization; social classes; arts and architecture; public works; writing
4. Before writing systems were developed, ideas, customs, technology, and news spread by word of mouth. Writing allowed such knowledge to be preserved and to spread more quickly and widely.
5. While defeat in war was painful, it ended conflicts between neighboring peoples and created common bonds, allowing powerful empires to expand.

Topic 1

Answers to TEKS Assessment

1. Student answers will vary but should note that the chart is a secondary source that lists the attributes of hominids. Students may also suggest that *Homo habilis* ("handy man") could have used agriculture because they created primitive tools for chopping and cutting plants. *Homo erectus*, who had larger brains and bones, are the most likely to have been an agricultural group because they were the first to use fire and develop a hand ax that could be used for digging. Evidence, such as being the first to wear clothing and develop a language, makes *Homo neanderthalensis* another group that could have practiced agriculture.

2. Student answers will vary but should include that historians study and write about the historical past. They study artifacts, such as tools and weapons made by humans, as well as documents and other written evidence. They evaluate this evidence, explain what it means, and try to place it in historical context. By explaining why things occurred in the past, historians can help us understand what happens today and what may happen in the future.

3. Student answers will vary but should include that people needed a steady supply of food. Learning how to domesticate plants and animals met this need. Agriculture probably began when people realized that seeds scattered on the ground produced plants the next year. Historians have found evidence that people began to farm in different parts of the world at different times and that not all of the plants were domesticated in each place. The evidence historians use includes artifacts, or objects made by man. Artifacts can include clothing, tools, and weapons.

4. Student answers will vary in part, but should be as follows:
   1. No, a high school student's Web site would not be a valid source, unless the Web site included content created by credible authors.
   2. Yes, if the article is accurately translated, it is a valid source.
   3. Yes, if the chart has a credible author and is on the university Web site, it is valid.
   4. Yes, if there is a valid source listed for the timeline in the description, but not valid if there is no credible source.
   5. Yes, the archaeologist has firsthand information from her findings.
   6. Yes, if the cave paintings are legitimate, then so are the photographs.

5. Student answers will vary but should include that domestication of plants and animals led to settled farming and permanent villages. One of the first Neolithic villages was Çatalhüyük, built circa 7000 B.C. Students should explain that by examining the remains of this village, archaeologists have determined that it had hundreds of rectangular mud-brick houses, all connected and all about the same size. Archaeologists would have excavated through several layers of earth to reach the remains. Artifacts would be analyzed, and their locations would be marked on a map. Different artifacts would suggest the activities of the villagers and where these activities took place. Archaeologists would determine whether certain artifacts provide information on a social structure for the community. Leaders would need to make decisions on planting and harvesting, or deciding what to do in case of a shortfall. In settled farming communities, men began to dominate family, economic, and political life.

TEKS ASSESSMENT

Attributes of Early Hominids

Ardipithecus ramidus
- lived 4.4 million years ago
- fossils first found between 1992 and 1994
- walked on two legs

Australopithecus afarensis
- lived 3.85-2.95 million years ago
- strong arms with curved fingers
- some were as tall as 5 feet
- walked on two legs

Homo habilis
- Lived 2.4 – 1.5 million years ago
- nicknamed "handy man"
- first to use primitive tools

Homo erectus
- lived 1.8 million- 143,000 years ago
- bones first found in Indonesia in 1893
- similar to modern humans

Homo neanderthalensis
- lived 200,000-28,000 years ago
- first to wear clothing
- might have been the first to have a spoken language

5 million years ago | 4 million years ago | 3 million years ago | 2 million years ago | 1 million years ago | Present

Source: Smithsonian Institution

1. **Identify Major Causes of Events** Identify major causes of events from 8000 B.C. to 500 B.C., including the development of agriculture. Explain the differences between primary and secondary sources, analyzing frame of reference and point of view. Using the Attributes of Early Hominines chart to gain a frame of reference, as well as lessons from this topic, write a paragraph identifying hominids who would most likely have used agriculture. Be sure to support your point of view. Include physical characteristics of hominids and the tools they may have made and used. **1.A, 29.C**
2. **Identify Characteristics of Civilizations** Identify the characteristics of civilizations by explaining how historians examine sources. Write a paragraph telling how historians identify the characteristics of early civilizations. Predict how knowing about the civilizations of the past can help civilizations of the future. Consider what historians do in your predictions. **2.B, 29.B**
3. **Identify and Describe Major Causes of Events** Identify and describe major causes of events from 8000 B.C. to 500 B.C., including the development of agriculture by identifying methods historians used to analyze evidence. Write a paragraph describing how early humans learned to plant crops, and draw conclusions about why certain plants were domesticated. Consider what people needed, how they most likely discovered that planting was a good idea, and which methods historians have used for studying evidence. **1.A, 29.A**
4. **Identify Major Causes of Events** Identify major causes of events from 8000 B.C. to 500 B.C., including the development of agriculture and of the river valley civilizations. Evaluate the validity of a source based on language, corroboration with other sources, and information about the author. Determine whether the following are valid sources about researching major events after the Neolithic Revolution: 1) A high school student creates a Web site called "Strategies for Survival." 2) An article about government is translated from early writing. 3) The author of a chart which lists the economy of the Neolithic Period is a college professor. The chart has several legitimate sources and is a link on the university's Web site. 4) A historical magazine has a timeline of the Neolithic Period. 5) An archaeologist finds remains of terraced farming areas and writes a paper on her findings. 6) A spelunker discovers a cave with early tools and paintings of hunting scenes. A scientist verifies that the tools and paintings are over 5,000 years old. The spelunker takes photos of the art and publishes them in a newsletter. Answers should include an explanation of why the source is valid or not. **1.A, 29.D**
5. **Identify Changes** Identify important changes in human life caused by the Neolithic Revolution. Also, identify methods used by archaeologists to analyze evidence. Write a paragraph identifying how the Neolithic Revolution led to the establishment of early villages, and give an example. Identify the methods used by archaeologists to analyze evidence about changes in human life. Consider the transition from nomadic life, examples and description of an early Neolithic village, archaeological process and analysis of artifacts, and indications of early social structure and decision-making. **17.A, 29.A**

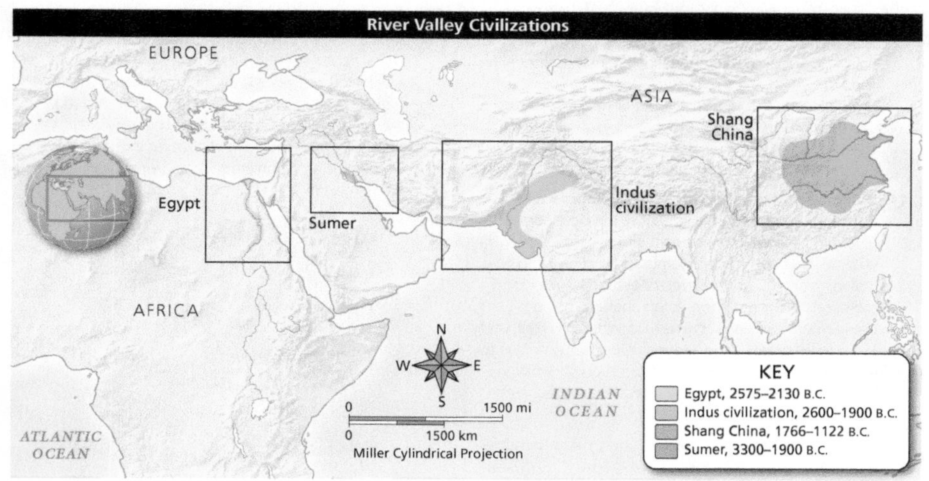

6. **Locate Regions and Places** Locate regions and places of historical significance directly related to major eras. Identify the regions and places of historical significance that are related directly to major eras. Look at the four civilizations that are highlighted on the map. In what range of dates did these four areas develop? Explain the features of these early civilizations. What generalizations can you make about the population and adequacy of food? Explain the transition of early villages to cities and the larger role of governments. **16.A**

7. **Identify Major Causes of Events** Identify major causes of events from 8000 B.C. to 500 B.C., including the development of agriculture. Explain the differences between primary and secondary sources analyzing historical context. Write a paragraph identifying why permanent villages would lead to new skills and technologies. Identify a primary source you might use to find out what technologies were invented at this time. Consider how permanent villages came to be, why these villages led to the development of technology, and a primary source you can use for research. **1.A, 29.C**

   "By producing their own food, people no longer needed to roam in search of animals, fish, or plants. For the first time, they could remain in one place throughout the year. As a result, early farmers settled the first permanent villages. They also developed entirely new skills and technologies."

8. **Describe Major Effects** Describe the major effects of events from 8000 B.C. to 500 B.C., including the development of agriculture. Use a decision-making process to gather information, identify options, predict consequences, and take action to implement a decision. Write a paragraph describing the effects of agricultural development from 8000 B.C. to 500 B.C. Then, use a decision-making process that Neolithic people may have used to determine issues related to building permanent settlements. Consider domestication of plants and animals and food production that led to permanent villages. **1.A, 31.B**

9. **Identify the Characteristics** Summarize the impact of the development of farming (Neolithic Revolution) on the creation of river valley civilizations. Analyze information by finding the main idea. Summarize the main reason the Neolithic Revolution was a time of dramatic changes. Consider what the Neolithic Revolution was and how it changed life. **2.A, 29.F**

6. Student answers will vary but should include that the four river valley civilizations started independently in this order: Sumer, Indus, Egypt, and Shang. Students can provide dates. All of these regions contributed to the development of river valley civilizations. Each river valley civilization had surpluses of food that could be stored. Food supplies were adequate enough to support increasingly large populations, and cities evolved. With larger populations, the social order became more complex, with people ranked according to their jobs. Organized governments coordinated public works projects to benefit the community, such as dikes and canals.

7. Student answers will vary but should include that domestication of plants and animals led to the first permanent villages. To farm successfully, people had to develop new technologies: to measure time in order to know when to plant and harvest; to measure seeds for planting; to create more efficient tools; to create pottery for cooking and storage; and to weave cloth from animal hair or vegetable fibers. Students should note that they could find more information about the tools and technologies by going to a museum and studying a primary source, such as tools that archaeologists have recovered from the period. A secondary source could be an encyclopedia or a book that describes these tools.

8. Student answers will vary but should include that during the Neolithic Revolution, nomadic people learned to domesticate plants and animals. Plant domestication may have begun with seeds scattered on the ground that produced plants the next year. People also domesticated animals and used them for food, skins, milk, or eggs. With stable food production, people could settle in permanent farming villages.

   Use the following steps to demonstrate how Neolithic people may have used a decision-making process to organize a permanent settlement that would best meet their needs:

   - Gather information: A leader or group of leaders would need to do some basic planning to provide food, shelter, and security. They would need to assess the number of people who would inhabit the settlement and which area would provide water and the most fertile soil to grow crops.
   - Identify options: Options could include locations with proximity to water for crops and people. The location would ideally be near a forest or similar area that could provide raw materials to make houses, tools for farming, and pottery used to store food. Also, the area selected would have to be big enough to accommodate any population growth, but small enough to be manageable and be secure for the community.
   - Predict consequences: The consequences of settling in an area would mean having a longer-term outlook for survival and potential community growth. It would require able-bodied people to provide security, such as a defensive wall, to protect the community from potential invaders. It might also require construction of dikes or canals to prevent natural calamities such as floods. Some type of basic government or leadership would be critical to completing these public works projects.
   - Take action to implement a decision: The government or leadership would make a decision to secure a permanent settlement for a population of several thousand people. The selected area could be fairly flat, approximately three to four acres, and near a stream or a larger body of water. The selected place would have fertile soil to grow crops and nearby raw materials to construct tools needed for agriculture. Raw material would also be available for housing construction and tools and supplies to build a solid wall around the village.

Answers to TEKS Assessment

9. Student answers will vary but should include that the Neolithic Revolution was the transition from nomadic life to settled farming, as people learned to domesticate plants and animals. This development led to the first permanent villages, which were often located in river valleys that provided water and fertile soil for farming. Men came to dominate family, economic, and political life and formed councils to make decisions about community issues. The end to a nomadic existence was a major change in the way people lived. Societies became more organized and developed more complex technological innovations.

10. Student answers will vary but should include a chart, which can be two columns with one to two words on the left side and a longer description on the right. For example:

    Geologists: Experts in earth science who determine the age of rocks near archaeological sites to help archaeologists estimate the age of artifacts found at the site.

    First villages: Jericho, built between 10,000 and 9000 B.C. Small village, surrounded by a huge stone wall. Geologists would analyze stones to help determine when the wall was built.

    Workshops: Villages had separate workshops where they made tools using materials such as stones, cloth, and clay. Geologists would analyze stones in tools to determine how and when they were made.

11. Student answers will vary but should include that, in river valleys, flood waters spread silt, tiny bits of rock and dirt, which made the soil fertile. This led to surplus food production that fed growing populations. Too much rain might lead to floods that damaged crop growth, leading to poor harvests and famines. Sudden changes in the environment could destroy crops, shelters, or natural resources needed for survival.

12. Student answers will vary but should include that this writing is a form of pictographs. The image is a type of pictograph called cuneiform. To interpret pictographs or cuneiform, a historian would analyze each symbol to figure out what object or idea the symbol represents. Then, the historian would compare and examine several pieces of writing to determine whether the different sources had similarities. Eventually, through these comparisons, the historian would develop a frame of reference to help determine what the symbols mean.

13. Student answers will vary but should include that the Indus Valley bordered a desert and a mountain range, and included plains. The Indus Valley was a good place to settle because the river valley had fertile soil for farming and there was a river that provided water and food, as well as travel and trade routes.

TEKS ASSESSMENT

10. **Create Charts** Create charts to demonstrate the relationship between geography and the historical development of a region or nation. Identify methods used by geographers to analyze evidence. Create a chart showing the relationship between geography and the historical development of a region. Be sure to include the following: what a geologist does, unearthing the first villages, and making tools. **15.A, 29.A**

11. **Summarize the Impact of the Development of Farming** Summarize the impact of the development of farming (Neolithic Revolution) on the creation of river valley civilizations. Write a paragraph summarizing how farming along rich soil at river valleys led to producing more food. Why did unexpected changes in the environment lead to problems? Consider why river valley soil is fertile and feeding expanding populations. Use at least one specific example from the excerpt below to infer the problems caused by unexpected changes in the environment. **2.A, 29.F**

    "Like their Stone Age ancestors, people living in early civilizations depended heavily on the physical environment. They needed ample rain and fertile soil to be able to produce crops. Resources such as stone, timber, or metals were also essential. Significant changes in the environment could have an immediate impact on people's lives."

12. **Describe the Major Effects** Describe the major effects of events from 8000 B.C. to 500 B.C., including the development of the river valley civilizations. Explain how historians, when examining sources, analyze frame of reference and point of view to interpret historical events. Write a paragraph explaining early writing in the picture. What is the general term for this type of writing? How would a person studying this writing possibly figure out its meaning? **1.A, 29.B**

13. **Interpret Maps to Explain Geography** Interpret maps to explain how geography influenced events and people in the past. Write a paragraph about the three landforms in and around the Indus Valley and why it was a good place to settle. **16.C**

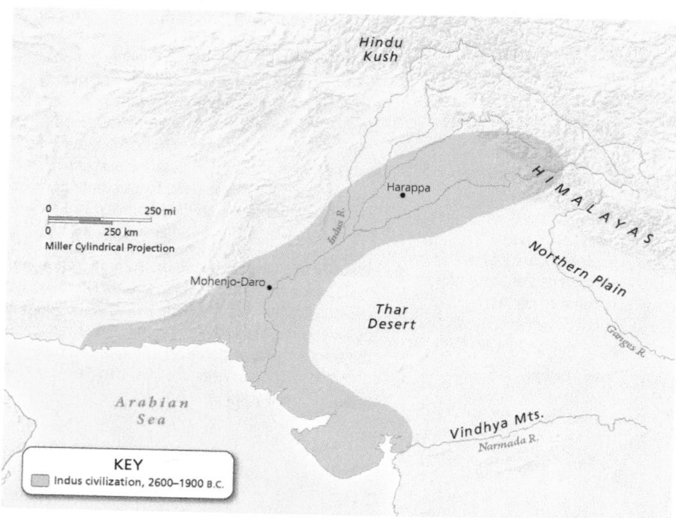

14. **Analyze the Influence of Geographic Factors** Analyze the influence of human and physical geographic factors on major events in world history, including the development of river valley civilizations. Write a paragraph analyzing the influence of human and physical geographic factors on the development of river valley civilizations. How did farmers make their work easier and more productive? Consider the effects of silt from the rivers. What did farmers do to control damages from potential flooding? 16.B

15. **Identify the Characteristics of Theocracies** Identify the characteristics of theocracies as forms of government in early civilizations. Write a paragraph identifying why the priests in early religions practiced certain rituals. Consider the types of rituals they practiced and why it was important to them. 19.A

16. **Identify the Characteristics of Political Systems** Identify the characteristics of political systems, including theocracy. Identify methods used by anthropologists to analyze evidence. Using the art and information from lessons, write a paragraph identifying why an anthropologist might study the statue of the priest king to learn more about the characteristics of a theocracy. Consider what anthropologists do and how the statue shows that religion was important. What might be some of the anthropologist's findings? 19.B, 29.A

17. **Reflect on the Essential Question Write an essay on the Essential Question: Why is culture important?** Use evidence from your study of this Topic to support your answer.

16. Student answers will vary but should include that anthropologists focus on the origins and development of human cultures. The statue shows a priest king. An anthropologist might say that the creation of the statue symbolizes the importance of religion to an ancient civilization. The date the statue was made and details from the statue would help anthropologists better understand the culture and the role of a priest king. A theocracy is a government run by religious leaders. Even in governments that were not theocracies, priests probably had the greatest power in the government.

14. Student answers will vary but should include that river valley civilizations were established because silt from the rivers made them fertile areas for farming. Because of the damage flooding could do, farmers cooperated to build dikes, canals, and irrigation systems to control flooding. Farmers also created tools and domesticated animals to make farming easier and more productive.

15. Student answers will vary but should include that priests practiced certain rituals such as ceremonies, dances, prayers, and hymns to gain favor with the gods. They wanted the gods to help them and their communities. People built temples, and priests guided sacrifices and other ceremonies to the gods to ensure divine help. They may have feared that bad things would happen if they didn't show respect to the gods.

Topic 1

Answers to TEKS Practice

1. B
2. H

Online To prepare for the End-of-Topic test, have students go online for additional Topic Review and Assessment questions or to review their notes in the **Interactive Reading Notepad** for the lessons in this Topic.

Benchmark Tests

Assign these benchmark tests as you complete the relevant topics to monitor student progress toward mastering the course content and as preparation for the End-of-Course Test.

Benchmark Test 1: Topics 1–5

Benchmark Test 2: Topics 6–10

Benchmark Test 3: Topics 11–15

Benchmark Test 4: Topics 16–21

TEKS PRACTICE

1

Archaeologists find a site
Excavation begins
Artifacts are analyzed to determine age
Data about the dig is entered into a computer

Study the chart that explains the process archaeologists follow when excavating for evidence of how early hominids lived. Which of the following is the missing step?

A Geologists examine seeds and animal bones at the site

B Archaeologists record the description and location of each artifact

C Botanists analyze blood stains found on artifacts

D Zoologists determine the age of the rocks surrounding the dig

---

2 During the Neolithic period, as people began working more closely together in farming communities, which of the following aspects of culture developed?

F Fire, tools, and boats

G Plowing, hunting, and cooking

H Calendars, weaving, and pottery

J Language, religion, and art

Test Taking Tips: Tip for Questions With Photographs or Drawings

1. Read the question.
2. Read any title or caption provided with the image. Note information about the time, place, objects, or people in the image that you can learn from the title or caption.
3. Determine who or what is shown in the image. Is an action or situation shown? If so, what is it? What aspects of the action or situation will help you answer the question?
4. Read the question again to be sure you understand what is being asked. Look at the image to find the answer to the question. Reread the title or caption if you need further information.
5. Answer the question in your own words.
6. Read the answer choices and select the best answer.

3

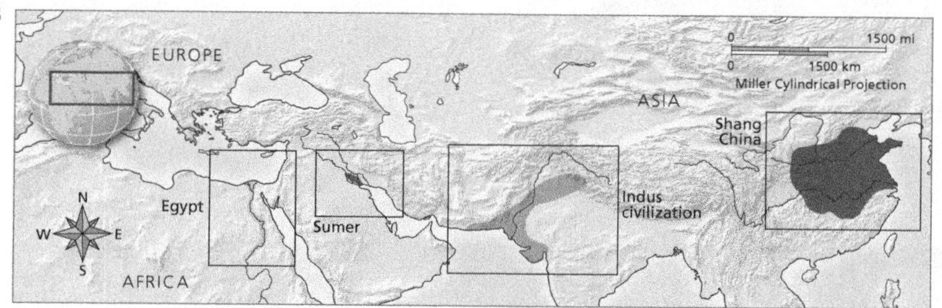

Which of the following generalizations is true for all of the places indicated on the map?

A They developed complex economies by trading wheat and corn with other societies.

B They developed cities with complex social classes.

C They were home to all of the people in the regions at the time.

D They invented terraced farming to grow enough food for their populations.

---

4 In an ancient civilization, a warrior king dies, and his son takes over his father's role in government. From whom did they claim their right to rule came from?

F Royal officials

G City artisans

H City nobles

J The gods

If you have trouble with...				
Question	1	2	3	4
See Lesson	1.1	1.2	1.3	1.3
TEKS	29.A	17.A	16.A	19.B

3. B
4. J

Online Use the **Topic Synthesize** to help students revisit and reflect on the Essential Question for this Topic.

Topic Inquiry

If students have done a Topic Inquiry for this Topic, have them complete the final step of the Inquiry now.

The Ancient Middle East and Egypt (3200 B.C.–500 B.C.)

TOPIC 2 ORGANIZER	PACING: APPROX. 1 PERIOD, .5 BLOCKS		
	PACING	**TEKS**	**ELPS**
Connect	1 period		
MY STORY VIDEO **Hatshepsut, the Woman Who Was King**	10 min.		
ESSENTIAL QUESTION ACTIVITY **How Much Does Geography Affect People's Lives?**	10 min.	16.B	
MAP ACTIVITY **The Ancient Middle East and Egypt**	10 min.	16.A, 16.B, 16.C	
TOPIC INQUIRY: DOCUMENT-BASED QUESTION **What is the Function of Law?**	20 min.		
Investigate	2–4 periods		
TOPIC INQUIRY: DOCUMENT-BASED QUESTION **What is the Function of Law?**	Ongoing		
LESSON 1 **A Civilization Emerges in Sumer**	30–40 min.	1.A, 2.C, 16.B, 19.A, 27.A	
LESSON 2 **Empires in Mesopotamia**	30–40 min.	1.B, 2.C, 3.A, 20.B, 27.A	1.G.1, 1.C.1
LESSON 3 **The Hebrews and the Origins of Judaism**	30–40 min.	1.B, 3.A, 20.A, 20.B, 22.B, 23.A, 23.B	1.D.1
LESSON 4 **Egyptian Civilization**	30–40 min.	1.A, 2.C, 16.B, 19.A, 24.A, 26.B, 27.A	1.E.1
Synthesize	1 period		
DIGITAL ACTIVITY **Reflect on the Essential Question and Topic**	10 min.	16.A, 16.B, 16.C	
TOPIC INQUIRY: DOCUMENT-BASED QUESTION **What is the Function of Law?**	20 min.		
Demonstrate	1–2 periods		
DIGITAL TOPIC REVIEW AND ASSESSMENT **The Ancient Middle East and Egypt**	10 min.		
TOPIC INQUIRY: DOCUMENT-BASED QUESTION **What is the Function of Law?**	20 min.		

AUTHOR'S NOTE

Hammurabi of Babylon

Hammurabi was born King of Babylon, the sixth in a line of otherwise undistinguished Amorite rulers of that city. He apparently governed his modest metropolis and its hinterland—at that time a city-state no more than fifty miles across—for some thirty years before he seized his chance to make Babylon great in the land. Then, late in his reign, he seems to have parlayed a combination of shrewd stagecraft, brilliant timing, and military force into a far wider power than any of his predecessors had enjoyed. For a brief time, he and his heirs held supreme authority over all the peoples of Mesopotamia.

The reputation of Hammurabi as a ruler in peace, however, considerably outshines his claim to fame as an empire builder. In the chronicles of the Near East, he lived on not as Hammurabi the Conqueror but as Hammurabi the Lawgiver.

The three hundred Sumerian and Akkadian laws of *Hammurabi's Code* cover a wide range of civil and criminal matters, from land law and business law to regulation of family relations, from personal injury to military service, from witchcraft to taxes. Many of the principles promulgated in the code seem harsh to the modern reader. The principle of an eye for an eye, a life for a life, is here commonly invoked, centuries before Moses. Mutilation and death are repeatedly prescribed as far and fitting punishments. And a clear sense of social hierarchy is reflected throughout; there is one law for slaves, another for their masters.

Yet the Code of Hammurabi does reveal a society with a highly developed belief in social justice. Even harsh punishment imposed by the state may be seen as an advance over the random retaliation of feuding clans that it replaced. And if the life of the slave is not rated as high in shekels of compensation as the life of a freeman, by the same token a nobleman may be punished more rigorously for the same of offense than his social inferiors. Perhaps most important, there is a clear conviction that might does not make right, that the law has a fundamental obligation to protect the weak from the strong. It was not the worst foundation for this early attempt at a larger social order, which reached beyond the city-state to govern a whole people.

—Anthony Esler, *The Human Venture: From Prehistory to the Present*, (Upper Saddle River, New Jersey: Pearson Education, 2004), p. 42

TOPIC INQUIRY: DOCUMENT-BASED QUESTION

What is the Function of Law?

TEKS 20.B, 22.A, 29.C, 29.F, 29.G, 29.H 30.B, 30.C

In this Topic Inquiry, students work individually to analyze five documents, both primary and secondary sources, expressing ideas about the function of the law. Students will answer questions about each document, reflect on the ideas, draw their own conclusions, and then write an essay on the following question: What is the function of the law?

STEP 1: CONNECT

Develop Questions and Plan the Investigation

Launch the DBQ Writing Activity

Have students write their definitions of a law. Refer them to the bulleted list of questions to get them started. If necessary, ask students to think about laws they have been affected by in their own lives. Suggest they keep this definition in mind as they read the documents, answer the questions, and write their essays.

Suggestion: Have volunteers read their definitions and have the rest of the class discuss them. Ask: What are some different things laws can be designed to do?

Generate Questions

Divide the class into small groups and have them record their questions about the function of laws.

Professional Development

Document Based Questions

Be sure to view the Document Based Questions resources in the online course.

Resources

- Student Instructions
- Need-to-Know Questions

PROFESSIONAL DEVELOPMENT

Document-Based Question

Be sure to view the Document-Based Question Professional Development resources in the online course.

STEP 2: INVESTIGATE

Apply Disciplinary Concepts and Tools

Read and Analyze Documents

Tell students that they will read and analyze five documents about some aspect of the law and its function in society. Then, they will write an essay and express their own opinions about what the function of the law is. Documents A and B are actual laws from two of the civilizations studied in this Topic. Document C is a discussion of the purpose and role of the law. Document D is a modern-day political cartoon. Document E is another actual law, but a modern one passed by the U.S. Congress.

At this time, discuss with students the differences between primary and secondary sources. Share these definitions:

A **primary source** is a historical record produced at the time of the event or period that it describes, or soon thereafter. These sources may include written accounts, such as diaries, speeches, government records, law codes, religious texts, and period cartoons, photographs, and artifacts.

A **secondary source** is a document that describes, interprets, or analyzes an event or person. Secondary sources are removed from the event, but can be written at about the same time as the event.

When using both primary and secondary sources, students must keep in mind the author's frame of reference and point of view, as well as the context in which the document was created.

Suggestion: Have students offer examples of other primary and secondary sources they have read and used.

Check Understanding

After students finish reading each individual document, have them answer the questions attached to each document. Review the questions and discuss the answers after students have answered the questions.

Resources

- Information Organizer

STEP 3: SYNTHESIZE

Evaluate Sources and Use Evidence to Formulate Conclusions

Write Your Essay

Now have students write their essays to express their own opinion about the question: What is the function of the law?

Suggestion: Have volunteers review their definitions of the law as a reminder before students begin on their essays.

Edit Your Essay

Have students read over their first drafts. Suggest they ask themselves these questions: Does it accurately express my viewpoint? Does it need more details? Then have students proofread and edit their essays, revising as needed. If time allows, have students exchange essays for a peer edit.

Suggestion: Remind students to check spelling and grammar in their essays.

Resources

- 21st Century Skill Tutorials: Write an Essay
- Writing Rubric
- 21st Century Skill Tutorials: Develop a Clear Thesis

STEP 4: DEMONSTRATE

Communicate Conclusions and Take Informed Action

Present Your Essay

Have students make a neat, clean copy of their essays. Then ask volunteers to read their essays aloud to the class.

Suggestion: As an alternative, have students publish their essays on a class website, bulletin board, or other online vehicle.

Reflect on the Project

After students briefly discuss what they found challenging in their essays and what they feel they did well, encourage them to use the lessons they learned writing this essay so they can write even more effectively in future writing projects.

Suggestion: As an extension activity, have students research the career of a leading American legal figure, focusing on his or her opinion about the function of law. Ask them to write a three-paragraph essay about the person's thoughts about the function of law. Suggest these jurists as starting points: John Marshall, Louis Brandeis, Oliver Wendell Holmes, Benjamin Cardozo, Felix Frankfurter, Thurgood Marshall, Sandra Day O'Connor, and Earl Warren. Ask students to share their essays with the class.

A Civilization Emerges in Sumer

Objectives

Objective 1: Understand how geography influenced the development of civilization in the Fertile Crescent.

Objective 2: Outline the main features of Sumerian civilization.

Objective 3: Explain how the advances in learning made by the Sumerians left a lasting legacy for later peoples to build on.

LESSON 1 ORGANIZER	PACING: APPROX. 1 PERIOD, .5 BLOCKS					
			RESOURCES			
	OBJECTIVES	PACING	Print	Online	TEKS	ELPS
Connect						
DIGITAL START UP ACTIVITY **The Fertile Crescent**		5 min.		●	1.A, 16.B	
Investigate						
READ **Civilizations Arise in the Fertile Crescent**	Objective 1	10 min.	●	●	1.A, 16.B	
INTERACTIVE MAP **Sumer and the Fertile Crescent**		10 min.		●	1.A, 16.B	
READ **Sumerian Civilization Develops**	Objective 2	10 min.	●	●	1.A, 16.B, 19.A	1.F.1
READ **Sumer's Legacy**	Objective 3	10 min.	●	●	2.C, 27.A	
INTERACTIVE GALLERY **Sumerian Civilization**		10 min.		●	2.C, 27.A	
Synthesize						
DIGITAL ACTIVITY **What is Civilization?**		5 min.		●	16.B	
Demonstrate						
DIGITAL QUIZ **Lesson Quiz and Class Discussion Board**		10 min.		●	1.A, 16.B, 19.A, 27.A	

PEARSON realize™ www.PearsonTexas.com Access your Digital Lesson

Focus on Texas Standards

Texas Essential Knowledge and Skills

1.A identify major causes and describe the major effects of the following events from 8000 BC to 500 BC: the development of agriculture and the development of the river valley civilizations

2.C explain how major river valley civilizations influenced the development of the classical civilizations

16.B analyze the influence of human and physical geographic factors on major events in world history, including the development of river valley civilizations, trade in the Indian Ocean, and the opening of the Panama and Suez canals

19.A identify the characteristics of monarchies and theocracies as forms of government in early civilizations

NOTES

Empires in Mesopotamia

Objectives

Objective 1: Outline the achievements of the first empires that arose in Mesopotamia

Objective 2: Understand how conquests brought new empires and ideas into the Middle East.

Objective 3: Describe the major political, religious, and cultural influences of Persia.

Objective 4: Summarize the contributions the Phoenicians made to the ancient Middle East.

LESSON 2 ORGANIZER	PACING: APPROX. 1 PERIOD, .5 BLOCKS					
			RESOURCES			
	OBJECTIVES	PACING	Print	Online	TEKS	ELPS
Connect						
DIGITAL START UP ACTIVITY **The Spreading of Ideas**		5 min.		●	2.C	
Investigate						
READ **Empires Emerge in Mesopotamia**	Objective	10 min.	●	●	2.C, 20.B	
READ **New Empires and Ideas**	Objective 2	10 min.	●	●	27.A	
INTERACTIVE GALLERY **Development of Civilizations**		10 min.		●	27.A	
READ **Rise of the Persian Empire**	Objective	10 min.	●	●	1.B, 3.A	1.G.1
READ **Phoenician Contributions**	Objective 4	10 min.	●	●	2.C	1.C.1
INTERACTIVE GALLERY **Mesopotamian Empires**		10 min.		●	2.C	
Synthesize						
DIGITAL ACTIVITY **Persian Influences**		5 min.		●	1.B, 3.A	
Demonstrate						
DIGITAL QUIZ **Lesson Quiz and Class Discussion Board**		10 min.		●	2.C, 3.A, 20.B, 27.A	

Focus on Texas Standards

Texas Essential Knowledge and Skills

1.B identify major causes and describe the major effects of the following events from 500 BC to AD 600: the development of the classical civilizations of Greece, Rome, Persia, India (Maurya and Gupta), China (Zhou, Qin, and Han), and the development of major world religions

2.C explain how major river valley civilizations influenced the development of the classical civilizations

3.A describe the major political, religious/philosophical, and cultural influences of Persia, India, China, Israel, Greece, and Rome, including the development of monotheism, Judaism, and Christianity

20.B identify the impact of political and legal ideas contained in the following documents: Hammurabi's Code, the Jewish Ten Commandments, Justinian's Code of Laws, Magna Carta, the English Bill of Rights, the Declaration of Independence, the U.S. Constitution, and the Declaration of the Rights of Man and of the Citizen

27.A identify the origin and diffusion of major ideas in mathematics, science, and technology that occurred in river valley civilizations, classical Greece and Rome, classical India, and the Islamic caliphates between 700 and 1200 and in China from the Tang to Ming dynasties

NOTES

The Hebrews and the Origins of Judaism

Objectives

Objective 1: Understand what made the ancient Israelites' belief system unique from others at the time.

Objective 2: Outline the main events in the early history of the Israelites.

Objective 3: Analyze the central moral and ethical ideas of Judaism.

LESSON 3 ORGANIZER	PACING: APPROX. 1 PERIOD, .5 BLOCKS					
			RESOURCES			
	OBJECTIVES	PACING	Print	Online	TEKS	ELPS
Connect						
DIGITAL START UP ACTIVITY **The Hebrew Bible**		5 min.		●	1.B, 23.A	
Investigate						
READ **The Ancient Israelites' Unique Belief System**	Objective 1	10 min.	●	●	3.A, 23.A	
READ **The Ancient Israelites**	Objective 2	10 min.	●	●	1.B, 3.A, 23.A	1.D.1
INTERACTIVE GALLERY **Origins of Judaism**	Objective 2	10 min.		●	23.A, 23.B	
READ **Law and Morality in Judaism**	Objective 3	10 min.	●	●	3.A, 20.A, 20.B, 22.B, 23.B	
INTERACTIVE CHART **The Ten Commandments and Modern Laws**	Objective 3	10 min.		●	20.A, 20.B, 23.A	
Synthesize						
DIGITAL ACTIVITY **Origins of Judaism**		5 min.		●	1.B, 23.A	
Demonstrate						
DIGITAL QUIZ **Lesson Quiz and Class Discussion Board**		10 min.		●	1.B, 3.A, 22.B, 23.A	

PEARSON realize™ www.PearsonTexas.com Access your Digital Lesson

Focus on Texas Standards

Texas Essential Knowledge and Skills

3.A describe the major political, religious/philosophical, and cultural influences of Persia, India, China, Israel, Greece, and Rome, including the development of monotheism, Judaism, and Christianity

20.A explain the development of democratic-republican government from its beginnings in the Judeo-Christian legal tradition and classical Greece and Rome through the English Civil War and the Enlightenment

20.B identify the impact of political and legal ideas contained in the following documents: Hammurabi's Code, the Jewish Ten Commandments, Justinian's Code of Laws, Magna Carta, the English Bill of Rights, the Declaration of Independence, the U.S. Constitution, and the Declaration of the Rights of Man and of the Citizen

22.B identify the influence of ideas regarding the right to a "trial by a jury of your peers" and the concepts of "innocent until proven guilty" and "equality before the law" that originated from the Judeo-Christian legal tradition and in Greece and Rome

NOTES

Egyptian Civilization

Objectives

Objective 1: Understand the ways in which geography helped shape ancient Egypt.

Objective 2: Explain how Egypt grew strong during the New Kingdom.

Objective 3: Describe the ways in which religious beliefs shaped the lives of ancient Egyptians.

Objective 4: Explain how the Egyptians organized their society.

Objective 5: Outline the advances that the Egyptians made in learning, the arts, science, and literature.

LESSON 4 ORGANIZER — **PACING: APPROX. 1 PERIOD, .5 BLOCKS**

	OBJECTIVES	PACING	RESOURCES: Print	RESOURCES: Online	TEKS	ELPS
Connect						
DIGITAL START UP ACTIVITY **The Nile River**		5 min.		●	16.B	
Investigate						
READ **Geography Shapes Egypt**	Objective 1	10 min.	●	●	1.A, 16.B	
READ **The Old Kingdom**	Objective 2	10 min.	●	●	1.A, 2.C, 16.B, 19.A	
READ **Middle and New Kingdom Egypt**		10 min.	●	●	1.A, 2.C	
INTERACTIVE MAP **Ancient Egyptian Lands**		10 min.		●	1.A, 2.C, 16.B	
READ **Religion Shapes Ancient Egyptian Life**	Objective 3	10 min.	●	●	19.A	1.E.1
INTERACTIVE 3-D MODEL **Pyramids**		10 min.		●	19.A	
READ **Organization of Egyptian Society**	Objective 4	10 min.	●	●	1.A, 24.A	
READ **Egyptian Learning Advances**	Objective 5	10 min.	●	●	2.C, 26.B, 27.A	
INTERACTIVE GALLERY **Hieroglyphics**		10 min.		●	2.C, 26.B	
Synthesize						
DIGITAL ACTIVITY **Egypt's Kingdoms**		5 min.		●	2.C	
Demonstrate						
DIGITAL QUIZ **Lesson Quiz and Class Discussion Board**		10 min.		●	1.A, 16.B, 26.B	

NOTES

TOPIC 2 **TEKS Mastery**

The Ancient Middle East and Egypt (3200 B.C.–500 B.C)

In this Topic, you will learn about the ancient Middle East and Egypt. You will also find lots of interesting ways to master the TEKS associated with this Topic.

Your study will help you master these TEKS:

TEKS

1.A, 1.B, 2.C, 3.A, 16.B, 19.A, 20.A, 20.B, 22.A, 22.B, 23.A, 23.B, 24.A, 24.B, 26.B, 27.A, 29.G, 30.A, 30.B, 30.C

LESSON OUTLINE

Connect

Connect with this Topic by watching a video about a fascinating person related to this Topic. You can think about how this Topic connects to your own life. And you'll encounter an intriguing Essential Question: How much does geography affect people's lives?

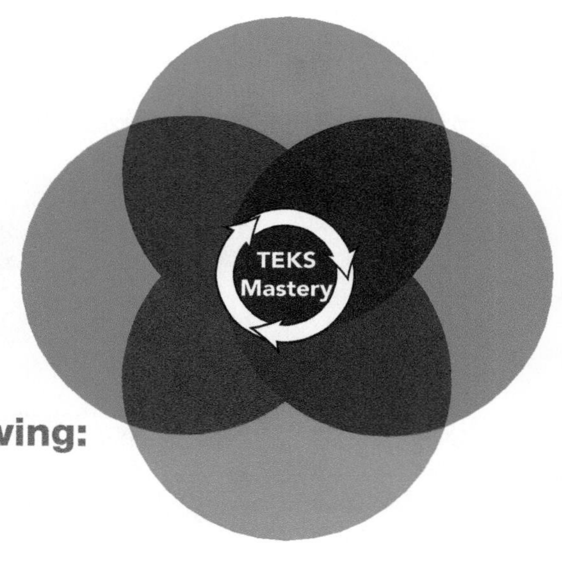

Begin your study by trying the following:

NBC LEARN Watch My Story Video:

Hatshepsut, the Woman Who Was King

Launch your Document-Based Question:

What is the Function of the Law?

Investigate

The Lesson Outline lists all the lessons you will investigate in this Topic. As you read and interact with key content, the story of the ancient Middle East and Egypt will come to life. Read the texts; try the interactivities. Investigate the fascinating story of the people who lived in the ancient Middle East and Egypt.

And keep working on your Document-Based Question to help build your mastery of the Topic TEKS.

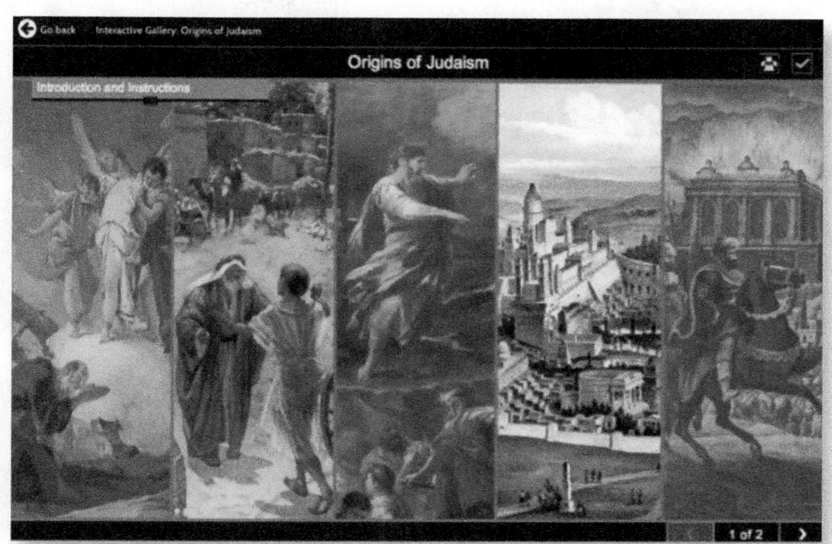

>> Digital interactivity from the online course

Synthesize

You will get a chance to pull together everything you have learned by thinking again about the Essential Question. Consider how you would answer the question now: How much does geography affect people's lives?

Demonstrate

Now you will get to show what you know. You will get a chance to complete the TEKS Review and Assessment pages, answering questions about every TEKS for this Topic. Or you can write an essay to show your response to the Document-Based Question. No matter which you do, it will be a real-world demonstration of the things you now understand about the Topic.

TEKS in Topic 2	Topic Review and Assessment Questions
1.A	1, 12, 16
1.B	5, 8
2.C	6, 7
3.A	6, 8, 11
16.B	2
19.A	9
20.A	10
20.B	4, 13
22.B	17
23.A	14
23.B	18
24.B	12
26.B	15
27.A	3
29.G	16
30.A	4, 8
30.B	4, 10, 14
30.C	11

Topic 2

The Ancient Middle East and Egypt (3200 B.C.–500 B.C.)

Introduction

The world's first civilizations emerged about 4,000 years ago in the Middle East in a region called the Fertile Crescent. Nearby, in Egypt, another powerful and influential empire flourished, while at the eastern shore of the Mediterranean, the civilization of the ancient Israelites was born. All of these civilizations were powerful influences on those that came later, affecting the future development of science, economics, culture, religion, politics, and government.

ESSENTIAL QUESTION

Ask students to think about the Essential Question for this Topic: How much does geography affect people's lives? Project the Essential Question activity from the course. Have a volunteer read each bulleted question. Discuss them as a class.

Identify Central Issues What geographical features might people settling in a place want to find? *(Answers may include a source of clean water, abundant food sources, a climate with an adequate growing season, access to building supplies such as timber or stone, and natural protection from invasions.)*

Classify What different ways of life would probably develop in different kinds of geographical areas? *(Possible answer: People who live near the sea would probably become sailors and traders and depend on fish for much of their diet. People who live in a desert would have to trade for things they need and cannot produce, such as food. They might also become herders, since some animals can live in harsh climates.)*

Generate Explanations What single geographical feature is the most important when settling in a place? Why? *(Answers will vary and may include usable water, a climate suitable for growing crops, safety from invasions, and access to transportation routes.)*

[**ESSENTIAL QUESTION**] How much does geography affect people's lives?

2 The Ancient Middle East and Egypt (3200 B.C.–500 B.C.)

Analyze Images

Ask students to examine the gold mask shown in this photograph. It was placed on the face of the deceased Egyptian king, Tutankhamen. Discuss what this mask might indicate about ancient Egyptians' beliefs about death.

>> Gold burial mask of King Tutankhamen

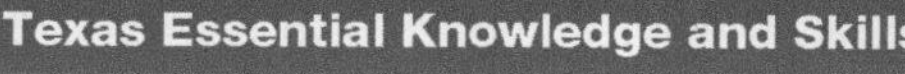

Texas Essential Knowledge and Skills

1.A, 1.B, 2.C, 3.A, 16.B, 19.A, 20.A, 20.B, 22.A, 22.B, 23.A, 23.B, 24.A, 24.B, 26.B, 27.A, 29.G, 30.A, 30.B, 30.C

Enduring Understandings

- A number of early civilizations and empires arose in the Fertile Crescent, a region of the Middle East that became a crossroads where people and ideas met and mingled.
- Sumerian city-states had distinct social structures, and Sumerian ideas and innovations influenced later civilizations.
- The ancient Israelites' belief in a single all-knowing, all-powerful God developed into Judaism, the world's first monotheistic religion and an influence on later religions and civilizations.
- Daily life in Egypt was strongly affected by religious beliefs, and Egyptians made many advances in art, literature, and learning.

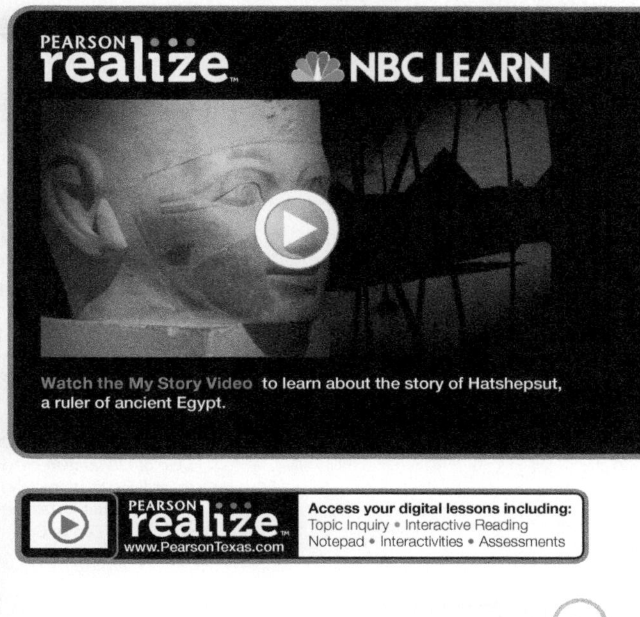

Watch the My Story Video to learn about the story of Hatshepsut, a ruler of ancient Egypt.

PEARSON realize www.PearsonTexas.com **Access your digital lessons including:** Topic Inquiry • Interactive Reading Notepad • Interactivities • Assessments

31

NBC LEARN MY STORY VIDEO

Project the My Story Video that introduces students to Hatshepsut, an ancient Egyptian ruler who declared herself king, or pharaoh.

Online My Story Video: **Hatshepsut, The Woman Who Was King**.

After viewing, ask students to respond to the following questions.

Check Understanding What about Hatshepsut was unprecedented in Egyptian history? *(She seized power and made herself king.)*

Hypothesize What does Hatshepsut's story reveal about the dangers of overgeneralizing about history? *(Hatshepsut's story contradicts the assumption of most people that the rulers of ancient civilizations were always male.)*

OVERVIEW ACTIVITY

Online Project **The Ancient Middle East and Egypt Map.** During this Topic students will learn about all of these places, but this map will provide a framework into which they can place the civilizations and events they learn about. Ask students to use the map to point out how location and geographical features might affect the development of these civilizations and the ways the people lived.

Analyze Maps What important geographical feature do Egypt and the civilizations of Mesopotamia have in common? *(a river)*

Topic Inquiry

If you choose to assign the Topic Inquiry, launch the DBQ activity after introducing the Topic.

D Differentiate Extra Support Have students locate Phoenicia on the map. Ask: What factor in Phoenicia's geography might have helped it develop into a trading civilization? *(It is located on the shore of a large sea, the Mediterranean, which meant it could easily sail to many different places to trade.)*

Topic 2 Lesson 1

A Civilization Emerges in Sumer

CONNECT

Preview Have students preview the **Lesson Objectives** and the list of **Key Terms**.

Students can also preview all the **Key Terms** and **Academic Vocabulary** using the **Interactive Reading Notepad** on the digital course or preview a summary of the lesson in the **Reading and Note Taking Study Guide**.

Online Use the **Editable Presentation** found on the digital course to present the main ideas for this lesson.

Start Up Activity

Remind students that the area known as Sumer was a river valley civilization located in Mesopotamia. As we learned previously, it was important for people to live near water sources in order to have access to drinking water as well as water for farming.

Predict Consequences Think back to the features of civilizations. Predict how Mesopotamia will develop into an early river valley civilization. *(Early people will settle there because of the rich farmland and develop cities with organized government to control the mass of people, which will result in other features of civilizations forming.)*

Online You can also project the **Start Up Activity** from the course.

INVESTIGATE

Have students read the section using the **Reading and Note Taking Study Guide** to help them take notes and understand the text as they read.

Civilizations Arise in the Fertile Crescent

The early civilizations of Mesopotamia depended on the region's two important rivers—the Tigris and the Euphrates. *Mesopotamia* means "between the rivers" in Greek and refers to the fertile farmland allowed for the rise of civilizations. Hunter-gatherer groups first settled in Mesopotamia and these people learned how to plant crops and to grow their own food on the fertile farmland. Plentiful food led to population growth and the formation of villages, which eventually developed into city-states and the world's first civilization.

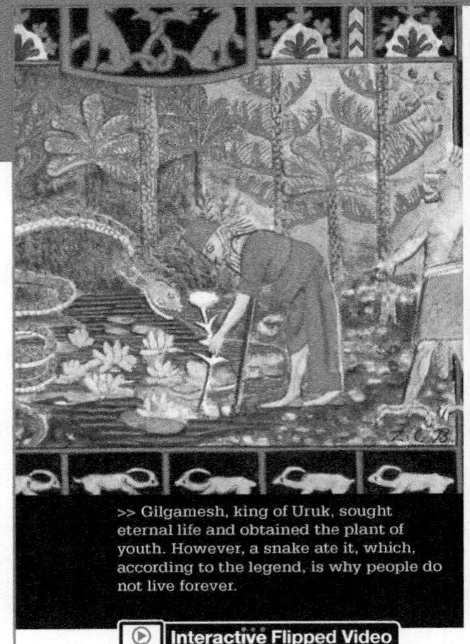

>> Gilgamesh, king of Uruk, sought eternal life and obtained the plant of youth. However, a snake ate it, which, according to the legend, is why people do not live forever.

Interactive Flipped Video

2.1 A desert climate dominates the land between the Persian Gulf and the Mediterranean Sea, yet a number of early civilizations arose here. The region of the Middle East is called the Fertile Crescent, named for its rich soils and golden wheat fields. Over time, nomadic herders, ambitious invaders, and traders easily overcame the region's few natural barriers. As a result, the region became a crossroads where people and ideas met and mingled. This region is often referred to as the "cradle of civilization." Many of the earliest human civilizations developed in this river valley region because of the availability of water and other agricultural resources.

TEKS
1.A, 2.C, 16.B, 19.A, 27.A

>> Objectives

Understand how geography influenced the development of civilization in the Fertile Crescent.

Outline the main features of Sumerian civilization.

Explain how the advances in learning made by the Sumerians left a lasting legacy for later peoples to build on.

>> Key Terms

Fertile Crescent
Mesopotamia
Sumer
The Epic of Gilgamesh
hierarchy
ziggurat
cuneiform

A Civilization Emerges in Sumer

Civilizations Arise in the Fertile Crescent

The Fertile Crescent curves from the Persian Gulf to the eastern coast of the Mediterranean Sea. Within the Fertile Crescent lies a region that the ancient Greeks later named **Mesopotamia,** which means "between the rivers." Mesopotamia is the area of land between the Tigris and Euphrates rivers, which flow from the highlands of modern-day Turkey through Iraq into the Persian Gulf. Around 3300 B.C., the world's first civilization developed in southeastern Mesopotamia, in a region called **Sumer.**

Sumerians Overcome Environmental Challenges Control of the Tigris and Euphrates was key to developments in Mesopotamia. The rivers frequently rose in terrifying floods that washed away topsoil and destroyed mud-brick villages. The Mesopotamian narrative poem *The Epic of Gilgamesh,* which was first told orally in Sumer, describes a great flood that destroys the world. Archaeologists have indeed found evidence that catastrophic floods occurred regularly in the ancient days of the Fertile Crescent.

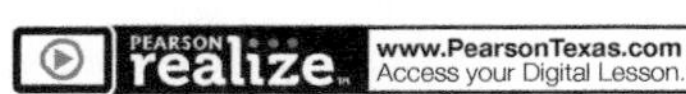

Vocabulary Builder

1. Have students pronounce the following academic vocabulary terms in this lesson and clarify the part of speech. For difficult or polysyllabic words, break them into syllables and pronounce them with the students.
2. Explain what the word means in common "student-friendly" language using synonyms and antonyms when possible. Provide concrete examples to clarify the meaning, and rephrase the definition.

ensure: to make sure that something will happen

evolve: to develop gradually into something

To survive and to protect their farmland, villagers along the riverbanks had to work together. Even during the dry season, the rivers had to be controlled in order to channel water to the fields. Temple priests or royal officials provided the leadership that was necessary to ensure cooperation. They organized villagers to work together on projects such as building dikes to hold back flood waters and irrigation ditches to carry water to their fields.

Sumerian City-States By 3000 B.C, Sumerians built a number of cities. Each city and the land surrounding formed a city-state. The Sumerians had few natural resources to build these cities, but they made the most of what they did have. They lacked building materials such as timber or stone, so they built with clay and water. They used the clay to make bricks, which they shaped in wooden molds and dried in the sun. These bricks were the building blocks for some of the world's first great cities, such as Ur and Uruk.

Trade brought riches to Sumerian cities. Traders sailed along the rivers or risked the dangers of desert travel to carry goods to distant regions. Although it is unclear where and when the wheel was invented, the Sumerians may have made the first wheeled vehicles. Archaeologists have found goods from as far away as Egypt and India in the rubble of Sumerian cities.

? IDENTIFY MAIN IDEAS How did geography influence the development of civilizations in the Fertile Crescent?

Sumerian Civilization Develops

Within a few hundred years of its beginning, Sumer included at least 12 separate city-states. Rival city-states often battled for control of land and water. For protection, people turned to war leaders. Over time, the practice of rule by war leaders evolved into hereditary rule. This resulted in the formation of monarchies. A monarchy is a government in which one person has complete authority to rule in peacetime and to lead soldiers in wartime.

Sumerian Government In each city-state, the ruler was responsible for maintaining the city walls and the irrigation systems. He led its armies in war, enforced the laws, and employed scribes to carry out functions such as collecting taxes and keeping records. The ruler was seen as the chief servant of the gods and led

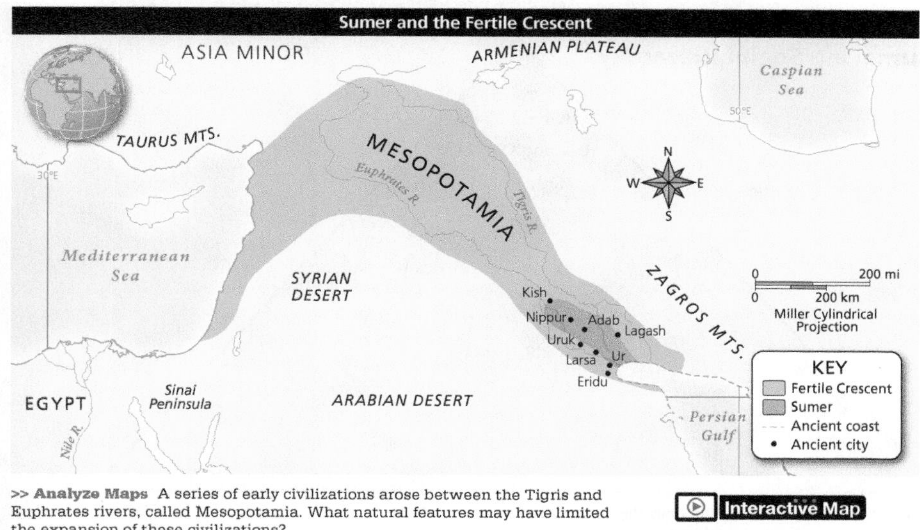

>> **Analyze Maps** A series of early civilizations arose between the Tigris and Euphrates rivers, called Mesopotamia. What natural features may have limited the expansion of these civilizations?

Interactive Map

The Ancient Middle East and Egypt 33 2.1 A Civilization Emerges in Sumer

Topic 2 Lesson 1

Online Project the **Interactive Map: Sumer and the Fertile Crescent.**

Early Sumerians faced the challenge of controlling the flow of river water to their fields. They worked together to control the waters, and over time city-states developed along with government, social hierarchy, religion, and other features. What made civilization possible in Mesopotamia? *(The two rivers created fertile farmland, which provided people a place to settle and eventually led to the development of civilizations.)*

ACTIVE CLASSROOM

Have students write a headline that captures the information displayed in the map. Instruct them to write a headline for this topic that captures the most important aspect that should be remembered. Allow time for them to share their headlines with a partner.

Key Terms

Ask students to find the key term **Mesopotamia** (in bold) in the text. Explain that the area, located between the Tigris and Euphrates rivers in modern-day Iraq and Turkey, was a fertile land that helped spur the world's first civilization.

Guided Reading and Discussion

Review the influence of geographic and human factors on the development of river valley civilizations.

Draw Conclusions Priests or officials organized large projects such as building dikes to hold back floodwaters. How might running large projects prepare people for running a government? *(It would provide them with organizational skills and the ability to organize and direct the work of a large group of people.)*

Answers

Analyze Maps *deserts and mountains*

Identify Main Ideas *The rich soil and the Tigris and Euphrates rivers created a rich farming region, especially for growing wheat. With a food supply from farms, Sumerians could form stable societies in the region instead of living a nomadic lifestyle.*

Topic 2 Lesson 1

Sumerian Civilization Develops

The main features of Sumerian civilization included an organized government, a distinct social hierarchy, an organized religion, and a writing system. Ancient Sumerians used a cuneiform writing system, which transformed pictorial drawings into signs that represented words. The famous *Epic of Gilgamesh*, a Sumerian tale of a man searching for eternal life, was written in cuneiform.

Guided Reading and Discussion

Ask students to review the features of Sumerian civilization, such as the formation of city-states leading to a government structure that consisted of an absolute monarchy with characteristics of theocracies, since the kings were seen as intermediaries between the human and the divine. Discuss the importance of a social structure within Sumerian society, again noting the highest class. Other features of Sumerian civilization were an organized religion and the cuneiform writing system.

Determine Relevance Sumerian scribes kept track of economic exchanges as well as social issues by recording details on clay tablets using cuneiform. How might the invention of cuneiform writing have strengthened Sumerian government and religious practices?

ceremonies meant to please them. Although Sumerian government consisted of an absolute monarchy, characteristics of theocracies were present since the kings were seen as intermediaries between the human and the divine.

Sumerian Society Each Sumerian city-state had a distinct social **hierarchy** (HY ur ahr kee), or system of ranking groups. The highest class included the ruling family, leading officials, and high priests. A small middle class was made up of lesser priests, scribes, merchants, and artisans. Artisans who practiced the same trade, such as weavers or carpenters, often lived and worked on the same street.

The majority of people were peasant farmers, and they formed the lowest level of society. Some had their own land, but most worked land belonging to the king or to temples. Sumerians also owned slaves. Most slaves had been captured in war. Some, though, had sold themselves into slavery to pay their debts.

The role of women in Mesopotamian society changed over time. In Sumer, goddesses were highly honored in religious practice. Perhaps because of the importance of female deities, women held a higher social standing in Sumer than in later civilizations of the region. However, Sumerian women never held legal rights equal to those of men. But some rulers' wives had supervisory powers, and a number wrote songs about their husbands, revealing to later scholars that they had learned writing and music. On rare occasion, a woman may have inherited property.

Sumerian Religion Like most ancient peoples, the Sumerians were polytheistic, worshiping many gods. These gods were thought to control every aspect of life, especially the forces of nature. Sumerian monarchs also served as the high priest, representing the city-state's chief deity, or god. The city-states were also theocracies where much of the land belonged to the local deity. Sumerians believed that gods and goddesses behaved like ordinary people—they ate, drank, married, and raised families. Although the gods favored truth and justice, they were also responsible for causing violence and suffering.

Sumerians believed their highest duty was to keep these divine beings happy and, by doing so, ensure the safety of their city-state. Each city built a **ziggurat** (ZIG oo rat), a large, stepped platform thought to have been topped by a temple dedicated to the city's chief god or goddess. Additionally, Sumerians celebrated holy days with ceremonies and processions. In one ritual, the king went through a symbolic wedding to Inanna, the life-giving goddess of love. This rite was meant to ensure a prosperous new year.

The Sumerians believed in an afterlife. In their view, all people lived after death in a grim underworld from

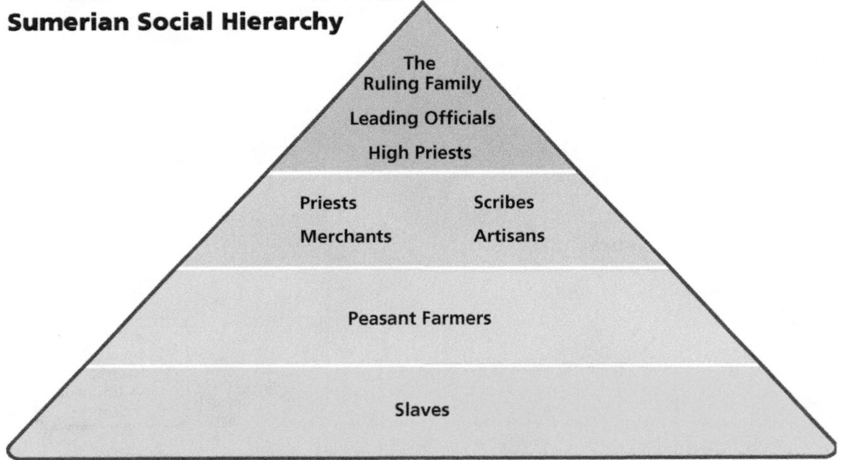

>> **Analyze Information** What does the information on the chart indicate about how Sumerian society supported itself?

History Background

Riches from a Tomb In the late 1920s, the world's imagination was captured by news accounts of discoveries being made in Iraq by British archaeologist Sir Leonard Woolley, at the site of the ancient city of Ur. Large, two-story homes were unearthed, some of which included a chapel for worship. The remains of the original ziggurat revealed that the ancient Sumerians were knowledgeable about such architectural forms as the column, the arch, the vault, and the dome. The most breathtaking discoveries, however, were unearthed in a royal cemetery, which contained artifacts of gold, silver, bronze, and semiprecious stones; musical instruments; mosaics; and other works of art. It was apparent from the evidence that Sumerian kings were buried with their court officials and servants—who, it was presumed, were expected to continue their service in the afterlife.

Answers

Analyze Information *The society was largely dependent on agriculture.*

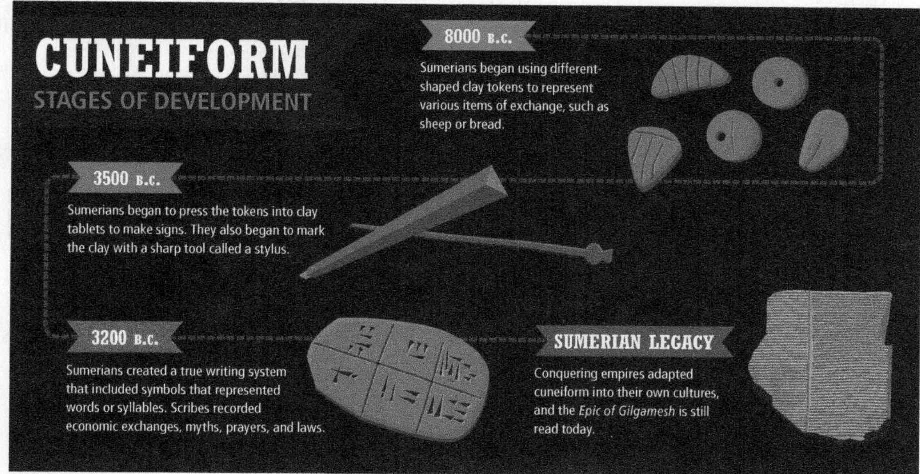

CUNEIFORM
STAGES OF DEVELOPMENT
8000 B.C.
Sumerians began using different-shaped clay tokens to represent various items of exchange, such as sheep or bread.
3500 B.C.
Sumerians began to press the tokens into clay tablets to make signs. They also began to mark the clay with a sharp tool called a stylus.
3200 B.C.
Sumerians created a true writing system that included symbols that represented words or syllables. Scribes recorded economic exchanges, myths, prayers, and laws.
SUMERIAN LEGACY
Conquering empires adapted cuneiform into their own cultures, and the *Epic of Gilgamesh* is still read today.

>> **Analyze Information** How did cuneiform writing allow Sumerians to communicate more effectively?

which there was no release. One character in *The Epic of Gilgamesh* describes the underworld as "the place where they live on dust, their food is mud, / . . . and they see no light, living in blackness / on the door and door-bolt, deeply settled dust."

Sumerian Writing By 3200 B.C., Sumerians had invented the earliest known writing. It was later called **cuneiform** (kyoo NEE uh fawrm), from the Latin word *cuneus* for "wedge," because scribes wrote by making wedge-shaped marks on clay tablets. Cuneiform grew out of a system of pictographs used to record goods brought to temple storehouses. Later, the Sumerians developed symbols to represent more complicated thoughts. As their writing evolved, the Sumerians used it to record not only economic exchanges but also myths, prayers, laws, and business contracts.

Sumerian scribes had to go through years of difficult schooling to acquire their skills. Discipline was strict. Untidy copying or talking in class could be punished by caning. Students who did well often learned about religion, mathematics, and literature as well.

SUMMARIZE Describe the three levels of Sumerian society.

ELPS **ELPS 1.F.1** Practice using words you already know to learn new words in *Sumerian Civilization Develops.*

Sumer's Legacy

Beginning around 2500 B.C., armies of conquering peoples swept across Mesopotamia and overwhelmed the Sumerian city-states. By 1900 B.C., the Sumerian civilization had been replaced by other civilizations and empires that you will read about in the next lesson.

Language and Culture However, Sumer left behind a lasting legacy. Newcomers to the region adopted many ideas and innovations from the Sumerians. For example, the Akkadians, Babylonians, and Assyrians adapted cuneiform so it could be used with their own languages. These peoples then helped spread Sumerian learning across the Middle East. The river-valley civilization that began in Sumer featured a number of elements, beyond a written language, that reappeared in other, later civilizations. Sumer's patriarchal family structure, agricultural-based economies, government structures, and the beginning of a trade base influenced later empires and the rise of classical civilizations, such as Greece and Rome. Later peoples also elaborated on Sumerian oral narratives, such as *The Epic of Gilgamesh*, which was written down in cuneiform by both the Akkadians and the Babylonians.

Astronomy and Mathematics Over the centuries, Sumerian scholars had begun to develop astronomy and mathematics. They studied the skies and recorded the

Sumer's Legacy

Sumerian knowledge and advances in language, culture, astronomy, mathematics, and technology passed to Greece and Rome through conquerors and traders and laid the foundation for technologies that still affect us today.

Online Project the **Interactive Gallery: Sumerian Civilization.** Display the photo of Sumerian jewelry and discuss the role of trade on Sumerian inventions and ideas. How was it possible for independent city-states to share similar cultures? *(Ideas, goods, and beliefs spread through trade between city-states.)*

ACTIVE CLASSROOM

Use the Write 1–Get 3 strategy. Ask a question with multiple possible answers, such as: What are some of Sumer's lasting legacies? Instruct students to fold a piece of paper into fourths and write one response in the first box. Ask to hear students' responses. Instruct students to record a response in each remaining box until they have four responses. Share responses with the class.

Guided Reading and Discussion

Explain that Sumer's advances, such as cuneiform, understanding of planetary movement, creation of a number system, the wheel, irrigation, and advances in metalworking, were adopted by civilizations such as the Babylonians after Sumer was defeated.

Determine Relevance Why was trade important to Sumerians? *(Trade gave Sumerians access to natural resources they lacked and allowed exchange of goods and ideas.)*

Answers

Analyze Information *Possible answer: wheel, plow, sails, metalwork, and numeral system*

Summarize *The three levels included rulers, officials, and high priests at the top; priests, merchants, scribes, and artisans in the middle; and peasants and slaves, the vast majority, at the bottom.*

Topic 2 Lesson 1

SYNTHESIZE

Online Ask students to consider the topic Essential Question, "How much does geography affect people's lives?" Remind them of Mesopotamia's location and the importance of the Tigris and Euphrates rivers. Have them use the Think-Pair strategy to answer the questions in the Digital Activity. Ask them to define *civilization*. Then have students explain how Sumer relates to this definition. Remind students to use details from the text to support their ideas.

Have partners think about the following question: Do you think geography is the most important factor for the development of early civilizations?

DEMONSTRATE

Online Assign the **Digital Lesson Quiz** for this lesson if you haven't already done so. Students will be offered automatic remediation or enrichment based on their score.

Pose the following questions to the class on the Discussion Board:

In "Civilization Emerges in Sumer," you read about events that led to the development of and the features of river valley civilizations in Mesopotamia.

Summarize Explain how geography influenced the development of Mesopotamian civilizations.

Evaluate Data Considering what you have learned in this lesson, do you think ancient civilizations would have prospered and grown without the access to trade? Why or why not?

Topic Inquiry

Have students continue their investigations for the Topic Inquiry.

>> The Standard of Ur is a small wooden panel covered on both sides with mosaics composed of stones and jewels. This image shows a banquet scene with the king and his servants.

movements of planets and stars. They also established a number system based on six, dividing the hour into 60 minutes and the circle into 360 degrees, as we still do today.

Although the weakened Sumerian city-states could no longer ward off attacks from surrounding peoples, their advances in mathematics and science did not die. Their achievements in these fields were diffused to other civilizations through trade and warfare, and also as succeeding rulers adapted Sumerian ideas and built upon them.

While the Akkadians, later known as Babylonians, controlled Sumer, Sumerians assimilated into Akkadian culture, and Akkadians adapted many Sumerian technological advances and culture.

Eventually, Babylonians considered themselves to be the inheritors of the Sumerian civilization. They adopted Sumerian history as their own and worshiped many of the same gods, continued Sumerian culture traditions, and used the Sumerian writing and number systems. The Babylonians also used Sumerian mathematical knowledge to develop basic algebra and geometry, to create accurate calendars, and to predict eclipses of the sun and moon.

Technology The Sumerians built the earliest known wheeled carts and wagons. They then developed the potter's wheel, which is used to shape wet clay into bowls and other kinds of pottery. They used bronze to make tools and weapons and developed looms to weave cloth. Equally important was the technology and engineering skills they invented to build irrigation systems and flood control projects.

Even though the Sumerian city-states were conquered and the Sumerian language disappeared, Sumerian inventions and ideas survived. As you will read, many peoples conquered the Middle East, including the Akkadians, Babylonians, Assyrians, and Persians.

These people preserved and furthered Sumerian knowledge and achievements. The rich heritage of Mesopotamian civilizations was later passed on to the Greeks and Romans. From them, this ancient legacy was carried to the Western world. In this way, developments and innovations made more than 5,000 years ago came to shape Western civilization today.

SYNTHESIZE What advances did the Sumerians make in mathematics and astronomy?

ASSESSMENT

1. **Describe** What are some Sumerian inventions and advances in learning that influenced the development of later civilizations?
2. **Determine Relevance** How might the invention of cuneiform writing have strengthened Sumerian government and religious practices?
3. **Compare** In what way was Sumer both a monarchy and theocracy?
4. **Summarize** What are some of the main features of Sumerian civilization?
5. **Synthesize** How did the geography of the Fertile Crescent affect the development of civilizations there?

Answers

Synthesize *The Sumerians recorded the movements of planets and stars and established a number system based on six.*

Assessment

1. Cities, monarchies, writing, astronomy, mathematics, the wheel, the sail, the plow, irrigation
2. Writing allowed the government to preserve records, laws, and achievements. Writing allowed priests to preserve prayers, rituals, and beliefs about gods, goddesses, and the afterlife.
3. Sumer was a monarchy and a theocracy because its government was led by kings who were also religious leaders.
4. A strong government led by kings, an organized social structure, an established religion, and an economy based on farming and trade were features that influenced development of the Sumerian civilization.
5. The Fertile Crescent not only had rich farmland that supported the development and growth of cities, it was also located between rivers, which made it accessible to multiple trade routes, giving Sumerians access to goods and enabling them to share and spread ideas.

2.2 Invasion and conquest were prominent features in the history of the ancient Middle East. Again and again, nomadic peoples or ambitious warriors descended on the rich cities of the Fertile Crescent. The region became a vital crossroads where warriors and traders met, clashed, and mingled. While many invaders simply looted and burned, some stayed to rule. Powerful leaders created large, well-organized empires, bringing peace and prosperity for a time to the region. Over several thousand years, these empires made advances in government, technology, and learning that influenced later civilizations from Greece and Rome to India and beyond.

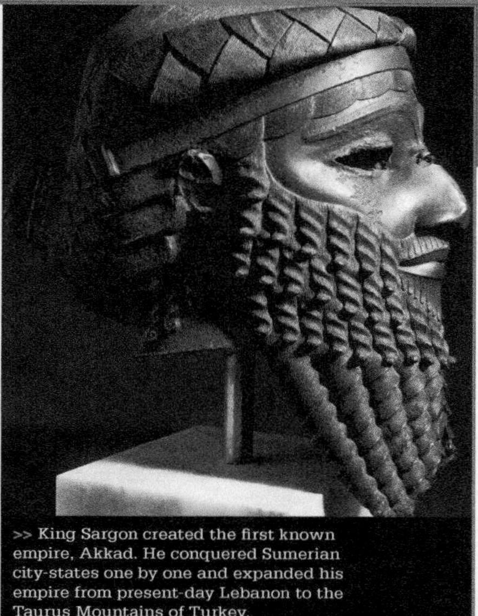

>> King Sargon created the first known empire, Akkad. He conquered Sumerian city-states one by one and expanded his empire from present-day Lebanon to the Taurus Mountains of Turkey.

Interactive Flipped Video

Empires in Mesopotamia

Empires Emerge in Mesopotamia

The First Empire About 2300 B.C., **Sargon,** the ruler of Akkad, invaded and conquered the neighboring city-states of Sumer. He continued to expand his territory, building the first empire known to history. He appointed local rulers, each of whom served as king of the land he oversaw. However, the world's first empire did not last long. After Sargon's death, other invaders swept into the wide valley between the rivers, tumbling his empire into ruin.

The Babylonian Empire In time, the Sumerian city-states revived, and they resumed their power struggles. Eventually, however, new conquerors followed in Sargon's footsteps and imposed unity over the Fertile Crescent. About 1790 B.C., **Hammurabi** (hah muh RAH bee), king of Babylon, brought much of Mesopotamia under the control of his empire. Hammurabi became king following the abdication of the throne by his father, Sin-Muballit, and formed an empire by winning a series of wars against neighboring kingdoms.

TEKS
1.B, 2.C, 3.A, 20.B, 27.A

>> Objectives

Outline the achievements of the first empires that arose in Mesopotamia

Understand how conquests brought new empires and ideas into the Middle East.

Describe the major political, religious, and cultural influences of Persia.

Summarize the contributions the Phoenicians made to the ancient Middle East.

>> Key Terms

Sargon
Hammurabi
codify
civil law
criminal law
Nebuchadnezzar
bureaucracy
barter economy
money economy
Zoroaster
colony
alphabet

PEARSON realize. www.PearsonTexas.com Access your Digital Lesson.

37

Empires in Mesopotamia

CONNECT

Preview Have students preview the **Lesson Objectives** and the list of **Key Terms**.

Students can also preview all the **Key Terms** and **Academic Vocabulary** using the **Interactive Reading Notepad** on the digital course or preview a summary of the lesson in the **Reading and Note Taking Study Guide**.

Online Use the **Editable Presentation** found on the digital course to present the main ideas for this lesson.

Start Up Activity

Tell students that the cultural, political, and economic influences of civilizations can be spread through military conquests or the trade of goods and services, and when people move and take their ways of life with them. Ask students: Which method do you think has the strongest, most long-lasting effect and why? *(Answers will vary. Students will probably argue that trade and other personal, willing contact has a more profound influence than military conquests.)*

Discuss Remind students that one feature of civilization is an organized government with laws. The set of laws known as Hammurabi's Code gave rise to important political and legal ideas, such as the principle that government has a responsibility for what happens in society. These ideas strongly influenced Mesopotamian civilizations and future civilizations as well. Ask students to discuss why laws are important.

Online You can also project the **Start Up Activity** from the course.

INVESTIGATE

Have students read the section using the **Reading and Note Taking Study Guide** to help them take notes and understand the text as they read.

Empires Emerge in Mesopotamia

Mesopotamian empires and kingdoms unified cities and created governments that served as a model for other governmental systems. The nations and empires of the region influenced each other in different ways.

Aa Vocabulary Builder

1. Have students pronounce the following academic vocabulary terms in this lesson and clarify the part of speech. For difficult or polysyllabic words, break them into syllables and pronounce them with the students.
2. Explain what the word means in common "student-friendly" language using synonyms and antonyms when possible. Provide concrete examples to clarify the meaning, and rephrase the definition.

emerge: to arise, appear, or occur
promote: to help something happen
various: several, many
diverse: different
represent: to be a sign or symbol for something else

Topic 2 Lesson 2

Analyze Images

Tell students that laws were used since Sumerian times, but Hammurabi made them public by carving them on a stone pillar. Ask students to look at the infographic and answer the question.

Guided Reading and Discussion

Be sure students understand the importance of unified cities and a strong government to ruling large groups of people. Discuss the Babylonian empire and the importance of established laws that maintained peace and stability within the empire.

Synthesize Explain a lasting legacy of Hammurabi's Code. *(the principle that government had a responsibility for what occurred in society)*

Hammurabi's Code Hammurabi's most ambitious and lasting contribution was his publication of a set of laws known as Hammurabi's Code. Most of the laws had been around since Sumerian times, but Hammurabi wanted to ensure that everyone in his empire knew the legal principles his government would follow. He had artisans carve nearly 300 laws on a stone pillar for all to see. Hammurabi's Code was the first important attempt by a ruler to **codify,** or arrange and set down in writing, all the laws that would govern a state.

Hammurabi's Code gave rise to an important political idea in Mesopotamian civilization that influenced future civilizations. The code developed the principle that government had a responsibility for what occurred in society. Hammurabi's Code is the first set of rules that is reflected in the principles of much later civilizations, such as the idea that the king did not have sole power over the people. Hammurabi's laws brought peace and stability to the Babylonian empire.

Hammurabi Establishes Civil Law One section of Hammurabi's Code codified **civil law.** This branch of law deals with private rights and matters, such as business contracts, property inheritance, taxes, marriage, and divorce. Much of Hammurabi's civil code dealt with property rights, but some of the laws were designed to protect the powerless, such as slaves or women. Some laws, for example, allowed a woman to own property and pass it on to her children. Another law spelled out the rights of a married woman, saying that if she was found to be blameless for the problems between herself and her husband, she could leave the marriage. If she were found to be at fault, however, the law instructed that she be thrown in the river.

In general, Babylonian civil law gave a husband both legal authority over his wife and a legal duty to support her. The code also gave a father nearly unlimited authority over his children. The Babylonians believed that an orderly household was necessary for a stable empire.

Some elements of Hammurabi's civil law are present in modern laws. For example, family law, which covers marriage and divorce, are addressed in the code. Many of his laws were adapted by succeeding rulers, and many scholars consider them early predecessors of Jewish and Islamic legal systems.

Criminal Law Hammurabi's Code also addressed **criminal law.** This branch of law deals with offenses against others, such as robbery, assault, or murder. Earlier traditions often permitted victims of crimes or their families to take the law into their own hands. By setting out specific punishments for specific offenses,

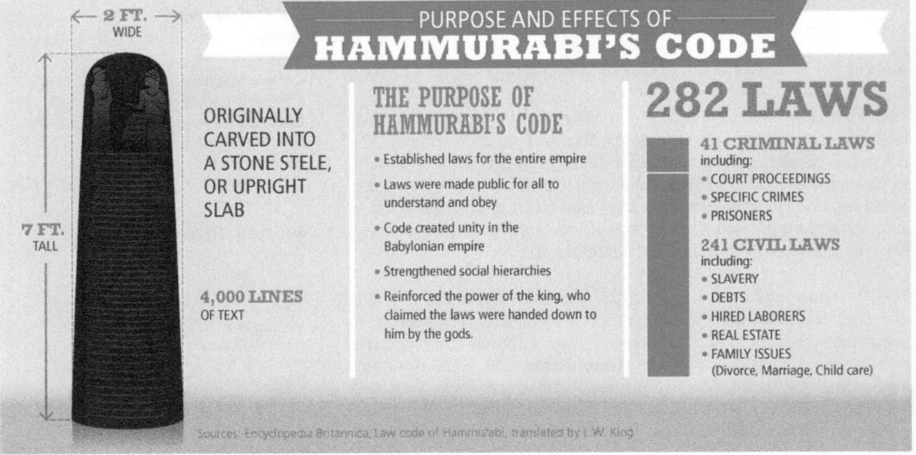

>> **Analyze Information** The purpose of Hammurabi's Code was to create common bonds among the diverse people of the society. Why was it important that Hammurabi's Code was a written legal code?

History Background

Flood Stories Around the World *The Epic of Gilgamesh* may be most famous for the story it tells of a great flood destroying the world. The story begins with the gods deciding to destroy the world and its wickedness. They instruct Utnapishtim to build a boat to save his family and every species of animal on the Earth from the rising waters. He sends out birds from his boat to search for dry land. Stories about floods that destroy the world are found in many cultures. In a tale from East Africa, a curious daughter-in-law ignores a warning not to touch a magical water pot. It breaks, and a huge flood drowns everyone. In an ancient Chinese flood story, Tse-gu-dzih sends a flood to destroy wicked humankind. Only the favored Du-mu, his family, and a few animals are saved in a hollowed-out log.

Answers

Analyze Information *Hammurabi had his code written on a stone stele, so all could see and be held accountable for following the laws.*

Topic 2 Lesson 2

Hammurabi's Code limited personal vengeance and encouraged social order.

Laws varied according to social class and gender. For example, fines for killing a slave woman or causing the death of her unborn child were less than for injuries to a free woman.

By today's standards, the punishments in Hammurabi's Code often seem cruel, following the principle of "an eye for an eye and a life for a life." For example, if a house collapsed because of poor construction and the owner died as a result, the house's builder could be put to death. Still, such a legal code imposed more social order than existed when individuals sought their own justice.

Hammurabi's Accomplishments Although most famous for his code of laws, Hammurabi took other steps to unite his empire. He improved the system of irrigation, organized a well-trained army, and ordered many temples to be repaired. To encourage religious unity across his empire, he promoted Marduk, the patron god of Babylon, over older Sumerian gods. In time, Marduk became the chief god of Babylonian worship.

DRAW CONCLUSIONS What was the most important and lasting legacy of Hammurabi's Code?

>> The Babylonian empire is known for the flourishing of art, science, music, mathematics, astronomy, and literature. This Babylonian roller seal was used on official documents.

New Empires and Ideas

Later empires shaped the Middle East in different ways. Some conquerors, such as the Hittites, brought new skills to the region's people. Other conquerors uprooted the peoples they defeated, which helped spread the ideas of the uprooted to new regions.

Hittites and the Secret of Ironworking The Hittites pushed out of Asia Minor into Mesopotamia in about 1400 B.C. They brought with them a major advancement—the knowledge of how to extract iron from ore. The tools and weapons they made with iron were harder and had sharper edges than those made out of bronze or copper. Because iron was plentiful, the Hittites were able to arm more people at less expense.

The Hittites tried to keep this valuable technology secret. But as their empire collapsed in about 1200 B.C., Hittite ironsmiths migrated to serve customers elsewhere.

Hittite migration, new conquerors, and traders contributed to the diffusion of technology throughout Mesopotamia and other river valley civilizations. The new knowledge thus spread across Asia, Africa, and Europe, ushering in the Iron Age.

>> The Hittites, known for their ironwork, adapted and improved the horse-drawn chariot. Hittite charioteers used lances, bows and arrows, and axes like the ones shown in the photo.

Interactive Gallery

New Empires and Ideas

Hittites, Assyrians, and Babylonians all built strong empires with new ideas to the Middle East. The Hittites brought their advanced knowledge of ironworking, which eventually spread across Asia, Africa, and Europe. Assyrian warriors created and maintained a well-ordered society. The Babylonian empire was vast with an impressive infrastructure. Each empire built on the preceding empire and introduced new ideas.

Online Project the **Interactive Gallery: Development of Civilizations**. Look at the picture of the Assyrian ruins of the library. Discuss cultural diffusion and how ideas spread throughout the Middle East by conquering empires, trade, and written records.

ACTIVE CLASSROOM

Use the See-Think-Wonder strategy. Pair students with a partner. Ask: What do you see? What does that make you think? What are you wondering about now that you've seen this? Share insights with the class.

Guided Reading and Discussion

Ask students to discuss diffusion of technologies such as ironworking across the Middle East, Africa, and Europe through conquest and trade. Assyrians adopted Hittite ironworking and became a military power. Babylonians adopted this technology from the Assyrians and established the New Babylonian Empire.

Summarize Each empire brought new ideas and spread them through conquest and trade. Describe a significant contribution made by the Hittites, Assyrians, and Babylonians. *(Hittites: ironworking; Assyrians: laws regulating life within the royal household; Babylonians: one of the largest cities in ancient Mesopotamia.)*

Answers

Draw Conclusions *The principle that government had a responsibility for what occurred in society*

Topic 2 Lesson 2

Remind students that the Persians eventually conquered Babylon and introduced many new ideas, including the idea of a money economy. The money economy enabled the vast Persian empire to expand commerce and promote international trade.

Synthesize Zoroastrian religious beliefs stressed an individual's free will to choose good or evil. Is this belief important in other religions you know of? Which ones? *(Three other religions, Judaism, Christianity, and Islam, also stressed the importance of individuals exercising their free will to choose between good or evil.)*

Key Terms

Ask students to find the key term **barter economy** (in bold) in the text. Explain that people traded one set of goods and services to obtain another set of goods or services they wanted.

Assyrian Warriors Build on Ancient Knowledge The Assyrians, who lived on the upper Tigris, also learned to forge iron weapons. They had established an empire by about 1350 B.C., and by 1100 B.C., they began expanding their empire across Mesopotamia. Over the course of 500 years, they earned a reputation for being among the most feared warriors in history.

Historians are unsure why warfare was so central to Assyrian culture. Was it to keep others from attacking, or to please their god Assur by bringing wealth to the region? Assyrian kings gave a vow to conquer new lands, lands that initially belonged to their central deity, Assur. Whatever the reason for the brutal warfare, Assyrian rulers boasted of their conquests. One told of capturing Babylon. He proclaimed, "The city and its houses, from top to bottom, I destroyed and burned with fire."

Despite their fierce reputation, Assyrian rulers encouraged a well-ordered society. They used riches from trade and war loot to pay for splendid palaces in their well-planned cities. They were also the first rulers to develop extensive laws regulating life within the royal household. For example, women of the palace were confined to secluded quarters and had to wear veils when they appeared in public.

At Nineveh (NIN uh vuh), King Assurbanipal (ahs ur BAH nee pahl) founded one of the world's first libraries. There, he kept cuneiform tablets that he ordered scribes to collect from all over the Fertile Crescent. Those tablets have offered modern scholars a wealth of information about the ancient Middle East.

The New Babylonian Empire In 612 B.C., shortly after Assurbanipal's death, neighboring peoples joined forces to crush the once-dreaded Assyrian armies. In their absence, Babylon—which a king named Nabopolassar had reestablished as a power in 625 B.C.—quickly revived under its aggressive and ruthless second king, **Nebuchadnezzar** (neb yuh kud NEZ ur). The new Babylonian empire stretched from the Persian Gulf to the Mediterranean Sea.

After nearly a thousand years of the city facing decline and destruction, Nebuchadnezzar oversaw the rebuilding of the canals, temples, walls, and palaces of Babylon. During his reign, the city became one of the largest and most highly regarded in the history of ancient Mesopotamia.

Nebuchadnezzar surrounded Babylon with a defensive moat and a brick wall that was 85 feet (26 meters) thick. Nine solid gateways dedicated to important gods allowed people to pass through the wall. The most famous one today, the Ishtar Gate, was made of bricks glazed bright blue and covered in lions representing the goddess Ishtar, dragons representing

>> **Analyze Maps** The Assyrian empire controlled much of the land in the ancient Middle East. What earlier empires did the Assyrians conquer in order to build their large empire?

Answers

Analyze Maps *Mesopotamian empires including Babylon and into Egypt*

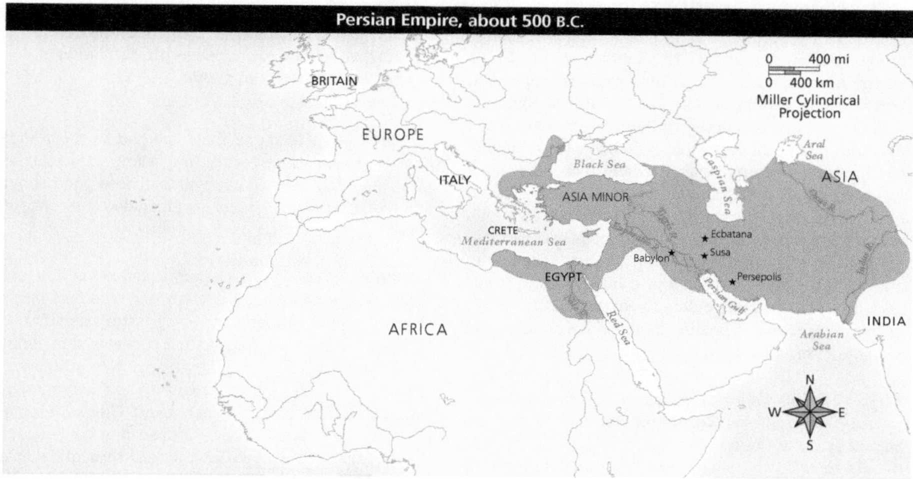

>> **Analyze Maps** Study the locations of the Persian capitals. Were they well placed for rule over the entire empire?

the god Marduk, and bulls representing the god Hadad. At the center of the city, Nebuchadnezzar enlarged and decorated the city's ziggurat to the gods and restored the temple honoring the city's chief god, Marduk.

Although their remains have not yet been found, Nebuchadnezzar may have built the famous Hanging Gardens—known as one of the "seven wonders of the ancient world"—near his main palace. The gardens were probably made by planting trees and flowering plants on the steps of a huge ziggurat. According to legend, Nebuchadnezzar had the gardens built to please his wife, who was homesick for the hills where she had grown up.

 **IDENTIFY** Name a significant contribution made by the Hittites, Assyrians, and Babylonians after each group's conquest in the Middle East.

Rise of the Persian Empire

The thick walls built by Nebuchadnezzar failed to hold back new conquerors. In 539 B.C., Babylon fell to the Persian armies of Cyrus the Great. Cyrus and his successors went on to build the largest empire yet seen, unifying the various tribes and clans under a single political structure.

The Persians eventually controlled a wide sweep of territory that stretched from Asia Minor to India, including present-day Turkey, Iran, Egypt, Afghanistan, and Pakistan. The Persian empire built a network of roads that increased the efficiency of the government and aided the development of the classical civilization of Persia. In general, Persian kings pursued a policy of tolerance, or acceptance, of the people they conquered. The Persians respected the customs of the diverse groups and built a strong, vast empire.

Darius Unites Many Peoples The real unification of the Persian empire was accomplished under the emperor Darius I, who ruled from 522 B.C. to 486 B.C. Darius set up a **bureaucracy,** or a system of government through departments and subdivisions administered by officials who follow set rules. The Persian bureaucracy became a model for later rulers.

Darius divided the empire into provinces, each called a satrapy and headed by a governor called a satrap. Each satrapy had to pay taxes based on its resources and wealth. Special officials visited each satrapy to check on the satraps. Darius created an efficient and successful government structure that was not under the day-to-day control of the king.

Darius adapted laws from the peoples he conquered and, like Hammurabi, drew up a single code of laws for the empire. To encourage unity, he had hundreds of miles of roads built or repaired. Roads made it easier to communicate with different parts of the empire.

Rise of the Persian Empire

The Persian empire was divided into departments and subdivisions, each administered by local officials who followed a set of procedures and rules. This bureaucracy allowed the large empire to run smoothly. Be sure that students understand that Zoroastrianism focused on two important elements: the struggle between good and evil, and the free will of the individual to choose one or the other.

Guided Reading and Discussion

Discuss with students how major ideas spread throughout the Mediterranean as a result of Phoenician trade. Discuss how the diffusion of ideas through trade also impacted the development of classical civilizations.

Summarize Ideas, advances in government, technology, and mathematics were spread through conquest and trade. Explain why the term *carriers of civilization* is used to describe Phoenicians. *(The Phoenicians traded goods and spread ideas throughout Mesopotamia and the Mediterranean, reaching Sicily, Spain, and Britain.)*

English Language Proficiency Standards

Learning Strategies 1.G.1 Read "Rise of the Persian Empire" aloud and have students complete one activity according to their English proficiency.

Beginning Read aloud formal and informal sentences about the section and have students indicate whether each sentence is formal or informal. Help students write one formal and one informal sentence about Darius I.

Intermediate Provide a set of formal and informal sentences about the section. Help volunteers read each sentence aloud and indicate whether the sentence is formal or informal. Have students write one formal and one informal sentence about Darius I.

Advanced Have small groups write three formal and three informal sentences about the section. Have a volunteer from each group read the sentences aloud.

Advanced High Have students work independently to write three formal and three informal sentences about the section. Have students read their sentences aloud in small groups of three or four.

Answers

Analyze Maps *Possible answer: Their distance from each other made it possible to govern a wider area.*

Identify *Hittites introduced ironworking, the Assyrians introduced laws regulating life within the royal household and founded the first library, and the Babylonians built one of the largest and most respected cities of ancient Mesopotamia.*

Topic 2 Lesson 2

Phoenician Contributions

The Phoenicians were from a string of cities along the eastern Mediterranean coast. Their location allowed them to develop manufacturing and trade. Phoenicians traded with people all around the Mediterranean Sea. They established colonies in North Africa, Sicily, and Spain as trading outposts, which also allowed them to spread ideas from Mesopotamia to faraway lands. As a result of their expansive trade routes, Phoenicians are known as "carriers of civilization" because they spread Middle Eastern ideas throughout the Mediterranean. Their most significant contribution to culture was their alphabet, which was later adapted by the Greeks and, with later adaptations, became the alphabet we use today.

Online Project the **Interactive Map: Mesopotamian Empires** and have students look at the map of the Phoenician trade routes. Discuss the extent of the Phoenician trade routes and their capabilities to learn and spread ideas and inventions through trade. The diffusion of ideas eventually influenced the development of classical civilizations such as Greece and Rome.

ACTIVE CLASSROOM

Use the Closer Look strategy. Project the map of Persian lands onto the board and divide it into four numbered quadrants. Have students count off from one to four. Then have them look closely at the part of the image in their quadrant. Have them tell their group what they see and what they learned as a result of their focus on one part of the map. Share insights with the class.

Persia's Economy Darius used his power as head of the Persian government to introduce many economic innovations and reforms. To improve trade, Darius set up a common set of weights and measures and introduced a system of taxation. He also encouraged the use of coins, which the Lydians of Asia Minor had first introduced. Most people continued to be part of the **barter economy,** which means they exchanged one set of goods or services for another. Coins, however, brought merchants and traders into an early form of a **money economy.** In this system, goods and services are paid for through the exchange of some token of an agreed value, such as a coin or a bill. By minting his own gold coins, Darius created economic links among his far-flung subjects, helping to expand commerce and promote international trade.

Birth of a New Religion Religious beliefs put forward by the Persian thinker **Zoroaster** (ZOH ruh as tur) also helped to unite the empire. Zoroaster lived about 600 B.C. He rejected the old Persian gods and taught that a single wise god, Ahura Mazda (AH hoo ruh MAHZ duh), ruled the world. Ahura Mazda, however, was in constant battle against Ahriman (AH rih mun), the prince of lies and evil. Each individual would have to choose which side to support.

In the end, taught Zoroaster, Ahura Mazda would triumph over the forces of evil. On a final judgment day, all individuals would be judged for their actions, as described below:

> Then the assembly . . . will meet, that is, all men of this earth will stand. In that assembly, every person will see his own good deeds and evil deeds. The righteous will be as conspicuous [obvious] amongst the wicked as a white sheep among the black. . . .
>
> They will then [carry] the righteous to the abode of harmony [heaven], and cast the wicked back to the wicked existence [hell]. . . . Then [the last savior] Soshyant by order of the Creator will give reward and recompense to all men in conformity with their deeds.
>
> —Bundahishn, Zoroastrian scripture

Three other religions that emerged in the Middle East, Judaism, Christianity and Islam, also stressed ideas of an individual's free will to choose good or evil, and the latter two religions also included the concepts of heaven, hell, and a final judgment day.

Persia's Legacy Persia's legacy to the rest of the world includes the first postal system and the first larger-scale network of roadways, both vital elements for establishing a well-organized and cohesive civilization. In addition, the Persian empire's practice of allowing conquered peoples to retain many of their own customs influenced later rulers. The ancient Greeks adopted religious, cultural, and political ideas from the Persians. Some of these ideas were later spread throughout their empire by the Romans, who admired the Greeks.

 **DESCRIBE** Describe the steps Darius took to unite the Persian empire.

Phoenician Contributions

While powerful rulers subdued large empires, many small states of the ancient Middle East made their own contributions to civilization. The Phoenicians (fuh NISH unz), for example, gained fame as both sailors and traders. They occupied a string of cities along the eastern Mediterranean coast, in the area that today is Lebanon and Syria.

Manufacturing and Trade Expands The coastal land, though narrow, was fertile and supported

Benefits of a Money Economy

SIMPLIFIED EXCHANGES	Only one party is purchasing an item rather than two.
EXACT VALUES	Comparison of items being considered for purchase is simplified because all items are given exact values.
NO LIMITATIONS	Money can be kept for use at a later time, whereas barter items such as live animals may not last.

>> **Analyze Information** Money economies developed as a result of the benefits they offered to the exchange process. What advantages did a money economy offer?

Answers

Describe *Darius had hundreds of miles of roads built or repaired to make communication within the empire easier. He also established a bureaucracy and a common set of weights and measures and encouraged the use of coins.*

Analyze Information *Money economies offered less complicated exchanges, and allowed economic links to develop over greater distances because currency had a stable value.*

Analyze Maps *They had several cities on the coast and were able to establish colonies across the Mediterranean near present-day Sicily, Sardinia, and Spain.*

Integrate Information *It is the foundation of the Greek alphabet, which is a basis of the alphabet we use today.*

English Language Proficiency Standards

Learning Strategies 1.C.1 Read "Phoenician Contributions" aloud. Have students work as a class, in pairs, or individually to complete a concept map.

Beginning Help the class create a concept map. Write *Phoenician Contributions* in the center circle and include circles with *manufacturing, trade, colony,* and *alphabet*. Ask students to define and find examples for each word, copy the map into their notebooks, and draw an image for each term.

Intermediate Follow instructions for Beginning activity but invite volunteers to suggest terms. Help students define terms and find examples and then copy the map into their notebooks.

Advanced Have pairs create a concept map, define the terms, and find an example for each. Ensure that all important terms are included.

Advanced High Have students work independently to create a concept map with definitions and examples for each term. Have students share completed maps with a partner.

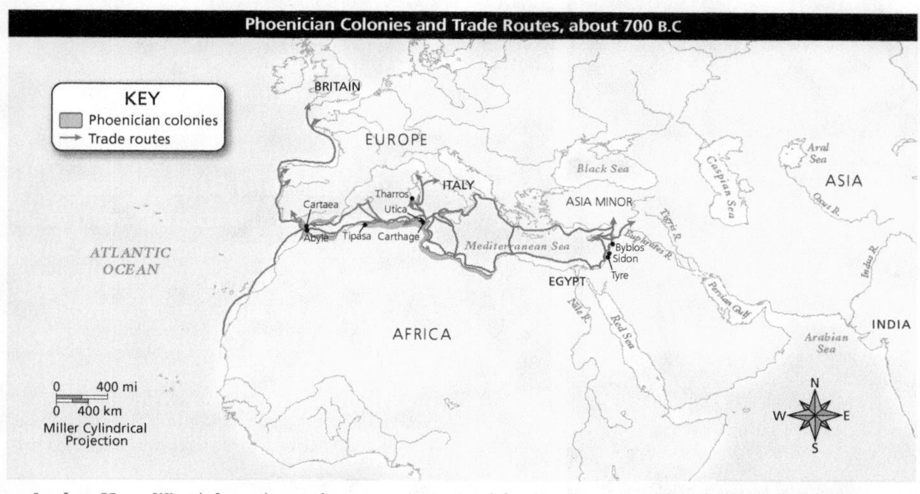

>> **Analyze Maps** What information on the map supports the claim that the Phoenicians were skilled sailors?

Interactive Map

farming. Still, because of their location near the sea, the resourceful Phoenicians became best known for manufacturing and trade. They made glass from coastal sand. From a tiny sea snail, they produced a widely admired purple dye, called "Tyrian purple" after the city of Tyre.

Phoenicians traded with people all around the Mediterranean Sea. To promote trade, they set up colonies from North Africa to Sicily and Spain.

A **colony** is a territory settled and ruled by people from another land. A few Phoenician traders braved the stormy Atlantic and sailed as far as Britain. There, they exchanged goods from the Mediterranean for tin.

The Phoenician Alphabet Historians have called the Phoenicians "carriers of civilization" because they spread Middle Eastern civilization around the Mediterranean. One of the most significant Phoenician contributions to culture was their alphabet. Unlike cuneiform, in which symbols represent syllables or whole words, an **alphabet** is a writing system in which each symbol represents a single basic sound, such as a consonant or vowel.

Phoenician traders developed an alphabetic system of 22 symbols that stood for consonant sounds. Later, the Greeks adapted the Phoenician alphabet and added symbols for the vowel sounds. From this Greek alphabet came the letters in which this sentence is written—that is, the alphabet we use today.

INTEGRATE INFORMATION How has the Phoenician development of an alphabet been a lasting contribution to civilization?

ELPS **ELPS 1.C.1** Use a concept map to learn about *Phoenician Contributions.*

ASSESSMENT

1. **Explain** Explain the importance of Babylonian achievements.
2. **Synthesize** How did the Hittites contribute to cultural diffusion of early Mesopotamian culture and ideas, and what was one of their important technological advancements?
3. **Synthesize** Describe some of the major influences of Persia.
4. **Compare** How did conquests contribute to the growth of well-organized empires?
5. **Synthesize** Explain how the Phoenicians spread ideas among different peoples in the ancient Middle East.

Topic 2 Lesson 2

SYNTHESIZE

Online Ask students to recall Persian influences, especially on politics, religion, and culture. Have them use the Think-Pair strategy to answer the questions in the Synthesize activity. Discuss that Persia became a strong and unified civilization because of its efficient government structure and by developing a money economy. Persia operated under a centralized government that was unified economically and applied the same laws to everyone.

Zoroastrian religious practices stressed the importance of the individual and free will. Have students write two to three sentences describing how Zoroastrianism advanced the importance of the individual. Remind students to use details from the text. *(Possible answer: Zoroastrianism was founded on the belief that individuals have free will and rights.)*

Have partners answer the following question: How did the size of the Persian empire strengthen its influence throughout the Middle East? *(Possible answer: Persia's government system divided the large empire into manageable subdivisions that could communicate effectively through the use of the postal and roadway systems.)* Have pairs share their answers with the class.

DEMONSTRATE

Online Assign the **Digital Lesson Quiz** for this lesson if you haven't already done so. Students will be offered automatic remediation or enrichment based on their score.

Pose the following on the Discussion Board:

Summarize List three different influences of the Persian empire. *(1. Development of a roadway system; 2. development of a money economy; and 3. the idea that individuals have free will and rights)*

Topic Inquiry

Have students continue their investigations for the Topic Inquiry.

Assessment

1. Hammurabi's Code created peace and stability and established the responsibility of government to protect rights and manage society. Babylonians also improved irrigation systems and established a well-trained army.
2. They migrated and brought knowledge and skills to new lands. They were also traders, which led to the diffusion of ideas. Hittite iron working had a large impact on tools and weapons.
3. Persians established a single code of law for the empire, built and maintained roads, and encouraged a money economy and tolerance for the diverse cultures within the empire.
4. As empires were conquered, their ideas blended with new ideas from conquering nations, and leaders established governments, law codes, and roads to create well-organized empires.
5. Phoenicians spread ideas through trade as they traveled throughout the Middle East and as far north as England.

The Hebrews and the Origins of Judaism

CONNECT

Preview Have students preview the **Lesson Objectives** and the list of **Key Terms**.

Students can also preview all the **Key Terms** and **Academic Vocabulary** using the **Interactive Reading Notepad** on the digital course or preview a summary of the lesson in the **Reading and Note Taking Study Guide**.

Online Use the **Editable Presentation** found on the digital course to present the main ideas for this lesson.

Start Up Activity

Read aloud the following quote from Exodus 20:2–3:

> I am the LORD thy God, who brought thee out of the land of Egypt, out of the house of bondage. Thou shalt have no other gods before Me.

Ask students what this quotation from the Hebrew Bible says that God did for the ancient Israelites, and what God demanded in return. *(God freed the Israelites from Egypt; the Israelites should worship God.)* Ask students what idea in this quotation refers to a belief that is different from most other cultures in the Fertile Crescent that they have read about in earlier lessons. *(There is one God.)*

Online You can also project the **Start Up Activity** from the course.

INVESTIGATE

Have students read the section using the **Reading and Note Taking Study Guide** to help them take notes and understand the text as they read.

The Ancient Israelites' Unique Belief System

One of the central ideas of Judaism is the existence of one God who is all-knowing and all-powerful. Israelites believed their God was present everywhere and that he had a plan for the Israelites. Students will learn about what Jews believe are the origins of Judaism: how the father of the Israelites and Judaism, Abraham, moved himself and his followers from the city-state Ur to the region of Canaan because he believed it was part of God's plan for him and his followers.

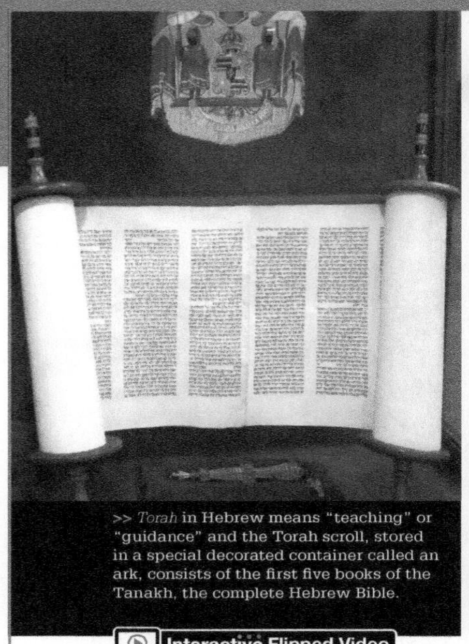

>> *Torah* in Hebrew means "teaching" or "guidance" and the Torah scroll, stored in a special decorated container called an ark, consists of the first five books of the Tanakh, the complete Hebrew Bible.

Interactive Flipped Video

2.3 The ancient land of Israel was located at the far western end of the Fertile Crescent, on the eastern coast of the Mediterranean Sea. The first ancient Israelites inhabited small villages in the hill country of central Israel, called at that time Canaan, sharing land and many cultural attributes with other Canaanites. Although archaeology teaches us that they shared a common physical culture, the ancient Israelites' worship of a single God was unique. About 4,000 years ago, the ancient Israelites developed the religion of Judaism, which became a defining feature of their culture. Today, Judaism is one of the world's major faiths.

TEKS
1.B, 3.A, 20.A, 20.B, 22.B, 23.A, 23.B

>> Objectives

Understand what made the ancient Israelites' belief system unique from others at the time.

Outline the main events in the early history of the Israelites.

Analyze the central moral and ethical ideas of Judaism.

>> Key Terms

monotheistic
Torah
Abraham
covenant
Moses
David
Solomon
patriarchal
Sabbath
prophet
ethics
Diaspora

The Hebrews and the Origins of Judaism

The Ancient Israelites' Unique Belief System

The beliefs of the ancient Israelites, also called the Hebrews for the first three generations, differed in basic ways from those of nearby peoples. The Israelites were **monotheistic,** believing that there was only one god. At the time, all other peoples worshiped many gods.

A few religious leaders, such as the Egyptian pharaoh Akhenaton, spoke of a single powerful god. However, such ideas did not have the lasting impact that Israelite beliefs did.

The Israelites believed in an all-knowing, all-powerful God who was present everywhere. In their views, history and faith were interconnected. Each event reflected God's plan for the people of Israel, and the Israelites' choices and actions made the plan unfold. The **Torah** (TOH ruh), their most sacred text, tells the history of the ancient Israelites and their continuing relationship with God. The Torah includes the first five books of the Hebrew Bible—that is, the books of Genesis, Exodus, Leviticus, Numbers, and Deuteronomy. The Hebrew Bible includes a total of 24 books. Additional laws, customs,

www.PearsonTexas.com Access your Digital Lesson.

Aa Vocabulary Builder

1. Have students pronounce the following academic vocabulary term in this lesson and clarify the part of speech. Break the word into syllables and pronounce it with the students.
2. Explain what the word means in common "student-friendly" language using synonyms and antonyms when possible. Provide concrete examples to clarify the meaning, and rephrase the definition.

undertake: to begin to do something

legends, and ethics written down much later make up another important lengthy text, the Talmud, containing over 12,000 pages.

SUMMARIZE How did the beliefs of ancient Israelites differ from those of other nearby peoples?

The Ancient Israelites

Abraham is considered the father of the Israelites and their religion, Judaism. According to the Torah, Abraham was born near Ur in Mesopotamia, in present-day Iraq, and moved to Haran in present-day Syria about 2000 B.C. According to Jewish belief, God called to Abraham in Haran. God made an offer to Abraham, telling him that if he left his home and his family, then God would make him the founder of a great nation and bless him. So he and his extended family migrated, herding their sheep and goats into a region called Canaan (KAY nun). Abraham believed that everything was created by a single God, and he began to teach this belief to others.

God's Covenant With the Israelites The Israelites believed that God had made the following **covenant,** or promise and agreement, with Abraham:

> You shall be the father of a multitude of nations. . . . I will make nations of you, and kings shall come forth from you. And I will establish my covenant between me and you and your descendants after you throughout their generations for an everlasting covenant, to be God to you and to your descendants after you. And I will give to you, and to your descendants after you, the land of your sojournings [short stay], all the land of Canaan. . . .
>
> —Genesis 17:4–8

God's covenant with Abraham included two declarations that became the basis of two key beliefs of Judaism. First, God declared that He would have a special relationship with Abraham and his descendants. The Israelites believed that God had chosen them to fulfill certain obligations and duties in the world. Second, God declared that Canaan would one day belong to the Israelites. As a result, the Israelites viewed Canaan as their "promised land."

As described in the Book of Genesis, Abraham and his descendants left their home in Ur and adopted a

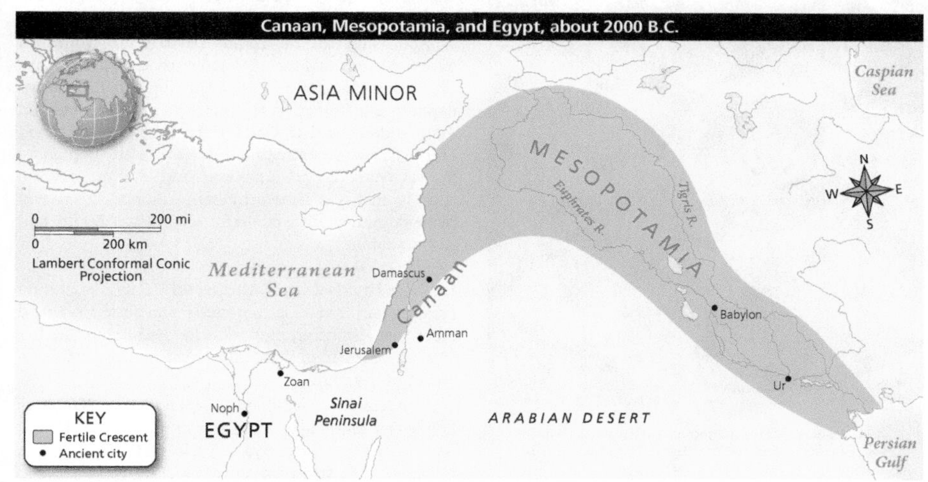

>> **Analyze Maps** What factors may have led to Canaan's becoming a crossroads in the ancient Middle East?

Guided Reading and Discussion

Discuss the central ideas of Judaism, highlighting monotheism, as the Israelites were the only people of the time who believed in one God.

Synthesize Explain the central ideas of Judaism. *(Judaism was built around the belief in one God who is all-knowing and powerful. The Israelites believed their God was present everywhere and that he had a plan for the Israelites.)*

Key Term

Ask students to find the key term **monotheistic** (in bold) in the text. Explain that *mono-* means "one" and *theos* means "god." Have them use that information to define the term. *(Possible answer: characterized by belief in one God)*

The Ancient Israelites

According to Jewish belief, the origins of Judaism can be traced back to Abraham, who made a covenant with God. Abraham and his descendants moved to the land of Canaan, where Abraham had a son named Isaac. Isaac fathered Jacob who was believed to have been blessed by God and given the name Israel. Jacob had twelve sons, and all his descendants are known as the children of Israel. The Israelites were eventually enslaved in Egypt, where they had fled during a famine. Moses led the Israelites back to their promised land. Eventually, Saul united the twelve tribes of Israel into the Kingdom of Israel. The kingdom eventually divided into two separate entities until the Assyrians conquered the northern Kingdom of Israel, followed by the Babylonians and then the Persians. However, Israelites, or Jews, always kept their strong belief in one God, and Judaism developed into one of the world's major religions.

Answers

Summarize *The Israelites believed in only one God, while other peoples believed in many gods.*

Analyze Maps *It is located between Mesopotamia and Egypt; it lies along the Mediterranean coast.*

Topic 2 Lesson 3

Online Project the **Interactive Gallery: Origins of Judaism** and click through the images with students. Look carefully at the fourth picture. Discuss the importance of the unification of the twelve tribes of Israel into the one kingdom of Israel.

ACTIVE CLASSROOM

Use the Sequence It strategy. Give students pieces of paper with the following events out of order: Abraham moves his descendants to Canaan, Jacob leads his family to Egypt, Moses receives the Ten Commandments, King David unites the twelve tribes of Israel and forms the Kingdom of Israel, Assyrians defeat the Kingdom of Israel. Allow students 3–5 minutes to put the events in the proper order.

Guided Reading and Discussion

Discuss how Judaism spread as a result of conquering nations. During the time of Babylonian occupation, Israelites were forced to leave Canaan and many settled back into Egypt and in the city of Babylon. Eventually, the Persian empire took control and allowed the Israelites to resettle in Canaan under Persian rule.

Summarize Moses led the Israelites back to the land of Canaan after they fled Egypt. Many Israelites returned to Canaan after the Persian empire took control. Why was Canaan a special location to the ancient Israelites? *(Canaan was considered the "promised land" because of God's covenant with Abraham.)*

>> In this 17th-century painting, Moses is depicted holding out his staff as the Red Sea is parted by God. According to the Bible, the Israelites were able to cross the sea and escape from Egypt.

Interactive Gallery

>> This mosaic from a synagogue wall in Jerusalem shows the symbols of the 12 tribes of Israel. Each tribe represents one of the twelve sons of Jacob.

nomadic lifestyle, traveling for many years. Late in life, Abraham and his wife Sarah had a son named Isaac. Isaac had two sons, one named Jacob. Jews believe that Jacob was blessed by God and given the name Israel. Jacob fathered 12 sons, and his many descendants are known as the children of Israel.

Jacob's son Joseph was placed in charge of Egypt's food supplies after he interpreted the pharoah's dream as predicting a famine. When a famine did strike, Jacob moved his entire family into Egypt, where the pharaoh welcomed them and they lived peacefully. After many years, a new pharaoh came to power. He feared the growing power and numbers of the children of Israel and made them slaves.

Years later, an Israelite named **Moses** renewed God's covenant with the Israelites. In the book of Exodus, Moses tells the Israelites that in return for faithful obedience to God, God will lead them out of bondage in Egypt and into the promised land.

Moses led the Israelites in their exodus, or departure, from Egypt, from slavery to freedom. After 40 years, they reached Canaan, although Moses died just before they arrived.

The Kingdom of Israel By 1000 B.C., the Israelites had set up the Kingdom of Israel. The Torah tells of twelve separate tribes of Israel that were not united before this time. Saul, the first king of Israel, united these tribes into a single nation. The strong and wise second king of Israel, **David,** established Jerusalem as its national capital and led successful military campaigns creating secure borders for Israel.

According to the Torah, David's son **Solomon** followed him as king. Solomon undertook the task of turning the city of Jerusalem into an impressive capital. Jerusalem was praised for its splendid Temple dedicated to God, which David had planned and Solomon constructed. Solomon also won fame for his wisdom and understanding. Additionally, he tried to increase Israel's influence around the region by negotiating with powerful empires in Egypt and Mesopotamia.

Israel Is Divided and Conquered Solomon's building projects required such high taxes and so much forced labor that revolts erupted after he died about 922 B.C. The kingdom then split into Israel in the north and Judah in the south.

The Israelites remained independent for 200 years but eventually fell to more powerful peoples. In 722 B.C., the Assyrians conquered the northern Kingdom of Israel. From this time, since most of the remaining Israelites came from the tribe of Judah and were now part of the Kingdom of Judah, they became known

English Language Proficiency Standards

Learning Strategies 1.D.1 Read "The Ancient Israelites" aloud to students. Then instruct students to complete one of the following activities based on their level of English proficiency.

Beginning Review this section, pausing to demonstrate requesting assistance in understanding the content. Then read the following sentences. Ask each student to read the sentences aloud and ask for help with information in the text.

- How do you say this word? Demonstrate pointing to a challenging word in the text: Can you explain _____ again, please?

Intermediate Review the first paragraph of this section, pausing to demonstrate requesting assistance in understanding the content. Have small groups generate their own questions to ask for assistance, and share their three best questions with other groups.

Advanced Have student pairs discuss why knowing how to ask for assistance is important for understanding the reading assignment. Then have pairs develop a list of questions and statements that can be used to request assistance.

Advanced High Have each student develop a list of questions and statements that can be used to request assistance, and share their three best with another student. Discuss as a group why knowing how to ask for assistance is an important skill when learning about history.

The Ten Commandments

The Ten Commandments helped shape American laws and people's ideas about right and wrong.	
COMMANDMENT	**EXPLANATION**
1st "Thou shalt not have strange gods before me."	to recognize God as the one and only God
2nd "Thou shalt not take the name of the Lord thy God in vain."	to speak the truth; seen today in legal oaths
3rd "Remember that you keep Holy the Sabbath Day."	to dedicate one day to worship
4th "Honor thy father and thy mother…"	to respect and love one's parents
5th "Thou shalt not kill."	to avoid killing others; seen today in laws about murder
6th "Thou shalt not commit adultery."	to ensure faithfulness to one's spouse; seen today in divorce laws
7th "Thou shalt not steal."	to prevent taking another person's belongings
8th "Thou shalt not bear false witness against thy neighbor."	to prevent lying; seen today by laws against testifying falsely in a court of law
9th "Thou shalt not covet thy neighbor's goods."	to prevent wanting other people's possessions
10th "Thou shalt not covet they neighbor's wife."	to help ensure that families are not broken up

>> Over time, the ideas in the Ten Commandments have influenced aspects of some modern legal and political systems.

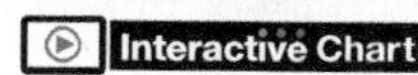

as *yehudi,* or Jews. In 586 B.C., Babylonian armies captured Judah. Nebuchadnezzar destroyed the great temple and forced many of those he defeated into exile in Babylon. This period of exile, called the Babylonian Captivity, lasted about 50 years.

In 539 B.C., the Persian ruler Cyrus the Great conquered Babylon and soon freed the Jews. Many Jews returned to Judah, where they rebuilt a smaller version of Solomon's Temple. However, like other groups in the region, they lived under Persian rule.

IDENTIFY MAIN IDEAS According to the Torah, where did the Israelites go once they left Egypt? What was special to them about their destination?

ELPS **ELPS 1.D.1** Practice asking for assistance to learn about *The Ancient Israelites.*

Law and Morality in Judaism

From early times, the concept of law was central to the Israelites. The Torah includes many laws and is thus often referred to as the Books of the Law. Some of the laws deal with everyday matters such as cleanliness and food preparation. Others define criminal acts. The Torah also establishes moral principles.

Like other early civilizations, Israelite society was **patriarchal,** which means that men held the greatest legal and moral authority. A family's oldest male relative was the head of the household, but women were respected and had more rights than women in many other ancient societies. A few outstanding women, such as the judge and military leader Deborah and the prophetess Miriam won great honor.

The Ten Commandments as a Guide At the heart of Judaism are the Ten Commandments, a set of laws that Jews believe God gave to them through Moses. The first four commandments stress religious duties toward God, such as keeping the **Sabbath,** a holy day for rest and worship. The rest address conduct toward others. They include "Honor your father and mother," "You shall not murder," and "You shall not steal." In addition to establishing a moral law, the Ten Commandments also helped develop the "rule of law," the idea that laws should apply to everyone equally. Finally, the Ten Commandments guided the ancient Jews in setting up their society and government, an influence that endures into our own time.

A Strong Code of Ethics Often in Jewish history, spiritual leaders emerged to interpret God's will. These **prophets,** such as Isaiah and Jeremiah, reminded the Jewish people of their duties.

Law and Morality in Judaism

The concept of law was central to the way of life of the ancient Israelites. The Torah included many laws, from dealing with cleanliness to criminal and civil laws. The Ten Commandments also served as a foundation for laws, and Jews believe God gave these laws to them. Judaism became one of the world's major religions and its influences can be found in the ethical, political, and legal traditions of most Western cultures, especially in the idea that all people are created equal.

Online Project the **Interactive Chart: The Ten Commandments and Modern Laws**. In many of our laws today, you can see the influence of the Ten Commandments. Through the Diaspora, Judaism and its ideas spread throughout the world along with the values of justice, fairness, and compassion in society and government. These ideas influenced the classical civilizations of Greece and Rome, and many of the commandments are reflected in our legal and political systems today. One example is in a U.S. court of law, where people swear to tell the truth "so help me God," as in the Second Commandment.

ACTIVE CLASSROOM

Use the Quick Write strategy. Instruct students to write what they know about the influences of the Ten Commandments. Allow them 45 seconds to write, then instruct students to share with a partner.

History Background

Seven Wonders of the Ancient World
This list of seven spectacular sites developed over time as various observers noted the most remarkable works created by humans during ancient times. Some say the list was first composed by the Greek historian Herodotus in the fifth century B.C. Only one of the original seven wonders still exists today: the pyramids of Giza in Egypt. The other wonders include the hanging gardens of Babylon in present-day Iraq—roof gardens atop a ziggurat; the 40-foot-high statue of Zeus on his throne at Olympia in Greece; the large and magnificently decorated temple of Artemis at Ephesus in Turkey; the Mausoleum of Halicarnassus in Turkey, which was topped by a pyramid and a four-horse marble chariot; the Greek colossus of Rhodes—a 105-foot-high bronze statue of the sun god Helios; and Pharos of Alexandria—the 350-foot-high Egyptian lighthouse.

Answers

Identify Main Ideas *They went back to Canaan, which they considered their "promised land" because of God's covenant with Abraham.*

Topic 2 Lesson 3

Guided Reading and Discussion

Tell students that today, Judaism is numbered among the world's major religions for its contributions to religious thought as well as its strong influence on two later religions, Christianity and Islam. All three of these monotheistic faiths emerged in the Middle East and spread to other parts of the world.

Discuss how Judaism influenced the Judeo-Christian legal traditions, especially the right to a trial by jury and the assumption of "innocent until proven guilty." Some people have suggested that Judeo-Christian traditions had an even more far-reaching impact on world history. They trace today's democratic-republican forms of government to the teachings of these religions, such as ideas about the worth of the individual, the importance of social responsibility, and the concept that all believers are equal before God.

Summarize During the Babylonian captivity, Israelites lived in Babylon and Egypt. Again, after Alexander the Great defeated the Persian empire, Jews were displaced. Describe the result of the Jewish Diaspora, the spreading of the Jews beyond their historic homeland. *(The influence of Jewish ideas and values is widely spread.)*

The prophets also taught a strong code of **ethics,** or moral standards of behavior. They urged both personal morality and social justice, calling on the rich and powerful to protect the poor and weak. All people, they said, were equal before God. Unlike many ancient societies in which the ruler was seen as a god, Jews saw their leaders as fully human and bound to obey God's law.

Scholars have been able to learn more about ancient Israelite culture and ethics as a result of the discovery of the Dead Sea Scrolls. The Scrolls are fragments of early Jewish religious documents. These documents have shed light on the way the Bible and Torah were transmitted to us and have illuminated the religious backgrounds of both Judaism and Christianity.

The spiritual ideas of the ancient Israelites later influenced Western culture, morality, ethics, and conduct. Judaism influenced both Christianity and Islam, two other monotheistic faiths that also arose in the Middle East. Jews, Christians, and Muslims alike honor Abraham, Moses, and the prophets, and they all teach the ethical worldview developed by the Israelites. Today, in the West, this shared heritage of Jews and Christians is known as the Judeo-Christian tradition.

Judaism Spreads For a 500-year period that began with the Babylonian Captivity, many Jews left Judah and moved to different parts of the world. This spreading out of the Jewish people was called the **Diaspora** (dy AS pur uh). Some Jews were exiled, others moved to farther reaches of the empires that controlled their land, and yet others moved because of discontent with political rulers. Wherever Jews settled, many maintained their identity as a people by living in close-knit communities and obeying their religious laws and traditions. These traditions helped them survive centuries of persecution, or unfair treatment inflicted on a particular group of people, which you will read about in later chapters.

Today, Judaism is numbered among the world's major religions for its contributions to religious thought as well as its strong influence on two later religions, Christianity and Islam. All three of these monotheistic faiths emerged in the Middle East and spread to other parts of the world. Although their beliefs differ in many ways, Jews, Christians, and Muslims all honor Abraham, Moses, and the Hebrew prophets. All three teach the ethical worldview developed by the Israelites.

Judeo-Christian Influences Some people have suggested that Judeo-Christian traditions had an even more far-reaching impact on world history. They trace today's democratic-republican forms of government to the teachings of these religions, such as ideas about

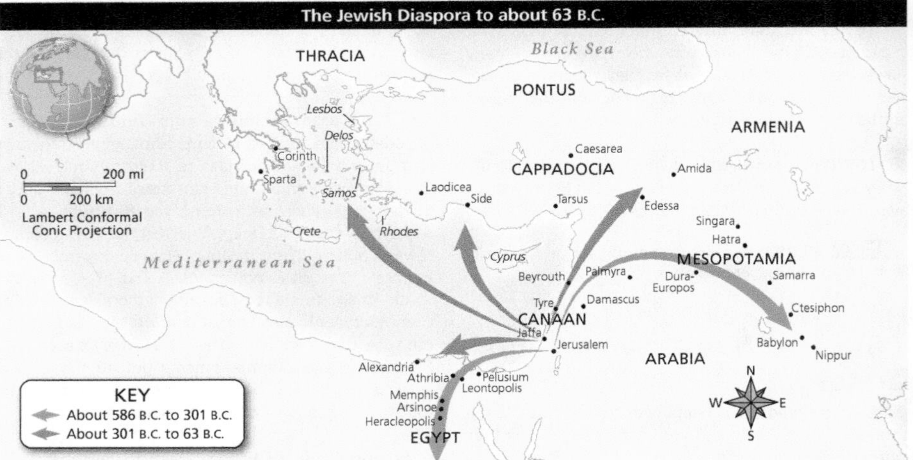

>> **Analyze Maps** The Jewish Diaspora began with the Babylonian Captivity in 6th century B.C. and has continued throughout history. How did the Diaspora contribute to the spread of Judaism?

Answers

Analyze Maps *As a result of the Diaspora, Judaism spread as Israelites left Israel to find refuge in other parts of the world. Originally they spread throughout the Middle East, and in later years north toward Europe. As Israelites moved around, they brought their beliefs and culture with them.*

the worth of the individual, the importance of social responsibility, and the concept that all believers were equal before God. They look to Judeo-Christian legal traditions for the origins of such rights and concepts as trial by jury and innocent until proven guilty. Indeed, the Ten Commandments, the teachings of the Hebrew prophets, and the historical traditions of the ancient Israelites helped shape Western culture, morality, ethics, and conduct over many centuries.

EXPLAIN How did the prophets help Jews uphold the law?

ASSESSMENT

1. **Identify Main Ideas** How did the religion of the ancient Israelites differ from those of its neighbors?
2. **Support Ideas with Examples** Name two events from Jewish history that reflect the Israelites' belief that God had a plan for the people of Israel.
3. **Identify Cause and Effect** Explain what happened to the Israelites after the death of Solomon.
4. **Summarize** Identify the points in Israel's early history when it was unified, divided, or ruled by outsiders.
5. **Synthesize** How did Judeo-Christian ideas influence legal traditions in Western countries?

Topic 2 Lesson 3

SYNTHESIZE

Online Project the **Digital Activity: Origins of Judaism**. Ask students to recall the origins of Judaism. Have them use the Think-Pair strategy to order the events on the Synthesize activity into chronological order. Then have students write two to three sentences describing the central ideas of Judaism. Remind students to use details from the text to support their ideas. *(Answers will vary. The central ideas of Judaism include the belief in one all-knowing and all-powerful God, who has a plan for the Israelites and who, through his covenant, will guide them. Students may also cite the belief in the equality of all people, along with other values enshrined in modern legal and ethical systems.)*

Have partners think about the following question: What evidence did ancient Israelites have that God had a plan for them? *(Answers will vary. God's covenant with Abraham was part of His plan to establish Canaan as the land of the ancient Israelites as well as the exodus from Egypt led by Moses.)* Have pairs share their answers with the class.

DEMONSTRATE

Online Assign the **Digital Lesson Quiz** for this lesson if you haven't already done so. Students will be offered automatic remediation or enrichment based on their score.

Remind students that, in this lesson, they read about the ancient Israelites' unique belief system and central ideas. They also learned how the political and legal ideas of Judaism influenced today's Judeo-Christian legal and ethical traditions.

Pose the following question to the class on the Discussion Board:

Summarize How did the worship of only one God shape Judaism? *(The ancient Israelites were the only people at the time to worship only one God, which helped them to maintain close communities even when forced to relocate.)*

Topic Inquiry

Have students continue their investigations for the Topic Inquiry.

Assessment

1. The Israelites were the only people to worship one God.
2. One example of their beliefs reflecting God's plan was when God established a covenant with Abraham and renewed it with Moses. Another event was Moses's Exodus from Egypt to Canaan.
3. Israelites were divided and split into two kingdoms, Israel and Judah.
4. Israel was unified under the rule of Kings David and Solomon, divided for 200 years after Solomon's death, and ruled by outsiders for about 300 years after its division.
5. Judeo-Christian beliefs in the rights of the individual helped shape legal traditions such as the right to a jury by peers, innocence until proven guilty, and equality before the law.

Answers

Explain *They taught a strong code of ethics that encouraged both personal morality and social justice.*

Topic 2 Lesson 4

Egyptian Civilization

CONNECT

Preview Have students preview the **Lesson Objectives** and the list of **Key Terms**.

Students can also preview all the **Key Terms** and **Academic Vocabulary** using the **Interactive Reading Notepad** on the digital course or preview a summary of the lesson in the **Reading and Note Taking Study Guide**.

Online Use the **Editable Presentation** found on the digital course to present the main ideas for this lesson.

Start Up Activity

Discuss Remind students about the advantages and disadvantages of living in Mesopotamia because of the Tigris and Euphrates rivers. Although the rivers provided fertile farmland, they also brought flooding. Discuss with students how the Nile River impacted the lives of ancient Egyptians.

Work with students to list pros and cons of living along the Nile River for ancient Egyptians. Ask students to write 1–2 sentences predicting how the Nile River likely affected ancient Egyptian civilization.

Online You can also project the **Start Up Activity** from the course.

INVESTIGATE

Have students read the section using the **Reading and Note Taking Study Guide** to help them take notes and understand the text as they read.

Geography Shapes Egypt

Like ancient Mesopotamians, ancient Egyptians had to learn to control the floodwaters by building dikes, reservoirs, and irrigation ditches. Menes, the king of Upper Egypt, was successful in uniting the two regions of Egypt by using the Nile as a highway to link the north and south. The Nile helped make Egypt one of the world's first unified states.

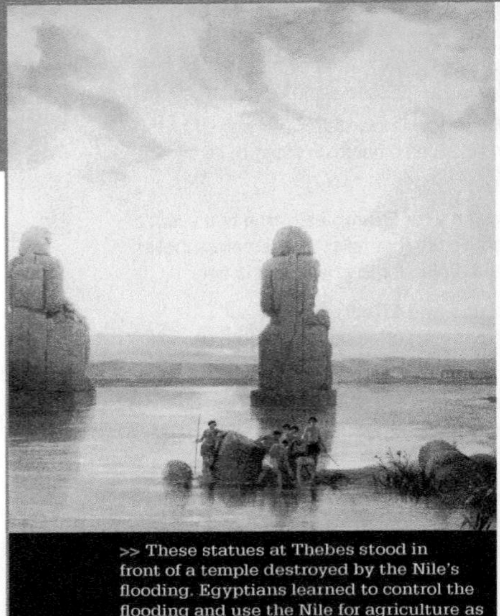

>> These statues at Thebes stood in front of a temple destroyed by the Nile's flooding. Egyptians learned to control the flooding and use the Nile for agriculture as well as transportation.

Interactive Flipped Video

2.4 **The fertile lands of the Nile Valley attracted Stone Age farmers. People migrated there from the Mediterranean area, from hills and deserts near the Nile, and from other parts of Africa. In time, a powerful civilization emerged that depended heavily on the control of river waters.**

TEKS
1.A, 2.C, 16.B, 19.A, 24.A, 26.B, 27.A

>> Objectives

Understand the ways in which geography helped shape ancient Egypt.

Explain how Egypt grew strong during the New Kingdom.

Describe the ways in which religious beliefs shaped the lives of ancient Egyptians.

Explain how the Egyptians organized their society.

Outline the advances that the Egyptians made in learning, the arts, science, and literature.

>> Key Terms

cataract
delta
dynasty
pharaoh
vizier
Hatshepsut
Thutmose III
Ramses II
Amon-Re
Osiris
Isis
Akhenaton
mummification
hieroglyphics
papyrus
decipher
Rosetta Stone

PEARSON realize. www.PearsonTexas.com Access your Digital Lesson.

Egyptian Civilization

Geography Shapes Egypt

"Egypt," said the ancient Greek historian Herodotus, "is wholly the gift of the Nile." Without the Nile, Egypt would be just the barren desert that surrounds the river. But while the desert protected Egypt from invasion, it also limited where people could settle.

In ancient times, as today, farming villages dotted the narrow band of land watered by the Nile. Beyond the rich, irrigated "Black Land," generally no more than ten miles wide, lay the "Red Land," a sun-baked desert that stretched across North Africa. Farmers took advantage of the fertile soil of the Nile Valley to grow wheat and flax, a plant whose fibers were used for clothing.

Benefits of Nile Flooding The Nile rises in the highlands of Ethiopia and the lakes of central Africa. Every spring, the rains in this interior region send water racing down streams that feed the Nile River. In ancient times, Egyptians eagerly awaited the annual flood. It soaked the land with life-giving water and deposited a layer of rich silt.

People had to cooperate to control the Nile's floods. Under the direction of early governments, they built dikes, reservoirs, and irrigation ditches to channel the rising river and store water for the dry season.

50

Aa Vocabulary Builder

1. Have students pronounce the following academic vocabulary term in this lesson and clarify the part of speech. Break the word into syllables and pronounce it with the students.
2. Explain what the word means in common "student-friendly" language using synonyms and antonyms when possible. Provide concrete examples to clarify the meaning, and rephrase the definition.

radical: favoring or making economic, political, or social changes of a sweeping or extreme nature

Two Regions United Ancient Egypt had two distinct regions, Upper Egypt in the south and Lower Egypt in the north. Upper Egypt stretched from the Nile's first **cataract,** or waterfall, to within 100 miles of the Mediterranean Sea. Lower Egypt covered the delta region where the Nile empties into the Mediterranean. A **delta** is a triangular area of marshland formed by deposits of silt at the mouth of some rivers.

About 3100 B.C., Menes, the king of Upper Egypt, united the two regions. He founded Egypt's first capital at Memphis, a site near where the Nile empties into its delta. Menes and his successors used the Nile as a highway linking north and south. They could send officials or armies to towns along the river. The Nile thus helped make Egypt one of the world's first unified states.

The river also served as a trade route. Egyptian merchants traveled up and down the Nile in sailboats and barges, exchanging the products of Africa, the Middle East, and the Mediterranean region.

? IDENTIFY MAIN IDEAS How did the yearly floods of the Nile influence life in ancient Egypt?

The Old Kingdom

Scholars divide the history of ancient Egypt into three main periods: the Old Kingdom (about 2575 B.C.–2130 B.C.), the Middle Kingdom (about 1938 B.C.–1630 B.C.), and the New Kingdom (about 1539 B.C.–1075 B.C.). Although power passed from one **dynasty,** or ruling family, to another, the land generally remained united.

A Structured Government During the Old Kingdom, Egyptian kings, later called **pharaohs** (FEHR ohz), organized and developed a strong, centralized state. Pharaohs held absolute power and played key roles in government and religion. Egyptians believed each pharaoh was a god. However, the pharaohs were also seen as human. People expected their pharaohs to behave morally and judged the pharaohs for their deeds.

Pharaohs of the Old Kingdom ruled by means of a bureaucracy. The pharaoh depended on a **vizier** (vih ZEER), or chief minister, to supervise the government. Under the vizier, various departments looked after tax collection, farming, and the all-important irrigation system. Thousands of scribes carried out the vizier's instructions.

Ptah-hotep (ptah HOH tep), who lived around 2450 B.C. in Egypt, was a vizier to a pharaoh who took an interest in training young officials. Based on his vast experience of government, he wrote a book, *Instructions*

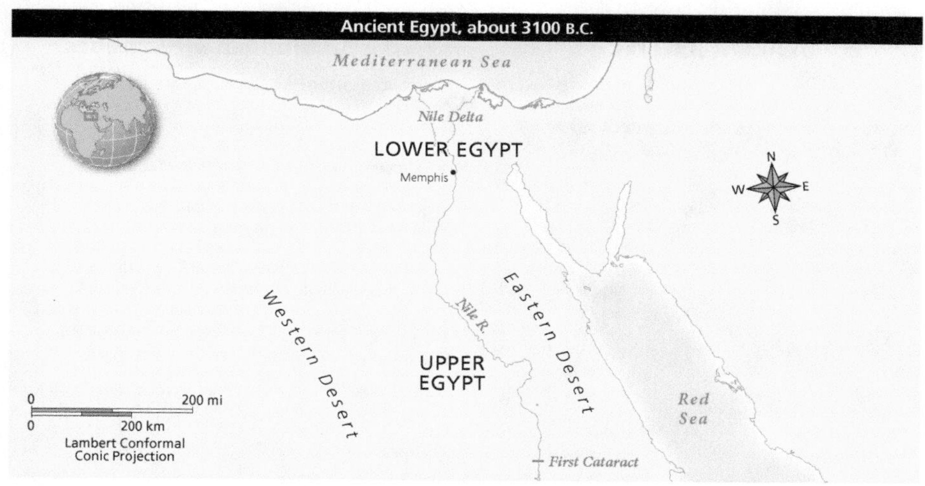

>> **Analyze Maps** The Nile extends another 3,600 miles south of its first cataract. What geographic features might have limited the expansion of civilization beyond the Nile Valley?

Topic 2 Lesson 4

The Old Kingdom

The history of ancient Egypt is divided into three main periods: the Old Kingdom, the Middle Kingdom, and the New Kingdom. During the Old Kingdom, the pharaohs, or Egyptian monarchs, created, organized, and developed a strong centralized state.

Guided Reading and Discussion

Discuss how Old Kingdom Egypt created a strong, organized government structure, allowing Egyptian civilization to flourish as a monarchy. Middle Kingdom Egypt, despite social and political turbulence, developed new areas of farmable land using the rich soil deposits from the Nile's floodwaters. The New Kingdom expanded the empire and brought advances in mathematical and scientific ideas that reached later classical civilizations such as Greece.

Summarize Old Kingdom pharaohs set up bureaucracies to administer a central government. Describe the government bureaucracy of ancient Egypt. *(The pharaoh was at the top; a chief administrator called a vizier led various departments, and scribes carried out his directives.)*

Key Terms

Ask students to find the key term **bureaucracy** (in bold) in the text. Explain that in ancient Egypt the pharaoh relied on government workers in specific departments and with varying degrees of authority. Modern governments also depend on bureaucracies.

History Background

Pharaoh, the King The word *pharaoh* derives from the Egyptian language. It means "great house" and originally referred to the royal palace. During the New Kingdom of ancient Egypt, it began to be used to refer to the Egyptian king, rather than the king's residence. Over time, it came to refer to any and all Egyptian kings, despite the fact that it was never part of the king's official title. Ancient Egyptians kept lists of pharaohs, called king lists, to keep track of important events in their history. Rather than numbering their years from a fixed date, the Egyptians numbered the years of each king's reign and began again with each new king. The most accurate of the surviving king lists is the tattered Turin Papyrus, in the Egyptian Museum in Turin, Italy. It dates from the reign of Ramses II (1279 B.C.–1213 B.C.) and lists kings of Egypt from earliest times to the nineteenth dynasty.

Answers

Identify Main Ideas *Egyptians relied on the floods for water and silt for farming. They also had to cooperate in order to channel and store the water.*

Analyze Maps *The Eastern and Western deserts.*

Middle and New Kingdom Egypt

The Middle Kingdom was a turbulent time, as corruption and rebellion were common. During the Middle Kingdom, the Hyksos took over Egypt and adopted Egyptian customs and beliefs. Hyksos rule came to an end when the Egyptian leaders from the New Kingdom regained control over Egypt. The New Kingdom flourished and Egypt became a large empire. The heightened prosperity brought advances in medicine, hygiene, dentistry, and craftsmanship during this period.

of the Vizier Ptah-hotep, in which he emphasized the importance of being humble and honest, obedient to one's father and superiors, and fair in dealing with other officials of all ranks.

Building the Great Pyramids During the Old Kingdom, Egyptian pharaohs built many necropolises (neh KRAHP uh lis iz), or cemeteries, containing majestic pyramids in the areas surrounding Memphis. Today, the best known are the Great Pyramids that still stand at Giza.

Tombs within the pyramids were considered homes in which the deceased would live for eternity. Because Egyptians believed in an afterlife, they preserved the bodies of their dead rulers and provided them with everything they would need in their new lives. Building each of the pyramids took so long that often a pharaoh would begin to build his tomb as soon as he came to power.

CHECK UNDERSTANDING How was the Egyptian government structured during the Old Kingdom?

Middle and New Kingdom Egypt

Power struggles, crop failures, and the cost of building the pyramids all contributed to the collapse of the Old Kingdom. Then, after more than a century of disunity, new pharaohs reunited the land, ushering in a new era, the Middle Kingdom.

The Middle Kingdom The Middle Kingdom was a turbulent period. The Nile did not rise as regularly as it had in the past. Corruption and rebellions were common. Despite the struggles, strong rulers were able to organize a large drainage project, creating vast new stretches of arable, or farmable, land. During this period, the central state ended the powers and privileges of the regional aristocrats. In addition, Egyptian armies occupied part of Nubia (also known as Kush), a gold-rich land to the south. Traders also had greater contacts with the peoples of the Middle East and the Mediterranean island of Crete.

About 1700 B.C., foreign invaders called the Hyksos (HIK sohs) occupied the Nile delta region. Although the Hyksos took over the governance of Egypt, there was little conflict between the new rulers and the Egyptian people. The Hyksos awed the Egyptians with their horse-drawn war chariots. In time, the Egyptians

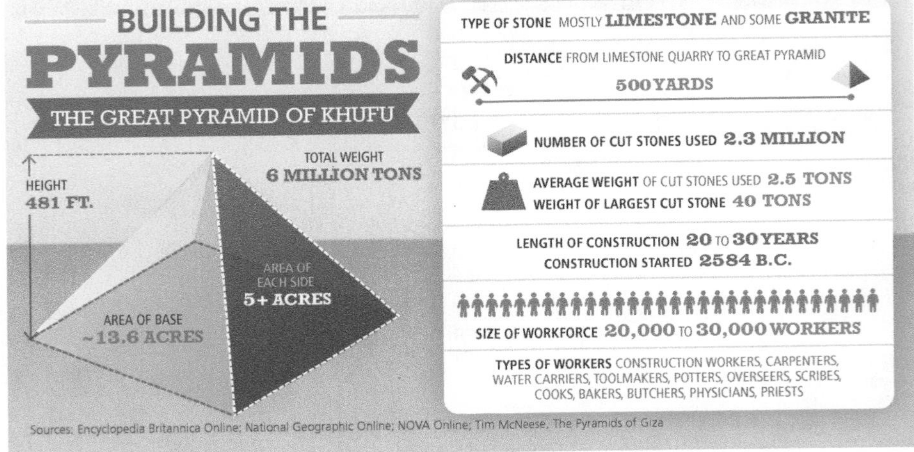

>> **Analyze Data** Pharaohs spent a great deal of resources and time building pyramids. Based on the information here, why do you think Giza pyramids built after Khufu's were not as large as his?

Answers

Check Understanding *Egyptian government was a bureaucracy, with the pharaoh at the top, vizier next, and various departments and scribes below the vizier.*

Analyze Data *Khufu's pyramid required too much labor and too many resources, taking almost 20–30 years to build.*

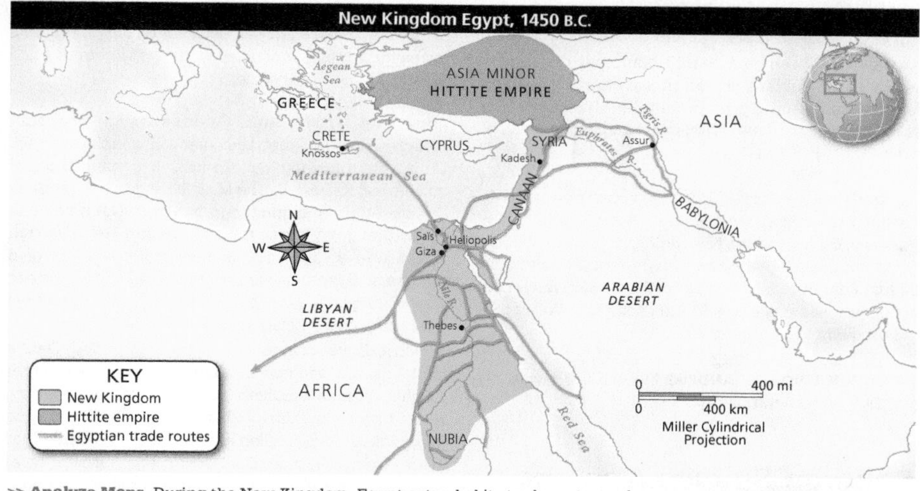

>> **Analyze Maps** During the New Kingdom, Egypt extended its trade routes and made peace with the Hittites to the north. How do you think the alliance with the Hittites helped Egypt reach its greatest extent?

Interactive Map

mastered this new military technology. The Hyksos, in turn, were impressed by Egyptian civilization. They soon adopted Egyptian customs, beliefs, and even names. Finally, after more than 100 years of Hyksos rule, new Egyptian leaders arose and established the New Kingdom.

The New Kingdom During the years of the New Kingdom, a number of powerful and ambitious pharaohs created a large empire. At its height around 1450 B.C., the Egyptian empire reached as far north as Syria and the Euphrates River. The New Kingdom proved to be an age of conquest that brought Egyptians into greater contact with peoples in southwestern Asia as well as other parts of Africa.

In addition to expanding the empire and extending trade routes, New Kingdom pharaohs initiated large-scale building campaigns. They also brought prosperity to the land under a strong central government. The prosperity led to advances in medicine, hygiene, and dentistry, and craftsmanship reached new heights. During the years of the New Kingdom, Egypt was a great and powerful civilization.

Egypt's Powerful Rulers Egypt's first female ruler took charge during the New Kingdom. Her name was **Hatshepsut** (haht SHEP soot), and she exercised all the rights of a pharaoh. From about 1472 B.C. to 1458 B.C., she encouraged trade with eastern Mediterranean lands and along the Red Sea coast of Africa. Her stepson, **Thutmose III** (thoot MOH suh), took over as pharaoh once he reached adulthood. A great military general, Thutmose III stretched Egypt's borders to their greatest extent ever.

Much later, **Ramses II** (RAM seez) became pharaoh of the New Kingdom. He ruled for 66 years, from 1279 B.C. to 1213 B.C., and during that time pushed Egyptian control northward again as far as Syria. He may be the best known of the Egyptian rulers because he boasted of his conquests on numerous temples and monuments, although his greatest reported victory may not actually have taken place.

Egypt Fights Its Neighbors During the reign of Ramses II, Egypt fought a number of fierce battles against the Hittites of Asia Minor. After years of fighting, the Egyptians and the Hittites signed a peace treaty, the first such document in history known to have survived. It declared that Egypt and the Hittites "shall be at peace and in brotherhood forever."

To the south of Egypt, Nubia had developed along the Nile. For centuries, Egyptians traded or fought with their southern neighbor. From Nubia, they acquired

Online Project the **Interactive Map: Ancient Egyptian Lands.** Look carefully at the map of the New Kingdom. Discuss the importance of trade during the New Kingdom and the relationships Egyptians made with the Hittites. Discuss the importance of the Greeks eventually taking over Egypt: this was the primary source of cultural diffusion and how ancient Egyptian culture was able to influence the development of classical civilizations, such as Greece.

ACTIVE CLASSROOM

Use the My Simile strategy. Give students the following prompt so they can create a simile based on the content of the New Kingdom text and map. This map shows that New Kingdom Egypt is like ____ because _____. Allow students time to write their simile and share with a partner.

Answers

Analyze Maps *Trade alliances probably helped build Egypt's wealth; making peace with the Hittite empire gave Egypt access to the resources in their lands as well.*

Topic 2 Lesson 4

Guided Reading and Discussion

Discuss how religion impacted the lives of ancient Egyptians. Tell students that ancient Egypt had characteristics of theocracies because pharaohs were seen as gods and as kings.

Summarize Describe how religion shaped the lives of ancient Egyptians. *(Ancient Egyptians believed that they would have eternal life after death, so they mummified people and built pyramids to protect the bodies of the dead and to give them a place to access their possessions after death. Ancient Egyptian pharaohs were also seen as gods as well as kings, which indicates the importance of religion in their lives.)*

Religion Shapes Ancient Egyptian Life

Religion was an essential part of ancient Egyptian life. Ancient Egyptians believed in many gods and goddesses and that these divine forces ruled the world and the afterlife. Ancient Egypt was a monarchy and had characteristics of a theocracy, as ancient Egyptians viewed their pharaohs as gods as well as kings. Most of what we know about ancient Egyptian religion today comes from inscriptions on tombs or monuments, which depict the importance of the afterlife for ancient Egyptians. Mummification and pyramids reflect ancient Egyptian views of the afterlife.

ivory, cattle, and slaves. During the New Kingdom, Egypt conquered Nubia.

Ramses II used gold from Nubia to pay charioteers in his army. Nubians served in Egyptian armies and left their mark on Egyptian culture. Much Egyptian art of this period shows Nubian soldiers, musicians, or prisoners.

Egypt Declines After 1100 B.C., Egyptian power slowly declined. Invaders, such as the Assyrians and the Persians, conquered the Nile region. In 332 B.C., the last Egyptian dynasty ended as the Greeks took control. In 30 B.C., Roman armies displaced the Greeks. Each new conqueror was eager to add the fertile Nile Valley to a growing empire.

CHECK UNDERSTANDING In what ways was the Middle Kingdom turbulent?

Religion Shapes Ancient Egyptian Life

Religious beliefs about gods, values, and life after death affected the daily lives of ancient Egyptians. Today, much of what we know about Egyptian religion comes from inscriptions on monuments and wall paintings in tombs. These inscriptions describe Egyptians appealing to the divine forces that they believed ruled this world and the afterlife.

>> The ancient Egyptians believed in many gods and goddesses, each of whom had a role in maintaining peace and prosperity across Egypt.

Important Gods and Goddesses In the sun-drenched land of Egypt, the chief god was the sun god. During the Old Kingdom, Egyptians worshiped a sun god named Re (ray). By the Middle Kingdom, Egyptians associated Re with another god, Amon (AH mun), and called this great lord of the gods **Amon-Re.** Although Egypt was a monarchy, it had characteristics of a theocracy. Egyptians viewed their pharaohs as gods as well as kings, and they believed the pharaohs received their right to rule from Amon-Re.

Most Egyptians related more to the god **Osiris** (oh SY ris) and the goddess **Isis** (EYE sis), whose story touched human emotions such as love and jealousy. According to mythology, Osiris ruled Egypt until his jealous brother, Set, killed him. Set then cut Osiris into pieces, which he tossed all over Egypt. Osiris's wife, Isis, saved him. She reassembled his body and brought him back to life. Because Osiris could no longer rule over the living, he became god of the dead and judge of souls seeking admission to the afterlife.

To Egyptians, Osiris was especially important because, in addition to ruling over the underworld, he was also god of the Nile. In that role, he controlled the annual flood that made the land fertile. Isis had special appeal for women, who believed that she had first taught women to grind corn, spin flax, weave cloth, and care for children. Like Osiris, Isis promised the faithful that they would have life after death.

An Attempt to Reshape Religion About 1380 B.C., a young pharaoh named Amenhotep IV (ah mun HOH tep) challenged the powerful priests of Amon-Re. He devoted his life to the worship of Aton, a minor god. The pharaoh took the name **Akhenaton** (ah keh NAH tun), meaning "he who serves Aton." He ordered priests to worship only Aton and to remove the names of other gods from their temples.

Akhenaton's radical ideas had little success. Priests of Amon-Re and of other gods resisted such revolutionary changes. The people, too, were afraid to abandon their old gods in favor of Aton. Nobles also deserted the pharaoh because he neglected his duty of defending the empire. After Akhenaton's death, priests of the old gods reasserted their power.

Egyptian Views of the Afterlife As you have read, Egyptians believed that Osiris and Isis had promised them eternal life after death. Belief in the afterlife

English Language Proficiency Standards

Use with the text "Religion Shapes Ancient Egyptian Life."

Learning Strategies 1.E.1 Read the text aloud. Display the words *gods, life,* and *death* and have students copy them into their notebooks. Have students complete one of the following based on their English proficiency.

Beginning Say the words aloud. Have students repeat them. Use each word in a sentence to describe Egyptian life.

Intermediate Say the words aloud. Have students repeat them. Help students use each word in a sentence to describe Egyptian life.

Advanced Assist with pronunciation as students say the words. Have pairs of students use each word in a sentence describing Egyptian life. Have pairs share their sentences with the class.

Advanced High Assist with pronunciation as students say the words. Have students use each word in a sentence describing Egyptian life, then share sentences with the class.

Answers

Check Understanding *During the Middle Kingdom, corruption and rebellions were common and foreigners took over the governance of Egypt, both factors in the rise of unrest.*

affected all Egyptians, from the highest noble to the lowest peasant.

The Egyptians believed that each soul had to pass a test to win eternal life. First, the dead soul would be ferried across a lake of fire to the hall of Osiris. Then the dead person's heart would be weighed against the feather of truth. Those Osiris judged to be sinners would be fed to the crocodile-shaped Eater of the Dead. Worthy souls would enter the Happy Field of Food, where they would live forever in bliss. To survive the dangerous journey through the underworld, Egyptians relied on the *Book of the Dead*. It contained spells, charms, and formulas for the dead to use in the afterlife.

Mummification Egyptians believed that the afterlife would be much like life on Earth. As a result, they buried their dead with everything they would need for eternity.

To give a soul use of its body in the afterlife, Egyptians perfected scientific skills in **mummification** (mum uh fih KAY shun), the preservation of dead bodies by embalming them and wrapping them in cloth. At first, mummification was a privilege reserved for rulers and nobles. Eventually, ordinary Egyptians also won the right to mummify their dead, including beloved pets.

King Tutankhamen's Tomb During the New Kingdom, many pharaohs were buried in a desolate valley known as the Valley of the Kings. Their tombs, known to be filled with fantastic riches, were a temptation to robbers in ancient times. As a result, most royal tombs were stripped of their treasures long ago. In 1922, however, British archaeologist Howard Carter unearthed the tomb of the young pharaoh Tutankhamen (toot ahng KAH mun), who was the son-in-law of Akhenaton. The tomb had remained almost untouched for more than 3,000 years. Its treasures have provided scholars with a wealth of evidence about Egyptian civilization.

The body of the 18-year-old "King Tut" had been placed in a solid-gold coffin, nested within richly decorated outer coffins. Today, the dazzling array of objects found in the tomb fills several rooms in the Egyptian Museum in Cairo. The treasures include chariots, weapons, furniture, jewelry, toys, and games. Tutankhamen was a minor king. We can only imagine what treasures must have filled the tombs of great pharaohs like Thutmose III or Ramses II.

 **DRAW CONCLUSIONS** How did mummification reflect Egyptian beliefs about the afterlife?

>> To complete a pyramid, workers quarried millions of huge limestone blocks. They transported the cut stones on barges along the Nile then pulled them up a ramp to build the pyramid.

Interactive 3-D Model

>> Tutankhamen, or "King Tut," reigned for only eight or nine years. However, his tomb has unraveled many mysteries about his life and death. His solid gold funeral mask is shown here.

Online Project the **Interactive 3-D Model: Pyramids.** Ask students to look carefully at the model of an ancient Egyptian pyramid. Discuss the importance Egyptians placed on the afterlife. Explain that ancient Egyptians wrote the *Book of the Dead* to help guide Egyptians into the afterlife successfully. Discuss the time it took to build pyramids, which is another indicator of the importance of religion in ancient Egypt's culture.

ACTIVE CLASSROOM

Use the See-Think-Wonder strategy. Pair students with a partner and have them select a part of the 3-D model to study closely. Ask them: What do you see? What does that make you think? What are you wondering about now that you've seen this? Share insights with the class.

Analyze Images

Ask students to look at the death mask of King Tut that was found in his tomb. Along with other artifacts, the golden mask gave scientists insight into the religious practices of the ancient Egyptians. Ask: Why do you think the ancient Egyptians filled the tombs of their leaders with such valuables and treasures? What does it say about the role the afterlife played in ancient Egypt?

Answers

Draw Conclusions *Because Egyptians believed that they would have eternal life after death and that the afterlife would be much like life on Earth, they mummified people so that they could use their bodies in the afterlife.*

Topic 2 Lesson 4

Organization of Egyptian Society

Explain that during the New Kingdom, social classes became more fluid as trade and warfare increased. Trade offered opportunities for social advancement to a growing merchant class and also allowed for ancient Egyptian ideas to spread via the trade routes. Many skilled craftsmen emerged during the New Kingdom as the need for fine jewelry, furniture, and fabrics for the palaces and tombs of pharaohs and nobles grew.

Analyze Images

Direct students to look at the chart about Egyptian social hierarchy. Introduce the chart by reminding students that peasant farmers made up the largest part of the population. Ask students to look at the chart and answer the question.

Guided Reading and Discussion

Discuss the importance of an organized social hierarchy in early civilizations. Stress how the middle class became more fluid and upwardly mobile as trade and warfare increased. Remind students that an organized social structure is a feature of early civilizations. Be sure that students notice the size of the lowest class and see the need for laborers in ancient Egypt, especially during the New Kingdom building booms.

Synthesize What does the much greater relative size of the lowest class tell you about the need for laborers in Egyptian society? *(Many workers were needed for such activities as building pyramids and other monuments and working in the farm fields.)*

Answers

Analyze Information *Since priests and priestesses were near the top of society, clearly religion was regarded highly.*

Organization of Egyptian Society

Like other early civilizations, Egypt had its own class system. As both a god and an earthly leader, the pharaoh stood at the top of society, along with the royal family. Directly under the pharaoh were government officials and the high priests and priestesses, who served the gods and goddesses. Next came a tiny class of merchants, scribes, and artisans. They provided for the needs of the rich and powerful. The bottom layer of society was the largest—made up of peasants who worked the land.

Peasant Farmers Most Numerous Most Egyptians were peasant farmers. Many were slaves. Men and women spent their days working the soil and repairing the dikes. One ancient record describes the life of a typical Egyptian peasant. "When the water is full he irrigates [the fields] and repairs his equipment. He spends the day cutting tools for cultivating barley, and the night twisting ropes."

In the off-season, peasant men were expected to serve the pharaoh, laboring to build palaces, temples, and tombs. Besides working in the fields, women also spent much time raising children, collecting water, and preparing food.

Changes to Social Structure During the New Kingdom, social classes became more fluid as trade and warfare increased. Trade offered new opportunities to the growing merchant class. Foreign conquests brought riches to Egypt, which in turn meant more business for artisans. These skilled craftworkers made fine jewelry, furniture, and fabrics for the palaces and tombs of pharaohs and nobles.

Higher Status for Egyptian Women Egyptian women generally enjoyed a higher status and greater independence than women elsewhere in the ancient world. For example, Ramses II declared, "The foot of an Egyptian woman may walk where it pleases her and no one may deny her." Under Egyptian law, women could inherit property, enter business deals, buy and sell goods, go to court, and obtain a divorce.

Although there were often clear distinctions between the occupations of women and men, women's work was not confined to the home. Women manufactured perfume and textiles, managed farming estates, and served as doctors. Women could also enter the priesthood, especially in the service of goddesses. Despite their many rights and opportunities, few women learned to read and write. Even if they did,

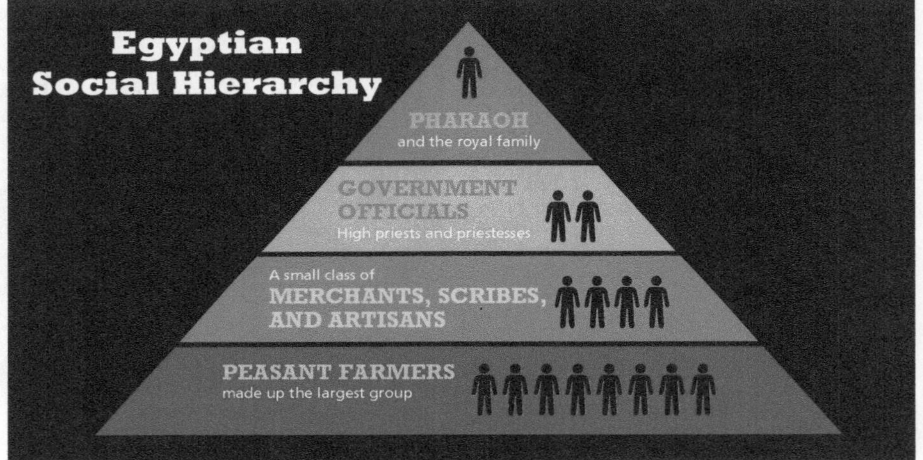

>> **Analyze Information** What does the structure of Egypt's class system tell you about the importance of religion in that society?

History Background

Discuss the role of women in Egyptian society. Besides working in the fields, peasant women also spent much time raising children, collecting water, and preparing food. Egyptian women generally enjoyed a higher status and greater independence than women elsewhere in the ancient world. Women could inherit property, enter business deals, buy and sell goods, go to court, and obtain a divorce. Although there were often clear distinctions between the occupations of women and men, women's work was not confined to the home. Women manufactured perfume and textiles, managed farming estates, and served as doctors. Women could also enter the priesthood, especially in the service of goddesses.

Egyptian Learning Advances

We know a lot about ancient Egypt today because of our ability to decipher ancient Egyptian writing, or hieroglyphics. The discovery of the Rosetta Stone allowed scholars to decipher the meaning of hieroglyphic passages. Discuss the advances ancient Egyptians made in mathematics and science and how they eventually influenced the classical civilization of Greece. Explain that Greek scholars traveled to Egypt to study and discuss ideas with Egyptian priests and scholars. The Greeks were impressed by Egyptian civilization and adopted many Egyptian ideas into their culture.

Online Project the **Interactive Gallery: Hieroglyphics.** Look carefully at the Rosetta Stone. Discuss the importance of the discovery of the Rosetta Stone and how it unlocked many secrets about ancient Egypt. Explain that the Rosetta Stone was written in hieroglyphics, demotic text, and Greek. Describe how Egyptian culture was diffused into Greece after the Greek emperor Alexander the Great conquered Egypt.

ACTIVE CLASSROOM

Use the See-Think-Wonder strategy. Pair students with a partner and have them select a part of the gallery to study closely. Ask them: What do you see? What does that make you think? What are you wondering about now that you've seen this? Share insights with the class.

they were excluded from becoming scribes or holding government jobs.

IDENTIFY Which social class grew in size as a result of trade and warfare?

Egyptian Learning Advances

Learned scribes played a central role in Egyptian society. Some kept records of ceremonies, taxes, and gifts. Others served government officials or the pharaoh. Scribes also acquired skills in mathematics, medicine, and engineering. With skill and luck, a scribe from a poor family might become rich and powerful.

Written Records Like people in other early civilizations, the ancient Egyptians developed writing. In fact, they developed multiple writing systems. The first was **hieroglyphics** (hy ur oh GLIF iks), a system in which symbols or pictures called hieroglyphs represent objects, concepts, or sounds. The Egyptians used hieroglyphs to record important economic, administrative, and royal information. Often, priests and scribes carved hieroglyphs in stone. Such inscriptions on temples and other monuments are records of Egyptian culture that have endured for thousands of years.

Around the time that hieroglyphics came into use, scribes also developed hieratic (hy ur AT ik) writing, a simpler script for everyday use. The hieratic script was a cursive form of writing created by simplifying the shapes of the hieroglyphs. Over time, hieratic script was replaced by a similar one called demotic.

The Egyptians also learned to make a paper-like writing material from **papyrus** (puh PY rus), a plant that grows along the banks of the Nile. (Paper would not be invented until about A.D. 100, in China.) Writing cursive scripts with reed pens and ink on the smooth surface of papyrus strips was much easier than chiseling words onto stone. When writing official histories, however, scribes continued to carve hieroglyphs. Invaders such as the Hyksos, along with an expanding Egyptian empire, helped spread the use of papyrus to other regions.

Greek scholars traveled to Egypt to learn about Egyptian civilization and took the use of papyrus, along with mathematics, medicine, engineering, and other knowledge, back to Greece with them.

The Rosetta Stone Unlocks Egyptian Writing After ancient Egypt declined, the meanings of ancient hieroglyphs were lost. Not until the early 1800s did

>> Since hieroglyphs, seen here, took a lot of time and care to write, Egyptian scribes also developed the cursive hieratic and demotic scripts for quicker use.

 Interactive Gallery

a French scholar, Jean Champollion (zhahn shahm poh LYOHN), unravel the then mysterious writings on Egypt's great monuments. Champollion did so by **deciphering,** or figuring out the meaning of, passages written on the **Rosetta Stone.** This flat, black stone presents the same passage carved in hieroglyphics, demotic script, and Greek. By comparing the three versions, Champollion worked out the meanings of many hieroglyphs. As a result of that breakthrough, scholars could begin to read the thousands of surviving records from ancient Egypt.

Egyptian Science and Mathematics The ancient Egyptians accumulated a vast store of knowledge in fields such as medicine, astronomy, and mathematics. Like most doctors until relatively recent times, Egyptian physicians believed in various kinds of magic. However, they learned a great deal about the human body through their knowledge of mummification. They also became skilled at observing symptoms, diagnosing illnesses, and finding cures.

Doctors also performed complex surgical operations, such as amputations, which we know about today because they are described on papyrus scrolls that survived through time. Many plant parts that Egyptian doctors prescribed as medicines—such as anise, castor beans, and saffron—are still used today for various

Topic 2 Lesson 4

Guided Reading and Discussion

Discuss how ancient Egyptians made advances in writing, through the use of hieroglyphics in science, through their knowledge of the human body from mummification, and in mathematics, especially geometry. Ancient Egyptian art in the forms of statues, paintings, sculptures, and architecture reflected its culture by emphasizing the importance placed on the gods, goddesses, and afterlife. Discuss how these advances in learning eventually influenced the classical civilizations of Greece and Rome through cultural diffusion.

Summarize Identify three important advances in learning made by the ancient Egyptians. *(Ancient Egyptians created hieroglyphics, advanced knowledge of the human body, and developed a sophisticated geometry.)*

SYNTHESIZE

Online Ask students to recall the strengths and weaknesses of each of ancient Egypt's three kingdoms. Have them use the Think-Pair strategy to answer the questions in the Synthesize activity. Then have students write two or three sentences describing the importance of each kingdom. Remind students to use details from the text to support their ideas. *(Answers will vary. The Old Kingdom was important because it developed a strong centralized government and state, the Middle Kingdom expanded farmable land, while the New Kingdom expanded Egyptian territory and made important advances in learning.)*

purposes. Egyptian medical ideas spread throughout the Middle East and Africa as traders, scholars, and conquerors adapted these ideas and techniques. Pharaohs also sent their personal physicians to serve other kings. For example, Ramses II sent physicians to the king of Hatti, and many rulers, including Persians, employed Egyptian doctors as medical staff. Egyptian medical theories influenced the Greeks, who, in turn often served as doctors in the Roman empire. Arab and European doctors then adapted Roman ideas about medicine and anatomy.

Egyptian priest-astronomers studied the heavens, mapping constellations and charting the movements of the planets. With this knowledge, they developed a calendar that included 12 months of 30 days each as well as 5 days added at the end of each year. With a few changes, this ancient Egyptian calendar became the basis for our modern calendar.

Egyptians developed mathematics partly in response to practical problems that they faced. Flooding Nile waters forced Egyptians to redraw the boundaries of their fields each year. To do this, scholars developed geometry in order to survey the land. Egyptian engineers also used geometry to calculate the exact size and location of each block of stone to be used in construction of a pyramid or temple. Huge projects such as building pyramids required considerable skills in design and engineering. These skills were passed on to other cultures as a result of foreign invasions of the New Kingdom of Egypt. These invasions helped spread Egyptian learning to other regions.

Specifically, Egyptian ideas were spread rapidly through the invasion led by Greece's Alexander the Great in 332 B.C. Alexander allowed for scholars to visit Egypt and work side by side with Egyptian scholars. Even before Alexander's invasion, mathematical and other scientific knowledge spread through trade and commerce.

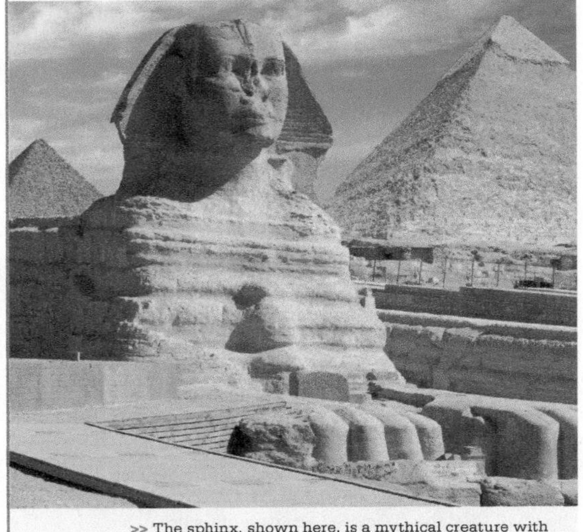

>> The sphinx, shown here, is a mythical creature with the body of a lion and a human head. The Egyptians thought of sphinxes as guardians at the entrances of temples or pyramids.

Egyptian Arts The Egyptians left behind them a rich legacy of art. Statues and paintings have given us a wealth of information about ancient Egyptian viewpoints and values.

The arts of ancient Egypt included statues, wall paintings in tombs, and carvings on temples. Some show everyday scenes of trade, farming, family life, or religious ceremonies. Others boast of victories in battle. Ancient Egyptian art and architecture is one way Egyptian history is understood today. Egyptian art reflects the history, culture, and society in which it was created. Much Egyptian art reflects the importance of religion, portraying Egyptians' beliefs about death and the afterlife.

Painting and sculpture styles remained almost unchanged for thousands of years. Artists always presented gods and pharaohs as much larger than other figures—size indicated the subject's importance, not his or her real size. Also, artists usually depicted people with their heads and limbs in profile but their eyes and shoulders facing the viewer.

Statues often showed people in stiff, standard poses. Some human figures have animal heads that represent special qualities. The Sphinx that crouches near the Great Pyramids at Giza portrays an early pharaoh as a powerful lion-man. Egyptians also erected many stone buildings and monuments, mostly tombs and temples.

Egyptian Literature The oldest Egyptian literature includes hymns and prayers to gods, proverbs, and love poems and reflects Egyptian culture. Other writings tell of royal victories in battle or, like Ptah-hotep's book, give practical advice.

In Egypt, as in other early societies, folk tales were popular, especially *The Tale of Sinuhe.* It relates the wanderings of Sinuhe (SIN oo hay), an Egyptian official forced to flee into what is now Syria. He fights his way to fame among the desert people, whom the Egyptians considered uncivilized. As he gets older, Sinuhe longs to return home. The story ends happily when the pharaoh welcomes him back to court. *The Tale of Sinuhe* helps us see how Egyptians viewed both themselves and the people of the surrounding desert.

? IDENTIFY What art forms were common in ancient Egypt?

ASSESSMENT

1. **Summarize** How did the Nile play an important role in uniting Egypt and allowing Egypt to expand during the New Kingdom?
2. **Draw Conclusions** Which details about the Egyptian gods show the importance of agriculture to Egyptian society?
3. **Determine Relevance** What does mummification reveal about ancient Egyptian religious views?
4. **Describe** Describe some of the main achievements of the ancient Egyptians.
5. **Describe** Describe the organization of Egyptian society.

Remind students how Greeks admired Egyptian civilization and that Greek scholars traveled to Egypt to study with Egyptian priests and scholars. Have partners think about the following question: What things and ideas of ancient Egypt do you think would have impressed visitors from other civilizations? *(Many students will cite impressive structures, such as the pyramids, sphinx, and great temples; others might point to the extensive irrigation networks, the well-organized society and hierarchy, or the art.)*

DEMONSTRATE

Online Assign the **Digital Lesson Quiz** for this lesson if you haven't already done so. Students will be offered automatic remediation or enrichment based on their score.

Pose the following question to the class on the Discussion Board:

In "Egyptian Civilization," you read about the importance of geography to the development of ancient Egypt as well as the contributions of the three kingdoms. Eventually, Egyptian ideas in mathematics and science were adopted by the Greeks and other cultures through both trade and conquest.

Summarize Name an achievement of the ancient Egyptians in each of the following fields: medicine, astronomy, and mathematics. *(In medicine, knowledge of the human body, illnesses, and surgery developed. In astronomy, ancient Egyptians were able to map constellations and chart planetary movements, as well as develop a 365-day calendar. In mathematics, ancient Egyptians developed geometry.)*

Topic Inquiry

Have students continue their investigations for the Topic Inquiry.

Answers

Identify *statues, paintings, sculpture, and architecture*

Assessment

1. The Nile was a link between Upper Egypt and Lower Egypt as well as a trade route with other regions. A series of ambitious and powerful pharaohs expanded the empire. Pharaohs conquered Nubia and obtained gold and soldiers from this region on the southern Nile.
2. The most important gods were associated with the sun and the Nile, both of which were key to agriculture. With a stable food supply, the population could grow and Egyptian civilization could flourish.

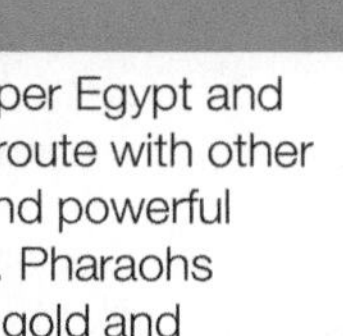

3. Egyptians wanted to preserve the body for use in the afterlife because they believed the afterlife would resemble life on Earth.
4. Technical achievements include creating dams and other flood-control techniques, building the Great Pyramids and other monuments, advances in mathematics and medicine, writing and keeping written records, and in the arts and literature.
5. The pharaoh was at the center of religion as well as government and the army. The pharaoh was considered a god. Below the pharaohs came high priests and priestesses and government officials, and then a small class of artisans, scribes, and merchants. The largest portion of the population was peasants or slaves who worked in agricultural production.

Topic 2

Answers to TEKS Assessment

1. Student answers will vary but should include that the land between the Persian Gulf and the Mediterranean Sea is called the Fertile Crescent. It was an ideal place to settle because of its rich soil and golden wheat fields. It was called the Fertile Crescent because an abundance of crops could be grown there.

2. Student answers will vary but should include that the Fertile Crescent had rich soil and wheat fields and was located near water sources, which made it a very popular location for settlement. Herders, traders, and nomads easily overcame the region's few natural barriers, including its desert climate. The region is referred to as the "cradle of civilization" because many of the earliest human civilizations developed there.

3. Student answers will vary, but the paragraph should say that Sumerians built the earliest known wheeled vehicles, including carts similar to the one shown, to help with farming and other day-to-day tasks. They also used irrigation and metalworking. Their ideas spread as trade increased. Although Sumer was conquered, Sumerian inventions and ideas spread to the peoples who conquered them. These and other ideas from Mesopotamian civilizations were eventually passed on to the ancient Greeks and Romans, and later to the Western world.

4. Student answers will vary but should include that Hammurabi wanted to be sure that everyone in his empire knew the laws that should be followed. It was the first important attempt by a ruler to codify laws. Hammurabi had artisans carve nearly 300 laws on a stone pillar for everyone to see. The only people who could really "see" the laws were the people who could read. This made knowledge of the laws inaccessible to some people.

5. Student answers will vary but should say that Darius I ruled from 522 B.C. to 486 B.C. He set up a bureaucracy, which is a system of government based on departments and subdivisions administered by people who follow set rules. He divided the empire into provinces, each with its own governor. Each province had to pay taxes based on its wealth, and special officials visited each province to check up on the governor.

6. Student answers will vary but should include that under Darius I, an efficient and successful government structure was set up. He adopted rules and laws from the peoples he conquered and, like Hammurabi, drew up a single code of laws for the empire. Darius set up a bureaucracy, a government in which departments and subdivisions administer the rules. Darius also set up a common system of weights and measures, which implemented an early form of a money economy. There was a religion as well, called Zoroastrianism, in which followers were taught that they had the individual freedom to choose between right and wrong. Like Christianity and Islam, two other religions that later emerged in the Middle East, Zoroastrianism stressed ideas about individual free will, heaven, hell, and a final judgment day.

7. Student answers will vary, but the outline should include the main headings 1. Philosophical, 2. Political, and 3. Religious. Under each heading, students should list at least two points. For example, under *Political,* students might note that Israeli political and legal ideas are found in most Western cultures.

8. Student answers will vary but should say that the Israelites lived in small villages in central Canaan. Although the ancient Israelites shared other aspects of culture with Canaanites, they practiced Judaism and worshiped a single god. Judaism developed around 4,000 years ago. At the time, most religions worshiped many gods, so this made Judaism unique.

TEKS ASSESSMENT

1. **Identify and Describe Major Events** Identify and describe major causes of events from 8000 B.C. to 500 B.C., including the development of the river valley civilizations. Write a paragraph that describes the Fertile Crescent and why the region was called the Fertile Crescent. In your paragraph, be sure to describe its location and what made it an ideal place for the rise of civilizations. 1.A

2. **Analyze the Influences of Human and Physical Geographic Factors** Analyze the influence of human and physical geographic factors on major events in world history, including the development of river valley civilizations. Write a paragraph analyzing how human and physical geographic factors led to the Fertile Crescent eventually being nicknamed the "cradle of civilization." Include information on the geography, how people overcame natural barriers, and the reason for the region's nickname. 16.B

3. **Identify Origin and Diffusion** Identify the origin and the diffusion of major ideas in technology that occurred in river valley civilizations. Write a paragraph identifying the origin and diffusion of technology in Sumer. Include information on particular inventions, passing technological skills to other cultures, and the legacy of Sumer. 27.A

4. **Identify the Impact of Political and Legal Ideas** Identify the impact of political and legal ideas contained in documents, including Hammurabi's Code. Write a paragraph identifying Hammurabi's effort to make sure that his laws were available for all to see, and tell why he wanted them to be seen. Using your knowledge of the period, explain how even if the laws were available for all to see, some would never really "see" them. Use correct social studies terminology and standard grammar. In your paragraph include a discussion of Hammurabi's Code and how the laws were published. 20.B, 30.A, 30.B

5. **Identify and Describe Major Events** Identify and describe major causes of events from 500 B.C. to A.D. 600, including the development of the classical civilization of Persia. Identify and describe how Darius I was vital to the development of this period. Include the time of his rule, his establishment of a bureaucracy, and his division of the empire. 1.B

6. **Explain How Major Civilizations Influenced Developments** Explain how major river valley civilizations influenced the development of Persia by describing Persia's major political and religious influences. Write a paragraph describing the development of Persia, including specific accomplishments of Darius I. Include information about Zoroastrianism and some of its central ideas. 2.C, 3.A

7. **Describe Major Philosophical and Political Influences** Describe the major philosophical, political, and religious influences of Israel. Create an outline describing these major influences by using three main headings and several supporting points under each heading. 3.A

8. **Describe the Development of Major Religions** Describe the development of major religious and philosophical influences of Israel, including the development of Judaism. Write a paragraph, using correct social studies terminology, and describe how the belief system of the ancient Israelites was unique to its time. Include information on the religion they practiced, where they lived, their beliefs, and about when their religion was developed. 1.B, 3.A, 30.A

9. **Identify the Characteristics of Monarchies and Theocracies** Identify the characteristics of monarchies and theocracies as forms of government in early civilizations. Using the passage below and the lessons from this topic, write a paragraph identifying the characteristics of early monarchies. 19.A

"Each Sumerian city-state had a distinct social hierarchy, or system of ranking groups."

10. **Explain the Development of Government** Explain the development of democratic-republican government from its beginnings in the Judeo-Christian legal tradition. Write a paragraph drawing your own conclusion about early Jewish teachings and how they contributed to the eventual development of Western culture. Include Jewish beliefs and the development of Western culture, and be sure to use standard, grammar, spelling, sentence structure, and punctuation. **20.A, 30.B**

11. **Describe the Development of Monotheism** Describe the development of monotheism by creating a written presentation using social studies information. Write a paragraph telling how the beliefs of the ancient Israelites eventually led to Judaism becoming one of the world's major faiths. Include information on ancient Israelites' differences from other peoples, monotheism, and the Torah. **3.A, 30.C**

12. **Identify Major Causes** Identify major causes of events from 8000 B.C. to 500 B.C., including the development of the river valley civilizations. Write a paragraph about Egypt's first female ruler shown above. How does the art depict her? How did she rule, and what were some of her notable accomplishments? **1.A, 24.B**

13. **Identify the Impact of Political and Legal Ideas** Identify the impact of political and legal ideas contained in documents, including the Jewish Ten Commandments. Write a paragraph explaining why the Ten Commandments are such an important part of Judaism, and include the origin of the commandments according to Jewish belief, what they stress, how they impact political and legal ideas, and why the Jewish people believed them. **20.B**

14. **Describe the Spread, Origins, and Ideas of Major Religious and Philosophical Traditions** Describe the spread, historical origins, and central ideas of major religious and philosophical traditions, including Judaism, using standard spelling. Read the excerpt below. Then write a paragrah (using standard spelling) describing God's covenant with Abraham and how that came to be a covenant with the Israelites, according to Genesis. Include what God told Abraham about his role and how God was going to take care of Abraham's descendants. **23.A, 30.B**

"You shall be the father of a multitude of nations. . . . I will make nations of you, and kings shall come forth from you. And I will establish my covenant between me and you and your descendants after you throughout their generations for an everlasting covenant, to be God to you and to your descendants after you. And I will give to you, and to your descendants after you, the land of your sojournings [short stay], all the land of Canaan. . . ."

—Genesis 17:4–8

9. Student answers will vary but should include that in early civilizations, the monarchs were responsible for maintaining city walls and irrigation systems as well as leading the army and enforcing the laws. In addition, the kings were seen as godlike. They were considered intermediaries between man and God.

10. Student answers will vary but should include that spiritual leaders, or prophets, such as Isaiah and Jeremiah, taught a strong code of ethics, including personal morality and social justice. Some people believe that these and other Judeo-Christian traditions, including the idea of social responsibility, the worth of the individual, and the idea that all believers were equal before God, helped shape Western culture, morality, and ethics over many centuries.

11. Student answers will vary but should include that the ancient Israelites were monotheistic, meaning that they believed in one God. This set them apart from other peoples of the time, who believed in many gods. The Torah, which includes the first five books of the Hebrew Bible, is the most sacred text for the people of Israel. It is meant to guide the Jewish people in their faith.

12. Student answers will vary but should include that Hatshepsut was pharaoh during the New Kingdom. She was Egypt's first female ruler. The art shows her as beautiful, with big, bright eyes and an ornate headpiece, which shows wealth. As pharaoh, she was known for building temples and monuments and reestablishing trade networks, which helped Egypt to flourish.

13. Student answers will vary but should include that, according to Jewish belief, God gave the Ten Commandments to Moses on Mount Sinai. The commandments are a set of laws that guide Judaism and aided the ancient Israelites in setting up their society and government. They also established moral law and the concept of the rule of law. The basic ideas of the commandments still endure today.

14. Student answers will vary but should include that, according to Genesis, God made a covenant with Abraham in which God said that Abraham would be a father of nations. Genesis also says that God would always have a relationship with Abraham and all of his descendants and that one day all of Abraham's descendants should go back to Canaan. As a result, the Israelites considered Canaan to be their promised land.

15. Student answers will vary, but the paragraph should say that Egyptians represented gods and other important figures as bigger than the common person. The size of a person in art didn't represent his or her actual size; it showed how important the subject was. The art also depicted mythical creatures, such as the sphinx in the sculpture shown. The sphinx had the head of a man but the body of lion, which represented the creature's strength and power.

16. Student answers will vary but may include a thesis such as "Pharaohs were Egyptian kings who held absolute power and played key roles in religion and politics. They were seen as gods, but they were also human and were expected by the people to behave morally. The vizier was a government supervisor. Under his supervision, taxes were collected and farms and irrigation were looked after."

The student should also provide an opinion as to whether or not the pharaohs were good rulers.

Answers to TEKS Assessment

17. Student answers will vary, but the chart should list all three rights and a definition as well as a current example of their use. For example, "innocent until proven guilty" means that the burden of proof is on the accuser, not on the accused. The accuser must have enough evidence to prove a person's guilt. Present-day use: any criminal trial found in the newspaper, heard on the news, etc. An example of a title might be "Ethical, Political, and Legal Traditions."

18. Student answers will vary but should include that a belief in the afterlife affected all Egyptians. They believed that each soul must pass a test to win eternal life. Tombs were considered homes where the dead could live for eternity. People preserved the bodies of the deceased and provided each tomb with everything a person would need in the next life. The tombs of pharaohs were housed in enormous, costly pyramids that took years to construct, and a pharaoh would often begin construction at the beginning of his reign.

TEKS ASSESSMENT

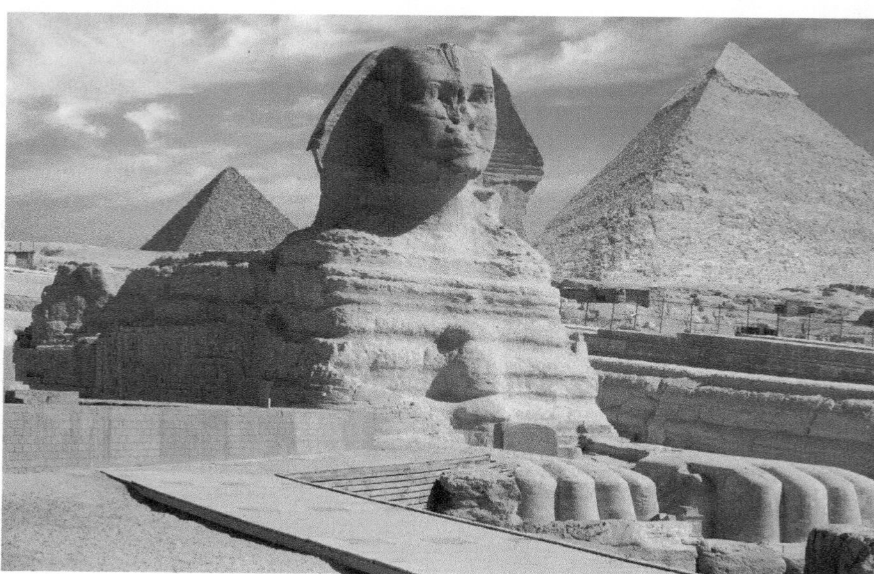

15. **Analyze Examples of Art** Analyze examples of how art reflects the history of the cultures in which it is produced. Look at the image above. Write a paragraph analyzing how Egyptian art represents the culture of ancient Egypt. Include how gods and pharaohs are represented, what can be seen in the art, and how the art reflects Egyptian culture. **26.B**

16. **Identify Major Causes** Identify major causes of events from 8000 B.C. to 500 B.C., including the development of the river valley civilizations by constructing a thesis on a social studies issue or event supported by evidence. Develop a thesis on the rule of the pharaohs in Egypt. Discuss the role of the pharaohs, and state whether or not you believe they were good rulers by considering what people expected of them. Include information on the role of the vizier and how he or she supported the pharaoh. **1.A, 29.G**

17. **Identify the Influence of Ideas** Identify the influence of ideas regarding the right to a "trial by a jury of your peers" and the concepts of "innocent until proven guilty" and "equality before the law" that some people believe originated from the Judeo-Christian legal tradition. Create a chart that defines these terms using the lessons of this topic, the statement below, and outside sources. In your chart, include a present-day example of when the rights of individuals have been protected by these laws. Using the statement below, write an engaging title for your chart and include the three rights, their definitions, and a current example of their use from a newspaper or other media. **22.B**

"Both Judaism and Christianity emphasize the worth of the individual and social responsibility. Judeo-Christian influences can be found in the ethical, political, and legal traditions of most Western cultures."

18. **Identify Examples** Identify examples of religious influence on various events referenced in the major eras of world history. Write a paragraph about the Egyptian belief in an afterlife and how that affected Egyptian society. Consider the construction of and items within tombs, including the tombs of the pharaohs within the pyramids. **23.B**

19. **Reflect on the Essential Question** **Write an essay on the Essential Question: How much does geography affect people's lives?** Use evidence from your study of this Topic to support your answer.

Topic 2

Topic 2

Answers to TEKS Practice

1. A
2. G

Online To prepare for the End-of-Topic test, have students go online for additional Topic Review and Assessment questions or to review their notes in the **Interactive Reading Notepad** for the lessons in this Topic.

Benchmark Tests

Assign these benchmark tests as you complete the relevant topics to monitor student progress toward mastering the course content and as preparation for the End-of-Course Test.

Benchmark Test 1: Topics 1–5

Benchmark Test 2: Topics 6–10

Benchmark Test 3: Topics 11–15

Benchmark Test 4: Topics 16–21

TEKS PRACTICE

1 Who was the ruler of Akkad, the first empire of Mesopotamia?

A Sargon
B Hammurabi
C Sin-Muballit
D Marduk

2

The image above is best representative of what?

F The Commandments
G Tribes of Israel
H The Exodus
J Abraham's descendents

Test Taking Tips: Tip for Multiple-Choice Tests

1. Read the question carefully. Make sure you understand the question.
2. Read all four answer choices. Even if you think you know the correct answer, check your choice.
3. If you do not understand the question, read it again. If you are still unsure of the answer, use the process of elimination. Begin by rejecting any answer choice that you know is wrong.
4. Look for answer choices that do not relate to the question. (Remember that some answer statements are true, but do not relate to the question.)
5. Look for clue words in the answer choices. Words such as *all, everyone, only,* or *completely* can be wrong because they are too general. A correct answer might use words such as *often, generally,* or *at times*.

3

> *"Finally, the Ten Commandments guided the ancient Jews in setting up their society and government, an influence that endures into our own time."*

What did the Jewish prophets teach?

A Men and women are equal in all respects.

B Rulers are not bound by God's law.

C People should adopt moral standards of behavior.

D Jews should spread out to the farthest reaches of their empire.

---

4 Anthropologists gave the hominid group Homo habilis this name because—

F they walked upright

G they could make fire

H they made their own tools

J they were the first to evolve

If you have trouble with...				
Question	1	2	3	4
See Lesson	2.2	2.3	2.3	1.1
TEKS	16.B	23.A	20.A	29.A

3. C
4. H

Online Use the **Topic Synthesize** to help students revisit and reflect on the Essential Question for this Topic.

Topic Inquiry

If students have done a Topic Inquiry for this Topic, have them complete the final step of the Inquiry now.

Ancient India and China (2600 B.C.–A.D. 550)

TOPIC 3 ORGANIZER	PACING: APPROX. 1 PERIOD, .5 BLOCKS		
	PACING	TEKS	ELPS
Connect	1 period		
MY STORY VIDEO **Shi Huangdi, First Emperor of a Unified China**	10 min.		
DIGITAL ESSENTIAL QUESTION ACTIVITY **How Are Religion and Culture Connected?**	10 min.	25.A	
DIGITAL TIMELINE ACTIVITY **Ancient India and China**	10 min.	25.A	
TOPIC INQUIRY: DOCUMENT-BASED QUESTION **What Makes an Ordered Society?**	20 min.		
Investigate	2–5 periods		
TOPIC INQUIRY: DOCUMENT-BASED QUESTION **What Makes an Ordered Society?**	Ongoing		
LESSON 1 **Early Civilization in South Asia**	30–40 min.	1.A, 3.A, 16.B, 26.B, 27.A	2.C.3
LESSON 2 **The Origins of Hinduism and Buddhism**	30–40 min.	1.A, 1.B, 3.A, 23.A, 23.B, 25.A	2.C.4
LESSON 3 **Powerful Empires Emerge in India**	30–40 min.	1.B, 3.A, 25.A, 27.A	2.D.1
LESSON 4 **Rise of Civilization in China**	30–40 min.	1.A, 1.B, 2.C, 3.A, 16.B, 23.A, 25.A, 27.A	2.D.2,, 2.C.1, 1.F.1
LESSON 5 **Strong Rulers Unite China**	30–40 min.	1.B, 3.A, 4.J, 27.A	2.C.2, 2.E.1
Synthesize	1 period		
DIGITAL ACTIVITY **Reflect on the Essential Question and Topic**	10 min.	25.A	
TOPIC INQUIRY: DOCUMENT-BASED QUESTION **What Makes an Ordered Society?**	20 min.		
Demonstrate	1–2 periods		
DIGITAL TOPIC REVIEW AND ASSESSMENT **Ancient India and China**	10 min.		
TOPIC INQUIRY: DOCUMENT-BASED QUESTION **What Makes an Ordered Society?**	20 min.		

AUTHOR'S NOTE

The Scholar Bureaucrats

The Han period also saw a crucial institutional development that made the authority of the imperial government much more than a theory. For in Han times, China's famous system of scholar bureaucrats began to evolve.

The great shift from government by an autonomous feudal aristocracy to government by appointed officials of the central government had had a brief, violent trial run under the Qin. But the Legalist rigor of Qin administrators had made the system too brutal for wide acceptance. Infused with the more moderate spirit of Confucianism—and with due concessions to the existing social elite of the countryside—China's administration under the Han dynasty became the most impressive in the world. . . . .

In the Han period . . . these officials were still members of wealthy landowning families.

Also under the Han, however, the system of civil-service examinations that would eventually undermine the remaining power of the landed magnates slowly took shape. Exams on Confucian principles and classics were given annually at Chang'an to young gentlemen nominated for office. To prepare them, an imperial university was established at the capital. Again, the children of the wealthy, who had money for books and tutors, were evidently the ones most likely to succeed. Nevertheless, the result was to produce a ruling elite of government administrators who had a common family background and whose heads were filled with common Confucian theories, shared historical understanding, and the same basic values—a powerful force for stability in the ancient Middle Kingdom.

Around 100 B.C.E. China's governmental bureaucracy divided into eighteen civil-service ranks, included upwards of 130,000 people—not many to govern tens of millions of Chinese, but an astonishing number of educated, centrally appointed officials for those days, when most of the world was still ruled by village elders, hereditary clan chieftains, and local princes.

—Anthony Esler, *The Human Venture: From Prehistory to the Present*, (Upper Saddle River, New Jersey: Pearson Education, 2004), p. 193

Topic 3

TOPIC INQUIRY: DOCUMENT-BASED QUESTION

What Makes an Ordered Society?

TEKS 1.B, 3.A, 23.A, 25.A, 29.C, 29.F, 29.G, 30.B

In this Topic Inquiry, students will analyze three primary source and two secondary source documents to draw their own conclusions on how Indian and Chinese religions contributed to the ordered structure of their society. The Topic Essential Question is "How are religion and culture connected?" This DBQ expands on that essential question and provides students an opportunity to consider some of the impact religion had on India and China's societal order.

STEP 1: CONNECT

Develop Questions and Plan the Investigation

Launch the DBQ Writing Activity

Show the flipped video on Shi Huangdi, First Emperor of Unified China. Lead a class discussion about the video, and then have students work together in partnerships to consider the following questions.

- What helps unify a society?
- How does a society govern itself?
- How does a society create a common purpose?

Generate Questions

Form small groups and have students record their questions about how religion affected the culture and society of India and China on the Need-to-Know Questions document.

Suggestion: Help students generate questions by referring to the 5 WQs and 1 H: Who? What? When? Where? Why? and How? Allot ten minutes for students to generate as many questions as possible. Select the questions that most target the DBQ question.

Professional Development

Document-Based Questions

Be sure to view the Document-Based Questions resources in the online course.

Resources

- Need-to-Know Questions
- Student Instructions

STEP 2: INVESTIGATE

Apply Disciplinary Concepts and Tools

Analyze the Documents

Instruct students to analyze the five documents before responding to the question, What makes an ordered society? Before students read the selections, point out the distinction between primary and secondary sources. Explain that Documents A and B are primary sources about Confucianism, and Document C is an image of Buddha, which represents the religion of Buddhism. Documents D and E are secondary sources articles on the impact of the Hindu caste system and how Confucian teachings can affect a country's culture and government.

Check Understanding

Students should answer the multiple-choice and short answer questions at the conclusion of each document.

Resources

- Information Organizer

STEP 3: SYNTHESIZE
Evaluate Sources and Use Evidence to Formulate Conclusions

Write Your Essay
Using the documents and their knowledge of history, have students write an essay on the following topic: What is an ordered society and which Indian and Chinese ideas contributed to such order?

Students should draw their own conclusions from reading the primary and secondary source evidence and viewpoints. Instruct students that their essays should have good organization and development, the criteria for which are found in their writing rubric. Remind students that they need to formulate clear topic sentences and use clearly identified supporting evidence from at least three of the documents. A conclusion should summarize the main concept and key points that provide proof of their hypothesis.

Suggestion: If students need assistance with organization, review the 5-paragraph essay: introduction of main idea, at least three paragraphs to develop key points, and a final paragraph to summarize the conclusion.

Edit Your Essay
Remind students that they should review the writing rubric and revise their first draft. Students should make necessary changes to the organization of their essay before turning it in. Peer editing may be an option before papers are finalized.

Resources
- Writing Rubric
- 21st Century Skill Tutorials: Draw Inferences

STEP 4: DEMONSTRATE
Communicate Conclusions and Take Informed Action

Reflect on the Project
When students have completed their essays, explain that the DBQ study on how ancient Indian and Chinese ideas contributed to their social order will become a basis for their understanding of how religion and culture are connected. Emphasize that they may revise their thinking on religion's role in culture, but they will have the knowledge of how to analyze multiple sources and process varying viewpoints in order to establish an educated, informed opinion.

PROFESSIONAL DEVELOPMENT

Document-Based Question
Be sure to view the Document-Based Question Professional Development resources in the online course.

Early Civilization in South Asia

Objectives

Objective 1: Describe the Indian subcontinent's geography.

Objective 2: Understand the clues archaeology has provided about the rise and fall of the Indus civilization.

Objective 3: Analyze the main characteristics of the Aryan civilization and the Vedic Age.

Objective 4: Explain what ancient Indian epics reveal about Aryan life.

LESSON 1 ORGANIZER		PACING: APPROX. 1 PERIOD, .5 BLOCKS				
			RESOURCES			
	OBJECTIVES	PACING	Print	Online	TEKS	ELPS
Connect						
DIGITAL START UP ACTIVITY **Ancient Civilizations, Modern Voices**		5 min.		●	16.B	
Investigate						
READ **Geography of the Indian Subcontinent**	Objective 1	10 min.	●	●	16.B	
INTERACTIVE MAP **Early Civilizations in South Asia**		10 min.		●	1.A, 2.C, 16.B	
READ **The Forgotten Indus Civilization**	Objective 2	10 min.	●	●	1.A, 2.C, 16.B	
INTERACTIVE GRAPHIC ORGANIZER **Technological Advances of the Indus Civilization**		10 min.		●	1.A, 2.C, 16.B	
READ **Aryan Civilization and the Vedas**	Objective 3	10 min.	●	●	3.A, 25.A	
READ **The Great Vedic Epics**	Objective 4	10 min.	●	●	3.A, 25.A	2.C.3
Synthesize						
DIGITAL ACTIVITY **Ancient Civilizations of the Indian Subcontinent**		5 min.		●	1.A, 2.C, 3.A, 16.B	
Demonstrate						
DIGITAL QUIZ **Lesson Quiz and Class Discussion Board**		10 min.		●	1.A, 3.B, 16.B, 25.A	

Focus on Texas Standards

Texas Essential Knowledge and Skills

1.A identify major causes and describe the major effects of the following events from 8000 BC to 500 BC: the development of agriculture and the development of the river valley civilizations

3.A describe the major political, religious/philosophical, and cultural influences of Persia, India, China, Israel, Greece, and Rome, including the development of monotheism, Judaism, and Christianity

16.B analyze the influence of human and physical geographic factors on major events in world history, including the development of river valley civilizations, trade in the Indian Ocean, and the opening of the Panama and Suez canals

26.B analyze examples of how art, architecture, literature, music, and drama reflect the history of the cultures in which they are produced

27.A identify the origin and diffusion of major ideas in mathematics, science, and technology that occurred in river valley civilizations, classical Greece and Rome, classical India, and the Islamic caliphates between 700 and 1200 and in China from the Tang to Ming dynasties

NOTES

The Origins of Hinduism and Buddhism

Objectives

Objective 1: Describe the origins and central beliefs of Hinduism.

Objective 2: Analyze and summarize how the caste system shaped India.

Objective 3: Describe the origins and central beliefs of Buddhism.

Objective 4: Explore how Buddhism grew and changed as it spread beyond India.

LESSON 2 ORGANIZER	PACING: APPROX. 1 PERIOD, .5 BLOCKS					
			RESOURCES			
	OBJECTIVES	PACING	Print	Online	TEKS	ELPS
Connect						
DIGITAL START UP ACTIVITY **Religion and Society**		5 min.		●	1.A, 1.B, 3.A, 23.A	
Investigate						
READ **Hinduism Beliefs Develop**	Objective 1	10 min.	●	●	1.B, 3.A, 23.A, 25.A	
INTERACTIVE GALLERY **The Origins of Hinduism**	Objective 1	10 min.		●	3.A, 23.A	
READ **The Caste System Shapes India**	Objective 2	10 min.	●	●	1.A, 1.B, 3.A, 23.A, 23.B, 25.A	
READ **The Buddha's Key Teachings**	Objective 3	10 min.	●	●	1.B, 3.A, 23.A, 23.B, 25.A	2.C.4
INTERACTIVE MAP **The Origins and Spread of Buddhism**	Objective 3	10 min.		●	1.B, 3.A, 23.A, 25.A	
READ **Buddhism Spreads**	Objective 4	10 min.	●	●	1.A, 1.B, 23.A, 25.A	
Synthesize						
DIGITAL ACTIVITY **Hinduism and Buddhism**		5 min.		●	1.A, 1.B, 3.A, 23.A, 25.A	
Demonstrate						
DIGITAL QUIZ **Lesson Quiz and Class Discussion Board**		10 min.		●	1.A, 1.B, 3.A, 23.A, 25.A	

PEARSON realize™ www.PearsonTexas.com Access your Digital Lesson

Focus on Texas Standards

Texas Essential Knowledge and Skills

1.A identify major causes and describe the major effects of the following events from 8000 BC to 500 BC: the development of agriculture and the development of the river valley civilizations

1.B identify major causes and describe the major effects of the following events from 500 BC to AD 600: the development of the classical civilizations of Greece, Rome, Persia, India (Maurya and Gupta), China (Zhou, Qin, and Han), and the development of major world religions

3.A describe the major political, religious/philosophical, and cultural influences of Persia, India, China, Israel, Greece, and Rome, including the development of monotheism, Judaism, and Christianity

23.A describe the historical origins, central ideas, and spread of major religious and philosophical traditions, including Buddhism, Christianity, Confucianism, Hinduism, Islam, Judaism, Sikhism, and the development of monotheism

23.B identify examples of religious influence on various events referenced in the major eras of world history

25.A summarize the fundamental ideas and institutions of Eastern civilizations that originated in China and India

NOTES

Powerful Empires Emerge in India

Objectives

Objective 1: Analyze how Mauryan rulers created a strong central government for their empire.

Objective 2: Explore the kingdoms that arose across the Deccan.

Objective 3: Explain why the period of Gupta rule in India is considered a golden age.

Objective 4: Understand how family and village life shaped Indian society.

LESSON 3 ORGANIZER — **PACING: APPROX. 1 PERIOD, .5 BLOCKS**

	OBJECTIVES	PACING	RESOURCES Print	RESOURCES Online	TEKS	ELPS
Connect						
DIGITAL START UP ACTIVITY **Powerful Rulers and The Golden Age in India**		5 min.		●		
Investigate						
READ **The Maurya Empire Builds a Strong Government**	Objective 1	10 min.	●	●	1.B, 25.A	
INTERACTIVE MAP **The Maurya and Gupta Empires**		10 min.		●	1.B	
READ **Deccan Kingdoms Arise**	Objective 2	10 min.	●	●	1.B, 3.A	
READ **A Golden Age Under Gupta Rule**	Objective 3	10 min.	●	●	1.B, 3.A, 25.A, 27.A	2.D.1
INTERACTIVE GALLERY **A Golden Age in the Arts**		10 min.		●	1.B, 3.A, 27.A	
READ **Family and Village Life Shape Indian Society**	Objective 4	10 min.	●	●	3.A	
Synthesize						
DIGITAL ACTIVITY **Maintaining Peace and Order**		5 min.		●	3.A	
Demonstrate						
DIGITAL QUIZ **Lesson Quiz and Class Discussion Board**		10 min.		●	1.B, 3.A, 25.A, 27.A	

PEARSON realize™ www.PearsonTexas.com Access your Digital Lesson

Focus on Texas Standards

Texas Essential Knowledge and Skills

1.B identify major causes and describe the major effects of the following events from 500 BC to AD 600: the development of the classical civilizations of Greece, Rome, Persia, India (Maurya and Gupta), China (Zhou, Qin, and Han), and the development of major world religions

3.A describe the major political, religious/philosophical, and cultural influences of Persia, India, China, Israel, Greece, and Rome, including the development of monotheism, Judaism, and Christianity

25.A summarize the fundamental ideas and institutions of Eastern civilizations that originated in China and India

27.A identify the origin and diffusion of major ideas in mathematics, science, and technology that occurred in river valley civilizations, classical Greece and Rome, classical India, and the Islamic caliphates between 700 and 1200 and in China from the Tang to Ming dynasties

NOTES

Rise of Civilization in China

Objectives

Objective 1: Understand how geography influenced early Chinese civilization.

Objective 2: Analyze how Chinese culture took shape under the Shang and Zhou dynasties.

Objective 3: Describe the origins, central ideas, and spread of Confucianism and Daoism.

Objective 4: List some achievements made in early China.

LESSON 4 ORGANIZER — **PACING: APPROX. 1 PERIOD, .5 BLOCKS**

	OBJECTIVES	PACING	RESOURCES Print	RESOURCES Online	TEKS	ELPS
Connect						
DIGITAL START UP ACTIVITY **Philosophy, Society, and Technology**		5 min.		●	23.A	
Investigate						
READ **Geography Influences Chinese Civilization**	Objective 1	10 min.	●	●	1.A, 2.C, 16.A, 16.B	2.D.2
READ **The Shang Dynasty Begins to Form China**	Objective 2	10 min.	●	●	2.C, 3.A, 19.A	2.C.1
READ **The Zhou Dynasty**		10 min.	●	●	1.B, 19.A	
READ **Religious Beliefs in Early China**	Objective 3	10 min.	●	●	3.A	
READ **Two Major Belief Systems Take Root**		10 min.	●	●	2.A	1.F.1
INTERACTIVE CHART **Confucianism and Daoism**		10 min.		●	1.B, 3.A, 23.A	
READ **A Time of Achievements in Early China**	Objective 4	10 min.	●	●	1.B, 3.A, 27.A	
INTERACTIVE GALLERY **Silk Making in Ancient China**		10 min.		●	27.A	
Synthesize						
DIGITAL ACTIVITY **Ancient Influences**		5 min.		●	23.A	
Demonstrate						
DIGITAL QUIZ **Lesson Quiz and Class Discussion Board**		10 min.		●		

NOTES

Strong Rulers Unite China

Objectives

Objective 1: Understand how Shi Huangdi unified China and established a Legalist government.

Objective 2: Outline why the Han period is considered a Golden Age of Chinese civilization.

Objective 3: Analyze how the Silk Road facilitated the spread of ideas and trade in China.

Objective 4: Analyze why Buddhism spread through China.

LESSON 5 ORGANIZER	PACING: APPROX. 1 PERIOD, .5 BLOCKS					
			RESOURCES			
	OBJECTIVES	PACING	Print	Online	TEKS	ELPS
Connect						
DIGITAL START UP ACTIVITY **Strong Rulers, New Civilizations**		5 min.		●	1.B	
Investigate						
READ **Shi Huangdi Unifies China**	Objective 1	10 min.	●	●	1.B, 3.A, 19.A	2.C.2
INTERACTIVE GALLERY **Terra Cotta Army of Emperor Qin**		10 min.		●	1.B, 3.A	
READ **The Han Dynasty Creates a Strong China**	Objective 2	10 min.	●	●	1.B, 3.A, 4.J	
INTERACTIVE GALLERY **The Silk Road Connects East and West**		10 min.		●	1.B, 3.A, 4.J	
READ **The Han Golden Age**	Objective 3	10 min.	●	●	1.B, 3.A, 27.A	2.E.1
READ **Buddhism Spreads in China**	Objective 4	10 min.	●	●	1.B	
Synthesize						
DIGITAL ACTIVITY **Changing Systems of Government**		5 min.		●	1.B, 3.A	
Demonstrate						
DIGITAL QUIZ **Lesson Quiz and Class Discussion Board**		10 min.		●	1.B, 3.A, 4.J, 19.A, 27.A	

PEARSON realize
www.PearsonTexas.com
Access your Digital Lesson

Focus on Texas Standards

Texas Essential Knowledge and Skills

1.B identify major causes and describe the major effects of the following events from 500 BC to AD 600: the development of the classical civilizations of Greece, Rome, Persia, India (Maurya and Gupta), China (Zhou, Qin, and Han), and the development of major world religions

3.A describe the major political, religious/philosophical, and cultural influences of Persia, India, China, Israel, Greece, and Rome, including the development of monotheism, Judaism, and Christianity

4.J analyze how the Silk Road and the African gold-salt trade facilitated the spread of ideas and trade

27.A identify the origin and diffusion of major ideas in mathematics, science, and technology that occurred in river valley civilizations, classical Greece and Rome, classical India, and the Islamic caliphates between 700 and 1200 and in China from the Tang to Ming dynasties

NOTES

Ancient India and China (2600 B.C.–A.D. 550)

In this Topic, you will learn about the ancient India and China. You will also find lots of ways to investigate the ideas of this Topic and to master the TEKS.

Your study will help you master these TEKS:

TEKS

1.A, 1.B, 2.C, 3.A, 4.J, 16.B, 19.A, 23.A, 23.B, 25.A, 26.B, 27.A, 29.C, 29.F, 29.H

LESSON OUTLINE

3.1: Early Civilization in South Asia 1.A, 3.A, 16.B, 25.A, 26.B, 27.A

3.2: The Origins of Hinduism and Buddhism 1.A, 1.B, 3.A, 23.A, 23.B, 25.A

3.3: Powerful Empires Emerge in India 1.B, 3.A, 25.A, 27.A

3.4: Ancient Civilization in China 1.A, 1.B, 2.C, 3.A, 16.B, 23.A, 25.A, 27.A

3.5: Strong Rulers Unite China 1.B, 3.A, 4.J, 27.A

Connect

You will start by connecting with the Topic through a video that tells a personal story about the times. You will start to think about how the Topic connects with your own experience or to what you have already learned. And you'll get a chance to think about a really big question, or Essential Question: How are religion and culture connected?

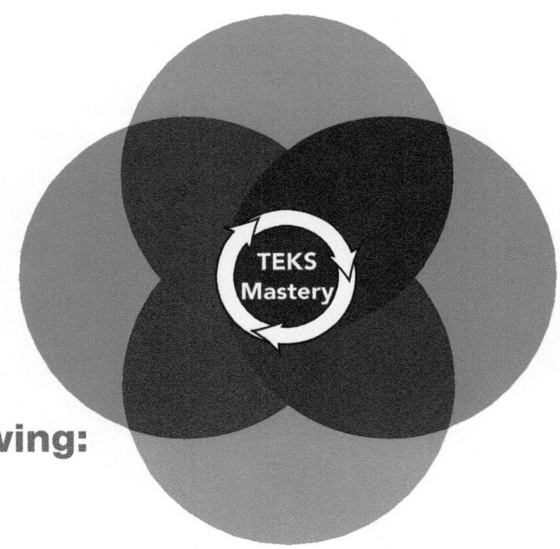

Begin your study by trying the following:

NBC LEARN Watch My Story Video:

Shi Huangdi, First Emperor of Unified China

Launch your Document-Based Question:

What Makes an Ordered Society?

Investigate

A group of lessons will help you investigate the Topic further. Each lesson has interesting text readings and fascinating interactivities. Together, they will bring the Topic to life and help you master the TEKS for this Topic.

And keep working on your Document-Based Question. You're almost ready to show what you have accomplished by completing the essay to show what you have learned.

>> Digital interactivity from the online course

Synthesize

You'll see that this Topic is about even more than fascinating texts and fun interactivities. It's really about how those things help you think about big ideas, like the Essential Question for this Topic.

Demonstrate

Completing this Topic is like practicing all your soccer skills or rehearsing the scenes in a play. Now you get a chance to pull it all together for the final game or the live performance. You can do this on the Topic Review and Assessment pages. Or you can complete work on the essay for your Document-Based Question, What Makes an Ordered Society?

TEKS in Topic 3	Topic Review and Assessment Questions
1.A	1
1.B	9, 11, 14
2.C	2
3.A	5, 12
4.J	14
16.B	6
19.A	13
23.A	3, 4, 7, 9, 12
23.B	5
25.A	9, 10, 13
27.A	8, 15, 16
29.F	5, 8
29.H	7

Topic 3

Ancient India and China (2600 B.C.–A.D. 550)

Introduction

In ancient India and China, complex civilizations developed with vast empires and powerful dynasties. They made great advances in the arts and sciences. In addition, the developing beliefs of Hinduism, Buddhism, Confucianism, and Daoism significantly affected ancient Indian and Chinese culture and governments. How did the religions and belief systems of this era help shape the way of life then and now?

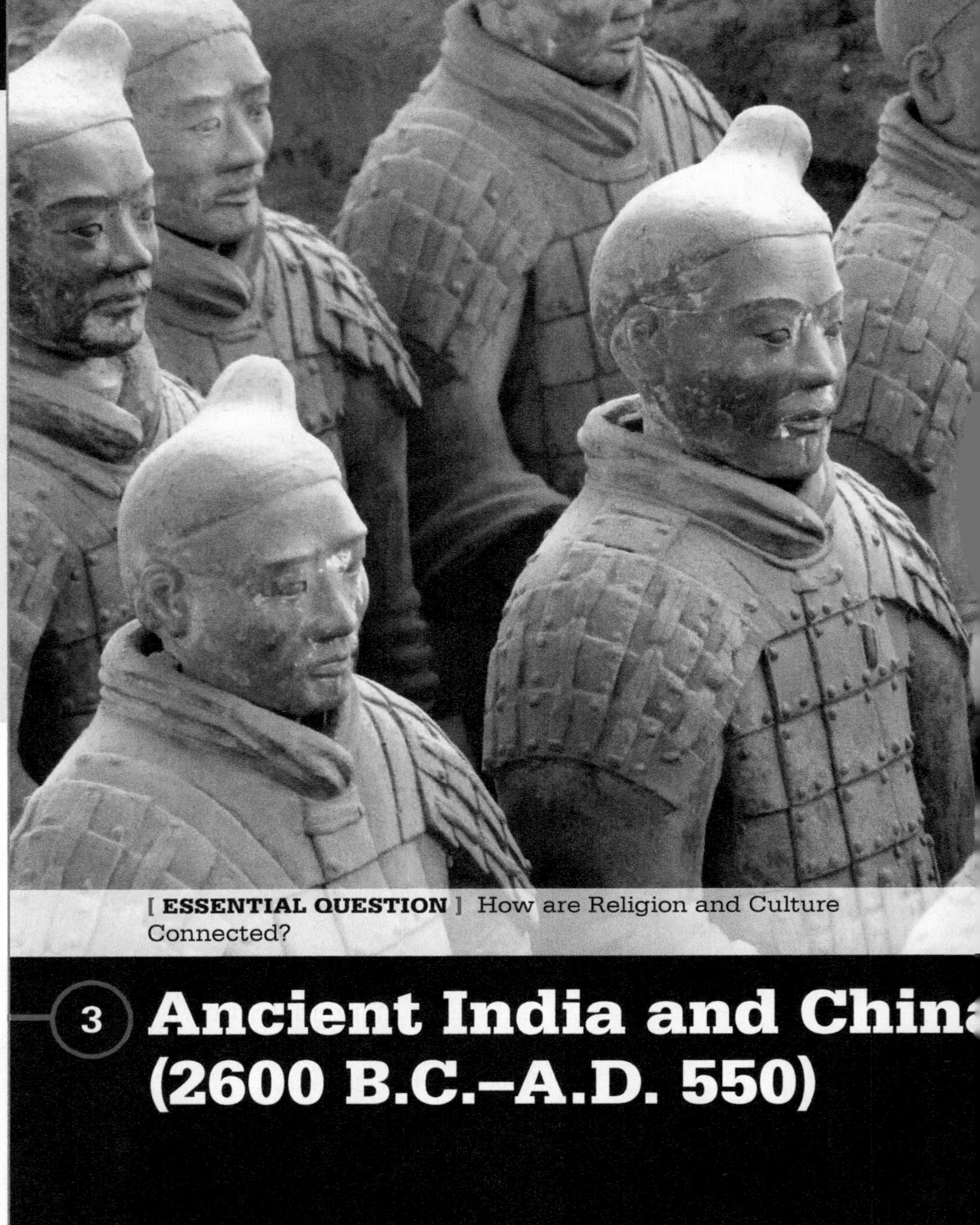
[ESSENTIAL QUESTION] How are Religion and Culture Connected?
3 Ancient India and China (2600 B.C.–A.D. 550)

ESSENTIAL QUESTION

Ask students to think about the Essential Question for this Topic: How are religion and culture connected? Project the Essential Question activity from the course. Remind students of what they read in Topic 1 about the growth of complex religions as early civilizations developed. Have students work with a partner to complete the activity. Then, as a class, go over the ideas students discussed with their partners. Ask what other connections they added. As a class, list and rank the five most important connections between religion and culture.

Support a Point of View With Evidence Why did you rank one of the connections as most important?

Identify Central Issues How might religion affect daily life? *(Possible answer: the role of family members, devotion to prayers, and ethical standards)*

Identify Cause and Effect How might religion affect government? *(Possible answer: A religion might have ethical or moral codes that get incorporated into legal codes. There might also be a correlation between religious and political hierarchy.)*

Analyze Images

Ask students to examine the statues shown in this photograph. They are made of terra cotta ("baked earth"), a kind of clay. Ask students what these statues represent, based on their outfits. *(soldiers; warriors)* Thousands of these terra cotta soldiers, along with horses, chariots, and weapons, were buried with China's first emperor. Discuss the belief system that might lead a culture to bury a terra cotta army with a dead ruler.

>> A terracotta army guards the tomb of China's first emperor

Texas Essential Knowledge and Skills

1.A, 1.B, 2.C, 3.A, 4.J, 16.B, 19.A, 23.A, 23.B, 25.A, 26.B, 27.A, 29.C, 29.F, 29.H

Enduring Understandings

- The Indus Valley civilization had large, well-planned cities and an organized government.
- Sacred texts known as the Vedas teach us about Aryan society.
- Hinduism and Buddhism emerged in ancient India and their ethical and spiritual messages shaped Indian civilization.
- The Maurya and Gupta empires united much of India; under the Guptas, India enjoyed a golden age of cultural achievement.
- Confucianism and Daoism are ancient Chinese belief systems that influenced China's culture for centuries.
- After Shi Huangdi unified China, the Han Golden Age brought advances in science, medicine, technology, and the arts.

PEARSON realize NBC LEARN

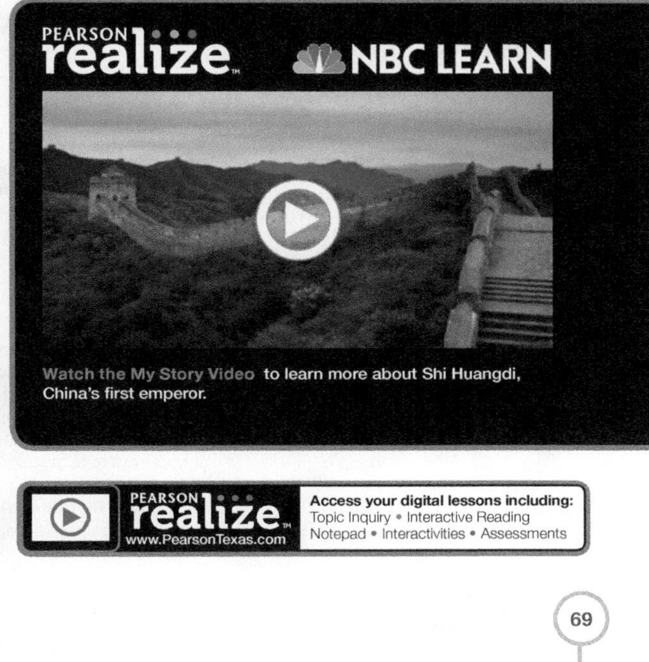

Watch the My Story Video to learn more about Shi Huangdi, China's first emperor.

PEARSON realize www.PearsonTexas.com

Access your digital lessons including: Topic Inquiry • Interactive Reading Notepad • Interactivities • Assessments

69

NBC LEARN MY STORY VIDEO

Project the My Story Video that introduces students to China's first emperor, who unified China through conquest.

Online My Story Video: **Shi Huangdi, First Emperor of Unified China**.

After viewing, ask students to respond to the following questions.

Check Understanding Why did Shi Huangdi seek to unify China? *(to end the warfare that was constantly breaking out among feudal warlords and rulers)*

Evaluate Data In what ways was Shi Huangdi great? What negative impact did he have? *(Shi Huangdi unified China for the first time, bringing stability. However, his harsh policies caused resentment among many Chinese.)*

OVERVIEW ACTIVITY

Online Project the **Ancient India and China Introduction Timeline** showing some of the major historical events in India and China between 2600 B.C. and A.D. 500. During this Topic study, students will learn about these events and many more. The timeline will provide a framework into which they can place the events.

Check Understanding Ask approximately how much time passed between when Hinduism was established in India and when the founder of Buddhism was born. *(around 900–934 years)*

Topic Inquiry

If you choose to assign the Topic Inquiry, launch the DBQ activity after introducing the Topic.

D Differentiate **Extra Support** For the Overview Activity, explain that there is no "zero" year, but that A.D. immediately follows B.C. Ask students to figure out the span of time between 2600 B.C. and A.D. 550. *(3,150 years)*

D Differentiate **Challenge** Ask students to make a copy of the timeline and add entries as they read. After reading all of the lessons, invite the students to share their new entries.

Topic 3 Lesson 1

Early Civilization in South Asia

CONNECT

Preview Have students preview the **Lesson Objectives** and the list of **Key Terms**.

Students can also preview all the **Key Terms** and **Academic Vocabulary** using the **Interactive Reading Notepad** on the digital course or preview a summary of the lesson in the **Reading and Note Taking Study Guide**.

Online Use the **Editable Presentation** found on the digital course to present the main ideas for this lesson.

Start Up Activity

Read aloud the following statement made in 1924 by Sir John Marshall, Director General of Archaeology in India:

> Not often has it been given to archaeologists . . . to light upon the remains of a long-forgotten civilization. It looks, however, at this moment, as if we were on the threshold of such a discovery in the plains of the Indus.

Ask students what types of items archaeologists might have found on the Indian subcontinent. *(Answers will vary. Students should show an understanding that archaeologists would find ruins and relics from an ancient and previously undiscovered civilization.)*

Online You can also project the **Start Up Activity** from the course.

INVESTIGATE

Have students read the section using the **Reading and Note Taking Study Guide** to help them take notes and understand the text as they read.

Geography of the Indian Subcontinent

The Indian subcontinent juts into the Indian Ocean with the tallest mountains in the world forming natural boundaries to the north and west.

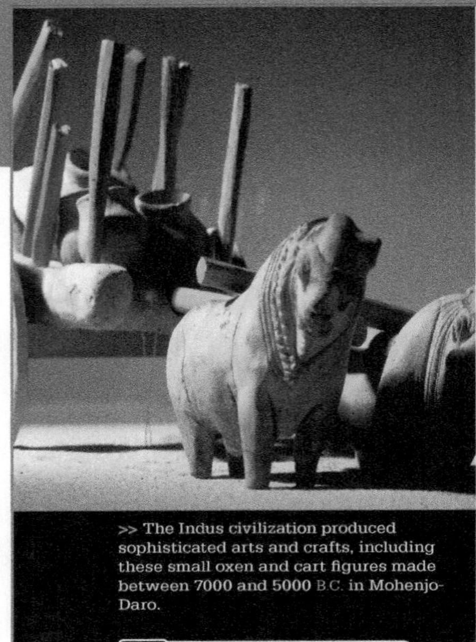

>> The Indus civilization produced sophisticated arts and crafts, including these small oxen and cart figures made between 7000 and 5000 B.C. in Mohenjo-Daro.

3.1 In the early 1900s, archaeologists digging in the Indus River valley of Pakistan made some startling discoveries. They unearthed bricks, small clay seals, figurines, and other artifacts dissimilar in style to any they had seen before. The archaeologists soon realized they had uncovered a civilization that had flourished 4,500 years earlier. It had been unknown to the world ever since.

TEKS 1.A, 3.A, 16.B, 26.B, 27.A

>> Objectives

Describe the Indian subcontinent's geography.

Understand the clues archaeology has provided about the rise and fall of the Indus civilization.

Analyze the main characteristics of the Aryan civilization and the Vedic Age.

Explain what ancient Indian epics reveal about Aryan life.

>> Key Terms

subcontinent
plateau
monsoon
Harappa
Mohenjo-Daro
veneration
acculturation
Vedas
rajah
Indra
brahman
mystic

Early Civilization in South Asia

Geography of the Indian Subcontinent

The Indus Valley is located in the region known as South Asia, or the Indian subcontinent. A **subcontinent** is a large landmass that juts out from a continent. The Indian subcontinent is a huge peninsula extending into the Indian Ocean.

Today, it includes three of the world's ten most populous countries—India, Pakistan, and Bangladesh—as well as the island nation of Sri Lanka (sree LAHNG kuh) and the mountain nations of Nepal and Bhutan.

Towering, snow-covered mountain ranges mark the northern border of the subcontinent, including the Hindu Kush and the Himalayas. These mountains limited contacts with other lands, leaving India's distinct culture to develop on its own. However, the mountains were not a complete barrier. Steep passes through the Hindu Kush served as gateways to migrating and invading peoples for thousands of years.

Mountains, Plateaus, and Plains of India The Indian subcontinent is divided into three major zones: the fertile Gangetic Plain in the

PEARSON realize www.PearsonTexas.com Access your Digital Lesson.

70

Aa Vocabulary Builder

1. Have students pronounce the following academic vocabulary term in this lesson and clarify the part of speech. Break the word into syllables and pronounce it with the students.
2. Explain what the word means in common "student-friendly" language using synonyms and antonyms when possible. Provide concrete examples to clarify the meaning, and rephrase the definition.

embody: to give a visible form for something abstract

north, the dry Deccan plateau, and the coastal plains on either side of the Deccan.

The Gangetic Plain lies just south of the Himalayas. This fertile region is watered by mighty rivers: the Indus, which gives India its name, the Ganges (GAN jeez), and the Brahmaputra (brah muh POO truh). These rivers and their tributaries carry melting snow from the mountains to the plains, making agriculture possible.

The Deccan is a **plateau,** or raised area of level land, that juts into the Indian Ocean. Much of it lacks the melting snows that feed the rivers of the north and provide water for irrigation. As a result, parts are arid, agriculturally unproductive, and sparsely populated.

The coastal plains are separated from the Deccan by low-lying mountain ranges, the Eastern and Western Ghats. Rivers and heavy seasonal rains provide water for farmers. Also, from very early times, people in this region used the seas for fishing and as highways for trade.

Life-Giving Monsoons A defining feature of life in the Indian subcontinent is the **monsoons,** or seasonal winds that regularly blow from a certain direction for part of the year. In October, the winter monsoons blow from the northeast, bringing hot dry air that withers crops. In mid-June, the summer monsoons blow from the southwest. They pick up moisture over the Indian Ocean and drench the land with downpours.

The monsoons have shaped Indian life. Each year, people welcome the rains that are desperately needed to water the crops. If the rains are late, famine and starvation may occur. However, if the rains are too heavy, rushing rivers will unleash deadly floods.

CHECK UNDERSTANDING What geographical feature limited the Indian subcontinent's contact with other peoples?

The Forgotten Indus Civilization

About 2600 B.C., the earliest South Asian civilization emerged in the Indus River valley, in present-day Pakistan. The Indus civilization flourished for about 700 years. However, only since the 1920s have its once-prosperous cities emerged beneath the archaeologists' picks and shovels.

Archaeologists have investigated numerous Indus sites. Unfortunately, they have not yet turned up any names of kings or queens, tax records, literature, or accounts of famous victories. The written remains of Indus civilization are found only rarely, usually on small clay seals that do not include any long passages. Still, we do know that the Indus Valley civilization covered the largest area of any civilization until the rise of Persia

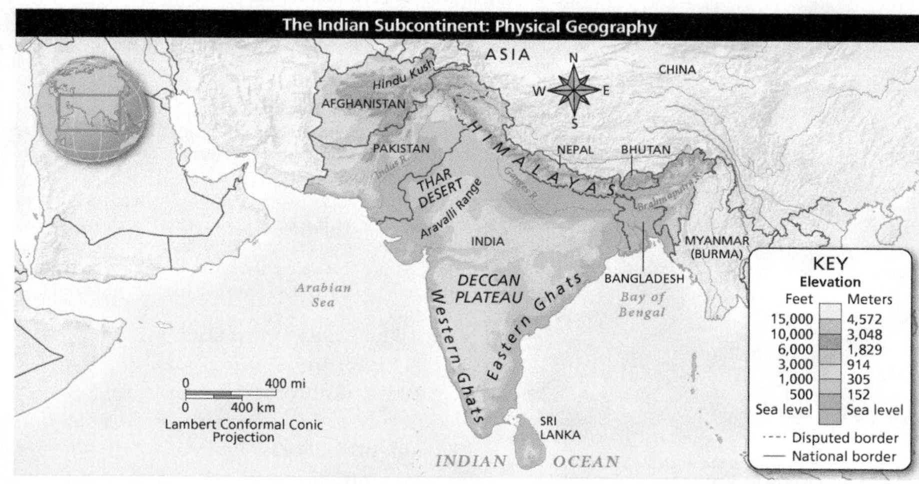

>> **Analyze Maps** The Indian subcontinent has a diverse range of geographic features. Where did most people in ancient India settle? Why?

Interactive Map

Topic 3 Lesson 1

Online Project the **Interactive Map: Early Civilizations in South Asia** and click through the key with students to show the physical geography of the Indian subcontinent, the area where the Indus civilization arose, and the path of the Aryan migration. Help students connect the physical geography of the subcontinent to the development of the Indus civilization *(It arose along the Indus River)*, and the Aryan migration *(The Aryans came through passes of the Hindu Kush mountains in northwestern India.)*.

ACTIVE CLASSROOM

Project the map and use a whiteboard tool to divide the physical geography layer into four main areas (northern mountains [Himalayas, Hindu Kush], Gangetic Plain, Deccan Plateau, Eastern and Western Ghats). Have students research images that depict the most important physical characteristics of these areas and present their findings to the class.

Guided Reading and Discussion

Ask students to describe the geographical features of the Indian subcontinent and speculate about how they might have affected the early peoples of the region.

Identify Cause and Effect Ask students to think about the map and what they have read in the lesson to determine the effect of water on how and where people lived.

History Background

The Significance of Seals When excavating the cities of Harappa and Mohenjo-Daro, archaeologists unearthed more than 2,000 small clay seals showing images and writing. The seals often bear images of animals, such as bulls. Other symbols with unknown meanings sometimes appear on seals, and they may have religious significance. Archaeologists believe that merchant families used their own seals to label their goods, and it is possible that the undeciphered writings found on some seals could be the merchants' names. Because seals are so durable, large numbers of them are often found during archaeological digs. The study of art history has benefited from the discovery of these seals, but the seals have also enriched cultural history because they provide pictorial details about a civilization's environment, clothing, and equipment.

Answers

Analyze Maps *Answers may vary but students should show an understanding of the regions where ancient Indians settled, and that these regions were in fertile river valleys that provided water and good farmland.*

Check Understanding *Possible answer: The mountain ranges of the Hindu Kush and the Himalayas were difficult for humans to cross. This meant that the people of the Indian subcontinent were isolated from their neighbors.*

Topic 3 Lesson 1

The Forgotten Indus Civilization

In the 1920s archaeologists found the remains of a great, complex civilization along the Indus River. This river valley civilization built impressive, carefully planned cities, created beautiful and intricate objects, and traded with distant lands.

Online Project the **Interactive Activity: Technological Advances of the Indus Civilization** and note each of the categories in this graphic organizer.

ACTIVE CLASSROOM

Ask students to record the technological advances of the Indus civilization using two different criteria: 1) according to which had the greatest long-term impact and 2) which was most important to the civilization at the time. Ask students to provide a justification for their rankings. Then ask them to work in pairs to share their rankings and justifications. Poll the class to see if there is agreement on the rankings.

Analyze Images

Direct students' attention to the photograph of Mohenjo-Daro. Ask students what skills the Indus Valley people needed to have in order to construct such a city. *(Possible answers: They needed to know how to make bricks; they needed masonry, or brick-laying, skills; they had to understand mathematics in order to design buildings and streets.)*

Key Terms

Ask students to find the key term **veneration** (in bold) in the text. Explain that some individuals—especially heroes or people considered to be holy, such as saints—are also venerated, or highly respected.

more than 1,000 years later. We know, too, that its cities rivaled those of Sumer.

Well-Planned Cities Reveal Organized Government Archaeologists' investigations in recent years have led them to believe that at least five large cities may have been prominent during the course of the civilization's history. A few hundred smaller sites have also been studied. Since their discovery in the 1920s, the Indus cities of **Harappa** and **Mohenjo-Daro** (moh HEN joh DAH roh) have been considered possible twin capitals of the civilization, or cities that ruled the area one after the other. Both were large, some three miles in circumference. Each was dominated by a massive hilltop structure whose exact purpose is unknown. Each city also included a huge warehouse used for storage.

A notable feature of Mohenjo-Daro and a few smaller sites is how carefully planned they were. Mohenjo-Daro was laid out in an organized pattern, with long, wide main streets and large rectangular blocks. Most of its houses were built with baked clay bricks of a standard size. At Harappa and other Indus sites mud and unbaked bricks were also common building materials.

In addition, Indus houses had complex plumbing systems, with baths, drains, and water chutes that led into sewers beneath the streets. Indus merchants used a uniform system of weights and measures. From such evidence, archaeologists have concluded that these Indus cities had a well-organized government.

>> Mohenjo-Daro, with a citadel in the background, was the largest Indus city. **Identify Main Ideas** Which important features of the Indus civilization does this image show?

Interactive Chart

Farmers, Traders, and Weavers As in other early civilizations, most people living in the Indus civilization were farmers. They grew a wide variety of crops, including wheat, barley, melons, and dates. They also may have been the first people to cultivate cotton and weave its fibers into cloth.

Some people were merchants and traders. Their ships carried cargoes of cotton cloth, grain, copper, pearls, and ivory combs to distant lands. By hugging the coast of the Arabian Sea and sailing up the Persian Gulf, Indus vessels reached the cities of Sumer.

Scholars think that this contact with Sumer may have prompted the people of the Indus Valley to develop their own system of writing; however, the Indus writing system is unique, showing no relationship to Sumerian cuneiform.

Indus Religious Beliefs From clues such as statues and images on small clay seals, archaeologists have speculated about the religious beliefs of Indus Valley people. Many think that, like other ancient peoples, the people of the Indus were polytheistic. A mother goddess, the source of creation, seems to have been widely honored, as perhaps was a leading male god. Indus people also seem to have viewed certain animals as sacred, including the buffalo and the bull. Some scholars think these early practices influenced later Indian beliefs, especially the **veneration** of, or special regard for, cattle.

A Mysterious Decline By 1900 B.C., the quality of life in the Indus Valley was declining. Crude pottery replaced the finer works of earlier days. The use of writing halted.

Mohenjo-Daro was entirely abandoned. The populations of the other Indus cities and towns also dwindled to small numbers. While people continued to live in the Indus Valley, the basic features of civilization dwindled away as they returned to simpler ways of life.

> The Indus Civilization remains an historical enigma [puzzle]. A remarkably uniform [culture] distributed over a vast geographical area utterly disappears without an apparent successor. Cities, writing, the high achievement of their crafts,

History Background

The *Mahabharata* This great Sanskrit epic of western India is probably based on fact—a war for control of the Ganges Valley around 1000 B.C. Twice the length of the Western epics the *Iliad* and the *Odyssey* combined, the *Mahabharata* is the longest poem ever created. In addition to the main story line—the struggle of five brothers to regain their kingdom—the *Mahabharata* gathers many myths, episodes, prayers, narratives, and stories. The principal teaching of the *Mahabharata's* stories is dharma, or devotion to one's duty. One element that has become very popular in the West is the *Bhagavad Gita*, a classic Hindu text of devotion that is analogous to Christ's Sermon on the Mount in that each work contains essential teachings of Hinduism and Christianity, respectively.

Answers

Identify Main Ideas *Answers may vary. Students might identify the citadel; the planned, organized pattern of buildings; and the uniform clay bricks.*

the use of standardized weights, long distance trade with the Gulf, and their exceptional system of urban sanitation simply disappear from the South Asian social landscape.

—Carl Lamberg-Karlovsky, archaeologist

Scholars do not know for sure what happened to the Indus civilization, but they have offered several explanations for its decline. They once thought that invaders attacked and overran the cities of the Indus, but this now seems unlikely. Some suggest that damage to the local environment was a factor. Possibly too many trees were cut down to fuel the ovens of brick makers. Tons of river mud found in the streets of Mohenjo-Daro suggest a major flood. Other evidence points to a devastating earthquake. Today scholars think that some of these events may have worked together to bring an end to Indus civilization.

CITE EVIDENCE What evidence shows that the Indus civilization included a well-organized government?

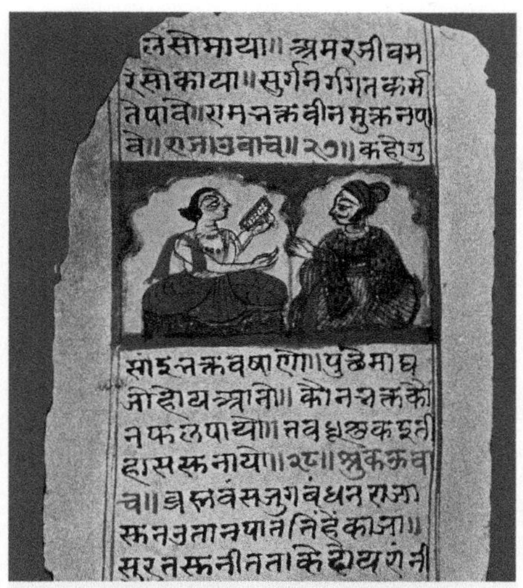

>> The Vedas were recited for many years before they were written down. This page is from the *Rig Veda,* or "Knowledge of the Hymns of Praise," the largest Veda, containing over 1,000 hymns.

Aryan Civilization and the Vedas

During the centuries between 2000 B.C. and 1500 B.C., waves of nomadic peoples migrated slowly with their herds of cattle and horses from Central Asia. They traveled through the mountain passes into northwestern India.

Aryan Migration into India These nomads belonged to one of many groups of speakers of Indo-European languages who migrated across Europe and Asia. The nomads intermarried with local peoples to form a group who called themselves Aryans. Through **acculturation,** or the blending of two or more cultures, the Aryans combined the cultural traditions of the nomads with those of earlier Indian peoples.

The early Aryans in India built no cities and left behind very little archaeological evidence. Most of what we know about them comes from the **Vedas,** a collection of hymns, chants, ritual instructions, and other religious teachings. Aryan priests memorized and recited the Vedas for a thousand years before they ever wrote down these sacred teachings. This period, from 1500 B.C. to 500 B.C., is often called the Vedic Age.

In the Vedas, the Aryans appear as warriors who fought in chariots with bows and arrows. They loved food, drink, music, chariot races, and dice games. These nomadic herders valued cattle, which provided them with food and clothing. Later, when they became settled farmers, families continued to measure their wealth in cows and bulls.

From Nomads to Farmers Gradually, the Aryans gave up their nomadic ways and settled into villages to cultivate crops and breed cattle. From local farmers, the Aryans learned to raise crops. They also took up other skilled crafts.

In time, the Aryans spread eastward to colonize the heavily forested Ganges basin. By about 800 B.C., they learned to make tools out of iron. Equipped with iron axes and weapons, restless pioneers carved farms and villages out of the rain forests of the northeast.

The Aryan people had a tribal political system that later formed the basis for the small independent kingdoms that formed in northwestern India. Aryan tribes were led by chiefs who were called **rajahs.** A rajah, who was often the most skilled war leader, had been elected to his position by an assembly of warriors. As he ruled, he considered the advice of a council of elders made up of the heads of families. Rajahs often fought with one another to control trade and territory across the Gangetic Plain. Some rajahs became

Guided Reading and Discussion

Ask students to list the various mysteries associated with the Indus Valley civilization. Use students' responses as a framework for discussing this ancient civilization.

Synthesize What other river valley civilizations have you read about? *(Students should note the river valley civilizations of Sumer, Mesopotamia, and Egypt.)*

Draw Conclusions Why would humans from such different areas of the world develop large civilizations along rivers? *(Students should understand that rivers provided access to a consistent water supply, fertile soil for farming, and transportation/trade routes, which helped people develop civilizations.)*

Aryan Civilization and the Vedas

Direct students' attention to the drawing of Purusha and lead them through a discussion about what it reveals about the Aryans and why the Aryans might have structured their society in this way.

Guided Reading and Discussion

Ask students to describe who the Aryans were and how they progressed from a nomadic culture to a more structured society. Help students understand the political and cultural influence of the Aryan civilization on India.

D Differentiate Extra Support For students who are having difficulty connecting the various river valley civilizations, show them a world map. Point out the rivers that are associated with each civilization. Then work with students to create a flowchart, which can help students connect all of the benefits of living next to a river to the growth of civilization.

Answers

Cite Evidence *Possible answer: cities laid out in a planned, organized pattern; uniform bricks for building; a system of standardized weights and measures; complex plumbing systems; huge warehouses*

The Great Vedic Epics

Remind students that the Vedic epics, the *Mahabharata* and the *Ramayana*, are the major texts of the Aryan civilization. Review how these texts reveal important aspects of the civilization, including religious beliefs and the immortality of the soul, the value of performing one's duty, and warfare between rival tribes.

Guided Reading and Discussion

Ask students how the Vedic epics reveal information about the political, religious, and cultural life of the Aryans. *(Possible answer: The stories of the Vedas reveal Aryan religious beliefs and the importance of duty. They teach lessons about correct moral behavior and echo the history of wars between the different Aryan tribes.)*

SYNTHESIZE

Online Project the **Digital Activity: Ancient Civilizations of the Indian Subcontinent**. Ask students to identify the significant achievements of the Indus and Aryan civilizations, and help them complete the graphic organizer. *(Technological advances, organized government, well-planned cities, and trade; literature, religion, and societal and political structures)*

powerful hereditary rulers, extending their influence over many villages.

Aryans Structure Society From the Vedas, we learn that the Aryans divided their society into ranked groups based on occupation.

The highest group was made up of the Brahmins, or priests. Next came the Kshatriyas (kuh SHAT ree yuhz), or warriors. Even though the Brahmins were the highest caste, the Kshatriyas were the rulers. The third group, the Vaisyas (VYS yuz), included herders, farmers, artisans, and merchants. The Aryans separated people who had little or no Aryan heritage into a fourth group, the Sudras (SOO druz). This group included farmworkers, servants, and other laborers. The lowest social group, the dalits (DAH lits), was considered outside of the caste system. These people did work that others wouldn't, such as making leather from animal skins.

The gods' creation of the universe is described in the *Rig Veda*. It says they divided the body of Purusha, the first man, into four parts to create the four social groups of ancient India.

The Aryan Religion The Aryans were polytheistic. They worshiped gods and goddesses who embodied natural forces such as sky, sun, storm, and fire.

The chief Aryan deity was fierce **Indra,** the god of war. Indra's weapon was the thunderbolt, which he used not only to destroy demons but also to announce the arrival of rain, so vital to Indian life. Other major gods included Varuna, the god of order and creation, and Agni, the god of fire and the messenger who communicated human wishes to the gods. The Aryans also honored animal deities, such as monkey and snake gods.

Brahmins offered sacrifices of food and drink to the gods. Through the correct rituals and prayers, the Aryans believed, they could call on the gods for health, wealth, and victory in war.

As the lives of the Aryans changed, so, too, did their beliefs. Some religious thinkers were moving toward the notion of **brahman,** a single spiritual power that existed beyond the many gods of the Vedas and that resided in all things. There was also a move toward mysticism. **Mystics** are people who seek direct communion with divine forces.

Aryan mystics practiced meditation and yoga, spiritual and bodily disciplines designed to enhance the attempt to achieve direct contact with the divine. The religions that emerged in India after the Vedic Age

PURUSHA AND THE STRUCTURE OF ARYAN SOCIETY

The Rig Veda says that when the gods created the universe, they divided the body of Purusha into four parts to create the four social groups of ancient India. When they divided Purusha, in how many different portions did they arrange him? What became of his mouth, what of his two arms? What were his two thighs and his two feet called? His mouth became the Brahmin; his two arms were made into the Rajanya [Kshastriya]; his two thighs the Vaisya; from his two feet the Sudra was born.

—Rig Veda, "Hymn of Man"

>> The Aryans divided their people into castes, or groups, based on occupation.
Infer How does the way Purusha's body is divided show the status of a particular group in Aryan Society?

English Language Proficiency Standards

Listening Strategies 2.C.3 Have students work with basic vocabulary terms in the text. As they listen to "The Great Vedic Epics" being read aloud, have them respond to the vocabulary. Explain how the terms relate to ancient India.

Beginning Display these terms: *poems, religion, epic,* and *moral lesson*. Read each word aloud and have students repeat. Define the words. Tell students to snap their fingers every time one is used as you read this section. Provide content-specific sentence stems and help students write a sentence for each word.

Intermediate Follow the instructions in the Beginning ELPS activity, but have students help define the words and generate examples before you read aloud. Guide students as they write a sentence for each word.

Advanced Have small groups review this section and write down new basic vocabulary words, using context clues and dictionaries to define them. Tell groups to take turns reading

Answers

Infer *Possible answer: The higher a group is on the body the more status they had. The Brahmins, from the head, were the highest, while the Sudras, from the feet, were the lowest.*

were influenced by both mysticism and the notion of brahman.

INFER What qualities led Indra to be the chief god of the Aryans?

The Great Vedic Epics

By 500 B.C., Indian civilization consisted of many rival kingdoms. Archaeologists have learned that cities were growing rapidly at this time as people left the countryside to practice skilled crafts. By this time, too, the written language, Sanskrit, that priests had used to write sacred texts began to flourish in literary usage.

The Aryans maintained a strong oral tradition as well. They continued to memorize and recite ancient hymns, as well as two long epic poems, the *Mahabharata* (muh hah BAH rah tuh) and the *Ramayana* (rah MAH yuh nuh). Like the Sumerian *Epic of Gilgamesh*, the Indian epics mix history, mythology, adventure, and religion.

***Mahabharata* Describes Warfare and Religion** The *Mahabharata* is India's greatest epic. Through its nearly 100,000 verses, we hear echoes of the battles that rival Aryan tribes fought to gain control of the Ganges region.

Five royal brothers, the Pandavas, lose their kingdom to their cousins. After a great battle that lasts 18 days, the Pandavas regain their kingdom and restore peace to India. One episode, a lengthy poem known as the *Bhagavad-Gita*(BUG uh vud GEE tuh), reflects important Indian religious beliefs about the immortality of the soul and the value of performing one's duty. In its verses, the god Krishna instructs Prince Arjuna on the importance of duty over personal desires and ambitions.

***Ramayana* Teaches Values** The *Ramayana* is much shorter but equally memorable. It recounts the fantastic deeds of the daring hero Rama and his beautiful bride Sita. Early on, Sita is kidnapped by the demon-king Ravana. The rest of the story tells how Rama finally rescues Sita with the aid of the monkey general Hanuman.

Like the Aryan religion, these epics evolved over thousands of years. Priest-poets added new morals to the tales to teach different lessons. For example, they pointed to Rama as a model of virtue or as an ideal king. Likewise, Sita came to be honored as an ideal woman who remained loyal and obedient to her husband through many hardships.

>> Artworks depicting scenes from the *Mahabharata* have been created since ancient times. This folk-art painting on cloth shows the god Krishna in a chariot pulled by horses.

DRAW CONCLUSIONS How do the Aryan epics relate Aryan history in India?

 **ELPS 2.C.3** Learn new basic vocabulary words from *The Great Vedic Epics*.

ASSESSMENT

1. **Identify Cause and Effect** How has geography affected where people live on the subcontinent?
2. **Make Generalizations** Why did the Indus civilization decline?
3. **Synthesize** How do cattle link the Indus Civilization, the Aryans, and modern India?
4. **Summarize** How were Aryan society and government structured?
5. **Connect** How do the Indian epics reveal the values of the Aryans, and what are some of those values?

Topic 3 Lesson 1

Compare and Contrast In what ways did the Indus civilization's settlement patterns seem to differ from the Aryan civilization's? *(The Indus civilization built large cities and seemed to be a unified civilization. The Aryan civilization developed separate states.)* Why might they have developed differently? *(The Indus civilization might have been developed by farmers who settled along the Indus River. The Aryans were originally nomadic.)*

DEMONSTRATE

Online Assign the **Digital Lesson Quiz** for this lesson if you haven't already done so. Students will be offered automatic remediation or enrichment based on their score.

Pose this question to the class on the Discussion Board:

Generate Explanations What discoveries by archaeologists in the Indus River valley led to the conclusion that they had found a previously unknown civilization? *(Possible answer: They found the ruins of large, carefully planned cities with complex plumbing, standardized bricks, weights and measures, and storage facilities. All of these elements showed that the Indus civilization had a well-organized government.)*

Topic Inquiry

Have students continue their investigations for the Topic Inquiry.

Answers

Infer *Possible answer: Indra was the god of war and the Aryans were a warrior-like society. Indra was also the god of rain, which was essential to life in India.*

Draw Conclusions *Possible answer: The battles described in the Mahabharata tell us that the Aryan tribes were war-like and fought battles to establish dominance of the Ganges region in India.*

aloud. When a student hears one of the words, they become the reader. Then lead a discussion on how these terms relate to ancient India.

Advanced High Follow the instructions in the Advanced ELPS activity, but with partners instead of groups. Switch readers whenever a term is used. Then follow final instructions for Advanced activity.

Assessment

1. People settled in fertile areas like the Gangetic Plain where they could easily grow crops. The coastal plains are more populated because the seasonal rains provide water for farmers and the seas allow fishing and trade.
2. Students should show an understanding that scholars have offered a number of causes for the disappearance of the Indus civilization, including invasion, environmental disasters, and depletion of natural resources.
3. All three held cows as sacred beings.
4. Aryan society was divided based on a person's occupation. The top group were the priests (Brahmins); the second were the warriors (Kshatriyas); the third were farmers and herders (Vaisyas); the fourth were non-Aryan servants or laborers (Sudras); and there was a group outside the system who performed the work no one else wanted to do (Dalits).
5. The Indian epics reveal Aryan values by giving the gods, kings, or heroes qualities that they admired, including duty and virtue in kings, and loyalty and obedience in women.

The Origins of Hinduism and Buddhism

CONNECT

Preview Have students preview the **Lesson Objectives** and the list of **Key Terms**.

Students can also preview all the **Key Terms** and **Academic Vocabulary** using the **Interactive Reading Notepad** on the digital course or preview a summary of the lesson in the **Reading and Note Taking Study Guide**.

Online Use the **Editable Presentation** found on the digital course to present the main ideas for this lesson.

Start Up Activity

Read the following quotation from the *Agni Puranam*, a Hindu sacred text: "The river Ganges is the earthly door to salvation to men who long for emancipation from this prison house of life." Ask students to think about what this quote says about the relationship between religion, society, and nature in Hindu cultures.

Discuss Ask students whether their culture bestows on any river the same kind of respect that Hindu culture bestows upon the Ganges. *(The religious nature of the respect that Indian culture has for the Ganges is absent, or at least rare, in Western cultures.)*

Online You can also project the **Start Up Activity** from the course.

INVESTIGATE

Have students read the section using the **Reading and Note Taking Study Guide** to help them take notes and understand the text as they read.

Hinduism Beliefs Develop

Hinduism developed in ancient India from the religious beliefs of the diverse groups who settled there. A mixture of gods, beliefs, and practices overlapped and were recorded in sacred texts called the Vedas. A basic belief of Hinduism is an all-powerful spiritual force called brahman. The goal of life for Hindus is to achieve moksha, or union with brahman.

Answers

Interpret *The artist has the men show respect for each other in their prayerful hand gestures.*

>> Interpret Visvamitra visits Vasishtha in ancient India. Both men wrote parts of the Vedas, the sacred texts about Hindu beliefs. How does the artist convey respect between the authors?

Interactive Flipped Video

3.2 Thousands of years ago, two major religions—Hinduism and Buddhism—emerged in ancient India. The ethical and spiritual messages of both religions profoundly shaped Indian civilization.

TEKS 1.A, 1.B, 3.A, 23.A, 23.B, 25.A

>> Objectives

Describe the origins and central beliefs of Hinduism.

Analyze and summarize how the caste system shaped India.

Describe the origins and central beliefs of Buddhism.

Explore how Buddhism grew and changed as it spread beyond India.

>> Key Terms

atman
moksha
reincarnation
karma
dharma
ahimsa
caste
Siddhartha Gautama
Four Noble Truths
Eightfold Path
nirvana
sect

The Origins of Hinduism and Buddhism

Hinduism Beliefs Develop

Unlike most major religions, Hinduism has no single founder and no single sacred text. Instead, it grew out of the overlapping beliefs of the diverse groups who settled India. The process probably began when the Aryans added the gods of the Indus civilization to their own. Later people brought other gods, beliefs, and practices. As a result, Hinduism became one of the world's most complex religions, with countless gods and goddesses and many forms of worship existing side by side. Despite this diversity, all Hindus share certain basic beliefs.

One Force Unites Everything "God is one, but wise people know it by many names." This ancient proverb reflects the Hindu belief that everything is part of the unchanging, all-powerful spiritual force called brahman. Hindus worship a variety of gods who give concrete form to brahman.

The most important Hindu gods are Brahma, the Creator; Vishnu, the Preserver; and Shiva, the Destroyer. Each can take many forms,

Aa Vocabulary Builder

1. Have students pronounce the following academic vocabulary term in this lesson and clarify the part of speech. If necessary, break it into syllables and pronounce it with the students.
2. Explain what the word means in common "student-friendly" language using synonyms and antonyms when possible. Provide concrete examples to clarify the meaning, and rephrase the definition.

aspiration: a desire or ambition to achieve something

human or animal, to represent the various aspects of brahman with which he is associated. Some Hindus also worship various forms of the powerful goddess Shakti. She is both kind and cruel, a creator and a destroyer.

Sacred Texts Show Hindu Beliefs Over many hundreds of years, Hindu teachings were recorded in the sacred texts of the Vedas. The Upanishads (oo PAN ih shadz) are a section of the Vedas that address mystical questions related to Hinduism. These sacred texts use vivid images to examine complex ideas about the human soul and the connectedness of all life. In addition, literary works such as the *Bhagavad-Gita*were also revered for their representations of Hindu beliefs.

Achieving Moksha Is the Goal of Life for Hindus To Hindus, every person has an essential self, or **atman** (AHT mun). Some view it as the same as brahman and others as a form of brahman. The ultimate goal of existence, Hindus believe, is achieving **moksha** (MAHK shuh), or union with brahman. To do that, individuals must free themselves from selfish desires that separate them from brahman. Most people cannot achieve moksha in one lifetime, but Hindus believe in **reincarnation,** or the rebirth of the soul in another bodily form. Reincarnation allows people to continue working toward moksha through several lifetimes.

In each existence, Hindus believe, a person can come closer to achieving moksha by obeying the law of karma. **Karma** refers to all the actions of a person's life that affect his or her fate in the next life. To Hindus, all existence is ranked. Humans are closest to brahman. Then come animals, plants, and objects like rocks or water.

People who live virtuously earn good karma and are reborn at a higher level of existence. Those who do evil acquire bad karma and are reborn into suffering at a lower level of existence. In Indian art, this cycle of death and rebirth is symbolized by the image of the wheel.

To escape the wheel of fate, Hinduism stresses the importance of **dharma** (DAHR muh), the religious and moral duties of an individual. These duties vary according to class, occupation, gender, and age. Another key moral principle of Hinduism is **ahimsa** (uh HIM sah), or nonviolence. To Hindus, all people and things are aspects of brahman and therefore deserve to be respected. Many Hindus try to follow the path of ahimsa.

Jainism Evolves From Hinduism About 500 B.C., the teacher Mahavira (mah hah VEE ruh) founded Jainism (JY niz um), a religion that grew out of Hindu traditions and that is still practiced today. Mahavira rejected the idea that Brahmin priests alone could perform certain sacred rites. Jain teachings emphasize meditation, self-denial, and an extreme form of ahimsa. To avoid accidentally killing a living thing, even an insect, Jains carry brooms to sweep the ground in front of their feet.

SUMMARIZE How do the Hindu gods relate to the concept of brahman?

The Caste System Shapes India

As you read in Section 1, the Aryans divided society into four groups. Non-Aryans held the lowest jobs. During the Vedic Age, class divisions moved more toward reflecting social and economic roles than ethnic differences between Aryans and non-Aryans. As these changes occurred, they led to a more complex system of **castes,** or social groups into which people are born and which can rarely be changed.

Complex Rules of the Caste System Caste was closely linked to Hindu beliefs. To Hindus, people in different castes were different species of beings.

>> A statue of the wheel of dharma, a Hindu symbol of life, death, and rebirth. In Hinduism, how does one escape the wheel of fate?

Interactive Gallery

Online Project the **Interactive Gallery: The Origins of Hinduism** and click through the images with students.

ACTIVE CLASSROOM

Use the See-Think-Wonder strategy with students working in partner pairs. Have each pair of students choose one image from the gallery. They should discuss with each other what they see in the image, what they think about it, and any questions they may have. Partners can then share highlights of their discussion with the class.

Key Terms

Ask students to find the key term **reincarnation** (in bold) in the text. Explain that *re-* means "again," *in-* means "into," and *carn-* refers to the body. Have them use that information to define the term. *(Possible answer: to enter again into bodily form)*

Guided Reading and Discussion

Ask students to list the most important principles of Hinduism. *(Possible answers: atman, an essential self; karma, one's actions that affect fate in the next life; dharma, the religious and moral duties of an individual; and ahimsa, nonviolence.)*

Analyze Images

Point out the photograph of the wheel of dharma sculpture, and tell students that Indian artists often incorporate the wheel into their work. Ask students what it says about Indian culture that the image of the wheel of fate commonly appears in works of art.

History Background

The *Tripitaka* The *Tripitaka* is the total canon of Theravada Buddhism, which is prevalent in Sri Lanka and Southeast Asia. It is viewed differently by Mahayana Buddhists, who see it as being a preliminary body of teachings similar to the Old Testament in Christianity. The first of the three texts, or "baskets," of the *Tripitaka* is the "Basket of Discipline." This basket contains rules for monastic life and is the earliest and shortest text. The second and largest basket is the "Basket of Discourse," which contains sermons and discussion of ethics and doctrine attributed to the Buddha or his disciples. The third basket, called the "Basket of Special Doctrine," is made up of additional doctrine. All three baskets contain legends and other narratives as well.

Answers

Summarize *The gods give concrete form to the concept of brahman. The various Hindu gods are representations of different aspects of brahman, such as a destroying, creating, or animal aspect.*

Wheel of Dharma *through karma and dharma*

The Caste System Shapes India

Hinduism contributed to the development of a caste system. To Hindus, people in different castes were different species and the law of karma determined caste. Higher castes were closer to moksha. The caste system also reflected and influenced social and economic roles; the "dirtiest" jobs were performed by the lowest castes. The caste system did ensure a stable social order, and castes were interdependent.

Guided Reading and Discussion

Ask students to explain why Hindus tended to accept whatever level of the caste system that they were born into.

The Buddha's Key Teachings

Siddhartha Gautama started life as a prince around 563 B.C. He renounced royal life when he discovered human suffering, and he searched for "the realm of life where there is neither suffering nor death." He gained enlightenment and became the Buddha, teaching others about the Four Noble Truths and the Eightfold Path. The Truths describe that life is suffering, the cause of suffering is nonvirtue, and the cure is to overcome nonvirtue.

Guided Reading and Discussion

Be sure students understand that the Buddha taught an Eightfold Path as a way to overcome nonvirtue and achieve nirvana. Ask students to explain the similarities between nirvana in Buddhism and moksha in Hinduism.

A high-caste Brahmin, for example, was purer and therefore closer to moksha than someone from a lower caste. To ensure spiritual purity, a web of complex caste rules governed every aspect of life—for example, where people lived, what they ate, how they dressed, and how they earned a living. Rules forbade marrying outside one's caste or eating with members of another caste.

High-caste people had the strictest rules to protect them from the spiritually polluted, or impure, lower castes. Because they had jobs such as digging graves, cleaning streets, or turning animal hides into leather, some people were considered so impure that they were called "untouchables."

For the untouchables, today called dalits, life was harsh and restricted. Other castes feared that contact with an untouchable could spread pollution. Untouchables had to live apart and to sound a wooden instrument called a clapper to warn of their approach.

Caste Affects Social Structure Despite its inequalities, caste ensured a stable social order. People believed that the law of karma determined their caste. While they could not change their status in this life, they could reach a higher state in a future life by faithfully fulfilling the duties of their present caste.

>> **Infer** Chair-bearers, or "dolavahi," were part of the caste of untouchables in ancient India and in later times, as shown in this 19th century image. Who in this image would be a higher caste person?

The caste system gave many people a sense of identity and interdependence. Each caste had its own occupation and its own leaders. Caste members cooperated to help one another. In addition, each caste had its own special role in Indian society as a whole. Although strictly separated, different castes depended on one another for their basic needs. A lower-caste carpenter, for example, built the home of a higher-caste scholar. The caste system also adapted to changing conditions.

Over time, many additional castes and subcastes evolved. As people migrated into the subcontinent, they formed new castes. Other castes grew out of new occupations and religions. This flexibility allowed people with diverse customs to live side by side in relative harmony. By modern times, there were thousands of major castes and subcastes.

? ANALYZE INFORMATION How did the caste system provide a sense of order in Indian society?

The Buddha's Key Teachings

In the foothills of the Himalayas, a reformer appeared named **Siddhartha Gautama** (sih DAHR tuh gow TUH muh). His teachings eventually spread across Asia to become the core beliefs of one of the world's most influential religions, Buddhism.

From Boy to Buddha Gautama's early life is known mostly through various religious writings and literature. He was born a prince about 563 B.C. According to tradition, his mother dreamed that a radiant white elephant descended to her from heaven. Signs such as this led a prophet to predict that the boy would someday become a wandering holy man. To prevent that—in hopes of his son one day becoming a ruler—Gautama's father kept him in the family's palaces, surrounded by comfort and luxury. At age 16, Gautama married a beautiful woman and enjoyed a happy life.

At age 29, Gautama's life changed. One day he took a ride beyond the palace gardens and saw an old man. On following rides, he also saw a sick person and a dead body. For the first time, Gautama became aware of human suffering. Deeply disturbed, he bade farewell to his family and left the palace, never to return. He set out to discover "the realm of life where there is neither suffering nor death."

Gautama wandered for years, seeking answers from Hindu scholars and holy men whose ideas failed to satisfy him. He fasted and meditated. At some point, he took a seat under a large tree, determined to stay there

Answers

Infer *Since chair-bearers were lowest caste, someone sitting in the covered chair or litter, or riding a horse, was most likely higher caste.*

Analyze Information *Although it was unequal, the caste system gave each person a specific place and role in society. It gave people a sense of identity and interdependence.*

English Language Proficiency Standards

Listening Strategies 2.C.4 Have students work with academic vocabulary from the text. As they listen to portions of "The Buddha's Key Teachings" being read aloud, have them respond to the use of the words. Guide students in their understanding of the meanings and usage of these terms.

Beginning Display the academic vocabulary *nirvana, prophet, sermon*, and *tradition*. Read each word aloud and define each. Tell students that as you read "The Buddha's Key Teachings," they should listen for and snap every time each term is read. Provide content-specific sentence stems and help students write one sentence with each academic word.

Intermediate Follow the instructions in the Beginning ELPS activity, but have students help define the words and, with your guidance, write one content-specific sentence with each academic word.

until he understood the mystery of life. Throughout the night, legend tells, evil spirits tempted Gautama to give up his meditations, but he fended them off. When he rose, he believed he understood the cause of and cure for suffering and sorrow. He was no longer Gautama; he had become the Buddha, or "Enlightened One."

Following the Four Noble Truths The Buddha spent the rest of his life teaching others what he had learned. In his first sermon after reaching enlightenment, he explained the **Four Noble Truths** that lie at the heart of Buddhism:

- All life is full of suffering, pain, and sorrow.
- The cause of suffering is nonvirtue, or negative deeds and mindsets such as hatred and desire.
- The only cure for suffering is to overcome nonvirtue.
- The way to overcome nonvirtue is to follow the Eightfold Path.

The Buddha described the **Eightfold Path** as "right views, right aspirations, right speech, right conduct, right livelihood, right effort, right mindfulness, and right contemplation." The first two steps involved understanding the Four Noble Truths and committing oneself to the Eightfold Path. Next, a person had to live a moral life, avoiding evil words and actions. Through meditation, a person might at last achieve enlightenment. For the Buddhist, the final goal is **nirvana,** or union with the universe and release from the cycle of rebirth.

The Buddha saw the Eightfold Path as a middle way between a life devoted to pleasure and one based on harsh self-denial. He stressed moral principles such as honesty, charity, and kindness to all living creatures.

Buddhism and Hinduism Buddhism grew from the same traditions as Hinduism. Both Hindus and Buddhists stressed nonviolence and believed in karma, dharma, and a cycle of rebirth. Yet the religions differed in several ways. Instead of focusing on the priests, formal rituals, and many gods of Hinduism, the Buddha urged each person to seek enlightenment through meditation. Buddhists also rejected the caste system, offering the hope of nirvana to all regardless of birth.

SEQUENCE EVENTS How did Siddhartha Gautama become the Buddha?

ELPS 2.C.4 Learn new academic vocabulary words from *The Buddha's Key Teachings.*

>> **Describe** This ancient statue of the Buddha in a meditating pose is in Sri Lanka. What does the Buddha's facial expression show?

Buddhism Spreads

The Buddha attracted many disciples, or followers, who accompanied him as he preached across northern India. Many men and women who accepted the Buddha's teachings set up monasteries and convents for meditation and study. Some Buddhist monasteries grew into major centers of learning.

Collecting the Teachings of Buddha Legend holds that at age 80, the Buddha ate spoiled food. As he lay dying, he told his disciples, "Decay is inherent in all things. Work out your own salvation with diligence." After the Buddha's death, his followers collected his teachings into the *Tripitaka,* or "Three Baskets of Wisdom." One of the "baskets" includes sayings like this one, which echoes the Hindu emphasis on duty: "Let a man, after he has discerned his own duty, be always attentive to his duty. " Other sayings give the Buddha's version of the golden rule: "Overcome anger by not growing angry. Overcome evil with good. Overcome the liar by truth."

Buddhism Spreads Beyond India and Divides Missionaries and traders spread Buddhism across India to many parts of Asia. Gradually, Buddhism split into two major **sects,** or subgroups. These were Theravada

Buddhism Spreads

The Buddha's teachings were collected by followers in a series of texts. Missionaries and traders spread Buddhism to other parts of Asia. Buddhism eventually split into two sects, or subgroups, known as Theravada and Mahayana. Theravada Buddhism spread to Sri Lanka and Southeast Asia. The Mahayana sect spread even more widely across Asia.

Online Project the **Interactive Map: The Origins and Spread of Buddhism** and click through the hotspots with students.

ACTIVE CLASSROOM

Use the A Closer Look strategy with small groups of students. Each group can be assigned to take a closer look at one country and the accompanying image. Have them tell you what they see and what they learned as a result of their focus on this part of the map. Collect insights from each group.

Guided Reading and Discussion

Ask students to identify the features of Mahayana Buddhism that increased its popularity in places like China and Japan.

Advanced Ask small groups to review "The Buddha's Key Teachings" to identify new academic words. Have them use context clues and dictionaries to define each word on their list. Instruct them to write two content-specific sentences that include one of the academic words each. Have the entire group listen as small groups read their sentences aloud, omitting each academic word. Then have the larger group determine which academic word correctly completes each sentence.

Advanced High Follow the instructions in the Advanced ELPS activity, but with pairs of students. Have partners write a content-specific paragraph that includes at least four of their academic words. Combine partners and have each listen as the other reads their paragraph aloud, omitting the academic words. Have the new partners determine which academic words correctly complete the paragraph.

Answers

Sequence Events *Gautama left his palace and wandered for years, seeking answers from scholars and holy men about the "realm of life with no suffering or death." One day, he sat under a tree to meditate. Although tempted by evil spirits, he discovered a spiritual path that he shared with others.*

Describe *Answers may vary. Students might notice peacefulness and serenity, which are goals of Buddhist meditation.*

SYNTHESIZE

Online Project the **Digital Activity: Hinduism and Buddhism**. Ask students to recall their predictions about the development of religion and society in ancient Indian cultures. Remind them that the development of society in India was intertwined with the development of the religions of Hinduism and Buddhism. Then use the Think-Pair-Share strategy to have students answer the questions in the activity and share them with a partner.

DEMONSTRATE

Online Assign the **Digital Lesson Quiz** for this lesson if you haven't already done so. Students will be offered automatic remediation or enrichment based on their score.

Pose these questions to the class on the Discussion Board:

Summarize According to the Buddha, how can people escape worldly suffering? *(They can do this by understanding the Four Noble Truths, following the Eightfold Path, living a moral life, and meditating.)*

Draw Conclusions What is a main way that Hinduism influenced a social and economic order in ancient and modern India? *(Hinduism still brings spiritual guidance to Indians, but the main way it influenced a social and economic order in India is in the development and following of a caste system.)*

Topic Inquiry

Have students continue their investigations for the Topic Inquiry.

Answers

Analyze Maps *China; Mahayana Buddhism*

Infer *Buddha's followers collected his teachings and sayings into a series of texts, which were transported by missionaries and traders to other countries beyond India.*

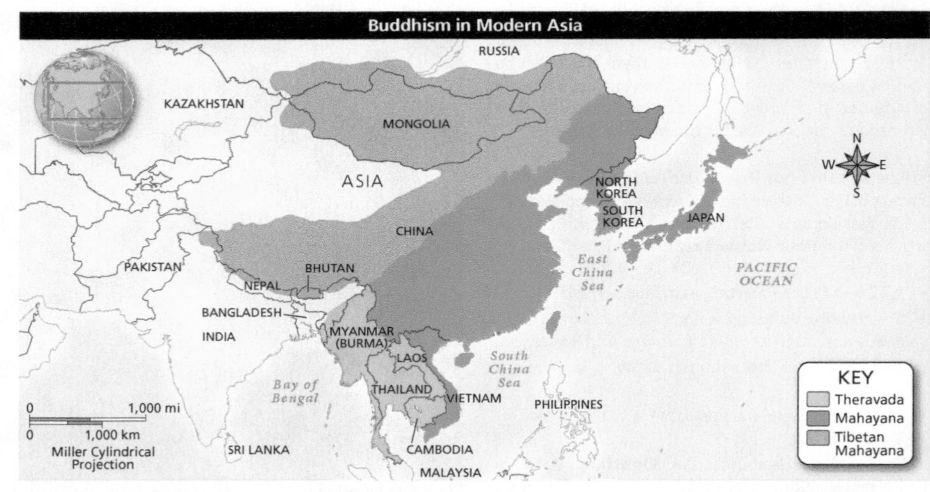

>> **Analyze Maps** What is one Asian country that has followers of both Mahayana Buddhism and Tibetan Mahayana Buddhism? Which do more countries follow, Mahayana Buddhism or Theravada Buddhism?

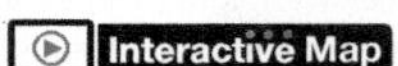
Interactive Map

(thehr uh VAH duh) Buddhism and Mahayana (mah huh YAH nuh) Buddhism.

Theravada Buddhism closely followed the Buddha's original teachings. It required a life devoted to hard spiritual work. Only the most dedicated seekers, such as monks and nuns, could hope to reach nirvana. The Theravada sect spread to Sri Lanka and Southeast Asia.

The Mahayana sect made Buddhism easier for ordinary people to follow. Even though the Buddha had forbidden followers to worship him, Mahayana Buddhists pictured him and other holy beings as compassionate gods. People turned to these gods for help in solving daily problems as well as in achieving salvation. While the Buddha had said little about the nature of nirvana, Mahayana Buddhists described an afterlife filled with many heavens and hells. Mahayana Buddhism spread to China, Tibet, Korea, and Japan.

Buddhism's Decline in India Although Buddhism took firm root across Asia, it slowly declined in India. Hinduism eventually absorbed some Buddhist ideas and made room for Buddha as another Hindu god. A few Buddhist centers survived until the 1100s, when they fell to Muslim armies that invaded India.

INFER How did the *Tripitaka* help Buddhism spread beyond India?

ASSESSMENT

1. **Summarize** In Hinduism, what is the role of reincarnation in achieving moksha?
2. **Identify Cause and Effect** How did Hinduism become a complex religion with many gods, goddesses, and forms of worship?
3. **Summarize** How did Hindu beliefs influence the development of different caste levels in India?
4. **Summarize** What is the final goal of Buddhists in their practice of the religion?
5. **Sequence Events** What sequence of events after Buddha's death caused Buddhism to spread beyond India?

Assessment

1. Hindus believe that it takes more than one lifetime to attain moksha, or union with brahman. Reincarnation, the rebirth of one's soul in future bodies, allows a person to continue working towards moksha through several lifetimes.
2. There was no single founder or single sacred text. Hinduism grew out of a combination of beliefs from diverse groups that settled in India. Aryans added gods of the Indus civilization to their own gods. Later migrants to India brought new gods, beliefs, and practices that blended with Hinduism.
3. Caste levels were related to spiritual levels people had reached according to Hindu beliefs. In the Hindu religion, the law of karma also determined what caste a person was born into. People could not change their caste level during their lifetime, but it was believed they could affect the caste levels of their future lives (reincarnation being another Hindu belief).
4. The final goal of Buddhists and Buddhism is to reach nirvana, a state of enlightenment that unites one with the universe and releases a person from the cycle of rebirth.
5. 1. Buddha's teachings were collected in a series of texts; 2. Missionaries and traders were able to spread the Buddha's teachings to other parts of Asia; 3. Buddhism gradually divided into two sects, helping it adapt in new places.

3.3 **Northern India was often a battleground where rival rajahs fought for control of the rich Ganges valley. But in 321 B.C., a young adventurer, Chandragupta Maurya (chun druh GUP tuh MOWR yuh), forged the first Indian empire.**

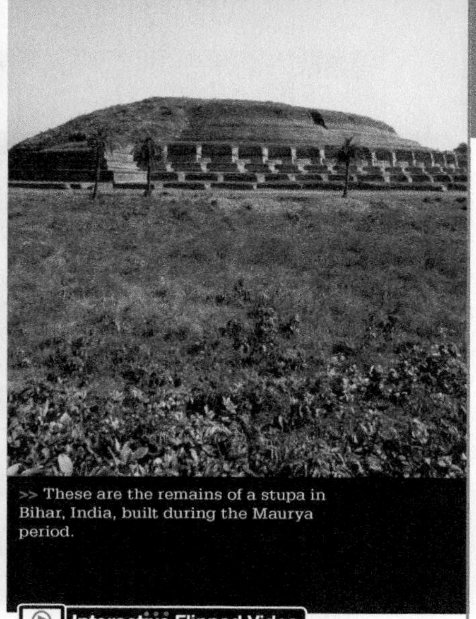

>> These are the remains of a stupa in Bihar, India, built during the Maurya period.

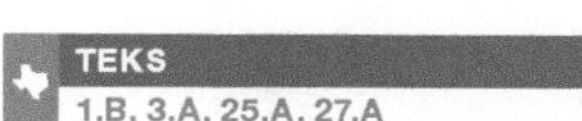

Powerful Empires Emerge in India

TEKS
1.B, 3.A, 25.A, 27.A

>> **Objectives**

Analyze how Mauryan rulers created a strong central government for their empire.

Explore the kingdoms that arose across the Deccan.

Explain why the period of Gupta rule in India is considered a golden age.

Understand how family and village life shaped Indian society.

>> **Key Terms**

Chandragupta Maurya
dissent
Asoka
missionaries
golden age
decimal system
joint family
dowry

The Maurya Empire Builds a Strong Government

We know about Chandragupta largely from reports written by Megasthenes (muh GAS thuh neez), a Greek ambassador to the Mauryan court. He described the great Maurya capital at Pataliputra. It boasted schools and a library as well as splendid palaces and temples. An awed Megasthenes reported that the wall around the city "was crowned with 530 towers and had 64 gates."

Chandragupta Forges an Empire Chandragupta first gained power in the Ganges valley. He then conquered northern India. His son and grandson later pushed south, adding much of the Deccan to their empire. From 321 B.C. to 185 B.C., the Maurya dynasty ruled over a vast, united empire.

Chandragupta maintained order through a well-organized bureaucracy. Royal officials supervised the building of roads and harbors to benefit trade. Other officials collected taxes and managed state-owned factories and shipyards. People sought justice in royal courts.

Aa Vocabulary Builder

1. Have students pronounce the following academic vocabulary term in this lesson and clarify the part of speech.
2. Explain what the word means in common "student-friendly" language using synonyms and antonyms when possible. Provide concrete examples to clarify the meaning, and rephrase the definition.

status: social standing or prestige

Topic 3 Lesson 3

Powerful Empires Emerge in India

CONNECT

Preview Have students preview the **Lesson Objectives** and the list of **Key Terms**.

Students can also preview all the **Key Terms** and **Academic Vocabulary** using the **Interactive Reading Notepad** on the digital course or preview a summary of the lesson in the **Reading and Note Taking Study Guide**.

Online Use the **Editable Presentation** found on the digital course to present the main ideas for this lesson.

Start Up Activity

Have students decide what they think about a king who believed that his subjects' happiness and welfare determined his own happiness and welfare. Ask: How would such a king likely treat his subjects? What kind of government would result from such a philosophy? *(Possible answers: He would probably treat his subjects with respect and kindness, and government would be fair and just.)* Have students predict whether such a king would be weak or strong.

Online You can also project the **Start Up Activity** from the course.

INVESTIGATE

Have students read the section using the **Reading and Note Taking Study Guide** to help them take notes and understand the text as they read.

The Maurya Empire Builds a Strong Government

The Maurya empire was one of the first major civilizations to develop in ancient India. As religion and government had shaped the Indus and Aryan civilizations before them, the Mauryan kings also relied on those two factors to shape their growing empire. However, the two greatest Mauryan kings took different approaches. Chandragupta, the first Mauryan king, built a strong central government and harshly enforced his policies. His grandson, Asoka, took a different path. He believed that rulers should lead by example and put the welfare of their subjects ahead of their own welfare. Asoka's reign also featured a strong government, but he promoted his policies much differently than his predecessors.

Topic 3 Lesson 3

Online Project the **Interactive Map: The Maurya and Gupta Empires** and click through the hotspots with students. Explain to students that one of the most important achievements of the Maurya empire was the unification of many warring states throughout India. A civilization cannot progress unless there is relative peace. Although the Gupta empire was smaller geographically, its stability encouraged other types of growth, such as in education and the arts.

ACTIVE CLASSROOM

Use the Conversation With History strategy and ask students to pretend they're having a conversation with either Chandragupta or Asoka. Have students write down a question they want to ask, then what that person would say and, finally, what the student would say in response. Discuss the results of the activity.

Guided Reading and Discussion

Explain that Chandragupta faced a formidable challenge in trying to create a cohesive empire out of a large geographic area. He chose to build a central government that maintained order by force and was supported by a well-organized bureaucracy.

Cause and Effect Ask students to describe the effects of Chandragupta's methods of government.

Key Terms

Ask students to find the key term **dissent** (in bold) in the text. Explain that harsh rulers throughout history have tried to suppress dissent.

>> The Maurya emperor Asoka went from warrior to Buddhist, and then ruled by moral example instead of excessive force.

Interactive Gallery

>> Asoka had stone pillars erected throughout India. Writing on the pillars provides moral advice and Asoka's promise of a just government for all.

Chandragupta's rule was effective but harsh. A brutal secret police force reported on corruption, crime, and **dissent**—that is, ideas that opposed those of the government. Fearful of his many enemies, Chandragupta had specially trained women warriors guard his palace.

Asoka Governs by Example The most honored Maurya emperor was Chandragupta's grandson, **Asoka** (uh SOH kuh). A few years after becoming emperor in 268 B.C., Asoka fought a long, bloody war to conquer the Deccan region of Kalinga.

Then, horrified at the slaughter—more than 100,000 people are said to have died—Asoka turned his back on further conquests. He converted to Buddhism, rejected violence, and resolved to rule by moral example.

True to the Buddhist principle of respect for all life, Asoka stopped eating most meats and limited Hindu animal sacrifices. He sent **missionaries,** or people sent on a religious mission, to spread Buddhism across India and to Sri Lanka. By doing so, he paved the way for the spread of Buddhism throughout Asia. Although Asoka promoted Buddhism, he also preached tolerance for other religions.

Asoka had stone pillars set up across India, offering moral advice and promising a just government. Asoka's rule brought peace and prosperity and helped unite the diverse peoples within his empire. He built hospitals and Buddhist shrines. To aid transportation, he built roads and rest houses for travelers. "I have had banyan trees planted on the roads to give shade to people and animals," he noted. "I have planted mango groves, and I have had [wells] dug and shelters erected along the roads."

Division and Disunity After Asoka's death, Mauryan power declined. By 185 B.C., the unity of the Maurya empire was shattered as rival princes again battled for power across the Gangetic Plain.

In fact, during its long history, India has seldom remained united for long. In ancient times, as today, the subcontinent was home to many peoples. Although northern India shared a common civilization, fierce local rivalries kept it divided. Meanwhile, distance and cultural differences separated the peoples of the north and the peoples of the Deccan in the south. Adding to the turmoil, foreigners frequently pushed through mountain passes into northern India. The divided northern kingdoms often proved incapable of resisting these conquerors.

ANALYZE INFORMATION What was the basic structure of Chandragupta's Mauryan government?

D Differentiate Extra Support Help students better understand the achievements of Chandragupta and Asoka by asking students to create an illustrated timeline depicting and describing the key events and achievements of each king's reign. Each entry on the timeline should include an illustration as well as a concise description of the event or achievement.

Answers

Analyze Information *He established an organized bureaucracy of royal officials who collected taxes, supervised road and harbor building, and managed government-owned factories and shipyards.*

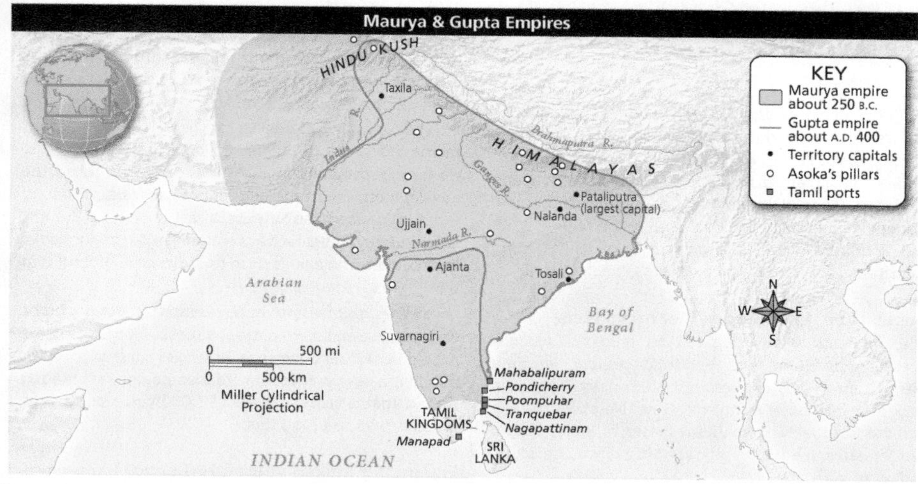

>> **Analyze Maps** Maurya and Gupta emperors united much of India under their rule. How did geography limit the northward expansion of both empires? What region of the Indian subcontinent remained separate from both empires?

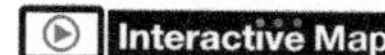

Deccan Kingdoms Arise

Like the Gangetic Plain, the Deccan was divided into many kingdoms after the decline of Mauryan power. Each kingdom had its own capital with magnificent temples and bustling workshops. The peoples of the Deccan were Dravidians with very different languages and traditions from the peoples of the north. Over the centuries, Hindu and Buddhist traditions and Sanskrit writings drifted south and blended with local cultures. Deccan rulers generally tolerated all religions as well as the many foreigners who settled in their busy ports.

In the Tamil kingdoms, which occupied much of the southernmost part of India, trade was important. The different Tamil kingdoms traded goods with each other, as well as with other countries. Tamil rulers improved harbors to support overseas trade.

Tamil merchants sent spices, fine textiles, and other luxuries westward to eager buyers in the Roman empire. And as the Roman empire declined, Tamil trade with China increased. The Tamil kingdoms left a rich and diverse literature. Tamil poets described fierce wars, heroic deeds, and festive occasions, along with the ordinary routines of peasant and city life.

 **DETERMINE RELEVANCE** How did trade help link the separate kingdoms of the Deccan?

A Golden Age Under Gupta Rule

Although many kingdoms flourished in the Deccan, the most powerful Indian states rose to its north. About 500 years after the Mauryas, the Gupta dynasty again united much of India. Gupta emperors organized a strong central government that promoted peace and prosperity. Under the Guptas, who ruled from A.D. 320 to about 540, India enjoyed a **golden age,** or period of great cultural achievement.

A Time of Peace and Prosperity Gupta rule was probably looser than that of the Mauryas. Much power was left in the hands of individual villages and city governments elected by merchants and artisans. Faxian (FAH shyahn), a Chinese Buddhist monk who visited India in the 400s, reported on the mild nature of Gupta rule:

> The people are numerous and happy; . . . only those who cultivate the royal land have to pay [a portion of] the grain from it. . . . The king governs without . . . corporal punishments. Criminals are simply fined, lightly or

Deccan Kingdoms Arise

With the fall of the Maurya empire and the unity it had achieved, India once again divided into separate small kingdoms, each with its own capital city and ruler. Over time, cultural and religious influences from the northern parts of India filtered down to the Deccan. The Tamil kingdoms' strong trade network ensured lively trade both locally and overseas.

Guided Reading and Discussion

Ask students why the collapse of the Maurya empire might have created less of an upheaval for the Tamil kingdoms than it did for northern areas. *(The Tamils' extensive trade network provided stability.)*

A Golden Age Under Gupta Rule

About 500 years after the Maurya empire fell, the Gupta dynasty formed in the north. It was built on the foundations of a strong central government and policies that promoted peace and prosperity. For about 200 years the Gupta dynasty maintained power and ushered in a golden age of trade and cultural and technological advancements.

Online Project the **Interactive Gallery: A Golden Age in the Arts** and click through the images with students.

ACTIVE CLASSROOM

Use the Quick Write strategy and give students 30 seconds to write what they know about the Interactive Gallery activity. They should write as if they were posting a Twitter statement. Therefore, their comment is limited to 140 characters. Ask students to share their statements.

English Language Proficiency Standards

Listening Strategies 2.D.1 Have students listen as you or others read aloud "A Golden Age Under Gupta Rule." Then monitor the listeners understanding of the vocabulary and content by having them answer questions asked of them by the reader.

Beginning Read aloud the "Gupta Rule Encourages Learning" subsection. Then retell the content, enhancing it with gestures, movement, and drawings. To monitor student understanding, have them complete sentence frames such as: _____ is an example of the Gupta advances in mathematics.

Intermediate Read aloud to students "A Golden Age Under Gupta Rule." Pause after reading the content of each subsection and ask content-specific questions. Have partners develop an answer to each question and share them with the group.

Advanced Have small groups listen as members take turns reading aloud "A Golden Age Under Gupta Rule." Instruct readers

Answers

Determine Relevance *The separate kingdoms bought each other's goods and interacted with each other through this trade.*

Analyze Maps *Expansion was blocked by some of the world's highest mountain ranges; the extreme south, Tamil kingdoms*

Topic 3 Lesson 3

Guided Reading and Discussion

Like the Maurya before them, the Gupta relied on a strong central government with a well-organized bureaucracy. However, unlike the Maurya, the Gupta allowed more local self-government than the Maurya. The Gupta dynasty allowed people to prosper in an era of relative peace. As a result, trade flourished and farming expanded into new types of crops. Artisans produced everything from cloth to metal wares for both domestic and foreign markets. Scholars and students attended schools that taught a wide variety of subjects such as mathematics, medicine, astronomy, literature, and other arts.

Draw Conclusions How did the stable government and economic prosperity of the Maurya and Gupta empires encourage growth in other areas such as education and trade? *(Stability and prosperity provided the security people needed to explore other areas of growth. They had the time to innovate and advance their cultures.)*

Analyze Images

Direct students' attention to the image of the Indian physician, and have them read the caption. Ask students whether the ancient medical practices described here seem at all familiar. Some students may realize that many modern physicians practice a similar "holistic" medicine, which focuses on balancing every part of a person's life.

heavily, according to the circumstances [of each case].

—Faxian, A Record of Buddhistic Kingdoms

Trade and farming flourished across the Gupta empire. Farmers harvested crops of wheat, rice, and sugar cane. The Gupta era saw advances in metal-working, especially in gold and silver. In cities, artisans produced cotton cloth, pottery, and metalware for local markets and for export to East Africa, the Middle East, and Southeast Asia. The prosperity of Gupta India contributed to a flowering in the arts and learning.

Gupta Rule Encourages Learning Under Gupta rule, students were educated in religious schools. However, in Hindu and Buddhist centers, learning was not limited to religion and philosophy. The large Buddhist monastery-university at Nalanda, which attracted students from many parts of Asia, taught mathematics, medicine, physics, languages, literature, and other subjects.

Indian advances in mathematics had a wide impact on the rest of the world. Gupta mathematicians devised the system of writing numbers that we use today. (However, these numerals are now called "Hindu-Arabic" numerals because Arabs carried them from India to the Middle East and Europe.) Indian mathematicians also originated the concept of zero and developed the **decimal system** of numbers based on ten digits, which we still use today. Indian technological advancements

The advances made in mathematics also helped increase knowledge in the science of astronomy. The work of Gupta mathematicians greatly influenced the development of Islamic astronomy in Persia, which, in time, influenced the science of astronomy in Europe. Indian technological advancements in the production of iron, copper, and zinc, cotton textiles, and shipbuilding were spread through trade.

By Gupta times, Indian physicians were using herbs and other remedies to treat illness. Surgeons were skilled in setting bones and in simple surgery to repair injuries. It seems that doctors also began vaccinating people against smallpox about 1,000 years before this practice was used in Europe.

Expanding India's Literature During Gupta times, many fine writers added to the rich heritage of Indian literature. They collected and recorded fables and folk tales in the Sanskrit language. In time, Indian fables were carried west to Persia, Egypt, and Greece.

The greatest Gupta poet and playwright was Kalidasa. His most famous play, *Shakuntala*(shahk oon TAH luh), tells the story of a king who marries the lovely orphan Shakuntala. Under an evil spell, the king forgets his bride. After many plot twists, he finally recovers his memory and is reunited with her.

The Decline of the Gupta Empire Eventually, Gupta India declined under the pressure of weak rulers, civil war, and foreign invaders. From central Asia came the White Huns, a nomadic people who overran the weakened Gupta empire, destroying its cities and trade. Once again, India split into many kingdoms. It would see no other great empire like those of the Mauryas or Guptas for almost 1,000 years.

DRAW CONCLUSIONS What role did religion play in influencing learning and the arts in Gupta India?

ELPS **ELPS 2.D.1** Listen as your partner or teacher reads *A Golden Age Under Gupta Rule* aloud. Then answer your partner's questions using what you just heard.

>> Indian physicians often used a medical system called Ayurveda, which treats illness by addressing every part of the patient's life, from diet and exercise to herbal remedies. This method is still used in India.

English Language Proficiency Standards

to pause after reading the content of each subsection and ask the group a question related to the content. Circulate among the groups to monitor their understanding of the vocabulary and content.

Advanced High Have partners take turns reading aloud "A Golden Age Under Gupta Rule." Instruct readers to pause after reading the content of each subsection and ask the listener a question related to the content. Circulate among the groups to monitor their understanding of the vocabulary and content.

Answers

Draw Conclusions *Students were educated in Hindu and Buddhist schools that stressed ways of living based on their specific religion. The arts often depicted religious subjects and themes, including Hindu gods and Buddhist stories and legends. This helped people recall and appreciate the significance of religious events.*

Family and Village Life Shape Indian Society

Most Indians knew nothing of the dazzling courts of the Mauryas or Guptas. The vast majority were peasants who lived in the villages that dotted the Indian landscape. In Indian society, everyday life revolved around the rules and duties associated with caste, family, and village.

Joint Family Structure The ideal family was a **joint family,** in which parents, children, and their offspring shared a common dwelling. Indian families were patriarchal—the father or oldest male in a family headed the household. Adult sons continued to live with their parents even after they married and had children. (A daughter would go to live with her husband and his family.) Often only the wealthy could afford such large households. Still, even when they did not share the same house, close ties linked brothers, uncles, cousins, and nephews.

A father was thought to have wisdom and experience, and he enjoyed great authority. Even so, his power was limited by sacred laws and tradition. Usually, he made decisions after consulting his wife and other family members. Property belonged to the whole family.

>> The ancient Indian ideal of a joint family—several generations of family members living under one roof—emphasizes the cultural importance of obligations within families.

Family Duties The family performed the essential function of training children in the traditions and duties of their castes. Thus family interests came before individual wishes. Children worked with older relatives in the fields or at a family trade. While still young, a daughter learned that as a wife she would be expected to serve and obey her husband and his family. A son learned the rituals to honor the family's ancestors. Such rites linked the living and the dead, deepening family bonds across the generations.

For parents, an important duty was arranging good marriages for their children based on caste and family interests. Marriage customs varied. In northern India, for example, a bride's family commonly provided a **dowry,** or payment to the bridegroom, and financed the costly wedding festivities. After marriage, the daughter left her home and became part of her husband's family.

Role of Women Changes Over Time In early Aryan society, women seem to have enjoyed a higher status than in later times. Aryan women even composed a few Vedic hymns. However, attitudes and customs affecting women varied across India and changed over time. By late Gupta times, upper-class women were increasingly restricted to the home. When they went outside the home, they were supposed to cover themselves from head to foot. Lower-class women, however, labored in the fields or worked at spinning and weaving.

Women were thought to have shakti, a creative energy that men lacked. In marriage, a woman's shakti helped to make the husband complete. Still, shakti might also be a destructive force. A husband's duty was to channel his wife's energy in the proper direction. Women had few rights within the family and society. Their primary duties were to marry and raise children.

For a woman, rebirth into a higher existence was gained through devotion to her husband. Often, a widow was expected to join her dead husband on his funeral pyre. In this way, a widow became a sati, or "virtuous woman." Some widows accepted this painful death as a noble duty that wiped out their own and their husbands' sins. Other women bitterly resisted the custom.

Typical Village Structure Throughout India's history, the village was at the heart of daily life. The size of villages varied, from a handful of people to hundreds of families. A typical village included a cluster of homes made of earth or stone. Beyond these dwellings stretched the fields, where farmers grew wheat, rice, cotton, sugar cane, or other crops according to region.

Topic 3 Lesson 3

Family and Village Life Shape Indian Society

The vast majority of the population during these times were peasants who lived a structured life dictated by caste, family, and village. The ideal family was a joint family, in which several generations lived within the same household. The patriarchal system placed the father at the head of the household, with women and children fulfilling specific duties and responsibilities. Within the village, a headman and council made decisions that affected the whole community.

Guided Reading and Discussion

Ask students to discuss the daily lives of most of the population, who were not directly involved in the activities of kings and government. They should describe families and village life.

SYNTHESIZE

Online Project the **Digital Activity: Maintaining Peace and Order**. Ask students to share their responses to the question about how the two rulers achieved peace. Discuss with students that there are modern examples of both leaders' approaches to government. Have students try to think of examples that reflect the political influences of the ancient Maurya and Gupta empires. Then ask students to describe the main factors common to the governments of both Chandragupta and Asoka. *(Both brought a period of peace and prosperity; both had strong central governments.)*

History Background

Kailasa Temple Indians considered caves holy and often built temples inside them. Inspired by this tradition, Indian stonemasons cut directly into rock cliffs to create Kailasa Temple. The temple's creators dedicated it to the Hindu god Shiva and made it appear like the god's sacred mountain home. It was painted white to emulate the snow-capped peaks of the Himalayas. The temple features many images of elephants, which are significant in several ways. Ganesh, the elephant-headed god, was the son of Shiva. Also, elephants were treasured throughout India for their power. Four pairs of elephants were believed to hold the dome of the Earth when time began. Elephants were the royal mounts of kings, and their size and strength made them formidable foes in war.

DEMONSTRATE

Online Assign the **Digital Lesson Quiz** for this lesson if you haven't already done so. Students will be offered automatic remediation or enrichment based on their score.

In this lesson, you read about two of the earliest empires of India and their political and cultural influences on the development of civilization on the Indian subcontinent. Pose these questions to the class on the Discussion Board:

Recognize Cause and Effect How did the formation of the Maurya and Gupta empires contribute to the development of civilization in India? *(Both empires united warring kingdoms into one kingdom with a strong central government and an effective bureaucracy. The relative peace and prosperity encouraged advances in agriculture, education, technology, and the arts. With the Gupta, India experienced a golden age of significant cultural growth in many areas.)*

Draw Conclusions What are some factors that encourage the advance of civilizations? *(Some of the factors are a unifying government, a good civil service, peace, and economic prosperity where people no longer have to spend the majority of their lives simply trying to survive. A civilization has to have people who have the time to help it grow.)*

Topic Inquiry

Have students continue their investigations for the Topic Inquiry.

Answers

Synthesize *Living in a common dwelling provided the structure needed to allow each member to learn their specific duties and roles within the family. It taught that the welfare of the family was more important than the wishes of individual family members.*

>> Both in ancient India and today, village members worked together on projects that benefited the community. Projects might include digging a well, working on a road, or building irrigation systems.

Each village included people of different castes who performed the necessary tasks of daily life. It ran its own affairs based on caste rules and traditions and faced little outside interference as long as it paid its share of taxes. A village headman and council made decisions. The council included the most respected people of the village.

In early times, women served on the council. As Hindu law began to place greater restrictions on women, they were later excluded. The headman and council organized villagers to cooperate on vital local projects such as building irrigation systems and larger regional projects like building roads and temples.

Agriculture and Trade Shape Life In most of India, farming depended on the rains brought by the summer monsoons. Too much or too little rain meant famine. Landlords owned much of the land. Farmers who worked the land had to give the owner part of the harvest. Often, what remained was hardly enough to feed the farmers and their families.

Villages usually produced most of the food and goods that they needed. However, they relied on trade for some essentials, such as salt and spices, as well as various manufactured goods. People regularly interacted with others from nearby villages while attending weddings, visiting relatives, or shopping at marketplaces. This continual interchange was crucial in the establishment of common ideas across the subcontinent.

? SYNTHESIZE Why was the joint family so important to everyday Indian life?

ASSESSMENT

1. **Compare and Contrast** Compare and contrast the approaches of Chandragupta and Asoka to ruling the Mauryan empire.
2. **Analyze Information** Choose three achievements of the Gupta period and explain why they made the Gupta period a golden age.
3. **Summarize** How did India's great rulers maintain peace and order?
4. **Explain** How did geography influence trade in the Tamil kingdoms?
5. **Draw Conclusions** What characteristics of family and village life shaped Indian society?

Assessment

1. Both rulers relied on a strong central government and a well-organized bureaucracy. Chandragupta conquered India through force and ruled harshly, using tactics like a secret police. Asoka ruled by example, hoping to lead and unite his people by teaching tolerance and the correct way to live.
2. Possible answer: Guptas made great advances in mathematics, including creating Hindu-Arabic numerals and the decimal system. They made contributions to astronomy, as well as medical advances, such as vaccinations. Contributions to the arts include plays and dances still performed today, and vibrant sculptures and paintings.
3. They had justice systems, used secret police, and stifled dissent. Asoka ruled by moral example. He rejected violence and promoted tolerance and unity. Strong Indian rulers resisted foreign invaders.
4. Many of the Tamil kingdoms had harbors on the Indian Ocean, which allowed Tamil ships to engage in overseas trade.
5. Each person in the family and village had specific responsibilities and duties based on their caste and place in the family or community. This made Indian society structured, with each member aware of exactly what they were expected to do.

3.4 In ancient times, the Chinese depended on rivers for irrigation and transportation. They highly valued the ability to control floodwaters and to develop irrigation systems. The Chinese also prized devotion to duty. The importance they placed on these skills played a key role in the development of Chinese civilization.

>> The Huang River is also called the Yellow River. Its color comes from the loess, or soil, that settles in the water. Great amounts of loess displace the water, causing the river to rise and flood.

Interactive Flipped Video

Ancient Civilization in China

Geography Influences Chinese Civilization

Long distances and physical barriers separated China from Egypt, the Middle East, and India. This isolation contributed to the Chinese belief that China was the center of Earth and the sole source of civilization. These beliefs in turn led the ancient Chinese to call their land Zhongguo (jahng gwoh), or the Middle Kingdom.

Geographic Barriers Set China Apart To the west and southwest of China, brutal deserts and high mountain ranges—the Tian Shan (tyen shahn) and the Himalayas—blocked the easy movement of people. To the southeast, thick rainforests divided China from Southeast Asia. To the north awaited a forbidding desert, the Gobi. To the east lay the vast Pacific Ocean.

Despite these formidable barriers, the Chinese did have contact with the outside world. They traded with neighboring people and, in time, Chinese goods reached the Middle East and beyond. More often, the outsiders whom the Chinese encountered were nomadic invaders. Such conquerors, however, were usually absorbed into the advanced Chinese civilization.

TEKS
1.A, 1.B, 2.C, 3.A, 16.B, 23.A, 25.A, 27.A

>> Objectives

Understand how geography influenced early Chinese civilization.

Analyze how Chinese culture took shape under the Shang and Zhou dynasties.

Describe the origins, central ideas, and spread of Confucianism and Daoism.

List some achievements made in early China.

>> Key Terms

loess
clan
dynastic cycle
feudalism
Confucius
Laozi
philosophy
filial piety
oracle bone
characters
calligraphy

87

www.PearsonTexas.com
Access your Digital Lesson.

Aa Vocabulary Builder

1. Have students pronounce the following academic vocabulary term in this lesson and clarify the part of speech. If necessary, break it into syllables and pronounce it with the students.
2. Explain what the word means in common "student-friendly" language using synonyms and antonyms when possible. Provide concrete examples to clarify the meaning, and rephrase the definition.

interact: to be or become involved in communication, work, or social activity with someone else

Ancient Civilization in China

CONNECT

Preview Have students preview the **Lesson Objectives** and the list of **Key Terms**.

Students can also preview all the **Key Terms** and **Academic Vocabulary** using the **Interactive Reading Notepad** on the digital course or preview a summary of the lesson in the **Reading and Note Taking Study Guide**.

Online Use the **Editable Presentation** found on the digital course to present the main ideas for this lesson.

Start Up Activity

Tell students that the ideas of the Chinese philosopher Confucius greatly influenced early Chinese culture. Those ideas included guidelines regarding the responsibilities of individuals and the behavior of rulers. Confucius advised rulers: "Deal with the common people as if you were officiating at an important sacrifice."

Discuss Ask students to make a prediction about the structure of early Chinese civilization, given the importance of Confucianism in Chinese society. *(Possible answer: The civilization would reflect Confucian ideas, including those related to responsibilities and behavior.)*

Online You can also project the **Start Up Activity** from the course.

INVESTIGATE

Have students read the section using the **Reading and Note Taking Study Guide** to help them take notes and understand the text as they read.

Geography Influences Chinese Civilization

Tell students that vast distances and geographical barriers in the form of high mountains, brutal deserts, and thick rainforests separated China from other areas of growing civilization, such as Egypt, the Middle East, and India. The first Chinese civilization developed around the Huang River.

Topic 3 Lesson 4

Guided Reading and Discussion

Ask students to explain how geography, especially the Huang River, influenced the development of a civilization in ancient China. *(Geographic barriers—high mountains, deserts, and dense rainforests—discouraged invaders, allowing the settlements along the Huang River to develop largely undisturbed. The river provided water and fertile soil, and its flooding forced people to work together, which encouraged the formation of a central government.)*

Key Terms

Ask students to find the key term **loess** (in bold) in the text. Explain that this windblown yellow soil was very fertile, and as a result the people of the Huang Valley could produce the crops needed to support a growing population.

The Shang Dynasty Begins to Form China

The Shang dynasty was the first dynasty for which solid archaeological evidence has been gathered. It ruled China for about 644 years. Its government began as a network of kings and loyal noblemen with the kings controlling a relatively small area, but depending on loyal noblemen to govern their clan areas. The Shang dynasty left behind artifacts that indicated the development of social classes.

The Varied Regions of China As the Chinese expanded over an enormous area, their empire came to include many regions. The Chinese heartland lay along the east coast and the valleys of the Huang, or Yellow, River and the Chang River. In ancient times, as today, these fertile farming regions supported the largest populations. Then, as now, the rivers provided water for irrigation and served as transportation routes.

Beyond the heartland are the outlying regions of Xinjiang (shin jyahng) and Mongolia. These regions have harsh climates and rugged terrain. Until recent times, they were mostly occupied by nomads and subsistence farmers. Nomads repeatedly attacked and plundered Chinese cities. At times, however, powerful Chinese rulers conquered or made alliances with the people of these regions and another outlying region, Manchuria. China also extended its influence over the Himalayan region of Tibet, which the Chinese called Xizang (shih dzahng).

Early Peoples Settle Along the "River of Sorrows" Chinese history began in the Huang River valley, where Neolithic people learned to farm. As in other places, the need to control the flow of the river through large water projects probably led to the rise of a strong central government and the founding of what is sometimes called the Yellow River civilization.

>> Shang dynasty artisans were skilled in creating detailed objects in a variety of materials, including bronze and jade. This is a ceremonial bronze axe head.

The Huang River got its name from the **loess,** or fine windblown yellow soil, that it carries eastward from Siberia and Mongolia. Long ago, the Huang River earned a bitter nickname, "River of Sorrows." As loess settles to the river bottom, it raises the water level. Chinese peasants labored constantly to build and repair dikes to prevent the river from overflowing. If the dikes broke, floodwaters burst over the land. Such disasters destroyed crops and brought mass starvation.

EXPLAIN What are some ways that geographical features shaped how people lived in ancient China?

ELPS **ELPS 2.D.2** Practice asking for clarification using *Geography Influences Chinese Civilization* by writing context sentences.

The Shang Dynasty Begins to Form China

About 1766 B.C., the first Chinese dynasty for which scholars have found solid evidence arose in a corner of northern China. This dynasty, the Shang, would dominate the region until about 1122 B.C.

Formation of Government Archaeologists have uncovered some of the large palaces and rich tombs of Shang rulers. The evidence indicates that from their walled capital city at Anyang, the Shang emerged to drive off nomads from the northern steppes and deserts.

Shang kings probably controlled only a small area. Loyal princes and local nobles governed most of the land. They were likely the heads of important **clans,** or groups of families who claim a common ancestor.

However, the sizes and richly furnished tombs of the kings showed that they were at the top of the social hierarchy. The most powerful of the Shang kings could muster armies of several thousand men, if needed.

In one Shang tomb, archaeologists discovered the burial place of Fu Hao (foo how), wife of the Shang king Wu Ding. Artifacts show that she owned land and helped to lead a large army against invaders. This evidence suggests that noblewomen may have had considerable status during the Shang period.

Social Classes Develop As in other early civilizations, the top level of Shang society included the royal family and a class of noble warriors. Shang warriors used leather armor, bronze weapons, and horse-drawn chariots. They may have learned of chariots from other Asian peoples with whom they interacted.

Early Chinese cities supported a class of artisans and merchants. Artisans produced goods for nobles,

Answers

Explain *Fertile areas around rivers and river valleys encouraged people to live as farmers. Desert and mountainous areas encouraged a nomadic lifestyle.*

English Language Proficiency Standards

Listening Strategies 2.D.2 Read or have students read "Geography Influences Chinese Civilization" aloud. Have them complete one activity.

Beginning Read the section aloud. Tell students to ask for clarification as you read, using stems such as: Can you reread the sentence about ____? What does the word ____ mean? Answer each question using accessible language.

Intermediate Read the section aloud. Tell students to ask for clarification on vocabulary or content as you read. Answer each question for students.

Advanced Have small groups take turns reading aloud. Then instruct them to develop questions to clarify any confusion and share their clarification questions with the class. Answer or allow the group to answer the questions.

Advanced High Perform the Advanced activity but with pairs of students, instead of small groups, and begin with pairs reading and discussing the section.

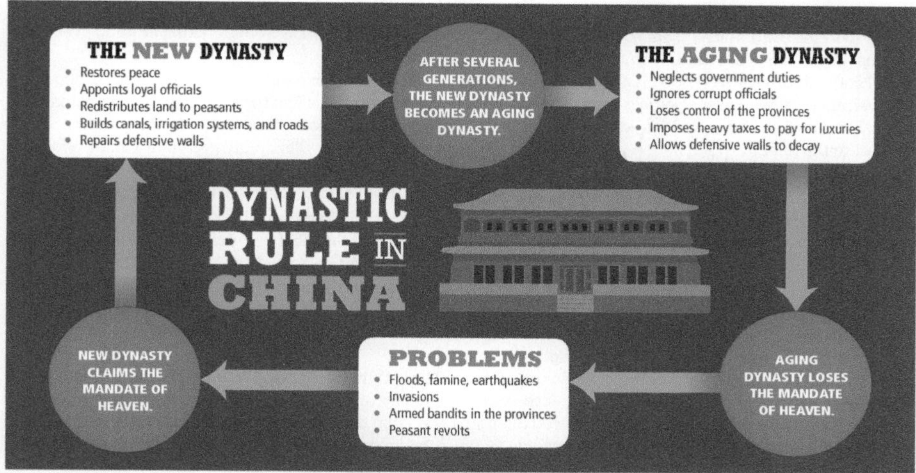
THE NEW DYNASTY
Restores peace
Appoints loyal officials
Redistributes land to peasants
Builds canals, irrigation systems, and roads
Repairs defensive walls
AFTER SEVERAL GENERATIONS, THE NEW DYNASTY BECOMES AN AGING DYNASTY.
THE AGING DYNASTY
Neglects government duties
Ignores corrupt officials
Loses control of the provinces
Imposes heavy taxes to pay for luxuries
Allows defensive walls to decay
DYNASTIC RULE IN CHINA
AGING DYNASTY LOSES THE MANDATE OF HEAVEN.
PROBLEMS
Floods, famine, earthquakes
Invasions
Armed bandits in the provinces
Peasant revolts
NEW DYNASTY CLAIMS THE MANDATE OF HEAVEN.

>> **Analyze Information** What causes a dynasty to lose the Mandate of Heaven?

including bronze weapons, silk robes, and jade jewelry. Merchants exchanged food and crafts made by local artisans for salt, certain types of shells, and other goods not found in northeastern China.

The majority of people in Shang China were peasants. They clustered together in farming villages. Many lived in thatch-roofed pit houses whose earthen floors were dug several feet below the surrounding ground.

Peasants led grueling lives. All family members worked in the fields, using stone tools to prepare the ground for planting or to harvest grain. When they were not in the fields, peasants had to repair the dikes. If war broke out between noble families, the men had to fight alongside their lords.

 **SUMMARIZE** How did the Shang kings govern China?

ELPS ELPS 2.C.1 Listen as your teacher or partner reads *The Shang Dynasty Begins to Form China* aloud. If you don't understand something you hear, ask the reader for clarification.

The Zhou Dynasty

In 1122 B.C., the battle-hardened Zhou (joh) people marched out of their kingdom on the western frontier to overthrow the Shang. They set up the Zhou dynasty, which lasted until 256 B.C.

The Zhou Claim the Mandate of Heaven To justify their rebellion against the Shang, the Zhou promoted the idea of the Mandate of Heaven, or the divine right to rule. They declared that the cruelty of the last Shang king had so outraged the gods that they had sent ruin on him. The gods then passed the Mandate of Heaven to the Zhou, who "treated the multitudes of the people well."

The Chinese later expanded the idea of the Mandate of Heaven to explain the **dynastic cycle,** or the rise and fall of dynasties. As long as a dynasty provided good government, it enjoyed the Mandate of Heaven. If the rulers became weak or corrupt, the Chinese believed that heaven would withdraw its support.

Floods, famine, or other catastrophes were signs that a dynasty had lost the favor of heaven. In the resulting chaos, an ambitious leader might seize power and set up a new dynasty. His success and strong government showed the people that the new dynasty had won the Mandate of Heaven. The dynastic cycle would then begin again.

Guided Reading and Discussion

Tell students that the formation of a cooperative and somewhat centralized government first emerged in early China during the Shang dynasty. Ask students to explain how the Shang dynasty contributed to the development of China's classical civilization. *(The system of cooperative government produced enough stability to support artisans. The Shang also established the beginnings of social classes.)*

The Zhou Dynasty

In 1122 B.C. the Zhou overthrew the Shang rulers to form the Zhou dynasty. The Zhou established feudalism as their system of government. Feudalism relied on local lords governing their own lands, but owing military service to the Zhou emperors. During the Zhou dynasty, which lasted about 850 years, China made major advances in technology.

Guided Reading and Discussion

Have students explain how the Zhou justified overthrowing the Shang dynasty. *(The Zhou claimed that poor governing by the Shang meant that the dynasty had lost the gods' favor—the Mandate of Heaven.)* Ask them to describe why the Zhou dynasty was successful. *(Its belief in the Mandate of Heaven and its feudal economic system brought stability, economic growth, and technological advancements.)*

English Language Proficiency Standards

Listening 2.C.1 Read aloud "The Shang Dynasty Begins to Form China." Students will learn new language structures by listening to classroom instructions and other students. Have them complete one activity according to their level of English proficiency.

Beginning Retell the content of this section in language that students easily understand. Display one of the blue headings from the text, explain that this is a fragment, and explain the difference between a complete sentence and a fragment. Display a sentence from the text that includes the fragment, and then have students listen as you read the fragment and then the sentence out loud. Finally, provide another fragment for students to use to create a new sentence.

Intermediate Follow the instructions in the Beginning ELPS activity, but have students use the text to create a sentence that includes the fragment. Students will listen as others read their fragments, and then their sentences, out loud. Finally, provide another fragment for students to use to create a new sentence.

Answers

Analyze Information *A corrupt or weak government that doesn't serve the needs of the people.*

Summarize *The kings controlled relatively small areas and relied on clan leaders, loyal princes, and nobles to govern most of the land.*

Topic 3 Lesson 4

Religious Beliefs in Early China

Complex religious beliefs had developed by the time of the Shang dynasty. The early Chinese religions were built around many gods and nature spirits, with Shang Di being the most powerful of these and only reachable through the royal family and nobles. Although they did not worship ancestors, the Chinese would ask the ancestors for help or to bring good fortune. In turn, they honored their ancestors in special ways.

Guided Reading and Discussion

Ask students how early Chinese religious beliefs might have reinforced the power of kings and other nobles. *(Possible answer: The Shang believed that spirits could influence the gods, who could ensure good harvests and victory in war. The gods would listen only to the spirits of the greatest mortals. Thus the king and other nobles, by praying to their spirits, could bring good fortune to all, and this power to sway the gods gave these nobles power.)*

Analyze Images

Direct students' attention to the photograph of the bronze coins. Tell them that anything can be used as money, as long as people are willing to accept it. Evidently, the ancient Chinese valued these objects enough to accept them in payment for goods.

A Feudal State Is Established The Zhou rewarded their supporters by granting them control over different regions. Thus, under the Zhou, China developed into a feudal state. **Feudalism** (FYOOD ul iz um) was a system of government in which local lords governed their own lands but owed military service and other forms of support to the ruler.

In theory, Zhou kings ruled China for more than 850 years. For about 250 of those years, they actually did enjoy great power and prestige. After the 800s B.C., however, feudal lords exercised the real power and profited from the lands worked by peasants within their domains.

Wuwang founded the Zhou dynasty in 1046 B.C. when he defeated the last of the Shang kings. Wuwang strengthened the new government by giving territory to relatives and supporters who acknowledged the Zhou kings as the supreme rulers. Considered a wise ruler, Wuwang even gave land to some of the defeated Shang as long as they recognized the new Zhou dynasty.

Economic Growth During the Zhou period, China's economy grew. Knowledge of iron working reached China in the 600s B.C. As iron axes and ox-drawn iron plows replaced stone, wood, and bronze tools, farmers produced more food. Peasants also began to grow new crops, such as soybeans. Some feudal lords organized large-scale irrigation works, making farming even more productive.

Commerce expanded too. The Chinese began to use money for the first time. Chinese copper coins were made with holes in the center so that they could be strung on cords. This early form of a money economy made trade easier. Merchants also benefited from new roads and canals that feudal lords constructed.

Economic expansion led to an increase in China's population. People from the Huang River heartland advanced into central China and soon began to farm the immense Chang River basin. Feudal nobles also expanded their territories and encouraged peasants to settle in the conquered territories.

Zhou Dynasty Ends By 256 B.C. China was a large, wealthy, and highly developed center of civilization. Yet the Zhou dynasty was too weak to control feudal lords who ignored the emperor and battled one another in savage wars. Out of these wars rose a ruthless leader who was determined to impose political unity. His triumphs brought an end to the Zhou dynasty and ushered in a new dynasty called the the Qin (chin) dynasty.

EXPLAIN What are three ways that China expanded during the Zhou dynasty?

>> The holes punched at the top of these bronze coins from the Zhou dynasty allowed the coins to be strung on cords, making it easier to carry money securely.

Religious Beliefs in Early China

By Shang times, the Chinese had developed complex religious beliefs, many of which continued to be practiced for thousands of years. The early Chinese prayed to many gods and nature spirits. Chief among them was the supreme god, Shang Di (shahng dee). The king was seen as the link between the people and Shang Di.

Gods as great as Shang Di, the Chinese believed, would not respond to the pleas of mere mortals. Only the spirits of the greatest people, such as the ancestors of the king, could possibly get the ear of the gods. Thus the prayers of rulers and nobles to their ancestors were thought to serve the community as a whole, ensuring such benefits as good harvests or victory in war.

At first only the royal family and other nobles had ancestors important enough to influence the gods. Gradually, other classes shared in these rituals. The Chinese called on the spirits of their ancestors to bring good fortune to the family. To honor their ancestors' spirits, they offered them sacrifices of food and other

English Language Proficiency Standards

Advanced Reread the section aloud. Have pairs of students discuss the difference between a fragment and a complete sentence, create three or four fragments that describe images in the reading, and listen to each other's fragments as they are read aloud. Then have pairs turn their fragments into sentences using the text. Have two pairs together listen to each other's fragments and sentences as they are read out loud.

Advanced High Reread the section aloud for students. Instruct students to create 3 to 4 word fragments that describe the images in the reading, and then trade their fragments with a partner. Students should use the text to turn their new fragments into complete sentences. Finally, have each partner listen as the other reads their fragments, and then their sentences out loud.

Answers

Explain *The dynasty expanded economic production by developing new iron tools that helped to produce more food. They grew new crops, and organized large-scale irrigation works. They expanded commerce by using money. Economic expansion led to an increase in population, which led to the settling and farming of new territories.*

necessities. When westerners reached China, they mistakenly called this practice "ancestor worship."

SUMMARIZE What steps did early Chinese communities take to ensure good harvests?

Two Major Belief Systems Take Root

During the late Zhou period, when war and social changes were disrupting old ways of life, new belief systems developed that would form the basis of China's culture and government for centuries to come. Thinkers such as **Confucius** (known by the Chinese as Kong Fuzi) and **Laozi** (LOW dzuh) put forward ideas on how to restore social order and maintain harmony with nature.

Confucius Spreads His Wisdom Confucius was born in 551 B.C. to a noble but poor family. A brilliant scholar, he dedicated himself to education and public service. He felt that educated people had a responsibility to serve in government so they could translate their good ideas into action. As such a person, Confucius hoped to become an adviser to a local ruler. He studied ancient texts to learn the rules of conduct that had guided the ancestors. For years, he wandered from court to court talking to rulers about how to govern.

Unable to find a permanent government position, he turned to teaching. As his reputation for wisdom grew, he attracted many students. Like two other influential thinkers who lived about the same time—Siddhartha Gautama in India and Socrates in Greece—Confucius never wrote down his ideas. Rather, his students collected many of his sayings in the *Analects*, a book of 497 verses compiled long after Confucius's death.

> The Master said, if out of the three hundred *Songs* I had to take one phrase to cover all my teaching, I would say 'Let there be no evil in your thoughts.'
>
> The Master said, Yu, shall I teach you what knowledge is? When you know a thing, to recognize that you know it, and when you do not know a thing, to recognize that you do not know it. That is knowledge.
>
> —*Analects*

>> A scholar and teacher, Confucius had an enormous cultural influence on early Chinese civilization.

Interactive Chart

Unlike the Buddha, Confucius took little interest in spiritual matters such as salvation. Instead, he developed a **philosophy,** or system of ideas, that was concerned with worldly goals, especially those of ensuring social order and good government.

Five Relationships Shape Behavior Confucius taught that harmony resulted when people accepted their place in society. He stressed five key relationships: ruler to subject, parent to child, husband to wife, elder brother to younger brother, and friend to friend. Confucius believed that, except for friendship, none of these relationships were equal. For example, he felt that older people were superior to younger ones and men were superior to women.

According to Confucius, everyone had duties and responsibilities. Superiors should care for their inferiors and set a good example, while inferiors owed loyalty and obedience to their superiors. Correct behavior, Confucius believed, would bring order and stability. Confucius put **filial piety,** or respect for parents, above all other duties. Other Confucian values included honesty, hard work, and concern for others. "Do not do to others," he declared, "what you do not wish yourself."

Confucius also taught that it was a ruler's responsibility to provide good government. In return, the people would be respectful and loyal subjects.

Two Major Belief Systems Take Root

Tell students that Confucianism and Daoism were two religions that evolved from different philosophies on the meaning of life and the guidelines one should follow to ensure a properly lived life. Confucius promoted good government and a social order based on specific relationships. He spoke of the responsibilities and duties people had toward one another and toward their ruler, depending on their place in society. Daoists promoted the idea that people should step away from daily issues, live in harmony with nature, and pursue a more spiritual life.

Guided Reading and Discussion

War and social changes late in the Zhou period disrupted old ways of life. New belief systems arose through the differing teachings of Confucius and Laozi. Confucianism had great appeal, because it provided practical answers to a multitude of social questions. Confucianism also promoted the idea of maintaining a balance between yin—essentially Earth and darkness, and yang—light and heaven. Laozi, who founded the philosophy of Daoism, took a more removed and spiritual approach, promoting the importance of balance and harmony with nature. Confucius encouraged involvement in life, but Laozi discouraged it, believing that the ways of society were unnatural. Over time, people blended the two philosophies and often practiced both.

D Differentiate Challenge/Gifted
Explain to students that this activity is called "Dear Confucius." After students have learned about Confucius and his teachings by reading the texts, ask them to apply the ideas of Confucius to modern-day situations. Students should write an advice column with questions for Confucius to respond to. Ask them to apply the ideas of Confucianism in crafting a plausible response that Confucius might have provided.

Answers

Summarize *They prayed to the spirits of their ancestors and offered them sacrifices of food and other necessities.*

Topic 3 Lesson 4

Compare and Contrast Ask students to describe the basic philosophies of Confucianism and Daoism, and to identify what is similar and what is different between the two beliefs. *(Both religions are based on the teachings of one individual, and both focus on the need for the correct balance or harmony in life. Confucianism: This religion has specific rules that govern behavior in all relationships, promotes involvement with life such as accepting one's place in the social order, and emphasizes the need to maintain balance and structure in all things. Daoism: This religion advocates that living in harmony with nature is most important, and that disengaging from social conflict and the unnatural structures of society is essential to spiritual growth.)*

Online Project the **Interactive Chart: Confucianism and Daoism** and click through the activity with students.

ACTIVE CLASSROOM

Use the Wallpaper strategy and have students review what they have learned about Confucianism and Daoism. Ask each student to design a piece of "wallpaper" that encapsulates the key ideas they've learned. Each piece of wallpaper is then posted. Students take a gallery "wisdom" walk and note what others have written or illustrated. New ideas or notes that build on existing wallpaper content can be added during the tour.

A Time of Achievements in Early China

Tell students that during the Shang and Zhou periods, the Chinese made several significant advancements in science, technology, and the arts. They ranged from astronomical observations to bronze making to a system of writing.

Confucius said the best ruler was a virtuous one who led people by good example. In addition, Confucius believed that government leaders and officials should be well educated. "By nature, men are pretty much alike," he said. "It is learning and practice that set them apart." He urged rulers to take the advice of wise, educated men.

Confucianism Has Great Influence In the centuries after Confucius died, his ideas influenced many aspects of Chinese life. Chinese rulers relied on Confucian ideas and chose Confucian scholars as officials. The Confucian emphasis on filial piety bolstered traditional customs such as reverence for ancestors. Confucianism also introduced a long-lasting Chinese belief that the universe reflected a delicate balance between two forces, yin and yang.

Yin was linked to Earth, darkness, and female forces, while yang stood for heaven, light, and male forces. To the Chinese, the well-being of the universe depended on maintaining balance between yin and yang. For example, the king should make the proper sacrifices to heaven while also taking practical steps to rule well.

>> The yin and yang symbol represents the Chinese belief that the universe reflects a delicate balance between yin, linked to earth, darkness, and female forces, and yang, which stands for heaven, light, and male forces.

Confucianism Spreads After Confucius's death, dedicated students of his teachings kept his ideas alive. One of these, Mencius, had been a student of the grandson of Confucius.

When a new dynasty established itself in China, Mencius traveled to many of its states to persuade the local nobility to adhere to Confucian teachings.

As Chinese civilization spread, hundreds of millions of people in Korea, Japan, and Vietnam accepted Confucian beliefs. Nearly one third of the world's population came under the influence of these ideas.

Daoism Teaches Harmony With Nature Laozi, or "Old Master," is said to have lived at the time of Confucius and to have founded a philosophy called Daoism (DOW iz um). Although little is known about Laozi, he has been credited with writing the *Dao De Jing*(dow duh jing), or *The Way of Virtue*, a book that had enormous influence on Chinese life.

Unlike Confucianism, Daoism was not concerned with bringing order to human affairs. Instead, Daoists sought to live in harmony with nature. Laozi stressed that people should look beyond everyday cares to focus on the Dao, or "the way" of the universe.

The Dao, he explained, was hard to understand fully or put into words. Thus he taught, "Those who know the Dao do not speak of it. Those who speak of it do not know it."

To know the Dao, one should reject conflict and strife. Daoists stressed the simple ways of nature and the virtue of yielding. Water, they pointed out, does not resist, but rather yields to outside pressure—yet it is an unstoppable force.

Many Daoists turned from the "unnatural" ways of society. Some became hermits, artists, or poets. Daoists viewed government as unnatural and, therefore, the cause of many problems. "If the people are difficult to govern," Laozi declared, "it is because those in authority are too fond of action." To Daoists, the best government was one that governed the least.

Confucianism and Daoism Evolve Although scholars kept to Daoism's original teachings, the philosophy also evolved into a popular religion with gods, goddesses, and magical practices. Chinese peasants turned to Daoist priests for charms to protect them from unseen forces. In addition, people gradually blended Confucian and Daoist teachings. Although the two belief systems differed, people took beliefs and practices from each. Confucianism showed them how

English Language Proficiency Standards

Learning Strategies 1.F.1 Read "Two Major Belief Systems Take Root" to the class. Students will use their language skills to learn words that they must know the meaning of in order to understand the core ideas of Confucianism and Daoism.

Beginning Write and display one essential word from the text, such as *education* or *responsibility* or *wisdom*. Use accessible language to define the word, and then use it in a simple sentence that relates to the content. Have students write the word, definition, and sentence in their notebooks. Finally, have students form their own sentences for the word, offering gentle feedback as needed to ensure correct grammar, fluency, and intonation.

Intermediate Follow the instructions in the Beginning ELPS activity, but write and display several essential words. After you define the words for students and they have copied the definitions into their notebooks, have groups of students work together to create and say a sentence for each essential word in the list.

to behave. Daoism influenced their view of the natural world.

CONTRAST Compare the basic ideas of Confucianism and Daoism in their approach to how people should live their lives.

ELPS 1.F.1 Practice identifying, defining and speaking about essential words in *Two Major Belief Systems Take Root.*

A Time of Achievements in Early China

The people of Shang and Zhou China are known for numerous cultural achievements. For example, Shang astronomers studied the movement of planets and recorded eclipses of the sun. Their findings helped them develop an accurate calendar with 365 and ¼ days. In addition, the Chinese also improved the art and technology of bronze-making, producing stunning bronze weapons and ritual vessels covered with intricate decorations.

Discovering the Secret of Making Silk By 2640 B.C. the Chinese had made a discovery with an extremely long-lasting impact: they had learned how to make silk thread from the cocoons of silkworms. Soon, the Chinese were cultivating both silkworms and the mulberry trees on which they fed. Women did the laborious work of tending the silkworms and processing the cocoons into thread. They then wove silk threads into a smooth cloth that was colored with brilliant dyes.

Only royalty and nobles could afford robes made from this luxurious silk. In time, silk became China's most valuable export. To protect their control of this profitable trade item the Chinese kept the process of silk making a secret for many hundreds of years.

A Complex System of Writing Is Developed Written Chinese took shape at least 4,000 years ago, if not earlier. Some of the oldest examples are found on **oracle bones.** These are animal bones or turtle shells on which Shang priests wrote questions addressed to the gods or to the spirit of an ancestor. Priests then heated each bone or shell until it cracked. They believed that by interpreting the pattern of cracks they could provide answers or advice from the ancestors.

Over time a writing system evolved that includes tens of thousands of **characters,** or written symbols. Each character represents a whole word or idea. To write a character requires a number of different brush

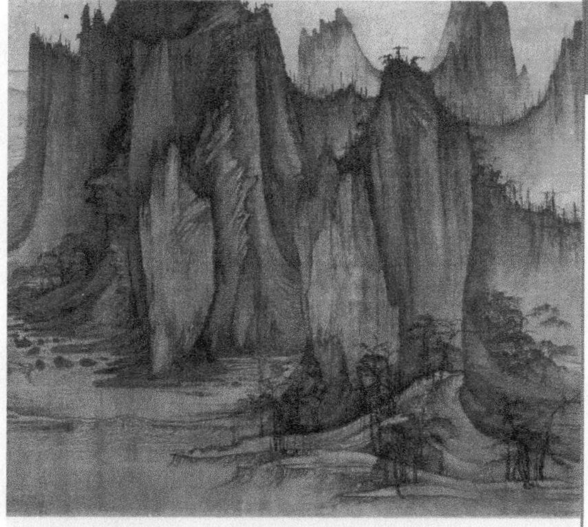

>> Living in harmony with nature is one of the central ideas of Daoism. Daoist paintings reflect that philosophy with a focus on trees, mountains, rivers, and other objects found in nature.

>> Silk thread or silk woven into magnificent fabrics were key trading items for the Chinese. Because of this, the process of converting raw silk to smooth cloth was a closely guarded secret.

Interactive Gallery

Online Project the **Interactive Gallery: Silk Making in Ancient China** and click through the images with students.

ACTIVE CLASSROOM

Use the Rank It strategy to help students recognize the significance of key achievements made in early China. List the following on the board: silk making, common written language, book making. Ask students to rank these achievements in order of greatest to least impact on the development of Chinese civilization. Then ask students to provide a justification for their ranking decisions. Group students in pairs to share their rankings and justifications. Poll the class to see if there is agreement on the ranking.

Guided Reading and Discussion

Explain to students that advances in technology do not always have to be in areas of science. Developing ways of farming silk worms, of spinning and weaving, and of fabric dyeing were all technological advances. Ask students to describe other key technological advances made in early China and explain why they were important.

Advanced Instruct students to scan the text to find essential words. Invite students to use classroom resources and context clues to define the words, and have them copy the definitions into their notebooks. Then have students create and say a sentence to a partner for each essential word. Tell students to work together to improve their pronunciation, fluency, and intonation.

Advanced High Follow the instructions in the Advanced ELPS activity, but tell students they will be sharing their sentences with the whole class. Encourage them to practice their pronunciation, fluency, and intonation before sharing with others.

Answers

Contrast *Confucianism taught people to accept their place in society and to live their lives according to the duties and responsibilities of their roles in the five key relationships. Daoism taught people to concentrate on living in harmony with nature.*

SYNTHESIZE

Online Project the **Digital Activity: Ancient Influences**. Ask students to share their predictions from the Start Up activity about how Chinese society would develop. Poll students to see which predictions were correct. Ask: How did the quote from the *Analects* of Confucius help you predict the types of social structures that arose in early China?

Draw Conclusions Why might Confucianism appeal to many different kinds of people? *(Possible answer: Confucianism provides a firm structure for almost any facet of life, especially proper behavior and the core relationships among people.)*

DEMONSTRATE

Online Assign the **Digital Lesson Quiz** for this lesson if you haven't already done so. Students will be offered automatic remediation or enrichment based on their score.

Pose this question to the class on the Discussion Board:

Describe What were the major religious and philosophical influences of China's early classical civilization, and why were they important? *(Answers should include an understanding of the impact on China's developing civilization by the types of government chosen by Shang and Zhou rulers, and of Confucianism and Daoism, the development of a common written language, and the techniques of making silk.)*

Topic Inquiry

Have students continue their investigations for the Topic Inquiry.

Answers

Analyze Information *Different languages were spoken throughout China. Since all of China used the same system of writing, it provided a way for all Chinese to communicate regardless of spoken language.*

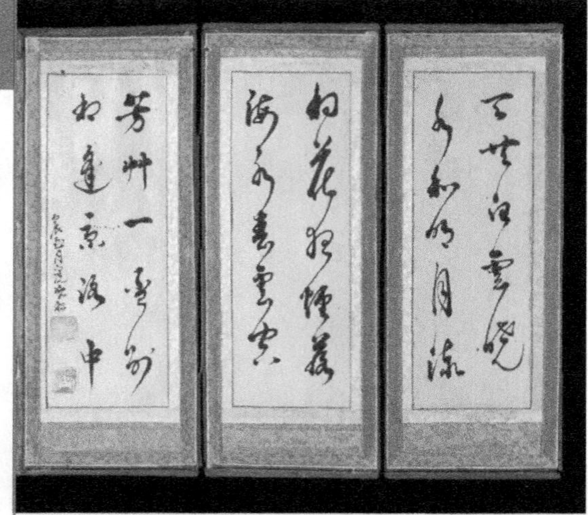

>> Poems and odes from the *Book of Songs* were put on strips of bamboo as part of a painting, or on wooden screens such as this one.

or pen strokes. In the past century the Chinese have simplified their characters, but Chinese remains one of the most difficult languages to learn to read and write. A person must memorize several thousand characters to read a newspaper. By contrast, languages such as English or Arabic, which are based on an alphabet, contain only about two dozen symbols that represent basic sounds.

Although it was complex, this written language fostered unity in early China. People in different parts of China often could not understand one another's spoken language, but they all used the same system of writing. Not surprisingly, in earlier times, only the well-to-do could afford the years of study needed to master the skills of reading and writing. Working with brush and ink, Chinese scholars later turned writing into an elegant art form called **calligraphy.**

Creating the First Books Under the Zhou, the Chinese made the first books. They bound thin strips of wood or bamboo together and then carefully drew characters on the flat surface with a brush and ink. Among the greatest Zhou works is the lovely *Book of Songs.* Many of its poems describe events like planting and harvesting in the lives of farming people. Other poems praise kings or describe court ceremonies. The book also includes tender or sad love songs.

ANALYZE INFORMATION How did a uniform system of writing benefit the Chinese?

ASSESSMENT

1. **Analyze Information** How did China's varied geography both help and hinder China's development as a country?
2. **Synthesize** What characteristics did the Shang and Zhou governments and social structures have in common?
3. **Analyze Information** What aspects of Confucianism and Daoism do you think contributed to their long-lasting influence?
4. **Synthesize** Why do you think that many Daoist painters featured water in paintings that represented Daoist beliefs?
5. **Describe** What are some of the most notable achievements of early China?

Assessment

1. In some places, natural barriers isolated China as a country, allowing it to develop on its own, without interference from foreign invasion. At the same time, fertile river valleys allowed people to grow enough food not only to eat and trade but also to expand their population and the economy during periods of peace and prosperity.
2. In both governments, kings had wealth, rich palaces, and status, but noble landowners had enough power to govern; both social structures were made up of nobles, warriors, artisans, merchants, and peasants.
3. Possible answer: The Confucian emphasis on achieving harmony by performing the duties associated with their roles gave people a sense of structure and a map for achieving a good life. Daoism's emphasis on living in harmony with nature and the virtue of yielding to the ways of the universe gave people a way of looking beyond everyday cares.
4. Daoists valued the ability to yield and flow with the rhythms of nature. Water, they pointed out, does not resist but rather yields to outside pressure—yet it is an unstoppable force.
5. a complex system of writing, creating the first books, silk making, astronomers helping develop an accurate calendar, bronze-metals technology

Strong Rulers Unite China

3.5 From his base in western China, the powerful ruler of the state of Qin rose to unify all of China. An ancient Chinese poet and historian described how Zheng (jeng) crushed all his rivals: "Cracking his long whip, he drove the universe before him, swallowing up the eastern and the western Zhou and overthrowing the feudal lords."

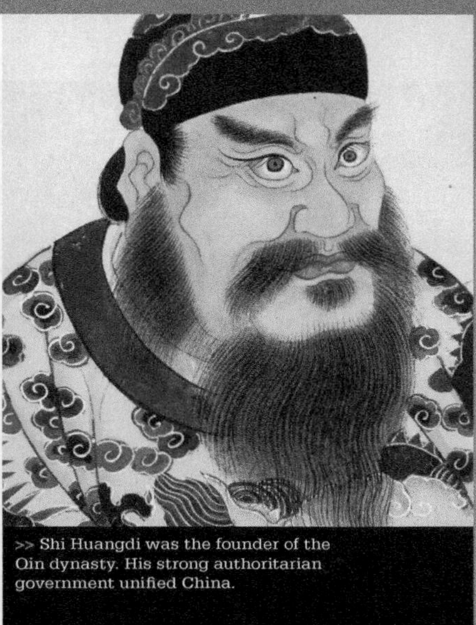

>> Shi Huangdi was the founder of the Qin dynasty. His strong authoritarian government unified China.

Interactive Flipped Video

Strong Rulers Unite China

TEKS
1.B, 3.A, 4.J, 27.A

>> Objectives

Understand how Shi Huangdi unified China and established a Legalist government.

Outline why the Han period is considered a Golden Age of Chinese civilization.

Analyze how the Silk Road facilitated the spread of ideas and trade in China.

Analyze why Buddhism spread through China.

>> Key Terms

Shi Huangdi
Wudi
monopoly
expansionism
civil servants
warlords
acupuncture

Shi Huangdi Unifies China

In 221 B.C., Zheng proclaimed himself **Shi Huangdi** (shur hwahng dee), or "First Emperor." Although his methods were brutal, he ushered in China's classical age—a term historians use when a civilization sets patterns in government, philosophy, religion, science, and the arts that serve as a framework for later cultures.

Shi Huangdi was determined to end the divisions that had splintered Zhou China. He spent nearly 20 years conquering most of the warring states. Then, imposing punishments for failure, he built the strong, authoritarian Qin government.

Legalism Establishes Harsh Rule Shi Huangdi centralized power with the help of Legalist advisers. Legalism was based on the teachings of Hanfeizi (hahn fay dzuh), who had died in 233 B.C. According to Hanfeizi, "The nature of man is evil. His goodness is acquired." Greed, he declared, was the motive for most actions and the cause of most conflicts. Hanfeizi insisted that the only way to achieve order was to pass strict laws and impose harsh punishments for crimes.

To Legalists, strength, not goodness, was a ruler's greatest virtue. "The ruler alone possesses power," declared Hanfeizi, "wielding it like

95

PEARSON realize. www.PearsonTexas.com Access your Digital Lesson.

CONNECT

Preview Have students preview the **Lesson Objectives** and the list of **Key Terms**.

Students can also preview all the **Key Terms** and **Academic Vocabulary** using the **Interactive Reading Notepad** on the digital course or preview a summary of the lesson in the **Reading and Note Taking Study Guide**.

Online Use the **Editable Presentation** found on the digital course to present the main ideas for this lesson.

Start Up Activity

Check students' prior knowledge of the Great Wall of China by having them answer these questions as they get settled: What is the Great Wall? Why was it built? How long did the construction take? Tell students that in this lesson they will learn the answers to these questions and much more, including how China was unified and when China experienced a golden age.

Online You can also project the **Start Up Activity** from the course.

INVESTIGATE

Have students read the section using the **Reading and Note Taking Study Guide** to help them take notes and understand the text as they read.

Shi Huangdi Unifies China

Zheng was the powerful ruler of the state of Qin in China. Using harsh and often brutal methods, he unified parts of China. For the first time, there was one ruler and one government. Zheng called himself Shi Huangdi, which means First Emperor. He established the short-lived Qin dynasty and used Legalism as the governing structure of Qin China. Shi Huangdi also oversaw construction of the Great Wall of China. He is also famous as the Qin emperor who ordered a life-size army of terra cotta soldiers, including horses and chariots, to be built to guard him in his tomb.

Aa Vocabulary Builder

1. Have students pronounce the following academic vocabulary term in this lesson and clarify the part of speech.
2. Explain what the word means in common "student-friendly" language using synonyms and antonyms when possible. Provide concrete examples to clarify the meaning, and rephrase the definition.

compile: to create by gathering things together

Online Project the **Interactive Gallery: Terra Cotta Army of Emperor Qin** and click through the images with students. Explain to students that the activity will introduce them to one of the most amazing Chinese archaeological finds of the modern era—an entire army made out of terra cotta, a type of baked clay. Uncovering this incredible piece of history took years of painstaking work to remove the soil surrounding the figures without damaging the figures themselves.

ACTIVE CLASSROOM

Use the Act it Out strategy and have students act parts to bring to life the image in the lesson showing the initial building phase of the Great Wall. Have different students play the overseers/soldiers, engineers, or laborers. Students should state what their characters are thinking about the endeavor in which they are involved.

Guided Reading and Discussion

Discuss Shi Huangdi's Legalism and the idea that the only way to achieve order was through strict laws and harsh punishments for criminals. Then have students summarize what Shi Huangdi did to unify China. *(He conquered the warring states. He replaced feudalism with military districts. Nobles were required to live in his capital. He promoted unity by standardizing weights and measures, replacing various coins with one currency, and creating uniformity in Chinese writing. He also improved transportation.)*

D Differentiate Challenge/Gifted

Explain to students that the Great Wall of China is considered one of the wonders of the world. Have students research aspects of the history of the wall, including the reasons for its construction. Students should present their research to the rest of the class.

>> Standardized weights and coins, such as this one, were part of the Qin dynasty's efforts to promote unity among various Chinese states.

>> Building the Great Wall required intense labor. Each stone was cut to a specific size and carried or dragged to the wall before being set in place.

lightning or like thunder." Many feudal rulers chose Legalism as the most effective way to keep order. Shi Huangdi made it the official policy of the Qin government. He then moved harshly against his critics. He tortured, killed, or enslaved many who opposed his rule. Hardest hit were the feudal nobles and Confucian scholars who loathed his laws.

To end dissent, Shi Huangdi approved a ruthless campaign of book burning, ordering the destruction of all writings other than manuals on topics such as medicine and agriculture. Policies such as this one were so cruel that later generations despised Legalism. Yet Legalist ideas survived for hundreds of years in laws that forced people to work on government projects and punished those who shirked their duties. Indeed, the policy of enslaving people as punishment for crimes lasted through most of the following dynasty, though only a very small percentage of Chinese were enslaved.

Emperor Forces Unity Shi Huangdi also abolished feudalism, which required little allegiance from local rulers to the central government. He replaced the feudal states with 36 military districts and appointed loyal officials to administer them. Shi Huangdi forced noble families to live in his capital at Xianyang (**shyahn yahng**), where he could monitor them. He distributed the lands of the displaced nobles to peasants. Still, peasants had to pay high taxes to support Shi Huangdi's armies and building projects.

To promote unity, the First Emperor standardized weights and measures and replaced the diverse coins of the Zhou states with Qin coins. He also had scholars create uniformity in Chinese writing. Workers repaired and extended roads and canals to strengthen the transportation system. A new law even required cart axles to be the same width so that wheels could run in the same ruts on all Chinese roads.

Building the Great Wall Shi Huangdi's most remarkable and costly achievement was the Great Wall. In the past, individual feudal states had built walls to defend their lands against raiders. Shi Huangdi ordered the walls to be joined. Hundreds of thousands of laborers worked for years through bitter cold and burning heat. They pounded earth and stone into a mountainous wall almost 25 feet high and topped with a wide brick road. Many workers died in the harsh conditions.

Over the centuries, the wall was extended and rebuilt many times. Eventually, it snaked for thousands of miles across northern China. While the wall did not keep invaders out of China, it did demonstrate the emperors' ability to mobilize China's vast resources. The Great Wall became an important symbol to the

English Language Proficiency Standards

Listening 2.C.2 Write the idiom "You can't fight City Hall" on the board and read it aloud. Then guide students through one of the following activities.

Beginning Act out the literal meaning of the idiom, then explain the idiom, focusing on its figurative meaning. Read the subsection "Legalism Establishes Harsh Rule" aloud and have students listen for content that reflects the idiom. Have students share their examples.

Intermediate Follow the instructions in the Beginning ELPS activity, but have a volunteer act out the idiom's literal meaning. After reading the subsection aloud, discuss how Legalism might have made the average Chinese person feel this way.

Advanced Instruct students to work in groups to figure out the idiom's meaning. Have a volunteer in each group read aloud the subsection as students listen for content that reflects the idiom. Then have groups discuss how Legalism might have made the average Chinese person feel this way.

Advanced High Have students repeat the Advanced activity working with a partner, taking turns reading the subsection and taking note of content that reflects the idiom. Then have pairs share their ideas with the group and discuss how Legalism may have made the average Chinese person feel this way.

Chinese people, dividing and protecting their civilized world from the nomadic bands north of the wall.

Qin Dynasty Collapses Although the Qin dynasty under Shi Huangdi had many achievements, those achievements came at a public cost. When Shi Huangdi died in 210 B.C., anger over heavy taxes, forced labor, and cruel policies exploded into revolts. As Qin power officially collapsed in 206 B.C., Gao Zu (gow dzoo), an illiterate peasant leader, defeated rival armies and founded the new Han dynasty four years later.

COMPARE How does Legalism differ from Confucianism?

ELPS 2.C.2 Examine common English expressions and apply them to *Shi Huangdi Unifies China.*

>> Shi Huangdi had a 20-square-mile compound built for his tomb. The emperor had himself buried with an army of about 8,000 life-size clay soldiers to guard him after his death. They carried actual weapons and were grouped in military formation.

Interactive Gallery

The Han Dynasty Creates a Strong China

As emperor, Gao Zu set about restoring order and justice to his empire. Although he continued earlier efforts to unify China, he lowered taxes and eased Legalist policies. In a key move, he appointed Confucian scholars as advisers. His policies created strong foundations for the Han dynasty, which lasted from 202 B.C. until A.D. 220.

Emperor Wudi Brings Great Changes The most famous Han emperor, **Wudi** (woo dee), took China to new heights. During his long reign from about 141 B.C. to 87 B.C., he strengthened the government and economy. Like Gao Zu, he chose officials from Confucian "men of wisdom and virtue." To train scholars, he set up an imperial university at Xian (shyahn).

Wudi furthered economic growth by improving canals and roads. He had granaries set up across the empire so the government could buy grain when it was abundant and sell it at stable prices when it was scarce. He reorganized finances and imposed a government monopoly on iron and salt. A **monopoly** is the complete control of a product or business by one person or group. The sale of iron and salt gave the government a source of income other than taxes on peasants.

Wudi followed a policy of **expansionism,** or expanding a country's territory, by increasing the amount of land under Chinese rule. He fought many battles to expand China's borders and to drive nomadic peoples beyond the Great Wall. Chinese armies added outposts in Manchuria, Korea, northern Vietnam, Tibet, and Central Asia. Soldiers, traders, and settlers slowly spread Chinese influence across these areas.

>> The Han emperor, Wudi, receives a letter from a messenger.

The Han Dynasty Creates a Strong China

Out of the chaos that followed Shi Huangdi's death, an illiterate peasant named Gao Zu took command. He defeated rival armies and established the Han dynasty. Easing the harsh Legalist system, he appointed Confucian scholars as government advisers. Later in the Han dynasty, the dynamic emperor Wudi created a network of trade routes that became known as the Silk Road, which stretched from China through deserts and mountains all the way to the Middle East. It included a sea route. The Silk Road delivered Chinese goods to the rest of the world and brought goods and cultural influences from the West to China.

Online Project the **Interactive Map: The Silk Road Connects East and West** and click through the hotspots with students.

ACTIVE CLASSROOM

Use the Make Headlines strategy and have students write a headline that captures the adventure that was the Silk Road. Ask: If you were to write a headline for this Topic right now that captured the most important aspect of the Silk Road that should be remembered, what would that headline be? Have students pass their headlines to partners for them to review.

Key Terms

Ask students to find the key term **expansionism** (in bold) in the text. Explain that throughout history, countries have tried to expand their territory. The United States began as thirteen states along the East Coast of North America but eventually expanded all the way to the West Coast.

History Background

An Unwelcome Exchange Commercial interaction between China and other areas of the world resulted in the beneficial exchange of goods and cultural items. However, such contact also resulted in the spread of deadly diseases. The caravans that traveled along the Silk Road and the ships that came to China from India transported all sorts of viruses and germs. Major epidemics of smallpox, measles, bubonic plague, and malaria frequently swept through China with appalling effects. When an epidemic struck in A.D. 317, the Chinese historian Sima Guang said that only one or two out of a hundred survived. The bubonic plague that decimated Europe in the 1300s was itself the result of international commerce. The plague began in Asia and traveled to Europe along the trade routes.

Answers

Compare *Confucianism focuses on the good in people and expects rulers to behave in a righteous manner towards those they rule in order to preserve social order. Legalists believe that people are basically evil and must learn goodness. Rulers must show strength and achieve order through strict, harsh laws.*

Topic 3 Lesson 5

Guided Reading and Discussion

Remind students that both the Qin and Han dynasties made significant contributions to the development of a classical civilization in China. With Shi Huangdi, the Qin Dynasty was the first to successfully unite the warring Chinese territories under one ruler and government. The successful unification by the Qin set the stage for the Han dynasty and its more progressive political policies. One of the most successful Han emperors was Wudi. His achievements included strengthening the government and economy, and supporting education. His expansionist policy added as much territory as possible to the Han empire. Of his many achievements, establishing the network of trade routes called the Silk Road was one of the greatest. It opened up China to an exchange of goods and ideas with Western nations far from its borders, including the Middle East, Rome, and Persia. The Silk Road expanded and eventually stretched for 4,000 miles. Ask students how the achievements of the Qin dynasty under Shi Huangdi differed from those of the Han dynasty under Wudi.

Cause and Effect Ask students why the Silk Road might have presented an opportunity for an exchange of ideas as well as goods. *(People from different cultures would travel the Silk Road. Even if they were traders, they would still bring their cultures, including religious beliefs and technologies, with them. Also, some travelers might have been scholars or priests from other countries.)*

The Silk Road Links China to the West The emperor Wudi opened up a network of trade routes, later called the Silk Road, that would link China and the West for centuries.

During the Han period, new foods such as grapes, figs, cucumbers, and walnuts flowed into China from western Asia. Lucky traders might return to China bearing furs from Central Asia, muslin from India, or glass from Rome. At the same time, the Chinese sent large quantities of silk westward to fill a growing demand for the prized raw silk and fabric.

Eventually, the Silk Road stretched for 4,000 miles, linking China to the Fertile Crescent in the Middle East. Few traders covered the entire distance, however. Instead, goods were relayed in stages from one set of traders to another. At the western end, trade was controlled by various peoples, including the Persians.

The Silk Road became a route for new ideas and technologies, as well as goods. Chinese inventions such as paper, gunpowder, and the magnetic compass all traveled west on the Silk Road, as did Confucian ideas. China absorbed cultural influences from its trading partners, including Buddhism from India and Islam from Persia. The Silk Road helped the growth of civilizations that engaged in this exchange of goods and ideas.

Scholar-Officials Run the Government Han emperors made Confucianism the official belief system of the state. They relied on well-educated scholars to run the bureaucratic government. A scholar-official was expected to match the Confucian ideal of a gentleman. He would be courteous and dignified and possess a thorough knowledge of history, music, poetry, and Confucian teachings.

The Han Civil Service System Han emperors adopted the idea that **civil servants**—that is, officials in the government—should win their positions by merit, rather than through family ties as had occurred in the past. In the Han civil service system, a young man would start in a clerical job. Once he proved his abilities, he would move up in local government. If he continued to excel, he would eventually be recruited into the civil service and might be tested on his knowledge of government policy. Essential to his studies were the Five Classics, a collection of histories, poems, and handbooks compiled by Confucius and others that served as a guide to conduct for about 2,000 years.

Much later, in the A.D. 580s, the Sui dynasty set up a formal system of civil service exams, which were given at the local, provincial, and national levels. In theory, any man could take the exams. In practice, only those

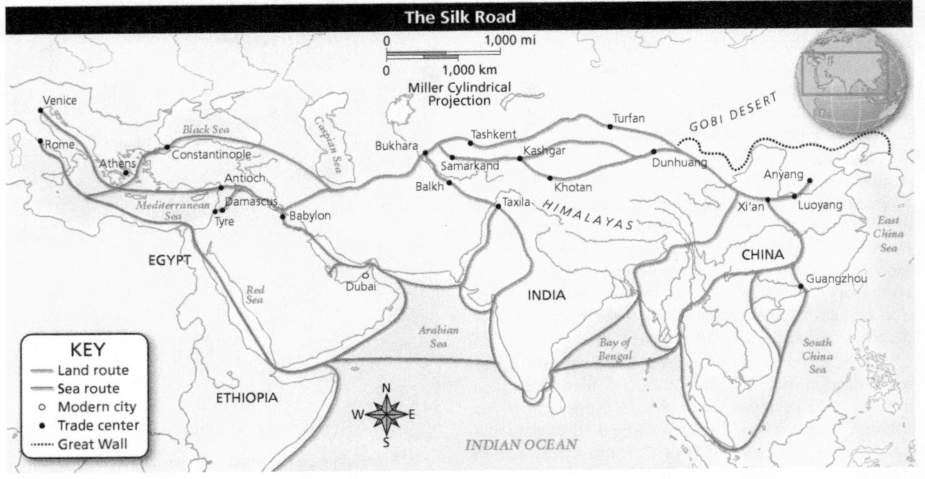

>> **Analyze maps** The Silk Road stretched from China to the Mediterranean. New ideas, as well as goods, were exchanged along the Silk Road. Describe two possible travel routes for a shipment of silk traveling from Taxila to Babylon.

Interactive Map

Answers

Analyze Maps *land/sea route: Taxila south to the western coast of India and by water and land to Babylon; land route: Taxila to Balkh then to Bukhara, from Bukhara to Babylon* who could afford years of study, such as the sons of wealthy landowners or officials, could hope to succeed.

Occasionally, a village or wealthy family might pay for the education of a brilliant peasant boy. If he passed the exams and obtained a government job, he, his family, and his clan all enjoyed immense prestige and moved up in society. Confucian teachings about filial piety and the superiority of men prevented women from taking the civil service exam. As a result, women were excluded from government jobs.

The civil service system remained in use until 1912. It put men trained in Confucian thought at every level of government and created an enduring system of values. Dynasties rose and fell, but Confucian influence survived.

The Han Empire Is Overthrown As the Han dynasty aged, signs of decay appeared. Court intrigues undermined emperors who could no longer control powerful **warlords,** or local military rulers. Weak emperors let canals and roads fall into disrepair. Burdened by heavy taxes and crushing debt, many peasants revolted. Thousands of rebellious peasants abandoned their villages and fled to the mountains. There they joined secret groups of bandits known by colorful names like the "Red Eyebrows" and the "Green Woodsmen."

In A.D. 220, ambitious warlords overthrew the last Han emperor. After 400 years of unity, China broke up into several kingdoms. Adding to the disorder, invaders poured over the Great Wall and set up their own states. In time, many of these newcomers were absorbed into Chinese civilization.

ANALYZE INFORMATION Why do you think the Silk Road is sometimes called the Road of Civilization?

>> During the Han dynasty, Confucianism became the official belief system of the state. Children attended classes at a young age under the watchful eye of a Confucian scholar.

The Han Golden Age

The Han period was one of the golden ages of Chinese civilization. Han China made such tremendous advances in so many fields that the Chinese later called themselves "the people of Han."

New Advances in Science and Medicine Han scientists wrote texts on chemistry, zoology, botany, and other subjects. Han astronomers carefully observed and measured movements of the stars and planets, which enabled them to improve earlier calendars and invent better timekeeping devices. One scientist invented a simple seismograph to detect and measure earthquakes.

>> Local chiefs and warlords overthrew the last of the Han emperors. The unity of the Han empire disintegrated, and China once again became a country of individual kingdoms.

The Han Golden Age

During the Han dynasty, China made tremendous advances in many fields. This political and cultural growth contributed to the development of China's classical civilization. The dynasty was also considered a golden age because of contributions in science, technology, government, and the arts. Many of the technological advances of the Han dynasty, such as the wheelbarrow and the making of paper from wood pulp, are still used today.

Guided Reading and Discussion

The era of the Han dynasty is considered a golden age of China because there were advancements in several areas. Ask students how the Han government and the Silk Road might have played a role in the achievements of this golden age. *(Possible answer: The stability of the Han government and the accessibility to trade and ideas offered by the Silk Road created an environment that supported scientific, cultural, and other achievements.)*

Identify Identify some of the inventions and other technological advances made during the Han dynasty. *(ship's rudder, wheelbarrow, bronze and iron stirrups, suspension bridges, paper made from wood pulp)*

English Language Proficiency Standards

Listening 2.E.1 Read "The Han Golden Age" aloud to the class. Have students complete one activity according to their level of English proficiency.

Beginning Retell the content in accessible language. Then compare the image of the seismoscope and its caption with the information in the text that you retold. Ask students simple questions to determine their understanding.

Intermediate Follow the instructions in the Beginning ELPS activity, but have students do the comparing of the text and image related to the seismoscope. Ask students questions about the connections between the image and the information in the text to determine their understanding.

Advanced Reread "The Han Golden Age" aloud. Then let small groups of students compare the image of the seismoscope to the information in the text. Provide groups with discussion questions about the connections between the image and the information in the text. Listen

Answers

Analyze Information *It was the way in which far-flung cultures exchanged goods and ideas. This exchange of ideas, goods, and technologies contributed to the growth of civilization.*

Topic 3 Lesson 5

Analyze Images

Direct students' attention to the seismoscope. Have them explain how the mechanism works. Tell them scientists have greatly refined such devices over the years but have still not created an instrument that can tell when an earthquake will strike.

Buddhism Spreads in China

By 100 A.D., Buddhism had spread to China from India by missionaries and merchants traveling the Silk Road. Mahayana Buddhism was welcomed by Chinese who saw the religion as a source of hope for eternal happiness and salvation if one lived a good life. By the end of the Han dynasty, Buddhism had spread throughout China.

Guided Reading and Discussion

Tell students that at first, Buddhism seemed like it would conflict with Confucian philosophy. Buddhism honored those who lived lives of solitude and prayer, while Confucianism stressed the importance of family loyalty. Eventually, though, many Chinese people embraced the merciful and hopeful premise of Buddhism. Ask students why Buddhism took solid root in China. *(It appealed to people who were living in uncertain times, because it promised escape from suffering and a path to eternal salvation. Buddhism represented mercy and compassion.)*

>> Zhang Heng developed the earliest known seismoscope to detect and measure earthquakes. Shock waves move a pendulum linked to a mechanism that opens the jaw of the dragon. The event is recorded when the ball falls from the dragon's mouth into the open mouth of the toad below.

>> Han dynasty artists created items of great beauty. This mythical beast, called a "Bixie," is made of bronze and was used to ward off evil spirits.

The scientist Wang Chong disagreed with the widely held belief that comets and eclipses showed heaven's anger. "On the average, there is one moon eclipse about every 180 days," he wrote, "and a solar eclipse about every 41 or 42 months. Eclipses . . . are not caused by political action." Wang Chong argued that no scientific theories should be accepted unless they were supported by proof.

Chinese physicians diagnosed diseases, developed anesthetics, and experimented with herbal remedies and other drugs. Many doctors promoted the use of **acupuncture.** In this medical treatment, developed about 2500 B.C., the doctor inserts needles into the skin at specific points to relieve pain or treat various illnesses.

New Ideas in Technology and Engineering In its time, Han China was the most technologically advanced civilization in the world. Cai Lun (ky loon), an official of the Han court, invented a method for making paper out of wood pulp. His basic method is still used to manufacture paper today. The Chinese also pioneered advanced methods of shipbuilding and invented the rudder to steer. Other practical inventions included bronze and iron stirrups, fishing reels, wheelbarrows, and suspension bridges. Some of these ideas moved west slowly, reaching Europe hundreds of years later.

The Arts Flourish The walled cities of Han China boasted splendid temples and palaces amid elegant parks. Although these wooden buildings have not survived, Han poets and historians have described their grandeur. In addition, artisans produced delicate jade and ivory carvings and fine ceramic figures. Bronze-workers and silk-makers improved on earlier techniques and set high standards for future generations.

Lessons for Women, a handbook of behavior written by Ban Zhao (bahn jow) around A.D. 100, carefully spells out the proper behavior for women and men. Ban Zhao favored equal education for boys and girls. However, she stressed that women should be obedient, respectful, and submissive. "Let a woman modestly yield to others," she advised. "Let her respect others."

 **CONNECT** What are some examples of Han inventions still used today?

English Language Proficiency Standards

to students' discussions to determine their understanding of the content.

Advanced High Have a student volunteer reread "The Han Golden Age" aloud. Then provide groups with discussion questions about the connections between the image and the information in the text. Listen to students' discussions to determine their understanding of the content.

Answers

Connect *basic paper-making, metal riding stirrups, wheelbarrows, boat or ship steering rudders, acupuncture, suspension bridges*

Buddhism Spreads in China

By A.D. 100, missionaries and merchants had spread Mahayana Buddhism from India into China. At first the Chinese had trouble with the new faith. For example, Chinese tradition valued family loyalty, while Buddhism honored monks and nuns who gave up the benefits of family life for a life of solitary meditation.

Despite obstacles such as this, Buddhism became increasingly popular, especially in times of crisis. Its great appeal was the promise of escape from suffering. Mahayana Buddhism offered the hope of eternal happiness and presented the Buddha as a compassionate, merciful god. Through prayer, good works, and devotion, anyone could hope to gain salvation. Neither Daoism nor Confucianism emphasized this idea of personal salvation.

By A.D. 400, Buddhism had spread throughout China. Buddhist monasteries became important centers of learning and the arts. Buddhism absorbed many Confucian and Daoist traditions. Chinese Buddhist monks stressed filial piety and honored Confucius.

Looking Ahead Shi Huangdi, Gao Zu, Wudi, and later Han rulers forged a vast and varied land into a united China. Han rulers created an empire roughly the size of the continental United States. During this period, Chinese officials established the system of administration that would survive until 1912. In coming centuries, China would undergo great changes. It would break up and be painfully reassembled over and over. On the whole, however, Chinese civilization would flourish. After periods of disunity, in A.D. 581 a new dynasty, the Sui, would turn to Confucian scholars to revive the days of Han greatness.

? ANALYZE INFORMATION Why did so many people in China find Buddhism appealing?

>> This giant statue of Buddha was carved directly into a sheer cliff that leads to a Buddhist temple in China.

ASSESSMENT

1. **Explain** How did Shi Huangdi impose allegiance to a central government?
2. **Summarize** Why was the Han period considered a Golden Age of Chinese civilization?
3. **Analyze Information** How was the Silk Road used to bring ideas to and from China?
4. **Analyze Information** Why was a well-ordered civil service of benefit to the Han government?
5. **Explain** What factors helped Buddhism spread through China?

SYNTHESIZE

Online Project the **Digital Activity: Changing Systems of Government**. Have students complete and share their graphic organizer results. Explain that both the Qin and Han dynasties had a profound impact on the development of classical civilization in China. Although the methods of the dynastic rulers differed, both contributed to the political, cultural, and technological advancements of their eras.

Draw Conclusions What are some of the key contributions made by the Qin and Han dynasties that had a long-lasting effect on China's development as a classical civilization?

DEMONSTRATE

Online Assign the **Digital Lesson Quiz** for this lesson if you haven't already done so. Students will be offered automatic remediation or enrichment based on their score.

Pose this question to the class on the Discussion Board:

Describe Describe some of the ways China's development as a classical civilization affected other countries. *(Answers will vary but should note the impact of the Silk Road in the exchange of ideas between China and the West. Some Chinese inventions, such as the wheelbarrow and the ship's rudder, had long-lasting global effects, as did the discoveries of Chinese astronomers and physicians.)*

Topic Inquiry

Have students continue their investigations for the Topic Inquiry.

Answers

Analyze Information *They welcomed the Buddhist promise that religious devotion could end suffering and lead to eternal happiness.*

Assessment

1. He abolished feudalism and replaced feudal states with military districts run by loyal government officials. He gave the nobles' lands to peasants and forced noble families to move to the capital so he could monitor them.
2. The Han period resulted in many advances and achievements in science, medicine, technology, engineering, and the arts. The Silk Road was established, and canals and roads improved.
3. Chinese inventions such as paper, printing, gunpowder, and the magnetic compass all traveled west on the Silk Road, as did Confucian ideas. Cultural influences, like Buddhism and Islam, were absorbed into China from its trading partners. New knowledge about astronomy and mathematics also spread to China from Arab, Indian, and European sources.
4. It created a network of government representatives who had won their positions through merit rather than family ties. This would suggest they were qualified and could do their jobs effectively. Also, it created a strong system of Confucian values within the government that was carried on through the years.
5. Buddhist missionaries from India had spread Mahayana Buddhism to China. Times of crisis in China made a religion that featured a merciful god and a promise of eternal happiness very appealing. Through prayer, good works, and devotion, anyone could hope to gain salvation.

Answers to TEKS Assessment

1. Students' responses will vary but should explain that the domestication of plants made agriculture possible and allowed people to settle permanently. River valleys provided water and fertile soil for farming, as well as transportation and trade routes. Surpluses of food led to growing populations. River valley civilizations developed cities that had organized governments, social classes, complex religions, public works, and job specialization.

2. Students' responses should demonstrate an understanding of major river valley civilizations, such as the Yellow River valley civilization, and their achievements in expanding agriculture to feed large populations. Surplus food meant that people could specialize in other jobs, leading to economic growth, as both commerce and farming expanded. All the river valley civilizations built dikes and dams to control flooding. Governments were needed to organize these public works projects. Students should understand that in early governments, priests had the greatest power and that leaders often claimed that their right to rule came from the gods. Students should understand how these developments in river valley civilizations contributed to the development of later, classical civilizations.

3. Students' answers should clearly explain that Hinduism grew out of the overlapping beliefs of the diverse groups that settled India, and that later followers added other gods, beliefs, and practices. Students should also note that Hindu teachings were recorded in the sacred texts of the Vedas. The Vedas were developed by early Aryans. Aryans moved toward the notion of Brahman, which influenced the development of Hinduism. Through the Vedas and other literary works, such as the "Bhagavad-Gita," which represents Hindu beliefs, Hinduism spread across India.

4. Students' responses should demonstrate an understanding of the formation of Eastern religious and philosophical systems, such as Confucianism. Confucianism was a philosophy that was concerned with ensuring social order and good government. Confucianism became the official belief system of China. Chinese rulers relied on Confucian ideas and Confucian scholars ran the government. Confucianism later spread to Korea, Japan, and Vietnam. Daoism was a belief system that urged people to live in harmony with nature. Many Daoists rejected the unnatural ways of society.

5. Students' answers should clearly explain that the caste system, like Hinduism, was developed by the Aryans. People were born into their castes, or social groups. The caste system was closely linked to Hindu beliefs. Each caste had its own occupation, its own leaders, and its own special role in Indian society. To ensure spiritual purity, complex caste rules governed every aspect of life: food, dress, occupation, and so forth. Students should also explain that people believed the law of karma determined their caste. Students should explain the religious reasons why castes were kept separate from each other and how the rules of each caste governed the lives of individuals living in India. Students should state specific rules relating to the caste system.

6. Students' responses should clearly explain that early Chinese civilizations were dependent on rivers for agriculture, transportation, and trade. Students should understand that mountain ranges, deserts, thick rain forests, and the Pacific Ocean formed physical barriers that isolated China from the rest of the world. Students should note that there were wide variations in regional climates and terrain. Nomads from

TEKS ASSESSMENT

1. **Identify Causes and Effects** Identify major causes and effects of events from 8000 B.C. to 500 B.C., including the development of the river valley civilizations. Write a paragraph that describes major events and one or two aspects of these events. Consider such factors as existing environment, the existing geography, and existing agricultural systems. How did these factors help in the types of developing permanent settlements? 1.A

2. **Explain How Major River Valley Civilizations Influenced Development** Explain how major river valley civilizations influenced the development of the classical civilizations. Write a paragraph discussing a major river valley civilization and describe its contribution to the advancement of later classical civilizations. Consider such factors as agricultural achievements, the role of government, the relationship between government and religion, and economic growth. 2.C

3. **Describe the Spread of Major World Religions** Describe the historical origins and spread of major religious and philosophical traditions, including Hinduism. Write a paragraph to describe the historical origins and spread of Hinduism. Consider the founder of Hinduism, its sacred texts, and its growth. How was Hinduism easily spread throughout India? 23.A

4. **Describe Historical Origins and Central Ideas** Describe the historical origins and central ideas of major religious and philosophical traditions, including Confucianism. Write a paragraph about the historical origins and ideas of Confucianism and Daoism. In your paragraph, consider such factors as historical context and need for social order. How did the origin and ideas of Confucianism influence Eastern culture? Explain man's relationship with nature in Daoism. 23.A

5. **Identify Examples of Religious Influence** Identify examples of religious influence on various events referenced in the major eras of world history, and describe the major religious and philosophical influences of India by analyzing information to draw inferences and conclusions. Write a paragraph describing the religious influences of Hinduism on the caste system in India. Consider factors such as the origin of the caste system, rules associated with each caste, and the spiritual meaning of each caste. 3.A, 23.B, 29.F

6. **Analyze the Influence** Analyze the influence of physical geographic factors on major events in world history, including the development of river valley civilizations in China. Using information from the lessons and the map below, write a paragraph analyzing the influence of geography on the development of China's river valley civilizations, including the Shang and Zhou dynasties. Consider the dependence on rivers, how geography isolated China, and variations in regional climates. How did the geography shown in the map affect the development of the Shang and Zhou dynasties? 16.B

Shang and Zhou Civilizations

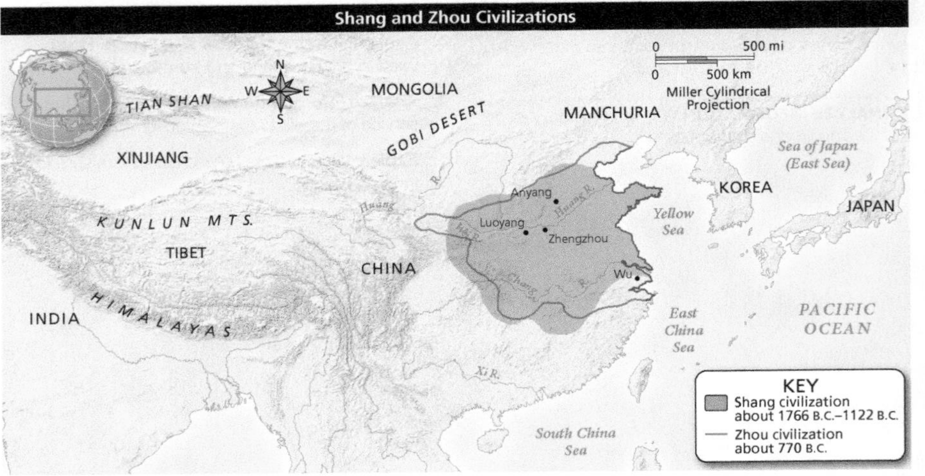

7. **Describe the Spread** Using appropriate reading skills to interpret social studies information, describe the spread of major religious and philosophical traditions, including Confucianism. Write a paragraph describing the spread of Confucianism and other religions in the region. Consider such factors as man-made borders, geographical borders, and national culture. How does the map above correlate to the spread of major Eastern religious and philosophical beliefs, such as Buddhism? **23.A, 29.H**
8. **Identify the Diffusion of Technology** Identify the diffusion of major ideas in technology that occurred in classical India. Write a paragraph identifying the diffusion of major ideas in technology in classical India, including the Maurya and Gupta empires. Consider the effects of trade, migration and conquest, and geography on the spread of technology. How was the diffusion of major ideas similar or different between the two empires? **27.A, 29.F**
9. **Describe the Development of Major World Religions** Describe the development and historical origins of major religious and philosophical traditions, including Buddhism. Summarize the fundamental ideas of Eastern civilizations that originated in India. Write a paragraph describing the development and philosophical traditions of Buddhism. Consider the religion's founder, his background, and his explanation of the Four Noble Truths. How can the origin and major ideas of Buddhism best be explained? **1.B, 23.A, 25.A**
10. **Summarize Institutions** Summarize the institutions of Eastern civilizations that originated in India. Write a paragraph summarizing the major institutions of Eastern civilization that have their roots in India. Describe two or more examples of Eastern institutions and consider the country's major religions, relationship between religion and politics, and introduction of technology. **25.A**
11. **Identify Causes and Effects of the Development of the Gupta Civilization** Identify major causes and effects of events from 8000 B.C. to 500 A.D., including the development of the Gupta classical civilization of India. Write a paragraph describing how the ideas expressed in the quote below characterized the general prosperity of the Gupta civilization. Consider the centralization and distribution of political power during the period, the state of the economy, and cultural developments of the Gupta civilization. **1.B**

"The people are numerous and happy; . . . only those who cultivate the royal land have to pay [a portion of] the grain from it. . . . The king governs without . . . corporal punishments. Criminals are simply fined, lightly or heavily, according to the circumstances [of each case]."

—Faxian, A Record of Buddhistic Kingdoms

these outer regions frequently attacked Chinese cities. The Shang drove off nomads from the northern steppes and deserts. The Zhou were from the western frontier and overthrew the Shang. The Zhou organized large-scale irrigation projects that improved farm production. The Zhou also advanced into central China and began to farm the immense Chang River basin.

7. Students' responses should clearly explain that religious and philosophical beliefs such as Buddhism and Confucianism spread throughout Eastern Asia. Students should note that as Chinese civilization spread, hundreds of millions of people in Korea, Japan, and Vietnam accepted Confucian beliefs. Buddhism also spread throughout East Asia, blended with other beliefs, and split into two major sects, Mahayana Buddhism and Theravada Buddhism. As the map indicates, Buddhism still thrives in East Asia.

8. Students' responses should clearly explain and identify that both the Maurya and Gupta empires ruled larger, more unified areas of India. The Maurya emperor Asoka built roads and rest houses, aiding travel and cultural diffusion. Both empires had periods of peace and prosperity that enabled cultural achievements and increased trade. However, Gupta rule allowed more self-government for villages and cities and exported goods such as metalware to more countries and regions than the Maurya. Additionally, the Gupta sponsored schools of learning that attracted students from many parts of Asia.

9. Students' answers should clearly explain that Siddhartha Gautama was the founder of Buddhism. When Gautama, a prince, first saw suffering, he left his palace to discover "the realm of life where there is neither suffering nor death." Students should also explain Gautama's journeys and the development of Buddhist teachings such as the Four Noble Truths and the Eightfold Path. Students should describe how Buddhism spread to become a major religion in Asia.

10. Students' responses will vary but should explain that early Indian civilizations had strong central governments and well-organized bureaucracies. Villages had councils that made decisions that affected their communities. Buddhism became a major religion in other Eastern civilizations. Hindu numerals are still used globally, as is the Indian decimal system. India's social order and caste system also spread.

11. Students' responses should clearly explain that Gupta rule ushered in a golden age of Indian civilization. Students should understand that the Guptas had a strong central government but gave much power to village and city governments. Trade and farming flourished. Artisans produced cotton cloth, pottery, and metalware for local use and export. This prosperity led to a flowering in the arts and learning. Impressive Gupta sculptures and art depicted religious subjects. Students should note that Buddhist centers of learning attracted students from all over Asia. There were also significant advancements in mathematics and medicine during the Gupta dynasty.

12. Students' answers should clearly explain how followers of the Buddha established monasteries for the study of Buddhism. These monasteries became centers of learning. The Buddha's followers also collected his teachings into the Tripitaka. Students should note that missionaries and traders spread Buddhism across Asia. Students should also describe the split of Buddhism into two sects: Mahayana and Theravada. Mahayana Buddhism was easier to follow, and appealed to more people because it offered the hope of salvation. Students should explain the basic beliefs and practices of each sect.

Answers to TEKS Assessment

13. Students' responses should clearly explain and demonstrate an understanding of important institutions, such as the the feudal system that developed during the Zhou dynasty. During this period, Confucianism began to influence many aspects of Chinese life. Confucianism later spread to other Asian countries. Responses should also include the development of the Mandate of Heaven, which justified a dynasty's divine right to rule. As long as a dynasty provided good government, it enjoyed the Mandate of Heaven.

14. Students' responses should clearly explain that the Han Dynasty created a stable and lasting state in China. The Han ushered in one of the golden ages of Chinese civilization. Students should note that Han Emperor Wudi made Confucianism China's official belief system and set up a civil service system based on merit. He strengthened the transportation system, promoted economic growth, and established a government monopoly on salt and iron to generate income. He followed a policy of expansionism, acquiring new territories. Wudi opened up a network of trade routes known as the Silk Road. The Silk Road extended all the way to the Middle East. Goods, including silk, as well as cultural and religious ideas were exchanged along these trade routes. Achievements of the Han Golden Age include: acupuncture, making paper out of wood pulp, the rudder, the wheelbarrow, fishing reels, suspension bridges, and a simple seismograph.

15. Students' responses should clearly explain that Buddhist centers of learning and religious schools probably influenced Indian achievements in mathematics during the Gupta dynasty. Students should understand that the numerals developed during the Gupta period are called Arabic numerals because Arabs carried them from India to the Middle East and Europe. Other Gupta mathematical advancements such as the concept of zero and the ten digit decimal system were probably diffused in a similar way. All of these Indian advancements in mathematics are still used today and have had a wide impact on the rest of the world.

16. Students' responses should clearly explain that the technology of making books, similar to the image shown, originated under the Zhou. Students should note that geographic barriers isolated China from many of its neighbors. Students should discuss how early Chinese civilizations relied on the rivers for transportation, which allowed them to trade and spread their ideas and technological advancements to other civilizations in the region.

TEKS ASSESSMENT

12. **Describe the Major Religious Influences of China** Describe the major religious and philosophical influences of China and the spread of major religious and philosophical traditions, including Buddhism. Write a paragraph explaining the traditions and influences of Buddhism as it spread to China and throughout Asia. Consider the centers established for meditation, collection of Buddhist teachings, and two divisions of Buddhism. What was the appeal of Mahayana Buddhism? **3.A, 23.A**

13. **Summarize the Institutions** Summarize the institutions of Eastern civilizations that originated in China. Identify the characteristics of monarchies as forms of government in early civilizations. Write a paragraph that summarizes the characteristics of monarchical government and early institutions that developed out of China's early dynasties. Consider such factors as the development of the feudal system, development of Confucianism, and the Mandate of Heaven. What aspects of Chinese monarchy and other institutions influenced other Eastern cultures? **19.A, 25.A**

14. **Describe Major Effects** Describe the major effects of events from 500 B.C. to A.D. 600, including the development of the Han Dynasty of China. Write a paragraph describing the rise of the Han dynasty and the reforms of Emperor Wudi that affected Chinese history. Consider the following: achievements including the civil service system, Confucianism, cultural importance, and economic growth as well as expansion and impact along the Silk Road. **1.B, 4.J**

15. **Identify Diffusion of Major Ideas of Mathematics** Identify the diffusion of major ideas in mathematics that occurred in classical India. Write a paragraph describing the importance and the spread of mathematical advances during the Gupta empire. Consider where mathematics developed in India, the path through which Gupta mathematics spread throughout the world, and the type of mathematics which gained greatest importance. Explain how Indian advancements in mathematics support the statement below. **27.A**

    "Indian advances in mathematics had a wide impact on the rest of the world."

16. **Identify the Origin and Diffusion** Identify the origin and diffusion of major ideas in technology that occurred in river valley civilizations. Write a paragraph that identifies and describes the technology pictured below and explain how these technologies originated and spread outside of the river valley civilizations in China. Consider the country's trade patterns, the geography, and borders. Why were rivers so important to the diffusion of major technological advancements? **27.A**

17. **Reflect on the Essential Question** **Write an essay on the Essential Question: How are religion and culture connected?** Use evidence from your study of this Topic to support your answer.

Topic 3

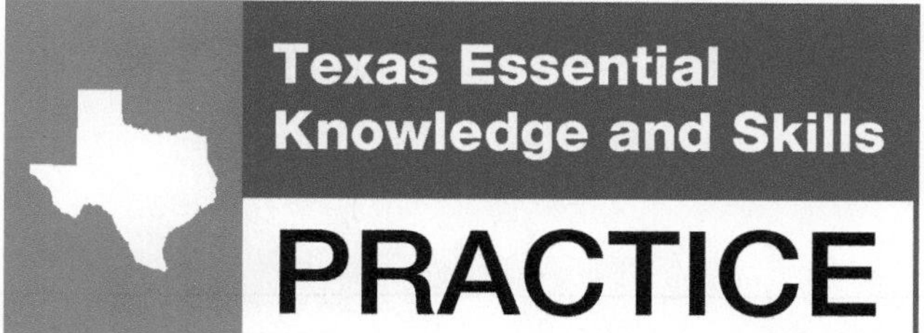
Texas Essential
Knowledge and Skills
PRACTICE

Topic 3

Answers to TEKS Practice

1. B
2. J

Online To prepare for the End-of-Topic test, have students go online for additional Topic Review and Assessment questions or to review their notes in the **Interactive Reading Notepad** for the lessons in this Topic.

Benchmark Tests

Assign these benchmark tests as you complete the relevant topics to monitor student progress toward mastering the course content and as preparation for the End-of-Course Test.

Benchmark Test 1: Topics 1–5

Benchmark Test 2: Topics 6–10

Benchmark Test 3: Topics 11–15

Benchmark Test 4: Topics 16–21

TEKS PRACTICE

1 Why would the Aryan civilization in the Indus Valley most likely have influenced the development of the civilization of early India?

A The telling and retelling of the conquest of numerous cities in the Vedas reminded earlier Indian people that the Aryans had settled in the Indus Valley, and so the Indians did too.

B The telling and retelling of the Vedas for hundreds of years allowed many of the cultural and religious beliefs of the Aryans to continue to be practiced by later cultures.

C The telling and retelling of famous battles in the Vedas allowed earlier Indian civilization to develop in peace because they believed the Aryans would always protect them.

D The telling and retelling of the Vedas for hundreds of years reminded the Indian civilization that the Aryans worshiped cattle, and so the Indians did too.

---

2 Why did ancient Chinese civilizations continue to develop along the Huang River even though it regularly flooded, destroying lands, crops, and villages?

F The river was essential for contact with the outside world, making increased communication worth the risk.

G The river was essential for its supply of loess, making the access to resources worth the risk.

H The river was essential for trade and troop movement, making the convenience worth the risk.

J The river was essential for irrigation and transportation, making the prosperity worth the risk.

Test Taking Tips: Tip for Questions With Graphs

1. Read the question.
2. Read the graph's title to determine what the graph shows.
3. Decide what information you need from the graph to answer the question.
4. Study the graph's labels. If the graph has a key, identify any symbols or shading used to show different information.
5. Read the question again to be sure you understand what is being asked. Answer the question in your own words using the information from the graph.
6. Read the answer choices and select the best answer.

3

Using the photo above, which statement best describes two examples of technology that originated in ancient Sumer?

A The umbrella has its origin as a status symbol, and the store is constructed from concrete, which has its origins in the clay used as the bonding between bricks.

B The automobile has its origin in the first wheeled carts, and the food is produced on farms where crops are watered using irrigation systems.

C The cloth sack has its origin in the first woven fabric panels, and the paved road originated on the Indian subcontinent.

D The wristwatch has its origin in a mathematical system based on the number six, and shoes have their origins in single pieces of cowhide laced together

---

4 Based on the information from the lessons, why did the Silk Road provide an advantage over other routes between China and the West?

F Traders no longer needed to make the entire journey from the West through China; they could ship their goods from trading station to trading station like an assembly line.

G Traders could make the entire journey from the West through China but access to nearby trading settlements was not always easy.

H Chinese traders had an advantage when using the Silk Road because their country owned it and they had a special passing lane.

J Traders no longer needed to make the entire journey from the West through China; they could wait at the end and the Chinese merchants would bring them the silk they wanted to buy.

If you have trouble with...				
Question	1	2	3	4
See Lesson	3.3	3.3	3.3	2.2
TEKS	2.C	1.A	4.J	27.A

3. A

4. G

Online Use the **Topic Synthesize** to help students revisit and reflect on the Essential Question for this Topic.

Topic Inquiry

If students have done a Topic Inquiry for this Topic, have them complete the final step of the Inquiry now.

The Americas (Prehistory–A.D. 1570)

TOPIC 4 ORGANIZER	PACING: APPROX. 1 PERIOD, .5 BLOCKS		
	PACING	TEKS	ELPS
Connect	1 period		
MY STORY VIDEO **Pachacuti, He Who Shakes the Earth**	10 min.		
DIGITAL START UP ACTIVITY **How Much Does Geography Affect People's Lives?**	10 min.	6.A	
DIGITAL TIMELINE ACTIVITY **Civilizations Develop in the Early Americas**	10 min.	26.B, 27.B	
TOPIC INQUIRY: PROJECT-BASED LEARNING **Create an Online Historical Atlas**	20 min.		
Investigate	1–3 periods		
TOPIC INQUIRY: PROJECT-BASED LEARNING **Create an Online Historical Atlas**	Ongoing		
LESSON 1 **Civilizations of Middle America**	30–40 min.	6.A, 26.B, 27.B	1.G.2, 2.E.2
LESSON 2 **The World of the Incas**	30–40 min.	6.A, 27.B	2.E.3
LESSON 3 **Peoples of North America**	30–40 min.	1.A, 16.A, 26.B	2.F.1
Synthesize	1 period		
DIGITAL ESSENTIAL QUESTION ACTIVITY **The Americas**	10 min.	6.A	
TOPIC INQUIRY: PROJECT-BASED LEARNING **Create an Online Historical Atlas**	20 min.		
Demonstrate	1–2 periods		
DIGITAL TOPIC TEST **The Americas**	10 min.		
TOPIC INQUIRY: PROJECT-BASED LEARNING **Create an Online Historical Atlas**	20 min.		

www.PearsonTexas.com
Access your Digital Lesson

AUTHOR'S NOTE

American Societies

The rise of the United States to prominence over the past two centuries has fostered a completely unhistorical sense of "natural" North American predominance in the western hemisphere. For most of the history of civilization in the New World, Middle and South America have in fact been the leaders, and North America the less developed continent of our hemisphere.

Population densities in the pre-Columbian Americas are an intensely debated subject, but there does seem to be some agreement that the south was much more heavily populated than the north. In both Middle America and northwestern South America, intensive advanced agriculture centering in corn, beans, squash, and, in South America, potatoes had produced a population base adequate to support societies more elaborate than any to be found north of the Rio Grande.

The Olmec culture of Mexico and the Chavín culture of Peru had begun the social evolution of Mesoamerica and South America during the first millennium before Christ. During the first thousand years C.E., that process of cultural evolution continued in Mexico and Central America on the one hand, and in northwestern South America on the other.

In both these areas, the process of state formation was a key element in this development. From agricultural villages linked by religion and culture, there evolved states with populations of tens and hundreds of thousands, specialization of labor, structured systems of social classes, and sometimes true cities and central governments as well. Unification into larger empires like those of the Aztecs and Incas of later centuries was rare. Nevertheless, during the classical period areas of advanced culture were scattered all over the highlands and lowlands of Mexico, Honduras, Guatemala, and through the central Andes and neighboring coastal lowlands of Peru.

While North America remained the preserve of hunting-and-gathering tribes and agricultural villages dominated by hereditary chiefs, impressive civilizations had thus emerged in Middle and South America.

—Anthony Esler, *The Human Venture: From Prehistory to the Present,* (Upper Saddle River, New Jersey: Pearson Education, 2004), p. 211

TOPIC INQUIRY: PROJECT-BASED LEARNING

Create an Online Historical Atlas

TEKS 15.A, 16.C, 29.F, 29.H, 30.B, 30.C, 30.D, 31.B

In this Topic Inquiry, students work in teams to create an online historical atlas that illustrates how geography impacted the lives and development of the Maya, Aztec, and Inca civilizations. Learning more about the impact of geography will deepen students' understanding of how the civilizations emerged and thrived and will contribute to the Topic Essential Question: How much does geography affect people's lives?

STEP 1: CONNECT

Develop Questions and Plan the Investigation

Launch the Project and Generate Questions

Display the *Entry Event*, which is a fictional assignment from a geographical society. Tell students that in this project they will learn about how geography affects human lives.

Divide the class into three groups, and assign each group one of the classical civilizations of the Americas: Maya, Aztec, or Inca. Explain that each group will research, plan, and create one section of an online historical atlas pertaining to their assigned civilization. Tell students that they must include and interpret at least one thematic map, one chart, and one graph to illustrate the relationship between the geography and historical development of their civilization. Then project and review the bullet-point list of additional components that they may include in their online atlases. If students are not familiar with atlases, you may want to project pages of an online atlas to help students better understand what they will be creating and how the elements work together.

Finally, allow students time to discuss the bullet-point list and begin to brainstorm ideas. Tell students to take notes as they brainstorm.

Prepare for Project Work

Before students begin researching, have them learn or review the essentials of working as a team by taking a tutorial and signing the *Project Contract*. Guide students as they complete the *Need-to-Know Questions* for their assigned civilization.

Resources

- Entry Event
- Project Tracker and Project Roles
- Need-to-Know Questions
- Rubric for an Online Historical Atlas
- Project Contract
- Student Instructions

STEP 2: INVESTIGATE

Apply Disciplinary Concepts and Tools

Collect Source Material

Have students do the 21st Century Skills Tutorial *Search for Information on the Internet* to learn tips on how to find information online. Then project the list of possible sources and discuss why these sites might be helpful. You may want to project one of the sites, such as the University of Texas: Perry-Castaneda Library, Historical Map Collection, to show students how to navigate the site and locate information and maps.

Suggest that students use the *Need-to-Know Questions* to help them focus their research. If time permits, allow students time to begin researching their civilizations. Direct students to continue researching outside of class.

Create and Edit Content, Maps, Charts, and Graphs

Review Google Map Maker and Google Earth. Explain that these tools will allow them to create maps with live GIS data. They will also be able to add and edit information on the maps.

Then review the different types of graphs and charts. Help students understand what type of graph or chart might be the most suitable for the information and data they have collected. For example, a line graph is often used for average temperatures. A bar graph is often used for population statistics or average rainfall.

Project the *Information Organizer: Online Historical Atlas of the Americas*. Explain that the first page of the handout is a flowchart template that will help them determine what details to include in their section of the atlas and how to organize it. Stress that each box represents one page of their Web site and that each line indicates the way the pages will be linked.

Resources

- Information Organizer: Online Historical Atlas of the Americas

STEP 3: SYNTHESIZE

Evaluate Sources and
Use Evidence to Formulate Conclusions

Build Your Web Site

Project the second page of the *Information Organizer: Online Historical Atlas of the Americas*. Explain that this sketch will help students design each page. Provide each group with several copies of the page, or tell students to make additional copies so they can design each page of their Web site.

Once they have sketched each page, have them return to the flowchart they created and use the sketches and flowchart to begin building their Web site. Stress that their Web site should be easy to navigate. Remind them that their goal is to focus on the relationship between the geography and historical development of the civilization.

Remind students to review *Getting Started With WordPress* for information on building a Web site using WordPress. Tell students that they are not required to use this tool. They can use Weebly or other Web-site-building tools to create their online atlas.

Write a Conclusion

Tell students that they should write a powerful conclusion that clearly expresses what they learned about their civilization based on the maps, graphs, charts, and content they created. Project and review the questions to help students focus their conclusions.

Remind students that their conclusions should include an interpretation of the maps, graphs, and charts they created. They may also want to include any inferences they made.

Resources

- Getting Started With WordPress

STEP 4: DEMONSTRATE

Communicate Conclusions
and Take Informed Action

Present Your Online Historical Atlas

Before students present their Web site, suggest that they review the 21st Century Skills Tutorial *Give an Effective Presentation*. Have students present their online atlases to the class or a larger audience. Allow time for comments, questions, and answers after each presentation.

Reflect on the Project

After students have finished creating and presenting their online atlases, provide your assessment, and help them go over what worked well and what did not work well so they can improve their results on the next project.

Resources

- 21st Century Skills Tutorial: Give an Effective Presentation
- Self Assessment

PROFESSIONAL DEVELOPMENT

Project-Based Learning

Be sure to view the Project-Based Learning Professional Development resources in the online course.

Civilizations of Middle America

Objectives

Objective 1: Explain when and where people first settled the Americas.

Objective 2: Analyze the rise of the Olmec civilization.

Objective 3: Describe the major developments of the Maya and Aztec civilizations.

Objective 4: Explain how prior civilizations influenced the Maya and Aztec.

LESSON 1 ORGANIZER		PACING: APPROX. 1 PERIOD, .5 BLOCKS				
			RESOURCES			
	OBJECTIVES	PACING	Print	Online	TEKS	ELPS
Connect						
DIGITAL START UP ACTIVITY **Civilizations in the Americas**		5 min.		●	6.A	
Investigate						
READ **Civilizations Develop in the Americas**	Objectives 1, 2	10 min.	●	●	6.A, 26.B, 27.B	2.E.2
INTERACTIVE MAP **Settlements of Civilizations of Mesoamerica**		10 min.		●	6.A, 27.B	
READ **The Maya**	Objectives 3, 4	10 min.	●	●	6.A, 26.B, 27.B	1.G.2
READ **Maya Cultural Life**	Objective 5	10 min.	●	●	6.A, 26.B, 27.B	
INTERACTIVE GALLERY **The Religious Life of the Maya**		10 min.		●	6.A, 26.B, 27.B	
READ **The Aztec**	Objective 6	10 min.	●	●	6.A, 26.B, 27.B	
INTERACTIVE 3-D MODEL **Aztec Temple**		10 min.		●	26.B, 27.B	
Synthesize						
DIGITAL ACTIVITY **The Rise of the Mesoamerican Civilizations**		5 min.		●	6.A	
Demonstrate						
DIGITAL QUIZ **Lesson Quiz and Class Discussion Board**		10 min.		●	6.A, 26.B, 29.F	

PEARSON realize™ www.PearsonTexas.com Access your Digital Lesson

Focus on Texas Standards

Texas Essential Knowledge and Skills

6.A compare the major political, economic, social, and cultural developments of the Maya, Inca, and Aztec civilizations and explain how prior civilizations influenced their development

26.B analyze examples of how art, architecture, literature, music, and drama reflect the history of the cultures in which they are produced

27.B summarize the major ideas in astronomy, mathematics, and architectural engineering that developed in the Maya, Inca, and Aztec civilizations

NOTES

Topic 4 Lesson 2

The World of the Incas

Objectives

Objective 1: Examine the early cultures of the Andes.

Objective 2: Understand how Inca emperors extended and maintained their empire.

Objective 3: Describe the major developments of Inca civilization.

LESSON 2 ORGANIZER	PACING: APPROX. 1 PERIOD, .5 BLOCKS					
			RESOURCES			
	OBJECTIVES	PACING	Print	Online	TEKS	ELPS
Connect						
DIGITAL START UP ACTIVITY **Government and Civilization**		5 min.		●	27.B	
Investigate						
READ **Cultures of the Andes**	Objective 1	10 min.	●	●	6.A, 16.A	
INTERACTIVE MAP **Civilizations of the Andes**	Objective 1	10 min.		●	6.A	
READ **The Powerful Inca Empire**	Objective 2	10 min.	●	●	6.A, 27.B	2.E.3
READ **Inca Life**	Objective 3	10 min.	●	●	6.A, 27.B	
INTERACTIVE GALLERY **Inca Culture**	Objective 3	10 min.		●	6.A	
Synthesize						
DIGITAL ACTIVITY **Three Great American Civilizations**		5 min.		●	6.A, 27.B	
Demonstrate						
DIGITAL QUIZ **Lesson Quiz and Class Discussion Board**		10 min.		●	6.A, 27.B	

Focus on Texas Standards

Texas Essential Knowledge and Skills

6.A compare the major political, economic, social, and cultural developments of the Maya, Inca, and Aztec civilizations and explain how prior civilizations influenced their development	**27.B** summarize the major ideas in astronomy, mathematics, and architectural engineering that developed in the Maya, Inca, and Aztec civilizations

NOTES

Peoples of North America

Objectives

Objective 1: Understand how groups of people adapted to the desert environment of the Southwest.

Objective 2: Analyze the evidence from which we have learned about the emergence of culture in eastern North America.

Objective 3: Examine the cultures that developed in three very different geographic regions.

LESSON 3 ORGANIZER	PACING: APPROX. 1 PERIOD, .5 BLOCKS					
			RESOURCES			
	OBJECTIVES	PACING	Print	Online	TEKS	ELPS
Connect						
DIGITAL START UP ACTIVITY **Climate and Civilization**		5 min.		●	16.A, 26.B	
Investigate						
READ **Cultures Develop in the Desert Southwest**	Objective 1	10 min.	●	●	1.A, 16.A, 26.B	
INTERACTIVE MAP **Native American Architecture**	Objective 1	10 min.		●	16.A, 26.B	
READ **Cultures Develop in the East**	Objective 2	10 min.	●	●	16.A, 26.B	
READ **Distinct Cultures Develop in Different Geographic Regions**	Objective 3	10 min.	●	●	16.A, 26.B	2.F.1
INTERACTIVE CHART **Native American Cultures**	Objective 3	10 min.		●	16.A, 26.B	
Synthesize						
DIGITAL ACTIVITY **Ancient Civilizations in the Americas**		5 min.		●	16.A	
Demonstrate						
DIGITAL QUIZ **Lesson Quiz and Class Discussion Board**		10 min.		●	1.A, 16.A, 26.B	

PEARSON realize

www.PearsonTexas.com
Access your Digital Lesson

Focus on Texas Standards

Texas Essential Knowledge and Skills

1.A identify major causes and describe the major effects of the following events from 8000 BC to 500 BC: the development of agriculture and the development of the river valley civilizations

16.A locate places and regions of historical significance directly related to major eras and turning points in world history

26.B analyze examples of how art, architecture, literature, music, and drama reflect the history of the cultures in which they are produced

NOTES

The Americas (Prehistory–A.D. 1570)

In this Topic, you will learn about the early civilizations in the Americas. You will also find lots of interesting ways to master the TEKS associated with this Topic.

Your study will help you master these TEKS:

TEKS

1.A, 6.A, 15.A, 16.A, 16.C, 26.B, 27.B, 29.F, 30.D

LESSON OUTLINE

4.1: Civilizations of Middle America 6.A, 26.B, 27.B

4.2: The World of the Incas 6.A, 16.A, 27.B

4.3: The Peoples of North America 1.A, 16.A, 26.B

Connect

Connect with this Topic by watching a video about a fascinating person or situation related to this Topic. You can think about how this Topic connects to your own life. And you'll encounter an intriguing Essential Question: How much does geography affect people's lives?

Begin your study by trying the following:

NBC LEARN Watch My Story Video:

Pachacuti, He Who Remakes the World

Launch your Project:

Create an Online Historical Atlas

Investigate

Then you will investigate the Topic through a group of lessons. The story of the early Americas will come to life as you read and interact with key content. You will get a chance to read about what happened and why. And you'll be able to interact with a lot of fascinating online materials.

You'll also keep working on your Project as you build further mastery of the Topic.

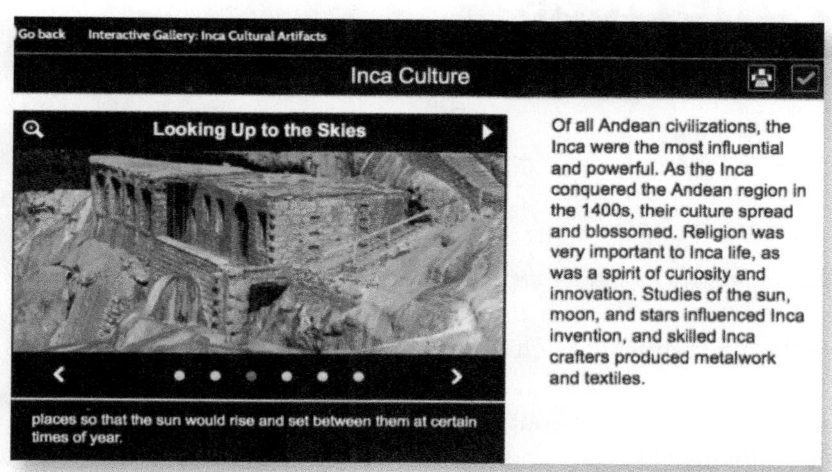

>> Digital interactivity from the online course

Synthesize

Next you will pull it all together by reflecting on the Essential Question. This will give you a chance to be the storyteller, to show how you would answer the big question.

Demonstrate

Finally, you can show what you know. You can write an essay, hold a discussion, or make a presentation. You can answer questions about every TEKS on the Topic Review and Assessment pages. Or you can finish your Project for this Topic and share it with the class.

TEKS in Topic 4	Topic Review and Assessment Questions
6.A	1, 2, 3, 4, 5, 7, 8, 11, 12, 13, 15
15.A	1, 5, 7, 11, 12
16.C	1, 3, 12, 13
26.B	14
27.B	6, 8, 9, 10, 14, 16
29.F	15, 16

Topic 4

The Americas (Prehistory–A.D. 1570)

Introduction

The earliest civilizations in the Americas arose in Mesoamerica, where the Olmec, the Maya, and the Aztec built pyramids and cities. Other parts of the Americas also saw the rise of civilizations, such as the Inca of South America and the Mississippians of North America. Each of these societies adapted to the landscape and climate of the places where they lived.

ESSENTIAL QUESTION

Ask students to think about the Essential Question for this Topic, How much does geography affect people's lives? Explain that many ancient civilizations developed along major rivers, which provided water for agriculture and transportation routes. In the Americas, however, civilizations often arose in much different environments.

Have students think about each environment below. Ask: What would people in each environment have to do to make agriculture—and thus civilization—possible? *(Possible answers: create terraces in mountains, clear land in jungles, drain the swampy lake, and form an irrigation network in the desert.)* Tell students to discuss their ideas with a partner.

- high valleys among steep mountains
- a dense tropical jungle
- scattered islands in the midst of a swampy lake
- a hot desert

Express Problems Clearly If a group of people wanted to farm in a desert, what do you think would be the main problem to overcome? *(Sample answer: getting enough water to grow crops)*

Support Point of View With Evidence Which of the environments do you think would be the most difficult to farm successfully? Explain your answer with details. *(Answers will vary. Some students might say: Mountains are the most difficult to farm because of the rocky terrain, steep hills, and lack of flat, fertile land for growing crops. On the other hand, a jungle and swampy lake has enough flat, fertile land. Trees just need to be cut or the lake drained. For the desert, providing water would create fertile land.)*

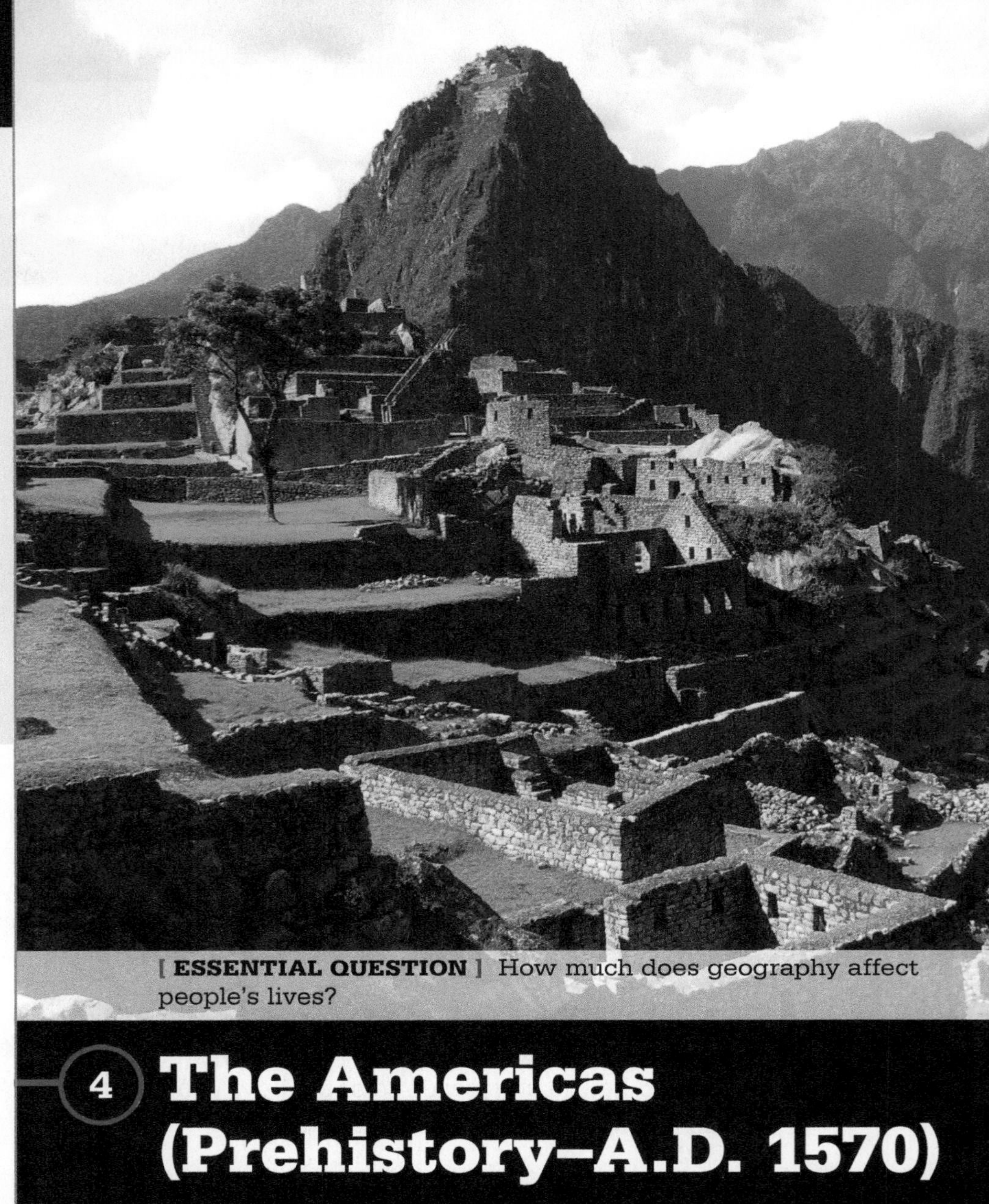

[ESSENTIAL QUESTION] How much does geography affect people's lives?

4 The Americas (Prehistory–A.D. 1570)

Analyze Images

Direct students' attention to the photograph. It shows Machu Picchu, a religious and agricultural center of the Inca civilization located high in the Andes Mountains of present-day Peru. Invite students to tell what they know about Machu Picchu and the Inca.

Texas Essential Knowledge and Skills

1.A, 6.A, 15.A, 16.A, 16.C, 26.B, 27.B, 29.F, 30.D

Enduring Understandings

- The Maya developed individual and powerful city-states, built towering buildings from stone, and made advances in mathematics and astronomy.
- In Mexico, the Aztecs built a large empire under a single ruler and used their knowledge of mathematics and astronomy to develop calendars.
- The most powerful civilization in the South American Andes was the Inca civilization, which had a well-organized society led by an all-powerful ruler.
- Native North Americans lived in places with very different landforms, weather, and vegetation, and each group developed a culture and a way of life that matched its resources.

>> Machu Picchu

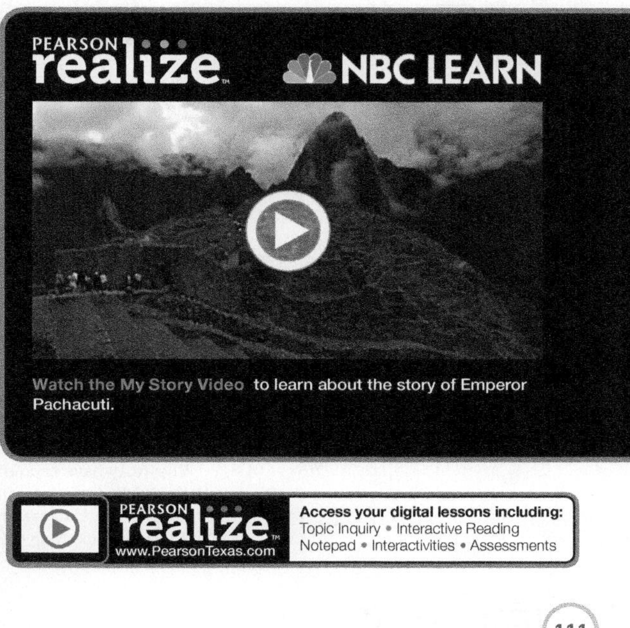

Watch the My Story Video to learn about the story of Emperor Pachacuti.

PEARSON realize www.PearsonTexas.com Access your digital lessons including: Topic Inquiry • Interactive Reading Notepad • Interactivities • Assessments

111

NBC LEARN MY STORY VIDEO

Project the My Story Video that introduces students to the Emperor Pachacuti, who expanded and strengthened the Inca empire.

Online My Story Video: **Pachacuti, He Who Shakes the Earth**.

After viewing, ask students to respond to the following questions.

Check Understanding What was the most powerful civilization in the Americas before the Europeans' arrival? *(Inca empire)*

Support a Point of View With Evidence Pachacuti's name meant "he who remakes the world." What evidence is there that his name was an appropriate one? *(He expanded the empire and strengthened it by building cities, roads, and bridges. He changed the Inca religion to focus on worship of the sun.)*

OVERVIEW ACTIVITY

Online Project the **Timeline: Civilizations Develop in the Early Americas** showing major events in the development of civilizations in the Americas. During this Topic, students will learn about all of these events and many more, but this timeline will provide a framework into which they can place the events they learn about.

Sequence Events Place the following in chronological order: Cahokia thrives, the Maya build large cities, the Iroquois League forms, and the Aztecs found Tenochtitlán. *(The Maya build large cities, Cahokia thrives, the Aztecs found Tenochtitlán, the Iroquois League forms.)*

Compare How are the Maya and Aztec civilizations similar? *(Both civilizations had cities.)*

Topic Inquiry

If you choose to assign the Topic Inquiry, launch the project after introducing the Topic.

D Differentiate Extra Support For the Overview Activity, remind students that B.C. dates run backwards from the point at which dates change, while A.D. dates go forward from that point. There is no year "zero"; A.D. 1 immediately follows 1 B.C.Then ask: How many years after the Maya built cities did the Puebloans settle in the American Southwest? *(400 years; the Maya built large cities around 300 B.C. and the Puebloans began to settle in the American Southwest around A.D. 100.)*

Topic 4 Lesson 1

Civilizations of Middle America

CONNECT

Preview Have students preview the **Lesson Objectives** and the list of **Key Terms**.

Students can also preview all the **Key Terms** and **Academic Vocabulary** using the **Interactive Reading Notepad** on the digital course or preview a summary of the lesson in the **Reading and Note Taking Study Guide**.

Online Use the **Editable Presentation** found on the digital course to present the main ideas for this lesson.

Start Up Activity

Tell students that scientists generally believe that people arrived in the Americas from Asia around 12,000 to 10,000 years ago. Ask students to answer the following question as they enter and get settled. Then have them share their ideas with another student in class or through a chat room or blog.

Discuss What would be the most influential item that an ancestor of a Mesoamerican who traveled from Asia to the Americas might carry to pass on to future generations? Explain. *(Answers will vary but could include rituals and religious practices, or carvings, shells, or rocks which might represent of a culture's traditions.)*

Tell students that in this lesson they will learn about some of the earliest civilizations that settled in Mesoamerica.

Online You can also project the **Start Up Activity** from the course.

INVESTIGATE

Have students read the lesson using the **Reading and Note Taking Study Guide** to help them take notes and understand the text as they read.

Civilizations Develop in the Americas

Explain that scholars have different theories about how humans migrated to Mesoamerica. One of those theories proposes that people crossed a land bridge from Asia into North America and moved south.

>> Maize was an important staple for early Native Americans, who ate it, made it into flour, and used it for ceremonial purposes.

Interactive Flipped Video

4.1 The Americas refers to two continents, North America and South America. Within these two regions is a cultural region that historians call Middle America or Mesoamerica, which is made up of Mexico and Central America. Some of the earliest civilizations in the Americas developed in Mesoamerica.

TEKS
6.A, 26.B, 27.B

>> Objectives

Explain when and where people first settled the Americas.

Analyze the rise of the Olmec civilization.

Describe the major developments of the Maya and Aztec civilizations.

Explain how prior civilizations influenced the Maya and Aztec.

>> Key Terms

Mesoamerica
maize
Olmec
stela
Valley of Mexico
Tenochtitlán
chinampa
tribute
Teotihuacán

Civilizations of Middle America

Civilizations Develop in the Americas

Scholars disagree about exactly when and how the first people reached the Americas. A common theory held that between 12,000 and 10,000 years ago, Paleolithic people reached North America from Asia. This migration took place during the last Ice Age, which lasted from about 100,000 years ago to about 10,000 years ago. At the time, so much water froze into thick ice sheets that the sea levels dropped, exposing a land bridge between Siberia and Alaska in the area that is now the Bering Strait.

Early evidence supported the theory that bands of hunters and food gatherers followed herds of bison and mammoths across the land bridge between Siberia and Alaska. They slowly moved south through North America, Central America, and South America. Recent evidence suggests that people may have reached the Americas much earlier. They may have paddled small boats and fished along the coasts. As archaeologists have discovered new evidence, they have modified their theories. Researchers now base the dates of migration into the Americas mostly on evidence found at prehistoric sites.

Aa Vocabulary Builder

1. Have students pronounce the following academic vocabulary term in this lesson and clarify the part of speech. Break the word into syllables and pronounce it with the students.
2. Explain what the word means in common "student-friendly" language using synonyms and antonyms when possible. Provide concrete examples to clarify the meaning, and rephrase the definition.

ingenious: clever, original, effective

Adapting to New Environments The first Americans faced a variety of environments in which they could settle. For example, great mountain chains—the Rockies, the eastern and western Sierra Madre, and the Andes—dominate the western Americas. In addition, through the continents flow three of the world's five longest rivers, the Amazon of South America and the Missouri and Mississippi rivers of North America.

Far to the north and south of the continents, people learned to survive in icy, treeless lands. Closer to the Equator, people settled in the hot, wet climate and dense vegetation of the Amazon rain forest. Elsewhere, hunters adapted to deserts like the Atacama of Chile, woodlands like those in eastern North America, and the fertile plains of both continents.

Farming Begins In the Americas, as elsewhere, the greatest adaptation occurred when people learned to domesticate plants and animals. These changes took place slowly between about 8500 B.C. and 2000 B.C. In Mesoamerica, Neolithic people cultivated a range of crops, including beans, sweet potatoes, peppers, tomatoes, squash, and **maize**—the Native American name for corn. People in South America cultivated crops such as maize and cassava and domesticated llamas and other animals valued for their wool. By 3000 B.C. in parts of South America and 1500 B.C. in parts of Mesoamerica, farmers had settled in villages. Populations then expanded, and some villages eventually grew into the great early cities of the Americas.

Olmec Civilization Emerges Many scholars consider the **Olmec** the first American civilization; it emerged in the fertile coastal areas along the Gulf of Mexico and lasted from about 1200 to 400 B.C. Compared to other civilizations such as the Maya, Aztec and Inca, archaeologists know little about the Olmec. We do not even know what they called themselves. In fact, Olmec is the name the Aztecs later used for these people. But rich tombs and temples suggest that they had a powerful class of priests. The Olmec did not build true cities, but rather priests and other leaders may have lived in ceremonial centers, while the common people lived in surrounding farming villages.

Olmec Culture and Trade Ceremonial centers had large pyramid-shaped temples and other important buildings. Much of Olmec art is carved stone. The smallest examples include jade figurines of people and gods. The most dramatic remains are 14 giant stone heads found at the major ceremonial centers of San Lorenzo and La Venta.

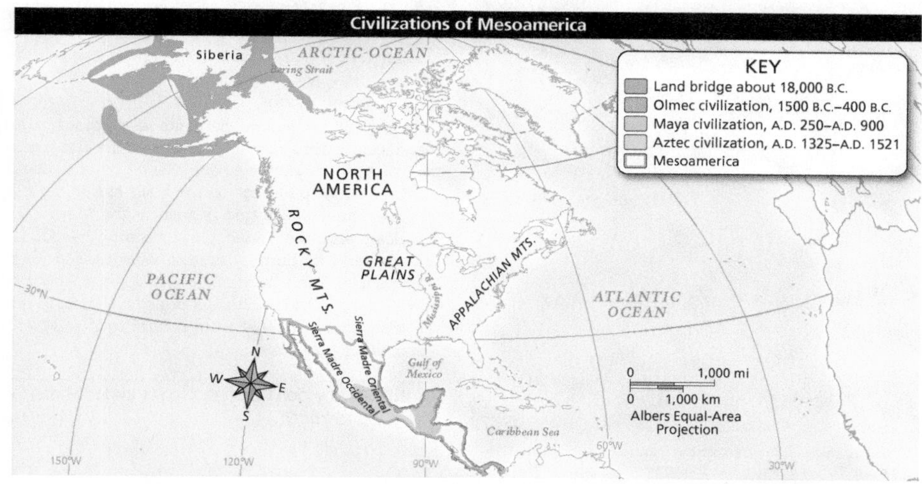

>> **Analyze Maps** Early people are thought to have crossed the Bering Strait from Asia to the Americas either on foot or in small boats. What might have been one of the biggest geographic influences on Mesoamerican civilizations?

Interactive Map

Guided Reading and Discussion

Ask students to describe how it is possible to understand what happened 12,000 to 10,000 years ago and rebuild a history based on that information. Ask students to write two to three sentences about how knowledge has been gained about the settlements and cultures of the Olmec, Maya, and Aztec. *(Answers will vary but may mention that archaeological excavations have provided historical insight. Artifacts found during the dig of a particular culture may provide evidence about that culture's time of existence, customs, religious practices, and agriculture. This information is shared globally and can help scholars form a solid theory about a civilization's way of life, which will be widely held until it is refuted by later scientific finds.)*

Online Project the **Interactive Map: Settlements of Civilizations of Mesoamerica** and click through the hotspots with students.

ACTIVE CLASSROOM

Use the Quickdraw strategy and pair students. Students have a short period to share what they know by writing with symbols or drawings. Have the first students tell their partners what they are going to draw or symbolize. Then, have the second students prepare the symbols or drawing. Use a document camera to scan drawings to add to the class blog.

Draw Comparisons Which civilizations were influenced by the Olmec, and how was this influence represented in the ways those later civilizations lived? *(There is evidence that both the Maya and the Aztec were influenced by the Olmec. The name Olmec is an Aztec name for that civilization, since the real name is unknown. The Olmec were the first to build the pyramid style of temples in Mesoamerica, a style later used by the Aztec and the Maya. The jaguars and serpents in Olmec art later appeared in the art of later Mesoamerican peoples.)*

Answers

Analyze Maps *the sea, as all the cultures were bordered by water to the east and west*

English Language Proficiency Standards

Listening 2.E.2 Read "Civilizations Develop in the Americas" aloud. Then have students complete one activity according to their English proficiency.

Beginning Explain how to use context clues by choosing a word students are unlikely to know. Use a Think Aloud strategy to model the use of context to support your understanding of the word. Continue reading and using context to define other unfamiliar words. Invite one or two volunteers to participate.

Intermediate Follow the instructions in the Beginning activity, but after you demonstrate once, ask students to use context clues to explain the meaning of additional words you identify.

Advanced Review context clues. Choose an unfamiliar word such as *scholars, migration, originally,* or *evidence,* and ask volunteers to demonstrate use of context clues to determine meaning. Have students continue reading the text with a partner, pausing to identify challenging words and using context clues by speaking aloud with their partner until they determine the meaning of the word.

Advanced High Follow the instructions in the Advanced activity, but have student partners choose two words to demonstrate how to use context clues.

Analyze Images

Point out to students the photograph of the stone head. Ask: Are there clues in this photograph that help you figure out how tall this stone sculpture is? *(The plants and trees offer some perspective but are not definitive.)* Tell them that the Olmec stone heads average about 6 feet in height. Ask: If you were taking a photograph of this stone sculpture, how would you show the viewer how tall it is? *(Possible answer: by including an adult standing beside the sculpture)*

>> Archaeologists discovered the giant Olmec stone heads, made of volcanic rock and weighing up to five tons each, during excavations. The Olmec moved them to ceremonial sites from distant quarries.

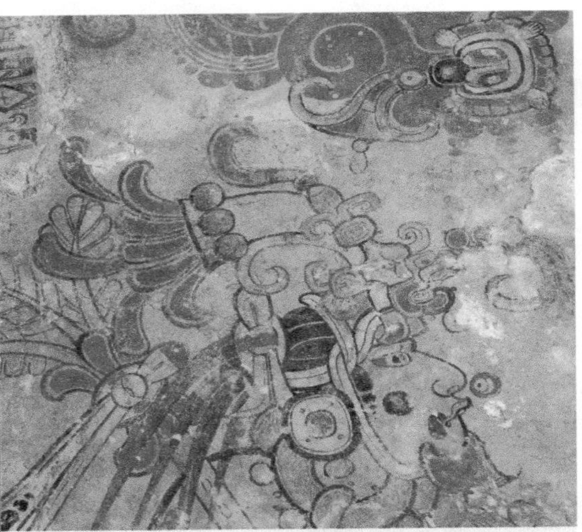

>> The ruins of San Bartolo have murals deep within the pyramidal complex of Las Pinturas.

Scholars think that these colossal heads, which the Olmec carved from 40-ton stones, are portraits of actual rulers. No one knows exactly how the Olmec moved these stones from distant quarries without wheeled vehicles or draft animals. Still, the evidence shows that the Olmec could mobilize a large labor force.

The Olmec also engaged in trading jade, obsidian, serpentine, mica, rubber, feathers, and pottery; through such trade, they influenced a wide area. The grinning jaguars and serpents that decorate many Olmec carvings appear in the arts of later Mesoamerican peoples. The Olmec also invented a calendar, and they carved hieroglyphic writing into stone. Recent archaeological excavations in Mexico indicate they may have developed a writing system, which would make them the first Mesoamerican civilization to do so.

Influence of the Olmec Through trade, Olmec influence spread over a wide area. Archaeologists have identified Olmec religious and artistic influences on two later Mesoamerican civilizations—the Mayas and Aztecs.

Both these civilizations built pyramid-shaped temples similar to those of the Olmec. Olmec ceremonial centers had the remains of ball courts linked to religious rituals. Similar ball courts have been found at Maya and later Aztec sites.

The ball game was fast paced and involved great skill on the part of the players. They had to keep a rubber ball in motion and send it through hoops high on a stone wall. The ball was not allowed to touch the ground. Archaeologists do not know the exact meaning of the game, but it had religious and political importance. It also was a source of entertainment for crowds of spectators.

The grinning jaguars, serpents, and other images that decorate Olmec carvings appear in the arts of later people. A figure similar to the Maya god of maize is found in Olmec paintings on the walls at San Bartolo, and the Olmec snake god is seen in the Maya gods Kukulcan and the Aztec Quetzalcoatl. The Olmec calendar and its number system were passed on to later people. Their most important legacy, however, may have been the tradition of priestly leadership and the religious rituals that were central to later Middle American civilizations.

INFER Why don't archaeologists know where the Olmec came from?

Answers

Infer *Archaeologists can only define history by evidence that has been confirmed. For the Olmec, in the absence of written records, the physical evidence of their past has not been sufficient to answer the question as to their origination. Recent excavations are reflecting new information and possibilities, but absolute knowledge on this question has not been established.*

History Background

Settlement Clues Excavations at Monte Verde, Chile, have contributed dramatic evidence to the debate over just how long ago the first migrations to the Americas occurred. In 1997, a team of scientists concluded that artifacts uncovered at Monte Verde were at least 12,500 years old. This was over 1,000 years older than previous discoveries had indicated. In addition, Monte Verde is about 10,000 miles south of the Bering Strait, while the earlier accepted "oldest" artifacts in New Mexico are much farther north. People would have needed many years to reach Monte Verde, so must have begun migrating much earlier than previously thought. More recently, scientists at Monte Verde have explored a second site that may indicate even older human activity.

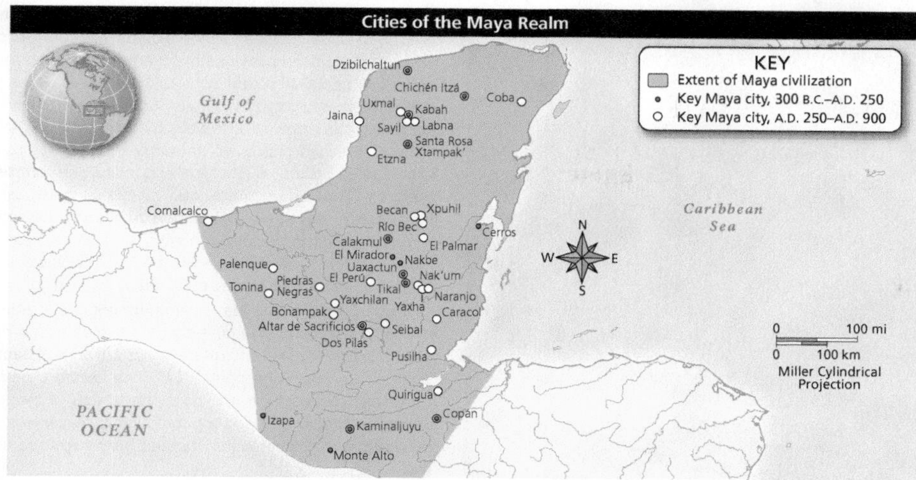

>> **Analyze Maps** Maya cities were centered around temples used for ceremonial purposes and for observations of the stars, from which the Maya calculated mathematics and astronomy. Where were most of the later cities established?

The Maya

Scholars have long thought that among the peoples the Olmec influenced were the Maya. New evidence suggests that the Maya may have developed ceremonial centers about the same time as the Olmec. By 300 B.C., the Maya were building large cities, such as El Mirador in Guatemala. By about A.D. 250, the Maya golden age—known as the Classic Period—began, with city-states flourishing from the Yucatán Peninsula in southern Mexico through much of Central America.

Farming Methods Before the Maya developed large population centers, like those later constructed by the Inca and Aztecs, they lived scattered across the land. They developed two farming methods that allowed them to thrive in the tropical environment. In many areas, farmers burned down forests and then cleared the land in order to plant on it. After a few years, the fields were no longer fertile. The Maya would then abandon these lands until they could be used once again.

In the meantime, farmers would burn and clear new lands for farming. In addition, along the banks of rivers, Maya farmers built raised fields to lift crops up above the annual floodwaters. These methods allowed the Maya to produce enough maize and other crops to support rapidly growing cities.

City-States Ruled Over the People The Maya cities that developed before and during the Classic Period never formed an empire. Instead, individual and powerful city-states evolved. The smaller city-states ruled over the people living directly within and near their borders. The largest ones reigned over neighboring areas as well—often requiring nearby cities to show allegiance to their kings and to participate in their ritual activities. Over the course of hundreds of years, many different city-states held power, with warfare and trade a constant theme of life among them. Cities such as Palenque, Copán, and Piedras Negras all carried great influence in their time, but the largest and most supreme power resided in the rulers of Tikal and Calakmul.

While the Maya were not united politically as later Aztec and Inca civilizations came to be, city-states maintained regular contact through a system of economic exchange, which generated much wealth. Traders carried valuable cargoes long distances by sea and along roads made of packed earth. Trade goods included items of daily use—such as honey, salt, and cotton—and nonessential but prized items such as feathers, jade, and jaguar pelts. These goods might have been used in ceremonies or to show status.

The Maya

The Maya began as an agricultural people. Over time they developed into an urban culture, with powerful city-states vying for dominance. These city-states never coalesced into an empire. They did, however, interact through a network of trade.

Guided Reading and Discussion

Ask students to name some of the largest Maya city-states and explain the relationship of city-states with one another. *(Possible answer: City-states included Palenque, Copàn, Piedras Negras, Tikal, and Calakmul. The largest city-states reigned over neighboring ones. They engaged in warfare with one another as well as extensive trade.)*

English Language Proficiency Standards

Learning Strategies 1.G.2 Read "The Maya" aloud and have students complete one of the following activities.

Beginning Use examples of formal and informal English about the Maya to explain the features of each type of writing. Give students another example and guide them in determining whether the writing is formal or informal.

Intermediate Follow instructions in the Beginning activity, but have students point out the features of each type of writing. Read an additional example aloud and ask them to identify formal and informal features.

Advanced Have small groups use classroom resources to locate examples of formal and informal writing about the Maya. Offer groups support in making the distinction between the two types of language. Have each group share an example of each type of writing with the class.

Advanced High Follow instructions in the Advanced activity, but have students work in pairs.

Answers

Analyze Maps *farther inland*

Topic 4 Lesson 1

Maya Cultural Life

The Maya are known for their impressive cities built of stone and decorated with stone sculpture. Central to the cities were temples, which sat at the top of pyramid-shaped stone platforms. There Maya priests performed rites and sacrifices. The priests were students of astronomy and mathematics. They invented a counting system based on three symbols: a dot to represent one, a bar for five, and a shell for zero. With these three symbols, they could keep track of events. The Maya were one of the only early civilizations to understand the concept of zero. The Maya also developed a hieroglyphic writing system. Scribes wrote on stone monuments and also on bark paper about important events, the study of astronomy, and their polytheistic religion.

Online Project the **Interactive Gallery: The Religious Life of the Maya** and click through the images with students.

ACTIVE CLASSROOM

Pair activity in which students have a short period (typically 30 seconds) to share what they know by writing with symbols or drawings. Use a document camera to scan drawings to add to the class blog.

Key Terms

Ask students to find the key term **stela** (in bold) in the text. Explain that this type of standing stone monument was used in ancient Greece and elsewhere, usually as a grave marker, but other cultures besides the Maya carved words and images on stelae to memorialize past events and rulers.

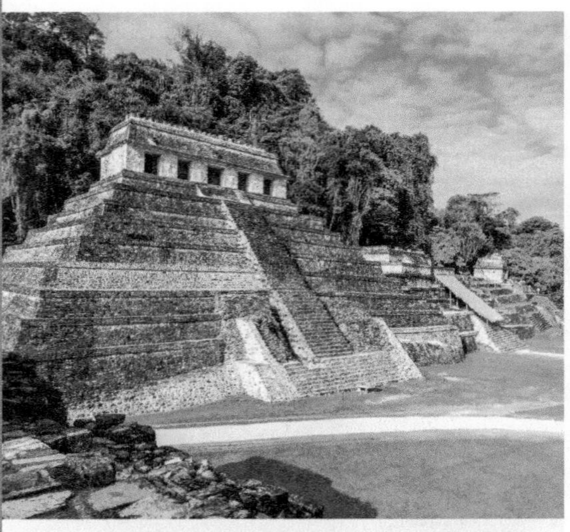

>> Maya temples were built in the shape of pyramids using hand-cut limestone blocks. The interior usually consisted of a few narrow rooms, indicating that they were intended for ceremonial purposes rather than for the public.

Interactive Gallery

>> Maya artifacts reflect their lifestyle and culture. Maya rulers and other nobles commissioned art such as this carved ceremonial mask.

Social Hierarchy Each Maya city had its own ruler, who was usually male. Maya records and carvings show that women occasionally governed on their own or in the name of young sons. Nobles served many functions in support of the ruler. Some were military leaders, while some collected taxes and enforced laws. Others managed public works, similar to the way the Olmec used collective labor for monument and temple building. Scribes, painters, and sculptors were also very highly respected. Merchants may have formed a middle class in society, though the wealthiest and most powerful merchants were certainly nobles, as they had been in the Olmec civilization.

The majority of the Maya were farmers. They grew maize, beans, and squash—the basic food crops of Mesoamerica—as well as fruit trees, cotton, and brilliant tropical flowers. To support the cities, farmers paid taxes on food and worked on construction projects. Some cities also included a population of slaves, who generally were commoners who had been captured in war.

EXPLAIN How did the Maya operate politically without a centralized government?

Maya Cultural Life

The cultural life of the Maya included impressive advances in learning and the arts. In addition, the Maya developed a complex polytheistic religion, perhaps inherited from the Olmec, that influenced their cultural life as well as their spiritual beliefs. Many Maya today maintain elements of the traditional religion established by the ancient Maya, such as the belief that each person's spirit is associated with a particular animal.

A Legacy in Stone The cities of the Maya are known today for their towering temples and palaces built from stone. Temples rested on pyramid-shaped platforms, reflective of the Olmecs' first pyramid, that were often quite large. Atop the temples, priests performed rites and sacrifices, while the people watched from the plazas below. Some temples also served as burial places for rulers, nobles, and priests. Palaces may have been used as royal residences as well as locations for meetings, courts, and other governmental activities. The multi-use aspect of royal residences is reminiscent of the Olmec ceremonial centers.

The Maya placed elaborately carved sculpture on many of their buildings. They also sculpted tall stone monuments, as did the Olmec, each of which is called a **stela** (STEE luh). These carvings preserve striking images of nobles, warriors in plumed headdresses, and

Answers

Explain *Individual city-states, each with its own ruler, held power. The city-states were not united politically, they maintained contact through economic exchange.*

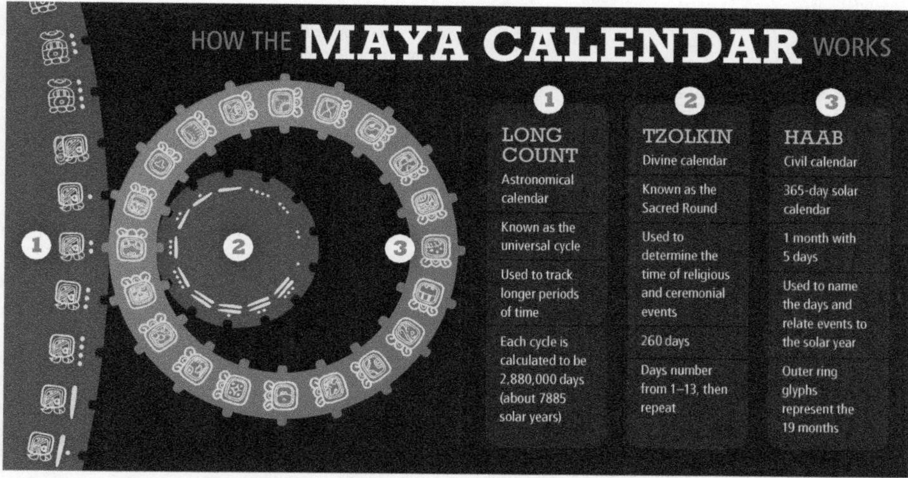

HOW THE MAYA CALENDAR WORKS
1
LONG COUNT
Astronomical calendar
Known as the universal cycle
Used to track longer periods of time
Each cycle is calculated to be 2,880,000 days (about 7885 solar years)
2
TZOLKIN
Divine calendar
Known as the Sacred Round
Used to determine the time of religious and ceremonial events
260 days
Days number from 1–13, then repeat
3
HAAB
Civil calendar
365-day solar calendar
1 month with 5 days
Used to name the days and relate events to the solar year
Outer ring glyphs represent the 19 months

>> **Analyze Information** The Maya calendar consists of three linked calendars. Which calendar is closest to the one we use today?

powerful rulers. They also represent the Maya gods, including the creator god Itzamna (et SAHM nah), the rain god Chac (chakh), and the sun god K'inich Ajaw (keen EECH ah HOW).

Scribes Record History The Maya also developed a hieroglyphic writing system, which scholars did not decipher until recent decades. Maya scribes carved inscriptions on stelae that include names of rulers, mentions of neighboring city-states, and dates and descriptions of events. They also wrote about astronomy, rituals, and other religious matters in books made of bark paper. Spanish conquerors later burned most of these books, considering any works that were written by non-Christians to be unacceptable. Three books, however, were taken to Europe and have survived into the present.

Astronomy and Mathematics Maya texts reveal that priests were dedicated students of astronomy and astrology, the study of the stars and planets that assumes heavenly bodies influence human affairs. Advances in astronomy were closely linked to mathematics. Maya priests needed to measure time accurately in order to produce an accurate calendar. They developed a 365-day solar calendar as well as a 260-day religious calendar, recording the correct timing for important ceremonies.

Maya priests also invented a counting system based on three symbols: a dot to represent one, a bar for five, and a shell for zero. With these three symbols, they could keep track of events. Even peasants could use this simple form of arithmetic for trade. The Maya were one of the only early civilizations to understand the concept of zero. Along with counting, the Maya developed other, more sophisticated concepts in mathematics.

Maya Civilization Declines About A.D. 900, the Maya abandoned many of their cities. In the Yucatán Peninsula, cities flourished for a few more centuries, but there, too, the Maya eventually stopped building them. By the time the Spanish arrived in the 1500s, the Maya mostly lived in farming villages. Archaeologists do not know for sure why Maya civilization declined, although theories abound. For example, frequent warfare may have taken its toll on society, or overpopulation could have led to over-farming and exhaustion of the soil.

Throughout the region, however, the remoteness of their jungle and mountain locations allowed many Maya to survive the encounter with the Spanish. Today, more than two million Maya people live in Guatemala and southern Mexico.

? EXPLAIN What made it important for Maya mathematicians and astronomers to work in unison?

Guided Reading and Discussion

Ask students to describe the role of stone in Maya culture. *(Answers will vary and may include: The Maya temple pyramids, palaces, walls, and residences were made of stone that remained for thousands of years. The Maya decorated their stonework with carving. They also made ceremonial masks of stone and carved colossal heads out of stone. Scribes preserved important events and information on tall stone stelae.)*

Summarize Ask students to explain the decline of the Maya civilization. *(Answers will vary. Students should note that in 900 B.C., the Maya began to disappear from their cities. Archaeologists do not have a solid explanation for this, but they do have theories. For example, warfare may have taken its toll on society, or the Maya may have exhausted their environment.)*

Answers

Analyze Information *the Haab, a 365-day solar calendar*

Explain *Life in Maya ancient times centered around religion. It became important for priests to hold religious ceremonies at accurate times. They collaborated with and became mathematicians and astronomers so that they could create a calendar system.*

The Aztec

The Aztec empire, in the Valley of Mexico, was centered on the city of Tenochtitlán, whose magnificent temples and royal palaces greatly impressed visitors. The city, located on an island in the middle of a swampy lake, grew steadily. The Aztecs supported their rising population by farming on chinampas, artificial islands built up in the shallow lake. The Aztecs were fierce warriors who gained control of a huge swath of Mexico through conquest and alliances. A single ruler led them, supported by nobles, priests, and military leaders. Religion played a large role in Aztec life. The Aztecs worshiped many gods, and priests regularly carried out rituals, including human sacrifice.

Online Project the **Interactive 3-D Model: Aztec Temple** and explore its architecture with students. Explain to students that they are looking at a cross-section of an Aztec temple. Tell students that rituals, and sometimes sacrifices, took place there. Architecturally, the temples were pyramid in shape and had stairs ascending from the foundation to the top. They had more than one worship area. Carvings found often included serpents.

ACTIVE CLASSROOM

After completing the activity, ask students to break into groups to answer the following question: How did the structure of the Maya and Aztec temples differ? Have students write as much as they can for one minute then switch with the person on their right. The next person tries to improve or elaborate the response where the other person left off. Continue to switch until the paper comes back to the first person. The group then decides which is the best response and shares that with the entire class.

The Aztec

Sometime shortly after about A.D. 1200, bands of nomadic people from the north migrated into the **Valley of Mexico,** which lies in the high plateau of central Mexico. These people identified themselves as separate tribes, such as the Mexica (may SHEE kah), from whom Mexico gets its name. All the tribes spoke one language—Nahuatl (NAH hwaht el)—and believed their origins began in the same legendary birthplace, Aztlan. Together, these tribes are known as the Aztecs.

Empire Building In A.D. 1325, the Aztecs founded their capital city, **Tenochtitlán** (teh nawch tee TLAHN). According to Aztec legend, the gods had told the Aztecs to search for an eagle holding a snake in its beak and perching atop a cactus. When they saw this sign, they would know where to build their capital.

Indeed, they finally saw the sign on a swampy island in Lake Texcoco (tesh KOH koh), and there they built their city. Today, Mexico City sits atop this same site.

As their population grew, the Aztecs found ingenious ways to create more farmland in their lake environment, just as the Maya had modified their environment by farming raised beds in the river valley. The Aztec built **chinampas,** artificial islands made of mud piled atop reed mats that were anchored to the shallow lake-bed with willow trees. On these "floating gardens," the Aztecs raised maize, squash, and beans, the same crops grown by their predecessors the Maya. They gradually filled in parts of the lake and created canals for transportation. Wide stone causeways linked Tenochtitlán to the mainland.

The Empire Expands In the 1400s, the Aztecs greatly expanded their territory. Through a combination of fierce conquests and shrewd alliances, they spread their rule across most of Mexico, from the Gulf of Mexico in the east to the Pacific Ocean in the west. By 1517, the Aztec empire numbered an estimated 5 to 6 million people.

Government and Society War brought immense wealth as well as power to the Aztec empire. **Tribute,** or payment from conquered peoples, helped the Aztecs turn their capital into a magnificent city. From its temples and royal palaces to its zoos and floating gardens, Tenochtitlán seemed a city of wonders. It was also the center of a complex, well-ordered empire.

Unlike the Maya city-states, each of which had its own king, the Aztec empire had a single ruler. However, like the Maya, the Aztecs had a clear social hierarchy. A council of nobles, priests, and military leaders elected the emperor, whose primary function was to lead in war. Below him, nobles served as officials, judges, and governors of conquered provinces. Next came the

Aztec Hierarchy

ELITE		
EMPEROR	COUNCIL OF NOBLES	PRIESTS/PRIESTESSES
elected by council of nobles, priests and military leaders; function was to lead war	officials, judges, governors of conquered provinces; owned/received land	peformed rituals to please the gods and prevent droughts and other disasters

COMMONER	
WARRIORS	MERCHANTS
military; could become nobles depending on victories in battle	Long-distance, not local, traveling traders; could become nobles depending on trades Artisans
PEASANT FARMERS	SERFS/SLAVES
could not own land	prisoners of war/debtors; slaves could own land and buy their freedom

>> **Analyze Information** In Aztec society, birth determined social status. Rank was visible in Aztec clothing. Nobles dressed in fine textiles, often cotton, and sandals. Where could a woman have influence in Aztec society?

Answers

Analyze Information *as a priestess, part of the elite*

warriors, who could rise to noble status by performing well on the battlefield. The priests were a class apart. They performed rituals to please the gods and prevent droughts or other disasters.

The Aztec had a powerful middle class, which included long-distance traders, who ferried goods across the empire and beyond. With goods from the highlands such as weapons, tools, and rope, they bartered for tropical products such as jaguar skins and cocoa beans.

The majority of people were commoners who farmed the land. At the bottom of society were serfs and slaves, who were mostly prisoners of war or debtors. Despite their low status, slaves' rights were clearly established by law. For example, slaves could own land and buy their freedom.

Religion and Mythology Like the Olmec and the Maya before them, the Aztecs believed in many gods. They revered Huitzilopochtli (weets ee loh POHCH tlee) as the patron god of their people. His temple towered above central Tenochtitlán.

The Aztecs also worshipped Quetzalcoatl (ket sahl koh AHT el), which was akin to the Olmec snake god and the Maya god Kukulcan, the feathered serpent who reigned over earth and water. The Aztecs also worshiped the other powerful gods of an earlier culture that had been centered at the city of Teotihuacán (tay oh tee wah KAHN.)

Teotihuacán had dominated life in the Valley of Mexico from about A.D. 200 to A.D. 750. The city was well planned, with wide roads, massive temples, and large apartment buildings to house its population of perhaps 200,000. Along the main avenue, the enormous Pyramid of the Sun and the Pyramid of the Moon rose majestically toward the sky.

Citizens of Teotihuacán worshiped gods such as Quetzalcoatl and Tlaloc (TLAH lohk), the rain god. After Teotihuacán fell, possibly to invaders, its culture survived and greatly influenced later peoples of Mesoamerica. The Aztecs, for example, believed that the gods had created the world multiple times. In their mythology, it was in Teotihuacán that the gods created the world in which the Aztecs lived.

In Aztec mythology, the gods frequently sacrificed themselves for the good of the people. They believed a god named Nanahuatzin (nah nah WAHTS een) had sacrificed himself to become the sun. To give the sun strength to rise each day, the Aztecs offered human sacrifices. Most of the victims were prisoners of war, who were plentiful because the Aztecs carried on almost continuous warfare.

>> Tenochtitlán was one of the largest cities in the world at the height of the Aztec empire, with some 200,000 inhabitants in the early 1500s. The city was laid out on a grid with intricately engineered canals, streets, and causeways.

>> An Aztec temple, like the one shown in this illustration, was the place priests went to pray and make ritualistic sacrifice. Unlike Maya temples, Aztec temples have stairs on only one side.

Interactive 3-D Model

Topic 4 Lesson 1

Guided Reading and Discussion

Ask students to explain the role of warfare in the Aztec empire. *(Warfare brought power and wealth, through tribute, to the Aztec. It also provided prisoners of war who could be sacrificed in religious rituals.)*

Draw Inferences Have students review the text about the Olmec and how they contributed to the later Maya and Aztec civilizations. Ask students to point out what the influences were for each civilization. *(Answers will vary but should reflect the knowledge that the Olmec are considered leaders among the Mesoamerican cultures. The Olmec traded long-distance. They had elaborate ceremonial centers and worshiped many gods. They were great engineers, creating early aqueducts.)*

SYNTHESIZE

Online Project the **Digital Activity: The Rise of Mesoamerican Civilizations**. Ask students to recall the five questions that they created at the beginning of the class. Tell students they have five minutes to answer the questions. Then ask them to pair with a partner and share their responses.

Tell the pairs to collaborate on an answer for this question: How were the early Maya and Aztecs able to carry their history with them over the centuries it took for them to settle in Mesoamerica? *(Answers may vary but should include that they consistently practiced the traditions, rituals, and religions of their ancestors.)*

DEMONSTRATE

Online Assign the **Digital Lesson Quiz** for this lesson if you haven't already done so. Students will be offered automatic remediation or enrichment based on their score.

Pose these questions to the class on the Discussion Board:

In "The Aztec," you read about how the Aztec empire expanded by conquest. Their immense wealth was used to build an infrastructure, including networks of streets and canals and elaborate cities with a worship center in the middle. As the empire expanded, the Aztecs incorporated some of the customs of the conquered peoples into their culture.

Recognize Cause and Effect Why might peoples conquered by the Aztecs become discontented? *(Possible answer: Many of the people conquered by the Aztec might have disliked the harsh demands of Aztec rule, for example, the demand for tribute and the use of prisoners of war as sacrificial.)*

Summarize What role did mathematics play in the life of the Maya and the Aztec? *(The Maya used mathematics to develop a method to hold their ceremonies at the appropriate times, and they created a numbering system. The Aztec used mathematics in their engineering to develop a massive city laid out on a grid, and temples that lasted centuries.)*

Topic Inquiry

Have students continue their investigations for the Topic Inquiry.

Answers

Summarize *The Aztec created floating gardens for growing crops, canals for transportation, wide-stone causeways, massive apartments to house their people, and enormous temples.*

>> Spanish explorers and invaders found the Aztec empire at the height of its size and power in the early 1500s. The Aztecs initially believed the Spanish to be descendants of the god Quetzalcoatl.

Keepers of Knowledge Priests were the keepers of Aztec knowledge. They recorded laws and historical events in the Aztec hieroglyphic writing system. Some priests ran schools. Others used their knowledge of astronomy and mathematics to foretell the future. The Aztecs, like the Maya, developed a 260-day ritual calendar and a 365-day solar calendar.

Like many other ancient peoples, the Aztecs believed that illness was a punishment from the gods. Still, Aztec priests used herbs and other medicines to treat fevers and wounds. Aztec physicians could set broken bones and treat dental cavities. They also prescribed steam baths as cures for various ills, a therapy still in use today.

Discontent Grows The Aztecs developed a sophisticated and complex culture. But among many of the peoples they conquered, discontent festered and rebellion often flared up. At the height of Aztec power, word reached Tenochtitlán that pale-skinned, bearded men had landed on the east coast. When these armies from Spain arrived, the Spanish found ready allies among peoples who were ruled by the Aztec empire.

SUMMARIZE How was the Aztec skill at engineering demonstrated in Mesoamerica after about 1300?

ASSESSMENT

1. **Compare Points of View** What are two possible theories about how people first settled the Americas?
2. **Identify Supporting Details** What evidence supports the idea that the Olmec developed an advanced civilization that was capable of organizing large pools of labor for important projects?
3. **Summarize** What methods of recording of history were used by the Maya and the Aztec?
4. **Contrast** What is the main difference between the Aztec and Maya regarding the governing of their societies?
5. **Identify Patterns** How did the Olmec influence the Maya and the Aztecs?

Assessment

1. One theory is that humans crossed a land bridge that existed in what is now the Bering Strait about 10,000 B.C. and then their descendants gradually migrated throughout the Americas by following herds of animals as they hunted. The other theory is that humans spread throughout the Americas more quickly by taking coastal routes.
2. The Olmec built large monuments and temples, and they transported huge blocks of stone to be carved into massive sculptures.
3. Both the Maya and the Aztecs developed hieroglyphic writing systems. Both also carved important records and images in stone. The Maya record reflects carvings of gods, warriors, and nobles, and their dress, names, dates, events, and neighboring city-states. The Aztec record was more advanced and included additional information about laws, and details that the priests taught in schools.
4. The Maya were not unified politically. Individual city-states each had a king who ruled that city-state. Some city-states were more powerful than others. In contrast, the Aztec built an empire that unified the Aztec people under a single ruler.
5. The Olmec built the first Mesoamerican pyramids, a form that both the Maya and the Aztecs later used. Olmec gods influenced Maya and Aztec gods; for example, the Olmec snake god is seen in the Maya god Kukulcan and the Aztec Quetzalcoatl. Evidence of the rubber ball games developed by the Olmec was found at Maya sites.

4.2 The first cultures of South America developed in the Andean region along the western edge of the continent. This region includes a variety of climates and terrains. The narrow coastal plain is a dry, lifeless desert crossed by occasional rivers. Further inland, the snow-capped Andes Mountains rise steeply, leveling off into high plateaus that bake by day and freeze at night. East of the Andes, dense jungles stretch from Peru into Brazil.

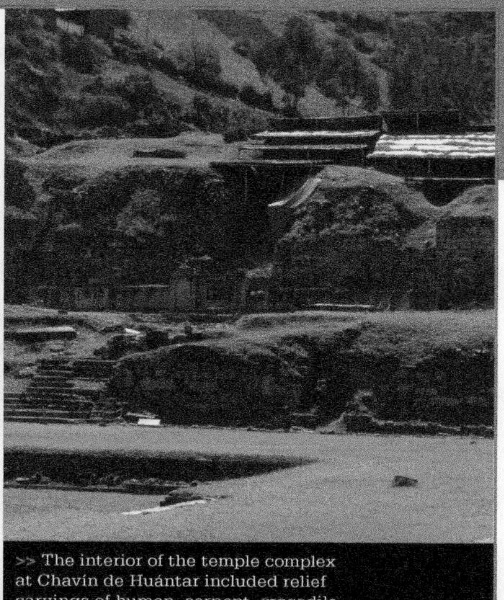

>> The interior of the temple complex at Chavín de Huántar included relief carvings of human, serpent, crocodile, feline, and bird images. Scholars believe that Chavín religious beliefs unified the surrounding region.

The World of the Incas

TEKS 6.A, 27.B

>> Objectives

Examine the early cultures of the Andes.

Understand how Inca emperors extended and maintained their empire.

Describe the major developments of Inca civilization.

>> Key Terms

Chavín
Moche
adobe
Nazca
Huari
Tiahuanaco
Pachacuti Inca Yupanqui
Sapa Inca
Cuzco
quipu
ayllu
Inti

Cultures of the Andes

Thousands of years ago, people settled in fishing villages along the desert coast of Peru and Chile. Gradually they expanded inland, farming the river valleys that run up into the highland plateaus. Using careful irrigation, they grew maize, cotton, squash, and beans. On mountain slopes, they cultivated potatoes, eventually producing 700 varieties. On high plateaus, they domesticated the llama and the alpaca. Eventually, they built large ceremonial centers and developed skills in pottery and weaving.

The Chavín Archaeologists have pieced together a chronology of various cultures that left their mark on the Andean region over the course of 2,000 years. The earliest of these was the **Chavín** (chah VEEN) culture, named for ruins at Chavín de Huantar (chah VEEN day WAHN tahr). There, in about 900 B.C., people built a huge temple complex. Archaeologists are not sure of the Chavín political structure, but they think the culture's religion unified people throughout northern and central Peru. Chavín arts and religion continued to influence later peoples of Peru as well.

www.PearsonTexas.com Access your Digital Lesson.

Topic 4 Lesson 2

The World of the Incas

CONNECT

Preview Have students preview the **Lesson Objectives** and the list of **Key Terms**.

Students can also preview all the **Key Terms** and **Academic Vocabulary** using the **Interactive Reading Notepad** on the digital course or preview a summary of the lesson in the **Reading and Note Taking Study Guide**.

Online Use the **Editable Presentation** found on the digital course to present the main ideas for this lesson.

Start Up Activity

Tell students that in the 1500s a Spanish explorer was amazed by the Inca road system, which ran through the valleys and high mountains of the Andes. He noted how clean the road was kept, and he admired the "lodgings, storehouses, Sun temples, and posts along the route."

Discuss What conclusions might a Spanish explorer in the 1500s have drawn regarding Inca competency in mathematics and engineering? *(Answers will vary but may include that he would be amazed at the sophistication of the architecture and the organizational and mathematical skills needed to govern the Inca empire.)*

Online You can also project the **Start Up Activity** from the course.

INVESTIGATE

Have students read the lesson using the **Reading and Note Taking Study Guide** to help them take notes and understand the text as they read.

Cultures of the Andes

Explain that the spread of civilization throughout the Andes was gradual. The earliest major civilization in the region was the Chavín, of northern and central Peru. The Moche settled along the northern coast of Peru. The Moche used canals to irrigate farmland, and their artisans produced fine textiles and ceramics.

Aa Vocabulary Builder

1. Have students pronounce the following academic vocabulary term in this lesson and clarify the part of speech.
2. Explain what the word means in common "student-friendly" language using synonyms and antonyms when possible. Provide concrete examples to clarify the meaning, and rephrase the definition.

network: a widely distributed group of things that work together as a unit or system

Topic 4 Lesson 2

Online Project the **Interactive Map: Civilizations of the Andes** and click through the screens with students.

ACTIVE CLASSROOM

Ask: How did the cultures of the Andes use the resources in their geographical region? Have students pair up and write their responses on sticky notes and then post them on the board or on chart paper. Lead a discussion on similarities and differences in the individual responses. *(Sample responses: Those near the ocean fished; those in river valleys used fresh water to irrigate crops; those in mountain regions grew potatoes and domesticated llamas and alpaca.)*

Guided Reading and Discussion

Ask: What contributions did the Chavín, Moche, and Nazca peoples make to Andean civilizations 2,000 years ago? Invite students to list one entry for each culture and then discuss their answers. *(Answers may include Chavín: temple complex or uniting peoples of northern and central Peru; Moche: adobe structures, roads, irrigation canals, or ceramics, textiles and gold work; Nazca: animal geoglyphs.)*

Key Terms

Ask students to find the key term **adobe** (in bold) in the text. Explain that this mixture of water, clay or mud, plant fibers such as straw, and often sand is especially good for warm climates because it absorbs heat during the day and releases it into the building at night.

The Moche Between A.D. 100 and A.D. 700, the **Moche** (MOH chay) people—named after their most famous city—forged a culture along the arid north coast of Peru. Skilled Moche farmers developed methods for fertilizing the soil and used canals to irrigate the land. Their leaders built roads and organized networks of relay runners to carry messages, ideas that a later Andean civilization, the Inca, would adopt.

At the city of Moche, builders constructed the largest adobe structure in the ancient Americas. **Adobe** is a mixture of clay and plant fibers that becomes hard as it dries in the sun. Moche artisans perfected skills in textile production, goldworking, and woodcarving and produced ceramic vessels in lifelike imitation of people and animals.

Nazca, Huari, and Tiahuanaco Many other Andean cultures emerged, and some left behind intriguing clues about their lives and beliefs. Between about 200 B.C. and A.D. 600 along the southern coast of Peru, the **Nazca** (NAHS kah) people etched geoglyphs in the desert. A geoglyph is a figure or line made on Earth's surface by clearing away rocks and soil.

The Nazca geoglyphs include straight lines that run for miles as well as giant birds, whales, and other animals. Most researchers think that the geoglyphs carried some sort of spiritual meaning.

The city of **Huari** (WAH ree) developed east of the Nazca culture. It controlled much of Peru's mountain and coastal areas. At the same time, a powerful city, **Tiahuanaco** (tee ah wah NAH koh), developed on the southern shores of Lake Titicaca, in modern-day Bolivia. It reigned over parts of modern-day Argentina, Chile, and Peru. Many of the same artistic styles appear at Huari and Tiahuanaco, leading scholars to think that these two southern powers shared religious or trade affiliations.

? IDENTIFY PATTERNS In what ways did the Chavín and the Moche influence later Andean cultures?

>> Pachacuti Sapa Inca was a master strategist who expanded the Inca empire by taking over enemy territory both by force and through peaceful negotiation.

Interactive Map

The Powerful Inca Empire

The most powerful of the Andean civilizations—the Inca civilization—came into being in the 1100s with the founding of its first dynasty. For the next three centuries, the Inca civilization stood out no more than any other. But in 1438, an historic change occurred. **Pachacuti Inca Yupanqui** (pahch ah KOO tee ING kuh yoo PANG kee), a skilled warrior and leader, proclaimed himself **Sapa Inca,** or emperor.

From his small kingdom at Cuzco in a high mountain valley, Pachacuti set out on a campaign of conquest. Once he subdued neighboring peoples, he enlisted them in his armies. His son, emperor Topa Inca Yupanqui, continued the expansion. With **Cuzco** as its capital, the resulting empire stretched more than 2,500 miles along the Andes, from Ecuador in the north to Chile in the south.

Inca Government The Sapa Inca held absolute power. Claiming to be divine, the son of the sun itself, he was also the empire's religious leader. Gold, considered the "sweat of the sun," served as his symbol. His queen, the Coya, carried out important religious duties and sometimes governed in his absence.

The Sapa Inca laid claim over all the land, herds, mines, and people of his empire. As the Inca people had no personal property, there was little demand for items for barter or sale, and trade played a much smaller role in the Inca economy than it had in the earlier Maya economy. Periodically, the Sapa Inca would call upon men of a certain age to serve as laborers for short periods, perhaps a few months. By so doing, he could access millions of laborers at once.

Inca rulers ran an efficient government. Nobles ruled the provinces along with local chieftains whom the Inca armies had conquered. Below them, officials

D Differentiate Extra Support While projecting the **Interactive Map: Civilizations of the Andes**, point out the region where each civilization resided. Ask students to list the civilizations named in the key that reside in the coastal regions, rivers valleys, plateaus and mountains. *(coastal and river valley regions: Moche, Nazca; plateaus: Chavín; mountains: Huari; Tiahuanaco)*

Answers

Identify Patterns *The arts and religion of the Chavín influenced later peoples of Peru. The Moche built roads and organized networks of relay runners to carry messages, ideas that the Inca would later adopt.*

English Language Proficiency Standards

Listening 2.E.3 Read "The Powerful Inca Empire" aloud. Then have students complete one activity according to their level of English proficiency.

Beginning Provide bilingual dictionaries. Write and display unfamiliar words from the selection, and then demonstrate how to look up the listed words. Write, display, and read their meanings. Have students copy the words and definitions in their notebooks and draw an illustration to help them remember the meaning of each word. Ask students to listen with the word meanings in mind as you reread the selection.

Intermediate Follow the instructions in the Beginning activity, but have students point out unfamiliar words as you read.

Advanced Provide dictionaries. Put students into groups and have one read aloud while the others write down unfamiliar words. Instruct each group to write the words and definitions in their notebooks and then reread the text and refer to their definitions to enhance their understanding of the text.

carried out the day-to-day business of enforcing laws and organizing labor.

Specially trained officials kept records on a **quipu,** a collection of colored strings that were knotted in different ways to represent various numbers. Scholars think that the Inca, who never invented a writing system, may have used quipus to record economic, bureaucratic, religious, and other information. The Inca then took the quipa and used it with the yupanas, a system of stone grids representing various mathematical values, to make complex calculations.

Uniting the Empire with Language and Roads To unite their empire, the Inca imposed their language, Quechua (KECH wuh) and their religion on the people they conquered. The Inca also created one of history's great road networks. At its greatest extent, it wound about 14,000 miles through mountains and deserts, passing through an area inhabited by almost 10 million people. Hundreds of bridges spanned rivers and deep gorges. Steps were cut into steep slopes and tunnels dug through hillsides. The expanse of the Inca road system was unmatched in the early Americas.

The roads allowed armies and news to move rapidly throughout the empire. At stations set regular distances apart, runners waited to carry messages.

Relays of runners could carry news of a revolt swiftly from a distant province to the capital. Inca soldiers stood guard at outposts throughout the empire. Within days of an uprising, they would be on the move to crush the rebels. Ordinary people were restricted from using the roads at all.

Cuzco as Capital All roads led through Cuzco. People from all the culture groups ruled by the empire lived in the city. Members of a given group lived in a particular part of the city and wore the traditional clothing and practiced the traditional crafts of their region of origin. In the heart of the city stood the great Temple of the Sun, its interior walls lined with gold. Like Inca palaces and forts—and like the temples and other buildings of the Maya and the Aztec—the temple was made of enormous stone blocks, each polished and carved to fit exactly in place without mortar used to secure it. Inca engineers were so precise that many of their buildings have survived severe earthquakes.

 **SYNTHESIZE** How did the Sapa Inca consolidate his power and keep control of his large empire?

>> Machu Picchu, built at the height of the Inca empire, is a complex located almost 8,000 feet above sea level. It is composed of some 220 structures that were used for agricultural, ceremonial, and astronomical purposes.

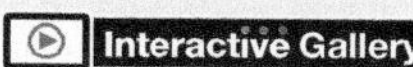
Interactive Gallery

Inca Life

The Inca strictly regulated the lives of millions of people within their empire. The leaders of each Inca village, called an **ayllu**(EYE loo), carried out government orders. They assigned jobs to each family and organized the community to work the land. Government officials arranged marriages to ensure that men and women were settled at a certain age.

Terraced Farming Inca farmers expanded step terraces built by earlier Andean peoples. They carved out flat strips of land on steep hillsides and built stone walls to hold the land in place. The terraces the Inca created kept rains from washing away the soil and made farming possible in places where naturally flat land was scarce.

Farmers spent part of each year working land for their community, and part working land for the emperor and the temples. The government allotted part of each harvest to specific groups of people or for particular purposes. It stored the rest in case of disasters such as famine.

Masters of Metalwork and Weaving The Inca were some of the most skilled metalworkers in the Americas.

The Powerful Inca Empire

In the 1400s, the Inca empire was born when the ruler of a small kingdom at Cuzco named Pachacuti set out on a campaign of conquest. Ultimately, this Andean empire stretched from Ecuador to Chile, more than 2,500 miles. Conquered peoples were required to speak the Inca language and accept the Inca religion which, along with an efficient road system, helped unify the empire.

Guided Reading and Discussion

Ask: How do we know the Inca used mathematics and were exacting engineers? *(Artifacts reveal the use of quipus and a system of stone grids to make complex calculations. Inca-built structures have survived earthquakes and lasted for centuries.)*

Inca Life

The Inca used their high altitude cities and towns to make astronomy an important part of their society, including not only religious rites, but also as a way to plan the harvesting of crops. The Inca were also masters of metalwork and skilled textile weavers.

Advanced High Follow the instructions in the Advanced activity, but have pairs of students work together.

Answers

Synthesize *The Sapa Inca held absolute power. He imposed the language and religion of the Inca on all parts of the empire. He owned all land, herds, mines, and people, so it would have been nearly impossible for any rivals to acquire the means to challenge him. The road system helped link the empire. Messengers quickly carried news of revolts, and armies could travel swiftly to put down any uprisings.*

Topic 4 Lesson 2

Online Project the **Interactive Gallery: Inca Culture** and click through the images with students.

ACTIVE CLASSROOM

Have students review what they have learned. Each student should design and post a piece of "wallpaper" that encapsulates their key learnings. Students then take a gallery/"wisdom" walk and note what others have written/illustrated. Students can jot down ideas as they occur. A video can be made of the wisdom walk and posted on YouTube.

Guided Reading and Discussion

Ask students to name features that characterized the bureaucratic nature of Inca civilization. *(Possible response: The Inca strictly regulated the lives of the people; government officials at the local and empire level made sure communities were organized to do what needed to be done; farmers, metalworkers, and weavers all contributed their skills and products.)*

D Differentiate Challenge/Gifted
The Inca offered incentives to those conquered. Have students research these incentives to create an advertisement convincing people to join the Inca empire. Advertisements should mention incentives and combine persuasive writing with maps or illustrations.

Answers

Analyze Information *Sample response: the worship of many gods*

Analyze Information *Tocricoq*

They learned to work and alloy, or blend, copper, tin, bronze, silver, and gold. While they employed copper and bronze for useful objects, they reserved precious metals for statues of gods and goddesses, eating utensils for the nobles, and decoration.

The Inca also mastered the art of weaving, a practice passed down to them from earlier Andean peoples. They raised cotton and sheared the wool from llamas and alpacas to create colorful textiles to be worn as clothing or as adornments, such as belts and bags.

Medical Practices The Inca developed important medical practices, including surgery on the human skull. In such operations, they cleaned the area to be operated on and then gave the patient a drug to make him or her unconscious—procedures similar to the modern use of antiseptics and anesthesia.

This is not dissimilar from the Aztec, whose doctors set bones and prepared prescriptions to cure illnesses. The Inca also used medical procedures to mummify the dead.

Religion and Ritual The Inca worshipped many gods linked to the forces of nature. People offered food, clothing, and drink to the guardian spirits of the home and the village. Each month had its own festival, from the great ripening and the dance of the young maize to the festival of the water. Festivals were celebrated with ceremonies, sports, and games.

A powerful class of priests served the gods. Chief among the gods was **Inti,**the sun god. His special attendants, the "Chosen Women," were selected from each region of the empire. During years of training, they studied the mysteries of the religion, learned to prepare ritual food and drink, and made the elaborate wool garments worn by the Sapa Inca and the Coya. After their training, most Chosen Women continued to serve Inti. Others joined the Inca's court or married nobles.

Comparing Three Civilizations The three major civilizations of the Americas differed in location, origins, and early history. Their customs, languages, and traditions differed, too. Still, like civilizations elsewhere, the Maya, Aztecs, and Inca shared key features: well-organized governments, complex religions, job specialization, social classes, architecture and arts, and public works. Of the three, only the Inca did not have a system of writing, although their quipu are thought to have preserved records. All built on the achievements of earlier peoples in their regions, but each created its own style in the arts, legends, and view of the world.

Characteristics of Inca Life

CHARACTERISTIC	DESCRIPTION
Farming	• Built terraced fields • Grew corn, potatoes, beans, squash, peanuts, avocados, cotton, coca (fought hunger, thirst, pain), rare orchids (for medicine)
Domesticated Animals	• Alpaca (for wool) • Llamas (carried goods)
Crafts	• Metal work (gold, silver, bronze): eating utensils for nobles, decoration • Weaving: colorful wool, cotton textiles with gold and feathers woven in • Goldwork: ornaments such as jewelry and objects for religious ceremonies • Pottery: coiled technique and used for everyday use and decoration
Counting/Record-keeping	• Quipu: a system of strings and tied knots
Medical practices	• Surgery • Early antiseptics/anesthesia • Mummification
Religion	• Worshipped many gods, most importantly sun god; • Females were attendants to gods
Made Clothing	• Two-piece loose tunics without sleeves slipped over the head • Cloaks as outer garments fastened at neck with pin • Caps for men, only; women pulled cloaks over head

>> **Analyze Information** Inca society was sophisticated, and much of daily life was structured and strictly regulated by government officials. How was their religion similar to many other cultures?

History Background

Quipus and Messages Inca quipus were complex and varied. They were constructed from a long rope with 48 smaller ropes attached and many even smaller ropes attached to the 48. Knots were placed in different locations on the ropes to represent 1, 10, or 100. Quipus were colored differently to represent different government interests, such as the labor tax, crop yields, or population information.

The Inca also used quipus to send messages. It is believed that they sent these messages with *chasquis*, or messengers. Chasquis served 15-day shifts, during which they lived in small roadside huts. Each runner had to know his section of road well enough to run it barefoot on a starless night. A message was relayed from one runner to the other, often moving at a rate of about 200 miles a day.

Inca Hierarchy

>> **Analyze Information** The highly structured Inca society allowed the government to regulate the lives of the millions of people who lived within the empire. Who had a higher position in Inca society, Tocricoq or Hatun Runa?

Within these broad features of civilizations, the Maya, Aztec, and Inca developed different political and economic patterns. While the Maya ruled city-states, the Aztecs and Inca built large empires. Although all three were polytheistic, each had its own gods, goddesses, and religious rituals. The Maya and Aztec developed their own form of the popular ball game that originated with the Olmec.

Each of these three civilizations adapted to its particular environment—like civilizations in Africa and Asia. The Maya built raised beds along flood-prone rivers. The Aztecs created chinampas in their swampy lake bed, and the Inca constructed terraced fields on steep mountainsides. All three depended on farming, but the Inca developed some different crops and were less involved in trade than the two Mesoamerican civilizations.

A Breakdown of Power At its height, the Inca civilization was a center of learning and political power. But in 1525, the emperor Huayna Capac (WY nuh kah PAHK) died suddenly of illness. Civil war broke out over which of his sons would reign next, weakening the empire at a crucial moment—the eve of the arrival of Spanish invaders.

CONNECT How did the Inca use and improve upon skills they learned from earlier peoples?

ASSESSMENT

1. **Solve Problems** How were the Moche able to farm along the arid north coast of Peru?
2. **Cite Evidence** Why do scholars think that the cities of Huari and Tiahuanaco were affiliated by either trade or religion?
3. **Explain** What features and policies of the Inca government helped the emperor control his empire?
4. **Identify Supporting Details** What were the major medical advances developed by the Inca?
5. **Identify** In what crafts and technical achievements did the Inca excel?

SYNTHESIZE

Online Project the **Digital Activity: Three Great American Civilizations**. Ask students to think about how the Inca, Maya, and Aztec compared. Students can complete the activity independently, in pairs, or in groups. (If necessary, review how to complete a Venn diagram.)

DEMONSTRATE

Online Assign the **Digital Lesson Quiz** for this lesson if you haven't already done so. Students will be offered automatic remediation or enrichment based on their score.

Pose these questions to the class on the Discussion Board:

Explain What medical contributions did the Inca offer society and how did this compare with the medicine of the Aztecs? *(Answers will vary but may include that the Inca performed operations, cleaned the area prior to surgery, gave anesthesia, and mummified bodies. Similarly, the Aztecs set bones and prescribed medications for healing.)*

Draw Conclusions What were some benefits of the Inca road system? *(The Inca road system zigzagged across mountains, went through tunnels and across bridges throughout the expanse of the empire. Armies and runners carrying information were able to get to their destinations more easily and with reasonable speed on prepared surfaces.)*

Topic Inquiry

Have students continue their investigations for the Topic Inquiry.

Answers

Connect *Inca farmers expanded step terraces built by earlier Andean peoples. They carved out flat strips of land on steep hillsides and built stone walls to hold the land in place. The Inca also mastered the art of weaving, a practice passed down to them from earlier Andean peoples. They raised cotton and sheared the wool from llamas and alpacas to create colorful textiles to be worn as clothing or as adornments, such as belts and bags.*

Assessment

1. Skilled Moche farmers developed methods for fertilizing the soil and used canals to irrigate the land.
2. Many of the same artistic styles appear at Huari and Tiahuanaco, leading scholars to think that these two southern powers shared religious or trade affiliations.
3. Inca Nobles ruled the provinces along with conquered local chieftains. Officials carried out the day-to-day business of enforcing laws and organizing labor. Records were kept on a quipu, a collection of colored knotted strings that represented various numbers. News of revolts were carried quickly along the extensive road system, and armies could travel swiftly to put down any uprisings.
4. The Inca developed important medical practices, including surgery on the human skull. In such operations, they cleaned the area to be operated on and made the patient unconscious with a drug—procedures similar to the modern use of antiseptics and anesthesia.
5. The Inca were some of the most skilled metalworkers in the Americas. They worked and alloyed copper, tin, bronze, silver, and gold. They also mastered weaving. Their engineers were so skilled at fitting stone blocks together that Inca structures have survived severe earthquakes.

Topic 4 Lesson 3

The Peoples of North America

CONNECT

Preview Have students preview the **Lesson Objectives** and the list of **Key Terms**.

Students can also preview all the **Key Terms** and **Academic Vocabulary** using the **Interactive Reading Notepad** on the digital course or preview a summary of the lesson in the **Reading and Note Taking Study Guide**.

Online Use the **Editable Presentation** found on the digital course to present the main ideas for this lesson.

Start Up Activity

Have students answer this question as they get settled: Why would a people choose to build their homes in the side of a cliff? *(Possible answer: to protect themselves from invaders)*

Discuss Did it make sense for the Ancestral Puebloans to build their homes in the river valley cliffs? *(Yes. This strategy did help protect them from raiders.)* Tell students that in this lesson they will learn about the Ancestral Puebloans and other early Native Americans that settled across North America.

Online You can also project the **Start Up Activity** from the course.

INVESTIGATE

Have students read the lesson using the **Reading and Note Taking Study Guide** to help them take notes and understand the text as they read.

Cultures Develop in the Desert Southwest

Explain that Native Americans migrated across North America and settled in different geographical locations. Many of them farmed the land. To survive, these cultures had to learn to adapt to the climates of and the resources available in their new regions. To farm in the desert, the Hohokam built a complex irrigation system that included numerous canals. The Ancestral Puebloans, or Anasazi, cut stone blocks to build their cliff dwellings.

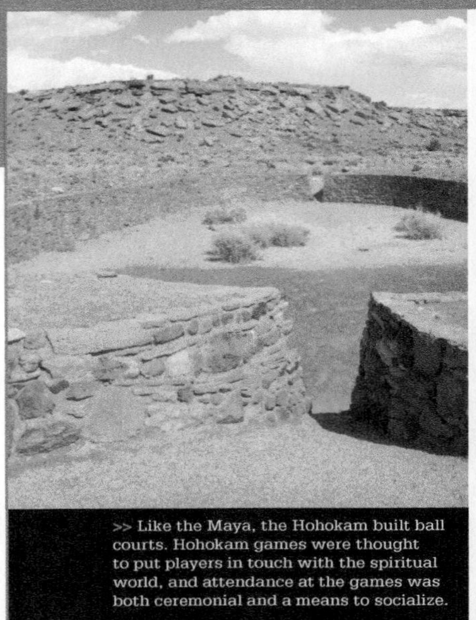

>> Like the Maya, the Hohokam built ball courts. Hohokam games were thought to put players in touch with the spiritual world, and attendance at the games was both ceremonial and a means to socialize.

Interactive Flipped Video

4.3 Hundreds of Native American cultural groups lived in North America before A.D. 1500 and the arrival of Europeans. Based on the environments in which people lived, scholars have categorized them into ten culture areas: Arctic, Subarctic, Northwest Coast, California, Great Basin, Plateau, Southwest, Plains, Southeast, and Northeast. In each area, people adapted to geographic conditions that influenced their ways of life.

TEKS
1.A, 16.A, 26.B

>> Objectives

Understand how groups of people adapted to the desert environment of the Southwest.

Analyze the evidence from which we have learned about the emergence of culture in eastern North America.

Examine the cultures that developed in three very different geographic regions.

>> Key Terms

Mesa Verde
pueblo
Pueblo Bonito
kiva
earthwork
Cahokia
potlatch
Iroquois League

The Peoples of North America

Cultures Develop in the Desert Southwest

For millennia, Native American groups lived by hunting, fishing, and gathering wild plants. After farming spread north from Mesoamerica, many people raised corn and other food crops. Some people farmed so successfully that they built large permanent settlements. Some of the earliest farming cultures arose in what is today the southwestern United States.

The Hohokam, Pima, and Papago Perhaps as long ago as 300 B.C., fields of corn, beans, and squash bloomed in the desert of present-day Arizona, near the Salt and Gila rivers. These fields were planted by a people later called the Hohokam, or "Vanished Ones," by their descendants, the Pima and the Papago. To farm in the desert, the Hohokam built a complex irrigation system that included numerous canals. The canals carried river water to fields as far as several miles away. The Hohokam also built temple mounds and ball courts similar in appearance to those of Mesoamerica. Evidence indicates that, for unknown reasons, the Hohokam left their settlements sometime during the A.D. 1400s.

www.PearsonTexas.com Access your Digital Lesson.

Aa Vocabulary Builder

1. Have students pronounce the following academic vocabulary term in this lesson and clarify the part of speech.
2. Explain what the word means in common "student-friendly" language using synonyms and antonyms when possible. Provide concrete examples to clarify the meaning, and rephrase the definition.

complex: a whole composed of various interrelated parts

The Ancestral Puebloans About A.D. 100, Ancestral Puebloans lived in what is today the Four Corners region of Arizona, New Mexico, Colorado, and Utah. Within a few hundred years, they were building villages, some inside caves and some outside.

Between A.D. 1150 and A.D. 1300, the Ancestral Puebloans (also known as Anasazi) built their famous cliff residences. Using hand-cut stone blocks, they constructed housing complexes on cliffs along canyon walls. Such cliffs offered protection from raiders. The largest of these cliff dwellings, at **Mesa Verde** (MAY suh VEHR dee) in present-day Colorado, included more than 200 rooms. People climbed ladders to reach their fields on the flatlands above or the canyon floor below.

The Ancestral Puebloans also built freestanding villages, which were similar in structure to the cliff dwellings. These communities, which the Spanish later called **pueblos** (PWEB lohs), were made of multi-floor houses that were connected to one another by doorways and ladders.

Remains of **Pueblo Bonito,** the largest such pueblo, still stands in New Mexico. The huge complex consisted of 800 rooms that could have housed about 3,000 people. Builders used stone and adobe bricks to erect a crescent-shaped compound rising five stories high. In the center of the great complex lay a plaza. There, the Ancestral Puebloans dug their **kiva** (KEE vuh), a large underground chamber used for religious ceremonies and political meetings. In the kiva, they carved out a small hole in the floor, which represented the birthplace of the tribe. They also painted the walls with geometric designs and scenes of ritual or daily life.

In the late 1200s, a long drought forced the Ancestral Puebloans to abandon their dwellings. Attacks by Navajos and Apaches—peoples from the north—may have contributed further to their decline. However, Ancestral Puebloan traditions survived among several groups of descendants. Known collectively as Pueblo Indians, many of these groups continue to live in the southwestern United States today.

INFER What does the nature of the Ancestral Puebloans' buildings tell you about the people who built them?

Cultures Develop in the East

Far to the east of the Ancestral Puebloans, in the Mississippi and Ohio river valleys, other farming cultures emerged after about 1000 B.C. They, too, left behind impressive constructions from which we can learn a great deal about their lives.

Native American Culture Areas

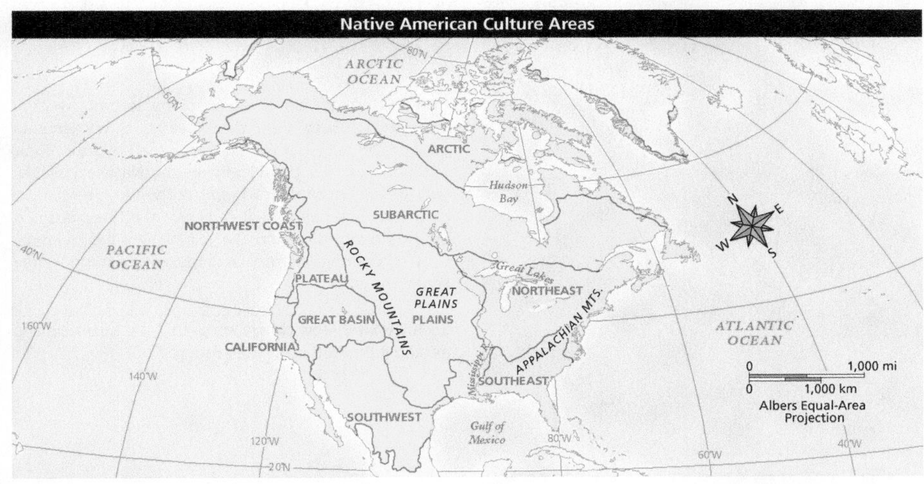

>> **Analyze Maps** Native Americans developed a wide variety of cultures. In each culture area, people shared fairly similar environments and ways of life. Which culture area was the farthest south?

Interactive Map

Topic 4 Lesson 3

Online Project the **Interactive Map: Native American Architecture** and click through the hotspots with students.

ACTIVE CLASSROOM

Put this question on the whiteboard: How did geography favor and frustrate the development of Native American settlements in North America? Ask students to spend three minutes writing their response to the question on sticky notes. Have students pair up and share their responses. Ask students to post their sticky notes on the board or on chart paper and then look at all the various responses. Finally, lead a class discussion on the similarities and differences in the individual responses. *(Possible answers: Native Americans of the Northwest lived in an environment of forest and ocean. Their access to these resources allowed them to flourish. The Inuit of the Arctic region lived in an extreme climate but were able to use the ocean and animals to support themselves. The Desert Southwest Native Americans were able to develop agricultural crops using river valley waters, but drought was a continual concern. Some cultures created cliff dwellings to protect themselves from raiders.)*

Guided Reading and Discussion

What is significant about our present-day knowledge that the Hohokam grew corn, beans, and squash as long ago as 300 B.C.? *(Possible answers: Irrigation agriculture was an organized event, perhaps calling for leadership or government; these specific crops were used to sustain a civilization; we can date the cultivation of these vegetables to around 300 B.C.)*

D Differentiate Extra Support While projecting the **Interactive Map: Native American Architecture**, ask students to select three regions from the map and list one resource or human-made artifact needed for the creation of a successful settlement. *(Possible answers: Arctic cultures needed structures to protect them from cold. Desert cultures needed water to grow crops. Northeast cultures needed tools to clear land for settlements.)*

Answers

Analyze Maps *Southwest*

Infer *Their complexes had hundreds of rooms, indicating their communities were quite large. They were organized, and built cliff dwellings, which protected them from enemies above and below. The communities built on the ground were multi-level and used stone and adobe, resources available in the area where they lived. They had the knowledge to make adobe. The paintings on the walls demonstrate an ability to communicate what they saw.*

Topic 4 Lesson 3

Cultures Develop in the East

Farming cultures that arose in the Ohio and Mississippi river valleys are known for their earthworks, which served as burial mounds, platforms for structures, and defensive walls. Early mound builders included the Adena and the Hopewell. Later mound builders included the Mississippians, known for their center at Cahokia, and the Natchez, known for their worship of the sun.

Guided Reading and Discussion Remind students that archaeologists believe the earthworks found at various sites in the Mississippi and Ohio river valleys were used as burial grounds, foundations, and walls. Ask students what those archaeologists might have based their conclusions on. *(Possible answer: They might have studied artifacts or the shape and size of the mounds.)*

Analyze Images

Direct attention to the photo of the Great Serpent Mound. Ask: Why do you think the Adena built this mound in the shape of a snake? *(Possible answer: Snakes may have had religious significance for this culture, as they did for cultures in Mesoamerica.)*

Key Terms

Explain that Cahokia was a center of Mississippian culture for centuries. The center of the city was surrounded by a stockade made of 20-foot-tall oak and hickory logs. Cahokia's population, at its peak, equaled or exceeded that of London at the time.

>> Cahokia was a large city with buildings constructed in rows, with a central plaza in the middle and agricultural land surrounding it. The reasons for Cahokia's decline are unknown, but theories have ranged from climate change to war or disease.

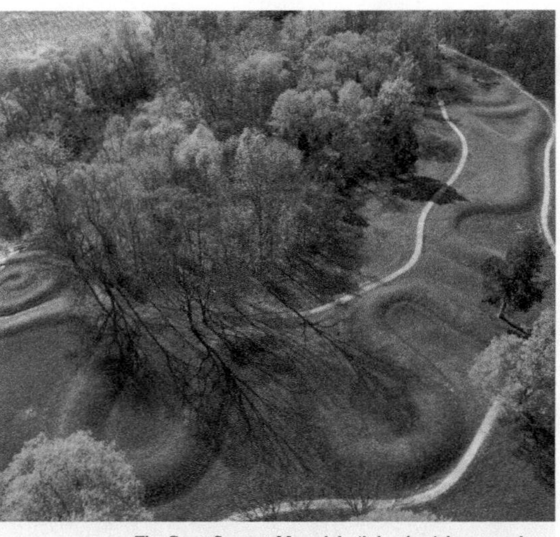

>> The Great Serpent Mound, built by the Adena people, is some 1300 feet long and ranges in width from three to twenty feet. Inside the mound, which is made of yellow clay, are hollow cave-like openings.

The Adena and Hopewell Both the Adena and the later Hopewell people of the Northeast are known for giant **earthworks** that they built for various purposes by heaping earth in piles and shaping them. Some of the earthworks were large burial mounds, others served as platforms for structures such as temples, and still others served as defensive walls. Mounds were usually cone-shaped, oval, or formed into the shape of an animal. The Adena's Great Serpent Mound in Ohio wriggles and twists in the shape of a snake for almost a quarter of a mile.

Some of the objects found in the Hopewell mounds show that traders extended their influence over a wide area. They acquired goods such as conch shells from the Gulf of Mexico, grizzly bear teeth and obsidian from the Rocky Mountains, and copper from the Great Lakes region. Skilled artisans then hammered and shaped the copper into fine ornaments.

The Mississippians By A.D. 800, these early eastern cultures had disappeared. A new people, whom today we refer to as the Mississippians, gained influence in the Southeast and Mississippi River valley regions. As their culture spread, the Mississippians built clusters of earthen mounds and ever larger towns and ceremonial centers.

The greatest Mississippian center, **Cahokia** in present-day Illinois housed as many as 20,000 people by about A.D. 1100. Cahokia boasted 120 mounds, atop some of which sat the homes of rulers and nobles. The largest mound probably had a temple on its summit, where priests and rulers offered prayers and sacrifices to the sun.

The Natchez The Mississippians left no written records. Artifacts from the remains of settlements such as Cahokia provide clues into their culture. Their traditions have survived among the Natchez people, who are known for their worship of the sun. They called their ruler, who held absolute power, the Great Sun. He and his family lived on the top of pyramid mounds. Society was divided into castes; the highest group was called the suns.

IDENTIFY How do we know that the Mississippians existed if they left no written record?

Answers

Identify *Many Mississippian settlements remain, and from these archaeologists can extrapolate information. Mississippian traditions were passed on to the Natchez people, and this legacy provides insight into their culture.*

>> The Inuit had to overcome the challenges of living in the harsh Arctic climate. They built kayaks with wood or whale bone, over which they stretched animal skins, and used harpoons and other weapons to hunt seals.

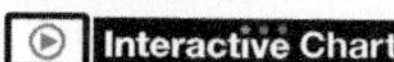

Distinct Cultures Develop in Different Geographic Regions

Distinct ways of life developed in each Native American culture area. Here, we examine three culture areas—the Arctic, the Northwest Coast, and the Eastern Woodlands—in which varied climates and natural environments helped unique cultures develop.

The Inuit In the far northern stretches of Canada, the Inuit (IN oo it; often called the Eskimo) adapted to the harsh climate of the Arctic. By about 2000 B.C., they had settled there, using the resources of the frozen land to survive. Small bands lived by hunting and fishing. Seals and other sea mammals provided them with food, skins for clothing, bones for needles and tools, and oil for cooking.

The Inuit paddled kayaks in open waters or used dog sleds to transport goods across the ice. In some areas, the Inuit constructed igloos, or dome-shaped homes made from snow and ice. In others, they built sod dwellings that were partly underground.

Cultures of the Northwest Coast The peoples of the Northwest Coast lived in an environment far richer in natural resources than the Inuit did. Rivers teemed with salmon, and the Pacific Ocean offered a supply of other fish and sea mammals. Hunters tracked deer, wolves, and bears in the forests. In this land of plenty, people built large permanent villages with homes made of wood. They traded their surplus goods, gaining wealth that was then shared in a ceremony called **potlatch.** At this ceremony, which is still practiced in Canada and the Northwest coast of the United States today, a person of high rank and wealth distributes lavish gifts to a large number of guests. By accepting the gifts, the guests acknowledge the host's high status.

The Iroquois On the other side of the continent, the Northeast was home to numerous Native American groups. Many of these spoke the Iroquois (IHR uh kwoy) language, shared similar traditions, and were known collectively as the Iroquois. Typically, the Iroquois cleared land and built villages in the forests. While women farmed, men hunted and frequently fought wars against rival groups.

According to Iroquois tradition, the prophet Dekanawidah (deh kan ah WEE dah) urged these rivals to stop their constant wars. In the late 1500s, he became one of the founders of the unique political system known as the **Iroquois League.** This was an alliance of five Iroquois groups—the Mohawk, Oneida, Onondaga, Cayuga, and Seneca—who were known as the Five Nations. The Iroquois League did not always succeed in keeping the peace. Still, it was the best-organized political group north of Mexico. Member nations governed their own villages, but met jointly in a council when they needed to address larger issues. Only men sat on the council, but each clan had a "clan mother" who could name or remove members of the council.

Distinct Cultures Develop in Different Geographic Regions

Explain to students that different regions of North America provided Native American cultures with life experiences that differed depending on what was naturally available in each locality. Varied climates and natural environments produced distinctly different cultures.

Online Project the **Interactive Chart: Native American Cultures** and match up names with regions along with students.

ACTIVE CLASSROOM

After completing the interactive activity, ask pairs of students the following questions: What did you discover? What does that make you think? What are you wondering about now that you've seen this? *(Sample responses: Some Native Americans survived by hunting salmon and hunting deer. These same activities were not available to the Ancestral Puebloans who lived in the desert. How the North American Native Americans survived was dependent on the resources available in their geographical region. For example, the Inuit built houses of ice and the Haida built homes of wood.)* After a few minutes of discussion, students should then share their insights with the class.

Guided Reading and Discussion What environmental advantages did the Native Americans of the Northwest have over some other North American groups? *(They lived in an environment of rivers, forests, and an ocean. Temperatures were mild, and it rained often. Their location allowed them to trade the animals they trapped and the fish they caught. Building materials were as near as the closest forest.)*

English Language Proficiency Standards

Listening 2.F.1 Have students watch (or listen to) the video clip about characteristics of Native American cultures in the Arctic, the Northwest Coast, and the Eastern Woodlands. Then have students complete one of these activities.

Beginning Have students make three sketches to show what they learned about each of the three culture groups.

Intermediate Follow the instructions in the Beginning ELPS activity. Have students write a one-sentence caption for each sketch.

Advanced Follow the instructions in the Beginning ELPS activity. Have students write a short paragraph to explain each sketch.

Advanced High After the video, have students write a paragraph describing what they learned about each of the three cultures. Then have them make three drawings to accompany their paragraphs. After they finish their work, have them share it with a partner.

Topic 4 Lesson 3

SYNTHESIZE

Online Project the **Digital Activity: Civilizations in the Americas**. Give students five minutes to explain how much geography affected the Native American groups discussed in these lessons. Then ask them to pair with a partner to share their responses.

DEMONSTRATE

Online Assign the **Digital Lesson Quiz** for this lesson if you haven't already done so. Students will be offered automatic remediation or enrichment based on their score.

Pose the following question to the class on the Discussion Board:

In "Peoples of North America," you learned about cultures that built settlements across North America and the Native Americans' resourcefulness in adapting to their geographical location.

Predict Consequences Consider what you have read about the civilizations of North America. What potential impact do you think the introduction of European explorers into North America would have on Native Americans? Explain your answer. *(The European explorers' interest in North America was largely for riches that would benefit their home country. They were well funded and had powerful weapons and armies. Initially, the Native Americans might help the explorers learn to live off the land and act as guides. Ultimately, the Europeans could disrupt the Native American way of life to a point of permanent change or destruction.)*

Topic Inquiry

Have students continue their investigations for the Topic Inquiry.

Answers

Summarize *They built igloo homes or homes made of sod, partially underground. The Inuit clothed themselves in heavy animal skins and also used them for blankets.*

The Iroquois League emerged at the same time that Europeans arrived in the Americas. Just as encounters with Europeans would topple the Aztec and Inca empires, so too would they take a fearful toll on the peoples of North America.

? SUMMARIZE How did the Inuit protect themselves from the harsh Arctic cold?

ASSESSMENT

1. **Draw Conclusions** How did the Ancestral Puebloans adapt their housing to the building materials that were available in the arid Southwest?
2. **Infer** What purposes did the earthwork mounds of the Adena and Hopewell serve? How can archaeologists know that?
3. **Summarize** How did the potlatch help the societies of the Northwest?
4. **Identify** What was the initial purpose of the Iroquois League in the Northeast?
5. **Support Ideas with Examples** How did climate and specific natural environments help the Native American peoples of the Arctic, the Northwest, and the Northeast develop distinct cultures?

Assessment

1. They built houses of stone blocks against canyon walls and built freestanding villages of stone and adobe brick. This was an adaptation to their desert environment.
2. Some were used for burial mounds; the presence of human remains would reveal that purpose. Others were used as building platforms; these may have had markings or debris that revealed what they were used for.
3. Peoples of the Northwest enjoyed bountiful fishing and hunting. They had forest lumber to build villages. They had surpluses to trade, and some people became quite wealthy. In the potlatch ceremony, wealth was redistributed across the tribes. Those who gave gifts were acknowledged as having high status, so the potlatch also reinforced social roles.
4. The purpose of the Iroquois League was to prevent war among tribes that of the Iroquois cultural group.
5. The Inuit lived in the frigid Arctic by fishing and hunting seals and bears. Their homes were of ice or sod. Those of the Northwest, which had bountiful resources, hunted, fished, and traded the surplus with others. Those in the Northeast cleared land and built wood villages in forests. They farmed and hunted.

1. **Compare Major Economic Developments** Compare the major economic developments of the Maya, Inca, and Aztec civilizations. Interpret graphs to demonstrate the relationship between geography and the historical development of a region. Interpret graphs to explain how geography has influenced people and events in the past. Write a paragraph explaining the role of geography and economic policies in the size of each civilization. Consider types of economic systems, trade, and wealth. How did economic policies contribute to the overall size of each civilization? **6.A, 15.A, 16.C**

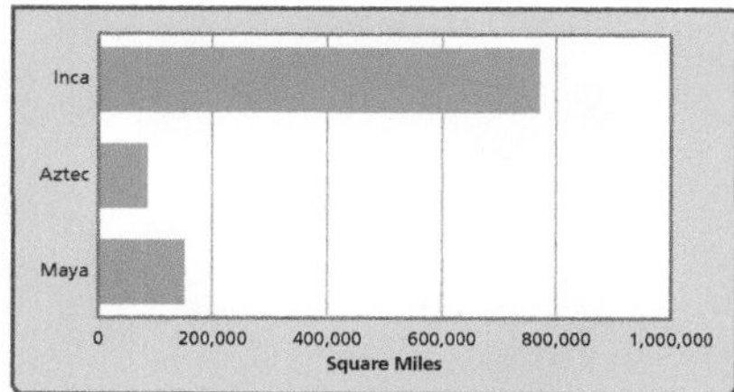

2. **Compare the Major Political Developments** Compare major political developments of the Maya, Inca, and Aztec civilizations. Write a paragraph to compare the major political developments of these three civilizations. Consider the types of leaders in each civilization, the role of nobles, and how each empire was unified. What similarities and differences existed in how the Maya, Inca, and Aztec civilizations were ruled? **6.A**

3. **Compare Social Developments** Interpret charts to explain how geography has influenced events in the past, and compare the major social developments of the Maya, Inca, and Aztec civilizations. Look at the chart above. Then, write a paragraph describing how the geography of ancient Mesoamerica and South America influenced the Maya, Inca, and Aztec people. Consider the size of each empire, what events caused each empire to decline, what role geography played in the decline of each empire, and why the Spanish soldiers played a role in one decline but not the others. **6.A, 16.C**

	MAYA	AZTEC	INCA
Governing structure	loosely organized city-states	rulers and nobles	divine ruler
Reason for the decline	abandoned cities	rebellion and the Spanish invasion	civil war

4. **Compare Major Cultural Developments** Compare the major economic and cultural developments of the Maya, Inca, and Aztec civilizations. Write a paragraph that compares the economic systems of the Maya, Inca, and Aztec civilizations. Consider how the Maya, Inca, and Aztec empires expanded, how the Maya, Inca, and Aztec citizens met basic needs, and how the Maya, Inca, and Aztec empires acquired wealth. **6.A**

5. **Compare Major Economic Developments and Create Graphs** Compare major economic developments of the Maya, Inca, and Aztec civilizations. Create graphs to demonstrate the relationship between geography and the historical development of a region. Read the passage below. Write a paragraph describing the major economic developments of the three civilizations that includes farming methods, trade, and taxes. Create a basic graph showing trends over time that represents the relationship between the geography of the Yucatán Peninsula and the economic development of the Maya civilization. **6.A, 15.A**

"The first Americans faced a variety of environments in which they could settle. For example, great mountain chains—the Rockies, the eastern and western Sierra Madre, and the Andes—dominate the western Americas.

In Mesoamerica, Neolithic people cultivated a range of crops, including beans, sweet potatoes, peppers, tomatoes, squash, and maize—the Native American name for corn. People in South America cultivated crops such as maize and cassava and domesticated llamas and other animals valued for their wool. By 3000 B.C. in parts of South America and 1500 B.C. in parts of Mesoamerica, farmers had settled in villages. Populations then expanded, and some villages eventually grew into the great early cities of the Americas."

6. **Summarize Major Ideas** Summarize the major ideas in mathematics that developed in Inca civilization. Write a paragraph that summarizes how the Inca use of the quipu demonstrated their understanding of major ideas in mathematics. Consider how the Inca recorded numbers, how the Inca advanced their scientific and astronomical knowledge, and how the Inca kept records with no written language. **27.B**

Answers to TEKS Assessment

1. Students' answers should clearly explain the following:

   The Maya allowed for each city-state to keep its own ruler while trading with each other. This would have created a large trade network.

   The Aztecs also used an extensive trade network and conquered other people to gain territory. Conquered people had to pay tributes to the Aztec leader, which helped increase the empire's wealth.

   The Inca gained all territory through conquest, not trade. While farmers and other laborers could not keep any of the goods or food that they produced, the emperor provided enough for everyone to eat. By ensuring that all of his people were fed, the emperor could rule vast territory.

2. Students' answers should clearly explain that nobles helped support the role of rulers by performing tasks, such as tax collecting, and observe that workers were organized to meet the needs of the whole group in all three civilizations. Students should also explain that the Aztecs and Inca both had powerful rulers and conquered other groups. Students should clearly explain how Maya city-states made the Maya different and explore the role of trade in each civilization. Students should explain how the Inca kept control over their empire and owned all of the wealth.

3. Students' answers will vary but should include information about what caused each empire to decline and the role geography played in each decline. Students should demonstrate understanding that the size of the empires contributed to their declines, and that the Aztec empire was most vulnerable to the Spanish because of its location.

4. Students' responses should clearly explain how the economic and cultural systems of the Maya, Inca, and Aztec empires differed, including the ways in which the needs of basic citizens were met. Students should demonstrate understanding that the Maya empire was based on trade and expanded due to trade, the Inca empire was based on dependence on the ruler who provided for the citizens' needs, and the Aztec empire was based on conquest and acquired wealth through tributes from conquered peoples.

5. Students' answers should clearly demonstrate that as farmers improved their techniques, crop production increased. Students should explain that techniques included burning down forests, clearing the land, and building raised fields to lift crops above floodwaters. Students should also explain that an increase in crops led to an increase in taxes collected and trade between city-states.

   Students' graphs should match this information. A bar graph, histogram, or line graph could be used to show changes over time.

6. Students' responses should clearly explain that quipu were colored, knotted strings used by the Inca to record numbers and transactions because they did not have a written language system. Students should demonstrate understanding that use of the quipu required advances in mathematics, such as a place-value system.

TEKS ASSESSMENT

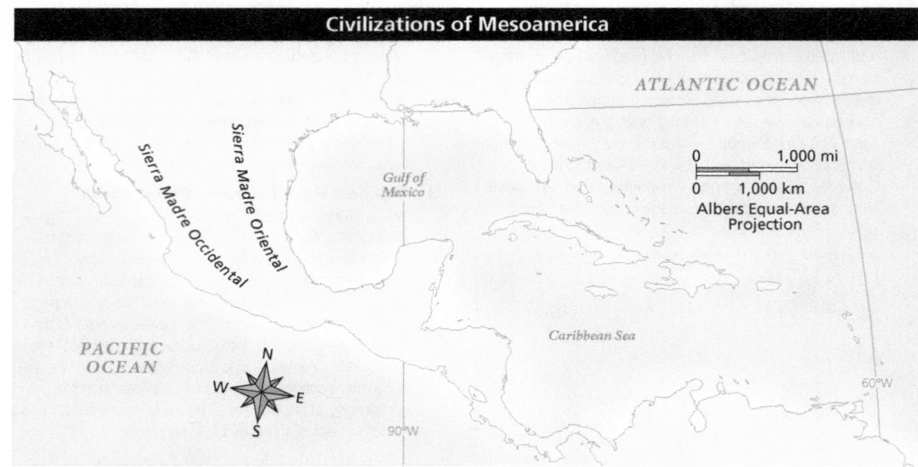

7. **Create and Interpret Thematic Maps** Create and interpret thematic maps to demonstrate the relationship between geography and the historical development of a region, and compare the major political developments of the Maya and Aztec civilizations. Review the above map. Use the information to help you create a map showing the location of each civilization by using shading and labels. Write a paragraph explaining how the leaders of each civilization helped unite their people and how each empire was able to grow and thrive. **6.A, 15.A**

8. **Summarize and Explain the Influence of Prior Civilizations on Maya Architectural Ideas** Summarize the major ideas in architectural engineering that developed in the Maya civilization, and explain how prior civilizations influenced the Maya's development. Write a paragraph discussing prior civilizations' influences on major ideas in architectural engineering that developed in the Maya civilization. Consider common forms in prior civilizations' architecture, types of buildings in Maya architecture, and how the Maya tried to increase the grandeur of some of their temples. How were the Olmec ideas about architecture apparent in examples of Maya architectural engineering? **6.A, 27.B**

9. **Summarize Major Ideas** Summarize the major ideas in mathematics that developed in Aztec civilization. Write a paragraph that summarizes major mathematical ideas that developed in Aztec civilization. Consider the types of calendars developed by priests, the cycles of celestial bodies measured, and the need for a workable system of value for trading. Give an example of how mathematical ideas were intertwined with Aztec culture. **27.B**

10. **Summarize Major Ideas** Summarize the major ideas in astronomy that developed in the Maya civilization. Write a paragraph that summarizes Maya astronomy. Consider the purpose of the Maya astronomers, the astronomical concepts that the Maya must have incorporated, and how their knowledge of astronomy was used. Using the excerpt below, how were Maya ideas about astronomy related to their culture? **27.B**

"The Maya calendar consists of three linked calendars, including an accurate 365-day solar calendar and a shorter calendar for religious and other rituals."

11. **Explain Previous Civilizations' Influence and Create Charts** Explain how previous civilizations influenced the Maya's development. Create charts to demonstrate the relationship between geography and the historical development of a region or nation. Write a paragraph and create a chart that illustrates how prior civilizations like the Olmecs influenced the Maya's development in art. Consider the use of the following in the prior cultures and in the Maya culture: materials, style, and subjects. **6.A, 15.A**

Answers to TEKS Assessment

7. Students' answers should clearly show each civilization shaded and labeled in the correct place on the map. Student answers should clearly explain that Maya rulers used trade to unify their civilization because each ruler controlled only his own city-state. Students should also explain that Aztec rulers conquered other lands and that the Aztecs formed alliances.

8. Students' responses should clearly summarize major ideas in architectural engineering that developed in the Maya civilization and explain how ideas from Olmec architectural engineering influenced Maya architectural engineering. Students should demonstrate understanding of common ideas from the two cultures, such as the pyramid in architectural engineering and knowledge of how these ideas were applied in Maya civilization.

9. Students' responses should clearly summarize the major mathematical ideas that developed in Aztec civilization, including the 260-day and 365-day calendars, advanced astronomical calculations, and the need for record keeping in the well-developed trading economy. Students should demonstrate understanding of how mathematical ideas were intertwined with Aztec culture, including the 260-day ritual calendar and the foretelling of the future based on astronomical calculations.

10. Students' responses should clearly explain how Maya astronomers used their knowledge to develop accurate calendars for both daily and religious purposes. Students should demonstrate understanding of major Maya ideas about astronomy, such as the relationship between passing time and the movements of the objects in the night sky.

11. Students' answers will vary but should compare the materials, styles, and subjects of art from both cultures and include the geographical connection, such as the availability of stone suitable for carving. Students' responses should include an applicable chart showing similar information. The chart should include rows or columns for both the Maya and the Olmec. Each row or column should be divided into several sections comparing the art of both cultures. The chart sections should include but are not limited to subjects (animals for the Olmec, people and gods for the Maya), materials (stone for both), and form of sculpture (tall stone monuments for both).

12. **Compare Social Developments** Interpret charts to demonstrate the relationship between geography and historical development and to explain how geography has influenced people in the past; compare the major social developments of the Maya, Inca, and Aztec civilizations. Look at the above chart. Write a paragraph that describes how the geography of each region influenced the farming practices of the Maya, Inca, and Aztec people. Consider the need for food for growing populations, the surrounding geography, the challenges it presented, and how the farmers creatively solved the problems the land presented. 6.A, 15.A, 16.C

	MAYA	AZTEC	INCA
Location	Central America	Mexico	Andes Mountains
Farming Technique	raised fields	floating gardens	terraced farming

13. **Interpret Thematic Maps and Compare Political Developments** Interpret thematic maps to explain how geography has influenced people and events in the past. Review the map below. Compare the major political developments of the Maya, Inca, and Aztec civilizations. Write a paragraph explaining how the Inca leader was able to unite such a large empire of diverse tribes. Consider the use of road, rulers of conquered territory, rules imposed on conquered tribes, and how conquered people were provided for. 6.A, 16.C

14. **Summarize Major Ideas and Analyze Examples** Summarize the major ideas in architecture that developed in the Aztec civilization, and analyze examples of how architecture reflects the history of the cultures in which it is produced. Write a paragraph that summarizes major architectural ideas in the Aztec civilization, and analyze an example of how the architecture reflects the history of its culture. Consider which architectural form was used by the Aztecs in their religious buildings, which culture originated that form, and how and why the Aztecs modified the form. 26.B, 27.B

15. **Explain and Analyze** Explain how prior civilizations influenced the Aztecs' development, and analyze information by developing connections between historical events over time. Write a paragraph showing how prior civilizations influenced the Aztecs and how historical events were connected with the formation of its culture. Consider historical events like inventions from the Olmec and the Maya, languages of prior civilizations, religious and historical beliefs of prior civilizations, and the Aztecs' method of expanding their empire. 6.A, 29.F

16. **Summarize Major Ideas and Analyze Cause-and-Effect Relationships** Summarize the major ideas in architectural engineering in the Inca civilization, and analyze information by identifying cause-and-effect relationships. Write a paragraph that describes major architectural ideas of the Incas, and tell how these ideas affected their buildings and subsequent cultures. Consider how Inca architecture was similar to and different from that of previous cultures, what architectural ideas can be traced to its culture, and how well their buildings have survived. 27.B, 29.F

"Like Inca palaces and forts—and like the temples and other buildings of the Maya and the Aztec—the temple was made of enormous stone blocks, each polished and carved to fit exactly in place without mortar used to secure it."

17. **Reflect on the Essential Question** **Write an essay on the Essential Question: How much does geography affect people's lives?** Use evidence from your study of this Topic to support your answer.

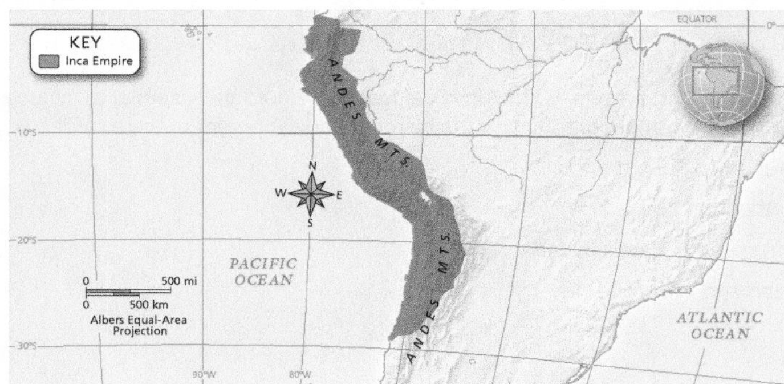

12. Students' answers will vary but should include the unique farming method (Maya raised beds, Aztec floating gardens, and Inca terraces) used by each group as well as an explanation of how this method was suited to the area's geographical features. Students should demonstrate understanding of the relationship between geography and social developments.

13. Students' answers should clearly explain that only armies and the emperor's messengers could use the roads, which helped them maintain order and obedience. Nobles who were loyal to the emperor ruled conquered territory along with a local chieftain. Students should also explain that the emperor forced all conquered people to adhere to the same religion and speak the same language and that the emperor provided for all of the needs of his people in exchange for labor.

14. Students' responses should clearly explain that the Aztecs borrowed the pyramid structure from the earlier Maya civilization and incorporated it into their temple design. Students should demonstrate an understanding that the Aztecs modified the original design by making it larger and grander and even built their pyramids on top of the pyramids built by their predecessors.

15. Students' responses should clearly explain the connection between prior civilizations, prior events, and the Aztec empire, including common language and beliefs, the development of agriculture, and the invention of writing. Students should demonstrate understanding that the growth of the Aztec empire had its foundation in previous historical events from earlier cultures and that it grew as it conquered other groups of people, some of whom had the same cultural background and roots.

16. Students' responses should clearly explain how Inca architecture, including precisely joined stones forming massive structures, is related to the long-term survival of their buildings. Students should demonstrate understanding of unique aspects of Inca architecture, such as construction of large and elaborate temples, use of massive building blocks with unmortared seams and joints, and precision in engineering.

Topic 4

Answers to TEKS Practice

1. A

2. H

Online To prepare for the End-of-Topic test, have students go online for additional Topic Review and Assessment questions or to review their notes in the **Interactive Reading Notepad** for the lessons in this Topic.

Benchmark Tests

Assign these benchmark tests as you complete the relevant topics to monitor student progress toward mastering the course content and as preparation for the End-of-Course Test.

Benchmark Test 1: Topics 1–5

Benchmark Test 2: Topics 6–10

Benchmark Test 3: Topics 11–15

Benchmark Test 4: Topics 16–21

TEKS PRACTICE

1 How did the major political developments of the Maya, Inca, and Aztec civilizations compare with one another?

A The Aztecs acquired new wealth and territory through war more frequently than the Maya and Inca.

B The Aztecs acquired new wealth and territory through trade with neighboring city-states, while the Inca and Maya were more warlike.

C The Inca acquired new wealth and territory through war more frequently than the Maya and Aztecs.

D The Inca acquired wealth and territory through trade with neighboring city-states, while the Maya and Aztecs were more warlike.

2

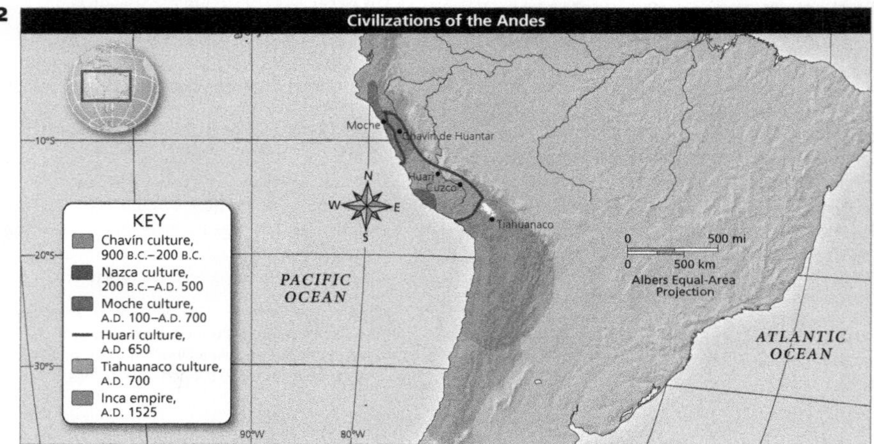

When creating a map of the Inca empire, which physical features would be essential to include to show the relationship between geography and the historical development of the empire?

F The Amazon River and Andes mountains

G The Pacific and Atlantic oceans

H The Andes mountains and Pacific Ocean

J The Atlantic Ocean and Amazon River

Test Taking Tips: Tip for Questions With Reading Passages

1. Read the question.
2. Read the title of the passage if it is provided.
3. Determine when the passage or quotation was written or spoken and by whom.
4. Carefully read the entire passage or quotation.
5. Read the question again to be sure you understand what is being asked. Identify details or ideas in the passage or quotation that you will use to answer the question.
6. Answer the question in your own words.
7. Read the answer choices and select the best answer.

www.PearsonTexas.com
Access additional practice questions

3 What three geographical features were significant in the historical development of the Inca empire?

A Amazon River, Andes Mountains, Coastal Desert
B Amazon Rainforest, Andes Mountains, Coastal Desert
C Amazon River, Andes Mountains, Prairie lands
D Amazon Rainforest, Andes Mountains, Prairie lands

4 Why would Chandragupta's ruling style influence the development of the Maurya civilization?
F He exercised military force to keep citizens honest.
G He ruled through a dictatorship to expand his territory.
H He executed a well thought-out plan to organize and rule the dynasty.
J He welcomed dissenting views to ensure personal freedoms of citizens.

If you have trouble with...				
Question	1	2	3	4
See Lesson	4.4	4.2	4.2	3.3
TEKS	6.A	27.B	27.B	1.B

3. B

4. H

Online Use the **Topic Synthesize** to help students revisit and reflect on the Essential Question for this Topic.

Topic Inquiry

If students have done a Topic Inquiry for this Topic, have them complete the final step of the Inquiry now.

Ancient Greece (1750 B.C.–133 B.C.)

TOPIC 5 ORGANIZER PACING: APPROX. 1 PERIOD, .5 BLOCKS	PACING	TEKS	ELPS
Connect	1 period		
MY STORY VIDEO **Pericles, The Golden Age of Athens**	10 min.		
DIGITAL ESSENTIAL QUESTION ACTIVITY **How Much Power Should the Government Have?**	10 min.	19.B, 21.B	
DIGITAL MAP ACTIVITY **Ancient Greece**	10 min.	16.A, 16.C	
TOPIC INQUIRY: CIVIC DISCUSSION **Athens or Sparta?**	20 min.		
Investigate	2–4 periods		
TOPIC INQUIRY: CIVIC DISCUSSION **Athens or Sparta?**	Ongoing		
LESSON 1 **Early Greece**	30–40 min.	3.A, 16.A, 26.B	2.F.2
LESSON 2 **The Greek City-States**	30–40 min.	1.B, 3.A, 16.A, 19.A, 19.B, 20.A, 21.B, 22.A, 22.B, 24.A, 25.B	2.B.1
LESSON 3 **Greek Thinkers, Artists, and Writers**	30–40 min.	1.B, 3.A, 25.B, 26.B, 26.C	2.C.1
LESSON 4 **Alexander the Great and the Legacy of Greece**	30–40 min.	1.B, 3.A, 20.A, 24.A, 26.B, 27.A, 27.E	2.C.2
Synthesize	1 period		
DIGITAL ESSENTIAL QUESTION ACTIVITY **Ancient Greece**	10 min.	19.B, 20.A, 21.B, 22.B, 25.B, 26.C, 27.A, 27.E	
TOPIC INQUIRY: CIVIC DISCUSSION **Athens or Sparta?**	20 min.		
Demonstrate	1–2 periods		
DIGITAL TOPIC TEST **Ancient Greece**	10 min.		
TOPIC INQUIRY: CIVIC DISCUSSION **Athens or Sparta?**	20 min.		

AUTHOR'S NOTE

Participatory Democracy in Athens

The history of Athens was in some ways similar to that of other Greek city-states. Its kings were replaced by a government of aristocratic councils early in the seventh century B.C.E. At the beginning of the sixth century the *archon* (magistrate) Solon—a member of the city's chief elected council—became Athens' most famous law-giver. The laws of Solon freed poor farmers from debt slavery and opened up public office to citizens of less than aristocratic birth. Later in the sixth century the tyrant Pisistratus destroyed the residual power of the old clan-based aristocracy and transferred land from the aristocrats to the landless farmers who supported him. Pisistratus also encouraged handicraft manufacture and foreign trade and began the vast program of temple building that Pericles would carry to a triumphant climax.

Paradoxically, it was the aristocratic Cleisthenes who, during the last decade of the sixth century, brought participatory democracy to Athens. Winning popular support in 508, Cleisthenes instituted a Council of Five Hundred, chosen by lot, which was given sweeping authority to guide foreign and domestic affairs, to control government finances, and to prepare the crucial agenda for assembly meetings. The assembly of citizens still elected archons, passed all new laws, voted on questions of peace and war. A citizen-jury system began to edge out the aristocratic Areopagus court in judicial power. *Demokratia*, the rule of the citizens, was from this time on—a dozen years before the onset of the Persian War—the basic political reality of Athens. . . .

These men of ancient Athens, with all their faults, had come as close to genuine self-government as any ancient people ever would. And they had found uses for their freedom that would seldom be matched, perhaps never exceeded.

—Anthony Esler, *The Human Venture: From Prehistory to the Present* (Upper Saddle River, New Jersey: Pearson Education, 2004), pp. 82–84

TOPIC INQUIRY: CIVIC DISCUSSION

Athens or Sparta?

TEKS 1.B, 3.A, 20.A, 21.B, 24.A, 25.B, 29.C, 29.D, 29.E, 29.F, 29.G, 29.H, 30.A, 30.C

In this Topic Inquiry, students work in teams to examine different perspectives on this issue by analyzing several sources, arguing both sides of a Yes/No question, then developing and discussing their own point of view on the question: Do you think it would have been better to live in Athens instead of Sparta?

STEP 1: CONNECT

Develop Questions and Plan the Investigation

Launch the Civic Discussion

Divide the class into groups of four students. Students can access the materials they'll need in the online course or you can distribute copies to each student. Read the main question and introduction with the students.

Have students complete Step 1 by reading the Discussion Launch and filling in Step 1 of the Information Organizer. The Discussion Launch provides YES and NO arguments on the main question. Students should extract and paraphrase the arguments from the reading in Step 1 of their Information Organizers.

Next, students share within their groups the arguments and evidence they found to support the YES and NO positions. The group needs to agree on the major YES and NO points and each student should note those points in their Information Organizer.

Resources

- Student Instructions
- Discussion Launch
- Information Organizer

PROFESSIONAL DEVELOPMENT

Civic Discussion

Be sure to view the Civic Discussion Professional Development resources in the online course.

STEP 2: INVESTIGATE

Apply Disciplinary Concepts and Tools

Examine Sources and Perspectives

Students will examine sources with the goal of extracting information and perspectives on the main question. They analyze each source and describe the author's perspective on the main question and key evidence the author provides to support that viewpoint in Information Organizer Step 2.

Ask students to keep in mind:

- **Author/Creator:** Who created the source? An individual? Group? Government agency?
- **Audience:** For whom was the source created?
- **Date/Place:** Is there any information that reveals where and when the source was created?
- **Purpose:** Why was the source created? Discuss with students the importance of this question in identifying bias.
- **Relevance:** How does the source support one argument or another?

Suggestion: Reading the source documents and filling in Step 2 of the Information Organizer could be assigned as homework.

Resources

- Student Instructions
- Source documents
- Information Organizer

STEP 3: SYNTHESIZE

Use Evidence to Formulate Conclusions

Formulate Compelling Arguments With Evidence

Now students will apply perspectives and evidence they extracted from the sources to think more deeply about the main question by first arguing one side of the issue, then the other. In this way students become more prepared to formulate an evidence-based conclusion on their own.

Within each student group, assign half of the students to take the position of YES on the main question and the others to take the position of NO. Students will work with their partners to identify the strongest arguments and evidence to support their assigned YES or NO position.

Present Yes/No Positions

Within each group, those assigned the YES position share arguments and evidence first. As the YES students speak, those assigned NO should listen carefully, take notes to fill in the rest of the Compelling Arguments Chart (Step 3 in Information Organizer), and ask clarifying questions.

When the YES side is finished, students assigned the NO position present while those assigned YES should listen, take notes, and ask clarifying questions. Examples of clarifying questions are:

- I think you just said [x]. Am I understanding you correctly?
- Can you tell me more about [x]?
- Can you repeat [x]? I am not sure I understand, yet.

Suggestion: You may want to set a 5-minute time limit for each side to present. Provide a two-minute warning so that students make their most compelling arguments within the time frame.

Switch Sides

The students will switch sides to argue the opposite point of view. To prepare to present the other position, partners who first argued YES will use the notes they took during the NO side's presentation, plus add any additional arguments and evidence from the reading and sources. The same goes for students who first argued the NO position.

STEP 4: DEMONSTRATE

Communicate Conclusions and Take Informed Action

Individual Points of View

Now the students will have the opportunity to discuss the main question from their own points of view. To help students prepare for this discussion, have them reflect on the YES/NO discussions they have participated in thus far and fill in Step 4 of their Information Organizers.

After all of the students have shared their points of view, each group should list points of agreement, filling the last portion of Step 4 on their Information Organizers.

Reflect on the Discussion

Ask students to reflect on the civic discussion, thinking about:

- The value of having to argue both the YES and NO positions.
- If their individual views changed over the course of the discussion and why.
- What they learned from participating in the discussion.

Resources

- Student Instructions
- Information Organizer

Early Greece

Objectives

Objective 1: Identify the influences on Minoan culture and how the civilization prospered.

Objective 2: Summarize how the Mycenaeans ruled the sea trade and started the Trojan War.

Objective 3: Describe the works of Homer and their influence on Greek culture.

LESSON 1 ORGANIZER		PACING: APPROX. 1 PERIOD, .5 BLOCKS				
			RESOURCES			
	OBJECTIVES	PACING	Print	Online	TEKS	ELPS
Connect						
DIGITAL START UP ACTIVITY **The Influence of Trade**		5 min.		●	1.B	
Investigate						
READ **Minoans Prosper From Trade**	Objective 1	10 min.	●	●	1.B, 16.A	
READ **Mycenaean Civilization**	Objective 2	10 min.	●	●	1.B, 26.B	
READ **Homer and the Great Greek Legends**	Objective 3	10 min.	●	●	25.B, 26.B	2.F.2
INTERACTIVE CHART **Values of Ancient Greek Culture**		10 min.		●	3.A, 25.B, 26.B	
Synthesize						
DIGITAL ACTIVITY **Icarus Flying High**		5 min.		●	1.B, 3.A, 25.B, 26.B	
Demonstrate						
DIGITAL QUIZ **Lesson Quiz and Class Discussion Board**		10 min.		●	1.B, 3.A, 25.B, 26.B	

PEARSON realize™ www.PearsonTexas.com Access your Digital Lesson

Focus on Texas Standards

Texas Essential Knowledge and Skills

3.A describe the major political, religious/philosophical, and cultural influences of Persia, India, China, Israel, Greece, and Rome, including the development of monotheism, Judaism, and Christianity

16.A locate places and regions of historical significance directly related to major eras and turning points in world history

26.B analyze examples of how art, architecture, literature, music, and drama reflect the history of the cultures in which they are produced

NOTES

The Greek City-States

Objectives

Objective 1: Understand how geography influenced the Greek city-states.

Objective 2: Explain how democracy and other forms of government developed in ancient Greece.

Objective 3: Describe the influence of ancient Greek concepts related to the rights and responsibilities of citizenship.

Objective 4: Identify the culture and values shared by Ancient Greeks.

Objective 5: Summarize how the Persian and Peloponnesian Wars affected Greece.

LESSON 2 ORGANIZER	PACING: APPROX. 1 PERIOD, .5 BLOCKS					
			RESOURCES			
	OBJECTIVES	PACING	Print	Online	TEKS	ELPS
Connect						
DIGITAL START UP ACTIVITY **By Mountains or the Sea**		5 min.		●	1.B, 16.A	
Investigate						
READ **Geography Shapes Greek City-States**	Objective 1	10 min.	●	●	1.B, 16.A	
INTERACTIVE CHART **Forms of Government**		10 min.		●	1.B, 19.A, 19.B	
READ **Discipline and Warfare in Sparta**	Objective 2	10 min.	●	●	1.B, 3.A, 19.A, 24.A	
READ **Democracy Evolves in Athens**		10 min.	●	●	1.B, 19.B, 20.A, 24.A	2.B.1
READ **Forces for Unity**	Objective 4	10 min.	●	●	1.B, 3.A, 23	
READ **Greek Wars With Persia**	Objective 5	10 min.	●	●	1.B, 3.A, 16.B	
INTERACTIVE MAP **Persian Wars, 490 B.C.–479 B.C.**		10 min.		●		
READ **Pericles, Democracy, and War**	Objectives 3, 5	10 min.	●	●	1.B, 19.B, 20.A, 21.B	
INTERACTIVE GALLERY **Athenian Democracy**		10 min.		●	1.B, 3.A, 19.B, 20.A, 21.B, 22.A, 22.B	
Synthesize						
DIGITAL ACTIVITY **Alliances: Cooperation for a Cause**		5 min.		●	1.B, 3.A	
Demonstrate						
DIGITAL QUIZ **Lesson Quiz and Class Discussion Board**		10 min.		●	1.B, 3.A, 16.A, 19.A, 19.B, 20.A, 21.B, 22.B	

Focus on Texas Standards

Texas Essential Knowledge and Skills

1.B identify major causes and describe the major effects of the following events from 500 BC to AD 600: the development of the classical civilizations of Greece, Rome, Persia, India (Maurya and Gupta), China (Zhou, Qin, and Han), and the development of major world religions

3.A describe the major political, religious/philosophical, and cultural influences of Persia, India, China, Israel, Greece, and Rome, including the development of monotheism, Judaism, and Christianity

16.A locate places and regions of historical significance directly related to major eras and turning points in world history

19.A identify the characteristics of monarchies and theocracies as forms of government in early civilizations

19.B identify the characteristics of the following political systems: theocracy, absolute monarchy, democracy, republic, oligarchy, limited monarchy, and totalitarianism

20.A explain the development of democratic-republican government from its beginnings in the Judeo-Christian legal tradition and classical Greece and Rome through the English Civil War and the Enlightenment

21.B describe the rights and responsibilities of citizens and noncitizens in civic participation throughout history

22.A summarize the development of the rule of law from ancient to modern times

22.B identify the influence of ideas regarding the right to a "trial by a jury of your peers" and the concepts of "innocent until proven guilty" and "equality before the law" that originated from the Judeo-Christian legal tradition and in Greece and Rome

24.A describe the changing roles of women, children, and families during major eras of world history

25.B summarize the fundamental ideas and institutions of Western civilizations that originated in Greece and Rome

NOTES

Greek Thinkers, Artists, and Writers

Objectives

Objective 1: Analyze the political and ethical ideas developed by ancient Greek philosophers.

Objective 2: Understand how balance and order governed ancient Greek art and architecture.

Objective 3: Identify the themes explored by ancient Greek writers and historians.

LESSON 3 ORGANIZER	PACING: APPROX. 1 PERIOD, .5 BLOCKS					
			RESOURCES			
	OBJECTIVES	PACING	Print	Online	TEKS	ELPS
Connect						
DIGITAL START UP ACTIVITY **A Lasting Legacy**		5 min.		●	1.B, 3.A, 25.B	
Investigate						
READ **Philosophers and the Pursuit of Wisdom**	Objective 1	10 min.	●	●	3.A, 23, 25.B	2.C.1
INTERACTIVE CHART **Understanding Greek Philosophers**		10 min.		●	3.A, 23, 25.B	
READ **Conveying Ideals in Art and Architecture**	Objective 2	10 min.	●	●	1.B, 3.A, 26.B	
INTERACTIVE GALLERY **Art and Architecture of Ancient Greece**		10 min.		●	1.B, 3.A, 26.B	
READ **Greek Literature**	Objective 3	10 min.	●	●	3.A, 25.B, 26.B, 26.C	
READ **Studying History**		10 min.	●	●	25.B, 26.B, 26.C	
Synthesize						
DIGITAL ACTIVITY **Remembering Greece**		5 min.		●	1.B, 3.A, 25.B, 26.C	
Demonstrate						
DIGITAL QUIZ **Lesson Quiz and Class Discussion Board**		10 min.		●	1.B, 3.A, 25.B, 26.B, 26.C	

Focus on Texas Standards

Texas Essential Knowledge and Skills

1.B identify major causes and describe the major effects of the following events from 500 BC to AD 600: the development of the classical civilizations of Greece, Rome, Persia, India (Maurya and Gupta), China (Zhou, Qin, and Han), and the development of major world religions

3.A describe the major political, religious/philosophical, and cultural influences of Persia, India, China, Israel, Greece, and Rome, including the development of monotheism, Judaism, and Christianity

25.B summarize the fundamental ideas and institutions of Western civilizations that originated in Greece and Rome

26.B analyze examples of how art, architecture, literature, music, and drama reflect the history of the cultures in which they are produced

26.C identify examples of art, music, and literature that transcend the cultures in which they were created and convey universal themes

NOTES

Alexander the Great and the Legacy of Greece

Objectives

Objective 1: Explain how Alexander the Great built an extensive empire.

Objective 2: Describe the empire's cultural impact.

Objective 3: Identify major Hellenic Greek scientists and their discoveries and innovations.

LESSON 4 ORGANIZER — **PACING: APPROX. 1 PERIOD, .5 BLOCKS**

	OBJECTIVES	PACING	RESOURCES: Print	RESOURCES: Online	TEKS	ELPS
Connect						
DIGITAL START UP ACTIVITY **The Golden Age**		5 min.		●	1.B, 3.A, 26.B	
Investigate						
READ **The New Era of Alexander the Great**	Objective 1	10 min.	●	●	1.B, 3.A	2.C.2
INTERACTIVE GALLERY **Alexander the Great's Conquests and Contributions**	Objective 1	10 min.		●	1.B, 3.A	
READ **Alexander's Legacy**	Objective 2	10 min.	●	●	1.B, 3.A	
READ **Hellenistic Arts and Sciences**	Objective 3	10 min.	●	●	3.A, 27.A	
INTERACTIVE GALLERY **Math, Science, and Technology in the Hellenistic Age**	Objective 3	10 min.		●	1.B, 3.A, 27.A	
Synthesize						
DIGITAL ACTIVITY **Effects of Size**		5 min.		●	3.A, 20.A	
Demonstrate						
DIGITAL QUIZ **Lesson Quiz and Class Discussion Board**		10 min.		●	1.B, 3.A, 20.A, 24.A, 27.A	

Focus on Texas Standards

Texas Essential Knowledge and Skills

1.B identify major causes and describe the major effects of the following events from 500 BC to AD 600: the development of the classical civilizations of Greece, Rome, Persia, India (Maurya and Gupta), China (Zhou, Qin, and Han), and the development of major world religions

3.A describe the major political, religious/philosophical, and cultural influences of Persia, India, China, Israel, Greece, and Rome, including the development of monotheism, Judaism, and Christianity

20.A explain the development of democratic-republican government from its beginnings in the Judeo-Christian legal tradition and classical Greece and Rome through the English Civil War and the Enlightenment

24.A describe the changing roles of women, children, and families during major eras of world history

26.B analyze examples of how art, architecture, literature, music, and drama reflect the history of the cultures in which they are produced

27.A identify the origin and diffusion of major ideas in mathematics, science, and technology that occurred in river valley civilizations, classical Greece and Rome, classical India, and the Islamic caliphates between 700 and 1200 and in China from the Tang to Ming dynasties

27.E identify the contributions of significant scientists such as Archimedes, Copernicus, Eratosthenes, Galileo, Pythagoras, Isaac Newton, and Robert Boyle

NOTES

Ancient Greece (1750 B.C.–133 B.C.)

In this Topic, you will learn about ancient Greece. You know the TEKS are very important, and this course will make it fun to learn about the things that will help you master them. Keep reading to see how.

Your study will help you master these TEKS:

TEKS

1.B, 3.A, 16.A, 19.A, 19.B, 20.A, 21.B, 22.A, 22.B, 24.A, 25.B, 26.B, 26.C, 27.A, 27.E, 29.F, 30.C

LESSON OUTLINE

5.1: Early Greece 3.A, 16.A, 26.B

5.2: The Greek City-States 1.B, 3.A, 16.A, 19.A, 19.B, 20.A, 21.B, 22.A, 22.B, 24.A, 25.B

5.3: Greek Thinkers, Artists, and Writers 1.B, 3.A, 25.B, 26.B, 26.C

5.4: Alexander the Great and the Legacy of Greece 1.B, 3.A, 20.A, 24.A, 26.B, 27.A, 27.E

Connect

Connect with this Topic by watching a video about a fascinating person or situation related to this Topic. You can think about how the legacy of ancient Greece connects to your own life. And you'll encounter an intriguing Essential Question: How much power should the government have?

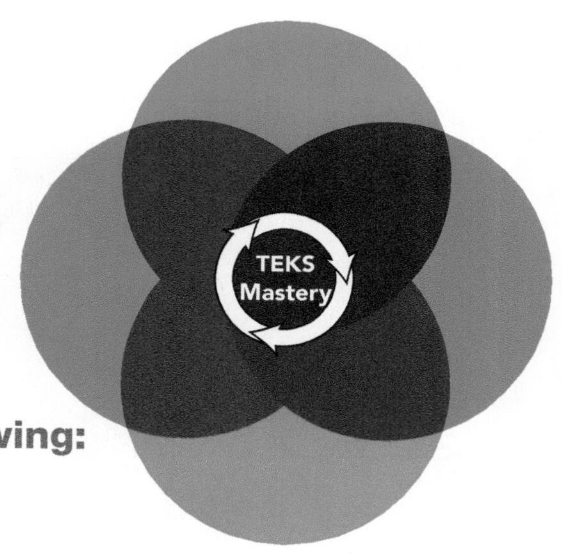

Begin your study by trying the following:

NBC LEARN Watch My Story Video:

Pericles, the Golden Age of Athens

Launch your Civic Discussion:

Athens or Sparta?

Investigate

The Lesson Outline lists all the lessons you will investigate in this Topic. As you read and interact with key content, the story of ancient Greece will come to life. Read the texts; try the interactivities. Investigate the fascinating story of this influential civilization.

And keep working on your Civic Discussion to help build your mastery of the Topic TEKS.

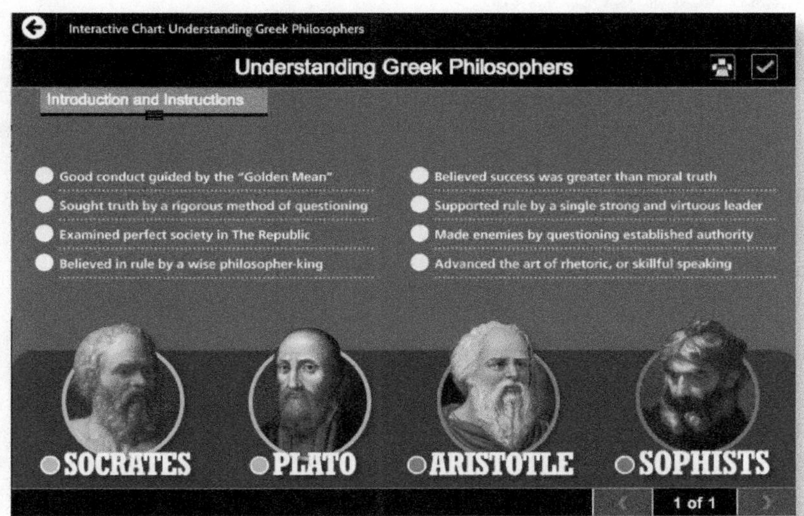

>> Digital interactivity from the online course

Synthesize

You will get a chance to pull together everything you have learned by thinking again about the Essential Question: How much power should the government have?

Demonstrate

Now you will get to show what you know. You will get a chance to complete the TEKS Review and Assessment pages, answering questions about every TEKS for this Topic. Or write an essay, share a project, or take part in a Civic Discussion No matter which you do, it will be a real-world demonstration of the things you now understand about the Topic.

TEKS in Topic 5	Topic Review and Assessment Questions
1.B	1
3.A	2
16.A	14
19.A	3
19.B	4
20.A	13
21.B	5
22.A	7
22.B	6
24.A	15
25.B	12
26.B	8
27.A	10
27.E	9, 11
29.F	5, 12
30.C	9

Topic 5

Ancient Greece (1750 B.C.–133 B.C.)

Introduction

From its modest beginnings as a small society of seafaring traders and small farmers, ancient Greece developed into one of the most influential civilizations in world history. The ancient Greeks pioneered scientific and medical discoveries by examining nature, and they made important contributions in philosophy, history, and the arts. Democracy was born in the city-state of Athens, where citizens participated in lawmaking and in the courts. Alexander the Great conquered an empire stretching from Egypt to India, helping to spread Greek culture and learning across a wide area.

ESSENTIAL QUESTION

Ask students to think about the Essential Question for this Topic: How much power should the government have? Project the Essential Question activity from the course. Have a volunteer read each bulleted suggestion. Discuss them as a class.

Predict Consequences What do you think would happen if the government did not have the power to enforce laws? *(Answers will vary. Students may predict chaos and the tyranny of the strong over the weak; others may argue that private mechanisms, such as private police forces, would develop to take over the role of law enforcement.)*

Connect Why do you think people disagree on the question of how much power a government should have? *(Answers will vary. Some students may claim that one's opinion about government responsibility depends on faith in the government to do good or on past experiences with government actions.)*

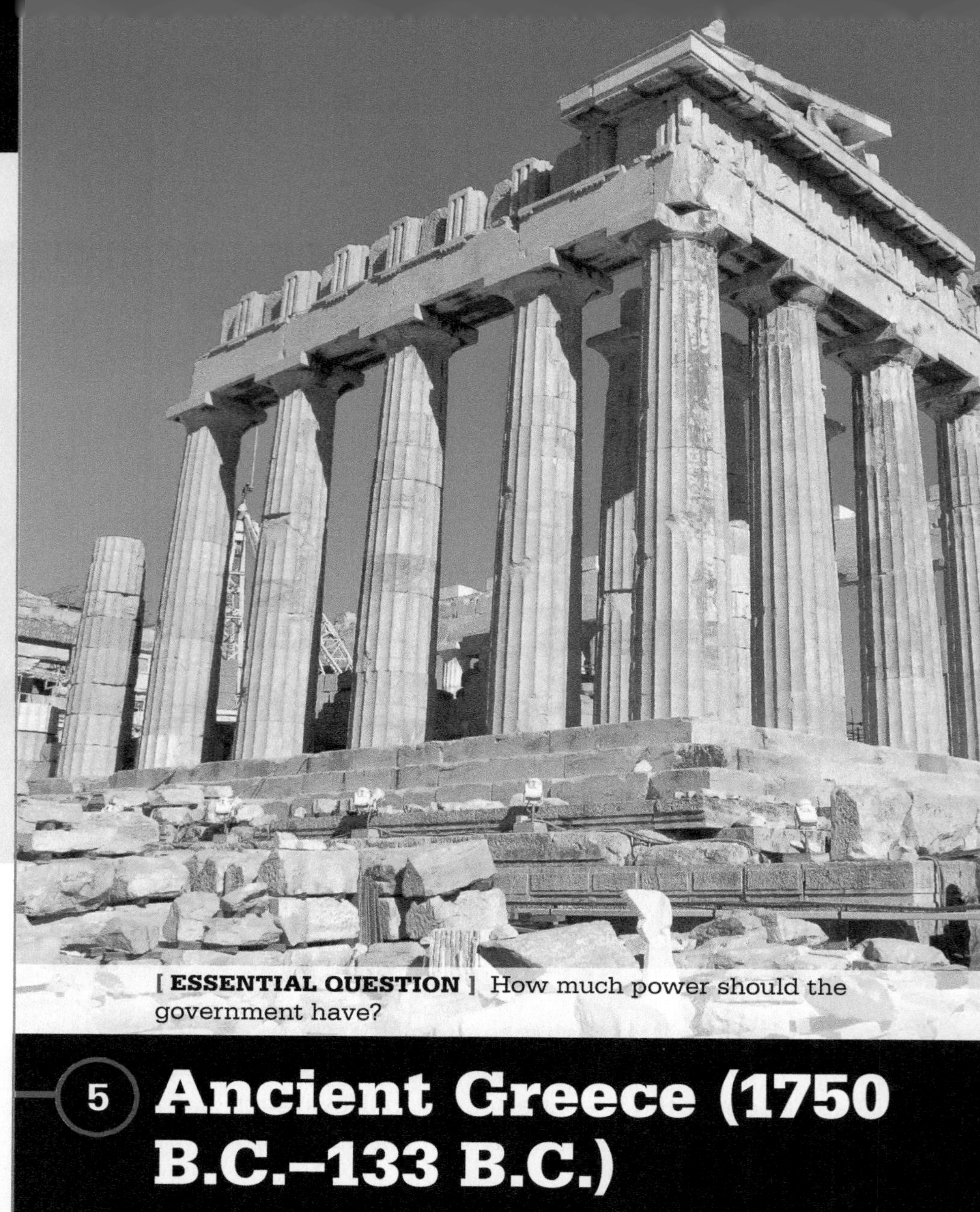

[**ESSENTIAL QUESTION**] How much power should the government have?

5 **Ancient Greece (1750 B.C.–133 B.C.)**

Analyze Images

Direct students' attention to the photograph of the Parthenon. Tell them that this temple, with its towering Doric columns, was built in the mid-400s B.C. on a hill in Athens, Greece. The temple was dedicated to the goddess Athena, whose massive gold-and-ivory statue was positioned inside. Discuss with students how this structure reflects not only the wealth of the Athenian empire but also the willingness of the citizens of this democratically governed state to fund such an impressive (and expensive) monument.

>> The Parthenon

Enduring Understandings

- Greek city-states experimented with different forms of government.
- Democracy developed in Athens, where citizens participated in lawmaking and in the courts.
- Greek city-states cooperated to defeat a threat from the Persian empire, but rivalry between Athens and Sparta led to a series of wars that weakened all of Greece.
- The ancient Greeks pioneered scientific and medical discoveries, and they made important contributions in philosophy, history, and the arts.
- Alexander the Great conquered an empire stretching from Egypt to India, helping to spread Greek culture and learning across a wide area.

PEARSON realize NBC LEARN

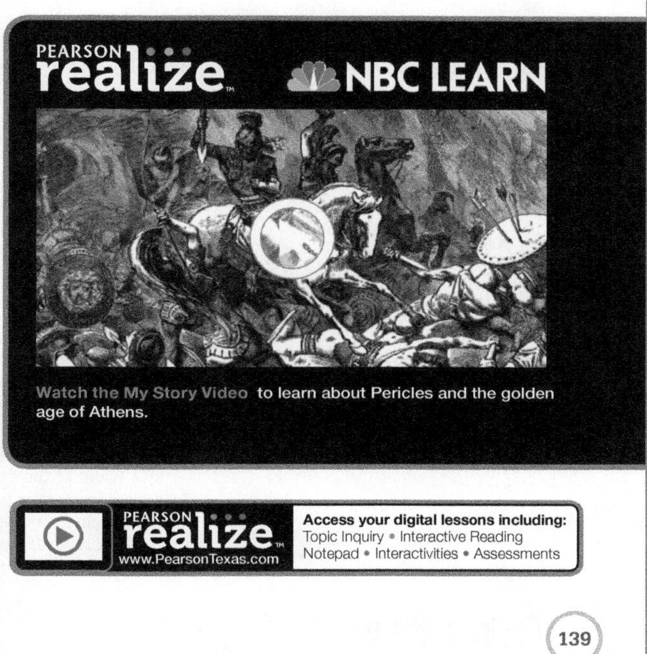

Watch the My Story Video to learn about Pericles and the golden age of Athens.

PEARSON realize www.PearsonTexas.com Access your digital lessons including: Topic Inquiry • Interactive Reading Notepad • Interactivities • Assessments

NBC LEARN MY STORY VIDEO

Project the My Story Video that introduces students to the influential Athenian leader Pericles and the role he played in changing Athenian life.

Online My Story Video: **Pericles, The Golden Age of Athens**.

After viewing, ask students to respond to the following questions.

Check Understanding How did Pericles change Athenian life? *(built stone monuments, reformed government, paid people who served on juries, emphasized freedom of speech, encouraged civic participation)*

Cite Evidence How do the ideals of Pericles live on today? *(His emphasis on civic responsibility and civic duty, as well as on freedom and equality, are values shared by modern-day democracies.)*

OVERVIEW ACTIVITY

Online Project the **Map: Ancient Greece** showing Greek settlements both east and west of the Aegean Sea. This map not only shows the key Greek settlements but also gives a sense of how geography affected ancient Greek history. This Topic will explore that history and examine how ancient Greek culture has influenced the Western world.

Analyze Maps How might the geography of ancient Greece have been an obstacle to unity? *(Sample response: The islands would have kept different peoples apart, more so than if they had lived on the same land mass; mountainous terrain would have made it harder to travel from place to place.)*

Topic Inquiry

If you choose to assign the Topic Inquiry, launch the discussion after introducing the Topic.

D Differentiate Extra Support For the Overview Activity, have students locate the Aegean Sea on the map. Ask in what way the Aegean Sea could be called the "Greek Lake." *(Sample response: It is almost totally surrounded by Greek settlements; it was probably heavily traveled by Greek ships.)*

Topic 5 Lesson 1

Early Greece

CONNECT

Preview Have students preview the **Lesson Objectives** and the list of **Key Terms**.

Students can also preview all the **Key Terms** and **Academic Vocabulary** using the **Interactive Reading Notepad** on the digital course or preview a summary of the lesson in the **Reading and Note Taking Study Guide**.

Online Use the **Editable Presentation** found on the digital course to present the main ideas for this lesson.

Start Up Activity

Tell students that early Greece was strongly influenced by trade. Crete, the island where the Minoans and later the Mycenaeans lived, was located in a region that allowed traders to reach areas in Africa and the Middle East, so these early Aegean civilizations, trading by sea, made contact with other great early civilizations. Ask students how contact with foreign peoples might have affected an early civilization. *(Contact with other groups might lead to learning new ways of doing things.)*

Discuss Ask students how the geography of trade routes affected the building and settlement of towns. *(People who wanted access to markets would build and live in towns close to trading routes.)* Tell students that in this lesson they will learn about early ancient Greek civilizations that grew up around the Aegean Sea and the great Greek legends of Homer's epic poems.

Online You can also project the **Start Up Activity** from the course.

INVESTIGATE

Have students read the lesson using the **Reading and Note Taking Study Guide** to help them take notes and understand the text as they read.

Minoans Prosper From Trade

Tell students that the brilliant Minoan civilization made its home on Crete, a rocky island in the Aegean Sea. The Minoan culture reached its greatest success between 1600 B.C. and 1500 B.C.

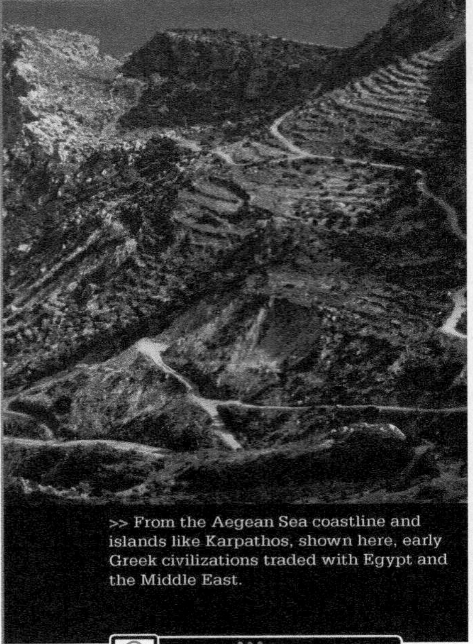

>> From the Aegean Sea coastline and islands like Karpathos, shown here, early Greek civilizations traded with Egypt and the Middle East.

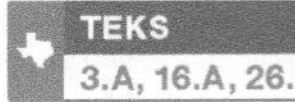

Interactive Flipped Video

5.1 The island of Crete (kreet) was the cradle of an early civilization that later influenced Greeks living on the European mainland. The people of Crete, however, had absorbed many ideas from the older civilizations of Egypt and Mesopotamia.

TEKS 3.A, 16.A, 26.B

>> Objectives

Identify the influences on Minoan culture and how the civilization prospered.

Summarize how the Mycenaeans ruled the sea trade and started the Trojan War.

Describe the works of Homer and their influence on Greek culture.

>> Key Terms

Knossos
shrine
fresco
Trojan War
strait
Homer

Early Greece

Minoans Prosper From Trade

Washed by the warm waters of the Aegean (ee JEE un) Sea, Crete was home to a brilliant early civilization. We do not actually know what the people who built this civilization called themselves. However, the British archaeologist who unearthed its ruins called them Minoans after Minos, a legendary king of Crete. Minoan civilization reached its height, or greatest success, between 1600 B.C. and 1500 B.C. The success of the Minoans was based on trade, not conquest. Minoan traders set up outposts throughout the Aegean world. From their island home in the eastern Mediterranean, they crossed the seas to the Nile Valley and the Middle East. Through contact with Egypt and Mesopotamia, they acquired ideas and technology in fields such as writing and architecture that they adapted to their own culture.

The Palace at Knossos The rulers of this trading empire lived in a vast palace at **Knossos** (NAHS us). It housed rooms for the royal family, banquet halls, and working areas for artisans. It also included religious **shrines,** areas dedicated to the honor of gods and goddesses.

The walls of the palace at Knossos were covered with colorful **frescoes,** watercolor paintings done on wet plaster. These frescoes tell us much about Minoan society. Leaping dolphins reflect the importance of the sea to the Minoan people. Religious images indicate that the Minoans worshiped the bull as well as a mother goddess.

PEARSON realize. www.PearsonTexas.com Access your Digital Lesson.

140

Aa Vocabulary Builder

1. Have students pronounce the following academic vocabulary term in this lesson and clarify the part of speech. If necessary, break it into syllables and pronounce it with the students.
2. Explain what the word means in common "student-friendly" language using synonyms and antonyms when possible. Provide concrete examples to clarify the meaning, and rephrase the definition.

eloquent: a manner of speech that is vivid and persuasive

Other frescoes show young men and women strolling through gardens or jumping through the horns of a charging bull. The paintings also suggest that women appeared freely in public and may have enjoyed more rights than women in most other ancient civilizations.

Minoan Civilization Vanishes By about 1400 B.C., Minoan civilization had disappeared. Archaeologists are not sure of the reasons for its vanishing. A sudden volcanic eruption on a nearby island may have rained flaming death on Knossos. Or perhaps an earthquake may have destroyed the palace, followed by an immense wave that drowned the inhabitants of the island. However, it is certain that invaders played some role in the destruction of Minoan civilization. These intruders were the Mycenaeans (my suh NEE unz), the first Greek-speaking people of whom we have a written record.

IDENTIFY How does the art at Knossos reflect Minoan culture?

Mycenaean Civilization

Like the Aryans who spread across India, the Mycenaeans spoke an Indo-European language. They conquered the Greek mainland before overrunning the island of Crete.

Trade by Sea Brings Wealth Mycenaean civilization dominated the Aegean world from about 1400 B.C. to 1200 B.C. Like the Minoans, the Mycenaeans were sea traders. They reached out beyond the Aegean to Sicily, Italy, Egypt, and Mesopotamia. The Mycenaeans learned many skills from the Minoans, including the art of writing. They, too, absorbed Egyptian and Mesopotamian customs, many of which they passed on to later Greeks.

The Mycenaeans lived in separate city-states on the mainland. In each, a warrior-king built a thick-walled fortress from which he ruled the surrounding villages. Wealthy rulers amassed treasure, including fine gold ornaments that archaeologists have unearthed from their tombs.

The Trojan War The Mycenaeans are best remembered for their part in the **Trojan War,** which took place around 1250 B.C. The conflict may have had its origins in economic rivalry between Mycenae and Troy, a rich trading city in present-day Turkey, that controlled the vital **straits,** or narrow water passages, connecting the Mediterranean and Black seas.

In Greek legend, however, the war had a more romantic cause. When the Trojan prince, Paris, kidnaps Helen, the beautiful wife of a Greek king, the Mycenaeans sail to Troy to rescue her. For the next 10 years, the two sides battle until the Greeks finally seize Troy and burn the city to the ground.

For centuries, most people regarded the Trojan War as pure legend. Then, in the 1870s, a wealthy German businessman, Heinrich Schliemann (HYN rik SCHLEE mahn), set out to prove that the legend was rooted in fact.

As Schliemann excavated the site of ancient Troy, he found evidence of fire and war dating to about 1250 B.C. Though most of the details remain lost in legend, modern scholars now agree that the Trojan War was an actual event.

DESCRIBE How did trade shape Mycenaean society?

Homer and the Great Greek Legends

Not long after their victory over Troy the Mycenaeans themselves came under attack from sea raiders and also from another Greek-speaking people, the Dorians, invading from the north. As Mycenaean power faded, their people abandoned the cities and trade declined.

>> Archaeologists rebuilt these room walls and stairway at the Minoan palace of Knossos on Crete.

Topic 5 Lesson 1

Guided Reading and Discussion Ask students to explain why the Minoan civilization was important. *(Sample response: The Minoans traded with older civilizations in Egypt and the Middle East, absorbing and adapting important ideas and technology. The Minoans influenced later Aegean civilizations.)*

Mycenaean Civilization

Tell students that by around 1400 B.C. the Minoan civilization ended and invading Mycenaeans helped destroy it. Also sea traders, the Mycenaeans learned skills from the Minoans and made contact with Sicily, Italy, Egypt, and Mesopotamia.

Guided Reading and Discussion

Ask students to suggest some specific things that might have caused the Mycenaeans to go to war with Troy. *(Sample response: Troy was a wealthy city and a trade rival of the Mycenaean city-states—and thus, perhaps, a tempting prize for conquest.)*

Homer and the Great Greek Legends

Ask students why the heroes of Homer's two epic poems, the *Iliad* and the *Odyssey,* inspired the ancient Greeks. *(Sample response: The heroes became famous and familiar examples of honor, courage, and eloquence.)*

D Differentiate Special Needs/Extra Support Tell students that Homer's epic poems, the *Iliad* and the *Odyssey*, tell us much of what we know about the Trojan War, how the ancient Greeks lived, and what they valued, such as honor and courage. Explain that an epic is a long poem or great story about the adventures of a hero. Invite students to list stories of today that might be considered epics. Ask how each tells something about the writer and the writer's culture.

Answers

Identify *The Knossos artwork illustrates the importance of the sea to the Minoan culture and provides details of the culture's daily life.*

Describe *Trade brought wealth and prosperity in addition to contact with the ideas and skills of other cultures. However, trade also brought conflict.*

Topic 5 Lesson 1

Online Project the **Interactive Chart: Values of Ancient Greek Culture** and answer the questions with students.

ACTIVE CLASSROOM

Pair students to have a "Conversation With History." Have the first student assume the role of a famous Greek artist. Have the second student assume the role of his or her visiting patron (supporter of the arts) who has asked for a painting of a myth or legend. The artist gives his or her patron a verbal "tour" of the painting. The patron makes comments and asks questions about the myth or legend presented by the painting. Ask students to record their conversation.

Guided Reading and Discussion Tell students that the *Iliad* begins with the mightiest Greek warrior, Achilles, refusing to fight because his commander has treated him unfairly and insulted him. What does this tell us about the values of the ancient Greeks?

Analyze Images

Direct students' attention to the photograph of the vase. Tell students that the only Greek paintings to survive are on pottery. They offer glimpses of the daily lives of Greek men and women or tell stories from popular myths and legend.

Key Terms

Ask students to find the key term **Homer** (in bold) in the text. Explain that scholars offer many theories concerning such mysteries as when and where Homer was born (or if he even existed). As to his birthplace, many scholars point to coastal Asia Minor (across the Aegean Sea from Greece) since his writing includes references to place names and cultural elements typical of that region.

>> In this scene from the *Illiad*, the water goddess Thetis, mother of Achilles, brings her son new divinely forged armor after his best friend Patroclus dies wearing Achilles's armor.

Interactive Gallery

>> Hundreds of years after Homer sang his epic poems, a sculptor carved into marble this idea of the poet's appearance.

People forgot many skills, including the art of writing. From the end of the Mycenaean civilization in about 1100 B.C. until about 900 B.C., Greek civilization seemed to step backward.

Two Epic Poems Much of what we know about the Trojan War and life during this period comes from two great epic poems, the *Iliad* and the *Odyssey*. These epics may have been the work of many people, but they are credited to the poet **Homer,** who probably lived about 750 B.C. According to tradition, Homer was a blind poet who wandered from village to village, singing of heroic deeds. Like the great Indian epics, Homer's tales were passed on orally for generations before they were finally written down.

The *Iliad* The *Iliad*, full as it is of gods, goddesses, and even a talking horse, is our chief source of information about the Trojan War. At the start of the poem, Achilles (uh KIL eez), the mightiest Greek warrior, has withdrawn from battle because he has been unfairly treated and insulted by his commander. The war soon turns against the Greeks, but Achilles stubbornly refuses to listen to pleas that he rejoin the fighting. Only after his best friend is killed does Achilles return to battle.

The *Odyssey* The *Odyssey* tells of the many struggles of the Greek hero Odysseus (oh DIS ee us) on his return home to his faithful wife, Penelope, after the fall of Troy. On his long voyage, Odysseus encounters a sea monster, a race of one-eyed giants, and a beautiful sorceress who turns men into swine.

The *Iliad* and *Odyssey* reveal much about the values and culture of the ancient Greeks. The heroes display honor, courage, and eloquence, as when Achilles rallies his troops:

> "Let not the Trojans," he cried, "keep you at arm's length, Achaeans, but go for them and fight them man for man. However valiant I may be, I cannot give chase to so many and fight all of them . . . nevertheless, so far as in me lies I will show no slackness of hand or foot nor want of endurance, not even for a moment . . ."
>
> —Homer, *Iliad* (translated by Samuel Butler)

For almost 3,000 years, the epics of Homer have inspired European writers and artists.

English Language Proficiency Standards

Listening 2.F.2 Obtain an audio recording of an excerpt from the *Iliad* or the *Odyssey*. Read this section aloud. Have students complete one activity.

Beginning After reading the text, provide students with a transcript of the excerpt. Display challenging words. Summarize the content and play the recording. Define and read aloud the words and have students repeat them.

Intermediate Follow the Beginning activity instructions, but skim the transcript, saying each challenging word. Have students repeat them. Summarize the content, play the recording, and review the challenging words and their meanings.

Advanced Follow the Intermediate activity instructions, but after playing the recording, have student pairs write and say six sentences with a challenging word to each other.

Advanced High Follow the Advanced activity instructions, but have student pairs underline challenging words.

Answers

Analyze Charts *The Minoan and Mycenaean civilizations were sea traders. They absorbed ideas from Egypt and Mesopotamia while trading in those lands.*

Describe *The values of the ancient Greeks with their depiction of honor, courage, and eloquence, as well as details of their religious beliefs and warfare*

Early Aegean Civilizations, c. 1600 B.C.–1000 B.C.

CIVILIZATION	CHARACTERISTICS	ACCOMPLISHMENTS
Minoan 1600 B.C.–1500 B.C. (Vanished by 1400 B.C.)	• Sea traders based on Crete • Absorbed ideas from Egypt, Mesopotamia • Worshiped bull and mother goddess	• Later influenced Greeks living on European mainland • Colorful, graceful frescos at Knossos palace; women perhaps enjoyed more rights than in most other ancient civilizations
Mycenaean 1400 B.C.–1200 B.C. (Ended around 1100 B.C.)	• Sea traders • Absorbed ideas from Egypt, Mesopotamia; also reached Italy, Sicily; learned from Minoans (including writing) • Lived in separate city-states on mainland; warrior kings rule surrounding villages from thick-walled fortresses	• First Greek-speaking culture which left written records, spoke Indo-European language • Fine gold ornaments found in their tombs • Conquered Greek mainland, then Crete; took part in Trojan War, around 1250 B.C.
Dorian 1100 B.C.–1000 B.C. Swept away Minoans and Mycenaeans, initiated cultural dark age	• Originated in northern and northwestern Greece, attacked Mycenaeans from the north • Conquered and settled cities of Sparta, Corinth, and Argos, as well as in today's Sicily, Italy, North Africa, and along the Black Sea coast	• Greek-speaking people, relatively low cultural level, inventors of iron slashing sword • Their restrained, powerful, monumental art an important influence on later Greek art

>> **Analyze Charts** A series of Greek civilizations grew, flourished, and fell on the mainland and islands of the eastern Mediterranean. Which civilizations absorbed ideas from Egypt and Mesopotamia? How did they learn about these ideas?

A Legacy for the Future After the Dorian invasions, the land of Greece passed several centuries in obscurity. The people lived in small isolated villages and had few contacts with the outside world. Over time they made the stories about Crete and Mycenae a part of their heritage, and they built upon the legacy of those and other civilizations to forge a new Greek civilization. When it emerged, this Greek civilization would not only dominate the region; it would ultimately extend the influence of Greek culture over most of the Western world.

 **DESCRIBE** What do Homer's epics reveal about Greek culture?

ASSESSMENT

1. **Identify Cause and Effect** How did the Minoans create a brilliant early Greek civilization?
2. **Draw Conclusions** How do frescoes on the walls of the palace of Knossos reflect the history of the Minoan culture in which they were produced?
3. **Infer** Why do you think the Minoans and Mycenaeans absorbed ideas, customs, and skills from other cultures?
4. **Hypothesize** Why do you think that for centuries most people thought the Trojan War was just a legend?
5. **Summarize** What is known about the causes of the Trojan War?

SYNTHESIZE

Online Project the **Digital Activity: Icarus Flying High**. Ask students, in groups, to read the description of a story from Greek mythology. Have them take 5 minutes to brainstorm and then write down brief answers to the questions shown. Have each group share its answers with the class.

DEMONSTRATE

Online Assign the **Digital Lesson Quiz** for this lesson if you haven't already done so. Students will be offered automatic remediation or enrichment based on their score.

Pose these questions to the class on the Discussion Board:

Compare and Contrast How were the Minoans and Mycenaeans alike and different? Explain. *(Sample response: Both were sea traders who learned and adapted skills and ideas from earlier peoples. The Minoans developed a culture that honored gods and goddesses, and women probably played an active public role. The Mycenaeans built massive walled fortresses and, according to Homer's poems, were led by warrior-kings.)*

Draw Inferences How do you think literature reflects the history of the culture in which it is produced? *(Sample response: by describing people who lived then, important events, and common daily activities)*

Topic Inquiry

Have students continue their investigations for the Topic Inquiry.

Assessment

1. With trading posts throughout the Aegean world, the Minoans built their civilization through adapted ideas and knowledge from other cultures like Egypt and Mesopotamia.
2. They portray a seafaring trading civilization, developed through contact with other cultures. Images of religious worship, pleasant gardens, athletics, and women suggest that a long period of peaceful development made this confident and expressive civilization possible.
3. Answers may vary. Students should mention that the Minoans and Mycenaeans might have learned that other cultures had useful ways to solve common problems or to improve the quality of their lives. They then chose to adapt these ideas to benefit themselves.
4. Answers may vary. Students may include that the stories in Homer's *Iliad* and the *Odyssey* included such exciting larger-than-life warriors, gods and goddesses, and famous dramatic scenes that people thought Troy itself must have been made up by a great storyteller.
5. Economic competition between Mycenae and Troy, which controlled the straits between the Mediterranean and Black seas, may have fueled the conflict that led to the Trojan War. According to Greek legend, Paris, a Trojan prince, kidnapped Helen, the beautiful wife of a Greek king. The Mycenaeans went to Troy and fought for ten years to bring her back.

Topic 5 Lesson 2

The Greek City-States

CONNECT

Preview Have students preview the **Lesson Objectives** and the list of **Key Terms**.

Students can also preview all the **Key Terms** and **Academic Vocabulary** using the **Interactive Reading Notepad** on the digital course or preview a summary of the lesson in the **Reading and Note Taking Study Guide**.

Online Use the **Editable Presentation** found on the digital course to present the main ideas for this lesson.

Start Up Activity

Have students think about how their community would be affected by living near mountains or the sea, or both. Tell them that ancient Greeks adapted to both conditions. Ask students how access to the sea could influence a country's trade, economy, and travel. *(The ease of shipping goods by sea might encourage trade with other countries and thus enhance the economy. Travel, especially foreign travel, would increase.)* How might mountains affect overland trade and political unity? *(Sample answer: Mountains would make overland trade more difficult, and if they isolated regions, they could make it more difficult to achieve political unity.)*

Online You can also project the **Start Up Activity** from the course.

INVESTIGATE

Have students read the lesson using the **Reading and Note Taking Study Guide** to help them take notes and understand the text as they read.

Geography Shapes Greek City-States

Part of Greece lies on a peninsula, divided by mountains into isolated valleys. Greece also contains hundreds of rocky islands. Separated by mountains and water, ancient Greeks built many small city-states that were initially governed by kings. The inherited central power of a monarch eventually shifted to noble landowners who won power for themselves and their families as military defenders. In time, as trade increased, oligarchies consisting of wealthy merchants, farmers, and artisans dominated some city-states.

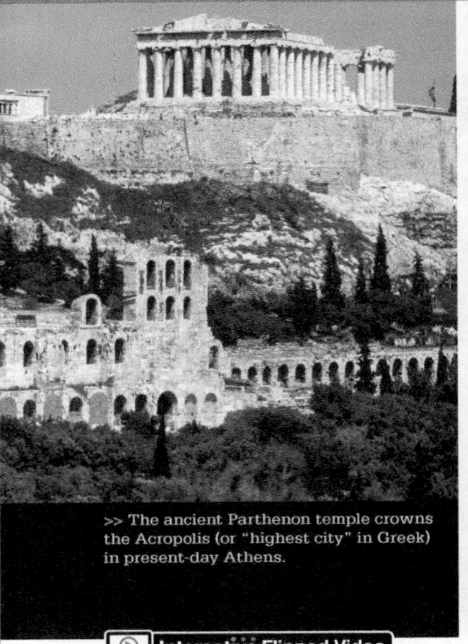

>> The ancient Parthenon temple crowns the Acropolis (or "highest city" in Greek) in present-day Athens.

Interactive Flipped Video

5.2 **The Mediterranean and Aegean seas were as central to the development of Greek civilization as the Nile was to the Egyptians. The ancient Greeks absorbed many ideas and beliefs from the older civilizations of Mesopotamia and Egypt. At the same time, they developed their own unique ways. In particular, the Greeks developed new ideas about how best to govern each individual Greek *polis* (POH lis), or city-state.**

TEKS
1.B, 3.A, 16.A, 19.A, 19.B, 20.A, 21.B, 22.A, 22.B, 24.A, 25.B

>> Objectives

Understand how geography influenced the Greek city-states.

Explain how democracy and other forms of government developed in Ancient Greece.

Describe the influence of Ancient Greek concepts related to the rights and responsibilities of citizenship.

Identify the culture and values shared by Ancient Greeks.

Summarize how the Persian and Peloponnesian Wars affected Greece.

>> Key Terms

polis
acropolis
citizen
monarchy
aristocracy
oligarchy
phalanx
Sparta
Athens
democracy
tyrant
legislature
alliance
Pericles
direct democracy
stipend
jury
ostracism

PEARSON realize www.PearsonTexas.com Access your Digital Lesson.

The Greek City-States

Geography Shapes Greek City-States

As you have read, the earliest civilizations rose in fertile river valleys. There, strong rulers organized irrigation works that helped farmers produce food surpluses needed to support large cities. A very different set of geographic conditions influenced the rise of Ancient Greek civilization.

Landscape Forms Political Borders Greece is part of the Balkan peninsula, which extends southward into the eastern Mediterranean Sea. Mountains divide the peninsula into isolated valleys. Beyond the rugged coast, hundreds of rocky islands spread toward the horizon.

The Greeks who farmed the valleys or settled on the scattered islands did not create a large empire such as that of the Egyptians or Persians. Instead, they built many small city-states, cut off from one another by mountains or water. Each included a city and its surrounding countryside. Greeks fiercely defended the independence of their small city-states, and endless rivalry frequently led to war.

144

Aa Vocabulary Builder

1. Have students pronounce the following academic vocabulary terms in this lesson and clarify the part of speech. For difficult or polysyllabic words, break them into syllables and pronounce them with the students.
2. Explain what the word means in common "student-friendly" language using synonyms and antonyms when possible. Provide concrete examples to clarify the meaning, and rephrase the definition.

impose: to place on or to make something compulsory

uniqueness: the quality of being without equal; individuality

Living by the Sea While mountains divided Greeks from one another, the seas provided a vital link to the world outside. With its hundreds of bays, the Greek coastline offered safe harbors for ships. The Greeks became skilled sailors and carried cargoes of olive oil, wine, and marble to ports throughout the eastern Mediterranean.

They returned not only with grains and metals but also with ideas, which they adapted to their own needs. For example, the Ancient Greeks adapted the Phoenician alphabet to meet their needs. The resulting alphabet in turn became the basis for all later Western alphabets.

By 750 B.C., rapid population growth forced many Greeks to leave their own overcrowded valleys. With fertile land limited, the Greeks expanded overseas. Gradually, a scattering of Greek colonies took root all around the Mediterranean from Spain to Egypt. Wherever they traveled, Greek settlers and traders carried their ideas and culture.

Rise of Greek City-States As their world expanded after 750 B.C., the Greeks evolved a unique version of the city-state, which they called the polis. The polis was made up of a major city or town and its surrounding countryside. Typically, the city itself was built on two levels.

On the top of a hill stood the **acropolis** (uh KRAH puh lis), or high city, with its great marble temples dedicated to different gods and goddesses. On flatter ground below lay the walled main city with its marketplace, theater, public buildings, and homes.

The population of each city-state was fairly small, which helped the **citizens,** or free residents, share a sense of responsibility for its triumphs and defeats. In the warm climate of Greece, free men spent much time outdoors in the marketplace, debating issues that affected their lives. The whole community joined in festivals honoring the city's special god or goddess. The rights of citizens were unequal, however, and male landowners held all the political power.

Types of Government Evolve Between 750 B.C. and 500 B.C. different forms of government evolved in Greece. At first, the ruler of the polis, like those in the river valley empires, was a king.

A government in which a hereditary ruler exercises central power is a **monarchy.** Slowly, however, power shifted to a class of noble landowners. Because only they could afford bronze weapons and chariots, these nobles were also the military defenders of the city-

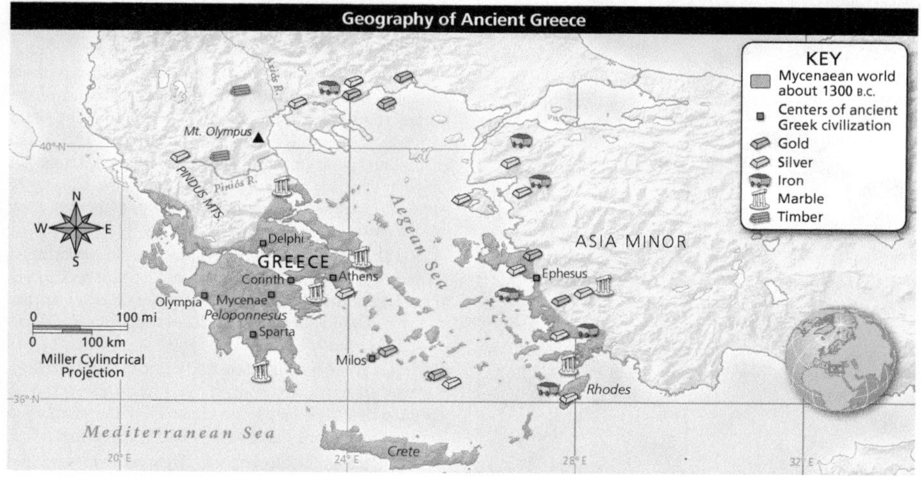

>> **Analyze Maps** Ancient Greek civilization was shaped by rugged mountainous terrain and surrounding seas. How did the geography of Greece present obstacles to unity? How did the geography of Greece differ from that of other ancient civilizations?

Online Project the **Interactive Chart: Forms of Government**. Move the colored dots representing the different forms of government to the text that defines or gives an example of that government type.

ACTIVE CLASSROOM

Group students. Give each group a three-column organizer with the headings Plus/Minus/Interesting for recording responses to three questions about forms of government. Ask each group to choose one form of government: monarchy, aristocracy, or oligarchy. Then have students answer these questions: 1. What are the positive ideas about the form of government you chose? 2. What are the negative ideas about it? 3. What is interesting about it? *(Sample response: Monarchy: positive ideas—one person clearly in charge, can make decisions and act right away; negative ideas—has total power, can be unfair or cruel, may not have intelligent or capable successors; interesting—how many countries were or are monarchies)*

Analyze Maps

Direct students' attention to the Geography of Ancient Greece map. Have students indicate the locations of Sparta, Mycenae, Corinth, Athens, and Ephesus. Ask: What do the locations of these cities have in common? *(They are all on a coast or very close to the sea.)* Point out that Greece itself is very mountainous and has limited natural resources, with the exception of marble.

Guided Reading and Discussion

What effect did the mountains and water have on Greek city-states? *(The Greeks were cut off from each other, developed their own systems of government, and fought frequently. Access to water helped Greeks become skilled sailors and traders.)*

D Differentiate Special Needs/Extra Support Students may use the map of the geography of Ancient Greece to learn more about Greece. Point out that Greece is made up of isolated valleys and small islands. Ask: How did its geography influence its economy? *(Because it was surrounded by the sea, the Greeks became great traders.)* How did its geography affect political divisions? *(It prevented the Greeks from building a large local empire. Instead they built small city-states.)*

Answers

Analyze Maps *Sample answer: The geography of mountains separated the Greek towns physically, and surmounting this separation made unifying the region difficult. Most ancient civilizations developed along river valleys.*

Key Terms

Ask students to find the key term **phalanx** (in bold) in the text. Explain that a Greek phalanx was a densely packed formation of foot soldiers, eight rows deep. Each soldier carried a sword and a spear. They overlapped their shields to form a protective barrier, with the spears of the front row extending forward toward the enemy.

Discipline and Warfare in Sparta

Conquered and settled by Dorian invaders from the north, Sparta developed into a powerful military state that placed little emphasis on trade, wealth, new ideas, or the arts. Its conquered population became state-owned slaves who worked the land. Sparta was ruled by kings.

Guided Reading and Discussion

Ask students to describe Sparta's form of government, including the responsibilities of its citizens. *(Sparta was a dual monarchy: two kings ruled, advised by a council of elders and an assembly of citizens who approved major decisions. Male citizens trained from childhood to fight for Sparta; female citizens trained to produce healthy sons and sometimes to run the family estates.)*

Infer What do you think daily life in Sparta was like? *(Sample response: Daily life was highly disciplined and difficult, with little or no time for personal freedom, contact between men and women, interests, leisure, or intellectual pursuits.)*

Predict Consequences How do you think Sparta's large enslaved population affected the daily life of its citizens? *(Sample response: Supplying the city-state's daily needs, especially food, depended on the reliable activity of this valuable underclass. Yet Spartan citizens would always be aware that their slaves might rise up against them.)*

states. At first these landowners defended the king. In time, however, they won power for themselves. The result was an **aristocracy,** or rule by a hereditary landholding elite.

New Ways of War Shape Greece Changes in military technology increased the power of the middle class. By about 650 B.C., iron weapons replaced bronze ones. Since iron was cheaper, ordinary citizens could afford iron helmets, shields, and swords. Meanwhile, a new method of fighting emerged—the **phalanx,** a massive tactical formation of heavily armed foot soldiers. It required long hours of drill to master. Shared training created a strong sense of unity among the citizen-soldiers.

As trade expanded, a new middle class of wealthy merchants, farmers, and artisans emerged in some cities. They challenged the landowning nobles for power and came to dominate some city-states. The result was a form of government called an **oligarchy.** In an oligarchy, power is in the hands of a small, wealthy elite.

By putting the defense of the city-state in the hands of ordinary citizens, the phalanx reduced class differences. The new type of warfare, however, led the two most influential city-states—Athens and Sparta—to develop very different ways of life. While Sparta stressed military virtues and stern discipline, Athens glorified the individual and extended political rights to more citizens.

>> The Spartans put great emphasis on the strength and agility of the human body. This sculpture from 530 B.C. shows a Spartan woman exercising, a task rarely expected of other Greek women.

IDENTIFY How did the sea coast contribute to Greek commerce?

Discipline and Warfare in Sparta

Dorian invaders from the north conquered Laconia, in the southern part of the Peloponnesus (pel uh puh NEE sus). The Dorians settled here and built the city-state of **Sparta.** The invaders turned the conquered people into state-owned slaves, called helots, and made them work the land. Because the helots greatly outnumbered their rulers, the Spartans set up a brutal system of strict control.

The Spartan government included two kings and a council of elders who advised the monarchs. An assembly made up of all citizens approved major decisions. Citizens were male, native-born Spartans over the age of 30. The assembly also elected five ephors, or officials, who ran day-to-day affairs.

Discipline Rules Daily Life From childhood, a Spartan prepared to be part of a military state. Officials examined every newborn, and sickly children were abandoned to die. Spartans wanted future soldiers and the future mothers of soldiers to be healthy.

At the age of seven, boys began training for a lifetime in the military. They moved into barracks, where they were toughened by a coarse diet, hard exercise, and rigid discipline. This strict and harsh discipline made Spartan youths excellent soldiers. To develop cunning and supplement their diet, boys were even encouraged to steal food. If caught, though, they were beaten severely.

At the age of 20, a man could marry, but he continued to live in the barracks for another 10 years and to eat there for another 40 years. At the age of 30, after further training, he took his place in the assembly.

Spartan Women Girls, too, had a rigorous upbringing. As part of a warrior society, they were expected to produce healthy sons for the army. They therefore were required to exercise and strengthen their bodies.

Like other Greek women, Spartan women had to obey their fathers or husbands. Yet under Spartan law, they had the right to inherit property. Because men were occupied with war, some women took on responsibilities such as running the family's estate.

Differentiate Extra Support Ask students to look up the definition of the word *spartan*. Then discuss how the definition reflects the philosophy of Sparta.

Differentiate Special Needs/Extra Support To help students learn how Sparta developed into a military society, have them create a flowchart that shows the steps. *(Sample chart text: 1. City-states emerge. 2. The kings lose power to the wealthy. 3. Changing technology means ordinary citizens can afford iron weapons. 4. The phalanx means more training and a greater sense of unity among citizens. 5. Spartans conquer Laconia and make its people helots. 6. The helots greatly outnumber the Spartans. 7. Spartans create a brutal system of strict control.)*

Answers

Identify *The sea coast encouraged the Greeks to become skilled sailors and traders.*

Sparta Stands Alone The Spartans isolated themselves from other Greeks. They looked down on trade and wealth, forbade their own citizens to travel, and had little use for new ideas or the arts. While other Greeks admired the Spartans' military skills, no other city-state imitated their rigorous way of life. "Spartans are willing to die for their city," some suggested, "because they have no reason to live."

EXPLAIN Why was discipline important in Sparta?

Democracy Evolves in Athens

Athens was located in Attica, just north of the Peloponnesus. As in many Greek city-states, Athenian government evolved from a monarchy into an aristocracy. By 700 B.C. landowners held power. They chose the chief officials, judged major court cases, and dominated the assembly.

Discontent Drives Change Under the aristocracy, Athenian wealth and power grew. Yet discontent spread among ordinary people. Merchants and soldiers resented the power of the nobles. They argued that their service to Athens entitled them to more rights. Foreign artisans, who produced many of the goods that Athens traded abroad, were resentful that foreigners were barred from becoming citizens. Farmers, too, demanded change. During hard times, many farmers were forced to sell their land to nobles. A growing number even sold themselves and their families into slavery to pay their debts.

As discontent spread, Athens moved slowly toward **democracy,** or government by the people. As you will see, the term had a different meaning for the ancient Greeks than it has for us today.

Solon Makes Reforms Solon, a wise and trusted leader, was appointed archon (AHR kahn), or chief official, in 594 B.C. Athenians gave Solon a free hand to make needed reforms. He outlawed debt slavery and freed those who had already been sold into slavery for debt. He opened high offices to more citizens, granted citizenship to some foreigners, and gave the Athenian assembly more say in important decisions.

Solon introduced economic reforms as well. He encouraged the export of wine and olive oil. This policy helped merchants and farmers by increasing demand for their products.

Despite Solon's reforms, citizenship remained limited, and many positions were open only to the wealthy. Continued and widespread unrest led to the

>> The Parthenon holds center stage on the ancient Athenian Acropolis. Originally a temple honoring the city's patron goddess, Athena, the Parthenon is one of the world's most famous and influential buildings.

>> Solon (630 B.C.–560 B.C.) became so famous for his wise political and economic reforms that today in English we call a wise and skillful lawgiver a *solon.*

Democracy Evolves in Athens

Athens slowly moved from an aristocracy to a democracy. Popular discontent continued despite significant government reforms under Solon's leadership. By making reforms to help merchants and the poor, tyrants gained their support to seize power. Then the reformer Cleisthenes expanded citizens' role in government, made the assembly a lawmaking body, and Athens became a limited democracy.

English Language Proficiency Standards

Listening 2.B.1 Read "Democracy Evolves in Athens" aloud to students. Then instruct students to complete one of the following activities based on their level of English proficiency.

Beginning Write and display the following words from the text: *Greek, Athens, chose, chief, wealth,* and *merchants*. Point to and say each consonant cluster in the displayed words. Then say each word aloud, emphasizing the consonant cluster, and have students repeat them. Scan the text for additional words with the consonant clusters *gr, ch,* and *th*. Repeat the procedure with the new words.

Intermediate Follow the instructions in the Beginning ELPS activity, but invite student volunteers to identify the consonant cluster in each word. Then say each word aloud, emphasizing the consonant cluster, and have students repeat them. Have students scan the text for additional words and repeat the procedure with the new words.

Answers

Explain *Every Spartan citizen had to be ready to fight since their slaves outnumbered them and would likely revolt if Spartans showed any signs of weakness. Discipline was vital in keeping Sparta secure.*

Topic 5 Lesson 2

Guided Reading and Discussion

Tell students that Athenian democracy, although limited by modern standards, did offer its citizens the opportunity to participate directly in the government of their polis. Remind students that more people were involved in decision making in Athens than in any other ancient civilization.

Discuss the role of families, including women and children in the society. Families played a vital role in ancient Greek culture, and women played their most significant public role in religion. Their participation in sacred processions and ceremonies was considered essential for the city's well-being. In well-to-do Athenian homes, women managed the entire household. They spun and wove, cared for their children, and prepared food, but lived a secluded existence and were rarely seen in public. Their slaves or children were sent to buy food and to fetch water from the public well. Only poor women went shopping alone in Athens. They worked outside the home, often beside their husbands.

Girls received little or no formal education, but boys attended school if their families could afford it. Besides learning to read and write, they studied music, memorized poetry, and studied public speaking because, as citizens in a democracy, they would have to voice their views. Although they received military training and participated in athletic contests, unlike Sparta, which put military training above all else, Athens encouraged young men to explore many areas of knowledge.

Classify Why is the democracy of ancient Athens considered a "limited one"? *(Though citizens had broad rights, few Athenians were actually citizens. Women and slaves were excluded from citizenship and thus any say in government, since only men could be citizens. Such a version of democracy was hardly representative of the population it ruled.)*

rise of **tyrants,** or people who gained power by force. Tyrants often won support from the merchant class and the poor by imposing reforms to help these groups. Although Greek tyrants often governed well, the word *tyrant*has come to mean a vicious and brutal ruler.

Citizens Share Power and Wealth The Athenian tyrant Pisistratus (py SIS truh tus) seized power in 546 B.C. He helped farmers by giving them loans and land taken from nobles. New building projects gave jobs to the poor. By giving poor citizens a greater voice, he further weakened the aristocracy.

In 507 B.C. another reformer, Cleisthenes (KLYS thuh neez), broadened the role of ordinary citizens in government. He set up the Council of 500, whose members were chosen by lot from among all citizens over the age of 30. The council prepared laws considered by the assembly and supervised the day-to-day work of government.

Cleisthenes made the assembly a genuine **legislature,** or lawmaking body, that debated laws before deciding to approve or reject them. All male citizens were members of the assembly and were expected to participate.

Cleisthenes's reforms advanced the principle of *isonomia*, or equal rights for all before the law. More citizens of Athens could now participate more actively in public life. This principle has influenced the development of democratic traditions of government throughout history.

Democracy Within Limits By modern standards, Athenian democracy was quite limited. Only citizens could participate in government—voting to choose officials and pass laws or holding office—and citizenship was restricted to landowning men over 30 years of age. Citizens had a responsibility to serve in government and fight for their polis as soldiers when needed. Women were excluded along with merchants and people whose parents were not citizens.

So were the tens of thousands of Athenian slaves who lacked political rights as well as personal freedom, although it was their labor that gave citizens the time to participate in government. Still, Athens gave more people a say in decision making than any other ancient civilization.

Foreign merchants and most other noncitizens could not own land or houses. Though usually provided basic hospitality, at first such noncitizens were not recognized as persons under the law and, without rights or access to legal process, could be robbed, cheated, or worse. This strongly discouraged trade, so city-states granted some rights to merchants and skilled craftsmen. City-

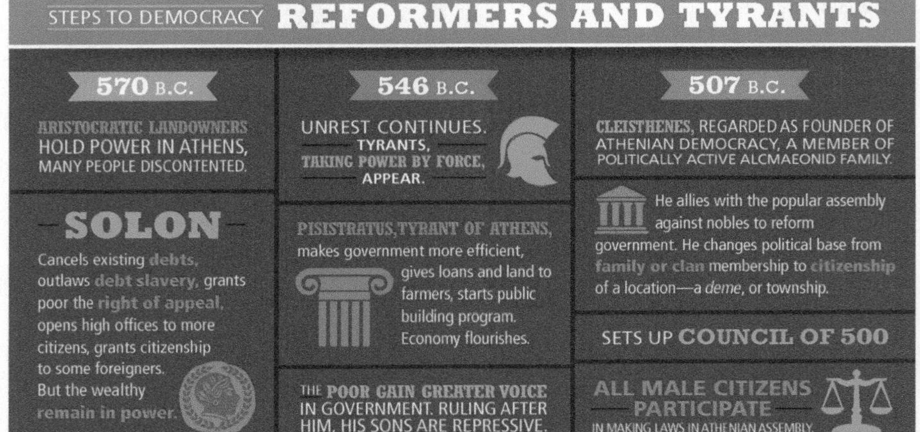

STEPS TO DEMOCRACY
REFORMERS AND TYRANTS
570 B.C.
ARISTOCRATIC LANDOWNERS HOLD POWER IN ATHENS, MANY PEOPLE DISCONTENTED.
SOLON
Cancels existing debts, outlaws debt slavery, grants poor the right of appeal, opens high offices to more citizens, grants citizenship to some foreigners. But the wealthy remain in power.
546 B.C.
UNREST CONTINUES. TYRANTS, TAKING POWER BY FORCE, APPEAR.
PISISTRATUS, TYRANT OF ATHENS, makes government more efficient, gives loans and land to farmers, starts public building program. Economy flourishes.
THE POOR GAIN GREATER VOICE IN GOVERNMENT. RULING AFTER HIM, HIS SONS ARE REPRESSIVE.
507 B.C.
CLEISTHENES, REGARDED AS FOUNDER OF ATHENIAN DEMOCRACY, A MEMBER OF POLITICALLY ACTIVE ALCMAEONID FAMILY.
He allies with the popular assembly against nobles to reform government. He changes political base from family or clan membership to citizenship of a location—a deme, or township.
SETS UP COUNCIL OF 500
ALL MALE CITIZENS PARTICIPATE IN MAKING LAWS IN ATHENIAN ASSEMBLY.

>> Motivated by widespread discontent with the aristocracy ruling Athens, political reforms by Solon, Pisistratus, and Cleisthenes were steps in Athenian democracy's evolution.

Interactive Chart

English Language Proficiency Standards

Advanced Tell students that they will be working with a partner to locate and write down words in the text with the following consonant clusters: *gr, ch,* and *th*. Have pairs sound out each word on their list. Circulate among students to provide support as necessary.

Advanced High Tell students that they will be working independently to locate and write down words in the text with the following consonant clusters: *gr, ch,* and *th*. Have students work with a partner to sound out each word on their list. Circulate among students to provide support as necessary.

states also sometimes made treaties that guaranteed rights and privileges to each other's citizens.

Athenian Women Families played a vital role in ancient Greek culture. As in other Greek city-states, however, women in Athens had no share in political life. According to Aristotle, "The man is by nature fitter for command than the female just as an older person is superior to a younger, more immature person."

Although some men disagreed, most Greeks accepted the view that women must be guided by men. In court, fathers or guardians represented women, as they did for children.

Greek playwrights such as Sophocles, and Aristophanes prominently featured women or families in their tragedies and comedies. Social, political, and religious issues often were played out within family dramas, as in Sophocles's *Antigone*, where a heroine's disobedience of a ruler's command puts her into conflict with her uncle and guardian. In Aristophanes's comedy, *The Clouds*, a father tries to take control of his spendthrift son.

Women played their most significant public role in religion. Their participation in sacred processions and ceremonies was considered essential for the city's well-being. In well-to-do Athenian homes, women managed the entire household. They spun and wove, cared for their children, and prepared food, but lived a secluded existence and were rarely seen in public. Their slaves or children were sent to buy food and to fetch water from the public well. Only poor women went shopping alone in Athens.

They worked outside the home, often beside their husbands. They obtained water, did the family wash in a stream, and tended sheep or worked as spinners, weavers, or potters.

Educating the Young Unlike girls, who received little or no formal education, boys attended school if their families could afford it. Besides learning to read and write, they studied music, memorized poetry, and studied public speaking because, as citizens in a democracy, they would have to voice their views. Although they received military training and participated in athletic contests, unlike Sparta which put military training above all else, Athens encouraged young men to explore many areas of knowledge.

DEFINE How was democracy limited in Athens?

>> On this oil flask, painted around 480 B.C., a young woman works with wool, a common domestic occupation of ancient Greek women.

>> **Compare** This drinking cup from 480 B.C. illustrates subjects Athenian boys studied: speech and playing the lyre. How does this image show the differences between Athenian and Spartan systems of education?

Draw Conclusions How do you think slavery may have contributed to the success of democracy in ancient Athens? *(Answers will vary and may include that many Athenians owned slaves, freeing them from spending time on daily chores or the routine work of commerce and manufacturing. Thus they had time they could dedicate to discussing public affairs in the marketplace, debating issues and voting on laws in the assembly, and holding public office.)*

Analyze Chart Direct students to the table of reformers and tyrants in ancient Greece. Have students identify the groups whose interests were favored by different leaders, as the government in ancient Athens gradually evolved into a democracy. *(Solon's reforms helped the poor, but the wealthy remained in power. Pisistratus helped farmers, merchants, and the poor. Cleisthenes worked with the popular assembly against the nobles, broadening the political role of ordinary citizens.)*

History Background

Training for Boys At age seven, by law, Spartan boys were taken from their mothers and placed in "packs" under the control of a "warden" of the city-state. They learned to read and write and even to sign and memorize poetry, but the focus of their education was to harden and discipline them for battle by instilling the values of fitness, obedience, and courage. Boys built their own beds from rushes using their bare hands rather than knives. They rarely bathed. At age twelve, they received but one cloak to wear each year. Packs of boys were trained to fight each other. Tests of courage were severe, forcing boys to run a gauntlet of whips or to survive alone for a time. Disobedience was severely punished by beatings. The result was that young Spartans learned to obey and respect their laws—which forbade them to flee in battle but required them to always stand firm: to conquer or die.

Answers

Define *Athenian democracy was limited because a voice in government was denied to many Athenians, including women and slaves.*

Compare *While Spartans valued physical training and toughness, the image shows that Athenians valued intellectual training and artistry.*

Topic 5 Lesson 2

Forces for Unity

The Greek city-states shared a common culture—a language, ancient heroes, gods, and festivals—despite their fiercely independent spirit and economic rivalry. As trade and colonies increased, the Greeks met foreigners and borrowed many ideas. Yet the Greeks retained a sense of their own uniqueness and superiority.

Guided Reading and Discussion

How do you think ancient Greek religion helped unify the Greeks and came to greatly influence later civilizations? *(Sample response: Having religious beliefs and practices in common, the ancient Greeks shared the same or similar values and could usually understand one another, even when they disagreed. Later civilizations absorbed the classical Greek religious values, embodied in traditional legends and myths, and through famous Greek works of art, such as poems, plays, and sculptures.)*

Greek Wars With Persia

In 499 B.C., Athens sent ships to help self-governing Greek city-states in Asia Minor fight against the Persian empire. This later led to the Persian Wars against Greece. The Greek city-states united to fight and ultimately defeat the Persians.

Forces for Unity

Strong local identification, an independent spirit, and economic rivalry led to fighting among the Greek city-states. Despite these divisions, Greeks shared a common culture. They spoke the same language, honored the same ancient heroes, participated in common festivals, and prayed to the same gods.

Myths and Beliefs Like most other ancient people, the Greeks were polytheistic, believing in more than one deity. According to their myths, or traditional stories that explain the ways of nature or the gods, the gods lived on Mount Olympus in northern Greece. In Greek myths, the most powerful Olympian was Zeus (zoos), who presided over the affairs of gods and humans. His children included Ares (EHR eez), god of war, and Aphrodite (af ruh DY tee), goddess of love. His daughter Athena (uh THEE nuh), goddess of wisdom, gave her name to Athens.

Greeks honored their gods with temples and festivals, which included processions, sacrifices, feasts, plays, choral singing, and athletic competitions. Greeks consulted oracles, who were priests or priestesses through whom the gods were thought to speak. However, some Greek thinkers came to believe that the universe was regulated not by the gods but by natural laws.

Greek religion greatly influenced later civilizations. Through its traditional legends and myths, related in Homer's epic poems, classical Greek plays, and portrayed in famous sculptures, Greek religious values and cultural ideas have been absorbed as a major part of the world's cultural heritage. For example, the Romans identified their gods with those of the Greeks, and many of the stories about Greek heroes and gods have influenced modern literature.

Greek View of Foreigners As trade and colonies expanded, the Greeks came in contact with people from foreign lands with different languages and customs. Greeks called them *barbaroi*, people who did not speak Greek, and felt superior to them.

The English word *barbarian* comes from this Greek term. These "barbarians" even included the Phoenicians and Egyptians, from whom the Greeks borrowed important ideas and inventions. This sense of uniqueness and superiority would help the Greeks when they were threatened by the mightiest power in the Mediterranean world—the Persian empire.

IDENTIFY What factors united the city-states of Greece?

>> At this Tholos Temple in Delphi, Greeks offered sacrifices to Athena, guardian of the famous oracle, before asking their questions. This *tholos*, or circular structure, was built about 400 B.C.

Greek Wars with Persia

The Greek city-states were often at odds with one another. Yet when the Persians threatened them, the Greeks briefly put aside their differences to defend their freedom.

The Persians had conquered a huge empire stretching from Asia Minor to the border of India. Their subjects included the Greek city-states of Ionia in Asia Minor. Though under Persian rule, these Ionian city-states were largely self-governing. Still, they resented their situation.

In 499 B.C., Ionian Greeks rebelled against Persian rule. Athens sent ships to help them. As the historian Herodotus wrote some years later, "These ships were the beginning of mischief both to the Greeks and to the barbarians."

Athens Wins at Marathon The Persians soon crushed the rebel cities. However, Darius I was furious at the role Athens played in the uprising.

In time, Darius sent a huge force across the Aegean to punish Athens for its interference. The mighty Persian army landed near Marathon, a plain north of Athens, in 490 B.C. The Athenians asked for help

Answers

Identify *their language and shared myths and religious beliefs and a general feeling of their uniqueness and superiority over other peoples*

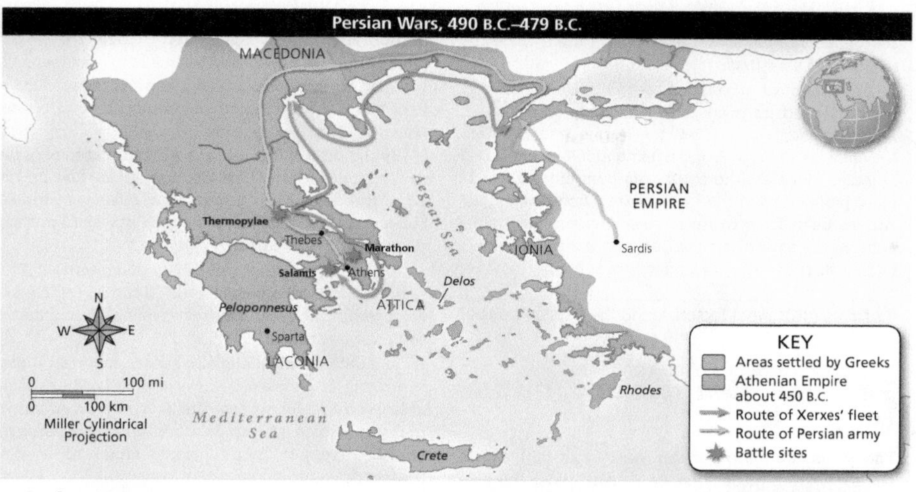

>> **Analyze Maps** When the Persian empire attacked Greece, the Greek city-states briefly joined forces for defense. Describe the routes of the Persian army and navy toward Athens.

Interactive Map

from neighboring Greek city-states, but received little support.

The Persians greatly outnumbered Athenian forces. Yet the invaders were amazed to see "a mere handful of men coming on at a run without either horsemen or archers." The Persians responded with a rain of arrows, but the Greeks rushed onward. They broke through the Persian line and engaged in fierce hand-to-hand combat. Overwhelmed by the fury of the assault, the Persians hastily retreated to their ships.

The Athenians celebrated their triumph. Still, the Athenian leader, Themistocles (thuh MIS tuh kleez), knew the victory at Marathon had bought only a temporary lull in the fighting. He urged Athenians to build a fleet of warships and prepare other defenses.

Greek City-States Join Together Darius died before he could mass his troops for another attack. But in 480 B.C. his son Xerxes (ZURK seez) sent a much larger force to conquer Greece. By this time, Athens had persuaded Sparta and other city-states to join in the fight against Persia.

Once again, the Persians landed in northern Greece. A small Spartan force guarded the narrow mountain pass at Thermopylae (thur MAHP uh lee). Led by the great warrior-king Leonidas (lee AHN ih dus), the Spartans held out heroically against the enormous Persian force but were defeated in the end. The Persians marched south and burned Athens. The city was empty, however. The Athenians had already withdrawn to safety.

The Greeks now put their faith in the fleet of ships that Themistocles had urged them to build. The Athenians lured the Persian navy into the narrow strait of Salamis (SAHL uh mis). Then Athenian warships, powered by rowers, drove into the Persian ships with submerged battering rams. On the shore, Xerxes watched helplessly as his mighty fleet sank.

The next year, the Greeks defeated the Persians on land in Asia Minor. This victory marked the end of the Persian invasions. In a brief moment of unity, the Greek city-states had saved themselves from the Persian threat.

Athens Leads the Delian League Victory in the Persian Wars increased the Greeks' sense of their own uniqueness. The gods, they felt, had protected their superior form of government—the city-state—against invaders from Asia.

Athens emerged from the war as the most powerful city-state in Greece. To continue to defend against Persia, it organized with other Greek city-states an **alliance,** or a formal agreement between two or more nations or powers to cooperate and come to one

Online Project the **Interactive Map: Persian Wars, 490 B.C.–479 B.C.** and click through the hotspots with students.

ACTIVE CLASSROOM

Pair students to have a "Conversation With History." Ask the first student to assume the role of a Spartan king. Have the second student assume the role of a visiting official messenger from Athens. The Spartan king listens as the messenger from Athens provides a verbal "tour" of a map of the Aegean, describing the Persian threat to Greece and requesting Spartan military assistance. The Spartan king listens and then asks questions such as: How large is the Persian army? When will the Persians arrive? How many cities will join together to defend Greece? Have students record their conversation so others in class can access it.

Infer Why do you think Xerxes' fleet hugged the Greek coastline instead of sailing directly across the Aegean Sea? *(Sample responses: Warships of the time were not built for deep-sea voyages; unpredictable weather or treacherous currents encouraged ships to travel near the coasts.)*

Guided Reading and Discussion

Ask students to describe the sequence of events leading to the Greek victory in the Persian Wars. *(Sample response: In 490 B.C., the Athenians defeated the Persians at Marathon. Athens then convinced Sparta and other city-states to band together for defense. In 480 B.C., the Persians burned Athens. However, the Athenians lured the Persian fleet into the straits of Salamis and destroyed it, ending the threat of Persian invasion.)*

History Background

Slavery and Democracy Ironically, the system of slavery in ancient Athens probably had a great deal to do with the success of democracy there. Since many Athenians owned slaves, they were freed from the necessity of daily chores and the routine work of commerce and manufacturing. Thus, they could devote their time to discussing affairs in the marketplace, debating issues and voting on laws in the assembly, and holding office.

Answers

Analyze Maps *The Persians followed two routes to Athens: one over land from the north and the second by sea, hugging the coastline and eventually approaching Athens from the south.*

Pericles, Democracy, and War

After the Persian Wars, Pericles led Athens in a golden age with a flourishing economy and a more democratic government. Athenian citizens from all social classes took part directly in their government's daily affairs. Greek concepts related to the rights and responsibilities of citizenship put into practice in Athens at this time set standards that influenced the laws and governments of many later societies.

Compare How does Athenian democracy compare to the democratic system of the United States? *(Sample response: Athenian democracy was a direct democracy unlike the representative democracy of the United States; however, the U.S. system could be considered more democratic in that most adult Americans can vote and therefore have a voice in government.)*

Online Project the **Interactive Gallery: Athenian Democracy** and click through the images with students.

ACTIVE CLASSROOM

Graffiti Concepts: Ask students to reflect on the meaning of one of these concepts—"trial by a jury of your peers," "impartial juries," "innocent until proven guilty," and "the rule of law"—and create a visual image and/or phrase that represents that concept. Allow approximately 3 to 5 minutes. Have students post their "graffiti" on the board or on chart paper. Ask students to look at the various responses. Then discuss similarities and differences in the responses as a group.

Guided Reading and Discussion

Ask students to compare and contrast the Persian and Peloponnesian wars, focusing on the outcomes.

another's defense. Modern scholars call this alliance the Delian League after Delos, the location where the league held meetings.

From the start Athens dominated the Delian League. It slowly used its position of leadership to create an Athenian empire. It moved the league treasury from the island of Delos to Athens, using money contributed by other city-states to rebuild its own city. When its allies protested and tried to withdraw from the league, Athens used force to make them remain. Yet, while Athens was enforcing its will abroad, Athenian leaders were championing political freedom at home.

DESCRIBE What factors led to the Persian defeat?

Pericles, Democracy, and War

The years after the Persian Wars from 460 B.C. to 429 B.C. were a golden age for Athens under the able statesman **Pericles** (PEHR uh kleez). Because of his wise and skillful leadership the economy thrived and the government became more democratic.

>> Pericles (c. 495 B.C.–429 B.C.), shown here in a Roman marble bust copied from a Greek original, came from a rich noble family. His father led the Athenian assembly and fought at Salamis.

Democracy in Athens Periclean Athens was a **direct democracy.** Under this system, citizens take part directly in the day-to-day affairs of government. By contrast, in most democratic countries today, citizens participate in government indirectly through elected representatives.

By the time of Pericles, the Athenian assembly met several times a month. A Council of 500, selected by lot, conducted daily government business. Pericles believed that all citizens, regardless of wealth or social class, should take part in government.

Athens therefore began to pay a **stipend,** or fixed salary, to men who participated in the Assembly and its governing Council. This reform enabled poor men to serve in government.

In addition, Athenians also served on juries. A **jury** is a group of people who have the authority to make a decision in a legal case. Unlike a modern American trial jury, which is usually made up of 12 members, an Athenian jury might include hundreds or even thousands of jurors.

Citizens over 30 years of age were chosen by lot to serve on the jury for a year. Effectively, Athenian citizens were tried by a jury of their peers, a basic legal principle echoed in England's Magna Carta, the U.S. Sixth Amendment, and in American jury trials today. Also, the fundamental legal concepts of the "rule of law" (all must obey the laws) and "innocent until proven guilty" were substantially embodied in the laws of Athens and Sparta.

Athenian citizens could also vote to banish, or send away, a public figure whom they saw as a threat to their democracy. This process was called **ostracism** (AHS truh siz um). The person with the largest number of votes cast against him was ostracized, meaning that that individual would have to live outside the city, usually for a period of 10 years.

Athenian Culture Thrives Athens prospered during the Age of Pericles. With the empire's riches, Pericles directed the rebuilding of the Acropolis, which the Persians had destroyed. With the help of an educated foreign-born woman named Aspasia (as PAY shuh), Pericles turned Athens into the cultural center of Greece. They encouraged the arts through public festivals, dramatic competitions, and building programs. Such building projects increased Athenians' prosperity by creating jobs for artisans and workers.

The Peloponnesian War Many Greeks outside Athens resented Athenian domination. Before long, the Greek world was split into rival camps.

To counter the Delian League, Sparta and other enemies of Athens formed the Peloponnesian League.

D Differentiate Special Needs/ Extra Support To reinforce student understanding of the development of direct democracy in Pericles' Athens, have students scan this text section and find the (bold) key terms and people. Ask students to write a simple explanation of each by illustrating the word, sketching a map, writing a definition, or any combination of these.

Assessment

1. Sample answer: The earliest civilizations rose in fertile river valleys with organized irrigation systems so that farmers could support large cities. Greece is divided by mountains and has a rugged coast and hundreds of islands. Within these geographic conditions, the ancient Greeks established numerous small city-states separated from each other by mountains or water.

Answers

Describe *Athenian assistance in the Ionian revolt, unification of the Greek city-states, Greek preparation*

In 431 B.C. warfare broke out between Athens and Sparta. This conflict, which became known as the Peloponnesian War, soon engulfed all of Greece. The fighting would last for 27 years.

Athens Defeated by Sparta Despite its riches and powerful navy, Athens faced a serious geographic disadvantage. Because Sparta was inland, Athens could not use its navy to attack. Sparta's powerful army, however, had only to march north to attack Athens. When the Spartan troops came near, Pericles allowed people from the countryside to move inside the city walls. The overcrowded conditions led to a terrible plague that killed many Athenians, including Pericles himself.

As the war dragged on each side committed savage acts against the other. Sparta even allied itself with Persia, the longtime enemy of the Greeks. Finally, in 404 B.C., with the help of the Persian navy, the Spartans captured Athens. The victors stripped the Athenians of their fleet and empire. However, Sparta rejected calls from its allies to destroy Athens.

The Decline of Greek Dominion The Peloponnesian War ended Athenian domination of the Greek world. The Athenian economy eventually revived and Athens remained the cultural center of Greece. However, its spirit and vitality declined. Meanwhile, as Greeks battled among themselves, a new power rose in Macedonia (mas uh DOH nee uh), a kingdom to the north of Greece. By 359 B.C. its ambitious ruler stood poised to conquer the quarrelsome Greek city-states.

DESCRIBE Describe Pericles' influence on Athens.

>> Athena, patroness of Athens and goddess of wisdom, observes citizens fulfilling one of their most important responsibilities in a democracy—voting.

Interactive Gallery

>> The Greek hoplite was named after his unique shield, the *hoplon*. These heavily armored soldiers were usually men from the middle class who could afford to purchase the armor and weapons.

ASSESSMENT

1. **Contrast** the earliest civilizations, which rose in fertile river valleys, with the geographical conditions that influenced the rise of ancient Greek civilization.
2. **Identify Steps in a Process** Explain how democracy evolved in ancient Greece from earlier forms of government in Greece.
3. **Draw Conclusions** How do you think Greek concepts related to the rights and responsibilities of citizenship influence modern societies?
4. **Infer** How do you think the culture and values shared by Greeks both united and divided them?
5. **Summarize** how the Persian and Peloponnesian Wars affected Greece.

Topic 5 Lesson 2

SYNTHESIZE

Online Project the **Digital Activity: Alliances: Cooperation for a Cause**. Have students work in pairs for five minutes to brainstorm and write down brief answers to each question in the activity. They should suggest why countries form alliances and what might be the resulting advantages, disadvantages, and tensions.

DEMONSTRATE

Online Assign the **Digital Lesson Quiz** for this lesson if you haven't already done so. Students will be offered automatic remediation or enrichment based on their score.

Pose these questions to the class on the Discussion Board:

Summarize How did the Persian Wars affect the Greek city-states? *(The Persian Wars united the Greek city-sates, increased the power and wealth of Athens, and led to the formation of the Delian League.)*

Identify Cause and Effect How did the growth of Athenian power lead to war? *(Resentment of Athenian power encouraged rivals to set up their own alliances, and the rivalry eventually escalated into war.)*

Topic Inquiry

Have students continue their investigations for the Topic Inquiry.

Answers

Describe *His leadership led Athens to its greatest achievements, which included a stable and prosperous economy, a more democratic government, and increased cultural development.*

2. Monarchy was the earliest form of Greek government, but power shifted to an aristocracy, in which an elite class of landowners rules and provides military defense. A wealthy middle class formed as trade increased and challenged the landowners, creating an oligarchy, where power is held by a small, wealthy elite. By 700 B.C., Athenian landowners held power, but people demanded more rights. Economic and political reforms increased their role in government and led to a limited democracy.
3. Sample answer: Greek concepts about the rights and responsibilities of citizenship set the standard by which we judge the claims and results of modern democratic governments and societies. The rights citizens have, such as equality before the law, and the responsibilities they fulfill, such as participating in public life or defending their country, go back to the ideals and practices of ancient Greece.
4. A shared language and religion resulted in a common Greek culture, but the independent attitude, local identification, and economic competition often led to fighting.
5. Victory in the Persian Wars affirmed the Greek sense of uniqueness. They felt the gods had protected the city-state from Asian invaders. Athens's powerful status, a result of the Persian Wars, was ended by defeat in the Peloponnesian War. The city-states then began to fight each other.

Greek Thinkers, Artists, and Writers

CONNECT

Preview Have students preview the **Lesson Objectives** and the list of **Key Terms**.

Students can also preview all the **Key Terms** and **Academic Vocabulary** using the **Interactive Reading Notepad** on the digital course or preview a summary of the lesson in the **Reading and Note Taking Study Guide**.

Online Use the **Editable Presentation** found on the digital course to present the main ideas for this lesson.

Start Up Activity

Tell students that they probably already have some knowledge of the philosophers, art and architecture, and literature of ancient Greece.

Discuss Ask students what they know about Greek art and architecture. *(They may be familiar with Greek sculpture or architectural design elements.)* Ask what they know about Greek philosophers. *(They may name Socrates, Plato, or Aristotle and may know of their ethical or political philosophies or of the Socratic method of teaching.)* Ask what they know about Greek poetry and drama. *(They may name Sappho, Sophocles, or Aristophanes and may be familiar with Greek masks of tragedy and comedy.)*

Online You can also project the **Start Up Activity** from the course.

INVESTIGATE

Have students read the lesson using the **Reading and Note Taking Study Guide** to help them take notes and understand the text as they read.

Philosophers and the Pursuit of Wisdom

Using observation and reasoning, Greek philosophers explored many subjects, including mathematics, music, ethics, and morality. Socrates, Plato, and Aristotle searched for laws that governed human behavior and the universe, seeking truth by questioning ideas and beliefs, including the authority of traditions. Plato and Aristotle established schools where they taught their ideas and examined many branches of knowledge.

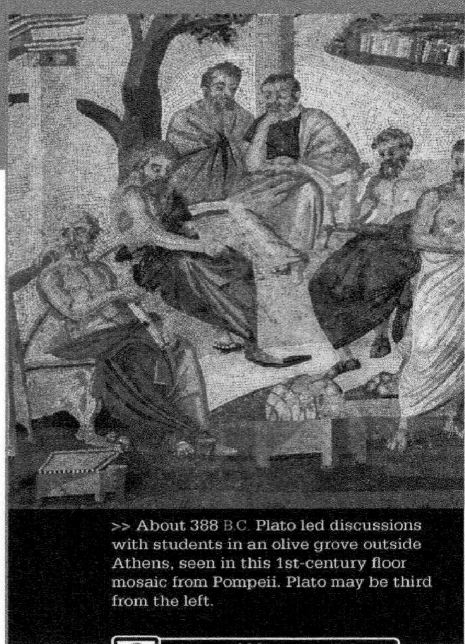

>> About 388 B.C. Plato led discussions with students in an olive grove outside Athens, seen in this 1st-century floor mosaic from Pompeii. Plato may be third from the left.

5.3 **Even in the midst of wars and political turmoil, Greeks had confidence in the power of the human mind. Driven by curiosity and a belief in reason, Greek thinkers, artists, and writers explored the nature of the universe and the place of people in it. To later admirers, Greek achievements in the arts represented the height of human development in the Western world. They looked back with deep respect on what one poet called "the glory that was Greece."**

TEKS
1.B, 3.A, 25.B, 26.B, 26.C

>> Objectives

Analyze the political and ethical ideas developed by ancient Greek philosophers.

Understand how balance and order governed ancient Greek art and architecture.

Identify the themes explored by ancient Greek writers and historians.

>> Key Terms

philosopher
logic
rhetoric
Socrates
Plato
Aristotle
Parthenon
tragedy
comedy
Herodotus

Greek Thinkers, Artists, and Writers

Philosophers and the Pursuit of Wisdom

As you have read, some ancient Greek thinkers challenged the belief that events were caused by the whims of gods. Instead, they used observation and reason to find causes for events. The Greeks called these thinkers **philosophers,** meaning "lovers of wisdom."

Greek philosophers explored many subjects, from mathematics and music to **logic,** or rational thinking. Through reason and observation, they believed, they could discover laws that governed the universe. Much modern science traces its roots to the Greek search for such principles.

Debating Morality and Ethics Some Greek philosophers were interested in ethics and morality. They debated such questions as what was the best kind of government and what standards should rule human behavior.

In Athens, the Sophists questioned accepted ideas. To them, success was more important than moral truth. They developed skills in **rhetoric,** the art of skillful speaking. Ambitious men could use clever and persuasive rhetoric to advance their careers. The turmoil of

Aa Vocabulary Builder

1. Have students pronounce the following academic vocabulary terms in this lesson and clarify the part of speech.
2. Explain what the word means in common "student-friendly" language using synonyms and antonyms when possible. Provide concrete examples to clarify the meaning, and rephrase the definition.

rigid: stiff; unbending; severe

bias: a mental leaning; prejudice; slant

the Peloponnesian War led many young Athenians to follow the Sophists. Older citizens, however, accused the Sophists of undermining traditional Greek values.

Socrates Challenges Tradition One outspoken critic of the Sophists was **Socrates,** an Athenian stonemason and philosopher. Most of what we know about Socrates comes from his student **Plato.** Socrates himself wrote no books. Instead he passed his days in the town square asking people about their beliefs.

Using a process we now call the Socratic method, he would pose a series of questions to a student or passing citizen, and challenge them to examine the implications of their answers. To Socrates, this patient examination was a way to help others seek truth and self-knowledge. To many Athenians, however, such questioning was a threat to accepted values and traditions.

When he was about 70 years old, Socrates was put on trial. His enemies accused him of corrupting the city's youth and failing to respect the gods. Standing before a jury of 501 citizens, Socrates offered a calm and reasoned defense. But the jurors condemned him to death.

Loyal to the laws of Athens, Socrates accepted the death penalty. He drank a cup of hemlock, a deadly poison.

Plato Describes a Perfect Society The execution of Socrates left Plato with a lifelong distrust of democracy. He fled Athens for 10 years. When he returned, he set up a school called the Academy. There, he taught and wrote about his own ideas. Like Socrates, Plato emphasized the importance of reason. Through rational thought, he argued, people could discover unchanging ethical values, recognize perfect beauty, and learn how best to organize society.

In his book *The Republic,* Plato described his vision of an ideal state. He rejected Athenian democracy because it had condemned Socrates just as it tended to other excesses. Instead, Plato argued that the state should regulate every aspect of its citizens' lives in order to provide for their best interests. He divided his ideal society into three classes: workers to produce the necessities of life, soldiers to defend the state, and philosophers to rule. This elite class of leaders would be specially trained to ensure order and justice. The wisest of them, a philosopher-king, would have the ultimate authority.

Plato thought that, in general, men surpassed women in mental and physical tasks, but that some women were superior to some men. Talented women, he said, should be educated to serve the state. The ruling elite, both men and women, would take military

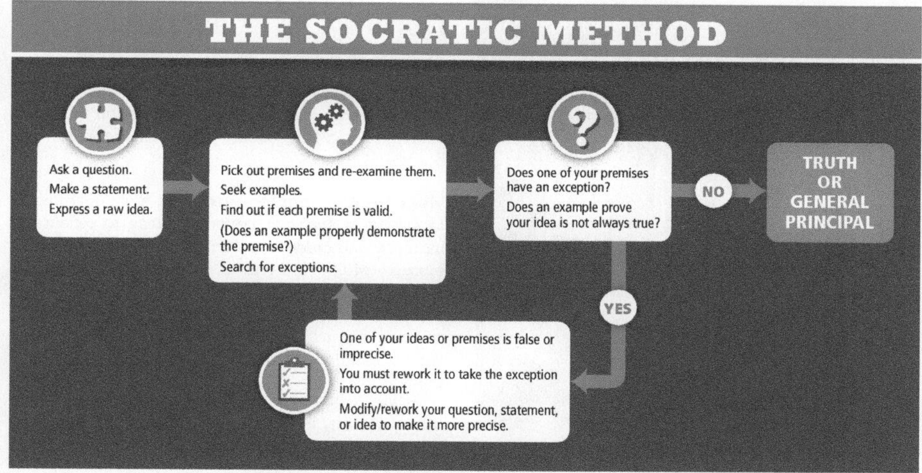
THE SOCRATIC METHOD
Ask a question.
Make a statement.
Express a raw idea.
Pick out premises and re-examine them.
Seek examples.
Find out if each premise is valid.
(Does an example properly demonstrate the premise?)
Search for exceptions.
Does one of your premises have an exception?
Does an example prove your idea is not always true?
NO
TRUTH OR GENERAL PRINCIPAL
YES
One of your ideas or premises is false or imprecise.
You must rework it to take the exception into account.
Modify/rework your question, statement, or idea to make it more precise.

>> The Socratic method uses questions and answers as steps in a reasoning process that aims to arrive at truths by logically examining the underlying assumptions and implications of statements.

Interactive Chart

Topic 5 Lesson 3

Online Project the **Interactive Chart: Understanding Greek Philosophers**. Look at each description individually and then the collection of descriptions as a whole.

ACTIVE CLASSROOM

Employ the Make Headlines Strategy with the interactive chart to explore the ideas and techniques of the ancient Greek philosophers. Ask: If you were to write a headline right now to capture the most important aspect that should be remembered about a Greek thinker, what would that headline be? Pass your headline to a partner for them to review—they can keep yours or ask for theirs back. *(Sample answers: "Socrates Seeks Truth With Questions," "Plato Describes Ideal State")*

Contrast How did the aims and techniques of the Sophists differ from the goals and approach of Socrates and Plato? *(Answers may vary but should include that the Sophists taught rhetoric, the art of skillful and persuasive speaking. Unlike Socrates and Plato, they believed that success was more important than moral truth.)*

Guided Reading and Discussion

Tell students that Socrates said, "The unexamined life is not worth living." Ask: How did his actions support this idea? *(Sample response: Although Socrates' constant questioning and examination brought public disapproval, he continued to do so because without this, for Socrates, life would not be worth living.)*

English Language Proficiency Standards

Listening 2.C.1 Read "Philosophers and the Pursuit of Wisdom" aloud. Instruct students to complete one of the following activities based on their level of English proficiency.

Beginning Identify independent and dependent clauses in the text. Say each sentence aloud and ask students to repeat. Then use a fact or term from the text to model creating these types of clauses. Say these clauses aloud and have students identify each as independent or dependent and say them aloud.

Intermediate Follow the Beginning activity instructions, but have students work together to create clauses about a fact or a term from the text. Write and display the sentences and have them identify the subject and verb and say the sentences aloud.

Advanced Review the difference between dependent and independent clauses. Have student pairs write four examples of each clause about the Greek philosophers. Have pairs share their writing with another pair. Students should take turns saying their clauses aloud, and the listeners will determine the type of clause. Then the groups should create complete sentences using all of their clauses and share them with the class.

Advanced High Ask students to explain the difference between dependent and independent clauses. Then follow the Advance activity instructions, but have individual students write clauses and share them with a partner.

Conveying Ideals in Architecture and Art

Greek architects and artists sought to express in created forms ideals of balance, order, and beauty. Reflecting the harmony and order of the universe, architects attempted to evoke a sense of perfect balance in buildings such as the Parthenon, which has been admired for centuries. Greek sculptors and painters also strived for the ideal by creating the most lifelike and graceful images of perfect human forms.

Online Project the **Interactive Gallery: Art and Architecture of Ancient Greece** and click through the images with students.

ACTIVE CLASSROOM

Have students describe the Parthenon's history or the history of another object shown in the interactive gallery using the If Photos Could Talk Strategy. Ask: What do you think the Parthenon (or other object) would say about the rise of Athens and the evolution of democracy there if it could talk? What's your evidence? Have students present their responses to the class. *(Sample response: "As a temple dedicated to this city's patron goddess, I watched people pray for my help in their lives—for their children, for success in war, for changes in leadership—and saw the shifting fortunes of Athens.")*

Guided Reading and Discussion

Tell students that the architecture and art of ancient Greece is considered "classic"—a standard of excellence against which other art forms are measured. Invite students to explain why. *(Greek architecture, sculpture, and painting embody perfect human form or portray ideal forms of balance, order, and beauty.)*

>> Aristotle (384 B.C.–322 B.C.) is counted among the greatest philosophers and scientists of Western history. His system of thought provided a framework for later Christian and Islamic philosophy.

training together and raise their children in communal centers for the good of the republic.

Aristotle Seeks the Golden Mean Plato's most famous student, **Aristotle,** developed his own ideas about government. He analyzed all forms of government, from monarchy to democracy, and found good and bad examples of each. Like Plato, he was suspicious of democracy, which he thought could lead to mob rule. In the end, he favored rule by a single strong and virtuous leader.

Aristotle also addressed the question of how people ought to live. In his view, good conduct meant pursuing the "golden mean," a moderate course between the extremes.

He promoted reason as the guiding force for learning. He set up a school, the Lyceum, for the study of all branches of knowledge. He left writings on politics, ethics, logic, biology, literature, and many other subjects. When the first European universities evolved some 1,500 years later, their courses were based largely on the works and ideas of Aristotle.

DRAW CONCLUSIONS Why might some of the philosophers' ideas be a threat to Greek tradition?

ELPS **ELPS 2.C.1** Practice identifying and creating complete sentences about *Philosophers and the Pursuit of Wisdom.*

>> The builders of the Parthenon (shown here), seeking to reflect a harmonious universe, used geometric proportions to convey a dignified sense of order that feels balanced.

Interactive Gallery

Conveying Ideals in Architecture and Art

Plato argued that every object on Earth had an ideal form. The work of ancient Greek artists and architects reflected a similar concern with balance, order, and beauty.

Monumental Architecture Greek architects sought to convey a sense of perfect balance to reflect the harmony and order of the universe. The most famous example of Greek architecture is the **Parthenon,** a temple dedicated to the goddess Athena. The basic plan of the Parthenon is a simple rectangle, with tall columns supporting a gently sloping roof. The delicate curves and placement of the columns add dignity and grace.

Greek architecture has been widely admired for centuries. Today, many public buildings throughout the world have incorporated Greek architectural elements, such as columns, in their designs.

D Differentiate **Special Needs/Extra Support** For visual learners and students who need help with basic skills, direct attention to the **Interactive Gallery: Art and Architecture of Ancient Greece**. Explain that these visuals show some of the finest examples of Greek art and architecture. Ask volunteers to explain how individual images demonstrate Greek ideals of beauty, balance, and order starting from the left-most image. *(For example, the image of the Parthenon shows a rectangular building with columns. It is built from simple geometric shapes—rectangles, a triangle—arranged in a graceful, orderly, and balanced way.)*

Answers

Draw Conclusions *Since the philosophers are perpetually questioning and examining aspects of life, it is possible that the results of their inquiries may challenge or disprove existing traditions and beliefs and thus be a threat to Greek traditions.*

Topic 5 Lesson 3

Crafting Lifelike Human Forms Early Greek sculptors carved figures in stiff, lifeless poses, similar in style to the art of ancient Egypt. By 450 B.C., however, Greek sculptors had developed a new style that emphasized more natural forms. While their work was lifelike, it was also idealistic. That is, sculptors carved gods, goddesses, athletes, and famous men in a way that showed human beings in their most perfect, graceful form.

The only Greek paintings to survive are on pottery. They offer intriguing views of everyday Greek life. Women carry water from wells, warriors race into battle, and athletes compete in javelin contests. Each scene is designed to fit the shape of the pottery.

DESCRIBE How did Greek art reflect the idea of an ideal form?

>> Thousands of surviving painted vases provide us with much of what we know about daily life in ancient Greece. This vase from the 300s B.C., for example, shows women in conversations at home.

Greek Literature

In literature, as in art, the ancient Greeks developed their own style. To later Europeans, Greek styles were a model of perfection. They admired what they called the "classical style," referring to the elegant and balanced forms of traditional Greek works of art.

Early Greek literature began with the epic poems of Homer, whose stirring tales inspired later writers. In later times, the poet Sappho sang of love and of the beauty of her island home, while the poetry of Pindar celebrated the victors in athletic contests.

Greek Tragedy Perhaps the most important ancient Greek contribution to literature was in the field of drama. The first Greek plays evolved out of religious festivals, especially those held in Athens to honor the god of fertility and wine, Dionysus (dy uh NY sus).

Plays were performed in large outdoor theaters with little or no set. Actors wore elaborate costumes and stylized masks. A chorus sang or chanted comments on the action taking place on stage. Greek dramas were often based on popular myths and legends. Through these familiar stories, playwrights discussed moral and social issues or explored the relationship between people and the gods.

The greatest Athenian playwrights were Aeschylus (ES kih lus), Sophocles (SAH fuh kleez), and Euripides (yoo RIP ih deez). All three wrote **tragedies,** plays that told stories of human suffering that usually ended in disaster. The purpose of tragedy, the Greeks felt, was to stir up and then relieve the emotions of pity and fear. For example, in his play *Oresteia* (aw res TEE uh), Aeschylus showed a powerful family torn apart by betrayal, murder, and revenge. Audiences saw how

>> A Roman fresco from Pompeii believed to be of the Greek poet Sappho (610 B.C.–570 B.C.). Over the ages, readers have been impressed with her writing style and lively personality.

Greek Literature

The ancient Greek writers created the elegant and balanced "classical style" admired by later Europeans. Homer's epic poems inspired later Greek poets who sang of love, beauty, and victorious athletes. In tragedies, Greek playwrights explored universal dramatic conflicts between people and the gods, within families, and between individual duty and laws of the state. Comic writers probed current social issues and poked fun at foolish customs.

Ancient Greek historians collected and recorded information about recent events from witnesses. They also carefully inquired and studied evidence from the past, traveling widely and sometimes taking part in the events they chronicled. Herodotus and Thucydides set critical standards in inquiry and presentation for future historians.

Analyze Images

Direct students' attention to the photograph of the fresco believed to show the Greek poet Sappho. Tell them that the ancient Greeks admiringly referred to Sappho as "the Poetess." Ask students what the person shown in the fresco appears to be doing. *(Possible response: She is thinking about something related to her writing.)*

History Background

The Parthenon The Athenian leader Pericles ordered the building of the Parthenon, dedicated to the goddess Athena Parthenos, in the mid-400s B.C. Colorful sculptures adorned the white marble building, which is 101 feet wide and 228 feet long. The Parthenon stood largely as built for some 800 years until, in the mid-400s A.D. it was turned into a Christian church. In 1460, after the Ottoman Turks took control of Athens, the Parthenon became a mosque, with a minaret built into one corner. During a battle between the Turks and an army from Venice, munitions stored in the Parthenon exploded, damaging the central part of the structure. After 1800, many sculptures, including the famed Elgin marbles, were removed to museums and other locations in Britain, France, Denmark, and elsewhere.

Answers

Describe *through symmetry and graceful geometry in architecture and through perfect and graceful depictions of lifelike forms in sculpture*

Guided Reading and Discussion

Remind students that the playwrights Sophocles and Euripides both survived the horrors of the Peloponnesian War, as did the historian Thucydides. How do you think firsthand experience of this event might have influenced their writing? Why? *(Possible responses: Sophocles and Euripides might have favored tragedies as a result of having experienced the horrors of war. Thucydides might also have adopted a tragic view of the events he experienced; or his personal experience might have motivated him to understand as much as possible about all aspects and points of view before writing his history of this war.)*

Key Terms

Have students locate the key term **comedies** (in bold) in the text. Ask students what, for them, is a typical comedy. Explain that the elements of Greek comedies were not so different from those of modern comedies. They ranged from slapstick to satire and often employed song, dance, and outlandish costumes.

"... it was not Zeus that had published me that edict [law]; not such are the laws set among men by the Justice who dwells with the gods below; nor deemed [judged] I that thy decrees were of such force, that a mortal could override the unwritten and unfailing statutes of heaven.

—Sophocles, *Antigone* (translated by Richard C. Jebb)

>> Modern versions of ancient Greek dramas and myths are often presented today. Shown here is a 2001 Italian production of *Persephone* with Isabella Rossellini.

even the powerful could be subject to horrifying misfortune and how the wrath of the gods could bring down even the greatest heroes.

> . . . it was not Zeus that had published me that edict [law]; not such are the laws set among men by the Justice who dwells with the gods below; nor deemed [judged] I that thy decrees were of such force, that a mortal could override the unwritten and unfailing statutes of heaven.
>
> —Sophocles, *Antigone* (translated by Richard C. Jebb)

In *Antigone* (an TIG uh nee), Sophocles explored what happens when an individual's moral duty conflicts with the laws of the state. Antigone is a young woman whose brother has been killed leading a rebellion. King Creon forbids anyone to bury the traitor's body. When Antigone buries her brother anyway, she is sentenced to death. She defiantly tells Creon that duty to the gods is greater than human law.

Like Sophocles, Euripides survived the horrors of the Peloponnesian War. That experience probably led him to question many accepted ideas of his day.

His plays suggested that people, not the gods, were the cause of human misfortune and suffering. In *The Trojan Women*, he stripped war of its glamour by showing the suffering of women who were victims of the war.

Greek Comedy Some Greek playwrights wrote **comedies,** humorous plays that mocked people or customs. Almost all the surviving ancient Greek comedies were written by Aristophanes (a rih STAHF uh neez). In *Lysistrata,* he shows the women of Athens banding together to force their husbands to end a war against Sparta. Unlike tragedy, which focused on events of the past, comedies ridiculed individuals of the day, including political figures, philosophers, and prominent members of society. Through ridicule,

D Differentiate Challenge/Gifted Have students consider the importance of Herodotus' and Thucydides' advances in writing history. Then ask them to work in pairs to write a short history of this class period, by collecting information from firsthand observers and presenting it without bias. Have students present their histories to the class.

Answers

Identify *Greek writers used familiar stories that explored the relationship between people and the gods to discuss morality through poetry and drama.*

Assessment

1. By carefully posing a series of questions to people about their beliefs, Socrates wanted people to think about the implications of their answers. The effect of such patient examination, he believed, could lead people to truth and self-knowledge.
2. Greek architects sought to embody in their buildings a sense of perfect balance that reflected the harmony and order of the universe. For example, the basic plan of the Parthenon, a temple dedicated to the goddess Athena, is a simple rectangle. Carefully placed tall columns support a gently sloping roof. The delicate curves of the columns contribute dignity and grace to the temple's overall appearance of balance.
3. Themes that Greek playwrights addressed include the consequences of family betrayal, murder, and revenge; the relationship between people and the gods; conflicts between an individual's moral duty and the state's laws; how people, not

comic playwrights sharply criticized society, much as political cartoonists do today.

IDENTIFY How was drama used to influence Greek society?

Studying History

The Greeks also applied observation, reason, and logic to the study of history. **Herodotus** is often called the "Father of History" in the Western world because he went beyond listing names of rulers or the retelling of ancient legends. Before writing *The Persian Wars,* Herodotus visited many lands, collecting information from people who remembered the actual events he chronicled. In fact, Herodotus used the Greek term *historie,* which means inquiry, to define his work. Our *history* comes from this word, but its definition has evolved today to simply mean the recording and study of past events.

Herodotus cast a critical eye on his sources, noting bias and conflicting accounts. However, despite this special care for detail and accuracy, his writings reflected his own view that the war was a clear moral victory of Greek love of freedom over Persian tyranny. He even invented conversations and speeches for historical figures.

Another historian, Thucydides, who was a few years younger than Herodotus, wrote about the Peloponnesian War, a much less happy subject for the Greeks. He had lived through the war and vividly described the war's savagery and corrupting influence on all those involved. Although he was an Athenian, he tried to be fair to both sides.

Both writers set standards for future historians. Herodotus stressed the importance of research. Thucydides showed the need to avoid bias.

IDENTIFY MAIN IDEAS Why is Herodotus considered the "Father of History"?

>> Herodotus (*c.* 484 B.C.–*c.* 425 B.C.) was born under Persian rule at Halicarnassus, a Greek city in Asia Minor. His *The Persian Wars* is famous as the ancient world's first great narrative history.

ASSESSMENT

1. **Identify Cause and Effect** Why did Socrates question Athenians about their beliefs?
2. **Cite Evidence** How did balance and order govern Greek architecture?
3. **Summarize** the themes explored by Greek playwrights.
4. **Contrast** the subject matters of Greek tragedy and Greek comedy.
5. **Determine Point of View** How do you think the points of view of Herodotus and Thucydides influenced their approaches to writing history?

SYNTHESIZE

Online Project the **Digital Activity: Remembering Greece**. Have students, using the Think-Pair-Share strategy, take 5 minutes to write down brief answers to the questions below and then share their answers with a partner. Ask partners to think about the following questions.

Which ideas and accomplishments of the ancient Greeks were familiar to you? Which were most impressive? Which did you know about before but did not know that they originated in ancient Greece? Did your impressions about Greece change after studying this lesson?

DEMONSTRATE

Online Assign the **Digital Lesson Quiz** for this lesson if you haven't already done so. Students will be offered automatic remediation or enrichment based on their score.

Pose these questions to the class on the Discussion Board:

Cite Evidence How do the roots of modern science go back to the ancient Greek philosophers? Support your answer with evidence from the text. *(Sample response: The Greek philosophers believed that by observation and reasoning they could find the laws that governed the universe. They also used observation, mathematics, and logic to search for and explore such laws or principles.)*

Topic Inquiry

Have students continue their investigations for the Topic Inquiry.

the gods, caused human misfortune; and foolish customs and behavior of prominent members of contemporary Greek society.

4. Greek tragedy focused on events of the past often taken from myths or legends, probing moral or social issues, or how people interacted with the gods. Greek comedy criticized the current state of affairs—politicians, philosophers, and other notable members of society—as well as customs of the day.
5. Sample answer: Thucydides had an insider's knowledge from experience of the Peloponnesian War's destructive effects. This would likely influence and perhaps bias his approach to writing. Herodotus was less personally involved in what he wrote about. He traveled and interviewed people who remembered the Persian wars. Such research, although perhaps limiting his insight, might also result in a more objective approach to writing history.

Answers

Identify Main Ideas *because he went beyond simply listing names and retelling ancient legends and tried to collect information from witnesses to relate history accurately*

Topic 5 Lesson 4

Alexander the Great and the Legacy of Greece

CONNECT

Preview Have students preview the **Lesson Objectives** and the list of **Key Terms**.

Students can also preview all the **Key Terms** and **Academic Vocabulary** using the **Interactive Reading Notepad** on the digital course or preview a summary of the lesson in the **Reading and Note Taking Study Guide**.

Online Use the **Editable Presentation** found on the digital course to present the main ideas for this lesson.

Start Up Activity

Explain to students that after the Peloponnesian War, Macedonian rulers conquered Greece. Ask: What do you think might be the fate of Greek arts and ideas? Will they disappear? *(Sample answer: The arts and ideas were so strong and significant that they will survive the conquest.)*

Tell students that in this lesson they will learn about how Alexander the Great conquered vast territories, founded cities, and spread Greek culture from Egypt to India.

Online You can also project the **Start Up Activity** from the course.

INVESTIGATE

Have students read the lesson using the **Reading and Note Taking Study Guide** to help them take notes and understand the text as they read.

The New Era of Alexander the Great

Alexander, at age 20, unexpectedly became ruler of the backward kingdom of Macedonia when his father was assassinated. During the next 12 years, he led his army in the conquest of an empire that stretched from Greece to India.

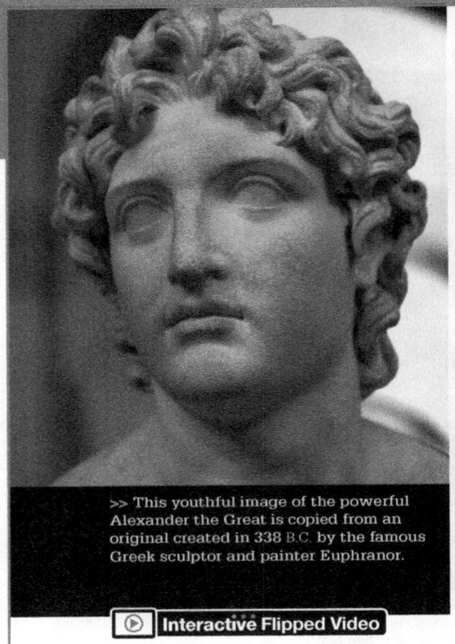

>> This youthful image of the powerful Alexander the Great is copied from an original created in 338 B.C. by the famous Greek sculptor and painter Euphranor.

5.4 In 338 B.C., Athens fell to the Macedonian army. Athens and the other Greek city-states lost their independence. Yet the disaster ushered in a new age in which Greek culture spread from the Mediterranean to the borders of India. The architect of this new era was the man who would eventually become known to history as Alexander the Great.

Interactive Flipped Video

TEKS 1.B, 3.A, 20.A, 24.A, 26.B, 27.A, 27.E

>> Objectives

Explain how Alexander the Great built an extensive empire.

Describe the empire's cultural impact.

Identify major Hellenic Greek scientists and their discoveries and innovations.

>> Key Terms

Alexander the Great
Philip II
assassination
assimilate
Alexandria
Pythagoras
heliocentric
Archimedes
Hippocrates

Alexander the Great and the Legacy of Greece

The New Era of Alexander the Great

To the Greeks, the rugged, mountainous kingdom of Macedonia was a backward, half-civilized land. The rulers of this frontier land, in fact, were of Greek origin and kept ties to their Greek neighbors. As a youth, **Philip II** had lived in Thebes and had come to admire Greek culture. Later, he hired Aristotle as a tutor to his young son Alexander.

Philip II Takes Control of Greece When Philip II gained the throne in 359 B.C. he dreamed of conquering the prosperous city-states to the south. He built a superb and powerful army. Through threats, bribery, and diplomacy, he formed alliances with many Greek city-states. Others he conquered. In 338 B.C., when Athens and Thebes joined forces against him, Philip II defeated them at the battle of Chaeronea (kehr uh NEE uh). He then brought all of Greece under his control.

Philip had a still grander dream—to conquer the Persian empire. Before he could achieve that plan, though, he was assassinated at his

PEARSON realize. www.PearsonTexas.com Access your Digital Lesson.

Aa Vocabulary Builder

1. Have students pronounce the following academic vocabulary terms in this lesson and clarify the part of speech. For difficult or polysyllabic words, break them into syllables and pronounce them with the students.
2. Explain what the word means in common "student-friendly" language using synonyms and antonyms when possible. Provide concrete examples to clarify the meaning, and rephrase the definition.

accumulate: to gather or collect over a period of time

elaborate: developed in great detail; highly ornamented

daughter's wedding. **Assassination** is the murder of a public figure, usually for political reasons. Philip's queen, Olympias, then outmaneuvered his other wives and children to put her own son, Alexander, on the throne.

Alexander Conquers Persia Alexander was only 20 years old. Yet he was already an experienced soldier who shared his father's ambitions. With Greece subdued, he began organizing the forces needed to conquer Persia. By 334 B.C. he had enough ships to cross the Dardanelles, the strait separating Europe from Asia Minor.

Persia was no longer the great power it had once been. The emperor Darius III was weak, and the provinces were often in rebellion against him. Still, the Persian empire stretched more than 2,000 miles from Egypt to India.

Alexander won his first victory against the Persians at the Granicus River. He then moved from victory to victory, marching through Asia Minor into Palestine and south to Egypt before turning east again to take Babylon in 331 B.C. Other cities followed. But before Alexander could capture Darius, the Persian emperor was murdered.

The March into India With much of the Persian empire under his control, the restless Alexander headed farther east. He crossed the Hindu Kush into northern India. There, in 326 B.C., his troops for the first time faced soldiers mounted on war elephants. Although Alexander never lost a battle, his soldiers were tired of the long campaign and refused to go farther east.

Reluctantly, Alexander agreed to turn back. After a long and difficult march, they reached Babylon, where Alexander began planning a new campaign.

The Early Death of Alexander Before he could set out again, the thirty-two-year-old fell victim to a sudden fever. As Alexander lay dying, his commanders asked to whom he left his immense empire. "To the strongest," he is said to have whispered.

No one leader proved strong enough to succeed Alexander. Instead, after years of disorder, three generals divided up the empire. Macedonia and Greece went to one general, Egypt to another, and most of Persia to a third. For the next 300 years, their descendants competed for power over the lands Alexander had conquered.

EXPLAIN Why was Alexander the Great able to conquer the Persian empire?

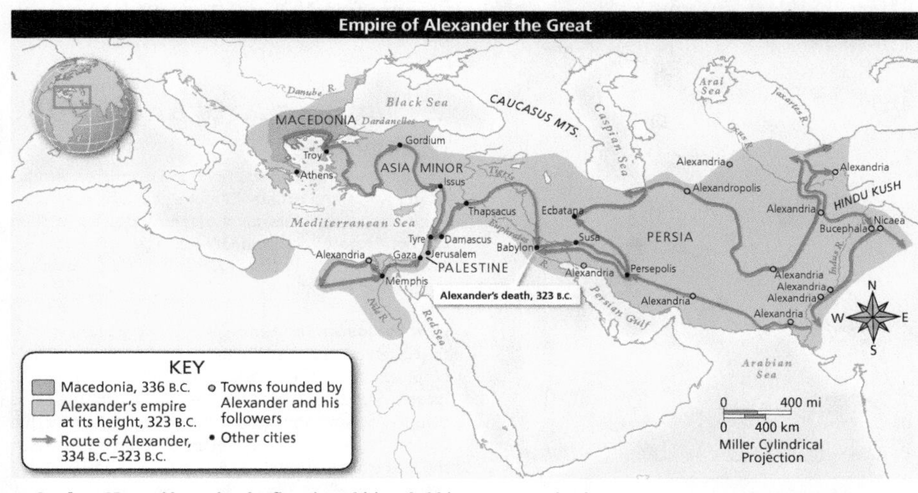

>> **Analyze Maps** Alexander the Great's ambitions led him to conquer lands across a vast area. Judging from this map, do you think his empire would be difficult to keep united? Explain your reasoning.

Interactive Map

Online Project the **Interactive Gallery: Alexander the Great's Conquests and Contributions** and click through the images with students.

ACTIVE CLASSROOM

You are having a conversation with Alexander the Great. Write down a question you'd like to ask, then what he would say to you, and what you would say in response. *(Possible answer: I ask Alexander, "Now that you've returned from India, what are you going to do next?" Alexander: "Conquer Africa and Asia and then set up cities and colonies there." Me: "So Greek civilization will continue to spread.")*

Guided Reading and Discussion

Remind students that after Darius was murdered, Alexander controlled much of the Persian empire. Ask them why they think he continued his conquests.

Answers

Analyze Maps *Sample answer: Keeping such a far-flung empire united would be challenging and require much organization, especially at a time when travel and communication were so difficult.*

Explain *The Persian empire was declining due to weak leadership.*

English Language Proficiency Standards

Listening 2.C.2 Read "The New Era of Alexander the Great" aloud. Then instruct students to complete one of the following activities based on their level of English proficiency.

Beginning Display the following phrase: *Alexander the Great*. Read it aloud and have students repeat it. Then explain the meaning of this phrase to students. Tell students that Alexander was not born with the name "the Great"; it was given to him later. Have students think about why Alexander was given this name, as you read the text aloud. Guide a discussion to explore Alexander's leadership characteristics.

Intermediate Follow the instructions in the Beginning activity, but, instead of explaining the meaning of the phrase, help students determine its meaning.

Advanced Follow the instructions in the Beginning activity, but ask small groups of students to discuss the meaning of this phrase and share their explanation with other groups. Then, using students' explanations, develop one explanation students can use to read about Alexander the Great. Ask groups to think about the kind of leader Alexander the Great was. Have groups share their opinions with the class.

Advanced High Follow the instructions in the Advanced activity, but with pairs of students discussing the meaning of the phrase and sharing explanations and opinions.

Alexander's Legacy

Alexander's empire soon fell apart, but his campaigns and conquests spread Greek culture from Persia to northern India. Greek soldiers, traders, and artisans settled in newly founded cities, introducing Greek ideas and traditions. Over time, a new Hellenistic culture arose.

Guided Reading and Discussion

Tell students that many of the new cities founded by Alexander or his followers were named Alexandria. One of them, the Alexandria in Egypt, became the greatest of Hellenistic cities. Ask students to explain why. *(Sample response: Alexandria's strategic location on sea lanes between Europe and Asia, great markets, mix of cultural resources and influences, and Alexander and his successors' encouragement of learning made it the greatest Hellenistic capital.)*

Identify Cause and Effect What factors shaped Hellenistic civilization? *(Alexander and his generals founded new cities settled by Greeks who brought their culture with them; local people assimilated Greek ideas; Greeks adopted local customs.)*

Hellenistic Arts and Sciences

Many new styles of art and architecture and important ideas in philosophy, math, science, and medicine emerged during the Hellenistic age. A number of these ideas, including the Pythagorean theorem, the heliocentric solar system, the water screw, and the Hippocratic oath, continue to be relevant today.

ELPS **ELPS 2.C.2** Learn how to *read between the lines* to learn more about Alexander the Great.

Alexander's Legacy

Although Alexander's empire soon crumbled following his premature death, he had unleashed changes that would ripple across the Mediterranean world and the Middle East for centuries. His most lasting achievement was the spread of Greek culture.

Cultures Blend Across his far-flung empire, Alexander founded many new cities, most of them named after him. The generals who succeeded him founded still more. Greek soldiers, traders, and artisans settled these new cities. From Egypt to the borders of India, they built Greek temples, filled them with Greek statues, and held athletic contests as they had in Greece. Local people **assimilated,** or absorbed, Greek ideas. In turn, Greek settlers adopted local customs.

Alexander had encouraged a blending of eastern and western cultures when he had married a Persian woman and urged his soldiers to follow his example. He had also adopted many Persian customs, including Persian dress. Gradually, after his death, a vital new culture emerged that blended Greek, Persian, Egyptian, and Indian influences. This Hellenistic civilization would flourish for several centuries.

>> The famous Pharos lighthouse in Alexandria was one of the Seven Wonders of the World. Built in 280 B.C., it stood 350 feet high until an earthquake destroyed it in the 1300s.

Alexandria: The Cultural Capital At the very heart of the Hellenistic world stood the city of **Alexandria,** Egypt. Located on the sea lanes between Europe and Asia, its markets boasted a wide range of goods, from Greek marble to Arabian spices to East African ivory. A Greek architect had drawn up plans for the city, which would become home to almost a million people. Among the city's marvelous sights was the Pharos, an enormous lighthouse that soared 440 feet into the air.

Alexander and his successors encouraged the work of scholars. The rulers of Alexandria built the great Museum as a center of learning. The Museum boasted laboratories, lecture halls, and a zoo. Its library had thousands of scrolls representing the accumulated knowledge of the ancient world. Unfortunately, the library was later destroyed in a fire.

Women Take New Roles Paintings, statues, and legal codes show that women were no longer restricted to their homes during the Hellenistic period. More women learned to read and write. Some became philosophers or poets. Royal women held considerable power, working alongside husbands and sons who were the actual rulers. In Egypt, the able and clever queen Cleopatra VII came to rule in her own right.

DESCRIBE How did Alexander encourage the blending of cultures?

Hellenistic Arts and Sciences

The cities of the Hellenistic world employed armies of architects and artists. Temples, palaces, and other public buildings were much larger and grander than the buildings of classical Greece. The elaborate new style reflected the desire of Hellenistic rulers to glorify themselves as godlike.

New Philosophies Emerge Political turmoil during the Hellenistic age contributed to the rise of new schools of philosophy. The most influential was Stoicism. Its founder, Zeno, urged people to avoid desires and disappointments by accepting calmly whatever life brought. Stoics preached high moral standards, such as the idea of protecting the rights of fellow humans. They taught that all people, including women and slaves, though unequal in society, were morally equal because

History Background

Realism and Color The classical statutes that we admire today are only pale reminders of a colorful past bleached white by the passage of time. Greek sculptors portrayed the human figure as accurately and realistically as possible. Facial lines and poses conveyed the physical beauty of the individual. Color heightened the realism and natural beauty even more. From the traces of paint that remain on the marble, art historians know that classical Greek statues were usually painted in bright colors.

Answers

Describe *by marrying a Persian woman and encouraging his soldiers to do the same; by adopting Persian customs; by encouraging scholarship*

all had the power of reason. Stoicism later influenced many Roman and Christian thinkers.

Math and Astronomy Advance During the Hellenistic age, scholars built on earlier Greek, Babylonian, and Egyptian knowledge. In mathematics, **Pythagoras** (pih THAG uh rus), who had studied in Egypt and Babylon, derived a formula to calculate the relationship between the sides of a right triangle. His interest in the principles of mathematics, the relations between numbers, and the idea of a proof influenced Plato, Aristotle, and later western thought.

Euclid, (YOO klid) wrote *The Elements,* a textbook that brilliantly compiled earlier works and became the basis for modern geometry. From stated axioms, or assumptions, Euclid built a logical and rigorous geometry. *The Elements* had a powerful impact on Islamic mathematics, and Latin translations of Arabic versions first made it known in Europe. Since it was first printed in 1482, more than a thousand editions have been published.

Using mathematics and careful observation, the astronomer Aristarchus (a ris TAHR kus) argued that Earth rotated on its axis and orbited the sun. This theory of a **heliocentric,** or sun-centered, solar system was not accepted by most scientists until almost 2,000 years later. His ideas about Earth's motion inspired the Polish astronomer Copernicus in the early 1500s. Aristarchus also used geometry to calculate the sizes and distances of the sun and the moon. Another Hellenistic astronomer, Eratosthenes (eh ruh TAHS thuh neez) showed that Earth was round and accurately calculated its circumference. His *On the measurement of the Earth* was lost, but other ancient authors preserved some details of his calculations.

The most famous Hellenistic scientist, **Archimedes** (ahr kuh MEE deez) of Syracuse, applied principles of physics to make practical inventions. He mastered the use of the lever and pulley and boasted, "Give me a lever long enough and a place to stand on, and I will move the world."

Then, to demonstrate the power of his invention, Archimedes used it to draw a ship over the land before a crowd of awed spectators. In 212 B.C., at the request of the King of Syracuse, Archimedes devised machines of war to defend his hometown against Roman attack. He also invented the Archimedes screw, a mechanical pump still used in many parts of the world to lift water to higher levels for irrigation.

Medical Practice Improves About 400 B.C. the Greek physician **Hippocrates** (hih PAH kruh teez) studied the causes of illnesses and looked for cures. The Hippocratic oath attributed to him set ethical standards for doctors.

>> Pythagoras and his followers speculated about using numbers to measure and compare things. They had intuitive feelings of the *harmonia* ("fitting together") of the *kosmos* ("order of things").

Interactive Gallery

>> Archimedes's screw is shown in a French illustration from the early 1700s. In this image, it uses a rotating spiral tube wound around an axis to raise water from *A* to *B*. Pulling the rope turns the tube.

Online Project the **Interactive Gallery: Math, Science, and Technology in the Hellenistic Age** and click through the images with students.

ACTIVE CLASSROOM

Have students jot down responses to this question on sticky notes: *What does the gallery tell you about Hellenistic advances? (Sample response: Greek scientists made many important and useful advances. For example, in medicine, a new theory proposed that illness had natural causes, rather than being caused by the gods.)* Ask students to post their sticky notes on the board and have students look at all the various responses, discussing similarities and differences.

Key Terms

Ask students to find the key term **heliocentric** (in bold) in the text. Explain that *helio-* comes from the Greek word for "sun" while *-centric* comes from the Greek *kentrikos*, "pertaining to the center." At the time that Aristarchus proposed his theory of a heliocentric solar system, most scientists accepted Egyptian astronomer Ptolemy's geocentric, or Earth-centered, solar system.

Guided Reading and Discussion

Remind students that Hellenistic era thinkers, mathematicians, and scientists added their accomplishments to important earlier Greek achievements in politics, philosophy, and the arts to form ancient Greece's legacy to later civilizations. Ask students which aspect of that ancient legacy they think is most important and why. *(Sample response: The Greek legacy in government—including citizens making laws, rule by majority vote, and trial by jury—is most important because it encourages people to participate in government, provides possibilities for change, and promotes fairness and justice.)*

Analyze Images

Tell students that Archimedes' screw had many uses in ancient times up to the present. Invite students to imagine how Archimedes' screw might be used in a terraced rice field; in a mine; in a ship.

D Differentiate Special Needs/Extra Support Students may use the examples of Hellenistic art and artifacts presented in this section to learn about Hellenistic civilization. Ask: What does each image show about the nature and achievements of the Hellenistic world? *(Sample response: They show the influence and spread of Greek culture, and the importance of science and technology throughout the Hellenistic world.)*

Topic 5 Lesson 4

SYNTHESIZE

Online Project the **Digital Activity: Effects of Size**. Have groups of students take 5 minutes to brainstorm and write down brief answers to the questions shown. *(Sample response: Aristotle would have termed neither the Persian empire nor Alexander's empire a polis. Both were far too large to allow for direct participation by citizens.)*

Discuss Would modern electronic communication change Aristotle's view? Why or why not? *(Students might note that direct participation would be easier but still not practical enough to make any modern political state a polis.)*

DEMONSTRATE

Online Assign the **Digital Lesson Quiz** for this lesson if you haven't already done so. Students will be offered automatic remediation or enrichment based on their score.

Pose this question to the class on the Discussion Board:

Predict Consequences How do you think Alexander's empire would have developed if he and his successors had not founded many Greek cities and encouraged Greek settlement? *(Possible answers: Such a large and varied empire would have soon split apart. Without the Greek influence, the empire would have produced fewer advances.)*

Topic Inquiry

Have students continue their investigations for the Topic Inquiry.

Answers

Identify *philosophy, mathematics, geometry, astronomy, physics, medicine*

THE GREEK LEGACY

GOVERNMENT
- Written code of laws
- Citizens bring charges of wrongdoing
- Trial by jury
- Citizenship expands to all free adult men, except foreigners
- Athenian assembly makes laws
- Direct democracy: male citizens rule by majority vote

CULTURE
- Greek language: many roots, prefixes, suffixes used in English
- Mythology about gods and goddesses
- Olympic games
- Philosophers searching for truth, apply reason, question tradition

ARTS
- Drama and poetry
- History: encouraging research, unbiased accounts
- Sculpture portraying lifelike human forms and ideal beauty
- Painted pottery with scenes of everyday Greek life and legendary tales
- Classical architecture embodies balance, grace

MATHEMATICS, SCIENCE, AND TECHNOLOGY
- Properties of numbers and proportion studied
- Disagreement whether sun or Earth at center of universe
- Accurate estimate of circumference of Earth
- Development of lever, pulley, pump
- Natural not divine causes and cures of illness sought, code of ethics for physicians

>> Ancient Greece's legacy has been as broad as it is deep, including major concepts, institutions, and inventions in government, culture, the arts, mathematics, the sciences, and technology.

Greek physicians swore to "help the sick according to my ability and judgment but never with a view to injury and wrong." Doctors today still take a similar oath.

A Remarkable Legacy With its conquest of Asia Minor in 133 B.C. Rome replaced Greece as the dominant power in the Mediterranean world. However, the Greek legacy remains. Greek works in the arts and sciences set a standard for later people of Europe. Greek ideas about law, freedom, justice, and government continue to influence political thinking to the present day.

Socrates, Plato, Aristotle, and other Greek philosophers developed an ideal of critical thought and self-examination that allowed people to question ideas and institutions. Citizens could participate and judge governments. Later, the founders of Western political systems, including of the United States, studied these ancient Greek ideas as part of their classical educations. The Athenian experiment in direct democracy by citizen participation thus had a deep and far-reaching impact on modern politics and governments.

These achievements and their impact were especially remarkable because they were produced by a scattering of tiny city-states whose rivalries left them too weak to defend themselves from conquest. Later, you will learn how the Greek legacy influenced the civilizations of Rome and of Western Europe.

IDENTIFY In what fields did Hellenistic civilization make advancements?

ASSESSMENT

1. **Identify Cause and Effect** How did Philip II take control of Greece?
2. **Infer** Why do you think Alexander the Great and his generals founded so many new cities?
3. **Cite Evidence** How did Alexander and his successors spread Greek culture through the Hellenistic world?
4. **Summarize** the contributions Aristarchus and Eratosthenes made to astronomy.
5. **Identify** Which Greek scientist invented a pump that continues to be used for irrigation in many parts of the world today? What does his invention do?

Assessment

1. Philip II assembled a strong and effective army. To form alliances with many Greek city-states, he employed threats, bribery, and diplomacy. He also conquered other city-states in battle.
2. Sample answer: They wanted to attract Greek settlers and extend Greek cultural influence into the lands they conquered. Perhaps they thought that such settlements would better secure and control these conquered territories.
3. Sample answer: They founded and built many new Greek cities, encouraging Greek soldiers, traders, and artisans to settle them; married non-Greek women; encouraged the work of scholars, building a learning center with a famous library at Alexandria in Egypt.
4. Aristarchus asserted that Earth rotated on its axis and orbited the sun, a heliocentric explanation for the solar system. He also calculated the sizes and distances of the sun and the moon. Eratosthenes demonstrated that Earth was round and accurately determined its circumference.
5. Archimedes; it lifts water to higher levels.

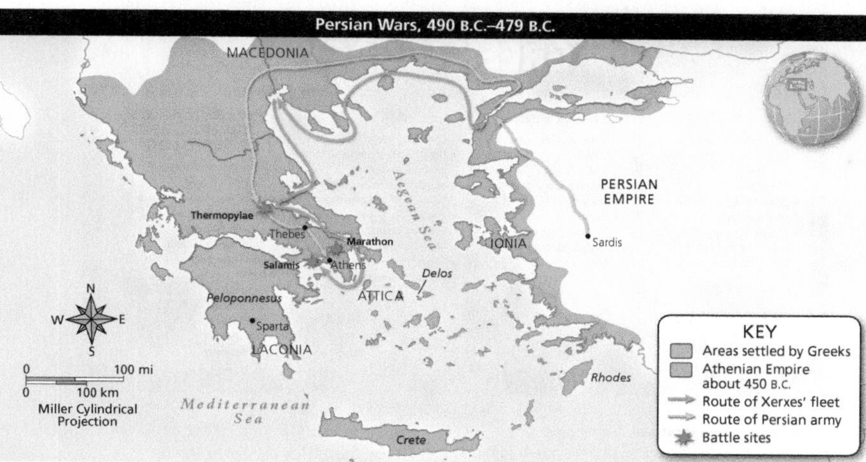

1. **Identify Major Causes and Describe Effects of Events** Identify major causes and describe major effects of events from 500 B.C. to A.D. 600, including the development of the classical civilization of Greece. Write a paragraph that identifies how wars with Persia influenced the development of ancient Greece. Use the map above to trace the route of the Persian army and explain the importance of a shift in Greek politics due to the Persian Wars. Consider the position of Greek city-states prior to the Persian Wars, role of Athens in the wars, and the Delian League. **1.B**
2. **Describe Major Influences** Describe the major political and religious/philosophical influences of Greece. Write a paragraph that identifies and describes some of the major influences of Greece by Solon and Cleisthenes as well as religious traditions. Consider Solon's reforms, Cleisthenes's principle of *isonomia*, or equal rights for all before the law, and the importance of Greek gods in daily life. **3.A**
3. **Identify Characteristics** Identify the characteristics of monarchies as forms of government in early civilizations. Write a paragraph that identifies the characteristics of Greek monarchies and why the Greeks moved away from them. Consider early Greek government, definition of monarchy, and why the Greeks shifted away from monarchies. Which other types of government did Greek society eventually have? **19.A**
4. **Identify Characteristics** Identify the characteristics of political systems, including democracy and oligarchy. Write a paragraph that identifies the differences between democracy and oligarchy in ancient Greece. Consider the definitions of democracy and oligarchy, and how these two forms of government influenced ancient Greek society. **19.B**
5. **Describe Rights and Analyze Information** Describe the rights of citizens and noncitizens throughout history, and analyze the information by categorizing. Draw a chart detailing the rights of citizens and noncitizens in ancient Greece. After organizing the chart, write a paragraph that describes the rights of both groups, including similarities and differences. Consider property rights, voting rights, and legal protection. **21.B, 29.F**
6. **Identify Influence of Ideas** Identify the influence of ideas regarding the right to a "trial by a jury of your peers" in ancient Greece. Write a paragraph that identifies the relevance of the excerpt below to the concept of "trial by a jury of your peers" in ancient Greece. Consider the meaning of direct democracy and the qualifications and responsibilities of citizenship in Athens. Be sure to include what expanded citizenship participation meant to citizens. **22.B**

"Pericles believed that all citizens, regardless of wealth or social class, should take part in government. Athens therefore began to pay a stipend, or fixed salary, to men who participated in the Assembly and its governing Council. This reform enabled poor men to serve in government."

Answers to TEKS Assessment

1. Students' responses should clearly explain that prior to the wars with Persia, ancient Greece was not united and that the Persian Wars were critical to the unification of Greek city-states. They should address the route of the Persian army on the map and explain its importance in the unification of Greece—that it was the wars with Persia, led by the Athenian win at Marathon, that changed the face of Greece. They should note that during a landmark battle against Xerxes, Athens called on other city-states to unite with it in order to defeat the Persians. They should explain that the new alliance, referred to as the Delian League, combined forces throughout Greece and helped guard against further Persian invasion.
2. Students' responses should clearly explain some of the reforms made by Solon, such as outlawing debt slavery, opening high offices to more citizens, granting citizenship to foreigners, and encouraging the export of such products as wine and olive oil. Students should be able to clearly explain Cleisthenes' principle of isonomia (equal rights for all) and how it influenced Athenian democracy. Students should also explain the religious traditions of the Greeks, with a mention of the gods of Mount Olympus, and demonstrate knowledge of Zeus, Aphrodite, and Athena and the importance of ritual in daily life in ancient Greece.
3. Students' responses should clearly explain the definition and history of monarchies, including the hereditary element, which contributed to continuity and stability, and the importance of monarchies in centralizing political power. Students should also mention that the gradual shift to aristocracy, oligarchy, and democracy was due to reactions against the limitations on political power and liberty that monarchies (and, later, other forms of government) placed on various groups of Greek citizens at a given time.
4. Students' responses should clearly explain the differences between oligarchy and democracy in ancient Greece. They should note that in an oligarchy, small groups of wealthy people rule the government and that this form of government was possible after changes in military technology that allowed a new middle class of traders to amass wealth. They should explain that a democracy is different from an oligarchy in that power is in the hands of many, not just a few, and the idea of democracy was to have a government by the people. However, in this early form of Athenian democracy only citizens of the state had power, and citizens were only men who owned land.
5. Students' responses should clearly explain the rights of citizens and noncitizens in ancient Greece. Answers should begin by creating a chart that categorizes rights.

Sample chart:

Citizen Rights	Noncitizen Rights
Recognized as persons under the law	Not recognized as persons
Owned land	Could not own land or houses
Could participate in government by voting	No voting rights
Could serve on juries	Only had protections through treaties in particular city-states

Then, students should clearly explain the material in the chart by stating that citizens had rights to be protected under law, to own land, to vote, and to serve on juries, while noncitizens were not even considered legal persons and were subject to slavery. Noncitizens were only protected by treaties if they were merchants or traders of value.

Topic 5

TEKS ASSESSMENT

THE GREEK LEGACY
GOVERNMENT
• Written code of laws
• Citizens bring charges of wrongdoing
• Trial by jury
• Citizenship expands to all free adult men, except foreigners
• Athenian assembly makes laws
• Direct democracy: male citizens rule by majority vote
CULTURE
• Greek language: many roots, prefixes, suffixes used in English
• Mythology about gods and goddesses
• Olympic games
• Philosophers searching for truth, apply reason, question tradition
ARTS
• Drama and poetry
• History: encouraging research, unbiased accounts
• Sculpture portraying lifelike human forms and ideal beauty
• Painted pottery with scenes of everyday Greek life and legendary tales
• Classical architecture embodies balance, grace
MATHEMATICS, SCIENCE, AND TECHNOLOGY
• Properties of numbers and proportion studied
• Disagreement whether sun or Earth at center of universe
• Accurate estimate of circumference of Earth
• Development of lever, pulley, pump
• Natural not divine causes and cures of illness sought, code of ethics for physicians

7. **Summarize Development** Summarize the development of the rule of law from ancient to modern times. Write a paragraph, using the chart above and information from the lessons, to summarize how the rule of law has developed from ancient Greece to the modern era. Consider the culture, concepts of citizenship, and importance of democracy, all in ancient Greece and modern times. **22.A**

8. **Analyze Architecture** Analyze examples of how architecture reflects the history of the cultures in which it is produced. Write a paragraph describing an example of ancient Greek architecture and explaining how it reflects the beliefs and values of the era. Consider the objective of a building, connection of a building to cultural values, and the role of Greek gods. **26.B**

9. **Identify the Contribution of Scientists; Interpret Written Presentations** Identify the contributions of significant scientists (Eratosthenes), and interpret written presentations of social studies information. Write a paragraph identifying how the observations of Eratosthenes described in the excerpt below led to his notable contribution to science. Consider what Eratosthenes is known to have discovered and how his findings are still relevant today. **27.E, 30.C**

"Eratosthenes used Aristotle's idea that, if the Earth was round, distant stars in the night sky would appear at different positions to observers at different latitudes. Eratosthenes knew that on the first day of summer, the Sun passed directly overhead at Syene, Egypt. At midday of the same day, he measured the angular displacement of the Sun from overhead at the city of Alexandria—5000 stadia away from Syene."

from the National Aeronautics and Space Administration

10. **Identify the Origin and Diffusion of Major Ideas** Identify the origin and diffusion of major ideas in science and technology that occurred in classical Greece. Write a paragraph identifying these ideas in ancient Greece, how they were used, and how they were spread to other cultures. Consider the contributions of Archimedes, contributions of Hippocrates, and how both their ideas spread to other cultures. **27.A**

11. **Identify Contributions of Scientists** Identify the contributions of significant scientists: Pythagoras. Write a paragraph explaining how the ideas of Pythagoras contributed to ancient Greece and are still relevant to modern society. Consider his specific contributions, influence on thought in ancient Greece, and applications of his contributions in modern times. **27.E**

12. **Summarize and Analyze the Origins of Western Institutions** Summarize and analyze the institutions of Western civilizations that originated in Greece by drawing inferences and conclusions. Write a paragraph that analyzes how government in Greek city-states formed the basis for modern democracy found in Western civilizations. Consider the evolution of Greek government from a monarchy to a direct democracy, reforms introduced by leaders Solon and Cleisthenes, reforms introduced by Pericles in Athens, and the democratic process in the United States today. **25.B, 29.F**

Answers to TEKS Assessment

6. Students' responses should clearly explain that because Pericles, the leader of Athens, felt all citizens had a responsibility to take part in government, the government stipend implemented during his rule allowed more men to take more active roles in government and as citizens. This allowed more of them to participate in jury groups, helping to support the concept of a "trial by a jury of your peers." Students should explain that being part of a direct democracy meant Athenian citizens took part in government's day-to-day matters and that a jury could be a panel of hundreds or even thousands of citizens, who were defined as males older than age 30.

7. Students' responses should clearly explain how ancient Greek society has influenced modern societies. Students should note influences on governments, such as citizenship, laws, and majority vote; the prevalence of Greek words in modern language; the Olympic Games; philosophical concepts by such scholars as Plato and Aristotle; and ancient influences on modern math and sciences.

8. Students' responses should clearly explain that the Greeks wanted to convey a sense of perfect balance in their architecture to reflect the harmony and order of the universe; for example, simple geometric shapes were often used, and decorated columns signifying balance were common. Students should also explain that the Greeks were very concerned with order, balance, and idealism, all of which were reflected in the shapes and style of their architecture. One example is the Parthenon. The builders sought to reflect a harmonious universe. Students should also explain that many buildings were dedicated to the gods, connecting them to cultural values.

9. Students' responses should identify that Eratosthenes deduced that Earth was round and correctly calculated its circumference. Students should explain that Eratosthenes used the angles of the shadows and his knowledge of the sun in the sky to correctly make his calculations. Students should also explain that Eratosthenes' findings eventually contributed to the development of successful modern space travel.

10. Students' responses should identify that Archimedes applied principles of physics to make practical inventions, such as the lever and pulley, and machines of war. Students should also identify that Hippocrates studied the causes of illnesses and looked for cures and that the Hippocratic oath attributed to him set ethical standards for doctors. Students should explain that these ideas were valuable to Greeks and other cultures and spread through interactions like trade and war, as well as through encouragement of scholarship by Alexander the Great and his successors, who promoted the Museum and library of Alexandria as a center of learning for all.

11. Students' responses should identify that Pythagoras developed a formula to calculate the relationship between the sides of a right triangle, that he speculated about using numbers to measure and compare things, and that his interest in the principles of mathematics, the relations between numbers, and the idea of a "proof" influenced Greek philosophers Plato and Aristotle. Students should note that Pythagoras's ideas are still used as a basis of study in all math classes today.

12. Students' responses should clearly explain how democracy originated in the desires of the people to have more say in the governance of the Greek city-states. Students should make connections to elements in the Greek direct democracy that still exist today. These elements may include, but are not limited to, councils selected to run day-to-day aspects of government, the responsibility of citizens to vote, paying a wage/stipend to council

13. **Explain Development** Explain the development of democratic-republican government from its beginnings in classical Greece. Using the chart below, write a paragraph that explains what important factors led to the development of a democratic-republican government in Athens. Consider property rights, citizenship, and major political influences in ancient Greece. 20.A

14. **Locate Places and Regions** Locate the places and regions of historical significance directly related to major eras and turning points in world history. Using the maps and information from the lessons, write a paragraph describing how the geography of regions in Greece was an asset in the Persian Wars. Consider how mountains helped the Greeks, how water played a significant role, and how the Spartans and Athenians used geography to their advantage in specific battles. How did all these factors relate to the outcome of the Persian Wars? 16.A

15. **Describe Roles** Describe the changing roles of families during major eras of world history. Write a paragraph that describes the role of families, and explain other factors that impacted families in ancient Greece. Consider traditional family roles, religious traditions, political factors, and the roles of Greek women. 24.A

16. **Reflect on the Essential Question** **Write an essay on the Essential Question: How much power should the government have?** Use evidence from your study of this Topic to support your answer.

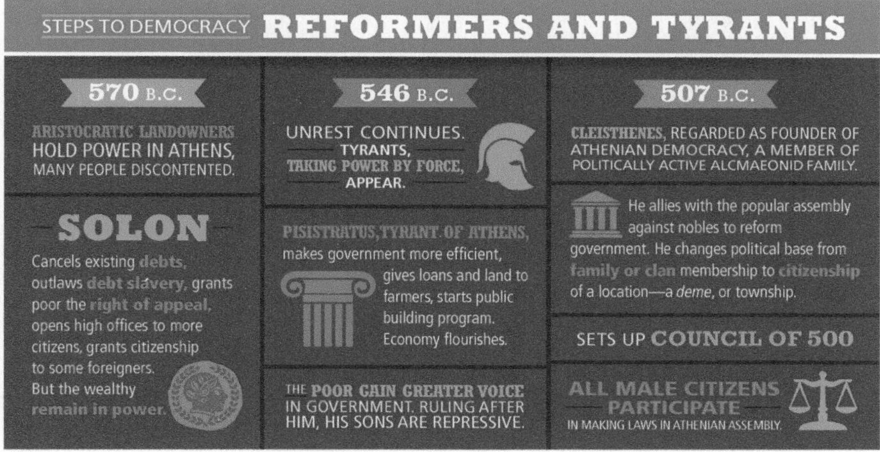
STEPS TO DEMOCRACY
REFORMERS AND TYRANTS
570 B.C.
ARISTOCRATIC LANDOWNERS HOLD POWER IN ATHENS, MANY PEOPLE DISCONTENTED.
SOLON
Cancels existing debts, outlaws debt slavery, grants poor the right of appeal, opens high offices to more citizens, grants citizenship to some foreigners. But the wealthy remain in power.
546 B.C.
UNREST CONTINUES. TYRANTS, TAKING POWER BY FORCE, APPEAR.
PISISTRATUS, TYRANT OF ATHENS, makes government more efficient, gives loans and land to farmers, starts public building program. Economy flourishes.
THE POOR GAIN GREATER VOICE IN GOVERNMENT. RULING AFTER HIM, HIS SONS ARE REPRESSIVE.
507 B.C.
CLEISTHENES, REGARDED AS FOUNDER OF ATHENIAN DEMOCRACY, A MEMBER OF POLITICALLY ACTIVE ALCMAEONID FAMILY.
He allies with the popular assembly against nobles to reform government. He changes political base from family or clan membership to citizenship of a location—a deme, or township.
SETS UP COUNCIL OF 500
ALL MALE CITIZENS PARTICIPATE IN MAKING LAWS IN ATHENIAN ASSEMBLY.

members to allow people from all social classes to participate in government, and the ability of the people to remove officials from office.

13. Students' responses should clearly explain Solon's shifts toward a more democratic state, the ability of the poor to gain a voice in politics, the role of Cleisthenes in promoting democracy, the shift in emphasis to citizenship instead of clan, the Council of 500, and the participation of men in assembly. Students should also explain that Athenian democracy developed from an aristocracy and oligarchy prior to the growth of democratic rule, and that changes occurred due to social unrest.

14. Students' responses should clearly explain that the Persians landed near Marathon and the rocky terrain kept the fighting isolated from other city-states, and therefore, the Persians were forced to make all attacks by crossing the sea and then coming over land. Students should also describe how the Spartans were cornered at Thermopylae and that their sacrifice at the mountain crossing point allowed all citizens to flee to safety before the Persians could cross the mountains. Students should explain that the Athenians lured Persians into the strait of Salamis and sank Persian ships because the Athenians knew the water better. The Persians did not have back-up troops in the area because, due to the terrain, they had to sail rather than march to battle.

15. Students' responses should clearly explain what the roles of families were in ancient Greece, particularly in religious rites. Students should note the importance of women in religious rites and running the home, as well as the fact that women ran estates when men departed for war. Students should note other information about families in Greek society, such as the importance of hereditary social class to monarchies and oligarchies, with less importance placed on one's bloodline when it came to citizenship and political office.

Topic 5

Answers to TEKS Practice

1. D

2. J

Online To prepare for the End-of-Topic test, have students go online for additional Topic Review and Assessment questions or to review their notes in the **Interactive Reading Notepad** for the lessons in this Topic.

Benchmark Tests

Assign these benchmark tests as you complete the relevant topics to monitor student progress toward mastering the course content and as preparation for the End-of-Course Test.

Benchmark Test 1: Topics 1–5

Benchmark Test 2: Topics 6–10

Benchmark Test 3: Topics 11–15

Benchmark Test 4: Topics 16–21

TEKS PRACTICE

1

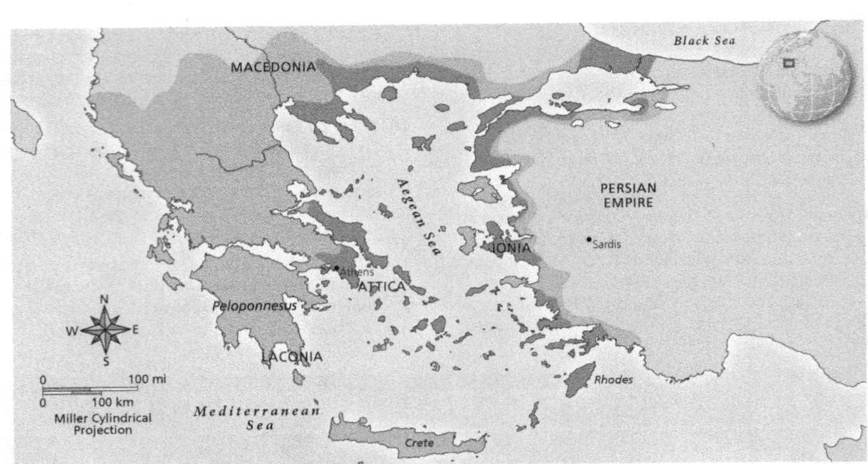

Use the map to identify the location that was home to the Minoans. How did this location affect their civilization?

A Attica; it granted easy access to the rest of the Aegean Sea

B Macedonia; it offered large plains for agricultural production

C Rhodes; it offered many trade opportunities with the Persian Empire

D Crete; it was central to trade routes in the Mediterranean Sea and Aegean Sea

2 How did the development of the classical civilization of Greece influence modern science?

F Greek mathematicians established principles still in use today.

G Greek historians pointed out the importance of accurate documentation of events.

H Greek rhetoricians revealed the importance of clever, persuasive speech to win arguments.

J Greek philosophers emphasized observation and reason to find laws governing the universe.

Test Taking Tips: Tip for Questions With Photographs or Drawings

1. Read the question.
2. Read any title or caption provided with the image. Note information about the time, place, objects, or people in the image that you can learn from the title or caption.
3. Determine who or what is shown in the image. Is an action or situation shown? If so, what is it? What aspects of the action or situation will help you answer the question?
4. Read the question again to be sure you understand what is being asked. Look at the image to find the answer to the question. Reread the title or caption if you need further information.
5. Answer the question in your own words.
6. Read the answer choices and select the best answer.

3 Which current U.S. institution was most likely influenced by the Athenian Council of 500?

A The Presidency

B Congress

C The Supreme Court

D The Electoral College

---

4 Characteristics of Mesoamerican and Andean Civilizations

INCA	MAYA	AZTEC
Empire	City-states	Empire
Emperor claimed descent from god.	Each city-state had its own king.	Emperor elected by nobles.
Lives of people strictly regulated.	City-states had their own priests and temples.	Empire grew wealthy through conquest.
All property owned by emperor.	Farmers worked the land independently.	Conquered peoples paid tribute to the empire.
Local chieftains organized citizen work parties.	Merchants and farmers paid taxes to city-state.	Religious and cultural life centered on capital city.
Government officials arranged marriages.		

Read the chart. Which statement **best** explains an important contrast between the Mayan society and the societies of the Incas and Aztecs?

F Mayan society built many large cities.

G Mayan society promoted the equality of all citizens.

H Mayan society had one class of priests for the entire civilization.

J Mayan society was not controlled by a single central government.

If you have trouble with...				
Question	1	2	3	4
See Lesson	5.1	5.3	5.2	4.4
TEKS	16.A	3.A	3.A	6.A

3. B
4. J

Online Use the **Topic Synthesize** to help students revisit and reflect on the Essential Question for this Topic.

Topic Inquiry

If students have done a Topic Inquiry for this Topic, have them complete the final step of the Inquiry now.

Ancient Rome and the Origins of Christianity (509 B.C.–A.D. 476)

TOPIC 6 ORGANIZER	PACING: APPROX. 1 PERIOD, .5 BLOCKS		
	PACING	TEKS	ELPS
Connect	1 period		
MY STORY VIDEO **Documentary: Biography of Augustus**	10 min.		
DIGITAL ESSENTIAL QUESTION ACTIVITY **What Makes a Government Successful?**	10 min.	3.A, 21.B, 29.F	
DIGITAL TIMELINE ACTIVITY **Ancient Rome**	10 min.	29.H	
TOPIC INQUIRY: DOCUMENT-BASED QUESTION **Why Empires Collapse**	20 min.		
Investigate	2–4 periods		
TOPIC INQUIRY: DOCUMENT-BASED QUESTION **Why Empires Collapse**	Ongoing		
LESSON 1 **The Roman Republic**	30–40 min.	1.B, 3.A, 19.B, 20.A, 21.B, 24.A	2.C.3
LESSON 2 **The Roman Empire: Rise and Decline**	30–40 min.	1.B, 1.C, 3.A, 3.B, 20.A, 25.B	2.C.4
LESSON 3 **The Legacy of Rome**	30–40 min.	1.B, 3.A, 22.A, 22.B, 25.B, 26.B, 27.A	2.D.1
LESSON 4 **The Origins of Christianity**	30–40 min.	1.B, 3.A, 20.A, 23.A	2.D.2
Synthesize	1 period		
DIGITAL ESSENTIAL QUESTION ACTIVITY **Ancient Rome and the Origins of Christianity**	10 min.	3.A, 21.B, 29.F	
TOPIC INQUIRY: DOCUMENT-BASED QUESTION **Why Empires Collapse**	20 min.		
Demonstrate	1–2 periods		
DIGITAL TOPIC REVIEW AND ASSESSMENT **Ancient Rome and the Origins of Christianity**	10 min.		
TOPIC INQUIRY: DOCUMENT-BASED QUESTION **Why Empires Collapse**	20 min.		

www.PearsonTexas.com
Access your Digital Lesson

AUTHOR'S NOTE

The Roman City-State

[The Romans] were, in their own judgment, a people made to rule. . . . In time, much of the Western world would come to accept that judgment—and that imperial sway.

There were many myths of Roman origins, among them Aeneas's flight from burning Troy, and Romulus and Remus suckled by a wolf. In fact the city of Rome seems to have been founded by descendants of a number of tribes—Latins, Sabines, Etruscans—living among the seven hills, meeting in the little valley that would become the Forum. Among these Latin tribes there were two important classes: *patricians*, who would become the better-off farmers, and *plebeians*, the poorer. The real centers of authority among them remained for a long time the old tribes and clans, whose heads were the chief men in the emerging Roman state.

Under the Etruscans Rome became a sizable city, important for trade and a power in that part of Italy. Probably sometime around 509 B.C.E., the traditional date of the founding of the Roman Republic, the Latin tribes overthrew their Etruscan kings. The constitution they established to replace the old Etruscan monarchy was dominated by the Senate, a patrician council composed of elder statesmen, former magistrates, and other leaders of the old clans. . . .

The city on the Tiber River extended its sway over the entire Italian peninsula quite rapidly. Fear impelled some of the neighboring states to accept the protection and sovereignty of Rome—fear of a resurgence of Etruscan power, or of the barbarian Goths who had once stormed down from the north. The primitive ethnic organization of the other Italian tribes favored the Romans too: The loosely structured tribal societies that surrounded Rome offered little resistance to the opposition of Roman authority. By the end of the third century, Rome was the undisputed master of the Italian peninsula. And the centuries of the Roman conquest were just beginning.

During the last three centuries before Christ, then, Rome became the political center of the Mediterranean world.

—Anthony Esler, *The Human Venture: From Prehistory to the Present*, (Upper Saddle River, New Jersey: Pearson Education, 2005), pp. 158–159

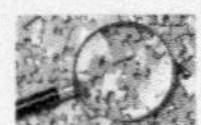

TOPIC INQUIRY: DOCUMENT-BASED QUESTION

Why Empires Collapse

In this Topic Inquiry, students work in teams to research and create a multimedia presentation about the collapse of the Roman empire, Han dynasty, and Inca empire. Learning more about these empires and their collapse will contribute to students understanding of the Topic Essential Question: What makes a government successful?

STEP 1: CONNECT

Develop Questions and Plan the Investigation

Launch the Project and Generate Questions

Display the invitation from the Committee for Global Hotspots. Tell students they will have to research and create a multimedia presentation about the Roman empire, Han dynasty, or Inca empire focusing on its rise to power and the reasons for its collapse. Have them review the *Rubric for a Group Presentation* to establish expectations.

Suggestion: To get started, have students discuss and take notes about what they already know.

Plan the Investigation

Form students into teams. Have students sign the *Project Contract*, and assign team roles using the roles document in *Project Tracker*. Give students examples of how to break down the Driving Question to begin the *Need-to-Know Questions*.

Suggestion: You can control the length of the project by removing some of the elements, such as the timeline or cultural achievements image gallery. Similarly, if you prefer that each student do more research, form more than three teams.

Resources

- Project Contract
- Need-to-Know Questions
- Project Tracker
- Student Instructions

PROFESSIONAL DEVELOPMENT

Document-Based Question

Be sure to view the Document-Based Question Professional Development resources in the online course.

STEP 2: INVESTIGATE

Apply Disciplinary Concepts and Tools

Conduct Research

Before students begin their investigation, have them review the Skills Tutorial, *Work In Teams*.

Teams will learn how to assign tasks and monitor their work with the *Project Tracker*. They will brainstorm how to approach their subject, keeping in mind the Driving Question, What causes empires to collapse?

To guide their research, teams will create a list of *Need-to-Know Questions* about their empire or dynasty. Refer students to helpful resources within the core content of the Topic to help answer their questions. For example, if they are researching cultural accomplishments, refer them to the readings and activities in Lesson 3. Help students begin to fill out the *Information Organizer*.

Suggestion: If your class has limited access to the Internet, you could make several books available to students, such as *The Ancient Romans* by Kathryn Hinds and *The Ancient Inca* by Patricia Calvert.

Write and Edit Presentation

The teams should plan how to present the information they have gathered. Next, students should write their presentation and create any visual elements, such as timelines and maps, that will be included in their presentation. When students do peer review of their work, remind them to offer detailed, constructive criticism.

Resources

- Project Tracker
- Information Organizer

STEP 3: SYNTHESIZE

Evaluate Sources and
Use Evidence to Formulate Conclusions

Create Your Presentation

Now have students get together to create their presentation. If students are having trouble sharing the work on this part of the project, remind them to review their *Roles for a Group Presentation* in the *Project Tracker*. Review each team's progress on their presentation to make sure they are on track. For students who are having trouble with their presentation, take a look at the Model Presentation as a class to get ideas.

Suggestion: For a less technology-dependent end product, have students assemble and organize the most important elements of their project and design a poster board to accompany their presentation. To take the technology a step further, have students incorporate audio or video into their presentation.

Review Your Presentation

Have students review one another's work and offer suggestions and edits to improve the text and visuals. Be prepared to offer advice on how to improve the teams' products.

Write a Conclusion

Have students write a conclusion about the Driving Question based on their work on the presentation. To help teams start, have each team member write down his or her answer to a different question listed in the *Student Instructions* and then share those answers with their team.

Resources

- 21st Century Skill Tutorials: Participate in a Discussion or Debate
- 21st Century Skill Tutorials: Give an Effective Presentation

STEP 4: DEMONSTRATE

Communicate Conclusions
and Take Informed Action

Give Your Presentation

Have students prepare their collapse of empire presentations, then watch the team presentations. To help the teams structure their time, set up a clock in the back of the room and alert them when they have only a few minutes left.

Compare Conclusions

Lead a class discussion about each team's conclusions. First, have students compare common elements of each government's collapse. Then lead a discussion about modern nations that might be experiencing similar issues. Each team should use the *Information Organizer II* to record its thoughts.

Have students revise their presentation's conclusion by adding a comparison between the collapse of the Roman empire, Han dynasty, and Inca empire. Next, have students write a letter to the Committee for Global Hotspots detailing their conclusions.

Reflect on the Project

After students have finished their Team Assessments, help them go over what they thought went well and what did not, so they can be even more effective in the future.

Suggestion: As an extension activity, have students research a government today and compare its problems to the common elements of government collapse they uncovered in their project.

Resources

- Group Presentation Rubric
- Self-Assessment
- Information Organizer II

The Roman Republic

Objectives

Objective 1: Describe the development of the classical civilization of Rome.

Objective 2: Outline how the Roman republic was structured and governed.

Objective 3: Understand the rights and religious practices that characterized Roman society.

Objective 4: Explain how the Roman republic grew and used its political influence.

LESSON 1 ORGANIZER	PACING: APPROX. 1 PERIOD, .5 BLOCKS					
			RESOURCES			
	OBJECTIVES	PACING	Print	Online	TEKS	ELPS
Connect						
DIGITAL START UP ACTIVITY **From Humble Beginnings**		5 min.		●	3.A, 21.B	
Investigate						
READ **The Rise of the Roman Civilization**	Objective 1	10 min.	●	●	1.B, 29.H	
READ **The Early Roman Republic**	Objective 2	10 min.	●	●	1.B, 3.A, 19.B	2.C.3
INTERACTIVE GALLERY **The Roman Cursus Honorum**		10 min.		●		
READ **Roman Society**	Objective 3	10 min.	●	●	1.B, 24.A	
READ **The Roman Republic Expands**	Objective 4	10 min.	●	●	1.B, 3.A, 20.A, 21.B	
INTERACTIVE MAP **Growth of the Roman Republic, 500 B.C. to 44 B.C.**		10 min.		●	1.B, 3.A, 21.B	
Synthesize						
DIGITAL ACTIVITY **Communication Is Key**		5 min.		●	1.B, 3.A, 20.A	
Demonstrate						
DIGITAL QUIZ **Lesson Quiz and Class Discussion Board**		10 min.		●	1.B, 3.A, 19.B	

Focus on Texas Standards

Texas Essential Knowledge and Skills

1.B identify major causes and describe the major effects of the following events from 500 BC to AD 600: the development of the classical civilizations of Greece, Rome, Persia, India (Maurya and Gupta), China (Zhou, Qin, and Han), and the development of major world religions

3.A describe the major political, religious/philosophical, and cultural influences of Persia, India, China, Israel, Greece, and Rome, including the development of monotheism, Judaism, and Christianity

19.B identify the characteristics of the following political systems: theocracy, absolute monarchy, democracy, republic, oligarchy, limited monarchy, and totalitarianism

20.A explain the development of democratic-republican government from its beginnings in the Judeo-Christian legal tradition and classical Greece and Rome through the English Civil War and the Enlightenment

21.B describe the rights and responsibilities of citizens and noncitizens in civic participation throughout history

24.A describe the changing roles of women, children, and families during major eras of world history

NOTES

The Roman Empire: Rise and Decline

Objectives

Objective 1: Identify the events leading to the decline of the Roman republic.

Objective 2: Summarize the fundamental ideas and institutions of Western civilizations that originated in Rome.

Objective 3: Explain how and why the Roman empire divided.

Objective 4: Identify the factors that led to the decline and fall of Rome.

LESSON 2 ORGANIZER		PACING: APPROX. 1 PERIOD, .5 BLOCKS				
	OBJECTIVES	PACING	RESOURCES Print	RESOURCES Online	TEKS	ELPS
Connect						
DIGITAL START UP ACTIVITY **Julius Caesar**		5 min.		●	3.A	
Investigate						
READ **Empire Building Through Conquest**	Objective 1	10 min.	●	●	1.B, 1.C, 3.A	2.C.4
READ **The Roman Republic Declines**	Objective 1	10 min.	●	●	1.B, 1.C, 3.A	
READ **The Roman Empire**	Objective 2	10 min.	●	●	1.B, 1.C, 3.A, 25.B	
INTERACTIVE TIMELINE **Roman Rulers Who Made History**	Objective 2	10 min.		●	1.B, 1.C, 3.A, 25.B	
READ **The Roman Empire Splits**	Objective 3	10 min.	●	●	1.B, 1.C	
READ **Rome Faces Invasions**	Objective 4	10 min.	●	●	1.B, 1.C	
READ **Why Did Rome Fall?**	Objective 4	10 min.	●	●	1.C	
INTERACTIVE MAP **Invasions of the Roman Empire, A.D. 378–533**	Objective 4	10 min.		●	1.C, 3.B	
Synthesize						
DIGITAL ACTIVITY **When Did Rome Fall?**		5 min.		●	1.C	
Demonstrate						
DIGITAL QUIZ **Lesson Quiz and Class Discussion Board**		10 min.		●	1.C, 3.A, 25.B	

PEARSON realize
www.PearsonTexas.com
Access your Digital Lesson

Focus on Texas Standards

Texas Essential Knowledge and Skills

1.B identify major causes and describe the major effects of the following events from 500 BC to AD 600: the development of the classical civilizations of Greece, Rome, Persia, India (Maurya and Gupta), China (Zhou, Qin, and Han), and the development of major world religions

1.C identify major causes and describe the major effects of the following important turning points in world history from 600 to 1450: the spread of Christianity, the decline of Rome and the formation of medieval Europe; the development of Islamic caliphates and their impact on Asia, Africa, and Europe; the Mongol invasions and their impact on Europe, China, India, and Southwest Asia

3.A describe the major political, religious/philosophical, and cultural influences of Persia, India, China, Israel, Greece, and Rome, including the development of monotheism, Judaism, and Christianity

3.B explain the impact of the fall of Rome on Western Europe

20.A explain the development of democratic-republican government from its beginnings in the Judeo-Christian legal tradition and classical Greece and Rome through the English Civil War and the Enlightenment

25.B summarize the fundamental ideas and institutions of Western civilizations that originated in Greece and Rome

NOTES

The Legacy of Rome

Objectives

Objective 1: Summarize the works of Roman literary figures, historians, and philosophers.

Objective 2: Describe the art and architecture developed by the Romans.

Objective 3: Understand how the Romans applied science and mathematics for practical use.

Objective 4: Explain how Rome's rule of law influenced modern legal systems.

Objective 5: Summarize the Roman ideas and institutions that have influenced Western civilization.

LESSON 3 ORGANIZER	PACING: APPROX. 1 PERIOD, .5 BLOCKS					
			RESOURCES			
	OBJECTIVES	PACING	Print	Online	TEKS	ELPS
Connect						
DIGITAL START UP ACTIVITY **Advances in Roman Culture**		5 min.		●	26.B	
Investigate						
READ **Roman Literature, History, and Philosophy**	Objective 1	10 min.	●	●	3.A, 26.B	2.D.1
READ **Roman Art, Architecture, and Drama**	Objective 2	10 min.	●	●	3.A, 26.B	
INTERACTIVE 3-D MODEL **The Pantheon**		10 min.		●	26.B	
READ **Roman Achievements in Science and Engineering**	Objective 3	10 min.	●	●	3.A, 25.B, 27.A	
INTERACTIVE GALLERY **Science and Technology in Ancient Rome**		10 min.		●	3.A, 27.A	
READ **Roman Law Unites the Empire**	Objectives 4, 5	10 min.	●	●	1.B, 3.A, 22.A, 22.B, 25.B	
INTERACTIVE CHART **The Influence of Roman Law**		10 min.		●	1.B, 22.A, 22.B, 25.B	
Synthesize						
DIGITAL ACTIVITY **Architecture in Ancient Rome**		5 min.		●	26.B	
Demonstrate						
DIGITAL QUIZ **Lesson Quiz and Class Discussion Board**		10 min.		●	3.A, 22.B, 26.B, 27.A	

PEARSON realize™ www.PearsonTexas.com Access your Digital Lesson

Focus on Texas Standards

Texas Essential Knowledge and Skills

1.B identify major causes and describe the major effects of the following events from 500 BC to AD 600: the development of the classical civilizations of Greece, Rome, Persia, India (Maurya and Gupta), China (Zhou, Qin, and Han), and the development of major world religions

3.A describe the major political, religious/philosophical, and cultural influences of Persia, India, China, Israel, Greece, and Rome, including the development of monotheism, Judaism, and Christianity

22.A summarize the development of the rule of law from ancient to modern times

22.B identify the influence of ideas regarding the right to a "trial by a jury of your peers" and the concepts of "innocent until proven guilty" and "equality before the law" that originated from the Judeo-Christian legal tradition and in Greece and Rome

25.B summarize the fundamental ideas and institutions of Western civilizations that originated in Greece and Rome

26.B analyze examples of how art, architecture, literature, music, and drama reflect the history of the cultures in which they are produced

27.A identify the origin and diffusion of major ideas in mathematics, science, and technology that occurred in river valley civilizations, classical Greece and Rome, classical India, and the Islamic caliphates between 700 and 1200 and in China from the Tang to Ming dynasties

NOTES

Topic 6 Lesson 4

The Origins of Christianity

Objectives

Objective 1: Understand the diverse religions included in the early Roman empire.

Objective 2: Describe the development and central ideas of Christianity.

Objective 3: Summarize the spread of Christianity.

Objective 4: Outline the development of the early Christian Church.

LESSON 4 ORGANIZER	PACING: APPROX. 1 PERIOD, .5 BLOCKS					
			RESOURCES			
	OBJECTIVES	PACING	Print	Online	TEKS	ELPS
Connect						
DIGITAL START UP ACTIVITY **A Roman Emperor Accepts Christianity**		5 min.		●	3.A, 23.A	
Investigate						
READ **Romans Accept Many Religions**	Objective 1	10 min.	●	●	1.B, 3.A, 23.A	
READ **The Teachings of Jesus**	Objective 2	10 min.	●	●	1.B, 3.A, 20.A, 23.A	2.D.2
INTERACTIVE GALLERY **Christian Symbols**		10 min.		●	1.B, 3.A, 23.A	
READ **Christianity Spreads**	Objective 3	10 min.	●	●	1.B, 3.A, 23.A	
INTERACTIVE MAP **The Spread of Christianity**		10 min.		●	23.A	
READ **The Growth of the Christian Church**	Objective 4	10 min.	●	●	3.A, 23.A	
Synthesize						
DIGITAL ACTIVITY **Key Roles in Early Christianity**		5 min.		●	1B, 3.A, 23.A	
Demonstrate						
DIGITAL QUIZ **Lesson Quiz and Class Discussion Board**		10 min.		●	1.B, 3.A, 23A	

Focus on Texas Standards

Texas Essential Knowledge and Skills

1.B identify major causes and describe the major effects of the following events from 500 BC to AD 600: the development of the classical civilizations of Greece, Rome, Persia, India (Maurya and Gupta), China (Zhou, Qin, and Han), and the development of major world religions

3.A describe the major political, religious/philosophical, and cultural influences of Persia, India, China, Israel, Greece, and Rome, including the development of monotheism, Judaism, and Christianity

20.A explain the development of democratic-republican government from its beginnings in the Judeo-Christian legal tradition and classical Greece and Rome through the English Civil War and the Enlightenment

23.A describe the historical origins, central ideas, and spread of major religious and philosophical traditions, including Buddhism, Christianity, Confucianism, Hinduism, Islam, Judaism, Sikhism, and the development of monotheism

NOTES

TOPIC 6 TEKS Mastery

Ancient Rome and the Origins of Christianity (509 B.C.–A.D. 476)

In this Topic, you will learn about the age of ancient Rome and the origins of Christianity. You will also find lots of ways to investigate the ideas of this Topic and to master the TEKS.

Your study will help you master these TEKS:

TEKS

1.B, 1.C, 3.A, 3.B, 3.C, 19.B, 20.A, 21.B, 22.A, 22.B, 23.A, 24.A, 25.B, 26.B, 27.A, 29.F, 29.H, 30.C, 30.D

LESSON OUTLINE

Connect

You will start by connecting with the Topic through a video that tells a personal story about the times. You will start to think about how the Topic connects with your own experience or to what you already know. And you'll get a chance to think about a really big question, or Essential Question: What makes a government successful?

Begin your study by trying the following:

NBC LEARN Watch My Story Video:

Augustus, the Pax Romana

Launch your Project:

Give a Presentation About the Collapse of Empires

Investigate

Then you will investigate the Topic through a group of lessons. The story of ancient Rome and Christianity's origins will come to life as you read and interact with key content. You will get a chance to read about what happened and why. And you'll be able to interact with a lot of engaging online materials.

And keep working on your Project. You're almost ready to show what you have accomplished by presenting your Project about the collapse of empires.

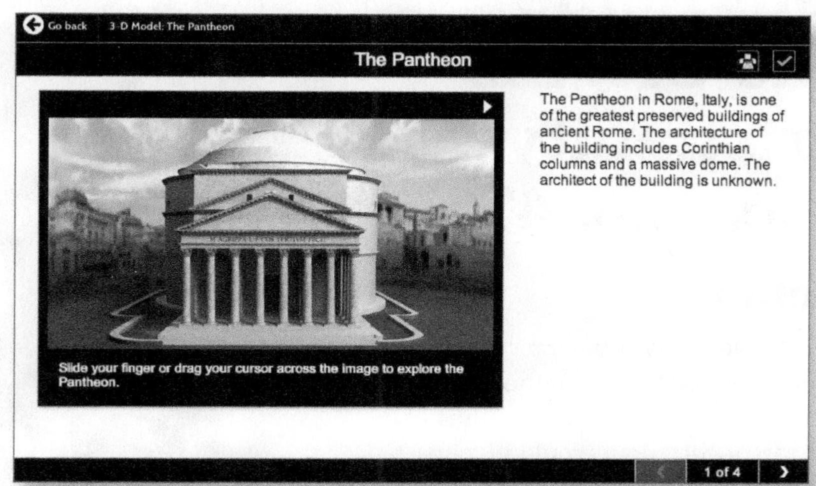

Go back
3-D Model: The Pantheon
The Pantheon
The Pantheon in Rome, Italy, is one of the greatest preserved buildings of ancient Rome. The architecture of the building includes Corinthian columns and a massive dome. The architect of the building is unknown.
Slide your finger or drag your cursor across the image to explore the Pantheon.
1 of 4

>> Digital interactivity from the online course

Synthesize

Next you will pull it all together by reflecting on the Essential Question. This will give you a chance to be the storyteller, to show how you would answer this big question.

Demonstrate

Completing this Topic is like practicing all your soccer skills or rehearsing the scenes in a play. Now you get a chance to pull it all together for the final game or the live performance. You can do this on the Topic Review and Assessment pages. Or you can complete work on your presentation about the collapse of empires.

TEKS in Topic 6	Topic Review and Assessment Questions
1.B	2
1.C	15
3.A	4, 5
3.B	12, 15
3.C	14
19.B	1
20.A	8
21.B	3
22.A	6
22.B	7
23.A	4, 11
25.B	10
26.B	9
27.A	13
29.F	14
30.C	4, 5
30.D	14

Topic 6

Ancient Rome and the Origins of Christianity (509 B.C.–A.D. 476)

Introduction

The Roman civilization grew from a city on the Tiber to become a republic that spanned Europe and the Mediterranean. Many of the features of Rome's republican government would inspire Western democratic governments centuries later. Rome embraced Greek learning and beliefs, creating a Greco-Roman culture that is considered the basis of Western civilization. When Augustus took power, Rome became an empire and an era of prosperity began. Later, internal unrest and a relentless series of invasions led to the fall of the western empire. During the Roman empire, a new religion arose in the territory of Judea. Based upon the teachings of Jesus, Christianity spread throughout the empire until it became its official religion.

[ESSENTIAL QUESTION] What Makes a Government Successful?

6 Ancient Rome and the Origins of Christianity (509 B.C.-A.D. 476)

ESSENTIAL QUESTION

Ask students to think about the Essential Question for this Topic: What makes a government successful? Project the Essential Question activity from the course. Have a volunteer read the quotation and another volunteer read the introduction and the items in the bulleted list. Ask students to rank each of the criteria of good government in importance. Then discuss the results as a class.

Support a Point of View With Evidence Why did you rank one of the criteria as most important? *(Answers will vary.)*

Identify Central Issues What role does a citizen have in making government a success? *(Answers may vary. A citizen can vote, serve in the government or the military, obey laws, pay taxes, serve on juries, and volunteer for community service.)*

Cause and Effect How would ensuring equal treatment of all citizens under the law contribute to a government's success? *(Answers may vary. Students might respond that citizens who perceive the law as fair would support the government and would be less likely to participate in civic unrest.)*

Analyze Images

Have students examine the photograph of the Colosseum. Explain that this stadium was built during the time of ancient Rome for spectator events. Discuss what the size, purpose, and longevity of this structure tell us about Roman society and the government that built infrastructure like it.

> The Colosseum in Rome

Enduring Understandings

- Rome was founded as a republic, which served as a model for later governments, including the United States.
- As Roman power grew, society became more unequal and the republic became an empire.
- During the Pax Romana, many fundamental ideas and institutions of Western civilization originated in Rome.
- Political violence and foreign invasions led to the fall of the Western Roman empire, while the eastern Byzantine empire survived.
- The Romans adapted Greek cultural achievements and Roman law influenced many modern legal systems.
- Jesus and his disciples founded Christianity and spread its message to many people.

PEARSON realize. NBC LEARN

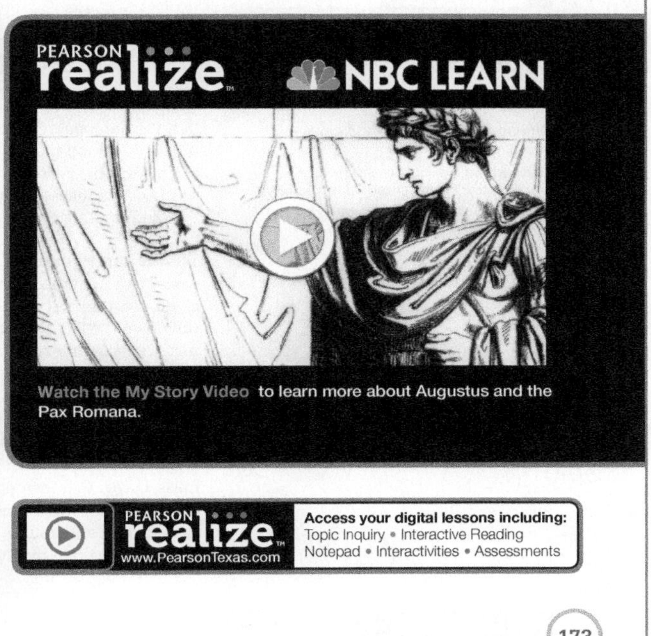

Watch the My Story Video to learn more about Augustus and the Pax Romana.

PEARSON realize. www.PearsonTexas.com Access your digital lessons including: Topic Inquiry • Interactive Reading Notepad • Interactivities • Assessments

173

NBC LEARN MY STORY VIDEO

Project the My Story Video that tells the story of Augustus.

Online My Story Video: **Augustus, the Pax Romana**.

After viewing, ask students to respond to the following questions.

Check Understanding Who was Augustus? *(the first emperor of Rome)*

Determine Point of View Augustus said, "I found Rome a city of bricks and left it a city of marble." What did he mean and how credible is his point of view? *(Augustus contributed to the growth of Rome's empire and to its prosperity. While it was in his interest to exaggerate his role, he is nevertheless viewed by scholars as one of the most significant figures in Roman history.)*

OVERVIEW ACTIVITY

Online Project the timeline showing the major events of ancient Rome. While exploring this Topic, students will learn about all of these events and many more, but this timeline will provide a framework into which they can place the events they learn about.

Check Understanding In what year did Christianity become the official Roman religion? *(A.D. 392)*

Topic Inquiry

If you choose to assign the Topic Inquiry, launch the project after introducing the Topic.

D Differentiate Extra Support For the Overview Activity, demonstrate to students how to read the timeline. How many years are there between the establishment of the republic and when Augustus becomes the first Roman emperor? *(482; The republic was founded in 509 B.C.; Augustus became emperor in 27 B.C.)*

Topic 6 Lesson 1

The Roman Republic

CONNECT

Preview Have students preview the **Lesson Objectives** and the list of **Key Terms**.

Students can also preview all the **Key Terms** and **Academic Vocabulary** using the **Interactive Reading Notepad** on the digital course or preview a summary of the lesson in the **Reading and Note Taking Study Guide**.

Online Use the **Editable Presentation** found on the digital course to present the main ideas for this lesson.

Start Up Activity

Write and read aloud the following quote from Roman poet Horace, describing his father:

> "For although he was a poor man, with only an infertile plot of land, he was not content to send me to [the school in his hometown].... My father had the courage to take his boy to Rome, to have him taught the same skills which any equestrian or senator would have his sons taught.... I could never be ashamed of such a father, nor do I feel any need, as many people do, to apologize for being a freedman's [former slave's] son."

Discuss What inferences can you make about Roman life based on the quote? *(Students may note that education was important in Roman society and that some people started off at a disadvantage because they were not born free or rich.)*

Online You can also project the **Start Up Activity** from the course.

Tell students they will be learning about the Roman republic's origin, structure, society, and evolution.

INVESTIGATE

Have students read the section using the **Reading and Note Taking Study Guide** to help them take notes and understand the text as they read.

The Rise of the Roman Civilization

Remind students that Roman ancestors, the Latins, migrated to Italy by 800 B.C. According to legend, the twin brothers Romulus and Remus founded the city that would become the heart of the classical civilization of Rome.

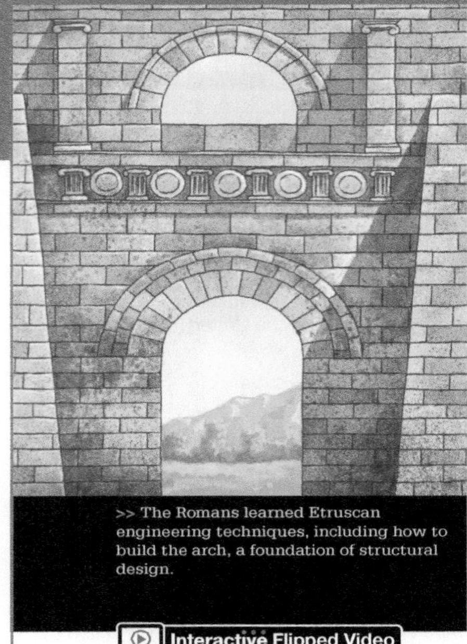

>> The Romans learned Etruscan engineering techniques, including how to build the arch, a foundation of structural design.

Interactive Flipped Video

6.1 Rome rose from a small city-state on the Italian peninsula to become the dominant power in the Mediterranean world. Roman law ruled over a vast, ethnically diverse empire. Rome's 1000-year history had many lasting effects, including the spread of important aspects of the civilizations of Greece, Egypt, and the Fertile Crescent into Europe.

TEKS
1.B, 3.A, 19.B, 20.A, 21.B, 24.A

>> Objectives

Describe the development of the classical civilization of Rome.

Outline how the Roman republic was structured and governed.

Understand the rights and religious practices that characterized Roman society.

Explain how the Roman republic grew and used its political influence.

>> Key Terms

Etruscans
republic
patrician
consul
dictator
plebeian
tribune
veto
legion

The Roman Republic

The Rise of the Roman Civilization

Italy is a peninsula that looks like a boot jutting into the Mediterranean Sea and kicking the island of Sicily toward Africa. The city of Rome sits toward the center of Italy. This location would benefit the Romans as they expanded—first within Italy and then into the lands bordering the Mediterranean.

The Italian Peninsula Because of its geography, Italy proved much easier to unify than Greece. Unlike Greece, Italy is not broken up into small, isolated valleys. In addition, the Apennine Mountains, which run down the length of the Italian peninsula, are less rugged than the mountains of Greece. Finally, Italy has broad, fertile plains in the north and the west. These plains supported the growing population.

Early Settlements in Italy By about 800 B.C., the ancestors of the Romans, called the Latins, had migrated into Italy. The Latins settled along the Tiber River in small villages scattered over seven low-lying hills. There, they herded and farmed. Their villages would in time grow together into Rome, the city on seven hills. Legend held that twin brothers, Romulus and Remus, had founded the city. Romans regarded this tale highly because the twins were said to be sons of

www.PearsonTexas.com Access your Digital Lesson.

174

Aa Vocabulary Builder

1. Have students pronounce the following academic vocabulary term in this lesson and clarify the part of speech. Break the term into syllables and pronounce it with the students.
2. Explain what the word means in common "student-friendly" language using synonyms and antonyms when possible. Provide concrete examples to clarify the meaning, and rephrase the definition.

dominate: have authority over

a Latin woman and the war god Mars, lending Rome a divine origin.

The Romans shared the Italian peninsula with other peoples. Among them were Greek colonists whose city-states dotted southern Italy and the **Etruscans** (ih TRUHS kuhnz), who lived mostly north of Rome. The origins of the Etruscan civilization are uncertain. One theory says they migrated from Asia Minor, while another suggests they came from the Alps. What is certain is that, for a time, the Etruscans ruled much of central Italy, including Rome.

The Romans learned much from Etruscan civilization. They adapted the alphabet that the Etruscans had earlier acquired from the Greeks. The Romans also learned from the Etruscans to use the arch in construction, and they adapted Etruscan engineering techniques to drain the marshy lands along the Tiber. Over time, the Romans adopted some Etruscan gods and goddesses who became merged with Roman deities.

? IDENTIFY MAIN IDEAS How did geography influence the origins and expansion of Rome?

The Early Roman Republic

In 509 B.C., the Romans drove out their Etruscan king. This date is traditionally considered to mark the founding of the Roman state. Determined never again to be ruled by a monarch, the Romans set up a new government in which officials were chosen by male citizens. They called it *res publica*, or "that which belongs to the people." This form of government, in which people choose their officials, is today called a **republic.** In a republic, Romans thought, no single individual would be able to gain too much power.

Structure of Rome's Republic In the early republic, the most powerful government body was the senate. It made the laws and controlled the government. At first, its 300 members were all **patricians,** or members of the landholding upper class.

Each year, the senators nominated two **consuls** from the patrician class. Their job was to supervise the business of government and command the armies. Consuls, however, could serve only one term and were expected to approve each other's decisions.

They were also expected to consult with the senate. By limiting their time in office and making them responsible to each other, Rome had a system of checks on the power of government.

In the event of war, the senate might choose a **dictator** or ruler who has complete control over a

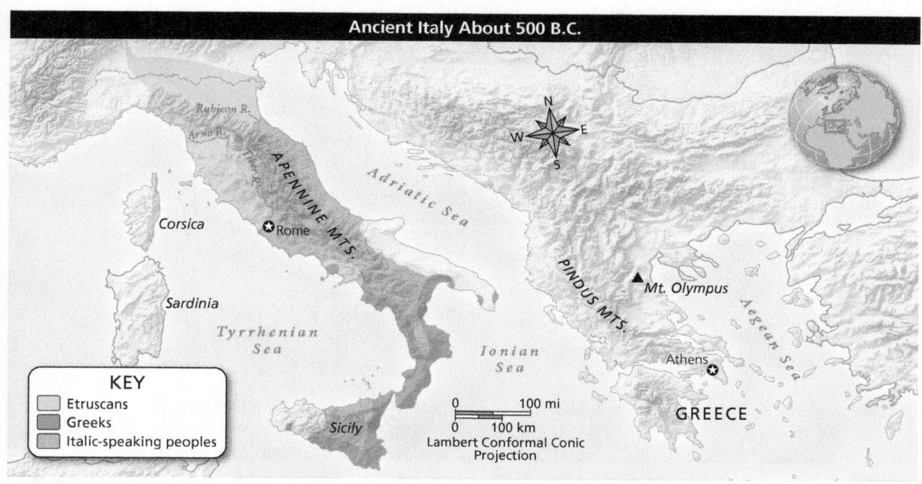

>> **Analyze Maps** Various ancient civilizations lived on the Italian peninsula around 500 B.C. What was one of Rome's geographical advantages?

Topic 6 Lesson 1

Guided Reading and Discussion

Ask students to describe the different civilizations on the Italian peninsula and their contributions to Roman culture.

Predict Consequences As Rome expands, what do you think its relationship will be with neighboring cultures? *(Sample response: Increased contact will create conflict, and Rome will want to conquer the Greeks and Etruscans.)*

Evaluate Impact How would the control of the Italian peninsula affect the development of Roman civilization? *(Sample response: Rome would have access to more ports, which would increase trade. Rome might try to expand its rule beyond the peninsula.)*

The Early Roman Republic

The Roman republic began when the Romans overthrew the Etruscan ruler in 509 B.C. Romans wanted a republic to prevent any individual from gaining too much power. Romans structured the republic by creating a senate, initially comprised of upper class patricians, to make laws and control the government. Over time, plebeians gained more access to power and were able to serve in the senate. The structure of the Roman government created checks and balances on power, an idea later adapted by the framers of the United States Constitution.

Key Terms

Ask students to find the key term **republic** (in bold) in the text. Explain that the term describes the government of the United States. In a republic, the people vote for individuals to represent their interests in government decisions.

History Background

Etruscan Civilization Although few Etruscan houses have survived, thousands of ancient Etruscan tombs remain intact. The Etruscans believed tombs were the dwelling places of the dead, so they built their tombs to look like the interiors of Etruscan homes. Tombs often had one or more rooms made of stone that contained Etruscan works of art. By examining the tomb artifacts and the construction of these rooms, archaeologists have learned a great deal about the Etruscans and their use of arches in construction.

Answers

Analyze Maps *Sample response: Rome had access to the Mediterranean, making trade easier. It was at the mouth of the Tiber River, which provided an inland water transportation route.*

Identify Main Ideas *Rome had a favorable central location on the Italian peninsula, access to the Mediterranean Sea, and fertile plains for farming.*

Topic 6 Lesson 1

Online Project the **Interactive Gallery: The Roman *Cursus Honorum*** and click through the images and hotspots. Each hotspot represents a position and details the career path of a senator.

ACTIVE CLASSROOM

Use the Conversation With History strategy. Have students select a senatorial position that interests them. Have them write one question that they would like to ask the senator. Then ask them to jot down how they think the senator will respond. Suggest their dialogue be posted as a video conversation on YouTube.

Guided Reading and Discussion

Ask students to describe how Rome's government changed over time and the effect of that change on its citizens. Help students understand that, over time, citizen plebeians gained political influence and eventually served in the senate. As a result, the senate represented more of the Roman people.

D Differentiate Challenge Help students understand that the development of the Roman government was a matter of trial and error. Two-thirds of the class will be patrician senators grouped in their respective hierarchy of office. The remainder of the class will be plebeians. Ask the plebeians to formulate an issue, based on the reading, that they want to present to the senate. In advance of their presentation, have them write down the issue and give it to patrician students. The plebeians and patricians will role-play their positions in a senate setting.

Answers

List *the incorporation of the Roman ideas of a senate, veto power, a system of checks and balances, and term limits*

Analyze Charts *Tables IV, V, VI, XI*

government. Each Roman dictator was granted power to rule for six months. After that time, he had to give up power. Romans particularly admired Cincinnatus(SIHN suh NA tuhs) as a model dictator.

Cincinnatus organized an army, led the Romans to victory over the attacking enemy, attended victory celebrations, and returned to work his fields—all within 15 days.

Plebeians Demand Equality At first, all government officials were patricians. **Plebeians** (plih BEE uhnz), the farmers, merchants, and artisans who made up most of the population, were citizens but had little influence. Plebeian demands for power shaped politics in the early republic.

The plebeians' first breakthrough came in 450 B.C., when the government had the laws of Rome inscribed on 12 tablets, which were set up in the Forum, Rome's marketplace. For the first time, the Laws of the Twelve Tables made it possible for plebeians to appeal a judgment handed down by a patrician judge.

In time, the plebeians gained the right to elect their own officials, called **tribunes,** to protect their interests. The tribunes could **veto,** or block, laws that they felt were harmful to plebeians. Little by little, plebeians forced the senate to choose plebeians as consuls, appoint them to high offices, and finally to admit them to the senate. These changes made Rome's government more representative.

A Lasting Legacy Although the senate still dominated the government, the common people had gained access to power and won safeguards for their rights without having to resort to war or revolution.

More than 2,000 years later, the framers of the United States Constitution would adapt such Roman ideas as the senate, the veto, and a system of checks and balances on political power.

? LIST How did the Roman republic influence the U.S. Constitution?

ELPS 2.C.3 Listen to your teacher or another student as they discuss the first section under the heading *The Early Roman Republic.* Note unfamiliar words and find their meanings through listening to discussions and asking questions.

Roman Society

The family was the basic unit of Roman society. Under Roman law, the male head of the household—usually the father—had absolute power in the family. He enforced strict discipline and demanded total respect for his authority. His wife was subject to his authority

LAWS OF THE TWELVE TABLES			
TABLE I	Procedure: for courts and trials	TABLE VII	Land rights
TABLE II	Trial continuance and evidence	TABLE VIII	Torts and delicts (Laws of injury)
TABLE III	Debt	TABLE IX	Public law
TABLE IV	Rights of fathers (paterfamilias) over the family; infanticide	TABLE X	Sacred law
TABLE V	Legal guardianship and inheritance laws	TABLE XI	Marriage between a patrician and a plebeian forbidden
TABLE VI	Acquisition and possession; marriage	TABLE XII	Binding law: power of the people

>> **Analyze Charts** Posting the Laws of the Twelve Tables in the Forum made Rome's laws accessible to all of its citizens. Which of the Twelve Tables laws dealt with family law?

Interactive Gallery

English Language Proficiency Standards

Listening 2.C.3 To help students learn basic vocabulary, tell them to listen carefully as others discuss vocabulary related to "The Early Roman Republic," such as *republic, senate, senator, patrician, nominate, consul,* and *dictator*. Read the terms and their definitions aloud. Then guide students in how to use these new terms to discuss Roman government.

Beginning Ask students to listen carefully as you rephrase vocabulary definitions using words with which they are familiar. Then reread sentences in the text that contain these words aloud. Have students keep a log of new words, creating definitions in familiar English words, drawings, or in their native language.

and was not allowed to administer her own affairs. The ideal Roman woman was loving, dutiful, dignified, and strong.

The Role of Women During the early Roman Republic, women had few rights. Later, they gained more freedom, and played a larger role in society than did Greek women. They could own property, and, in later Roman times, women from all classes ran a variety of businesses, from small shops to major shipyards. Aristocratic women earned respect by supporting the arts or paying for public festivals. However, most women worked at home, raising their families, spinning, and weaving.

Over the centuries, Roman women gained even greater freedom and influence. Patrician women went to the public baths, dined out, and attended the theater or other forms of public entertainment with their husbands. Some women, such as Livia (LIHV ee uh) and Aggripina the Younger (ag ruh PY nuh), had highly visible public roles and exercised significant political influence.

Roman Education Girls and boys from the upper and lower classes learned to read and write. By the later years of the republic, many wealthy Romans hired private tutors, often Greeks, to educate their children. Children memorized major events in Roman history. Boys who wanted to pursue political careers studied rhetoric.

Roman Mythology and Religion The Romans believed in many gods and goddesses, who resembled those of the Etruscans and Greeks. Like the Greek god, Zeus, the Roman god Jupiter ruled over the sky and the other gods. According to Roman myths, his wife Juno, like the Greek goddess Hera, protected marriage. Romans also prayed to Neptune, god of the sea, whose powers were the same as those of the Greek god Poseidon. On the battlefield, they turned to Mars, the god of war.

The Roman calendar was full of feasts and other celebrations to honor the gods and goddesses and to ensure divine favor for the city. As loyal citizens, most Romans joined in these festivals, which inspired a sense of community. Throughout Rome, dozens of temples housed statues of the gods. In front of these temples, Romans took part in ritual activities such as worshipping the gods and asking for divine assistance.

IDENTIFY What social rights did women have in the republic?

>> Roman life was centered on the family and religious practice. Religious worship included sacrifices to the gods.

>> Paying homage to a variety of gods and goddesses was an integral part of Roman life. Minerva was the goddess of wisdom, whom Romans prayed to for guidance.

Topic 6 Lesson 1

Roman Society

Tell students that Roman society was centered on the family. The father was the authoritative figure, and the wife raised the family and usually worked at home. Discuss the role of women and children in Roman society. Romans placed a significant emphasis on education for both girls and boys.

Guided Reading and Discussion

Ask students to discuss Greek contributions to Roman culture.

Apply Concepts Describe religious worship and practice in ancient Rome. *(The worship of gods and goddesses was an important part of Roman society. Honoring them was thought to ensure divine favor. Roman citizens showed their loyalty by attending religious festivals that centered on paying homage to any one to a number of gods.)*

Intermediate Have volunteers describe the role of the senate in the Roman republic. Then have them complete these oral sentence frames: The role of the senate was ________. Senators were from the class of ________. Consuls were nominated by ________. Their job was ________.

Advanced Have pairs take turns listening to each other explain each term as it relates to the Roman republic. Then have them work together to write a few sentences describing the government of the Roman republic. Ask volunteers to read their sentences aloud and answer questions from the group.

Advanced High Have pairs take turns listening to each other explain each term as it relates to the Roman republic. Then have them construct a graphic organizer explaining the different roles of a senator, a consul, and a dictator in the Roman republic. Ask them to share it with the group and answer questions.

Answers

Identify *Initially, Roman women had few rights. Later, they could own property and businesses, go to public baths, dine out, and attend the theater or other entertainments with their husbands.*

Topic 6 Lesson 1

The Roman Republic Expands

By 270 B.C., Rome controlled most of the Italian peninsula. Rome's legions of citizen-soldiers won many victories. Rome allowed conquered persons to retain their customs, money, and local government. In return, the conquered had to acknowledge the authority of Rome and contribute to the republic. For example, they paid taxes and supplied soldiers for the Roman army. Although most were non-citizens, some conquered groups were granted partial or full citizenship.

Online Project the **Interactive Map: Growth of the Roman Republic, 500 B.C. to 44 B.C.** and click through the layers. Explain to students that each layer of the map reflects lands conquered by the Romans.

ACTIVE CLASSROOM

Use the Make Headlines strategy with the Interactive Map to explore the invasions' impact. Ask: If you were to write a headline right now to capture the most important aspect that should be remembered about any invasion, what would that headline be? Tell students they can post their ideas on Twitter.

Guided Reading and Discussion

Ask students to discuss what attributes of Roman rule helped it conquer and maintain control over many lands.

Interpret What steps did Rome take to govern its new territories? *(The senate instituted laws to determine how the conquered lands would be governed. Conquered persons could keep their customs, money, and local government. They had to acknowledge Rome's authority and contribute to the republic.)*

The Roman Republic Expands

The Roman Republic lasted almost 500 years, During that time, its armies expanded Roman power across Italy. First, they conquered their neighbors in central Italy, including the Etruscans. Then they overpowered the Greek city-states in the south. By about 270 B.C., Rome controlled most of the Italian peninsula.

Citizen-Soldiers Rome's success was due to skillful diplomacy and to its loyal, well-trained army. The basic military unit was the **legion,** each of which included about 5,000 men. As in Greece, Roman armies consisted of citizen-soldiers who supplied their own weapons and fought without pay. Eventually, they received a small stipend, or payment, but their main compensation was always a share of the spoils of victory. Well-trained in military skills and raised to value loyalty and courage, Roman soldiers chalked up a series of brilliant victories.

To ensure success, Roman commanders mixed rewards with harsh punishment. Young soldiers who showed courage in action won praise and gifts. If a unit fled from battle, however, one out of every ten men from the disgraced unit was put to death.

Rome's Treatment of Conquered People Rome's armies could be ruthless, killing or enslaving those who resisted. However, if surrender was negotiated, terms could be more favorable. Conquered peoples had to acknowledge Roman leadership, pay taxes, and supply soldiers for the Roman army. In return, Rome let them keep their own customs, money, and local government. Once its rule was established, Rome generally treated its conquered peoples with justice, provided they did not rebel.

To a few privileged groups among the conquered people, Rome gave the highly prized right of full citizenship. Others became partial citizens, who were allowed to marry Romans and carry on trade in Rome. As a result of such generous policies, most conquered lands remained loyal to Rome even in troubled times.

Building Unity To protect its conquests, Rome posted soldiers throughout the land. It also built a network of all-weather military roads to link distant territories to Rome. As trade and travel increased, local peoples incorporated Latin into their languages and adopted many Roman customs and beliefs. Slowly, Italy began to unite under Roman rule.

? DESCRIBE What rights and responsibilities did Rome extend to conquered peoples?

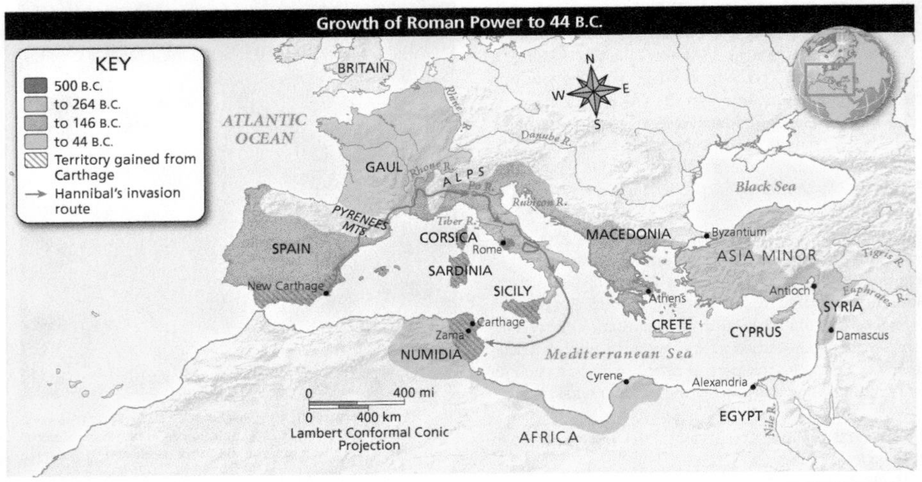

>> **Analyze Maps** Roman power and influence increased as its armies conquered new territories. Which territories were gained by Rome from 264 to 44 B.C.?

Interactive Map

Answers

Describe *Sample response: Rome has a prime location, with water access to the interior and a port for maritime trade. In times of war, Romans could move troops by land or by sea.*

Analyze Maps *In 264 B.C., Rome controlled most of the Italian peninsula. By 146 B.C., they had added Macedonia and Spain. By 44 B.C., Rome had gained Gaul, Numidia, Asia Minor, and Crete.*

History Background

Laws of the Twelve Tables The Twelve Tables were the earliest written form of Roman law. Before their publication, judgments of the courts were based on unwritten custom. Until the plebeians demanded a written law code, a small group of patrician scholars were the only people who had exact knowledge of these customs. The code was probably engraved on bronze tablets. It described in clear, simple, and exact language the rights and duties of citizens. Although the Laws of the Twelve Tables were a step toward the rule of law, it was a harsh code that maintained class divisions by banning marriage between patricians and plebeians. The code also gave fathers the legal right to whip, imprison, sell, or kill their children.

ASSESSMENT

1. **Identify** How did the classical civilization of Rome develop? Describe some aspects of its culture.
2. **Explain** How did the republic's structure of government change and develop over time?
3. **Summarize** What Roman principles of government were incorporated into the United States Constitutions?
4. **Interpret** What was Cincinnatus's contribution to Roman history? How does he reflect some of the ideals of Roman civilization?
5. **Paraphrase** What attributes of Rome's citizen-soldiers made them so important to the republic's growth?

SYNTHESIZE

Online Project the **Digital Activity: Communication Is Key**. Using Think-Pair-Share, suggest students review the initial Synthesize Activity and answer the following questions. They should share their answers with their partner.

How did well-built roads contribute to Rome's success? *(Roman roads improved communication and allowed faster movement of troops, which helped Rome conquer and govern its territories.)*

How might the Internet and Roman roads be similar in their effect on culture and the economy? *(The Internet and Roman roads improved the ability to share ideas; to spread language, customs, and beliefs, and to facilitate trade.)*

DEMONSTRATE

Online Assign the **Digital Lesson Quiz** for this lesson if you haven't already done so. Students will be offered automatic remediation or enrichment based on their score.

Pose these questions to the class on the Discussion Board:

In "The Early Roman Republic," you read about the beginning of the republic's government, how it changed with challenges from the common people, which fundamental structures became a legacy for future generations, and how Rome expanded its control across the Italian peninsula.

Draw Inferences Do you think Rome will continue to conquer new territories? If so, where? Hint: Look at the map Ancient Italy About 500 B.C.

Predict Consequences Consider what you have read about Greece. What new challenges will the Roman republic face?

Topic Inquiry

Have students continue their investigations for the Topic Inquiry.

Assessment

1. The Latins built Rome along the Tiber River. Roman culture adopted elements, such as the alphabet, engineering techniques, and religious beliefs, from the Etruscans and the Greeks. Rome became the dominant power on the Italian peninsula. As a republic, Rome developed a political system that influenced many modern governments. Family, education, religion, and civic duty were important aspects of Roman society.
2. Initially, only patricians could serve in the government. Plebeians demanded representation and gained the right to select their own officials. Later, plebeians were permitted to be members of the senate, which made Rome's government more democratic.
3. The idea of a senate made up of representatives of the people, veto power, a system of checks and balances, and term limits
4. Cincinnatus was chosen as dictator during a time of crisis. He organized an army, defeated the enemy, celebrated his victory, then returned to his farmlands. Cincinnatus represents the ideal Roman citizen, serving the republic as needed with efficiency and success.
5. Rome's citizen-soldiers valued loyalty, courage, and respect for authority. They initially served without pay and used their own weapons. As a result, Rome had a dedicated and disciplined army at little cost. Its strong military helped the republic to expand.

Topic 6 Lesson 2

The Roman Empire: Rise and Decline

CONNECT

Preview Have students preview the **Lesson Objectives** and the list of **Key Terms**.

Students can also preview all the **Key Terms** and **Academic Vocabulary** using the **Interactive Reading Notepad** on the digital course or preview a summary of the lesson in the **Reading and Note Taking Study Guide**.

Online Use the **Editable Presentation** found on the digital course to present the main ideas for this lesson.

Start Up Activity

Give students background information about Julius Caesar: Julius Caesar was a military leader who later became the dictator of Rome. Long after Caesar died, his name became a symbol for power and authority. Many languages adapted Caesar's name to create titles for their leaders. In Germany, the nation's ruler became known as the *kaiser*. The Russian word *tsar* also comes from *Caesar*.

Discuss What does the use of Caesar's name in other languages tell you about Caesar as a leader? How might an absolute ruler change the Roman republic?

Online You can also project the **Start Up Activity** from the course.

INVESTIGATE

Have students read the section using the **Reading and Note Taking Study Guide** to help them take notes and understand the text as they read.

Empire Building Through Conquest

The Roman Republic Declines

Remind students that once Rome controlled the Italian peninsula, it expanded westward and came into conflict with Carthage. After its victory in the Third Punic War, Roman conquest continued until Rome controlled most of the Mediterranean region. Rome had gained great power and wealth, but expansion created internal issues that threatened the republic. Small farmers could not compete with the latifundia. Unemployment and a growing gap between the rich and the poor led to social unrest.

>> Praetorian Guards were skilled and loyal bodyguards who protected generals during the time of the late republic. Later, they became an elite guard for Roman emperors.

Interactive Flipped Video

6.2 After conquering the Italian peninsula, Rome began to build an empire around the Mediterranean Sea. This expansion brought great riches but created conflicts that divided Roman society and weakened and finally crushed the republic. Out of the rubble, however, rose the Roman empire and a new chapter in Rome's long history.

TEKS
1.B, 1.C, 3.A, 3.B, 20.A, 25.B

>> Objectives

Identify the events leading to the decline of the Roman republic.

Summarize the fundamental ideas and institutions of Western civilizations that originated in Rome.

Explain how and why the Roman empire divided.

Identify the factors that led to the decline and fall of Rome.

>> Key Terms

imperialism
latifundia
census
Huns
inflation
Constantine
Constantinople
mercenaries
Tiberius
Gaius Gracchus
Julius Caesar
Augustus
Hadrian
Diocletian

The Roman Empire: Rise and Decline

Empire Building Through Conquest

Rome's conquest of the Italian peninsula brought it into contact with Carthage, a city-state on the coast of North Africa. Settled by Phoenician traders and people from North Africa, Carthage ruled over a vast trading empire that stretched across North Africa and the western Mediterranean, including parts of Spain. As Rome spread into the Mediterranean, conflict between these two powers became inevitable.

The Punic Wars Between 264 B.C. and 146 B.C., Rome fought three wars against Carthage. They are called the Punic Wars, from *Punicus*, the Latin word for Phoenician. In the First Punic War, Rome defeated Carthage and won the islands of Sicily, Corsica, and Sardinia.

The Carthaginians sought revenge in the Second Punic War. In 218 B.C., the Carthaginian general Hannibal (HA nuh buhl) led his army, including dozens of war elephants, on an epic march across the Pyrenees, through France, and over the Alps into Italy. The trek cost Hannibal one-third of his army. But Hannibal still managed to surprise the Romans, who had expected an invasion from the south.

PEARSON realize. www.PearsonTexas.com Access your Digital Lesson.

Aa Vocabulary Builder

1. Have students pronounce the following academic vocabulary terms in this lesson and clarify the part of speech. For difficult or polysyllabic words, break them into syllables and pronounce them with the students.
2. Explain what the word means in common "student-friendly" language using synonyms and antonyms when possible. Provide concrete examples to clarify the meaning, and rephrase the definition.

suppress: use force to put an end to something

prestige: the power to impress or influence because of success or wealth

For 15 years, Hannibal and his army moved across Italy, winning battle after battle.

However, the Carthaginians failed to capture Rome itself. In the end, the Romans outflanked Hannibal by sending an army to attack Carthage. Hannibal returned to defend his homeland, where the Romans defeated him at last. Under the peace terms ending the war, Carthage had to give up all its lands outside of Africa and pay a huge tribute, or tax, to Rome. Victory gave Rome mastery of the Mediterranean.

Carthage Is Destroyed Despite Hannibal's defeat, many Romans still feared their old rival. They wanted revenge for the terrible destruction that Hannibal's army had brought to Italy. For years, the Roman senator Cato ended his every speech declaring, "Carthage must be destroyed."

Finally, in the Third Punic War, Rome completely destroyed the 700-year-old city of Carthage. Survivors were killed or sold into slavery. The Romans poured salt over the earth so that nothing would grow there again. Carthage and the region surrounding it became the new Roman province of Africa.

Ruler of the Mediterranean World "The Carthaginians fought for their own preservation and the sovereignty of Africa," observed a Greek witness to the fall of Carthage; "the Romans, for supremacy and world domination." Like other ancient powers, the Romans followed a policy of **imperialism,** or establishing control over foreign lands and peoples. While Rome fought Carthage in the west, it was also expanding into the eastern Mediterranean. There, Romans confronted the Hellenistic rulers who had divided up the empire of Alexander the Great.

Sometimes to defend Roman interests, sometimes simply for plunder, Rome launched a series of wars in the area. One by one, Macedonia, Greece, and parts of Asia Minor surrendered and became Roman provinces. Other regions, such as Egypt, allied with Rome. By 133 B.C., Roman power extended from Spain to Egypt. Truly, the Romans were justified in calling the Mediterranean *Mare Nostrum*, or "Our Sea."

Conquests Impact Rome Conquests and greatly expanded trade brought incredible riches into Rome. Generals, officials, and traders amassed fortunes from loot, taxes, and commerce. A new class of wealthy Romans emerged. They built lavish mansions and filled them with luxuries imported from the east. Wealthy families bought up huge farming estates, called **latifundia**(LA tuh FUHN dee uh).

With every new conquest, Rome acquired more slaves. Some were well-educated Greeks or other highly skilled people. Romans brought enslaved Greeks into their homes as teachers for their children. Unskilled slaves, however, faced brutally harsh lives.

The growth of slavery greatly changed Rome. The widespread use of slave labor hurt small farmers, who were unable to produce food as cheaply as the latifundia could. The farmers' problems grew when huge quantities of grain pouring in from the conquered lands drove down grain prices. Many farmers fell into debt and had to sell their land.

In despair, landless farmers flocked to Rome and other cities looking for jobs. There, they joined an already restless class of unemployed people. As the gap between rich and poor widened, angry mobs began to riot. In addition, the new wealth led to increased corruption. Greed and self-interest replaced the virtues of the early republic, such as simplicity, hard work, and devotion to duty.

Attempts at Reform Bring Violence Two young plebeians, brothers named **Tiberius** (ty BIHR ee uhs) and **Gaius Gracchus** (GAY us GRAK us), were among the first to attempt reform. Tiberius, elected a tribune in 133 B.C., called on the state to distribute land to poor farmers. Gaius, elected a tribune ten years later, sought a wider range of reforms, including the use of public funds to buy grain to feed the poor. The reforms of the

>> In the second Punic War, Hannibal's army used elephants to battle the Romans.

Guided Reading and Discussion

Have students discuss Caesar's accomplishments as a dictator and the effects of his assassination. Students should note that Caesar created jobs for the unemployed, gave public land to the poor, reorganized the governments of the provinces, and granted citizenship to more people.

Draw Conclusions Why could the Punic Wars be considered a turning point for Rome? *(Sample response: They proved that Rome could challenge a powerful empire. The defeat of Carthage is the beginning of Rome's political and cultural domination of the Mediterranean region.)*

Evaluate Impact How did imperialism threaten the stability of the republic and foreshadow the decline of Rome? *(As it conquered more lands, Rome gained great wealth and more slaves. Small farmers could not compete with the latifundia. This led to unemployment and a growing gap between the rich and the poor. The disparity led to social unrest. Republican virtues declined as greed and corruption increased. These internal problems worsened as Rome expanded.)*

Analyze Information Which of Caesar's political reforms have influenced Western civilization? *(He created a program of public works to employ the jobless, a policy that many Western governments have implemented in times of economic hardship.)*

Key Terms

Ask students to find the key term **imperialism** (in bold) in the text. Explain that many countries have practiced imperialism throughout history. Imperialist governments can control foreign lands in many ways, including establishing colonies.

Topic 6 Lesson 2

The Roman Empire

Augustus's reign marked the end of the Roman republic and the beginning of the Roman empire. The 200-year period of peace and prosperity that followed is known as the *Pax Romana*.

Guided Reading and Discussion

Explain that *Pax Romana* is Latin for "Roman Peace." During this period, Roman rule brought peace, order, unity, and prosperity to lands stretching from the Euphrates River to Britain.

Hypothesize Briefly review some of the fundamental principles of the Roman republic and the Interactive Timeline. Then ask students if they think the citizens of the republic would have viewed the Roman empire favorably or not. *(Answers will vary. Favorable: Some reforms made government more fair. The empire's prosperity increased the mobility of goods, people, and ideas. Unfavorable: Without the checks and balances of the republic, corrupt and incompetent emperors contributed to Rome's decline.)*

>> The brothers Tiberius and Gaius Gracchus tried to reform Rome's government.

>> Caesar dictated his commentaries on war to scribes who recorded his words.

Gracchus brothers angered the senate, which saw them as a threat to its power. The brothers and thousands of their followers were killed in waves of street violence set off by senators and their hired thugs.

IDENTIFY What economic challenges did Rome face while building an empire around the Mediterranean Sea?

ELPS **ELPS 2.C.4** Listen for the terms conflict, distribute, expand, and series as your teacher or partner reads *Empire Building Through Conquest* aloud. Raise your hand every time you hear one of these words read.

The Roman Republic Declines

A century of turmoil and civil wars engulfed Rome after the murders of the Gracchus brothers, whose attempts to bring reforms had failed. At issue was who should hold power—the senate, which wanted to govern as it had in the past, or popular political leaders, who wanted to weaken the senate and enact reforms.

The turmoil sparked slave uprisings at home and revolts among Rome's allies. Meanwhile, the old legions of Roman citizen-soldiers became professional armies whose first loyalty was to their commanders. Once rival commanders had their own armies, they could march into Rome to advance their ambitions. Power struggles among ambitious generals would help weaken the republic and lead to its overthrow.

Caesar's Bid for Power Out of this chaos emerged **Julius Caesar,** an ambitious military commander. For a time, Caesar and another brilliant general, Pompey, dominated Roman politics.

In 58 B.C., Caesar set out with his army to make new conquests. After nine years of fighting, he completed the conquest of Gaul—the area that is now France and Belgium. Jealous and fearful of Caesar's success, Pompey persuaded the senate to order Caesar to disband his army and return to Rome. Caesar defied the order. Acting swiftly and secretly, he led his army across the Rubicon River into northern Italy and headed toward Rome. Once again, Rome was plunged into civil war.

Caesar crushed Pompey and his supporters. He then swept around the Mediterranean, suppressing rebellions. "Veni, vidi, vici"—"I came, I saw, I conquered"—he announced after one victory. Later, returning to Rome, he forced the senate to make him dictator. Although he maintained the senate and other features of the republic, he was in fact the absolute ruler of Rome.

English Language Proficiency Standards

Listening 2.C.4 Have students work with academic vocabulary from the text. As they listen to "Empire Building Through Conquest" read aloud, have them respond to the use of the words. Guide students in their understanding of the meanings and usage of these terms.

Beginning Display the words: *conflict*, *distribute*, *expand*, and *series*. Read each word aloud and define it. As you read, have students listen for each word and raise their hands at every instance. Then provide students with sentence stems that allow them to use the academic word within the context of the Roman empire.

Intermediate Display the words: *conflict*, *distribute*, *expand*, and *series*. Read each word aloud and help students define it. As you read, have them listen for each word and raise their hands at every instance. Then ask content-specific questions that allow students to use the academic word in their answer.

Answers

Identify *As Rome expanded, it added people, in the form of slaves, to the population. Cheap slave labor and imported grain hurt the small farmers. When farmers could no longer compete, they lost their land and became unemployed. Trade created immense wealth for merchants and others, but the growing division between rich and poor led to dissension and social unrest.*

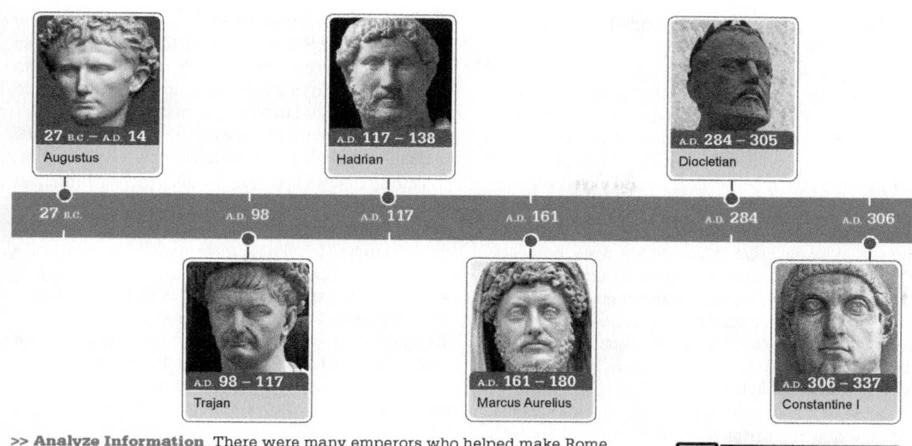

>> **Analyze Information** There were many emperors who helped make Rome great during the period 27 B.C. to A.D.306. What is the main difference between the rule of Augustus and that of Diocletian?

Interactive Timeline

Caesar's Reforms Between 48 B.C. and 44 B.C., Caesar pushed through a number of reforms intended to deal with Rome's many problems. He launched a program of public works to employ the jobless and gave public land to the poor. He also reorganized the government of the provinces and granted Roman citizenship to more people.

Caesar's most lasting reform was the introduction of a new calendar based on that of the Egyptians. The Roman calendar, later named the Julian calendar, was used in Western Europe for more than 1,600 years. With minor changes, it is still our calendar today.

The Death of Caesar Caesar's enemies worried that he planned to make himself king of Rome. To save the republic, they plotted against him. In March of 44 B.C., as Caesar arrived in the senate, his enemies stabbed him to death.

The death of Julius Caesar plunged Rome into a new round of civil wars. Mark Antony, Caesar's chief general, and Octavian (ahk TAH vee uhn), Caesar's grandnephew, joined forces to hunt down the murderers. The two men soon quarreled, setting off another bitter struggle for power. In 31 B.C.,Octavian finally defeated Antony and his powerful ally, Queen Cleopatra of Egypt.

IDENTIFY What central issue sparked the warfare that led to the decline of the Roman republic?

The Roman Empire

The senate gave the triumphant Octavian the title of **Augustus** (aw GUHS tuhs), or Exalted One, and declared him princeps, or first citizen. Although he was careful not to call himself king, a title that Romans had hated since Etruscan times, Augustus exercised absolute power and named his successor, just as a king would do.

Under Augustus, who ruled until A.D. 14, the 500-year-old republic came to an end. Romans did not know it at the time, but a new age had dawned—the age of the Roman empire. Augustus was its first emperor.

Augustus Reforms Government Through firm but moderate policies, Augustus laid the foundation for a stable government, helping Rome to recover from its endless civil wars. He left the senate in place and created an efficient, well-trained civil service to enforce the laws. High-level jobs were open to men of talent, regardless of their class. In addition, he cemented the allegiance of cities and provinces to Rome by allowing them a large amount of self-government.

Augustus also undertook economic reforms. To make the tax system more fair, he ordered a **census,** or population count, of the empire so there would be records of all who should be taxed. He set up a postal service and issued new coins to make trade easier. He

Online Project the **Interactive Timeline: Roman Rulers Who Made History**. Click through the hotspots and discuss institutions or ideas that originated during that emperor's rule of Rome.

ACTIVE CLASSROOM

After projecting the timeline, use the Cartoon It activity to have students create a quick copy of one compelling emperor's image on a piece of paper. Then have them turn it into a political cartoon that illustrates a key concept or main idea of that emperor's accomplishments. Use a document camera to scan the political cartoons to add to a class blog.

Analyze Information Ask students to identify each emperor's most important achievement. *(Answers may vary. Augustus: civil service, self-government, census; Trajan: built aqueduct; Hadrian: codified Roman law; Marcus Aurelius: abolished harsh civil law; Diocletian: split the empire and slowed inflation; Constantine: supported tolerance for Christians)*

Go over the answers and then take a poll on which emperor had the greatest role in the development of Roman civilization.

Advanced Work with students to review "Empire Building Through Conquest" to identify new academic words. Have partners use context clues and dictionaries to define each word on their list. Instruct them to write two content-specific sentences that each include one of the academic words. Have the group listen as pairs read their sentences aloud, omitting each academic word. Then have the group determine which academic words complete the sentences.

Advanced High Have pairs review "Empire Building Through Conquest" to identify new academic words and define each. Have them write a content-specific paragraph that includes at least four of their academic words. Instruct partners to turn to another pair to listen as they read their paragraph aloud, omitting the academic words. Have the new partners determine which academic words correctly complete the paragraph.

Answers

Analyze Information *Sample response: Augustus built a strong, stable government by creating a civil service, a census, and public works projects. Diocletian came into an empire that was in decline. He divided the empire to make it easier to govern and fixed prices to stop inflation.*

Identify *The question of who should gain power, the senate or popular political leaders.*

Topic 6 Lesson 2

The Roman Empire Splits

After the death of Marcus Aurelius, the empire entered a period of political violence and social unrest. The depth of the crisis is highlighted by the fact that in 50 years, there were 26 emperors.

Identify Cause and Effect Have students read the infographic "The Roman Empire Declines" on p. 185. Tell students to take a few minutes to review the categories listed for the causes of the empire's decline. Then discuss the reasons listed as causes and effects. Ask each student to look at all the categories and rank the causes of decline in importance with an explanation of the ranking. *(Possible answer: Political turbulence because civil war weakened the empire and negatively affected the economy, society, and military: Cause: high taxes; Effect: oppressive society.)*

put the jobless to work building roads and temples and sent others to farm the land.

The government that Augustus organized functioned well for 200 years. Still, a serious problem kept arising: Who would rule after an emperor died? Romans did not accept the idea of power passing automatically from father to son. As a result, the death of an emperor often led to intrigue and violence.

Emperors after Augustus Not all Augustus' successors were great rulers. Some were weak and incompetent. Two early emperors, Caligula (kuh LIH gyuh luh) and Nero, were considered evil and perhaps insane. Caligula, for example, appointed his favorite horse as consul. Nero viciously persecuted Christians and was even blamed for setting a great fire that destroyed much of Rome.

Between A.D. 96 and A.D. 180, the empire benefited from the rule of a series of "good emperors." **Hadrian** (HAY dree uhn), for example, codified Roman law, making it the same for all provinces. He also had soldiers build a wall across Britain to hold back attackers from the non-Roman north.

Marcus Aurelius (MAHR kuhs uh REE le uhs), who read philosophy while on military campaigns, was close to being Plato's ideal of a philosopher king. His *Meditations* show his commitment to duty: "Hour by hour resolve firmly . . . to do what comes to hand with correct and natural dignity."

The Pax Romana The 200-year span that began with Augustus and ended with Marcus Aurelius is known as the period of the *Pax Romana*, or "Roman Peace." During that time, Roman rule brought peace, order, unity, and prosperity to lands stretching from the Euphrates River in the east to Britain in the west, an area roughly equal in size to the continental United States.

During the Pax Romana, Roman legions maintained and protected the roads, and Roman fleets chased pirates from the seas. Trade flowed freely to and from distant lands. Egyptian farmers supplied Romans with grain. From other parts of Africa came ivory and gold, as well as lions and other wild animals used for public entertainment. From India came spices, cotton, and precious stones. Trade caravans traveled along the great Silk Road, bringing silk and other goods from China. People, too, moved easily within the Roman empire, spreading ideas and knowledge, especially the advances of the Hellenistic east.

Bread and Circuses Throughout the empire, rich and poor alike loved spectacular forms of entertainment. At the Circus Maximus, Rome's largest racecourse, chariots thundered around an oval course, making dangerously tight turns at either end. Fans bet feverishly on their favorite teams—the Reds, Greens, Blues, or Whites—and successful charioteers were hailed as heroes.

Comparing Structures of Government

ROMAN REPUBLIC		ROMAN EMPIRE
HIGHEST OFFICIALS		**HIGHEST OFFICIALS**
Two Consuls • annually elected • held equal power	**Dictator** • appointed in times of emergency • held office for 6 months only	**Emperor** • inherited power • served for life • if served well, was worshipped as a god after death
GOVERNING BODIES		**GOVERNING BODIES**
Senate • issued advisory decrees to magistrates and people • in practice, held enormous power • had about 300 members	**Popular Assemblies** • two assemblies: centuriate (miltary), tribal (nonmilitary) • elected magistrates, held legislative power, made key decisions	**Senate** • issued binding decrees, acted as a high court, elected magistrates • in practice, held little power as compared to the emperor • had about 600 members

>> **Analyze Charts** There were significant differences between the governments of the Roman republic and the Roman empire. For a plebeian, which of the two structures of government would be preferable?

Answers

Analyze Charts *Students may argue that plebians fared better in the republic because they were able to elect their own officials and gradually force the government to represent them.*

THE ROMAN EMPIRE DECLINES

	CAUSE	EFFECT
POLITICAL TURBULENCE	Government oppression; corrupt officials	Government loses popular support
	Political violence leads to 26 emperors in 50 years	Empire becomes unstable
	Eastern Byzantine Empire becomes center of power	Roman Empire is divided into eastern and western halves
ECONOMIC TURBULENCE	Over-cultivated farmland; slave labor	Abandonment of land, reduced agricultural productivity; unemployment
	High taxes; epidemic diseases	Civil unrest; decline in population
SOCIAL TURBULENCE	Decline in patriotism, discipline and devotion to duty	Citizen-soldiers replaced with less loyal mercenaries; upper-class no longer provides leaders
	"Bread and circuses"	Self-reliance of masses is undermined
MILITARY ATTACKS	Invading Huns attack Germanic peoples on Rome's borders	Germanic peoples seek safety in Roman Empire
	Weakened Roman legions cannot stop invaders	Roman Empire surrenders territories to German invaders
	German invaders conquer Italy and attack Rome	German leader Odoacer ousts Roman emperor; Eastern Byzantine Empire lasts for another 1,000 years

>> **Analyze Information** There were many factors that led to the decline of the Roman empire. What were some of the effects of over-cultivated farmland and slave labor?

Gladiator contests were even more popular. Many gladiators were slaves who had been trained to fight. In the arena, they battled one another, either singly or in groups. Crowds cheered a skilled gladiator, and a good fighter might even win his freedom. But if a gladiator made a poor showing, sometimes the crowd turned thumbs down, a signal that he should be killed.

During the Pax Romana, the general prosperity hid underlying social and economic problems. To the emperors who paid for them with taxes they collected, these amusements were a way to distract the city's restless mobs. In much the same spirit, the government provided free grain to feed the poor. Critics warned against this policy of "bread and circuses," but few listened. Later Roman emperors, however, would face problems that could not be brushed away with "bread and circuses."

? EXPLAIN How did Augustus lay the foundation for stable government in the Roman empire?

The Roman Empire Splits

After ruling the Mediterranean for hundreds of years, the Roman empire faced threats from inside and outside. Political and economic problems, along with foreign invasions, shook the empire. In fact, these problems had existed since the late republic. Roman greatness did not end overnight. As decay set in, some emperors tried to halt the decline. But no ruler was able to reverse the long, slow collapse.

Political Violence Political turmoil rocked the Roman empire. The long Roman Peace ended when power struggles led to a new pattern in politics. Violence replaced the orderly succession to power. One after another, ambitious generals seized power with the support of their legions. The successful general ruled for a few months or years and then was overthrown or assassinated by a rival, who then made himself emperor. In one 50-year period, at least 26 emperors reigned. Political violence and instability had become the rule.

Economic and Social Issues At the same time, the empire was shaken by disturbing economic and social trends. High taxes to support the army and the bureaucracy placed heavy burdens on business people and small farmers. Some farmlands had been over-cultivated and lost their productivity.

As a result, many poor farmers left their land and sought protection from wealthy landowners. Living on large estates, they worked for the landowners and

Guided Reading and Discussion

Have students use cause-and-effect organizers to list the causes and effects of the Roman empire's economic decline. Causes may include government instability, over-cultivated farmland, and an influx of conquered people. Effects may include burdensome taxes, runaway inflation, worthless land, lack of goods for sale, lack of competition, and unemployment.

Identify Central Issues The Roman empire was imploding in decay, corruption, and violence when Diocletian became emperor. Ask students to identify what steps Diocletian took to combat the empire's decline and the reason for each. *(divided the empire in two for better management; appointed a co-emperor to split the responsibilities; fixed prices to slow inflation)*

Evaluate Impact Constantine I continued Diocletian's reforms and made some of his own. What were the effects of these reforms? *(These two reforms changed European history. When Constantine I granted freedom of worship to Roman citizens, Christianity grew, as people could openly practice and preach their religion. Constantine I established a new capital, Constantinople, shifting the empire's center of power to the east.)*

D Differentiate Extra Support As students discuss Diocletian, have them compare him to a modern day businessperson taking over a failing company. He had to assess the problems and come up with solutions. Write the following: *Problem: the company (empire) was too large to administer effectively with one owner (emperor).* Then ask students what they would write for Solution. *(Possible solution: Divide the company (empire) and share ownership (power) with Maximian.)*

Answers

Analyze Information *Sample answer: reduced employment opportunities, which led to rising unemployment*

Explain *He created an efficient, well-trained civil service to enforce the laws of the empire; allowed Roman cities and provinces to self-govern; created a fair tax system; set up a postal service; issued new coins to make trade easier; and put the poor to work building roads and temples and tending farms.*

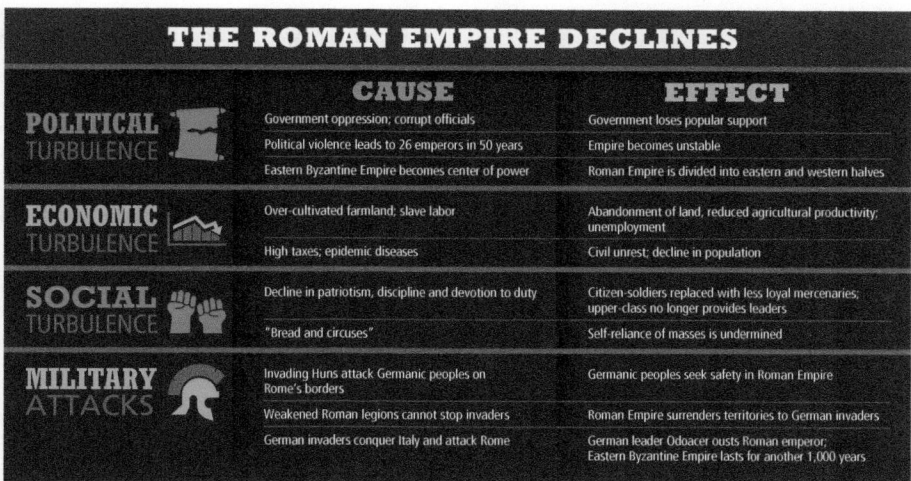

Topic 6 Lesson 2

Rome Faces Invasions

Why Did Rome Fall?

The fall of Rome was a major turning point in the history of Western civilization. The empire's long decline is attributed to multiple causes that generally fit into four categories: military assaults, political turbulence, economic issues, and social decay.

Online Project the map, **Interactive Map: Invasions of the Roman Empire, A.D. 378–533**. Point out that Rome had faced attacks for centuries, but as the empire declined, its legions struggled to stop the invaders. Explain to students that each layer of the map shows the battles of that invader. Step through the layers on the map and discuss the impact that the invasions had on the Roman empire.

ACTIVE CLASSROOM

Have students form an Opinion Line to answer the following question: Were invasions the major cause of the decline of Rome? Yes or no? *(Possible answers: Yes: the massive number of invasions drained resources from the empire to provide for its defense, disrupted trade, displaced people, and resulted in the loss of land. No: Rome had repelled attacks in the past, but the military began using mercenaries rather than citizen-soldiers. If the economy was strong and the government was unified and popular, Rome could have continued to successfully defend its borders.)*

farmed small plots for themselves. Although technically free, they were not allowed to leave the land.

The Empire Is Divided In 284, the emperor **Diocletian** (DY uh KLEE shuhn) set out to restore order. To better handle the challenge of governing the huge empire, he divided it into two parts. He kept control of the wealthier eastern part for himself and appointed a co-emperor, Maximian (mak SIH mee uhn), to rule the weaker western provinces.

Diocletian also took steps to end the empire's economic decay. To slow **inflation,** or the rapid rise of prices, he fixed the prices of many goods and services. Other laws forced farmers to remain on the land. In cities, sons were required to follow their fathers' occupations. These rules were meant to ensure steady production of food and other goods.

Constantinople Becomes the Center of Power In A.D 312, the talented general **Constantine** gained the throne. As emperor, Constantine continued Diocletian's reforms. More important, he took two steps that changed the course of European history. First, he granted toleration to Christians. Second, he set up a new capital at the centuries-old city of Byzantium, located near the Black Sea in what is now Turkey. He renamed it **Constantinople** (KAHNSTAN tuhn OH puhl). With this "New Rome," he made the already wealthier and more populated eastern half of the empire the center of power.

Reforms Fail The reforms of Diocletian and Constantine had mixed results. They revived the economy, and by increasing the power of government, they helped hold the empire together for another century. Still, the reforms failed to stop the long-term decline. In the end, internal problems, along with attacks from the outside, brought the empire down.

ANALYZE How did Rome's unstable government affect the economy?

Rome Faces Invasions

For centuries, Rome had faced attacks from the Germanic peoples who lived along its borders. When Rome was powerful, its legions on the frontiers held back the invaders. Some of the Germanic tribes along the borders of the empire had learned Roman ways and become allies.

Migrating Nomads Attack As early as A.D 200, wars in East Asia set off a chain of events that would eventually overwhelm Rome, thousands of miles to the

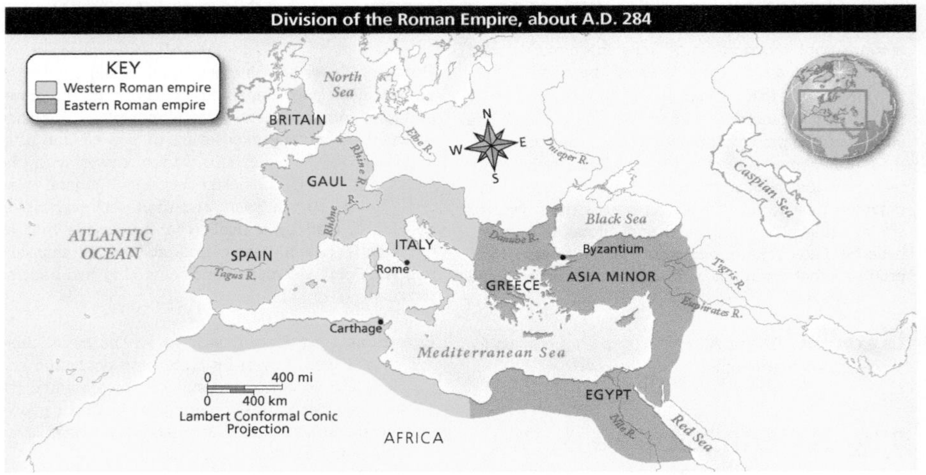

>> **Analyze Maps** Diocletian divided the empire into eastern and western halves to make governing more manageable. Why might the eastern Roman empire be considered more desirable?

Answers

Analyze *Instability made trade difficult or dangerous, led to burdensome taxes which were difficult to collect, and to runaway inflation. Unstable government also resulted in inconsistent economic policies.*

Analyze Maps *Sample answer: Constantinople linked the Black Sea and the Mediterranean Sea, and thus the riches of the east.*

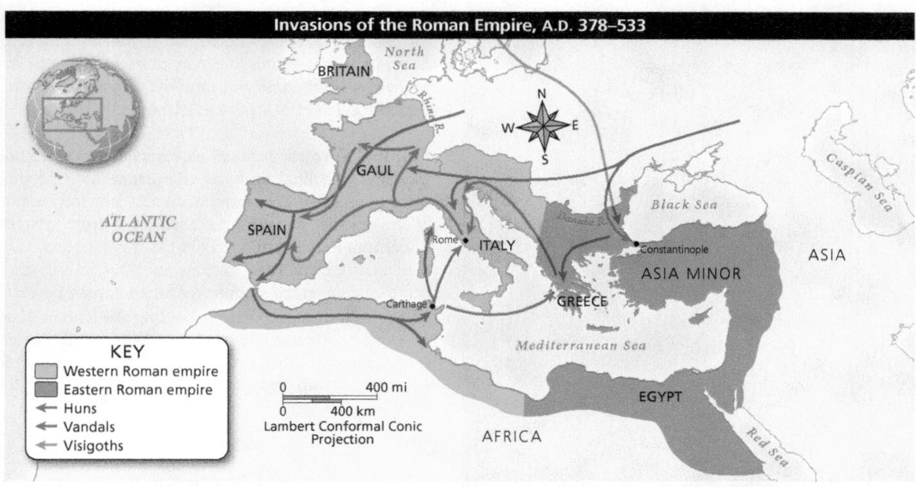

>> **Analyze Maps** The empire's weakened borders made it vulnerable to invasions by tribal groups from across Europe. What appears to be the common goal of all the tribes' invasions?

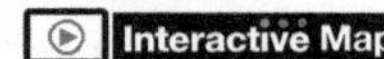

west. Those wars sent a nomadic people, the **Huns,** migrating from central Asia toward eastern Europe, which they reached by A.D 370. These skilled riders fought fierce battles to dislodge the Germanic peoples in their path. The Visigoths, Ostrogoths, and other Germanic peoples sought safety by crossing into Roman territory.

As the empire declined, Rome was hard pressed to halt the invaders. Slowly, Roman legions pulled back from the borderlands. Under pressure from attacks, Rome had to withdraw its legions, first from Britain, then from France and Spain. In time, invaders pushed into Italy and threatened Rome itself.

Rome Is Attacked In A.D 378, when a Roman army tried to turn back the Visigoths at Adrianople, it suffered a stunning defeat. Roman power was fading. New waves of invaders were soon hammering at Rome's borders, especially in the west. In A.D 410, the Visigoth general Alaric overran Italy and plundered Rome. Other invaders, the Vandals, took over Spain and North Africa before sacking Rome. Gradually, other Germanic peoples occupied large parts of the western Roman empire.

For Rome, the worst was yet to come. Starting in A.D 434, Hun leader Attila (uh TIHL luh) embarked on a savage campaign of conquest across much of Europe. Christians called Attila the "scourge of God" because they believed his attacks were a punishment for the sins of humankind. The Hun invasions sent still more Germanic peoples fleeing into the lands of the Roman empire.

Finally, in A.D 476, Odoacer (OH duh WAY suhr), a Germanic leader, ousted the emperor in Rome. Later, historians referred to that event as the "fall" of Rome. By then, however, the Roman empire had already lost many of its territories, and Roman power in the west had ended. By contrast, the Roman empire in the east would continue to flourish for centuries to come.

IDENTIFY MAIN IDEAS How did the Hun invasion weaken the Roman empire?

Why Did Rome Fall?

The "fall" of Rome is often seen as an important event in the history of Western civilization. Why did Rome "fall"? Modern historians identify a number of interrelated causes.

Military Causes Perhaps the most obvious cause of Rome's fall was the invasions. Still, these attacks were successful partly because Roman legions of the late empire lacked the discipline and training from

Guided Reading and Discussion

Have students list the causes of Rome's fall and categorize them as military, political, economic, or social causes.

Generate Explanations Review the text on the Roman defeat at Adrianople. What is the significance of Rome losing this battle? *(Adrianople was on the eastern edge of the Roman empire. By the time invaders had pierced this border, the northern borders of Britain, France, and Spain had already been overrun. The invaders had now claimed the territories that surrounded Italy on the northern side of the Mediterranean and were pressing in on Rome.)*

Express Ideas Clearly Military assaults are considered to be one of the most obvious causes of the fall of Rome. What happened to the Roman army that made it incapable of defending the empire? *(It lacked discipline, training, and the sheer number of soldiers that were representative of the earlier legions. To bolster the number of soldiers, Rome hired mercenaries who may not have been loyal to Rome.)*

Evaluate Impact Diocletian divided the empire to help restore order and better govern it. How did this decision contribute the decline of Rome? *(It weakened the empire, and the wealthier eastern half did little to help the western half.)*

Answers

Analyze Maps *Sample answer: All three tribes wanted to conquer Rome.*

Identify Main Ideas *The Huns ravaged large areas of the Roman empire and left Italy open to attack.*

Economic Causes

Paraphrase As the empire declined, there were increased numbers of political, economic, and social problems. How did they contribute to Rome's decline? *(The people lost faith in their leaders. Corruption was rampant, and the authoritative nature of the government was oppressive. As the reign changed from emperor to emperor, the stability of the empire eroded. A growing tax burden; reliance on slave labor; and the decline of values such as patriotism, discipline, and self-reliance also contributed to Rome's decline.)*

SYNTHESIZE

Online Project the **Synthesize Activity: When Did Rome Fall?** Ask students to count off as 1 or 2. Then pair students. Ask one person to review the Brown quote and the other the Gibbons quote. Then direct students to write down their answers to the following questions.

What about Rome's end most surprises Gibbons? How does Brown differ with Gibbons on this point? *(Gibbons is surprised that the empire lasted as long as it did, while Brown states that the empire actually endured longer than its supposed date of collapse.)*

In a partner-to-partner dialogue, students should try to persuade their partner that their opinion is correct. *(Possible arguments: Brown supporters: The Roman empire declined over a very long period of time. During the decline, people continued to live their daily life with little change. Gibbons supporters: On the surface the empire appeared affluent, but beneath it was in decay. What had brought the empire great wealth, its conquests, and vast territory, would inevitably lead to its collapse.)*

Discuss The partners should share and discuss their answers with the class.

>> Romans line up to pay their taxes. The government, desperate for funds to support its massive army, imposed oppressive taxes on Rome's citizens.

>> Wealthy Romans enjoyed lavish lifestyles but often neglected their civic duties. The gap between rich and poor weakened the empire.

which earlier Roman armies had benefited. To meet its need for soldiers, Rome hired **mercenaries,** or foreign soldiers serving for pay, to defend its borders. Many were Germanic warriors who, according to some historians, felt little loyalty to Rome.

Political Turmoil Political problems also contributed to Rome's decline. First, as the government became more oppressive and authoritarian, it lost the support of the people. Growing numbers of corrupt officials undermined loyalty, too. So did the frequent civil wars over succession. Rival armies battling to put their commanders on the throne weakened Roman power.

Perhaps most important, dividing the empire when it was under attack may have weakened it beyond repair. Faced with its own invasions, the richer and stronger eastern Roman empire did little to help the west.

Economic Causes

Rome faced widespread economic problems, including an ever greater tax burden on its people. To support the huge government bureaucracy and military that ruled the empire, Rome imposed heavy taxes. As the wealth of the empire declined, over-taxed farmers abandoned their land and the middle class sank into poverty. At the same time, reliance on slave labor discouraged Romans from exploring new technology. Rome, rich from its conquests, also lost a vital source of income as it lost territories. Finally, the population itself declined as war and epidemic diseases swept the empire.

Social Causes For centuries, worried Romans pointed to the decline in values such as patriotism, discipline, and devotion to duty on which the empire was built. The upper class, which had once provided leaders, devoted itself to luxury and prestige. Besides being costly, providing "bread and circuses" may have undermined the self-reliance of the masses.

Did Rome Fall? Although we talk of the "fall" of Rome, the Roman empire did not disappear from the map in A.D 476. An emperor still ruled the eastern Roman empire, which later became known as the Byzantine Empire and lasted for another 1,000 years.

The phrase "the fall of Rome" is, in fact, shorthand for a long, slow change from one way of life to another. In Italy, people continued to live much as they had before, though under new rulers. Many still spoke Latin and obeyed Roman laws.

Over the next centuries, however, Germanic customs and languages replaced much of Roman culture. Old Roman cities crumbled, and Roman roads disappeared. Still, the Christian Church, which had become the official religion of Rome, preserved many elements of Roman civilization. Far from disappearing with the "fall" of Rome, Roman civilization and Christian traditions eventually gave rise to medieval civilization in Western Europe.

 **SUMMARIZE** What social problems contributed to the decline of the Roman empire?

ASSESSMENT

1. **Identify Main Ideas** Why did Diocletian decide to split the empire?
2. **Identify Cause and Effect** What led to the Punic Wars, and how did they affect Rome?
3. **Draw Conclusions** What factors caused Rome to plunge into civil wars and how did they weaken the republic?
4. **Analyze Information** Why did a new class of wealthy Romans emerge after the conquests?
5. **Summarize** What reforms did Caesar make to address Rome's many problems?

Topic 6 Lesson 2

DEMONSTRATE

Online Assign the **Digital Lesson Quiz** for this lesson if you haven't already done so. Students will be offered automatic remediation or enrichment based on their score.

While the causes of the fall of the Roman empire are still debated, it is certain that classical Rome had a lasting political influence on Western civilization.

Summarize What Roman institutions or ideas are incorporated into American culture and government? *(Possible answers: Institutions of the senate, the postal service, census, taxes, public works projects to employ the jobless, expanding citizenship, Julian calendar, civil service based on merit, codified law, and religious tolerance)*

Topic Inquiry

Have students continue their investigations for the Topic Inquiry.

Answers

Summarize *A decline in values such as patriotism, discipline, and devotion to duty. Citizen soldiers were replaced with mercenaries who had little loyalty. Expensive entertainments, used to mask the social divide, depleted government funds at a rapid rate. Also, few members of the upper class were willing to assume leadership positions.*

Assessment

1. Since the Roman empire was so vast, it was easier to restore order and govern a smaller empire.
2. The two empires came into conflict as they sought to expand. Rome won Sicily, Corsica, and Sardinia in the first Punic War. Carthage launched the second war led by Hannibal, who attacked from the north and won many battles as he moved down the Italian peninsula. Hannibal returned to Carthage when it was attacked by the Roman army. In the last Punic War, Rome destroyed Carthage. As a result, Rome became the dominant power in the western Mediterranean.
3. Confusion about who should govern. The senate wanted to govern as it had in the past. Popular political leaders wanted to weaken the senate and enact reforms.
4. New conquests increased trade and control over trade routes. Trade, taxes, and commerce brought riches to generals, officials, and traders, creating a new class of wealthy Romans.
5. Caesar's reforms included reorganizing the governments of the provinces, granting Roman citizenship to more people, instilling a public works program to employ the jobless, and giving land to the poor.

Topic 6 Lesson 3

The Legacy of Rome

CONNECT

Preview Have students preview the **Lesson Objectives** and the list of **Key Terms**.

Students can also preview all the **Key Terms** and **Academic Vocabulary** using the **Interactive Reading Notepad** on the digital course or preview a summary of the lesson in the **Reading and Note Taking Study Guide**.

Online Use the **Editable Presentation** found on the digital course to present the main ideas for this lesson.

Start Up Activity

Explain to students that Cicero was a politician and philosopher who often criticized Julius Caesar. But when Caesar came to power, he forgave Cicero, saying it was "more glorious to have enlarged the limits of the Roman mind than the boundaries of Roman rule."

Discuss What does this story say about Caesar's view of culture? *(Sample response: Caesar forgave Cicero out of respect for his intellectual achievements. He placed a higher value on enlightening the mind than expanding a nation.)*

Tell students that in this lesson they will be learning the origin, diffusion, and lasting influence of the Roman empire.

Online You can also project the **Start Up Activity** from the course.

INVESTIGATE

Have students read the section using the **Reading and Note Taking Study Guide** to help them take notes and understand the text as they read.

Roman Literature, History, and Philosophy

Remind students that the Romans adapted Greek and Hellenistic ideas to create a Greco-Roman civilization. Tell students that many Roman poets, such as Virgil, and historians, such as Livy, used their writing to promote patriotism. Roman writers focused on the greatness of Rome. The Hellenistic philosophy of Stoicism, which showed concern for the well-being of all people and stressed the importance of duty and acceptance of one's fate, impressed Roman thinkers.

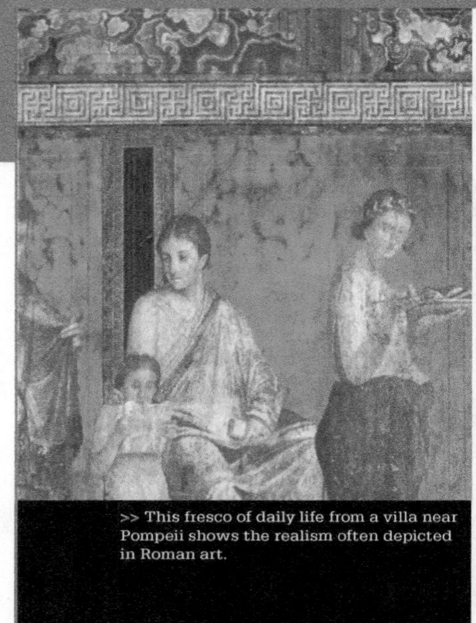

>> This fresco of daily life from a villa near Pompeii shows the realism often depicted in Roman art.

Interactive Flipped Video

6.3 Through war and conquest, Romans spread their Latin language and Roman civilization to distant lands. Yet the civilization that developed was not simply Roman. Rather, it blended Greek, Hellenistic, and Roman achievements.

TEKS
1.B, 3.A, 22.A, 22.B, 25.B, 26.B, 27.A

>> Objectives

Summarize the works of Roman literary figures, historians, and philosophers.

Describe the art and architecture developed by the Romans.

Understand how the Romans applied science and mathematics for practical use.

Explain how Rome's rule of law influenced modern legal systems.

Summarize the Roman ideas and institutions that have influenced Western civilization.

>> Key Terms

Virgil
satirize
mosaic
engineering
aqueduct
Ptolemy

The Legacy of Rome

Roman Literature, History, and Philosophy

Greco-Roman Civilization In its early days, Rome absorbed ideas from Greek colonists in southern Italy, and it continued to borrow heavily from Greek culture after it conquered Greece. To the Romans, Greek art, literature, philosophy, mathematical, and scientific genius represented the height of cultural achievement. Their admiration never wavered, leading the Roman poet Horace to note, "Greece has conquered her rude conqueror."

Over time, Romans adapted Greek and Hellenistic achievements, just as the Greeks had once absorbed ideas from Egypt and the Fertile Crescent. The blending of Greek, Hellenistic, and Roman traditions produced what is known as Greco-Roman civilization. During the Pax Romana, trade and travel helped spread this vital new civilization.

Roman Writers In literature, the Romans greatly admired, and owed a debt to the Greeks. Many Romans spoke Greek and imitated Greek styles in prose and poetry. Still, the greatest Roman writers used Latin to create their own literature.

In his epic poem the *Aeneid*, **Virgil** tried to show that Rome's past was as heroic as that of Greece. He linked his epic to Homer's work by

PEARSON realize. www.PearsonTexas.com Access your Digital Lesson.

190

Aa Vocabulary Builder

1. Have students pronounce the following academic vocabulary terms in this lesson and clarify the part of speech. For difficult or polysyllabic words, break them into syllables and pronounce them with the students.
2. Explain what the word means in common "student-friendly" language using synonyms and antonyms when possible. Provide concrete examples to clarify the meaning, and rephrase the definition.

utilize: to make use of something

idealistic: aiming for perfection

legacy: something handed down by a predecessor

Topic 6 Lesson 3

telling how Aeneas escaped from Troy to found Rome. Virgil wrote the *Aeneid* soon after Augustus came to power. He hoped it would arouse patriotism and help unite Rome after years of civil wars.

Other poets used verse to **satirize,** or make fun of, Roman society. Horace's satires were gentle, using playful wit to attack human folly. Those of Juvenal and Martial were more biting. Martial's poems, for example, were so harsh that he had to use fictitious names to protect himself from retribution.

Roman Historians Roman historians pursued their own theme—the rise and fall of Roman power. Like the poet Virgil, the historian Livy sought to arouse patriotic feeling and restore traditional Roman virtues by recalling images of Rome's heroic past. In his history of Rome, Livy recounted tales of great heroes, such as Horatius and Cincinnatus. In this passage, Livy comments on the importance of studying history:

> . . . in history you have a record of the infinite variety of human experience plainly set out for all to see; and in that record you can find for yourself and your country both examples and warnings: fine things to take as models, base things, rotten through and through, to avoid.
>
> —Livy, *The History of Rome*

Another historian, Tacitus, wrote bitterly about Augustus and his successors, who, he felt, had destroyed Roman liberty. He admired the simple culture of the Germans who lived on Rome's northern frontier and would later invade the empire.

Roman Philosophers Romans borrowed much of their philosophy from the Greeks. The Hellenistic philosophy of Stoicism impressed Roman thinkers such as the emperor Marcus Aurelius. Stoics stressed the importance of duty and acceptance of one's fate. They also showed concern for the well-being of all people, an idea that would later be reflected in Christian teachings.

IDENTIFY MAIN IDEAS How did Roman writers promote patriotism?

ELPS **ELPS 2.D.1** Listen as your teacher or partner reads *Roman Literature, History, and Philosophy* aloud. Then discuss the influence the Greeks had on Roman culture.

>> The fight between Aeneas and King Turnus, from Virgil's epic poem, the *Aeneid*.

>> Livy's writings featured Roman heroes such as Horatius. Horatius defended Rome's Sublician bridge against the entire Etruscan army.

Key Terms

Ask students to find the key term **satirize** (in bold) in the text. Explain that to satirize is to use satire, which is a form of humor. Satire pokes fun at others, especially those in politics or others in the public eye. Comedians and writers use satire to make a point about the weaknesses of the subject or subjects.

Guided Reading and Discussion

Review the Roman achievements and the themes of Roman literature. Help students analyze how Roman literature reflected their admiration of the Greeks.

Be sure that students understand that Romans imitated Greek prose and borrowed Greek ideas. However, the greatest Roman literature was written in Latin. The use of satire was also popular with Roman poets.

Analyze Information Ask students how literature reflects the history of the culture in which it is produced. *(Writers often incorporate the values, opinions, and characteristics of the culture they are most closely associated with.)* Have students provide examples of modern literature, cinema, or television series that reflect characteristics of our culture.

English Language Proficiency Standards

Listening 2.D.1 Read aloud or have students read "Roman Literature, History, and Philosophy." Encourage students to focus on how Greek culture influenced that of Rome. Then monitor students' understanding of the vocabulary and content as they discuss the two cultures.

Beginning Read aloud. Pause after each sentence to clarify any questions about unfamiliar vocabulary, using drawings or gestures when necessary. Tell students to think about how the Romans learned from Greek culture. Then monitor their understanding by having them answer using a sentence frame such as: The Romans copied Greek ________.

Intermediate Read aloud. Monitor student understanding by asking questions about key words and important points from the reading. For example, "What did the Romans admire about ancient Greek civilization?" Instruct students to use complete sentences when answering.

Answers

Identify Main Ideas *In his epic, the Aeneid, the poet Virgil portrays Rome's past as heroic and links his country's history to Homer's Greek epics. Livy's history of Rome recalls images of Rome's heroic past and tells tales of great Roman heroes.*

Roman Art, Architecture, and Drama

Roman art, architecture, and drama all had Greek influences. Roman art and drama depicted idealism, daily life, and humor. Art and architecture reflected the history of Rome and its values. While the Greeks had a simple, elegant style of architecture, Roman architecture often reflected the majesty and grandeur of the Roman empire. The Colosseum and the Pantheon are examples of imposing Roman architecture.

Online Project the **Interactive Flipbook: The Pantheon** and click through the hotspots.

Guided Reading and Discussion

Ask students to analyze how art, drama, and architecture reflect Roman history. *(Art included both idealism and realism. Some plays were based on legends about the glory of Rome. Others were about the daily life of Romans. Roman architecture exemplified the power of the empire with immense structures.)*

Roman Achievements in Science and Engineering

Remind students that many Roman ideas in science and mathematics originated from Greek ones. Roman engineers put Greek principles in mathematics and science to practical use in their technology. Romans are noted for their engineering projects. They built roads, bridges, harbors, and aqueducts that lasted for generations. Romans also compiled scientific encyclopedias. Tell students that this transfer of information from one culture to another is called cultural diffusion.

Roman Art, Architecture, and Drama

Rome left a vast legacy of art and architecture across its empire. To a large degree, Roman art and architecture were based on Greek and Etruscan models. However, as with their literature, Romans adapted these influences to develop their own style.

Roman Art Expresses Realism The Romans imported Greek statues to decorate their homes, gardens, and public monuments. Roman sculptors adapted the realistic style of Hellenistic works, showing subjects with warts or veins in place. The Romans also broke new ground, creating portraits in stone or on coins that revealed a person's character. A statue might capture an expression of smugness or haughty pride.

Some Roman sculpture was more idealistic, in the tradition of the classic Greek statues of gods and athletes. Sculptors transformed Augustus, who was neither handsome nor imposing, into a symbol of power and leadership.

Wealthy Romans displayed fine works of art, such as colorful frescoes, or murals, in their homes. They also hired artists to depict scenes from daily life or Roman myths in **mosaics,** or pictures made from chips of colored stone. Examples of Roman murals, mosaics, and other decorative items were preserved in Pompeii, a city buried by volcanic ash after Mount Vesuvius erupted in A.D. 79.

>> Attending the theater was a popular pastime in Rome. Here, actors don costumes and masks before a performance.

Roman Theater The Romans loved to attend theater. Some playwrights, like the Roman philosopher and dramatist Seneca, based their plays, such as *Hercules Furens*, on myths and legends. Roman audiences enjoyed comedies, including those by Plautus. His comedies were based on Roman life and featured songs and dances, along with slapstick and mistaken identity.

Roman Architecture From England to Spain, to North Africa and the Middle East, Roman buildings still stand today. Roman architecture combined both Greek and Roman elements. Roman builders used Greek columns, but where the Greeks aimed for simple elegance, the Romans emphasized grandeur. Immense palaces, temples, stadiums, and victory arches stood as monuments to Roman power.

The Romans improved on building devices such as columns and arches. They invented concrete, which was used as a building material, and developed the rounded dome to roof large spaces. The most famous domed structure is the Pantheon, a temple that honored all the Roman gods. It still stands in Rome today.

Another famous Roman building, the Colosseum, was a public arena that stood 12 to 15 stories high (159 feet) and could hold as many as 50,000 spectators. A system of tunnels and stairs allowed crowds to exit the building quickly. Many of today's sports stadiums have similar features.

Roman advances in architecture, such as the use of concrete, arches, and domes, were passed to other cultures. First in Europe and later in North America, builders looked to Roman models. In Washington, D.C., public buildings such as the Jefferson Memorial and the Capitol use elements of Roman architecture.

CONTRAST How did Roman architecture differ from Greek architecture?

Roman Achievements in Science and Engineering

The Romans generally left scientific research to the Greeks, who were citizens of the Roman empire. While Greek scientists and mathematicians sought to learn more about the world, the Romans put science to practical uses. They used Greek principles to construct roads and bridges and to make advances in medical care.

English Language Proficiency Standards

Advanced Have small groups read aloud. Then have them discuss the quotation, "Greece has conquered her rude conqueror" and debate whether or not they agree with this statement. To monitor student understanding, circulate to correct mistakes and ask questions.

Advanced High Have students read. Then have partners discuss the quotation, "Greece has conquered her rude conqueror" and debate whether or not they agree with this statement. To monitor student understanding, have partners summarize the results of their discussion.

Answers

Contrast *The Greeks aimed for simple elegance in architecture. The Romans aimed for grandeur, building huge palaces, temples, and stadiums as monuments to Roman power.*

Science and Engineering The Romans excelled in **engineering,** or the application of science and mathematics to develop structures and machines. They perfected engineering skills as they built roads, bridges, and harbors across the empire. Roman roads were so solidly built that many remained in use long after Rome fell.

Roman engineers built immense **aqueducts,** or bridge-like stone structures that carried water from the hills into Roman cities. The availability of fresh water was important to the Romans. Wealthy homes piped in water. Almost every city had public baths for men and women. Here, people gathered not only to bathe, but to hear the latest news and exchange gossip.

New Ideas in Science In Roman times, Alexandria, Egypt, remained a center of learning, where Hellenistic scientists exchanged ideas freely. It was there that astronomer-mathematician **Ptolemy** proposed his theory that the Earth was the center of the universe, a mistaken idea that was accepted in the Western world for nearly 1,500 years.

The Greek doctor Galen advanced the frontiers of medical science by insisting on experiments to prove a conclusion. Galen compiled a medical encyclopedia summarizing what was known in the field at the time. It remained a standard text for more than 1,000 years.

While the Romans rarely did original scientific investigations, they did put science to practical use. They applied geography to make maps and medical knowledge to help doctors improve public health. Like Galen, they collected knowledge into encyclopedias.

Pliny the Elder, a Roman scientist, compiled volumes on geography, zoology, botany, and other topics, all based on other people's works. In his 37-volume *Natural History*, he explained that his goal was to "set forth in detail all the contents of the entire world." Even into the Middle Ages, copies of his work could be found in the larger libraries of Europe.

In A.D. 79, Pliny's eagerness for knowledge led to his death. He ventured too close to Mount Vesuvius as the volcano near Pompeii was erupting. He was smothered to death in hot ashes.

IDENTIFY MAIN IDEAS How did Romans put science to practical use?

Roman Law Unites the Empire

"Let justice be done," proclaimed a Roman saying, "though the heavens fall!" Probably the greatest legacy of Rome was its commitment to the rule of law and to

>> The Pont du Gard in France was a Roman aqueduct built in 19 B.C. The three tiers of arches rise about 155 feet (47 m).

Interactive 3-D Model

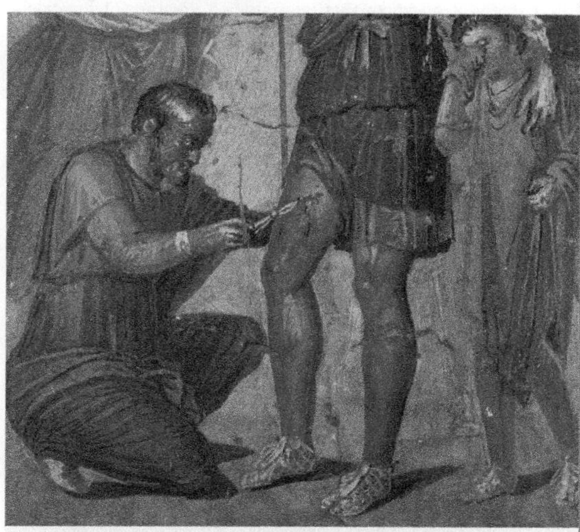

>> Romans valued medical knowledge. The army had medical officers, physicians provided healthcare for the poor, and hospitals were built.

Interactive Gallery

Online Project the **Interactive Gallery: Science and Technology in Ancient Rome** and click through the images.

ACTIVE CLASSROOM

Use the Cartoon It activity to have students do a quick copy of a compelling example of science or technology in ancient Rome. Then have them turn it into a cartoon that illustrates the use, importance, or significance of the item.

Guided Reading and Discussion

Ask students to summarize some of the scientific accomplishments of Greek citizens of the Roman empire.

Draw Conclusions What evidence supports the idea that Romans perfected their engineering skills? *(Roman roads, buildings, bridges can still be found intact today.)*

Roman Law Unites the Empire

Online Project the **Interactive Chart: The Influence of Roman Law** and click through the topics.

List the following on the board: rule of law, use of solid evidence, laws apply to citizens and non-citizens, the right to face the accuser, the right to offer a defense, and innocent until proven guilty. Ask students to rank the ideas according to what they think had the greatest influence on future civilizations.

Guided Reading and Discussion

Ask students to summarize the development of rule of law in ancient Rome. (*Rome developed civil law that only applied to its citizens. As more people became part of the empire, the law of nations emerged. It applied to all, citizens and non-citizens. In time, the two systems merged.*)

History Background

The Colosseum Nowhere is the Roman love of grandeur more apparent than in the giant amphitheater known as the Colosseum. The Colosseum was a stone-and-concrete building 12 to 15 stories high. It could hold as many as 50,000 spectators. Large crowds came to watch combat between gladiators, fights between men and animals, and fabulous spectacles that included mock naval engagements. For the naval battles, workers removed the heavy wooden floor and made artificial lakes by flooding the lowest level. A system of tunnels and staircases allowed large crowds to exit the building in minutes.

Answers

Identify Main Ideas *They applied geography to make maps and medical knowledge to improve public health. They also compiled Greek scientific research into encyclopedias.*

Topic 6 Lesson 3

SYNTHESIZE

Online Project the **Digital Activity: Architecture in Ancient Rome**. Ask students to identify the image and take a few minutes to write down some of the ideas they think of when they see the image, keeping in mind the history of the Romans. Then have students share their responses with a partner.

Discuss Ask students to think about the Connect activity at the beginning of this lesson. Ask if they can think of specific examples of how Romans valued cultural achievements.

DEMONSTRATE

Online Assign the **Digital Lesson Quiz** for this lesson if you haven't already done so. Students will be offered automatic remediation or enrichment based on their score.

Pose these questions to the class on the Discussion Board:

In "The Legacy of Rome," you read about Roman culture and its influences on other cultures. Roman art, architecture, and basic principles continue to influence the modern world.

Draw Inferences With its Greco-Roman civilization, Rome demonstrated it could integrate other cultures. What were some other ways Rome demonstrated its adaptability?

Predict Consequences How do you think Roman civilization will affect the rest of Europe?

Topic Inquiry

Have students continue their investigations for the Topic Inquiry.

Answers

Summarize *The accused is presumed innocent until proven guilty; the accused is allowed to face the accuser and offer a defense; guilt has to be established using solid evidence*

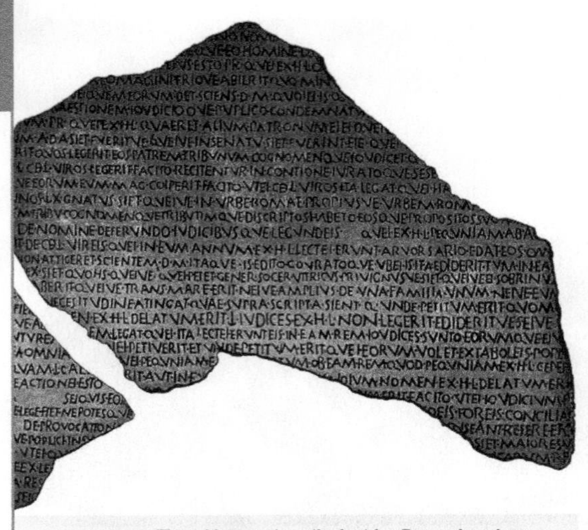

>> The tablets are inscribed with a Roman law that protects citizens from extortion.

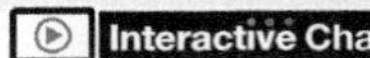

Interactive Chart

justice—ideas that later shaped Western civilization. Many centuries later, key principles of Roman law became the basis for legal systems throughout the world, including that of the United States.

Rome's System of Law Emerges During the republic, Rome developed a system of law, known as the civil law, that applied to its citizens. As Rome expanded, however, it ruled many foreigners who were not covered under the civil law. Gradually, a second system of law, known as the law of nations, emerged. It applied to all people under Roman rule, both citizens and non-citizens. Later, when Rome extended citizenship across the empire, the two systems merged.

Principles of Roman Law As Roman law developed, certain basic principles evolved. Many of these principles are familiar to Americans today. Among the most important was that an accused person is presumed innocent until proven guilty. A second principle ensured that the accused was allowed to face the accuser and mount a defense against the charge. A third idea was that guilt must be established "clearer than daylight," using solid evidence. Still another idea was that judges interpret the laws and make fair decisions.

Many other principles of Roman law were later adapted by the Western world. The idea of a trial by jury is sometimes traced to Roman law practices. Cases where the accused faced the death penalty might be tried in front of hundreds of people from the community.

Some Roman principles differed from today's laws. Penalties varied according to social class, and lower-class defendants could be treated more harshly. The idea of equality before the law for all would take centuries to be accepted.

SUMMARIZE What basic principles of Roman law were a foundation for laws in the United States?

ASSESSMENT

1. **Identify Central Ideas** Identify examples of how literature reflects the history of Rome.
2. **Support Ideas with Examples** Describe the architectural elements developed or adapted by the Romans. Provide examples of its influence on Western architecture.
3. **Identify** What was the origin and diffusion of major ideas in mathematics, science, and technology that occurred in classical Rome?
4. **Summarize** Explain the concept of "trial by jury" that is sometimes traced back to Rome.
5. **Analyze Information** Give two examples of American legal principles that had their foundation in Roman law.

Assessment

1. The rise and fall of Roman power was a theme frequently used by writers such as Virgil and Livy, who wanted to arouse patriotism and unite Rome. They told stories of Roman heroes, Rome's past, and how some Roman emperors had destroyed liberty.
2. They adapted and used the dome, arch, and concrete in their architecture—elements which later spread to other civilizations. Buildings today such as sports stadiums, the United States Capitol, and the Jefferson Memorial were influenced by Roman architecture.
3. Many Roman ideas in these areas originated from Greek ones. In their technology, Roman engineers put Greek principles in mathematics and science to practical use. They built roads, bridges, harbors, and aqueducts throughout the empire. Romans also compiled scientific encyclopedias that could be found centuries later in European libraries.
4. It is based on the idea that some Roman death penalty cases were tried and judged in front of hundreds in the community.
5. Student answers should include two of the following: a person is presumed innocent until proven guilty; the accused can offer a defense in court against the accuser; guilt must be established through evidence; judges are expected to make fair decisions.

6.4 Early in the Pax Romana, a new religion, Christianity, arose in a distant corner of the Roman empire. At first, Christianity was one of many religions practiced in the empire. But the new faith grew rapidly, and by A.D. 395 it had been declared the official religion of the Roman empire.

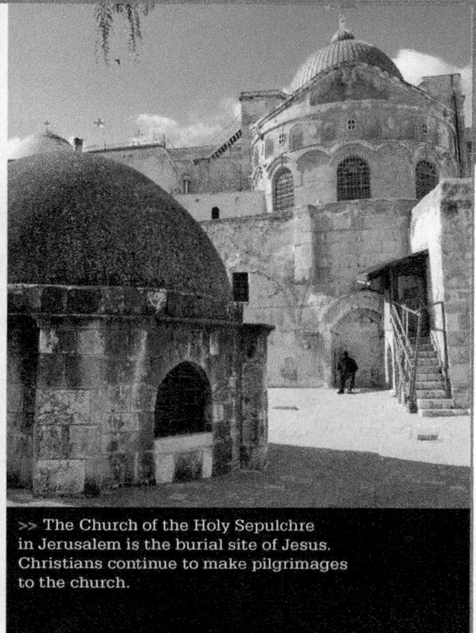

>> The Church of the Holy Sepulchre in Jerusalem is the burial site of Jesus. Christians continue to make pilgrimages to the church.

Interactive Flipped Video

The Origins of Christianity

TEKS
1.B, 3.A, 20.A, 23.A

>> Objectives

Understand the diverse religions included in the early Roman empire.

Describe the development and central ideas of Christianity.

Summarize the spread of Christianity.

Outline the development of the early Christian Church.

>> Key Terms

messiah
apostle
Paul
martyr
clergy
bishop
patriarch
pope
heresy
Augustine
Christian Bible
Constantine

Romans Accept Many Religions

As it gained strength and spread through the empire, Christianity reshaped Roman beliefs. When the Roman empire fell, the Christian Church took over much of its role, becoming the central institution of Western civilization for nearly 1,000 years.

Rome Tolerates Diversity Within the vast Roman empire, numerous religious beliefs thrived. Generally, Rome tolerated these varied religious traditions. As long as citizens showed loyalty by honoring Roman gods such as Jupiter and Mars and by accepting the divinity of the emperor, they were allowed to worship as they pleased. Since most people were polytheistic, they were content to worship the Roman gods alongside their own.

As Rome expanded, people came into contact with different religious traditions, including those in Egypt and the Fertile Crescent. Especially during turbulent times, a growing number of people turned to the so-called mystery religions, which emphasized secret rituals and promised special rewards to believers. Among the most popular of these was the cult of Isis, which originated in Egypt and offered women equal status with men. Roman soldiers favored the cult of the

PEARSON realize. www.PearsonTexas.com Access your Digital Lesson.

Topic 6 Lesson 4

The Origins of Christianity

CONNECT

Preview Have students preview the **Lesson Objectives** and the list of **Key Terms**.

Students can also preview all the **Key Terms** and **Academic Vocabulary** using the **Interactive Reading Notepad** on the digital course or preview a summary of the lesson in the **Reading and Note Taking Study Guide**.

Online Use the **Editable Presentation** found on the digital course to present the main ideas for this lesson.

Start Up Activity

Explain to students that it was almost 300 years before a Roman emperor fully supported Christianity. A legend stated that the emperor Constantine—just before a battle—saw a cross in the sky along with the words, "By this you shall conquer." He had his troops mark their shields with the Christian symbol. After winning the battle, he fully embraced Christianity.

Discuss Why is this legend important? *(It exemplifies the growing importance of Christianity and monotheism in ancient Rome.)*

Tell students that in this lesson they will learn about the development and the central ideas of Christianity. They will also read how Christianity spread throughout the Roman empire.

Online You can also project the **Start Up Activity** from the course.

INVESTIGATE

Have students read the section using the **Reading and Note Taking Study Guide** to help them take notes and understand the text as they read.

Romans Accept Many Religions

Remind students that the Romans were usually tolerant of other religious beliefs. Tell them this tolerance of local beliefs helped Rome govern its diverse territories. Point out that freedom of religion was not, however, a basic right for citizens like it is in the United States today.

Aa Vocabulary Builder

1. Have students pronounce the following academic vocabulary term in this lesson and clarify the part of speech. Break the word into syllables and pronounce it with the students.
2. Explain what the word means in common "student-friendly" language using synonyms and antonyms when possible. Provide concrete examples to clarify the meaning, and rephrase the definition.

comply: to obey or conform to something

Topic 6 Lesson 4

Guided Reading and Discussion

Display a cause-and-effect graphic organizer and work as a class to explain the causes and effects of the Jewish revolt against Rome. Causes may include the fact that Jewish zealots rebelled against Roman rule. Effects may include the fact that Romans crushed the rebels, captured Jerusalem, and destroyed the Jewish temple.

Identify Cause and Effect Review the section under the heading "Divisions in Judea." Why were some Jews concerned that their religion was weakening? *(Many Jews absorbed Greek customs and ideas.)*

Analyze Information Why did the role of rabbis become more important after many Jews left Judea? *(Rabbis extended and preserved Jewish law since many Jews were scattered in communities around the Mediterranean.)*

The Teachings of Jesus

Christianity emerged as a religion in the Roman territory of Judea. It started as people followed the teachings of a Jew named Jesus. His teachings reflected Jewish law and traditions. Jesus believed in one God and accepted the Ten Commandments and the teachings of the Jewish prophets. Echoing the teachings of Judaism, Jesus emphasized God's love and taught the need for justice, morality, and service to others. Jesus also preached new beliefs. According to his followers, he called himself the Son of God. Jesus said his mission was to bring spiritual salvation and eternal life to anyone who believed in him. Note that shared Judeo-Christian beliefs about the just treatment of individuals and equality before the law would later influence Western legal systems as well as the governments of many Western democracies.

Persian god Mithras, who championed good over evil and offered life after death.

Divisions in Judea Among the many peoples within the Roman empire were the Jews. By 63 B.C., the Romans had conquered Judea. The Romans tolerated the religion of the Jews and even excused Jews, who were monotheistic, from worshiping Roman gods.

Among the Jews themselves, however, religious ferment was creating deep divisions. During the Hellenistic age, many Jews absorbed Greek customs and ideas. Concerned about the weakening of their religion, Jewish conservatives rejected these influences and called for strict obedience to Jewish laws and traditions.

The turmoil also had a political side. While most Jews were reluctantly willing to live under Roman rule, others, called zealots, were not. They called on Jews to revolt against Rome and reestablish an independent state. Some Jews believed that a **messiah,** or anointed king sent by God, would lead the Jewish people to freedom.

Rome Crushes the Jewish Revolt In A.D. 66, discontent flared into rebellion. Four years later, Roman forces crushed the rebels, captured Jerusalem, and destroyed the Jewish Temple. When revolts broke out again in the next century, Roman armies leveled Jerusalem. Thousands of Jews were killed in the fighting, and many others were enslaved and transported to various parts of the empire.

>> The Roman destruction of Jerusalem's temple in A.D.70 was one of the devastating consequences of the Jewish rebellion.

Faced with a devastated land and defeated in their efforts to regain political independence, many other Jews decided to leave Judea. They joined Jewish communities around the Mediterranean, or in other parts of the Roman empire. Some Jews remained in the northern part of Judea, near the Galilee.

Over the centuries, Jewish religious teachers called rabbis extended and preserved the Jewish law and began to record their discussions in the Talmud. They developed the form of Judaism still practiced today, focusing on the study of the Torah, prayer, and acts of kindness. Despite the loss of the Temple in Jerusalem, Judaism survived.

CHECK UNDERSTANDING What were citizens expected to do in exchange for toleration of their religious beliefs and practices?

The Teachings of Jesus

As turmoil engulfed the Jews in Judea, a new religion, Christianity, arose among them. It began among the followers of a Jew named Jesus. Almost all the information we have about the life of Jesus comes from the Gospels, the first four books of the New Testament of the **Christian Bible.** Early Christians attributed the writing of these accounts to four followers of Jesus—Matthew, Mark, Luke, and John.

Early Life and Teachings Jesus was born about 4 B.C. in Bethlehem, near Jerusalem. According to the Gospels, he was a descendant of King David of Israel. The Gospels say an angel visited a young woman named Mary—referred to by many Christians as the Virgin Mary—and told her that she would give birth to the messiah. "He will be great," said the angel, "and will be called the Son of the Most High God."

Many Christians believe that God is the father of Jesus and that Jesus was the incarnation, or human form, of God. The doctrine of the Trinity reflects the Christian belief that there is one God made up of three beings: the Father, the Son, and the Holy Spirit.

Growing up in the small town of Nazareth, Jesus worshiped God and followed Jewish law. As a young man, he may have worked as a carpenter. At the age of 30, the Gospels relate, he began preaching to villagers near the Sea of Galilee. Large crowds gathered to hear his teachings, especially when word spread that he had performed miracles of healing. Jesus often used

D Differentiate Challenge/Gifted After students finish reading and have completed the activity, have them write and perform a speech. The topic of the speech can be the development of Christianity, the development of monotheism, the central ideas in Christianity, or the historical origins of Christianity.

Answers

Check Understanding *Show loyalty to Rome by honoring Roman gods and acknowledging the divine spirit of the emperor.*

English Language Proficiency Standards

Listening 2.D.2 Read "The Teachings of Jesus" aloud. As you read, allow students to ask for clarification of vocabulary or content they do not understand.

Beginning Read "The Teachings of Jesus" aloud. Allow students to interrupt you with requests for clarification using the following: Could you explain what ____ means? Answer each question using accessible language. Encourage students to seek clarification using this method as needed during class time.

Intermediate Read "The Teachings of Jesus" aloud. As they listen, allow students to interrupt you with requests for clarification using the following: I don't understand what you mean when you say __________. Does it mean ____? Answer each question. Encourage students to seek clarification using this method as needed during class time.

Advanced Read "The Teachings of Jesus" aloud. As they listen, allow students to interrupt you with requests for clarification by explaining what parables, or short stories with simple moral lessons, to communicate his ideas.

According to the Gospels, Jesus recruited 12 disciples, or close followers, to help him in his mission. They were called **apostles,** a name that in Greek means "a person sent forth." After three years, Jesus and his disciples went to Jerusalem to spread his message there.

The Message of Jesus Jesus' teachings were firmly rooted in Jewish tradition. Jesus believed in one God and accepted the Ten Commandments. He preached obedience to the laws of Moses and defended the teachings of the Jewish prophets. However, Jesus also preached new beliefs. According to his followers, he called himself the Son of God. Many people believed Jesus was the long-anticipated messiah. Jesus proclaimed that his mission was to bring spiritual salvation and eternal life to anyone who believed in him.

In the Sermon on the Mount, Jesus summarized his ethical message, which echoed Jewish ideas of mercy and sympathy for the poor and helpless:

> "Blessed are the meek, for they shall inherit the earth.
>
> Blessed are those who hunger and thirst for righteousness, for they shall be satisfied.
>
> Blessed are the merciful, for they shall obtain mercy.
>
> Blessed are the pure of heart, for they shall see God.
>
> Blessed are the peacemakers, for they will be called sons of God."
>
> —Matthew 5:5-9

Jesus emphasized God's love and taught the need for justice, morality, and service to others. According to Jesus, a person's major duties were to observe the Jewish command to "love the Lord your God with all your heart" and to "love your neighbor as yourself." Jesus also emphasized the importance of forgiveness. Shared Judeo-Christian beliefs about the just treatment of individuals and equality before the law would later influence Western legal systems as well as the governments of many Western democracies.

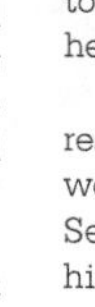

>> The apostles accompanied Jesus and later spread his teachings.

Interactive Gallery

Condemned and Crucified According to the Gospels, Jesus traveled to Jerusalem near the time of the Jewish festival of Passover, a celebration of the exodus from Egypt. To the Roman authorities, Jesus was a threat because his speeches could inflame those eager to end Roman rule.

The Gospels state that Jesus was betrayed by one of his disciples. He was arrested by the Romans, tried, and condemned to death by crucifixion. In this method of execution, which the Romans often used, a person was nailed or bound to a cross and left to die. Jesus' crucifixion threw his disciples into confusion.

But then rumors spread through Jerusalem that Jesus was not dead at all. The Gospels report that his disciples saw and talked with Jesus, who was resurrected, or raised from the dead. The Gospels go on to say that Jesus, after commanding his disciples to spread his teachings to all people, ascended into heaven.

According to the Gospels, before his crucifixion and resurrection, Jesus prophesied, or predicted, that he would return. In this return to Earth, now known as the Second Coming, Jesus said he would bring salvation to his followers and that they would always be with him.

SUMMARIZE Summarize the main ideas of Jesus' teachings.

Topic 6 Lesson 4

Online Project the **Interactive Gallery: Christian Symbols** and click through the images.

Analyze Images What does the image of the dove shown in the gallery represent in Christianity? *(The dove symbolizes the Holy Spirit. Doves are also associated with the birth and baptism of Jesus.)*

ACTIVE CLASSROOM

Have students complete a Walking Tour activity. Post images from the Interactive Gallery or passages from the text around the room. Have groups tour the room and discuss each image or passage. Have students describe the central idea of Christianity exhibited at each stop.

Guided Reading and Discussion

Ask students to summarize the central ideas of Christianity. Students should mention the following ideas: the belief in one god and the Ten Commandments; Jesus as the son of God who will bring spiritual salvation and eternal life to his followers; and a belief that mercy, sympathy, and forgiveness are all important traits.

Draw Conclusions What is significant about the fact that Jesus emphasized mercy, sympathy, and forgiveness? Consider what you have read about the Roman empire. Why might the emphasis on these qualities appeal to many of his followers? *(These traits were not always supported by religions and governments. The emphasis on these traits may have drawn people who felt that they were treated harshly or unfairly.)*

they understood and asking for confirmation or correction. Encourage students to seek clarification using this method as needed during class time.

Advanced High Read "The Teachings of Jesus" aloud. As they listen, allow students to interrupt you with requests for clarification by restating what they understood. Encourage students to seek clarification using this method as needed during class time.

Answers

Summarize *Jesus proclaimed that his mission was to bring spiritual salvation and eternal life to those who believed in him. He emphasized God's love and taught the need for justice, morality, and service to others. Jesus also stressed the importance of forgiveness.*

Topic 6 Lesson 4

Christianity Spreads

Remind students that Christianity spread as missionaries traveled the Roman empire. At first, the apostles preached only among the Jews. Paul decided to spread Jesus' teachings to non-Jews, marking the beginning of Christianity as a world religion. Despite persecution, the religion drew followers with its message of love, teachings of equality, dignity, and the promise of a better life after death. Some missionaries used Greek philosophy to explain Jesus' message. Romans who had embraced Greek philosophy were drawn to a religion that incorporated the discipline and moderation of this philosophy. Once Rome officially embraced Christianity, it grew in importance and number of followers.

Online Project the **Interactive Map: The Spread of Christianity**. Click through the map. Point out that it shows the spread of the religion from A.D. 325 through A.D. 476.

Draw Conclusions Point out that today, Christianity is practiced on every continent. Ask students how Christianity may have continued to spread. *(Sample response: When people migrated, they brought their beliefs with them, introducing the religion into new lands.)*

ACTIVE CLASSROOM

Use the See-Think-Wonder activity with students. Project the final map from the Interactive Map on the whiteboard. Ask: What do you see? What does that make you think? What are you wondering about now that you've seen this? Ask volunteers to share their insights with the class.

ELPS **ELPS 2.D.2** Listen as your teacher reads *The Teachings of Jesus* aloud. If you don't understand something you hear, ask your teacher for clarification.

Christianity Spreads

After Jesus' death, the apostles and other disciples spread his message. At first, they preached only among the Jews of Judea. Others traveled to the communities of the Jewish diaspora, including Rome. According to tradition, the apostle Peter traveled to Rome to spread the word of Jesus.

At first, a few Jews accepted the teaching that Jesus was the messiah, or the Christ, from the Greek word for "anointed one." They were the first Christians. These early Christians remained a small group within Judaism. Then **Paul,** a Jew from Asia Minor, began the wider spread of the new faith, and Christianity took root across the Roman world.

The Work of Paul Paul had never met Jesus. In fact, he had been among those who persecuted Jesus' followers. According to his writings, Paul had a vision in which Jesus spoke to him. He immediately converted to the new faith and made an important decision. He would spread Jesus' teachings beyond Jewish communities to gentiles, or non-Jews.

Paul's missionary work set Christianity on the road to becoming a world religion. A tireless traveler, Paul journeyed around the Mediterranean and set up churches in Asia Minor and Greece. In long letters to these Christian communities, Paul explained Christian teachings. He answered questions from believers and judged disputes.

Paul emphasized that Jesus had sacrificed his life to atone, or make amends, for the sins of humankind. Paul taught that those who believed Jesus was the son of God and complied with his teachings would achieve salvation, or eternal life. His letters became part of the New Testament.

Persecution of Christians Rome's tolerant attitude toward religion did not extend to Christians. Roman officials suspected Christians of disloyalty to Rome because they refused to honor the emperor with sacrifices or honor the Roman gods. When Christians met in secret to avoid persecution, rumors spread that they were engaged in evil practices.

In times of trouble, persecution increased. Roman rulers, like Nero, used Christians as scapegoats, blaming them for social or economic ills. Over the centuries, thousands of Christians became **martyrs,** or people who suffer or die for their beliefs. According to tradition, both Peter and Paul were martyred in Rome during the reign of Nero.

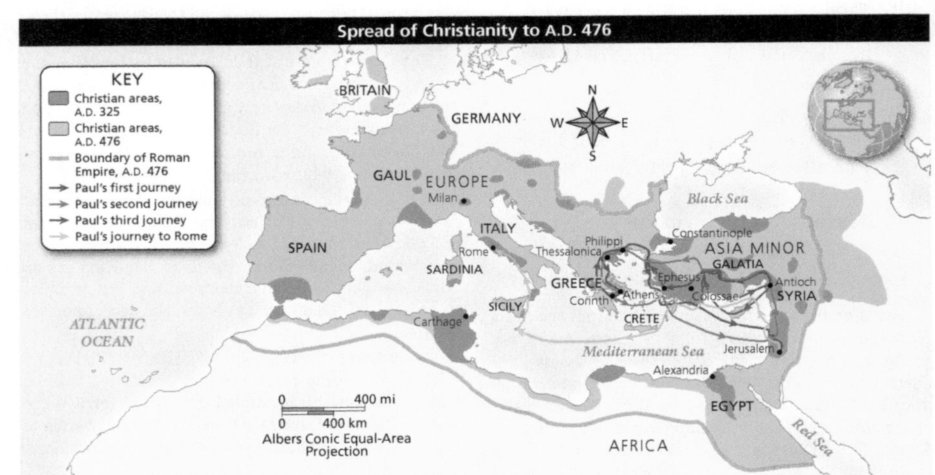

>> **Analyze Maps** How did the extent of Christianity in A.D. 325 compare to that in A.D. 476?

Interactive Map

History Background

Surviving in the Diaspora Over the centuries, many Jews left or were forced to leave their homeland in Judea. They settled in lands around the Mediterranean and elsewhere. In time, many of those who migrated began to speak Greek. Two Greek words became important parts of Jewish history. The Greek word *diaspora,* which means "scattering," refers to the fact that most Jews were forced to migrate and settle in various parts of the world. The Greek word *synagogue*, which means "a bringing together," became the term for a place where Jews gather to read their most sacred book, the Torah. Synagogues have helped Jewish culture survive and thrive in the diaspora.

Answers

Analyze Maps *By A.D. 476, Christianity had spread to a large part of southern and western Europe, Egypt, and Southwest Asia.*

The Message Wins Converts Despite the attacks, Christianity continued to spread throughout the Roman world. The reasons were many. Jesus had welcomed all people, especially the lowly, the poor, and the oppressed. These people found comfort in his message of love, as well as in Christian teachings about equality and a better life beyond the grave.

As they did their work, Christian missionaries like Paul added ideas from Plato, the Stoics, and other Greek thinkers to explain Jesus' message. Educated Romans, in particular, were attracted to a religion that incorporated the discipline and moderation of Greek philosophy.

The unity of the Roman empire also eased the work of missionaries. Christians traveled along Roman roads and across the Mediterranean Sea, which was protected by Roman fleets. Early Christian documents were usually written in Greek or Latin, languages that many people across the empire understood.

Even persecution brought new converts. People who witnessed the willingness of Christians to die for their religion were impressed by the strength of their beliefs. "The blood of the martyrs is the seed of the [Christian] Church," noted one Christian.

>> Renaissance painter Raphael depicts the cross in the sky that Constantine saw before a battle. After his victory, Constantine ended the persecution of Christians.

Rome Embraces Christianity The persecution of Christians finally ended in A.D. 313, when the emperor **Constantine** issued the Edict of Milan. It granted freedom of worship to all citizens of the Roman empire. By the end of the century, the emperor Theodosius (thee uh DOH shus) had made Christianity the official religion of the Roman empire and repressed the practice of other faiths. Gradually, the Christian Church emerged as a well-organized, powerful force in the Roman world, sending missionaries to distant lands to win more converts to the faith.

IDENTIFY SUPPORTING DETAILS What factors enabled Christianity to spread throughout the Roman empire?

The Growth of the Christian Church

Early Christian communities shared a common faith in the teachings of Jesus and a common way of worship. Only gradually did these scattered communities come together under the authority of a well-organized Christian Church.

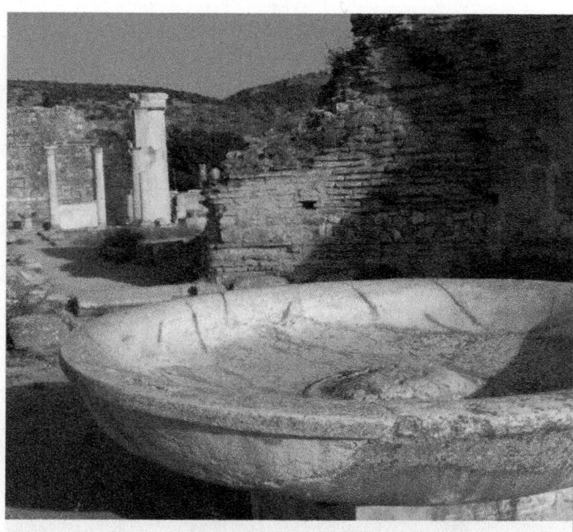

>> This baptismal font survives among the ruins of the Church of St. Mary in Ephesus, Turkey.

Early Christian Communities To join the Christian community, a person had to be baptized, or blessed with holy water. Baptism at first signified acceptance

Guided Reading and Discussion

Ask students to read aloud and summarize the information under the heading "The Message Wins Converts."

Analyze Information How did Paul contribute to Christianity becoming a world religion? *(He preached to non-Jews, started churches, and clarified Christian doctrine.)*

Describe How did Christianity continue to spread when Christians were persecuted? *(The teachings of love, equality, dignity, and a promise of a better life appealed to people. In addition, Jesus had welcomed all people, especially the poor or oppressed. People also were drawn to the discipline and moderation of Greek philosophy that was part of the missionaries' message. The martyrs and the strength of their beliefs also impressed Romans.)*

Identify Cause and Effect Have students think about the actions of Theodosius. Then ask them to describe Rome's influence on Christianity. *(With Christianity the official religion of Rome, the religion grew and would likely continue to grow. The church would also gain more power as more churches were developed throughout the empire.)*

The Growth of the Christian Church

Have students read the information on the chart "The Christian Clergy" on the next page. Introduce the chart by telling students that as Christianity spread, the church became more organized and eventually became the central institution in the region.

History Background

Paul's Letters to the Corinthians Paul wrote two letters, or epistles, to the Christian community he founded at Corinth in Greece. This passage is part of a longer letter that Paul sent to the Corinthians to discuss problems within the community that arose after Paul's first missionary visit to Corinth. At that time there were conflicts among the converts who followed the teachings of various apostles. Paul uses this letter to answer questions the Corinthian Christians have asked him about such issues as marriage and celibacy, the conduct of women, and the Eucharist service. Paul later wrote another letter to the Corinthians, known as Corinthians II. Paul's writings are found in the New Testament.

Answers

Identify Supporting Details *The unity of the Roman empire, the Roman-protected Mediterranean, and Rome's network of roads made it easy for missionaries to travel. Also, Greek and Latin, languages common throughout the empire, were used in documents and aided in the spread of Christianity.*

Topic 6 Lesson 4

Guided Reading and Discussion

Call attention to the history and relevance of Christian traditions in the reading before asking the following questions.

Summarize Discuss the roles of different members of the clergy. Ask students to summarize the role of women. *(At first women served as teachers and administrators. Later they were not allowed to serve in official roles; however, women could still carry on the tradition of missionary work.)* In the early Christian church, which officials were considered to be equal successors to the apostles? *(bishops)*

Identify Central Issues Why did church leaders seek a structure for the church? *(to ensure uniformity in beliefs, practices, and rituals so that local priests or bishops did not act independently, and to provide an orderly way to make decisions and settle conflicts over doctrine or practices)*

Key Terms

Ask students to find the key term **patriarchs** (in bold) in the text. Explain that, in addition to describing figures from early Christian history, the word *patriarch* can describe the male leader of any family or tribe. Some people refer to the oldest male relative in their extended family as the family's patriarch.

of Christian teachings along with purification, or the forgiveness of sins. Members of the community were considered equals, and they addressed each other as "brother" or "sister." Early Christians gathered on Sunday for a ceremony of thanksgiving that included elements of Jewish traditions and Christian beliefs. They celebrated the sacred rite of the Eucharist, in which they consumed bread and wine, taken in memory of Jesus, whose last supper is described in the Gospels.

The Role of Women Many women welcomed Christianity's promise that in the Christian faith, "there is neither Jew nor Greek . . . neither slave nor free . . . neither male nor female." In early Christian communities, women served as teachers and administrators. Even when they were later barred from any official role in the Christian Church, they still worked to win converts and supported Christian communities across the Roman world.

The Structure of the Christian Church During the first centuries A.D., Christian communities developed a formal church structure with its own **clergy,** or people who conduct worship services. At first, the Christian clergy included priests and **bishops,** the highest-ranking Church officials. A bishop presided over a diocese, which included a number of Christian communities and their priests.

As the church expanded, archbishops were appointed to oversee the bishops. An archbishop's territory was called a province.

This type of organization in which officials are arranged according to rank is called a hierarchy.

As the Christian Church grew more organized, women lost their influence. They could not become priests or conduct Mass, the Christian worship service. Still, they continued to work as missionaries and even suffered martyrdom for their faith.

In time, the bishops of the most important cities in the Roman empire—Rome, Antioch, Alexandria, Jerusalem, and Constantinople— gained greater authority and were called **patriarchs.** Like all bishops, they traced their spiritual authority to the apostles and Jesus. Eventually, in the Latin-speaking western empire, the bishop of Rome assumed a dominant position, claiming that the apostle Peter had made Rome the center of the Christian Church. He took the title **pope,** or father of the Church. Patriarchs in the eastern Roman empire rejected the pope's claim to be supreme ruler of the Church.

Rivalries Within the Church Together, the clergy, including archbishops, bishops, and priests, helped keep Christianity alive in the early years of persecution. They also maintained order and discipline in the Church.

Despite its strong structure, the Church faced constant battles against **heresies,** or beliefs said to be

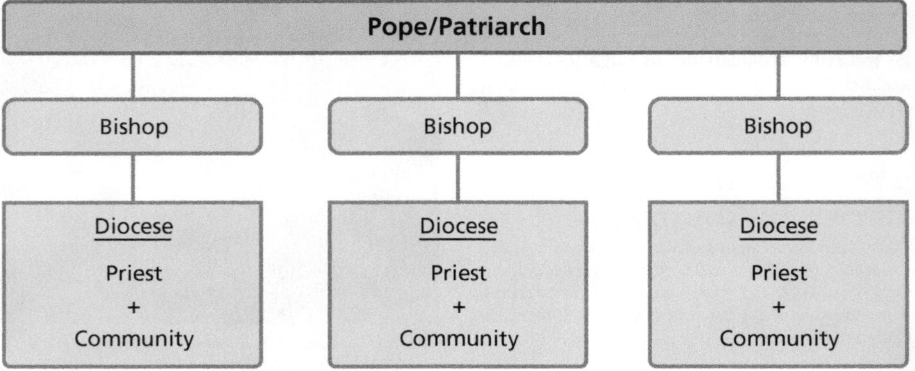

>> **Analyze Charts** Over time, the clergy of the Christian church developed into a hierarchy. What are some positive and negative elements that may arise from this type of organizational structure?

Answers

Analyze Charts *Sample answer: positive elements: a more comprehensive structure to the clergy, a ranking of spiritual authority; negative elements: an authoritarian church, a distancing of the Christian community from the clergy*

Describe *At the local level, each Christian community had its own priest. Over each priest was a bishop responsible for all Christians within an area called a diocese. In time, the bishops of the most important cities in the Roman empire gained greater authority over all other bishops in their area and assumed the honorary title of patriarchs.*

contrary to official Church teachings. To end disputes over questions of faith, councils of Church leaders met to decide which ideas or practices the Church would accept. Among the most important was the Council of Nicaea in Asia Minor, where they drew up the Nicene Creed, a statement of basic Christian beliefs.

Scholars Further Define Christian Teachings For centuries, Christian scholars debated issues of theology, or the study of religious faith and practice. Two leading scholars of the early Church were Clement and Origen. Both worked as teachers in Alexandria, Egypt, a major center of learning in the Roman world.

Perhaps the best known Christian theologian was **Augustine,** bishop of Hippo in North Africa. His writings have greatly influenced Christian thought and philosophy up to the present. In *City of God*, Augustine defended Christianity against critics who claimed the sack of Rome in A.D.410 was a punishment for abandoning their traditional gods.

>> Augustine was the bishop of Hippo in North Africa. A noted Church scholar, he combined Christian doctrine with the philosophy of Plato.

 **DESCRIBE** How was the early Christian clergy organized?

ASSESSMENT

1. **Summarize** What were the historical origins of Christianity, and how did that reflect the development of monotheism in the Roman empire?
2. **Describe** How was the work of missionaries vital in the spread of Christianity through the Roman empire?
3. **Identify Main Ideas** What were the central ideas in Christianity?
4. **Identify** What was the role of women in early Christian communities?
5. **Draw Conclusions** Why might Romans be receptive to Augustine's ideas?

SYNTHESIZE

Online Project the **Digital Activity: Key Roles in Early Christianity**. As students work through the chart, ask them which of the key roles they would categorize as part of the central ideas in Christianity and which would fall into the category of the spread of Christianity. *(Central ideas in Christianity: Jesus and apostles; spread of Christianity: Jesus, apostles, Paul, and missionaries)*

DEMONSTRATE

Online Assign the **Digital Lesson Quiz** for this lesson if you haven't already done so. Students will be offered automatic remediation or enrichment based on their score.

Pose these questions to the class on the Discussion Board:

Predict Consequences How do you think the fall of Rome will affect the church and Western Europe? *(Some students might respond that the church will lose power without the unity that Rome brought to Western Europe. Others might predict that the church will have a chance to fill the power vacuum left by the fall of Rome.)*

Draw Inferences What do you think will be the biggest challenge to the growth of Christianity? *(Students might respond that as Christianity spreads its followers will come into conflict with those who hold different beliefs. Others might note that the church will have an increase in internal divisions.)*

Topic Inquiry

Have students continue their investigations for the Topic Inquiry.

Assessment

1. Christianity arose in Judea during a period of conflict and rebellion. The new religion began among the followers of a Jew named Jesus. His teachings were grounded in Jewish traditions, including the belief in one god—monotheism. Missionaries spread Christianity, although Roman emperors did not accept it for many years. Eventually, Christianity became the official religion of the Roman empire, with the result that monotheism became widely practiced and replaced polytheism.
2. After Jesus' death, his apostles and disciples, such as Peter and Paul, dedicated their lives to spreading his teachings. They traveled throughout the empire explaining Jesus' teachings and guiding his followers.
3. In Christianity, Jesus taught the idea of one God as a Trinity—the Father, the Son, and the Holy Spirit. He said the he was the son of God and would bring salvation and eternal life to his followers. Jesus also expressed the importance of justice, morality, equality, service, and forgiveness.
4. Women served as teachers and administrators. Although they were later barred from any official role, they continued to work as missionaries.
5. Answers will vary, but students should understand that Augustine combined Christian doctrine with Greco-Roman learning. This would likely make the doctrine more familiar to Romans.

Answers to TEKS Assessment

1. The more democratic republic featured a lawmaking senate that controlled the government and representation for plebeians. The empire was an absolute monarchy ruled by an emperor with total power and no limit on his term. Both nobles and plebeians had a role under the republic, but the latter had no role in the empire. As the Roman republic conquered more lands, inequality grew and led to social unrest. Government corruption increased. This led to a series of power struggles and civil wars over who should rule and contributed to the republic's decline.

2. The rise of the Roman republic brought great riches to the new wealthy class. Slave labor and imported grains, along with latifundias, meant small farmers couldn't compete and lost their farms. The gap between rich and poor grew. The Gracchus brothers started a movement for social reform, but were murdered. The question of who would lead the government led to power struggles and civil wars. Julius Caesar seized leadership and enacted reforms before his assassination.

3. Initially, the male patricians of the senate created laws and controlled government. The senate voted tor consuls, who supervised the business of government. Plebeians at first had no power in the government before eventually winning the right to elect their own officials, or tribunes, and later earned the right to be consuls and senators. During the Roman republic, noncitizens had few opportunities for civic participation until Rome later granted citizenship privileges.

4. Christianity is based on Judaism, monotheism, and just treatment of individuals and equality before the law; differences from Judaism: spiritual salvation and eternal life. Christians were persecuted by Roman officials; Christianity spread via Jesus's apostles.

5. Romans worshiped many gods and goddesses. Romans honored their traditional gods to receive divine favor from them, such as assistance on the battlefield from Mars, the god of war. The worshiping rituals and celebrations inspired a sense of community. Due to the size of the empire, Romans tolerated worship of other gods as long as the subjects also honored Roman gods and acknowledged the divine spirit of the emperor.

6. The Romans were committed to the rule of law and to justice, believing it fostered unity and stability. The legacy of Roman law is that many Roman legal principles, like the presumption of innocence, right to a defense, and the need for solid evidence to convict, became the basis for legal systems throughout the world, including that of the United States.

TEKS ASSESSMENT

Comparing Structures of Government

ROMAN REPUBLIC		ROMAN EMPIRE
HIGHEST OFFICIALS		**HIGHEST OFFICIALS**
Two Consuls • annually elected • held equal power	**Dictator** • appointed in times of emergency • held office for 6 months only	**Emperor** • inherited power • served for life • if served well, was worshipped as a god after death
GOVERNING BODIES		**GOVERNING BODIES**
Senate • issued advisory decrees to magistrates and people • in practice, held enormous power • had about 300 members	**Popular Assemblies** • two assemblies: centuriate (miltary), tribal (nonmilitary) • elected magistrates, held legislative power, made key decisions	**Senate** • issued binding decrees, acted as a high court, elected magistrates • in practice, held little power as compared to the emperor • had about 600 members

1. **Identify Characteristics** Identify the characteristics of political systems, including a republic. Write a paragraph identifying the characteristics of the political systems of both the Roman republic and the Roman empire, and compare their government structures. Consider primary differences in the structures, civic participation by nobles and plebeians, and weaknesses that led to the fall of the republic. **19.B**

2. **Describe Major Effects of Events** Describe the major effects in the transition from the Roman republic to the Roman empire. Write a paragraph describing several effects of this transition, and answer the following questions: What consequences did conquests bring to the Roman republic? What role did the Gracchus brothers play in the Roman republic? What events followed before the decline of the republic? **1.B**

3. **Describe the Responsibilities of Citizens and Noncitizens** Describe the responsibilities of citizens and noncitizens in civic participation throughout history. Write a paragraph that describes the responsibilities of citizens and noncitizens in civic participation in the Roman republic. Consider the concept of *res publica*; civic participants in the senate, consuls, and tribunes; gradual rights for plebeians; and the status of noncitizens. **21.B**

4. **Describe Central Ideas and Major Religious/Philosophical Influences** Describe the central ideas and major religious/philosophical influences of Israel, including the development of Christianity. Write a paragraph on the central ideas and major religious influences of Christianity. What beliefs was Christianity based on? How were Christian beliefs different from Judaism? How was Christianity tolerated and what was its influence? **3.A, 23.A, 30.C**

5. **Describe a Major Cultural Influence** Describe the major cultural influence of Rome. Create oral and visual presentations of social studies information. Write a speech that describes how the Roman belief in many gods and goddesses was a major cultural influence. Research examples of art, photos, or museum pictures to enhance your speech. Consider the reasons for worship of multiple gods and goddesses, example of deities, sense of community, and explain why Romans still tolerated religious diversity. **3.A, 30.C**

6. **Summarize the Development** Summarize the development of the rule of law from ancient to modern times. Use the information from the lessons in this topic to summarize the development of the rule of law from the Roman era to modern times. Consider the importance of the Roman rule of law and justice, some principles, and its legacy. **22.A**

7. **Identify the Influence of Ideas** Identify the influence of ideas regarding the concept of "innocent until proven guilty" in Rome. Write a newspaper article about a criminal trial (either one you know about or one you make up) identifying how the idea of "innocent until proven guilty" is used. Consider the meaning of "innocent until proven guilty," what a person could be accused of, what might prove a person guilty of the crime, and what might prove the person innocent of the crime. **22.B**

8. **Explain the Development** Explain the development of democratic-republican government from its beginnings in the Judeo-Christian legal tradition and in classical Rome. Write a paragraph to explain Judeo-Christian beliefs about this type of government, and include the influence of just treatment of individuals, influence of equality before the law, basic Roman legal principles, and ideas from Rome's republican form of government. **20.A**

9. **Analyze Examples** Analyze examples of how Roman art reflects the history of Roman culture. Write a paragraph analyzing the types of art that Romans created. Include answers to the following questions: Which art adaptations were mainly used by the Romans? What types of new art styles did the Romans develop? What types of artwork did wealthy Romans typically have? **26.B**

7. A person accused of a crime is considered innocent until proven guilty; is entitled to a trial before a judge; can offer a defense; and must be proved guilty using solid evidence. Students should mention a crime and should lay out evidence that would lead to a verdict of either guilty or not guilty.

8. Judeo-Christian beliefs about the just treatment of individuals and equality before the law and basic Roman legal principles, such as the presumption of innocence and the right to a defense, would later influence legal systems and governments of Western democracies. Ideas from Rome's republican form of government, such as the senate, the veto, and checks on political power, were adopted into the U.S. Constitution.

9. Roman architecture emphasized grandeur. Roman literature focused on the history of Rome and its heroes and accomplishments, borrowing from Greek literature. Roman sculptures broke new ground. The sculptures emphasized realism, reflecting a subject's character. Wealthy Romans had

10. Summarize Fundamental Ideas and Institutitons Summarize the fundamental ideas and institutions of Western civilizations that originated in Rome. Write a paragraph summarizing Rome's fundamental ideas and institutions that are a part of Western civilizations: Rome's legal system; civil service, postal service, and census; and self-government of its territories. 25.B

11. Describe Historical Origins Describe the historical origins of major religious and philosophical traditions, including the development of monotheism. Write a paragraph describing the historical origins of Judaism and Christianity and their development of monotheism, including information about the traditions of both religions. What was the Roman attitude toward monotheism? 23.A

12. Explain Impacts Explain the impact of the fall of Rome on Western Europe. Write a paragraph explaining why the fall of Rome is seen as an important event in Western Europe. Consider such things as Rome's status before its decline; territorial invasions and lack of leadership; and military, economic, and social reasons. 3.B

13. Identify Diffusion of Major Ideas Identify the diffusion of major ideas in mathematics and technology that occurred in classical Rome. Write a paragraph that describes how the diffusion of mathematics and technology in classical Rome benefited its empire. Consider how mathematics and technology were used in practical ways, how structures and machines were built, and the quality and longevity of engineering constructions. 27.A

14. Compare the Factors Compare the factors that led to the collapse of Rome and Han China. Analyze information by making generalizations and predictions, and transfer information from one medium to another. Make up a chart, and then write a paragraph generalizing and predicting the reasons for the fall of the Han dynasty in China and of the Roman empire. Consider the size and control of the empires, role of the military, economic instability and excessive taxation, and political and social unrest. What similarities do you see? 3.C, 29.F, 30.D

15. Describe Major Effects of Events Describe the major effects of the following important turning points in world history from 600 to 1450: the decline of Rome. Explain the impact of the fall of Rome on Western Europe. Using the map below and information from the lessons, describe the major effects of the decline of the Roman empire and its impact on Western Europe. Who divided the Roman empire and why? How did Constantinople became the center of power and change the course of European history? 1.C, 3.B

16. Reflect on the Essential Question Write an essay on the Essential Question: What makes a government successful? Use evidence from your study of this Topic to support your answer.

Division of the Roman Empire, about A.D. 284

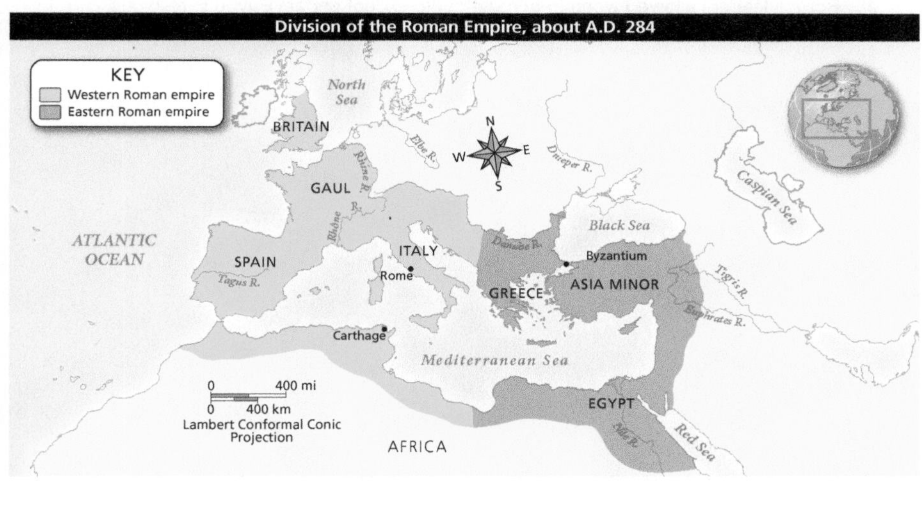

decorative frescoes, murals, or mosaics—pictures made from chips of colored stone or glass—in their homes.

10. Many aspects of Rome's legal system, such as the rule of law, the presumption of innocence, and the right of the accused to offer a defense, were adopted by later Western civilizations. Rome also had a civil service, a postal service, a census, standardized coins, and public works programs. Rome allowed its territories a large degree of self-government. All of these ideas and institutions continue to be used in Western civilizations.

11. Judaism and Christianity were both monotheistic religions. Romans were polytheists, but tolerant of diverse religions. Jews were excused from worshiping Roman gods. After Rome suppressed a Jewish uprising and destroyed the temple in Jerusalem, Jewish rabbis ensured preservation of Jewish law and traditions. Christianity was developed from the teachings of Jesus, and was firmly rooted in the laws of Moses and the teachings of the Jewish prophets. Jesus believed in one God and said he was the son of God. He also preached new beliefs about spiritual salvation and eternal life that are a part of Christian values and tradition. After Jesus's death, Christians gathered on Sundays for a ceremony of thanksgiving to God and celebrated the Eucharist in honor of Jesus.

12. At one time Rome was a dominant power in Europe. Before the fall, the empire was split and weakened. Roman government became more authoritarian and lost the support of its people. Corruption and civil wars led to instability. High taxes to support the government and military, which now consisted of mercenaries who had less loyalty to Rome, were too high for farmers, who abandoned their land. The gap between the rich and the poor grew. The army could not protect the empire from bands of invaders. Rome had to surrender Britain, then France and Spain to foreign invaders.

13. The size of the Roman empire necessitated improvements in transportation for better communication. Romans adapted much scientific and technological knowledge from the Greeks and put it to practical use. The Romans excelled in engineering, or using science and mathematics to build structures. The Romans built roads, aqueducts, bridges, and harbors. They pioneered the use of concrete as a building material, and developed the rounded dome as a roof for large spaces. Many Roman structures like roads and aqueducts were built so solidly that they lasted for centuries.

14. Controlling and governing these large empires would be difficult, and border attacks would be an issue. A large military to control and protect the empires would require high taxes, which, in both empires, would have been paid mostly by peasants. This led to political and social unrest by poor peasants who revolted. Powerful local military rulers could not be controlled. Weak emperors were unable to stop outside invasions, leading to the decline of the empires.

15. Diocletian divided the empire into western and eastern parts to better govern it. After Diocletian, Constantine served as emperor. Constantine granted tolerance to Christians and set up a new capital in the eastern part of the empire called Constantinople. This eastern half of the empire, known as the Byzantine empire, was stronger and wealthier than the western half and became the center of power. It flourished for another 1,000 years.

Answers to TEKS Practice

1. D

2. H

Online To prepare for the End-of-Topic test, have students go online for additional Topic Review and Assessment questions or to review their notes in the **Interactive Reading Notepad** for the lessons in this Topic.

Benchmark Tests

Assign these benchmark tests as you complete the relevant topics to monitor student progress toward mastering the course content and as preparation for the End-of-Course Test.

Benchmark Test 1: Topics 1–5

Benchmark Test 2: Topics 6–10

Benchmark Test 3: Topics 11–15

Benchmark Test 4: Topics 16–21

TEKS PRACTICE

1

> *"The Carthaginians fought for their own preservation and the sovereignty of Africa; the Romans, for supremacy and world domination"*

Explain the significance of the statement "The Carthaginians fought for their own preservation and the sovereignty of Africa; the Romans, for supremacy and world domination" which was made after the end of the Punic Wars.

A Carthage was the last holdout of the Roman conquests before the height of its empire.

B Citizens celebrated major military victories as an example of Roman domination.

C Rome gained religious converts after gaining the coveted islands of Sicily, Corsica, and Sardinia.

D The fall of Carthage was a turning point in Roman domination of the Mediterranean and northern Africa.

---

2 Explain the status of religion in Rome before Christianity was declared the official religion.

F Roman leaders promoted monotheism for a more civilized Roman life.

G Citizens resisted being forced to worship the emperor's divine gods.

H Most people were polytheistic, worshipping Roman gods and their own religions.

J Roman leaders allowed worship of most gods, except certain Egyptian religions.

Test Taking Tips: Tip for Questions With Maps

1. Read the question.
2. Read the map title and look at the map to determine what is shown in the map.
3. Look at the key or legend. What symbols, shades, or patterns are used to show information on the map? Find examples of each symbol, shade, or pattern on the map.
4. Read the question again. What information do you need from the map to answer the question? Use the information in the map title, the key or legend, and on the map itself to find the answer.
5. Answer the question in your own words.
6. Read the answer choices and select the best answer.

3

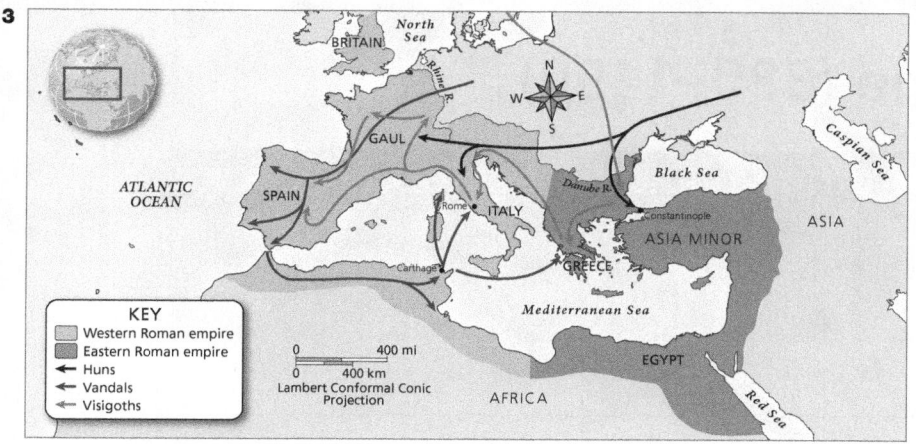

Using the map, how did the Huns and other tribes invade the Roman empire to gain control?

A Rome's weakened borders in the north, west, and northern Africa resulted in its defeat.

B The Visogoths and the Vandals regained Carthage and some Greek islands before taking over Rome.

C The Vandals made periodic invasions close to Asia Minor that defeated Rome's eastern capital.

D Migrating Huns from the north pushed their way to Spain and joined forces with other tribes.

---

4 How did Greek literature reflect the history of the culture in which it was produced?

F Greek tragedies often mocked leading political figures and prominent members of society.

G Historians like Herodotus emphasized research of actual events before writing Greek comedies.

H Greek dramas were often based on myths and legends to discuss moral issues and human suffering.

J Greek philosophers used the art of skillful speaking to stage important plays about ethics and morality.

If you have trouble with...				
Question	1	2	3	4
See Lesson	6.2	6.4	6.2	5.3
TEKS	1.B	3.A	1.c	26.B

Topic 6

3. A
4. H

Online Use the **Topic Synthesize** to help students revisit and reflect on the Essential Question for this Topic.

Topic Inquiry

If students have done a Topic Inquiry for this Topic, have them complete the final step of the Inquiry now.

Medieval Christian Europe (330–1450)

TOPIC 7 ORGANIZER	PACING: APPROX. 1 PERIOD, .5 BLOCKS		
	PACING	TEKS	ELPS
Connect	1 period		
MY STORY VIDEO **Guédelon, A Medieval Castle in the Making**	10 min.		
DIGITAL ESSENTIAL QUESTION ACTIVITY **What Should Governments Do?**	10 min.	20.A, 20.B, 20.C	
DIGITAL TIMELINE ACTIVITY **Medieval Christian Europe**	10 min.	3.B, 4.A, 4.B, 4.C, 4.E, 4.G, 20.A, 20.B, 23.A, 26.B	
TOPIC INQUIRY: PROJECT-BASED LEARNING **Create a Graphic Novel Spread About Medieval Christian Europe**	20 min.		
Investigate	4–8 periods		
TOPIC INQUIRY: PROJECT-BASED LEARNING **Create a Graphic Novel Spread About Medieval Christian Europe**	Ongoing		
LESSON 1 **The Early Middle Ages**	30–40 min.	1.C, 3.B, 20.B	2.E.2
LESSON 2 **Feudalism and the Manor Economy**	30–40 min.	4.C	2.E.3
LESSON 3 **The Medieval Christian Church**	30–40 min.	1.C, 4.A, 4.B, 4.E	2.H.2
LESSON 4 **Economic Expansion and Change: The Crusades and After**	30–40 min.	4.D, 4.E, 4.G, 16.A, 23.B, 24.A	2.I.1, 2.F.2
LESSON 5 **The Feudal Monarchs and the Church**	30–40 min.	4.A, 20.B	2.G.1, 2.I.2
LESSON 6 **Learning, Literature, and the Arts of the Middle Ages**	30–40 min.	4.A, 20.C, 24.A, 26.B	2.G.2, 2.I.3
LESSON 7 **The Late Middle Ages: A Time of Upheaval**	30–40 min.	4.G	2.G.3, 2.I.4
LESSON 8 **Russia and Eastern Europe**	30–40 min.	1.C, 4.K, 15.A, 23.B	2.G.4, 2.I.5
Synthesize	1 period		
DIGITAL ESSENTIAL QUESTION ACTIVITY **Medieval Christian Europe**	10 min.	20.A, 20.B, 20.C	
TOPIC INQUIRY: PROJECT-BASED LEARNING **Create a Graphic Novel Spread About Medieval Christian Europe**	20 min.		

TOPIC 7 ORGANIZER	PACING: APPROX. 1 PERIOD, .5 BLOCKS		
	PACING	TEKS	ELPS
Demonstrate	1–2 periods		
ONLINE TEST **Medieval Christian Europe**	10 min.		
TOPIC INQUIRY: PROJECT-BASED LEARNING **Create a Graphic Novel Spread About Medieval Christian Europe**	20 min.		

AUTHOR'S NOTE

The Crusades: Rehearsal for Empire

The beginnings were small enough. The First Crusade began in 1095, sending tens of thousands of Christian holy warriors swarming into the Near East to liberate from Islam the lands where Christ had lived. . . .

The First Crusaders did "liberate" Jerusalem, massacring most of its Jewish and Muslim population in the process. They then set up a series of Crusader States stretching along the eastern end of the Mediterranean from Gaza through Lebanon. European pilgrim traffic, Italian trading colonies, and a steady flow of men and money maintained this Western toehold in the Near East for two hundred years (though Jerusalem fell to the famous Muslim leader Saladin in less than a century). European taste for Asian spices and other luxury goods and Christian zeal for spreading the faith by force of arms were both whetted by the Crusades. The Western money economy of the High Middle Ages was stimulated by the expanded trade with the East, and Europeans learned to tax themselves and to organize large-scale overseas ventures while mounting these international military campaigns.

All the later Crusades were costly failures, however, and the movement dwindled to talk and minor skirmishes after 1250. It would be another two and a half centuries before Europeans would again reach out for spices and converts, land and booty, beyond the confines of their own end of Eurasia. But the dynamism, the organizing ability, the ruthlessness, courage, and greed of the West had been demonstrated in this first rehearsal for empire.

—Anthony Esler, *The Human Venture: From Prehistory to the Present*, (Upper Saddle River, New Jersey: Pearson Education, 2004), p. 240

TOPIC INQUIRY: PROJECT-BASED LEARNING

Create a Graphic Novel Spread About Medieval Christian Europe

TEKS 4.C, 4.G, 30.C, 30.D

In this Topic Inquiry, students work in teams to research and create an eight-panel graphic novel about life in Europe in the Middle Ages.

STEP 1: CONNECT

Develop Questions and Plan the Investigation

Launch the Project, Generate Questions, and Examine Graphic Novels

Tell students that they will research life in medieval Europe and use this knowledge, along with special software, to create a two-page spread from a graphic novel. Display the Project Launch and refer students to the bulleted list "What Makes a Graphic Novel Good?"

Suggestion: Have students describe favorite graphic novels and point out how they succeed in various categories such as characters, plot, setting, and text. Suggest they compare and contrast various graphic novels they have read and enjoyed.

Plan the Investigation

Form students into teams. Have them learn about working as a team by reviewing a skills tutorial. Then have each team sign the *Project Contract*, assign team roles using the *Project Tracker*, and begin the *Need-to-Know Questions*.

Suggestion: To spur discussion about various elements of a graphic novel and how they use visuals and text to present the author's ideas, ask team members to take turns describing a graphic novel they enjoy.

Resources

- Project Launch
- Project Contract
- Project Tracker
- Need-to-Know Questions
- Student Instructions
- Rubric for a Graphic Novel
- Skills Tutorial: *Search for Information on the Internet*
- Skills Tutorial: *Work in Teams*

STEP 2: INVESTIGATE

Apply Disciplinary Concepts and Tools

Identify Topic

Teams will learn how to assign tasks and monitor their work, then, with your help, choose a subject for their graphic novel spread. They will brainstorm how to approach their subject, keeping in mind the driving question, What was life like in the Middle Ages for people at different economic and social levels?

Suggestion: To ensure that a variety of subjects from different aspects of medieval life are portrayed, assign topics. Possible topics might include family life in either rural areas or cities, different kinds of work, the arts, kings and queens, the Church, science and technology, transportation, operating a manor, and the Crusades.

Conduct Research

There are two research tasks for this project: finding and learning how to use the graphic novel software to produce the spread and researching the Middle Ages to write the text and design the art. To guide their research, teams will create a list of *Need-to-Know Questions* about their subject and about the graphic novel software they plan to use. Refer students to helpful resources within the Topic to help answer their questions. If they are researching Gothic cathedrals, refer them to the text and activities in Lesson 6. Help students fill out the *Information Organizer*.

Suggestion: Preview some of the suggested graphic novel construction websites to make sure they fit students' needs. Also, see if your school has subscribed to any sites that might be appropriate for the project.

Write, Edit, and Storyboard Your Spread

Students write and edit their text and storyboard their visual ideas. Emphasize that the storyboard is a kind of draft where they can try out different visual elements before deciding on a final version.

Suggestion: Create a sample storyboard to show students how to create one.

STEP 3: SYNTHESIZE

Evaluate Sources and Use Evidence to Formulate Conclusions

Create the Graphic Novel Spread

Now have students get together to create their graphic novel spreads. If students are having trouble sharing the work on this part of the project, remind them to review their *Project Tracker* document to see how they planned to divide the work. Review each team's spread to make sure they are on track. For students who are having trouble, walk them through *Information Organizer: Plan Your Graphic Novel* as a class to get ideas.

Suggestion: For a less technology-dependent end product, have students use art materials to create a graphic novel spread by hand. To take the technology a step further, have students animate their spreads with audio or movement.

Review the Graphic Novel Spread

Have students edit each other's work and offer suggestions to improve the text and visuals. Be prepared to offer advice on how to improve the teams' products.

State Conclusion About the Driving Question

Have students state a conclusion about the driving question based on their work with the graphic novel spread. They should produce a written paragraph to accompany their graphic novel spread.

Suggestion: Consider leading a short discussion on how the driving question relates to the teams' individual subjects.

Resources

- Information Organizer: Plan Your Graphic Novel Spread

STEP 4: DEMONSTRATE

Communicate Conclusions and Take Informed Action

Present the Graphic Novel

Have students prepare their graphic novel spread presentations, then watch the team presentations. To help the teams structure their time, set up a clock in the back of the room, and alert them when they have only a few minutes left.

Reflect on the Project

After students have finished their Team Assessments, help them go over what they thought went well and what did not, so they can be even more effective in the future.

Suggestion: As an extension activity, have students create a "Then and Now" chart that compares aspects of life, including people's relationship with various governments, during the Middle Ages and today.

Resources

- Give an Effective Presentation Skills Tutorial
- Graphic Novel Spread Rubric
- Self-Assessment

PROFESSIONAL DEVELOPMENT

Project-Based Learning

Be sure to view the Project-Based Learning Professional Development resources in the online course.

Resources

- Skills Tutorial: *Work in Teams*
- Skills Tutorial: *Search for Information on the Internet*
- Need-to-Know Questions
- Project Tracking Sheet
- Information Organizing Worksheet

The Early Middle Ages

Objectives

Objective 1: Summarize ways in which the Byzantine empire flourished after the decline of Rome.

Objective 2: Explain the impact of the fall of Rome on Western Europe.

Objective 3: Describe how Germanic tribes carved Europe into small kingdoms.

Objective 4: Explain how Charlemagne briefly reunited much of Western Europe and what happened to his empire after his death.

LESSON 1 ORGANIZER — **PACING: APPROX. 1 PERIOD, .5 BLOCKS**

	OBJECTIVES	PACING	RESOURCES: Print	RESOURCES: Online	TEKS	ELPS
Connect						
DIGITAL START UP ACTIVITY **A Sovereign City**		5 min.		●	1.C	
Investigate						
READ **The Byzantine Empire Thrives**	Objective 1	10 min.		●	1.C	
READ **The Age of Justinian**		10 min.		●	1.C, 20.B	2.E.2
INTERACTIVE GALLERY **Hagia Sophia**		10 min.		●	1.C	
READ **Changes in Western Europe**	Objective 2	10 min.		●	1.C, 3.B	
READ **Germanic Kingdoms**	Objective 3	10 min.		●	1.C	
READ **Charlemagne Builds an Empire**	Objective 4	10 min.		●	1.C, 4.A	
READ **New Invasions Pound Europe**		10 min.		●	1.C	
INTERACTIVE MAP **Invasions of Europe 700–1000**		10 min.		●	1.C	
Synthesize						
DIGITAL ACTIVITY **Cooperation: The European Union**		5 min.		●	1.C	
Demonstrate						
LESSON QUIZ **Lesson Quiz and Class Discussion Board**		10 min.		●	1.C, 3.B, 4.A	

PEARSON realize™ www.PearsonTexas.com Access your Digital Lesson

Focus on Texas Standards

Texas Essential Knowledge and Skills

1.C identify major causes and describe the major effects of the following important turning points in world history from 600 to 1450: the spread of Christianity, the decline of Rome and the formation of medieval Europe; the development of Islamic caliphates and their impact on Asia, Africa, and Europe; the Mongol invasions and their impact on Europe, China, India, and Southwest Asia	**3.B** explain the impact of the fall of Rome on Western Europe **20.B** identify the impact of political and legal ideas contained in the following documents: Hammurabi's Code, the Jewish Ten Commandments, Justinian's Code of Laws, Magna Carta, the English Bill of Rights, the Declaration of Independence, the U.S. Constitution, and the Declaration of the Rights of Man and of the Citizen

NOTES

Feudalism and the Manor Economy

Objectives

Objective 1: Describe the development of the political and social system of feudalism.

Objective 2: Summarize the life of knights and nobles.

Objective 3: Analyze how the economic system of manorialism worked and how it affected peasants and nobles.

LESSON 2 ORGANIZER	PACING: APPROX. 1 PERIOD, .5 BLOCKS					
			RESOURCES			
	OBJECTIVES	PACING	Print	Online	TEKS	ELPS
Connect						
DIGITAL START UP ACTIVITY **Knighted on the Battlefield**		5 min.		●	4.C	
Investigate						
READ **Feudalism Develops**	Objective 1	10 min.		●	4.C	
READ **Nobles, Knights, and Warfare**	Objective 2	10 min.		●	4.C	2.E.3
INTERACTIVE GALLERY **Defending a Castle**		10 min.		●	4.C	
READ **Manorialism**	Objective 3	10 min.		●	4.C	
INTERACTIVE CHART **The Medieval Manorial System**		10 min.		●	4.C	
Synthesize						
DIGITAL ACTIVITY **A Powerful Woman**		5 min.		●	4.C	
Demonstrate						
LESSON QUIZ **Lesson Quiz and Class Discussion Board**		10 min.		●	4.C	

Focus on Texas Standards

Texas Essential Knowledge and Skills

4.C describe the major characteristics of and the factors contributing to the development of the political/social system of feudalism and the economic system of manorialism

NOTES

The Medieval Christian Church

Objectives

Objective 1: Explain how the Christian Church shaped medieval life.

Objective 2: Understand monastic life and the influence of medieval monks and nuns. .

Objective 3: Analyze how the power of the Church grew during the Middle Ages and how reformers worked for change in the Church.

Objective 4: Describe the situation of Jews in medieval Europe.

Objective 5: Analyze how Christianity in the Byzantine empire differed from Christianity in the West.

LESSON 3 ORGANIZER			PACING: APPROX. 1 PERIOD, .5 BLOCKS			
			RESOURCES			
	OBJECTIVES	PACING	Print	Online	TEKS	ELPS
Connect						
DIGITAL START UP ACTIVITY **The Medieval Christian Church**		5 min.		●	1.C	
Investigate						
READ **The Church Shapes Everyday Life**	Objective 1	10 min.		●	1.C, 4.A, 23.A	2.H.2
INTERACTIVE MAP **Spread of Christianity in Europe**		10 min.		●	1.C, 23.A	
READ **Life in Monasteries and Convents**	Objective 2	10 min.		●	1.C, 4.A	
INTERACTIVE 3-D MODEL **Medieval Monastery**		10 min.		●	1.C	
READ **The Growth of Church Power**	Objective 3	10 min.		●	1.C, 4.A, 23.A	
READ **The Church Faces Calls to Reform**		10 min.		●	1.C, 4.A, 23.A	
READ **Jewish Communities in Medieval Europe**	Objective 4	10 min.		●	4.E	
READ **The Christian Church Is Divided**	Objective 5	10 min.		●	1.C, 4.A, 4.B	
INTERACTIVE CHART **The Church Divides**		10 min.		●	4.A, 4.B	
Synthesize						
DIGITAL ACTIVITY **Role of the Church**		5 min.		●	1.C, 4.A, 23.A	
Demonstrate						
LESSON QUIZ **Lesson Quiz and Class Discussion Board**		10 min.		●	1.C, 4.A, 4.B, 4.E, 23.A	

PEARSON realize™ www.PearsonTexas.com Access your Digital Lesson

Focus on Texas Standards

Texas Essential Knowledge and Skills

1.C identify major causes and describe the major effects of the following important turning points in world history from 600 to 1450: the spread of Christianity, the decline of Rome and the formation of medieval Europe; the development of Islamic caliphates and their impact on Asia, Africa, and Europe; the Mongol invasions and their impact on Europe, China, India, and Southwest Asia

4.A explain the development of Christianity as a unifying social and political factor in medieval Europe and the Byzantine Empire

4.B explain the characteristics of Roman Catholicism and Eastern Orthodoxy

4.E describe the interactions among Muslim, Christian, and Jewish societies in Europe, Asia, and North Africa

NOTES

Economic Expansion and Change: The Crusades and After

Objectives

Objective 1: Summarize how new technologies sparked an agricultural revolution, and the revival of trade led to the growth of towns and cities.

Objective 2: Explain how a commercial revolution changed society and how guilds led to the rise of the middle class.

Objective 3: Explain the causes and effects of the Crusades.

Objective 4: Summarize how Christians in Spain carried out the Reconquista.

LESSON 4 ORGANIZER — **PACING: APPROX. 1 PERIOD, .5 BLOCKS**

	OBJECTIVES	PACING	RESOURCES: Print	RESOURCES: Online	TEKS	ELPS
Connect						
DIGITAL START UP ACTIVITY **Power of the Church**		5 min.		●	4.E	
Investigate						
READ **Changes in Agriculture Transform Europe**	Objective 1	10 min.	●	●	1.C	2.I.1
READ **Trade Expands and Towns Grow**	Objective 1	10 min.	●	●	1.C	
INTERACTIVE GALLERY **The Growth of Towns**	Objective 1	10 min.		●	1.C	
READ **Economic Changes**	Objective 2	10 min.	●	●	1.C	
READ **A New Middle Class**	Objective 2	10 min.	●	●	1.C, 24.A	2.F.2
READ **The Crusades**	Objective 3	10 min.	●	●	4.G, 16.A	
INTERACTIVE MAP **The Crusades 1096–1204**	Objective 3	10 min.		●	4.G	
READ **The Effects of the Crusades**	Objective 3	10 min.	●	●	4.G	
READ **The Reconquista**	Objective 4	10 min.	●	●	4.D, 4.E	
Synthesize						
DIGITAL ACTIVITY **Power of the Church**		5 min.		●	4.E	
Demonstrate						
LESSON QUIZ **Lesson Quiz and Class Discussion Board**		10 min.		●	1.C, 4.D, 4.E, 4.G	

PEARSON realize™ www.PearsonTexas.com Access your Digital Lesson

Focus on Texas Standards

Texas Essential Knowledge and Skills

4.D explain the political, economic, and social impact of Islam on Europe, Asia, and Africa

4.E describe the interactions among Muslim, Christian, and Jewish societies in Europe, Asia, and North Africa

4.G explain how the Crusades, the Black Death, the Hundred Years' War, and the Great Schism contributed to the end of medieval Europe

16.A locate places and regions of historical significance directly related to major eras and turning points in world history

23.B identify examples of religious influence on various events referenced in the major eras of world history

24.A describe the changing roles of women, children, and families during major eras of world history

NOTES

Topic 7 Lesson 5

The Feudal Monarchs and the Church

Objectives

Objective 1: Learn how monarchs gained power over nobles and the Christian Church, and how English kings strengthened their power.

Objective 2: Describe how traditions of government evolved under King John and later English monarchs.

Objective 3: Explain how strong monarchs unified France.

Objective 4: Describe the formation of the Holy Roman Empire and how some emperors struggled with the papacy to control specific religious and secular issues.

Objective 5: Analyze how the Church reached the height of its power under Pope Innocent III.

LESSON 5 ORGANIZER — **PACING: APPROX. 1 PERIOD, .5 BLOCKS**

	OBJECTIVES	PACING	RESOURCES: Print	RESOURCES: Online	TEKS	ELPS
Connect						
DIGITAL START UP ACTIVITY **A Challenge to Power**		5 min.		●	20.B	
Investigate						
READ **Feudal Monarchs Begin to Centralize Power**	Objective 1	10 min.	●	●	1.C, 4.A	
READ **English Kings Expand Their Power**		10 min.	●	●	1.C, 4.A, 4.B	2.G.1
READ **Developing New Traditions of Government**	Objective 2	10 min.	●	●	19.B, 20.B	
READ **Growth of the French Monarchy**	Objective 3	10 min.	●	●	4.A, 19.B	
INTERACTIVE MAP **The Growth of France 987–1328**		10 min.		●	4.A, 19.B	
READ **The Holy Roman Empire**	Objective 4	10 min.	●	●	4.A, 19.B	2.I.2
READ **A Pope and Emperor Feud**		10 min.	●	●	4.A, 19.B	
READ **The Battle for Italy**		10 min.	●	●	4.A, 19.B	
INTERACTIVE GALLERY **Battle for Power – Monarchs and Popes**		10 min.		●	4.A, 19.B	
READ **Church Power Reaches Its Peak**	Objective 5	10 min.	●	●	4.A, 19.B	
Synthesize						
DIGITAL ACTIVITY **Different Paths Develop Different Governments**		5 min.		●	4.A	
Demonstrate						
LESSON QUIZ **Lesson Quiz and Class Discussion Board**		10 min.		●	1.C, 4.A, 19.B	

Focus on Texas Standards

Texas Essential Knowledge and Skills

4.A explain the development of Christianity as a unifying social and political factor in medieval Europe and the Byzantine Empire	**20.B** identify the impact of political and legal ideas contained in the following documents: Hammurabi's Code, the Jewish Ten Commandments, Justinian's Code of Laws, Magna Carta, the English Bill of Rights, the Declaration of Independence, the U.S. Constitution, and the Declaration of the Rights of Man and of the Citizen

NOTES

Learning, Literature, and the Arts of the Middle Ages

Objectives

Objective 1: Explain the emergence of universities and their importance to medieval life.

Objective 2: Understand how newly translated writings from the past and from other regions influenced medieval thought.

Objective 3: Describe the literature, architecture, and art of the High and Late Middle Ages.

Objective 4: Examine the lasting heritage of the Byzantine Empire.

LESSON 6 ORGANIZER	PACING: APPROX. 1 PERIOD, .5 BLOCKS					
			RESOURCES			
	OBJECTIVES	PACING	Print	Online	TEKS	ELPS
Connect						
DIGITAL START UP ACTIVITY **A Hero's Tale**		5 min.		●	26.B	
Investigate						
READ **The Rise of Medieval Universities**	Objective 1	10 min.	●	●	4.A, 24.A	2.G.2
READ **New Knowledge Reaches Europe**	Objective 2	10 min.	●	●	20.C, 26.B	2.I.3
INTERACTIVE GALLERY **Medieval Innovation in Europe**		10 min.		●	26.B	
READ **Medieval Literature**	Objective 3	10 min.	●	●	26.B	
READ **Architecture and Art**		10 min.	●	●	26.B	
INTERACTIVE GALLERY **A Gothic Cathedral**		10 min.		●	26.A, 26.B	
READ **The Byzantine Heritage**	Objective 4	10 min.	●	●	26.B	
Synthesize						
DIGITAL ACTIVITY **Reach for the Sky**		5 min.		●	4.A, 26.B	
Demonstrate						
LESSON QUIZ **Lesson Quiz and Class Discussion Board**		10 min.		●	4.A, 20.C, 26.B	

Focus on Texas Standards

Texas Essential Knowledge and Skills

4.A explain the development of Christianity as a unifying social and political factor in medieval Europe and the Byzantine Empire

20.C explain the political philosophies of individuals such as John Locke, Thomas Hobbes, Voltaire, Charles de Montesquieu, Jean Jacques Rousseau, Thomas Aquinas, John Calvin, Thomas Jefferson, and William Blackstone

24.A describe the changing roles of women, children, and families during major eras of world history

26.B analyze examples of how art, architecture, literature, music, and drama reflect the history of the cultures in which they are produced

NOTES

Topic 7 Lesson 7

The Late Middle Ages: A Time of Upheaval

Objectives

Objective 1: Understand how the Black Death caused social and economic decline.

Objective 2: Describe the problems facing the Church in the late Middle Ages and how the Church reacted.

Objective 3: Summarize the causes, turning points, and effects of the Hundred Years' War.

LESSON 7 ORGANIZER		PACING: APPROX. 1 PERIOD, .5 BLOCKS				
	OBJECTIVES	PACING	RESOURCES Print	RESOURCES Online	TEKS	ELPS
Connect						
DIGITAL START UP ACTIVITY **The Black Death Approaches**		5 min.		●	4.G	
Investigate						
READ **The Black Death Spreads Across Europe**	Objective 1	10 min.	●	●	4.G	2.G.3
INTERACTIVE MAP **The Black Death**	Objective 1	10 min.		●		
READ **Crisis in the Church**	Objective 2	10 min.	●	●	4.G	
READ **The Hundred Years' War**	Objective 3	10 min.	●	●	4.G	2.I.4
INTERACTIVE MAP **The Hundred Years' War**	Objective 3	10 min.		●	4.G	
Synthesize						
DIGITAL ACTIVITY **Epidemics: Science vs. Fears**		5 min.		●	4.G	
Demonstrate						
LESSON QUIZ **Lesson Quiz and Class Discussion Board**		10 min.		●	4.G	

Focus on Texas Standards

Texas Essential Knowledge and Skills

4.G explain how the Crusades, the Black Death, the Hundred Years' War, and the Great Schism contributed to the end of medieval Europe

NOTES

Topic 7 Lesson 8

Russia and Eastern Europe

Objectives

Objective 1: Describe how geography influenced the rise of Russia, and how Kiev grew to be the center of the first Russian state.

Objective 2: Explain how Mongol rule affected Russia.

Objective 3: Describe how Moscow took the lead in Russia and how its rulers developed authoritarian control.

Objective 4: Describe how geography influenced the development of Eastern Europe.

Objective 5: Understand how migration contributed to cultural diversity in Eastern Europe, and learn about three early Eastern European kingdoms.

LESSON 8 ORGANIZER — **PACING: APPROX. 1 PERIOD, .5 BLOCKS**

	OBJECTIVES	PACING	RESOURCES Print	RESOURCES Online	TEKS	ELPS
Connect						
DIGITAL START UP ACTIVITY **Clans and Factions**		5 min.		●	1.C	
Investigate						
READ **The Geography of Russia**	Objective 1	10 min.	●	●	15.A	2.G.4
READ **Early Russia**	Objective 1	10 min.	●	●	4.B	
INTERACTIVE MAP **The Growth of Russia**	Objective 1	10 min.		●	4.B, 15.A, 16.C	
READ **The Mongols Conquer Russia**	Objective 2	10 min.	●	●	1.C, 4.K	
READ **Moscow Surpasses Kiev**	Objective 3	10 min.	●	●	4.K, 23.B	
READ **The Geography of Eastern Europe**	Objective 4	10 min.	●	●	15.A, 16.A, 23.B	2.I.5
READ **Migrations Increase Diversity**	Objective 5	10 min.	●	●	23.B	
READ **Early Kingdoms of Eastern Europe**	Objective 5	10 min.	●	●	23.B	
INTERACTIVE MAP **Jewish Migrations and Expulsions 500–1650**	Objective 5	10 min.		●		
Synthesize						
DIGITAL ACTIVITY **The Impact of the Mongols**		5 min.		●	1.C, 4.K	
Demonstrate						
LESSON QUIZ **Lesson Quiz and Class Discussion Board**		10 min.		●	1.C, 4.K, 15.A, 16.C, 23.B	

PEARSON realize™ www.PearsonTexas.com Access your Digital Lesson

Focus on Texas Standards

Texas Essential Knowledge and Skills

1.C identify major causes and describe the major effects of the following important turning points in world history from 600 to 1450: the spread of Christianity, the decline of Rome and the formation of medieval Europe; the development of Islamic caliphates and their impact on Asia, Africa, and Europe; the Mongol invasions and their impact on Europe, China, India, and Southwest Asia

4.K summarize the changes resulting from the Mongol invasions of Russia, China, and the Islamic world

15.A create and interpret thematic maps, graphs, and charts to demonstrate the relationship between geography and the historical development of a region or nation

23.B identify examples of religious influence on various events referenced in the major eras of world history

NOTES

Medieval Christian Europe (330–1450)

In this Topic, you will learn about life in Medieval Christian Europe. You know the TEKS are very important, and this course will make it fun to learn about the things that will help you master them. Keep reading to see how.

Your study will help you master these TEKS:

TEKS

1.C, 3.B, 4.A, 4.B, 4.C, 4.D, 4.E, 4.G, 4.K, 15.A, 16.A, 16.C, 19.B, 20.A, 20.B, 20.C, 23.A, 23.B, 24.A, 26.B, 29.F, 29.H, 30.C, 30.D

LESSON OUTLINE

Connect

My Story Video and Topic Essential Question—see how they connect to your past experience or to what you have already learned. The Essential Question for this Topic is: What should government do?

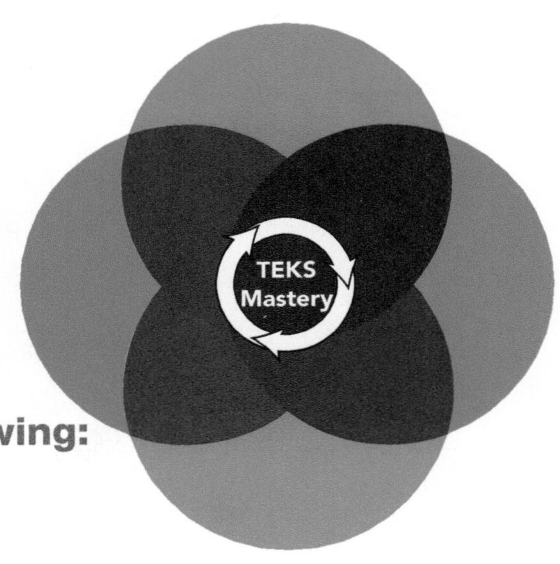

Begin your study by trying the following:

NBC LEARN Watch My Story Video:

Guédelon, a Medieval Castle

Launch your Project:

Create a Graphic Novel About Medieval Europe

Investigate

Then you will investigate the Topic through a group of lessons. The story of Medieval Christian Europe will come to life as you read and interact with key content. You will get a chance to read about what happened and why. And you'll be able to interact with a lot of fascinating online materials.

You'll also keep working on your Project as you build further mastery of the Topic TEKS.

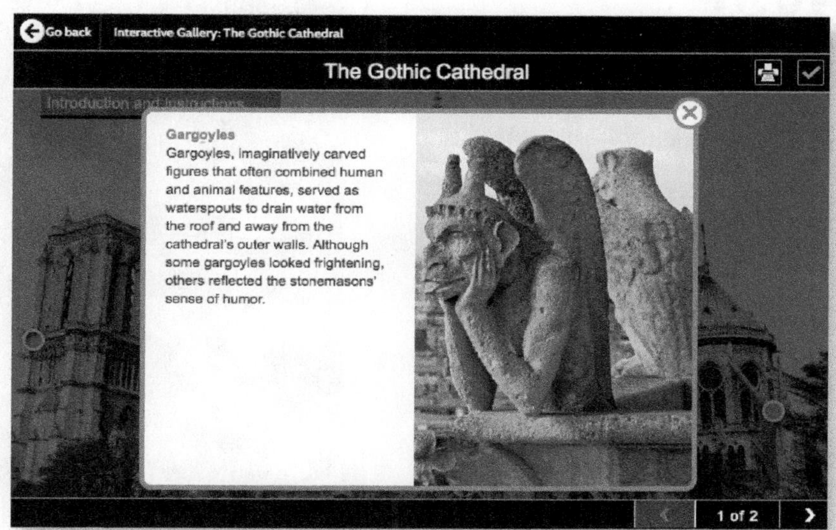

>> Digital interactivity from the online course

TEKS in Topic 7	Topic Review and Assessment Questions
1.C	2, 3
3.B	2
4.A	5
4.B	4
4.C	1, 6
4.D	17
4.E	16
4.G	22
4.K	7
15.A	14
16.A	19
19.B	9
20.A	11
20.B	10
20.C	12
23.A	13
23.B	15
24.A	18
26.B	8, 20
29.F	21
29.H	21
30.C	23
30.D	1

Synthesize

Next you will pull it all together by reflecting on the Essential Question. This will give you a chance to be the storyteller, to show how you would answer the big question.

Demonstrate

Finally, you can show what you know. You can write an essay, hold a discussion, or make a presentation. You can answer questions about every TEKS on the Topic Review and Assessment pages. Or you can finish your graphic novel about Medieval Europe.

Topic 7

Medieval Christian Europe (330–1450)

Introduction

After the decline of Rome, Western Europe entered a period of political, social, and economic disorder as waves of invaders swept across the region. A decentralized political and economic structure known as feudalism developed, and the Church became powerful. Improvements in agriculture, growing towns and cities, and a new middle class helped plant the seeds of our modern world.

ESSENTIAL QUESTION

Ask students to think about the Essential Question for this Topic: What should governments do? Project the Essential Question activity from the course. Ask students to decide which of the six activities they feel is an appropriate government activity. Then go over the results as a class.

Support a Point of View With Evidence Which activities did you consider an appropriate government activity? Why? What evidence did you use to make your judgment? *(historical records, facts about actual attempts of government and private elements to perform the tasks, reasoned judgments of experts)*

Identify Central Issues If not government at some level, who should take on these responsibilities? Do you think nongovernmental groups might do a better job in some cases than the government? *(Answers will vary. Some students may cite private nongovernmental groups as more cost-effective, while others may argue that some jobs are too big for anything but government to address.)*

Distinguish Among Fact, Opinion, and Reasoned Judgment Many people have strong opinions about some of the six responsibilities listed. What criteria can you use to separate facts from opinions if a topic is controversial? *(Criteria should include facts and historical records and awareness of special interests that could affect someone's stance on a position.)*

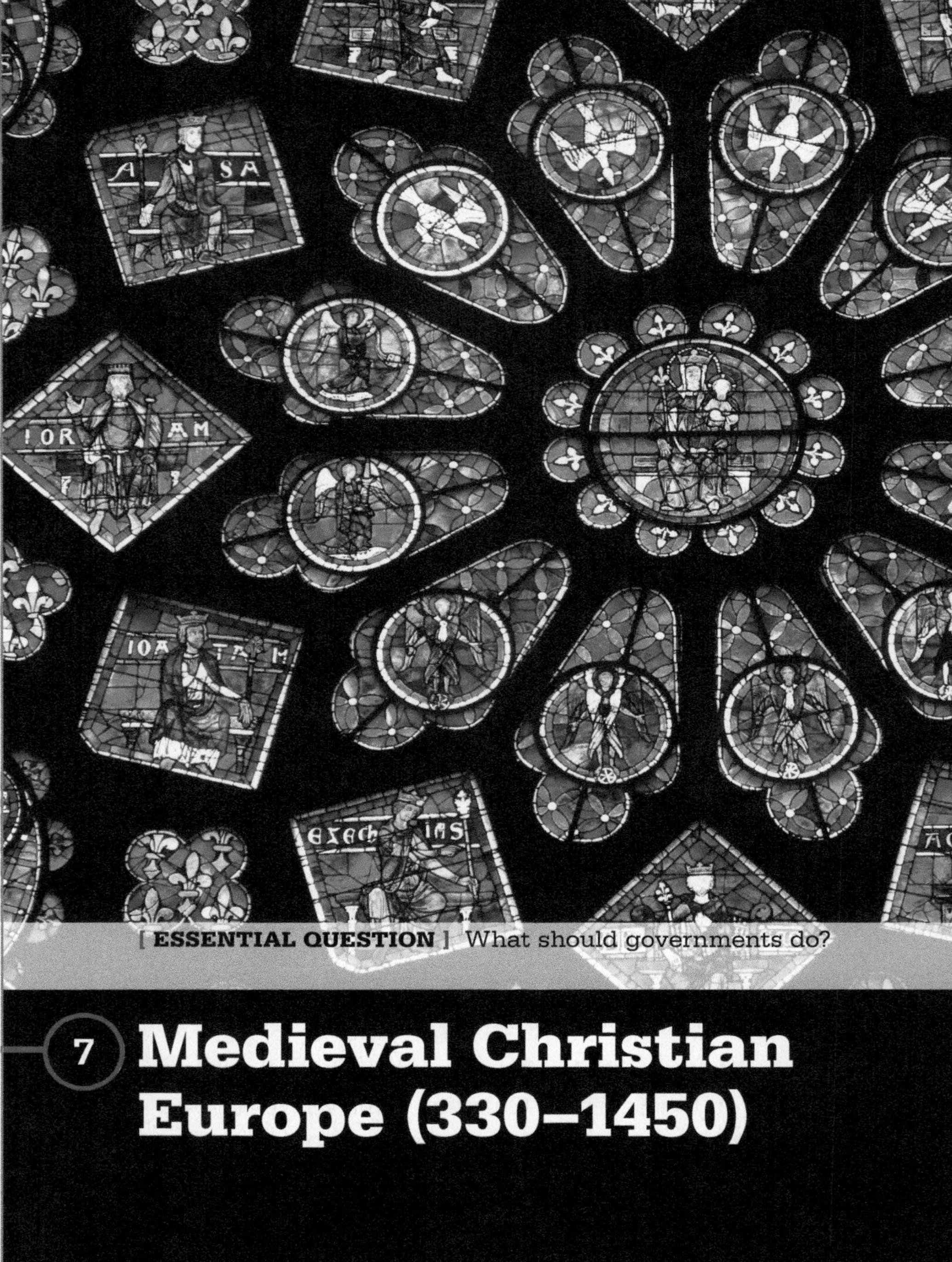
[ESSENTIAL QUESTION] What should governments do?
7 Medieval Christian Europe (330–1450)

Analyze Images

Ask students to examine the colorful image on this page. Explain that this is part of a stained-glass window in Chartres Cathedral in France, located about 50 miles southwest of Paris. The current building was mostly constructed between 1194 and 1220. Ask students to predict what this image tells us about the power and influence of the Catholic Church in Medieval Europe.

> Stained-glass window, Chartres Cathedral

Texas Essential Knowledge and Skills

1.C, 3.B, 4.A, 4.B, 4.C, 4.D, 4.E, 4.G, 4.K, 15.A, 16.A, 16.C, 19.B, 20.A, 20.B, 20.C, 23.A, 23.B, 24.A, 26.B, 29.F, 29.H, 30.C, 30.D

Enduring Understandings

- After the decline of Rome, Western Europe entered a period of disorder as invaders swept across the region.
- Medieval Europe saw the development of a political and economic structure known as feudalism.
- Improvements in agriculture led to a growing population and the revival of trade and travel.
- Religion shaped the lives of European Christians, and the Church came to wield considerable power.
- In the Crusades, Christians battled Muslims for control of the Holy Land in the Middle East.
- Changing conditions and the growing power of monarchs began to build the framework for the modern nation-state.

PEARSON realize NBC LEARN

Watch the My Story Video to see modern craftspeople build a castle using medieval tools and techniques.

PEARSON realize www.PearsonTexas.com

Access your digital lessons including: Topic Inquiry • Interactive Reading Notepad • Interactivities • Assessments

209

NBC LEARN MY STORY VIDEO

Project the My Story Video, which shows modern craftspeople building a castle using medieval techniques and materials.

Online My Story Video: **Guédelon, a Medieval Castle in the Making**.

OVERVIEW ACTIVITY

Project the **Timeline Activity: Medieval Christian Europe** showing the major events of the Middle Ages. During this Topic students will learn about all of these events and many more, but this timeline will provide a framework into which they can place the events they learn about.

Check Understanding In what year did the Black Death first appear in Europe? *(1347)*

Topic Inquiry

If you choose to assign the Topic Inquiry, launch the project after introducing the Topic.

D Differentiate Extra Support Ask a volunteer to point out the time intervals on the timeline and the overall range of time covered by this timeline. Ask: How many years are there between the launching of the First Crusade and the election of Innocent III as pope? *(103; First Crusade began in 1095; Innocent III became pope in 1198)*

The Early Middle Ages

CONNECT

Preview Have students preview the **Lesson Objectives** and the list of **Key Terms**.

Students can also preview all the **Key Terms** and **Academic Vocabulary** using the **Interactive Reading Notepad** on the digital course or preview a summary of the lesson in the **Reading and Note Taking Study Guide**.

Online Use the **Editable Presentation** found on the digital course to present the main ideas for this lesson.

Start Up Activity

Tell students that, in 1203, when the Crusaders arrived in Constantinople, they were amazed by its immense richness and vast size. Read aloud the statement attributed to 13th century knight and historian Geoffrey de Villehardouin.

> [T]hose who had never seen Constantinople opened wide eyes now; for they could not believe that so rich a city could be in the whole world, when they saw her lofty walls and her stately towers wherewith she was encompassed, and these stately palaces and lofty churches, so many in number as no man might believe who had not seen them, and the length and breadth of this town which was sovereign over all others.

Discuss If you were first seeing Constantinople in 1203, how would you have felt about such a vast city? What do you think makes such cities grow rich and successful, and then later decline?

Online You can also project the **Start Up Activity** from the course.

INVESTIGATE

Have students read the section using the **Reading and Note Taking Study Guide** to help them take notes and understand the text as they read.

The Byzantine Empire Thrives

Explain to students that as German invaders pounded the Roman empire in the west, Roman emperor Constantine and his successors shifted their base to the eastern Mediterranean. The center of this eastern Roman empire was Constantinople, rebuilt from the Greek city of Byzantium by emperor Constantine and made capital in 330 of what would be called the Byzantine empire.

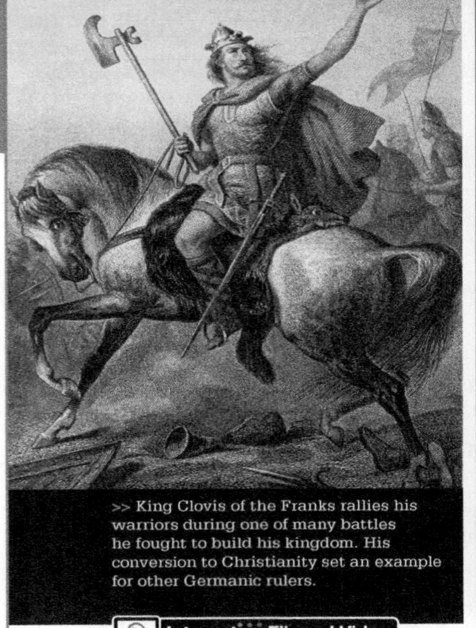

>> King Clovis of the Franks rallies his warriors during one of many battles he fought to build his kingdom. His conversion to Christianity set an example for other Germanic rulers.

Interactive Flipped Video

7.1 In European history, the thousand-year span between the fall of the Roman empire and the Renaissance beginnings of modern history is known as the Middle Ages. Perhaps best remembered today for knights on horseback and towering Gothic cathedrals, this medieval period began with the collapse of the western Roman empire.

TEKS
1.C, 3.B, 20.B

>> Objectives

Summarize ways in which the Byzantine empire flourished after the decline of Rome.

Explain the impact of the fall of Rome on Western Europe.

Describe how Germanic tribes carved Europe into small kingdoms.

Explain how Charlemagne briefly reunited much of Western Europe and what happened to his empire after his death.

>> Key Terms

Constantinople
Justinian
Justinian's Code
autocrat
Theodora
Clovis
medieval
Franks
Charles Martel
battle of Tours
Charlemagne
Magyars
Vikings

The Early Middle Ages

The Byzantine Empire Thrives

You have read that as German invaders pounded the Roman empire in the west, the Roman emperor Constantine and his successors shifted their base to the eastern Mediterranean. Constantine rebuilt the Greek city of Byzantium and then renamed it after himself—**Constantinople.** By 330, he made Constantinople the new capital of the empire. From this "New Rome," roads fanned out to the Balkans, to the Middle East, and to North Africa. In time, the eastern Roman empire became known as the Byzantine empire.

Constantinople Grows The vital center of the empire was Constantinople. The city was located on the shores of the Bosporus, a strait that links the Mediterranean and Black seas. Constantinople had an excellent harbor and was guarded on three sides by water. Emperors after Constantine built an elaborate system of land and sea walls to bolster its defenses.

Equally important, Constantinople commanded key trade routes linking Europe and Asia. For centuries, the city's favorable location made it Europe's busiest marketplace. There, merchants sold silks

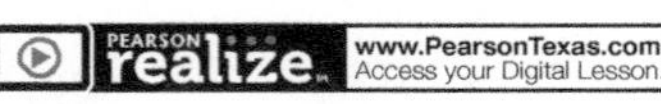

Aa Vocabulary Builder

1. Have students pronounce the following academic vocabulary terms in this lesson and clarify the part of speech. For difficult or polysyllabic words, break them into syllables and pronounce them with the students.
2. Explain what the word means in common "student-friendly" language using synonyms and antonyms when possible. Provide concrete examples to clarify the meaning, and rephrase the definition.

luxurious: of the finest and richest kind
embroidered: ornamented with needlework
unify: to combine into one

from China, wheat from Egypt, gems from India, spices from Southeast Asia, and furs from Viking lands in the north.

At the center of the city, Byzantine emperors and empresses lived in glittering splendor. Dressed in luxurious silk, they attended chariot races at the Hippodrome arena. Crowds cheered wildly as rival charioteers careened around and around in their vehicles. The spectacle was another reminder of the city's glorious Roman heritage.

A Blending of Cultures After rising to spectacular heights, the Byzantine empire eventually declined to a small area around Constantinople itself. Yet it was still in existence nearly 1,000 years after the fall of the western Roman empire. As the heir to Rome, it promoted a brilliant civilization that blended ancient Greek, Roman, and Christian influences with other traditions of the Mediterranean world.

? IDENTIFY Why did Constantinople become a rich and powerful city?

The Age of Justinian

The Byzantine empire reached its greatest size under the emperor **Justinian,** who ruled from 527 to 565. Justinian was determined to revive ancient Rome by retaking lands that had been overrun by invaders.

Led by the brilliant general Belisarius, Byzantine armies reconquered North Africa, Italy, and the southern Iberian peninsula. However, the fighting exhausted Justinian's treasury and weakened his defenses in the east. Moreover, the victories were only temporary. Justinian's successors would lose the bitterly contested lands, one after the other.

Hagia Sophia Justinian left a more lasting monument in the structures of his capital. In 532, riots and a devastating fire swept Constantinople. Many buildings were destroyed and many lives were lost.

To restore Roman glory, Justinian launched a program to make Constantinople grander than ever. His great triumph was rebuilding the church of Hagia Sophia (AH yee uh suh FEE uh), which means "Holy Wisdom."

Hagia Sophia's immense, arching dome improved on earlier Roman buildings. The interior glowed with colored marble and embroidered silk curtains. Seeing this church, the emperor recalled King Solomon's temple in Jerusalem. "Glory to God who has judged me

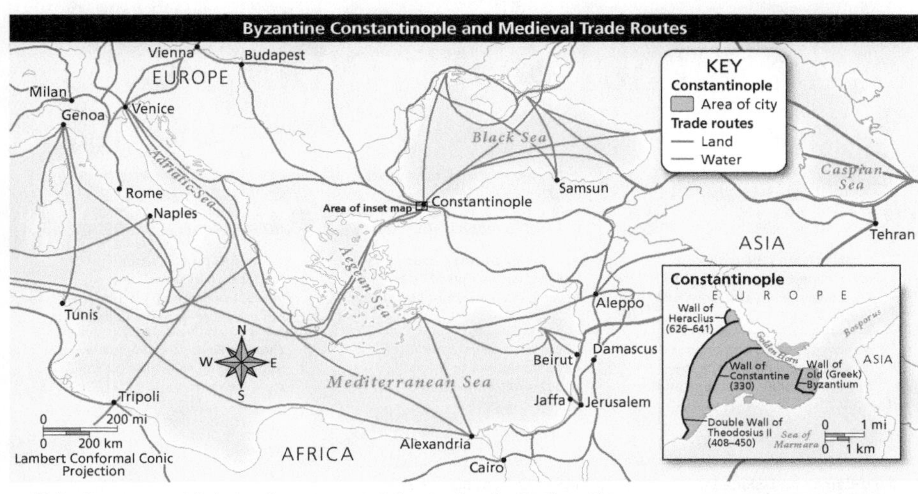

>> Major European and Asian trade routes met at Constantinople. **Analyze Maps** Summarize Constantinople's protective advantages.

Interactive Gallery

Topic 7 Lesson 1

The Age of Justinian

Explain to students that Justinian ruled the Byzantine empire from 527 to 565. Justinian's attempt to revive ancient Rome by retaking lands overrun by invaders brought the empire to its largest size under his reign. Justinian's desire to restore Roman glory can also be seen in the church of Hagia Sophia, which he had rebuilt, along with other parts of Constantinople, after a devastating fire in 532.

Online Project the **Interactive Gallery: Hagia Sophia**. Explain that Constantine's magnificent rebuilding of Hagia Sophia and much of Constantinople provides an example of how the Byzantine empire flourished after the decline of Rome. Point out that the history of this building reflects the interactions between Christian and Muslim societies. Click through the hotspots on the gallery and discuss the building's important architectural features as a church and as a mosque.

ACTIVE CLASSROOM

Have students describe Hagia Sophia's history using the If Photos Could Talk strategy. Ask: What do you think Hagia Sophia (the exterior photo in the Interactive Gallery) would say about the flourishing Byzantine empire and the years that followed if it could talk? What's your evidence? Have students present their responses to the class. *(Sample response: "As a church and mosque, I watched thousands of people from many different cultures praying, was destroyed and rebuilt luxuriously several times, and saw Constantinople's fortunes shift.")*

History Background

The Nika Revolt The fire that devastated Constantinople in 532 was not accidental. It was set purposefully by rioters during the Nika revolt. *Nika* was the word for "conquer" or "win," and was shouted by the crowds at the Hippodrome chariot races. Rival fans, known as the Blues and Greens, united in protest against the emperor and his government. They set fire to several important buildings, including part of the palace and the Church of the Holy Wisdom that adjoined it. The rioters demanded the dismissal of two of Justinian's ministers. Although Justinian acquiesced to their demands, the Blues and Greens were not appeased and proclaimed a new emperor, Hypatius. The empress Theodora convinced Justinian to fight back, and the general Belisarius crushed the revolt, killing thousands.

Answers

Identify *Protected by walls and water, it commanded key trade routes linking Europe and Asia, making it Europe's busiest marketplace.*

Analzye Maps *Sample answer: surrounded on three sides by water: the Bosporus, the Golden Horn, and the Sea of Marmara; protected by a system of defensive land and sea walls*

Topic 7 Lesson 1

Guided Reading and Discussion

One of Justinian's greatest achievements was his reform of the law. Early in his reign, he set up a commission to collect, revise, and organize all the laws of ancient Rome. The result is known as Justinian's Code.

Analyze Chart Make sure students understand how Justinian's organization of Roman laws helped unify the Byzantine empire and the impact of the Code's political and legal ideas on later rulers and the development of systems of law.

Draw Inferences Have students review the text and Justinian's Code. Ask: What was the impact of political and legal ideas contained in Justinian's Code of laws? *(Student answers may vary. Students should include that by gathering, organizing, and simplifying Roman laws, the Code helped unify Justinian's vast empire; its political and legal principles served as models for later Western European rulers' laws, helping leaders consolidate their power; and the Code became the main Roman law source, often borrowed from to develop civil and international legal systems in Western Europe, Latin America, Africa, and the United States.)*

Key Terms

Ask students to find the key term **autocrat** (in bold) in the text. Explain that the word describes a ruler who holds unlimited power and is answerable to no one. Tell students that people also use the word to refer to a bossy or domineering person.

worthy of accomplishing such a work as this!" Justinian exclaimed. "O Solomon, I have surpassed you!"

Justinian's Code and Its Impact Even more important than expanding the empire and rebuilding its capital was Justinian's reform of the law. Early in his reign, he set up a commission to collect, revise, and organize all the laws of ancient Rome.

The result was the Corpus Juris Civilis, or "Body of Civil Law," popularly known as **Justinian's Code.** This massive collection included laws passed by Roman assemblies or decreed by Roman emperors, as well as the legal writings of Roman judges and a handbook for students.

Justinian's Code had a legal and political impact far beyond the Byzantine empire. By the 1100s, it had reached Western Europe. There, monarchs modeled their laws on its principles, which would slowly, over many centuries, help them to centralize their power. Later, the code also guided legal thinkers who began to put together the international law in use today.

Justinian Rules With Absolute Power To Justinian, the law was a means to unite the empire. Yet he himself was an **autocrat,** or sole ruler with complete authority. Like earlier Roman emperors, he had a large bureaucracy to carry out his orders.

The emperor also had power over the Church. He was deemed Christ's co-ruler on Earth.

As a Byzantine official wrote, "The emperor is equal to all men in the nature of his body, but in the authority of his rank he is similar to God, who rules all." His control was aided by his wife, **Theodora.** A shrewd politician, she served as advisor and co-ruler to Justinian. At times, she even challenged the emperor's orders and pursued her own policies.

Economic and Military Power The Byzantine empire flourished under a strong central government, which exercised strict control over a prosperous economy. Peasants formed the backbone of the empire, working the land, paying taxes, and providing soldiers for the military. In the cities of the empire, trade and industry flourished. As coined money disappeared from areas once ruled by the Roman empire in the west, the Byzantine empire preserved a healthy money economy. The bezant, the Byzantine gold coin stamped with the emperor's image, circulated from England to China.

A prosperous economy allowed the Byzantines to build one of the strongest military forces in the world. Soldiers, ships, and sailors protected the empire, and fortifications protected its capital. The Byzantines also relied on a secret weapon called Greek fire, a liquid that probably contained petroleum. Thrown toward an

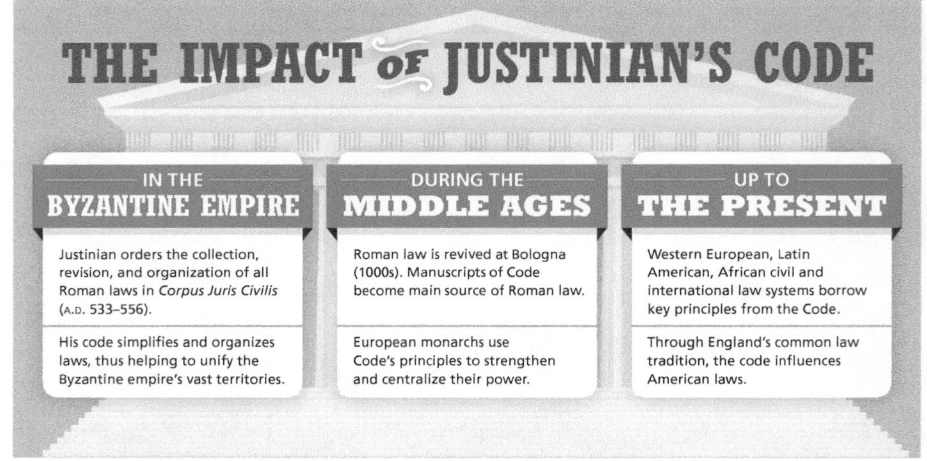

THE IMPACT OF JUSTINIAN'S CODE
IN THE BYZANTINE EMPIRE
Justinian orders the collection, revision, and organization of all Roman laws in Corpus Juris Civilis (A.D. 533–556).
His code simplifies and organizes laws, thus helping to unify the Byzantine empire's vast territories.
DURING THE MIDDLE AGES
Roman law is revived at Bologna (1000s). Manuscripts of Code become main source of Roman law.
European monarchs use Code's principles to strengthen and centralize their power.
UP TO THE PRESENT
Western European, Latin American, African civil and international law systems borrow key principles from the Code.
Through England's common law tradition, the code influences American laws.

>> Justinian commissioned an important reform of ancient Rome's laws. **Analyze Charts** How did Justinian's Code help rule the Byzantine empire? Why did the Code become so valuable later?

Answers

Analyze Charts *Sample answers: By providing a simpler, organized body of laws that applied to all Byzantine territories, Justinian's Code helped unify the empire; The Code became the main source for Roman law. Later, European leaders employed its principles to consolidate their power. Principles borrowed from the Code also played an important role in the development of international legal systems.*

English Language Proficiency Standards

Use with the reading "The Age of Justinian."

Listening 2.E.2

Beginning Read "The Age of Justinian" aloud. Point out appositives, and explain that the information following the comma provides additional information about what is being described. Help students find the appositives in a section of the text and identify which part of the sentence is the description and what is being described. Have students practice using appositives in conversation with these sentence frames.

I try to do my homework for my most difficult class, _____, before I get tired at night.

I try to eat my favorite food, _____, at least once a week.

Intermediate Use the Beginning activity, but have students identify which section of the sentence is the description and which section is being described before they practice using appositives in conversation with the sentence frames.

>> The Byzantine empire reached its greatest size by 565. **Analyze Maps** Describe the Byzantine empire's extent in 1020. **Infer** What does the empire's size in 565 suggest about Justinian's rule?

enemy, it would ignite on contact, and its fire could not be put out with water. For centuries, Greek fire was an effective and terrifying weapon of the Byzantine navy.

The Empire Declines The fortunes of the Byzantine empire rose and fell in the centuries after Justinian. Time and again, its skilled forces held off attacks by invaders. The empire withstood successive attacks by Persians, Slavs, Vikings, Huns, Arabs, and Turks. The empire thus served as a buffer for Western Europe by absorbing the brunt of invasions from the east. Among the fiercest attacks came from the Arab armies that were carrying a new religion, Islam, into the Mediterranean world and beyond.

In the 600s and 700s, Arab armies overran the wealthy Byzantine provinces of Egypt and Syria before advancing on Constantinople. The city held out, eventually turning back the attacks. By resisting the Arab advance, the Byzantine empire gave a measure of security to the small, weak Germanic kingdoms that had divided up Western Europe after the fall of Rome.

? DESCRIBE What were Justinian's accomplishments?

Changes in Western Europe

In Europe, the centuries after the fall of Rome are called the Middle Ages, which lasted from about 500 to 1350. The Middle Ages refers to the time between the ancient and modern worlds. During this long stretch of time, Western Europe passed through two distinct phases: the early Middle Ages, lasting from about 500 to 1050, and the late Middle Ages, lasting from about 1050 to 1350.

A Shift to the North At its height, the Roman empire included much of Western Europe. Rome unified the region and spread classical ideas, the Latin language, and Christianity to the tribal peoples of Western Europe. But Rome was a Mediterranean power. The Germanic peoples who ended Roman rule in the west shifted the focus to the north. There, the peoples of Europe would begin to create a new civilization, building on the legacy of Rome.

Despite the disorder and decay that came with the fall of Rome, Western Europe was a place of great potential. It had fertile land and other resources, such as timber, furs, and tin. In the early Middle Ages, gradual changes took place that would eventually bring a measure of order.

Changes in Western Europe

Tell students that after the western Roman empire fell, the lack of a centralized Roman state and powerful army had a strong impact on Western Europe. The populations of many cities declined during the period following the collapse of the western Roman empire.

Guided Reading and Discussion

Predict Consequences Have students imagine that a large country no longer has a centralized government or a strong army. What impact would that have on the country? Tell students to write three or four consequences that they predict would occur. List their predictions on the board. *(Sample responses: Regions become politically divided, become isolated from other regions, face rapid drops in trade, are threatened by invaders, and experience large declines in city populations.)*

Summarize Ask students to explain the impact of the fall of Rome on Western Europe. *(Answers will vary. Students should include that after the collapse of the western Roman empire, no centralized state backed by a strong army existed to maintain law and keep the peace in former Roman territories. Western Europe became politically divided, isolated, overrun by invaders, and experienced steep declines in trade and urban populations.)*

Advanced Working in pairs, have students read "The Age of Justinian." Point out one appositive in the text, explaining that what follows the comma can explain information before the comma. Have pairs find the appositives in the rest of the section, either highlighting them or copying them into a notebook. Ask students to practice using appositives as they discuss what they read with their partner.

Advanced High Explain appositives to students, focusing on an example from the text. After students read "The Age of Justinian" have them identify 2 or 3 appositives and explain how they enhance understanding of the content. Finally, ask students to turn to a partner and practice using appositives as they discuss how Constantinople was rebuilt after the devastation in 532.

Answers

Analyze Maps *Sample answer: It had shrunk to include southern Italy, the Balkans, Asia Minor, Crete, and Cyprus.*

Infer *Sample answer: that he was very successful and interested in acquiring territory*

Describe *rebuilt Constantinople; with autocratic rule unified and enlarged the empire to its greatest size; built the strongest military force in the world; restored Roman glory by rebuilding the Church of Hagia Sophia; reformed the laws of ancient Rome and created a "body of civil law" known as Justinian's Code*

Topic 7 Lesson 1

Germanic Kingdoms

Germanic tribes, such as the Goths, Vandals, Saxons, and Franks, divided up Western Europe into many small kingdoms. The former Roman province of Gaul, for example, was conquered in 486 by Clovis, king of the Franks, a Germanic tribe. Clovis converted to Christianity but also followed Frankish and Roman customs.

Guided Reading and Discussion

Analyze Information Remind students that Clovis chose to change his religion to that of his subjects in Gaul. Ask students to discuss the reasons for his conversion to Christianity. Then have students form small groups to research Clovis and present their findings to the class. *(Answers will vary. Students should include Clovis's personal beliefs, family traditions, and his intentions to gain support for his leadership from his subjects and the pope.)*

Infer Point out that Frankish tribes in Gaul included both pagans and Christians. Ask: How did the conversion to Christianity by Clovis impact his efforts to politically and socially unite his kingdom? Students may wish to research Clovis's reign. *(Answers will vary. Students should understand Gaul was a formerly religiously diverse region that was undergoing Christian conversion. Clovis's conversion could both distance him from pagan leaders and their communities and bring him closer to Christian leaders and their groups.)*

Be sure that students understand that Clovis and the Franks represent only one among many small kingdoms that appeared in Western Europe after the fall of the western Roman empire.

A Time of Decline As Rome declined and withdrew from its provinces in Western Europe, these lands suffered severe blows. Waves of invaders swept in, and Roman civilization slowly disappeared. Wars raged constantly. Trade slowed to a trickle, towns emptied, and learning virtually ceased.

The early Middle Ages was a harsh and difficult time for the peoples of Europe. Much later, some people looked back on this time and called it the "dark ages" because of the disorder and loss of Roman civilization. Today, historians recognize that the Middle Ages were, in fact, a time of new beginnings. During this long period, Greek, Roman, Germanic, and Christian traditions were slowly blended and gave rise to a new **medieval** civilization. *Medieval* comes from the Latin term for "middle age."

? DESCRIBE What was Western Europe like after the collapse of the western Roman empire?

Germanic Kingdoms

The Germanic tribes that conquered parts of the Roman empire included the Goths, Vandals, Saxons, and **Franks.** Their culture was very different from that of the Romans. They were mostly farmers and herders, so they had no cities or written laws. Instead, they lived in small communities governed by unwritten customs. Their kings were elected leaders, chosen by tribal counsels. Warriors swore loyalty to the king in exchange for weapons and a share in the plunder taken from defeated enemies. Between 400 and 700, these Germanic tribes carved Western Europe into small kingdoms.

>> In this illustration from the 1800s, Charles Martel swings his hammer (or "martel") against Muslim invaders in the battle of Tours, stopping their further advance into Europe.

The Kingdom of the Franks The strongest and most successful kingdom was that of the Franks. In 486, **Clovis,** king of the Franks, conquered the former Roman province of Gaul. Later, this area would be known as France.

Clovis ruled his new lands according to Frankish custom. At the same time, however, he managed to preserve much of the Roman legacy in Gaul.

Clovis took an important step when he converted to Christianity, the religion of his subjects in Gaul. In doing so, he not only earned their support, but he also gained a powerful ally in the pope, leader of the Christian Church of Rome.

Muslim Armies Advance Into Europe As the Franks and other Germanic peoples carved up Europe, a powerful new force, Islam, swept out of the Middle East across the Mediterranean world. Islam is a religion that began in Arabia around 622. Over the next 200 years, Muslims, or believers in Islam, built a huge empire and created a major new civilization.

The pope and the Christian kingdoms in Europe watched with alarm as Muslim armies overran Christian lands from Palestine to North Africa and Spain. When a Muslim army crossed into France, **Charles Martel** rallied Frankish warriors.

At the **battle of Tours** in 732, Christian warriors triumphed. To them, the victory was a sign that God was on their side.

Muslims advanced no farther into Western Europe, although they continued to rule most of what is now Spain. To European Christians, the Muslim presence in Spain and around the Mediterranean was a source of anxiety and anger. Even when the Muslim armies were no longer a threat, Christians continued to have a hostile view of the Muslim world. Still, medieval Europeans did learn from the Arabs, whose knowledge in many areas, especially science and mathematics, was extensive and exceeded their own.

? IDENTIFY How did the Germanic tribes govern their kingdoms?

D Differentiate Challenge/Gifted
Ask students to do additional research on Clovis, his conquest of Gaul, and his conversion to Christianity and present their findings.

Answers

Describe *politically divided, rural; little trade or contact with other regions*

Identify *Small communities were governed by unwritten customs. Warriors swore loyalty to the king in exchange for weapons and plunder.*

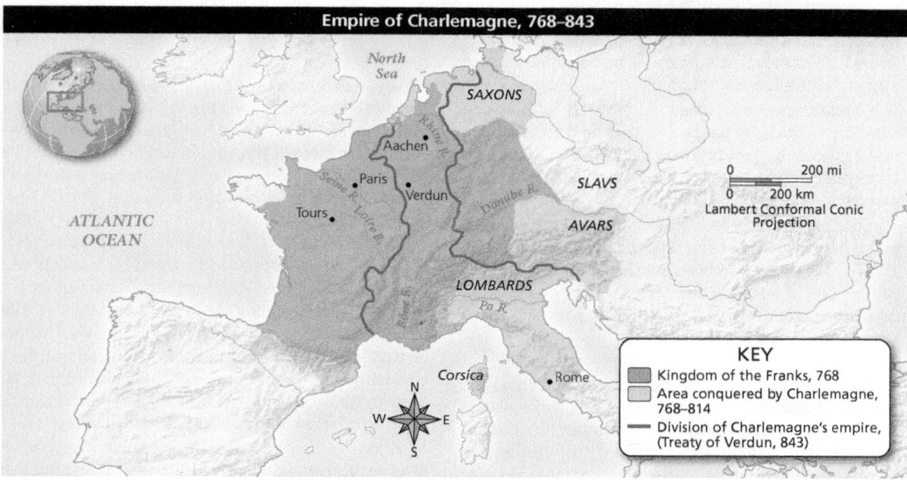

>> Charlemagne built an empire his descendants could not hold together. **Locate** Charlemagne's empire in 814. **Predict Consequences** What might be one result of the division of his empire? Explain.

Charlemagne Builds an Empire

In 768, the grandson of Charles Martel became king of the Franks. He built an empire reaching across what is now France, Germany, and part of Italy. The founder of this empire became known as **Charlemagne** (SHAHR luh mayn), or Charles the Great.

Charlemagne spent much of his 46-year reign fighting Muslims in Spain, Saxons in the north, Avars and Slavs in the east, and Lombards in Italy. Charlemagne loved battle and was a successful conqueror who reunited much of the old Roman empire in Europe.

Emperor of the Romans In 799, Pope Leo III asked Charlemagne for help against rebellious nobles in Rome. Charlemagne aided the pope against his attackers. On Christmas Day in the year 800, the pope showed his gratitude by placing a crown on Charlemagne's head and proclaiming him Emperor of the Romans.

This ceremony would have enormous significance. A Christian pope had crowned a Germanic king successor to the Roman emperors. In doing so, Pope Leo III revived the ideal of a united Christian community, which came to be called Christendom.

The pope's action also outraged the eastern Roman emperor in Constantinople. The Byzantine emperor saw himself as the sole Roman ruler. In the long run, the crowning of Charlemagne would deepen an already growing split between the eastern and western Christian worlds. Perhaps even more important, the crowning sowed the seeds for a long and desperate power struggle between later popes and Germanic emperors.

Creating a Unified Christian Empire Charlemagne set out to exercise control over his lands and create a united Christian Europe. Many of his subjects were pagans, as non-Christians were called. Charlemagne worked closely with the Church to spread Christianity to the conquered peoples on the fringes of his empire. During his reign, missionaries won converts among the Saxons and Slavs.

Like other Germanic kings, Charlemagne appointed powerful nobles to rule local regions. He gave them land so they could offer support and supply soldiers for his armies. To keep control of these provincial rulers, he sent out officials called *missi dominici* (MIH see daw mih NEE chee) to check on roads, listen to grievances, and see that justice was done. Charlemagne instructed the *missi* to "administer the law fully and justly in the case of the holy churches of God and of the poor, of wards and of widows, and of the whole people."

Charlemagne Builds an Empire

Throughout his long rule, Charlemagne, king of the Franks, conquered tribes and fought off invaders to forge an empire unified by Christianity in what became present-day France, Germany, and Italy. He established a strong government, spread Christianity—allying with the pope—revived Latin learning, and built schools. After Charlemagne's death in 814, his sons vied for power, his grandsons divided his empire, and new invaders, the Magyars and Vikings, threatened Europe.

Compare and Contrast Ask: How did Clovis and Charlemagne spread Christianity and employ it as a unifying social and political force in their kingdoms? Write responses on the board under "Clovis" and "Charlemagne." *(Answers may vary. Clovis: converts to Christianity, thus unifying his Christian subjects, gains support of pope; Charlemagne: a Christian, allies with Church, crowned by Pope Leo III as Emperor of the Romans, sends out missionaries)*

Guided Reading and Discussion

Identify Cause and Effect Why did Charlemagne support the creation of local schools and seek to revive Latin learning? *(Answers may vary but should include that Charlemagne felt education would help unify his kingdom. To govern effectively, his officials would need to write reports and keep careful records. Charlemagne also hoped to revive Rome's glory at his court in Aachen, where he brought Europe's top scholars to his Palace School.)*

D Differentiate Extra Support Ask students to read "Charlemagne Builds an Empire" aloud. As they read, list Charlemagne's accomplishments on the board. Ask students to use the notes to write a short obituary commemorating Charlemagne. Follow up by discussing why Charlemagne was considered the greatest ruler of early medieval Europe.

Answers

Locate *Review location with students: includes much of present-day France, Germany, and part of Italy.*

Predict Consequences *Sample answer: not as strong so more open to invasion; harder to carry on trade*

Topic 7 Lesson 1

New Invasions Pound Europe

Online Project the **Interactive Map: Invasions of Europe, 700–1000**. Point out that for three hundred years various groups both attacked and settled in Europe. Step through the layers on the map and discuss the impact that the invasions had on medieval society.

Analyze Images Ask: Where did the Magyars, Vikings, and Muslims come from?

ACTIVE CLASSROOM

Employ the Make Headlines strategy with the **Interactive Map: Invasions of Europe, 700–1000** to explore the invasions' impact. Ask: If you were to write a headline right now to capture the most important aspect that should be remembered about any invasion, what would that headline be? Pass your headline to a partner for review—that person can keep yours or ask for his or hers back. *(Sample response: "Vikings Strike from the Sea! Some Stay to Settle")*

Compare Have students consider how the collapse of Charlemagne's empire was similar to the collapse of the Roman empire. *(weakened when divided, then suffered attacks by outside plundering tribes)*

Charlemagne Revives Latin Learning Charlemagne hoped to make his capital at Aachen (AH kun) a "second Rome." To achieve this goal, he made a determined effort to revive Latin learning.

Charlemagne could read but not write. He is said to have kept a slate by his bed so that he could practice making letters. For him, education also served to strengthen his empire as he saw the need for records and clear reports.

To ensure a supply of educated officials, Charlemagne set up a palace school and brought scholars there from all over. He asked a famous scholar, Alcuin of York, to run his palace school. There, scholars were set to work copying ancient manuscripts including the Bible and Latin works of history and science.

Charlemagne's Legacy Although Charlemagne's empire crumbled, the great Frankish ruler left a lasting legacy. He extended Christian civilization into northern Europe and furthered the blending of Germanic, Roman, and Christian traditions. He also set up a system for strong, efficient government. Later medieval rulers looked to his example when they tried to strengthen their own kingdoms.

DESCRIBE How did Charlemagne unify Europe?

New Invasions Pound Europe

After Charlemagne died in 814, his son Louis I took the throne. Later, Louis's sons battled for power. Finally, in 843, Charlemagne's grandsons drew up the Treaty of Verdun, which split the empire into three regions. The empire was divided just at a time when these lands were faced with new waves of invasions.

Three Sources of Attack Between about 700 to about 1000, Western Europe was battered by invaders from other lands. Muslims, Magyars, and Vikings conquered lands across the region. Even after their defeat at Tours in 732, Muslim forces kept up their pressure on Europe. In the late 800s, they conquered the island of Sicily, which became a thriving center of Muslim culture. Not until the 900s, when power struggles erupted in the Middle East, did Muslim attacks finally subside.

About 900, a new wave of nomadic people, the **Magyars,** overran Eastern Europe and attacked the Byzantine empire. They moved on to plunder Germany, parts of France, and Italy. Finally, after about 50 years, they were turned back and settled in what is today Hungary.

>> **Analyze Maps** Use the map to find total distances the invaders traveled and number of routes taken. Rank the invaders from longest to shortest total distances traveled and most to least routes taken.

Interactive Map

Answers

Describe *He brought more land under his control, spread Christianity throughout his empire, sent missi to control provincial rulers and administer justice, and encouraged education.*

Analyze Maps *Sample answer: total distances: Vikings, Magyars, Muslims; number of routes: Vikings, Muslims, Magyars*

Describe *Muslims conquered Sicily. The Magyars overran a large area of Europe but eventually retreated back to present-day Hungary. Vikings from Scandinavia invaded, looted, and burned European communities, but also settled in parts of Western Europe where they mixed with local populations.*

Assessment

1. Justinian rebuilt Constantinople, formed a strong central government, reformed the laws of ancient Rome, built a powerful military, and preserved a healthy money economy throughout the Byzantine empire.
2. Justinian's Code provided principles on which Western European monarchs, from the 1100s on, modeled their laws. This helped rulers strengthen and centralize their power. Legal thinkers centuries later used the code as a guide to creating today's international law.
3. After Rome's collapse, its centralized state and powerful military no longer maintained the rule of law or kept the peace within its territories. Western Europe went into political, social, and economic decline. It became politically divided, predominantly rural as towns emptied, and cut off from advanced civilizations in the Middle East and Asia. Trade slowed and nearly ceased.

Viking Raids from the North The most destructive raiders, however, were the **Vikings.** At home, they were independent farmers ruled by land-owning chieftains. When they took to the seas, they snapped the last threads of unity in Charlemagne's empire. These expert sailors and ferocious fighters burst out of Scandinavia, a northern region that now includes Norway, Sweden, and Denmark. They looted and burned communities along the coasts and rivers of Europe from Ireland to Russia.

The Vikings were not just fierce warriors. They were traders and explorers as well. In their far-ranging voyages, they sailed around the Mediterranean Sea and crossed the Atlantic Ocean.

Leif Erikson set up a short-lived Viking colony on the continent of North America in about the year 1000. Other Vikings opened trade routes that linked northern Europe to Mediterranean lands. Vikings also settled in England, northern France (Normandy), Ireland, and parts of Russia.

DESCRIBE What European invasions took place after Charlemagne's death?

>> An illustration from the 1800s shows Charlemagne sitting back to listen as scholars and lords at his court read aloud to him, engage in lively discussion, and write in their manuscripts.

ASSESSMENT

1. **Summarize** In what ways did Justinian contribute to the flourishing of the Byzantine empire after the decline of Rome?
2. **Identify** What was the impact of political and legal ideas contained in Justinian's Code?
3. **Explain** What impact did the fall of Rome have on Western Europe?
4. **Describe** How did Germanic tribes carve Europe into small kingdoms?
5. **Explain** How did Charlemagne briefly reunite much of Western Europe, and what happened to his empire after his death?

SYNTHESIZE

Online Have students use the Think-Pair-Share strategy to answer the question in the Cooperation: The European Union activity. Ask them to take five minutes to write down some brief answers to the questions below, and then share their answers with a partner.

Ask partners to think about the following questions. What do you think were obstacles in unifying the nations in the European Union? How do you think these obstacles were similar to those Charlemagne encountered as he tried to unify his empire? Have pairs share their answers with the class.

Discuss Have students describe what they think governments should do to encourage cooperation as they try to unify diverse peoples into kingdoms or groups of nations, whether during the Middle Ages or today.

DEMONSTRATE

Online Assign the **Digital Lesson Quiz** for this lesson if you haven't already done so. Students will be offered automatic remediation or enrichment based on their score.

Pose these questions to the class on the Discussion Board:

Recognize Cause and Effect Why did the collapse of the western Roman empire lead to the formation of medieval Europe?

Draw Conclusions Why do you think that Charlemagne encouraged the spread of Christianity in his empire?

Topic Inquiry

Have students continue their investigations for the Topic Inquiry.

Classical learning almost disappeared. Waves of invaders swept through the region.

4. Germanic tribes, including the Goths, Vandals, Saxons, and Franks, lived in small communities. They were led by kings elected by tribal councils. These kings established their kingdoms by conducting wars of conquest. In exchange for weapons and a share in plunder taken from conquered peoples warriors swore loyalty to the king.
5. Charlemagne expanded his Kingdom of the Franks across today's France, Germany, and part of Italy by wars of conquest. Allied with the Pope, he sent missionaries to spread Christianity to the far reaches of his realm. This helped unify his empire because different regions and groups now shared a common religion. Charlemagne also sent out officials called *missi dominici* to keep control over his provincial rulers. In addition, he encouraged a revival of Latin learning and built local schools. After Charlemagne's death, his son Louis I ruled the empire. In 843, Charlemagne's grandsons divided his empire into three parts.

Topic 7 Lesson 2

Feudalism and the Manor Economy

CONNECT

Preview Have students preview the **Lesson Objectives** and the list of **Key Terms**.

Students can also preview all the **Key Terms** and **Academic Vocabulary** using the **Interactive Reading Notepad** on the digital course or preview a summary of the lesson in the **Reading and Note Taking Study Guide**.

Online Use the **Editable Presentation** found on the digital course to present the main ideas for this lesson.

Start Up Activity

Describe the following situation to students: A young man of good family, trained in warfare, has proven himself in battle. He has bravely assisted the knight he serves. As another battle looms, his knightly master now tells the young squire to kneel. The knight strikes the young man on the shoulder with the flat of his sword or his glove, and says, "I make you knight." As his sponsor, the older knight also presents the young man with a sword and spurs. Now the young man is ready to fight for his lord: he has become a knight.

Discuss If you lived in Europe during the Middle Ages, how would you have felt if your brother or friend trained and became a knight? How do you think the relationship between medieval squires and knights is similar to or different from the relationships between soldiers today?

Online You can also project the **Start Up Activity** from the course.

INVESTIGATE

Have students read the section using the **Reading and Note Taking Study Guide** to help them take notes and understand the text as they read.

Feudalism Develops

Explain to students that the political and social system of feudalism developed in response to the great need for protection Europeans felt during invasions by Vikings, Muslims, and Magyars. When kings and emperors could not maintain law and order, a loosely organized system of relationships arose between lords and vassals based on the exchange of land for loyalty and military service.

>> A monarch dubs a kneeling young man a knight. Two knights sponsor and stand by him in this French illustration from the late 1200s.

Interactive Flipped Video

7.2 In the face of invasions by Vikings, Muslims, and Magyars, kings and emperors were too weak to maintain law and order. People needed protection for themselves, their homes, and their lands. In response to this basic need for protection, a decentralized political and economic structure evolved, known as feudalism. Feudalism was a loosely organized system of rule in which powerful local lords divided their landholdings among lesser lords. In exchange, these lesser lords, or vassals, pledged service and loyalty to the greater lord.

TEKS
4.C

>> Objectives

Describe the development of the political and social system of feudalism.

Summarize the life of knights and nobles.

Analyze how the economic system of manorialism worked and how it affected peasants and nobles.

>> Key Terms

feudalism
vassal
feudal contract
fief
knight
tournament
chivalry
troubadour
manor system
Eleanor of Acquitaine
manor
serf

Feudalism and the Manor Economy

Feudalism Develops

In practice, feudalism varied greatly from place to place, and its traditions changed over time. Overall, however, feudalism became the basis for the political and economic system that governed life during the Middle Ages and beyond.

Mutual Obligations Medieval society involved a network of mutual obligations between the ruler and the ruled. The relationship between lords and vassals was both political and economic. It was based on the exchange of land for loyalty and military service. These vows were conducted publicly in front of witnesses.

The relationship between lord and vassal grew out of custom and tradition and involved an exchange of pledges known as the **feudal contract.** Under this system, a powerful lord granted his vassal a **fief** (feef), or estate. Fiefs ranged from a few acres to hundreds of square miles. In addition to the land itself, the fief included peasants to work the land, as well as any towns or buildings on it.

As part of this agreement, the lord promised to protect his vassal. In return, the vassal pledged loyalty to his lord. He also agreed to

PEARSON realize www.PearsonTexas.com Access your Digital Lesson.

Aa Vocabulary Builder

1. Have students pronounce the following academic vocabulary term in this lesson and clarify the part of speech. If necessary, break it into syllables and pronounce it with the students.
2. Explain what the word means in common "student-friendly" language using synonyms and antonyms when possible. Provide concrete examples to clarify the meaning, and rephrase the definition.

aristocrat: member of the nobility

provide the lord with 40 days of military service each year, certain money payments, and advice.

A Complex System Everyone had a place in medieval feudal society. At the top of the power structure stood the monarch. Below the monarch were the most powerful lords, who might have had titles such as duke or count. They held the largest fiefs. Each of these lords had vassals, and these vassals in turn had their own vassals. In many cases, the same man was both vassal and lord—vassal to a more powerful lord above him and lord to a less powerful vassal below him.

Because vassals often held fiefs from more than one lord, relationships between them grew very complex. A vassal who had pledged loyalty to several lords could have serious problems if his overlords quarreled with each other. What was he to do if both demanded his aid? To solve this problem, a vassal usually had a liege lord to whom he owed his first loyalty.

IDENTIFY What was the relationship between lords and vassals?

ELPS **ELPS 2.E.3** Use various types of support to understand the text as it is read aloud.

Nobles, Knights, and Warfare

During the Middle Ages, warfare was constant. For medieval lords and vassals, it was a way of life. Rival lords battled constantly for power. Both greater and lesser nobles trained from boyhood for a future occupation as a **knight,** or mounted warrior.

The Life of a Knight At the age of seven, a boy slated to become a knight was sent away to the castle of his father's lord. There, he learned to ride and fight. He also learned to keep his armor and weapons in good condition. Training was difficult and discipline was strict. Any laziness was punished with an angry blow or even a severe beating.

With his training finished, the youth was named a knight, often in a public ceremony. An older knight or the boy's future lord said words like these: "In the name of God, Saint Michael, and Saint George, I dub thee knight; be brave and loyal." Then the young knight took his place beside other warriors.

Knights usually fought on horseback using swords, axes, and lances, which were long poles. They wore armor and carried shields for protection. Other soldiers fought on foot using daggers, spears, crossbows, and longbows.

As the fierce fighting of the early Middle Ages lessened in the 1100s, **tournaments,** or mock battles, came into fashion. A powerful lord would invite knights from the area to a tournament to enter contests of fighting skill. At first, tournaments were as dangerous as real battles. In time, they acquired more ceremonies and ritual.

Castles and War During the early Middle Ages, powerful lords fortified their homes to withstand attack. The strongholds gradually became larger and grander. By the 1100s, monarchs and nobles owned sprawling stone castles with high walls, towers, and drawbridges over wide moats.

Castles were fortresses. Wars often centered on seizing castles that commanded strategic river crossings, harbors, or mountain passes. Castle dwellers stored up food and water so they could withstand a long siege. In time of war, peasants from nearby villages might take refuge within the castle walls.

The Lives of Noblewomen Noblewomen played active roles in this warrior society. While her husband or father was off fighting, the "lady of the manor" took over his duties. She supervised vassals, managed the household, and performed necessary agricultural and

>> The Frankish knight Godfrey of Bouillon helped lead the First Crusade. He refused the title of king of Jerusalem but accepted the crown. Songs described him as a "perfect Christian knight."

Interactive Gallery

Guided Reading and Discussion

Predict Consequences Ask students to write brief answers to this question: Do the major characteristics of the political and social system of feudalism encourage or discourage conflict? Have students form two panels and conduct a feudalism debate.

Draw Conclusions Why do you think land ownership became an increasing source of power for lords in the political and social system of feudalism?

Differentiate: Extra Support After students have read the section, write the terms *king, lord, knight,* and *peasant* on the board. Write "Responsibilities" and "Privileges" under each. Have students share examples of responsibilities and privileges of each level of European feudal society. Write examples on the board and ask students to copy them into their notebooks.

Nobles, Knights, and Warfare

Warfare was a way of life for medieval nobles. From an early age, boys trained to fight and ride as knights. To protect their homes, powerful lords built castles to withstand attacks.

Online Project the **Interactive Gallery: Defending a Castle**. Click through the hotspots around the castle. Introduce the gallery by telling students that under the political system of feudalism, lords could summon vassals to join them on military campaigns.

ACTIVE CLASSROOM

Pair students for an Audio Tour of the *Defending a Castle* gallery. Have the first student give the second a verbal "tour" of the castle—What does it show? Have the second student explain to the first what it means.

English Language Proficiency Standards

Listening 2.E.3 Read "Nobles, Knights, and Warfare" aloud. Then have students complete one activity according to their level of English proficiency.

Beginning Provide students with bilingual dictionaries. Reread "The Life of a Knight," pausing to write and display unfamiliar words. After reading one paragraph, demonstrate how to look up the listed words. Write, display, and read their meanings. Have students copy the words and definitions in their notebooks and draw an illustration to help them remember the meanings of the words. Then ask students to listen again with the word meanings in mind as you reread the paragraph.

Intermediate Provide students with bilingual dictionaries. Reread "The Life of a Knight" and ask students to raise their hands when they encounter unfamiliar words. Write and display these words. After reading one paragraph, assist students as they look up the listed words. Write, display, and read their meanings.

Answers

Identify *They had mutual obligations; lords provided land and protection; vassals provided loyalty, military service, money, and advice.*

Guided Reading and Discussion

Contrast How do you think the opportunities available to a noblewoman and a peasant woman differed within the political and social system of feudalism?

Make Generalizations Ask students: What positive effects do you think the code of chivalry might have had on the political and social system of feudalism?

Manorialism

During the Middle Ages, the economic system of manorialism supported the political and social structure of feudalism. On a lord's manor, or estate, mutual obligations tied together peasants and their lords.

Online Project the **Interactive Chart: The Medieval Manorial System**. Point out that the tiles on the chart represent rights and responsibilities exchanged by lords and peasants in the manorial system. Move the tiles to the appropriate column.

ACTIVE CLASSROOM

Have students imagine a conversation with a lord or peasant about shared rights and responsibilities on a manor. Ask students to write a question they would like to ask, what the lord or peasant would say, and what the student would say in response. *(Sample response: Student: "How does your lord protect you?" Peasant: "When raiders come, his soldiers guard our fields. We can stay safe in his castle." Student: "That must be a great relief.")*

medical tasks. Sometimes she might even have to go to war to defend her estate.

Some medieval noblewomen, like **Eleanor of Aquitaine,** took an active hand in politics. Eleanor inherited vast lands in southwestern France.

Through two marriages, she became queen of France and, later, queen of England. For more than 50 years, Eleanor was a leading force in European affairs.

A woman's right to inheritance was severely restricted under the feudal system, although women did sometimes inherit fiefs. Land usually passed to the eldest son in a family. A woman frequently received land as part of her dowry, and fierce marriage negotiations swirled around an unmarried or widowed heiress. If her husband died before her, a woman gained her rights to her land.

Like their brothers, the daughters of nobles were sent to friends or relatives for training. Before her parents arranged her marriage, a young woman was expected to know how to spin and weave and how to supervise servants. A few learned to read and write. In her role as wife, a noblewoman was expected to bear many children and be dutiful to her husband.

The Code of Chivalry In the later Middle Ages, knights adopted a code of conduct called **chivalry.** Chivalry required knights to be brave, loyal, and true to their word. In warfare, they had to fight fairly. For example, a knight agreed not to attack another knight before the opponent had a chance to put on his armor. Warriors also had to treat a captured knight well or even release him if he promised to pay his ransom. Chivalry had limits, though. Its elaborate rules applied to nobles only, not to commoners.

But chivalry also dictated that knights protect the weak, and that included both peasants and noblewomen. Few real knights could live up to the ideals of chivalry, but they did provide a standard against which a knight's behavior could be measured.

Chivalry raised women to a new status. In theory, if not always in practice, chivalry placed women on a pedestal. **Troubadours,** or wandering musician-poets, composed their love songs, praising the beauty and wit of women throughout the ages.

In epic stories and poems, they told stories of brave knights and their devotion to a beloved woman. Much later, ideas of chivalry would shape our modern ideas of romantic love.

DESCRIBE How was warfare central to life in the Middle Ages?

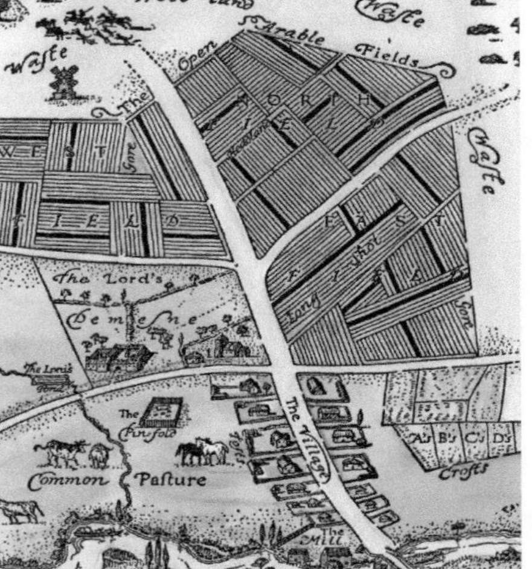

>> This diagram of the lands of a manor during Middle Ages shows where the lord's family and peasants' families live. **Contrast** How does this compare with the bird's-eye view shown later in the lesson?

Manorialism

The heart of the medieval economy was the **manor,** or lord's estate. Most manors included one or more villages and the surrounding lands. Peasants, who made up the majority of the population in medieval society, lived and worked on the manor.

An Economic System Under the **manor system,** also called the manorial system, the lord of the manor exercised legal and economic power over the peasants who lived on the estate. The lord administered justice and provided land and protection. In return, peasants owed their lord labor and goods.

Most peasants on a manor were **serfs,** bound to the land. Serfs were not slaves who could be bought and sold. Still, they were not free. They could not leave the manor without the lord's permission. If the manor was granted to a new lord, the serfs went along with it.

The Mutual Obligations of Lords and Peasants Peasants and their lords were tied together by mutual rights and obligations. Peasants had to work several days a week farming the lord's lands. They also repaired his roads, bridges, and fences. Peasants had to ask

Answers

Describe *Rival lords battled constantly for power and also fought invaders. This gave rise to a class of warriors called knights and to the development of the castle, used as a fortress for protection during warfare.*

Contrast *The lord's family lives in a large manor house set apart on the lord's home, or demesne. Peasant families live in small cottages and huts placed near each other. In both the diagram and the bird's-eye view, peasant homes are much smaller than the lord's house. They also are grouped closely together along a road rather than set on a large separate plot of land.*

English Language Proficiency Standards

Have students copy the words and definitions in their notebooks. Then ask students to listen again with the word meanings in mind as you reread the paragraph. Continue this activity with the rest of "Nobles, Knights, and Warfare."

Advanced Provide students with dictionaries. Ask students to work together in small groups to reread "The Life of a Knight." As one student reads out loud, the other students should write down any unfamiliar words. Instruct each group to write the words and their definitions in their notebooks. Groups should then reread the text and refer to their list of definitions as necessary to enhance their understanding of the text.

Advanced High Follow the instructions in the Advanced ELPS activity but have students work with a partner instead of a small group.

>> A bird's-eye view of a typical medieval manor, which might include a manor house, a village church, a grain mill, storage barns, a blacksmith's shop, clustered peasant huts, and fields for crops and grazing.

the lord's permission to marry. Peasants paid the lord a fee when they inherited their father's acres or when they used the local mill to grind grain. Other payments fell due at Christmas and Easter. Because money had largely disappeared in late Roman times, peasants had to pay fees with products such as grain, honey, eggs, or chickens.

In return for a lifetime of labor, peasants had the right to farm a certain amount of land for themselves. Under the system of mutual obligations, they were entitled to their lord's protection from raids or warfare. Although they could not leave the manor without permission, they also could not be forced off it. In theory, at least, they were guaranteed food, housing, and land.

The manor system supported feudalism. Lords and knights relied on their estates to provide them with food, lodging, horses, armor, weapons, money, and time to train for warfare.

A Self-Sufficient World During the early Middle Ages, the manor was generally self-sufficient. That is, the peasants who lived there produced almost everything they needed, from food and clothing to simple furniture and tools. Most peasants never ventured more than a few miles from their village. They had no schooling and no knowledge of a larger world outside.

A typical manor included cottages and huts clustered close together in a village. Nearby stood a water mill to grind grain, a church, and the lord's manor house. The fields surrounding the village were divided into narrow strips. Each family had strips of land in different fields so that good land and bad land were shared evenly.

Beyond the fields for growing crops, there were pastures for animals and meadows that provided hay. Only the lord had the right to chop wood or hunt animals in the forests that lay beyond the cleared land.

The Life of a Peasant For most peasants, life was harsh. Men, women, and children worked long hours, from sunup to sundown. During planting season, a man might guide an ox-drawn plow through the fields while his wife walked alongside, urging the ox on with a pointed stick. Children helped in the fields, planting seeds, weeding, and taking care of pigs or sheep.

The peasant family ate a simple diet of black bread with vegetables such as cabbage, turnips, or onions. They seldom had meat—that was reserved for the lord. Peasants who poached, or illegally killed wild game on their lord's manor, risked harsh punishment. If they lived near a river, peasants might add fish to their diet. At night, the family and their livestock—cows, chickens, pigs, or sheep—slept together in their hut.

Seasons and Celebrations Like farmers everywhere, peasants in Europe plowed in spring and autumn. In

Key Terms

Ask students to find the key term **serf** (in bold) in the text. Explain that serfs could not be bought and sold like slaves, but had to work in exchange for protection from the lord of the manor, who ruled and administered justice.

Guided Reading and Discussion

Identify Cause and Effect How might the decline of trade during the early Middle Ages have contributed to the self-sufficiency of the economic system of manorialism? *(The limited amount of outside goods available during those times made it necessary for communities to produce everything they needed.)*

Analyze Information Ask: What benefits did the medieval economic system of manorialism provide to serfs living on a manor? What drawbacks were there? *(Answers will vary. Benefits: fulfilled basic food, shelter, and protection needs; offered security along with the feeling of belonging to a community; Drawbacks: limited freedom, exhausting labor, minimal awareness of the outside world, poor living conditions)*

Identify Steps in a Process Have pairs of students research why manors had plantings in the spring and fall, and why a field was left fallow. *(Spring and fall plantings produced food that was available all year. A field was left fallow to replenish its soil nutrients.)*

SYNTHESIZE

Online Project the **Digital Activity: A Powerful Woman**. Have students work in small groups for five minutes to brainstorm and write down brief answers to the following questions. They should suggest what characteristics of the political and social system of feudalism made it possible for women like Eleanor of Aquitaine and some young men to achieve places of honor in the medieval world.

Draw Inferences Ask students to evaluate the roles available to medieval noblewomen, such as Eleanor of Aquitaine, and knights in the political and social system of feudalism.

DEMONSTRATE

Online Assign the **Digital Lesson Quiz** for this lesson if you haven't already done so. Students will be offered automatic remediation or enrichment based on their score.

Pose these questions to the class on the Discussion Board:

Make Comparisons Compare the rights and obligations of noblemen and noblewomen during the Middle Ages.

Draw Conclusions How did the manor serve the needs of peasants during the early Middle Ages? *(Answers may vary. Students should include that it provided land to farm; necessary services, such as milling grain; and safety and security during raids and war.)*

Topic Inquiry

Have students continue their investigations for the Topic Inquiry.

Answers

Describe *Lords granted land to peasants in return for their labor and certain fees. Lords also provided protection to peasants. Peasant labor on farms and as artisans made the manor self-sufficient during the early Middle Ages.*

summer, they harvested and hayed. At other times, they weeded and repaired. Hunger was common, especially in late winter when the harvest was exhausted. Disease took a heavy toll, and few peasants lived beyond the age of 35.

Still, peasants found occasions to celebrate, such as marriages and births. Welcome breaks came on holidays, such as Christmas and Easter. At these times, people might butcher an animal for a feast. There would also be dancing and rough sports, from wrestling to ball games.

 **DESCRIBE** How did the manor system operate?

ASSESSMENT

1. **Describe** Why did feudalism develop as a political and social system?
2. **Summarize** How did the lives of knights and nobles demonstrate the importance of warfare in the Middle Ages?
3. **Describe** What did noblewomen contribute to medieval warrior society?
4. **Analyze** How did the economic system of manorialism work, and how did it affect peasants and nobles?
5. **Identify Cause and Effect** What do you think caused peasants working on medieval manors to die so young?

Assessment

1. People needed protection for themselves, their homes, and their lands in the face of outside invaders. The system of feudalism evolved as a decentralized structure of mutual obligations between lords and vassals. By custom, tradition, and an exchange of pledges, land was exchanged for loyalty and military service.
2. Lords constantly fought each other for power. From an early age, many nobles trained to become knights. In the castle of their father's lord, they learned to ride, fight, and maintain their equipment. Knights fought in armor on horseback, using shields, swords, axes, and lances. Many nobles built and owned castles that served as homes and fortresses. Knights lived in the castles they defended.
3. Medieval noblewomen took over their husbands' lordly duties if they were away, brought inherited lands to their marriages, and ran the daily life of the manor or castle.
4. Mutual rights and obligations tied peasants and their lords together. Most peasants were bound to the land as serfs. They lived on the lord's land; worked the lord's fields; repaired roads, bridges, and fences; and paid fees, usually in the form of products. In return, lords gave peasants land to farm and provided protection.
5. Peasants on manors worked very hard, had poor diet, and sanitation, and were very vulnerable to disease.

7.3 Religion was woven into the fabric of the medieval world. Indeed, the Middle Ages has often been called Europe's "age of faith." The commanding force behind that faith was the Christian Church.

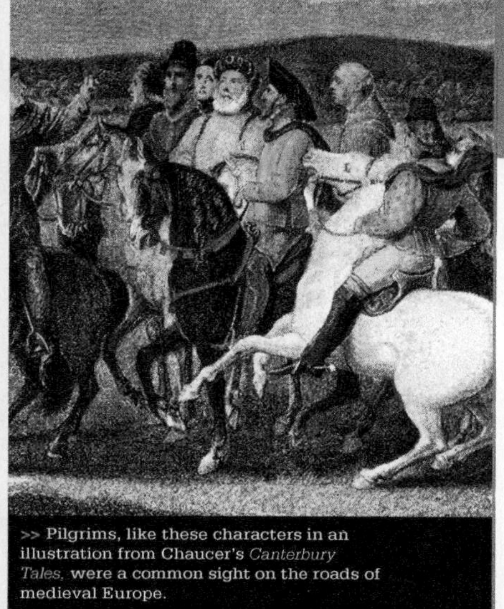

>> Pilgrims, like these characters in an illustration from Chaucer's *Canterbury Tales*, were a common sight on the roads of medieval Europe.

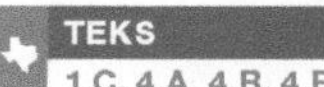

Interactive Flipped Video

The Medieval Christian Church

TEKS
1.C, 4.A, 4.B, 4.E

>> **Objectives**

Explain how the Christian Church shaped medieval life.

Understand monastic life and the influence of medieval monks and nuns.

Analyze how the power of the Church grew during the Middle Ages and how reformers worked for change in the Church.

Describe the situation of Jews in medieval Europe.

Analyze how Christianity in the Byzantine empire differed from Christianity in the West.

>> **Key Terms**

sacrament
Benedictine Rule
secular
papal supremacy
canon law
excommunication
interdict
friar
St. Francis of Assisi
icon
Great Schism
anti-Semitism
usury
schism

The Church Shapes Everyday Life

The Spread of Christianity During the early Middle Ages, the Church sent missionaries to spread Christianity to the diverse peoples of Europe. In 597, Pope Gregory I sent Augustine to convert the Anglo-Saxons in England. Other missionaries carried Christianity to Germanic tribes elsewhere in Europe.

By the late Middle Ages, Western Europe had built a civilization based on Christianity. Differences in language, culture, and government divided the peoples of Europe, but they shared a common faith and viewed non-Christians with suspicion and hostility.

The Parish Priest Christian rituals and faith were part of the fabric of everyday life. In villages, the priest of the parish, or local region, was often the only contact people had with the Church. The priest celebrated the mass and administered the other **sacraments**, the sacred rites of the Church. Christians believed that they needed the sacraments to achieve salvation, or the deliverance from sin into everlasting life. Priests passed on Church teachings and helped the

PEARSON realize. www.PearsonTexas.com Access your Digital Lesson.

Topic 7 Lesson 3

The Medieval Christian Church

CONNECT

Preview Have students preview the **Lesson Objectives** and the list of **Key Terms**.

Students can also preview all the **Key Terms** and **Academic Vocabulary** using the **Interactive Reading Notepad** on the digital course or preview a summary of the lesson in the **Reading and Note Taking Study Guide**.

Online Use the **Editable Presentation** found on the digital course to present the main ideas for this lesson.

Start Up Activity

Tell students that, during the medieval period, monasteries produced elaborately illustrated works known as illuminated manuscripts. These books, often religious in nature, were beautifully decorated by monks who specialized in the laborious process of copying by hand. Ask students to answer the following questions, and then have them share their ideas with a partner.

Discuss The monks believed their work on the illuminated manuscripts was a way of "fighting the Devil by ink and pen." What does this statement mean? How can illustrations "fight" against evil? *(The pictures in religious texts were a way to reinforce Christian beliefs, especially for those unable to read. From a Christian standpoint, this helped to spread Christianity and thus "fight evil.")*

Tell students that in this lesson they will learn that as Christianity spread, the Christian Church played a vital role in the everyday lives of medieval Europeans.

Online You can also project the **Start Up Activity** from the course.

INVESTIGATE

Have students read the section using the **Reading and Note Taking Study Guide** to help them take notes and understand the text as they read.

The Church Shapes Everyday Life

Explain to students the spread of Christianity throughout medieval Europe between 476 and 1050 was an important turning point in world history.

Aa Vocabulary Builder

1. Have students pronounce the following academic vocabulary terms in this lesson and clarify the part of speech. For difficult or polysyllabic words, break them into syllables and pronounce them with the students.
2. Explain what the word means in common "student-friendly" language using synonyms and antonyms when possible. Provide concrete examples to clarify the meaning, and rephrase the definition.

doctrine: something taught as the principle of a religion

abbot: head of a monastery

abbess: head of a convent

graven image: object of worship

divergent: differing from each other.

Topic 7 Lesson 3

Online Project the **Interactive Map: Spread of Christianity in Europe**. Introduce the activity by explaining that the spread of Christianity throughout medieval Europe was an important turning point in world history. Use the slider to view how Christianity spread across Europe between 476 and 1050.

ACTIVE CLASSROOM

After viewing the Interactive Map, ask students to pair up with a partner for a Circle Write. Ask students to answer the following questions: What do you see? What does that make you think? What are you wondering about now that you've seen this? *(Sample responses: Christianity spread to the east and north across medieval Europe. Christianity was an important part of people's lives. Why did so many people become Christians?)*

Analyze Maps In what directions did Christianity spread? How did Christianity spread across Europe? *(westward and northward; through the establishment of monasteries, by missionaries, and by monarchs deciding to become Christians)*

Guided Reading and Discussion

Why might Sweden, northern Scotland, and northwestern Russia around the Baltic Sea have been the last areas to be Christianized? *(It was more difficult for missionaries to reach these areas; the people and/or their rulers may have been less inclined to become Christians.)*

Predict Consequences Ask students to predict what they think the effects of the spread of Christianity in medieval Europe will be. *(Sample response: The different people in various regions will be united by their faith and religious practices.)*

sick and needy. If he could read or write, the local priest served as the only teacher in the village.

Priests also collected the tithe, or tax paid each year to the Church. The Church required Christians to pay a tithe, or tax equal to a tenth of their income. In the early Middle Ages, the tithe supported the local parish. Later, increasing amounts of money were sent to Rome.

The Village Church By the later Middle Ages, the church had grown into a social center as well as a place of worship, in part because it was the largest building in a village. Life revolved around the church calendar, which included holidays such as Easter and other holy days dedicated to important saints, or deceased people recognized for their holiness or virtue by the Church. The main events of a person's life took place at the church. The sacrament of baptism was a ceremony that admitted a person to the Christian community. Marriage, another sacrament, was performed at the entrance to a church. The dying received yet another sacrament, and when dead, were buried in the churchyard.

At first the village church was a simple building. Later, prosperous communities built larger churches of stone, rather than wood. Some churches housed relics, or the possessions or remains of saints and other holy figures. During the Middle Ages, many people made pilgrimages, or journeys to a sacred place, to pray or touch the relics.

The medieval writer Geoffrey Chaucer noted that, when spring comes,

> Then people long to go on pilgrimages . . .
>
> To seek the stranger strands
>
> Of far-off saints, hallowed in sundry lands
>
> —Geoffrey Chaucer, *The Canterbury Tales*

The Rise of Cathedrals Bishops, who supervised parish priests, managed larger churches called cathedrals. These magnificent buildings were a source of pride to the communities that built them. Cities all over Europe competed to build grander, taller cathedrals. Members of the Church contributed money, labor, and skills to help build these monuments glorifying their God.

Women and the Church The Church taught that men and women were equal before God. But on Earth, women were viewed as weak and easily led into sin. Thus, they needed the guidance of men.

At the same time, the Church offered the ideal woman, modest and pure in spirit, as reflected in Mary, whom Christians believed was the mother of Jesus. Many churches were dedicated to Mary, called the "mother of God" and the "queen of heaven." During the Middle Ages, Mary was a popular figure with many Christians who saw her as a sympathetic figure with the powers to help them in their struggles.

The Church tried at times to protect women. It set a minimum age for marriage. Church courts sometimes fined men who seriously injured their wives. Yet the medieval Church upheld a double standard, punishing women more harshly than men for similar offenses.

>> This mosaic from the 800s shows Mary, the baby Jesus, and two saints.

Interactive Map

SUPPORT IDEAS WITH EVIDENCE What was the role of the Church in everyday life during the Middle Ages?

Answers

Support Ideas With Evidence *The church was the social center of the village. Daily life revolved around the Christian calendar. People were baptized, married, and buried at their church. Some people went on pilgrimages and everyone was required to pay a tithe to the Church. The Church had the power to administer the sacraments.*

English Language Proficiency Standards

Listening 2.H.2 Read "The Church Shapes Everyday Life" aloud. Have students complete one activity according to their level of English proficiency.

Beginning Create an outline for students to complete. Read each subsection slowly, allowing for questions. Review content so that students may complete outlines. Provide assistance to students. Students may also include sketches.

Intermediate Follow the Beginning ELPS activity, but help students create an outline. Read each subsection, allowing time for students to add to their outlines. Students may use dictionaries and other references.

Advanced Have students take turns reading the section aloud, then creating an outline using the subsections as a guide. Have students read each subsection slowly so that students can complete their outlines. Provide reference materials.

Advanced High Have groups read and outline the subsections of the section. Have students discuss each subsection. Provide reference materials.

>> Medieval monasteries were centers of religious, educational, and community life in medieval Europe.

Life in Monasteries and Convents

During the Middle Ages, some men and women withdrew from worldly life to become monks and nuns. Behind the walls of monasteries and convents, they devoted their lives to spiritual goals.

The Benedictine Rule About 530, a monk named Benedict organized the monastery of Monte Cassino in central Italy. He created rules to regulate monastic life. In time, the **Benedictine Rule** was used by monasteries and convents across Europe.

Under the Benedictine Rule, monks and nuns took three vows. The first was obedience to the abbot or abbess who headed the monastery or convent. The second was poverty, or giving up worldly goods, and the third was chastity, or purity. Each day was divided into periods for worship, work, and study.

Benedict believed in the spiritual value of manual labor and required monks to work in the fields or at other physical tasks. Like peasants all over Europe at the time, monks and nuns cleared and drained land. They also experimented with crops. By helping to develop new farming methods, they contributed to the gradual improvement in the farm economy, which supported medieval life.

A Life of Service In a world without hospitals, public schools, or social programs, monasteries and convents often provided basic social services. Monks and nuns looked after the poor and sick and set up schools for children. Travelers, especially Christian pilgrims traveling to holy shrines, could find food and a night's lodging at many monasteries and convents.

Some monks and nuns worked in the outside world as missionaries. During the Middle Ages, men and women risked their lives to spread Christian teachings across Europe. Patrick was a monk who set up the Church in Ireland. Augustine was a missionary to the Angles and Saxons in England. Later, the Church honored some of its missionaries by declaring them saints.

Centers of Learning Monasteries and convents performed a vital cultural function by preserving the writings of the ancient world. Their libraries contained Greek and Roman works, which monks and nuns copied as a form of labor. Most monks and nuns had little education, but some were well educated. They wrote and taught Latin or Greek, the languages of the ancient world. In England, the Venerable Bede wrote the most important history of England in the early Middle Ages.

Convents Offer Opportunities for Women During the Middle Ages, many women entered convents. For

Life in Monasteries and Convents

Explain to students that the establishment of monasteries was a major force in the spread of Christianity. Monasteries also played an important role in medieval European villages by providing care for the sick and needy, forming schools, improving agricultural methods, and preserving knowledge.

Online Project the image of the **Interactive 3-D Model: Medieval Monastery**. Review the instructions and demonstrate to students how the model can be viewed from different angles. Click on the hotspots to learn more information about life in a monastery.

ACTIVE CLASSROOM

Ask students to break up into pairs and do an audio tour. Have the first student give the second a verbal "tour" of the monastery–what does it show? Have the second student give the first an explanation of what it means. *(Sample response: First student points out the dormitory and explains that monks lived very humbly and were not allowed personal possessions. Second student describes the Benedictine Rule and how living humbly and devoting their lives to their faith set a moral example for the community.)*

Guided Reading and Discussion

Draw Conclusions Monasteries and convents made important contributions to medieval society. Which contribution do you think was most useful to medieval society as a whole? Explain. *(Possible response: They preserved and protected knowledge, copied manuscripts, and contributed their own scholarship. Without them, this knowledge could have been lost.)*

Compare How did convents and monasteries help to unify medieval Europe? *(The services they provided to surrounding communities attracted Christian converts. The people were unified by the vital roles the Church played in their daily lives.)*

History Background

Marking Time Beginning in 1582, the Julian calendar established by Julius Caesar in 45 B.C. was replaced by the Gregorian calendar. Pope Gregory XIII's new calendar adjusted for a miscalculation of the Julian calendar in the length of the solar year. The Gregorian calendar is in general use in non-Muslim countries around the world today. During medieval times, the calendar was interspersed with holy days (from which comes our modern word *holiday*) and religious festivals. Some controversy exists as to whether the church purposely overlaid these holidays on the old pagan feast days, so as to make conversion easier for new Christians. Christmas occurs at the time of the ancient feast of the winter solstice, and the word *Easter* may derive from the Old English word for the goddess of spring and fertility, Eostre.

The Growth of Church Power

Explain to students that as Christianity spread, the Church's social, economic, and political power expanded as well.

Guided Reading and Discussion

Ask students to think about the causes and effects of the Church's growth in power. Explain how the spread of Christianity and the power of the Church affected one another. Review the problems of corruption within the church.

Compare and Contrast Ask students to explain the difference between interdict and excommunication. Then have them compare and contrast friars and monks. *(Excommunicated persons could not receive the sacraments or a Christian burial, while an interdict was an order excluding an entire town, region, or kingdom from receiving most sacraments and Christian burial; friars were monks who wandered the countryside and towns helping and preaching to poor people instead of living in monasteries.)*

Make Generalizations In what ways were Church authority and secular authority intertwined? *(Feudal rulers appointed highly educated Church officials to government positions. Church officials were often relatives of secular rulers. High clergy were usually nobles and had their own territories and armies.)*

Key Terms

Ask students to find the key term **canon law** (in bold) in the text. Explain that this term refers to a set of laws and regulations, established by Church authorities, for governing the Church and its members. The word *canon* refers to a measuring line or rule in Latin.

some capable and inquiring women, convents offered an escape from the restrictions of medieval society. In the 1100s, Hildegard of Bingen served as abbess, heading her own convent. She composed religious music, wrote scholarly books, and had visions of the future. As reports of her prophecies spread, popes and rulers sought her advice.

By the late Middle Ages, the Church had begun to restrict the activities of nuns. The Church withdrew rights nuns had once had, such as to hear confessions. It frowned on too much learning for women, preferring them to accept Church authority.

? DRAW CONCLUSIONS How did monks and nuns contribute to their surrounding communities.

The Growth of Church Power

During the Middle Ages, the Church became the most powerful institution in Western Europe. The Church not only controlled the spiritual life of Christians but also exercised enormous influence over **secular,** or nonreligious, affairs.

>> This illustration of Pope Sylvester II, who reigned from 999 to 1003, shows the power and pomp of medieval European popes.

A Spiritual and Worldly Empire During the Middle Ages, the Christian Church split into eastern and western churches. The western church, headed by the pope in Rome, became known as the Roman Catholic Church. The Roman Catholic Church grew stronger and wealthier during the Middle Ages.

The pope was the spiritual leader of Roman Catholic Christians but also ruled vast lands in central Italy, later called the Papal States. As the spiritual heir and representative of Christ on Earth, according to Church teachings, the medieval pope eventually claimed **papal supremacy,** or authority over all secular rulers.

The pope headed an army of clergy who not only supervised church activities but also influenced political affairs. The high clergy, such as bishops and archbishops, were usually nobles. Like other feudal lords, they had their own territories and armies. Since they were often well educated, feudal rulers appointed them to administer their own governments.

Church officials were closely linked to secular rulers. Churchmen were often highly educated, so feudal rulers appointed them to government positions. In addition, Church officials were often relatives of secular rulers.

Church Law and Authority The Church had complete power over spiritual matters and determined who could receive the sacraments. Without the sacraments, Christians believed that they faced everlasting suffering after death. The Church also developed its own body of laws, known as **canon law,** and had its own courts. Canon law was based on religious teachings and governed many aspects of life, from the behavior of the clergy to morals, marriages, and wills.

Anyone who disobeyed Church law faced a range of penalties. The most severe and terrifying penalty was **excommunication.** People who were excommunicated were cut off from the Church and its sacraments.

A powerful noble who opposed the Church could face the **interdict,** an order excluding an entire town, region, or kingdom from receiving most sacraments and Christian burial. Even the strongest ruler was likely to give in rather than face the interdict, which might cause revolts by the people under his rule.

Working for Peace By about 1000, the Church had begun to use its authority to limit feudal warfare. It tried to enforce periods of peace known as the Truce of God. It demanded that fighting stop between Fridays and Sundays and on religious holidays. Such efforts may have contributed to the gradual decline in private feudal wars that had raged in Europe for centuries.

Answers

Draw Conclusions *The monks and nuns improved the economy through better agricultural practices, established schools, cared for the sick and needy, preserved knowledge through libraries and copying books, provided spiritual leadership.*

CRITICISMS OF THE CHURCH	
Church Political Power Grows	The Church accumulated vast amounts of wealth and even controlled its own armies.
Simony	Simony involved the selling of Church land, spiritual offices, holy relics, or sacred property. The practice gave spiritual authority to people interested in monetary or political gain.
Selling of Indulgences	A complex system was developed to calculate earthly penance for sins and the required time a person must spend in purgatory, a physical place in which the soul was punished for sins on Earth, after death. Priests would reduce a person's penance or time in purgatory in exchange for contributions to the Church.
Growth of Church Wealth	Everyone was required to pay a tithe, or one-tenth, of his or her income to the Church. Peasants lacking money were required to provide goods, food, or livestock and regularly work on the Church's land without pay.

>> **Analyze Charts** Which criticism do you think common people felt most strongly? Why?

The Legacy of Judeo-Christian Teachings By the late Middle Ages, traditions that had grown out of Christianity and Judaism had helped shape many aspects of life in Western Europe. The blending of Jewish and Christian teachings much later were called Judeo-Christian ideas. The teachings of these religions, along with ancient Greek and Roman ideas about law and government, would lead to new ways of thought. In time, these ideas became the basis for republican forms of government in the modern world that emphasized democracy and human rights and rejected the power of hereditary rulers.

Judeo-Christian teachings emphasized the value of the individual and the importance of social responsibility, or the idea of people helping one another, especially those in need. These teachings also included the idea of free will, or the freedom of humans to make choices for themselves. Christianity emerged in the Greco-Roman world, where it absorbed ideas of equality before the law, consent of the governed, and individual liberty.

IDENTIFY CENTRAL IDEAS How did the Church gain secular power?

The Church Faces Calls to Reform

The very success of the medieval Church brought problems. As its wealth and power grew, discipline weakened. Powerful clergy grew more worldly, and many lived in luxury. Monks and nuns often ignored their vows. Priests, who were allowed to marry during this time, sometimes devoted more time to the interests of their families than to Church duties. The growing corruption and decay led to calls for reform.

Reform Movements In the early 900s, Abbot Berno set out to reform his monastery of Cluny in eastern France. First, he revived the Benedictine Rule, which required vows of obedience, poverty, and chastity. He then encouraged monks to follow solely religious pursuits and refused to allow nobles or bishops to interfere in monastery affairs. Instead, Cluny was placed under the direct protection of the pope. Over the next 200 years, many monasteries and convents copied these reforms.

In 1073, Gregory VII, a former monk, became pope and extended the Cluniac reforms throughout the entire Church. He prohibited simony (**SY** muh nee), or the selling of Church offices, and outlawed marriage for priests. Gregory then called on Christians to renew their faith. To end outside influence, he insisted that the Church, and not kings and nobles, choose Church officials. That policy would lead to a bitter battle of wills with the German emperor.

The Church Faces Calls to Reform

As its wealth and power grew, the Church became increasingly corrupt. As a result, reformers in the Church sought to change the situation.

Guided Reading and Discussion

Review the problems of corruption and the role of reformers within the Church.

Paraphrase Why did reformers find it problematic for priests to live lives of luxury? *(Because it was at the expense of the majority of the people. Individual wealth was accumulated due to corruption and abuse of power.)*

Answers

Analyze Charts *Perhaps the common people most resented the growth of Church wealth, in the face of their own poverty.*

Identify Central Ideas *Because the Church had absolute power over religious matters, any Christian could be penalized for disobeying. Entire regions could be punished for the actions of a ruler, causing revolts by the people.*

Topic 7 Lesson 3

Jewish Communities in Medieval Europe

Review how interactions between Jewish and Christian communities changed over time during the medieval period. Jews were treated differently in different geographic locations.

Guided Reading and Discussion

Ask what students know about anti-Semitism and discuss other kinds of religious, ethnic, and racial prejudice. Note the change in attitudes toward Jews in medieval Europe.

Summarize How were Jews treated in Muslim Spain? *(Muslim rulers were somewhat tolerant of other religions, and Jews flourished there.)*

Identify Central Issues Why might it have been difficult for Jews to celebrate their own religious holidays during the Middle Ages? *(Sample response: Because they could be viewed as outsiders for celebrating holidays that were not part of the Christian religious calendar. Since the majority of people within a village were Christian, Jewish celebrations would be conspicuous and reinforce the idea that Jews were not a part of the social structure.)*

The Christian Church is Divided

As in Western Europe, Christianity was also a strong unifying political and social factor in the Byzantine empire. The Church was a significant influence in the daily lives of the majority of Eastern Europeans. They worshiped and celebrated holy days according to the Church's religious calendar and looked to the heads of the Byzantine Church for leadership. Many revered holy religious images, or icons. Most people spoke Greek, the language of the Eastern Church. The religious philosophies introduced in Western Europe following the fall of Rome were not adopted in the East.

Preaching Orders A different approach to reform was taken by **friars**, or monks who traveled widely preaching to the poor, especially in Europe's growing towns. The first order of friars, the Franciscans, was founded by a wealthy Italian later known as **St. Francis of Assisi.** Giving up a comfortable life, he devoted himself to preaching the Gospels and teaching by his own example of good works.

The Spanish reformer St. Dominic also set up a preaching order of friars to work in the larger world. He called on friars to live in poverty, as the early Christians had. Dominic was particularly concerned about the spread of heresies, or religious beliefs that differed from accepted Church teachings. The Dominicans worked to teach people about official Christian doctrines so they would not be tempted into heresies.

Some women responded to the call for reform. They became Dominican nuns or joined orders like the Poor Clares, which was linked to the Franciscans. Often these orders welcomed only well-born women whose families gave a dowry, or gift, to the church. Another group, the Beguines (BEHG eenz), welcomed poor women who could not be accepted by other religious orders.

? SUPPORT IDEAS WITH EXAMPLES How did monks contribute to reforming the Church?

>> A Jewish religious procession winds its way through a medieval European street in the 1400s.

Jewish Communities in Medieval Europe

Medieval Europe was home to numerous Jewish communities. During Roman times, Jewish communities had sprung up all around the Mediterranean. After Rome put down the Jewish uprising in A.D. 70, Jews scattered farther afield. In their new homes, Jews preserved the oral and written laws that were central to their faith.

Communities in Spain and Northern Europe Many Jewish communities thrived in Spain. The Arab Muslims who gained control of Spain in the 700s were generally tolerant of both Christians and Jews. Jewish culture flowered in Muslim Spain, which became a major center of Hebrew scholarship. Jews also served as officials in Muslim royal courts.

Jews also lived in northern Europe. During the early Middle Ages, Christians and Jews often lived side by side in relative peace. Many Christian rulers valued and protected Jewish communities, although they taxed them heavily. Early German kings had given educated Jews positions in their royal courts.

Persecution Often, however, medieval Christians persecuted Jews. During the Middle Ages, the Church and local rulers barred Jews from many occupations such as trade and handicrafts. More damaging, the Church forbade Jews from owning land. Popes and rulers still turned to Jews as financial advisers and physicians, but in much of Europe, Jews lived in increasingly isolated communities.

By the late 1000s, as the Church's power had increased, **anti-Semitism,** or prejudice against Jews, grew. Christians blamed Jews for disasters such as epidemic diseases, famine, or economic hardship. Christians saw Jews as unfamiliar people and were suspicious of their culture and beliefs.

In some areas, Jews were required to wear identifying clothing, or to live in a specific crowded and forcibly segregated part of a city called a ghetto.

The Church forbade Christians from **usury,** or the practice of lending money at interest. Because Jews were barred from so many other professions, some Jews became moneylenders. Moneylenders played a key role as the medieval economy grew, but nobles and others who borrowed heavily resented their debts, which further added to anti-Semitism.

Between 1096 and 1450, Jews were persecuted and expelled from major European cities and states, including England, France, and parts of what is today Germany, Italy, Austria, and Hungary. In response to growing persecution, and after these expulsions, many

Answers

Support Ideas With Examples *They traveled around Europe's growing towns as friars, preaching to the poor and teaching by example.*

The Church Divides

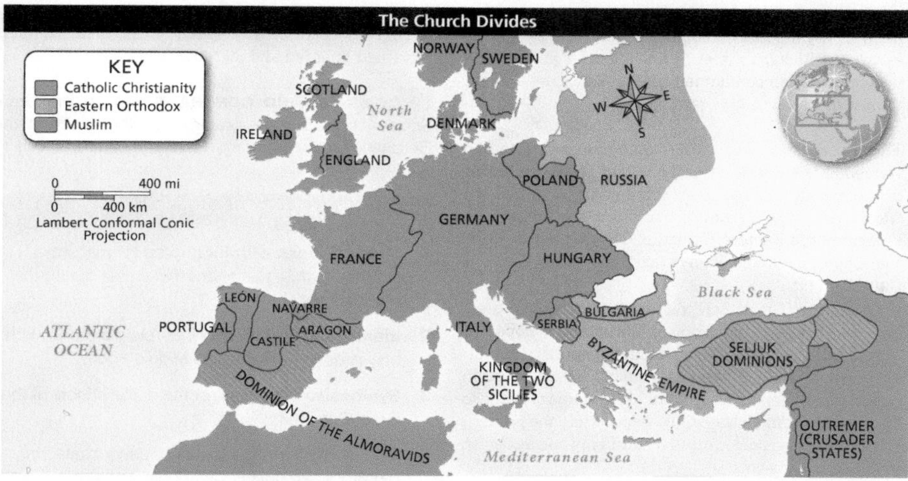

>> **Analyze Maps** What part of Europe was influenced by both the Roman Catholic and Eastern Orthodox Churches?

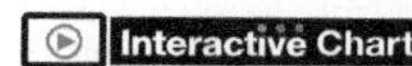

thousands of Jews migrated into Eastern Europe. Some local rulers there welcomed their skills and knowledge. Jewish communities grew, experiencing times of relative tolerance and prosperity, as well as periods of persecution.

DRAW CONCLUSIONS Why did prejudice against Jews increase as Christianity spread in the later Middle Ages?

The Christian Church Is Divided

During the Middle Ages, a growing divide split Christendom, as the Christian world was sometimes called. The divide opened up differences between Byzantine Christians in the east and Roman Catholics in lands to the west.

In general, Christians in both regions originally shared a common theology, or set of beliefs, and the same holy days in the Christian calendar, such as Christmas and Easter. Over time, however, the practices of Christians in the east and west grew apart. Long simmering controversies broke into open conflict, leading to a **schism,** or great divide, within the Christian world.

Differences East and West Since early Christian times, differences had emerged over Church leadership. Although the Byzantine emperor was not a priest, he controlled Church affairs and appointed the patriarch, or highest Church official, in Constantinople. Byzantine Christians rejected the pope's claim to authority over all Christians.

Other differences emerged during the Middle Ages. While reform movements in the West ended up forbidding the clergy to marry, Byzantine priests were allowed to marry. Greek, not Latin, was the language of the Byzantine Church. As in the Roman Church, the most significant Byzantine holy day was Easter, celebrated as the day Jesus rose from the dead. However, Byzantine Christians placed somewhat less emphasis on Christmas—the celebration of the birth of Jesus—compared to Christians in the West.

Dispute Over Icons Differences in customs and celebrations were a growing sign of the divide. A huge controversy erupted in the 700s over the issue of **icons,** or holy images. This dispute contributed further to the divide.

Many Byzantine Christians prayed to images of Jesus, Mary, and the saints. In 730, however, a Byzantine emperor outlawed the veneration, or honoring, of icons, saying it violated God's commandment against worshiping "graven images." The ban set off violent

Online Project the **Interactive Chart: The Church Divides**. Remind students that the Great Schism created the Roman Catholic Church in the West and the Orthodox Church in the East. Ask students to review the different beliefs, customs, and practices listed. Then drag and drop each one of the characteristics of Roman Catholicism and Eastern Orthodoxy into one of the two columns of the chart.

ACTIVE CLASSROOM

After completing the activity, ask students to break into groups to answer the following question: What are reasons the Eastern and Western Churches differed? Have students write as much as they can for one minute, and then switch with the person on their right. The next person tries to improve or elaborate the response where the other person left off. Continue to switch until the paper comes back to the first person. The group then decides which is the best response and shares that with the entire class.

Guided Reading and Discussion

Draw Conclusions Ask students to explain why the development of Christianity unified medieval Europe. Then have them discuss how the schism divided different parts of Christian Europe.

D Differentiate Special Needs
Remind students that the use of icons was a significant factor in teaching about Christianity to an illiterate population. Ask students to draw a picture that conveys a message without using words. The final illustrations should be understood by anyone without prior understanding.

Answers

Draw Conclusions *Jews were not part of the local parish, which influenced the everyday lives of Christian Europeans. Christians were suspicious of a culture they did not understand.*

Analyze Maps *The eastern part of Serbia was influenced by both the Roman Catholic and Eastern Orthodox Churches.*

Compare and Contrast *The Byzantine church used Greek instead of Latin. Byzantine Christians celebrated the use of holy icons. Papal supremacy was rejected in the Byzantine Church. Priests could be married in the Byzantine Church. Rejection of the* filioque *clause helped ignite the flames that caused the Great Schism.*

Topic 7 Lesson 3

SYNTHESIZE

Online Project the **Digital Activity: Role of the Church**. Review how to create a graphic organizer. Ask students to think about the types of power held by the Church and how it was used. Students can complete the activity independently, in pairs, or in groups. Discuss student answers from their graphic organizers. Ask students to evaluate the role of the medieval Church. How did it affect the everyday life of medieval Europeans? Explain how these events, as well as the Church's role in them, helped create unity in medieval Europe.

Evaluate Ask students to create a list of the different events in a person's life that were influenced by the Church.

DEMONSTRATE

Online Assign the **Digital Lesson Quiz** for this lesson if you haven't already done so. Students will be offered automatic remediation or enrichment based on their score.

Pose these questions to the class on the Discussion Board:

Summarize What roles did the Church play in daily life?

Compare and Contrast What was one difference between the Roman and Byzantine Churches before the Great Schism?

Draw Conclusions What institution, if any, fills the same role for people today that the medieval Church filled for Europeans in the Middle Ages? Have them cite evidence to support their claims.

Topic Inquiry

Have students continue their investigations for the Topic Inquiry.

battles within the Byzantine empire. The pope took a hand in the dispute, excommunicating the Byzantine emperor. Although a later Byzantine ruler restored the use of icons, the conflict left great resentment against the pope.

The Great Schism By 1054, other controversies had worsened the divide, leading to the **Great Schism,** or the permanent split between eastern and western Christianity. The Byzantine Christian Church became known as the Eastern Orthodox Church. In the west, the Church became known as the Roman Catholic Church.

After the Great Schism, other differences grew between the two branches of Christianity. Popes in Rome had long asserted their claim to papal supremacy. The patriarchs in the eastern Christian Church continued to reject this claim. The Roman Catholic Church had a single leader, the pope, while the Eastern Orthodox Church recognized a number of patriarchs, or high-ranking clergy.

During the many controversies that erupted between the Roman Catholic and Eastern Orthodox churches, popes and patriachs excommunicated each other. Although both churches still followed the same faith, the centers of power saw each other as rivals. During the Middle Ages and after, their contacts remained guarded and distant.

? COMPARE AND CONTRAST Prior to the Great Schism, how did the practice of Christianity in the Byzantine empire differ from that in Western Europe?

ASSESSMENT

1. **Support Ideas with Examples** In what ways did the Church gain economic power during the Middle Ages?
2. **Identify Central Ideas** What role did the Church play in daily life during the Middle Ages?
3. **Synthesize** What were some of the effects of the Great Schism?
4. **Draw Conclusions** How were Jews treated in Muslim Spain during the Middle Ages?
5. **Support Ideas with Examples** What were Church attitudes towards women in medieval Europe?

Assessment

1. The Church owned large tracts of land. Wealthy people willed riches to the Church. Agricultural and commercial activity in monasteries provided income.
2. The local parish was the center of most communities, performing marriages, baptisms, and funerals for the faithful. They provided mass and administered the sacraments, essential to avoiding an eternity in hell, according to Christian beliefs. Churches provided aid to the needy and moral guidance for society. Christians also shared a religious calendar, celebrating many of the same fasts, feasts, and festivals across Europe.
3. The pope and the patriarch excommunicated each other. The Church divided into the Roman Catholic branch in Western Europe, and the Orthodox Church in Eastern Europe.
4. Muslim rulers were somewhat tolerant of other religions, and Jews flourished there.
5. Doctrine taught they needed the guidance of men because the Church viewed women as weak and easily led into sin. The Church's ideal woman was embodied in Mary. The Church protected women by setting a minimum age for marriage and Church courts fined men who seriously injured their wives. Women often were punished more severely than men who committed similar crimes.

7.4 By about 1000, Europe was undergoing an economic revival. Over the next few centuries, remarkable changes greatly strengthened Western Europe. These changes began in the countryside, where peasants adopted new farming technologies that made their fields more productive. The result was an agricultural revolution that transformed Europe.

>> New farming technologies changed medieval Europe. In the fields, a new type of harness distributed pressure along the shoulders of the horse, which allowed the plowing of heavier soils.

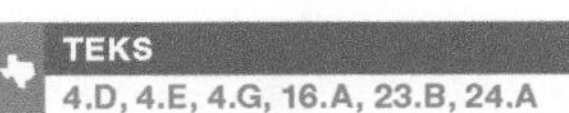

Economic Expansion and Change: The Crusades and After

TEKS
4.D, 4.E, 4.G, 16.A, 23.B, 24.A

Changes in Agriculture Transform Europe

Farming Technology Improves By about 800, peasants were using iron plows that carved deep into the heavy soil of northern Europe. These plows were an improvement over wooden plows, which were designed for light Mediterranean soils rather than heavier northern soils.

Also, a new kind of harness allowed peasants to use horses rather than oxen to pull the plows. Faster moving horses could plow more land in a day than oxen could, so peasants could enlarge their fields and plant more crops.

Food Output and Population Grow Other changes brought still more land into use. Peasants adopted a new way of rotating crops: the three-field system. They planted one field with grain; a second with legumes, such as peas and beans; and the third they left unplanted.

>> Objectives

Summarize how new technologies sparked an agricultural revolution, and the revival of trade led to the growth of towns and cities.

Explain how a commercial revolution changed society and how guilds led to the rise of the middle class.

Explain the causes and effects of the Crusades.

Summarize how Christians in Spain carried out the Reconquista.

>> Key Terms

- charter
- capital
- partnership
- tenant farmer
- middle class
- guild
- apprentice
- journeyman
- Holy Land
- Pope Urban II
- Reconquista
- Ferdinand and Isabella
- Inquisition
- Crusades

www.PearsonTexas.com
Access your Digital Lesson.

Topic 7 Lesson 4

Economic Expansion and Change: The Crusades and After

CONNECT

Preview Have students preview the **Lesson Objectives** and the list of **Key Terms**.

Students can also preview all the **Key Terms** and **Academic Vocabulary** using the **Interactive Reading Notepad** on the digital course or preview a summary of the lesson in the **Reading and Note Taking Study Guide**.

Online Use the **Editable Presentation** found on the digital course to present the main ideas for this lesson.

Start Up Activity

Tell students that later in this lesson, they will be reading about how the Pope called on European Christian knights to join a Crusade to free the Holy Land from control of the Turks.

Predict Given what you now know about the medieval Christian Church, predict whether Europeans will respond to the Pope's call to free the Holy Land from Muslim control. Why or why not? We'll come back to your predictions at the end of the lesson.

Online You can also project the **Start Up Activity** from the course.

INVESTIGATE

Have students read the section using the **Reading and Note Taking Study Guide** to help them take notes and understand the text as they read.

Changes in Agriculture Transform Europe

Trade Expands and Towns Grow

Explain to students that most towns and villages in the early Middle Ages were small, sparsely populated, and spread out over a fairly large geographic area. Over time, more efficient agricultural methods and tools lead to increased food production in Europe, which lead to population growth. As the population grew and warfare declined, trade increased to meet people's needs for goods and services that were not available on the manor.

Aa Vocabulary Builder

1. Have students pronounce the following academic vocabulary terms in this lesson and clarify the part of speech. For difficult or polysyllabic words, break them into syllables and pronounce them with the students.
2. Explain what the word means in common "student-friendly" language using synonyms and antonyms when possible. Provide concrete examples to clarify the meaning, and rephrase the definition.

stimulate: make more active
profitable: providing a financial gain
diverse: varied; different
undermine: weaken or ruin

Topic 7 Lesson 4

Online Project the **Interactive Gallery: Growth of Towns in the Middle Ages**, and move the slider to see how a typical town in the Middle Ages might have grown. Ask students to identify what has changed and why. Then ask students to think of instances where similar types of growth have taken place in their communities.

ACTIVE CLASSROOM

Use the Word Wall strategy and ask students to choose one of the vocabulary terms for the lesson and create a visual image with a definition. Allow approximately three to five minutes. Then ask students to post their words on the board or on chart paper and look at all the various responses. As a group, discuss similarities and differences in the responses, pick a favorite, and post it on the Class Word Wall for the year.

Guided Reading and Discussion

Discuss the causes and effects of the population growth in medieval Europe from 1000 A.D. to 1300 A.D. Provide historical background on the expansion of trade by pointing out that transportation was a major obstacle to trade in medieval Europe. Well-maintained concrete roads built at the height of the Roman empire had fallen into decay even though they remained in use. The lords who owned the lands through which the roads traveled were inconsistent in the roads' maintenance. They also could not provide adequate protection for merchant travelers from highwaymen. Travel by water was an alternative. Merchants from international ports such as Constantinople and Venice used sea routes, while other European merchants used rivers to transport goods.

Answers

Check Understanding *better plow and harness, increased acreage to farm, three-field system*

The legumes restored fertility to the soil and added protein to the peasants' diet. The new method allowed peasants to plant two thirds of their land, rather than half. In addition, lords who wanted to boost the incomes of their manors had peasants clear forests, drain swamps, and reclaim wasteland for farming and grazing.

All these improvements allowed farmers to produce more food. With more food available, the population began to grow. Between about 1000 and 1300, the population of Europe almost tripled.

CHECK UNDERSTANDING Why did agricultural production improve?

Trade Expands and Towns Grow

Europe's growing population needed goods that were not available on the manor. Peasants needed iron for farm tools. Wealthy nobles wanted fine wool, furs, and spices from distant lands. As foreign invasions and feudal warfare declined, traders reappeared, crisscrossing Europe to meet the growing demand for goods.

New Trade Routes Enterprising traders formed merchant companies that traveled in armed caravans for safety. They followed regular trade routes, many of which had hardly been used for centuries. Along these routes, merchants exchanged local goods for those from remote markets in the Middle East and from still farther east in Asia.

In Constantinople, merchants bought Chinese silks, Byzantine gold jewelry, and Asian spices. They shipped these goods by sea to Venice, where traders loaded their wares onto pack mules and headed north to Flanders. There, other traders bought the goods at trade fairs and sent them to England and lands along the Baltic Sea. Northern Europeans paid for these goods with products such as honey, furs, cloth, tin, and lead.

Trade Fairs and the Hanseatic League Annual trade fairs were an early sign of economic revival. Traders from all over Europe met at fairs near navigable rivers or where trade routes met. Trading lasted for weeks. The fairs became elaborate events with entertainments as well as goods.

The trade fairs gradually declined, in part because of competition from the Hanseatic League, an association of towns in northern Germany that banded together to protect their trading interests. The league used its shipping fleets to clear the northern seas of pirates and boost trade in furs, timbers, and fish.

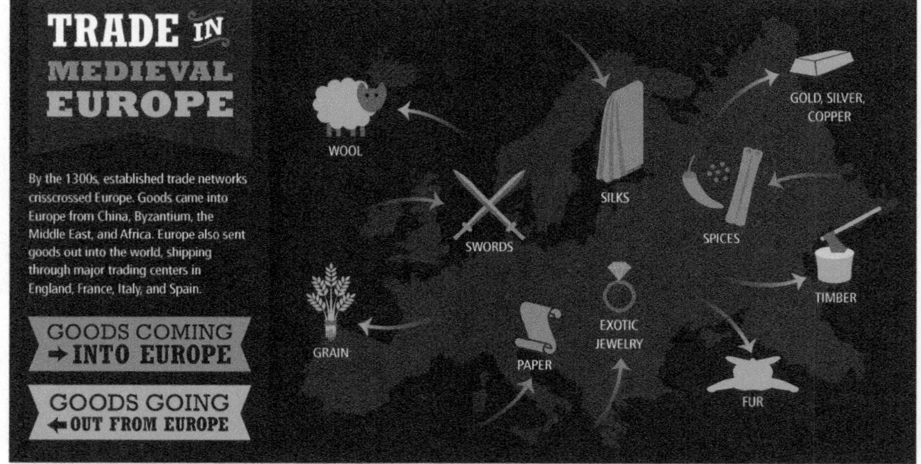

>> Active trade routes brought in new ideas as well as new goods.

English Language Proficiency Standards

Listening 2.I.1 Tell students that they will be creating a summary of the new technologies that caused an agricultural revolution. Read "Changes in Agriculture Transform Europe" aloud to students. Have students complete one activity according to their level of English proficiency.

Beginning As you read, use pictures and diagrams that help explain the text. Have students summarize by using these sentence frames:

- Old wooden plows were replaced by _____.
- Farmers could use horses to pull their plows because _____.
- The three-field system _____.

Intermediate As you read, define difficult terms and concepts for students. Have students summarize the material by creating a list of key words and phrases to explain the changes and new technologies that led to the agricultural changes in Europe.

>> **Analyze Visuals** Population growth in medieval towns led to growth and changes in many other areas as well. What evidence do you see of change that supports population growth?

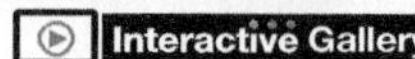

Towns and Cities Expand Many trade fairs closed in the autumn, when the weather made roads impassable. Merchants might wait out the winter near a castle or in a town. These settlements attracted artisans who made goods that merchants could sell.

Slowly, these small centers of trade and handicraft became the first medieval cities. Some boasted populations of 10,000, and by the fourteenth century, a few topped 100,000. Europe had not seen towns of this size since Roman times. The richest cities emerged in northern Italy and Flanders—the two ends of the profitable north-south trade route. Both areas were centers of the wool trade and had prosperous textile industries.

To protect their interests, the merchants who set up a new town asked the local lord, or the king himself, for a **charter.** This written document set out the rights and privileges of the town. In return, merchants paid the lord or the king a large sum of money, a yearly fee, or both.

Although charters varied from place to place, they almost always granted townspeople the right to choose their own leaders and control their own affairs. A common saying of the late Middle Ages was "Town air makes free."

Town and City Life Medieval towns and cities were surrounded by high, protective walls. As a city grew, space within the walls filled to overflowing, and newcomers had to settle in the fields outside the walls. Because of overcrowding, city dwellers added second and third stories to their houses and shops. Therefore, a typical medieval city was a jumble of narrow streets lined with tall houses.

Most towns were filthy, smelly, noisy, and crowded—a perfect breeding ground for disease. Even a rich town had no garbage collection or sewer system, so residents simply flung their wastes into the street. Fire was a constant danger with wooden houses so closely packed together. Despite the drawbacks of town and city life, people were attracted to the opportunities available there.

 **CHECK UNDERSTANDING** How and why did medieval towns and cities grow?

Economic Changes

During the turmoil of the early Middle Ages, coined money largely disappeared. As trade revived after 1000, money again appeared in circulation, coined by rulers. In time, the need for **capital,** or money for investment, grew. Merchants, for example, needed capital to buy goods, so they borrowed from moneylenders. Over time, the need for capital led to the growth of banking houses.

Draw Inferences What types of towns would be likely to attract the greatest variety of merchants? *(towns with good transportation systems, adequate security against robbers, and a large enough population to make the trip profitable for the merchant)*

Analyze Maps Direct students' attention to the map on the previous page showing trade in medieval Europe. Discuss the variety of goods represented. Ask students to think about the links between the producers of goods in Europe and producers of goods in other countries like Asia and the Byzantine empire. How did trade benefit everyone involved?

Key Terms

Ask students to find the key term **capital** (in bold) in the text. Explain that capital in an economic sense is material wealth in the form of money or property and is a resource that can be used to generate economic wealth.

Advanced As you read, have students note difficult terms and give them a dictionary or other resource to define them. Have students summarize the material by writing one sentence about each of the three main developments that improved agriculture.

Advanced High Follow the instructions from the Advanced activity, but have students write a short paragraph describing the new developments.

Answers

Analyze Visuals *There are more people, houses, boats on the river, more carts on the roads carrying goods and people.*

Check Understanding *Towns grew because of increased trade, the growth of trade fairs, the decline of serfdom, and the increased use of money.*

Topic 7 Lesson 4

Economic Changes

A New Middle Class

Explain that the growth of trade led to more people choosing to make trade the source of their livelihoods. This included people who produced goods, such as weavers, ironworkers, and goldsmiths. As tradespeople, these skilled individuals lived in towns where making goods or selling them would be part of each day rather than just a few trade fairs each year. The opportunities available in towns allowed some to earn more money than they had as farmers. They were not nobles, but they were not peasants either; they were in a new economic group – the middle class. This commercial revolution also affected women and children in families. Women and children often helped in what had become the family business. Some women were able to trade on their own. This was a dramatic change from life in the fields. Town life also presented educational opportunities for children.

>> This image shows banking operations in the 1400s. The man at the right is depositing a bag of gold.

>> Letters of credit worked like medieval credit cards. Purchases or cash withdrawals could be made without money actually changing hands.

New Ways of Doing Business To meet the needs of the changing economy, Europeans developed new ways of doing business. Groups of merchants joined together in **partnerships.** They pooled their funds to finance a large-scale venture that would have been too costly for any individual trader. This practice made capital more easily available. It also reduced the risk for any one partner because no one had to invest all his or her capital in the company.

Later, merchants developed a system of insurance to help reduce business risks. For a small fee, an underwriter insured the merchant's shipment. If the shipment was lost or destroyed, the underwriter paid the merchant most of its value. If the goods arrived safely, the merchant lost only the insurance payment.

Europeans adopted some practices from Arab and Muslim merchants with whom they traded. Among the most important were bills of exchange and letters of credit. With a bill of exchange, a merchant would deposit money with a banker in his home city. The banker would issue a bill of exchange, which the merchant could exchange for cash in a distant city. The merchant could thus travel without carrying gold coins, which were easily stolen. A letter of credit guaranteed payment of a set sum of money after the seller met certain conditions.

Changes Affect Medieval Society These new business practices were part of a commercial revolution that transformed the medieval economy. Slowly, they also reshaped medieval society.

For example, the use of money undermined serfdom. Feudal lords needed money to buy fine goods. As a result, many peasants began selling farm products to townspeople and paying rent to their lord in cash rather than in labor. By 1300, most peasants in Western Europe were either **tenant farmers,** who paid rent for their land, or hired farm laborers.

In growing towns, the old social order of nobles, clergy, and peasants also changed. By 1000, a new class appeared that included merchants, traders, and artisans. They formed a **middle class,** standing between nobles and peasants.

DESCRIBE Describe three economic changes in medieval Europe.

A New Middle Class

In the growing towns and cities of medieval Europe, a new middle class emerged. The middle class, made up of merchants, artisans, and tradespeople, stood outside the old feudal order. Although they ranked between

Answers

Describe *partnerships, insurance, bills of exchange, or how money undermined serfdom*

English Language Proficiency Standards

Listening 2.F.2 Read aloud, or have students read, "A New Middle Class." Then read the French apprenticeship agreement, 1248, as Peter Borre might speak the words to Peter Feissac as he gives his son to the weaver's care and instruction. Have students complete one of the activities according to their level of English proficiency.

Beginning Reread the passage, helping students to understand the meaning of each phrase as well as the overall meaning of the legal document. Choose one sentence in the agreement and have students repeat it until they are able to speak it with ease and fluency.

Intermediate Follow the instructions in the Beginning activity, but have students repeat the entire agreement.

Advanced Have students reread the passage silently to identify any difficult words or phrases. Define any unfamiliar words and explain any unfamiliar concepts to students. Have students practice reading the agreement with a partner until they are able to speak it with ease and fluency.

nobles and peasants, their status was not tied to the farming economy, but to business and commerce.

Nobles and the clergy often despised the new middle class. To nobles, towns were a disruptive influence beyond their control. To the clergy, the profits that merchants and bankers made from usury, or lending money at interest, were immoral.

Guilds Shape Town Life In medieval towns, the middle class gained economic and political power. First, merchants and artisans formed associations known as **guilds.** Merchant guilds appeared first. They dominated town life, passing laws and levying taxes. They also decided whether to spend funds to pave the streets with cobblestones or make other town improvements.

In time, artisans came to resent the powerful merchants. They organized craft guilds. Each guild represented workers in one occupation, such as weavers, bakers, or goldsmiths. In some towns, struggles between craft guilds and the wealthier merchant guilds led to riots.

Guild members cooperated to protect their own economic interests. To prevent competition, they limited guild membership. No one except guild members could work in any trade. Guilds made rules to protect the quality of their goods, regulate hours of labor, and set prices. Guilds also provided social services. They operated schools and hospitals, looked after the needs of their members, and provided support for the widows and orphans of their members.

Becoming a Guild Member Becoming a guild member took many years of hard work. At the age of seven or eight, a child might become an **apprentice,** or trainee, to a guild master. The apprentice usually spent seven years learning the trade. The guild master paid no wages, but was required to give the apprentice food and housing. These arrangements were usually part of a formal legal document that bound both the apprentice and the guild master.

> I, Peter Borre, in good faith and without guile, place with you, Peter Feissac, weaver, my son Stephen, for the purpose of learning the trade or craft of weaving, to live at your house, and to do work for you . . . for four continuous years, promising you by this agreement to take care that my son does the said work, . . .

>> This Italian painting from the 1300s shows guild members meeting to discuss issues important to the guild and the town.

>> A guild master oversees apprentices in the making of coins. The scale is used to ensure that the coins have the proper amount of gold in them.

Guided Reading and Discussion

Explain that medieval guilds served as models for today's trade unions. The first guilds, though, were merchant guilds, and they exerted a great deal of power over town life. The merchant guilds levied taxes and passed town laws. They also built bridges and paved roads within the towns. Artisan guilds also formed to protect the rights of workers in a particular occupation. To keep wages and prices favorable, the artisan guilds restricted membership. Guilds built hospitals and schools and tried to look after the needs of their members. Ask students to think about how guilds and modern unions are alike and how they differ.

Compare How are guilds similar to modern trade unions? *(Guilds made rules to ensure product quality, regular hours of labor, and set prices. They provided support for their members or for their widows and orphans.)*

Advanced High Follow the instructions in the Advanced activity, but have students practice reading the agreement aloud to the class as if they were Peter Borre.

The Crusades

The Effects of the Crusades

The Crusades were a series of wars in which Christians battled Muslims for control of land in the Middle East.

Online Project the **Interactive Map: The Crusades, 1096–1204**. Explain that there were four separate Crusades that took place over a period of 200 years. During this time, Western Europeans learned that the world was much larger than they had ever dreamed. The ideas brought back by crusaders accelerated change in Europe. By the end of the Fourth Crusade, social, economic, and political changes contributed to the end of medieval Europe. Trade with the Middle East increased, kings became stronger, and new ideas pushed Europe into a new era. Click on the button for each Crusade to present key information about that Crusade.

ACTIVE CLASSROOM

Use the Audio Tour strategy and pair students who will tour the map. Have the first student give the second a verbal "tour" of the map – what does it show? Then have the second student give the first an explanation of what it means.

will neither steal nor take anything away from you, or fleen or depart from you for any reason, until he has completed his apprenticeship.

—French apprenticeship agreement, 1248

Few apprentices ever became guild masters unless they were related to one. Most worked for guild members as **journeymen,** or salaried workers. Journeymen often accused masters of keeping their wages low so that they could not save enough to open a competing shop.

Women in the Guilds Women worked in dozens of crafts. A woman often engaged in the same trade as her father or husband and might inherit his workshop if he died. Because she knew the craft well, she kept the shop going and sometimes became a guild master herself. Young girls became apprentices in trades such as ribbon-making and paper-making. Women dominated some trades and even had their own guilds.

In Paris, they far outnumbered men in the profitable silk and wool guilds. A third of the guilds in Frankfurt were composed entirely of women.

>> These women and children are working at a wool weaving loom. Many women belonged to weaving guilds.

Middle Class Family Life Family life in the towns and cities differed in some ways from the lives of peasants on farms. Unlike peasants, middle class families did not grow their own food. Instead, they bought food and other goods in the town's market. Although the calendar still determined everyday life from harvests to holidays, artisans, merchants, and other townspeople saw the seasons differently. They had to make or sell goods during all seasons.

In towns, children were apprenticed out or worked in the business of their parents, rather than in the fields. Some middle class families sent their boys to schools, which were more common in towns than on the manor. Boys might attend a local church school, learning the basics of reading and writing. A few privileged boys might even get the chance for a higher education. In a world where most people were illiterate, or unable to read and write, a basic education was a valuable skill.

CHECK UNDERSTANDING Why were guilds important in town life?

The Crusades

By 1050, Western Europe was just emerging from centuries of isolation. For the first time since the fall of Rome, Western Europeans were strong enough to break out of their narrow world and take the offensive against other lands.

Starting in 1096, thousands of Europeans took part in the **Crusades,** a series of wars in which Christians battled Muslims for control of land in the Middle East. During these wars, both sides committed bloody acts. The First Crusade freed Jerusalem from Muslim rule and established a string of European-ruled Crusader states. They were surrounded by Muslim-ruled lands, however, and Arab counterattacks reconquered the last European outpost in 1291.

Conflict in the Holy Land By the 1050s, the once prosperous Byzantine empire was facing a serious threat from the Seljuk Turks.

The Turks had migrated from Central Asia into the Middle East, where they converted to Islam. Before long, the Seljuks had overrun most Byzantine lands in Asia Minor (present-day Turkey) and extended their power over the **Holy Land.** This area included Jerusalem and other places where Christians believe Jesus had lived and preached. For centuries, Christians had made pilgrimages to the Holy Land.

Although Muslims had controlled the Holy Land before, the conflict between the Seljuk Turks and the Byzantines disrupted travel to the Holy Land and was

D Differentiate Extra Support The Church offered incentives to those who joined the Crusades. Have students research these incentives to create an advertisement convincing people to join the Crusades. Advertisements should mention incentives and combine persuasive writing with maps or illustrations.

Answers

Check Understanding *They played a large role in government, levied taxes, and made improvements that benefited the whole town.*

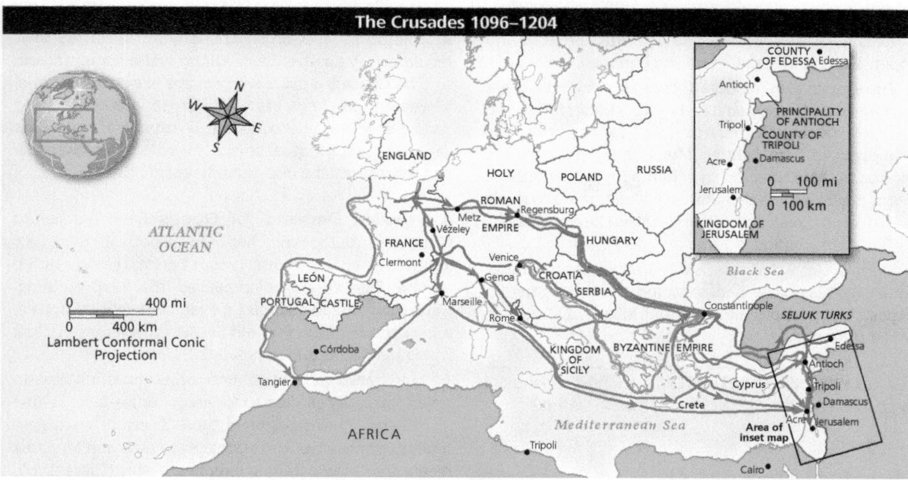

>> **Analyze Maps** Urged on by Pope Urban II, thousands of Europeans joined the Crusades to expel Muslims from the Holy Land. What route did English crusaders take? Why do you think they took that route?

threatening the very survival of the Byzantine empire. In 1095, the Byzantine emperor Alexius I urgently asked **Pope Urban II** for Christian knights to help him fight the Muslim Turks. Although Roman popes and Byzantine emperors were longtime rivals, Urban agreed.

The Pope Calls for War At the Council of Clermont in 1095, Urban incited bishops and nobles to action. "From Jerusalem and the city of Constantinople comes a grievous report," he began. "An accursed race . . . has violently invaded the lands of those Christians and has depopulated them by pillage and fire." Urban then called for a crusade to free the Holy Land.

> Both knights and footmen, both rich and poor . . . [must] strive to help expel [the Seljuk] from our Christian lands before it is too late. . . . Christ commands it. Remission of sins will be granted for those going thither.
>
> —Fulcher of Chartres, *Chronicle of the First Crusade*

"God wills it!" roared the assembly. By 1096, thousands of knights were on their way to the Holy Land. As the crusading spirit swept through Western Europe, armies of ordinary men and women inspired by fiery preachers also left for the Holy Land. Few returned.

Why did so many people embark on the Crusades? Religious reasons played a large role. Yet many knights hoped to win wealth and land. Some crusaders sought to escape troubles at home. Others yearned for adventure.

The pope, too, had mixed motives. In addition to his religious motivations, Urban hoped to increase his power in Europe and perhaps heal the schism, or split, between the Roman and Byzantine churches. He also saw lands in the Middle East as an outlet for Europe's growing population of knights. Sending Christian knights to fight Muslims instead of one another would help ease warfare at home.

Waves of Crusaders Head Eastward Only the First Crusade came close to achieving its goals. After a long and bloody campaign, Christian knights captured Jerusalem in 1099 and killed the Muslim and Jewish residents of the city.

The crusaders divided their captured lands into four small states, called crusader states. The Muslims repeatedly sought to destroy these Christian states, prompting Europeans to launch new crusades.

By 1187, Jerusalem had fallen to the able Muslim leader Salah al-Din, known to Europeans as Saladin.

Draw Conclusions Why did the Fourth Crusade essentially "stall" in Constantinople? *(The crusaders ended up fighting the Byzantines in Constantinople because the Venetian merchants funding much of the Crusade wanted to control this important trading site.)*

Guided Reading and Discussion

Each of the Crusades was launched for different reasons. On the surface, the main reason for the Crusades was to regain control over lands in the Middle East under control of the Muslims. One of these areas was Jerusalem, or the Christian Holy Land, and the major roads that allowed Christian pilgrims to safely go there and return. However, the Crusades also had a political component. With the First Crusade, Urban hoped to reunite a divided Christian church. By the Fourth Crusade, kings had gained more power and securing profitable trading centers was as much a goal as securing safe passages for pilgrims. Trade increased with the Muslim nations in the Middle East and new ideas in science and medicine from Islamic countries traveled back with the crusaders as well.

Draw Comparisons What factors contributed to the vast difference in how the four Crusades were conducted? *(Answers should include at least two of the following: changing roles of monarchial power over 200 years, growing power and influence of Venetian traders, personalities of the individual nobles involved, weakening of the Byzantine empire, and changing role of the Church.)*

Answers

Analyze Maps *Sample answer: They sailed. It was probably easier to go by sea than on bad roads overland. They could avoid lands controlled by hostile rulers.*

The Reconquista

Explain that most of Spain had been under Muslim control for more than 300 years. During this time, Spain had experienced the political, economic, and social impact of Islam. The early years of Muslim rule encouraged education in philosophy, medicine, and science. Different religions were tolerated, allowing people of different faiths to worship as they chose.

Analyze Maps Direct students' attention to the map showing the Reconquista. Explain to students that over time, Muslim control weakened in Spain. Christian kingdoms in the north of Spain took advantage of this to reconquer and return territory to Christian Spain. As the Reconquista progressed, it also led to the expulsion of Muslims and Jews from Spain.

On the Third Crusade, Europeans failed to retake Jerusalem. After negotiations, though, Saladin did reopen the holy city to Christian pilgrims.

Europeans also mounted crusades against other Muslim lands, especially in North Africa. All ended in defeat. During the Fourth Crusade, the crusaders were diverted from fighting Muslims to fighting other Christians. After helping merchants from the northern Italian city of Venice defeat their Byzantine trade rivals in 1204, crusaders captured and looted Constantinople, the Byzantine capital.

Meanwhile, Muslim armies overran the crusader states. By 1291, they had captured the last Christian outpost, the port city of Acre, and killed its Christian residents.

ANALYZE INFORMATION Did the Christian kings of Europe achieve their goals during the Crusades?

The Effects of the Crusades

The Crusades failed in their chief goal—the conquest of the Holy Land. They also left a bitter legacy of religious hatred. In the Middle East, both Christians and Muslims committed atrocities in the name of religion. In Europe, crusaders sometimes turned their religious fury against Jews, killing entire communities.

The Crusades did have positive effects on Europe, however. They began just as Europe was undergoing major economic and political changes, and the Crusades helped quicken the pace of those changes, contributing to the end of medieval Europe.

A Growing Demand for Goods Even before the Crusades, Europeans had developed a taste for luxuries that merchants brought from the Byzantine empire. The Crusades increased the level of trade. Returning crusaders brought even more fabrics, spices, and perfumes from the Middle East to a larger market. Trade increased and expanded.

Merchants in Venice and other northern Italian cities built large fleets to carry crusaders to the Holy Land. They later used those fleets to open new markets in the crusader states. Even after the Muslims recaptured Acre, Italian merchants kept these trade routes open. Our words *sugar*, *cotton*, and *rice*, which were borrowed from Arabic, show the range of trade goods brought back to Europe.

The Crusades further encouraged the growth of a money economy. To finance a journey to the Holy Land, nobles needed money. They therefore allowed peasants to pay rents in money rather than in grain or labor. Peasants began to sell their goods in towns to earn money, a practice that helped to undermine serfdom.

Changes for Monarchs and the Church The Crusades helped to increase the power of monarchs. They managed to gain the power to levy, or collect, taxes in order to support the Crusades.

Some rulers, such as the French king Louis IX and the English king Richard I, called the Lionheart, led crusades, which added greatly to their prestige.

Enthusiasm for the Crusades brought papal power to its greatest height. The growing power of the Church, however, soon brought popes into a bitter struggle with feudal rulers in Europe. Also, the Crusades did not end the split between the Roman and Byzantine churches as Pope Urban had hoped. In fact, Byzantine resentment against the West hardened as a result of the Fourth Crusade, which ended in the sack of Constantinople.

Europe Gains a Wider View of the World Contacts with the Muslim world led Christians to realize that millions of people lived in regions they had never even known existed. Soon, a few curious Europeans left to explore far-off places such as India and China.

In 1271, a young Venetian, Marco Polo, set out for China with his merchant father and uncle. After many

>> Crusaders returned to Europe with spices, perfumes, and other trade goods from the Middle East, and trade began to grow.

Answers

Analyze Information *The Crusades succeeded briefly in capturing Jerusalem and controlling the Holy Land, but ultimately the kings were not successful in achieving their goals.*

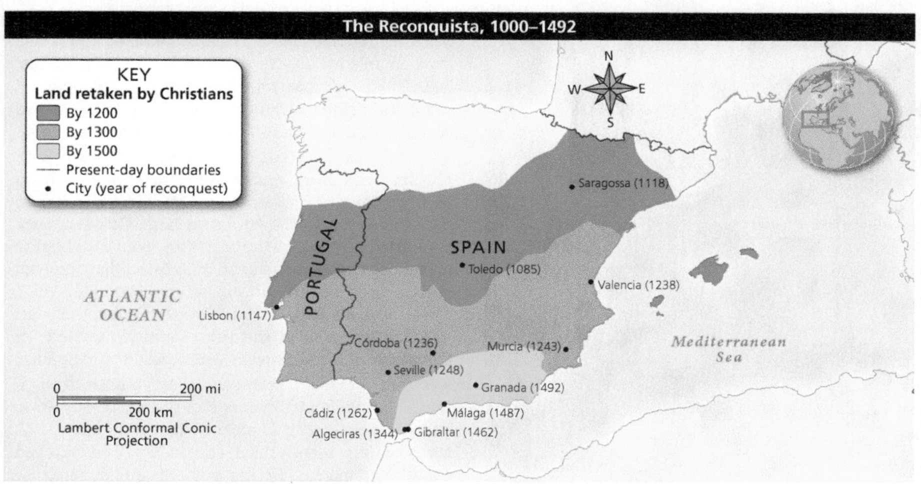

>> **ANALYZE MAPS** The Reconquista took many years and reflected political changes in Spain. The union of Ferdinand and Isabella and their countries gave their forces the power to take back most of Spain. How did the union of the countries of Castile and Aragon help the Reconquista?

years in China, he returned to Venice and wrote a book about the wonders of Chinese civilization. Europeans who heard his stories dubbed him a liar, rejecting his incredible tales of government mail service and black stones (coal) that were burned to heat homes.

The experiences of crusaders and of travelers like Marco Polo expanded European horizons and contributed to the end of medieval Europe by bringing Europe into a wider world from which it had been cut off since the fall of Rome. By the 1400s, a desire to trade directly with India and China would lead Europeans to a new age of exploration.

Impact on the Middle East and the Byzantine Empire The Crusades occurred during a time when Muslims in the Middle East were locked in frequent local power struggles. On occasion, rival Muslim rulers joined forces to fight the European invaders. Saladin briefly united lands from Egypt to Syria, but divisions soon reappeared.

The Fourth Crusade further weakened the Byzantine empire, which had already lost most of its lands. As the empire continued to decline, it faced a new threat, this time from the Ottoman Turks. In 1453, finally fell to the invaders led by Mehmet II.

SUMMARIZE Summarize the effects of the Crusades.

The Reconquista

The crusading spirit continued long after the European defeat at Acre. It flourished especially in Spain, where Christian warriors had been battling Muslims since the time of Charlemagne.

Spain is part of the Iberian peninsula, which also includes present-day Portugal. During the 700s, Muslims from North Africa had conquered most of the peninsula. These Muslims, called Moors by Christian Europeans, carried Islamic civilization to Spain. In the north, several tiny Christian kingdoms survived the Muslim conquest. They slowly expanded their borders, taking over Muslim lands. Their campaign to drive Muslims from Spain became known as the **Reconquista,** or "reconquest."

Christian Forces Advance Efforts by Christian warriors to expel Muslims began in the 700s. Their first

Guided Reading and Discussion

The Reconquista ushered in enormous changes for Spain. This included political, economic, and social changes that affected the general population. To help students explore the effects of the Reconquista, have pairs of students write a news story that describes its effects in Spain. Encourage students to explore the different facets of the Reconquista. What specific things changed? What were the results of these changes? Ask student teams to read aloud their news stories.

Synthesize What did the Reconquista ultimately achieve? *(A more united Spain, but one that lost positive contributions from the cultural and religious diversity of its people.)*

SYNTHESIZE

Online Project the **Digital Activity: Power of the Church**. Take a poll to see how many students made the correct prediction about whether the people of Europe would respond to the Church's call for Crusades. Ask these students to explain why they predicted as they did. Then, ask the students who predicted incorrectly why they believed that there would be no response to the Crusades.

Answers

Analyze Maps *Sample answer: It created a new united country called Spain that had the goal of driving the Muslims out of the area. The two countries combined armies, money, and a sense of purpose.*

Summarize *The Crusades left a legacy of religious hatred. However, they spurred trade and a money economy and strengthened monarchs and popes. They expanded European horizons and encouraged exploration.*

Draw Conclusions What was the extent of the Church's power and influence during this time? *(The Church was very powerful in that it was able to persuade national leaders to conduct a war to reclaim the Holy Land.)*

DEMONSTRATE

Online Assign the **Digital Lesson Quiz** for this lesson if you haven't already done so. Students will be offered automatic remediation or enrichment based on their score.

Pose these questions to the class on the Discussion Board:

Draw Conclusions What were some positive and negative effects of the Crusades? *(They were positive in that ideas and trade came back with the crusaders and negative in that a great deal of money and bloodshed was spent in a cause that ultimately failed to capture the Holy Land from Muslim control. Whether the Crusades were positive or negative also depends on which side one fought.)*

Summarize What factors influenced the growth of cities and towns? *(greater wealth, greater trade, safer trade routes, more productivity, and people leaving agriculture and moving into trades)*

Topic Inquiry

Have students continue their investigations for the Topic Inquiry.

>> A later illustration shows prisoners being led to the stake during the Inquisition.

real success did not come, however, until 1085, when they captured the city of Toledo.

During the next 200 years, Christian forces pushed slowly and steadily southward. By 1300, Christians controlled the entire Iberian Peninsula except for Granada. Muslim influences remained strong, though, and helped shape the arts and literature of Christian Spain.

In 1469, the marriage of Ferdinand of Aragon and Isabella of Castile created the unified state called Spain. Using their combined forces, **Ferdinand and Isabella** made a final push against the Muslim stronghold of Granada. In 1492, Granada fell. The Reconquista was complete. Ferdinand and Isabella then set out to impose unity on their diverse peoples. Isabella was determined to bring religious as well as political unity to the kingdom.

Spain Forces Non-Christians to Leave Under Muslim rule, Spanish Christians, Jews, and Muslims lived in relative peace, worshipping as they chose. Isabella ended that tolerance. With the support of the **Inquisition,** a Church court set up to try people accused of heresy, Isabella launched a new crusade.

Conditions for Muslims and Jews worsened. Both Muslims and Jews were ordered to accept baptism as Christians or go into exile. Many were baptized but secretly followed their former faith. Converts were often tried by the Inquisition. If they were found guilty of practicing their old religion, they faced punishments such as torture or burning at the stake. In 1492, Queen Isabella expelled all Jews who did not convert to Christianity. Over the next century, hundreds of thousands of Muslims were also expelled from Spain.

Spain achieved religious unity, but at a high price. Hundreds of thousands of people, mostly Jews and Muslims, fled into exile in the years after 1492. Many of them were skilled, educated people who had contributed much to Spain's economy and culture.

? CHECK UNDERSTANDING What was the Reconquista?

ASSESSMENT

1. **Draw Conclusions** Why was the invasion of the Byzantine empire by the Seljuk Turks in the 1050s significant?
2. **Determine Relevance** How did the Crusades accelerate change in Europe?
3. **Recognize Cause and Effect** How did improvements in agriculture in the countryside likely affect the lives of townspeople?
4. **Draw Inferences** What were the advantages of living in a medieval city? Would you rather have lived in the country or a city in medieval Europe? Why?
5. **Draw Conclusions** Why was the revival of trade so important?

Assessment

1. It led to the Byzantine emperor's call for help from Pope Urban and thus to the Crusades.
2. Crusaders brought goods and ideas back with them, trade increased a money economy, serfdom began to be undermined, and ships that carried Crusaders were available for trade and exploration.
3. They had more and better food and their cities may have become more crowded as peasants left the country to find work in the cities.
4. Answers will vary. Students choosing the country may cite less crowding and healthier living conditions and the chance to grow food, while those choosing the city may point to increased opportunities for work other than farming and easier access to goods.
5. Trade spurred the growth of towns, increased the use of money, and undermined the manor system. It led to an exchange of ideas and a wider worldview.

Answers

Check Understanding *The Reconquista was the Christian campaign to drive the Muslims from the Iberian penninsula, which was accomplished in 1492.*

7.5 During the early Middle Ages, hundreds of feudal nobles ruled over territories of varying size. Feudal nobles had their own courts and armies and collected their own taxes. Most feudal lords acknowledged a king or other overlord, but royal rulers had little power. The Church, too, was a center of power with its own laws, system of justice, and methods of raising money. Both nobles and the Church could at times have as much power as a monarch.

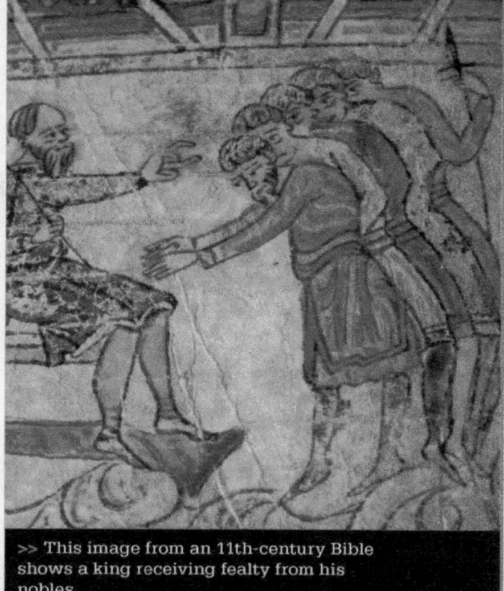

>> This image from an 11th-century Bible shows a king receiving fealty from his nobles.

Interactive Flipped Video

The Feudal Monarchs and the Church

TEKS
4.A, 20.B

Feudal Monarchs Begin to Centralize Power

From about 1000 to 1300, sometimes called the High Middle Ages, the balance of power slowly shifted. Feudal monarchs began to exert royal authority over their nobles and the Church. Some feudal monarchs succeeded in centralizing power and built the framework for nation-states such as Britain and France. (A nation-state refers to an independent political unit that has a single government and usually shares a common culture and history.)

Monarchs used various means to centralize power. First, they sought to extend royal law and justice over their kingdoms. To do so, they had to crush the power of rival courts of justice run by feudal nobles and the Church. To provide efficient government and a steady source of income, feudal monarchs set up government bureaucracies that administered justice and taxation. With a larger income, monarchs could afford to support a standing army, rather than rely on the military service of their nobles.

>> Objectives

Learn how monarchs gained power over nobles and the Christian Church, and how English kings strengthened their power.

Describe how traditions of government evolved under King John and later English monarchs.

Explain how strong monarchs unified France.

Describe the formation of the Holy Roman Empire and how some emperors struggled with the papacy to control specific religious and secular issues.

Analyze how the Church reached the height of its power under Pope Innocent III.

>> Key Terms

William the Conqueror
common law
King John
Magna Carta
due process of law
habeas corpus
Parliament
Louis IX
Holy Roman Empire
Henry IV
Gregory VII
lay investiture
Frederick Barbarossa
Pope Innocent III

PEARSON realize. www.PearsonTexas.com Access your Digital Lesson.

The Feudal Monarchs and the Church

CONNECT

Preview Have students preview the **Lesson Objectives** and the list of **Key Terms**.

Students can also preview all the **Key Terms** and **Academic Vocabulary** using the **Interactive Reading Notepad** on the digital course or preview a summary of the lesson in the **Reading and Note Taking Study Guide**.

Online Use the **Editable Presentation** found on the digital course to present the main ideas for this lesson.

Start Up Activity

Tell students that in 1215, English nobles forced King John to sign the Magna Carta, a document that established certain rights for nobles (and eventually all citizens) and that stated that the king had to obey the law.

Discuss Why do you think John agreed to sign the charter (Magna Carta)? *(John knew the nobles could seize power if he did not do what they asked.)* What were the nobles demanding from King John? *(Sample response: new laws and liberties for the nobles)* What liberties or rights do you feel are the most essential in our society today? Why? *(Sample response: The right to free speech and the right to elect our leaders are our most important rights today because they give us the opportunity to protest against or change the government if we don't like it. This controls the power of the government.)*

Online You can also project the **Start Up Activity** from the course.

INVESTIGATE

Have students read the section using the **Reading and Note Taking Study Guide** to help them take notes and understand the text as they read.

Feudal Monarchs Begin to Centralize Power

Explain to students that strong monarchs who wanted to have total control over their domains would likely have a conflict with strong popes who wanted the Church to control as much as it could. This conflict included clerical issues, but also influenced secular issues that the Church felt would intrude on its authority.

Aa Vocabulary Builder

1. Have students pronounce the following academic vocabulary terms in this lesson and clarify the part of speech. For difficult or polysyllabic words, break them into syllables and pronounce them with the students.
2. Explain what the word means in common "student-friendly" language using synonyms and antonyms when possible. Provide concrete examples to clarify the meaning, and rephrase the definition.

domain: territory under one ruler

descendant: coming from an ancestor

confronted: came face to face with; opposed boldly

prestige: someone's standing in the eyes of people

English Kings Expand Their Power

English monarchs not only gained power over nobles and the Christian Church, but also were able to strengthen their hold on England, keeping the nation united.

Guided Reading and Discussion

Review the reigns of William the Conqueror and Henry II. Engage students in a discussion to decide if William's and Henry's efforts resulted in an increase or decrease in their power.

Identify Central Issues What has to happen for one power to extend its authority over another power? *(The second power has to agree to give up authority or it has to be taken by force.)*

Support Ideas With Examples What events show that the Christian Church acted to politically unify medieval European nations? *(At this time, the ruling class and most citizens of European nations were Christian. As such, they were under the religious authority of the pope. That authority united the different kingdoms under Christianity.)*

The growth of towns and the money economy also strengthened royal rulers. Townspeople in the middle class often turned to monarchs, rather than nobles, who could ensure peace that was necessary for successful commerce.

CHECK UNDERSTANDING During the High Middle Ages, how did the balance of power shift between kings, noblemen, and the Church?

English Kings Expand Their Power

During the early Middle Ages, Angles, Saxons, and Vikings invaded and settled in England. Although feudalism emerged in England, as it did elsewhere in Europe, English monarchs generally kept their kingdoms united.

The Norman Conquest of England In 1066, however, the Anglo-Saxon king, Edward, died without an heir. His death triggered a power struggle that changed the course of English history. A council of nobles chose Edward's brother-in-law Harold to rule. But William, Duke of Normandy, in what is present-day France, also claimed the throne. The answer to the rival claims lay on the battlefield.

In France, William raised an army and won the support of the pope. He then sailed across the English Channel to England.

At the Battle of Hastings, William and his Norman knights triumphed over Harold. **William the Conqueror,** as he was now called, became king of England on Christmas Day 1066.

>> William of Normandy, called the Conqueror, ended Anglo-Saxon rule in England.

Interactive Gallery

William Exerts Firm Control Once in power, William exerted firm control over his new lands. Like other feudal monarchs, he granted fiefs to the Church and to his Norman lords, or barons, but he also kept a large amount of land for himself. He monitored who built castles and where. He required every vassal to swear first allegiance to him rather than to any other feudal lord.

To learn about his kingdom, William had a complete census of its land and livestock taken in 1086. The result was the (pronounced "doomsday"), which listed every castle, field, and pigpen in England.

As the title suggests, the survey was as thorough and inevitable as doomsday, believed to be God's final day of judgment that no one could escape. Information in the Domesday Book helped William and later English monarchs build an efficient system of tax collection.

Although William's French-speaking Norman nobles dominated England, the country's Anglo-Saxon population survived. Over the next 300 years, there was a gradual blending of Norman French and Anglo-Saxon customs, languages, and traditions.

Extending Royal Power William's successors strengthened two key areas of government, finance and law. They created the royal exchequer, or treasury, to collect taxes, fees, fines, and other dues. In 1154, an energetic, well-educated king, Henry II, inherited the English throne. He broadened the system of royal justice. As a ruler, he could not simply write new laws but had to follow accepted customs. Henry, however, found ways to expand old customs into laws. He then sent out traveling justices to enforce these royal laws.

The decisions of the royal courts became the basis for **common law,** or a legal system based on custom and court rulings. Unlike local feudal laws, it was "common," meaning that it was the same for all the people. In time, people brought their disputes to royal courts rather than to those of nobles or the Church. Since the royal courts charged fees, the exchequer benefited from the growth of royal justice.

The Early Jury System Under Henry II, England also developed an early jury system. When traveling justices

English Language Proficiency Standards

Listening 2.G.1 Read "English Kings Expand Their Power." Then have students participate in the following activities to explore the vocabulary words *martyr*, *saint*, and *pilgrim*.

Beginning Tell students the story of Thomas Becket. Use images to supplement students' understanding of the conflict between Henry II and the Church. Explain the meanings of the vocabulary words using the story of Thomas Becket as an example.

Intermediate Tell students the story of Thomas Becket. Ask students to think about a time when they had a conflict with a good friend. Use this real-world example and images from the text to help students understand the conflict between Henry II and the Church. Explain the meanings of the vocabulary words using the story of Thomas Becket as an example. Students may use a bilingual dictionary to aid understanding.

Advanced Have students describe a time when they had a conflict with a close friend. Then have them use this experience for reference as they listen to the story of Henry II and Thomas Becket. Explain the meanings of the vocabulary

Answers

Check Understanding *Monarchs gained power, while lords and the Church lost power.*

visited an area, local officials collected a jury, or group of men sworn to speak the truth. These early juries determined which cases should be brought to trial and were the ancestors of today's grand jury. Later, another jury developed that was composed of 12 neighbors of an accused person. It was the ancestor of today's trial jury.

A Tragic Conflict with the Church Henry's efforts to extend royal power over the clergy led to a bitter dispute with the Church. Henry claimed the right to try clergy in royal courts. Thomas Becket, the archbishop of Canterbury and once a close friend of Henry, fiercely opposed the king on this issue.

The conflict simmered for years. At last, Henry's fury exploded. "What cowards I have brought up in my court," he cried. "Who will rid me of this meddlesome priest?" Four hot-headed knights took Henry at his word. In 1170, they murdered Archbishop Thomas Becket in his own cathedral. Henry denied any part in the attack. Still, to make peace with the Church, he eased his attempts to regulate the clergy. Meanwhile, Becket was honored as a martyr and declared a saint. Pilgrims flocked to his tomb at Canterbury, where miracles were said to occur.

>> This image shows prisoners brought before judges and a jury. The men sitting at the table writing on scrolls are recording the court activities, much like today's court reporters.

DESCRIBE What was Henry II's argument with the Church?

Developing New Traditions of Government

Later English rulers repeatedly clashed with nobles and the Church as they tried to raise taxes or to impose royal authority over traditional feudal rights. Out of those struggles evolved traditions of government that would have great influence on the modern world.

King John Battles Powerful Enemies A son of Henry II, **King John** was a clever, cruel, and untrustworthy ruler. During his reign, he faced three powerful enemies: King Philip II of France, Pope Innocent III, and his own English nobles. He lost each struggle.

Ever since William the Conqueror, Norman rulers of England had held vast lands in France. In 1205, John suffered his first setback when he lost a war with Philip II and had to give up lands in Anjou and Normandy.

Next, John battled with Innocent III over selecting a new archbishop of Canterbury. When John rejected the pope's nominee, the pope excommunicated him, or prevented him from participating in the sacraments and services of the Church.

>> In this illustration from the 1800s, King John lays a token of his submission before the feet of Pope Innocent III's representative, conceding defeat.

Developing New Traditions of Government

Introduce the text by explaining that the Magna Carta is one of the most important charters, or agreements, in European history. It was the first time noblemen successfully challenged the right of the king to rule as he chose. The Magna Carta spelled out some of what the nobles considered to be their basic rights. These "rights" would have been unheard of even a generation earlier, especially if the king disagreed. In centuries to come, the English people would frequently refer to the Magna Carta to support their efforts to establish a limited monarchy.

Guided Reading and Discussion

The political and legal ideas contained in the Magna Carta inspired future efforts to establish a representative government that ensured the rights of its citizens.

words using the story of Thomas Becket as an example.

Advanced High Have small groups of students discuss examples of conflicts they have had with a close friend or loved one. Then ask students to listen to the story of Henry II and Thomas Becket. Have students discuss the similarities and differences between their own experiences and the story of Henry II and Thomas Becket in small groups. Finally, ask student groups to explain the meanings of the vocabulary words using the story of Thomas Becket as an example.

D Differentiate Extra Support Explain that the British model of Parliament was a model for the United States Congress. Ask: How are the United States' legislature and Britain's Parliament alike? How are they different? *(Alike: both possess the exclusive power to tax, both are two-house bodies, both can limit the power of the monarch or president; Different: the House of Lords consists of nobles and clergy, while neither house of the United States Congress is for specific classes of people.)*

Answers

Describe *Henry believed the royal court had the right to try clergymen accused of crimes. The Church said clergymen could be tried only by the Church.*

Draw Inferences What ideas in the Magna Carta have influenced the development of the U.S. legal and governmental systems? *(Many of the same rights, including habeas corpus and due process, are central to U.S. legal traditions. Other ideas in the Magna Carta, such as rulers must obey the law, people should have a voice in decisions about taxation, and all people have specific rights, have strongly influenced American ideas about government and what it should and should not do.)*

Growth of the French Monarchy

While England was moving toward restrictions on the monarchy, France was moving in the other direction.

Key Terms

Ask students to find the key term **due process** (in bold) in the text. Due process safeguards the legal rights of citizens. Ask students how due process plays a role in modern society.

Innocent also placed England under the interdict, which forbade Church services to the entire kingdom. Even the strongest ruler was likely to give in to that pressure. To save himself and his crown, John had to accept England as a fief of the papacy and pay a yearly fee to Rome.

The Magna Carta Finally, John angered his own nobles with oppressive taxes and other abuses of power. In 1215, a group of rebellious barons cornered John and forced him to sign the **Magna Carta,** or great charter. In this document, the king affirmed a long list of feudal rights. Besides protecting their own privileges, the barons included a few clauses recognizing the rights of townspeople and the Church.

The Magna Carta contained two very important ideas that in the long run would shape political and legal traditions in England. First, it asserted that the nobles had certain rights. Over time, these rights that had been granted to nobles were extended to all English citizens. Second, the Magna Carta made it clear that the monarch must obey the law.

Among other clauses in the Magna Carta that would have lasting impact were those that protected freemen from arbitrary arrest, imprisonment, and other legal actions, except "by legal judgment of his peers or by the law of the land." This clause would much later become the basis of the right we know today as **due process of law,** which safeguarded the legal rights of the individual.

Over the centuries, the English would rely on the Magna Carta to develop other political and legal ideas and traditions. In the 1600s, the idea of protecting people from arbitrary arrest and imprisonment would evolve into the right of **habeas corpus,** the principle that no person can be held in prison without first being charged with a specific crime.

In the Magna Carta, King John also had to agree not to raise new taxes without first consulting his Great Council of lords and clergy. Many centuries later, American colonists would claim that those words meant that any taxation without representation was unjust. In 1215, though, neither the king nor his lords could have imagined such an idea.

>> This image from the 1200s shows Edward I attending an English parliamentary meeting.

Parliament Develops During the 1200s, English rulers often called on the Great Council for advice. Eventually, this council evolved into **Parliament,** which later became England's legislature. As Parliament acquired a larger role in government, it helped unify England.

In 1295, King Edward I summoned Parliament to approve money for his wars in France. "What touches all," he declared, "should be approved by all." He had representatives of the "common people" join with the lords and clergy. The "commons" included two knights from each county and representatives of the towns.

Much later, this assembly became known as the Model Parliament because it set up the framework for England's legislature. In time, Parliament developed into a two-house body: the House of Lords with nobles and high clergy and the House of Commons with knights and middle-class citizens.

Over the centuries, Parliament gained the crucial "power of the purse": the right to approve any new taxes. With that power, Parliament could insist that the monarch meet its demands before voting for taxes. In this way, it could check, or limit, the power of the monarch.

DESCRIBE What was the political, legal, and economic impact of the ideas contained in the Magna Carta?

Growth of the French Monarchy

Unlike William the Conqueror in England, monarchs in France did not rule over a unified kingdom. The successors to Charlemagne had little power over a

Answers

Describe *The Magna Carta strengthened the role of nobles and townspeople in government, asserted that nobles and freemen had rights, and declared that kings had to consult Parliament about levying taxes.*

History Background

Although Henry II used juries to dispense justice, many Western European monarchs and nobles doled out harsh punishments without the benefit of juries. A thief might have his hand cut off. A woman who verbally abused family or friends could be punished by being forced to wear a bridle whose bit held her tongue. Hanging was a common punishment. It was used not only for serious offenses such as murder, but also for rioting and robbery. Public punishments were common. For fighting, a person might be whipped or confined in a stock. A man accused of assault might be ordered to stand for a day in the pillory and then be branded on the forehead with a red-hot iron so that he was marked for the rest of his life.

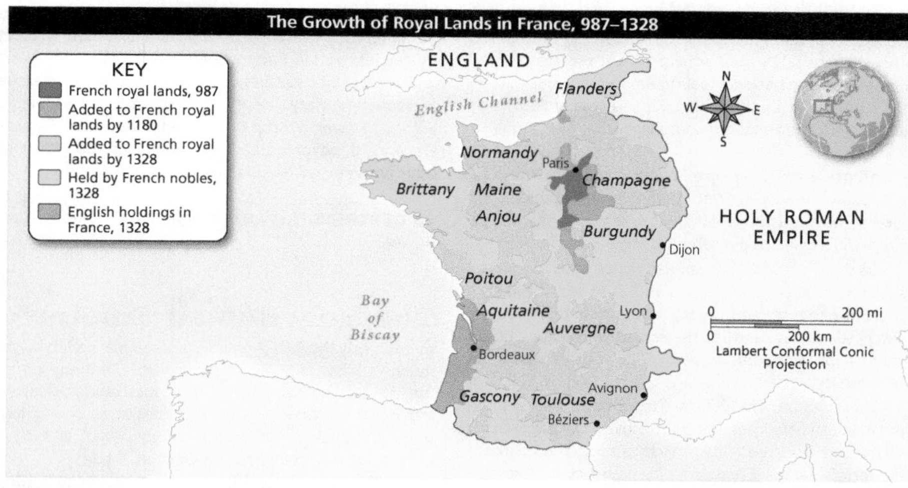

>> Capetian kings gradually extended royal control over more than half of France. **Analyze Maps** What overall trend in French royal power does the map show? Where and by whom might that power be challenged after 1328? Explain your answer.

patchwork of French territories ruled by powerful feudal lords.

France Under the Capetians In 987, these feudal nobles elected Hugh Capet, the count of Paris, to fill the vacant French throne. They may have chosen him because they thought he was too weak to pose a threat to them. Hugh's own lands around Paris were smaller than those of many of his vassals.

Nevertheless, Hugh and his heirs slowly increased royal power. First, they made the throne hereditary, passing it from father to son. The Capetian dynasty lasted for 300 years, making the kingdom more stable. Next, they added to their lands by playing rival nobles against each other. They also won the support of the Church.

Perhaps most important, the Capetians built an effective bureaucracy. Government officials collected taxes and imposed royal law over the king's lands. By establishing order, they increased their prestige and gained the backing of the new middle class.

Philip Augustus Increases Power and Prosperity In 1179, Philip II became king of France. Called Philip Augustus, he was a shrewd and able ruler. He strengthened royal government in many ways. Instead of appointing nobles to government jobs, he used paid middle-class officials who owed their loyalty to him. He granted charters to many new towns and introduced a new national tax.

Philip also quadrupled royal land holdings. Through trickery, diplomacy, and war, he gained control of English-ruled lands in Normandy, Anjou, and elsewhere. He then began to take over southern France. At the pope's request, he sent knights to suppress a heresy among the Albigensians (al buh JEN see unz) in the south and then added this vast area to his domain. Before his death in 1223, Philip had become the most powerful ruler in Europe.

Louis IX: A Model Monarch Perhaps the most admired French ruler of this time was **Louis IX,** grandson of Philip Augustus. Louis embodied the ideal of the medieval monarch—he was generous, noble, and devoted to justice and the rules of chivalry.

A deeply religious man, Louis pursued religious goals that Christians admired at the time. He persecuted heretics and Jews and led thousands of French knights in two wars against Muslims. Within 30 years of his death, the Church declared him a saint.

Louis did much to improve royal government. Like Charlemagne, he sent out traveling officials to check on local administrators. He expanded the royal

Online Project the **Interactive Map: The Growth of France 987–1328**. As you look at the map, explain that during this period, France's monarchs consolidated power and territory until more than half of France was controlled by one monarch.

ACTIVE CLASSROOM

Use the Audio Tour strategy and pair students for this activity. Have the first student give the second a verbal "tour" of the map – what does it show? Have the second student give the first an explanation of what it means.

Determine Relevance Why is the Capetian kings' success at expanding their territory important to European history at this time? *(France was put on a different path than England in terms of how the country would be governed. This difference affected the future direction of both countries in everything from their relationship to the papacy to how wars were fought and paid for.)*

Guided Reading and Discussion

Draw Conclusions Why did the election of a French pope lead to a split in the papacy? *(The French pope was perceived as being more loyal to France than to the papacy. The pope's move of the papal court close to the French border angered other Church leaders. They elected a different pope, which contributed to the Great Schism.)*

Compare and Contrast What are some similarities and differences between the development of the French and English monarchies? *(English and French kings both developed centralized governments that took power away from nobles while giving some power to common citizens. However, the English monarch was weak, and French monarchs never gave up any power.)*

Answers

Analyze Maps *Royal lands grew during this period; The English would challenge the French king on lands bordering their own. The French nobles would be likely to do the same.*

Topic 7 Lesson 5

The Holy Roman Empire

With the formation of the Holy Roman Empire, some emperors struggled with the papacy to control specific religious and secular issues.

Online Project the **Interactive Gallery: Battle for Power – Monarchs and Popes.** Explain that monarchs and popes were individuals who had absolute rule over their specific areas. The monarch ruled the secular activities of people, while the pope ruled the religious activities. At times, there was conflict regarding exactly where the boundaries were between the secular and religious worlds. When this happened, a struggle for power would ensue between a monarch and a pope.

ACTIVE CLASSROOM

Use the Conversation with History strategy and ask students to pretend they are having a conversation with one of the people in the Interactive Gallery. Students should write down a question they'd like to ask their chosen historical person, then what the person would say to them and, finally, how the student would respond.

Discuss Ask students to share their conversations with the class. What types of responses did students get from the historical person to whom they posed their question?

courts, outlawed private wars, and ended serfdom in his personal domain. To ensure justice, he even heard cases himself. His enormous personal prestige helped create a strong national feeling among his subjects. By the time of his death in 1270, France was emerging as an efficient centralized monarchy.

Conflicts with the Pope Louis's grandson, Philip IV, ruthlessly extended royal power. Always pressed for money, he tried to collect new taxes from the clergy. These efforts led to a clash with Pope Boniface VIII.

Declaring that "God has set popes over kings and kingdoms," the pope forbade Philip to tax the clergy without papal consent. Philip threatened to arrest any clergy who did not pay. As their quarrel escalated, Philip sent troops to capture Boniface. The pope escaped, but he died soon afterward.

Shortly after, in 1305, a Frenchman was elected pope. Four years later, the pope moved the papal court to Avignon (ah vee NYOHN), just outside the southern border of France. There, French rulers could exercise more control over the Church in their kingdom. The move to Avignon later sparked a crisis in the Church when a rival pope was elected in Rome. The rival popes each claimed to be the true leader of the Church.

>> The Estates General did not limit the power of the French king. However, it did give townspeople (at right) a voice equal to nobles (center) and clergy (left).

The King Sets Up the Estates General During this struggle with the pope, Philip rallied French support by setting up the Estates General in 1302. This body had representatives from all three estates, or classes of French society: clergy, nobles, and townspeople. Although later French kings consulted the Estates General, it never gained the power of the purse or otherwise served as a balance to royal power.

DESCRIBE How did French kings increase royal power?

The Holy Roman Empire

In the early Middle Ages, Charlemagne had brought much of what is today the nation of Germany under his rule. After his death, these German lands dissolved into a patchwork of separate states ruled by counts and dukes. In time, the dukes of Saxony began to extend their power over neighboring German lands.

In 936, Duke Otto I of Saxony took the title King of Germany. Like other feudal monarchs, he and his successors set out to increase royal power. In doing so, they came into fierce conflict with the Church. The longest and most destructive of these power struggles pitted Otto's successors, who ruled over lands called the **Holy Roman Empire,** against the pope in Rome.

Otto I Becomes Emperor Like Charlemagne, Otto I worked closely with the Church. He appointed bishops to top government jobs. He also took an army into Italy to help the pope defeat rebellious Roman nobles. In 962, a grateful pope crowned Otto emperor of the German states of Central Europe. Later, Otto's successors took the title Holy Roman emperor—"holy" because they were crowned by the pope, and "Roman" because they saw themselves as heirs to the emperors of ancient Rome.

German Emperors Face a Challenge The Holy Roman Emperor had the potential to be the strongest monarchy in Europe. German emperors claimed authority over much of central and eastern Europe as well as parts of France and Italy. In fact, the real rulers of these lands were the emperor's vassals— hundreds of nobles and Church officials. For German emperors, the challenge was to control their vassals. It was a challenge they never met.

The Conflict with the Church Begins The close ties between Otto and the Church held the seeds of conflict. Holy Roman emperors saw themselves as protectors of Italy and the pope. They repeatedly intervened in

English Language Proficiency Standards

Listening 2.I.2 Read "The Holy Roman Empire" aloud. Then have students complete one activity according to their level of English proficiency.

Beginning Summarize aloud a short section of "The Holy Roman Empire" for students using simple sentences. Match each sentence with a visual aid. Then present written copies of the sentences for students and help them match each sentence with its corresponding visual aid. Assist students as necessary to ensure understanding of the spoken content.

Intermediate Summarize aloud a short section of "The Holy Roman Empire" for students using simple sentences. Then present written copies of the sentences to students. Display a set of visual aids that correspond to the section. Then have students match each sentence with its corresponding visual aid and arrange them in order. Assist students as necessary to ensure understanding of the spoken content.

Advanced Read a short section of "The Holy Roman Empire" aloud to students. Have students give a summary of the section using simple sentences. If necessary, have students supplement their summaries with visual aids that correspond to the section. Assist students as necessary to ensure understanding of the spoken content.

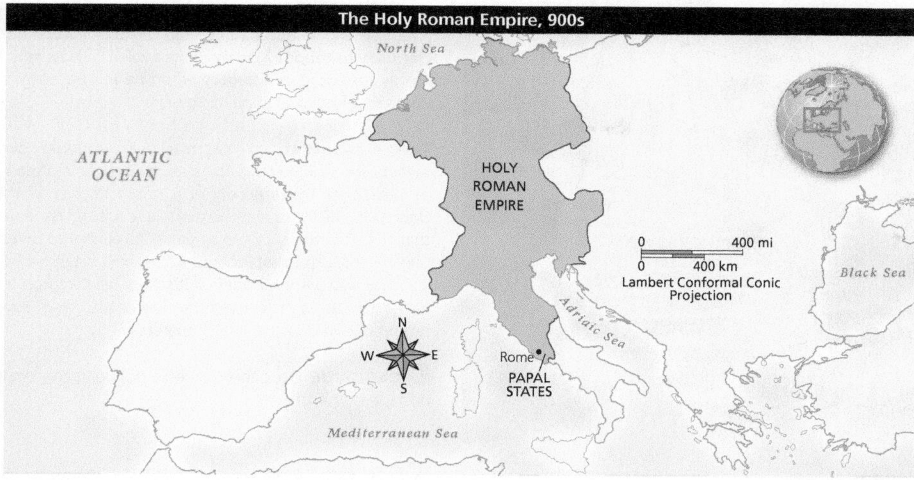

>> The Holy Roman Empire was a vast kingdom that bordered several important bodies of water. This aided in trade as well as defense. **Analyze Maps** Locate: (a) the North Sea, (b) the Adriatic Sea, (c) the Mediterranean Sea

Italian affairs and were tempted by the growing rich cities of northern Italy.

A key conflict between emperors and popes involved who would control appointments to high Church office. Like rulers in England and France, the Holy Roman emperor often appointed bishops and abbots. As popes sought to reform the Church, they tried to end such outside interference by secular rulers.

DESCRIBE Describe the Holy Roman Empire.

ELPS **ELPS 2.I.2** Practice your listening comprehension by listening to and summarizing sections of *The Holy Roman Empire.*

A Pope and an Emperor Feud

Under the reforming pope **Gregory VII,** the conflict between emperors burst into flames. Gregory was one of the greatest medieval popes. He was also one of the most controversial. Pope Gregory ruled at the same time as the German emperor **Henry IV.** These two strong-willed rulers clashed over competing claims to power.

Gregory Undertakes Reforms Gregory was determined to make the Church independent of secular rulers. To achieve this goal, he banned the practice of **lay investiture.** Under this practice, the emperor or another lay person (a person who is not a member of the clergy) "invested," or presented, bishops with the ring and staff that symbolized their office. Only the pope, said Gregory, had the right to appoint and install bishops in office.

The Emperor Responds Pope Gregory's ban brought an angry response from the Holy Roman emperor, Henry IV. He argued that bishops held their lands as royal fiefs. Since he was their overlord, Henry felt entitled to give them the symbols of office. The feud heated up as the two men exchanged insulting letters. Meanwhile, rebellious German princes undermined Henry by supporting the pope.

In 1076, Gregory excommunicated Henry, freeing Henry's subjects from their allegiance to the emperor. The pope then headed north to crown a new emperor. Faced with revolts, Henry was forced to make peace.

Henry Repents In January 1077, he presented himself to the pope as a repentant sinner. Gregory knew that Henry was just trying to save his throne. But according to tradition and Church law, the pope, as a priest, had

A Pope and an Emperor Feud

The actions of Pope Gregory VII made the political influence of the Church very clear. Although the initial issue with Emperor Henry IV appeared to be strictly concerned with Church doctrines and policies, it was more complicated because the clergymen involved held lands as royal fiefs and, therefore, owed allegiance to the emperor. The fact that the pope ultimately "won" because Henry IV was forced to humble himself is critical to what future popes expected from monarchs.

Guided Reading and Discussion

Draw Inferences Why was it important that Henry IV was finally forced to give in to Pope Gregory? *(It implied the pope had more power than even the Holy Roman Emperor. Other monarchs noticed this feud and its result, which likely affected how they would deal with future popes.)*

Advanced High Have students work in pairs and read different sections of "The Holy Roman Empire" independently. Then have students explain the sections they read to their partners. After the explanation, partners should summarize the information that they listened to. To check comprehension, have students read the sections read by their partners to make sure their summaries make sense.

Answers

Describe *Capetian kings made the monarchy hereditary, played the nobles off each other, won support of the Church, built bureaucracy; Phillip II paid middle-class officials, granted town charters, introduced national tax, extended royal lands; Philip IV formed the Estates General.*

Analyze Maps *North Sea is between England and Holy Roman Empire; Adriatic Sea is east of Rome & Papal States; Mediterranean is south of Holy Roman Empire.*

Describe *The Holy Roman Empire included much of central and eastern Europe and parts of France and Italy. But the emperor had little real control over his vassals, the real rulers of these lands.*

The Battle for Italy

Italy became ground zero in the struggle between popes and emperors as ambitious German rulers sought to control the Italian peninsula.

>> Pope Gregory VII stands above Henry IV, who is wearing the clothing of a penitent and humbling himself in the snow before the pope.

>> Frederick Barbarossa, or Frederick Red-Beard, leads soldiers in battle against the Seljuk Turks.

to forgive a confessed sinner. Gregory then lifted the order of excommunication, and Henry returned to Germany to subdue his rebellious nobles. In later years, he took revenge on Gregory when he led an army to Rome and forced the pope into exile.

The Concordat of Worms The struggle over investiture dragged on for almost 50 years. Finally, in 1122, both sides accepted a treaty known as the Concordat of Worms (vawrmz). This treaty declared that the Church had the sole power to elect and invest bishops with spiritual authority. The emperor, however, still invested them with fiefs. Although this compromise ended the investiture struggle, new battles were soon raging between popes and emperors.

? DESCRIBE Describe the feud between the pope and the emperor.

The Battle for Italy

The struggle between popes and emperors moved from the battle over investiture to a battle for Italy. During the 1100s and 1200s, ambitious German emperors sought to control Italy. As they headed south across the Alps, they came into conflict not only with the pope but also with the wealthy cities of northern Italy.

German Emperors In Italy The Holy Roman emperor Frederick I, called **Frederick Barbarossa,** or "Red Beard," dreamed of building an empire from the Baltic to the Adriatic. For years, he fought to bring the wealthy cities of northern Italy under his control. With equal energy, they resisted. By joining forces with the pope in the Lombard League, they finally managed to defeat Barbarossa's armies.

Barbarossa did succeed, however, in arranging a marriage between his son Henry and Constance, the heiress to Sicily and southern Italy. That move entangled German emperors even more deeply in Italian affairs.

Frederick II Barbarossa's grandson, Frederick II, was raised in Sicily, a rich island kingdom in the Mediterranean. Frederick was bright and well educated. An able but arrogant leader, he was willing to use any means to achieve his ends.

As Holy Roman emperor, Frederick spent little time in Germany. Instead, he pursued his ambitions in Italy, clashing repeatedly and unsuccessfully with several popes. Like his grandfather, Frederick also tried but failed to subdue the cities of northern Italy.

Answers

Describe *The emperor claimed the right of lay investiture—the right to appoint, or invest, bishops; the pope said only the pope had the right to appoint high Church officials.*

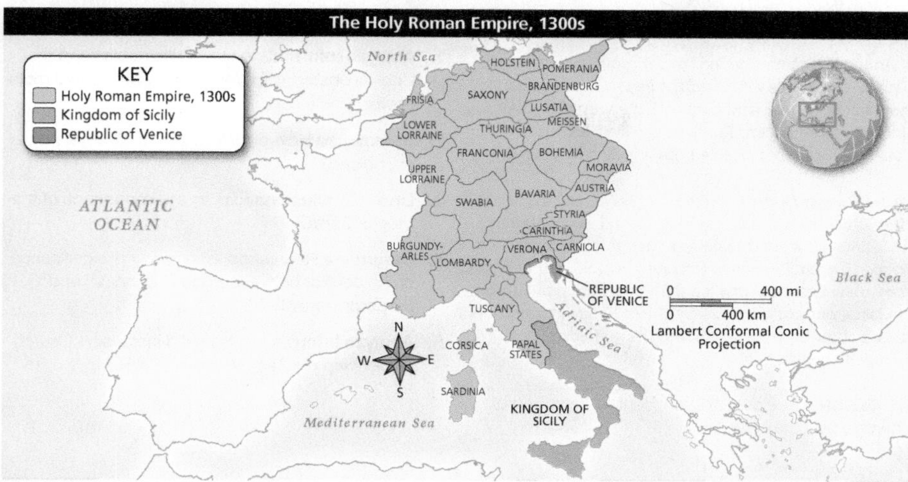

>> Frederick II spent much of his rule fighting for territory around the Kingdom of Sicily. **Analyze Maps** Why do you think that the barons and nobility of areas such as Saxony and Bavaria were successful in breaking into independent states?

Effects of the Struggle While Frederick II was occupied in Italy, German nobles grew more independent. The Holy Roman Empire survived, but remained a patchwork of feudal states. Unlike France and England, Germany would not become a nation-state for another 600 years.

Southern Italy and Sicily also faced centuries of upheaval. There, popes turned to the French to overthrow Frederick's heirs.

A local uprising against French rule in Sicily led to 200 years of chaos as French and Spanish rivals battled for power. The region that had once been a thriving center of culture was left in ruins.

? DESCRIBE What obstacles did German emperors face in Italy?

Church Power Reaches Its Peak

In the 1200s, the Roman Catholic Church reached the height of its political power. Reforming popes like Gregory VII claimed the right to depose kings and emperors. Gregory's successors greatly expanded papal power. In addition, a more powerful Church was able to spread its influence to new areas, increasing religious unity in Europe.

Popes Assert Their Power **Pope Innocent III,** who took office in 1198, embodied the triumph of the Church. As head of the Church, Innocent III claimed supremacy over all other rulers. The pope, he said, stands "between God and man, lower than God but higher than men, who judges all and is judged by no one."

Innocent III clashed with all the powerful rulers of his day, and he usually won. As you have read, when King John of England dared to appoint an archbishop of Canterbury without the pope's approval, Innocent excommunicated the king and placed his kingdom under interdict. Innocent ordered the same punishment for France when Philip II tried unlawfully to annul, or invalidate, his marriage. The Holy Roman emperor Frederick II also felt the wrath of the powerful pope.

In 1209, Innocent, aided by Philip II, launched a brutal crusade against the Albigensians in southern France. The Albigensians wanted to purify the Church and return to the simpler ways of early Christianity. The Church saw them as heretics because they rejected Catholic beliefs and rituals. Knights from all over western Europe took part in the fighting.

Church Power Reaches Its Peak

Introduce the reading by explaining that Pope Innocent III's claim that the pope was superior to all men and second only to God was a dramatic step to take. Other popes had not made such an explicit claim, and it angered many monarchs and some clergy. At the same time, others accepted it. Innocent's claim also opened the door for popes succeeding him to make the same claim. This added the potential for more conflict between future monarchs and popes.

Guided Reading and Discussion

The popes reached the height of their political power during the 13th century under Pope Innocent III, one of the most powerful of all medieval popes. He introduced the controversial idea that the pope was the direct link to God, subordinate only to God and, therefore, under no temporal authority. In other words, the pope was the one individual on Earth above even the mightiest of kings. This led to Innocent's use of religious power, such as excommunication and interdict, to impose his will on kings who chose to challenge him.

Draw Conclusions How did Innocent's claim that the pope judged all but was judged by no one reflect the Church's political power? *(He won in his clashes with King John of England over appointing bishops and with Philip of France over an annulment of a marriage. In both cases, he asserted the power of the pope over that of the monarch.)*

Answers

Describe *the resistance of wealthy Italian cities and their alliance with the pope in the Lombard League*

Analyze Maps *Sample answer: Sicily was far away from northern Europe. While Frederick was occupied with Sicily, it would be easier for the barons in the furthest northern areas of the Holy Roman Empire to strengthen their claims for independent territories.*

Topic 7 Lesson 5

SYNTHESIZE

Online Ask students to share their responses to the Synthesize question. Explain that the Church developed enormous power in relation to European monarchies and that it was often the source of serious conflicts that affected the people of the countries, as well as the monarchs. For example, Pope Innocent III's interdict on the entire country of England punished regular citizens who were innocent of wrongdoing. The political power of the Church would continue to be a source of contention and spur efforts toward reform.

DEMONSTRATE

Online Assign the **Digital Lesson Quiz** for this lesson if you haven't already done so. Students will be offered automatic remediation or enrichment based on their score.

Pose these questions to the class on the Discussion Board:

Analyze Information How were nobles and the Church obstacles for monarchs who wanted more power? *(Nobles and popes fought for power. Nobles forced King John to sign the Magna Carta. Pope Innocent III forced King John to yield in regard to appointing bishops. In France, King Philip IV failed in his goal to tax clergy when the pope refused and said the pope was above "kings and kingdoms." Pope Gregory VII's clash with the Holy Roman Emperor Henry IV led nobles to take advantage of the situation to create further political unrest. The popes thus proved that they could, and would, get involved in political issues or use their religious authority to impose their will on kings.)*

Determine Relevance What was the significance of the conflict between Pope Gregory VII and Emperor Henry IV? *(It was central to the struggle for power between popes and secular rulers during the High Middle Ages.)*

Topic Inquiry

Have students continue their investigations for the Topic Inquiry.

Tens of thousands of people were slaughtered in the Albigensian Crusade.

Innocent strengthened papal power within the Church as well. He extended the Papal States, reformed the Church courts, and changed the way that Church officials were chosen. Finally, he called a council that issued decrees that justified the pope's new power.

Papal Power Begins to Decline For almost a century after Innocent's death, popes pressed their claim to supremacy. During this period, though, the French and English monarchies grew stronger. In 1296, Philip IV of France successfully challenged Pope Boniface VIII on the issue of taxing the clergy. After Philip engineered the election of a French pope, the papacy entered a period of decline.

DESCRIBE How did Innocent III embody the Church's political power?

ASSESSMENT

1. **Analyze Information** How were nobles and the Church obstacles for monarchs who wanted more power?
2. **Summarize** How did William increase royal power in England?
3. **Draw Conclusions** Explain the importance of the Magna Carta.
4. **Determine Relevance** What was the significance of the conflict between Pope Gregory VII and Emperor Henry IV?
5. **Analyze Information** How did increasing Church power help create political unity in Europe?

Answers

Describe *He won out in his clashes with King John of England over appointing bishops and with Philip of France over an annulment of a marriage—in both cases asserting the power of the pope over that of the monarch. He put down heretical groups such as the Albigensians.*

Assessment

1. Nobles and popes fought for power. Nobles forced King John to sign the Magna Carta. Pope Innocent III forced King John to yield in regard to appointing bishops.
2. He kept land for himself, required first allegiance of all barons, monitored castles, and made a detailed census.
3. The Magna Carta established the principles that the monarch must obey the law and that nobles and freemen have certain rights.
4. It was central to the struggle for power between popes and secular rulers during the High Middle Ages.
5. A stronger Church was able to standardize practices throughout Christian Europe; popes claimed supremacy over secular rulers, creating a feeling of belonging to Christendom as well as to a kingdom or nation.

7.6 By the 1100s, Europe was experiencing dynamic changes. No longer was everyone preoccupied with the daily struggle to survive. A more reliable food supply and the revival of trade and growth of towns were signs of increased prosperity.

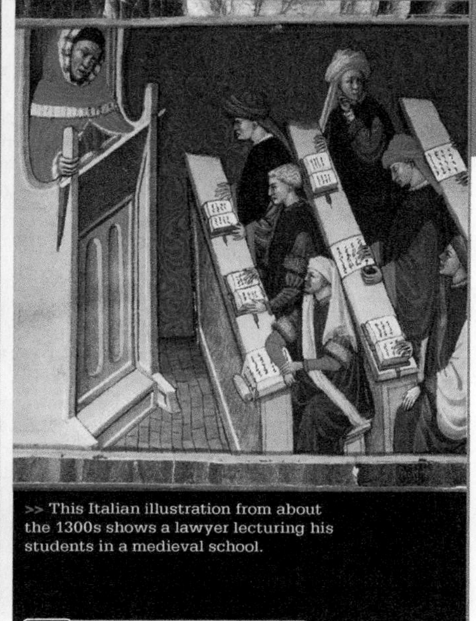

>> This Italian illustration from about the 1300s shows a lawyer lecturing his students in a medieval school.

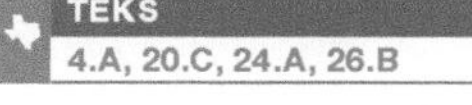

Learning, Literature, and the Arts of the Middle Ages

TEKS
4.A, 20.C, 24.A, 26.B

>> Objectives

Explain the emergence of universities and their importance to medieval life.

Understand how newly translated writings from the past and from other regions influenced medieval thought.

Describe the literature, architecture, and art of the High and Late Middle Ages.

Examine the lasting heritage of the Byzantine Empire.

>> Key Terms

scholasticism
Thomas Aquinas
vernacular
Dante Alighieri
Geoffrey Chaucer
Gothic style
flying buttresses
illumination
icon
Christine de Pisan

The Rise of Medieval Universities

As economic and political conditions improved in the High Middle Ages, the need for education expanded. The Church wanted better-educated clergy. Royal rulers also needed literate men for their growing bureaucracies. By acquiring an education, the sons of wealthy townspeople might hope to qualify for high positions in the Church or with royal governments.

Early Universities By the 1000s, schools had sprung up around the great cathedrals to train the clergy. Some of these cathedral schools evolved into the first universities. They were organized like guilds, with charters to protect the rights of members and set standards for training.

As early as the 900s, Salerno in Italy had a respected medical school. Bologna's university, set up in 1158, became famous for legal studies. Paris and Oxford founded universities in the later 1100s. In the next century, other cities rushed to organize universities. Students often traveled from one university to another to study different subjects.

www.PearsonTexas.com
Access your Digital Lesson.

Aa Vocabulary Builder

1. Have students pronounce the following academic vocabulary terms in this lesson and clarify the part of speech. For difficult or polysyllabic words, break them into syllables and pronounce them with the students.
2. Explain what the word means in common "student-friendly" language using synonyms and antonyms when possible. Provide concrete examples to clarify the meaning, and rephrase the definition.

dictate: speak or read words for another person to write down

initiate: start; introduce

depict: show

chronicle: to present a record of

Topic 7 Lesson 6

Learning, Literature and the Arts of the Middle Ages

CONNECT

Preview Have students preview the **Lesson Objectives** and the list of **Key Terms**.

Students can also preview all the **Key Terms** and **Academic Vocabulary** using the **Interactive Reading Notepad** on the digital course or preview a summary of the lesson in the **Reading and Note Taking Study Guide**.

Online Use the **Editable Presentation** found on the digital course to present the main ideas for this lesson.

Start Up Activity

Discuss Treachery and betrayal are often also part of heroic stories. Why do you think Ganelon betrayed his king and caused Roland's death? *(Since he conspired with Marsil, Ganelon might have hoped for part of Charlemagne's kingdom if Charlemagne lost the war.)* How was the idea of betrayal, but with the just winning in the end, an important theme for the people of medieval Europe? *(Warfare was almost constant. The belief, especially within the Christian context, that the "good" cause would win eventually gave the people hope that things would be right in the end, even if that "end" was death.)*

Online You can also project the **Start Up Activity** from the course.

INVESTIGATE

Have students read the section using the **Reading and Note Taking Study Guide** to help them take notes and understand the text as they read.

The Rise of Medieval Universities

Universities had their beginnings as church or monastery schools. These centers of learning were one of the ways medieval Christianity acted as a unifying social force. For a largely illiterate society, the Church and Christianity were the center of people's lives.

Topic 7 Lesson 6

Guided Reading and Discussion

Historians now recognize that a new culture was emerging in the early Middle Ages. Education meant the introduction of new ideas from many different cultures, including ancient cultures such as the Greeks and Romans. Students studying medicine would become familiar with both Muslim and Greek writings. Those studying law would learn about the history of legal systems, as well as the local legal codes. With education, a broader worldview started to emerge, especially in areas where foreign trade was common and ideas arrived along with trade goods.

Identify Cause and Effect Why did an improving economy lead to the growth of universities? *(As some people became wealthy, they looked for opportunities for their children in government bureaucracies and the Church, which required education.)*

Draw Inferences How did women get an education? *(Very few did. Of those, most would have gotten their education in convents or with private schools or tutors.)*

Refer to the map Medieval Universities. Explain that most schools and universities had their beginnings as church or monastery schools.

Medieval universities brought prestige and profit to the cities in which they were located. Local merchants provided students with housing, food, clothing, and entertainment. But students could also create problems for university communities. The priest Jacques de Vitry complained, "They were always fighting and engaging in scuffles."

Student Life University life offered few comforts. A bell wakened students at about 5 A.M. for prayers. Students then attended classes until 10 A.M., when they had their first meal of the day.

Afternoon classes continued until 5 P.M. Students usually ate a light supper and then studied until bedtime. Since the first medieval universities did not have permanent buildings, classes were held in rented rooms or in the choir loft of a church. Students sat for hours on hard benches as the teacher dictated and then explained Latin texts. Students were expected to memorize what they heard.

A program of study covered the seven liberal arts: arithmetic, geometry, astronomy, music, grammar, rhetoric, and logic. There were separate programs for the further study of law, medicine, and theology. To show mastery of a subject, students took an oral exam. Earning a degree as a bachelor of arts took between three and six years. Only after several more years of study could a man qualify to become a master of arts and a teacher. Theology was the longest course of study.

> They tell me that, unlike everyone else, you get out of bed before the first bell sounds in order to study, that you are the first into the classroom and the last to leave it. And when you get back home you spend the whole day going over what you were taught in your lessons . . . Many people make themselves permanently ill through excessive study; some of them die and others . . . waste away day after day.
>
> —Boncomagno da Sigma

Women and Education During the Middle Ages, women were expected to pursue their "natural" gifts at home—raising children, managing the household, and doing needlework. Only men were expected to seek an education or write books. Women were not allowed to attend universities. This exclusion seriously affected their lives. Since most did not even attend school, they

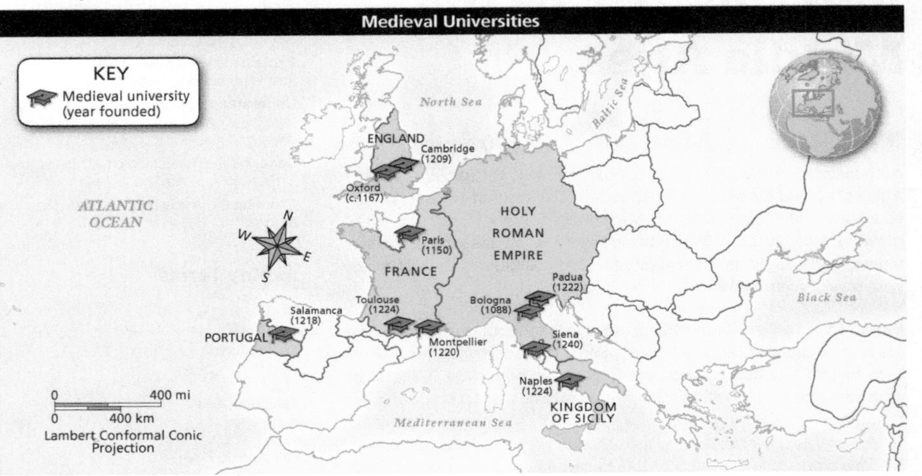

>> Most medieval universities were supported by a church or monastery. **Analyze Maps** Locate: (a) Paris, (b) Rome, (c) London. Which area had the greatest number of universities? What factors do you think contributed to this?

History Background

The Game of Chess Chess is thought to have originated in India around the 6th century A.D. At that time, the game was called *chaturanga* and although it involved four players, it included features found in all subsequent versions of chess, including different pieces with varying powers and the need to vanquish one piece (today's king) in order to win. It is believed that Muslims brought the game to North Africa, Sicily, and Spain; Eastern Slavs carried it to Kievan Rus, and Vikings introduced chess to Iceland and England. The game has been favored by nobility and the wealthy and it is from this fact that chess gained its nickname, the "royal game." The modern term *checkmate* derives from the Persian *shah mat*, which means "the king is dead."

Answers

Analyze Maps *Rome and surrounding areas had the greatest number of universities, followed by Paris. The first universities were part of monasteries or churches. Rome was the center of the papacy and Italy would have more monasteries and churches than elsewhere. Paris had a relatively large number of monasteries and churches as well.*

were deprived of the mental stimulation that was an important part of an educated person's life. Without a university education, women could not become doctors, lawyers, or church officials.

Despite restrictions, a few women did get an education. Most convents educated girls. Some nuns became scholars and writers. Still, women like **Christine de Pisan**(duh pee ZAHN) were the exceptions. In *The City of Ladies*, she asks whether women are less capable of learning and understanding, as men insist, and a character replies.

> If it were customary to send daughters to school like sons, and if they were then taught the same subjects, they would learn as thoroughly and understand the subtleties of all arts and sciences as well as sons.
>
> —Christine de Pisan

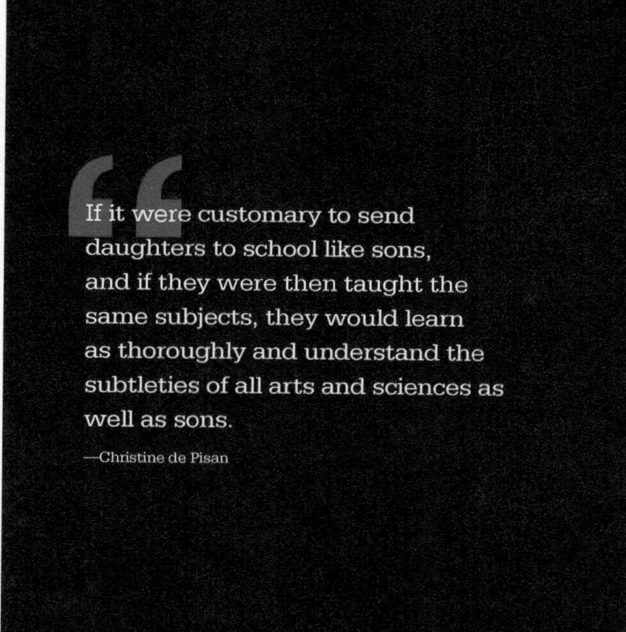

If it were customary to send daughters to school like sons, and if they were then taught the same subjects, they would learn as thoroughly and understand the subtleties of all arts and sciences as well as sons.
—Christine de Pisan

>> The daughter of a physician, and a widow by age 25, Christine de Pisan was far more educated than most women of her time. She used her eduction to write about women's social issues.

Learning for Children Few children in the Middle Ages received any education. At home, and perhaps in the parish church, they learned basic Christian beliefs.

Overall, education for most children was informal. They learned by doing. Within the family, they were assigned tasks appropriate to their age. Older children looked after younger ones. Children often took on demanding tasks in the fields or towns where they lived. They carried heavy loads, cleared land, or learned skilled trades if they were apprenticed out by their families.

 **DESCRIBE** What was university life like in medieval Europe?

New Knowledge Reaches Europe

Universities received a further boost from an explosion of knowledge that reached Europe in the High Middle Ages. Many of the "new" ideas had originated in ancient Greece but had been lost to Western Europeans after the fall of Rome.

New Knowledge Reaches Europe

The High Middle Ages was a time of exciting ideas and inventions that changed how people lived.

Guided Reading and Discussion

Explain that the Greek philosopher, Aristotle, produced a work called *Ethics*. The main ideas of this work include: the importance of the soul in defining humans, finding the mean or middle between extremes, living a life of moderation, and the importance of developing virtue by maintaining positive behavior and habits. Other Greek philosophers emphasized the existence of natural and universal laws that are independent of laws passed by people. Christian scholars and philosophers, such as Thomas Aquinas, were often able to find common ground with these secular teachings.

Compare Where did Aquinas find the important similarities between Aristotle's philosophy and Christian religious beliefs? *(Answers will vary but should include an understanding that the specific examples given of Aristotle's philosophy mirror basic Christian teachings concerning humans having a soul, adopting personal behaviors that are not indulgent or gluttonous, and the importance of living a virtuous life according to Church doctrine.)*

Answers

Describe *Boys studied the seven liberal arts. The hours of study were very long and students had to memorize what they heard from the teacher. Students paid for room and board at places within the town.*

English Language Proficiency Standards

Listening 2.G.2 Read aloud, or have students read, "The Rise of Medieval Universities." Focus on the quotation from Christine de Pisan and have students participate in the following activities.

Beginning Before you read the quotation aloud, identify challenging words and phrases. Read slowly, with natural expression. Help students look up challenging words in a bilingual dictionary and complete this sentence frame:

Christine de Pisan believed that daughters and sons _____.

Intermediate Before you read the quotation aloud, identify challenging words and phrases. Read slowly, with natural expression. Direct students to look up identified words in a bilingual dictionary.

Advanced Before you read the quotation aloud, have students skim the text to identify challenging words and phrases. Direct students to look up words they identify in a bilingual dictionary.

Advanced High Before students read the quotation aloud, have them skim the text to identify challenging words and phrases. Direct students to look up difficult words in a bilingual dictionary. Have a volunteer read the quote slowly, with natural expression.

Topic 7 Lesson 6

Online Project the **Interactive Gallery: Medieval Innovation in Europe.** Click on each invention for a brief explanation of what it was and its impact on medieval life of the time. Discuss how seemingly minor innovations, such as an iron plow, could have far-reaching effects. Ask students for examples of modern inventions that impact their daily lives.

ACTIVE CLASSROOM

Use the Rank It strategy to have students decide which inventions had the greatest impact on medieval life. List the inventions on the board. Ask students to rank the inventions and provide a justification for ranking decisions they made. Then ask students to work in pairs to discuss their rankings and justifications. Poll the class to see if there is agreement on the rankings. Discuss any significant differences in poll results.

Ancient Learning Is Brought to Europe In the Middle East, Muslim scholars had translated the works of Aristotle and other Greek thinkers into Arabic. Their translations and commentaries on these ancient texts spread across the Muslim world. In Muslim Spain, Jewish and Christian scholars translated these works into Latin, the language of Christian European scholars.

Aristotle's Ideas Challenge Christian Thinkers In the 1100s, these new translations were reaching Western Europe. There, they set off a revolution in the world of learning.

The writings of the ancient Greeks posed a challenge to Christian scholars. Aristotle taught that people should use reason to discover basic truths. Christians, however, accepted many ideas on faith. They believed that the Church was the final authority on all questions. How could they use the logic of Aristotle without undermining their Christian faith?

Christian scholars, called scholastics, tried to resolve the conflict between faith and reason. Their method, known as **scholasticism,** used reason to support Christian beliefs. Scholastics studied the works of the Muslim philosopher Averroës (uh VEER uh weez) and the Jewish rabbi Maimonides (my MAHN uh deez). These thinkers, too, used logic to resolve the conflict between faith and reason.

>> Metal-framed eyeglasses like these were the result of new knowledge that resulted in a variety of inventions during the Middle Ages.

Interactive Gallery

Thomas Aquinas The writings of these philosophers influenced the famous scholastic **Thomas Aquinas** (uh KWY nus). In a monumental work, *Summa theologica*, Aquinas concluded that faith and reason exist in harmony.

Aquinas's work concluded that both lead to the same truth, that God rules over an orderly universe. Aquinas thus brought together Christian faith and classical Greek philosophy.

Aquinas also wrote about government and natural law, or a set of unwritten moral principles based on fairness and reason. Aquinas believed that government should work for the "common good" that benefits all. He also argued that people are not obliged to obey unjust laws or the rulers who enact them.

The ideas Aquinas developed about natural law, unjust laws, and rebellion influenced European philosophers in the 1600s and 1700s. Their ideas, in turn, influenced the men like Thomas Jefferson who wrote the American Declaration of Independence and others who authored the U.S. Constitution.

Science and Mathematics Scientific works, translated from Arabic and Greek, also reached Europe from Spain and the Byzantine empire. Christian scholars studied Hippocrates on medicine and Euclid on geometry, along with works by Arab scientists. They saw, too, how Aristotle had used observation and experimentation to study the physical world.

Yet science made little real progress in Europe in the Middle Ages because most scholars still believed that all true knowledge must fit with Church teachings. It would take many centuries before Christian thinkers changed the way they viewed the physical world.

In mathematics, Europeans adopted Hindu-Arabic numerals, commonly called Arabic numerals. In fact, the Arabs had adapted these numerals from India. Hindu-Arabic numerals were much easier to use than the cumbersome system of Roman numerals that Europeans had used for centuries. In time, but long after the Middle Ages, the use of Hindu-Arabic numerals allowed both scientists and mathematicians to make extraordinary advances in their fields.

DESCRIBE What were some elements of the new learning of medieval Europe?

ELPS **ELPS 2.I.3** Practice listening and following directions as you learn about the contributions of Arabic thinkers to science and mathematics in Europe.

English Language Proficiency Standards

Listening 2.I.3 Ask students to find the section "Science and Mathematics" in the text "New Knowledge Reaches Europe."

Beginning Read the section aloud, using a variety of linguistic supports, to help students understand the content.

Intermediate Repeat the Beginning activity, and then ask students to identify two contributions from the Arab world that improved the way European thinkers viewed science and mathematics.

Advanced Repeat the Intermediate activity. Then ask students to discuss the contributions they identified in a small group.

Advanced High Read the section aloud to students, making sure students have an opportunity to ask any questions they may have about the language or the content of the section.

Answers

Describe *It was a blend of Greek learning, Muslim learning, and the efforts of European thinkers to reconcile these ideas with their religious faith.*

Medieval Literature

While Latin remained the written language of scholars and churchmen, new writings began to appear in the **vernacular,** or the everyday languages of ordinary people, such as French, German, and Italian. These writings captured the spirit of the late Middle Ages. Medieval literature included epics, or long narrative poems, about feudal warriors and chivalry as well as tales of the common people.

Heroic Epics Capture the Imagination Across Europe, people began writing down oral traditions in the vernacular. French pilgrims traveling to holy sites loved to hear the chansons de geste, or "songs of heroic deeds." The most popular was the *Song of Roland,* written around 1100, which praises the courage of one of Charlemagne's knights. A true chivalric hero, Roland loyally sacrifices his life out of a sense of honor.

Spain's great epic, *Poem of the Cid*, tells the story of Rodrigo Díaz de Vivar, a bold and fiery Christian lord who fought both with and against Muslim forces. His nickname, El Cid, comes from the Arabic word for "lord."

Heroic epics that told thrilling tales of heroism appealed to Christians across Europe. Nobles in the late Middle Ages adopted ideas about honor and chivalry in theory, if not in practice. Epic tales found a ready audience among all classes of medieval society. The tales varied from region to region, but people took pride in their great heroes.

>> Rodrigo Diaz de Vivar, known as El Cid, was an epic hero in Spanish medieval literature. Like Roland, his story features bravery in battle and personal honor.

Dante's Journey "In the middle of the journey of life, I found myself in a dark wood, where the straight way was lost." So begins the *Divine Comedy,* written in the early 1300s by the Italian poet **Dante Alighieri** (DAHN tay ah leeg YEH ree). The poem takes the reader on an imaginary journey into hell and purgatory, where souls await forgiveness. Finally, Dante describes a vision of heaven.

"Abandon all hope, ye that enter here" is the warning Dante receives as he approaches hell. There, he talks with people from history who tell how they earned a place in hell.

Dante's *The Divine Comedy* contains both humor and tragedy rooted in the familiar medieval quest for spiritual understanding. As he journeys through heaven and hell, he reflects on moral and ethical questions that Christians faced and shows how people's actions in life determine their fate in the afterlife.

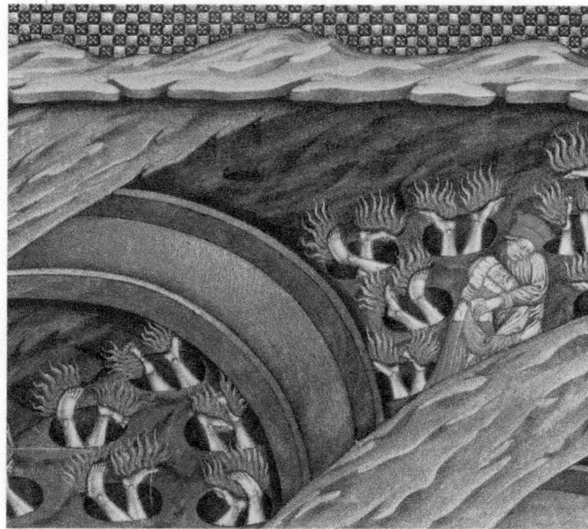

>> In *The Divine Comedy,* Dante, shown here in the red hat, is carried to a level of the underworld where he learns the terrible fate of two popes who abused their powers when alive.

Chaucer's *Canterbury Tales* In the *Canterbury Tales,* the English writer **Geoffrey Chaucer** follows a band of English pilgrims traveling to Thomas Becket's tomb. In brilliant word portraits, he sketches a range of

Medieval Literature

Medieval writers wrote such works as *The Divine Comedy* and *The Canterbury Tales* in a long, narrative style. Medieval writings also included poems about chivalrous warriors and rich stories about common people.

Guided Reading and Discussion

Medieval literature in the vernacular grew from several traditions. Traditional stories that had withstood the test of time were valued over original stories. Therefore, medieval authors often adapted themes and stories similar to those used by their Greek and Roman predecessors. Several of these works became the first examples of national literature, helping to define emerging European nations. These include the stories of King Arthur (Britain), The Song of Roland (France), and El Cid (Spain). However, there were also works that offered readers humor or a "slice of life" that opened a window on the lives of a wide variety of people.

Draw Comparisons How is a popular work like *The Canterbury Tales* like a medieval version of a modern-day TV reality show? *(Chaucer tried to represent different general types or categories of people as they actually were. Their opinions and actions reflect the reality of a person of that class or station in life.)*

Architecture and Art

The High Middle Ages was a time of both technical and artistic change in architecture. Builders used engineering skills to construct vast cathedrals that would have been structurally impossible even a generation earlier.

The Byzantine Heritage

The Byzantine empire, especially Constantinople, was an important center of learning. Schools of law, philosophy, and religion attracted students from all over the known world. Heavily influenced by ancient Roman civilization, the Byzantines often integrated classical concepts with emerging Christian beliefs.

Draw Inferences Why is integrating different cultural influences a major factor in the development of art, literature, and architecture? *(The combination of different perspectives represented by the cultures creates a unique piece of art, literature, or architecture that reflects the time in which it is created.)*

>> This scene from Chaucer's *Canterbury Tales* shows the merchant, nun, and priest, who are among several who tell stories during the pilgrimage.

>> Romanesque churches like this one reflect the most common form of church architecture throughout Europe.

characters, including a knight, a plowman, a merchant, a miller, a monk, and a nun. Each character tells a story to entertain the group. Whether funny, romantic, or bawdy, each tale adds to our picture of medieval life.

DESCRIBE What were three works of medieval literature? What were their subjects?

Architecture and Art

"In the Middle Ages," wrote French author Victor Hugo, "men had no great thought that they did not write down in stone." Those "writings" were the great buildings of the Middle Ages. With riches from trade and commerce, townspeople, nobles, and monarchs indulged in a flurry of building. Their greatest achievements were the towering stone cathedrals that served as symbols of their wealth and religious devotion.

Romanesque Buildings In the year 1000, monasteries and towns were building solid stone churches that reflected Roman influences. These Romanesque churches looked like fortresses with thick walls and towers. The roofs were so heavy that they required massive stone walls with no windows or only tiny slits of windows. Larger windows, builders feared, would weaken the support for the roof. As a result, the interiors of Romanesque churches were dark and dimly lit.

Graceful Gothic Cathedrals About 1140, Abbot Suger (SOOZHAY) wanted to build a new abbey church at St. Denis near Paris. He hoped that it "would shine with wonderful and uninterrupted light." There, builders developed what became known as the **Gothic style** of architecture.

A key feature of the new Gothic style was the **flying buttresses,** or stone supports that stood outside the church. These supports allowed builders to construct higher, thinner walls and leave space for large stained-glass windows. Gothic churches soared to incredible heights. Their graceful spires and tall windows carried the eye upward to the heavens. "Since their brilliance lets the splendor of the True Light pass into the church," declared a medieval visitor, "they enlighten those inside."

Splendid Art in Stone and Glass As churches rose, stonemasons carved sculptures to decorate them inside and out. Sculptures included portraits and scenes from the lives of saints and illustrated stories from the Bible. Sculptors also carved plants and animals, both real and imaginary. Some stone pieces were gargoyles, grotesque figures with a spout that carried water

Answers

Describe *Choices are:* The Canterbury Tales, The Divine Comedy, The Song of Roland, Poem of the Cid. Song of Roland *and* Poem of the Cid *are heroic epics.* The Canterbury Tales *is meant to be entertaining, but also give us an idea of what medieval life was like.* The Divine Comedy *is an imaginary journey through purgatory, hell, and heaven as imagined by a traveler to each place.*

off the roof and away from the walls of the building. They also carved whimsical or frightening images of mythical creatures such as dragons and unicorns.

Other skilled craft workers created the colorful stained-glass windows that added to the splendor of Gothic churches. Stained-glass windows illustrated dramatic scenes from the Bible and other Christian beliefs. Stained-glass windows and carvings in stone served an essential purpose. They helped educate the masses of people who could not read about the Christian faith.

Paintings and Tapestries Medieval artists created other works, including splendid altarpieces that decorated the space behind the church altar. Altarpieces could be paintings, relief sculptures, or both.

Like stained-glass windows, they illustrated Christian subjects and were designed to inspire devotion among the faithful. Most altarpieces hung in churches, although wealthy families might have a chapel and altarpiece in their homes.

Both churches and the houses of the rich were decorated with "paintings" in thread. Stone churches and castles were cold, drafty places. Tapestries, or woven wall hangings, added color and warmth. The famous Bayeux Tapestry is an embroidery piece that illustrates in detail the story of William the Conqueror and the Battle of Hastings in 1066. Although no one knows who wove it or exactly when, it has been used to learn details of the event.

Illuminated Manuscripts Throughout the Middle Ages, monks, nuns, and other skilled artisans decorated the handwritten books of the time with elaborate designs and illustrations, known as **illumination.** The most spectacular deocrations in these books were made of gold and silver.

Some illuminations depicted biblical scenes. Others, such as prayer books called Books of Hours, showed scenes of daily life in towns and castles with peasants in the field along with nobles on horseback.

DESCRIBE What types of artistic works were found in medieval churches?

The Byzantine Heritage

The Byzantine empire contributed to the civilizations of the eastern Mediterranean and of Western Europe. Byzantine civilization rose out of many traditions, blending Christian beliefs with Greek philosophy,

>> The multicolored and multipaned Rose window in Notre Dame Cathedral in Paris thrilled medieval church-goers.

Interactive Gallery

>> This panel of the Bayeaux Tapestry shows a scene from the Battle of Hastings in 1066.

Online Project the **Interactive Gallery: The Gothic Cathedral.** Click on each hotspot to show students the amazing architectural and artistic skills represented by a Gothic cathedral. Artisans were brought in from all over Europe to produce wondrous works of art in stained-glass windows. These windows reflected the power of the Church and portrayed Bible episodes for illiterate Christians. Italian stonemasons often traveled far from home to create the intricate statues of saints or fanciful gargoyles.

ACTIVE CLASSROOM

Use the See-Think-Wonder strategy to have students take a closer look at the many architectural and artistic wonders present in a Gothic cathedral. Ask students: What do you see? What does that make you think? What are you wondering about now that you've seen this?

Draw Conclusions Why was the flying buttress such an important architectural advance? *(It allowed for greater open spaces and light in cathedrals.)*

Key Terms

Ask students to find the key term **icons** (in bold) in the text. Explain that many churches use images to invoke the presence of God. Ask students what might be considered an icon of a country such as the United States.

Answers

Describe *stained-glass windows, paintings and sculptures with religious themes; carvings of plants, animals, and mythical creatures*

Describe *religious art and architecture; preserved the ancient Greek, Roman, and Christian heritage blended with other traditions of the Mediterranean world; produced important literature; contributed to the European Renaissance*

Topic 7 Lesson 6

SYNTHESIZE

Online Have students use the Think-Pair-Share strategy to answer the questions in the Reach for the Sky activity. Ask them to take five minutes to write down some brief answers to the following questions and then share their answers with a partner.

How did increasing access to education affect architecture and art in the Middle Ages?

Discuss What is the role of government in providing education? *(Answers may vary. Students may argue that access to education is a human right that should not be limited to those who are wealthy or to specific genders and races. They may claim that education is a key to progress and, as such, it is the responsibility of government to ensure that there is equal access to quality education for all people.)*

DEMONSTRATE

Online Assign the **Digital Lesson Quiz** for this lesson if you haven't already done so. Students will be offered automatic remediation or enrichment based on their score.

Pose these questions to the class on the Discussion Board:

In "Learning, Literature, and the Arts of the Middle Ages," you learned about how the rise of medieval universities and education in general had a profound effect on people of various social and economic backgrounds. Education led to a re-emergence of philosophical thought that challenged theologians such as Thomas Aquinas. This inquiry led to greater intellectual growth within the Church while maintaining basic religious concepts. Education also influenced art and architecture, with both areas flourishing. Advanced techniques made it possible to build the Gothic cathedral, which would have a major impact on Christian houses of worship for many centuries. Finally, you learned about the extensive influence of the Byzantine empire on the new educational growth in Europe. Byzantine scholars moved to Europe to teach, and there was a renewal of interest in classical thought. Ideas from the Middle East also influenced art and architecture.

Draw Conclusions How do art, literature, and architecture reflect the history of the cultures in which they are produced? *(Art, literature, and architecture are creative as well as technical. The creativity that allows people to produce these works is a function of what they experience on a personal or observed level. The cultures in which the artisans live will affect how they view things and, therefore, what and how they create.)*

Topic Inquiry

Have students continue their investigations for the Topic Inquiry.

>> This religious icon showing Mary and the baby Jesus showcases the Byzantine style.

science, and the arts. It also extended Roman achievements in engineering and law.

As the medieval world expanded, so did its contacts with Byzantine civilization, and Byzantine influence radiated across Europe. Even though the Byzantine empire fell to the Ottomans in 1453, the conquerors adapted features of Byzantine government, arts, and culture.

Contributions in the Arts Byzantine artists made unique contributions, especially in religious art and architecture, that influenced Western styles. **Icons,** images designed to evoke the presence of God, gave viewers a sense of personal contact with the sacred.

Mosaics brought scenes from the Bible to life. In architecture, Byzantine palaces and churches blended Greek, Roman, Persian, and other Middle Eastern styles.

Preserving and Spreading Knowledge Byzantine scholars preserved the classic works of ancient Greece and Rome. In addition, they produced their own great books, especially in the field of history.

Like the Greek historians Herodotus and Thucydides, Byzantine historians were mostly concerned with writing about their own times. Procopius, an advisor to the general Belisarius, chronicled the Byzantine campaign against Persia. In his *Secret History*, Procopius savagely criticized the Emperor Justinian and the Empress Theodora. He called the emperor "both an evil-doer and easily led into evil . . . never of his own accord speaking the truth."

Anna Comnena is considered by many scholars to be the Western world's first important female historian. In the *Alexiad*, she analyzed the reign of her father, Emperor Alexius I. Comnena's book portrayed Latin Crusaders as greedy barbarians.

As the Byzantine empire tottered in the 1400s, many Greek scholars left Constantinople to teach at Italian universities. They took valuable Greek manuscripts to the West, along with their knowledge of Greek and Byzantine culture. The work of these scholars contributed to the cultural flowering in Europe that became known as the Renaissance.

DESCRIBE What were some Byzantine contributions to art and learning?

ASSESSMENT

1. **Analyze Information** How did new knowledge, based on Aristotle and other Greek thinkers, pose a challenge to Christian scholars?
2. **Synthesize Information** Why were heroic epics in the vernacular popular with medieval Europeans?
3. **Identify Central Issues** How was religion central to the art and architecture of the Middle Ages?
4. **Predict Consequences** How might universities that drew students from many places affect European life in the future?
5. **Demonstrate Reasoned Judgment** Why was the Byzantine empire so important to Western Europe?

Medieval Christian Europe 258 7.6 Learning, Literature, and the Arts of the Middle Ages

Assessment

1. Aristotle taught that people should use reason to discover truth; the Church taught that faith and the Church were the final authority.
2. People could understand the stories whose heroes embodied their own ideals.
3. The major architectural advance of the Middle Ages was the Gothic cathedral. Stained-glass windows, painting, and sculpture often had religious themes.
4. As students traveled from place to place, they might help spread new ideas and blend local cultures into a more general, unified European culture.
5. Byzantine scholars helped preserve ancient Greek and Roman works and ideas and spread them to the West. This was an important contribution to the European Renaissance.

7.7 To Europeans in the mid-1300s, the end of the world seemed to have come. First, widespread crop failures brought famine and starvation. Then plague and war ravaged populations. Europe eventually recovered from these disasters. Still, the upheavals of the 1300s and 1400s marked the end of the Middle Ages and the beginning of the early modern age.

>> This medieval illustration shows a man dying of the plague. Boils erupting all over the body was a sign that the plague would likely claim more victims because the disease spread through contact.

 Interactive Flipped Video

The Late Middle Ages: A Time of Upheaval

TEKS
4.G

>> **Objectives**

Understand how the Black Death caused social and economic decline.

Describe the problems facing the Church in the late Middle Ages and how the Church reacted.

Summarize the causes, turning points, and effects of the Hundred Years' War.

>> **Key Terms**

Black Death
epidemic
longbow

The Black Death Spreads Across Europe

The Arrival In the autumn of 1347, a fleet of Genoese trading ships loaded with grain left the Black Sea port of Caffa and set sail for Messina, Sicily. By midvoyage, sailors were falling sick and dying. Soon after the ships tied up at Messina, townspeople, too, began to fall sick and die.

Within months, the disease that Europeans called the **Black Death** was raging through Italy. By 1348, it had reached Spain and France. From there, it ravaged the rest of Europe. One in three people died—a death rate worse than in any war in history.

A Global Epidemic The deadly illness was bubonic plague, a disease spread by fleas carried on rats. In the pre-modern world, rats infested ships, towns, and even the homes of the rich and powerful. Bubonic plague had broken out before in Europe, Asia, and North Africa but

  www.PearsonTexas.com Access your Digital Lesson.

Aa Vocabulary Builder

1. Have students pronounce the following academic vocabulary terms in this lesson and clarify the part of speech. For difficult or polysyllabic words, break them into syllables and pronounce them with the students.
2. Explain what the word means in common "student-friendly" language using synonyms and antonyms when possible. Provide concrete examples to clarify the meaning, and rephrase the definition.

authorize: give official power to perform an act

venture: business enterprise or other undertaking involving some risk

ravaged: badly damaged

hysteria: uncontrollable outburst of emotion or fear

Topic 7 Lesson 7

The Late Middle Ages: A Time of Upheaval

CONNECT

Preview Have students preview the **Lesson Objectives** and the list of **Key Terms**.

Students can also preview all the **Key Terms** and **Academic Vocabulary** using the **Interactive Reading Notepad** on the digital course or preview a summary of the lesson in the **Reading and Note Taking Study Guide**.

Online Use the **Editable Presentation** found on the digital course to present the main ideas for this lesson.

Start Up Activity

Discuss When Gethin describes the arrival of death as "black smoke" and "a rootless phantom," what types of feelings and images does that evoke in you? *(Sample responses: mysterious, frightening, something uncontrollable)* How do you think your neighbors and friends would react to a mysterious, fatal illness that swept through the community? *(Sample responses: fearfulness, chaos, blaming a person or group)* How might public services, such as electricity, water, and fuel, be affected if almost half the population of a city or town suddenly disappeared? *(Sample response: Services would stop because no one could run them.)*

Online You can also project the **Start Up Activity** from the course.

INVESTIGATE

Have students read the section using the **Reading and Note Taking Study Guide** to help them take notes and understand the text as they read.

The Black Death Spreads Across Europe

The Black Death had an enormous impact on every aspect of medieval society. It spread far and fast, sometimes eradicating entire villages.

Online Project the **Interactive Map: The Black Death.** Click on each time period to show how fast and how far the Black Death spread. Discuss the effects of the Black Death on medieval society and how it contributed to the end of medieval Europe.

ACTIVE CLASSROOM

Have students write a headline and then a three-sentence introduction to a television special on the Black Death. Ask volunteers to present their introductions. Discuss which aspects of the Black Death contributed the most to the end of medieval Europe's social structure and economy.

Guided Reading and Discussion

The significance of the plague is not solely in the outbreak of disease, but in the profound political, social, and economic consequences of high rates of mortality throughout Europe.

Identify Cause and Effect How did the high mortality rate affect the feudal and manorial systems in medieval Europe? *(These systems began to collapse, giving serfs and peasants freedom to seek work where it was available.)*

Crisis in the Church

After the devastation of the Black Death, survivors were asking difficult questions of their Church leaders. Strong Church leadership was sorely needed. However, the Church was dealing with serious internal conflicts.

Key Terms

Ask students to find the key term **epidemic** (in bold) in the text. Explain that an epidemic is a fast-spreading disease. Ask them to give an example of a modern-day epidemic.

D Differentiate Challenge/Gifted After reviewing students' headlines and program introductions, have students complete the exercise by creating a script for a short documentary on the plague. Some students can write the script. Others can be the actors in a video presentation to the rest of the class.

had subsided. One strain of the disease, though, had survived in Mongolia.

In the 1200s, Mongol armies conquered much of Asia, probably setting off the new **epidemic,** or outbreak of rapid-spreading disease. In the early 1300s, rats spread the plague in crowded Chinese cities, killing about 35 million people there. Fleas jumped from those rats to infest the clothes and packs of traders traveling west. As a result, the disease spread from Asia to the Middle East and then to Europe.

Social Upheaval In Europe, the plague brought terror and bewilderment, as people had no way to stop the disease. Some people turned to magic and witchcraft for cures. Others plunged into wild pleasures, believing they would soon die anyway. Still others saw the plague as God's punishment. They beat themselves with whips to show that they repented their sins. Normal life broke down as people fled cities or hid in their homes to avoid contracting the plague from neighbors and relatives.

Some Christians blamed Jews for the plague, charging unjustly that they had poisoned the wells to cause the disease. In the resulting hysteria, thousands of Jews were murdered.

Economic Impact As the plague kept recurring in the late 1300s, the European economy plunged to a low ebb. When workers and employers died, production declined. Survivors demanded higher wages, but as the cost of labor soared, prices rose, too.

Landowners and merchants pushed for laws to limit wages. To limit rising costs, landowners converted croplands to land for sheep raising, which required less labor. Villagers forced off the land looked for work in towns. There, guilds limited opportunities for advancement.

Coupled with the fear of the plague, these restrictions sparked explosive revolts. Angry peasants rampaged in England, France, Germany, and elsewhere. In the cities, artisans fought for more power, usually without success. Revolts erupted on and off through the 1300s and 1400s. The plague had spread death and social unrest. It would take Western Europe more than 100 years to fully recover from its effects.

The plague returned repeatedly during the later Middle Ages and into early modern times. Daniel Defoe's *Journal of the Plague Year* vividly chronicled the impact of mass deaths in England in the 1600s.

CHECK UNDERSTANDING How did the Black Death affect Europe?

>> This image is of an angry mob storming a nobleman's fortress. Because of the plague, crops often rotted in the field. Peasants often blamed the lord of the manor for leaving fields fallow.

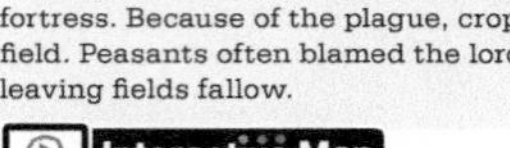

Crisis in the Church

The late Middle Ages brought spiritual crisis, scandal, and division to the Roman Catholic Church. Many priests and monks died during the plague. Their replacements faced challenging questions. Survivors asked, "Why did God spare some and kill others?"

Divisions in the Church The Church was unable to provide the strong leadership needed in this desperate time. In 1309, Pope Clement V had moved the papal court to Avignon outside the border of southern France. It remained there for about 70 years under French domination. This period is often called the Babylonian Captivity of the Church, referring to the time when the ancient Hebrews were held captive in Babylon.

In Avignon, popes reigned over a lavish court. Critics lashed out against the worldly, pleasure-loving papacy, and anticlerical sentiment grew. Within the Church itself, reformers tried to end the "captivity."

In 1378, reformers within the Church elected their own pope to rule from Rome. French cardinals responded by choosing a rival pope. The election of two and sometimes even three rival popes created a schism, or divide, in the Church. This second Great Schism, like the earlier split into eastern and western

English Language Proficiency Standards

Listening 2.G.3 Use with the reading "The Black Death Spreads Across Europe." To help students understand the effects of the bubonic plague, have them complete one of these activities.

Beginning Ask students to recall a time when they were worried about something. Have one or two volunteers offer their experiences. Help students feel empathy for the people who suffered the Black Death, or bubonic plague. To help students understand the effects of the bubonic plague, consider providing a video clip about the difficulties of life at this time.

Intermediate Ask students to describe to a partner a time when they were worried about something. Have a few volunteers offer their experiences to the class. Some students will have a personal context for this; others will not. Ask students to identify words that describe how they would feel if they lived at this time.

Advanced Ask students to describe to a partner a time when they were worried about something. Ask students to write one or two sentences to describe how people living during this time might feel about all the death and sadness around them.

Advanced High Ask students to share a time when they were worried about something. Consider providing a video clip about the difficulties of life at this time. Have students discuss in a small group how people might have felt about all the death and sadness around them.

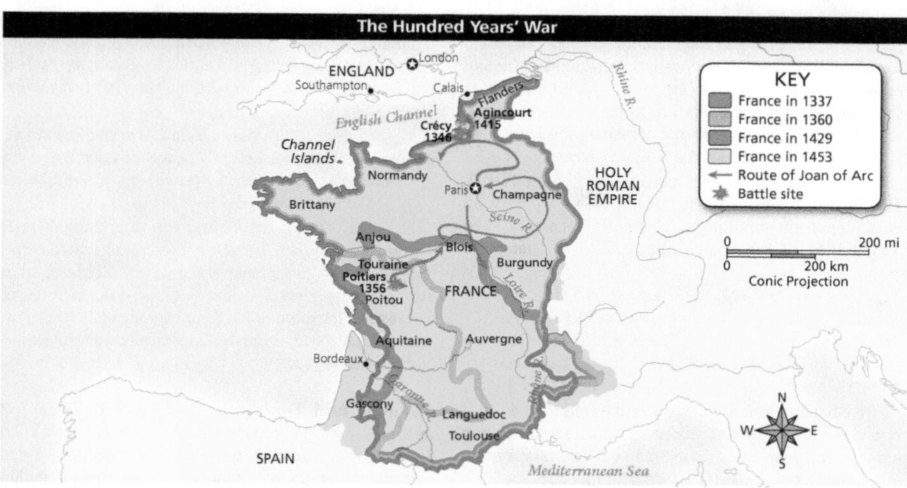

>> The English and French battled for control of France. **Analyze Maps** What regions of France did England gain between 1337 and 1429?

Interactive Map

branches of Christianity, hurt the Church and weakened its moral authority, contributing to the gradual end of medieval Europe. Not until 1417 did a Church council at Constance finally end the crisis.

New Heresies Threaten the Church With its moral standing and leadership in decline, the Church faced still more problems. Popular preachers challenged its power. In England, John Wycliffe, an Oxford professor, attacked corruption in the Church.

Wycliffe insisted that the Bible, not the Church, was the source of all Christian truth. He supported the idea of translating the Bible into English so that people could read it themselves rather than rely on the clergy to read and interpret it for them. Czech students at Oxford carried Wycliffe's ideas to Bohemia—today's Czech Republic. There, Jan Hus led the call for reforms, supported by his followers, known as Hussites.

The Church responded to these calls for reform by persecuting Wycliffe and his followers and suppressing the Hussites. Hus was tried for preaching heresy—ideas contrary to Church teachings. Found guilty, he was burned at the stake in 1415.

The ideas of Wycliffe and Hus survived. Their calls for reform had taken root in response to the worldliness of the Church and feuds among its leaders. These reformers looked on the Bible, rather than the pope or bishops, as the source of Christian faith. In the next century, other reformers echoed similar demands, calling for the faithful to rely on the Bible and for limiting the role of the clergy. This new reform movement would split the Roman Catholic Church forever and transform Western Europe.

 **DESCRIBE** Describe two threats to Church power.

The Hundred Years' War

On top of the disasters of famine, plague, and economic decline came a long, destructive war. Between 1337 and 1453, England and France engaged in a series of conflicts, known as the Hundred Years' War. The fighting devastated France and drained England.

Rival Powers: England and France English rulers had battled for centuries to hold on to the French lands of their Norman ancestors. But French kings were intent on extending their own power in France. When Edward III of England claimed the French crown in 1337, war erupted anew between these rival powers. Once fighting started, economic rivalry and a growing sense of national pride made it hard for either side to give up the struggle.

Early Victories for England At first, the English won a string of victories—at Crécy in 1346, Poitiers in

Guided Reading and Discussion

When France forced the pope to move from Rome to Avignon, a period of intense rivalry and confusion began within the Church. The pope moved back to Rome in 1377 and died a year later. The policies of the next pope, Urban VI, were unpopular, and he was considered mentally ill. The cardinals elected another pope, Clement VII, who moved back to Avignon because Urban would not relinquish the papal throne. This began the Great Schism, or Western Schism, with rival popes excommunicating each other and their followers. In 1409, a Church council elected a third pope and added to the confusion.

Draw Inferences Why did the Church react so harshly to reformers like Wycliffe and Hus? *(Once the papacy was restored, the Church moved to regain the political and social control it had had before the Great Schism. Reformers like Wycliffe threatened the status quo.)*

The Hundred Years' War

Explain that England and France were at war from 1337 to 1453. Drastic changes in weapons technology affected several key battles. Political changes also set England and France on different paths.

Online Project the **Interactive Map: The One Hundred Years' War.** Click through the key periods on the map and discuss the changes to medieval Europe.

ACTIVE CLASSROOM

Using the Ranking strategy, have students rank events on the Interactive Map that had the greatest impact in the Hundred Years' War. Ask students to justify their decisions, and then ask them to work in pairs to share their rankings and justifications.

History Background

Dark Days The events of the 14th century created a religious crisis that left people wondering if they were following the "true" pope. These concurrent events led to a sense of pessimism and helplessness that pervaded European society and culture. Art became darker, with a greater focus on death. Many people felt that the end of the world was near. Groups of flagellants tried to purify themselves by whipping and self-mutilation. Others resorted to witchcraft or became immoral, living only for pleasure. The church condemned all these practices and later used the Inquisition to try to put an end to them.

Answers

Check Understanding *It killed one third of the population, caused the breakdown of normal life, hysteria, and persecution; social unrest; and economic decline.*

Analyze Maps *Brittany, Normandy, Flanders, and Burgundy*

Describe *Answers should include two of the following: the Black Death, the Babylonian Captivity, anti-clergy reformist sentiment, the schism, Wycliffe and Hus heresies.*

Topic 7 Lesson 7

Guided Reading and Discussion

The 14th century was a watershed for Europe. The century was marked by tremendous upheaval: The Hundred Years' War combined with the Black Death and the crisis in the Church led to a sense of pessimism and hopelessness that pervaded European society and culture. People lost confidence in their rulers and in the Church. In England, the people, in the form of Parliament, felt emboldened to restrict the war activities of the king through denying funds for war.

Analyze While the Hundred Years' War led to greater parliamentary strength in England, it led to a stronger monarchy in France. The French people suffered a great deal during the constant fighting. Why do you think they continued to support a strengthened monarchy instead of pushing for a greater voice in government? *(After so many reverses, the French won back enormous amounts of territory. This inspired strong nationalistic feeling and, with it, a reinforced belief in the monarchy and established forms of government.)*

SYNTHESIZE

Online Have students use the Think-Pair-Share strategy to answer the questions in the A Challenge for Science: Epidemics activity. Ask them to take five minutes to write brief answers to these questions and then share their answers with a partner.

Why do you think epidemics continue to pose threats? How are the ways epidemics spread today similar to the ways the plague spread in the 1300s?

Answers

Analyze Charts *Edward III of England claimed the French crown in 1337.*

1356, and Agincourt in 1415. They owed much of their success not to braver or more skillful knights but to the **longbow,** a powerful new weapon wielded by English archers. The longbow was six feet long and took years to master. But it could discharge three arrows in the time a French archer with his crossbow fired just one. Its arrows pierced all but the heaviest armor.

The English victories took a heavy toll on French morale, or spirit. England, it seemed, was likely to bring all of France under its control. Then, in what seemed like a miracle to the French, their fortunes were reversed.

Joan of Arc In 1429, a 17-year-old peasant woman, Joan of Arc, appeared at the court of Charles VII, the uncrowned king of France. She told him that God had sent her to save France. She convinced the desperate French king to let her lead his army against the English.

To Charles's amazement, Joan inspired the battered and despairing French troops to fight anew. In one astonishing year, she led the French to several victories and planted the seeds for future triumphs.

Joan paid for success with her life. She was taken captive by allies of the English and turned over to her enemies for trial. To discredit her, the English had Joan tried for witchcraft. She was convicted and burned at the stake. That action, however, only strengthened her value to the French, who saw her as a martyr. Much later, the Church declared her a saint.

Results of the Long War After Joan's death, the French took the offensive. With a powerful new weapon, the cannon, they attacked English-held castles. By 1453, the English held only the port of Calais in northwestern France.

In the end, the Hundred Years' War set France and England on different paths. The war created a growing sense of national feeling in France and allowed French kings to expand their power.

On the other hand, during the war, English rulers turned repeatedly to Parliament for funds, which helped that body win the "power of the purse." England ended up losing its French lands, but that setback was not disastrous for them. With their dreams of a continental empire shattered, English rulers turned to new trading ventures overseas.

Change and Recovery The Hundred Years' War brought many changes to the late medieval world. The longbow and cannon gave common soldiers a new importance on the battlefield and undermined the value of armored knights on horseback. Although neither nobles nor commoners knew it then, feudal society was changing and medieval Europe was coming to an end. Knights and castles were doomed to disappear. Strong monarchs needed large armies, not feudal vassals, to fight their wars.

As Europe recovered from the Black Death, the population expanded, and manufacturing grew. These

CAUSES	EFFECTS
• Long-standing English and French rivalry over lands in France • Edward III of England Claims the French throne • Edward III's armies invade France	• English monarchy is weakened; French monarchy strengthened • Knights displaced as main fighting force; replaced with soldiers for hire • Weapons become more technologically advanced

>> This shows the causes and effects of the Hundred Years' War. **Analyze Charts** What event began the Hundred Years' War?

English Language Proficiency Standards

Listening 2.I.4 Read "Joan of Arc" aloud. Have students complete one activity according to their level of English proficiency. Then ask students to identify historic and modern individuals who took risks for something they believed in.

Beginning Using linguistic aids, help students understand "Joan of Arc" as you read aloud. Have students formulate opinions about Joan's role in the Hundred Years' War.

Intermediate Ask pairs of students to identify reasons that Joan of Arc was canonized. Provide resources to find word meanings, and have them help each other with vocabulary.

Advanced Ask students whether the Church should have canonized Joan of Arc. Help groups develop the vocabulary to name reasons for and against canonization. Have volunteers read their lists.

Advanced High Have small groups discuss and analyze why Joan of Arc was canonized.

changes led to increased trade. Italian cities flourished as centers of trade and shipping. Europeans borrowed and developed new technologies. This recovery set the stage for further changes during the Renaissance, the Reformation, and the Age of Exploration.

IDENTIFY What effect did the Hundred Years' War have on medieval warfare?

ELPS **ELPS 2.1.4** Practice listening to and speaking with your classmates as you discuss the reasons why Joan of Arc was canonized a saint by the Church.

ASSESSMENT

1. **Recognize Cause and Effect** What were three effects of the Black Death on late medieval Europe?
2. **Draw Conclusions** What were some of the factors that allowed the Black Death to spread so quickly and with such deadly results?
3. **Draw Inference** How did the second Great Schism affect Church authority and power and contribute to the end of medieval Europe?
4. **Cause and Effect** How did Joan of Arc's execution affect the French forces?
5. **Compare** Compare the effects of the Hundred Years' War on France and England.

Topic 7 Lesson 7

Discuss What is the role of government in preventing epidemics? *(Answers should discuss the importance of scientific cooperation between nations, of governments taking the lead in preventive research, and of medical and sanitary standards.)*

DEMONSTRATE

Online Assign the **Digital Lesson Quiz** for this lesson if you haven't already done so. Students will be offered automatic remediation or enrichment based on their score.

Pose these questions to the class on the Discussion Board:

In "The Late Middle Ages: A Time of Upheaval," you learned about three major crises facing the medieval world. These included the Black Death, the Great Schism, and the Hundred Years' War. The combination of these crises brought about the end of medieval Europe.

Recognize Cause and Effect In what specific ways did these crises bring about the end of medieval Europe? *(The Black Death changed the basic structure of medieval life. The Hundred Years' War brought on larger, more temporary armies and improved weapons technology. The crisis in the Church led people to question Church leadership and, eventually, to reform movements.)*

Topic Inquiry

Have students continue their investigations for the Topic Inquiry.

Answers

Identify *Castles and armored knights were doomed to disappear because their defenses could not stand up to the more deadly firepower of the longbow and the cannon; monarchs needed large armies, not feudal vassals, to fight their wars.*

Assessment

1. Answers should include three of the following: the death of one third of Europe's population, the breakdown of normal life, hysteria, persecution, social unrest, decline of production, unemployment, rioting, economic decline.
2. Rats were common on trading ships and in the countryside and towns. The fleas on the rats that carried the plague could easily move from the rats to people. Traders carried fleas in their goods. Conditions in towns were unsanitary, and crowding and fleas were a part of life. There was no known medical treatment for infected people and no one really knew how the plague spread.
3. It weakened the Church's authority, created disarray in the hierarchy of the Church, and led reformers to question if the Church's true authority lay in its members and in the Bible, rather than in popes, cardinals, and bishops.
4. They saw her as a martyr and they quickly took the offensive against the English forces, attacking English-held castles. The French eventually pushed the English forces to Calais, the only remaining English-held castle in France.
5. France: created pride and national feeling; England: power began to shift to Parliament, away from the monarchy.

Topic 7 Lesson 8

Russia and Eastern Europe

CONNECT

Preview Have students preview the **Lesson Objectives** and the list of **Key Terms**.

Students can also preview all the **Key Terms** and **Academic Vocabulary** using the **Interactive Reading Notepad** on the digital course or preview a summary of the lesson in the **Reading and Note Taking Study Guide**.

Online Use the **Editable Presentation** found on the digital course to present the main ideas for this lesson.

Start Up Activity

What parallels can you find between the Slavs that Ibrahim-Ibn-Yaqub described and the conflicts that exist in the world today? Use examples you have seen in the news to develop your response. *(Answers will vary. Students might refer to conflicts in the Middle East, such as the Arab Spring; conflicts in various nations regarding growing immigrant populations; or unrest in areas such as Africa, where different factions are fighting for control.)*

Online You can also project the **Start Up Activity** from the course.

INVESTIGATE

Have students read the section using the **Reading and Note Taking Study Guide** to help them take notes and understand the text as they read.

The Geography of Russia

Russia as we know it today is far different from the Russia of the 14th century. Russia's growth was influenced by its geography, its early trading traditions, the Mongol invasion, and the influence of Byzantine culture.

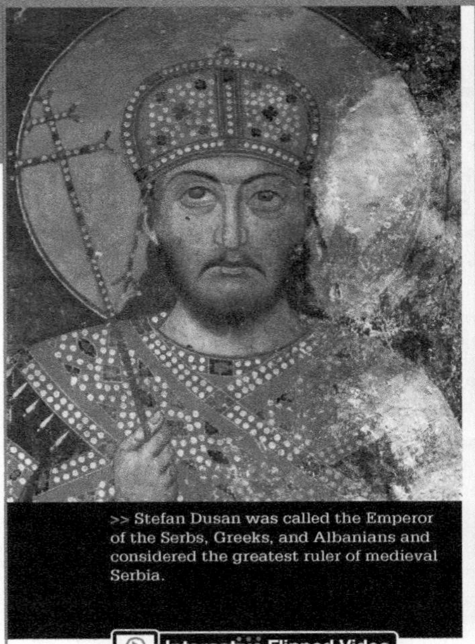

>> Stefan Dusan was called the Emperor of the Serbs, Greeks, and Albanians and considered the greatest ruler of medieval Serbia.

Interactive Flipped Video

7.8 **While feudalism and the Roman Catholic Church were shaping Western Europe in the Middle Ages, another culture was emerging in Russia to the east. Russia lies on the vast Eurasian plain that stretches from Europe to the borders of China. Although mapmakers use the Ural Mountains to mark the boundary between Europe and Asia, these ancient mountains were long ago worn away to wooded hills. They posed no great obstacle to the movement of peoples who were constantly migrating from Asia into Russia.**

TEKS
1.C, 4.K, 15.A, 23.B

>> Objectives

Describe how geography influenced the rise of Russia, and how Kiev grew to be the center of the first Russian state.

Explain how Mongol rule affected Russia.

Describe how Moscow took the lead in Russia and how its rulers developed authoritarian control.

Describe how geography influenced the development of Eastern Europe.

Understand how migration contributed to cultural diversity in Eastern Europe, and learn about three early Eastern European kingdoms.

>> Key Terms

steppe
Kiev
Cyrillic
Ivan the Great
Ivan the Terrible
Balkan Peninsula
ethnic group
diet
Golden Bull of 1222

Russia and Eastern Europe

The Geography of Russia

During the Middle Ages, Russia—like Western Europe—was battered by invasions. Russia, however, had never been part of the Roman empire, and its early rulers looked to the Byzantine world, adapting much of its advanced civilization.

Three Regions Three broad regions with different climates and resources helped shape early Russian life. The first included the northern forests, which supplied lumber for building and fuel. Fur-bearing animals attracted hunters, but poor soil and a cold, snowy climate hindered farming. Farther south lay a second zone of fertile land, where farmers settled and grew crops. This region, which includes what is today Ukraine, was home to Russia's first civilization. The fertile soil and relatively mild climate of this region would eventually make it the "breadbasket" of Russia because of the vast fields of wheat grown there.

A third region, the southern **steppe,** is an open, treeless grassland. It offered splendid pasture for the herds and horses of nomadic peoples. With no natural barriers, the steppe was a great highway along which streams of nomads migrated.

PEARSON realize www.PearsonTexas.com Access your Digital Lesson.

264

Aa Vocabulary Builder

1. Have students pronounce the following academic vocabulary terms in this lesson and clarify the part of speech. For difficult or polysyllabic words, break them into syllables and pronounce them with the students.
2. Explain what the word means in common "student-friendly" language using synonyms and antonyms when possible. Provide concrete examples to clarify the meaning, and rephrase the definition.

tolerate: recognize and not suppress the different beliefs or practices of other people

dominate: to have control, power, or authority over somebody or something

buffer: a protective barrier

ambitious: showing a great desire for fame or power.

Rivers Russia's network of rivers provided transportation for both people and goods. The Dneiper (NEE puhr) and Volga rivers became productive trade routes. Major rivers ran from north to south, linking Russia early on to the advanced Byzantine world to the south.

? ANALYZE CONTEXT How did geography affect Russian settlement and growth?

Early Russia

Russia's early history was similar to that of much of Western Europe. Migrating peoples settled on the land, which was fragmented into many small kingdoms. Early Russia included a collection of small cities that were in time united into an empire.

Slavs and Vikings During Roman times, migrating Slavic peoples expanded into southern Russia. Like the Germanic people who pushed into Western Europe, the Slavs had no political organization more complex than the clan. They lived in small villages, farmed, and traded along the rivers connecting the Baltic in the north to the Black Sea in the south.

In the 700s and 800s, while some Viking leaders pushed into Western Europe, others steered their long ships out of Scandinavia into Russia. These Vikings, whom the Russians later called Varangians, traveled south along the rivers, trading with and collecting tribute, or forced payment, from the Slavs.

The Vikings also conducted a thriving trade with Constantinople. Located at the heart of this trade was the city of **Kiev,** which would later become the center of the first Russian state. Within a few generations, the Varangians who had settled among the Slavs were absorbed into the local culture. Viking names like Helga and Waldemar became the Slavic names Olga and Vladimir.

Byzantine Influences Trade had already brought Kiev into the Byzantine orbit. In the 800s, Constantinople sent Christian missionaries to convert the Slavs. About 863, two Greek brothers, Cyril and Methodius, adapted the Greek alphabet so they could translate the Bible into the Slavic tongue. This **Cyrillic** (suh RIL ik) alphabet became the written script that is still used today in Russia, Ukraine, Serbia, Bulgaria, and other countries of Eastern Europe.

In 957, Olga, the reigning princess of Kiev, converted to Byzantine Christianity. But it was not until the reign of Olga's grandson Vladimir that the religion spread widely. After his conversion, Vladimir married the sister of a Byzantine emperor. Soon, Greek priests

>> The vast, rolling plain made invasions easy, contributing to the early diversity of the Russian culture.

>> This reconstruction of a Viking ship unearthed in Russia is an example of the swift Viking trading ships that traveled Russia's many rivers.

Online Project the **Interactive Map: Growth of Russia.** Click on each period of time to show how Russia's boundary changed. Ask students what key events affected Russia's growth.

ACTIVE CLASSROOM

Use the Walking Tour strategy. Post passages from the text on individual pages around the room. Form students into groups and ask the groups to tour the room, discuss each passage, and then summarize.

Early Russia

Like other countries in Europe, early Russia was settled by migrants who divided the land into small kingdoms and cities that were ultimately united into one empire.

Guided Reading and Discussion

The Byzantine empire established an early trading presence in Russia due to Russia's river geography and because, at the time, the Byzantine empire was more stable than Western Europe. This early relationship with the Byzantine world would have far-reaching effects on how Russia developed, including its eventual connections with Eastern Orthodox Christianity.

Draw Inferences How did the introduction of Cyrillic script influence Russian culture? *(Cyrillic provided a common link between everyday language and published laws and government documents. The translation of the Bible into Cyrillic made Christianity a stronger presence in people's lives. Use of a different script from that of western Europe also helped to isolate Russia from the West.)*

D Differentiate Special Needs *Steppe* is a key word in this text. Have pairs of students practice geographic terms by looking at a map of Russia. Ask pairs to locate each geographic feature mentioned in the text. After they have pointed out each feature, have them explain to their partner how each one influenced the rise of Russia.

English Language Proficiency Standards

Listening 2.G.4 Read "The Geography of Russia" aloud, focusing on "Three Regions." Have students complete one activity according to their level of English proficiency.

Beginning Describe the three regions of Russia, using a visual. Describe each zone with a few key words. Help students use linguistic aids to develop their understanding of the vocabulary.

Intermediate Present one picture for each zone. Describe the characteristics of each of the regions with simple sentences.

Advanced Describe each of the three zones. Present one picture for each zone. Have students identify which picture describes each zone. Have students describe the characteristics of each in simple sentences.

Advanced High Follow the instructions in the Advanced activity, but have students describe the characteristics to a partner.

Answers

Analyze Context *The Eurasian plain was easily accessible; southern steppes encouraged migration from Asia into Europe; a network of rivers supported transportation and trade; northern forests supplied food and fuel; a southern band of fertile land attracted farmers.*

Topic 7 Lesson 8

The Mongols Conquer Russia

The initial Mongol invasion swept through Russia like a firestorm. The extensive slaughter terrorized the inhabitants and gave the Mongol dynasty control of Russia for the next 150 years. However, once the system of tribute was established, the Mongols' general policies allowed the Russian nobility to grow in strength and eventually push out the Mongols and extend Russian territory.

Guided Reading and Discussion

Explain that once the Mongol forces were established in Russia, they were tolerant of diversity in religion and culture, as long as the Mongols profited from Russian growth through paid tributes. The Russians were left to develop their own authoritarian government and evolve in culture and religion. The Mongol army's presence ensured peace on trade routes, which encouraged Russia to establish even closer ties with Byzantium and other eastern markets.

Analyze Information How did the Russians benefit from the Mongol invasion? What did they forfeit? *(Gained: stability, trade routes, freedom to develop their culture; Forfeited: participation in scientific advances being made in Europe because of lack of contact through trade)*

arrived in Kiev to preside over the mass baptisms organized by Vladimir.

With Byzantine Christianity came many changes. As Russians adopted their new written language, a class of educated Russian priests emerged. Russians adapted Byzantine religious art, music, and architecture. Byzantine domes, capped with colorful, carved "helmets," became the onion-shaped domes of Russian churches.

Byzantine Christianity set the pattern for close ties between Church and state. Kievan princes, like the Byzantine emperor, controlled the Church and made it dependent on them. As the Russian Orthodox Church evolved, it remained a pillar of state power, not a rival as in Western Europe.

Kiev's Golden Age Under Yaroslav Kiev enjoyed a golden age under Yaroslav the Wise, who ruled from 1019 to 1054. To improve justice, he issued a written law code.

A scholar, he translated Greek works into his language. He arranged marriages between his children and the families of royal rulers in Western Europe.

Kiev declined in the 1100s, as rival families battled for the throne. Also, Russian trading cities like Kiev declined because Byzantine prosperity was fading. As Russian princes continued to feud among themselves, Mongol invaders from central Asia struck the final blow.

CHECK UNDERSTANDING Why did Kiev become an important city?

The Mongols Conquer Russia

In the early 1200s, a young leader united the nomadic Mongols of central Asia. As his mounted bowmen overran lands from China to eastern Europe, he took the title Genghis Khan (GENG is kahn), or "World Emperor."

Between 1236 and 1241, Batu, the grandson of Genghis, led Mongol armies into Russia. Known as the Golden Horde because of the color of their tents, these invaders looted and burned Kiev and other Russian towns. So many inhabitants were killed, declared a Russian historian, that "no eye remained to weep for the dead."

>> Skilled warriors, Mongol armies swept through southwest Russia. They were called the Golden Horde because of the color of their tents that presented a sea of golden cloth that stretched for miles.

Mongol Rule From their capital on the Volga, the Golden Horde ruled Russia for more than 150 years. Areas that were not directly controlled by the Mongols were raided by Mongol armies.

The Mongols, while fierce conquerors, were generally tolerant rulers. Russian princes had to acknowledge the Mongols as their overlords and pay heavy tribute. But as long as the tribute was paid, the Mongols left the Russian princes to rule without much other interference.

Effects of Mongol Conquest Historians have long debated how Mongol rule affected Russia. Peasants felt the burden of heavy taxes to pay tribute to the Mongols. Some fled to remote regions, while others sought protection from Mongol raids by becoming serfs of Russian nobles. Even though the Mongols had converted to Islam, they tolerated the Russian Orthodox Church, which grew more powerful during this period. The Mongol conquest also brought peace to the huge swath of land between China and Eastern Europe, and Russian merchants benefited from new trade routes across this region.

The absolute power of the Mongols served as a model for later Russian rulers. Russian princes developed a strong desire to centralize their own power without interference from nobles, the clergy, or wealthy merchants. Perhaps most important, Mongol rule cut Russia off from contacts with Western Europe at a time

Answers

Check Understanding *Its location at the center of a vital trade network between the Baltic and Black seas, Byzantine and Christian influences, and a strong economy.*

>> **Analyze Maps** Between 1300 and 1584, Russian lands expanded from a small area around Moscow to a large territory. In which period did Novgorod come under Moscow's rule?

Interactive Map

when Europeans were making rapid advances in the arts and sciences.

DESCRIBE What are some aspects of Mongol rule of Russia?

Moscow Surpasses Kiev

During the Mongol period, the princes of Moscow steadily increased their power. Their success was due in part to the city's location near important river trade routes. They also used their positions as tribute collectors for the Mongols to subdue neighboring towns. When the head of the Russian Orthodox Church made Moscow his capital, the city became Russia's religious center as well as its political center.

As Mongol power declined, the princes of Moscow took on a new role as defenders of Russia against foreign rule. In 1380, they rallied other Russians and defeated the Golden Horde at the battle of Kulikovo (koo lih KOH vuh). Although the Mongols continued their terrifying raids, their strength was much reduced.

Ivan the Great A driving force behind Moscow's successes was Ivan III, known as **Ivan the Great.** Between 1462 and 1505, he brought much of northern Russia under his rule.

Ivan built the framework for absolute rule. He tried to limit the power of the *boyars*, or great landowning nobles. After he married a niece of the last Byzantine emperor, Ivan adopted Byzantine court rituals to emphasize Russia's role as the heir to Byzantine power.

Like the Byzantine emperors, he used a double-headed eagle as his symbol and sometimes referred to himself as tsar, the Russian word for Caesar. In 1504, a Russian church council echoed Byzantine statements, declaring, "By nature, the tsar is like any other man, but in power and office he is like the highest God."

Ivan the Terrible In 1547, Ivan IV, grandson of Ivan the Great, became the first Russian ruler officially crowned tsar. He further centralized royal power by limiting the privileges of the old boyar families and granting land to nobles in exchange for military or other service. At a time when the manor system was fading in Western Europe, Ivan IV introduced new laws that tied Russian serfs to the land.

About 1560, Ivan IV became increasingly unstable. He trusted no one and became subject to violent fits of rage. In a moment of madness, he even killed his own son.

He organized the *oprichniki* (ah PREECH nee kee), agents of terror who enforced the tsar's will. Dressed in black robes and mounted on black horses, they

Connect to Our World

Connections to Today Today, Moscow is the capital of Russia and covers 386 square miles. At the center of the city stands the Kremlin, a fortified red-brick enclosure crowned by 20 towers. The Kremlin was built by Italians at the invitation of Ivan the Great in the fifteenth century. Russians across the country set their clocks and watches to the radio broadcasts of the chiming of the clock in the belfry of the Savior Tower. Engineering and metalworking are the leading industries in Moscow, including several notable vehicle production plants. Moscow's famous GUM department store traces its roots back to medieval trade fairs.

Moscow Surpasses Kiev

Moscow steadily increased its power during the Mongol period because of the city's location on important river trade routes.

Guided Reading and Discussion

Moscow's rise as the center of Russia was based on the strong leadership of Ivan the Great and Ivan the Terrible and the choice of Moscow to be the capital of the Russian Orthodox Church. With one city as the center of both religious and secular rule, Moscow was able to surge ahead of all other Russian cities. As power coalesced in Moscow, so did the Russian desire to rid itself of foreign rule. After a decisive victory against the Mongols, Russian rulers continued to consolidate their power and their form of government – absolute monarchy.

Draw Conclusions How were Ivan the Great and Ivan the Terrible able to wrest control from the Mongols and ensure the success of their regimes? *(They rallied Russians against foreign rule, limited the influences of competing factions, centralized royal power, and exercised total control.)*

Online Project the **Interactive Map: Growth of Russia.** Project the map on the whiteboard. Click on each period of time to show how Russia's boundary changed.

ACTIVE CLASSROOM

Use the Walking Tour strategy. Post passages from the text on individual pages around the room. Form students into groups and ask the groups to tour the room, discuss each passage, and then summarize.

Answers

Analyze Maps *between 1462 and 1533*

Describe *brought peace; Russian merchants benefited from new trade routes; exacted heavy taxes; Russian princes ruled without much interference; tolerated Orthodox Church grew more powerful; cut Russia off from contacts with Western Europe; absolute power a model for later Russian rulers*

The Geography of Eastern Europe

Explain that Eastern Europe's isolation was reinforced by a wide diversity in local cultural influences. Some areas were more influenced by Europe, while other areas were influenced by the Byzantine world. The separately developing cultural identities impeded strong national feeling and unity. The geography of the area kept ethnic groups fairly isolated from each other for extended periods of time.

Guided Reading and Discussion

The term *Balkanization* is used to describe the breaking up of an area into separate ethnic regions. The Balkan conflicts during the 1990s, following the breakup of Yugoslavia, pitted Eastern Orthodox Serbs, Bosnian Muslims, and Catholic Croats against each other. In 1998, Christian Serbs and Muslims of Albanian heritage clashed in Kosovo. These wars echo ethnic struggles that have existed for more than 600 years in the Balkans as different ethnic and religious groups have dispersed through the region. The conflicts had their beginnings during the time studied in this text, as the various areas were influenced by different cultural and religious factors.

Identify Supporting Details What influenced the development of different religious and cultural areas in the Balkans? *(The geography of the Balkans placed groups close to those areas that eventually influenced their religion and culture.)*

slaughtered rebellious boyars and sacked towns where people were suspected of disloyalty. Their saddles were decorated with a dog's head and a broom, symbols of their constant watchfulness to sweep away their master's enemies.

The tsar's awesome power, and the ways he used it, earned him the title **Ivan the Terrible.** When he died in 1584, he left a land seething with rebellion. But he had introduced Russia to a tradition of extreme absolute power that would shape Russia into modern times.

DESCRIBE How did Ivan III and Ivan IV establish authoritarian power?

The Geography of Eastern Europe

Many peoples and nations flourished in Eastern Europe over the centuries. In part because of its location, the region was often shaped by migration and foreign conquest.

Location The region called Eastern Europe refers to a wide swath of territory between German-speaking Central Europe to the west and Russia to the east. It reaches from the chilly Baltic Sea down through the plains of Poland and Hungary into the mountainous **Balkan Peninsula.** Often called the Balkans, this roughly triangular area juts southward into the warm Mediterranean.

Diverse Cultural Influences In the early Middle Ages, Slavs migrated into Eastern Europe. Like the Germanic peoples who settled Western Europe, the Slavs were a diverse group of tribes. Other peoples also migrated into Eastern Europe, enriching its culture. In the 900s, Ibrahim-ibn-Yaqub, a Spanish-Jewish traveler, left this account of the region:

> The lands of the Slavs stretch from the Syrian Sea to the Ocean in the north . . . They comprise numerous tribes, each different from the other . . . if not for the disharmony amongst them, caused by the multiplication of factions and by their fragmentation into clans, no people could match them for strength.
>
> —Ibrahim-Ibn-Yaqub

>> **Analyze Maps** Locate on the map regions where Eastern Europe meets Asia. What might happen in these regions?

Answers

Describe *Ivan III recovered lost territories, limited the power of* boyars, *emphasized Russia's role as heir to Byzantine power, and set a framework for absolute rule. Ivan IV further limited the power of* boyars, *reinforced serfdom, increased military strength, organized* oprichniki, *and centralized royal power.*

Analyze Maps *Possible answers may include cultural tensions, war, and conflict, but also cultural exchange, increased trade, and inter-migration of peoples.*

Geographic Features Shape Eastern Europe Much of the region lies on the great European Plain that links up with the steppes of southern Russia. Its main rivers, such as the Danube and the Vistula (VISH chuh luh), flow either south into the Black Sea or north into the Baltic Sea.

Goods and cultural influences traveled along these river routes. As a result, the Balkans in the south felt the influence of Byzantine civilization and Eastern Orthodox Christianity, which also shaped Russia. Later, the Muslim Ottoman empire brought other cultural influences. In contrast, the northern regions of Eastern Europe that bordered Germany and the Baltic Sea forged closer links to Western Europe.

CHECK UNDERSTANDING How did Eastern Europe's rivers affect the region?

ELPS **ELPS 2.I.5** Practice listening to and taking notes about the influence of geography on the development of Eastern Europe.

Migrations Increase Diversity

Eastern Europe has long been a crossroads and buffer. Many peoples migrated into the region, which had no difficult geographic barriers such as high mountains or wide deserts. As a result, Eastern Europe today includes a wealth of languages and cultures.

Often, migrating peoples and even invaders stopped their advances in Eastern Europe. By absorbing waves of newcomers, Eastern Europe served as a barrier protecting Western Europe.

A Mix of Peoples During the early Middle Ages, various groups of Slavs migrated into Eastern Europe. The West Slavs filtered into present-day Poland and the Czech and Slovak republics. The South Slavs occupied the Balkans, where they became some of the ancestors of the Serbs, Croats, and Slovenes.

Other ethnic groups settled in the Balkans. (An **ethnic group** is a group of people who share the same language and cultural heritage.) Waves of Asian peoples migrated into Eastern Europe, among them the Huns, Avars, Bulgars, Khazars, and Magyars. Vikings and other Germanic peoples added to the mix.

Diverse Religious Influences Powerful neighboring states brought different religions to the region. Byzantine missionaries spread Eastern Orthodox Christianity throughout the Balkans. German knights and missionaries from the West brought Roman

>> *Oprichnik* is the Russian word for guardsman. Totally loyal to the tsar, the oprichniki terrorized whomever the tsar saw as an enemy.

>> The Danube had been a major river trading route from the time of the Vikings. It continued to be a water highway to and from the Byzantine markets to the south.

Topic 7 Lesson 8

Migrations Increase Diversity

Eastern Europe has always been a crossroads for people migrating to the region. As a result, many cultures with differing languages populate the region today.

Guided Reading and Discussion

A great variety of people migrated to Eastern Europe because of the lack of geographic barriers. These groups included Slavs from Belarus, several groups from Asia, Vikings, Germans, and Jews. Later migrations had political or religious incentives.

Draw Inferences How did the migration of many diverse peoples into Eastern Europe change the region? *(As different groups migrated into Eastern Europe, they brought their languages, cultures, and religions with them.)*

English Language Proficiency Standards

Listening 2.I.5 Read "The Geography of Eastern Europe" aloud. Describe how geography has influenced the development of Eastern Europe. Then have students complete one activity according to their level of English proficiency.

Beginning Provide a list of key terms with bilingual definitions, including *migrating, plain, climate, hindered, fertile,* and *steppe*. Use visual aids. Have students take notes.

Intermediate Follow the instructions in the Beginning activity, then have students review their notes for areas of concern.

Advanced Follow the instructions in the Intermediate activity, but have students share notes with a partner to locate errors.

Advanced High Have students take notes and point out any confusing terms or concepts. Focus on these confusing terms or concepts. Have students share their notes with a partner to locate errors.

Answers

Check Understanding *Trade routes along the rivers brought goods and diverse ideas and cultures into Eastern Europe.*

Online Project the **Interactive Map: Jewish Migrations and Expulsions.** Ask students to make generalizations about the information the map shows. *(Most of the places the Jews left are in Western Europe, while those they went to are in Eastern Europe; many of the routes they took are water routes, probably because it was easier and safer to travel by water.)*

ACTIVE CLASSROOM

Use the See-Think-Wonder strategy with the map. Pair students. Ask each pair: What do you see? What does that make you think? What are you wondering about now that you've seen this? Ask each pair to share insights with the class.

Early Kingdoms of Eastern Europe

During the Middle Ages, Eastern Europe included many kingdoms and small states. Internal shifts in political power had an impact on a kingdom's ability to survive. While a monarch provided a central power able to act decisively, the movement toward assemblies of nobles holding power often resulted in fragmented government.

Catholic Christianity to Poland, Hungary, the Czech area, and the western Balkans. In the 1300s, the Ottomans invaded the Balkans and brought Islam to the region.

Jews Settle in Eastern Europe By about 1100, Jews had begun to settle in Eastern Europe. Settlements were probably organized by merchants. Jews carried on trade along routes that connected what is today Poland, Hungary, and the Balkans.

In the late Middle Ages, Eastern Europe had become a refuge for Jews. Christians in Western Europe launched attacks on Jewish communities during the Crusades and the Black Death. To escape persecution, Jews fled east. As monarchs centralized power in England, France, and Spain, they expelled Jews from their lands. These groups, too, migrated eastward.

A growing number of Jews settled in Poland. By 1264, Jews had gained a charter, or official document, from Prince Boleslaw of Krakov. The charter protected the rights of Jews in his territory. Over the next 500 years, other Polish towns gave shelter to Jews. By about 1650, about 500,000 Jews lived in Poland and Lithuania, the largest population of Jews in Europe. Although some Polish leaders encouraged Jews to settle in their lands, Jews still faced persecution throughout Eastern Europe.

Jewish merchants and scholars contributed to the economic and cultural development of Poland and other parts of Eastern Europe where they settled. Owing to their ties with Jewish communities abroad, Jewish merchants were very successful in European and overseas trade. Merchants often mastered many languages, including Arabic. Educated Jews had studied Greek and Latin as well as Hebrew. Jews expelled from Spain in 1492 brought a large range of skills to their new homes.

DESCRIBE How did three major religions spread to Eastern Europe?

Early Kingdoms of Eastern Europe

During the Middle Ages, wars constantly shifted boundaries in Eastern Europe. Sometimes strong empires absorbed national groups. Alliances or royal marriages might bind others together. The histories of three kingdoms—Poland, Hungary, and Serbia—illustrate the shifting fortunes that the peoples of Eastern Europe faced.

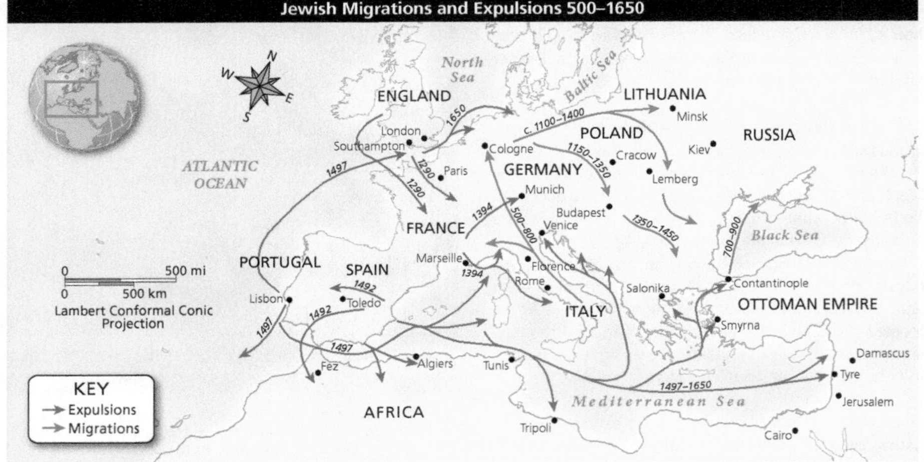

>> **Analyze Maps** The constantly changing treatment of Jews throughout medieval Europe led to periods of migration and expulsion for the Jewish people. Was the movement of Jews into Eastern Europe a result of migration or expulsion?

Interactive Map

Answers

Describe *Christian missionaries spread the beliefs of the Orthodox and Roman Catholic Churches, Ottoman invaders contributed Islam, and refugees from persecution brought Judaism.*

Analyze Maps *migration*

Poland Missionaries brought Roman Catholicism to the West Slavs of Poland in the 900s. Within a century, the first Polish king was crowned. To survive, Poland often had to battle Germans, Russians, and Mongols.

Poland's greatest age came after a royal marriage united Poland and Lithuania in 1386. Under the Jagiello (yahg YEH loh) dynasty, Poland-Lithuania was the largest state in Europe. Its empire stretched from the Baltic to the Black Sea.

Unlike in Russia or Western Europe, where royal rulers limited the power of nobles, Polish nobles gradually gained power at the expense of the monarch. They met in a **diet,** or assembly, where the vote of a single noble could block the passage of a law. This *liberum veto*, or "free veto," made it hard for the government to take decisive action.

Without a strong central government, Poland-Lithuania declined. It enjoyed a final moment of glory in 1683 when the Polish king Jan Sobieski (yahn soh BYEH skee) broke the Ottoman siege of Vienna. In the next century, however, Poland and Lithuania were gobbled up by ambitious neighbors.

Hungary Hungary was settled by the Magyars, who had raided Europe from the Asian steppes. About 970, the Magyar adopted Roman Catholic Christianity.

In the Middle Ages, Hungary was larger than it is today. Its rulers controlled present-day Slovakia, Croatia, and parts of Romania.

Like King John of England, the Hungarian king was forced to sign a charter recognizing nobles' rights. Known as the **Golden Bull of 1222,** it strictly limited royal power.

The Mongols overran Hungary in 1241, killing as much as half its population. These invaders soon withdrew, so the Mongol invasion did not have the lasting impact on Hungary that it had on Russia. The expansion of the Ottoman Turks, though, did end Hungarian independence in 1526. Later, the Austrian Hapsburgs replaced the Ottomans as rulers of Hungary.

Serbia During the 600s, South Slavs settled in the mountainous Balkans. Serbs, Croats, Slovenes, and other Slavic peoples in the Balkans had different histories during the Middle Ages. The Serbs accepted Orthodox Christianity. By the late 1100s, they set up their own state, which reached its height under Stefan Dusan (STEH vahn DOO shahn). He battled the Byzantine empire and conquered Macedonia in the 1300s. Yet Dusan encouraged Byzantine culture and even modeled his law code on that of Justinian.

Dusan's successors lacked his political gifts, however, and Serbia could not withstand the advance of Ottoman Turks. At the battle of Kosovo in 1389, Serbs fought to the death, a memory still honored by their descendants. During almost 500 years of Ottoman rule, Serbs preserved a sense of their own identity.

? **SYNTHESIZE** How did Poland, Hungary, and Serbia lose their independence?

ASSESSMENT

1. **Cause and Effect** How did Russia's geography affect its early history?
2. **Determine Relevance** How important was Byzantine influence on Russia?
3. **Synthesize Information** What were major causes and effects of Mongol rule on Russia's economy and political structure?
4. **Analyze Information** How did a tradition of absolute rule develop in Russia?
5. **Identify Central Issues** How did Eastern Europe become home to so many ethnic groups?

SYNTHESIZE

Online Ask students to share their responses to the Synthesize exercise.

Point out that the Mongol invasion and occupation of Russia and parts of Eastern Europe had far-reaching effects, such as the absolute monarchy model used by Russia and the destabilizing of Hungary when the invasion resulted in the death of about half of Hungary's population. Despite the devastation left in their wake, the Mongols also brought a controlled peace that allowed trade between Russia and Byzantium and a cultural exchange that continued into modern times.

DEMONSTRATE

Online Assign the **Digital Lesson Quiz** for this lesson if you haven't already done so. Students will be offered automatic remediation or enrichment based on their score.

Pose these questions to the class on the Discussion Board:

Identify Key Steps in a Process How did the early Russian state develop? *(Trade routes that included Asian traders, Vikings, and Byzantine merchants plied the rivers throughout western Russia. Trading towns developed in the larger cities of Kiev and Moscow. After the Mongol invasion, Russian leaders paid tribute while they worked to push out the Mongols and extend Russia's borders.)*

Summarize How did the great diversity of migrating groups affect Eastern Europe? *(Each group brought its own culture, religion, and language, along with knowledge and skills.)*

Topic Inquiry

Have students continue their investigations for the Topic Inquiry.

Assessment

1. Proximity to the steppe aided migration, fertile land attracted farmers, the river network encouraged migration and trade.
2. Byzantine Christianity set the pattern for close ties between Church and state; Russians adapted Byzantine religious art, music, and architecture.
3. High taxation rates contributed to the growth of serfdom as people sought protection of Russian lords; it encouraged autocratic rule and absolute power.
4. Ivan III tried to limit the power of the *boyars* and saw himself as a tsar; Ivan IV further centralized royal power.
5. Its geography and location facilitated migration and made it a cultural crossroads.

Answers

Synthesize *In Poland, an ineffective central government was unable to defend itself against aggressive neighbors; in Hungary, Turkish armies took control of Hungarian territory; in Serbia, less-talented political successors to Stefan were not able to ward off the Turks.*

Topic 7

Answers to TEKS Assessment

1. Student answers will vary but can include something similar to the following:

   Monarch
   Only one in a feudal society; the most powerful member of a feudal society

   Lords
   There were many lords; lifetime loyalty to the monarch; may be a duke or count

   Knights
   Knights were the lords' vassals; their loyalty was to the lords

   Peasants
   Lowest people on the social scale; largest of the social groups; also did the majority of the work

2. Student answers will vary but should include that invaders took over and wars were constantly being fought. Trade slowed down considerably, and towns nearly disappeared. Learning ceased. It was a very difficult time period for people, and later writers referred to it as the "dark ages" because of the chaos. Historians refer to it as a time of great change. Traditions of many different civilizations such as Greek, German, and Roman blended and began a new civilization.

3. Student answers will vary but should include that the pope and others sent missionaries to spread Christianity throughout Europe. By the late Middle Ages, Western Europe had become a diverse Christian community. Europeans had many different languages, cultures, and governments, but most were linked by a common faith—Christianity.

4. Student answers will vary but should include that Roman Catholics considered the Pope supreme, whereas the Eastern Orthodox considered the emperor supreme. A Byzantine emperor outlawed praying to icons, saying it was against one of God's commandments, but later restored it after he was excommunicated by the Pope. Both branches of Christianity celebrate the seven sacraments.

5. Students' answers will vary but should include that by the 1050s, the Byzantine empire was facing a serious threat from the Seljuk Turks, who had overrun most of the Byzantine lands in Asia Minor and had extended their power into the Holy Land. For centuries, Christians had made pilgrimages to the Holy Land. Because the very survival of the Byzantine empire was being threatened by the Seljuk Turks, Byzantine ruler Alexius I asked Pope Urban II for Christian knights to help fight the Muslim Turks. Students should go on to point out that even though Roman popes and Byzantine emperors were longtime rivals due to their religious differences, Pope Urban II agreed to help Alexius. Thus, Christianity helped unify Western Europeans and the Byzantine empire against the Seljuk Turks, who were Muslim.

6. Student answers will vary but should include that the lord held legal and economic power over the peasants who lived on the estate. The peasants worked the land for protection. Most peasants were serfs. They couldn't leave the manor without permission, and if there was a new lord, the serfs had to honor his power. Peasants did many jobs for the lord. They farmed the land and mended roads, bridges, and fences. Even though they couldn't leave, they also couldn't be forced out, so they were always guaranteed food, housing, and land.

TEKS ASSESSMENT

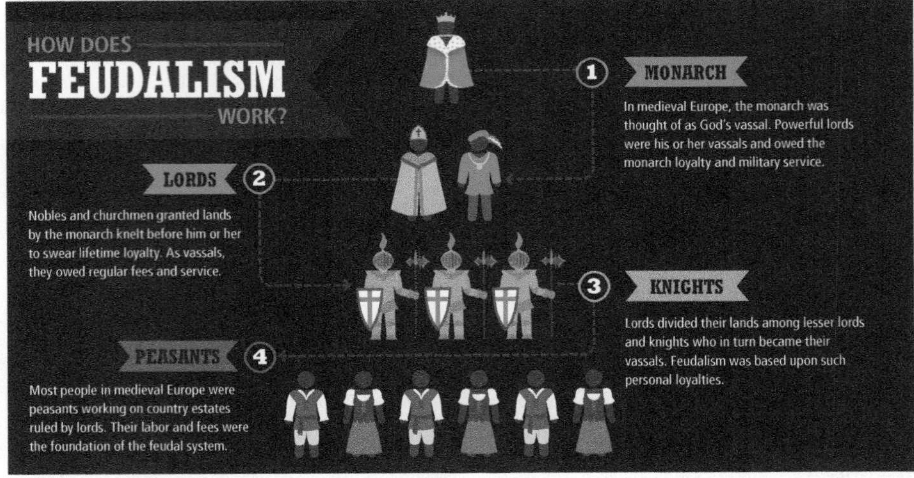

1. **Describe Characteristics** Describe the major characteristics of and the factors contributing to the development of the political/social system of feudalism. Transfer information from one medium to another. Study the graphic shown, and write a short description of the monarch, lords, knights, and peasants. Be sure to read the description given and look at the art, use your own words when writing, and place your description in a graphic organizer. **4.C, 30.D**
2. **Identify Major Effects and Explain the Impact** Describe the major effects and explain the impact of the following important turning points in world history from 600 to 1450: the decline of Rome. Write a paragraph explaining the impact as Rome declined and withdrew from Europe. Consider supporting evidence like unrest and war, trade and the reaction of people at the time, and how historians view the decline. **1.C, 3.B**
3. **Identify Major Causes** Identify major causes of the following turning points in world history from 600 to 1450: the spread of Christianity. Write a paragraph identifying how Christianity was spread throughout Europe. Include information about missionaries, diversity, and commonality. **1.C**
4. **Explain Characteristics** Explain the characteristics of Roman Catholicism and Eastern Orthodoxy. Write a paragraph comparing Roman Catholicism and Eastern Orthodoxy. Consider the following: supreme leaders, use of icons, and celebration of sacraments. **4.B**
5. **Explain the Development** Explain the development of Christianity as a unifying political factor in the Byzantine empire. Write a paragraph explaining how Christianity helped to unify the Byzantine empire from attacks by the Seljuk Turks. What religion were the Seljuk Turks? How was this a factor in the roles played by Byzantine emperor Alexius I and Pope Urban II? **4.A**
6. **Describe Characteristics and Factors** Describe the major characteristics of and the factors contributing to the development of the economic system of manorialism. Write a paragraph describing the organization and factors contributing to manorialism. Consider the power of the lord, the role and the life of serfs (peasants), and how workers were provided for. **4.C**
7. **Summarize Changes** Summarize the changes resulting from the Mongol invasions of Russia. Write a paragraph summarizing how the Mongol invasions of Russia resulted in social and economic changes. Consider how peasants were affected and where trade routes were expanded. How did the Mongols' absolute power affect Russian interaction with Western Europe? **4.K**

8. **Analyze Examples** Analyze examples of how literature reflected the history of the cultures in which it was produced. Write a paragraph analyzing how Geoffrey Chaucer's *Canterbury Tales* reflects the Middle Ages. Scenes from the *Canterbury Tales* brings together a group of various classes of society. The merchant, nun, priest, and knight are among those who tell stories during the pilgrimage. What do the stories and characters tell us? 26.B
9. **Identify Characteristics** Identify the characteristics of political systems, including absolute monarchy. Write a paragraph identifying how feudal monarchs began to develop absolute monarchy by expanding royal authority over their nobles and the church. Consider how monarchs centralized power, set up government, and the reaction of the townspeople. 19.B
10. **Identify Impact** Identify the impact of political and legal ideas contained in documents, including the Magna Carta. Write a paragraph identifying the impact of important concepts contained in the Magna Carta. Consider the rights for nobles and rules affecting the monarchs, due process of law, and habeas corpus. How was taxation affected under King John's rule at the time? 20.B
11. **Explain Development** Explain the development of democratic-republican government from its beginnings in the Judeo-Christian legal tradition. Explain how Jewish and Christian traditions helped shape many aspects of life in Western Europe. Consider what republican government emphasized, social responsibilities, and the concept of free will under Judeo-Christian teachings. 20.A
12. **Explain Political Philosophies** Explain the political philosophies of individuals: Thomas Aquinas. Write a paragraph explaining the political philosophy of Thomas Aquinas. Consider the work called *Summa Theologica,* his writing on the role of governments and natural law, and his influence on Thomas Jefferson. 20.C
13. **Describe the Spread of Traditions** Describe the spread of major religious and philosophical traditions, including Christianity. Write a paragraph describing Church law and authority under Christianity. Consider the importance of the sacraments, excommunication, and how feudal warfare was limited. 23.A
14. **Interpret Thematic Maps** Interpret thematic maps to demonstrate the relationship between geography and the historical development of a region or nation. Write a paragraph demonstrating the relationship between Moscow's location and the growth of Russia. Include information on Moscow's location and political gains, land growth, and the effects on Mongol power. 15.A
15. **Identify Examples** Identify examples of religious influence on various events referenced in the major eras of world history. Write a paragraph identifying examples of how Eastern Europe became a refuge for Jews during the late Middle Ages. Include information about attacks on Jewish people by Christians and others in Western Europe, protection in Poland, and Jewish growth in Europe. 23.B
16. **Describe Interactions** Describe the interactions among Muslim, Christian, and Jewish societies in Europe and Asia. Write a paragraph describing these interactions among the Muslims, Christians, and Jews in Europe and Asia following the Crusade. Consider the results of religious hatred, how the world became "bigger," and Jewish persecution in Europe. 4.E

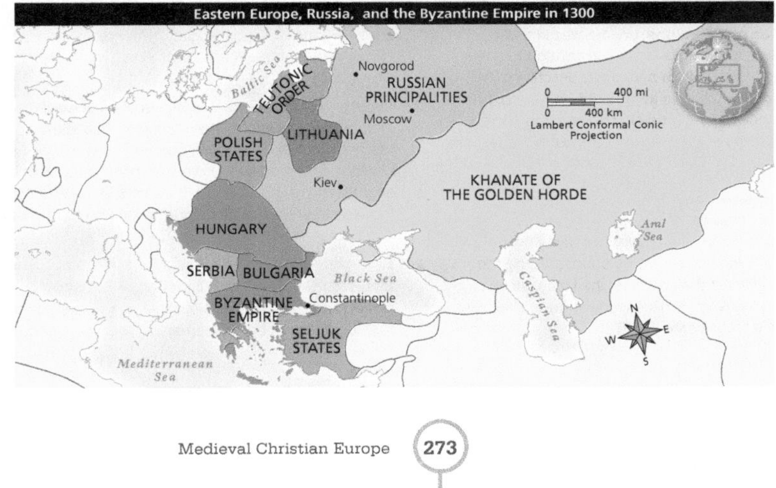

7. Student answers will vary but should include that after the Mongol invasions, peasants were taxed very heavily. Some fled to remote regions, and others became serfs to Russian nobles. Peace between China and Eastern Europe was also a result of the Mongol invasions, allowing more trade routes. The Mongols ruled with absolute power, and they were able to cut Russia off from the rest of Western Europe. This would limit Russian knowledge of technological and other advances happening in Western Europe at the time.

8. Student answers will vary but should include that Chaucer created a cast of characters traveling to a tomb. He included a knight, a plowman, a merchant, a miller, a monk, and a nun. As they travel, each character has a funny tale to tell. The *Canterbury Tales* offers us a peek into medieval life.

9. Student answers will vary, but the paragraph should include that feudal monarchs crushed the power of feudal nobles and of the church. They were then able to set up their own systems of government that administered justice and collected taxes. Townspeople turned to monarchs because the monarchs could ensure peace, which was necessary for commerce and maintaining their middle-class status.

10. Student answers will vary but should include that the Magna Carta included two important ideas. One was that the nobles had certain rights; the second was that the monarch must obey the law. Due process of law protected men from arbitrary arrest, imprisonment, or any legal action except by legal judgment of his peers or the law of the land. It protected the legal rights of individuals. The right of habeas corpus said that no prisoner could be imprisoned without first being charged with a crime. The king of England at the time, King John, couldn't raise any taxes without consulting with his Great Council of lords and clergy. These political and legal concepts shaped English government in the future.

11. Student answers will vary but should include that some concepts of the republican form of government were based on Judeo-Christian ideas, which emphasized human rights and rejected hereditary rulers. Judeo-Christian teachings also stressed the value of individuals, the belief that people have a social responsibility to help those in need, and the concept of free will—the idea that people have the ability to make their own decisions.

12. Student answers will vary but should include that in the work *Summa Theologica,* Thomas Aquinas said that faith and reason exist in harmony, and that God rules over an orderly universe. He wrote about government based on natural laws of fairness and reason. He believed that government should work for good that benefits all. People should not feel obliged to obey unfair laws or the rulers who enact them. Aquinas's laws influenced European philosophers in the 1600s and 1700s and even influenced Thomas Jefferson when he wrote the Declaration of Independence.

13. Student answers will vary but should include that Christians believed that without the sacraments, they would be sure to have everlasting suffering after death. Anyone who disobeyed the Church laws faced excommunication, or being cut off from the church and its sacraments. A person of authority could face the interdict, meaning his whole town would be excommunicated. This caused many rulers to give in to Christian law rather than face the revolts from the people under his rule. To limit feudal warfare, the Church demanded that fighting stop between Fridays and Sundays and on religious holidays. These periods of peace may have contributed to the gradual end of feudal warfare altogether.

Answers to TEKS Assessment

14. Student answers will vary but should include that Moscow was located near important trade routes. It was also named the capital of Russia, and this helped increase its political and religious power. Russia expanded from a small area around Moscow to a much larger territory. This was due to Moscow's proximity to river trade routes. As Russia continued to gain more and more land, the Mongols' strength decreased.

15. Student answers will vary but should include that Christians in Western Europe attacked Jews during the Crusades and the Black Death. Monarchs began to expel Jews from England, France, and Spain. The persecuted and expelled Jews moved east. Many settled in Poland, where they were protected by a charter from Prince Boleslaw of Krakov. By about 1650, more than 500,000 Jews lived in Poland and Lithuania. These areas had the largest concentration of Jews in Europe.

16. Student answers will vary but should include that following the Crusades, Muslims and Christians were brutal to each other in the name of religion. In Europe, religion also motivated the killings of entire communities of Jews. Because of the Crusades, Christians realized that people lived in regions of the world that they had never seen. They wanted to learn about these Muslim lands. Explorers began to venture out of Europe and into China and India.

17. Students' answers will vary but should include that Europeans traded with Muslims and eventually adopted some Muslim practices. These practices included the use of money, which had a huge impact on social order. Feudal lords needed money to buy things. Peasants began selling farm products and paying rent in cash instead of products. Peasants eventually became tenant farmers, using cash to pay for their land, and they also hired laborers. Over time, a new middle class of merchants, traders, and artisans developed. Now there was a social group between nobles and peasants.

18. Student answers will vary but should include that people in cities and towns lived differently than those on farms. People on farms grew their own food, but the people in towns and cities went and bought their food from the merchants who sold them. For artisans, merchants, and other townspeople, there was no difference between certain seasons and harvests. They had to sell or make goods during all seasons. Farmers still had harvest seasons when the growing stopped and the picking and harvesting began.

19. Student answers will vary but should state that the English crusaders left southwestern England and traveled south into the Atlantic Ocean along the coasts of France and Portugal. As they sailed past Tangier, they entered the Mediterranean Sea and sailed northeast to Marseille. From Marseille, they traveled eastward through the Mediterranean past Sicily, the Byzantine empire, Crete, and Cyprus, before arriving in the Holy Land.

20. Student answers will vary but should include that in the Middle Ages, the most important examples of architecture in many towns were religious buildings, reflecting the importance of Christianity in medieval Europe. In the year 1000, monasteries and towns were building stone churches that reflected Roman influences. They were solid buildings with thick walls and towers. The roofs and walls were so thick that windows any larger than slits might weaken the support for the roof. Over time, builders developed great cathedrals built in the Gothic style, with stone supports on the outside that allowed large stained-glass windows to be built. The graceful spires and tall windows of Gothic cathedrals carried the eye upward to the heavens in an attempt to inspire and enlighten people inside.

TEKS ASSESSMENT

The Crusades, 1096–1204

KEY
- Predominantly Muslim lands, 1095
- First Crusade, 1096–1099
- Second Crusade, 1147–1149
- Third Crusade, 1189–1192
- Fourth Crusade, 1202–1204

Lambert Conformal Conic Projection

17. **Explain Social Impact** Explain the social impact of Islam on Europe. Write a paragraph explaining European interactions with Muslims. Consider the adoption of Muslim practices, how the use of money changed the social order, and who the players were in the new middle class. **4.D**

18. **Describe Changing Roles** Describe the changing roles of families during major eras of world history. Write a paragraph describing the role of family life in the Middle Ages. Include the differences between city or town families and farm families. How did the seasons impact both groups in food production and jobs? **24.A**

19. **Locate Places and Regions** Locate places and regions of historical significance directly related to major eras. Using the map, write a paragraph describing the route that English crusaders took to the Holy Land. Consider the point of departure in England, the bodies of water that were involved, and which countries the crusaders traveled to reach the Holy Land. **16.A**

20. **Analyze Examples** Analyze examples of how architecture reflected the history of the cultures in which it was produced. Write a paragraph analyzing how the architecture of religious buildings produced during the Middle Ages reflected the culture of the times. Include information on the Roman influence and gradual transition to the Gothic style. **26.B**

21. **Analyze Information** Analyze information by developing connections between historical events over time. Use appropriate reading and mathematical skills to interpret social studies information. Write a paragraph analyzing the three Crusades. Approximately how many years passed between each of the Crusades? How was the situation similar or different in Jerusalem each time? **29.F, 29.H**

22. **Explain Contributions** Explain how the Hundred Years' War contributed to the end of medieval Europe. Write a paragraph explaining how the countries involved and years spanned in the Hundred Years' War contributed to the end of medieval Europe. What were some changes in feudal society? How did new trade routes and technology advancements also impact the changes? **4.G**

23. **Create Presentations** Create visual presentations of social studies information. Create a slide show of the geography of Eastern Europe. You may use photographs or pictures from valid primary or secondary sources or create your own. Be sure to include captions for each visual, examples of the various types of terrain, and bodies of water. **30.C**

24. **Reflect on the Essential Question** **Write an essay on the Essential Question: What should governments do?** Use evidence from your study of this Topic to support your answer.

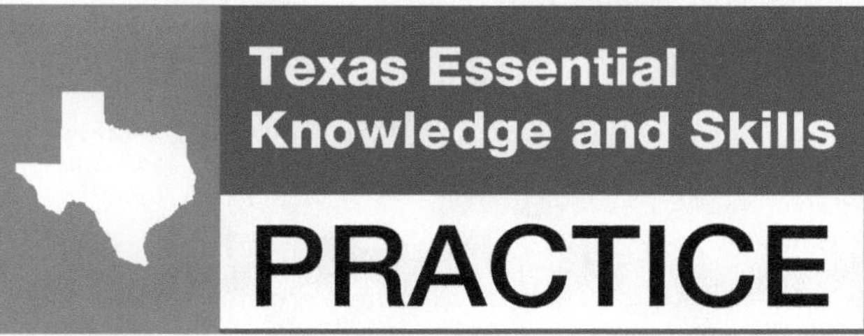

21. Student answers will vary but should include that the Crusades began in 1096, and by 1291, 195 years later, the Arabs reconquered the last European outpost. The Crusades were a series of battles between Christians and Muslims for control of the Middle East. The First Crusade reached its goal, with Christians capturing Jerusalem in 1099. But by the time of the Second Crusade in 1187, Jerusalem had fallen to the Muslims again. On the Third Crusade, Europeans again failed to take over Jerusalem; however, after negotiations, the city was opened to Christian pilgrims.

22. Student answers will vary but should include that the Hundred Years' War was a series of bitter battles fought between England and France between 1337 and 1453. Feudal society changed, as monarchs needed strong armies to fight the wars rather than relying on feudal vassals to fight. Trade routes were constantly expanding, and new technologies, including new weapons, were developed. All this would eventually contribute to the end of medieval Europe.

23. Student answers will vary but should include a reasonable caption for each photo or illustration. Visuals should include the land masses, plains and mountains, and bodies of water, including the Mediterranean Sea, Danube and Vistula Rivers, the Black Sea, and the Baltic Sea.

Topic 7

Answers to TEKS Practice

1. B
2. F

Online To prepare for the End-of-Topic test, have students go online for additional Topic Review and Assessment questions or to review their notes in the **Interactive Reading Notepad** for the lessons in this Topic.

Benchmark Tests

Assign these benchmark tests as you complete the relevant topics to monitor student progress toward mastering the course content and as preparation for the End-of-Course Test.

Benchmark Test 1: Topics 1–5

Benchmark Test 2: Topics 6–10

Benchmark Test 3: Topics 11–15

Benchmark Test 4: Topics 16–21

TEKS PRACTICE

1 What was the impact of political ideas contained in Justinian's Code of Laws?

A Present-day international law attacked its rigid principles.

B Western European monarchies justified centralizing their power.

C Constantine used it to justify the spread of Christianity.

D Ancient Roman cities were revived as centers of learning.

2

Which factor contributed to the development of manorialism?

F Security for peasants and labor for the lord's lands.

G Peasants and their lords were tied together by the same religion.

H Fees paid entitled serfs to the lord's protection from warfare.

J Estates became self-sufficient under authority from monarchs.

Test Taking Tips: Tip for Questions About Timelines

1. Read the question.
2. Read the title of the timeline to determine what it is about. Note whether the dates covered by the timeline are included in the title.
3. Look at the beginning and end points of the timeline. Notice the intervals of time indicated by the markers between the beginning and end points.
4. Read all the events on the timeline. Notice when each event happened and its relationship to the other events.
5. Read the question again and answer it in your own words using the information on the timeline.
6. Read the answer choices and select the best answer.

PEARSON realize™ www.PearsonTexas.com Access additional practice questions

Topic 7

3 A Divided Church

What effect did the Great Schism in 1054 have in medieval Europe?

A The split between eastern and western Christianity upset cultural unity.

B Actions of the Eastern Orthodox Church disrupted the papal hierarchy.

C Excommunication of religious leaders led to several local wars.

D Modifications in icon use caused a permanent rift.

4 Describe outside influences in Roman literature and philosophy.

F Most of Roman philosophy was based on Latin influences that were passed down.

G Roman literature included a mixture of Greek and Hellenistic influences as well as Latin.

H Roman philosophy was mostly from Germanic influences from Rome's northern borders.

J Classic Roman literature usually had themes of Greek and Roman competition.

If you have trouble with...				
Question	1	2	3	4
See Lesson	7.1	7.2	7.3	6.3
TEKS	20.B	4.C	4.G	3.A

3. A
4. G

Online Use the **Topic Synthesize** to help students revisit and reflect on the Essential Question for this Topic.

Topic Inquiry

If students have done a Topic Inquiry for this Topic, have them complete the final step of the Inquiry now.

The Muslim World and Africa (730 B.C.–A.D. 1500)

TOPIC 8 ORGANIZER	PACING: APPROX. 1 PERIOD, .5 BLOCKS		
	PACING	TEKS	ELPS
Connect	1 period		
MY STORY VIDEO **Ibn Battuta, Traveler**	10 min.		
DIGITAL ESSENTIAL QUESTION ACTIVITY **How are religion and culture connected?**	10 min.	4.D	
DIGITAL TIMELINE ACTIVITY **The Muslim World and Africa**	10 min.	4.D	
TOPIC INQUIRY: CIVIC DISCUSSION **The Battle of Tours**	20 min.		
Investigate	4–8 periods		
TOPIC INQUIRY: CIVIC DISCUSSION **The Battle of Tours**	Ongoing		
LESSON 1 **The Origins of Islam**	30–40 min.	4.D, 23.A, 24.A, 25.D	
LESSON 2 **A Muslim Empire**	30–40 min.	1.C, 4.D, 4.E, 4.K, 16.A, 23.A, 23.B	2.G.6
LESSON 3 **Achievements of Muslim Civilization**	30–40 min.	4.D, 26.B, 27.A	3.B.2
LESSON 4 **The Ottoman and Safavid Empires**	30–40 min.	1.D, 7.D	3.B.3
LESSON 5 **Early Civilizations of Africa**	30–40 min.	1.C, 4.E, 16.C	
LESSON 6 **Kingdoms of West Africa**	30–40 min.	4.D, 4.J	
LESSON 7 **Trading States of East Africa**	30–40 min.	4.D, 16.B	3.C.3
LESSON 8 **Diverse Peoples and Traditions in Africa**	30–40 min.	24.A, 26.B	
Synthesize	1 period		
DIGITAL ESSENTIAL QUESTION ACTIVITY **The Muslim World and Africa**	10 min.	4.D	
TOPIC INQUIRY: CIVIC DISCUSSION **The Battle of Tours**	20 min.		

TOPIC 8 ORGANIZER	PACING: APPROX. 1 PERIOD, .5 BLOCKS		
	PACING	TEKS	ELPS
Demonstrate	1–2 periods		
DIGITAL TOPIC TEST **The Muslim World and Africa**	10 min.		
TOPIC INQUIRY: CIVIC DISCUSSION **The Battle of Tours**	20 min.		

AUTHOR'S NOTE

The Splendors of Baghdad

Through all the conflicts and transformations, the Arab Empire did much to advance the welfare of their subjects. The spread of a common culture across a wide swatch of the Old World encouraged trade, by caravan and swift Arab dhow, from Spain to India.

A common language and religion, a Muslim law code based on the life of the merchant, and the caravan town all encouraged commercial development. And commerce in turn contributed to the development of handicraft industry; Damascus steel, Córdoba leather, and silks and cottons from the East were all internationally known. The tales of *The Arabian Nights* include mouthwatering descriptions of Baghdad bazaars heaped with good things, from Syrian apples and Arabian peaches to perfumes and incense, aloewood, musk, and candle of Alexandria wax.

Baghdad itself—"City of Peace, Gift of God, Paradise on Earth"—was one of the wonders of the age. Built up by the Abbasids from a small market town on the Tigris, the third capital of Islam (after Mecca and Damascus) grew into a city that rivaled even Constantinople in size, wealth, and beauty. Arabs, Persians, Turks, and all the rest of the empire's kaleidoscope of peoples mingled in the streets of the city. There were many libraries, a House of Wisdom for the study of theology, and an observatory for the study of the stars.

At the courts of the caliphs, poetry, music, and the other arts all flourished, along with the self-indulgence indigenous to the courts of princes. At first glance there would seem to be little connection between that paradise and the lives of the majority of the faithful the caliphs claimed to rule. But there were crucial connections nonetheless. . . .

Whether they knew it or not, the life of the farmers tending their immemorial water wheels was the better for the men who ruled in Baghdad, for the commerce, the protection, the Law of the Prophet—the good things that Baghdad symbolized in the varying degrees provided over the centuries.

—Anthony Esler, *The Human Venture: From Prehistory to the Present* (Upper Saddle River, New Jersey: Pearson Education, 2004), pp. 261–262

TOPIC INQUIRY: CIVIC DISCUSSION

The Battle of Tours

TEKS 1.C, 4.D, 4.E, 29.C, 29.D, 29.E, 29.F, 29.G, 29.H, 30.A, 30.C

In this Topic Inquiry, students work in teams to examine different perspectives on this issue by analyzing several sources, arguing both sides of a Yes/No question, then developing and discussing their own point of view on the question: Was the Battle of Tours the decisive event stopping the spread of Islam in Europe?

STEP 1: CONNECT

Develop Questions and Plan the Investigation

Launch the Civic Discussion

Divide the class into groups of four students. Students can access the materials they'll need in the online course or you can distribute copies to each student. Read the main question and introduction with the students.

Have students complete Step 1 by reading the Discussion Launch and filling in Step 1 of the Information Organizer. The Discussion Launch provides YES and NO arguments on the main question. Students should extract and paraphrase the arguments from the reading in Step 1 of their Information Organizers.

Next, students share within their groups the arguments and evidence they found to support the YES and NO positions. The group needs to agree on the major YES and NO points and each student should note those points in their Information Organizer.

Resources

- Student Instructions
- Discussion Launch
- Information Organizer

PROFESSIONAL DEVELOPMENT

Civic Discussion

Be sure to view the Civic Discussion Professional Development resources in the online course.

STEP 2: INVESTIGATE

Apply Disciplinary Concepts and Tools

Examine Sources and Perspectives

Students will examine sources with the goal of extracting information and perspectives on the main question. They analyze each source and describe the author's perspective on the main question and key evidence the author provides to support that viewpoint in Information Organizer Step 2.

Ask students to keep in mind:

- **Author/Creator:** Who created the source? An individual? Group? Government agency?
- **Audience:** For whom was the source created?
- **Date/Place:** Is there any information that reveals where and when the source was created?
- **Purpose:** Why was the source created? Discuss with students the importance of this question in identifying bias.
- **Relevance:** How does the source support one argument or another?

Suggestion: Reading the source documents and filling in Step 2 of the Information Organizer could be assigned as homework.

Resources

- Student Instructions
- Source documents
- Information Organizer

STEP 3: SYNTHESIZE

Use Evidence to Formulate Conclusions

Formulate Compelling Arguments With Evidence

Now students will apply perspectives and evidence they extracted from the sources to think more deeply about the main question by first arguing one side of the issue, then the other. In this way students become more prepared to formulate an evidence-based conclusion on their own.

Within each student group, assign half of the students to take the position of YES on the main question and the others to take the position of NO. Students will work with their partners to identify the strongest arguments and evidence to support their assigned YES or NO position.

Present Yes/No Positions

Within each group, those assigned the YES position share arguments and evidence first. As the YES students speak, those assigned NO should listen carefully, take notes to fill in the rest of the Compelling Arguments Chart (Step 3 in Information Organizer), and ask clarifying questions.

When the YES side is finished, students assigned the NO position present while those assigned YES should listen, take notes, and ask clarifying questions. Examples of clarifying questions are:

- I think you just said [x]. Am I understanding you correctly?
- Can you tell me more about [x]?
- Can you repeat [x]? I am not sure I understand, yet.

Suggestion: You may want to set a 5-minute time limit for each side to present. Provide a two-minute warning so that students make their most compelling arguments within the time frame.

Switch Sides

The students will switch sides to argue the opposite point of view. To prepare to present the other position, partners who first argued YES will use the notes they took during the NO side's presentation, plus add any additional arguments and evidence from the reading and sources. The same for students who first argued the NO position.

STEP 4: DEMONSTRATE

Communicate Conclusions and Take Informed Action

Individual Points of View

Now the students will have the opportunity to discuss the main question from their own points of view. To help students prepare for this discussion, have them reflect on the YES/NO discussions they have participated in thus far and fill in Step 4 of their Information Organizers.

After all of the students have shared their points of view, each group should list points of agreement, filling in the last portion of Step 4 on their Information Organizers.

Reflect on the Discussion

Ask students to reflect on the civic discussion, thinking about:

- The value of having to argue both the YES and NO positions.
- If their individual views changed over the course of the discussion and why.
- What they learned from participating in the discussion.

Resources

- Student Instructions
- Information Organizer

The Origins of Islam

Objectives

Objective 1: Understand how Muhammad spread Islam.

Objective 2: Describe the central ideas of Islam.

Objective 3: Explain how Islam helped shape the way of life of its believers.

LESSON 1 ORGANIZER			PACING: APPROX. 1 PERIOD, .5 BLOCKS			
			RESOURCES			
	OBJECTIVES	PACING	Print	Online	TEKS	ELPS
Connect						
DIGITAL START UP ACTIVITY **Mecca**		5 min.		●	23.A	
Investigate						
READ **Muhammad and Early Islam**	Objective 1	10 min.	●	●	4.D, 23.A	
INTERACTIVE TIMELINE **The Origins of Islam**		10 min.		●	4.D, 23.A	
READ **Teachings of Islam**	Objective 2	10 min.	●	●	23.A	
INTERACTIVE GALLERY **The Five Pillars of Wisdom**		10 min.		●	23.A	
READ **Islam as a Way of Life**	Objective 3	10 min.	●	●	4.D, 23.A, 25.D	
Synthesize						
DIGITAL ACTIVITY **Foundations of Islam**		5 min.		●	23.A, 25.D	
Demonstrate						
DIGITAL QUIZ **Lesson Quiz and Class Discussion Board**		10 min.		●	4.D, 23.A, 25.D	

PEARSON realize™ www.PearsonTexas.com Access your Digital Lesson

Focus on Texas Standards

Texas Essential Knowledge and Skills

4.D explain the political, economic, and social impact of Islam on Europe, Asia, and Africa

23.A describe the historical origins, central ideas, and spread of major religious and philosophical traditions, including Buddhism, Christianity, Confucianism, Hinduism, Islam, Judaism, Sikhism, and the development of monotheism

24.A describe the changing roles of women, children, and families during major eras of world history

25.D explain how Islam influences law and government in the Muslim world

NOTES

A Muslim Empire

Objectives

Objective 1: Describe the spread of Islam.

Objective 2: Identify the divisions that emerged within Islam.

Objective 3: Describe the rise of the Umayyad and Abbasid dynasties.

Objective 4: Explain why the Abbasid empire declined.

LESSON 2 ORGANIZER	PACING: APPROX. 1 PERIOD, .5 BLOCKS					
			RESOURCES			
	OBJECTIVES	PACING	Print	Online	TEKS	ELPS
Connect						
DIGITAL START UP ACTIVITY **Nomadic Raids**		5 min.		●	23.A	
Investigate						
READ **Islam Faces Challenges**	Objective 1	10 min.	●	●	1.C, 4.D, 23.A	
READ **The Dome of the Rock**		10 min.		●	26.B	
READ **Divisions Split Islam**	Objective 2	10 min.	●	●	1.C, 4.D, 23.A	
READ **Umayyad Caliphs Create an Arab Empire**	Objectives 1, 3	10 min.	●	●	1.C, 4.D, 4.E, 23.A	2.G.6
INTERACTIVE MAP **Spread of Islam**		10 min.		●	1.C, 23.A	
READ **New Rule Under the Abbasid Dynasty**		10 min.	●	●	1.C, 4.D, 23.A	
INTERACTIVE TIMELINE **Rise and Decline of an Arab Empire**		10 min.		●	1.C, 4.D, 23.A	
READ **Decline of the Arab Empire**	Objective 4	10 min.	●	●	1.C, 4.D, 4.K	
Synthesize						
DIGITAL ACTIVITY **The Umayyad and Abbasid Caliphates**		5 min.		●	1.C, 4.D, 23.A	
Demonstrate						
DIGITAL QUIZ **Lesson Quiz and Class Discussion Board**		10 min.		●	1.C, 4.D, 4.E, 23.A	

PEARSON realize™ www.PearsonTexas.com Access your Digital Lesson

Focus on Texas Standards

Texas Essential Knowledge and Skills

4.D explain the political, economic, and social impact of Islam on Europe, Asia, and Africa

4.E describe the interactions among Muslim, Christian, and Jewish societies in Europe, Asia, and North Africa

23.A describe the historical origins, central ideas, and spread of major religious and philosophical traditions, including Buddhism, Christianity, Confucianism, Hinduism, Islam, Judaism, Sikhism, and the development of monotheism

NOTES

Achievements of Muslim Civilization

Objectives

Objective 1: Describe the role of trade in Muslim civilization.

Objective 2: Identify the traditions that influenced Muslim art, architecture, and literature.

Objective 3: Describe the major ideas in mathematics, science, and technology that occurred in Muslim civilization.

LESSON 3 ORGANIZER — **PACING: APPROX. 1 PERIOD, .5 BLOCKS**

	OBJECTIVES	PACING	RESOURCES Print	RESOURCES Online	TEKS	ELPS
Connect						
DIGITAL START UP ACTIVITY **Inspiration From Aristotle**		5 min.		●	26.B	
Investigate						
READ **Economic and Social Changes**	Objective 1	10 min.	●	●	4.D, 23.A	
READ **Literature, Art, and Architecture**	Objective 2	10 min.		●	TX 26.B	
INTERACTIVE GALLERY **Islamic Art and Architecture**	Objective 2	10 min.		●	TX 26.B	
READ **An Emphasis on Knowledge**	Objective 3	10 min.	●	●	4.D, 27.A	3.B.2
INTERACTIVE GALLERY **Muslim Advances in Technology, Math, and Science**	Objective 3	10 min.		●	27.A	
Synthesize						
DIGITAL ACTIVITY **Accomplishments in Medicine, Literature, History, and Mathematics**		5 min.		●	26.B, 27.A	
Demonstrate						
DIGITAL QUIZ **Lesson Quiz and Class Discussion Board**		10 min.		●	4.D, 23.A, 26.B, 27.A	

PEARSON realize™ www.PearsonTexas.com Access your Digital Lesson

Focus on Texas Standards

Texas Essential Knowledge and Skills

4.D explain the political, economic, and social impact of Islam on Europe, Asia, and Africa

26.B analyze examples of how art, architecture, literature, music, and drama reflect the history of the cultures in which they are produced

27.A identify the origin and diffusion of major ideas in mathematics, science, and technology that occurred in river valley civilizations, classical Greece and Rome, classical India, and the Islamic caliphates between 700 and 1200 and in China from the Tang to Ming dynasties

NOTES

The Ottoman and Safavid Empires

Objectives

Objective 1: Explain the impact of the Ottoman empire on Eastern Europe.

Objective 2: Describe the characteristics of Ottoman culture.

Objective 3: Explain how Abbas the Great strengthened the Safavid empire.

LESSON 4 ORGANIZER	PACING: APPROX. 1 PERIOD, .5 BLOCKS					
	OBJECTIVES	PACING	RESOURCES Print	RESOURCES Online	TEKS	ELPS
Connect						
DIGITAL START UP ACTIVITY **Constantinople Falls**		5 min.		●		
Investigate						
READ **Growth of the Ottoman Empire**	Objective 1	10 min.	●	●	1.D, 7.D	
INTERACTIVE GALLERY **Ottoman Empire Under Suleiman**		10 min.		●	1.D	
READ **Ottoman Society**	Objective 2	10 min.	●	●	1.D, 4.D, 7.D, 23.A, 26.B	3.B.3
READ **The Rise of the Safavids**	Objective 3	10 min.	●	●	4.D, 23.A	
INTERACTIVE MAP **Growth of the Ottoman and Safavid Empires**		10 min.		●	1.D, 4.D	
Synthesize						
DIGITAL ACTIVITY **The Ottoman and Safavid Empires**		5 min.		●	1.D, 4.D, 23.A	
Demonstrate						
DIGITAL QUIZ **Lesson Quiz and Class Discussion Board**		10 min.		●	1.D, 4.D, 7.D, 23.A, 26.B	

PEARSON realize™ www.PearsonTexas.com Access your Digital Lesson

Focus on Texas Standards

Texas Essential Knowledge and Skills

1.D identify major causes and describe the major effects of the following important turning points in world history from 1450 to 1750: the rise of the Ottoman Empire, the influence of the Ming dynasty on world trade, European exploration and the Columbian Exchange, European expansion, and the Renaissance and the Reformation	**7.D** explain the impact of the Ottoman Empire on Eastern Europe and global trade

NOTES

Early Civilizations of Africa

Objectives

Objective 1: Understand how geography affected migration, cultural development, and trade in Africa.

Objective 2: Describe the rise and decline of Nubia.

Objective 3: Explain how outside influences led to change in North Africa.

LESSON 5 ORGANIZER — **PACING: APPROX. 1 PERIOD, .5 BLOCKS**

	OBJECTIVES	PACING	RESOURCES Print	RESOURCES Online	TEKS	ELPS
Connect						
DIGITAL START UP ACTIVITY **Danger in the Desert**		5 min.		●	16.B	
Investigate						
READ **The Geography of Africa**	Objective 1	10 min.	●	●	16.C	
INTERACTIVE MAP **Africa's Vegetation Regions**		10 min.		●	16.C	
READ **Migration of People and Ideas**		10 min.	●	●	16.C	
READ **Egypt and Nubia Flourish**	Objective 2	10 min.	●	●	1.A, 16.B, 26.B	
INTERACTIVE GALLERY **Nubian Art and Culture**		10 min.		●	26. B	
READ **North Africa in the Ancient World**	Objective 3	10 min.	●	●	1.C, 4.E	
Synthesize						
DIGITAL ACTIVITY **Revisit the Essential Question**		5 min.		●	1.C, 4.E	
Demonstrate						
DIGITAL QUIZ **Lesson Quiz and Discussion Board**		10 min.		●	1.C, 4.E	

PEARSON realize™ www.PearsonTexas.com Access your Digital Lesson

Focus on Texas Standards

Texas Essential Knowledge and Skills

1.C identify major causes and describe the major effects of the following important turning points in world history from 600 to 1450: the spread of Christianity, the decline of Rome and the formation of medieval Europe; the development of Islamic caliphates and their impact on Asia, Africa, and Europe; the Mongol invasions and their impact on Europe, China, India, and Southwest Asia

4.E describe the interactions among Muslim, Christian, and Jewish societies in Europe, Asia, and North Africa

16.C interpret maps, charts, and graphs to explain how geography has influenced people and events in the past

NOTES

Topic 8 Lesson 6

Kingdoms of West Africa

Objectives

Objective 1: Analyze how the gold and salt trade in Africa facilitated the spread of ideas and trade.

Objective 2: Describe how the rulers of Ghana, Mali, and Songhai built strong kingdoms.

Objective 3: Summarize how other West African societies developed.

LESSON 6 ORGANIZER	PACING: APPROX. 1 PERIOD, .5 BLOCKS					
	OBJECTIVES	PACING	RESOURCES: Print	RESOURCES: Online	TEKS	ELPS
Connect						
DIGITAL START UP ACTIVITY **Trade in Mali**		5 min.		●	4.J	
Investigate						
READ **Trade Grows Across the Sahara**	Objective 1	10 min.	●	●	4.J	
INTERACTIVE MAP **Trans-Saharan Trade (750 B.C.)**	Objective 1	10 min.		●	4.D, 4.J	
READ **Ghana**	Objective 2	10 min.	●	●	4.D, 4.J	
READ **Mali**	Objective 2	10 min.	●	●	4.D, 4.J	
READ **Songhai**	Objective 2	10 min.	●	●	4.D, 4.J	
INTERACTIVE GALLERY **Artifacts From West Africa's Great Kingdoms**	Objective 2	10 min.		●	26.B	
READ **Small Societies and Kingdoms of West Africa**	Objective 3	10 min.	●	●	4.D, 4.J	
Synthesize						
DIGITAL ACTIVITY **Reflect on the Essential Question**		5 min.		●	4.D, 4.J	
Demonstrate						
DIGITAL QUIZ **Lesson Quiz and Class Discussion Board**		10 min.		●	4.D, 4.J	

Focus on Texas Standards

Texas Essential Knowledge and Skills

4.D explain the political, economic, and social impact of Islam on Europe, Asia, and Africa	**4.J** analyze how the Silk Road and the African gold-salt trade facilitated the spread of ideas and trade

NOTES

Trading States of East Africa

Objectives

Objective 1: Explain how religion influenced the development of Axum and Ethiopia.

Objective 2: Understand how trade affected the city-states in East Africa.

Objective 3: Describe the economy of Great Zimbabwe.

LESSON 7 ORGANIZER	PACING: APPROX. 1 PERIOD, .5 BLOCKS					
			RESOURCES			
	OBJECTIVES	PACING	Print	Online	TEKS	ELPS
Connect						
DIGITAL START UP ACTIVITY **Trading States of East Africa**		5 min.		●	1.C, 23.B	
Investigate						
READ **Axum**	Objective 1	10 min.	●	●	1.C, 4.D, 4.E, 16.B	
READ **Ethiopia**		10 min.	●	●	1.C, 4.E, 16.B	3.C.3
READ **City-States of East Africa**	Objective 2	10 min.	●	●	4.D, 4.E, 16.B	
INTERACTIVE MAP **Journeys of Ibn Battuta**		10 min.		●	4.D, 16.B	
READ **Great Zimbabwe**	Objective 3	10 min.	●	●	26.B	
INTERACTIVE GALLERY **Architecture of the African Kingdoms**		10 min.		●	26.B	
Synthesize						
DIGITAL ACTIVITY **Kingdoms and Trading States of East Africa**		5 min.		●	4.D, 16.B	
Demonstrate						
DIGITAL QUIZ **Lesson Quiz and Class Discussion Board**		10 min.		●	4.D, 4.E, 16.B, 26.B	

PEARSON realize www.PearsonTexas.com Access your Digital Lesson

Focus on Texas Standards

Texas Essential Knowledge and Skills

4.D explain the political, economic, and social impact of Islam on Europe, Asia, and Africa	**16.B** analyze the influence of human and physical geographic factors on major events in world history, including the development of river valley civilizations, trade in the Indian Ocean, and the opening of the Panama and Suez canals

NOTES

Diverse Peoples and Traditions in Africa

Objectives

Objective 1: Identify the different ways that the family influenced medieval African cultures.

Objective 2: Describe the variety of forms of medieval African governments.

Objective 3: Understand the role of religion and art in medieval societies.

LESSON 8 ORGANIZER — **PACING: APPROX. 1 PERIOD, .5 BLOCKS**

	OBJECTIVES	PACING	RESOURCES: Print	RESOURCES: Online	TEKS	ELPS
Connect						
DIGITAL START UP ACTIVITY **The Dama**		5 min.		●	26.B	
Investigate						
READ **Many Cultures and Patterns of Life**	Objective 1	10 min.	●	●	24.A	
INTERACTIVE CHART **Family Patterns in African Society**		10 min.		●	24.A	
READ **Government and Power**	Objective 2	10 min.		●		
READ **Religion**	Objective 3	10 min.	●	●	4.E, 26.B	
READ **Art and Literature**		10 min.	●	●	26.B	
INTERACTIVE GALLERY **African Art and Culture**		10 min.		●	26.B	
Synthesize						
DIGITAL ACTIVITY **African Society**		5 min.		●	4.E, 24.A	
Demonstrate						
DIGITAL QUIZ **Lesson Quiz and Class Discussion Board**		10 min.		●	4.E, 24.A, 26.B	

Focus on Texas Standards

Texas Essential Knowledge and Skills

24.A describe the changing roles of women, children, and families during major eras of world history	**26.B** analyze examples of how art, architecture, literature, music, and drama reflect the history of the cultures in which they are produced

NOTES

TOPIC 8 **TEKS Mastery**

The Muslim World and Africa (730 B.C–A.D. 1500)

In this Topic, you will learn about the Muslim world and Africa. You will also find lots of interesting ways to master the TEKS associated with this Topic.

Your study will help you master these TEKS:

TEKS

1.C, 1.D, 4.D, 4.E, 4.J, 4.K, 7.D, 16.A, 16.B, 16.C, 23.A, 23.B, 24.A, 25.D, 26.B, 27.A, 29.F

LESSON OUTLINE

8.1: The Origins of Islam **4.D, 23.A, 24.A, 25.D**

8.2: A Muslim Empire **1.C, 4.D, 4.E, 4.K, 16.A, 23.A, 23.B**

8.3: Achievements of Muslim Civilization **4.D, 26.B, 27.A**

8.4: Correlation The Ottoman and Safavid Empires **1.D, 4.D, 7.D**

8.5: Early Civilizations of Africa **1.C, 4.E, 16.C**

8.6: Kingdoms of West Africa **4.D, 4.J**

8.7: Trading States of East Africa **4.D, 16.B, 26.B**

8.8: Diverse Peoples and Traditions in Africa **24.A, 26.B**

Connect

Connect with this Topic by watching a video about a fascinating person related to this Topic. You can think about how this Topic connects to your own life. And you'll encounter an intriguing Essential Question: How are religion and culture connected?

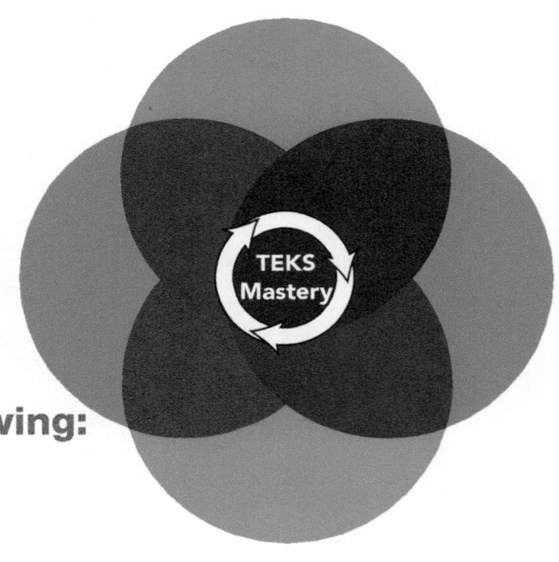

Begin your study by trying the following:

NBC LEARN Watch My Story Video:

Ibn Battuta, Traveler

Launch your Civic Discussion:

The Battle of Tours

Investigate

A group of lessons will help you investigate the Topic further. Each lesson has interesting text readings and fascinating interactivities. Together, they will bring Africa and the Muslim world to life and help you master the TEKS for this Topic.

And keep working on your Civic Discussion. You're almost ready to show what you have accomplished by expressing your position on the Battle of Tours using the evidence you have gathered.

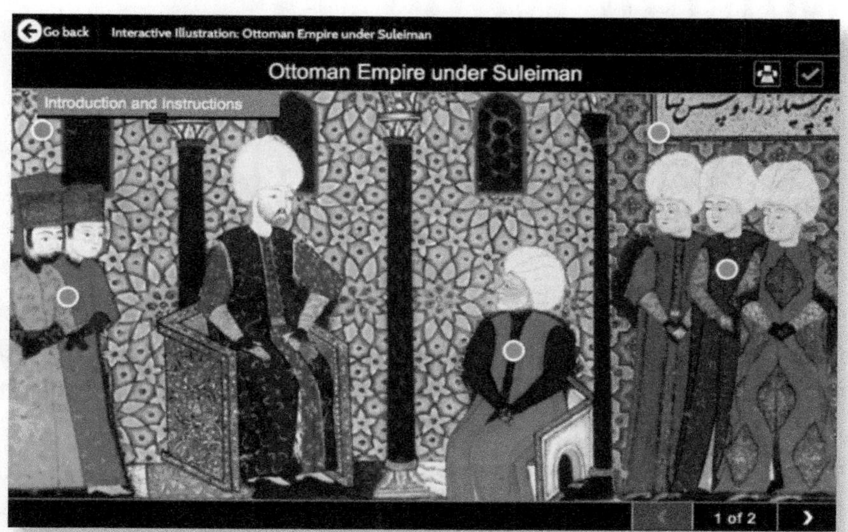

>> Digital interactivity from the online course

Synthesize

You will get a chance to pull together everything you have learned by thinking again about the Essential Question. Consider how you would answer the question now: How are religion and culture connected?

Demonstrate

Now you will get to show what you know. You will get a chance to complete the TEKS Review and Assessment pages, answering questions about every TEKS for this Topic. Or you can write an essay, take part in a discussion, or share your Project. No matter which you do, it will be a real-world demonstration of the things you now understand about the Muslim World and Africa.

TEKS in Topic 8	Topic Review and Assessment Questions
1.C	**2, 5, 8**
1.D	**15**
4.D	**6, 7**
4.E	**10**
4.J	**9**
4.K	**2**
7.D	**16**
16.B	**1**
23.A	**3, 6**
24.A	**11**
25.D	**3**
26.B	**14**
27.A	**12, 13**
29.F	**12**

Topic 8

The Muslim World and Africa (730 B.C.–A.D. 1500)

Introduction

A new major world religion emerged in the Arabian Peninsula with the teachings of Muhammad. As Arabs united under Islam, a Muslim empire arose and expanded. Under the caliphates, and then later the Ottoman and Safavid empires, Muslim civilization developed a rich and diverse culture. Arab traders in the flourishing gold and salt trade routes in Africa helped spread Islam to the region. The kingdoms and trading states of Africa, influenced by the continent's wide range of climate, vegetation, and terrain, had a variety of unique cultures and societies. While there were some isolated but flourishing smaller societies, areas with abundant resources and access to trade routes grew into vast and wealthy empires.

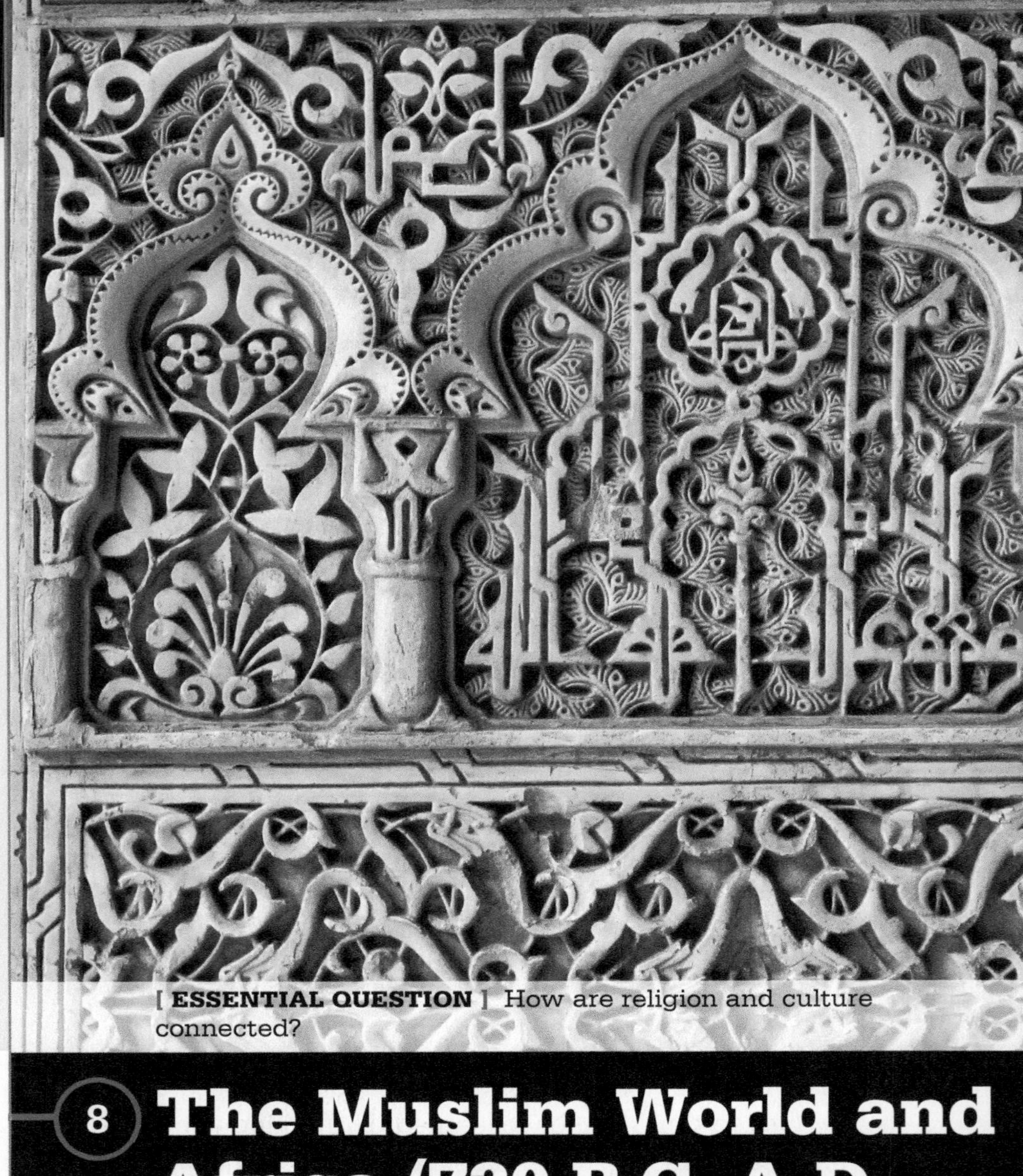

[**ESSENTIAL QUESTION**] How are religion and culture connected?

8 The Muslim World and Africa (730 B.C.-A.D. 1500)

ESSENTIAL QUESTION

Ask students to think about the Essential Question for this Topic: How are religion and culture connected? Project the Essential Question activity from the course. Read the information about Muhammad and the items in the bulleted list. If students have not already done so, ask them to list which of the connections has the most influence on society. Then discuss the results as a class.

Identify Central Issues Why does religion often play a central role in the cultural development of a society? *(Answers may vary. Religion can affect many aspects of a society, ranging from the most personal—the beliefs of the individual, family roles, and daily life—to the broadest—law, economics, and government.)*

Cause and Effect How might religion be a unifying force? *(Answers may vary. Students might respond that if most members of a society practice the same religion, then they might share similar cultural values.)*

Analyze Images

Have students examine the photograph of the decorative carving from the Alhambra, a fortress and palace complex in southern Spain. This carving shows a style of Islamic art. Ask students to describe ways that artists can represent their religious beliefs in their work.

Texas Essential Knowledge and Skills

1.C, 1.D, 4.D, 4.E, 4.J, 4.K, 7.D, 16.A, 16.B, 16.C, 23.A, 23.B, 24.A, 25.D, 26.B, 27.A, 29.F

Decorative carving at the hambra palace complex, Spain

Enduring Understandings

- The prophet of Islam was Muhammad, who preached his beliefs and built up the Muslim faith.
- After Muhammad's death, Islam spread across Southwest Asia and to many other parts of the world.
- Art, architecture, and literature flourished in the Muslim empires, and Muslims made advances in many fields of learning.
- In Africa, trade of food, gold, and salt developed into a trans-Saharan trade network, and rulers created powerful kingdoms.
- Christianity and Islam spread to many regions of Africa, and people who adopted those religions often blended them with their local practices and beliefs.

PEARSON realize NBC LEARN

Watch the My Story Video to learn about the travels of Ibn Battuta.

PEARSON realize www.PearsonTexas.com — Access your digital lessons including: Topic Inquiry • Interactive Reading Notepad • Interactivities • Assessments

281

NBC LEARN MY STORY VIDEO

Project the My Story Video that describes the travels of Ibn Battuta.

Online My Story Video: **Ibn Battuta, Traveler**.

After viewing, ask students to respond to the following questions.

Check Understanding Why is Ibn Battuta's journey considered one of the greatest in history? *(In the fourteenth century, he visited the lands of every Muslim ruler at the time.)*

Hypothesize What impact might the news of Ibn Battuta's travels have had on people of the time? *(a desire to travel, a desire to learn more about other lands, eagerness to exchange ideas and goods with other peoples)*

OVERVIEW ACTIVITY

Online Project the timeline showing the major events in Muslim civilization and Africa. These are just some of the events that students will learn about while exploring this Topic. The timeline will provide a framework into which they can place the events they learn about.

Check Understanding How many years after the hijra did Mansa Musa complete his hajj to Mecca? *(702; Mohammad traveled to Medina in 622 and Mansa finished his hajj in 1324.)*

Topic Inquiry

If you choose to assign the Topic Inquiry, launch the discussion with students after introducing the Topic.

D Differentiate Extra Support Ask a volunteer to point out the time intervals on the timeline and the overall range of time covered by this timeline. Ask, how many years are there between the establishment of the Abbasid dynasty and the reign of Shah Abbas in the Safavid empire? *(838; Abu al-Abbas establishes the Abbasid dynasty in 750; Shah Abbas begins reign in 1588.)*

Topic 8 Lesson 1

The Origins of Islam

CONNECT

Preview Have students preview the **Lesson Objectives** and the list of **Key Terms**.

Students can also preview all the **Key Terms** and **Academic Vocabulary** using the **Interactive Reading Notepad** on the digital course or preview a summary of the lesson in the **Reading and Note Taking Study Guide**.

Online Use the **Editable Presentation** found on the digital course to present the main ideas for this lesson.

Start Up Activity

Have students look at the photograph and caption at the bottom of the next page.

Discuss What might the image and caption reveal about the role of pilgrimage and the significance of Mecca in Islam? *(Sample response: Pilgrimage likely plays an important part in Islam, and Mecca is probably an important religious site for Muslims.)*

Online You can also project the **Start Up Activity** from the course.

Tell students that in this lesson they will learn about the origins, religious beliefs, and spread of Islam.

INVESTIGATE

Have students read the section using the **Reading and Note Taking Study Guide** to help them take notes and understand the text as they read.

Muhammad and Early Islam

Mecca was an important pilgrimage site, home to the Kaaba, an ancient pagan temple. Tell students that Muhammad, a successful merchant troubled by the moral ills of Mecca, went to meditate in a cave on Mount Hira. There, according to Islamic belief, he was called to be the messenger of God. In Mecca, people rejected Muhammad's call to worship Allah—the Arabic word for *God*—instead of their pagan gods. Fearing for his life, Muhammad traveled to Medina, a journey called the hijra. In Medina, Muhammad gathered many followers and helped unite Arabs into a larger Muslim community. He returned to Mecca and rededicated the Kaaba to Allah, making it the holiest site in Islam.

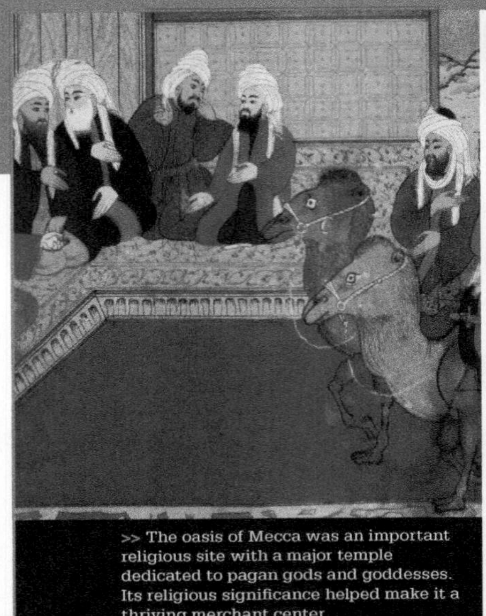

>> The oasis of Mecca was an important religious site with a major temple dedicated to pagan gods and goddesses. Its religious significance helped make it a thriving merchant center.

Interactive Flipped Video

8.1 **The religion of Islam, whose followers are called Muslims, emerged in the Arabian Peninsula. This region of southwestern Asia is mostly desert, yet it was home to many Arab tribes in the A.D. 500s. Nomadic herders called Bedouins (BED oo inz) moved through the desert to reach seasonal pasturelands for their camels, goats, and sheep. Competition for water and grazing land often led to warfare. Bedouins also traded with settled Arab tribes in oasis towns and protected the caravan trading routes.**

TEKS
4.D, 23.A, 24.A, 25.D

>> Objectives

Understand how Muhammad spread Islam.

Describe the central ideas of Islam.

Explain how Islam helped shape the way of life of its believers.

>> Key Terms

Bedouin
Muhammad
Mecca
Yathrib
hijra
Medina
Kaaba
Quran
mosque
hajj
Sharia

The Origins of Islam

Muhammad and Early Islam

Muhammad's Early Life Muhammad, an Arab man whom Muslims honor as the prophet of Islam, was born in the oasis town of Mecca around A.D. 570. **Mecca** was a bustling market town at the crossroads of several caravan routes. It was also a thriving pilgrimage center. Many Arabs came to pray at the **Kaaba,** an ancient temple that housed statues of pagan gods and goddesses. The pilgrims helped make Mecca's merchants wealthy. All weapons had to be laid down near the temple, making Mecca a safe and peaceful place to do business.

Arabia's deserts and trade centers shaped Muhammad's early life. In his youth, he worked as a shepherd among the Bedouins. Later, he led caravans across the desert and became a successful merchant. When he was about 25, Muhammad married Khadija (ka DEE jah), a wealthy widow who ran a prosperous caravan business. According to tradition, Muhammad became known for his honesty in business and was a devoted husband and father.

Muhammad the Messenger Muhammad was troubled by the moral ills of Meccan society, especially greed. He often went to a cave in the hills near Mecca to meditate. According to Muslim belief, when he was about 40 years old he heard the voice of the angel Gabriel

PEARSON realize. www.PearsonTexas.com Access your Digital Lesson.

282

Aa Vocabulary Builder

1. Have students pronounce the following academic vocabulary terms in this lesson and clarify the part of speech. For difficult or polysyllabic words, break them into syllables and pronounce them with the students.
2. Explain what the word means in common "student-friendly" language using synonyms and antonyms when possible. Provide concrete examples to clarify the meaning, and rephrase the definition.

mediate: to act as a go-between
affirm: to judge as valid

calling him to be the messenger of God. Muhammad was terrified and puzzled. How could he, an illiterate merchant, become the messenger of God?

Khadija encouraged him to accept the call. She became the first convert to the faith called Islam, from the Arabic word that means "to submit to God." Muhammad devoted his life to spreading Islam. He urged Arabs to give up their worship of pagan gods and to instead worship God. In Arabic, the word for God is *Allah*.

The Hijra: From Mecca to Medina At first, few people listened to Muhammad's teachings. His rejection of traditional Arab gods angered Mecca's merchants, who feared that neglect of their gods would disrupt the pilgrim trade. Facing persecution, in 615 some of Muhammad's followers left Mecca for Axum, located across the Red Sea, where they received protection from Axum's Christian king.

In 622, faced with the threat of murder, Muhammad and his followers left Mecca for **Yathrib,** a journey known as the **hijra** (HIJ ruh). Later, Yathrib was renamed **Medina,** or "city of the Prophet," and 622 became the first year of the Muslim calendar.

The hijra was a turning point for Islam. In Medina, local people welcomed Muhammad and agreed to follow his teachings. They became a community of Muslims, or *umma*. Loyalty to the umma was based on Islam instead of old family rivalries. Muhammad created rules that governed and united Muslims and brought peace among the clans of Medina. As his reputation grew, thousands of Arabs adopted Islam. Meanwhile, Meccan leaders grew more hostile toward the Muslims, seizing Muslim property. After Muslims attacked several Meccan caravans, the Meccans prepared for war.

Return to Mecca After winning battles with the Meccans, Muhammad triumphantly returned to Mecca in 630. He destroyed the Arab icons in the Kaaba, the temple that he believed Abraham had built to worship the one true God. He rededicated the Kaaba to Allah, and it became the most holy place in Islam. For the next two years, Muhammad worked to unite the Arabs under Islam. Muhammad died in 632, but the faith that he proclaimed continued to spread. Today, Islam is one of the world's major religions.

SEQUENCE EVENTS What sequence of events led to Muhammad devoting his life to the spread of Islam?

>> When Muhammad came to Medina, he not only drew thousands to the new religion of Islam but also showed how Islam could be a unifying force for Arabs in the region. This would be a key strength in the growth of the Muslim empire.

>> This modern photograph shows Muslim pilgrims at the Kaaba, located in the center of the Haram Sharif Great Mosque in Mecca. More than two million Muslims make a pilgrimage to Mecca each year.

Interactive Timeline

Topic 8 Lesson 1

Online Project the **Interactive Timeline: The Origins of Islam** and click through the images and hotspots that describe the origins and spread of Islam on the Arabian Peninsula.

ACTIVE CLASSROOM

Have students complete a See-Think-Wonder activity as they look at the images of the hijra. With a partner, students should think about these questions: What do you see? What does it make you think about? What are you wondering about now that you have seen this?

D Differentiate Challenge/Gifted Ask students to do extra research on the hijra and present their findings to the class. Suggest they also think about the geography of the region and the role it played in Muhammad's life.

Guided Reading and Discussion

Review with students Muhammad's actions in Medina, particularly the initial acceptance of his teachings, the unification of the Arab community there, the thousands who came to adopt Islam, and the role it played in conquering Mecca.

Draw Conclusions How important do you think Medina is in Islam? *(Sample response: Because of its central role in establishing the Islamic faith, Medina might be a holy site and place of pilgrimage. In addition, the fact that Muhammad's arrival in Medina is the start of the Muslim calendar is a reflection of its significance to Muslims.)*

Key Terms

Ask students to find the key term **Mecca** (in bold) in the text. Ask them to think about and describe the people and lifestyles of an oasis town located on trade routes.

Background

The Kaaba Muslims believe that the Kaaba was built by Adam and rebuilt by Abraham. Located in Mecca, it is the holiest temple of Islam. The black silk cloth that covers the ancient stone masonry building is changed each year. The word *kaaba* means "cube." At one corner is a black stone, probably a meteorite. The marble walls inside are inset with verses from the Quran. During the *hajj,* or period of pilgrimage, the *kaaba* is surrounded by white-robed pilgrims.

Answers

Sequence Events *First, Muhammad meditated about problems in Meccan society. According to Muslim belief, he heard the angel Gabriel ask him to serve as a messenger to God. Then he embarked on the hijra from Mecca to Yathreb, or Medina. Muhammad spent the rest of his life spreading the word of Islam.*

Topic 8 Lesson 1

Teachings of Islam

Be sure students understand the central ideas of Islam. Remind them that Islam is a monotheistic religion, that the Quran is the sacred text that preaches that God is all-powerful and compassionate, and that Muslims perform five duties, called the Five Pillars of Wisdom.

Online Project the **Interactive Gallery: The Five Pillars of Wisdom** and click through the hotspots that describe the five duties central to Islam: the declaration of faith, prayer five times daily, alms for the poor, fasting during Ramadan, and the hajj.

ACTIVE CLASSROOM

Ask the following question using the Sticky Note strategy: Viewed together, what do these images tell you about an important aspect of Islam? *(Sample response: Many of these images show group activities, which demonstrate the strong community ties in Muslim traditions.)*

Guided Reading and Discussion

Tell students that for Muslims the Quran is the sacred word of God as revealed to Muhammad. It is the final authority, teaches God's will, and sets ethical standards.

Draw Conclusions How might the importance of the Quran inspire Muslims to learn Arabic, and how might that affect the Muslim community? *(Sample response: Because it is considered the sacred word of God, many Muslims learn Arabic, which provides a unifying language for Muslims.)*

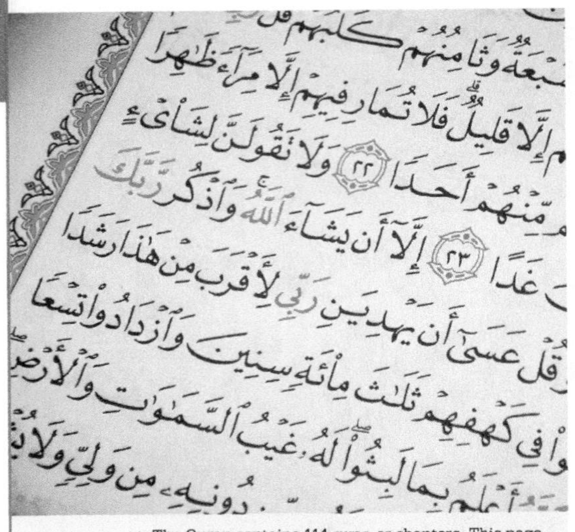

>> The Quran contains 114 *suras,* or chapters. This page shows a portion of the Cave Sura, named after its story about God protecting persecuted people by causing them to sleep safely in a cave.

>> The Muslim declaration of faith—written here—expresses the importance of monotheism in the religion.

Interactive Gallery

Teachings of Islam

Like Judaism and Christianity, Islam is monotheistic, based on belief in one God. The **Quran** (koo RAHN), the sacred text of Islam, teaches that God is all-powerful and compassionate. It also states that people are responsible for their own actions. Islam does not require priests to mediate between the people and God. Muslims believe that God had sent other prophets, including Abraham, Moses, and Jesus, but that Muhammad was the last and greatest prophet.

The Quran To Muslims, the Quran contains the sacred word of God as revealed to Muhammad. It is the final authority on all matters discussed in the text. The Quran teaches about what Muslims believe to be God's will and provides a guide to life. Its ethical standards emphasize honesty, generosity, and social justice.

It sets harsh penalties for crimes such as stealing or murder. According to the Quran, each individual will stand before God on the final judgment day to face either eternal punishment in hell or eternal bliss in paradise.

Muslims believe that the Quran is the direct, unchangeable word of God and that its meaning and poetic beauty reside in its original language of Arabic. For that reason, all Muslims, including converts to Islam, are expected to learn the Quran and required prayers in Arabic. This shared language has helped unite Muslims from many regions throughout the world.

The Five Pillars of Islam All observant Muslims perform five basic duties, known as the Five Pillars of Islam. The first is to make a declaration of faith. The Muslim profession of faith states, "There is no god but God; Muhammad is the messenger of God." The second is to pray five times daily. After a ritual washing, Muslims face the holy city of Mecca to pray.

Although Muslims may pray anywhere, they often gather in houses of worship called masjids or **mosques.** A mosque official called a muezzin (moo EZ in) calls the faithful to prayer.

The third pillar is to give charity to the poor. The fourth is to fast from sunrise to sunset during the holy month of Ramadan—the month in which Muslims believe Muhammad received his first revelations from God. The fifth pillar is to make the **hajj,** or pilgrimage to Mecca, if a person is able. Pilgrims participate in ceremonies commemorating the actions of Muhammad, Abraham, and Abraham's family. Their simple attire symbolizes the abandonment of the material world for the sake of God.

Background

Quran *Quran* means "recitation," and Muhammad, who was illiterate, orally recited the words as they were revealed to him. They were later written down by his followers. The Quran contains rhymed or semi-rhymed verses whose grace and poetry are difficult to translate. Devout Muslims try to memorize the entire book. Before touching the Quran, Muslims ritually cleanse and prepare in mind, body, and spirit. Veneration of the Quran is also expressed in the ornate calligraphy and decoration of each page. The Quran includes the teachings of and about earlier leaders from Jewish and Christian texts such as Noah, Moses, Abraham, Solomon, Jesus, and John the Baptist. Many Qurans have a wide margin so readers may turn the pages without touching the words.

"People of the Book" According to Muslim belief, Muslims, Jews, and Christians worship the same God. The Quran teaches that Islam is God's final and complete revelation, while Hebrew scriptures and the Christian Bible contain portions of earlier revelations. Muslims consider Jews and Christians to be "People of the Book," spiritually superior to polytheistic idol worshipers. Although Jews and Christians did not have the same rights as Muslims in early Muslim societies, they often enjoyed religious freedom.

INFER Why do Muslims follow the Five Pillars of Islam?

Islam as a Way of Life

Islam is both a religion and a way of life. Its teachings shape the lives of Muslims around the world. Islamic law governs daily life, and Muslim traditions determine ethical behavior and influence family relations.

Islamic Law Over time, Muslim scholars developed the **Sharia,** a body of law that includes interpretation of the Quran, examples of behavior from Muhammad's life, and Muslim traditions. Similar to Jewish law, the Sharia regulates moral conduct, family life, business practices, government, and other aspects of individual and community life. It does not separate religion from criminal or civil law, but applies religious principles to all legal situations.

Women in Early Muslim Society Before Islam, the position of women in Arab society varied. In some communities, women were active in religion, trade, or politics. As in most societies at that time, however, most women had limited rights. Arab women could not inherit property and had to obey a male guardian. Among a few tribes, unwanted daughters were sometimes killed at birth.

Islam extended rights and protection to women by affirming the spiritual equality of all Muslims. The Quran teaches that "Whoever does right, whether male or female, and is a believer, all such will enter the Garden." The Quran prohibited the killing of daughters, granted women the right to inherit, and allowed women to reject a marriage offer. Islam also encouraged education for men and women so that all Muslims could study the Quran.

Although spiritually equal under Islam, men and women had different roles and rights. For example, women inherited less than men and had a more difficult time getting a divorce.

>> This illustration shows a beggar asking for alms. Muslims are expected to give charity, or aid, to the poor.

>> Reading the Quran is an important aspect of Muslim beliefs, so many Muslims study the Quran to better understand and practice their religion.

Islam as a Way of Life

Tell students that Islam is both a religion and a way of life, having both a political and social impact. Islam, through its law and codes of ethics, shapes daily and family life for Muslims throughout the world. Go over how the Sharia is a body of law that interprets the Quran and provides guidance for Muslims in conducting all aspects of their lives, from community to business to government to family life.

Summarize How do the Quran and the Sharia unify Muslims? *(Sample response: The Quran unifies Muslim beliefs while the Sharia provides a unifying legal framework for Muslims throughout the world.)*

Guided Reading and Discussion

Review the role of women in Islam with students. Note that while women had certain rights, such as the right to inherit or to reject a marriage offer, women and men had different rights and roles in Muslim society. Then read students the following quote from the Quran: "Whoever does right, whether male or female, and is a believer, all such will enter the Garden."

Cite Evidence What does this quote suggest about the spiritual role of women in the Islamic faith? *(Sample response: It suggests that men and women are spiritually equal.)*

Answers

Infer *Muslims believe that the individual duties of the Five Pillars are the most important requirements for practicing the Islamic faith.*

Topic 8 Lesson 1

SYNTHESIZE

Online Project the **Digital Activity: Foundations of Islam**. Have students work through it with a partner and compare their answers. Then go over the graphic organizer as a class and discuss these three important aspects of the Islamic faith—the Quran, the Sharia, and the Five Pillars of Wisdom—and the role they play in unifying Muslims.

DEMONSTRATE

Online Assign the **Digital Lesson Quiz** for this lesson if you haven't already done so. Students will be offered automatic remediation or enrichment based on their score.

Pose this question to the class:

Make Predictions How might Islam spread beyond the Arabian Peninsula? *(Sample response: With its rules, legal traditions, and common language, it might provide a unifying element and appeal to people as it is introduced through trade and conquest to other regions.)*

Topic Inquiry

Have students continue their investigations for the Topic Inquiry.

Islamic Practices Change As Islam spread throughout Asia, Africa, and Europe, Muslims adopted practices of conquered peoples. For example, the practices of veiling upper-class women and secluding them in a separate part of the home were Persian customs. The Quran says that women should dress modestly, which has been interpreted in multiple ways. Still, women's lives varied according to region and class. In rural areas, peasant women often needed to work and did not wear a veil, but took care to dress modestly.

? CONTRAST How are the Quran and Sharia different?

ASSESSMENT

1. **Identify Cause and Effect** According to Muslim belief, in what way did meditation lead toward Muhammad becoming a prophet?
2. **Apply Concepts** Why was the hijra a turning point for Islam?
3. **Draw Conclusions** Why is declaring faith the first of the Five Pillars of Islam?
4. **Infer** How do the Quran and Sharia guide Muslims?
5. **Draw Conclusions** Why might women in Arab society have welcomed Islam?

Answers

Contrast *To Muslims, the Quran contains the sacred word of God as revealed to Muhammad; Sharia is a body of law that includes interpretations of the Quran, examples from the life of Muhammad, and Muslim traditions applied to family, business, and community life.*

Assessment

1. During meditation, Muhammad heard the call to become a messenger of God, according to Islamic belief.
2. In Medina, Muhammad found many people willing to accept him as God's messenger, convert to Islam, and follow his teachings.
3. Accepting that there is one God and that Muhammad is the last and final prophet are essential beliefs of all Muslims.
4. The Quran is the sacred text of Islam and provides a guide to life, including ethical standards of behavior. While the Quran unifies Muslim beliefs, the Sharia interprets the Quran and unites Muslims under a common legal framework.
5. Islam extended many rights and protections to Arab women that they may not have had previously.

8.2 The death of Muhammad plunged his followers into grief. Muhammad had been a pious man and a powerful leader. No one else had ever been able to unify so many Arab tribes. Could the community of Muslims survive without him?

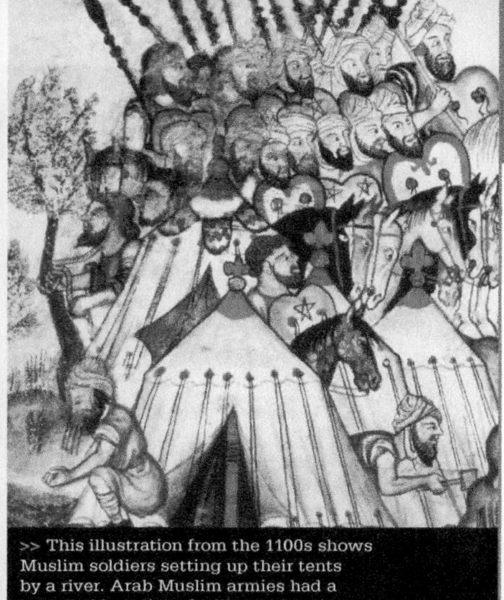

>> This illustration from the 1100s shows Muslim soldiers setting up their tents by a river. Arab Muslim armies had a remarkable series of military victories under Abu Bakr and his successors.

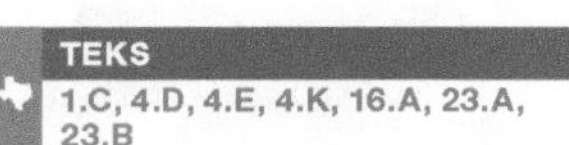

A Muslim Empire

TEKS
1.C, 4.D, 4.E, 4.K, 16.A, 23.A, 23.B

Islam Faces Challenges

Muslims faced a problem when Muhammad died because he had not named a successor to lead the community. Eventually, they agreed that **Abu Bakr** (uh BOO BAK ur), Muhammad's father-in-law and an early convert to Islam, should be the first **caliph,** or successor to Muhammad. Abu Bakr sternly told the faithful, "If you worship Muhammad, Muhammad is dead. If you worship God, God is alive."

Arabs Join Together Under Islam Abu Bakr faced an immediate crisis. The loyalty of some Arab tribal leaders had been dependent on Muhammad's personal command. They refused to follow Abu Bakr and withdrew their loyalty to Islam. After several battles with the wavering tribes, Abu Bakr succeeded in reuniting the Muslims, based on their allegiance to Islam.

Once reunited, the Muslims set out on a remarkable series of military campaigns. They began by converting the remaining Arab tribes to Islam, which ended warfare between Arabs and united them under one leader.

Arab Muslims Win Victories Then, under the first four caliphs, the Arab Muslims marched from victory to victory against the neighboring Byzantine and Persian empires, capturing territory in parts of Asia, Europe, and Africa. The Byzantines and Persians had competed with

>> Objectives

Describe the spread of Islam.

Identify the divisions that emerged within Islam.

Describe the rise of Umayyad and Abbasid dynasties.

Explain why the Abbasid empire declined.

>> Key Terms

Abu Bakr
caliph
Sunni
Shiite
Sufi
Umayyad
Abbasid
Baghdad
minaret
sultan

Topic 8 Lesson 2

A Muslim Empire

CONNECT

Preview Have students preview the **Lesson Objectives** and the list of **Key Terms**.

Students can also preview all the **Key Terms** and **Academic Vocabulary** using the **Interactive Reading Notepad** on the digital course or preview a summary of the lesson in the **Reading and Note Taking Study Guide**.

Online Use the **Editable Presentation** found on the digital course to present the main ideas for this lesson.

Start Up Activity

Write and read aloud the following quote from the historian W. Montgomery Watt, included in his book *The Influence of Islam on Medieval Europe:*

> "For centuries, nomadic Arab tribes had been in the habit of making raids, or razzias, on other tribes. The usual aim was to drive off the camels or other livestock of the opponents. . . . After experiencing one or more such raiding expeditions, the inhabitants of the countries traversed usually surrendered and became protected allies."

Discuss How could new alliances affect the spread of Islam? *(Most students will say something about surprise raids and subduing the other tribes, leading to new alliances; over time, many tribes decided to convert to Islam.)*

Tell students they will learn about how the Arab empire grew and about the divisions within Islam.

Online You can also project the **Start Up Activity** from the course.

INVESTIGATE

Have students read the section using the **Reading and Note Taking Study Guide** to help them take notes and understand the text as they read.

Islam Faces Challenges

After Muhammad died, his successor needed to unite Arab tribes who had been dependent on Muhammad's personal command. They did this through military campaigns and converting tribes to Islam. Abu Bakr, Muhammad's father-in-law, was Islam's first caliph after Muhammad died.

Aa Vocabulary Builder

1. Have students pronounce the following academic vocabulary terms in this lesson and clarify the part of speech. For difficult or polysyllabic words, break them into syllables and pronounce them with the students.
2. Explain what the word means in common "student-friendly" language using synonyms and antonyms when possible. Provide concrete examples to clarify the meaning, and rephrase the definition.

schism: a formal division or separation

mystic: a person who seeks divine wisdom and spiritual truth

Topic 8 Lesson 2

Online Project the **3D Model: The Dome of the Rock**. As students study the model, have them identify different components of the building. Tell students that the Dome of the Rock was built around 691 after the Muslims captured Jerusalem to mark the site of Muhammad's ascent into heaven. Be sure they understand the importance of the building to both Muslims and Jews.

ACTIVE CLASSROOM

Use the See-Think-Wonder strategy with students as they view images of the Dome of the Rock. Ask them: What do you see? What does it make you think? What are you wondering about now that you've seen this? *(Possible answer: I see a very ornate building, colorful and large. It makes me think that it would have taken a lot of people a lot of time to build it. I wonder how long it took to build, where the materials came from, and how was it accomplished.)*

Guided Reading and Discussion

Ask students to find the word *caliph* in the text. Ask them to predict what criteria Muslims might have used to select a caliph.

Draw Conclusions Why was it important that Muslims accepted Abu Bakr as Muhammad's successor? *(Possible answer: It was important to keep Muslims unified and to ensure that Muhammad was seen as a messenger of God and a leader rather than be worshipped himself.)*

Determine Central Ideas What was the purpose of the early raids on Arab tribes? *(Possible response: The purpose of the raids was to take livestock from other tribes and to push into new lands.)*

Remind students that when the Arabs united they were able to win victories against the Byzantine and Persian empires, which had been weakened from fighting each other.

>> The Dome of the Rock in Jerusalem is the oldest surviving Islamic building. Construction began soon after Muslims captured the city. According to Muslim teaching, Muhammad ascended to heaven from the rock inside this building.

Interactive 3-D Model

>> Medina is the second holiest site in Islam. Like Mecca, it is an important part of the hijra and Muhammad's journey. Both sites attract many pilgrims.

each other over control of lands in the Middle East. Once the Arabs united, they surprised their neighbors, conquering great portions of the Byzantine empire and defeating the Persians entirely. First, they took the provinces of Syria and Palestine from the Byzantines, including the cities of Damascus and Jerusalem. Then they captured the weakened Persian empire and swept into Byzantine Egypt.

INFER Why do you think the Byzantines and Persians were surprised by the strength of the Arab Muslims?

Divisions Split Islam

When Muhammad died, Muslims disagreed about who should be chosen to be the leader of the community. The split between **Sunni** (SOO nee) and **Shiite** (SHEE yt) Muslims had a profound impact on later Islamic history.

Differing Ideas About Leaders One group of Muslims felt that Muhammad had designated his son-in-law, Ali, to be his successor. They were called Shiites, after *shi'at Ali*, or followers of Ali. Shiites believe that the true successors to Muhammad are the descendants of Ali and Muhammad's daughter, Fatima. They believe that these descendants, called Imams, are divinely inspired religious leaders, who are empowered to interpret the Quran and the actions of Muhammad.

Another group felt that any good Muslim could lead the community, since there could be no prophet after Muhammad. This group soon divided and fought among themselves as well as with others over issues of who could be defined as a "good" Muslim.

The majority of Muslims eventually compromised around the view that the successor to Muhammad should be a pious male Muslim from Muhammad's tribe. This successor is called a caliph and is viewed as a political leader of the religious community, without any divine or prophetic functions.

Members of the compromise group, which forms the majority of Muslims in the world today, are known as Sunnis, since they follow the custom of the community, or *sunna*. The Sunni believe that inspiration comes from the example of Muhammad as recorded by his early followers.

Sunni and Shiite Beliefs Like the schism between Roman Catholic and Eastern Orthodox Christians, the division between Sunni and Shiite Muslims has survived to the present day.

D Differentiate On-Level After they look at the 3D model, have students research the history of the Dome of the Rock and develop a written report or digital presentation with the information they find. They should include topics such as how it was built and how long it took.

Answers

Infer *The newly united Arab Muslims had not posed a threat before.*

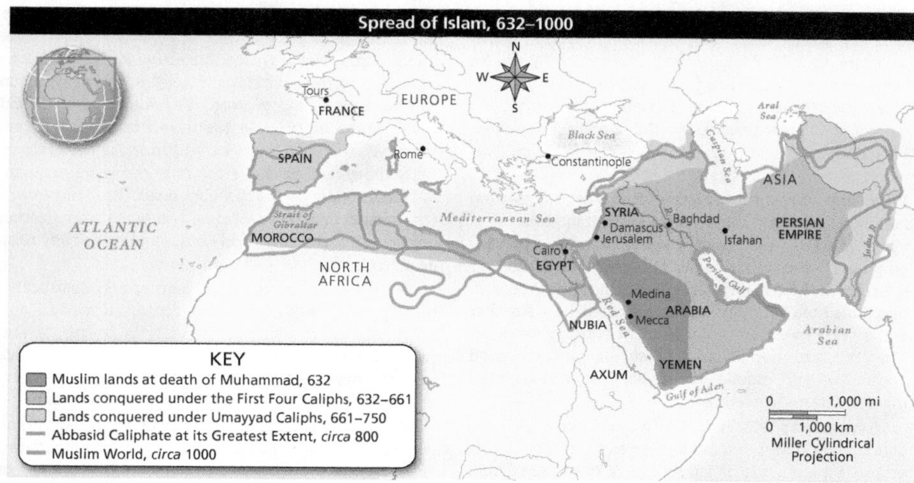

>> **Analyze Maps** Islam spread across northern Africa and into the Mediterranean. Near what important city was the further spread of Islam into Europe stopped?

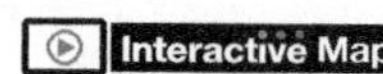

Members of both branches of Islam believe in the same God, look to the Quran for guidance, and follow the Pillars of Islam. However, Sunnis and Shiites differ in such areas as religious practice, law, and daily life. Today, about 90 percent of Muslims are Sunni. Most Shiites live in Iran, Lebanon, Iraq, and Yemen. The Shiite branch itself has further split into several different subgroups.

Over the centuries, the division between Sunnis and Shiites has sometimes been a source of conflict. When Sunni rulers held power, they often favored other Sunnis and deprived Shiites of wealth and power. When Shiites gained power, Sunnis often stood to lose. This sometimes bitter rivalry remains a source of tension in the Middle East today.

Sufis Emerge In both the Sunni and Shiite branches of Islam, a group called the **Sufis** emerged. Sufis are Muslim mystics who sought communion with God through meditation, fasting, and other rituals. Sufis were respected for their piety and some were believed to have miraculous powers.

Like Christian monks and nuns, some Sufis helped spread Islam by traveling, preaching, and being good examples to others. They carried the faith to remote villages, where they blended local traditions and beliefs into Muslim culture.

CONTRAST How did ideas about leadership differ between Shiites and Sunnis?

Umayyad Caliphs Create an Arab Empire

After the death of Ali, a powerful Meccan clan set up the **Umayyad** (oo MY ad) caliphate, a dynasty of Sunni caliphs that ruled the Muslim empire until 750. From their capital at Damascus in Syria, they directed the conquests that extended Arab rule from Spain and Morocco in the west to the Indus River Valley in the east. Although Islam also spread peacefully through trade and cultural exchange—reaching East Africa as early as the mid-700s—these conquests further enabled the spread of Muslim civilization and had an impact on Europe, Asia, and Africa.

The Muslim Empire Expands From Egypt, Arab Muslim armies moved west, defeating Byzantine forces across North Africa.

In 711, Muslim forces crossed the Strait of Gibraltar and conquered Spain. In 731, a Muslim army moved

Divisions Split Islam

Tell students that divisions emerged within Islam, forming the Sunni and Shiite branches. The Sunnis wanted a caliph who was a political leader. The Shiites wanted a caliph who was a descendent of Muhammad's daughter Fatima and son-in-law Ali, and a religious leader. Later on, the two groups developed different practices and laws. One group, the Sunnis, compromised around a leader who would be a political leader of the religious community and not a prophet.

Guided Reading and Discussion

Have students discuss the role of Sufis in the spread of Islam and possible outcomes of the schism between Sunni and Shiite Muslims.

Identify Main Ideas Describe the Sufis. To which branch of Islam do they belong? How do they differ from other Muslims? *(Sample response: Sufis are Muslim mystics that can belong to either the Sunni or Shiite branch of Islam. Sufis differ in some beliefs and practices. They helped spread Islam by traveling, preaching, and being good examples to others. They blended local traditions and beliefs into Muslim culture.)*

Predict Consequences Ask students to predict long-term issues that might arise from the division within Islam. *(Possible answer: Continued conflict could result in discrimination and regional conflicts.)*

History Background

Sufi Mystics Sufis differ in some beliefs and practice, but they believe that basic teachings on divine love underlie every religion. An early and highly influential Sufi mystic, Rabia al-Adawivva, was a woman and former slave from Basra. Rabia lived an ascetic life of poverty, fasting, and prayer in a desert cave, striving for a direct experience of God and God's love. A later Sufi mystic, Jalal al-Din Rumi, wrote lyric poems to God, whom he called the Beloved. His work includes poems, stories, and reflections, both humorous and profound, designed to illustrate Sufi beliefs. Rumi also founded a school of Sufism that, unlike mainstream Islam, emphasized dancing and music. Due to the modern translations by Tennessee poet Coleman Barks, Rumi is widely read in the United States today.

Answers

Analyze Maps *Sample response: The spread of Islam stopped around Constantinople, where Muslim forces failed to take the Byzantine capital.*

Contrast *The Shiites believed that only descendants of Ali and Fatima could lead, while the Sunnis believed that any pious male from Muhammad's tribe could lead.*

Umayyad Caliphs Create an Arab Empire
New Rule Under the Abbasid Dynasty

Online Project the **Interactive Map: Spread of Islam** and click through the layers. Tell students that in less than 150 years, Muslim rule spread from Arabia across southwest Asia and North Africa and into Europe. Be sure students can point out Damascus, Baghdad, Persia, Cairo, Constantinople, Cordoba, and Tours on the map.

Make Predictions Muslim armies conquered Spain and remained in control there until 1492. Frankish forces defeated Muslims at the battle of Tours in France and Muslim forces advanced no farther into Europe. If Muslim forces had been successful in France, where might they have advanced next? What might the advancement of Muslims farther into Europe have meant for the area? *(Sample response: The Muslim armies may have moved into more areas around the Mediterranean and Black seas, thus giving them control of all areas surrounding the Mediterranean.)*

Identify Central Ideas How might the spread of the Muslim empire have contributed to an increase in trade? *(Possible response: Muslim control of the land around the Mediterranean allowed merchants to travel safely through the region. Many Muslims learned Arabic, making communication easier.)*

ACTIVE CLASSROOM

Use the See-Think-Wonder strategy with students as they examine the Interactive Map: Spread of Islam. Ask them: What do you see? What does it make you think? What are you wondering about now that you've seen this?

north into France to settle new areas. There, Christian Frankish forces defeated the Muslims at the battle of Tours in 732. Muslims ruled parts of Spain for centuries, but advanced no farther into Europe. Elsewhere, Muslim forces besieged the Byzantine capital of Constantinople, but failed to take the well-defended city.

Why the Muslim Empire Succeeded Several factors help explain the series of Muslim victories. One factor was the weakness of the Byzantine and Persian empires. The longtime rivals had fought each other to exhaustion. Many people also welcomed the Arabs as liberators from harsh Byzantine or Persian rule. Another factor was the Arabs' bold, efficient fighting methods. The Bedouin camel and horse cavalry mounted aggressive and mobile offensives that overwhelmed more traditional armies.

Another key reason for the Arab success was the common faith Muhammad had given his people. Islam united a patchwork of tribes into a determined and unified state. Belief in Islam and certainty of paradise for those who fell in battle spurred Arab armies to victory.

>> This gold dinar, dating from 695–6, shows a Umayyad caliph dressed in traditional Arab head-dress and robes and holding a sword. On the other side of the coin is a design modified from the image of a Byzantine cross on steps.

Conquered People Under Islamic Rule The advancing Arabs brought many people under their rule in Asia, North Africa, and beyond. These Arabs imposed certain restrictions and a special tax on non-Muslims, but allowed Christians, Jews, and Zoroastrians to practice their own faiths and follow their own religious customs within those restrictions. Early Umayyads did not attempt to convert these non-Muslims, because the tax supported the Arab troops who settled in conquered areas. As Muslim civilization developed, many Jews and Christians played key roles as officials, doctors, and translators.

Muslim leaders prohibited looting and destruction of conquered lands, ensuring continued wealth and prosperity for the empire in the form of tribute and taxes. However, the rulers also urged Arab settlers to stay separate from the native populations, which created an Arab upper class throughout the empire.

In time, many non-Muslims converted to Islam. Some converted to gain political or economic advantages. However, many were drawn to Islam's simple and direct message, and they saw its triumph as a sign of God's favor. Many of the nomadic peoples in North Africa and Central Asia chose Islam immediately. Unlike some religions, Islam had no religious hierarchy or class of priests. In principle, it emphasized the equality of all believers, regardless of race, gender, class, or wealth. In later centuries, Turkish and Mongol converts helped spread Islam far across Asia.

Impact on North Africa The Islamic presence in North Africa—or the Maghrib, as early Muslims called the region—led to rapid change. Arab Muslims destroyed Carthage and built a new city called Kairouan, which became known as a holy city of Islam.

They built many mosques throughout North Africa. Many of the peoples of North Africa who quickly converted to Islam, including the Berber people, also adopted some Arab customs.

The Umayyad Caliphate Declines As military victories and negotiation expanded the Muslim empire, the Umayyads faced numerous problems. First, Arabs had to adapt from living in the desert to ruling large cities and huge territories. In many ways, the caliphs ruled like powerful tribal leaders, rather than kings with large bureaucracies. To govern their empire, the Umayyads often relied on local officials. Although they helped govern the empire, non-Arabs often did not have the same privileges that Arabs had, even if they converted to Islam.

While conquests continued, vast wealth flowed into Umayyad hands. When conquests slowed in the 700s, economic tensions increased between wealthy Arabs

English Language Proficiency Standards

Listening 2.G.6 Read aloud, or have students read, "Conquered People Under Islamic Rule." Discuss the concept of tolerance with students. Follow the instructions and then discuss the connections between modern examples of tolerance and tolerance shown by Muslim leaders.

Beginning Using short phrases, write, display, and explain the main points of the paragraph. Identify the supporting details for each main point. Explain the concept of tolerance, using modern-day examples.

Intermediate Demonstrate for students how to locate a main point and a detail to support it in the subsection. Then have small groups identify the remaining main points and supporting details. Review the concept of tolerance.

Advanced Have small groups identify the main points and supporting details in this subsection. Have them share one main point and detail aloud. Ask the groups to discuss an example of modern-day tolerance.

Advanced High Have students identify the main points and supporting details in this subsection. Have partners describe them in their own words. Have them compare how Muslim leaders showed tolerance toward their people and how it is demonstrated in modern times.

and those who had less. In addition, more and more resources were used to support the caliphs' luxurious lifestyle. By the eighth century, many Muslims criticized the court at Damascus for abandoning the simple ways of the early caliphs. Shiites considered the Umayyad caliphs to be illegitimate rulers of the Islamic community. Unrest also grew among non-Arab converts to Islam, who had fewer rights than Arabs.

SUMMARIZE What factors contributed to the success of the Ummayad conquests?

New Rule Under the Abbasid Dynasty

Discontented Muslims found a leader in Abu al-Abbas, descended from Muhammad's uncle. With strong support from Shiite and non-Arab Muslims, he captured Damascus in 750. Soon after, he had members of the defeated Umayyad family killed. Only one survived, escaping to Spain. Abu al-Abbas then founded the **Abbasid** (uh BAS id) dynasty, which lasted until 1258.

>> Mesue the Elder, a Christian Persian physician, was received by the Caliph Haroun-al-Raschid, the fifth and most famous ruler of the Abbasid dynasty. Mesue was personal physician to four caliphs.

The Abbasids Make Changes The Abbasid dynasty tried to create an empire based on the equality of all Muslims. The new rulers halted the large military conquests, ending the dominance of the Arab military class. The empire of the caliphs reached its greatest wealth and power under the early Abbasids, and Muslim civilization flourished.

Under the Abbasids, Islam became a more diverse religion because discrimination against non-Arab Muslims ended. Official policy encouraged conversion to Islam and treated all Muslims equally. The Abbassids created a more sophisticated bureaucracy and encouraged learning.

The Abbasids also moved the capital from Damascus to Baghdad, a small market town on the banks of the Tigris river. This move into Persian territory allowed Persian officials to hold important offices in the caliph's government. It also allowed Persian traditions to influence the development of the caliphate. Although these traditions strongly influenced Arab culture, Islam remained the religion of the empire and Arabic its language. The most important official was known as the vizier, or the head of the bureaucracy, a position that had existed in Persian government.

The Amazing City of Baghdad The second Abbasid caliph, al-Mansur, chose **Baghdad** as the site of his new capital. The walls formed a circle, with the caliph's palace in the center. Poets, scholars, philosophers, and entertainers from all over the Muslim world flocked to the Abbasid court. Under the Abbasids, Baghdad exceeded Constantinople in size and wealth. Visitors no doubt felt that Baghdad deserved its title "City of Peace, Gift of God, Paradise on Earth."

The city was beautiful, with many markets, gardens, and mosques. Domes and **minarets** (min uh RETS), slender towers of the mosques, loomed overhead. Five times each day, muezzins climbed to the tops of the minarets and called the faithful to prayer. Merchants sold goods from Africa, Asia, and Europe. The palace of the caliph bustled with activity.

A Muslim State in Spain The surviving member of the Umayyad family had fled to Spain and established an independent Muslim state. There, Muslim rulers presided over brilliant courts, where the arts and learning thrived. In general, they were tolerant of other religions. At centers of learning, such as the city of Córdoba, rulers employed Jewish officials and welcomed Christian scholars to study science and philosophy. Architects built grand buildings, such as the Alhambra, a fortified palace in Granada. Its lovely gardens, reflecting pools, and finely decorated marble

Guided Reading and Discussion

Online Project the **Interactive Timeline: Rise and Decline of an Arab Empire** and step through the events. Point out the changes from Sunni to Shiite rule. Tell students that after the death of Ali, a powerful clan set up the Umayyad caliphate, a dynasty of Sunnis that ruled the Muslim empire until 750. This caliphate extended the Muslim world into Spain and farther into Central Asia and North Africa, where they built many mosques. Many of the peoples of North Africa quickly converted to Islam. The Umayyads were successful because they unified the tribes and created an empire with an orderly system of administration. The Umayyads faced problems in governing their large territories, including criticism of their rule and the lavish lifestyles of the caliphs. Abu al-Abbas, a descendent from Muhammad's uncle, won strong support from Shiite and non-Arab Muslims who were discontented with Umayyad rule. He captured Damascus in 750 and founded the Abbasid dynasty that lasted until 1258.

Compare and Contrast How was the Abbasids' treatment of non-Muslims similar to that of the Umayyads'? How was it different? *(Sample response: They were both tolerant of non-Muslims, but the Abbasids didn't tax them as the Umayyads had. All Muslims were treated equally, and converts weren't discriminated against.)*

ACTIVE CLASSROOM

Quick Write—Have students write what they know about the timeline of Islamic History for 30 seconds. Challenge them to keep the length to 140 characters.

Answers

Summarize *Years of conflict had weakened both the Byzantines and the Persians. Many people looked to the Umayyads as liberators. The Umayyads used bold and efficient fighting methods.*

Topic 8 Lesson 2

Decline of the Arab Empire

Have students study the map of the Mongol invasions on p. 292. Point out to students that the Abbasids never ruled Spain and began to lose control over the rest of the Muslim empire starting around 850. The caliph's power began to fade in some areas, and Shiite rulers came to power. Invasions by the Seljuk Turks weakened the Abbasid rule of Central and Southwest Asia. Genghis Khan and other Mongol leaders led a number of Mongol invasions of Southwest Asia, seeking to expand their lands. In the invasions, they destroyed Baghdad and killed the last Abbasid caliph. Later Mongol rulers, such as Tamerlane, converted to Islam and helped restore influence to Muslims, and mosques were built throughout the empire.

Guided Reading and Discussion

Identify Cause and Effect Why did the empire of the Abbasid caliphs decline and eventually break up? *(Sample response: The Abbasid empire became fragmented into many small states and was further weakened by invasions from Seljuk Turks, crusaders, and Mongols.)*

Cite Evidence What strategies did the Seljuk Turks and the Mongols use to gain control in Central Asia? Why was their strategy important? *(Sample response: They adopted Islam as they mingled with local inhabitants to build trust and unity.)*

Key Terms

Ask students to find the key term **sultan** (in bold) in the text and define its meaning. Ask them to compare a sultan with a caliph. *(Both ruled Muslim states, but a sultan was not a religious leader.)*

columns mark a high point of Muslim civilization in Spain. Muslim rule endured in parts of Spain until 1492.

DRAW CONCLUSIONS Why did the Abbasids make changes to the Arab Muslim empire?

Decline of the Arab Empire

Starting about 850, Abbasid control over the rest of the empire fragmented. In Egypt and elsewhere, independent dynasties ruled states that had been part of a unified empire. As the caliph's power faded in some regions, Shiite rulers came to power. Between 900 and 1400, a series of invasions added to the chaos.

Seljuk Turks Gain Control In the 900s, Seljuk Turks migrated into the Middle East from Central Asia. They adopted Islam and built a large empire across the Fertile Crescent. By 1055, a Seljuk **sultan,** or ruler, controlled Baghdad, but he kept the Abbasid caliph as a figurehead. As the Seljuks pushed into Asia Minor, they threatened the Byzantine empire. The conflict prevented Christian pilgrims from traveling to Jerusalem, leading Pope Urban II to call for the First Crusade in 1095.

Mongols Advance Through Central Asia In 1216, Genghis Khan led the Mongols out of Central Asia across Southwest Asia. Mongol armies returned again and again.

In 1258, Hulagu, the grandson of Genghis, burned and looted Baghdad, killing the last Abbasid caliph. Later, the Mongols living in central and southwest Asia adopted Islam as they mingled with local inhabitants.

In the late 1300s, another Mongol leader, Timur the Lame, or Tamerlane, led his armies into the Middle East. Though he was a Muslim, Tamerlane's ambitions led him to conquer Muslim as well as non-Muslim lands. His armies overran Southwest Asia before invading Russia and India.

The Mongols' physical destruction of Baghdad brought an end to the city's glories. But even with the end of the Arab caliphate, Islam continued to expand from West Africa to South and Southeast Asia.

The end of the last Arab caliphate meant the loss of Islamic influence on government. Muslims at times faced persecution while Christians in the region had increased status. The conversion of Mongol rulers to Islam helped restore influence to Muslims. Mosques rose up throughout the empire.

A Divided Muslim World By the late 1200s, the Arab empire had fragmented. Independent Muslim caliphates and states were scattered across North

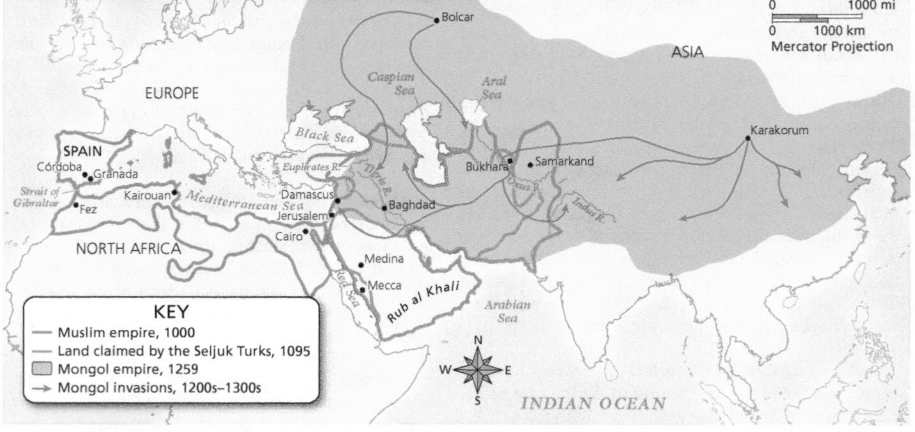

>> **Analyze Maps** Repeated invasions from the Mongols, first led by Genghis Khan, weakened the Abbasid caliphates. Where did the invaders come from?

Interactive Timeline

Answers

Draw Conclusions *They wanted to appeal to all classes of Muslims, to people of different religions, and to conquered Persians.*

Analyze Maps *from the north and west*

Cause and Effect *The Abbasid dynasty fragmented, and other peoples gained control.*

Africa and Spain, including the Mamluk state in Egypt and Syria, while a Mongol khan ruled much of the Muslim Middle East. After five centuries, Dar al-Islam—the world of Islam—was as politically divided as the Christian world.

Even though the Arab empire crumbled, Islam continued to link diverse people across an enormous area. Other Muslim empires emerged to rule the Middle East and India. Muslims also benefited from the advanced civilization that had taken root under the Abbasids.

 **CAUSE AND EFFECT** What events led to the decline of the Abbasid dynasty?

ASSESSMENT

1. **Cause and Effect** What effect did Abu Bakr have on the spread of Islam?
2. **Compare and Contrast** In what ways are Sunni and Shiite beliefs alike and different?
3. **Draw Conclusions** How might the Umayyads have retained control of the Muslim empire?
4. **Contrast** In what way was the rise of the Umayyads and the rise of the Abbasids different?
5. **Cause and Effect** How might a greater interest in the military have helped preserve the Abbasids' empire?

Topic 8 Lesson 2

SYNTHESIZE

Online Project the **Digital Activity: The Umayyad and Abbasid Caliphates**. Have students work in pairs to complete the Graphic Organizer. Have them think about the type of leadership structure and economic development during each caliphate as they think about which one was more successful. *(Responses will vary; students should use the information from their graphic organizer as their reasons. Umayyad accomplishments: • Expanded Islam (North Africa and Spain; Southwest Asia) • Created unified state • Treated non-Muslims well, but taxed them; Reasons for decline: • Too large a territory to control • Too much reliance on local non-Arabs • Tensions between Arabs and non-Arab Muslims • Luxurious lifestyle of caliphs; Abbasid accomplishments: • Arab and non-Arab Muslims treated equally • Encouraged learning • Baghdad as capital city; Reasons for decline: • Seljuk Turks invaded • Mongols invaded)*

DEMONSTRATE

Online Assign the **Digital Lesson Quiz** for this lesson if you haven't already done so. Students will be offered automatic remediation or enrichment based on their score.

Pose these questions to the class:

Cause and Effect What were some of the effects of the Shiite and Sunni divisions? *(Sample response: While Islam was a strong unifying force among Muslims, the split created unrest and divisions within the Arab empire that eventually weakened it and contributed to its decline.)*

Identify Main Ideas How did Muslims treat Christian and Jewish peoples in conquered lands? *(Sample response: They generally tolerated conquered peoples who followed monotheistic religions, but they taxed them and did not provide equal rights or opportunities.)*

Topic Inquiry

Have students continue their investigations for the Topic Inquiry.

Assessment

1. By uniting Arab Muslims, he enabled them to set out on a campaign of conquest.
2. Both groups believe in the same God and look to the Quran as the ultimate religious authority, but Shiites believe the true successor of Muhammad descended from Ali and Fatima.
3. by not expanding the empire to so large a size, by having a centralized government, and by distributing wealth more fairly
4. The Umayyads defeated other peoples and created a new Muslim empire based on Islam. The Abbasids replaced another Muslim caliphate and promised to improve the empire rather than expand it.
5. The Abbasids would have been more prepared to fend off attacks.

Answers

Cause and Effect *The Abbasid dynasty fragmented, and other peoples gained control.*

Topic 8 Lesson 3

Achievements of Muslim Civilization

CONNECT

Preview Have students preview the **Lesson Objectives** and the list of **Key Terms**.

Students can also preview all the **Key Terms** and **Academic Vocabulary** using the **Interactive Reading Notepad** on the digital course or preview a summary of the lesson in the **Reading and Note Taking Study Guide**.

Online Use the **Editable Presentation** found on the digital course to present the main ideas for this lesson.

Start Up Activity

Write and read aloud the following story:

> One night, Caliph al-Mamun had a dream about the great Greek philosopher Aristotle. The caliph asked Aristotle questions about ethics, reason, and religion. After al-Mamun awoke, he had scholars translate the great works of the classical world into Arabic. By the year 830, the caliph had set up a library and university in Baghdad.

Discuss What fields of study do you think the caliph might have in his university? *(Possible responses: art, architecture, literature, history, medicine, philosophy)*

Online You can also project the **Start Up Activity** from the digital course.

Tell students that in this lesson they will learn about the social, economic, and cultural advances made by Muslim civilization.

INVESTIGATE

Have students read the section using the **Reading and Note Taking Study Guide** to help them take notes and understand the text as they read.

Economic and Social Changes

Muslim civilization blended traditions from the various cultures in the empire. Between 750 and 1350, merchants built a trading network across Europe, Asia, and Africa. Trade spread products, technologies, knowledge, and culture. Arabic grew as a common language, and many people converted to Islam. Banking grew as a new industry. Manufactured goods such as carpets became valued, and agricultural production increased. Many people were able to move up in social class.

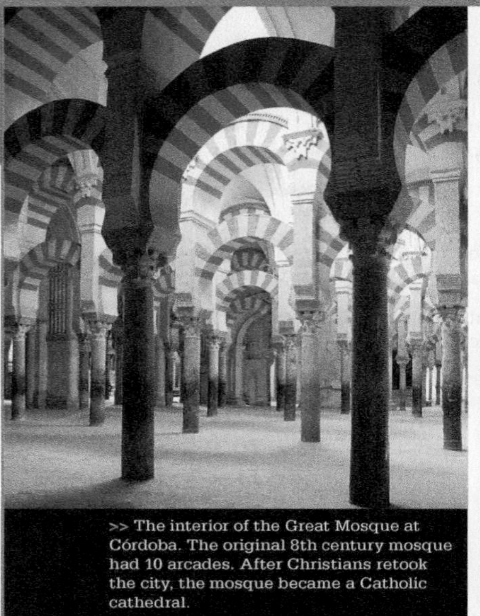

>> The interior of the Great Mosque at Córdoba. The original 8th century mosque had 10 arcades. After Christians retook the city, the mosque became a Catholic cathedral.

Interactive Flipped Video

8.3 Under the Abbasids, Muslim civilization absorbed traditions from many cultures. In the process, a flourishing new civilization arose in cities from Baghdad to Córdoba. It incorporated all the people who lived under Muslim rule, including Jews and Christians.

TEKS
4.D, 26.B, 27.A

>> Objectives

Describe the role of trade in Muslim civilization.

Identify the traditions that influenced Muslim art, architecture, and literature.

Describe the major ideas in mathematics, science, and technology that occurred in Muslim civilization.

>> Key Terms

social mobility
Firdawsi
Omar Khayyám
calligraphy
Ibn Rushd
Ibn Khaldun
al-Khwarizmi
Muhammad al-Razi
Ibn Sina

Achievements of Muslim Civilization

Economic and Social Changes

Diffusion of Learning The great works produced by scholars of the Abbasid period shaped Muslim culture and civilization. Through contacts in Spain and Sicily, Christian European scholars began to study Muslim philosophy, art, and science. Muslim scholars also reintroduced knowledge of Greco-Roman civilization to later Europeans.

Muslim ideas spread to other regions as well. In North Africa, for example, Arab Muslims settled and spread Arab customs, traditions, and language.

Muslim rulers united diverse cultures, including Arab, Persian, Egyptian, African, and European. Later, Mongols, Turks, Indians, and Southeast Asians joined the Muslim community. Muslim civilization absorbed and blended many of their traditions.

Trade in the Muslim World Merchants were honored in Muslim culture, in part because Muhammad had been a merchant. A traditional collection of sayings stated:

www.PearsonTexas.com Access your Digital Lesson.

Aa Vocabulary Builder

1. Have students pronounce the following academic vocabulary term in this lesson and clarify the part of speech. Break the word into syllables and pronounce it with the students.
2. Explain what the word means in common "student-friendly" language using synonyms and antonyms when possible. Provide concrete examples to clarify the meaning, and rephrase the definition.

anecdote: a short, entertaining story, often historical

I commend the merchants to you, for they are the couriers of the horizon and God's trusted servants on Earth.

—Sayings of the Prophet

Between 750 and 1350, merchants built a vast trading network across Muslim lands and beyond. Caravans crossed the Sahara into West Africa, where West Africans traded gold and enslaved persons for salt, bronze, cloth, books, and ceramics. In turn, North Africans traded gold to Europe in exchange for European goods such as beads and utensils, and provided the gold used in European buildings, art, and coins.

Muslim, Jewish, and Christian traders traveled the Silk Road toward China and were a vital link in the exchange of goods between East Asia and Europe. Monsoon winds carried Arab ships from East Africa to India and southeast Asia. Some traders made great fortunes.

Spreading Products and Ideas Trade spread products, technologies, knowledge, and culture. Muslim merchants introduced an Indian number system to Europe, where they became known as Hindu-Arabic numerals, or Arabic numerals. Traders also carried sugar from India and papermaking from China, introducing Islam to many new regions. As more people converted to Islam and learned Arabic, the common language and religion helped the global exchange grow and thrive.

Extensive trade and a money economy led Muslims to pioneer new business practices. They created partnerships, bought and sold on credit, formed banks to change currency, and invented the ancestors of today's bank checks. In fact, the English word *check* comes from the Arabic word *sakk*. Bankers developed a sophisticated system of accounting. They opened branch banks in all major cities, so that a check written in Baghdad might be cashed in Cairo. These economic ideas eventually spread to Europe, where they influenced the rise of modern economic systems.

High Demand for Manufactured Goods Muslim artisans produced a wealth of fine goods. Steel swords from Damascus, leather goods from Córdoba, cotton textiles from Egypt, and carpets from Persia were highly valued. Workshops also turned out fine glassware, furniture, and tapestries.

As in medieval Europe, handicraft manufacturing in Muslim cities was typically organized by guilds. The heads of the guilds, chosen by their members, often had the authority to regulate prices, weights and measures,

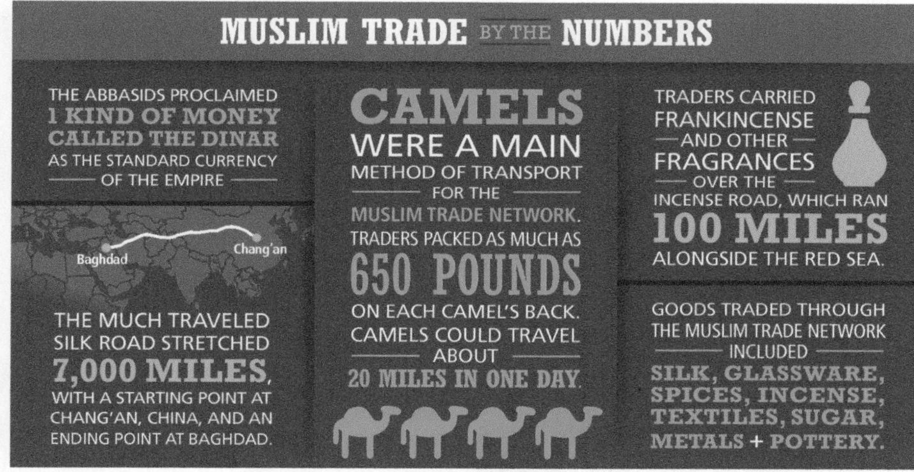

MUSLIM TRADE BY THE NUMBERS
THE ABBASIDS PROCLAIMED 1 KIND OF MONEY CALLED THE DINAR AS THE STANDARD CURRENCY OF THE EMPIRE
Baghdad
Chang'an
THE MUCH TRAVELED SILK ROAD STRETCHED 7,000 MILES, WITH A STARTING POINT AT CHANG'AN, CHINA, AND AN ENDING POINT AT BAGHDAD.
CAMELS WERE A MAIN METHOD OF TRANSPORT FOR THE MUSLIM TRADE NETWORK.
TRADERS PACKED AS MUCH AS 650 POUNDS ON EACH CAMEL'S BACK.
CAMELS COULD TRAVEL ABOUT 20 MILES IN ONE DAY.
TRADERS CARRIED FRANKINCENSE AND OTHER FRAGRANCES OVER THE INCENSE ROAD, WHICH RAN 100 MILES ALONGSIDE THE RED SEA.
GOODS TRADED THROUGH THE MUSLIM TRADE NETWORK INCLUDED SILK, GLASSWARE, SPICES, INCENSE, TEXTILES, SUGAR, METALS + POTTERY.

>> **Analyze Data** Trade across the desert brought great wealth to Muslim merchants. How do you think having a standard currency in the Abbasid caliph affected trade?

Guided Reading and Discussion

Discuss with students the social and economic impact of Islam as the Muslim empire spread across Europe, Asia, and Africa. Brainstorm a list of advances with students and list them on the board. Describe the significance of each. Advances might include trade, the use of Arabic numerals, new business practices, the use of banks, new manufactured goods, the growth of agriculture, and social mobility.

Be sure students understand the significance of the economic and social advances made during this period. Merchants, workers, and farmers could all prosper due to the increase in trade and improved farming practices. Slavery was discouraged and people had the ability to improve their social class. There was the acceptance of a variety of different groups of people in society.

Draw Conclusions How did the start of a banking system have a positive economic impact on merchants? *(Possible response: It standardized currency, and it protected merchants on long journeys from carrying large sums of money that cold be stolen.)*

Identifying Supporting Details Detail an example of social mobility in Muslim society in the eighth and ninth centuries. *(Possible responses: Slaves could be freed as an act of charity, a child born of a slave mother but a free father was considered freeborn, and slave-soldiers loyal to the caliph could rise to high government positions.)*

Answers

Analyze Data *Sample response: A single currency within a large empire would facilitate trade by providing a common way to value and conduct transactions, and in turn make further trade.*

Key Terms

Ask students to find the key term **social mobility** (in bold) in the text and define its meaning. Ask them to explain how increased social mobility might benefit all of society. *(Possible response: Talented people who were not born into rich families could end up in important roles anyway. The ability to do better in society would motivate many people to work harder and better.)*

Literature, Art, and Architecture

In Muslim cultures, religion shaped the arts, architecture, and literature of the civilization. The great work of Islamic literature was the Quran, which banned the worship of idols. Artists were forbidden to portray God or human figures in religious art pieces. This made Muslim artists perfect geometric designs and calligraphy. Human and animal figures appeared in nonreligious art and in science illustrations. Arabs and Persians also had a rich history of oral poetry and tales of adventure including stories such as "Aladdin and His Magic Lamp" and "Ali Baba and the Forty Thieves." Arab writers were great storytellers and their writing included romances, fables, adventures, and humorous writings. Domed mosques and tall minarets became symbols of Muslim architecture. Nonreligious art included human and animal figures in scientific works as well as intricate miniatures painted to illustrate stories and poems.

methods of production, and the quality of the product. Most labor was done by wage workers.

Agriculture Flourishes Outside the cities, agriculture flourished across a wide variety of climates and landforms. Both Umayyad and Abbasid rulers took steps to preserve and extend agricultural land. Small farming communities in desert areas faced a constant scarcity of water. To improve farm output, the Abbasids organized massive irrigation projects and drained swamplands between the Tigris and Euphrates rivers. In addition to other crops raised for food, farmers cultivated sugar cane, cotton, medicinal herbs, and flowers that were sold in far-off markets. Farmers began to grow crops that came from different regions.

The deserts continued to support nomads who lived by herding. Still, nomads and farmers shared economic ties. Nomads bought dates and grain from settled peoples, while farming populations acquired meat, wool, and hides from the nomads. Pastoral groups also provided pack animals and guides for the caravan trade.

Social Structure and Slavery Muslim society in the 700s and 800s was more open than that of medieval Christian Europe. Muslims enjoyed a certain degree of **social mobility,** or the ability to move up in social class. People could improve their social rank through religious, scholarly, or military achievements.

As in many earlier societies, slavery was a common institution in Muslim lands, though Islamic law encouraged the freeing of slaves as an act of charity. Slaves were often from conquered lands because Muslims were not supposed to enslave other Muslims.

Some slaves bought their freedom, often with the help of charitable donations or even state funds. However, if non-Muslim slaves converted to Islam, they did not automatically become free. A female slave who bore a child by her Muslim owner gained freedom upon her master's death. Children born of a slave mother and free father were also considered freeborn.

Most slaves worked as household servants, while some were skilled artisans. To help break down the tribal system, Abbasid caliphs also created a class of Turkish slave-soldiers who were loyal only to the caliph. Often educated in Islamic law and government, some of these men rose to high positions in the government, such as vizier. This set the stage for the Turks to become powerful later in the Abbasid era.

DESCRIBE What new business practices did merchants introduce in Muslim lands?

>> Many copies of the Quran were richly illustrated with elaborate designs and detailed patterns.

Literature, Art, and Architecture

Muslim art and literature reflected the diverse traditions of the various peoples who lived under Muslim rule, including Greeks, Romans, Persians, Indians, and North Africans. As in Christian Europe and Hindu India, religion shaped the arts and literature of Muslim civilization. The great work of Islamic literature was the Quran itself. Because the Quran strictly banned the worship of idols, Muslim religious leaders forbade artists to portray God or human figures in religious art. This gave Islamic art a distinctive style.

A Rich Tradition of Literature Long before Muhammad, Arabs had a rich tradition of oral poetry. In musical verses, poets chanted the dangers of desert journeys, the joys of battle, or the glories of their clans.

Their most important themes—chivalry and the romance of nomadic life—recurred in Arab poetry throughout the centuries. Later Arab poets developed elaborate formal rules for writing poetry and explored both religious and worldly themes. The poems of Rabiah al-Adawiyya expressed Sufi mysticism and encouraged the faithful to worship God selflessly without hope of reward. "If I worship Thee in hope of Paradise / Exclude me from Paradise," she wrote in one prayer poem.

Answers

Describe *They introduced partnerships, credit, banks, bank checks, accounting system, and branch banks.*

Persians also had a fine poetic tradition. **Firdawsi** (fur DOW see) wrote in Persian using Arabic script. His masterpiece, the *Shah Namah*, or *Book of Kings*, tells the history of Persia. **Omar Khayyám** (OH mahr ky AHM), famous in the Muslim world as a scholar and an astronomer, is best known for *The Rubáiyát* (roo by AHT). In this collection of four-line stanzas, Khayyám meditates on fate and the fleeting nature of life:

> The Moving Finger writes; and having writ,
> Moves on; nor all your Piety nor Wit
> Shall lure it back to cancel half a line,
> Nor all your Tears wash out a word of it.
>
> —Omar Khayyám, The Rubáiyát

Arab writers also prized the art of storytelling. Along with ancient Arab tales, they gathered and adapted stories from Indian, Persian, Greek, Jewish, Egyptian, and Turkish sources. The best-known collection is *The Thousand and One Nights*, a group of tales narrated by a fictional princess. They include romances, fables, adventures, and humorous anecdotes, many set in Harun al-Rashid's Baghdad. Later versions filtered into Europe, where children heard about "Aladdin and His Magic Lamp" or "Ali Baba and the Forty Thieves."

Religion Shapes Architecture The main purpose of early mosques was to serve as community centers for the faithful. These simple buildings were hubs for social interaction, Islamic study, and group prayer. Later, domed mosques and high minarets dominated Muslim cities. Adapted from Byzantine buildings, domes and arches became symbolic of Muslim architecture.

Just as Islam is an important part of the daily life of Muslims, so too is it integral to Muslim architecture. While Islamic religious buildings had some elements borrowed from Christian building styles, they were designed to meet the needs of Muslims, with places to call people to worship and large halls for prayer. Each mosque also featured a mihrab, an indented wall that faced toward Mecca. Completed in 715, the Great Mosque of Damascus includes minarets, a large area for prayer, and a mihrab.

Art in the Muslim Empire Early Muslims believed that God should be worshiped directly, not through representations. Early artists avoided picturing God or

>> This courtyard is in the Umayyad Mosque, or Great Mosque of Damascus, which was built in the early 700s.

 Interactive Gallery

Muhammad, believed to be God's messenger. Instead, they emphasized the importance of God's word.

They used **calligraphy,** the art of beautiful handwriting, to add physical beauty to the spiritual words of the Quran. Religious artists decorated the handwritten pages with borders containing geometric shapes and arabesques, or flowered patterns.

The Muslim style of religious art could be seen in mosques across the empire. Inside, the walls and ceilings of mosques were decorated with elaborate abstract, geometric patterns. They worked the flowing Arabic script, especially verses from the Quran, into decorations on buildings. The Dome of the Rock in Jerusalem, completed around 692, provides exquisite examples of early Muslim art.

Some Muslim artists painted human and animal figures in nonreligious art. Arabic scientific works, including those of the human body, were often lavishly illustrated. Literary works sometimes showed stylized figures. Later Persian, Turkish, and Indian artists excelled at painting miniatures to illustrate books of poems and fables.

IDENTIFY Which traditions influenced Muslim literature, art, and architecture?

Topic 8 Lesson 3

Online Project the **Interactive Gallery: Islamic Art and Architecture** and click through the images.

Analyze Images Examine each of the images and identify the aspects of Muslim art and architecture that you see. *(Answers will vary. Students should identify aspects such as domes, minarets, horseshoe arches, geometric patterns, calligraphy, and arabesques.)*

ACTIVE CLASSROOM

Ask students to review information they have learned in this lesson and design a piece of wallpaper that encapsulates key learnings. Post the wallpaper and have students take a gallery/"wisdom" walk and note what others have written/illustrated.

Guided Reading and Discussion

Summarize What is calligraphy, and where can it be found? *(beautiful writing that can be found in books and on buildings)*

Distinguish Between Fact and Opinion Is the statement "Muslim art, literature, and architecture is the most original in the world" a fact or an opinion? Support your answer. *(Sample response: Students should identify the statement as an opinion. Muslim art, literature, and architecture have all been influenced by the traditions of the people who have lived under Muslim rule. This includes Greeks, Romans, Persians, and Indians.)*

English Language Proficiency Standards

Speaking 3.B.2 Before beginning this activity, read "An Emphasis on Knowledge" aloud to the class. Have students complete one of the following activities according to their level of English proficiency.

Beginning After reading "An Emphasis on Knowledge" aloud, turn students' attention to the image depicting Hindu-Arabic numerals. Model using new English vocabulary, like the words *numerals* and *traders*, as you explain the importance of these numerals. Have students use simple words and phrases to retell the information shown in this visual in their own words.

Intermediate Reread "An Emphasis on Knowledge" aloud to students, pausing frequently to model retelling the meaning of the text in your own words. Have students examine the visual depicting Hindu-Arabic numerals. Ask students to explain what they have learned from studying the visual in their own words.

Answers

Identify *Influences on literature and art included traditions of the Greeks, Romans, Persians, and Indians as well as Arabs. Christian traditions influenced early Muslim architecture, but Muslim architects also included elements related to their belief in Islam.*

An Emphasis on Knowledge

Although Muhammad could not read or write, he inspired Muslims to respect learning, and great advances were made in philosophy, history, mathematics, and the sciences. Boys and girls attended school, where reading and writing were emphasized, so Muslims could study the Quran. Many advances were made in the field of astronomy by advancing tools designed by the Greeks. Medicine advanced and included improvements in the area of public heath. Medical texts written by two Muslim doctors became standards in European schools. A Muslim mathematician wrote an algebra book that became the standard in Muslim areas and Europe when translated to English.

Online Project the **Interactive Gallery: Muslim Advances in Technology, Math, and Science** and click through the images.

ACTIVE CLASSROOM

Have students form groups and generate a response to this prompt, "Summarize the scientific contributions of Muslim civilization." Have students write as much as they can for one minute then switch with the person on their right. The next person tries to elaborate on where the other person left off. Continue to switch until the paper comes back to the first person. The group then decides which is the best response and shares with the class.

Guided Reading and Discussion

Have students reflect on how things may have been different if Muslims had disregarded the learning of the past.

Evaluate Data Muslims made advances in medicine and public health by building on the knowledge of the ancient Greeks. What does this tell you about their acceptance of information from different sources? *(Sample answer: Muslim scholars respected scholars of earlier civilizations.)*

Cite Evidence How did Muslim scholars preserve and build on the learning of earlier civilizations? *(Sample answer: They placed writings in libraries, translated them into Arabic, and expanded on them.)*

SYNTHESIZE

Online Project the **Digital Activity: Accomplishments in Medicine, Literature, History, and Mathematics**. Ask students to complete the Graphic Organizer identifying the accomplishments of the Muslim civilization in medicine, history, literature, and mathematics.

Answers

Summarize *tests for physicians, hospitals, emergency rooms, the idea of treating both mind and body, and advances in diagnosing and curing diseases*

An Emphasis on Knowledge

Although Muhammad could neither read nor write, his respect for learning inspired Muslims to make great advances in philosophy, history, mathematics, and the sciences. Wealthy families might educate their boys and even allow their girls to learn to read and write in order to study the Quran. Most people, however, were illiterate, and they memorized the Quran. Institutions of higher learning included schools for religious instruction and for the study of Islamic law.

Muslim Centers of Learning The caliph Al-Mamun and his successors established Baghdad as the greatest Muslim center of learning. Its libraries attracted well paid and highly respected scholars. Other cities, like Cairo, Córdoba, and Timbuktu, were also known as centers of learning. In these places, scholars made advances in philosophy, science, mathematics, medicine, and other fields. They also preserved the learning of earlier civilizations by translating ancient Persian, Sanskrit, and Greek texts into Arabic.

>> This image shows Jabir ibn Hayyan, or Geber, a Spanish Muslim alchemist during the 700s and 800s. Geber, who is sometimes known as the Father of Chemistry, invented equipment that can still sometimes be found in laboratories today.

Interactive Gallery

Studying Philosophy and History Muslim scholars translated the works of the Greek philosophers, as well as many Hindu and Buddhist texts. Scholars tried to harmonize Greek ideas about reason with religious beliefs based on divine revelation. In Córdoba, the philosopher **Ibn Rushd**—known in Europe as Averroës—put all knowledge except the Quran to the test of reason. His writings on Aristotle were translated into Latin and influenced Christian scholastics in medieval Europe.

Another Arab thinker, **Ibn Khaldun** (IB un kal DOON), set standards for the scientific study of history. He stressed economics and social structure as causes of historical events. He also warned about common causes of error in historical writing, such as bias, exaggeration, and overconfidence in the accuracy of sources. Ibn Khaldun urged historians to trust sources only after a thorough investigation.

Advances in Mathematics and Astronomy One of the greatest Muslim mathematicians was **al-Khwarizmi** (al KWAHR iz mee). He pioneered the study of algebra (from the Arabic word *al-jabr*). In the 800s, he wrote a book that was translated into Latin and became a standard mathematics textbook in Europe. Like many scholars of the time, al-Khwarizmi contributed to other fields too. He developed a set of astronomical tables based on Greek and Indian discoveries.

Muslim scholars studied the works of the ancient Greeks, such as Euclid and Ptolemy. They translated these and other ancient mathematical works into Arabic and used them as a basis for a complete system of mathematics, including an organized method for equations. Soon, Muslim works on mathematics spread to Europe, where they were studied with interest.

Over time, Europeans in all fields of business adopted Hindu-Arabic numerals and used them in their day-to-day lives. They also adopted new tools and technologies developed or improved by Muslim astronomers, including the quadrant and the astrolabe. These two instruments were used to observe the positions of stars and aid in navigation.

Improvements in Medicine Building on the knowledge of the ancient Greeks, Muslims made remarkable advances in medicine and public health. Under the caliphs, physicians and pharmacists had to pass a test before they could practice their professions. The government set up hospitals, where injured people could get quick treatment at a facility similar to today's emergency room. Some physicians traveled to rural areas to provide healthcare to those who could not get to a city, while others regularly visited jails.

The Muslim World and Africa 298 8.3 Achievements of Muslim Civilization

English Language Proficiency Standards

Advanced Have students reread "An Emphasis on Knowledge" aloud in small groups. Remind students to pause frequently to check their understanding of the text by retelling what they have read in their own words. Then have small groups focus on the visual showing Hindu-Arabic numerals. Ask each group to explain what information is communicated by the visual.

Advanced High Have pairs of students focus on the visual showing Hindu-Arabic numerals. Ask each pair to retell the information they see in the image. Ask each pair to discuss how a universal set of numbers improves trade and communication across cultures. Have pairs report on their discussion to the group to share what they have learned.

One of the most original medical thinkers was **Muhammad al-Razi,** head physician at Baghdad's chief hospital. He wrote many books on medicine, including a pioneering study of measles and smallpox. He also challenged accepted medical practices. Treat the mind as well as the body, he advised young doctors. He theorized that if doctors were hopeful with their patients, recovery would be faster.

The famous Persian physician **Ibn Sina** (IB un SEE nah) was known in Europe as Avicenna. By the age of 16, he was a doctor to the Persian nobility. His great work was the *Canon on Medicine*, a huge encyclopedia of what the Greeks, the Arabs, and he himself had learned about diagnosing and treating diseases. The book includes many prescriptions, made with such ingredients as mercury from Spain, myrrh from East Africa, and camphor from India.

Other Muslim surgeons developed a way to treat cataracts, drawing fluid out of eye lenses with a hollow needle. For centuries, surgeons around the world used this method to save patients' eyesight. Arab pharmacists were the first to mix bitter medicines into sweet-tasting syrups and gums.

Eventually, these and other Muslim medical ideas spread to Europe. European physicians began to attend Muslim universities in Spain. Arabic medical texts were translated into Latin, and the works of Avicenna and al-Razi became the standard medical textbooks at European schools for 500 years. Through this diffusion of ideas, Europeans were introduced to the concepts of training physicians and creating hospitals.

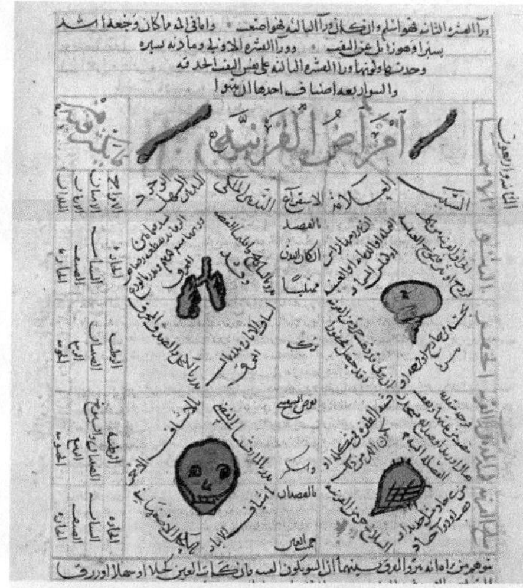

>> The *Canon of Medicine* served as an encyclopedia recording the findings of Greeks and Arabs, as well as Ibn Sina's own observations.

SUMMARIZE What ideas about medicine were developed during the time of the Muslim empire?

ELPS 3.B.2 Practice explaining and retelling information by discussing the visual of Hindu-Arabic Numerals provided in *An Emphasis on Knowledge*.

ASSESSMENT

1. **Draw Conclusions** Why did trade play such an important role in the Muslim empire?
2. **Contrast** What is an important difference between medieval Muslim and Christian art?
3. **Infer** In what ways did Islamic art and literature show diversity, and what important trait do they have in common?
4. **Cite Evidence** What evidence supports the fact that learning was important in the Arab Muslim empire?
5. **Draw Conclusions** Why were Europeans interested in the ideas of Mathematician al-Khwarizmi and physicians Muhammad al-Razi and Ibn Sina?

Discuss Have students compare answers and share with the class. What do the accomplishments reveal about the Muslim civilization? *(Answers will vary. Students should comment on the importance of reason and innovation; willingness to change; and promotion of religious tolerance.)*

DEMONSTRATE

Online Assign the **Digital Lesson Quiz** for this lesson if you haven't already done so. Students will be offered automatic remediation or enrichment based on their score.

In "Achievement of Muslim Civilization," you learned about how trade and commerce benefited Muslim civilization. Muslims absorbed traditions from many cultures and made many advances in art, economics, literature, and science.

Cite Evidence Describe the advances in medicine that were made by Muslim physicians. *(Sample answer: They set up hospitals and rural health care, learned and wrote about diagnoses and treatments, and improved medical practices.)*

Draw Conclusions Muhammad said "the ink of the scholar is holier than the blood of the martyr." What do you think he meant? How might this attitude have contributed to the development of Muslim civilization? *(Possible answer: Knowledge is more important than sacrificing one's life. Muslim scholars pursued learning.)*

Topic Inquiry

Have students continue their investigations for the Topic Inquiry.

Assessment

1. Muslims had high regard for the merchant profession. Trade was a way to earn money and to gain access to resources and products, knowledge, and new ideas.
2. Muslim art was noted for use of calligraphy, geometric shapes, and the arabesque style in religious art and architecture. In contrast, Christian art used scenes from the Bible and the lives of the saints in sculptures, stained glass, and paintings to decorate churches.
3. Islamic art and literature showed diversity because they were influenced by different cultures. They both follow the requirements of Islam.
4. Muhammad respected learning. Both girls and boys received an education. Centers of learning were established throughout the empire. Scholars studied ancient learning.
5. They relayed the ideas of the ancient Greeks to Europeans of their time and made their own advances in mathematics and medicine, which the Europeans borrowed.

Topic 8 Lesson 4

The Ottoman and Safavid Empires

CONNECT

Preview Have students preview the **Lesson Objectives** and the list of **Key Terms**.

Students can also preview all the **Key Terms** and **Academic Vocabulary** using the **Interactive Reading Notepad** on the digital course or preview a summary of the lesson in the **Reading and Note Taking Study Guide**.

Online Use the **Editable Presentation** found on the digital course to present the main ideas for this lesson.

Start Up Activity

Relay the following information about Constantinople: When Mehmet II became Ottoman sultan in 1451, his goal was to conquer Constantinople, which was all that was left of the once-mighty Byzantine empire. The Byzantines sought help from the pope and European princes as Mehmet's grip tightened. In 1453, Mehmet began a 54-day siege of Constantinople. Eventually, Constantinople fell to the Ottomans, who made the city the capital of their Muslim empire.

Discuss Why was the fall of Constantinople a powerful symbol? *(Possible answer: It meant the capture by Muslims of a major Christian city—once the capital of the eastern Roman empire—in a strategic location at the doorway of Europe.)*

Online You can also project the **Start Up Activity** from the course.

INVESTIGATE

Have students read the section using the **Reading and Note Taking Study Guide** to help them take notes and understand the text as they read.

Growth of the Ottoman Empire

Tell students that the Ottoman empire controlled major trade routes between Europe, Africa, and Asia. As a result, Istanbul became one of the great trading capitals of the world. In 1533, Suleiman created an enormous fleet that dominated all trade in the eastern Mediterranean. European countries eventually commanded new trade routes around Africa and ended Ottoman control of both land and sea routes.

>> Until the Ottomans invaded, the high, thick walls and well-positioned defenses of Constantinople had repelled invaders for a thousand years.

Interactive Flipped Video

8.4 By the 1400s, two powerful new empires had emerged in the Middle East: the Ottoman and the Safavid empires. Both were Muslim empires, and both ruled diverse peoples. Most important, both owed their success in part to a new military technology, gunpowder. For this reason, the Ottoman and Safavid empires are often called "gunpowder empires." Gunpowder led to the use of new weapons such as cannons that blasted through defensive walls. Later, muskets made a new kind of army possible, giving firepower to ordinary foot soldiers and reducing the importance of mounted warriors.

TEKS 1.D, 7.D

>> Objectives

Explain the impact of the Ottoman empire on Eastern Europe.

Describe the characteristics of Ottoman culture.

Explain how Abbas the Great strengthened the Safavid empire.

>> Key Terms

Ottoman
Istanbul
Suleiman
janizary
Safavid
shah
Isfahan
Qajar
Tehran

The Ottoman and Safavid Empires

Growth of the Ottoman Empire

The Ottomans Conquer Constantinople Like the Seljuks, the **Ottomans** were a Turkish-speaking nomadic people who had migrated from Central Asia into northwestern Asia Minor. By the 1300s, they were spreading across Asia Minor and into Eastern Europe's Balkan Peninsula.

Ottoman expansion threatened the crumbling Byzantine empire. After several failed attempts to capture Constantinople, the Ottoman sultan Mehmet II finally succeeded in 1453. In a surprise move, the Ottomans hauled ships overland and launched them into the harbor outside Constantinople. After a nearly two-month siege, Ottoman cannons finally blasted gaps in the great defensive walls of the city, and it became the new capital of the Ottoman empire. From Constantinople, renamed **Istanbul,** the Ottoman Turks continued their conquests for the next 200 years.

Suleiman the Magnificent The Ottoman empire enjoyed a golden age under the sultan **Suleiman** (soo lay MAHN), who ruled from 1520

www.PearsonTexas.com Access your Digital Lesson.

Aa Vocabulary Builder

1. Have students pronounce the following academic vocabulary terms in this lesson and clarify the part of speech. For difficult or polysyllabic words, break them into syllables and pronounce them with the students.
2. Explain what the word means in common "student-friendly" language using synonyms and antonyms when possible. Provide concrete examples to clarify the meaning, and rephrase the definition.

edict: an order or command having the force of law

sagacious: having good judgment

to 1566. His people called him "the Lawgiver," while Europeans called him Suleiman the Magnificent.

A brilliant general, Suleiman modernized the army and conquered many new lands. He extended Ottoman rule eastward into the Middle East, and also into Kurdistan and Georgia in the Caucasus Mountain region. In the west, Suleiman advanced deeper into Europe through a combination of diplomacy and warfare. In 1529, his armies besieged the Austrian city of Vienna, sending fear through the kingdoms of Western Europe.

Although they failed to take Vienna, the Ottoman armies threatened the divided kingdoms of Europe, which feared invasion from the east. While European powers formed alliances to keep Suleiman from expanding further into Europe, France tried to weaken its rivals by signing a treaty with the Ottomans.

French leaders hoped to take advantage of Ottoman pressure to weaken the Hapsburg empire, which included the Holy Roman Empire and the Netherlands. The treaty also allowed French merchants to travel and trade throughout the Ottoman empire—unlike traders from other European countries.

Ottomans Control Trade The Ottoman empire controlled major trade routes between Europe, Africa, and Asia. As a result, Istanbul became one of the great trading capitals of the world.

The Ottoman empire strengthened its trading position by bringing merchants into Istanbul, particularly European Jewish traders. European navies had taken control of the Mediterranean Sea from Venice, but in 1533, Suleiman created an enormous fleet that dominated all trade in the eastern Mediterranean. Eventually, the Portuguese and other European navies commanded new trade routes around Africa and ended Ottoman control of both land and sea routes.

Ottoman Government Still, the Ottomans ruled the largest, most powerful empire in both Europe and the Middle East for centuries. At its height, the empire stretched from Hungary to Arabia and Mesopotamia and across North Africa. Suleiman felt justified in claiming to be the rightful heir of the Abbasids and caliph of all Muslims. To the title of "Emperor," he added the symbolic name of "Protector of the Sacred Places" (Mecca and Medina).

Suleiman was a wise and capable ruler. He strengthened the government of the rapidly growing empire and improved its system of justice. As sultan, Suleiman had absolute power, but he ruled with the help of a grand vizier and a council. A huge bureaucracy supervised the business of government, and the powerful military kept the peace. Ottoman law was based on the Sharia, supplemented by royal edicts. Government officials worked closely with religious scholars who interpreted the law.

? ANALYZE CONCEPTS The Ottoman empire took Constantinople and then threatened Eastern Europe. Which European power did the Ottoman sign a treaty with, and what did that country gain?

Ottoman Society

Ottoman society was divided into classes, each with its appointed role. At the top were "men of the sword"—soldiers who guarded the sultan and defended the state—and "men of the pen"—scientists, lawyers, judges, and poets. Below them were "men of negotiation," such as merchants, tax collectors, and artisans who carried out trade and production. Finally, there were "men of husbandry," or farmers and herders who produced food for the community.

Religion in Ottoman Society The Ottomans ruled diverse peoples of many religions. The men of the sword and men of the pen were almost all Muslims, but the other classes included non-Muslims. The people were organized into millets, or religious communities.

>> The Ottomans attempted to expand their empire west into Hungary and Vienna, but they could not keep a large invading force well supplied so far from Istanbul.

Interactive Illustration

Online Project the **Interactive Illustration: Ottoman Empire Under Suleiman** and click through the hotspots. Explain to students that Suleiman's power came through diplomacy as well as war, expanding the empire from the Balkan peninsula into Eastern Europe, including much of Hungary.

ACTIVE CLASSROOM

Have students create a political cartoon from one image in this lesson to include in a class blog. The caption should provide details about the image. *(Possible example: Students may choose the image of a member of one social class such as a merchant. The caption should describe the life of a merchant in the Ottoman social structure.)*

Guided Reading and Discussion

The Ottomans captured Constantinople and renamed it Istanbul. Be sure students understand Europeans feared the Ottomans because they were getting very close to Western Europe, and they were very powerful. They were also Muslim, not Christian.

Identify Supporting Details Find details in the text supporting the statement that new weapon technology allowed the Ottomans to successfully expand their empire. *(Possible response: Cannons blasted gaps in the defensive walls of Constantinople. Muskets gave greater firepower to foot soldiers, reducing the need for mounted warriors.)*

Ottoman Society

Tell students that Ottoman society was organized into classes, each with its own role. The soldiers who guarded the sultan and defended the state held the top role in the society. The farmers held the bottom role. The Ottoman empire began to decline after Suleiman's death in 1566.

D Differentiate Extra Support As students read the lesson, have them make a table identifying key characteristics of the Ottoman and Safavid empires. *(The tables should be constructed so students find characteristics for the Ottomans and Safavids for the following: Capital, Dates, Strongest Ruler, Extent of Empire, Branch of Islam, and Relationship With Europe.)*

Answers

Analyze Concepts *France signed a treaty with the Ottomans to get special privileges for its traders and also used the threat of the Ottoman invasion to weaken its enemies in Europe.*

Topic 8 Lesson 4

Guided Reading and Discussion

Be sure students understand that the Ottomans organized religious groups into millets—Muslims, Greek Christians, Armenian Christians, and Jews. The millets each had their own leaders and brought ideas and connections to the Ottoman empire. Many of these ideas and connections allowed the Ottoman empire to expand.

Cite Evidence The Ottomans ruled people of many religions. How did Islam grow in the Ottoman empire? *(Possible answer: The Ottomans required Christian families to turn over their young sons for government service and often converted them to Islam.)*

>> The Selimiye Mosque, in Turkey displays the glory of Ottoman culture as the empire reached its height.

>> The janizaries, or the elite military force made up mostly of converted Christians, suppressed any revolt within the Ottoman empire because they controlled the military, even dethroning Sultan Beyezid II.

These included Muslims, Greek Christians, Armenian Christians, and Jews.

Each millet had its own leaders who were responsible for education and some legal matters. The Jewish millets included many Jews who had been expelled from Spain in 1492. They brought international banking connections with them, plus a new technology for making cloth that helped the Ottoman empire finance its expansion.

Treatment of Conquered Peoples Like earlier Muslim empires, the Ottomans recruited officers for the army and government from among the huge populations of conquered peoples in their empire. The Ottomans levied a "tax" on Christian families in the Balkans, requiring them to turn over their young sons for government service.

The boys were converted to Islam and put into rigorous military training at the palace school. The best soldiers won a prized place in the **janizaries** (JAN ih sehr eez), the elite force of the Ottoman army. The brightest students received special education to become government officials. They might serve as judges, poets, or even grand vizier.

Like the boys, non-Muslim girls from eastern Europe served as slaves in wealthy Muslim households. There, they might be accepted as members of the household. Some of the enslaved girls were freed after the death of their masters.

Literature and the Arts The arts blossomed under Suleiman. Ottoman poets adapted Persian and Arab models to produce works in Turkish. Influenced by Persian artistic styles, Ottoman painters produced detailed miniatures and illuminated manuscripts.

The royal architect Sinan, a janizary military engineer, designed hundreds of mosques and palaces. He compared his most famous building, the Selimiye Mosque at Edirne, to the greatest church of the Byzantine empire. "With God's help and the Sultan's mercy," Sinan wrote, "I have succeeded in building a dome for the mosque which is greater in diameter and higher than that of Hagia Sophia."

Decline of the Ottomans After Suleiman's death in 1566, Ottoman government and society began to change slowly. Suleiman had killed two of his most able sons because he suspected them of treason. His son and successor Selim II left most of the governing to his ministers, and government bureaucracy became corrupt.

By the 1700s, European advances in both commerce and military technology were leaving the Ottomans behind. Russia and other European powers captured

D Differentiate Challenge/Gifted Have students use Internet sources to find examples of detailed miniatures and illuminated manuscripts produced by Ottoman painters or research the work of the royal architect Sinan, who designed hundreds of mosques and palaces. Students should write a sentence or two analyzing how the art or architecture reflects the history of the Ottoman empire. Have them share their findings with the class with a digital poster or slide show. They can also post their findings on the class Web site or blog.

English Language Proficiency Standards

Speaking 3.B.3 Before beginning this activity, read "Ottoman Society" aloud. Display these directions:

- Locate the heading "Ottoman Society."
- Find the four divisions of Ottoman society.
- Draw a sketch to show your understanding of each of the four divisions.

Beginning Read directions one at a time. Help students as needed by demonstrating what each direction tells them to do. Allow time for students to accomplish each task.

Intermediate Have volunteers read directions one at a time. Help students as needed by having volunteers demonstrate what each direction tells them to do. Allow time for students to accomplish each task.

Advanced Instruct students to read each task and follow the directions. Circulate to support their understanding as needed. When tasks are complete, have students share final sketches and captions.

Advanced High Instruct students to read and follow the directions. Circulate to support their understanding as needed. When tasks are complete, have students share final sketches and captions.

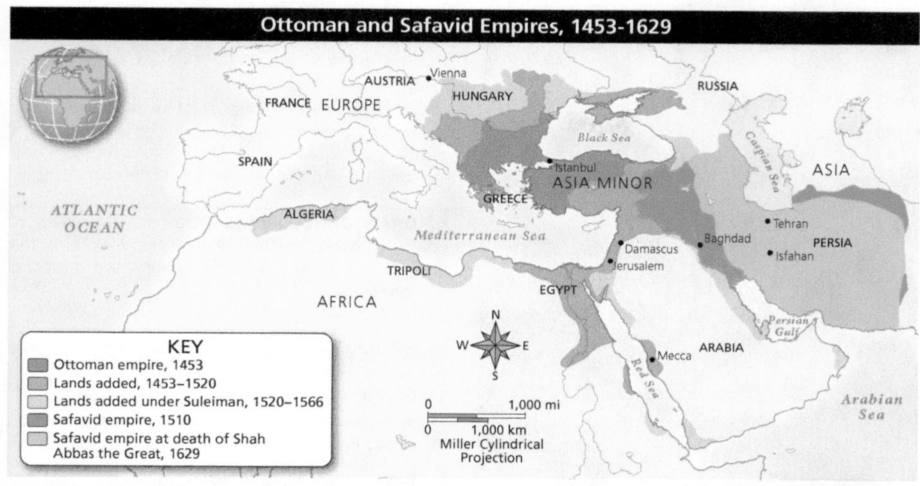

>> **Analyze Maps** At its greatest extent, the Ottoman empire stretched across three continents, while the Safavid empire controlled most of what is today Iran. Into what regions did the Ottoman empire expand under Suleiman?

Interactive Map

Ottoman lands, while local rulers in North Africa and elsewhere broke away from Ottoman control. Sultans tried to revive Ottoman power with limited success.

CATEGORIZE Who were the men of the sword, the men of the pen, the men of negotiation, and the men of husbandry, and what was their overall purpose?

ELPS **ELPS 3.B.3** Practice understanding and following directions in the activity that focuses on *Ottoman Society.*

The Rise of the Safavids

By the early 1500s, the **Safavid** (sah FAH vid) dynasty had united an empire in Persia (present-day Iran). Sandwiched between two expansionist powers—India and the Ottoman empire—the Safavids often engaged in warfare. Religion played a role in the conflict. The Safavids were Shiite Muslims who enforced their beliefs in their empire. The Ottomans were Sunni Muslims who viewed the Shiites as heretics.

Abbas the Great The most outstanding Safavid ruler, or **shah,** was **Shah Abbas the Great,** who revived the glory of ancient Persia. From 1588 to 1629, he centralized the government and created a powerful military force modeled on the Ottoman janizaries. Abbas used a mixture of force and diplomacy against the Ottomans. He also sought alliances with European states that had reason to fear Ottoman power.

To strengthen the economy, Abbas reduced taxes on farmers and herders and encouraged the growth of industry. Unlike earlier Safavids, Abbas tolerated non-Muslims and valued their economic contributions. He built a new capital at **Isfahan** (is fah HAHN), which eventually reached a population of one million, with hundreds of mosques, schools, parks, libraries, and public baths.

A Center of Art and Trade Under Shah Abbas, Isfahan flourished. It became a center for the arts and architecture, and the shah welcomed artists, poets, and scholars to his court. Palace workshops produced magnificant paintings, metalwork, textiles, and rugs.

Isfahan also became a center of the international silk trade. Armenians controlled the trade, so Abbas brought thousands of Armenians to Isfahan. He had a settlement built for these Christians just outside the capital, where they governed themselves.

The Decline of the Safavid Empire Safavid glory slowly faded after the death of Shah Abbas and under continuing pressure from Ottoman armies. Shiite

The Rise of the Safavids

Online Project the **Interactive Map: Growth of the Ottoman and Safavid Empires** and click through the hotspots. Tell students that at its greatest extent, the Ottoman empire stretched across three continents. The Safavid empire controlled most of what is modern-day Iran.

ACTIVE CLASSROOM

Use the headline strategy. Have students write a headline that captures the essence of the interactive map. Ask: If you were to write a headline for this topic or issue right now that captured the most important aspect that should be remembered, what would that headline be? Exchange headlines with a partner and review. *(Possible answers: "Heading toward Europe," "Prosperity Increases Size of Kingdom," "Gaining Ground Quickly")*

Guided Reading and Discussion

The Safavid empire flourished under the reign of Shah Abbas. He tolerated non-Muslims and valued their economic contributions. During the reign of Shah Abbas, a new capital was built at Isfahan and it became the center of the international silk trade. The arts also flourished during this time.

Summarize How did the Savafid empire decline? *(Possible answer: Shiite scholars challenged the shah's authority and persecuted religious minorities, causing the Sunnis to rebel. This ultimately led to a new dynasty, the Qajars, taking control of the area.)*

Key Terms

Ask students to find the key term **shah** (in bold) in the text. Explain that the term was used throughout history to name kings of Persia and later Iran. The last man named the shah of Iran was Mohammad Reza Pahlavi, who was the ruler when the monarchy was overthrown in the 1970s.

Answers

Categorize *They were the four divisions of Ottoman society that helped the empire to function smoothly. They included soldiers (sword); scientists, poets, and lawyers (pen); merchants, artisans (negotiation); farmers and herders (husbandry).*

Analyze Maps *Tripoli, Algeria, Hungary, and lands bordering Persia*

Draw Conclusions *It enabled him to revive the glory of ancient Persia and establish the Safavid empire to dominate the Middle East.*

Topic 8 Lesson 4

SYNTHESIZE

Online Project the **Digital Activity: The Ottoman and Safavid Empires**. Ask students to complete the Graphic Organizer comparing the Ottoman and Safavid empires. They should then compare with a partner. Have them discuss what differences in rule may have made a difference in the fate of each of the empires. *(Ottoman empire: ruled by Suleiman the Magnificent; modernized army; class system; growth of the arts; Sunni Islam was primary religion; Safavid empire: ruled by Shah Abbas; centralized government and powerful military; alliances with European cities; Isfahan was a center for arts and manufacturing; Shiite Islam was primary religion)*

DEMONSTRATE

Online Assign the **Digital Lesson Quiz** for this lesson if you haven't already done so. Students will be offered automatic remediation or enrichment based on their score.

In "The Ottoman and Safavid Empires" you read about the rise and fall of both the Ottoman and Safavid empires. Each empire made contributions to the belief systems, culture, and arts of their respective empires.

Draw Conclusions Why do you think Ottoman and Safavid rulers had some tolerance of other religious groups? *(Possible answer: The successful rulers realized that non-Muslim groups made important economic and cultural contributions to their empires.)*

Predict Consequences How do you think Safavid shahs might have been able to halt or slow the decline of their empire after the reign of Abbas the Great? *(Possible answer: by strengthening the army, centralizing political and religious authority, and/or practicing tolerance of religious minorities)*

Topic Inquiry

Have students continue their investigations for the Topic Inquiry.

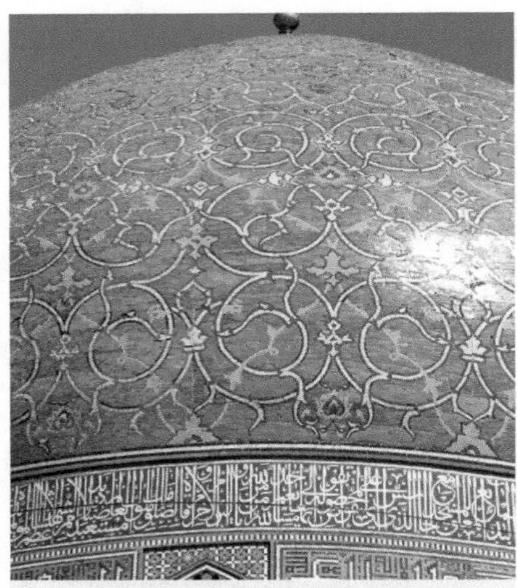

>> Under Shah Abbas, art, architecture, and learning flourished. Tile mosaics combined with mathematical precision created this masterpiece, the Shah (Imam) Mosque in Isfahan, Iran.

scholars also challenged the authority of the shah by stressing their own authority to interpret law and determine government policy. They encouraged persecution of religious minorities, pushing Sunni Afghans to rebel. The rebels defeated imperial armies, captured Isfahan, and forced the last Safavid ruler to abdicate in 1722.

In the late 1700s, a new dynasty, the **Qajars** (kuh JAHRZ), won control of Iran. They made **Tehran** their capital and ruled until 1925. Still, the Safavids left a lasting legacy. They established Shiism firmly in Iran and gave Persians a strong sense of their own identity.

DRAW CONCLUSIONS What was the effect of Shah Abbas centralizing the government and the economy, creating a powerful military, and tolerating non-Muslims?

ASSESSMENT

1. **Identify Central Ideas** How did Shah Abbas strengthen the Safavid empire and leave a lasting legacy in Persia?
2. **Draw Conclusions** Which were the important characteristics of the Ottoman and Safavid empires?
3. **Identify Cause and Effect** What was one of the characteristics of the Ottoman empire under the rule of Suleiman "the Lawgiver"?
4. **Infer** Why do you think the Ottoman and Safavid rulers allowed some religious tolerance?
5. **Summarize** What were the two greatest impacts on the non-Muslim peoples of the Ottoman empire in eastern Europe?

Assessment

1. By establishing a strong empire, he helped define the identity of all Persians and also firmly established Shiism in the region.
2. The Sunni Ottomans and Shiite Safavids expanded their empires under strong rulers and Islamic law and created centralized societies and flourishing cultures in which non-Muslims participated.
3. The Ottoman empire under Suleiman established a stable legal system and the bureaucracy to run it and a strong military to enforce the laws.
4. The rulers may have recognized that non-Muslims made important economic and cultural contributions to their empires.
5. Non-Muslims had to give up their sons and daughters to serve as warriors, government workers, or slaves. Non-Muslims were not part of the empire but were organized into millets, or religious communities.

8.5 Africa is the world's second largest continent, larger than Europe, China, and the United States combined. Its geography is immensely varied, but certain features have had a major impact on its development. Its size and location have contributed to its range of climates, vegetation, and terrains as well as the diverse cultures that developed within Africa.

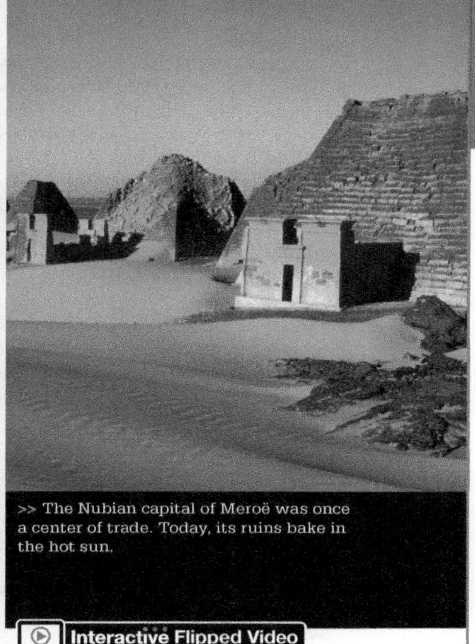

>> The Nubian capital of Meroë was once a center of trade. Today, its ruins bake in the hot sun.

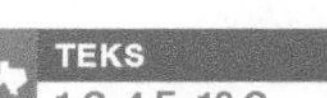
Interactive Flipped Video

Early Civilizations of Africa

TEKS
1.C, 4.E, 16.C

>> **Objectives**

Understand how geography affected migration, cultural development, and trade in Africa.

Describe the rise and decline of Nubia.

Explain how outside influences led to change in North Africa.

>> **Key Terms**

Sahara
savanna
cataract
desertification
Bantu
Nubia
Meroë
Piankhi
Septimius Severus

The Geography of Africa

Climate and Vegetation Zones As shown on the map, Africa's vegetation regions create wide bands that stretch across the continent. Along the equator is a band of tropical rain forest. Moving north and south from this band are the continent's largest and most populated regions, the **savannas,** or grassy plains. Beyond the savannas lies the **Sahara,** the largest desert in the world. Although the Sahara did become a highway for migration and trade, its size and harsh terrain limited movement. The Kalahari and Namib deserts in the south are smaller but equally forbidding.

Although the Sahara did become a highway for migration and trade, its size and harsh terrain limited movement. The Kalahari and Namib deserts in the south are smaller but equally forbidding.

Along the Mediterranean coast of North Africa and the tip of southern Africa lie areas of fertile farmland. The fertile Nile Valley, for example, offered a favorable environment to early farmers.

Geographic Features In addition to deserts and rain forests, other geographic features have acted as barriers to easy movement of people

PEARSON realize www.PearsonTexas.com Access your Digital Lesson.

Early Civilizations of Africa

CONNECT

Preview Have students preview the **Lesson Objectives** and the list of **Key Terms**.

Students can also preview all the **Key Terms** and **Academic Vocabulary** using the **Interactive Reading Notepad** on the digital course or preview a summary of the lesson in the **Reading and Note Taking Study Guide**.

Online Use the **Editable Presentation** found on the digital course to present the main ideas for this lesson.

Start Up Activity

Explain that, in 1325, a young Moroccan named Ibn Battuta began a pilgrimage to Mecca. Read aloud his description of crossing the Sahara:

> That desert . . . make[s] sport of him [the traveler] and disorder(s) his mind, as that he loses his way and perishes. For there is no visible road or track . . . nothing but sand blown hither and thither by the wind. You see hills of sand in one place, and afterwards you will see them moved to quite another place.

Discuss What do you think Moroccan traveler Ibn Battuta was saying about life in the Sahara? How might Africa's climate and geography have affected the development of early North African societies? *(Students may say it was dangerous and that the vast desert made travel difficult and acted as a barrier to movement.)*

Online You can also project the **Start Up Activity** from the course.

INVESTIGATE

Have students read the section using the **Reading and Note Taking Study Guide** to help them take notes and understand the text as they read.

The Geography of Africa

Tell students that Africa's early civilizations were diverse and formed in part because of the continent's geography and climate. Tell students that Africa's geographic features acted not only as barriers to trade and cultural development, but also as passageways linking many kingdoms and villages.

Aa Vocabulary Builder

1. Have students pronounce the following academic vocabulary terms in this lesson and clarify the part of speech. For difficult or polysyllabic words, break them into syllables and pronounce them with the students.
2. Explain what the word means in common "student-friendly" language using synonyms and antonyms when possible. Provide concrete examples to clarify the meaning, and rephrase the definition.

utilize: to put to practical use

migrate: to move from one area to another

Topic 8 Lesson 5

Online Project the **Interactive Map: Africa's Vegetation Regions** and click through the hotspots.

ACTIVE CLASSROOM

Think of yourself as a merchant living on the Mediterranean coast just north of the Libyan Desert. A trader from the Great Rift Valley wants to do business with you. What would you like to ask the trader about the products he or she wants to trade and what life is like in that part of Africa?

Guided Reading and Discussion

Discuss Ask students to evaluate and explain the influence of camels on trade in the Sahara. *(Camels allowed traders to move goods over great distances with little water.)*

Apply Concepts Ask students to explain how each of the following geographic features influenced ways of life: desert; rain forest; savanna. *(Students may say: In the desert, the lack of rainfall prevented farming and herding; in the rain forest, diverse plants and animals allowed for a variety of ways of life to flourish; in the savanna, fertile soil permitted farming and herding.)*

Migration of People and Ideas

Tell students that Neolithic people, skilled as hunter-gatherers, began to cultivate the Nile Valley. This farming led to the development of villages along the river valley and the Sahara, which was then a well-watered area. Desertification prompted migration, which contributed to the rich diversity of cultures in Africa.

Key Terms

Ask students to find the key term **desertification** (in bold) in the text. Ask students what problems might confront people living in an area that was undergoing desertification. *(difficulty in finding food and water; inability to farm or raise animals; lack of shelter)*

and goods. Although Africa is surrounded by oceans and seas, it has few good natural harbors. Also, much of the interior is a high plateau. As rivers flow down to the coast, they cascade through a series of rapids and **cataracts,** or waterfalls, that hinder travel between the coast and the interior. Within the interior, though the same rivers, including the Zambezi, Congo, and Niger, serve as open highways.

Despite geographic barriers, people did migrate, both within Africa and to neighboring continents. Like the rivers, the Great Rift Valley of East Africa served as an interior corridor. People also traveled across the savanna lands. The Red Sea and Indian Ocean linked East Africa to the Middle East and other Asian lands, while North Africa formed the southern rim of the Mediterranean world.

Resources and Trade Africa sits atop great mineral and other natural resources. Since ancient times, mineral wealth spurred trade among various regions. Salt, gold, iron, and copper were important items in early trade networks. Much later, in the 1800s, desire for gold and diamonds was one cause that led Europeans to seek control of lands in Africa.

Trade between Africa and Asia increased with the introduction of the camel. By A.D. 200, camels had been brought to North Africa from Asia. These hardy "ships of the desert" revolutionized trade across the Sahara. Although daring traders had earlier made the difficult desert crossing in horse-drawn chariots, camel caravans created new trade networks.

Camels could carry loads of up to 500 pounds and could plod 20 or 30 miles a day, often without water. The caravan brought great profits to merchants on both sides of the Sahara.

>> At first, trade in the Sahara Desert was hindered by inhospitable conditions, but new forms of transportation, including the use of the camel, revolutionized commerce in the region.

Interactive Map

CHECK UNDERSTANDING How did geographic features affect movement in Africa?

Migration of People and Ideas

Archaeologists have uncovered evidence that points to the Great Rift Valley as home to some of the earliest ancestors of modern people. Gradually, their descendants migrated out of Africa and beyond to people in every corner of the Earth.

Stone Age Cultures In Africa, as elsewhere, Paleolithic people developed skills as hunters and food gatherers. By 5500 B.C., Neolithic farmers had learned to cultivate the Nile Valley and to domesticate animals. As farming spread across North Africa, Neolithic villages even appeared in the Sahara, which was then a well-watered area. Scientists have found ancient rock paintings that show a Sahara covered with rich grasslands and savanna.

About 2500 B.C., a climate change slowly dried the Sahara. As the land became parched, the desert spread. This process of **desertification** devoured thousands of acres of cropland and pastureland. The ever-expanding desert forced many people to move, or migrate, to seek new areas in order to maintain their ways of life.

The Bantu Migrations Over thousands of years, the migration of people throughout Africa contributed to the continent's rich diversity of cultures. Scholars have traced these migrations by studying language patterns. They have learned, for example, that West African farmers and herders migrated to the south and east between about 1000 B.C. and A.D. 1000. Like the Indo-European peoples of Europe and Asia, these West African peoples spoke a variety of languages deriving from a single common language. The root language is called **Bantu,** which gives this movement its name—the Bantu migrations.

As the Bantu-speakers migrated into southern Africa, they spread their skills in farming, ironworking, and domesticating animals. Some existing cultures

D Differentiate Extra Support When discussing the Interactive Map, point out that traders provide goods that people need by bringing them from other areas, including different countries. Ask students to list three modern examples of products from a different region or country.

Answers

Check Understanding *Movement across Africa was hindered by its deserts, tropical rain forests, and cataracts along interior rivers. However, Africa's Great Rift Valley, along with the Mediterranean and Red seas, provided easy access to overseas trade routes.*

merged with those of the Bantu-speakers wherever they settled. The influence of the Bantu-speakers is still found in the languages of the region today.

ANALYZE INFORMATION What was the effect of the Bantu migrations on the development of African culture?

Egypt and Nubia Flourish

While Egyptian civilization was developing along the northern Nile River, another African civilization took shape on a wide band of fertile land of the southern Nile. The ancient kingdom of **Nubia,** also called Kush, was located in present-day Sudan. Archaeologists and historians have just begun to document the shifting tides of Nubia's 4,000-year history.

Nubia and Egypt: Two Great Powers From time to time, ambitious Egyptian pharaohs subdued Nubia, but the Nubians always regained their independence. As a result of conquest and trade, Nubian rulers adopted many Egyptian traditions. They built palaces and pyramids modeled on Egyptian style. They used Egyptian titles and worshiped Egyptian deities.

About 730 B.C., the Nubian king **Piankhi** (PYAHN kee) conquered Egypt. For a century, Nubian kings ruled Egypt. But Nubian armies could not match the iron weapons of the Assyrians who invaded from southwest Asia. Forced to retreat from Egypt, the Nubians returned to the south.

Nubian Trade and Iron By 500 B.C., Nubian rulers had moved their capital from Napata to **Meroë** (MEHR uh wee). Meroë eventually commanded both the Nile's north-south trade route and the east-west trade route from the Red Sea to North Africa. Along this wide trade network, Nubia sent gold, ivory, animal skins, perfumes, and slaves to the Mediterranean world and Southwest Asia. Meroë's location was a major reason for its development into a successful center of commerce.

Equally important, however, was the region's resources. Meroë was rich in iron ore. Fueled by the region's large quantities of timber, the smelting furnaces of Meroë produced the iron tools and weaponry needed to feed, control, and defend the kingdom. Today, giant heaps of iron waste remain as evidence of ancient Meroë's industry.

Splendor and Decline Although Nubia absorbed much from Egypt, Nubian culture later followed its own course. For example, after gaining independence from Egypt, Nubians worshiped their own gods, including Apedemak, a lion-headed warrior god. At Meroë, artistic styles reflected a greater sense of freedom than Egyptian styles did. Nubians also created their own system of writing, using an alphabet instead of hieroglyphics. Unfortunately, the Nubian alphabet has not yet been deciphered.

>> Nubians and Egyptians worshiped many of the same gods and goddesses, including Amon, the king of all the gods, who was often depicted as a ram.

Interactive Gallery

After the joint reign of King Natakamani and Queen Amanitere in the first century A.D., the splendor of Nubia's golden age dimmed. Finally, about A.D. 350, King Ezana's armies from the kingdom of Axum overwhelmed Nubia.

APPLY CONCEPTS How did trade affect Nubia and North Africa?

North Africa in the Ancient World

Early African civilizations had strong ties to the Mediterranean world. Trade linked Egypt with Greece and Mesopotamia. Later, Egypt was ruled, in turn, by the Greeks and Romans. These powers also knew of the rich civilization that lay south of Egypt and valued Nubian exports. Over time, however, Nubia lost touch with the Mediterranean world.

Guided Reading and Discussion

Discuss Ask students to evaluate and explain the impact that farming had on Neolithic culture and trade in Africa. *(Students may say farming resulted in the production of surplus food, which led to trade and the establishment of villages and trading centers along trade routes.)*

Draw Inferences What impact did the Bantu migration have on language in southern Africa? *(As the Bantu migrated south, many cultures absorbed the Bantu language.)*

Egypt and Nubia Flourish

Explain that Nubia, located along the Nile River valley, was one of the great kingdoms of ancient Africa. Its culture and religion were influenced heavily by Egypt. After invasions from the Assyrians, Nubians moved their capital to Meroë, where it commanded vital trade routes and had great natural resources. There it thrived until it was overwhelmed by Axum's armies.

Online Project the **Interactive Gallery: Nubian Art and Culture** and click through the images.

ACTIVE CLASSROOM

Use the See-Think-Wonder strategy and pair students and ask them to review all the images in the photo gallery. Ask students: What do you see in each image? What does that make you think? What are you wondering about now that you've seen this? Have students share their insights with the class.

Guided Reading and Discussion

Identify Cause and Effect Analyze and describe how Egypt's geographic location influenced Nubia. *(Students may say that Egypt's proximity led to trade and the sharing of ideas. As a result, the Nubians adapted many Egyptian traditions including religion.)*

History Background

Human Contribution to Desertification
Ironically, Nubia's great economic success probably played a significant role in its downfall. The needs of the iron industry resulted in overexploitation of the natural environment. To fuel their iron furnaces, the Nubians needed to burn massive amounts of charcoal. To produce that charcoal, they had to cut down huge areas of timber. They cut down the trees more quickly than new ones could grow. This left the land without trees to hold in the topsoil. When rains came, erosion washed the soil away. The once-fertile lands of Nubia became barren as they gradually succumbed to the process of desertification.

Answers

Analyze Information *As the Bantu migrated, they spread their language, skills, and beliefs.*

Apply Concepts *Trade brought contact with other regions, people, and ideas, but also a rivalry with Egypt and conflict over the control of each region's natural resources.*

North Africa in the Ancient World

Refer to the map of Islam, Christianity, and Judaism in Africa on p. 308. Remind students that early Africa had strong ties to the regions across the Mediterranean and Red seas. Explain that the Phoenicians, Romans, and Muslim Arabs all affected African history.

Analyze Maps After studying the map, in which area(s) do you think Muslims, Jews, and Christians might have interacted? Which religion had expanded into the largest geographic location by A.D. 1000? *(Students may say that Muslims, Jews, and Christians would have interacted along the Mediterranean coast. Students may also say that by A.D. 1000, Islam had the greatest geographical influence of all three religions.)*

Guided Reading and Discussion

Have students answer the following question: In what ways did outside influences contribute to the spread of Islam, Christianity, and Judaism in North Africa? *(Answers may vary, but students should show an understanding that early African civilizations had strong ties to regions across the Mediterranean, and that these outside influences, including the interactions with Romans and Muslim Arabs, brought changes in religion and other aspects of life.)*

Phoenicians and Carthage As Nubia thrived along the Nile, Carthage began to rise as a great North African power. Founded by Phoenician traders as a port on the Mediterranean coast, Carthage came to dominate trade in the western Mediterranean. From 800 B.C. to 146 B.C., Carthage forged an empire that stretched from present-day Tunisia, Algeria, and Morocco to southern Spain and beyond.

As Rome expanded, territorial and trade rivalries erupted between the two powers. After a series of fierce wars, Rome eventually defeated Carthage and totally destroyed the capital city.

Rome Controls North Africa Rome expanded its rule over much of North Africa from the coast to the Sahara and into Egypt. There, the Romans built roads, dams, aqueducts, and cities. They developed North African farmlands to harvest bumper crops of grain, fruit, and other foods. From North Africa, they imported lions and other fierce animals to Rome to do battle with gladiators. North Africa also provided soldiers for the Roman army, including **Septimius Severus,** who would later become a Roman emperor.

Under Roman rule, Christianity spread to the cities of North Africa. In fact, Augustine, the most influential Christian thinker of the late Roman empire, was born in present-day Algeria. From A.D. 395 to A.D. 430, Augustine was bishop of Hippo, a city located near the ruins of ancient Carthage.

Islam Spreads In the 690s, Muslim Arabs conquered and occupied the cities of North Africa. By the early 700s, they had successfully conquered the Berbers, a largely nomadic North African people. Islam also spread peacefully as, over time, Muslim traders from North Africa carried Islam into West Africa. Muslim civilization blossomed in cities such as Cairo, Fez, and Marrakesh, which became famous for their mosques and universities.

Muslim, Jewish, and Christian traders and merchants lived, bartered, and interacted with one another as commerce expanded throughout North and West Africa. Jewish communities formed near Muslim and Christian enclaves, including those in Ghana, Mali, and, later, Songhai. Some African societies adopted aspects of the religions into their cultures, while many Africans continued to practice traditional religions such as ancestor worship.

Islam eventually became the dominant religion in many regions of Africa, and Muslim caliphates governed many African kingdoms. The caliphates established a centralized system of government and a vast trade network to India and China, which allowed

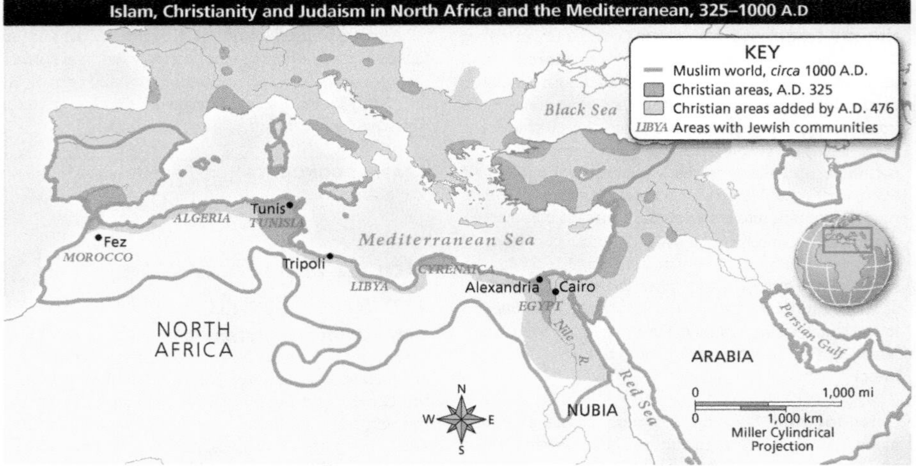

>> **Analyze Maps** Islam, Judaism, and Christianity all influenced African culture. By looking at the map, what can you generalize about each of the three religions?

Answers

Analyze Maps *Sample answer: Each religion flourished at first along the Mediterranean coast.*

the movement of goods between both regions to flourish.

IDENTIFY CAUSE AND EFFECT Describe the role trade played in the development of culture in North Africa.

ASSESSMENT

1. **Draw Conclusions** How did Africa's geographic features influence migration, cultural development, and trade?
2. **Identify** In what ways did outside influences affect Nubian development?
3. **Identify Main Ideas** What factors contributed to the prosperity of the kingdom of Nubia?
4. **Identify Central Issues** What major changes occurred in North Africa from around 800 B.C. to A.D. 700?
5. **Determine Relevance** How did the Bantu migrations contribute to African cultural diversity?

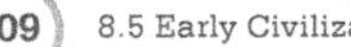

SYNTHESIZE

Online Project the **Digital Activity: Revisit the Essential Question**. Ask students to reconsider the Essential Question: How are religion and culture connected? Using the Rank It strategy, ask students to rank (from most important to least important) the interaction of religion, trade, and geography with African culture. Ask students to provide a justification for their ranking. Then ask students to work in pairs to share their rankings and justifications. Poll the class to see if there is any agreement on the ranking.

DEMONSTRATE

Online Assign the **Digital Lesson Quiz** for this lesson if you haven't already done so. Students will be offered automatic remediation or enrichment based on their score.

In "Early Civilizations of Africa," you read about the influence of geography on early Africa; you studied the interactions among Muslim, Christian, and Jewish societies; and you read how art reflects the history of cultures.

Pose this question to the class:

Describe What effect did trade have on the cities of North Africa? *(Success in trade allowed the Carthaginians to build a mighty empire, but led to war. Trade with Rome helped spur the adoption of Christianity. Later, trade promoted the development of Muslim culture and the adoption of Islam.)*

Topic Inquiry

Have students continue their investigations for the Topic Inquiry.

Answers

Identify Cause and Effect *Trade brought many outsiders to the region, which influenced the development of African culture, religion, government, and agriculture.*

Assessment

1. The continent's geographic features acted as either barriers or highways to ease movement of people, goods, and ideas.
2. Nubians adopted many Egyptian traditions when they were under Egypt's control. Assyrian conquest forced the Nubians back to the south where they setted in Meroë and prospered.
3. Nubia prospered by controlling trade and by utilizing natural resources to produce iron tools and weapons.
4. Carthage, built by Phoenicians, dominated the western Mediterranean trade until conquered by Rome. Under Roman rule, Christianity spread to North African cities. These cities were eventually conquered by Muslim Arabs, and Islam became the dominant religion.
5. The Bantu-speaking peoples spread their culture and technology to other areas and merged with local peoples. The influence of Bantu speakers is still found in the region's languages today.

Topic 8 Lesson 6

Kingdoms of West Africa

CONNECT

Preview Have students preview the **Lesson Objectives** and the list of **Key Terms**.

Students can also preview all the **Key Terms** and **Academic Vocabulary** using the **Interactive Reading Notepad** on the digital course or preview a summary of the lesson in the **Reading and Note Taking Study Guide**.

Online Use the **Editable Presentation** found on the digital course to present the main ideas for this lesson.

Start Up Activity

Read aloud the following quote from Hassan ibn Muhammad, who published an account of his travels through North and West Africa in 1526. Here he describes the value of goods traded in a city in the African kingdom of Mali:

> "It is a wonder to see what plenty of merchandise is daily brought hither, and how costly and sumptuous [lavish] all things be. Horses bought in Europe for ten ducats [coins] are here sold again for forty . . . and spices are sold at a high rate; but of all other commodities salt is most extremely dear [expensive]."

Discuss What can you conclude about the need for salt in West Africa? *(Salt was very important in West Africa.)*

Online You can also project the **Start Up Activity** from the course.

Tell students they will be learning about how the gold and salt trade influenced various cultures in West Africa and how leaders of those kingdoms built strong societies.

INVESTIGATE

Have students read the section using the **Reading and Note Taking Study Guide** to help them take notes and understand the text as they read.

Trade Grows Across the Sahara

Remind students that salt is important to human health, and while abundant in the Sahara, it was rare in many other regions of Africa. In West Africa, gold was widely available. Trade networks that originally dealt in surplus agriculture expanded and became dominated by these two commodities.

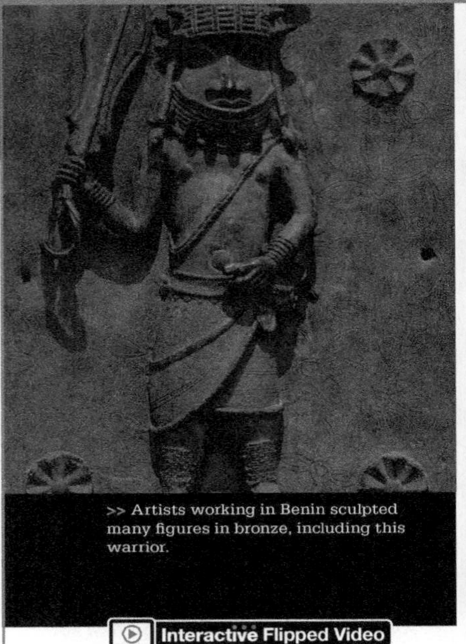

>> Artists working in Benin sculpted many figures in bronze, including this warrior.

Interactive Flipped Video

8.6 As the Sahara dried out in Neolithic times, people were forced to migrate. Some moved into the savanna, the grasslands area that offered land for farming and pasturing herds. There, farmers grew beans, melons, and a variety of grains. Men cleared the land and prepared fields for planting. Women weeded, transplanted seeds, and threshed or ground grains.

TEKS
4.D, 4.J

>> Objectives

Analyze how the gold and salt trade in Africa facilitated the spread of ideas and trade.

Describe how the rulers of Ghana, Mali, and Songhai built strong kingdoms.

Summarize how other West African societies developed.

>> Key Terms

surplus
commodity
Ghana
Sundiata
Mali
Mansa Musa
Songhai

Kingdoms of West Africa

Trade Grows Across the Sahara

By A.D. 100, settled farming villages were expanding, especially along the Senegal and Niger rivers and around Lake Chad. In time, these villages grew into towns with local rulers creating governments over growing populations.

Trading Patterns Emerge Farming villages began to produce a **surplus;** that is, more food than they needed. They began to trade their surplus food for products from other villages. Gradually, a trade network emerged across the savanna. It linked the savanna to the forest lands in the south and then funneled goods across the Sahara to the Mediterranean world and the Middle East. From West Africa, caravans crossed the Sahara carrying leather goods, kola nuts, cotton cloth, and enslaved people. From North Africa, Arab and Berber merchants brought silk, metal, beads, and horses to the peoples south of the Sahara. They also spread their beliefs and ideas

Trading Gold for Salt Two products, gold and salt, dominated the Sahara trade. Gold was widely available in the area of present-day Ghana, Nigeria, and Senegal. The precious metal was found in the

PEARSON realize. www.PearsonTexas.com Access your Digital Lesson.

310

Aa Vocabulary Builder

1. Have students pronounce the following academic vocabulary terms in this lesson and clarify the part of speech. For difficult or polysyllabic words, break them into syllables and pronounce them with the students.
2. Explain what the word means in common "student-friendly" language using synonyms and antonyms when possible. Provide concrete examples to clarify the meaning, and rephrase the definition.

administer: to manage or direct

tolerance: fair and objective attitude toward opinions and practices which differ from one's own soil along rivers in various forms, including nuggets and dust. The gold was carried to the markets of North Africa and eventually made its way into Europe.

In exchange, West Africans traded for an equally important **commodity,** or valuable product—salt. Salt was rare in some regions of Africa. However, people need salt in their diet to prevent dehydration, especially in tropical areas. Salt is also used to preserve food. The Sahara had an abundance of salt. In fact, at Taghaza, in the central Sahara, people built homes out of blocks of salt. But in the savanna, several hundred miles south, salt was scarce. It was easily worth its weight in gold, pound for pound.

As farming and trade prospered, cities developed on the northern edges of the savanna. Soon strong monarchs arose, gaining control of the most profitable trade routes, and building powerful kingdoms. As the gold and salt trade expanded, so did the spread of ideas and religion. Traders brought their customs and ideas with them as they traveled throughout Africa, helping to spread Islam and the Arabic language to many places. Neighboring kingdoms strengthened their trading partnerships, which helped the region maintain peaceful relationships.

EXPLAIN In what ways did farming affect the growth of African villages and cities?

Ghana

Between about 800 and 1600, several powerful kingdoms won control of the prosperous Sahara trade. The first of these kingdoms was **Ghana,** located on the broad "V" made by the Niger and Senegal rivers.

Ghana means ruler and was the name used for this kingdom by Arab traders. The modern nation of Ghana is not located on the site of the ancient kingdom, but stands several hundred miles to the south. Ancient Ghana occupied lands in what is today northern Senegal and southern Mauritania.

Gold Wealth of Ghana By 800, the rulers of the Soninke people had united many farming villages to create the kingdom of Ghana. Given their favorable location, the rulers of Ghana controlled the gold-salt trade across West Africa. Two streams of trade came together in the marketplaces of Ghana, where the king collected tolls on all goods entering or leaving his land. So great was the flow of gold that Arab writers called Ghana "the land of gold."

The King and His Court Ghana may have had several large cities that served as capitals during its long history. The last great capital was called Kumbi Saleh, and according to the custom of the time, it included two separate walled towns. The first town was the

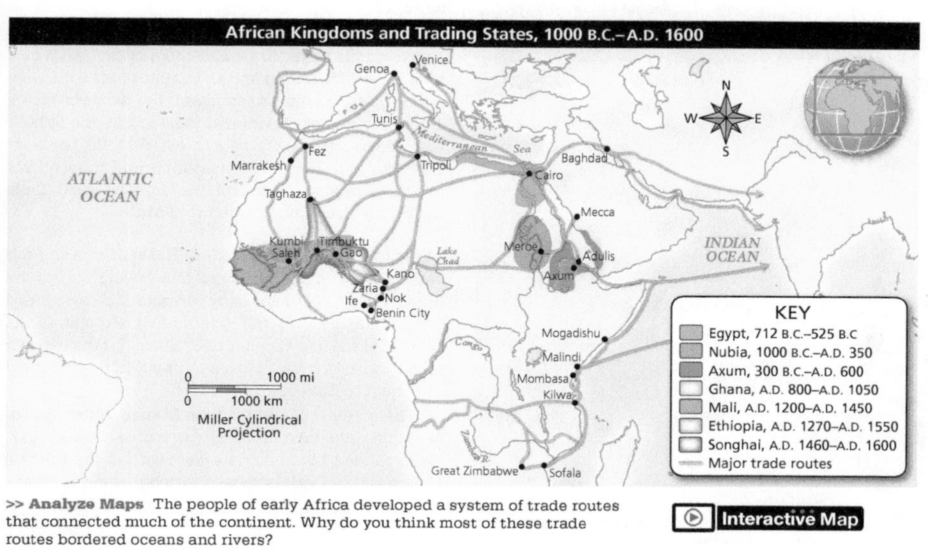

>> **Analyze Maps** The people of early Africa developed a system of trade routes that connected much of the continent. Why do you think most of these trade routes bordered oceans and rivers?

Interactive Map

Online Project the **Interactive Map: Trans-Saharan Trade (750 B.C.–A.D. 1600)** and click through the boxes. Introduce the map activity by telling students that in West and East Africa a series of kingdoms developed as trade extended beyond village borders. Some of the cities along trade routes became wealthy international commercial centers.

ACTIVE CLASSROOM

Using the A Closer Look strategy, divide the map into four numbered quadrants. Have students count off from 1 to 4. Next, have them look closely at the part of the image in their quadrant. Have them discuss what they see. Ask students why the trade routes in their quadrant are shaped as they are. Have them explain how these trade routes facilitated the spread of ideas and goods. Ask students what geographic factors might have impeded or helped spur trade.

Guided Reading and Discussion

Evaluate Ask students to explain how trade might have allowed Islam to spread among the kingdoms of West Africa and what impact Islam had on those kingdoms. *(The ideas and religion of Muslim merchants traveling to West African kingdoms would have impacted the political, economic, and social fabric of those communities.)*

Key Terms

Ask students to find the key terms **surplus** and **commodity** (in bold) in the text and explain their meanings. Tell them to write a sentence that uses both terms. Ask volunteers to read their sentences aloud.

D Differentiate Challenge After they study the map, pair students and explain to them they are going to assume the role of traders. Have the students negotiate for 5 minutes with each other over goods that they have and that the other trader might want, such as pencils, erasers, etc. Then ask each pair whether they were able to successfully complete a deal. Ask them to explain the problems they encountered and the benefits of the trade.

Answers

Explain *Villages began to produce surplus food, which they traded with other areas. The growth of trade helped those towns develop into cities.*

Analyze Maps *Sample answer: Water provided a highway of sorts for the movement of goods and people.*

Topic 8 Lesson 6

Ghana
Mali
Songhai

Tell students that the control of gold-salt trade routes across West Africa made the kingdom of Ghana very wealthy. Its capital was divided into two walled towns, one dominated by the court, the other with prosperous Muslim merchants. Muslim traders brought the Arabic language and writing, coinage, and new business methods. While Muslims introduced their culture to Ghana and were influential in court as counselors and officials, Islam was slow to spread. The Almoravid caliphate overwhelmed Ghana around 1050 but was unable to maintain control of the region. The kingdom of Mali emerged in the region, and its greatest ruler, Mansa Musa, converted to Islam.

Refer to the infographic of Mansa Musa's journey on p. 313 and note the role he played promoting Mali's reputation and helping Timbuktu become a center of learning. Discuss how the Songhai empire arose in the region after the kingdom of Mali weakened. Draw comparisons to the importance Islam played in both kingdoms and the ties it forged to the Muslim world.

Online Project the **Interactive Gallery: Artifacts From West Africa's Great Kingdoms** and click through the images. Tell students that trade made the kingdoms of West Africa rich and that evidence of their prosperity and culture can be found in the art, textiles, ideas, and literature that each society left behind.

Analyze Images What do you think the fourth image in the gallery—a brass figurine used to weigh gold dust—says about trade and the kingdom's wealth? *(Answers will vary. Students might say that Ghana's gold lured merchants from a variety of places, making the kingdom a bustling center of trade and power.)*

home of the king and included the royal palace. The second was home to Muslim merchants and traders.

The royal palace was surrounded by a complex of domed buildings. Here, in a court noted for its wealth and splendor, the king of Ghana presided over elaborate ceremonies. To his people, the king was a godlike figure who administered justice and kept order. In the second town of Kumbi Saleh, prosperous Muslim merchants from north of the Sahara lived in luxurious stone buildings. Lured by the gold wealth of Ghana, these merchants helped make Kumbi Saleh a bustling center of trade.

Islam's Influence Even before the rise of Ghana, Muslim traders had brought their faith to West Africa. As Ghana flourished, Muslim merchants and traders came to play an important role in the kingdom. The king employed Muslims as counselors and officials. Over time, Ghana's rulers adapted some military technology and ideas about government and law from the Muslim world.

The gold-salt trade and other trade with the Muslim world brought other ideas and customs to West Africa. Muslim merchants introduced their Arabic language and writing, coinage, and business methods. From the Islamic world came an emphasis on education and learning. Islamic clerics and scholars traveled with Muslim traders into West Africa and other parts of the continent. Muslim scholars built libraries and schools. Educated Muslims became advisors to West African rulers. Some rulers embraced Islam, which led their people to convert to the new religion. Many African converts to Islam combined aspects of their new faith with some of their traditional beliefs.

As Islam spread across Africa, its teachings and beliefs based on the Quran influenced how people lived. For example, some African Muslim rulers imposed the *zakat,* or a yearly tax on certain kinds of property that was used for charitable purposes. The zakat reflected the Islamic practice of alms giving, or charity.

Ghana Declines About 1050, the Almoravids (al muh RAH vuds), pious Muslims from North Africa, launched a campaign to spread their form of Islam and seize control of Ghana's trade routes. After conquering parts of North Africa and Spain, they pushed south across the Sahara. The Almoravids conquered Ghana, but were unable to maintain control over their extended empire for long. Ghana survived, but its empire declined in the late 1100s. In time, it was swallowed up by a rising new West African power, the kingdom of Mali.

DESCRIBE What impact did trade have on the West African kingdom of Ghana?

>> **Draw Conclusions** In this 1325 world map, Mali ruler Mansa Musa is offering gold to a trader. What does this image say about Mansa Musa and the Mali empire?

Mali

Amid the turmoil of Ghana's collapse, the Mandinka people on the upper Niger suffered a bitter defeat by a rival leader. Their king and all but one of his sons were executed. According to tradition, the survivor was a sickly boy named **Sundiata,** regarded by his father's enemies as too weak to be a threat. By 1235, however, Sundiata had become a great king and crushed his enemies, seizing control of the lucrative gold trade routes, and founding the empire of **Mali.**

Mansa Musa: Mali's Greatest Ruler *Mali* is an Arab version of the Mandinka word that means "where the king dwells." The *mansas,* or kings of Mali, expanded their influence over the gold-mining regions to the south and the salt supplies of Taghaza. Where caravan routes crossed, towns such as Timbuktu mushroomed into great trading cities.

The greatest Mali ruler was **Mansa Musa** (MAHN sah MOO sah), who came to the throne around 1312. He expanded Mali's borders westward to the Atlantic Ocean and pushed northward to conquer many cities.

During his 25-year reign, Mansa Musa worked to ensure peace and order in his empire. He converted to Islam and based his system of justice on the Quran.

Answers

Draw Conclusions *Sample answer: The image shows that Mali was rich in gold.*

Describe *Trade made Ghana prosperous as trading cities arose. In addition, trade gave Ghana's rulers new ideas about government as they were introduced to Islam.*

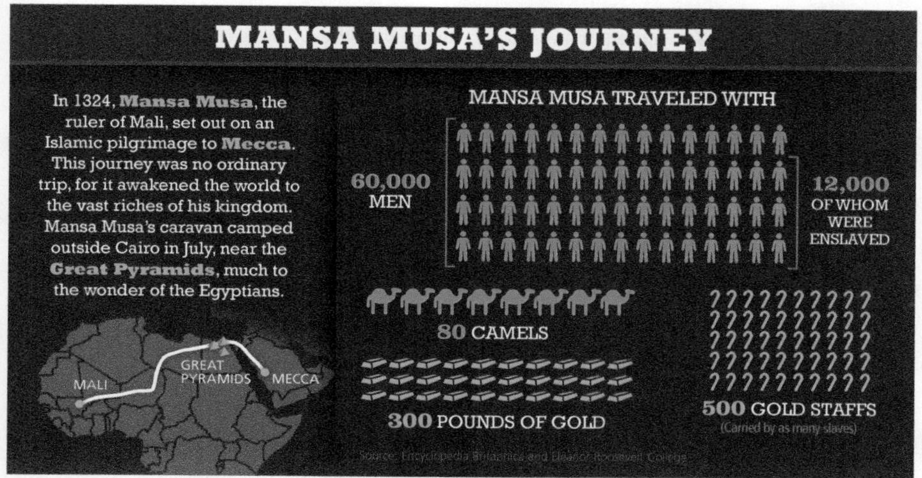

MANSA MUSA'S JOURNEY
In 1324, Mansa Musa, the ruler of Mali, set out on an Islamic pilgrimage to Mecca. This journey was no ordinary trip, for it awakened the world to the vast riches of his kingdom. Mansa Musa's caravan camped outside Cairo in July, near the Great Pyramids, much to the wonder of the Egyptians.
MANSA MUSA TRAVELED WITH
60,000 MEN
12,000 OF WHOM WERE ENSLAVED
80 CAMELS
300 POUNDS OF GOLD
500 GOLD STAFFS
(Carried by as many slaves)
MALI
GREAT PYRAMIDS
MECCA

>> **Analyze Data** Mansa Musa's pilgrimage to Mecca in 1324 was a sight to behold as he traveled in grand style. Based on the numbers, what percentage of those who traveled with him were enslaved?

However, in order to ensure prosperity and peace in his kingdom, he did not impose Islam on the people, but promoted religious freedom and tolerance.

Mansa Musa's Pilgrimage In 1324, Mansa Musa fulfilled one of the Five Pillars of Islam by making the hajj, or pilgrimage, to Mecca. Through his pilgrimage, Mansa Musa showed his devotion to Islam, but the visit also allowed him to forge new diplomatic and economic ties with other Muslim states. Mansa Musa returned home with Muslim scholars, architects, and teachers. The newcomers introduced Arab styles in the palaces and mosques of Mali. They also helped promote Islamic education in Mali.

As a result of Mansa Musa's pilgrimage, word of Mali's great wealth spread across the Muslim world and filtered into Europe. The news sparked the interest of European rulers in African gold, especially since they had recently begun to use gold coins.

Growth of Timbuktu As he returned home from Mecca, Mansa Musa stopped in the busy city of Timbuktu, where he built a palace and mosque. Timbuktu had grown from a small settlement into a major center of trade and Islamic learning. Its diverse population included Muslim and non-Muslim merchants from West Africa and Arabs from North Africa and elsewhere.

For hundreds of years, the city drew some of the best scholars from the Muslim world, including doctors, priests, and judges. Even before Mansa Musa, Timbuktu had won fame for its thriving university that reportedly had 25,000 students from Africa and the Muslim world. The university reflected the Islamic emphasis on education and showed how Islam spread peacefully through trade and centers of learning.

DRAW CONCLUSIONS What were some of Mansa Musa's accomplishments when he ruled Mali?

Songhai

In the 1400s, disputes over succession weakened Mali. Subject peoples broke away, and the empire shriveled. By the 1460s, the wealthy trading city of Gao (gow) had become the capital of the emerging West African kingdom of **Songhai** (SAWNG hy).

An Empire Expands Songhai developed on fertile ground at the bend of the Niger River in present-day Mali and Niger. Between 1464 and 1492, the soldier-king Sonni Ali built the largest state that had ever existed in West Africa. Sonni Ali brought trade routes

History Background

The City of Timbuktu Timbuktu was an important learning center for Muslims of Africa and beyond. The city's scholars, many of whom had studied in Mecca or Egypt, attracted students from diverse areas. But as a result of the Moroccan conquest of Songhai, Timbuktu suffered a rapid decline. The new Moroccan rulers doubted the loyalty of the city's scholars and ordered they be arrested. Some were killed and many others were exiled. In the years ahead, Timbuktu continued to experience invasions and political instability, and its importance as an educational center declined.

ACTIVE CLASSROOM

In 1324, Mansa Musa made a hajj, or pilgrimage, to Mecca. People at the time said that his traveling caravan was one of the most wondrous sights they had ever seen. Let's say that you were a reporter traveling with Mansa Musa. Write down a series of questions you'd like to ask him and what you would expect him to say to you.

Guided Reading and Discussion

Discuss Explain how Sonni Ali made Songhai a wealthy kingdom after Mali's empire shriveled. *(Students might say that Sonni Ali made Songhai a powerful kingdom by bringing trade routes and wealthy cities under his control.)*

Compare and Contrast Compare the influence of Islam on the political and economic life in Mali and Songhai. *(Students might say that in Mali, Islam was important to forging economic and political ties with other Muslim nations, although the country's rulers did not impose Islam on the population. In Songhai, the kingdom first followed traditional religious beliefs. Over time, Islam greatly influenced the kingdom's government and economy.)*

Answers

Analyze Data *20 percent*

Draw Conclusions *He expanded the kingdom and worked to ensure peace and order. He based his system of justice on the Quran. He also forged ties with other Muslim lands and promoted education.*

Topic 8 Lesson 6

Small Societies and Kingdoms of West Africa

Remind students that smaller kingdoms flourished in West Africa in the period from 500 to 1500. They included the forest kingdom of Benin, and the city-states of the Hausa. Tell students that a three-mile-long wall surrounded the capital of Benin and that their king was a political, judicial, and religious leader. The queen mother and a council of chiefs were also important. Discuss the impact Ife artisans had on the development of brass and bronze sculptures in Benin. The walled cities of the Hausa, built for protection from invaders, expanded into thriving commercial centers with vast trade networks. Some of the city-states had kings who were Muslims, resulting in an Islamic influence on the region. Some of the cities were ruled by women.

Summarize Ask students to explain how the walled cities of the Hausa impacted trade. *(Students might say the walled cities provided merchants and traders protection, which allowed cities to expand and thrive.)*

Guided Reading and Discussion

Ask students to analyze the interaction between Ife and Benin and how this relationship impacted Benin. *(Students might say Ife taught Benin how to cast bronze and brass, which allowed Benin sculptors to develop their own unique style.)*

Answers

Identify *In addition to expanding its territory, Askia Muhammad improved the kingdom's government and forged stronger ties with the Muslim world.*

and wealthy cities like Timbuktu under his control. Unlike the rulers of Mali, he did not adopt Islam, but instead followed traditional religious beliefs.

Soon after Sonni Ali's death in 1492, however, the emperor Askia Muhammad set up a Muslim dynasty. He further expanded the territory of Songhai and improved its government.

To run the empire more efficiently, he set up a bureaucracy with separate departments for farming, the military, and the treasury. Officials appointed by the emperor supervised each department.

Like Mansa Musa, Askia Muhammad made a pilgrimage to Mecca that led to stronger ties with the wider Muslim world. Scholars from Muslim lands flocked to Askia Muhammad's court at Gao. In towns and cities across Songhai, he built mosques and opened schools for the study of the Quran.

Invaders from the North Songhai continue to prosper after Askia Muhammad died in 1528, but disputes over succession led to frequent changes in leadership. In 1586, a dispute erupted that led to civil war. Soon after, the ruler of Morocco sent his armies south to seize the West Africa gold mines. The invaders used gunpowder weapons to defeat the disunited forces of Songhai.

Like the Almoravids who conquered Ghana, the Moroccans were not able to rule an empire that reached so far south of the Sahara. With the downfall of Songhai, this part of West Africa splintered into many small kingdoms. Memories of the splendid gold kingdoms of the region survived.

IDENTIFY In which ways did Askia Muhammad shape the Songhai empire?

Small Societies and Kingdoms of West Africa

In the period from 500 to 1500, other kingdoms and societies flourished in various part of West Africa. The kingdom of Benin (beh NEEN) developed in the rain forest, while the fertile northern lands of modern-day Nigeria were home to the Hausa (HOW suh) people. They were both successful farmers and traders.

Benin: A Forest Kingdom South of the savanna, Benin rose in the rain forests of the Guinea coast. The forest peoples built farming villages and traded pepper and ivory—and later, slaves—to their neighbors in the savanna.

The rulers of Benin organized their kingdom in the 1300s, probably building on the achievements of earlier forest cultures. Their *oba*, or king, was a political, judicial, and religious leader. Still, much power was

THE GREAT CITY OF TIMBUKTU

Timbuktu was one of the grandest and greatest cities in West Africa. Founded in the 5th century, the city was a great cultural, religious, and economic center. The city reached the zenith of its power in the 1400s and 1500s.

CENTER OF TRADE	Salt from Taghaza came into Timbuktu by camel in 200-pound (90.7 kg) blocks. Once it arrived, merchants in Timbuktu dispersed the salt throughout western Africa. Merchants from Ghudāmis traveled to Timbuktu to buy gold and slaves
CENTER OF LEARNING	University of Sankore encompassed 180 Quranic schools with 25,000 students. Sacred Muslim texts were carried into Timbuktu , so scholars from Cairo, Baghdad, and Persia could study them.
LOOKING TO THE STARS	Astronomers in Timbuktu charted the movement of the stars while physicians studied the healing properties of plants.
CITY OF READING	In the mid-1500s, an Islamic scholar named Mohammed abu Bakr al-Wangariai amassed thousands of manuscripts and books on subjects ranging from history to astronomy.
THE FALL	The city began its decline in the 1500s when Moroccan invaders arrested or exiled the Muslim scholars and trading patterns began to shift to the coasts.

>> Founded in the 5th century, Timbuktu was a great cultural, religious, and economic center. The city reached the height of its power in the 1400s and 1500s.

History Background

Royal Administration in Africa In several kingdoms of West Africa, rulers brought about a major change in how leaders were chosen. Traditionally, the position of chief was an inherited one, as was the case with the lands and titles of European nobles of the Middle Ages. Rulers of Songhai and some Hausa city-states changed these patterns. They began to name officials, both political and military. By doing so, they tried to achieve greater control over decision making—and greater loyalty. The people they named, after all, owed their positions to the rulers and could be expected to act in accordance with the rulers' wishes. This change also had a parallel in Europe, as monarchs there used the power of appointment and the creation of bureaucracies to consolidate their own power and weaken that of nobles.

spread among other figures, including the queen mother and a council of hereditary chiefs.

A three-mile-long wall surrounded the capital, Benin City, where a great palace was decorated with elaborate brass plaques and sculptures. Artisans from Ife (EE fay), a neighboring forest society, taught the people of Benin how to cast bronze and brass. Benin sculptors developed their own unique style for representing the human face and form. Their works depicted warriors, queen mothers, and the oba himself. Later, the sculptures showed helmeted and bearded Portuguese merchants, who began to arrive in growing numbers in the 1500s.

Walled City-States of the Hausa By the 1300s, the Hausa had built a number of independent clay-walled cities. Walls were designed to protect the people from invasions.

While these cities remained independent of one another, in time, the walled cities expanded into thriving commercial centers. In the cities, cotton weavers and dyers, leatherworkers, and other artisans produced goods for sale. Merchants traded with Arab and Berber caravans from north of the Sahara. Hausa goods were sold as far away as North Africa and southern Europe.

Kano was the most prosperous Hausa city-state. Its walls, over 12 miles in circumference and up to 50 feet high, protected a population of more than 30,000. Kano's greatest king, Muhammad Rumfa, was a Muslim, as were many of the city's merchants and officials. During his reign, the Hausa developed a writing system influenced by Arabic script, and Islamic law influenced government.

Many Hausa rulers were women, including Amina of the city-state of Zazzau, located in present-day Nigeria. In the late 1500s, she conquered Kano and other regions, expanding the boundary of Zaria as far as the Niger River. Under Amina, the Hausa came to dominate many Saharan trade routes.

SUMMARIZE Describe how other cultures influenced Benin and the Hausa city-states.

>> The mud walls of Hausa cities have survived the centuries. The walls helped the cities expand into thriving centers of commerce.

Interactive Gallery

ASSESSMENT

1. **Identify Cause and Effect** Why did the gold-salt trade develop between West Africa and North Africa?
2. **Compare** How was the reign of Mansa Musa in Mali similar to that of Askia Muhammad in Songhai?
3. **Draw Conclusions** How did the walls of Benin city and the other Hausa city-states contribute to their development and success?
4. **Identify Central Ideas** What did Timbuktu contribute to Mali's importance as a kingdom?
5. **Check Understanding** How did the gold-salt trade affect the kingdom of Ghana?

SYNTHESIZE

Ask students to recall the Topic Essential Question: How are religion and culture connected? Ask students to spend three minutes writing down a response to this question on a sticky note. Have students post their sticky notes on the board. Ask students to look at all the various responses from other students then discuss similarities and differences in the responses as a group.

DEMONSTRATE

Online Assign the **Digital Lesson Quiz** for this lesson if you haven't already done so. Students will be offered automatic remediation or enrichment based on their score.

Pose the following question to students:

Predict Consequences Do you think West Africa would have developed differently had Muslim traders not dominated trade on the continent? *(Students might say that many African societies might have been more influenced by other outsiders, such as those from Europe, had Muslim traders not brought Islam to Africa.)*

Identify What impact did Islam have on education, government, and economics in West Africa? *(Students might say that in many West African kingdoms, Islamic schools were built; new ideas about governments were introduced; and Islam helped many nations forge trading ties with other Muslim lands.)*

Topic Inquiry

Have students continue their investigations for the Topic Inquiry.

Answers

Summarize *Benin's rulers built on the achievements of earlier forest cultures. They also learned from Ife's artisans how to cast bronze and brass. In addition, the Arabic alphabet influenced the Hausa writing system.*

Assessment

1. Farming villages in the savanna region began producing a surplus of food that they traded with the people in the forests to the south. Each region had goods the other needed, especially when it came to salt from the Sahara region and gold from West Africa.
2. Both expanded the borders of their kingdoms; both made pilgrimages to Mecca that helped strengthen ties with the Muslim world; and both attracted scholars from other Muslim lands to their kingdoms.
3. In a region of frequent conflict and invasion, the walls could protect people within the cities and help merchants feel safer and more willing to trade.
4. The city was the center of trade, culture, and education in the ever-expanding Muslim world, and as a result, made Mali a formidable kingdom.
5. Ghana controlled the gold-salt trade routes across West Africa, bringing it great wealth. As Muslim merchants traded and lived in the region, they brought their religion and culture with them. The king incorporated some of their ideas in government and military technology. Eventually, some people adopted Islam, combining it with aspects of their traditional religions.

Topic 8 Lesson 7

Trading States of East Africa

CONNECT

Preview Have students preview the **Lesson Objectives** and the list of **Key Terms**.

Students can also preview all the **Key Terms** and **Academic Vocabulary** using the **Interactive Reading Notepad** on the digital course or preview a summary of the lesson in the **Reading and Note Taking Study Guide**.

Online Use the **Editable Presentation** found on the digital course to present the main ideas for this lesson.

Start Up Activity

Read aloud the following quote by King Ezana of Ethiopia, speaking about his conquest of Nubia:

> "May the Lord of Heaven make my kingdom stronger! And as He has this day conquered my enemy for me may He Conquer for me wherever I go. . . . I will rule the people with righteousness and justice, and will not oppress them . . . I have set up this throne by the might of the Lord of Heaven."

Discuss What does this quote say about the role of religion in Ethiopia and in King Ezana's life? *(King Ezana was a very religious person who believed God was on his side. The king's religious attitudes reflected the importance of religion in Ethiopia.)*

Online You can also project the **Start Up Activity** from the course.

INVESTIGATE

Have students read the section using the **Reading and Note Taking Study Guide** to help them take notes and understand the text as they read.

Axum

Explain that Axumite kings frequently called Axum Ethiopia, a term the Greeks used for the region. Tell students that Axum was a major center of trade that allowed the kingdom to grow and prosper. Greek, Egyptian, Arab, and Jewish merchants interacted with one another. Eventually, Christianity would greatly influence the region, even after Axum's power faded. Note that Christianity, which had once strengthened Axum's ties to its trading partners, isolated it as Islam spread to much of the region.

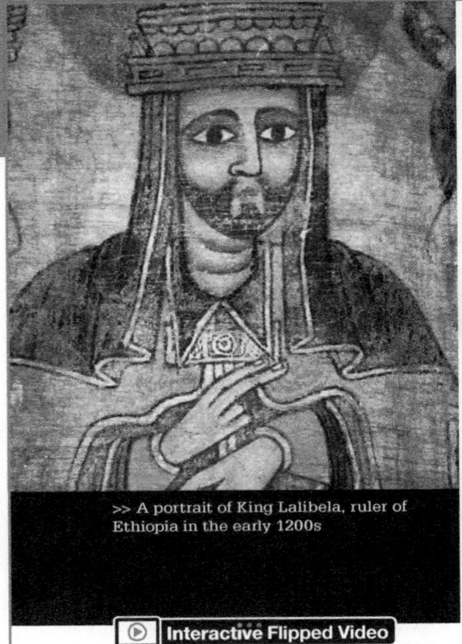

>> A portrait of King Lalibela, ruler of Ethiopia in the early 1200s

Interactive Flipped Video

8.7 After 100 B.C., the kingdom of Axum expanded across the northern Ethiopian highlands. By about A.D. 1, Axum had gained control of the Red Sea coast in present-day Eritrea. By controlling the Red Sea trade with Rome and Persia, Axum grew rich.

TEKS
4.D, 16.B

>> Objectives

Explain how religion influenced the development of Axum and Ethiopia.

Understand how trade affected the city-states in East Africa.

Describe the economy of Great Zimbabwe.

>> Key Terms

Axum
Adulis
Ethiopia
Lalibela
Swahili
Great Zimbabwe

Trading States of East Africa

Axum

An Ideal Location for Trade Located to the southeast of Nubia, Axum extended from the mountains of present-day Ethiopia to the sun-bleached shores of the Red Sea in present-day Eritrea. The peoples of Axum were descended from African farmers and people from the Middle East who brought Jewish traditions through Arabia. This merging of cultures gave rise to a unique written and spoken language, Geez.

The kingdom of Axum profited from the strategic location of its two main cities, the port of **Adulis** on the Red Sea, and the upland capital city of Axum. By A.D. 400, the kingdom commanded a triangular trade network that connected Africa, India, and the Mediterranean world.

A great variety of goods and enslaved people funneled in and out of the markets of these two cities. From the interior of Africa, traders brought ivory, animal hides, and gold to the markets of Axum. Goods from farther south and across the Indian Ocean came to the Red Sea harbor of Adulis. There, the traders and markets offered iron, spices, precious stones, and cotton cloth from India and other lands beyond the Indian Ocean. Ships carried these commodities up the Red Sea,

PEARSON realize. www.PearsonTexas.com Access your Digital Lesson.

316

Aa Vocabulary Builder

1. Have students pronounce the following academic vocabulary terms in this lesson and clarify the part of speech. For difficult or polysyllabic words, break them into syllables and pronounce them with the students.
2. Explain what the word means in common "student-friendly" language using synonyms and antonyms when possible. Provide concrete examples to clarify the meaning, and rephrase the definition.

unify: to form a single unit

complex: a group of connected buildings that form a single whole where they collected goods from Europe and countries along the Mediterranean.

Christianity Takes Hold In these great centers of international trade, Greek, Egyptian, Arab, and Jewish merchants mingled with traders from Africa, India, and other regions. Ideas spread as these goods were traded. By the 300s, Christianity had reached the region. After converting to the new religion, Axum's King Ezana made Christianity the official religion of his kingdom. As Christianity took hold among Axum's people, they replaced older temples with Christian churches decorated with intricately designed religious images and murals painted on wood panels.

Islam Spreads At first, Christianity strengthened the ties between Axum, North Africa, and the Mediterranean world. In the 600s, however, Islam began to spread across North Africa and other regions surrounding Axum. Many African rulers embraced this new faith, creating strong cultural ties across much of the continent. Axum, which remained Christian, grew isolated from its own trade network—by distance from Europe and by religion from many former trading partners. As civil war and economic decline combined to weaken Axum, the kingdom slowly declined.

SYNTHESIZE Describe how the spread of Christianity and Islam affected the kingdom of Axum.

Ethiopia

Though Axum's political and economic power faded, its cultural and religious influence did not disappear. This legacy survived among the peoples of the interior uplands, in what is today northern Ethiopia. Although Axum's empire was only a portion of the present-day nation, when referring to their kingdom as a whole, the Axumite kings frequently used **Ethiopia,** a term the Greeks used for the region.

A Distinctive Culture Medieval Ethiopia was protected by rugged mountains, and the descendants of the Axumites were able to maintain their independence for centuries. Their success was due in part to the unifying power of their Christian faith, which gave them a unique sense of identity and helped establish a culture distinct from that of neighboring peoples.

Kingdom of Axum 300 B.C. to A.D. 600

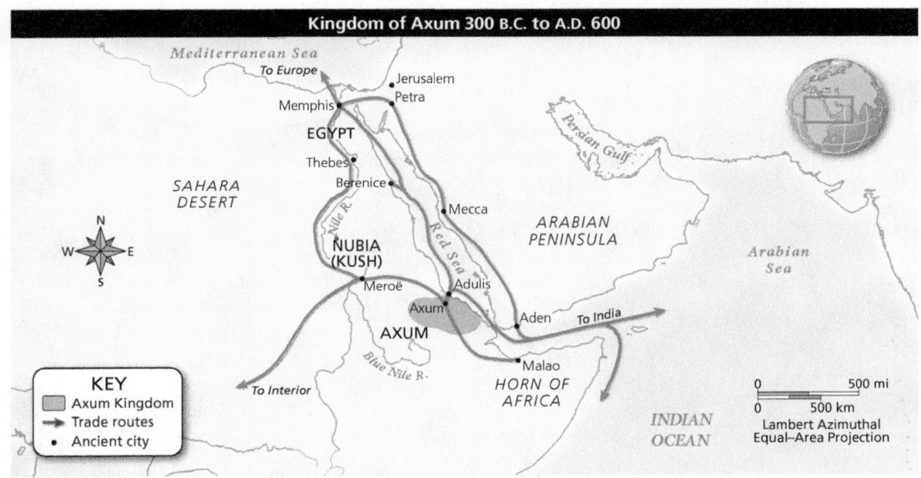

>> **Analyze Maps** Axum's location allowed the kingdom to become a hub of trade in East Africa. Based on the map, why did Axum become a favorite center for maritime traders?

Guided Reading and Discussion

Draw Conclusions What was it about Axum's location that allowed religion to influence the region? *(Students may say that Axum's location allowed trade routes to develop that brought people from different cultures and different religions to the region.)*

Ethiopia

In medieval Ethiopia, which was protected by mountains, the descendants of Axumites maintained their independence for centuries. Their Christian faith was a unifying force, creating a cultural identity different from those of neighboring peoples.

Guided Reading and Discussion

Identify Cause and Effect Explain how Islam influenced Ethiopia's development. *(Sample response: Ethiopia, which was a Christian kingdom, grew isolated from its own trade network as its trading partners began to embrace Islam.)*

Key Terms

Ask students to find the key term **Lalibela** (in bold) in the text on p. 318. Have students take note that *Lalibela* is the name of both an Ethiopian kingdom's ruler and the city named for him.

English Language Proficiency Standards

Speaking 3.C.3 Before beginning this activity, read "Ethiopia" aloud to the class. Then have students practice saying different types of sentences according to their level of English proficiency.

Read the following examples based on "Ethiopia."

- Ethiopia was separated from other cultures by mountains.
- Why did Ethiopian Jews leave the mountains in the late 1900s?
- Look at the photos of medieval Ethiopia.
- Lalibela's churches were built down into the ground!

Beginning Review the four types of sentences. Then read the sentences above and have students repeat them. Listen to make sure that students are pronouncing each word correctly and help them make corrections as needed. Then ask students to say one declarative sentence about what they learned from reading "Ethiopia." Assist them as needed.

Answers

Synthesize *At first, Christianity strengthened Axum's relationship with its North African neighbors and the Mediterranean world. As its neighbors and trading partners converted to Islam, however, Axum, which remained Christian, lost its influence in the region. As a result, civil war and economic decline weakened the kingdom.*

Analyze Maps *Sample answer: Axum's location on the Red Sea allowed seafaring traders from as far away as Asia to visit the kingdom.*

City-States of East Africa

Tell students that the city-states along the coast of East Africa reflected the diversity of the merchants who traded there, such as the Muslim communities that were established. Point out that the monsoon winds were critical to the shipping between Africa and India across the Indian Ocean, leading to trade that stretched from the interior of Africa to India, Southeast Asia, and China. Discuss the development of the slave trade and explain that demand for enslaved people as a source of labor led Indian Ocean traders to purchase slaves who had been captured during raids in the East African interior as well as in coastal African areas. Discuss the emergence of Swahili as a culture and language, including the contributions of traders from the Middle East and Asia who settled in the coastal cities.

Online Project the **Interactive Map: Journeys of Ibn Battuta** and click through the hotspots. Introduce the map activity by telling students that Ibn Battuta was a Muslim man who at the age of 21 decided to make a pilgrimage to Mecca in Saudi Arabia. During his journey, Battuta visited much of Southwest Asia, East Africa, and other regions.

ACTIVE CLASSROOM

Let's say you were traveling with Ibn Battuta on his trip. After studying the hotspots on the map, do additional research on all of the regions and write a travel blog that you can either post online or print out for your classmates to read. In your blog, explain what life was like in each location, and what you might have seen had you actually traveled with Battuta.

One example of Ethiopia's distinct culture is the unique churches of Lalibela. In the early 1200s, King **Lalibela** came to power in Ethiopia.

During his reign, he directed the building of eleven remarkable churches that workers had carved from ground level downward into the solid rock of the mountains. These amazing structures still exist today and illustrate the architectural and artistic skill of the craftsmen who created them.

Despite their isolation, Ethiopian Christians kept ties with the Holy Land. In fact, some made pilgrimages to Jerusalem. They also were in touch with Christian communities in Egypt. Over time, Ethiopian Christianity absorbed many local customs. Traditional East African music and dance were adapted, and their influence is still felt in Ethiopian church services today. In addition, the services are still conducted in the ancient language of Geez.

Judaism in Ethiopia The kings of Ethiopia claimed descent from the Israelite king Solomon and the queen of Sheba. This belief was recorded in an ancient Ethiopian book called *The Glory of Kings* and reinforced by the fact that Ethiopians observe some of the Jewish holidays and dietary laws.

Some Ethiopians practiced Judaism, not the predominant Christianity. These Ethiopian Jews lived in the mountains of Ethiopia until the late 1900s, when most evacuated to Israel due to famine and persecutions.

IDENTIFY How did Ethiopia's geographic isolation shape its culture?

ELPS **ELPS 3.C.3** Practice speaking about *Ethiopia* using each of the four sentence types.

City-States of East Africa

While Axum declined, a string of commercial cities—including Kilwa, Mogadishu, Mombasa, and Sofala—gradually arose along the East African coast. Since ancient times, Phoenician, Greek, Roman, and Indian traders had visited this region. Under the protection of local African rulers, Arab and Persian merchants set up Muslim communities beginning in the 600s. Port cities, as well as offshore islands such as Lamu and Zanzibar, were ideally located for trade with Asia. As a result, Asian traders and immigrants from as far away as Indonesia soon added to the rich cultural mix.

Trade in the Indian Ocean By the 600s, sailors had learned that the annual monsoon winds could carry sailing ships plying the waters of the Indian Ocean between India and Africa. On the East African coast,

>> Traders from Europe, Asia, and the interior of Africa descended on East Africa to trade enslaved people and ivory, gold, and other goods.

English Language Proficiency Standards

Intermediate Provide students with the four sentence types listed above. Instruct students to say two declarative and two interrogative sentences to a partner about what they learned from reading "Ethiopia." Provide additional examples and assistance as needed.

Advanced Have pairs work together to identify each of the four sentence types as the examples above are read aloud. Then instruct students to say three declarative, three interrogative, and three imperative sentences about the information they learned from reading "Ethiopia." Encourage students to speak using increasingly complex sentences.

Advanced High Have students identify each of the four sentence types as the examples above are read aloud. Then have students work with a partner to take turns saying several sentences of each type. The sentences should relate to the information students learned from reading "Ethiopia."

Answers

Identify *Ethiopia's geographic isolation allowed the kingdom to remain independent while helping it develop a unique sense of identity based largely on religion.*

rulers took advantage of the opportunities for trade that these winds of the Indian Ocean provided.

They welcomed ships from Arabia, Persia, and China. Traders acquired ivory, leopard skins, iron, copper, gold, and enslaved people from the interior of Africa, as well as from coastal regions. From India, Southeast Asia, and China came cotton cloth, silk, spices, porcelain, glassware, and swords.

Trade was beneficial to the merchants, and it also helped local rulers build strong, independent city-states. Although they competed for trade, relations between the city-states were generally peaceful. A Muslim visitor described Kilwa, the most successful city-state, as "one of the most beautiful and well-constructed towns in the world." Its royal palace still stands on cliffs that today overlook the ocean. The complex consists of courtyards, terraces, and nearly 100 rooms. Built of coral and cut stone, the structure is evidence of the old city's splendor.

Trade Influences Swahili The successful East African international trade system led to the emergence of a vibrant culture and language known as **Swahili.** By the 1000s, many East African coastal cities had not only grown in wealth but also in size. Traders from the Middle East and Asia began to settle permanently in flourishing trading cities such as Kilwa.

As more settlers arrived, the local East African culture absorbed cultural elements from these new residents. For example, the architecture of private houses and palaces illustrated a blend of East African and Arabic designs that created unique and elegant Swahili buildings and furniture. Over time, many Arabic words were absorbed into the local Bantu-based language. In fact, the term *swahili* comes from an Arabic word meaning "of the coast." The language itself was eventually written in Arabic script.

The Travels of Ibn Battuta The journey of Ibn Battuta tells us much about travel and trade in East Africa, the Indian Ocean, and beyond. Battuta was born in Tangier to a Berber family of the Muslim faith. After completing his education at the age of 21, Battuta made the hajj, or the pilgrimage to Mecca that Muslims are expected to make if they are able. His trek became one of the greatest journeys of medieval times. The 30-year sojourn took Battuta to Southwest Asia, West Africa, Southern Russia, India, and China. Along the way, he gained fame and wealth and met kings, sheiks, and holy men. He wrote a book called the *Rihlah*, or *Travels*, in which the following passage describes the unique trading tradition of Mogadishu.

>> **Determine Point of View** Beta Ghiorgis, which means House of George, is one of King's Lalibela's solid rock churches. Why would King Lalibela build a church in the shape of a cross?

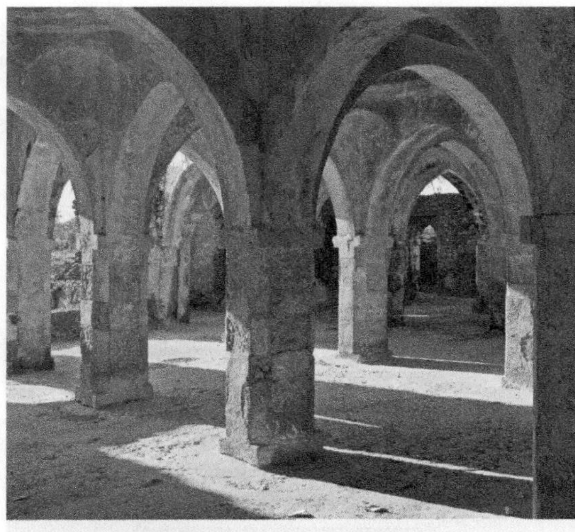

>> Trade brought great wealth and different cultural influences to the region. The Great Mosque in Kilwa reflects the prosperity and the spread of Islam that trade brought to the area.

Interactive Gallery

Compare and Contrast Compare the travels of Ibn Battuta with the travels of Mansa Musa from the previous lesson. Are there any similarities? Are there any differences? *(Sample response: Similarities: Both men were Muslim. Both showed their devotion to Islam by making a pilgrimage to Mecca. Differences: Mansa Musa traveled mostly in North Africa and Saudi Arabia; Battuta traveled not only across Saudi Arabia, but throughout Asia and East Africa. Mansa Musa traveled with a great caravan that showed Mali's wealth.)*

Guided Reading and Discussion

Describe Describe the impact Islam had on the city-states of East Africa. *(Sample response: Arab and Persian traders descended on the East African city-states and set up Muslim communities in those areas. Local culture, such as language and architecture, also reflects Arabic influence.)*

Answers

Determine Point of View *The cross is a symbol of Christianity, which the people of medieval Ethiopia identified with strongly.*

Great Zimbabwe

Online Project the **Interactive Gallery: Architecture of the African Kingdoms** and click through the images. Tell students that the various architectural forms in Africa differed greatly from society to society and from geographic region to geographic region. In some places, architecture reflected a community's culture or wealth, while in other cases, it showcased the influence of religion.

Analyze Images Study the photo of the Gede ruins and the image of Ethiopia's sculpted churches of Lalibela. How did religion influence the design of these buildings? *(Sample responses: In Gede, the ancient mosques underscored the importance of Islam in that prosperous Swahili community, while Ethiopia's sculpted churches reflected Christianity's influence on that kingdom.)*

ACTIVE CLASSROOM

Using the See-Think-Wonder strategy, pair students and ask them to review each image in the photo gallery. Ask them: What do you see? What does that make you think? What are you wondering about now that you've seen this? Have students share their insights with the class.

Guided Reading and Discussion

Ask students to analyze how people lived, worked, and played in Great Zimbabwe by doing additional research on the kingdom. Have students print out pictures of any relics that they might have found that underscore the importance of Great Zimbabwe as a trading center.

. . . we sailed for fifteen days and came to Maqdashaw [Mogadishu], which is an enormous town. Its inhabitants are merchants . . . When a vessel reaches the port, it is met by *sumbuqs*, which are small boats, in each of which are a number of young men, carrying a covered dish containing food. He presents this to one of the merchants on the ship saying "This is my guest" . . . Each merchant on disembarking goes only to the house of the young man who is his host . . . the host then sells his goods for him and buys for him, and if anyone buys anything from him at too low a price, or sells to him in the absence of his host, the sale is regarded by them as invalid.

—Ibn Battuta, the *Rihlah*

IDENTIFY CENTRAL IDEAS What was the impact of trade on the city-states of East Africa?

Great Zimbabwe

To the south and inland from the coastal city-states, massive stone ruins sprawl across rocky hilltops near the great bend in the Limpopo River. The looming walls, large palace, and cone-shaped towers were once part of the powerful and prosperous capital of a great inland empire. Today, these impressive ruins are known as **Great Zimbabwe.**

An Inland Trading Center The word *zimbabwe* comes from a Bantu-based word that means "stone houses." In fact, Great Zimbabwe was built by a succession of Bantu-speaking peoples who settled in the region between 900 and 1500. These newcomers brought iron, mining methods, and improved farming skills. Early settlers raised cattle and built stone enclosures to protect their livestock. In time, these settlers improved

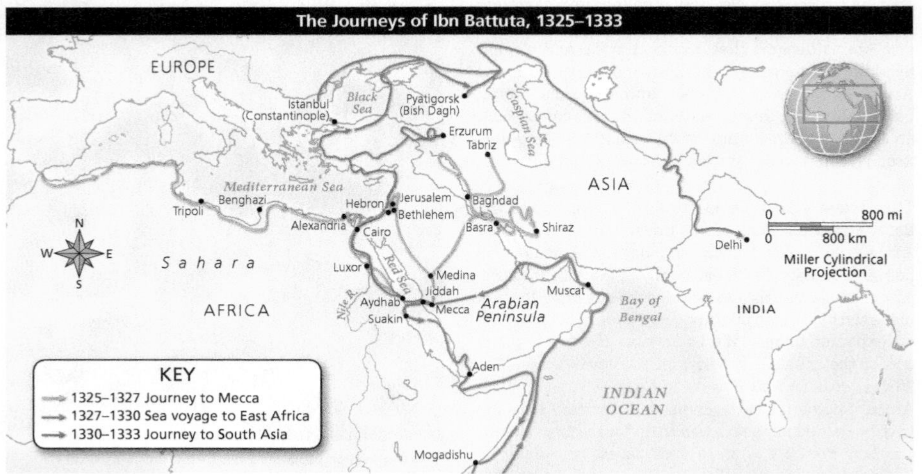

>> **Analyze Maps** In 1325, a Moroccan named Ibn Battuta began one of the greatest trips of medieval times, visiting Asia, parts of Europe, and the Middle East. In which general direction did Ibn Battuta travel from the Caspian Sea to Delhi?

Interactive Map

Answers

Identify Central Ideas *Trade was responsible for bringing different cultures to the cities, which led to the spread of Islam. Trade also helped change the region's architecture and assisted in the development of the Swahili language.*

Analyze Maps *southeast*

Explain *The size of the ruins, coupled with evidence of skilled artisans and the presence of trade goods from India and China, all reflect the capital's former prosperity.*

D Differentiate Challenge Ask students to create and perform a fictional reader's theater based on the society of Great Zimbabwe. The parts for the reader's theater can include a narrator, a king, a Muslim merchant, a trader from China, a skilled artisan, and a member of Zimbabwe's community. The play should revolve around Great Zimbabwe as a hub of trade in East Africa.

their building methods and erected large walls and palaces.

The capital probably reached its height about 1300. By then, it had tapped nearby gold resources and created profitable commercial links with coastal cities such as Sofala. Archaeologists have found beads from India and porcelain from China, showing that Great Zimbabwe was part of a trade network that reached across the Indian Ocean. In addition, they have found artifacts that indicate that Great Zimbabwe had artisans skilled in making jewelry and weaving cotton cloth.

Very little is known about the government in Great Zimbabwe. However, after studying the architecture and artifacts of the ruins, some scholars have suggested that the ruler was a god-king who presided over a large court. Below the king, a central bureaucracy may have ruled an inner ring of provinces, while appointed governors had authority in more distant villages. Although there is much about Great Zimbabwe that remains unknown, as archaeologists continue their research, we are learning more about how the capital and empire developed.

Zimbabwe Declines By 1500, Zimbabwe was in decline. Some scholars suggest that the population had grown too great. Civil war and dwindling trade probably contributed as well.

By then, Portuguese traders were pushing inland to find the region's source of gold. They failed to discover the gold mines, but their attempts further weakened the small states that formed in the region as Zimbabwe declined. Some scholars believe that the environment also played a role in Great Zimbabwe's decline. Overgrazing and drought on the Zimbabwe Plateau, coupled with a decline in land productivity, may have eventually led to famine.

 **EXPLAIN** Explain how the ruins of Great Zimbabwe reflected the capital's wealth.

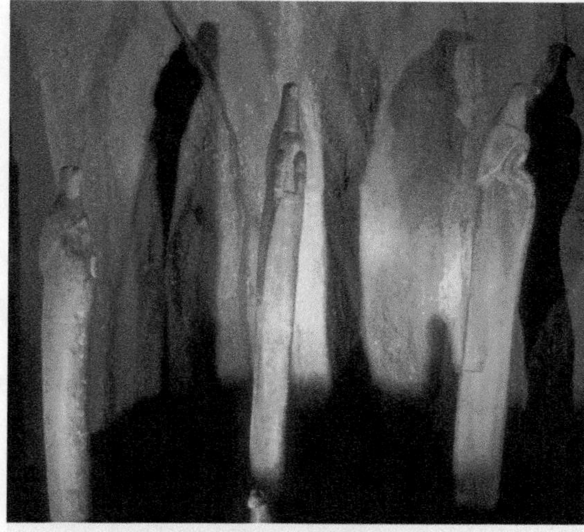

>> These figurines were crafted by artisans of Great Zimbabwe and show the wealth of detail in that advanced society.

ASSESSMENT

1. **Synthesize** How did geography and religion influence Ethiopia's development?
2. **Infer** How did the Swahili language affect trade in the East African city-states?
3. **Test Conclusions** What does archeological evidence suggest about Great Zimbabwe's economy?
4. **Identify Central Ideas** How did religion and trade affect the development of East Africa?
5. **Identify Cause and Effect** What role did religion play in the rise and decline of Axum?

Topic 8 Lesson 7

SYNTHESIZE

Ask students to recall the Topic Essential Question: How are religion and culture connected? Ask students to create a Concept Web to show the relationship.

Online Project the **Digital Activity: Kingdoms and Trading States of East Africa**. Explain to students that trade was essential to the development of many East African societies, including Axum, Ethiopia, the Coastal City-States, and Great Zimbabwe. As you discuss the causes and effects with students, have them fill in the chart.

DEMONSTRATE

Online Assign the **Digital Lesson Quiz** for this lesson if you haven't already done so. Students will be offered automatic remediation or enrichment based on their score.

Pose the following questions to students:

Predict Consequences Do you think Ethiopia would have developed differently had the nation embraced Islam as opposed to Christianity? *(Students might say that if Ethiopia had embraced Islam, it would not have found itself isolated from its one-time trading partners.)*

Compare and Contrast Describe any similarities between the trade routes in East Africa and the trade routes in West Africa. *(Sample response: Each region had trade routes that linked Africa to the Mediterranean world; both traded in gold.)*

Topic Inquiry

Have students continue their investigations for the Topic Inquiry.

Assessment

1. Ethiopia was physically isolated from other areas by surrounding mountains, which helped it maintain independence. It also developed a strong unifying culture based on the Christian faith.
2. Since Swahili has both Arabic and Bantu elements, it made trading easier between both groups in the cities of East Africa.
3. Artifacts, such as beads from India and porcelain from China, have been found among the ruins of Great Zimbabwe, as well as artifacts created by skilled artisans. These artifacts indicate that Great Zimbabwe was a part of a large trade network.
4. Trade brought wealth and the Christian religion to Axum. East Africa's trading cities also had a rich mix of people from many cultures. Each prospered through trade. As a result, East Africa became a mixed culture representing the influences of many societies.
5. As Christianity took hold among the people, it became a unifying influence and strengthened ties with Axum's trading partners. After Islam became the dominant religion in the region, the Christian kingdom of Axum became isolated from its trade network, leading to economic decline.

Diverse Peoples and Traditions in Africa

CONNECT

Preview Have students preview the **Lesson Objectives** and the list of **Key Terms**.

Students can also preview all the **Key Terms** and **Academic Vocabulary** using the **Interactive Reading Notepad** on the digital course or preview a summary of the lesson in the **Reading and Note Taking Study Guide**.

Online Use the **Editable Presentation** found on the digital course to present the main ideas for this lesson.

Start Up Activity

Read aloud the following description:

> In West Africa, the dama is an ancient celebration that usually lasts for three days. During that time, dozens of dancers don flowing costumes and masks, the most important of which is the sirige. Carved from a single tree, the sirige links the Dogon people with their ancestors. Among other things, the Dogon believed that their deceased ancestors watched over and protected their villages. The dama is a way for the Dogon to ask the spirits of their ancestors to create peace and harmony within the village.

Discuss What does the dama tell you about the Dogon's relationship with their ancestors in some parts of West Africa? *(Sample response: The Dogon valued family relationships, and rituals were important connections to the past.)*

Online You can also project the **Start Up Activity** from the course.

Tell students that they will learn about family patterns and different forms of government in medieval African cultures, and how religion and art impacted African society.

INVESTIGATE

Have students read the section using the **Reading and Note Taking Study Guide** to help them take notes and understand the text as they read.

Many Cultures and Patterns of Life

Tell students that there were several types of family relationships in African society. Explain that in some communities, the nuclear family was the main family unit, while in others, extended families dominated society.

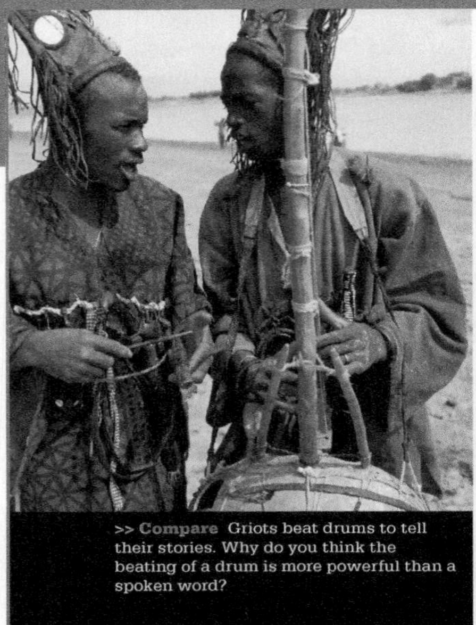

>> Compare Griots beat drums to tell their stories. Why do you think the beating of a drum is more powerful than a spoken word?

Interactive Flipped Video

8.8 Across the immense African continent, a variety of cultures emerged, ranging from wealthy trading kingdoms to nomadic herding societies to small farming communities. As people adapted to different environments and landscapes, their ways of life differed. Across Africa, communities varied in size, economic activity, family patterns, and forms of government. Still, they all had these features as well as their own religious beliefs, art, and technology.

TEKS 24.A, 26.B

>> Objectives

Identify the different ways that the family influenced medieval African cultures.

Describe the variety of forms of medieval African governments.

Understand the role of religion and art in medieval societies.

>> Key Terms

nuclear family
patrilineal
matrilineal
lineage
consensus
griot

Diverse Peoples and Traditions in Africa

Many Cultures and Patterns of Life

Early Communities As you have read, the worldwide Neolithic Revolution led to the beginning of settled farming communities located in areas with fertile soil and proximity to water. These farming settlements grew as surpluses increased, enabling artisans to develop specialized skills.

Advancements in transportation, such as the use of the camel, increased a community's reach beyond its borders, and this exchange allowed villages to grow into towns. Extended trade brought additional wealth, leading to the creation of individual states and kingdoms. Throughout Africa, communities varied in size, environment, and economics. However, each society developed around four common elements—family, government, religion, and art.

Family Patterns Across Africa, as elsewhere around the globe, the family was the basic unit of society. Patterns of family life varied greatly. In some small societies, the basic family unit was the **nuclear family,** or parents and children living and working together as a

 www.PearsonTexas.com Access your Digital Lesson.

322

Aa Vocabulary Builder

1. Have students pronounce the following academic vocabulary term in this lesson and clarify the part of speech.
2. Explain what the word means in common "student-friendly" language using synonyms and antonyms when possible. Provide concrete examples to clarify the meaning, and rephrase the definition.

complex: made up of different parts connected in a way that is hard to understand unit. In other communities, family units included the extended family—parents, children, and several generations such as grandparents and uncles—who lived and worked together to ensure the success of the family group.

Women were valued as wives and mothers. Women contributed to the economy in settled farming societies, where they worked the fields.

Even in herding societies, women raised food in small gardens while men and boys tended the herds. Often, women were respected for their wisdom and skills in many areas. In a few societies, women served a soldiers, and, as you will read, served as rulers or in other government jobs.

Children were highly valued for the work they performed within the family and community and, most importantly, for the link they served between the past and future. Parents depended on children to care for them in old age and educated their children in the customs, skills, and ways of their society.

Kinship Ties Family organization varied in many ways across Africa. Some families were **patrilineal.** In these families, important kinship ties such as inheritance were passed through the father's side. Other families were **matrilineal,** with inheritance traced through the mother's side. In a patrilineal culture, a bride would move to her husband's village and become part of his family. In matrilineal culture, the husband joined his wife's family in her village.

Matrilineal cultures forged strong ties between brothers and sisters. Brothers were expected to protect their sisters, and sons were expected to help their mother's brothers whenever needed.

Wider Ties Each family belonged to a **lineage,** or group of households who claimed a common ancestor. Several lineages formed a clan that traced its descent to an even more remote and often legendary ancestor. Belonging to a particular family, lineage, or clan gave people a sense of community with shared responsibilities to that community.

An individual's place in some African societies was also determined by a system of age grades. An age grade included all girls or boys born in the same year. Each age grade had particular responsibilities and privileges. As they moved up from one age grade to another, children began to take part in village activities, which created social ties beyond the family.

 **IDENTIFY CENTRAL IDEAS** How did a person's kinship affect his or her place in society?

>> This ornately crafted bronze wine bowl was made in eastern Nigeria around the 800s.

Interactive Gallery

>> In many African societies, older people were revered and looked upon as sources of wisdom. Today, family ties are often still an important part of modern African life.

Interactive Chart

Online Project the **Interactive Chart: Family Patterns in African Society** to show the variety of family patterns in different communities.

ACTIVE CLASSROOM

Using the Graffiti Concept strategy, have students reflect on each of the family relationships in African society. Next, have students create a visual image that represents each concept. Allow 3 to 5 minutes. When time is up, ask students to post their "graffiti" on the board. Have the class look at the various responses, and discuss any similarities or differences between each family relationship.

Guided Reading and Discussion

Identify Ask students to describe the roles of children in some medieval African cultures. *(Sample response: In some cultures, an individual's place was determined by a system of age grades that included all the children born in a particular year. Those age grades determined a child's responsibilities in that society.)*

Key Terms

Ask students to find the key terms **patrilineal, matrilineal,** and **lineage** (in bold) in the text. Ask students what word root is found in all three terms. *(line)* How is that word related to each term? *(All three terms describe the bloodlines that connect people to others in their families.)*

D Differentiate Challenge After working with the Interactive Chart, have students learn about their own families by creating a timeline of their family's history. Have students interview family members and record such things as marriages, immigration dates, births, deaths, and divorces.

Answers

Compare *Sample answer: A beating drum appeals to a human's visceral sense of rhythm.*

Identify Central Ideas *Kinship defined inheritance, where one lived, and what a person's responsibilities to his or her family and society were.*

Government and Power

Remind students that in larger kingdoms, villages had to obey decisions and pay taxes and provide soldiers to a centralized, and often distant, court. In some kingdoms, a monarch's power was somewhat limited. Unlike larger African kingdoms, the governments of smaller medieval African societies were often organized through power-sharing arrangements rather than centralized in the hands of a single leader. While in some societies a chief had a good deal of authority, most decisions were made collectively. Explain that consensus was a common method of decision making, with the wisdom of older men and women carrying the most weight in many village decisions.

Guided Reading and Discussion

Summarize How does a power-sharing government in Africa work? *(Answers may vary. Students should have an understanding that in a power-sharing system, members of a village would make decisions based on consensus.)*

Draw Inferences Why might the opinions of older individuals carry more weight than the opinions of younger people? *(Answers may vary. Some students may say that the experience and wisdom of older people carried the greatest weight.)*

Compare and Contrast What differences existed between the form of government found in an African kingdom and the form of government found in a smaller village? *(Answers may vary. Students should have an understanding that in a kingdom, taxes were collected through local governors, and the king had to rule according to traditional laws. The governments of smaller villages were led generally by a chief with limited power, and the main decision-making body was often a group of village elders.)*

Answers

Explain *In these societies, power was usually shared by several people. Often groups of elders made decisions by consensus.*

Government and Power

Farming peoples generally lived in tight-knit communities and helped one another in tasks such as clearing the land, planting, and harvesting. Both men and women planted, but usually were responsible for different crops. Political patterns varied, depending in part on the size of the community that the land could support.

Shared Power In farming societies, power was usually shared among a number of people rather than centralized in the hands of a single leader. In some villages, a chief had a good deal of authority, but in many others, elders made the major decisions. Sometimes, older men supervised religious ceremonies linked to the government, while younger men made decisions about war. In some places, especially in parts of West Africa, women took the dominant role in the marketplace or acted as official peacemakers in the village.

Villages often made decisions by a process known as **consensus,** or general agreement. In open discussions, people whose opinions were valued voiced their views before a final agreement was reached. Because of the experience and wisdom of older men and women, their opinions usually carried the greatest weight.

>> King Alvaro II, ruler of Kongo, made alliances and trade agreements with Europeans, such as the Dutch depicted in this illustration.

In villages that were part of a large kingdom such as Songhai, decisions made at a distant court had to be obeyed. These villagers, therefore, had to pay taxes and provide soldiers to the central, and frequently distant, government.

Kingdom of Kongo Many different forms of government developed in Africa. An example of one kind of government organization was the kingdom of Kongo. It flourished about A.D. 1500 in the forest zone of west-central Africa. The kingdom consisted of many villages grouped into districts and provinces and governed by officials appointed by the king. Each village had its own chief, a man chosen on the basis of the descent of his mother's family.

In theory, the king of Kongo had absolute power. In fact, that power was limited. The king was chosen by a board of electors and had to govern according to traditional laws. Unlike rulers of West Africa states, who maintained strong standing armies, kings of Kongo depended on a system of military service that called upon men to fight only in times of need. The king ruled through local governors who collected taxes either in goods or in cowrie shells, a common currency in Africa.

The organization of Kongo was just one type of African government. In many regions, people belonged to small local societies without a centralized government.

EXPLAIN How did power-sharing work in small African societies?

Religion

Across Africa, religious beliefs and practices were varied and complex. As elsewhere, religion helped to unite a society. Through religion, people learned about their origins. Oral traditions and myths taught important moral truths about right and wrong. Dancing, singing, and playing musical instruments were part of religious celebrations.

Like ancient Greeks and Romans, village Africans worshiped many gods and goddesses. Along with all ancient peoples, they identified the forces of nature with divine spirits and tried to influence those forces through rituals and ceremonies.

Traditional Beliefs Many African peoples believed that a single, unknowable supreme being stood above all the other gods and goddesses. This supreme being was the creator and ruler of the universe and was helped by the lesser gods and spirits, who were closer to the people.

Some African peoples believed, like the Chinese, that the spirits of their ancestors could help, warn, or punish their descendants on Earth. To honor and please their ancestors, they said prayers or performed rituals.

Like the followers of traditional religions in other parts of the world, many African peoples believed that every object on Earth is filled with a living spirit. They respected nature because they believed that the supreme being had created all things.

In some African societies, diviners and healers held places of honor. These men and women were well educated in the traditions of their societies. Diviners served as interpreters between people and the divine world. They might explain the cause of misfortune such as illness. The healer might then help a person find a solution to a problem. Diviners and healers also had knowledge of herbal medicines.

Christianity and Islam Spread By A.D. 1000, both Christianity and Islam had spread into Africa. African converts often associated the God of Christians and Muslims with their traditional supreme being. In this way, Christianity and Islam absorbed many local African practices and beliefs.

Over time, Islam played a dominant role in commerce, education, and government in large parts of Africa. Jewish communities had existed in North Africa since ancient times. Later, many Jews moved to North Africa after they were expelled from Spain in 1492. As you have read, a community of Ethiopian Jews lasted for centuries, while Ethiopian Christian communities also survived for more than 1,500 years. In areas where Islam was dominant, Christians and Jews continued to practice their faiths as protected "people of the Book." Christians and Jews developed their own institutions within the context of the Islamic community, in some cases acting as advisors in the courts of the early caliphs.

DESCRIBE Describe the various religious belief systems in medieval Africa.

Art and Literature

African artistic traditions extend far back in time to the ancient rock paintings of the Sahara, which were created by about 1000 B.C., and the over-4,000-year-old pyramids of Egypt and Nubia. More recently, but still about 1,000 years ago, the rock churches of Ethiopia and the palace of Great Zimbabwe were built. These accomplishments bear lasting witness to the creative power of these early and medieval civilizations.

>> Jews in many communities in Africa lived side by side with Muslims and Christians and worshiped in temples such as this one in Egypt.

Visual Arts African artists worked in many materials, including gold, ivory, wood, bronze, and cloth. They created many decorative items such as woven cloth, inscribed jugs and bowls, or jewelry simply for their beauty. Even so, art usually served social and religious purposes as well.

Art strengthened bonds within the community and linked the makers and the users of the work. Patterns used to decorate textiles, baskets, swords, and other objects had important meanings or special messages that the artisan or owner wanted to convey. Often, they identified an object as the work of a particular clan or the possession of royalty. One example is kente cloth, a traditional West African textile woven of silk and cotton. When it was made in bright gold and blue colors, the symbols of power, only the ruling elite and the wealthy were allowed to wear it.

In Africa, as elsewhere, much art was closely tied to religion. Statues and other objects were used in religious rites and ceremonies. In some rituals, for example, leaders wore elaborately carved masks decorated with cowrie shells or grass. Once the mask was in place, both the wearer and the viewers could feel the presence of the spiritual force it represented.

Religion

Art and Literature

Online Project the **Interactive Gallery: African Art and Culture**. Tell students that art's important role in the culture of many communities can be seen in African jewelry, dance, music, and literature. Click through the images in the gallery. Then explain to students that religion and art were important to the development of medieval African societies. Tell students that the religious beliefs that existed before the arrival of Islam and Christianity were often complex and varied. Some Africans worshiped multiple gods and goddesses; others believed, as Muslims and Christians did, in one supreme being. In other African cultures, ancestor worship dominated.

ACTIVE CLASSROOM

After reviewing all the images in the Interactive Gallery, use the Act it Out strategy to make the images come to life. Have students choose one of the images and create a story around that image.

Describe Ask students to explain how literature, art, and religion influenced medieval African society. *(Students should have an understanding that literature, religion, and art encouraged a sense of community and common values.)*

Guided Reading and Discussion

Draw Inferences Why do you suppose many African societies believed that their deceased ancestors could impact the lives of those living on Earth? *(Family relationships were very important to many Africans, and as a result, deceased family members could positively influence their lives.)*

Determine Central Ideas Why were Christianity and Islam able to absorb some of the beliefs of many African religions? *(Those who adopted these religions often associated the God of Christians and Muslims with their traditional supreme being.)*

D Differentiate Challenge Have students connect to the past by creating their own oral histories. Encourage students to record interviews with older family members about a specific event in their lives, such as living through a war or some other event. Students can also interview family members about family history. When the assignment is completed, call on students to talk about what they learned about their family's history.

Answers

Describe *Some Africans believed in many gods, while others believed that a single, supreme being stood above all other gods. Those who adopted Christianity or Islam often linked them with traditional practices.*

Topic 8 Lesson 8

SYNTHESIZE

Online Project the **Digital Activity: African Society**. Review how to create a concept web. Students can complete the activity independently, in pairs, or in groups.

Ask students to list the different ways families, government, and religion were connected to African society. Next, have them rank which concept they believe was the most important. Have them explain their reasons for the ranking. *(Students' answers should reflect an understanding of the various family, religious, and governmental relationships discussed in the lesson.)*

DEMONSTRATE

Online Assign the **Digital Lesson Quiz** for this lesson if you haven't already done so. Students will be offered automatic remediation or enrichment based on their score.

Evaluate How did kinship ties influence daily life in medieval Africa? *(Sample response: Kinship ties were an important factor in determining the people an individual identified with, lived with, worked with, and supported and could expect support from.)*

Summarize How can artistic traditions identify a community and its environment? *(Sample response: Art was created using locally available materials, and often illustrated the community's beliefs.)*

Topic Inquiry

Have students continue their investigations for the Topic Inquiry.

Answers

Identify Central Ideas *Literature related the history of the people and provided moral guidance.*

Literature Early African societies preserved their histories and values through both written and oral literature. Ancient Egypt, Nubia, and Axum left written records of their past. Later, Arabic provided a common written language in those parts of Africa influenced by Islam. African Muslim scholars gathered in cities such as Timbuktu and Kilwa. Documents in Arabic offer invaluable evidence about the law, religion, and history of the time.

Oral traditions date back many centuries. In West Africa, **griots** (GREE ohz), or professional storytellers, recited ancient stories. Griots preserved both histories and traditional folk tales in the same way that the epics of Homer or Aryan India were passed orally from generation to generation. The histories praised the heroic deeds of famous ancestors or rulers. Griots often used riddles to sharpen the wits of audiences.

Oral traditions also passed down folk tales, which blended fanciful stories with humor and sophisticated word play. Such stories often taught important moral lessons. Oral literature, like religion and art, thus encouraged a sense of community and common values in the diverse societies across the African continent.

? IDENTIFY CENTRAL IDEAS How did literature help to reinforce social ties?

ASSESSMENT

1. **Identify Cause and Effect** How did an individual's family ties affect life in medieval African societies?
2. **Determine Relevance** What was the importance of art in medieval African cultures?
3. **Identify Central Ideas** What role did religion play in medieval Africa communities?
4. **Summarize** What were the forms of government in medieval Africa?
5. **Interpret** Why might it be beneficial for an African village to have more than one person sharing a leadership role?

Assessment

1. Belonging to a particular family, lineage, or clan gave people a sense of community, a sense of responsibility, and the ability to create social ties beyond the family.
2. As well as being decorative, art served a social purpose, linking the makers and users of the work. In addition, statues and other objects were used in religious rites and ceremonies.
3. Strong religious beliefs helped bind the members of society together and inspire a sense of unity.
4. In smaller societies, power was often shared and decisions were made by consensus. Some villages gave greater power to a chief, while others left decisions to the elders. In larger societies, kingdoms grouped villages into districts and provinces governed by officials appointed by the king.
5. A village that had multiple leaders had people with different experiences and talents that could increase their chance of solving problems.

TEKS ASSESSMENT

Topic 8

1. **Analyze the Influence** Analyze the influence of human geographic factors on major events in world history, including trade in the Indian Ocean. Write a paragraph analyzing the influence of human geographic factors during trade with East Africa as described by Ibn Battuta in his travels. What part did Islam play in Battuta's travels? According to the map, what was the scope of his journeys? What does the excerpt from his book state about the importance of human relationships and integrity in trade? **16.B**

"...we sailed for fifteen days and came to Maqdashaw [Mogadishu], which is an enormous town. Its inhabitants are merchants... When a vessel reaches the port, it is met by sumbuqs, which are small boats, in each of which are a number of young men, carrying a covered dish containing food. He presents this to one of the merchants on the ship saying "This is my guest" ... Each merchant on disembarking goes only to the house of the young man who is his host...the host then sells his goods for him and buys for him, and if anyone buys anything from him at too low a price, or sells to him in the absence of his host, the sale is regarded by them as invalid."

—Ibn Battuta, *the Rihlah*

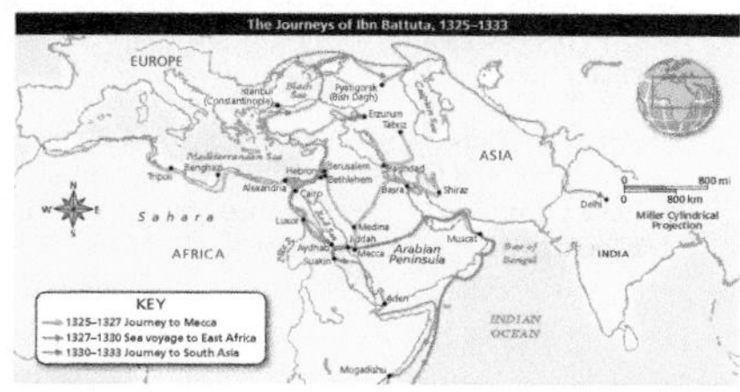

2. **Describe the Major Effects and Summarize Changes** Describe the major effects of the following important turning points in world history from 600 to 1450: the Mongol invasions of Europe and southwest Asia; also, summarize the changes resulting from the Mongol invasions of the Islamic world. Write a paragraph describing the effects of the Mongol invasions from the 1200s to the 1400s in Europe and southwest Asia, including changes to the Islamic world. Consider the impact of the destruction of Baghdad and the conversion of Mongol rulers to Islam. **1.C, 4.K**

3. **Describe the Spread** Describe the spread of major religious and philosophical traditions, including Islam and the development of monotheism. Write a paragraph describing the spread of Islam. Include information on the origin of Islam in the early A.D. 600s, monotheism, Islam in Medina, and the growth of the Muslim empire. **23.A**

4. **Explain Influences** Explain how Islam influences law and government in the Muslim world. Write a paragraph explaining how the Sharia influences Islamic law and government. Consider Islam's dual role and the influence of the Sharia. Can laws that apply religious principles to criminal and civil law be subject to interpretation? **25.D**

5. **Identify Major Causes and Effects** Identify major causes and effects of the following turning points in world history from 600 to 1450: the impact of medieval Islamic caliphates on Europe. Write a paragraph identifying major causes and effects of the impact of the Umayyad caliphate on Europe. Consider the Arab empire's expansion into Europe, how a unified Islamic state came to be, characteristics of rule in Spain, and significance of the battle of Tours. **1.C**

6. **Describe the Spread and Explain the Impact** Describe the spread of major religious and philosophical traditions and explain the political and social impact of Islam on Europe. Write a paragraph describing the spread of Islam in Spain by an Umayyad caliphate, and explain its political and social impact. What was the impact on the arts, learning, and architecture? What was the Muslim policy toward Jews and Christians? **4.D, 23.A**

7. **Explain the Impact** Explain the political, economic, and social impact of Islam on Asia. Write a paragraph explaining how Islam affected Muslim lives in southwest Asia. Consider the impact of the unification of the Byzantine and Persian empires. How did Islam spread, and what was the influence of the Sharia on business practices? **4.D**

8. **Identify Major Causes and Effects** Identify major causes and effects of the following turning points in world history from 600 to 1450: the impact of medieval caliphates on Africa. Write a paragraph identifying the impact of the Umayyad caliphate on Africa in the 700s. Consider their empire expansion into North Africa and how they spread Islam. What was the status of conquered people, and why did many people convert to Islam? **1.C**

Answers to TEKS Assessment

1. Student answers will vary but should include information on how human relationships established from trading were important in building strong city-states in the East African port cities. Battuta, a Muslim, made a pilgrimage to Mecca during a 30-year journey (southwest Asia, West Africa, southern Russia, India, and China) where he met all types of people and documented it in his book called *Rihlah*, or *Travels*.

2. Student answers will vary but should include information on how starting in 1216 through the 1300s, Genghis Khan and his successors led the Mongols from Central Asia to conquer Russia and other parts of present-day Eastern Europe and southwest Asia; the last Abbasid caliph was killed. Destroying Baghdad meant the end of Islamic cultural influence and loss of government power. However, Mongols adopted Islam and restored its influence.

3. Student answers will vary but should include information on how Islam began in the early A.D. 600s. When Muhammad fled to Medina, people there began converting to Islam and worshiping, according to Muslim belief, the one true God. Muhammad's army fought with Arab tribes and destroyed their idols. Thousands of Arabs adopted Islam as Muhammad created rules that governed Muslims and brought peace to the clans of Medina. Muhammad triumphantly returned to Mecca in 630 and destroyed the idols in the Kaaba, and continued to work to unite the Arabs under Islam. The spread of Islam continued after Muhammad's death in 632; today it is one of the major religions of the world.

4. Student answers will vary but should include information on how Islam is both a religion and way of life. The Sharia is a set of laws that is taken from the Quran, Muhammad's life, and Muslim traditions; it regulates moral conduct, family life, and business life, both in private and public lives. The Sharia is a common legal framework for both criminal and civil law.

5. Student answers will vary but should include information on the causes for Muslim expansion, which included weakened Byzantine and Persian empires, the bold fighting methods of the Muslim armies, and the fact that many people welcomed the Arabs as liberators. An Umayyad caliphate (of Sunnis) ruled in Europe by expanding into Spain beginning in 711; Muslims ruled parts of Spain for centuries, until 1492, in an age of arts and learning. In 731 Muslims moved into France but their defeat at the battle of Tours prevented them from expanding farther into Western Europe.

6. Student answers will vary but should include information on how a surviving member of the Umayyad family fled to Spain and set up an independent Muslim state. During that era, arts and learning thrived, Muslim rulers generally tolerated other religions, and Jewish officials and Christian scholars were accepted in the court. Architectural wonders, especially in Granada, showcased Muslim civilization until its decline in Spain in 1492.

7. Student answers will vary but should include information on how Islam's teachings affect the religious and nonreligious lives of Muslims. After Muhammad's death, Arabs (through the first four caliphs) unified politically and economically through conquest of the Byzantine and Persian empires in southwest Asia. During the conquests, the caliphates became wealthy; when conquests declined, economic tensions ensued. Through trade and cultural exchange, the caliphates spread Muslim civilization. The Sharia, a body of law that interprets the Quran, also regulated business practices and government.

Topic 8

Answers to TEKS Assessment

8. Student answers will vary but should include information on the Sunni Umayyad caliphate that ruled until 750 in North Africa (Syria, Morocco). The Umayyads had a significant impact on North Africa; they destroyed Carthage and built a new city called Kairouan. They built mosques throughout North Africa, where many people converted to Islam and adopted Arab customs. Many of the nomadic peoples in North Africa liked the fact that Islam emphasized the equality of all believers, with no religious hierarchy or class of priests. Non-Muslims were allowed to practice their own faiths but paid a special tax and had certain restrictions.

9. Student answers will vary but should include information on how trading centers developed in Africa as trade expanded due to a surplus of food or other products. Primary trading items were gold from West Africa (Ghana, Nigeria, and Senegal) and salt from the Sahara. Between 500 and 1600, much gold was exported annually from West Africa. Cities developed as farming and trade prospered. Traders spurred the spread of ideas and religion, such as Islam and the Arabic language, in their travels throughout Africa.

10. Student answers will vary but should include information on the belief of many Africans in a supreme being, which helped them to adopt the monotheism of Christianity and Islam. Although Islam became the dominant religion, traders especially interacted with Jews and Christians. Jews established colonies in North Africa, especially those who had migrated from Europe to Morocco and Libya. Christians and Jews developed their own institutions within the context of Islam. Christians often advised the courts of the early caliphs.

11. Student answers will vary but should include information on how African families were either nuclear or extended families; also they were patrilineal (familial ties passed on through father's side) or matrileaneal (familial ties passed on through mother's side). Families belonged to a lineage that claimed a common ancestor; several formed a clan that could trace its descent to remote or legendary ancestors. It was important that families support each other as families or within the communities.

12. Student answers will vary but should include information on how al-Khwarizmi, a great Muslim mathematician, pioneered the study of algebra in the 800s; his book became a standard math text in Europe. He also developed astronomical tables based on other discoveries. Other Muslim scholars studied mathematical works of ancient Greeks, particularly in geometry, and translated them to Arabic. Probably the Arabs learned about Hindu numerals from trading with India; these were translated to Arabic, and then these and other works of mathematics spread to Europe.

13. Student answers will vary but should include information on how Muslim advances in medicine included setting up hospitals and emergency rooms; pioneering studies of medical ideas; diagnosis and treatment; and new advances for treating eye diseases. Muhammad al-Razi wrote medical books that challenged traditional medicine. Ibn Sina wrote *Canon on Medicine*, an encyclopedia of diagnosis and treatment of disease. All these ideas spread to Europe: Surgeons used Muslim methods for eye surgery, physicians attended Muslim universities in Spain, and medical texts were translated into Latin and were the standard textbooks in Europe for 500 years.

14. Student answers will vary but should include information on how Arabs historically had oral poetry that spoke of journeys, battles, and the glories of their

TEKS ASSESSMENT

9. **Analyze How Trade Facilitated the Spread** Analyze how the African gold-salt trade facilitated the spread of ideas and trade. Write a paragraph analyzing how the development of trading centers in African gold-salt trade influenced the spread of ideas and trade. Consider the availability and trade of gold and salt products in different African regions, how traders spread ideas, and the start of cities. **4.J**

10. **Describe the Interactions** Describe the interactions among Muslim, Christian, and Jewish societies in North Africa. Write a paragraph describing how Christians and Jews interacted within the dominant Muslim society in North Africa. Consider African beliefs in a supreme being, spread of Christianity and Islam by A.D. 1000, Jewish colonies in North Africa, and roles of Christians in the courts of early caliphs. **4.E**

11. **Describe Changing Roles** Describe the changing roles of families during major eras of world history. Write a paragraph describing the changing roles of families from farming communities to more structured societies in medieval Africa. Include information on the basic societal unit, nuclear families, patrilineal or matrilineal families, and the importance of extended lineages. **24.A**

12. **Identify the Origin and Diffusion of Major ideas** Identify the origin and diffusion of major ideas in mathematics and science that occurred in the Islamic caliphates between 700 and 1200. Also, analyze information by making generalizations and predictions. Write a paragraph identifying important contributions in mathematics and astronomy that occurred in the Islamic caliphates. Consider advances in algebra, geometry, and astronomy, and scholarly works. Using the image above and information from the lessons, generalize and predict how Hindu numerals found their way to Arab scholars and then to Europe. **27.A, 29.F**

ORIGIN OF HINDU-ARABIC NUMERALS

Eastern Muslim Regions	Western Muslim Regions	Modern Western
١	1	1
٢	2	2
٣	3	3
۴	ع	4
۵	y	5
٦	6	6
٧	7	7
٨	8	8
٩	9	9
٠	0	0

13. **Identify the Origin and the Diffusion of Major ideas** Identify the origin and diffusion of major ideas in technology that occurred in the Islamic caliphates between 700 and 1200. Write a paragraph identifying the reputation and spread of Muslim ideas in medical technology that occurred in the Islamic caliphates. Consider advances in diagnosis and treatment and public health, Muslim medical books, and how and where advances in the medical field spread. **27.A**

14. **Analyze Examples** Analyze examples of how literature reflected the history of the cultures in which it was produced. Write a paragraph analyzing examples of how religion shaped the literature of Muslim civilization. Consider oral poetry by Arabs, poetry from Persia, and storytelling by Arabs, and include specific authors or literary examples. **26.B**

15. **Identify Major Causes** Identify major causes of the following important turning points in world history from 1450 to 1750: the rise of the Ottoman empire. Write a paragraph identifying major causes of the rise of the Ottoman empire. Include an explanation of the "age of gunpower empires" and how this affected the fall of Constantinople in 1453. **1.D**

16. **Explain the Impact** Explain the impact of the Ottoman empire on Eastern Europe, including global trade. Write a paragraph explaining how trade expansion led to the dominance of the Ottoman empire in the Middle East and parts of Eastern Europe. Consider the geography of the trade routes and trade expansion in the eastern Mediterranean. **7.D**

17. **Reflect on the Essential Question** **Write an essay on the Essential Question: How are religion and culture connected?** Use evidence from your study of this Topic to support your answer.

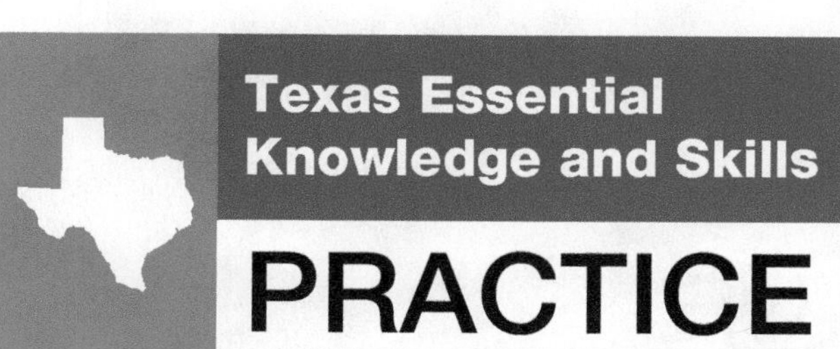

clan. Two famous Persian poets include Firdawsi (epic literature, *Book of Kings*, about the history of Persia) and Omar Khayyám (*The Rubáiyát*). Storytelling by Arabs was especially popular, with stories from various sources (Indian, Persian, Greek, and others). Examples include a collection of tales in *The Thousand and One Nights* which includes romance, adventures, and fables; "Aladdin and His Magic Lamp" is one story.

15. Student answers will vary but should include information on how the Ottomans had new military technology that reduced the number of mounted warriors, and included cannons and muskets. The Ottomans hauled ships overland to Constantinople's harbor and eventually used their cannons to blast through Constantinople's defensive walls, capturing the great city.

16. Student answers will vary but should include information on how the expansion of the Ottoman empire dominated the Middle East and parts of Eastern Europe. Ottomans controlled major trade routes between Europe, Africa, and Asia. They brought merchants into Istanbul, particularly European Jewish traders, and dominated trade in the eastern Mediterranean.

Topic 8

Answers to TEKS Practice

1. B
2. G

Online To prepare for the End-of-Topic test, have students go online for additional Topic Review and Assessment questions or to review their notes in the **Interactive Reading Notepad** for the lessons in this Topic.

Benchmark Tests

Assign these benchmark tests as you complete the relevant topics to monitor student progress toward mastering the course content and as preparation for the End-of-Course Test.

Benchmark Test 1: Topics 1–5

Benchmark Test 2: Topics 6–10

Benchmark Test 3: Topics 11–15

Benchmark Test 4: Topics 16–21

TEKS PRACTICE

1 How did the Abbasid caliphates differ from the Umayyads in their rule from 750 to the 1250s?

A They discriminated against local non-Arab Muslims and their laws.

B They focused on creating an empire rather than on military conquests.

C They urged Arabs to abandon Persian traditions.

D They adopted a simple lifestyle with a focus on religion.

2

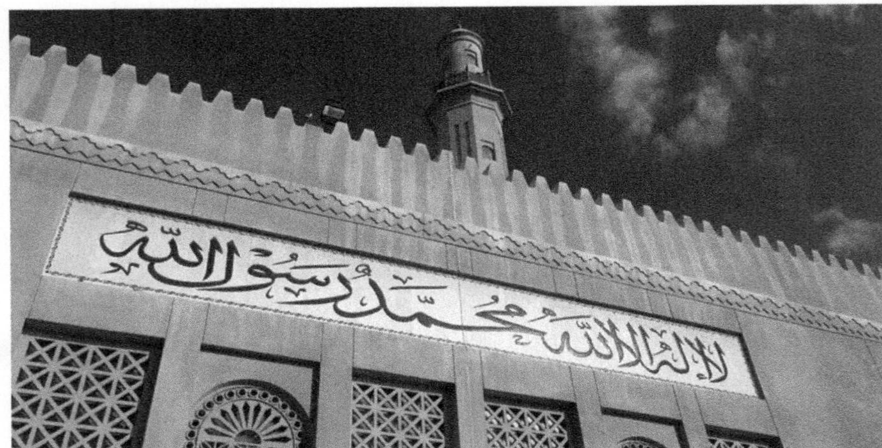

Look at the picture of a Muslim building. How did the architecture of early mosques reflect the history of the Islam culture?

F The fine writing in the exterior is a symbol of religious diversity.

G Simple buildings became social centers for Muslim worship.

H All mosques faced Mecca as Muslims must face it during prayer.

J Ornate mosque styles differed from plain Byzantine churches.

Test Taking Tips: Tip for Questions to Compare Viewpoints

1. Read the question.
2. Identify the authors of the passages you will compare. What do you know about the authors, or what information is provided about them? Note information about when and where the authors wrote or spoke if that is provided.
3. Read the passages carefully. Identify the main ideas and supporting details for each passage.
4. Read the question again. What does the question ask you to compare?
5. Identify the words or phrases in each passage that allow you to make the comparison the question requires. Answer the question in your own words.
6. Read the answer choices and select the best answer.

www.PearsonTexas.com
Access additional practice questions

3 Which of these was a key impact of the Ottoman empire on global trade?

A Its greatest contribution was increased activity along the Silk Road.
B Wars with Europeans resulted in new trade routes around Africa.
C It encouraged commerce rather than wars with European countries.
D It dominated trade in the eastern Mediterranean from Istanbul.

4 

Describe the political situation that led to the rise of feudalism.

F Strong monarchs depended on lords for local conquests.
G Weak monarchs could not maintain law and order.
H Economic instability forced monarchs to provide leadership.
J Fiefdoms provided protection from religious intolerance.

If you have trouble with...				
Question	1	2	3	4
See Lesson	8.2	8.3	8.4	7.2
TEKS	1.C	23.A, 26.B	7.D	4.C

3. D
4. G

Online Use the **Topic Synthesize** to help students revisit and reflect on the Essential Question for this Topic.

Topic Inquiry

If students have done a Topic Inquiry for this Topic, have them complete the final step of the Inquiry now.

Civilizations of Asia (500–1650)

TOPIC 9 ORGANIZER	PACING: APPROX. 1 PERIOD, .5 BLOCKS		
	PACING	TEKS	ELPS
Connect	1 period		
MY STORY VIDEO **Genghis Khan, Conqueror**	10 min.	1.C, 4.K	
DIGITAL ESSENTIAL QUESTION ACTIVITY **What Distinguishes One Culture From Another?**	10 min.	23.A, 25.A, 26.B, 27.A	
DIGITAL MAP ACTIVITY **Civilizations of Asia**	10 min.	1.B, 15.A, 15.B, 16.B, 16.C	
TOPIC INQUIRY: CIVIC DISCUSSION **Genghis Khan**	20 min.		
Investigate	3–6 periods		
TOPIC INQUIRY: CIVIC DISCUSSION **Genghis Khan**	Ongoing		
LESSON 1 **The Delhi Sultanate and Mughal India**	30–40 min.	1.C, 4.D, 4.F, 23.A, 25.A, 26.A, 26.B	3.C.4
LESSON 2 **Golden Ages in China: Tang and Song Dynasties**	30–40 min.	4.H, 4.J, 25.A, 26.B, 27.A	2.I.2, 3.D.1
LESSON 3 **The Mongol Empire and Ming China**	30–40 min.	1.C, 1.D, 4.K, 7.E, 25.A, 27.A	2.I.3, 3.D.2
LESSON 4 **Korea and Its Traditions**	30–40 min.	3.A, 4.H, 23.A, 25.A, 26.A, 27.A	2.I.4, 3.E.1
LESSON 5 **The Island Kingdom of Japan**	30–40 min.	4.H, 24.A, 25.A, 26.B	3.F.1, 2.I.5
LESSON 6 **The Many Cultures of Southeast Asia**	30–40 min.	16.B, 23.A	3.F.2
Synthesize	1 period		
DIGITAL ESSENTIAL QUESTION ACTIVITY **The Many Cultures of Southeast Asia**	10 min.	23.A, 25.A, 26.B, 27.A	
TOPIC INQUIRY: CIVIC DISCUSSION **Genghis Khan**	20 min.		
Demonstrate	1–2 periods		
DIGITAL TOPIC TEST **Civilizations of Asia**	10 min.		
TOPIC INQUIRY: CIVIC DISCUSSION **Genghis Khan**	20 min.		

AUTHOR'S NOTE

Japan and the Chinese Model

In the sixth century Chinese Buddhism reached Japan through Korea, bringing Chinese culture with it. In the seventh and eighth centuries, reforming Japanese regimes sent repeated embassies, including many students and monks, to Tang China to acquire the skills and learn the ways of the East Asian colossus. Powerful Japanese statesmen encouraged this procedure. The famous Prince Shotoku, in particular, preached centralized government and court hierarchy and even imported the Chinese calendar.

The resulting changes seemed likely to turn Japan into another small version of the Tang state. Japanese rulers and *uji* chiefs, some of whom were more powerful than their sovereign, nevertheless preached centralized rule by an absolute emperor and urged a Confucian sense of duty and Buddhist reverence. Centralized bureaus were established, a Chinese-style law code was promulgated, and attempts were made to establish the equal-field system and centralized taxation of Tang China. . . .

Beneath these transformations at the top of Nara society, however, Japan remained in many ways the Japan of old. The *uji* aristocracy preserved much of its former feudal independence despite the emperor's exalted claims. The economy remained comparatively simple; money, for example, was still rare, barter far more common. And the great Chinese invention of an educated civil service based on merit was never adopted at all beyond the Sea of Japan.

Then, as Tang China declined and crumbled into chaos in the ninth century, Japan turned away from its great model and began to develop its own distinct style of civilization. The Heian period (roughly 800–1200), when the Japanese capital was at Heian (present-day Kyoto), was the period when this return to older ways was strongest. In three dynamic centuries, Japan's ruling elite had absorbed all they could learn from China. The following four hundred years were given over to digesting and modifying these cultural acquisitions in terms of Japan's older narrative heritage.

—Anthony Esler, *The Human Venture: From Prehistory to the Present* (Upper Saddle River, New Jersey: Pearson Education, 2004), pp. 308–309

TOPIC INQUIRY: CIVIC DISCUSSION

Genghis Khan

TEKS 1.C, 4.K, 29.C, 39.D, 29.F, 29.G, 29.H, 30.A, 30.C

In this Topic Inquiry, students work in teams to examine different perspectives on this issue by analyzing several sources, arguing both sides of a Yes/No question, then developing and discussing their own point of view on the question: **Does Genghis Khan deserve to be known primarily for his cruelty and ruthlessness?**

STEP 1: CONNECT

Develop Questions and Plan the Investigation

Launch the Civic Discussion

Divide the class into groups of four students. Students can access the materials they'll need in the online course or you can distribute copies to each student. Read the main question and introduction with the students.

Have students complete Step 1 by reading the Discussion Launch and filling in Step 1 of the Information Organizer. The Discussion Launch provides YES and NO arguments on the main question. Students should extract and paraphrase the arguments from the reading in Step 1 of their Information Organizers.

Next, students share within their groups the arguments and evidence they found to support the YES and NO positions. The group needs to agree on the major YES and NO points and each student should note those points in their Information Organizer.

Resources

- Student Instructions
- Information Organizer
- Discussion Launch

PROFESSIONAL DEVELOPMENT

Civic Discussion

Be sure to view the Civic Discussion Professional Development resources in the online course.

STEP 2: INVESTIGATE

Apply Disciplinary Concepts and Tools

Examine Sources and Perspectives

Students will examine sources with the goal of extracting information and perspectives on the main question. They analyze each source and describe the author's perspective on the main question and key evidence the author provides to support that viewpoint in Information Organizer Step 2.

Ask students to keep in mind:

- **Author/Creator:** Who created the source? An individual? Group? Government agency?
- **Audience:** For whom was the source created?
- **Date/Place:** Is there any information that reveals where and when the source was created?
- **Purpose:** Why was the source created? Discuss with students the importance of this question in identifying bias.
- **Relevance:** How does the source support one argument or another?

Suggestion: Reading the source documents and filling in Step 2 of the Information Organizer could be assigned as homework.

Resources

- Student Instructions
- Information Organizer
- Source documents

STEP 3: SYNTHESIZE

Use Evidence to Formulate Conclusions

Formulate Compelling Arguments With Evidence

Now students will apply perspectives and evidence they extracted from the sources to think more deeply about the main question by first arguing one side of the issue, then the other. In this way students become more prepared to formulate an evidence-based conclusion on their own.

Within each student group, assign half of the students to take the position of YES on the main question and the others to take the position of NO. Students will work with their partners to identify the strongest arguments and evidence to support their assigned YES or NO position.

Present Yes/No Positions

Within each group, those assigned the YES position share arguments and evidence first. As the YES students speak, those assigned NO should listen carefully, take notes to fill in the rest of the Compelling Arguments Chart (Step 3 in Information Organizer), and ask clarifying questions.

When the YES side is finished, students assigned the NO position present while those assigned YES should listen, take notes, and ask clarifying questions. Examples of clarifying questions are:

- I think you just said [x]. Am I understanding you correctly?
- Can you tell me more about [x]?
- Can you repeat [x]? I am not sure I understand, yet.

Suggestion: You may want to set a 5-minute time limit for each side to present. Provide a two-minute warning so that students make their most compelling arguments within the time frame.

Switch Sides

The students will switch sides to argue the opposite point of view. To prepare to present the other position, partners who first argued YES will use the notes they took during the NO side's presentation, plus add any additional arguments and evidence from the reading and sources. The same goes for students who first argued the NO position.

STEP 4: DEMONSTRATE

Communicate Conclusions and Take Informed Action

Individual Points of View

Now the students will have the opportunity to discuss the main question from their own points of view. To help students prepare for this discussion, have them reflect on the YES/NO discussions they have participated in thus far and fill in Step 4 of their Information Organizers.

After all of the students have shared their points of view, each group should list points of agreement, filling in the last portion of Step 4 on their Information Organizers.

Reflect on the Discussion

Ask students to reflect on the civic discussion, thinking about:

- The value of having to argue both the YES and NO positions.
- If their individual views changed over the course of the discussion and why.
- What they learned from participating in the discussion.

Resources

- Student Instructions
- Information Organizer

The Delhi Sultanate and Mughal India

Objectives

Objective 1: Describe the effects of the Delhi sultanate on India.

Objective 2: Explain how Muslim and Hindu civilizations interacted in India.

Objective 3: Describe the historical origins and central ideas of Sikhism.

Objective 4: Summarize the policies of Akbar that strengthened Mughal India.

LESSON 1 ORGANIZER		PACING: APPROX. 1 PERIOD, .5 BLOCKS				
			RESOURCES			
	OBJECTIVES	PACING	Print	Online	TEKS	ELPS
Connect						
DIGITAL START UP ACTIVITY **Akbar the Great Speaks on Religion**		5 min.		●	4.F, 25.A	
Investigate						
READ **The Delhi Sultanate**	Objective 1	10 min.	●	●	1.C, 4.D, 23.A, 25.A	
INTERACTIVE MAP **The Delhi Sultanate and Mughal Empire**	Objective 1	10 min.		●	1.C, 4.D	
READ **The Meeting of Islam and Hinduism**	Objective 2	10 min.	●	●	4.D, 4.F, 23.A, 25.A	3.C.4
READ **Sikhism Emerges**	Objective 3	10 min.	●	●	23.A	
READ **Mughal India**	Objective 4	10 min.	●	●	1.C, 4.D, 4.F, 23.A, 25.A, 26.A, 26.B	
INTERACTIVE GALLERY **The Art of the Mughal Empire**	Objective 4	10 min.		●	26.A, 26.B	
Synthesize						
DIGITAL ACTIVITY **Cultures Meet in India**		5 min.		●	4.F, 25.A	
Demonstrate						
DIGITAL QUIZ **Lesson Quiz and Class Discussion Board**		10 min.		●	1.C, 4.D, 4.F, 23.A, 25.A	

PEARSON realize www.PearsonTexas.com Access your Digital Lesson

Focus on Texas Standards

Texas Essential Knowledge and Skills

1.C identify major causes and describe the major effects of the following important turning points in world history from 600 to 1450: the spread of Christianity, the decline of Rome and the formation of medieval Europe; the development of Islamic caliphates and their impact on Asia, Africa, and Europe; the Mongol invasions and their impact on Europe, China, India, and Southwest Asia

4.D explain the political, economic, and social impact of Islam on Europe, Asia, and Africa

4.F describe the interactions between Muslim and Hindu societies in South Asia

23.A describe the historical origins, central ideas, and spread of major religious and philosophical traditions, including Buddhism, Christianity, Confucianism, Hinduism, Islam, Judaism, Sikhism, and the development of monotheism

25.A summarize the fundamental ideas and institutions of Eastern civilizations that originated in China and India

26.A identify significant examples of art and architecture that demonstrate an artistic ideal or visual principle from selected cultures

26.B analyze examples of how art, architecture, literature, music, and drama reflect the history of the cultures in which they are produced

NOTES

Topic 9 Lesson 2

Golden Ages in China: Tang and Song Dynasties

Objectives

Objective 1: Summarize how the Tang dynasty reunified China.

Objective 2: Explain how the Song dynasty grew rich and powerful despite military setbacks.

Objective 3: Understand how China created an ordered society.

Objective 4: Describe the major cultural developments in the Tang and Song dynasties.

LESSON 2 ORGANIZER	PACING: APPROX. 1 PERIOD, .5 BLOCKS					
	OBJECTIVES	PACING	RESOURCES Print	RESOURCES Online	TEKS	ELPS
Connect						
DIGITAL START UP ACTIVITY **Fireworks and Gunpowder**		5 min.		●	4.J, 27.A	
Investigate						
READ **The Tang Dynasty Restores China to Glory**	Objective 1	10 min.	●	●	4.H, 25.A	
READ **The Song Dynasty**	Objective 2	10 min.	●	●	1.C, 4.H, 4.J, 27.A	2.I.2
INTERACTIVE GALLERY **Technology in the Tang and Song Dynasties**		10 min.		●	25.A, 27.A	
READ **An Ordered Society**	Objective 3	10 min.	●	●	4.H	
READ **The Rich Culture of Tang and Song China**	Objective 4	10 min.	●	●	4.H, 25.A, 26.B	3.D.1
INTERACTIVE GALLERY **Chinese House and Compound**		10 min.		●	26.B	
Synthesize						
DIGITAL ACTIVITY **Tang China**		5 min.		●	4.H	
Demonstrate						
DIGITAL QUIZ **Lesson Quiz and Class Discussion Board**		10 min.		●	1.C, 4.H, 4.J, 25.A, 26.B, 27.A	

Focus on Texas Standards

Texas Essential Knowledge and Skills

4.H summarize the major political, economic, and cultural developments in Tang and Song China and their impact on Eastern Asia

4.J analyze how the Silk Road and the African gold-salt trade facilitated the spread of ideas and trade

25.A summarize the fundamental ideas and institutions of Eastern civilizations that originated in China and India

26.B analyze examples of how art, architecture, literature, music, and drama reflect the history of the cultures in which they are produced

27.A identify the origin and diffusion of major ideas in mathematics, science, and technology that occurred in river valley civilizations, classical Greece and Rome, classical India, and the Islamic caliphates between 700 and 1200 and in China from the Tang to Ming dynasties

NOTES

The Mongol Empire and Ming China

Objectives

Objective 1: Summarize how Mongol armies built an empire.

Objective 2: Describe China under Mongol rule.

Objective 3: Understand how the Ming restored Chinese rule.

Objective 4: Explain why the Ming explored the seas for only a brief period.

LESSON 3 ORGANIZER	PACING: APPROX. 1 PERIOD, .5 BLOCKS					
			RESOURCES			
	OBJECTIVES	PACING	Print	Online	TEKS	ELPS
Connect						
DIGITAL START UP ACTIVITY **Warriors on Horseback**		5 min.		●	1.C	
Investigate						
READ **Mongols Build an Empire**	Objective 1	10 min.	●	●	1.C, 4.K	
INTERACTIVE MAP **The Mongol Empire**	Objective 1	10 min.		●	1.C, 4.K	
READ **Mongols Rule China**	Objective 2	10 min.	●	●	1.C, 4.K	2.I.3
INTERACTIVE GALLERY **Marco Polo and Life Under the Mongols**	Objective 2	10 min.		●	1.C, 4.K	
READ **Chinese Rule Restored by the Ming**	Objective 3	10 min.	●	●	1.D, 7.E, 25.A, 26.B, 27.A	3.D.2
INTERACTIVE 3-D MODEL **Ming Vase**	Objective 3	10 min.		●	1.D, 7.E, 26.B	
READ **Chinese Fleets Explore the Seas**	Objective 4	10 min.	●	●	1.D, 7.E	
Synthesize						
DIGITAL ACTIVITY **Timeline of Mongol Empire in China**		5 min.		●	1.C, 4.K	
Demonstrate						
DIGITAL QUIZ **Lesson Quiz and Class Discussion Board**		10 min.		●	1.C, 1.D, 4.K.B, 7.E	

PEARSON realize
www.PearsonTexas.com
Access your Digital Lesson

Focus on Texas Standards

Texas Essential Knowledge and Skills

4.K summarize the changes resulting from the Mongol invasions of Russia, China, and the Islamic world

7.E explain Ming China's impact on global trade

25.A summarize the fundamental ideas and institutions of Eastern civilizations that originated in China and India

27.A identify the origin and diffusion of major ideas in mathematics, science, and technology that occurred in river valley civilizations, classical Greece and Rome, classical India, and the Islamic caliphates between 700 and 1200 and in China from the Tang to Ming dynasties

NOTES

Korea and Its Traditions

Objectives

Objective 1: Describe how geography affected life on the Korean peninsula.

Objective 2: Understand the influence of China and Buddhism on Korea.

Objective 3: Explain the major achievements of the Choson dynasty.

LESSON 4 ORGANIZER	PACING: APPROX. 1 PERIOD, .5 BLOCKS					
			RESOURCES			
	OBJECTIVES	PACING	Print	Online	TEKS	ELPS
Connect						
DIGITAL START UP ACTIVITY **Korea and Its Traditions**		5 min.		●	3.A.iii, 3.A.xix, 4.H.vii	
Investigate						
READ **The Geography of Korea**	Objective 1	10 min.	●	●	3.A.iii, 3.A.xix, 4.H.vii, 23.A.xix, 25.A.i, 25.A.iii	2.I.4
READ **The Silla and Koryo Dynasties Develop**	Objective 2	10 min.	●	●	3.A.iii, 3.A.xix, 4.H.vii, 23.A.xvii, 23.A.xix, 25.A.i, 25.A.iii, 26.A.ii, 26.B, 27.A.xxxv	
INTERACTIVE MAP **Korea's Three Kingdoms**	Objective 2	10 min.		●	3.A.iii, 26.A.ii, 26.B	
READ **The Choson Dynasty**	Objective 3	10 min.	●	●	3.A.iii, 26.A.ii, 26.B	3.E.1
INTERACTIVE CHART **Silla, Koryo, and Choson Dynasties**	Objective 3	10 min.		●	3.A.iii, 23.A.xix, 25.A.i, 25.A.iii	
Synthesize						
DIGITAL ACTIVITY **Korean Civilization**		5 min.		●	3.A.iii, 3.A.xix	
Demonstrate						
DIGITAL QUIZ **Lesson Quiz and Class Discussion Board**		10 min.		●	3.A, 4.H, 23.A, 25.A, 26.A, 26.B, 27.A	

Focus on Texas Standards

Texas Essential Knowledge and Skills

4.H summarize the major political, economic, and cultural developments in Tang and Song China and their impact on Eastern Asia

23.A describe the historical origins, central ideas, and spread of major religious and philosophical traditions, including Buddhism, Christianity, Confucianism, Hinduism, Islam, Judaism, Sikhism, and the development of monotheism

25.A summarize the fundamental ideas and institutions of Eastern civilizations that originated in China and India

27.A identify the origin and diffusion of major ideas in mathematics, science, and technology that occurred in river valley civilizations, classical Greece and Rome, classical India, and the Islamic caliphates between 700 and 1200 and in China from the Tang to Ming dynasties

NOTES

The Island Kingdom of Japan

Objectives

Objective 1: Explain how geography set Japan apart.

Objective 2: Understand how China influenced Japan, and describe the Heian period.

Objective 3: Summarize the Japanese feudal system.

Objective 4: Explain how the Tokugawas united Japan.

Objective 5: Identify how Zen Buddhism shaped culture in Japan.

LESSON 5 ORGANIZER — **PACING: APPROX. 1 PERIOD, .5 BLOCKS**

	OBJECTIVES	PACING	RESOURCES Print	RESOURCES Online	TEKS	ELPS
Connect						
DIGITAL START UP ACTIVITY **Devastating Tsunamis**		5 min.		●	16.B	
Investigate						
READ **Japan's Geography**	Objective 1	10 min.	●	●	16.C	3.F.1
READ **Early Japan**	Objective 2	10 min.	●	●	25.A	
READ **Chinese Influence in Japan**		10 min.	●	●	23.A, 26.B	
READ **Japanese Culture in the Heian Period**		10 min.	●	●	24.A, 25.A, 26.A, 26.B	2.I.5
READ **Japan's Feudal Age**	Objective 3	10 min.	●	●	4.C, 4.H	
INTERACTIVE CHART **Feudal Society in Japan**		10 min.		●	4.C	
READ **A United Japan**	Objective 4	10 min.	●	●	25.A	
READ **Japanese Feudal Culture Evolves**	Objective 5	10 min.	●	●	4.C, 4.H, 23.A, 25.A, 26.A, 26.B	
INTERACTIVE GALLERY **Japanese Art and Theater**		10 min.		●	26.A, 26.B	
Synthesize						
DIGITAL ACTIVITY **Japan During the Heian and Tokugawa Periods**		5 min.		●	24.A, 26.B	
Demonstrate						
DIGITAL QUIZ **Lesson Quiz and Class Discussion Board**		10 min.		●	4.H, 7.B, 7.E, 16.B, 23.A, 25.A, 25.B, 25.C, 26.B, 27.A	

PEARSON realize™ www.PearsonTexas.com Access your Digital Lesson

Focus on Texas Standards

Texas Essential Knowledge and Skills

4.H summarize the major political, economic, and cultural developments in Tang and Song China and their impact on Eastern Asia

24.A describe the changing roles of women, children, and families during major eras of world history

25.A summarize the fundamental ideas and institutions of Eastern civilizations that originated in China and India

26.B analyze examples of how art, architecture, literature, music, and drama reflect the history of the cultures in which they are produced

NOTES

Topic 9 Lesson 6

The Many Cultures of Southeast Asia

Objectives

Objective 1: Describe the geography of Southeast Asia.

Objective 2: Understand the impact of India on the history of Southeast Asia.

Objective 3: Summarize the characteristics of the new kingdoms and empires in Southeast Asia.

Objective 4: Explain the emergence of Vietnam.

LESSON 6 ORGANIZER — **PACING: APPROX. 1 PERIOD, .5 BLOCKS**

	OBJECTIVES	PACING	RESOURCES Print	RESOURCES Online	TEKS	ELPS
Connect						
DIGITAL START UP ACTIVITY **Geography of Southeast Asia**		5 min.		●	16.B	
Investigate						
READ **The Geography of Southeast Asia**	Objective 1	10 min.	●	●	16.B	
INTERACTIVE MAP **Topography of Southeast Asia**	Objective 1	10 min.		●	16.B	
READ **Indian Culture Spreads**	Objective 2	10 min.	●	●	23.A, 25.A, 26.B	3.F.2
READ **Kingdoms and Empires**	Objective 3	10 min.	●	●	16.B, 23.A, 25.A, 26.B, 27.A	
INTERACTIVE GALLERY **Angkor City and Angkor Wat**	Objective 3	10 min.		●	23.A, 25.A, 26.B	
READ **The Rise of Vietnam**	Objective 4	10 min.	●	●	16.B, 23.A, 25.A	
Synthesize						
DIGITAL ACTIVITY **The Impact of Geography**		5 min.		●	16B	
Demonstrate						
DIGITAL QUIZ **Lesson Quiz and Class Discussion Board**		10 min.		●	3.A.ii, 16.B.ii, 16.B.vi, 23.A.i, 23.A.iii, 23.A.ix, 23.A.xi, 23.A.xvii, 23.A.xx, 23.A.xxii, 23.A.xxiv, 23.B.i, 24.A.i, 25.A.i, 25.A.ii, 25.A.iv, 26.B.ii	

PEARSON realize™ www.PearsonTexas.com Access your Digital Lesson

Focus on Texas Standards

Texas Essential Knowledge and Skills

16.B analyze the influence of human and physical geographic factors on major events in world history, including the development of river valley civilizations, trade in the Indian Ocean, and the opening of the Panama and Suez canals

23.A describe the historical origins, central ideas, and spread of major religious and philosophical traditions, including Buddhism, Christianity, Confucianism, Hinduism, Islam, Judaism, Sikhism, and the development of monotheism

NOTES

Civilizations of Asia (500–1650)

In this Topic, you will learn about civilizations of Asia. You will also find lots of ways to investigate the ideas of this Topic and to master the TEKS.

Your study will help you master these TEKS:

TEKS

1.C, 1.D, 3.A, 4.D, 4.F, 4.H, 4.J, 4.K, 7.E, 16.B, 23.A, 24.A, 25.A, 26.A, 26.B, 27.A, 29.H

LESSON OUTLINE

9.1: The Delhi Sultanate and Mughal India **1.C, 4.D, 4.F, 23.A, 25.A, 26.A, 26.B**

9.2: Golden Ages in China: Tang and Song Dynasties **4.H, 4.J, 25.A, 26.B, 27.A**

9.3: The Mongol Empire and Ming China **1.C, 1.D, 4.K, 7.E, 25.A, 27.A**

9.4: Korea and Its Traditions **3.A, 4.H, 23.A, 25.A, 26.A, 27.A**

9.5: The Island Kingdom of Japan **4.H, 24.A, 25.A, 26.B**

9.6: The Many Cultures of Southeast Asia **16.B, 23.A**

Connect

My Story Video and Topic Essential Question—see how they connect to your past experience or to what you have already learned. The Essential Question for this Topic is: What distinguishes one culture from another?

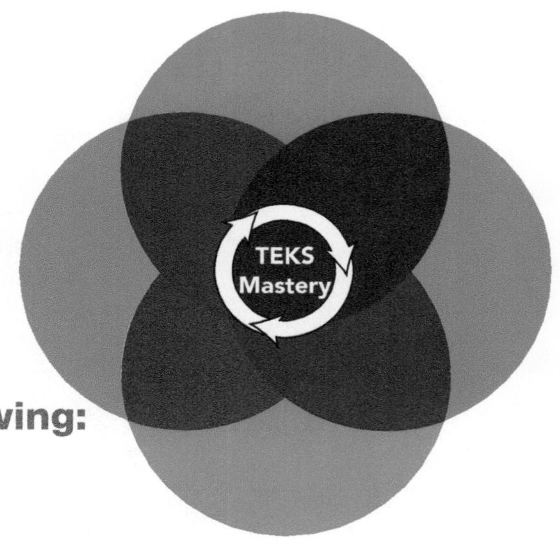

Begin your study by trying the following:

NBC LEARN Watch My Story Video:

Genghis Kahn, Conqueror

Launch your Civic Discussion:

Genghis Kahn

Investigate

The Lesson Outline lists all the lessons you will investigate in this Topic. As you read and interact with key content, the story of civilizations in Asia will come to life. Read the texts; try the interactivities. Investigate the fascinating story of Asian civilizations.

And keep working on your Civic Discussion to help build your mastery of the Topic TEKS.

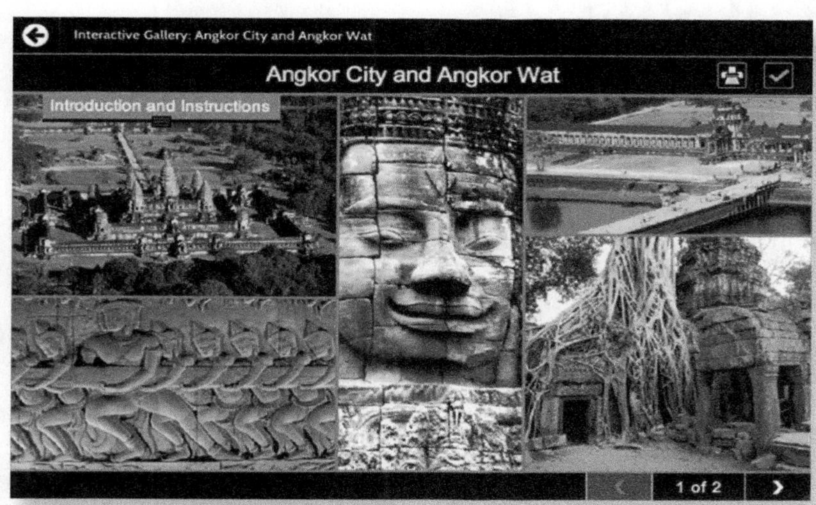

>> Digital interactivity from the online course

Synthesize

Next you will pull it all together by reflecting on the Essential Question. This will give you a chance to be the storyteller, to show how you would answer this big question: What distinguishes one culture from another?

Demonstrate

Finally, you can show what you know. You can write an essay, hold a discussion, or make a presentation. You can answer questions about every TEKS on the Topic Review and Assessment pages. Or you can take part in the Civic Discussion on Genghis Kahn.

TEKS in Topic 9	Topic Review and Assessment Questions
1.C	6
1.D	9
4.D	10
4.F	12
4.H	1, 2
4.J	3
4.K	7
7.E	9
16.B	11
23.A	15
25.A	13
26.A	8
26.B	4, 14
27.A	5
29.H	4

Topic 9

Civilizations of Asia (500–1650)

Introduction

Various civilizations developed in Asia, including those in India, China, Korea, and Japan. Each civilization developed its own unique culture and institutions, but each was also strongly influenced by outside forces. Islam had a strong impact on India, the Mongols influenced China, and China itself influenced the cultures of Japan and Korea. As a result, there was a blending of ideas and knowledge that revealed itself in the artistic, scientific, social, and religious elements of each civilization.

ESSENTIAL QUESTION

Ask students to think about the Essential Question for this topic: What distinguishes one culture from another? Project the Essential Question activity from the course. Have volunteers read the bulleted questions. Discuss them as a class.

Contrast What do you think makes American culture different from other cultures in the world? What are the most important differences? *(American history, religion, popular culture elements, or other factors; differences include the importance of individual liberties, free enterprise, or equality)*

Compare What are some ways American culture is like other cultures? *(Examples: the importance of family, admiration of success, or strong religious beliefs)*

Analyze What are some ideas, customs, and traditions that American culture has adopted from other cultures? What are some reasons that one culture borrows from another? How does this occur? *(Discuss ideas about government, society, and economics and customs involving food, language, dress, the arts, and religion.)*

Make Generalizations Are some values, beliefs, or ideas shared by all cultures? *(Students might agree that some values, beliefs, and ideas, such as family love, patriotism, and desire to be useful, are shared by all cultures.)*

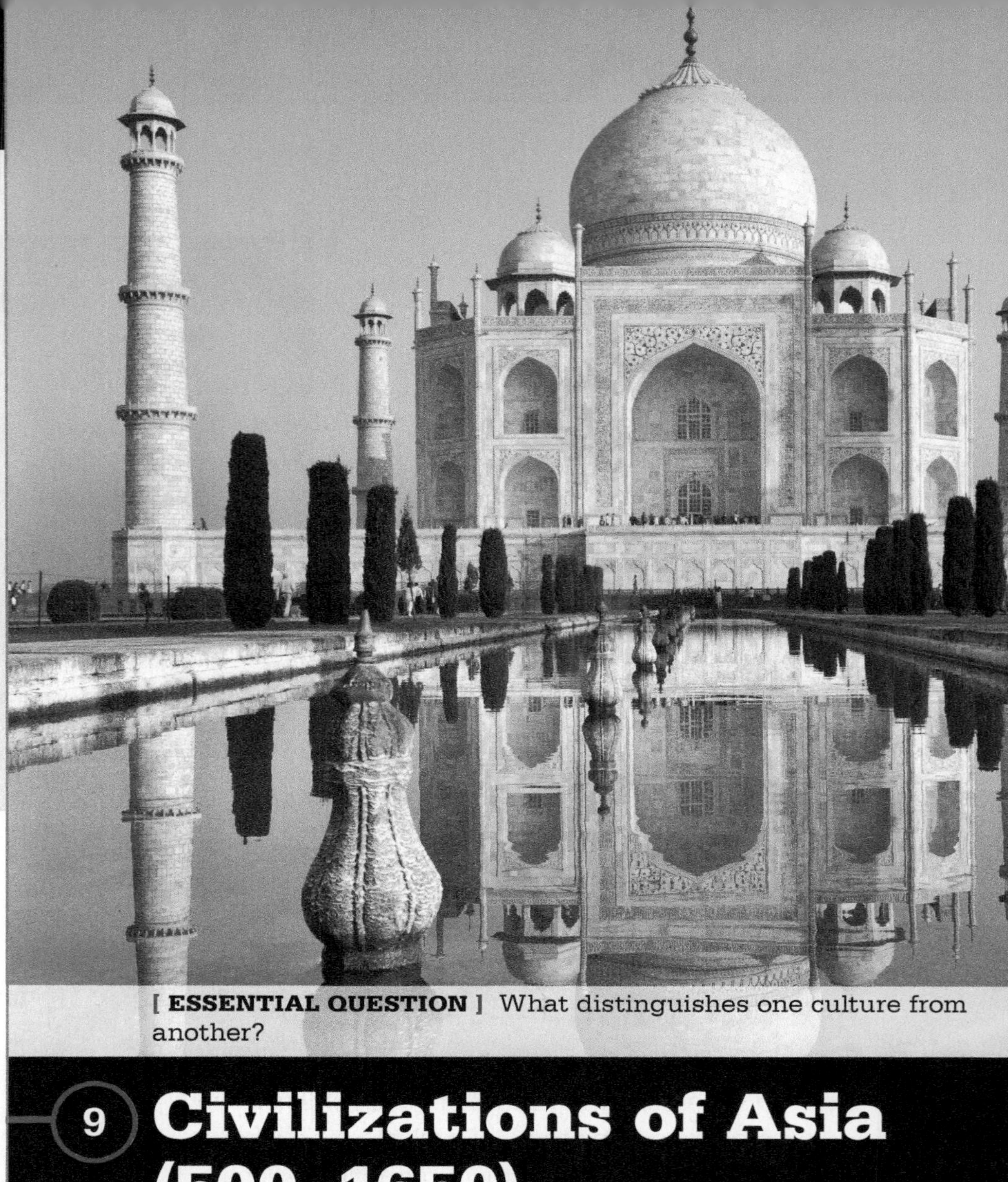

[**ESSENTIAL QUESTION**] What distinguishes one culture from another?

9 **Civilizations of Asia (500–1650)**

Analyze Images

Ask students to look at the photo of the Taj Mahal, the marble tomb built in the 1600s by Indian emperor Shah Jahan in memory of his wife. It mixes Islamic, Indian, and Persian architectural styles. Ask students what distinguishes the Taj Mahal from a typical structure in the United States. *(Students might point out the towers, the arches, or the overall "look." Some may note that state capitols often have domes.)*

>> Taj Mahal, India

Texas Essential Knowledge and Skills

1.C, 1.D, 3.A, 4.D, 4.F, 4.H, 4.J, 4.K, 7.E, 16.B, 23.A, 24.A, 25.A, 26.A, 26.B, 27.A, 29.H

Enduring Understandings

- The arrival of Islam brought great changes to India.
- Under the Tang and Song dynasties, China was a well-ordered society with a rich culture.
- The Mongols built a mighty empire in China under Genghis Khan and Kublai Khan, but the Ming dynasty restored Chinese rule and revived arts and literature.
- Korea received many cultural and technological influences from China, but it maintained its own culture under the three dynasties that ruled the country after the 600s.
- Medieval Japan was a feudal, warrior-dominated society, until the Tokugawas united much of Japan and imposed a central government.

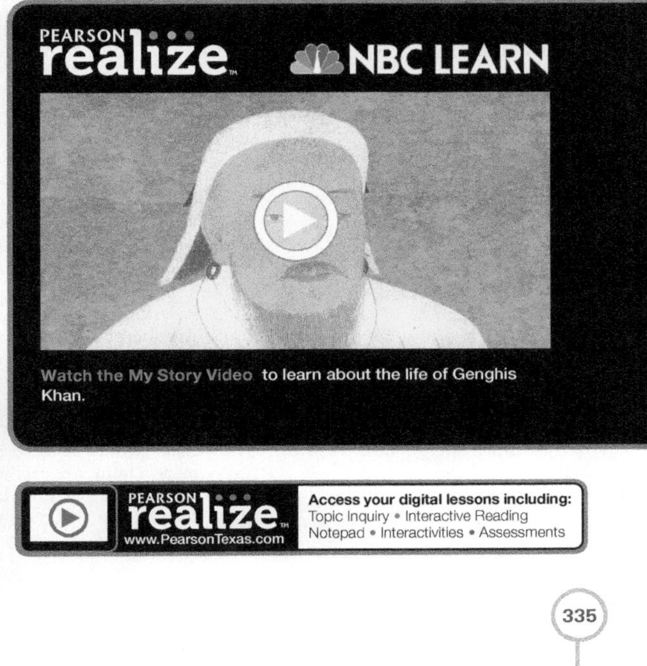

Watch the My Story Video to learn about the life of Genghis Khan.

PEARSON realize www.PearsonTexas.com Access your digital lessons including: Topic Inquiry • Interactive Reading Notepad • Interactivities • Assessments

335

NBC LEARN MY STORY VIDEO

Project the My Story Video that introduces students to Genghis Khan, a Mongol chieftain who united warring tribes and led them on a series of conquests across Asia.

Online My Story Video: **Genghis Khan, Conqueror**

After viewing, ask students to respond to the following questions.

Check Understanding From what part of the world did Genghis Khan come? *(from the remote grasslands of Mongolia)*

Identify Central Issues Genghis Khan's name means "Universal Ruler." Why is that an appropriate name? *(Genghis Khan conquered and ruled a vast empire, stretching from the Pacific to the Caspian Sea.)*

OVERVIEW ACTIVITY

Online Project the **Map: Civilizations in Asia**, which locates ancient civilizations of South and East Asia. During this topic students will learn about cultural interactions among India, China, Japan, and Korea. Ask students to use the map to point out how location and geographic features might affect the development of these civilizations.

Analyze Maps From what other countries might cultural influences on Cambodia and Vietnam come? Why? *(Possible answers: from China because it is the closest civilization to Cambodia and Vietnam; from India because it would have been easy to sail across the Bay of Bengal)*

Topic Inquiry

If you choose to assign the Topic Inquiry, launch the discussion after introducing the Topic.

D Differentiate Extra Support Have students locate Japan on the map. Ask them what factor in Japan's location might have helped it remain isolated from influences from other countries. *(It is an island.)*

Topic 9 Lesson 1

The Delhi Sultanate and Mughal India

CONNECT

Preview Have students preview the **Lesson Objectives** and the list of **Key Terms**.

Students can also preview all the **Key Terms** and **Academic Vocabulary** using the **Interactive Reading Notepad** on the digital course or preview a summary of the lesson in the **Reading and Note Taking Study Guide**.

Online Use the **Editable Presentation** found on the digital course to present the main ideas for this lesson.

Start Up Activity

Read the following prayer of the sixteenth-century Mughal empire ruler known as Akbar the Great:

> O God, in every temple, I see people that seek You. In every language I hear spoken, people praise You. If it be a mosque, people murmur the holy prayer. If it be a Christian church, they ring the bell for love of You. . . . It is You whom I seek from temple to temple.

Have students consider the meaning of Akbar's words. Then have them answer the following question.

Discuss Akbar recognized that his subjects are a diverse group of people with different beliefs about seeking God. What else does he understand about their beliefs? *(They all sought the same basic thing, even though their religious practices differed.)*

Online You can also project the **Start Up Activity** from the course.

INVESTIGATE

Have students read the lesson using the **Reading and Note Taking Study Guide** to help them take notes and understand the text as they read.

Analyze Visuals Have students look at the image and identify elements that show Akbar was considered a great and powerful ruler. *(Sample response: He is in the center of the picture.)*

The Delhi Sultanate

Muslims who invaded India around 1000 A.D. defeated Hindu armies and went on to conquer much of India. Around 1200, one Muslim ruler established a sultanate centered in Delhi. The Delhi sultanate would hold power in northern India for more that 300 years.

>> Akbar's tolerance of different Indian cultures and his willingness to include them in government was one of his strengths as a ruler.

Interactive Flipped Video

9.1 **Invasions and migrations had long shaped the Indian subcontinent, contributing to its diverse cultures. Centuries after the rise of Islam in the Middle East, Muslim invaders conquered much of northern India. The arrival of Islam brought changes to India as great as those caused by the Aryan migrations 2,000 years earlier. As Muslims mingled with Indians, each civilization absorbed elements from the other.**

TEKS
1.C, 4.D, 4.F, 23.A, 25.A, 26.A, 26.B

>> Objectives

Describe the effects of the Delhi sultanate on India.

Explain how Muslim and Hindu civilizations interacted in India.

Describe the historical origins and central ideas of Sikhism.

Summarize the policies of Akbar that strengthened Mughal India.

>> Key Terms

sultan
Delhi
rajah
Sikhism
Babur
Mughal
Akbar
Nur Jahan
Shah Jahan
Taj Mahal

The Delhi Sultanate and Mughal India

The Delhi Sultanate

Struggles for Power After the Gupta empire fell in about 550, India again fragmented into many local kingdoms. Rival princes battled for control of the northern plain. Despite power struggles, Indian culture flourished. Hindu and Buddhist rulers spent huge sums to build and decorate magnificent temples. Trade networks linked India to the Middle East, Southeast Asia, and China.

Although Arabs conquered the Indus Valley in 711, they advanced no farther into the subcontinent. Then around 1000, Muslim Turks and Afghans pushed into India. They were fierce warriors with a tradition of conquest. Sultan Mahmud of Ghazni pillaged much of the north, but he did not settle there.

Muslim Invaders Triumph In the late 1100s, the **sultan,** or Muslim ruler, of Ghur defeated Hindu armies across the northern plain and made **Delhi** his capital. From there, his successors organized a sultanate, or land ruled by a sultan. The Delhi sultanate, which lasted from 1206 to 1526, marked the start of Muslim rule in northern India.

PEARSON realize www.PearsonTexas.com Access your Digital Lesson.

336

Aa Vocabulary Builder

1. Have students pronounce the following academic vocabulary term in this lesson and clarify the part of speech.
2. Explain what the word means in common "student-friendly" language using synonyms and antonyms when possible. Provide concrete examples to clarify the meaning, and rephrase the definition.

policy: a plan for action

Why did the Muslim invaders triumph? They won on the battlefield in part because Muslim mounted archers had far greater mobility than Hindu forces, who rode slow-moving war elephants. Also, Hindu princes wasted resources battling one another instead of uniting against a common enemy. In some places, large numbers of Hindus, especially from low castes, converted to Islam. In the Hindu social system, people were born into castes, or social groups, from which they could not change.

Changes Under the Delhi Sultanate Muslim rule brought significant changes to Indian government and society. Sultans introduced Muslim traditions of government. Many Turks, Persians, and Arabs migrated to India to serve as soldiers or officials. Trade between India and Muslim lands increased. During the Mongol raids of the 1200s, many scholars and adventurers fled from Baghdad to India, bringing Persian and Greek learning. The newcomers helped create a brilliant civilization at Delhi, where Persian art and architecture flourished.

Northern India Fragments The Delhi sultanate collapsed in 1398 when Mongol armies under the command of Tamerlane invaded India. He plundered the northern plain and smashed into Delhi. "Not a bird on the wing moved," reported stunned survivors.

Thousands of artisans were enslaved to build Tamerlane's capital at Samarkand. Delhi, an empty shell, slowly recovered. The sultans no longer controlled a large empire, however, and northern India again fragmented, this time into rival Hindu and Muslim states.

ANALYZE INFORMATION How did the Delhi sultanate change Indian government and society?

The Meeting of Islam and Hinduism

At its worst, the Muslim conquest of northern India resulted in disaster for Hindus and Buddhists. The widespread destruction of Buddhist monasteries contributed to the drastic decline of Buddhism as a major religion in India. During the most violent onslaughts, many Hindus were killed. In time, though, relations became more peaceful.

Hindu-Muslim Differences The Muslim advance brought two utterly different religions and cultures face to face. Hinduism was an ancient religion that had evolved over thousands of years. Hindus recognized many sacred texts and prayed before statues

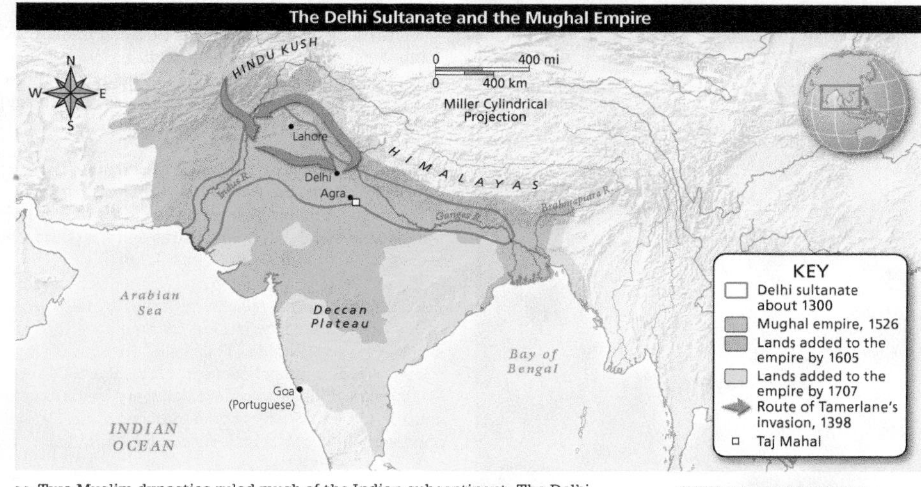

>> Two Muslim dynasties ruled much of the Indian subcontinent. The Delhi sultanate lasted more than 300 years before the Mughal dynasty replaced it. **Analyze Maps** Describe Tamerlane's route into India.

Interactive Map

Online Project the **Interactive Map: The Delhi Sultanate and the Mughal Empire**. Explain that two Muslim dynasties ruled much of India. The first, the Delhi sultanate, held power for more that 300 years, when it was replaced by the Mughal dynasty, founded by the famous Mongol general Tamerlane. Click through the hotspots with students.

ACTIVE CLASSROOM

Use the Write Headlines strategy. Ask students to write a headline that captures the main focus of the interactive map. Ask: If you were to write a headline for this topic or issue right now that captured the most important aspect that should be remembered, what would that headline be? Pass your headline to a partner for them to review. They can keep yours or ask for theirs back.

Guided Reading and Discussion

Identify Cause and Effect Ask students to work with a partner to identify causes and effects of the Mongol invasion of India. Taking turns, have one student list a cause and the other provide an effect. Share this example: Cause: Muslim archers rode swift horses, while Hindu defenders rode slow-moving elephants. Effect: Muslim invasions were successful.

The Meeting of Islam and Hinduism

Interactions between Muslims and Hindus in the Indian subcontinent resulted in important exchanges of cultural, political, religious, social, and artistic ideas. These exchanges have led to the multicultural India we know today.

Answers

Analyze Maps *Tamerlane came from the northwest, through the Hindu Kush, across the northern plain.*

Analyze Information *Muslim traditions of government replaced Hindu rule; Turks, Arabs, and Persians migrated to India and influenced Indian life; trade increased; Persian art and architecture flourished.*

Topic 9 Lesson 1

Guided Reading and Discussion

Ask students why some Hindus converted to Islam during the Delhi sultanate, but far fewer Muslims converted to Hinduism. *(Some lower-caste Hindus preferred Islam because it rejected the caste system. Some higher-caste Hindus chose to adopt Islam because they served in the Muslim government. Hindu merchants often converted to enhance trade links with Muslim lands. Muslims had fewer incentives to convert in a society ruled by Muslims.)*

Key Terms

Ask students to find the key term **rajahs** (in bold) in the text. Explain that the term *rajah* (also spelled *raja*) denotes a Hindu prince, or a person of the nobility. Rajahs had political power and often great wealth. Higher-ranking princes were known as maharajas, or "great princes."

Sikhism Emerges

Tell students that the Sikh religion has its historical origins in the Punjab, a region that includes northwestern India and part of Pakistan today. It was founded in the 1400s by a man named Nanak, who after a religious experience spent many years traveling throughout South Asia spreading the Sikh faith and way of life. During the 1500s and 1600s, his teachings and those of his nine successors shaped the core beliefs of Sikhism, which spread throughout the region and developed into a major religion. Sikh beliefs include the equality of all people in the eyes of God, regardless of their race, gender, social class, or religion.

representing many gods and goddesses. Islam, by contrast, was a newer faith with a single sacred text. Muslims were devout monotheists who saw the statues and carvings in Hindu temples as an offense to their belief in one God.

Hindus accepted differences in caste status and honored Brahmans as a priestly caste. Muslims taught the equality of all believers before God and had no religious hierarchy. Hindus celebrated religious occasions with music and dance, a practice condemned by many strict Muslims.

Tolerance Grows Eventually, the Delhi sultans grew more tolerant of their Hindu subjects. Some Muslim scholars argued that behind the many Hindu gods and goddesses was a single god. Hinduism was thus accepted as a monotheistic religion. As a protected subject group, Hindus were allowed to practice their religion as long as they paid a poll tax. Some sultans even left **rajahs,** or local Hindu rulers, in place.

Cultural Sharing Indian converts to Islam kept many Hindu traditions, especially marriage customs and caste. Living side by side, Hindus and Muslims developed a common life.

Hindus and Muslims came to honor each other's saints. Muslims adopted many Hindu practices, including clothing, food, music, and dance. At the same time, the Muslim custom of secluding women was adopted by Hindus.

In response to the spread of Islam, conservative Hindus strengthened some practices, especially caste rules. In the centuries after the arrival of Islam, the Hindu caste system became more rigid. Muslims in India also became divided on the basis of caste.

Finally, cultural blending led to a new language, Urdu, which combined Persian and Arabic with the Indian language spoken in Delhi. Artistic styles, too, changed as local Indian artisans applied Persian styles to Indian subjects.

EXPLAIN How did Muslim and Hindu cultures interact?

ELPS **ELPS 3.C.4** Practice saying sentences about *The Meeting of Islam and Hinduism* with connecting words.

>> Portraits of Guru Nanak held places of honor in Sikh homes. This tradition continues today.

Sikhism Emerges

In the late 1400s, a young man named Nanak founded the religion of **Sikhism** (SIK iz um) in the Punjab region of India. According to Sikh beliefs, Nanak had entered a trance while swimming and was presumed drowned, but he emerged after three days and said that he had experienced a spiritual revelation. Based on his experience, Nanak preached a faith recognizing one God for all people. He became known as Guru Nanak, after a word meaning spiritual guide.

Guru Nanak spent many years traveling throughout South Asia spreading the Sikh faith and way of life. During the 1500s and 1600s, his teachings and those of his successors shaped the core beliefs of Sikhism, which grew into one of the region's major religions.

A Message of Equality and Tolerance In the Punjabi language, the word *Sikh* (SIK) means "disciple." Sikhs consider themselves disciples of God who follow the teachings of the Ten Sikh Gurus and the guidance of the Sikh scripture, *Guru Granth Sahib.*

In addition to the belief in one God for all humanity, the basic Sikh beliefs include the equality of all people in the eyes of God, regardless of their race, gender, social class, or religion. This belief in equality and tolerance was a radical concept during the 1500s and 1600s, when Sikhism was developing and beginning to spread. At the time, strict division among social classes and inequality for women were common in India.

Taking New Names During the early years of Sikhism in India, a person's last name often indicated that person's social status, or caste. The tenth Sikh

Answers

Explain *The Muslim and Hindu religions and cultures differed. Hindus believed in many gods and sacred texts, social castes, and reincarnation; Muslims believed in one God, equality of all believers, and an afterlife. Cultures blended as the sultans became more tolerant of Hindu subjects and adopted some Hindu customs. Urdu, a new language, combined Indian languages with Persian and Arabic.*

English Language Proficiency Standards

Speaking 3.C.4 Read "The Meeting of Islam and Hinduism" aloud to the class. Then have students complete one of the following depending on their level of English proficiency.

Beginning Say these sentences aloud and have students repeat them after you.

- The Muslim conquest of northern India resulted in disaster for Hindus and Buddhists.
- Some sultans even left rajahs, or local Hindu rulers, in place.
- Muslims believed that all people were equal before God, but Hindus accepted differences in caste status.

Explain when to use the conjunctions *and*, *but*, and *or*. Have students say one sentence using *and*, *but*, or *or*.

Intermediate Help students scan the text for sentences that include *and*, *but*, or *or*. Help them say each sentence using correct pronunciation and increased fluency. Have them generate a short summary sentence using the word *and*.

Guru, Gobind Singh, wanted to remove these barriers between people and promote tolerance of others. He sought to reinforce the idea of equality by giving all Sikh men the last name of Singh, which means *lion* in the Punjabi language. All women were given the last name Kaur, which means *princess*.

The "Five Ks" Some Sikhs aspire to take Amrit, which is a special initiation ceremony where individuals commit themselves to actively practicing the essential Sikh values of truthfulness, trust, loyalty, productive labor, sharing, integrity, and spirituality. Upon completing the Amrit, these Sikhs become part of the community of initiates called the Khalsa.

The Khalsa, as well as many Sikhs who have not been initiated, wear distinctive clothing that identifies them as Sikh. The clothing includes the five Sikh articles of faith, called the "Five Ks" among English-speaking Sikhs because they each begin with the English letter *k*.

The Five Ks are Kesh, which is uncut hair kept covered by a turban; the Kirpan (kir PAHN), a religious sword representing the dual responsibilities to God and community; the Kara (KEHR a), a metal bracelet; Kanga (KANG a) a comb; and the Kachera (kuh TSHERA), special underclothing.

As articles of faith, each object holds a deep personal and religious meaning for the Sikh wearing it. They are worn to honor the Sikh Gurus and to remind the wearer of the Sikh way of life. They also publicly proclaim the person to be a follower of Sikhism.

This outward demonstration of faith has been a part of the spread of Sikhism through the centuries. It is now the fifth-largest religion in the world.

EXPLAIN Why were the Sikh beliefs a radical change from existing Indian beliefs and customs?

Mughal India

In 1526, Turkish and Mongol armies again poured through mountain passes into India. At their head rode **Babur** (BAH bur), who claimed descent from Genghis Khan and Tamerlane. Babur was a military genius, a poet, and the author of a detailed book of memoirs.

Babur Founds the Mughal Dynasty Just north of Delhi, Babur met a huge army led by the sultan Ibrahim. "I placed my foot in the stirrup of resolution and my hands on the reins of confidence in God," recalled Babur. His force was small but had cannons, which he put to good use.

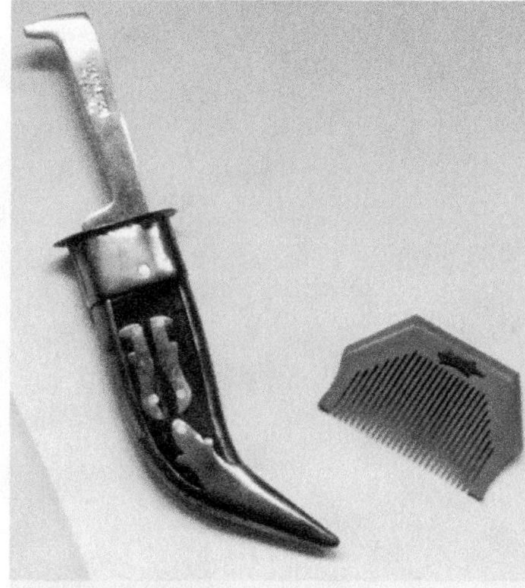

>> These two items, a comb and knife, are outward symbols of the Sikh faith and show the wearer's devotion.

>> Sikh men, wearing turbans to cover their uncut hair, pray during a Sikh ceremony.

Guided Reading and Discussion

Synthesize Discuss with students why Sikhism was a radical set of ideas in the early 1500s. Ask: What ideas made it different from most customs and traditions of the time? *(Sample response: Most people at the time, in both the East and West, believed in some kind of hierarchy of society, rigid social classes with some people on top and most on the bottom; they did not believe in social equality; they did not consider women equal to men; they did not believe in one God for all people.)*

Transfer Information Have students work with a partner to write a dialogue between a Sikh and a Muslim or Hindu, set either in the 1500s or today, based on information in this lesson. Ask volunteers to share their dialogues with the class and discuss issues they raise.

Mughal India

Tell students that in the 1500s, a military genius named Babur invaded northern India, overthrew the Delhi sultanate, and established the Mughal empire. Babur's grandson Akbar later strengthened the growing Mughal empire by creating a strong central government, by increasing trade, and by gaining the trust of Hindus and other non-Muslims through a policy of tolerance. Akbar's grandson Shah Jahan, who built the Taj Mahal, continued Akbar's tolerance of other religions. Shah Jahan's son Aurangzeb, however, rejected that policy, and in the late 1600s, the empire began to decline.

Advanced Instruct pairs of students to scan the text for sentences with connecting words and phrases like *and, or, but, in fact, for example*, and *however*. Have students pause and take turns saying each sentence aloud to their partner.

Advanced High Follow the instructions in the Advanced activity, but have each pair write and say three sentences about the information in "The Meeting of Islam and Hinduism" using connecting words in each one.

Answers

Explain *The Sikhs believe that all people are equal regardless of race, gender, social status, or religious beliefs. This differed from the Indian caste system and the traditional inequality between men and women.*

Online Project the **Interactive Gallery: The Art of the Mughal Empire** and, as you click through the images, discuss their significance and how the art reflects Mughal India.

ACTIVE CLASSROOM

Employ the See-Think-Wonder strategy with the interactive gallery. Pair students with a partner. Have them take turns explaining. What do you see? What does that make you think? What are you wondering about now that you've seen this? Have volunteers share insights with the class.

Guided Reading and Discussion

Identify Main Ideas Remind students that Akbar decided to promote religious and cultural diversity in the Mughal empire. Ask them to describe how he did this and to explain the impact of this decision on the strength of his rule. *(Although a Muslim, Akbar won the support of Hindu subjects through his policy of tolerance. He opened government jobs to Hindus of all castes and treated Hindu princes as his partners in ruling the vast empire. Akbar ended the tax on non-Muslims, and he married a Hindu princess. By promoting religious harmony through tolerance and recognizing India's diversity, Akbar placed Mughal power on a firm footing.)*

Support Ideas With Evidence Why was the Taj Mahal built? In what ways does it reflect the Islamic culture of the Mughal ruler Shah Jahan? *(It was built as tomb for the wife of the Mughal ruler Shah Jahan; it was designed by a Persian architect with domes and minarets, or prayer towers, and has verses from the Quran on its walls.)*

Analyze Images

Ask students to look at the image of Babur assembling his army. Ask: Which figure in the picture is Babur? How can you tell? *(Possible answers: the figure with the umbrella-like object over his head; he is in the center of the picture and all the other people are looking at him)*

> "The sun had mounted spear-high when the onset began, and the battle lasted till midday, when the enemy was completely broken and routed. By the grace and mercy of Almighty God, this difficult affair was made easy to me, and that mighty army . . . was crushed in the dust.
>
> —Babur, Memoirs

>> Babur assembles his army for his battle with Sultan Ibrahim to win control of Delhi.

In little time, Babur swept away the remnants of the Delhi sultanate and set up the **Mughal** dynasty, which ruled from 1526 to 1857. (*Mughal* is the Persian word for "Mongol.") Babur and his heirs conquered an empire that stretched from the Himalayas to the Deccan Plateau.

The chief builder of the Mughal empire was Babur's grandson **Akbar.** During his long reign, from 1556 to 1605, he created a strong central government and earned the title Akbar the Great.

Akbar the Great Akbar was a leader of unusual abilities. Although a Muslim, he won the support of Hindu subjects through his policy of tolerance. He opened government jobs to Hindus of all castes and treated Hindu princes as his partners in ruling the vast empire. Akbar ended the tax on non-Muslims, and he married a Hindu princess.

Akbar could not read or write, but he consulted leaders of many faiths, including Muslims, Hindus, Buddhists, and Christians. Like the early Indian leader Asoka, he hoped to promote religious harmony through tolerance. By recognizing India's diversity, Akbar placed Mughal power on a firm footing.

Akbar strengthened his empire in other ways as well. To improve government, he used paid officials in place of hereditary officeholders. He modernized the army, encouraged international trade, standardized weights and measures, and introduced land reforms.

Akbar's Heirs Akbar's son Jahangir (juh HAHN geer) was a weaker ruler than his father. He left most details of government in the hands of his wife, **Nur Jahan.** Fortunately, she was an able leader whose shrewd political judgment was matched only by her love of poetry and royal sports. Nur Jahan was the most powerful woman in Indian history until the 1900s.

The high point of Mughal literature, art, and architecture came with the reign of **Shah Jahan,** Akbar's grandson. When his wife, Mumtaz Mahal, died at age 39 after having borne 14 children, Shah Jahan was distraught. "Empire has no sweetness," he cried, "life itself has no relish left for me now."

Taj Mahal To honor his favorite wife, Shah Jahan ordered the building of a magnificent tomb, the **Taj Mahal** (tahzh muh HAHL). Designed by a Persian architect, it has spectacular white domes and graceful minarets mirrored in clear blue reflecting pools. Verses from the Quran adorn its walls, and pleasant gardens surround the entire structure. The Taj Mahal stands as perhaps the greatest monument of the Mughal empire.

Shah Jahan planned to build a twin structure to the Taj Mahal as a tomb for himself. However, before he could do so, his son Aurangzeb usurped the throne in 1658. Shah Jahan was kept imprisoned until he died several years later.

Mughal Decline In the late 1600s, the emperor Aurangzeb rejected Akbar's tolerant policies and resumed persecution of Hindus. With this policy, the Mughals lost the support of India's majority Hindu population. Economic hardships grew worse under heavy taxes, and discontent sparked revolts.

Against this background, European traders began to gain small footholds in India. The Mughal empire survived into the 1800s, but was weakened by wars among rivals to the throne and local rulers who controlled their lands like independent kingdoms. In the end, the once-powerful empire dwindled to a small area around Delhi.

? ANALYZE INFORMATION How did the policies Akbar put in place help to strengthen his empire?

>> An architectural masterpiece, the Taj Mahal is an enduring symbol of the glory of the Mughal empire and of India itself.

Interactive Gallery

ASSESSMENT

1. **Identify Cause and Effect** How did the Delhi Sultanate affect Indian government and society?
2. **Analyze Information** How did the relationship between Muslims and Hindus change over time?
3. **Analyze Information** Why might Sikhism appeal to many Indians during the 1600s?
4. **Determine Cause and Effect** How did Akbar win the support of his Hindu subjects, thus creating a more united society?
5. **Explain** What were some of Akbar's policies that resulted in a stronger government in Mughal India?

SYNTHESIZE

Online Project the **Digital Activity: Cultures Meet in India.** Have students list steps Akbar took to unify and strengthen his rule. *(He removed the taxes on non-Muslims, invited Hindus to become government officials, worked with the Hindu rajahs to govern, and married a Hindu princess. He also paid government officials, increased trade, and put land reforms into place.)*

Discuss Ask students to recall the quotation from the beginning of this lesson by Akbar about the religious diversity of his subjects and his understanding of the common elements in all religions. Ask what Akbar did to show that he valued this religious and cultural diversity. *(Answers may include introduction of Islam into greater Indian society, conversion of lower-caste Hindus to Islam, centralized government, greater trade opportunities, blending of cultures, and advanced art and architecture that reflected the blended culture.)*

DEMONSTRATE

Online Assign the **Digital Lesson Quiz** for this lesson if you haven't already done so. Students will be offered automatic remediation or enrichment based on their score.

Pose the following question to the class:

Predict Consequences After learning about India, what can you predict about how it will change?

Topic Inquiry

Have students continue their investigations for the Topic Inquiry.

Answers

Analyze Information *He created a strong central government with paid officials, recognized and tolerated diversity, modernized the army, encouraged trade, standardized weights and measures, and introduced land reforms.*

Assessment

1. Persians brought ancient Greek learning to the area, while Turks, Persians, and Arabs arrived to work within the government. Trade increased. Persian styles influenced Indian art and architecture.
2. At first, the relationship was very violent, with Muslims fighting Hindus. Over time, Muslims became more tolerant of their Hindu subjects, some Hindus converted to Islam, and Muslims adopted some elements of Hindu culture.
3. It promoted equality among all, regardless of race, gender, and social position. It might be especially appealing to those of the lowest Indian castes as Sikhism rejected the caste system. Women were viewed as equal with men, which would give women more opportunities.
4. He removed the taxes on non-Muslims, invited Hindus to become government officials, worked with the Hindu rajahs to govern, and married a Hindu princess.
5. He paid government officials instead of relying on the traditional inheritance of government posts. He increased trade and put land reforms into place.

Golden Ages in China: Tang and Song Dynasties

CONNECT

Preview Have students preview the **Lesson Objectives** and the list of **Key Terms**.

Students can also preview all the **Key Terms** and **Academic Vocabulary** using the **Interactive Reading Notepad** on the digital course or preview a summary of the lesson in the **Reading and Note Taking Study Guide**.

Online Use the **Editable Presentation** found on the digital course to present the main ideas for this lesson.

Start Up Activity

Tell students that gunpowder originated in China, perhaps as early as the ninth century. Ask students the following question: How might the introduction of gunpowder have changed that society?

Discuss How has gunpowder changed the history of the world? Overall, has this invention had a positive or negative influence? Why? *(Answers will vary, but should show evidence of careful thought about gunpowder's effects on societies. Students might say that gunpowder itself is neither negative nor positive, but the uses to which it has been put determine its overall effects.)*

Online You can also project the **Start Up Activity** from the course.

INVESTIGATE

Have students read the lesson using the **Reading and Note Taking Study Guide** to help them take notes and understand the text as they read.

The Tang Dynasty Restores China to Glory

After the Han dynasty collapsed in 220, China broke apart and remained divided for nearly 400 years. The Tang dynasty, founded in 618, ushered in a period of stability. Tang rulers strengthened their rule by centralizing power, rebuilding the bureaucracy, enlarging the civil service system, and introducing land reforms. Tang rulers also sent their armies into neighboring countries, forcing them to acknowledge Chinese dominance and pay tribute to China.

>> Wu Zhao rose from a lowly position at court to a position of influence over the Tang emperor. Upon his death, she became the first woman to claim the throne.

Interactive Flipped Video

9.2 **In the late 600s, Wu Zhao (woo jow) became the only woman to rule China in her own name. She proved herself to be a capable empress. Her strong rule helped guide China through one of its most brilliant periods. At a time when Europe was fragmented into many small feudal kingdoms, two powerful dynasties—the Tang and the Song—restored unity in China.**

TEKS
4.H, 4.J, 25.A, 26.B, 27.A

>> Objectives

Summarize how the Tang dynasty reunified China.

Explain how the Song dynasty grew rich and powerful despite military setbacks.

Understand how China created an ordered society.

Describe the major cultural developments in the Tang and Song dynasties.

>> Key Terms

Tang dynasty
Tang Taizong
tributary state
land reform
Song dynasty
gentry
dowry
pagoda

Golden Ages in China: Tang and Song Dynasties

The Tang Dynasty Restores China to Glory

The Han Dynasty Collapses After the Han dynasty collapsed in 220, China broke apart and remained divided for nearly 400 years. Yet China escaped the decay that disrupted Western Europe after the fall of Rome. Farm production expanded and technology slowly improved. Buddhism spread, while learning and the arts continued to flourish. Even Chinese cities survived. Although invaders stormed into northern China, they often adopted Chinese civilization rather than demolishing it.

Meanwhile, various dynasties rose and fell in the south. During the brief Sui (swee) dynasty (589–618), the emperor Sui Wendi reunited the north and south. But China was not restored to its earlier glory until the emergence of the **Tang dynasty** in 618.

PEARSON realize. www.PearsonTexas.com Access your Digital Lesson.

Aa Vocabulary Builder

1. Have students pronounce the following academic vocabulary terms in this lesson and clarify the part of speech. For difficult or polysyllabic words, break them into syllables and pronounce them with the students.
2. Explain what the word means in common "student-friendly" language using synonyms and antonyms when possible. Provide concrete examples to clarify the meaning, and rephrase the definition.

compel: to force to do something

economy: the prosperity or earnings of a place

redistribute: divide and give out again

establish: bring something about

symbol: something used to represent something else

Building an Empire The first Tang emperor, Li Yuan (lee yoo AHN), was a general under the Sui dynasty. When the Sui began to crumble, Li Yuan's ambitious 16-year-old son, Li Shimin, urged him to lead a revolt. Father and son crushed all rivals and established the Tang dynasty. Eight years later, Li Shimin compelled his aging father to step down and mounted the throne himself, taking the name **Tang Taizong** (ty DZUNG). A brilliant general, government reformer, historian, and master of the calligraphy brush, Tang Taizong would become China's most admired emperor.

Later Tang rulers carried empire-building to new heights, conquering territories deep into Central Asia. Chinese armies forced the neighboring lands of Vietnam, Tibet, and Korea to become **tributary states.** That is, while these states remained self-governing, their rulers had to acknowledge Chinese supremacy and send regular tribute to the Tang emperor. At the same time, students from Korea and Japan traveled to the Tang capital to learn about Chinese government, law, and arts.

>> Tang Taizong, the first Tang emperor, meets with his councilors at his court.

Strengthening the Government and Economy Tang rulers, such as Empress Wu Zhao, helped restore the Han system of uniform government throughout China. They rebuilt the bureaucracy and enlarged the civil service system to recruit talented officials trained in Confucian philosophy. They also set up schools to prepare male students for the exams and developed a flexible new law code.

Tang emperors instituted a system of **land reform** in which they broke up large agricultural holdings and redistributed the land to peasants. This policy strengthened the central government by weakening the power of large landowners. It also increased government revenues, since the peasants who farmed their own land would be able to pay taxes.

Decline of the Dynasty Like earlier dynasties, the Tang eventually weakened. Later Tang emperors lost territories in Central Asia to the Arabs. Corruption, high taxes, drought, famine, and rebellions all contributed to the downward swing of the dynastic cycle. In 907, a rebel general overthrew the last Tang emperor. This time, however, the chaos following the collapse of a dynasty did not last long.

ANALYZE INFORMATION How did the Tang dynasty re-unify China?

>> Bustling markets were important to the local economy. Food, tools, cloth, and other items were bought and sold at a market like this one.

Guided Reading and Discussion

Discuss with students how the Tang dynasty came to power in China and how it built a strong empire. *(The Tang came to power by overthrowing the Sui dynasty. The Tang improved the system of government, recruited talented officials through a revamped civil service system, set up schools to prepare male students to take civil service exams, developed a flexible law code, and engaged in land reform.)*

Analyze Images

Have students look at the illustration of the market. What signs of prosperity and a well-run government and society can you see in this image? *(Sample response: lots of goods for sale, different classes of people interacting peacefully, some people expensively dressed)*

Draw Conclusions Ask students to think about why some governments are able to rule well, while others are not. What factors contribute to a well-run government such as the Tang? Which factors can a government control? Which factors can it not control? *(Students may cite the innate ability, education, and training of rulers and government officials, external factors such as threats of invasion and climate issues, organization of society, the economy, and the willingness of the people to be ruled or not.)*

Identify Cause and Effect What factors led to the decline of the Tang dynasty? *(loss of territory in central Asia, corruption, high taxes, drought and resulting famine, rebellions)*

Key Terms

Ask students to find the key term **tributary states** (in bold) in the text. Have them define it. Then ask students what a tributary is in geography, perhaps by having a volunteer draw a river with several tributary streams flowing into it. Discuss how the geographical term can help them better understand the historical term.

Answers

Analyze Information *Tang rulers conquered territories, restored a uniform government, and enlarged the civil service systems.*

Topic 9 Lesson 2

The Song Dynasty

Tell students that after the fall of the Tang dynasty in 907, a short period of disorder ended with the founding of the Song dynasty in 960. In spite of suffering military defeats and controlling less territory than the Tang, Song rulers were able to create a society of great wealth, cultural achievement, and economic and political influence. Like the Tang, the Song was a period of technological, scientific, and mathematical advancement.

Online Project the **Interactive Gallery: Technology in the Tang and Song Dynasties** and click through the images with students.

Support Ideas With Examples What would have made these inventions attractive to people in other countries? *(Sample response: Inventions such as block type would appeal to other countries because it would make possible the printing of many more books and other documents.)*

ACTIVE CLASSROOM

Use the Rank It strategy. Ask students to rank the inventions shown in the interactive gallery according to which had the greatest impact on world civilizations. In a class discussion, ask students to provide a justification for the ranking decisions they made. Then poll the class to see if there is agreement on the ranking. Make a tally of the top inventions.

>> The invention of gunpowder made possible the cannon, such as this one with a dragon head at its mouth.

Interactive Gallery

>> The Song dynasty used a network of rivers and canals to improve local trade. Ships carried items from different parts of China to trading ports.

The Song Dynasty

In 960, a scholarly general named Zhao Kuangyin reunited much of China and founded the Song (sung) dynasty. The Song ruled for 319 years, slightly longer than the Tang, but they controlled less territory than the Tang. The Song also faced the constant threat of invaders in the north. In the early 1100s, the battered Song retreated south of the Huang River. There, the southern Song continued to rule for another 150 years. However, in the late 1200s Mongol invaders from the north attacked and overthrew the Song.

Song Achievements Despite military setbacks, the Song period was a time of great achievement. China's wealth and culture dominated East Asia even when its armies did not. Under the Song, the Chinese economy expanded because of improved farming methods and open border policy. The latter allowed a new type of faster-growing rice to be imported from Southeast Asia. Farmers were now able to produce two crops a year, one of rice and one of a cash crop to sell.

The rise in productivity created surpluses, allowing more people to pursue commerce, learning, or the arts. As people became more educated, they developed technology such as an improved compass, shipbuilding innovations, and gunpowder.

The Growth of Trade Under the Tang and Song, foreign trade flourished. Merchants arrived by land and seas from India, Persia, and the Middle East. The Chinese built better ships, and their merchants carried goods to Southeast Asia in exchange for spices and special woods. Tea was introduced to China from Southeast Asia, while Song porcelain has been found as far away as East Africa. To improve trade, the government issued paper money. China's cities, which had been mainly centers of government, now prospered as centers of trade. Several cities boasted populations over one million.

Trade spread ideas as well as goods. Merchants traveled in both directions along the 4,000-mile Silk Road, which linked China to India, Persia, and the Middle East. They helped spread technologies, advances in science and mathematics, religious beliefs, music, and artistic styles. Advances made in China were slowly carried westward to the Mediterranean world. At the same time, Chinese Buddhist monks headed west to India, the birthplace of Buddhism. There, they studied Indian culture.

Within China itself, the government promoted trade through a system of canals. From China's earliest history, rulers had supported the building of canals to improve transportation across large areas. The Grand Canal, completed under the Sui, linked areas in the

English Language Proficiency Standards

Listening 2.I.2 Have students practice retelling and summarizing the information they learn from reading "The Song Dynasty" according to their level of English proficiency.

Beginning Slowly and clearly read aloud the subsection "The Growth of Trade." After each sentence, pause to retell what was read using accessible language. Ask students to draw a picture to summarize this subsection. Then help them create a simple sentence to describe the picture and speak the sentence aloud. Assist as needed with pronunciation.

Intermediate Read aloud the first few sentences from "The Growth of Trade," pausing after each to retell what was read. Ask students to retell the remaining sentences. Then have students draw a picture and write a descriptive caption to summarize this subsection. Have them explain their picture and speak the caption aloud.

Advanced Have students listen and take notes as "The Song Dynasty" is read aloud. Pause after each subsection so they can summarize the text to a partner. When all of the subsections have been read, have students work with their partners to write and share a few sentences to summarize the text.

Advanced High Have students complete the Advanced task, but have students summarize the reading to a partner only after all subsections have been read.

south of China to the north. It allowed food, troops, and military supplies to reach the capital in the north. Under the Song, vast amounts of grain were shipped along the Grand Canal, spurring economic activity and the growth of cities along the route.

Advances in Science and Technology Under Tang and Song rulers, China enjoyed a golden age in science and technology. Using earlier advances, close observation, and analysis, the Chinese made breakthroughs in astronomy, agriculture, medicine, and military technology. Astronomers produced accurate star maps and calendars. Expert engineers developed irrigation and flood control projects. The human-operated water wheel was invented as well as new plows and rice-growing technologies.

By the mid-800s, the Chinese had discovered the chemistry of making explosives. At first, the new technology was used for fireworks. In time, gunpowder was put to military purposes for canons and other firearms. The Chinese pioneered the use of movable type to print books. The invention made printed books available more cheaply and spread learning, especially medical knowledge. During this time, the Chinese improved on their ancient practice of acupuncture to treat many ailments. The magnetic compass invented in China helped sailors at sea. The Chinese also developed mechanical clocks to tell exact time.

>> Candidates take the rigorous civil service exam during the Song dynasty. Students studied for years in preparation for the exam, which usually led to an honored position as a civil servant in the bureaucracy.

? CHECK UNDERSTANDING How was the Song dynasty able to continue its prosperity despite threats from the north?

 **ELPS 2.1.2** Practice retelling and summarizing the information in *The Song Dynasty.*

An Ordered Society

Under the Tang and Song, China was a well-ordered society. At its head was the emperor, whose court was filled with aristocratic families. The court stood at the center of a huge bureaucracy from which officials fanned out to every province and county in China. The bureaucracy oversaw China's huge population, made up of the **gentry,** or wealthy landowners, and peasants.

The Bureaucracy Under the Tang and Song rulers, the Chinese bureaucracy, which had begun under the Han, continued to develop. Aristocratic families had less influence. Instead, officials came from the scholar-gentry, the educated landowning class.

The bureaucracy included a variety of government-funded departments. Some of these departments oversaw tax collecting and government revenue. Other departments were devoted to the study of disciplines such as medicine, astronomy, and mathematics.

Important mathematical texts were written during the Tang and Song dynasties that recorded existing arithmetic, algebra, and geometry knowledge and helped these ideas spread. Later mathematicians used these books as references for their own discoveries.

The Gentry China's gentry class stood at the top of Chinese society. They valued scholarship more than physical labor. Most scholar-officials at court came from this class because they alone could afford to spend years studying the Confucian ideas. Only a few lucky men passed the grueling civil service exam and won the most honored positions in government.

The Song scholar-gentry supported a revival of Confucian thought. Scholars searched out old Confucian texts and new schools of thinkers reinterpreted Confucian ideas that emphasized social order, duty, rank, and proper behavior. This Confucian revival stressed traditions of the past. Although corruption and greed existed among the civil servants, the ideal Confucian official was a wise, kind, selfless, virtuous scholar who knew how to ensure harmony in society.

Guided Reading and Discussion

Remind students that the Song economy expanded in part from improved agricultural technology. Have them explain how trade also benefited Song China. *(It allowed new ideas and products, such as the new type of rice, to come into China; it also helped China gain economic, political, and cultural influence in other countries.)*

D Differentiate Challenge/Gifted Ask students to research the modern-day effects of food production on economic development, focusing on one less-developed country. You may want to offer this list of possible countries to research: India, Pakistan, Bangladesh, North Korea, Sudan, Mali, Niger, and Chad. Have students answer this question: How has the lack of availability of food helped or hindered economic development in this country? Ask students to share their research with the class.

An Ordered Society

Ask students to identify and describe well-ordered societies they have read about *(medieval Europe, ancient Egypt, ancient Rome)* and ask what they have in common *(strictly arranged hierarchy with a few monarchs, nobles, and religious leaders at the top and the vast majority of peasants and other laborers at the bottom)* Explain that Tang and Song China were similarly ordered societies, with one key difference from some other highly ordered societies. Challenge students to look for this difference as they read through this text.

History Background

Sunglasses in China Sunglasses were invented in China, but they were used for a different purpose than they are used for today. The Chinese made the lenses for their glasses from clear quartz. To make sunglasses, those lenses were tinted, or darkened, by exposing them to smoke. They became so dark that they kept other people from seeing the eyes of the person wearing them—which was exactly what the Chinese wanted. These darkened lenses were worn by judges in Chinese courts. The tinted lenses prevented people from reading the expression in the judges' eyes. That kept them from tailoring their statements to try to sway the judges' decisions.

Answers

Check Understanding *Rising productivity in farming created surpluses that could be sold. This strengthened China's economy, which allowed people to pursue commerce, learning, or the arts.*

Topic 9 Lesson 2

Guided Reading and Discussion

Remind students that Chinese society was based on a strict hierarchy of social classes. Have them identify the four levels of the Tang and Song social structure. *(The emperor stood at the top, followed by the gentry, peasants, and merchants.)* Ask students to describe how a peasant boy could overcome this rigid social hierarchy. *(If he received an education and was able to pass the difficult civil service exams, he could rise in the social hierarchy, bringing his family up with him.)*

Identify Central Issues Ask students: How did the status of women change from Tang and early Song times to the later Song dynasty? *(Their status was higher during the earlier times.)* Then have students explain the connection between foot binding and Chinese society's ideas about the role and value of women. *(Chinese society valued women who were delicate and subordinate, and foot binding locked women into a subservient role. It reinforced the idea that women should stay inside the home, since many were unable to walk without assistance after their feet were deformed.)*

Pose and Ask Have pairs of students write a dialogue/interview between a modern news reporter and a Chinese woman of the Song dynasty gentry, based on what they have learned in this text. Have volunteers read their dialogues to the class. Discuss issues raised.

Peasants Most Chinese were peasants who worked the land, living on what they produced. Drought and famine were a constant threat, but new tools and crops did improve the lives of many peasants.

To add to their income, some families produced handicrafts such as baskets or embroidered items. They carried these products to nearby market towns to sell or trade for salt, tea, or iron tools.

Peasants lived in small, largely self-sufficient villages that managed their own affairs. "Heaven is high," noted one Chinese saying, "and the emperor far away." Peasants relied on one another rather than the government. When disputes arose, a village leader and council of elders put pressure on the parties to resolve the problem. Only if such efforts failed did villagers take their disputes to the emperor's county representative.

In China, even peasants could move up in society through education and government service. If a bright peasant boy received an education and passed the civil service examinations, both he and his family rose in status. Slaves in early China, however, did not have such opportunities. As in many other parts of the world, slavery played a role in early China, though a limited one.

>> Despite the importance of trade, merchants had low social status in Chinese society. This was a result of the influence of Confucianism in Chinese life.

Merchants: Prosperous but Lowly In market towns and cities, some merchants acquired wealth. Still, according to Confucian tradition, merchants had an even lower social status than peasants since their riches came from the labor of others. An ambitious merchant, therefore, might buy land and educate one son to enter the ranks of the scholar-gentry.

The Confucian attitude toward merchants affected economic policy. Some rulers favored commerce but sought to control it. They often restricted where foreign merchants could live and even limited the activities of private traders. Still, Chinese trade flourished during Song times.

Status of Women Women had higher status in Tang and early Song times than they did later. Within the home, women were called upon to run family affairs. A man's wife and his mother had great authority, managing servants and family finances. Still, families valued boys more than girls. When a young woman married, she became a part of her husband's family. She could not keep the **dowry,** or the payment a woman brings to a marriage. If widowed, she could never remarry.

Women's subordinate position was reinforced in late Song times when the custom of foot binding emerged. The custom probably began at the imperial court but later spread to the lower classes. The feet of young girls were bound with long strips of cloth, producing a lily-shaped foot about half the size of a foot that was allowed to grow normally. Tiny feet and a stilted walk became a symbol of nobility and beauty. Foot binding was extremely painful, yet the custom survived. Even peasant parents feared that they could not find a husband for a daughter with large feet.

Not all girls in China had their feet bound. Peasants who needed their daughters to work in the fields did not accept the practice. Yet most women did have to submit to foot binding. Women with bound feet often could not walk without help. Thus, foot binding reinforced the Confucian tradition that women should remain inside the home.

? CHECK UNDERSTANDING How did the Confucian attitude towards merchants affect some Chinese economic policies?

Answers

Check Understanding *As the lowest members of society, their activities were restricted, including where they could live and sell their goods.*

English Language Proficiency Standards

Speaking 3.D.1 Before beginning this activity, remind students that special words used in history class are history vocabulary words. Explain that knowing these words can help improve their understanding of the topics. Then have students complete one of the following activities depending on their level of English proficiency.

Beginning Provide students with examples of vocabulary words from "The Rich Culture of Tang and Song China," such as *culture, scholar,* and *gentry*. Model using a bilingual dictionary to define these terms. Then read the text aloud, pausing to highlight any vocabulary terms. Help students use the bilingual dictionary to define the terms aloud and help students understand them in the context of the section.

Intermediate Read "The Rich Culture of Tang and Song China" aloud. Ask students to raise their hands when they hear an unfamiliar history vocabulary word. Pause to highlight these terms. Assist students as they use the bilingual

>> Homes of the nobility and wealthy were often designed along the lines of Buddhist temples. The homes included lovely courtyards and gardens, as well as guest rooms and banquet halls.

The Rich Culture of Tang and Song China

A prosperous economy supported the rich culture of Tang and Song China. Writers produced brilliant works of poetry and prose, while the works of artists survived the centuries.

Seeking Balance and Harmony in Nature Along with poetry, painting and calligraphy were essential skills for the scholar-gentry. In both of these arts, they sought balance and harmony through the mastery of simple strokes and lines. The Song period saw the triumph of Chinese landscape painting. Steeped in the Daoist tradition, painters sought to capture the spiritual essence of the natural world. "When you are planning to paint," instructed a Song artist, "you must always create a harmonious relationship between heaven and earth."

Misty mountains and delicate bamboo forests dominated Chinese landscapes. Yet Chinese painters also produced realistic, vivid portraits of emperors or lively scenes of city life.

Sculpture and Architecture Buddhist themes dominated sculpture and influenced Chinese architecture. Chinese sculptors created striking statues of the Buddha. These statues created such a strong impression that many people today picture the Buddha as a Chinese god rather than an Indian holy man.

In China, the Indian stupa evolved into the graceful Chinese **pagoda,** a multistoried temple with eaves that curve up at the corners. Although the splendid royal palaces of Chinese emperors were long ago destroyed, statues and pagodas survived.

Porcelain The Chinese perfected techniques in making porcelain, a shiny, hard pottery that was prized as the finest in the world. They developed beautiful glazes to decorate vases, tea services, and other objects that Westerners would later call "chinaware."

Artists also produced porcelain figures of camels, elegant court ladies playing polo, and bearded foreigners newly arrived from their travels on the Silk Road.

Chinese Literature Prose and poetry flowed from the brushes of Tang and Song writers. Scholars produced works on philosophy, religion, and history. Short stories that often blended fantasy, romance, and adventure made their first appearance in Chinese literature. Among the gentry, poetry was the most respected form of Chinese literature. Confucian scholars were expected to master the skills of poetry. We know the names of some 200 major and 400 minor Tang and Song poets. Their works touched on Buddhist and Daoist themes

The Rich Culture of Tang and Song China

Explain to students that a prosperous economy made possible the cultural achievements of the Tang and Song dynasties. Various influences, including Daoism, Buddhism, admiration of nature, and respect for older traditions, shaped the art and literature of this rich period. In turn, art influenced everyday life, as Chinese gentry chose to live in beautiful homes that reflected their artistic values.

Online Project the **Interactive Gallery: Chinese House and Compound** and click through the images with students.

Analyze Images How does the Chinese house reflect ideas about art, nature, and respect for traditions? *(Answers will vary. Students may cite the space set aside for ancestor worship as reflecting respect for traditions, the many garden spaces as reflecting the love of nature, and the careful arrangement of all the rooms and spaces as reflecting the love of harmony.)*

ACTIVE CLASSROOM

Use the Audio Tour strategy. Pair students. Have the first student give the second a verbal "tour" of the house—what does it show? Have the second student give the first an explanation of what it means. If you have suitable technology, have students make an mp3 of their audio tour and share it with other students.

Guided Reading and Discussion

Apply Concepts Ask students to review the major themes of the three poets discussed in the text and then look at the images of artworks. Have half the students choose one of the themes and write a poem. Have the other half read one of the poems and make a drawing to accompany it. Display the poems and drawings.

dictionary to define the terms and then read their definitions aloud. Help them understand the terms in context.

Advanced Instruct pairs of students to scan the text to make a list of at least four grade-level history vocabulary words. Then have pairs define each word on their list and read the definitions to each other. Encourage students to reread the text while using their list of definitions as a reference.

Advanced High Have students scan the text for grade-level content vocabulary words and create a glossary for their words. Glossaries should include a definition, the part of speech, and an example sentence for each word. Then have students read their glossary to a partner.

Topic 9 Lesson 2

SYNTHESIZE

Online Project the **Digital Activity: Tang China**. Have students fill out the chart and then discuss how each factor helped the Tang dynasty gain and maintain power.

Discuss Ask students if they agree with the Tang that a strong central government is the key to a well-run country. *(Some students will agree, based on their knowledge of U.S. history, but others may favor a system with more local control.)*

DEMONSTRATE

Online Assign the **Digital Lesson Quiz** for this lesson if you haven't already done so. Students will be offered automatic remediation or enrichment based on their score.

Make the following observation to the class, then pose the question:

In "Golden Ages in China: Tang and Song Dynasties" you read about how the Tang and Song represent two golden ages, marked by advances in science, technology, the arts, and government.

Support a Point of View With Evidence The Song dynasty survived despite military setbacks in part because it supported innovation and trade. Do you think countries can be strong without a powerful army? Explain. *(Some students may argue that a strong military is necessary to defend a nation's vital interests; others may point out that economic power can be a powerful weapon as well.)*

Topic Inquiry

Have students continue their investigations for the Topic Inquiry.

>> The famous Tang poet Li Bao is shown dining with friends. Such enjoyments were often the subject of his poems.

as well as on social issues. Many poems reflected on the shortness of life and the immensity of the universe.

Probably the greatest Tang poet was Li Bo (lee boh). A zestful lover of life and freedom, he moved about from one place to another for most of his life.

He wrote some 2,000 poems celebrating harmony with nature or lamenting the passage of time. A popular legend says that Li Bo drowned when he tried to embrace the reflection of the moon in a lake.

> You ask me why I dwell in the green mountain; I smile and make no reply for my heart is free of care. As the peach-blossom flows down stream and is gone into the unknown, I have a world apart that is not among men.
>
> —From "Green Mountain" by Li Bo

More realistic and less romantic were the poems of Li Bo's friend Du Fu. His verses described the horrors of war or condemned the lavishness of the court. A later poet, Li Qingzhao (lee ching jow), described the experience of women left behind when loved ones went off to war. Her poems reflect a time when invasion threatened to bring the brilliant Song dynasty to an end.

SUMMARIZE What themes did Tang and Song arts address?

ELPS **ELPS 3.D.1** Find and define vocabulary words in *The Rich Culture of Tang and Song China.*

ASSESSMENT

1. **Draw Conclusions** In what ways did the rise of the Tang dynasty unify and benefit China?
2. **Determine Relevance** What was the significance of the Grand Canal to the Song dynasty?
3. **Describe** Describe the social structure of China under the Tang and Song dynasties.
4. **Recognize Ideologies** How did the social structure of the Tang and Song dynasties reflect Confucian traditions?
5. **Analyze Information** What ideas and traditions were reflected in Chinese paintings?

Answers

Summarize *Buddhist and Daoist themes as well as social issues*

Assessment

1. China enjoyed political stability, efficient government, thriving agriculture, expanding trade, and artistic achievements, all of which helped create a stronger sense of national identity and purpose.
2. The Grand Canal allowed the Chinese to ship grain from southern China to northern China. The availability of more and better-distributed food allowed the Song to maintain its prosperity in spite of foreign military threats.
3. At the top were the emperor and royal family followed by the gentry, peasants, and merchants.
4. It was a stable social order based on rank and the duties associated with each rank. For women, the Confucian tradition emphasized the woman's role in the home.
5. balance, harmony, and the Daoist tradition of seeking the spiritual essence of the natural world

9.3 In the early 1200s, a new wave of invaders swept into China from the north and overran Song lands. The invaders were the Mongols, who had burst out of Central Asia to conquer a vast empire across Asia and Europe.

>> Mongol archers on horseback, as shown in this Ming illustration, were tough warriors who could swiftly shoot arrows at enemies from all sides.

Interactive Flipped Video

The Mongol Empire and Ming China

TEKS
1.C, 1.D, 4.K, 7.E, 25.A, 27.A

>> Objectives

Summarize how Mongol armies built an empire.

Describe China under Mongol rule.

Understand how the Ming restored Chinese rule.

Explain why the Ming explored the seas for only a brief period.

>> Key Terms

steppe
Genghis Khan
Kublai Khan
Yuan dynasty
Marco Polo
Ming dynasty
abacus
Zheng He

Mongols Build an Empire

The Mongols were a nomadic herding people who grazed their horses and sheep on the **steppes,** or vast, treeless plains, of Central Asia. Rival Mongol clans spent much of their time warring with one another. In the early 1200s, however, a brilliant Mongol chieftain united these warring tribes. This chieftain took the name **Genghis Khan,** meaning "Universal Ruler." Under his leadership, Mongol forces conquered a vast empire that stretched from the Pacific Ocean to Eastern Europe.

Mongols Conquer China Genghis Khan imposed strict military discipline and demanded absolute loyalty. His highly trained, mobile armies had some of the most skilled horsemen in the world. Genghis Khan had a reputation for fierceness. He could order the massacre of an entire city. Yet he also could be generous, rewarding the bravery of a single fighter.

Mongol armies conquered the Asian steppe lands with some ease, but as they turned on China, they encountered the problem of attacking walled cities. Chinese and Turkish military experts taught them to use cannons and other new weapons. The Mongols and Chinese launched missiles against each other from metal tubes filled

PEARSON realize. www.PearsonTexas.com Access your Digital Lesson.

Topic 9 Lesson 3

The Mongol Empire and Ming China

CONNECT

Preview Have students preview the **Lesson Objectives** and the list of **Key Terms**.

Students can also preview all the **Key Terms** and **Academic Vocabulary** using the **Interactive Reading Notepad** on the digital course or preview a summary of the lesson in the **Reading and Note Taking Study Guide**.

Online Use the **Editable Presentation** found on the digital course to present the main ideas for this lesson.

Start Up Activity

Have students answer this question as they get settled: What do you know about the Mongols? Have them share their ideas with another student.

Discuss Tell students that the Mongols were skilled horsemen who could shoot arrows while riding on horseback. How do you think an attacking army of such horsemen would affect an enemy army of foot soldiers? *(Possible answers: astonishment, determination, terror, or flight)*

Online You can also project the **Start Up Activity** from the course.

INVESTIGATE

Have students read the lesson using the **Reading and Note Taking Study Guide** to help them take notes and understand the text as they read.

Mongols Build an Empire

Mongols—nomadic warriors from the north of China—swept across Central Asia, conquering vast territory, attacking China, and building an empire that stretched from the Pacific Ocean to eastern Europe.

Aa Vocabulary Builder

1. Have students pronounce the following academic vocabulary terms in this lesson and clarify the part of speech. For difficult or polysyllabic words, break them into syllables and pronounce them with the students.
2. Explain what the word means in common "student-friendly" language using synonyms and antonyms when possible. Provide concrete examples to clarify the meaning, and rephrase the definition.

dominate: to have control of or power over someone or something

annihilate: to destroy someone or something completely; to defeat someone completely

oppressive: very cruel or unfair

technique: a way of doing something by using special knowledge or skill

subdue: to get control of a violent or dangerous person or group by using force, punishment, etc.

eliminate: to remove something that is not wanted or needed

integrate: to combine two or more things to form or create something

Topic 9 Lesson 3

Online Project the **Interactive Map: The Mongol Empire** and step through the layers on the map.

ACTIVE CLASSROOM

Employ the Make Headlines strategy with the Interactive Map to explore the Mongol invasions' impact. Ask: If you were to write a headline right now to capture the most important aspect that should be remembered about any of these invasions, what would that headline be? Pass your headline to a partner for them to review—they can keep yours or ask for theirs back. *(Possible answer: "Mongol Horsemen Strike From the Steppes!")*

Draw Conclusions Why did Genghis Khan impose strict discipline and demand absolute loyalty from his armies? *(Possible answer: Strong discipline and absolute loyalty kept his warriors, who came from many different clans, focused on conquering enemy forces rather than fighting among themselves to settle old feuds.)*

Guided Reading and Discussion

Tell students that Genghis Khan could be both cruel and kind. Ask them to discuss how these contrasting characteristics were reflected in the way the Mongols conquered versus the way they ruled. *(In conquest, the Mongols were highly destructive; yet they were tolerant and even respectful of people they ruled.)*

Mongols Rule China

Tell students that Genghis Khan's grandson, Kublai Khan, overthrew China's Song dynasty in 1279. Under Mongol rule, China was linked by trade with Europe and other conquered lands. The Mongols tried to maintain their own ways, but a mix of Chinese and foreign customs developed.

with gunpowder. This use of cannons in warfare would soon spread westward to Europe.

Genghis Khan did not live to complete the conquest of China. His heirs, however, continued to expand the Mongol empire. For the next 150 years, they dominated much of Asia. Their furious assaults toppled empires and spread destruction from southern Russia through Muslim lands in Southwest Asia to China. In China, the Mongols devastated the flourishing province of Sichuan (see chwahn), and annihilated its great capital city of Chengdu.

Impact of Mongol Rule Once conquest was completed, the Mongols were not oppressive rulers. Often, they allowed conquered people to live much as they had before—as long as they regularly paid tribute to the Mongols.

Genghis Khan had set an example for his successors by ruling conquered lands with toleration and justice. Although the Mongol warrior had no use for city life, he respected scholars, artists, and artisans. He listened to the ideas of Confucians, Buddhists, Christians, Muslims, Jews, and Zoroastrians.

The Mongol Peace In the 1200s and 1300s, the sons and grandsons of Genghis Khan established peace and order within their domains. Today, many historians refer to this period of order as the *Pax Mongolica*, or Mongol Peace.

Political stability set the stage for economic growth. Under the protection of the Mongols, who now controlled the great Silk Road, trade flourished across Eurasia.

According to a contemporary, Mongol rule meant that people "enjoyed such a peace that a man might have journeyed from the land of sunrise to the land of sunset with a golden platter upon his head without suffering the least violence from anyone."

Cultural exchanges increased as foods, tools, inventions, and ideas spread along the protected trade routes. From China, the use of gunpowder moved westward into Europe. Techniques of papermaking also reached parts of Europe, and crops and trees from the Middle East were carried into East Asia.

DESCRIBE How did the Mongol rulers change once their conquests were complete?

Mongols Rule China

Although Genghis Khan had subdued northern China, the Mongols needed nearly 70 more years to conquer the south. Genghis Khan's grandson, **Kublai Khan** (KOO bly KAHN), finally toppled the last Song emperor in 1279. From his capital at Khanbaliq, present-day

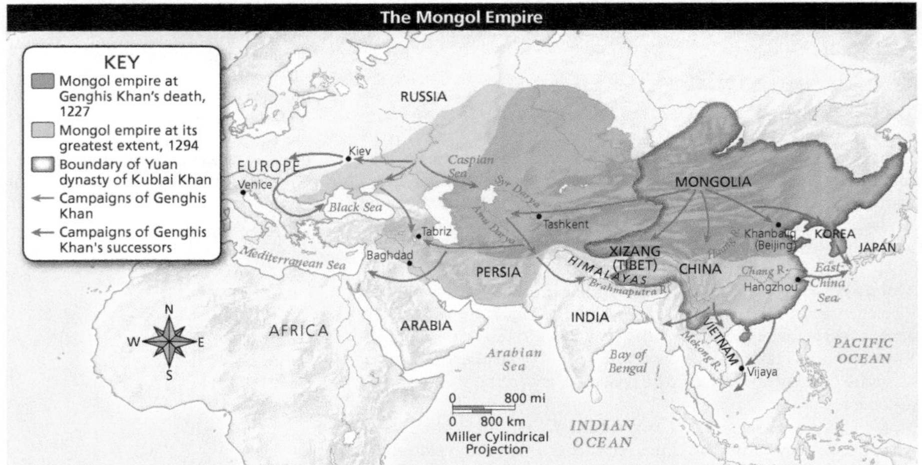

>> **Analyze Maps** At its height, the Mongol empire was the world's largest up to that time. Describe the growth of the empire between 1227 and 1294. Did Genghis Khan or his successors conquer the most land?

Interactive Map

Answers

Analyze Maps *The empire expanded to include more of China and Persia and parts of Russia and eastern Europe; Genghis Khan.*

Describe *They were not oppressive but allowed people to live much as they had before, as long as they paid tribute.*

English Language Proficiency Standards

Listening 2.I.3 Have students listen as "Mongols Rule China" is read aloud. As the selection is read, pause and ask *how* questions about the text. Ask students to respond using single words, phrases, and sentences.

Beginning Reread the section aloud to students, pausing to explain challenging vocabulary and concepts. Retell the content in more accessible language. Then ask students to listen to each of the following questions before completing the sentence frames below: How did Kublai Khan keep Mongols and Chinese separated? What was the Chinese name of Kublai Khan's dynasty? How did Kublai Khan show tolerance for many cultures?

- Kublai Khan kept Mongols and Chinese separate by _____.
- The Chinese name of Kublai Khan's dynasty was _____.
- Kublai Khan showed tolerance for many cultures by _____.

Beijing, Kublai Khan ruled all of China as well as Korea, Tibet, and Vietnam.

Government Kublai Khan tried to prevent the Mongols from being absorbed into Chinese civilization as other conquerors of China had been. He decreed that only Mongols could serve in the military. He also reserved the highest government jobs for Mongols or for other non-Chinese officials whom he employed. Still, because there were too few Mongols to control so vast an empire, Kublai allowed Chinese officials to continue to rule in the provinces.

Under Mongol rule, an uneasy mix of Chinese and foreign customs developed. Kublai adopted a Chinese name for his dynasty, the **Yuan** (yoo AHN), and turned Khanbaliq into a Chinese walled city. At the same time, he had Arab architects design his palace, and many rooms reflected Mongol steppe dwellings. Kublai rebuilt and extended the Grand Canal to his new capital, which made the shipment of rice and other goods easier. He also welcomed many foreigners to his court, including the African Muslim world traveler Ibn Battuta.

As long as the Mongol empire prospered, contacts between Europe and Asia continued. The Mongols tolerated a variety of beliefs. The pope sent Christian priests to Beijing, while Muslims set up their own communities in China. Meanwhile, some Chinese products moved toward Europe. They included gunpowder, porcelain, and playing cards.

Marco Polo Describes China The Italian merchant **Marco Polo** was one of many visitors to China during the Yuan dynasty. Although there is some debate on whether Marco Polo reached China, most historians acknowledge that he did indeed reach Cathay (northern China). In 1271, Polo left Venice with his father and uncle. He crossed Persia and Central Asia to reach China. He then spent 17 years in Kublai's service. Finally, he returned to Venice by sea, visiting Southeast Asia and India along the way.

In his writings, Marco Polo left a vivid account of the wealth and splendor of China. He described the royal palace of Kublai Khan and also described China's efficient royal mail system, with couriers riding swift ponies along the empire's well-kept roads. Furthermore, he reported that the city of Hangzhou was 10 or 12 times the size of Venice, one of Italy's richest city-states. In the next centuries, Polo's reports sparked European interest in the riches of Asia.

>> Marco Polo is welcomed at the court of Kublai Khan during the 1200s, as depicted in this hand-colored European illustration from the 1800s.

Interactive Gallery

>> Kublai Khan, the emperor of China, is portrayed as he was in the 1260s, an alert, vigorous, simply attired man. He wears the symbolic white robes of a Mongol shaman.

DESCRIBE How did Kublai Khan organize Mongol rule in China?

Online Project the **Interactive Gallery: Marco Polo and Life Under the Mongols** and click through the hotspots with students. Explain that Marco Polo was among many foreign visitors to the court of Kublai Khan during the Yuan dynasty.

ACTIVE CLASSROOM

Use the Conversation With History strategy. Have students think about having a conversation with Marco Polo or Kublai Khan. Tell them: Write down a question you'd like to ask, then what that person would say to you, and what you would say in response. *(Possible answer: I ask Marco Polo, "What did people in Venice say when you told them about China?" Polo: "They thought I made everything up or was crazy." Me: "So then you wrote it all down in your book.")*

Guided Reading and Discussion

Point out that the Mongols conquered huge territories and dominated many different groups. Ask students why they think the Mongols did not oppress conquered peoples and allowed them to live much as they did before. *(Possible answer: The Mongols were nomads organized by clans, not city dwellers or administrators. They wanted to receive tribute, not change beliefs or cultural traditions. Also, there were not enough Mongols to control fully all the areas they had conquered.)*

Predict Consequences Have students consider the ways an empire such as that of the Mongols can change over time. Tell students to write three or four consequences that they predict would occur. List their predictions on the board. *(Possible answers: empire expands (perhaps too far), leadership weakens, corruption occurs, internal conflicts arise, rival groups fight for power, external enemies attack, territory becomes divided up)*

Intermediate Reread the section aloud. Pause after reading each paragraph of the text to retell the content in more accessible language. Help students with any challenging vocabulary or concepts. Ask students to listen to the same questions and complete the same sentence frames as in the Beginning ELPS activity.

Advanced Have students reread the text aloud to a partner, alternating after each paragraph. Have pairs demonstrate their listening comprehension by summarizing each paragraph after it is read. Then ask student pairs to answer the following questions: How did Kublai Khan keep Mongol and Chinese cultures from merging? What did Kublai Khan do that showed tolerance for many cultures?

Advanced High Have students listen as volunteers read the text aloud, then summarize each subsection. Then instruct students to discuss the questions from the Advanced ELPS activity.

Answers

Describe *He allowed only Mongols to serve in the military and kept the highest government jobs for Mongols, though Chinese officials still ruled in the provinces.*

Topic 9 Lesson 3

Chinese Rule Restored by the Ming

Tell students that the Chinese finally pushed back the Mongols and founded a new dynasty, the Ming, in 1368. Ming rulers revived the civil service system, repaired the canal system, and promoted agriculture and industry. To purchase highly valued Ming porcelain, silk, and other trade goods, European traders brought huge quantities of precious metals to China. The arts and literature flourished, as did scholarship.

Guided Reading and Discussion

Explain that major ideas in mathematics, science, and technology—such as abacus calculation, gunpowder, and the magnetic compass—originated and were first applied in China long before diffusing through Asia and beyond. At this time, use of the abacus rapidly spread inside and beyond China. Then ask: How did the Chinese apply European science to solve one of their own problems? *(Chinese scholars applied Western astronomy and technology to improve the accuracy of their calendar.)*

Key Terms

Ask students to find the key term **abacus** (in bold) in the text. Explain that an abacus is a device for making calculations manually. It typically consists of a rectangular frame containing beads that slide along vertical rods, which are attached to the frame. It can be used to quickly perform not only addition, subtraction, multiplication, and division but also square roots.

ELPS **ELPS 2.I.3** Practice listening comprehension by summarizing and answering questions about *Mongols Rule China*.

Chinese Rule Restored by the Ming

The Yuan dynasty declined after the death of Kublai Khan, which occurred in 1294. Most Chinese despised the foreign Mongol rulers. Confucian scholars retreated into their own world, seeing little to gain from the barbarians. Heavy taxes, corruption, and natural disasters led to frequent uprisings. Finally, Zhu Yuanzhang (dzoo YOO AHND zahng), a peasant leader, forged a rebel army that toppled the Mongols and pushed them back beyond the Great Wall. In 1368, he founded a new Chinese dynasty, which he called the **Ming,** meaning "brilliant."

Ming Policies Early Ming rulers sought to reassert Chinese greatness after years of foreign rule. They initially moved the capital to Nanjing, which they felt possessed more characteristics of the Chinese, but eventually moved it back to present-day Beijing. The Ming restored the civil service system, and Confucian learning again became the road to success. The civil service exams became more rigorous than ever. A board of censors watched over the bureaucracy, eliminating corruption and disloyalty.

>> Zhu Yuanzhang ousted the Mongols and led China as the Hongwu emperor, shown here, for 30 years. He founded the Ming dynasty, which ruled China for almost 300 years.

Interactive 3-D Model

Economic Revival Economically, Ming China was very productive. The fertile, well-irrigated plains of eastern China supported a population of more than 100 million. In the Chang River valley, peasants produced huge rice crops. Better methods of fertilizing helped to improve farming. Reshaping the landscape helped as well. Some farmers cut horizontal steps called terraces into steep hillsides to gain soil in which to grow crops. In the 1500s, new crops reached China from the Americas, especially corn and sweet potatoes.

Chinese cities, such as Nanjing, were home to many industries, including porcelain, paper, and tools. The Ming repaired the extensive canal system that linked various regions, made trade easier, and allowed cities to grow. New technologies increased output in manufacturing. Better methods of printing, for example, led to the production of a flood of books.

During this period, the Ming also carefully limited the extent and duration of trade with Europeans. Over time, one Chinese trade practice significantly impacted global trade. By accepting only silver or gold in exchange for goods in high demand in Europe, such as silk, tea, and porcelain, the Ming caused a massive flow of precious metals into China. First, China traded silk and tea for silver from Japan. Then, in the 1500s, vast quantities of silver from Spain's new territories in the Americas were shipped across the Pacific to the Philippines (claimed by Spain in 1565) to purchase Chinese goods.

Flourishing Culture Ming China also saw a revival of arts and literature. Ming artists developed their own styles of landscape painting and created brilliant blue and white porcelain. Ming vases were among the most valuable and popular Chinese products exported to the West.

Confucian scholars continued to produce classical poetry. At the same time, new forms of popular literature to be enjoyed by the common people began to emerge. Ming writers composed novels, including *The Water Margin* about an outlaw gang that tries to end injustice by corrupt officials. Ming writers also produced the world's first detective stories.

Ming Math, Science, and Technology In the late fifteenth century, China was the richest civilization in the world, possessing science and technology far beyond that of Europe. Gunpowder, papermaking,

D Differentiate Challenge/Gifted Ask students to do additional research on major Ming Chinese trade goods, such as porcelain, silk, or tea, and present their findings.

English Language Proficiency Standards

Speaking 3.D.2 Read "Chinese Rule Restored by the Ming" aloud to the class. Then review a few content area vocabulary words with students by providing examples like *mathematical achievements* and *technological achievements*. Explain that it helps to study new vocabulary words when learning new concepts in history. Then have students complete one of the following activities depending on their level of English proficiency.

Beginning Display the words *mathematical achievements*. Say the phrase and ask students to repeat it. Then define the phrase. Have students whisper-read the section "Ming Math, Science, and Technology" as you read it aloud. Ask students to identify information about Ming mathematical achievements using one- or two-word responses. Help them say one sentence to show that they understand the effect of Chinese developments in mathematics.

Intermediate Display the words *technological achievements*. Have students define the phrase and then say the phrase and definition to a partner. Instruct pairs to identify how the

Topic 9 Lesson 3

the magnetic compass, horse collars, cast iron, textile machinery, and many other technologies originated and were used in China long before spreading elsewhere.

In mathematics, after the brilliant Song and Yuan achievements in theory, research turned more to popular and practical application. Many earlier achievements were lost or forgotten. Taking the place of traditional Chinese counting rods for calculations, the **abacus,** invented much earlier, spread rapidly within and beyond China. To explain arithmetic on the abacus, Cheng Dawei wrote the *Suanfa tongzong* ("Systematic Treatise on Mathematics," 1592) and included his summary of contemporary mathematical knowledge.

Ming scholars at this time sought to integrate their own traditions with the Western mathematics and science they were learning from Jesuit missionaries. Knowing that the Chinese calendar had become increasingly inaccurate, the scholar Xu Guangqi thought of a way to repair it. In 1629, the emperor approved his plan to reform the Chinese calendar by employing Western astronomy and technology—including telescopes—to gather information about the heavenly bodies.

Xu Guangqi led the imperial research program. Telescopes and other instruments were constructed, allowing Chinese scholars, helped by Jesuit priests, to make observations, translate manuscripts, and produce star atlases and a catalog. By using the new data and tools, movements of the sun, moon, and planets could be more accurately predicted and the calendar could be corrected.

IDENTIFY How did Ming rulers restore an earlier style of Chinese government?

ELPS ELPS 3.D.2 Practice using content vocabulary by identifying and summarizing information from *Chinese Rule Restored by the Ming.*

Chinese Fleets Explore the Seas

Early Ming rulers sent Chinese fleets into distant waters. The most extraordinary of these ventures were the voyages of the Chinese admiral and diplomat **Zheng He** (jeng he).

The Great Fleets of Zheng He Between 1405 and 1433, Zheng He made seven expeditions at the head of large fleets. His goal was to promote trade and collect tribute from lesser powers across the "western seas." He departed at the head of a fleet of 62 huge ships and

>> This illustration from an 1825 French book shows a Chinese merchant calculating with an abacus, or *suan pan* ("calculating plate").

>> Xu Guangqi (1562–1633), shown with colleague Matteo Ricci in this engraving from about 1600, converted to Christianity and was the first Chinese person to translate European books into Chinese.

Chinese Fleets Explore the Seas

Make sure that students understand that extensive voyages of exploration and trade such as Zheng He's took place during the early part of the long Ming dynasty (1368–1644), when China's rulers sought to reaffirm the greatness of their country. The aim of these voyages was to show the glory of the Ming government and to collect tribute from lesser foreign powers, as well as to promote trade.

Ming used astronomy and technology. Have pairs write, then say, one or two sentences to summarize Ming technological advancements.

Advanced Have students define *astronomy* and *technology*. Instruct them to review the text to identify how the Ming used astronomy and technology. Then have students analyze how these advances helped the Ming connect with Western cultures. Finally, have students share their ideas with a partner.

Advanced High Have students summarize Ming mathematical and technological achievements using classroom resources. Instruct them to identify how the Ming used astronomy and technology. Have them analyze how these advances allowed them to connect with Western cultures and share their ideas with the group.

Answers

Identify *They restored the civil service system, and Confucian learning again became the road to success.*

Topic 9 Lesson 3

Analyze Images

Have students examine the infographic The Seven Voyages of Zheng He. Look at the section for each voyage and the sequence of voyages as a whole. Remind students that soon after the fleet's final voyage the Ming ruler stopped the building of seagoing ships, ending overseas trading and exploration expeditions. His reasons are unknown but may have included cost, lack of profits, or opposition from Confucian scholars at court who, lacking interest in such activities, felt their civilization was superior to all others and wanted to preserve China's ancient traditions.

Draw Inferences In what ways do you think Zheng He's voyages affected the places he visited? Cite information from the text and infographic to support your answer. *(Zheng He's voyages had a significant impact wherever his fleets visited. He often provided the first contact with China and its valuable trade goods. After his voyages, Chinese merchants established their permanent presence in the trading centers of Southeast Asia and India. He also helped open diplomatic relations with foreign nations by attending an Indian king's inauguration, visiting heads of state, and transporting ambassadors to and from China.)*

Guided Reading and Discussion

Predict Consequences Ask students what they think the long-term effects on global trade would have been if China had not closed down its overseas exploration and trade in 1435. Tell students to write three or four consequences that they predict would occur. List their predictions on the board. *(Sample answers: Chinese goods and influence would have been greater and more widespread earlier; European and African goods and influence in China would have been greater; Chinese explorers and traders might have reached and colonized Australia, the Pacific islands, and the Americas.)*

> "The countries beyond the horizon and from the ends of the earth have all become subjects. . . . We have traversed immense waterspaces and have beheld in the ocean huge waves like mountains rising sky high, and we have set eyes on barbarian regions far away . . . while our sails loftily unfurled like clouds day and night continued their course, traversing those savage waves as if we were treading on a public throughfare."
>
> —Zeng He, quoted in *The True Dates of the Chinese Maritime Expeditions in the Early Fifteenth Century* (Duyvendak)

>> Zheng He and his crew and ships are portrayed in this colorful relief at the Gedong Batu Temple in Semarang, Java Indonesia. An annual celebration commemorates his visit.

over 200 smaller ones, carrying a crew of about 28,000 sailors. The largest ships measured 400 feet long.

Between 1405 and 1433, Zheng He explored the coasts of Southeast Asia and India and the entrances to the Red Sea and the Persian Gulf. He also visited many ports in East Africa.

In the wake of these expeditions, Chinese merchants settled in Southeast Asia and India and became a permanent presence in their trading centers. Exotic animals, such as giraffes, were imported from foreign lands as well. The voyages also showed local rulers the power and strength of the Chinese empire.

Zheng He set up an engraved stone tablet listing the dates, places, and achievements of his voyages. The tablet proudly proclaimed that the Ming had unified the "seas and continents" even more than the Han and Tang had done.

> "The countries beyond the horizon and from the ends of the earth have all become subjects. . . . We have traversed immense waterspaces and have beheld in the ocean huge waves like mountains rising sky high, and we have set eyes on barbarian regions far away . . . while our sails loftily unfurled like clouds day and night continued their course, traversing those savage waves as if we were treading on a public throughfare."
>
> —Zeng He, quoted in *The True Dates of the Chinese Maritime Expeditions in the Early Fifteenth Century* (Duyvendak)

The Ming Turn Inward In 1435, the Ming emperor suddenly banned the building of giant seagoing ships like the ones Zheng He had commanded. In time, ships with more than two masts were forbidden. In the 1500s, when Europeans first reached China by sea, the Ming carefully limited the extent and duration of trade. They did, however, demand silver or gold in exchange for Chinese products that Europeans wanted, such as silk, tea, and porcelain. This policy led to a flood of silver and gold into China.

Assessment

1. Genghis Khan united the warring Mongol clans, forged them into highly trained, mobile armies, and led them to conquer a vast empire. His heirs continued to add to the empire and dominated much of Asia for the next 150 years.
2. The Mongols maintained peace and order. They were not oppressive but allowed people to live much as they had before. Only Mongols could serve in the military and in the highest government positions. Chinese officials were allowed to continue to rule in the provinces. A mix of Mongol and Chinese customs developed, and a variety of beliefs were tolerated. Foreign visitors were welcomed, and trade flourished on the Silk Road.
3. Early Ming rulers moved the capital to Nanjing, which they felt was more characteristically Chinese. They restored the civil service system and once again gave prominence to Confucian learning.

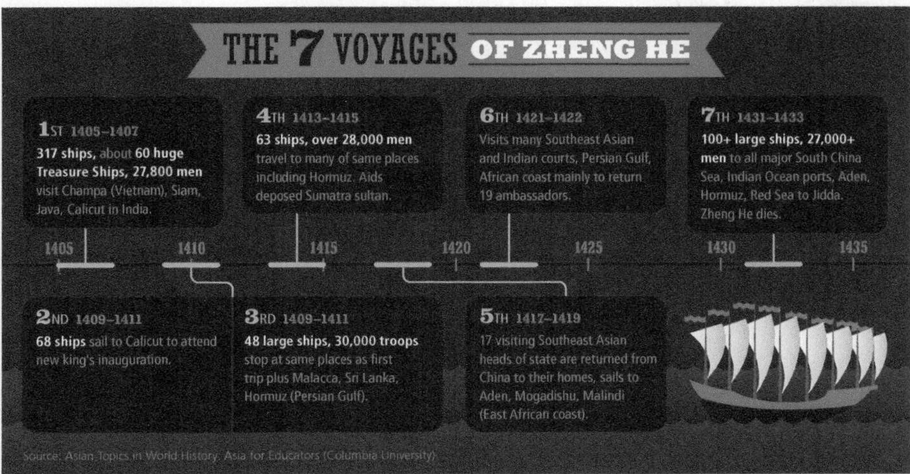

THE 7 VOYAGES OF ZHENG HE
1ST 1405–1407
317 ships, about 60 huge Treasure Ships, 27,800 men visit Champa (Vietnam), Siam, Java, Calicut in India.
4TH 1413–1415
63 ships, over 28,000 men travel to many of same places including Hormuz. Aids deposed Sumatra sultan.
6TH 1421–1422
Visits many Southeast Asian and Indian courts, Persian Gulf, African coast mainly to return 19 ambassadors.
7TH 1431–1433
100+ large ships, 27,000+ men to all major South China Sea, Indian Ocean ports, Aden, Hormuz, Red Sea to Jidda. Zheng He dies.
1405
1410
1415
1420
1425
1430
1435
2ND 1409–1411
68 ships sail to Calicut to attend new king's inauguration.
3RD 1409–1411
48 large ships, 30,000 troops stop at same places as first trip plus Malacca, Sri Lanka, Hormuz (Persian Gulf).
5TH 1417–1419
17 visiting Southeast Asian heads of state are returned from China to their homes, sails to Aden, Mogadishu, Malindi (East African coast).
Source: Asian Topics in World History, Asia for Educators (Columbia University)

>> Zheng He's epic voyages were multipurpose expeditions of exploration, diplomacy, and trade to Southeast Asia, India, and Africa. **Analyze Data** Which voyage had the largest number of ships?

Why did China, with its advanced naval technology, turn its back on overseas exploration? The fleets were costly and did not produce any profits. Also Confucian scholars at court had little interest in overseas ventures. To them, Chinese civilization was the most successful in the world. They wanted to preserve its ancient traditions, which they saw as the source of stability.

Eventually, this rigid loyalty to tradition would weaken China. Less than 60 years after China halted overseas expeditions, the explorer Christopher Columbus would sail west from Spain to find a sea route to Asia.

 **IDENTIFY** What occurred in 1435 that changed China's relationship with the rest of the world?

ASSESSMENT

1. **Summarize** Summarize how Mongol armies built an empire.
2. **Describe** Describe China under Mongol rule.
3. **Draw Conclusions** How did the Ming restore Chinese rule?
4. **Identify Cause and Effect** How did Ming China impact global trade?
5. **Explain** Why did the Ming explore the seas for only a brief period?

SYNTHESIZE

Online Project the **Digital Activity: Timeline of the Mongol Empire in China**. Have students take five minutes to answer the questions in the activity and then share their responses with a partner. Discuss with students how keeping track of the sequence of historical events can help them connect those events and determine causes and effects.

DEMONSTRATE

Online Assign the **Digital Lesson Quiz** for this lesson if you haven't already done so. Students will be offered automatic remediation or enrichment based on their score.

Make the following observation to the class, then pose the questions:

In "The Mongol Empire and Ming China" you read about how the Mongol armies built their conquests into an empire that included China. During the Ming dynasty's restoration of Chinese rule, the country's economy expanded and its arts and literature revived.

Predict Consequences What do you think might have happened if Kublai Khan had allowed Chinese, not just Mongols, to serve in the Mongol army? *(Sample response: Chinese soldiers might have shared their culture with the Mongols, thus lessening Chinese resentment of Mongol rule.)*

Draw Inferences How do you think the contact that Zheng He's fleets made with distant lands affected Ming China? *(Answers will vary. Some students might suggest that Zheng He's voyages did not have a great impact on most of Ming China during this flourishing period. Other students, however, may say that there might have been enough potential foreign influence to disturb Confucian scholars at court, causing them to oppose further seagoing ventures.)*

Topic Inquiry

Have students continue their investigations for the Topic Inquiry.

They also sent Chinese fleets on long exploration and trading voyages to display the glory and power of their government.

4. The Ming strictly limited the access of foreign traders to China. And by accepting only silver or gold in exchange for Chinese goods, such as silk, tea, and porcelain, the Ming caused a huge flow of silver into China. In the 1500s, the Spanish shipped vast quantities of silver across the Pacific from their mines in the Americas.
5. Historians are uncertain why. Scholars hypothesize that the great cost of the Chinese fleets was not matched by profits made from the voyages. Moreover, Confucian scholars at the imperial court had no interest in overseas exploration or trade. They felt that their own civilization was far superior to all others and wished to protect the source of their culture's stability: China's ancient traditions.

Answers

Analyze Data *the first*

Identify *The Ming emperor banned the building of seagoing ships and halted expeditions, thereby ending overseas exploration.*

Topic 9 Lesson 4

Korea and Its Traditions

CONNECT

Preview Have students preview the **Lesson Objectives** and the list of **Key Terms**.

Students can also preview all the **Key Terms** and **Academic Vocabulary** using the **Interactive Reading Notepad** on the digital course or preview a summary of the lesson in the **Reading and Note Taking Study Guide**.

Online Use the **Editable Presentation** found on the digital course to present the main ideas for this lesson.

Start Up Activity

Tell students that Korea is a small country surrounded by larger, more powerful countries. Ask them to think of other countries or peoples they have studied about who were surrounded by larger, more powerful neighbors, such as those living near the Roman empire. Ask: How did the nearness of such neighbors affect the people who lived in these smaller countries? Make a prediction about how Korea might have been influenced by neighbors such as China and Japan.

Online You can also project the **Start Up Activity** from the course.

INVESTIGATE

Have students read the lesson using the **Reading and Note Taking Study Guide** to help them take notes and understand the text as they read.

The Geography of Korea

Explain that Korea's geography has played an important role in its development. Almost 70 percent of the Korean peninsula is covered by mountains, making farming difficult. Most Koreans lived and live on the coastal plains and depend on the sea for food. Equally influential is Korea's location. Its northern neighbor China has exerted many cultural, religious, political, and technological influences on Korea. Because it lies between China and its other larger neighbor, Japan, Korea has often served as a bridge linking China and Japan.

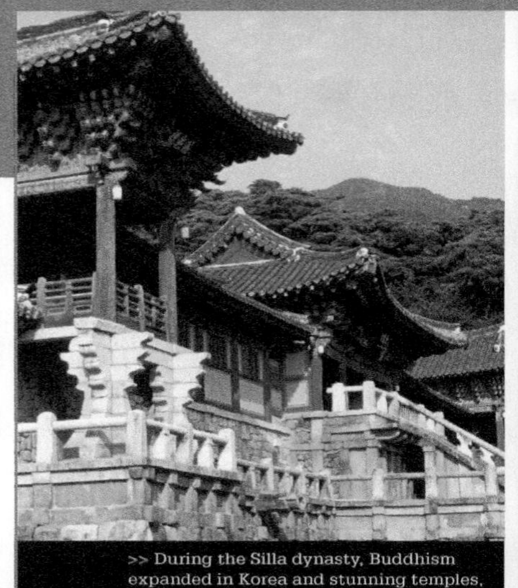

>> During the Silla dynasty, Buddhism expanded in Korea and stunning temples, such as the Pulguksa Temple shown here, were built. It is considered the most famous Buddhist temple in Korea.

Interactive Flipped Video

9.4 As early as Han times, China expanded its influence to a ring of states and peoples on the border of the Middle Kingdom. To the northeast, Korea lay within the Chinese zone of influence. While Korea absorbed many Chinese traditions over the centuries, it also maintained its own identity.

TEKS
3.A, 4.H, 23.A, 25.A, 26.A, 27.A

>> Objectives

Describe how geography affected life on the Korean peninsula.

Understand the influence of China and Buddhism on Korea.

Explain the major achievements of the Choson dynasty.

>> Key Terms

Silla dynasty
Koryo dynasty
celadon
Choson dynasty
King Sejong
hangul
literacy rate

Korea and Its Traditions

The Geography of Korea

The Korean Peninsula Korea is located on a peninsula that juts south from the Asian mainland and points toward Japan. At the northern end of the peninsula, mountains and the Yalu River separate Korea from China.

An early visitor once compared Korea's landscape to "a sea in a heavy gale." Low but steep mountains cover nearly 70 percent of the Korean peninsula.

The most important range is the T'aebaek (ta bak). It runs from north to south along the eastern coast, with smaller chains branching off to form hilly areas. Because farming is difficult on the mountains, most people live along the western coastal plains, Korea's major farming region.

Korea has a 5,400-mile coastline with hundreds of good harbors. In addition, the offshore waters feature thousands of islands. Since early times, Koreans have depended upon seafood for most of the protein in their diet. Today, South Korea has one of the largest fishing industries in the world.

PEARSON realize www.PearsonTexas.com Access your Digital Lesson.

356

Aa Vocabulary Builder

1. Have students pronounce the following academic vocabulary term in this lesson and clarify the part of speech.
2. Explain what the word means in common "student-friendly" language using synonyms and antonyms when possible. Provide concrete examples to clarify the meaning, and rephrase the definition.

evolve: develop gradually

The Impact of Location Korea's location on China's eastern border has played a key role in its development. From its powerful mainland neighbor, Korea received many cultural and technological influences. At various times in history, China extended political control over the Korean peninsula. Korea has also served as a cultural bridge linking China and Japan. Koreans have, from early times, adapted and transformed Chinese traditions before passing them on to the Japanese.

The earliest Koreans probably migrated southeastward from Siberia and northern Manchuria during the Stone Age. They spoke a language unrelated to Chinese and evolved their own ways of life long before any Chinese influences reached the peninsula.

About 108 B.C., the Han emperor, Wudi, conquered the northern part of the peninsula and set up a military colony there. For almost 400 years, the Han administered the area around what is today Pyongyang. From this outpost, Confucian traditions and Chinese ideas about government, as well as Chinese writing and farming methods, spread into Korea.

EXPLAIN How did the relative location of the Korean peninsula influence the development of Korean civilization?

ELPS ELPS 2.I.4 Practice listening comprehension by listening to *The Geography of Korea* and creating drawings to demonstrate what you have learned.

The Silla and Koryo Dynasties Develop

Between 100 B.C. and A.D. 676, powerful local rulers forged three separate kingdoms: Koguryo in the north, Paekche in the southwest, and Silla in the southeast. Although they shared the same language and cultural background, the three kingdoms often warred with one another or with China.

Chinese Influences Still, Chinese influences continued to arrive. Missionaries spread Mahayana Buddhism, which took root among the rulers and nobles. Korean monks then traveled to China and India to learn more about Buddhism. They brought home the arts and learning of China. A Korean writer of the time explained the benefits that he believed Buddhism could bring to his country:

"If you teach people to rely on this teaching [Buddhism] and practice it,

Korea's Three Kingdoms, A.D. 300–A.D. 600

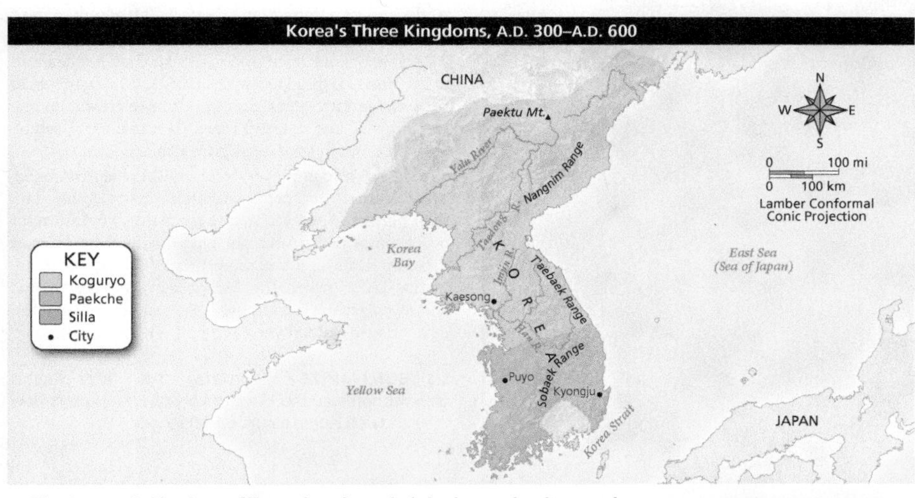

>> The three early kingdoms of Korea shared an ethnic background, culture, and language, although they were frequently at war with each other. **Analyze Maps** Which of these kingdoms was probably most influenced by Chinese civilization? Why?

Interactive Map

Guided Reading and Discussion

Identify Central Issues Ask students to define "cultural bridge." *(Sample response: a geographic location that allows people, ideas, trade, armies, and other elements to pass easily from one country to another)* Ask why Korea fits this definition. *(Sample response: It is only a short distance from the island nation of Japan; it also shares a border with China.)* Then ask students to identify other places they have read about that might be considered cultural bridges and why. *(Sample responses include north Africa, Sicily, and Italy.)*

Predict Consequences Ask students to make a prediction about Korea's relationship with China over the thousand years covered in this lesson. Have them explain on what they base their prediction.

The Silla and Koryo Dynasties Develop

In this reading, students will learn about Korea's two early dynasties and the way that China, Confucian ideas, and Buddhism shaped Korean life, culture, politics, religion, and technology. Confucian China had a strong influence on the political, religious, philosophical, cultural, and technological development of Korea. Korean culture reflected the Confucian emphasis on the family, and the Silla set up a Confucian academy to train young men. Buddhism, founded in India and brought to Korea from China, became the dominant religion in Korea.

Answers

Explain *Because it was near China, Korea was influenced by Chinese culture and technology and sometimes came under Chinese political control.*

Analyze Maps *Koguryo; it shared a long border with China.*

English Language Proficiency Standards

Listening 2.I.4 Have students demonstrate their listening comprehension by producing a drawing based on the information in "The Geography of Korea."

Beginning Retell the information in the text in accessible language. Have student pairs draw a picture of the Korean landscape. If possible, provide a basic map of Korea. Help students label their drawings with details from the text.

Intermediate Read the text aloud and allow students to ask clarifying questions. Have students draw a picture of the Korean landscape with a partner. If possible, provide large sheets of paper and a variety of drawing implements. Allow students to use other classroom resources for research. Help students write a few sentences to serve as captions.

Advanced Follow the instructions in the Intermediate ELPS activity, but have a volunteer read the text aloud. Instruct student pairs to include details in their drawings, and then write a brief description of their drawings to share.

Advanced High Instruct student pairs to take turns reading paragraphs from the text aloud. Have them use the descriptions to develop three drawings to show the country's three geographical areas: mountains, farmland, and coastal regions. Allow students to use other classroom resources for research. Then have each pair write a description of each region to share.

Topic 9 Lesson 4

Online Project the **Interactive Map: Korea's Three Kingdoms** and click through the hotspots with students. Have volunteers read each description. Ask students to look for evidence in the images of the influences of China and of Buddhism.

ACTIVE CLASSROOM

Invite pairs of students to compile an Audio Tour of the interactive map. Have the first student give the second a verbal "tour" of the map—what does it show? Have the second student give the first an explanation of what it means. If technology allows, have students make an mp3 file of their tour and share it with others.

Guided Reading and Discussion

Identify Bias Have students read the quotation about bringing Buddhism to Korea. Review the claims that Gihwa makes for adopting Buddhism. Then ask students why Gihwa thought these were valid reasons for a country adopting a specific religion.

Determine Central Ideas Ask a group of students to review the information in the text and write a one-minute TV news report about the influence of China on Silla Korea. Have them specify an image to accompany the report. Have another group of students do the same for the influence of Buddhism. *(News reports and images should show understanding of the powerful cultural influence of both China and Buddhism on Korea.)*

Analyze Images

Point out the photo of the celadon porcelain statue. Ask students who they think the image represents. *(It is likely the Buddha.)* Ask how Koreans came to practice Buddhism. *(It came from China.)* Remind them that Koreans learned to make porcelain from China, and tell them that Koreans adapted a Chinese-style kiln to produce celadon.

then their minds can be corrected, and their bodies can be cultivated. You can regulate your family, you can govern the state, and you can bring peace to the world."

—Gihwa, *The Exposition of the Correct*

The Silla Unite Korea By 688, backed by the Tang ruler Wu Zhao, the Silla kingdom had defeated Paekche and Koguryo and united Korea. From this time until 1910, Korea had only three dynasties. The **Silla dynasty** ruled a unified Korea from 668 to 935, the Koryo from 935 to 1392, and the Choson from 1392 to 1910. During much of its history, Korea was a tributary state, acknowledging Chinese power but preserving its independence.

Under Silla rule, Korea prospered and the arts flourished. Koreans made advances in medicine, astronomy, metal casting, and textile manufacturing.

Chinese influences remained strong, and Koreans adopted many features of Confucian China. Korean culture reflected the Confucian emphasis on the family as the foundation of the state. Women's public roles were restricted, and their position within the family became subordinate to the male head of the household.

The Silla built a capital city, Kyongju, modeled on the Tang capital. Buddhist influence grew and spread, and the Silla supported the building of Buddhist temples. A brisk trade encouraged links between Korea and China. Koreans used Chinese written characters and studied Chinese ideas about government.

>> Celadon is created with a slip, or wash of liquid clay, that contains iron and is applied before glazing. When the pottery is fired at a high temperature, the iron colors the surface.

Interactive Chart

Koreans Adapt Chinese Influences At the same time, Koreans adapted and modified Chinese ideas. For example, the Silla set up a Confucian academy to train young men to become high officials. They even adapted the Chinese civil service examination, but the Korean civil service system reflected their own system of inherited ranks. In China, even a peasant could win political influence by passing the exam. In Korea, where rank was important, only aristocrats were permitted to take the test.

The Koryo Dynasty After a century of conflicts disrupted Silla rule, a rebel general finally seized power and set up the **Koryo dynasty** in 935. The English word "Korea" comes from the name of this dynasty.

During the Koryo age, Buddhism reached its greatest influence in Korea, while Korea developed more on its own than it had under the Silla. Confucian traditions remained strong, however. Koreans wrote histories and poems based on Chinese models, while artists created landscape paintings that reflected Chinese principles about harmony and balance.

Koreans used woodblock printing they had learned from China to produce a flood of Buddhist texts. In time, Korean investors took the Chinese invention one step further and created movable metal type, which allowed them to print large numbers of books.

Koreans also improved on other Chinese inventions. They learned to make porcelain from China, and then perfected the technique for making **celadon**, or porcelain with an unusual blue-green glaze. Korean celadon vases and jars were prized throughout Asia. In the 1200s, when the Mongols overran Korea and destroyed many industries, the secret of making celadon was lost forever.

SUMMARIZE Summarize two technological achievements of the Koryo dynasty and explain how they showed Korea's cultural influences.

English Language Proficiency Standards

Speaking 3.E.1 Read "The Choson Dynasty." Then have students complete one of the following activities depending on their level of English proficiency.

Beginning Reread the text aloud and retell the content as necessary. Then support students as they take turns stating one fact they learned from the text. Make sure each student contributes at least once.

Intermediate Follow the instructions in the Beginning ELPS activity, but without retelling the content, and allow students to continue stating facts until all of the content has been covered.

Advanced Have students face one another in two concentric circles. Students will hear a question and discuss it for a minute with their partner. Then students in the outside circle will rotate to the left and discuss a new question with their new partner for the next minute. Repeat the procedure for the third question.

Answers

Summarize *Movable metal type was adapted from a Chinese invention, wood block printing, and allowed better and faster printing of books, while celadon pottery was a refinement of Chinese porcelain.*

KOREAN AND CHINESE CALLIGRAPHY

KOREAN

HANGUL, THE KOREAN WRITING SYSTEM, HAS 24 LETTERS (14 CONSONANTS AND 10 VOWELS). THE LETTERS ARE COMBINED TO FORM SYLLABLES.

ABOUT 70% OF KOREAN VOCABULARY COMES FROM CHINESE. KOREAN GRAMMAR IS SIMILAR TO JAPANESE.

CHINESE

CHINESE HANJA, HOWEVER, HAS MORE THAN 50,000 CHARACTERS.

A PERSON NEEDS TO KNOW ABOUT 3,000 CHARACTERS TO READ A NEWSPAPER.

>> Korean hangul is used for nearly all written communication in both South and North Korea today. **Analyze Data** How might the introduction of hangul affect literacy rates?

The Choson Dynasty

The Mongols invaded Korea between 1231 and the 1250s. In 1258, the Koryo made peace with the Mongols, but a lack of tax income weakened the kingdom. In 1392, the brilliant Korean general Yi Song-gye (yee sung gyeh) overthrew them and set up the **Choson dynasty.** This was the last and longest-lived of Korea's three dynasties. General Yi reduced Buddhist influence and set up a government based upon Confucian principles.

The Invention of Hangul Despite Chinese influence, Korea preserved its distinct identity. In 1443, **King Sejong** decided to replace the Chinese system of writing that had never worked well for the Korean language. "The language of this land," he noted, "is different from China's." Sejong had experts develop **hangul,** the Korean phonetic alphabet that uses symbols to represent the sounds of spoken Korean.

Although Confucian scholars and Koreans of the upper classes rejected hangul at the outset, its use quickly spread. Hangul was easier for Koreans to use than the thousands of characters of written Chinese. Its use led to an extremely high **literacy rate,** or percentage of people who can read and write.

Koreans Battle Japanese Invaders In the 1590s, an ambitious Japanese ruler decided to invade China by way of Korea. Japanese armies landed and for years looted and burned across the peninsula. To stop the invaders at sea, the Korean Admiral Yi Sun-shin used metal-plated "turtle ships" to beat back the invaders at sea. These turtle-shaped ships were the world's first ironclad warships. They had great mobility and firepower and helped Koreans win sea battles.

After six years of devastating war, the Japanese armies finally withdrew from Korea. As they left, however, they carried off many Korean artisans to introduce their skills to Japan.

EXPLAIN Why did Korea want to develop its own system of writing?

ELPS 3.E.1 Practice sharing information from *The Choson Dynasty* by participating in different cooperative activities.

The Choson Dynasty

Tell students that the Mongols invaded Korea between 1231 and the 1250s. However, by the late 1300s, the Koreans had overthrown them. Korea's longest-lived dynasty, the Choson, lasted from 1392 until the early 1900s.

Online Project the **Interactive Chart: Silla, Koryo, and Choson Dynasties** and complete the chart with students. Then ask: What general statements can you make about Korean civilization? *(Possible answers: It was strongly influenced by China; Buddhism was an important influence on Korean culture, art, and architecture.)*

ACTIVE CLASSROOM

Ask students to Take a Stand on the following question: Has the influence of China on Korean civilization mostly been positive or negative? Why? *(Answers will vary. Mostly positive: the transfer of technology and ideas about good government, efficient civil service, and religion; mostly negative: military and political dominance that stifled Korea's independent development)*

Guided Reading and Discussion

Contrast Direct students' attention to the infographic. Ask students to explain how hangul is different from hanja. *(Sample response: Hangul uses symbols to represent the sounds of the Korean language; hanja characters represent ideas or things.)*

Key Terms

Ask students to find the key term **literacy rate** (in bold) in the text. Explain that this measure reflects not just the educational level of a country but also its level of economic development, especially as technology becomes more sophisticated.

- Why is General Yi Song-gye important to Korean history?
- Discuss the differences between written Chinese and Korean languages. Which language is easier to learn and why?
- How did the Japanese invasion of the 1590s damage Korea and its culture?

Advanced High Follow the instructions for the Advanced ELPS activity, but after each rotation, have students give their new partners a brief summary of their previous discussion.

Answers

Analyze Data *Sample response: It had far fewer letters to learn than Chinese, making it more accessible for the average person to learn to read.*

Explain *Koreans wanted an alphabet that better reflected its own language and was not based on Chinese; it wanted to assert its unique national character and show its independence from China.*

Topic 9 Lesson 4

SYNTHESIZE

Online Project the **Digital Activity: Korean Civilization**. Ask students to take out the graphic organizer with predictions about how Korea might be influenced by its neighbors. After they fill in the remaining columns, have volunteers read a prediction to the class, state whether it was accurate or not, and share the text evidence they found to support or disprove the prediction.

DEMONSTRATE

Online Assign the **Digital Lesson Quiz** for this lesson if you haven't already done so. Students will be offered automatic remediation or enrichment based on their score.

Pose the following question to the class:

Predict Consequences What can you predict about Korea and its relationship with China in the years after 1500? *(Sample response: Because China will always be near and large, its influence on Korea will continue to be strong, unless China decides to isolate itself.)*

Support Ideas With Evidence Choose either movable metal type for printing or celadon pottery and explain how it illustrates Koreans' talent for improving on foreign inventions. *(Sample response: Koreans adapted Chinese printing blocks into movable metal type, better suited to Korea's hangul system.)*

Topic Inquiry

Have students continue their investigations for the Topic Inquiry.

ASSESSMENT

1. **Synthesize** How are Korea's history and culture linked to those of China and Japan?
2. **Make Generalizations** Why might Korea's location be of strategic importance to other countries?
3. **Identify Main Ideas** What are two examples of how Korea adapted or modified Chinese ideas?
4. **Evaluate Data** Today, Hangul Day is a holiday in South Korea. Why do you think Koreans celebrate this holiday?
5. **Identify Bias** Reread the quotation from the fourth-century writer Gihwa. What evidence can you find that he sympathized with the rulers and the upper class?

Assessment

1. Korea was influenced by many cultural and technological achievements in China and served as a cultural bridge that linked China and Japan. It also came under the political control of China at times and had to fight off a Japanese invasion.
2. Its location next to China gives it access to that country for trade, cultural exchange, or invasion.
3. Koreans modified the Chinese civil service so that only aristocrats could take the qualifying exam. They made books using movable type to allow easier printing of books. They adapted Chinese ceramic techniques to make celadon. They modified the Chinese alphabet to make it simpler to use.
4. Hangul, the Korean alphabet, is an important symbol of their national identity.
5. He states that if people are taught Buddhism, it will make the state easier to govern.

9.5 Japan is an archipelago (ahr kuh PEL uh goh), or chain of islands, about 100 miles off the Asian mainland and east of the Korean peninsula. Its four main islands are Hokkaido, Honshu, Kyushu, and Shikoku.

>> Prince Shotoku was an advisor to Empress Suiko. He revolutionized Japan by creating a government based on Chinese practices and Buddhist teachings.

 Interactive Flipped Video

The Island Kingdom of Japan

TEKS 4.H, 24.A, 25.A, 26.B

>> **Objectives**

Explain how geography set Japan apart.

Understand how China influenced Japan, and describe the Heian period.

Summarize the Japanese feudal system.

Explain how the Tokugawas united Japan.

Identify how Zen Buddhism shaped culture in Japan.

>> **Key Terms**

archipelago
tsunami
Shinto
selective borrowing
kana
samurai
bushido
Zen
Murasaki Shikibu

Japan's Geography

Like Korea, Japan felt the powerful influence of Chinese civilization early in its history. At the same time, the Japanese continued to maintain their own distinct culture.

A Mountainous Land Japan is about the size of Montana, but most of its land is too mountainous to farm. As a result, most people settled in narrow river valleys and along the coastal plains. A mild climate and sufficient rainfall, however, helped Japanese farmers make the most of the limited arable land. As in ancient Greece, the mountainous terrain at first was an obstacle to unity.

The Sea Sets Japan Apart The surrounding seas have both protected and isolated Japan. The country was close enough to the mainland to learn from Korea and China, but too far away for the Chinese to conquer. Japan thus had greater freedom to accept or reject Chinese influences than did other East Asian lands. At times, the Japanese sealed themselves off from foreign influences, choosing to go their own way.

  www.PearsonTexas.com Access your Digital Lesson.

361

Aa Vocabulary Builder

1. Have students pronounce the following academic vocabulary term in this lesson and clarify the part of speech.
2. Explain what the word means in common "student-friendly" language using synonyms and antonyms when possible. Provide concrete examples to clarify the meaning, and rephrase the definition.

stress: to emphasize

Topic 9 Lesson 5

The Island Kingdom of Japan

CONNECT

Preview Have students preview the **Lesson Objectives** and the list of **Key Terms**.

Students can also preview all the **Key Terms** and **Academic Vocabulary** using the **Interactive Reading Notepad** on the digital course or preview a summary of the lesson in the **Reading and Note Taking Study Guide**.

Online Use the **Editable Presentation** found on the digital course to present the main ideas for this lesson.

Start Up Activity

Tell students that Japan consists of a chain of islands off the eastern coast of Asia. Much of its land is covered by mountains. Based on these geographical features, have students make predictions about the development of Japan's culture and history.

Discuss Remind students that geography affects development. Have them compare one aspect of Japan's geography to that of another region they've studied. *(Sample response: Rome used its sea power to conquer and trade in the Mediterranean region.)*

Online You can also project the **Start Up Activity** from the course.

INVESTIGATE

Have students read the lesson using the **Reading and Note Taking Study Guide** to help them take notes and understand the text as they read.

Japan's Geography

Discuss with students how Japan's location—fairly close to the mainland yet separated from it by the Sea of Japan—might have helped shape its development. *(The islands of Japan were close enough to the mainland to be influenced by China and Korea, but separated enough for Japan to remain as isolated as it wished to be.)* Be sure students understand that Japan is located in an area of the Pacific Ocean that has many volcanoes and is subject to frequent earthquakes.

Topic 9 Lesson 5

Guided Reading and Discussion

Ask students how volcanoes, earthquakes, and other dramatic forces of nature might have affected Japan's history and development. *(Sample response: A major earthquake might destroy cities; if the rulers failed to respond adequately, they might lose the support of the people.)* Tell students that on more than one occasion, storms and tsunamis actually prevented invasions of Japan.

Key Terms

Ask students to find the key term **tsunami** (in bold) in the text. Explain that a major offshore earthquake in 2011 generated a tsunami whose 30-foot-high waves caused enormous destruction along the northeast coast of Japan. The tsunami killed more than 15,000 people and nearly caused a catastrophic meltdown at the Fukushima nuclear power plant.

The seas that helped Japan preserve its identity also served as trade routes. The Inland Sea was an especially important link among various Japanese islands. The seas also offered plentiful food resources and the Japanese developed a thriving fishing industry.

The Pacific Ring of Fire Japan lies in a Pacific region known as the Ring of Fire, which also includes the Philippines, Indonesia, and parts of Australia, and South America. The region is subject to frequent earthquakes and volcanoes.

Violent underwater earthquakes can launch killer tidal waves, called **tsunamis,** that sweep over the land without warning, wiping out everything in their path.

Throughout their long history, the Japanese came to fear and respect the dramatic forces of nature. Today, as in the past, soaring Mount Fuji, with its snow-capped volcanic crater, is a sacred symbol of the beauty and the majesty of nature.

INTEGRATE INFORMATION How did Japan avoid being dominated by Chinese armies and influences?

ELPS **ELPS 3.F.1** Practice using high frequency words and/or content vocabulary to ask questions about *Japan's Geography.*

>> Since A.D. 500, the Japanese emperor has traced his lineage through one clan. Here, the Japanese royal family poses around 1900.

Early Japan

The people we know today as the Japanese probably migrated from the Asian mainland more than 2,000 years ago. They slowly pushed the earlier inhabitants, the Ainu, onto the northernmost island of Hokkaido.

The Yamato Clan Early Japanese society was divided into *uji*, or clans. Each *uji* had its own chief and a special god or goddess who was seen as the clan's original ancestor. Some clan leaders were women, suggesting that women enjoyed a respected position in society.

By about A.D. 500, the Yamato clan came to dominate a corner of Honshu, the largest Japanese island. For the next 1,000 years, the Yamato Plain was the heartland of Japanese government. The Yamato set up Japan's first and only dynasty. They claimed direct descent from the sun goddess, Amaterasu, and chose the rising sun as their symbol. Later Japanese emperors were revered as living gods. While this is no longer the case, the current Japanese emperor still traces his roots to the Yamato clan.

Shinto: A Religion of Nature Early Japanese clans honored kami, or superior powers that were natural or divine beings. The worship of the forces of nature became known as **Shinto,** meaning "the way of kami." Although Shinto has not evolved into an international religion like Christianity, Buddhism, or Islam, its traditions survive to the present day in Japan. Hundreds of Shinto shrines dot the Japanese countryside. Though simple in design, they are generally located in beautiful, natural surroundings. Shinto shrines are dedicated to special sites or objects such as mountains or waterfalls, ancient gnarled trees, or even oddly shaped rocks.

Contact With Korea The Japanese language is distantly related to Korean but completely different from Chinese. From early on, Japan and Korea were in continuous contact with each other.

Korean artisans and metalworkers settled in Japan, bringing sophisticated skills and technology. Japanese and Korean warriors crossed the sea in both directions to attack each other's strongholds. Some of the leading families at the Yamato court claimed Korean ancestors.

By about A.D. 500, missionaries from Korea had introduced Buddhism to Japan. With it came knowledge of Chinese writing and culture that sparked a sustained period of Japanese interest in Chinese civilization.

CONNECT How did the Yamato clan affect Japan?

Answers

Integrate Information *The sea kept China from invading and also isolated Japan, allowing it a choice to accept Chinese influences.*

Connect *The Yamato clan lived on and dominated an area of the largest island, which became the center of Japanese government. The clan was also important because it established Japan's only dynasty.*

English Language Proficiency Standards

Speaking 3.F.1 Read "Japan's Geography" aloud to the class. Then have students complete one of the following activities depending on their level of English proficiency.

Beginning Display several high-frequency world history words such as *trade routes, mountainous, civilization*, and *geography*. Say each word aloud, and have students repeat. Model forming simple questions about the text with each word, and have students repeat the questions. Help students form their own question using one high-frequency word.

Intermediate Follow the instructions in the Beginning ELPS activity, but have students write three simple questions about the text using one high-frequency word in each question.

Advanced Have students find content-based vocabulary words such as *archipelago* and *tsunami* in the text. Ask them to generate questions using these words. Then have student pairs answer each other's questions.

Advanced High Have students reread the text and ask their classmates questions using content-based vocabulary. Have one student pose a question and call on another to answer it. The respondent should ask the next one, and so on, until everyone has asked and answered a question.

Chinese Influence in Japan

In the early 600s, Prince Shotoku of the Yamato clan decided to learn about China directly instead of through Korean sources. He sent young nobles to study in China. Over the next 200 years, many Japanese students, monks, traders, and officials visited the Tang court.

Japan Imports Ideas from Tang China Each mission to China spent a year or more there—negotiating, trading, but above all studying. On their return to Japan, they were eager to spread Chinese thought, technology, and arts. They also imported Chinese ideas about government. Japanese rulers adopted the title "Heavenly Emperor" and claimed absolute power. They strengthened the central government, set up a bureaucracy, and adopted a law code similar to that of China. Still, the new bureaucracy had little real authority beyond the royal court. Out in the countryside, the old clans remained strong.

In 710, the Japanese emperor built a new capital at Nara, modeled on the Tang capital at Chang'an. There, Japanese nobles spoke Chinese and dressed in Chinese fashion. Their cooks prepared Chinese dishes and served food on Chinese-style pottery. Tea drinking, along with an elaborate tea ceremony, was imported from China. Japanese officials and scholars used Chinese characters to write official histories. Tang music and dances became very popular, as did gardens designed using Chinese influences.

As Buddhism spread, the Japanese adopted pagoda architecture. Buddhist monasteries grew rich and powerful. Confucian ideas and ethics also took root. They included an emphasis on filial piety, the careful management of relationships between superior and inferior, and respect for learning.

Selective Borrowing In time, the initial enthusiasm for everything Chinese died down. The Japanese kept some Chinese ways but discarded or modified others.

This process is known as **selective borrowing.** Japan, for example, never accepted the Chinese civil service examination to choose officials based on merit. Instead, they maintained their tradition of inherited status through family position. Officials were the educated sons of nobles.

By the 800s, as Tang China began to decline, the Japanese court turned away from its model. After absorbing all they could from China, the Japanese spent the next 400 years digesting and modifying these cultural borrowings to produce their own unique civilization. The Japanese asserted their identity by

>> During the Heian period, the wealthy aristocracy established a refined world that led to achievements in art and literature.

revising the Chinese system of writing and adding **kana,** or phonetic symbols representing syllables. Japanese artists developed their own styles.

 **GENERATE EXPLANATIONS** Why did Japanese nobles, students, monks, traders, and officials visit China?

Japanese Culture in the Heian Period

This blending of cultures of Chinese influences with Japanese culture occurred during the Heian (hay ahn) period in Japan, which lasted from 794 to 1185. During this time, the imperial capital was located in Heian, present-day Kyoto. There, emperors performed traditional religious ceremonies, while wealthy court families like the Fujiwara wielded real power. The Fujiwara married their daughters to the heirs of the throne, thus ensuring their authority.

An Elegant Court At the Heian court, an elegant and sophisticated culture blossomed. Noblewomen and noblemen lived in a fairy-tale atmosphere of beautiful

Topic 9 Lesson 5

Early Japan

Chinese Influence in Japan

Japanese Culture in the Heian Period

Chinese culture was introduced to Japan by Korea. In the early 600s, Japanese students, monks, traders, and officials visited China and brought back Chinese customs, architecture, government, and bureaucracy. The Japanese continued to selectively borrow elements of Chinese culture and modify them to produce their own civilization. During the Heian period (794–1185), wealthy families, not the emperor, dominated Japan. Elegance and sophistication were the norm at the Heian court. Heian women produced important works of literature. One, Lady Murasaki, wrote the world's first full-length novel.

Guided Reading and Discussion

Make Generalizations Ask students to explain how Korea and China influenced the Japanese culture. *(Korea introduced Buddhism to Japan as well as Chinese writing and culture.)*

Make Predictions Think about the early influences of China on Japanese society. What do you think might have happened if the Japanese did not practice selective borrowing of Chinese ways? *(Possible answers: The Japanese government would have been different; the Japanese might not have developed their own style of art.)*

Answers

Generate Explanations *They wanted to learn about Chinese culture and bring back ideas to Japan.*

English Language Proficiency Standards

Listening 2.I.5 Tell students that they will be taking notes in this activity. Remind them that note taking is a good way to improve listening skills. Then tell them to listen carefully as you read "Japanese Culture in the Heian Period" aloud.

Beginning Reread the text aloud, pausing after each main idea and important detail so students can write it down. Remind students that taking notes is not the same as copying every piece of information.

Intermediate Follow the instructions in the Beginning ELPS activity, but pause after every few sentences so students can take notes.

Advanced Reread the text aloud. Tell students to take notes on the main idea and important details as you read. Remind students that taking notes is not the same as copying every piece of information. Encourage them to use abbreviations and shorter phrases. Then have students revisit their notes and work with a partner to fill in information or make corrections.

Advanced High Follow the instructions in the Advanced ELPS activity. Then have students write a one- or two-sentence summary of their notes to share with the class.

Analyze Images

Have students study the images of the Heian period in this text. Discuss the style of dress and hairstyles shown. Ask students if these clothing styles probably made it easy or difficult for a person to work. *(Lead students to infer that the people who wore these clothes did not engage in manual labor but lived lives of elegant leisure.)*

Support Ideas With Evidence Women were very important in court in Japan during the Heian period. Identify two examples that support this statement. *(Women wrote important literary works during this time period. Sei Shonagon wrote* The Pillow Book, *and Lady Murasaki wrote* The Tale of Genji.*)*

D Differentiate Special Needs Write the following questions on the board: What did I read about in this text? What did I learn from the text? What do I not understand? What conclusions can I draw from the text? Have students apply these questions to the text readings in this Topic to help them increase their understanding.

Japan's Feudal Age

Tell students that in the 1400s, warfare swept Japan, and social disorder continued through the following century. Despite the turmoil, a new Japanese feudal social system arose. As in the feudal world of medieval Europe, a warrior aristocracy dominated Japanese society during this time. Remind students that the emperor remained at the head of the feudal society, but he was a mostly powerless figurehead. The shogun, or supreme military commander, was the true ruler. He had the obedience of powerful vassals called daimyo, who were, in turn, supported by local warrior lords called samurai. Far below the samurai in the social hierarchy were the peasants and artisans, with merchants at the bottom.

pavilions, gardens, and lotus pools. Elaborate rules of etiquette governed court ceremony.

Courtiers dressed with extraordinary care in delicate, multicolored silk. Draping one's sleeve out a carriage window was a fine art.

Although men at court still studied Chinese, women were forbidden to learn the language. Despite these restrictions, it was Heian women who produced the most important works of Japanese literature of the period.

In the 900s, Sei Shonagon, a lady-in-waiting to the empress, wrote *The Pillow Book*. In a witty series of anecdotes and personal observations, she provides vivid details of court manners, amusements, decor, and dress.

Lady Murasaki Writes the World's First Novel The best-known Heian writer was Shonagan's rival, **Murasaki Shikibu.** Her monumental work, *The Tale of Genji*, was the world's first full-length novel. Even though learning by girls was considered improper, she studied with her brother and learned how to read and write. She served as a lady-in-waiting at court, where she observed its customs.

>> This illustration from *The Tale of Genji* shows the Heian court at leisure, a world Lady Muraski depicted through her tale of human emotions and the beauty of nature.

Composed in 1010, *The Tale of Genji* recounts the adventures and loves of the fictional Prince Genji and his son. In one scene, Genji moves with ease through the festivities at an elaborate "Chinese banquet." After dinner, "under the great cherry tree of the Southern court," the entertainment begins. The main event of the evening is a Chinese poetry contest. Genji and other guests are given a "rhyme word," which they must use to compose a poem in Chinese. Genji's poem is the hit of the banquet.

Heian Poetry The novel includes 800 poems about the Heian court, known as *waka*. They provide a detailed portrait of the life of the Japanese court at the time, including descriptions of members of the court creating poetry, music, and calligraphy. Lady Murasaki uses her complex tale to comment on life in the court.

The Heian romances like that of Murasaki are haunted by a sense of sadness. Writers of poems lament that love does not last, and beauty is soon gone. Perhaps this feeling of melancholy was prophetic. Outside the walls of the elegant Heian court, clouds of rebellion and civil war were gathering.

? CHECK UNDERSTANDING What was significant about the rise of Japanese literature during the Heian Period?

ELPS **ELPS 2.I.5** Practice listening comprehension by taking notes on *Japanese Culture in the Heian Period.*

Japan's Feudal Age

While the emperor presided over the splendid court at Heian, rival clans battled for control of the countryside. Local warlords and even some Buddhist temples formed armed bands loyal to them rather than to the central government. As these armies struggled for power, Japan evolved a feudal system. As in the feudal world of medieval Europe, a warrior aristocracy dominated Japanese society.

A Feudal Society Emerges In theory, the emperor stood at the head of Japanese feudal society. In fact, he was a powerless, though revered, figurehead. Real power lay in the hands of the shogun, or supreme military commander. Minamoto Yoritomo was appointed shogun in 1192. He set up the Kamakura shogunate, the first of three military dynasties that would rule Japan for almost 700 years.

Often the shogun controlled only a small part of Japan. He distributed lands to vassal lords who agreed to support him with their armies in time of need. These great warrior lords were later called daimyo (DY myoh).

History Background

Elegant Life in the Heian Court The Heian court was among the most elegant and elaborate in history. Lively social gatherings took place in the beautiful gardens of the "dwellers among the clouds," as the nobles of the court were called. During these parties, poetry was recited and composed, and courtiers might rise or fall in rank depending on their skill in turning a line. As it was indelicate for a woman to be seen standing upright, couples lounged on the ground. They often stationed themselves beside winding streams of cool mountain water. Occasionally, a cup of wine floated by. Guests would take a sip and return the cup to the water so it could continue downstream to be available for other guests.

Answers

Check Understanding *The most important works were created by women.*

They, in turn, granted land to lesser warriors called **samurai,** meaning "those who serve." Samurai were the fighting aristocracy of a war-torn land.

Bushido: Way of the Warrior Like medieval Christian knights, samurai were heavily armed and trained in the skills of fighting. Over time, they developed their own code of values. Known as **bushido,** or the "way of the warrior," the code emphasized honor, bravery, and absolute loyalty to one's lord.

The true samurai had no fear of death. Samurai prepared for hardship by going hungry or walking barefoot in the snow. A samurai who betrayed the code of bushido was expected to commit seppuku (she POO koo), or ritual suicide, rather than live without honor.

Bushido set values for the samurai and showed them how to live even when they were not fighting. It reflected ideas from Buddhism, Confucianism, and Shintoism. Bushido stressed Buddhist teachings about discipline and the importance of moderation along with Confucian emphasis on loyalty and duty.

Women in Feudal Society During the age of the samurai, the position of well-born women declined. At first, some women in feudal society trained in the military arts or supervised their family's estate. A few even became legendary warriors. As fighting increased, though, inheritance was limited to sons.

Unlike the European ideal of chivalry, the samurai code did not set women on a pedestal. The wife of a warrior had to accept the same hardships as her husband and owed the same loyalty to his overlord.

Other Classes Far below the samurai in the social hierarchy were the peasants, artisans, and merchants. Peasants, who made up 75 percent of the population, formed the backbone of feudal society in Japan. Peasant families cultivated rice and other crops on the estates of samurai. Some peasants also served as foot soldiers in feudal wars.

On rare occasions, an able peasant soldier might rise through the ranks to become a samurai himself.

Artisans, such as armorers and sword-makers, provided necessary goods for the samurai class. Merchants had the lowest rank in Japanese society, reflecting the Confucian view of them as people who were interested only in profits and who made these profits off the goods made by others. However, while peasants had a higher status, merchants often had much greater wealth.

Mongol Invaders Threaten Japan During the feudal age, most fighting took place between rival warlords, but the Mongol conquest of China and Korea also threatened Japan. When the Japanese refused to accept Mongol rule, Kublai Khan launched an invasion from Korea in 1274. A fleet carrying 30,000 troops arrived, but shortly afterwards a typhoon wrecked many Mongol ships and drove the invaders back to the mainland.

>> Over 13,000 invaders drowned in the first tsunami that saved Japan. Almost all of the 4,400 ships and 140,000 Chinese invaders were lost in the second tsunami.

In 1281, the Mongols landed an even larger invasion force, but again a typhoon destroyed much of the Mongol fleet. The Japanese credited their miraculous delivery to the kamikaze (kah muh KAH zee), or divine winds. The Mongol failure reinforced the Japanese sense that they were a people set apart who enjoyed the special protection of the gods.

APPLY CONCEPTS How did honor, bravery, and absolute loyalty to one's lord affect Japanese feudal society?

A United Japan

The Kamakura shogunate crumbled in the aftermath of the Mongol invasions. A new dynasty took power in 1338, but the level of warfare increased after 1450. To defend their castles, daimyo armed peasants as well

Online Project the **Interactive Chart: Feudal Society in Japan** and click through the different levels of Japanese society.

ACTIVE CLASSROOM

Employ the Conversation With History strategy with the interactive chart. Have students imagine they are having a conversation with one of the people in the interactive chart about Japanese feudalism. Ask them to write down a question they'd like to ask, then what that person would answer, and what they would say in response. Have volunteers share their questions and responses with the class.

Guided Reading and Discussion

Compare and Contrast Have students compare and contrast the positions and roles of the members of feudal Japanese society. Be sure students understand the hierarchy of feudal society in Japan. Point out that the only way to move up in society was to be a warrior able to rise through the ranks to become a samurai. Review the terms *feudalism* and *vassal*. *Feudalism* is a loosely organized system of government in which local lords governed their own lands but owed military service to a greater lord. *Vassal* refers to a person granted land in exchange for service to a greater lord.

A United Japan

Explain that after years of unrest, several powerful warriors united large parts of Japan. In 1600 the daimyo Tokugawa Ieyasu defeated all rivals to become master of Japan. He was named shogun and his dynasty would rule Japan until 1868. The Tokugawas maintained the outward forms of feudal society but imposed central government control on all Japan and created a unified, orderly society. A strict moral code was enforced, transportation improved, trade flourished, and the economy grew.

Answers

Apply Concepts *These values created a warrior class ready to fight in a time of war.*

Topic 9 Lesson 5

Summarize the changes in Japanese society during the Tokugawas' rule. *(The Tokugawas ended feudal warfare and imposed a central government on Japan, replacing a weak government and country overrun with fighting warlords; the position of women declined; and the economy boomed after the fighting ended.)*

Guided Reading and Discussion

Identify Cause and Effect How did the end of warfare allow the economy of Japan to grow? *(Sample response: Men worked on farms and in businesses rather than fighting wars.)* Be sure students understand the concept of centralized feudalism. The feudal society still existed, with people assigned a position in the hierarchy, but the government was centralized. Have students discuss the differences between this type of feudalism and the feudalism in place before the Tokugawa rule. *(The positions of the people in the hierarchy stayed the same, but the daimyos had less power and were subjected to more controls.)*

Japanese Feudal Culture Evolves

Tell students that during the feudal age a Buddhist sect known as Zen became popular in Japan. Zen emphasized self-reliance, meditation, and devotion to duty. Some Zen teachings were contradictory, but the love of beauty and nature powerfully influenced the evolution of art and drama.

>> After the Battle of Sekigahara in 1600, Tokugawa Ieyasau seized control of central Japan. He used strict administrative regulations to control anyone who challenged his power.

Interactive Chart

>> Edo, now called Tokyo, was once a small fishing village. This changed when Shogun Tokugawa built his castles in Edo and created the new capital, with the Imperial Palace at its center.

as samurai, which led to even more ruthless fighting. A saying of the time declared, "The warrior does not care if he's called a dog or beast. The main thing is winning."

Warriors Gradually Unite Japan Gradually, several powerful warriors united large parts of Japan. By 1590, the ambitious and successful general Toyotomi Hideyoshi (hee day YOH shee), a commoner by birth, had brought most of Japan under his control. He then tried, but failed, to control Korea. After his death, another ambitious warrior, the daimyo Tokugawa Ieyasu (toh koo gah wah ee AY ah soo) defeated his rivals to become master of Japan.

Centralized Feudalism In 1603, Tokugawa was named shogun. The Tokugawa shogunate would last until 1868. The Tokugawa shoguns were determined to end feudal warfare. To do so, they kept the outward forms of feudal society, but imposed central government control on all of Japan. For this reason, their system of government is called centralized feudalism.

The Tokugawas created a unified, orderly society. To control the daimyo, they required these great lords to live in the shogun's capital at Edo (present-day Tokyo) every other year. A daimyo's wife and children had to remain in Edo full time, giving the shogun a powerful check on the entire family. The shogun also forbade daimyo to repair their castles or marry without permission.

New laws fixed the old social order rigidly in place and upheld a strict moral code. Only samurai were allowed to serve in the military or hold government jobs.

They were expected to follow the traditions of bushido. Peasants had to remain on the land. People in lower classes were forbidden to wear luxuries such as silk clothing.

A Booming Economy While the shoguns tried to hold back social change, the Japanese economy grew by leaps and bounds. With peace restored to the countryside, agriculture improved and expanded. New seeds, tools, and the use of fertilizer led to a greater output of crops.

Food surpluses supported rapid population growth. Towns sprang up on the lands around the castles of daimyo. Edo grew into a booming city, where artisans and merchants flocked to supply the needs of the daimyo and their families.

Trade flourished within Japan. New roads linked castle towns and Edo. Each year, daimyo and their servants traveled to and from the capital, creating a demand for food and services along the route. In the

History Background

The Japanese Invasion of Korea Japan's invasion of Korea by general Toyotomi Hideyoshi in the 1590s had long-lasting consequences for all three nations involved. For Ming China, which aided Korea early in the war, the large cost weakened the dynasty, which was already in decline. When the Manchus later challenged the Ming dynasty, the Ming did not have the resources to successfully fight back. In Korea, towns and temples were destroyed. Cultural objects were ransacked or stolen, and the conflict hardened Korean feelings against foreigners. Japan is the only country to have benefited from the fighting. The stolen books and artwork aided scholastic development, as did the movable type printing machine, which they stole and imitated. They also took Korean prisoners, including potters and weavers who helped build Japan's growing ceramic and textile industries.

cities, a wealthy merchant class emerged. Despite their low social status under Confucian traditions, merchants gained influence by lending money to daimyo and samurai. Some merchants further improved their social position by marrying their daughters into the samurai class.

APPLY CONCEPTS After the Tokugawas forced daimyo and their wives and children to live in certain places, what happened?

Japanese Feudal Culture Evolves

During Japan's feudal age, a Buddhist sect from China won widespread acceptance among samurai. Known in Japan as **Zen,** it emphasized self-reliance, meditation, and devotion to duty.

Zen Beliefs Zen had seemingly contradictory traditions. Zen monks were great scholars, yet they valued the uncluttered mind and stressed the importance of reaching a moment of "non-knowing." Zen stressed compassion for all, yet samurai fought to kill. In Zen monasteries, monks sought to experience absolute freedom, yet rigid rules gave the Zen master complete authority over his students.

Zen Buddhists believed that people could seek enlightenment through meditation and through the precise performance of everyday tasks. For example, the elaborate rituals of the tea ceremony reflected Zen values of peace, simplicity, and love of beauty. Zen reverence for nature also influenced the development of fine landscape paintings.

Artistic Traditions Change Under the Tokugawas, cities such as Edo and Osaka were home to an explosion in the arts and theater. At stylish entertainment quarters, sophisticated nobles mixed with the urban middle class. Urban culture emphasized luxuries and pleasures and differed greatly from the feudal culture that had dominated Japan for centuries.

New Drama Develops In the 1300s, feudal culture had produced Noh plays performed on a square, wooden stage without scenery. Men wore elegant carved masks while a chorus chanted important lines to musical accompaniment. The action was slow, and each movement had a special meaning. Many Noh plays presented Zen Buddhist themes, emphasizing the need to renounce selfish desires. Others recounted fairy tales or the struggles between powerful feudal lords.

>> This painting, *Flowers of the Four Seasons* (ink and watercolor on gold leafed paper), by Shiko Watanabe (1683–1755) demonstrates the Zen ideal of subtle suggestion.

In the 1600s, towns gave rise to a popular new form of drama called Kabuki. Kabuki was influenced by Noh plays, but it was less refined and included comedy or melodrama in portraying family or historical events. Dressed in colorful costumes, actors used lively movements and exaggerated facial expressions. Kabuki originated with a temple dancer named Okuni, who became famous for her performances of warrior roles. However, the government soon banned women from performing on stage.

Puppet plays, known as bunraku, were also enormously popular in towns. A narrator told a story while handlers silently manipulated near-life-sized puppets. Bunraku plays catered to popular middle-class tastes.

Literature The feudal age produced stories like the *Tale of the Heike* about a violent conflict between two families. Other prose works dealt with Buddhist themes such as the fleeting nature of worldly things.

The Japanese also adapted Chinese poetry models, creating miniature poems, called haiku. In only three lines—totaling 17 syllables in the Japanese language—these tiny word pictures express a feeling, thought, or idea.

Online Project the **Interactive Gallery: Japanese Art and Theater** and click through the images and text with students.

ACTIVE CLASSROOM

Employ the See-Think-Wonder strategy with the interactive gallery. Pair students with a partner. Have them take turns explaining: What do you see? What does that make you think? What are you wondering about now that you've seen this? Have volunteers share insights with the class.

Guided Reading and Discussion

Identifying Supporting Details Zen Buddhism had contradictory traditions. Have students identify some of these in a chart format. *(Sample response: Zen monks were great scholars, yet they valued the uncluttered mind and the importance of "not-knowing"; Zen stressed compassion for all, yet the samurai fought to kill; Zen monks wanted absolute freedom yet lived with strict rules.)* Explain to students that the samurai were a group most likely to embrace Zen Buddhism because the religion's values were already important to the samurai culture.

Identify Main Ideas Have students summarize the new art and theater traditions that developed during this period. *(Possible answer: A new form of drama called Kabuki was developed that appealed to more middle-class tastes. Wood-block printing became very popular.)*

Identify Cause and Effect New drama and art forms that appealed to the middle class developed. Why do you think this happened? *(The economy improved so that more people had access to these things. The culture changed and nobles and the middle class mixed together more.)*

Answers

Apply Concepts *The Tokugawas established a centralized form of feudalism.*

Topic 9 Lesson 5

SYNTHESIZE

Online Project the **Digital Activity: Japan During the Heian and Tokugawa Periods**. Ask students to complete their graphic organizer and discuss the cultural and political changes between the Heian period and Tokugawa rule.

Discuss Have students think about how geography influenced Japan's development. Ask: How might Japan have developed differently if it shared a land border with India or China?

DEMONSTRATE

Online Assign the **Digital Lesson Quiz** for this lesson if you haven't already done so. Students will be offered automatic remediation or enrichment based on their score.

Pose the following questions to the class:

Determine Central Ideas How did life in Japan change under the Tokugawas? *(The central government strengthened and the social order became rigidly fixed. Merchants improved their social status, but women faced greater restrictions.)*

Identify Cause and Effect A new form of drama developed in the 1600s called Kabuki. Why was this new form of drama so popular? *(Kabuki appealed to the middle class as well as the upper class. It was popular as it had a wider audience.)*

Topic Inquiry

Have students continue their investigations for the Topic Inquiry.

Answers

Recall *They appealed to a growing middle class that now had time and money for new artistic traditions.*

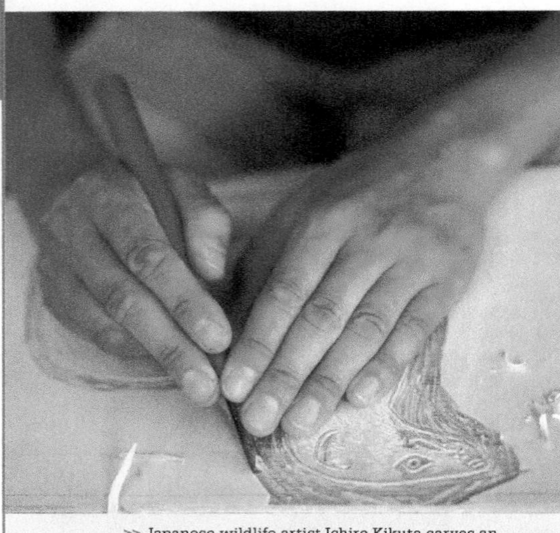

>> Japanese wildlife artist Ichiro Kikuta carves an image of a mongoose to make a woodblock print.

Interactive Gallery

Painting and Printmaking Japanese paintings often reflected the influence of Chinese landscape paintings, yet Japanese artists developed their own styles. On magnificent scrolls, painters boldly recreated historical events, such as the Mongol invasions.

In the 1600s, the vigorous urban culture produced a flood of colorful woodblock prints to satisfy middle-class tastes. Some woodblock artists produced humorous prints. Their fresh colors and simple lines give us a strong sense of the pleasures of town life in Japan.

RECALL Why did Kabuki and Noh theater as well as puppet plays and colorful woodblock prints gain popularity?

ASSESSMENT

1. **Identify Cause and Effect** How did geography affect the development of Japan and set it apart from its neighbors?
2. **Check Understanding** Describe some of the ways China influenced Japan's political and cultural development.
3. **Analyze Information** Describe the structure of Japanese society under the feudal system.
4. **Check Understanding** How did the Tokugawas unite Japan, and what was the effect on the economy?
5. **Generate Explanations** How did Zen Buddhism help shape Japanese culture?

Assessment

1. Its proximity to China and Korea led to some cultural blending, but its island location made it easier to avoid being conquered, close itself off from foreign influence, and establish trade routes.
2. Japanese who visited China returned with many ideas about politics and government, including the absolute power of an emperor, a strong central government bureaucracy, a code of law, and, during the Heian period, Confucian ideals. Japan also adopted many elements of Chinese culture, including Chinese language and writing, cooking and tea drinking, and music and literature.
3. The emperor was at the top of the social system, but the shogun held the real power and was supported by the armies of vassal lords, to whom he gave land. Local warlords, or daimyo, led clans that struggled for power and gave their land to samurai. Most of the population made up the peasants and artisans below them in the social system. Merchants were at the bottom.
4. The strong central government of the Tokugawas was able to end feudal war and create a strong unified society. The economy boomed and trade flourished in the absence of constant war.
5. Zen, which emphasized self-reliance, meditation, and devotion to duty, helped create a strong belief in the importance of performing everyday tasks with precision. Zen values such as peace, simplicity, and love of beauty also proved a powerful influence on Japanese art, particularly landscape painting, printmaking, and Noh drama.

9.6 Located between China and India, the region known today as Southeast Asia was strongly influenced by both of these powerful neighbors. Even so, the distinct cultures of Southeast Asia retained their own unique identities.

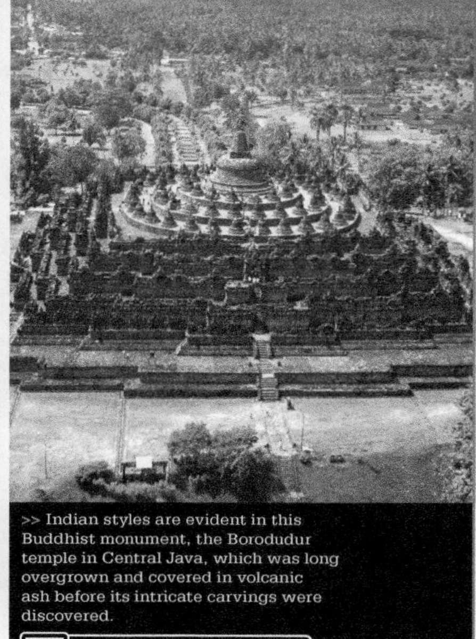

>> Indian styles are evident in this Buddhist monument, the Borodudur temple in Central Java, which was long overgrown and covered in volcanic ash before its intricate carvings were discovered.

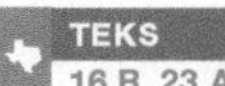 Interactive Flipped Video

The Many Cultures of Southeast Asia

 TEKS
16.B, 23.A

>> Objectives

Describe the geography of Southeast Asia.

Understand the impact of India on the history of Southeast Asia.

Summarize the characteristics of the new kingdoms and empires in Southeast Asia.

Explain the emergence of Vietnam.

>> Key Terms

stupa
paddy
King Suryavarman II

The Geography of Southeast Asia

Two Major Regions Southeast Asia is made up of two major regions. The first, mainland Southeast Asia, includes several peninsulas that jut south between India and China. Today, this region is home to Myanmar, Thailand, Cambodia, Laos, Vietnam, and part of Malaysia. The second region, island Southeast Asia, consists of more than 20,000 islands scattered between the Indian Ocean and the South China Sea. It includes the present-day nations of Indonesia, Singapore, Brunei (broo NY), and the Philippines.

Separated by Mountains The mainland is separated from the rest of Asia by mountains and high plateaus. Still, traders and invaders did push overland into the region. Mountains also separate the four main river valleys of Southeast Asia—the Irrawaddy (ihr uh WAH dee), Chao Phraya (chow PRY uh), Mekong, and Red. These river valleys were home to early civilizations.

Trade in the Southern Seas Island Southeast Asia has long been of strategic importance. All seaborne trade between China and India

Aa Vocabulary Builder

1. Have students pronounce the following academic vocabulary term in this lesson and clarify the part of speech.
2. Explain what the word means in common "student-friendly" language using synonyms and antonyms when possible. Provide concrete examples to clarify the meaning, and rephrase the definition.

impact: effect

Topic 9 Lesson 6

The Many Cultures of Southeast Asia

CONNECT

Preview Have students preview the **Lesson Objectives** and the list of **Key Terms**.

Students can also preview all the **Key Terms** and **Academic Vocabulary** using the **Interactive Reading Notepad** on the digital course or preview a summary of the lesson in the **Reading and Note Taking Study Guide**.

Online Use the **Editable Presentation** found on the digital course to present the main ideas for this lesson.

Start Up Activity

Direct students' attention to the map on page 371, "Empires and Kingdoms of Southeast Asia." Point out that Southeast Asia lies to the south of China and to the east of India. Geographically, Southeast Asia consists of a large peninsula on the Asian mainland and a collection of large and small islands spread across the region where the Pacific and Indian oceans meet. Ask them to predict which culture—India or China—had the greater influence on Southeast Asia. *(Possible answer: India may have had better access via land and sea routes.)*

Online You can also project the **Start Up Activity** from the course.

INVESTIGATE

Have students read the lesson using the **Reading and Note Taking Study Guide** to help them take notes and understand the text as they read.

The Geography of Southeast Asia

Tell students that Southeast Asia can be divided into two main regions, the mainland and the more than 20,000 islands. The mainland is mountainous, and although traders and invaders found routes through the mountains, much of the intercultural contact occurred via sea travel. Explain that before India and China had begun to exert influence over Southeast Asia, the peoples of this region had developed their own cultures.

Topic 9 Lesson 6

Online Project the **Interactive Map: Topography of Southeast Asia** and click through the hotspots. Ask students to give their initial impressions of the area. Ask them to make predictions about how the geography of the region will influence its development. *(People, trade, and ideas may move more easily across water than land barriers.)*

ACTIVE CLASSROOM

Use the strategy called A Closer Look. Project the map of Southeast Asia and use a whiteboard tool to divide it into four numbered quadrants. Have students count off 1 to 4. Then have them look closely at the part of the map in their quadrant. Have them tell you what they see and what they learned as a result of their focus on this part of the image. Collect insights for each quadrant.

Guided Reading and Discussion

Review the geography of Southeast Asia with students. Ask how location and climate affected the way the region developed. *(Trade routes through the islands gave straits enormous strategic value. While waiting for the monsoon winds to stop, trading ships remained in ports, increasing cultural, religious, and economic exchange.)*

Identify Cause and Effect Ask students to explain how culture developed on some of the more isolated islands and villages in Southeast Asia.

Indian Culture Spreads

Indian culture came to Southeast Asia by way of trade and religion. Indian merchants and Hindu priests came first, followed by Buddhist monks and scholars. Indian influence was seen in writing, law, government, art, architecture, and farming. Indian influence reached its peak between 500 and 1000. Along with Hinduism and Buddhism, Indians brought Islamic beliefs and Muslim culture to the area.

had to pass through either the Malacca or Sunda straits. Whoever commanded these straits controlled rich trade routes.

The monsoons, or seasonal winds, shaped trading patterns in the southern seas. Ships traveled northeast in summer and southwest in winter. Between seasons, while waiting for the winds to shift, merchants harbored their vessels in Southeast Asian ports, which became important centers of trade and culture. Soon, an international trade network linked India, Southeast Asia, and China to East Africa and the Middle East.

The key products of Southeast Asia were spices. In coastal towns from India to Southeast Asia, merchants bought and sold cloves, nutmeg, ginger, pepper, and other spices. Only a fraction of the spices traded in the region went to markets in Europe. Most cargoes were carried to East Asia, the Middle East, and East Africa.

Early Traditions The peoples of Southeast Asia developed their own cultures before Indian or Chinese influences shaped the region. At Bang Chiang in Thailand, archaeologists have found jars and bronze bracelets at least 5,000 years old. This evidence is challenging old theories about when civilization began in the region.

Over the centuries, diverse ethnic groups speaking many languages settled in Southeast Asia. Living in isolated villages, they followed their own religious and cultural patterns. Many societies were built around the nuclear family rather than the extended families of India and China.

Role of Women Women had greater equality in Southeast Asia than elsewhere in Asia. Female merchants took part in the spice trade, gaining fame for their skill in bargaining, finance, and languages. In some port cities, they gained enough wealth and influence to become rulers.

Matrilineal descent, or inheritance through the mother, was an accepted custom in Southeast Asia. Women also had some freedom in choosing or divorcing their marriage partners. Even after Indian and Chinese influences arrived, women retained their traditional rights.

IDENTIFY CAUSE AND EFFECT How did Southeast Asia's location and climate affect the region's development and significance?

>> King Anawrahta built the Shwezigon Pagoda with an Indian bell-shaped stupa design above a terraced pyramid topped with a golden umbrella encrusted with jewels. The interior of the pagoda is also richly decorated.

Indian Culture Spreads

Indian merchants and Hindu priests filtered into Southeast Asia, slowly spreading their culture. Later, Buddhist monks and scholars introduced Theravada beliefs. Following the path of trade and religion came the influence of writing, law, government, art, architecture, and farming.

Indian Influence Increases In the early centuries A.D., Indian traders settled in Southeast Asian port cities in growing numbers. They gave presents to local rulers and married into influential families. Trade brought prosperity as merchants exchanged products such as cotton cloth, jewels, and perfume for raw materials such as timber, spices, and gold.

In time, local Indian families exercised considerable power. Also, people from Southeast Asia visited India as pilgrims or students. As these contacts increased, Indian beliefs and ideas won widespread acceptance. Indian influence reached its peak between 500 and 1000.

Arrival of Islam Long after Hinduism and Buddhism took root in Southeast Asia, Indians carried a third religion, Islam, into the region. By the 1200s, Muslims ruled northern India. From there, traders spread Islamic

English Language Proficiency Standards

Speaking 3.F.2 Read "Indian Culture Spreads" aloud. Have students complete one of the following activities depending on their level of English proficiency.

Beginning Display several high-frequency world history words, such as *merchants, port, traders,* and *products*. Point to each word, say it aloud, and ask students to repeat it. Model answering simple questions about how Indian culture spread, using each word. Have students repeat the answers. Help them formulate their own answers using one high-frequency word in a sentence.

Intermediate Follow the instructions in the Beginning ELPS activity, but don't point to the word before you say it. Model answering simple questions with one or two of the example words. Have students repeat the answers. Have students write three simple questions and answers about the reading using one high-frequency word in each question.

Advanced Have students review the text to look for content-based vocabulary words like *monks, scholars,* and *pilgrims*. Ask students to read the information and work with a partner to provide

Answers

Identify Cause and Effect *Location: nearness to cultural centers India and China and on trade route between India and China. Climate: monsoon winds favored regional trade.*

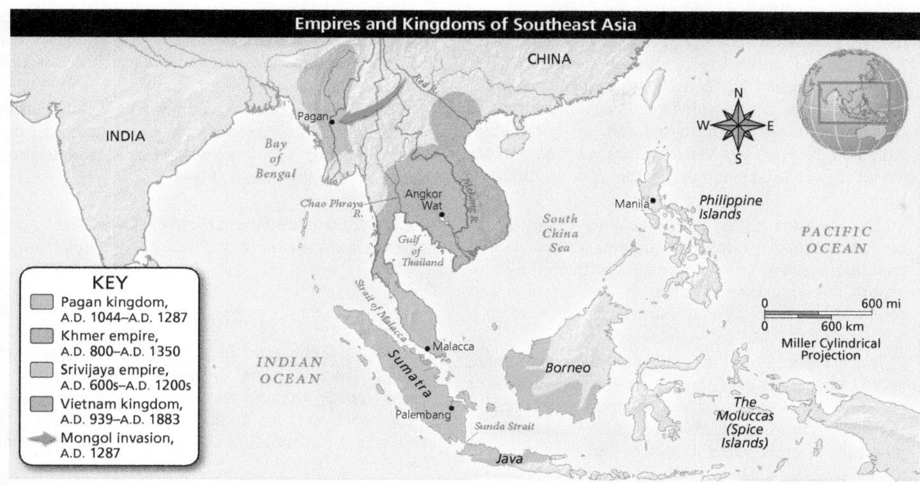

>> **Analyze Maps** From which direction did the Mongol invasion take place?

beliefs and Muslim culture throughout the islands of Indonesia and as far east as the Philippines. Today, Indonesia has the largest Muslim population of any nation in the world.

Arab merchants, too, spread the new faith. The prevalence of Islam in lands surrounding the Indian Ocean contributed to the growth of a stable, thriving trade network.

GENERATE EXPLANATIONS How did Hinduism, Buddhism, and Islam become established in Southeast Asia?

ELPS **ELPS 3.F.2** Practice using high frequency words and/or content vocabulary to answer questions about *Indian Culture Spreads.*

Kingdoms and Empires

The blend of Indian influences with local cultures in time produced a series of kingdoms and empires in Southeast Asia. Some of these would rival those of India.

The Pagan Kingdom The kingdom of Pagan (puh GAHN) arose in the fertile rice-growing Irrawaddy Valley in present-day Myanmar. In 1044, King Anawrahta (an ow RAHT uh) united the region. He is credited with bringing Buddhism to the Burman people. Buddhism had reached nearby cultures long before, but Anawrahta made Pagan a major Buddhist center.

Anawrahta filled his capital city with magnificent **stupas,** or dome-shaped shrines, at about the same time that people in medieval Europe were beginning to build Gothic cathedrals. Stupas originated in India, but in Pagan they took on a distinctly different form. These stupas were designed as sacred mountains of bricks and stone with stairways and terraces that turned them into large temples.

Painting, carvings, and sculpture told the life of the Buddha. The great Anada temple at Pagan dates from 1090 A.D. and is still in use. Over time, many stupas have been built over smaller stupas.

Pagan flourished for some 200 years after Anawrahta's death, but fell in 1287 to conquering Mongols. When the Burmans finally threw off foreign rule, they looked back with pride to the great days of Pagan.

The Khmer Empire Indian influences also helped shape the Khmer (kuh MEHR) empire, which reached its peak between 800 and 1350. Its greatest rulers controlled much of present-day Cambodia, Thailand, and Malaysia. The Khmer people adapted Indian writing, mathematics, architecture, and art. Khmer rulers became pious Hindus. Like the princes and emperors of India, they saw themselves as god-kings. Most ordinary people, however, preferred Buddhism.

Guided Reading and Discussion

Support a Point of View With Evidence *"Southeast Asia would not be the same today without the influence of Indian culture."* Write a paragraph agreeing or disagreeing with this statement. Explain your reasoning with evidence from the text. *(Possible answer: Indians brought Islam and Muslim culture to the area. Indonesia has the largest Muslim population in the world.)*

Analyze Images

Turn students' attention to the map. Tell them that in the 1500s and 1600s, European powers would seek to control lands in Southeast Asia. Have them find a clue on the map to explain why. *(Spices—the Moluccas were also known as the Spice Islands.)*

Kingdoms and Empires

Tell students that the blend of Indian influences and local cultures produced a series of kingdoms and empires in Southeast Asia. The kingdom of Pagan (in present-day Myanmar) became a major center of Buddhism. Rulers of the Khmer empire (covering much of present-day Cambodia, Thailand, and Malaysia) adopted Hinduism, although the people preferred Buddhism.

Key Terms

Ask students to find the key term **stupas** (in bold) in the text. Explain that stupas began as homes for sacred relics from the Buddha or his disciples. People worshiped by walking around the stupa in a clockwise direction.

three details about how Indian culture spread. Have partners share their information with other pairs in the group.

Advanced High Have students reread the text and then ask their classmates questions about it, using content-based vocabulary. Have one student pose a question and call on another to answer it. The respondent should ask the next question, and so on, until everyone has asked and answered a question.

Answers

Generate Explanations *Indian traders, missionaries, and others brought Indian religions to the area.*

Analyze Maps *north or northeast, from China*

Topic 9 Lesson 6

Online Project the **Interactive Gallery: Angkor City and Angkor Wat** and click through the hotspots with students.

ACTIVE CLASSROOM

Have students complete a See-Think-Wonder strategy as they look at the images in the interactive gallery. With a partner, students should think about these questions: What do you see? What does it make you think about? What are you wondering about now that you have seen this? *(Sample response: The size of Angkor Wat suggests that the civilization that built it had many resources and a strong ruler.)*

Guided Reading and Discussion

Draw Conclusions Direct students' attention back to the map on the previous page. Ask students to explain how culture developed on some of the more isolated islands and villages in Southeast Asia. *(Sample response: Isolated groups with different customs gradually formed because of the geographic barriers to easy travel.)*

The Rise of Vietnam

Vietnam was more heavily influenced by China than India, having adopted Confucian ideas and the Chinese civil service system and governmental structure before the collapse of the Tang dynasty freed it of Chinese rule.

Guided Reading and Discussion

Draw Conclusions Unlike the rest of Southeast Asia, Vietnam was influenced by China more than India. Provide reasons why this may have occurred. *(Sample response: Vietnam borders China; China sent military forces to take control of Vietnam.)*

In the 1100s, **King Suryavarman II** (sur yuh VAHR mun) built the great temple complex at Angkor Wat. The ruins that survive today, though overgrown with jungle and pocked by the bullets of recent wars, are among the most impressive in the world. Hundreds of carved figures tell Hindu myths and glorify the king. Although the images of Vishnu, Shiva, and the Buddha reflect strong Indian influence, the style is uniquely Khmer.

The temples at Angkor Wat were intended to be Suryavarman's tomb. He and other royal family members wanted to be associated with the gods to ensure their immortality. Many of the carvings and sculptures there show the Hindu god Vishnu with Suryavarman's features.

Angkor Wat is part of a larger city, Angkor, which served as the center of the Khmer empire and was at one time one of the wealthiest and most sophisticated capitals in the world. Its artwork and design have been preserved despite being abandoned to the jungles in the 1300s.

The Srivijaya Empire In Indonesia, the trading empire of Srivijaya (sree wih JAW yuh) flourished from the 600s to the 1200s. Srivijaya controlled the Strait of Malacca, which was vital to shipping. Both Hinduism and Buddhism reached this island empire. As elsewhere in Southeast Asia, however, the local people often blended Indian beliefs into their own forms of worship based on nature spirits.

Later, Islam spread to Sumatra, Java, and other islands. Local rulers adopted the new religion, which cemented commercial links with other Muslim trading centers around the Indian Ocean.

CITE EVIDENCE How did India influence the Pagan kingdom and the Khmer and Srivijaya empires?

>> The magnificent temple complex at Angkor Wat in northern Cambodia is a striking blend of Indian and Khmer, as well as Hindu and Buddhist, artistic influences.

Interactive Gallery

The Rise of Vietnam

In most of Southeast Asia, Indian influence was stronger than Chinese influence. Indian traditions spread mostly through trade rather than conquest. China, however, sent military forces to conquer the neighboring state of Annam (now the northern part of Vietnam).

The heart of northern Vietnam was the Red River delta, around present-day Hanoi. There, the river irrigated fertile rice **paddies,** or fields, which provided food for a growing population.

Chinese Domination In 111 B.C., Han armies conquered the region, and China remained in control for the next 1,000 years. During that time, the Vietnamese absorbed Confucian ideas. They adopted the Chinese civil service system and built a government bureaucracy similar to that found in China. Vietnamese nobles learned to speak and read Chinese.

Unlike the rest of Southeast Asia, where Theravada Buddhism had the strongest impact, Vietnam adopted Mahayana Buddhist beliefs from China. Daoism also helped shape Vietnamese society.

Resistance Despite these powerful Chinese influences, the Vietnamese preserved a strong sense of their separate identity. In A.D. 39, two noble sisters, Trung Trac and Trung Nhi, led an uprising that briefly drove the Chinese occupiers from the land. They tried to restore a simpler form of government based on ancient Vietnamese traditions. To this day, the Trung sisters are remembered as great martyrs and heroes.

Finally, in 939, as the Tang dynasty collapsed in China, Vietnam was able to break free from China. The Vietnamese turned back repeated Chinese efforts to reconquer their land, but Vietnam still remained a tributary state of China. Ties between the two lands remained so strong that, while China was the "large

D Differentiate Challenge/Gifted Ask students to do extra research on Angkor Wat and present their findings to the class. Challenge them to present their findings in a multimedia format.

Answers

Cite Evidence *India helped shape their culture and religion, but individual peoples interpreted Indian styles in their own way. The Khmer empire also adapted Indian writing, mathematics, architecture, and art.*

Assessment

1. Pagan and its capital became a major Buddhist center filled with beautiful stupas. In the Khmer empire, the influence of various religions led to Hindu rulers and a mostly Buddhist population, and is reflected by the temple complex at Angkor Wat.
2. Unlike other parts of Southeast Asia, Vietnam was influenced more by China than by India, absorbing Confucian ideas, Mahayana beliefs, and Daoism.

dragon" of East Asia, Vietnam became known as the "smaller dragon."

IDENTIFY CAUSE AND EFFECT How did the government, language, and religion of Vietnam show outside influences?

ASSESSMENT

1. **Compare** What role did religion play in the Pagan kingdom and Khmer empire?
2. **Identify Cause and Effect** What key difference separated Vietnam's development from that of other parts of Southeast Asia?
3. **Generate Explanations** How did the geography of Srivijaya affect its cultural and religious development?
4. **Summarize** What are some ways India influenced the countries of Southeast Asia?
5. **Identify Central Ideas** Describe the geography of Southeast Asia and explain how geographic features affected the development of the region.

>> The Trung sisters and other Vietnamese led revolts against China, but without peasant support, supplies, or trained troops, they only briefly freed Vietnam.

Topic 9 Lesson 6

SYNTHESIZE

Online Project the **Digital Activity: The Impact of Geography**. If students do not have access to the digital Start Up Activity, have students, in pairs, look at the map, "Empires and Kingdoms of Southeast Asia," on page 371. Have each partner choose a country, kingdom, or empire and explain, using the text information and map key information, how geography affected the place's development, culturally, economically, politically, or religiously. Have them take 5 minutes for this activity. Have them share their responses in a class discussion.

DEMONSTRATE

Online Assign the **Digital Lesson Quiz** for this lesson if you haven't already done so. Students will be offered automatic remediation or enrichment based on their score.

Pose these questions to the class:

Compare and Contrast How were the countries of Southeast Asia similar and different? *(Similar: Other civilizations influenced them; women had significant freedoms. Different: Some relied more on trade; they adopted various religions.)*

Support Ideas With Evidence Architectural advances were made in civilizations with strong leaders. Where is this evident in Southeast Asia? *(Sample answer: King Suryavarman built the temple complex at Angkor Wat; King Anawrahta built a capital city and many stupa shrines.)*

Topic Inquiry

Have students continue their investigations for the Topic Inquiry.

Answers

Identify Cause and Effect *Vietnam modeled its civil service system after China's, its upper classes spoke Chinese, and its people adopted a Chinese form of Buddhism.*

Nobility spoke and wrote in Chinese. Vietnam eventually broke away from China after the collapse of the Tang dynasty.

3. Srivijaya's control of the Strait of Malacca made the empire a vital part of the region's major shipping routes, and brought to the empire religious and cultural ideas, including Hinduism, Buddhism, and Islam, the last of which helped strengthen ties between Srivijaya and other trading centers around the Indian Ocean.
4. Traders brought Indian goods, beliefs, and ideas, including Hinduism, Buddhism, and Islam, to the region. The Khmer empire adapted Indian writing, mathematics, architecture, and art.
5. There is the mainland, which consists of several major peninsulas, and island Southeast Asia, which consists of 20,000 islands. The mainland is separated from the rest of Asia by mountains and high plateaus, helping keep out invaders. Early settlements sprang up in the four river valleys. Island Southeast Asia controlled much of the regional trade because of its control of sea lanes. The monsoon winds shaped the trading patterns, helping Southeast Asia become not only an important part of international trade routes but also a trading center.

Answers to TEKS Assessment

1. The Song dynasty helped unify China after the collapse of the Han dynasty. The Song continued the Tang dynasty's well-ordered society under a hierarchy, with the imperial court at the top and the scholar-gentry class just below. They instituted a strong political bureaucracy that had government-funded departments that oversaw tax collecting and revenues. The Song dynasty achieved economic expansion from farm improvements and open border policies that permitted imports of faster-growing rice, which allowed them to have two rice crops a year. Trade expanded with completion of a system of canals built during the Sui dynasty. The Silk Road helped allow the diffusion of Chinese cultural and religious ideas as far away as East Africa.

2. China in this period had several social classes: the gentry at the top, then peasants, and finally the merchants. The gentry usually supplied the scholar-officials who formed society's elite. Since the positions were based on merit, through passing exams on Confucian classics, men from other classes had opportunities for social mobility. Scholar-officials, representing Confucian values, headed up China's huge bureaucracy and also served in the provinces. Confucian values and civil service exams were also adopted in East Asian countries, notably Japan and Korea.

3. Along with trade goods, merchants from Southwest Asia and India also brought their ideas, religions, and cultures from travel on the Silk Road. Chinese merchants used other routes to exchange goods for spices and special woods from Southeast Asia. Buddhist priests traveled to India to study at temples. Foreign music and art were brought to China.

4. The Tang and Song writers produced prose, poetry, and nonfiction works covering philosophy, religion, and history. Li Bo was a prolific Tang writer, producing 2,000 poems with themes of harmony with nature and lamenting the passage of time. Du Fu described the horrors of war or criticized lavish court expenses. Li Qingzhao wrote realistic poems about the experiences of women left behind during times of war.

5. During the Tang and Song dynasties, the emperor's court included various government-funded departments to study different disciplines, including astronomy. During the Ming dynasty, Chinese scholars received ideas of Western science from Jesuit missionaries. They then started their own research in subjects like astronomy to integrate their findings into the prevailing knowledge of science. They used telescopes and other technology to study heavenly bodies and reform the Chinese calendar; this was a major undertaking led by Xu Guangqi in the imperial research program that later produced star atlases and a catalog.

6. The Mongols swept into China, ending the Song dynasty, with skilled horsemen and advanced military weapons. However, once in power, they ruled with peace and order (*Pax Mongolica*: Mongol Peace) and were tolerant of the conquered people and their religions and cultures. This increased economic growth and cultural exchanges along the trade routes, including the spread of gunpowder and paper making to Europe and crops and trees to East Asia.

7. Kublai Khan ruled after conquering southern China. Kublai used Chinese officials to rule the provinces and Mongols in the military and for top government positions. Chinese and foreign customs blended, including in his use of Arab architects to design his palace, which featured Mongol steppe dwellings. He rebuilt and extended the Grand Canal to facilitate trade, and met with foreigners, including Ibn Battuta and Marco Polo. Religious exchanges were common.

TEKS ASSESSMENT

1. **Summarize Developments** Summarize the major political and economic developments in Song China. Write a paragraph summarizing the major political and economic achievements in Song China, circa A.D. 960. Consider the Song's political bureaucracy, including the scholar-gentry class; economic expansion from farming improvements; and growth of trade, including impact of the Silk Road. **4.H**

2. **Summarize Developments** Summarize the major cultural developments in Tang and Song China and summarize their impact on Eastern Asia. Write a paragraph summarizing the major cultural developments in Tang and Song China and how their values were adopted in East Asian countries. Consider the status of scholar-officials, Confucian exams, and emphasis on social order. How could peasants and merchants gain social mobility? **4.H**

3. **Analyze Facilitation** Analyze how the Silk Road facilitated the spread of trade and ideas. Write a paragraph analyzing the importance of the Silk Road in the exchange of trade and other ideas. Consider the start and end points of the route and how traders exchanged views on religion and culture, among other ideas. Other than traders, who else might have used the Silk Road or other comparable roads? **4.J**

4. **Analyze Examples** Analyze examples of how literature reflected the history of the cultures in which it was produced. Also, use appropriate reading skills to interpret social studies information. Write a paragraph, using appropriate reading skills, to analyze how Li Bo's poem is a reflection of the Tang and Song cultures. What types of literature, subjects, or themes did other Tang and Song writers like Du Fu and Li Qingzhao produce? **26.B, 29.H**

"You ask me
why I dwell in the green mountain; I smile
and make no reply for my heart is
free of care.

As the peach-blossom flows down
stream and is gone into the unknown, I have
a world apart that is not among
men."

—From "Green Mountain" by Li Bo

5. **Identify the Origin and Diffusion** Identify the origin and diffusion of major ideas in science and technology that occurred in China from the Tang to the Ming dynasties. Write a paragraph about astronomy research that occurred in China from the Tang to the Ming dynasties. Consider how government-funded departments studied astronomy and how research was conducted to reform their calendar. What role did Jesuit priests play in the diffusion of scientific ideas? **27.A**

6. **Identify Major Effects** Identify major effects of the following turning points in world history from 600 to 1450: the Mongol invasions and their impact on China. Write a paragraph identifying how the Mongols ended Song dynasty rule and their impact on China in the 1200s and 1300s. Consider *Pax Mongolica*, economic growth and cultural exchanges, and policy toward conquered people. **1.C**

7. **Summarize the Changes** Summarize the changes resulting from the Mongol invasions of China. Write a paragraph summarizing how Kublai Khan influenced China during Mongol rule. Consider Mongol and Chinese roles in government, including the provinces. Explain the results of the Mongol attitude toward religion and foreign influences. **4.K**

8. **Identify Significant Examples** Identify significant examples of architecture that demonstrate an artistic ideal or visual principle from selected cultures. Write a paragraph identifying a significant example of architecture in Korea influenced by China. Look at the picture of the Pulguksa Temple that was built in the capital of the Silla dynasty. Explain the Chinese influence, particularly the Buddhist theme. **26.A**

9. **Identify Major Causes and Effects** Identify major causes and effects or impact of the following important turning points in world history from 1450 to 1750: the influence of the Ming dynasty on world trade. Write a paragraph identifying influential events of the Ming dynasty on global trade. Consider what factors contributed to economic growth, including the transportation system. Explain why Ming China limited its trade with Europe and why precious metals flowed into the country. **1.D, 7.E**

10. **Explain the Political and Social Impact** Explain the political and social impact of Islam on Asia. Write a paragraph explaining the political and social impact of Islam in India under the Delhi sultanate. Consider the Muslim conquest of northern India, introduction of Muslim traditions of government, and the impact of scholars from the Middle East. **4.D**
11. **Analyze the Influence** Analyze the influence of physical geographic factors on major events in world history, including trade in the Indian Ocean. Write a paragraph analyzing the influence of the monsoons in the southern seas on trade in the Indian Ocean. Consider the strategic importance of the southern seas, how monsoons help shape trading patterns, and the extent of the trading network. **16.B**
12. **Describe the Interactions** Describe the interactions between Muslim and Hindu societies in South Asia. Write a paragraph describing interactions between Muslims and Hindus under the Muslim empire of the Delhi sultanate from the 1200s to the 1500s. Consider religious and cultural tensions and how these were overcome. Which groups served in the government? Explain the extent of Muslim absorption of Hindu culture. **4.F**
13. **Summarize the Fundamental Ideas** Summarize the fundamental ideas and institutions of Eastern civilizations that originated in India. Write a paragraph summarizing the origins of Hinduism in India and how Muslim rulers grew more tolerant of Hindu traditions. Consider the features of Hinduism, including polytheism, sacred texts, and the caste system. Describe the extent of how religious tolerance spread Hindu traditions under Muslim rule. **25.A**
14. **Analyze Examples** Analyze examples of how drama reflected the history of the cultures in which it was produced. Write a paragraph analyzing examples of how Noh plays and Kabuki drama reflected Japanese culture in the 1300s to 1600s. Describe the origins and differences of Noh plays and Kabuki. In the picture, why do Noh plays have no scenery, and what is the significance of the mask? **26.B**

15. **Describe the Historical Origins and Central Ideas** Describe the historical origins, central ideas, and spread of major religious and philosophical traditions, including Sikhism. Write a paragraph describing the historical origins, central ideas, and spread of Sikhism. Consider the role of Guru Nanak and the central ideas of Amrit and the Khalsa. Of what significance are the turban, sword, and comb in the pictures? **23.A**

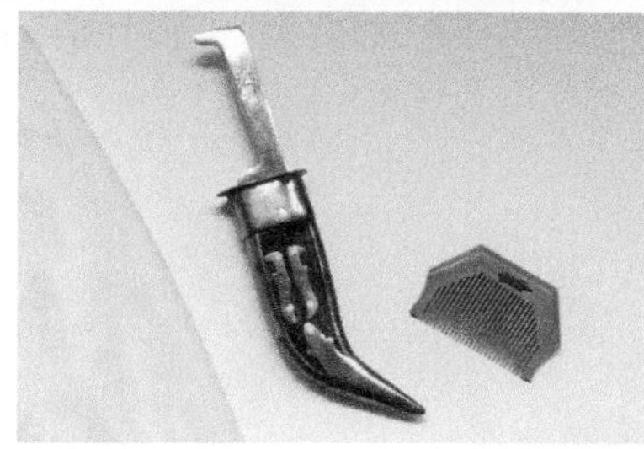

16. **Reflect on the Essential Question** **Write an essay on the Essential Question: What distinguishes one culture from another?** Use evidence from your study of this Topic to support your answer.

Along with increased trade between India and Muslim lands, scholars from the Middle East went to India and brought Persian and Greek learning.

11. The southern seas acted like a crossroads for trade between China and India as ships had to use either the Malacca or Sunda strait. Monsoons shaped trading patterns, with ships harboring vessels in the off-season in Southeast Asian trading centers or traveling with the help of the seasonal winds. The international trade network included Southeast Asia, India, China, East Africa, and the Middle East.

12. The Delhi sultanate established a Muslim empire in India that lasted for several centuries. Tensions between Hinduism (a polytheistic religion) and Islam (a monotheistic religion) gradually gave way to religious tolerance and conversion. Some Hindus served in the Muslim government and others wanted to participate in the trading between Muslim lands. Muslims in India also absorbed some aspects of Hindu culture in marriage customs, caste ideas, language, art, and music.

13. Hinduism was an ancient religion founded in India that had evolved over thousands of years. It has many sacred texts and worships many deities; religious occasions are marked with music and dance. Hindus accepted differences in caste status and honored Brahmans as a priestly caste. Despite these differences from Islam, after Muslims conquered India and initial violence had passed, Muslim rulers grew more tolerant of Hinduism; Hindus could continue to practice their faith as long as they paid a poll tax. Indian converts to Islam kept many Hindu traditions, including marriage customs and the caste system. Muslims also adopted Hindu practices in music, dance, and art.

14. Japanese feudal culture in the 1300s produced slow-paced Noh plays with men in carved masks, presented with Zen Buddhist themes or as fairy tales or struggles between feudal lords. In the absence of scenery, the emphasis is on the stylized actions of the actors who wear masks to portray different characters. In the 1600s, Kabuki drama was influenced by Noh plays but acting styles were less refined and livelier. Exaggerated styles emerged to portray different emotions.

15. Guru Nanak founded Sikhism, a major religion, in the late 1400s and spread the word along with his nine successors. Sikhism believes in equality and tolerance for all people. Sikh believers can commit to Amrit, or practicing Sikh values, and can become part of the Khalsa, a community of those who are initiated, wearing special clothing that includes the five articles of faith. Today Sikhism is the world's fifth-largest religion.

8. Chinese architecture with Buddhist themes influenced the Silla dynasty. Many temples were built, and one in particular, the Pulguksa Temple, is a prime example. Modeled after the Tang capital in Chang'an, China, and constructed in the capital city of Kyongju, the temple with its opulent roof and other features reflects the extravagance that the capital was then noted for.

9. Several causes reflected Ming China's influence on world trade: A stable, growing economy, cities that were home to varied industries and new technology, and canal system repairs all facilitated trade. Major effects included China limiting the extent and duration of trade with Europeans and eventually accepting only silver or gold payments in exchange for goods. This resulted in a massive flow of precious metals into China, particularly in trade with Japan and Spanish territories.

10. Islam spread to different parts of India after Muslims conquered northern India. Sultans changed Indian government and society by introducing Muslim traditions.

Answers to TEKS Practice

1. A
2. H

Online To prepare for the End-of-Topic test, have students go online for additional Topic Review and Assessment questions or to review their notes in the **Interactive Reading Notepad** for the lessons in this Topic.

Benchmark Tests

Assign these benchmark tests as you complete the relevant topics to monitor student progress toward mastering the course content and as preparation for the End-of-Course Test.

Benchmark Test 1: Topics 1–5

Benchmark Test 2: Topics 6–10

Benchmark Test 3: Topics 11–15

Benchmark Test 4: Topics 16–21

TEKS PRACTICE

1 Using the lessons from this topic answer the following question: Which of these situations would allow Genghis Khan and his successors to conquer a vast area, including China?

A Uniting tribes from across the region under a skilled military

B An absence of rivers in Mongolia that hindered the economy

C An absence of rugged mountain ranges

D A desire for access to Indian Ocean trade with East Africa

2

	LAST NAME	MEANING
SIKH MEN	Singh	lion
SIKH WOMEN	Kaur	princess

According to the values of Sikhism, why do all male believers have the same last name?

F To show a higher social status for men over women

G To show religious tolerance and abide by monotheism

H To reinforce the idea of equality and tolerance for all people

J To commit themselves to the Five Ks before taking Amrit

Test Taking Tips: Tip for Questions With Maps

1. Read the question.
2. Read the map title and look at the map to determine what is shown in the map.
3. Look at the key or legend. What symbols, shades, or patterns are used to show information on the map? Find examples of each symbol, shade, or pattern on the map.
4. Read the question again. What information do you need from the map to answer the question? Use the information in the map title, the key or legend, and on the map itself to find the answer.
5. Answer the question in your own words.
6. Read the answer choices and select the best answer.

3 What Chinese influences led the Korean Silla dynasty to set up a Confucian academy to train high officials?

A It started recognizing Theravada Buddhism and religious art.

B Government officials were needed to oversee growing trade.

C It was preparing to convert its language to the Chinese alphabet.

D It instituted civil service exams modeled after those in China.

4

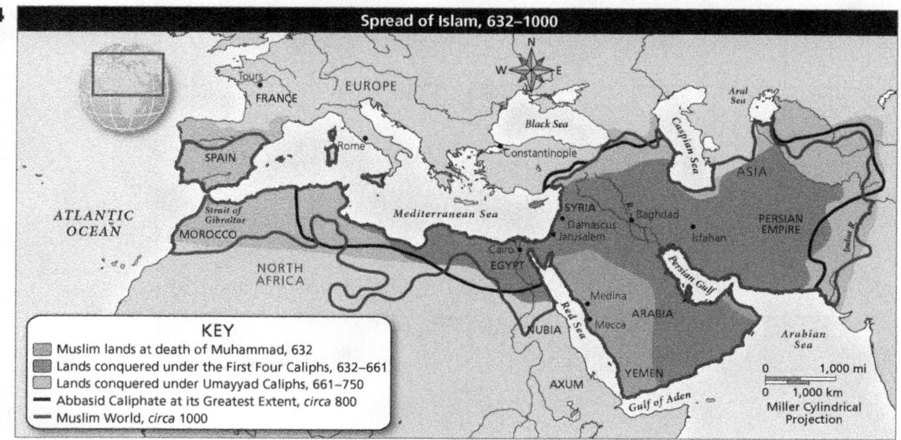

Looking at the map, which of these accurately describes the spread of the Muslim world?

F Cairo remained the physical and spiritual center of the Muslim territory.

G Muslim lands at the death of Muhammad were reduced in size, circa 1000.

H The Abassids and Umayyads together conquered lands from 632 to 661.

J The Umayyad Caliph spread Islam from Spain to beyond Persia, circa 750.

If you have trouble with...				
Question	1	2	3	4
See Lesson	9.3	9.1	9.4	8.2
TEKS	1.C	23.A	25.A	4.D, 23.A

Topic 9

3. D
4. J

Online Use the **Topic Synthesize** to help students revisit and reflect on the Essential Question for this Topic.

The Renaissance and Reformation (1300–1650)

TOPIC 10 ORGANIZER	PACING: APPROX. 1 PERIOD, .5 BLOCKS		
	PACING	TEKS	ELPS
Connect	1 period		
MY STORY VIDEO **Leonardo da Vinci, Renaissance Man**	10 min.		
DIGITAL ESSENTIAL QUESTION ACTIVITY **Why is Culture Important?**	10 min.	5.A	
DIGITAL TIMELINE ACTIVITY **The Renaissance and Reformation**	10 min.	5.A, 27.C, 27.D, 27.E	
TOPIC INQUIRY: PROJECT-BASED LEARNING **Create a Hall of Fame Web Site**	20 min.		
Investigate	2–5 periods		
TOPIC INQUIRY: PROJECT-BASED LEARNING **Create a Hall of Fame Web Site**	Ongoing		
LESSON 1 **The Italian Renaissance**	30–40 min.	1.D, 5.A, 25.C, 26.A, 26.B, 26.C	3.G.1
LESSON 2 **The Renaissance in Northern Europe**	30–40 min.	1.D, 5.A, 26.B, 26.C, 27.C	3.B.2, 3.G.2
LESSON 3 **The Protestant Reformation**	30–40 min.	1.D, 5.A, 5.B, 19.B, 20.C, 23.B, 25.C, 27.C	3.B.3
LESSON 4 **Reformation Ideas Spread**	30–40 min.	1.D, 5.B, 23.B, 24.B, 25.C	
LESSON 5 **The Scientific Revolution**	30–40 min.	1.E, 27.D, 27.E	
Synthesize	1 period		
DIGITAL ESSENTIAL QUESTION ACTIVITY **Reflect on the Essential Question and Topic**	10 min.	5.A	
Demonstrate	1–2 periods		
DIGITAL TOPIC TEST **The Renaissance and Reformation**	10 min.		
TOPIC INQUIRY: PROJECT-BASED LEARNING **Create a Hall of Fame Web Site**	20 min.		

AUTHOR'S NOTE

The Renaissance of Western Art

The word *renaissance* means "rebirth," and the age was so called by its own leading intellectual lights, the classical scholars of Renaissance Italy. They thought of their era as one of cultural rebirth, a revival of the wisdom and art of what was for them Europe's greatest age—the ancient world of Periclean Greece and Augustan Rome. The legacy of ancient Rome especially enthralled them. They did a splendid job of imbuing Renaissance culture with Latin literature and Roman history and mythology. Indeed, it is almost impossible to read Renaissance literature or look at much Renaissance art without some knowledge of ancient Rome.

The study of classical culture, in contrast with the study of things divine, was known in the Renaissance as *humanism*. The men who began to read the Latin classics seriously again after a thousand years were called humanists. They were a varied lot of classical scholars—teachers and writers, poets and philosophers, pious Christians and libertines. The first of them, the fourteenth-century Italian poet Petrarch, wrote Renaissance love poems and medieval meditations on death with equal enthusiasm. The most famous sixteenth-century humanist, Erasmus, was equally admired for his editions of the New Testament and for his worldly satires on every aspect of Renaissance life, including the sins of organized religion.

The humanists as a group performed one great service for the modern West. They recovered much of our Western heritage of ancient Greek and Roman literature, lost and moldering in forgotten corners of obscure monastic libraries, unhonored and unread. They also attempted, with more modest success, to "civilize" the sword-swinging medieval nobility by a strong infusion of ancient culture. They did not produce the race of Platonic philosopher-kings they hoped for. But they did produce the first really literate aristocracy Europe had for ten centuries—a first step at least toward matching the more cultivated courtier classes of the Muslim East or China's Confucian scholar bureaucrats.

—Anthony Esler, *The Human Venture: From Prehistory to the Present* (Upper Saddle River, New Jersey: Pearson Education, 2004), p. 372

Create a Hall of Fame Web Site

TEKS 1D, 5.A, 26.A, 26.B, 26.C, 27.D, 27.E

In this Topic Inquiry, students work in teams to research the lives of important figures of the Renaissance and the Scientific Revolution and build a Hall of Fame Web site honoring their lives and the significance of their work. Learning about these individuals will contribute to students' understanding of the Topic Essential Question: Why is culture important?

STEP 1: CONNECT

Develop Questions and Plan the Investigation

Launch the Project and Generate Questions

Display the letter from the European Museum of Culture and Science. Tell students that for their project, each team will need to research, nominate, and select ten inductees for a Renaissance Hall of Fame. They will then write Hall of Fame profiles for these key figures of the Renaissance and Scientific Revolution. They will build a Hall of Fame Web site that will include the inductee profiles, as well as additional material on the era.

Plan the Investigation

Form students into teams. Have them learn about working as a team by taking a tutorial, signing the *Project Contract*, and beginning the *Need-to-Know Questions*.

Suggestion: You can control the length of the project by assigning either fewer or more inductees. Similarly, if you prefer that each student research and write an inductee entry as well as doing some of the other roles, either form groups of three or have larger groups research more inductees.

Resources

- Entry Event
- Rubric for a Group Web Site
- Student Instructions
- Need-to-Know Questions
- Project Contract

PROFESSIONAL DEVELOPMENT

Project-Based Learning

Be sure to view the Project-Based Learning Professional Development resources in the online course.

STEP 2: INVESTIGATE

Apply Disciplinary Concepts and Tools

Identify Potential Hall of Fame Inductees

Teams will work together to decide the criteria for admittance to the Hall of Fame, who should be nominated, and who should be inducted into their Web site. Help students to determine the significance of a nominee's work in the Renaissance or Scientific Revolution if they are having trouble choosing their inductees. You can also direct them to other Hall of Fame Web sites, such as the Baseball or Rock-n-Roll Hall of Fame, if students need more examples.

Suggestion: If your class has limited access to the Internet, you could make several books available to students, such as *Leonardo and His Times* by Dorling Kindersley and *William Shakespeare: Playwright and Poet* by Compass Point Books.

Conduct Research on the Inductees

Have students research their inductees. To guide their research, teams will create a list of *Need-to-Know Questions* about the people they have chosen for the Hall of Fame. Refer students to helpful resources within the core content of the Topic to help answer their questions. Help students begin to fill out the *Information Organizer*.

Write and Edit the Hall of Fame Profiles

The teams should plan how to present the information they have gathered.

Next, students should write their inductees' entries and do some peer review of one another's writing. Remind students to offer detailed, constructive criticism of one another's work.

Resources

- Project Tracker
- Information Organizer

STEP 3: SYNTHESIZE

Evaluate Sources and
Use Evidence to Formulate Conclusions

Build Your Web Site

Now have students get together to build their Web sites. If students are having trouble sharing the work of this part of the project, remind them to review their *Project Tracker and Project Roles* document to make sure they are on track. For students who are having trouble, walk them through *Plan Your Web Site* to get ideas.

Suggestion: For a less technology-dependent end product, have students write their inductees' Hall of Fame profiles and create a Hall of Fame exhibit with the information they have gathered. To take technology a step further, have students set up a mock blog and conduct discussions using their inductees as online personas.

Write a Conclusion

Ask teams to review their Web sites and draw conclusions about what they have learned. To help teams start, have each team member write down their answer to a different question listed in the *Student Instructions* and then share those answers with the group. Have students work their conclusions into the selection criteria of the Web site.

STEP 4: DEMONSTRATE

Communicate Conclusions
and Take Informed Action

Present Your Hall of Fame Web Site

Have students prepare their Web site presentations, then watch the team presentations. To help the teams structure their time, set up a clock in the back of the room and alert them when they have only a few minutes left.

Reflect on the Project

After students have finished their Team Assessments, help them go over what they thought went well and what did not, so they can be even more effective in the future.

Resources

- Web Site Rubric
- Self Assessment

The Italian Renaissance

Objectives

Objective 1: Describe the characteristics of the Renaissance and understand why it began in Italy.

Objective 2: Identify Renaissance artists and explain how new ideas affected the arts of the period.

Objective 3: Understand how writers of the time addressed Renaissance themes.

Objective 4: Explain the impact of the Renaissance.

LESSON 1 ORGANIZER	PACING: APPROX. 1 PERIOD, .5 BLOCKS					
			RESOURCES			
	OBJECTIVES	PACING	Print	Online	TEKS	ELPS
Connect						
DIGITAL START UP ACTIVITY **Michelangelo's *David***		5 min.		●		
Investigate						
READ **The Italian Renaissance**	Objective 1	10 min.	●	●	1.D, 5.A, 26.B	
READ **The Renaissance Begins in Italy**		10 min.	●	●	1.D, 5.A, 26.B	
INTERACTIVE MAP **Renaissance Italy's City-States**		10 min.		●	1.D, 5.A, 26.A, 26.B	
READ **Art Flourishes in the Renaissance**	Objectives 2, 4	10 min.	●	●	1.D, 5.A, 26.A, 26.B, 26.C	3.G.1
BEFORE AND AFTER **The Discovery of Perspective**		10 min.		●	5.A, 26.A, 26.B, 26.C	
3-D MODEL **Duomo in Florence**		10 min.		●	5.A, 26.A, 26.B	
READ **New Books Reflect Renaissance Themes**	Objective 3	10 min.	●	●	5.A, 26.B	
Synthesize						
DIGITAL ACTIVITY **Sistine Chapel**		5 min.		●	5.A, 26.A, 26.B	
Demonstrate						
LESSON QUIZ **Lesson Quiz and Class Discussion Board**		10 min.		●	1.D, 5.A, 26.B	

Focus on Texas Standards

Texas Essential Knowledge and Skills

1.D identify major causes and describe the major effects of the following important turning points in world history from 1450 to 1750: the rise of the Ottoman Empire, the influence of the Ming dynasty on world trade, European exploration and the Columbian Exchange, European expansion, and the Renaissance and the Reformation

5.A explain the political, intellectual, artistic, economic, and religious impact of the Renaissance

25.C explain the relationship among Christianity, individualism, and growing secularism that began with the Renaissance and how the relationship influenced subsequent political developments

26.A identify significant examples of art and architecture that demonstrate an artistic ideal or visual principle from selected cultures

26.B analyze examples of how art, architecture, literature, music, and drama reflect the history of the cultures in which they are produced

26.C identify examples of art, music, and literature that transcend the cultures in which they were created and convey universal themes

NOTES

The Renaissance in Northern Europe

Objectives

Objective 1: Describe the themes that northern European artists, humanists, and writers explored.

Objective 2: Explain how the printing revolution shaped European society.

LESSON 2 ORGANIZER		PACING: APPROX. 1 PERIOD, .5 BLOCKS				
			RESOURCES			
	OBJECTIVES	PACING	Print	Online	TEKS	ELPS
Connect						
DIGITAL START UP ACTIVITY **An Expanding World**		5 min.		●	1.D, 5.A, 27.C	
Investigate						
READ **Artists of the Northern Renaissance**	Objective 1	10 min.	●	●	1.D, 5.A, 26.B	
READ **Northern Renaissance Humanists and Writers**	Objective 1	10 min.	●	●	1.D, 5.A, 26.B, 26.C	
INTERACTIVE GALLERY **Realism in Northern Europe Renaissance Art**	Objective 1	10 min.		●	5.A, 26.B	
INTERACTIVE GALLERY **Shakespeare: "For All Time"**	Objective 1	10 min.		●	26.B, 26.C, 27.C	
READ **The Printing Revolution**	Objective 2	10 min.	●	●	1.D, 5.A, 27.C	3.B.2, 3.G.2
Synthesize						
DIGITAL ACTIVITY **Erasmus**		5 min.		●	1.D, 5.A, 26.B, 27.C	
Demonstrate						
LESSON QUIZ **Lesson Quiz and Class Discussion Board**		10 min.		●	1.D, 5.A, 26.B, 26.C, 27.C	

Focus on Texas Standards

Texas Essential Knowledge and Skills

1.D identify major causes and describe the major effects of the following important turning points in world history from 1450 to 1750: the rise of the Ottoman Empire, the influence of the Ming dynasty on world trade, European exploration and the Columbian Exchange, European expansion, and the Renaissance and the Reformation

5.A explain the political, intellectual, artistic, economic, and religious impact of the Renaissance

26.B analyze examples of how art, architecture, literature, music, and drama reflect the history of the cultures in which they are produced

26.C identify examples of art, music, and literature that transcend the cultures in which they were created and convey universal themes

27.C explain the impact of the printing press on the Renaissance and the Reformation in Europe

NOTES

The Protestant Reformation

Objectives

Objective 1: Summarize the factors that encouraged the Protestant Reformation.

Objective 2: Explain the impact of the printing press on the Reformation.

Objective 3: Analyze Martin Luther's role in shaping the Protestant Reformation.

Objective 4: Explain the teachings and impact of John Calvin.

LESSON 3 ORGANIZER — **PACING: APPROX. 1 PERIOD, .5 BLOCKS**

	OBJECTIVES	PACING	RESOURCES: Print	RESOURCES: Online	TEKS	ELPS
Connect						
DIGITAL START UP ACTIVITY **Launching the Protestant Reformation**		5 min.		●	1.D	
Investigate						
READ **Causes of the Reformation**	Objective 1	10 min.	●	●	1.D, 5.B, 25.C	3.B.3
READ **Martin Luther's Protests Bring Change**	Objectives 2, 3	10 min.	●	●	1.D, 5.B, 23.B, 27.C	
BEFORE AND AFTER **Illuminated Manuscripts to Printed Pages**		10 min.		●	5.B, 27.C	
INTERACTIVE GALLERY **Reformation Art**		10 min.		●	5.B	
READ **John Calvin Challenges the Church**	Objective 4	10 min.	●	●		
Synthesize						
DIGITAL ACTIVITY **Technology: The Communications Revolution**		5 min.		●	1.D, 27.C	
Demonstrate						
DIGITAL QUIZ **Lesson Quiz and Class Discussion Board**		10 min.		●	5.A, 5.B, 23.C, 27.C	

Focus on Texas Standards

Texas Essential Knowledge and Skills

1.D identify major causes and describe the major effects of the following important turning points in world history from 1450 to 1750: the rise of the Ottoman Empire, the influence of the Ming dynasty on world trade, European exploration and the Columbian Exchange, European expansion, and the Renaissance and the Reformation

5.A explain the political, intellectual, artistic, economic, and religious impact of the Renaissance

5.B explain the political, intellectual, artistic, economic, and religious impact of the Reformation

19.B identify the characteristics of the following political systems: theocracy, absolute monarchy, democracy, republic, oligarchy, limited monarchy, and totalitarianism

20.C explain the political philosophies of individuals such as John Locke, Thomas Hobbes, Voltaire, Charles de Montesquieu, Jean Jacques Rousseau, Thomas Aquinas, John Calvin, Thomas Jefferson, and William Blackstone

23.B identify examples of religious influence on various events referenced in the major eras of world history

25.C explain the relationship among Christianity, individualism, and growing secularism that began with the Renaissance and how the relationship influenced subsequent political developments

27.C explain the impact of the printing press on the Renaissance and the Reformation in Europe

NOTES

Reformation Ideas Spread

Objectives

Objective 1: Describe the new ideas that Protestant sects embraced.

Objective 2: Understand why England formed a new church.

Objective 3: Analyze how the Catholic Church reformed itself.

Objective 4: Explain why many groups faced persecution during the Reformation.

Objective 5: Explain the impact of the Reformation.

LESSON 4 ORGANIZER	PACING: APPROX. 1 PERIOD, .5 BLOCKS					
			RESOURCES			
	OBJECTIVES	PACING	Print	Online	TEKS	ELPS
Connect						
DIGITAL START UP ACTIVITY **Reformation Ideas Reach England**		5 min.		●	5.B, 23.B	
Investigate						
READ **An Explosion of Protestant Sects**	Objectives 1, 5	10 min.	●	●	1.D, 5.B, 23.B, 25.C	
READ **The English Reformation**	Objectives 2, 5	10 min.		●	1.D, 5.B, 23.B, 24.B, 25.C	
INTERACTIVE TIMELINE **Timeline of the English Reformation**		10 min.		●	1.D, 5.B, 23.B, 24.B, 25.C	
READ **The Catholic Reformation**	Objectives 3, 5	10 min.	●	●	1.D, 5.B, 23.B, 25.C	
INTERACTIVE MAP **Major European Religions, About 1600**		10 min.		●	1.D, 5.B, 23.B, 25.C	
READ **Religious Persecution Continues**	Objective 4	10 min.	●	●	1.D, 5.B	
Synthesize						
DIGITAL ACTIVITY **Spread and Impact of the Protestant Reformation**		5 min.		●	1.D, 5.B, 23.B	
Demonstrate						
LESSON QUIZ **Lesson Quiz and Class Discussion Board**		10 min.		●	1.D, 5.B	

www.PearsonTexas.com
Access your Digital Lesson

Focus on Texas Standards

Texas Essential Knowledge and Skills

1.D identify major causes and describe the major effects of the following important turning points in world history from 1450 to 1750: the rise of the Ottoman Empire, the influence of the Ming dynasty on world trade, European exploration and the Columbian Exchange, European expansion, and the Renaissance and the Reformation

5.B explain the political, intellectual, artistic, economic, and religious impact of the Reformation

23.B identify examples of religious influence on various events referenced in the major eras of world history

24.B describe the major influences of women such as Elizabeth I, Queen Victoria, Mother Teresa, Indira Gandhi, Margaret Thatcher, and Golda Meir during major eras of world history

25.C explain the relationship among Christianity, individualism, and growing secularism that began with the Renaissance and how the relationship influenced subsequent political developments

NOTES

The Scientific Revolution

Objectives

Objective 1: Explain how new discoveries in astronomy changed the way people viewed the universe.

Objective 2: Understand the new scientific method and how it developed.

Objective 3: Identify the contributions that Galileo, Copernicus, Newton, and other scientists made to the Scientific Revolution.

LESSON 5 ORGANIZER — **PACING: APPROX. 1 PERIOD, .5 BLOCKS**

	OBJECTIVES	PACING	RESOURCES: Print	RESOURCES: Online	TEKS	ELPS
Connect						
DIGITAL START UP ACTIVITY **A New Way of Thinking**		5 min.		●	1.E, 27.D, 27.E	
Investigate						
READ **Changing Views of the Universe**	Objective 1	10 min.	●	●	1.E, 25.C, 27.D, 27.E	
INTERACTIVE GALLERY **Changing Views of the Universe**	Objective 1	10 min.		●	1.E, 27.D, 27.E	
READ **A New Scientific Method**	Objective 2	10 min.	●	●	1.E, 25.C, 27.D	
READ **Breakthroughs in Medicine and Chemistry**	Objective 3	10 min.	●	●	1.E, 27.D, 27.E	
INTERACTIVE GALLERY **A Scientific Revolution in Medicine**	Objective 3	10 min.		●	1.E, 27.D, 27.E	
Synthesize						
DIGITAL ACTIVITY **Important People of the Scientific Revolution**		5 min.		●	27.E	
Demonstrate						
DIGITAL QUIZ **Lesson Quiz and Class Discussion Board**		10 min.		●	1.E, 27.D, 27.E	

PEARSON realize™ www.PearsonTexas.com Access your Digital Lesson

Focus on Texas Standards

Texas Essential Knowledge and Skills

1.E identify major causes and describe the major effects of the following important turning points in world history from 1750 to 1914: the Scientific Revolution, the Industrial Revolution and its impact on the development of modern economic systems, European imperialism, and the Enlightenment's impact on political revolutions

27.D describe the origins of the Scientific Revolution in 16th century Europe and explain its impact on scientific thinking worldwide

27.E identify the contributions of significant scientists such as Archimedes, Copernicus, Eratosthenes, Galileo, Pythagoras, Isaac Newton, and Robert Boyle

NOTES

The Renaissance and Reformation (1300–1650)

In this Topic, you will learn about the Renaissance and the Reformation. You know the TEKS are very important, and this course will make it fun to learn about the things that will help you master them. Keep reading to see how.

Your study will help you master these TEKS:

TEKS

1.D, 1.E, 5.A, 5.B, 19.B, 20.C, 23.B, 24.B, 25.C, 26.A, 26.B, 26.C, 27.C, 27.D, 27.E, 29.H

LESSON OUTLINE

Connect

Connect with this Topic by watching a video about a fascinating person related to the Renaissance. You can think about how this Topic connects to your own life. And you'll encounter an intriguing Essential Question: Why is culture important?

Begin your study by trying the following:

NBC LEARN Watch My Story Video:

Leonardo da Vinci, Renaissance Man

Launch your Project:

Build a Hall of Fame Website

Investigate

The Lesson Outline lists all the lessons you will investigate in this Topic. As you read and interact with key content, the story of the Renaissance and the Reformation will come to life. Read the texts; try the interactivities. Investigate the story of these fascinating eras in history.

And keep working on your Project to help build your mastery of the Topic TEKS.

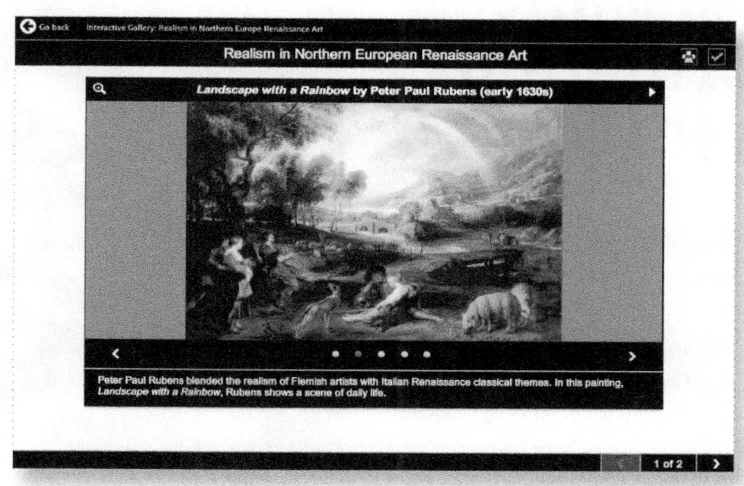

>> Digital interactivity from the online course

Synthesize

Next you will pull it all together by reflecting on the Essential Question. This will give you a chance to be the storyteller, to show how you would answer this big question: Why is culture important?

Demonstrate

Completing this Topic is like practicing all your soccer skills or rehearsing the scenes in a play. Now you get a chance to pull it all together for the final game or the live performance. You can do this on the Topic Review and Assessment pages. Or you can complete your work on your Hall of Fame Website.

TEKS in Topic 10	Topic Review and Assessment Questions
1.D	2, 7, 9
1.E	13, 14
5.A	4, 7, 11
5.B	11
19.B	10
20.C	10
23.B	9
24.B	5
25.C	8
26.A	3
26.B	6
26.C	1
27.C	12
27.D	13
27.E	15

Topic 10

The Renaissance and Reformation (1300–1650)

Introduction

The Renaissance was an era marked by a new way of thinking and a burst of artistic creativity. It spread from Italy to northern Europe, where a remarkable number of artists and writers produced great works. The invention of the printing press not only helped spread Renaissance ideas, but also made the Bible widely available. When Martin Luther challenged some practices of the Catholic Church, it marked the beginning of the Protestant Reformation. It spread throughout Europe, often sparking bloody religious wars, and forever broke the unity of the Church in Europe. The Catholic Reformation stemmed the spread of Protestantism and reasserted its power in much of Europe. The Church faced other challenges as scientists, spurred by a new approach called the scientific method, made exciting new discoveries.

[ESSENTIAL QUESTION] Why is Culture Important?

10 **The Renaissance and Reformation (1300–1650)**

ESSENTIAL QUESTION

Ask students to think about the Essential Question for this Topic: Why is culture important?

Project the Essential Question activity from the course, or you may choose to read or display this list of cultural connections: politics; economics; the arts; science; religion. Ask students to list the connections in order of importance. Then go over the results as a class.

Support a Point of View With Evidence Ask: Why did you rank this cultural connection as most important? *(Students should understand that the Renaissance affected not only the arts, but also politics, religion, and science.)*

Identify Cause and Effect Why might scientific discoveries impact culture? *(Possible answer: If a new scientific discovery challenges commonly held beliefs, it will require people to reevaluate how they think about their world.)*

Analyze Images

Point out that the painting on p. 380 is the *Mona Lisa*, an oil portrait created by Leonardo da Vinci in Italy between 1503 and 1506. It is one of the world's most famous paintings, but the identity of the woman pictured and the meaning of her expression are unknown. Have students point out details that they notice about the painting's content and style.

Texas Essential Knowledge and Skills

1.D, 1.E, 5.A, 5.B, 19.B, 20.C, 23.A, 23.B, 24.B, 25.C, 26.A, 26.B, 26.C, 27.C, 27.D, 27.E, 29.H

Enduring Understandings

- The Renaissance, a time of great creativity and cultural changes, marked the transition from medieval times to the modern world.
- Renaissance thinkers looked to classical learning for a deeper understanding of human life, and Renaissance artists treated both religious and secular subjects in a new realistic style.
- The Protestant Reformation began when Martin Luther protested against corruption in the Catholic Church.
- During the Reformation, Protestant ideas spread while Catholic leaders sought to reform the Church.
- The Scientific Revolution led to dramatic breakthroughs in the study of the physical world.

>> The *Mona Lisa*, a painting by Leonardo da Vinci

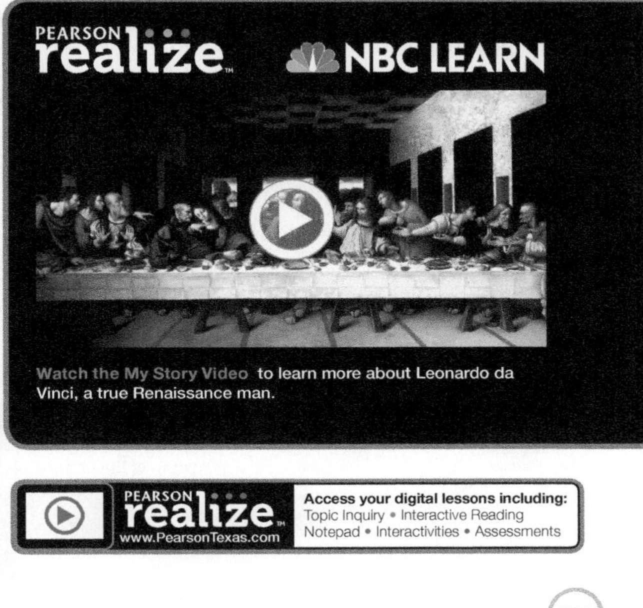

Watch the My Story Video to learn more about Leonardo da Vinci, a true Renaissance man.

PEARSON realize www.PearsonTexas.com — Access your digital lessons including: Topic Inquiry • Interactive Reading Notepad • Interactivities • Assessments

381

NBC LEARN MY STORY VIDEO

Project the My Story Video that tells about one of the leading figures of the Renaissance, Leonardo da Vinci.

Online My Story Video: **Leonardo da Vinci, Renaissance Man**

After viewing, ask students to respond to the following questions.

Check Understanding Why did Renaissance artists use the new technique of perspective? *(To show depth and distance on a flat surface; perspective introduced new levels of realism to art.)*

Apply Concepts Leonardo da Vinci said, "The knowledge of all things is possible." How did this statement reflect Renaissance thinking? *(The Renaissance was a time when people in Europe took great interest in art, literature, and learning.)*

OVERVIEW ACTIVITY

Online Display the timeline showing major events of the Renaissance and Reformation as well as the Scientific Revolution. These are just some of the events that students will learn about while exploring this Topic. The timeline will provide a framework into which students can place the events they learn about.

Check Understanding How many years after Martin Luther posted his Theses did the English Parliament pass the Act of Supremacy? *(17; Theses posted in 1517; Act of Supremacy was passed in 1534)*

Topic Inquiry

If you choose to assign the Topic Inquiry, launch the project with students after introducing the Topic.

D Differentiate Extra Support For the overview activity, demonstrate to students how to read the timeline. How many years passed between the first printed Bible and Martin Luther posting his 95 Theses? *(61, Bible printed in 1456; 95 Theses posted in 1517)*

Topic 10 Lesson 1

The Italian Renaissance

CONNECT

Preview Have students preview the **Lesson Objectives** and the list of **Key Terms**.

Students can also preview all the **Key Terms** and **Academic Vocabulary** using the **Interactive Reading Notepad** on the digital course or preview a summary of the lesson in the **Reading and Note Taking Study Guide**.

Online Use the **Editable Presentation** found on the digital course to present the main ideas for this lesson.

Start Up Activity

If available, show students an image of Michelangelo's statue *David*. Explain: The Renaissance was a time of artistic and intellectual curiosity. An artist named Michelangelo completed a statue in 1504 showing the hero David from the Bible, a shepherd who kills the giant Goliath. Renaissance art was influenced by earlier styles but also reflected a new emphasis on the individual.

Discuss How do you think Renaissance art styles might differ from medieval art? *(Sample answer: Renaissance art could have religious themes, which was common in medieval European art, but the focus was more on individual identity.)*

Online You can also project the **Start Up Activity** from the course.

INVESTIGATE

Have students read the section using the **Reading and Note Taking Study Guide** to help them take notes and understand the text as they read.

The Italian Renaissance

The Renaissance was a time of rebirth for the arts and culture in Europe, beginning in Italy in the 1300s. During the Renaissance, Western Europe witnessed the growth of cities and trade. There was renewed interest in classical learning and arts from Greece and Rome, along with technological innovations, an interest in humanism, and realism in the arts. In Italy, wealthy merchants and the powerful Catholic Church helped the arts flourish by their patronage of art.

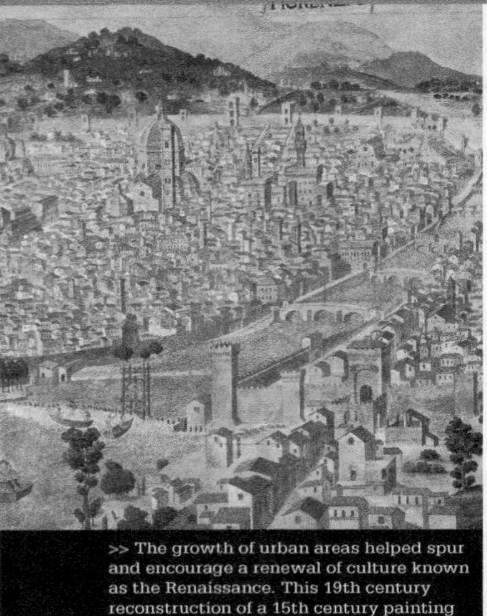

>> The growth of urban areas helped spur and encourage a renewal of culture known as the Renaissance. This 19th century reconstruction of a 15th century painting shows Florence, Italy, in 1490.

Interactive Flipped Video

10.1 From the 1300s to the 1500s, Western Europe enjoyed a golden age in the arts and literature, known as the Renaissance. The word literally means "rebirth." The Renaissance was a time of great creativity and change in many areas—economic, political, social, and above all, cultural.

TEKS
1.D, 5.A, 25.C, 26.A, 26.B, 26.C

>> Objectives

Describe the characteristics of the Renaissance and understand why it began in Italy.

Identify Renaissance artists and explain how new ideas affected the arts of the period.

Understand how writers of the time addressed Renaissance themes.

Explain the impact of the Renaissance.

>> Key Terms

humanism
humanities
Petrarch
Florence
patron
perspective
Leonardo da Vinci
Michelangelo
Raphael
Baldassare Castiglione
Niccolò Machiavelli
vernacular

The Italian Renaissance

The Italian Renaissance

The Renaissance marked the transition between medieval and early modern times. During the Renaissance, Western Europe witnessed the growth of cities and trade, which greatly extended people's horizons.

A New Worldview Most important, the Renaissance changed the way people saw themselves and their world. Spurred by a reawakened interest in the learning of ancient Greece and Rome, creative Renaissance minds set out to transform their own age. Their era, they felt, was a time of rebirth after the disorder and disunity of the medieval world.

Renaissance Europe did not really break with its medieval past. Much of the classical heritage had survived, including the Latin language and knowledge of ancient thinkers such as Euclid and Aristotle. Yet the Renaissance did produce new attitudes toward culture and learning. Unlike medieval scholars, who debated the nature of life after death, Renaissance thinkers were eager to explore the richness and variety of human experience in the here and now.

PEARSON realize. www.PearsonTexas.com Access your Digital Lesson.

382

Aa Vocabulary Builder

1. Have students pronounce the following academic vocabulary terms in this lesson and clarify the part of speech. For difficult or polysyllabic words, break them into syllables and pronounce them with the students.
2. Explain what the word means in common "student-friendly" language using synonyms and antonyms when possible. Provide concrete examples to clarify the meaning, and rephrase the definition.

comprehend: understand; take in
emerge: develop; rise from; become known

During the Renaissance, there was a new emphasis on individual achievement. Indeed, the Renaissance ideal was a person with talents and skills in many fields.

A Spirit of Adventure and Curiosity The Renaissance supported a spirit of adventure and curiosity that led people to explore new worlds or to reexamine old ones. Columbus, who sailed to the Americas in 1492, represented that spirit. So, too, did the scientists who looked at the universe in new ways.

An Italian thinker, Pico della Mirandola, captured this spirit of adventure and confidence in human abilities when he wrote: "To [man] it is granted to have whatever he chooses, to be whatever he wills."

Renaissance Humanism At the heart of the Italian Renaissance was an intellectual movement known as **humanism**. Humanist scholars studied classical Greek and Roman cultures, hoping to use the wisdom of the ancients to increase their understanding of their own times. Though most humanists were pious Christians, they focused on worldly, or secular, subjects rather than on the religious issues that had occupied medieval thinkers.

Humanists believed that education should stimulate the individual's creative powers. They emphasized the **humanities**—subjects such as grammar, rhetoric (the study of using language effectively), poetry, and history—that had been taught in ancient Greek and Roman schools.

Francesco **Petrarch** (PEE trahrk), who lived in Florence, a city in north Italy in the 1300s, was an early Renaissance humanist. From monasteries and churches, he hunted down and assembled a library of Greek and Roman manuscripts. Through his efforts, and those who followed his example, the speeches of Cicero, the poems of Homer and Virgil, and Livvy's *History of Rome* again became known to Western Europeans.

Petrarch also wrote poetry. His *Sonnets to Laura* are love poems, inspired by a woman he knew only at a distance, but their style greatly influenced writers of his time. Petrarch wrote in the **vernacular**, or everyday language of ordinary people, as well as in Latin.

DESCRIBE What were some important characteristics of the Renaissance?

>> The Church was an important patron of Renaissance art, commissioning paintings and sculptures. Here, the pope meets with artist Michelangelo.

>> Francesco Petrarch, an Italian Renaissance scholar, poet, and humanist.

Guided Reading and Discussion

Writers also benefited from the wealth and flourishing culture in Italy. Renaissance writers like Francisco Petrarch were pious Christians who focused on worldly subjects and emphasized humanism. Petrarch valued education and the classics in his work as a scholar, poet, and humanist.

Compare What were some characteristics of the Renaissance that can be seen in Francesco Petrarch and his work? *(Possible answer: Petrarch was multi-talented and had varied interests, a characteristic of Renaissance men. He stressed education and valued the classics, both Renaissance characteristics. He advocated humanism, also typical of the Renaissance.)*

Answers

Describe *Important characteristics of the Renaissance included a "rebirth" of culture; a new worldview based on human experience; an emphasis on education and humanism; the end of medieval times; a gradual shift from rural to urban societies; the growth of trade; new technologies; and a spirit of adventure, creativity, and curiosity.*

Topic 10 Lesson 1

The Renaissance Begins in Italy

Online Project the **Interactive Map: Renaissance Italy's City-States** and click each hotspot to bring up images and text about the various city-states, artists, and sea trade. Tell students that the city-states had some similarities.

ACTIVE CLASSROOM

Use the strategy A Closer Look and explain that students will study the role of arts in various Italian city-states or along a trade route. Divide the class into six groups. Project the Interactive Map. Have each group focus on one hotspot area of the map. Have them tell you what they learned as a result of their focus on this section. Collect insights for each map section.

Guided Reading and Discussion

Identify Causes What were some economic causes of the Italian Renaissance? *(Possible answer: Italy's location allowed sea trade, which made Italian merchants and merchant families wealthy. Wealthy families became patrons of the arts. The Roman Catholic Church also gave financial support to artists and scholars.)*

Analyze Images

Have students look at the map Italy's City-States and Sea Trade. Ask: Why did the Renaissance develop in Italy before other European countries? *(Possible answer: Wealthy merchants and the Roman Catholic Church financed artists; other factors were art and artifacts from ancient Rome and knowledge gleaned from trade with Muslims, who had preserved classic works of Greece and Rome.)*

The Renaissance Begins in Italy

The Renaissance began in Italy in the mid-1300s and later spread north to the rest of Europe. It reached its height in the 1500s. The Renaissance emerged in Italy for several reasons.

Italy's History and Geography The Renaissance was marked by a reawakened interest in the culture of ancient Rome. Since Italy was the center of ancient Roman civilization, it was only natural for this reawakening to begin there. Architectural remains, antique statues, coins, and inscriptions were all daily reminders of the glory of ancient Rome.

Italy differed from the rest of Europe in another important way. Italy's cities had thrived during the Middle Ages. In the north, city-states like Florence, Milan, Venice, and Genoa grew into prosperous centers of trade and manufacturing. Rome and Naples, along with many smaller city-states, also contributed to the Renaissance cultural revival.

At trading ports along Italy's coastlines, ships brought goods, people, and ideas from the Muslim world, which had preserved much learning from ancient Greece and Rome. Many texts—and much knowledge—that had been lost in Europe were recovered through these trading contacts.

A class of wealthy and powerful merchants emerged in Italy's city-states, and they promoted the cultural rebirth. These merchants exerted both political and economic leadership, and their attitudes and interest helped to shape Renaissance Italy. They stressed education and individual achievement. They also spent lavishly to support the arts.

Florence and the Medicis Florence, perhaps more than any other city, came to symbolize the Italian Renaissance. Like ancient Athens, it produced a dazzling number of gifted poets, artists, architects, scholars, and scientists in a short space of time.

In the 1400s, the Medici (MED dee chee) family of Florence organized a banking business. Their business prospered, and the family expanded into manufacturing, mining, and other ventures. Soon, the Medicis ranked among the richest merchants and bankers in Europe. Money translated into cultural and political power. Cosimo de' Medici gained control of the Florentine government in 1434, and the family continued as uncrowned rulers of the city for many years.

The best known Medici was Cosimo's grandson, Lorenzo, known as "the Magnificent." Lorenzo represented the Renaissance ideal. A clever politician, he held Florence together through difficult times. He was also a generous **patron**, or financial supporter, of

>> **Analyze Maps** The states and kingdoms of Italy lay at the center of Europe's sea trade. Why were so many banking centers located in Italy?

Interactive Map

Answers

Analyze Maps *The central location of Italy and its prominence in sea trade made it ideal for providing loans to traders.*

the arts. At Lorenzo's invitation, poets and philosophers frequently visited the Medici palace. Artists learned their craft by sketching ancient Roman statues displayed in the Medici gardens.

IDENTIFY CAUSE AND EFFECT Why did Italy's historic legacy make it an ideal place for the Renaissance to begin?

Art Flourishes in the Renaissance

The Renaissance attained its most glorious expression in its paintings, sculpture, and architecture. Wealthy patrons played a major role in this artistic flowering. Popes and princes, along with successful merchants, supported the work of hundreds of artists.

Art Reflects New Ideas and Attitudes Renaissance art reflected humanist concerns. Like the artists of the Middle Ages, Renaissance artists portrayed religious figures, such as Mary and Jesus. However, they often set these figures against Greek or Roman backgrounds.

Painters also produced portraits of well-known figures of the day, reflecting the humanist interest in individual achievement. Renaissance artists also painted scenes from Greek and Roman mythology and depicted historical events.

Renaissance artists studied ancient Greek and Roman works and revived many classical forms. The sculptor Donatello, for example, created a life-size statue of a soldier on horseback. It was the first such figure done since ancient times.

New Techniques and Styles Ancient Roman art was realistic, a style that was abandoned in the Middle Ages. Renaissance painters developed new techniques for representing humans and landscapes in a realistic way. They discovered the rules of **perspective**, which allowed them to represent a three-dimensional world—what people see—onto a two-dimension surface, such as wood or canvas. By making distant objects smaller than those close to the viewer, artists gave the impression of space and depth on a flat surface.

Artists also used shadings of light and dark to make objects look round and real, making scenes more dramatic. Renaissance artists studied human anatomy and drew from live models. This made it possible to portray the human body more accurately than medieval artists had done.

>> In this painting by Italian Renaissance artist Tintoretto, Mary Magdalene anoints the feet of Jesus. Classical columns in the background reflect the Renaissance style.

>> **Analyze Information** Leonardo da Vinci used perspective in his painting, *The Last Supper*, completed in 1498. What techniques bring the viewer's eye to the central figure of Jesus?

Interactive Illustration

Topic 10 Lesson 1

Art Flourishes in the Renaissance

Remind students that even today, some of the world's most famous and influential artists—like Leonardo da Vinci, Michelangelo, and Raphael—are from the Italian Renaissance. These artists represented the ideals of their time: reviving classical forms, using innovative techniques, and focusing on humanism and realism in addition to religious themes. One example of Renaissance impact is Michelangelo's dome design for St. Peter's Cathedral, which, centuries later, was an inspiration for the United States Capitol's dome.

Online Project the **Interactive Art: The Discovery of Perspective**. Look at each image individually and view the transition between the two images. Let students know that another way artists added perspective to drawings was to make distant objects in the picture smaller than those closest to the viewer.

ACTIVE CLASSROOM

Use the Quickdraw strategy with students working in pairs. Give students a short period to share what they understand about perspective by trying to create their own sketches that show perspective.

Background

Italian Renaissance Society Not all people experienced the Renaissance in the same way. While the upper class enjoyed lives made easier by wealth and enriched by art and ideas, most Italians of the time lived and worked much as they always had: from hand to mouth. Only slowly were the lives of the working classes affected by the Renaissance.

In addition, the Renaissance occurred against a background of extreme violence. Families within city-states feuded and fought, as Shakespeare immortalized in his late-1500s play *Romeo and Juliet*. Italian city-states were constantly at war with one another. Yet none of this social conflict dampened the spirit of the Renaissance. Indeed, people looked to new, innovative Renaissance ideas to help them solve the problems of their time.

Answers

Identify Cause and Effect *Renaissance thinkers were interested in reviving classical art, philosophy, and architecture from ancient Rome. Ancient Roman artifacts abounded in Italy. Some of ancient Rome's history was preserved by Muslim scholars, who traded with Italians. The Catholic Church in Rome also supported the arts.*

Analyze Information *elegant clothing, servants, the counting of money*

Topic 10 Lesson 1

Key Terms

Ask students to find the key term **humanism** (in bold) in the text. Explain that the increased interest in humanism led artists to look for new techniques that would let them draw, paint, and sculpt more realistically during the Renaissance.

Guided Reading and Discussion

Create a two-column chart listing the artists Leon Alberti, Filippo Brunelleschi, Leonardo da Vinci, Michelangelo, and Raphael in the left-hand column. Label the right-hand column *Accomplishments*. As a class, review the names of Renaissance artists and architects and their accomplishments and fill in the graphic organizer as you go.

Summarize How did the Renaissance worldview affect Renaissance artists and writers? *(They adopted a new realism and a new emphasis on humanity.)*

Online Project the **3-D Model: Duomo in Florence**. Look at the model from various views and at the interactive aspects of the cathedral dome. Note that Brunelleschi, the dome's architect, was a Renaissance man—he designed the dome, invented perspective, and built some machines used in the dome's construction.

ACTIVE CLASSROOM

Use the See-Think-Wonder strategy and have each student pair with a partner. Ask them: What do you notice about the dome? What does that make you think? What are you wondering about now that you've seen this? Share insights with the class.

>> The Duomo, a dome atop a cathedral in Florence, was designed by Renaissance architect Filippo Brunelleschi. Completed in 1496, it was modeled on the dome of the Pantheon, built in ancient Rome.

Interactive 3-D Model

>> **Analyze Information** Ceiling frescoes done by Michelangelo in the Vatican's Sistine Chapel in Rome. How do the paintings show aspects of Renaissance humanism?

Renaissance Architecture Renaissance architects rejected the Gothic style of the late Middle Ages. To them, it was disorderly. Instead, they adopted the columns, arches, and domes used by the ancient Greeks and Romans. To top the cathedral in Florence, Filippo Brunelleschi (broo nay LAYS kee) created a majestic dome, modeled on the dome of the ancient Pantheon in Rome.

Like so many other Renaissance artists, Brunelleschi had many talents. He had studied sculpture with Donatello and was an accomplished engineer, inventing many of the machines used to construct his dome.

Leonardo da Vinci Florence was home to many outstanding painters and sculptors. Among the most brilliant was **Leonardo da Vinci** (DAH VIHN chee), who was born in 1452. His endless curiosity fed a genius for invention. He sketched objects in nature and dissected corpses to learn how bones and muscles work. Today, people admire Leonardo's paintings for their freshness and realism. Most popular is the *Mona Lisa*, a portrait of a woman whose mysterious smile has baffled viewers for centuries.

Another masterpiece, *The Last Supper*, which shows Jesus and his disciples, is a deceptively simple painting and a brilliant example of the use of perspective. To create it, Leonardo used a new type of paint, which decayed over time. However, the painting has been restored.

Although Leonardo thought of himself as an artist, his interests extended to botany, anatomy, optics, music, architecture, and engineering. He sketched flying machines and undersea boats centuries before the first airplane or submarine was built. His many notebooks filled with sketches are a testament to his genius.

Michelangelo Like Leonardo, **Michelangelo** was a many-sided genius. He was a sculptor, engineer, painter, architect, and poet. Born in 1475, he came under the wing of the Medicis in Florence. As a young man, he shaped marble into masterpieces like the *Pieta*, which captures the sorrow of Mary as she cradles the dead Jesus on her knees. *David*, Michelangelo's statue of the biblical shepherd who killed the giant Goliath, recalls the harmony and grace of ancient Greek sculptures.

In 1508, Michelangelo started a new project, painting a series of murals on the vast curved ceiling of the Sistine Chapel in Rome. During the next four years, he worked to complete scenes from the biblical book of *Genesis* along with figures of prophets who had foretold the coming of Jesus.

Later, as an architect, Michelangelo drew a design for the enormous dome of St. Peter's Cathedral in

English Language Proficiency Standards

Speaking 3.G.1 Have students examine the images of Renaissance art in the text. Have them select a favorite or least favorite and share their opinions.

Beginning Display each image and have students describe what they see. Then ask students to choose a favorite piece. Have them express their opinion using the following sentence frame: My favorite piece is ________ because ____________.

Intermediate Follow the instructions in the Beginning activity, but have students create their own sentences expressing their opinions.

Advanced Have pairs share their opinions on the pieces that they chose. Encourage students to use varied and rich language to describe their opinions to their partner.

Advanced High Have students express their opinions and reasoning to the group. Encourage students to use varied and rich language.

Answers

Analyze Information Answers may vary but could include: *Jesus appears in the center, in front of light windows, with an arch above the window directly behind his head. Most apostles look toward him. Converging lines draw the viewer's eye to the center and to Jesus.*

Rome. Although he did not live to see it, the dome was completed based on his exact design. The dome served as a model for many later structures, including the Capitol in Washington, D.C.

Raphael A few years younger than Leonardo and Michelangelo, **Raphael** (rah fah EL) studied the works of those great masters. His paintings blend Christian and classical styles. Among his best-known works is *School of Athens*, which pictures an imaginary gathering of great thinkers and scientists, including Plato, Aristotle, Socrates, and the Arab philosopher Averroës. In typical Renaissance fashion, Raphael included Michelangelo, Leonardo, and himself.

IDENTIFY Which artistic technique was developed during the Renaissance and used in *The Last Supper*?

ELPS 3.G.1 Practice sharing your opinions about the art described in *Art Flourishes in the Renaissance*.

>> **Analyze Information** In *School of Athens*, Italian painter Raphael imagines a gathering of great thinkers and scientists. Why did he include Renaissance artists in the scene?

New Books Reflect Renaissance Themes

Poets, artists, and scholars mingled with politicians at the courts of Renaissance rulers. A literature of "how to" books sprang up to help ambitious men and women who wanted to rise in the Renaissance world.

Castiglione's Ideal Courtier The most widely read of these handbooks was *The Book of the Courtier*, by **Baldassare Castiglione** (kahs teel YOH nay). In it, he describes the manners, skills, learning, and virtues that a member of the court should have.

The ideal differed for men and women. The ideal man, wrote Castiglione, is athletic but not overactive. He is good at games but not a gambler. He plays a musical instrument and knows literature and history but is not arrogant. The ideal woman offers a balance to men. She is graceful and kind, lively but reserved. She is beautiful, "for outer beauty," wrote Castiglione, "is the true sign of inner goodness."

Machiavelli's Advice to Princes **Niccolò Machiavelli** (mahk ee uh VEL ee) wrote a different kind of handbook. He had served Florence as a diplomat and had observed kings and princes in foreign courts. He had also studied ancient Roman history. In *The Prince*, published in 1513, Machiavelli offered a guide to rulers on how to gain and maintain power. It combined his personal experience of politics with his knowledge of the past.

>> This 1474 painting by Italian Renaissance artist Andrea Mantegna is called *The Court of Mantua*. An Italian nobleman was Mantegna's patron and commissioned art works like this.

New Books Reflect Renaissance Themes

Like Italian Renaissance artists, the writers of the time also showed curiosity, creativity, scholarship, and humanism. For example, Machiavelli and Castiglione both wrote "how-to" type books that were designed to help their fellow men. Some writers like Machiavelli had an impact beyond their own generation, influencing politicians for centuries.

Guided Reading and Discussion

Draw Conclusions What Renaissance idea appears in writing by Castiglione? *(Possible answer: He wrote about the ideal man having multiple talents and skills, which was a popular idea in the Renaissance.)*

Identify Effects How did Machiavelli's book, *The Prince,* have political impact many years after Machiavelli's life? *(Possible answer: Later readers argued that Machiavelli provided a realistic look at politics. His work is still read today for its study of government and power.)*

SYNTHESIZE

Online Project the **Digital Activity: Sistine Chapel**. Tell students the enormous project of painting the Sistine Chapel ceiling still impresses artists today. The Italian Renaissance had a lasting impact on art and architecture.

Have students answer the questions in this activity, then discuss their answers with a partner.

Have partners think about the following question: Why is culture important? Have pairs share their answers with the class.

Discuss The Sistine Chapel painting was commissioned by a pope for a church. Wealthy merchant families in Renaissance Italy were patrons of the arts. In today's modern American culture, where can you find examples of important art and architecture?

D Differentiate Challenge After students review the Renaissance artists and architects, have them research the design of the United States Capitol. Also have them research Michelangelo's design for the St. Peter's Cathedral dome in Rome. Have students compare the two buildings, since the Capitol was modeled on Michelangelo's dome. Students may wish to draw a picture of one or both buildings to illustrate similarities.

Answers

Identify *The new technique used was perspective. Leonardo da Vinci painted* The Last Supper. *He also used new types of paints.*

Analyze Information *Renaissance artists had self-confidence to consider their own artistic creations as valuable to society, on par with contributions by great thinkers and scientists. They recognized that their own time period was special and revolutionary.*

Topic 10 Lesson 1

DEMONSTRATE

Online Assign the **Digital Lesson Quiz** for this lesson if you haven't already done so. Students will be offered automatic remediation or enrichment based on their score.

Pose the following question to the class on the Discussion Board:

In "The Italian Renaissance," you read that Italy's ancient history, geography, and thriving city-states contributed to the development of a new age and a new way of thinking. The Italian Renaissance and its artists, writers, and architects shared some characteristics such as an emphasis on humanism, realism, and multiple talents. They also all had an impact on later time periods.

Predict Consequences How might the Renaissance worldview and characteristics such as humanism eventually influence other areas, such as religion? *(Possible answer: A student might predict correctly that a focus on humanism could lessen the power and influence of organized religion and the Catholic Church.)*

Topic Inquiry

Have students continue their investigations for the Topic Inquiry.

>> **Analyze Information** Niccolò Machiavelli, the Italian Renaissance political philosopher and writer. Would Machiavelli have considered *The Court of Mantua* painting as realistic or not? Why?

The Prince did not discuss leadership in terms of high ideals, as Plato had. Instead, it looked at real rulers in an age of ruthless power politics. Machiavelli stressed that the end justifies the means. He urged rulers to use whatever methods were necessary to achieve their goals.

Machiavelli saw himself as an enemy of oppression and corruption, but critics attacked his cynical advice. (In fact, the term "Machiavellian" came to refer to the use of deceit in politics.) Later students of government, however, argued that Machiavelli provided a realistic look at politics. His work continues to spark debate because it raises important ethical questions about the nature of government and the use of power.

 **IDENTIFY** How did Renaissance writings express realism?

ASSESSMENT

1. **Analyze Information** What were some of the characteristics of the Italian Renaissance?
2. **Identify Cause and Effect** How did Italy's trade with the Muslim world contribute to the Italian Renaissance?
3. **Analyze Information** What new ideas and techniques resulted in more realistic and accurate portrayals of people in Renaissance paintings?
4. **Draw Conclusions** What Renaissance theme appears in Machiavelli's book *The Prince?*
5. **Identify Central Ideas** What was the impact of the Italian Renaissance in the field of architecture?

Answers

Analyze Information *Possible answer: Yes, because some figures in the painting appear to be whispering or exchanging glances as though they are plotting against other figures.*

Identify *Writers focused on the human experience in the world around them.*

Assessment

1. Student answers may include a "rebirth" of culture; the end of medieval times; a time of creativity, inquiry, and exploration; and an emphasis on the humanities.
2. Trade with Muslim countries in North Africa brought ancient Greek and Roman scientific and technical knowledge (which Muslim scholars had preserved) to Italy and helped shape the Italian Renaissance.
3. Renaissance artists studied human anatomy and live models. Leonardo dissected corpses to study bones and muscles. The Renaissance emphasis on humanism also contributed to more realistic portrayals of people in art. These new ideas and techniques gave Renaissance paintings of human bodies more realism and accuracy.
4. Machiavelli applied the Renaissance theme of realism to describe power politics.
5. Architects adopted features such as columns, arches, and domes from ancient Greece and Rome. Renaissance architects created beautiful buildings that inspired future generations of architects. For example, the U.S. Capitol was modeled on Michelangelo's dome for St. Peter's Cathedral in Rome.

10.2 In the mid-1300s, the Black Death had reduced the population of Europe by one-third and brought the economy to a standstill. Italy recovered fairly quickly and was soon the center of the Renaissance and its creative upsurge. Only after 1450 did northern Europe enjoy the economic growth that had earlier supported the Renaissance in Italy.

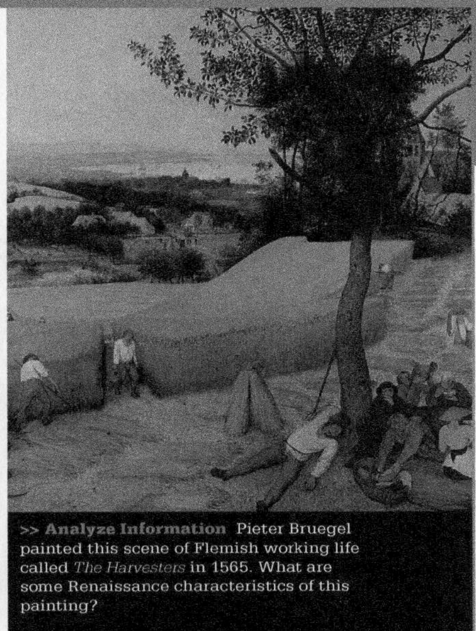

>> **Analyze Information** Pieter Bruegel painted this scene of Flemish working life called *The Harvesters* in 1565. What are some Renaissance characteristics of this painting?

Interactive Flipped Video

The Renaissance in Northern Europe

TEKS
1.D, 5.A, 26.B, 26.C, 27.C

>> **Objectives**

Describe the themes that northern European artists, humanists, and writers explored.

Explain how the printing revolution shaped European society.

>> **Key Terms**

Johannes Gutenberg
Flanders
Albrecht Dürer
engraving
Erasmus
Sir Thomas More
utopian
Shakespeare

Artists of the Northern Renaissance

The northern Renaissance began in the prosperous cities of **Flanders**, a region that included parts of what is today northern France, Belgium, and the Netherlands. Flanders was a thriving center of trade for northern Europe. From Flanders, the Renaissance spread to Spain, France, Germany, and England, which enjoyed cultural rebirths during the 1500s.

Flemish Painters Among the many talented artists of Flanders in the 1400s, Jan van Eyck stands out. His portrayals of townspeople as well as religious scenes abound in rich details that add to the realism of his art. Van Eyck developed new techniques for using oil paint. He and other Flemish artists used these new methods to produce strong colors and a hard-surfaced paint that could survive for centuries.

A leading Flemish painter of the 1500s was Pieter Bruegel (BROY gul). He used vibrant colors to portray lively scenes of peasant life, earning him the nickname "Peasant Bruegel." Although Bruegel produced works on religious and classical themes, his secular art

389

PEARSON realize www.PearsonTexas.com Access your Digital Lesson.

Aa Vocabulary Builder

1. Have students pronounce the following academic vocabulary term in this lesson and clarify the part of speech. Break the word into syllables and pronounce it with the students.
2. Explain what the word means in common "student-friendly" language using synonyms and antonyms when possible. Provide concrete examples to clarify the meaning, and rephrase the definition.

prosperous: successful; wealthy

Topic 10 Lesson 2

The Renaissance in Northern Europe

CONNECT

Preview Have students preview the **Lesson Objectives** and the list of **Key Terms**.

Students can also preview all the **Key Terms** and **Academic Vocabulary** using the **Interactive Reading Notepad** on the digital course or preview a summary of the lesson in the **Reading and Note Taking Study Guide**.

Online Use the **Editable Presentation** found on the digital course to present the main ideas for this lesson.

Start Up Activity

Explain that by the mid-1400s, the Renaissance was spreading from Italy into northern Europe. The newly invented printing press made books cheaper and more plentiful. All over Europe, knowledge was expanding.

Discuss How does the effect of the printing press compare with the effects of a modern technology? Explain. *(Possible answer: Like the printing press, the Internet lets information travel all over the world faster than ever before.)*

Online You can also project the **Start Up Activity** from the course.

INVESTIGATE

Have students read the section using the **Reading and Note Taking Study Guide** to help them take notes and understand the text as they read.

Artists of the Northern Renaissance

The northern Renaissance began in the trading cities of Flanders. Artists who had traveled to Italy also carried Renaissance ideas north. Like the Italians, northern European artists explored realism and humanism. Northern writers also examined these themes, and some were critical of organized religion. The works of playwright William Shakespeare exemplified the Renaissance and had a lasting cultural impact.

Answers

Analyze Information *It shows a scene of realism and focuses on the daily lives of common people.*

Online Project the **Interactive Gallery: Realism in Northern Europe Renaissance Art** and look at and discuss each image individually. Explain how northern European artists like Jan van Eyck pioneered the technique of oil painting to reflect light, achieve depth, and create realistic details in their works. Northern Renaissance artists brought new realism to paintings of peasant life, religious scenes, and landscapes.

ACTIVE CLASSROOM

Use the Quickdraw strategy with students working in pairs. Have each pair work on a sketch to show an understanding of realism. One student can research an Internet image of an animal or something else from nature; the other student can try to realistically recreate that image in a sketch.

Northern Renaissance Humanists and Writers

Analyze Information How did northern Renaissance artists blend Italian Renaissance ideas with their own? *(Dürer used Italian painting techniques along with his own ideas for engraving. Flemish artists used oil paintings to achieve depth, create realistic details, and express humanist themes.)*

>> This 1511 woodcut print by Albrecht Dürer is called *St. Christopher.*

Interactive Gallery

>> Desiderius Erasmus was a Dutch priest and humanist scholar who was active during the Northern European Renaissance. He believed an individual's chief duties were to be open-minded and to show good will toward others.

influenced later Flemish artists, who painted scenes of ordinary people in their daily lives.

Albrecht Dürer: A "German Leonardo" Among the most influential artists of the northern Renaissance was the German painter and printmaker **Albrecht Dürer** (DYOOR ur). In 1494, he made the first of several trips to Italy to study the works and techniques of Italian masters. At home, he employed the new methods in his own paintings, engravings, and prints. Through these works as well as his essays, Dürer helped spread Renaissance ideas to northern Europe.

Dürer had a keen, inquiring mind. Because of his wide-ranging interests, which extended far beyond art, he is sometimes called the "German Leonardo."

Dürer is well-known for applying the painting techniques he had learned in Italy to **engraving**, a method of making prints from metal plates. In an engraving, an artist etches a design on a metal plate with acid. The artist then uses the plate to make prints. Many of Dürer's engravings and paintings portray religious upheaval of the time.

IDENTIFY What were some important artistic themes in the Northern European Renaissance?

Northern Renaissance Humanists and Writers

Like the Italian humanists, northern European humanist scholars stressed education and classical learning. At the same time, they emphasized religious themes. They believed that the revival of ancient learning should be used to bring about religious and moral reform.

Although most humanist scholars wrote mainly in Latin, other writers began to write in the vernacular, or everyday language of ordinary people. In this way, their works were accessible to the new middle class audience living in towns and cities.

Erasmus The great Dutch humanist Desiderius **Erasmus** (ih RAZ mus), became a priest in 1492. He used his knowledge of classical languages to produce a new Greek edition of the New Testament and a much-improved Latin translation of the Bible. At the same time, Erasmus called for a translation of the Bible into the vernacular.

"I disagree very much with those who are unwilling that Holy Scripture, translated into the vernacular, be read by the uneducated." For him, "the strength of the Christian religion" should not be based on people's

English Language Proficiency Standards

Speaking 3.B.2 Read aloud or have students read "The Impact of the Printed Book." Have them practice retelling, using the information and the image, to a partner or the group. Guide them to an understanding of the term *mass production.*

Beginning Have students describe images from the text and choose a favorite piece. Have them express their opinion using this sentence frame: My favorite piece is ______ because _________.

Intermediate Follow the instructions in the Beginning activity, but have students create their own sentences.

Advanced Have students reread "The Impact of the Printed Book" and take turns retelling to a partner, using the illustration for support. Have pairs discuss the meaning of *mass production* and share a summary of their discussion.

Advanced High Follow the instructions in the Advanced activity, but have students retell the information to a group and discuss the importance of *mass production* as it relates to the printed book.

Answers

Identify *Realism in the human form and in daily life, religious upheaval, and classical themes.*

ignorance of it, but on their ability to study it on their own.

Erasmus used his pen to call for reforms in the Church. He challenged the worldliness of the Church and urged a return to early Christian traditions. His best-known work, *In Praise of Folly*, uses humor to explore the ignorant, immoral behavior of people. Erasmus taught that an individual's chief duties were to be open-minded and show good will toward others.

Sir Thomas More Erasmus's friend, the English humanist **Sir Thomas More**, also pressed for social and economic reforms. In *Utopia*, More describes an ideal society in which men and women live in peace and harmony. Private property does not exist. No one is idle, all are educated, and justice is used to end crime rather than to eliminate criminals. Today, the word **utopian** has come to describe any ideal society, with the implication that such a society is impractical.

Rabelais's Comic Masterpiece The French humanist François Rabelais (rab uh LAY) had a varied career as a monk, a physician, a Greek scholar, and an author. Unlike Erasmus and More, Rabelais wrote in the French vernacular. In *Gargantua and Pantagruel*, he chronicles the adventures of two gentle giants. On the surface, the novel is a comic tale of travel and war. But Rabelais uses his characters to offer opinions on religion, education, and other serious subjects.

Shakespeare Explores Universal Themes The towering figure of Renaissance literature was the English poet and playwright **William Shakespeare**. Between 1590 and 1613, he wrote 37 plays that are still performed around the world. Shakespeare's genius was in expressing universal themes in everyday realistic settings. His work explores Renaissance ideals such as the complexity of the individual and the importance of the classics. At the same time, his characters speak in language that common people can understand and appreciate.

Shakespeare's comedies, such as *A Midsummer Night's Dream*, laugh at the follies and joys of young people in love. His history plays, such as *Richard III*, chronicle the power struggles of English kings. His tragedies show human beings crushed by powerful forces or their own weakness. In *Romeo and Juliet*, two teenagers fall victim to an old family feud. In *Othello*, a noble soldier is driven mad by jealousy, while *Macbeth* depicts an ambitious couple whose desire for political power leads them to murder.

Shakespeare's love of words vastly enriched the English language. More than 1,700 words appeared for

>> **Draw Conclusions** Boats sit in front of the island Utopia, from More's 1516 book *Utopia*. On the island, "... men and women of all ranks, go to hear lectures of one sort or other." More advocated for an education system available to all.

>> William Shakespeare (1564–1616), English author, playwright, and poet

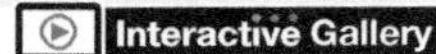
Interactive Gallery

Topic 10 Lesson 2

Key Terms

Ask students to find the key term **utopian** (in bold) in the text and read its meaning. Ask students to discuss why one connotation of a utopian society is impracticality.

Online Project the **Interactive Gallery: Shakespeare: "For All Time."** Click each hotspot individually. Explain how Shakespeare's plays reflected their own Renaissance time period. For example, they often included some religious characters. His plays also transcend time by addressing universal themes such as family, power, and love.

ACTIVE CLASSROOM

Use the Act It Out strategy with students working in small groups. Have each group choose one of the hotspot images to act out. Their choice might include lines from *Hamlet*, a short biography of Shakespeare, or an image from his other plays. They can find scenes from his plays online to get more lines to enact.

Guided Reading and Discussion

Besides Shakespeare, other northern European Renaissance writers included Sir Thomas More, Desiderius Erasmus, and François Rabelais. These three writers were humanists, addressing society's problems and advocating for social reforms and better education.

Summarize How did popular writers like Shakespeare help spread humanist ideas? *(They wrote in the vernacular so everyday people could read their works. They focused on stories about individuals and their human problems and emotions.)*

English Language Proficiency Standards

Speaking 3.G.2 Read aloud or have students read "The Printing Revolution." Encourage students to discuss their ideas as to why printing had such a great effect at the time.

Beginning Help students create a list of the effects of the printing press on the board. Have them express their ideas about the printing revolution by completing these sentence frames:

- The printing revolution _____ Europe.
- The changes that the printing revolution caused include _____.

Intermediate Follow the instructions in the Beginning activity, but have students create their own sentences.

Advanced Have pairs review the text and list the effects of the printing press on everyday life in northern Europe. Have pairs discuss in groups the effect printing had on society.

Advanced High Follow the instructions in the Advanced activity, but have students work alone before starting a class discussion.

The Printing Revolution

Tell students that around 1455, Johannes Gutenberg invented a printing press in Germany. The first book he printed was a Bible. Many Bibles soon followed; the press allowed books to be produced at a much faster rate than medieval handwriting methods. The Italian Renaissance, already spreading to northern Europe, expanded quickly throughout Europe due to the increased knowledge and education nurtured by the printing revolution and books.

Guided Reading and Discussion

Infer Why was the Christian Bible the first book that Gutenberg printed? *(Possible answer: It was the most widely used book of the time, and even Renaissance humanists were still influenced by Christianity and religious themes.)*

Analyze Images

Ask students to look at the chart Effects of the Printing Press. Ask: Do you think that the Renaissance would have spread as quickly throughout northern Europe if the presses printed only Bibles? *(Answers may vary, but the best prediction is probably no. Through other books, readers gained access to a broad range of knowledge, from medicine and law to mining. Other printed books exposed educated Europeans to new ideas and places, including Renaissance ideas from Italy.)*

the first time in his works, including *bedroom, lonely, generous, gloomy, heartsick, hurry,* and *sneak.*

? COMPARE What Renaissance themes are explored in Shakespeare's works?

The Printing Revolution

The great works of Renaissance literature reached a large audience. The reason for this was a crucial breakthrough in technology—the development of printing in Europe.

The New Technology In 1456, **Johannes Gutenberg** (GOOT un burg) of Mainz, Germany, printed a complete edition of the Christian Bible using a printing press with movable metal type. With the Gutenberg Bible, the European age of printing had begun. Within a few years, printing presses using Gutenberg's technology sprang up in Italy, Germany, the Netherlands, and England.

The development of printing set off revolutionary changes that would transform Europe. Before the printing press, there had been only a few thousand books in all of Europe. These books had been slowly copied out by hand. By 1500, according to some estimates, 15 to 20 million volumes had been produced on new printing presses. In the next century, between 150 and 200 million books went into circulation.

The Impact of the Printed Book The printing revolution ushered in a new era of mass production of books. It also affected the price of books. Books printed with movable type on rag paper were easier to produce and cheaper than hand-copied works. As books became readily available, more people learned to read and write. They thus gained access to a broad range of knowledge as presses churned out books on topics from medicine and law to astrology, mining, and geography.

Printing influenced both religious and secular, or nonreligious, thought. "The preaching of sermons is speaking to a few of mankind," noted an English author, "but printing books is talking to the whole world." With printed books, educated Europeans were exposed to new ideas that greatly expanded their horizons.

The new printing presses contributed to the religious turmoil that engulfed Europe in the 1500s. By then, many Christians could read the Bible for themselves. As a result, the ideas of religious reformers spread faster and to a larger audience than ever before.

? CHECK UNDERSTANDING Why was it hard for the general population to access books before the printing press?

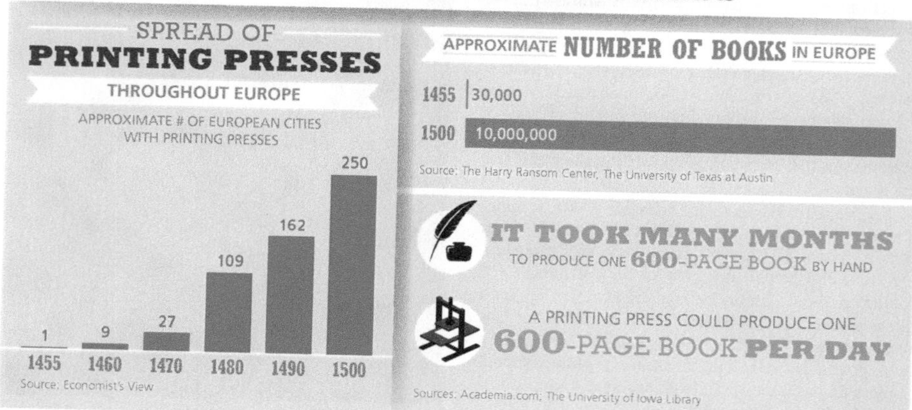

>> **Analyze Charts** The chart shows the effects of the printing press in Europe. Is it likely or unlikely that in 1500, only the largest European capital cities had printing presses?

Answers

Compare *Renaissance themes explored in works by Shakespeare include realism, the complexity of individuals (humanism), and the importance of the classics and of history.*

Check Understanding *Books were hand-copied and rare, with only a few thousand copies in Europe. After the printing press, millions of books became available to the general public.*

Analyze Charts *unlikely, because there were many fewer than 250 large capital cities in Europe*

ELPS **ELPS 3.G.2** Practice sharing ideas in *The Printing Revolution* with your classmates.

ELPS **ELPS 3.B.2** Retell the story of the printing press to understand the term *mass production*.

ASSESSMENT

1. **Identify Cause and Effect** What effects did the invention of the printing press have on European society?
2. **Draw Conclusions** How did the Flemish painters Jan van Eyck and Pieter Bruegel's realistic portrayals of townspeople and peasants reflect common themes in Renaissance art?
3. **Compare** Why is the German artist Albrecht Dürer compared to the Italian Renaissance figure Leonardo da Vinci?
4. **Identify Central Ideas** What intellectual topics did the Renaissance humanist Sir Thomas More explore?
5. **Analyze Information** How does Shakespeare's play about a historical figure like Julius Caesar reflect an important aspect of the Renaissance?

Topic 10 Lesson 2

SYNTHESIZE

Online Project the **Digital Activity: Erasmus**. Have students complete the questions in the Digital Activity and share their answers with partners.

Discuss Why did humanists like Erasmus call for translating the Bible into the vernacular? *(He believed that all people should have access to religious and classical learning.)*

DEMONSTRATE

Online Assign the **Digital Lesson Quiz** for this lesson if you haven't already done so. Students will be offered automatic remediation or enrichment based on their score.

Pose the following questions to the class on the Discussion Board:

In "The Renaissance in Northern Europe," you read about the printing revolution and its effect on helping spread Renaissance ideals such as humanism and education. You also learned about northern European Renaissance artists and writers, the techniques they used, and the themes they explored.

Identify Effects What political impacts did writers like More, Rabelais, and Erasmus hope to achieve in their own time and for future generations? *(Possible answer: They wanted to reform societies to be more fair and just, with widespread literacy and education. More envisioned an ideal utopian society. They challenged the political power of the Church by critiquing corruption in organized religion.)*

Predict Consequences What impact might the printing press have had on religious reform movements of the 1500s? *(Possible answer: Religious reformers could use the printing press to spread their ideas to a large number of people quickly and cheaply.)*

Topic Inquiry

Have students continue their investigations for the Topic Inquiry.

Assessment

1. Printed books became cheaper and easier to produce, which resulted in millions more books in circulation. More people learned to read and were therefore better educated and better informed.
2. Most Renaissance artists were interested in humanity in general and in capturing realistic human anatomy, living conditions, and emotions.
3. Both were painters and artists with wide-ranging interests that went beyond art. They studied art in Italy and were innovators in artistic techniques.
4. More explored topics such as social reform, improving society, education, and the justice system.
5. Many Renaissance artists and writers used ancient Greek and Roman cultures for inspiration and ideas.

Topic 10 Lesson 3

The Protestant Reformation

CONNECT

Preview Have students preview the **Lesson Objectives** and the list of **Key Terms**.

Students can also preview all the **Key Terms** and **Academic Vocabulary** using the **Interactive Reading Notepad** on the digital course or preview a summary of the lesson in the **Reading and Note Taking Study Guide**.

Online Use the **Editable Presentation** found on the digital course to present the main ideas for this lesson.

Start Up Activity

Explain that German monk Martin Luther nailed his 95 Theses to a church door This was Luther's attempt to force Church authorities to defend religious policies that more and more people were finding objectionable. The Church's response to Luther's challenge would help launch the Protestant Reformation.

Discuss What does Luther's demand that Church authorities defend policies that had been in place for centuries tell you about his attitude toward the Church? *(By inviting the Church to debate, Luther showed that he was willing to work for change within the structure of the Church.)*

Online You can also project the **Start Up Activity** from the course.

INVESTIGATE

Have students read the section using the **Reading and Note Taking Study Guide** to help them take notes and understand the text as they read.

Causes of the Reformation

As in Renaissance Italy, life in northern Europe at this time was filled with uncertainty. The changing economy and uncertain times pushed society toward social and religious reform. The humanist stress on education resulted in people questioning traditional ways of doing things. Renaissance humanist ideas added to a spirit of reform. This was especially true of religious traditions, as abuses within the Church became common. All of these factors encouraged protests and calls for reform.

>> Although the clergy had been selling indulgences for years, this practice sparked the first serious steps toward reform.

Interactive Flipped Video

10.3 During the Renaissance, Christians from all levels of society grew impatient with the corruption of the clergy and the worldliness of the Roman Catholic Church. In the words of one unhappy peasant, "Instead of saving the souls of the dead and sending them to Heaven, [the clergy] gorge themselves at banquets after funerals . . . They are wicked wolves! They would like to devour us all, dead or alive."

TEKS
1.D, 5.A, 5.B, 19.B, 20.C, 23.B, 25.C, 27.C

>> Objectives

Summarize the factors that encouraged the Protestant Reformation.

Explain the impact of the printing press on the Reformation.

Analyze Martin Luther's role in shaping the Protestant Reformation.

Explain the teachings and impact of John Calvin.

>> Key Terms

indulgence
Martin Luther
Wittenberg
Charles V
diet
John Calvin
predestination
Geneva
theocracy

www.PearsonTexas.com
Access your Digital Lesson.

The Protestant Reformation

Causes of the Reformation

From such bitterness sprang new calls for reform. During the Middle Ages, the Church had renewed itself from within. In the 1500s, however, the movement for reform unleashed forces that would shatter Christian unity in Europe. This reform movement is known as the Protestant Reformation.

Abuses Within the Church Beginning in the late Middle Ages, the Church had become increasingly caught up in worldly affairs. Popes competed with Italian princes for political power. They fought long wars to protect the Papal States against invasions by secular rulers. They plotted against powerful monarchs who tried to seize control of the Church within their lands.

Popes, like other Renaissance rulers, led lavish lives. When Leo X, a son of Lorenzo the Magnificent, was elected pope, he is said to have exclaimed, "God has given us the papacy—let us enjoy it." Like other Renaissance rulers, popes were patrons of the arts. They hired painters and sculptors to beautify churches and spent vast sums to rebuild the Cathedral of St. Peter in Rome.

394

Aa Vocabulary Builder

1. Have students pronounce the following academic vocabulary terms in this lesson and clarify the part of speech. For difficult or polysyllabic words, break them into syllables and pronounce them with the students.
2. Explain what the word means in common "student-friendly" language using synonyms and antonyms when possible. Provide concrete examples to clarify the meaning, and rephrase the definition.

radical: extreme, calling for change
doctrine: practice; teaching

To finance such projects, the Church increased fees for services such as marriages and baptisms. Some clergy also promoted the sale of indulgences.

An **indulgence** was a type of pardon that lessened the time of punishment a soul faced for sins committed during a person's lifetime. In the Middle Ages, the Church had granted indulgences only for good deeds. By the late 1400s, however, indulgences could be bought with money or a gift to the Church.

Many Christians protested such practices. In Northern Europe, especially, religious piety deepened even as interest in secular things was growing. Christian humanists such as Erasmus urged a return to the simplicity of the early Christian church. They stressed Bible study and rejected Church pomp and ceremony.

Early Reformers Even before the Protestant Reformation, a few religious thinkers had called for change. In England in the late 1300s, John Wycliffe attacked corruption in the Church. He also questioned some Church doctrines. He is probably best remembered for supporting the translation of the Bible into English. After his death, Wycliffe was condemned for heresy, but not before his ideas had spread to other lands.

A Czech priest and philosopher, John Hus, was a follower of Wycliffe. Like Wycliffe, Hus believed Christians should be allowed to read the Bible in their own language. He rejected some Church teachings, including indulgences. Put on trial for his activities, he was condemned and burned at the stake. His followers continued to operate in Eastern Europe, despite Church efforts to destroy the movement.

ANALYZE INFORMATION What factors worked together to set the groundwork for the Protestant Reformation?

ELPS **ELPS 3.B.3** Practice using words that are important to compare eras and describe changes over time.

Martin Luther's Protests Bring Change

Protests against the Church continued to grow. In 1517, these protests erupted into a full scale revolt. The man who triggered the revolt was a German monk and professor of theology named **Martin Luther**.

Raised in a middle-class German family, Martin Luther had been slated by his father for a career as a lawyer. As a youth, however, he had a powerful religious experience that changed his life. One day, during a violent storm, a terrified Luther cried out to St. Anne for help. He promised to become a monk if he were spared.

True to his word, Luther entered a monastery. There, he prayed, fasted, and tried to lead a holy life. Still, he suffered from doubts. He believed he was a sinner, doomed to eternal damnation.

He also grew increasingly disillusioned with what he saw as the corruption and worldliness of the Church. An incident in his native town of **Wittenberg,** Germany, prompted him to act.

95 Theses Challenge the Church In 1517, a German priest, Johann Tetzel, set up a pulpit on the outskirts of Wittenberg. With the approval of the pope, he sold indulgences to any Christian who contributed money for the rebuilding of the Cathedral of St. Peter in Rome. Tetzel claimed that purchase of these indulgences would assure entry into heaven not only for the buyers but for their dead relatives as well.

To a pious man like Luther, Tetzel's actions were an outrage. Luther was furious that people could pay for indulgences and think they were saved instead of seeking true repentance for their sins. Besides, only the rich could afford indulgences.

>> Martin Luther nails his 95 Theses to the church door in Wittenberg. The theses also contained an invitation to church leaders to debate Luther on the issues raised by his theses. The invitation was ignored.

Interactive Illustration

Topic 10 Lesson 3

Guided Reading and Discussion

Be sure students understand that the economic changes to a market economy resulted in an unequal distribution of wealth, which, in turn, contributed to Renaissance ideas of social reform.

When the Church began to condone the selling of indulgences for money instead of awarding them for good works, many people began to think that the Church was corrupt and was losing its moral authority. Some people questioned why they should follow the practices of such a Church instead of the simpler practices of the early Christian church.

Analyze Information Popes had led lavish lifestyles for centuries. Why would people find that lifestyle objectionable at this point in history? *(Possible answer: Renaissance ideas promoted the concepts of social reform and the return of the Church to its simpler Christian roots.)*

Martin Luther's Protests Bring Change

The Protestant Reformation was a response to several conditions that existed in northern Europe. Luther's objections to Church practices sparked a full-scale revolt, leading to his excommunication. One of his important teachings was that people have access to God through faith and the Bible, which was more readily available as a result of the printing press. Reformation ideas were also expressed through the visual medium of the arts, with painters expressing Reformist ideas on canvas.

Answers

Analyze Information *Factors included anger about Church practices such as lavish papal lifestyles, popes exercising political power, and the selling of indulgences; societal upheaval as a result of a changing economy; humanist philosophies from the Renaissance; and the ability of the printing press to spread ideas quickly.*

English Language Proficiency Standards

Speaking 3.B.3 Have students explore terms used to indicate contrasts over time, such as *during, by, since,* and *however* in "Causes of the Reformation" to understand how changes over time contributed to the Reformation.

Beginning Read the first two paragraphs of the section aloud. Point out vocabulary that is used in the first paragraph to compare the Middle Ages to the 1500s, such as *during* and *however*. Help students find similar words used to compare indulgences in the second paragraph.

Intermediate Follow the instructions in the Beginning activity, but have students identify the comparative vocabulary.

Advanced Have pairs identify words and phrases that compare the Middle Ages to the Reformation. Have them construct complex sentences using words and phrases such as *since, by the time of,* and *before then*.

Advanced High Follow the instructions in the Advanced activity, but have students work in groups to create sentences using words and phrases for comparison.

Guided Reading and Discussion

Make sure students understand the importance of the printing press to the success of the Protestant Reformation. Whereas earlier reform movements were more localized, the printing press allowed Martin Luther and other reformers to publish their views throughout northern Europe and beyond, in a relatively short period of time. Printed versions of Luther's 95 Theses made the critical questions and challenges to Church authority accessible to many people. This gave people an opportunity to discuss these new ideas and, often, to support reform movements.

Online Project the **Before and After: Illuminated Manuscripts to Printed Pages**. Project the slider image. Explain how the interaction works by demonstrating the slider feature that allows students to compare a handwritten, illuminated text with a similar text produced by a printing press from the 1500s.

ACTIVE CLASSROOM

Use the Make Headlines strategy and ask students to write a headline that captures the most important aspect about the printing press and its impact on the Protestant Reformation. Have students share their headlines with the rest of the class.

Draw Inferences How did the Renaissance and Reformation emphasis on greater education help the Protestant Reformation? *(The Renaissance humanists encouraged education, and Luther, along with other reformers, strongly promoted education for all. The printing press provided affordable books and other writings that allowed people to read about these issues.)*

Analyze Images

Ask students to look at the image of Luther appearing before Charles V. Ask: Do you think the artist sympathizes with Luther or with the king? Explain your answer. *(Possible answer: Luther, because he is shown closer to the viewer and appears upright and courageous while the king is distant and surrounded by wealth.)*

In response, Luther drew up a list of 95 Theses, or arguments, against indulgences. Following the custom of the time, he posted the list on the door of Wittenberg's All Saints Church. In the 95 Theses, he argued that indulgences had no basis in the Bible, that the pope had no authority to release souls from purgatory (where sinners atoned for their sins), and that Christians could be saved only through faith.

> I have cast the die. . . . I will not reconcile myself to them [the Roman Catholic Church] for all eternity. . . . Let them condemn and burn all that belongs to me; in return I will do as much for them. . . . Now I no longer fear, and I am publishing a book in the German tongue about Christian reform, directed against the pope, in language as violent as if I were addressing the Antichrist.
>
> —Martin Luther, 1520

>> Charles V summoned the excommunicated Luther to the Diet of Worms. When Luther refused to recant, Charles V declared him an outlaw. This made it a criminal offense for anyone to help Luther in any way.

A Firestorm Begins Almost overnight, copies of Luther's 95 Theses were printed and distributed across Europe, where they stirred furious debate. The Church called on Luther to recant, or give up his views. Luther refused. Instead, he developed even more radical doctrines. Before long, he was urging Christians to reject the tyranny of Rome. He wrote that the Church could only be reformed by secular, or non-Church, authorities.

In 1521, Pope Leo X excommunicated Luther. Later that year, the new Holy Roman emperor, **Charles V**, summoned Luther to the **diet**, or assembly, of German princes at the city of Worms (**vohrms**). Luther went, expecting to defend his writings. Instead, the emperor simply ordered him to give them up. Luther again refused.

Charles declared Luther an outlaw, making it a crime for anyone in the empire to give him food or shelter. Still, Luther had many powerful supporters. One of them let Luther hide in his castle. Throughout Germany, thousands hailed him as a hero. They accepted his teachings and, following his lead, renounced the authority of the pope.

Luther's Teachings At the heart of Luther's teachings were several beliefs. First, he argued that salvation could be achieved through faith alone. He thus rejected the Church doctrine that good deeds were necessary for salvation. Second, Luther declared that the Bible was the sole source of religious truth. He denied other traditional authorities, such as Church councils or the pope.

Third, Luther rejected the idea that priests and the Church hierarchy had special powers. He talked, instead, of the "priesthood of all believers." All Christians, he said, have equal access to God through faith and the Bible. Luther translated the Bible into the German vernacular so that ordinary people could study it. Every town, he said, should have a school where children could learn to read the Bible.

Luther wanted to change or modify other church practices. He rejected five of the seven sacraments because the Bible did not mention them. He banned indulgences, confession, pilgrimages, and prayers to saints. He simplified the elaborate ritual of the mass and instead emphasized the sermon. And Luther permitted the clergy to marry. These, and other changes, were adopted by the Lutheran churches set up by his followers.

Luther's Reforms Gain Support The new printing presses spread Luther's writings throughout Germany and Scandinavia, prompting him to declare that "printing was God's highest act of grace." Fiery

Topic 10 Lesson 3

preachers denounced Church abuses. By 1530, the Lutherans were using a new name, *Protestant*, for those who "protested" papal authority.

The "protests" were also expressed in some artists' work. Lucas Cranach was a court painter to Frederick the Wise, one of the electors of Saxony. Cranach befriended Luther and painted portraits of him and other Protestant notables. Cranach's work promoted the Protestant cause and its leaders.

Luther's ideas won widespread support for many reasons. Many clergy saw Luther's reforms as the answer to corruption in the Roman Catholic Church.

A number of German princes, however, embraced Lutheran beliefs for more selfish reasons. Some saw Lutheranism as a way to throw off the rule of both the Church and the Holy Roman emperor. Others welcomed a chance to seize valuable Church property in their territories. Still other Germans supported Luther because of feelings of national loyalty. They were tired of German money going to support churches and clergy in Italy.

The Peasants' Revolt Many peasants also took up Luther's call for reform. They hoped to gain his support for social and economic change as well. In 1524, a Peasants' Revolt erupted across Germany. The rebels demanded an end to serfdom and for other changes to ease their harsh lives. However, Luther strongly favored social order and respect for political authority. As the Peasants' Revolt grew more violent, Luther denounced it. With his support, nobles suppressed the rebellion with great brutality, killing as many as 100,000 people and leaving thousands more homeless.

The Peace of Augsburg During the 1530s and 1540s, Charles V tried to force Lutheran princes back into the Catholic Church, but with little success. Finally, after a number of brief wars, Charles and the princes reached a settlement. The Peace of Augsburg, signed in 1555, allowed each prince to decide which religion—Catholic or Lutheran—would be followed in his lands. Most northern German states chose Lutheranism. The southern German states remained largely Catholic.

DRAW CONCLUSIONS What effects did Martin Luther's teachings have on Northern Europe?

John Calvin Challenges the Church

In the wake of Luther's revolt against the Church, other reformers challenged Church authority. The most important was **John Calvin**, who lived in what is

>> This 1545 woodcut by Lucas Cranach the Elder is an example of how Reformation art expressed the differences between Protestantism and Catholicism. Cranach wrote that the work was meant to show the difference between the "true religion" and the "false idolatrous teaching."

Interactive Gallery

>> The leaders of Germany's Peasants' Revolt of 1524 hoped for Luther's support. Instead, Luther sided with the authorities because of his belief in social order and the rule of law.

Online Project the **Interactive Gallery: Reformation Art**. Click on one of the hotspots for an explanation of what that area of the painting is communicating. Ask students to examine the different parts of the painting before they click on the hotspot.

ACTIVE CLASSROOM

Use the See-Think-Wonder strategy and have students pair with a partner. Students should study the Cranach painting. Ask them: What do you see? What does it make you think? What are you wondering about now that you've seen this? Have the student pairs share their insights with the class.

D Differentiate Extra Support Help students understand why someone who had dedicated his life to the Church would then decide to protest against it. First, ask students to think about groups that they belong to. Then ask them to think of a time when they disagreed with the group's decision. How did they feel about the group? Did they speak out? If so, what was their motivation? *(Possible answer: to bring about change)* Reinforce that Luther's goal was not to bring down the Church but, rather, to change it because he did not agree with some of its practices.

Background

Luther's German Bible Luther's translation of the Bible into German has been called his noblest achievement. Luther spent many years on this translation. In order to get just the right German words for describing animal sacrifices in the Old Testament, he visited butcher shops and asked what the various parts of a goat or sheep were called. In describing Biblical events, Luther often made them seem as if they had taken place in the forests and castles of Germany. His work made the Bible come alive to people for whom it had previously been distant and strange.

Answers

Draw Conclusions *Luther's teachings led to the establishment of a new church and sparked a period of social upheaval and violence as some people fought over religious differences.*

Topic 10 Lesson 3

John Calvin Challenges the Church

Tell students that the Reformation included the founding of many different Protestant sects. Calvinism became one of the largest. John Calvin and his followers established a theocracy in Geneva. A theocracy is a government run by religious leaders. It was the only political system of this type in Europe. Along with this theocratic political system, the Calvinist belief in predestination set them apart from the other main Protestant faiths.

Key Terms

Ask students to find the key term **theocracy** (in bold) in the text. Ask students to recall other forms of government, such as democracy and monarchy, and compare the definitions.

Guided Reading and Discussion

Calvinism and the doctrine of predestination appealed to many people because it provided a preordained structure in a time of uncertainty. If people lived good lives, it was evidence that they had attained salvation because only those chosen would live good lives in the first place. While Calvinism had a strong following, it faced a great deal of opposition from both Catholics and Lutherans, which led to religious wars throughout Europe.

Draw Conclusions Why might Calvin's belief in a theocracy as the ideal form of government lead to persecution of Calvinists? *(Possible answer: The secular leaders of other European countries would see a theocracy as a threat because it suggests that a secular government would prevent a truly Christian society.)*

today Switzerland. Calvin had a razor-sharp mind, and his ideas had a profound effect on the direction of the Protestant Reformation.

Calvin's Teachings Calvin was born in France and trained as a priest and lawyer. In 1536, Calvin published the *Institutes of the Christian Religion*, which was widely read. In it, he set forth his religious beliefs. He also provided advice on how to organize and run a Protestant church.

Like Luther, Calvin believed that salvation was gained through faith alone. He, too, regarded the Bible as the only source of religious truth. But Calvin put forth a number of ideas of his own.

Calvin taught that God was all-powerful and that humans were by nature sinful. God alone, he said, decided whether an individual achieved eternal life. This idea that God had long ago determined who would gain salvation was known as **predestination**.

To Calvinists, the world was divided into two kinds of people—saints and sinners. Calvinists tried to live like saints, believing that only those who were saved could live truly Christian lives.

Calvin's Geneva In 1541, Protestants in the city-state of **Geneva** in Switzerland asked Calvin to lead their community. In keeping with his teachings, Calvin set up a **theocracy**, or government run by church leaders.

Calvin's followers in Geneva came to see themselves as a new "chosen people" entrusted by God to build a truly Christian society. Calvinists stressed hard work, discipline, thrift, honesty, and morality. Citizens faced fines or other harsher punishments for offenses such as fighting, swearing, laughing in church, or dancing. To many Protestants, Calvinist Geneva seemed like a model community.

Calvinist Ideas Spread Reformers from all over Europe visited Geneva and then returned home to spread Calvinist ideas. By the late 1500s, Calvinism had taken root in Germany, France, the Netherlands, England, and Scotland. This new challenge to the Roman Catholic Church set off bloody wars of religion across Europe.

In Germany, Catholics and Lutherans opposed Calvinists. In France, wars raged between French Calvinists and Catholics. Calvinists in the Netherlands organized the Dutch Reformed Church. In Scotland, a Calvinist preacher named John Knox led a religious rebellion, overthrowing the Catholic queen and establishing the Scottish Presbyterian Church.

SUMMARIZE How did Calvin and his supporters implement his ideas?

Catholicism, Lutheranism, and Calvinism

	CATHOLOCISM	LUTHERANISM	CALVINISM
SALVATION	Salvation is achieved through faith and good works.	Salvation is achieved through faith.	God alone predetermines who will be saved.
SACRAMENTS	Priests perform seven sacraments, or rituals—baptism, confirmation, marriage, ordination, communion, anointing of the sick, and repentance.	Accepts some of the sacraments, but rejects others because rituals cannot erase sin—only God can.	Accepts some of the sacraments, but rejects others because rituals cannot erase sin—only God can.
HEAD OF CHURCH	Pope	Elected councils	Council of elders
IMPORTANCE OF THE CHRISTIAN BIBLE	Bible is one source of truth; Church tradition is another.	Bible alone is source of truth.	Bible alone is source of truth.
HOW BELIEF IS REVEALED	Priests interpret the Bible and Church teachings for the people.	People read and interpret the Bible for themselves.	People read and interpret the Bible for themselves.

>> **Analyze Charts** Who served as head of the Lutheran Church? Why was this an important difference from the organization of the Catholic Church?

Answers

Summarize *Calvinists set up a theocracy in Geneva. In other places, Calvinists established churches and led reformist rebellions.*

Analyze Charts *elected councils; because it means that members of the church derived their own authority from God and the Bible rather than from the pope*

Topic 10 Lesson 3

ASSESSMENT

1. **Identify Central Ideas** How did rebellions against the Roman Catholic Church affect northern European society?
2. **Analyze Information** Why did the sale of indulgences become a critical point of focus during the Renaissance but not during the Middle Ages?
3. **Analyze Information** How did Luther's ideas provide the catalyst for the Protestant Reformation?
4. **Summarize** How did Calvin see predestination as a means to a Christian life?
5. **Cite Evidence** Why was the printing press essential to the success of the Protestant Reformation?

SYNTHESIZE

Discuss How is the impact of the modern technology chosen similar to the impact of the printing press? *(Possible answer: Communication over large areas is much quicker than it was in the past. The printing press was as revolutionary in this regard as television, cellphones, computers, or the Internet.)*

DEMONSTRATE

Online Assign the **Digital Lesson Quiz** for this lesson if you haven't already done so. Students will be offered automatic remediation or enrichment based on their score.

Pose the following questions to the class on the Discussion Board:

Analyze Main Idea What were the causes of the Protestant Reformation? *(Reasons include changing social structure and economic roles; a greater emphasis on humanism after the Renaissance; and dissatisfaction with the abuses of the Church.)*

Summarize What impact did the printing press have on the Protestant Reformation? *(It allowed new ideas to spread more quickly than before and made them available to more sectors of society.)*

Topic Inquiry

Have students continue their investigations for the Topic Inquiry.

Assessment

1. People began to question traditional Church doctrine and practices and the role of religion in general. This led to the spread of Protestantism.
2. During the Middle Ages, people accepted the authority of the Church without question. Renaissance humanist thought influenced people to look more critically at questionable Church practices.
3. Luther emphasized direct examination of the Bible and personal relationships to God, opposing traditional teachings of the Church and opening the door to change, or reform.
4. Calvin believed that only those who were saved could live good Christian lives. Therefore, living that type of life would be proof that the person was a saint, or one who is saved.
5. It allowed reformist ideas to reach a greater number of people in a short period of time. People were able to react to the ideas more quickly as well.

Topic 10 Lesson 4

Reformation Ideas Spread

CONNECT

Preview Have students preview the **Lesson Objectives** and the list of **Key Terms**.

Students can also preview all the **Key Terms** and **Academic Vocabulary** using the **Interactive Reading Notepad** on the digital course or preview a summary of the lesson in the **Reading and Note Taking Study Guide**.

Online Use the **Editable Presentation** found on the digital course to present the main ideas for this lesson.

Start Up Activity

Have students consider the following questions: A revolutionary idea can grow and change over time. What are some of the things that might influence how an idea changes? Which of these things is most important?

As students share, you may wish to keep a list of answers. Students should understand that many things can influence how one idea is reshaped to fit specific circumstances or requirements. Explain that the Reformation that began in northern Germany sparked a series of other Reformations, both within and outside Europe.

Online You can also project the **Start Up Activity** from the course.

INVESTIGATE

Have students read the section using the **Reading and Note Taking Study Guide** to help them take notes and understand the text as they read.

An Explosion of Protestant Sects

Tell students that as the Reformation spread from northern Germany, different Protestant sects emerged throughout Europe. Some of these sects, like the Anabaptists, were considered quite radical even by other Protestants. While most of the new Protestant movements were peaceful, some spurred violence as reformers clashed with other reformers.

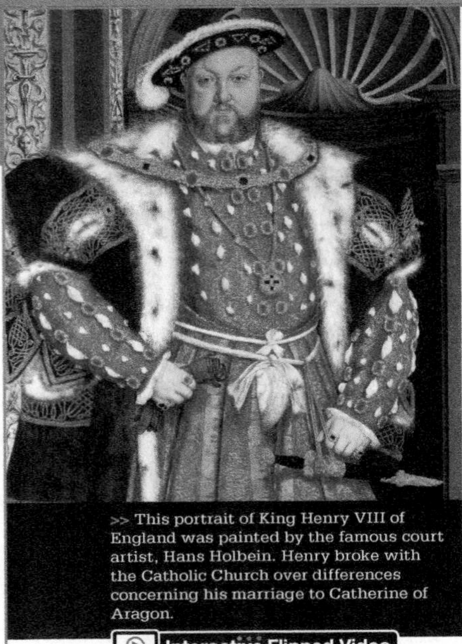

>> This portrait of King Henry VIII of England was painted by the famous court artist, Hans Holbein. Henry broke with the Catholic Church over differences concerning his marriage to Catherine of Aragon.

Interactive Flipped Video

(10.4) **Henry III, the Catholic king of France, was deeply disturbed by the Calvinist reformers in Geneva. "It would have been a good thing," he wrote, "if the city of Geneva were long ago reduced to ashes, because of the evil doctrine which has been sown from that city throughout Christendom."**

TEKS 1.D, 5.B, 23.B, 24.B, 25.C

>> Objectives

Describe the new ideas that Protestant sects embraced.

Understand why England formed a new church.

Analyze how the Catholic Church reformed itself.

Explain why many groups faced persecution during the Reformation.

Explain the impact of the Reformation.

>> Key Terms

sect
Henry VIII
Mary Tudor
Thomas Cranmer
Elizabeth
canonize
compromise
Council of Trent
Ignatius of Loyola
St. Teresa of Avila
ghetto

Reformation Ideas Spread

An Explosion of Protestant Sects

Henry was not alone in his anger. Across Europe, Catholic monarchs and the Catholic Church fought back against the Protestant challenge. They also took steps to reform the Church and to restore its spiritual leadership in the Christian world.

As the Reformation continued, hundreds of new Protestant **sects**, or religious groups, sprang up. Some sects developed their own versions of the teachings of Luther or Calvin, or followed the teachings of another Swiss reformer, Ulrich Zwingli. Others developed ideas that were increasingly radical.

Radical Reformers A number of groups, for example, rejected the practice of infant baptism. Infants, they argued, are too young to understand what it means to accept the Christian faith. Only adults, they felt, should receive the sacrament of baptism. Because of this belief, they became known as Anabaptists.

Most Anabaptists, however, were peaceful. In an age of religious intolerance, they called for religious toleration. They also put forward the idea of the separation of church and state. Despite harsh persecution for their threat to the traditional order, these groups

PEARSON realize www.PearsonTexas.com Access your Digital Lesson.

400

Aa Vocabulary Builder

1. Have students pronounce the following academic vocabulary terms in this lesson and clarify the part of speech. For difficult or polysyllabic words, break them into syllables and pronounce them with the students.
2. Explain what the word means in common "student-friendly" language using synonyms and antonyms when possible. Provide concrete examples to clarify the meaning, and rephrase the definition.

variations: differences
suppress: forcefully push down
denounce: publicly condemn
moderate: within reasonable limits; not extreme
rigorous: strict, thorough

influenced Protestant thinking in many countries. Today, the Baptists, Mennonites, and Amish all trace their religious ancestry to the Anabaptists.

EXPLAIN In what ways did Anabaptist sects differ from other Protestant sects?

The English Reformation

In England, religious leaders like John Wycliffe had called for Church reform as early as the 1300s. By the 1520s, some English clergy were exploring Protestant ideas. The break with the Catholic Church, however, was the work not of religious leaders but of King **Henry VIII**. For political reasons, Henry wanted to end papal control over the English Church.

Henry VIII Seeks an Annulment At first, Henry VIII stood firmly against the Protestant revolt. The pope even awarded him the title "Defender of the Faith" for a pamphlet that Henry wrote denouncing Luther.

In 1527, however, an issue arose that set Henry at odds with the Church. After 18 years of marriage, Henry and his Spanish wife, Catherine of Aragon, had only one surviving child, **Mary Tudor**. Henry felt that England's stability depended on his having a male heir. He wanted to divorce Catherine and marry a new wife, hoping she would bear him a son. Because Catholic law does not permit divorce, he asked the pope to annul, or cancel, his marriage.

Popes had annulled royal marriages before. But this pope refused. He did not want to offend the Holy Roman emperor Charles V, Catherine's nephew. He therefore refused Henry's request.

Henry VIII Breaks with the Church Henry was furious. Spurred on by his advisers, many of whom leaned toward Protestantism, he decided to take over the English Church. Henry had Parliament pass a series of laws that took the English Church from the pope's control and placed it under Henry's rule. The most notable of these laws was the Act of Supremacy, passed in 1534. It made Henry "the only supreme head on Earth of the Church of England."

By then, Henry had appointed **Thomas Cranmer** archbishop. Cranmer had annulled the king's marriage to Catherine. Henry married Anne Boleyn, a noble lady-in-waiting to Catherine. Soon, Anne gave birth to a daughter, **Elizabeth**. In the years that followed, Henry married four more times, but had only one son, Edward.

Many loyal Catholics refused to accept the Act of Supremacy and were executed for treason. Among them was the well-known English humanist, Sir Thomas More. More was later **canonized**, or recognized as a saint, by the Catholic Church.

The Church of England Between 1536 and 1540, Henry ordered the closing of all convents and monasteries in England and seized their lands and wealth for the crown. This became know as the dissolution, the dissolving, or ending, of Catholic monasteries in England.

This move brought new wealth to the royal exchequer. Henry shrewdly granted some church lands to nobles and other high-ranking citizens, thereby securing their support for the Anglican Church, as the new Church of England was called. Henry used much of his newly acquired wealth to pursue wars in Europe.

Despite Henry's actions in rejecting the pope's authority, he was not a religious radical. He had no use for most Protestant doctrines. Aside from breaking away from Rome and allowing use of the English Bible, he kept most Catholic forms of worship.

Religious Turmoil When Henry died in 1547, his nine-year-old son, Edward VI, inherited the throne. The young king's advisers were devout Protestants who pushed for Calvinist reforms. Thomas Cranmer drew up the *Book of Common Prayer* to be used in the Anglican

>> Monks were forced to leave monasteries as part of the dissolution ordered by King Henry VIII. Henry ordered that Catholic convents and monasteries be closed, claiming they were centers of immorality.

Interactive Timeline

Guided Reading and Discussion

During this period, groups protesting traditional Catholic authority took the opportunity to develop religious systems that fit their specific needs. The Anabaptists, who opposed infant baptism, were considered the most radical sect. They also had more radical groups within their own sect that sought sweeping social change as well as religious change. Disagreement over religion erupted into violence in some places and earned the condemnation of Reformation leaders like Martin Luther.

Identify Cause and Effect What was one of the effects of the Protestant Reformation on religion in Europe? *(Europe had more religious diversity as a variety of religious sects developed.)*

Compare What belief did all Protestant reformers share, regardless of sect? *(The Catholic Church had no spiritual or moral authority over Christians.)*

The English Reformation

The English Reformation ended with a compromise and a Protestant England with a state church that was similar to the Catholic Church in terms of hierarchy. The differences between the two churches, though, were substantial enough to cause conflict through the reigns of four consecutive English monarchs.

Online Project the **Interactive Timeline: Timeline of the English Reformation**. Look at each image individually, and then view the timeline as a whole.

ACTIVE CLASSROOM

Use the Ranking Strategy to have students go through the events in the timeline and rank which ones had the greatest impact on the English Reformation.

Answers

Explain *Anabaptists rejected the idea of infant baptism. Some wanted to speed up Judgment Day by violent means. Others wanted to abolish private property, while many preached religious tolerance and the separation of church and state.*

Topic 10 Lesson 4

Guided Reading and Discussion

Read aloud Henry VIII's statement to the pope and give students a few minutes to think about it. ". . . we believe that no duty is more incumbent on a Catholic sovereign than to preserve and increase the Catholic faith . . . so when we learned that the pest of Martin Luther's heresy had appeared in Germany and was raging everywhere . . . we bent all our thoughts and energies on uprooting (those heresies) in every possible way."

Explain that Henry VIII considered himself a Catholic monarch of a Catholic country. Explore with students how Henry's actions could be so different from his earlier words.

Predict Would Henry still have broken with the Church if Luther's teachings had not become as popular as they were? *(Possible answer: It's unlikely he would have broken from the Church. Had Luther's teachings not gained traction, a break from the Church would likely have been an unpopular move among Henry's subjects.)*

The Catholic Reformation

Despite the spread of Protestantism, Europe remained mostly Catholic. The Catholic Reformation is also called the Counter-Reformation because it was driven by the Church's desire to counter the Protestant Reformation that had spread so quickly throughout parts of Europe. There had long been Catholic reformers in the Church who wanted to effect change. The challenge of the Protestant Reformation gave impetus to these internal reform efforts and the goal of stopping Protestantism from spreading.

>> Although Protestant, Queen Elizabeth showed more tolerance for Catholics and other Protestant sects in an effort to end religious conflicts. The Elizabethan settlement went far in achieving that goal.

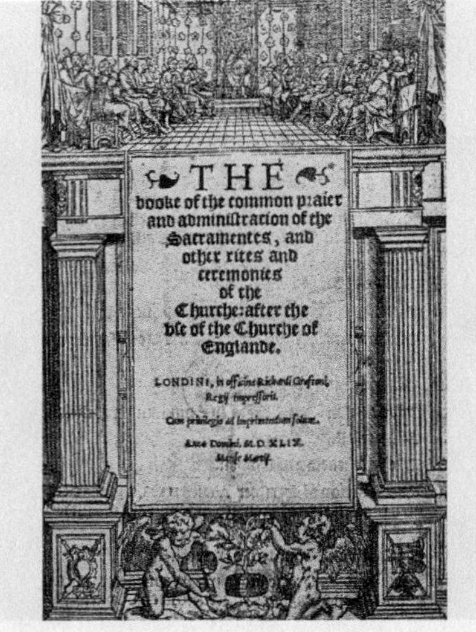

THE
booke of the common praier
and administracion of the
Sacramentes, and
other rites and
ceremonies
of the
Churche: after the
use of the Churche of
Englande.

LONDINI, in officina Richardi Graftoni,
Regij impressoris.

Cum privilegio ad imprimendum solum.

Anno Domini. M.D.XLIX.
Mense Martij.

>> The *Book of Common Prayer* was written in English, rather than Latin. This is the title page from the 1549 first edition.

Church. It imposed a moderate form of Protestant service but preserved many Catholic doctrines. Even so, it sparked uprisings that were harshly suppressed.

When Edward died in his teens, his half-sister Mary Tudor came to the throne. A pious Catholic, she was determined to make England Catholic once more. She failed, but not before hundreds of English Protestants, including Archbishop Cranmer, were burned at the stake for heresy.

The Elizabethan Settlement On Mary's death, the throne passed to her Protestant half-sister, Elizabeth. For years, Elizabeth had survived court intrigues, including the religious swings under Edward and Mary. As queen, Elizabeth adopted a policy of religious **compromise**, or acceptable middle ground. She moved cautiously at first but gradually enforced reforms that both moderate Catholics and Protestants could accept. This policy of compromise was later known as the Elizabethan settlement.

Under Elizabeth, English replaced Latin as the language of the Anglican service. The *Book of Common Prayer* was restored, although it was revised to make it more acceptable to Catholics. Much of the Catholic ritual was kept. The Church of England also kept the old hierarchy of bishops and archbishops, but Elizabeth quickly affirmed that the monarch, not the pope, was the head of the Anglican Church.

Even though Elizabeth preserved many traditional Catholic ideas, she firmly established England as a Protestant nation. During a long and skillful reign, she worked to restore unity, and England escaped the kinds of religious wars that tore apart other European countries in the 1500s.

? ANALYZE INFORMATION What factors led to the formation of the Church of England?

The Catholic Reformation

As the Protestant Reformation swept across northern Europe, a vigorous reform movement took hold within the Catholic Church. The leader of this movement, known as the Catholic Reformation, was Pope Paul III. (Protestants often called it the Counter-Reformation.)

During the 1530s and 1540s, the pope set out to revive the moral authority of the Church and roll back the Protestant tide. To end corruption within the papacy, he appointed reformers to top posts. They and their successors led the Catholic Reformation for the rest of the century.

Answers

Analyze Information *Henry VIII wanted a male heir. He believed that wasn't possible with his wife, Catherine of Aragon. When the pope refused to annul their marriage, Henry established the Church of England as separate and independent from Rome.*

The Council of Trent Passes Reforms To establish the direction that reform should take, the pope called the **Council of Trent** in 1545. It met off and on for almost 20 years. The council reaffirmed the traditional Catholic views that Protestants had challenged. The council believed that salvation comes through faith and good works. It declared that the Christian Bible, while a major source of religious truth, is not the only source.

The council also took steps to end abuses in the Church. It provided stiff penalties for worldliness and corruption among the clergy. It also established schools to create a better-educated clergy who could challenge Protestant teachings.

The Inquisition Is Strengthened To deal with the Protestant threat more directly, Pope Paul strengthened the Inquisition. The Inquisition was a Church court set up during the Middle Ages. To battle Protestant ideas, the Inquisition used secret testimony, torture, and execution to root out what the Church considered heresy. It also prepared the *Index of Forbidden Books*, a list of works considered too immoral for Catholics to read. The list included books by Luther and Calvin and even some books by Italian humanists.

The Jesuits In 1540, the pope recognized a new religious order, the Society of Jesus, or Jesuits. Founded by **Ignatius of Loyola**, the Jesuit order was dedicated to combating heresy and spreading the Catholic faith.

Ignatius was a Spanish knight whose military career ended abruptly when his leg was shattered in battle. During a long and painful recovery, he found comfort reading about Christian saints who had overcome mental and physical torture. He then vowed to become a "soldier of God."

Ignatius drew up a strict program for the Jesuits. It included spiritual and moral discipline, rigorous religious training, and absolute obedience to the Church. Led by Ignatius, the Jesuits embarked on a crusade to defend and spread the Catholic faith worldwide.

To further the Catholic cause, Jesuits became advisers to Catholic rulers, helping them combat heresy in their lands. They set up schools that taught humanist and Catholic beliefs and enforced discipline and obedience. Daring Jesuits slipped into Protestant lands in disguise to minister to Catholics. Jesuit missionaries spread their Catholic faith to Asia, Africa, and the Americas.

Teresa of Avila As the Catholic Reformation spread, many Catholics experienced renewed feelings of intense faith. Among those who experienced religious

>> Pope Paul III meets with Catholic religious leaders at the Council of Trent, where he called for a series of reforms to correct abuses within the Church.

>> Ignatius of Loyola founded the Jesuits and was one of the key individuals of the Catholic Reformation. He represented the Church's new commitment to religious education, moral reform, and strict obedience to Church teachings.

Online Project the **Interactive Map: Major European Religions, About 1600**.

ACTIVE CLASSROOM

Use the Audio Tour strategy and pair students to work with the map. Have the first student give the second a verbal "tour" of the map—what does it show? Have the second student give the first an explanation of what it means.

Guided Reading and Discussion

Remind students that many elements of the Catholic Reformation were a response to the rapid spread of Protestantism. The Catholic Reformation's goals included not only stopping that spread but also bringing those who had left the Church back into the faith as well as reforming the Church itself. Empowering the Inquisition to root out Protestant heretics, a reaffirmation of religious piety, and an active support of humanist and Catholic education were three major efforts of the Catholic Reformation.

Draw Conclusions What does the term *Counter-Reformation* imply about the causes of the Catholic Reformation? *(that it was a specific response to the Protestant Reformation)*

Topic 10 Lesson 4

Key Terms

Ask students to find the key term **ghetto** (in bold) in the text and find its meaning. Then ask them where they have heard the term used and how it was used. Ask them to compare what they understand the word to mean to what it meant during this period in history.

Religious Persecution Continues

A dramatic increase in religious persecution followed the rise in religious fervor among Catholics and Protestants. Throughout Europe, witch hunts were common, with tens of thousands of men and women perishing. Jews in Europe were forced to live in ghettos, separate, segregated parts of a town or city, even in regions that had been relatively tolerant.

Guided Reading and Discussion

Students should understand that the religious intolerance that spread throughout Europe was a direct result of heightened tensions between Protestants and Catholics. Protestantism was strengthening in certain parts of Europe, and Catholicism was attempting to stem the tide and win back some who had converted.

Draw Inferences Why was persecution of Jews and "witches" especially harsh? *(In a time of insecurity, people looked for others to blame, especially those most unlike themselves.)*

Analyze Images

Ask students to look at the map of major European Religions in 1600. Ask: Which areas of Europe had the *least* religious diversity at this time? *(Possible answer: the northwestern Ottoman empire)*

renewal was **Teresa of Avila**. Born into a wealthy Spanish family, Teresa entered a convent in her youth. The convent routine was not strict enough for her strong religious nature. So she set up her own order of nuns. They lived in isolation, eating and sleeping very little and dedicating themselves to prayer and meditation.

Impressed by her spiritual life, her superiors in the Church asked Teresa to reorganize and reform Spanish convents and monasteries. Teresa was widely honored for her work, and after her death the Church made her a saint. Her spiritual writings rank among the most important Christian texts of her time and are still widely read today.

Results of the Catholic Reformation By 1600, the majority of Europeans remained Catholic. Tireless Catholic reformers, like Francis de Sales in France, had succeeded in bringing Protestants back into the Catholic Church. Across Catholic Europe, piety, charity, and religious art flourished, and church abuses were reduced from within.

The reforms of the Catholic Reformation did stop the Protestant tide and even returned some areas to the Catholic Church. Still, Europe remained divided into a Catholic south and a Protestant north. This division would fuel conflicts that lasted for centuries, although later, the goals were more political than religious.

? ANALYZE INFORMATION What were some of the specific results of the Catholic Reformation?

Religious Persecution Continues

During this period of heightened religious passion, persecution was widespread. Both Catholics and Protestants fostered intolerance. The Inquisition executed many people accused of heresy. Catholic mobs attacked and killed Protestants. Protestants killed Catholic priests and destroyed Catholic churches. Both Catholics and Protestants persecuted radical sects like the Anabaptists.

Witch Hunts The religious fervor of the time contributed to a wave of witch hunting. Between 1450 and 1750, tens of thousands of women and men died as victims of witch hunts. Often, those accused of being witches, or agents of the devil, were women.

Scholars have offered various reasons for this savage persecution, but most agree that it had to do with people's beliefs in magic and spirits. At the time,

>> **Analyze Maps** By 1600, the spread of Protestantism had transformed Catholic Europe. What was the main religion in France? Why were most people in each region practicing that religion by 1600?

Interactive Map

Background

Evidence of Witchcraft As the witchcraft mania spread in Europe, popular superstitions came to be treated as legal truths. Until the late 1600s, most magistrates accepted that there were physical tests for witchcraft. If the body of the accused exhibited unusual marks, the person was considered to be a witch. If the accused had body parts that were insensitive to the prick of a needle, the person was judged to be a witch. Storms and diseases were also taken as signs of sorcery. Witch hunts also took place across the Atlantic in the English colonies. In 1692, a witch hunt broke out in the town of Salem, Massachusetts. Accusations spread like wildfire throughout the town. Before the witch hunt ended the following year, at least 200 people had been named as witches. Twenty of them had been executed.

Answers

Analyze Information *It reaffirmed traditional Catholic doctrine and its differences from Protestant beliefs. Europe remained mostly Catholic. The Church ended abuses, such as the selling of indulgences, and developed a greater sense of piety among believers and in the arts.*

Analyze Maps *Catholic; Political leaders in each region had adopted that religion and persecuted members of other religions* people saw a close link between magic and heresy. Witches, they believed, were in league with the devil and were thus anti-Christian.

In troubled times, people looked for scapegoats. Typically, people accused of witchcraft were social outcasts—beggars, poor widows, midwives blamed for infant deaths, or herbalists whose potions and cures were seen as gifts of the devil.

In the charged religious atmosphere of the Reformation, many people were convinced that witchcraft and devil worship were on the rise. Most victims of witch hunts died in the German states, Switzerland, and France, all centers of religious conflict. When the wars of religion came to an end, the persecution of witches also declined.

Persecution of Jews The Reformation brought hard times to Europe's Jews. For many Jews in Italy, the early Renaissance had been a time of relative prosperity. Unlike Spain, which had expelled its Jews in 1492, Italy allowed them to remain. Some Jews followed the traditional trades they had been restricted to in medieval times. They were goldsmiths, artists, traders, and moneylenders. Others expanded into law, government, and business. A few well-educated Jews served as advisers to powerful rulers.

Yet the pressure remained strong on Jews to convert. By 1516, Jews in Venice had to live in a separate quarter of the city called the **ghetto**. Other Italian cities set up walled ghettos in which Jews were forced to live.

At first, Luther hoped that Jews would be converted to his teachings. When they did not convert, he called for them to be expelled from Christian lands and for their synagogues to be burned.

During the Reformation, restrictions on Jews increased. Some German princes expelled Jews from their lands. All German states confined Jews to ghettos or required them to wear a yellow badge if they traveled outside the ghetto.

In the 1550s, Pope Paul IV reversed the lenient policy of Renaissance popes and restricted Jewish activities. After 1550, many Jews migrated to Poland-Lithuania and to parts of the Ottoman Empire. Dutch Calvinists also tolerated Jews, taking in families who were driven out of Portugal and Spain.

 **SYNTHESIZE** How did the increased religious fervor among Protestants and Catholics lead to persecutions?

>> People gather on a street in a Jewish ghetto in Rome. The gate at the end of the street would likely be closed and locked at sundown. This was for the protection of the Jewish residents from mobs bent on violence.

ASSESSMENT

1. **Explain** Why did some consider the Anabaptist sects radical?
2. **Identify Cause and Effect** What roles did Henry VIII and Elizabeth I play in bringing the Reformation to England?
3. **Analyze Information** What steps did the Catholic Church take to reform and to stop the growth of Protestantism?
4. **Distinguish** Why did the Reformation see an increase in persecution of people of different beliefs or religions?
5. **Synthesize** What was the religious impact of the Reformation in Europe?

SYNTHESIZE

Online Project the **Digital Activity: Spread and Impact of the Protestant Reformation**. Ask students to review their flowcharts on the spread and impact of the Protestant Reformation. Have them use the Think-Pair-Share strategy to compare their graphic organizers.

Have partners think about the following question: What are three causes/effects that you believe made the greatest impact on the Protestant or Catholic Reformation movements? Have them share their answers with the class.

Discuss What characteristics did the two reformation movements share? What were the most important differences? Explain that both movements were a result of a situation that one or more people wanted to change. That is essentially what it means to reform something.

DEMONSTRATE

Online Assign the **Digital Lesson Quiz** for this lesson if you haven't already done so. Students will be offered automatic remediation or enrichment based on their score.

Pose the following question to the class on the Discussion Board:

Analyze Main Idea How did Reformation ideas take root in England? Why did the Church respond with its Catholic Reformation?

Topic Inquiry

Have students continue their investigations for the Topic Inquiry.

Answers

Synthesize *People of both religions were intense and passionate in their beliefs. This led to greater intolerance for those who held different religious beliefs. They were seen as outcasts. They were persecuted, expelled, or even executed.*

Assessment

1. Anabaptists advocated rapid social change, and their interpretations of the Bible were very different from mainstream Protestant sects.
2. Henry VIII broke from the Catholic Church and founded the Protestant, or Anglican, Church of England. Elizabeth I reached a compromise between Catholic and Protestant practices but kept England a Protestant country with no allegiance to the pope and the Catholic Church.
3. It led a vigorous reform movement known as the Catholic Reformation. It outlined the differences between Catholic and Protestant doctrine, levied heavy penalties against corrupt clergy, stopped the sale of indulgences, and encouraged a new sense of piety and commitment to the Church.
4. Many regions had bloody religious conflicts, which often resulted in a greater intolerance for those who held different religious beliefs or who were seen as social outcasts. Widespread persecution occurred against sects like the Anabaptists, those accused of witchcraft, and Jews.
5. It established Protestantism as an alternative to Catholicism. It broke the centuries-long authority of the Church over many European nations. But most of Europe remained Catholic.

The Scientific Revolution

CONNECT

Preview Have students preview the **Lesson Objectives** and the list of **Key Terms**.

Students can also preview all the **Key Terms** and **Academic Vocabulary** using the **Interactive Reading Notepad** on the digital course or preview a summary of the lesson in the **Reading and Note Taking Study Guide**.

Online Use the **Editable Presentation** found on the digital course to present the main ideas for this lesson.

Start Up Activity

Explain: The Renaissance emphasis on education and a desire to learn more about the physical world transformed the sciences. In 1609, a new Dutch invention, the telescope, inspired Italian astronomer Galileo Galilei to build his own telescope. When he pointed it at the night sky, he saw mountains on the moon, fiery spots on the sun, and four moons circling the planet Jupiter. Discoveries by Galileo and others created a Scientific Revolution that continues to this day.

Discuss What might your reaction have been had you been in Galileo's place? *(Answers will vary. Answers should reflect an understanding of how astonishing and thrilling such a discovery must have been.)*

Online You can also project the **Start Up Activity** from the course.

INVESTIGATE

Have students read the section using the **Reading and Note Taking Study Guide** to help them take notes and understand the text as they read.

Changing Views of the Universe

Changes in science happened at the same time as the social, political, and artistic changes of the Renaissance. The Scientific Revolution was spurred by scientists' interest in the natural world and their desire to know more about it. The invention of the telescope allowed astronomers to examine the moon and identify planetary bodies invisible to the naked eye. This ability to observe eventually changed the way people viewed the universe.

>> The ancient Greek astronomer Ptolemy believed that the Earth was at the center of the universe and the sun and stars revolved around it. This is an image of Ptolemy's Geocentric Universe.

Interactive Flipped Video

10.5 **Both the Renaissance and the Reformation looked to the past for models. Humanists turned to ancient classical learning. Religious reformers looked to the Bible and early Christian times for inspiration. The Renaissance spirit of inquiry led scientists to explore beyond the knowledge of the ancients.**

TEKS
1.E, 27.D, 27.E

>> Objectives

Explain how new discoveries in astronomy changed the way people viewed the universe.

Understand the new scientific method and how it developed.

Identify the contributions that Galileo, Copernicus, Newton, and other scientists made to the Scientific Revolution.

>> Key Terms

Nicolaus Copernicus
heliocentric
Tycho Brahe
Johannes Kepler
Galileo
Francis Bacon
René Descartes
scientific method
hypothesis
Robert Boyle
Isaac Newton
gravity
calculus

The Scientific Revolution

Changing Views of the Universe

Beginning in the 1500s, profound changes took place in the sciences that pointed toward a future shaped by a new way of thinking about the physical universe. These new understandings about the physical world became part of what is now called the Scientific Revolution.

Old Views Until the mid-1500s, European scholars accepted the ideas set out by ancient Greek thinkers like Aristotle. The Greek astronomer Ptolemy had taught that Earth was the center of the universe.

European scholars long accepted this view because it seemed to agree with common sense. It also followed the teachings of the Church. In the 1500s and 1600s, startling discoveries radically changed the way Europeans viewed the physical world.

Copernicus Offers a New Theory In 1543, Polish scholar **Nicolaus Copernicus** (koh PUR nih kus) published *On the Revolutions of the Heavenly Spheres.* In it, he proposed a **heliocentric**, or sun-centered, model of the universe. The sun, he said, stands at the center of the universe. Earth is just one of several planets that revolve around the sun.

PEARSON realize. www.PearsonTexas.com Access your Digital Lesson.

406

Aa Vocabulary Builder

1. Have students pronounce the following academic vocabulary terms in this lesson and clarify the part of speech. For difficult or polysyllabic words, break them into syllables and pronounce them with the students.
2. Explain what the word means in common "student-friendly" language using synonyms and antonyms when possible. Provide concrete examples to clarify the meaning, and rephrase the definition.

contradict: to go against

philosopher: a person who is an expert in the study of knowledge

Most experts rejected this revolutionary theory, which contradicted both Church teachings and the teachings of Ptolemy. In Europe, all scientific knowledge and many religious teachings were based on the arguments developed by classical thinkers. If Ptolemy's reasoning about the planets was wrong, then the whole system of human knowledge might be called into question.

In the late 1500s, the Danish astronomer **Tycho Brahe** (TEE koh BRAH uh) provided evidence to support Copernicus's theory. Brahe set up an astronomical observatory. Every night for years, he carefully observed the sky, accumulating data about the movement of the heavenly bodies.

After Brahe's death, his assistant, the brilliant German astronomer and mathematician **Johannes Kepler** used Brahe's data to calculate the orbits of the planets revolving around the sun. His calculations supported Copernicus's heliocentric view. At the same time, however, they showed that each planet does not move in a perfect circle, as both Ptolemy and Copernicus believed, but in an oval-shaped orbit called an ellipse.

The Church Rejects Galileo's Discoveries Scientists from many different lands built on the work of Copernicus and Kepler. In Italy, **Galileo Galilei** used new technology to assemble an astronomical telescope. With this instrument he became the first person to see mountains on the moon. He observed that the four moons of Jupiter move slowly around that planet—exactly, he realized, the way Copernicus said that Earth moves around the sun.

Galileo's discoveries caused an uproar. Other scholars attacked him because his observations contradicted ancient views about the world. The Church condemned him because his ideas challenged the Christian teaching that the heavens were fixed, unmoving, and perfect.

In 1633, Galileo was tried before the Inquisition, and spent the rest of his life under house arrest. Threatened with death unless he withdrew his "heresies," Galileo agreed to state publicly in court that Earth stood motionless at the center of the universe. However, legend has it that as he left the court he muttered, "And yet it moves."

ANALYZE INFORMATION Why were the discoveries of astronomers like Galileo seen as radical and a threat to Church authority?

A New Scientific Method

Despite the opposition of the Church, by the early 1600s a new approach to science had emerged. Unlike most earlier approaches, it started not with Aristotle or Ptolemy or even the Bible but with observation and experimentation. Most important, complex mathematical calculations were used to convert the observations and experiments into scientific laws. In time, this approach became known as the **scientific method.**

Revolutionary Scientific Thinkers The new scientific method was really a revolution in thought. Two giants of this revolution were the Englishman **Francis Bacon** and the Frenchman **René Descartes** (day KAHRT). Each devoted himself to understanding how truth is determined.

Both Bacon and Descartes, writing in the early 1600s, rejected Aristotle's scientific assumptions. They also challenged the medieval scholars who sought to make the physical world fit in with the teachings of the Church. Both argued that truth is not known at the beginning of inquiry but at the end, after a long process of investigation.

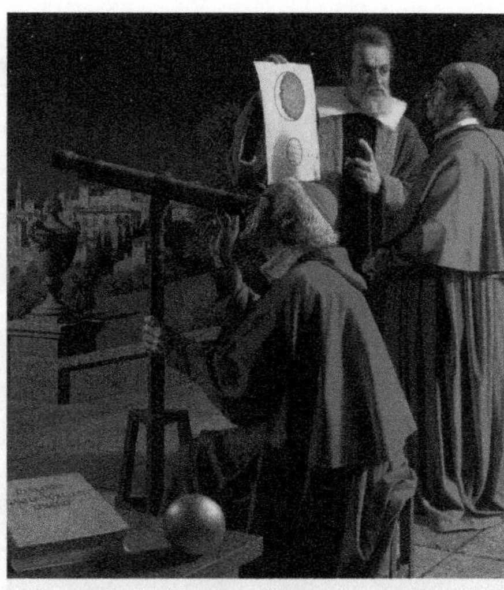

>> Galileo explains to skeptical church officials that the moon's phases reflect its relation to the earth and the sun. Galileo studied the moon through a special telescope he built for the purpose.

Interactive Gallery

Online Project the **Interactive Gallery: Changing Views of the Universe**. Show students that clicking on each photo will open a box that contains key information about each man.

ACTIVE CLASSROOM

Use the Make Headlines strategy and have students write a headline about one of the scientists covered in the Interactive Gallery. Ask: If you were to write a headline capturing the most important aspect of this person's discovery, what would that headline be? Have students pass their headline to a partner to review.

Guided Reading and Discussion

Scientific discoveries represented a search for a truth that often contradicted traditional thought and led even nonscientists to change how they viewed the universe and their place in it. For these people, changing the way they thought would affect every part of their lives. The Reformation extended Renaissance ideas and encouraged the questioning of traditional beliefs. The astronomers of the Scientific Revolution were some of the first to actively explore a new approach to conventionally accepted truths.

Infer Why would Galileo's discovery that the universe is heliocentric threaten the Catholic Church? *(After the sweeping changes of the religious Reformation, it was one more challenge to the Church's authority and traditional teachings.)*

A New Scientific Method

The development of a structured, step-by-step process of inquiry into the physical world grew from the belief of the philosophers Francis Bacon and René Descartes that truth is found not at the beginning of an inquiry, but at the end. The scientific method that eventually developed incorporates this belief as well as Bacon's emphasis on experimentation and observation.

Background

Kepler's Laws Johannes Kepler wanted to know why Mars didn't appear where it was supposed to, based on mathematical calculations. Thanks to exact measurements by his mentor, Tycho Brache, Kepler had excellent records of how Mars's position in the sky seemed to change. But the positions seemed wrong. They didn't fit any known theory of planetary movement. Racking his brain to work out a better theory, he finally came up with three principles of planetary motion, now known as Kepler's laws.

Answers

Analyze Information *The astronomers' conclusions contradicted Church teachings that the universe is ordered and doesn't change. They suggested that physical laws controlled the universe and that man could rely on observations, experiments, and results to make sense of the world.*

Topic 10 Lesson 5

Guided Reading and Discussion

Be sure that students understand that a method of inquiry that relies on experimentation and observation would have to have some type of structure in order to have lasting value.

Compare How did the scientific method differ from traditional methods of finding truth? *(Traditional methods relied on people just accepting what they were told to be truth. The scientific method relies on personal experimentation and observation.)*

Breakthroughs in Medicine and Chemistry

Changes in science extended to the new science of chemistry and to real exploration of how the human body functions. Medical trailblazers helped people to better understand anatomy, chemistry, and microorganisms.

Key Terms

Ask students to find the key term **hypothesis** (in bold) in the text. Have students discuss the difference between a hypothesis and a random guess. If needed, explain that a hypothesis, unlike a guess, is solidly based on gathered information and data and is something that can be tested.

Analyze Images

Ask students to study the diagram showing the steps of the scientific method. Ask: At what point does a scientist draw conclusions? *(step 6)* On what do you think the conclusions should be based? *(data collected and analyzed in step 5)*

Bacon and Descartes differed in their methods, however. Bacon stressed experimentation and observation. He wanted science to make life better for people by leading to practical technologies. Descartes emphasized human reasoning as the best road to understanding. His *Discourse on Method* explains how he decided to discard all traditional authorities and search for provable knowledge. Left only with doubt, he concluded that doubt was the only thing he could not question, and that in order to doubt he had to exist as a rational, thinking being. At that point, he made his famous statement, "I think, therefore I am."

A Step-By-Step Process Over time, the scientific method evolved into a step-by-step process of discovery. Scientists collected and accurately measured data. To explain the data, scientists used reasoning to propose a logical **hypothesis,** or possible explanation. They then tested the hypothesis with further observation or experimentation.

For the first time, mathematical calculations were used to convert the observations and experiments into scientific laws. After reaching a conclusion, scientists repeated their work at least once—and usually many times—to confirm and refine their hypotheses or formulate better ones.

Thinkers like Bacon and Descartes helped bring the scientific method to the pursuit of all knowledge. Their pioneering approaches to thought opened the way to even more revolutionary ways of thinking in the 1700s.

EXPLAIN How did the ideas of Francis Bacon and René Descartes lead to a new scientific method?

Breakthroughs in Medicine and Chemistry

The 1500s and 1600s saw dramatic changes in many of the sciences, especially medicine and chemistry. Like Copernicus, Bacon, and Descartes, scientists rejected long-held assumptions. They relied on new technology, such as the microscope, and benefited from better communication, especially the availability of printed books.

Exploring Human Anatomy Medieval physicians relied on the works of the ancient Greek physician Galen. Galen, however, had made many errors, in part because he had limited knowledge of human anatomy. During the Renaissance, physicians made new efforts to study the human body.

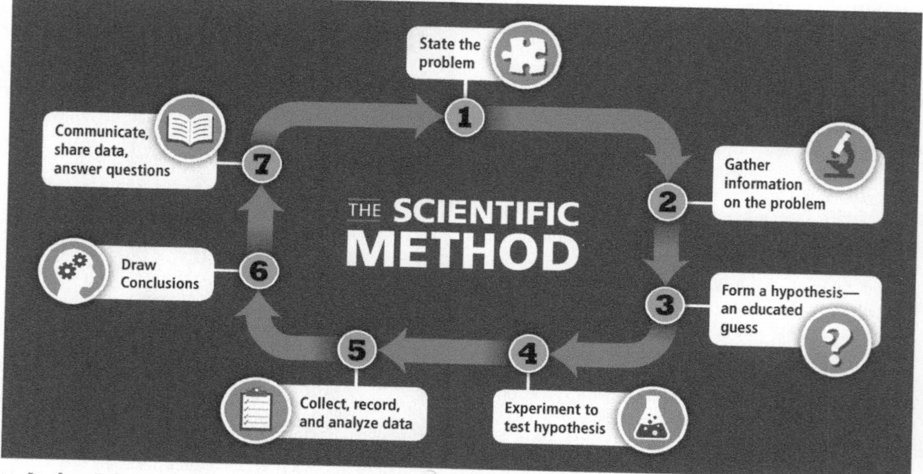

>> **Analyze Information** The scientific method, still used today, is based on careful observation and measurement of data. Why do you think it's critical to follow each step in sequence and to follow the same procedure for each step?

Answers

Analyze Information *Possible answer: Following a specific procedure and doing the steps in order limits the variables in an experiment and makes the results something that can be reproduced by other scientists.*

Explain *Bacon and Descartes believed that truth could only be discovered through a process of investigation. Bacon emphasized experimentation and observation, while Descartes emphasized human reasoning. The scientific method is a process in which truth is pursued through defined steps of discovery.*

Background

Telescope Improvements in a single tool can help in the advancement of science over centuries. In the early 1600s, Galileo used a homemade refracting telescope to map landforms on Earth's moon, discover four of Jupiter's moons, and study nearby stars. Steady improvements since then have resulted in sophisticated modern telescopes that are helping scientists look back at the early universe to see how stars, galaxies, and planetary systems evolved.

However, these telescopes have a problem: Earth's atmosphere distorts the images they receive. In 1990, space-shuttle technology allowed NASA to place the Hubble Space Telescope into orbit above the distorting atmosphere. Since then, its amazingly sharp images have helped scientists measure the rate of expansion of the universe, prove the existence of black holes, and observe in greater detail the birth and death of stars.

In 1543, Andreas Vesalius (vuh SAY lee us) published *On the Structure of the Human Body*, the first accurate and detailed study of human anatomy. Vesalius's careful and clear drawings corrected errors inherited from ancient classical authorities.

About the same time, French physician Ambroise Paré (pa RAY) made many practical advances. He developed a new, more effective ointment for preventing infection and better ways to seal wounds during surgery. He introduced the use of artificial limbs and invented several scientific instruments.

In the early 1600s, William Harvey, an English scholar, described the circulation of the blood for the first time. He showed how the heart serves as a pump to force blood through veins and arteries. Pioneering scientists like Harvey opened the way for further advances.

The Microscope Later in the 1600s, the Dutch inventor Anton van Leeuwenhoek (LAY wun hohk) perfected the single-lens microscope. Van Leeuwenhoek worked on grinding lenses as a hobby. He used them to examine tiny objects such as lice or the mouths of bees.

Peering through his microscope at drops of water, he was surprised to see tiny organisms, which he called "very little animalcules." Van Leeuwenhoek thus became the first human to see cells and microorganisms such as bacteria. For this work, he is often called the founder of microbiology. Over time, the microscope would lead to still more startling discoveries.

The New Science of Chemistry The branch of science today called chemistry was known as alchemy in medieval times. Alchemists believed that one substance could be transformed into another substance and tried to turn ordinary metals into gold. During the Scientific Revolution, chemistry slowly freed itself from the magical notions of alchemy. Still, scientists benefited from some of the alchemists' practical knowledge, such as the manipulation of metals and acids.

In the 1600s, English chemist **Robert Boyle** explained that all matter was composed of tiny particles that behave in knowable ways. Boyle distinguished between individual elements and chemical compounds and explained the effect of temperature and pressure on gases. Boyle's work opened the way to modern chemical analysis of the composition of matter.

Isaac Newton Links the Sciences As a student at Cambridge University in England, **Isaac Newton** devoured the works of the leading scientists of his day. By age 24, he had formed a brilliant theory to explain why the planets moved as they did. According

>> English surgeon John Banister dissects a corpse to teach students about human anatomy. New approaches to scientific investigation helped to change how physicians learned about the human body.

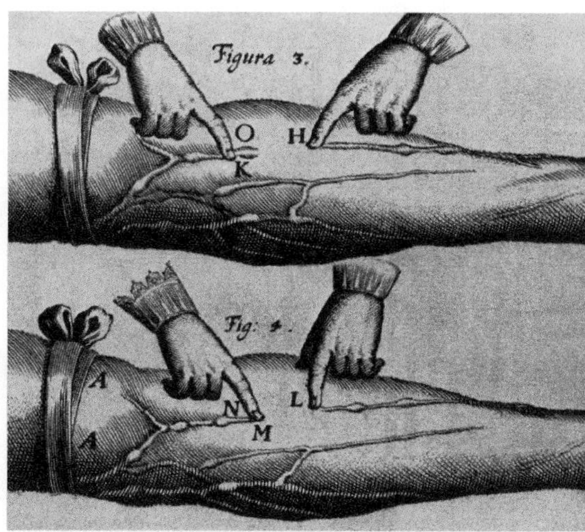

>> An illustration of the circulatory system from William Harvey's book, *On the Motions of the Heart and Blood*. Harvey revolutionized medicine by suggesting that blood circulates continuously throughout the body.

Topic 10 Lesson 5

Online Project the **Interactive Gallery: A Scientific Revolution in Medicine**. Click on one of the images to demonstrate how doing so brings up additional information about each scientist.

ACTIVE CLASSROOM

Use the Conversation With History strategy and have students pretend they are having a conversation with one of the scientists featured in the Interactive Gallery. Ask students to write down a question they'd like to ask and how that person would respond to the question. Students would also offer a response.

Guided Reading and Discussion

Isaac Newton put his considerable intellect into the study of a variety of scientific disciplines. He specialized in mathematics and physics but also studied alchemy, the precursor to chemistry. Robert Boyle's discoveries in chemistry and his formulas expressing the relationship between gases and pressure are still used today. The discoveries of anatomists like Andreas Vesalius and William Harvey changed how people viewed the human body.

Test Conclusions The discoveries of Galileo, Newton, and other leaders of the Scientific Revolution are often described as evidence of human progress. Evaluate whether this is an accurate description. *(Answers may agree with this description because the discoveries made by these scientists and others of the period advanced human knowledge of the natural world. Other answers may suggest that most people did not benefit greatly from the period's progress and still lived in poverty.)*

Answers

Explain *He established that all matter is composed of tiny particles that behave in knowable ways and identified chemicals as the building blocks of life. He made the distinction between joined chemicals (compounds) and individual elements.*

Topic 10 Lesson 5

SYNTHESIZE

Online Project the **Digital Activity: Important People of the Scientific Revolution**. Ask students to recall the section focus question: How did discoveries in science lead to a new way of thinking for Europeans? Ask them to take 5 minutes to write down some brief answers to the question, and then to share their answers with a partner.

Have partners think about the following question: What are three discoveries that you believe made the greatest impact on society? Have pairs share their answers with the class.

DEMONSTRATE

Online Assign the **Digital Lesson Quiz** for this lesson if you haven't already done so. Students will be offered automatic remediation or enrichment based on their score.

Pose the following question to the class on the Discussion Board:

Analyze the Main Idea How did the Scientific Revolution build on the spirit of the Reformation? *(The Reformation was a time of challenging long-held religious beliefs and the authority of the Church on these matters. The Scientific Revolution also challenged traditional beliefs about the natural world and challenged Church authority in the process.)*

Topic Inquiry

Have students continue their investigations for the Topic Inquiry.

>> Isaac Newton performs an experiment to analyze how light is made up of a spectrum of different colors.

to one story, Newton saw an apple fall from a tree. He wondered whether the force that pulled that apple to Earth also controlled the movements of the planets.

Over the next 20 years, Newton perfected his theory. To do so, he developed the basis for **calculus**, a branch of mathematics. Using mathematics, he showed that a single force keeps the planets in their orbits around the sun. He called this force **gravity**.

In 1687, Newton published *Mathematical Principles of Natural Philosophy*, explaining the law of gravity and other workings of the universe. Nature, argued Newton, follows uniform laws. All motion in the universe can be measured and described mathematically.

To many people, Newton's work seemed to link the sciences of physics and astronomy with mathematics, just as gravity bound the universe together.

For more than 200 years Newton's laws held fast, until the early 1900s, when a revolution in physics once more transformed the way people saw the universe. Still, Newton's work, ranging from the laws of motion and gravity to mathematics, makes him one of the most influential scientists of all time.

EXPLAIN How did Boyle's research transform chemistry into a real science?

ASSESSMENT

1. **Recognize Ideologies** How did the theories of Copernicus and Galileo change the way people understood the universe?
2. **Make Generalizations** In what ways did the scientific method differ from earlier approaches to learning?
3. **Identify Cause and Effect** What impact did Reformation ideas have on medicine?
4. **Synthesize** How did Newton use the ideas of Plato?
5. **Infer** How did the Reformation help spur the Scientific Revolution?

Assessment

1. Their theories challenged traditional beliefs, as well as Church teachings about the universe and how it functions. The discoveries of Copernicus and Galileo raised questions about those teachings and proved that some were in error. This opened up the possibility of people further questioning how the physical world works.
2. Before, people learned accepted truths, dictated by tradition or religion. The scientific method was based on the idea that truth could come only through investigation.
3. The Reformation worldview led people to explore the human body in new ways to see how it really worked. This sparked new discoveries in anatomy and medicine.
4. He used Plato's emphasis on mathematics and reality to discover nature's laws.
5. The Reformation launched a period of questioning and change within the Christian Church. This trend of inquiry continued in the secular world and encouraged scientists and philosophers to challenge traditional thought in many areas.

TEKS ASSESSMENT

1. **Identify Examples** Identify examples of literature that convey universal themes and transcend the cultures in which they were created. Write a paragraph identifying examples of literature from northern Renaissance writers and their universal themes. Give examples and describe the works of humanists Sir Thomas More or François Rabelais. Identify common themes and the scope of William Shakespeare's works. **26.C**

Humanist Author	Universal Theme Addressed
Sir Thomas More	
François Rabelais	
William Shakespeare	

2. **Identify Major Causes** Identify the major causes of the following important turning points in world history from 1450 to 1750: the Renaissance. Write a paragraph identifying the major causes of the Renaissance from the 1300s to the 1500s. Consider agricultural vs. urban society, factors that fueled the Renaissance, and the invention of the printing press. **1.D**
3. **Identify Examples** Identify examples of art that transcend the cultures in which they were produced, convey universal themes, and demonstrate an artistic ideal or visual principle from selected cultures. Write a paragraph describing how the works of Michelangelo and Leonardo da Vinci related to Renaissance ideals of humanism. Did they share any common themes? **26.A**
4. **Explain the Impact** Explain the political and economic impact of the Renaissance. Write a paragraph explaining the influence of the powerful merchant families who controlled the Italian city-states. Consider how trading growth supported the arts during the Renaissance, and describe the growth of the financial and manufacturing networks. **5.A**
5. **Describe Influences** Describe the major influences of women during major eras of world history: Elizabeth I. Write a paragraph describing the major influences of Queen Elizabeth I during the Protestant Reformation in England. Explain England's religious turmoil before Elizabeth I arrived on the throne. What were the results of her compromises under the Elizabethan Settlement? **24.B**
6. **Analyze Examples** Analyze examples of how literature reflected the history of the cultures in which it was produced. Write a paragraph analyzing examples of how literary works reflected common Renaissance themes, like the works of Baldassare Castiglione and Machiavelli. Describe the interest in philosophy and learning and the interest in guidebooks to achieve success. **26.B**
7. **Describe Major Effects** Describe the major effects of the following important turning points in world history from 1450 to 1750: the Renaissance, and explain the intellectual and artistic impact. Write a paragraph describing the impact of individualism and creative thinking during the European Renaissance. Consider the effect of the shift to urbanization and how humanist ideas resulted in a rebirth of artistic and intellectual thinking. **1.D, 5.A**

Europe Shifts from Medieval to Renaissance Era

MEDIEVAL EUROPE	RENAISSANCE EUROPE
APPROXIMATELY 400s to 1300s	APPROXIMATELY 1300s to 1500s
Agricultural society	Urban society
Less long-distance trade between countries	Long-distance trade increases
Focus on religion for studies	Focus on humanities in studies
Individual achievement less highly valued	Celebrates individual achievements
Classical works are preserved, but not focus of scholars	Scholars and others have a renewed interest in classical works of ancient Greece and Rome

8. **Explain the Relationship and Explain the Influence** Explain the relationship among Christianity, individualism, and growing secularism that began with the Renaissance, and explain how the relationship influenced subsequent political developments. Write a paragraph explaining the Christian challenge to the Roman Catholic Church and the growing secularism that began with the Renaissance. Explain how this influenced Martin Luther and the Protestant Reformation. What type of works did artists at this time produce? **25.C**
9. **Identify Major Effects and Examples** Identify major effects, including examples of religious influence, of the following important turning points in world history from 1450 to 1750: the Reformation, including the religious influence of Lutheranism during the Reformation. Write a paragraph identifying major effects of Lutheranism during the Reformation. Consider why Martin Luther issued his 95 Theses, how Lutheranism differed from Catholicism on sacraments, and other fundamental differences with Catholicism. **1.D, 23.B**
10. **Explain the Philosophies and Identify Characteristics** Explain the political philosophies of individuals: John Calvin, and identify the characteristics of political systems, including theocracy. Write a paragraph explaining the beliefs of John Calvin, including theocracy. Consider Calvin's decision about the Church, predestination concept, and the focus of his model society in Geneva. **19.B, 20.C**

Answers to TEKS Assessment

1. Student answers will vary but should include information on how Renaissance humanists focused on themes such as education, social reform, and classical learning. Sir Thomas More advocated social reform in his work *Utopia*. Rabelais offered opinions on religion and education through characters in his book *Gargantua and Pantagruel*. Shakespeare wrote 37 plays, including tragedies, comedies, and histories, among them *Romeo and Juliet, Richard II, Henry IV,* and *Henry V.* Shakespeare's works express universal themes, such as the complexity of the individual, in everyday settings.

2. Student answers will vary but should include information on how the Renaissance was caused by a number of factors. A shift from an agricultural to an urban society occurred. It was a time when creative thinking and new technology let people understand and describe their world more accurately. Renaissance thinkers and artists were influenced by the learnings of classical Greece and Rome. The Renaissance emphasized individual achievement. Trade was important, as it spread ideas and the wealth that fueled the Renaissance. In particular, powerful city-state merchant families exerted both political and economic leadership and were patrons of the arts, commissioning artworks. The Catholic Church was another patron of the arts. The invention of a new technology, the printing press, produced inexpensive printed books that enabled Renaissance ideas to spread quickly.

3. Student answers will vary but should include information on how two of the world's greatest artists left their mark during the Renaissance. Artistic works by da Vinci and Michelangelo both transcend their times, and reflect the idea of humanism by emphasizing both religious themes and individual achievement. Michelangelo's versatility was evident in his marble masterpiece *David,* which depicted the Biblical shepherd who killed Goliath. It recalls the harmony and grace of ancient Greek sculptures. In the *Pietà*, he captures Mary's sorrow as she cradles the dead Jesus, a universal theme. Michelangelo is also known for painting the biblical history of the world on the Sistine Chapel ceiling in Rome. He was also an architect, designing the dome of St. Peter's Cathedral. Da Vinci's paintings *Mona Lisa* and *The Last Supper* reflect realism as well as religious themes. *The Last Supper* is a masterpiece of perspective, the new Renaissance technique that made paintings appear three-dimensional. Leonardo was also a scientist with many accomplishments in botany, music, and engineering. His notebooks, in which he made sketches of flying machines and submarines centuries before they were built, still survive today.

4. Student answers will vary but should include information on how Italian city-states were controlled by wealthy, powerful merchant families. These city-states became centers of trade. Trade flourished, and these merchants provided financial support and patronage for the arts, helping to shape the Italian Renaissance. Banking, manufacturing, and merchant networks supported the increased trade. Printed books had an impact, helping to facilitate the spread of new ideas.

5. Student answers will vary but should include information on how Elizabeth I faced religious turmoil upon her ascension to the throne. Henry VIII had thrown off the Catholic Church to have his marriage annulled and named himself the supreme head of the Church of England. Catholic convents and monasteries were closed, and Protestant reforms began. Queen Mary wanted England to be Catholic again and persecuted Protestants. The Elizabethan Settlement was a compromise that preserved some Catholic rituals and the hierarchy of bishops, but accepted Protestant doctrine and used English in church services. Because of Elizabeth's sensible compromises, Britain remained a Protestant nation and did not face endless religious wars.

Topic 10

Answers to TEKS Assessment

6. Student answers will vary but should include information on how Italian writers reflected the Renaissance curiosity and interest in the humanities. Baldassare Castiglione wrote works of philosophy dealing with humanism. His handbook *The Book of the Courtier* describes the skills and learning that court members should have. His ideal courtier was an aristocrat who was educated, had manners, was athletic, played musical instruments, and had mastered other fields. Women, in his opinion, should focus more on a kind personality and beautiful looks. Machiavelli was representative of writers who wrote guidebooks to help ambitious Renaissance people become successful. He wrote about how rulers can realistically gain and maintain power in *The Prince* and stressed using whatever means are necessary to achieve goals, even though he himself disliked corruption.

7. Student answers will vary but should include that urbanization created a better environment for an exchange of ideas. The Renaissance emphasis on individualism and creative thinking produced many gifted poets, artists, architects, scholars, and scientists. An intellectual movement called humanism renewed interest in education and the classical Greek and Roman cultures. Humanists studied these cultures to increase understanding of their own times, but they focused on secular subjects rather than the religious issues of the past. They believed that education should stimulate creativity and thus emphasized study of the humanities, including grammar, poetry, and history. Art, in particular, reflected the new ideas and attitudes of humanism, including individual achievement.

8. Student answers will vary but should include information on how Christians began to challenge the worldliness and corruption of the Roman Catholic Church. During the Renaissance, many Christians focused on secular, or worldly, subjects instead of religious issues. Society placed a new emphasis on individual achievement. Renaissance artists produced works that reflected the humanist interest in individual achievements. A desire for reform led to protests against the Church that resulted in the Protestant Reformation. It was triggered by Martin Luther, a German monk and professor, whose ideas were spread by new printing presses. Luther emphasized a return to simplicity and Bible study rather than Church pomp and ceremony. He said that all Christians have access to God through faith and the Bible. The Peace of Augsburg (1555) allowed German princes to decide which religion they would follow; most northern German states chose Lutheranism, and southern German states chose Catholicism.

9. Student answers will vary but should include that Martin Luther challenged Catholic Church teachings and Church abuses, such as the selling of indulgences, by issuing his 95 Theses. Lutheranism accepted some Catholic Church sacraments but rejected others because rituals cannot erase sin, only God can. Other fundamental differences include that Lutheranism supports people's direct interpretation of the Bible instead of interpretations by priests; that councils lead the church instead of the pope; and that the Bible is the sole source of truth. Luther also simplified the mass, emphasizing the sermon, and changed other Church practices, banning confessions, pilgrimages, and prayers to saints.

10. Student answers will vary but should include information on how John Calvin shared Martin Luther's beliefs and broke away from the Catholic Church. Calvin wrote a book on how to organize and run a Protestant church. Calvin preached predestination, the idea that God had already determined who would gain salvation. In 1541, Calvin set up a theocracy (a government run by religious leaders) in the city-state of Geneva, Switzerland, with followers who wanted a model Christian society. Calvinists tried to live like saints and saw themselves as chosen people.

TEKS ASSESSMENT

11. **Explain the Impact** Explain the religious impact of the Renaissance and the Reformation. Write a paragraph analyzing examples of the reaction of the Catholic Church to the Protestant Reformation. Consider the Catholic Counter-Reformation, Council of Trent, Catholic Inquisition, and the status of Catholicism in Europe by 1600. **5.A, 5.B**

12. **Explain the Impact** Explain the impact of the printing press on the Renaissance in Europe. Write a paragraph explaining the impact of the printing press on the Renaissance in northern Europe. Consider the impact on price and quantity of books, impact on literacy rates, and exposure to new ideas. What happened to the status of cities that had printing presses? **27.C**

13. **Describe the Major Effects and Explain Its Impact** Describe the major effects of the following important turning points in world history from 1750 to 1914: the Scientific Revolution, and explain its impact on scientific thinking worldwide. Write a paragraph describing the worldwide effects of the Scientific Revolution. Looking at the chart below, describe the scientific method. How were the contributions of Francis Bacon and René Descartes key to the scientific process? After step 7 in the chart, what did scientists usually do to gain credibility? **1.E, 27.D**

14. **Describe Major Causes and Effects** Describe the major causes and effects of the following important turning points in world history from 1750 to 1914: the Scientific Revolution. Write a paragraph describing the dramatic changes in thinking during the Scientific Revolution. Consider the focus on the physical universe governed by mathematical laws; contributions of Copernicus, Brahe, and Kepler; and the use and features of a new scientific method. **1.E**

15. **Identify the Contributions** Identify the contributions of significant scientists: Galileo. Write a paragraph that identifies the contributions of Galileo. Using the excerpt and lesson information, answer the following: Who is condemning Galileo's work? What were Galileo's beliefs that angered people? How serious were the accusations, and what actually occurred after his condemnation? **27.E**

"The Sentence of the Inquisition on Galileo.

"We, the undersigned, by the Grace of God, Cardinals of the Holy Roman Church, Inquisitors General throughout the whole Christian Republic, Special Deputies of the Holy Apostolical Chair against heretical depravity,

"Whereas you, Galileo, son of the late Vincenzo Galilei of Florence, aged seventy years, were denounced in 1615 to this Holy Office, for holding as true a false doctrine taught by many, namely, that the sun is immoveable in the centre of the world, and that the earth moves, and also with a diurnal motion; also, for having pupils whom you instructed in the same opinions; also, for maintaining a correspondence on the same with some German mathematicians; also for publishing certain letters on the solar spots, in which you developed the same doctrine as true; . . .

"But whereas being pleased at that time to deal mildly with you, it was decreed in the Holy Congregation, held before His Holiness on the 25th day of February, 1616, that His Eminence the Lord Cardinal Bellarmine should enjoin you to give up altogether the said false doctrine; if you should refuse, that you should be ordered by the Commissary of the Holy Office to relinquish it, not to teach it to others, nor to defend it, nor ever mention it, and in default of acquiescence that you should be imprisoned; . . . "

16. **Reflect on the Essential Question Write an essay on the Essential Question: Why is culture important?** Use evidence from your study of this Topic to support your answer.

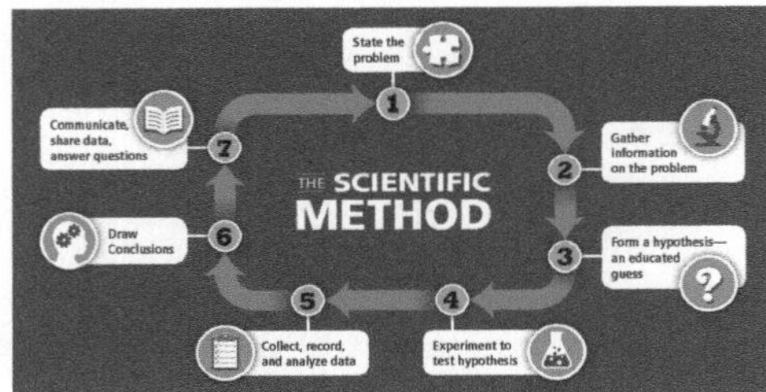

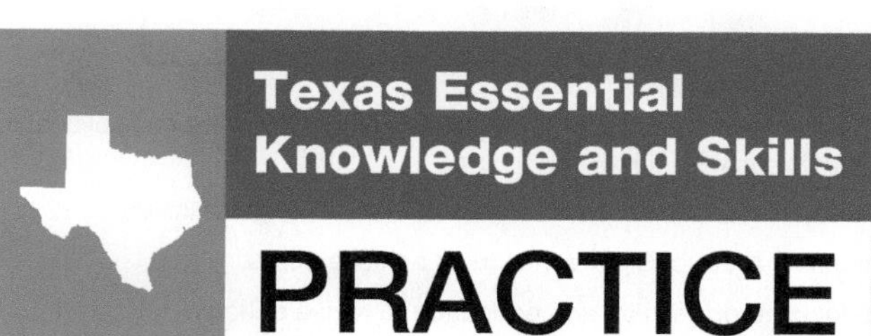

They emphasized hard work, honesty, and thriftiness, and faced fines or other punishments for offensive activities like fighting, dancing, or laughing in church. Reformers from all over Europe came to Geneva to observe and returned home to spread Calvin's ideas.

11. Student answers will vary but should include information on how the Protestant Reformation led Catholics to fight back with their own reformation, or the Counter-Reformation. Since the Protestants had revealed many abuses within the Church, the Pope attempted to end corruption and bring back Protestant converts. To that end, the Council of Trent established reforms but still reaffirmed the Catholic views that the Protestants had challenged. The Catholic Inquisition (Church court) was strengthened and used torture and execution to root out heresy. The Catholic Reformation had some success, and by 1600, Europeans were still mainly Catholic.

12. Student answers will vary but should include information on how the invention of the printing press by Johannes Gutenberg in 1456 transformed Europe by increasing the number of books from a few thousand to approximately 15–20 million by 1500. The cheaper price and the fact that more books were available encouraged people to learn to read and increased literacy rates, leading to the spread of knowledge and new Renaissance ideas. Cities with printing presses attracted more people and grew more quickly than those without.

13. Student answers will vary but should include that at the heart of the Scientific Revolution was the belief that mathematical laws governed nature and the universe. Scientists now focused on experimentation and observations as a new approach to science. The scientific method required scientists to use a step-by-step process to collect and accurately measure data, formulate hypotheses, and then test those hypotheses with further experimentation. It used mathematical calculations to reach a conclusion, and experiments were repeated and refined (after step 7). Bacon stressed experimentation, and Descartes emphasized human reasoning. Both argued that truth is not known at the beginning of an inquiry, but at the end, after a long process of investigation.

14. Student answers will vary but should include information on how the Renaissance cast aside medieval thinking. Renaissance scientists made profound shifts in thinking about the physical universe. A new spirit of inquiry focused on how mathematical laws governed nature and the universe. As for effects, three scholars and astronomers (Copernicus, Brahe, and Kepler) disproved that the Earth is the center of the universe. Copernicus proposed that the universe is heliocentric, or sun-centered. Others (Bacon and Descartes) helped establish the beginnings of a new scientific method that focused on step-by-step procedures based on observation, experimentation, careful measurement of data, and a hypothesis, or possible explanation.

15. Student answers will vary but should include that the cardinals of the Catholic Church and the Church hierarchy condemned Galileo's work. Galileo, using a telescope, proved Copernicus's theory about the Earth revolving around the sun, and that the phases of the moon reflect its position relative to the Earth and sun. The Church and other scholars believed the heavenly bodies were fixed in position relative to the Earth. Galileo's discovery contradicted Church teachings. The charges were serious enough that Galileo was tried before the Inquisition and forced to renounce his heresies. He had to publicly state that Earth stands motionless at the center of the universe in order to avoid a death sentence. In 1633, Galileo was sentenced to house arrest for the rest of his life.

Topic 10

Answers to TEKS Practice

1. A
2. H

Online To prepare for the End-of-Topic test, have students go online for additional Topic Review and Assessment questions or to review their notes in the **Interactive Reading Notepad** for the lessons in this Topic.

Benchmark Tests

Assign these benchmark tests as you complete the relevant topics to monitor student progress toward mastering the course content and as preparation for the End-of-Course Test.

Benchmark Test 1: Topics 1–5

Benchmark Test 2: Topics 6–10

Benchmark Test 3: Topics 11–15

Benchmark Test 4: Topics 16–21

TEKS PRACTICE

1 Europe Shifts from Medieval to Renaissance Era

MEDIEVAL EUROPE	RENAISSANCE EUROPE
APPROXIMATELY 400s to 1300s	APPROXIMATELY 1300s to 1500s
Agricultural society	Urban society
Less long-distance trade between countries	Long-distance trade increases
Focus on religion for studies	Focus on humanities in studies
Individual achievement less highly valued	Celebrates individual achievements
Classical works are preserved, but not focus of scholars	Scholars and others have a renewed interest in classical works of ancient Greece and Rome

According to the chart and information from the lessons, what were the political and economic effects of the Renaissance?

A An urban society and increased trade helped the exchange of ideas.

B Medieval thinking produced more individual achievements.

C Humanists focused on religion and education to revive education.

D Renewed focus on classical Greco-Roman philosophy energized thinkers.

2

> *"The second half of Henry's reign was dominated by two issues very important for the later history of England and the monarchy: the succession and the Protestant Reformation, which led to the formation of the Church of England."*

What is the relationship between the two issues referenced in the quote?

F The Church of England seized the lands that belonged to Henry VIII.

G The Church of England investigated abuses of power committed by Henry VIII.

H Henry VIII broke with the Catholic Church to obtain an annulment in part to have a male heir.

J Henry VIII wanted to abdicate the throne and turn over absolute power to the Catholic Church.

Test Taking Tips: Tip for Questions With Maps

1. Read the question.
2. Read the map title and look at the map to determine what is shown in the map.
3. Look at the key or legend. What symbols, shades, or patterns are used to show information on the map? Find examples of each symbol, shade, or pattern on the map.
4. Read the question again. What information do you need from the map to answer the question? Use the information in the map title, the key or legend, and on the map itself to find the answer.
5. Answer the question in your own words.
6. Read the answer choices and select the best answer.

3 How did European departure from its medieval past affect the Scientific Revolution?

- **A** Church agreement about using experimentation changed thinking.
- **B** Astronomy became the leading scientific field led by Galileo.
- **C** New advances in medicine became accepted beliefs.
- **D** People thought about the physical universe in a new way.

4 Which of these were fundamental ideas and institutions of China that spread to Korea?

- **F** Chinese alphabet and paper printmaking techniques
- **G** Theravada Buddhism and architecture with religious themes
- **H** Civil service exams and managing government bureaucracy
- **J** New military technology and improved walled fortresses

If you have trouble with...				
Question	1	2	3	4
See Lesson	10.1	10.4	10.5	9.3
TEKS	1.D, 5.A	1.D	1.E	25.A

3. D
4. H

Online Use the **Topic Synthesize** to help students revisit and reflect on the Essential Question for this Topic.

Topic Inquiry

If students have done a Topic Inquiry for this Topic, have them complete the final step of the Inquiry now.

New Global Connections (1415–1796)

TOPIC 11 ORGANIZER	PACING: APPROX. 1 PERIOD, .5 BLOCKS		
	PACING	TEKS	ELPS
Connect	1 period		
MY STORY VIDEO **Hernán Cortés and Moctezuma, The Conquest of a Golden City**	10 min.		
DIGITAL ESSENTIAL QUESTION ACTIVITY **Why Do People Move?**	10 min.	1.D, 7.A	
DIGITAL TIMELINE ACTIVITY **New Global Connection**	10 min.	1.D, 6.B	
TOPIC INQUIRY: DOCUMENT-BASED QUESTION **What Was the Impact of the Columbian Exchange?**	20 min.		
Investigate	3–6 periods		
TOPIC INQUIRY: DOCUMENT-BASED QUESTION **What Was the Impact of the Columbian Exchange?**	Ongoing		
LESSON 1 **Europeans Explore Overseas**	30–40 min.	1.D, 7.A	3.H.3, 3.C.3
LESSON 2 **Europeans Gain Footholds in Asia**	30–40 min.	1.D, 16.B	3.C.4
LESSON 3 **European Conquests in the Americas**	30–40 min.	1.D, 6.B, 7.A	3.D.1
LESSON 4 **European Colonies in North America**	30–40 min.	1.D, 7.A	3.D.2
LESSON 5 **The Slave Trade and Its Impact on Africa**	30–40 min.	1.D, 4.I, 7.A, 7.C	3.E.1
LESSON 6 **Effects of Global Contact**	30–40 min.	1.D, 7.B, 7.F, 18.F	3.F.1
Synthesize	1 period		
DIGITAL ESSENTIAL QUESTION ACTIVITY **Reflect on the Essential Question and Topic**	10 min.		
TOPIC INQUIRY: DOCUMENT-BASED QUESTION **What Was the Impact of the Columbian Exchange?**	20 min.		
Demonstrate	1–2 periods		
ONLINE TEST **New Global Connections**	10 min.		
TOPIC INQUIRY: DOCUMENT-BASED QUESTION **What Was the Impact of the Columbian Exchange?**	20 min.		

AUTHOR'S NOTE

The Western Predominance

The degree of global sovereignty exercised by Western people at this point in history remains debatable. . . . Many historians detect a systematic European global dominance emerging over these early centuries. Other scholars, however, emphasize the much greater degree of western power achieved during the second great wave of imperial conquest in the 1800s and early 1900s.

Between 1500 and 1800, these specialists assert, most non-Western peoples were still affected by the long reach of Western ships and guns, soldiers, traders, and missionaries. The millions of Native Americans and Africans who became subjects or slaves of Europeans after 1500 would certainly have disagreed with this view. But European intercontinental empires would in fact impact many more peoples during the New Imperialism of the nineteenth century and twentieth centuries, when Western predominance turned almost all of Africa and most of Asia into Western colonies, protectorates, or spheres of influence. . . .

The global power balance, however, did shift dramatically between 1500 and 1800. In 1500 the most powerful nation in the world was certainly China. The most dynamic expanding culture was probably that of the Muslim center of Eurasia. In Africa and the Americas, independent centers of empire were developing in the Western Sudan, Mexico, and Peru. Pluralism prevailed, and Europe was by no means the greatest of world civilizations.

As 1800 approached, all this had clearly changed. European power had destroyed the American empires, and the African kingdoms had declined in a welter of wars and slave trading. The Western nations, meanwhile, had repulsed and outflanked the Islamic lands, pushed into an Indian Ocean formerly dominated by Muslim traders, and replaced Muslim power in Southeast Asia with European power. The rulers of India were being slowly sucked into the maw of European dependency. Everywhere except East Asia, the weight of Western political predominance was being felt as the eighteenth century drew to a close.

—Anthony Esler, *The Human Venture: From Prehistory to the Present* (Upper Saddle River, New Jersey: Pearson Education, 2004), pp. 468–469

TOPIC INQUIRY: DOCUMENT-BASED QUESTION

What Was the Impact of the Columbian Exchange?

TEKS 1.F, 7.B, 7.C

In this Topic Inquiry, students analyze six primary and secondary source documents to draw their own conclusions on how the Columbian Exchange had a lasting impact on Europe and the Americas. This DBQ on the Columbian Exchange expands on that essential question and provides students an opportunity to consider some of the consequences of human migration, which address the Topic Essential Question: "Why do people move?"

STEP 1: CONNECT

Develop Questions and Plan the Investigation

Launch the DBQ Writing Activity

Show the flipped video "Cortés and Moctezuma," which deals with early encounters between Europeans and Native Americans and the resulting Columbian Exchange. Use the questions to lead a class discussion about the video, or have students work in pairs to answer the questions.

Suggestion: Give more context for the video by explaining that Mexico City is built upon the ruins of the Aztec capital of Tenochtitlán. In its people and culture, today's Mexico City reflects the enduring impact of the Columbian Exchange.

Generate Questions

Divide the class into small groups and have them use the Need-to-Know Questions document to record their questions about how the Columbian Exchange affected Europe and how it affected the Americas.

Suggestion: Help students generate questions by reminding them of the five Ws and one H used by journalists: *Who? What? When? Where? Why?* and *How?* Suggest that students take 10 minutes to brainstorm as many questions as possible and then select the ones most relevant to the broader DBQ question.

Resources

- Need-to-Know Questions
- Student Instructions

STEP 2: INVESTIGATE

Apply Disciplinary Concepts and Tools

Analyze the Documents

Have students analyze the six documents to start building their response to the question "How did the Columbian Exchange affect both Europe and the Americas?" Before students read the material, you may wish to point out that Documents A through D are all secondary sources, while Documents E and F are primary sources. Another distinction is that Documents A and C are both charts that provide data on the migration of people, plants, and animals, while the other documents all express a viewpoint on the effects of these migrations. Remind students that as they analyze these, they should be aware of any biases that the authors might have.

Suggestion: Document E contains some words that the translator left in the original Spanish. You may wish to help students use context to understand the meaning of these words. Or you might use a Spanish dictionary to provide English translations for these words.

Check Understanding

Students should answer the multiple-choice and short-answer questions that follow each document.

PROFESSIONAL DEVELOPMENT

Document-Based Question

Be sure to view the Document-Based Question Professional Development resources in the online course.

STEP 3: SYNTHESIZE

Evaluate Sources and Use Evidence to Formulate Conclusions

Write Your Essay

Have students consider all of the evidence and viewpoints and draw their own conclusions. Using the documents and their knowledge of history, have them write an essay on the following topic: How did the Columbian Exchange affect both Europe and the Americas?

Remind students that their essays should have the following characteristics: a topic sentence that states their view; evidence from at least *three* of the documents, clearly identified; relevant facts; an explanation and rebuttal of at least one opposing viewpoint; and logical organization, including an introduction and a conclusion. Be sure that students use social studies terminology correctly and use standard grammar, spelling, sentence structure, and punctuation.

Suggestion: If students struggle with organization, review the structure of a five-paragraph essay. The first paragraph is the introduction. The body consists of three paragraphs, each of which explores a key point. The conclusion should restate the main idea and summarize the key points.

Edit Your Essay

Remind students that they should revise their first draft and create a final draft of their essay before turning it in. You may want to suggest that they ask a classmate to peer edit their essay.

Resources

- Writing Rubric

STEP 4: DEMONSTRATE

Communicate Conclusions and Take Informed Action

Reflect on the Project

After students have finished their essays, explain that the work they did on this DBQ on the Columbian Exchange will serve as a foundation for their understanding of human migration and the variety of effects that can result from it. In the future, they may refine or revise ideas they developed here on migration, but they can use a similar process for considering multiple sources of evidence and points of view to form an educated and carefully reasoned opinion.

Suggestion: Help students connect this inquiry project to their world today by reminding them that the impact of human migration is still a significant global issue. For example, in our own country, citizens and government leaders are often concerned with the issue of immigration. Throughout the world, the movement of people affects the region from which they move and the region to which they move.

Europeans Explore Overseas

Objectives

Objective 1: Understand the major causes of European exploration.

Objective 2: Analyze early Portuguese and Spanish explorations and expansion.

Objective 3: Describe how the Portuguese established footholds on Africa's coasts.

Objective 4: Describe European searches for a direct route to Asia.

LESSON 1 ORGANIZER	PACING: APPROX. 1 PERIOD, .5 BLOCKS					
	OBJECTIVES	PACING	RESOURCES: Print	RESOURCES: Online	TEKS	ELPS
Connect						
DIGITAL START UP ACTIVITY **The Search for Spices**		5 min.		●	1.D	
Investigate						
READ **Causes of European Exploration**	Objective 1	10 min.	●	●	1.D	
READ **Portugal Explores the Seas**	Objectives 2, 3	10 min.	●	●	1.D, 7.A	3.H.3
INTERACTIVE MAP **Early Voyages of European Exploration, 1487–1522**		10 min.		●	1.D	
READ **Columbus Searches for a Route to Asia**	Objectives 2, 4	10 min.	●	●	1.D, 7.A	3.C.3
INTERACTIVE 3-D MODEL **Explorer's Ship**		10 min.		●		
READ **The Search for a Route to the Pacific**	Objective 4	10 min.	●	●	1.D	
INTERACTIVE GALLERY **Navigating the World**		10 min.		●	1.D	
Synthesize						
DIGITAL ACTIVITY **The Wealth of Asia**		5 min.		●	1.D, 7.A	
Demonstrate						
LESSON QUIZ **Lesson Quiz and Class Discussion Board**		10 min.		●	1.D, 7.A, 16.B	

Focus on Texas Standards

Texas Essential Knowledge and Skills

1.D identify major causes and describe the major effects of the following important turning points in world history from 1450 to 1750: the rise of the Ottoman Empire, the influence of the Ming dynasty on world trade, European exploration and the Columbian Exchange, European expansion, and the Renaissance and the Reformation	**7.A** analyze the causes of European expansion from 1450 to 1750

NOTES

Europeans Gain Footholds in Asia

Objectives

Objective 1: Summarize how Portugal built a trading empire in South and Southeast Asia.

Objective 2: Analyze the rise of Dutch and Spanish dominance in Asia and the Indian Ocean.

Objective 3: Understand how the decline of Mughal India affected European traders in the region.

Objective 4: Describe European contacts with Ming and Qing China.

Objective 5: Summarize Korea's and Japan's attitudes toward contact with the outside world.

LESSON 2 ORGANIZER — **PACING: APPROX. 1 PERIOD, .5 BLOCKS**

	OBJECTIVES	PACING	RESOURCES: Print	RESOURCES: Online	TEKS	ELPS
Connect						
DIGITAL START UP ACTIVITY **Gunfire Over Malacca**		5 min.		●	1.D, 7.A, 16.B	
Investigate						
READ **Portugal Builds an Empire in Asia**	Objective 1	10 min.	●	●	1.D, 7.A, 16.B	
READ **Rise of the Dutch and the Spanish**	Objective 2	10 min.	●	●	1.D, 7.A, 16.B	
READ **European Trade in Mughal India**	Objectives 1, 2, 3	10 min.	●	●	1.D, 7.A, 16.B	
INTERACTIVE CHART **European Footholds in the Eastern Hemisphere**		10 min.		●	1.D, 7.A, 16.B	
READ **Ming China and Europe**	Objective 4	10 min.	●	●	1.D, 7.E	3.C.4
READ **The Manchus Conquer China**		10 min.	●	●	1.D	
INTERACTIVE MAP **Trade Among Europe, Africa, and Asia**		10 min.		●	1.D, 7.A	
READ **Korea and Japan Choose Isolation**	Objective 5	10 min.	●	●	1.D	
Synthesize						
DIGITAL ACTIVITY **International Trade: Different Approaches**		5 min.		●	1.D, 7.A, 16.B	
Demonstrate						
LESSON QUIZ **Lesson Quiz and Class Discussion Board**		10 min.		●	1.D, 7.A, 16.B	

PEARSON realize
www.PearsonTexas.com
Access your Digital Lesson

Focus on Texas Standards

Texas Essential Knowledge and Skills

1.D identify major causes and describe the major effects of the following important turning points in world history from 1450 to 1750: the rise of the Ottoman Empire, the influence of the Ming dynasty on world trade, European exploration and the Columbian Exchange, European expansion, and the Renaissance and the Reformation	**16.B** analyze the influence of human and physical geographic factors on major events in world history, including the development of river valley civilizations, trade in the Indian Ocean, and the opening of the Panama and Suez canals

NOTES

European Conquests in the Americas

Objectives

Objective 1: Analyze the results of the first encounters between the Spanish and Native Americans.

Objective 2: Explain how the Aztec and Inca empires were impacted by Spanish conquistadors and European colonization.

Objective 3: Describe how Portugal and other European nations challenged Spanish power.

Objective 4: Analyze the major features of Spanish colonial government, society, and culture.

Objective 5: Describe the impact of Spanish colonization of the Americas.

LESSON 3 ORGANIZER — **PACING: APPROX. 1 PERIOD, .5 BLOCKS**

	OBJECTIVES	PACING	RESOURCES Print	RESOURCES Online	TEKS	ELPS
Connect						
DIGITAL START UP ACTIVITY **Moctezuma Is Filled with Terror**		5 min.		●	1.D, 6.B	
Investigate						
READ **First Encounters**	Objective 1	10 min.	●	●	1.D	
READ **Cortés Conquers the Aztecs**	Objective 2	10 min.	●	●	1.D, 6.B, 16.A	
READ **The Incan Empire and Beyond**	Objectives 2, 3	10 min.	●	●	1.D, 6.B	
INTERACTIVE MAP **Spanish and Portuguese Colonies in the Americas**	Objectives 2, 3	10 min.		●	1.D, 6.B	
READ **Governing the Spanish Empire**	Objective 4	10 min.	●	●	1.D, 7.A	3.D.1
READ **Society and Culture in Spanish America**	Objective 4	10 min.	●	●	1.D	
READ **The Impact of Spanish Colonization**	Objective 5	10 min.	●	●	1.D	
INTERACTIVE CHART **Causes and Effects of Spanish Colonization**	Objective 5	10 min.		●	1.D	
Synthesize						
DIGITAL ACTIVITY **Unexpected Impacts**		5 min.		●	1.D, 6.B	
Demonstrate						
DIGITAL QUIZ **Lesson Quiz and Class Discussion Board**		10 min.		●	1.D, 6.B, 7.A	

PEARSON realize™ www.PearsonTexas.com Access your Digital Lesson

Focus on Texas Standards

Texas Essential Knowledge and Skills

1.D identify major causes and describe the major effects of the following important turning points in world history from 1450 to 1750: the rise of the Ottoman Empire, the influence of the Ming dynasty on world trade, European exploration and the Columbian Exchange, European expansion, and the Renaissance and the Reformation

6.B explain how the Inca and Aztec empires were impacted by European exploration/colonization

7.A analyze the causes of European expansion from 1450 to 1750

NOTES

European Colonies in North America

Objectives

Objective 1: Explain why the colony of New France grew slowly.

Objective 2: Analyze the establishment and growth of the English colonies.

Objective 3: Understand why Europeans competed for power in North America and how their struggle affected Native Americans.

LESSON 4 ORGANIZER	PACING: APPROX. 1 PERIOD, .5 BLOCKS					
			RESOURCES			
	OBJECTIVES	PACING	Print	Online	TEKS	ELPS
Connect						
DIGITAL START UP ACTIVITY **Competing for a Continent**		5 min.		●	1.D	
Investigate						
READ **New France**	Objective 1	10 min.	●	●	1.D, 7.A	
INTERACTIVE MAP **European Colonization of North America, About 1700**	Objective 1	10 min.		●	1.D, 7, 7.A	
READ **The 13 English Colonies**	Objective 2	10 min.	●	●	1.D, 7.A	
READ **A Power Struggle Begins**	Objective 3	10 min.	●	●	1.D, 7.A	3.D.2
INTERACTIVE CHART **Characteristics of French and English Colonies**	Objective 3	10 min.		●		
Synthesize						
DIGITAL ACTIVITY **A Conquest of the Greatest Importance**		5 min.		●	1.D	
Demonstrate						
DIGITAL QUIZ **Lesson Quiz and Class Discussion Board**		10 min.		●	1.D, 7.A	

PEARSON realize™ www.PearsonTexas.com Access your Digital Lesson

Focus on Texas Standards

Texas Essential Knowledge and Skills

1.D identify major causes and describe the major effects of the following important turning points in world history from 1450 to 1750: the rise of the Ottoman Empire, the influence of the Ming dynasty on world trade, European exploration and the Columbian Exchange, European expansion, and the Renaissance and the Reformation	**7.A** analyze the causes of European expansion from 1450 to 1750

NOTES

The Slave Trade and Its Impact on Africa

Objectives

Objective 1: Summarize the expansion of the African slave trade.

Objective 2: Explain how triangular trade worked.

Objective 3: Understand the nature of the Middle Passage and describe its effects.

Objective 4: Analyze the impact of the Atlantic slave trade on West Africa and the Americas.

LESSON 5 ORGANIZER		PACING: APPROX. 1 PERIOD, .5 BLOCKS				
	OBJECTIVES	PACING	RESOURCES Print	RESOURCES Online	TEKS	ELPS
Connect						
DIGITAL START UP ACTIVITY **Slave Ships From West Africa**		5 min.		●	7.C	
Investigate						
READ **The African Slave Trade Expands**	Objective 1	10 min.	●	●	1.D, 4.I, 7.A, 7.C	
READ **The Atlantic Slave Trade**	Objective 2	10 min.	●	●	1.D, 4.I, 7.C	
INTERACTIVE MAP **Triangular Trade Routes**		10 min.		●		
READ **Horrors of the Middle Passage**	Objective 3	10 min.	●	●	1.D, 7.C	
READ **Impact of the Slave Trade**	Objective 4	10 min.	●	●	7.C	3.E.1
INTERACTIVE CHART **Effects of Slavery**		10 min.		●	7.C	
Synthesize						
DIGITAL ACTIVITY **Trade**		5 min.		●	7.C	
Demonstrate						
DIGITAL QUIZ **Lesson Quiz and Class Discussion Board**		10 min.		●		

NOTES

Effects of Global Contact

Objectives

Objective 1: Explain how European exploration led to the Columbian Exchange.

Objective 2: Explain new economic factors and principles that contributed to the success of the commercial revolution.

Objective 3: Understand the impact of mercantilism on European and colonial economies.

LESSON 6 ORGANIZER	PACING: APPROX. 1 PERIOD, .5 BLOCKS					
			RESOURCES			
	OBJECTIVES	PACING	Print	Online	TEKS	ELPS
Connect						
DIGITAL START UP ACTIVITY **Uniting Distant Parts of the World**		5 min.		●	1.D, 7.B	
Investigate						
READ **The Columbian Exchange**	Objective 1	10 min.	●	●	1.D, 7.A, 7.B	3.F.1
INTERACTIVE MAP **The Columbian Exchange**	Objective 1	10 min.		●	1.D, 7.A, 7.B	
READ **A Commercial Revolution**	Objective 2	10 min.	●	●	1.D, 7.F, 18.F	
INTERACTIVE CHART **Economic Concepts**	Objective 2	10 min.		●	1.D, 7.F, 18.F	
READ **Mercantilism**	Objective 3	10 min.	●	●	7.F	
Synthesize						
DIGITAL ACTIVITY **Capitalism and Mercantilism**		5 min.		●	7.B, 7.F, 18.F	
Demonstrate						
DIGITAL QUIZ **Lesson Quiz and Class Discussion Board**		10 min.		●	1.D, 7.B, 7.F, 18.F	

Focus on Texas Standards

Texas Essential Knowledge and Skills

1.D identify major causes and describe the major effects of the following important turning points in world history from 1450 to 1750: the rise of the Ottoman Empire, the influence of the Ming dynasty on world trade, European exploration and the Columbian Exchange, European expansion, and the Renaissance and the Reformation

7.B explain the impact of the Columbian Exchange on the Americas and Europe

7.F explain new economic factors and principles that contributed to the success of Europe's Commercial Revolution

18.F formulate generalizations on how economic freedom improved the human condition, based on students' knowledge of the benefits of free enterprise in Europe's Commercial Revolution, the Industrial Revolution, and 20th-century free market economies, compared to communist command communities

NOTES

New Global Connections (1415–1796)

In this Topic, you will learn about Global Connections from the early 1400s to the late 1700s. You will also find lots of ways to investigate the ideas of this Topic and to master the TEKS.

Your study will help you master these TEKS:

TEKS

1.D, 4.F, 4.I, 6.B, 7.A, 7.B, 7.C, 7.E, 7.F, 16.A, 16.B, 18.F

LESSON OUTLINE

11.1: Europeans Explore Overseas **1.D, 7.A, 16.B**

11.2: Europeans Gain Footholds in Asia **1.D, 7.A, 16.B**

11.3: European Conquests in the Americas **1.D, 6.B, 7.A, 16.A**

11.4: European Colonies in North America **1.D, 7.A**

11.5: The Slave Trade and Its Impact on Africa **1.D, 4.I, 7.A, 7.C**

11.6: Effects of Global Contact **1.D, 7.B, 7.F, 18.F**

Connect

Connect with this Topic by watching a video about a person related to global connections. You can think about how this Topic connects to your own life. And you'll encounter an intriguing Essential Question: Why do people move?

Begin your study by trying the following:

NBC LEARN Watch My Story Video:

Hérnán Cortés and Moctezuma, The Conquest of a Golden City

Launch your Document-Based Question:

Columbian Exchange

Investigate

Then you will investigate the Topic through a group of lessons. The story of global connections will come to life as you read and interact with key content. You will get a chance to read about what happened and why. And you'll be able to interact with a lot of fascinating online materials.

And keep working on your Document-Based Question to help build your mastery of the Topic TEKS.

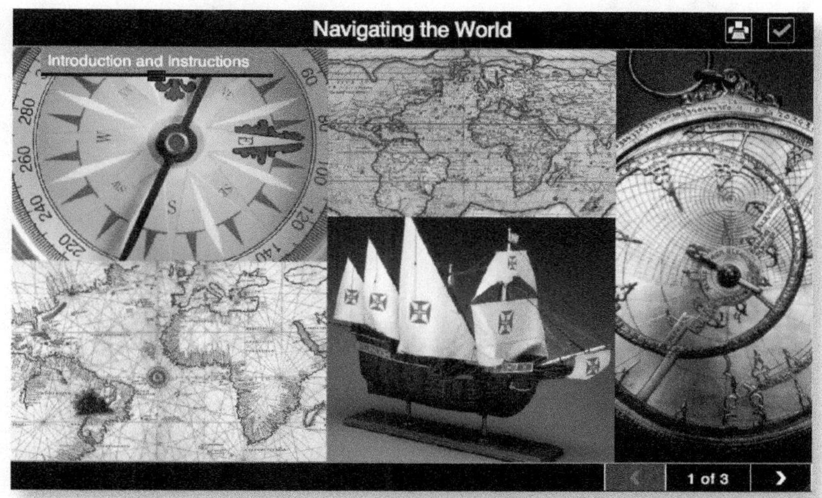

>> Digital interactivity from the online course

Synthesize

Next you will pull it all together by reflecting on the Essential Question. This will give you a chance to be the storyteller, to show how you would answer this big question: Why do people move?

Demonstrate

Finally, you can show what you know. You can write an essay, hold a discussion, or make a presentation. You can answer questions about every TEKS on the Topic Review and Assessment pages. Or you can finish essay on the Columbian Exchange.

TEKS in Topic 11	Topic Review and Assessment Questions
1.D	1, 2, 3, 4, 6, 7, 8, 13, 14
4.F	11
4.I	15
6.B	3, 4
7.A	3, 13
7.B	6
7.C	12, 14
7.E	10
7.F	5
16.A	1
16.B	9
18.F	5

Topic 11

New Global Connections (1415–1796)

Introduction

Beginning in the 1400s, European voyages of exploration ushered in an era of new global connections. Migration and commerce across the Indian and Atlantic Ocean led to European expansion, the Columbian Exchange, and the Atlantic slave trade. These and other developments affected people in Europe, Africa, Asia, and the Americas. As a result, some civilizations increased in power and wealth, while others declined. How did the movement of people during this era of global connections shape the world we live in today?

ESSENTIAL QUESTION

Ask students to think about the Essential Question for this Topic: Why do people move? Have them explain in writing the reasons that the following factors might cause people to move: conflict, environmental change, economic conditions, religious differences, and political or social conditions.

Express Ideas Clearly Invite volunteers to share their ideas with the class, expressing clearly how one or more of the factors cause movement of people.

Express Problems Clearly What problems might people have to overcome in order to successfully move? *(Sample responses: long distance, cost of travel, harsh weather and geography, attacks along the way)* After they have moved, what new problems might arise? *(Sample responses: conflict with native inhabitants, inadequate supplies, unfamiliar territory, need to establish new home)*

Hypothesize Based on what students have learned about European civilization around the 1400s, why do they think Europeans began to move beyond their own continent? *(Sample responses: Renaissance spirit of curiosity, to flee harsh rulers, to find more profitable work, to trade with other regions)*

Analyze Images

Tell students that this map of the world dates to the late 1500s. Ask students to identify areas of the map that look accurate, and what the shapes of North America, South America, and Australia indicate to them.

Texas Essential Knowledge and Skills

1.D, 4.F, 4.I, 6.B, 7.A, 7.B, 7.C, 7.E, 7.F, 16.A, 16.B, 18.F

Enduring Understandings

- During the Renaissance, Europeans sought to profit from trade with Asian lands, and new technologies made long ocean trading voyages possible.
- Desire for wealth led European nations to establish colonies in the Americas. In North America, colonial rivalries led to war.
- The transatlantic slave trade began as Spain sought labor for its American colonies, and the Middle Passage brought misery to millions of enslaved Africans.
- The voyages of European explorers eventually led to the growth of capitalism, the adoption of the economic policy of mercantilism, and other economic changes in Europe.

>> Map of the world, late 1500s

Watch the My Story Video to learn about the Spanish conquest of Mexico.

PEARSON realize www.PearsonTexas.com **Access your digital lessons including:** Topic Inquiry • Interactive Reading Notepad • Interactivities • Assessments

419

NBC LEARN MY STORY VIDEO

Project the My Story Video that introduces students to the Spanish conquest of Mexico.

Online My Story Video: **Hernán Cortés and Moctezuma, The Conquest of a Golden City**

After viewing, ask students to respond to the following questions.

Check Understanding What factors helped the Spanish defeat the Aztecs? *(alliances with other native peoples, the death of Moctezuma, disease)*

Hypothesize How might history have been different if Moctezuma had not believed Cortés to be the god Quetzalcoatl? *(He might not have welcomed the strangers but, with his superior numbers, have driven them out of his land.)*

OVERVIEW ACTIVITY

Online Project the **Timeline: New Global Connections** showing some major events of the era of new global connections. During their work on this Topic, students will learn about all of these events and many more, but this timeline will provide a framework into which they can place the events they learn about.

Check Understanding About how much time passed between the arrival of Europeans in the Caribbean and Britain's establishment of dominance in North America? *(about 270 years)*

Topic Inquiry

If you choose to assign the Topic Inquiry, launch the DBQ Activity with students after introducing the Topic.

D Differentiate Challenge/Gifted During the overview activity, suggest that students copy the timeline onto their own paper and add entries to it as they read the chapter. Have them make a final, clean copy after they read all six lessons, and discuss the new entries as a class.

Topic 11 Lesson 1

Europeans Explore Overseas

CONNECT

Preview Have students preview the **Lesson Objectives** and the list of **Key Terms**.

Students can also preview all the **Key Terms** and **Academic Vocabulary** using the **Interactive Reading Notepad** on the digital course or preview a summary of the lesson in the **Reading and Note Taking Study Guide**.

Online Use the **Editable Presentation** found on the digital course to present the main ideas for this lesson.

Start Up Activity

Tell students that spices were a vital part of the world economy in the 1400s. Europeans were desperate to find and secure supplies of these spices. However, Arab merchants and traders controlled the spice trade. Ask students to answer the following question.

Discuss If you were a king or queen in Europe during the 1400s, how do you think you would respond when an explorer asked for your help to pay for a voyage to find a direct route to the Asian source of spices? *(Students may say that the potential prestige and profits outweigh the costs and risks.)*

Tell students that in this lesson they will learn why and how Europeans began to explore Africa, Asia, and the Americas.

Online You can also project the **Start Up Activity** from the course.

INVESTIGATE

Have students read the lesson using the **Reading and Note Taking Study Guide** to help them take notes and understand the text as they read.

Causes of European Exploration

There were several causes of European exploration in the 1400s. A main reason was that Europeans wanted to find a direct sea route to access the valuable spices of East Asia. Other causes of exploration were the Renaissance spirit of curiosity, the desire to spread Christianity, and competition with other European powers.

Key Terms

Have students find the key term **Moluccas** (in bold) in the text on this page and identify its European name. Then have students locate the islands on the map on this page.

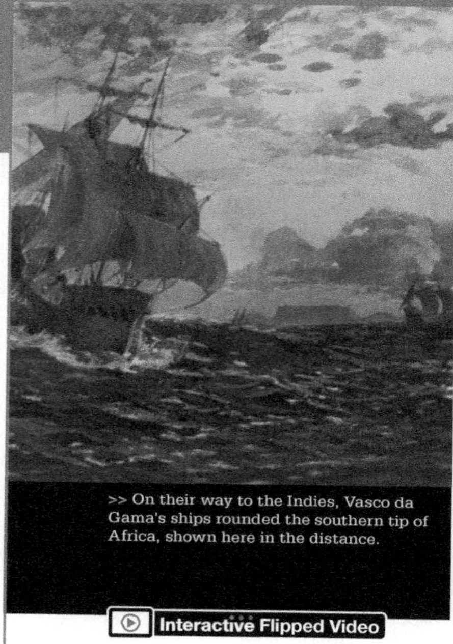

>> On their way to the Indies, Vasco da Gama's ships rounded the southern tip of Africa, shown here in the distance.

Interactive Flipped Video

11.1 **Starting in the 1400s, Europeans undertook a flurry of exploration, mapping new sea routes around the world. This great age of exploration was fueled by many causes, but at first, the most important cause was the search for spices.**

TEKS
1.D, 7.A

>> Objectives

Understand the major causes of European exploration.

Analyze early Portuguese and Spanish explorations and expansion.

Describe how the Portuguese established footholds on Africa's coasts.

Describe European searches for a direct route to Asia.

>> Key Terms

Moluccas
Prince Henry
cartographer
Mombasa
Malindi
Vasco da Gama
Christopher Columbus
Line of Demarcation
Treaty of Tordesillas
Ferdinand Magellan
circumnavigate
Cape Town
Boers

PEARSON realize www.PearsonTexas.com Access your Digital Lesson.

Europeans Explore Overseas

Causes of European Exploration

European Trade with Asia Europeans had traded with Asia long before the Renaissance. During the Middle Ages, the Crusades introduced Europeans to many luxury goods from Asia. When the Mongol empire united much of Asia in the 1200s and 1300s, Asian goods flowed to Europe along complex overland trade routes.

The Black Death and the breakup of the Mongol empire disrupted Asian trade routes, but by the 1400s, Europe's population was growing—as was the demand for goods from Asia. The most valued trade items were spices, such as cloves, cinnamon, and pepper. People used spices to preserve and add flavor to food, and to make medicines and perfumes.

The chief source of spices was the **Moluccas,** an island chain in present-day Indonesia. Europeans called the Moluccas the Spice Islands.

The Drive to Explore In the 1400s, Arab and Italian merchants controlled most trade between Asia and Europe. Muslim traders brought spices and other goods to Mediterranean ports in Egypt,

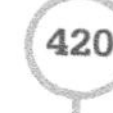

Aa Vocabulary Builder

1. Have students pronounce the following academic vocabulary terms in this lesson and clarify the part of speech. For difficult or polysyllabic words, break them into syllables and pronounce them with the students.
2. Explain what the word means in common "student-friendly" language using synonyms and antonyms when possible. Provide concrete examples to clarify the meaning, and rephrase the definition.

authority: the power to give commands and enforce obedience

affluent: having a large amount of money and owning many expensive things

demarcation: delimiting or setting apart

immigrant: a person who comes to a country to take up permanent residence

Syria, and Turkey. From there, Italian traders carried them to European markets. Each time goods passed from one trader to another, prices increased.

Europeans wanted to cut out the Muslim and Italian middlemen and gain direct access to the riches of Asia. To do so, the Atlantic powers sought a new route to Asia, one that bypassed the Mediterranean.

Many explorers hoped to get rich by entering the spice trade or conquering other lands. Yet the desire for wealth was not the only motive that lured them to sea. Some missionaries and soldiers ventured overseas to win new converts to Christianity. The Renaissance spirit of curiosity also fed a desire to learn more about lands beyond Europe.

Improved Technology Improvements in technology helped Europeans cross vast oceans. Cartographers, or mapmakers, created more accurate maps and sea charts. European sailors also learned how to use the astrolabe, an instrument used to determine latitude at sea. The astrolabe was first developed by the ancient Greeks and later perfected by the Arabs.

Along with more reliable navigational tools, Europeans designed larger and better ships. The Portuguese developed the caravel, which combined the square sails of European ships with Arab lateen, or triangular, sails. Caravels also adapted the sternpost rudder and numerous masts of Chinese ships. The new rigging made it easier to sail across, or even into, the wind. Finally, European ships added more armaments, including sturdier cannons.

? IDENTIFY What were the major causes of European exploration?

Portugal Explores the Seas

Portugal, a small nation on the western edge of Spain, led the way in exploration. As in Spain, Christian knights in Portugal had fought to end Muslim rule. By the 1400s, Portugal was strong enough to expand into Muslim North Africa. In 1415, the Portuguese seized Ceuta (SAY oo tah) on the North African coast. The victory sparked the imagination of **Prince Henry,** known to history as Henry the Navigator.

The African Coast Mapped Prince Henry saw great promise in Africa. The Portuguese could convert Africans—most of whom practiced either Islam or native religions—to Christianity. He also believed that in Africa he would find the sources of the gold Muslim traders controlled.

Finally, Prince Henry hoped to find an easier way to reach Asia that bypassed the Mediterranean, which

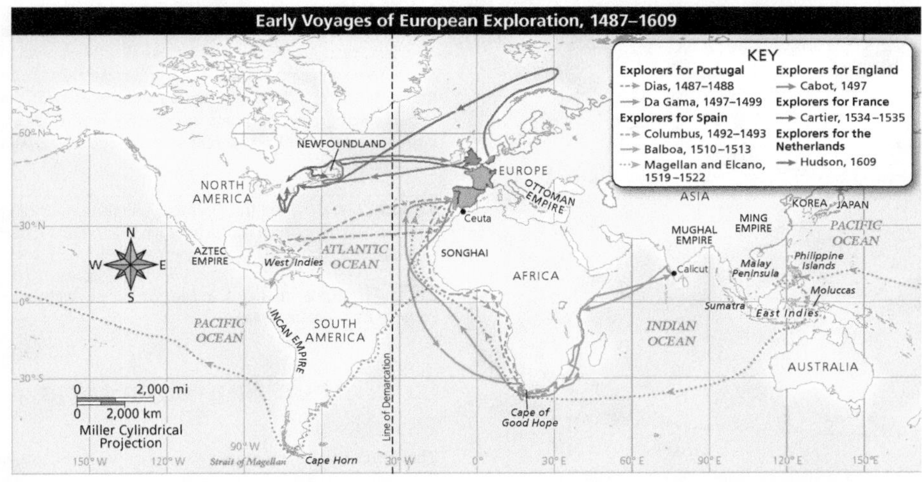

>> **Analyze Maps** Portugal led the way in exploring the world by ship. Spain and other countries soon followed. How did Magellan's route to Asia differ from the routes of other explorers?

 Interactive Map

Topic 11 Lesson 1

Guided Reading and Discussion

Ask students to explain the importance of the spice trade and how it affected global trade.

Identify Supporting Details Ask students to identify details that explain why Europeans valued spices so highly. *(They wanted spices to flavor food and to make medicines and perfumes.)*

Infer Why do you think Arab and Italian traders were able to retain control of the spice trade? *(Students may infer that Arabs controlled the overland routes to the Middle East and that Italian merchant ships controlled trade across the eastern Mediterranean Sea.)*

Portugal Explores the Seas

Tell students that Portuguese ships under Prince Henry's sponsorship were the first Europeans to venture far out into the Atlantic Ocean. They were soon followed by the Spanish. The Portuguese applied their growing naval knowledge and technology to exploration. They built forts and trading posts along the African coast, sailed across the Indian Ocean to India, and gained control of the spice trade.

Online Project the **Interactive Map: Early Voyages of European Exploration, 1487–1522** and check the boxes in the key to locate different explorers' routes. If students do not have access to the Interactive Map, have them view the map "Early Voyages of European Exploration" on this page.

Analyze Maps Ask students to describe the spice trade route that Arab and Italian merchants dominated. Ask: Which European countries sent explorers into the Atlantic Ocean? Why?

English Language Proficiency Standards

Speaking 3.H.3 Read "Portugal Explores the Seas" aloud. Tell students that explaining what they learn shows that they understand a topic.

Beginning Reread the passage aloud. Have students use words and phrases from the text to explain how Portuguese explorers influenced East African trade. Create a sentence or two from the words and phrases as a model. If possible, have students create their own sentences.

Intermediate Reread the passage aloud. Have students explain how Portuguese explorers influenced East African trade, using vocabulary from the text and paraphrasing what they read.

Advanced Have student pairs reread the passage. Ask pairs to explain why the Portuguese empire in Africa declined. Challenge students to use detailed information.

Advanced High Have students work alone to complete the Advanced High activity. Challenge them to use detailed information.

Answers

Identify *desire to gain direct access goods in Asia, to spread Christianity, to gain wealth, and to satisfy Renaissance curiosity by learning more about lands beyond Europe*

Analyze Maps *Unlike other explorers, who traveled east around Africa, Magellan reached Asia by traveling west, around South America, across the Pacific, to Asia.*

Topic 11 Lesson 1

ACTIVE CLASSROOM

Have students write and then discuss several headlines that capture the action in the Interactive Map "Early Voyages of European Discovery." Ask: If you were to tweet news headlines that captured the most important events of this Topic, what would those headlines be? Exchange your headlines with a partner to review and improve. *(Sample headlines: Prince Henry gathers navigation and technology experts; Portuguese explore west coast of Africa; Bartholomeu Dias reaches southern tip of Africa; Vasco da Gama reaches India; Portuguese seize control of Indian Ocean spice trade)*

D Differentiate Extra Support Ask students to create a chart with two columns labeled "Explorer" and "Accomplishments." Then have them complete the chart with the names of Portuguese explorers and their major accomplishments. Then discuss how each person's accomplishments were based on the previous accomplishments.

Guided Reading and Discussion

Ask students to explain the Portuguese military and commercial presence in Africa.

Draw Conclusions Why do you think the Portuguese limited their footholds in Africa to coastal forts and trading posts and did not explore much into the interior? *(Sample response: The Portuguese were only interested in trading profitably in Africa. They had little desire to settle or colonize the interior. African groups resisted Portuguese efforts to explore the interior and take control of the gold trade.)*

meant going around Africa. The Portuguese felt that with their expert knowledge and technology, they could accomplish this feat. At Sagres, in southern Portugal, Henry gathered scientists, **cartographers,** or mapmakers, and other experts. They redesigned ships, prepared maps, and trained captains and crews for long voyages.

Henry then sent ships that slowly worked their way south to explore the coast of West Africa. Henry died in 1460, but the Portuguese continued their quest.

Portuguese Footholds in Africa The Portuguese built small forts in West Africa to collect food and water and to repair their ships. They also established trading posts to trade muskets, tools, and cloth for gold, ivory, hides, and slaves. These were not colonies peopled by settlers. Instead, the Portuguese left just enough men and firepower to defend their forts.

From West Africa, the Portuguese sailed around the continent. In 1488, Bartholomeu Dias rounded the southern tip of Africa.

Despite the turbulent seas around it, the tip became known as the Cape of Good Hope because it opened the way for a trade route through the Indian Ocean to Asia.

>> **Identify** This colored woodcut, "World Map According to Ptolemy" (1541), shows early European geographic knowledge. Which regions are shown most inaccurately? Explain.

The Portuguese continued to establish forts and trading posts, but they also attacked East African coastal cities such as **Mombasa** and **Malindi,** which were hubs of international trade. With cannons blazing, they expelled the Arabs who controlled the East African trade network and took over this thriving commerce for themselves. Each conquest added to their growing trade empire.

Over the next two centuries, some Portuguese explorers managed to reach parts of present-day Congo, Zambia, and Zimbabwe, establishing limited trade. In general, however, the Portuguese did not venture far from Africa's coasts. They knew little about the interior of Africa, and they lacked accurate maps or other resources to help them explore there. Furthermore, Africans in the interior, who wanted to control the gold trade, resisted such exploration.

Beyond Africa: Reaching India In 1497, Portuguese navigator **Vasco da Gama** followed in Dias's footsteps, leading four ships around the Cape of Good Hope. Da Gama, however, had plans to go farther. After a ten-month voyage, da Gama reached the great spice port of Calicut on the west coast of India. On the long voyage home, the Portuguese lost half their ships, and many sailors died of hunger, thirst, and scurvy, a disease caused by a lack of vitamin C in the diet.

Despite the suffering, the venture proved highly profitable to survivors. In India, da Gama had acquired a cargo of spices that he sold at an enormous profit. He quickly outfitted a new fleet, seeking greater profits. In 1502, he forced a treaty on the ruler of Calicut. Da Gama then left Portuguese merchants there whose job was to buy spices when prices were low and store them until the next fleet could return. Before long, the Portuguese began seizing other outposts around the Indian Ocean, building a vast trading empire and making Portugal a world power.

? EXPLAIN How did the Portuguese create a trading empire stretching from Africa through the Indian Ocean to India?

ELPS **ELPS 3.H.3** Practice explaining details of *Portugal Explores the Seas.*

Columbus Searches for a Route to Asia

The profitable Portuguese voyages spurred other European nations to seek a sea route to Asia. An Italian navigator from the port of Genoa, **Christopher Columbus,** wanted to reach the East Indies—a group

English Language Proficiency Standards

Speaking 3.C.3 Read "Columbus Searches for a Route to Asia" aloud to students. Ask students to practice recognizing and speaking different types of sentences by completing the activities according to their English proficiency.

Beginning Write and display a declarative sentence from the passage. Then slowly read it aloud and have students repeat it. Modify the sentence to turn it into an interrogative sentence. Write and display the interrogative sentence, read it, and have students repeat it. Finally, turn this question into a declarative sentence and have students repeat it.

Intermediate Write and display several declarative sentences from the passage. Have students say the sentences aloud. Then help students turn the sentences into interrogative sentences. Write and display these questions. Point out the similarities and differences between the types of sentences. Then have students choose a declarative sentence from the text and modify it to create their own interrogative sentence.

Answers

Explain *The Portuguese explored and discovered a sea route around Africa to India, established forts and trading posts along the African coast, seized key ports around the Indian Ocean, and sent merchant ships to and from India.*

Identify *Sample response: Africa's shape is distorted. The Indian subcontinent appears very small compared to its actual size.*

The Treaty of Tordesillas, 1494

CAUSES	KEY PROVISIONS OF TREATY	EFFECTS
• Columbus explored Caribbean islands. • Spain, seeking wealth and power, claimed control of the islands. • Portugal, with its own ambitions, disputed Spain's claims. • Aided by Pope Alexander IV, Spain and Portugal negotiated a treaty.	• Lands discovered west of a meridian 370 leagues west of the Cape Verde Islands would belong to Spain. • Lands discovered east of a meridian 370 leagues west of the Cape Verde Islands would belong to Portugal.	• Treaty favored Spain: most of Americas was west of the line. • Spain claimed much of the Americas. • Spanish colonies yielded incredible wealth for Spain, especially silver and gold. • Spanish language and culture became key elements of Latin American culture. • Brazil became a Portuguese colony and retains much Portuguese culture today. • England, France, and other countries did not recognize the agreement and established their own colonies in the Americas.

>> **Analyze Charts** The Treaty of Tordesillas resolved a major territorial dispute between Spain and Portugal. Whose rights and claims were not addressed by this treaty?

of islands in Southeast Asia, today part of Indonesia—by sailing west across the Atlantic. Like most educated Europeans, Columbus knew that Earth was a sphere. A few weeks sailing west, he reasoned, would bring a ship to eastern Asia. His plan made sense, but Columbus greatly underestimated Earth's size—and he had no idea that two continents, North and South America, lay in his path.

Reaching Faraway Lands Portugal refused to sponsor him, but Columbus persuaded Ferdinand and Isabella of Spain to finance his voyage. To increase their authority, the Spanish rulers had taken radical measures, including expelling Jews from Spain. They hoped their actions would strengthen Catholicism. However, the loss of some of Spain's most affluent and cultured people weakened the nation. The rulers hoped Columbus's voyage would bring wealth and prestige.

On August 3, 1492, Columbus sailed west with three small ships, the *Niña*, the *Pinta*, and the *Santa María*. Although the expedition encountered good weather and a favorable wind, no land came into sight for many weeks. Provisions ran low, and the crew became anxious. Finally, on October 12, land was spotted.

Columbus spent several months cruising the islands of the Caribbean. Because he thought he had reached the Indies, he called the people of the region "Indians." In 1493, he returned to Spain to a hero's welcome. In three later voyages, Columbus remained convinced that he had reached the coast of east Asia. Before long, though, other Europeans realized that Columbus had found a route to previously unknown continents.

Spain and Portugal Divide Up the World Spain and Portugal each pressed rival claims to the islands Columbus explored. With the support of the pope, the two countries agreed to settle their claims and signed the **Treaty of Tordesillas** in 1494. It set a **Line of Demarcation,** dividing the non-European world into two zones. Spain had trading and exploration rights in any lands west of the line, including most of the Americas. Portugal had the same rights east of the line. The actual Line of Demarcation was unclear because geography at the time was not precise. However, the treaty allowed Spain and Portugal to claim vast areas in their zones. It also spurred other European nations to challenge Spanish and Portuguese claims and build their own trade empires.

Naming the Western Hemisphere An Italian sea captain named Amerigo Vespucci wrote a journal describing his voyage to Brazil. In 1507, a German cartographer named Martin Waldseemüller used Vespucci's descriptions of his voyage to publish a map of the region, which he labeled "America." Over time, the term "Americas" came to be used for both

Advanced Have student pairs write down three declarative sentences from the passage. Have partners say each sentence aloud together. Instruct partners to modify each declarative sentence into an interrogative sentence, an imperative sentence, and an exclamatory sentence. Finally, have each pair share their favorite set of sentences with the class.

Advanced High Have students discuss the passage with a partner. Ask students to use at least one declarative, one interrogative, one imperative, and one exclamatory sentence. Remind students to use rich and varied vocabulary. Finally, have each pair choose their favorite sentence(s) from their discussion to share with the class.

Columbus Searches for a Route to Asia

Explain to students that Columbus believed the world was round and that he could reach the spices of the East Indies by sailing west. Spain financed his voyage, hoping to gain riches and glory. Columbus landed not in the Indies, but in the Americas. Soon after, Spain and Portugal agreed to a treaty dividing the newly discovered lands into two zones, one for Spain and one for Portugal.

Guided Reading and Discussion

Ask students to explain the reasons for European voyages of exploration.

Point out to students that Portugal refused to sponsor Columbus, while Spain did not. Have students make a list of possible reasons why Portugal refused. *(Sample response: The Portuguese did not feel the need. They had already explored the coast of Africa. They hoped to reach the spice trade by sailing around Africa into the Indian Ocean. One year after Columbus reached the Americas, da Gama sailed across the Indian Ocean and reached India.)*

Hypothesize If Spain's rulers had known of the existence of the Americas and the actual size of the world, would they still have financed Columbus's voyage? Why or why not? *(Sample response: Yes, because they were eager to gain direct access to the spice trade, to gain wealth and glory for Spain, and to spread Christianity)*

Answers

Analyze Charts *Sample response: The treaty did not address territorial rights and claims of Native Americans or other European nations.*

The Search for a Route to the Pacific

European Expansion in Africa

The search for direct water routes to Asia continued. European explorers looked for ways through or around the Americas. Ferdinand Magellan led an expedition that sailed from Spain, around South America, and on to Asia. Meanwhile, Britain, France, and the Netherlands also joined the search and began developing their own trade networks.

Online Project the **Interactive Gallery: Navigating the World** and click through the hotspots. Discuss how such improvements in naval technology affected European exploration and expansion.

ACTIVE CLASSROOM

Tell students that they are explorers in the late 1400s or early 1500s. Ask them to rank the items from the Interactive Gallery according to which they think will be most useful on a voyage to find a route to the Pacific. Have students provide a justification for the rankings they make. Poll the class to see if there is agreement on the rankings.

Guided Reading and Discussion

Ask students to explain the reasons Europeans were looking for a route to the Pacific and the outcome of Magellan's voyage.

Analyze Images

Have students examine the infographic "To Sail Around the World: Magellan's Voyage, 1519–1522." Ask: Judging from the items and amounts shown, what skills and resources would be needed to assemble these materials?

continents of the Western Hemisphere. The islands Columbus had explored in the Caribbean became known as the West Indies.

INFER Why were Spanish rulers pleased with the Treaty of Tordesillas and Line of Demarcation?

ELPS **ELPS 3.C.3** Practice recognizing and saying sentences of different lengths in *Columbus Searches for a Route to Asia.*

The Search for a Route to the Pacific

Once Europeans realized that the Americas blocked a sea passage to India, they hunted for a route around or through the Americas in order to reach Asia. The English, Dutch, and French explored the coast of North America unsuccessfully for a "northwest passage," or a route from the Atlantic Ocean to the Pacific through the Arctic islands. Meanwhile, in 1513, the Spanish adventurer Vasco Núñez de Balboa, helped by local Indians, hacked a passage westward through the tropical forests of Panama. From a ridge on the west coast, he gazed at a huge body of water. The body of water that he named the South Sea was in fact the Pacific Ocean.

Magellan Sets Sail On September 20, 1519, a minor Portuguese nobleman named **Ferdinand Magellan** set out from Spain with five ships to find a way to reach the Pacific. Magellan's ships sailed south and west, through storms and calms and tropical heat. At last, his fleet reached the coast of South America. Carefully, they explored each bay, hoping to find one that would lead to the Pacific. In November 1520, Magellan's ships entered a bay at the southern tip of South America. Amid brutal storms, rushing tides, and unpredictable winds, Magellan found a passage that later became known as the Strait of Magellan. The ships emerged into Balboa's South Sea. Magellan renamed the sea the Pacific, from the Latin word meaning *peaceful.*

The Long Way Home Their mission accomplished, most of the crew wanted to return to Spain the way they had come. Magellan, however, insisted that they push on across the Pacific to the East Indies. Magellan underestimated the size of the Pacific. Three more weeks, he thought, would bring them to the Spice Islands. Magellan was wrong.

For nearly four months, the ships plowed across the uncharted ocean. Finally, in March 1521, the fleet reached the Philippines, where Magellan was killed. On September 8, 1522, nearly three years after setting out, the survivors—one ship and 18 sailors—reached

>> Months of careful planning, provisioning, and loading of supplies went into preparing for Magellan's voyage. Even so, during the long voyage, regular stops for fresh food and water were required.

Interactive 3-D Model

Answers

Infer *Spain gained exclusive exploration and trading rights over half the world, which helped expand its wealth and power and limited competition from rival European powers.*

Infer *Balboa established Spain's claim to the Pacific Ocean and surrounding land and spurred Magellan to seek a direct sea route to the Pacific and East Indies.*

Spain. The survivors had been the first people to **circumnavigate,** or sail around, the world. Antonio Pigafetta, one of the few survivors of the expedition, observed: "I believe of a certainty that no one will ever again make such a voyage."

INFER What was the significance of Balboa's discovery?

European Expansion in Africa

Following the Portuguese and Spanish examples, several other European powers sought to expand their trade networks. By the 1600s, the French, English, and Dutch all had footholds along the coast of West Africa. These outposts often changed hands as European countries battled for control of the new trade routes. Like the Portuguese, they used these footholds to protect and expand their trade routes in Africa, the Indian Ocean, and India.

The Dutch Settle Cape Town In 1652, Dutch settlers began to arrive at the southern tip of the continent. They built **Cape Town,** the first permanent European settlement in Africa, to supply ships sailing to or from the East Indies.

Dutch farmers, called **Boers,** settled around Cape Town. Over time, they ousted, enslaved, or killed the people who lived there. The Boers held a Calvinist belief that they were the elect, or chosen, of God. They looked on Africans as inferiors. In the 1700s, Boer herders and ivory hunters began to push north from the Cape Colony. As they did so, they battled powerful African groups like the Zulus who had settled in southern Africa.

The British and French Explore By the mid-1600s, the British and French had both reached present-day Senegal. The French established a fort in the region around 1700. In the late 1700s, stories about British explorers' search for the source of the Nile River sparked an interest in Africa among Europeans, especially the French and British. In 1788, the British established the African Association, an organization that sponsored explorers to Africa. Over the next century, European exploration of Africa would explode.

IDENTIFY Why did the European presence in Africa expand?

>> In the late 1600s, the Dutch colony at Cape Town was busy with arriving and departing ships.

Interactive Gallery

ASSESSMENT

1. **Identify Cause and Effect** Why did Europeans explore Africa, Asia, and the Americas beginning in the 1400s?
2. **Identify Steps in a Process** Describe how the Portuguese gained dominance of the spice trade.
3. **Draw Conclusions** How did competition between European countries such as Portugal and Spain affect overseas exploration and expansion?
4. **Summarize** Summarize European searches for a direct route across the Atlantic Ocean to Asia.
5. **Cite Evidence** How did religious beliefs cause Dutch immigrants to aggressively expand their settlements in southern Africa?

Identify Cause and Effect How did the need to replenish supplies and make repairs on the long voyages to Asia cause European expansion? *(Sample response: European countries established outposts along the routes of the long journeys, in Africa, the Americas, and eventually on islands in the Pacific.)*

SYNTHESIZE

Online Project the **Digital Activity: The Wealth of Asia**. Have students form small groups to write down brief answers to these questions: According to Boorstin, why did the Portuguese establish control over trade in the Indian Ocean? What trading powers lost power and wealth because of the new Portuguese trade routes? How would future international trade be different because of Western European countries developing new trade routes? Have the groups present their answers to the class.

DEMONSTRATE

Online Assign the **Digital Lesson Quiz** for this lesson if you haven't already done so. Students will be offered automatic remediation or enrichment based on their score.

Pose this question to the class:

Predict Consequences How will European exploration and expansion during this time affect much of the world? *(European colonization, expansion of the slave trade, or a blending of cultures)*

Topic Inquiry

Have students continue their investigations for the Topic Inquiry.

Answers

Identify *Various European powers took over Portuguese forts to expand their power in Africa, the Indian Ocean, and India.*

Assessment

1. Europeans explored Africa, Asia, and the Americas to find a direct route to Asian spices. Explorers also wished to spread Christianity and learn more about lands beyond Europe.
2. The Portuguese led Europe in early exploration for new trade routes by sea. They found a sea route around Africa to India. They built coastal forts and trading posts, conquered local peoples, made treaties, and established trade.
3. European nations competed to control ports and coastal territory and therefore control trade.
4. In 1492, Columbus sailed west from Spain and reached the Caribbean islands. The English, Dutch, and French unsuccessfully explored the coast of North America for a "northwest passage" from the Atlantic Ocean to the Pacific. Balboa hacked his way through Panama's tropical forests to find the Pacific. Magellan journeyed southwest from Spain and found a passage around South America's southern tip into the Pacific Ocean. His ships eventually reached Asia before continuing around the world.
5. The Boers were Calvinists who believed that they were God's chosen ones. They considered Africans inferior. They believed that they had the right to expand into southern Africa and push the native African people off their land.

Europeans Gain Footholds in Asia

CONNECT

Preview Have students preview the **Lesson Objectives** and the list of **Key Terms**.

Students can also preview all the **Key Terms** and **Academic Vocabulary** using the **Interactive Reading Notepad** on the digital course or preview a summary of the lesson in the **Reading and Note Taking Study Guide**.

Online Use the **Editable Presentation** found on the digital course to present the main ideas for this lesson.

Start Up Activity

Tell students that in 1511, a Portuguese fleet dropped anchor off Malacca, a port that controlled the sea route linking India, Southeast Asia, and China. It eventually opened fire.

Discuss Why do you think the fleet attacked Malacca? *(The Portuguese wanted control of the spice trade.)*

Tell students that in this lesson they will learn how Europeans built trading empires and established footholds in Asia.

Online You can also project the **Start Up Activity** from the course.

INVESTIGATE

Have students read the lesson using the **Reading and Note Taking Study Guide** to help them take notes and understand the text as they read.

Portugal Builds an Empire in Asia

Explain that Afonso de Albuquerque continued the exploration and expansion begun by Vasco da Gama, growing the Portuguese trading empire in India, the Indian Ocean, and Southeast Asia through a mixture of diplomacy and violence.

>> The experienced general and admiral Afonso de Albuquerque spearheaded Portugal's efforts to build a trade empire around the Indian Ocean.

Interactive Flipped Video

11.2 Portugal was the first European power to gain a foothold in Asia. The Portuguese ships were small in size and number, but the firepower of their shipboard cannons was unmatched. In time, this superior firepower helped them win control of the rich Indian Ocean spice trade and build a trading empire in Asia.

TEKS
1.D, 16.B

>> Objectives

Summarize how Portugal built a trading empire in South and Southeast Asia.

Analyze the rise of Dutch and Spanish dominance in Asia and the Indian Ocean.

Understand how the decline of Mughal India affected European traders in the region.

Describe European contacts with Ming and Qing China.

Summarize Korea's and Japan's attitudes toward contact with the outside world.

>> Key Terms

Afonso de Albuquerque
Mughal empire
Goa
Malacca
outpost
Dutch East India Company
sovereign
Philippines
sepoy
Macao
Guangzhou
Matteo Ricci
Manchus
Qing
Qianlong
Lord Macartney
Tokugawa
Nagasaki
Malacca

www.PearsonTexas.com Access your Digital Lesson.

Europeans Gain Footholds in Asia

Portugal Builds an Empire in Asia

Albuquerque in India After Vasco da Gama's voyage, the Portuguese, under **Afonso de Albuquerque's** command, burst into the Indian Ocean. By that time, Muslim rulers, originally from central Asia, had established the **Mughal empire** throughout much of India.

The southern regions of India, however, were still controlled by a patchwork of local princes. The Portuguese won these princes to their side with promises of aid against other Europeans. With these southern footholds, Albuquerque and the Portuguese hoped to end Muslim power and turn the Indian Ocean into a "Portuguese lake."

Trading Outposts Around the Indian Ocean In 1510, the Portuguese seized the island of **Goa** off the coast of India, making it their major military and commercial base. Albuquerque burned coastal towns and crushed Arab fleets at sea. The Portuguese took the East Indies port of **Malacca** in 1511, killing the city's Muslim inhabitants.

In less than 50 years, the Portuguese had built a trading empire with military and merchant **outposts,** or distant areas under their control, around the Indian Ocean. They used the cities they had seized

426

Aa Vocabulary Builder

1. Have students pronounce the following academic vocabulary terms in this lesson and clarify the part of speech. For difficult or polysyllabic words, break them into syllables and pronounce them with the students.
2. Explain what the word means in common "student-friendly" language using synonyms and antonyms when possible. Provide concrete examples to clarify the meaning, and rephrase the definition.

strategic: important to carrying out a plan of action

convert: to bring over from one belief, view, or party to another; to bring about a religious conversion

prosperous: marked by success or economic well-being

overseas: in or to a foreign country that is across a sea or ocean

multitude: a great number of things or people

porcelain: a hard, white substance that is very delicate and that is made by baking clay

imperial: relating to an empire or emperor

acknowledge: to say that you accept or do not deny the truth or existence of (something)

turbulent: full of confusion, violence, or disorder; not stable or steady

allegiance: loyalty or devotion to a cause or person

on the east coast of Africa to resupply and repair their ships. For most of the 1500s, Portugal controlled the spice trade between Europe and Asia.

Limits Impact Despite their sea power, the Portuguese remained on the fringe of Asian trade. They had neither the strength nor the resources to conquer much territory on land. In India and China, where they faced far stronger empires, they merely sought permission to trade.

The intolerance of Portuguese missionaries caused resentment. In Goa, they attacked Muslims, destroyed Hindu temples, and introduced the Inquisition. Portuguese ships even sank Muslim pilgrim ships on their way to Mecca. While the Portuguese disrupted some older trade patterns, exchanges continued among the peoples of Asia. Some bypassed Portuguese-controlled towns. Others traded with the newcomers.

In the late 1500s, Portuguese power declined overseas. By the early 1600s, other Europeans were vying to replace the Portuguese in the rich spice trade.

INFER How did the Portuguese use geographic factors to help them control the spice trade?

Rise of the Dutch and the Spanish

The Dutch were the first Europeans to challenge Portuguese domination of Asian trade. Their homeland (in the present-day Netherlands) was a group of provinces and prosperous trading cities which fell under Spanish rule in the early 1500s. Later, the Protestant northern provinces won independence and soon competed against Portugal to control the rich spice trade of the Indies.

Dutch Sea Power In 1599, a Dutch fleet returned to Amsterdam from Asia carrying a rich cargo of pepper, cloves, and other spices. This successful voyage led to a frenzy of overseas activity. Dutch warships and trading vessels soon made the Dutch leaders in European commerce. They used their sea power to set up colonies and trading posts around the world, including a strategic settlement at Cape Town.

The Dutch Dominate Indian Ocean Trade In 1602, a group of wealthy Dutch merchants formed the **Dutch East India Company.** Unlike Portuguese and Spanish traders, whose expeditions were tightly controlled by government, the Dutch East India Company had full **sovereign** powers. With its power to build armies, wage war, negotiate peace treaties, and govern overseas territory, it came to dominate the region.

In 1641, the Dutch captured Malacca from the Portuguese, opened trade with China, and soon enforced a monopoly in the Spice Islands. They controlled shipments to Europe as well as much of the trade within Southeast Asia. Like the Portuguese, the Dutch used military force to further their trading goals. Yet they forged closer ties with local rulers than the Portuguese had. Many Dutch merchants married Asian women. In the 1700s, however, the growing power of England and France contributed to a decline in the Dutch overseas trading empire.

Spain Captures the Philippines While the Portuguese and Dutch set up bases on the fringes of Asia, Spain took over the **Philippines.** Magellan had claimed the archipelago for Spain in 1521. Within about 50 years, Spain had conquered and colonized the islands, renaming them for the Spanish king Philip II. Unlike most other peoples of Southeast Asia, the Filipinos were not united. As a result, they could be conquered more easily.

In the spirit of the Catholic Reformation, Spanish priests set out to convert the Filipino people to Christianity. Later, missionaries from the Philippines tried to spread Catholic teachings in China and Japan.

>> This hand-colored woodcut illustration shows Dutch merchant galleons at sea during the 1600s. Note these ships' great storage capacity for trade goods.

Key Terms

Have students locate the term **sovereign** (in bold) in the text. Call on a volunteer to explain what the term means in the context of the paragraph. Then, point out to students that sovereignty—independent power and authority—is typically held only by a national government.

Guided Reading and Discussion

Compare How did Vasco da Gama's achievements compare with those of Afonso de Albuquerque? *(They were quite similar. Da Gama pioneered the route to India, forced a treaty on Calicut's ruler, and made highly profitable voyages. Albuquerque increased Portuguese power in India, went on to Southeast Asia, attacked coastal towns, destroyed Arab fleets, and seized the port of Malacca. Da Gama and Albuquerque built a Portuguese trading empire around the Indian Ocean and Southeast Asia.*

Rise of the Dutch and the Spanish

Tell students that Portugal's dominance of trade with Asia ended due to stiff competition. After Dutch warships defeated the Portuguese and seized Malacca, the Dutch East India Company dominated the spice trade. Meanwhile, Spain seized the Philippine Islands in the Pacific and established a trade network from the Americas through the Philippines to China.

History Background

Still Life in Holland In the 1600s, Holland enjoyed a golden age of art. After years of war in the Low Countries, there was finally peace at home, and the wealth provided by the overseas trade created a consumer class with enough disposable income to support the arts. Affluent burghers bought paintings and portraits to hang in their homes.

Amsterdam became not only a major commercial port, but also a rich cultural center that attracted artists such as Johannes Vermeer, Rembrandt von Rijn, and Willem Kalf. Rembrandt and his students developed the genre of the still life, depicting inanimate objects such as fruit or flowers. While other artists focused on religious or courtly themes, the Dutch turned toward nature. So prominent were these new kinds of paintings during the 1600s that the Dutch words *stilleven* and *landschap* were adapted into English as "still life" and "landscape."

Answers

Infer *They used force and diplomacy to establish coastal trading posts and take control of key ports around the Indian Ocean so that they could control the spice trade and establish a trading empire.*

Guided Reading and Discussion

Distinguish Ask students: What were key differences between the Portuguese presence in India and the Spanish presence in the Philippines? *(Sample response: The Portuguese did not move far beyond the coast and had limited impact. The Spanish conquered the Philippines and brought Catholic missionaries to convert people to Christianity.)*

Identify Steps in a Process Ask students to draw a diagram identifying the steps in the Spanish trade system that linked the Spanish colonies in the Americas, the Spanish Philippines, and China. *(Sample response: step 1: mine silver and gold in Americas; step 2: ship precious metals to Philippines; step 3: use gold and silver to buy goods in China; step 4: ship goods to Spain, colonies, and other countries)*

Europeans Trade in Mughal India

Remind students that a series of European powers gained footholds in Asia from the 1500s through the 1700s. Many were achieved and held by force. Diplomacy during changes in local political power also played an important role.

Online Project the **Interactive Chart: European Footholds in the Eastern Hemisphere** on the whiteboard and have students place the reason for each country's interest into the appropriate location.

ACTIVE CLASSROOM

Have students spend 3 minutes jotting down their response to this question on sticky notes: *What does this chart tell you about European expansion in the Eastern Hemisphere?* Ask students to post their sticky notes on the board and then look at all the responses, discussing similarities and differences as a group. *(Sample responses: Europeans established footholds in Africa and Asia to gain trade, establish bases, and compete against rival European powers.)*

>> In this Mughal illustration painted on fine cotton, a servant is at work, standing on a richly decorated carpet. Indian carpets and other textiles were highly prized trade goods.

Interactive Chart

>> In 1712, the Mughal emperor Shah Jahan gave this reception for Jan Joshua Ketelaer, an envoy from the Dutch East India Company envoy.

The Spanish Trade Network The Philippines became a key link in Spain's overseas trading empire. The Spanish shipped silver mined in Mexico and Peru across the Pacific to the Philippines. From there, they used the silver to buy goods in China. In this way, large quantities of American silver flowed into the economies of East Asian nations.

COMPARE AND CONTRAST How did Dutch expansion and trade in Asia differ from Portuguese and Spanish expansion and trade?

Europeans Trade in Mughal India

For two centuries, the Mughal empire had enjoyed a period of peace, strength, and prosperity. European merchants were dazzled by India's splendid Mughal court and its many luxury goods.

A Thriving Trade Center Mughal India was the center of the valuable spice trade. It was also the world leader in textile manufacturing, exporting large quantities of silk and cotton cloth. The Mughal empire was larger, richer, and more powerful than any kingdom in Europe. When Europeans sought trading rights, Mughal emperors saw no threat in granting them. The Portuguese—and later the Dutch, English, and French—thus were permitted to build forts and warehouses in Indian coastal towns.

Turmoil and Decline Over time, the Mughal empire weakened. Later rulers ended an earlier policy of religious toleration, rekindling conflicts between Hindu and Muslim princes. Civil war drained Mughal resources. Rulers then increased taxes, sparking peasant rebellions. Several weak rulers held the throne in the early 1700s. Corruption became widespread, and the central government slowly faded.

British-French Rivalry in India As Mughal power faltered, French and English traders fought for power. Like the Dutch, entrepreneurs in England and France had set up the English and French East India companies. These companies made alliances with local officials and independent rajahs, or princely rulers. Each company organized its own army of **sepoys,** or Indian troops.

By the mid-1700s, the British and the French had become locked in a bitter struggle for global power. The fighting involved both nations' lands in Asia and the Americas. In India, the British East India Company used an army of British troops and sepoys to drive

English Language Proficiency Standards

Speaking 3.C.4 Read "Ming China and Europe" aloud and have students practice using connecting words as they speak about the topic.

Beginning Write and display these sentences for students, with the connecting word underlined: *European interest in China and other parts of East Asia continued to grow. The Portuguese wanted Chinese silks and porcelains but had little to offer in exchange.* Explain that connecting words, or conjunctions (*and, but, or*), connect ideas within a sentence. Read each sentence above and have students repeat it. Explain how *and* connects ideas, while *but* shows contrast.

Intermediate Have partners skim the text for connecting words. Remind students that connecting words connect ideas within a sentence. Have partners use the example sentences they find to say their own sentences about the text with *and*, *but*, and *or*.

Answers

Compare and Contrast *Dutch traders were not under the strict control of their government. The Dutch set up the Dutch East India Company, which had sovereign powers.*

out the French. The company then forced the Mughal emperor to recognize its right to collect taxes in the northeast. By the late 1700s, it had used its great wealth to dominate most of India.

EXPLAIN How did the British gain control of India?

Ming China and Europe

Portuguese ships first reached China from their base in Malacca in 1514. To the Chinese, the Portuguese and all other foreigners were barbarians because they lacked the civilized ways of the Chinese. Europeans, by contrast, wrote enthusiastically about China. In 1590, a visitor described Chinese artisans "cleverly making devices out of gold, silver and other metals," and wrote with approval: "They daily publish huge multitudes of books."

Trade with Ming China European interest in China and other parts of East Asia continued to grow. The Ming, however, had no interest in Europe—since, as a Ming document proclaimed, "Our empire owns the world." The Portuguese wanted Chinese silks and porcelains, but had little to offer in exchange. European textiles and metalwork were inferior to Chinese products. The Chinese therefore demanded payment in gold or silver.

The Ming eventually allowed the Portuguese a trading post at **Macao** near Canton, present-day **Guangzhou** (GWAHNG joh). Later, they let the Dutch, English, and other Europeans trade with Chinese merchants. Foreigners could trade only at Canton under the supervision of imperial officials. When each year's trading season ended, they had to sail away.

Christian Missionaries Portuguese missionaries arrived in China along with the traders. In later years, the Jesuits—from Spain, Italy, and Portugal—arrived. Most Jesuits had a broad knowledge of many subjects, and the Chinese welcomed the chance to learn about Renaissance Europe from these scholars. A few European scholars, like the brilliant Jesuit priest **Matteo Ricci** (mah TAY oh REE chee) did make an impression on Ming China. In the 1580s, Ricci learned to speak Chinese and adopted Chinese clothing. His goal was to convert upper-class Chinese to Christianity. He hoped that they, in turn, would spread Christian teachings to the rest of China.

Ricci won friends among the scholarly class in China by sharing his knowledge of the arts and sciences of Renaissance Europe. The Chinese were fascinated by new European technologies, including maps. They were also open to European discoveries

>> Europeans desired fine Ming goods, such as porcelain vases with intricate designs.

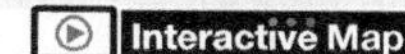

Interactive Map

>> The Jesuit missionary priest Matteo Ricci impressed Chinese scholars with his knowledge and appreciation for Chinese culture.

Guided Reading and Discussion

Ask students to explain why European merchants were strongly attracted to trade with the Mughal empire.

Sequence Events Ask students to create a timeline identifying when individual European powers acquired their footholds in the Eastern Hemisphere. *(Portugal first: Goa, 1510; and Malacca, 1511; then Spain: the Philippines, claimed in 1521; next, the Netherlands: Malacca, taken from the Portuguese, 1641; and Cape Town, 1652; finally, the British and French in India during the 1700s)*

Ming China and Europe

Explain to students that European merchants desired Chinese trade goods. The Chinese economy thrived under the Ming and Qing dynasties, but both dynasties limited trade with Europeans. The Ming allowed the Portuguese to set up a trading post at Guangzhou. They later permitted Europeans to trade with Chinese merchants only at Canton, supervised by imperial officials, and only during a yearly trading season.

Online Project the **Interactive Map: Trade Among Europe, Africa, and Asia**. Click through the hotspots on the map with students to learn more about some of the goods that were traded.

ACTIVE CLASSROOM

For this "Act it Out" activity, divide the class into four groups (Portugal, Spain, the Netherlands, and Great Britain). Groups should role-play explorers and merchants of the late 1400 through the 1700s and write a short speech to convince others to invest in their profit-seeking voyage to Asia. A spokesperson should then deliver the speech. *(Speeches should describe destination and trade goods.)*

Advanced Have students reread the text and write and say four sentences about the text to a partner, using connecting words and transitional phrases. Give students examples of transitional words and phrases, such as *in fact*, *however*, *by the way*, and *for example*.

Advanced High Follow the instructions for the Advanced activity, but have students write eight sentences that they will say to the group.

Answers

Explain *The British East India Company made alliances with local leaders and organized armies of sepoys to drive out the French; it used its wealth to weaken the Mughal empire.*

The Manchus Conquer China

Guided Reading and Discussion

Identify Steps in a Process What steps did the Ming take to limit trade with European merchants? *(The Ming demanded payment in gold or silver. They allowed the Portuguese to set up a trading post at Guangzhou. They later permitted Europeans to trade with Chinese merchants only at Canton, supervised by imperial officials, and only during a yearly trading season.)*

Draw Conclusions What effects do you think Ming restrictions had on global trade? *(Sample response: a large flow of gold and silver into China; Because of the limited supply, there was probably increased worldwide demand and higher prices for Chinese goods, and hence intense competition among European merchants.)*

Analyze Images

Tell students to examine the infographic "The Chinese Tribute System" and look at the sections for every step, including the information about Lord Macartney's 1793 mission to the Qing court. What step did Macartney fail to perform? *(kowtow)*

Predict Consequences What do you think would have resulted in China and Britain if Lord Macartney had performed the required kowtow before the Qing emperor Qianlong? *(Sample response: Britain might have been granted trading privileges in China.)*

in astronomy and mathematics. While Chinese rulers welcomed Ricci and other Jesuits from Europe for their learning, the priests had little success in spreading their religious beliefs.

IDENTIFY CAUSE AND EFFECT How did Ming China's policies toward Europeans affect global trade?

ELPS **ELPS 3.C.4** Practice creating and saying sentences using conjunctions and transitional phrases.

The Manchus Conquer China

By the early 1600s, the aging Ming dynasty was decaying. Revolts erupted, and Manchu invaders from the north pushed through the Great Wall. The **Manchus** ruled a region in the northeast, Manchuria, that had long been influenced by Chinese civilization. In 1644, the Manchus seized Beijing and made it their capital.

The Qing Dynasty Rises The Manchus set up a new dynasty called the **Qing** (ching), which means "pure." The Manchus won the support of Chinese scholar-officials because they adopted the Confucian system of government. For each top government position, the Qing chose two people, one Manchu and one Chinese. Local government remained in the hands of the Chinese, but Manchu troops stationed across the empire ensured loyalty.

Two rulers oversaw the most brilliant age of the Qing. Kangxi (kahng shee), who ruled from 1661 to 1722, was an able administrator and military leader. He extended Chinese power into central Asia and promoted Chinese culture. Kangxi's grandson **Qianlong** (chyahn lung) had an equally successful reign from 1736 to 1796. He expanded China's borders to rule the largest area in the nation's history. Qianlong retired after 60 years because he did not want to rule longer than his grandfather had.

Peace and Prosperity Spread The Chinese economy expanded under both emperors. New crops from the Americas, such as potatoes and corn, had been introduced into China. These crops boosted farm output, which in turn contributed to a population boom. China's population rose from 140 million in 1740 to over 300 million by 1800. The silk, cotton, and porcelain industries expanded. Internal trade grew, as did the demand for Chinese goods from all over the world.

The Qing Limit Foreign Traders The Qing maintained the Ming policy of restricting foreign traders. Still, Europeans kept pressing to expand

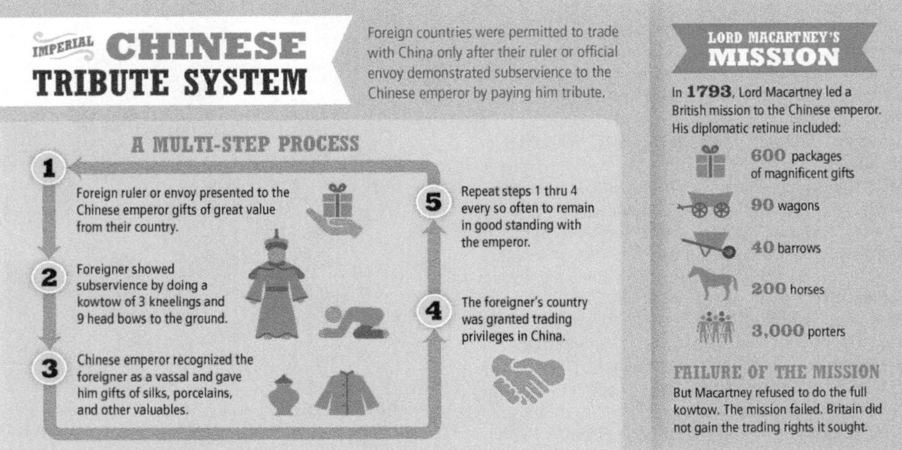

>> European trade activities in China were strictly limited. Only countries that observed the rules of the imperial tribute system could hope for permission to trade.

Answers

Identify Cause and Effect *The Chinese were not interested in any European trade items, which were inferior to Chinese products. They demanded payment for Chinese goods in gold or silver and limited trade with European merchants, which reduced the volume of global trade.*

trade to cities other than Guangzhou. In 1793, **Lord Macartney** arrived in China at the head of a British diplomatic mission. He brought samples of British-made goods to show the Chinese the advantages of trade with Westerners. The Chinese, who looked on the goods as rather crude products, thought they were gifts offered as tribute to the emperor.

Further misunderstandings followed. Macartney insisted on an audience with the emperor. The Chinese told Macartney he would have to perform the traditional kowtow, touching his head to the ground to show respect to the emperor. Macartney refused. He also offended the Chinese by speaking of the natural superiority of the English. The negotiations faltered.

At the time, Qianlong's attitude seemed justified by China's successes. After all, he already ruled the world's greatest empire. Why should he negotiate with a nation as distant as Britain?

In the long run, however, his policy proved disastrous. Even in the late 1700s, there was much the Chinese could have learned from the West. In the 1800s, China would discover to its regret the cost of ignoring the West and rejecting its advances—especially in military technology.

>> A brightly colored formal portrait of the Kangxi, Emperor of the Qing dynasty. Kangxi ascended the throne as a boy and reigned from 1662 to 1722.

SUMMARIZE How did the Qing respond to Britain's diplomatic mission?

Korea and Japan Choose Isolation

Before the 1500s, Korean traders had far-reaching contacts across East Asia. A Korean map from the 1300s accurately outlines lands from Japan to the Mediterranean. Koreans probably acquired this knowledge from Arab traders who had visited Korea.

Invaders Attack Korea In 1592, and again in 1597, the Japanese invaded Korea. The Japanese were driven out in 1598, but the invasions proved disastrous for Korea. Villages were burned to the ground, famine and disease became widespread, and the population decreased. Then, in 1636, before the country was fully recovered, the Manchus invaded Korea. When the Manchus set up the Qing dynasty in China, Korea became a tributary state. It was run by its own government but forced to acknowledge China's supremacy.

>> Outnumbered Korean ships destroy an invading Japanese fleet at the Battle of Myeongnyang in 1597, as depicted by an artist in the 1900s.

Korea Limits Contact With the World Devastated by the two invasions, Korean rulers adopted a policy of isolation, excluding foreigners except the Chinese and a few Japanese. When European sailors were shipwrecked on Korean shores, they were imprisoned

Korea and Japan Choose Isolation

Tell students that Korea, after invasion by Japan and conquest by China, did not welcome many foreigners. From the 1500s on, it preferred a policy of isolationism. Japan at first welcomed contact with Portuguese, Spanish, and Dutch traders, and even showed interest in Christianity. However, after Spanish conquest of the Philippines and a rise in conversion to Christianity, Japanese rulers began to fear foreigners and turned to isolationism.

Guided Reading and Discussion

Identify Steps in a Process What actions did the Tokugawas take against foreign influences on Japan? *(Answers may vary. Students may include many of the following: They expelled foreign missionaries, persecuted Japanese Christians, barred European merchants, forbade Japanese to travel abroad, and outlawed the building of large ships, which effectively closed off foreign trade.)*

Identify Supporting Details Explain that in many ways Japan thrived despite its policy of isolationism. Ask students to identify details from the text that support this statement. *(Sample response: Japanese arts flourished, internal trade thrived, cities grew in population, and a merchant class grew in wealth.)*

D Differentiate Challenge/Gifted Ask two students or two small groups of students to conduct a class presentation debating the positives and negatives of Japan choosing a policy of isolationism.

Answers

Summarize *The Qing emperor received Lord Macartney but felt offended by the British diplomat and rejected Britain's requests.*

Topic 11 Lesson 2

SYNTHESIZE

Online Project the **Digital Activity: International Trade: Different Approaches**. Ask students to take 5 minutes to brainstorm and write down brief answers to this question: Why did Europeans take different approaches—including military force and diplomacy—to establishing trade in Asia?

DEMONSTRATE

Online Assign the **Digital Lesson Quiz** for this lesson if you haven't already done so. Students will be offered automatic enrichment based on their score.

Pose these questions to the class:

Predict Consequences How do you think European policies in Asia at this time would affect future relations between Europe and Asia? *(Students may think that European influence and trade in Asia will grow and bring wealth to both. However, in the long term, governments and people of Asia may resent the violence and force that were used.)*

Analyze Information Which European country do you think was most successful in establishing a trade empire and good long-term relationships with people in Asia? Why? *(Sample response: The Dutch drove out the Portuguese and set up successful trading posts and colonies across South and Southeast Asia. I think their closer relationships with local people led to long-term success for the Dutch.)*

Topic Inquiry

Have students continue their investigations for the Topic Inquiry.

Answers

Identify Patterns *They came to see Europeans as a threat to their independence. They feared invasion and foreign domination.*

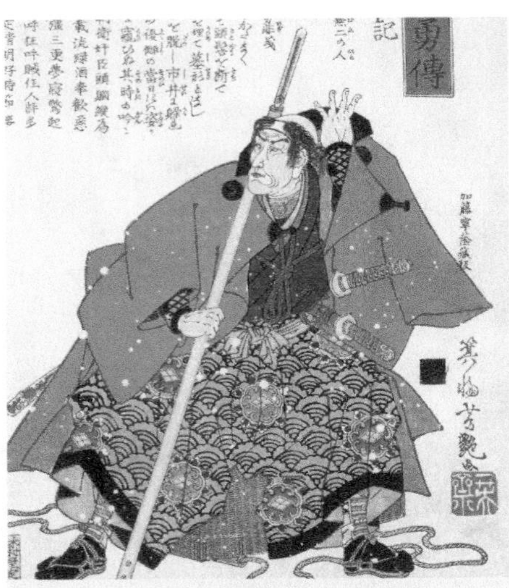

>> This portrait of a fierce daimyo, or Japanese feudal warlord, was made by Utagawa Toyokuni (1769–1825), well known for his wood-block print portraits.

and held as spies. Although Korea had few contacts with much of the world for almost 250 years, Koreans on tribute missions brought back maps, as well as books on scientific discoveries. This was also a great age for Korean arts and literature.

Westerners Arrive in Japan Unlike the Chinese or Koreans, the Japanese at first welcomed Western traders. In 1543, the Portuguese reached Japan, followed by the Spanish, Dutch, and English. They arrived at a turbulent time, when Japanese daimyo were struggling for power. The daimyo, powerful warrior lords, quickly adopted Western firearms, which may have helped the **Tokugawa** shoguns centralize power and impose order.

Japan was much more open to Christian missionaries than China. Jesuits, such as the Spanish priest Francis Xavier, found the Japanese curious and eager to learn about Christianity.

A growing number of Japanese adopted the new faith. The Japanese also welcomed the printing press the Jesuits brought.

The Tokugawa shoguns, however, grew increasingly hostile toward foreigners. After learning that Spain had seized the Philippines, they may have seen the newcomers as threats. They also worried that Japanese Christians—who may have numbered as many as 300,000—owed their allegiance to the pope, rather than to Japanese leaders. In response, the Tokugawas expelled foreign missionaries. They brutally persecuted Japanese Christians, killing many thousands of people.

Tokugawas Bar Foreigners By 1638, the Tokugawas had turned against European traders as well. Japan barred all European merchants and forbade Japanese citizens from traveling abroad. To further their isolation, the Japanese outlawed the building of large ships, thereby ending foreign trade. In order to keep informed about world events, they permitted just one or two Dutch ships each year to trade at a small island in **Nagasaki**harbor.

Japan remained isolated for more than 200 years. Art and literature flourished, and internal trade boomed. Cities grew in size and importance, and some merchant families gained wealth and status. By the early 1700s, Edo (present-day Tokyo) had a million inhabitants, more than either London or Paris.

 **IDENTIFY PATTERNS** Why did both Korea and Japan pursue a policy of isolationism?

ASSESSMENT

1. **Identify Steps in a Process** Summarize the steps by which Portugal built a trading empire in Asia around the Indian Ocean.
2. **Identify Cause and Effect** How did dominating the Philippines benefit Spain?
3. **Draw Conclusions** How did the decline of Mughal India aid European traders in the region?
4. **Synthesize** How successful were European attempts to establish missions and trade in Ming and Qing China?
5. **Compare and Contrast** Why did both Korea and Japan's attitudes toward contact with the outside world change?

Assessment

1. After Vasco da Gama's voyage to India, Afonso de Albuquerque led a Portuguese fleet into the Indian Ocean, captured Goa, destroyed coastal towns, and demolished Arab fleets. In 1511, the Portuguese took Malacca. The Portuguese won the loyalty of local southern Indian princes and used ports seized on Africa's east coast for their ships.
2. The Philippines linked the Spanish trading empire because silver shipped from mines in Mexico and Peru could be used to purchase trade goods in China.
3. Civil war drained Mughal resources, and the empire was unable to stop French and British traders from setting up East India companies that allied with local officials and independent princes.
4. Europeans gained limited trade concessions at Guangzhou, which included restrictions continued by the Qing. The Ming required payment in gold and silver.
5. Invasions by Japan and China led Korea to distrust foreigners and isolate itself. The Japanese at first welcomed European contact, with many adopting Christian beliefs. But in the 1600s, the Tokugawa shoguns saw Spain seize control of the Philippines and then persecuted Japanese Christians, banned European traders, and forbade Japanese travel abroad.

11.3 In 1492, Columbus landed in the islands that are now called the West Indies. In later voyages, he claimed all the lands he visited for Spain. Columbus's voyages set Spain on a course of exploration and colonization in the Americas. Before long, Spain conquered and ruled a vast empire that included the West Indies, much of South America, Central America, Mexico, and other parts of North America. The Spanish conquests transformed the Americas and would have a huge impact on Europe, and even on distant lands in Asia.

>> *First Tribute to Columbus* (1892) by Spanish artist José Garnelo y Alda represents the first meeting with the Taíno. **Hypothesize** Do you think the encounter actually appeared like this? Why or why not?

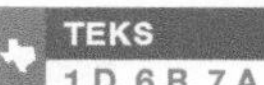

European Conquests in the Americas

TEKS
1.D, 6.B, 7.A

>> Objectives

Analyze the results of the first encounters between the Spanish and Native Americans.

Explain how the Aztec and Inca empires were impacted by Spanish conquistadors and European colonization.

Describe how Portugal and other European nations challenged Spanish power.

Analyze the major features of Spanish colonial government, society and culture.

Describe the impact of Spanish colonization of the Americas.

>> Key Terms

Taíno
conquistador
immunity
Hernán Cortés
Tenochtitlán
Malinche
alliance
Moctezuma
Francisco Pizarro
civil war
viceroy
encomienda
Bartolomé de Las Casas
peon
peninsular
creole
mestizo
mulatto
privateer

First Encounters

The Taínos Meet Columbus When Columbus first arrived in the West Indies in 1492, he encountered the **Taíno** (TY noh) people. The Taínos lived in villages and grew corn, yams, and cotton, which they wove into cloth. They were friendly and open toward the Spanish. Columbus noted that they were "generous with what they have, to such a degree as no one would believe but he who had seen it."

Friendly relations soon evaporated. Columbus's men assaulted Taíno men and women, seized some to take back to the Spanish king, and claimed their land for Spain. The Spanish killed any Taínos who dared to resist. Columbus later required each Taíno to give him a set amount of gold. Any Taíno who failed to deliver was tortured or killed.

A wave of Spanish **conquistadors** (kahn KEES tuh dawrz), or conquerors, who soon arrived in the Americas repeated Columbus's encounter. They first settled on the islands of Hispaniola (now the Dominican Republic and Haiti), Cuba, and Puerto Rico. Throughout the region, the conquistadors seized the Native Americans' gold ornaments and then made them pan for more gold. At the same time, the Spanish forced the Native Americans to convert to Christianity.

Topic 11 Lesson 3

European Conquests in the Americas

CONNECT

Preview Have students preview the **Lesson Objectives** and the list of **Key Terms**.

Students can also preview all the **Key Terms** and **Academic Vocabulary** using the **Interactive Reading Notepad** on the digital course or preview a summary of the lesson in the **Reading and Note Taking Study Guide**.

Online Use the **Editable Presentation** found on the digital course to present the main ideas for this lesson.

Start Up Activity

Tell students that in 1519, Aztec ruler Moctezuma received word from messengers that strangers had arrived in the region—people with white skin and yellow hair, clad in iron, who rode "deer" as tall as a house and had dogs with burning yellow eyes.

Discuss How would you have felt if you were Moctezuma?

Tell students that in this lesson they will learn about European colonization in the Americas and the effects of expansion on both Europeans and Native Americans.

Online You can also project the **Start Up Activity** from the course.

INVESTIGATE

Have students use the **Reading and Note Taking Study Guide** to take notes and understand the text.

First Encounters

Columbus's encounters with the Taíno had far-reaching effects. Spanish conquistadors seized the property of Native Americans and urged or forced them to accept Christianity.

Aa Vocabulary Builder

1. Have students pronounce the following academic vocabulary terms in this lesson and clarify the part of speech. For difficult or polysyllabic words, break them into syllables and pronounce them with the students.
2. Explain what the word means in common "student-friendly" language using synonyms and antonyms when possible. Provide concrete examples to clarify the meaning, and rephrase the definition.

encounter: meeting

ornament: a small, fancy object that is put on something else to make it more attractive

influenza: a common illness that is caused by a virus and that causes fever, weakness, severe aches and pains, and breathing problems

turquoise: bluish-green stone used in jewelry

negotiate: to discuss something formally in order to make an agreement

monitor: to watch, keep track of, or check (something) usually for a special purpose over a period of time

symbolize: to represent, express, or identify by a symbol, an action, object, event, etc., that expresses or represents a particular idea or quality

Topic 11 Lesson 3

Guided Reading and Discussion

Compare and Contrast Direct students to compare Columbus's first meeting with the Taínos with his relations with them. How do they compare? *(At first, Columbus was welcomed. But afterwards, Columbus imprisoned some of them and claimed their land for Spain.)*

Generate Explanations Remind students that the early conquistadors were greatly outnumbered by the Native Americans. Ask students to explain why the conquistadors were successful at conquering the Native Americans. *(The Spanish had horses and superior weapons, which Native Americans did not have. Also, many Native Americans died from European diseases that they had no immunity against.)*

Cortés Conquers the Aztecs

In 1519, Hernán Cortés and his soldiers landed in Mexico and marched to Tenochtitlán, the Aztec capital. After friendly first encounters, the Spanish tried to convert the Aztecs to Christianity and take their riches. They imprisoned the emperor Moctezuma, battled the Aztecs, and demolished Tenochtitlán.

Draw Inferences Why do you think Cortés thought he could conquer the Aztecs? *(Sample response: Cortés was a very determined person. Although greatly outnumbered, he thought his men, with their armor, guns, swords, and horses, could terrify and dominate the Aztecs.)*

>> After fighting with Tlaxcalans, Cortés and his men were welcomed into Tlaxcala. The Tlaxcalans became allies of the Spanish in the conflict with the Aztecs.

>> A Spanish conquistador with his helmet, body armor, and sword rides on horseback in this hand-colored illustration from the 1800s.

Guns, Horses, and Disease Although Spanish conquistadors only numbered in the hundreds as compared to millions of Native Americans, they had many advantages. Their guns and cannons were superior to the Native Americans' arrows and spears, and European metal armor provided them with better protection. They also had horses, which not only were useful in battle and in carrying supplies, but also frightened the Native Americans, who had never seen a horse.

Most important, an invisible invader—disease—helped the conquistadors take control of the Taínos and other Native Americans. Europeans unknowingly carried diseases, such as smallpox, measles, and influenza, to which Native Americans had no **immunity,** or resistance. These diseases spread rapidly and wiped out village after village. As a result, the Native American population of the Caribbean islands declined by as much as 90 percent in the 1500s. Millions of Native Americans died from disease as Europeans made their way inland.

DESCRIBE How did Spanish conquistadors treat the Taínos?

Cortés Conquers the Aztecs

From the Caribbean, Spanish explorers probed the coasts of the Americas. From local peoples, they heard stories of empires rich in gold, but the first explorers also told about fierce fighters they had encountered. Attracted by the promise of riches as well as by religious zeal, a flood of adventurers soon followed.

Cortés Arrives in Mexico Among the earliest conquistadors was **Hernán Cortés.** Cortés, a landowner in Cuba, heard of Spanish expeditions that had been repelled by Indians. He believed that he could succeed where none had before. In 1519, he landed on the coast of Mexico with about 600 men, 16 horses, and a few cannons. He began an inland trek toward **Tenochtitlán** (teh nawch tee TLAHN), the capital of the Aztec empire.

A young Indian woman named **Malinche** (mah LEEN chay), called Doña Marina by the Spanish, served as his translator and advisor. Malinche knew both the Maya and Aztec languages, and she learned Spanish quickly.

Malinche told Cortés that the Aztecs had gained power by conquering other groups of people. The Aztecs sacrificed thousands of their captives to the Aztec gods each year. Many conquered peoples hated

Answers

Hypothesize *Sample response: No, the Spanish probably were more afraid and cautious than shown here.*

Describe *The Spanish assaulted Taíno men and women, seized some to take back to the Spanish king, and claimed their land for Spain.*

History Background

La Malinche Also known as Doña Marina, La Malinche was the daughter of Aztec nobles. Her mother sold her into slavery as a young girl; eventually, she and 19 other slaves were given to Cortés when he arrived in the Yucatán.

Cortés had been relying on a Spanish priest who spoke Mayan to interpret for him, but the priest could not speak the Aztec language. Malinche could. She spoke various Mayan dialects along with her native Aztec language and quickly learned Spanish. Her work as Cortés's interpreter helped save thousands of lives since it allowed him to negotiate rather than fight.

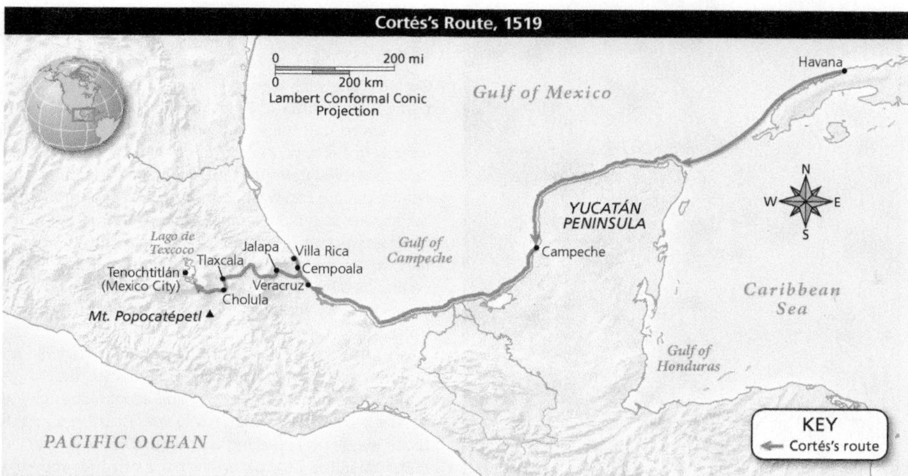

>> **Analyze Maps** Why do you think Cortés's ships sailed so close to the Mexican coast?

their Aztec overlords, so Malinche helped Cortés arrange **alliances** with them. They agreed to help Cortés fight the Aztecs.

Moctezuma's Dilemma Meanwhile, messengers brought word about the Spanish to the Aztec emperor **Moctezuma** (mahk tih ZOO muh). The Aztec ruler hesitated. Was it possible, he wondered, that the leader of the pale-skinned, bearded strangers might be Quetzalcoatl (ket sahl koh AHT el), an Aztec god-king who had long ago vowed to return from the East? To be safe, Moctezuma sent gifts of turquoise, feathers, and other goods with religious importance, but urged the strangers not to continue to Tenochtitlán.

Cortés, however, had no intention of turning back. He was not interested in the Aztec religious objects, but was extremely interested in the gold and silver ornaments that Moctezuma began sending him.

Cortés became more determined than ever to reach Tenochtitlán. Fighting and negotiating by turns, Cortés led his forces inland toward the capital. At last, the Spanish arrived in Tenochtitlán, where they were dazzled by the grandeur of the city.

Cortés Takes Tenochtitlán Moctezuma welcomed Cortés to his capital. However, relations between the Aztecs and Spaniards soon grew strained. The Spanish scorned the Aztecs' religion and sought to convert them to Christianity. At the same time, as they remained in the city, they saw more of the Aztec treasure. They decided to imprison Moctezuma so they could gain control of the Aztecs and their riches.

Cortés compelled Moctezuma to sign over his land and treasure to the Spanish. In the meantime, a new force of Spanish conquistadors had arrived on the coast to challenge Cortés. In the confusion that followed—with various groups of Spanish, Aztecs, and Native Americans all fighting for control—the Aztecs drove the Spanish from the city. More than half of the Spanish were killed in the fighting, as was Moctezuma.

Cortés retreated to plan an assault. In 1521, in a brutal struggle, Cortés and his Native American allies captured and demolished Tenochtitlán. The Spanish later built Mexico City on the ruins of Tenochtitlán. As in the Caribbean, disease had aided their cause. Smallpox had spread among the Aztecs from the 1519 encounter, decimating the population.

 **IDENTIFY CAUSE AND EFFECT** Why did Cortés want to conquer the Aztecs?

Analyze Images

Direct students' attention to the map of Cortés's route to Tenochtitlán on this page. Ask students to describe the route. *(He traveled by sea from Cuba to the Yucatán Peninsula of Mexico. His ships then hugged the coast until they reached Veracruz. From there, they marched inland to Tenochtitlán.)* Ask students to explain how this route benefited Cortés. *(Sample response: The Spanish could travel more quickly and safely by sea. They avoided marching a long distance over rough terrain and fighting Native Americans along the way.)*

Guided Reading and Discussion

Compare How were the character and impact of Cortés and Columbus alike? *(Sample response: Both Cortés and Columbus were very courageous and determined and led successful expeditions. Despite being at first welcomed by Native Americans, they both used force against them, claimed their land, and sought to convert them to Christianity.)*

Support Ideas With Evidence Tell students that Cortés was flexible and used both peaceful diplomacy and military force to achieve his goals. Ask students to provide evidence from the text that supports this idea. *(Cortés used force against the Aztecs but cooperated with Malinche and formed alliances with other Native American groups.)*

Answers

Analyze Maps *Sample responses: to explore the coast, to avoid treacherous currents and other hazards in little-known and perhaps poorly charted waters, to remain close to sources of food and fresh water*

Identify Cause and Effect *He wanted their land and riches, and he wanted to convert them to Christianity.*

The Incan Empire and Beyond

The success of Cortés in Mexico inspired the Spanish and other Europeans to pursue conquests and colonization. In South America, the Spanish conquistador Francisco Pizarro conquered the Incas, killed their ruler, and captured Peru. From Peru, the Spanish added much of South America to their empire. Meanwhile, the Portuguese developed a large colony in Brazil. The English, French, and Dutch made some small efforts to challenge Spanish and Portuguese dominance in the region.

Online Project the **Interactive Map: Spanish and Portuguese Colonies in the Americas, About 1700**. Look at each image individually and then the collection of images as a whole. Where were the Spanish and Portuguese colonies in the Americas located? Which nation claimed the most territory? *(Spain: Viceroyalty of New Spain consisted of Florida, Cuba, and other Caribbean islands, as well as Mexico, Central America, and a northern portion of South America. Viceroyalty of Peru: much of the west coast of South America; parts of today's Chile and Argentina; all of Peru, Ecuador, and Bolivia; and parts of Columbia, Paraguay, and Uruguay. Portugal's Brazil: the northern and eastern coastal regions of present-day Brazil. Spain claimed the most territory.)*

ACTIVE CLASSROOM

Pair students to have a "Conversation With History." Have the first student assume the role of a Spanish colonial official. Have the second student assume the role of a visiting royal official from Spain. The colonial official gives the official from Spain a verbal "tour" of the map—what does it show? The official from Spain makes comments and asks questions about the benefits and challenges for Spain. Ask students to record their conversation so others in the class can access it.

>> Atahualpa, portrayed here by an unknown painter in the 1500s, was the thirteenth and last Incan ruler.

>> The conquistador Francisco Pizarro appears in full armor in this hand-colored woodcut from the 1800s.

The Incan Empire and Beyond

Cortés's success inspired other adventurers. Among them was Spaniard **Francisco Pizarro** (pee SAHR oh). Pizarro had heard rumors about a fabulously rich empire in Peru, with even more gold than the Aztecs. Pizarro arrived in Peru in 1532, just after the Incan ruler Atahualpa (ah tah WAHL puh) had won the throne from his brother in a bloody **civil war.** A civil war is fought between groups of people in the same nation. The war had weakened the Incas, and they had also begun to be affected by European diseases. In the end, however, it was trickery that helped Pizarro defeat the Incas.

Atahualpa Resists When Pizarro and his small force of about 200 men reached the Inca leader, they urged him to convert to Christianity and accept Charles V as sovereign. When Atahualpa refused, Pizarro tricked the Incan leader into meeting with him. Then with the help of Indian allies, he took the emperor prisoner and killed thousands of Incas.

For a time, the Spanish held Atahulpa captive. Pizarro's secretary described him as:

> a man of thirty years, good-looking and poised, somewhat stout, with a wide, handsome, and ferocious face, and the eyes flaming with blood . . .
>
> —Francisco de Xerez

Pizarro Triumphs Despite continuing resistance, Pizarro and his followers overran the Incan heartland. He had superior weapons, and the Incan people were weakened by European diseases. From Peru, Spanish forces surged across Ecuador and Chile. Before long, Spain had added much of South America to its growing empire. Pizarro himself was killed by a rival Spanish faction a few years after he established the city of Lima.

Beyond Spain's Empire As in the Spanish empire, the Native Americans who lived in Brazil—the Tupian Indians—had been largely wiped out by disease. In the 1530s, Portugal began to issue grants of land to Portuguese nobles, who agreed to develop the land and share profits with the crown. Landowners sent settlers to build towns, plantations, and churches.

Unlike Spain's American colonies, Brazil offered no instant wealth from silver or gold. However, early settlers cut and exported brazilwood. The Portuguese named the colony after this wood, which was used to

D Differentiate Special Needs/Extra Support Ask students to work in a group to briefly jot down three or more similarities between the actions of Cortés and Pizarro. *(Both conquered Native American civilizations, killed their rulers, claimed their land, and took their riches.)*

Topic 11 Lesson 3

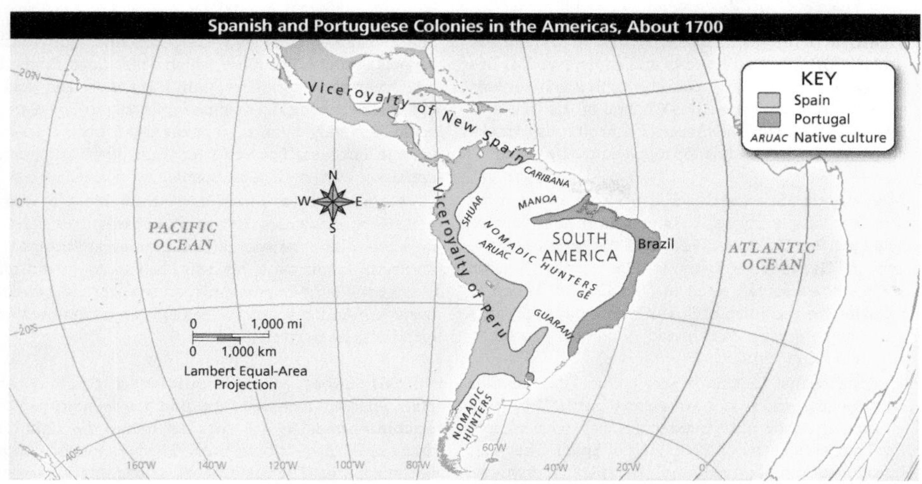

>> **Analyze Maps** What do all the European land claims in South America have in common? Which country settled the easternmost region?

produce a valuable dye. Soon they turned to plantation agriculture and raising cattle.

Like the Spanish, the Portuguese forced Indians and Africans to clear land for plantations. As many as four million Africans were sent to Brazil. As in Spanish America, a new culture emerged in Brazil that blended European, Native American, and African elements.

Challenges to Portugal and Spain In the 1500s, the wealth of the Americas helped make Spain the most powerful country in Europe, with Portugal not far behind. The jealous English and Dutch shared the resentment that French king Francis I felt when he declared, "I should like to see Adam's will, wherein he divided the Earth between Spain and Portugal."

To get around those countries' strict control over colonial trade, smugglers traded illegally with Portuguese and Spanish colonists. In the Caribbean and elsewhere, Dutch, English, and French pirates preyed on treasure ships from the Americas. Some pirates, called **privateers,** even operated with the approval of European governments. Other European explorers continued to sail the coasts of the Americas, hunting for gold and other treasure, as well as a northwest passage to Asia.

COMPARE AND CONTRAST How was Pizarro's treatment of the Incas similar to Cortés's treatment of the Aztecs?

Governing the Spanish Empire

Spanish settlers and missionaries followed the conquistadors to the Americas. In time, the huge Spanish empire stretched from California in the north to Argentina in the south. Spain divided these lands into four provinces, including New Spain (Mexico) and Peru.

Spain imposed its culture, language, religion, and way of life on millions of new subjects in its empire. The Spanish built new Spanish-style cities on top of the ruins of Native American cities. "Christianizing" Native Americans, however, turned out to be more complex. In the end, though, Spain imposed its will by force.

Royal Officials Rule the Provinces Spain was determined to maintain strict control over its empire. To achieve this goal, the king set up the Council of the

Guided Reading and Discussion

Integrate How did the Portuguese empire in the Americas differ from the Spanish empire? *(Sample response: The Portuguese empire was much smaller, limited to coastal areas of Brazil. The Portuguese colony did not have much gold and silver. But they developed a profitable colony. Settlers cut and exported brazil wood, established plantations, and raised cattle.)*

Summarize How did Britain, France, and the Netherlands compete with the Spanish and Portuguese in South America? *(The French and Dutch had very small colonies in northeastern South America. Pirates and privateers preyed on treasure ships from the Americas. All three European nations sent explorers to search the Americas' coasts for riches.)*

Governing the Spanish Empire

Society and Culture in Spanish America

The Spanish monarchy sent royal officials to direct the government and economy of its American colonies. Catholic missionary priests spread Christianity and Spanish culture. Under the encomienda system, Native Americans were forced to work under brutal conditions. The Spanish brought enslaved Africans to work in mines and on plantations. Cultural blending occurred, but there was a layered society of unequal classes based on ethnicity and wealth.

Answers

Analyze Maps *Sample response: They all extend along coasts; Portugal, in Brazil*

Compare and Contrast *Like Cortés, Pizarro used military force to defeat the Native Americans, kill their leader, and seize their land and riches.*

Analyze Images

Have students quickly view all the images and captions for this lesson. Ask: What were four key characteristics of Spain's colonies in the Americas? Have students take a piece of paper and fold it into quarters, write down one response in the first box, and then go around the room asking other students for their responses. If they think a response is correct, they should write it in another one of their boxes until they have four different responses on their page. Ask volunteers to read their responses to the class and post them on the whiteboard.

Indies to pass laws for the colonies. He also appointed **viceroys,** or representatives who ruled in his name, in each province. Lesser officials and audiencias (ow dee EN see ahs), or advisory councils of Spanish settlers, helped the viceroy rule. The Council of the Indies in Spain closely monitored these colonial officials to make sure they did not assume too much authority.

Missionaries Spread Christianity To Spain, winning souls for Christianity was as important as gaining land. The Catholic Church worked with the government to convert Native Americans to Christianity. Church leaders often served as royal officials and helped to regulate the activities of Spanish settlers. As Spain's American empire expanded, Church authority expanded along with it.

Franciscans, Jesuits, and other missionaries baptized thousands of Native Americans. They built mission churches and worked to turn new converts into loyal subjects of the Catholic king of Spain. They also introduced European clothing, the Spanish language, and new crafts such as carpentry and locksmithing. Where they could, the Spanish missionaries forcibly imposed European culture over Native American culture.

Regulation of Trade To make the empire profitable, Spain closely controlled its economic activities, especially trade. The most valuable resources shipped from Spanish America to Spain were silver and gold. Colonists could export raw materials only to Spain and could buy only Spanish manufactured goods. Laws forbade colonists from trading with other European nations or even with other Spanish colonies.

When sugar cane was introduced into the West Indies and elsewhere, it quickly became a profitable resource. The cane was refined into sugar, molasses, and rum. Sugar cane, however, had to be grown on plantations, large estates run by an owner or the owner's overseer. And plantations needed large numbers of workers to be profitable.

Forced Labor: The Encomienda System At first, Spanish monarchs granted the conquistadors **encomiendas** (en koh mee EN dahs), the right to demand labor or tribute from Native Americans in a particular area. The conquistadors used this system to force Native Americans to work under the most brutal conditions. Those who resisted were hunted down and killed. Disease, starvation, and cruel treatment caused drastic declines in the Native American population.

The encomienda system was used in the mines as well as on plantations. By the 1540s, tons of silver

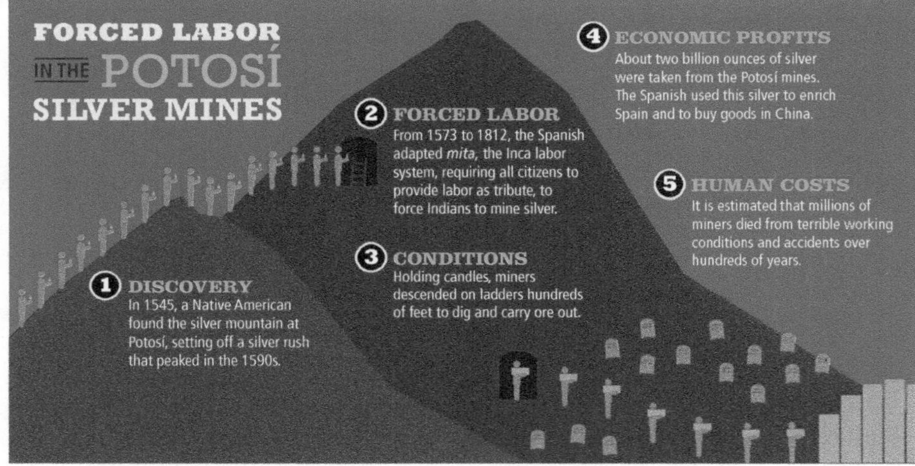

FORCED LABOR IN THE POTOSÍ SILVER MINES
1 DISCOVERY
In 1545, a Native American found the silver mountain at Potosí, setting off a silver rush that peaked in the 1590s.
2 FORCED LABOR
From 1573 to 1812, the Spanish adapted mita, the Inca labor system, requiring all citizens to provide labor as tribute, to force Indians to mine silver.
3 CONDITIONS
Holding candles, miners descended on ladders hundreds of feet to dig and carry ore out.
4 ECONOMIC PROFITS
About two billion ounces of silver were taken from the Potosí mines. The Spanish used this silver to enrich Spain and to buy goods in China.
5 HUMAN COSTS
It is estimated that millions of miners died from terrible working conditions and accidents over hundreds of years.

>> While the process of extracting silver from the Potosí mines was terribly destructive for Native American and other forced laborers, it proved immensely profitable for Spain.

English Language Proficiency Standards

Speaking 3.D.1 Explain that content-area vocabulary is specific to each academic discipline. Read "Governing the Spanish Empire" aloud to students. Then have students practice defining and using content-area vocabulary as they speak about the topic.

Beginning Provide students with a few content-area vocabulary terms from the text, such as *empire*, *colony*, and *settler*. Say each word and have students repeat it. Then model how to use context clues and a dictionary to determine the meaning of each word. Share each meaning with students and help them read it aloud. Ask students to describe the meaning of one term.

Intermediate Help pairs of students find three grade-level content-area vocabulary terms from the text. Then help them use dictionaries, context clues, and glossaries to create a definition for each word. Ask pairs to use the words in phrases or simple sentences to describe the text.

Advanced Instruct students to find six grade-level content-area terms from the text. Have them create a definition for each word. Ask pairs to use the terms in complete sentences in a discussion about the text.

Advanced High Have students perform the Advanced activity and then write a sentence using each term correctly and share their sentences aloud with a partner. Ask pairs to have a discussion about the text, using the terms in complete sentences.

from the Potosí region of Peru and Bolivia filled Spanish treasure ships. Year after year, thousands of Native Americans were forced to extract the rich ore from dangerous shafts deep inside the Andes Mountains. As thousands of Native Americans died from the terrible conditions, they were replaced by thousands more.

A Spanish Priest Condemns the Abuses A few bold priests, like **Bartolomé de Las Casas** (bahr toh loh MAY deh lahs KAHS ahs), condemned the evils of the encomienda system. In vivid reports to Spain, Las Casas detailed the horrors that Spanish rule had brought to Native Americans and pleaded with the king to end the abuse.

Prodded by Las Casas, Spain passed the New Laws of the Indies in 1542. The laws forbade enslavement and abuse of Native Americans, but Spain was too far away to enforce them. Many Native Americans were forced to become **peons,** workers forced to labor for a landlord in order to pay off a debt. Landlords advanced them food, tools, or seeds, creating debts that workers could never pay off in their lifetime.

Bringing Workers from Africa To fill the labor shortage, Las Casas urged colonists to import workers from Africa. He believed that Africans were immune to tropical diseases and had skills in farming, mining, and metalworking.

Las Casas later regretted that advice because it furthered the brutal African slave trade.

The Spanish began bringing Africans to the Americas as slave laborers by the 1530s. As demand for sugar products skyrocketed, the settlers imported millions of Africans as slaves. They were forced to work as field hands, miners, or servants in the houses of wealthy landowners. Others became skilled artists and artisans.

Within a few generations, Africans and their American-born descendants greatly outnumbered European settlers throughout the Americas. In the cities, some enslaved Africans earned enough money to buy their freedom. Others resisted slavery by rebelling or running away. You will learn more about slavery in the Americas in a later lesson.

DEFINE What was the encomienda system?

ELPS **ELPS 3.D.1** Practice creating and saying sentences using conjunctions and transitional phrases.

>> This Mexican painting from the 1700s shows a Spanish man with his Native American wife and their mestizo child, who is trying on a new pair of shoes.

Society and Culture in Spanish America

In Spanish America, a diverse mix of peoples gave rise to a new society. The blending of Native American, African, and European peoples and traditions resulted in a culture distinct to the Americas.

A Society of Unequal Classes Spanish colonial society was made of distinct social classes. At the top were **peninsulares** (peh neen soo LAY rayz), people born in Spain. (The term *peninsular* referred to the Iberian Peninsula, on which Spain is located.) Peninsulares filled the highest positions in both colonial governments and the Catholic Church. Next came **creoles,** American-born descendants of Spanish settlers. Creoles owned most of the plantations, ranches, and mines.

Other classes stood lower in the social order and reflected the mixing of populations. They included **mestizos,** people of Native American and European descent, and **mulattoes,** people of African and European descent. Native Americans and people of African descent formed the lowest social classes.

Guided Reading and Discussion

A new social structure and culture arose in Spanish America as Native American, African, and European peoples and traditions interacted. Various crops, foods, farming methods, cooking styles, religions, and artistic expressions blended together. Spanish colonial society consisted of distinct social classes: peninsulares, creoles, mestizos, mulattoes, Native Americans, and people of African descent.

Key Terms

Have students find and define the key terms **peninsular, creole, mestizo**, and **mulatto**. Ask them to analyze what the use of such specific terms says about Spanish colonial society.

Predict Consequences Divide students into groups and ask them to consider what they have learned about Spanish colonial life. Do they predict that there will be social and political stability in the future or social and political conflict? Why? *(Answers may vary. Students may predict rebellion and revolution as colonists try to be free of the strict rule of the Spanish monarchy or change the unequal society where only a few have the most freedom, power, and wealth.)*

Answers

Define *It was a system in which the Spanish monarchs granted the conquistadors the right to demand labor or tribute from Native Americans. Native Americans were forced to work on plantations, in mines, and elsewhere.*

Topic 11 Lesson 3

The Impact of Spanish Colonization

Spanish exploration and colonization in the Americas had far-reaching effects. Ships carried people, goods, and ideas along the sea routes that now connected many parts of the world for the first time. Spain grew in wealth and power. However, Native American civilizations and populations declined greatly.

Online Project the **Interactive Chart: Causes and Effects of Spanish Colonization**. Have students complete the chart and discuss the overall impact of Spanish colonization.

ACTIVE CLASSROOM

Group students. Give each group a three-column organizer with headings “Plus/Minus/Interesting” to record responses to these questions: 1. What are the positives of Spanish colonization? *(Sample responses: brings new animals, European ideas and technologies)* 2. What are the negatives of Spanish colonization? *(plunders and destroys cultures, brings lethal diseases)* 3. What is interesting about the impact of Spanish colonization? *(Interaction creates a new society and culture.)*

Guided Reading and Discussion

As Spain profited from the resources and goods taken from the Americas, Native Americans suffered and resisted. The Maya, Incas, and other Native Americans fought and resisted Spanish rule for centuries, preserving as much as they could of their own cultures.

Analyze Graphs Discuss the population graph on the facing page with the class. Ask: During which interval did the Native American population of Central Mexico decline the most? Why? *(1500–1540; war and diseases)* the least? *(1580–1620)* What is the estimated total population decline between about 1520 and 1600? *(about 25 million people)*

Thriving Towns and Cities Spanish settlers generally lived in towns and cities. The population of Mexico City grew so quickly that by 1550 it was the largest Spanish-speaking city in the world. Colonial cities were centers of government, commerce, and European culture. Around the central plaza, or square, stood government buildings and a Spanish-style church. Broad avenues and public monuments symbolized European power and wealth. Cities were also centers of intellectual and cultural life. Architecture and painting, as well as poetry and the exchange of ideas, flourished in Spanish cities in the Americas.

Educational Opportunities To meet the Church's need for educated priests, the colonies built universities. The University of Mexico was established as early as 1551. A dozen Spanish American universities were already educating young men long before Harvard was founded in 1636 as the first college in the 13 English colonies.

Women desiring an education might enter a convent. One such woman was Sor Juana Inés de la Cruz (sawr HWAN uh ee NES deh lah krooz). Refused admission to the University of Mexico because she was female, Juana entered a convent at around the age of 18. There, she devoted herself to study and the writing of poetry. She earned a reputation as one of the greatest poets ever to write in the Spanish language.

>> Sor Juana Inés de la Cruz, a Catholic nun, appears at her desk in this painting from the 1700s by Miguel Cabrera. She defended women's right to learn and was recognized as an important writer.

A Blending of Cultures Although Spanish culture was dominant in the cities, the blending of diverse traditions changed people's lives throughout the Americas. Settlers learned Native American styles of building, ate foods native to the Americas, and traveled in Indian-style canoes. Indian artistic styles influenced the newcomers. At the same time, Europeans taught their religion to Native Americans. They also introduced animals, especially the horse, thereby transforming the lives of many Native Americans.

Africans contributed to this cultural mix with their farming methods, cooking styles, and crops. African drama, dance, and song heightened Christian services. In Cuba, Haiti, and elsewhere, Africans forged new religions that blended African and Christian beliefs.

? DRAW CONCLUSIONS In Spanish colonial society, what determined a person's social rank?

The Impact of Spanish Colonization

Spanish exploration, colonization, and expansion had a long-lasting impact on Native Americans, Europeans, and others beyond these two groups. By establishing an empire in the Americas, Spain dramatically changed the pattern of global encounter first set in motion by European exploration of Africa's coasts. For the first time, much of the world was now connected by sea routes, on which traveled ships carrying goods, people, and ideas.

Spain Wins Wealth and Power In the 1500s, Spain acquired enormous wealth from its American colonies. Every year treasure fleets sailed to Europe loaded with gold and silver. These riches helped make Spain the most powerful country in Europe. At the same time, the French, English, and Dutch jealously eyed the Spanish treasure fleets and defied Spain's claims to the Americas.

Native American Suffering and Resistance The conquest of the Americas brought suffering and death to many Native American peoples. Although many converted to Christianity and adopted some Spanish ways, others resisted Spanish rule for centuries. For centuries, the Maya fought Spanish rule in Mexico and Central America. Long after the death of Atahualpa, revolts erupted among the Incas.

D Differentiate Special Needs/Extra Support Have students make a graphic organizer, such as a concept web with four circles, and then jot down characteristics of Spanish colonial government in one circle, and so forth, for economy, culture, and society.

Answers

Draw Conclusions *their ethnic background*

Describe *The Maya and the Incas fought or rebelled for years. Native Americans resisted by preserving aspects of their traditional cultures.*

Native American Population of Central Mexico

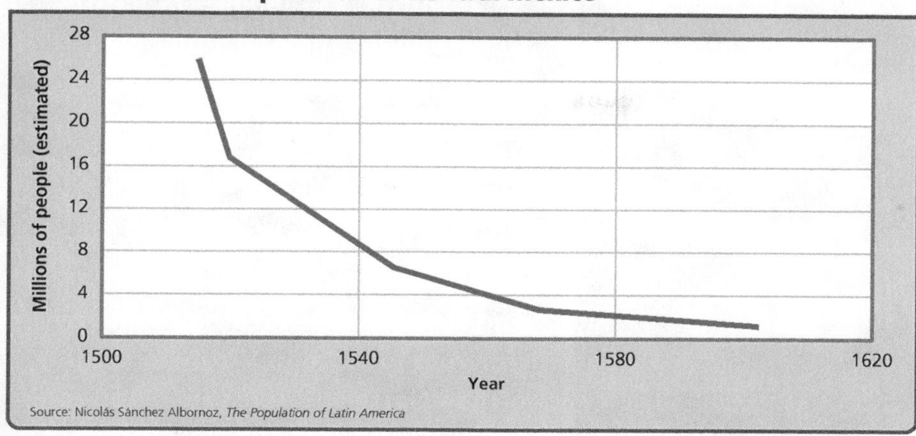

>> **Analyze Graphs** What is the estimated population decline between 1519 and 1540? How does it compare with the population change between 1540 and 1580? Why?

Resistance did not always take the form of military action. Throughout the Americas, Native Americans resisted Europeans by preserving their own cultures, languages, religious traditions, and skills, such as weaving and pottery. As you will read later, European exploration and colonization had tremendous global impact even beyond the Americas by connecting people, goods, and ideas around the world.

 **DESCRIBE** In what ways did Native Americans resist European influence?

ASSESSMENT

1. **Identify Patterns** Describe the common effects of the first encounters between the Spanish and Native Americans in Mexico, Peru, and elsewhere.
2. **Draw Conclusions** Why were Native Americans unable to defeat the Spanish conquistadors?
3. **Identify Main Ideas** Describe the main characteristics of government, religion, and economics in Spain's colonies in the Americas.
4. **Categorize** Explain how the people of Spanish colonial society were categorized into different social classes.
5. **Predict Consequences** How do you think other European nations will threaten Spanish and Portuguese power in the Americas?

Topic 11 Lesson 3

SYNTHESIZE

Online Have students use the Think-Pair-Share strategy to work on the Synthesis Activity titled "Unexpected Impacts." Then ask them to create their Venn diagram on the impacts of European exploration and expansion in the Americas. Invite volunteers to present their diagrams.

Discuss How is the impact of conquest and colonization by the Spanish and other Europeans still visible in the Americas today? *(Possible answer: Native American poverty)*

DEMONSTRATE

Online Assign the **Digital Lesson Quiz** for this lesson if you haven't already done so. Students will be offered automatic remediation or enrichment based on their score.

Pose these questions to the class:

Compare and Contrast How were the ways the Spanish treated Native Americans and Africans alike or different? Explain. *(Sample response: The Spanish used both Native Americans and Africans as forced labor. Native Americans had their homes invaded, but Africans were taken from theirs.)*

Draw Inferences Why do you think rebellion attempts by the Maya, the Incas, and other Native American groups usually failed? *(Sample response: The strength and circumstances of Native American groups varied. Many were decimated by disease and warfare and did not have the strength to face European soldiers.)*

Topic Inquiry

Have students continue their investigations for the Topic Inquiry.

Assessment

1. The Spanish conquered Native Americans and plundered their lands for wealth. Thousands of Native Americans died from disease and war. The Spanish tried to force Native Americans to abandon their culture.
2. Spanish soldiers had guns and horses. European diseases reduced the Native American population. Sometimes the Spanish were able to enlist the aid of other Native American groups.
3. Spain divided its empire into four provinces and set up the Council of the Indies to oversee its officials. Roman Catholicism was the main religion. Spain regulated the economy and exported gold and silver from the colonies. Native Americans were often used as forced laborers.
4. Peninsulares, people from Spain, were at the top, followed by creoles, or people of Spanish descent born in the Americas. Mulattoes were people of mixed African and European descent, while mestizos were of mixed Native American and European descent; these groups were in the middle. Native Americans and people of African descent were among the lowest social classes.
5. Other European nations resented Spanish and Portuguese power and wealth in the Americas. Dutch, English, and French pirates attacked and captured treasure ships from the Americas. It is likely that wars will erupt in the future.

European Colonies in North America

CONNECT

Preview Have students preview the **Lesson Objectives** and the list of **Key Terms**.

Students can also preview all the **Key Terms** and **Academic Vocabulary** using the **Interactive Reading Notepad** on the digital course or preview a summary of the lesson in the **Reading and Note Taking Study Guide**.

Online Use the **Editable Presentation** found on the digital course to present the main ideas for this lesson.

Start Up Activity

Read this quotation aloud: "Gentlemen, there is no time to be lost; the French seem to have advanced further towards making themselves masters of this continent within these last five or six years than they have done ever since the first beginnings of their settlements upon it."—William Shirley, Royal Governor of Massachusetts, April 2, 1754

Ask: Why is Governor Shirley concerned? *(He is fearful that French expansion threatens his colony and other English colonies in North America.)*

Discuss Ask students to predict how the colonization of North America will be similar to and different from the colonization of Latin America. *(Similarities: European competition; conflict with Native Americans. Difference: France and England will engage in more conflict with each other than Spain and Portugal did.)*

Tell students that in this lesson they will learn about French and English competition for colonies in North America and how their struggle affected Native Americans.

Online You can also project the **Start Up Activity** from the course.

INVESTIGATE

Have students read the section using the **Reading and Note Taking Study Guide** to help them take notes and understand the text as they read.

New France

Explain that the colonies of France and England in North America were very different from each other and from Spanish colonies in geography, government, economy, and culture.

>> French explorer Jacques Cartier found that the St. Lawrence River was a gateway into a vast territory of rich forests, with an abundance of fish and animals that could provide wealth from trade.

Interactive Flipped Video

11.4 During the 1600s, France, the Netherlands, England, and Sweden joined Spain in settling North America. At first, Europeans were disappointed that North America did not yield gold treasure or offer a water passage to Asia, as they had hoped. Before long, though, the English and French were turning profits by growing tobacco in Virginia, fishing off the North Atlantic coast, and trading furs from New England and Canada with Europe.

TEKS
1.D, 7.A

>> Objectives

Explain why the colony of New France grew slowly.

Analyze the establishment and growth of the English colonies.

Understand why Europeans competed for power in North America and how their struggle affected Native Americans.

>> Key Terms

New France
revenue
Pilgrim
compact
French and Indian War
Treaty of Paris
Jacques Cartier
Samuel de Champlain
John Cabot

European Colonies in North America

New France

By 1700, France and England controlled large parts of North America. As their colonies grew, they developed their own governments that differed from each other and from that of Spanish America.

French Exploration Begins By the early 1500s, French fishing ships were crossing the Atlantic each year to harvest rich catches of cod off Newfoundland, Canada. Within 200 years, the French had occupied or claimed nearly half of North America.

French claims in Canada—which the French called **New France**—quietly grew while French rulers were distracted by wars at home in Europe. In 1534, **Jacques Cartier** (zhahk kahr tee AY) began exploring the coastline of eastern Canada, eventually discovering the St. Lawrence River. Traveling inland on the river, he claimed much of present-day eastern Canada for France.

French explorers and fur traders gradually traveled inland with the help of Native American allies, who sought support against rival Native American groups. Jesuits and other missionaries soon followed the explorers. They advanced into the wilderness, trying with little success to convert the Native Americans they met to Christianity.

PEARSON realize. www.PearsonTexas.com Access your Digital Lesson.

442

Aa Vocabulary Builder

1. Have students pronounce the following academic vocabulary term in this lesson and clarify the part of speech. Break the word into syllables and pronounce it with the students.
2. Explain what the word means in common "student-friendly" language using synonyms and antonyms when possible. Provide concrete examples to clarify the meaning, and rephrase the definition.

prevail: to triumph

Topic 11 Lesson 4

New France Grows Slowly The population of New France grew slowly. The first permanent French settlement was not established until 1608, when Samuel de Champlain established a colony in Quebec. Wealthy landlords bought huge tracts, or areas of land, along the St. Lawrence River. They sought settlers to farm the land, but the harsh Canadian climate, with its long winters, attracted few French peasants.

Many who went to New France soon abandoned farming in favor of the more profitable fur trapping and trading. They faced a hard life in the wilderness, but the soaring European demand for fur ensured good prices. Fishing was another industry that supported settlers, who exported cod and other fish to Europe.

Royal Power and Economic Growth In the late 1600s, the French king Louis XIV set out to strengthen royal power and boost **revenues,** or income, from taxes from his overseas empire. He appointed officials to oversee economic activities in New France.

He also sent soldiers and more settlers—including women—to North America. However, Louis, who was Catholic, prohibited Protestants from settling in New France.

By the early 1700s, French forts, missions, and trading posts stretched from Quebec to Louisiana, and the population was growing. Yet the population of New France remained small compared to that of the English colonies that were expanding along the Atlantic coast.

EXPRESS PROBLEMS CLEARLY Why was the growth of New France slow?

The 13 English Colonies

At the time of Columbus and throughout the centuries ahead, the English sailed westward, hoping to find a sea passage to India. In 1497, John Cabot, a Venetian explorer, commanded an English expedition that reached the rich fishing grounds off Newfoundland. He claimed the region for England. Dozens of other English explorers continued to search for a northwest passage to Asia, without success. In the 1600s, England turned its attention instead to building colonies along the Atlantic seaboard of North America.

Jamestown The English built their first permanent colony at Jamestown, Virginia, in 1607. Its early years were filled with disaster. Many settlers died of starvation and disease. The rest survived with the help of friendly Native Americans.

Plymouth In 1620, another group of English settlers landed at Plymouth, Massachusetts. They were **Pilgrims,** or English Protestants who rejected the

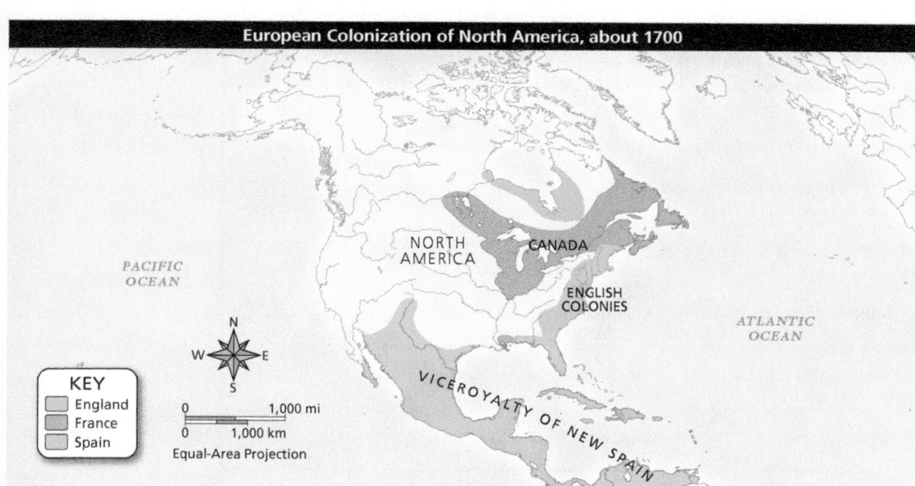

>> England, France, and Spain controlled large parts of North America. Their colonies differed from each other in a number of ways.

Interactive Map

Online Project the **Interactive Map: European Land Claims in North America, About 1700** and click through the hotspots.

ACTIVE CLASSROOM

Put this question on the whiteboard: How did geography benefit and hinder the development of New France? Ask students to spend 3 minutes writing their response to the question on sticky notes. Ask students to post their sticky notes on the board or on chart paper, and then lead a class discussion on the similarities and differences in the individual responses. *(Cold winters limited farming and kept population down; abundant wildlife supported fishing and fur industries; rivers and lakes aided hunters, trappers, and missionaries; large geographic area made it difficult to govern.)*

Guided Reading and Discussion

Ask students to explain the main economic activities of New France.

Draw Inferences How did the policies of the French king Louis XIV benefit and hinder the development of New France? *(Louis XIV helped development by sending more soldiers, settlers, and women to new France, but he also prohibited Protestants from settling in New France.)*

The 13 English Colonies

Explain that the English colonies had a variety of climates and that economic activities therefore varied by region. English colonists enjoyed some self-government based on English traditions and rights.

Analyze Images

Ask students to examine the map. Ask: In which part of North America was New France located? *(in what is now Canada)*

History Background

Jacques Cartier In 1534, Jacques Cartier sailed to North America on behalf of France. His commission was to find spices, gold, and a passage to Asia. Cartier found none of these things, despite several attempts, and ended his career in relative obscurity. During his own lifetime, no one guessed the impact that Cartier's voyages would have. In his thousand-mile trek into Canada's interior, he staked France's later claim to a huge amount of North American territory. His legacy also lives on in the Canadian place names he coined, such as the St. Lawrence River and the name *Canada*—derived from an Iroquois word meaning "village" or "settlement."

Answers

Express Problems Clearly *Wars in Europe distracted the attention of French rulers. Canada's long and harsh winters made farming difficult, and therefore French people were reluctant to move there. France's Catholic monarchs would not allow Protestants to settle in New France.*

Topic 11 Lesson 4

Analyze Images

Direct students to the charts on the Mayflower Compact and the roots of democracy in English colonial government. Ask students to identify the influences that contributed to self-government in the English colonies. *(Sample response: Judeo-Christian ideals, Greco-Roman models, English tradition of rights, English parliamentary tradition)*

Key Terms

Ask students to find the key term **compact** (in bold) in the text and explain its meaning. Point out that the Pilgrims wrote the Mayflower Compact because they had landed far north of Virginia in a place outside the authority of the English government. What **compacts** can students think of that people still make today?

Guided Reading and Discussion

Ask students to explain English colonial government and regional economies.

Compare How did the economies of New England and the South differ? *(New England's economy relied on shipbuilding, fishing, and timber. Southern colonies developed a plantation economy based on cash crops such as rice and tobacco.)*

Church of England. They sought religious freedom rather than commercial profit. Before coming ashore, they signed the Mayflower Compact, in which they set out guidelines for governing their North American colony. A **compact** is an agreement among people. Today, we see this document as an important early step toward self-government.

Many Pilgrims died in the early years of the Plymouth colony. Local Native Americans, however, taught them to grow corn and helped them survive in the new land. Soon, a new wave of English Protestant immigrants arrived to establish the Massachusetts Bay Colony.

Expansion and Prosperity In the 1600s and 1700s, other groups and individuals founded colonies for England. Some colonies, like Virginia and New York, were commercial ventures, organized for profit.

Others, like Massachusetts, Pennsylvania, and Maryland, were set up as havens for persecuted religious groups. Still others, like Georgia and South Carolina, were gifts from the king of England to loyal supporters.

Geographic conditions helped shape different ways of life in the New England, Middle, and Southern colonies. At first, settlers in each colony just struggled to survive. Early on, they abandoned dreams of finding riches like the Spanish had in Mexico and Peru. Instead, they learned to create wealth by using the resources native to their surroundings.

In New England, many settlers were farmers who recreated in North America their village life from England. They took advantage of fishing and timber resources, and some colonists set up shipbuilding industries. In the Middle Colonies, farmers grew large quantities of grain on the abundant land. In the Southern Colonies, a plantation economy emerged. Cash crops, such as rice and tobacco, grew well in the warm climate. They therefore developed a plantation economy to grow these crops.

As in New Spain, the English colonists needed workers to clear land and raise crops. The English tried using Native American labor, but the Native Americans fled or died of diseases. Before long, the colonists began to rely on the work of Africans who were brought to the colonies and sold as slaves. In several colonies in the South, enslaved Africans and their descendants would eventually outnumber people of European descent.

Limited Self-Government Like the rulers of Spain and France, English monarchs asserted control over their American colonies. They appointed royal governors to oversee colonial affairs and had Parliament pass laws to regulate colonial trade. Yet, compared with settlers in the Spanish and French colonies, English colonists enjoyed a large degree of self-government. Each colony

THE MAYFLOWER COMPACT NOVEMBER 21, 1620
• First written framework of government in English colonies
• Signed by all 41 adult males aboard the Mayflower
• Signers agreed to form a civil government and obey its laws
• Signers agreed to enact "just and equal laws" for the general good of the colony
• Based on English traditions of self-government
• Served as inspiration for later more complex frameworks of government

>> In the Mayflower Compact the Pilgrims agreed to form a government and obey its laws. The idea of self-government would later become a founding principle of the United States.

D Differentiate Extra Support To help students remember the regional variations of the English colonies, ask them to write down one unique fact about each of the three regions.

English Language Proficiency Standard

Speaking 3.D.2 Read "Britain and France in a Global Struggle" aloud to students. Then have students partner up, and ask pairs to explain the rivalry between Britain and France in their own words. Have students discuss with their partner why the countries struggled and give examples of how that struggle affected North America.

Beginning Ask students to use short sentences to respond. Provide them with model sentence starters: *Britain and France struggled because _____. This struggle affected North America*

Roots of Democracy

TRADITIONS INFLUENCING ENGLISH COLONIAL SELF- GOVERNMENT
JUDEO-CHRISTIAN IDEALS
Jewish and Christian traditions emphasized the value of the individual, the importance of social responsibility, and the idea of free will, or the freedom of humans to make choices for themselves
GRECO-ROMAN MODELS
Ancient Greek democracy and Roman republicanism served as ancient models of limited self-government and influenced ideas about equality before the law and individual liberty
ENGLISH TRADITION OF GUARANTEED RIGHTS
The Magna Carta (1215) and the English Bill of Rights (1689) guaranteed certain rights to citizens, including the right to trial by jury and individual liberty
ENGLISH PARLIAMENTARY TRADITION
Beginning with the Magna Carta, the two houses of Parliament played an increasing role in representing the English people and making English laws

>> The ideas of democracy and representative government have a long history. They are based on traditions that are far older than the English colonies that gave birth to the United States.

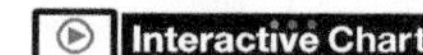

had its own representative assembly, elected by men who owned property, that advised the governor and made decisions on local issues.

The tradition of consulting representative assemblies grew out of the English experience. Beginning in the 1200s, Parliament had begun to play an important role in English affairs. Slowly, too, English citizens had gained certain legal and political rights. England's American colonists expected to enjoy the same rights. When colonists later protested British policies in North America, they viewed themselves as "freeborn Englishmen" who were defending their traditional rights.

IDENTIFY CENTRAL IDEAS Why did the English colonies have a large degree of self-government?

A Power Struggle Begins

By the 1600s, Spain, France, England, and the Netherlands all had colonies in North America. They began to fight—both in the colonies and around the world—to protect and expand their interests.

A Race for Colonies By the late 1600s, French claims included present-day Canada as well as much of the present-day central United States. The Spanish had moved north, making claims to present-day Texas and Florida. Meanwhile, the English and Dutch maintained colonies along the East Coast. Native Americans throughout the colonies entered the conflict, hoping to play the Europeans against one another.

Competition was also fierce in the Caribbean, as European nations fought to acquire the profitable sugar-producing colonies. By the 1700s, the French and English Caribbean islands, worked by enslaved Africans, had surpassed the whole of North America in exports to Europe.

Britain and France in a Global Struggle By the 1700s, Britain and France emerged as bitter rivals for power around the globe. Their clashes in Europe often ignited conflicts in the Caribbean, North America, India, and Africa.

In 1754, fighting broke out between the French and British in North America. In the British colonies, it marked the beginning of the **French and Indian War.** By 1756, that regional conflict was linked to the Seven Years' War in Europe. The war soon spread to India and other parts of the globe.

Although France held more territory in North America, the British colonies had more people. Trappers, traders, and farmers from the British colonies were pushing west into the Ohio Valley, a region claimed

when _____. Have students draw illustrations to go with their sentences.

Intermediate Ask students to give three examples of how the struggle between Britain and France affected North America. Encourage open-ended discussion. Provide a sentence starter: *The struggle between Britain and France affected North America when* _____.

Advanced Encourage students to have an open-ended discussion about the struggle between Britain and France during the 1700s. Encourage them to use complex sentences with connecting words such as *and, but,* and *because* in their examples.

Advanced High After students discuss the rivalry between Britain and France, ask them to discuss the impact of the Treaty of Paris on the rivalry. Ask them to give examples to support their statements.

A Power Struggle Begins

European countries often clashed over colonial territories and trade in North America. In the mid-1700s, the British battled the French in the French and Indian War. Some Native American groups fought on the French side, while others fought on the British side. The British won the war, and the French had to give up Canada.

Online Project the **Interactive Chart: Characteristics of French and British Colonies** and click through each tile individually.

Hypothesize Ask students to hypothesize how the differences between the French and British colonies might have helped the British win. *(The British colonies had a larger population and a larger fighting force; a long coast and easier access to aid shipped from Britain; and a more compact territory that was easier to defend.)*

ACTIVE CLASSROOM

Ask students to think about what it might be like to have a conversation with one of the people in this lesson. Have them write down a question they would like to ask, a response the person might make to the question, and then a comment the student might make in return. Encourage students to act out their conversations and post videos or sound files.

Guided Reading and Discussion

Ask students to describe in detail why conflict broke out among global powers during the 1700s.

Be sure that students understand that the French and Indian War was part of a larger European power struggle called the Seven Years' War. Ask: What was the outcome of the 1763 Treaty of Paris? *(France ceded all of Canada and its land east of the Mississippi River to Britain, and the Louisiana Territory to Spain. France regained islands in the Caribbean and African outposts that Britain had seized during the war.)*

Answers

Identify Central Ideas *England had a long tradition of representative assemblies dating back to the development of Parliament in the 1200s.*

Summarize *Native Americans entered into the wars, allying themselves with one European nation or another. Native American nations therefore engaged in conflict with one another.*

Topic 11 Lesson 4

SYNTHESIZE

Online Ask students to recall the Topic Essential Question, "Why do people move?" Tell students they have 5 minutes to answer the questions in the A Conquest of Great Importance activity. Then ask them to pair with a partner and share their responses.

Tell the pairs to collaborate on an answer for the following question: "How might the outcome of the French and Indian War cause movement among French colonists, British colonists, and Native Americans?" *(Sample response: French colonists might move back to France or to other French colonies; British colonists might move west and north into the French territories that they gained in the war; as British settlers advance, Native Americans might have to move away.)*

DEMONSTRATE

Online Assign the **Digital Lesson Quiz** for this lesson if you haven't already done so. Students will be offered automatic remediation or enrichment based on their score.

Pose the following question to the class on the Discussion Board:

In "European Colonies in North America," you learned about French and British competition for colonies in North America, their struggle for dominance, and how that struggle affected Native Americans.

Draw Inferences How does the British victory in the French and Indian War have a lasting impact on North America today? *(Sample response: The primary language of Canada and the United States is English. Both countries have democratic governments based on British traditions. A French-speaking population remains in Canada, especially in the province of Quebec. Native American populations in the eastern United States are much smaller than they used to be.)*

Topic Inquiry

Have students continue their investigations for the Topic Inquiry.

by France. The French, who had forged alliances with Native Americans, fought to oust the intruders.

During the war, British soldiers and colonial troops launched a series of campaigns against the French in Canada and on the Ohio frontier. In 1759, the British captured Quebec, capital of New France, and then Montreal. Although the war dragged on until 1763, the British had won control of Canada.

The 1763 **Treaty of Paris** officially ended the worldwide war and ensured British dominance in North America. France ceded all of Canada and its lands east of the Mississippi River to Britain. It handed the Louisiana Territory over to Spain. However, France did regain the rich sugar-producing islands in the Caribbean and the slave-trading outposts in Africa that the British had seized during the war.

? **SUMMARIZE** How did wars between European powers in the Americas affect Native Americans?

ELPS 3.D.2 Give examples of how the rivalry between Britain and France affected North America.

ASSESSMENT

1. **Generate Explanations** Why did European countries compete to expand their power in North America?
2. **Summarize** How were the Pilgrims' goals for religious freedom hampered during the early years of the Plymouth colony, and how did they overcome the obstacles?
3. **Compare and Contrast** How were conditions in New France and the English colonies different?
4. **Identify Patterns** How did the various regions of the British colonies become prosperous in different ways?
5. **Identify Central Issues** How was the French and Indian War caused by European expansion and competition on a global scale?

Assessment

1. European countries wanted wealth from raw materials such as fur, fish, lumber, and agricultural produce; to spread Christianity; and to keep their European rivals from gaining territory.
2. The Pilgrims were unprepared for harsh winters and lacked techniques to use the natural resources surrounding them. Many died from starvation and disease. Friendly Native Americans taught them to grow corn and work the land.
3. New France had poor farming conditions, a small population, and firm royal control. English colonies had better farming conditions, a fast-growing population, and limited self-government.
4. New England had fishing, timber, and shipbuilding industries. People of the middle colonies relied on farming. In the South, plantation cash crops provided large profits.
5. During the 1700s, Britain and France competed for wealth and power around the world. The French and Indian War began in 1754 as a battle over control of North America. But their war gradually spread to Europe, India, and Africa. Britain won, and gained considerable power.

11.5 In the 1400s and 1500s, as you have read, Europeans set up small forts on the coast of West Africa in order to resupply their ships and profit from local trade, especially in gold. As Europeans built colonies in the Americas, they needed large numbers of laborers to make their colonies profitable. By the 1600s, they increasingly turned to Africa to provide that labor.

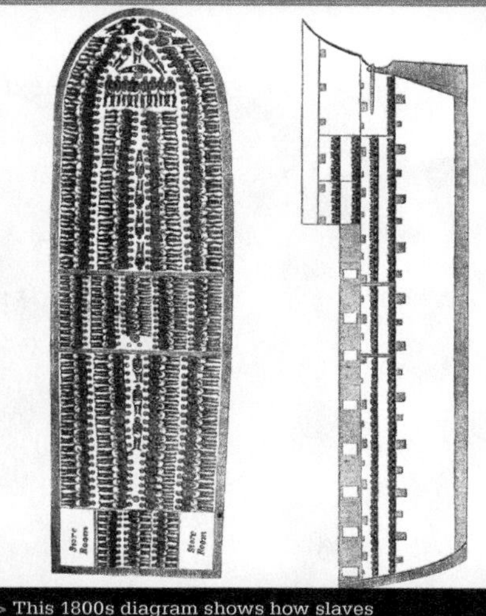

>> This 1800s diagram shows how slaves were so tightly crammed in small spaces that they had to lie side by side with little room to move for many hours at a time.

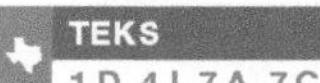
Interactive Flipped Video

The Slave Trade and Its Impact on Africa

The African Slave Trade Expands

Slavery Throughout History Slavery has existed all over the world since ancient times: ancient Egypt, Greece, and Rome, as well as China, Persia, the Aztecs, and other societies had enslaved people. The English word *slave* comes from *Slav*, the people of Eastern Europe who were often sold into slavery in the Middle Ages.

The Arabs also used slave labor. Some were captives taken from Africa.

In the Middle East, enslaved Africans worked on large farming estates or large-scale irrigation projects. Others became artisans, soldiers, or merchants.

European Traders Enter the Slave Trade In the 1400s and early 1500s, the Portuguese and other Europeans brought a few Africans back to Europe as slaves. There, Africans were seen as exotic servants of the rich. As European colonies in the Americas grew, however, Europeans turned to slave laborers to clear **plantations,** or the large estates run by an owner or an owner's overseer.

TEKS
1.D, 4.I, 7.A, 7.C

>> Objectives

Summarize the expansion of the African slave trade.

Explain how triangular trade worked.

Understand the nature of the Middle Passage and describe its effects.

Analyze the impact of the Atlantic slave trade on West Africa and the Americas.

>> Key Terms

Osei Tutu
Oyo empire
plantation
missionary
Asante kingdom
monopoly
triangular trade
Middle Passage
mutiny
Afonso I
Olaudah Equiano

447

PEARSON realize. www.PearsonTexas.com Access your Digital Lesson.

The Slave Trade and Its Impact on Africa

CONNECT

Preview Have students preview the **Lesson Objectives** and the list of **Key Terms**.

Students can also preview all the **Key Terms** and **Academic Vocabulary** using the **Interactive Reading Notepad** on the digital course or preview a summary of the lesson in the **Reading and Note Taking Study Guide**.

Online Use the **Editable Presentation** found on the digital course to present the main ideas for this lesson.

Start-Up Activity

Read this quotation describing the first ship of African slaves to arrive in Portugal from West Africa in 1444.

"Some kept their heads low and their faces bathed in tears, looking at each other . . . others struck themselves in the face and threw themselves to the ground; and others sang sad songs—although we did not understand their words, the sound told of their great sorrow. . . . The mothers threw themselves flat on the ground. They were beaten but they refused to give up their children."—From *Chronicle of the Discovery and Conquest of Guinea*

Determine Author's Point of View What was the writer's opinion of slave trading? *(The author thought slave trading was cruel and inhumane.)*

Tell students that in this lesson they will be learning about the expansion and impact of the African slave trade.

Online You can also project the **Start Up Activity** from the course.

INVESTIGATE

Have students read the section using the **Reading and Note Taking Study Guide** to help them take notes and understand the text as they read.

The African Slave Trade Expands

The African slave trade grew because of high demand for cheap slave labor, much of it for plantations in the Americas. Some African leaders tried to resist, but profits for slave traders and plantation owners were high, and demand grew.

Aa Vocabulary Builder

1. Have students pronounce the following academic vocabulary terms in this lesson and clarify the part of speech. For difficult or polysyllabic words, break them into syllables and pronounce them with the students.
2. Explain what the word means in common "student-friendly" language using synonyms and antonyms when possible. Provide concrete examples to clarify the meaning, and rephrase the definition.

convert: cause to change

dominate: to rule or control by superior power

unified: combined into one

commodity: anything bought and sold

restrain: to keep under control; to keep from action

Identify Steps in a Process Ask students to create a flowchart describing the process by which Africans were enslaved and shipped to plantations in the Americas. *(African traders seized captives in the interior, transported them to the coast, and traded slaves for European goods; European traders shipped slaves across the Atlantic to plantations in the Americas.)*

Guided Reading and Discussion

Ask students to describe how some African leaders tried to resist the transatlantic slave trade.

Compare Ask students to compare the African slave trade before and after the involvement of the Portuguese and other Europeans. What differences do they note? *(Sample response: Before European involvement: Arab and African traders, lower volume of trade; After European involvement: European, Arab, and African traders, greater volume of trade, slaves transported across Atlantic, slaves in Americas had little hope of improving their status.)*

>> The African slave trade expanded in response to Europeans' increasing use of enslaved workers on plantations in the Americas.

>> Portuguese soldiers and missionaries are received by the king of Kongo. Afonso I of Kongo welcomed Portuguese missionaries and scholars and sent his son to Portugal to learn about Christianity.

Europeans lacked the resources to travel inland to seize slaves. Instead, they relied on local African rulers and traders to bring captives—usually from other African nations—to coastal trading posts. There, the traders exchanged captured Africans for weapons, gunpowder, textiles, iron, and other goods.

In the 1500s, the slave trade was relatively small. Over the next 300 years, however, it grew into a huge, profitable business.

By the 1700s and 1800s, traders had shipped tens of thousands of enslaved Africans across the Atlantic to work on tobacco and sugar plantations in the Americas. These slaves were property.

African Resistance As the slave trade grew, some African leaders tried to slow it down or even stop it altogether. They used different forms of resistance, but in the end, the system that supported the trade was too strong for them to resist.

An early critic of the slave trade was **Afonso I,** ruler of Kongo in west-central Africa. As a young man, Afonso had been tutored by Portuguese **missionaries,** who baptized him to Christianity.

Impressed by his early contacts with the Portuguese, Afonso hoped to build a Christian state in Kongo. After becoming king in 1505, he called on Portuguese missionaries, teachers, and technical experts to help him develop Kongo and increase his own power. He sent his sons to Portugal to be educated in Christian ways.

Afonso grew worried as more and more Portuguese came to Kongo to buy slaves. Afonso wanted to maintain contact with Europe but end the slave trade. His appeal failed, and the slave trade continued.

In the late 1700s, another African ruler tried to halt the slave trade in his lands. He was the almany (religious leader) of Futa Toro, in present-day Senegal. Since the 1500s, French sea captains had bought slaves from African traders in Futa Toro. To end this trade, the almany issued a law in 1788. It forbade anyone to transport slaves through his land to sell abroad. However, the inland slave traders simply worked out a new route to the coast. Sailing to this new market, the French captains easily purchased the slaves that the almany had prevented them from buying in Futa Toro.

IDENTIFY CAUSE AND EFFECT Why did the African slave trade expand?

D Differentiate Challenge/Gifted Tell students that slavery and slave trading are still problems in the world today. Ask them to do some quick online research on this topic and share their findings with the class.

Answers

Identify Cause and Effect *As a result of European exploration and expansion, European traders arrived in Africa and entered the slave trade. These merchants shipped tens of thousands of enslaved Africans to work on plantations in European colonies in the Americas.*

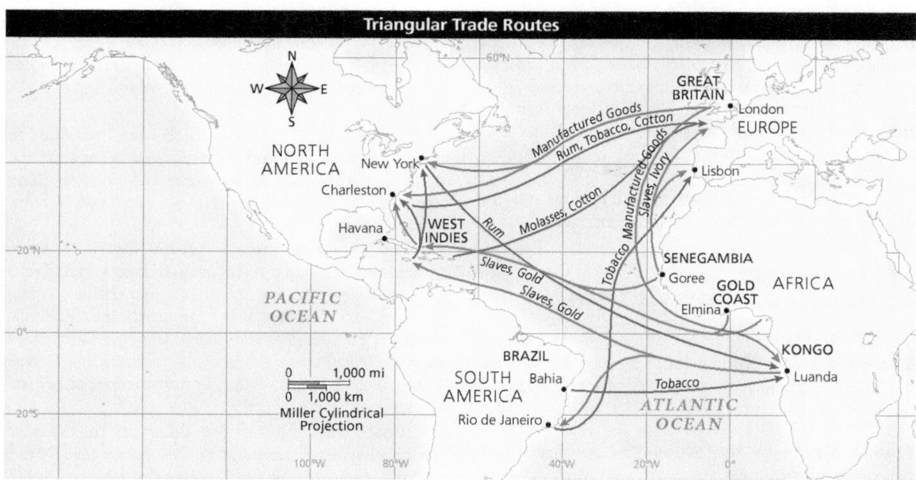

>> **Analyze Maps** This map shows triangular trade routes that started in the 1500s. What trade goods were slaves exchanged for in North America?

Interactive Map

The Atlantic Slave Trade

In the 1750s, a young 11-year-old boy named **Olaudah Equiano** was seized from his Nigerian village by slave traders. He was then transported as human cargo from West Africa to the Americas. In later years, he wrote about the experience in his autobiography:

> The first object which saluted my eyes when I arrived on the coast was the sea, and a slave ship which was then riding at anchor and waiting for its cargo. These filled me with astonishment, which was soon converted into terror when I was carried on board.
>
> —Olaudah Equiano

Enslaved Africans like Olaudah Equiano formed part of an international trade network that arose during the 1500s. The Spanish were the first major European partners in the slave trade, buying slaves to labor in Spain's South American empire.

As other European powers established colonies in the Americas, the slave trade—and with it the entire international trade network—intensified.

Triangular Trade The Atlantic slave trade formed one part of a three-legged international trade network known as **triangular trade.** This was a triangle-shaped series of Atlantic trade routes linking Europe, Africa, and the Americas.

Triangular trade worked in the following way. On the first leg, merchant ships brought European goods—including guns, cloth, and cash—to Africa. In Africa, the merchants traded these goods for slaves. On the second leg, known as the **Middle Passage,** the slaves were transported to the Americas. There, the enslaved Africans were exchanged for sugar, molasses, and other products manufactured at plantations owned by Europeans.

On the final leg, merchants carried sugar, molasses, cotton, and other American goods such as furs, salt fish, and rum made from molasses. These goods were shipped to Europe, where they were traded at a profit for the European commodities that merchants needed to return to Africa.

Merchants, Industries, and Cities Thrive Triangular trade was immensely profitable for many people. Merchants grew wealthy. Even though there were risks such as losing ships at sea, the money to be made from valuable cargoes usually outweighed the risks. Certain industries that supported trade thrived. For example, a shipbuilding industry in New England grew to support the shipping industry. Other colonial industries, such as fishing, raising tobacco, and processing sugar, became hugely successful.

Thriving trade led to successful port cities. European cities such as Nantes, France, and Bristol, England,

Topic 11 Lesson 5

Key Terms

Ask students to find the key term **triangular trade** (in bold) in the text. Explain that many people profited both directly and indirectly from the traffic of human slaves, the second leg of the triangular route—merchants and port cities in Africa, the Americas, and Europe; shipbuilders in New England; planters in the West Indies; and so on.

The Atlantic Slave Trade

Starting in the 1500s, a triangular trade system linked Europe, Africa, and the Americas. Ships went from Europe to Africa carrying trade items such as guns, cloth, and cash, which were exchanged for slaves. Ships then took African slaves to the Americas, where they were exchanged for cash, sugar, molasses, cotton rum, or other goods. These American products were then shipped to Europe and sold for profit.

Online Project the **Interactive Map: Triangular Trade Routes** and bring up the different layers showing each of the three legs of the triangular trade.

ACTIVE CLASSROOM

Use the "A Closer Look" strategy with the Interactive Map. Have students divide into three groups. Each group should more closely investigate one leg of the triangular trade map and then share what they learned.

Guided Reading and Discussion

Ask students to describe the general sequence of events in triangular trade.

Identify Cause and Effect Be sure students understand that the triangular trade connected Europe, Africa, and the Americas. Ask: Which social classes and regions within continents profited the most from the triangular trade? *(Answers may vary. Sample response: shipping merchants, plantation owners, manufacturers and merchants in port towns and cities)*

History Background

African-born or Not? Recent scholarship suggests that Olaudah Equiano may not have been born in Africa. Though historians agree that he was a slave and became a leading spokesperson for the abolitionist movement in the United States, there is evidence (a U.S. Naval document) that suggests he was actually born in South Carolina. This would make his account of his youth in Africa and on the Middle Passage voyage a composite creation, drawn from the lives of others he knew. Some historians believe that Equiano may in fact have lied to the Navy about his birthplace in order to present himself, for reasons unknown, as American-born. If this is the case, the story of his Igbo life in Africa would be true. Even if Equiano was not African-born, historians agree that his story of eighteenth-century African society is accurate and remains a unique and effective way of understanding the past.

Answers

Analyze Maps *rum, tobacco, cotton, molasses*

Horrors of the Middle Passage

The Middle Passage was the central leg of the triangular trade route. Enslaved Africans were transported from Africa to the Americas on slave ships. Up to half the Africans onboard died.

Generate Explanations Why did so many enslaved Africans die over the course of the Middle Passage? *(They died from disease and physical mistreatment.)*

Guided Reading and Discussion

Ask students to describe some details of the Middle Passage journey that made it a horror for Africans aboard slave ships.

Identify Supporting Details What were some ways that Africans tried to resist the Middle Passage? *(While being marched to the coast, some tried to escape. On the ships, slaves sometimes tried to join in mutinies or take over the ships.)*

Impact of the Slave Trade

Some African kingdoms participated in slavery and used their wealth to conquer weaker states. But slavery also destroyed many African states. Millions of Africans died or lived in the terrible conditions of slavery. In the Americas, plantation owners and merchants in port cities and towns profited from slavery. Eventually, slavery was one of the leading causes of the American Civil War.

grew prosperous because of triangular trade. In North America, even newly settled towns such as Salem, Massachusetts, and Newport, Rhode Island, quickly grew into thriving cities. Even though few slaves were imported directly to northern cities in North America, the success of the port cities there was made possible by the Atlantic slave trade.

IDENTIFY CAUSE AND EFFECT How did the Atlantic slave trade affect colonial economies?

Horrors of the Middle Passage

To merchants, the Middle Passage was just one leg of triangular trade. For enslaved Africans, the Middle Passage was a horror.

Forced March to the Ships The terrible journey began before the slave ships set sail. Most Africans were taken from inland villages. After they were enslaved, they were forced to march to coastal ports. Men, women, and children were bound with ropes and chains, often to one another, and forced to walk distances as long as a thousand miles. They might be forced to carry heavy loads, and often the men's necks were encircled with thick iron bands.

Many captives died along the way. Others tried to escape, and were often quickly recaptured and brutally punished.

Those who survived the march were restrained in coastal holding pens and warehouses in slave shipping ports such as Elmina, Ghana, or Gorée, Senegal. They were held there until European traders arrived by ship.

>> Europeans built fortresses in ports along the west coast of Africa, such as the town of Elmina in Ghana, shown here. **Hypothesize** What was one probable use of the fortress?

Packed Aboard the "Floating Coffins" Once purchased, Africans were packed below the decks of slave ships, usually in chains. Hundreds of men, women, and children were crammed into a single vessel for voyages that lasted from three weeks to three months. The ships faced many perils, including storms at sea, raids by pirate ships, and **mutinies,** or revolts, by the captives.

Disease was the biggest threat to the lives of the captives and the profit of the merchants. Of the slaves who died, most died of dysentery. Many died of smallpox. Many others died from apparently no disease at all. Whatever the cause, slave ships became "floating coffins" on which up to half the Africans on board died from disease or brutal mistreatment.

Some enslaved Africans resisted, and others tried to seize control of the ship and return to Africa. Suicide, however, was more common than mutiny. Many Africans believed that in death they would be returned to their home countries. So they hanged themselves, starved themselves, or leapt overboard.

SUMMARIZE Why did so many enslaved Africans die during the Middle Passage?

Impact of the Slave Trade

Historians continue to debate how many Africans were carried to the Americas during the Atlantic slave trade. Some historians estimate that about 2,000 Africans were sent to the Americas each year during the 1500s. In the 1780s, when the slave trade reached its peak, that number approached 80,000 a year. By the mid-1800s, when the overseas slave trade was finally ended, an estimated 11 million enslaved Africans had been forcibly carried to the Americas. Another 2 million probably died under the brutal conditions of the Middle Passage.

The slave trade brought great profits to many and provided the labor needed by colonial economies. Yet the slave trade had a devastating impact on African societies. Millions of people in Africa were brutalized

Answers

Identify Cause and Effect *Slave labor made European colonies wealthy and more productive. Colonial industries became prosperous. Port cities in the Americas thrived.*

Summarize *Enslaved Africans were treated cruelly, chained, and crammed tightly into ships. Many died from disease and mistreatment.*

Hypothesize *Sample response: Fortresses were used to defend European trading interests and as holding areas for slaves awaiting ships to the Americas.*

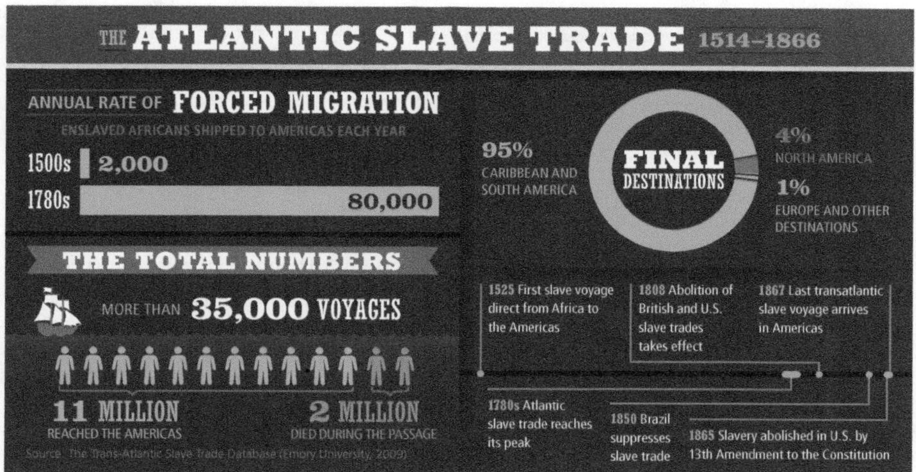

>> **Analyze Charts** Based on this information, what percentage of slaves died during passage to the Americas? Where in the Americas did most slaves end up?

by the slave trade and slavery itself. Many others died during the horrific Middle Passage.

The Asante Kingdom In some parts of Africa, the slave trade had little or no impact. In other areas, it disrupted whole societies. The slave trade triggered wars, increased tensions among neighboring peoples, and led to the rise of strong new states. The rulers of these states battled rivals for control of the slave trade.

The **Asante kingdom** (uh SAHN teh) emerged in the area occupied by present-day Ghana. In the late 1600s, an able military leader, **Osei Tutu,** won control of the trading city of Kumasi. From there, he conquered neighboring peoples and unified the Asante kingdom. The Asante faced a great challenge in the Denkyera, a powerful neighboring enemy kingdom. Osei Tutu realized that in order to withstand the Denkyera, the people of his kingdom needed to be firmly united. To do this, he claimed that his right to rule came from heaven, and that people in the kingdom were linked by spiritual bonds. This strategy paid off when the Asante defeated the Denkyera in the late 1600s.

Under Osei Tutu, government officials, chosen by merit rather than by birth, supervised an efficient bureaucracy. They managed the royal monopolies on gold mining and the slave trade. A **monopoly** is the exclusive control of a business or industry. The Asante traded with Europeans on the coast, exchanging gold and slaves for firearms. They also played rival Europeans against one another to protect themselves. In this way, they built a wealthy, powerful state.

The Oyo Empire The **Oyo empire** arose from successive waves of settlement by the Yoruba people of present-day Nigeria. It began as a relatively small forest kingdom. Beginning in the late 1600s, however, its leaders used wealth from the slave trade to build up an impressive army. The Oyo empire used the army to conquer the neighboring kingdom of Dahomey. At the same time, it continued to gain wealth by trading with European merchants at the port city of Porto-Novo.

Slavery and the Americas The slave trade brought millions of Africans to the Americas. The descendants of the early captives knew life only as slaves and had limited or no information about their African ancestors. By the late 1700s and throughout the 1800s, reformers in Britain, the United States, and elsewhere called for abolition, or ending slavery and the slave trade.

In 1807, Britain abolished the slave trade throughout its empire and abolished slavery itself in 1833. In the United States, the issue of the spread of slavery into new territories helped fuel tensions that ultimately led to the Civil War. In 1865, when the Thirteenth Amendment was ratified, slavery was officially ended in all parts of the United States.

Online Project the **Interactive Chart: Effects of Slavery** and discuss the questions on the chart.

ACTIVE CLASSROOM

Use the "Make Headlines" strategy, and have each student select one cell of the chart and write a headline based on it. Ask: If you were to write a headline on the most important aspect of this topic, what would it be?

Guided Reading and Discussion

Ask students to compare and contrast short-term effects of slavery on West Africa with longer-term effects of slavery in the Americas.

Analyze Images

Ask students to use the infographic "The Atlantic Slave Trade" to write a sentence summarizing a key idea supported by a set of the data. *(Sample responses: The slave trade volume peaked in the 1780s. Eleven million enslaved Africans were shipped to the Americas. Most went to South America and the Caribbean. The transatlantic slave trade ended in the 1800s.)*

D Differentiate **Special Needs/Extra Support** Have students work in pairs to identify three words in the text that they do not fully understand and three questions that they have about the effects of the slave trade. Provide guidance to help them with these questions.

English Language Proficiency Standards

Speaking 3.E.1 Arrange groups of four and assign jobs: timekeeper, reader, discussion leader, and scribe. Read "Impact of the Slave Trade" aloud and ask: *What was the impact of the slave trade?*

Beginning Encourage students to use information from the text to answer the question. Make sure each group member gives a different answer. Help groups choose their two best answers to share with the class.

Intermediate Perform the Beginning activity, but have students share their answers and direct each group to choose three answers.

Advanced Have students reread "Impact of the Slave Trade." Discussion leaders should ensure that each student gives a different answer. Scribes should guide their groups in writing a summary of their three best answers.

Advanced High Perform the Advanced activity, but add this question: How did the slave trade affect the development of the economies in the Americas?

Answers

Analyze Charts *about 18% (2 million out of 11 million); Most ended up in the Caribbean and South America.*

Contrast *Some African states lost so many people to slavery that they disappeared forever. Other African states participated in the slave trade and gained wealth that they used to increase their power and conquer weaker neighboring states.*

Topic 11 Lesson 5

SYNTHESIZE

Online The Essential Question for this Topic is: "Why do people move?" Ask students to take 5 minutes to write down some brief answers to these questions: Why did Europeans go to Africa? Why did Africans go to the Americas? Have pairs share their answers with the class.

Hypothesize After existing for centuries, the transatlantic slave trade's volume peaked in the 1780s, just a few decades before the United States and Britain passed laws abolishing it. Why do you think there was such a short amount of time between the slave trade's peak and abolition? *(Sample response: The period of high volume made the slave trade and its horrors very visible, and increased calls to abolish it. The ideals of the American and French revolutions increased abolitionism. Slave traders anticipated the abolition laws and increased their volume to make more money and provide customers with more slaves.)*

DEMONSTRATE

Online Assign the **Digital Lesson Quiz** for this lesson if you haven't already done so. Students will be offered automatic remediation or enrichment based on their score.

Pose this question to the class on the Discussion Board:

Identify Causes and Effects How has the transatlantic slave trade affected the history, society, and culture of the United States from the 1700s to today? *(Answers will vary. Students may mention the plantation culture of the American South, the Civil War, the struggle for civil rights, the ethnic diversity of the United States, or the African influence on American culture.)*

Topic Inquiry

Have students continue their investigations for the Topic Inquiry.

Slavery continued longer elsewhere in the Americas, notably in Brazil. Over the centuries, about 80 percent of all enslaved Africans were brought to Brazil or the Caribbean.

In Brazil, the profitable sugar industry along with other businesses relied on slave labor. Only in 1888 was slavery officially ended in Brazil.

The Atlantic slave trade brought people from different societies in Africa to the Americas. Although most came from West Africa, that region was home to diverse communities from small chiefdoms to larger states and kingdoms. A rich variety of African traditions, languages, beliefs, stories, music, and other cultural elements were added to the emerging new cultures of the Americas.

? **CONTRAST** How did the slave trade damage some African states, but help others?

ELPS **ELPS 3.E.1** Participate in a cooperative group activity to analyze *Impact of the Slave Trade.*

ASSESSMENT

1. **Compare and Contrast** How was the African slave trade before European involvement different from the African slave trade after European involvement?
2. **Identify Cause and Effect** How did the Atlantic slave trade affect the Asante kingdom and the Oyo empire?
3. **Identify Steps in a Process** How did the three steps of the triangular trade network function?
4. **Infer** Why was disease the leading cause of death of enslaved Africans on the Middle Passage?
5. **Summarize** Write a short summary explaining how the Atlantic slave trade impacted West Africa and the Americas.

Assessment

1. Before European involvement, Arab and African traders traded for enslaved people to work on farms or irrigation projects in the Middle East, but some became soldiers or merchants and could rise in rank.
2. Both states gained wealth and strength by trading slaves for firearms and gold. They used their wealth to conquer other African states.
3. Merchant ships transported European goods from Europe to Africa to exchange for slaves. The Middle Passage carried enslaved Africans to be exchanged for sugar, molasses, cotton, tobacco, and other products. These goods were shipped across the Atlantic for sale in Europe.
4. Limited space, inadequate food, and poor conditions encouraged spread of disease.
5. The slave trade brought wealth to traders in Africa and plantation owners in the Americas, but some West African societies were decimated by the abduction and death of thousands of people. Millions of Africans were enslaved in the Americas.

11.6 The European voyages of exploration in the 1500s and 1600s set off a chain of events that brought major changes to the world. Over the next centuries, European exploration and expansion overseas affected people from Asia, Africa, and the Americas to Europe itself.

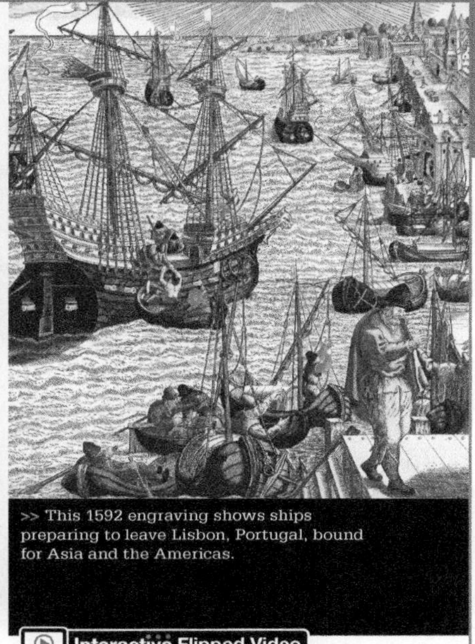

>> This 1592 engraving shows ships preparing to leave Lisbon, Portugal, bound for Asia and the Americas.

Effects of Global Contact

TEKS
1.D, 7.B, 7.F, 18.F

>> **Objectives**

Explain how European exploration led to the Columbian Exchange.

Explain new economic factors and principles that contributed to the success of the commercial revolution.

Understand the impact of mercantilism on European and colonial economies.

>> **Key Terms**

Columbian Exchange
inflation
price revolution
capitalism
entrepreneur
mercantilism
tariff
Commercial Revolution
free enterprise system

The Columbian Exchange

A Global Exchange When Columbus returned to Spain in March 1493, he brought with him plants and animals that he had found in the Americas. Later that year, Columbus returned to the Americas with some 1,200 settlers and a collection of European animals and plants. In this way, Columbus began a vast global exchange that would profoundly affect the world. Because this exchange began with Columbus, we call it the **Columbian Exchange.**

Exchanging Foods and Animals In the Americas, Europeans found a variety of foods that were new to them, including tomatoes, pumpkins, and peppers. They eagerly transported these to Europe. Two of these new foods, corn and potatoes, became important foods in the Old World. Easy to grow and store, potatoes helped feed Europe's rapidly growing population. Corn spread all across Europe and to Africa and Asia, becoming one of the world's most important cereal crops.

Europeans also carried a wide variety of plants and animals to the Americas, including wheat and grapes from Europe and bananas

www.PearsonTexas.com Access your Digital Lesson.

Topic 11 Lesson 6

Effects of Global Contact

CONNECT

Preview Have students preview the **Lesson Objectives** and the list of **Key Terms**.

Students can also preview all the **Key Terms** and **Academic Vocabulary** using the **Interactive Reading Notepad** on the digital course or preview a summary of the lesson in the **Reading and Note Taking Study Guide**.

Online Use the **Editable Presentation** found on the digital course to present the main ideas for this lesson.

Start Up Activity

Tell students that in the late 1700s, economist Adam Smith wrote about the European exploration that began in the 1400s:

"The discovery of America, and that of a passage to the East Indies by the Cape of Good Hope, are the two greatest and most important events recorded in the history of mankind. By uniting, in some measure, the most distant parts of the world, by enabling them to relieve one another's wants, to increase one another's enjoyments, and to encourage one another's industry, their general tendency would seem to be beneficial." —Adam Smith, *The Wealth of Nations*, 1776

Did Smith think increased global contact was a good thing or a bad thing? *(He thought it was good. He said European voyages were the "greatest and most important events.")* Ask students if they agree.

Tell students that in this lesson they will learn about the effects of increased global contact and new economic ideas.

Online You can also project the **Start Up Activity** from the course.

INVESTIGATE

Have students read the section using the **Reading and Note Taking Study Guide** to help them take notes and understand the text as they read.

The Columbian Exchange

Christopher Columbus's voyage started a global exchange of people, plants, animals, ideas, and technology now called the Columbian Exchange. This exchange profoundly impacted the Americas, Europe, Africa, and Asia.

Aa Vocabulary Builder

1. Have students pronounce the following academic vocabulary terms in this lesson and clarify the part of speech. For difficult or polysyllabic words, break them into syllables and pronounce them with the students.
2. Explain what the word means in common "student-friendly" language using synonyms and antonyms when possible. Provide concrete examples to clarify the meaning, and rephrase the definition.

dispersal: gathering; spreading of

migration: movement from one country or place to another

investment: the outlay of money

export: to send goods to other countries or places for sale

exploited: made full use of, often selfishly

Topic 11 Lesson 6

Online Project the **Interactive Map: The Columbian Exchange**. Bring up each image and text and discuss.

ACTIVE CLASSROOM

Use the "Audio Tour" strategy with student pairs. Have one student give the other a verbal "tour" of the map and hotspots. What do they show? Have the second student give the first an explanation of the lasting impact associated with each hotspot area. Pairs may want to audio record their tours to share with the class.

Guided Reading and Discussion

Ask students to explain the causes and effects of the Columbian Exchange.

Draw Inferences Choose an item that was transported as part of the Columbian Exchange. Explain how life in the hemisphere it traveled to might be different if the Columbian Exchange had not occurred. *(Many in the Eastern Hemisphere would have died from malaria without quinine, which came from the Western Hemisphere.)*

A Commercial Revolution

As the result of increased trade between Europe, Asia, Africa, and the Americas, Europe underwent a period of economic growth and colonialism. Lasting from about the 1500s until the early 1700s, the Commercial Revolution, as it is known, included the growth of capitalism, banking, and investing.

D Differentiate Extra Support Have students identify three items that moved from one hemisphere to another. Ask them to trace this movement on the Interactive Gallery and explain how each item was good or bad for the people in the hemisphere to which it moved.

and sugar cane from Africa and Asia. Cattle, pigs, goats, and chickens, unknown before the European encounter, joined the Native American diet. Horses and donkeys transported people and goods quickly. Horses also provided the nomadic peoples of western North America with a new, more effective way to hunt buffalo.

Population Growth The transfer of food crops from continent to continent took time. By the 1700s, however, corn, potatoes, manioc, beans, and tomatoes were contributing to population growth around the world. While other factors help account for the population explosion that began at this time, the dispersal of new food crops from the Americas was certainly a key cause.

Movement of People and Ideas The Columbian Exchange resulted in the migration of millions of people. Shiploads of Europeans sailed to the Americas in search of new opportunities. Others settled on the fringes of Africa and Asia. As you have read, the Atlantic slave trade forcibly brought millions of Africans to the Americas. Native American populations, however, declined drastically in the years after European arrival, largely as a result of diseases. Some American diseases traveled to Europe.

The vast movement of people led to the diffusion, or transfer, of ideas and technologies. Europeans and Africans brought their beliefs and customs to the Americas. In Europe and elsewhere, people adapted ideas and inventions from distant lands. Language also traveled. Words such as *pajama* (from India) and *hammock* or *canoe* (from the Americas) entered European languages as evidence of the global exchange.

? IDENTIFY CAUSE AND EFFECT How did the Columbian Exchange affect global population?

ELPS ELPS 3.F.1 Develop an understanding of concrete and abstract vocabulary in *The Columbian Exchange.*

A Commercial Revolution

The opening of direct links with Asia, Africa, and the Americas had far-reaching economic consequences for Europeans and their colonies. Europe underwent a period of economic growth and change known as the **Commercial Revolution,** which spurred the growth of modern capitalism, banking, and investing.

The Price Revolution By the 1500s, prices began to rise in many parts of Europe. At the same time, there was much more money in circulation. Earnings were often retained in banks or reinvested in the economy.

A rise in prices that is linked to a sharp increase in the amount of money available is called **inflation.** The

The Columbian Exchange

TRANSFERRED FROM THE WESTERN HEMISPHERE		TRANSFERRED FROM THE EASTERN HEMISPHERE	
Corn	Turkeys	Wheat	Coffee
Potatoes	Pineapples	Sugar	Horses
Sweet Potatoes	Tomatoes	Bananas	Pigs
Beans	Cocoa	Rice	Cows, oxen
Peanuts	Cassava/manioc	Oats	Goats
Squash	Silver	Barley	Chickens
Pumpkins	Quinine	Rye	Smallpox
Chili peppers	Sunflowers	Grapes	Typhus

>> **Analyze Charts** The Columbian Exchange affected people around the world. What livestock were introduced to the Americas by the Columbian Exchange?

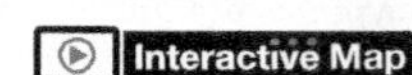

Answers

Identify Cause and Effect *The exchange of food crops and animals boosted global food production and helped increase population in Europe and other world regions. Millions of Europeans and enslaved Africans moved to the Americas. Some populations declined due to the transfer of disease, especially Native American populations.*

Analyze Charts *horses, pigs, cattle, goats, chickens*

English Language Proficiency Standards

Speaking 3.F.1 Explain the differences between concrete and abstract vocabulary. Read "The Columbian Exchange" aloud and have students complete one activity.

Beginning Provide concrete vocabulary terms from the text. Say each word for students to repeat. Have them create a pictorial dictionary. Have them write a simple interrogative sentence with each word and read them to a partner.

Intermediate Have students identify concrete vocabulary terms and create a pictorial dictionary. Have students write interrogative sentences with the words and use them in conversation.

Advanced Provide a few abstract vocabulary terms from the text. Have students develop definitions using context clues and work with a partner to improve them. Discuss definitions as a group.

Advanced High Complete the Advanced activity, but have students find the terms.

TULIPMANIA PRICE BUBBLE 1636–1637 

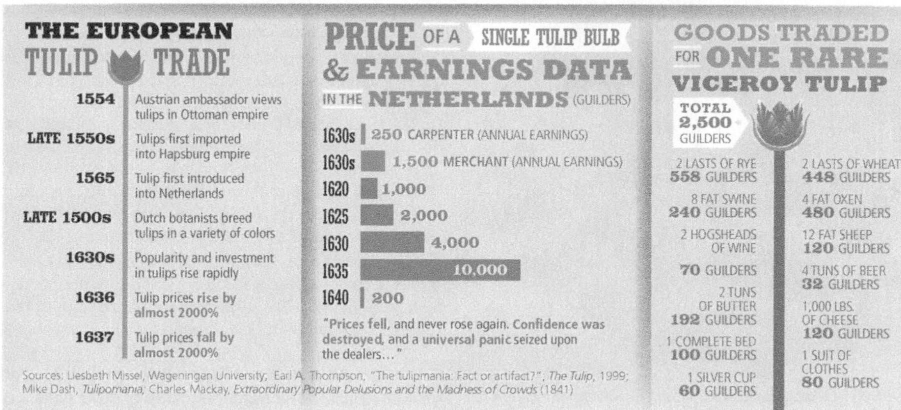

>> **Analyze Charts** Tulipmania is an example of an inflationary price bubble. From an investment standpoint, which year was the worst to buy a tulip? Explain.

period in European history when inflation rose rapidly is known as the **price revolution.** Inflation was fueled by the enormous amount of silver and gold flowing into Europe from the Americas by the mid-1500s. When prices began to rise, output also increased.

Free Enterprise Expanded trade and the push for overseas empires spurred the growth of European **capitalism,** or the investment of money to make a profit. In a capitalist economy, also called a **free enterprise system,** most businesses are privately owned and economic decisions are made between buyers and sellers based on supply and demand. Other key elements of capitalism include the accumulation and investment of capital (money) and competition within a free market.

During the Commercial Revolution, **entrepreneurs,** or enterprising business people, organized, managed, and took on the risks of doing business. Entrepreneurs provided jobs for workers and paid for raw materials, transport, and other costs of production. They pushed for predictable laws and secure contracts to protect their property and investments from unfair seizure or taxes.

As trade increased, entrepreneurs sought to expand into overseas ventures. Distant markets could be risky since governments were often small or weak in those places, but capitalists, because of their resources, were more willing to take risks.

As a result, the price revolution of the early modern age gave a boost to capitalism. Supply and demand began to control markets and prices rather than the more traditional medieval concept of a just, or fair, price. Entrepreneurs and capitalists made up a new business class devoted to the goal of making profits. Together, they helped change local European economies into an international trading system.

New Business Methods Early European capitalists discovered new ways to create wealth. From the Arabs, they adapted methods of bookkeeping to show profits and losses from their ventures. During the late Middle Ages, as you have read, banks increased in importance, allowing wealthy merchants to lend money at interest. Businesses could more easily obtain short-term loans because of expanded credit.

The joint stock company, which had also emerged in the late Middle Ages, grew in importance. It allowed people to pool large amounts of capital needed for overseas trading voyages. Individuals who invested in a joint stock company shared in the profits a company made. If a venture failed, investors lost only the amount they had put into the voyage, not the entire cost of the voyage.

Entrepreneurs Bypass the Guilds The growing demand for goods led merchants to find ways to increase production. Traditionally, guilds controlled

Online Project the **Interactive Chart: Economic Concepts** and work through it with students.

ACTIVE CLASSROOM

Use the "Sticky Notes" strategy. Have each student choose an economic term and write responses to this question on sticky notes: "What were some effects of this particular economic event or system?" Compare and contrast the responses as a group.

Guided Reading and Discussion

Point out that the capitalist free enterprise system provided new economic freedoms. Ask students to discuss these economic freedoms.

Identify Main Ideas Ask students to name some of the benefits of capitalism. *(Sample response: Consumers and producers can make free choices; prices are not set but determined by free market conditions.)*

Analyze Images

Direct students' attention to the infographic "Tulipmania Price Bubble." Say that at the height of the mania, a painting of tulips by a Dutch master cost less than one tulip bulb. Then ask: By what year did the price of a single tulip bulb equal more than six times the salary of a carpenter in the 1630s? *(1625)*

D Differentiate Extra Support For students who have trouble understanding some of the economic terms in the text, help them list some modern-day examples of capitalism, entrepreneurs, inflation, and cottage industries. *(Examples of capitalism are the stock market and companies competing for consumers. Local entrepreneurs include babysitters, lawn service providers, and people who own and operate stores. Rising gas prices are an example of inflation. Modern-day cottage industries include people who sell their crafts online.)*

Answers

Analyze Charts *1636 was the worst year to buy. Prices plunged in 1637, resulting in large losses for investors.*

Topic 11 Lesson 6

Mercantilism

European countries adopted the policy of mercantilism. This policy sought to increase national wealth by exporting more than importing. Colonies supplied the parent country with raw materials and served as a market for the parent country's exports. Tariffs, or taxes on imported goods, were used to limit imports.

Compare How was mercantilism consistent or inconsistent with capitalist principles? *(It was inconsistent in that mercantilist governments regulated trade and used tariffs to limit free trade.)*

Guided Reading and Discussion

Discuss the steps that governments took to impose mercantilism. Lead students in a discussion of whether or not the Commercial Revolution was beneficial to society.

Predict Consequences Why might mercantilist policies be a reason for colonies to rebel against parent countries? *(Sample response: Mercantilist laws prevented colonies from starting their own industries or buying goods from a foreign country, which limited their economic freedom.)*

>> These Irish women are boiling flax and spinning yarn to make linen cloth. Enterprising capitalists employed peasant cottagers like these in the "putting-out" system.

Interactive Chart

>> As European rulers embraced mercantilism and expanded trade, their ports became thriving centers of commerce. This painting depicts the crowded port of Toulon, France, in the mid-1700s.

the manufacture of goods. But guild masters often ran small-scale businesses without the capital to produce for large markets. They also had strict rules regulating quality, prices, and working conditions.

Enterprising capitalists devised a way to bypass the guilds called the "putting-out" system. It was first used to produce textiles but later spread to other industries. Under this system, for example, a merchant capitalist distributed raw wool to peasant cottages. Cottagers spun the wool into thread and then wove it into cloth. Merchants bought the wool cloth from the peasants and sent it to the city for finishing and dyeing. Finally, the merchants sold the finished product for a profit.

The "putting-out" system, also known by the term "cottage industry," separated capital and labor for the first time. In the 1700s, this system would lead to the capitalist-owned factories of the Industrial Revolution.

COMPARE AND CONTRAST How did capitalism, or free enterprise, differ from the medieval guild system?

Mercantilism

European monarchs enjoyed the benefits of the Commercial Revolution. In the fierce competition for trade and empire, they adopted a new economic policy, known as **mercantilism,** which was aimed at strengthening their national economies. Mercantilists believed that a nation's real wealth was measured in its gold and silver treasure. To build its supply of gold and silver, they said, a nation must export more goods than it imported.

The Value of Colonies To mercantilists, overseas colonies existed for the benefit of the parent country. They provided resources and raw materials not available in Europe. In turn, they enriched a parent country by serving as a market for its manufactured goods. To achieve these goals, European powers passed strict laws regulating trade with their colonies. Colonists could not set up their own industries to manufacture goods. They were also forbidden from buying goods from a foreign country. In addition, only ships from the parent country or the colonies themselves could be used to send goods into or out of the colonies.

Increasing National Wealth Mercantilists urged rulers to adopt policies that they believed would increase national wealth and government revenues. To boost production, governments exploited mineral and timber resources, built roads, and backed new industries. They imposed national currencies and established standard weights and measures.

Answers

Compare and Contrast *Guild masters often ran small businesses without the capital to produce for large markets. Guilds strictly regulated quality, prices, and working conditions. Free enterprise allowed the economic forces of supply and demand to set prices. Capitalists hired non-guild peasants to do the labor in their cottages. In time, the capitalists expanded their businesses into factories.*

Describe *Mercantilism amassed wealth for Europe with the principle of exporting more than was imported, thereby earning more gold and silver for Europe. Mercantilism relied on using colonies as a place to sell exports and as a source of resources and raw materials.*

Economics Background

Trade Wars Mercantilist policies favored the imposition of tariffs on imported goods. Tariffs remain a subject of debate today because some believe they "interfere" with free trade. They can also be used in retaliation against a nation for favoring one source of a good over another. In the 1990s, for example, a trade war over bananas broke out between the United States and the European Union. The European Union wanted to buy bananas from small banana growers in its former colonies in Africa and the Caribbean. The EU gave these growers special deals within the EU market, which protected them from competition from Latin American banana growers, many of which were U.S.-based multinational corporations. The United States argued that these deals violated the principles of free trade. U.S. leaders responded by heavily taxing common European imports such as French cheese. In 2001, an agreement was reached that ended the trade war.

Governments also sold monopolies to large producers in certain industries as well as to big overseas trading companies. Finally, they imposed **tariffs,** or taxes on imported goods. Tariffs were designed to protect local industries from foreign competition by increasing the price of imported goods. All of these measures led to the rise of national economies, in which national governments had a lot of control over their economies. However, modern economists debate whether mercantilist measures actually made nations wealthier.

Impact on European Society By the 1700s, European societies were still divided into distinct social classes. Merchants who invested in overseas ventures acquired wealth, while the price revolution hurt nobles, whose wealth was in land.

Economic changes took generations, even centuries, to be felt by the majority of Europeans, who were still peasants. The merchants and skilled workers of Europe's growing cities thrived. Middle-class families enjoyed a comfortable life. In contrast, hired laborers and those who served the middle and upper classes often lived in crowded quarters on the edge of poverty.

? **DESCRIBE** How did mercantilism and colonialism contribute to the success of Europe's Commercial Revolution?

>> At the Customs House of London, government officials supervised regulations on overseas trade. Customs officers collected the tariffs that were due on imported goods.

ASSESSMENT

1. **Analyze Information** How was the impact of the Columbian Exchange positive in some ways, but negative in other ways?
2. **Identify Cause and Effect** What economic factors and principles contributed to the success of Europe's Commercial Revolution?
3. **Make Generalizations** What economic changes came during the Commercial Revolution?
4. **Identify Steps in a Process** How did the "putting out" system work?
5. **Compare Points of View** How did capitalists and mercantilists have different points of view on government regulation of the economy?

SYNTHESIZE

Online Project the Digital Activity: **Capitalism and Mercantilism**. Have students complete the chart in this activity and then share their chart with a partner and discuss their answers.

Discuss Based on your chart showing advantages and disadvantages of free enterprise and mercantilism, who were some people that benefited from those economic developments? Who were some people who experienced problems because of the economic developments? *(Sample response: Middle- and upper-class entrepreneurs profited the most. Their hired laborers earned wages but were often poorly paid.)*

DEMONSTRATE

Online Assign the **Digital Lesson Quiz** for this lesson if you haven't already done so. Students will be offered automatic remediation or enrichment based on their score.

Pose these questions to the class on the Discussion Board:

Identify Cause and Effect What were some effects of the Columbian Exchange on Native Americans? *(Positives include the introduction of horses and new food sources that improved nutrition. Negatives include diseases and the imposition of European culture on Native Americans.)*

Apply Concepts What are some benefits and problems of the American free enterprise system? *(Benefits include economic freedoms, innovation, business and investment opportunities, social mobility; problems may include excessive regulations, high prices, unbalanced distribution of wealth, poverty for some.)*

Topic Inquiry

Have students continue their investigations for the Topic Inquiry.

Assessment

1. A positive was the exchange of foods that enriched people's diet. Negatives were that many people died from diseases and enslaved Africans were forcibly moved to the Americas.
2. Contributions to the success of Europe's Commercial Revolution included expanding trade with new colonies, vast amounts of gold and silver flowing into Europe, an increased money supply, the growth of capitalist free enterprise, new business methods, replacing guild regulations with the principles of supply and demand, and mercantilism.
3. Capitalist free enterprise principles gradually replaced economic systems of the past. Individuals were free to make more economic choices. The profit motive spurred more investment, more business, and more jobs.
4. Under this system, a capitalist might distribute raw wool to peasant cottages. Cottagers spun the wool into thread and then wove it into cloth. Merchants bought the wool cloth from the peasants and sent it to the city for finishing and dyeing. Finally, the merchants sold the finished product for a profit. Merchants provided the capital, or money, to invest in the business, and cottagers did the labor.
5. Capitalists preferred the principles of free enterprise. Mercantilists generally favored government regulations that would regulate colonial economies to increase the national wealth of the parent country.

Topic 11

TEKS ASSESSMENT

1. **Identify Major Causes and Effects and Locate Places and Regions** Identify major causes and effects of the following important turning points in world history from 1450 to 1750: European expansion; also locate regions and places of historical significance. Write a paragraph identifying how Spain benefited from its expansion in the Americas. Which Spaniards came to the Americas after the explorers and why? On the map below, locate the areas of the Spanish empire and summarize its scope; how did the areas under viceroys affect local rule? How were Native Americans treated under Spanish rule? **1.D, 16.A**

2. **Identify Major Causes** Identify major causes of the following important turning points in world history from 1450 to 1750: European exploration. Write a paragraph identifying how demographic factors in Europe starting in the 1400s contributed to European exploration. Consider the demand for new goods and spread of Christianity. Which region was the primary motivation of exploration, and why? **1.D**

3. **Identify and Analyze Major Causes and Explain the Impact** Identify and analyze the major causes of the following important turning points in world history from 1450 to 1750: European exploration and colonization; also explain how the Aztec empire was impacted by it. Write a paragraph identifying and analyzing Spanish exploration that led to colonizing the Aztec empire. Consider the actions of Spanish explorer Hernán Cortés, the Aztec capital of Tenochtitlán, and consequences to Native Americans. **1.D, 6.B, 7.A**

4. **Describe Major Effects and Explain the Impact** Describe major effects and explain how the Inca empire was impacted by the following important turning points in world history from 1450 to 1750: European exploration and colonization. Write a paragraph explaining how the Inca empire was impacted by Spanish exploration and colonization. How did explorer Francisco Pizarro conquer the Incas? How were Native Americans treated? Explain the encomienda system of labor and subsequent slave trade. **1.D, 6.B**

5. **Explain New Factors and Principles; Formulate Generalizations** Explain new economic factors and new principles that contributed to the success of Europe's Commercial Revolution. Also formulate generalizations on how economic freedom improved the human condition, based on the benefits of free enterprise in Europe's Commercial Revolution. Write a paragraph explaining how Europe's global trading links contributed to the success of Europe's Commercial Revolution. Consider bank loans; joint stock companies, bookkeeping methods, and the putting-out system. Also, generalize about how entrepreneurs benefited from the free enterprise system and what risks they took. **7.F, 18.F**

6. **Explain the Impact and Describe the Effects** Explain the impact and describe the effects of the Columbian Exchange on the Americas and Europe. Write a paragraph explaining the impact and describing the effects of the Columbian Exchange. Consider the products and contributions exchanged and the effect on the Native Americans and growth of agriculture. **1.D, 7.B**

7. **Describe Major Effects** Describe the major effects of the following important turning points in world history from 1450 to 1750: European exploration. Write a paragraph describing the effects of European exploration in Asia in the 1600s. What was the importance of establishing ports in the East African coastal areas and Cape Town? Which countries had the greatest and least presence in Indian Ocean trade? **1.D**

8. **Identify Major Causes** Identify major causes of the following important turning points in world history from 1450 to 1750: the Columbian Exchange. Write a paragraph identifying the major causes of the Columbian Exchange in the 1500s and 1600s. How did the voyages of Christopher Columbus lead to the two-way Columbian Exchange? What were some of the major items that were exchanged? **1.D**

9. **Analyze the Influence** Analyze the influence of human geographic factors on major events in world history, including trade in the Indian Ocean. Write a paragraph analyzing the influence of human geographic factors on trade by the Dutch East India Company in the Indian Ocean. Consider the impact of its full sovereign powers, trade with China and in the Spice Islands, and the relationship with local Asian people. **16.B**

Answers to TEKS Assessment

1. Spanish settlers and missionaries came to work the land and spread Christianity. The Spanish colonies extended from Mexico to the southeastern coast of South America. Mexico and eastern South America were ruled by Spanish viceroys, who tightly regulated trade. Spain won wealth and power as it took silver, gold, and raw materials from the Americas. Native Americans suffered under forced labor. Some converted to Christianity.

2. The growing population in Europe caused demand for goods that were unavailable in Europe, which became an incentive for worldwide exploration. In particular, spices were in high demand for food flavoring and for making medicine and perfumes. Although overland routes to Asia had been used, competing European nations wanted to find more profitable, direct access routes to Asia; spread Christianity; and gain glory for their country.

3. Spanish explorers went to the Americas looking for gold and other riches. In the 1500s, explorer Hernán Cortés conquered the Aztec empire and claimed their land and treasures. Cortés demolished the Aztec capital Tenochtitlán, later rebuilt as present-day Mexico City. Spanish explorers also inadvertently brought diseases, which killed tens of thousands of Native Americans.

4. Spaniard Francisco Pizarro arrived in Peru in 1532 and captured and killed thousands of the Incas with superior weapons. He then conquered and claimed Ecuador and Chile for Spain. Tens of thousands of Native Americans died of diseases inadvertently brought by the explorers. Pizarro added much of South America to the Spanish empire. Settlers to the area used the encomienda system to demand labor from Native Americans, and many died as a result. After Spain forbade enslavement and abuse of Native Americans, Spanish colonists used enslaved workers from Africa as laborers.

5. Europe's global trading links resulted in a commercial revolution that eventually led to the development of modern capitalism, banking, and investing. Prices began to rise along with inflation. Free enterprise spurred the growth of entrepreneurs who took on financial risks and developed overseas trading ventures. Bookkeeping methods were adapted, banks lent more money, and joint stock companies allowed investors limited risks. Capitalists developed the putting-out system, or cottage industry, as a way to bypass the guilds, separating capital and labor for the first time.

6. The Americas introduced corn and potatoes; both became staples in European diets and contributed to population growth in Europe. Europeans introduced plants and animals like horses that changed transportation. Sugar cane became an important cash crop in the Americas. Europeans also inadvertently brought smallpox and typhus, which killed off many Native Americans. Increased migration to the Americas led to agricultural growth that was enabled by the labor of enslaved Africans.

7. East African port cities were established by the Portuguese as a springboard to trade with India and Macao (southern China). The Dutch set up a port city in Cape Town, which was their springboard to establishing trading bases in Southeast Asia, the center of the spice trade. They dominated Indian Ocean trade in the 1600s. France had the least presence.

8. European exploration of the Americas marked the beginning of European domination of the globe. Columbus took plants and animals from America back to Spain. He then returned with European plants and animals, which was the start of a global exchange among the Americas and Europe, Africa, and Asia. Corn, potatoes, and other foods were taken to the Eastern Hemisphere; horses, pigs, wheat, smallpox, and typhus were brought back to the Americas.

10. **Explain Impact** Explain Ming China's impact on global trade. Write a paragraph explaining Ming China's impact on global trade in the 1500s and 1600s. Consider Portuguese attempts to trade with China and the trading post at Macao in southern China. How did the Chinese belief that they were the center of the world, or the "Middle Kingdom," relate to their opinion of European goods in that era? 7.E

11. **Describe Interactions** Describe the interactions between Muslim and Hindu societies in South Asia. Write a paragraph describing how the British used the conflicts between Muslim and Hindu societies to gain entry into and dominate most of India by the late 1700s. Consider the location of the Mughal empire, conflicts between Hindus and Muslims, decline of the Mughal empire, and the role of the British East India Company. 4.F

12. **Explain Impact** Explain the impact of the Atlantic slave trade on the Americas. Write a paragraph about the economic impact of Atlantic slave trade on the Americas, including the people and industries who benefited the most. Why did Brazil become the largest destination point for slaves? Before slavery ended, approximately how many slaves came to the Americas? 7.C

13. **Identify, Describe, and Analyze Major Causes and Effects** Identify, describe, and analyze major causes and effects of the following important turning points in world history from 1450 to 1750: European expansion. Write a paragraph about the French and British expansion in North America from 1450 to 1750. Why did the French and British settle in North America? What industries were profitable for New France and for the British colonies? 1.D, 7.A

14. **Describe Effects and Explain Impact** Describe the major effects of the following important turning point in world history from 1450 to 1750: European expansion. Explain the impact of the Atlantic slave trade on the Americas. Write a paragraph describing the major effects of the European expansion in Africa, and explain the impact of the slave trade on the Americas. Consider the different parts of the triangular trade and what types of goods were exchanged. Where did most of the 11 million slaves end up working? When was slavery abolished throughout the Americas, and what was the impact of slaves on the cultures of the Americas? 1.D, 7.C

15. **Explain Development and Impact** Explain the development and the impact of the Atlantic slave trade on West Africa. Write a paragraph explaining the development and impact of the Atlantic slave trade on West Africa. Consider the roles of the African rulers and the impact of the slave trade on the population. On the map below, locate the slave trading regions, including the Asante kingdom and the Oyo empire. What did these two regions do with the wealth they gained? 4.I

16. Reflect on the Essential Question **Write an essay on the Essential Question: Why do people move?** Use evidence from your study of this Topic to support your answer.

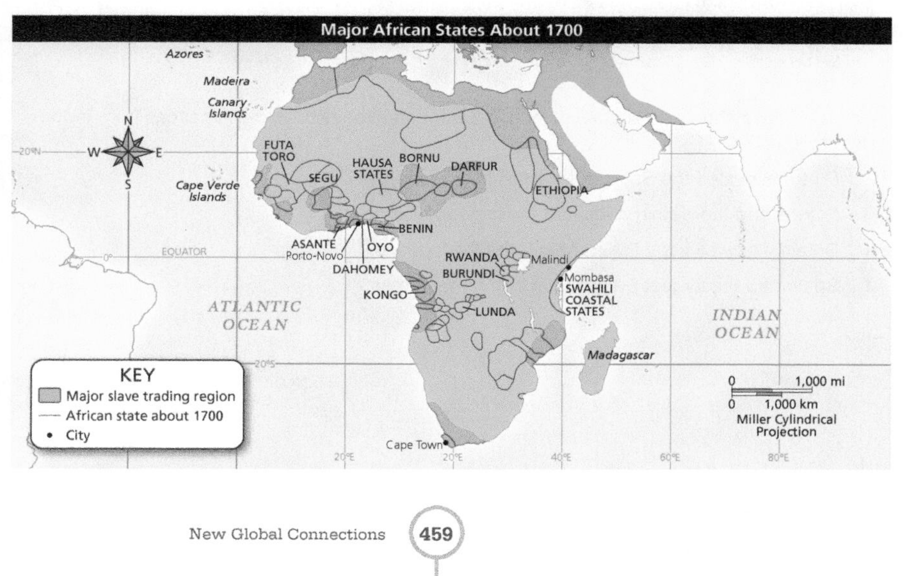

9. The Dutch East India Company claimed supremacy in Indian Ocean trade. It could build armies, wage war, negotiate peace treaties, and govern overseas territory. In the 1600s the Dutch captured Malacca, opened trade with China, and monopolized trade in the Spice Islands, controlling shipments to Europe and in Southeast Asia. Despite using military force to advance trading goals, they were more integrated with the local people and rulers.

10. The Portuguese reached China, hoping to buy silks and porcelain. However, the Chinese did not want European goods in exchange, only gold or silver payments. The Ming government allowed a restricted trading post at Macao, near Canton, in southern China. Although the Portuguese were unsuccessful in converting locals to Christianity, Chinese contact with Christian missionaries led to the exchange of ideas.

11. The Mughal empire was a center of valuable spice trade and, thus, a destination for European explorers. However, the empire was weakened by conflicts between Hindus and Muslims, which took a financial toll. Raising taxes then sparked more chaos, leading to a government collapse. European nations tried to assert their power on the area. The British East India Company fought off the French to establish domination.

12. The slave trade was very profitable for many people, including merchants and those in the New England shipbuilding industry, as well as the fishing, tobacco, and sugar industries. Ports along the North American coast grew into thriving cities. By the mid-1800s, near the end of the overseas slave trade, almost 11 million Africans had been forcibly transported to the Americas, while another 2 million had died onboard ships. Approximately 80 percent of African slaves ended up in the Caribbean and Brazil, which had a thriving sugar industry in need of labor.

13. The French and the British settlements in North America were approximately equal in size. The French explored and settled in North America, where they focused on fishing and fur trapping. The British also did not find a northwest passage to Asia. After John Cabot landed in Newfoundland, the British focused on establishing colonies along the present-day eastern United States. Subsequent colonies were mostly established either as religious havens or as commercial ventures. Fishing, shipbuilding, and cash crops were the key industries.

14. Europeans traded manufactured goods to African rulers and traders in exchange for enslaved Africans. During the Middle Passage, slaves were transported in horrific conditions to the Americas to work on sugar cane and tobacco plantations. In exchange, slave traders received goods like rum and tobacco and shipped those products to Europe on the final leg of the triangular trade. Almost 11 million enslaved Africans were in the Americas by the mid-1800s. Over time, slavery caused tensions that contributed to the American Civil War, and it was later abolished. In Brazil and the Caribbean, which had 80% of the slaves, slavery ended later, in the late 1800s. A variety of traditions from enslaved Africans added to the diverse cultures of the Americas.

15. European traders used African rulers, willingly, and traders to seize captives in Africa in exchange for manufactured goods. Although some African rulers tried to stop the slave trade, they were unsuccessful; a steep population decline occurred in Africa, and some new states arose that depended economically on the slave trade. The Asante kingdom is located in present-day Ghana. In the 1600s it managed the monopoly on gold mining and the slave trade. The Oyo empire is located in present-day Nigeria. It used wealth from the slave trade to build up its military in the late 1600s.

Topic 11

Answers to TEKS Practice

1. C

2. J

Online To prepare for the End-of-Topic test, have students go online for additional Topic Review and Assessment questions or to review their notes in the **Interactive Reading Notepad** for the lessons in this Topic.

Benchmark Tests

Assign these benchmark tests as you complete the relevant topics to monitor student progress toward mastering the course content and as preparation for the End-of-Course Test.

Benchmark Test 1: Topics 1–5

Benchmark Test 2: Topics 6–10

Benchmark Test 3: Topics 11–15

Benchmark Test 4: Topics 16–21

TEKS PRACTICE

1 Which human geographic factors led the British to take over trade in the Indian Ocean after the Mughal empire?

A Old transportation networks were rebuilt from the earlier days of the Mughal empire.

B The working population had migrated to centers of trade after famine destroyed crops.

C Local rulers who controlled the textile trade established key business alliances with the British.

D Advances in medicine gradually allowed the British to tolerate the warmer climate.

---

2 **European Migration to the Americas, 1492–1640**

PLACE OF ORIGIN	BEFORE 1580	1580–1640
Spain	139,000	188,000
Portugal	58,000	110,000
Britain	0	87,000
France	0	4,000
Netherlands	0	2,000

Source: Based on David Ellis, ed., Coerced and Free Migration: Global Perspectives (Stanford University Press, 2002. Note: Data are scholar's estimates.)

Which of these shows an accurate trend in European expansion in the Americas from before 1580 to 1640?

F Portugal rivaled the Spanish for most migrations.

G France and the Netherlands had the largest drop.

H Britain was well established before the Portuguese.

J Spain had the largest presence in both time frames.

Test Taking Tips: Tip for Answering Multiple-Choice Questions

1. Try answering the question before looking at the choices. If your answer is one of the choices, select that choice.
2. Eliminate the obviously incorrect answers, crossing them out if you are allowed to write on the test paper. Then choose the best answer from the remaining choices.
3. Change a question into a statement by inserting your answer. See if the statement makes sense.
4. Restate the question in your own words to make sure you understand it.
5. Before you read the paragraph, preview the question or questions. Think about the questions as you read.

3 Which of these statements is true about the impact of the Atlantic slave trade on commerce in North America?

A Many industries, directly or indirectly, benefited from the slave trade.

B Hot weather caused fewer deaths for slaves in the sugar cane fields.

C Cash crops, such as tobacco, required the fewest number of slaves.

D The most profitable industries paid the most for African slaves.

4

> *"By the mid-15th century, Johann Gutenberg's invention of the printing press revolutionized the world, making the printed word accessible to the literate public."*

How did the printing press impact urbanization during the Renaissance in Europe?

F Cities became more powerful than city-states, which declined in population.

G Cities with printing presses could charge a tax on books that funded schools.

H More people migrated to cities, creating an increased exchange of ideas.

J Decentralized governments allowed construction of centers of learning.

If you have trouble with...				
Question	1	2	3	4
See Lesson	11.2	11.3	11.5	10.2
TEKS	16.B	1.D	7.C	27.C

Topic 11

3. A
4. H

Online Use the **Topic Synthesize** to help students revisit and reflect on the Essential Question for this Topic.

Absolutism and Revolution (1550–1850)

TOPIC 12 ORGANIZER	PACING: APPROX. 1 PERIOD, .5 BLOCKS		
	PACING	TEKS	ELPS
Connect	1 period		
MY STORY VIDEO **Biography: Louis XIV, An Absolute Monarch**	10 min.	19.B	
DIGITAL ESSENTIAL QUESTION ACTIVITY **How Much Power Should the Government Have?**	10 min.	19.B, 30.B, 30.C	
DIGITAL TIMELINE ACTIVITY **Absolutism and Revolution**	10 min.	29.F	
TOPIC INQUIRY: DOCUMENT-BASED QUESTION **What Rights Should Everyone Have?**	20 min.		
Investigate	4–8 periods		
TOPIC INQUIRY: DOCUMENT-BASED QUESTION **What Rights Should Everyone Have?**	Ongoing		
LESSON 1 **Absolute Monarchy in Spain and France**	30–40 min.	19.B, 26.B	3.G.1, 4.B.1
LESSON 2 **Rise of Austria, Prussia, and Russia**	30–40 min.	16.A, 24.B	4.C.1, 3.G.2
LESSON 3 **Triumph of Parliament in England**	30–40 min.	19.B, 20.A, 20.B	4.C.2
LESSON 4 **The Enlightenment**	30–40 min.	1.E, 18.A, 20.A, 20.C, 21.C, 25.C, 26.B, 26.C	3.H.1, 4.C.3
LESSON 5 **The American Revolution**	30–40 min.	1.E, 9.D, 19.B, 20.B, 20.C, 21.B, 22.F	4.C.3
LESSON 6 **The French Revolution Begins**	30–40 min.	1.E, 9.D, 20.B	4.D.1, 3.H.3
LESSON 7 **A Radical Phase**	30–40 min.	9.A	4.E.1
LESSON 8 **The Age of Napoleon**	30–40 min.	9.B	4.F.1
Synthesize	1 period		
DIGITAL ESSENTIAL QUESTION ACTIVITY **Reflect on the Essential Question and Topic**	10 min.	1.E, 19.B	
TOPIC INQUIRY: DOCUMENT-BASED QUESTION **What Rights Should Everyone Have?**	20 min.		
Demonstrate	1–2 periods		
DIGITAL TOPIC TEST **Absolutism and Revolution**	10 min.		
TOPIC INQUIRY: DOCUMENT-BASED QUESTION **What Rights Should Everyone Have?**	20 min.		

AUTHOR'S NOTE

"I am the State"

No ruler of the age embodied the spirit of royal absolutism as did Louis XIV (1643–1715), for whom the age is named. Who but the Sun King, the Grand Monarch, could have interrupted a diplomat's pompous references to "the French state" with an impatient but quite accurate *"l' état, c'est moi"*—"*I* am the state"—and have historians nodding sagely ever since?

Building royal power meant undermining local and regional power centers, and this Louis did with a will. The old independent-minded French aristocrats were turned into tame courtiers at Louis's court. Town officials became royal appointees. Royal regulations were imposed upon medieval guilds. Provincial courts called *parlements* were compelled to rubberstamp royal decrees. The Estates General, France's embryonic Parliament, became a dead letter by virtues of never being summoned to meet during Louis's long reign.

In place of medieval regional autonomy, centralized royal institutions grew up. Central councils presided over by the king formulated government policies. Powerful royal masters such as the Marquis de Louvois, minister of war, and above all Jean Baptiste Colbert (1619–1683), chief minister for finances and many other matters, elaborated and then implemented them in the provinces, collecting taxes and army conscripts, regulating the economy, and providing at least some government protection in the countryside.

Perhaps the most impressive achievement of absolutism under Louis XIV, however, was the elaborate system of mercantilist regulation of the national economy developed by Colbert. The traditional goals of mercantilism were to increase a national production, secure a favorable balance of trade in the goods produced, and thus guarantee a flow of payments in gold and silver bullion in the country. . . .

Under Colbert, then, an intricate structure of monopolies, chartered companies, protective tariffs, controls on wages, prices, and product quality, and colonial regulations was established to achieve these ends. All major powers practice mercantilistic regulation of their economies. But few did so as efficiently and wholeheartedly as Louis and his first minister, Colbert.

—Anthony Esler, *The Human Venture: From Prehistory to the Present* (Upper Saddle River, New Jersey: Pearson Education, 2004), pp. 475–476

 TOPIC INQUIRY: DOCUMENT-BASED QUESTION

What Rights Should Everyone Have?

TEKS 20.C, 21.C, 29.C, 29.F, 29.G, 30.B, 30.C

In this Topic Inquiry, students work individually to analyze six documents expressing ideas about the rights of people. Students will reflect on the six viewpoints, draw their own conclusions, and then write an essay on the following question: What rights should everyone have? Learning about different philosophies on human rights will contribute to students' understanding of the Topic Essential Question: How much power should the government have?

STEP 1: CONNECT

Develop Questions and Plan the Investigation

Launch the DBQ Writing Activity

Have students watch the video of President Barack Obama talking about human rights, and then discuss the video in class or have students discuss it with a partner. Have students address the questions from the *Student Instructions* about the video. Make sure they understand that China has often been criticized for restricting individual rights, which is why President Obama refers to Americans' belief in the universality of some rights.

Generate Questions

Have students use the *Need-to-Know Questions* document to record their questions about the rights of individuals.

Resources

- Need-to-Know Questions
- Student Instructions

PROFESSIONAL DEVELOPMENT

Document-Based Question

Be sure to view the Document-Based Question Professional Development resources in the online course.

STEP 2: INVESTIGATE

Apply Disciplinary Concepts and Tools

Read and Analyze Documents

Tell students that they will read and analyze six documents about human rights. Then, they will write an essay and express their own opinions about human rights. Documents A and D express the views of absolute monarchs. Documents B and C express the views of Enlightenment thinkers. Document E is taken from the Bill of Rights of the U.S. Constitution, and Document F is a modern-day political cartoon.

Help students begin to fill out the *Information Organizer*. Point out that the organizer will help them keep track of the various views about the rights of people in the documents they read. Suggest that students paraphrase or summarize the information as they fill out the organizer.

Suggestion: Review each student's *Information Organizer* as he or she is completing it to make sure students are on track.

Check Understanding

After students finish reading each individual document, have them answer the multiple-choice and short-answer questions attached to each document. Review the questions and discuss the answers after students have answered the questions for all the documents.

Resources

- Information Organizer

STEP 3: SYNTHESIZE

Evaluate Sources and Use Evidence to Formulate Conclusions

Write Your Essay

Now have students write their essays to express their own opinions about the question: What rights should everyone have? If students are having trouble getting started, remind them to review their *Information Organizer* and reflect on the information.

Suggestion: Review each student's essay as he or she is writing it to make sure students are on track.

Edit Your Essay

Have students read over their first drafts. Suggest they ask themselves these questions: Does it accurately express my viewpoint? Does it need more details? Then have students proofread and edit their essays, revising as needed. If time allows, have students exchange essays for a peer edit.

Suggestion: Have students use a thesaurus to better describe their viewpoint and to make the essay more interesting.

Resources

- Writing Rubric

STEP 4: DEMONSTRATE

Communicate Conclusions and Take Informed Action

Present Your Essay

Have students make a neat, clean copy of their essays. Then ask volunteers to read their essays aloud to the class.

Suggestion: As an alternative, have students read one or more of their classmates' essays on their own.

Reflect on the Project

After students have finished their essays, help them go over what they thought went well in their essays and what did not so they can be even more effective in the future.

Suggestion: As an extension activity, have students research human rights issues around the world today. Ask them to write a three-paragraph essay in which they compare the limitations on rights during the period of absolute monarchies versus those in modern-day countries. Ask students to share their comparisons with the class.

Absolute Monarchy in Spain and France

Objectives

Objective 1: Identify the characteristics of absolute monarchy, including the concept of divine right.

Objective 2: Explain how Spanish power grew under Charles V and Philip II.

Objective 3: Understand how France built a centralized monarchy after the wars of religion.

Objective 4: Evaluate Louis XIV as an absolute monarch.

Objective 5: Describe how the arts flourished in Spain and France.

LESSON 1 ORGANIZER	PACING: APPROX. 1 PERIOD, .5 BLOCKS					
			RESOURCES			
	OBJECTIVES	PACING	Print	Online	TEKS	ELPS
Connect						
DIGITAL START UP ACTIVITY **Defining Absolute Monarchy**		5 min.		●	19.B, 29.F	
Investigate						
READ **Ruling with Absolute Power**	Objective 1	10 min.	●	●	19.B, 29.G, 30.C	
READ **Spain and the Hapsburg Empire**	Objective 2	10 min.	●	●	24.B	
READ **Philip II Becomes an Absolute Monarch**		10 min.	●	●	16.A, 24.B	3.G.1
READ **Arts and Literature of Spain's Golden Century**	Objective 5	10 min.	●	●	26.B, 30.C	
INTERACTIVE GALLERY **Art of Spain's Golden Century**		10 min.		●	26.B	
READ **Royal Power Expands in France**	Objective 3	10 min.	●	●	19.B, 30.C	
READ **Louis XIV, an Absolute Monarch**	Objective 4	10 min.	●	●	19.B, 26.B	
READ **The Royal Palace at Versailles**		10 min.	●	●		4.B.1
READ **The Legacy of Louis XIV**		10 min.	●	●		
INTERACTIVE GALLERY **The Palace of Versailles**		10 min.		●	26.B, 30.C	
Synthesize						
DIGITAL ACTIVITY **Graphic Organizer: Techniques of Absolutism**		5 min.		●	19.B, 29.G	
Demonstrate						
LESSON QUIZ **Lesson Quiz and Class Discussion Board**		10 min.		●	19.B, 26.B	

PEARSON realize

www.PearsonTexas.com
Access your Digital Lesson

Focus on Texas Standards

Texas Essential Knowledge and Skills

19.B identify the characteristics of the following political systems: theocracy, absolute monarchy, democracy, republic, oligarchy, limited monarchy, and totalitarianism	**26.B** analyze examples of how art, architecture, literature, music, and drama reflect the history of the cultures in which they are produced

NOTES

Rise of Austria, Prussia, and Russia

Objectives

Objective 1: Outline the causes and results of the Thirty Years' War.

Objective 2: Understand how Austria and Prussia emerged as great powers.

Objective 3: Explain the steps Peter the Great took to modernize Russia.

Objective 4: Describe how Russia grew under Peter the Great and Catherine the Great.

Objective 5: Describe how European nations tried to maintain a balance of power.

LESSON 2 ORGANIZER	PACING: APPROX. 1 PERIOD, .5 BLOCKS					
			RESOURCES			
	OBJECTIVES	PACING	Print	Online	TEKS	ELPS
Connect						
DIGITAL START UP ACTIVITY **Experiencing the Thirty Years' War**		5 min.		●		
Investigate						
READ **The Thirty Years' War**	Objective 1	10 min.	●	●	15.A, 16.A	4.C.1
READ **Hapsburg Austria Expands**	Objective 2	10 min.	●	●	19.B, 24.B	
READ **Prussia Emerges**		10 min.	●	●		
INTERACTIVE MAP **Maps of Europe, 1648 and 1700**		10 min.		●	15.A	
READ **Peter the Great Modernizes Russia**	Objective 3	10 min.	●	●	19.B	
INTERACTIVE GALLERY **The Achievements of Peter the Great**		10 min.		●	19.B	
READ **Expanding Russia's Borders**	Objective 4	10 min.	●	●	19.B, 29.G	
READ **Catherine the Great**		10 min.	●	●	15.A, 19.B, 24.B	3.G.2
READ **Five Great European Powers**	Objective 5	10 min.	●	●	15.A, 16.A	
Synthesize						
DIGITAL ACTIVITY **Mini-DBQ: Absolutism in Prussia and Russia**		5 min.		●	19.B	
Demonstrate						
LESSON QUIZ **Lesson Quiz and Class Discussion Board**		10 min.		●	19.B, 24.B	

PEARSON realize™ www.PearsonTexas.com Access your Digital Lesson

Focus on Texas Standards

Texas Essential Knowledge and Skills

16.A locate places and regions of historical significance directly related to major eras and turning points in world history	**24.B** describe the major influences of women such as Elizabeth I, Queen Victoria, Mother Teresa, Indira Gandhi, Margaret Thatcher, and Golda Meir during major eras of world history

NOTES

Topic 12 Lesson 3

Triumph of Parliament in England

Objectives

Objective 1: Describe the relationship between Parliament and the monarchy under the Tudors and Stuarts.

Objective 2: Explain how English government developed after the English Civil War.

Objective 3: Identify the causes of the Glorious Revolution and the ideas contained in the English Bill of Rights.

Objective 4: Identify the characteristics of limited monarchy and constitutional government in England.

LESSON 3 ORGANIZER		PACING: APPROX. 1 PERIOD, .5 BLOCKS				
			RESOURCES			
	OBJECTIVES	PACING	Print	Online	TEKS	ELPS
Connect						
DIGITAL START UP ACTIVITY **Compare Rulers**		5 min.		●	20.A	
Investigate						
READ **Tudor Monarchs Work with Parliament**	Objective 1	10 min.	●	●	19.B	
READ **Stuart Monarchs Clash with Parliament**	Objective 1	10 min.	●	●	19.B	
READ **The English Civil War**	Objective 2	10 min.	●	●	20.A	
READ **Cromwell and the Commonwealth**	Objective 2	10 min.	●	●		
INTERACTIVE TIMELINE **England Divided: The Monarchy and Parliament Fight for Power**	Objective 2	10 min.		●	20.A	
READ **From Restoration to Glorious Revolution**	Objective 3	10 min.	●	●	19.B, 20.B	
INTERACTIVE GALLERY **Protections of the English Bill of Rights**	Objective 3	10 min.		●	20.B	
READ **England's Constitutional Government Evolves**	Objective 4	10 min.	●	●	19.B	4.C.2
Synthesize						
DIGITAL ACTIVITY **Steps Toward Liberty**		5 min.		●	20.B	
Demonstrate						
LESSON QUIZ **Lesson Quiz and Class Discussion Board**		10 min.		●	19.B, 20.A, 20.B	

PEARSON realize™ www.PearsonTexas.com Access your Digital Lesson

Focus on Texas Standards

Texas Essential Knowledge and Skills

19.B identify the characteristics of the following political systems: theocracy, absolute monarchy, democracy, republic, oligarchy, limited monarchy, and totalitarianism

20.A explain the development of democratic-republican government from its beginnings in the Judeo-Christian legal tradition and classical Greece and Rome through the English Civil War and the Enlightenment

20.B identify the impact of political and legal ideas contained in the following documents: Hammurabi's Code, the Jewish Ten Commandments, Justinian's Code of Laws, Magna Carta, the English Bill of Rights, the Declaration of Independence, the U.S. Constitution, and the Declaration of the Rights of Man and of the Citizen

NOTES

The Enlightenment

Objectives

Objective 1: Describe how science led to the Enlightenment.

Objective 2: Explain the political philosophies of Hobbes, Locke, Voltaire, Montesquieu, and Rousseau.

Objective 3: Summarize the economic ideas of the physiocrats and Adam Smith.

Objective 4: Describe how Enlightenment ideas spread and influenced the arts.

Objective 5: Understand the role of enlightened despots.

LESSON 4 ORGANIZER	PACING: APPROX. 1 PERIOD, .5 BLOCKS					
			RESOURCES			
	OBJECTIVES	PACING	Print	Online	TEKS	ELPS
Connect						
DIGITAL START UP ACTIVITY **Salons Spread Ideas**		5 min.		●	26.B	
Investigate						
READ **Scientific Revolution Leads to the Enlightenment**	Objective 1	10 min.	●	●	1.E, 25.C	3.H.1
READ **Hobbes and Locke on the Role of Government**	Objective 2	10 min.	●	●		4.C.3
READ **The *Philosophes***		10 min.	●	●		
INTERACTIVE CHART **Thinkers of the Enlightenment**		10 min.		●	20.A, 20.C, 21.C	
READ **New Economic Ideas**	Objective 3	10 min.	●	●	18.A, 21.C	
READ **Spread of Enlightenment Ideas**	Objective 4	10 min.	●	●	1.E, 20.C, 23.B, 25.C, 26.B	
READ **Arts and Literature of the Enlightenment**		10 min.	●	●	23.B, 26.B	
INTERACTIVE GALLERY **Music of the Enlightenment**		10 min.		●	23.B, 26.B, 26.C	
READ **The Enlightened Despots**	Objective 5	10 min.	●	●	20.A	
Synthesize						
DIGITAL ACTIVITY **Enlightenment Ideas: Then and Now**		5 min.		●	20.A	
Demonstrate						
LESSON QUIZ **Lesson Quiz and Class Discussion Board**		10 min.		●	1.E, 18.A, 20.A, 20.C, 26.B	

Focus on Texas Standards

Texas Essential Knowledge and Skills

18.A identify the historical origins and characteristics of the free enterprise system, including the contributions of Adam Smith, especially the influence of his ideas found in The Wealth of Nations

20.A explain the development of democratic-republican government from its beginnings in the Judeo-Christian legal tradition and classical Greece and Rome through the English Civil War and the Enlightenment

20.C explain the political philosophies of individuals such as John Locke, Thomas Hobbes, Voltaire, Charles de Montesquieu, Jean Jacques Rousseau, Thomas Aquinas, John Calvin, Thomas Jefferson, and William Blackstone

21.C identify examples of key persons who were successful in shifting political thought, including William Wilberforce

25.C explain the relationship among Christianity, individualism, and growing secularism that began with the Renaissance and how the relationship influenced subsequent political developments

26.B analyze examples of how art, architecture, literature, music, and drama reflect the history of the cultures in which they are produced

26.C identify examples of art, music, and literature that transcend the cultures in which they were created and convey universal themes

NOTES

The American Revolution

Objectives

Objective 1: Describe how Britain became a global power.

Objective 2: Understand the events and ideas leading up to the American Revolution, including the impact of the Enlightenment.

Objective 3: Summarize key events of the American Revolution.

Objective 4: Identify the political and legal ideas in the Declaration of Independence and the United States Constitution.

LESSON 5 ORGANIZER			PACING: APPROX. 1 PERIOD, .5 BLOCKS			
	OBJECTIVES	PACING	RESOURCES Print	RESOURCES Online	TEKS	ELPS
Connect						
DIGITAL START UP ACTIVITY **The Unalienable Rights of Citizens**		5 min.		●	9.D, 19.B, 20.B	
Investigate						
READ **Britain Becomes a Global Power**	Objective 1	10 min.	●	●		4.C.3
READ **The British Colonies in America**	Objective 1	10 min.	●	●	9.D, 21.B	
READ **Discontent in the Colonies**	Objective 2	10 min.	●	●	1.E, 9.D, 20.B, 20.C	
INTERACTIVE IMAGE **From Words to Action—Ideology in the American Revolution**	Objective 2	10 min.		●	9.D, 19.B, 20.C, 21.C	
READ **The American Revolution**	Objective 3	10 min.	●	●	9.D	
READ **The United States Constitution**	Objective 4	10 min.	●	●	1.E, 20.B, 20.C, 21.B	
INTERACTIVE CHART **Checks and Balances**	Objective 4	10 min.		●	20.B	
Synthesize						
DIGITAL ACTIVITY **The United States Constitution**		5 min.		●	9.D, 19.B, 20.B, 21.B, 22.F	
Demonstrate						
LESSON QUIZ **Lesson Quiz and Class Discussion Board**		10 min.		●	9.D, 20.B	

PEARSON realize
www.PearsonTexas.com
Access your Digital Lesson

Focus on Texas Standards

Texas Essential Knowledge and Skills

1.E identify major causes and describe the major effects of the following important turning points in world history from 1750 to 1914: the Scientific Revolution, the Industrial Revolution and its impact on the development of modern economic systems, European imperialism, and the Enlightenment's impact on political revolutions

9.D identify the influence of ideas such as separation of powers, checks and balances, liberty, equality, democracy, popular sovereignty, human rights, constitutionalism, and nationalism on political revolutions

19.B identify the characteristics of the following political systems: theocracy, absolute monarchy, democracy, republic, oligarchy, limited monarchy, and totalitarianism

20.B identify the impact of political and legal ideas contained in the following documents: Hammurabi's Code, the Jewish Ten Commandments, Justinian's Code of Laws, Magna Carta, the English Bill of Rights, the Declaration of Independence, the U.S. Constitution, and the Declaration of the Rights of Man and of the Citizen

20.C explain the political philosophies of individuals such as John Locke, Thomas Hobbes, Voltaire, Charles de Montesquieu, Jean Jacques Rousseau, Thomas Aquinas, John Calvin, Thomas Jefferson, and William Blackstone

21.B describe the rights and responsibilities of citizens and noncitizens in civic participation throughout history

22.F assess the degree to which American ideals have advanced human rights and democratic ideas throughout the world

NOTES

The French Revolution Begins

Objectives

Objective 1: Describe the social divisions of France's old order.

Objective 2: Trace the causes of the French Revolution.

Objective 3: Identify the reforms enacted by the National Assembly, including the Declaration of the Rights of Man and the Citizen.

LESSON 6 ORGANIZER	PACING: APPROX. 1 PERIOD, .5 BLOCKS					
	OBJECTIVES	PACING	RESOURCES Print	RESOURCES Online	TEKS	ELPS
Connect						
DIGITAL START UP ACTIVITY **The Rights of Citizens**		5 min.		●	1.E, 9.D	
Investigate						
READ **The Old Regime in France**	Objective 1	10 min.	●	●		4.D.1
INTERACTIVE CARTOON **Characteristics of the Three Estates**	Objective 1	10 min.		●	1.E, 9.D	
READ **France's Economic Crisis**	Objective 2	10 min.	●	●	1.E, 9.D	
READ **Louis XVI Calls the Estates-General**	Objective 2	10 min.	●	●	1.E, 9.D	3.H.3
READ **Storming the Bastille**	Objective 2	10 min.	●	●		
READ **Revolts in Paris and the Provinces**	Objective 2	10 min.	●	●		
READ **The National Assembly**	Objective 3	10 min.	●	●		
READ **Reforms of the National Assembly**	Objective 3	10 min.	●	●		
INTERACTIVE DOCUMENT **Declaration of the Rights of Man**	Objective 3	10 min.		●	1.E, 9.A, 20.B	
Synthesize						
DIGITAL ACTIVITY **Events of the French Revolution**		5 min.		●		
Demonstrate						
LESSON QUIZ **Lesson Quiz and Class Discussion Board**		10 min.		●	1.E, 9.A, 9.D	

PEARSON realize™ www.PearsonTexas.com Access your Digital Lesson

Focus on Texas Standards

Texas Essential Knowledge and Skills

1.E identify major causes and describe the major effects of the following important turning points in world history from 1750 to 1914: the Scientific Revolution, the Industrial Revolution and its impact on the development of modern economic systems, European imperialism, and the Enlightenment's impact on political revolutions

9.D identify the influence of ideas such as separation of powers, checks and balances, liberty, equality, democracy, popular sovereignty, human rights, constitutionalism, and nationalism on political revolutions

20.B identify the impact of political and legal ideas contained in the following documents: Hammurabi's Code, the Jewish Ten Commandments, Justinian's Code of Laws, Magna Carta, the English Bill of Rights, the Declaration of Independence, the U.S. Constitution, and the Declaration of the Rights of Man and of the Citizen

NOTES

A Radical Phase

Objectives

Objective 1: Explain why the French Revolution entered a more radical phase.

Objective 2: Understand how radicals abolished the French monarchy.

Objective 3: Analyze the causes and course of the Reign of Terror.

Objective 4: Describe France under the Directory.

Objective 5: Identify how the French Revolution changed life in France.

LESSON 7 ORGANIZER	PACING: APPROX. 1 PERIOD, .5 BLOCKS					
			RESOURCES			
	OBJECTIVES	PACING	Print	Online	TEKS	ELPS
Connect						
DIGITAL START UP ACTIVITY **Violence in the Name of Revolution**		5 min.		●		
Investigate						
READ **Radicals Gain Strength**	Objective 1	10 min.	●	●	9.A	
READ **The Monarchy Is Abolished**	Objective 2	10 min.	●	●		
READ **The Reign of Terror**	Objective 3	10 min.	●	●	9.D	4.E.1
INTERACTIVE GALLERY **The Reign of Terror**		10 min.		●	9.D	
READ **Reaction and the Directory**	Objective 4	10 min.	●	●		
READ **The Revolution Transforms France**	Objective 5	10 min.	●	●	9.A	
INTERACTIVE TIMELINE **The French Revolution Enters a More Radical Phase**		10 min.		●		
Synthesize						
DIGITAL ACTIVITY **The Reign of Terror**		5 min.		●		
Demonstrate						
LESSON QUIZ **Lesson Quiz and Class Discussion Board**		10 min.		●		

PEARSON realize™ www.PearsonTexas.com Access your Digital Lesson

Focus on Texas Standards

Texas Essential Knowledge and Skills

9.A compare the causes, characteristics, and consequences of the American and French revolutions, emphasizing the role of the Enlightenment, the Glorious Revolution, and religion

NOTES

Topic 12 Lesson 8

The Age of Napoleon

Objectives

Objective 1: Describe how Napoleon Bonaparte rose to power.

Objective 2: Explain the impact of Napoleon and the Napoleonic Wars.

Objective 3: Identify the reasons for Napoleon's fall from power.

Objective 4: Understand how the Congress of Vienna tried to restore order to Europe.

LESSON 8 ORGANIZER	PACING: APPROX. 1 PERIOD, .5 BLOCKS					
			RESOURCES			
	OBJECTIVES	PACING	Print	Online	TEKS	ELPS
Connect						
DIGITAL START UP ACTIVITY **Enter Napoleon Bonaparte**		5 min.		●	9.B	
Investigate						
READ **Napoleon on the Rise**	Objective 1	10 min.	●	●	9.B	
READ **Napoleon Reforms France**	Objective 2	10 min.	●	●	9.B	
READ **The Napoleonic Wars**	Objective 2		●	●		
INTERACTIVE MAP **Napoleon's Europe (1804–1815)**	Objective 2	10 min.		●	9.B	
READ **Challenges to the French Empire**	Objective 3	10 min.	●	●	9.B	
READ **Napoleon Falls from Power**	Objective 3		●	●		
INTERACTIVE TIMELINE **The Rise and Fall of Napoleon**	Objective 3	10 min.		●	9.B	
READ **The Congress of Vienna**	Objective 4	10 min.	●	●	9.B	4.F.1
Synthesize						
DIGITAL ACTIVITY **The Age of Napoleon**		5 min.		●	9.B	
Demonstrate						
LESSON QUIZ **Lesson Quiz and Class Discussion Board**		10 min.		●	9.B	

Focus on Texas Standards

Texas Essential Knowledge and Skills

9.B explain the impact of Napoleon Bonaparte and the Napoleonic Wars on Europe and Latin America

NOTES

Absolutism and Revolution (1550–1850)

In this Topic, you will learn about absolute rulers and revolutions. You will also find lots of ways to investigate the ideas of this Topic and to master the TEKS.

Your study will help you master these TEKS:

TEKS

1.E, 9.A, 9.B, 9.D, 15.A, 16.A, 18.A, 19.B, 20.A, 20.B, 20.C, 21.B, 21.C, 22.F, 23.B, 24.B, 25.C, 26.B, 26.C, 29.C, 29.E, 29.F, 29.G, 30.B, 30.C

LESSON OUTLINE

12.1: Absolute Monarchy in Spain and France 19.B, 26.B

12.2: Rise of Austria, Prussia, and Russia 16.A, 24.B

12.3: Triumph of Parliament in England 19.B, 20.A, 20.B

12.4: The Enlightenment 1.E, 18.A, 20.A, 20.C, 21.C, 25.C, 26.B, 26.C

12.5: The American Revolution 1.E, 9.D, 19.B, 20.B, 20.C, 21.B, 22.F

12.6: The French Revolution Begins 1.E, 9.D, 20.B

12.7: A Radical Phase 9.A

12.8: The Age of Napoleon 9.B, 16.A

Connect

My Story Video and Topic Essential Question—see how they connect to your past experience or to what you have already learned. The Essential Question for this Topic is: How much power should the government have?

Begin your study by trying the following:

NBC LEARN Watch My Story Video:

Louis XIV, An Absolute Monarch

Launch your Document-Based Question:

What Rights Should Everyone Have?

Investigate

The Lesson Outline lists all the lessons you will investigate In this Topic,. As you read and interact with key content, the story of absolute monarchs and revolutions will come to life. Read the texts; try the interactivities. Investigate the fascinating story of these rulers and revolutions.

And keep working on your Document-Based Question to help build your mastery of the Topic TEKS.

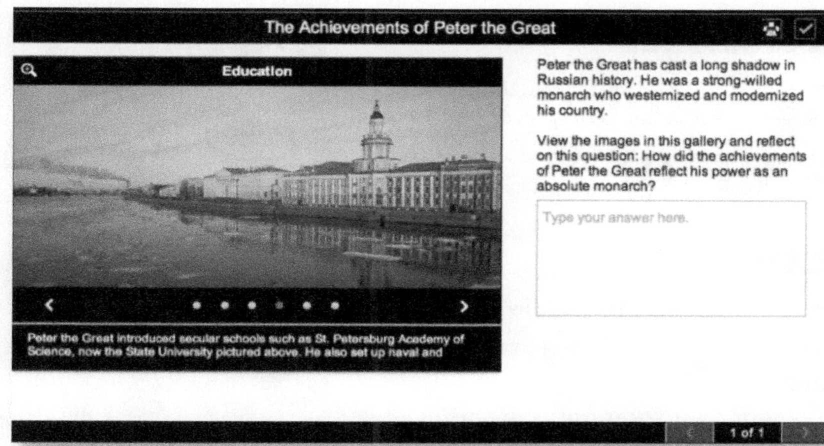

>> Digital interactivity from the online course

Synthesize

Next you will pull it all together by reflecting on the Essential Question. This will give you a chance to be the storyteller, to show how you would answer this big question: How much power should the government have?

Demonstrate

Now you will get to show what you know. You will get a chance to complete the TEKS Review and Assessment pages, answering questions about every TEKS for this Topic. Or complete a Project, take part in a discussion, or you can write an essay. No matter which you do, it will be a real-world demonstration of the things you now understand about absolutism and revolutions.

TEKS in Topic 12	Topic Review and Assessment Questions
1.E	20
9.A	17, 19, 21
9.B	12
9.D	7, 14
15.A	12, 18
16.A	1, 12, 18
18.A	11
19.B	2
20.A	3, 7
20.B	14
20.C	6, 8, 9, 15
21.C	8
22.F	16
23.B	17
24.B	10
25.C	24
26.B	4
26.C	5
29.C	6, 9, 22
29.E	6
29.F	22
29.G	13
30.B	1, 19, 21
30.C	9, 23

Topic 12

Absolutism and Revolution (1550–1850)

Introduction

After feudalism died out in Europe, strong nation-states emerged. Most of these were absolute monarchies, where strong rulers held complete power over their nations and people. However, by the 1700s, Enlightenment thinkers introduced new ideas about liberty and human rights. What role did the Enlightenment have in the government we have in the United States today?

ESSENTIAL QUESTION

Ask students to think about the Essential Question for this Topic: How much power should the government have? Governments around the world have different levels of power. How much power is enough?

Project the Essential Question activity from the course. Read the introduction. Ask students to make their decisions. Allow volunteers to share their decisions, and the reasons for them, with the class.

Identify Central Issues What level of government power do you think might be problematic? *(Sample responses: too much power; too little power)*

Predict Consequences What do you think might be some unintended negative consequences of a government having too much or too little power? Explain. *(Sample response: Too much power might lead to oppression of the people; too little power might make society unorganized and dangerous.)*

Infer Why do you think the period of governments having too much power in Europe was followed by revolutions? *(Sample response: because people became tired of social inequality and limited rights)*

[**ESSENTIAL QUESTION**] How much power should the government have?

12 Absolutism and Revolution

Analyze Images

Direct students' attention to the painting of the execution of Queen Marie Antoinette during the French Revolution. Have students list the ways that people are reacting and then speculate about why people might have these different perspectives. Then ask students to speculate about the perspective of the artist and justify their responses.

>> The execution of Queen Marie Antoinette during the French Revolution

Enduring Understandings

- Absolute monarchs such as Louis XIV of France exerted complete authority over their kingdoms.
- England developed a limited monarchy with a written constitution.
- Enlightenment philosophers applied reason to political, social, and economic problems.
- Ideas such as natural rights shaped the American Revolution and the U.S. Constitution.
- An unequal social system sparked the French Revolution, in which the monarchy was replaced by a republic.
- As emperor of France, Napoleon Bonaparte began a series of wars that had lasting effects on Europe and the Americas.

Watch the My Story Video to learn about King Louis XIV of France, the greatest of the absolute monarchs.

PEARSON realize www.PearsonTexas.com Access your digital lessons including: Topic Inquiry • Interactive Reading Notepad • Interactivities • Assessments

NBC LEARN MY STORY VIDEO

Project the My Story Video about France's King Louis XIV, the greatest of the absolute monarchs.

Online My Story Video: **Louis XIV, An Absolute Monarch**

After viewing, ask students to respond to the following questions.

Check Understanding What is the meaning of the expression "divine right of kings"? *(the right to rule comes from God, not from people)*

Generate Explanations Why did Louis XIV build Versailles? *(He built the lavish palace at Versailles as a symbol of his kingdom's wealth and power.)*

OVERVIEW ACTIVITY

Online Display the **Absolutism and Revolution: Introduction Timeline** showing the major events in the age of absolutism and revolution. During the Topic, students will learn about all of these events and many more, but this timeline will provide a framework into which they can place the events they learn about.

Check Understanding How many years after Louis XIV became king of France did the French Revolution begin? *(146 years)*

Topic Inquiry

If you choose to assign the Topic Inquiry, launch the DBQ Activity after introducing the Topic.

D Differentiate Challenge/Gifted After the Overview Activity, suggest that students copy the timeline onto their own paper and add entries to it as they read the Topic. If they want, they can make a final, clean copy to share with the class after they have read all eight lessons.

Topic 12 Lesson 1

Absolute Monarchy in Spain and France

CONNECT

Preview Have students preview the **Lesson Objectives** and the list of **Key Terms**.

Students can also preview all the **Key Terms** and **Academic Vocabulary** using the **Interactive Reading Notepad** on the digital course or preview a summary of the lesson in the **Reading and Note Taking Study Guide**.

Online Use the **Editable Presentation** found on the digital course to present the main ideas for this lesson.

Start Up Activity

Have students define the words *absolute* and *monarchy. (absolute: total, complete; monarchy: rule by a leader who gains his or her crown by being born to it)*. Then, using those two definitions, have students write down what an absolute monarchy is *(when a monarch has total control of his or her subjects).*

Discuss After students have answered individually, have them share their ideas with another student, either in class or through a chat room or blog. Possible follow-up questions: What would it be like to live under an absolute monarchy? Is an absolute monarchy fair to the people living in it?

Online You can also project the **Start Up Activity** from the course.

INVESTIGATE

Have students read the section using the **Reading and Note Taking Study Guide** to help them take notes and understand the text as they read.

Ruling with Absolute Power

Explain to students that during the Age of Absolutism, the kings and queens of Europe ruled their countries with absolute authority given to them by God himself. They used this theory to justify their power.

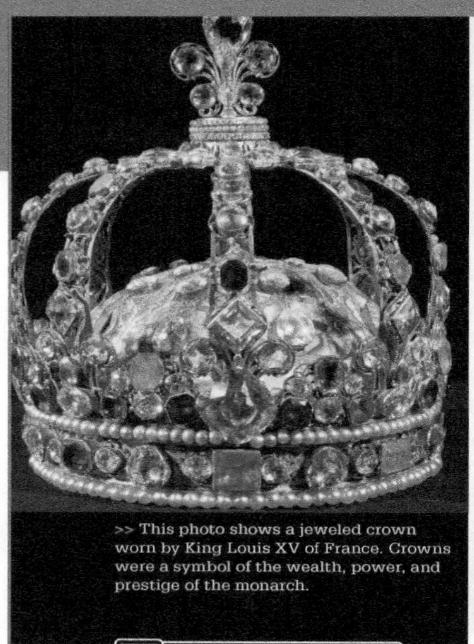

>> This photo shows a jeweled crown worn by King Louis XV of France. Crowns were a symbol of the wealth, power, and prestige of the monarch.

Interactive Flipped Video

12.1 During the Renaissance and Reformation, European rulers continued to centralize power at the expense of their nobles and the clergy. As wars of religion raged in many European lands, monarchs battled to impose royal law and restore order in their kingdoms.

TEKS
16.A, 19.B, 24.B, 26.B

>> Objectives

Identify the characteristics of absolute monarchy, including the concept of divine right.

Explain how Spanish power grew under Charles V and Philip II.

Understand how France built a centralized monarchy after the wars of religion.

Evaluate Louis XIV as an absolute monarch.

Describe how the arts flourished in Spain and France.

>> Key Terms

Hapsburg empire
Charles V
Philip II
absolute monarchy
armada
El Greco
Miguel de Cervantes
Huguenots
Henry IV
Edict of Nantes
Cardinal Richelieu
Louis XIV
intendant
Jean-Baptiste Colbert
Versailles
levée
balance of power
divine right

PEARSON realize. www.PearsonTexas.com Access your Digital Lesson.

Absolute Monarchy in Spain and France

Ruling with Absolute Power

Between about 1500 and 1800, the old feudal order gave way to individual nation-states with strong central governments. Monarchs presided over government bureaucracies that enforced the law and collected taxes. They used income not only to support lavish Renaissance courts but also to strengthen their military power.

Powerful States and Rulers The emergence of strong unified nation-states occurred at different times in different parts of Europe.

The rulers of some countries, such as Spain and France, set up **absolute monarchies.** The chief characteristic of this political system is that a ruler has complete authority over the government and the lives of the people.

During the Age of Absolutism, as this period is called, powerful new dynasties emerged. The Hapsburgs in Spain and the Bourbons in France passed power from generation to generation within the family while they added lands to their kingdoms through skillfully arranged marriages.

Absolute monarchs often had parliaments or other bodies, but these bodies had no real power. The ruler could dissolve them at

466

Aa Vocabulary Builder

1. Have students pronounce the following academic vocabulary terms in this lesson and clarify the part of speech. For difficult or polysyllabic words, break them into syllables and pronounce them with the students.
2. Explain what the word means in common "student-friendly" language using synonyms and antonyms when possible. Provide concrete examples to clarify the meaning, and rephrase the definition.

cumbersome: hard to handle because of size, weight, or many parts

erode: wear away or disintegrate

will. In theory, absolute monarchs had total power, but in practice, to preserve power, they had to balance the interests of different groups from nobles and clergy to the middle class and peasants.

Divine Right to Rule During the Age of Absolutism, European monarchs embraced the idea of **divine right,** meaning that their authority to rule came directly from God. They used divine right theory to justify their power. As God's representative on Earth, monarchs could command absolute obedience from their subjects. In the 1600s, a French bishop and court preacher, Jacques Bossuet (bah soo WAY) defended the theory of divine right and royal absolutism, saying that absolute power was necessary to protect the people.

> "The royal power is absolute.... Without this absolute authority the king could neither do good nor repress evil. It is necessary that his power be such that no one can escape him."
>
> —Jacques Bossuet, "Politics Drawn from the Very Words of Scripture," 1679

Still, absolute monarchs who claimed to rule by divine right were expected to act for the good of their people.

By 1700, absolute monarchs reigned over most of the great powers in Europe, except England. In time, however, thinkers and others challenged divine right theory along with the entire system of absolute monarchy. They called, instead, for limits on government power and for governments to be responsible to the people.

IDENTIFY What are the characteristics of an absolute monarchy?

Spain and the Hapsburg Empire

By the 1500s, Spain had emerged as the first modern European power. Through their marriage, Queen Isabella and King Ferdinand had unified the country. They pursued a policy of imposing religious unity and financed Columbus's voyage,

"The royal power is absolute.... Without this absolute authority the king could neither do good nor repress evil. It is necessary that his power be such that no one can escape him."

—Jacques Bossuet, "Politics Drawn from the Very Words of Scripture," 1679

>> Portrait of French bishop Jacques Bossuet, who supported the theory of the divine right of kings.

Analyze Images

Direct attention to the image of Bishop Bossuet, seventeenth-century French cleric, and read or invite a volunteer to read the quotation on the image. Ask: According to Bossuet, what type of power does the king have, and why? What are the limits on his power? *(absolute power; to do good and repress evil; there are no limits to his power.)*

Guided Reading and Discussion

Break students into groups of four. Then, ask students what kind of government we have in the United States. *(democratic republic)* Ask them to write a definition of a democratic republican form of government. Have students compare this definition to that of an absolute monarchy from the **Start Up Activity.** Discuss the differences. Have students write a short essay explaining the differences between our system of government and an absolute monarchy.

Spain and the Hapsburg Empire

Spain was the first modern European power, unified by the marriage of Queen Isabella and Ferdinand. Spain grew rich and powerful after financing expeditions to the New World, and Spain continued to grow the empire by forming alliances through marriages. When the king and queen's grandson, Charles, took the throne, he became the ruler of a large swath of territories known as the Holy Roman Empire, which included the Hapsburg empire.

History Background

The Divine Right of Europe's Monarchs Since the Middle Ages, Europe's monarchs had struggled to assert power over feudal lords. Some early monarchs were elected, but over time Europe's royal families retained power by making monarchy hereditary—passed down within families. They also developed an ideology to support their claims to absolute power. It reached its height in the 1600s when Jacques-Benigne Bossuet, a French bishop who admired Louis XIV, formulated the concept of the divine right of kings. Bossuet argued that monarchs were chosen by god and therefore should be obeyed absolutely. This idea allowed European kings and queens to bring all aspects of government, trade, and religion under their rule.

Answers

Identify *The monarch has complete authority over the government and people, usually inherits the throne by lineage and right of birth, and often claims a divine right to rule.*

Philip II Becomes an Absolute Monarch

Tell students that by the 1580s, Spain's King Philip saw England's Queen Elizabeth I as his chief Protestant enemy. She sided with the Dutch against Spain and encouraged English captains, known as sea dogs, to plunder Spanish treasure ships and loot Spanish cities in the Americas. Philip eventually sent the armada to attack England, only to be humbled by defeat.

Key Terms

Ask students to find the key term **Hapsburg empire** (in bold) in the text. Explain that the central European empire lasted from the 1400s to the 1900s.

Guided Reading and Discussion

Ask the following questions: Is it ever a good idea to go to war over religion? To extend territory? Why or why not? *(Answers will vary, but students might mention that religious wars typically put one religion over another and don't respect people's differences, and wars over territory affect not only control over land, but also the people who live on it.)* Students should first share their answers with their neighbor. Then, have pairs participate in a full-group discussion.

which would lead to the Spanish conquest of the Americas. Wealth from the Americas would help Spain to become the most powerful nation in Europe.

Charles V Wears Two Crowns In 1516, Ferdinand and Isabella's grandson, Charles I, became king of Spain, and thereby ruler of the Spanish colonies in the Americas as well. When his other grandfather died in 1519, Charles I also became heir to the sprawling **Hapsburg empire,** which included the German states of the Holy Roman Empire and the Dutch Netherlands. As ruler of the Hapsburg empire, Charles took the name **Charles V,** the title by which historians now usually refer to him.

Ruling two empires involved Charles in constant warfare. He continued a long Hapsburg struggle with France over rival claims in Italy.

As a devout Catholic, he fought to suppress Protestantism in the German states. After years of religious conflict, however, Charles was forced to allow the German princes to choose their own religion.

His greatest foe was the Ottoman empire, which at the time controlled the Balkans in southeastern Europe. Under Suleiman, Ottoman forces advanced across central Europe to the walls surrounding Vienna, Austria. Although Austria held firm during the siege, the Ottomans occupied much of Hungary following their crushing victory at the Battle of Mohács. Ottoman naval forces also continued to challenge Spanish power in the Mediterranean.

The Empire Is Divided The Hapsburg empire proved to be too scattered and cumbersome for any one person to rule. Exhausted, Charles gave up his titles in 1556 and entered a monastery. He divided his empire, leaving the Hapsburg lands in central Europe to his brother Ferdinand, who became Holy Roman emperor. He gave Spain, the Netherlands, some southern Italian states, and Spain's overseas empire to his son Philip, who became Philip II.

SUMMARIZE Why did Charles V divide the Hapsburg Empire?

>> This painting shows the abdication of Charles V 1555. He divided the Hapsburg empire between his son, Philip II of Spain, and his brother, Holy Roman Emperor Ferdinand I. **Infer** What types of problems could have contributed to Charles V's decision to resign?

Philip II Becomes an Absolute Monarch

During his 42-year reign, **Philip II** expanded Spanish influence, strengthened the Catholic Church, and made his own power absolute. Thanks in part to silver from Spanish colonies in the Americas, he made Spain the foremost power in Europe.

A Dedicated Ruler Philip surpassed Ferdinand and Isabella in making every part of the government responsible to him. He reigned as an absolute monarch, claiming divine right. Like his father, he was hard working, devout, and ambitious. Unlike many other monarchs, Philip devoted most of his time to government work. He seldom hunted, never jousted, and lived as simply as a monk. The king's isolated, somber palace outside Madrid, known as the Escorial (es kohr YAHL), reflected his character. It served as a church, a residence, and a tomb for the royal family.

Philip saw himself as the guardian of the Roman Catholic Church. The great undertaking of his life was to defend the Catholic Reformation and turn back the rising Protestant tide in Europe. Within his empire, Philip enforced religious unity, turning the Inquisition against Protestants and other people thought to be heretics.

The Wars of Philip II Philip fought many wars to advance Spanish Catholic power. In the Mediterranean, Spain and its Italian allies soundly defeated an Ottoman fleet at the Battle of Lepanto in 1571. Although Christians hailed this as a great victory, the

Answers

Summarize *It was too difficult for one person to rule effectively.*

Infer *Sample answer: territory too large to control, issues of religious unity, too many wars*

>> **Integrate Information** Which country divided Philip's empire? Based on the map, why was England in a position to disrupt Spanish shipping?

Ottoman Empire would remain a major power in the Mediterranean region for three more centuries.

During the last half of his reign, Philip battled Protestants and other rebels in the Netherlands. At the time, the region included 17 provinces that are today Belgium, the Netherlands, and Luxembourg. It was the richest part of Philip's empire.

Protestants in the region resisted Philip's efforts to crush their faith. Protestants and Catholics alike opposed high taxes and autocratic Spanish rule, which threatened local traditions of self-government.

In the 1560s, riots against the Inquisition sparked a general uprising in the Netherlands. Savage fighting raged for decades. In 1581, the northern, largely Protestant provinces declared their independence from Spain and became known as the Dutch Netherlands. They did not gain official recognition, however, until 1648. The southern, mostly Catholic provinces of the Netherlands remained part of the Spanish Empire.

The Spanish Armada By the 1580s, Philip saw England's Queen Elizabeth I as his chief Protestant enemy. First secretly, then openly, Elizabeth had supported the Dutch against Spain. She encouraged English captains, known as sea dogs, to plunder Spanish treasure ships and loot Spanish cities in the Americas. To Philip's dismay, Elizabeth made Francis Drake, the most daring sea dog, a knight instead of punishing him as a pirate.

To end English attacks and subdue the Dutch, Philip prepared a huge **armada,** or fleet, to carry a Spanish invasion force to England. In 1588, the Spanish Armada sailed with more than 130 ships, 20,000 men, and 2,400 pieces of artillery. The Spanish were confident of victory. "When we meet the English," predicted one Spanish commander, "God will surely arrange matters so that we can grapple and board them, either by sending some strange freak of weather or, more likely, just by depriving the English of their wits."

This prediction did not come to pass. In the English Channel, lumbering Spanish ships were outmaneuvered by the lighter, faster English ships. Strong winds favored the English, scattering the Armada. After further disasters at sea, the tattered remnants limped home in defeat.

Decline of the Spanish Empire While the defeat of the Spanish Armada ended Philip's plan to invade England, it had little short-term effect on his power. In the long-term, however, Spanish power slowly faded. The decline was due in part to Philip's successors, who were less able rulers than he.

Economic problems were also to blame. Costly overseas wars drained wealth out of Spain almost as fast as it came in. Treasure from the Americas led Spain

Analyze Maps Direct students' attention to the map The Wars of Philip II: 1571–1588. Ask students the following questions: With whom did Philip II go to war? *(the Netherlands, Ottoman Empire, England)* What were the main reasons for these wars? *(religion, extension of territory)* Ask students why they think religion mattered so much to Philip II. *(Sample response: His father was very religious and became a monk, and the Reformation was a threat to his country's stability.)*

Tell students that by the 1580s, Philip saw England's Queen Elizabeth I as his chief Protestant enemy. She sided with the Dutch against Spain and encouraged English captains, known as sea dogs, to plunder Spanish treasure ships and loot Spanish cities in the Americas. Philip eventually sent the armada to attack England, only to be humbled by defeat.

English Language Proficiency Standards

Speaking 3.G.1 **Beginning** Display and read aloud the following sentence: *King Philip II of Spain was a good king who ruled every part of his empire fairly.* Have students complete this sentence stem: I agree/disagree with this statement because_______.

Intermediate Allow students to think about whether King Philip II was a good or bad king. Then have students turn to a partner to express their opinion, making sure to include one reason to support it.

Advanced Have groups discuss the benefits and drawbacks of having a king who rules with the intensity and focus of Philip II. Have them share their opinions of Phillip II's reign.

Advanced High Form groups with each student filling a role: a resident of Madrid, a Roman Catholic priest, a Spanish colonist, and a Dutch Protestant. Have them express their persona's opinion of Philip II's reign.

Answers

Integrate Information *Sample answer: France is located between Spain and the Netherlands; any ships passing from Spain to the Netherlands would have to sail through the English Channel.*

Arts and Literature of Spain's Golden Century

Historians often refer to the period from 1550 to 1650 as the Golden Age of Spain because of its vast accomplishments in the arts and literature. King Phillip II was an enthusiastic patron of the arts, as well as science and mathematics.

Online Project the **Interactive Gallery: Art of Spain's Golden Century**. Click through the images in the gallery, reading (or having student volunteers read) the captions. Ask students how the history and values of sixteenth-century Spain are reflected in its art. *(royalty, religion, expansion/war)* Students' answers can be written individually, shared with a neighbor, or shared on the board.

ACTIVE CLASSROOM

Ask students to write a headline that captures the most important aspect that should be remembered about sixteenth-century Spanish culture. Post a quick print of one of the images from the gallery on the whiteboard or elsewhere in the room. Have students write their headline on a sticky note and place it on the image. Alternatively, students could tweet their responses. Discuss the similarities and differences in responses.

Guided Reading and Discussion

List two of Philip II's goals ("Expansion of Territory" and "Strengthening Catholic Religion") on the whiteboard. Have students go through the images in the gallery and decide which of these motivations is evident in each (some works can appear in both lists). Ask students if they see any other cultural values represented in the art. You could also ask them: Can a culture as a whole value something that its leader does not? Discuss as a class.

>> The Spanish painter El Greco was born Domenikos Theotokopoulos in Greece. The *View of Toledo*, shown here, was one of the very few landscapes done by El Greco. It shows his elongated, dramatic style.

Interactive Gallery

>> This Spanish gold coin features the images of Ferdinand and Isabella of Spain. The Spanish conquerors plundered the gold of the Americas and transported most of it to Europe.

to neglect farming and commerce. The government heavily taxed the small middle class, weakening a group that in other European nations supported royal power. The expulsion of Muslims and Jews from Spain deprived the economy of many skilled artisans and merchants. Finally, the influx of American gold and silver led to soaring inflation. As Spain's power dwindled in the 1600s and 1700s, Dutch, English, and French fleets challenged—and eventually surpassed—Spanish power both in Europe and around the world.

SUMMARIZE What were Philip II's motivations for waging war?

ELPS **ELPS 3.G.1** Listen to your teacher read *Philip II Becomes an Absolute Monarch,* and discuss your opinion of his reign.

Arts and Literature of Spain's Golden Century

The century from 1550 to 1650 is often referred to as Spain's *siglo de oro* (SEEG loh day OHR oh), or "golden century," for the brilliance of its arts and literature. Philip II was an enthusiastic patron of the arts and also founded academies of science and mathematics.

Painting Among the famous painters of this period was a man known as **El Greco,** meaning "the Greek." Though not Spanish by birth, El Greco became a master of Spanish painting. Born on the Greek island of Crete, El Greco had studied in Italy before settling in Spain. He produced haunting religious pictures and striking portraits of Spanish nobles, done in a dramatically elongated style.

El Greco's use of vibrant colors influenced the work of Diego Velázquez (vuh LAHS kes), court painter to King Philip IV. Velázquez is perhaps best known for his vivid portraits of Spanish royalty.

Literature Spain's golden century produced several outstanding writers. Lope de Vega (LOH pay duh VAY guh), a peasant by birth, wrote more than 1,500 plays, including witty comedies and action-packed romances.

During Spain's golden age, **Miguel de Cervantes** (sur VAN teez) wrote Europe's first modern novel. *Don Quixote* pokes fun at medieval tales of chivalry. The elderly Don Quixote has read too many tales of days when fictional knights were bold. Imagining himself a medieval knight, he sets out across the Spanish countryside dressed in rusty armor. By his side is his practical servant, Sancho Panza.

D Differentiate Extra Support Have students list three individuals who contributed to arts and literature during Spain's golden century and write two to three sentences describing how their works reflect the times. *(Some works reflect religion; others reflect absolutism.)* Discuss how arts and literature reflect the times.

Answers

Summarize *advancing Catholicism and increasing Spain's power*

Don Quixote mocks the traditions of Spain's feudal past. At the same time, Cervantes depicts with affection both the earthy realism of Sancho and the foolish but heroic idealism of Don Quixote.

DESCRIBE What was the *siglo de oro*?

Royal Power Expands in France

Like Philip II in Spain, French rulers were determined to expand royal power. France was torn apart by wars of religion in the late 1500s. Then a new dynasty, the Bourbons, rose to power and built the foundations for an absolute monarchy in France.

Wars of Religion After the Hundred Years' War, French kings slowly consolidated power over their lands. In the 1500s, rivalry with Spain and the Protestant Reformation posed new challenges for France. Religious wars between the Catholic majority and French Protestants, called **Huguenots** (HYOO guh nahts), tore France apart. Leaders on both sides used the strife to further their own ambitions.

Each side committed terrible acts of violence. The worst began on St. Bartholomew's Day (a Catholic holiday), August 24, 1572.

While Huguenot and Catholic nobles were gathered for a royal wedding, a Catholic plot led to the massacre of 3,000 Huguenots. In the next few days, thousands more were slaughtered. For many, the St. Bartholomew's Day Massacre symbolized the complete breakdown of order in France.

Henry IV Restores Order In 1589, a Huguenot prince inherited the French throne as **Henry IV.** Henry was the first ruler in the Bourbon dynasty. As a Huguenot, Henry had battled Catholic forces. Once on the throne, he realized he would face severe problems ruling a largely Catholic country, so he converted to Catholicism. "Paris is well worth a Mass," he is supposed to have said. To protect Protestants, however, he issued the **Edict of Nantes** in 1598. It granted the Huguenots religious toleration and other freedoms.

Henry IV then set out to restore royal power and rebuild a land shattered by war. His goal, he said, was not the victory of one sect over another, but "a chicken in every pot"—a good Sunday dinner for every peasant. Under Henry, the government reached into every area of French life.

Royal officials administered justice, improved roads, built bridges, and revived agriculture. By building the

>> *Don Quixote*, Europe's first modern novel, was written by Miguel de Cervantes. It is a satirical tale about chivalry. This illustration shows the novel's main characters, Don Quixote (left) and his squire Sancho Panza.

>> The St. Bartholomew's Day Massacre began at a royal wedding in Paris in 1572. Thousands of French Huguenots were massacred.

Royal Power Expands in France

In the last half of the fifteenth century, France enjoyed a period of peace after driving out the English. French kings solidified their power, but in the 1500s, France's rivalry with Charles V of Spain, along with other religious conflicts, plunged the kingdom into turmoil.

Tell students to look at the image of the St. Bartholomew's Day Massacre and reread the statistics on this massacre. *(Three thousand Huguenots were killed initially, and a few thousand more were killed in the days that followed.)* Then discuss Henry IV's conversion and his quotation: "Paris is well worth a mass." Ask students: Did Henry IV do the right thing by converting? Why or why not? *(Some students may respond that compromise led to less conflict, while others may say that it's best to stick with your beliefs.)*

Guided Reading and Discussion

Ask students: How did Henry IV's attitude toward religion differ from Philip II's? *(Henry IV was more tolerant of different religions than Philip II was.)* What did Philip gain from his attitude toward religion? *(He was a devout Catholic, so he defended the Catholic Reformation, and strengthened his power to rule by claiming divine right.)* What did Henry gain? *(He was able to protect Protestants and unite France.)* List these responses on the whiteboard. Then, ask students to write a letter from Henry IV to a Huguenot supporter who is upset by his conversion, explaining his reasons for conversion. *(Students' letters will vary but should include that Henry IV converted to Catholicism to end conflict with Catholics. They might also mention that he issued the Edict of Nantes in order to protect Protestants.)*

D Differentiate Extra Support After asking students to take a stand, ask them to think of a time when they had to compromise to get what they wanted. Why is it sometimes a good idea to compromise? What can be gained by compromise? Have students work in groups to create a list of compromises and share the list with the class.

Answers

Describe *It was a golden century of Spanish arts and literature, from 1550 to 1650.*

Topic 12 Lesson 1

Louis XIV, an Absolute Monarch

Louis XIV ruled France for 72 years. When he was crowned, Louis spent many hours attending to government affairs, solidifying his power, and strengthening the state. "I am the state," Louis said.

Guided Reading and Discussion

Ask students: What are some possible consequences—both positive and negative—of Louis XIV's power as an absolute monarch? List some of the principles of absolutism on the whiteboard and have students brainstorm possible consequences of each. List the results on the whiteboard. Discuss.

>> Cardinal Richelieu, one of the architects of French absolutism, was principle advisor to Louis XIII. The Siege of La Rochelle, shown here, was a battle in Richelieu's campaign to bring the Huguenots under royal authority.

>> Louis XIV, who came to the throne at a young age, ruled France for more than 72 years. He believed in the divine right of kings and was a powerful absolute monarch.

royal bureaucracy and reducing the influence of nobles, Henry IV laid the foundations for royal absolutism.

Richelieu Strengthens Royal Authority When Henry IV was killed by an assassin in 1610, his nine-year-old son, Louis XIII, inherited the throne. For a time, nobles reasserted their power. Then, in 1624, Louis appointed **Cardinal Richelieu** (ree shul YOO) as his chief minister. This cunning, capable leader devoted the next 18 years to strengthening the central government.

Richelieu was determined to destroy the power of two groups that defied royal authority—nobles and Huguenots. He defeated the private armies of the nobles and destroyed their fortified castles. While reducing their independence, Richelieu tied the nobles to the king by giving them high posts at court or in the royal army. At the same time, he smashed the walled cities of the Huguenots and outlawed their armies. Yet he allowed them to continue to practice their religion.

Richelieu handpicked his able successor, Cardinal Mazarin (ma za RAN). When five-year-old **Louis XIV** inherited the throne in 1643, the year after Richelieu's death, Mazarin was in place to serve as chief minister. Like Richelieu, Mazarin worked tirelessly to extend royal power.

IDENTIFY SUPPORTING DETAILS How did the Edict of Nantes affect Huguenots?

Louis XIV, an Absolute Monarch

Soon after Louis XIV became king, disorder again swept France. In an uprising called the *Fronde*, nobles, merchants, peasants, and the urban poor each rebelled in order to protest royal power or preserve their own. On one occasion, rioters drove the boy king from his palace. It was an experience Louis would never forget.

When Mazarin died in 1661, the 23-year-old Louis resolved to take complete control over the government himself. "I have been pleased to entrust the government of my affairs to the late Cardinal," he declared. "It is now time that I govern them myself."

"I Am the State" Like his great-grandfather Philip II of Spain, Louis XIV firmly believed in his divine right to rule. He took the sun as the symbol of his absolute power.

Just as the sun stands at the center of the solar system, he argued, so the Sun King stands at the center of the nation. Louis is often quoted as saying,

D Differentiate Challenge/Gifted Break students into groups. Have them write a set of questions for Louis XIV about his tactics and motivations for controlling the nobles and unifying religion. Ask the students to then conduct an interview of Louis (one student should write the questions, the other should play Louis). This activity could involve costumes and could be performed in front of the class or recorded and posted to YouTube.

D Differentiate Extra Support Have students look at the photo of Louis XIV. Tell them he was called the "Sun King." Ask them to consider his quote: "I am the state." Ask: What do the image and the statement have in common? *(Everything revolves around the sun; If you ARE the state, everything revolves around you.)*

Answers

Identify Supporting Details *It guaranteed them religious toleration and other rights.*

LOUIS XIV STRENGTHENS HIS ABSOLUTE MONARCHY
FOLLOWED THE PROVEN POLICIES OF CARDINAL RICHELIEU
EXPANDED THE BUREAUCRACY
GAVE MANY JOBS TO WEALTHY MIDDLE-CLASS MEN TO CEMENT HIS TIES WITH THE MIDDLE CLASS
APPOINTED INTENDANTS WHO COLLECTED TAXES, RECRUITED SOLDIERS, AND CARRIED OUT POLICIES
SPENT MANY HOURS EACH DAY ATTENDING TO GOVERNMENT AFFAIRS
BUILT THE FRENCH ARMY INTO THE STRONGEST IN EUROPE

>> **Make Generalizations** What do all Louis XIV's efforts to strenghen absolutism have in common?

"L'état, c'est moi" (lay TAH seh MWAH), which in English translates as "I am the state."

During his reign, Louis did not once call a meeting of the Estates General, the medieval assembly made up of representatives of all French social classes. In fact, the Estates General did not meet between 1614 and 1789. Thus, the Estates General played no role in checking royal power.

Louis Centralizes Power Louis spent many hours each day attending to government affairs. To strengthen the state, he followed the policies of Richelieu. He expanded the bureaucracy and appointed **intendants,** royal officials who collected taxes, recruited soldiers, and carried out his policies in the provinces.

The king often appointed wealthy middle-class men to government jobs. In this way, Louis cemented ties with the middle class and limited the influence of nobles.

Under Louis XIV, the French army became the strongest in Europe. The state paid, fed, trained, and supplied up to 300,000 soldiers. Louis used this highly disciplined army to enforce his policies at home and abroad.

Colbert Strengthens the Economy The French economy grew under the king's brilliant finance minister, **Jean-Baptiste Colbert** (kohl behr). Colbert had new lands cleared for farming, encouraged mining and other basic industries, and built up luxury trades such as lacemaking. To protect French manufacturers, Colbert put high tariffs on imported goods.

Colbert also fostered overseas colonies, such as New France in North America and several colonies in India. Imposing mercantilist policies, he regulated trade with the colonies to enrich the royal treasury.

Colbert's policies helped make France the wealthiest state in Europe. Yet not even his financial genius could produce enough income to support the huge costs of Louis's court and his many foreign wars.

 **RECALL** Why did Louis XIV choose the sun as his symbol?

The Royal Palace at Versailles

In the countryside near Paris, Louis XIV turned a royal hunting lodge into the immense palace of **Versailles** (ver SY). There, he presided over both his court and the government. Versailles became the perfect symbol of the power of the Sun King.

Louis spared no expense in making Versailles the most magnificent building in Europe. Its halls and salons displayed the finest paintings and statues.

The Royal Palace at Versailles

In the countryside near Paris, Louis XIV turned a royal hunting lodge into a beautiful, ornate palace called Versailles. In its halls hung the finest paintings and the grandest sculptures. Millions of flowers bloomed in the garden. It became the king's home and office, where nobles, officials, and servants also lived.

Answers

Make Generalizations *Possible answer: They centralize power.*

Recall *It symbolized his role as the all-powerful center of the nation.*

English Language Proficiency Standards

Reading 4.B.1 Tell students that they will be reading the first paragraph from the text "The Royal Palace at Versailles." Have students demonstrate their understanding of how to recognize and read English sentences from left to right and from the top of a paragraph to the bottom by completing the following tasks:

Beginning Ask students to point at the word in the paragraph that they will read first. Then have them point at the word in the paragraph that they will read last. Then have students read the first sentence of the paragraph aloud to you while running their finger along below the words as they read them.

Intermediate Have students point at the first word in each sentence in the paragraph. Then have them read the first three sentences in the paragraph aloud as they run their fingers along below the words.

Advanced Have students explain to a partner where the paragraph begins and ends. Then have students take turns reading the paragraph aloud to each other.

Advanced High Have students write and read aloud a sentence to explain the directionality of English reading. Then ask students to read the paragraph aloud to a small group. Other members of the small group should offer pronunciation and vocabulary support as necessary.

Topic 12 Lesson 1

Online Project the **Interactive Gallery: The Palace of Versailles**. Ask students to make a graphic organizer using a piece of paper, with the paper divided into five sections. Click each hotspot on the image gallery, without reading the captions. Ask students to write a one-word response to each image and record it on the graphic organizer. Click through the images again, this time reading the captions. Ask students to answer (for each slide) this question: What does this image say about Louis XIV and his goals?

ACTIVE CLASSROOM

Speaking: Audio Tour Pair students. Have one student give the other a verbal "tour" of the interior of Versailles. Have the second student give the first an explanation of how the interior of the palace reflects absolutism. Then, have the second student give the first a verbal "tour" of the exterior of Versailles. Ask the first student to give the second an explanation of how the exterior of the palace reflects absolutism.

The Legacy of Louis XIV

Under Louis XIV, France became the most dominant state in Europe, as well as the focal point for culture and art. However, Louis used a vast amount of France's treasury to wage costly wars, which would become problematic for France in later years.

>> The Hall of Mirrors is one of the most famous rooms at the Versailles Palace. This elaborate palace was the principal residence of Louis XIV and a monument to his power.

Interactive Gallery

>> English troops fight the French in this 1704 battle in the War of the Spanish Succession, one of the many foreign wars of Louis XIV.

Some depicted the king as Apollo, the ancient Greek god of the sun. Chandeliers and mirrors glittered with gold. In the royal gardens, millions of flowers, trees, and fountains were set out in precise geometric patterns, reflecting royal power over nature.

Elaborate Court Ceremonies Louis XIV perfected elaborate ceremonies that emphasized his own importance. Each day began in the king's bedroom with a ritual known as the **levée** (luh VAY), or rising. High-ranking nobles competed for the honor of holding the royal washbasin or handing the king his diamond-buckled shoes. At night, the ceremony was repeated in reverse. Wives of nobles vied to serve women of the royal family.

Rituals such as the levée served a serious purpose. French nobles were descendants of the feudal lords who had held power in medieval times. At liberty on their estates, these nobles were a threat to the power of the monarchy. By luring nobles to Versailles, Louis turned them into courtiers angling for privileges rather than rival warriors battling for power. His tactic worked because he carefully protected their prestige and continued their privilege of not paying taxes.

A Flowering of French Culture The king and his court supported a "splendid century" of the arts. The king sponsored musical entertainments and commissioned plays by the best writers. The age of Louis XIV came to be known as the classical age of French drama.

In painting, music, architecture, and decorative arts, French styles became the model for all Europe. A new form of dance drama, ballet, gained its first great popularity at the French court. As a leading patron of culture, Louis sponsored the French Academies, which set high standards for both the arts and the sciences.

 **SUMMARIZE** How did Louis XIV secure support from the nobility?

The Legacy of Louis XIV

Louis XIV ruled France for 72 years—far longer than any other monarch. During that time, French culture, manners, and customs set the standard for European tastes. The Sun King made France the strongest state in Europe. In both foreign and domestic affairs, however, many of Louis's policies were costly failures.

Costly Wars Louis XIV poured vast resources into wars meant to expand French borders. However, rival rulers joined forces to check these ambitions. Led by the Dutch or the English, these alliances fought to

Answers

Summarize *He kept them tied to the court and continued their privilege of not paying taxes.*

Identify Cause and Effect *Waging war drained his treasury; expelling Huguenots removed some of his most productive subjects.*

History Background

Court Etiquette The strictness of etiquette at Versailles made it almost impossible to relax. A noble would never consider walking out of his court-appointed place in a royal procession. Knocking on a door was forbidden. Instead, one was to scratch on the door with the fingernail of the little finger. Any digression from court etiquette subjected one to open derision and ridicule for days and might even result in banishment from court. One duchess who sat down at a gaming table when she was not playing was never invited to the Palace of Versailles again.

maintain the **balance of power.** The goal was to maintain a distribution of military and economic power to prevent any one country from dominating Europe.

In 1700, Louis's grandson Philip V inherited the throne of Spain. To maintain the balance of power, neighboring nations led by England fought to prevent the union of France and Spain.

The War of the Spanish Succession dragged on until 1713, when an exhausted France signed the Treaty of Utrecht (YOOtrekt). Philip remained on the Spanish throne, but France agreed never to unite the two crowns.

Huguenots Face Persecution Perhaps Louis's most costly mistake was his treatment of the Huguenots. Louis saw the Protestant minority as a threat to religious and political unity. In 1685, he revoked, or withdrew, the Edict of Nantes.

Facing renewed persecution, more than 100,000 Huguenots fled France. They settled mainly in England, the Netherlands, Germany, Poland, and the Americas. The Huguenots had been among the hardest working and most prosperous of Louis's subjects. Their loss was a serious blow to the French economy, just as the expulsion of Spanish Muslims and Jews had hurt Spain.

>> Huguenot families like these fled France in large numbers under Louis's persecution. Many Huguenots had been prosperous members of the middle class, and their departure hurt France economically.

? IDENTIFY CAUSE AND EFFECT How did Louis's actions weaken the French economy?

ASSESSMENT

1. **Identify** What factors led to the rise of absolute monarchies?
2. **Summarize** How did Spanish power grow under Charles V? under Philip II?
3. **Identify Supporting Details** How did France build a centralized monarchy after the wars of religion?
4. **Support a Point of View with Evidence** Would you consider Louis XIV a successful absolute monarch? Give examples from the text to support your answer.
5. **Connect** What impact did Spanish king Philip II and French king Louis XIV have on the arts?

Topic 12 Lesson 1

SYNTHESIZE

Online Ask students to recall the Topic Essential Question, "How much power should the government have?" First, have students fill out the graphic organizer for Louis XIV. His accomplishments will fit into all six areas. Then, have them fill out the chart for Philip II, whose accomplishments do not fit all six. Discuss the differences.

Compare and Contrast Have students use evidence from the chart to write a two-paragraph essay comparing and contrasting the two leaders. *(Students' essays should include both how the two leaders were alike and how they were different; similarities include persecution of Protestants, wars, monuments; differences include how they handled the nobles and the economy.)*

DEMONSTRATE

Online Assign the **Digital Lesson Quiz** for this lesson if you haven't already done so. Students will be offered automatic remediation or enrichment based on their score.

Pose the following to the class on the Discussion Board:

Remind students that in "Absolute Monarchy in Spain and France," they read about the characteristics of absolute monarchy and how different absolute monarchs sought to gain and keep power. They also read about some of their accomplishments and some of their failures.

Main Ideas Identify three characteristics that helped solidify the power of absolute monarchs. *(Possible answers: claimed divine right, controlled nobles, controlled economy, organized bureaucracy, unified religion, expanded territory, formed alliances)* Now list some general failures. *(overly ambitious, fought too many wars and used too many resources to fight them, taxed too heavily, expelled different groups)*

Topic Inquiry

Have students continue their investigations for the Topic Inquiry.

Assessment

1. Strong rulers centralized power, reduced the influence of nobles and the church, fought wars to increase territory, and used the doctrine of divine right to justify absolute power.
2. Spanish power grew under Spanish King Charles V when he inherited the Hapsburg empire. It grew under King Philip II because he expanded Spanish influence, strengthened the Catholic Church, made his own power absolute, and took possession of silver in the Spanish colonies in the Americas.
3. French King Henry IV built a centralized monarchy by creating a royal bureaucracy and reducing the influence of nobles.
4. Louis XIV was a successful absolute monarch. He was a shrewd ruler who centralized royal power and kept the nobility in check.
5. Both were enthusiastic patrons of the arts. As a result, literature and the arts flourished in Spain and France.

Topic 12 Lesson 2

Rise of Austria, Prussia, and Russia

CONNECT

Preview Have students preview the **Lesson Objectives** and the list of **Key Terms**.

Students can also preview all the **Key Terms** and **Academic Vocabulary** using the **Interactive Reading Notepad** on the digital course or preview a summary of the lesson in the **Reading and Note Taking Study Guide**.

Online Use the **Editable Presentation** found on the digital course to present the main ideas for this lesson.

Start Up Activity

Ask students what they think it would be like to live through 30 years of war. Have them write three to five sentences explaining what life might have been like for someone their age during the war and directly after it. Ask: How would your family have been affected? What would you have done with your days? What would you have eaten? *(Students might write about the need to take care of oneself, the daily hardship of finding food, the risk of death, or catching a disease.)*

Discuss When the Thirty Years' War ended, the German states were decimated. Farmland was destroyed, and people had lost their faith. Discuss the possible effects of loss of population, loss of economic security, and loss of faith of the people. *(likely hardships include lack of food, illness, conflict among people, financial insecurity)*

Online You can also project the **Start Up Activity** from the course.

INVESTIGATE

Have students read the section using the **Reading and Note Taking Study Guide** to help them take notes and understand the text as they read.

The Thirty Years' War

At the time of the Thirty Years' War, Europe was a fragmented continent, a patchwork of several hundred small states ruled by the Holy Roman emperor, who had very little authority over rival princes. This power vacuum contributed to the outbreak of the war, which was actually a series of wars.

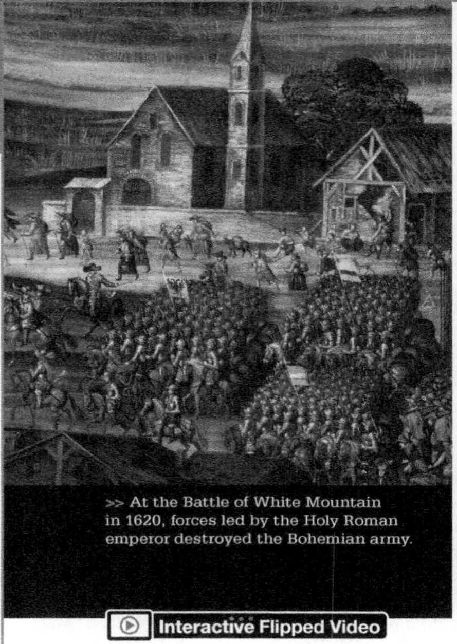

>> At the Battle of White Mountain in 1620, forces led by the Holy Roman emperor destroyed the Bohemian army.

12.2 During the Reformation, the many German-speaking states within the Holy Roman Empire were plunged into religious wars. Some princes remained loyal to the Roman Catholic Church. Others accepted the teachings of Protestant reformers like Martin Luther or John Calvin. By the early 1600s, war raged across much of the Holy Roman Empire.

Interactive Flipped Video

TEKS
16.A, 19.B, 24.B

>> Objectives

Outline the causes and results of the Thirty Years' War.

Understand how Austria and Prussia emerged as great powers.

Explain the steps Peter the Great took to modernize Russia.

Describe how Russia grew under Peter the Great and Catherine the Great.

Describe how European nations tried to maintain a balance of power.

>> Key Terms

elector
mercenary
depopulation
Peace of Westphalia
Maria Theresa
War of the Austrian Succession
Prussia
Frederick William I
Frederick II
Peter the Great
westernization
boyar
autocratic
warm-water port
St. Petersburg
Catherine the Great
partition

PEARSON realize. www.PearsonTexas.com Access your Digital Lesson.

Rise of Austria, Prussia, and Russia

The Thirty Years' War

A Fragmented "Empire" By early modern times, as the French philosopher Voltaire later observed, the Holy Roman Empire was neither holy, nor Roman, nor an empire. Instead, by the seventeenth century it had become a patchwork of several hundred small, separate states.

In theory, these states were ruled by the Holy Roman emperor, who was chosen by seven leading German princes called **electors.** In practice, the emperor had little power over the many rival princes. This power vacuum contributed to the outbreak of the Thirty Years' War.

Religion further divided the German states. The north had become largely Protestant, while the south remained Catholic.

Conflict Erupts The Thirty Years' War was actually a series of wars. It began in Bohemia, the present-day Czech Republic. Ferdinand, the Catholic Hapsburg king of Bohemia, sought to suppress Protestants and to assert royal power over nobles.

476

Aa Vocabulary Builder

1. Have students pronounce the following academic vocabulary terms in this lesson and clarify the part of speech. For difficult or polysyllabic words, break them into syllables and pronounce them with the students.
2. Explain what the word means in common "student-friendly" language using synonyms and antonyms when possible. Provide concrete examples to clarify the meaning, and rephrase the definition.

aspired: aimed; sought

stipulated: made a specific demand

In May 1618, a few rebellious Protestant nobles tossed two royal officials out of a castle window in Prague. This act, known as the Defenestration of Prague, sparked a general revolt, which Ferdinand moved to suppress. As both sides sought allies, what began as a local conflict widened into a general European war.

The following year, Ferdinand was elected Holy Roman Emperor. With the support of Spain, Poland, and other Catholic states, he tried to roll back the Reformation by force. Early on, he defeated rebellious Bohemians and their Protestant allies. Alarmed, Protestant powers like the Netherlands and Sweden sent troops into Germany.

Political motives quickly outweighed religious issues. Catholic and Protestant rulers shifted alliances to suit their own interests. At one point, Catholic France joined Lutheran Sweden against the Catholic Hapsburgs.

A Time of Chaos The fighting took a terrible toll. Roving armies of **mercenaries,** or soldiers for hire, burned villages, destroyed crops, and killed without mercy. Murder and torture were followed by famine and disease. Wolves, not seen in settled areas since the Middle Ages, stalked the deserted streets of once-bustling villages.

The war led to a severe **depopulation,** or reduction in population. Exact statistics do not exist, but historians estimate that as many as one third of the people in the German states may have died as a result of the war.

Peace Is Restored Finally, in 1648, the exhausted combatants accepted a series of treaties, known as the **Peace of Westphalia.** Because so many powers had been involved in the conflict, the treaties ended with a general European peace and settled other international problems.

Among the combatants, France emerged a clear winner, gaining territory on both its Spanish and German frontiers. The Hapsburgs were not so fortunate. They had to accept the almost total independence of all the princes of the Holy Roman Empire. In addition, the Netherlands and the Swiss Federation (present-day Switzerland) won recognition as independent states.

The Thirty Years' War left German lands divided into more than 360 separate states—"one for every day of the year." These states still acknowledged the rule of the Holy Roman emperor. Yet each state had its own government, currency, church, armed forces, and foreign policy.

The German-speaking states, if united, had the potential to become the most powerful nation in Europe.

>> **Analyze Maps** After the Thirty Years' War, the Peace of Westphalia redrew the map of Europe. Who controlled Bohemia after 1648?

 Interactive Map

Topic 12 Lesson 2

Online Project the **Interactive Map: Maps of Europe, 1648 and 1700**. Focus students' attention on the area of the Holy Roman Empire on the 1648 map. Slide to the 1700 map, asking students to keep their eyes on the same region. Which two states grew the most from 1648 to 1700? *(Austria and Prussia)* On the whiteboard, draw a T-chart (students could also construct their own graphic organizer) and list Maria Theresa and Frederick William I on the chart. Ask students to list how both Maria Theresa and Frederick William I consolidated their power. *(Maria Theresa: reorganized bureaucracy, taxed nobles and clergy, used German-speaking officials to help unify; Frederick William I: built up army, gave Junkers positions in Army, created an efficient bureaucracy)*

ACTIVE CLASSROOM

Speak: A Close Look Part 1: Project the 1648 map on the whiteboard and use a whiteboard tool to divide it into four numbered quadrants. Have students count off 1 to 4. Ask them to look closely at the part of the map in their quadrant. Ask students to list what they see. Part 2: Repeat with the 1700 map. Part 3: Ask students to focus on any changes they see in their quadrant and list them. Collect insights and list them on the board or on chart paper.

Answers

Analyze Maps *the Austrian Hapsburgs*

English Language Proficiency Standards

Reading 4.C.1 Instruct students to look at the red headers of "The Thirty Years' War" for sight vocabulary. Ask students to create a list of the words and explain what each means.

Beginning Guide students as they look at the red headings for words that they know by sight. Display the list of words with definitions. Have pairs take turns providing a word or phrase, explaining what each sight word means. Provide the following sentence frame: ________ means ________.

Intermediate Complete the Beginning activity, but have students write sentences using each word instead of completing the sentence frame.

Advanced Have students look through the red headings in Lesson 2 for sight vocabulary. Instruct students to make flashcards of each of their sight words. Have them write a short definition and a sentence on the back of each card. Have students quiz each other on the meaning of each word.

Advanced High Have students look through the red headings in Lesson 2 for sight vocabulary. Have them define each sight word and write a sentence using each word. Ask them to exchange lists and sentences with another pair and peer edit their work.

Topic 12 Lesson 2

Guided Reading and Discussion

Ask students to look again at the 1700 map. Which states have the most coastline? *(Spain, France, England, Sweden)* Why would having a longer coastline be a benefit to the state? *(more ports, more shipping, more trade)* Which states have the least coastline? *(Austria, Poland, Russia)* What do you think they might do to increase their access to the sea? *(invade other countries, develop alliances)*

Hapsburg Austria Expands

Although the Hapsburgs were weakened by war, they still sought to expand their territory, which they would later do by adding parts of Poland, Italy, Bohemia, and Hungary.

They remained fragmented, however, and would not be joined into a single nation for another 223 years.

? IDENTIFY CAUSE AND EFFECT What were some effects of the Peace of Westphalia?

ELPS ELPS 4.C.1 Demonstrate your understanding of root words to decode the meanings of vocabulary words used in this section.

Hapsburg Austria Expands

The Thirty Years' War took a terrible toll on the people of the German states. Out of the ashes, however, rose two great German-speaking powers: Austria and Prussia. Like Louis XIV in France, their rulers tried to centralize power and rule as absolute monarchs.

A Diverse Empire Though weakened by war, the Hapsburgs still wanted to create a strong united state. They kept the title "Holy Roman emperor" but focused their attention on expanding their own lands. To Austria, their base of power, they added Bohemia, Hungary, and, later, parts of Poland and some Italian states.

>> The War of the Austrian Succession challenged Maria Theresa's right to rule the Holy Roman Empire. In 1745, French forces defeated British and Austrian troops at the Battle of Fontenoy, shown here.

Uniting these lands proved difficult. Not only were they divided by geography, they included a number of diverse peoples and cultures as well. By the 1700s, the Hapsburg Empire included Germans, Magyars, Slavs, and others. In many parts of the empire, people had their own languages, laws, political assemblies, and customs.

The Hapsburgs did exert some control over these diverse peoples. They sent German-speaking officials to Bohemia and Hungary and settled Austrians on lands they had seized in these provinces. They also put down revolts in Bohemia and Hungary. Still, the Hapsburgs never developed a fully centralized governmental system like that of France.

Empress Maria Theresa In the early 1700s, a new challenge threatened Hapsburg Austria. Emperor Charles VI had no male heir. His daughter, **Maria Theresa,** was intelligent and capable, but no woman had yet ruled Hapsburg lands in her own name. Charles persuaded other European rulers to recognize his daughter's right to succeed him. When he died, however, many ignored their pledge.

Shortly after Charles's death in 1740, Frederick II of Prussia seized the rich Hapsburg province of Silesia. This action sparked the eight-year **War of the Austrian Succession.**

Maria Theresa set off for Hungary to appeal for military help from her Hungarian subjects. The Hungarians were ordinarily unfriendly to the Hapsburgs. But she made a dramatic plea before an assembly of Hungarian nobles. According to one account, the nobles rose to their feet and shouted, "Our lives and blood for your Majesty!" She eventually got further help from Britain and Russia.

Reforms of an Absolute Monarch Maria Theresa never succeeded in forcing Frederick out of Silesia. Still, she did preserve her empire and win the support of most of her people. Equally important, she strengthened Hapsburg power by reorganizing the bureaucracy and improving tax collection. She forced nobles and clergy to pay taxes and tried to ease the burden of taxes and labor services on peasants.

Maria Theresa was an absolute monarch who believed that her decisions were for the good of her subjects. Like other rulers at the time, she strengthened royal authority by limiting the power of nobles and the Church.

? IDENTIFY CAUSE AND EFFECT What caused the War of the Austrian Succession?

D Differentiate Extra Support Have students look closely at the 1648 map and identify the Dutch Netherlands, Spanish Netherlands, Hungary, and Westphalia. Then ask: (1) What is controlled by Spain? *(Spain, Spanish Netherlands, Sardinia, Sicily, boot of Italy, regions in north of Italy and Holy Roman Empire)* (2) Which state has land on the coast of Poland? *(Prussia)*

Slide map to reveal the 1700 map. Ask students: (1) Have Spain's lands decreased, increased, or stayed the same? *(stayed the same)* (2) Which other state (besides Spain, Austria, and Prussia) has land in the Holy Roman Empire? *(Sweden)*

Answers

Identify Cause and Effect *France gained land, the Hapsburgs lost land, the Netherlands and Swiss Federation gained independence, and the German lands were even more divided.*

Identify Cause and Effect *Maria Theresa's succession to the throne and Frederick II's invasion of Silesia*

Prussia Emerges

While Austria was molding a strong Catholic state, **Prussia** emerged as a new Protestant German-speaking power in the north. In the 1600s, the Hohenzollern (HOH un tsahl urn) family ruled scattered lands across north Germany. After the Peace of Westphalia, ambitious Hohenzollern rulers united their holdings by taking over states between them. Like absolute rulers elsewhere, they imposed royal power on all their subjects and reduced the independence of their nobles, called Junkers (YOON kerz).

Creating an Efficient Bureaucracy To achieve their goals, Hohenzollern rulers set up an efficient central bureaucracy and forged one of the best-trained armies in Europe. One Prussian military leader boasted, "Prussia is not a state which possesses an army, but an army which possesses a state."

Emperor **Frederick William I,** who came to power in 1713, gained the loyalty of the Junkers by giving them positions in the army and government. His tactic reduced the nobles' independence and increased his own control. By 1740, Prussia was strong enough to challenge its rival Austria.

Frederick the Great That year, young **Frederick II** inherited the throne. From an early age, Frederick was trained in the art of war, as his father insisted.

> His tutor must take the greatest pains to imbue my son with a sincere love for the soldier's profession and to impress upon him that nothing else in the world can confer upon a prince such fame and honor as the sword.
>
> —Frederick William I

However, Frederick preferred playing the flute and writing poetry. His father despised these pursuits and treated the young prince so badly that he tried to flee the country. Discovering these plans, Frederick William put his son in solitary confinement. Then he forced the 18-year-old prince to watch as the friend who had helped him was beheaded.

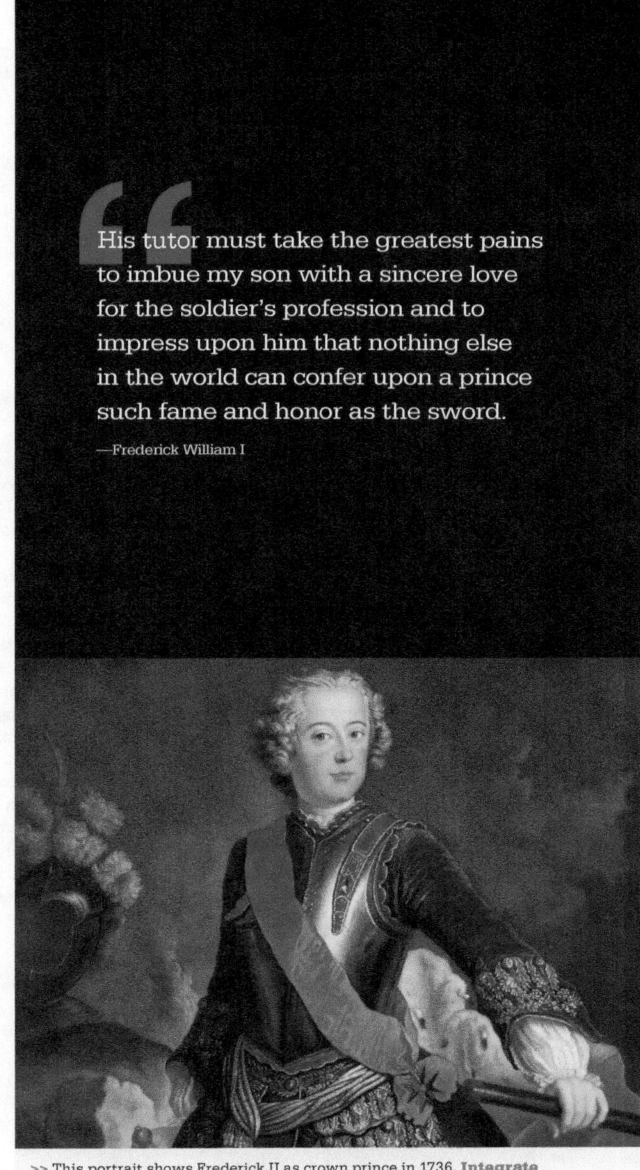
His tutor must take the greatest pains to imbue my son with a sincere love for the soldier's profession and to impress upon him that nothing else in the world can confer upon a prince such fame and honor as the sword.
—Frederick William I

>> This portrait shows Frederick II as crown prince in 1736. **Integrate Information** Why might Frederick have been painted dressed in armor?

Topic 12 Lesson 2

Prussia Emerges

For over 200 years, the German states were extremely divided. Two strong states—Prussia and Austria—emerged to fill the void, but many other German states remained independent until the middle of the nineteenth century.

Key Terms

Ask students to find the key term **Frederick William I** (in bold) in the text. Explain that he was the second Prussian king who helped transform his country into a prosperous state.

D Differentiate Challenge Break students into small groups and assign each group one of the larger states—Bavaria, Saxony, Hesse-Kassel, Wurttemberg, Hanover, or Baden. Ask them to research the history of that state from 1648 to 1800 and the type of government in each. Presentations can be made using PowerPoint or could use digital media and be posted on a Web site. Follow with a discussion of the similarities and differences of the stories from each state.

History Background

Frederick William King Frederick William of Prussia led a militaristic lifestyle that was impassioned, and at times, bizarre. In public, he always wore his military uniform. Like a good soldier, he regularly began his work day at five or six in the morning. At ten in the morning, he usually reported to the parade ground to drill or inspect the troops. Any lapse in military discipline might trigger his violent temper.

Frederick William had an unusual admiration for tall soldiers, whom he regarded as possessing superior strength and stamina. Like a fanatical basketball coach seeking the championship, he sent scouts throughout much of Europe. Their mission was to entice, buy, and even kidnap the tallest soldiers for service in the Prussian army.

Answers

Integrate Information *He's dressed in armor because his father wants him to be a soldier.*

Topic 12 Lesson 2

Peter the Great Modernizes Russia

By the end of the 1600s, a new tsar emerged in Russia and used his power to make that nation a great and modern power. Peter the Great, as he became known, pushed through economic and social reforms, strengthened the military, and even simplified the Russian alphabet.

Guided Reading and Discussion

Ask students to answer the following questions: 1) How did Peter the Great westernize Russia? Cite three pieces of evidence from the text. *(modernized the military, forced the Boyars to westernize their dress, improved education, built western city [St. Petersburg])* 2) What challenges did Peter the Great face when he tried to westernize Russia? Cite three pieces of evidence from the text. *(building a world-class navy from nothing, the resistance of the Boyars, the difficulties building St. Petersburg)*

Frederick's harsh military training had an effect. After becoming king in 1740, Frederick II lost no time in using his army. He boldly seized Silesia from Austria, sparking the War of the Austrian Succession.

In several later wars, Frederick continued to brilliantly use his disciplined army, forcing all to recognize Prussia as a great power. His exploits and his power as an absolute monarch earned him the name Frederick the Great.

? SUMMARIZE How did Frederick William increase his power?

Peter the Great Modernizes Russia

From 1604 to 1613, Russia was in a period of disorder, plagued by foreign invasions and internal rebellion. The rise of the first Romanov tsar restored a measure of order. Still, Russia remained a medieval state, untouched by the Renaissance or Reformation and largely isolated from Western Europe.

At the end of the century, a tsar emerged who was strong enough to regain the absolute power of earlier tsars. Just 10 years old when he took the throne in 1682, Peter I took control of the government seven years later. **Peter the Great,** as he came to be called, used his power to put Russia on the road to becoming a great modern power.

>> Peter the Great, shown here as a young man, worked to restore order in Russia and make it a great modern power.

Peter Visits the West The young tsar was a striking figure, nearly seven feet tall, with a booming laugh and a furious temper. Although he was not well educated, he was immensely curious. He spent hours in the Moscow neighborhood where many Dutch, Scottish, English, and other foreigners lived. There, he heard of the new technology that was helping Western European monarchs forge powerful empires.

In 1697, Peter set out to learn about Western technology and ways for himself. He spent hours walking the streets of European cities, noting the manners and homes of the people. He visited factories and art galleries, learned anatomy from a doctor, and even had a dentist teach him how to pull teeth.

In England, Peter was impressed by Parliament. "It is good," he said, "to hear subjects speaking truthfully and openly to their king."

The Westernization of Russia Returning to Russia, Peter brought a group of technical experts, teachers, and soldiers he had recruited in Europe. He then embarked on a policy of **westernization,** the adoption of Western ideas, technology, and culture.

Some changes had a symbolic meaning. He forced the **boyars,** or landowning nobles, to shave their traditional beards and wear Western-style clothes. To end the practice of secluding upper-class women in separate quarters, he held grand parties at which women and men were expected to dance together. Russian nobles opposed this radical mixing of the sexes in public, but they had to comply.

To impose his will, Peter became the most **autocratic** of Europe's absolute monarchs, meaning that he ruled with unlimited authority. Determined to centralize royal power, he brought the Russian Orthodox Church under his control. He forced the haughty boyars to serve the state in civilian or military jobs.

Extending Serfdom Peter knew that nobles would serve the state only if their own interests were protected. Therefore, he passed laws ensuring that nobles retained control over their lands. This included the serfs who were tied to those lands.

Under Peter's rule, serfdom spread in Russia at a time when it was dying out in Western Europe. Further, he forced some serfs to become soldiers or to work as laborers on roads, canals, and other government projects.

History Background

Siberia Russia's absolute monarchs needed a place to exile both criminals and political opponents for long periods of time. What place was better than the arctic region of Siberia? Siberia was far away from everything Russian and had an extremely inhospitable climate; temperatures could average -59°F (–51°C) in winter. There was little chance of escape, as it was almost impossible to survive alone in the vast, frozen, sparsely population region. In fact, 10 to 15 percent of exiles never made it to Siberia; they died along the way. The number of exiles grew from a trickle in the early 1600s to 2,000 a year by the early 1800s. After a revolt in 1825, the tsar sent 150,000 people off to their freezing fate. Today, the expression "sent to Siberia" still implies that a person is being punished or has become an outcast.

Answers

Summarize *He controlled the Junkers, created an efficient bureaucracy, and established a strong army.*

A Harsh, Effective Ruler Peter showed no mercy to any who resisted his new order. When elite palace guards revolted, he had more than 1,000 of the rebels tortured and executed. Then, as an example of his power, he left their rotting corpses outside the palace walls for months.

Peter was known not only for cruelty but also for remaking Russia. He imported Western technology, simplified the Russian alphabet, and set up academies for the study of mathematics, science, and engineering. To pay for his reforms, Peter adopted mercantilist policies, such as encouraging exports. He improved waterways and canals, developed mining and textile manufacturing, and backed new trading companies. Peter succeeded in refashioning Russia from a medieval backwater into a rising European—and Asian—power.

CATEGORIZE What policies did Peter use to solidify his control over the nobles?

>> In this image, Peter the Great is studying the building plans for St. Petersburg. The establishment of the city was one of his most important and long-lasting achievements.

Interactive Gallery

Expanding Russia's Borders

From his earliest days as tsar, Peter worked to build Russia's military power. He created the largest standing army in Europe, built a world-class navy from scratch, and set out to extend Russian borders to the west and south. To achieve these goals meant fighting Russia's neighbors.

Seeking a Warm-Water Seaport Peter's chief goal was to win a **warm-water port,** a port that was not frozen in winter. Russian seaports, located along the Arctic Ocean, were covered in ice most of the year. A warm-water port would increase Russia's ability to trade with the West.

The nearest warm-water coast was located along the Black Sea. To gain control of this territory, Peter had to push through the powerful Ottoman Empire. In the end, Peter was unable to defeat the Ottomans and gain his warm-water port. The drive to achieve this goal motivated future Russian tsars, and by the late 1700s, Catherine the Great would succeed.

The Great Northern War In 1700, Peter began a long war against the kingdom of Sweden, which at the time dominated the Baltic region. Early on, Russia suffered humiliating defeats. A Swedish force of only 8,000 men defeated a Russian army five times its size. Undaunted, Peter rebuilt his army, modeling it after European armies.

>> Peter wanted to gain access to a warm-water port and the open sea. His first step toward this goal was to capture Azov, a town in what is now southwestern Russia, from the Turks. This painting shows the successful capture of Azov in 1696.

Online Project the **Interactive Gallery: The Achievements of Peter the Great**. Read the caption copy as you click through the images. Remind students about the techniques of absolutism (control nobles, control economy, centralize bureaucracy, unify religion, increase military strength/expand territory, build monuments to self). Ask students: How did the achievements of Peter the Great reflect his strength as an absolute monarch? Cite at least three pieces of specific information from the images and captions. *(improved trade, regulated churches, built St. Petersburg, strengthened navy)*

ACTIVE CLASSROOM

Group students. Give each group a three-column organizer with the headings Plus/Minus/Interesting for recording responses to these three questions: (1) What were the positive effects of Peter the Great's achievements? (2) What were the negative effects? (3) What is interesting about them? Each column must have at least one entry. Record students' responses on the whiteboard or on charting paper. Discuss the answers as a class.

Expanding Russia's Borders

Peter the Great eventually expanded Russia's borders and created a large standing army and a world-class navy.

D Differentiate Challenge Group students, and give each group a copy of the image of Peter the Great cutting off the beards of the Boyars. Ask students to use this image to create a political cartoon about the tactics Peter used to westernize Russia. Groups will need to write (1) a title; (2) a caption; and (3) word bubbles for Peter and the Boyars.

Answers

Categorize *He forced them to change their customs and serve the state. He also won their support by strengthening serfdom.*

Topic 12 Lesson 2

Catherine the Great

Catherine the Great continued Peter the Great's efforts to westernize Russia but was also a ruthless leader in the old Russian mold.

Guided Reading and Discussion

Ask students to give examples of Catherine the Great's reforms and her ruthlessness in a paragraph in which they assess Catherine's achievements as an absolute monarch. *(Answers will vary. Examples of westernizing: French language and customs, education for both boys and girls, reorganizing government, making the laws more clear/systematic—"codifying" them; Examples of ruthlessness: harsh treatment of serfs, giving more rights to nobles [Boyars], and exempting nobles from taxation)*

Finally, in 1709, he defeated the Swedes and won territory along the Baltic Sea. On this land, Peter would build a magnificent new capital city, **St. Petersburg.**

A "Window on the West" St. Petersburg became the great symbol of Peter's desire to forge a modern, Western-oriented Russia nation. Seeking to open a "window on the West," he located the city along the swampy shores of the Neva River, near the Baltic coast. He forced tens of thousands of serfs to drain the swamps. Many thousands died, but Peter's plan for the city succeeded.

On his journey to the West, Peter had visited Louis XIV's splendid new palace of Versailles. Like the Sun King, Peter invited the best European architects and artisans to design and build the palaces for his new city. Peter even planned the city's parks and boulevards himself, modeling them on those he had seen at Versailles.

Expanding to the East Peter also expanded the Russian empire eastward toward the Pacific. Russian traders and raiders also crossed the plains and rivers of Siberia. Under Peter, Russia signed a treaty with China that recognized Russia's claim to lands north of China and defined the common border of the two empires.

>> The Bering expedition brought the Russians to the west coast of North America.

In the early 1700s, Peter hired the Danish navigator Vitus Bering to explore what became known as the Bering Strait between Siberia and Alaska. After Peter's death, Russian traders built outposts in Alaska and northern California. Few Russians moved east of the Ural Mountains at this time, but the expansion made Russia the largest country in the world. It still is today, nearly 300 years later.

A Mixed Legacy When Peter died in 1725, he left a mixed legacy. He had expanded Russian territory, gained ports on the Baltic Sea, and created a mighty army. He had also ended Russia's long period of isolation. From the 1700s on, Russia would be increasingly involved in the affairs of Western Europe. Yet many of Peter's ambitious reforms died with him. Nobles, for example, soon ignored his policy of service to the state.

Like earlier tsars, Peter the Great had used terror to enforce his absolute power. His policies contributed to the growth of serfdom, which served only to widen the gap between Russia and the West that Peter had sought to narrow.

IDENTIFY CAUSE AND EFFECT What impact did Peter's defeat of Sweden have on Russia's expansion?

Catherine the Great

Peter's successors in the Romanov dynasty were ineffective rulers. Russian nobles quickly reasserted their independence. Then a new monarch took the reins of power firmly in hand. She became known to history as **Catherine the Great.**

A German Princess Becomes Tsar A German princess by birth, Catherine came to Russia at the age of 15 to wed the heir to the Russian throne. She learned Russian, embraced the Russian Orthodox faith, and won the loyalty of the people.

In 1762, a group of Russian army officers loyal to her deposed and murdered her mentally unstable husband, Tsar Peter III. Whether or not Catherine was involved in the assassination is uncertain. In any case, with the support of the military, she ascended the Russian throne.

Catherine Embraces Reform Catherine proved to be an efficient, energetic empress. She reorganized the provincial government, codified laws, and began state-sponsored education for both boys and girls.

Like Peter the Great, Catherine embraced Western ideas and worked to bring Russia fully into European

History Background

Bering's Explorations Young Vitus Bering, a Danish navigator, joined the newly created Russian navy in 1703. In 1725 he was sent by Peter the Great to explore Asia's northeast coast. It took two years to move men and supplies across Siberia. Finally, he sailed through what is now the Bering Strait, proving that Russia was not connected to North America. On his return across Siberia, he became ill, but in 1741 he set off again, this time to explore the northwest coast of North America. He discovered the Aleutian Islands, but then he fell ill again, and Bering and 28 of his men died there on a barren island. Following his expedition, Spain rushed to establish settlements on North America's west coast. Russia, however, was more interested in the fur trade than in expanding onto a third continent.

Answers

Identify Cause and Effect *It gained Russia territory along the Baltic Sea, including the land for his new capital, St. Petersburg.*

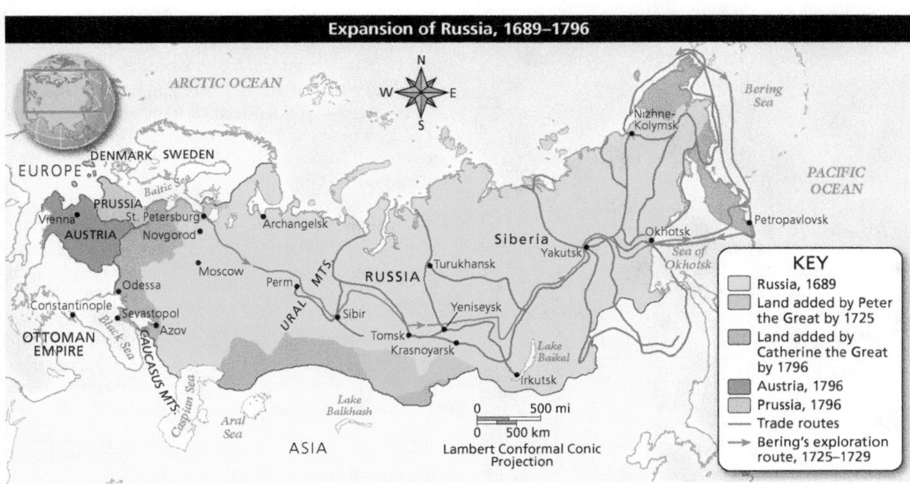

>> **Analyze Maps** Russia expanded its borders from 1689 to 1796. Which five cities could probably serve as warm-water ports?

cultural and political life. At court, she encouraged French language and customs, wrote histories and plays, and organized performances. She was also a serious student of the French thinkers who led the intellectual movement known as the Enlightenment.

An Absolute Monarch Like rulers in France and Spain, Catherine was an absolute monarch. Like them, she could be ruthless. She granted a charter to the boyars outlining important rights, such as exemption from taxes. She also allowed them to increase their stranglehold on the peasants. When peasants rebelled against the harsh burdens of serfdom, Catherine harshly suppressed the uprisings. Under Catherine, conditions grew even worse for Russian peasants and serfdom continued to spread.

Like Peter the Great, Catherine was determined to expand Russia's borders. After a war against the Ottoman Empire, she achieved the Russian dream of a warm-water port on the Black Sea. She also took steps to seize territory from neighboring Poland.

The Partitions of Poland Poland-Lithuania had once been a great European power. However, its rulers were unable to centralize their power or diminish the influence of the Polish nobility. In the 1770s, three powerful neighboring monarchs—Catherine of Russia, Frederick II of Prussia, and Joseph II of Austria—hungrily eyed Poland.

To avoid fighting one another, the three monarchs agreed in 1772 to **partition,** or divide up, Poland. Poland was partitioned three times between the 1770s and 1790s. Russia took the eastern part, where many Russians and Ukrainians lived. Austria and Prussia divided up the rest. By 1795, the independent kingdom of Poland had vanished from the map. Not until 1919 would a free Polish state reappear.

COMPARE How were Catherine's goals similar to those of Peter?

ELPS 3.G.2 Read, or listen to your teacher read *Catherine the Great* and discuss the positive and negative outcomes of her reign.

Five Great European Powers

By 1750, five European powers had come to dominate European affairs. They were Austria, Prussia, France, Britain, and Russia. All five had strong centralized governments. Although Spain and the Ottoman Empire ruled parts of Europe, these once powerful empires were in decline.

Analyze Images

Have students examine the map of Russia's expansion, 1689–1796. Ask students to locate Sweden, the Baltic Sea, St. Petersburg, Siberia, and the Bering Sea. Ask them: (1) Why do you think Peter the Great wanted to improve his navy? *(It would help him expand Russia's borders.)* (2) How might this map look different if Peter the Great had not developed a modern navy? *(Sample response: Russia might look smaller.)* (3) What do the lands that were added during Catherine's reign have in common? *(Catherine succeeded in gaining a warm-water port that Peter wanted badly.)*

Five Great European Powers

In the 1740s, the alliances between the major European powers shifted. England and France were in opposition, as were Austria and Prussia. The Seven Years' War was fought between these powers, and it was the first European war to be fought on four continents.

Answers

Analyze Maps *Odessa, Sevastopol, and Azov on the Black Sea; Petropavlovsk on the Pacific Ocean; and Okhotsk on the Sea of Okhotsk*

Compare *They both wanted to increase the power of the monarchy, extend Russia's borders, and make it a modern European country.*

English Language Proficiency Standards

Speaking 3.G.2 **Beginning** Read "Catherine the Great" aloud. Help students identify positive and negative aspects of her reign, supporting them with simple phrases and words to help them formulate and communicate their ideas. Have students use sentence frames such as the following to express their ideas: The reign of Catherine the Great was good/bad for Russia because ________.

Intermediate Have partners create a list of words to describe Catherine the Great and her reign. Then ask the pairs to discuss whether these words describe Catherine's reign as positive or negative. Have pairs share their ideas with the class, using supporting details from the text.

Advanced Have students work together in small groups to discuss the life of Catherine the Great and to develop a list of positive and negative outcomes that define her reign. Have students discuss their ideas on how Catherine's reign affected Russia and its people.

Advanced High Divide students into two groups. Have students in each group discuss the influence of Catherine the Great. Have one group develop a list of positive outcomes of her reign, and have the other develop a list of negative outcomes. Then have groups debate their positions, supporting their ideas with evidence from the text.

Topic 12 Lesson 2

SYNTHESIZE

Remind students of the Topic Essential Question: How much power should the government have? Project the **Mini-DBQ: Absolutism in Prussia and Russia**. Have students read the documents and then answer these questions: How was the absolute rule of Peter the Great, Frederick II, and Catherine the Great different from earlier European absolute monarchs? How was it similar?

Encourage students to cite the documents and the lesson to support their answers. *(Sample answer: Peter the Great: Different: worked with his hands; admired the constitution and religion. Frederick II: Different: Leader is the head of the state, should be honest, hardworking, and worthy. Catherine the Great: Similar: obedience to authority; assumes religious unity.)*

DEMONSTRATE

Online Assign the **Digital Lesson Quiz** for this lesson if you haven't already done so. Students will be offered automatic remediation or enrichment based on their score.

Remind students that in "Rise of Austria, Prussia, and Russia," they read about the Thirty Years' War, how Austria and Prussia emerged as powers, the reigns of Peter the Great and Catherine the Great, and the five great European powers that existed by 1750.

How did Austria, Prussia, and Russia expand their power and territory to become three of the most powerful countries in eighteenth-century Europe? *(Their leaders ruled as absolute monarchs, expanded their armies, and in some cases, formed alliances.)* In your opinion, which country was most successful, and why?

Topic Inquiry

Have students continue their investigations for the Topic Inquiry.

Answers

Describe *European nations maintained a balance of power through wars and shifting alliances.*

>> The Seven Years' War in Europe pitted Europe, Prussia, and Britain against Austria, France, Russia, and Sweden. This painting shows a December 1757 battle in which the Prussians defeated the Austrians.

Struggles for Power As these five nation-states competed with one another, they formed various alliances to maintain the balance of power. Though nations sometimes switched partners, two basic rivalries persisted. Prussia battled Austria for control of the German-speaking states. At the same time, Britain and France competed for power and influence both in Europe and in their growing overseas empires.

On occasion, these rivalries resulted in worldwide conflict. The Seven Years' War, which lasted from 1756 until 1763, was fought on four continents.

In Europe, Prussia and Britain battled Austria, France, Russia, and Sweden. Britain and France also battled for power in India, Africa, and North America, where the conflict became known as the French and Indian War.

Absolutism at Its Peak Absolutism reached its peak in the mid-1700s. Four of the five great European powers were ruled by absolute monarchs. Britain, with its strong Parliament, was the only exception.

At the same time, new ideas were circulating about natural rights and the role of government. In time, demands for change and reform would topple French absolutism, revolutionize European societies, and transform the balance of power in Europe.

? DESCRIBE How did European nations maintain a balance of power?

ASSESSMENT

1. **Identify Cause and Effect** What were the causes and results of the Thirty Years' War?
2. **Identify** How were the goals of Austria and Prussia similar?
3. **Describe** How did European nations try to maintain a balance of power?
4. **List** What steps did Peter the Great take to modernize Russia?
5. **Describe** How did Russia grow under Peter the Great and Catherine the Great?

Assessment

1. *Causes*: The Holy Roman emperor had little power over the many rival princes. *Results*: The treaties brought about a general European peace. France gained territory on both its Spanish and German frontiers. The Hapsburgs had to accept the almost total independence of all the princes of the Holy Roman Empire. The Netherlands and the Swiss Federation won recognition as independent states. The Thirty Years' War left German lands divided into more than 360 separate states.
2. Both sought to consolidate power, build a strong state, and extend their territory.
3. They often ended up fighting wars to maintain a balance of power.
4. Using autocratic methods, Peter pushed through social and economic reforms. He imported Western technology; improved education; simplified the Russian alphabet; and set up academies for the study of mathematics, science, and engineering. He improved waterways and canals and developed mining and textile manufacturing.
5. Russia grew under Peter the Great because he adopted a policy of westernization, controlled the Church and the nobles, built up a strong army, and expanded Russia's borders. It grew under Catherine the Great because she embraced Russian culture, organized the provincial government, and seized territory.

12.3 During the age of absolutism, English monarchs, like rulers on the continent, tried to increase royal power and claim the divine right to rule. Their efforts, however, ran into the obstacle of Parliament, which during the Middle Ages had acquired the power of the purse. Only Parliament could grant monarchs the funds they needed to pursue their ambitions. And Parliament at times stood firm against royal absolutism.

>> Henry VIII consulted with Parliament frequently. Here, he presides as chairman over the House of Lords.

Interactive Flipped Video

Triumph of Parliament in England

TEKS
19.B, 20.A, 20.B

>> Objectives

Describe the relationship between Parliament and the monarchy under the Tudors and Stuarts.

Explain how English government developed after the English Civil War.

Identify the causes of the Glorious Revolution and the ideas contained in the English Bill of Rights.

Identify the characteristics of limited monarchy and constitutional government in England.

>> Key Terms

James I
dissenter
Puritan
Charles I
Oliver Cromwell
English Bill of Rights
limited monarchy
constitutional government
cabinet
prime minister
oligarchy

Tudor Monarchs Work with Parliament

Henry VIII From 1485 to 1603, England was ruled by Tudor monarchs. Although the Tudors believed in divine right, they shrewdly recognized the value of good relations with Parliament. When Henry VIII broke with the Roman Catholic Church, he turned to Parliament to legalize his actions. Parliament approved the Act of Supremacy, making the monarch head of the Church of England.

A constant need for money led Henry to consult Parliament frequently. Although he had inherited a bulging treasury, he quickly used up his funds fighting overseas wars. To levy new taxes, the king had to seek the approval of Parliament. Members of Parliament tended to vote as Henry's agents instructed. Still, they became accustomed to being consulted on important matters.

485

PEARSON realize. www.PearsonTexas.com Access your Digital Lesson.

Aa Vocabulary Builder

1. Have students pronounce the following academic vocabulary terms in this lesson and clarify the part of speech. For difficult or polysyllabic words, break them into syllables and pronounce them with the students.
2. Explain what the word means in common "student-friendly" language using synonyms and antonyms when possible. Provide concrete examples to clarify the meaning, and rephrase the definition.

suppressed: kept from being revealed; put down by force

justification: the state of having shown to be just, right, or reasonable

tolerate: to respect others' beliefs without sharing them

Triumph of Parliament in England

CONNECT

Preview Have students preview the **Lesson Objectives** and the list of **Key Terms**.

Students can also preview all the **Key Terms** and **Academic Vocabulary** using the **Interactive Reading Notepad** on the digital course or preview a summary of the lesson in the **Reading and Note Taking Study Guide**.

Online Use the **Editable Presentation** found on the digital course to present the main ideas for this lesson.

Start Up Activity

Ask students to answer the questions below as they enter and get settled. Then have them share their ideas with another student, either in class or through a chat room or blog.

Discuss What do these portraits suggest about these two men and how they ruled? *(Sample response: King James's clothing and throne are symbols of his power as king. Cromwell shows a more military focus.)*

Draw Inferences Cromwell did not come from a poor family, so his simple dress was a matter of choice. Why do you think this choice might have influenced those who followed Cromwell? *(The common people could identify with Cromwell more easily.)*

Online You can also project the **Start Up Activity** from the course.

INVESTIGATE

Have students read the section using the **Reading and Note Taking Study Guide** to help them take notes and understand the text as they read.

Tudor Monarchs Work with Parliament

The tradition of the English Parliament set England apart from other European nations with absolute monarchs. English monarchs had to work with Parliament, and each had developed his or her own method for dealing with its members.

Topic 12 Lesson 3

Analyze Images

Discuss the image of Henry VIII and Parliament at the beginning of the lesson. What does the image suggest about the relationship between the king and Parliament? *(That the king and Parliament are one governing body; they act in concert with each other.)*

Predict Consequences What might be a likely outcome when an absolute monarch clashes with a Parliament that is growing in strength? *(One or the other would have to back down. If both refuse, a civil war or other armed conflict might result.)*

Stuart Monarchs Clash with Parliament

When James Stuart ascended the English throne, he brought with him strong views about the power of the monarchy, which did not sit well with Parliament.

D Differentiate Challenge/Gifted Ask students to research and prepare a short presentation about English political philosopher Thomas Hobbes, who favored an absolute monarchy. Have students concentrate on why Hobbes believed that an absolute monarchy was the correct system of government. Part of the presentation should include a comparison of Hobbes's beliefs and the beliefs of those who supported a much more limited monarchy.

>> James I, the first Stuart king of England, ruled England from 1603 to 1625.

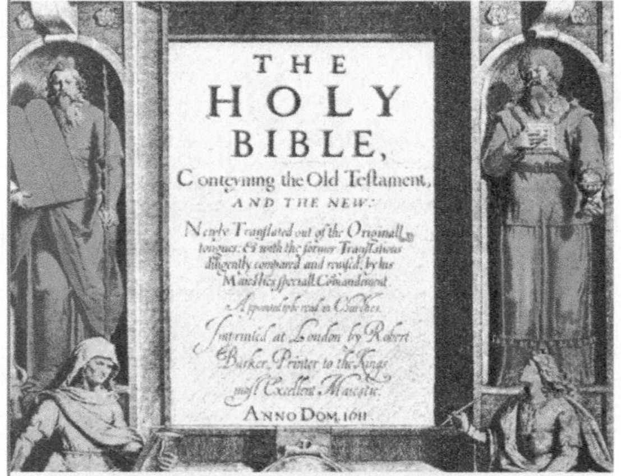

>> King James gave Greek and Hebrew scholars specific instructions for translating the Christian Bible into English. The King James Bible is considered a literary masterpiece.

Elizabeth I When Henry's daughter Elizabeth I gained the throne, she too both consulted and controlled Parliament. In theory, the monarch called Parliament for advice. In practice, Elizabeth rarely asked for its view. During her 45-year reign, she summoned Parliament only 13 times. All but one time, she asked for money.

When Parliament met, the queen's advisers conveyed her wishes. Certain subjects, such as foreign policy or the queen's marriage, were forbidden. Her skill in handling Parliament helped make "Good Queen Bess" a popular and successful ruler.

CHECK UNDERSTANDING Why did Henry VIII work with Parliament?

Stuart Monarchs Clash with Parliament

Elizabeth died childless in 1603. The throne passed to her relatives the Stuarts, the ruling family of Scotland. The Stuarts were neither as popular as the Tudors nor as skillful in dealing with Parliament. They also inherited problems that Henry and Elizabeth had long suppressed. The result was a "century of revolution" that pitted the Stuart monarchs against Parliament.

James I Asserts Divine Right When the first Stuart monarch, **James I,** took the throne, he agreed to rule according to English laws and customs. Soon, however, he was lecturing Parliament about divine right. In 1610, the king made a speech in Parliament.

> The state of Monarchy is the supremest thing upon earth; for kings are not only God's lieutenants upon earth and sit upon God's throne, but even by God himself they are called gods. . . . Kings are justly called gods for that they exercise a manner or resemblance of Divine power on earth . . . And to the King is due both the affection of the soul and the service of the body of his subjects....
>
> —King James I

Parliament was not impressed with the king's claim to rule by divine right. Instead, James faced repeated clashes with Parliament, mostly over money and foreign policy that involved the king's wars in Europe. James

Answers

Check Understanding *He needed Parliament's approval to levy new taxes and to obtain a divorce.*

History Background

The King James Bible A positive result of the king's dispute with the Puritans was his support of the Puritans' call for a new translation of the Bible. This version, known as the King James, appeared in 1611 and has had a lasting influence on English language and literature. The King James Version of the Bible represents one of the great literary achievements in English. The translators' mission was to create a text that both Anglicans and Puritans could use, expressed in the language of the day. Today scholars argue about the version's accuracy, but its poetic style and imagery still resonate in familiar excerpts, such as "Yea, though I walk through the valley of the shadow of death, I will fear no evil . . ." (Psalm 23).

lived extravagantly and had to ask Parliament for funds to finance his lavish court.

More than once, when members wanted to discuss foreign policy before voting funds, James dissolved Parliament and raised money without their consent. These actions poisoned relations between the king and Parliament.

James also found himself embroiled in religious disputes. He clashed with **dissenters,** Protestants who differed with the Church of England. One group were called **Puritans** because they sought to "purify" the English church of Catholic practices. Puritans called for simpler services and a more democratic church without bishops. James rejected their demands, vowing to "harry them out of this land or else do worse."

Charles I Clashes with Parliament In 1625, **Charles I** inherited the throne. Like his father, Charles behaved like an absolute monarch. He imprisoned his foes without trial and squeezed the nation for money. By 1628, however, his need to raise taxes forced Charles to summon Parliament. Before voting any funds, Parliament insisted that Charles sign the Petition of Right.

This document prohibited the king from raising taxes without Parliament's consent or from jailing anyone without legal justification.

Charles did sign the Petition, but he then dissolved Parliament in 1629. For 11 years, he ignored the Petition and ruled without Parliament. During that time, he created bitter enemies, especially among Puritans. His Archbishop of Canterbury, William Laud, tried to force all clergy to follow strict Anglican rules, dismissing or imprisoning dissenters. Many people felt that the archbishop was trying to revive Catholic practices.

In 1637, Charles and Laud tried to impose the Anglican prayer book on Scotland. The Calvinist Scots revolted. To get funds to suppress the Scottish rebellion, Charles once again had to summon Parliament in 1640. When it met, however, Parliament launched its own revolt.

The Long Parliament Begins The 1640 Parliament became known as the Long Parliament because it lasted on and off until 1653.

Its actions triggered the greatest political revolution in English history. In a mounting struggle with Charles I, Parliament tried and executed his chief ministers, including Archbishop Laud. It called for the abolition of bishops and declared that the Parliament could not be dissolved without its own consent.

Charles lashed back. In 1642, he led troops into the House of Commons to arrest its most radical leaders.

>> Charles I and his troops stormed into the House of Commons to arrest radicals.

Interactive Timeline

They escaped through a back door and soon raised their own army. The clash now moved to the battlefield.

DESCRIBE What was the Petition of Right?

The English Civil War

The civil war that followed lasted from 1642 to 1651. Like the Fronde that occurred about the same time in France, the English Civil War posed a major challenge to absolutism. But while the forces of royal power won in France, in England the forces of revolution triumphed.

Cavaliers and Roundheads At first, the odds seemed to favor the supporters of Charles I, called Cavaliers. Many Cavaliers were wealthy nobles, proud of their plumed hats and fashionably long hair. Well trained in dueling and warfare, the Cavaliers expected a quick victory. But their foes proved to be tough fighters with the courage of their convictions.

The forces of Parliament were composed of country gentry, town-dwelling manufacturers, and Puritan clergy. They were called Roundheads because their hair was cut close around their heads. The Roundheads found a leader of genius in **Oliver Cromwell.** A Puritan member of the lesser gentry, Cromwell proved himself to be a skilled general.

Guided Reading and Discussion

Elizabeth's deft handling of Parliament did not continue with James Stuart. The radical difference between Elizabeth's approach to working with Parliament and James's insistence on his right to rule without interference set the monarchy up against Parliament. When Charles I ascended the throne, he was committed to ruling as his father had. This attitude brought him into continued direct conflict with Parliament, resulting in the Long Parliament and, eventually, the English Civil War.

Identify Cause and Effect What could Charles have done to avoid a war? *(He could have been more willing to work with Parliament instead of constantly overriding it and treating the members of Parliament as enemies.)*

The English Civil War

The English Civil War lasted from 1642 until 1651, posing a major challenge to the English monarchy.

Online Project the **Interactive Timeline: England Divided: The Monarchy and Parliament Fight for Power**. Review the events presented on the timeline. Click on the hotspots for information on especially important points. Ask students to think about the stages at which a war might have been avoided. What actions would each side have had to take?

ACTIVE CLASSROOM

Use the Wallpaper strategy to have students review what they have learned. Ask each student to design a piece of "wallpaper" that encapsulates the key items they have learned. Then post each piece of the wallpaper. Invite students to take a "wisdom" walk and note what others have written or illustrated.

History Background

Good Queen Bess When Elizabeth took the throne, England had suffered decades of religious and political turmoil. An observer noted: "The Queen poor. The realm exhausted. The nobility poor and decayed. Want of good captains and soldiers. The people out of order. Justice not executed." Due to Elizabeth's skillful management and striking speeches, England was a great power at the time of her death. In 1588, as English forces mustered to combat the Spanish Armada, she gave a stirring speech: "I am come amongst you . . . resolved in the midst and heart of battle, to live and die amongst you all. . . . I know I have the body but of a weak and feeble woman, but I have the heart and stomach of a king and of a King of England too."

Answers

Describe *It was a legal document that prohibited the king from raising taxes without Parliament's consent or imprisoning people who had not violated laws.*

Guided Reading and Discussion

Explain that there was a specific sequence of events that led to the English Civil War. The Cavaliers expected a quick and easy victory. When the Roundheads rallied and eventually won, it was a shock not only to the Cavaliers but also to the absolute monarchs in Europe.

Analyze Information Why did the Cavaliers expect a quick victory? *(They were well-trained and experienced soldiers who saw themselves as far superior to the Roundheads in military ability.)*

Cromwell and the Commonwealth

After the Roundhead victory in the civil war, the House of Commons abolished the monarchy and the House of Lords and declared England a republic, also known as the Commonwealth.

>> Charles I was beheaded in January 1649. It was the first time a ruling monarch had been tried and executed by his own people.

>> Oliver Cromwell held power in England during the "kingless decade" from 1649 until his death in 1658.

He organized the "New Model Army" for Parliament into a disciplined fighting force. Cromwell's army defeated the Cavaliers in a series of decisive battles. By 1647, the king was in the hands of parliamentary forces.

Execution of the King Eventually, Parliament set up a court to put the king on trial. It condemned him to death as "a tyrant, traitor, murderer, and public enemy." On a cold January day in 1649, Charles I stood on a scaffold surrounded by his foes. "I am a martyr of the people," he declared. Showing no fear, the king told the executioner that he himself would give the sign for him to strike. After a brief prayer, Charles knelt and placed his neck on the block. On the agreed signal, the executioner severed the king's neck with a single stroke.

The execution sent shock waves throughout Europe. In the past, a king had occasionally been assassinated or killed in battle. But for the first time, a ruling monarch had been tried and executed by his own people. The parliamentary forces had sent a clear message that, in England, no ruler could claim absolute power and ignore the rule of law.

IDENTIFY CAUSE AND EFFECT What was the result of the English Civil War?

Cromwell and the Commonwealth

After the execution of Charles I, the House of Commons abolished the monarchy and the House of Lords, and established the Church of England. It declared England a republic, known as the Commonwealth, under the leadership of Oliver Cromwell.

Challenges to the Commonwealth The new government faced many threats. Supporters of Charles II, the uncrowned heir to the throne, attacked England by way of Ireland and Scotland. Cromwell led forces into Ireland and brutally crushed the uprising. He then took harsh measures against the Irish Catholic majority that are still vividly remembered in that nation today. In 1652, Parliament passed a law exiling most Catholics to barren land in the west of Ireland. Any Catholic found disobeying this order could be killed on sight.

Squabbles also splintered forces within the Commonwealth. One group, called Levellers, thought that poor men should have as much say in government as the gentry, lawyers, and other leading citizens. "The poorest he that is in England hath a life to live as the greatest he," wrote one Leveller. In addition, woman

Answers

Identify Cause and Effect *Parliament won and had Charles I executed.*

THE
PURITAN INFLUENCE

After the execution of Charles I, Puritans and reformers controlled Parliament. They believed that it was time to encourage seriousness of purpose. Puritans did dance and sing, but they did so only in private gatherings. Their objection was not so much to the music and dancing as to the "public disorder" to which those frivolities contributed.

>> **Analyze Information** The Puritans sought societal and moral reforms. How did Puritans feel about education?

Levellers asserted their right to petition Parliament. These ideas horrified the gentry, who dominated Parliament.

Cromwell suppressed the Levellers, as well as more radical groups who threatened ownership of private property. In 1653, as the challenges to order grew, Cromwell took the title Lord Protector. From then on, he ruled as a virtual dictator, using the army to back up his orders.

England Under the Puritans Under the Commonwealth, Puritan preachers tried to root out godlessness and impose a "rule of saints." The English Civil War thus ushered in a social revolution as well as a political one.

Parliament enacted a series of laws designed to make sure that Sunday was set aside for religious observance.

Anyone over the age of 14 who was caught "profaning the Lord's Day" could be fined. To the Puritans, theaters were frivolous. So, like John Calvin in Geneva, Cromwell closed all theaters. Puritans also frowned on taverns, gambling, and dancing.

Puritans felt that every Christian, rich and poor, must be able to read the Bible. To spread religious knowledge, they encouraged education for all people. By mid-century, families from all classes were sending their children to school, girls as well as boys.

Puritans pushed for changes in marriage to ensure fidelity. In addition to marriages based on business interests, they encouraged marriages based on love. Still, as in the past, women were seen mainly as subordinate to men.

Although Cromwell did not tolerate open worship by Roman Catholics, he believed in religious freedom for other Protestant groups. He even welcomed Jews back to England after more than 350 years of exile.

Puritan Rule Ends Oliver Cromwell died in 1658. Soon after, the Puritans lost their grip on England. Many people were tired of military rule and strict Puritan ways. In 1660, a newly elected Parliament invited Charles II to return to England from exile.

England's "kingless decade" ended with the Restoration, or return of the monarchy. Yet Puritan ideas about morality, equality, government, and education endured. These ideas were already shaping England's colonies in North America, where many Puritans had settled.

 **DESCRIBE** What was the Commonwealth?

Infer Why did Cromwell and the Roundheads decide to execute Charles instead of just imprisoning him or sending him into exile? *(As long as Charles was alive, there would be supporters who would encourage him to try to win back his crown. This would have led to constant warfare. Also, his execution made a clear statement that no one, not even a king, was above the law established by the people.)*

Identify Cause and Effect Explain how the English Civil War led to the development of a democratic-republican government. *(Limiting the authority of the monarch and giving greater authority to a partially elected body such as Parliament led to a representative system of government.)*

History Background

British Redcoats Cromwell was a fiery member of Parliament who proved a brilliant military strategist despite his lack of military training. He chose soldiers not for their social standing (as the king did) but for their proficiency. He instituted discipline and high moral standards in his New Model Army. He paid soldiers regularly, provided good weapons, and gave them brilliant red uniforms. In the heat of battle, the bright red coats helped soldiers tell friend from foe. The red color also camouflaged bloodstains from wounds, helping to keep morale high. He trained soldiers to regroup quickly in battle for a new charge. It was Britain's first professional army. After Cromwell's demise, Charles II kept the professional army, the discipline, and the red coats, which would become a symbol of British power around the world.

Answers

Analyze Information *They believed in education for all.*

Describe *The Commonwealth was the republic of England under Cromwell.*

Topic 12 Lesson 3

From Restoration to Glorious Revolution

The Glorious Revolution and the English Bill of Rights created a limited monarchy in England. The English Bill of Rights gave citizens certain civil rights that could not be abridged. The English Bill of Rights was the foundation for the U.S. Bill of Rights.

Guided Reading and Discussion

Habeas corpus is one of the rights included in the English Bill of Rights and in the U.S. Constitution. *Habeas corpus* is Latin for "you may have the body," and requires that a prisoner be charged with a crime before a judge or released. In the United States and other nations, there are provisions for suspending this right in times of rebellion or war.

Analyze Information Can a "right" be a "right" if it can be legally taken away? *(Some students may argue that rights cannot be taken away. Others may argue that the authority given to the president or other governing body to restrict a "right" comes from the will of the people.)*

Direct students' attention to the chart on the influence of the Glorious Revolution. Introduce the concepts of limited monarchy and constitutional government. Point out that the institutions of the cabinet and the prime minister were part of the evolution of Britain's constitutional government that includes a limited monarchy.

Draw Conclusions What are the characteristics of an oligarchy? Since Britain's constitutional government provided for a House of Commons as well as a House of Lords, how could the government be an oligarchy? *(An oligarchy is a government ruled by a small group of people. Even though the Commons was intended to represent "common" people, it was largely wealthy individuals who were representatives. Therefore, the British government remained a government by the privileged few.)*

From Restoration to Glorious Revolution

In late May 1660, cheering crowds welcomed Charles II back to London. An observer described the celebration as a triumph.

> This day came in his Majesties Charles the Second to London after a sad, and long Exile . . . with a Triumph of above 20,000 horse and [soldiers], brandishing their swords, and shouting with inexpressible joy; the [ways strewn] with flowers, the bells ringing, the streets hung with [tapestry].
>
> —John Evelyn, Diary

A Popular King With his charm and flashing wit, young Charles II was a popular ruler. He reopened theaters and taverns and presided over a lively court in the manner of Louis XIV.

Charles restored the official Church of England but encouraged toleration of other Protestants such as Presbyterians, Quakers, and Baptists. Although Charles accepted the Petition of Right, he shared his father's belief in absolute monarchy and secretly had Catholic sympathies. Still, he shrewdly avoided his father's mistakes in dealing with Parliament.

>> Crowds welcomed Charles II back after the monarchy was restored.

Charles was a strong supporter of science and the arts. He helped found the Royal Society, a group formed to advance scientific knowledge. Its early members, such as Isaac Newton, Robert Hooke, and Robert Boyle, advanced the study of mathematics, biology, physics, and chemistry. Charles was equally supportive of the arts, especially architecture. After the Great Fire of 1666 destroyed much of London, Charles appointed the great architect, Sir Christopher Wren, to rebuild the city.

The Glorious Revolution Charles's brother, James II, inherited the throne in 1685. Unlike Charles, James practiced his Catholic faith openly. He angered his subjects by suspending laws on a whim and appointing Catholics to high office. Many English Protestants feared that James would restore the Roman Catholic Church.

In 1688, alarmed parliamentary leaders invited James's Protestant daughter, Mary, and her Dutch Protestant husband, William III of Orange, to become rulers of England. When William and Mary landed with their army, James II fled to France. This bloodless overthrow of the king became known as the Glorious Revolution.

The English Bill of Rights Before they could be crowned, William and Mary had to accept several acts passed by Parliament in 1689 that became known as the **English Bill of Rights.** The Bill of Rights ensured the superiority of Parliament over the monarchy. It required the monarch to summon Parliament regularly and ensured that the House of Commons kept control over spending. A king or queen could no longer interfere in parliamentary debates or suspend laws. The Bill of Rights also barred any Roman Catholic from sitting on the throne.

The Bill of Rights also restated the traditional legal rights of English citizens, such as trial by jury. It abolished excessive fines and cruel or unjust punishment. It affirmed the principle of habeas corpus. That is, no person could be held in prison without first being charged with a specific crime. The legal ideas contained in the English Bill of Rights would later have a strong influence on the United States.

Soon after, the separate Toleration Act of 1689 granted limited religious freedom to Puritans, Quakers, and other Protestant dissenters. Still, only members of the Church of England could hold public office. And Catholics were allowed no religious freedom.

A Limited Monarchy The Glorious Revolution turned England into a **limited monarchy,** a type of government in which a constitution or legislative body

History Background

Parliamentary Democracy The first model for a parliament was Rome's senate, a council of the elite. During feudal times, lords met to decide whether to support the king, leading in the 1300s to England's Magna Carta and its first parliament. A parliamentary democracy has a constitution, a parliament, and both a head of state (a monarch or, today, a president), which is a ceremonial positions with limited powers, and a head of government (a prime minister), who is chosen by the parliament's ruling party from among its members. The prime minister, therefore, is not directly elected by the people and can be removed by the parliament. Because the executive and legislative branches are led by the same party, it is easier to pass reforms than in a republic. Most parliaments today include ordinary people as well as the elite and represent all the nation's people.

Topic 12 Lesson 3

Influence of the Glorious Revolution

	English Bill of Rights	Writings of John Locke	Constitutional Government
OUTCOME IN ENGLAND	• People elect representatives to Parliament, which is supreme over the monarch. • All citizens have natural rights.	• People have natural rights such as life, liberty, and property. • There is a social contract between people and government.	• Government is limited and defined by law. • Political parties, the cabinet, and the office of prime minister arise.
IMPACT ON THE UNITED STATES	• Colonists believed that they too had rights, including the right to elect people to represent them.	• Locke's ideas shaped the American Revolution and the writing of the Declaration of Independence and the Constitution.	• Government is limited and defined by law. • The new nation formed a constitutional government with two parties and even stronger provisions for the separation of powers.

>> **Analyze Charts** A common protest during the American Revolution was "no taxation without representation." Which outcome in England influenced that idea?

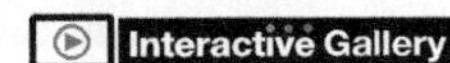

limits the monarch's powers. English rulers still had much power, but they had to obey the law and govern in partnership with Parliament. In an age of absolute monarchy elsewhere in Europe, the limited monarchy in England was quite radical.

Among the people who lived at the time of the Glorious Revolution was the political thinker, John Locke. Events in England helped shape his philosophy. Much later, Locke's ideas about government and natural rights would influence the Americans who drew up the Declaration of Independence and the United States Constitution.

DEFINE What was the Glorious Revolution?

England's Constitutional Government Evolves

In the century following the Glorious Revolution, three new political institutions arose in Britain: political parties, the cabinet, and the office of prime minister. The appearance of these institutions was part of the evolution of Britain's **constitutional government**—that is, a government whose power is defined and limited by law.

Political Parties In the late 1600s, political parties emerged in England as a powerful force in politics. At first, there were just two political parties—Tories and Whigs.

Tories were generally aristocrats who sought to preserve older traditions. They supported broad royal powers and a dominant Anglican Church.

Whigs backed the ideas embodied in the Glorious Revolution. They were more likely to reflect urban business interests, support religious toleration, and favor Parliament over the crown. For much of the 1700s Whigs dominated Parliament.

The Cabinet System The cabinet, another new feature of government, evolved in the 1700s after the British throne passed to a German prince. George I spoke no English and relied on the leaders in Parliament to help him rule. Under George I and his German-born son George II, a handful of parliamentary advisors set policy. They came to be referred to as the **cabinet** because of the small room, or "cabinet," where they met.

In time, the cabinet gained official status. It was made up of leaders of the majority party in the House of Commons. The cabinet remained in power so long as it enjoyed the support of the Commons.

If the Commons voted against a cabinet decision, the cabinet resigned. The cabinet system (also called a parliamentary system) was later adopted by other countries in Europe and elsewhere around the globe.

Online Project the **Interactive Gallery: Protections of the English Bill of Rights**. Introduce the activity by having students identify the main characteristic of a limited monarchy. *(A legislative body or written constitution limits the powers of the monarch.)*

ACTIVE CLASSROOM

Use the Make Headlines strategy and have students write a headline that captures the impact of the ideas in the English Bill of Rights. Pass your headline to a partner for him or her to review. Ask your partner if he or she agrees or disagrees with your headline, and why.

England's Constitutional Government Evolves

The powers of a constitutional government are defined and limited by law. By the 1600s, political parties formed in England, while the cabinet and the prime minister eventually became part of the government.

Key Terms

Ask students to find the key term **limited monarchy** (in bold) in the text. Explain that the term refers to a government in which a constitution or legislative body limits the monarch's powers. Ask students to name a current limited monarchy.

English Language Proficiency Standards

Reading 4.C.2 Write *Environmental Print*, and have students say it. Remind them that *environmental print* refers to printed materials (signs, billboards, logos, etc.). Tell students they will create their own environmental print based on "England's Constitutional Government Evolves."

Beginning Have students examine the image of London's eighteenth-century market scene and list the environmental print they see. Have pairs exchange lists.

Intermediate Have students reread the last paragraph of "Rule by an Oligarchy." Have pairs design a business sign with a name and logo for one of the types of middle-class workers (merchants, craftspeople, manufacturers).

Advanced Have students reread "Political Parties." Have groups make modern text-only campaign signs for the Tories or Whigs.

Advanced High Complete the Advanced activity, and then have the groups show their logos and how they might be used in London.

Answers

Analyze Charts *the English Bill of Rights*

Define *the bloodless overthrow of James II and the installation of William and Mary as monarchs*

SYNTHESIZE

Have students use the Think-Pair-Share strategy to answer the questions in the **Steps Toward Liberty** activity. Ask them to take 5 minutes to write down some brief answers to the following question and then share their answers with a talking partner.

What form of government did the developments listed in your flowchart create?

Discuss Remind students of the Topic Essential Question: How much power should the government have? Ask them to respond to the question while considering the outcome of the English Civil War. *(Answers may vary. Students should demonstrate an understanding that whatever power a government has must come from the people who elected that government. In the English Civil War, the power of the monarchy lessened, while the power of the more-representative Parliament grew.)*

DEMONSTRATE

Online Assign the **Digital Lesson Quiz** for this lesson if you haven't already done so. Students will be offered automatic remediation or enrichment based on their score.

Pose this question to the class on the Discussion Board:

Draw Conclusions Why do you think the people didn't immediately try to set up a constitutional monarchy with houses of Parliament after Cromwell's death? *(Answers will vary but should demonstrate an understanding that the English Civil War was a time of upheaval as well as progress. Many people wanted stability and were willing to re-establish a system of government with which they were familiar, like the monarchy under Charles II. However, during this time, people took advantage of relative peace to coalesce and reaffirm what they had achieved with the Commonwealth. They put these ideas into practice as soon as they could with William and Mary.)*

Topic Inquiry

Have students continue their investigations for the Topic Inquiry.

Answers

Interpret *by their clothes*

Check Understanding *political parties, the cabinet, and the office of prime minister*

>> The marketplace brought different classes of people together, but the classes differed widely in terms of political power. **Interpret** In this painting, how can you tell the different classes apart?

The Prime Minister Over time, the head of the cabinet came to be known as the **prime minister.** This person was always the leader of the majority party in the House of Commons.

Eventually, the prime minister became the chief official of the British government and the prime minister's power would exceed that of the monarch. From 1721 to 1742, the able Whig leader Robert Walpole molded the cabinet into a unified body by requiring all members to agree on major issues. Although the title was not yet in use, Walpole is often called Britain's first prime minister.

Rule by an Oligarchy Even as Parliament and the cabinet assumed new powers, British government was far from democratic. Rather, it was an **oligarchy**—a government in which the ruling power belongs to a few people.

Landowning aristocrats were believed to be the "natural" ruling class. The highest nobles held seats in the House of Lords. Other wealthy landowners and rich business leaders in the cities controlled elections to the House of Commons. The right to vote was limited to a relatively few male property owners, whose votes were often openly bought.

The lives of most people contrasted sharply with those of the ruling elite. The majority made a meager living from the land.

In the 1700s, even that poor existence was threatened. Wealthy landowners, attempting to increase agricultural production, bought up farms and took over common lands, evicting tenant farmers and small landowners. Because they controlled Parliament, they easily passed laws ensuring that their actions were legal. A small but growing middle class included successful merchants and manufacturers. These prosperous and often wealthy people controlled affairs in the towns and cities. Some improved their social standing by marrying into the landed gentry. The middle class also produced talented inventors and entrepreneurs who would soon help usher in the Industrial Revolution.

CHECK UNDERSTANDING What were the new political institutions that developed as a result of Britain's constitutional government?

ELPS **ELPS 4.C.2** Think of all the signs, billboards, labels, and business logos you see every day. Show your understanding of these types of printed materials by completing the activities given to you by your teacher.

ASSESSMENT

1. **Check Understanding** Why was James I resistant to working with Parliament?
2. **Define** What was the Long Parliament?
3. **Recall** Who was Oliver Cromwell?
4. **Describe** What did the English Bill of Rights mean to Parliament?
5. **Identify Central Ideas** What is the main feature of a constitutional government?

Assessment

1. He believed that kings were given their authority by God and were second only to God in power on Earth.
2. It was a Parliament called in 1640 that met off and on until 1653. Its struggles with Charles I led to the English Civil War.
3. He was a Puritan and minor gentry. He led the Roundhead forces against King Charles I and his Cavaliers during the English Civil War. His victory led to the establishment of a 10-year Commonwealth in England.
4. It ensured that Parliament had superiority over the monarchy. It required the monarch to summon Parliament on a regular basis and prevented the monarch from interfering in Parliamentary debates or disbanding Parliament against its will.
5. It is a government whose power is defined and limited by law.

12.4 During the Scientific Revolution of the 1500s and 1600s, European scholars made advances in physics, chemistry, biology, and medicine. Like ancient scholars, the thinkers of the Scientific Revolution relied on reason, but they also developed a new "scientific method" to test their theories and observations. Using mathematics and the scientific method, they discovered a series of laws that governed the physical universe.

>> Sir Isaac Newton was a key figure in the Scientific Revolution. Among his many discoveries was gravity.

Interactive Flipped Video

The Enlightenment

Scientific Revolution Leads to the Enlightenment

The Scientific Revolution, in turn, helped spark the Enlightenment in which thinkers emphasized the use of reason to uncover "natural" laws that governed human life. During the Enlightenment of the 1600s and 1700s, thinkers developed new ideas about government and basic human rights.

While scientists and mathematicians developed laws about natural phenomena like the law of gravity, European thinkers searched for similar laws that governed human life. Like scientists, they emphasized the power of reason, rather than religious beliefs. During the 1600s and 1700s, these thinkers developed new ideas about **natural laws**—unchanging principles, discovered through reason, that govern all human conduct.

Using the methods of the Scientific Revolution, European thinkers and reformers set out to study human behavior and solve the problems of society. The German philosopher Immanuel Kant used the word *enlightenment* to describe this new approach. During the Enlightenment, also called the Age of Reason, philosophers emphasized the power of human reason to uncover general laws of nature that shape all of human experience.

TEKS
1.E, 18.A, 20.A, 20.C, 21.C, 23.B, 25.C, 26.B, 26.C

>> Objectives

Describe how science led to the Enlightenment.

Explain the political philosophies of Hobbes, Locke, Voltaire, Montesquieu, and Rousseau.

Summarize the economic ideas of the physiocrats and Adam Smith.

Describe how Enlightenment ideas spread and influenced the arts.

Understand the role of enlightened despots.

>> Key Terms

natural law
Thomas Hobbes
John Locke
social contract
natural rights
philosophe
Montesquieu
Voltaire
Jean-Jacques Rousseau
laissez faire
Adam Smith
free market
free enterprise system
censorship
salon
baroque
rococo
enlightened despot
Joseph II

PEARSON realize. www.PearsonTexas.com Access your Digital Lesson.

Topic 12 Lesson 4

The Enlightenment

CONNECT

Preview Have students preview the **Lesson Objectives** and the list of **Key Terms**.

Students can also preview all the **Key Terms and Academic Vocabulary** using the **Interactive Reading Notepad** on the digital course or preview a summary of the lesson in the **Reading and Note Taking Study Guide**.

Online Use the **Editable Presentation** found on the digital course to present the main ideas for this lesson.

Start Up Activity

Tell students that, beginning in the 1600s in Europe, new literature, the arts, science, and philosophy reflected Enlightenment ideas. They were regular topics of discussion in salons, or informal social gatherings at which writers, artists, *philosophes,* and others exchanged ideas. Tell students to compare these salons with social media today. Ask: What do they share in common? How are they different from each other? Can you think of any other modern-day "salons"? *(Answers will vary, but students may point out that salons and social media are alike in that people share ideas and opinions in both. They are different in that salons were gatherings of Enlightenment thinkers but social media can include anyone. Coffee shops might be a type of modern-day "salon.")*

Discuss Ask students to talk about how people share new and enlightening ideas today. *(the Internet, television, print)*

Online You can also project the **Start Up Activity** from the course.

INVESTIGATE

Have students read the lesson using the **Reading and Note Taking Study Guide** to help them take notes and understand the text as they read.

Scientific Revolution Leads to the Enlightenment

Previously, people accepted things based on faith or unquestioning beliefs. Scientific successes convinced many educated Europeans to accept the power of reason, which is thought based on logic. Many people's long-held beliefs were challenged.

Aa Vocabulary Builder

1. Have students pronounce the following academic vocabulary terms in this lesson and clarify the part of speech. For difficult or polysyllabic words, break them into syllables and pronounce them with the students.
2. Explain what the word means in common "student-friendly" language using synonyms and antonyms when possible. Provide concrete examples to clarify the meaning, and rephrase the definition.

philosophy: love of, or the search for, wisdom or knowledge

evolved: developed gradually over time

Topic 12 Lesson 4

Guided Reading and Discussion

Infer Through the Renaissance, Scientific Revolution, and Enlightenment, European thinkers increasingly relied on principles of natural law rather than religious authority to address social, economic, and political problems. Thinkers also placed greater emphasis on individual rights. How might the relationship among Christianity, individualism, and growing secularism have influenced subsequent political developments? *(Possible answer: The Enlightenment caused people to question many areas of their lives, including the idea of divine right. Church influence in government declined.)*

Infer Who might have objected to people using reason to challenge long-held ideas? *(Possible answers: the Church, noblemen, political leaders)*

Hobbes and Locke on the Role of Government

The *Philosophes*

During the 1600s, the ideas of English thinkers Thomas Hobbes and John Locke, particularly on human nature and the role of government, would become the basis for the Enlightenment. In the following century, French *philosophes,* including Voltaire and Montesquieu, expressed ideas about government, law, and society that would eventually spread beyond Europe.

The Enlightenment continued a trend that began during the Renaissance. During the Middle Ages, Europe had been dominated by the Church. Feudal monarchs, like later absolute rulers, looked to the Church to justify their royal authority. The Renaissance placed a new emphasis on secularism and individual achievement.

The Scientific Revolution and Enlightenment also stressed science and natural law rather than religious authority. Enlightenment thinkers turned away from absolutism and divine right toward democracy and individual rights. Their ideas would encourage revolutionary leaders in Europe and the Americas. Though Christianity would remain a strong force in western culture, most governments became increasingly secular. The French Revolution in particular would see a radical decline in Church influence on government.

EXPLAIN How was the Scientific Revolution directly related to the development of the concept of natural law?

>> This illustration from Thomas Hobbes's book *Leviathan* reflects his belief in a powerful ruler. The monarch rises above all society, just as the mythological Leviathan, or sea monster, rises above all the seas.

Interactive Chart

Hobbes and Locke on the Role of Government

During the 1600s, two English thinkers, **Thomas Hobbes** and **John Locke,** set forth ideas that were to become key to the Enlightenment. Both men lived through the upheavals of the English Civil War. Yet they reached different conclusions about human nature and the purpose and proper role of government.

Hobbes Argues for Powerful Government In 1651, Thomas Hobbes outlined his ideas in a work titled *Leviathan.* In it, he argued that people were naturally cruel, greedy, and selfish. If not strictly controlled, they would fight, rob, and oppress one another. Life in the "state of nature"—without laws or other control—would be "solitary, poor, nasty, brutish, and short."

To escape that "brutish" life, said Hobbes, people entered into a **social contract,** an agreement by which they gave up their freedom for an organized society. Hobbes believed that only a powerful government could ensure an orderly society. For him, such a government was an absolute monarchy, which could impose order and compel obedience. Not surprisingly, Hobbes had supported the Stuart kings in their struggle against Parliament.

Locke Focuses on Natural Rights John Locke had a more optimistic view of human nature. He thought people were basically reasonable and moral.

Further, they had certain **natural rights,** or rights that belonged to all humans from birth. These included the right to life, liberty, and property.

In *Two Treatises of Government,* Locke argued that people formed governments to protect their natural rights. The best kind of government, he said, had limited power and was accepted by all citizens. Thus, unlike Hobbes, Locke rejected absolute monarchy.

Locke proposed a radical idea about this time. A government, he said, has an obligation to the people it governs. If a government fails its obligations or violates people's natural rights, the people have the right to overthrow that government. Given these ideas, Locke supported the overthrow of James II in the Glorious Revolution of 1688. In Locke's view, the king deserved to lose his throne because he had violated the rights of the English people.

Locke's idea would one day influence leaders of the American Revolution, such as Benjamin Franklin, Thomas Jefferson, and James Madison. Locke's idea of

Answers

Explain *Scientific successes and breakthroughs reflected the new reliance on reason and the application of scientific principles.*

English Language Proficiency Standards

Speaking 3.H.1 Read the text "Scientific Revolution Leads to the Enlightenment," and complete the activities below.

Beginning Have students point to words and phrases in the text that show an understanding of how the Scientific Revolution gave rise to the Enlightenment. Help students put those words and phrases into a logical order showing the progression from the Scientific Revolution to the Enlightenment. Have them say their lists aloud.

Intermediate Help students create a list of ideas showing how the Scientific Revolution led to the Enlightenment. Help students develop two or three simple sentences from their lists. Have students practice speaking their sentences aloud.

Advanced Have students review the section with a partner and create a list of ideas that show how the Scientific Revolution led to the Enlightenment. Then have two pairs of students form a group. Have each group develop a paragraph on the progression of European thought from the Scientific Revolution to the Enlightenment. Have the groups narrate this progression for the class.

Advanced High Have students review the text. Ask students to create a list of ideas and events that demonstrate how the Scientific Revolution led to the Enlightenment. Ask each student to prepare a creative way to "tell the story" of how the Scientific Revolution gave rise to the Enlightenment.

Montesquieu: Separation of Powers

	FUNCTION	EXAMPLES IN U.S. GOVERNMENT	EXAMPLES IN BRITISH GOVERNMENT
LEGISLATIVE	Creates law	Congress	Parliament
EXECUTIVE	Enforces law	President	Prime minister
JUDICIAL	Applies law	Supreme Court	U.K. Supreme Court

>> **Analyze Charts** Montesquieu believed in the separation of the powers of government into branches. Who currently heads the executive branch of government in the United States?

the right of revolution would also echo across Europe and Latin America in the centuries that followed.

CONTRAST How did Hobbes and Locke differ in their views on the role of government?

ELPS **ELPS 4.C.3** Many terms are used frequently in certain academic subjects. In history, some of those words include government, laws, revolution, society, and political. Read *Hobbes and Locke on the Role of Government* and complete the activity to gain a better understanding of the context of these terms at the beginning of the Enlightenment.

The *Philosophes*

In the 1700s, France saw a flowering of Enlightenment thought. French ***philosophes*** (fee loh ZOHFS), or philosophers, felt that nothing was beyond the reach of human reason. As they examined ideas about government, law and society, they called for reforms to protect people's natural rights. Their ideas, like those of Locke, would shift political thought and strongly influence the development of democratic-republican government.

Montesquieu Calls for Separation of Powers An early and influential *philosophe* was Baron de **Montesquieu** (MAHN tus kyoo). Montesquieu studied the governments of Europe, from Italy to England. He read about ancient and medieval Europe, and learned about Chinese and Native American cultures. He sharply criticized absolute monarchy.

In 1748, Montesquieu published *The Spirit of the Laws,* in which he discussed governments throughout history. Montesquieu felt that the best way to protect liberty was to divide the various functions and powers of government among three branches: the legislative, executive, and judicial.

He also felt that each branch of government should be able to serve as a check on the other two, an idea that we call checks and balances. Montesquieu's beliefs would influence the Framers of the United States Constitution.

Voltaire Supports Freedom of Thought Probably the most famous of the *philosophes* was François-Marie Arouet, who took the name **Voltaire.** "My trade," said Voltaire, "is to say what I think." He used biting wit as a weapon to expose the abuses of his day. He targeted corrupt officials and idle aristocrats. With his pen, he battled inequality, injustice, and superstition. He detested the slave trade and deplored religious prejudice.

Voltaire's outspoken attacks offended both the French government and the Catholic Church. He was imprisoned and forced into exile. Even as he saw

Online Project the **Interactive Chart: Thinkers of the Enlightenment**. and introduce the activity by reviewing the contributions of each of the men listed. Students should use the chart to list the key ideas of each man.

D Differentiate Extra Support Complete the Interactive Chart as a group or a class. Provide students with the ideas and achievements. Then, ask them to sort the list items into the appropriate column according to the Enlightenment thinker to which each corresponds.

ACTIVE CLASSROOM

Ask students to have a Conversation With History with one of the thinkers listed in the Interactive Chart. Have students write down a question they would like to ask, what that person would say in response, and how they would reply to the thinker's response.

Guided Reading and Discussion

Compare Hobbes's and Locke's political philosophies. Discuss the meanings of a social contract *(an agreement by which people gave up their freedom to a powerful government in order to avoid chaos)* and a natural right *(a right that belongs to all humans from birth, such as life, liberty, or property)*.

Draw Conclusions How did Locke's ideas shift political thought in Europe? *(His theory of natural rights contradicted the theory of divine rights.)*

Make Predictions What might be the long-term effect of these ideas? *(They influenced revolutions across the globe.)*

English Language Proficiency Standards

Reading 4.C.3 Read "Hobbes and Locke on the Role of Government," and point out the following frequently used social studies terms: *government, laws, revolution, society, political*.

Beginning Have students reread the text. Then point to each vocabulary term. Say each word aloud, and have students repeat the word after you. Define the words, using images and context to support students' understanding.

Intermediate Correct students' pronunciation when necessary. Help students define each word by establishing contextual support from the text and visual images.

Advanced Provide students with dictionaries to assist them in learning the definition of each term. Remind students to use context clues from the text.

Advanced High Have students define each term and explain how the terms relate to one another, using context clues from the text.

Answers

Contrast *Hobbes believed that the government needed to impose order and compel obedience. Locke thought governments should have limited power and be sanctioned by all citizens.*

Analyze Charts *Students should name the current President.*

Summarize Ask students how the political philosophies of the *philosophes* helped to shift political thought by creating new assumptions about the proper use of power and the attributes of a just government. *(Possible answer: They proposed that a government's power was dependent upon the consent of the governed, that government should have limited power and that its power should be separated by a system of checks and balances, that the goal of government was material well-being and social justice, that the purpose of government was to protect natural rights, and that the people have the right to overthrow the government when it fails.)*

New Economic Ideas

Natural law could be applied to economics. Mercantilists favored government regulation and believed in building wealth through trade, while physiocrats opposed government regulation and believed in building wealth through land productivity. Economist Adam Smith built upon these ideas with his ideas about the free enterprise system.

>> Diderot's *Encyclopedia* was a collection of articles written by famous Enlightenment thinkers. It represented the rational approach of Enlightenment thinkers.

>> Writer Mary Wollstonecraft was a passionate advocate for social and educational equality for women.

his books outlawed and sometimes even burned, he continued to defend the principle of freedom of speech.

Diderot Edits the *Encyclopedia* Denis Diderot (DEE duh roh) worked for years to produce a 28-volume set of books called the *Encyclopedia*. As the editor, Diderot did more than just compile articles. His purpose was "to change the general way of thinking" by explaining ideas on topics such as government, philosophy, and religion.

Diderot's *Encyclopedia* included articles by leading thinkers of the day, including Montesquieu and Voltaire. In these articles, the *philosophes* denounced slavery, praised freedom of expression, and urged education for all. They attacked divine-right theory and traditional religions.

The French government viewed the *Encyclopedia* as an attack on public morals, and the pope threatened to excommunicate Roman Catholics who bought or read the volumes. Despite these and other efforts to ban the *Encyclopedia*, more than 4,000 copies were printed between 1751 and 1789.

Rousseau Promotes the Social Contract The most controversial *philosophe* was **Jean-Jacques Rousseau** (roo SOH). Rousseau believed that people in their natural state were basically good. This natural innocence, he felt, was corrupted by the evils of society, especially the unequal distribution of property.

In 1762, Rousseau set forth his ideas about government and society in *The Social Contract*. Rousseau felt that society placed too many limitations on people's behavior. He believed that some controls were necessary, but that they should be minimal. Additionally, only governments that had been freely elected should impose these controls. Rousseau put his faith in the "general will," or the best conscience of the people. The good of the community as a whole, he said, should be placed above individual interests. Woven through Rousseau's work is a hatred of all forms of political and economic oppression.

Women and the Enlightenment The Enlightenment slogan "free and equal" did not apply to women. Though the *philosophes* said women had natural rights, their rights were limited to the areas of home and family.

By the late 1700s, a small but growing number of women protested this view. Germaine de Staël in France and Mary Wollstonecraft in Britain argued that women were being excluded from the social contract itself. Their arguments, however, were ridiculed and often sharply condemned.

Wollstonecraft was a British writer and thinker. She accepted that a woman's first duty was to be a good

History Background

Science and Philosophy Sociology, the study of human behavior and the development of human societies, came out of the science practiced by the eighteenth-century *philosophes,* in particular Baron de Montesquieu. He can legitimately be called the father of sociology. In his treatise, *The Spirit of the Laws,* Montesquieu wrote that religion shapes politics, that political climate controls behavior, and that the extent of freedom in a society is determined by its institutions. He examined laws, customs, and behaviors of various societies. His method of study was to compare the features of past and present societies. This is similar to the methods of comparative sociology today.

mother but felt that a woman should be able to decide what was in her own interest without depending on her husband. In her book *A Vindication of the Rights of Woman*, Wollstonecraft called for equal education for girls and boys. Only education, she argued, could give women the tools they needed to participate equally with men in public life. Her ideas would influence the women's rights movement that emerged in the next century.

IDENTIFY SUPPORTING DETAILS What political philosophies did Jean-Jacques Rousseau set forth in *The Social Contract*?

New Economic Ideas

French thinkers known as physiocrats focused on economic reforms. Like the *philosophes*, physiocrats based their thinking on natural laws. The physiocrats claimed that their rational economic system was based on the natural laws of economics.

Laissez-Faire Economics Physiocrats rejected mercantilism, which required government regulation of the economy to achieve a favorable balance of trade. Instead, they urged a policy of **laissez faire** (les ay FEHR), allowing business to operate with little or no government interference. Physiocrats supported free trade and opposed tariffs.

Adam Smith and *The Wealth of Nations* Scottish economist **Adam Smith** greatly admired the physiocrats. In his influential work *The Wealth of Nations*, he argued that the **free market,** the natural forces of supply and demand, should be allowed to operate and regulate business. Smith favored a **free enterprise system** in which commerce and business compete for profit with little or no government interference.

Smith tried to show how manufacturing, trade, wages, profits, and economic growth were all linked to the market forces of supply and demand. Wherever there was a demand for goods or services, he said, suppliers would seek to meet that demand in order to gain profits.

Smith was a strong supporter of laissez faire. However, he felt that government had a duty to protect society, administer justice, and provide public works. Adam Smith's ideas about free enterprise would help to shape productive economies in the 1800s and 1900s.

COMPARE AND CONTRAST How is laissez-faire policy different from mercantilism?

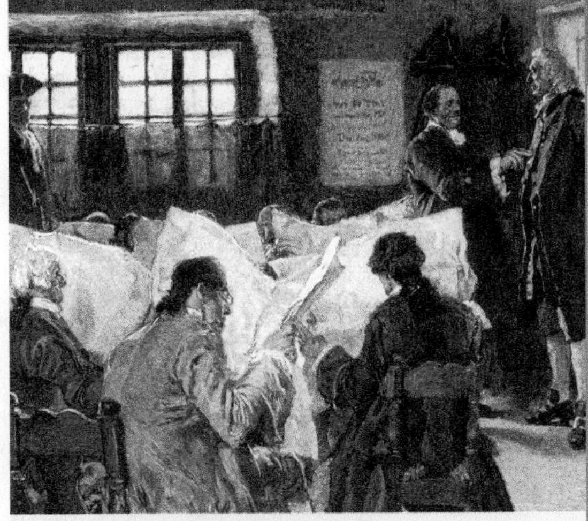

>> Enlightenment ideas spread through the printing of pamphlets and newspapers available to citizens.

Spread of Enlightenment Ideas

From France, Enlightenment ideas flowed across Europe and beyond. Everywhere, thinkers examined traditional beliefs and customs in the light of reason and found them flawed. Literate people eagerly read Diderot's *Encyclopedia* as well as small pamphlets turned out by printers that discussed a broad range of issues. More and more people came to believe that reform was necessary in order to achieve a just society.

During the Middle Ages, most Europeans had accepted without question a society based on divine-right rule, a strict class system, and a belief in heavenly reward for earthly suffering. In the Age of Reason, such ideas seemed unscientific and irrational. A just society, Enlightenment thinkers taught, should ensure social justice and happiness in this world. While many people embraced these new ideas, other groups rejected calls for change.

Writers Confront Censorship Most, but not all, government and church authorities felt they had a sacred duty to defend the old order. They believed that God had set up the old order.

To protect against the attacks of the Enlightenment, they waged a war of **censorship,** or restricting access

Topic 12 Lesson 4

Guided Reading and Discussion

Help students identify the contributions of Adam Smith and the characteristics of the free enterprise system. Discuss how Adam Smith believed that the free market should be allowed to regulate business activity with minimal government interference, and that the economy should be ruled by the market forces of supply and demand. Review Smith's argument from *The Wealth of Nations* that the market will create a balance between supply and demand that affects the quantity of products and services available as well as their prices.

Summarize What are the characteristics of the free enterprise system? *(a free market in which the government has minimal interference with business activity)*

Apply Concepts According to Smith, a characteristic of the free enterprise system is that the quantity and prices of goods and services are dependent upon demand. Smith argued that as the supply of a product increases but demand remains unchanged, prices fall. What will happen if supply decreases but demand increases? *(The price will rise.)*

Spread of Enlightenment Ideas

The ideas of the Enlightenment would soon spread far from Europe. As these ideas migrated, they challenged preexisting institutions.

History Background

Satire and Society Enlightenment writers tried to bring about reform by satirizing corruption in society. Their satires often presented a premise that, when carried to its logical extreme, was absurd. The Anglo-Irish author Jonathan Swift used this method in his essay "A Modest Proposal." The essay, which may be found in many anthologies of English literature, protested English domination of Ireland.

Swift's satire suggests that the starving masses of Ireland could be satisfied if unwanted children were raised and slaughtered for food and accessories. Swift's shocking plain is meant to get the reader to recognize the cannibalism of Ireland by England, a domination he found no less scandalous than the barbarism of his proposal.

Answers

Identify Supporting Details *Rousseau felt that controls on people's behavior should be minimal and that only governments that had been freely elected should impose these controls.*

Compare and Contrast *Laissez-faire policy dictates that the free market should be allowed to regulate business activity, while mercantilism requires government regulation of the economy to achieve a favorable balance of trade.*

Guided Reading and Discussion

Ask students to predict why the government and Church authorities would want to censor the new ideas of the Enlightenment. Explain the ways in which Enlightenment ideas spread. Review how government restricted access to information by banning books and imprisoning writers. Discuss how the *philosophes* disguised their ideas in works of fiction and exchanged ideas in private at salons to try to avoid censorship.

Summarize Why would people defend the old order? *(Many government and Church officials felt they had a sacred duty to defend the old order that God had established.)*

Arts and Literature of the Enlightenment

People's taste in art changed as the ideas of the Enlightenment spread. The middle class emerged as a new audience for the arts because they could now afford to attend operas and commission works of music and art. Their tastes were different from those of the royal court, and the music and art reflected this new influence.

to ideas and information. They banned and burned books and imprisoned writers.

To avoid censorship, writers like Montesquieu and Voltaire sometimes disguised their ideas in works of fiction. In the *Persian Letters*, Montesquieu used two fictional Persian travelers, named Usbek and Rica, to mock French society. The hero of Voltaire's satirical novel *Candide*, published in 1759, travels across Europe and even to the Americas and the Middle East in search of "the best of all possible worlds." Voltaire slyly uses the tale to expose the corruption and hypocrisy of European society.

In England, Jonathan Swift published *Gulliver's Travels* in 1726. The story uses fantasy to satirize, or make fun of, English political life.

In a famous scene, Gulliver is bound by the Lilliputians, tiny six-inch-tall characters, and is unable to move. The harder Gulliver tries to break free, the more the Lilliputians attack him. Swift uses the story to comment on the pettiness of nations and their rulers.

Salons Spread Ideas New literature, the arts, science, and philosophy were regular topics of discussion in **salons,** or informal social gatherings at which writers, artists, *philosophes,* and others exchanged ideas. The salon originated in the 1600s, when a group of noblewomen in Paris began inviting a few friends to their homes for poetry readings. By the 1700s, some middle-class women began holding salons. There, middle-class citizens met with nobles on an equal basis to discuss Enlightenment ideas.

Through the salons, Enlightenment ideas spread among the educated people of Europe. Madame Geoffrin (zhoh FRAN) ran one of the most respected salons. In her home on the Rue St. Honoré (roo sant ahn ur AY), she brought together the brightest and most talented people of her day.

The young musical genius Wolfgang Amadeus Mozart played for her guests, and Diderot was a regular at her weekly dinners for philosophers and poets.

>> During the Enlightenment, Madame Geoffrin's salons were popular gatherings for intellectual discussions.

Slow Change for the Majority At first, most Europeans were untouched by the spread of Enlightenment ideas. They remained what they had always been—peasants living in small rural villages. Echoes of serfdom still remained throughout Europe despite advances in Western Europe. Centuries-old traditions continued to shape European society, which only very slowly began to change.

By the late 1700s, ideas about equality and social justice had finally seeped into peasant villages across Europe. Some peasants welcomed ideas about equality and an end to the old order. Others did not. Upheavals in France and elsewhere quickened the pace of change. By the early 1800s, war and changing economic conditions began to transform life for people across Europe.

IDENTIFY CENTRAL IDEAS How did those opposed to Enlightenment ideas try to stop the spread of information?

Arts and Literature of the Enlightenment

In the 1600s and 1700s, the arts evolved to meet changing tastes. As in earlier periods, artists and composers had to please their patrons, the men and women who commissioned works from them or gave them jobs.

Changing Styles in Art and Architecture In the age of Louis XIV, courtly art and architecture were either in the Greek and Roman tradition or in a grand, ornate style known as **baroque.** Baroque paintings were huge, colorful, and full of excitement. They glorified historic battles or the lives of saints. Such works matched the grandeur of European courts at that time.

By the mid-1700s, architects and designers developed a new style that reflected changing tastes.

D Differentiate Challenge/Gifted Remind students that several of the *philosophes* shared their ideas on reform with the enlightened despots. It was Diderot, after all, who nicknamed Frederick II—Frederick the Great. Have students take the role of a *philosophe* and write a letter to one of the enlightened despots. Letters should address both the arts and politics of the day and should suggest a reform. Then have students exchange letters and compose a letter in response from the viewpoint of that ruler, explaining whether or not they will enact the suggested reform. Students should explain their reasoning.

Answers

Identify Central Ideas *They banned and burned books and imprisoned writers.*

Unlike the heavy splendor of the baroque, **rococo** art was lighter, more personal, elegant and charming. Rococo furniture and tapestries featured delicate shells and flowers, and more pastel colors were used. Portrait painters showed noble subjects in charming rural settings, surrounded by happy servants and pets. Although this style was criticized by the *philosophes* for its superficiality, it was popular with the upper and middle classes.

New Trends in Music During the Enlightenment, composers and musicians developed new forms of music. Their music followed ordered structured forms well suited to the Age of Reason. At the same time, their work transcended, or rose above, the culture of the Enlightenment and remains popular all over the world today.

Ballets and opera—plays set to music—were performed at royal courts, and opera houses sprang up from Italy to England. In the past, only the highest people in society could afford to commission new works of music. By the mid-1700s, wealthy middle class people commissioned works and hired musicians to perform them. Among the towering musical figures of the era was Johann Sebastian Bach.

A devout German Lutheran, Bach wrote beautiful religious works for organ and choirs. His skills playing the organ and harpsichord were recognized during his lifetime, but he is now generally regarded as one of the greatest composers in history. Bach was a master of counterpoint, a technique that weaves two or more independent melodies together to create a new harmony.

Another German-born composer, George Frideric Handel, spent much of his life in England, where his music was extremely popular with the general public. There, he wrote *Water Music* and other pieces for King George I, as well as more than 30 operas. His most celebrated choral work, the *Messiah*, is often performed at Christmas and Easter. The stirring "Hallelujah Chorus" from the *Messiah* conveys universal themes of joy and celebration.

In 1761, a six-year-old prodigy, Wolfgang Amadeus Mozart, burst onto the European scene. He gained instant celebrity as a composer and performer.

During his brief life, the young man from Salzburg in Austria composed an amazing variety of music with remarkable speed. His operas reflected Enlightenment criticism of a class-ridden world full of hypocrisy and lies. At age 35, Mozart died in poverty, leaving a musical legacy that thrives today.

The Novel Takes Shape By the 1700s, literature developed new forms and a wider audience. Middle-

>> *The Swing,* by French painter Jean-Honore Fragonard, is a masterpiece of rococo art.

>> Johann Sebastian Bach plays the piano with his family in a 1870 painting. Many of Bach's children became important musicians.

 Interactive Gallery

Online Project the **Interactive Gallery: Music of the Enlightenment**. Introduce the activity by explaining that music reflects the history of the cultures in which it is produced. Ask students to listen to the audio selections. Discuss the characteristics of the music and how it differed from the heavy, ornamental music of the Baroque period. Ask students to identify an example of music from this period that transcended Enlightenment culture and expressed universal themes. *(Possible answer: All these composers remain popular. Handel's Messiah reflects universal themes of joy and celebration.)*

ACTIVE CLASSROOM

After completing the activity, ask students to break into pairs to discuss the music selections. Have students each do a Quick Write activity in which they take 30 seconds to write their observations about the music they listened to. Once they are finished, ask them how the music reflected the Enlightenment period. *(There was a transition in music from the Baroque style to rococo. An elegant style of music known as "classical" followed. Also, music was accessible to more of the general public.)* Then have them compare it to popular music today. *(Answers will vary but could compare instruments used or the fact that classical music is typically instrumental in nature.)*

Key Terms

Ask students to find the key term **rococo** (in bold) in the text. The rise of this new style reflected changes in French society brought about by the Enlightenment. As the French elite became more involved in the salons of the day (numbering about 800 in Paris), they competed with each other for the most fashionable home in which to host their intellectual discussions.

History Background

Opera Opera is generally considered a European art form—traditionally, operas are performed in Italian, French, or German. It would take many years for well-known operas to come out of the United States. The best-known American opera, *Porgy and Bess,* was written in 1935 by George Gershwin and DuBose Howard. The opera, based on Howard's book *Porgy,* is the story of a black fishing town in South Carolina and the unlikely relationship between Bess, a woman with a sordid past, and Porgy, an old, crippled man. At first, critics did not accept the work as an opera, and Gershwin himself chose to have it open on Broadway. Eventually, though, it was accepted as an opera and is performed at major opera houses worldwide.

The Enlightened Despots

Some absolute monarchs used their power to bring about political changes. Review the reforms enacted by these "enlightened despots" and their goals in affecting change. *(Frederick the Great of Prussia reduced the use of torture, allowed free press, and increased government efficiency and religious tolerance; Catherine II of Russia made limited government reforms, abolished torture, established religious tolerance, and granted nobles a charter of rights; Maria Theresa of Austria improved peasants' way of life; and Joseph II of Austria supported religious equality for Protestants and Jews, sold the property of monasteries and gave funds to those who helped the poor or sick, and abolished serfdom.)*

Guided Reading and Discussion

Explain to students that some rulers who believed in absolute power also saw value in political and social reform. Because the *philosophes* wanted reform, they tried to persuade rulers to accept their ideas, and the rulers had the power to effect change. Ask students to offer speculations on the rulers' motivations for accepting the *philosophes'* ideas. *(Rulers might be motivated toward reform because they believed it would keep them in power, or they believed in a more just society.)*

Analyze Information What did Fredrick the Great mean when he said, "In my kingdom, everyone can go to heaven in his own fashion"? *(freedom of religion)*

Predict Consequences What actions might peasants take as they learn more about ideas such as equality? *(Possible answer: Peasants might begin to expect more equality or perhaps protest to fight for equality.)*

class readers, for example, liked stories about their own times told in straightforward prose. One result was an outpouring of novels, or long works of prose fiction.

English novelists wrote many popular stories. Daniel Defoe wrote *Robinson Crusoe*, an exciting tale about a sailor shipwrecked on a tropical island. In a novel called *Pamela*, Samuel Richardson used a series of letters to tell a story about a servant girl. This technique was adopted by other authors of the period.

? DRAW CONCLUSIONS How did literature change as Enlightenment ideas spread?

The Enlightened Despots

Discussions of Enlightenment theories enlivened the courts of Europe. *Philosophes* hoped to convince European rulers to adopt their ideas and introduce reforms. Some monarchs did accept Enlightenment ideas. They became **enlightened despots,** or absolute rulers who used their power to bring about political and social change.

Frederick the Great As king of Prussia from 1740 to 1786, Frederick II exerted extremely tight control over his subjects. Still, he saw himself as the "first servant of the state," with a duty to work for the common good.

Frederick openly praised Voltaire's work and invited him to Berlin. He asked French scientists to help him set up a Prussian academy of science. As king, he tried to reduce the use of torture and allowed a free press. He also tolerated religious differences, welcoming victims of religious persecution. "In my kingdom," he said, "everyone can go to heaven in his own fashion."

Most of Frederick's reforms were directed at making the Prussian government more efficient. To do this, he reorganized the government's civil service and simplified laws. Although Frederick did believe in enlightened reform, his efforts to improve government meant more power for himself.

>> Catherine the Great expressed an interest in many Enlightenment ideas. She often met with scholars to learn more. **Interpret** What type of scholar do you think she is meeting in this painting? Explain.

Catherine the Great Catherine II, empress of Russia, read the works of the *philosophes* and exchanged letters with Voltaire and Diderot. She praised Voltaire as someone who had "fought the united enemies of humankind: superstition, fanaticism, ignorance, trickery." Catherine believed in the Enlightenment ideas of equality and liberty.

Catherine experimented with implementing Enlightenment ideas. Early in her reign, she made some limited reforms in law and government. Catherine abolished torture and established religious tolerance in her lands. She granted nobles a charter of rights and spoke out against serfdom. Still, like Frederick in Prussia, Catherine did not intend to give up power. Her main political contribution to Russia was an expanded empire.

Joseph II The most radical of the enlightened despots was **Joseph II** of Austria, the son and successor of Maria Theresa. Joseph was an eager student of the Enlightenment, and he traveled in disguise among his subjects to learn of their problems.

Like his mother, Joseph worked to modernize Austria's government. He chose talented middle-class officials rather than nobles to head departments and imposed a range of political and legal reforms. Despite opposition, Joseph granted toleration to Protestants and Jews in his Catholic empire. He ended censorship by allowing a free press and attempted to bring the Catholic Church under royal control. He sold the property of many monasteries that were not involved in education or care of the sick and used the proceeds to build hospitals. Joseph even abolished serfdom. Like

D Differentiate Extra Support Organize students into groups of three and assign each group an enlightened despot. *(Maria Theresa, Joseph II, Catherine the Great, or Frederick the Great)* Each group should write or illustrate five of their ruler's accomplishments on posterboard. Ask students to explain how Enlightenment ideas affected each ruler's actions.

Answers

Draw Conclusions *Literature developed new forms and more readers.*

Interpret *Sample answer: The man is a scientist because he is demonstrating an experiment.*

many of his other reforms, however, this measure was canceled after his death.

? ANALYZE INFORMATION What did Frederick the Great mean by, "In my kingdom, everyone can go to heaven in his own fashion"?

ASSESSMENT

1. **Explain** Explain the influence of scientific ideas on the progression of thought from the Scientific Revolution to the Enlightenment.
2. **Identify Central Ideas** What are some ways in which Enlightenment ideas spread?
3. **Identify Central Ideas** Explain the components of the free-enterprise system.
4. **Draw Conclusions** Why might some absolute monarchs have been willing to consider Enlightenment ideas, while others were not?
5. **Identify Central Ideas** In what way were the ideas of John Locke and Jean-Jacques Rousseau similar?

SYNTHESIZE

Online Project the **Digital Activity: Enlightenment Ideas: Then and Now**. Remind students of the Topic Essential Question: How much power should the government have? Each of the bullet points can be related to the power of government. Review the list. Ask students to discuss their opinions regarding the importance of each.

Draw Conclusions How did ideas of a "just society" change during the Enlightenment? How might these ideas lead to the development of a new form of government? *(A just society should ensure justice before the law and happiness for the people.)*

DEMONSTRATE

Online Assign the **Digital Lesson Quiz** for this lesson if you haven't already done so. Students will be offered automatic remediation or enrichment based on their score.

Pose these questions to the class on the Discussion Board:

Predict Consequences How might Enlightenment thinkers later inspire revolutionaries? *(They might question what existed and strive for a more just society and government.)*

Compare and Contrast Salons originated in the 1600s with a group of noblewomen and a few friends. How had salons changed by the 1700s, and why was this change significant? *(By the 1700s, middle-class citizens were able to discuss ideas with the nobility on equal footing.)*

Topic Inquiry

Have students continue their investigations for the Topic Inquiry.

Answers

Analyze Information *He believed in freedom of religion.*

Assessment

1. As scientists discovered the laws that governed the physical world, philosophers began to seek natural laws that governed society.
2. Educated people all over Europe read works such as Diderot's *Encyclopedia* and other pieces by the *philosophes,* along with small, inexpensive pamphlets on a broad range of issues. Different ways of thinking also spread to the arts, which were more widely enjoyed by different groups of people.
3. A free enterprise economic system is one in which markets operate freely, allowing the forces of supply and demand to regulate the market with little government interference.
4. Answers will vary. Some may say that some monarchs were compassionate about the suffering of their subjects. Others may say that monarchs believed that reforms were necessary to maintain control.
5. Locke and Rousseau both emphasized the rights of the people with regard to their government. Locke believed that government had an obligation to the people it governed, and that people could overthrow an unjust government. Rousseau thought only a freely elected government was just.

Topic 12 Lesson 5

The American Revolution

CONNECT

Preview Have students preview the **Lesson Objectives** and the list of **Key Terms**.

Students can also preview all the **Key Terms and Academic Vocabulary** using the **Interactive Reading Notepad** on the digital course or preview a summary of the lesson in the **Reading and Note Taking Study Guide**.

Online Use the **Editable Presentation** found on the digital course to present the main ideas for this lesson.

Start Up Activity

Remind students that in 1776, the Second Continental Congress declared the American colonies independent from Britain. The Declaration of Independence outlined the colonists' complaints as well as the obligations of a government to its citizens. Ask: In the Declaration of Independence, what did the colonists mean when they said "We hold these truths to be self-evident"? Why did they believe that "life, liberty and the pursuit of happiness" were "unalienable rights"? Why was the phrase "governments are instituted among men, deriving their just powers from the consent of the governed" a novel concept in the 1700s? *(Americans, as colonists under a monarchy, had no rights. The words reflect their belief that government should protect its citizens' basic rights and that its power comes from the people who create it.)*

Online You can also project the **Start Up Activity** from the course.

INVESTIGATE

Have students read the lesson using the **Reading and Note Taking Study Guide** to help them take notes and understand the text as they read.

Britain Becomes a Global Power

The British Colonies in America

On the eve of the American Revolution, King George III was eager to recover the powers the monarchy had lost during the Glorious Revolution. With the help of Parliament, he introduced polices that would prove disastrous to Britain, especially in relation to its North American colonies.

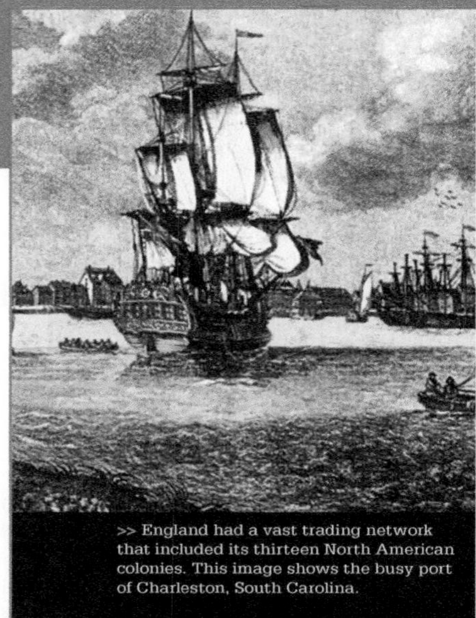

>> England had a vast trading network that included its thirteen North American colonies. This image shows the busy port of Charleston, South Carolina.

Interactive Flipped Video

12.5 By the 1770s, Britain was a major power in Europe with territories around the globe. Although upheavals in the 1600s had created a limited monarchy, a new king was eager to recover powers the crown had lost.

TEKS 1.E, 9.D, 19.B, 20.B, 20.C, 21.B, 21.C, 22.F

>> Objectives

Describe how Britain became a global power.

Understand the events and ideas leading up to the American Revolution, including the impact of the Enlightenment.

Summarize key events of the American Revolution.

Identify the political and legal ideas in the Declaration of Independence and the United States Constitution.

>> Key Terms

George III
Stamp Act
George Washington
Benjamin Franklin
Thomas Jefferson
popular sovereignty
Yorktown, Virginia
Treaty of Paris
James Madison
federal republic
checks and balances

PEARSON realize. www.PearsonTexas.com Access your Digital Lesson.

The American Revolution

Britain Becomes a Global Power

Trade and Commerce Britain's rise to global prominence had multiple causes. England's location and long seagoing tradition placed it in a position to build a vast trading network. By the 1600s, England had trading outposts and colonies in the West Indies, North America, and India. A new merchant class expanded trade and competed vigorously with Spanish, Portuguese, and Dutch traders.

During the 1700s, thousands of settlers sailed to North America to build colonies. At the same time, British merchants expanded into the profitable slave trade, carrying enslaved people from West Africa to the Americas.

Britain's economic policies added to its prosperity. England offered a climate favorable to business and commerce. It put fewer restrictions on trade than some of its neighbors, such as France.

Territorial Expansion In the 1700s, Britain was generally on the winning side in European conflicts. In the Treaty of Utrecht, which ended the War of the Spanish Succession, France gave Nova Scotia and Newfoundland to Britain. As a result of the French and Indian

502

Aa Vocabulary Builder

1. Have students pronounce the following academic vocabulary terms in this lesson and clarify the part of speech. For difficult or polysyllabic words, break them into syllables and pronounce them with the students.
2. Explain what the word means in common "student-friendly" language using synonyms and antonyms when possible. Provide concrete examples to clarify the meaning, and rephrase the definition.

assert: to insist on being recognized
monopoly: control of market supply
fundamental: basic; central
supreme: above all others; in highest degree

War, Britain gained all of French Canada, as well as rich islands in the Caribbean in 1763.

At home, England grew by merging with neighboring Scotland. In 1701, the Act of Union united the two countries in the United Kingdom of Great Britain. The union brought economic advantages.

Free trade between both lands created a larger market for farmers and manufacturers. The United Kingdom also included Wales, and in 1801 Ireland would be added to Great Britain.

George III Takes Power In 1760, **George III** began a 60-year reign. Unlike his German father and grandfather, the new king was born in England. He spoke English and loved Britain. But George was eager to recover the powers the crown had lost since the Glorious Revolution. Following his mother's advice, "George, be a king!" he set out to reassert royal power. He wanted to end Whig domination, choose his own ministers, dissolve the cabinet system, and make Parliament follow his will.

Gradually, George found seats in Parliament for "the king's friends." With their help, he began to assert his leadership. Many of his policies, however, would prove disastrous. He angered colonists in North America, leading 13 English colonies to declare independence.

Britain's loss of its American colonies discredited the king. Increasingly, too, he suffered from bouts of mental illness. By 1788, cabinet rule was restored in Britain.

ANALYZE INFORMATION What were some of the elements that led to Britain's rise to global prominence in the 1700s?

ELPS **ELPS 4.C.4** Read the first paragraph under the heading "George III Takes Power" and locate the quotation marks in the paragraph. Then complete the activity as instructed.

The British Colonies in America

By 1750, a string of prosperous colonies stretched along the eastern coast of North America. They were part of Britain's growing empire. Colonial cities such as Boston, New York, and Philadelphia were busy commercial centers that linked North America to the West Indies, Africa, and Europe. Colonial shipyards produced many vessels for this trade.

Britain applied mercantilist policies to its colonies in an attempt to strengthen its own economy by exporting more than it imported. To this end, in the 1600s, Parliament had passed the Navigation Acts to regulate colonial trade and manufacturing. For the most part, however, these acts were not rigorously enforced.

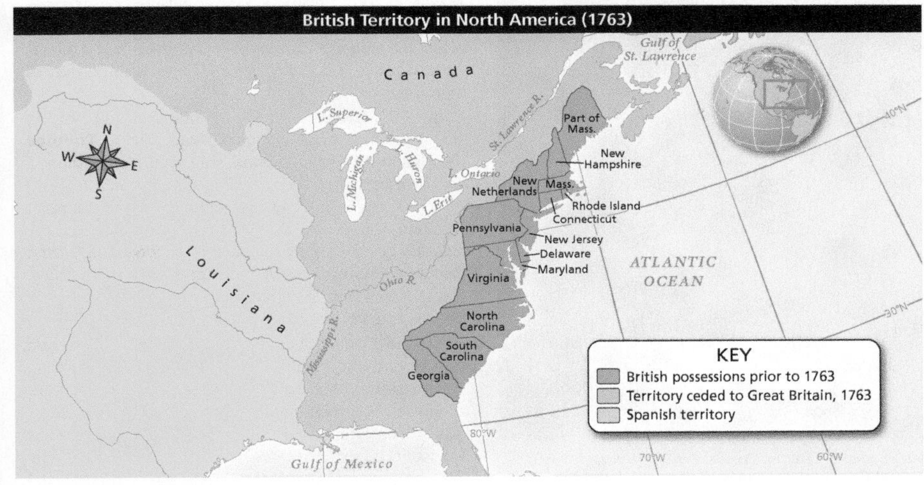

>> **Analyze Maps** What do all of the colonies on this map have in common?

Absolutism and Revolution  503 12.5 The American Revolution

Guided Reading and Discussion

Point out to students that by the mid-1700s, the colonies were home to diverse religious and ethnic groups. Wealthy landowners and merchants dominated government and society, but class differences were less rigid than those in Europe. Colonists felt free to discuss politics and other topics. Their colonial assemblies had a great deal of control over local affairs. Colonists began to feel entitled to the rights of English citizens.

Hypothesize How might having more local control over colonial affairs have changed colonists' ideas about their rights compared with those of British citizens? *(Sample response: Colonists probably began to feel that they should have the same rights as British citizens because they were part of the British colonies. Having local control over affairs gave them direct experience with making decisions about government.)*

Answers

Analyze Information *Britain became a world power based mostly on its location, the power of its military, the influence of its merchant class, and the lack of restrictions on business.*

Analyze Maps *Students may say that all of them were located on the Atlantic coast, across the ocean from England.*

English Language Proficiency Standards

Reading 4.C.3 Tell students that they will be using the third paragraph from the text "Britain Becomes a Global Power" for this activity. Have students demonstrate their understanding of how quotation marks are used in the context of this paragraph.

Beginning Begin by explaining the role of quotation marks. Ask students to skim the paragraph and point to the two quotation marks that frame the sentence, *"George, go be a king!"* Expressively read the paragraph to demonstrate how the quotation marks affect the reading of the text. Instruct students to listen to the paragraph with their eyes closed and to raise their hands when they think the quotation has begun and lower them when they believe the quotation has ended. Then ask each student to read the sentence containing the quotation aloud.

Intermediate Have students skim the paragraph and point out the locations of the quotation marks. Then have students read the paragraph aloud to a partner, paying special attention to the quotation.

Advanced Have students first read the paragraph silently to themselves, and then read it aloud to a partner.

Advanced High Have students read the paragraph aloud to the group. Before reading, have students work in pairs to discuss the role of quotation marks in this paragraph.

Topic 12 Lesson 5

Discontent in the Colonies

The ideas of the Enlightenment, combined with the political philosophies of the country's founders, gave rise to American independence and the formation of a government that derives its power from the people.

Online Project the **Interactive Image: From Words to Action—Ideology in the American Revolution**, and click through all the hotspots so students can read about several of the country's founders.

ACTIVE CLASSROOM

Ask students to reflect on the meaning of "liberty" and create a collage of images that depict the concept. Have students post their "graffiti" on the board so they can discuss similarities and differences.

Guided Reading and Discussion

Ask students how the political philosophies of individuals, such as Thomas Jefferson, impacted the ideas contained in the Declaration of Independence. *(Students might answer that Jefferson and others believed that it was important to put in the Declaration the philosophy that people are by nature equally free and independent with inherent political and legal rights. They also believed governments existed only through the will of the people. When a government fails to protects its citizens' rights, such as the right to have a say in government or the right to trial by jury, the people have a right to change their government.)*

Apply Concepts How did the Enlightenment concept of popular sovereignty influence the American Revolution? *(Students might answer that the founders were influenced by the idea that citizens have the right to alter or abolish unjust governments.)*

Therefore, activities like smuggling were common and not considered crimes by the colonists.

By the mid-1700s, the colonies were home to diverse religious and ethnic groups. Social distinctions were more blurred than in Europe, although wealthy landowners and merchants dominated government and society. In politics, as in much else, there was a good deal of free discussion.

Colonists felt entitled to the rights of English citizens, and their colonial assemblies exercised much control over local affairs. Many also had an increasing sense of their own destiny separate from Britain.

DESCRIBE Why did Americans believe they had the same rights as English citizens?

Discontent in the Colonies

The French and Indian War had drained the British treasury. George III and his advisors insisted that colonists pay the costs of their own defense, including troops still stationed in frontier posts.

Growing Tensions Parliament passed new taxes on the colonies. The Sugar Act of 1764 taxed imports, while the **Stamp Act** of 1765 taxed items such as newspapers and pamphlets. Although the new taxes were not burdensome, colonists bitterly resented them as an attack on their rights. "No taxation without representation," they protested. Since they had no representatives in Parliament, they believed that Parliament had no right to tax them. Parliament repealed the Stamp Act, but asserted its right to tax the colonists.

A series of violent clashes intensified the colonists' anger. In March 1770, British soldiers in Boston opened fire on a crowd that was pelting them with stones and snowballs. Colonists called the death of five protesters the Boston Massacre.

Then, in December 1773, a handful of colonists hurled a cargo of recently arrived British tea into the harbor to protest a tax on tea. The incident became known as the Boston Tea Party. When Parliament passed harsh laws to punish Massachusetts, other colonies rallied to help Massachusetts.

As tensions rose, representatives from 12 colonies gathered in Philadelphia in 1774. At the First Continental Congress, representatives discussed how to respond to Britain's harsh moves against Massachusetts.

Among the participants were the radical but fair-minded John Adams, the Virginia planter and soldier **George Washington,** and **Benjamin Franklin,** a leading figure of the American Enlightenment.

>> Benjamin Franklin, Thomas Jefferson, John Adams, Robert R. Livingston, and Roger Sherman served as the committee to draft the Declaration of Independence.

Interactive Illustration

Declaring Independence In April 1775, the crisis between the colonists and the British exploded into war. At the battles of Lexington and Concord in Massachusetts, colonists clashed with British troops—the opening shots of the American Revolution. Soon after, the Second Continental Congress met and set up a Continental Army with George Washington in command.

In 1776, Congress took a momentous step, voting to declare independence from Britain. Young **Thomas Jefferson** of Virginia was the principal author of the Declaration of Independence. Jefferson's political philosophy was heavily influenced by Enlightenment thinkers, especially John Locke. The document clearly reflects Locke's political and legal ideas, including the idea of natural law. It announced that people have "certain inalienable rights, that among them are life, liberty, and the pursuit of happiness."

In the Declaration, Jefferson further stated that people had the right "to alter or to abolish" unjust governments, echoing Locke's ideas about the right to revolt. He then carefully detailed the colonists' grievances against Britain, such as imposing taxes without consent, dissolving colonial legislatures at will, and depriving many colonists of their legal right to trial by jury. Because Parliament had trampled colonists'

D Differentiate Extra Support Have students scan the headings and visuals in the section. Then create two columns on the board, labeled *Britain* and *The American Colonies*. Have students volunteer information comparing and contrasting the two regions in the 1700s. Then ask students to use this chart to explain why the colonists would seek independence in 1776.

Answers

Describe *Most Americans considered themselves English citizens and, therefore, believed they should enjoy the same rights.*

natural rights, he argued, the colonists had the right to rebel and set up a new government to protect them.

The document spelled out the political principle of **popular sovereignty,** the idea that all government power comes from the people. Aware of the risks involved, on July 4, 1776, American leaders signed the Declaration, pledging "our lives, our fortunes, and our sacred honor" to the cause of the United States of America.

DRAW CONCLUSIONS Why did the colonists object so strongly to the idea of taxation without representation?

The American Revolution

At first, the American cause looked bleak. The colonists themselves were divided. About one third of the American colonists were Loyalists, or those who supported Britain. Many others refused to fight for either side.

Military Strengths and Weaknesses The colonists faced severe military disadvantages as well. The British had a large number of trained soldiers, a huge fleet, and plentiful money. They occupied most major American cities. The Americans lacked military resources, had little money to pay soldiers, and did not have a strategic plan.

Still, the colonists had some advantages. They were battling for their own independence on their own familiar home ground. Although the British held New York and Philadelphia, colonists controlled the countryside. And they had a strong, inspiring military leader in George Washington.

As the war unfolded, the British relied on Loyalists as well as Native American groups, some of whom sided with them. The British also sought support among African Americans held in slavery. They offered freedom to any who would join their side.

Alliance with France The first turning point in the war came in 1777, when the Americans triumphed over the British at the Battle of Saratoga. This victory persuaded France to join the Americans against its old rival, Britain. The alliance brought the Americans desperately needed supplies, trained soldiers, and French warships. Spurred by the French example, the Netherlands and Spain added their support.

Hard times continued, however. In the brutal winter of 1777–1778, Continental troops at Valley Forge suffered from cold, hunger, and disease. Throughout this crisis

>> George Washington encouraged his men to fight on despite heavy odds.

and others, Washington was patient, courageous, and determined. He held the ragged army together.

Victory for the Americans Finally, in 1781, with the help of a French fleet, Washington forced the surrender of a British army at **Yorktown, Virginia.** With that defeat, the British war effort crumbled.

Two years later, American, British, and French diplomats signed the **Treaty of Paris,** ending the war. Britain formally recognized the independence of the United States of America. Britain also accepted the new nation's western frontier as the Mississippi River.

GENERATE EXPLANATIONS Why was the selection of George Washington as head of the American army essential to the ultimate success of the American Revolution?

The United States Constitution

The Articles of Confederation was the new nation's first constitution. It proved to be too weak to rule effectively. To address this problem, the nation's leaders gathered once more. Among them were George Washington, **James Madison,** and Benjamin Franklin. During

The American Revolution

Remind students that times were often bleak for the American army during the Revolution. However, George Washington's leadership held the army together until the French ultimately came to America's aid.

Guided Reading and Discussion

Ask students: How did ideas such as human rights, liberty, and equality influence the American patriots? *(Students might say that American patriots believed that British policies, especially as they related to trade and taxes, were unfair.)*

The United States Constitution

The U.S. Constitution was written because the Articles of Confederation were weak. The framers replaced the system under the Articles with a federal republic in which power was divided between the federal, or national, government and the states.

Key Terms

Ask students to find the key term **Treaty of Paris** (in bold) in the text. This was one of a set of treaties, known as the Peace of Paris, that ended the Revolutionary War between Great Britain and the United States of America. Great Britain had separate treaties with France, Spain, and the Dutch Republic, who had also supported the American cause.

D Differentiate Challenge/Gifted Have students create a storyboard to represent key military events in the American Revolution. Ask them to either sketch the storyboard by hand or use a computer program.

History Background

Spreading the Word After the Declaration of Independence was adopted on July 4, 1776, the Continental Congress had to get the word out. They brought the approved version to John Dunlap, the official printer to Congress, who printed the first copies. These copies, in turn, were dispatched to the various assemblies and conventions and to the officers of the Continental Army. George Washington ordered that it be read to his troops. Newspapers spread the message to the rest of the colonies. With the first week, five broadsheets in Philadelphia alone had reprinted the Declaration.

Answers

Draw Conclusions *The British government was imposing its laws on the colonies without any say from the colonists.*

Generate Explanations *Washington's leadership abilities allowed him to hold the bedraggled American army together during many trying times.*

Topic 12 Lesson 5

Online Project the **Interactive Chart: Checks and Balances**. Explain the importance of the idea of separation of powers among the legislative, executive, and judicial branches, with checks and balances to limit the power of each branch. Study the role each branch of government plays in the U.S. government by participating as a group to complete the activity.

ACTIVE CLASSROOM

Ask students to assume the role of reporters covering the Constitutional Convention. Have them write headlines that capture the outcome. Tell them to make sure that their headlines identify the impact of the convention's proceedings, such as the creation of the three branches of government. Then, have them pass their headlines to a partner for him or her to review.

Guided Reading and Discussion

The Declaration of Independence and the Constitution put forth the idea that everyone holds certain rights. The Bill of Rights states that citizens have basic rights that the government must protect, including freedom of religion, speech, and the press. It also protects the right to trial by jury. Point out that in 1789, most countries in Europe were ruled by hereditary absolute monarchs who did not give people these rights. The United States became an inspiration to Europeans, who took up the cry for liberty and freedom.

Analyze Images

Direct students to the image of the United States Constitution. Ask: How did the ideals of democracy and human rights put forth in the Declaration and the Constitution impact people in parts of the world outside of the United States? *(The idea that government is created by people, who by nature have certain basic human rights, spread to other parts of the world. People overthrew oppressive regimes and tried to form their own constitutional governments.)*

>> James Madison is known as the father of the U.S. Constitution because he was instrumental in drafting the document.

>> The U.S. Constitution, shown here, set up a series of checks and balances in which each branch of government can limit the powers of the other branches.

the hot summer of 1787, they hammered out the Constitution of the United States. This framework for a strong, flexible government has remained in place for more than 200 years.

The Impact of the Enlightenment The Framers of the Constitution had absorbed the ideas of Locke, Montesquieu, and Rousseau. Like Rousseau, the framers saw government in terms of a social contract among members of the community. A central feature of the new federal government—the separation of powers among the legislative, executive, and judicial branches—was borrowed directly from Montesquieu.

The framers were also influenced by the ideas of an English legal scholar of the 1700s, William Blackstone, who shared many of Locke's ideas. Blackstone's writings greatly informed the legal ideas contained in the Constitution and a good portion of American law to the present day. For example, his famous statement that "the law holds it better that ten guilty persons escape, than that one innocent party suffer" is reflected in the Constitutional rights given to people accused of crimes.

A Framework of Government The Constitution created a **federal republic,** with power divided between the federal, or national, government and the states. It provided for both an elected legislature and an elected president.

To prevent any branch of government from becoming too powerful, the Constitution set up a series of **checks and balances.** Under this system, each branch of the government has the right to monitor and limit each of the other branches.

The Bill of Rights, or the first ten amendments to the Constitution, recognized the idea that citizens have basic rights that the government must protect. These included freedom of religion, speech, and the press.

It also affirmed legal ideas, such as the right to trial by jury and the principle that no one may be forced to testify against him- or herself. The Bill of Rights, like the Constitution, put Enlightenment ideas into practice.

Symbol of Freedom From the start, the new republic was a symbol of freedom for many. The Declaration of Independence, along with the Bill of Rights, put forth the idea that there are certain rights that belong to everyone.

In 1789, most countries in Europe were ruled by hereditary absolute monarchs. The United States stood out as a beacon to Europeans who took up the cry for liberty and freedom.

Demands for written constitutions and a limit to royal power would bring great changes to Europe by

History Background

A Soldier's Philosophy The philosophical writings of the Enlightenment certainly influenced leading Americans such as Thomas Jefferson and Benjamin Franklin. However, more fundamental thoughts motivated many of the soldiers of the Continental Army. When Captain Levi Preston was asked if he joined the fight for independence because of having read the writings of Locke and others on liberty, he said he had never heard of Locke, but that he and the other soldiers of the Continental Army fought the "red coats" because Americans had always governed themselves and intended that they always would govern themselves.

the decades ahead. Revolutionaries in Latin America were also inspired by the example of the United States.

Under the Constitution, citizens enjoy many rights, but they also have many responsibilities. They are expected to vote, sit on juries, and keep informed on topics of local and national interest. Noncitizens who reside in the United States also enjoy its constitutional rights and protections and have responsibilities such as paying taxes and abiding by local, state, and federal laws.

ANALYZE CONTEXT How did the ideas of the Enlightenment influence the United States Constitution and the Bill of Rights?

ASSESSMENT

1. **Identify Main Ideas** How did trade play a role in Britain's becoming a global power?
2. **Identify Cause and Effect** Why did North America's geography make it difficult for the British to win the war?
3. **Check Understanding** Why did colonists wait to declare independence from Britain?
4. **Hypothesize** Why do you think many countries over time have emulated the principles outlined in the Declaration of Independence and the U.S. Constitution?
5. **Describe** In what way does the Bill of Rights put the ideas of the Enlightenment into practice?

SYNTHESIZE

Online Project the **Digital Activity: The United States Constitution**. Ask students to recall the Topic Essential Question, "How much power should the government have?" Break students into equal groups of four or five. Tell students they are going to debate the powers of the federal government. Half of the groups will debate the merits of a strong federal government; the other half will debate the merits of a weak federal government. Tell them to consider these questions: Should the government be able to pass laws curtailing a person's civil rights in a national emergency? Should state governments not follow federal laws that the states think unfair?

DEMONSTRATE

Online Assign the **Digital Lesson Quiz** for this lesson if you haven't already done so. Students will be offered automatic remediation or enrichment based on their score.

Pose this question to the class on the Discussion Board:

Predict Consequences Do you think the American Revolution was inevitable, or do you think it could have been avoided? *(Students might say that had Britain taken a more moderate approach to running its North American colonies, the rebellion might never have happened. Others might say that America was so far removed from Britain that war was inevitable.)*

Topic Inquiry

Have students continue their investigations for the Topic Inquiry.

Answers

Analyze Context *The Enlightenment emphasized the ideas of basic human rights and that all government should be based upon a treaty or social contract with its citizens.*

Assessment

1. England's location placed it in a position to control trade. It eventually established dominance over trade in the West Indies, North America, and India through its colonies. It profited from the slave trade.
2. The colonists were fighting on their own soil, which made fighting the British a bit easier. The colonists knew the woods, the roads, and the mountains. The British found it difficult to fight on such terrain.
3. At first, the Americans struggled to preserve their rights as citizens of Britain, but they later decided to expand the struggle, citing the cause of human freedom.
4. The principles contained in the Declaration of Independence and the U.S. Constitution have shown the world that a free people can govern themselves and that a stable government is one that protects the rights of citizens, including the rights to freedom of speech, assembly, and the press.
5. The Bill of Rights put into writing the Enlightenment principles that government derives its power from the people and that citizens have certain freedoms that the government must protect and cannot take away.

The French Revolution Begins

CONNECT

Preview Have students preview the **Lesson Objectives** and the list of **Key Terms**.

Students can also preview all the **Key Terms and Academic Vocabulary** using the **Interactive Reading Notepad** on the digital course or preview a summary of the lesson in the **Reading and Note Taking Study Guide**.

Online Use the **Editable Presentation** found on the digital course to present the main ideas for this lesson.

Start Up Activity

Present students with an excerpt from *Encyclopedia,* edited by Denis Diderot, one of the French *philosophes* of the Enlightenment:

> "No man has received from nature the right to give orders to others. Freedom is a gift from heaven, and every individual of the same species has the right to enjoy it as soon as he is in enjoyment of his reason."

Ask students to restate the main ideas in this excerpt. Ask: In what ways might these ideas appeal to the French revolutionaries who stressed that government exists to protect the natural rights of citizens? *(Students' answers will vary but should mention that freedom is a natural-born right, and no one is born with the power to give orders to others. These ideas might have inspired the revolutionaries because they oppose the idea of the absolute power of a monarch.)*

Online You can also project the **Start Up Activity** from the course.

INVESTIGATE

Have students read the lesson using the **Reading and Note Taking Study Guide** to help them take notes and understand the text as they read.

The Old Regime in France

In the late 1700s, French society was divided into three social classes: the First Estate, consisting of the clergy; the Second Estate, consisting of the nobility; and the Third Estate, composed of the middle class and peasants.

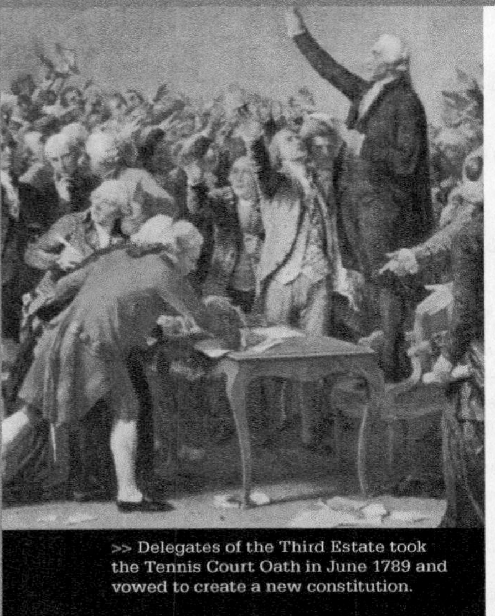

>> Delegates of the Third Estate took the Tennis Court Oath in June 1789 and vowed to create a new constitution.

Interactive Flipped Video

12.6 On April 28, 1789, unrest exploded at a Paris wallpaper factory. A rumor had spread that the factory owner was planning to cut wages even though bread prices were soaring. Enraged workers vandalized the owner's home and then rioted through the streets.

TEKS
1.E, 9.A, 9.D, 20.B

>> Objectives

Describe the social divisions of France's old order.

Trace the causes of the French Revolution.

Identify the reforms enacted by the National Assembly, including the Declaration of the Rights of Man and the Citizen.

>> Key Terms

ancien régime
estates
bourgeoisie
deficit spending
Louis XVI
Jacques Necker
Estates-General
cahiers
Tennis Court Oath
Bastille
faction
Marquis de Lafayette
Olympe de Gouges
Marie Antoinette

The French Revolution Begins

The Old Regime in France

The rioting reflected growing unrest in Paris and throughout France. In 1789, France faced not only an economic crisis but also widespread demands for far-reaching changes. By July, the hungry, unemployed, poorly paid people of Paris were taking up arms against the government, a move that would trigger the French Revolution.

In 1789, France, like the rest of Europe, still clung to an outdated social system that had emerged in the Middle Ages. Under this **ancien régime,** or old order, everyone in France belonged to one of three social classes, or **estates.** The First Estate was made up of the clergy; the Second Estate was made up of the nobility; and the Third Estate comprised the vast majority of the population.

First Estate: the Clergy During the Middle Ages, the Church had exerted great influence throughout Christian Europe. In 1789, the French clergy still enjoyed enormous wealth and privilege. The Church owned about 10 percent of the land, collected tithes, and paid no direct taxes to the state. High Church leaders such as bishops and abbots were usually nobles who lived very well. Parish priests,

PEARSON realize. www.PearsonTexas.com Access your Digital Lesson.

508

Aa Vocabulary Builder

1. Have students pronounce the following academic vocabulary terms in this lesson and clarify the part of speech. For difficult or polysyllabic words, break them into syllables and pronounce them with the students.
2. Explain what the word means in common "student-friendly" language using synonyms and antonyms when possible. Provide concrete examples to clarify the meaning, and rephrase the definition.

urban: of, relating to, or characteristic of a city

tithe: one tenth of a person's income paid annually to support a church

feudal: relating to the political and economic system in which a powerful lord granted his vassal a fief, or an estate, to work on in exchange for a pledge of loyalty

proclaimed: announced officially

however, often came from humble origins and might be as poor as their peasant congregations.

The First Estate did provide some social services. Nuns, monks, and priests ran schools, hospitals, and orphanages. But during the Enlightenment, *philosophes* targeted the Church for reform.

They criticized the idleness of some clergy, the Church's interference in politics, and its intolerance of dissent. In response, many clergy condemned the Enlightenment for undermining religion and moral order.

Second Estate: the Nobility The Second Estate was the titled nobility of French society. In the Middle Ages, noble knights had defended the land. In the 1600s, Richelieu and Louis XIV had crushed the nobles' military power but had given them other rights—under strict royal control. Those rights included top jobs in government, the army, the courts, and the Church.

At Versailles, ambitious nobles competed for royal appointments while idle courtiers enjoyed endless entertainments. Many nobles, however, lived far from the center of power. Though they owned land, they received little financial income. As a result, they felt the pinch of trying to maintain their status in a period of rising prices.

Many ambitious nobles came to hate absolutism and resented the royal bureaucracy that employed middle-class men in positions that once had been reserved for them. They feared losing their traditional privileges, especially their freedom from paying taxes.

Third Estate: From Middle Class to Peasantry The Third Estate was the most diverse social class. At the top sat the **bourgeoisie** (boor zhwah ZEE), or middle class. The bourgeoisie included prosperous bankers, merchants, and manufacturers, as well as lawyers, doctors, journalists, and professors.

The bulk of the Third Estate, however, consisted of rural peasants. Some were prosperous landowners who hired laborers to work for them. Others were tenant farmers or day laborers.

Among the poorest members of the Third Estate were urban workers. They included apprentices, journeymen, and others who worked in industries such as printing or cloth making.

Many women and men earned a meager living as servants, construction workers, or street sellers of everything from food to pots and pans. A large number of the urban poor were unemployed. To survive, some turned to begging or crime.

Widespread Discontent From rich to poor, members of the Third Estate resented the privileges enjoyed by

>> **Analyze Political Cartoons** What does this cartoon say about the relationship between the three social classes in France?

Interactive Cartoon

>> Merchants were among the bourgeoisie, France's middle class.

Online Project the **Interactive Cartoon: Characteristics of the Three Estates**. Click through each hotspot, and read the characteristics of each estate. Have students discuss what these characteristics might mean for French society.

ACTIVE CLASSROOM

Organize students into groups. Have groups look again at the political cartoon of France's Three Estates. Then ask them to create speech bubbles on sticky notes to reflect what each of the characters in the cartoon might be saying. Tell them to post their "graffiti" on the whiteboard, next to the appropriate characters. Tell students to look at each group's work and then discuss the similarities and differences of the captions as a group.

D Differentiate Challenge/Gifted Using the information contained in the Interactive Cartoon, divide the class into groups representing each of France's three pre-revolutionary estates. Give each group some sticky notes. Have groups spend 3 minutes writing down their response to this question: What do you think life was like for a member of your group in pre-revolutionary France? Have students post their sticky notes next to the previous exercise on the board. Discuss the similarities and differences among the groups as a class.

English Language Proficiency Standards

Reading 4.D.1 Have students preread the red headings in "The Old Regime in France" and examine the political cartoon to identify the three estates and the groups that belong to each.

Beginning On the board, write *First Estate, Second Estate, Third Estate* in one column and *nobility, bourgeoisie, peasants,* and *clergy* in another. Then have students match each group with the estate to which it belongs.

Intermediate Complete the Beginning activity.

Advanced Have students create a graphic organizer that lists the three estates and the groups that belong to each. Ask students to check their work and add details to their graphic organizer.

Advanced High Have students examine the political cartoon and create a graphic organizer that lists the estates and the groups that belong to each. Ask students to check their work.

Answers

Analyze Political Cartoons *Students might say the cartoon represents how the Third Estate was throwing off the chains of oppression, much to the alarm of the other two estates.*

Topic 12 Lesson 6

Guided Reading and Discussion

Summarize Ask students to briefly describe how a desire for equality and greater rights affected France's social classes in the years leading up to the Revolution. *(Students might say that the lower classes suffered the most from the social and economic inequality of pre-revolutionary France. As a result, they would be in conflict with the upper classes, who generally wanted to continue the status quo.)*

France's Economic Crisis

Explain to students that France's pre-revolutionary government was deeply in debt due to years of deficit spending. To bridge the gap between income and expenses, the government of King Louis XVI borrowed heavily. The country's economic problems hurt the poor in France the most. Tell students that as the crisis deepened, the public demanded that the king summon the Estates-General in the hope that reforms might be enacted.

their social "betters." Wealthy bourgeois families in the Third Estate could buy political office and even titles, but the best jobs were still reserved for nobles. Urban workers earned miserable wages. Even the smallest rise in the price of bread, their main food, brought the threat of greater hunger or even starvation. In 1775, before the French Revolution, peasants rioted over the high price of bread in an event called the "Flour War."

Because of traditional privileges, the First and Second Estates paid almost no taxes. Peasants were burdened by taxes on everything from land to soap to salt. Though they were technically free, many owed fees and services that dated back to medieval times, such as the corvée (KAWR VAY), which was unpaid labor to repair roads and bridges.

Peasants were also incensed when nobles, hurt by rising prices, tried to reimpose old manor dues. In towns and cities, Enlightenment ideas about equality led people to question the inequalities of the old regime. Why, people demanded, should the first two estates have such great privileges at the expense of the majority? Throughout France, the Third Estate called for the privileged classes to pay their share.

CONTRAST How did the lives of the Third Estate differ from the lives of clergy and nobles?

ELPS **ELPS 4.D.1** Examine the political cartoon about the three estates in the text *The Old Regime in France* to understand the relationships between the three estates.

France's Economic Crisis

Along with social unrest, France faced economic woes, especially a mushrooming financial crisis. The crisis was caused in part by years of **deficit spending.** This occurs when a government spends more money than it takes in.

A Nation in Debt Louis XIV had left France deeply in debt. The Seven Years' War and the American Revolution strained the treasury even further. Costs generally had risen in the 1700s, and the lavish court soaked up millions. To bridge the gap between income and expenses, the government borrowed more and more money. By 1789, half of the government's income from taxes went to paying the interest on this enormous debt.

To solve the financial crisis, the government would have to increase taxes, reduce expenses, or both. However, the nobles and clergy fiercely resisted any attempt to end their exemption from taxes.

A Crumbling Economy Other economic woes added to the crisis. A general economic decline began in the 1770s. Then in the late 1780s, bad harvests set food prices soaring and brought hunger to poorer peasants and city dwellers.

Hard times and lack of food inflamed these people. In towns, people rioted, demanding bread. In the

FRANCE IN ECONOMIC CRISIS

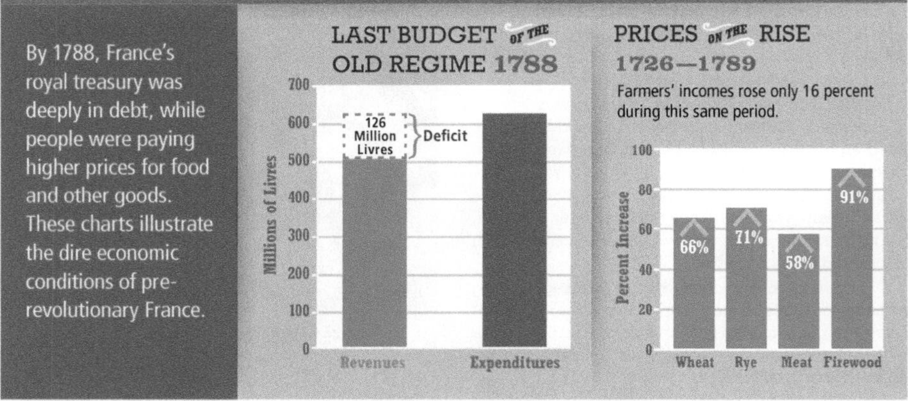

>> **Analyze Charts** As France's deficit grew, so did the suffering of the poor. How much did the price of firewood rise between 1726 and 1789?

History Background

Louis XVI as a Young Prince Indecisive and easily influenced, Louis XVI was ill-prepared to guide France through turbulent times. When he was born in 1754, he was the fourth in line for the throne. By age 10, he was the direct heir. Uneasy with this responsibility, he set out to prepare himself emotionally and mentally for his duties. As a student, he was only average, but he possessed an excellent memory, was interpreted in history and languages, and demonstrated skill as a locksmith. Nevertheless, he still preferred the quiet of the nearby woods to the pressures and politics of the court. When he became king at the young age of 20, he apparently said, "I am the unhappiest of men."

Answers

Analyze Charts *91 percent*

Contrast *The Third Estate paid nearly all of the taxes in pre-revolutionary France. Members of the Third Estate were mostly poor and did not occupy positions of authority, as the other two estates did.*

countryside, peasants began to attack the manor houses of nobles.

Failure of Reform The heirs of Louis XIV were not the right men to solve the economic crisis that afflicted France. Louis XV, who ruled from 1715 to 1774, pursued pleasure before serious business and ran up more debts.

The next king, **Louis XVI**, was well-meaning but weak and indecisive. He did wisely choose **Jacques Necker,** a financial expert, as an advisor. Necker urged the king to reduce extravagant court spending, reform government, and abolish burdensome tariffs on internal trade. When Necker proposed taxing the First and Second Estates, however, the nobles and high clergy forced the king to dismiss him.

As the crisis deepened, the pressure for reform mounted. The wealthy and powerful classes demanded, however, that the king summon the **Estates-General,** the legislative body consisting of representatives of the three estates, before making any changes. No French king had called the Estates-General for 175 years. They feared that nobles would try to recover the feudal powers they had lost under absolute rule.

To reform-minded nobles, the Estates-General seemed to offer a chance of carrying out changes like the ones the English had achieved through the Glorious Revolution. They hoped to bring the absolute monarch under the control of nobles and guarantee their own privileges.

DESCRIBE What were some of the main reasons France was in serious economic trouble in the late 1700s?

Louis XVI Calls the Estates-General

As 1788 came to a close, France tottered on the verge of bankruptcy. Bread riots were spreading, and nobles, fearful of taxes, were denouncing royal tyranny. A baffled Louis XVI finally summoned the Estates-General to meet at Versailles the following year.

The Cahiers In preparation, Louis had all three estates prepare **cahiers** (kah YAYZ), or notebooks, listing their grievances. Many cahiers called for reforms such as fairer taxes, freedom of the press, or regular meetings of the Estates-General. In one town, shoemakers denounced regulations that made leather so expensive they could not afford to make shoes. Servant girls in the city of Toulouse demanded the right to leave service when they wanted and insisted that "after a girl has served her master for many years, she receive some reward for her service."

>> The poor made up the majority of the Third Estate. Here, they are shown rioting during the "Flour War," a brief 1775 uprising brought on by higher bread prices.

The cahiers testified to boiling class resentments. One called tax collectors "bloodsuckers of the nation who drink the tears of the unfortunate from goblets of gold." Another one of the cahiers condemned the courts of nobles as "vampires pumping the last drop of blood" from the people. Yet another complained that "20 million must live on half the wealth of France while the clergy . . . devour the other half."

The Tennis Court Oath Delegates to the Estates-General from the Third Estate were elected, though only propertied men could vote. Thus, the delegates were mostly lawyers, middle-class officials, and writers. They were familiar with the writings of Voltaire, Rousseau, and other *philosophes*, as well as with the complaints in the cahiers. They went to Versailles not only to solve the financial crisis but also to insist on reform.

The Estates-General convened in May 1789. From the start, the delegates were deadlocked over the issue of voting. Traditionally, each estate had met and voted separately. Each group had one vote.

Under this system, the First and Second Estates always outvoted the Third Estate two to one. This time, the Third Estate wanted all three estates to meet in a

Analyze Images

Direct students' attention to the chart, "France in Economic Crisis," on the previous page. Ask students to study the chart and discuss these questions: How did the cost of certain products and the mounting national debt impact each of the three estates? Why would the French ask King Louis XVI to initiate economic reforms? Which group(s) do you think were impacted the most by rising prices?

Answers

Describe *The country, which had borrowed heavily to finance two wars, was deeply in debt. In addition, the royal government was not serious about lowering the debt, opting instead to spend more money, mostly frivolously. Moreover, bad harvests sent food prices soaring.*

Topic 12 Lesson 6

Louis XVI Calls the Estates-General
Storming the Bastille
Revolts in Paris and the Provinces

Louis XVI called the Estates-General into session to deal with France's economic crisis, which coincided with the worst famine in memory. In June 1789, claiming to represent the people of France, members of the Third Estate declared themselves a National Assembly. Tell students that the National Assembly pushed for a just constitution. Explain that the situation in France was so tense that more than 800 Parisians challenged the power of the king when they stormed the Bastille, a prison in Paris. At the same time, tales of attacks on villages and towns fueled the panic felt by peasants. Many took their frustration out on nobles who were trying to assert medieval dues.

D Differentiate Challenge/Gifted Have students work with a partner to outline the main ideas in these three sections. Ask pairs to write the headings from their outlines on the whiteboard, and discuss the results as a class.

single body, with votes counted "by head." After weeks of stalemate, delegates of the Third Estate took a daring step. In June 1789, claiming to represent the people of France, they declared themselves to be the National Assembly. A few days later, the National Assembly found its meeting hall locked and guarded. Fearing that the king planned to dismiss them, the delegates moved to a nearby indoor tennis court.

As curious spectators looked on, the delegates took their famous **Tennis Court Oath.** They swore "never to separate and to meet wherever the circumstances might require until we have established a sound and just constitution." When reform-minded clergy and nobles joined the Assembly, Louis XVI grudgingly accepted it.

At the same time, though, royal troops gathered around Paris. Rumors spread that the king planned to dissolve the Assembly.

DESCRIBE Why did the Third Estate want the Estates-General to meet as a single body?

ELPS ELPS 3.H.3 Explain why members of the Third Estate wanted to vote at the same time as the First and Second estates.

>> The storming of the Bastille on July 14, 1789, was the opening event of the French Revolution.

Storming the Bastille

On July 14, 1789, the city of Paris seized the spotlight from the National Assembly meeting in Versailles. The streets buzzed with rumors that royal troops were going to occupy the capital. More than 800 Parisians assembled outside the **Bastille,** a grim medieval fortress used as a prison for political and other prisoners. The crowd demanded weapons and gunpowder believed to be stored there.

The commander of the Bastille refused to open the gates and opened fire on the crowd. In the battle that followed, many people were killed. Finally, the enraged mob broke through the defenses. Thomas Jefferson was at the time American minister to France and described the scene as one of chaos and violence.

> The people rushed against the place, and almost in an instant were in possession of a fortification, defended by 100 men, of infinite strength, which in other times had stood several regular sieges and had never been taken. . . . They took all the arms, discharged the prisoners and such of the garrison as were not killed in the first moment of fury, carried the Governor and Lieutenant governor to the Greve (the place of public execution), cut off their heads, and set them through the city in triumph to the Palais royal.
>
> —Thomas Jefferson, letter to John Jay, July 14, 1789

The mob killed the commander and five guards and released the handful of prisoners who were being held there. However, they found no weapons.

For the French, the Bastille was a powerful symbol of the tyranny, inequalities, and injustices of the old order. The storming of the Bastille signaled the end of the absolute monarchy and a step toward freedom. It also marked the beginning of the French Revolution. Today, July 14 is a national holiday when the French celebrate the birth of modern France.

IDENTIFY CENTRAL IDEAS What was the main motivation behind the Parisians' attack on the Bastille?

Answers

Describe *Each Estate had one vote in the Estates-General, and the First and Second Estate always banded together to wield power to the detriment of the Third Estate by voting two to one. By meeting as a single body, each delegate would have a vote. The Third Estate, which had most of the delegates, could then flex its political muscle.*

Identify Central Ideas *They wanted guns and ammunition to fight off royal troops who were rumored to be on their way to Paris.*

English Language Proficiency Standards

Reading 3.H.3 Read aloud or have students read the section "Louis XVI Calls the Estates-General." Have students explain to the group the events that led up to and occurred during the meeting.

Beginning After reading the section to students, ask students to explain the Tennis Court Oath using the following sentence frames:

The Third Estate wanted to meet as a single body because _____.

The Tennis Court Oath was taken to make sure that _____.

Intermediate After reading the section to students, ask students to explain the Tennis Court Oath using the following sentence frames:

The Third Estate wanted _____.

The Tennis Court Oath was _____.

Advanced Have students read the section. Then have students work in small groups to discuss and explain why the Third Estate felt

Revolts in Paris and the Provinces

The political crisis of 1789 coincided with the worst famine in memory. Starving peasants roamed the countryside or flocked to towns, where they swelled the ranks of the unemployed. As grain prices soared, even people with jobs had to spend as much as 80 percent of their income on bread.

The "Great Fear" In such desperate times, rumors ran wild and set off what was later called the "Great Fear." Tales of attacks on villages and towns spread panic. Other rumors asserted that government troops were seizing peasant crops.

Inflamed by famine and fear, peasants unleashed their fury on nobles who were trying to reimpose medieval dues. Defiant peasants set fire to old manor records and stole grain from storehouses. The attacks eventually died down, but they clearly showed peasant anger with the injustice of the old order.

Paris in Arms Paris, too, was in turmoil. As the capital and chief city of France, it was the revolutionary center. A variety of factions competed to gain power. A **faction** is a group or clique within a larger group that has different ideas and opinions than the rest of the group.

Moderates looked to the **Marquis de Lafayette,** the aristocratic "hero of two worlds" who had fought alongside George Washington in the American Revolution. Lafayette headed the National Guard, a largely middle-class militia organized in response to the arrival of royal troops in Paris. The Guard was the first group to don the tricolor—a red, white, and blue badge that was eventually adopted as the national flag of France.

A more radical group, the Paris Commune, replaced the royalist government of the city. It could mobilize whole neighborhoods for protests or violent action to further the revolution. Newspapers and political clubs—many even more radical than the Commune—blossomed everywhere.

Some demanded an end to the monarchy and spread scandalous stories about the royal family and members of the court.

IDENTIFY MAIN IDEAS What stoked the "Great Fear"?

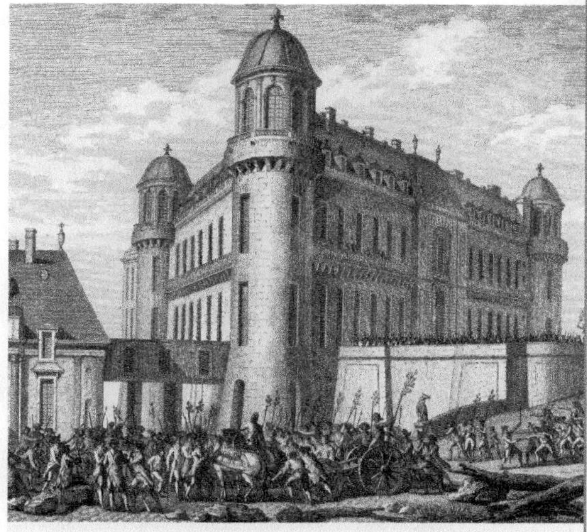

>> Peasant rebellions during the Great Fear began amid rumors that the king and other aristocrats wanted to overthrow the Third Estate.

The National Assembly

Peasant uprisings and the storming of the Bastille stampeded the National Assembly into action. On August 4, in a combative all-night meeting, nobles in the National Assembly voted to end their own privileges. They agreed to give up their old manorial dues, exclusive hunting rights, special legal status, and exemption from taxes.

An End to Special Privilege "Feudalism is abolished," announced the proud and weary delegates at 2 A.M. As the president of the Assembly later observed, "We may view this moment as the dawn of a new revolution, when all the burdens weighing on the people were abolished, and France was truly reborn."

Were nobles sacrificing much with their votes on the night of August 4? Both contemporary observers and modern historians note that the nobles gave up nothing that they had not already lost. In the months ahead, the National Assembly turned the reforms of August 4 into law, meeting a key Enlightenment goal—the equality of all male citizens before the law.

Declaration of the Rights of Man In late August, as a first step toward writing a constitution, the Assembly issued the Declaration of the Rights of Man

Guided Reading and Discussion

Discuss What role did taxes play in the discontent among members of French society prior to the Revolution? *(Taxes were mostly spent on debt from the Seven Years' War and the American Revolution, so the government had no money and needed to raise taxes; the nobles and the clergy opposed making them subject to taxes, which Louis XVI's adviser told him to do; those in the Third Estate who paid taxes demanded fairer taxes.)*

Compare and Contrast Compare the crisis in pre-revolutionary France to the crisis in the American colonies prior to the American Revolution. What were the differences? What were the similarities? *(Students might say class divisions were not an issue during the American Revolution, which was based more on the abuses of the British monarchy and the desire for self-rule. In France, decades of class division were one of the major reasons for the revolution. Both revolutions were influenced by the Enlightenment.)*

Key Terms

Ask students to find the key term **faction** (in bold) in the text and explain its meaning. Have students brainstorm the advantages and disadvantages of having many different factions.

that it was not being properly represented in the Estates-General and how this led to the Tennis Court Oath.

Advanced High Have students read the section. Then have students prepare a short presentation explaining why the Third Estate felt that it was not being properly represented in the Estates-General. Students should include how this led to the Tennis Court Oath and why it was so important to French citizens.

Answers

Identify Main Ideas *Amid the turmoil of the worst famine in history, rumors of violence perpetrated by royal troops and others fanned the flames of the "Great Fear."*

Topic 12 Lesson 6

The National Assembly

Peasant revolts and the storming of the Bastille forced the National Assembly to take action. On August 4, 1789, the National Assembly voted to end their own privileges and took the first steps toward writing a new constitution and transforming French society.

Online Project the **Interactive Document: Declaration of the Rights of Man**. Have students click through the political and legal principles contained in the Declaration. Explain to students that at the height of the French Revolution, the Declaration put into words the Enlightenment ideas of political freedom and equality before the law.

ACTIVE CLASSROOM

Divide the class into equal groups. Have each group discuss and rank what each believes are the most important political and legal ideas contained in the Declaration of the Rights of Man and the Citizen. When they are finished, ask each group to provide a justification for the ranking decisions they made. Poll the class to see if there is agreement on the ranking.

Guided Reading and Discussion

Identify Central Issues How did the Declaration of the Rights of Man and the Citizen impact the rights of French men? *(It made all male citizens equal before the law.)*

>> The ideals of the Enlightenment inspired the Declaration of the Rights of Man and the Citizen.

Interactive Illustration

>> On October 5, 1789, thousands of women marched on the royal palace at Versailles hoping to draw attention to their poor living conditions.

and the Citizen. The document was modeled in part on the American Declaration of Independence, written 13 years earlier. All men, the French declaration announced, were "born and remain free and equal in rights." They enjoyed natural rights to "liberty, property, security, and resistance to oppression." Like the writings of Locke and the *philosophes*, the declaration insisted that governments exist to protect the natural rights of citizens.

The declaration further proclaimed that all male citizens were equal before the law. Every French man had an equal right to hold public office "with no distinction other than that of their virtues and talents."

It affirmed the legal idea that no person could be arrested, tried or imprisoned except according to the law. In addition, the declaration asserted freedom of religion and called for taxes to be levied according to ability to pay. Its principles were captured in the enduring slogan of the French Revolution, "Liberty, Equality, Fraternity."

Some women were disappointed that the Declaration of the Rights of Man did not grant equal citizenship to them. In 1791, **Olympe de Gouges** (oh LAMP duh GOOZH) demanded equal rights in her Declaration of the Rights of Woman and the Female Citizen. "Woman is born free," she proclaimed, "and her rights are the same as those of man." She called for all citizens, men or women, to be equally eligible for all public offices. De Gouges and other women who pushed the cause of women's rights were often ridiculed or sometimes imprisoned and executed.

Women March on Versailles Louis XVI did not want to accept the reforms of the National Assembly. Nobles continued to enjoy gala banquets while people were starving.

By autumn, anger again turned to action. On October 5, about six thousand women marched 13 miles in the pouring rain from Paris to Versailles. "Bread!" they shouted. They demanded to see the king.

Much of the crowd's anger was directed at the queen, **Marie Antoinette.** She was the daughter of Maria Theresa of Austria. Ever since she had married Louis, she had come under attack for being frivolous and extravagant. She eventually grew more serious and even advised the king to compromise with moderate reformers. Still she remained a source of scandal. "Death to the Austrian!" the women who marched on Versailles shouted.

Lafayette and the National Guard eventually calmed the crowd. Still the women refused to leave Versailles until the king met their most important demand—to return to Paris. Not too happily, the king agreed. The next morning, the crowd, with the king and his family

History Background

Origins of the Declaration of the Rights of Man and the Citizen In addition to being influenced by the American Declaration of Independence and the English Bill of Rights, the French Declaration of the Rights of Man and the Citizen drew its content from other sources as well. The constitutions of individual states such as New Hampshire and Virginia also influenced the Declaration.

The impact of Enlightenment *philosophes* is clearly seen in the document, too. Montesquieu's notion of separation of powers is represented, as are Locke's ideas on natural rights and Rosseau's theories on the general will and national sovereignty. The physiocrats' ideas about private property and Voltaire's notions of protecting individuals against arbitrary police action are also included.

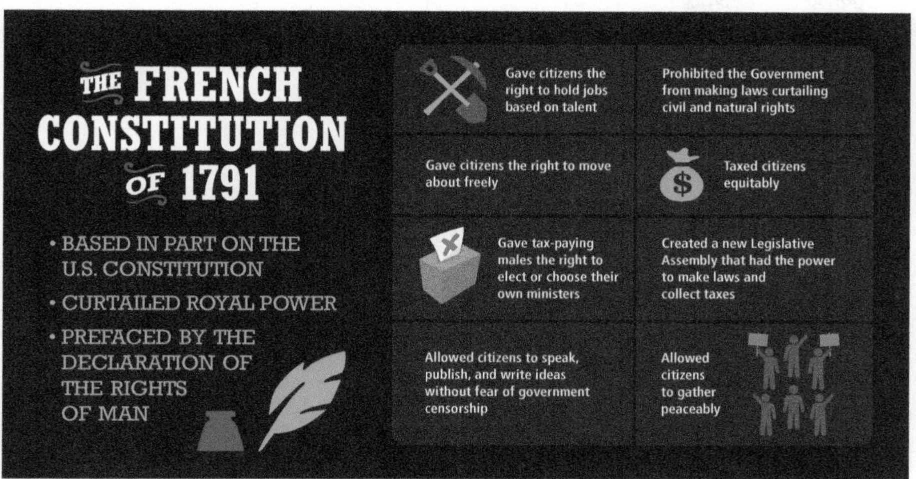

THE FRENCH CONSTITUTION OF 1791
• BASED IN PART ON THE U.S. CONSTITUTION
• CURTAILED ROYAL POWER
• PREFACED BY THE DECLARATION OF THE RIGHTS OF MAN
Gave citizens the right to hold jobs based on talent
Prohibited the Government from making laws curtailing civil and natural rights
Gave citizens the right to move about freely
Taxed citizens equitably
Gave tax-paying males the right to elect or choose their own ministers
Created a new Legislative Assembly that had the power to make laws and collect taxes
Allowed citizens to speak, publish, and write ideas without fear of government censorship
Allowed citizens to gather peaceably

>> **Analyze Charts** The Constitution of 1791 turned France upside down by destroying the old order. What powers did the Legislative Assembly now have?

in tow, set out for the city. At the head of the procession rode women perched on the barrels of seized cannons. Crowds along the way cheered the king, who now wore the tricolor.

In Paris, the royal family moved into the Tuileries (TWEE luh reez) palace. For the next three years, Louis was a virtual prisoner.

DESCRIBE Why did the women who marched on Versailles want King Louis XVI to return to Paris?

Reforms of the National Assembly

The National Assembly soon followed the king to Paris. Its largely bourgeois members worked to draft a constitution and to solve the continuing financial crisis.

Controlling the Church To pay off the huge government debt—much of it owed to the bourgeoisie—the Assembly voted to take over and sell Church lands. In an even more radical move, the National Assembly put the French Catholic Church under state control. Under the Civil Constitution of the Clergy, issued in 1790, bishops and priests became elected, salaried officials. The Civil Constitution ended papal authority over the French Church and dissolved convents and monasteries.

Reaction to the Civil Constitution was swift and angry. Many bishops and priests refused to accept the document while the pope condemned it.

Large numbers of French peasants, who were conservative concerning religion, also rejected the changes. When the government punished clergy who refused to support the Civil Constitution, a huge gulf opened between revolutionaries in Paris and the peasantry in the provinces.

The Constitution of 1791 The National Assembly completed its main task by producing a constitution. The Constitution of 1791 set up a limited monarchy in place of the absolute monarchy that had ruled France for centuries. A new Legislative Assembly had the power to make laws, collect taxes, and decide on issues of war and peace. Lawmakers would be elected by tax-paying male citizens over age 25.

To make government more efficient, the constitution replaced the old provinces with 83 departments of roughly equal size. It abolished the old provincial courts, and it reformed laws.

To moderate reformers, the Constitution of 1791 seemed to complete the revolution. Reflecting Enlightenment goals, it ensured equality before the law for all male citizens and ended Church interference

Reforms of the National Assembly

The National Assembly voted to take and sell Church land to pay off the huge government debt, and to place the French Catholic Church under state control. The National Assembly also produced a new constitution, which called for many reforms, including a limited monarchy and a Legislative Assembly made up of members elected into office by male citizens over age 25.

Guided Reading and Discussion

Compare and Contrast Ask students to recall what they learned about the freedoms protected under the new U.S. Constitution, such as freedom of speech, in the lesson on the American Revolution. Have students review the lesson to discern the role religion played in post-revolutionary America versus its role in revolutionary France. How did each government deal with religion in its respective country? Why might these two countries' religious provisions be different? *(Answers will vary, but students might say that the U.S. Constitution's First Amendment prevented the government from supporting a particular religion, while in France, the clergy became employees of the state. The French state wanted to control the influence of religion and even banned public worship, whereas many American colonies were established because colonists were pursuing religious freedom.)*

History Background

Catholic Protest Many historians consider the Civil Constitution of the Clergy to be the first major blunder of the National Assembly. Less than half the French clergy and only seven of the more than 100 French bishops took the oath to support the Civil Constitution. Though the government declared that clerics who opposed the Constitution were "refractory" and removed them from office, these clerics defiantly continued to perform their duties. Pope Pius VI condemned the Civil Constitution of the Clergy and declared all of its provisions void. French Catholics therefore faced a conflict between political loyalty and religious devotion. This caused a divide in the French population between those who supported the constitutional priests and those who followed the refractory glory.

Answers

Describe *They felt the king, who lived a life of luxury at Versailles, was out of touch with what was really happening in the country.*

Analyze Charts *Sample answer: A New Legislative Assembly had the power to make laws and collect taxes.*

Describe *The National Assembly put the Church under state control and sold off its lands. It also made priests and bishops paid government officials, and dissolved convents and monasteries.*

Topic 12 Lesson 6

SYNTHESIZE

Online Project the **Digital Activity: Events of the French Revolution**. Fill out the organizer with information as a class. *(The graphic organizer should include these stages: Louis XVI Calls the Estates-General; Tennis Court Oath; Storming the Bastille; Constitution of 1791.)* Ask students the critical-thinking question: Do you think the French Revolution was inevitable? *(Answers will vary but might mention that if the king had not been ineffective with regard to economic challenges, the outcome might have been different.)*

Ask students to recall the Topic Essential Question, "How much power should the government have?" Direct students' attention to the infographic "The French Constitution of 1791." Ask students to rank each provision by what they believe is important in relation to government power. Discuss their answers as a class.

DEMONSTRATE

Online Assign the **Digital Lesson Quiz** for this lesson if you haven't already done so. Students will be offered automatic remediation or enrichment based on their score.

Pose these questions to the class on the Discussion Board:

Predict Consequences Do you think that King Louis XVI could have enacted any social or economic reforms that might have prevented the Revolution? What might those reforms have been? *(Students might mention more equitable taxation, equality under the law, and more of a say in the workings of government policy.)*

Summarize What specific role did the American Revolution play in the direction the French Revolution took? *(Students might say that the American Revolution was the first time that the ideals of the Enlightenment were put into practice. As a result, the French were determined to also create a government based on the ideals of liberty, freedom, and popular sovereignty.)*

Topic Inquiry

Have students continue their investigations for the Topic Inquiry.

>> Revolutionaries captured King Louis XVI as he tried to escape.

in government. At the same time, it put power in the hands of men with the means and leisure to serve in government.

The Royal Family Tries to Escape Meanwhile, Marie Antoinette and others had been urging the king to escape their humiliating situation. Louis finally gave in. One night in June 1791, a coach rolled north from Paris toward the border. Inside sat the king disguised as a servant, the queen dressed as a governess, and the royal children.

The attempted escape failed. In a town along the way, Louis's disguise was uncovered by someone who held up a piece of currency with the king's face on it. A company of soldiers escorted the royal family back to Paris, as onlooking crowds hurled insults at the king. In place of the old shouts of "Long Live the King!" people cried, "Long Live the Nation." To many, Louis's dash to the border showed that he was a traitor to the revolution. As new crises arose, the French Revolution entered a new, more radical phase.

? DESCRIBE How did the National Assembly try to reform the French Catholic Church?

ASSESSMENT

1. **Apply Concepts** How did France's social divisions in the late 1700s contribute to the revolution?
2. **Draw Conclusions** Why was the conflict between the clergy and the Third Estate the most divisive in the course of the revolution?
3. **Compare** How might the complaints of a peasant and a merchant compare during the revolution?
4. **Identify Cause and Effect** What characteristics of the Third Estate helped fuel the Revolution?
5. **Connect** What did the Tennis Court Oath foretell about the coming events of the French Revolution?

Assessment

1. Social and economic inequity between the classes created a great deal of friction.
2. Most French were skeptical of the Church. The clergy exerted great influence on the government and enjoyed enormous wealth and privilege, including owning 10 percent of the land and paying no direct taxes. The resulting tax burden on the Third Estate was great.
3. While both would want more equality, the peasant might want better wages and the merchant might want a more active political role in the nation's affairs.
4. Most of those in the Third Estate were poor. They suffered the most when things went financially out of control or when famine rocked the country.
5. The oath underscored that the majority of Frenchmen would stand together until the government produced a new constitution that contained reforms.

12.7 The outbreak of the French Revolution stirred debate all over Europe and the United States. Supporters of the Enlightenment, such as Thomas Jefferson, saw the French experiment as the dawn of a new age for justice and equality. European rulers and nobles, however, denounced the French Revolution.

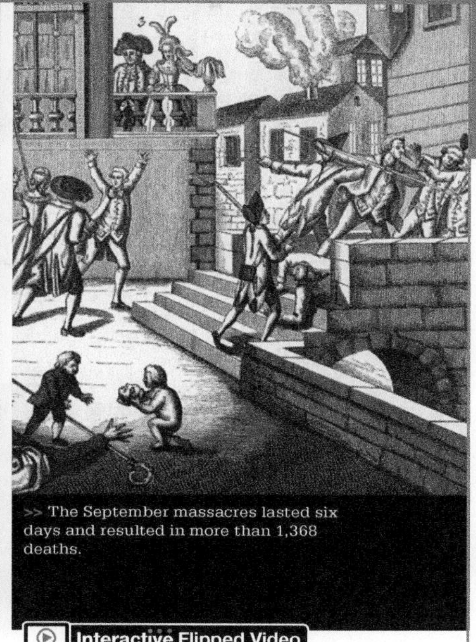

>> The September massacres lasted six days and resulted in more than 1,368 deaths.

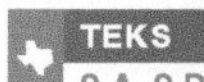

Interactive Flipped Video

A Radical Phase

TEKS 9.A, 9.D

>> **Objectives**

Explain why the French Revolution entered a more radical phase.

Understand how radicals abolished the French monarchy.

Analyze the causes and course of the Reign of Terror.

Describe France under the Directory.

Identify how the French Revolution changed life in France.

>> **Key Terms**

émigré
sans-culottes
Jacobin
suffrage
Maximilien Robespierre
Reign of Terror
guillotine
Napoleon Bonaparte
Nationalism
Marseilles

Radicals Gain Strength

Fear of the "French Plague" European rulers were horrified by the French Revolution, which threatened absolute monarchy. They increased border patrol to stop the spread of the "French plague." Fueling those fears were the horror stories that were told by **émigrés** (EM ih grayz)—nobles, clergy, and others who had fled France. Émigrés reported attacks on their privileges, their property, their religion, and even their lives. Even "enlightened" rulers turned against France. Catherine the Great of Russia burned Voltaire's letters and locked up critics.

Edmund Burke, a British statesman who earlier had defended the American Revolution, bitterly condemned revolutionaries in Paris. He predicted all too accurately that the revolution would become more violent. "When ancient opinions and rules of life are taken away," he warned, "we have no compass to govern us."

Threats from Abroad The failed escape of Louis XVI brought further hostile rumblings from abroad. In August 1791, the king of Prussia and the emperor of Austria—who was Marie Antoinette's brother—issued the Declaration of Pilnitz. In this document, the two monarchs threatened to protect the French monarchy.

517

PEARSON realize www.PearsonTexas.com Access your Digital Lesson.

Aa Vocabulary Builder

1. Have students pronounce the following academic vocabulary terms in this lesson and clarify the part of speech. For difficult or polysyllabic words, break them into syllables and pronounce them with the students.
2. Explain what the word means in common "student-friendly" language using synonyms and antonyms when possible. Provide concrete examples to clarify the meaning, and rephrase the definition.

radical: extreme departure from the usual or traditional

moderates: those in politics who are not excessive or unreasonable

dictatorial: imposing will on others

suppressed: prevented something from happening

Topic 12 Lesson 7

A Radical Phase

CONNECT

Preview Have students preview the **Lesson Objectives** and the list of **Key Terms**.

Students can also preview all the **Key Terms and Academic Vocabulary** using the **Interactive Reading Notepad** on the digital course or preview a summary of the lesson in the **Reading and Note Taking Study Guide**.

Online Use the **Editable Presentation** found on the digital course to present the main ideas for this lesson.

Start Up Activity

The only member of the royal family to survive the French Revolution was the king and queen's young daughter, Marie-Therese Charlotte de France. Read this excerpt from her memoirs describing her brother's life in prison: "The young prince was left to the brutal treatment of that monster Simon, a former shoe-maker. . . . During the winter, my brother suffered several attacks of fever; he was always close to the fire. . . . He grew weaker and weaker and died in agony. . . . I do not believe he was poisoned."

Ask: What picture did Marie-Therese paint of her brother's life in prison? Was this a just or an unjust way to treat a former ruler's family? Explain. *(Students' answers will vary. Some will focus on the violence that the king's family faced, while others might focus on the injustices of the monarchy.)*

Discuss What was her motivation in writing the letter about her family's treatment in prison? What bias does she have? What does the letter say about the radical turn the French Revolution took? *(Possible answer: Marie-Therese's letter was biased because she wanted to portray her family sympathetically. Her letter also underscores the brutality of the revolutionaries as the Revolution took a more radical turn.)*

Online You can also project the **Start Up Activity** from the course.

INVESTIGATE

Have students read the lesson using the **Reading and Note Taking Study Guide** to help them take notes and understand the text as they read.

Radicals Gain Strength

The French Revolution had taken a more radical turn by the summer of 1791. By this time, the Revolution had stirred debate across Europe.

Topic 12 Lesson 7

Key Terms

Ask students to find the key term **sans-culottes** (in bold) in the text. The term distinguished radical members of the working class, who wore long trousers *(pantalons)*, from more moderate, often middle-class revolutionaries, who wore knee breeches *(culottes)*.

Guided Reading and Discussion

Ask: Why did European rulers and nobles denounce the French Revolution? *(They feared that ideas of revolution would spread to their countries and bring an end to their power and privileges.)* What factors lead to the radical phase of the Revolution? *(continuing economic problems and hostile factions competing for power)*

The declaration may have been mostly a bluff, but revolutionaries in France took the threat seriously and prepared for war. The revolution was about to enter a new, more radical phase.

Radicals Seek Power In October 1791, the newly elected Legislative Assembly took office. Faced with crises at home and abroad, it survived for less than a year. Economic problems fed renewed turmoil.

Assignats (AS ig nats), the revolutionary currency, dropped in value, causing prices to rise rapidly. Uncertainty about prices led to hoarding and caused additional food shortages.

In Paris and other cities, working-class men and women, called **sans-culottes** (sanz koo LAHTS), pushed the revolution into more radical action. Sans-culottes means "without breeches." Men wore long trousers instead of the fancy knee breeches that men of the upper class wore. By 1791, many sans-culottes demanded an end to the monarchy and the creation of a republic. They also wanted the government to guarantee them a living wage.

Within the Legislative Assembly, several hostile factions competed for power. The sans-culottes found support among radicals, especially the Jacobins. A revolutionary political club, the **Jacobins** were mostly middle-class lawyers or intellectuals. They used pamphleteers and sympathetic newspaper editors to advance the republican cause.

Opposing the radicals were moderate reformers and officials who wanted no more reforms at all. The radicals soon held the upper hand in the Legislative Assembly.

War Breaks Out In April 1792, the war of words between French revolutionaries and European monarchs moved onto the battlefield. Eager to spread the revolution and destroy tyranny abroad, the Legislative Assembly declared war first on Austria and then on Prussia, Britain, and other states. The great powers expected to win an easy victory against France, a land divided by revolution. In fact, the fighting that began in 1792 lasted on and off until 1815.

The war abroad heightened tensions in Paris. Well-trained Prussian forces were cutting down raw French recruits. In addition, royalist officers were deserting the French army, joining émigrés and others hoping to restore the king's power.

CITE EVIDENCE How did the monarchs of Europe react to the French Revolution?

>> Europe in the 1790s was dominated by monarchies. **Analyze Maps** Why do you suppose France's neighbors were afraid of the French Revolution?

Absolutism and Revolution 518 12.7 A Radical Phase

D Differentiate Challenge/Gifted Ask students to act as an American tourist in France during the radical days of the Revolution. Have them write a letter home describing their feelings about what they are witnessing. Have them compare the French Revolution to the American Revolution, listing any differences or similarities.

Answers

Cite Evidence *Europe's monarchs denounced the Revolution, fearing its ideals would spread. The king of Prussia and the emperor of Austria, for example, threatened to intervene to protect the French monarchy.*

Analyze Maps *Students might say the proximity of France to the surrounding monarchies caused great fear throughout Europe.*

The Monarchy Is Abolished

In 1793, the Revolution entered a radical phase. For a year, France experienced one of the bloodiest regimes in its long history as determined leaders sought to extend and preserve the Revolution.

New Outbreaks of Violence Battle disasters overseas quickly inflamed revolutionaries in Paris. They thought the king was in league with the enemies. On August 10, 1792, a crowd of Parisians stormed the royal palace of the Tuileries and slaughtered the king's guards. The royal family fled to the Legislative Assembly.

A month later, citizens attacked prisons that held nobles and priests accused of political offenses. More than 1,000 prisoners were killed, including many ordinary criminals.

Historians disagree about the people who carried out these "September massacres." Some call them bloodthirsty mobs. Others describe them as patriots defending France. In fact, most were ordinary citizens fired to fury by real and imagined grievances.

The National Convention Backed by Paris crowds, radicals then took control of the Assembly. Radicals called for the election of a new legislative body called the National Convention. **Suffrage**, the right to vote, was to be extended to all male citizens, not just to property owners.

The Convention that met in September 1792 was a more radical body than earlier Assemblies. It voted to abolish the monarchy and establish a republic. Deputies then drew up a new constitution. The Jacobins, who controlled the Convention, set out to erase all traces of the old order. They seized lands of nobles and abolished titles of nobility. All men and women were called "Citizen." Louis XVI became Citizen Capet, from the dynasty that ruled France during the Middle Ages.

Execution of a King and Queen During the early months of the Republic, the Convention also put Louis XVI on trial as a traitor to France. The king was convicted by a single vote and sentenced to death.

On a foggy morning in January 1793, Louis mounted a scaffold in a public square in Paris. He started to speak, "Frenchmen, I die innocent. I pardon the authors of my death. I pray God that the blood about to be spilt will never fall upon the head of France. . . ." Then a roll of drums drowned out his words. Moments later, the king was beheaded. The executioner lifted the king's head by its hair and held it before the crowd.

In October, Marie Antoinette was also executed. The popular press celebrated her death. The queen, however, showed great dignity as she went to her death. Her son, who might once have become Louis XVII, died of unknown causes in the dungeons of the Revolution.

>> Marie Antoinette's lavish lifestyle and disregard for the masses contributed to her unpopularity and later execution.

CONTRAST What was the main difference between earlier Assemblies and the National Convention, which met in September 1792?

The Reign of Terror

By early 1793, danger threatened France on all sides. The country was at war with much of Europe, including Britain, the Netherlands, Spain, and Prussia. In the Vendée (vahn DAY) region of France, royalists and priests led peasants in rebellion against the government.

In Paris, the sans-culottes demanded relief from food shortages and inflation. The Convention itself was bitterly divided between Jacobins and a rival group, the Girondins.

Committee of Public Safety To deal with the threats to France, the Convention created the Committee of Public Safety. The 12-member committee had almost absolute power. Preparing France for all-out war, it ordered all citizens to contribute to the war effort. They

Topic 12 Lesson 7

The Monarchy Is Abolished

Remind students that the radicals of the French Revolution tried to export the ideals of the Revolution to other countries and attempted to destroy Europe's monarchies. Explain that by 1792, the radicals controlled the National Convention. One of the Convention's first moves was to abolish the monarchy and establish a republic.

Analyze Images

Direct students' attention to the image of Marie Antoinette on this page. Ask students to take a stand on the following question: Should France's revolutionaries have executed Louis XVI and his family—yes or no? Ask students to divide into two groups based on their answer and move to separate areas of the classroom. Ask a representative from each side to present and defend the group's point of view.

Guided Reading and Discussion

Apply Concepts What ideas of the Enlightenment did the National Assembly put into action in 1792? *(Students might answer that the National Assembly extended suffrage and also established a republic.)*

The Reign of Terror

In the fall of 1793 and well into 1794, the French Revolution took a radical turn. The Committee of Public Safety rounded up suspected persons, sentencing many to death for being traitors to the Revolution.

Answers

Contrast *Controlled by the Jacobins, the Convention was more radical than previous Assemblies, as it was set up to erase all traces of the old French order.*

Online Project the **Interactive Gallery: The Reign of Terror**, and click through all the hotspots so students can become familiar with the Reign of Terror.

ACTIVE CLASSROOM

Pair students to complete this activity. One student should act as a foreign journalist in France interviewing Robespierre about the Reign of Terror. The other student should act as Robespierre. When the interview is over, have students share the questions and answers with the class.

Guided Reading and Discussion

Identify Cause and Effect Define *nationalism*. Ask students to explain the influence of nationalism on the French Revolution during its most radical phase. *(Nationalism is loyalty to one's country. Nationalism spread as the radicals tried to purify the Revolution, which ultimately led to the Reign of Terror.)*

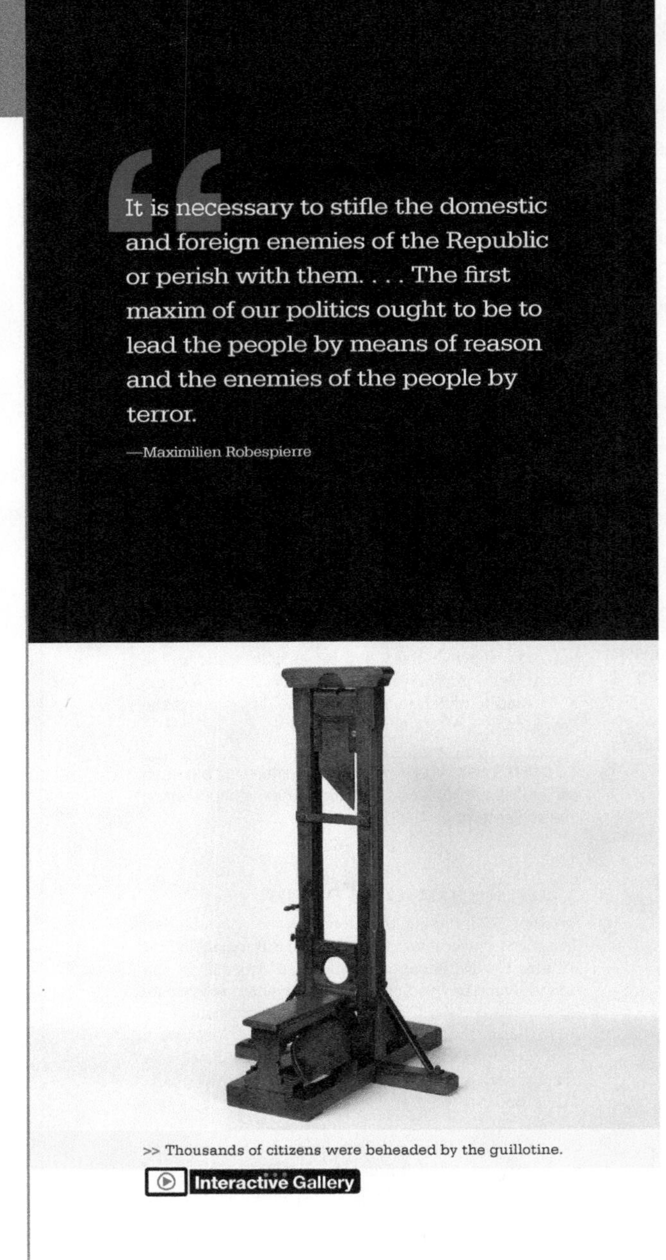
“It is necessary to stifle the domestic and foreign enemies of the Republic or perish with them. . . . The first maxim of our politics ought to be to lead the people by means of reason and the enemies of the people by terror.
—Maximilien Robespierre

>> Thousands of citizens were beheaded by the guillotine.

Interactive Gallery

urged young men to go into battle, women to make tents or serve in hospitals, and children to turn old lint into linen.

Spurred by revolutionary fervor, recruits marched off to defend the republic. Young officers developed effective tactics to win battles with masses of ill-trained but patriotic forces. Soon, French armies overran the Netherlands. They later invaded Italy. At home, they crushed peasant revolts. European monarchs shuddered as the revolutionaries carried "freedom fever" into conquered lands.

Robespierre, the Incorruptible At home, the government battled counterrevolutionaries under the guiding hand of **Maximilien Robespierre** (ROHBZ pyehr). Robespierre, a shrewd lawyer and politician, quickly rose to the leadership of the Committee of Public Safety. Among Jacobins, his selfless dedication to the revolution earned him the nickname "the incorruptible." His enemies called him a tyrant.

"Death to the Traitors" Robespierre was one of the chief architects of the **Reign of Terror**, which lasted from September 1793 to July 1794. Revolutionary courts conducted hasty trials. Spectators greeted death sentences with cries of "Hail the Republic!" or "Death to the traitors!" In a speech given on February 5, 1794, Robespierre explained that the terror was necessary to protect the Revolution and achieve its goals.

During the Reign of Terror, about 300,000 citizens were arrested. About 17,000 were executed. They included nobles and clergy, peasants, and sans-culottes, along with middle-class citizens who had once supported the Revolution.

> It is necessary to stifle the domestic and foreign enemies of the Republic or perish with them. . . . The first maxim of our politics ought to be to lead the people by means of reason and the enemies of the people by terror.
>
> —Maximilien Robespierre

Many were victims of mistaken identity or were falsely accused by their

English Language Proficiency Standards

Reading 4.E.1

Beginning Read aloud (or provide) a translated version of the introductory paragraph of "The Reign of Terror" to students. Then read the same paragraph in English. Have students repeat each sentence after you read it aloud. Allow students to use the translation or ask for help to clarify the meanings of challenging vocabulary. Have students summarize the text using a word or phrase in English.

Intermediate Before reading aloud in English, provide students with a translated version of the introductory paragraph of "The Reign of Terror." Then read the paragraph aloud in English, reading each sentence separately. Have students summarize the text in one sentence in English.

Advanced Read aloud the introductory paragraph of "The Reign of Terror." Then have students read the paragraph aloud together. Have partners take turns reading aloud. Let students work with bilingual dictionaries to support their understanding of unfamiliar words. Then, as a group, write a two- or three-sentence summary of the text.

Advanced High Have students take turns reading "The Reign of Terror" aloud to a partner. Partners should listen to and correct any mistakes in pronunciation and pacing. Let the partners write a brief summary of the text and read it to the group.

Topic 12 Lesson 7

neighbors. Many more were packed into hideous prisons, where deaths from disease were common.

The engine of the Terror was the **guillotine** (GIL uh teen). Its fast-falling blade extinguished life instantly. A member of the legislature, Dr. Joseph Guillotin (gee oh TAN), had introduced it as a more humane method of beheading than the uncertain ax. Still, the guillotine quickly became a symbol of horror.

Within a year, the Terror consumed those who initiated it. Weary of bloodshed and fearing for their own lives, members of the Convention turned on the Committee of Public Safety. On the night of July 27, 1794, Robespierre was arrested. The next day he was executed. After the heads of Robespierre and other radicals fell, executions slowed dramatically.

DRAW CONCLUSIONS How did radicals such as Robespierre justify the use of terror?

ELPS 4.E.1 Use a translation of the text or a bilingual dictionary to help you understand the content covered in *The Reign of Terror.*

>> The French Revolution began with the burning of the Bastille in 1789 and continued through the Reign of Terror. After the Terror, it moved into a third phase in which the government was headed by a five-man Directory.

Interactive Timeline

Reaction and the Directory

In reaction to the Terror, the Revolution entered a third stage. Middle class and professional people dominated this stage of the Revolution.

Moving away from the excesses of the Convention, moderates produced another constitution, the third since 1789. The Constitution of 1795 set up a five-man Directory and a two-house legislature elected by male citizens of property. The Directory held power from 1795 to 1799.

Weak, but willing to use force against its enemies, the Directory faced many challenges. Although France made peace with Prussia and Spain, the war continued with Austria and Great Britain. Corrupt leaders lined their own pockets but failed to solve pressing problems. When rising bread prices stirred hungry sans-culottes to riot, the Directory quickly suppressed them.

Another threat to the Directory was the revival of royalist feeling. Many émigrés were returning to France, and devout Catholics, who resented measures that had been taken against the Church, were welcoming them. In the election of 1797, supporters of a constitutional monarchy won the majority of seats in the legislature.

Despite its failings, the Directory consolidated many reforms of the National Convention. It set up a system of elite schools and helped the French economy to recover from the upheavals of the Terror. During the Directory, France had strengthened its armies and won several important battles.

As chaos threatened, politicians turned to **Napoleon Bonaparte,** a popular military hero who had won a series of brilliant victories against the Austrians in Italy. The politicians planned to use him to advance their own goals. To their dismay, however, before long Napoleon would outwit them all to become ruler of France.

IDENTIFY CAUSE AND EFFECT Why did Catholics welcome the return of the émigrés?

The Revolution Transforms France

By 1799, the 10-year-old French Revolution had dramatically changed France. It had dislodged the old social order, overthrown the monarchy, and brought the Church under state control.

New symbols such as the red "liberty caps" and the tricolor confirmed the liberty and equality of all male citizens. The new title "citizen" applied to people of all social classes. Elaborate fashions and powdered wigs gave way to the practical clothes and simple haircuts of the sans-culottes.

Reaction and the Directory

Explain to students that in 1795 there was a new constitution in France, which set up a five-man Directory. The Directory, however, was weak and corrupt. It faced many internal and external challenges. The Directory's failings eventually led to the rise of Napoleon Bonaparte.

Guided Reading and Discussion

Identify Cause and Effect Define *émigré*. Ask students to explain how returning émigrés presented a threat to the Directory. *(Students might say that many émigrés were devout Catholics who resented the measures France's revolutionaries took against the Church. As a result, the émigrés wanted the monarchy to return.)*

The Revolution Transforms France

Remind students that the French Revolution was a series of events that upended the old order in France. The monarchy was abolished, the French Catholic Church was put under state control, and a republic was established.

Online Project the **Interactive Timeline: The French Revolution Enters a More Radical Phase**, and have students place the correct event in the correct time period.

ACTIVE CLASSROOM

List these changes to French society: abolishing monarchy; curtailing Church power; abolishing the feudal system; creating equality before the law; opening careers to talent; creating a sense of national pride; creating a government based on popular sovereignty. Tell students that they will perform a Rank It activity in which they rank the items based on their importance. Ask students to provide justification for the ranking they made.

History Background

Women in the Revolution As the revolution progressed, women's right to express their views in public came under attack. In 1793, a committee of the National Convention declared that women lacked "the moral and physical strength necessary to practice political rights." Women's revolutionary clubs were banned and violators were arrested. Women were imprisoned and sent to the guillotine.

However, women did gain some rights for a time. The government made divorce easier, a move that was aimed at weakening Church authority. Government officials also allowed women to inherit property, hoping to undermine the tradition of nobles leaving large estates to their oldest sons. However, these reforms and others did not last long after Napoleon gained power.

Answers

Draw Conclusions *Only through the use of terror, the revolutionaries said, could France achieve the ideal republic.*

Identify Cause and Effect *Catholics resented the impact the Revolution had had on the Church and thought that welcoming the émigrés, who supported the monarchy, would mean a return to the old order and restore the power of the Church.*

Topic 12 Lesson 7

Guided Reading and Discussion

Explain that the French Revolution came after the American Revolution. In both, revolutions grew out of Enlightenment ideals such as liberty, freedom, and the rights of citizens; calls for reform led to a complete change of government; and people opposed oppressive monarchies and high taxes.

Ask: What kind of government did both countries set up? *(a republican form of government)* How was the American experience with republican government different from that of France? *(In France, the first republic did not last, but in the United States, it has lasted until the present.)* Tell students that the revolutions differed in other ways as well. American colonists saw themselves as citizens of Britain and entitled to the rights guaranteed by the Magna Carta and the Glorious Revolution.

Compare and Contrast How did American and French revolutionaries deal with the role of the church in their respective societies? *(Students might say that the Civil Constitution of the Clergy put the French Catholic Church under state control. In America, revolutionary leaders kept the church and state separate, forbidding the state from establishing a church or interfering with freedom of religion.)*

Nationalism Spreads Revolution and war gave the French people a strong sense of national identity. In earlier times, people had felt loyalty to local authorities. As monarchs centralized power, loyalty shifted to the king or queen. Instead, the government rallied sons and daughters of the Revolution to defend the nation itself.

Nationalism, a strong feeling of pride in and devotion to one's country, spread throughout France. The French people attended civic festivals that celebrated the nation and the Revolution. A variety of dances and songs on themes of the Revolution became immensely popular.

By 1793, France was a nation in arms. From the port city of **Marseilles** (mahr say), troops marched to a rousing new song. It urged the "children of the fatherland" to march against the "bloody banner of tyranny." This song, "La Marseillaise" (mahr say ez), would later become the French national anthem.

Social Reform Revolutionaries pushed for social reform and religious toleration. They set up state schools to replace religious ones and organized systems to help the poor, old soldiers, and war widows. With a major slave revolt raging in the colony of St. Domingue (Haiti), the government also abolished slavery in France's Caribbean colonies.

Religion and the Revolution During the Revolution, different governments pursued different policies toward religion. The Civil Constitution of the Clergy put the Catholic Church under state control. Unlike the United States whose Constitution forbade the establishment of any official state church, France supported the French Catholic Church by paying the salaries of the clergy.

Many revolutionaries embraced the ideas of religious toleration. Yet this Enlightenment ideal often fell victim to politics. During the radical phase, leaders banned public religious worship and removed the names of saints from streets and buildings. Any who opposed these moves faced persecution or death. This effort to de-Christianize France had little popular support. In the end, the Catholic Church was restored with limited rights.

Comparison with the American Revolution The French Revolution came on the heels of the American Revolution. The two revolutions had both similarities and differences.

Both grew out of Enlightenment ideals such as liberty, freedom, and the rights of citizens. Both began with calls for reform, but ended up with a complete change of government. In the colonies and in France, people rose up against oppressive monarchies and high taxes. Each revolution broke out after years of increasing

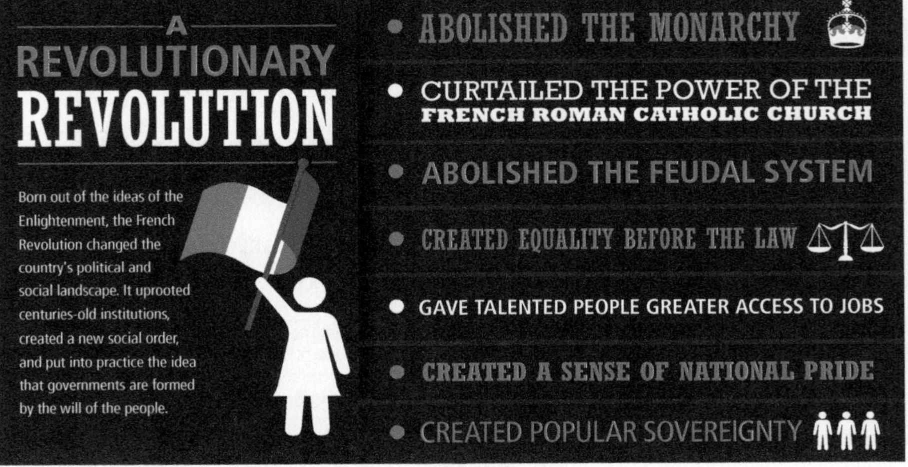

A
REVOLUTIONARY
REVOLUTION
Born out of the ideas of the Enlightenment, the French Revolution changed the country's political and social landscape. It uprooted centuries-old institutions, created a new social order, and put into practice the idea that governments are formed by the will of the people.
ABOLISHED THE MONARCHY
CURTAILED THE POWER OF THE FRENCH ROMAN CATHOLIC CHURCH
ABOLISHED THE FEUDAL SYSTEM
CREATED EQUALITY BEFORE THE LAW
GAVE TALENTED PEOPLE GREATER ACCESS TO JOBS
CREATED A SENSE OF NATIONAL PRIDE
CREATED POPULAR SOVEREIGNTY

>> **Analyze Charts** The French Revolution changed the country's political and social landscape. How did the Revolution change the social order?

Assessment

1. In the view of the radicals, the only way a popular government could remain in control was to terrorize its enemies. In reaction, moderates moved away from the excesses of the Revolution, producing a new constitution.
2. Because the Committee of Public Safety was tasked with dealing with threats to the Revolution and was granted almost absolute power. The Committee was put in charge of trials and executions, which resulted in the Terror.

Answers

Analyze Charts *Students should understand that the French Revolution did away with the old social order. Among other things, the Revolution made sure all citizens now enjoyed equal rights, while providing equitable taxation. The Church no longer dominated life, nor did the monarchy.*

discontent with powerful rulers who imposed their will on the people.

In both countries, the people set up a republican form of government. In France, the first republic did not last, but in the United States, it has lasted until the present. The political traditions and social climate of France and the colonies differed. Colonists saw themselves as citizens of Britain and entitled to the rights won long ago by the British people through the Magna Carta and the Glorious Revolution. In France, absolute monarchs had ruled for centuries.

In both England and pre-revolutionary France, the state supported an official church. In America, although many of the leaders of the Revolution were deeply religious, the First Amendment to the Constitution forbade the establishment of any state-supported church. In France, a state-supported Catholic Church remained a powerful force for more than a century.

ANALYZE INFORMATION Describe several ways the Revolution changed French society.

>> During the radical phase of the French Revolution, many Christian churches were renamed Temples of Reason. Religious symbols were covered. On some churches, the revolutionary motto "Liberté, egalité, fraternité" was inscribed on the stone facade.

ASSESSMENT

1. **Compare and Contrast** Compare and contrast the views of France's radical revolutionaries to the views of its moderates.
2. **Check Understanding** Why was the Committee of Public Safety allowed to terrorize France during the Reign of Terror?
3. **Describe** How did the Directory's actions ultimately lead to the rise of Napoleon?
4. **Describe** What actions did the French take after the Revolution to show their patriotism?
5. **Identify Cause and Effect** What was it about the nature of the French Revolution that led to political and social reform?

Topic 12 Lesson 7

SYNTHESIZE

Online Project the **Digital Activity: The Reign of Terror**. Have students fill out the graphic organizer for the events of the Reign of Terror. *(Possible answers: Individuals/Groups: Robespierre, Jacobins, National Assembly, King Louis XVI, émigrés, sans-culottes, Committee of Public Safety, Directory, bourgeoisie; Events: September massacres, execution of Louis XVI and Marie Antoinette, creation of the Committee of Public Safety, Robespierre gains power, trials, imprisonment and executions of those considered traitors to the Revolution; Outcomes: Revolution enters a third stage, new constitution sets up five-person Directory, public backlash against the Terror, Robespierre and other radicals lose their heads, the Age of Napoleon begins)* Then ask: Do you think the Reign of Terror helped or hindered the cause of reform in revolutionary France? *(Students might say it hindered the cause because of the Reign of Terror's indiscriminate violence. Some students might say it helped the cause because the Reign of Terror resulted in a more reformist constitution.)*

DEMONSTRATE

Online Assign the **Digital Lesson Quiz** for this lesson if you haven't already done so. Students will be offered automatic remediation or enrichment based on their score.

Pose these questions to the class on the Discussion Board:

Classify List the three most important aspects of the Reign of Terror. Which was most important, and why? How did the Reign of Terror lead to the emergence of Napoleon as France's leader? *(Students may mention the backlash against the Terror and the need for a strong leader amid the chaos.)*

Topic Inquiry

Have students continue their investigations for the Topic Inquiry.

3. The Directory was weak but dictatorial. Its leaders were corrupt and failed to solve the country's pressing problems. Faced with a revival of royalist feelings, the election of 1797 led to supporters of a constitutional monarchy winning the majority of seats in the legislature. The result was political chaos, which led to the rise of Napoleon.
4. When the Revolution ended, a feeling of nationalism swept the countryside. People showed their patriotism with festivals, songs, and dances relating to revolutionary themes. They did away with the fancy clothes and powdered wigs of the old order.
5. The French Revolution sprung from the seeds of the Enlightenment. As a result, the revolt replaced an unresponsive government with a government that was more in touch with the needs of its citizens, who pushed for social change and religious tolerance.

Answers

Analyze Information *Among other things, the Revolution abolished the French monarchy; put the Catholic Church under state control; overthrew the country's social order; and created a sense of nationalism.*

Topic 12 Lesson 8

The Age of Napoleon

CONNECT

Preview Have students preview the **Lesson Objectives** and the list of **Key Terms**.

Students can also preview all the **Key Terms** and **Academic Vocabulary** using the **Interactive Reading Notepad** on the digital course or preview a summary of the lesson in the **Reading and Note Taking Study Guide**.

Online Use the **Editable Presentation** found on the digital course to present the main ideas for this lesson.

Start Up Activity

Read the following statement made by influential French writer Madame de Staël:

"I do not believe that when Bonaparte became head of the government he had yet formulated the plan for a universal monarchy, but I do believe what he himself said to one of my friends, a few days after the 18 Brumaire [the date Napoleon overthrew the Directory]. 'It is necessary,' he said, 'to do something new every three months, in order to captivate the imagination of the French nation, with whom any-one who stands still is lost.' His system was to encroach [intrude] daily upon France's liberty and Europe's independence. . . . By alternating between cunning and force he has subjugated [conquered] Europe."

Ask students to describe the writer's viewpoint. *(Madame de Staël is critical of Napoleon and makes him sound like a tyrant.)*

Online You can also project the **Start Up Activity** from the course.

INVESTIGATE

Have students read the lesson using the **Reading and Note Taking Study Guide** to help them take notes and understand the text as they read.

Napoleon on the Rise

Explain to students that from 1799 to 1815, Napoleon Bonaparte dominated France and Europe. During the French Revolution, Napoleon had become a military hero, ultimately returning to France and crowning himself emperor. Napoleon's rise to power was fueled by his success on the battlefield, his personal political ambition, and his popularity with the French people.

>> Napoleon was a military genius who dominated Europe for more than a decade.

Interactive Flipped Video

12.8 From 1799 to 1815, Napoleon Bonaparte dominated France and Europe. A hero to some, an evil force to others, he gave his name to the final phase of the French Revolution—the Age of Napoleon.

TEKS
9.B

>> Objectives

Describe how Napoleon Bonaparte rose to power.

Explain the impact of Napoleon and the Napoleonic Wars.

Identify the reasons for Napoleon's fall from power.

Understand how the Congress of Vienna tried to restore order to Europe.

>> Key Terms

plebiscite
Napoleonic Code
Napoleonic Wars
annex
Continental System
guerrilla warfare
abdicate
Congress of Vienna
legitimacy
Concert of Europe

The Age of Napoleon

Napoleon on the Rise

Early Years Napoleon was born in Corsica, a French-ruled island in the Mediterranean. At age nine, he was sent to France to be trained for a military career. When the revolution broke out, he was an ambitious 20-year-old lieutenant, eager to make a name for himself.

Napoleon favored the Jacobins and republican rule. However, he found the conflicting ideas and personalities of the French Revolution confusing. He wrote to his brother in 1793: "Since one must take sides, one might as well choose the side that is victorious, the side which devastates, loots, and burns. Considering the alternative, it is better to eat than be eaten."

Military Success During the turmoil of the Revolution, Napoleon rose quickly in the army. In December 1793, he drove British forces out of the French port of Toulon (too LOHN).

He then went on to win several dazzling victories against the Austrians, capturing most of northern Italy and forcing the Hapsburg emperor to make peace. Hoping to disrupt British trade with India, he led an expedition to Egypt in 1798. The Egyptian campaign proved to be a disaster, but Napoleon managed to hide stories of the worst losses from his admirers in France.

PEARSON realize. www.PearsonTexas.com Access your Digital Lesson.

524

Aa Vocabulary Builder

1. Have students pronounce the following academic vocabulary terms in this lesson and clarify the part of speech. For difficult or polysyllabic words, break them into syllables and pronounce them with the students.
2. Explain what the word means in common "student-friendly" language using synonyms and antonyms when possible. Provide concrete examples to clarify the meaning, and rephrase the definition.

anticipate: to foresee or expect

coronation: a ceremony in which a member of a royal family becomes king or queen

despotism: the use of power in a cruel and unreasonable way

Success fueled Napoleon's ambition. By 1799, he moved from victorious general to political leader. That year, he helped overthrow the weak Directory and set up a three-man governing board known as the Consulate. Another constitution was drawn up, but Napoleon soon took the title First Consul. In 1800, he forced Spain to return Louisiana Territory to France. In 1802, Napoleon had himself named consul for life.

Napoleon Crowns Himself Emperor Two years later, Napoleon had acquired enough power to assume the title Emperor of the French. He invited the pope to preside over his coronation in Paris. During the ceremony, however, Napoleon took the crown from the pope's hands and placed it on his own head. By this action, Napoleon meant to show that he owed his throne to no one but himself.

At each step on his rise to power, Napoleon had held a **plebiscite** (PLEB uh syt), or popular vote by ballot. Each time, the French strongly supported him, even after he had assumed absolute power as emperor. To understand why, we must look at his policies.

CITE EVIDENCE How did Napoleon rise to power so quickly in France?

>> At Napoleon's coronation, he placed the crown on his own head to show that he was the source of his own power, not the pope.

Napoleon Reforms France

Napoleon consolidated his power by strengthening the central government. Order, security, and efficiency replaced liberty, equality, and fraternity as the slogans of the new regime.

Social and Economic Reforms To restore economic prosperity, Napoleon controlled prices, encouraged new industry, and built roads and canals. He set up a system of public schools under strict government control to ensure well-trained officials and military officers.

At the same time, Napoleon backed off from some of the Revolution's social reforms. He made peace with the Catholic Church in the Concordat of 1801. The Concordat kept the Church under state control but recognized religious freedom for Catholics. Revolutionaries who opposed the Church denounced the agreement, but Catholics welcomed it.

Napoleon won support across class lines. He encouraged émigrés to return, provided they take an oath of loyalty. Peasants were relieved when he recognized their right to lands they had bought from the Church and nobles during the Revolution.

The middle class, who had benefited most from the Revolution, approved of Napoleon's economic reforms and the restoration of order after years of chaos.

>> In 1798, the French army invaded Egypt, hoping to disrupt British trade routes to India.

Topic 12 Lesson 8

Analyze Images

Direct students' attention to the image of a young Napoleon on the previous page. Have them compare this with the image on this page of Napoleon dressed in luxurious robes and with a crown on his head. Ask students to describe the differences between the two images.

Guided Reading and Discussion

Discuss Have students explain the following statement made by Napoleon after one of his earliest victories in Lodi, Italy: "From that moment, I foresaw what I might be. Already I felt the earth flee from beneath me, as if I were being carried into the sky." *(Students might say that after that victory, Napoleon believed he was destined for great things.)*

Napoleon Reforms France

Tell students that Napoleon undertook social and economic reforms at home, particularly through the Napoleonic Code.

D Differentiate Challenge Ask students to write a diary entry from the perspective of a soldier in Napoleon's army about the soldier's feelings regarding Napoleon as emperor of France. Have them describe what Napoleon meant to them on the battlefield and what he could mean to France as its ruler.

Answers

Cite Evidence *Napoleon's rise to power was fueled in part by his success on the battlefield, his personal political ambition, and his popularity with the French people.*

Topic 12 Lesson 8

Key Terms

Ask students to find the key term **Napoleonic Code** (in bold) in the text and explain its meaning. Point out that previous proclamations and laws in France, America, and England were not referred to by the name of any particular leader (the Declaration of the Rights of Man and the Citizen is one example). Have students predict what having Napoleon's name attached to the Napoleonic Code might indicate about its laws.

ACTIVE CLASSROOM

Direct students' attention to the chart on this page that outlines some of the aspects of the Napoleonic Code. Divide the class into three or four groups, and give members of each group a sticky note. Ask each member of the groups to come up with a law that embodies the principles of the Enlightenment, including equality of all citizens before the law and religious toleration. Group members should then put their laws together into a "code." Have each group share its code with the rest of the class.

Guided Reading and Discussion

Ask: What do you think was the main reason Napoleon was able to gain absolute power in France? *(Sample answer: He had the support of the French people.)* Why do you think Napoleon was so popular? *(Sample answer: He was popular with all classes; he took charge when people longed for order.)*

Napoleon also opened jobs to all, based on talent, a popular policy among those who remembered the old aristocratic monopoly of power.

The Napoleonic Code Among Napoleon's most lasting reforms was a new code of laws, popularly called the **Napoleonic Code**. It embodied Enlightenment principles such as the equality of all citizens before the law, religious toleration, and the abolition of feudalism.

At the same time, the Napoleonic Code undid some reforms of the French Revolution. Women, for example, lost most of their newly gained rights and could not exercise the rights of citizenship. Male heads of households regained complete authority over their wives and children. Again, Napoleon valued order and authority over individual rights.

DESCRIBE What were some of the reforms Napoleon introduced?

The Napoleonic Wars

From 1804 to 1812, Napoleon furthered his reputation on the battlefield. In a series of conflicts known as the **Napoleonic Wars,** he battled the combined forces of the greatest European powers. He took great risks and even suffered huge losses. "I grew up on the field of battle," he once said, "and a man such as I am cares little for the life of a million men." By 1812, his Grand Empire reached its greatest extent.

As a military leader, Napoleon valued rapid movements and made effective use of his large armies. He developed a new plan for each battle so opposing generals could never anticipate what he would do next. His enemies paid tribute to his leadership. Napoleon's presence on the battlefield, said one, was "worth 40,000 troops."

Redrawing the Map of Europe As Napoleon created a vast French empire, he redrew the map of Europe. He **annexed**, or incorporated, into his empire the Netherlands, Belgium, and parts of Italy and Germany.

He also abolished the tottering Holy Roman Empire and created a 38 member Confederation of the Rhine under French protection. He cut Prussian territory in half, turning part of old Poland into the Grand Duchy of Warsaw.

Napoleon controlled much of Europe through forceful diplomacy. One tactic was placing friends and relatives on the thrones of Europe. For example, after unseating the king of Spain, he placed his own brother, Joseph Bonaparte, on the throne. He also forced alliances on European powers from Madrid to Moscow. At various times, the rulers of Austria, Prussia, and Russia reluctantly signed treaties with the "Corsican ogre," as defeated monarchs called him.

In France, Napoleon's successes boosted the spirit of nationalism. Great victory parades filled the streets

Napoleon Reforms the French Legal System

THE NAPOLEONIC CODE	
Before the French Revolution, France did not have a set of single laws. In 1804, Napoleon set out to reform the nation's legal system as it related to the ideals of the French Revolution. The result was the Napoleonic Code, which guided almost every aspect of life.	
EXAMPLES OF THE CODE	
• all French men will have civil rights; • foreigners in France will enjoy the same civil rights as French men; • husbands are obligated to protect their wives;	• any French man who joins the military of a foreign power is no longer a French citizen; • property rights are absolute; • a woman can make a will without her husband's permission

>> **Analyze Charts** The Napoleonic Code was Napoleon's attempt to reshape France's legal system. Whose civil rights were guaranteed under the Napoleonic Code?

Answers

Describe *He built roads and canals and set up public schools; he recognized religious freedom; he opened jobs to all based on talent; he made sure all citizens were equal before the law.*

Analyze Charts *All Frenchmen (male) and foreigners in France*

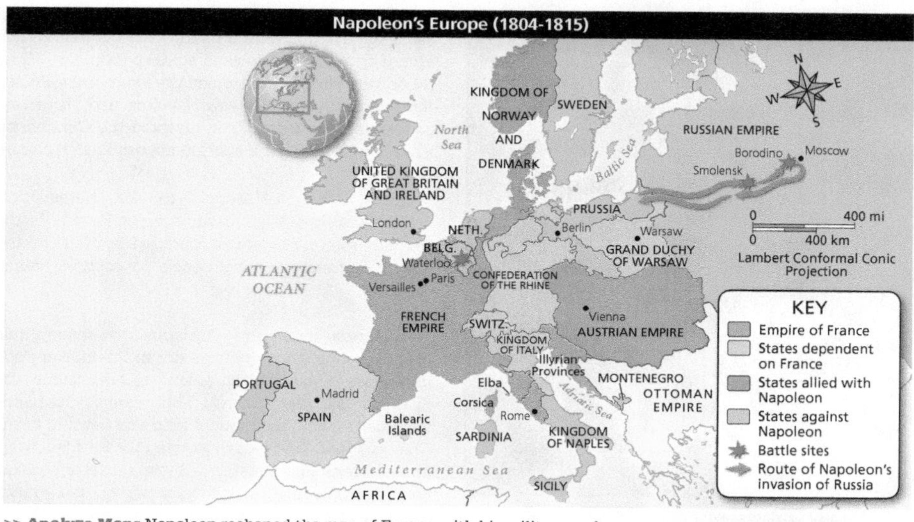

>> **Analyze Maps** Napoleon reshaped the map of Europe with his military and political conquests. Who were Napoleon's allies?

of Paris with cheering crowds. The people celebrated the glory and grandeur that Napoleon had gained for France.

The Continental System Of all the major European powers, Britain alone remained outside Napoleon's European empire. With only a small army, Britain relied on its sea power to stop Napoleon's drive to rule the continent. In 1805, Napoleon prepared to invade England. But at the Battle of Trafalgar, fought off the southwest coast of Spain, British Admiral Horatio Nelson smashed the French fleet.

With an invasion ruled out, Napoleon struck at Britain's lifeblood, its commerce. He waged economic warfare through the **Continental System**, which closed European ports to British goods. Britain responded with its own blockade of European ports. A blockade involves shutting off ports to keep people or supplies from moving in or out.

During their long struggle, both Britain and France seized neutral ships suspected of trading with the other side. British attacks on American ships sparked anger in the United States and eventually triggered the War of 1812.

In the end, Napoleon's Continental System failed to bring Britain to its knees. Although British exports declined, Britain's powerful navy kept vital trade routes open to the Americas and India. Meanwhile, trade restrictions created a scarcity of goods in Europe, sent prices soaring, and intensified resentment against French power.

Impact of Napoleon's Conquests French armies under Napoleon spread ideas of the revolution across Europe. They backed liberal reforms in the lands they conquered. In some places, they helped install revolutionary governments that abolished titles of nobility, ended Church privileges, opened careers to men of talent, and ended serfdom and manorial dues. The Napoleonic Code, too, influenced countries in continental Europe and Latin America.

 **IDENTIFY CAUSE AND EFFECT** How did Napoleon come to dominate most of Europe by 1812?

Challenges to the French Empire

In 1812, Napoleon continued his pursuit of European domination and invaded Russia. This campaign began a chain of events that eventually led to his downfall. Napoleon's final defeat brought an end to the era of the French Revolution.

The Napoleonic Wars

Napoleon furthered his reputation on the battlefield in a series of conflicts known as the Napoleonic Wars. Those wars redrew the map of Europe from 1804 to 1812.

Online Project the **Interactive Map: Napoleon's Europe (1804–1815)**. Click through the hotspots and introduce each of the maps for each period of time. Ask students to describe Napoleon's influence in different areas, identify places where he did not hold power, and compare the map from one period of time to the next.

Guided Reading and Discussion

Identify Cause and Effect What impact did the Napoleonic Wars and Napoleon's use of "forceful diplomacy" have on Europe? *(In addition to conquering other nations, Napoleon put relatives and friends on many European thrones. He also forced other countries to sign treaties with France.)*

How did geography both help and hurt Britain during its war with France? *(With the English Channel separating it from the rest of Europe, Britain was more difficult to attack. However, the Channel hurt Britain because a complete naval blockage could prevent any shipping to or from other countries.)*

Historical Background

A Double Victory At the Battle of Austerlitz, in 1805, Napoleon won not only on the field of battle. After his victory, Napoleon made a grand gesture that won him the loyalty and adoration of the masses. He announced in a public speech that he would adopt the children of all the French soldiers killed in battle—a number that was in the thousands. To fulfill his promise, he ordered the state to pay for the children's support and education, to arrange marriages for the girls, and to find jobs for the boys. One final provision was perhaps the most cherished—he permitted these children to add the name Napoleon to theirs.

Answers

Analyze Maps *Austrian Empire and Kingdom of Norway and Denmark*

Identify Cause and Effect *Napoleon's army conquered many territories and annexed others. He installed family members in many of those conquered lands, while other nations reluctantly signed treaties with France.*

Topic 12 Lesson 8

Challenges to the French Empire

Tell students that, in 1812, Napoleon continued his pursuit of European domination and invaded Russia. These actions set off a chain of events that would ultimately lead to Napoleon's downfall.

Guided Reading and Discussion

Have students discuss the challenges Napoleon faced in Spain, Austria, and Russia. Ask: How did nationalism both help and harm Napoleon? *(Nationalism helped Napoleon in France, where it boosted morale and encouraged the army and the people to support him. In other countries, nationalism prompted people to oppose and fight against the rule of a foreign invader.)*

>> Spanish patriots bravely resisted French invaders. In his famous painting *Third of May 1808*, Spanish artist Francisco Goya shows the execution of Spanish resistance leaders by French troops.

>> Napoleon, shown here crossing the Alps on horseback, attempted to spread French culture across Europe.

Seeds of Defeat Napoleon's successes contained seeds of defeat. Although nationalism spurred French armies to success, it worked against them, too. Many Europeans who had welcomed the ideas of the French Revolution nevertheless saw Napoleon and his armies as foreign oppressors. They resented the Continental System and Napoleon's effort to impose French culture on them.

From Rome to Madrid to the Netherlands, nationalism unleashed revolts against France. In the German states, leaders encouraged national loyalty among German-speaking people to counter French influence.

Resistance in Spain Resistance to foreign rule bled French-occupying forces dry in Spain. Napoleon introduced reforms that sought to undermine the Spanish Catholic Church. But many Spaniards remained loyal to their former king and devoted to the Church. When the Spanish resisted the invaders, well-armed French forces responded with brutal repression. Far from crushing resistance, however, the French response further inflamed Spanish nationalism. Efforts to drive out the French intensified.

Spanish patriots conducted a campaign of **guerrilla warfare**, or hit-and-run raids, against the French. (In Spanish, guerrilla means "little war.") Small bands of guerrillas ambushed French supply trains or troops before retreating into the countryside. These attacks kept large numbers of French soldiers tied down in Spain when Napoleon needed them elsewhere.

Austria Seeks Revenge Spanish resistance encouraged Austria to resume hostilities against the French. In 1805, at the Battle of Austerlitz, Napoleon had won a crushing victory against an Austro-Russian army of superior numbers. Now, in 1809, the Austrians sought revenge. But once again, Napoleon triumphed—this time at the Battle of Wagram. By the peace agreement that followed, Austria surrendered lands populated by more than three million subjects.

Napoleon Invades Russia Tsar Alexander I of Russia was once an ally of Napoleon. The tsar and Napoleon planned to divide Europe if Alexander helped Napoleon in his Continental System. Many countries objected to this system, and Russia became unhappy with the economic effects of the system as well. Yet another cause for concern was that Napoleon had enlarged the Grand Duchy of Warsaw that bordered Russia on the west.

These and other issues led the tsar to withdraw his support from the Continental System. Napoleon responded to the tsar's action by assembling an army

Historical Background

Napoleon's Retreat From Russia In June 1812, Napoleon eagerly took on the challenge of conquering Russia. A few months later, he would see things differently. After a disheartening battle outside Moscow, Napoleon hurried back to Paris to squelch rumors that he had been killed, leaving his shrinking army to retreat after him in the brutal Russian winter. French troops experienced temperatures as low as –40°F. In their desperation to find shelter in the blinding snow, soldiers resorted to building huts using the frozen corpses of their fallen comrades, stacking them like logs to create walls. In June, Napoleon had crossed into Russia with more than 400,000 troops. By December, there were only 10,000 soldiers left.

with soldiers from 20 nations, known as the Grand Army.

In 1812, with about 600,000 soldiers and 50,000 horses, Napoleon invaded Russia. To avoid battles with Napoleon, the Russians retreated eastward, burning crops and villages as they went. This scorched-earth policy left the French hungry and cold as winter came.

Napoleon entered Moscow in September. His triumph, however, was short-lived.

The Retreat from Moscow Even as French troops entered Moscow, Napoleon realized that he would not be able to feed and supply his army through the long Russian winter. In October, he turned homeward.

The 1,000-mile retreat from Moscow turned into a desperate battle for survival. Russian attacks and the brutal Russian winter took a terrible toll. Fewer than 20,000 soldiers of the once-proud Grand Army survived. Many died. Others deserted. French general Michel Ney sadly concluded, "General Famine and General Winter, rather than Russian bullets, have conquered the Grand Army."

Napoleon rushed to Paris to raise a new force to defend France. His reputation for success had been shattered.

>> The French invasion of Russia became a disaster when the lack of food and supplies combined with a hard winter to nearly destroy Napoleon's army.

ANALYZE INFORMATION What led to Napoleon's disaster in Russia?

Napoleon Falls from Power

The disaster in Russia changed the course of the Napoleonic Wars. Russia, Britain, Austria, and Prussia formed a new alliance against a weakened France. In 1813, they defeated Napoleon in the Battle of the Nations at Leipzig.

Napoleon Abdicates Briefly The next year, Napoleon **abdicated**, or stepped down from power. The victors exiled him to Elba, an island in the Mediterranean. They then recognized Louis XVIII, brother of Louis XVI, as king of France.

The restoration of Louis XVIII did not go smoothly. He agreed to accept the Napoleonic Code and honor the land settlements made during the Revolution. However, many émigrés rushed back to France bent on revenge. An economic depression and the fear of a return to the old regime helped rekindle loyalty to Napoleon.

As the victorious allies gathered in Vienna for a general peace conference, Napoleon escaped his island exile and returned to France. Soldiers flocked to his banner. As citizens cheered Napoleon's advance, Louis XVIII fled. In March 1815, Napoleon entered Paris in triumph.

Napoleon Is Defeated at Waterloo Napoleon's triumph was short-lived. His star soared for only 100 days, while the allies reassembled their forces. On June 18, 1815, the opposing armies met near the town of Waterloo in Belgium. British forces under the Duke of Wellington and a Prussian army commanded by General Blücher crushed the French in an agonizing day-long battle. Once again, Napoleon was forced to abdicate and to go into exile on St. Helena, a lonely island in the South Atlantic. This time, he would not return.

Napoleon's Legacy Napoleon died in 1821, but his legend lived on in France and around the world. His contemporaries as well as historians today have long debated his legacy. Was he "the Revolution on horseback," as he claimed? Or was he a traitor to the Revolution?

No one, however, questions Napoleon's impact on France and on Europe. The Napoleonic Code consolidated many changes of the Revolution. The France of Napoleon was a centralized state with a constitution. Elections were held with expanded, though limited, suffrage. Many more citizens had rights

Napoleon Falls from Power

After Napoleon's defeat in Russia, the countries of Russia, Britain, Austria, and Prussia forged a new alliance, which would ultimately defeat Napoleon at Waterloo and lead to Napoleon's permanent exile.

Online Project the **Interactive Timeline: The Rise and Fall of Napoleon**, and have students place the correct event in the correct time period. Introduce the activity by telling students that the end for Napoleon began in 1812 when he invaded Russia.

ACTIVE CLASSROOM

Have students use the timeline to compare the image of Napoleon being crowned emperor to the image of Napoleon's army retreating from Russia. Have them predict what might happen after each of these events. Ask students to state what the people in the images might be thinking. Tell them to write a script for each image, and then have volunteers act out their scripts for the class.

Guided Reading and Discussion

Have students describe the events that led to Napoleon's ultimate fall from power. Ask: Do you think Napoleon was the "revolution on horseback" or a traitor to the revolution? Explain. *(Students should give reasons for their opinions.)*

D Differentiate Challenge Have students research Napoleon's defeat at the Battle of Waterloo (1815) and produce a battle map showing the movements of allied and French troops. Students should show how elements of each army advanced and/or retreated during the battle.

History Background

Geography and the Battle of Waterloo To this day, the term *Waterloo* symbolizes utter defeat. On the morning of the battle, Napoleon felt certain of victory, but both weather and terrain conspired against him. First, he held off his attack until the rain-soaked ground could dry. (Cannonballs just stick in mud; they can do more damage bouncing along dry ground.) These lost hours gave the enemy time to move in more troops. Second, Napoleon ordered a frontal attack against an enemy position on an upward slope. The crest of its ridge helped shield the opposition from French artillery barrages. At Waterloo, more than 20,000 French soldiers died, and Napoleon suffered his final defeat.

Answers

Analyze Information *When France invaded Russia, the Russians undertook a scorched-earth policy that left the French army cold and hungry. This, combined with constant fighting and a brutal winter, defeated Napoleon.*

The Congress of Vienna

Explain that, after the Battle of Waterloo, the Congress of Vienna met to reestablish stability and order in Europe after years of war. The Congress met for 10 months, from September 1814 to June 1815. The Congress redrew the map of Europe (see facing page) and restored hereditary monarchies that the French Revolution or Napoleon had unseated. Explain to students that the Congress kept the peace for nearly 100 years.

Guided Reading and Discussion

Austria, Russia, Prussia, and Great Britain extended their wartime alliance and pledged to act together to maintain the balance of power. The powers also met periodically at the Concert of Europe to discuss any problems affecting peace. Ask students to describe what the shortcomings of the Congress's plans were. *(Students should mention that the leaders did not anticipate the strength of nationalism.)*

Summarize Ask students to summarize and explain the impact of Napoleon Bonaparte on Europe. *(Sample answers: the Napoleonic Code, the damage that his Continental System did to the economy, and the toppling of rulers)*

Answers

Analyze Information *An economic depression and the fear of a return to the old regime helped rekindle loyalty.*

Analyze Maps *to keep France from expanding*

to property and access to education than under the old regime. Still, French citizens lost many rights promised so fervently by republicans during the Convention.

On the world stage, the Napoleonic Wars spread the ideas of the French Revolution. He failed to make Europe into a French empire. Instead, he sparked nationalist feelings across Europe. The abolition of the Holy Roman Empire would eventually help in creating a new Germany.

Napoleon's impact also reached across the Atlantic. In 1803, his decision to sell France's vast Louisiana Territory to the American government doubled the size of the United States and ushered in an age of American expansion.

? ANALYZE INFORMATION Why were the French so eager for Napoleon to return to France after his escape from Elba?

The Congress of Vienna

After Waterloo, diplomats and heads of state again sat down at the **Congress of Vienna**. They faced the monumental task of restoring stability and order in Europe after years of war.

>> Prince Metternich of Austria, shown in this illustration, was a key figure during the Congress of Vienna.

The Congress met for 10 months, from September 1814 to June 1815. It was a brilliant gathering of European leaders. Diplomats and royalty dined and danced, attended concerts and ballets, and enjoyed parties arranged by their host, Emperor Francis I of Austria. The work fell to Prince Clemens von Metternich of Austria, Tsar Alexander I of Russia, and Lord Robert Castlereagh of Britain. Defeated France was represented by Prince Charles Maurice de Talleyrand.

Goals of the Congress The chief goal of the Vienna decision makers was to create a lasting peace by establishing a balance of power and protecting the system of monarchy. Each of the leaders also pursued his own goals. Metternich, the dominant figure at the Congress, wanted to restore things to the way they were in 1792. Alexander I urged a "holy alliance" of Christian monarchs to suppress future revolutions.

Lord Castlereagh was determined to prevent a revival of French military power. The aged diplomat Talleyrand shrewdly played the other leaders against one another so France would be accepted as an equal partner.

Restoring Peace and Order The peacemakers redrew the map of Europe. To contain French ambitions, they ringed France with strong countries. In the north, they added Belgium and Luxembourg to Holland to create the kingdom of the Netherlands. To prevent French expansion eastward, they gave Prussia lands along the Rhine River. They also allowed Austria to reassert control over northern Italy.

To turn back the clock to 1792, the architects of the peace promoted the principle of **legitimacy**, restoring hereditary monarchies that the French Revolution or Napoleon had unseated. Even before the Congress began, they had put Louis XVIII on the French throne. Later, they restored "legitimate" monarchs in Portugal, Spain, and the Italian states.

Successes and Failures To protect the new order, Austria, Russia, Prussia, and Great Britain extended their wartime alliance. In the Quadruple Alliance, the four nations pledged to act together to balance power and suppress uprisings. They then set up the **Concert of Europe**, a loose organization whose goal was to preserve the agreements set up by the Congress of Vienna. The four great powers—and later France—worked to suppress any uprising inspired by the French Revolution. The Concert of Europe was the first modern international peace keeping organization.

The Vienna statesmen achieved their immediate goals in creating a lasting peace. Peace lasted in Europe for the next 100 years. Although smaller wars

English Language Proficiency Standards

Reading 4.F.1 Examining the headings, images, and captions under "The Congress of Vienna" can provide context and visual clues to support the text.

Beginning Point out the main head and subheads in the text. Have students read the first paragraph under each head. Explain how each heading provides context for the content that follows. Ask students to look at the map. Help students recognize how the map supports the text.

Intermediate Have students point out the main head and subheads in the text. Then read the subhead "Restoring Peace and Order," and ask students to use the subhead to form a question about the content. Next, read that section aloud, and help students answer their question. Then ask students to look at how the map supports the text.

Advanced Have students work in pairs to read the boldface headings in the text and use those headings to create questions about the text that follows. Then have students read each subsection, using their questions as a guide. Next, have students examine the map and use that information to help them understand the text.

Advanced High Complete the Advanced activity, but have students work individually, answer their questions after reading, and explain how the map helps them understand the corresponding text.

>> **Analyze Maps** Why did the Congress of Vienna enlarge some of the countries around France?

broke out, Europe would not see war on a Napoleonic scale until 1914. They failed, however, to foresee how powerful new forces such as nationalism would shake the foundations of Europe and Latin America in the future.

 **ANALYZE INFORMATION** What was the chief goal of the Congress of Vienna?

ELPS **ELPS 4.F.1** Practice using special features in the text, like bolded headings and maps, to better understand the content that is presented.

ASSESSMENT

1. **Identify** What political views did Napoleon spread in Europe that angered monarchs?
2. **Describe** In what way was the Continental System an act of economic warfare? Why did it fail?
3. **Describe** In what way did Napoleon's actions doom his dream of creating a French empire in Europe?
4. **Compare and Contrast** Compare and contrast the goals of Prince Clemens von Metternich of Austria and Britain's Lord Castlereagh during the Congress of Vienna.
5. **Draw Conclusions** Why might some of the French have resisted a return to a monarchy?

SYNTHESIZE

Online Project the **Digital Activity: The Age of Napoleon**. Have students complete the graphic organizer regarding Napoleon's rise to power and defeat. *(Possible answers: overthrows Directory and crowns himself emperor; reforms France's political and social systems; pursues French domination of Europe; invades Russia; abdicates the throne in 1814; is exiled to Elba; escapes, regains power, and is defeated in 1815.)*

Then ask them to answer the following critical-thinking question: How might Napoleon have avoided his eventual downfall? Tell them to explain their answers. *(Possible answers: making peace with the allied nations of Europe after returning to France; stopping his quest to dominate Europe)*

DEMONSTRATE

Online Assign the **Digital Lesson Quiz** for this lesson if you haven't already done so. Students will be offered automatic remediation or enrichment based on their score.

Pose these questions to the class on the Discussion Board:

Predict Consequences How might Napoleon have achieved ultimate success in Europe? *(Students might mention not being too overly ambitious in warfare and territorial expansion.)* How might Europe have looked if Napoleon's conquest of the continent was successful? *(Students may say that even if he were successful at the time, nationalist movements might still have overthrown his rule at a later date.)*

Topic Inquiry

Have students continue their investigations for the Topic Inquiry.

Answers

Analyze Information *to create a lasting peace by establishing a balance of power and protecting the monarchy*

Assessment

1. Napoleon helped spread the ideals of the French Revolution, such as equal rights before the law.
2. By closing European ports to British goods, Napoleon hoped to bring Great Britain to its knees. The Continental System failed because Britain's navy blockaded European ports, which kept supplies from moving in or out.
3. Most nations resented Napoleon's Continental System and his effort to impose French culture on them.
4. Each wanted a lasting peace by establishing a balance of power in Europe. However, Lord Castlereagh was determined to prevent a revival of French military power, while Metternich wanted to restore Europe to the way it was in 1792.
5. French citizens who experienced life without a social hierarchy during the French Revolution and the Age of Napoleon would not want to return to living in a society based on social classes in which a king held absolute power.

Topic 12

Answers to TEKS Assessment

1. Students' answers will vary but should include information on how the Holy Roman Empire included all or part of present-day Germany, Slovakia, the Czech Republic, Austria, and the Netherlands. Switzerland was also part of the Roman empire. The Holy Roman Empire shared the Atlantic Ocean border with Western European countries. It also bordered the Baltic and North Seas. Students should go on to point out that from studying the world map, they can see that the Holy Roman Empire was nearly right in the center of Europe.

2. Students' answers will vary but should include information on Bach's composition of religious works for organ and choirs and Mozart's opera themes reflecting Enlightenment criticism of a class-ridden world. The stirring "Hallelujah Chorus" from Handel's *Messiah* is still popular today and conveys universal themes of joy and celebration.

3. Students' answers will vary but should explain how Parliament had slowly increased its power since King John signed the Magna Carta in 1215. Under the Stuarts, Parliament and the monarchy fought for power. During the English Civil War, King Charles I was executed and a period of republican rule followed. After the Restoration and Glorious Revolution, Parliament limited the power of the monarch. The British developed a constitutional government with a cabinet system and a prime minister whose power would exceed that of the monarch. Enlightenment thinker John Locke believed that government should protect the natural rights of man; other Enlightenment thinkers talked about liberty, equality, and separation of powers.

4. Students' answers will vary but could show how writers avoided censorship by using fiction to attack or expose the inequality and corruption of European society. Writers such as Jonathan Swift satirized English political life to comment on governments and monarchies as he did in his novel *Gulliver's Travels*. New Enlightenment ideas were discussed in salons or social gatherings. Writers, artists, and philosophers exchanged ideas. The rise of a new middle class led to the development of the novel, as middle-class readers wanted to read stories about their own lives.

5. Students' answers will vary but should mention that in an oligarchy, the rule belongs to a small ruling elite. In England, the wealthy controlled the House of Commons, and the highest nobles held seats in the House of Lords. Wealthy landowners bought up all the land, often evicting the poor tenant farmers. Because they held all the power, they justified their actions as legal and passed laws to say so. The growing middle class were successful merchants and manufacturers, and some even married into wealthier families. Middle-class people were also inventors and engineers.

6. Students' answers will vary but should include information on how Locke believed that people were basically reasonable and moral and had natural rights from birth (right to life, liberty, and property). His ideal type of government was one that had limited power and was accepted by all citizens; furthermore, if a government did not fulfill its obligations, people had a right to overthrow that government and erect a new one. Locke's bias here is against governments with absolute power, especially single leaders with absolute power. The types of reactions to a public reading of the Treatise would probably have varied in the colonies, but in the period they were published, support for the crown and monarchy in general was still strong, and such statements would likely have been shouted down by many colonists in the late seventeenth century.

TEKS ASSESSMENT

1. **Locate Regions** Locate regions of historical significance directly related to major eras. Using standard sentence structure and punctuation, write a paragraph about the geographical location of countries that were part of the Holy Roman Empire in 1600. Look for the following information on the map: eastern, western, northern, and southern borders, bodies of water, present-day countries, and location on the continent. **16.A, 30.B**
2. **Analyze Examples** Analyze examples of how music reflected the history of the cultures in which it was produced, and identify examples of music that conveyed universal themes and transcended the cultures in which they were created. Write a paragraph analyzing examples of how famous composers and their music reflected the history of the Age of Reason and transcended that era. Consider Bach, Handel, and Mozart's musical works and themes. **26.C**
3. **Explain Development** Explain the development of democratic-republican government through the English Civil War and the Enlightenment. Write a paragraph explaining how the English Civil War and Enlightenment affected the development of the British system of government. Consider the ideas of John Locke and other Enlightenment thinkers, changing role of the British Parliament through the English Civil War, and British constitutional government. **20.A**
4. **Analyze Examples** Analyze examples of how literature reflected the history of the cultures in which it was produced. Write a paragraph analyzing how Enlightenment literature reflected the inequality and corruption of European society. Give a specific example of an author or literary work. Consider censorship and how writers avoided it, spread of Enlightenment ideas, and how social change led to the rise of the novel. **26.B**
5. **Identify Characteristics** Identify the characteristics of political systems including oligarchy. Write a paragraph about England's rule by oligarchy in the 1600s and 1700s. Consider the definition of oligarchy, the people who held power, the contrast of the lives of the ruling elite with the poor, and the rise of the middle class. **19.B**
6. **Explain the Political Philosophies** Explain the political philosophies of individuals: John Locke. Examine sources to analyze point of view and historical context and identify bias in written and oral materials. Use valid primary and secondary sources to write a paragraph explaining the political philosophy of John Locke. Consider Locke's views about human nature and the ideal type of government. According to the excerpt below, under what conditions did Locke advocate a revolution? What bias for or against particular forms of government, if any, do you detect in the opening sentence of this excerpt? What reactions might the statements in this excerpt have provoked if read publicly in the American colonies in 1690? **20.C, 29.C, 29.E**

Chapter XIX. Of the Dissolution of Government

"Sect. 219. There is one way more whereby such a government may be dissolved, and that is, when he who has the supreme executive power, neglects and abandons that charge, so that the laws already made can no longer be put in execution. This is demonstratively to reduce all to anarchy, and so effectually to dissolve the government: . . .

Sect. 220. In these and the like cases, when the government is dissolved, the people are at liberty to provide for themselves, by erecting a new legislative, differing from the other, by the change of persons, or form, or both, as they shall find it most for their safety and good: . . ."

— The Second Treatise of Civil Government, 1690. By John Locke

7. **Identify the Influence and Explain the Development** Identify the influence of the idea of democracy on political revolutions, and explain the development of democratic-republican government through the Enlightenment. Write a paragraph explaining Enlightenment thinking on the development of a democratic-republican government. Consider emphasis on natural laws rather than religious beliefs, solving society's problems, and rejecting absolutism for new political ideas. **20.A, 9.D**

8. **Identify Examples** Identify examples of key persons who were successful in shifting political thought, including the political philosophies of Baron de Montesquieu. Write a paragraph identifying how Montesquieu was successful in changing political ideas. Include his ideas on absolute monarchy, publication of *The Spirit of the Laws*, and influence in democratic governments. **20.C, 21.C**

9. **Explain Political Philosophies of Individuals** Explain the political philosophies of individuals: Thomas Hobbes. Examine sources to analyze point of view and create a written and an oral presentation. Use valid primary and secondary sources to write an interview having Thomas Hobbes explain his political philosophy. With a partner, choose one person to play the part of the interviewer and the other to play the part of Hobbes. Ask and answer questions for a group. Include these suggestions: Hobbes's concept on the social contract, his beliefs about the role of government, and his views on human nature. **20.C, 29.C, 30.C**

10. **Describe Major Influences of Women** Describe the major influences of women during major eras of world history. Write a paragraph describing the influence of Mary Wollstonecraft, a British writer and philosopher, during the Enlightenment. Include Enlightenment ideas about woman's natural rights and their limitations, Wollstonecraft's beliefs about women's capabilities, and her advocacy for women. **24.B**

11. **Identify Origins, Influences, and Contributions** Identify the historical origins of the free enterprise system by referring to Adam Smith's contributions and his ideas and influences as found in *The Wealth of Nations*. Write a paragraph about Adam Smith and his writings on free enterprise. Consider the reasoning behind his beliefs, including supply and demand concepts and free competition. **18.A**

12. **Explain the Impact** Explain the impact of Napoleon Bonaparte and the Napoleonic Wars on Europe using thematic maps to locate places directly related to major eras and world history. Using information from the lessons and the map below, write a paragraph explaining the impact of Napoleon Bonaparte and the Napoleonic Wars on Europe. Consider his domination of Europe, the status of the Holy Roman Empire, and the spread of revolutionary ideas through the expanded French empire. **9.B, 15.A, 16.A**

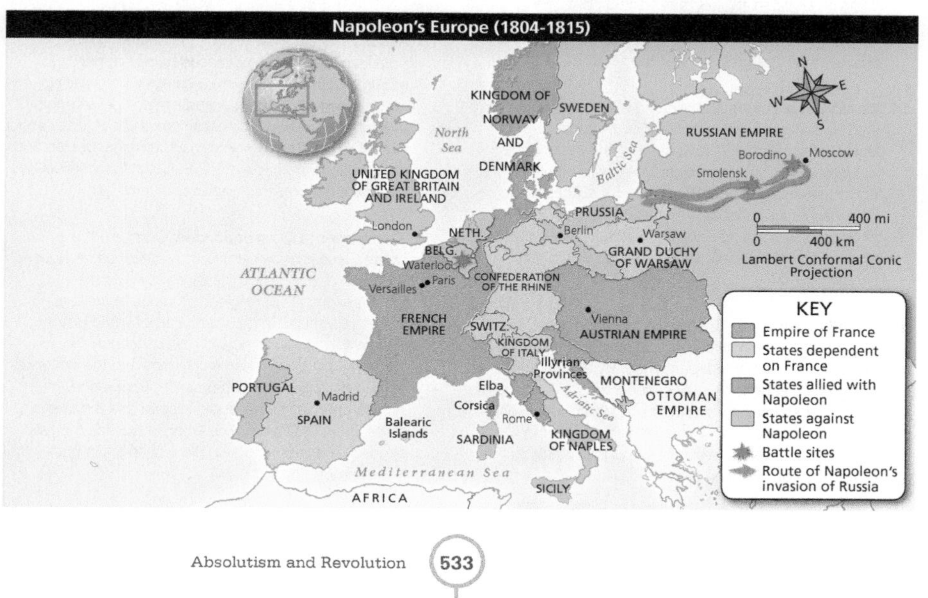

7. Students' answers will vary but should include information on how Enlightenment thinkers developed new ideas about natural laws and the study of human behavior to solve society's problems. This thinking eventually led to new political ideas of democracy and individual rights.

8. Students' answers will vary but should include information on how Baron de Montesquieu studied early governments extensively. He was strongly against monarchies. In 1748, he published *The Spirit of the Laws*. It was the history of government. He was the first person to suggest dividing the powers of government into three branches: the legislative, executive, and judicial branches. This idea of separation of powers had a worldwide influence and became part of the frame of government created by the U.S. Constitution.

9. Students' answers will vary but should include information on how Hobbes believed that people were naturally cruel and selfish and so needed a social contract, an agreement giving up their freedom for an organized society. Hobbes believed a strong government, such as an absolute monarchy, could ensure an orderly society.

10. Students' answers will vary but should include information on how Enlightenment thinkers said women had natural rights, but those rights were limited to home and family. Wollstonecraft felt that women should decide their best interests without depending on men and advocated equal education for boys and girls. Although her ideas were ridiculed in her lifetime, she would influence the later women's rights movement.

11. Students' answers will vary but should explain that Adam Smith wrote *The Wealth of Nations*. In this work, he proved he was an advocate for a free enterprise system. Businesses should compete for profit with little or no influence from government. Smith stated that manufacturing, trade, and wages were all related to supply and demand. Whenever there was a demand for services, suppliers would meet that demand to gain profits. The system would keep the economy moving. Free competition would keep prices low as suppliers competed for business.

12. Students' answers will vary but should include information on Napoleon's domination of Europe, including defeating the Austrian, Prussian, and Russian armies; abolishing the Holy Roman Empire; and spreading ideas of revolution across Europe. He redrew the map of Europe by creating a vast French empire.

Answers to TEKS Assessment

13. Students' answers will vary but should include information on how the Congress of Vienna in 1814–1815 sought to create a lasting peace in Europe by establishing a balance of power and protecting the system of monarchy. The Concert of Europe (Austria, Russia, Prussia, and Great Britain) was an international peacekeeping organization that pledged to act together to balance power and suppress uprisings; peace lasted in Europe for a century.

14. Student answers will vary but may include a thesis such as this: Peter the Great visited western Europe to learn the modern ways of the people living there. He then returned to Russia and used his education to make Russia more modern and make it culturally like the west of Europe. Making Russia more modern is evident when Peter the Great learns about Western technology, including learning anatomy from a doctor and how to extract teeth from a dentist. He also brought a group of experts, teachers, and soldiers back to Russia with him to help Russia in its modernization.

15. Students' answers will vary but should include information stating that popular sovereignty is the idea that government gets its authority to govern from the people. The Declaration stated that the people therefore had the right to change a government that violated their natural rights. When American leaders signed the Declaration of Independence, they pledged their lives and honor to the United States of America.

16. Students' answers will vary but should include information on how Thomas Jefferson wrote most of the Declaration of Independence. He took many of the ideas of John Locke, including the idea of natural rights that all people should have. These rights include life, liberty, and happiness. He argued that people had the right to revolt against an unjust government. Jefferson also wrote about the idea that all government power comes from the people, a principle known as popular sovereignty.

17. Student answers will vary but should include information on how the Declaration of Independence and the Constitution advanced the ideas of John Locke, who asserted that all people had natural rights such as liberty, property, and security. The Declaration of the Rights of Man and the Citizen was modeled after the American Declaration of Independence. The U.S. Constitution influenced many people in Europe and in Latin America to demand written constitutions that guaranteed their rights.

18. America established a permanent democratic republic with its own constitution and three branches of government. The French abolished its feudal system, placed the Catholic Church under state control, had more religious tolerance, and established a republic that was temporary. The Glorious Revolution and the English Bill of Rights had a direct influence on the American Revolution but played a relatively small role in the French Revolution.

TEKS ASSESSMENT

13. **Locate Places of Historical Significance** Locate places of historical significance directly related to major eras. Interpret thematic maps to demonstrate the relationship between geography and the historical development of a region or nation. Write a paragraph explaining the redrawn map of Europe set up by the Congress of Vienna. Consider the goals of the Congress, establishment of the Concert of Europe, and effects of the Congress of Vienna. 15.A, 16.A

14. **Construct a Thesis** Construct a thesis on a social studies issue or event supported by evidence. Using lesson information and valid primary and secondary sources, construct a thesis on whether or not Peter the Great's westernization of Russia was a success that benefited Russia. Consider his trip to western Europe and activities upon his return to Russia. What evidence shows Peter the Great's seriousness to westernize Russia? 29.G

15. **Identify Influences** Identify the influence of the idea of popular sovereignty on political revolutions as stated in the Declaration of Independence. Write a paragraph identifying the ideas and consequences of the principle of popular sovereignty as written into the Declaration of Independence. Include the definition of popular sovereignty and how popular sovereignty relates to the Declaration of Independence. 9.D, 20.B

16. **Explain Philosophies** Explain the political philosophies of Thomas Jefferson. Write a paragraph explaining the political philosophies of Jefferson. Include his role in writing the Declaration of Independence, the ideas of natural rights and popular sovereignty, and how his writing reflects the ideas of John Locke. 20.C

17. **Assess the Degree** Assess the degree to which American ideals have advanced human rights throughout the world. Write a paragraph assessing which American ideals have advanced human rights throughout the world. Consider the origin of ideas about human rights, the Declaration of the Rights of Man and of the Citizen, and how the U.S. Constitution influenced important documents in other countries. 22.F

18. **Compare the Consequences** Compare the consequences of the American and French revolutions, emphasizing the role of the Glorious Revolution. Identify examples of religious influence on various events referenced in the major eras of world history. Write a paragraph comparing the consequences of the American and French revolutions and the influence of the Glorious Revolution on each. For France, include changes in the feudal system and the status of the Catholic Church. For America, include the type of government established. Were changes in both countries long-lasting? 9.A, 23.B

19. Compare Characteristics Compare the characteristics of the American and French revolutions; use standard grammar, spelling, sentence structure, and punctuation. Write a paragraph comparing the characteristics of the American and French revolutions. Be sure to proof your work, fixing any grammar, spelling, sentence structure, or spelling errors. Consider when the revolutions took place, how the revolutions were fought, and the goal of the revolutionary leaders in each country. 9.A, 30.B

20. Identify and Describe Major Effects Identify and describe major effects of the following important turning points in world history from 1750 to 1914: the Scientific Revolution. Write a paragraph about the influence of the Scientific Revolution on European thinking. Consider the fundamental basis of the Scientific Revolution and how this influenced Enlightenment thinkers. What were the changes in religious beliefs at that time? 1.E

21. Compare Consequences Compare the consequences of the American and French revolutions; use standard grammar. Write a paragraph comparing the changes in government after the American and French revolutions. Be sure to proof your work and fix any grammar errors. Include information on each country's constitution and government role. 9.A, 30.B

22. Identify the Influence of Ideas Identify the influence of the idea of human rights on political revolutions by examining sources to analyze frame of reference by comparing and contrasting. Using lesson information and valid primary and secondary sources, list the rights all humans have according to the United States Constitution and the English Bill of Rights. Compare the two lists, making note of at least one difference between the two countries. 29.C, 29.F

23. Create Visual Presentations Create visual presentations of social studies information. Using valid primary and secondary sources and lesson information, create a slide show or PowerPoint presentation with captions providing information about the Committee of Public Safety formed during France's Reign of Terror. Consider the kinds of power the committee had and its specific orders. 30.C

24. Explain Relationships Explain how the relationship among Christianity, individualism, and growing secularism influenced subsequent political developments. Using information from the graphic below and the lessons, write a paragraph explaining Puritan life in England and the influence of Christianity on secular politics. Consider the Puritan way of worship, punishment for non-observers, shunned activities under Puritan beliefs, and how politics were influenced. Why did Puritans place an emphasis on education? 25.C

25. Reflect on the Essential Question **Write an essay on the Essential Question: How much power should the government have?** Use evidence from your study of this Topic to support your answer.

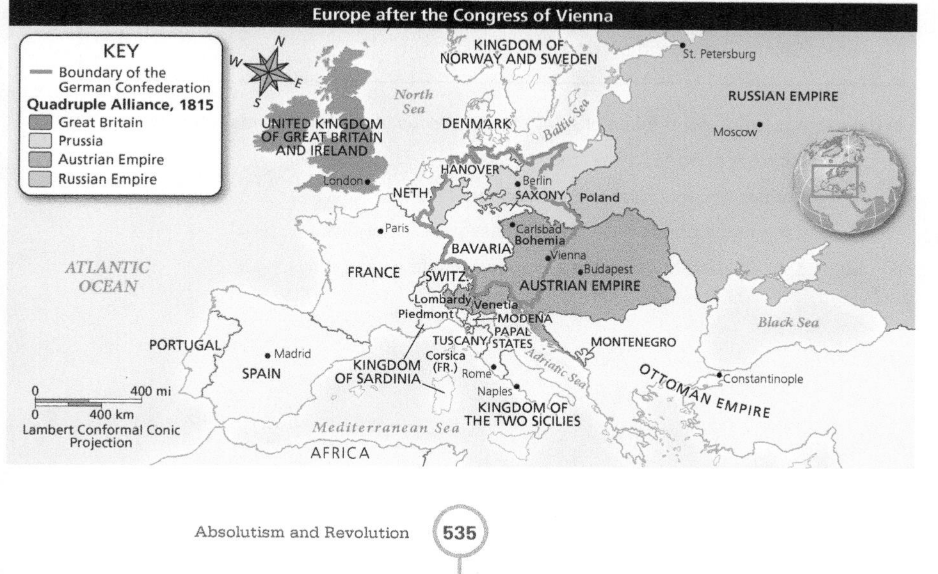

19. The French Revolution took place after the American Revolution. Revolutionary leaders in each country wanted a change in government, an end to unfair taxes, and greater political freedom. The Americans wanted freedom from British rule, and the French wanted an end to feudalism. In France, the revolution led to the "Great Fear." Attacks on villages and towns were common, and crops were being stolen from peasants. The American Revolution was fought on the countryside, which was an advantage since the soldiers knew the terrain better than the British did. Students should also note that there was no American equivalent to the Reign of Terror in France, as the Americans were able to set up a stable government.

20. European scholars made advances in scientific fields, such as physics and medicine, and relied on reason and scientific methods. These advances in turn sparked Enlightenment thinkers who used reason to develop new ideas about laws and basic human rights. Enlightenment thinkers emphasized reason rather than religion.

21. The French Constitution eliminated absolute monarchy and implemented a limited monarchy. France had a newly elected legislature to make laws, collect taxes, and decide on war and peace. However, due to the Reign of Terror and the Napoleonic Wars, France ended up with the monarchy restored. The U.S. Constitution implemented a separation of powers among the three legislative branches. Instead of a monarchy, the United States would have a federal republic. The power was divided between the federal government and the states and provided for an elected legislature and an elected President.

22. Possible lists and answers include the following: United States: religion, speech, the press, right to a jury of your peers, no cruel and unusual punishment; England: trial by jury, abolished excessive fines, cruel and unjust punishment, cannot be held in prison without being accused of a crime, limited religious freedom. The biggest difference between the U.S. Bill of Rights and the English Bill of Rights was in religious freedom. In the United States, the Bill of Rights provided for absolute religious freedom. In England, at the time, the religious freedom of Catholics was limited.

23. Students' answers may vary, and they may choose to render their own art or find art on the Internet or in other sources. The slide show images should include captions for a 12-member committee; young men in battle; women making tents or serving in hospitals; and children making linen from old lint.

24. The Puritans believed in leading a life of godliness. Parliament passed laws setting aside Sunday for religious observances at the Puritans' request. Anyone over the age of fourteen who broke the law was fined. Puritans looked down on dancing, gambling, and going to the theater. Cromwell took it upon himself to close all theaters. Puritans felt everyone needed to be educated so that they could read the Bible.

Topic 12

Answers to TEKS Practice

1. B

2. F

Online To prepare for the End-of-Topic test, have students go online for additional Topic Review and Assessment questions or to review their notes in the **Interactive Reading Notepad** for the lessons in this Topic.

Benchmark Tests

Assign these benchmark tests as you complete the relevant topics to monitor student progress toward mastering the course content and as preparation for the End-of-Course Test.

Benchmark Test 1: Topics 1–5

Benchmark Test 2: Topics 6–10

Benchmark Test 3: Topics 11–15

Benchmark Test 4: Topics 16–21

TEKS PRACTICE

1 What is the importance of popular sovereignty in forming the basis of many democratic-republican governments?

A Liberty and equality must coexist in equal amounts.

B Government is created with the consent of the people.

C Government must also have human rights to protect natural rights.

D A social contract is necessary to guarantee rights to life and liberty.

2

> *"The actual price at which any commodity is commonly sold is called its market price. It may either be above, or below, or exactly the same with its natural price. The market price of every particular commodity is regulated by the proportion between the quantity which is actually brought to market, and the demand of those who are willing to pay the natural price of the commodity. . . . A competition will immediately begin among them, and the market price will rise more or less above the natural price, according as either the greatness of the deficiency, or the wealth and wanton luxury of the competitors, happen to animate more or less the eagerness of the competition."*
>
> *—Adam Smith:* The Wealth of Nations, *1776*

In the excerpt, what is the focus of Adam Smith's ideas about the free market system?

F Competition is good for the economic system.

G Market prices above actual prices need regulation.

H Favorable market conditions can alter laissez-faire policies.

J Let supply and demand rule the economy, with few exceptions.

Test Taking Tips: Tip for Questions With Reading Passages

1. Read the question.
2. Read the title of the passage if it is provided.
3. Determine when the passage or quotation was written or spoken and by whom.
4. Carefully read the entire passage or quotation.
5. Read the question again to be sure you understand what is being asked. Identify details or ideas in the passage or quotation that you will use to answer the question.
6. Answer the question in your own words.
7. Read the answer choices and select the best answer.

3

> *"That whenever any Form of Government becomes destructive of these ends, it is the Right of the People to alter or to abolish it . . ."*

In this excerpt from the Declaration of Independence, it shows that events during the American Revolution and the French Revolution were partly based on which Enlightenment ideas?

A The evils of divine-right theory listed in Diderot's encyclopedia articles

B Western opinions about religious prejudice and the slave trade

C A social contract giving up organized society for individual freedoms

D Locke's theory about the right to overthrow a government if it fails its duties

---

4 How did Ming dynasty rulers respond to the initial European expansion in China in the late 1500s?

F Many European nations were encouraged to start trading with China using gold or silver payments.

G A trading post near Canton was opened with limited, supervised trading, first with Portugal and then with a few other nations.

H Chinese traders purchased European textiles and other goods that were in huge demand.

J Portuguese merchants convinced the Chinese to buy their goods and established Christian churches.

If you have trouble with...				
Question	1	2	3	4
See Lesson	12.4	12.4	12.5	11.2
TEKS	9.D, 20.A	18.A	1.E, 9.A	1.D

3. D
4. G

Online Use the **Topic Synthesize** to help students revisit and reflect on the Essential Question for this Topic.

Topic Inquiry

If students have done a Topic Inquiry for this Topic, have them complete the final step of the Inquiry now.

The Industrial Revolution

TOPIC 13 ORGANIZER	PACING: APPROX. 1 PERIOD, .5 BLOCKS		
	PACING	TEKS	ELPS
Connect	1 period		
MY STORY VIDEO **Lucy Larcom, Weaving Opportunity**	10 min.		
DIGITAL ESSENTIAL QUESTION ACTIVITY **How Do Science and Technology Affect Society?**	10 min.	1.E, 28.A, 28.E	
DIGITAL TIMELINE ACTIVITY **The Industrial Revolution**	10 min.	28.A, 28.E	
TOPIC INQUIRY: DOCUMENT-BASED QUESTION **Who Should Control Economic Decisions?**	20 min.		
Investigate	2–4 periods		
TOPIC INQUIRY: DOCUMENT-BASED QUESTION **Who Should Control Economic Decisions?**	Ongoing		
LESSON 1 **The Industrial Revolution Begins**	30–40 min.	1.E, 8.A, 15.A, 15.B, 16.A, 16.C, 28.A, 28.E	4.F.2, 3.J.1
LESSON 2 **Social Impact of Industrialism**	30–40 min.	1.E, 8.B, 8.E, 17.A, 17.B, 18.A, 18.B, 18.C, 18.F, 24.A	4.F.3
LESSON 3 **The Second Industrial Revolution**	30–40 min.	8.B, 8.E, 17.A, 17.B, 28.A, 28.E	
LESSON 4 **Changing Ways of Life and Thought**	30–40 min.	8.B, 17.A, 24.A, 26.B, 26.C	4.F.5
Synthesize	1 period		
DIGITAL ACTIVITY **Reflect on the Essential Question and Topic**	10 min.		
TOPIC INQUIRY: DOCUMENT-BASED QUESTION **Who Should Control Economic Decisions?**	20 min.		
Demonstrate	1–2 periods		
ONLINE TEST **The Industrial Revolution**	10 min.		
TOPIC INQUIRY: DOCUMENT-BASED QUESTION **Who Should Control Economic Decisions?**	20 min.		

AUTHOR'S NOTE

Causes of the Industrial Revolution

Attempts to explain the Industrial Revolution that began in the eighteenth century, like explanations of the European overseas empires that emerged in the sixteenth, are many and controversial. Traditional accounts celebrated a handful of English inventors as the heroes of the great transformation. More theoretical economic explanations emphasized the concentration of large amounts of capital to pay for the costly process of industrialization. Some emphasized character traits seen as typically European, including rationality, individualism, or "industriousness," while others pointed to alleged weaknesses in other societies, from poor tropical soils or unproductive elites to "oriental despotism" in government. One widely discussed recent analysis, on the other hand, could find no major differences between the British and Chinese economies beyond coal and colonial supplies of cotton.

The issue, in short, is still being debated vigorously. Here, we will offer a number of causal factors, all centered in Britain, where the Industrial Revolution did in fact begin. While no one of these factors was unique to eighteenth-century Britain, all of them together may have combined to generate the first industrial "take-off" in history. This complex combination includes natural resources, labor, demand, capital, technology, and entrepreneurship.

Natural resources, especially coal and iron, were essential. So was a substantial labor force free from agricultural labor. An increased demand from a growing population is often cited, as is capital accumulation to pay the huge initial cost of tooling up for industrial production. Invention undoubtedly played a part, though in the more systematic form of an ongoing process of technological development. Perhaps most important, there was the role of the entrepreneur, the catalytic agent that brought all the other elements together, added a touch of factory management and marketing skills—and made the Industrial Revolution happen.

—Anthony Esler, *The Human Venture: From Prehistory to the Present* (Upper Saddle River, New Jersey: Pearson Education, 2004), pp. 488–489

TOPIC INQUIRY: DOCUMENT-BASED QUESTION

Who Should Control Economic Decisions?

TEKS 18.A, 18.B, 18.C, 18.E

In this Topic Inquiry, students analyze documents to contrast the views of Adam Smith, other laissez-faire economists, Karl Marx, and socialist thinkers. Learning how economists explained the ways the Industrial Revolution affected the economy and society as a whole will contribute to students' understanding of the Topic Essential Question: How do science and technology affect society?

STEP 1: CONNECT

Develop Questions and Plan the Investigation

Launch the DBQ Writing Activity

Display the Winston Churchill quotation, and point out that it mentions two of the economic systems discussed in this Topic. Use the questions to lead a class discussion about the quotation, or have students work in pairs to answer the questions.

Suggestion: Give more context for the quotation by explaining that Winston Churchill was one of the most important world leaders of the mid-1900s. He served as British prime minister from 1941 to 1945 and again from 1951 to 1955. During his second term of office, the world experienced a great deal of tension between capitalist Western nations and the communist Soviet Union.

Generate Questions

Divide the class into small groups and have them use the Need-to-Know Questions document to record their questions about how the various economic systems work and who controls economic decisions in each one.

Suggestion: Help students generate questions by reminding them of the five Ws and one H used by journalists: *Who? What? When? Where? Why?* and *How?* Suggest that students take 10 minutes to brainstorm as many questions as possible and then select the ones most relevant to the broader DBQ question.

Resources

- Need-to-Know Questions
- Student Instructions

STEP 2: INVESTIGATE

Apply Disciplinary Concepts and Tools

Analyze the Documents

Have students analyze the six documents to see how they relate to the question, "Who should control economic decisions?" Before students read the documents, you may wish to remind them that Adam Smith and David Ricardo advocated laissez-faire capitalism, Robert Owen is considered a utopian socialist, and Karl Marx's writings are the basis for communism. The photograph is one taken of Moscow shoppers waiting in line to buy produce in 1965. The piece on the mixed economy was published by the State Department and is intended to help people in other countries understand how the U.S. economy works.

Suggestion: You can control the length of the DBQ by having students read just three representative documents: Document A to represent laissez-faire capitalism, Document B to represent utopian socialism, and Document D to represent communism.

Check Understanding

Students should answer the multiple-choice and short-answer questions that follow each document.

Resources

- Information Organizer

PROFESSIONAL DEVELOPMENT

Document-Based Question

Be sure to view the Document-Based Question Professional Development resources in the online course.

STEP 3: SYNTHESIZE

Evaluate Sources and Use Evidence to Formulate Conclusions

Write Your Essay

Have students consider all of the evidence and viewpoints and draw their own conclusions. Using the documents and their knowledge of history, have them write an essay on the following topic: **Who should control economic decisions?**

Remind students that their essays should have the following characteristics: a topic sentence that states their view; evidence from at least *three* of the documents, clearly identified; relevant facts; an explanation and rebuttal of at least one opposing viewpoint; logical organization, including an introduction and a conclusion; and correct spelling, grammar, and punctuation.

Suggestion: If students struggle with organization, review the structure of a five-paragraph essay. The first paragraph is the introduction. The body consists of three paragraphs, each of which explores a key point. The conclusion should restate the main idea and summarizes the key points.

Edit Your Essay

Remind students that they should revise their first draft and create a final draft of their essay before turning it in. You may want to suggest that they ask a classmate to peer-edit their essay.

Resources

- Writing Rubric

STEP 4: DEMONSTRATE

Communicate Conclusions and Take Informed Action

After students have finished their essays, explain that the work they did on this DBQ will serve as a foundation for the economic understanding they will need as adults. In the future, they may refine or revise the economic ideas they developed here, but they can use a similar process for considering multiple sources of evidence and points of view to form an educated and carefully reasoned opinion.

Suggestion: Help students connect this inquiry to real life by reminding them that the question of who should control economic decisions is still hotly debated today. For example, in the 2012 presidential elections, many campaign issues involved questions of how much the free market should be regulated and whether certain government programs are examples of socialism. This DBQ will help students make informed decisions later in their lives when they have to vote and communicate with elected officials.

The Industrial Revolution Begins

Objectives

Objective 1: Describe how changes in agriculture helped spark the Industrial Revolution.

Objective 2: Analyze why the Industrial Revolution began in Britain.

Objective 3: Explain the role of steam technology and textile manufacturing in the Industrial Revolution.

Objective 4: Describe how the factory system and transportation revolution advanced industry.

Objective 5: Trace how the Industrial Revolution spread.

LESSON 1 ORGANIZER — **PACING: APPROX. 1 PERIOD, .5 BLOCKS**

	OBJECTIVES	PACING	RESOURCES Print	RESOURCES Online	TEKS	ELPS
Connect						
DIGITAL START UP ACTIVITY **Compare Life Before and After Industrialization**		5 min.		●	17.A, 17.B	
Investigate						
READ **New Ways of Working Change Life**	Objective 1	10 min.	●	●	17.A, 17.B	
READ **A New Agricultural Revolution**		10 min.	●	●	1.E, 8.A	
READ **Coal, Steam, and the Energy Revolution**	Objective 2	10 min.	●	●	8.A, 28.E	
READ **Why Did the Industrial Revolution Start in Britain?**		10 min.	●	●	1.E, 8.A, 16.A	
READ **Textile Industry Initiates Industrialization**	Objective 3	10 min.	●	●	28.E	4.F.2
INTERACTIVE GALLERY **The Industrial Revolution and the Textile Industry**		10 min.		●	28.A	
READ **A Revolution in Transportation**	Objective 4	10 min.	●	●	28.A	
INTERACTIVE MAP **Advances in Transportation in England, 1800s**		10 min.		●	16.A, 28.A	
READ **Industrialization Spreads**	Objective 5	10 min.	●	●	8.B, 16.A, 17.B	3.J.1
Synthesize						
DIGITAL ACTIVITY **Causes of the Industrial Revolution**		5 min.		●	1.E, 8	
Demonstrate						
LESSON QUIZ **Lesson Quiz and Class Discussion Board**		10 min.		●	8.A, 8.B, 28.A, 28.E	

Focus on Texas Standards

Texas Essential Knowledge and Skills

1.E identify major causes and describe the major effects of the following important turning points in world history from 1750 to 1914: the Scientific Revolution, the Industrial Revolution and its impact on the development of modern economic systems, European imperialism, and the Enlightenment's impact on political revolutions

8.A explain how 17th and 18th century European scientific advancements led to the Industrial Revolution

28.A explain the role of textile manufacturing and steam technology in initiating the Industrial Revolution and the role of the factory system and transportation technology in advancing the Industrial Revolution

28.E identify the contributions of significant scientists and inventors such as Marie Curie, Thomas Edison, Albert Einstein, Louis Pasteur, and James Watt

NOTES

Social Impact of Industrialism

Objectives

Objective 1: Outline the growth of industrial cities and the emergence of new social classes.

Objective 2: Describe the working conditions in factories and mines.

Objective 3: Analyze the benefits and challenges of industrialism.

Objective 4: Describe the ideas of Adam Smith and other thinkers regarding free enterprise.

Objective 5: Identify the origins and characteristics of socialism and communism.

LESSON 2 ORGANIZER — **PACING: APPROX. 1 PERIOD, .5 BLOCKS**

	OBJECTIVES	PACING	RESOURCES: Print	RESOURCES: Online	TEKS	ELPS
Connect						
DIGITAL START UP ACTIVITY **Working Conditions**		5 min.		●	8.B, 17.A, 17.B	
Investigate						
READ **Industry Causes Urban Growth**	Objective 1	10 min.	●	●	1.E, 8.B, 17.B	
READ **The Rise of New Social Classes**	Objective 1	10 min.	●	●	1.E, 8.B, 17.B	4.F.3
READ **Harsh Conditions in Factories and Mines**	Objective 2	10 min.	●	●		
INTERACTIVE GALLERY **Life of the Working Class**	Objective 2	10 min.		●	8.B, 17.A, 17.B	
READ **Benefits of the Industrial Revolution**	Objective 3	10 min.	●	●		
READ **Laissez-Faire Economics**	Objective 4	10 min.	●	●	21.C	
READ **Utilitarians Support Limited Government**	Objective 4	10 min.	●	●	21.C	
READ **Socialist Thought Emerges, Marx and the Origins of Communism**	Objective 5	10 min.	●	●	1.E, 8.B, 17.B, 18.A, 18.B, 21.C	
INTERACTIVE CHART **Comparing Economic Systems**	Objective 5	10 min.		●	18.A, 18.B, 18.C	
Synthesize						
DIGITAL ACTIVITY **Economic Schools of Thought**		5 min.		●	18.A, 18.B, 18.C, 21.C	
Demonstrate						
LESSON QUIZ **Lesson Quiz and Class Discussion Board**		10 min.		●	8.B, 17.A, 17.B, 18.A, 18.C, 18.F, 24.A	

PEARSON realize™ www.PearsonTexas.com Access your Digital Lesson

Focus on Texas Standards

Texas Essential Knowledge and Skills

1.E identify major causes and describe the major effects of the following important turning points in world history from 1750 to 1914: the Scientific Revolution, the Industrial Revolution and its impact on the development of modern economic systems, European imperialism, and the Enlightenment's impact on political revolutions

8.B explain how the Industrial Revolution led to political, economic, and social changes in Europe

8.E explain the effects of free enterprise in the Industrial Revolution

17.A identify important changes in human life caused by the Neolithic Revolution and the Industrial Revolution

17.B summarize the role of economics in driving political changes as related to the Neolithic Revolution and the Industrial Revolution

18.A identify the historical origins and characteristics of the free enterprise system, including the contributions of Adam Smith, especially the influence of his ideas found in *The Wealth of Nations*

18.B identify the historical origins and characteristics of communism, including the influences of Karl Marx

18.C identify the historical origins and characteristics of socialism

18.F formulate generalizations on how economic freedom improved the human condition, based on students' knowledge of the benefits of free enterprise in Europe's Commercial Revolution, the Industrial Revolution, and 20th-century free market economies, compared to communist command economies

24.A describe the changing roles of women, children, and families during major eras of world history

NOTES

The Second Industrial Revolution

Objectives

Objective 1: Describe the impact of new technology on industry, transportation, and communication.

Objective 2: Understand how big business emerged.

Objective 3: Summarize the impact of medical advances in the later 1800s.

Objective 4: Describe how cities changed and grew.

Objective 5: Explain how conditions for workers gradually improved.

LESSON 3 ORGANIZER — **PACING: APPROX. 1 PERIOD, .5 BLOCKS**

	OBJECTIVES	PACING	RESOURCES: Print	RESOURCES: Online	TEKS	ELPS
Connect						
DIGITAL START UP ACTIVITY **Predict the Future**		5 min.		●	1.E, 17.B	
Investigate						
READ **Science and Technology Change Industry**	Objective 1	10 min.	●	●	1.E, 8.B, 28.A, 28.E	
READ **Advances in Transportation and Communication**	Objective 1	10 min.	●	●	1.E, 8.B, 28.A, 28.E	
INTERACTIVE TIMELINE **Transportation Milestones**	Objective 1	10 min.		●	1.E, 8.B	
READ **The Rise of Big Business**	Objective 2	10 min.	●	●	8.B, 17.B	
READ **Better Medicine, Nutrition, and Health**	Objective 3	10 min.	●	●	17.A, 28.E	
INTERACTIVE GALLERY **Advances in Medicine During the Industrial Age**	Objective 3	10 min.		●	17.A, 28.E	
READ **City Life Changes**	Objective 4	10 min.	●	●	17.A	
3-D MODEL **Living in a Tenement**	Objective 4	10 min.		●	17.A	
READ **The Working Class Wins New Rights**	Objective 5	10 min.	●	●	8.B, 17.A	
Synthesize						
DIGITAL ACTIVITY **Birth of the Industrial City**		5 min.		●		
Demonstrate						
LESSON QUIZ **Lesson Quiz and Class Discussion Board**		10 min.		●	1.E, 8.B, 17.A, 28.A	

Focus on Texas Standards

Texas Essential Knowledge and Skills

8.B explain how the Industrial Revolution led to political, economic, and social changes in Europe

8.E explain the effects of free enterprise in the Industrial Revolution

17.A identify important changes in human life caused by the Neolithic Revolution and the Industrial Revolution

17.B summarize the role of economics in driving political changes as related to the Neolithic Revolution and the Industrial Revolution

28.A explain the role of textile manufacturing and steam technology in initiating the Industrial Revolution and the role of the factory system and transportation technology in advancing the Industrial Revolution

28.E identify the contributions of significant scientists and inventors such as Marie Curie, Thomas Edison, Albert Einstein, Louis Pasteur, and James Watt

NOTES

Changing Ways of Life and Thought

Objectives

Objective 1: Identify what values shaped the new social order.

Objective 2: Describe how the role of women changed in the Industrial Revolution.

Objective 3: Explain the impact of education, new scientific ideas, and religion.

Objective 4: Analyze how romanticism, realism, and impressionism reflected the culture of the Industrial Age.

LESSON 4 ORGANIZER	PACING: APPROX. 1 PERIOD, .5 BLOCKS					
			RESOURCES			
	OBJECTIVES	PACING	Print	Online	TEKS	ELPS
Connect						
DIGITAL START UP ACTIVITY **Changing Attitudes and Values**		5 min.		●	1.E, 24.A	
Investigate						
READ **The New Social Order**	Objectives 1, 2	10 min.	●	●	1.E, 8.B, 18.F	
READ **The Struggle for Women's Rights**		10 min.	●	●	24.A	4.F.5
INTERACTIVE GALLERY **The New Social Order and Changing Roles of Women**		10 min.		●	1.E, 8.B, 18.F, 24.A	
READ **The Rise of Public Education**	Objective 3	10 min.	●	●	1.E, 8.B, 17.A	
READ **New Directions in Science**		10 min.	●	●	1.E, 17.A	
READ **The Role of Religion**		10 min.	●	●	8.B	
READ **The Romantics Turn from Reason**	Objective 4	10 min.	●	●	8.B, 17.A, 26.B, 26.C	
READ **Artists Represent Real Life**		10 min.	●	●	8.B, 17.A, 26.B	
READ **New Directions in the Visual Arts**		10 min.	●	●	8.B, 17.A, 26.B	
INTERACTIVE GALLERY **Artistic Movements During the Industrial Revolution**		10 min.		●	26.B	
Synthesize						
DIGITAL ACTIVITY **Art Reflects Culture**		5 min.		●	26.B	
Demonstrate						
LESSON QUIZ **Lesson Quiz and Class Discussion Board**		10 min.		●	17.A, 26.B	

PEARSON realize™ www.PearsonTexas.com Access your Digital Lesson

Focus on Texas Standards

Texas Essential Knowledge and Skills

8.B explain how the Industrial Revolution led to political, economic, and social changes in Europe

17.A identify important changes in human life caused by the Neolithic Revolution and the Industrial Revolution

24.A describe the changing roles of women, children, and families during major eras of world history

26.B analyze examples of how art, architecture, literature, music, and drama reflect the history of the cultures in which they are produced

26.C identify examples of art, music, and literature that transcend the cultures in which they were created and convey universal themes

NOTES

TOPIC 13 **TEKS Mastery**

The Industrial Revolution (1750–1914)

In this Topic, you will learn about the Industrial Revolution. You know the TEKS are very important, and this course will make it fun to learn about the things that will help you master them. Keep reading to see how.

Your study will help you master these TEKS:

TEKS

1.E, 8.A, 8.B, 8.E, 15.A, 15.B, 16.A, 16.C, 17.A, 17.B, 18.A, 18.B, 18.C, 18.E, 18.F, 21.C, 24.A, 26.B, 26.C, 28.A, 28.E, 29.E

LESSON OUTLINE

Connect

You will start by connecting with the Topic through a video that tells a personal story about the Industrial Revolution. You will start to think about how the Topic connects with your own experience or to what you have already learned. And you'll get a chance to think about a really big question, or Essential Question: How do science and technology affect society?

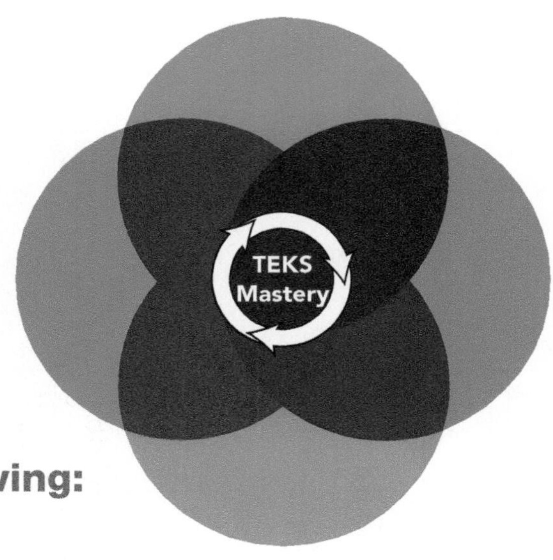

Begin your study by trying the following:

NBC LEARN Watch My Story Video:

Lucy Larcom, Weaving Opportunity

Launch your Document-Based Question:

Who Should Control Economic Decisions?

Investigate

The Lesson Outline lists all the lessons you will investigate in this Topic. As you read and interact with key content, the story of the Industrial Revolution will come to life. Read the texts; try the interactivities. Investigate the story of how changes in industry affected the lives of workers, business leaders, and consumers.

And keep working on your Document-Based Question to help build your mastery of the Topic TEKS.

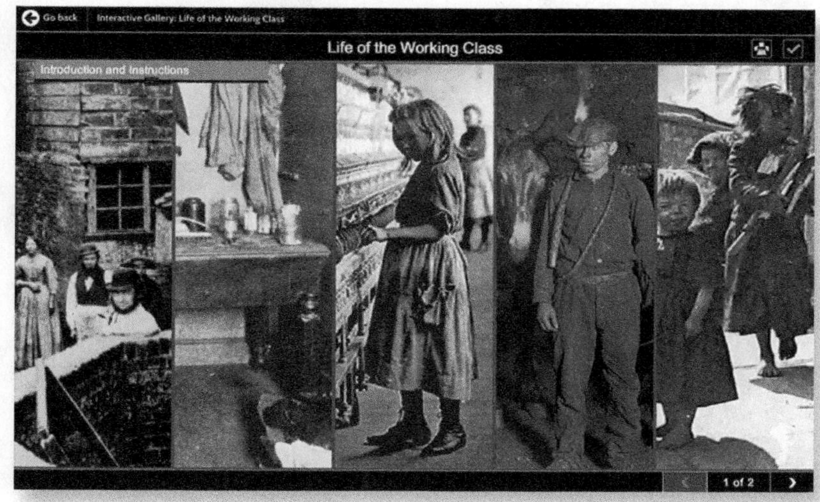

>> Digital interactivity from the online course

Synthesize

Next you will pull it all together by reflecting on the Essential Question. This will give you a chance to be the storyteller, to show how you would answer this big question: How do science and technology affect society?

Demonstrate

Completing this Topic is like practicing all your soccer skills or rehearsing the scenes in a play. Now you get a chance to pull it all together for the final game or the live performance. You can do this on the Topic Review and Assessment pages. Or you can complete your essay about who should control economic decisions.

TEKS in Topic 13	Topic Review and Assessment Questions
1.E	**3, 5, 14**
8.A	**5**
8.B	**6, 12, 14**
8.E	**7, 16**
17.A	**9, 15**
17.B	**12**
18.A	**16, 17**
18.B	**1**
18.C	**2**
18.E	**4**
18.F	**7**
21.C	**1**
24.A	**18**
26.B	**10, 13**
26.C	**13**
28.A	**11**
28.E	**8**
29.E	**12**

The Industrial Revolution

Introduction

During the 1700s, life in Europe began to change rapidly. People learned new and better ways of farming, which increased food production and made the population grow. Business owners wanted to find ways to produce more goods. These two trends combined to transform the world's economy. What role did the Industrial Revolution play in creating the world we live in today?

ESSENTIAL QUESTION

Ask students to think about the Essential Question for this Topic: How do science and technology affect society? New technologies have both positive and negative effects. How can technology have unintended consequences?

Project the Essential Question activity from the course. Read the introduction and the questions. Ask students to make their predictions, then allow volunteers to share their ideas with the class.

Identify Central Issues What do you expect to be the main areas in which the Industrial Revolution will cause change? *(Sample response: industry, work, transportation, medicine, city life)*

Predict Consequences What do you think might be some unintended negative consequences of the Industrial Revolution? Explain. *(Sample response: Unemployment rises as machines throw people out of work; pollution from factory smoke and chemical waste increases.)*

Infer Why do you think the development of industry is called a "revolution"? *(Sample response: because it overthrew an older way of life or because it radically changed the economy)*

[**ESSENTIAL QUESTION**] How do science and technology affect society?

13 The Industrial Revolution

Analyze Images

Point out that the image of the painting shows a furnace for manufacturing iron in England. Explain that iron is found naturally in the Earth and has been used as a building material since before 2000 B.C. During the Industrial Revolution, however, new inventions allowed people to melt iron, producing steel. Ask students to analyze the mood of the painting to determine what the artist might have thought about this technology.

>> A furnace for manufacturing iron in England

Texas Essential Knowledge and Skills

1.E, 8.A, 8.B, 8.E, 15.A, 15.B, 16.A, 16.C, 17.A, 17.B, 18.A, 18.B, 18.C, 18.E, 18.F, 21.C, 24.A, 26.B, 26.C, 28.A, 28.E, 29.E

Enduring Understandings

- Agricultural changes, the factory system, and steam power sparked the Industrial Revolution.
- Effects of industrialization included rapid urbanization and the rise of a new middle class.
- Early working conditions in factories and mines were harsh, but later improved.
- Laissez-faire economists like Adam Smith favored free enterprise and limited government control, while Karl Marx called for workers to control means of production.
- In the second Industrial Revolution, technology revolutionized production, transportation, and communication.
- Differing responses to industrial society led to new artistic movements.

PEARSON realize NBC LEARN

Watch the My Story Video to share the experiences of a worker in an early 19th century textile mill.

PEARSON realize www.PearsonTexas.com
Access your digital lessons including: Topic Inquiry • Interactive Reading Notepad • Interactivities • Assessments

541

NBC LEARN MY STORY VIDEO

Project the My Story Video that tells about Lucy Larcom, a worker in an early nineteenth-century Lowell textile mill.

Online My Story Video: **Lucy Larcom, Weaving Opportunity**

After viewing, ask students to respond to the following questions.

Check Understanding Where did many of the workers in the early textile mills come from? *(farms)*

Determine Point of View What may have accounted for the change in Lucy Larcom's view of mill work? *(Once she had grown accustomed to mill work, the novelty of it wore off. She grew to dislike the constant noise, and refused to become a slave to machines. The tedium of the labor and the need constantly to service the machines no doubt accounted for her change in view.)*

OVERVIEW ACTIVITY

Online Display the **The Industrial Revolution Introduction Timeline** showing major events in the Industrial Revolution. During the Topic, students will learn about all of these events and many more, but this timeline will provide a framework into which they can place the events they learn about.

Check Understanding About how many years after Watt's invention of the steam engine was the first successful steamboat developed? *(about 40)*

Topic Inquiry

If you choose to assign the Topic Inquiry, launch the DBQ activity with students after introducing the Topic.

D Differentiate Challenge/Gifted
Suggest that students copy the timeline onto their own paper and add entries to it as they read the chapter. Have them make a final, clean copy after they read all four lessons, and discuss the new entries as a class.

Topic 13 Lesson 1

The Industrial Revolution Begins

CONNECT

Preview Have students preview the **Lesson Objectives** and the list of **Key Terms**.

Students can also preview all the **Key Terms** and **Academic Vocabulary** using the **Interactive Reading Notepad** on the digital course or preview a summary of the lesson in the **Reading and Note Taking Study Guide**.

Online Use the **Editable Presentation** found on the digital course to present the main ideas for this lesson.

Start Up Activity

Explain: The Industrial Revolution brought radical change to people's lives. Before industrialization, people lived in villages and farmed. Women in particular often worked at home. The economy was based on farming and craftwork. By the late 1800s, the economy had shifted. Manufacturing by machine in factories and urbanization became commonplace.

Discuss In what ways do you think the Industrial Revolution changed daily life for the average person? *(Sample response: The rise of industry meant people would be more likely to work in manufacturing and live in cities near the factories. New inventions and mass production would improve the quality of life.)*

Online You can also project the **Start Up Activity** from the course.

INVESTIGATE

Have students read the section using the **Reading and Note Taking Study Guide** to help them take notes and understand the text as they read.

New Ways of Working Change Life

A New Agricultural Revolution

Remind students that the Scientific Revolution that took place in Europe in the seventeenth and eighteenth centuries paved the way for the Industrial Revolution. Improvements in farming led to increased food production and population growth. At the same time, farms needed fewer laborers, so workers had to find other kinds of jobs. These developments helped spark the rise of industry.

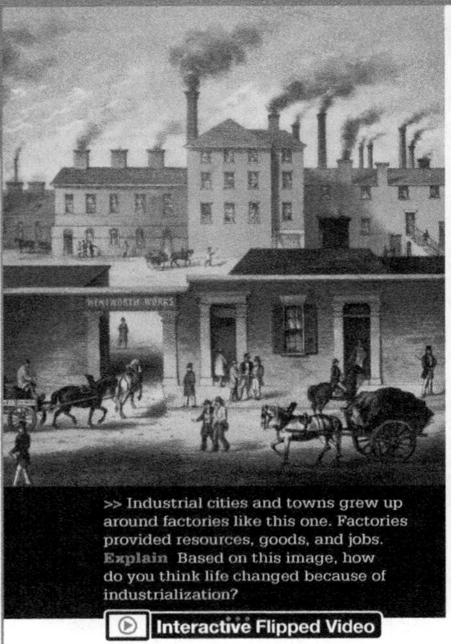

>> Industrial cities and towns grew up around factories like this one. Factories provided resources, goods, and jobs. **Explain** Based on this image, how do you think life changed because of industrialization?

Interactive Flipped Video

13.1 **For thousands of years following the rise of civilization, most people lived and worked in small farming villages. Then a chain of events set in motion in the mid-1700s changed that way of life. Today, we call this period of economic change the Industrial Revolution. Production shifted from simple hand tools to complex machines, and sources of energy shifted from human and animal power to steam and, later, electricity.**

TEKS
1.E, 8.A, 15.A, 15.B, 16.A, 16.C, 28.A, 28.E

>> Objectives

Describe how changes in agriculture helped spark the Industrial Revolution.

Analyze why the Industrial Revolution began in Britain.

Explain the role of steam technology and textile manufacturing in the Industrial Revolution.

Describe how the factory system and transportation revolution advanced industry.

Trace how the Industrial Revolution spread.

>> Key Terms

Industrial Revolution
anesthetic
enclosure
James Watt
smelt
capital
enterprise
entrepreneur
putting-out system
Eli Whitney
turnpike
Liverpool
Manchester

PEARSON realize. www.PearsonTexas.com Access your Digital Lesson.

The Industrial Revolution Begins

New Ways of Working Change Life

Like the Enlightenment, which occurred around the same time, the Industrial Revolution was partly an outgrowth of the Scientific Revolution of the 1600s and 1700s. The Scientific Revolution focused attention on the physical world, and thinkers used the scientific method to conduct controlled experiments. This scientific approach helped inventors to devise new technologies to improve life. These technologies would change the way work was done.

In contrast with most political revolutions, the Industrial Revolution was neither sudden nor swift. It was a long, slow, uneven process. Yet it affected people's lives as much as previous political changes and revolutions had. From its beginnings in Britain, it spread to the rest of Europe, to North America, and around the globe.

A Rural Way of Life In 1750, most people worked the land, using handmade tools. They lived in simple cottages lit by firelight and candles. They made their own clothing and grew their own food. In nearby towns, they might exchange goods at a weekly outdoor market.

542

Aa Vocabulary Builder

1. Have students pronounce the following academic vocabulary terms in this lesson and clarify the part of speech. For difficult or polysyllabic words, break them into syllables and pronounce them with the students.
2. Explain what the word means in common "student-friendly" language using synonyms and antonyms when possible. Provide concrete examples to clarify the meaning, and rephrase the definition.

illuminate: to light up; to give light to

dominate: to rule or control by power or influence

Like their ancestors, these people knew little of the world that existed beyond their village. The few who left home traveled only as far as their feet or a horse-drawn cart could take them. Those bold adventurers who dared to cross the seas were at the mercy of the winds and tides.

Growing Cities With the onset of the Industrial Revolution, the rural way of life began to disappear. By the 1850s, many country villages had grown into industrial towns and cities. Those who lived there were able to buy clothing and food that someone else produced.

Industrialization Brings Great Change Unlike earlier times, industrial-age travelers were able to move rapidly between countries and continents by train or steamship. Urgent messages flew along telegraph wires. New inventions and scientific "firsts" poured forth each year.

Between 1830 and 1855, for example, an American dentist first used an **anesthetic,** or drug that prevents pain during surgery; an American inventor patented the first sewing machine; a French physicist measured the speed of light; and a Hungarian doctor introduced antiseptic methods to reduce the risk of women's dying in childbirth. By the early 1900s, our familiar world of skyscraper cities and carefully planned suburbs had begun to emerge.

How and why did these great changes occur? Historians point to a series of interrelated causes that helped trigger the industrialization of the West. The "West" referred originally to the industrialized countries of western Europe and North America, but today includes many more.

IDENTIFY MAIN IDEAS How did the Industrial Revolution lead to social and economic changes in Europe?

A New Agricultural Revolution

Oddly enough, the Industrial Revolution was made possible in part by a change in the farming fields of western Europe. The first agricultural revolution took place some 11,000 years ago, when people learned to farm and domesticate animals. Then, about 300 years ago, a second agricultural revolution took place that greatly improved the quality and quantity of farm products.

Farmers Reclaim Land and Renew Soil The Dutch led the way in this new agricultural revolution. They built earthen walls known as dikes to reclaim land from the sea. They also combined smaller fields into larger ones to make better use of the land, and they used fertilizer from livestock to renew the soil.

In the 1700s, British farmers expanded on Dutch agricultural experiments.Educated farmers exchanged news of experiments through farm journals. Some farmers mixed different kinds of soils to get higher crop yields. Others tried out new methods of crop rotation.

Lord Charles Townshend urged farmers to grow turnips, which restored exhausted soil. Jethro Tull invented a new mechanical device, the seed drill, to aid farmers. It deposited seeds in rows to maximize land use rather than scattering them over land, a practice that wasted seeds by spacing plants irregularly.

Wealthy Landowners Enclose Lands Meanwhile, wealthy landowners pushed ahead with a practice called **enclosure.** Enclosure is the process of taking over and consolidating, or combining, lands formerly shared by peasant farmers. In the 1500s, landowners had enclosed land to gain more pastures for sheep in order to increase wool output. By the 1700s, they wanted to create larger fields that could be cultivated

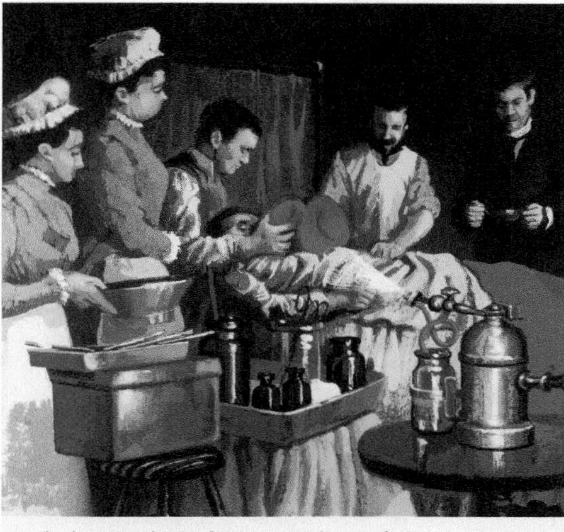

>> An American dentist demonstrates the use of ether as a surgical anesthetic in 1846.

Guided Reading and Discussion

Compare Have students compare life before and after industrialization to identify the impact of the Industrial Revolution on humanity.

Identify Cause and Effect Explain how the agricultural revolution contributed to a healthier population. *(Improvements to agriculture, such as rotating crops, building dikes, experimenting with soil, and enclosing land, provided more and better-quality food and reduced famine, leading to a healthier population.)*

Identify Cause and Effect As students discuss the agricultural revolution, be sure that they identify how agricultural advancements helped lead to industrialization. Once students have an understanding of agriculture's role in industrialization, ask: What was life like before the Industrial Revolution? *(Students may say that life was more rural, and people relied mostly on themselves or their small communities for necessary goods.)*

Answers

Explain *Sample answer: People now worked in large factories in industrial cities. These factories created pollution, such as the smoke coming from the smokestacks in the image.*

Identify Main Ideas *The Industrial Revolution changed people's way of life. A rural lifestyle that had existed for thousands of years disappeared as people moved to towns and cities and could purchase manufactured goods made in factories. Also, many technological and scientific advances changed the quality of life.*

Topic 13 Lesson 1

Coal, Steam, and the Energy Revolution

Why Did the Industrial Revolution Start in Britain?

Tell students that Great Britain was the first country to industrialize to a significant degree. It had land and resources, labor, capital, and entrepreneurship, all of which businesses need to produce goods and to grow.

more efficiently. The British Parliament passed laws that made it easier for landowners to enclose lands.

As millions of acres were enclosed, farm output rose. Profits also rose because consolidated fields needed fewer workers. However, such progress had a human cost. Many farm laborers were thrown out of work, and small farmers were forced off their land because they could not compete with large landholders. Villages shrank when people left in search of work.

This shift in the labor force became a key factor in industrialization. Jobless farm workers migrated to towns and cities. Many found work in the new factories, tending to the machines of the Industrial Revolution.

Population Grows Because of Better Farming Not only did people move to towns and cities, but an overall boom in population also occurred. The improved farming practices of the agricultural revolution contributed to this rapid population growth. Precise population statistics for the 1700s are rare, but those that do exist are striking. Britain's population, for example, soared from about 5 million in 1700 to almost 9 million in 1800.

The population of Europe as a whole shot up from roughly 120 million to about 180 million during the same period. Such growth had never before been seen.

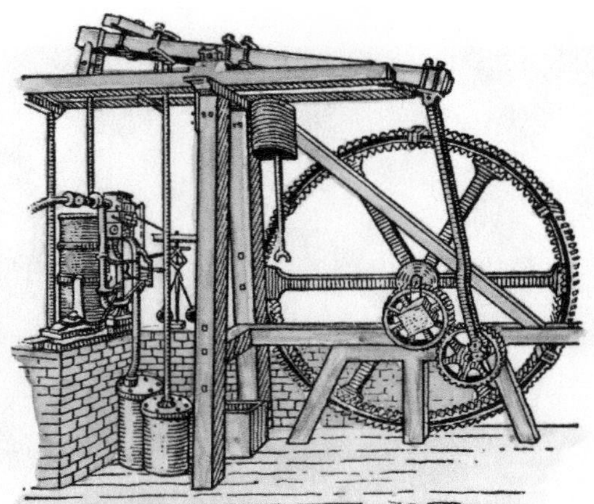

>> Watt's engine used steam and atmospheric pressure to power pistons and rods that moved machinery. It had a separate condenser to keep the water hot, conserving energy.

Why did this population increase occur? The population boom was due more to declining death rates than to rising birth rates. The agricultural revolution reduced the risk of famine. Since people ate better, they were healthier. Also, by the late 1800s, better hygiene and sanitation, along with improved medical care, further slowed deaths from disease. During the Industrial Revolution, this growing population tended the machines and bought the goods produced by factories.

CHECK UNDERSTANDING How did an agricultural revolution contribute to population growth?

Coal, Steam, and the Energy Revolution

Another major factor that contributed to the Industrial Revolution was an "energy revolution." In the past, the energy for work came mostly from the muscles of humans and animals. In the 1700s, inventive minds found ways to use water power more efficiently and harnessed new sources of energy. Among the most important energy sources was coal, which was used to develop the steam engine.

James Watt and the Steam Engine In 1712, inventor Thomas Newcomen developed a steam engine powered by coal to pump water out of mines. Later, in 1764, Scottish engineer **James Watt** looked at Newcomen's invention and set out to make improvements on the engine in order to make it more efficient. Watt's engine would become a vital power source of the Industrial Revolution.

The steam engine was first used to power machines, but later was adapted to power locomotives and steamships.

Producing Better Iron Coal was also a vital source of fuel in the production of iron, a material needed for the construction of machines and steam engines. The Darby family of Coalbrookdale, England, pioneered new methods of producing iron. In 1709, Abraham Darby used coal instead of charcoal to **smelt** iron, or separate iron from its ore.

Darby's experiments led him to produce less expensive and better-quality iron, which was used to produce parts for the steam engines. Both his son and grandson continued to improve on his methods. In fact, Abraham Darby III built the world's first iron bridge. In the decades that followed, high-quality iron was used

Answers

Check Understanding *There was more food of better quality, reducing famine and helping people live longer.*

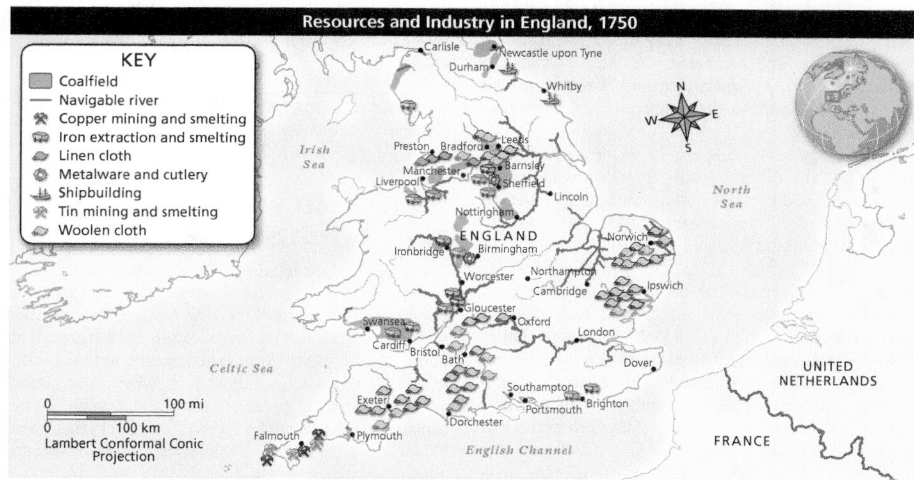

>> **Analyze Maps** Notice where various resources and industries were located in 1750. Why is the location of navigable rivers important to resources and industry?

more and more widely, especially after the world turned to building railroads.

IDENTIFY SUPPORTING DETAILS What did the Darby family contribute to the Industrial Revolution?

Why Did the Industrial Revolution Start in Britain?

Historians have fiercely debated why the Industrial Revolution began in Britain in the 1700s. They have identified a number of advantages Britain had. No single one was unique to Britain, but taken together they helped Britain take an early lead. This complex combination included natural resources, labor, capital, and entrepreneurship. Economists call these the four factors of production; that is, the elements necessary to produce goods. In addition to these factors, growing demand for goods and new technology provided the essential building blocks for Britain's leap forward.

Natural Resources and Geography During the 1700s, Britain began to take greater advantage of its abundant natural resources. Although Britain was a relatively small nation, it had large supplies of coal to power steam engines. Britain also had plentiful iron, which was used to build machines.

Britain's geography also provided an advantage. As an island nation with many ports, Britain had long benefited from trade. Its ships brought raw materials from its overseas empire and exported finished goods. Britain also had streams and rivers that could be harnessed to provide water power. Many rivers were later developed with canals and then used to transport goods to internal markets.

Labor and Capital A large number of workers were needed to mine the coal and iron, build the factories, and run the machines. The agricultural revolution of the 1600s and 1700s freed many men and women from farm labor. The population boom that resulted from changes in agriculture further swelled the available work force. The growing population also increased the demand for goods, which industry supplied.

To develop mining and other industries, capital was needed. **Capital** is money used to invest in enterprises. An **enterprise** is a business organization in an area such as shipping, mining, railroads, or factories. Many businesspeople were ready to risk their profits in new ventures. The capital that helped Britain industrialize came from landowners, banks, and merchants who profited from overseas trade, including the slave trade.

Guided Reading and Discussion

After you read the section "Coal, Steam, and the Energy Revolution," discuss how the innovations of the 1700s revolutionized energy. Energy sources such as coal and steam provided much more power than the labor of humans and animals. As you read the section "Why Did the Industrial Revolution Start in Britain?", be sure students understand that Britain had the four factors of production—natural resources, labor, capital, and entrepreneurship—necessary to produce goods. The demand for goods and new technology also contributed to Britain's rapid industrialization.

Draw Inferences Why was coal a vital power source? What effect might it have on employment? *(Coal was needed to provide the energy to power the new machines, especially steam engines. As a result, coal mining became an important job that employed many people in order to supply enough coal to factories.)*

Draw Conclusions How did Britain's overseas empire contribute to its role in starting the Industrial Revolution? *(Because Britain had an empire overseas, it had trading partners and access to more raw materials. The additional trade provided the capital that was needed to develop new businesses.)* What role did the British navy play in Britain's industrialization? *(The navy protected the empire, including shipping and overseas trade routes. This protection further encouraged entrepreneurs to invest in new ventures in Britain.)*

Analyze Images

Direct students' attention to the map "Resources and Industry in England, 1750." Point out the resources available in England in 1750. Discuss how each resource was used for industrialization. *(Iron was used to build machines and rails, coal-powered steam engines, etc.)* Why were resources a factor in Britain's role as the starting point of industrialization? *(Britain had an abundance of natural resources, providing the raw materials needed to industrialize.)*

Answers

Analyze Maps *Sample answer: The rivers were used to help transport natural resources to factories. They also helped transport finished goods to market. The rivers, together with the variety of resources available, helped industrialization start in England.*

Identify Supporting Details *They contributed new, improved methods of producing iron, which was used to make steam engines, bridges, and railroads.*

Textile Industry Initiates Industrialization

The creation of new machinery in the textile industry led to the demise of the putting-out system. Instead, the new factory system brought workers and machines together in one place. This advanced the Industrial Revolution by making manufacturing more efficient.

Online Project the **Interactive Gallery: The Industrial Revolution and the Textile Industry**. Look at each image. Direct students' attention to the diagram of the clothing manufacturing process and the inventions timeline in the gallery. How did advances in one part of the textile process spur other innovations? *(New machines helped weavers make cloth faster, increasing the demand for thread, which created the need for a machine to make thread faster.)*

ACTIVE CLASSROOM

Have students break into groups. Provide the following writing prompt: What might life be like today if James Watt had not invented his steam engine? Have students write as much as they can for a minute, and then pass the paper to the person on their right. The next person should try to improve or elaborate upon the response. Continue to switch until the paper comes back to the first person. The group should then decide which response is the best.

Key Terms

Ask students to find the key term **entrepreneur** (in bold) in the text and find its meaning. Then ask what kinds of social and political conditions are favorable to entrepreneurs and new technology.

Guided Reading and Discussion

Explain that once innovations in technology occurred, each new invention created demand for more innovations. Explain how that pattern played out in the textile industry. In this way, textile manufacturing initiated the Industrial Revolution.

Explain Why did Eli Whitney develop the cotton gin? *(to reduce costs and labor in processing cotton)*

Make Generalizations Ask: Why is technology developed? *(New inventions help solve a problem or make a process easier.)*

Answers

Make Predictions *Sample answer: Once new machines are able to do the textile work that was done at home in the putting-out system, most workers will move to factories and stop producing goods at home.*

Check Understanding *Answers include plentiful resources, a ready supply of labor and capital, and a government that encouraged business.*

Entrepreneurs and Inventors Britain also had plenty of skilled mechanics. They developed practical new inventions and partnered with entrepreneurs to profit from them. An **entrepreneur** is someone who manages and assumes the financial risks of starting new businesses.

Technology was important to the Industrial Revolution, but did not cause it. Only when other necessary conditions existed, including demand and capital, did technology pave the way for industrialization.

A Favorable Climate for Business In addition to the advantages already cited, Britain had a stable government that supported economic growth. Other countries in Europe imposed heavy river tolls and other barriers to growth. Britain had far fewer blocks to the movement of goods. The government built a strong navy that protected its empire, including shipping and overseas trade.

Social attitudes adjusted to changing economic conditions. Although members of the upper class looked down on business and business people, they did not reject the great wealth produced by the new entrepreneurs. Religious groups encouraged thrift and hard work. These goals led inventors, bankers, and other risk-takers to devote their energies to new enterprises.

>> Generations of women made textiles at home as part of the putting-out system. These women are making lace. **Make Predictions** What impact do you think machines and industrialization will have on the putting-out system?

CHECK UNDERSTANDING What conditions in Britain paved the way for the Industrial Revolution?

Textile Industry Initiates Industrialization

The Industrial Revolution first took hold in Britain's largest industry—textiles. In the 1600s, cotton cloth imported from India had become popular. British merchants tried to organize a cotton cloth industry at home. They developed the **putting-out system,** also known as the cottage industry, in which raw cotton was distributed to peasant families who spun it into thread and then wove the thread into cloth in their own homes. Skilled artisans in the towns then finished and dyed the cloth.

Technology Speeds Production Under the putting-out system, production was slow. The process of using manually operated machines for spinning and weaving took time. As the demand for cloth grew, inventors came up with a series of remarkable devices that revolutionized the British textile industry. For example, John Kay's flying shuttle enabled weavers to work so fast that they soon outpaced spinners. James Hargreaves solved that problem by producing the spinning jenny in 1764, which spun many threads at the same time. Five years later, Richard Arkwright patented the water frame, a spinning machine that could be powered by water.

Meanwhile, in America, these faster spinning and weaving machines presented a challenge—how to produce enough cotton to keep up with England. Raw cotton grown in the South had to be cleaned of dirt and seeds by hand, which is a time-consuming task. To solve this, **Eli Whitney** invented a machine called the cotton gin that separated the seeds from the raw cotton at a fast rate. He finished the cotton gin in 1793, and cotton production increased at a rapid rate.

The First Factories The new machines doomed the putting-out system. They were too large and expensive to be operated at home. Instead, manufacturers built long sheds to house the machines. At first, they located the sheds near rapidly moving streams, harnessing the water power to run the machines. Later, machines were powered by steam engines.

Spinners and weavers now came each day to work in these first factories, which brought together workers

English Language Proficiency Standards

Reading 4.F.2 Have students refer to the images on these pages to enhance their understanding of the development of the textile industry as a major accomplishment of the Industrial Revolution.

Beginning Explain the term *cottage industry*, and point out that *cottage* is another word for *small house*. Read aloud the text about cottage industry and the factory system. Help students understand how the visuals enhance the concept that the textile industry eventually outgrew homes.

Intermediate Have students use context clues from the first image to develop a working definition of the term *cottage industry*. Adjust and support student understanding of this term until it is accurate. Engage students in a discussion to explain why the textile industry needed more and more space to create cloth. Have students use evidence from the visuals to support their ideas.

Advanced Have students complete the Intermediate activity in pairs before discussing as a class.

and machines to produce large quantities of goods. Early observers were awed at the size and output of these establishments. One onlooker noted: "The same [amount] of labor is now performed in one of these structures which formerly occupied the industry of an entire district."

IDENTIFY CAUSE AND EFFECT What technology brought about advances in the British textile industry?

ELPS **ELPS 4.F.2** Use the images in *Textile Industry Intiates Industrialization* to enchance your understanding of how the textline industry grew and changed over time.

A Revolution in Transportation

As production increased, entrepreneurs needed faster and cheaper methods of moving goods from place to place. Some capitalists invested in **turnpikes,** private roads built by entrepreneurs who charged travelers a toll, or fee, to use them. Goods traveled faster as a result, and turnpikes soon linked every part of Britain. Other entrepreneurs had canals dug to connect rivers together or to connect inland towns with coastal ports. Engineers also built stronger bridges and upgraded harbors to help the expanding overseas trade.

Canals Improve Transportation During the late 1700s and early 1800s, British factories needed an efficient, inexpensive way to receive coal and raw materials and then to ship finished goods to market. In 1763, when the Bridgewater Canal opened, it not only made a profit from tolls, but it shortened the trip enough to cut in half the price of coal in Manchester.

The success of this canal set off a canal-building frenzy. Entrepreneurs formed companies to construct canals for profit. Not all the canals that were built had enough traffic to support them, however, and bankruptcy often resulted. Then, beginning in the 1830s, canals lost their importance as steam locomotives made railroads the new preferred form of transportation.

The Steam Locomotive Drives Railroads It was the invention of the steam locomotive that made the growth of railroads possible. In the early 1800s, pioneers like George Stephenson developed steam-powered locomotives to pull carriages along iron rails. The railroad did not have to follow the course of a river. This meant that tracks could go places where rivers did not, allowing factory owners and merchants to ship goods swiftly and cheaply over land. The world's

>> Workers and machines filled the early factories of the Industrial Revolution. Machines dramatically increased the quantity of goods that could be produced.

Interactive Gallery

>> Steam locomotives made travel faster than ever before. The locomotives burned coal to produce steam and traveled overland routes on iron rails.

 Interactive Map

A Revolution in Transportation

Explain that the steam engine led to other transportation advances.

Online Project the **Interactive Map: Advances in Transportation in England, 1800s**. Raw materials and finished goods were transported first on steamships by canal, and then by steam locomotive on railroad tracks. Have students look at the system of canals on the map, and then at the railroads.

Draw Conclusions Describe how transportation improvements helped advance industry. *(Industry relied on transportation to deliver raw materials to make goods and fuel to power the machines. Industries also transported finished goods to market. Steamboats and trains helped transport goods more quickly and cheaply, allowing industry to expand.)*

ACTIVE CLASSROOM

Ask students to pair with a partner to look at the map. Have them use the map layers on the key to reveal all of the data. Partners should then ask each other: What do you see? What does that make you think? What are you wondering about now that you've seen this? Share responses with the class or by posting the map and comments on Pinterest, Glogster, or Flickr.

Guided Reading and Discussion

Be sure that students understand that as production increased, business owners needed to be able to move their goods more quickly and efficiently from place to place. This led to the development of turnpikes, canals, bridges, and railroads.

Analyze Interactions Explain how iron production and railroading are interrelated. *(Because both trains and tracks are made of iron, railroading is dependent on the production of iron.)*

Advanced High Have students use the visuals to understand and describe the textile industry's development from cottage industry to a factory-based process with fewer skilled workers. Once students have had a chance to read the text and examine the supporting visuals, have them explain the development of the industry to the rest of the group.

Answers

Identify Cause and Effect *New machines sped up the process of spinning thread and weaving cloth, allowing textiles to be manufactured in large quantities in factories.*

Industrialization Spreads

Remind students that the Industrial Revolution began in the textile industry in Britain. Explain that it wasn't long before industrialization affected other industries and other countries.

Analyze Maps Direct students' attention to the map "Centers of Industry, 1871." Ask students to list the centers of industry in Europe. Explain that these cities are where the Industrial Revolution spread. The cities grew as they became economic centers. Then draw students' attention to the inset map of the United States. Point out that when industrialization reached the United States, it took off quickly because of the amount of resources available to fuel industry.

D Differentiate **Extra Support** Explain to students why coal and iron are on the map key. Remind them of the importance of these resources to industry. Point out that iron was needed to manufacture machines, rails, and trains. Coal was used to create the steam that worked the machines.

Answers

Analyze Maps *Possible cities: Glasgow, Newcastle, Liverpool, Barcelona; Portugal and Italy*

Draw Conclusions *Unlike shipping, railroads didn't rely on the location of rivers and canals. They could be built across the land using the best routes available. Therefore trains could deliver goods more quickly and cheaply.*

first major rail line, from **Liverpool** to **Manchester,** opened in England in 1830.

In the following decades, railroad travel became faster and railroad building boomed. By 1870, rail lines crisscrossed Britain, Europe, and North America.

Cheaper Goods Lead to More Demand As the Industrial Revolution got under way, it triggered a chain reaction. Once inventors developed machines that could produce large quantities of goods more efficiently, prices fell. Lower prices made goods more affordable and thus attracted more consumers. Additional consumers then further fed the demand for goods. This new cycle caused a wave of economic and social changes that dramatically affected the way people lived.

? DRAW CONCLUSIONS How did the development of railroads advance the Industrial Revolution?

Industrialization Spreads

The start of industrialization had largely been forged from iron, powered by steam engines, and driven by the British textile industry. By the mid-1800s, the Industrial Revolution entered a second phase. By then, it had spread outside Britain. New industrial powers emerged. Factories powered by electricity used innovative processes to turn out new products. Changes in business organization contributed to the rise of giant companies. As the twentieth century dawned, this second Industrial Revolution transformed the economies of the Western world.

Other Nations Industrialize During the early Industrial Revolution, Britain stood alone as the world's industrial giant. To protect its head start, Britain tried to enforce strict rules against exporting inventions.

For a while, the rules worked. Then, in 1807, British mechanic William Cockerill opened factories in Belgium to manufacture spinning and weaving machines. Belgium became the first European nation after Britain to industrialize. By the mid-1800s, other nations had joined the race, and several newcomers were challenging Britain's industrial supremacy.

How were other nations able to catch up with Britain so quickly? First, nations such as Germany, France, and the United States had more abundant supplies of coal, iron, and other resources than Britain did. Also, they had the advantage of being able to follow Britain's lead. Like Belgium, latecomers often borrowed British experts or technology. The first American textile factory was built in Pawtucket, Rhode Island, with plans smuggled out of

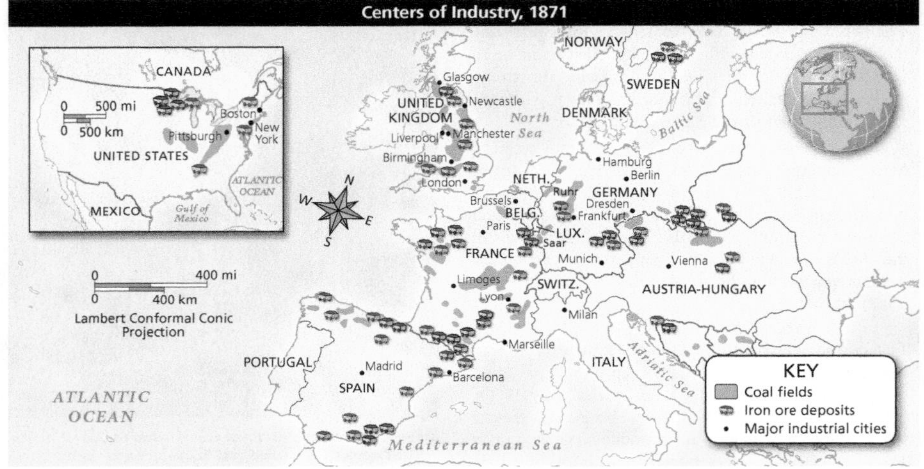

>> **Analyze Maps** By 1871, industrialization had spread through Europe and across the Atlantic to America. Which major industrial cities were probably shipping centers as well? Identify two nations that were at a disadvantage for industrialization.

English Language Proficiency Standards

Speaking 3.J.1 Have students read "Industrialization Spreads" according to their skill level and respond to the following activities and questions.

Beginning Read the text with students, taking time to examine the map that shows the spread of industrialization to other nations. Help students understand the concept that industrialization began in Britain but soon spread across much of the Western Hemisphere by using the sentence frames that follow to give an oral response.

- The British textile industry _____. *(began industrialization)*
- Natural resources in Germany and the United States _____. *(helped industrialization develop)*

Intermediate Have student volunteers take turns reading the text aloud. Then examine the map. Have students write ideas to explain why and how industrialization spread from Britain to other parts of Europe and the United States so quickly. Encourage each student to read his or her response.

Advanced Have groups read the text aloud and discuss why industrialization spread from Britain to other parts of the world. Have them report the main points of their discussion.

Advanced High After reading the text, have pairs make a list of reasons for the spread of the Industrial Revolution and how each contributed to the rise in industrialization. Have each pair share their list.

Britain. American inventor Robert Fulton powered his steamboat with one of James Watt's steam engines.

Two countries in particular—Germany and the United States—thrust their way to industrial leadership. Germany united into a powerful nation in 1871. Within a few decades, it became Europe's leading industrial power. Across the Atlantic, the United States advanced even more rapidly, especially after the Civil War.

With a large labor force, plenty of resources, and entrepreneurs who had capital, by 1900 the United States was manufacturing about 30 percent of the world's industrial goods. It had surpassed Britain as the leading industrial nation.

Industry Spreads Unevenly Other nations industrialized more slowly, particularly those in eastern and southern Europe. These nations often lacked natural resources or the capital to invest in industry. Although Russia did have resources, social and political conditions slowed its economic development. Only in the late 1800s, more than 100 years after Britain, did Russia move toward industrialization.

In East Asia, however, Japan offered a remarkable success story. Although Japan lacked many basic resources, it industrialized rapidly after 1868 because of a political revolution that made modernization a priority. Canada, Australia, and New Zealand also built thriving industries during this time.

Social, Economic, and Political Changes Like Britain, the new industrial nations underwent social changes, such as rapid urbanization. Early in the history of industrialization, men, women, and children worked long hours in difficult and dangerous conditions. By 1900, however, these conditions had begun to improve in many industrialized nations.

The factory system produced huge quantities of new goods at lower prices than ever before. In time, ordinary workers were buying goods that in earlier days only the wealthy could afford. The demand for goods created jobs, as did the building of cities, railroads, and factories. Politics changed, too, as leaders had to meet the demands of an industrial society.

Globally, industrial nations competed fiercely, altering patterns of world trade. Because of their technological and economic advantage, the Western powers came to dominate the world more than ever before.

ANALYZE INFORMATION What factors allowed other nations to industrialize after Britain?

>> This paddle steamer traveled the Potomac River in the United States around 1860. River travel was slow before steam engines because boats relied on sails or water currents. Steamers revolutionized water travel.

>> A street scene in Chicago, Illinois, from the early 1900s shows how the urban landscape was altered by industrialization. **Compare and Contrast** How is the scene similar to and different from a typical city street today?

Guided Reading and Discussion

Use these questions to spark class discussion about the spread of the Industrial Revolution.

Predict Consequences Ask students to brainstorm what the result might have been if Britain had been successful at preventing the knowledge about new textile inventions to spread to other countries. *(Answers will vary but students should demonstrate an understanding of the immense economic power Britain wanted to maintain and how some of that power was lost when industrialization spread.)*

Make Generalizations Have students refer to the "Centers of Industry" map and note that the United States is also included. Point out that individual countries in Europe are smaller in size than the United States. Ask students to generalize why land mass and resources in America are important to the discussion of industrialization. *(America's large size means that it may have more resources and labor to fuel its industries and that it also has a huge domestic market. These features give it an economic advantage over smaller countries.)*

Answers

Compare and Contrast *Sample answer: Student responses will vary but they should point out distinguishing characteristics in the photo that correspond to urban life today—such as tall buildings, pedestrians, shops—as well as characteristics unique to the era—such as the clothing and the horse-drawn carriages.*

Analyze Information *Despite British attempts to maintain the industrial lead, other nations learned the new technology and could follow Britain's example. They also had more resources than Britain, so they could industrialize quickly.*

Topic 13 Lesson 1

SYNTHESIZE

Online Project the **Digital Activity: Causes of the Industrial Revolution**. Ask students to take turns filling out a class version of the graphic organizer on the whiteboard.

Discuss Ask students to pick one of the causes listed on the board and create an argument for the importance of that cause. Then, conduct a debate in class. *(Responses will vary according to the opinions of the class, but encourage students to see how all the causes of the Industrial Revolution worked together to bring about industrialization.)*

DEMONSTRATE

Online Assign the online **Digital Lesson Quiz** for this lesson if you haven't already done so. Students will be offered automatic remediation or enrichment based on their score.

Pose this question to the class on the Discussion Board:

Make Predictions Based on what you have learned about the move away from a rural way of life and the subsequent growth of cities, what do you think living and working conditions were like in England in the 1800s? *(Students may have prior knowledge of tenements and slum conditions as well as long work hours and child labor practices. Encourage all suggestions and let students know they will find out about the impact of the Industrial Revolution on humanity in the next lesson.)*

Topic Inquiry

Have students continue their investigations for the Topic Inquiry.

ASSESSMENT

1. **Identify Patterns** What would you identify as the important changes in human life caused by the Industrial Revolution?
2. **Identify Cause and Effect** How did technological advances in agriculture affect the Industrial Revolution?
3. **Generate Explanations** Why was a supply of coal crucial to the Industrial Revolution?
4. **Synthesize** How did the four factors of production determine which nations were able to industrialize after Britain? Cite specific examples from the text.
5. **Cite Evidence** How did industrialization enable Western powers to dominate world affairs?

The Industrial Revolution  13.1 The Industrial Revolution Begins

Assessment

1. Before the Industrial Revolution, most people lived in farming villages. Then, increasing numbers of people moved to cities as men, women, and children began to work in factories, putting in long hours in difficult and dangerous conditions. Mass production lowered prices, so more people were able to afford items that only the wealthy had previously.
2. Wealthy landowners began to consolidate farms by enclosing them to have larger pastures. Better farming equipment and better practices helped increase the supply and quality of food. The better food supply created a population boom. More workers were available to fill jobs, providing the labor for the Industrial Revolution.
3. Coal was used as fuel to power steam engines, and it was used in the process of smelting iron, which was needed to build machines.
4. Nations that had all four factors of production available were able to follow Britain's lead and industrialize. Nations that lacked one or more of the factors of production did not. For example, many nations in southern and eastern Europe lacked either resources or capital.
5. The technological advances that led to industrialization started in the West, generating profits and an economic advantage.

13.2 The Industrial Revolution brought great riches to most of the entrepreneurs who helped set it in motion. It also provided employment for farmers and farmhands displaced by the changes in agriculture. But these jobs came with a heavy price. Millions of workers who crowded into the new factory towns endured dangerous working conditions, unsanitary and overcrowded housing, and unrelenting poverty.

>> Men, women, and children worked side by side in many factories. Conditions in cotton mills could be cramped, as this photograph inside a mill in Lancashire shows.

Social Impact of Industrialism

TEKS
1.E, 8.B, 8.E, 17.A, 17.B, 18.A, 18.B, 18.C, 18.F, 24.A

>> Objectives

Outline the growth of industrial cities and the emergence of new social classes.

Describe the working conditions in factories and mines.

Analyze the benefits and challenges of industrialism.

Describe the ideas of Adam Smith and other thinkers regarding free enterprise.

Identify the origins and characteristics of socialism and communism.

>> Key Terms

urbanization
tenement
labor union
standard of living
social mobility
free market
Thomas Malthus
Jeremy Bentham
utilitarianism
socialism
means of production
Robert Owen
Karl Marx
communism
proletariat
social democracy

Industry Causes Urban Growth

In time, reforms would curb many of the worst abuses of the early Industrial Age in Europe and the Americas. As standards of living increased, people at all levels of society would benefit from industrialization.

The Industrial Revolution brought rapid **urbanization,** or the movement of people to cities. Changes in farming, soaring population growth, and an ever-increasing demand for workers led masses of people to migrate from farms to cities. Almost overnight, small towns around coal or iron mines mushroomed into cities. Other cities grew up around the factories that entrepreneurs built in once-quiet market towns.

The British market town of Manchester numbered 17,000 people in the 1750s. Within a few years, it exploded into a center of the textile industry. Its population soared to 40,000 by 1780 and 70,000 by 1801. Visitors described the "cloud of coal vapor" that polluted the air, the pounding noise of steam engines, and the filthy stench of its river.

PEARSON realize. www.PearsonTexas.com Access your Digital Lesson.

Aa Vocabulary Builder

1. Have students pronounce the following academic vocabulary terms in this lesson and clarify the part of speech. For difficult or polysyllabic words, break them into syllables and pronounce them with the students.
2. Explain what the word means in common "student-friendly" language using synonyms and antonyms when possible. Provide concrete examples to clarify the meaning, and rephrase the definition.

contaminated: unclean and impure; polluted

formulated: devised or developed, as in a theory or plan

stressed: emphasized

Social Impact of Industrialism

CONNECT

Preview Have students preview the **Lesson Objectives** and the list of **Key Terms**.

Students can also preview all the **Key Terms** and **Academic Vocabulary** using the **Interactive Reading Notepad** on the digital course or preview a summary of the lesson in the **Reading and Note Taking Study Guide**.

Online Use the **Editable Presentation** found on the digital course to present the main ideas for this lesson.

Start Up Activity

Direct students' attention to the photograph of child mineworkers later in this lesson and read the caption. Then have students write a journal entry describing a typical day from the perspective of a worker in conditions like those in the photo. Encourage students to share their journals with a partner.

Discuss If you were a teenager in 1850, how would you feel about working a 12-hour day in a factory or coal mine? *(Students will likely respond that it would be difficult and give them little time for doing anything else.)* Why do you think children were expected to work? *(Sample response: Children worked to help out their families. They earned money to help pay for rent and food.)*

Tell students that in this section they will learn about the social and political effects of the Industrial Revolution.

Online You can also project the **Start Up Activity** from the course.

INVESTIGATE

Have students read the section using the **Reading and Note Taking Study Guide** to help them take notes and understand the text as they read.

Industry Causes Urban Growth

The Rise of New Social Classes

Before the Industrial Revolution, European society generally had two classes: the landed nobility and peasants. The economy was based almost entirely on agriculture. The Industrial Revolution changed all that.

Topic 13 Lesson 2

Analyze Images

Direct students' attention to the infographic. What caused the rise of the middle class? *(New business opportunities and economic growth expanded the middle class.)* Ask students to describe ways that the Industrial Revolution led to social changes in Europe. *(Students should identify how the growing cities differed from rural villages and describe the harsh living and working conditions that industrialization created.)*

Guided Reading and Discussion

Identify Cause and Effect Ask students to describe the major effects of the Industrial Revolution. They should focus on the link between industry and urban growth. *(Cities grew around the factories that entrepreneurs built. Towns near coal and iron mines also expanded as demand for these resources increased.)*

Analyze Images Have students look at the photo of Manchester on the facing page. Ask students to describe what life might be like in an urban industrial place like this. *(Students should support their opinion with details from the image.)* Then ask students to identify important changes in human life caused by the Industrial Revolution. If students need help describing the changes, have them compare this urban scene to what they know about life before industrialization. *(Students should identify how rural and urban ways of life differ and describe the harsh living and working conditions that industrialization brought about.)*

Answers

Identify Supporting Details *changes in farming, a population boom, and demand for workers in cities*

Analyze Charts *Sample answer: The part of the upper class that was noble from birth was unaffected by industrialization.*

This growth of industry and rapid population growth dramatically changed the location and distribution of two resources—labor and people.

? IDENTIFY SUPPORTING DETAILS What led to the massive migration of people from farms to cities?

ELPS **ELPS 4.F.3** Demonstrate your understanding of vocabulary words from this section by defining them with both pictures and words.

The Rise of New Social Classes

The Industrial Revolution helped create both a new middle class and a new urban working class. The middle class included entrepreneurs and others who profited from the growth of industry and the rise of cities. The middle class enjoyed a comfortable lifestyle.

When farm laborers and others moved to the new industrial cities, they took jobs in factories or mines. In rural villages, they had strong ties to a community, where their families had lived for generations. In the cities, they felt lost and bewildered. In time, though, factory and mine workers developed their own sense of community.

The Lives of the New Middle Class Those who benefited most from the Industrial Revolution were the entrepreneurs who set it in motion. The Industrial Revolution created this new middle class, or bourgeoisie (boor zhwah ZEE), whose members came from a variety of backgrounds. Some were merchants who invested their profits in factories. Others were inventors or skilled artisans who developed new technologies. Some rose from "rags to riches," a pattern that the age greatly admired. Middle-class families lived in well-built, well-furnished homes. In time, middle-class neighborhoods had paved streets and a steady water supply. These families dressed and ate well. The new middle class took pride in their hard work and their determination to "get ahead." Only a few had sympathy for the poor.

As a sign of their new and improved status, middle-class women sought to imitate the wealthy women of the upper classes. They did not do physical labor or work outside the home. They hired maidservants to care for their homes and look after their children.

The Lives of the Working Class While the wealthy and the middle class lived in pleasant neighborhoods, vast numbers of poor struggled to survive in foul-smelling slums. They packed into tiny rooms in **tenements,** or multistory buildings divided into

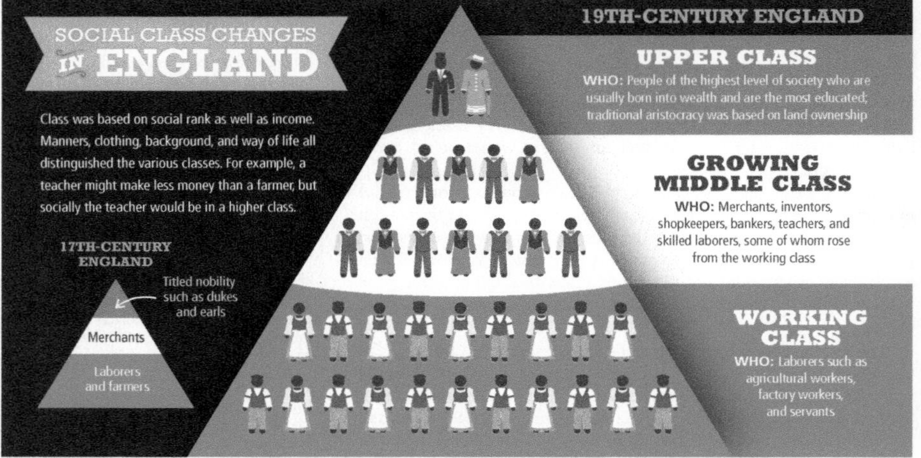

>> The expanding middle class included working-class people who found new opportunities because of industrialization. **Analyze Charts** Which class changed the least due to industrialization?

English Language Proficiency Standards

Reading 4.F.3 There are plenty of challenging vocabulary words that are not part of a lesson's vocabulary list. Remind students to use dictionaries, glossaries, and context clues to improve their vocabularies.

Beginning Display the term *urbanization*. Help students use the picture of Manchester to define the term. Point out the smokestacks of the factories and the growth of the city in the middle of the countryside. Read the third paragraph of "Industry Causes Urban Growth" aloud, stressing the definition given of *urbanization*. Point out the word *mushroomed* in the same paragraph. Ask students to visualize a mushroom growing, and help them use context clues to understand that *mushroomed* means "grew rapidly."

Intermediate Display the term *urbanization*. Ask students to point out details in the picture of Manchester that help them understand what *urbanization* means. Read aloud the text that contains the word's definition. Then ask apartments. These tenements had no running water, only community pumps. Early industrial cities had no sewage or sanitation systems, so waste and garbage rotted in the streets.

Sewage was also dumped into rivers, which created an overwhelming stench and contaminated drinking water. This led to the spread of diseases such as cholera.

Workers' Protests During the early Industrial Revolution, there were no **labor unions,** organizations of workers who bargained for better pay and working conditions. As the Industrial Revolution began, weavers and other skilled artisans resisted the new "labor-saving" machines that were replacing their jobs.

From 1811 to 1813, protesting workers, called Luddites (LUD yts), smashed machines and burned factories. The Luddites were harshly crushed. Although frustrated workers continued to protest, they were forbidden to form worker associations and strikes were outlawed.

Methodists Help the Poor Many working-class people found comfort in a religious movement called Methodism. John Wesley had founded the Methodist movement in the mid-1700s. Wesley stressed the need for a personal sense of faith. He encouraged his followers to improve themselves by adopting sober, moral ways.

Methodist meetings featured hymns and sermons promising forgiveness of sin and a better life to come. Methodist preachers took this message of salvation into the slums. There, they tried to rekindle hope among the working poor. They set up Sunday schools where followers not only studied the Bible but also learned to read and write. Methodists helped channel workers' anger away from revolution and toward reform.

MAKE GENERALIZATIONS How did members of the working class react to their new experiences in industrial cities?

Harsh Conditions in Factories and Mines

The heart of the new industrial city was the factory. There, the technology of the machine age imposed a harsh and dangerous way of life on workers. The miners who supplied the coal and iron for the Industrial Age faced equally unsafe working conditions.

Hazards of the Factory System Working in a factory system differed greatly from working on a farm. In rural

>> This picture shows Manchester, England, around 1850. Fields still surround the crowded city, but by the 1900s, the city had become almost entirely industrialized.

>> John Wesley, founder of Methodism, is shown preaching at his father's grave in a churchyard in Epworth, Lincolnshire, where he was born and raised.

Harsh Conditions in Factories and Mines

Review that the earliest factories housed machines used to make textiles. One of the most common types of mine in Great Britain was the coal mine.

Online Project the **Interactive Gallery: Life of the Working Class** and click on each of the images. Ask for students' reactions to the images.

Make Generalizations Have students describe the working conditions in factories, basing their responses on the text and the images in the slideshow. Then ask students to explain the role of the factory system in advancing the Industrial Revolution. *(Factories were centers of manufacturing. Using new technology and machines, workers in factories churned out goods. Conditions in factories were often harsh, however. Loud machines ran during the long workdays. Hazards included potential fires and dangerous machines.)*

Formulate Questions Then have students choose an industry's working conditions that they would like to learn more about. Have them write several questions they would like to have answered.

ACTIVE CLASSROOM

Have students choose an image in the interactive gallery and Cartoon It. Be sure students understand that political cartoons often use exaggeration to emphasize an opinion on a topic. Students should identify a key concept or main idea and emphasize it with their political cartoon. Post their cartoons in the classroom or include them in a class blog on the effects of the Industrial Revolution.

students to use context to create a glossary definition for the term *mushroomed*, including an illustration.

Advanced Display the term *urbanization*. Have students independently look at the picture of Manchester and read the text that contains the definition of *urbanization*. Then ask students to create a glossary page for the term *mushroomed*, including a definition, an illustration, and a sentence.

Advanced High Have students skim "Industry Causes Urban Growth" and create a list of unfamiliar terms. Then, have students create a pictorial glossary that includes a definition, a sketch, and a sentence for each term. Have students share their mini-glossaries.

Answers

Make Generalizations *The working class felt lost in the industrial cities and experienced difficult living conditions that led to protests and finding comfort in religion.*

Guided Reading and Discussion

Predict Consequences Have students list the working conditions men, women, and children faced due to industrialization. Use this list to discuss the impact of the Industrial Revolution on humanity. *(Students should recognize that industrialization brought about intense social change.)* Why did children work, too? *(Families needed the extra income and children had worked on farms, so it wasn't unusual for them to work.)*

Make Decisions Ask students to think about what they would do if faced with similar working conditions. *(Students' answers will vary, but they should demonstrate understanding of the obstacles people faced.)*

D Differentiate Challenge After students answer the discussion questions, remind them that reformers focused attention on child labor. Have student pairs conduct interviews, with one person in the pair serving as a reform committee member and the other as a child laborer. Then, have them switch roles as interviewer and subject. Tell them they can read firsthand accounts of working conditions online to enrich the content of their interviews.

villages, people worked long hours for low wages, but their work varied according to the season. Life was also hard for poor rural workers who were part of the putting-out system. If they worked too slowly, they did not earn enough, but at least they worked at their own pace. In the factories of industrial towns, workers faced a rigid schedule set by the factory whistle.

Working hours in early factories were long, with shifts lasting from 12 to 16 hours, six or seven days a week. A factory whistle announced time to eat a hasty meal, then quickly sent them back to the machines. Exhausted workers suffered accidents from machines that had no safety devices. They might lose a finger, a limb, or even their lives.

In textile mills, workers constantly breathed air filled with lint, which damaged their lungs. Those workers who became sick or injured lost their jobs.

At first, women made up much of the new industrial work force. Employers often preferred to hire women workers. They thought women could adapt more easily to machines and were easier to manage than men. More important, they were able to pay women less than men, even for the same work.

Factory work created a double burden for women. Their new jobs took them out of their homes for 12 hours or more a day. They then returned to their tenements, which might consist of one damp room with a single bed. They had to feed and clothe their families, clean, and cope with such problems as sickness and injury.

>> Before child labor laws, working-class children like these boys in Pennsylvania worked long hours on hazardous jobs. Many of these mineworkers were aged 10 or even younger. **Hypothesize** Why did mine owners hire children for certain jobs?

Interactive Gallery

Dangers in the Mines As the demand for coal and iron grew, more mines were opened. Although miners were paid more than factory workers, conditions in the mines were even harsher than in the factories. Miners worked in darkness, and the coal dust destroyed their lungs. There were always the dangers of explosions, flooding, and collapsing tunnels.

Women and children worked in mines, carting heavy loads of coal. Children were frequently hired to work in mines because they could climb through narrow shafts. Many spent their days on all fours or carried heavy baskets of coal up flimsy ladders.

Children Perform Risky Work Children had always worked on rural farms or as servants and apprentices. However, child labor took on new dimensions during the Industrial Revolution. Since children had helped with farm work, parents accepted the idea of child labor. The wages children earned were needed to keep their families from starving.

Factories and mines hired many boys and girls. These children often started working at age seven or eight, a few as young as five. Nimble-fingered and quick-moving, they changed spools in the hot and humid textile mills where sometimes they could not see because of all the dust. They also crawled under machinery to repair broken threads in the mills.

Conditions were even worse for children who worked in the mines. Some sat all day in the dark, opening and closing air vents. Others hauled coal carts in the extreme heat.

In the early 1800s, Parliament passed a series of laws, called "factory acts," to reform child labor practices. These early efforts were largely ignored. Then, in 1833, Michael Sadler headed up a committee to look into the conditions of child workers in the textile industry. The Sadler Report contained firsthand accounts of child labor practices and helped bring the harsh labor conditions to light. As a result, Parliament passed new regulations to ease working conditions for children.

An 1833 law forbade the hiring of children under the age of nine and limited the working hours of older children in the textile industry. Over time, Parliament passed other laws to improve working conditions in both factories and mines and to limit the work day of both adults and children to 10 hours. It also enacted

History Background

The Peterloo Massacre On August 16, 1819, a crowd of more than 50,000 men, women, and children in their Sunday best gathered in St. Peter's Field in Manchester. Speakers argued simply that workers had the right to vote and to be represented in Parliament. At the time, less than 5 percent of the men—mainly the rich gentry—could vote. Residents of Manchester and other new industrial cities had no representation at all. Local officials panicked at the size of the crowd. Troops on horseback waved their sabers and charged into the crowd, killing eleven and injuring hundreds. The speakers were arrested. Some were sent to prison for up to two years. Journalists who printed news of the event were also jailed, but one dubbed it the Peterloo Massacre, after the Battle of Waterloo, which had occurred four years earlier.

Answers

Hypothesize *Sample answer: Mine shafts were small and narrow. Boys could fit where men could not.*

laws to require the education of children and to stop the hiring of children and women in mines.

DRAW CONCLUSIONS How did the Industrial Revolution change the lives of men, women, and children?

Benefits of the Industrial Revolution

Since the 1800s, people have debated whether the Industrial Revolution was a blessing or a curse. The early Industrial Age brought great hardships and much misery. Although the first factories did provide jobs and wages to displaced farm workers, the conditions under which they labored were generally terrible. In time, however, reformers, along with labor unions, pushed for laws to improve working conditions in factories, mines, and other industries. Despite the negative aspects of industrialization, the new industrial world eventually brought many advantages.

Better Standards of Living The factory system produced huge quantities of new goods at lower prices than ever before. In time, as wages and working conditions improved, ordinary workers were able to buy goods that in earlier days only the wealthy had been able to afford. Slowly, too, the **standard of living** rose for workers. The standard of living refers to the level of material goods and services available to people in a society. Families ate more varied diets, lived in better homes, and dressed in inexpensive, mass-produced clothing. Advances in medicine ensured healthier lives.

New job opportunities opened up for skilled and unskilled workers. The building of cities, railroads, and factories provided jobs. The demand for goods and the growth of new industries, such as railroads and eventually automobiles, created more job opportunities.

New Worlds for Entrepreneurs The new industrial world was more open to change and innovation than the old rural world. Enterprising people opened new businesses and invented new products. The British potter Josiah Wedgwood, for example, was an entrepreneur who combined science and new industrial methods of production. Wedgwood experimented with new materials to improve the quality of his pottery. He set up a factory that gave each different job to a specially skilled worker. Wedgwood also used his pottery to spread ideas about social justice, especially the abolition of the slave trade. His factory cast antislavery medallions, worn by many, that carried the

>> Many middle-class families enjoyed newly afforded leisure activities, such as taking in a play.

image of a slave in chains with the words "Am I not a man and a brother?"

Social and Political Impact The Industrial Revolution opened new opportunities for success and increased **social mobility,** or the ability of individuals or groups to move up the social scale. In the past, birth determined a person's rank in society. Although birth still gave nobles their status, some families were able to move up the social ladder through successful enterprise. By the late 1800s, many people embraced the "rags to riches" idea, whereby a person could achieve great wealth and status through hard work and thrift.

With social mobility came greater political rights. As the middle class expanded, its members pushed for political influence. Gradually throughout the 1800s, working-class men gained the right to vote. From 1831 to 1885, the number of voters in England and Wales increased from 366,000 to almost 8 million. The growing number of voters gave the working class more power as politicians began to have to appeal to their concerns. Later, women also earned the right to vote.

Benefits of the Industrial Revolution

Remind students that they have already learned about some of the negative results of industrialism: Workers put in long hours under harsh, sometimes dangerous conditions. Counter this by explaining that industrialism also brought benefits, such as jobs, increased incomes, cheaper goods, and the creation of a middle class.

Direct students' attention to the image of a couple enjoying a play, and explain that the emerging middle class had more leisure time and disposable income because of the Industrial Revolution.

Guided Reading and Discussion

Remind students of the challenges of industrialism. Students should then contrast these challenges with the benefits presented in "Better Standards of Living" and "New Worlds for Entrepreneurs."

Identify Main Ideas Have students make a table of the challenges and benefits of industrialization in order to evaluate industrialization's effect on society. *(Challenges: long hours, dangerous working conditions, and low pay for some. Benefits: jobs, economic opportunities, cheaper goods, higher standard of living for others.)*

Make Generalizations Review the negative and positive effects of the Industrial Revolution, and ask students whether they think the benefits of industrialization outweigh the costs. *(Answers will vary. Some might point out that most of the technology we have today wouldn't have been possible without the Industrial Revolution.)*

Answers

Draw Conclusions *Unlike farm work, which varied with seasons and could be done at the worker's own pace, in factories, working hours were long and jobs were dangerous; women were expected to work long hours, do housework, and tend to the sick; children also worked in dangerous conditions for long hours because their families needed the extra income.*

Laissez-Faire Economics

Utilitarians Support Limited Government

Identify the characteristics of the free enterprise system: a free market with unregulated exchange of goods and services and no government interference in the economy.

Apply Concepts Remind students that according to Enlightenment ideals, "natural law" is a set of principles derived from nature. It is common to and binding upon all human beings. Ask students to explain how natural law relates to free enterprise. *(Free market economists believed that the market operated according to a set of natural laws. Therefore, a free market economy does not need government regulation or interference.)*

Guided Reading and Discussion

Evaluate Sources Show students the following quotation. Help them with any unfamiliar vocabulary.

"POLITICAL ECONOMY . . . proposes two distinct objects; first, to provide a plentiful revenue or subsistence for the people, or, more properly, to enable them to provide such a revenue or subsistence for themselves; and, secondly, to supply the state or commonwealth with a revenue sufficient for the public services." —Adam Smith, *The Wealth of Nations*

Paraphrase Ask students to restate the purpose of political economy according to Smith. *(The object of political economy is to provide sufficient money or goods for people to live and to provide sufficient revenue for the government to provide public services.)*

Apply Concepts Ask students to use what they know about laissez-faire economics to explain how a free market fulfills the object of political economy, according to Adam Smith. *(A free market allows people and the state to have sufficient means. Price is determined by the free market, which responds to supply and demand without interference.)*

Labor unions won the right to bargain with employers for better wages, hours, and working conditions.

? CHECK UNDERSTANDING Why was the Industrial Revolution seen as both a blessing and a curse?

Laissez-Faire Economics

Many thinkers and economists tried to understand the staggering changes taking place in the early Industrial Age. As heirs to the Enlightenment, these thinkers looked for natural laws to explain the world of business and economics. Their ideas would influence governments down to the present. Among the most influential schools of thought were laissez-faire economics, utilitarianism, and socialism.

Adam Smith and Laissez-Faire Economics During the Enlightenment, thinkers looked for natural laws that governed the world of business and economics. Physiocrats argued that natural laws should be allowed to operate without interference. As part of this philosophy, they believed that government should not interfere in the free operation of the economy. In the early 1800s, middle-class business leaders embraced this laissez-faire, or "hands-off," approach.

>> In *The Wealth of Nations,* Adam Smith proposed ideas about free market competition that are still applied today.

The main proponent of laissez-faire economics was Adam Smith, author of the bestseller *The Wealth of Nations.* Smith asserted that a **free market,** or unregulated exchange of goods and services, would come to help everyone, not just the rich. The free market, Smith said, would produce more goods at lower prices, making them affordable to everyone. A growing economy would also encourage capitalists to reinvest profits in new ventures. Supporters of this free-enterprise capitalism pointed to the successes of the Industrial Age, in which government had played no part.

Malthus on Population Growth Like Smith, **Thomas Malthus** was a laissez-faire thinker whose writings influenced economic ideas for generations. In his 1798 book *An Essay on the Principle of Population,* he grimly predicted that poverty was unavoidable because the population was increasing faster than the food supply.

Malthus wrote: "The power of population is [far] greater than the power of the Earth to produce subsistence for man." He thought that the only checks on population growth were nature's "natural" methods of war, disease, and famine. As long as population kept increasing, he went on, the poor would suffer. He thus urged families to have fewer children and discouraged charitable handouts and vaccinations.

During the early 1800s, with industrial workers living and working in harsh conditions, many people accepted Malthus's bleak view. His view was proved wrong, however. Although the population boom did continue, the food supply grew even faster.

As the century progressed, living conditions in the Western world slowly improved, and people eventually did begin to have fewer children. By the 1900s, population growth was no longer a problem in the West, but it did continue to afflict many nations elsewhere.

Ricardo and the "Iron Law of Wages" Another influential British laissez-faire economist, David Ricardo, dedicated himself to economic studies after reading Smith's *The Wealth of Nations.* Like Malthus, Ricardo claimed that the poor had too many children and had little chance to escape poverty. In his "Iron Law of Wages," Ricardo noted that when wages were high, families had more children. But more children increased the supply of labor, which led to lower wages and higher unemployment. Because of such gloomy predictions, economics became known as the "dismal science."

Neither Malthus nor Ricardo was a cruel man. Still, both opposed any government help for the poor. In their view, the best cure for poverty was not government

History Background

Adam Smith and the Workers After his death in 1790, Adam Smith's laissez-faire economic theory was used as an argument against reforms. But Smith had been concerned about the welfare of factory workers. In *The Wealth of Nations,* he argued that performing one specialized action all day was harmful to the mental well-being and happiness of workers. In his earlier *Theory of Moral Sentiments,* Smith asserted that mind-numbing work harmed a person's ability to make moral judgments, which had adverse effects on society. He observed that government must try to prevent this from happening to the working poor. He also argued for public education, a radical idea at the time.

Answers

Check Understanding *Although factory work introduced harsh conditions for the working class, there were numerous benefits to industrialization as well, including a new middle class with more opportunities than before.*

relief but the unrestricted "laws of the free market." They felt that individuals should be left to improve their lot through thrift, hard work, and limiting the size of their families.

IDENTIFY CAUSE AND EFFECT How did the ideas that Adam Smith discussed in *The Wealth of Nations* support the free enterprise system?

Utilitarians Support Limited Government

Other thinkers sought to modify laissez-faire doctrines to justify some government intervention. By 1800, British philosopher and economist **Jeremy Bentham** was advocating **utilitarianism,** or the idea that the goal of society should be "the greatest happiness for the greatest number" of its citizens. To Bentham, all laws or actions should be judged by their "utility." In other words, did they provide more pleasure or happiness than pain? Bentham strongly supported individual freedom, which he believed guaranteed happiness. Still, he saw the need for government to become involved under certain circumstances.

Bentham's ideas influenced the British philosopher and economist John Stuart Mill. Although he believed strongly in individual freedom, Mill wanted the government to step in to improve the hard lives of the working class.

"The only purpose for which power can be rightfully exercised over any member of a civilized community, against his will," Mill wrote, "is to prevent harm to others." Therefore, while middle-class business and factory owners were entitled to increase their own happiness, the government should prevent them from doing so in a manner that would harm workers.

Mill further called for giving the vote to workers and women. These groups could then use their political power to win reforms. Most middle-class people rejected Mill's ideas. Only in the later 1800s were his views slowly accepted. Today's democratic governments, however, have absorbed many ideas from Mill and the other utilitarians.

CHECK UNDERSTANDING What did John Stuart Mill see as the proper role of government?

Socialist Thought Emerges

While the champions of laissez-faire economics favored the free market and individual rights, other thinkers focused on social inequality and what they claimed were the evils of industrial capitalism. They argued that industrialization had created an unjust gulf between rich and poor.

>> Philosopher and economist John Stuart Mill supported extending suffrage. Mill believed that political power through voting could lead to necessary reforms.

The Socialist Point of View To end poverty and injustice, some thinkers offered a radical solution—socialism. Under **socialism,** the people as a whole rather than private individuals would own and operate the **means of production**—the farms, factories, railways, and other large businesses that produced and distributed goods. In practice, when socialist governments gained power in the 1900s, they tended to regulate the production and distribution of goods, which often proved inefficient.

Socialism grew out of the Enlightenment faith in progress and human nature and its concern for social justice. Socialist thinkers developed a number of different ideas about how to achieve their goals. The early experiments in socialism differed greatly from what later socialist governments would do.

Owen and Utopian Socialism A number of early socialists established communities in which all work was shared and all property was owned in common. When there was no difference between rich and poor, they said, fighting between people would disappear.

Socialist Thought Emerges

Marx and the Origins of Communism

Remind students what they have learned about free enterprise, socialism, and communism, and briefly review the definitions of each.

Online Project the **Interactive Chart: Comparing Economic Systems**. Have volunteers take turns identifying where each statement should be moved.

Analyze Charts When the chart is completed, ask students to compare and contrast the three economic systems. Because socialism and communism have similarities, make sure students can distinguish between them. *(Capitalism: a free market where individuals own the means of production; Socialism: the community as a whole owns the means of production and cooperates together; Communism: like socialism, the means of production are not individually owned; however, the change to communism is revolution with the workers united to overthrow owners.)*

Key Terms

Ask students to find the key term **socialism** (in bold) in the text and read its meaning. Point out the word's root, *social,* and that it was supposed to lead to *social* good, a system that was good for all of society.

D Differentiate Extra Support This section includes references to economic concepts with which students may not be familiar. Have students write down unfamiliar terms. Have them call out the terms, and others can suggest possible definitions. Clarify the meanings so that students understand the main concepts of this lesson.

Answers

Identify Cause and Effect *Smith asserted that a free market—the unregulated exchange of goods and services—would come to help everyone, not just the rich. The free market would produce more goods at lower prices, making them affordable. A growing economy would encourage capitalists to reinvest profits in new ventures.*

Check Understanding *He believed the government should prevent harm to others and improve the lives of the working class.*

Topic 13 Lesson 2

Guided Reading and Discussion

Integrate Information Ask students to summarize how changes to the economy resulting from the Industrial Revolution affected political change. *(The Industrial Revolution quickly expanded the economic power of industrialized countries, leading to new economic theories that eventually drove political decisions.)*

Cite Evidence Have students fill out the following statement three times to identify the historical origin of the three economic systems covered in this lesson. "__________ developed from views about __________." *(free enterprise: views about laissez-faire economics from Smith, Malthus, and Ricardo; socialism: views about class, injustice, and shared means of production; communism: views about the proletariat rising up to overthrow the bourgeoisie, as predicted by Karl Marx)*

Compare Points of View Verify that students understand the origins of contemporary economic systems by having them conduct a class debate. Divide the class into three groups and assign an economic system to each group. Groups should research the origins, benefits, and drawbacks of their economic system. Groups can take turns presenting arguments for or against their economic system.

These early socialists were called Utopians. To critics, the name implied that they were impractical dreamers.

One of these social reformers was **Robert Owen.** Owen himself was an industrial success story. He started life as a poor Welsh boy and became a successful mill owner. Unlike most industrialists at the time, Owen refused to use child labor. He campaigned vigorously for laws that limited child labor and encouraged the organization of labor unions.

Like other Utopians, Owen believed there was a way he could change society for the better. To prove his point, he set up a model community around a mill in New Lanark, Scotland, to put his own ideas into practice. At his factory in New Lanark, he built homes for workers, opened a school for children, and generally treated employees well. He wanted to show that an employer could offer decent living and working conditions and still run a profitable business.

IDENTIFY What were the characteristic beliefs of early socialists?

>> This well-known Marxist poster proclaims in German, "Workers of all countries, unite!" **Determine Point of View** Why should workers unite, according to Marx?

Interactive Chart

Marx and the Origins of Communism

In the 1840s, **Karl Marx,** a German philosopher, condemned the ideas of the Utopians as unrealistic idealism. He formulated a new theory, "scientific socialism," which he claimed was based on a scientific study of history. He teamed up with another German socialist, Friedrich Engels, whose father owned a textile factory in England.

Marxist Theory Marx and Engels wrote a pamphlet, *The Communist Manifesto*, which they published in 1848. "A spectre [ghost] is haunting Europe," it began, "the spectre of communism." According to Marx, **communism** would bring a classless society in which the means of production would be owned in common for the good of all.

In fact, wherever communism came to be practiced in the 1900s, it brought a system of government in which the state led by a small elite controlled all economic and political life and exercised authoritarian control over the people.

In *The Communist Manifesto*, Marx theorized that economics was the driving force in history. He argued that there was "the history of class struggles" between the "haves" and the "have-nots." The "haves" had always owned the means of production and thus controlled society and all its wealth. In industrialized Europe, Marx said, the "haves" were the bourgeoisie. The "have-nots" were the **proletariat,** or working class.

According to Marx, the modern class struggle pitted the bourgeoisie against the proletariat. In the end, he predicted, the proletariat would be triumphant. Workers would then take control of the means of production and set up a classless, communist society. In such a society, the struggles of the past would end because wealth and power would be shared equally.

Marx despised capitalism. He believed it created prosperity for only a few and poverty for many. He called for an international struggle to bring about its downfall. "Workers of all countries," he urged, "unite!"

Marxism Finds Support At first, Marxist ideas had little impact. In time, however, they would gain supporters around the world. In western Europe, communist political parties emerged and promoted the goals of violent revolution to achieve a classless society. Marx's ideas would never be practiced exactly as he imagined. Even so, Karl Marx remains a key historic figure, not only in his lifetime but in the century to come.

Answers

Identify *Early socialists believed that all people, not private individuals, should own the means of production.*

Determine Point of View *Sample answer: Marx wanted to end capitalism, which he believed created wealth for only a few and poverty for many. He thought that if all workers, or the proletariat, united together, they could overthrow the bourgeoisie, or wealthy who controlled society, and end capitalism.*

Analyze Charts *46 years*

Check Understanding *Marx believed the proletariat would triumph over the bourgeoisie and take control under a classless socialist system.*

History Background

Friedrich Engels Engels was born in Germany in 1820. His father was the wealthy owner of a textile mill. When Engels moved to a town near Manchester, England, in 1842, he was already interested in radical politics. He took a position in a cotton plant that was partially owned by his father. Engels used his firsthand knowledge of the hardships of factory workers and his excellent writing skills to portray their lives. Like *Uncle Tom's Cabin,* Engels's book outraged readers. Just four years later, Engels helped Karl Marx write *The Communist Manifesto,* one of the most influential books in history. They both believed that through revolution the new industrial working class would rise to power and transform society. In later years, Engels was a successful businessman (and capitalist) who used his income to support Marx and his writing.

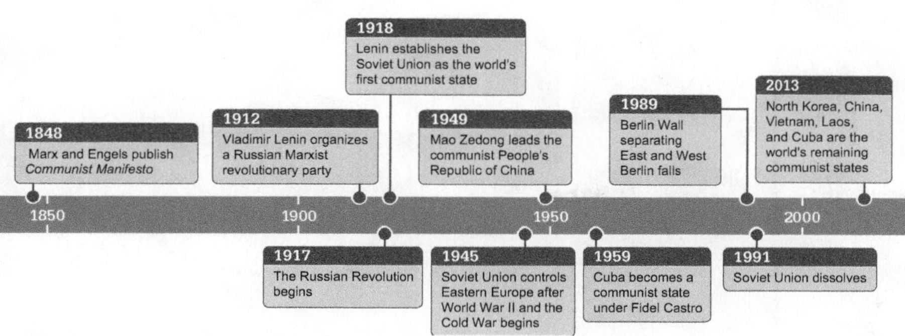
1848
Marx and Engels publish *Communist Manifesto*
1912
Vladimir Lenin organizes a Russian Marxist revolutionary party
1918
Lenin establishes the Soviet Union as the world's first communist state
1949
Mao Zedong leads the communist People's Republic of China
1989
Berlin Wall separating East and West Berlin falls
2013
North Korea, China, Vietnam, Laos, and Cuba are the world's remaining communist states
1850
1900
1950
2000
1917
The Russian Revolution begins
1945
Soviet Union controls Eastern Europe after World War II and the Cold War begins
1959
Cuba becomes a communist state under Fidel Castro
1991
Soviet Union dissolves

>> Since Marx's lifetime, communism has spread globally and then declined. **Analyze Charts** How much time elapsed between the Soviet Union's gaining control of Eastern Europe and the end of the Soviet Union?

In the 1860s, German socialists adapted Marx's beliefs to form **social democracy,** a political ideology in which there is a gradual transition from capitalism to socialism instead of a sudden violent overthrow of the system. By the late 1800s, a rift formed between strict Marxists, who believed in revolution to end capitalism, and social democrats, who believed in the possibility of peaceful reform.

In the late 1800s, Russian socialists embraced Marxism and formed a communist party to bring about revolution. In 1917, the Russian Revolution set up a communist government there that lasted until 1991. During the 1900s, revolutionaries in countries from China to Cuba adapted Marxist ideas to their own situations and needs. Independence leaders in Asia, Latin America, and Africa often experimented with Marxist ideas.

Marxism Loses Its Appeal Marx claimed that his ideas were based on scientific laws. However, many of his ideas turned out to be wrong. He predicted that the misery of the proletariat would touch off a world revolution. Instead, by 1900, the standard of living of the working class improved in industrially developed countries. He also predicted that workers would unite across national borders to wage class warfare.

Instead, people continued to feel stronger ties to their own countries than to any international workers' movement. Finally, by the late 1900s, the few nations that had experimented with communism were moving away from government control of the economy and were adding elements of free-market capitalism.

 **CHECK UNDERSTANDING** What did Marx predict was the future of the proletariat?

ASSESSMENT

1. **Summarize** How did the middle class live during the Industrial Revolution?
2. **Describe** What was life like for working-class women during the Industrial Revolution?
3. **Cite Evidence** What key social and economic changes did industrialization bring about, both for the better and for the worse? Explain your answer with evidence from the text.
4. **Identify Main Ideas** What were the historical origins and characteristics of the free enterprise system?
5. **Identify Patterns** How did the Industrial Revolution impact the development of modern economic systems? In your answer, identify the economic systems that arose during that period.

SYNTHESIZE

Online Project the **Digital Activity: Economic Schools of Thought**.

Discuss Ask the following for each of the economic systems in the organizer. In what way does __________ address the distribution of wealth brought on by industrialization? *(Free market: The market will regulate itself and provide equal opportunity; Utilitarian: The economy should be based on what is best for the most people; Socialism: People should cooperate and share the means of production; Communism: Workers should unite and overthrow the wealthy.)*

DEMONSTRATE

Online Assign the online **Digital Lesson Quiz** for this lesson if you haven't already done so. Students will be offered automatic remediation or enrichment based on their score.

Pose this question to the class on the Discussion Board:

Apply Concepts Why are economic systems fundamental to studying the Industrial Revolution? *(The Industrial Revolution changed the distribution of wealth and brought attention to class distinctions. New economic systems of thought developed to answer questions about how to distribute the profits from industry. In addition, inequities in society grew, and some thinkers proposed different systems to deal with this change.)*

Topic Inquiry

Have students continue their investigations for the Topic Inquiry.

Assessment

1. They lived in pleasant neighborhoods in spacious homes on paved streets. They had a supply of clean water. Women raised children at home instead of working or employing servants to raise them.
2. They worked long hours under harsh conditions in factories, and then when they went home, they had to tend to their families.
3. People moved to cities, creating problems with poor living conditions. The lower class worked long, hard hours. However, industrialization provided jobs to unemployed farmers. Overall, the standard of living increased for many, and there were new opportunities for social mobility.
4. The free enterprise system has its origins in the economic changes that occurred shortly before and during the Industrial Revolution. A free market is based on laissez-faire economic theory, in which the government does not need to interfere in the economy.
5. The free enterprise system developed as entrepreneurs invested in business during the Industrial Revolution. Socialists reacted to abuses that occurred during the Industrial Revolution. They proposed that the government or the people should own the means of production. Marx did not think socialists went far enough and developed the theory of communism; it stated that workers would rise up to create a classless society.

Topic 13 Lesson 3

The Second Industrial Revolution

CONNECT

Preview Have students preview the **Lesson Objectives** and the list of **Key Terms**.

Students can also preview all the **Key Terms** and **Academic Vocabulary** using the **Interactive Reading Notepad** on the digital course or preview a summary of the lesson in the **Reading and Note Taking Study Guide**.

Online Use the **Editable Presentation** found on the digital course to present the main ideas for this lesson.

Start Up Activity

Explain that during the second Industrial Revolution, advances in science, technology, and big business prompted industrial growth and revolutionized the way people lived. Have students write predictions, based on the questions below, about the role of science and technology in the second Industrial Revolution

Predict How will advances in technology impact business? *(Answers will vary. Students may say that more industries will become mechanized, so that a wider variety of goods become affordable. Others may say that businesses will grow from small local companies to huge national corporations.)*

Predict What technological advances do you think will change daily life? *(Answers will vary. Students might say that daily life was affected by inventions like the light bulb and the automobile.)*

Online You can also project the **Start Up Activity** from the course.

INVESTIGATE

Have students read the section using the **Reading and Note Taking Study Guide** to help them take notes and understand the text as they read.

Science and Technology Change Industry

Advances in Transportation and Communication

Advances in transportation technology changed the way people traveled and transported goods. These innovations also changed cities by introducing subway systems, elevated trains, paved roads, and bridges.

>> Henry Ford introduced the moving assembly line in 1913. These men are assembling the flywheel magneto—the first part of the Model T to be manufactured on a moving assembly line.

Interactive Flipped Video

13.3 The first phase of industrialization was forged from iron, powered by steam engines, and driven by the British textile industry. By the mid-1800s, the Industrial Revolution was entering a new phase in which new factories powered by new sources of energy used new processes to turn out new products. At the same time, new forms of business organization led to the rise of giant new companies.

TEKS
8.B, 8.E, 17.A, 17.B, 28.A, 28.E

>> Objectives

Describe the impact of new technology on industry, transportation, and communication.

Understand how big business emerged.

Summarize the impact of medical advances in the later 1800s.

Describe how cities changed and grew.

Explain how conditions for workers gradually improved.

>> Key Terms

Henry Bessemer
Alfred Nobel
Michael Faraday
dynamo
Thomas Edison
interchangeable parts
assembly line
Orville and Wilbur Wright
Guglielmo Marconi
stock
corporation
cartel
germ theory
Louis Pasteur
Robert Koch
Florence Nightingale
Joseph Lister
urban renewal
mutual-aid society

PEARSON realize. www.PearsonTexas.com Access your Digital Lesson.

The Second Industrial Revolution

Science and Technology Change Industry

During the early Industrial Revolution, inventions such as the steam engine were generally the work of gifted tinkerers. They experimented with simple machines to make them better.

During the second Industrial Revolution, the pace of change quickened as companies hired professional chemists and engineers to create new products and machinery. The union of science, technology, and industry spurred economic growth.

The Bessemer Process Transforms Steel British engineer **Henry Bessemer** and American inventor William Kelly independently developed a new process for making steel from iron. In 1856, Bessemer patented this process. Steel was lighter, harder, and more durable than iron, so it could be produced very cheaply. Steel quickly became the major material used in tools, bridges, and railroads. As steel production soared, industrialized countries measured their success in steel output. In 1880, for example, the average German steel mill produced less than 5 million metric tons of steel a year. By 1910, that figure had reached nearly 15 million metric tons.

560

Aa Vocabulary Builder

1. Have students pronounce the following academic vocabulary term in this lesson and clarify the part of speech. For difficult or polysyllabic words, break them into syllables and pronounce them with the students.
2. Explain what the word means in common "student-friendly" language using synonyms and antonyms when possible. Provide concrete examples to clarify the meaning, and rephrase the definition.

illuminate: to lighten or brighten

Innovations in Chemistry During the same period, chemists created hundreds of new products, from medicines such as aspirin to perfumes and soaps. Newly developed chemical fertilizers played a key role in increasing food production.

In 1866, the Swedish chemist **Alfred Nobel** invented dynamite, an explosive much safer than others used at the time. It was widely used in construction and, to Nobel's dismay, in warfare. Dynamite earned Nobel a huge fortune, which he willed to fund the famous Nobel prizes that are still awarded today.

Electricity Replaces Steam Power In the late 1800s, a new power source—electricity—replaced steam as the dominant source of industrial power. Scientists like Benjamin Franklin had tinkered with electricity a century earlier. The Italian scientist Alessandro Volta developed the first battery around 1800. Later, the English chemist **Michael Faraday** created the first simple electric motor and the first **dynamo,** a machine that generates electricity. Today, all electrical generators and transformers work on the principle of Faraday's dynamo.

In the 1870s, the American inventor **Thomas Edison** made the first electric light bulb. Soon, Edison's "incandescent lamps" illuminated whole cities. The pace of city life quickened, and factories could continue to operate after dark. By the 1890s, cables carried electrical power from dynamos to factories.

Improved Methods of Production The basic features of the factory system remained the same during the 1800s. Factories still used large numbers of workers and power-driven machines to mass-produce goods. To improve efficiency, however, manufacturers designed products with **interchangeable parts,** identical components that could be used in place of one another. Interchangeable parts simplified both the assembly and repair of products. By the early 1900s, manufacturers had introduced another new method of production, the **assembly line.**

Workers on an assembly line add parts to a product that moves along a belt from one work station to the next. A different person performs each task along the assembly line. While not all factories used assembly lines, the factory system always relied on the division of labor. Each worker was assigned one task, such as putting the sole on a shoe or sewing a collar on a shirt. Once that task was done, the worker handed the product to the next person, who then performed his or her task. Interchangeable parts, the division of labor, and the assembly line all made production more

Steel Production, 1880–1910

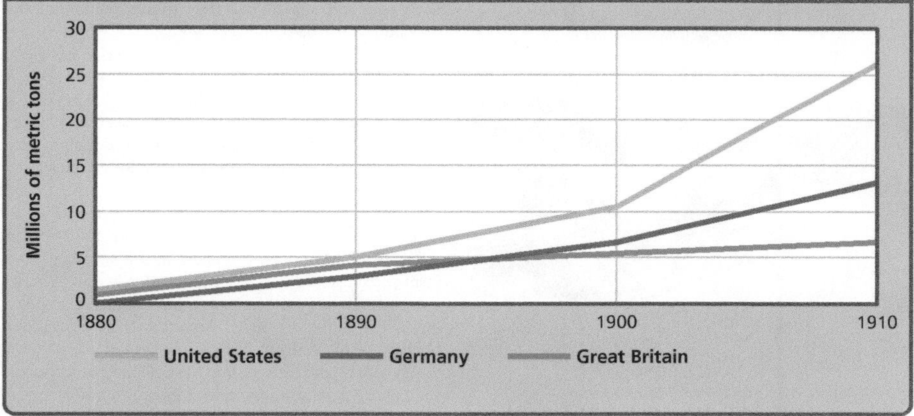

>> By the late 1800s, steel was the major material used in manufacturing tools. **Analyze Graphs** Between 1890 and 1910, which nation had the greatest increase in steel production? The smallest?

History Background

The Slow Acceptance of Electricity Like the development of steam power and the railroad before it, the development of electricity caused fear and apprehension. People were concerned about health hazards from the new, untested technology. Poorly insulated wires were placed next to gas mains, causing frightening explosions that made the front page of the papers. Accidental electrocutions also made the front page. At first, electricity was unreliable and repairs were slow, as there were not enough technicians. People also did not understand the new technology; Mark Twain and L. Frank Baum both satirized the fear that electricity would fall into the wrong hands. Consequently, the use of electricity spread slowly. Advertisements of the 1920s were still trying to convince people that electricity was safe and beneficial.

Topic 13 Lesson 3

Online Project the **Interactive Timeline: Transportation Milestones**. Click through each hot spot on the timeline, and discuss the impact each development had on society and the role it played in advancing the Industrial Revolution.

ACTIVE CLASSROOM

List the following innovations on the board: electricity, dynamo, automobile, airplane, internal combustion engine, radio, telephone, telegraph, interchangeable parts, and assembly line. Ask students to rank them according to which they think had the greatest impact on society and business. Ask students to provide a justification for the ranking based on how each development led to social changes. Then have students work in pairs to share their ideas. *(Answers will vary. Students should provide reasons for their ranking that include specific effects on society, such as greater mobility or instant communications, or improvements in the factory system leading to lower prices for goods.)*

D Differentiate Challenge/Gifted After students complete their ranking, have them write a short opinion essay explaining the reasons for their top ranking. Remind students to use evidence to support their claim. Have students exchange their essays with a partner and discuss their claim and evidence.

Guided Reading and Discussion

Have students discuss the causes and effects of the Industrial Revolution. Fill in a cause-and-effect graphic organizer on the board with students' responses.

Identify the contributions of Thomas Edison and other inventors. How did these inventions advance the Industrial Revolution? *(Sample response: Edison invented the electric light bulb, which allowed factories to stay open longer and made city streets safer. Faraday invented the dynamo, which was essential for later inventions. Otto invented the internal combustion engine, later used in cars, airplanes, and farming equipment.)*

Answers

Analyze Graphs *Unites States; Great Britain*

Topic 13 Lesson 3

Explain the global impact of advances in communications and transportation technology and how they led to economic changes. *(Sample response: Business leaders could communicate more quickly and ship their goods farther, including to foreign countries. New inventions, such as cars, meant more jobs and money because people had to produce the cars.)*

Make Predictions Divide students into small groups and have them write predictions about the additional changes the Industrial Revolution will bring about. Have them explain how these changes will further affect society, business, and the economy. Then discuss their ideas as a class. Have them keep these predictions in mind as they continue reading.

The Rise of Big Business

New technologies and methods of production led to economic changes in Europe and the United States. Entrepreneurs, such as John D. Rockefeller, Alfred Krupp, and Andrew Carnegie, formed big businesses and began to finance, manufacture, and distribute goods on a large scale. These big businesses soon dominated industry. In order to get the money they needed, owners began selling stock in their companies. Some powerful leaders created monopolies that controlled entire industries or sectors of the economy.

>> In 1903, Orville and Wilbur Wright tested their flying machine at Kitty Hawk, North Carolina. By 1905, they had built an airplane that could stay in the air for 39 minutes.

Interactive Timeline

>> Construction of the Trans-Siberian Railroad began in 1891. Work continued on various parts of the line until 1916.

efficient. They also lowered the price of factory goods, making them affordable to more people.

IDENTIFY CAUSE AND EFFECT How did the assembly line and division of labor affect manufacturing?

Advances in Transportation and Communication

During the second Industrial Revolution, transportation and communications were transformed by technology. Steamships replaced sailing ships, and railroad building took off. In Europe and North America, rail lines connected inland cities and seaports, mining regions, and industrial centers. In the United States, a transcontinental railroad provided rail service from the Atlantic to the Pacific. In the same way, Russians built the Trans-Siberian Railroad, linking Moscow in European Russia to Vladivostok on the Pacific. Railroad tunnels and bridges crossed the Alps in Europe and the Andes in South America. Passengers and goods rode on rails in India, China, Egypt, and South Africa.

The Age of the Automobile The transportation revolution took a new turn when a German engineer, Nikolaus Otto, invented a gasoline-powered internal combustion engine. In 1886, Karl Benz received a patent for the first automobile, which had three wheels. A year later, Gottlieb Daimler (DYM lur) introduced the first four-wheeled automobile. People laughed at the "horseless carriages," but they quickly changed the way people traveled.

The French nosed out the Germans as early automakers. Then the American Henry Ford started making models that reached the breathtaking speed of 25 miles per hour. In the early 1900s, Ford began using the assembly line to mass-produce cars, making the United States a leader in the automobile industry.

The First Airplane The invention of the internal combustion engine changed life and industry in other ways. Motorized threshers and reapers boosted farm production. Even more dramatically, the internal combustion engine made possible sustained, pilot-controlled flight. In 1903, American bicycle makers **Orville and Wilbur Wright** designed and flew a flimsy airplane at Kitty Hawk, North Carolina. Although their flying machine stayed aloft for only a few seconds, it ushered in the air age.

Soon, daredevil pilots were flying airplanes across the English Channel and over the Alps. Commercial

Answers

Identify Cause and Effect *Using an assembly line and the division of labor forced workers to specialize in and repeatedly complete one specific task. Specializing in one task made workers more efficient because they did not have to master every task that needed to be done, particularly in producing complex products such as automobiles.*

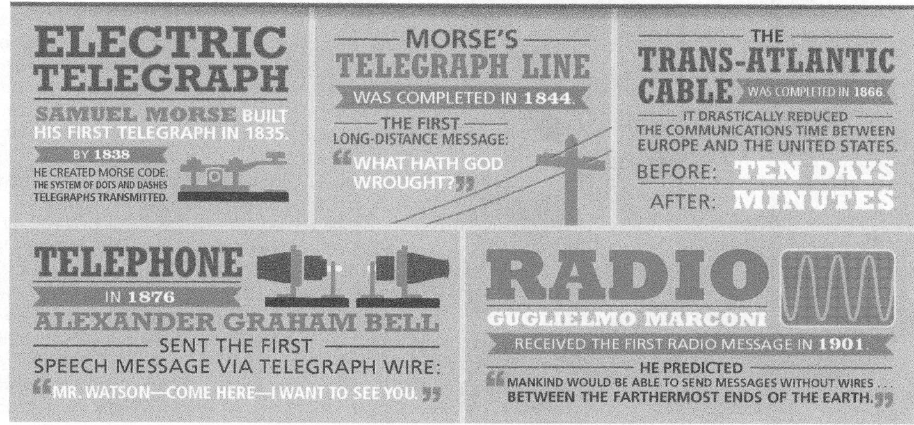

ADVANCES IN COMMUNICATION DURING THE INDUSTRIAL REVOLUTION
ELECTRIC TELEGRAPH
SAMUEL MORSE BUILT HIS FIRST TELEGRAPH IN 1835.
BY 1838
HE CREATED MORSE CODE: THE SYSTEM OF DOTS AND DASHES TELEGRAPHS TRANSMITTED.
MORSE'S TELEGRAPH LINE
WAS COMPLETED IN 1844.
THE FIRST LONG-DISTANCE MESSAGE:
"WHAT HATH GOD WROUGHT?"
THE TRANS-ATLANTIC CABLE
WAS COMPLETED IN 1866.
IT DRASTICALLY REDUCED THE COMMUNICATIONS TIME BETWEEN EUROPE AND THE UNITED STATES.
BEFORE: TEN DAYS
AFTER: MINUTES
TELEPHONE
IN 1876
ALEXANDER GRAHAM BELL
SENT THE FIRST SPEECH MESSAGE VIA TELEGRAPH WIRE:
"MR. WATSON—COME HERE—I WANT TO SEE YOU."
RADIO
GUGLIELMO MARCONI
RECEIVED THE FIRST RADIO MESSAGE IN 1901.
HE PREDICTED
"MANKIND WOULD BE ABLE TO SEND MESSAGES WITHOUT WIRES . . . BETWEEN THE FARTHERMOST ENDS OF THE EARTH."

>> **Analyze Information** How did the Trans-Atlantic cable affect communications?

passenger travel, however, would not begin until the 1920s.

A Communications Revolution A revolution in communications also made the world smaller. An American inventor, Samuel F. B. Morse, developed the telegraph, which could send coded messages over wires by means of electricity. His first telegraph line went into service between Washington, D.C., and Baltimore in 1844. By the 1860s, an undersea cable was relaying messages between Europe and North America. This trans-Atlantic cable was an amazing engineering accomplishment for its day.

Communication soon became even faster. In 1876, the Scottish-born American inventor Alexander Graham Bell patented the telephone. By the 1890s, the Italian pioneer **Guglielmo Marconi** had invented the radio, which allowed wireless communication over long distances. In 1901, Marconi received a radio message, using Morse code, sent from Britain to Canada. As Marconi had predicted, radio soon became a key part of a global communications network that linked every corner of the world.

 **IDENTIFY CAUSE AND EFFECT** How did Nikolaus Otto's invention of the internal combustion engine affect the Industrial Revolution? What can you infer about its impact on Western nations?

The Rise of Big Business

By the late 1800s, what we call "big business" came to dominate industry. Big business refers to an establishment that is run by entrepreneurs who finance, manufacture, and distribute goods or services on a large scale. As time passed, some big businesses came to control entire industries.

Investors Form Corporations The latest technologies required the investment of large amounts of money, or capital. To get the needed capital, owners sold **stock,** or shares in their companies, to investors. Each stockholder became owner of a tiny part of a company. Large-scale companies, such as steel foundries, needed so much capital that they sold hundreds of thousands of shares. These businesses formed giant **corporations,** businesses that are owned by many investors who buy shares of stock. With large amounts of capital, corporations could expand into many areas.

Monopolies Dominate Industry Some powerful business leaders created monopolies and trusts, huge corporate structures that controlled entire industries or areas of the economy. In Germany, Alfred Krupp inherited a steelmaking business from his father. He bought up coal and iron mines along with the supply lines that carried raw materials to feed the steel

Analyze Images

Direct students' attention to the political cartoon on the next page. Some critics believed the growth of monopolies had a dangerous effect on society. What does this political cartoon show? Why do you think the cartoonist represented monopolies this way? *(The cartoon shows a monopoly as an octopus-like monster that is taking over businesses. The cartoonist most likely opposed monopolies because they crushed their competitors.)*

Guided Reading and Discussion

To extend understanding of this section, discuss how business, monopolies, and cartels impacted the economies of Europe and the United States. *(Monopolies took over whole industries. Cartels were able to fix prices, set production quotas, and control markets. Monopolies and cartels put many small companies out of business. Big business also created the stock market and a new way to invest money.)*

Explain an Argument Why was there a debate over the growth of big business? Explain both sides of the argument. Cite textual evidence to support your response. *(Sample response: The growing power and wealth of business leaders concerned many people. Those who supported big business claimed that business leaders invested their wealth in worldwide ventures and employed thousands. Those who opposed big business claimed that leaders were putting many people out of business and damaging the free-market economy.)*

D Differentiate Challenge/Gifted Ask students to create their own political cartoons representing big business or monopolies. Remind them that political cartoons express an opinion about an issue. Have students post their cartoons on a Web site or in the classroom.

Answers

Analyze Information *Sample answer: It reduced the communications time between Europe and the United States from ten days to a few minutes.*

Identify Cause and Effect *It powered automobiles, threshers, reapers, and airplanes, which improved transportation and farm production. The invention helped the economies of industrialized Western nations that produced these products.*

Better Medicine, Nutrition, and Health

The population in Europe exploded during the Industrial Revolution. The rapid increase in population was the direct result of better nutrition and sanitation and major advances in medicine. The discoveries and contributions of many people, such as scientist Louis Pasteur, helped combat disease and create safer, cleaner hospitals.

Key Terms

Ask students to find the key term **germ theory** (in bold) in the text. Ask: Why was it important to know that certain microbes cause disease? *(Once the link was known, scientists and doctors could work on finding preventions and cures.)*

Online Project the **Interactive Gallery: Advances in Medicine During the Industrial Age**. Look at each image individually and then the collection of images as a whole.

ACTIVE CLASSROOM

Have students choose two images from the gallery and write headlines that capture the action in each image or the information in the captions. Then divide the class into small groups and have students discuss their headlines. Have groups synthesize their ideas to write a revised headline for each image.

Guided Reading and Discussion

Advances in medicine and science led to important changes in human life. New vaccines and antiseptic operations meant people lived longer than ever before. Improved sanitation in hospitals was particularly important for the poor because they could not afford to be treated at home.

>> This 1899 American political cartoon shows a monopoly as an octopus-like monster covering a city. **Analyze Political Cartoons** Which side of the debate about the effects of monopolies does this cartoon support? Explain.

>> Alfred Krupp was the first industrialist to use the Bessemer process in Europe. Known as the "Cannon King," Krupp produced cast-steel cannons and other weapons of war.

business. Later, he and his son acquired plants that made tools, railroad cars, and weapons.

In the United States, John D. Rockefeller dominated the petroleum industry by gaining control of oil wells, oil refineries, and oil pipelines. Andrew Carnegie, who started out as a poor immigrant from Scotland, worked his way up to build an American steel empire. He later used his wealth to fund libraries, universities, and other charities.

Sometimes, a group of corporations would join forces and form a **cartel,** an association to fix prices, set production quotas, or control markets. In Germany, a single cartel fixed prices for 170 coal mines.

Opposing Views of Big Business The rise of big business sparked a stormy debate. Admirers saw the Krupps, Rockefellers, and Carnegies as "captains of industry" and praised their vision and skills. They pointed out that capitalists invested their wealth in worldwide ventures, such as railroad building, that employed thousands of workers and added to the general prosperity. They also claimed that monopolies increased efficiency by driving out less efficient corporations.

To critics, the aggressive magnates were "robber barons" who ruthlessly destroyed competing companies in pursuit of profit. With the competition gone, they were free to raise prices. Destroying competition, critics argued, damaged the free-enterprise system. Reformers called for laws to prevent monopolies and regulate large corporations. By the early 1900s, some governments did move against monopolies. However, the political and economic power of business leaders often hindered efforts at regulation.

DRAW CONCLUSIONS Why was there a move toward developing monopolies?

Better Medicine, Nutrition, and Health

The population explosion that had begun during the 1700s continued through the 1800s. Between 1800 and 1900, the population of Europe more than doubled. This rapid growth was not due to larger families. In fact, families in most industrializing countries had fewer children. Instead, populations soared because the death rate fell. Nutrition improved, thanks in part to improved methods of farming, food storage, and distribution. Medical advances and improvements in public sanitation also slowed death rates.

D Differentiate Extra Support While looking through the interactive gallery, help students understand the different types of medical advances. Explain any terms that might be unfamiliar, such as *vaccines, unsanitary, antiseptics,* and *sterilize*. Ask students why it would be important for doctors to wash their hands and instruments. *(Dirty hands and instruments can lead to infection.)*

Answers

Analyze Political Cartoons *Sample answer: The cartoon supports the reformer's beliefs that monopolies were damaging the free enterprise system because the octopus is covering all of the businesses in the city.*

Draw Conclusions *Business leaders who dominated entire industries could squeeze out competing companies and then charge any price for a product or service.*

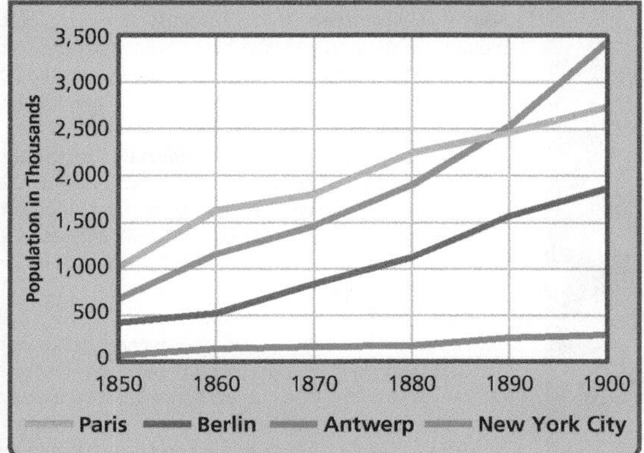

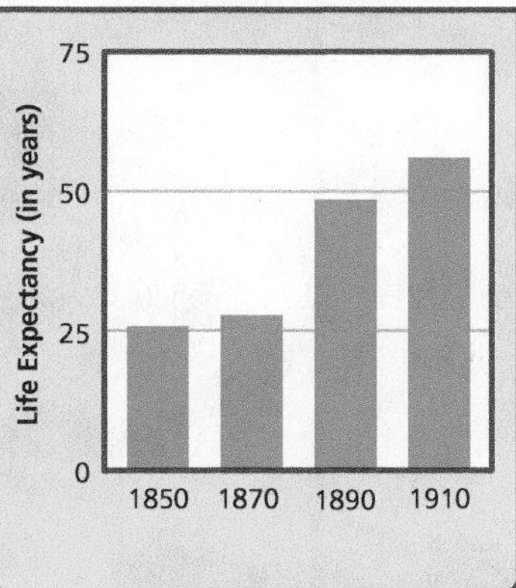

>> Longer life expectancies contributed to population booms in major cities. **Analyze Graphs** Which city's population grew the most? How did life expectancy change between 1850 and 1910?

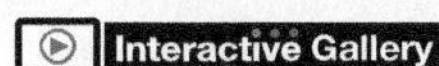

Combating Disease Since the 1600s, scientists had known of microscopic organisms, or microbes. Some scientists speculated that certain microbes might cause specific infectious diseases. Yet most doctors scoffed at this **germ theory.** Not until 1870 did French chemist **Louis Pasteur** (pas TUR) clearly show the link between microbes and disease. Pasteur went on to make other major contributions to medicine, including the development of vaccines against rabies and anthrax. He also discovered a process called pasteurization that killed disease-carrying microbes in milk.

In the 1880s, the German doctor **Robert Koch** identified the bacterium that caused tuberculosis, a respiratory disease that claimed about 30 million human lives in the 1800s. The search for a tuberculosis cure, however, took half a century. By 1914, yellow fever and malaria had been traced to microbes carried by mosquitoes.

As people understood how germs caused disease, they bathed and changed their clothes more often. In European cities, better hygiene helped decrease the rate of disease.

Improving Hospital Care By the 1840s, anesthesia was being widely used to relieve pain during surgery. The use of anesthetic gas allowed doctors to experiment with operations that had never before been possible.

Yet, throughout the century, hospitals could be dangerous places. Surgery was performed with dirty instruments in dank rooms. Often, a patient would survive an operation, only to die days later of infection. For the poor, being admitted to a hospital was often a death sentence. Wealthy or middle-class patients insisted on treatment in their own homes.

"The very first requirement in a hospital," said British nurse **Florence Nightingale,** "is that it should do the sick no harm." As an army nurse during the Crimean War, Nightingale insisted on better hygiene in field hospitals. After the war, she worked to introduce sanitary measures in British hospitals. She also founded the world's first school of nursing.

The English surgeon **Joseph Lister** discovered how antiseptics prevented infection. He insisted that surgeons sterilize their instruments and wash their hands before operating. Eventually, the use of antiseptics drastically reduced deaths from infection.

 **DRAW CONCLUSIONS** Why was the improvement in hospital care especially important to the poor?

City Life Changes

As industrialization progressed, cities came to dominate the West. Cities grew as rural people streamed into urban areas for work. By the end of the

Topic 13 Lesson 3

Express Ideas Clearly Florence Nightingale said, "The very first requirement in a hospital is that it should do the sick no harm." To what is she referring? What did she believe was necessary in hospitals? *(Sample response: She means that the conditions in hospitals and the actions of doctors should not make patients sicker. She believed that proper sanitation could reduce the death rate and prevent the spread of infection.)*

City Life Changes

The Industrial Revolution did not just change the way goods were produced and shipped and the way people communicated and traveled. It also changed the way people lived and the way cities looked. Large cities came to have paved streets lined with electric lights, large buildings, skyscrapers, apartments, and department stores. Sewer systems were installed to improve sanitation and water quality. New forms of transportation, such as trams and electric trains, allowed wealthier people to move away from the city center.

Online Project the **3-D Model: Living in a Tenement.** Click at the various locations to reveal what life in a tenement was truly like. For each, ask students to declare whether it shows a positive or a negative aspect of tenement life. Then challenge students to connect that aspect of tenement life to larger social issues affecting women, children, and immigrants caused by rapid urban growth (e.g., sanitation, fire, conflict).

ACTIVE CLASSROOM

Tell students that they can learn more about life in a tenement if they Act it Out. Review the images and information about tenements and tenement living. Then challenge students to create a short sketch that brings the picture to life by depicting appropriate challenges faced by tenement dwellers (e.g., overcrowding, conflict, fetching water).

History Background

Wash Your Hands In 1848, physician Ignaz Philipp Semmelweis of Hungary noted that fewer patients died when doctors washed their hands frequently. He ordered students in his clinic to wash their hands using a solution of chlorinated lime, which disinfected their hands. Semmelweis believed that infection was caused by microscopic particles. Yet his theories were largely ignored, because health professionals believed that disease was caused by mysterious vapors and that cleanliness practices were irrelevant. When Louis Pasteur discovered microorganisms, the world was finally ready to believe that they might play a role in disease. Today, doctors and patients both know that sterilizing wounds and medical instruments is paramount in preventing disease.

Answers

Analyze Graphs *Sample answer: New York City; life expectancy increased more than 25 years.*

Draw Conclusions *While wealthier patients could be treated at home, the poor were admitted to hospitals that were often unsanitary. Improved sanitary measures and antiseptics that prevented infection increased patients' rate of recovery and survival.*

Guided Reading and Discussion

Analyze Images Look at the picture of Paris. Why was urban renewal important? How does this image of Paris help you understand urban renewal? *(Urban renewal was the rebuilding of poor areas of a city. The image of Paris shows that it was transformed to create a city center, wide boulevards, and streets lined with buildings. It looks cleaner, more organized, and safer.)*

Compare How do cities during the late Industrial Revolution compare with cities today? *(Early industrial cities like Paris and London look much like cities today. They have skyscrapers, large buildings, public transportation, and wide streets.)*

>> This aerial view shows Paris around 1870, after being redesigned by Georges Haussmann.

>> Engineer Joseph Bazalgette (standing, top right) designed the London sewer system. The massive underground sewer pipes improved sanitation and combated disease.

1800s, European and American cities had begun to take on many of the features of cities today.

New Cityscapes Growing wealth and industrialization altered the basic layout of European cities. City planners created spacious new squares and boulevards. They lined these avenues with government buildings, offices, department stores, and theaters.

The most extensive **urban renewal,** or rebuilding of the poor areas of a city, took place in Paris in the 1850s. Georges Haussmann, chief planner for Napoleon III, destroyed many tangled medieval streets full of tenement housing. In their place, he built wide boulevards and splendid public buildings.

The project was designed after Paris had experienced frequent uprisings, where poor city dwellers and their leaders set up barricades across narrow streets to battle the authorities. Haussmann's plan provided jobs, and the wide new boulevards made it harder for rebels to block streets and easier for troops to move around the city.

Gradually, settlement patterns shifted. In most American cities, the rich lived in pleasant neighborhoods on the outskirts of the city. The poor crowded into slums near the city center, within reach of factories. Trolley lines made it possible to live in one part of the city and work in another.

Safety, Sanitation, and Skyscrapers Paved streets made urban areas much more livable. First gas lamps, and then electric street lights illuminated the night, increasing safety. Cities organized police forces and expanded fire protection.

Beneath the streets, sewage systems made cities much healthier places to live. City planners knew that clean water supplies and better sanitation methods were needed to combat epidemics of cholera and tuberculosis.

In Paris, sewer lines expanded from 87 miles (139 kilometers) in 1852 to more than 750 miles (1200 kilometers) by 1911. The massive new sewer systems of London and Paris were costly, but they cut death rates dramatically.

By 1900, architects were using steel to construct soaring buildings. The Eiffel Tower became the symbol of Paris and the heights to which modern structures could reach. American architects like Louis Sullivan pioneered a new structure, the skyscraper. In large cities, single-family middle-class homes gave way to multistory apartment buildings.

Life in the Slums Despite efforts to improve cities, urban life remained harsh for the poor. Some working-class families could afford better clothing, newspapers,

D Differentiate Challenge/Gifted After discussion, have students think about the different people who planned and lived in industrial cities. Have them choose one person, such as a city planner, an architect designing a skyscraper, a police officer, or a factory worker. Have them conduct research, and then create a list of interview questions and the answers they believe the person would give. Finally, have them write a short newspaper article based on the interview.

or tickets to a music hall. But they went home to small, cramped row houses or tenements in overcrowded neighborhoods.

In the worst tenements in cities such as London and New York, whole families were often crammed into a single room that had little light and almost no ventilation. Less than one foot of space separated the buildings, and most tenements did not have running water. Bathrooms outside in the back might be shared by as many as twenty people.

Unsanitary conditions and overcrowding meant diseases spread quickly. Unemployment or illness meant lost wages that could ruin a family, leaving it homeless. High rates of crime and alcoholism were a constant curse. Conditions had improved somewhat from the early Industrial Revolution, but slums remained a fact of city life.

The Lure of City Life Despite their drawbacks, cities attracted millions. New residents were drawn as much by the excitement as by the promise of work. For tourists, too, cities were centers of action.

Music halls, opera houses, and theaters provided entertainment for every taste. Museums and libraries offered educational opportunities. Sports, from tennis to bare-knuckle boxing, drew citizens of all classes. Tree-lined parks offered a chance for fresh air, walks, and picnics, while reminding people of life in the country.

DRAW CONCLUSIONS How did industrialization change the face of cities?

The Working Class Wins New Rights

Workers tried to improve the harsh conditions of industrial life. They protested low wages, long hours, unsafe conditions, and the constant threat of unemployment. At first, business owners and governments tried to silence protesters. By mid-century, however, workers began to make progress.

The Growth of Labor Unions Workers formed **mutual-aid societies,** self-help groups to aid sick or injured workers. Men and women joined socialist parties or organized unions. In 1830 and 1848, revolutions had broken out across Europe, sparked by political and social unrest. The revolts left vivid images of widespread worker discontent that governments could no longer ignore.

By the late 1800s, most Western countries had granted all men the vote. Workers also won the right

>> It was not uncommon for more than one family to share a tiny apartment in tenement buildings. **Analyze Images** What evidence does this photograph provide about the lives of the urban poor?

>> Sports became popular pastimes for all social classes in the early 1900s. These women pose with tennis rackets before a match.

Topic 13 Lesson 3

The Working Class Wins New Rights

One negative effect of the Industrial Revolution and the growth of factories was that factory workers and miners earned low wages and worked long, grueling hours in hazardous conditions. In the late 1800s, many workers joined mutual-aid societies and labor unions and began demanding changes. By the early 1900s, millions of workers in Europe belonged to labor unions. Why did workers join unions? *(Forming unions gave them representation and helped workers strike and demand improvements.)*

Guided Reading and Discussion

Although the Industrial Revolution began in the 1700s, workers had little success organizing until the late 1800s and did not win many rights until the early 1900s. Discuss working conditions and labor unions.

Draw Conclusions Why do you think working conditions were so harsh? *(Sample response: Some factory and business owners cared more about profit than about employees. Owners wanted to produce as much as possible for as little as possible, which meant low wages, long hours, and little concern for safety.)*

SYNTHESIZE

Online Project the **Digital Activity: Birth of the Industrial City**. Have students take five minutes to answer the questions. Then divide the class into small groups, and have each group discuss its responses.

Quick Write Have each group write a short response explaining how Dickens's quotation addresses the Essential Question. Discuss their responses as a class.

Answers

Draw Conclusions *With industrialization came more jobs, urban renewal, better sanitation, and entertainment, but industrialization also created slum conditions and higher crime rates.*

Analyze Images *Sample answer: The poor lived in overcrowded, dirty buildings. You can see how close the buildings are and that many people shared small apartments with very few windows.*

Topic 13 Lesson 3

DEMONSTRATE

Online Assign the online **Digital Lesson Quiz** for this lesson if you haven't already done so. Students will be offered automatic remediation or enrichment based on their score.

Pose this to the class on the Discussion Board:

In "The Second Industrial Revolution," you read about the ways advances in science, technology, transportation, and communications affected industry and then altered the economy, society, and human life. The changes brought about by the Industrial Revolution continue to affect us today.

Identify Cause and Effect Identify three causes of the Industrial Revolution. Describe three economic or social effects. *(Sample responses: Causes: growing population, new sources of energy, improved technology, demand for mass-produced goods; Effects: rise of big business, new methods of production, new forms of transportation, urbanization, growing slums)*

Draw Conclusions How does the Industrial Revolution continue to affect the world? *(Sample responses: The population has continued to grow; more nations have industrialized; new sources of energy have been found; many innovations—such as cars and factories—have polluted the air and water; there is now a global economy.)*

Topic Inquiry

Have students continue their investigations for the Topic Inquiry.

>> Miners and steelworkers go on strike in Belgium. **Draw Conclusions** Who do you think the men on horseback are? Why are they there? Explain.

to organize unions to bargain on their behalf. Germany legalized labor unions in 1869. Britain, Austria, and France followed. By 1900, Britain had about three million union members, and Germany had about two million.

The main tactic of unions was the strike, or work stoppage. Workers used strikes to demand better working conditions, wage increases, or other benefits from their employers. Violence was often a result of strikes, particularly if employers called in the police or hired nonunion workers to keep their operations going.

Pressured by unions, reformers, and working-class voters, governments passed laws to regulate working conditions. Early laws forbade employers to hire very young children. Later laws outlawed child labor entirely and banned the employment of women in mines. Other laws limited work hours and improved safety. By 1909, British coal miners had won an eight-hour day, setting a standard for workers in other countries.

In Germany, and then elsewhere, Western governments established old-age pensions, as well as disability insurance for workers who were hurt or became ill. These programs protected workers from dying in poverty once they were no longer able to work.

An Improved Standard of Living Wages varied throughout the industrialized world, with unskilled laborers earning less than skilled workers. Women received less than half the pay of men doing the same work. Farm laborers barely scraped by during the economic slump of the late 1800s. Periods of unemployment brought desperate hardships to industrial workers and helped boost union membership.

Overall, though, standards of living for workers did rise. Working-class people began to benefit from higher wages and better working conditions. They, too, were able to afford a larger variety of goods and services. Many benefited from the growing movement to provide public education. Some were able to get access to health care. Efforts to curb diseases led to vaccination programs that reached into poor communities. Some workers were able to move out of overcrowded slums into the outer ring of cities and travel to work on subways and trolleys. Despite improvements in the standard of living, however, a large gap divided workers from the middle class.

? DRAW CONCLUSIONS What were some ways that life improved for workers?

ASSESSMENT

1. **Identify Main Ideas** Identify the major effects of new technology and transportation on industry during the Industrial Revolution.
2. **Draw Conclusions** Why did big business emerge during the Industrial Revolution, and how did it affect free enterprise?
3. **Identify Central Issues** How did the Industrial Revolution bring about important changes to human life in cities? Identify changes for the better and for the worse.
4. **Apply Concepts** How did the working class begin to improve its conditions during the late 1800s?
5. **Identify** Describe the contributions of Louis Pasteur and how they impacted society during the Industrial Revolution.

Answers

Draw Conclusions *Possible answer: police called in to frighten or attack striking miners*

Draw Conclusions *Answers include higher wages, improved health care, more affordable goods and services, and greater access to education.*

Assessment

1. New technology, such as electricity, sparked industrial growth and made production faster and less expensive. New forms of transportation moved goods farther and faster.
2. New technologies required the investment of more money; big, powerful corporations allowed more people to invest in business.
3. Better: safety increased, police and fire departments were better organized, disease declined, standards of living rose. Worse: neighborhoods were overcrowded, the number of slums increased.
4. They formed unions and used strikes to demand better working conditions and wage increases. Unions, reformers, and working-class voters pressured government to pass laws to regulate working conditions, reduce the work hours, improve safety, and ban child labor.
5. Pasteur identified the causes of many diseases, including rabies, anthrax, smallpox, and chicken cholera, and then developed vaccines to prevent these diseases. One of his most important vaccines was the rabies vaccine. He also invented the process of pasteurization for wine, beer, milk, and vinegar. His inventions lowered the death rate.

13.4 The Industrial Revolution slowly changed the old social order in the Western world. For centuries, the two main classes were nobles and peasants. While middle-class merchants, artisans, and lawyers played important roles, they still had a secondary position in society. With the spread of industry, a more complex social structure emerged.

>> Until the late 1800s, the only education available for British students was at either religious schools or "ragged schools," which were schools for poor children. The Education Act of 1902 established a system of public grammar schools.

Interactive Flipped Video

Changing Ways of Life and Thought

TEKS 8.B, 17.A, 24.A, 26.B, 26.C

The New Social Order

The New Class Structure By the late 1800s, a new upper class emerged in western Europe. It came to include not only the old nobility but also wealthy families who had acquired their riches from business and industry. Rich entrepreneurs married into aristocratic families, gaining the status of noble titles. Nobles needed the money brought by the industrial rich to support their lands and lifestyle. By tradition, the upper class held the tops jobs in government and the military.

Below this tiny elite, a growing middle class was pushing its way up the social ladder. At its highest rungs were the upper middle class, made up of mid-level business people and professionals such as doctors and scientists. With comfortable incomes, they enjoyed a wide range of material goods. Next came the lower middle class, which included teachers, office workers, shop owners, and clerks. On much smaller incomes, they struggled to keep up with their "betters."

Industrial workers and rural peasants were at the base of the social ladder. The size of this working class varied across Europe. In highly industrialized Britain, workers made up more than 30 percent of the population in 1900. In western Europe and the United States, the

>> Objectives

Identify what values shaped the new social order.

Describe how the role of women changed in the Industrial Revolution.

Explain the impact of education, new scientific ideas, and religion.

Analyze how romanticism, realism, and impressionism reflected the culture of the Industrial Age.

>> Key Terms

cult of domesticity
temperance movement
Elizabeth Cady Stanton
women's suffrage
Sojourner Truth
John Dalton
Charles Darwin
racism
social gospel
William Wordsworth
romanticism
Lord Byron
Victor Hugo
Ludwig van Beethoven
realism
Charles Dickens
Gustave Courbet
Louis Daguerre
impressionism
Claude Monet
Vincent van Gogh

PEARSON realize www.PearsonTexas.com Access your Digital Lesson.

569

Topic 13 Lesson 4

Changing Ways of Life and Thought

CONNECT

Preview Have students preview the **Lesson Objectives** and the list of **Key Terms**.

Students can also preview all the **Key Terms** and **Academic Vocabulary** using the **Interactive Reading Notepad** on the digital course or preview a summary of the lesson in the **Reading and Note Taking Study Guide**.

Online Use the **Editable Presentation** found on the digital course to present the main ideas for this lesson.

Start Up Activity

Business and industry were not the only things revolutionized during the Industrial Age. The class structure was redefined, gender roles were questioned, education changed, and scientists rocked long-held traditions and beliefs. Have students make predictions about the lesson.

Discuss Why do you think education and equal rights became important issues during the Industrial Revolution? *(Sample response: The social order was changing, and women wanted to have the same rights as men in order to advance in an industrialized and modernized world.)* What other issues and changes do you expect to learn about? *(Sample response: how families changed; how technology impacted daily life; how cities changed)*

Online You can also project the **Start Up Activity** from the course.

INVESTIGATE

Have students read the section using the **Reading and Note Taking Study Guide** to help them take notes and understand the text as they read.

The New Social Order

The Struggle for Women's Rights

The Industrial Revolution created new jobs, industries, businesses, and investment prospects. For some people, these new opportunities brought wealth and power. Soon, a new social structure emerged consisting of an upper class, middle class, and working class. The roles of members in a family—particularly women and children—also began to change.

Aa Vocabulary Builder

1. Have students pronounce the following academic vocabulary terms in this lesson and clarify the part of speech. For difficult or polysyllabic words, break them into syllables and pronounce them with the students.
2. Explain what the word means in common "student-friendly" language using synonyms and antonyms when possible. Provide concrete examples to clarify the meaning, and rephrase the definition.

speculate: to think about

controversial: that is or can be argued about or debated

emphasis: special attention given to something to make it stand out

intense: very strong or deep

Online Project the **Interactive Gallery: The New Social Order and Changing Roles of Women**. Introduce the activity by reminding students that the Industrial Revolution created new jobs, industries, businesses, and investment prospects. For some people, these new opportunities brought wealth and power. Soon, a new social structure emerged consisting of an upper class, middle class, and working class. The roles of members in a family—particularly women and children—also began to change. Click through the hot spots on the image. Ask students how the images help them understand what life might have been like for the different classes.

ACTIVE CLASSROOM

Conversation With History Have students select one of the people in one of these images. Ask students to jot down questions they would like to ask that person about his or her life. Then have students work together to write answers to some of their questions.

D Differentiate Extra Support Have students work with an on-level partner and create a chart with one column for each social class. Then have students list the types of jobs or roles members of each class might have and describe what their lives might be like.

Key Terms

Ask students to find the key term **temperance movement** (in bold) in the text and read its meaning. Ask students if they would have supported the temperance movement if they had been alive then.

number of farmworkers dropped, but many families still worked the land. The rural population was higher in eastern and southern Europe, where industrialization was more limited.

Middle Class Values By midcentury, the growing middle class had developed its own way of life. A strict code of etiquette governed social behavior.

Rules dictated how to dress for every occasion, how to give a dinner party, how to pay a social call, when to write letters, and how long to mourn for relatives who had died.

Parents strictly supervised their children, who were expected to be "seen but not heard." A child who misbehaved was considered to reflect badly on the entire family. Servants, too, were seen as a reflection of their employers. Even a small middle-class household was expected to have at least a cook and a housemaid.

The Ideal Home and Family Middle-class families tended to include just the nuclear family, parents and children, rather than the larger extended families of the past. They lived in a large house, or perhaps one of the new apartment houses. Rooms were crammed with large, overstuffed furniture. Clothing reflected middle-class tastes for luxury and respectability.

>> In industrialized cities, many members of the working class lived in tenement buildings like this. **Infer** What can you infer about working-class life from the way these people are dressed indoors?

Within the family, the division of labor between wife and husband changed. Earlier, middle-class women had helped run family businesses out of the home.

By the later 1800s, most middle-class husbands went to work in an office or shop. A successful husband was one who earned enough to keep his wife at home. Women spent their time raising children, directing servants, and doing religious or charitable service.

Books, magazines, and popular songs supported a **cult of domesticity** that idealized women and the home. Women and girls stitched sayings like "home, sweet home" into needlework that was hung on parlor walls. The ideal woman was seen as a tender, self-sacrificing caregiver who provided a nest for her children and a peaceful refuge for her husband to escape from the hardships of the working world.

This ideal rarely applied to the bottom rungs of the social ladder. Lower-middle-class women might work alongside their husbands in stores. Working-class women labored for low pay in garment factories or worked as domestic servants. Young women might leave domestic service after they married, but often had to seek other employment. Despite long days working for wages, they were still expected to take full responsibility for child care and homemaking.

IDENTIFY MAIN IDEAS How did the roles of men and women in middle-class households change as a result of the Industrial Revolution?

The Struggle for Women's Rights

Some individual women and women's groups protested restrictions on women's lives. They sought a broad range of rights. Across Europe and the United States, politically active women campaigned for fairness in marriage, divorce, and property laws. Women's groups also supported the **temperance movement,** a campaign to limit or ban the use of alcoholic beverages. Temperance leaders pointed out that drinking threatened family life. They also argued that banning alcohol would create a more productive and efficient workforce.

These reformers faced many obstacles. In Europe and the United States, women could not vote. They were barred from most schools and had little, if any, protection under the law. A woman's husband or father controlled all of her property.

The Campaign Begins In the late 1700s, women such as Olympe de Gouges in France and Mary Wollstonecraft in England had begun to call for women's rights. Later,

Answers

Identify Main Ideas *Most husbands went to work in an office or shop, while most wives stayed at home to raise their children.*

Infer *Sample answer: There was little or no heat in their building.*

Identify Main Ideas *Women were too emotional to be allowed to vote; women needed to be protected from politics; a woman's place was traditionally at home and not out in society.*

History Background

The Proper Victorians In England, the period from 1837 to 1902 is known as the Victorian Era because Queen Victoria's long reign spanned those years. Middle-class Victorians had a strict code of manners.

- In respectable Victorian homes, fabric drapes concealed piano legs, which, like women's legs, were considered immodest if shown.
- A widow was expected to dress in black from head to toe and never to remarry. In contrast, a widower wore a black crepe band around his hat or sleeve and was expected to find a new wife quickly.
- Wealthy businessmen wore knee-length frock coats and silk top hats to the office.
- Women wore suffocating corsets pulled tightly enough to achieve the ideal waist measurement of 18 to 20 inches.

their successors—mostly from the middle class—took up the struggle. In the United States, Lucretia Mott, **Elizabeth Cady Stanton,** and Susan B. Anthony campaigned for the abolition of slavery. In the process, they realized the severe restrictions on their own lives. They became the founders of the American women's rights movement.

Over time, women began to break the barriers that kept them out of universities and professions. By the late 1800s, a few women trained as doctors or lawyers. Others became explorers, researchers, or inventors, often without recognition. For example, Julia Brainerd Hall worked with her brother to develop an aluminum-producing process. Their company became hugely successful, but Charles Hall received almost all of the credit.

The Suffrage Movement By the late 1800s, married women in some countries had won the right to control their own property. The struggle for political rights proved far more difficult. In the United States, the Seneca Falls Convention of 1848 demanded that women be granted the right to vote. In Europe, groups dedicated to **women's suffrage,** or women's right to vote, emerged in the later 1800s.

Among men, some liberals and socialists supported women's suffrage. In general, though, suffragists faced intense opposition. Some critics claimed that women were too emotional to be allowed to vote. Others argued that women needed to be "protected" from grubby politics or that a woman's place was in the home, not in government.

To such claims, **Sojourner Truth,** an African American suffragist, is credited with replying, "Nobody ever helps me into carriages, or over mud puddles, or gives me any best place! And ain't I a woman?"

On the edges of the Western world, women made faster strides. In New Zealand, Australia, and some western territories of the United States, women won the vote by the early 1900s. There, women who had "tamed the frontier" alongside men were not dismissed as weak and helpless. In the United States, Wyoming became the first state to grant women the right to vote. In much of the Western world, however, the women's suffrage struggle took much longer. By 1920, women in Britain and the United States had finally won the vote.

? IDENTIFY MAIN IDEAS What were the arguments against women's suffrage?

ELPS **ELPS 4.F.5** Demonstrate your understanding of how to use pictures and other visuals to deepen your understanding of the suffrage movement.

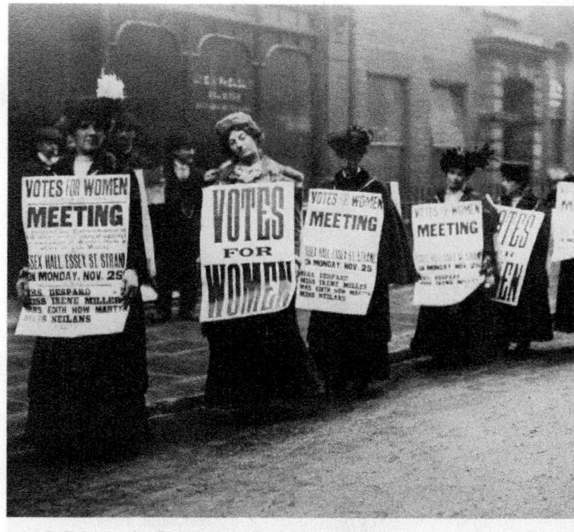

>> In Britain, the first petition for women's suffrage was presented to Parliament in 1867. The suffragist movement continued until Parliament finally granted women over 30 the right to vote in 1918. Women gained the same voting rights as men in 1928.

Interactive Gallery

The Rise of Public Education

By the late 1800s, reformers persuaded many governments to set up public schools and require basic education for all children. Teaching "the three Rs"—reading, writing, and 'rithmetic—was thought to produce better citizens. In addition, industrialized societies recognized the need for a literate workforce. Schools taught punctuality, obedience to authority, disciplined work habits, and patriotism. In European schools, children also received basic religious education.

Improving Public Schools At first, elementary schools were primitive. Many teachers had little schooling themselves. In rural areas, students attended class only during the times when they were not needed on the farm or in their parents' shops.

By the late 1800s, a growing number of children were in school, and the quality of elementary education improved. Teachers received training at normal schools, where the latest "norms and standards" of educational practices were taught. By the late 1800s, more schools

Guided Reading and Discussion

The roles of women also changed outside the home. Because most middle-class women did not have to work, they often became involved in charities, religious organizations, and women's groups. Some women became politically active and supported the temperance movement, campaigned for fairness in marriage and property laws, and fought for the right to vote.

Draw Conclusions Why might economic and social changes have encouraged women to fight for political change? *(Sample response: Women realized that they had important roles in society as mothers, wives, and workers. Women wanted to make sure their voices were heard and that they and their children were protected.)*

Identify Cause and Effect How did economic freedom improve the human condition? *(Sample response: Middle- and upper-class women had time to fight for equal rights. Middle-class women were able to spend more time shopping and raising their children.)*

English Language Proficiency Standards

Reading 4.F.5 Explain that using visuals can help students develop background knowledge, making it easier to understand the context in which events occurred. Have students use the text and photo in "The Struggle for Women's Rights" to deepen their understanding of the women's suffrage movement.

Beginning Display the term *women's suffrage movement* and break it down into individual words (*suffrage* refers to the right to vote and *movement* indicates a widespread organization). Read the text aloud and have students look at the photo. Point out details in the photo: The clothing suggests wealth; the signs suggest an organized movement; women march in front of watching men.

Intermediate Complete the Beginning activity, but have the students break down the term, read the text, and point out details.

Advanced Have pairs read and discuss the photo to determine how women shared their beliefs on suffrage with others. Then have sets of pairs discuss how the photo deepens their understanding.

Advanced High Have groups read, examine the photo, and discuss what it reveals about the fight for women's rights. Have them discuss why examining photos is an important part of the study of history. Have the groups share a summary of the discussion.

Topic 13 Lesson 4

The Rise of Public Education
New Directions in Science
The Role of Religion

Before 1870, the only formal education available for the majority of British children was in religious schools or "ragged schools," which taught poor children basic skills, such as reading. Schools in other countries were similar in their teaching methods and subjects. The rapid advances in technology and production, as well as new employment opportunities, led to social changes and drastically impacted the education system. In the late 1800s, universities added science and engineering courses to prepare students for life in an industrial world. At the same time, radical new theories in science challenged long-held beliefs. Despite this challenge, religion continued to be an important—and necessary—part of life and society.

Draw Conclusions Have students work in groups to generate a list of reasons why reforms and social services were needed and what religious groups could do to help fill this need. Have student groups share their lists with the class or post them on a blog. *(Sample response: Reform was needed to help the working poor deal with the harsh realities of industrialization. Religious leaders helped influence political changes. Religious organizations and social services provided charity.)*

Answers

Draw Conclusions *Fewer children were needed to work on farms or in their parents' shops; the growing number of middle-class families could afford to send their children to school.*

were being set up in western Europe and elsewhere to train teachers.

In England, schooling girls and boys between the ages of five and ten became compulsory after 1881. At the same time, governments began to expand secondary schools, known as high schools in the United States. In secondary schools, students learned the "classical languages," Latin and Greek, along with history and mathematics.

In general, only middle-class families could afford to have their sons attend these schools, which trained students for more serious study or for government jobs. Middle-class girls were sent to school primarily in the hope that they might marry well and become better wives and mothers. Generally, girls' schools did not teach much science or mathematics, which were considered unnecessary and inappropriate for young women.

Higher Education Grows Colleges and universities expanded in this period, too. Most university students were the sons of middle or upper-class families. The university curriculum emphasized ancient history and languages, philosophy, religion, and law. By the late 1800s, universities added courses in the sciences, especially in chemistry and physics. At the same time, engineering schools trained students who would have the knowledge and skills to build the new industrial society.

>> This image shows Dmitri Mendeleyev's 1869 manuscript of the periodic table. In 1871, he created a version with gaps where he believed elements that had not yet been discovered would fit.

Some women sought greater educational opportunities. By the 1840s, a few small colleges for women opened, including Bedford College in England and Mount Holyoke in the United States. In 1863, the British reformer Emily Davies campaigned for female students to be allowed to take the entrance examinations for Cambridge University. She succeeded, but as late as 1897, male Cambridge students rioted against granting degrees to women.

? DRAW CONCLUSIONS Why did more children attend school in the late 1800s than before?

New Directions in Science

Science in the service of industry brought great changes in the later 1800s. At the same time, researchers advanced startling theories about the natural world. Their new ideas challenged long-held beliefs.

Modern Atomic Theory A crucial breakthrough in chemistry came in the early 1800s when the English Quaker schoolteacher **John Dalton** developed modern atomic theory. The ancient Greeks had speculated that all matter was made of tiny particles called atoms. Dalton showed that each element has its own kind of atoms. Earlier theories put forth the idea that all atoms were basically alike. Dalton also showed how different kinds of atoms combine to make all chemical substances. In 1869, the Russian chemist Dmitri Mendeleyev (men duh LAY ef) drew up a table that grouped elements according to their atomic weights. His table became the basis for the periodic table of elements used today.

The Question of Earth's Age The new science of geology opened avenues of debate. In *Principles of Geology*, Charles Lyell offered evidence to show that Earth had formed over millions of years. His successors concluded that Earth was at least two billion years old and that life had not appeared until long after Earth was formed. These ideas did not seem to agree with biblical accounts of creation.

Archaeology added other pieces to an emerging debate about the origins of life on Earth. In 1856, workers in Germany accidentally uncovered fossilized Neanderthal bones. Later scholars found fossils of other early modern humans. These archaeologists had limited evidence and often drew mistaken conclusions. But as more discoveries were made, scholars developed new ideas about early humans.

Darwin's Theory of Natural Selection Some of the most controversial new ideas came from the British naturalist **Charles Darwin.** In 1859, after years of research, he published *On the Origin of Species.* Darwin argued that all forms of life, including human beings, had evolved into their present state over millions of years. To explain the extremely long, slow process of evolution, he put forward a startling new theory.

Darwin adopted Thomas Malthus's idea that all plants and animals produced more offspring than the food supply could support. As a result, he said, members of each species constantly competed to survive. Natural forces "selected" those with physical traits best adapted to their environment to survive and to pass the trait on to their offspring. Darwin called this process natural selection. Later, some people called it "survival of the fittest."

The Uproar Over Darwin Like the ideas of Nicolaus Copernicus and Isaac Newton in earlier times, Darwin's theory ignited a furious debate between scientists and theologians. To many Christians, the Bible contained the only true account of creation. It told that God created the world and all forms of life within seven days. Darwin's theory, they argued, reduced people to the level of animals and undermined belief in God and the soul. While some Christians eventually came to accept the idea of evolution, others did not. Controversy over Darwin's theories has continued to the present day.

Social Darwinism Although Darwin himself never promoted any social ideas, some thinkers used his theories to support their own beliefs about society. The idea that natural selection applied to human society, especially to warfare and economic competition, became known as Social Darwinism. It was British philosopher Herbert Spencer who coined the phrase "survival of the fittest."

Social Darwinists argued that industrial tycoons earned their success because they were more "fit" than those they put out of business. War brought progress by weeding out weak nations. Victory was seen as proof of superiority.

Social Darwinism encouraged **racism,** the unscientific belief that one racial group is superior to another, and had horrific consequences for people throughout the world. For example, Social Darwinism was used to justify harsh treatment of the mentally ill and countless acts of violence toward people of "different" religions, races, and ethnicities. By the late 1800s, many Europeans and Americans claimed that the success of Western civilization was due to

>> Darwin's theories about evolution sparked much debate. **Analyze Political Cartoons** How does the portrayal of Darwin as a monkey relate to his theories? Do you think the cartoonist accepts the theories?

>> Charles Darwin challenged traditional thinking with his new ideas about how forms of life developed and evolved. The specimens he collected during his five-year voyage on the HMS *Beagle* helped him develop this theory of evolution.

Guided Reading and Discussion

Be sure that students understand the impact new advances and theories in science had on society.

Draw Inferences While these advances had immediate effects, they also had long-term effects. Have students make inferences about the long-term impact of the following: atomic theory, periodic table, geological and archaeological findings and theories, and natural selection. *(Sample response: Scientists continued to experiment and research to build on these ideas and findings. The atomic theory advanced chemistry, and Mendeleyev's periodic table remains the basis for the modern periodic table. Darwin's theory changed the way people thought about species and led to the study of DNA. Archaeological findings helped scholars develop new ideas about humans and their ancestors.)*

D Differentiate Challenge/Gifted
Review the political cartoon about Darwin's theory. Have students create their own political cartoon based on the debate over his theory. Have them post their cartoons in the class or on a Web site.

Answers

Analyze Political Cartoons *Sample answer: The cartoonist portrayed Darwin as a monkey to mock the idea that humans evolved from lower primates. The mocking attitude makes it clear that the cartoonist does not support Darwin's theories.*

Draw Inferences Tell students that although advances in science and technology were rapidly changing society, many people continued to find comfort in religion and never gave up their beliefs. Priests, rabbis, and other religious leaders formed labor unions and political parties. Protestant churches urged people to provide social services. Why do you think religious leaders became involved in politics? What did they hope to achieve? *(Sample response: Religious leaders felt it was their duty to represent the poor and to try to help them. The poor did not have a voice in politics, so it was difficult for them to fight for their own rights. Religious leaders hoped they could use their influence and social standing to pressure the government to pass reforms for the working class and improve their housing, health care, and education.)*

The Romantics Turn from Reason

Throughout the 1800s, writers, poets, musicians, and painters were influenced by the ways the Industrial Revolution impacted society and human life. Some of them turned away from the harsh realities of the age, instead idealizing nature and intense feelings. These artists belonged to a cultural movement known as romanticism.

the supremacy of the white race. Such powerful ideas would have a long-lasting impact on world history.

IDENTIFY CENTRAL IDEAS How did science begin to challenge existing beliefs in the late 1800s?

The Role of Religion

Despite the challenge of new scientific ideas, religion continued to be a major force in Western society. Christian churches and Jewish synagogues remained at the center of communities. Religious leaders influenced political, social, and educational developments.

The grim realities of industrial life stimulated feelings of compassion and charity. Christian and Jewish labor unions and political parties pushed for reforms. Individuals, church groups, and Jewish organizations all tried to help the working poor. Catholic priests and nuns set up schools and hospitals in urban slums. Many Protestant churches backed the **social gospel,** a movement that urged Christians to social service. They campaigned for reforms in housing, healthcare, and education.

Motivated by their religious values, Christians and Jews founded many organizations to help those in need. In Paris, Frédéric Ozanum established the St. Vincent de Paul Society in 1833. By 1878, William and Catherine Booth had set up the Salvation Army in London.

It both spread Christian teachings and provided social services. Their daughter, Evangeline Booth, later helped bring the Salvation Army to North America. In 1881, the Jewish community in New York founded the Hebrew Immigrant Aid Society, which provided shelter, food, employment, and education to many new immigrants.

IDENTIFY SUPPORTING DETAILS What social services did religious organizations provide?

>> The hardships of industrial life led to the creation of numerous charitable organizations, including the Salvation Army, which provided many services to the needy.

The Romantics Turn from Reason

The Industrial Age shaped the arts as well as society and science. Many writers turned away from the harsh realities of industrial life to celebrate the peace and beauty of nature. These writers were part of a cultural movement called romanticism. **Romanticism** emphasized imagination, freedom, and emotion. (Romance, in the sense of romantic love, was not the focus of the movement.) From the late 1700s to 1850, romanticism shaped much of Western literature and arts.

Romantic Poetry Romantic writers, artists, and composers rebelled against the Enlightenment emphasis on reason, order, and emotional restraint. Instead, romantic writers focused on simple, direct language that conveyed intense feelings and glorified nature.

English poet **William Wordsworth** helped launch this cultural movement with the publication of *Lyrical Ballads* in 1789. Wordsworth rejected formal styles and conventions, and instead experimented with poetic forms and focused on common people and subjects, like the peace and beauty of the sunset.

> It is a beauteous evening, calm and free,
>
> The holy time is quiet as a Nun
>
> Breathless with adoration; the broad sun
>
> Is sinking down in its tranquility
>
> —William Wordsworth, *Complete Poetical Works*

Answers

Identify Central Ideas *The research of Lyell and Darwin challenged traditional and biblical views of creation.*

Identify Supporting Details *They supplied clothing and food to the urban poor and provided funds for hospitals and schools.*

Topic 13 Lesson 4

Poets such as William Blake, Samuel Taylor Coleridge, John Keats, and Percy Bysshe Shelley were also leading lights of the romantic movement.

Mysterious Heroes Romantic writers created a new kind of hero—a mysterious, melancholy figure who felt out of step with society. "My joys, my grief, my passions, and my powers, / Made me a stranger," wrote Britain's George Gordon, **Lord Byron.** He himself was a larger-than-life figure equal to those he created.

After a rebellious, wandering life, he joined Greek forces battling for independence from Turkish rule. When he died of a fever there, his legend bloomed. Moody, isolated romantic heroes came to be described as "Byronic."

The romantic hero often hid a guilty secret and faced a grim destiny. German writer Johann Wolfgang von Goethe (GUR tuh) wrote the dramatic poem *Faust*. The aging scholar Faust makes a pact with the devil, exchanging his soul for youth. After much agony, Faust wins salvation by accepting his duty to help others. In *Jane Eyre*, British novelist Charlotte Brontë weaves a tale about a quiet governess and her brooding, Byronic employer, whose large mansion conceals a terrifying secret.

Glorifying the Past Romantic writers combined history, legend, and folklore. Sir Walter Scott's novels and ballads evoked the turbulent history of Scottish clans or medieval knights. Alexandre Dumas (doo MAH) and **Victor Hugo** re-created France's past in novels like *The Three Musketeers* and *The Hunchback of Notre Dame*.

Architects, too, were inspired by old styles and forms. Churches and other buildings, including the British Parliament, were modeled on medieval Gothic styles. To people living in the 1800s, medieval towers and lacy stonework conjured up images of a glorious past.

Romanticism in Music The orchestra, as we know it today, took shape in the early 1800s. The first composer to take full advantage of the broad range of instruments was the German composer **Ludwig van Beethoven.** Beethoven's stirring music transcended his own time and culture by conveying universal emotions such as love, loss, death, joy, and fear. For example, the famous opening of his Fifth Symphony conveys the sense of fate knocking on one's door.

His Sixth Symphony captures a joyful day in the countryside, interrupted by a violent thunderstorm. In all, Beethoven produced nine symphonies, five piano concertos, a violin concerto, an opera, two masses, and dozens of shorter pieces that are still popular today.

>> Romantic paintings often focused on nature and emotion. Note the romantic features of this portrait of William Wordsworth. His arms are crossed, and his head is down as though he is brooding about something. A dramatic landscape looms behind him.

>> Lord Byron was a well-known, dashing romantic poet. One of his most famous works is the poem *Don Juan*, a satirical social commentary based on the literary hero Don Juan.

Guided Reading and Discussion

Remind students that writers and poets were not the only artists to create art that reflected the time. Musicians also composed pieces, such as symphonies and concertos, to convey the times in which they lived. Some musicians, such as Ludwig van Beethoven, composed music that conveyed universal themes that transcended the time and place during which they were created by expressing universal emotions.

Discuss Ask students if they have ever been to the symphony, listened to classical music, or played classical music. Have them discuss how the music stirred their emotions and what themes they felt were expressed in the compositions. If possible, play some of Beethoven's most well-known pieces, such as his Fifth Symphony or Sixth Symphony. Have students listen carefully and then discuss their reaction to the pieces.

Draw Inferences What themes inspired many romantic writers and architects? Why might they have found these ideas inspirational? *(Sample response: They were inspired by history, legend, folklore, old styles, and forms. These things represented simpler times and the glorious past—a time before the Industrial Revolution, growth of materialism, and loss of identity.)*

Topic 13 Lesson 4

Artists Represent Real Life

New Directions in the Visual Arts

In addition to romanticism, three other major movements emerged, each rejecting or reacting to previous artistic movements in order to reflect the culture of the age.

Online Project the **Interactive Gallery: Artistic Movements During the Industrial Revolution**. Look at each painting and discuss each movement.

Analyze Images

Have students analyze each image to identify how the artist's work reflects the culture. They should consider the subject, the colors, and the style when discussing each artist's work. Remind them also to consider the goals of each movement. Does the artist stay true to the movement? How?

ACTIVE CLASSROOM

Have students form an Opinion Line to answer the following question: Which painting or stylistic movement do you like the best? Once students have found their places in line, ask several to explain their response using details from the images and the text. *(Answers will vary. Students should support their responses with clear explanations and reasons.)*

Answers

Analyze Images *Sample answer: The brushstrokes, color, and composition—the tiny people in a valley surrounded by mountains and trees—show the power of nature over humans.*

Identify Cause and Effect *Romanticism appealed to emotion rather than reason, progress, and science, and it turned away from the harsh realities of urban life and factory work to celebrate nature and beauty.*

>> In many of his paintings, romantic artist J.M.W. Turner focused on the effects of light and color. **Analyze Images** How does *A View on the Rhine* exemplify the characteristics of romantic art?

>> Romantic painter Eugene Delacroix turned to foreign lands and ancient times to portray the exotic or simpler ways of life. Although the painting focuses on peasant musicians rather than nature, it still seems idealized rather than harshly realistic.

Romantic composers also tried to stir deep emotions. The piano music and passionate playing of the Hungarian composer Franz Liszt moved audiences to laugh or weep. Other composers wove traditional folk music into their works to glorify their nations' past. In his piano works, Frederic Chopin (shoh PAN) used Polish peasant dances to convey the sorrows and joys of people living under foreign occupation.

Romanticism in Art Painters, too, broke free from the discipline and strict rules of the Enlightenment. Landscape painters like J.M.W. Turner sought to capture the beauty and power of nature. Using bold brush strokes and colors, Turner often showed tiny human figures struggling against sea and storm.

Romantics painted many subjects, from simple peasant life to medieval knights to current events. Bright colors conveyed violent energy and emotion. The French painter Eugène Delacroix (deh luh KRWAH) filled his canvases with dramatic action. In *Liberty Leading the People,* the Goddess of Liberty carries the revolutionary tricolor as French citizens rally to the cause.

IDENTIFY CAUSE AND EFFECT How was romanticism a reaction to the Enlightenment and the Industrial Revolution?

Artists Represent Real Life

By the mid-1800s, a new artistic movement, **realism,** took hold in the West. Realism was an attempt to represent the world as it was, without the heightened sentiment and idealized emotions of the romantics. Realists often stressed the harsh side of life in urban slums or peasant villages. Many writers and artists were committed to improving the lot of the unfortunates whose lives they depicted.

Novelists Expose Social Wrongs The English novelist **Charles Dickens** vividly portrayed the lives of slum dwellers and factory workers, including children. In *Oliver Twist,* Dickens tells the story of a nine-year-old orphan raised in a grim poorhouse. When a desperately hungry Oliver asks for more food, he is smacked in the head by his well-fed master and sent off to work. Later, he runs away to London. There he is taken in by Fagin, a villain who trains homeless children to become pickpockets.

The book shocked many middle-class readers with its picture of poverty, mistreatment of children, and urban crime. Yet Dickens's humor and colorful

D Differentiate Extra Support While discussing the images in the interactive gallery, redefine each movement. Be sure students understand that romanticism has nothing to do with love or relationships (romance), but rather with a desire to express oneself and idealize nature. To help students understand the difference between the movements, point out various aspects of each painting and compare it to the previous movement. For example, note the difference in subject matter between the realist Courbet and the romantic Constable. Ask students why Courbet might have painted realistic-looking peasants. What does this say about his beliefs or goals in reflecting the Industrial Age? *(He wanted to represent real life and the effects of industrialization rather than an idealized image of life or nature.)*

characters made him one of the most popular novelists in the world.

French novelists also portrayed the ills of their time. With *Les Misérables* (lay miz ehr AHB), Victor Hugo moved from romanticism to realism. The novel showed how hunger drove a good man to crime and how the law hounded him ever after. The novels of Émile Zola painted an even grimmer picture. In *Germinal,* Zola exposed class warfare in the French mining industry. To Zola's characters, neither the Enlightenment faith in reason nor the romantic emphasis on feelings mattered at all.

Realism on Stage Norwegian dramatist Henrik Ibsen brought realism to the stage. His plays attacked the hypocrisy he observed around him. *A Doll's House* shows a woman caught in a straitjacket of social rules. In *An Enemy of the People,* a doctor discovers that the water in a local spa is polluted. Because the town's economy depends on its spa, the citizens denounce the doctor and suppress the truth. Ibsen's realistic dramas had a wide influence in Europe and the United States.

Realism in Art Realist painters also rejected the romantic emphasis on imagination. Instead, they focused on ordinary subjects, especially working-class men and women. "I cannot paint an angel," said the French realist **Gustave Courbet** (koor BAY), "because I have never seen one." Instead, he painted works such as *The Stone Breakers,* which shows two rough laborers on a country road. Later in the century, *The Gross Clinic,* by American painter Thomas Eakins, shocked viewers with its realistic depiction of an autopsy conducted in a medical classroom.

CONTRAST How did realism differ from romanticism?

New Directions in the Visual Arts

By the 1840s, a new art form, photography, was emerging. **Louis Daguerre** (dah GEHR) in France and William Fox Talbot in England had improved on earlier technologies to produce successful photographs. At first, many photos were stiff, posed portraits of middle-class families or prominent people. Other photographs reflected the romantics' fascination with faraway places.

In time, photographers used the camera to present the grim realities of life. During the American Civil War, Mathew B. Brady preserved a vivid, realistic record of the corpse-strewn battlefields. Other photographers

>> This poster shows characters from a play based on Victor Hugo's novel *Les Misérables*. In the center is Jean Valjean, who was arrested for stealing a loaf of bread to keep his sister's child from starving.

>> In 1839, Louis Daguerre perfected an effective method of photography. His camera changed both art and society.

Guided Reading and Discussion

Identify Cause and Effect How did members of the middle class respond to the realist movement? Why did they respond this way? *(Sample response: They were shocked by the grim depictions of the lives of the poor and working class, and many considered realists to be immoral. While people were aware of these social problems, they tried to ignore them or pretend they didn't exist. The realists forced them to accept the harsh reality of life in the Industrial Age.)*

Draw Conclusions How was photography used to support reform efforts? Why do you think it was an effective tool? *(Photographers were able to capture real life, which made the harsh lives of the working class and the dangers of factory work more difficult to ignore. Before the invention of the camera, artists were only able to imagine the lives of their subjects. Now artists could present actual proof of social ills.)*

SYNTHESIZE

Online Project the **Digital Activity: Art Reflects Culture**. Ask students to recall the Topic Essential Question, "How do science and technology affect society?" Remind students that science and technology also affected the arts. Artists focused on different styles and subject matters in response to the changes they witnessed due to the Industrial Revolution.

Have students take 5 minutes to answer the questions in the activity. Then divide the class into small groups, and have each group discuss its responses.

History Background

The Value of Art Like other artists, impressionist painters still had to make a living. Many impressionists came to rely on Paul Durand-Ruel, a Paris art dealer who became one of the movement's earliest supporters. He tirelessly promoted impressionism, and eventually patronage began to build. Many of the initial collectors were middle-class businessmen drawn to the world depicted in the paintings. Americans, in particular, became reliable purchasers of impressionist art. The first museum exhibit devoted to impressionism was held at the Musée de Luxembourg in 1897. The impressionists received further exposure at the World's Fair in 1900. Today, the style pioneered by a few artistic renegades is one of the most popular styles in the world.

Answers

Contrast *Realism represented the realities of industrialization and rejected the romantic emphasis on imagination and sentiment.*

Topic 13 Lesson 4

Discuss Ask students whether they have read books by authors from each literary movement or seen movies or television shows based on those books. Discuss their reactions to these works. Then ask them if they view these works differently or understand them better based on what they have learned in this lesson. Have students explain their responses.

DEMONSTRATE

Online Assign the online **Digital Lesson Quiz** for this lesson if you haven't already done so. Students will be offered automatic remediation or enrichment based on their score.

Pose this to the class on the Discussion Board:

In "Changing Ways of Life and Thought," you read about the ways the Industrial Revolution affected human life and society. A new social order emerged, public education was transformed, and scientists introduced radical theories that challenged long-held beliefs. Artists also responded to this changing society and found ways to reflect the culture of the Industrial Age.

Make Connections Some historians have suggested that we are now in the third phase of the Industrial Revolution, characterized by information technology and computers. Do you agree or disagree? How have these advances in technology affected ways of life and thought? How might they continue to change the way we live, work, socialize, and think?

Topic Inquiry

Have students continue their investigations for the Topic Inquiry.

>> After being rejected by France's most prestigious art exhibition, a group of painters held their own exhibition in 1874. One of the paintings, Claude Monet's *Impression: Sunrise,* gave the impressionist movement its name.

Interactive Gallery

showed the harsh conditions in industrial factories or slums.

The Impressionists Photography posed a challenge to painters. Why try for realism, some artists asked, when a camera could do the same thing better?

By the 1870s, a group of painters took art in a new direction, seeking to capture the first fleeting impression made by a scene or object on the viewer's eye. The new movement, known as **impressionism,** took root in Paris, capital of the Western art world.

Since the Renaissance, painters had carefully finished their paintings so that no brush strokes showed. But impressionists like **Claude Monet** (moh NAY) and Edgar Degas (day GAH) brushed strokes of color side by side without any blending. According to new scientific studies of optics, the human eye would mix these patches of color.

By concentrating on visual impressions rather than realism, artists achieved a fresh view of familiar subjects. Monet, for example, painted the cathedral of Rouen (roo AHN), France, dozens of times from the same angle, capturing how it looked in different lights at different times of day.

The Postimpressionists Later painters, called postimpressionists, developed a variety of styles. Georges Seurat (suh RAH) arranged small dots of color to define the shapes of objects.

Vincent van Gogh experimented with sharp brush lines and bright colors. His unique brushwork lent a dreamlike quality to everyday subjects. Desperately poor, he sold few paintings in his short, unhappy life. Today, Van Gogh's masterpieces sell for millions of dollars each.

Paul Gauguin (goh GAN) also developed a bold, personal style. He rejected the materialism of Western life and went to live on the island of Tahiti in the South Pacific. His most famous works depict the people of Tahiti. In his paintings, people look flat, as in "primitive" folk art. But his brooding colors and black outlining of shapes convey intense feelings and images.

CONNECT How did photography influence the development of painting?

ASSESSMENT

1. **Identify Cause and Effect** In what ways were the new artistic styles of the 1800s a reaction to changes in society?
2. **Draw Conclusions** Why did the movement to change women's roles in society face strong opposition?
3. **Infer** Why did reformers think free public education would lead to social change?
4. **Identify Supporting Details** How did the Industrial Revolution change the old social order and long-held traditions in the Western world?
5. **Infer** Referring to *Oliver Twist*, Charles Dickens wrote that "to show [criminals] as they really are, for ever skulking uneasily through the dirtiest paths of life . . . would be a service to society." How does his claim reflect the goals of realism?

Answers

Connect *The realism of photography made some artists turn away from realistic painting.*

Assessment

1. Each movement reacted to the developments in industry and technology. Romantics sought to escape or ignore the industrial society around them. Realists sought to expose the evils of the urban world and working poor. Impressionists responded to the development of photography.
2. Most men thought a woman's place was in the home. Giving women more power or new rights would change their role in society and the family. Men generally did not see women as equals, so they did not want women to have the same powers or rights they had.
3. Free public education would provide working-class children with some knowledge and skills that would give them more opportunities and improve their way of life.
4. Three distinct social classes emerged; middle-class tastes and values became a measuring stick for the working classes; women sought a political voice, the right to vote, and the chance to attend universities; scientists shook long-held religious beliefs.
5. By portraying the criminal world, he may inspire society to solve problems and institute reform or change.

TEKS ASSESSMENT

1. **Identify the Historical Origins, Characteristics, and Influences** Identify the historical origins, characteristics, and influences of communism, including the role of Karl Marx, who was successful in shifting political thought. Write a paragraph about how Karl Marx influenced communism with his theory of a classless society. Consider principles from *The Communist Manifesto*, ideas of communal ownership, and the methods to achieve global communism. 18.B, 21.C

2. **Identify the Historical Origins and Characteristics** Identify the historical origins and characteristics of socialism. Write a paragraph identifying the historical origins and characteristics of socialism during the Industrial Revolution. Consider poverty and injustice during the Industrial Revolution, group ownership of production, social justice, and contributions of Robert Owen. 18.C

3. **Identify Major Causes** Identify major causes, and describe the major effects of the following important turning points in world history from 1750 to 1914: the Industrial Revolution. Write a paragraph identifying changes in the way work was done during the Industrial Revolution. Consider the influence of Scientific Revolution thinking, innovations from the agricultural and energy revolutions, and the availability of capital. 1.E

4. **Explain the Collapse** Explain why communist command economies collapsed in competition with free market economies at the end of the twentieth century. Write a paragraph explaining why a united global revolution for communist countries did not materialize at the end of the twentieth century. Consider communism's global influence in the 1900s and why Marxism lost its appeal. How did workers feel about an international workers' movement? 18.E

5. **Explain Scientific Advancements** Explain how seventeenth- and eighteenth-century European scientific advancements led to the Industrial Revolution. Write a paragraph explaining how European scientific inventions led to the Industrial Revolution. Consider the scientific focus on the physical world and new technologies, such as water power. 1.E, 8.A

6. **Explain Political and Economic Changes** Explain how the Industrial Revolution led to political and economic changes in Europe. Write a paragraph explaining how the Industrial Revolution led to the growth of labor unions and changes in European laws. Consider the causes of revolutions in the mid-1800s, growth of labor unions, and the effects of voting rights on labor reform. 8.B

7. **Formulate Generalizations** Formulate generalizations on how economic freedom improved the human condition based on what you have learned about the benefits of free enterprise in the Industrial Revolution. Write a paragraph formulating generalizations on how free enterprise created successful business opportunities. Consider better standards of living, entrepreneurship, increased social mobility, and greater political rights. 8.E, 18.F

8. **Identify Contributions** Identify the contributions of significant scientists and inventors such as Marie Curie, Thomas Edison, Albert Einstein, Louis Pasteur, and James Watt. Write a paragraph identifying the contributions of Louis Pasteur. Explain his method of killing bacteria and his discovery of using vaccines. How did his contributions help human life? 28.E

9. **Identify Important Changes** Identify important changes in human life caused by the Industrial Revolution. Write a paragraph identifying the declining death rates caused by the Industrial Revolution. Consider the population explosion and death rate trend, factory illnesses, and better health and nutrition improvements. 17.A

Answers to TEKS Assessment

1. Student answers will vary but should include information on how Karl Marx, along with Friedrich Engels, proposed a new theory about a classless society that would jointly own the means of production for the common good. Eventually this theory influenced supporters around the world and spawned communist political parties. Some believed in violent revolutions to end capitalism, and others wanted a gradual, peaceful reform. Communism became prominent in Asia, Latin America, Africa, and Eastern Europe in the 1900s.

2. Student answers will vary but should include information on how industrialization brought on problems like poverty and injustice. Socialists believed that people as a whole should own and operate the means of production that produced and distributed goods. Early socialists believed in communities in which people shared work and owned property together to achieve social justice. Owen campaigned for laws limiting child labor and established a model community in Scotland for workers and their families.

3. Student answers will vary but should include information on how the Scientific Revolution focused on the physical world and helped inventors with new technologies to change the way work was done. The agricultural revolution produced innovations in farming methods and products. The energy revolution produced alternate sources of energy that powered new sources of energy, such as the steam engine. Entrepreneurs and inventors partnered together with capital and technical know-how to provide technology.

4. Student answers will vary but should include information on how communism spread globally, especially in Asia, Latin America, and Eastern Europe. However, Marx's ideas about a united world revolution and better standard of living for communist countries did not materialize. Workers had stronger ties to their country than to an international workers' movement, and free market capitalism reigned as communism declined by the end of the 1900s.

5. Student answers will vary but should include information on how scientific inventions in the 1600s and 1700s focused attention on the physical world as scientific methods were used to conduct experiments. New technologies included water power in the 1700s, the steam engine in 1764 (James Watt), and the use of coal for iron production in the 1700s.

6. Student answers will vary but should include information on how revolutions in Europe were sparked by discontented workers for political and social reasons. Most men in Western countries could vote by the late 1800s and tried to overturn negative working conditions. Unions were organized in Germany, Britain, Austria, and France. Governments then passed laws to regulate working conditions.

7. Student answers will vary but should include information on how the new industrial world was more open to innovation, and how under free enterprise no government interference hindered new businesses and inventions. With success came opportunities to move up socially through hard work, rather than through birth status. This in turn resulted in voting and political influence for the working class.

8. Student answers will vary but should include information on how Louis Pasteur, a French chemist, invented a process to kill microbes in milk. He also developed vaccines against rabies and anthrax. His contributions helped to advance medicine and led to declining death rates.

Topic 13

Answers to TEKS Assessment

9. Student answers will vary but should include information on how population in Europe more than doubled between 1800 and 1900 due to declines in death rates. Factory work itself caused many illnesses. However, the death rate declined overall due to better nutrition from improved farming methods and food storage. Better health from better medicine and sanitation improvements were also factors.

10. Student answers will vary but should include information on how romanticism, the leading genre, emphasized imagination, freedom, and emotion. William Wordsworth and other poets (William Blake, John Keats, Percy Bysshe Shelley) rejected formal styles and conventions. Lord Byron, Johann Wolfgang von Goethe (*Faust*), and Charlotte Brontë (*Jane Eyre*) featured mysterious figures in their literature. Some writers wrote about history, legend, and folklore, like Victor Hugo's *The Three Musketeers*.

11. Student answers will vary but should include information on how faster and cheaper transportation methods, such as turnpikes, canals, and steam-powered railroads, moved raw materials and helped ship finished goods to market. Railroads were especially efficient, as they did not have to be built alongside rivers. Cheaper goods led to more demand.

12. Student answers will vary but should include information on how technology required large amounts of financing, which was achieved by selling stock ownership in companies to investors. Huge corporations eventually dominated entire industries, such as Alfred Krupp in steel or John D. Rockefeller in the petroleum industry. Antimonopoly critics believed that those companies suppressed the competition so they could raise prices, destroying free enterprise. In the early 1900s, some governments moved to regulate monopolies, despite their political clout.

TEKS ASSESSMENT

10. Analyze Examples Analyze examples of how literature reflected the history of the cultures in which it was produced. Write a paragraph analyzing romanticism in the late 1700s to 1850. Include the features of romanticism, some leading authors and poets and their works, and the creation of mysterious heroes or legendary roles. **26.B**

"The consequence was, that when the moon, which was full and bright (for the night was fine), came in her course to that space in the sky opposite my casement, and looked in at me through the unveiled panes, her glorious gaze roused me. Awaking in the dead of night, I opened my eyes on her disk—silver-white and crystal clear. It was beautiful, but too solemn; I half rose, and stretched my arm to draw the curtain.

Good God! What a cry!

The night—its silence—its rest, was rent in twain by a savage, a sharp, a shrilly sound that ran from end to end of Thornfield Hall.

My pulse stopped: my heart stood still; my stretched arm was paralysed. The cry died, and was not renewed."

—*from Jane Eyre, Chapter 20*

11. Explain the Role Explain the role of transportation technology in advancing the Industrial Revolution. Using information from the lessons and the map below, write a paragraph explaining the importance of transportation during the Industrial Revolution in England. Consider turnpikes, canals, steam locomotive, and railroads. How did efficient transportation affect the price and demand for goods? **28.A**

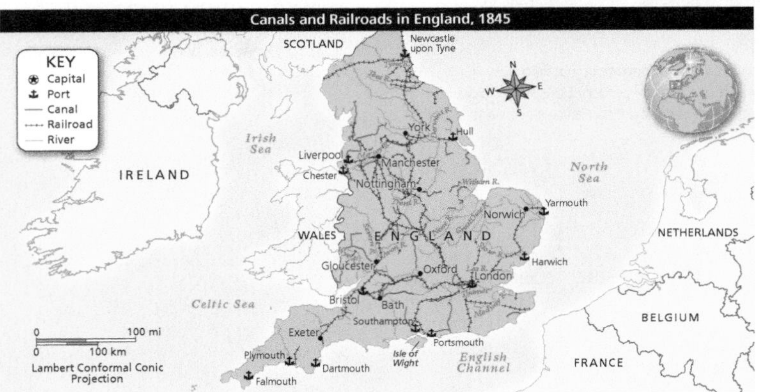

12. Explain Economic Changes and Identify Bias Explain the role of economics in driving political changes as related to the Industrial Revolution, and identify bias in written, oral, and visual material. Write a paragraph explaining how the advantages of a corporation led to the rise of big business and monopolies during the Industrial Revolution. Consider investors forming corporations and threats to competition. Does the image show any bias toward corporations and the changes during the Industrial revolution? Looking at the chart, do you think forming a corporation has any disadvantages? By looking at the image, can you tell if big-business monopolies have any positives? **8.B, 17.B, 29.E**

ADVANTAGES OF A CORPORATION

- Legally regarded as a single entity
- Can raise capital through selling shares of stock
- Able to transfer ownership of shares
- Continues to exist after original owner or owners die
- Limits the liability to stockholders

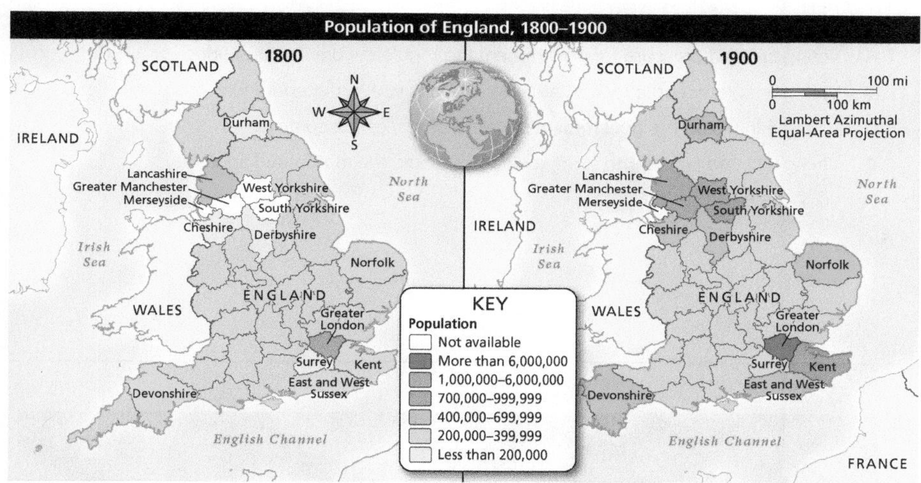

13. **Analyze and Identify Examples** Analyze and identify examples of how music reflected the history of the cultures in which it was produced. Also identify examples of music that transcended these cultures and expressed universal themes. Write a paragraph analyzing the romanticism genre in music during the Industrial Revolution. Identify examples of music that transcended these cultures, including works by Beethoven, Franz Liszt, and Frederic Chopin. **26.B, 26.C**

14. **Describe Major Effects** Describe the major effects of the following important turning points in world history from 1750 to 1914: the Industrial Revolution, and explain how the Industrial Revolution led to political, economic, and social changes in Europe. Write a paragraph describing the major effects of the Industrial Revolution. Look at the above map. Consider population growth and urbanization, demand for more goods, availability of cheaper goods, and workers' demands for better benefits. **1.E, 8.B**

15. **Identify Important Changes in Human Life** Identify important changes in human life caused by the Neolithic Revolution and the Industrial Revolution. Use standard grammar, spelling, sentence structure, and punctuation. Write a paragraph identifying how the Industrial Revolution improved upon the agricultural revolution of the Neolithic Revolution. Consider the gains made during the second agricultural revolution in the 1700s and the effect of land enclosures on farms and urbanization. **17.A**

16. **Identify the Historical Origins and Characteristics** Identify the historical origins and characteristics of the free enterprise system. Write a paragraph identifying economic thinking, particularly of Adam Smith, during the Industrial Revolution. Consider natural laws and laissez-faire economics, Smith's concept of free enterprise, and the impact of free markets during the Industrial Revolution. **8.E, 18.A**

17. **dentify the Contributions and Influence** Identify the contributions and influence of Adam Smith's ideas found in *The Wealth of Nations*. Write a paragraph identifying the contributions and influence of Adam Smith's ideas. Consider free market concepts and the relationship between price and supply. How would new ventures be financed? **18.A**

18. **Describe the Changing Roles** Describe the changing roles of children during major eras of world history. Write a paragraph describing the changing roles of working children during the Industrial Revolution in England. Consider young children doing factory work and legislation to improve working conditions. Which children attended school in the 1800s? **24.A**

19. **Reflect on the Essential Question Write an essay on the Essential Question: How do science and technology affect society?** Use evidence from your study of this Topic to support your answer.

13. Student answers will vary but should include information on how romanticism was the leading genre in music during the Industrial Revolution and did not focus on emotional restraint. Beethoven's music conveyed universal emotions and passions, for example, in his Fifth Symphony; pianist Franz Liszt portrayed passion in his compositions; Frederic Chopin used traditional folk music to glorify national pride and everyday sorrows and joys. All three musicians are listened to today.

14. Student answers will vary but should include information on how population growth led to urbanization, with a surplus of workers in farming communities. In the cities, entire families often worked in factories. Population growth increased demand for goods produced in factories, which benefited everyone with cheaper prices. Industrialization also produced political changes as workers demanded better benefits that resulted in the growth of unions and suffrage movements.

15. Student answers will vary but should include information on how during the Neolithic Revolution (considered the first agricultural revolution), people learned to farm and domesticate animals. A second agricultural revolution had further improvements in the quantity and quality of farm products in the 1700s. Land enclosures allowed more efficient land cultivation but threw people out of work; workers then migrated to urban areas to work in factories.

16. Student answers will vary but should include information on how physiocrats and economists looked for natural laws to explain the economics of the Industrial Revolution. Laissez-faire economics, proposed by Adam Smith in *The Wealth of Nations,* focused on the free market, an exchange of goods and services unregulated by the government. During the Industrial Revolution, free markets benefited people and investors.

17. Student answers will vary but should include information on how Adam Smith proposed in *The Wealth of Nations* that free markets (laissez-faire economics) would benefit everyone. The free enterprise system is based on production of more goods at lower prices, leading to a growing economy that would encourage reinvestments into new ventures.

18. Student answers will vary but should include information on how many young children worked in factories for less pay and became sick from long hours in poorly ventilated and unsafe factories and mines. In 1833, the British laws regulated hiring of children under nine and limiting working hours. In the 1800s more children were in school, but these children were mostly from middle-class families.

The Industrial Revolution 581

Topic 13

Answers to TEKS Practice

1. A
2. G

Online To prepare for the End-of-Topic test, have students go online for additional Topic Review and Assessment questions or to review their notes in the **Interactive Reading Notepad** for the lessons in this Topic.

Benchmark Tests

Assign these benchmark tests as you complete the relevant topics to monitor student progress toward mastering the course content and as preparation for the End-of-Course Test.

Benchmark Test 1: Topics 1–5

Benchmark Test 2: Topics 6–10

Benchmark Test 3: Topics 11–15

Benchmark Test 4: Topics 16–21

TEKS PRACTICE

1 Why was it important for workers to gain voting rights during the Industrial Revolution?

A Voting created pressure for governments to regulate working conditions.

B Voting enabled people to start strikes or revolts without interference.

C Voting minimized the government's feeling of worker discontent.

D Voting allowed workers to form societies such as the mutual-aid society.

2

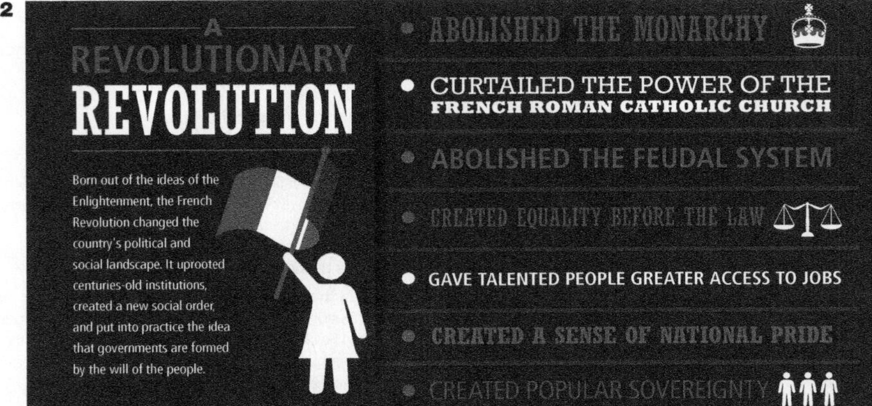

A
REVOLUTIONARY
REVOLUTION
Born out of the ideas of the Enlightenment, the French Revolution changed the country's political and social landscape. It uprooted centuries-old institutions, created a new social order, and put into practice the idea that governments are formed by the will of the people.
ABOLISHED THE MONARCHY
CURTAILED THE POWER OF THE FRENCH ROMAN CATHOLIC CHURCH
ABOLISHED THE FEUDAL SYSTEM
CREATED EQUALITY BEFORE THE LAW
GAVE TALENTED PEOPLE GREATER ACCESS TO JOBS
CREATED A SENSE OF NATIONAL PRIDE
CREATED POPULAR SOVEREIGNTY

Look at the chart that shows the end of the monarchy during the French Revolution. How did the French people react to this event?

F Opposition to dismantling the feudal system prematurely

G Sense of national pride instead of loyalty to a king or queen

H Growing opposition to the new republican government

J Relief that the constitution created social reform and jobs

Test Taking Tips: Tip for Questions With Reading Passages

1. Read the question.
2. Read the title of the passage if it is provided.
3. Determine when the passage or quotation was written or spoken and by whom.
4. Carefully read the entire passage or quotation.
5. Read the question again to be sure you understand what is being asked. Identify details or ideas in the passage or quotation that you will use to answer the question.
6. Answer the question in your own words.
7. Read the answer choices and select the best answer.

3

> *"Betty Harris, age 37: I was married at 23, and went into a colliery when I was married. I used to weave when about 12 years old; can neither read nor write. I work for Andrew Knowles, of Little Bolton (Lancs), and make sometimes 7s a week, sometimes not so much. I am a drawer, and work from 6 in the morning to 6 at night. Stop about an hour at noon to eat my dinner; have bread and butter for dinner; I get no drink. I have two children, but they are too young to work. I worked at drawing when I was in the family way. I know a woman who has gone home and washed herself, taken to her bed, delivered of a child, and gone to work again under the week."*

Read the excerpt. Which of these helped to change the roles of working-class women during the Industrial Age?

A Efforts of political activists successfully changed work conditions.

B Changes in laws guaranteed income for women with children.

C Women's suffrage in the late 1800s empowered women.

D Women had a large voice in the labor union movements.

---

4 How did factory systems enhance industrialization efforts?

F Expensive interchangeable parts improved parts repair.

G New inventions were tested by the government before use.

H Assembly line methods were efficient with division of labor.

J Division of labor excluded women and children from risky jobs.

If you have trouble with...				
Question	1	2	3	4
See Lesson	13.2	13.1	13.4	12.7
TEKS	8.B	28.A	24.A	9.D

Topic 13

3. A
4. H

Online Use the **Topic Synthesize** to help students revisit and reflect on the Essential Question for this Topic.

Topic Inquiry

If students have done a Topic Inquiry for this Topic, have them complete the final step of the Inquiry now.

Nationalism and the Spread of Democracy (1790–1914)

TOPIC 14 ORGANIZER	PACING: APPROX. 1 PERIOD, .5 BLOCKS		
	PACING	TEKS	ELPS
Connect	1 period		
MY STORY VIDEO **Simón Bolívar, The Liberator**	10 min.	9.B, 9.C, 9.D	
DIGITAL ESSENTIAL QUESTION ACTIVITY **What are the Challenges of Diversity?**	10 min.	9.D, 21.A	
DIGITAL TIMELINE ACTIVITY **Nationalism and the Spread of Democracy**	10 min.	9.C, 9.D, 21.A	
TOPIC INQUIRY: CIVIC DISCUSSION **The Irish Potato Famine**	20 min.		
Investigate	4–8 periods		
TOPIC INQUIRY: CIVIC DISCUSSION **The Irish Potato Famine**	Ongoing		
LESSON 1 **Revolutions Sweep Europe**	30–40 min.	9.D, 18.A, 21.A	4.F.6
LESSON 2 **Latin American Nations Win Independence**	30–40 min.	9.B, 9.C, 9.D, 21.A, 21.C	4.C.1, 4.F.7
LESSON 3 **The Unification of Germany**	30–40 min.	8.B, 9.B, 9.D, 18.C	4.C.2, 4.F.8
LESSON 4 **The Unification of Italy**	30–40 min.	9.D	4.C.3, 4.F.9
LESSON 5 **Democratic Reforms in Britain**	30–40 min.	8.B, 18.A, 21.A, 21.B, 21.C, 24.A, 24.B	4.C.4, 4.F.10
LESSON 6 **Divisions and Democracy in France**	30–40 min.	21.A	4.D.1
LESSON 7 **Growth of the United States**	30–40 min.	21.A	4.G.2, 4.E.1
LESSON 8 **Nationalism in Eastern Europe and Russia**	30–40 min.	9.D, 21.A	4.F.1, 4.G.3
Synthesize	1 period		
DIGITAL ESSENTIAL QUESTION ACTIVITY **Nationalism and the Spread of Democracy**	10 min.	21.A	
TOPIC INQUIRY: CIVIC DISCUSSION **The Irish Potato Famine**	20 min.		
Demonstrate	1–2 periods		
ONLINE TEST **Nationalism and the Spread of Democracy**	10 min.		
TOPIC INQUIRY: CIVIC DISCUSSION **The Irish Potato Famine**	20 min.		

AUTHOR'S NOTE

The Birth of Modern Ideologies: Nationalism

In some ways *nationalism* blazed even more brightly than liberalism across the nineteenth-century sky. Nineteenth-century nationalists built on the teachings of the eighteenth-century German cultural nationalists who preached the importance of each people's national spirit. They also drew on the model of the French Revolution, which had unleashed powerful patriotic energies, both in France and in nations conquered by Napoleon. Nationalists in the nineteenth century dedicated their energies to unifying divided peoples such as the Italians and the Germans. Or they labored to win national self-determination for oppressed minorities such as the Eastern European, mostly Slavic peoples ruled by the Austrian, Russian, and Ottoman emperors. Later in the century, however, nationalism turned chauvinistic. It began to be used to justify the aggressive or expansionist policies of German or French or British governments.

Nationalists believed that common language and literature, history and custom welded a people into a larger whole—the nation. Some of them believed in a folk soul or folk spirit uniting a people spiritually. Many saw a national character that they shared with their fellow nationals: Frenchmen were naturally more civilized and artistic than other peoples, Germans more philosophical or scientific, Britons better at government and more practical, and so forth.

These apostles of nationality preached their patriotic creed in terms of native soil and blood—the black earth of Russia, for instance, or German or Anglo-Saxon blood. They expressed their loyalty with reverence for such concrete symbols as the national flag or the national anthem. They wept when the French Tricolor or the British Union Jack passed by, and they sang the "Marseillaise," "Britannia Rules the Waves," or "Germany Over All" with passion.

—Anthony Esler, *The Human Venture: From Prehistory to the Present* (Upper Saddle River, New Jersey: Pearson Education, 2004), pp. 492

TOPIC INQUIRY: CIVIC DISCUSSION

The Irish Potato Famine

TEKS 1.E, 8.C, 8.D, 29.C, 29.D, 29.E, 29.F, 29.G, 29.H, 30.A, 30.C

In this Topic Inquiry, students work in teams to examine different perspectives on this issue by analyzing several sources, arguing both sides of a Yes/No question, and then developing and discussing their own point of view on the question: **Was the Irish potato famine caused by British policy?**

STEP 1: CONNECT

Develop Questions and Plan the Investigation

Launch the Civic Discussion

Divide the class into groups of four students. Students can access the materials they'll need in the online course or you can distribute copies to each student. Read the main question and introduction with the students.

Have students complete Step 1 by reading the Discussion Launch and filling in Step 1 of the Information Organizer. The Discussion Launch provides YES and NO arguments on the main question. Students should extract and paraphrase the arguments from the reading in Step 1 of their Information Organizers.

Next, students share within their groups the arguments and evidence they found to support the YES and NO positions. The group needs to agree on the major YES and NO points and each student should note those points in their Information Organizer.

Resources

- Student Instructions
- Information Organizer
- Discussion Launch

PROFESSIONAL DEVELOPMENT

Civic Discussion

Be sure to view the Civic Discussion Professional Development resources in the online course.

STEP 2: INVESTIGATE

Apply Disciplinary Concepts and Tools

Examine Sources and Perspectives

Students will examine sources with the goal of extracting information and perspectives on the main question. They analyze each source and describe the author's perspective on the main question and key evidence the author provides to support that viewpoint in the Information Organizer, Step 2.

Ask students to keep in mind:

- **Author/Creator:** Who created the source? An individual? A Group? A Government agency?
- **Audience:** For whom was the source created?
- **Date/Place:** Is there any information that reveals where and when the source was created?
- **Purpose:** Why was the source created? Discuss with students the importance of this question in identifying bias.
- **Relevance:** How does the source support one argument or another?

Suggestion: Reading the source documents and filling in Step 2 of the Information Organizer could be assigned as homework.

Resources

- Student Instructions
- Information Organizer
- Source documents

STEP 3: SYNTHESIZE

Use Evidence to Formulate Conclusions

Formulate Compelling Arguments With Evidence

Now students will apply perspectives and evidence they extracted from the sources to think more deeply about the main question by first arguing one side of the issue and then the other. In this way students become more prepared to formulate an evidence-based conclusion on their own.

Within each student group, assign half of the students to take the position of YES on the main question and the other half to take the position of NO. Students will work with their partners to identify the strongest arguments and evidence to support their assigned YES or NO position.

Present Yes/No Positions

Within each group, those assigned the YES position share arguments and evidence first. As the YES students speak, those assigned NO should listen carefully, take notes to fill in the rest of the Compelling Arguments Chart (Step 3 in the Information Organizer), and ask clarifying questions.

When the YES side is finished, students assigned the NO position present while those assigned YES should listen, take notes, and ask clarifying questions. Examples of clarifying questions are:

- I think you just said [x]. Am I understanding you correctly?
- Can you tell me more about [x]?
- Can you repeat [x]? I am not sure I understand, yet.

Suggestion: You may want to set a five-minute time limit for each side to present. Provide a two-minute warning so that students make their most compelling arguments within the time frame.

Switch Sides

The students will switch sides to argue the opposite point of view. To prepare to present the other position, partners who first argued YES will use the notes they took during the NO side's presentation and add any additional arguments and evidence from the reading and sources. The same goes for students who first argued the NO position.

STEP 4: DEMONSTRATE

Communicate Conclusions and Take Informed Action

Individual Points of View

Now the students will have the opportunity to discuss the main question from their own points of view. To help students prepare for this discussion, have them reflect on the YES/NO discussions they have participated in thus far and fill in Step 4 of their Information Organizers.

After all of the students have shared their points of view, each group should list points of agreement, filling in the last portion of Step 4 on their Information Organizers.

Reflect on the Discussion

Ask students to reflect on the civic discussion thinking about:

- The value of having to argue both the YES and NO positions.
- If their individual views changed over the course of the discussion and why.
- What they learned from participating in the discussion.

Resources

- Student Instructions
- Information Organizer

Revolutions Sweep Europe

Objectives

Objective 1: Compare the goals of conservatives and liberals in 19th century Europe.

Objective 2: Identify the influence of liberty, equality, and nationalism on political revolutions.

Objective 3: Describe the causes and results of the revolutions of 1830 and 1848.

LESSON 1 ORGANIZER		PACING: APPROX. 1 PERIOD, .5 BLOCKS				
			RESOURCES			
	OBJECTIVES	PACING	Print	Online	TEKS	ELPS
Connect						
DIGITAL START UP ACTIVITY **The Revolutions of 1830 and 1848**		5 min.		●	9.D	
Investigate						
READ **A Clash of Ideologies**	Objective 1	10 min.	●	●	21.A	
READ **Liberalism and Nationalism Spur Revolts**	Objective 1	10 min.	●	●		
INTERACTIVE CARTOON **Metternich Resists Liberal Ideas**	Objective 1	10 min.		●	9.D, 21.A	
READ **Rebellions Erupt in Eastern Europe**	Objective 2	10 min.	●	●	9.D	
READ **Revolutions of 1830 and 1848**	Objective 2	10 min.	●	●	9.D, 21.A	
READ **Demands for Reform Spread**	Objective 3	10 min.	●	●	9.D, 21.A	4.F.6
READ **The Revolution of 1848 in France**	Objective 3	10 min.	●	●		
READ **Revolution Spreads Across Europe**	Objective 3	10 min.	●	●		
INTERACTIVE MAP **Revolutionary Uprisings, 1830–1848**	Objective 3	10 min.		●	9.D, 21.A	
Synthesize						
DIGITAL ACTIVITY **"Central Shaft of the Mine"**		5 min.		●	9.D, 21.A	
Demonstrate						
LESSON QUIZ **Lesson Quiz and Class Discussion Board**		10 min.		●	9.D	

PEARSON realize™ www.PearsonTexas.com Access your Digital Lesson

Focus on Texas Standards

Texas Essential Knowledge and Skills

9.D identify the influence of ideas such as separation of powers, checks and balances, liberty, equality, democracy, popular sovereignty, human rights, constitutionalism, and nationalism on political revolutions

18.A identify the historical origins and characteristics of the free enterprise system, including the contributions of Adam Smith, especially the influence of his ideas found in The Wealth of Nations

21.A describe how people have participated in supporting or changing their governments

NOTES

Latin American Nations Win Independence

Objectives

Objective 1: List the causes of growing discontent in Latin America, including the influence of the Enlightenment.

Objective 2: Trace the influence of the American and French Revolutions on Latin America.

Objective 3: Describe the revolutions in Haiti, Mexico, and Central America.

Objective 4: Explain how South American nations won independence, including the role of Simón Bolívar.

LESSON 2 ORGANIZER			PACING: APPROX. 1 PERIOD, .5 BLOCKS			
			RESOURCES			
	OBJECTIVES	PACING	Print	Online	TEKS	ELPS
Connect						
DIGITAL START UP ACTIVITY **An Oath of Freedom**		5 min.		●	9.C, 9.D, 21.C	
Investigate						
READ **Latin America Ripe for Revolution**	Objectives 1, 2	10 min.	●	●	9.B, 9.C, 9.D	4.C.1
READ **Haiti Fights for Freedom**	Objective 3	10 min.	●	●	9.B, 9.D, 21.A, 21.C	
READ **Revolts in Mexico and Central America**		10 min.	●	●		
INTERACTIVE GALLERY **Latin American Independence Movements**		10 min.		●	9.C, 9.D, 21.A, 21.C	
READ **Discontent Sparks Revolts in South America**	Objective 4	10 min.	●	●	9.C, 9.D, 21.A, 21.C	4.F.7
INTERACTIVE MAP **Latin American Independence**		10 min.		●	9.D, 21.A, 21.C	
Synthesize						
DIGITAL ACTIVITY **The "Liberator's" Dream Doesn't Come True**		5 min.		●	9.D, 21.A, 21.C	
Demonstrate						
LESSON QUIZ **Lesson Quiz and Class Discussion Board**		10 min.		●	9.D	

PEARSON realize
www.PearsonTexas.com
Access your Digital Lesson

Focus on Texas Standards

Texas Essential Knowledge and Skills

9.B explain the impact of Napoleon Bonaparte and the Napoleonic Wars on Europe and Latin America

9.C trace the influence of the American and French revolutions on Latin America, including the role of Simón Bolivar

9.D identify the influence of ideas such as separation of powers, checks and balances, liberty, equality, democracy, popular sovereignty, human rights, constitutionalism, and nationalism on political revolutions

21.A describe how people have participated in supporting or changing their governments

21.C identify examples of key persons who were successful in shifting political thought, including William Wilberforce

NOTES

The Unification of Germany

Objectives

Objective 1: Identify the factors that promoted German nationalism.

Objective 2: Analyze how Bismarck achieved German unification.

Objective 3: Describe the German empire under Bismarck.

Objective 4: Explain the policies of Kaiser William II.

LESSON 3 ORGANIZER	PACING: APPROX. 1 PERIOD, .5 BLOCKS					
			RESOURCES			
	OBJECTIVES	PACING	Print	Online	TEKS	ELPS
Connect						
DIGITAL START UP ACTIVITY **Nationalist Pride**		5 min.		●	9.D, 21.A	
Investigate						
READ **Moving Toward a Unified Germany**	Objective 1	10 min.	●	●	9.B, 9.D, 21.A	4.C.2
READ **Bismarck Becomes the Architect of German Unity**	Objective 2	10 min.	●	●	9.D, 21.A	4.F.8
INTERACTIVE TIMELINE **German Unification**	Objective 2	10 min.		●	9.D, 21.A	
READ **Germany Becomes an Industrial Giant**	Objective 3	10 min.	●	●	8.B	
READ **The Iron Chancellor**	Objective 3	10 min.	●	●		
INTERACTIVE CARTOON **A Political Game of Chess**	Objective 3	10 min.		●	21.A	
READ **Kaiser William II**	Objective 4	10 min.	●	●		
Synthesize						
DIGITAL ACTIVITY **The Price of Nationalism**		5 min.		●	9.D, 21.A	
Demonstrate						
LESSON QUIZ **Lesson Quiz and Discussion Board**		10 min.		●	8.B, 9.D, 18.C, 21.A	

Focus on Texas Standards

Texas Essential Knowledge and Skills

8.B explain how the Industrial Revolution led to political, economic, and social changes in Europe

9.B explain the impact of Napoleon Bonaparte and the Napoleonic Wars on Europe and Latin America

9.D identify the influence of ideas such as separation of powers, checks and balances, liberty, equality, democracy, popular sovereignty, human rights, constitutionalism, and nationalism on political revolutions

18.C identify the historical origins and characteristics of socialism

NOTES

Topic 14 Lesson 4

The Unification of Italy

Objectives

Objective 1: List the key obstacles to Italian unity.

Objective 2: Evaluate the roles played by Cavour and Garibaldi in Italian unification.

Objective 3: Describe the challenges that faced the new nation of Italy.

LESSON 4 ORGANIZER — **PACING: APPROX. 1 PERIOD, .5 BLOCKS**

	OBJECTIVES	PACING	RESOURCES Print	RESOURCES Online	TEKS	ELPS
Connect						
DIGITAL START UP ACTIVITY **Stirrings of Nationalism**		5 min.		●	9.D	
Investigate						
READ **First Steps to Italian Unity**	Objective 1	10 min.	●	●	9.D	4.F.9
INTERACTIVE MAP **Italian Regions Before Unification**	Objective 1	10 min.		●	9.D	
READ **The Struggle for Italy**	Objective 2	10 min.	●	●	9.D	
INTERACTIVE GALLERY **Leaders of Italian Unification**	Objective 2	10 min.		●	9.D	
READ **Italy Faces New Challenges**	Objective 3	10 min.	●	●	9.D	4.C.3
Synthesize						
DIGITAL ACTIVITY **Unity Leads to Turmoil**		5 min.		●	9.D	
Demonstrate						
LESSON QUIZ **Lesson Quiz and Class Discussion Board**		10 min.		●	9.D	

Focus on Texas Standards

Texas Essential Knowledge and Skills

9.D identify the influence of ideas such as separation of powers, checks and balances, liberty, equality, democracy, popular sovereignty, human rights, constitutionalism, and nationalism on political revolutions

NOTES

Democratic Reforms in Britain

Objectives

Objective 1: Understand how political reforms in Britain affected suffrage and the nature of Parliament.

Objective 2: Identify the influence of Queen Victoria and the values she represented.

Objective 3: Describe social and economic reforms enacted by Parliament in the 1800s.

Objective 4: Describe the efforts by British women to win the vote.

Objective 5: Explain the struggle for Irish home rule and the impact of famine on Ireland.

LESSON 5 ORGANIZER — **PACING: APPROX. 1 PERIOD, .5 BLOCKS**

	OBJECTIVES	PACING	RESOURCES Print	RESOURCES Online	TEKS	ELPS
Connect						
DIGITAL START UP ACTIVITY **Harsh Working and Living Conditions Lead to Government Reforms**		5 min.		●	8.B, 21.A	
Investigate						
READ **"Two Nations": The Rich and the Poor**	Objective 1	10 min.	●	●	21.A	
READ **The Victorian Age**	Objective 2	10 min.	●	●	21.A, 24.B	4.C.4
READ **Reforms Increase Parliamentary Democracy, Economic and Social Reforms, Victories for the Working Class**	Objective 3	10 min.	●	●	8.B, 21.A	
INTERACTIVE TIMELINE **Britain Reformed**	Objective 3	10 min.		●	21.A	
READ **Women Struggle for the Vote**	Objective 4	10 min.	●	●	21.A, 21.B, 24.A, 24.B	
READ **The Irish Question**	Objective 5	10 min.	●	●	21.A, 21.C	4.F.10
INTERACTIVE GALLERY **Famine Changes Ireland**	Objective 5	10 min.		●	21.A	
Synthesize						
DIGITAL ACTIVITY **Democratic Transition**		5 min.		●	21.A	
Demonstrate						
LESSON QUIZ **Lesson Quiz and Class Discussion Board**		10 min.		●	21.A, 21.C, 24.B	

PEARSON realize™ www.PearsonTexas.com Access your Digital Lesson

Focus on Texas Standards

Texas Essential Knowledge and Skills

8.B explain how the Industrial Revolution led to political, economic, and social changes in Europe

18.A identify the historical origins and characteristics of the free enterprise system, including the contributions of Adam Smith, especially the influence of his ideas found in The Wealth of Nations

21.A describe how people have participated in supporting or changing their governments

21.B describe the rights and responsibilities of citizens and noncitizens in civic participation throughout history

21.C identify examples of key persons who were successful in shifting political thought, including William Wilberforce

24.A describe the changing roles of women, children, and families during major eras of world history

24.B describe the major influences of women such as Elizabeth I, Queen Victoria, Mother Teresa, Indira Gandhi, Margaret Thatcher, and Golda Meir during major eras of world history

NOTES

Topic 14 Lesson 6

Divisions and Democracy in France

Objectives

Objective 1: List the domestic and foreign policies of Napoleon III.

Objective 2: Describe the challenges and political reforms of the Third Republic.

Objective 3: Explain how the Dreyfus affair divided France and contributed to the growth of the Zionist movement.

LESSON 6 ORGANIZER — **PACING: APPROX. 1 PERIOD, .5 BLOCKS**

	OBJECTIVES	PACING	RESOURCES Print	RESOURCES Online	TEKS	ELPS
Connect						
DIGITAL START UP ACTIVITY **A Different Point of View**		5 min.		●	21.A	
Investigate						
READ **Napoleon III and the Second Empire**	Objective 1	10 min.	●	●	21.A	
INTERACTIVE GALLERY **The Siege of Paris**	Objective 1	10 min.		●	21.A	
READ **The Third Republic Faces New Struggles**	Objective 2	10 min.	●	●	21.A	
INTERACTIVE CARTOON **The Boulanger Scandal**	Objective 2	10 min.		●	21.A	
READ **The Dreyfus Affair**	Objective 3	10 min.	●	●	21.A	
READ **Reforms in France**	Objective 2	10 min.	●	●	21.A	4.D.1
Synthesize						
DIGITAL ACTIVITY **The Dreyfus Affair**		5 min.		●		
Demonstrate						
LESSON QUIZ **Lesson Quiz and Class Discussion Board**		10 min.		●	21.A	

Focus on Texas Standards

Texas Essential Knowledge and Skills

21.A describe how people have participated in supporting or changing their governments

NOTES

Growth of the United States

Objectives

Objective 1: Describe the territorial expansion of the United States.

Objective 2: Summarize the causes and effects of the Civil War.

Objective 3: Explain how American democracy grew in the 1800s.

Objective 4: Analyze the impact of economic growth and social reform on the United States.

LESSON 7 ORGANIZER — **PACING: APPROX. 1 PERIOD, .5 BLOCKS**

	OBJECTIVES	PACING	RESOURCES Print	RESOURCES Online	TEKS	ELPS
Connect						
DIGITAL START UP ACTIVITY **A Shining Beacon**		5 min.		●		
Investigate						
READ **The United States Expands**	Objective 1	10 min.	●	●	18.A	4.G.2
INTERACTIVE MAP **Expansion of the United States, 1783–1898**	Objective 1	10 min.		●		
READ **Expanding Democracy**	Objective 3	10 min.	●	●	21.A, 24.A	
INTERACTIVE TIMELINE **The Women's Rights Movement**	Objective 3	10 min.		●	21.A, 24.A	
READ **The Civil War**	Objective 2	10 min.	●	●	21.A	4.E.1
READ **Economic Growth and Reform**	Objective 4	10 min.	●	●	18.A	
Synthesize						
DIGITAL ACTIVITY **The Growth of the United States**		5 min.		●	21.A	
Demonstrate						
LESSON QUIZ **Lesson Quiz and Class Discussion Board**		10 min.		●	18.A, 21.A	

Focus on Texas Standards

Texas Essential Knowledge and Skills

21.A describe how people have participated in supporting or changing their governments

NOTES

Nationalism in Eastern Europe and Russia

Objectives

Objective 1: Explain how nationalism challenged Austria and the Ottoman Empire.

Objective 2: Summarize major obstacles to progress in Russia.

Objective 3: Describe the cycle of absolutism, reform, and reaction followed by the tsars.

Objective 4: Explain how industrialization contributed to the outbreak of revolution in 1905.

LESSON 8 ORGANIZER	PACING: APPROX. 1 PERIOD, .5 BLOCKS					
			RESOURCES			
	OBJECTIVES	PACING	Print	Online	TEKS	ELPS
Connect						
DIGITAL START UP ACTIVITY **Outside Influences**		5 min.		●	9.D, 21.A	
Investigate						
READ **Nationalism Endangers Old Empires**	Objective 1	10 min.	●	●	9.D, 21.A	4.F.1
READ **The Dual Monarchy**		10 min.	●	●		
READ **The Ottoman Empire Declines**		10 min.	●	●		
INTERACTIVE MAP **The Balkan Powder Keg**		10 min.		●	9.D, 21.A	
READ **Russia Tries Reform**	Objective 2	10 min.	●	●	9.D, 21.A	
INTERACTIVE GALLERY **Tug of War: Reform and Repression by the Russian Tsars**		10 min.		●	9.D, 21.A	
READ **Emancipation and Stirrings of Revolution**	Objective 3	10 min.	●	●	9.D, 21.A	
READ **The Beginnings of Industrialization**	Objective 4	10 min.	●	●	9.D, 21.A	4.G.3
READ **The Road to Revolution**		10 min.	●	●	9.D, 21.A	
Synthesize						
DIGITAL ACTIVITY **The People Fight Back**		5 min.		●	9.D, 21.A	
Demonstrate						
LESSON QUIZ **Lesson Quiz and Class Discussion Board**		10 min.		●	9.D, 21.A	

PEARSON realize™ www.PearsonTexas.com Access your Digital Lesson

Focus on Texas Standards

Texas Essential Knowledge and Skills

9.D identify the influence of ideas such as separation of powers, checks and balances, liberty, equality, democracy, popular sovereignty, human rights, constitutionalism, and nationalism on political revolutions	**21.A** describe how people have participated in supporting or changing their governments

NOTES

TOPIC 14 TEKS Mastery

Nationalism and the Spread of Democracy (1790–1914)

In this Topic, you will learn about the creation of new nations and the spread of democracy. You will also find lots of interesting ways to master the TEKS associated with this Topic.

Your study will help you master these TEKS:

TEKS

8.B, 9.B, 9.C, 9.D, 18.A, 18.C, 21.A, 21.B, 21.C, 24.A, 24.B

LESSON OUTLINE

Connect

Connect with this Topic by watching a video about a fascinating person related to this Topic. You can think about how this Topic connects to your own life. And you'll encounter an intriguing Essential Question: What are the challenges of diversity?

Begin your study by trying the following:

NBC LEARN Watch My Story Video:

Simón Bolívar, The Liberator

Launch your Civic Discussion:

The Irish Potato Famine

Investigate

A group of lessons will help you investigate nationalism and democracy further. Each lesson has interesting text readings and fascinating interactivities. Together, they will bring the new nations and young democracies alive and help you master the TEKS for this Topic.

And keep working on your Civic Discussion. You're almost ready to show what you have accomplished by expressing your position on the Irish Potato Famine using the evidence you have gathered.

>> Digital interactivity from the online course

Synthesize

You will get a chance to pull together everything you have learned by thinking again about the Essential Question. Consider how you would answer the question now: What are the challenges of diversity?

Demonstrate

Completing this Topic is like practicing all your soccer skills or rehearsing the scenes in a play. Now you get a chance to pull it all together for the final game or the live performance. You can do this on the Topic Review and Assessment pages. Or you can complete your work your Civic Discussion, the Irish Potato Famine.

TEKS in Topic 14	Topic Review and Assessment Questions
8.B	1
9.B	2
9.C	2, 3
9.D	1, 3, 4, 5, 6, 7, 13
18.A	14
18.C	15, 16
21.A	1, 7, 8, 9, 10
21.C	11
24.B	12

Topic 14

Nationalism and the Spread of Democracy

Introduction

During the 1800s, nationalism and democratic ideals spread through Europe and Latin America. Nationalism led to the creation of new nation-states and threatened the unity of multinational empires. In Britain and the United States, democracy expanded. In other countries, people used a variety of methods, including revolution, to change their governments and gain democratic rights and freedoms. How did the ideas of nationalism and democracy affect people and their governments in the 1800s?

ESSENTIAL QUESTION

Ask students to think about the Essential Question for this Topic: What are the challenges of diversity? Share the following with students: When people in a society have diverse cultural backgrounds and differing beliefs, opinions, and ideas, societal challenges can result. Again and again, citizens and rulers have had to make tough choices on difficult issues about the powers of government and human rights. Think about the issues listed below. Which side of the issue would rulers likely support? Which side would the common people likely support?

- One national language or a diversity of languages
- One national religion or a diversity of religions
- Strong monarchy or representative government
- Large, diverse state or many small countries, each identifying with a particular ethnic group

Ask volunteers to share their ideas with the class.

Predict Consequences How do you think nationalism might affect empires with people of diverse ethnic and religious backgrounds? *(Sample response: People belonging to particular groups or regions might want to break away from the empire.)*

Identify Cause and Effect Why do you think revolutions and civil wars occurred in the 1800s? *(Sample response: Wars broke out because people wanted more rights, they identified with their own cultural group or region, and they wanted self-government.)*

[**ESSENTIAL QUESTION**] What are the Challenges of Diversity?

14 Nationalism and the Spread of Democracy (1790–1914)

Analyze Visuals

Ask students to examine the statue shown in the photograph. Explain that the statue is a likeness of Simón Bolívar, also known in Spanish as El Libertador, or "The Liberator." Discuss why Bolívar might have been known as the Liberator. Have students predict from which perspective this nickname comes and whom Bolívar might have been liberating.

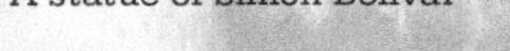
>> A statue of Simón Bolívar

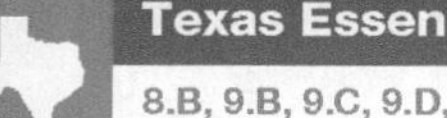

Texas Essential Knowledge and Skills

8.B, 9.B, 9.C, 9.D, 18.A, 18.C, 21.A, 21.B, 21.C, 24.A, 24.B

Enduring Understandings

- After Napoleon's defeat, conservatives tried to restore monarchies while liberals called for constitutional governments.
- Nationalism and liberalism led to a series of revolutions in Europe.
- Influenced by the American and French revolutions, Latin American colonies won independence.
- Nationalism led to the unification of Germany and Italy but threatened the Austrian and Ottoman empires.
- In Britain and the United States, democracy expanded as more people won the right to vote.
- After France's defeat by Prussia, the Third Republic was established.
- In Russia, the cycle of reform and repression led to instability.

Watch the My Story Video to learn more about The Liberator, Simón Bolívar.

PEARSON realize www.PearsonTexas.com **Access your digital lessons including:** Topic Inquiry • Interactive Reading Notepad • Interactivities • Assessments

587

NBC LEARN MY STORY VIDEO

Project the My Story Video that introduces students to Latin American independence leader Simón Bolívar.

Online My Story Video: **Simón Bolívar, An American Liberator**

Check Understanding What was Simón Bolívar's greatest achievement? *(He helped Latin America gain independence from Spain.)*

Identify Central Issues How did Enlightenment ideas influence Bolívar? *(The concepts of liberty, equality, and fraternity and of representative government were Enlightenment ideas that influenced Bolívar. So too were the examples of the American and French revolutions.)*

OVERVIEW ACTIVITY

Online Project the **Timeline: Nationalism and the Spread of Democracy** showing the major events having to do with nationalism and the spread of democracy in the 1800s. During this topic, students will learn about all of these events and many more, but this timeline will provide a framework into which they can place the events they learn about.

Analyze Timelines Between what years of the mid-1800s did many revolutions occur in Europe? *(between 1830 and 1848)*

Topic Inquiry

If you choose to assign the Topic Inquiry, launch the Civic Discussion with students after introducing the Topic.

D Differentiate Extra Support Suggest that students copy the timeline from the Overview Activity onto their own paper and add entries to it as they read the chapter. Help students draw the timeline correctly and add years for the late 1800s. Point out to them that some of the events they are seeing on the timeline were directly influenced by an event that happened in their own country—the American Revolution.

Topic 14 Lesson 1

Revolutions Sweep Europe

CONNECT

Preview Have students preview the **Lesson Objectives** and the list of **Key Terms**.

Students can also preview all the **Key Terms** and **Academic Vocabulary** using the **Interactive Reading Notepad** on the digital course or preview a summary of the lesson in the **Reading and Note Taking Study Guide**.

Online Use the **Editable Presentation** found on the digital course to present the main ideas for this lesson.

Start Up Activity

Tell students that the mid-1800s marked a time of protest and revolution in Europe. Liberals and nationalists challenged conservative European monarchies. Before the revolutions, many intellectuals had predicted the inevitable uprisings. Read the quotation and answer the question that follows:

[I hear] the dull sound of revolution, still deep down in the earth, pushing out under every kingdom in Europe its subterranean galleries from the central shaft of the mine which is Paris.—Victor Hugo, author of *Les Miserables*

Discuss What was Hugo predicting with his words, "pushing out under every kingdom in Europe"? *(Hugo was predicting that all of Europe would revolt, not just the French.)*

Tell students that in this lesson they will be learning about the causes of the Revolutions of 1848.

Online You can also project the **Start Up Activity** from the course.

INVESTIGATE

Have students read the section in the **Reading and Note Taking Study Guide** to help them take notes and understand the text as they read.

A Clash of Ideologies

Explain that Metternich and other conservatives opposed change and wanted to keep the old political order and social structure. They wanted to support the established monarchies and maintain order by using military force to stop nationalist and democratic political revolutions.

>> Prince Metternich served as the foreign minister of Austria from 1809 to 1848. To suppress revolutionary ideas, he urged conservatives to censor the press and crush protests in their countries.

Interactive Flipped Video

14.1 At the Congress of Vienna in 1815, the powerful rulers of Europe sought to suppress revolutionary ideas, preserve their own power, and set up a lasting peace. Prince Clemens von Metternich, a commanding force at the congress, warned of the dangers of the "revolutionary seed" spread by the French Revolution and Napoleon. Revolutionary ideas, he warned, not only threatened Europe's monarchs, but also undermined the values of the old social order.

TEKS
9.D, 18.A, 21.A

>> Objectives

Compare the goals of conservatives and liberals in 19th century Europe.

Identify the influence of liberty, equality, and nationalism on political revolutions.

Describe the causes and results of the revolutions of 1830 and 1848.

>> Key Terms

ideology
universal manhood suffrage
autonomy
radical
Louis Philippe
recession
Napoleon III
Louis Kossuth
absolutism

Revolutions Sweep Europe

A Clash of Ideologies

> Passions are let loose. . .to overthrow everything that society respects as the basis of its existence: religion, public morality, laws, customs, rights, and duties, all are attacked, confounded [defeated], overthrown, or called in question.
>
> —Prince Clemens von Metternich

Unlike the monarchs attending the Congress of Vienna, other voices loudly opposed Metternich's views. In the decades after 1815, people with opposing **ideologies,** or systems of thought and belief, plunged Europe into turmoil.

Conservatives Favor Old Order The Congress of Vienna was a victory for the conservative forces, which included monarchs and their officials, noble landowners, and church leaders. To preserve the old political and social order, European monarchs worked together to ensure stability and prevent revolution. This arrangement is sometimes called the Concert of Europe. In addition to the conservative

www.PearsonTexas.com Access your Digital Lesson.

Aa Vocabulary Builder

1. Have students pronounce the following academic vocabulary terms in this lesson and clarify the part of speech. For difficult or polysyllabic words, break them into syllables and pronounce them with the students.
2. Explain what the word means in common "student-friendly" language using synonyms and antonyms when possible. Provide concrete examples to clarify the meaning, and rephrase the definition.

agitator: someone who attempts to arouse feeling for or against something

denounce: to express harsh criticism of something or somebody

emerge: to arise, appear, or come out of

ruling class of Europe, conservative ideas appealed to peasants, who wanted to preserve traditional ways.

Conservatives of the early 1800s wanted to return to the way things had been before 1789. They had benefited under the old order. They wanted to restore royal families to the thrones they had lost when Napoleon swept across Europe. They supported a social hierarchy in which lower classes respected and obeyed their social superiors.

Conservatives also backed an established church—Catholic in Austria and southern Europe, Protestant in northern Europe, and Eastern Orthodox in eastern Europe.

Conservatives believed that talk about natural rights and constitutional government could lead only to chaos, as in France in 1789. If change had to come, they argued, it must come slowly. Conservatives felt that their own interest in peace and stability benefited everyone. Conservative leaders like Metternich opposed freedom of the press, which could spread revolutionary ideas. Metternich urged monarchs to crush protests in their own lands and help others to douse the flames of rebellion wherever they erupted.

IDENTIFY MAIN IDEAS What was the primary goal of conservatives in the Concert of Europe?

>> **Analyze Political Cartoons** A determined Prince Metternich stands firm, with an angry crowd behind him. Who does the crowd represent, and what do they want?

Interactive Cartoon

Liberalism and Nationalism Spur Revolts

Challenging the conservatives at every turn were the liberals. Liberals embraced the ideas of the Enlightenment and the French Revolution. Their goals, and the rising tide of nationalism, ignited revolts across Europe.

Liberals Defend Natural Rights Because liberals spoke mostly for the bourgeoisie, or middle class, their ideas are sometimes called "bourgeois liberalism." Liberals included business owners, bankers, and lawyers, as well as politicians, newspaper editors, writers, and others who helped to shape public opinion.

Liberals wanted governments to be based on written constitutions and separation of powers. They opposed the old notion of the divine right of monarchs and the tradition of a ruling aristocracy. Liberals called for rulers elected by the people and responsible to them. Thus, most liberals favored a republican form of government over a monarchy, or at least wanted the monarch to be limited by a constitution.

Liberals defended natural rights such as liberty and equality. They stood for property rights and freedom of religion. Liberals of the early 1800s saw the role of

>> **Compare** After the Congress of Vienna, liberals repeatedly protested and rebelled against the conservative order. How do the liberal protesters in this image differ in appearance from the image of the conservative leader Metternich in the previous text?

Online Project the **Interactive Cartoon: Metternich Resists Liberal Ideas**. Click through the hotspots and ask students to interpret the political cartoon.

ACTIVE CLASSROOM

Have students create a Quickdraw of a banner someone in the crowd might hold to oppose Metternich's ideas. The banner should be of a symbol or a drawing that highlights the ideas of liberals or nationalists between 1815 and 1848. *(Possible symbols: money, a written constitution, a ballot box)*

Guided Reading and Discussion

Tell students that Metternich feared that the French Revolution and the Age of Napoleon had planted a seed that would grow into revolution. Ask students to explain the ideologies of conservatives and to whom they appealed. *(Conservatives wanted to protect the old political and social order and an established church; their ideas appealed to the ruling class and to peasants.)*

Liberalism and Nationalism Spur Revolts

Next tell students that liberals and nationalists were influenced by the Enlightenment ideas of liberty, equality, and human rights, and they challenged conservatives by trying to change the government. The conflict of ideas was a major cause of the political revolutions between 1830 and 1848.

D Differentiate Challenge Ask students to draw a new banner representing other aspects of liberal ideology, such as social equality and human rights. Have students write a short opinion essay explaining what the banner represents. Remind students to use evidence to support their claims. Have students exchange their essays with a partner and then discuss their claims and evidence.

Answers

Analyze Political Cartoons *Sample answer: The crowd represents liberals and other reformers supporting natural rights; representative, constitutional governments; separation of powers; and an end to absolute monarchies.*

Identify Main Ideas *Conservatives supported the political and social order of monarchies that existed before the French Revolution and Napoleon.*

Compare *Sample answer: Metternich appears calm, content, and in control. The liberal protesters look agitated and angry as they chase the carriage of a conservative politician to show their opposition to the old order.*

Topic 14 Lesson 1

Guided Reading and Discussion

Tell students that in a free enterprise system, business owners set prices of goods and services based on supply and demand. Ask students to explain why liberals might have favored the free enterprise system.

Analyze Images

Tells students that the chart "Goals of Liberals and Conservatives" shows the main differences between the political and social ideals of these two groups. Ask: What did each group think about political revolution? *(Liberals supported it as a means to an end for political and social change; conservatives wanted to protect the old order and opposed revolution.)*

Rebellions Erupt in Eastern Europe

Explain that during the early 1800s the ideas of liberty, equality, and nationalism sparked many revolutions in Europe. Metternich and other conservative rulers succeeded in stopping most of the uprisings but not in suppressing the ideas of liberalism and nationalism. Ask: Where did revolutions occur, and why? *(Greece, Serbia, Spain, Portugal, various states in Italy; for rights and freedoms and the nationalist desire for self-rule)*

government as limited to protecting these basic rights. In their view, only male property owners or others with a financial stake in society should have the right to vote. Not until later in the 1800s did liberals support the principle of **universal manhood suffrage,** giving all adult men the right to vote.

Liberals also strongly supported the laissez-faire economics of Adam Smith and David Ricardo. They saw the free market as an opportunity for capitalist entrepreneurs to succeed. As capitalists, and often employers, liberals had different goals from those of workers laboring in factories, mines, and other enterprises of the early Industrial Revolution.

Nationalism Grows Another challenge to Metternich's conservative order came from the rise of nationalist feelings. Like liberalism, nationalism was an outgrowth of the Enlightenment and the French Revolution. Nationalism, like liberalism, would feed the flames of revolt against the established order.

For centuries, European rulers had gained or lost lands through wars, marriages, and treaties. They exchanged territories and the people in them like pieces in a game. As a result, by 1815 Europe had several empires that included many nationalities. The Austrian, Russian, and Ottoman empires, for example, each included diverse peoples.

During the 1800s, national groups who shared a common heritage demanded their own states. Each group had its own leaders who inspired and organized the struggle. Although nationalism gave people a sense of identity and the goal of achieving an independent homeland, it also had negative effects. It often bred intolerance and led to persecution of other ethnic or national groups.

HYPOTHESIZE Why would nationalism lead to intolerance and persecution of other ethnic or national groups?

Rebellions Erupt in Eastern Europe

Spurred by the ideas of liberalism and nationalism, revolutionaries fought against the old order. Although these ideas stirred unrest in Western Europe, the first successful nationalist revolts occurred in Eastern Europe. Eastern Europe was home to a mix of peoples and religions. In the early 1800s, several Balkan peoples in southeastern Europe rebelled against the Ottomans, who had ruled them for more than 300 years.

Serbia Gains Independence The first Balkan people to revolt were the Serbs. From 1804 to 1817, the Serbian independence leaders Karageorge (ka rah JAWR juh) and Milos Obrenovic (oh BRAY noh vich) battled Ottoman forces in two major uprisings.

Although Serbs had support from Russia, which shared its Slavic heritage and Eastern Orthodox

Goals of Liberals and Conservatives

LIBERALS	CONSERVATIVES
Ideas appealed to middle class of educated business people and professionals.	Ideas appealed to royalty, nobility, church leaders, and uneducated peasants.
GOALS:	**GOALS:**
Governments based on written constitutions	Royal families on their thrones
Separation of powers	Traditional social hierarchy
Natural rights of individuals (liberty, equality, and property)	Authority of established churches
Republican form of government	Respect and obedience to authority
Laissezfaire economics	Stability and order
Revolution, if necessary, to achieve goals	Suppression of revolutions

>> **Analyze Charts** Conservatives and liberals had very different ideas about the role of government. How did their different ideologies affect European politics in the early-to-mid-1800s?

Answers

Hypothesize *Many different ethnic groups lived within empires, and each group was fiercely loyal to its own members. People wanted a true sense of national identity, and this led to intolerance and persecution of other ethnic groups.*

Analyze Charts *Sample answer: Liberals wanted governments based on constitutions, with separation of powers and natural rights. Conservatives favored the old order. Liberals and nationalists challenged the existing order through protests and rebellions. Since conservatives were unwilling to compromise, it led to revolutions throughout Europe.*

D Differentiate Extra Support Guide students in using word relationships to help learn key terms. Tell them that *conservative* comes from the same Latin root as *conserve*, which means "to preserve." *Liberal* comes from the same Latin root as *liberate*, which means "to free." *Nationalism* comes from *nation*. Have students write a definition of each ideology using a root or related word.

Christianity, the Serbs faced a terrible struggle. The fighting took a huge toll. During this period, Serbian literature and culture flourished, further strengthening Serbian nationalism.

Gradually, Serbia gained a degree of **autonomy,** or self-rule, within the Ottoman empire. An 1830 agreement gave Serbs complete control over their own internal affairs, although European countries did not recognize Serbia's independence until 1878. Serbia continued its close ties with Russia, which it saw as a protector of its hard-won freedom.

Greeks Revolt Against Ottoman Rule In 1821, the Greeks revolted, seeking to end centuries of Ottoman rule. At first, the Greeks were badly divided. But years of suffering in long, bloody wars of independence helped shape a national identity. Leaders of the rebellion justified their struggle as "a national war, a holy war, a war the object of which is to reconquer the rights of individual liberty." The Greeks had the support of romantic writers such as English poet Lord Byron, who went to Greece to aid the fight for independence.

The Greek rebels won the sympathy of even the conservative powers of Europe. In the late 1820s, Britain, France, and Russia forced the Ottomans to grant independence to some Greek provinces. By 1830, Greece was independent. The European powers, however, pressured the Greeks to accept Otto von Wittelsbach, a German prince, as their king. This move was meant to show that the European powers did not support nationalist revolutions.

Other Challenges to the Old Order During the 1820s, other revolts erupted along the fringe of Europe. In Spain, Portugal, and several Italian states, rebels demanded constitutional governments. The unrest posed a challenge to the conservative rulers of Europe. Spurred on by Metternich, a French army marched over the Pyrenees to suppress a revolt in Spain. Austrian forces crossed the Alps to smash Italian rebels.

Troops dampened the fires of liberalism and nationalism, but could not smother them. In the next decades, sparks would flare anew. Added to liberal and nationalist demands were the goals of the new industrial working class. By the mid-1800s, social reformers and agitators were urging workers to support socialism or other ways of reorganizing property ownership, further contributing to the unrest of this period.

 **HYPOTHESIZE** Why would a monarch order his army to suppress an uprising in another country?

>> Uprisings flared up repeatedly across Europe, especially in Paris.

Revolutions of 1830 and 1848

In the 1820s, conservative forces quickly suppressed the liberal uprisings in Spain, Portugal, and the Italian states. They could not, however, end Europe's age of revolutions. Liberal French leader Alexis de Tocqueville warned that the revolutions of the 1820s were not over.

> We are sleeping on a volcano. . . Do you not see that the Earth trembles anew? A wind of revolution blows, the storm is on the horizon.
>
> —Alexis de Tocqueville

Conservatives and Liberals in France The Congress of Vienna had restored Louis XVIII to the French throne. The new ruler wisely issued a constitution, the Charter of French Liberties. It created a two-house legislature and allowed limited freedom of the press. Still, the king retained much power.

Louis's efforts at compromise satisfied few people. Ultra royalists despised constitutional government and wanted to restore the old regime. These "ultras" included many high clergy and émigré nobles who had returned to France after the revolution.

Guided Reading and Discussion

Remind students that Metternich predicted the outbreak of rebellions challenging the old order. Ask students to provide examples of how the ideas of liberty and equality sparked these rebellions.

Identify Supporting Details How did nationalism influence the political revolutions? *(The participants wanted to establish independent nation-states with constitutional governments. They wanted to create nations based on shared cultures and identities.)*

Revolutions of 1830 and 1848

Though the revolutions of the 1820s were suppressed, revolutionary thought was not. Dissatisfaction with the royal government of France among radicals and liberals led to uprisings in July 1830 that resulted in the king's abdication. Liberals then chose Louis Philippe as king.

Guided Reading and Discussion

Tell students that Louis Philippe was known as the "citizen king." Ask them to describe how Louis Philippe came to power, why he was given this nickname, and what policies he favored.

Draw Conclusions Read the quotation by Alexis de Tocqueville in the text. What does he mean when he says, "We are sleeping on a volcano"? *(Students should indicate that revolutionary thought has not gone away and will erupt in rebellions again.)*

History Background

Comparative Theories of Revolution
Political theorists have tried to come up with a comprehensive theory of revolutions. Theda Skocpol and other theorists have pointed to three main conditions. First, the state must be vulnerable. A vulnerable state is one that is facing external as well as internal pressures, such as war and economic problems. Second, there must be an elite group that is well positioned to oppose the government (for example, nobles or middle-class liberals in a legislative body). Third, there must be a rural or a peasant population that can be mobilized. Some theorists, such as Jack Goldstone, add that revolution occurs only when many people believe there is something wrong or unjust in the way the country is being governed.

Answers

Hypothesize *to prevent revolutionary ideas and uprisings from spreading to his or her own country*

Topic 14 Lesson 1

Key Terms

Ask students to find the key term **radical** (in bold) in the text and explain its meaning. Tell them that the word *radical* comes from the Latin for *root*. Note that in 1830, many radicals wanted to tear out the entire political system at its roots, not just fix it.

Demands for Reform Spread

The July Revolution in Paris inspired revolutions elsewhere in Europe. Though many failed, some were successful. Even unsuccessful revolutions often frightened rulers into making reforms.

Guided Reading and Discussion

Tell students that the Belgians successfully revolted against their government in 1830, but the Poles did not. Ask students to describe these revolutions—who led them and why.

Describe What caused the initial discontent in Belgium? *(the uniting of the Austrian Netherlands and the Kingdom of Holland under the Dutch king)*

Ask students to examine the map "Revolutions of 1830." Ask: Which northern European country gained independence during the period 1830–1831? *(Belgium)* Where was revolution suppressed? *(Cracow)*

Opposing the ultras were the liberals. They wanted to extend suffrage and win a share of power for middle-class citizens like themselves. Another group, the **radicals,** or people who favor extreme change, called for a republic like France had in the 1790s. The working class still wanted what it had hoped to win in 1789: decent pay and bread the people could afford.

Citizens Lead the July Revolution When Louis XVIII died in 1824, his younger brother, Charles X, inherited the throne. Charles, a strong believer in **absolutism,** rejected the very idea of the charter. In July 1830, he suspended the legislature, limited the right to vote, and restricted the press.

In Paris, angry citizens threw up barricades across the narrow streets. From behind the barricades, people fired on the soldiers and pelted them with stones and roof tiles. Within days, rebels controlled Paris. The revolutionary tricolor flew from the towers of Notre Dame cathedral. A frightened Charles X abdicated and fled to England.

Louis Philippe, the "Citizen King" Radicals and liberals who had united against Charles X disagreed over a new government. Radicals wanted to set up a republic. Liberals, however, insisted on a constitutional monarchy and chose **Louis Philippe** as king. Louis Philippe was a cousin of Charles X and in his youth had supported the revolution of 1789.

>> French rebels erected barricades in the streets using household items and whatever else they could find that might offer protection during battles with government soldiers.

The French called Louis Philippe the "citizen king" because he owed his throne to the people. Louis got along well with the liberal bourgeoisie. He dressed like them in a frock coat and top hat. Sometimes he strolled the streets, shaking hands with well-wishers. Liberal politicians filled his government.

Under Louis Philippe, the upper bourgeoisie prospered. Louis extended suffrage, but only to France's wealthier citizens. The vast majority of the people still could not vote. The king's other policies also favored the middle class at the expense of the workers.

RECALL What actions did Charles X take in 1830, and how did French rebels respond?

Demands for Reform Spread

The July Revolution in Paris inspired uprisings elsewhere in Europe. Metternich later said, "When France sneezes, Europe catches cold." Most of the uprisings were suppressed. But here and there, rebels did force changes on conservative governments. Even when they failed, revolutions frightened rulers badly enough to encourage reforms later in the century.

Belgium Wins Independence The one notable success in 1830 took place in Belgium. In 1815, the Congress of Vienna had united the Austrian Netherlands (present-day Belgium) and the Kingdom of Holland under the Dutch king. The Congress had wanted to create a strong barrier to help prevent French expansion in the future.

The Belgians resented the new arrangement. The Belgians and Dutch had different languages, religions, and economic interests. The Belgians were Catholic, while the Dutch were largely Protestant. The Belgian economy was based on manufacturing, while the Dutch relied on trade.

News of the 1830 Paris uprising ignited a revolutionary spark in Belgium. Students and workers, along with other citizens, threw up barricades in Brussels, the capital. The Dutch king hoped for help from Britain and France. These two countries backed Belgian demands for independence, expecting to benefit from the separation of Belgium and Holland. As a result, in 1831, Belgium became an independent state with a liberal constitution. Soon after, the major European powers signed a treaty recognizing Belgium as a "perpetually neutral state."

History Background

Poland Has Not Yet Perished When Poland was partitioned by Prussia, Austria, and Russia in 1795, Poland ceased to exist as an independent state, but the Polish national spirit lived on. The country's national anthem, which begins with the words "Poland has not yet perished," was written in 1797. Parts of Poland became provinces of the Austrian Empire and of Prussia, which later became part of Germany. However, the largest portion of Poland lay within the Russian empire, and the Russian province of Poland carried on the name of the divided nation. Russian Poland staged several armed revolts against Russian rule, including the 1830 uprising. Poles under German, Austrian, and Russian rule never abandoned their quest for reunification and independence. They finally achieved their goal in 1918, when Poland was reborn as an independent, united nation at the end of World War I.

Answers

Recall *After Charles X disbanded the legislature and limited the press, the rebels put up barricades, fired at soldiers, and gained control of Paris.*

>> **Analyze Maps** What were the results of the revolutions of 1830?

Polish Nationalists Defeated Nationalists in Poland also staged an uprising in 1830. But, unlike the Belgians, the Poles failed to win independence for their country.

In the late 1700s, Russia, Austria, and Prussia had divided up Poland. Poles had hoped that the Congress of Vienna would restore their homeland in 1815. Instead, the great powers handed most of Poland to Russia.

In 1830, Polish students, army officers, and landowners rose in revolt. The rebels failed to gain widespread support, however, and were brutally crushed by Russian forces. Some survivors fled to Western Europe and the United States, where they kept alive the dream of freedom.

COMPARE AND CONTRAST How were the Belgian and Polish revolutions of 1830 different?

ELPS 4.F.6 Work together with your teacher and your classmates to read and understand *Demands for Reform Spread.*

The Revolution of 1848 in France

By the 1840s, discontent in France was again reaching a boiling point. The Industrial Revolution was changing life in France, especially in the cities. Politically, France remained divided. Radicals still wanted a republic. Utopian socialists called for an end to private ownership of property. Even liberals denounced Louis Philippe's government for corruption.

Discontent grew when a **recession,** or period of reduced economic activity, hit France. Factories closed and workers lost their jobs. Poor harvests led to rising bread prices. Newspapers blamed the government for these problems. In Paris, conditions were ripe for revolution.

Violence Erupts During "February Days" In February 1848, the government took steps to silence critics and prevent public meetings. This action sent angry crowds into the streets of Paris. During the "February Days," overturned carts, paving stones, and toppled trees again blocked the streets. Church bells rang alarms, while women and men on the barricades sang the revolutionary

anthem "La Marseillaise." A number of demonstrators clashed with royal troops and were killed. As the turmoil spread, Louis Philippe abdicated. A group of liberal, radical, and socialist leaders proclaimed the Second Republic. The First Republic had lasted from 1792 until 1804, when Napoleon became emperor.

From the start, deep differences divided the new government. Middle-class liberals wanted moderate political reforms. Socialists wanted far-reaching social and economic change and forced the government

The Revolution of 1848 in France

Tell students that by the 1840s, political divisions and discontent remained in France. Differences about the structure and powers of government, combined with an economic recession, led to violent uprisings during "February Days." Louis Philippe was forced to abdicate, and liberals, radicals, and socialists proclaimed the Second Republic.

Guided Reading and Discussion

Ask students to describe how the French people participated in changing their government in 1848.

Identify Supporting Details List two reasons why the French working class still wanted change after the "February Days." *(The working class still demanded better working conditions and was fearful after the liberals shut down the national workshops.)*

English Language Proficiency Standards

Reading 4.F.6 Provide students with support to help them understand the main idea of the text "Demands for Reform Spread."

Beginning Read the text aloud. Have students repeat the first two sentences. Focus on the meaning of "When France sneezes, Europe catches cold." Point out the two subheadings and the map showing the revolutions of 1830. Have them identify the countries that "caught a cold" from France.

Intermediate Complete the Beginning activity, but have students read the text and interpret the quotation on their own.

Advanced Have students read, focusing on headings and visuals. Have pairs or groups explain the quotation. Have them identify the countries that "caught a cold" from France.

Advanced High Ask students to perform the Advanced activity independently.

Answers

Analyze Maps *Sample answer: Belgium and Greece became independent. France, Belgium, and Greece gained new constitutional monarchies. The uprising in Poland failed.*

Compare and Contrast *Belgians won their independence. Belgium became an independent state with a liberal constitution. Polish nationalists were brutally defeated by Russian forces and did not win their independence.*

Revolution Spreads Across Europe

Explain that after the 1848 French Revolution, the ideals of liberty, equality, and nationalism inspired other revolutionaries to revolt in an attempt to change their governments. They opposed conservatives who supported the existing governments.

Online Project the **Interactive Map: Revolutionary Uprisings, 1830–1848**. Click on the numbered hotspots to learn more about the revolutions and their results.

ACTIVE CLASSROOM

Organize students into pairs. Have the first student give the second student an Audio Tour of the map, explaining what is shown on the map. *(For example: I see a battle star on Paris.)* Have the second student give the first an explanation of what the different parts of the map mean. *(For example: Paris was the site of uprisings in 1830 and 1848, and so on.)*

to set up national workshops to provide jobs for the unemployed.

Workers Lose Out During "June Days" By June, however, upper- and middle-class interests had won control of the government. They saw the national workshops as a waste of money and shut them down. Furious, workers again took to the streets of Paris. This time, however, bourgeois liberals turned violently against the protesters. Peasants, who feared that socialists might take their land, also attacked the rioting workers. At least 1,500 people were killed before the government crushed the rebellion.

The fighting of the "June Days" left a bitter legacy. The middle class both feared and distrusted the socialists, while the working class harbored a deep hatred for the bourgeoisie.

Louis Napoleon is Elected President By the end of 1848, the National Assembly was dominated by members who wanted to restore order. They issued a constitution for the Second Republic. It created a strong president and a one-house legislature. But it also gave the vote to all adult men, the widest suffrage in the world at the time. Nine million Frenchmen could now vote, compared with only 200,000 who had that right before.

>> During the Second Republic, the National Assembly issued a constitution that gave the vote to all adult men.

When elections for president were held, the overwhelming winner was Louis Napoleon, nephew of Napoleon Bonaparte. The "new" Napoleon attracted the working classes by presenting himself as a man who cared about social issues such as poverty. At the same time, his famous name, linked with order and past French glory, helped him with conservatives.

Napoleon III Establishes the Second Empire Once in office, Louis Napoleon used his position as a stepping-stone to greater power. By 1852, he had proclaimed himself emperor, taking the title **Napoleon III.** Thus ended the short-lived Second Republic.

Like his celebrated uncle, Napoleon III used a plebiscite, or ballot in which voters have a direct say on an issue, to win public approval for his seizure of power. A stunning 90 percent of voters supported his move to set up the Second Empire. Many thought that a monarchy was more stable than a republic or hoped that Napoleon III would restore the glory days of Napoleon Bonaparte.

Napoleon III, like Louis Philippe, ruled at a time of rapid economic growth. For the bourgeoisie, the early days of the Second Empire brought prosperity and contentment. In time, however, Napoleon III would embark on foreign adventures that would bring down his empire and end French leadership in Europe.

CONTRAST How did the French governments created after the Revolutions of 1830 and 1848 differ?

Revolution Spreads Across Europe

The Revolution of 1848 in France triggered a wave of revolutions across Europe, just as it had in 1830. For opponents of the old order, it was a time of such hope that they called it the "springtime of the peoples." Although events in France touched off the revolts, grievances had been piling up for years.

European middle-class liberals wanted a greater share of political power for themselves, as well as protections for the basic rights of all male citizens. Workers demanded relief from the miseries of the Industrial Revolution. And nationalists of all classes ached to throw off foreign rule.

Revolts Shake the Austrian Empire In the Austrian empire, revolts broke out in the major cities, starting in Vienna. Metternich, who had long dominated Austrian politics, tried to suppress the revolts. Even though he censored the press, books were smuggled to universities throughout the empire. Students demanded change.

D Differentiate Extra Support After giving students the instructions for the Active Classroom, allow students five minutes to think about each of the sites on the map. Tell them to write down two details about each location shown on the map. Then continue the group activity.

Answers

Contrast *The revolt of 1830 resulted in a constitutional monarchy; in 1848, the result was the Second Republic, which had a constitution, a strong president, and universal suffrage for men.*

>> **Analyze Maps** France's successful 1848 uprising sparked revolutions throughout Europe. How does the map show the difficulties conservatives had in stopping the spread of revolutionary ideas?

Interactive Map

When workers joined the students on the streets of Vienna, Metternich resigned and fled in disguise.

Revolution quickly spread to other parts of the Austrian empire. In Budapest, Hungarian nationalists led by journalist **Louis Kossuth** demanded an independent government, an end to serfdom, and a written constitution. In Prague, the Czechs made similar demands. Overwhelmed by events, the Austrian government agreed to the reforms. The gains were temporary, however. Austrian troops soon regained control of Vienna and Prague and smashed the rebels in Budapest.

Revolts in Italy Uprisings also erupted in the Italian states. Nationalists wanted to end Hapsburg domination. As elsewhere, nationalist goals were linked to demands for liberal reforms such as constitutional government. Workers suffering economic hardships demanded even more radical changes.

From Venice in the north to Naples in the south, Italians set up independent republics. Revolutionaries expelled the pope from Rome. Before long, the forces of reaction returned, backed by military force. Austrian troops ousted the new governments in northern Italy. A French army restored the pope to power. Elsewhere, liberal reforms were canceled.

Rebellion in the German States In the German states, university students demanded national unity and liberal reforms. Economic hard times and a potato famine brought peasants and workers into the struggle. In Prussia, liberals forced King Frederick William IV to accept a constitution written by an elected assembly. Within a year, though, he dissolved the assembly.

Throughout 1848, delegates from German states met in the Frankfurt Assembly. Divisions soon emerged over whether Germany should be a republic or a monarchy and whether to include Austria in a united German state.

Finally, the assembly offered Prussia's Frederick William IV the crown of a united Germany. To their dismay, the conservative king rejected the offer because it came not from the German princes but from the people—"from the gutter," as he described it.

Failed Revolutions By 1850, rebellion faded, ending the age of liberal revolution that had begun in 1789. Why did the uprisings fail? In general, revolutionaries did not have mass support. Another reason was that opposing goals divided liberals, who wanted moderate political reforms, and workers, who sought radical economic changes. Also, rulers did not hesitate to use force to crush the uprisings.

Guided Reading and Discussion

The revolutions of 1848, known as the "springtime of the people," were a series of political revolutions. But within a year, conservatives regained control. Ask students to write three short paragraphs describing the revolutions in the Austrian empire, Italy, and the German states.

Identify Main Ideas What were some of the demands made by rebels in the 1848 revolutions? *(Sample response: a greater share of political power, protection of rights, an independent government, an end to serfdom, a written constitution)*

Describe Why were the revolutions unsuccessful? *(Conservatives took military action against revolutionaries, and the revolutionaries did not have mass public support.)*

Answers

Analyze Maps *Sample answer: Revolutions surged throughout Europe. While conservative forces stopped many of the protests and rebellions, they could not stop liberal ideas or nationalism from spreading. People wanted more political power, protection of natural rights, and freedom from foreign rule.*

Topic 14 Lesson 1

SYNTHESIZE

Online Project the **Digital Activity: "Central Shaft of the Mine."** Ask students to share their paragraphs with a partner. Have volunteers read their paragraphs aloud.

Then have students think about the Essential Question: What are the challenges of diversity? Then ask them the following question: How did the events of 1848 portray the challenges of diversity? *(Nationalism among diverse groups was one of the challenges to governments.)*

Discuss People in Europe were ready for change in 1848. Many wanted to replace divine-right monarchies with governments that were based on written constitutions. Even though conservatives regained control of most monarchies, how did Europe change forever? *(The events of 1848 popularized the ideals of liberty, equality, and fraternity. Several governments with elected representatives and written constitutions were formed. Citizens recognized that they could shift political thought and change their government.)*

DEMONSTRATE

Online Assign the **Digital Lesson Quiz** for this lesson if you haven't already done so. Students will be offered automatic remediation or enrichment based on their scores.

Pose these questions to the class on the Discussion Board:

Draw Conclusions What were the conditions under which the people of France lived that led to revolution rather than to peace? *(absolute rule, government corruption, and extreme poverty)*

Predict Consequences What do you predict will happen in European politics in the late 1800s and beyond? *(Sample response: Europeans will continue to oppose the old order and seek democratic rights and freedoms, and conflict will continue.)*

Topic Inquiry

Have students continue their investigations for the Topic Inquiry.

At mid century, although Metternich was gone, his conservative system remained in force. In the decades ahead, liberalism, nationalism, and socialism would win successes not through revolution, but through political activity.

? INTEGRATE INFORMATION Describe the role nationalism played in European revolutions in 1848.

ASSESSMENT

1. **Explain** Explain why peasants would support Conservative control of government.
2. **Describe** How did a history of outside rule lead to the Serbs' fight for independence?
3. **Draw Conclusions** What conditions led the French people to revolt?
4. **Cite Evidence** Why did most of the revolutions of 1848 fail to achieve their goals?
5. **Identify Main Ideas** Explain the main ideologies that led to the uprisings throughout Europe.

Answers

Integrate Information *Nationalists wanted to throw off foreign rule. In Budapest and Prague, nationalists wanted to be free from Austrian control and form new governments to protect basic rights. Nationalists in Italy wanted to end Hapsburg control, unify, and establish a constitutional government. Germans wanted national unity and liberal reforms as well.*

Assessment

1. Peasants were uneducated and feared change and the loss of their few possessions. They favored keeping the traditional ways.
2. The Serbs lived in the Balkans, along with peoples of different religions and ethnicities. Growing Serbian nationalism led the Serbs to revolt against the Ottomans, who had ruled them for hundreds of years.
3. The French people lived under absolute rule with government corruption and no representation. Many also lived in extreme poverty, worsened by recessions.
4. They lacked mass support, disagreed on their revolutionary goals, and were crushed by the armies of the European powers.
5. Liberals wanted constitutional governments that gave them more rights. Nationalists wanted unified states that represented their cultural identities. Socialists wanted equal rights for all and an end to social classes and private-property ownership.

14.2 By the late 1700s, the revolutionary fever that gripped Western Europe had spread to Latin America. There, discontent was rooted in the social, racial, and political system that had emerged during 300 years of Spanish rule. By 1825, most of Latin America was freed from colonial rule.

>> Simón Bolívar was a Venezuelan-born military and political leader. Inspired by Enlightenment ideals, he led revolutions to end Spanish rule in Latin America.

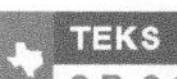 Interactive Flipped Video

Latin American Nations Win Independence

TEKS
9.B, 9.C, 9.D, 21.A, 21.C

Latin America Ripe for Revolution

A Complex Social Structure Spanish-born **peninsulares,** members of the highest social class, dominated Latin American political and social life. Only they could hold top jobs in government and the Church. Many **creoles**—the European-descended Latin Americans who owned the haciendas, ranches, and mines—bitterly resented their second-class status. Merchants fretted under mercantilist policies that tied the colonies to Spain.

Meanwhile, a growing population of **mestizos,** people of Native American and European descent, and **mulattoes,** people of African and European descent, were angry at being denied the status, wealth, and power that were available to whites. Native Americans suffered economic misery under the Spanish, who had conquered the lands of their ancestors. In the Caribbean region and parts of South America, masses of enslaved Africans who worked on plantations longed for freedom.

>> Objectives

List the causes of growing discontent in Latin America, including the influence of the Enlightenment.

Trace the influence of the American and French Revolutions on Latin America.

Describe the revolutions in Haiti, Mexico, and Central America.

Explain how South American nations won independence, including the role of Simón Bolívar.

>> Key Terms

peninsular
creole
mestizo
mulatto
Simón Bolívar
Toussaint L'Ouverture
Father Miguel Hidalgo
Father José Morelos
José de San Martín
Dom Pedro

 www.PearsonTexas.com Access your Digital Lesson.

Topic 14 Lesson 2

Latin American Nations Win Independence

CONNECT

Preview Have students preview the **Lesson Objectives** and the list of **Key Terms**.

Students can also preview all the **Key Terms** and **Academic Vocabulary** using the **Interactive Reading Notepad** on the digital course or preview a summary of the lesson in the **Reading and Note Taking Study Guide**.

Online Use the **Editable Presentation** found on the digital course to present the main ideas for this lesson.

Start Up Activity

Tell students that like many wealthy Latin Americans, young Simón Bolívar was sent to Europe to complete his education. Read this statement, made by Bolívar while he was a student there: "I swear before God and by my honor never to allow my hands to be idle nor my soul to rest until I have broken the chains that bind us to Spain."

Ask students to explain how the American and French Revolutions might have inspired Bolívar. *(Sample response: They showed him that it was possible to win independence from colonial control and to fight for the ideals of liberty, equality, and self-government.)*

Tell students that in this lesson they will be learning about the fight for independence in Latin America.

Online You can also project the **Start Up Activity** from the course.

INVESTIGATE

Have students use the **Reading and Note Taking Study Guide** to help them take notes and understand the text as they read.

Key Terms

Write the terms **peninsulares, creoles, mestizos,** and **mulattoes** on the board. Ask students to find them in the text and explain their meanings. Discuss which of these groups would be least content.

Latin America Ripe for Revolution

Explain to students that the Spanish controlled most of Latin and South America. Tell them that the colonists lived with unfair laws and taxes similar to those of the Americans during the time of the American Revolution.

Aa Vocabulary Builder

1. Have students pronounce the following academic vocabulary terms in this lesson and clarify the part of speech. For difficult or polysyllabic words, break them into syllables and pronounce them with the students.
2. Explain what the word means in common "student-friendly" language using synonyms and antonyms when possible. Provide concrete examples to clarify the meaning, and rephrase the definition.

cement: to secure or form a strong bond
proclaim: to announce publically or formally

Topic 14 Lesson 2

Guided Reading and Discussion

Tell students that there were many factors that led to the Latin American revolutions. Ask them to describe these factors in a paragraph.

Express Ideas Clearly Explain the influence of the idea of equality on Latin American revolutions. *(The social structure in Latin America wasn't equal. Many people resented their status and wanted equality.)*

Haiti Fights for Freedom

Tell students that in 1791, revolution erupted in a French-ruled colony on the island of Hispaniola, now known as Haiti. French planters there owned very profitable sugar plantations worked on by enslaved Africans, who they often mistreated. The island's slaves rose up in revolt, led by Toussaint L'Ouverture.

Guided Reading and Discussion

Ask students to describe the outcome of the rebellion in Haiti.

Then tell students that in 1802, Napoleon Bonaparte sent a large army to retake the colony. Toussaint was captured during the fighting.

Analyze Images

Have students study the drawing of Toussaint and his army in battle. What does the drawing suggest about the difficulties Toussaint's army faced? *(They had no uniforms and were fighting well-equipped and well-trained soldiers in close combat.)*

Enlightenment Ideas Reach Latin America In the 1700s, educated creoles read the works of Enlightenment thinkers. They watched colonists in North America throw off British rule and were inspired by their success. Translations of the Declaration of Independence and the Constitution of the United States circulated among the creole elite.

During the French Revolution, young creoles like **Simón Bolívar** (boh LEE vahr) traveled in Europe and were inspired by the ideals of "liberty, equality, and fraternity." Yet, despite their admiration for Enlightenment ideas and revolutions in other lands, most creoles were reluctant to act.

The Uprisings Begin The spark that finally ignited widespread rebellion in Latin America was Napoleon's invasion of Spain in 1808. Napoleon ousted the Spanish king and placed his brother Joseph on the Spanish throne. In Latin America, leaders saw Spain's weakness as an opportunity to reject foreign domination and demand independence from colonial rule.

? CHECK UNDERSTANDING In what ways did the American and French Revolutions influence Latin Americans?

>> **Draw Conclusions** Toussaint's army defeated British, Spanish, and French armies to end slavery in Haiti and win independence from France. Why would the British and Spanish join the fight against the rebels?

ELPS ELPS 4.C.1 Skim the portion of text titled *Enlightenment Ideas Reach Latin America*. Then locate, practice saying, and recall the meaning of sight words that you recognize.

Haiti Fights for Freedom

Even before Spanish colonists hoisted the flag of freedom, revolution had erupted in a French-ruled colony on the island of Hispaniola. In Haiti, as the island is now called, French planters owned very profitable sugar plantations worked by nearly a half million enslaved Africans. Sugar plantations were labor-intensive. The slaves were overworked and underfed.

Toussaint L'Ouverture Leads a Slave Revolt Embittered by suffering and inspired by the talk of liberty and equality, the island's slaves rose up in revolt in 1791. The rebels were fortunate to find an intelligent and skillful leader in **Toussaint L'Ouverture** (too SAN loo vehr TOOR), a self-educated former slave. Although untrained, Toussaint was a brilliant general and inspiring commander.

Toussaint's army of former slaves faced many enemies. Some mulattoes joined French planters against the rebels. France, Spain, and Britain all sent armies against them.

The fighting took more lives than any other revolution in the Americas. But by 1798, the rebels had achieved their goal: Slavery was abolished, and Toussaint's forces controlled most of the island.

Haitian Independence In 1802, Napoleon Bonaparte sent a large army to reconquer the former colony. Toussaint urged his countrymen to take up arms once again to resist the invaders. In April 1802 the French agreed to a truce, but then they captured Toussaint and carried him in chains to France. He died there in a cold mountain prison a year later.

The struggle for freedom continued, however, and late in 1803, with yellow fever destroying their army, the French surrendered. In January 1804, the island declared itself an independent country under the name of Haiti. In the following years, rival Haitian leaders fought for power. Finally, in 1820, Haiti became a republic.

? CHECK UNDERSTANDING What conditions led to the Haitian fight for independence?

Answers

Check Understanding *Many Latin Americans had read the works of Enlightenment writers and observed the outcomes of these revolutions. They hoped to put in place the ideas of self-government and a democratic society in their own countries.*

Draw Conclusions *Sample answer: They wanted to suppress revolutionary ideas from spreading to their colonies in the Americas and to protect their colonial economic interests.*

Check Understanding *Haitian slaves on French sugar plantations were overworked and underfed. They rose up to end their suffering, hoping to gain liberty and equality.*

English Language Proficiency Standards

Reading 4.C.1 Have students skim "Enlightenment Ideas Reach Latin America" to find sight vocabulary. Have them say the words and explain their meanings.

Beginning Help students skim the first paragraph for social studies words that they recognize, such as *colonist*, *rule*, *independence*, and *declaration*. Say each word and review its purpose or meaning.

Intermediate Complete the Beginning activity, but have students say each word and explain its purpose or meaning.

Advanced Have students complete the Intermediate activity on their own.

Advanced High Complete the Advanced activity using both paragraphs in the section. Have students write a one-sentence summary of the content to share with the group.

Topic 14 Lesson 2

Revolts in Mexico and Central America

The slave revolt in Haiti frightened creoles in Spanish America. Although they wanted power themselves, most had no desire for economic or social changes that might threaten their way of life. In 1810, however, a creole priest in Mexico, **Father Miguel Hidalgo** (hee DAL goh), raised his voice for freedom.

>> Father Hidalgo led the Mexican independence movement, battling Spanish forces for almost a year before his capture and execution.

Mexico's Battle for Independence Begins Father Hidalgo presided over the poor rural parish of Dolores. On September 15, 1810, he rang the church bells summoning the people to prayer. When they gathered, he startled them with an urgent appeal, "My children, will you be free?" Father Hidalgo's speech became known as "el Grito de Dolores"—the cry of Dolores. It called Mexicans to fight for independence.

A ragged army of poor mestizos and Native Americans rallied to Father Hidalgo and marched to the outskirts of Mexico City. At first, some creoles supported the revolt. However, they soon rejected Hidalgo's call for an end to slavery and his plea for reforms to improve conditions for Native Americans. They felt that these policies would cost them power.

After some early successes, the rebels faced growing opposition. Less than a year after he issued the "Grito," Hidalgo was captured and executed, and his followers scattered.

José Morelos Continues the Fight Another priest picked up the banner of revolution. **Father José Morelos** was a mestizo who called for wide-ranging social and political reform. He wanted to improve conditions for the majority of Mexicans, abolish slavery, and give the vote to all men. For four years, Morelos led rebel forces before he, too, was captured and shot in 1815.

Spanish forces, backed by conservative creoles, hunted down the surviving guerrillas. They had almost succeeded in ending the rebel movement when events in Spain had unexpected effects.

Mexico Wins Independence In Spain in 1820, liberals forced the king to issue a constitution. This move alarmed Agustín de Iturbide (ee toor BEE day), a conservative creole in Mexico. He feared that the new Spanish government might impose liberal reforms on the colonies as well.

Iturbide had spent years fighting Mexican revolutionaries. Suddenly, in 1821, he reached out to them. Backed by creoles, mestizos, and Native Americans, he overthrew the Spanish viceroy. Mexico was independent at last. Iturbide took the title Emperor Agustín I. Soon, however, liberal Mexicans toppled the would-be monarch and set up the Republic of Mexico.

New Republics in Central America Spanish-ruled lands in Central America declared independence in the early 1820s. Iturbide tried to add these areas to his Mexican empire. After his overthrow, local leaders set up a republic called the United Provinces of Central America. The union soon fragmented into the separate republics of Guatemala, Nicaragua, Honduras, El Salvador, and Costa Rica.

HYPOTHESIZE Why do you think Mexico's first two independence leaders were priests?

Discontent Sparks Revolts in South America

In South America, Native Americans had rebelled against Spanish rule as early as the 1700s, though with limited results. It was not until the 1800s that discontent among the creoles sparked a widespread drive for independence.

History Background

Tupac Amarú Even before Toussaint L'Ouverture's slave revolt and the creole revolutions of the 1800s, a Native American named Tupac Amarú led a rebellion in Latin America. He claimed to be the great-grandson of the last Inca who had fought against the Spaniards in the 1500s, also named Tupac Amarú. Tupac Amarú II demanded an end to the brutal system of forced Indian labor. Spanish officials reject the demand. In 1780, Tupac Amarú organized a revolt. A large army crushed the rebellion and killed its leader, but his rebellion did call attention to the system of forced labor, which was eventually abolished.

Revolts in Mexico and Central America

Tell students that in the first part of the 1800s, Latin America was still part of Spain's vast empire, but by 1825, it was free. Independence might never have been won without the leadership of those ready to fight for liberty and equality.

Online Project the **Interactive Gallery: Latin American Independence Movements** and click through the gallery.

ACTIVE CLASSROOM

Have students choose one of the leaders from the gallery. Ask them to create an analogy using the following prompt: This image shows that __________ is like __________ because __________.

Guided Reading and Discussion

Ask students to describe the outcome of the struggles of Father Hidalgo and Father Morelos.

Identify Steps in a Process Describe how the people of Mexico participated in changing their government. *(Mexicans fought for independence against the Spanish and stopped the control of creole elites.)*

Discontent Sparks Revolts in South America

Remind students that the French and American revolutions inspired Latin American leaders to fight for independence. During the French Revolution, Simón Bolívar traveled through Europe and learned about Enlightenment ideas. Latin American leaders were also inspired by the American Revolution and seeing colonial control overthrown.

D Differentiate **Extra Support** Ask students to choose one of the leaders from the Interactive Gallery, and have them make a list of words that describe the leader. Then tell them to use their list to think of similar objects in order to create the analogy from the Active Classroom activity.

Answers

Hypothesize *Priests were well educated and had close contact with the poor and Native Americans. They saw their living conditions and felt compassion for the injustices these people suffered.*

Topic 14 Lesson 2

Online Project the **Interactive Map: Latin American Independence** and move the slider to compare maps of Latin America before and after the majority of the revolutions.

ACTIVE CLASSROOM

Organize students into pairs. Make sure all students have seen both maps in the interactive map activity. Then ask students to do a See-Think-Wonder activity with the maps. Ask them: What do you see in the maps? What do the changes in the maps make you think? What are you wondering about now that you've seen the two maps? Allow them to discuss their insights with one another, and have a few pairs share with the class.

Guided Reading and Discussion

Tell students that in the early 1800s, discontent spread across South America. Ask them to describe how the liberators of South America participated in changing their governments.

Identify Cause and Effect List two causes and two effects of the Latin American revolutions. *(Causes: divided social structure and the weakening of Spain. Effects: creation of independent countries and civil war to create new boundaries.)*

Identify Supporting Details How did the American and French Revolutions influence the Latin American revolutions? *(The French Revolution ideals of liberty, equality, and fraternity inspired Latin American leaders, as did the success of Americans in establishing a democratic republic.)*

>> Bolívar leads his army against Spanish troops in the struggle to free South America from Spanish control.

Interactive Gallery

>> It took José de San Martín and his army several weeks to cross the Andes from Argentina to Chile. After defeating Spanish forces in Chile, he carried the fight to Peru.

Bolívar Fights for Independence In the early 1800s, discontent spread across South America. As you read earlier, educated creoles like Simón Bolívar admired the French and American revolutions. They dreamed of winning their own independence from Spain.

In 1808, when Napoleon Bonaparte occupied Spain, Bolívar and his friends saw the occupation as a signal to act. In 1810, Bolívar led an uprising that established a republic in his native Venezuela. Bolívar's new republic was quickly toppled by conservative forces, however. For years, civil war raged in Venezuela. The revolutionaries suffered many setbacks. Twice Bolívar was forced into exile on the island of Haiti.

Then, Bolívar conceived a daring plan. He would march his army across the Andes and attack the Spanish at Bogotá, the capital of the viceroyalty of New Granada (present-day Colombia). First, he cemented an alliance with the hard-riding llañeros, or Venezuelan cowboys. Then, in a grueling campaign, he led an army through swampy lowlands and over the snowcapped Andes. Finally, in August 1819, he swooped down to take Bogotá from the surprised Spanish.

Other victories followed. By 1821, Bolívar had succeeded in freeing Caracas, Venezuela. "The Liberator," as he was now called, then moved south into Ecuador, Peru, and Bolivia. There, he joined forces with another great leader, **José de San Martín.**

San Martín Joins the Fight Like Bolívar, San Martín was a creole. He was born in Argentina but went to Europe for military training. In 1816, this gifted general helped Argentina win freedom from Spain. He then joined the independence struggle in other areas.

He, too, led an army across the Andes, from Argentina into Chile. He defeated the Spanish in Chile before moving into Peru to strike further blows against colonial rule. San Martín turned his command over to Bolívar in 1822, allowing Bolívar's forces to win the final victories against Spain.

Civil Wars Break Out The wars of independence ended by 1824. Bolívar then worked tirelessly to unite the lands he had liberated into a single nation, called Gran Colombia. Bitter rivalries, however, made that dream impossible. Before long, Gran Colombia split into four independent countries: Colombia, Panama, Venezuela, and Ecuador.

Bolívar faced another disappointment as power struggles among rival leaders triggered destructive civil wars. Before his death in 1830, a discouraged Bolívar wrote, "We have achieved our independence at the expense of everything else." Contrary to his dreams, South America's common people had simply exchanged one set of masters for another.

English Language Proficiency Standards

Reading 4.F.7 Help students build an understanding of descriptive vocabulary for reading the text *Discontent Sparks Revolts in South America*. Provide them with a list of key descriptive words and perform one of the activities.

Beginning Read the text aloud. Help students use dictionaries to develop a bilingual glossary for the words. Ask pairs to reread the text with those definitions in mind.

Intermediate Help students work with a partner to develop the bilingual glossary. Ask them to reread the text with those definitions in mind.

Advanced Have students work in pairs or small groups and use a dictionary to confirm the meaning of the words. Ask them to reread the text with those definitions in mind.

Advanced High Have students work in pairs to develop working definitions for the terms. Then have pairs reread the text and use context clues to gather more information and confirm the meanings.

D Differentiate Challenge After students discuss the map with their partner, have them write a short speech about the map of Latin America in 1845, from the point of view of Simón Bolívar. Remind students that Simon Bolívar's plan was to establish one united nation, Gran Colombia.

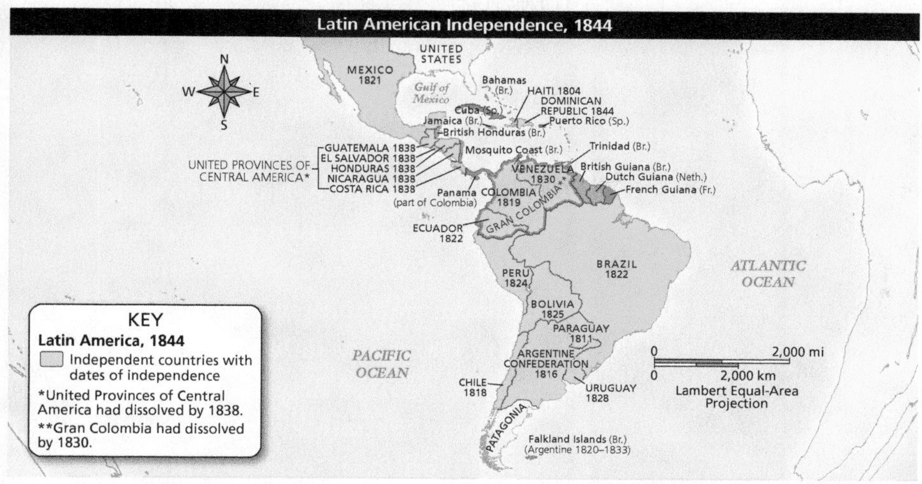

>> **Analyze Maps** What was Gran Colombia? Why is it not on maps of present-day South America?

Interactive Map

Brazil Gains Independence When Napoleon's armies conquered Portugal, the Portuguese royal family fled to Brazil. When the king returned to Portugal, he left his son **Dom Pedro** to rule Brazil. "If Brazil demands independence," the king advised Pedro, "proclaim it yourself and put the crown on your own head."

In 1822, Pedro followed his father's advice. A revolution had brought new leaders to Portugal who planned to abolish reforms and demanded that Dom Pedro return. Dom Pedro refused to leave Brazil. Instead, he became emperor of an independent Brazil. He accepted a constitution that provided for freedom of the press, freedom of religion, and an elected legislature. Brazil remained a monarchy until 1889, when social and political turmoil led it to become a republic.

COMPARE AND CONTRAST How did the goals of the Latin American revolutions differ from their results?

 **ELPS 4.F.7** Work with your teacher and classmates to build understanding of descriptive vocabulary words that will help you develop a deeper understanding of the reading *Discontent Sparks Revolts in South America.*

ASSESSMENT

1. **Draw Conclusions** How did the social structure contribute to discontent in Latin America?
2. **Identify Central Issues** Explain why creoles did not support Hidalgo or Morelos and how this affected the fight for independence.
3. **Draw Conclusions** What advantages did the Haitian slaves have over the French soldiers?
4. **Identify Main Ideas** Describe the challenges Simón Bolívar faced while liberating South America.
5. **Check Understanding** How do we know that Bolívar's political goals for South America were not achieved?

SYNTHESIZE

Online Project the **Digital Activity: The "Liberator's" Dream Doesn't Come True**. Ask students to recall the Topic Essential Question, What are the challenges of diversity? Have students use the Think-Pair-Share strategy to answer the questions in the activity. Ask them to take five minutes to write down some brief answers to the questions, and then share their answers with a partner. Then have students work with their partner to order the events in the activity in chronological order.

Discuss How do these events portray the challenges of diversity?

DEMONSTRATE

Online Assign the **Digital Lesson Quiz** for this lesson if you haven't already done so. Students will be offered automatic remediation or enrichment based on their score.

Pose the following question to the class on the Discussion Board:

In "Latin American Nations Win Independence," you read about the influences of other revolutions, Enlightenment ideals, and key people who led the fight for independence. These battles for independence ended Spanish control in the New World and created several new, independent nations.

Draw Inferences Do you think the tensions between the social classes will dissolve now that the independent nations are free to establish their own governments?

Topic Inquiry

Have students continue their investigations for the Topic Inquiry.

Assessment

1. Economic and political power was concentrated in the hands of a small number of colonial Europeans, which caused resentment and bitterness among the other classes.
2. Creoles did not want to give up power to mestizos or Native Americans. Without creole support, Hidalgo and Morelos had a weaker army and almost lost the fight for independence.
3. The Haitian slaves were motivated to fight for freedom, used to the conditions on the island, and familiar with the terrain.
4. Simón Bolívar faced discontent from the conservative order, which repeatedly tried to retake Venezuela. He was exiled twice.: Bolivar was also impeded by the swampy lowlands, Andes Mountains, and long distances of travel.
5. Gran Colombia was divided into Venezuela, Panama, Colombia, and Ecuador and did not remain one united nation.

Answers

Compare and Contrast *The revolutions won independence but failed to unite the lands or win social or democratic reforms.*

Analyze Maps *Sample answer: Gran Colombia was the single nation that Bolívar created. Gran Colombia became the independent nations of Ecuador, Colombia, Panama, and Venezuela.)*

Topic 14 Lesson 3

The Unification of Germany

CONNECT

Preview Have students preview the **Lesson Objectives** and the list of **Key Terms**.

Students can also preview all the **Key Terms** and **Academic Vocabulary** using the **Interactive Reading Notepad** on the digital course or preview a summary of the lesson in the **Reading and Note Taking Study Guide**.

Online Use the **Editable Presentation** found on the digital course to present the main ideas for this lesson.

Start Up Activity

Tell students that European leaders fought to create unified nations during the late 1800s by harnessing patriotic feelings. Ask students which sentence below they most agree with and why.

- Pride in one's country is a citizen's responsibility.
- Little pride in one's country makes a person a troublemaker.
- Too much pride in one's country can be dangerous.
- Expressing pride in one's country—in any fashion—is a citizen's right.

Discuss How do you think nationalism will play a role in unifying Germany? *(Nationalism brought German-speaking people in different states together.)*

Tell students that in this lesson they will learn about the unification of Germany and the role of nationalism.

Online You can also project the **Start Up Activity** from the course.

INVESTIGATE

Have students use the **Reading and Note Taking Study Guide** to help them take notes and understand the text as they read.

Moving Toward a Unified Germany

Point out the image of Napoleon riding into Berlin. Explain that German nationalism was a reaction to Napoleon's reorganization of German states under French control. Have students discuss with a partner why the conservatives at the Congress of Vienna didn't create a united Germany.

>> Napoleon rides triumphantly into Berlin. French rule inspired German nationalism and demands for a unified German state.

Interactive Flipped Video

14.3 In the early 1800s, German-speaking people lived in a number of small and medium-sized states, as well as in Prussia and the Austrian Hapsburg empire. Napoleon's invasions unleashed new forces in these lands, especially a sense of German nationalism. Early efforts to unify Germany failed, but by 1862 a strong-willed Prussian official, Otto von Bismarck, set out to build a strong, unified German state.

TEKS
8.B, 9.B, 9.D, 18.C

>> Objectives

Identify the factors that promoted German nationalism.

Analyze how Bismarck achieved German unification.

Describe the German empire under Bismarck.

Explain the policies of Kaiser William II.

>> Key Terms

Otto von Bismarck
chancellor
Realpolitik
annex
kaiser
Reich
Kulturkampf
William II
social welfare

The Unification of Germany

Moving Toward a Unified Germany

Impact of Napoleonic Invasions Between 1806 and 1812, Napoleon made important territorial changes in German-speaking lands. He annexed lands along the Rhine River for France. He dissolved the Holy Roman Empire by forcing the emperor of Austria to agree to the lesser title of king. He also organized a number of German states into the Rhine Confederation.

At first, some Germans welcomed the French emperor as a hero with enlightened, modern policies. He encouraged freeing the serfs, made trade easier, and abolished laws against Jews. However, not all Germans appreciated Napoleon and his changes. As people fought to free their lands from French rule, a sense of German nationalism emerged. They began to demand a unified German state.

Napoleon's defeat did not resolve the issue. At the Congress of Vienna, Metternich opposed nationalist demands. A united Germany, he argued, would require dismantling the governments of the many German states. Instead, conservative peacemakers created the German Confederation, a weak alliance headed by Austria.

Aa Vocabulary Builder

1. Have students pronounce the following academic vocabulary terms in this lesson and clarify the part of speech. For difficult or polysyllabic words, break them into syllables and pronounce them with the students.
2. Explain what the word means in common "student-friendly" language using synonyms and antonyms when possible. Provide concrete examples to clarify the meaning, and rephrase the definition.

edit: to make additions, deletions, or other changes to a piece of writing

synthetic: prepared or made artificially

coordinate: to design or adjust to create harmonious action

New Efforts to Bring Unity In the 1830s, Prussia created an economic union called the Zollverein (TSAWL fur yn). It dismantled tariff barriers between many German states. Still, Germany remained politically fragmented.

In 1848, liberals meeting in the Frankfurt Assembly again demanded German political unity. They offered the throne of a united German state to Frederick William IV of Prussia. The Prussian ruler, however, rejected the notion of a throne offered by "the people."

DESCRIBE What impact did the Napoleonic Wars have on Germany?

ELPS **ELPS 4.C.2** Examine U.S. currency and follow your teacher's instructions to learn how economic conditions affected German national unity.

Bismarck Becomes the Architect of German Unity

Where others had failed in uniting Germany, **Otto von Bismarck** succeeded. Bismarck came from Prussia's Junker (YOONG kur) class, made up of conservative landowning nobles. Bismarck first served Prussia as a diplomat in Russia and France, and then as prime minister to King William I. In 1871, he became **chancellor,** or the highest official, of a united Germany.

Blood and Iron In his "blood and iron" speech delivered in 1862, Otto von Bismarck set the tone for his future policies. He wanted Prussian legislators to vote for more money to build up the army. Liberal members opposed the move. Bismarck rose and dismissed their concerns with a speech that has become known as the "blood and iron" speech.

> Germany does not look to Prussia's liberalism, but to her power. . . .The great questions of the day are not to be decided by speeches and majority resolutions—that was the mistake of 1848 and 1849—but by blood and iron!
>
> —Otto von Bismarck, 1862

Master of Realpolitik Bismarck's success was due in part to his strong will. He was a master of **Realpolitik** (ray AHL poh lee teek), or realistic politics based on the needs of the state. In the case of Realpolitik, power was more important than principles.

Although Bismarck was the architect of German unity, he was not really a German nationalist. His

>> **Analyze Maps** By 1871, Germany had been unified. In what year was the North German Confederation formed?

Topic 14 Lesson 3

Guided Reading and Discussion

Tell students that German-speaking people lived in many small states and empires. Have students explain why it was difficult for the German nationalists to create a unified Germany.

Analyze Visuals

Direct attention to the map of German states on this page. Tell students that in the mid-1800s, people in German-speaking states had developed a national identity. Why might Austrian influence have been greater among southern German states than in northern ones? *(Austria-Hungary was geographically closer to southern states.)*

Bismarck Becomes the Architect of German Unity

Tell students that the main architect of unification was Otto von Bismarck. As Prussia's prime minister, Bismarck pursued an aggressive foreign policy that paved the way for German unity. Ask students to read the text and take note of the sequence of events leading to German unification.

Key Terms

Ask students to find the key term **Realpolitik** (in bold) in the text and explain it. Ask student whether they think governments today follow the ideas of Realpolitik. Are leaders justified in taking any action—even those that are illegal or immoral—that strengthens the nation?

Answers

Describe *Napoleon annexed German lands along the Rhine River and organized a number of German states into the Rhine Confederation. People opposed French rule and demanded a unified German state. At the Congress of Vienna, the German Confederation was created.*

Analyze Maps *1867*

English Language Proficiency Standards

Reading 4.C.2 Explain that *environmental print* is the printed material of everyday life. Display a dollar bill and a quarter and explain that every state in the United States uses a common currency, while the German states of the 1800s used several. Read, or have students read, "New Efforts to Bring Unity" and explain how the *Zollverein* aided German unification.

Beginning Point out symbols on the U.S. currency. Have students read aloud words on the currency. Explain that a system of currency helps unify a country and that the symbols and words reflect this. Explain that having multiple currencies was a cause of Germany's lack of unity.

Intermediate Have students read aloud the words on the currency and point out symbols. Discuss their meaning. Continue as directed in the Beginning activity.

Advanced Discuss the words and symbols on the currency in groups. Explain how having one system of currency benefits a country. Discuss why multiple currencies might be a problem for Germany.

Advanced High Have pairs discuss the words and symbols on the currency. Have them explain how the currency system of the United States benefits our country, and how multiple currencies were a problem for Germany in a few sentences.

Online Project the **Interactive Timeline: German Unification** and have individual students drag and drop the events into their proper place along the timeline, or call on them to provide the correct answers.

ACTIVE CLASSROOM

Ask students to take a stand on the following question: Do you think Bismarck, the master of Realpolitik, should have changed the telegram that reported on a meeting between King William I and the French ambassador? Yes or no? Then ask students to divide into two groups based on their answers and move to separate areas in the classroom. Ask students to talk with each other to compare their reasons for answering yes or no. Then have a representative from each side present and defend the group's point of view.

Guided Reading and Discussion

Tell students that in 1871, German nationalists celebrated the birth of the Second Reich. William I of Prussia took the title of Kaiser and made Bismarck his chancellor. Have students explain how nationalism played a role in unifying Germany.

Identify Supporting Details Describe the importance of the Austro-Prussian War. *(Prussia defeated Austria and annexed several north German states. Bismarck dissolved the Austrian-led German Confederation and created a new confederation under Prussian control.)*

Make sure students understand Bismarck's blood and iron policy and how that was reflected in the three wars Prussia fought prior to German unification.

main goal was to increase Prussia's power, not to fulfill German nationalist aims. Bismarck's primary loyalty was to the Hohenzollerns (hoh un TSAWL urnz), the ruling dynasty of Prussia. Through unification, he hoped to bring more power to the Hohenzollerns.

A Powerful Military As Prussia's prime minister, Bismarck first moved to build up the Prussian army. Despite Bismarck's "blood and iron" speech, the liberal legislature refused to vote for funds for the military. In response, Bismarck strengthened the army with money that had been collected for other purposes. With a powerful, well-equipped military, he was then ready to pursue an aggressive foreign policy. Over the next decade, Bismarck led Prussia into three wars. Each war increased Prussian prestige and power and paved the way for German unity.

War with Denmark and Austria Bismarck's first maneuver was to form an alliance in 1864 with Austria. Prussia and Austria then seized the provinces of Schleswig and Holstein from Denmark. After a brief war, Prussia and Austria "liberated" the two provinces and divided up the spoils. Austria was to administer Holstein and Prussia was to administer Schleswig.

In 1866, Bismarck invented an excuse to attack Austria. The Austro-Prussian War lasted just seven weeks and ended in a decisive Prussian victory. Prussia then **annexed,** or took control of, several other north German states.

Bismarck dissolved the Austrian-led German Confederation and created a new confederation dominated by Prussia. Austria and four other southern German states remained independent. Bismarck's motives, as always, were strictly practical. Attempting to conquer Austria might have meant a long and risky war for Prussia.

>> Bismarck used war with France as a way to unite the German states. Here, a triumphant Prussian army enters Paris.

Interactive Timeline

The Franco-Prussian War In France, the Prussian victory over Austria angered Napoleon III. A growing rivalry between the two nations led to the Franco-Prussian War of 1870.

Germans recalled only too well the invasions of Napoleon I some 60 years earlier. Bismarck played up the image of the French menace to spur German nationalism. For his part, Napoleon III did little to avoid war, hoping to mask problems at home with military glory.

Bismarck furthered the crisis by rewriting and then releasing to the press a telegram that reported on a meeting between King William I and the French ambassador. Bismarck's editing of the "Ems dispatch" made it seem that William I had insulted the Frenchman. Furious, Napoleon III declared war on Prussia, as Bismarck had hoped.

A superior Prussian force, supported by troops from other German states, smashed the badly organized and poorly supplied French soldiers. Napoleon III, old and ill, surrendered within a few weeks. France had to accept a humiliating peace. The Franco-Prussian War left a bitter legacy for the French and a strong desire for revenge against Germany.

The German Empire Is Created Delighted by the victory over France, princes from the southern German states and the North German Confederation persuaded William I of Prussia to take the title **kaiser** (KY zur), or emperor. In January 1871, German nationalists celebrated the birth of the Second **Reich,** or empire. They called it that because they considered it heir to the Holy Roman Empire, set up in the 900s and abolished by Napoleon I in 1806.

A constitution drafted by Bismarck set up a two-house legislature. The Bundesrat (BOON dus raht), or upper house, was appointed by the rulers of the German states. The Reichstag (RYKS tahg), or lower house, was elected by universal male suffrage. Still, the new German nation was far from democratic. Because the Bundesrat could veto any decisions of the Reichstag,

D Differentiate Extra Support After asking students to take a stand, allow students five minutes to think about the question individually. Tell them to write down their response *(yes or no)* and two reasons why they answered that way. Then continue with the group activity.

real power remained in the hands of the emperor and his chancellor.

EXPLAIN How did Bismarck unify the German states?

ELPS 4.F.8 Create a glossary for a list of key terms from *Bismarck Becomes the Architect of German Unity.*

Germany Becomes an Industrial Giant

In January 1871, German princes gathered in the glittering Hall of Mirrors at the French palace of Versailles. They had just defeated Napoleon III in the Franco-Prussian War. Once home to French kings, the palace seemed the perfect place to proclaim the new German empire. To the winners as well as to the losers, the symbolism was clear: French domination of Europe had ended. Germany was now the dominant power in Europe.

In the aftermath of unification, the German empire emerged as the industrial giant of the European continent. By the late 1800s, German chemical and electrical industries were setting the standard worldwide. Among the European powers, German shipping was second only to Britain's.

>> Germany became a leader in various industries, including the production of chemicals, electronics, steel, weapons, and optical equipment.

Economic Progress Germany, like Great Britain, had several factors that helped it industrialize. Germany's spectacular growth was due in part to ample iron and coal resources, the basic ingredients for industrial development. A disciplined and educated workforce also helped the economy. The German middle class and educated professionals helped to create a productive and efficient society that prided itself on its sense of responsibility and deference to authority. Germany's rapidly growing population—from 41 million in 1871 to 67 million by 1914—also provided a huge home market along with a larger supply of industrial workers.

The new nation also benefited from earlier progress. During the 1850s and 1860s, German entrepreneurs had founded large companies and built many railroads. The house of Krupp (kroop) boomed after 1871, becoming an enormous industrial complex that produced steel and weapons for a world market.

Between 1871 and 1914, the business tycoon August Thyssen (TEES un) built a small steel factory of 70 workers into a giant empire with 50,000 employees. Optics was another important industry. German industrialist and inventor Carl Zeiss built a company that became known for its telescopes, microscopes, and other optical equipment.

Promoting Economic Growth German industrialists were the first to see the value of applied science in developing new products such as synthetic chemicals and dyes. Industrialists, as well as the government, supported research and development in the universities and hired trained scientists to solve technological problems in their factories.

The German government promoted economic development. After 1871, it issued a single currency for Germany, reorganized the banking system, and coordinated railroads built by the various German states. When a worldwide depression hit in the late 1800s, Germany raised tariffs to protect home industries from foreign competition. The leaders of the new German empire were determined to maintain economic strength as well as military power.

DESCRIBE What factors did Germany possess that made industrialization possible?

Germany Becomes an Industrial Giant

Tell students that after unification, Germany emerged as an industrial powerhouse. Ask students to list the factors that helped Germany industrialize. *(ample coal and iron resources, a disciplined and educated workforce, a productive and efficient society, a growing population, successful entrepreneurial ventures)*

Guided Reading and Discussion

Tell students that in addition to these factors that contributed to Germany's industrialization, the German government promoted economic growth. Ask them to describe what steps the German government took to further economic development.

Identify Supporting Details What role did applied science play in Germany's industrialization? *(It led to new products and increased spending on research and development by industrialists and the government.)*

English Language Proficiency Standards

Reading 4.F.8 Help students create a glossary of challenging vocabulary from "Bismarck Becomes the Architect of German Unity."

Beginning Have students find three difficult terms from the text. Help them develop a bilingual glossary for the terms.

Intermediate Have students complete the Beginning activity but have them include a sentence using each word in their glossaries.

Advanced Have groups complete the Intermediate activity but include more than three words in their glossaries.

Advanced High Have students complete the Advanced activity individually.

Answers

Explain *Bismarck used Realpolitik, deception, and military power to unify the German states. He led three wars on the road to German unification and used deception and German nationalism to begin and win the Franco-Prussian war.*

Describe *Germany had ample coal and iron resources, a disciplined and educated workforce, and a growing population. It had made previous progress in building industries and railroads. Also, Germany put much effort into research and development in the applied sciences.*

The Iron Chancellor

Explain that Bismarck implemented a policy known as *Kulturkampf*, or "cultural struggle," to reduce the role and power of the Roman Catholic Church in Prussia. Bismarck believed that Germans' loyalty to their nation should come before anything else.

Online Project the **Interactive Cartoon: A Political Game of Chess**. Click on each of the hotspots to help students interpret the political cartoon.

ACTIVE CLASSROOM

Have students role-play and engage in an interview with either the pope or Bismarck. Have them write down a question they'd like to ask and then have a partner answer what either the pope or Bismarck would say in response.

>> Bismarck was a leader in international affairs, using a mix of force and diplomacy to further German interests. Bismarck (center) at the 1878 Congress of Berlin.

>> **Analyze Political Cartoons** In this political game of chess, Bismarck and Pope Pius IX try to checkmate each other. How does this image reflect the relationship between Bismarck and the Pope? How would each player define victory?

Interactive Cartoon

The Iron Chancellor

As chancellor of the new German empire, Bismarck pursued several foreign-policy goals. He wanted to keep France weak and isolated while building strong links with Austria and Russia. He respected British naval power but did not seek to compete in that arena. "Water rats," he said, "do not fight with land rats." Later, however, he would take a more aggressive stand against Britain as the two nations competed for overseas colonies.

On the domestic front, Bismarck applied the same ruthless methods he had used to achieve unification. The Iron Chancellor, as he was called, sought to erase local loyalties and crush all opposition to the imperial state. He targeted two groups—the Catholic Church and the Socialists. In his view, both posed a threat to the new German state.

Bismarck Challenges the Catholic Church After unification, Catholics made up about a third of the German population. Bismarck, who was Lutheran, distrusted Catholics—especially the clergy— whose first loyalty, he believed, was to the pope instead of to Germany.

In response to what he saw as the Catholic threat, Bismarck launched the ***Kulturkampf*** (kool TOOR kahmpf), or "battle for civilization," which lasted from 1871 to 1878. His goal was to make Catholics put loyalty to the state above allegiance to the Church. The chancellor had laws passed that gave the state the right to supervise Catholic education and approve the appointment of priests. Other laws closed some religious orders, expelled the Jesuits from Prussia, and made it compulsory for couples to be married by civil authority.

Bismarck's moves against the Catholic Church backfired. The faithful rallied behind the Church, and the Catholic Center party gained strength in the Reichstag. A realist, Bismarck saw his mistake and worked to make peace with the Church.

Bismarck Attacks the Socialists Bismarck also saw a threat to the new German empire in the growing power of socialism. Under socialism, the people are supposed to own and operate the means of production. Socialism had support among some Germans. By the late 1870s, German Marxists had organized the Social Democratic party, which called for parliamentary democracy and laws to improve conditions for the working class. Bismarck feared that socialists would undermine the loyalty of German workers and turn them toward revolution. Bismarck had laws passed that dissolved socialist groups, shut down their newspapers, and banned their meetings. Once again,

D Differentiate Extra Support After students choose either the pope or Bismarck, give them five minutes to write a question and an answer that contains two points that either the pope or Bismarck would make about their question. Then continue with the group activity.

Answers

Analyze Political Cartoons *Sample answer: Bismarck and the Pope have a strategic and competitive relationship. They are constantly thinking about how to maintain control and power. Bismarck would view victory as ensuring Germans put their nation above everything else, even above the church. The Pope would view victory as maintaining the power and faith of the Catholic congregation, reversing Bismarck's changes and maintaining power within Germany.*

repression backfired. It served to unite workers to support the socialist cause.

Bismarck Changes Course Bismarck then changed course. He set out to woo workers away from socialism by sponsoring laws to protect them. By the 1890s, Germans had health and accident insurance as well as old-age insurance to provide retirement benefits. Thus, under Bismarck, Germany was a pioneer in social reform. Its system of economic safeguards became the model for other European nations.

Although workers benefited from Bismarck's plan, they did not abandon socialism. In fact, the Social Democratic party continued to grow in strength. By 1912, it held more seats in the Reichstag than any other party. Yet Bismarck's program showed that conditions for workers could be improved without the upheaval of a revolution. Later, Germany and other European nations would build on Bismarck's social policies, greatly increasing government's role in providing for the needs of its citizens.

CHECK UNDERSTANDING Why did Bismarck try to dissolve socialist groups?

>> **Analyze Political Cartoons** Bismarck tries to push the scary looking "Socialist Jack" back into the box. What did Bismarck do after his anti-socialist laws strengthened the socialist cause?

Kaiser William II

In 1888, **William II** succeeded his grandfather as kaiser. The new emperor was supremely confident in his abilities and wished to put his own stamp on Germany. In 1890, he shocked Europe by asking the dominating Bismarck to resign. "There is only one master in the Reich," he said, "and that is I." William II seriously believed that his right to rule came from God.

> My grandfather considered that the office of king was a task that God had assigned to him. . . . That which he thought I also think. . . . Those who wish to aid me in that task . . . I welcome with all my heart; those who oppose me in this work I shall crush.
>
> —William II

>> Otto von Bismarck leaves his Berlin office in 1890 after Kaiser William II forced him to resign as chancellor.

Social Welfare Not surprisingly, William resisted efforts to introduce democratic political reforms. At the same time, however, his government continued the idea of **social welfare,** or programs provided by the state for the benefit of its citizens. These programs, designed to combat support for socialists, helped

Guided Reading and Discussion

Tell students that Bismarck was known as the Iron Chancellor because he was fierce and that nothing came before his loyalty to Prussia. Ask students to summarize Bismarck's role in German unification.

Identify Supporting Details Why did Bismarck attack the Socialists? *(He was fearful that they would spread ideas of revolution.)*

Kaiser William II

Explain that William II had different views on foreign policy than Bismarck had. He forced Bismarck to resign and focused on strengthening the German military. Why do you think William II wanted to strengthen the German navy? *(William II was a nationalist and wanted to show Germany's military strength. He expanded the German navy to win an overseas empire.)*

Guided Reading and Discussion

After William II became Kaiser, Bismarck's days of controlling Germany came to an end. Have students summarize the policies of Kaiser William II.

Hypothesize Why do you think William resisted efforts to introduce democratic reforms? *(William believed he was given the right to rule from God. Democratic reforms meant that he would have to share his power. As he said, "There is only one master in the Reich, and that is I.")*

History Background

Bismarck's Appointment The decision to make Bismarck prime minister came in the midst of a government crisis. Liberals in Prussia's parliament had blocked King William I's plans to reorganize and increase the army. After months of disagreement between king and parliament, the king was about to abdicate his throne in favor of his son. Then advisors suggested he turn to Bismarck. The two met and discussed the situation. Bismarck assured the king that he believed parliamentary government should be avoided at all costs. Convinced that Bismarck would support his claims to royal power, William named him prime minister.

Answers

Check Understanding *Bismarck was afraid the government would lose the support of the working class and that they would turn to revolution under socialism. After a failed assassination attempt on the Kaiser, he passed anti-socialist laws.*

Analyze Political Cartoons *Sample answer: Bismarck sponsored social welfare laws to woo German workers away from socialism. By the 1890s, Germans had health, accident, and old-age insurance.*

SYNTHESIZE

Online Project the **Digital Activity: Price of Nationalism**. Ask students to recall the Topic Essential Question, "What are the challenges of diversity?" Have them use the Think-Pair-Share strategy to answer these questions: Do you think Otto von Bismarck would have agreed with Crown Prince Friedrich? Why or Why not? *(Sample response: Otto von Bismarck believed in the importance of "blood and iron" and thought military and political strength would bring Germany respect. He wanted Germany to be feared, but he also helped to build Germany as a strong industrial nation. He also implemented social reform. Therefore, Bismarck would agree that Germany should be feared, but he might also think Germany should be respected.)*

Then have students think about the Essential Question and have them work with their partners to list three to four events that illustrate the challenges of diversity in unifying Germany.

Discuss How do these events portray the challenges of diversity? *(The events show the struggle that different groups, such as German-speaking states, Catholics, and socialists, had in the process of unifying Germany.)*

DEMONSTRATE

Online Assign the **Digital Lesson Quiz** for this lesson if you haven't already done so. Students will be offered automatic remediation or enrichment based on their scores.

Pose the following question to the class on the Discussion Board:

Draw Inferences How did Bismarck's government initially hold on to its power in Germany? *(through militarism and diplomacy)*

Topic Inquiry

Have students continue their investigations for the Topic Inquiry.

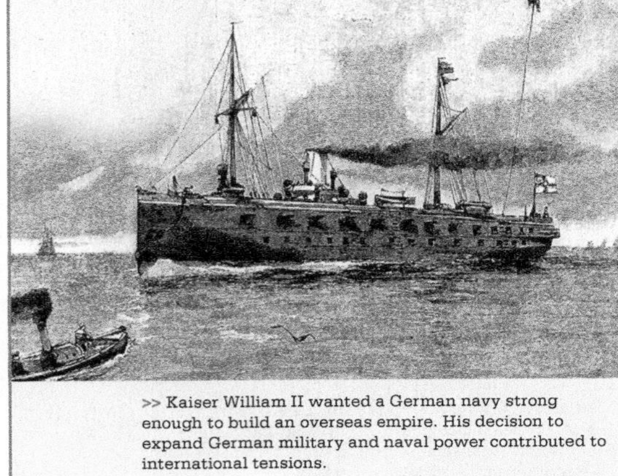

>> Kaiser William II wanted a German navy strong enough to build an overseas empire. His decision to expand German military and naval power contributed to international tensions.

improve conditions not only for workers and the elderly, but also German

society in general. His government also provided services such as cheap transportation and electricity.

An excellent system of public schools, which had flourished under Bismarck, taught students obedience to the emperor along with reading, writing, and mathematics.

Strengthening the Military Like his grandfather, William II lavished funds on the German military machine, already the most powerful in Europe. He also launched an ambitious campaign to expand the German navy and win an overseas empire to rival those of Britain and France. William's nationalism and aggressive military stance helped increase tensions on the eve of World War I.

RECALL Why did William II ask Bismarck to resign?

ASSESSMENT

1. **Recall** Describe Germany's economic changes after unifying in 1871.
2. **Describe** Why did Germany pioneer social reform under Bismarck?
3. **Connect** Why did the German government issue a single currency for all of Germany?
4. **Compare** How did Kaiser William II continue Bismarck's policies?
5. **Identify Main Ideas** Why do you think the German empire was committed to maintaining its economic strength?

Answers

Recall *William II wanted to be the sole ruler of the German empire.*

Assessment

1. Germany emerged as an industrial giant. German chemical and electrical industries became world leaders. Steel and optics were large industries. Germany also reorganized its banking system and coordinated its railroads. Germany's economic stability led to social reforms.
2. Bismarck wanted the working class to support the German government and reject socialism. As a result, the German government provided health and accident insurance, as well as disability and old age insurance.
3. Before unification, Germany was made up of several states. After unifying, Germany created a single currency to make trade within the nation easier, promoting economic development.
4. He continued to provide social welfare programs and to build up the military.
5. Economic strength helps support political stability.

14.4 **Although the peoples of the Italian peninsula spoke the same language, they had not been politically united since Roman times. Over the centuries, ambitious foreign conquerors had turned Italy into a battleground, occupying parts or all of the peninsula. By the early 1800s, nationalism inspired Italian patriots to dream of ousting foreign rulers and reuniting Italy.**

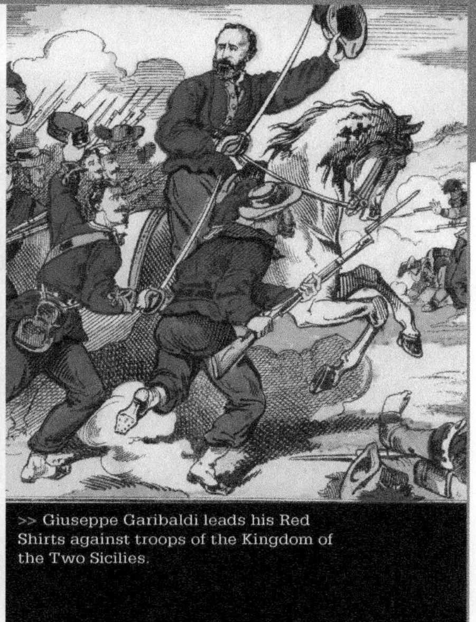

>> Giuseppe Garibaldi leads his Red Shirts against troops of the Kingdom of the Two Sicilies.

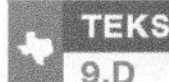 Interactive Flipped Video

The Unification of Italy

TEKS 9.D

>> Objectives

List the key obstacles to Italian unity.

Evaluate the roles played by Cavour and Garibaldi in Italian unification.

Describe the challenges that faced the new nation of Italy.

>> Key Terms

Camillo Cavour
Giuseppe Garibaldi
anarchist
emigration

First Steps to Italian Unity

Obstacles to Unity Frequent warfare and foreign rule had led people to identify with local regions. The people of Florence considered themselves Tuscans, those of Venice Venetians, those of Naples Neapolitans, and so on. But as in Germany, the invasions of Napoleon had sparked dreams of national unity.

The Congress of Vienna, however, ignored the nationalists who hoped to end centuries of foreign rule and achieve unity. To Prince Metternich of Austria, Italy was merely a "geographical expression," not a nation. Moreover, a divided Italy suited Austrian interests. At Vienna, Austria took control of much of northern Italy, while Hapsburg monarchs ruled various other Italian states. In the south, a French Bourbon ruler was put in charge of Naples and Sicily.

In response, nationalists organized secret patriotic societies and focused their efforts on expelling Austrian forces from northern Italy. Between 1820 and 1848, nationalist revolts exploded across the region. Each time, Austria sent in troops to crush the rebels.

609

 PEARSON realize. www.PearsonTexas.com Access your Digital Lesson.

Aa Vocabulary Builder

1. Have students pronounce the following academic vocabulary terms in this lesson and clarify the part of speech. For difficult or polysyllabic words, break them into syllables and pronounce them with the students.
2. Explain what the word means in common "student-friendly" language using synonyms and antonyms when possible. Provide concrete examples to clarify the meaning, and rephrase the definition.

constitute: to set up; establish

agitation: the attempt to arouse public feeling about an issue

successor: a person who succeeds another to an office or rank

Topic 14 Lesson 4

The Unification of Italy

CONNECT

Preview Have students preview the **Lesson Objectives** and the list of **Key Terms**.

Students can also preview all the **Key Terms** and **Academic Vocabulary** using the **Interactive Reading Notepad** on the digital course or preview a summary of the lesson in the **Reading and Note Taking Study Guide**.

Online Use the **Editable Presentation** found on the digital course to present the main ideas for this lesson.

Start Up Activity

Tell students that during the early 1800s, supporters of a united Italy rebelled unsuccessfully against Austrian rule in northern Italy. Many rebels fled, fearing for their safety. Giuseppe Mazzini described his reaction to the events:

"He (a rebel) held out a white handkerchief, merely saying, 'For the refugees of Italy.' My mother . . . dropped some money into the handkerchief . . . . That day was the first in which a confused idea presented itself to my mind . . . an idea that we Italians could and therefore ought to struggle for the liberty of our country."—Giuseppe Mazzini, *Life and Writings*

Discuss What did this experience spark in young Mazzini? *(He believed Italians should free themselves from foreign rule.)*

Tell students that in this lesson they will learn how Italians overcame obstacles to change their government and build a united, independent Italy.

Online You can also project the **Start Up Activity** from the course.

INVESTIGATE

Have students read the section using the **Reading and Note Taking Study Guide** to help them take notes and understand the text as they read.

First Steps to Italian Unity

Explain that the Italian peninsula had been divided into independent states for centuries. Italy's history was one of succeeding occupations by foreign powers. Thus, people tended to identify with their region rather than with the country as a whole.

Topic 14 Lesson 4

Online Project the **Interactive Map: Italian Regions Before Unification** and click on each area.

ACTIVE CLASSROOM

Have students do a Quick Write about the obstacles that impeded Italian unification and how individual citizens might participate in changing the governments of Italy.

Guided Reading and Discussion

Explain that even though Mazzini's attempt at revolution failed, he and his followers inspired others. Ask students to describe how nationalists tried to overcome the obstacles to unity.

Support a Point of View with Evidence Nationalists believed that a united Italy would bring greater economic prosperity than a collection of smaller states could. Ask students to describe some potential benefits of economic unity.

Key Terms

Ask students to find the name **Camillo Cavour** (in bold) in the text and identify him. Ask students how Cavour was different from and similar to Otto von Bismarck as they read.

The Struggle for Italy

Introduce the activity by explaining that the success of the Italian unification movement depended on people of many different social backgrounds and regions putting aside their differences. Nationalist leaders encouraged all Italians to work together to bring about change in their government.

Answers

Check Understanding *Due to warfare and foreign rule, many people saw themselves not as Italians but as citizens of local regions. Foreign rulers who controlled these Italian regions quickly crushed revolts.*

>> Giuseppe Mazzini, the founder of Young Italy, dreamed of a unified Italian republic. Due to his failed attempts at revolution, he spent many years in exile but continued to inspire Italian nationalism.

Interactive Map

Mazzini's Young Italy In the 1830s, the nationalist leader Giuseppe Mazzini founded Young Italy. The goal of this secret society was "to constitute Italy, one, free, independent, republican nation." In 1849, Mazzini helped set up a revolutionary republic in Rome, but French forces soon toppled it. Like many other nationalists, Mazzini spent much of his life in exile, plotting and dreaming of a united Italy.

Nationalism Spreads "Ideas grow quickly," Mazzini once said, "when watered by the blood of martyrs." Although revolution had failed, nationalist agitation had planted seeds for future harvests.

To nationalists like Mazzini, a united Italy made sense not only because of geography, but also because of a common language and shared traditions. Nationalists reminded Italians of the glories of ancient Rome and the medieval papacy. To others, unity made practical economic sense. It would end trade barriers among the Italian states and stimulate industry.

CHECK UNDERSTANDING What forces hindered Italian unity?

ELPS 4.F.9 Identify introductory clauses and explain their purpose using examples from *First Steps to Italian Unity.*

>> Prime Minister Cavour (middle) served Sardinia's King Victor Emmanuel II (right) with great success. Cavour improved the economy and brought other Italian states under Sardinian rule.

Interactive Gallery

The Struggle for Italy

After 1848, leadership of the Risorgimento (ree sawr jee MEN toh), or Italian nationalist movement, passed to the kingdom of Sardinia, which included Piedmont, Nice, and Savoy as well as the island of Sardinia. Its constitutional monarch, Victor Emmanuel II, hoped to join other states to his own, thereby increasing his power.

Cavour, a Crafty Politician In 1852, Victor Emmanuel made Count **Camillo Cavour** (kah VOOR) his prime minister. Cavour came from a noble family but favored liberal goals. He was a flexible, practical, crafty politician, willing to use almost any means to achieve his goals. Like Bismarck in Prussia, Cavour was a monarchist who believed in Realpolitik.

Once in office, Cavour moved first to reform Sardinia's economy. He improved agriculture, had railroads built, and encouraged commerce by supporting free trade. Cavour's long-term goal, however, was to end Austrian power in Italy and annex the provinces of Lombardy and Venetia.

Cavour Plots with France In 1855, Sardinia, led by Cavour, joined Britain and France against Russia in

English Language Proficiency Standards

Reading 4.F.9 Share with students the following: *To nationalists like Mazzini, a united Italy made sense not only because of geography, but also because of a common language and history.* Tell students that the introductory clause, *to nationalists like Mazzini,* provides background information. Point out other introductory clauses in sentences from the text.

Beginning Identify introductory clauses and main parts of the other sentences. For the first example above, explain how the introductory clause gives readers the clue that nationalists wanted a united Italy. Ask students to reread the text to find another sentence with an introductory clause.

Intermediate Explain how the introductory clause tells readers that nationalists shared a desire for a united Italy. Then provide students with other introductory clauses from the text and ask them to identify the background information they provide.

Advanced Have small groups identify the introductory clauses for sentences from the text and explain how each helps make the meaning of the sentence clearer.

Advanced High Have students identify introductory clauses in the text and explain how each makes the meaning of the sentence clearer. Have them write three sentences with introductory clauses about the obstacles facing Italian unity.

the Crimean War. Sardinia did not win territory, but it did have a voice at the peace conference. Sardinia also gained the attention of Napoleon III.

In 1858, Cavour negotiated a secret deal with Napoleon, who promised to aid Sardinia in case it faced a war with Austria. A year later, the shrewd Cavour provoked that war. With help from France, Sardinia defeated Austria and annexed Lombardy. Meanwhile, nationalist groups overthrew Austrian-backed rulers in several other northern Italian states. These states then joined with Sardinia.

Garibaldi's "Red Shirts" Next, attention shifted to the Kingdom of the Two Sicilies in southern Italy. There, **Giuseppe Garibaldi** (gah ree BAHL dee), a longtime nationalist and an ally of Mazzini, was ready for action.

Like Mazzini, Garibaldi wanted to create an Italian republic. He did not hesitate, however, to accept aid from the monarchist Cavour. By 1860, Garibaldi had recruited a force of 1,000 red-shirted volunteers. Cavour provided weapons and allowed two ships to take Garibaldi and his "Red Shirts" south to Sicily. With surprising speed, Garibaldi's forces won control of Sicily, crossed to the mainland, and marched triumphantly north to Naples.

Unity Achieved Garibaldi's success alarmed Cavour, who feared that the nationalist hero would set up his own republic in the south. To prevent this, Cavour urged Victor Emmanuel to send Sardinian troops to deal with Garibaldi. Instead, the Sardinians overran the Papal States and linked up with Garibaldi and his forces in Naples.

In a patriotic move, Garibaldi turned over Naples and Sicily to Victor Emmanuel. Shortly afterward, southern Italy voted to approve the move, and in 1861, Victor Emmanuel II was crowned king of Italy.

Two areas remained outside the new Italian nation: Rome and Venetia. Cavour died in 1861, but his successors completed his dream. Italy formed an alliance with Prussia in the Austro-Prussian War and won the province of Venetia. Then, during the Franco-Prussian War in 1870, France was forced to withdraw its troops from Rome. For the first time since the fall of the Roman empire, Italy was a united land.

DESCRIBE What steps did Cavour take to promote Italian unity?

>> **Analyze Political Cartoons** Garibaldi suggests that Pope Pius IX trade his papal cap for the cap of "liberty" that he offers. What does Garibaldi want? How do you think the Pope feels about the offer?

Italy Faces New Challenges

The new Italian nation faced a host of problems. Like the German empire that Bismarck cemented together out of many states, Italy had no tradition of political unity. Few Italians felt ties to the new nation. Strong regional rivalries left Italy unable to solve critical national issues.

Regional Differences The greatest regional differences were between the north and the south. The north was richer and had more cities than the south. For centuries, northern Italian cities had flourished as centers of business and culture. The south, on the other hand, was rural and poor. Its population was booming, but illiterate peasants could extract only a meager existence from the exhausted farmland.

Conflict with the Papal States Hostility between Italy and the Roman Catholic Church further divided the nation. Popes bitterly resented the seizure of the Papal States and of Rome. The government granted the papacy limited rights and control over church properties. Popes, however, saw themselves as

Online Project the **Interactive Gallery: Leaders of Italian Unification** and click on each image.

ACTIVE CLASSROOM

Ask students to use the Conversation With History strategy to write a question they would ask a leader of Italian unification, what the leader might say in response, and what the students might then reply.

Guided Reading and Instruction

Tell students that Garibaldi and Cavour were worlds apart in terms of social status and training. Ask students to write short descriptions of each man.

Italy Faces New Challenges

Eventually, Italy was united but faced serious challenges. Regionalism continued between prosperous northern Italy and rural southern Italy. There was tension between the Italian government and the Catholic Church. Also, socialists and anarchists opposed the constitutional monarchy.

Guided Reading and Discussion

Ask students to describe the regional differences between northern and southern Italy.

D Differentiate Extra Support To help students track the work of different Italian leaders, have them create a two-column chart labeled *Leader* and *Contribution*. As they read, have them note leaders' contributions to Italian unification.

English Language Proficiency Standards

Reading 4.C.3 Using the section "Italy Faces New Challenges," help students identify and define these common social studies terms: *unity, nation, regional, culture, population, political*.

Beginning Help students read and define each word, using bilingual resources. Highlight each social studies term from the list above and have students draw a pictorial representation of each word.

Intermediate Complete the Beginning activity, but have students find the words in the section.

Advanced Have students locate each social studies term in the section. Have them define each word, using a dictionary or a glossary, as needed.

Advanced High Complete the Advanced activity, but have students write a new sentence for each word as it is used in the context of the section.

Answers

Analyze Political Cartoons *Garibaldi wants the Papal States to unite with the rest of Italy; the pope appears unhappy with the offer. He does not support unification.*

Describe *He used Realpolitik to form an alliance with France and to provoke a war with Austria. He supported Garibaldi's efforts by providing weapons and transport.*

Topic 14 Lesson 4

SYNTHESIZE

Online Project the **Digital Activity: Unity Leads to Turmoil**. Ask students to recall the Topic Essential Question, "What are the challenges of diversity?" Have students use the Think-Pair-Share strategy to answer these questions: What does this image show? How does it relate to the unrest that followed Italian unity?

Then have students think about the Essential Question and Italian unification. Have them list examples portraying the challenges of diversity in Italian unification.

DEMONSTRATE

Online Assign the **Digital Lesson Quiz** for this lesson if you haven't already done so. Students will be offered automatic remediation or enrichment based on their scores.

Pose these questions to the class on the Discussion Board:

Identify Cause and Effect What did the Italian government do to distract those who opposed the government and helped to build Italian prestige and power? *(Italy began to build an overseas empire by trying to colonize Ethiopia.)*

Infer How might the economic problems and population boom in Italy benefit the United States, Canada, and Latin America? *(Many Italians emigrated and contributed to the economies, cultures, and governments of the United States, Canada, and many Latin American countries.)*

Topic Inquiry

Have students continue their investigations for the Topic Inquiry.

>> Italian emigrant families with their baggage and belongings wait to board a ship at this crowded port. **Draw Conclusions** Why did many Italians emigrate to other countries in the early 1900s?

"prisoners" and urged Italian Catholics—almost all Italians—not to cooperate with their new government.

Political and Social Turmoil Under Victor Emmanuel, Italy was a constitutional monarchy with a two-house legislature. The king appointed members to the upper house, which could veto bills passed by the lower house. Although the lower house consisted of elected representatives, only a small number of men had the right to vote.

In the late 1800s, unrest increased as radicals on the left struggled against a conservative government. Socialists organized strikes while **anarchists,** people who want to abolish all government, turned to sabotage and violence.

Slowly, the government extended suffrage to more men and passed laws to improve social conditions. Still, the turmoil continued. To distract attention from troubles at home, the government set out to win an overseas empire in Ethiopia.

Economic Progress Despite its problems, Italy did develop economically, especially after 1900. Although the nation lacked important natural resources such as coal, industries did sprout up in northern regions. Industrialization, of course, brought urbanization as peasants flocked to the cities to find jobs in factories. As in other countries, reformers campaigned to improve education and working conditions.

The population explosion of this period created tensions, but an important safety valve was **emigration,** or movement away from their homeland. Many Italians left for the United States, Canada, and Latin American nations.

By 1914, the country was significantly better off than it had been in 1861. But it was hardly prepared for the great war that broke out in that year.

? DESCRIBE What problems did Italians face after unification?

ELPS **ELPS 4.C.3** Identify and define the following vocabulary words commonly used in social studies texts: *unity, nation, regional, culture, population,* and *political,* which are used in *Italy Faces New Challenges.*

ASSESSMENT

1. **Analyze Context** Why would Prince Metternich of Austria oppose the idea of Italian unification?
2. **Describe** How did Cavour's appointment as prime minister of the kingdom of Sardinia help the cause of Italian unification?
3. **Analyze Information** Garibaldi could easily have kept the Kingdom of the Two Sicilies with himself as king. Why do you think he turned over control to Victor Emmanuel II instead?
4. **Cite Evidence** Why did conflict in Italy continue even after unification?
5. **Explain** Why do you think Rome and Venetia initially remained separate after unification?

Answers

Describe *The government faced opposition, regional divisions, and disputes with the Catholic Church. Italians experienced limited suffrage, social unrest, urbanization, and rapid population growth.*

Draw Conclusions *Sample answer: A population explosion in Italy made it difficult to find work. Italians moved to other countries to escape political turmoil and to search for new opportunities.*

Assessment

1. Metternich hoped to keep control over the northern regions of Italy.
2. Cavour, who supported Italian nationalists and allied with other countries that aided unification, worked secretly with the French to push Austria out of Italy.
3. Garibaldi, a supporter of unification, realized that Victor Emmanuel II was the best choice to bring Italy together.
4. There were still many regional differences; social unrest increased as anarchists and others used violence to oppose the government; the pope urged Italians to resist the new government.
5. Rome was under the control of the pope, who hoped to maintain control over certain territories. Venetia, lacking nationalistic fervor, had strong ties to Austria and it was in the best interest of its powerful families to stay independent.

14.5 In his 1845 novel, *Sybil, or The Two Nations*, Benjamin Disraeli describes the tremendous gap between the living conditions of the rich and the poor. In one scene, a man boasts to a stranger that Queen Victoria "reigns over the greatest nation that ever existed."

>> **Draw Conclusions** Poor living conditions, such as in this London slum, were a common sight in British industrial cities in the early 1800s. How do you think scenes like this affected British government leaders?

Democratic Reforms in Britain

TEKS
8.B, 18.A, 21.A, 21.B, 21.C, 24.A, 24.B

>> Objectives

Understand how political reforms in Britain affected suffrage and the nature of Parliament.

Identify the influence of Queen Victoria and the values she represented.

Describe social and economic reforms enacted by Parliament in the 1800s.

Describe the efforts by British women to win the vote.

Explain the struggle for Irish home rule and the impact of famine on Ireland.

>> Key Terms

rotten borough
electorate
secret ballot
Queen Victoria
Benjamin Disraeli
William Gladstone
parliamentary democracy
free trade
repeal
abolition
capital offense
penal colony
absentee landlord
home rule

"Two Nations": The Rich and the Poor

> Which nation? asks one of the strangers, "for she reigns over two... Two nations; between whom there is no [communication] and no sympathy; who are as ignorant of each other's habits, thoughts, and feelings, as if they were ... inhabitants of different planets.
>
> What are these "two nations," Egremont asks. "The Rich and the Poor," the stranger replies.
>
> —Benjamin Disraeli, *Sybil*

Benjamin Disraeli and other British leaders worked to bridge the gap between the "two nations" by expanding democratic rights and introducing social reforms to end deeply rooted inequalities. Unlike

www.PearsonTexas.com
Access your Digital Lesson.

613

Topic 14 Lesson 5

Democratic Reforms in Britain

CONNECT

Preview Have students preview the **Lesson Objectives** and the list of **Key Terms**.

Students can also preview all the **Key Terms** and **Academic Vocabulary** using the **Interactive Reading Notepad** on the digital course or preview a summary of the lesson in the **Reading and Note Taking Study Guide**.

Online Use the **Editable Presentation** found on the digital course to present the main ideas for this lesson.

Start Up Activity

The Industrial Revolution brought innovation, new products, and higher standards of living to much of the British population. Many entrepreneurs and business owners gained great wealth. However, rapid urbanization, population growth, and lack of regulation also created harsh working and living conditions. Have students examine the drawing on this page. Ask: What kinds of jobs might the people living in this area have? What might a middle-class neighborhood look like? What do you think are the dangers posed by deep divisions between the classes?

Discuss If you lived in Britain in the 1800s during the Industrial Revolution and were a member of the poor working class, what would you do to bring about social change? *(Sample responses: strike, protest march, petition government)*

Tell students that in this lesson they will learn how the British people made their government more democratic and gained social and economic reforms.

INVESTIGATE

Have students use the **Reading and Note Taking Study Guide** to help them take notes and understand the text as they read.

"Two Nations": The Rich and the Poor

Explain to students that in the early 1800s British government was not fully democratic. Most people could not vote, and the upper-class House of Lords could veto any bill passed by the House of Commons.

Answers

Draw Conclusions *Scenes like this made politicians more aware of the social injustices and spurred them to pass reform laws.*

Aa Vocabulary Builder

1. Have students pronounce the following academic vocabulary terms in this lesson and clarify the part of speech. For difficult or polysyllabic words, break them into syllables and pronounce them with the students.
2. Explain what the word means in common "student-friendly" language using synonyms and antonyms when possible. Provide concrete examples to clarify the meaning, and rephrase the definition.

allocate: to distribute according to a plan
drastic: severe, harsh, extreme

Guided Reading and Discussion

Explain to students that at the beginning of the nineteenth century, more than one fifth of the seats in Parliament were in rotten boroughs. Fifty of the representatives had fewer than 50 voters in their district, while new cities formed by the Industrial Revolution were not allowed any representation. Ask them to describe the effect of the "rotten borough."

Support Ideas With Evidence Have students list and describe specific reform efforts and laws that extended suffrage and eliminated rotten boroughs. *(Students should list and describe end of religious restrictions, Reform Act of 1832, Chartist movement.)*

some of its neighbors in Europe, Britain generally achieved change through reform rather than revolution.

Parliament In Need of Reform In 1815, Britain was a constitutional monarchy with a parliament and two political parties. Still, it was far from democratic. Parliament was made up of the House of Lords and the House of Commons. The House of Lords were hereditary nobles and high-ranking clergy in the Church of England. They had the right to veto any bill passed by the House of Commons.

Members of the Commons were elected, but less than five percent of the people could vote. Wealthy country squires, or landowners, along with nobles, dominated politics and heavily influenced voters. In addition, old laws banned Catholics and non-Anglican Protestants from voting or serving in Parliament. In the 1820s, after fierce debates, Parliament finally ended these religious restrictions.

Pressure for Reform Builds An even greater battle soon erupted over making Parliament more representative. During the Industrial Revolution, centers of population shifted. Some rural towns lost so many people that they had few or no voters. Yet local landowners in these **rotten boroughs** still sent members to Parliament.

At the same time, populous new industrial cities like Manchester and Birmingham had no seats in Parliament because they had not existed as population centers in earlier times.

>> During the early 1800s, the British Parliament was not very democratic. The House of Lords, shown here around 1830, could veto any bill passed by the House of Commons.

Reform Act of 1832 In the 1830s, as revolts flared in France and elsewhere, Whigs and Tories were battling over a bill to reform Parliament.

The Whig Party largely represented middle-class and business interests. The Tory Party spoke for nobles, landowners, and others whose interests and income were rooted in agriculture. In the streets, supporters of reform chanted, "The Bill, the whole Bill, and nothing but the Bill!" Their shouts seemed to echo the cries of revolutionaries on the continent.

Parliament finally passed the Great Reform Act in 1832. It redistributed seats in the House of Commons, giving representation to large towns and cities and eliminating rotten boroughs. It also enlarged the **electorate,** the body of people allowed to vote, by granting suffrage to more men. The act did, however, keep a property requirement for voting.

The Reform Act of 1832 did not bring full democracy, but it did give a greater political voice to middle-class men. Land-owning nobles, however, remained a powerful force in the government and in the economy.

The Chartist Movement The reform bill did not satisfy the demands of more radical reformers like the Chartists, who stood for working class interests. In the 1830s, they drew up the People's Charter, a petition setting out their goals. They demanded universal male suffrage, annual parliamentary elections, and salaries for members of Parliament. Another key demand was for a **secret ballot,** which would allow people to cast their votes without announcing them publicly.

Twice the Chartists presented petitions with over a million signatures to Parliament. Both petitions were ignored. In 1848, as revolutions swept Europe, the Chartists prepared a third petition and organized a march on Parliament. Fearing violence, the government banned the march.

Soon after, the unsuccessful Chartist movement declined. In time, however, Parliament would pass most of the major reforms proposed by the Chartists.

ANALYZE INFORMATION How did reformers' efforts make the British parliament more democratic?

History Background

Unfair Representation Before the passage of the Reform Act of 1832, more than one fifth of the seats in Parliament were rotten boroughs. Fifty of the representatives had fewer than 50 voters in their districts. Some members represented even fewer people. Thomas Paine, an English political thinker, described a condition in which one town had fewer than three houses but sent two members to Parliament, while the 60,000-person town of Manchester sent none. In addition to rotten boroughs, Britain also had "pocket boroughs," which were said to be in the pocket of the people or family who controlled them. They used coercion or bribes to influence the vote.

Answers

Analyze Information *Religious restrictions were eased, allowing non-Anglican Protestants and Catholics to vote; representation in the House of Commons was expanded to large towns and cities; more men gained suffrage through the Great Reform Act of 1832; Chartists' demands for reforms, such as for universal male suffrage, were eventually passed.*

The Victorian Age

From 1837 to 1901, the great symbol in British life was **Queen Victoria.** Her reign was the longest in British history. Although she exercised little real political power, she set the tone for what is now called the Victorian age.

Victorian Ideals As queen, Victoria came to embody the values of her age. These Victorian ideals included duty, thrift, honesty, hard work, and above all respectability. Victoria herself embraced a strict code of morals and manners. As a young woman, she married a German prince, Albert, and they raised a large family.

Although she outranked Albert, she treated him with the devotion a dutiful wife was expected to have for her husband. When he died in 1861, Victoria went into deep mourning and dressed in black for the rest of her long reign. She was fond of her 36 grandchildren, some of whom later became ruling monarchs.

Growing British Confidence Under Victoria, the British middle class—and growing numbers of the working class—felt great confidence in the future. That confidence grew as Britain expanded its already huge empire. Victoria, the empress of India and ruler of some 300 million subjects around the world, became a revered symbol of British might.

During her reign, Victoria witnessed growing agitation for social reform. The queen herself commented that the lower classes "earn their bread and riches so deservedly that they cannot and ought not to be kept back." As the Victorian era went on, reformers continued the push toward greater social and economic justice.

>> Queen Victoria in 1887. Her reign began in 1837 and lasted till her death at age 81 in 1901.

DRAW CONCLUSIONS When Queen Victoria stated that the lower classes "earn their bread and riches so deservedly that they cannot and ought not to be kept back," what did she mean?

ELPS **ELPS 4.C.4** Use the layout and structure of the text to better understand the main ideas of *The Victorian Age.*

Reforms Increase Parliamentary Democracy

In the 1860s, a new era dawned in British politics. The old political parties regrouped under new leadership. Benjamin Disraeli forged the Tories into the modern Conservative Party. The Whigs, led by **William Gladstone,** evolved into the Liberal Party. Between

>> **Hypothesize** In the 1800s and early 1900s, Parliament passed laws to extend and protect suffrage for men. Why were private booths and a police officer needed in this English polling station?

Interactive Timeline

English Language Proficiency Standards

Reading 4.C.4 Demonstrate that understanding the text's organization can help in understanding its content.

Beginning Have students read the main headings and subheadings under "The Victorian Age." Point out that the main heading is the largest, indicating it is the main topic. Explain that each paragraph has a main idea. Have students create a concept map using the headings.

Intermediate Point out the main heading, subheadings, and paragraphs. Have pairs discuss why the main heading is the largest, why most of the content is under subheadings, and why the text is arranged in paragraphs. Have them create summaries of parts of the text and share them.

Advanced Have pairs identify the main heading, subheadings, and paragraphs. Complete the Intermediate activity but have students create an outline of the text.

Advanced High Have students create an outline of the text individually.

Topic 14 Lesson 5

The Victorian Age

Explain to students that Queen Victoria had a significant influence on British society. Be sure students understand that she represented Victorian ideals, inspired confidence that British power and wealth would expand, and favored social reform.

Guided Reading and Discussion

Discuss the Victorian values and ideals that the queen represented. Ask students to describe them in a few sentences.

Evaluate Impact Point out Queen Victoria's comment that the lower classes "earn their bread and riches so deservedly that they cannot and ought not to be kept back." Ask students to explain how this comment probably influenced British society. *(They encouraged the British to enact social and economic reforms.)*

Reforms Increase Parliamentary Democracy

In the 1860s, new leadership brought important reforms to the political process in Britain. Suffrage was extended to most men, and by the end of the century, Britain had become a true parliamentary democracy.

Guided Reading and Discussion

Ask students to write a paragraph detailing the changes that the parties of Disraeli and Gladstone brought to the political process.

Predict Consequences By the end of the 1800s Britain had almost-universal manhood suffrage. Ask students what this means and what many British might demand next to extend democracy in Britain.

Answers

Draw Conclusions *The lower classes deserve social and economic reform.*

Hypothesize *The booths were needed because it was a secret ballot. To prevent threats and bribery, a police officer was present.*

Topic 14 Lesson 5

Key Terms

Ask students to find the key term **free trade** (in bold) and explain its meaning. Ask: How did mercantilism differ from free trade? *(In mercantilism, governments blocked colonies from trading with other countries and put tariffs on imported goods, while in free trade there were no restrictions.)*

Economic and Social Reforms

Tell students that during the early to mid-1800s, Parliament passed a series of economic and social reforms designed to help alleviate problems for members of the working class. Some of the reforms centered on the issue of free trade, which pitted the working and middle classes against landowners and farmers, who typically supported protective tariffs.

Express Ideas Clearly Why did liberals and middle-class business leaders oppose the Corn Laws? *(They believed that a free enterprise system would increase prosperity. If tariffs were abolished, merchants would have larger markets, and consumers would benefit from open competition and lower prices.)*

Guided Reading and Discussion

Ask students to explain how Britain finally abolished the slave trade.

Explain In what way did the punishment for capital offenses change during mid-1800s? *(The number of crimes that were punishable by death was strictly limited to only a few serious crimes.)*

1868 and 1880, as the majority in Parliament swung between the two parties, Gladstone and Disraeli alternated as prime minister. Both fought for important reforms.

Expanding Male Suffrage Disraeli and the Conservative Party pushed through the Reform Bill of 1867. By giving the vote to many working-class men, the new law almost doubled the size of the electorate.

In the 1880s, it was the turn of Gladstone and the Liberal Party to extend suffrage. Their reforms gave the vote to farmworkers and most other men.

By century's end, almost-universal male suffrage, the secret ballot, and other Chartist ambitions had been achieved. Britain had truly transformed itself from a constitutional monarchy to a **parliamentary democracy,** a form of government in which the executive leaders (usually a prime minister and cabinet) are chosen by and responsible to the legislature (parliament), and are also members of it.

Victory for Democracy In the early 1900s, many bills passed by the House of Commons met defeat in the House of Lords. In 1911, a Liberal government passed measures to restrict the power of the Lords, including their power to veto tax bills. The Lords resisted. Finally, the government threatened to create enough new lords to approve the law, and the Lords backed down.

People hailed the change as a victory for democracy. In time, the House of Lords would become a largely ceremonial body with little power. The elected House of Commons would reign supreme.

COMPARE AND CONTRAST What were the origins of the Liberal and Conservative parties? Which groups did they represent?

>> London dock workers unload tea from cargo ships. British customs officials monitored such activities and collected tariffs on foreign imports. **Summarize** Who opposed tariffs, and why?

Economic and Social Reforms

During the early and mid-1800s, Parliament passed a series of social and economic reforms. Many laws were designed to help working class families whose labor supported the new industrial society. Among the most controversial reforms was the issue of **free trade,** or trade between countries without quotas, tariffs, or other restrictions. It pitted landowners and farmers against the middle and working classes.

Abolishing the Corn Laws Britain, like other European nations, taxed foreign imports in order to protect local economies. By the early 1800s however, supporters of free trade, usually middle-class business leaders, wanted to end these protective tariffs. Like Adam Smith, they argued that a laissez-faire policy would increase prosperity for all. Without tariffs they said, merchants would have larger markets in which to sell their goods, and consumers would benefit from open competition.

Some British tariffs were repealed in the 1820s. However, fierce debate erupted over the Corn Laws, which imposed high tariffs on imported grain. (In Britain, "corn" refers to all cereal grains, such as wheat, barley, and oats.) Farmers and wealthy landowners supported the Corn Laws because they kept the price of British grain high. Free traders, however, wanted Parliament to **repeal,** or cancel, the Corn Laws. They argued that repeal of these laws would lower the price of grain, make bread cheaper for workers, and open up trade in general.

Parliament finally repealed the Corn Laws in 1846, after widespread crop failures swept many parts of Europe. Liberals hailed the repeal as a victory for free trade and laissez-faire capitalism. However, in the late 1800s, economic hard times led Britain and other European countries to impose protective tariffs on many goods again.

Answers

Compare and Contrast *The Liberals evolved from the Whigs and represented middle-class and business interests. The Conservatives evolved from the Tories and represented nobles, landowners, and others whose interests and income were rooted in agriculture.*

Summarize *Sample response: Free traders, middle-class business leaders, and other supporters of laissez-faire and free trade principles opposed tariffs because they wanted prices to go down.*

D Differentiate Extra Support To help students explain the argument against the Corn Laws, have them first use the glossary or a dictionary to define *laissez faire, free enterprise system, tariffs,* and any other unfamiliar terms.

Abolition of Slavery During the 1700s, Enlightenment thinkers had turned the spotlight on the evils of the slave trade. At the time, British ships were carrying more Africans to the Americas than any other European country. Middle-class reformers in Britain increased pressure for **abolition,** calling for an end to slavery and the slave trade.

In Parliament, William Wilberforce led the movement to end the slave trade. A dedicated social reformer, Wilberforce also held strong religious convictions. Wilberforce helped shift political thought by persistently introducing anti-slavery motions for decades in Parliament. Finally, in 1807, Britain became the first European power to abolish the slave trade.

Banning the slave trade did not end slavery. Although the Congress of Vienna condemned slavery, it had taken no action. In Britain, liberals preached the immorality of slavery. Finally, in 1833, Parliament passed a law banning slavery in all British colonies.

Crime and Punishment Other reforms were aimed at the criminal justice system. In the early 1800s, more than 200 crimes were punishable by death. Such **capital offenses** included not only murder but also shoplifting, sheep stealing, and impersonating an army veteran.

In practice, some juries refused to convict people charged with crimes, because the punishments were so harsh. Executions were public occasions, and the hanging of a well-known murderer might attract thousands of curious spectators. By 1868 however, Parliament banned public hangings, and executions then took place behind prison walls. Afterward, instead of receiving a proper burial, the criminal's body might be given to a medical college for dissection.

Reformers began to reduce the number of capital offenses. By 1850, the death penalty was reserved for murder, piracy, treason, and arson. Many petty criminals were instead transported to **penal colonies,** or settlements for convicts, in the new British territory of Australia. Additional reforms improved prison conditions and outlawed imprisonment due to debt.

DRAW CONCLUSIONS How did the Corn Laws affect the lower classes?

>> **Analyze Political Cartoons** In this cartoon, the British prime minister opens a particular gate. What change in policy does the cartoon depict? Explain.

>> Harsh working conditions and deadly accidents were common in British coal mines. With the Mines Act of 1842, Parliament prohibited all females and boys under age 10 from working in underground mines.

Victories for the Working Class

"Four [ghosts] haunt the Poor: Old Age, Accident, Sickness and Unemployment," declared Liberal politician David Lloyd George in 1905. "We are going to [expel] them."

Analyze Visuals

Ask students to examine the political cartoon on this page. Point out that political cartoons were and still are a popular form of political expression. Ask: Who does the figure holding the banner represent, and what is he being allowed to do? *(Free trade; he is being allowed to enter what was once a monopoly.)*

Victories for the Working Class

Tell students that beginning in the 1840s, Parliament passed laws benefiting the working class. These reforms continued to be passed in the late 1800s and early 1900s. Working conditions improved, and workers gained more rights.

Online Project the **Interactive Timeline: Britain Reformed** and click on the hotspots.

ACTIVE CLASSROOM

Have students Make Headlines that summarize the timeline's main idea. Ask: If you were to write a headline that captured the most important aspect of this timeline, what would that headline be? Exchange headlines with a partner for him or her to review and improve.

Guided Reading and Discussion

Ask students to describe other social reforms that were made during this period. How did workers gain greater protection under the law?

Identify Cause and Effect What were some results of interactions between British labor unions, socialists, and government leaders? *(Sample response: Working conditions improved, and socialists and union members formed the powerful Labour Party. Because of these reforms, Marxism had only limited appeal to the British working class.)*

Answers

Analyze Political Cartoons *Sample answer: Parliament's repeal of the Corn Law tariffs on imported grains*

Draw Conclusions *The Corn Laws kept the price of grains in Britain high. Repealing them would increase competition, lower prices, and enable the poor to buy bread.*

Topic 14 Lesson 5

Women Struggle for the Vote

Trace the developments of the women's suffrage movement, and review with students how reformers used increasingly drastic tactics to change their government. Point out that many people did not agree with the idea of women voting. Even those who agreed that women should have the vote did not agree on how to achieve their goals. Emphasize that reformers would not win suffrage for all British women until the mid-1900s.

Guided Reading and Discussion

Explain that hunger strikes and illegal actions were drastic measures taken by reformers. Ask students to describe reasons why some people felt those actions were required to change their government's policies.

Support a Point of View With Evidence In 1918, Parliament finally granted suffrage to women over the age of 30. If you were a 25-year-old suffragist in 1918, would you support the law passed that year? Use examples from the text to support your opinion. *(Possible answers: Support—Partial suffrage was a first step, similar to the incremental steps towards suffrage for men in the 1800s. Reject—Younger women deserved the right to vote just as much as older women; the age limit was arbitrary.)*

Make Generalizations Why would supporters of the women's suffrage movement use hunger strikes as a form of protest? *(Possible answers: Some suffragists concluded that only aggressive actions would help them get the vote. They may have hoped that physically suffering for their cause would garner public sympathy.)*

As early as the 1840s, Parliament passed some laws aimed at improving conditions for workers. Later in the 1800s and early 1900s, Parliament passed additional reforms, designed to help the working class whose labor supported the new industrial society.

Working Conditions Improve As you have read, working conditions in the early industrial age were grim and often dangerous. Gradually, Parliament passed laws to regulate conditions in factories and mines. In 1842, for example, mine owners were forbidden to employ women or children under age 10. An 1847 law limited women and children to a 10-hour day. Later in the 1800s, the government regulated many safety conditions in factories and mines—and sent inspectors to see that the laws were enforced. Other laws set minimum wages and maximum hours of work.

Labor Unions Expand Early in the Industrial Revolution, labor unions were outlawed. Under pressure, government and business leaders slowly accepted worker organizations. Trade unions were made legal in 1825 but it remained illegal to go on strike until later in the century.

Despite restrictions, unions spread, and gradually they won additional rights. Between 1890 and 1914, union membership soared. Besides winning higher wages and shorter hours for workers, unions pressed for other laws to improve the lives of the working class.

Other Social Reforms During the late 1800s and early 1900s, both political parties enacted social reforms to benefit Britain's citizens. Disraeli sponsored laws to improve public health and housing for workers in cities. Under Gladstone, an education act called for free elementary education for all children. Gladstone also pushed to open up government jobs based on merit rather than on birth or wealth.

Another force for reform was the Fabian Society, a socialist organization founded in 1883. The Fabians promoted gradual change through legal means rather than by violence. Though small in number, the Fabians had a strong influence on British politics.

The Labour Party Emerges In 1900, socialists and union members backed the formation of a new political party, which became the Labour Party. (*Labour* is the British spelling of *labor*.) The Labour Party would quickly grow in power and membership until, by the 1920s, it surpassed the Liberal Party and became one of Britain's two major parties.

In the early 1900s, Britain began to pass social welfare laws modeled on those Bismarck had introduced in Germany. They protected workers with accident, health, and unemployment insurance as well as old-age pensions. One result of such reforms was that the Marxist idea of a communist revolution gained only limited support among the British working class. The middle class hailed reforms as proof that democracy was working.

IDENTIFY CENTRAL IDEAS What reforms improved the lives of children in Britain?

Women Struggle for the Vote

In Britain, as elsewhere, women struggled against strong opposition for the right to vote. Women themselves were divided on the issue. Some women opposed suffrage altogether. Queen Victoria, for example, called the women's suffrage struggle "mad, wicked folly." Even women in favor of suffrage disagreed about how best to achieve it.

Radicals Take Action By the early 1900s, Emmeline Pankhurst, a leading suffragist, had become convinced that even more aggressive tactics were necessary to bring victory. Pankhurst and other radical suffragists interrupted speakers in Parliament, shouting, "Votes for women!" until they were carried away. They collected petitions and organized huge public demonstrations.

When mass meetings and other peaceful efforts brought no results, some women turned to more drastic, violent protests. They smashed windows or even burned buildings. Pankhurst justified such tactics as necessary to achieve victory. "There is something that governments care for far more than human life," she declared, "and that is the security of property, so it is through property that we shall strike the enemy." Many suffragists went on hunger strikes, risking their lives to achieve their goals.

Some titled women, like Lady Constance Lytton, joined the protests. Imprisoned after a demonstration, Lytton gave a false name and vowed to stay on a hunger strike until women won the vote. A doctor, unaware of her identity, force-fed Lytton through a tube. The painful ordeal failed to weaken Lytton's resolve. "No surrender," she whispered. "No surrender."

The Tide Turns Even middle-class women who disapproved of such radical and violent actions increasingly demanded votes for women. Still, Parliament refused to grant women's suffrage. Not until 1918 did Parliament finally grant suffrage to women

Answers

Identify Central Ideas *laws prohibiting children under age 10 from working in mines and from working longer than 10 hours per day, along with laws that improved public health and housing and provided free elementary education*

over age 30. Younger women did not win the right to vote for another decade.

DRAW CONCLUSIONS Why might some women have disagreed with the idea of giving women the vote?

>> When some jailed English suffragists went on hunger strikes, prison officials force-fed them to keep them alive. The suffragists used posters like this to gain popular support for their cause.

The Irish Question

Throughout the 1800s, Britain faced the ever-present "Irish question." The English had begun conquering Ireland in the 1100s. In the 1600s, English and Scottish settlers colonized Ireland, taking possession of much of the best farmland.

The Irish never accepted English rule. They bitterly resented settlers, especially **absentee landlords** who owned large estates but did not live on them. Many Irish peasants lived in desperate poverty, while paying high rents to landlords living in England. In addition, the Irish, most of whom were Catholic, had to pay tithes to support the Church of England. Under these conditions, resistance and rebellion were common.

Irish Nationalism Grows Like the national minorities in the Austrian empire, Irish nationalists campaigned vigorously for freedom and justice in the 1800s. Nationalist leader Daniel O'Connell, nicknamed "the Liberator," organized an Irish Catholic League and held mass meetings to demand repeal of unfair laws. "My first object," declared O'Connell, "is to get Ireland for the Irish."

Under pressure from O'Connell and other Irish nationalists, Britain slowly moved to improve conditions in Ireland. In 1829, Parliament passed the Catholic Emancipation Act, which allowed Irish Catholics to vote and hold political office. Yet many injustices remained. Absentee landlords could evict tenants almost at will. Other British laws forbade the teaching and speaking of the Irish language.

Irish Home Rule The famine in Ireland caused by the potato blight left the Irish with a legacy of bitterness and distrust toward Britain. The Great Hunger fueled movements in Ireland that pitted radicals, such as the Fenians, who wanted an independent Ireland, against moderates who called for **home rule,** or local self-government.

In the 1870s, moderates found a rousing leader in the Irish nationalist, Charles Stewart Parnell. He rallied Irish members of Parliament to work for home rule. The "Irish question" disrupted British politics for decades. At times, political parties were so deeply split over the

>> The Irish potato blight caused great hardship, famine, and death. Without potatoes to sell, thousands of tenants could not pay rent and were evicted.

Interactive Gallery

Topic 14 Lesson 5

The Irish Question

Explain that the Irish rejected English rule and wanted Irish home rule. Absentee English landlords charged high rents, leaving Irish families with little money for food. The Irish potato famine further deteriorated the social, economic, and political situation in Ireland.

Online Project the **Interactive Gallery: Famine Changes Ireland** and click through the images.

ACTIVE CLASSROOM

Have students Quickwrite short messages, such as those sent via Twitter, that capture the tragedy of the Irish potato famine. Ask: If you were to tweet the most important aspect that should be remembered about the Irish potato famine, what would your message be? *(Students should clearly state at least one of the effects of the famine, such as human suffering or emigration, and show understanding of the lack of help from the British government.)*

Guided Reading and Discussion

Ask students to discuss the Irish potato famine. Have them write a few sentences describing the causes and effects of the famine.

Identify Cause and Effect Why did many Irish people distrust the British after the Great Famine? *(The British continued to export food from Ireland while hundreds of thousands starved. This situation, combined with harsh British laws, outraged many, and they supported Irish nationalism and independence.)*

English Language Proficiency Standards

Reading 4.F.10 Explain that developing background knowledge on a topic makes understanding academic language easier. Display a historical map of the United Kingdom of Great Britain and Ireland and the headings "Democratic Reforms in Britain," "The Irish Question," "Irish Nationalism Grows," and "Irish Home Rule."

Beginning Brainstorm ideas that connect with the topic. Cover the relationship between Ireland and Great Britain. Have the class develop background knowledge on "The Irish Question."

Intermediate Have groups complete the Beginning activity. Make sure the background knowledge covers tensions between the Irish and British.

Advanced Have pairs or groups brainstorm about the relationship between Ireland and Great Britain. Make sure their work covers the tension between the Irish people and British rule.

Advanced High Ask students to work in pairs to perform the Advanced activity. Have them confirm and build their background knowledge through research.

Answers

Draw Conclusions *Many believed that women should continue to be subordinate to men. They thought that women's focus should remain on domestic issues.*

SYNTHESIZE

Online Project the **Digital Activity: Democratic Transition**. Ask students to recall the Topic Essential Question, What are the challenges of diversity? Remind them that they were asked to predict how the British government would resolve the deep divisions between the classes during the Victorian era. Ask them to review the Synthesize image and answer these questions: Was your prediction accurate? Why or why not? How did political reforms make the British government more democratic? Why do you think Britain was able to largely avoid the violence seen in other countries attempting to transition to a democratic form of government?

Next, have students use the "Think-Pair-Share" strategy to answer this question: How did diversity in the United Kingdom affect democratic reforms in Britain?

DEMONSTRATE

Online Assign the **Digital Lesson Quiz** for this lesson if you haven't already done so. Students will be offered automatic remediation or enrichment based on their score.

Pose this question to the class on the Discussion Board:

Draw Conclusions Identify two examples of key persons who were successful in shifting political thought during the period. Describe how each changed government *(Possible answer: William Wilberforce and Emmeline Pankhurst. Wilberforce served in the House of Commons and persistently introduced anti-slavery legislation for 18 years. Pankhurst used radical protest tactics to gain attention for the women's suffrage movement.)*

Topic Inquiry

Have students continue their investigations for the Topic Inquiry.

Irish question that they could not take care of other business.

As prime minister, Gladstone pushed for reforms in Ireland. He ended the use of Irish tithe money to support the Anglican church and tried to ease the hardships of Irish tenant farmers. New laws prevented landlords from charging unfair rents and protected the rights of tenants to the land they worked.

Finally, in 1914, Parliament passed a home rule bill. But it delayed putting the new law into effect when World War I broke out that year. As you will read, the dream of the Fenians was partly achieved in 1921, when the southern counties of Ireland finally became an independent nation.

MAKE GENERALIZATIONS How did absentee landlords feed the growth of Irish nationalism?

ELPS 4.F.10 Work together with classmates and your teacher to develop background knowledge on the historic relationship between Ireland and Great Britain.

ASSESSMENT

1. **Identify Central Issues** Which groups would benefit from repealing the high tariffs known as the Corn Laws? Why?
2. **Draw Conclusions** How did the political, social, and economic reforms of the early 1800s in Britain reflect the growing power of the middle class?
3. **Support Ideas with Examples** Why did many people view the criminal justice system in Britain during the 1800s as unjust? Provide specific examples.
4. **Draw Conclusions** How did the Fabian Society reflect Victorian ideals?
5. **Identify Central Issues** What were two of the reforms that improved conditions in Ireland?

Answers

Make Generalizations *High rents paid to absentee landlords and their ability to evict Irish tenants for nearly any reason fed the Irish hatred of British authority.*

Assessment

1. Middle-class traders would benefit from more customers. Food would be more affordable for the lower class.
2. As the middle class grew, it gained influence to affect reforms that reflected middle-class values.
3. Crimes such as shoplifting and sheep stealing were capital offenses; offenders were hanged; debtors were imprisoned; criminals were sent to penal colonies; people got away with crimes because juries refused to inflict extremely harsh punishments.
4. Its reforms emphasized equal treatment for all classes and sought change through legal means.
5. Examples include ending the requirement that Irish tithe money to the Anglican church, preventing unfair rents, and protecting the rights of tenants.

14.6 After the revolution of 1848, Napoleon III, nephew of Napoleon Bonaparte, rose to power and set up the Second Empire. His appeal cut across lines of class and ideology. The bourgeoisie saw him as a strong leader who would restore order. His promise to end poverty gave hope to the lower classes. People of all classes were attracted by his name, a reminder of the days when France had towered over Europe. Unlike his famous uncle, however, Napoleon III would bring France neither glory nor an empire.

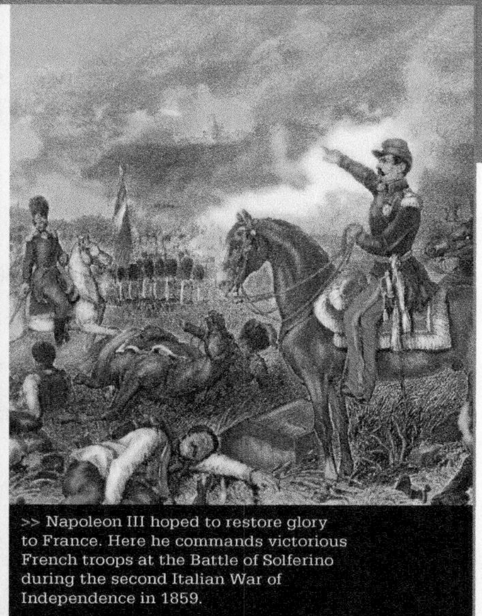

>> Napoleon III hoped to restore glory to France. Here he commands victorious French troops at the Battle of Solferino during the second Italian War of Independence in 1859.

 Interactive Flipped Video

Divisions and Democracy in France

TEKS 21.A

>> Objectives

List the domestic and foreign policies of Napoleon III.

Describe the challenges and political reforms of the Third Republic.

Explain how the Dreyfus affair divided France and contributed to the growth of the Zionist movement.

>> Key Terms

Napoleon III
Suez Canal
premier
coalition
Dreyfus Affair
libel
Zionism

Napoleon III and the Second Empire

Napoleon III Limits Liberties On the surface, the Second Empire looked like a constitutional monarchy. In fact, Napoleon III ruled almost as a dictator, with the power to appoint his cabinet, the upper house of the legislature, and many officials. Although the assembly was elected by universal male suffrage, appointed officials "managed" elections so that supporters of the emperor would win. Debate was limited, and newspapers faced strict censorship.

In the 1860s, Napoleon III began to ease controls. He lifted some censorship and gave the legislature more power. He even issued a new constitution that extended democratic rights.

Economic Growth Like much of Europe, France prospered at mid-century. Napoleon III promoted investment in industry and large-scale ventures such as railroad building and the urban renewal of Paris. During this period, a French entrepreneur, Ferdinand de Lesseps (LAY seps), organized the building of the **Suez Canal** in Egypt to link the Mediterranean with the Red Sea and the Indian Ocean.

 www.PearsonTexas.com Access your Digital Lesson.

Aa Vocabulary Builder

1. Have students pronounce the following academic vocabulary terms in this lesson and clarify the part of speech. For difficult or polysyllabic words, break them into syllables and pronounce them with the students.
2. Explain what the word means in common "student-friendly" language using synonyms and antonyms when possible. Provide concrete examples to clarify the meaning, and rephrase the definition.

repress: to put down, subdue
bourgeoisie: middle class
satellite: a country that is controlled by another country
fervor: extreme feeling or emotion

Topic 14 Lesson 6

Divisions and Democracy in France

CONNECT

Preview Have students preview the **Lesson Objectives** and the list of **Key Terms**.

Students can also preview all the **Key Terms** and **Academic Vocabulary** using the **Interactive Reading Notepad** on the digital course or preview a summary of the lesson in the **Reading and Note Taking Study Guide**.

Online Use the **Editable Presentation** found on the digital course to present the main ideas for this lesson.

Start Up Activity

Tell students that France and Prussia went to war in 1870. Read aloud the quotation from Georges Clemenceau, a young French politician who rallied Parisians as Prussian troops advanced on the city.

"Citizens, must France destroy herself and disappear, or shall she resume her old place in the vanguard of nations? . . . Each of us knows his duty. We are children of the Revolution. Let us seek inspiration in the example of our forefathers in 1792, and like them we shall conquer. *Vive la France!* (Long live France!)" —Georges Clemenceau

Ask: What specific words and phrases does Clemenceau use to appeal to his countrymen? *(Sample responses: "Citizens," "Each of us knows his duty," and "We are children of the Revolution.")*

Tell students that in this lesson they will learn about the Siege of Paris, the divisions in French society, and the challenges that democracy faced in France.

INVESTIGATE

Have students read the section using the **Reading and Note Taking Study Guide** to help them take notes and understand the text as they read.

Napoleon III and the Second Empire

As leader of France, Napoleon III limited human rights and liberties. He restricted popular sovereignty by appointing legislators and by "fixing" elections. His foreign policy led France to suffer a disastrous defeat in the Franco-Prussian War.

Online Project the **Interactive Gallery: The Siege of Paris**. Click through the hot spots on the screen.

Analyze Visuals Based on the Interactive Gallery images, how do you think the French people felt about their present and future government? *(Possible answers: They blamed Napoleon III for the defeat; they wanted to change their government to make it more democratic.)*

ACTIVE CLASSROOM

Use the Rank It strategy to have students review the major policies of Napoleon III and rank them in order from the most positive to the most negative. Ask students to provide justification for the ranking. Then ask students to work in pairs to share their ideas. Poll the class to see if there is agreement on the rankings.

Guided Reading and Discussion

Ask students to write several sentences about the government of Napoleon III, its political reforms, and its foreign policy with the class.

Predict Consequences Ask students to predict what the new French government, the Third Republic, will be like. *(Sample response: The Third Republic will be a democracy, and it will help France become a strong nation.)*

The Third Republic Faces New Struggles

The leaders of the Third Republic brought to France a more democratic government. France had many political parties, which formed coalitions to govern. Gradual social reforms benefited workers, women, and children. But the government faced many challenges, including corruption scandals and political divisions.

Workers enjoyed some benefits of economic growth. Napoleon legalized labor unions, extended public education to girls, and created a small public health program. Still, in France, as in other industrial nations, many people lived in great poverty.

Foreign Affairs Napoleon's worst failures were in warfare and foreign affairs. In the 1860s, he tried to place Maximilian, an Austrian Hapsburg prince, on the throne of Mexico. Through Maximilian, Napoleon hoped to turn Mexico into a French satellite. But after a large commitment of troops and money, the venture failed. Mexican patriots resisted fiercely, and the United States protested. After four years, France withdrew its troops. Maximilian was overthrown and shot by Mexican patriots.

Napoleon's successes were almost as costly as his failures. He helped Italian nationalists defeat Austria, and in return, the regions of Nice (nees) and Savoy were ceded to France. But this victory soon backfired when a united Italy emerged as a rival on France's border. And, though France and Britain won the Crimean War, France had little to show for its terrible losses except a small foothold in the Middle East.

Defeat in the Franco-Prussian War At this same time, France was growing increasingly concerned about the rise of a great European rival, Prussia. The Prussian leader Otto von Bismarck shrewdly manipulated the French and lured Napoleon into war in July 1870.

The Franco-Prussian War was a disaster for France. Napoleon III was forced to surrender to the Germans, ending the Second Empire. A brutal four-month siege of Paris by Prussian forces reduced residents to near starvation. People ate rats and killed circus animals for food. During the siege, Parisians used carrier pigeons and balloons to communicate with the outside world.

In 1871, a newly elected French Assembly accepted a harsh peace with Germany. France had to surrender the provinces of Alsace and Lorraine and pay a huge sum to Germany. The sting of defeat left the French burning to avenge their loss.

The Franco-Prussian War ended a long period of French domination of Europe that had begun under Louis XIV. Yet a Third Republic rose from the ashes of the Second Empire of Napoleon III. Economic growth, democratic reforms, and fierce nationalism all played a part in shaping modern France.

DESCRIBE the government of France during the Second Empire.

>> During the Prussian siege of Paris, the French government established municipal canteens to provide low-cost food for the starving people of the city.

Interactive Gallery

The Third Republic Faces New Struggles

At the end of the Franco-Prussian War, a new government, known as the Third Republic, was set up in France. Even as a new National Assembly took power and made peace with Germany, France was plunged into a new crisis. Once again, the crisis was centered in Paris.

The Paris Commune In early 1871, an uprising broke out in Paris. Rebels set up the Paris Commune. Like the radical government during the French Revolution, its goal was to save the Republic from royalists. Communards, as the rebels were called, included workers and socialists as well as bourgeois republicans. As patriots, they rejected the harsh peace that the National Assembly had signed with Germany. Radicals dreamed of creating a new socialist order.

The National Assembly ordered the Paris Commune to disband. When the Communards refused, the government sent troops to retake Paris. For weeks, civil war raged. As government troops advanced, the rebels set fire to several government buildings, toppled Paris

History Background

The Communards The Communards who did not die in the bloody Paris street fights faced trial for crimes against the state. Some were executed or imprisoned. Thousands more were sentenced to servitude in the penal colony of New Caledonia.

France had acquired this Pacific island in 1853 and used it as a penal colony until 1897. Located about 700 miles east of Australia, it is rich in minerals and has nearly one quarter of the world's known nickel reserves. In 1956, it became an overseas territory of France. In response to separatist protests in the 1980s, France promised that a referendum on self-determination would take place in 1998. The referendum did not pass, so the island remains an overseas territory of France.

Answers

Describe *The Second Empire was officially a constitutional monarchy. However, the emperor ran the government like a dictatorship. Debate was limited and newspapers were censored. Later in his reign, Napoleon III extended democratic rights and eased censorship.*

monuments, and slaughtered a number of hostages. Finally, government forces butchered some 30,000 Communards. The suppression of the Paris Commune left bitter memories that deepened social divisions within France.

Coalition Governments Despite its shaky beginnings, the Third Republic remained in place for 70 years. The new republic had a two-house legislature. The powerful lower house, or Chamber of Deputies, was elected by universal male suffrage. Together with the Senate, it elected the president of the republic. However, the president had little power and served mostly as a figurehead. Real power was in the hands of the **premier** (prih MIR), or prime minister.

Unlike Britain, with its two-party system, France had many parties, reflecting the wide splits within the country. Among them were royalists, constitutional monarchists, moderate republicans, and radicals. With so many parties, no single party could win a majority in the legislature. In order to govern, politicians had to form **coalitions,** or alliances of various parties. Once a coalition controlled enough votes, it could then name a premier and form a cabinet.

Multiparty systems and coalition governments are common in Europe. Such alliances allow citizens to vote for a party that most nearly matches their own beliefs. Coalition governments, however, are often unstable. If one party deserts a coalition, the government might lose its majority in the legislature. The government then falls, and new elections must be held. In the first 10 years of the Third Republic, 50 different coalition governments were formed and fell.

Scandals Rock the Third Republic Despite frequent changes of governments, France made economic progress. It paid Germany the huge sum required by the peace treaty and expanded its overseas empire. By the beginning of the twentieth century, France was the largest democratic country in Europe, with a constitution that protected basic rights. Its overseas empire was second only to that of Britain. But in the 1880s and 1890s, a series of political scandals shook public trust in the government.

One crisis involved the minister of war, General Georges Boulanger (boo lahn zhay), who rallied royalists, workers, the military, and ultranationalists eager for revenge on Germany. Accused of plotting to overthrow the republic, Boulanger fled to Belgium. In another scandal, a nephew of the president was caught selling nominations for the Legion of Honor, France's highest award. The president was forced to resign.

>> The Paris Commune, determined to save the Republic from royalists, rebelled against the new National Assembly. The Communards erected barricades throughout Paris.

>> **Analyze Political Cartoons** The Boulanger scandal rocked France. Boulanger leads as his supporters follow. What does the image of the man with the large banner suggest about Boulanger's goals?

Interactive Cartoon

Topic 14 Lesson 6

Key Terms

Ask students to find the word **coalitions** (in bold) in the text. Ask students to discuss the advantages and disadvantages of having to form coalitions in order to rule. *(Sample response: An advantage might be that more viewpoints may be taken into consideration when decisions are made; a disadvantage is that disagreements can lead to the destruction of the coalition and an inability to rule.)*

Online Project the **Interactive Cartoon: The Boulanger Scandal**. As a class, discuss the details of the Boulanger scandal and how it portrays the corruption and divisions in the French government. Click through the hot spots on the screen, discussing the pop-up text and what it tells students about the scandal.

ACTIVE CLASSROOM

Explain that France had an excessive number of political parties. During one 10-year period, 50 different coalition governments were formed and fell. Have students use the Cartoon It strategy to create a political cartoon that conveys the instability and confusion resulting from such a political system. Have each student show his or her cartoon to a partner and have the partner decipher its meaning.

Guided Reading and Discussion

Ask students to compare the points of view of the Communards and the National Assembly and examine why their differences led to a civil war.

Remind students to keep in mind what they learned about the French Revolution. Discuss why the suppression of the Commune deepened social divisions within France.

D Differentiate Challenge/Gifted Use the political cartoon as an opportunity to reinforce student understanding of concepts such as irony, metaphor, and hyperbole. Explain to students that a political cartoon is not meant to show a literal event, but to convey an opinion through visual metaphor.

Answers

Analyze Political Cartoons *Sample answer: The banner reads, "Long live the emperor," which suggests that Boulanger's goal was to become emperor, not president or prime minister, of France.*

The Dreyfus Affair

The French military forged evidence and convicted Captain Alfred Dreyfus of treason in an unfair trial rooted in anti-Semitism. This scandal was known as the Dreyfus Affair. Even after evidence revealed that another man was the spy, Dreyfus was not released from prison. He was finally cleared of all charges in 1906.

Identify Cause and Effect How did the Dreyfus Affair contribute to the growth of Zionism? *(It convinced Theodor Herzl that Jews needed a separate state to guarantee their rights.)*

Guided Reading and Discussion

Ask students to discuss how the Dreyfus Affair revealed anti-Semitism in France.

Infer What were the goals of the Dreyfusards? *(They wanted justice and freedom for Alfred Dreyfus.)*

D Differentiate Challenge/Gifted Point out the political cartoon. Have students research its meaning. Challenge students to answer this question: Why is Dreyfus shown as a lindworm? *(In European mythology, a lindworm is a dragon or serpent with a poisonous bite. The cartoon portrays Dreyfus as a dangerous traitor to France.)*

Reforms in France

Explain that France passed major reform laws in the early 1900s that regulated wages, hours, and safety conditions for workers. They set up a system of free public elementary schools. The government also tried to limit or end Church involvement in government.

Even more disturbing was a crisis that began in 1894. Known as the Dreyfus Affair, it scarred French politics and society for decades.

? DESCRIBE a coalition government.

The Dreyfus Affair

The most serious and divisive scandal began in 1894. The scandal involved a French army officer, Captain Alfred Dreyfus, who was charged with treason. His trial and conviction ignited a decades-long controversy known as the **Dreyfus Affair.**

Dreyfus on Trial Alfred Dreyfus was accused of spying for Germany. After a military trial, Dreyfus was convicted of treason. The military claimed to have plenty of written evidence against Dreyfus. Yet neither Dreyfus nor his lawyer was allowed to see it. The army claimed secrecy was needed to protect France.

The injustice was rooted in anti-Semitism. The military elite detested Dreyfus, the first Jewish person to reach such a high position in the army. Although Dreyfus proclaimed his innocence, he was convicted and condemned to life imprisonment on Devil's Island, a desolate penal colony off the coast of South America.

>> **Analyze Political Cartoons** This 1899 caricature, *The Traitor,* shows Dreyfus as a lindworm, a mythical dragon or serpent with a poisonous bite. Why was this figure used to represent Dreyfus?

A Long Struggle for Justice The Dreyfus Affair scarred French politics and society for decades. Royalists, ultranationalists, and Church officials charged Dreyfus supporters, or "Dreyfusards," with undermining France. Paris echoed with cries of "Long live the army!" and "Death to traitors!" Dreyfusards, mostly liberals and republicans, upheld ideals of justice and equality in the face of massive public anger.

By 1896, new evidence pointed to another officer, Ferdinand Esterhazy, as the spy. Still, the army refused to grant Dreyfus a new trial.

In 1898, French novelist Émile Zola joined the battle. In an article headlined *J'Accuse!* (I Accuse!), he charged the army and government with suppressing the truth. As a result, Zola was convicted of **libel,** or the knowing publication of false and damaging statements. He fled into exile.

Eventually, the Dreyfusards made progress, and the army had to release its evidence against Dreyfus. Much of it turned out to be forged. In 1906, a French court cleared Dreyfus of all charges and reinstated him in the army. Even though justice had triumphed, the Dreyfus Affair left lasting scars.

Growing Anti-Semitism The Dreyfus case reflected the rise of anti-Semitism in Europe. The Enlightenment and the French Revolution had spread ideas about religious toleration. In Western Europe, some Jews had gained jobs in government, universities, and other areas of life. Others had achieved success in banking and business, but most struggled to survive in the ghettos of Eastern Europe or the slums of Western Europe.

By the late 1800s, however, anti-Semitism was again on the rise. Anti-Semites were often members of the lower middle class who felt insecure in their social and economic position. Steeped in the new nationalist fervor, they adopted an aggressive intolerance for outsiders and a violent hatred of Jews.

The Rise of Zionism The Dreyfus case and pogroms in Russia stirred Theodor Herzl (HURT sul), a Hungarian Jewish journalist living in France. In the face of growing anti-Semitism, Herzl called for Jews to set up their own nation state. He helped spur the growth of **Zionism,** a nationalist movement devoted to rebuilding a Jewish state in the Jews' ancient homeland. Many Jews had kept this dream alive since the destruction of the temple

English Language Proficiency Standards

Reading 4.D.1 Preview "Reforms in France" by creating a graphic organizer that shows the text's main idea and details. Have students read the text and add additional details to the organizer.

Beginning Demonstrate how to skim the first paragraph for details. Skim the rest of the reading and help students create a main idea organizer. Allow students to add drawings for clarity.

Intermediate Complete the Beginning activity, but have students identify and define challenging terms.

Advanced Have pairs fill in the organizer as they skim the text. Have them identify and define challenging terms.

Advanced High Have students skim the text, fill in the organizer, and compare their work to a partner's, correcting any errors. Have pairs identify and define challenging terms.

Answers

Describe *In a coalition government, various political parties agree to a ruling alliance because no single party has enough votes to control the government.*

Analyze Political Cartoons *Sample answer: It portrays Dreyfus as an evil, treasonous figure who threatens France.*

in Jerusalem by the Romans. In 1897, Herzl organized the First Zionist Congress in Basel, Switzerland.

? DRAW CONCLUSIONS What solution did Zionists propose to address widespread anti-Semitism?

Reforms in France

Although shaken by the Dreyfus affair, France achieved serious reforms in the early 1900s. Like Britain, France passed laws regulating wages, hours, and safety conditions for workers. It set up a system of free public elementary schools. Creating public schools was also part of a campaign to reduce the control of the Roman Catholic Church over education in France.

Separation of Church and State Like Bismarck in Germany, French reformers tried to limit or even end Church involvement in government. Republicans viewed the Church as a conservative force that opposed progressive policies. In the Dreyfus Affair, it had backed the army and ultranationalists.

From 1899 to 1905, the government enacted a series of reforms. It closed Church schools, along with many convents and monasteries. In 1905, it passed a law to separate church and state and stopped paying the salaries of the clergy. Catholics, Protestants, and Jews all enjoyed freedom of worship, but the new laws ensured that none had any special treatment from the government.

Rights for Women Under the Napoleonic Code, French women had few rights. By the 1890s, a growing women's rights movement in France sought legal reforms. It made some gains, such as an 1896 law giving married women the right to their own earnings.

In 1909, Jeanne-Elizabeth Schmahl founded the French Union for Women's Suffrage. Schmahl and other women sought to win the vote through legal means. Yet even liberal men were reluctant to grant women suffrage. They feared that women would vote for Church and conservative causes. In the end, French women did not win the vote until 1946.

? DESCRIBE How did French women try to change their role in French society in the late 1800s?

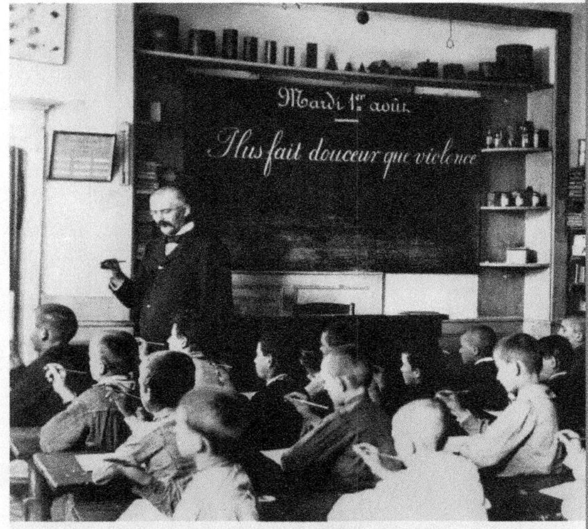

>> One of the many reforms in early 1900s France was the establishment of free public elementary schools.

ELPS **ELPS 4.D.1** Create a graphic organizer to help you preview the reading *Reforms in France* by identifying the main idea and supporting details.

ASSESSMENT

1. **Identify Main Ideas** What political changes did the end of the Franco-Prussian War bring to France?
2. **Draw Conclusions** Explain the effect of Napoleon III's foreign policy failures.
3. **Explain** How did coalition governments affect France?
4. **Draw Conclusions** Why was the Dreyfus Affair an important event in French history?
5. **Analyze Information** Why did French women not get the vote until 1946?

Topic 14 Lesson 6

Guided Reading and Discussion

Ask students to note how the French participated in changing their government.

SYNTHESIZE

Online Project the **Digital Activity: The Dreyfus Affair.** Review the details of the Dreyfus Affair with students. Then move forward to the second and third screens and have a student read each primary source aloud.

Discuss Have the class discuss the perspectives of Dreyfus and Zola. Though they were on the same side of the issue, they had different points of view. Dreyfus was the victim of injustice, while Zola was a famous writer expressing his outrage.

DEMONSTRATE

Online Assign the **Digital Lesson Quiz** for this lesson if you haven't already done so. Students will be offered automatic remediation or enrichment based on their score.

Pose these questions to the class on the Discussion Board:

Predict Consequences The Third Republic ends with the beginning of World War I. How will France's government change after the war? *(France will still be a republic but with a new constitution.)*

Draw Conclusions During the Second Empire, France had one stable government. During the Third Republic, governing coalitions were unstable, and there were 50 coalition governments in the first 10 years. Does this mean that Napoleon's government was better than the Republic's? Why or why not? *(Sample response: No, having a stable government is not better if that government does not represent the people.)*

Topic Inquiry

Have students continue their investigations for the Topic Inquiry.

Assessment

1. The Third Republic, which had a two-house legislature, many parties, and universal male suffrage, was formed.
2. The effort to install Maximilian as the king of Mexico failed, and the Franco-Prussian War led to the siege of Paris, the loss of the provinces of Alsace and Lorraine, and the burden of huge war reparations.
3. Coalitions led to unstable governments, but allowed French citizens to vote for a party that reflected their own political beliefs,
4. It divided French society and revealed growing anti-Semitism and injustice in France. It helped inspire later reforms that separated church and state. As a result, Zionism and calls for an independent Jewish state increased.
5. French men feared that women would vote for the Church and conservative causes.

Answers

Draw Conclusions *Zionists wanted to form a Jewish state that would provide rights denied them in Europe.*

Describe *French women sought legal reforms to protect their rights and win the right to vote.*

Topic 14 Lesson 7

Growth of the United States

CONNECT

Preview Have students preview the **Lesson Objectives** and the list of **Key Terms**.

Students can also preview all the **Key Terms** and **Academic Vocabulary** using the **Interactive Reading Notepad** on the digital course or preview a summary of the lesson in the **Reading and Note Taking Study Guide**.

Online Use the **Editable Presentation** found on the digital course to present the main ideas for this lesson.

Start Up Activity

In the 1800s, the United States welcomed hundreds of thousands of immigrants. In 1886, the Statue of Liberty was unveiled on an island in New York Harbor. It was one of the first things many immigrants saw as they arrived.

Have students answer these questions.

- What do you think the statue symbolized for the immigrants arriving at Ellis Island to a new life in America?
- Do you know where the Statue of Liberty came from? *(the French government)*
- Why might the statue's origins have special meaning for immigrants coming to America?

Discuss What monuments or symbols of American democracy and freedom do you see in your daily life? How do they make you feel?

Tell students that in this lesson they will learn about the expansion of the United States and American democracy in the 1800s.

INVESTIGATE

Have students use the **Reading and Note Taking Study Guide** to help them take notes and understand the text as they read.

The United States Expands

During the nineteenth century, the United States acquired the territory that makes up the country today.

>> Most people migrating west traveled in wagons, like the settlers moving through this mountain pass.

Interactive Flipped Video

14.7 In the 1800s, the United States was a beacon of hope for many people. The American economy was growing rapidly, offering jobs to newcomers. The Constitution and the Bill of Rights held out the hope of political and religious freedom. Not everyone shared in the prosperity or the ideals of democracy. Still, by the early 1900s, the United States had undertaken reforms to ensure equality for all its citizens.

TEKS
21.A

>> Objectives

Describe the territorial expansion of the United States.

Summarize the causes and effects of the Civil War.

Explain how American democracy grew in the 1800s.

Analyze the impact of economic growth and social reform on the United States.

>> Key Terms

expansionism
Louisiana Purchase
Manifest Destiny
secede
segregation

Growth of the United States

The United States Expands

Territorial Gains From the earliest years of its history, the United States had followed a policy of **expansionism,** or extending the nation's boundaries. At first, the United States stretched only from the Atlantic coast to the Mississippi River. In 1803, President Thomas Jefferson bought the Louisiana territory from France. In one stroke, the **Louisiana Purchase** virtually doubled the size of the nation.

By 1846, the United States had expanded to include Florida, Oregon, and the Republic of Texas. The Mexican War (1846–1848) added California and the Southwest.

Manifest Destiny With growing pride and confidence, Americans claimed that their nation was destined to spread across the entire continent, from sea to sea. This idea became known as **Manifest Destiny.** Some expansionists even hoped to absorb Canada and

PEARSON realize. www.PearsonTexas.com Access your Digital Lesson.

Aa Vocabulary Builder

1. Have students pronounce the following academic vocabulary terms in this lesson and clarify the part of speech. For difficult or polysyllabic words, break them into syllables and pronounce them with the students.
2. Explain what the word means in common "student-friendly" language using synonyms and antonyms when possible. Provide concrete examples to clarify the meaning, and rephrase the definition.

annex: to add a country or other territory into an existing country or state

resolution: a formal showing of an intent voted by an official group

monopoly: sole ownership or control over a commodity, product, or service

dominate: to rule or control by superior power or influence

Mexico. In fact, the United States did go far afield. In 1867, it bought Alaska from Russia and in 1898, annexed the Hawaiian Islands.

DESCRIBE Describe the United States' territorial gains during the 1800s.

ELPS **ELPS 4.G.2** Practice summarizing information found in *Territorial Gains* with classmates and with your teacher.

Expanding Democracy

In 1800, the United States had the most liberal suffrage in the world, but still only white men who owned property could vote. States slowly chipped away at requirements. By the 1830s, most white men had the right to vote. Democracy was still far from complete, however.

By mid-century, reformers were campaigning for many changes. Some demanded a ban on the sale of alcoholic beverages. Others called for better treatment of the mentally ill or pushed for free elementary schools. But two campaigns stood out above all others because they highlighted the limits of American democracy—the abolition movement and the women's rights movement.

The Abolition Movement In the early 1800s, a few Americans began to call for an immediate and complete end to slavery. One of these abolitionists was William Lloyd Garrison, who pressed the antislavery cause through his newspaper, the *Liberator*. Another was Frederick Douglass.

He had been born into slavery and escaped, and he spoke eloquently in the North about the evils of the system.

By the 1850s, the battle over slavery had intensified. As each new state entered the union, proslavery and antislavery forces met in violent confrontations to decide whether slavery would be legal in the new state. Harriet Beecher Stowe's novel *Uncle Tom's Cabin* helped convince many northerners that slavery was a great social evil.

Women Seek Equality Women worked hard in the antislavery movement. Lucretia Mott and Elizabeth Cady Stanton traveled to London for the World Antislavery Convention—only to find they were forbidden to speak because they were women. Gradually, American women began to protest the laws and customs that limited their lives. In 1848, Mott and Stanton organized the Seneca Falls Convention, the first women's rights convention, to address the problems faced by women.

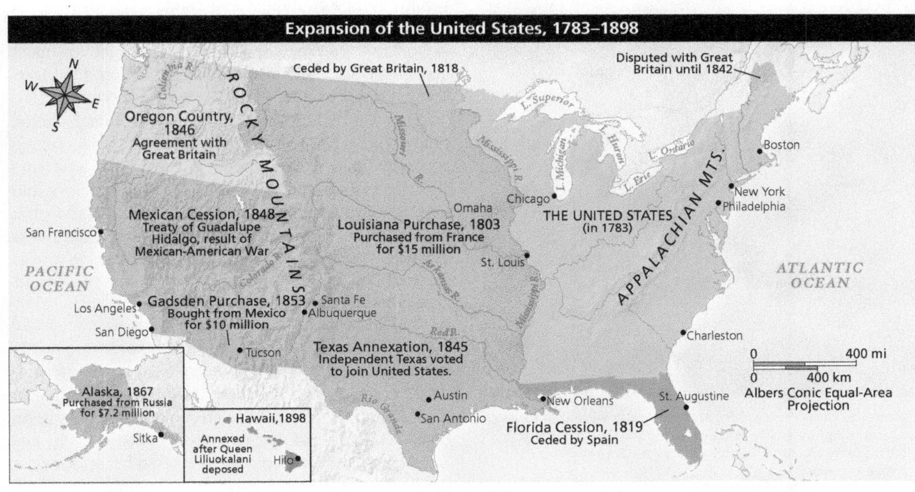

>> **Analyze Maps** Over the course of two centuries, the United States expanded its territory from east of the Mississippi River to the Pacific Ocean and beyond. How did the United States acquire territory on the Pacific coast?

Interactive Map

Topic 14 Lesson 7

Online Project the **Interactive Map: The Expansion of the United States, 1783–1898**. Click through the key to show the expansion of the United States, and discuss how each section of land was acquired. Relate these discussions to the concept of Manifest Destiny.

ACTIVE CLASSROOM

Have students pair off. Ask each pair to take turns doing a chronological Audio Tour of the map. The first student shows and describes the extent of U.S. territory in 1783. Then the other student shows and describes what territory was added in 1803. Have students continue taking turns in this way until they have covered all of the territories gained by the United States.

Guided Reading and Discussion

Be sure that students understand the term *Manifest Destiny*. Discuss with students how the belief in Manifest Destiny might have affected the acquisition of territory.

Infer Engage students in a discussion on how they think the American free enterprise system benefited the development and expansion of the United States. *(It promoted entrepreneurship, provided a network of communications and transportation technologies, and encouraged economic competition and growth.)*

Expanding Democracy

In the 1800s, two major movements expanded American democracy: the antislavery, or abolitionist, movement and the women's rights movement. Both sought to extend democratic rights to large portions of the population.

English Language Proficiency Standards

Reading 4.G.2 Read the first paragraph under "The United States Expands." Have students identify important details and write a summary sentence using the stem *In the 1800s* _____.

Beginning Read "Territorial Gains" aloud. Define challenging terms. Demonstrate how to summarize the first paragraph. Have students point to three important details in the second paragraph. Help them summarize using the details and read the summaries aloud.

Intermediate Complete the Beginning activity, but have students define challenging terms on their own and write a one-sentence summary.

Advanced Have pairs read the text and define challenging terms. Have one student summarize the first paragraph and the other summarize the second. Have two pairs exchange summaries and give each other feedback.

Advanced High Complete the Advanced activity, but have students work alone before sharing summaries as a group.

Answers

Describe *It extended its boundaries by buying the Louisiana territory and adding Florida, Texas, and other territories west of the Louisiana Purchase. It also acquired Hawaii and Alaska.*

Analyze Maps *by an agreement with Great Britain and a war with Mexico*

Topic 14 Lesson 7

Online Project the **Interactive Timeline: The Women's Rights Movement**, and advance through the screens.

ACTIVE CLASSROOM

Use the Conversation With History strategy to engage students in the timeline. Have students imagine that they are having a conversation with one of the people in the timeline. Have them write down a question they'd like to ask, then what that person would say in response, and how they would reply to the response.

Guided Reading and Discussion

Ask students to discuss how the people of the United States and their political leaders participated in changing their government.

The Civil War

Abraham Lincoln believed that slavery should not be allowed in new territories. Others said that the citizens of each territory should vote to decide whether or not to allow slavery. When Lincoln was elected President, southern states seceded and the Civil War began.

Key Terms

Ask students to find the key term **seceded** (in bold) on the page. Tell them that some Southerners believed they had a right to secede based on the Declaration of Independence, which says citizens have the right to dissolve their government and form a new one. Ask: Do you think states should be allowed to leave the nation if they disagree with national policies? Why or why not?

D Differentiate Challenge/Gifted Ask students to do some quick online research on how African American women might have been treated in the women's movement and report back to the class.

>> Lucretia Mott organized the Seneca Falls Convention with Elizabeth Cady Stanton in 1848.

Interactive Timeline

>> In the Union army, African Americans served in units commanded by white officers. Here, the famous black 54th Massachusetts Regiment attacks Fort Wagner in South Carolina.

The convention passed a resolution, based on the Declaration of Independence. It began, "We hold these truths to be self evident: that all men and women are created equal."

The women's rights movement set as its goals equality before the law, in the workplace, and in education. Some women also demanded the right to vote. The idea of women's suffrage sparked controversy. Many Americans, both women and men, thought it was ridiculous. Support for this idea, however, slowly grew.

DRAW CONCLUSIONS How did the abolitionist and women's rights movements highlight the limits of American democracy?

The Civil War

By the mid-1800s, the South and the North were developing along different paths. While the South remained largely rural and agricultural, the North was industrializing and had rapidly growing cities. Along with economic differences, the issue of slavery was increasingly driving a wedge between North and South.

The division reached a crisis in 1860 when Abraham Lincoln was elected president. Lincoln opposed extending slavery into new territories. Southerners feared that he would eventually abolish slavery altogether and that the federal government would infringe on their states' rights.

A Costly Civil War Soon after Lincoln's election, most southern states **seceded,** or withdrew, from the Union and formed the Confederate States of America.

This action sparked the Civil War, which lasted from 1861 to 1865. From 1861 to 1865, the agonizing ordeal of civil war divided families as well as a nation.

The South had fewer resources, fewer people, and less industry than the North. Still, Southerners fought fiercely to defend their cause. At first, the South won victories. At one point, Confederate armies under General Robert E. Lee drove northward as far as Gettysburg, Pennsylvania, before being driven back. In the last years of the war, Lincoln's most successful general, Ulysses S. Grant, used the massive resources of the North in a full-scale offensive against the South.

After devastating losses, the Confederacy finally surrendered in 1865. The struggle cost more than 600,000 lives—the largest casualty figures of any American war. Although the war left a bitter legacy, it did guarantee that the nation would remain undivided.

History Background

The Economies of the North and South The economies and infrastructure of the North and South were vastly different. Along with industrialization in the North came investment in new modes of transportation such as canals, roads, and steamboats, and a widespread communications network of newspapers and other periodicals. The addition of the telegraph in the 1840s made communications that much more immediate. Southerners, on the other hand, chose to invest mainly in slaves, land, and growing commercial crops like cotton, which had jumped tremendously in value in the 1850s. As prices for cotton grew, slaves' value also grew. At the time of the Civil War, the per capita income of northerners was half that of southern whites, and more than half of the wealthiest Americans lived in the South.

Answers

Draw Conclusions *They pointed out that some people—slaves and women—did not have all the rights that white males enjoyed.*

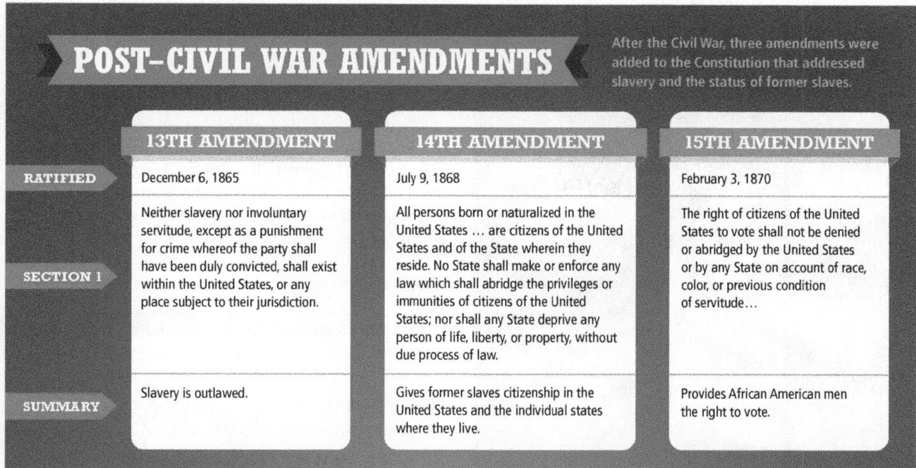

POST-CIVIL WAR AMENDMENTS
After the Civil War, three amendments were added to the Constitution that addressed slavery and the status of former slaves.
13TH AMENDMENT
14TH AMENDMENT
15TH AMENDMENT
RATIFIED
December 6, 1865
July 9, 1868
February 3, 1870
SECTION 1
Neither slavery nor involuntary servitude, except as a punishment for crime whereof the party shall have been duly convicted, shall exist within the United States, or any place subject to their jurisdiction.
All persons born or naturalized in the United States … are citizens of the United States and of the State wherein they reside. No State shall make or enforce any law which shall abridge the privileges or immunities of citizens of the United States; nor shall any State deprive any person of life, liberty, or property, without due process of law.
The right of citizens of the United States to vote shall not be denied or abridged by the United States or by any State on account of race, color, or previous condition of servitude…
SUMMARY
Slavery is outlawed.
Gives former slaves citizenship in the United States and the individual states where they live.
Provides African American men the right to vote.

>> After the Civil War, three amendments to the Constitution changed America. **Analyze Charts** What was the purpose of these amendments, and why were they necessary?

African Americans After the Civil War During the war, Lincoln issued the Emancipation Proclamation, a declaration freeing enslaved African Americans in the Confederate states. After the war, three amendments to the Constitution banned slavery throughout the country and granted political rights to African Americans. Under the Fifteenth Amendment, African American men won the right to vote.

Despite these amendments, African Americans faced many restrictions. In the South, state laws imposed **segregation,** or legal separation of the races, in hospitals, schools, and other public places. These laws were often called "Jim Crow laws." Other state laws imposed conditions for voter eligibility that, despite the Fifteenth Amendment, prevented African Americans from voting.

African Americans also faced economic hardships. Newly freed African Americans had no land, and many ended up working as tenant farmers. Some headed west to work as cowhands or buy farmland. Others migrated to northern cities to find jobs in factories.

SYNTHESIZE How did the Fifteenth Amendment expand democracy in the United States?

ELPS ELPS 4.E.1 As you read *The Civil War,* create a list of unfamiliar terms. Then use a bilingual dictionary to find the meanings of these words.

Economic Growth and Reform

As in Western Europe, the Industrial Revolution was transforming the United States at mid-century. By 1900, it led the world in industrial and agricultural output, thanks to many factors. It had vast natural resources, a stable government, and a growing population—supplied mostly by immigrants.

The free enterprise system and the protection of property rights allowed entrepreneurs to invest in expanding businesses. The building of railroads and new technologies that improved communication further helped farming and industry.

Business and Labor By 1900, giant monopolies controlled whole industries. Scottish-born Andrew Carnegie built the nation's largest steel company, while John D. Rockefeller's Standard Oil Company dominated the world's petroleum industry. Big business enjoyed tremendous profits. The growing prosperity was not shared by all. In factories, wages were low and conditions were often brutal. To defend their interests, American workers organized labor unions such as the American Federation of Labor. Unions sought better wages, hours, and working conditions. Struggles

Topic 14 Lesson 7

Guided Reading and Discussion

Ask students to discuss the causes and effects of the Civil War.

Analyze Images

Review the infographic on the Civil War amendments to the U.S. Constitution. Engage the class in a discussion about the failures and successes of the amendments. Challenge students with the following question: After the Civil War, were African Americans truly free?

Economic Growth and Reform

After the Civil War the United States became a world economic leader and a destination for millions of immigrants fleeing poverty, war, and persecution around the world.

Guided Reading and Discussion

Discuss with students how economic growth prompted social reform. Review the rise of monopolies such as those started by Andrew Carnegie and John D. Rockefeller. Help students understand the effects of monopolies on the market, and why efforts were made to control them.

Express Problems Clearly Ask students to describe working conditions for many industrial workers in the United States and how those conditions led to the push for reform. *(Sample response: Workers were not being paid very much, they had to work very long hours, and they faced dangerous working conditions.)* How did people try to change their situations? *(Sample response: They formed labor unions, they formed political parties, and they fought for voters to have more power.)*

English Language Proficiency Standards

Reading 4.E.1 Read, or have students read, "The Civil War." Help students understand the content.

Beginning Help students list challenging words from the text. Show them how to use a bilingual dictionary to find the meanings of these words. Reread the section. Provide sentence stems for students to complete.

Intermediate Have students use a bilingual dictionary to define unfamiliar words from the text. Reread the section. Have students answer who, where, what, why, and how questions about the text in complete sentences.

Advanced Have pairs read the text and use bilingual dictionaries to define unfamiliar words. Have them write answers to who, where, what, why, and how questions in complete sentences.

Advanced High Have students the text individually, using bilingual dictionaries to define unfamiliar words. Have them write a brief summary of the issues and events of the Civil War.

Answers

Analyze Charts *Sample answer: These amendments were passed to ensure that former slaves had rights. They were needed because they outlawed slavery, granted citizenship to former slaves, and gave African American men the vote.*

Synthesize *The Fifteenth Amendment gave African American men the right to vote.*

Topic 14 Lesson 7

SYNTHESIZE

Online Project the **Digital Activity: The Growth of the United States**. Have partners work together to answer the following questions: How did the United States acquire most of its territory west of the Mississippi? *(It purchased most of its territory from European countries.)* Did territorial expansion have a part in starting the Civil War? Why or why not? *(The question of whether new states would be slave or free states increased tensions prior to the Civil War.)*

Remind students that the Topic Essential Question is "What are the challenges of diversity?" Have them use the Think-Pair-Share strategy to discuss how diversity affected territorial growth and expansion of democracy in the United States. *(Students should discuss various topics, such as the women's rights movement or slavery versus abolitionism.)*

DEMONSTRATE

Online Assign the **Digital Lesson Quiz** for this lesson if you haven't already done so. Students will be offered automatic remediation or enrichment based on their score.

Pose this question to the class on the Discussion Board:

Hypothesize How would America be different if there hadn't been the extension of democratic ideals or social reform? Why? *(America would not be truly free and would not be a world power, because expanding democratic ideals and instituting social reforms helped build a strong and confident nation, provided economic opportunities, and helped ensure equality and human rights.)*

Topic Inquiry

Have students continue their investigations for the Topic Inquiry.

Answers

Draw Conclusions *Large numbers of immigrants worked for low wages, which helped U.S. industry expand.*

>> **The Pullman Strike** Members of the Illinois National Guard fire on striking railroad workers during the Pullman strike of 1894. Industrial workers struggled to convince management to improve labor conditions.

with management sometimes erupted into violent confrontations. Slowly, however, workers made gains.

The Push for Reform When economic hard times hit in the late 1800s, the farmers also organized to defend their interests. In the 1890s, they joined city workers to support the new Populist party. The Populists never became a major party, but their platform of reforms, such as an eight-hour workday, eventually became law.

By 1900, reformers known as Progressives pressed for change. They sought laws to ban child labor, limit working hours, regulate monopolies, and give voters more power. In addition Progressives backed women's suffrage. After a long struggle, American suffragists finally won the vote in 1920, when the Nineteenth Amendment went into effect.

 **DRAW CONCLUSIONS** How did immigration help economic growth after the Civil War?

ASSESSMENT

1. **Describe** What was Manifest Destiny and how did it affect the United States?
2. **Describe** How did a free enterprise system aid the growth of the United States?
3. **Connect** How did the expansion of the United States set the stage for the Civil War?
4. **Analyze Information** What was the impact of economic growth on the United States?
5. **Synthesize** What problems did workers face during the late 1800s and early 1900s and how did they try to enact change?

Assessment

1. Manifest Destiny, the belief that the U.S. was destined to spread across the continent, inspired the acquisition of territory by war or treaty.
2. The free enterprise system allowed people to try new things, start businesses, and take chances. This led to business and economic growth.
3. Contention arose over whether slavery would be allowed in new states and territories. Slave owners believed Lincoln would abolish slavery because of his resistance to extending slavery into new states.
4. The U.S. led the world in industrial and agricultural production. Big business enjoyed huge profits. Economic growth made the United States more confident and powerful, and inspired immigrants to settle in the country to find work.
5. Workers joined unions and political parties to combat long hours, low wages, and unsafe conditions.

14.8 In Eastern and Central Europe, the Austrian Hapsburgs and the Ottoman Turks ruled lands that included diverse ethnic groups. During the 1800s, nationalist feelings spread among these subjected people, which contributed to tensions in Europe. Nationalism, which had brought unity to countries like Germany and Italy, would undermine multi-ethnic empires like that of the Austrian Hapsburgs and the Ottoman Turks. Why did nationalism bring new strength to some countries and weaken others?

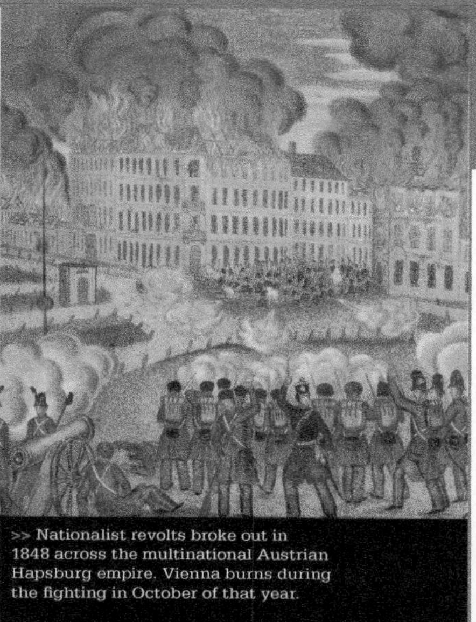

>> Nationalist revolts broke out in 1848 across the multinational Austrian Hapsburg empire. Vienna burns during the fighting in October of that year.

Interactive Flipped Video

Nationalism in Eastern Europe and Russia

TEKS
9.D, 21.A

>> Objectives

Explain how nationalism challenged Austria and the Ottoman Empire.

Summarize major obstacles to progress in Russia.

Describe the cycle of absolutism, reform, and reaction followed by the tsars.

Explain how industrialization contributed to the outbreak of revolution in 1905.

>> Key Terms

Francis Joseph
Ferenc Deák
Dual Monarchy
colossus
Alexander II
Crimean War
emancipation
zemstvo
pogrom
refugee
Duma
Peter Stolypin

Nationalism Endangers Old Empires

The Lands of the Hapsburg Empire The Hapsburgs were the oldest ruling house in Europe. In addition to their homeland of Austria, over the centuries they had acquired the territories of Bohemia and Hungary, as well as parts of Romania, Poland, Ukraine, and northern Italy. By the 1800s, ruling such a vast empire made up of many nationalities posed a challenge for the Hapsburg monarchs, especially as the tide of nationalism rose.

Austrian Hapsburgs Face Challenges Since the Congress of Vienna, the Austrian emperor Francis I and his foreign minister Metternich had upheld conservative goals against liberal forces. "Rule and change nothing," the emperor told his son. Under Francis and Metternich, newspapers could not even use the word constitution, much less discuss this key demand of liberals. The government also

Nationalism in Eastern Europe and Russia

CONNECT

Preview Have students preview the **Lesson Objectives** and the list of **Key Terms**.

Students can also preview all the **Key Terms** and **Academic Vocabulary** using the **Interactive Reading Notepad** on the digital course or preview a summary of the lesson in the **Reading and Note Taking Study Guide**.

Use the **Editable Presentation** found on the digital course to present the main ideas for this lesson.

Start Up Activity

As the forces of nationalism grew, old European empires were threatened, while reformers' efforts to modernize Russia met with little success. Read this quotation aloud:

"How is it that they [European powers] cannot understand that less and less is it possible . . . to direct the destinies of the Balkans from outside? We are growing up, gaining confidence, and becoming independent." —Bulgarian statesman, on the first Balkan War and the European powers

Have students write a few sentences to answer these questions: How does this quote relate to events in today's world? Can you think of current examples of groups or countries that do not want their destinies determined by "outside" forces? *(Students may discuss nationalities struggling to gain independence or independent countries opposing foreign intervention and fighting for self-determination.)*

Tell students that in this lesson they will learn about nationalism in Eastern Europe and the challenges facing the Austrian, Ottoman, and Russian empires.

INVESTIGATE

Have students use the **Reading and Note Taking Study Guide** to help them take notes and understand the text as they read.

Nationalism Endangers Old Empires

In the late 1800s and early 1900s nationalism challenged the Austrian empires as various nationalities sought to break away and form their own independent nation-states.

Aa Vocabulary Builder

1. Have students pronounce the following academic vocabulary terms in this lesson and clarify the part of speech. For difficult or polysyllabic words, break them into syllables and pronounce them with the students.
2. Explain what the word means in common "student-friendly" language using synonyms and antonyms when possible. Provide concrete examples to clarify the meaning, and rephrase the definition.

fraternal: brotherly

radical: a person who favors great changes or reforms

persecution: harassment or hostile treatment of a group or person because of belief

Guided Reading and Discussion

Ask students to discuss how nationalism affected the Hapsburgs.

Identify Cause and Effect What key event forced Francis Joseph to make limited political reforms? *(defeat by France and Sardinia in war)*

Key Terms

Ask students to find the key term **Dual Monarchy** (in bold) in the text and explain what it was. Have them predict if this compromise would help restore or further erode Austrian power.

The Dual Monarchy

The Dual Monarchy of Austria-Hungary faced continuing unrest. Hungarians welcomed the political compromise of the creation of the dual monarchy but wanted even more power. Slavic groups also had national aspirations.

Guided Reading and Discussion

Ask students to discuss the structure of the Austro-Hungarian state.

Explain the significance of Ferenc Deák to Austria-Hungary. *(He was a moderate Hungarian leader who proposed the Dual Monarchy.)*

tried to limit industrial development, which would threaten traditional ways of life.

The Hapsburgs, however, could not hold back the changes that were engulfing Europe. By the 1840s, factories were springing up. Soon, the Hapsburgs found themselves facing the problems of industrial life that had long been familiar in Britain—the growth of cities, worker discontent, and the stirrings of socialism.

Nationalist Demands Equally disturbing to the old order were the urgent demands of nationalists. The Hapsburgs presided over a multinational empire. Of its 50 million people at mid-century, fewer than a quarter were German-speaking Austrians. Almost half belonged to different Slavic groups, including Czechs, Slovaks, Poles, Ukrainians, Serbs, Croats, and Slovenes. Often, rival groups shared the same region. The empire also included large numbers of Hungarians and Italians. The Hapsburgs ignored nationalist demands as long as they could. When nationalist revolts broke out in 1848, the government crushed them.

Reforms of Francis Joseph Amid the turmoil, 18-year-old **Francis Joseph** inherited the Hapsburg throne. He would rule until 1916, presiding over the empire during its fading days.

>> Francis Joseph inherited the Hapsburg throne while still a teenager. He made some limited reforms, but not enough to save his empire.

An early challenge came when Austria suffered its humiliating defeat at the hands of France and Sardinia in 1859. Francis Joseph realized he needed to strengthen the empire at home. Accordingly, he made some limited reforms. He granted a new constitution that set up a legislature. This body, however, was dominated by German-speaking Austrians.

The reforms thus satisfied none of the other national groups that populated the empire. The Hungarians, especially, were determined to settle for nothing less than self-government.

HYPOTHESIZE What alternatives might Francis Joseph have had in responding to nationalist demands?

The Dual Monarchy

Austria's disastrous defeat in the 1866 war with Prussia brought renewed pressure for change from Hungarians within the empire. One year later, **Ferenc Deák** (DEH ahk), a moderate Hungarian leader, helped work out a compromise that created a new political power known as the **Dual Monarchy** of Austria-Hungary.

The Creation of Austria-Hungary Under the agreement, Austria and Hungary were separate states. Each had its own constitution and parliament. Francis Joseph ruled both, as emperor of Austria and king of Hungary. The two states also shared ministries of finance, defense, and foreign affairs, but were independent of each other in all other areas.

Nationalist Unrest Increases Although Hungarians welcomed the compromise, other subject peoples resented it. Restlessness increased among various Slavic groups, especially the Czechs in Bohemia.

Some nationalist leaders called on Slavs to unite, insisting that "only through liberty, equality, and fraternal solidarity" could Slavic peoples fulfill their "great mission in the history of mankind." By the early 1900s, nationalist unrest often left the government paralyzed in the face of pressing political and social problems.

DRAW CONCLUSIONS Why did the Dual Monarchy fail to end nationalist demands?

Answers

Hypothesize *Francis Joseph could have made sure his new legislature represented all the different multinational groups in his empire rather than just German-speaking Austrians.*

Draw Conclusions *Only Hungarian nationalist demands were addressed by the Dual Monarchy. Other ethnic groups were not consulted, and their needs and demands were not addressed.*

English Language Proficiency Standards

Reading 4.F.1 Use the map showing the nationalities and political boundaries of Eastern Europe to help students understand how nationalism challenged Austria and the Ottoman Empire.

Beginning Point out that the colors on the map represent ethnicities in the region. Trace the political boundaries of the Austrian Empire. Ask students to identify the number of ethnicities. Explain that nationalism often kept ethnic groups from working together. Then ask students to think about the problems this could cause for the Austrian Empire. Read the section aloud.

Intermediate Have students complete the Beginning activity. As you read, ask students to explain the connections between the map and the text using simple, short sentences.

Advanced Have students work individually to read the text and examine the map. Then have students work in pairs to identify the various ethnicities that lived in the Austrian Empire and the problems this could cause. Finally, have

>> **Analyze Maps** By 1914, there were several new, independent countries in the Balkans, such as Serbia, Bulgaria, and Romania. Based on the map, do you think the people of these new countries felt that their independence was secure? Explain.

Interactive Map

The Ottoman Empire Declines

Like the Hapsburgs, the Ottomans ruled a multinational empire. It stretched from Eastern Europe and the Balkans to North Africa and the Middle East. There, as in Austria, nationalist demands tore at the fabric of the empire.

Nationalism in the Balkans In the Balkans, Serbia won autonomy in 1830, and southern Greece won independence during the 1830s. But many Serbs and Greeks still lived in the Balkans under Ottoman rule. The Ottoman empire was also home to other national groups, such as Bulgarians and Romanians. During the 1800s, various subject peoples staged revolts against the Ottomans, hoping to set up their own independent states.

Dividing Ottoman Lands Such nationalist stirrings became mixed up with the ambitions of the great European powers. In the mid-1800s, Europeans came to see the Ottoman empire as "the sick man of Europe." Eagerly, they scrambled to divide up Ottoman lands. Russia pushed south toward the Black Sea and Istanbul, which Russians still called Constantinople.

Austria-Hungary took Bosnia and Herzegovina, angering Serbs. They had ambitions to expand their influence in the area. Meanwhile, Britain and France set their sights on other Ottoman lands in the Middle East and North Africa.

Balkan Wars In the end, a complex web of competing interests contributed to a series of crises and wars in the Balkans. Russia fought several wars against the Ottomans. France and Britain sometimes joined the Russians and sometimes the Ottomans.

Germany supported Austrian authority over the discontented national groups. But Germany also encouraged the Ottomans because of their strategic location in the eastern Mediterranean. In between, the subject peoples revolted and then fought among themselves. By the early 1900s, observers were referring to the region as the "Balkan powder keg." The explosion that came in 1914 helped set off World War I.

DRAW CONCLUSIONS How did Balkan nationalism contribute to the decline of the Ottoman Empire?

ELPS **ELPS 4.F.1** Use the map of Eastern Europe to help you understand where different groups lived and how nationalism challenged Austria and the Ottoman Empire.

Analyze Images

Draw students' attention to the map. Point out that not only were there many ethnicities in the Balkans, there were also more than ten different languages spoken. Ask: Which language dominates the northwestern part of the Balkans? *(German)*

The Ottoman Empire Declines

Tell students that the Ottoman Empire also ruled a multinational empire. It became the "sick man of Europe" as nationalist groups broke away to form their own countries.

Online Project the **Interactive Map: The Balkan Powder Keg**, and show and discuss the map layers.

ACTIVE CLASSROOM

Divide the ethnicities layer of the Interactive Map into four numbered quadrants. Have students count off 1 to 4 and then study their quadrant. Ask students to note the languages and ethnicities in their quadrant. Engage the slider to show the map's political layer. Have students note which group had political control of their quadrant. Ask students to describe their comparisons and predict the effects of nationalism.

Guided Reading and Discussion

Ask students to describe other European countries' reactions to the Ottoman Empire's weaknesses.

Draw Inferences How did the newly independent countries of Serbia and Greece influence nationalism among other subject peoples of the Ottoman Empire? *(Sample response: Other peoples were inspired to fight for their own freedom and independence.)*

students share ideas about how nationalism endangered multinational empires.

Advanced High Have students work with a partner to examine the map and predict possible problems of multinational diversity. Have pairs read the text, revise their prediction if needed, and list three supporting details that explain how nationalism threatened the old empires of Eastern Europe.

Answers

Analyze Maps *Sample answer: Probably not, because they were surrounded by large empires as well as other newly independent countries*

Draw Conclusions *Different nationalist groups in the Balkans rebelled against the Ottoman Empire, causing instability. The instability led to European powers trying to acquire Ottoman territory. A series of small wars resulted, further weakening the empire.*

Topic 14 Lesson 8

Russia Tries Reform

The Russian empire was huge, stretching from Eastern Europe to the Pacific. The rigid social structure of tsar, nobles, and serfs ensured that reform and progress came slowly, if at all, to Russia.

Online Project the **Interactive Gallery: Tug of War: Reform and Repression by the Russian Tsars**, and click through the hotspots.

ACTIVE CLASSROOM

Project the "Tug of War" Interactive Gallery. Write down a question you'd like to ask of one of the people in the image gallery visuals or in the lesson text, and then what that person might say to you, and what you would say in response.

Guided Reading and Discussion

Ask students to explore which factors in Russian society led to its lack of progress.

Compare Remind students that in Western Europe, industrialization, development of free enterprise, and the rise of the middle class all contributed to liberal democratic reforms. Ask students to compare conditions in Russia to those in Western Europe. Why was Russia slow to enact reforms? *(Sample response: The Russian nobles controlled a traditional agricultural economy. The tsars ruled with absolute power. The tsars and nobles were reluctant to allow economic and political reforms. The serfs were not emancipated until 1861.)*

D Differentiate Extra Support Ask students to create a two-column chart to compare social, economic, and political conditions. In the first column, list conditions in Britain and France. In the second column, list conditions in Russia. Fill in some information for them to help them get started.

Russia Tries Reform

During the 1800s, Russia expanded its empire eastward into Asia but faced rising demands for reform at home. Reformers hoped to bring Enlightenment ideals such as constitutional government and social justice. They called for an end to autocratic rule and urged the tsar to modernize Russia. Under pressure, tsars introduced some reforms, but soon reverted to repression when ongoing unrest threatened their throne.

Russia Expands By 1815, Russia was not only the largest, most populous nation in Europe but also a great world power. Since the 1600s, explorers, soldiers, and traders seeking furs had expanded Russia's empire eastward across Siberia to the Pacific.

In their efforts to gain warm water ports, Peter the Great and Catherine II added lands on the Baltic and Black seas. During the 1800s, as tsars sought to contain the Ottoman and British empires, they expanded into the Caucasus region and Central Asia. In the process, Russia acquired a vast multi-national empire over parts of Europe and Asia.

Other European powers, including Britain and France, watched the Russian **colossus,** or giant, anxiously. Russia had immense natural resources. Its vast size gave it global influence. But Western Europeans disliked its autocratic government and feared its expansionist aims. At the same time, Russia remained economically undeveloped.

>> Russian nobles celebrate the coronation of Tsar Nicholas II in 1896. Russian royalty and nobility lived lives of wealth and luxury.

Obstacles to Progress By the 1800s, tsars saw the need to modernize but resisted reforms that would undermine their absolute rule. While they wavered, Russia fell further behind the West in economic and social developments.

A great obstacle to progress was the rigid social structure. Landowning nobles dominated society and rejected any change that would threaten their privileges. The middle class was small and weak.

Most Russians were serfs, or laborers bound to the land and to the landowners who controlled them. While serfdom had almost disappeared in Western Europe by the 1700s, it had survived and even spread in Russia.

Russian Serfdom Most serfs were peasants. Others were servants, artisans, or soldiers forced into the tsar's army. As industry expanded, some masters sent serfs to work in factories but took much of their pay.

Enlightened Russians knew that serfdom was inefficient. As long as most people had to serve the whim of their masters, Russia's economy would remain backward. Landowning nobles had no reason to improve agriculture and took little interest in industry.

The Tsars Have Absolute Power For centuries, tsars had ruled with absolute power, imposing their will on their subjects. On occasion, the tsars made limited attempts at liberal reform, such as easing censorship or making legal and economic reforms to improve the lives of serfs. However, in each instance the tsars drew back from their reforms when they began to fear losing the support of nobles.

In short, the liberal and nationalist changes brought about by the Enlightenment and the French Revolution had almost no effect on Russian autocracy.

The tsarist motto was the "three pillars of absolutism." They were: orthodoxy, or strong ties between the Russian Orthodox Church and the government; autocracy, or absolute government; and nationality, or Russian nationalism, which called for respect for Russian traditions and suppression of non-Russian groups within the empire.

 **IDENTIFY CENTRAL ISSUES** Why did industrialization and reform come more slowly to Russia than to Western Europe?

History Background

Serfs The daily life of Russian serfs was scarcely better than that of workhorses or other animals. They lived in dirt-floored huts. Windows were covered with pigs' bladders, which allowed no light to enter. Pigs and calves slept in the huts along with the people. Fires that burned for warmth and cooking filled the homes with thick smoke. The labor requirements on serfs had changed little over the centuries. They still had to work several days a week on their masters' estates, usually doing farm work. They also spent part of the year building roads, canals, and railways for the state. When Russia began to industrialize, serfs were compelled to live and work in factory towns under quasi-military discipline.

Answers

Identify Central Issues *Powerful and wealthy landowning nobles had no desire for reform or industrialization, and tsars needed the support of the nobles to stay in power.*

Topic 14 Lesson 8

Emancipation and Stirrings of Revolution

During much of the 1800s, tsars moved back and forth between reform and repression. In mid-century, the tsar **Alexander II** moved toward reform, but his death at the hands of an assassin led to a return to repression.

The Crimean War Alexander II came to the throne during the **Crimean War.** The war had broken out after Russia tried to seize Ottoman lands along the Danube River. Britain, France, and Sardinia stepped in to help the Ottomans by sending armies into the Russian Crimea, a peninsula that juts into the Black Sea.

The war, which ended in a Russian defeat, revealed the country's backwardness. Russia had only a few miles of railroads, and the military bureaucracy was hopelessly inefficient.

Emancipation of the Serfs Russia's defeat in the Crimean War triggered widespread calls for change. Russian liberals demanded changes, and students demonstrated, seeking reform. Pressed from all sides, Alexander II finally agreed to reforms. In 1861, he issued a royal decree that required **emancipation,** or freeing, of the serfs.

Freedom brought problems. Former serfs had to buy the land they had worked, but many were too poor to do so. Also, the lands allotted to peasants were often too small to farm efficiently or to support a family. Peasants remained poor, and discontent festered.

Still, emancipation was a turning point. Many peasants moved to the cities, taking jobs in factories and building Russian industries. Equally important, freeing the serfs boosted the drive for further reform.

Limited Reforms Along with emancipation, Alexander II set up a system of local government. Elected assemblies, called **zemstvos,** were made responsible for matters such as road repair, schools, and agriculture. Through this system, Russians gained some experience of self-government at the local level.

The tsar also introduced legal reforms such as trial by jury. He eased censorship and tried to reform the military. A soldier's term of service was reduced from 25 years to 15, and brutal discipline was limited. Alexander also encouraged the growth of industry in Russia.

Dissent Continues Alexander's reforms failed to satisfy many Russians. Peasants had freedom but not land. Liberals wanted a constitution and an elected legislature. Radicals, who had adopted socialist ideas from the West, demanded even more revolutionary changes. The tsar, meanwhile, moved away from reform and toward repression.

>> The 1881 assassination of Alexander II prompted further repression by his son and successor, Alexander III.

Interactive Gallery

In the 1870s, some socialists went to live and work among peasants, preaching reform and revolution. They had little success. The peasants scarcely understood them and sometimes turned them over to the police.

The failure of this movement, combined with renewed government repression, sparked anger among radicals, leading some to embrace violence. On March 13, 1881, terrorists assassinated Alexander II.

Return to Repression Alexander III responded to his father's assassination by returning to repression. To wipe out liberals and revolutionaries, he increased the power of the secret police, restored strict censorship, and exiled critics to Siberia.

The tsar also launched a program of Russification aimed at suppressing the cultures of non-Russian peoples within the empire. Alexander insisted on one language, Russian, and one church, the Russian Orthodox Church. Poles, Ukrainians, Finns, Armenians, Muslims, Jews, and many others suffered persecution.

Persecution and Pogroms Russia had acquired a large Jewish population when it carved up Poland

Emancipation and Stirrings of Revolution

The reigns of Alexander II and Alexander III exemplify the tsarist cycle of periods of reform followed by periods of repression.

Identify Patterns Have pairs of students work together to create circular flowcharts to show the tsarist cycle of reform and repression. They should fill in the chart with specific details from the text. *(Freedom for serfs led to discontent because serfs were still poor, which led to movement to cities, which led people to drive for further reform; many Russians remained dissatisfied, which led to increased repression by the tsar, especially after the assassination of Alexander II.)*

Draw Conclusions What was the long-term effect of the cycle of repression and reform? *(Sample response: It made people even angrier and more radical as they were given a taste of reform followed by harsh measures of strict repression.)*

Guided Reading and Discussion

Guide students through a discussion of how emancipation affected the serfs.

Hypothesize Why did Alexander III think Russification would stifle dissent? *(Alexander's goal was to suppress the cultures of non-Russian peoples in the empire, uniting Russians against these outsiders. His Russification policy did lead to persecution of non-Russians in the empire.)*

The Beginnings of Industrialization

Tell students that by the late 1800s, Russia had finally entered the industrial age. Use the text and image of Russian industrialization to discuss Russia's industrialization. Then tell students that Russia's new class of industrial workers suffered low pay and poor working conditions. Socialists preached the revolutionary ideas of Karl Marx.

Guided Reading and Discussion

Ask students to discuss the Russian industrialization process.

Compare How were the social problems experienced during Russian industrialization similar to those that occurred in other nations during industrialization? *(Cities became flooded with migrants, who came looking for jobs and a better life. Working conditions were poor, and hours were long. Slums developed, and poverty and disease were widespread.)*

>> Jewish men view the damage done to their sacred Torah scrolls during an 1881 pogrom. Pogroms targeted Jewish communities in Russia.

>> An iron foundry in Lysva, Russia, in 1900. **Draw Conclusions** How did industrialization affect demands for reform in Russia?

and expanded into Ukraine. Under Alexander III, the persecution of Russia's Jewish population increased.

The tsar limited the number of Jews allowed to study in universities or practice certain professions. He revived old laws that forced Jews to live in restricted areas.

Official persecution encouraged **pogroms,** or violent mob attacks on Jewish people. Gangs beat and killed Jewish people and looted and burned their homes and stores. Faced with savage persecution, many left Russia. They became **refugees,** or people who flee their homeland to seek safety elsewhere. Large numbers of Russian Jews went to the United States.

IDENTIFY CAUSE AND EFFECT Why did emancipation fail to meet the needs of the serfs and lead to continued discontent?

The Beginnings of Industrialization

By the late 1800s, Russia had finally entered the industrial age under Alexander III and his son Nicholas II. Russia had several factors of production needed to industrialize. It had vast natural resources, including land and minerals. Its large population included peasants and the beginnings of an urban working class. Over time, a new industrial class emerged with the capital and drive to invest in economic development.

In the 1890s, the government focused on economic development. It encouraged the building of railroads to connect iron and coal mines with factories and to transport goods across Russia.

It secured foreign capital to invest in transportation and industry. Loans from France helped Russia build the Trans-Siberian Railway, which stretched 5,000 miles from European Russia to the Pacific Ocean.

Political Turmoil Grows Industrialization increased social and political problems. Government officials and business leaders applauded economic growth. Nobles opposed it, fearing the changes it brought.

Industrialization also created new social ills as peasants flocked to cities to work in factories. Instead of a better life, they found long hours and low pay in dangerous conditions. In the slums around the factories, poverty, disease, and discontent multiplied. These conditions provided fertile ground for radicals, who sought supporters among the new industrial workers. At factory gates, Socialists often handed out pamphlets that preached the revolutionary ideas of

Answers

Identify Cause and Effect *Serfs were too poor to buy land to farm. If they were given land, it was too small to allow them to grow enough food to survive. So their freedom only brought them continued or worse poverty and frustration.*

Draw Conclusions *Sample answer: Industrialization brought low wages, long workdays, dangerous working and living conditions, and overcrowding in urban slums. All of these issues increased demands for reform.*

English Language Proficiency Standards

Reading 4.G.3 Read with students, or have students read (in pairs or independently), the text "The Beginnings of Industrialization." Define any challenging terms for students, or have them define them.

Beginning Assist students with these questions.

1. How did industrialization affect Russian peasants? Industrialization caused Russian peasants to move to cities to get jobs in _____. *(factories)*
2. What were conditions like in Russian factories? Factory workers worked _____ hours for _____ pay. *(long; low)*
3. What was the political impact of factory conditions in Russia? Bad conditions in factories caused a rise in _____. *(radicalism)*

Intermediate Guide students as they respond.

1. How did industrialization affect Russian peasants? Industrialization caused Russian peasants to move to cities because _____. *(they needed jobs)*

Karl Marx, who won support among the new industrial workers.

HYPOTHESIZE Why did industrialization increase radicalism among Russian peasants?

ELPS 4.G.3 After reading the text section titled *The Beginnings of Industrialization*, demonstrate your understanding by answering questions about the effects of industrialization in Russia.

The Road to Revolution

When war broke out between Russia and Japan in 1904, Nicholas II called on his people to fight for "the Faith, the Tsar, and the Fatherland." Despite patriotic slogans and great sacrifices, the Russians suffered one humiliating defeat after another.

Bloody Sunday News of the military disasters unleashed pent-up discontent created by years of oppression. Protesters poured into the streets. Workers went on strike, demanding shorter hours and better wages. Liberals called for a constitution and reforms to overhaul the government.

As the crisis deepened, a young Orthodox priest, Father George Gapon, organized a peaceful march for Sunday, January 22, 1905. He felt certain that the tsar would help his people if only he understood their sufferings. Marchers flowed through the streets of St. Petersburg toward the tsar's Winter Palace. Chanting prayers and singing hymns, workers carried holy icons and pictures of the tsar. They also brought a petition for justice and freedom.

Fearing the marchers, the tsar had fled the palace and called in soldiers. As the people approached, they saw troops lined up across the square. Suddenly, gunfire rang out. Hundreds of men and women fell dead or wounded in the snow. One woman stumbling away from the scene moaned: "The tsar has deserted us! They shot away the orthodox faith." Indeed, the slaughter marked a turning point for Russians. "Bloody Sunday" killed the people's faith and trust in the tsar.

Unrest Explodes into Revolution In the months that followed Bloody Sunday, discontent exploded across Russia. Strikes multiplied. In some cities, workers took over local government. In the countryside, peasants revolted and demanded land. Minority nationalities called for autonomy. Terrorists targeted officials, and some assassins were cheered as heroes by discontented Russians.

>> Russian soldiers fire on peaceful protesters in front of the Winter Palace in St. Petersburg in January 1905. This event came to be known as Bloody Sunday.

At last, the clamor grew so great that Nicholas was forced to announce sweeping reforms. In the October Manifesto, he promised "freedom of person, conscience, speech, assembly, and union." He agreed to summon a **Duma,** or elected national legislature. No law, he declared, would go into effect without approval by the Duma.

Post-Revolution Reforms The manifesto won over moderates, leaving Socialists isolated. These divisions helped the tsar, who had no intention of letting strikers, revolutionaries, and rebellious peasants challenge him.

In 1906, the first Duma met, but the tsar quickly dissolved it when leaders criticized the government. Nicholas then appointed **Peter Stolypin** (stuh LIP yin) a conservative, as his prime minister. Arrests, pogroms, and executions followed as the conservative Stolypin sought to restore order.

Stolypin realized that Russia needed reform, not just repression. To regain peasant support, he introduced moderate land reforms. He strengthened the zemstvos and improved education before he was assassinated in 1911.

Several more Dumas met during this period, but new voting laws made sure they were conservative. By

The Road to Revolution

Military disasters abroad led to the outbreak of hostilities at home. A peaceful demonstration designed to show the tsar the extent of the people's suffering turned into "Bloody Sunday" on January 22, 1905, when hundreds of protesters were killed by the tsar's army. Revolution erupted in 1905.

Guided Reading and Discussion

Ask students to discuss the significance of Bloody Sunday as a turning point toward revolution in Russia.

Identify Cause and Effect Work with students to examine the specific causes and effects of the 1905 revolution. *(Sample answers: causes: absolutism, industrialization, years of oppression, Bloody Sunday, inequality, nationalism, appeals of liberalism and socialism, military defeat by Japan; effects: a constitution limiting the tsar's power, establishment of an elected legislature, and the protection of basic human rights)*

Hypothesize Why did the attack on the marchers on Bloody Sunday spur people to change their government with the Revolution of 1905? *(Sample response: Because it was a peaceful march led by a priest, and the excessive violence of the tsar's forces caused outrage and a loss of faith and trust in the tsar.)*

Draw Conclusions How successful were the Russian people in pursuing reform efforts and changing their government? *(Sample response: By striking, protesting, demanding reforms, and revolting, the Russians forced the tsar to agree to a new constitution, but the democratic reforms were largely temporary.)*

2. Why were Russian factory workers discontented? Factory workers were unhappy because _____. *(they worked long hours for low pay)*
3. Why did the ideas of Karl Marx gain support in Russia? A growing number of Russian workers liked the ideas of Karl Marx because _____. *(they were unhappy with working and living conditions)*

Advanced Ask: 1. As industrialization began in Russia, where did peasants move and why? *(to cities for factory jobs)*

2. How did Russian factory workers feel about their lives? *(They were unhappy because they worked long hours for low pay in poor conditions.)*
3. Why were the areas around slums and factories popular with radicals? *(People were unhappy with their lives and wanted change.)*

Advanced High Have students respond to the Advanced questions aloud and work in small groups to discuss their answers.

Answers

Hypothesize *Conditions for industrial workers were very bad, which led to even greater discontent. Political radicals tried to influence the new industrial workers, many of whom were peasants who had flocked to the cities looking for work.*

Topic 14 Lesson 8

SYNTHESIZE

Online Project the **Digital Activity: The People Fight Back**. Ask students to recall the Topic Essential Question: What are the challenges of diversity? Ask students to describe how this question relates to the lesson. Then have partners work together to answer the Synthesize questions: What is the artist stating with this cartoon about the possible effect the 1905 Revolution might have on monarchies throughout Europe? How does this relate to nationalism in Eastern Europe? *(The artist is showing that the 1905 Revolution would inspire other people to revolt against their kings. Many nationalists in Eastern Europe would have looked to the revolution as proof that they could successfully revolt.)*

DEMONSTRATE

Online Assign the **Digital Lesson Quiz** for this lesson if you haven't already done so. Students will be offered automatic remediation or enrichment based on their score.

Pose these questions to the class on the Discussion Board:

In "Nationalism in Eastern Europe and Russia," you learned about the rise of nationalism in Eastern Europe and the decline of the aging Austrian and Ottoman empires. You also learned about Russia's failed efforts to institute lasting reform. The lesson ends with a powder keg ready to explode in Eastern Europe and a conservative Dumas in Russia.

Draw Conclusions Do you think Russia will finally succeed in instituting democratic reforms? Will the Dumas become more representative of the people? Why or why not? *(Sample response: The Dumas will not become more representative. The cycle of reform and repression is too strong and will be repeated.)* Will nationalist groups reach their goals in the Balkans? Why or why not? *(Sample response: Nationalist groups in the Balkans will succeed because the age of empires is ending.)*

Topic Inquiry

Have students continue their investigations for the Topic Inquiry.

Answers

Draw Conclusions *Bloody Sunday shows how disconnected the tsar was from his subjects. The march on the tsar's palace was peaceful. People did not want to bring down the tsar. The tsar's reaction shows that he thought the people had reason to harm him and he was therefore afraid of them.*

1914, Russia was still an autocracy, but one simmering with unrest.

? DRAW CONCLUSIONS What does Bloody Sunday suggest about the relationship between the tsar and the Russian people?

ASSESSMENT

1. **Identify Cause and Effect** What effect did nationalism have on the Hapsburg and Ottoman empires?
2. **Synthesize** How did the concept of liberty influence nationalism and revolution in Eastern Europe?
3. **Integrate Information** How did the struggle for basic human rights such as life, liberty, and freedom of expression influence the Revolution of 1905?
4. **Analyze Information** Tsar Alexander II declared that it is "better to abolish serfdom from above than to wait until it will be abolished by a movement from below." Explain his statement.
5. **Hypothesize** Why would a policy such as "Russification" lead to increased nationalism?

Assessment

1. It destabilized and weakened the Ottoman and Hapsburg empires, forcing them to spend resources containing nationalist movements; it also created power vacuums that European powers used to gain territory.
2. Nationalist and revolutionary groups were able to gather people to their cause and point out that the current governments were denying people their liberties.
3. People in Russia had been fighting for rights, but when the guards fired on peaceful protesters on Bloody Sunday, they felt their right to life and free expression had been attacked, resulting in the 1905 Revolution.
4. He meant that if he did not abolish serfdom, then someday the serfs would free themselves.
5. It prompts people to prioritize and fight for their own cultural and national identity.

TEKS ASSESSMENT

1. **Explain Political Changes** Explain how the Industrial Revolution led to political changes in Europe, and describe how people have participated in changing their governments. Write a paragraph explaining how conditions from the Industrial Revolution contributed to political revolutions in Europe in 1848. Consider economic hardships from the Industrial Revolution, middle class desires for a greater political voice, nationalists wanting to get rid of foreign rule, and revolts in Austria, Italy, and the German states. **8.B, 9.D, 21.A**

2. **Explain the Impact** Explain the impact of the American and French revolutions, Napoleon Bonaparte, and the Napoleonic Wars in Latin America. Write a paragraph explaining the impact of the American and French revolutions on Simón Bolívar and the fight for South American independence. Consider the influence of the revolutions and Enlightenment ideas on South American hopes for independence, Napoleon's invasion of Spain in 1808, the uprising in Venezuela, and Bolívar's liberation of other South American nations. **9.B, 9.C**

3. **Trace the Influence** Trace the influence of the American revolutions on Latin America, including the ideas of liberty and equality. Write a paragraph identifying the influence of the American Revolution on Haiti's fight for freedom. Consider French rule in Haiti, enslaved Africans, and the outcome of Toussaint L'Ouverture's leadership during Haiti's revolt. **9.C, 9.D**

4. **Identify the Influence of Ideas** Identify the influence of nationalism on political revolutions. Write a paragraph identifying the influence of German nationalism on their reaction to Napoleon's rule. Consider Napoleon's rule over German states in the early 1800s, Napoleon's policies, and nationalist demands for a unified Germany. **9.D**

5. **Identify Influence** Identify the influence of ideas on political revolutions: equality and democracy. Write a paragraph identifying the influence of equality and democratic ideas on European political revolutions. Consider ideas from the Enlightenment and French Revolution, rejection of absolute monarchies, and the attraction of laissez-faire market principles. **9.D**

6. **Identify Influence** Identify the influence of ideas on political revolutions: nationalism. Write a paragraph identifying the influence of nationalism on unifying Italy. In your paragraph, explain the political make-up of the Italian peninsula, including foreign rulers. What were some obstacles to unity? How did Italian nationalists eventually unify Italy, and who played some prominent roles? **9.D**

7. **Identify Influence and Describe Participation** Identify the influence of ideas on political revolutions: liberty, and describe how people have participated in changing their governments. Write a paragraph identifying how people in Mexico participated in their independence movement. Consider the treatment of mestizos and Native Americans, the roles of Father Miguel Hidalgo and Father José Morelos, and the 1820 events that led to a Spanish constitution. How did these events influence the eventual establishment of the Mexican republic in 1921? **9.D, 21.A**

8. **Describe How People Participated** Describe how people have participated in changing their governments. Using lesson information and valid primary and secondary sources, write a paragraph describing how the Russian people participated in demanding government reforms. Consider Bloody Sunday, peasant strikes and revolts, reforms by Tsar Nicholas II, and establishment of a Duma. **21.A**

9. **Describe People's Participation** Describe how people have participated in changing their governments. Write a paragraph describing Simón Bolívar's attempts to unify Latin American countries under Gran Colombia. Consider the subsequent civil wars, national rivalries, and the formation of new independent countries. **21.A**

10. **Describe How People Have Participated** Describe how people have participated in supporting their governments. Write a paragraph describing how reformers in the United States formed the Progressive Party to press for change. Consider support of laws to better the workplace, regulating business monopolies, and backing women's suffrage. **21.A**

11. **Identify Examples** Identify examples of key persons, such as William Wilberforce, who were successful in shifting political thought. Write a paragraph about William Wilberforce whose efforts led to ending slavery in the British colonies. Consider the role of Britain in transporting slaves, Wilberforce's anti-slavery efforts in Parliament, and the significance of the year 1833. **21.C**

Answers to TEKS Assessment

1. Student answers will vary but should note that the Industrial Revolution brought low pay and poor working conditions. In 1840, a recession shut factories down and led to unemployment. In 1848, the French government's efforts to prevent public meetings led to uprisings in Paris. The king abdicated, and French leaders proclaimed the Second Republic. Revolutions flared across Europe. The middle class sought a greater share of power and protection of basic rights. Nationalists in Hungary, Czechoslovakia, and the Italian states rebelled against Austrian rule. Austrian troops crushed these rebellions. In the German states, protesters forced King Frederick William IV to issue a constitution written by an elected assembly. When the king was offered the crown of a united Germany, he rejected it.

2. Student answers will vary but should include information on how educated creoles such as Bolívar and other South American leaders wanted independence from Spanish rule. They were inspired by Enlightenment ideas, the American Revolution, and ideas from the French revolution, such as liberty, equality, and fraternity. Napoleon's invasion of Spain in 1808 showed that Spain was vulnerable. Latin American leaders saw an opportunity to demand independence. In 1808, Simón Bolívar led an uprising that established a republic in Venezuela. It was quickly toppled. However, in 1810, Bolívar and his army used daring maneuvers to free Venezuela and then liberate a number of other South American nations: Colombia, Ecuador, Peru, and Bolivia.

3. Student answers will vary but should include information on how the French-ruled colony of Haiti had large, very profitable sugar plantations worked by enslaved Africans. The slaves were overworked and underfed. They were inspired by talk of the American Revolution and the ideas of liberty and equality. Haitian slaves revolted in 1791. Toussaint L'Ouverture, their general, proved to be a brilliant leader. His army of former slaves defeated the French, abolished slavery, and won control of most of the island.

4. Student answers will vary but should include information on how Napoleon's rule over German states between 1806 and 1812 resulted in stronger German nationalism. Napoleon encouraged freeing the serfs, made trade easier, and abolished laws against Jews. Despite this, German nationalists fought to free themselves from French rule and demanded a unified German state. It would be half a century before Otto von Bismarck would unify Germany in 1862.

5. Student answers will vary but should include information on how liberals were influenced by Enlightenment ideals and the "liberty, equality, and fraternity" of the French Revolution. They rejected absolute monarchies; they wanted elections and governments based on written constitutions and separation of powers. They believed in natural rights, including democracy and equality. Liberals also supported free market enterprise under the laissez-faire principles of Adam Smith. These ideas influenced political revolutions in Serbia, Greece, France, and other European countries.

6. Student answers will vary but should include information on how the Italian peninsula was made up of regional states. Austria controlled northern Italy, a French Bourbon leader ruled some southern states, and Hapsburg monarchs ruled various other Italian states. People in Italy identified with their regional states. Students should note that the northern Italian states were richer and had more cities, while the south was rural and poor. By the 1800s, nationalists hoped to unify Italy by ousting foreign rulers. They organized secret patriotic societies like Young Italy, founded by nationalist leader Giuseppe Mazzini. From the 1820s to the 1840s, nationalists revolted to expel foreign rule, particularly Austrian forces. Through the efforts of nationalists such as Mazzini, Camillo Cavour, and Giuseppe Garibaldi, Italy was united in 1870 for the first time since the fall of the Roman empire.

Topic 14

Answers to TEKS Assessment

7. Student answers will vary but should include that slavery, poverty, and the poor treatment of mestizos and Native Americans in Spanish-ruled Mexico caused tensions that led to an independence movement. In 1810, Father Miguel Hidalgo urged mestizos and Native Americans to fight for freedom. Another priest, Father José Morelos, continued the fight, calling for abolition of slavery, better conditions for Mexicans, and voting rights for all men. Both priests were captured and executed. In 1820, liberals in Spain forced the Spanish king to issue a constitution. This event led to a coalition of Mexican revolutionaries and nationalists overthrowing the Spanish viceroy in Mexico. In 1921, Mexico gained independence and the Republic of Mexico was established.

8. Student answers will vary but should include information on how Russian workers had been oppressed for years, suffering poor living and working conditions. In 1905, after Russia was defeated in its war against Japan, workers went on strike, demanding better wages and working conditions. Liberals called for a constitution and government reforms. Peaceful protesters marched to the tsar's winter palace in St. Petersburg. Troops shot down hundreds of these protesters in an event that became known as Bloody Sunday. After that, discontent exploded across Russia, with strikes, takeovers of local governments, and peasant revolts and demands for land. Tsar Nicholas II announced sweeping reforms, promising "freedom of person, conscience, speech, assembly, and union." The tsar established a Duma, an elected national legislature, but dissolved it after it criticized the government.

9. Student answers will vary but should include information on how Simón Bolívar tried to organize the newly independent Latin American countries into one unified nation called Gran Colombia. However, bitter rivalries soon split Gran Colombia into four independent countries: Colombia, Panama, Venezuela, and Ecuador. Power struggles among rival leaders led to civil wars and created instability. Bolívar felt that South America's common people had exchanged one set of masters for another, saying, "We have achieved our independence at the expense of everything else."

10. Student answers will vary but should include information on how reformers in the Progressive Party worked for changes in the workplace. Progressives sought laws to ban child labor and limit working hours. They also wanted to regulate monopolies that controlled whole industries. Progressives wanted to empower voters and obtain voting rights for women. In 1920, the Nineteenth Amendment gave women the right to vote.

TEKS ASSESSMENT

Central American Independence

KEY
Independent Mexico and Central America
1821 Date of independence
*United Provinces of Central America had dissolved by 1838.

UNITED STATES
MEXICO 1821
Mexico City
PACIFIC OCEAN
Gulf of Mexico
Bahamas (Br.)
Cuba (Sp.)
DOMINICAN REPUBLIC 1844
Puerto Rico (Sp.)
Jamaica (Br.)
British Honduras (Br.)
HAITI 1804
ATLANTIC OCEAN
Caribbean Sea
Mosquito Coast (Br.)
*UNITED PROVINCES OF CENTRAL AMERICA
GUATEMALA 1838
EL SALVADOR 1838
HONDURAS 1838
NICARAGUA 1838
COSTA RICA 1838
Panama (part of Colombia)
COLOMBIA 1819
Bogotá
Caracas
VENEZUELA 1830
Trinidad (Br.)
British Guiana (Br.)
Dutch Guiana (Neth.)
French Guiana (Fr.)
0 1,000 mi
0 1,000 km
Lambert Equal-Area Projection

12. **Describe Major Influences** Describe the major influences of women, such as Queen Victoria, during major eras of world history. Write a paragraph describing Queen Victoria's support of reforms during the Industrial Revolution. Consider her status with the people under her reign, the growing British middle class, and eventual reforms. **24.B**

13. **Identify the Influence** Identify the influence of democracy and human rights on political revolutions. Using information from the lessns and the map above, write a paragraph identifying the influence of democratic ideals on political revolutions in Central America. Consider the overthrow of the Spanish viceroy, Mexico's revolution and its efforts to control lands in Central America, and the eventual status of countries like Guatemala, Nicaragua, and others. **9.D**

14. **Identify the Characteristics** Identify the characteristics of the free enterprise system. Write a paragraph about the controversies of the free enterprise system in Britain during the 1800s. Consider the supporters of free trade, supporters of tariffs and their reasons, and the debate and subsequent change in the Corn Law tariffs. How would ending tariffs decrease prices and affect trade? **18.A**

15. **Identify the Historical Origins** Identify the historical origins of socialism. Write a paragraph identifying the historical origins of socialism in Britain. Consider the impact of poverty and injustice during the Industrial Revolution, activities of the Fabian Society, and its influence on British social welfare laws. **18.C**

16. **Identify Origins** Identify the historical origins of socialism. Write a paragraph identifying how the socialism in Germany led to better worker benefits by the government. Consider the efforts of the German Marxists and the Social Democratic party, opposition and reversal by Chancellor Otto von Bismarck, and the impact of socialist reforms on other European nations. **18.C**

17. **Reflect on the Essential Question** **Write an essay on the Essential Question: What are the challenges of diversity?** Use evidence from your study of this Topic to support your answer.

11. Student answers will vary but should include information on how British ships were transporting more Africans to the Americas than any other European country. Enlightenment thinkers focused on the evils of the slave trade. William Wilberforce, a deeply religious member of Parliament, shifted political thought by persistently introducing anti-slavery motions for decades in Parliament. In 1807, Britain became the first European power to abolish the slave trade. In 1833, Parliament passed a law banning slavery in all British colonies.

12. Student answers will vary but should include how Queen Victoria was a symbol of British values such as duty, thrift, honesty, hard work, and respectability. During Victoria's reign, the middle class was growing and had confidence in the future, as Britain expanded its huge empire to include India. Victoria supported reforms, saying that the lower classes "earn their bread and riches so deservedly that they cannot and ought not to be kept back." As the Victorian era went on, reformers continued the push toward greater economic and social justice.

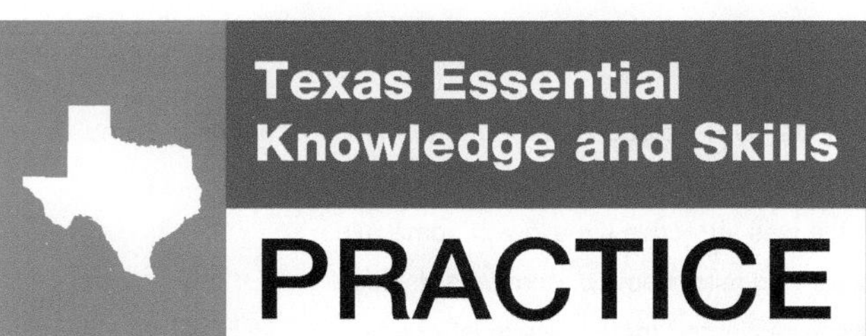

Nationalism and the Spread of Democracy 

13. Student answers will vary but should include information on how Mexican leaders took up arms and called for freedom and social and political reforms. A coalition of Mexican rebels eventually overthrew the Spanish viceroy, and Mexico became a republic in 1821. Spanish-ruled lands in Central America declared independence in the 1820s. Although Mexico tried to claim these Central American lands, local leaders set up a new republic called the United Provinces of Central America. However, it soon fragmented into the separate republics of Guatemala, Nicaragua, Honduras, El Salvador, and Costa Rica.

14. Student answers will vary but should include how the issue of free trade caused controversies in the early 1800s. The British taxed foreign imports to protect local economies. Supporters of free trade (middle-class business leaders) wanted to end those tariffs. They cited Adam Smith's policy of laissez faire, saying that abolishing tariffs would give merchants larger markets and that consumers would benefit from open competition. They believed a free enterprise system with a laissez-faire policy would increase prosperity for everyone. One big debate was the attempt to repeal the Corn Laws, protective tariffs on imported grains. Free traders argued that repeal of the Corn Laws would lower the price of grain, making bread less expensive, and open up trade in general. The Corn Laws were repealed in 1846.

15. Student answers will vary but should include how industrialization created problems such as poverty, injustice, and poor living and working conditions. Socialists believed that the people as a whole should own all property and operate all businesses. In Britain, the Fabian Society, a socialist organization founded in 1883, supported gradual reform through legal means. The Fabians had a strong influence on British politics. In 1900, socialists and union members formed the Labour Party, which quickly became one of Britain's two major parties. In the early 1900s, Britain began to pass social welfare laws to protect workers as well as the poor and disadvantaged.

16. Student answers will vary but should include how German Marxists had organized the Social Democratic Party by the late 1870s. They called for parliamentary democracy and better working conditions. Students should note that Chancellor Bismarck feared that socialists would undermine the loyalty of German workers, so he passed laws that dissolved socialist groups, banned their meetings, and shut down their newspapers. However, workers were unified in their support of the socialist cause. Bismarck then did an about-face and sponsored social welfare laws to protect workers. In fact, Germany pioneered social reform, providing health, accident, and retirement benefits to workers. It became a model for other European nations. Workers continued to support the socialist cause; in 1912, the Social Democratic Party had more seats in the Reichstag than any other party.

Topic 14

Answers to TEKS Practice

1. D
2. H

Online To prepare for the End-of-Topic test, have students go online for additional Topic Review and Assessment questions or to review their notes in the **Interactive Reading Notepad** for the lessons in this Topic.

Benchmark Tests

Assign these benchmark tests as you complete the relevant topics to monitor student progress toward mastering the course content and as preparation for the End-of-Course Test.

Benchmark Test 1: Topics 1–5

Benchmark Test 2: Topics 6–10

Benchmark Test 3: Topics 11–15

Benchmark Test 4: Topics 16–21

TEKS PRACTICE

1 What was the major influence on Latin American independence when Napoleon Bonaparte ousted the Spanish king in 1808?

- **A** Latin American independence movements feared French involvement.
- **B** Latin American leaders wanted to copy Napoleon's military strategy.
- **C** Latin American leaders feared delays in their own independence.
- **D** Spain's weakness showed that Latin America could also overthrow foreign rule.

2 How did the Industrial Revolution contribute to political changes in Europe?

- **F** Nations wanted to establish profitable overseas colonies.
- **G** Foreign rule was attractive if it allowed home rule.
- **H** Workers wanted relief from economic hardships.
- **J** Textile workers wanted more voice in labor unions.

Test Taking Tips: Tip for Questions About Timelines

1. Read the question.
2. Read the title of the timeline to determine what it is about. Note whether the dates covered by the timeline are included in the title.
3. Look at the beginning and end points of the timeline. Notice the intervals of time indicated by the markers between the beginning and end points.
4. Read all the events on the timeline. Notice when each event happened and its relationship to the other events.
5. Read the question again and answer it in your own words using the information on the timeline.

www.PearsonTexas.com
Access additional practice questions

Topic 14

3

> *"Never, never will we desist till we extinguish every trace of this bloody traffic."*
> *—William Wilberforce*

What is the significance of William Wilberforce's quote?

A Wilberforce fought to abolish slavery.

B Wilberforce worried about the loss of human life on the battlefield.

C Wilberforce raised concerns about the dangerous conditions in factories.

D Wilberforce opposed the use of military force to support national interests.

4

1848 Marx and Engels publish *Communist Manifesto*
1912 Vladimir Lenin organizes a Russian Marxist revolutionary party
1917 The Russian Revolution begins
1918 Lenin establishes the Soviet Union as the world's first communist state
1945 Soviet Union controls Eastern Europe after World War II and the Cold War begins
1949 Mao Zedong leads the communist People's Republic of China
1959 Cuba becomes a communist state under Fidel Castro
1989 Berlin Wall separating East and West Berlin falls
1991 Soviet Union dissolves
2013 North Korea, China, Vietnam, Laos, and Cuba are the world's remaining communist states
1850 1900 1950 2000

Looking at the chart, what was the influence of Karl Marx and communism up to the present?

F Communism attracted the poorest countries in the world.

G Eastern European countries were slow to adapt to communism.

H Communism spread globally and then was reduced to a few countries.

J The Soviet Union was the dominant, but short-lived, communist country.

If you have trouble with...				
Question	1	2	3	4
See Lesson	14.2	14.1	14.5	13.2
TEKS	9.B	8.B	21.C	18.B, 18.E

3. A
4. H

Online Use the **Topic Synthesize** to help students revisit and reflect on the Essential Question for this Topic.

Topic Inquiry

If students have done a Topic Inquiry for this Topic, have them complete the final step of the Inquiry now.

The Age of Imperialism (1800–1914)

TOPIC 15 ORGANIZER	PACING: APPROX. 1 PERIOD, .5 BLOCKS		
	PACING	TEKS	ELPS
Connect	1 period		
MY STORY VIDEO **Menelik II, Independence in the Age of Imperialism**	10 min.		
DIGITAL ESSENTIAL QUESTION ACTIVITY **Why Do People Move?**	10 min.	1.E, 8.C, 8.D	
DIGITAL OVERVIEW ACTIVITY **The Age of Imperialism**	10 min.	8.D	
TOPIC INQUIRY: DOCUMENT-BASED QUESTION **What Was the Impact of Imperialism on India?**	20 min.		
Investigate	4–8 periods		
TOPIC INQUIRY: DOCUMENT-BASED QUESTION **What Was the Impact of Imperialism on India?**	Ongoing		
LESSON 1 **The New Imperialism**	30–40 min.	1.E, 8.C, 8.D, 28.B	4.F.2, 4.G.4
LESSON 2 **European Colonies in Africa**	30–40 min.	1.E, 8.C, 28.B	4.F.3
LESSON 3 **Europe and the Muslim World**	30–40 min.	1.E, 8.C, 16.B, 22.C	4.F.4, 4.H.2
LESSON 4 **India Becomes a British Colony**	30–40 min.	1.E, 8.C, 8.D, 16.B, 28.B	
LESSON 5 **China and the West**	30–40 min.	1.E, 28.B	4.F.6
LESSON 6 **The Modernization of Japan**	30–40 min.	1.E, 28.B	4.F.7, 4.J.1
LESSON 7 **Southeast Asia and the Pacific**	30–40 min.	1.E, 8.C, 16.B, 28.B	4.F.2
LESSON 8 **The Americas in the Age of Imperialism**	30–40 min.	1.E, 8.C, 16.B	4.F.9
Synthesize	1 period		
DIGITAL ESSENTIAL QUESTION ACTIVITY **The Age of Imperialism**	10 min.	1.E, 8.D	
TOPIC INQUIRY: DOCUMENT-BASED QUESTION **What Was the Impact of Imperialism on India?**	20 min.		

TOPIC 15 ORGANIZER	PACING: APPROX. 1 PERIOD, .5 BLOCKS		
	PACING	TEKS	ELPS
Demonstrate	1–2 periods		
DIGITAL TOPIC TEST **The Age of Imperialism**	10 min.		
DIGITAL TEKS MASTERY TEST **TEKS Mastery Test**	10 min.		
TOPIC INQUIRY: DOCUMENT-BASED QUESTION **What Was the Impact of Imperialism on India?**	20 min.		

AUTHOR'S NOTE

Material Impact of Imperialism

Materially, the New Imperialism thrust its way into other people's cultures as the Old Imperialism seldom had. The makers of the New Imperialism exploited and developed colonial regions with unmatched thoroughness and intensity. They reaped harvests, tapped trees, dug mines, drilled for oil from Brazil to Borneo. They unrolled barbed wire, strung up telegraph lines, laid rails, constructed harbor facilities. They built processing plants and even manufacturing plants in the colonies to turn raw materials into something closer to the use objects the Europeans, the Americans, and their other customers wanted.

The material impact was vast, cumulative, and accelerating. Irreplaceable natural resources—Congo copper, Arab oil—began to be drained from the land. Patterns of agriculture were drastically changed. Cash crops replaced subsistence farming until populations that formerly fed themselves came to depend on imported food for sheer survival.

Local industries were ruined by the competition of cheap Western machine-made alternatives. The Indian cotton industry was the world's leader in the seventeenth century. It was driven to the brink of extinction by the cotton mills of Manchester and Birmingham in the nineteenth.

—Anthony Esler, *The Human Venture: From Prehistory to the Present* (Upper Saddle River, New Jersey: Pearson Education, 2004), pp. 586–587

TOPIC INQUIRY: DOCUMENT-BASED QUESTION

What Was the Impact of Imperialism on India?

TEKS 1.E, 8.D

In this Topic Inquiry, students will work individually to analyze six documents describing India under British imperialist rule. Students will reflect on the six documents, draw their own conclusions, and then write an essay on the following question: What was the impact of imperialism on India? Learning about India's experience during the Age of Imperialism will contribute to students' understanding of the Topic Essential Question: Why do people move?

STEP 1: CONNECT

Develop Questions and Plan the Investigation

Launch the DBQ Writing Activity

Have students examine the photograph of the polo team in British India. Explain that polo originated in Persia, but the first Europeans to play the game were the British in Assam, India. This team is made up of British army officers and Indian princes. Discuss the image in class, or have students discuss it with a partner.

Analyze Images What elements of British culture are evident in the photo? *(Sample response: the uniforms and mallets and the British players)* What elements of Indian culture are evident? *(Sample response: the turbans of the Indian players)*

Draw Conclusions What does the photograph tell you about the nature of British rule in India? *(Sample response: The British sometimes cooperated with Indians in positions of power or influence.)*

Generate Questions

Have students examine the question, "What was the impact of imperialism on India?" Ask a volunteer to paraphrase the question. *(Sample response: How did imperialism affect India?)* Then have students work with a partner to make a list of 5–10 questions that could help them answer the essay question. The questions should be specific, such as "How did imperialism affect India's economy?" Encourage students to look for answers to these questions and to add to their list of questions as they examine each document.

Resources

- Student Instructions
- Need-to-Know Questions

STEP 2: INVESTIGATE

Apply Disciplinary Concepts and Tools

Read and Analyze Documents

Tell students that they will read and analyze six documents about India under British rule. Then, they will write an essay and express their own opinions about the impact of imperialism on India. Documents A and B express the views of men who lived in British-ruled India. Document C expresses the view of a British artist of the era about events in India. Documents D and F express the opinions of modern historians, and Document E is a pair of graphs with economic data.

Remind students to read or study each document and make sure they understand what the document says. As part of their analysis, students should determine the point of view of the person who created the document and make a judgment about the reliability of the information.

Suggestion: If possible, encourage students to highlight, circle, or mark the area of each document that helps them answer the essay question.

Check Understanding

After students finish reading each individual document, have them answer the multiple-choice and short-answer questions attached to each document. Review the questions and discuss the answers after students have answered the questions for all the documents.

Resources

- Information Organizer

STEP 3: SYNTHESIZE

Evaluate Sources and
Use Evidence to Formulate Conclusions

Write Your Essay

Now have students write their essays to express their own opinion about the question: What was the impact of imperialism on India? If students are having trouble getting started, have them begin by writing one or two sentences that give a basic answer to the essay question. Then have them create an outline that expands on that answer and incorporates details from the documents.

Encourage students to include specific historical details and comments about the documents in their essays.

Suggestion: Before students plan and write their essay, review the scoring rubric. Make sure students understand the components of an effective Document-Based Question essay so they can incorporate those elements in their own writing.

Edit Your Essay

Have students read over their first drafts. Suggest they ask themselves these questions: Does it accurately express my viewpoint? Does it need more details? Then have students proofread and edit their essays, revising as needed. If time allows, have students exchange essays for a peer edit.

Suggestion: Have students use a thesaurus to better describe their viewpoint and to make the essay more interesting.

Resources

- Writing Rubric

STEP 4: DEMONSTRATE

Communicate Conclusions
and Take Informed Action

Present Your Essay

Have students make a neat, clean copy of their essays. Then ask volunteers to read their essays aloud to the class.

Suggestion: As an alternative, have students read one or more of their classmates' essays on their own.

Reflect on the Project

Help students go over what they thought went well in their essays and what did not, so they can be even more effective in the future.

Suggestion: As an extension activity, have students research the impact of imperialism on another country, such as Vietnam (Indochina) or Kenya. Ask them to write a three-paragraph essay in which they compare that country's experience with India's. Have volunteers share their comparisons with the class.

PROFESSIONAL DEVELOPMENT

Document-Based Question

Be sure to view the Document-Based Question Professional Development resources in the online course.

The New Imperialism

Objectives

Objective 1: Explain the political, economic, and social causes of European imperialism.

Objective 2: Understand how technology and other factors contributed to the spread of imperialism.

Objective 3: Describe the characteristics of imperial rule.

Objective 4: Summarize the cultural, political, and social effects of imperialism.

LESSON 1 ORGANIZER	PACING: APPROX. 1 PERIOD, .5 BLOCKS					
			RESOURCES			
	OBJECTIVES	PACING	Print	Online	TEKS	ELPS
Connect						
DIGITAL START UP ACTIVITY **Empire Builders**		5 min.		●	8.C	
Investigate						
READ **Motivations for the New Imperialism**	Objective 1	10 min.	●	●	1.E, 8.C	4.F.2
INTERACTIVE MAP **The New Imperialism**	Objective 1	10 min.		●	8.C	
READ **Western Imperialism Spreads Rapidly**	Objective 2	10 min.	●	●	1.E, 8.D, 28.B	
INTERACTIVE GALLERY **Technology Advances Imperialism**	Objective 2	10 min.		●	28.B	
READ **Types of Imperial Rule**	Objective 3	10 min.	●	●	1.E, 8.C, 8.D, 28.B	4.G.4
READ **The Effects of Imperialism**	Objective 4	10 min.	●	●	1.E, 8.D, 28.B	
Synthesize						
DIGITAL ACTIVITY **Imperialism—Different Opinions**		5 min.		●	1.E, 8.C, 8.D	
Demonstrate						
DIGITAL QUIZ **Lesson Quiz and Class Discussion Board**		10 min.		●	1.E, 8.C, 8.D, 28.B	

Focus on Texas Standards

Texas Essential Knowledge and Skills

1.E identify major causes and describe the major effects of the following important turning points in world history from 1750 to 1914: the Scientific Revolution, the Industrial Revolution and its impact on the development of modern economic systems, European imperialism, and the Enlightenment's impact on political revolutions

8.C identify the major political, economic, and social motivations that influenced European imperialism

8.D explain the major characteristics and impact of European imperialism

28.B explain the roles of military technology, transportation technology, communication technology, and medical advancements in initiating and advancing 19th century imperialism

NOTES

European Colonies in Africa

Objectives

Objective 1: Describe the forces that shaped Africa in the early 1800s.

Objective 2: Explain why European contact with Africa increased.

Objective 3: Analyze how European nations carved up Africa.

Objective 4: Describe African resistance to imperialism.

LESSON 2 ORGANIZER — **PACING: APPROX. 1 PERIOD, .5 BLOCKS**

	OBJECTIVES	PACING	RESOURCES: Print	RESOURCES: Online	TEKS	ELPS
Connect						
DIGITAL START UP ACTIVITY **Resisting Imperialism**		5 min.		●	1.E, 8.D	
Investigate						
READ **Africa Before Imperialism**	Objective 1	10 min.	●	●	1.E	
INTERACTIVE MAP **Effects of Imperialism on African Regions**	Objective 1	10 min.		●	1.E, 8.D	
READ **European Contact Increases**	Objective 2	10 min.	●	●	8.C, 28.B	4.F.3
READ **European Nations Scramble for Colonies**	Objective 3	10 min.	●	●	1.E, 8.C, 8.D	
INTERACTIVE MAP **European Imperialism in Africa**	Objective 3	10 min.		●	1.E, 8.D	
READ **African Resistance**	Objective 4	10 min.	●	●	1.E	
Synthesize						
DIGITAL ACTIVITY **European Domination in Africa**		5 min.		●	1.E	
Demonstrate						
DIGITAL QUIZ **Lesson Quiz and Class Discussion Board**		10 min.		●	1.E, 8.C, 8.D, 28.B	

PEARSON realize
www.PearsonTexas.com
Access your Digital Lesson

Focus on Texas Standards

Texas Essential Knowledge and Skills

1.E identify major causes and describe the major effects of the following important turning points in world history from 1750 to 1914: the Scientific Revolution, the Industrial Revolution and its impact on the development of modern economic systems, European imperialism, and the Enlightenment's impact on political revolutions

8.C identify the major political, economic, and social motivations that influenced European imperialism

28.B explain the roles of military technology, transportation technology, communication technology, and medical advancements in initiating and advancing 19th century imperialism

NOTES

Europe and the Muslim World

Objectives

Objective 1: Explain how internal and external pressures shaped the Muslim world.

Objective 2: Identify the challenges facing the Ottoman empire and Persia.

Objective 3: Describe the ways Egypt tried to modernize, including the opening of the Suez Canal.

LESSON 3 ORGANIZER	PACING: APPROX. 1 PERIOD, .5 BLOCKS					
			RESOURCES			
	OBJECTIVES	PACING	Print	Online	TEKS	ELPS
Connect						
DIGITAL START UP ACTIVITY **The Egyptian Campaign**		5 min.		●	1.E	
Investigate						
READ **Unrest in Muslim Regions**	Objective 1	10 min.	●	●	1.E, 8.D	4.F.4
READ **The Ottoman Empire Declines**	Objective 2	10 min.	●	●	8.D, 9.D, 22.C	
INTERACTIVE GALLERY **European Powers and the Ottoman Empire**	Objective 2	10 min.		●	1.E, 8.D	
READ **Modernization in Egypt**	Objective 3	10 min.	●	●	1.E, 8.C, 8.D, 16.B	4.H.2
INTERACTIVE GALLERY **The Suez Canal**	Objective 3	10 min.		●	16.B	
READ **European Imperialism in Persia**	Objective 2	10 min.	●	●	1.E, 8.C, 8.D	
Synthesize						
DIGITAL ACTIVITY **Effects of Europeans in Muslim Regions**		5 min.		●		
Demonstrate						
DIGITAL QUIZ **Lesson Quiz and Class Discussion Board**		10 min.		●		

PEARSON realize™ www.PearsonTexas.com Access your Digital Lesson

Focus on Texas Standards

Texas Essential Knowledge and Skills

1.E identify major causes and describe the major effects of the following important turning points in world history from 1750 to 1914: the Scientific Revolution, the Industrial Revolution and its impact on the development of modern economic systems, European imperialism, and the Enlightenment's impact on political revolutions

8.C identify the major political, economic, and social motivations that influenced European imperialism

16.B analyze the influence of human and physical geographic factors on major events in world history, including the development of river valley civilizations, trade in the Indian Ocean, and the opening of the Panama and Suez canals

22.C identify examples of politically motivated mass murders in Cambodia, China, Latin America, the Soviet Union, and Armenia

NOTES

India Becomes a British Colony

Objectives

Objective 1: Understand the causes and effects of the Sepoy Rebellion.

Objective 2: Explain the impact of British rule on India.

Objective 3: Describe how the British and Indians viewed one another.

Objective 4: Trace the origins of Indian nationalism.

LESSON 4 ORGANIZER	PACING: APPROX. 1 PERIOD, .5 BLOCKS					
			RESOURCES			
	OBJECTIVES	PACING	Print	Online	TEKS	ELPS
Connect						
DIGITAL START UP ACTIVITY **Critical of British Rule**		5 min.		●	8.D	
Investigate						
READ **The British East India Company**	Objective 1	10 min.	●	●	1.E, 8.C, 8.D	
INTERACTIVE GALLERY **The Sepoy Rebellion**		10 min.		●	1.E, 8.D	
READ **India Under British Rule**	Objective 2	10 min.	●	●	1.E, 8.C, 8.D, 16.B	
INTERACTIVE IMAGE **The Imperial Durbar, 1877**		10 min.		●	1.E, 8.C, 8.D	
READ **Diverse Views on Culture**	Objective 3	10 min.	●	●	8.D, 9.D	
READ **The Growth of Indian Nationalism**	Objective 4	10 min.	●	●	1.E, 8.D, 28.B	
Synthesize						
DIGITAL ACTIVITY **Positives and Negatives for India**		5 min.		●	1.E, 8.C, 8.D	
Demonstrate						
DIGITAL QUIZ **Lesson Quiz and Class Discussion Board**		10 min.		●	1.E, 8.D, 9.D	

PEARSON realize™ www.PearsonTexas.com Access your Digital Lesson

Focus on Texas Standards

Texas Essential Knowledge and Skills

1.E identify major causes and describe the major effects of the following important turning points in world history from 1750 to 1914: the Scientific Revolution, the Industrial Revolution and its impact on the development of modern economic systems, European imperialism, and the Enlightenment's impact on political revolutions

8.C identify the major political, economic, and social motivations that influenced European imperialism

8.D explain the major characteristics and impact of European imperialism

16.B analyze the influence of human and physical geographic factors on major events in world history, including the development of river valley civilizations, trade in the Indian Ocean, and the opening of the Panama and Suez canals

28.B explain the roles of military technology, transportation technology, communication technology, and medical advancements in initiating and advancing 19th century imperialism

NOTES

Topic 15 Lesson 5

China and the West

Objectives

Objective 1: Describe how Westerners tried to gain trade rights in China.

Objective 2: Explain how reformers tried to strengthen China.

Objective 3: Understand why the Qing dynasty fell.

LESSON 5 ORGANIZER	PACING: APPROX. 1 PERIOD, .5 BLOCKS					
			RESOURCES			
	OBJECTIVES	PACING	Print	Online	TEKS	ELPS
Connect						
DIGITAL START UP ACTIVITY **Trading Opium for Tea**		5 min.		●	8.D	
Investigate						
READ **Economic Interest in China**	Objective 1	10 min.	●	●	1.E, 8.C, 8.D, 28.B	4.F.6
INTERACTIVE MAP **Imperialist Spheres of Influence in China**		10 min.		●		
READ **The Taiping Rebellion and a Weakened China**	Objective 2	10 min.	●	●	8.D	
READ **Reform Efforts in China**		10 min.	●	●	1.E, 8.D	
READ **The Fall of the Qing Dynasty**	Objective 3	10 min.	●	●	1.E, 8.D, 9.D	
INTERACTIVE GALLERY **The Boxer Rebellion**		10 min.		●		
Synthesize						
DIGITAL ACTIVITY **The Decline of the Qing Dynasty**		5 min.		●	1.E, 8.D	
Demonstrate						
DIGITAL QUIZ **Lesson Quiz and Class Discussion Board**		10 min.		●	1.E, 8.C, 8.D	

Focus on Texas Standards

Texas Essential Knowledge and Skills

1.E identify major causes and describe the major effects of the following important turning points in world history from 1750 to 1914: the Scientific Revolution, the Industrial Revolution and its impact on the development of modern economic systems, European imperialism, and the Enlightenment's impact on political revolutions	**28.B** explain the roles of military technology, transportation technology, communication technology, and medical advancements in initiating and advancing 19th century imperialism

NOTES

The Modernization of Japan

Objectives

Objective 1: Identify the problems faced by Tokugawa Japan.

Objective 2: Explain how the United States opened Japan to the outside world.

Objective 3: Analyze the causes and effects of the Meiji Restoration.

Objective 4: Describe how Japan began to build an empire.

LESSON 6 ORGANIZER			PACING: APPROX. 1 PERIOD, .5 BLOCKS			
	OBJECTIVES	PACING	RESOURCES Print	RESOURCES Online	TEKS	ELPS
Connect						
DIGITAL START UP ACTIVITY **Adopting Western Ways**		5 min.		●	1.E	
Investigate						
READ **Unrest in Tokugawa Japan**	Objective 1	10 min.	●	●	1.E, 28.B	
READ **The Opening of Japan**	Objective 2	10 min.	●	●	1.E, 8.D, 28.B	4.F.7
INTERACTIVE IMAGE **Commodore Perry's Expedition to Japan**		10 min.		●	28.B	
READ **Transformation during the Meiji Period**	Objective 3	10 min.	●	●	1.E, 8.D, 28.B	4.J.1
INTERACTIVE GALLERY **The Meiji Restoration, 1868–1912**		10 min.		●	1.E, 8.D	
READ **Japan Builds an Empire**	Objective 4	10 min.	●	●	8.D, 28.B	
Synthesize						
DIGITAL ACTIVITY **The Meiji Restoration**		5 min.		●	1.E, 8.D	
Demonstrate						
DIGITAL QUIZ **Lesson Quiz and Class Discussion Board**		10 min.		●	1.E, 8.D, 28.B	

Focus on Texas Standards

Texas Essential Knowledge and Skills

1.E identify major causes and describe the major effects of the following important turning points in world history from 1750 to 1914: the Scientific Revolution, the Industrial Revolution and its impact on the development of modern economic systems, European imperialism, and the Enlightenment's impact on political revolutions	**28.B** explain the roles of military technology, transportation technology, communication technology, and medical advancements in initiating and advancing 19th century imperialism

NOTES

Southeast Asia and the Pacific

Objectives

Objective 1: Describe how Europe and the United States built colonies in Southeast Asia.

Objective 2: Explain how imperialism spread to the islands of the Pacific.

Objective 3: Analyze how Australia and New Zealand achieved self-rule.

LESSON 7 ORGANIZER		PACING: APPROX. 1 PERIOD, .5 BLOCKS				
			RESOURCES			
	OBJECTIVES	PACING	Print	Online	TEKS	ELPS
Connect						
DIGITAL START UP ACTIVITY **Europeans in Southeast Asia**		5 min.		●	1.E, 8.D	
Investigate						
READ **European Imperialism in Southeast Asia**	Objective 1	10 min.	●	●	1.E, 8.C, 8.D, 28.B	
READ **Military Might and the Philippines**	Objective 1	10 min.	●	●		
INTERACTIVE MAP **Imperialism in Southeast Asia, 1900**	Objective 1	10 min.		●		
READ **Strategic Holdings in the Pacific Islands**	Objective 2	10 min.	●	●	1.E, 8.C, 8.D, 16.B, 28.B	
READ **Europeans in Australia**	Objective 3	10 min.	●	●	1.E, 8.C, 8.D	4.F.8
READ **New Zealand's Story**	Objective 3	10 min.	●	●		
INTERACTIVE CHART **Colonization of Australia and New Zealand**	Objective 3	10 min.		●		
Synthesize						
DIGITAL ACTIVITY **The United States and the Philippines**		5 min.		●	1.E, 8.C, 8.D	
Demonstrate						
DIGITAL QUIZ **Lesson Quiz and Class Discussion Board**		10 min.		●	1.E, 8.C, 8.D	

PEARSON realize™ www.PearsonTexas.com Access your Digital Lesson

Focus on Texas Standards

Texas Essential Knowledge and Skills

1.E identify major causes and describe the major effects of the following important turning points in world history from 1750 to 1914: the Scientific Revolution, the Industrial Revolution and its impact on the development of modern economic systems, European imperialism, and the Enlightenment's impact on political revolutions

8.C identify the major political, economic, and social motivations that influenced European imperialism

16.B analyze the influence of human and physical geographic factors on major events in world history, including the development of river valley civilizations, trade in the Indian Ocean, and the opening of the Panama and Suez canals

28.B explain the roles of military technology, transportation technology, communication technology, and medical advancements in initiating and advancing 19th century imperialism

NOTES

The Americas in the Age of Imperialism

Objectives

Objective 1: Identify the political problems faced by new Latin American nations.

Objective 2: Describe Mexico's struggle to achieve stability.

Objective 3: Explain why Latin America entered a cycle of economic dependence.

Objective 4: Analyze the influence of the United States on Latin America, including the opening of the Panama Canal.

Objective 5: Analyze how Canada achieved self-rule.

LESSON 8 ORGANIZER	PACING: APPROX. 1 PERIOD, .5 BLOCKS					
			RESOURCES			
	OBJECTIVES	PACING	Print	Online	TEKS	ELPS
Connect						
DIGITAL START UP ACTIVITY **The United States and Latin America**		5 min.		●	1.E, 8.D	
Investigate						
READ **Political Problems Linger**	Objective 1	10 min.	●	●	1.E, 8.D, 28.B	
READ **Mexico's Search for Stability**	Objective 2	10 min.	●	●	1.E, 8.C, 8.D	4.F.9
READ **The Economics of Latin America's Dependence**	Objective 3	10 min.	●	●	1.E, 8.C, 8.D	
READ **The United States Wields Power and Influence**	Objective 4	10 min.	●	●	1.E, 8.C, 16.B, 28.B	
INTERACTIVE CARTOON **Uncle Sam Takes Off—United States Imperialism**		10 min.		●	8.D	
INTERACTIVE GALLERY **The Panama Canal**		10 min.		●	16.B, 28.B	
READ **Canada Achieves Self-Rule**	Objective 5	10 min.	●	●	1.E, 8.C, 8.D	
Synthesize						
DIGITAL ACTIVITY **Canada and Latin America**		5 min.		●	1.E, 8.D	
Demonstrate						
LESSON QUIZ **Lesson Quiz and Class Discussion Board**		10 min.		●	1.E, 8.D, 16.B	

Focus on Texas Standards

Texas Essential Knowledge and Skills

1.E identify major causes and describe the major effects of the following important turning points in world history from 1750 to 1914: the Scientific Revolution, the Industrial Revolution and its impact on the development of modern economic systems, European imperialism, and the Enlightenment's impact on political revolutions

8.C identify the major political, economic, and social motivations that influenced European imperialism

16.B analyze the influence of human and physical geographic factors on major events in world history, including the development of river valley civilizations, trade in the Indian Ocean, and the opening of the Panama and Suez canals

NOTES

The Age of Imperialism (1800–1914)

In this Topic, you will learn about the age of imperialism. You will also find lots of ways to investigate the ideas of this Topic and to master the TEKS.

Your study will help you master these TEKS:

TEKS
1.E, 8.C, 8.D, 9.D, 16.B, 22.C, 28.B, 29.D, 29.E, 29.F, 29.G

LESSON OUTLINE

- **15.1:** The New Imperialism **1.E, 8.C, 8.D, 28.B**
- **15.2:** European Colonies in Africa **1.E, 8.C, 28.B**
- **15.3:** Europe and the Muslim World **1.E, 8.C, 16.B, 22.C**
- **15.4:** India Becomes a British Colony **1.E, 8.C, 8.D, 16.B, 28.B**
- **15.5:** China and the West **1.E, 28.B**
- **15.6:** The Modernization of Japan **1.E, 28.B**
- **15.7:** Southeast Asia and the Pacific **1.E, 8.C, 16.B, 28.B**
- **15.8:** The Americas in the Age of Imperialism **1.E, 8.C, 16.B**

Connect

You will start by connecting with the Topic through a video that tells a personal story about imperialism. You will start to think about how the Topic connects with your own experience or to what you already know. And you'll get a chance to think about a really big question, or Essential Question: Why do people move?

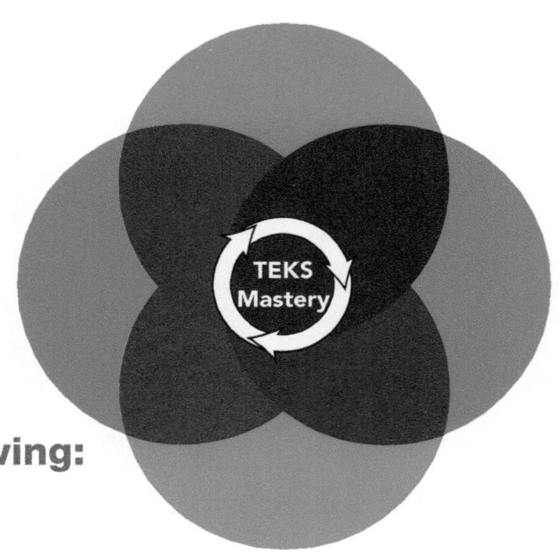

Begin your study by trying the following:

NBC LEARN Watch My Story Video:

Menelik II, Independence in the Age of Imperialism

Launch your Document-Based Question:

What was the Impact of Imperialism on India?

Investigate

The Lesson Outline lists all the lessons you will investigate in this Topic. As you read and interact with key content, the story of imperialism will come to life. Read the texts; try the interactivities. Investigate the fascinating story of how nations competed to conquer territory all over the world.

And keep working on your Document-Based Question to help build your mastery of the Topic TEKS.

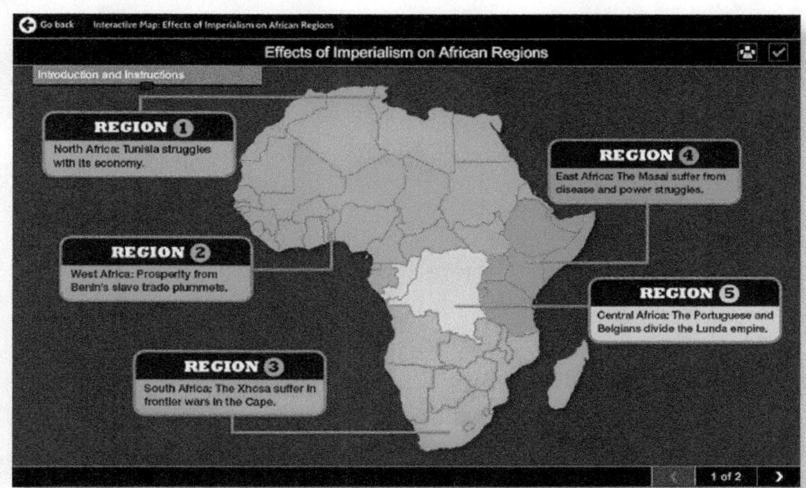

>> Digital interactivity from the online course

Synthesize

Next you will pull it all together by reflecting on the Essential Question. This will give you a chance to be the storyteller, to show how you would answer this big question: Why do people move?

Demonstrate

Finally, you can show what you know. You can write an essay, hold a discussion, or make a presentation. You can answer questions about every TEKS on the Topic Review and Assessment pages. Or you can finish your essay on the impact of imperialism on India.

TEKS in Topic 15	Topic Review and Assessment Questions
1.E	**3, 4**
8.C	**5, 6, 14**
8.D	**7, 8, 9**
9.D	**1, 2**
16.B	**10**
22.C	**11**
28.B	**12, 13, 15, 16**
29.G	**16**

Topic 15

The Age of Imperialism (1800–1914)

Introduction

The Industrial Revolution pushed the nations of Europe to move out into the world. Motivated by economic needs, nationalist ambitions, and the desire to spread European culture, Britain, France, and Germany established colonies in Africa and Asia. The United States and Japan quickly followed Europe's example.

ESSENTIAL QUESTION

Ask students to think about the Essential Question for this Topic: Why do people move? Share the following with students: During the Age of Imperialism, powerful countries established colonies abroad. The people who migrated to those colonies from their home countries moved for many reasons, including economic and political ones.

Hypothesize Think about each of these groups of people: soldiers, traders, government officials, missionaries. What was the motivation for each of these groups to go to the colonies? What roles did each group play? How might the goals of these groups conflict with one another? Would one group have a better chance at success than the others? Explain your opinion. *(Answers will vary. Students should recognize that each group had different goals. Traders, for example, hoped to make profits, and missionaries wanted to spread religious ideas. These goals could conflict with one another if two groups, such as soldiers and missionaries, tried to accomplish different ends among the same group of people. Students should be able to clearly state an opinion about chances of success and provide examples to support it.)*

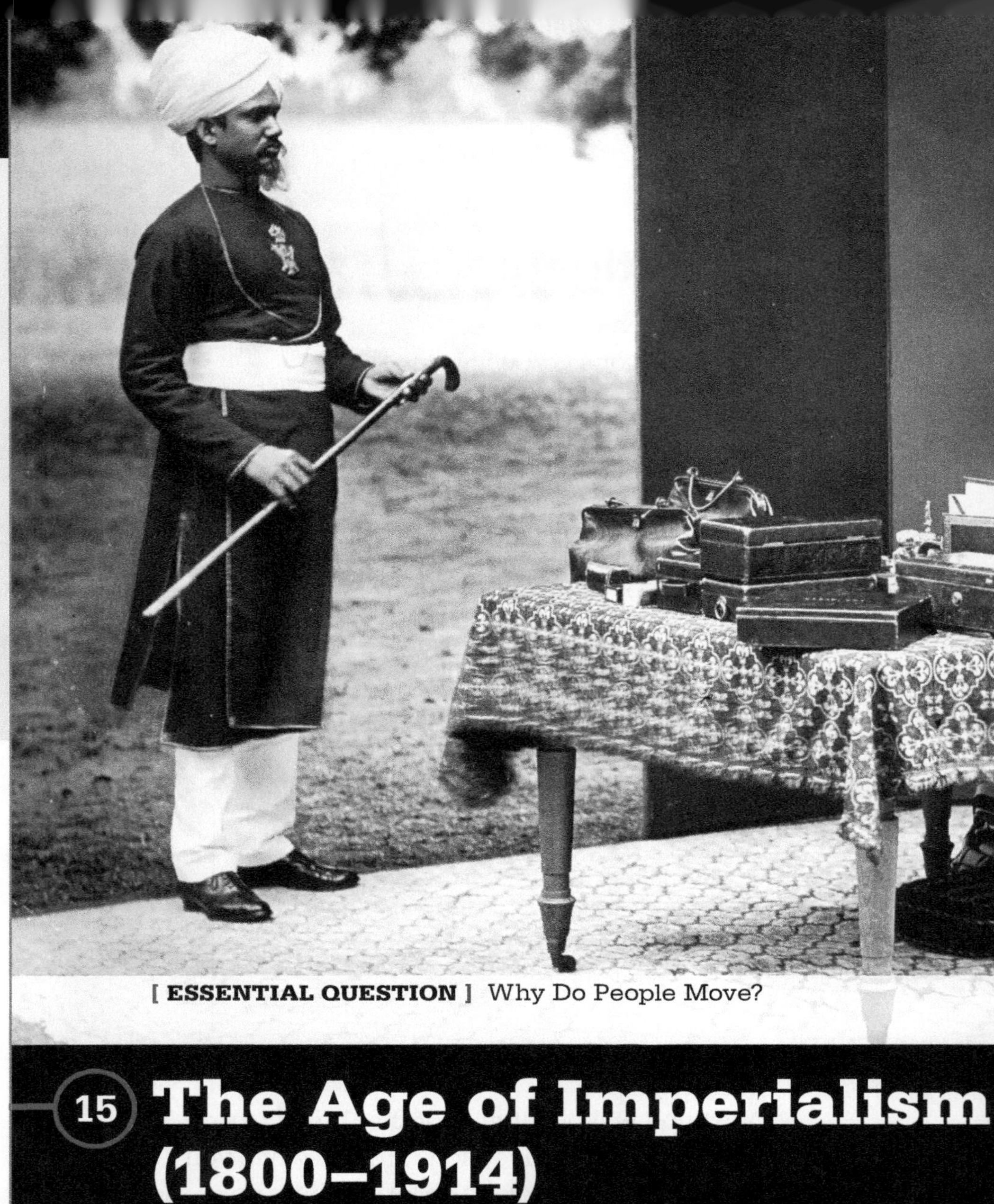

[**ESSENTIAL QUESTION**] Why Do People Move?

15 **The Age of Imperialism (1800–1914)**

Analyze Images

Ask students to examine the photograph, which shows Queen Elizabeth of Great Britain being "attended" by Hafiz Abdul Karim. Ask them where they think the man in the photograph comes from and what his job appears to be. *(His name and his dress suggest that he is a Muslim from South Asia. The presence of Queen Victoria in the photo, his demeanor, and the caption suggest that he is one of the queen's servants.)* Tell students that at the time, Britain ruled India as a colony.

>> Hafiz Abdul Karim attends to Queen Victoria, 1893

Enduring Understandings

- Motives for imperialism included the need for natural resources and new markets, racism, and the desire to spread Christianity.
- Using superior military technology, European powers divided up most of Africa and Southeast Asia, while India became a British colony.
- Many people resisted European rule, but Ethiopia and Siam avoided colonization.
- As Chinese power declined, western nations established spheres of influence in China.
- Japan responded to outside influences by rapidly modernizing and becoming an imperialist power.
- Latin American nations faced economic imperialism and the influence of the United States.

PEARSON realize
NBC LEARN
Watch the My Story Video to learn how Menelik II helped Ethiopia resist colonization during the Age of Imperialism.

PEARSON realize www.PearsonTexas.com

Access your digital lessons including: Topic Inquiry • Interactive Reading Notepad • Interactivities • Assessments

647

Topic Inquiry

If you choose to assign the Topic Inquiry, launch the DBQ Activity after introducing the Topic.

NBC LEARN MY STORY VIDEO

Project the My Story Video that introduces students to the Ethiopian leader Menelik II and his efforts to maintain his country's independence.

Online My Story Video: **Menelik II, Independence in the Age of Imperialism**.

After viewing, ask students to respond to the following questions:

Check Understanding What European country tried to colonize Ethiopia? *(Italy)*

Hypothesize What was the likely reaction to the news that Menelik's forces had defeated a European army in battle? *(Europeans, whose strength had enabled them to divide up most of Africa fairly easily, would have been shocked by news of the battle. Africans would have been encouraged by the news of Italy's failed effort to colonize Ethiopia.)*

OVERVIEW ACTIVITY

Online Project the **Timeline: The Age of Imperialism** showing important events during the Age of Imperialism. During this Topic, students will learn about these events and many more, but the timeline will provide a framework into which they can place the events they learn about.

Interpret When did the United States force Japan to open to trade? *(1854)* How long after that did Japan begin building its empire? *(40 years)*

Infer The events for the years 1854 and 1899 both use the word *forces*. What does that tell you about the events? *(Sample response: that the events happened against the will or wishes of Japan and China)*

Topic 15 Lesson 1

The New Imperialism

CONNECT

Preview Have students preview the **Lesson Objectives** and the list of **Key Terms**.

Students can also preview all the **Key Terms** and **Academic Vocabulary** using the **Interactive Reading Notepad** on the digital course or preview a summary of the lesson in the **Reading and Note Taking Study Guide**.

Online Use the **Editable Presentation** found on the digital course to present the main ideas for this lesson.

Start Up Activity

A British imperialist, Frederick Lugard, justified colonization of Africa because of the need "to provide for our ever-growing population." Colonies, he said, offered land for British settlers, jobs for British workers, and markets for British goods. Ask students what Lugard's statements imply about his attitude toward Africans. *(He seems to believe that Africans are less important than the British, that the rights of the British outweigh Africans' rights.)*

Online You can also project the **Start Up Activity** from the course.

INVESTIGATE

Have students read the lesson using the **Reading and Note Taking Study Guide** to help them take notes and understand the text as they read.

Motivations for the New Imperialism

Remind students that the first phase of imperialism, starting in the 1500s, involved Portugal, Spain, Britain, France, and the Netherlands. Tell them that the new imperialism was driven by the advancements of the Industrial Revolution, which created a need for raw materials and new markets. Europeans who believed in their own cultural and racial superiority wanted to spread Western civilization and dominate those they considered weaker races.

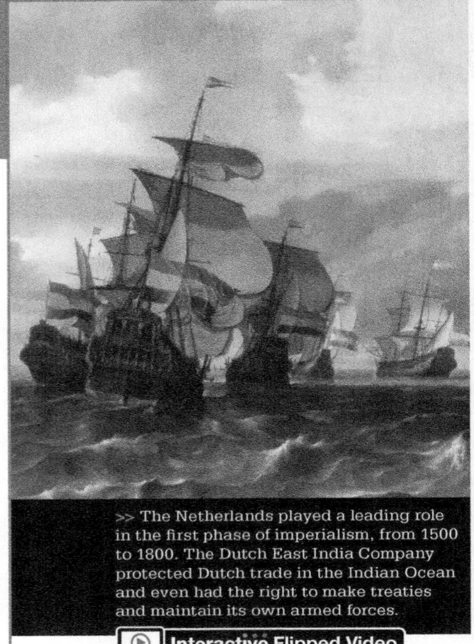

>> The Netherlands played a leading role in the first phase of imperialism, from 1500 to 1800. The Dutch East India Company protected Dutch trade in the Indian Ocean and even had the right to make treaties and maintain its own armed forces.

Interactive Flipped Video

15.1 The Industrial Revolution transformed the West. Advances in science and technology, industry, transportation, and communication provided Western nations with many advantages. Armed with new economic and political power, Western nations set out to dominate the world, building extensive overseas empires in the late 1800s.

TEKS
1.E, 8.C, 8.D, 28.B

>> Objectives

Explain the political, economic, and social causes of European imperialism.

Understand how technology and other factors contributed to the spread of imperialism.

Describe the characteristics of imperial rule.

Summarize the cultural, political, and social effects of imperialism.

>> Key Terms

imperialism
protectorate
sphere of influence

The New Imperialism

Motivations for the New Imperialism

European imperialism did not begin in the 1800s. **Imperialism** is the domination by one country of the political, economic, or cultural life of another country or region. As you have learned, European states won empires in the Americas after 1492, established colonies in South Asia, and gained toeholds on the coasts of Africa and China. Despite these gains, between 1500 and 1800, Europe had little influence on the lives of the peoples of China, India, or Africa.

By the 1800s, however, Europe had gained considerable power. Strong, centrally governed nation-states had emerged, and the Industrial Revolution had greatly enriched European economies. Encouraged by their new economic and military strength, Europeans embarked on a path of aggressive expansion that today's historians call the "new imperialism."

In just a few decades, beginning in the 1870s, Europeans brought much of the world under their influence and control. Like other key developments in world history, the new imperialism exploded out of a combination of causes.

Need for Resources Drives Further Expansion Capitalism was a driving force behind the new imperialism. The Industrial Revolution

PEARSON realize. www.PearsonTexas.com Access your Digital Lesson.

648

Aa Vocabulary Builder

1. Have students pronounce the following academic vocabulary term in this lesson and clarify the part of speech. Break the term into syllables and pronounce it with the students.
2. Explain what the word means in common "student-friendly" language using synonyms and antonyms when possible. Provide concrete examples to clarify the meaning, and rephrase the definition.

prestige: the power to impress or influence because of success or wealth created needs and desires that spurred overseas expansion. Manufacturers wanted access to natural resources such as rubber, petroleum, manganese for steel, and palm oil for machinery. They also hoped for new markets of consumers to whom they could sell their factory goods.

Bankers sought ventures in which to invest their profits. In addition, colonies offered a valuable outlet for Europe's growing population.

Political and Military Causes Political and military issues were closely linked to economic motives. Steam-powered merchant ships and naval vessels needed bases around the world to take on coal and supplies. Industrial powers seized islands or harbors to satisfy these needs.

Nationalism played an important role, too. When France, for example, moved into West Africa, rival nations like Britain and Germany seized lands nearby to halt further French expansion. Western leaders claimed that colonies were needed for national security. They also felt that ruling a global empire increased a nation's prestige around the world.

Humanitarian and Religious Motives Many Westerners felt a genuine concern for their "little brothers" beyond the seas. Missionaries, doctors, and colonial officials believed they had a duty to spread what they saw as the blessings of Western civilization, including its medicine, law, and Christian religion.

Social Darwinism's Impact Behind the idea of the West's civilizing mission was a growing sense of racial superiority. Many Westerners had embraced the ideas of Social Darwinism. They applied Darwin's ideas about natural selection and survival of the fittest to human societies. European races, they argued, were superior to all others, and imperial domination of weaker races was simply nature's way of improving the human species. As a result, millions of non-Westerners were robbed of their cultural heritage.

SUMMARIZE What main factors contributed to European imperialism in the 1800s?

ELPS **ELPS 4.F.2** Practice using visuals to enhance your understanding of *Motivations for the New Imperialism.*

Western Imperialism Spreads Rapidly

From about 1870 to 1914, imperialist nations gained control over much of the world. Leading the way were soldiers, merchants, settlers, missionaries, and explorers. In Europe, imperial expansion found favor with all classes, from bankers and manufacturers to workers. Western imperialism expanded rapidly for a number of reasons.

Vulnerable Non-Western States While European nations had grown stronger in the 1800s, several older civilizations were in decline, especially the Ottoman Middle East, Mughal (MOO gul) India, and Qing (ching) China. In West Africa, wars among African peoples and the damaging effect of the slave trade had undermined established empires, kingdoms, and city-states. Newer African states were not strong enough to resist the Western onslaught.

Western Advantages European powers had the advantages of strong economies, well-organized governments, and powerful armies and navies. Superior technology, including riverboats and the telegraph, as well as improved medical knowledge also

>> The growth of European industrial economies required raw materials to fuel its factories. New colonies provided both natural resources and new markets for European manufactured goods.

Interactive Map

Topic 15 Lesson 1

Online Project the **Interactive Map: The New Imperialism**, and click through the screens with students.

ACTIVE CLASSROOM

Use the Make Headlines strategy to have students write a headline that captures the most important aspect of the new imperialism. Have them pass their headline to a partner for them to review.

Guided Reading and Discussion

Ask students to identify the motivations of the new imperialism. *(Motivations included the need for raw materials and for new markets for manufactured goods; the need for naval bases; and the desire to spread Christianity. Social Darwinism played a role by helping justify imperialism; so did nationalism.)*

Infer How could nationalism lead to competition and conflict among imperialist powers? *(Sample response: Imperialist powers could fight over a particular colony, especially if that colony were rich in natural resources.)*

Western Imperialism Spreads Rapidly

Tell students that Western imperialism spread very quickly in the years between 1870 and 1914 for a number of reasons, including weaknesses in non-Western states and Western technological advantages.

English Language Proficiency Standards

Reading 4.F.2 Using the selection "Need for Resources Drives Further Expansion" and the image of an industrialized city in Europe in the late 1800s, have students complete one of the following:

Beginning Draw attention to the image. Read the caption aloud. Retell the content of the selection and use a Think Aloud strategy to model how an image improves understanding.

Intermediate Use the Beginning activity, but ask students to describe the image and explain how it improves understanding of the selection.

Advanced Have students describe the image. Invite a volunteer to read the caption. Have students reread the selection. Discuss how the image improves understanding of the content.

Advanced High Have groups of students examine the image, read the caption aloud, and work together to describe the image. Have groups reread the selection and discuss how the image improves understanding of the content.

Answers

Summarize *economic motives, political and military missions, humanitarian and religious beliefs, and Social Darwinist ideas*

Topic 15 Lesson 1

Online **Project the Interactive Gallery: Technology Advances Imperialism**. Examine each photo individually, and then view the gallery as a whole. Have students answer the question at the end individually, in small groups, or as a class.

ACTIVE CLASSROOM

Ask students to Take a Stand on this question: Could the new imperialism have occurred without the advances of the Industrial Revolution? Ask students to divide into two groups based on their answer and move to separate areas. Have each group discuss the reasons behind their answer and choose three to five details that best support their opinion. Ask a representative from each side to present and defend the group's stance.

Guided Reading and Discussion

Ask students to explain why Western imperialism expanded as quickly as it did. *(Sample response: The West had many technological advantages in medicine, weapons, communications, and transportation. Also, many of the areas that became colonies had been weakened by the slave trade, civil war, or the decline of a ruling empire.)*

Types of Imperial Rule

Tell students that under the new imperialism, European control of colonies took different forms: direct rule (officials and soldiers ruled the colony), indirect rule (colonized people helped rule), protectorate (local rulers were left in place but answered to the imperialist), and spheres of influence (the imperialist had exclusive trading privileges, but the country remained independent).

Key Terms

Call students' attention to the term **protectorate** (in bold) in the text. Point out the base word *protect,* and tell students that in this form of rule, the imperialist power claimed that it would protect the colony.

>> American author Mark Twain was an outspoken critic of both imperialism and the brutal Belgian rule in the Congo. In 1905, he published *King Leopold's Soliloquy,* which brought international attention to the situation.

played a role. Quinine and other new medicines helped Europeans survive deadly tropical diseases. And, of course, advances such as Maxim machine guns, repeating rifles, and steam-driven warships were very strong arguments in persuading Africans and Asians to accept Western control.

Some Resist Imperialism Africans and Asians strongly resisted Western expansion into their lands. Some people fought the invaders, even though they had no weapons to equal the Maxim gun. Ruling groups in certain areas tried to strengthen their societies against outsiders by reforming their own Muslim, Hindu, or Confucian traditions. Finally, many Western-educated Africans and Asians organized nationalist movements to expel the imperialists from their lands.

Critics at Home In the West itself, a small group of anti-imperialists emerged. Some argued that colonialism was a tool of the rich. Others said it was immoral. Westerners, they pointed out, were moving toward greater democracy at home but were imposing undemocratic rule on other peoples.

EXPLAIN How did Western imperialism spread through Africa and Asia so quickly?

>> The French practiced direct rule in their colonies. Here, French soldiers speak with an Algerian man. **Infer** What were the costs and benefits of direct rule?

Types of Imperial Rule

The leading imperial powers developed several kinds of colonial rule. Each of the different types reflected different goals for their colonies.

Direct and Indirect Rule The French practiced direct rule, sending officials and soldiers from France to administer their colonies. Their goal was to impose French culture on their colonies and turn them into French provinces.

The British, by contrast, often used a system of indirect rule. To govern their colonies, they used sultans, chiefs, or other local rulers. They then encouraged the children of the local ruling class to get an education in Britain. In that way, they groomed a new "Westernized" generation of leaders to continue indirect imperial rule and to spread British civilization. Like France and other imperialist nations, however, Britain could still resort to military force if its control over a colony was threatened.

Other Types of Imperial Rule In a **protectorate** local rulers were left in place but were expected to follow the advice of European advisers on issues such as trade or missionary activity. A protectorate cost less

English Language Proficiency Standards

Reading 4.G.4 Read "Types of Imperial Rule" aloud to the class. Have students complete one activity according to their level of English proficiency.

Beginning Reread the subsection "Direct and Indirect Rule" aloud to students. Demonstrate how to take notes on direct rule. Then ask students to help you take notes on indirect rule. Write and display notes for students, and instruct them to copy the notes into their notebooks.

Intermediate Reread the subsection "Direct and Indirect Rule" aloud. Invite small groups of students to share ideas for notes on this section. Write and display notes. Discuss which notes most accurately reflect the text. Once a set of notes has been decided upon, instruct students to copy them into their notebooks.

Advanced Have students work with a partner to reread and take notes on "Types of Imperial Rule." Circulate among students to offer support

Answers

Explain *Westerners had stronger economies, governments, and technology, along with the necessary military power.*

Infer *Sample response: costs: expensive to administer because you would need all French administrators; benefits: more control*

to run than a colony did and usually did not require a large commitment of military forces.

A third form of Western control was the **sphere of influence,** an area in which an outside power claimed exclusive investment or trading privileges. Europeans carved out these spheres in China and elsewhere to prevent conflicts among themselves.

COMPARE AND CONTRAST Compare and contrast how Britain and France ruled their colonies.

ELPS **ELPS 4.G.4** Take notes on *Types of Imperial Rule.*

>> In China, Western nations had trading centers on the waterfront in Shanghai. **Classify** Which form of imperialism was used in China?

The Effects of Imperialism

Western imperialism had an enormous impact around the world. It affected different places in different ways, but there were some common effects in colonized territories.

Cultural Changes Missionaries spread Christianity and European languages to colonized people as they established schools and hospitals. Some colonized peoples came to believe in Western superiority and lost confidence in their own culture. Economic and political disruption weakened pre-colonial traditions in some areas, especially where family members were forced to travel long distances to find work.

Political Changes New colonial administrations changed traditional political units. In India, for example, British officials worked with local rulers to meet their goals.

Colonizers often defined the borders of their new colonies without an understanding of the local political or ethnic situations. Colonized people took on European ideas of nationalism and agitated for their own independence.

Economic Changes In order to meet the export goals of their colonial rulers, colonized people often grew cash crops instead of food they could eat. As they became part of a money-driven capitalist economy, some colonized people were forced to work for their colonial rulers so that they could pay their taxes. Imports of machine-made goods destroyed indigenous cottage industries.

 **CATEGORIZE** How is migrating to find work a cultural as well as an economic effect of imperialism?

>> Missionaries brought not only religion, but cultural change. Girls at this French missionary school in China learn Christmas carols. **Analyze Context** What evidence can you find in the photo that this is a missionary school?

Topic 15 Lesson 1

Guided Reading and Discussion

Have students discuss which form of imperial rule would be most effective, especially in terms of cost and level of control—direct, indirect, or protectorate. *(Students should identify benefits and potential problems of each form and should support their choice with examples.)*

Analyze Images

Point out the image of the Shanghai waterfront and have students read the caption. Ask: What does the image tell you about foreigners in China during the Age of Imperialism? *(Sample responses: Foreigners maintained their own businesses and trading houses. Foreigners were more interested in China's trade than in controlling it as a colony.)*

The Effects of Imperialism

Explain to students that imperialism had a huge impact worldwide, including cultural changes such as the spread of Christianity and the loss of older cultures, political changes such as the redrawing of borders without regard for local ethnic situations, and economic changes such as conversion to economies based on cash crops and destruction of local industries.

Guided Reading and Discussion

Review with students the changes that imperialism brought to the world. Have them classify each change as positive or negative. *(Positive: more global communities; imperialist states got very rich and powerful; Western ideas of government were exported. Negative: decline of local cultures; cash crops grown instead of food; local cottage industries declined; workers and resources exploited for the benefit of imperialist powers.)*

and feedback. Instruct students to make sure their notes accurately reflect the information in the text.

Advanced High Have students reread and take notes on "Types of Imperial Rule." Circulate among students to offer support and feedback. Then have students share their notes with a partner to ensure accuracy.

Answers

Classify *spheres of influence*

Compare and Contrast *France practiced direct rule, whereas Britain often used indirect rule, through a local ruling class.*

Analyze Context *Sample response: There is a nun wearing a habit; students wear uniforms.*

Categorize *Pre-colonial traditions were weakened when many community members migrated to find work to pay their taxes.*

Topic 15 Lesson 1

SYNTHESIZE

Online Project the **Digital Activity: Imperialism—Different Opinions**. Have students answer the questions. *(Sample responses: 1. Rhodes reasons that the English are superior to other races and should spread across the world. 2. Kabongo declares that Africans elect their own leaders and make their own rules. 3. Rhodes believed he was part of a superior race, which justified imperialism. Kabongo is angry with the Westerners who seized power from the local people.)*

DEMONSTRATE

Online Assign the **Digital Lesson Quiz** for this lesson if you haven't already done so. Students will be offered automatic remediation or enrichment based on their score.

Pose this question to the class on the Discussion Board:

In "The New Imperialism," you read about the causes and effects of Western imperialism in the 1800s. Driven by economic, political, and social motivations, Europeans brought new political systems, economic systems, and cultural ideas to Africa and Asia.

Predict Consequences What would the world be like if there hadn't been an "Age of Imperialism"? *(Responses will vary. Some students may focus on a lack of unity in world languages, religions, etc.; others may suggest that African and Asian countries would have become stronger if they hadn't lost their independence.)*

Topic Inquiry

Have students continue their investigations for the Topic Inquiry.

ASSESSMENT

1. **Identify Cause and Effect** How did the Industrial Revolution lead to the new imperialism?
2. **Cite Evidence** How did Western nations come to dominate much of the world in the late 1800s?
3. **Distinguish** Why was Social Darwinism important to the new imperialism?
4. **Summarize** What were the long-term effects of imperialism on the colonized peoples?
5. **Predict Consequences** How might grouping several rival ethnic groups into one political unit cause friction once that region gains independence?

Assessment

1. As Western nations industrialized, they needed to acquire sources of raw materials and new markets for their products. The colonies provided these raw materials, as well as new customers.
2. Western scientific, technological, and economic progress during the Industrial Revolution led to strong economies, well-organized governments, and powerful militaries that allowed Western nations to dominate much of the world.
3. It gave Westerners a belief that they were racially superior to colonized peoples and justified their rule.
4. Their culture was changed to reflect Western beliefs, they adopted European ideas of nationalism, and their economies focused on cash crops. Many non-Westerners were robbed of their cultural heritage.
5. Sample response: The rivals might fight each other when not restricted by colonial rule.

15.2 **In the late 1800s, Britain, France, Germany, and other European powers began a scramble for African territories. Within about 20 years, the Europeans had carved up the continent and dominated millions of Africans. Although colonial peoples resisted, they could not prevent European conquest.**

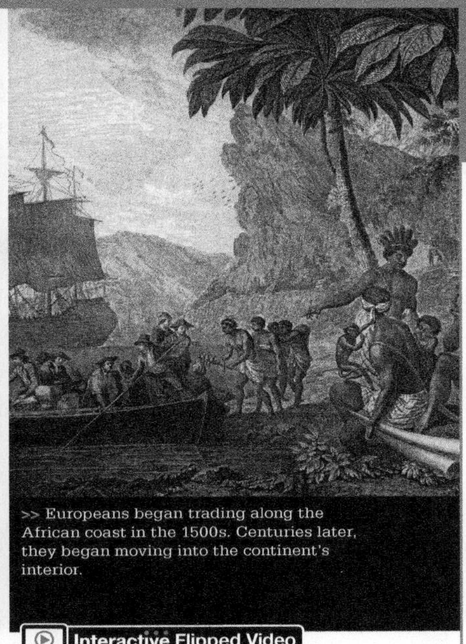

>> Europeans began trading along the African coast in the 1500s. Centuries later, they began moving into the continent's interior.

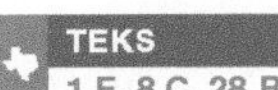

Interactive Flipped Video

European Colonies in Africa

TEKS
1.E, 8.C, 28.B

>> Objectives

Describe the forces that shaped Africa in the early 1800s.

Explain why European contact with Africa increased.

Analyze how European nations carved up Africa.

Describe African resistance to imperialism.

>> Key Terms

Usman dan Fodio
Shaka
paternalistic
David Livingstone
Henry Stanley
Leopold II
Boer War
Samori Touré
Yaa Asantewaa
Nehanda
Menelik II
elite

Africa Before Imperialism

To understand the impact of European domination, we must look at Africa in the early 1800s, before the scramble for colonies began. Africa is a huge continent, nearly three times the size of Europe. Across its many regions, people spoke hundreds of languages and had developed varied governments. Some people lived in large centralized states, while others lived in village communities.

North Africa North Africa includes the enormous Sahara and the fertile land along the Mediterranean. Since long before 1800, the region was a part of the Muslim world. In the early 1800s, much of North Africa remained under the rule of the declining Ottoman empire.

Islamic Conquest in West Africa By the early 1800s, an Islamic revival spread across West Africa. It began among the Fulani people in northern Nigeria. The scholar and preacher **Usman dan Fodio** (oo SMAHN dahn foh DEE oh) denounced the corruption of the local Hausa rulers. He called for social and religious reforms based on the sharia, or Islamic law. Usman inspired Fulani herders and Hausa townspeople to rise up against their European rulers.

PEARSON realize. www.PearsonTexas.com Access your Digital Lesson.

Topic 15 Lesson 2

European Colonies in Africa

CONNECT

Preview Have students preview the **Lesson Objectives** and the list of **Key Terms**.

Students can also preview all the **Key Terms** and **Academic Vocabulary** using the **Interactive Reading Notepad** on the digital course or preview a summary of the lesson in the **Reading and Note Taking Study Guide**.

Online Use the **Editable Presentation** found on the digital course to present the main ideas for this lesson.

Start Up Activity

Tell students that many Africans opposed Western attempts to dominate them. Have them read this statement from the leader of the Yao people to a German officer.

> "If it be friendship that you desire, then I am ready for it . . . but to be your subject, that I cannot be . . . I do not fall at your feet, for you are God's creature just as I am."

Ask students to predict what this chief would have done if Europeans had tried to force him and his people to submit.

Online You can also project the **Start Up Activity** from the course.

INVESTIGATE

Have students read the lesson using the **Reading and Note Taking Study Guide** to help them take notes and understand the text as they read.

Africa Before Imperialism

Tell students that before the European scramble for African colonies, the continent's population was diverse in language, government, and culture. North Africa was under weakening Muslim rule. Powerful states were emerging in West Africa. South Africa was caught in a series of wars, and the slave trade shaped life in both East and West Africa.

Aa Vocabulary Builder

1. Have students pronounce the following academic vocabulary terms in this lesson and clarify the part of speech. For difficult or polysyllabic words, break them into syllables and pronounce them with the students.
2. Explain what the word means in common "student-friendly" language using synonyms and antonyms when possible. Provide concrete examples to clarify the meaning, and rephrase the definition.

domain: territory over which rule or control is exercised

exploited: taken advantage of

Topic 15 Lesson 2

Online Project the **Interactive Map: Effects of Imperialism on African Regions**, and click through the regions with students.

ACTIVE CLASSROOM

Project the image of Benin's leaders in Region 2. Use a whiteboard tool to divide it into four numbered quadrants. Have students count off 1 to 4. Then ask them to take A Closer Look at the part of the image in their quadrant. Have groups describe what they see. Then, ask a representative of each group to present the group's findings. As a class, develop a full description of the process of trading on the African coast.

Guided Reading and Discussion

Have students summarize the situations in the different regions of Africa in the early 1800s. *(The Ottoman empire was declining in North Africa; in West Africa, Muslims were gaining power; in East Africa, they traded slaves and goods with India; and in South Africa, the Boers, white settlers who had been in South Africa since the 1600s, were fighting the Zulus.)*

European Contact Increases

Tell students that before the Age of Imperialism, Europeans traded with Africans but were prevented from moving into Africa's interior by African resistance, geographic obstacles, and disease. Medical advances and river steamships changed all that in the 1800s. The arrival of explorers and Christian missionaries such as Dr. David Livingstone opened the African continent to European imperialism.

Usman and his successors set up a powerful Islamic state in northern Nigeria. Under their rule, literacy increased, local wars quieted, and trade improved. Their success inspired other Muslim reform movements in West Africa. Between about 1780 and 1880, more than a dozen Islamic leaders rose to power, replacing old rulers or founding new states in the western Sudan.

In the forest regions, strong states like the Asante (uh SAHN teh) kingdom had arisen. The Asante traded with Europeans and Muslims and controlled several smaller states. However, these tributary states were ready to turn to Europeans or others who might help them defeat their Asante rulers.

East Africa Islam had long influenced the east coast of Africa, where port cities like Mombasa (mahm BAH suh) and Kilwa (KEEL wah) carried on profitable trade. The cargoes were often slaves. Captives were marched from the interior to the coast to be shipped as slaves to the Middle East. Ivory and copper from Central Africa were also exchanged for goods such as cloth and firearms from India.

Southern Africa In the early 1800s, the Zulus emerged as a major force in southern Africa under a ruthless and brilliant leader, **Shaka.** Between 1818 and 1828, Shaka waged relentless war and conquered many nearby peoples. He absorbed their young men and women into Zulu regiments. By encouraging rival groups to forget their differences, he cemented a growing pride in the Zulu kingdom.

>> East African port cities often served as centers for the slave trade. This slave market was on the island of Zanzibar.

Interactive Map

His conquests, however, set off mass migrations and wars, creating chaos across much of the region. Groups driven from their homelands by the Zulus then migrated north, conquering still other peoples and creating their own powerful states. By the 1830s, the Zulus faced a new threat, the arrival of well-armed, mounted Boers, descendants of Dutch farmers who were migrating north from the Cape Colony.

In 1814, the Cape Colony had passed from the Dutch to the British. Many Boers resented British laws that abolished slavery and otherwise interfered with their way of life. To escape British rule, they loaded their goods into covered wagons and started north. Several thousand Boer families joined this "Great Trek."

As the migrating Boers came into contact with Zulus, fighting quickly broke out. At first, Zulu regiments held their own. But in the end, Zulu spears could not defeat Boer guns. The struggle for control of the land would rage until the end of the century.

The Effect of the Slave Trade In the early 1800s, European nations began to outlaw the transatlantic slave trade, though it took years to end. Meanwhile, the East African slave trade continued to Asia.

Some people helped freed slaves resettle in Africa. In 1787, the British organized Sierra Leone in West Africa as a colony for former slaves. Later, some free blacks from the United States settled in nearby Liberia. By 1847, Liberia had become an independent republic.

? SUMMARIZE What factors shaped each of the main regions of Africa during the early 1800s?

European Contact Increases

From the 1500s through the 1700s, Europeans traded along the African coast. Africans wanted to trade with Europeans but did not want to "house them." Resistance by Africans, difficult geography, and diseases all kept Europeans from moving into the interior regions of the continent. Medical advances and river steamships changed all that in the 1800s.

Explorers Move into Africa's Interior In the early 1800s, European explorers began pushing into the interior of Africa. Explorers like Mungo Park and Richard Burton set out to map the course and sources of the great African rivers such as the Niger, the Nile, and the

Answers

Summarize *In Muslim North Africa, the Ottoman empire was declining. In West Africa, new Muslim leaders and strong kingdoms like the Asante held power. In East Africa, the slave trade continued. In South Africa, Zulus and Boers battled for control.*

Recall *Medical advances and steamships allowed explorers and missionaries to push deep into Africa's interior.*

Congo. They were fascinated by African geography, but they had little understanding of the peoples they met. All, however, endured great hardships while exploring Africa.

Missionaries Follow Explorers Catholic and Protestant missionaries followed the explorers. All across Africa, they sought to win people to Christianity. The missionaries were sincere in their desire to help Africans. They built schools and medical clinics alongside churches. They also focused attention on the evils of the slave trade. Still, missionaries, like most Westerners, took a **paternalistic** view of Africans, meaning they saw them as children in need of guidance. To them, African cultures and religions were "degraded." They urged Africans to reject their own traditions in favor of Western civilization.

Livingstone's Explorations The best-known explorer and missionary was Dr. **David Livingstone.** For 30 years, he crisscrossed Africa. He wrote about the many peoples he met with more sympathy and less bias than did most Europeans.

He relentlessly opposed the slave trade, which remained a profitable business for some African rulers and foreign traders. The only way to end this cruel traffic, he believed, was to open up the interior of Africa to Christianity and trade.

Livingstone blazed a trail that others soon followed. In 1869, the journalist **Henry Stanley** trekked into Central Africa to find Livingstone, who had not been heard from for years. He finally tracked him down in 1871 in what is today Tanzania, greeting him with the now-legendary question "Dr. Livingstone, I presume?"

RECALL Why did European contact with Africa increase in the late 1800s?

ELPS 4.F.3 Practice using context clues to understand new words in *European Contact Increases.*

>> Freetown, Sierra Leone, was settled by freed slaves from all over the world. Many had their origins in regions of Africa. Sierra Leone became a center of education for Africans.

European Nations Scramble for Colonies

Shortly afterward, King **Leopold II** of Belgium hired Stanley to explore the Congo River basin and arrange trade treaties with African leaders. Publicly, Leopold spoke of a civilizing mission to carry the light "that for millions of men still plunged in barbarism will be the dawn of a better era." Privately, he dreamed of conquest and profit. Leopold's activities in the Congo set off a scramble by other nations. Before long, Britain, France, and Germany were pressing rival claims to the region.

Conference in Berlin To avoid bloodshed, European powers met at an international conference in 1884. It took place not in Africa but in Berlin, Germany. No Africans were invited to the conference. At the Berlin Conference, European powers recognized Leopold's private claims to the Congo Free State but called for free trade on the Congo and Niger rivers. They further agreed that a European power could not claim any part of Africa unless it had set up a government office there. This principle led Europeans to send officials who would exert their power over local rulers and peoples.

The rush to colonize Africa was on. In the 20 years after the Berlin Conference, the European powers partitioned almost the entire continent. As Europeans carved out their claims, they established new borders and frontiers. They redrew the map of Africa with little regard for traditional patterns of settlement or ethnic boundaries.

Leopold's Horror in the Congo Leopold and other wealthy Belgians exploited the riches of the Congo, including its copper, rubber, and ivory. Soon, there were horrifying reports of Belgian overseers brutalizing villagers. Forced to work for almost nothing, laborers were savagely beaten or mutilated. The overall population declined drastically.

Guided Reading and Discussion

Have groups of students each make a list of pros and cons about missionaries in Africa. *(Sample pros: Missionaries established schools and hospitals and worked to end the slave trade. Sample cons: Local people lost some of their own culture and traditions; missionaries treated Africans like children.)*

D Differentiate **Extra Support** Give students a two-column chart to help with the Guided Reading activity. Have them label one column "Pros" and the other "Cons," making sure they know what those terms mean.

Key Terms

Call students' attention to the term **paternalistic** (in bold) in the text. Explain that the Latin word *pater* means "father." Thus people with a paternalistic view of others acted like a father toward them.

Analyze Images

Have students examine the image of Freetown, Sierra Leone, and read the caption. Tell them that Freetown, founded in the late 1700s, had an excellent harbor. Discuss with students how this image reflects the spirit of people who had once been slaves but now are free, and why they focused on education.

European Nations Scramble for Colonies

Tell students that the European scramble for African colonies began when King Leopold II of Belgium seized the Congo. His actions led to the Berlin Conference, in which European leaders established ground rules for colonizing Africa.

English Language Proficiency Standards

Reading 4.F.3 Explain that using context clues—the words and phrases around a new vocabulary word—can help students understand the meaning of the word. Then read "European Contact Increases" aloud. Instruct students to complete one of the following activities based on their level of English proficiency.

Beginning Read the following sentences aloud, and have students repeat them. Use a Think Aloud to model how to use context clues to determine the meaning of the word *missionaries*.

Catholic and Protestant missionaries followed the explorers. All across Africa, they sought to win people to Christianity.

Intermediate Follow the instructions in the Beginning activity, but lead students through the process of using context clues to determine the meaning of the word *missionaries*.

Advanced Invite a student volunteer to read the following sentences aloud. Ask small groups of students to work together to develop and explain the steps they took to use context clues to determine the meaning of the word *missionaries*. Then have students share their processes with their peers.

Catholic and Protestant missionaries followed the explorers. All across Africa, they sought to win people to Christianity.

Advanced High Follow the instructions in the Advanced activity, but ask pairs of students to work together.

Topic 15 Lesson 2

Online Project the **Interactive Map: European Imperialism in Africa**, and move the slider with students.

ACTIVE CLASSROOM

Discuss the image of the Asante people on the next page. Ask each student to choose one person from the photo. Then ask them to use the If Photos Could Talk strategy to write a description of what that person had been doing in the 10 minutes before the picture was taken, and what he did in the 10 minutes after it was taken. To extend this, you could ask them to state what their person was thinking.

Guided Reading and Discussion

Tell students that at the Berlin Conference, European leaders agreed that a European power could not claim any part of Africa unless it had set up a government office there. Ask students to explain what this principle led to. *(a rush to colonize Africa—European nations sent officials who would exert their power over local rulers and peoples—and the partitioning of nearly the whole continent)*

African Resistance

Tell students that many Africans resisted European imperialism, including the Algerians, the Zulus, and the Asante. One kingdom that fought the Europeans was the Ethiopians, who defeated the Italians trying to claim their land. In other parts of Africa, European education helped create an African elite that established nationalist movements to achieve self-determination.

Guided Reading and Discussion

Remind students that Europeans used their advanced technology to spread imperialism. How did Menelik II use European technology to stop the spread of imperialism in Ethiopia? *(Menelik modernized his country's transportation system with European-built railroads and his army with European weapons and training. He used these modernizations to fight off an Italian invasion.)*

Eventually, international outrage forced Leopold to turn over his personal colony to the Belgian government. It became the Belgian Congo in 1908. Under Belgian rule, the worst abuses were ended. Still, the Belgians regarded the Congo as a possession to be exploited. Africans were given little or no role in the government, and the wealth of their mines went out of the country to Europe.

France Expands Its Territory France took a giant share of Africa. In the 1830s, it had invaded and conquered Algeria in North Africa. The victory cost tens of thousands of French lives and killed many times more Algerians. In the late 1800s, France extended its influence along the Mediterranean into Tunisia. It also won colonies in West and Central Africa. At its height, the French empire in Africa was as large as the continental United States.

Britain's Share Britain's share of Africa was more scattered than that of France. However, it included more heavily populated regions with many rich resources. Britain took chunks of West and East Africa. It gained control of Egypt and pushed south into the Sudan.

Cecil Rhodes was a British industrialist and mine owner who became very wealthy from his investments in Africa. However, money was not his real interest. "I care nothing about money for its own sake," he once wrote, "but it is a power—and I do like power." Rhodes helped Britain extend its African empire by 1,000,000 square miles and had a British colony, Rhodesia (now Zimbabwe), named after him.

In southern Africa, Britain clashed with the Boers, who were descendants of Dutch settlers. As you have read, Britain had acquired the Cape Colony from the Dutch in 1814. At that time, many Boers fled British rule, migrating north and setting up their own republics. In the late 1800s, however, the discovery of gold and diamonds in the Boer lands led to conflict with Britain. The **Boer War,** which lasted from 1899 to 1902, involved bitter guerrilla fighting. The British won in the end, but at great cost.

In 1910, the British united the Cape Colony and the former Boer republics into the Union of South Africa. The new constitution set up a government run by whites and laid the foundation for a system of complete racial segregation that would remain in force until 1993.

Others Nations Join the Scramble Other European powers joined the scramble for colonies, in part to bolster their national image, while also furthering their economic growth and influence. The Portuguese carved out large colonies in Angola and Mozambique. Italy reached across the Mediterranean to occupy Libya and then pushed into the "horn" of Africa, at the southern end of the Red Sea. The newly united German empire took lands in eastern and southwestern African, including Cameroon and Togo. A German politician, trying to ease the worries of European rivals, explained, "We do not want to put anyone in the shade, but we also demand our place in the sun."

IDENTIFY CAUSE AND EFFECT How did King Leopold II set off a scramble for colonies in Africa?

>> French troops capture the city of Mascara in December 1835, during the French–Algerian War. **Infer** What advantages do the Algerian troops have? What advantages do the French troops have?

African Resistance

Europeans met armed resistance across the continent. The Algerians battled the French for years. **Samori Touré** (sah MAWR ee too RAY) fought French forces in West Africa, where he was building his own empire. The British battled the Zulus in southern Africa and the Asante in West Africa. When their king was exiled, the Asante put themselves under the command of their queen, **Yaa Asantewaa** (YA uh ah sahn TAY wuh). She led the fight against the British in the last Asante war.

Another woman who became a military leader was **Nehanda** (neh HAHN duh), of the Shona in Zimbabwe. Although a clever tactician, Nehanda was captured and

History Background

The Maxim Gun This weapon provided Western powers with a significant advantage in battle. Invented by Hiram Maxim in 1885, it was the first fully automatic machine gun. It could fire 500 rounds per minute, about as many as 100 rifles. A later model was called the "Devil's Paintbrush" because of the way it mowed down charging soldiers. In 1893, fifty British soldiers with four Maxim guns fought off 5,000 warriors in what is now Zimbabwe. The Austrian, German, Italian, and Russian armies also bought Maxim guns.

Answers

Infer *Algerians are on horseback and know the territory; French troops have guns.*

Identify Cause and Effect *by sending explorers to the Congo and trying to establish treaties to dominate trade*

executed. However, the memory of her achievements inspired later generations to fight for freedom.

In East Africa, the Germans fought wars against the Yao and Herero (huh REHR oh). Fighting was especially fierce in the Maji-Maji Rebellion of 1905. The Germans triumphed only after burning acres and acres of farmland, leaving thousands of local people to die of starvation.

Ethiopia Remains Independent One ancient Christian kingdom in East Africa, Ethiopia, managed to resist European colonization and maintain its independence. Like feudal Europe, Ethiopia had been divided up among a number of rival princes who ruled their own domains.

In the late 1800s, however, a reforming ruler, **Menelik II,** began to modernize his country. He hired European experts to plan modern roads and bridges and set up a Western school system. He imported the latest weapons and European officers to help train his army. Thus, when Italy invaded Ethiopia in 1896, Menelik was prepared. At the battle of Adowa (AH duh wuh), the Ethiopians smashed the Italian invaders. Ethiopia was the only African nation, aside from Liberia, to preserve its independence.

A New African Elite During the Age of Imperialism, a Western-educated African **elite,** or upper class, emerged. Some middle-class Africans admired Western ways and rejected their own culture. Others valued their African traditions and condemned Western societies that upheld liberty and equality for whites only. By the early 1900s, African leaders were forging nationalist movements to pursue self-determination and independence.

? **DESCRIBE** How did Ethiopians resist imperialism?

>> During the Age of Imperialism, some Africans adopted Western dress. The man wearing a Western jacket behind the Asante king was an Asante official.

ASSESSMENT

1. **Describe** Name one development in each region of Africa in the early 1800s.
2. **Identify Cause and Effect** How did imperialist European powers claim control over most of Africa by the end of the 1800s?
3. **Analyze Information** What impact did explorers and missionaries have on Africa?
4. **Infer** Why do you think the Europeans did not invite Africans to the Berlin Conference?
5. **Summarize** How did Africans resist European imperialism?

SYNTHESIZE

Online Project the **Digital Activity: European Domination in Africa**. Encourage students to use the completed graphic organizer to help them explain how imperialist European powers claimed control over most of Africa by the end of the 1800s. *(Typical methods included trade agreements, participation in African natural resource markets, conspiring to decide the rules for dividing up the continent, military invasion, and colonization.)*

DEMONSTRATE

Online Assign the **Digital Lesson Quiz** for this lesson if you haven't already done so. Students will be offered automatic remediation or enrichment based on their score.

Pose this question to the class on the Discussion Board:

In "European Colonies in Africa," you read about how Africa was colonized in the late 1800s by European nations, especially Britain and France. You learned that Africa was carved up by European nations and that Africans resisted being colonized.

Predict Consequences What are some potential long-term consequences of African colonization by European nations? *(Sample responses: conflict between European countries over colonies; conflict between ethnic groups placed together by European-drawn boundaries; continued exploitation of African resources; nationalist revolts against colonizers)*

Topic Inquiry

Have students continue their investigations for the Topic Inquiry.

Answers

Describe *Menelik II modernized and westernized both his country and his army, so Ethiopia was prepared to fight Western troops. Ethiopians defeated the Italian invasion and remained independent.*

Assessment

1. Sample response: In North Africa, the Ottoman empire was declining. In West Africa, new Muslim leaders held power. In East Africa, the slave trade continued. In South Africa, Zulus, Boers, and the British battled for control.
2. Explorers and missionaries penetrated Africa. Per the Berlin Conference, European powers had to set up a government office before claiming territory in Africa. European countries divided and conquered Africa with superior arms.
3. Explorers opened Africa's interior to other Europeans. Missionaries built churches, schools, and clinics but undermined African cultures by urging Africans to adopt Western ways.
4. Sample response: They believed they had a right to decide Africa's fate.
5. Many Africans battled the European invaders (the Ethiopians were successful), and the new African elite began organizing for independence.

Topic 15 Lesson 3

Europe and the Muslim World

CONNECT

Preview Have students preview the **Lesson Objectives** and the list of **Key Terms**.

Students can also preview all the **Key Terms** and **Academic Vocabulary** using the **Interactive Reading Notepad** on the digital course or preview a summary of the lesson in the **Reading and Note Taking Study Guide**.

Online Use the **Editable Presentation** found on the digital course to present the main ideas for this lesson.

Start Up Activity

Tell students that in 1798, Napoleon Bonaparte invaded Egypt. Read aloud this quotation, which suggests his motivation:

> "Europe is a molehill. . . . We must go to the East. . . . All great glory has been acquired there."

Discuss Why do you think Napoleon viewed the East as a place for glory? *(Sample response: It was the location of previous empires, the pyramids, and spectacular art.)* What might conquering Egypt mean for him? *(Sample response: It would allow him to extend his empire and claim the region before the British.)*

Online You can also project the **Start Up Activity** from the course.

INVESTIGATE

Have students read the lesson using the **Reading and Note Taking Study Guide** to help them take notes and understand the text as they read.

Unrest in Muslim Regions

Tell students that in the 1500s, three giant Muslim empires ruled large areas of the world—the Ottomans in the Middle East, the Safavids in Persia, and the Mughals in India. By the 1700s, all three Muslim empires were in decline, in part because of weakened central governments, corruption, and Muslim discontent. Reform movements arose, stressing religious piety and strict rules of behavior. For example, in the Sudan, Muhammad Ahmad announced that he was the Mahdi, the long-awaited savior of the faith. The Mahdi and his followers fiercely resisted British expansion into the region.

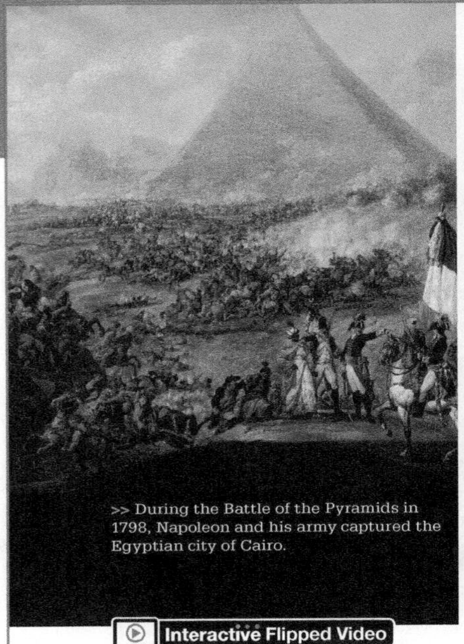

>> During the Battle of the Pyramids in 1798, Napoleon and his army captured the Egyptian city of Cairo.

15.3 Muslim lands extended from western Africa to Southeast Asia. In the 1500s, three giant Muslim empires—the Ottomans in the Middle East, the Safavids (sah FAH vidz) in Persia, and the Mughals in India—ruled much of this land.

Interactive Flipped Video

TEKS 1.E, 8.C, 16.B, 22.C

>> Objectives

Explain how internal and external pressures shaped the Muslim world.

Identify the challenges facing the Ottoman empire and Persia.

Describe the ways Egypt tried to modernize, including the opening of the Suez Canal.

>> Key Terms

Muhammad Ahmad
Mahdi
pasha
sultan
genocide
Muhammad Ali
concession

Europe and the Muslim World

Unrest in Muslim Regions

Napoleon Bonaparte invaded Egypt, a province of the Ottoman empire, in 1798. His Egyptian campaign highlighted Ottoman decline and opened a new era of European contact with Muslim regions of the world. At first, European countries just nibbled at the edges of Muslim countries. Before long, they would strike at their heartland.

Declining Empires By the late 1700s, all three Muslim empires were in decline. The decay of the once-vast Muslim empires had many causes.

Central governments had lost control over powerful groups such as landowning nobles, military elites, and urban craft guilds. Corruption was widespread. In some places, Muslim scholars and religious leaders were allied with the state. In other areas, they helped to stir discontent against the government.

Muslim Reform Efforts In the 1700s and 1800s, reform movements sprang up across various Muslim regions of Africa and Asia. Most stressed religious piety and strict rules of behavior. Usman dan Fodio led the struggle to reform Muslim practices in northern Africa. In the

 PEARSON realize www.PearsonTexas.com Access your Digital Lesson.

Aa Vocabulary Builder

1. Have students pronounce the following academic vocabulary terms in this lesson and clarify the part of speech. For difficult or polysyllabic words, break them into syllables and pronounce them with the students.
2. Explain what the word means in common "student-friendly" language using synonyms and antonyms when possible. Provide concrete examples to clarify the meaning, and rephrase the definition.

bureaucracy: government staffed by administrators who follow rigid rules

intervening: becoming involved in events in order to have influence on outcome

output: yield

successor: the person who takes a position after another has left

Sudan, **Muhammad Ahmad** (AHK mud) announced that he was the **Mahdi** (mahk DEE), the long-awaited savior of the faith. The Mahdi and his followers fiercely resisted British expansion into the region.

Another Islamic reform movement, the Wahhabi (wah HAHB ee) movement in Arabia, rejected the schools of theology and law that had emerged in the Ottoman empire. In their place, they wanted to recapture the purity and simplicity of Muhammad's original teachings.

Although the revolt was put down, the Wahhabi movement survived. Its teachings remain influential in the kingdom of Saudi Arabia today.

European Imperialism In addition to internal decay and stress, the three Muslim empires faced powerful threats from Western imperialists. Through diplomacy and military threats, European powers won treaties giving them favorable trading terms. They then demanded special rights for Europeans residing in Muslim lands. At times, European powers protected those rights by intervening in local affairs.

EXPLAIN How did Western powers gain the upper hand in Muslim regions of the world?

The Ottoman Empire Declines

At its height, the Ottoman empire had extended across North Africa, southeastern Europe, and the Middle East. By the early 1800s, however, it faced serious challenges. Ambitious **pashas,** or provincial rulers, had increased their power. Economic problems and corruption added to Ottoman decay.

Nationalist Revolts As ideas of nationalism spread from Western Europe, internal revolts weakened the multiethnic Ottoman empire. Subject peoples in North Africa, Eastern Europe, and the Middle East threatened to break away. In the Balkans, Greeks, Serbs, Bulgarians, and Romanians gained their independence. Revolts against Ottoman rule also erupted in Arabia, Lebanon, and Armenia. The Ottomans suppressed these uprisings, but Egypt slipped out of their control.

Increasing European Pressure European states sought to benefit from the slow crumbling of the Ottoman empire. After seizing Algeria in the 1830s, France hoped to gain more Ottoman territory. Russia schemed to gain control of the Bosporus (BAHS puh rus) and the Dardanelles. Control of these straits would give the Russians access to the Mediterranean Sea.

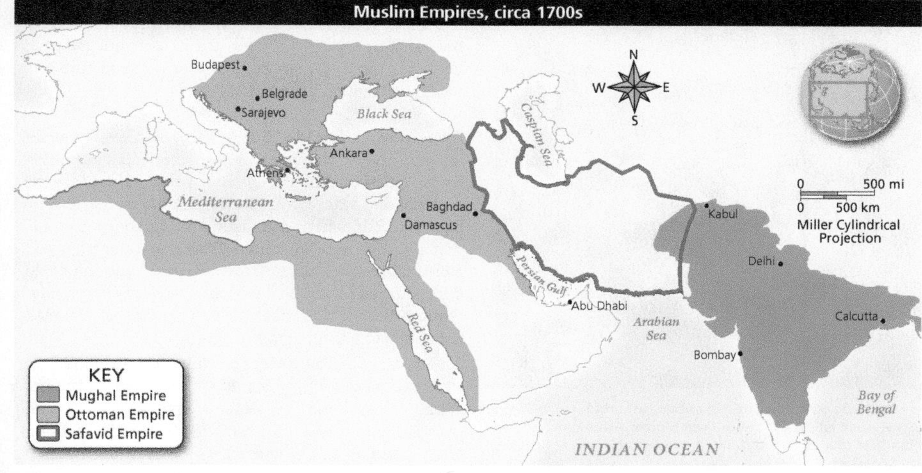

>> **Analyze Maps** Western imperialism gained steam at a time when the three major Muslim empires were in decline. In which empire might ethnic diversity have created internal challenges? Why?

Topic 15 Lesson 3

Guided Reading and Discussion

Ask students to explain how corruption, the spread of Western ideas, and the threat of European imperialism destabilized the Ottoman empire. *(Corruption allowed provincial rulers to gain power, sultans reacted to the spread of Western ideas by rejecting reform, and European imperialism threatened Ottoman territory.)*

Analyze Images

Point out the painting of the Battle of the Pyramids. Ask students to describe the mood of the painting. What feelings do the colors evoke? Do they think the artist favored the French or the Ottomans? After students offer their interpretations, tell them a French artist painted it not long after the battle.

The Ottoman Empire Declines

At its height, the Ottoman empire extended across North Africa, southeastern Europe, and parts of the Middle East. When economic problems, the spread of Western ideas, and internal revolts weakened the empire, European states grabbed territory. Tension between Turkish nationalists and minority groups led to a brutal genocide of Christian Armenians.

Answers

Analyze Maps *the Ottoman empire, because it controlled territory in Europe, North Africa, and the Middle East, giving the empire many different ethnic groups that might want independence*

Explain *Europeans exploited stresses in Muslim regions, schemed to increase their influence, gained concessions and debts, and then sent troops to take control and protect their interests.*

English Language Proficiency Standards

Reading 4.F.4 Explain the components of complex sentences. Then read "Unrest in Muslim Regions" aloud. Instruct students to complete one of the following activities.

Beginning Display the following sentence, read it aloud, and have students repeat it. Underline the subordinate clause and circle the independent clause in the sentence. Use a Think Aloud to explain why the subordinate clause cannot stand alone as a complete sentence.

Although the revolt was put down, *the Wahhabi movement survived.*

Intermediate Follow the instructions in the Beginning activity, but have students underline the subordinate clause, circle the independent clause, and use a Think Aloud to explain why the subordinate clause cannot stand alone.

Advanced Follow the instructions in the Beginning activity, but have student volunteers complete each part of the activity. Then have pairs of students identify other complex sentences in the text and repeat the underlining and circling process with each. Have students share their work with the class.

Advanced High Follow the instructions in the Advanced activity, but have students work individually to identify and mark up other complex sentences and then share their work with a partner.

Topic 15 Lesson 3

Online Project the **Interactive Gallery: European Powers and the Ottoman Empire**, and click through the hotspots with students.

ACTIVE CLASSROOM

Ask students to examine the political cartoon in the Interactive Gallery and create their own visual concept that represents the same idea. Invite them to post their Graffiti Concepts on the board or on chart paper. Then discuss the similarities and differences among the responses.

Guided Reading and Discussion

Ask students to identify and describe the main causes of Ottoman decline. *(government corruption, nationalist revolts, economic problems, European pressure, efforts to Westernize, the Young Turks movement, problems with Armenians)*

Key Terms

Call students' attention to the term **genocide** (in bold) in the text. Explain that the word part *geno-* means "race" and the word part *-cide* means "kill." Have them put the parts together to create a rough literal definition *("kill a race")*. Then review the broader definition supplied in the text.

Modernization in Egypt

Tell students that in the early 1800s, Egypt was a semi-independent province of the Ottoman empire. Muhammad Ali, the "father of modern Egypt," introduced a number of political and economic reforms. He also conquered the neighboring lands of Arabia, Syria, and Sudan. Before he died in 1849, he had set Egypt on the road to becoming a major Middle Eastern power. His successors were less skilled, however, and in 1882 Egypt became a protectorate of Britain.

SALLE A MANGER
Thanksgiving on the other side—No. 1
Thanksgiving on the other side—No. 2
THE POWERS WAITING TO DIVIDE THE TURKEY WHICH RUSSIA IS STILL PURSUING

>> **Analyze Political Cartoons** The European powers hoped to carve up the crumbling Ottoman empire for themselves. How do you know which figure in the cartoon represents the Ottoman empire?

Interactive Gallery

>> Tensions between Turkish nationalists and Armenians led to a brutal persecution of Armenians. In this 1915 image, Armenian widows and children wait to be deported.

Britain tried to thwart Russia's ambitions, which it saw as a threat to its own power in the Mediterranean and beyond to India. And in 1898, the new German empire hoped to increase its influence in the region by building a Berlin-to-Baghdad railway.

Efforts to Westernize Since the late 1700s, several Ottoman rulers had seen the need for reform and looked to the West for ideas. They reorganized the bureaucracy and system of tax collection. They built railroads, improved education, and hired Europeans to train a modern military. Young men were sent to the West to study science and technology. Many returned with Western political ideas about democracy and equality.

The reforms also brought improved medical care and revitalized farming. These improvements, however, created a different set of problems. Better health care resulted in a population explosion that increased the already intense competition for the best land and led to unrest.

The adoption of Western ideas also increased tension. Many officials objected to changes that were inspired by a foreign culture. For their part, repressive **sultans,** rulers of the Ottoman Turkish empire, rejected reform and tried to rebuild the autocratic power enjoyed by earlier rulers.

The Young Turks In the 1890s, a group of liberals formed a movement called the Young Turks. They insisted that reform was the only way to save the empire. In 1908, the Young Turks overthrew the sultan. Before they could achieve their planned reforms, however, the Ottoman empire was plunged into the world war that erupted in 1914.

Armenian Genocide Traditionally, the Ottomans had let minority nationalities live in their own communities and practice their own religions. By the 1890s, however, nationalism was igniting new tensions, especially between Turkish nationalists and minority peoples who sought their own states. These tensions triggered a brutal genocide of the Armenians, a Christian people concentrated in the eastern mountains of the empire. **Genocide** is a deliberate attempt to destroy a racial, political, or cultural group.

The Muslim Turks accused Christian Armenians of supporting Russian plans against the Ottoman empire. When Armenians protested repressive Ottoman policies, the sultan had tens of thousands of them slaughtered. Over the next 25 years, between 600,000

D Differentiate Challenge/Gifted Ask students to learn more about the Young Turks and their revolutionary movement, including its key leaders, the chronology of events leading up to the overthrow of the sultan, and its main goals. Have them identify another, similar group of individuals in history. Students should then write an editorial for a newspaper or magazine with the information they find.

Tell students that the term *Young Turks* has come to represent individuals or a group inside an organization that tries to take control or pursues liberal or progressive policies or reforms.

Answers

Analyze Political Cartoons *The figure being chased is a turkey—a play on words because the Ottoman empire originated and was centered in Turkey. The turkey also wears a Turkish hat called a fez.*

The Age of Imperialism (1800–1914) 660 Europe and the Muslim World and 1.5 million Armenians were killed or died from disease and starvation.

DESCRIBE How were efforts to Westernize problematic for the Ottoman empire?

Modernization in Egypt

In the early 1800s, Egypt was a semi-independent province of the Ottoman empire, making great strides toward reform. Its success was due to **Muhammad Ali,** an ambitious soldier appointed governor of Egypt by the Ottomans. Ali used the opportunity created by Napoleon's invasion and the civil war that followed to seize power in 1805.

Reform Efforts Muhammad Ali is sometimes called the "father of modern Egypt." He introduced a number of political and economic reforms, including improving tax collection, reorganizing the landholding system, and backing large irrigation projects to increase farm output. By expanding cotton production and encouraging the development of many local industries, Ali increased Egyptian participation in world trade.

Muhammad Ali also brought Western military experts to Egypt to help him build a well-trained, modern army. He conquered the neighboring lands of Arabia, Syria, and Sudan. Before he died in 1849, he had set Egypt on the road to becoming a major Middle Eastern power.

The Suez Canal Muhammad Ali's successors lacked his skills, and Egypt came increasingly under foreign control. In 1858, a French entrepreneur, Ferdinand de Lesseps (LAY seps), organized a company to build the Suez Canal, a waterway connecting the Mediterranean and Red Seas. The waterway would reduce the travel time between Europe and Asia. European nations gained power over the Ottomans by extending loans at high interest rates. In 1875, the ruler of Egypt was unable to repay loans he had contracted for the canal and other projects. To pay his debts, he sold his shares in the canal. The British, seeing the Suez Canal as an important tool in maintaining their vast colonial empire, bought the shares. The shares gave the British a controlling interest in the canal.

Becoming a British Protectorate When Egyptian nationalists revolted against foreign influence in 1882, Britain made Egypt a protectorate. In theory, the governor of Egypt was still an official of the Ottoman government. In fact, he followed policies dictated by Britain. Under British influence, Egypt continued to

>> Muhammad Ali, the Ottoman governor of Egypt, sought to make Egypt a modern state.

>> The British used their military strength to protect their interest in the Suez Canal. These troops were sent to Egypt during the 1882 Anglo-Egyptian War. **Identify Cause and Effect** Why would the British want to protect their control of the Suez Canal?

Interactive Gallery

Topic 15 Lesson 3

Online Project the **Interactive Gallery: The Suez Canal**, and click through the images with students.

ACTIVE CLASSROOM

Have students use what they have learned about the Suez Canal to use the Cartoon It strategy to create a political cartoon about one event in the canal's early history. Give students the option of using an image from the Interactive Gallery as the foundation of their cartoon.

Guided Reading and Discussion

Ask students to explain how Britain gained control of the Suez Canal. *(Egypt was unable to repay its loans for the canal, so Britain bought Egypt's shares and gained controlling interest in the canal.)* Discuss the legitimacy of this action.

European Imperialism in Persia

Tell students that Persia—now Iran—faced major challenges, much like those of the Ottoman empire. The Qajar shahs exercised absolute power. Foreign nations, especially Russia and Britain, wanted to control Iran's oil fields, increasing the reach of European imperialism. They were granted concessions and sent troops to protect their interests. These actions outraged Iranian nationalists.

Guided Reading and Discussion

Ask students to explain why foreign nations became interested in Persia in the early 1900s and identify the issues that arose from this interest. *(Oil was found in the area, and both Russia and Britain wanted control of the oil fields. Both countries sent troops to the area, causing unrest among Persian nationalists.)*

English Language Proficiency Standards

Reading 4.H.2 Have students complete one activity according to their level of English proficiency.

Beginning Remind students that when reading silently, they should not move their lips or murmur the words. Read "Modernization in Egypt" aloud. Instruct students to reread the subsection "The Suez Canal" silently. Ask questions to determine comprehension. Review challenging words or concepts.

Intermediate Complete the Beginning activity, but when students reread the subsection, have small groups share one fact they learned from reading silently.

Advanced Ask students to read "Modernization in Egypt" silently. Have partners outline the text, and then share their outlines with the class and make any needed corrections.

Advanced High Ask students to read "Modernization in Egypt" silently. Then have them write an outline of the text and share it with a partner.

Answers

Describe *They led to a population explosion that increased competition for the best land and led to conflict over foreign influence.*

Identify Cause and Effect *Sample response: The canal made it easier for the British to manage and trade with their colonies in South and East Asia.*

Topic 15 Lesson 3

SYNTHESIZE

Online Project the **Digital Activity: Effects of Europeans in Muslim Regions**. Have students fill in the concept web. *(Sample responses: foreign intervention in local affairs; spread of Western ideas; nationalist outrage and uprisings; less control of trade routes; construction of a Berlin-to-Baghdad railroad; loss of control of the Suez Canal; Western education of young men; overpopulation)*

DEMONSTRATE

Online Assign the **Digital Lesson Quiz** for this lesson if you haven't already done so. Students will be offered automatic remediation or enrichment based on their score.

Pose these questions to the class on the Discussion Board:

In "Europe and the Muslim World," you read about the internal and external pressures that shaped the Muslim world and the challenges faced by the Ottoman empire and Persia from European imperialism. Modernization brought issues as well as greater influence from outside nations.

Draw Conclusions What motivated European imperialists in both Africa and the Muslim world? *(the desire for new resources)* How did European nations take advantage of stresses in the Muslim world? *(Through diplomacy, economic investments, the introduction of Western ideas, and the threat of force, European nations expanded their control.)*

Topic Inquiry

Have students continue their investigations for the Topic Inquiry.

modernize. However, nationalist discontent simmered and flared into protests and riots.

GENERATE EXPLANATIONS How did Egypt fall under British control?

European Imperialism in Persia

Like the Ottoman empire, Persia faced major challenges in the 1800s. The Qajar (kah JAHR) shahs, who ruled Persia from 1794 to 1925, exercised absolute power. Still, they did take steps to introduce reforms. The government helped build telegraph lines and railroads and experimented with a liberal constitution. Reform, however, did not save Persia from Western imperialism. Russia wanted to protect its southern frontier and expand into Central Asia. Britain wanted to protect its interests in India.

For a time, each nation set up its own sphere of influence in Persia. The discovery of oil in the early 1900s heightened foreign interest in the region. Both Russia and Britain plotted for control of Persian oil fields. They persuaded the Persian government to grant them **concessions,** or special rights given to foreign powers.

To protect their interests, they sent troops into Persia. Persian nationalists were outraged. The nationalists included two very different groups. Some Persians wanted to move swiftly to adopt Western ways. Others, led by Muslim religious leaders, condemned the Persian government and Western influences.

ANALYZE INFORMATION For what reason did Persia attract foreign interest in the early 1900s?

ASSESSMENT

1. **Make Generalizations** What was the goal of the Wahhabi reform movement?
2. **Identify Cause and Effect** What effect did nationalism have on the Ottoman empire during the 1800s?
3. **Express Ideas Clearly** Who was Muhammad Ali, and why was he a significant figure?
4. **Summarize** How did Britain gain control of the Suez Canal?
5. **Generate Explanations** Why did foreign interest in Persia increase in the early 1900s?

Answers

Generate Explanations *Britain gained an economic foothold, and then, when Egyptian nationalists revolted, Britain made Egypt a protectorate.*

Analyze Information *Oil was discovered.*

Assessment

1. Its members wanted to recapture the purity and simplicity of Muhammad's original teachings.
2. Nationalism caused internal revolts and weakened the multi-ethnic Ottoman empire.
3. Muhammad Ali is known as the "father of modern Egypt." He introduced political and economic reforms, increased Egyptian trade across the world, reformed the military, and conquered neighboring lands.
4. Britain bought control of the canal from the Ottoman ruler.
5. Oil was discovered there in the early 1900s.

15.4 For more than 200 years, Mughal rulers governed a powerful empire in India. By the mid-1700s, however, the Mughal empire was collapsing from a lack of strong rulers. Britain then turned its commercial interests in the region into political ones.

>> **Draw Conclusions** In this painting from the early 1800s, an official of the British East India Company rides in an Indian procession. How does the painting convey the power of the British?

 Interactive Flipped Video

India Becomes a British Colony

TEKS
1.E, 8.C, 8.D, 16.B, 28.B

>> Objectives

Understand the causes and effects of the Sepoy Rebellion.

Explain the impact of British rule on India.

Describe how the British and Indians viewed one another.

Trace the origins of Indian nationalism.

>> Key Terms

sati
sepoy
viceroy
deforestation
Ram Mohun Roy
purdah

The British East India Company

In the early 1600s, the British East India Company won trading rights on the fringe of the Mughal empire. As Mughal power declined, the company's influence grew. By the mid-1800s, it controlled three fifths of India.

Exploitation of Indian Diversity The British were able to conquer India by exploiting its diversity. Even when Mughal power was at its height, India was home to many people and cultures. As Mughal power crumbled, India became fragmented.

Indians with different traditions and dozens of different languages were not able to unite against the newcomers. The British took advantage of Indian divisions by encouraging competition and disunity among rival princes. Where diplomacy or intrigue did not work, the British used their superior weapons to overpower local rulers.

Implementation of British Policies The East India Company's main goal in India was to make money, and leading officials often grew rich. At the same time, the company did work to improve roads, preserve peace, and reduce banditry.

663

www.PearsonTexas.com
Access your Digital Lesson.

Aa Vocabulary Builder

1. Have students pronounce the following academic vocabulary terms in this lesson and clarify the part of speech. For difficult or polysyllabic words, break them into syllables and pronounce them with the students.
2. Explain what the word means in common "student-friendly" language using synonyms and antonyms when possible. Provide concrete examples to clarify the meaning, and rephrase the definition.

overall: total

incorporate: join with something that already exists

distinctions: separations into different groups

Topic 15 Lesson 4

India Becomes a British Colony

CONNECT

Preview Have students preview the **Lesson Objectives** and the list of **Key Terms**.

Students can also preview all the **Key Terms** and **Academic Vocabulary** using the **Interactive Reading Notepad** on the digital course or preview a summary of the lesson in the **Reading and Note Taking Study Guide**.

Online Use the **Editable Presentation** found on the digital course to present the main ideas for this lesson.

Start Up Activity

Tell students that Indians called Britain's system of rule over India "the knife of sugar." Have them discuss what this seemingly contradictory phrase likely meant about relations between the British and the Indians. *(Sample response: The British, on the surface, treated Indians relatively well, but their "sweetness" masked the fact that if necessary, they would use force to keep control of India. Relations, therefore, likely always included some level of tension.)*

Online You can also project the **Start Up Activity** from the course.

INVESTIGATE

Have students read the lesson using the **Reading and Note Taking Study Guide** to help them take notes and understand the text as they read.

The British East India Company

Tell students that in the mid-1800s, the British East India Company controlled most of India. Company officials made rules for Indian soldiers, or sepoys, in its service that were not popular with the sepoys. The sepoys rebelled against British officers. The Sepoy Rebellion was eventually put down by England, but it led to reforms and changes in rule: the British government took charge of India.

Answers

Draw Conclusions *Answers will vary but could include: The lone British official is the largest figure among all the many Indian people. He rides a horse, unlike most of the Indian people, who walk. He wears a fancy uniform and hat.*

Topic 15 Lesson 4

Online Project the **Interactive Gallery: The Sepoy Rebellion**, and click through the images with students.

ACTIVE CLASSROOM

Use the Make Headlines strategy with the Interactive Gallery. Have students pick one image and use it to write a headline that might have appeared at the time, describing or summarizing an event that led to or occurred during the Sepoy Rebellion. Students can read their headlines to small or large class groups.

Guided Reading and Discussion

Ask students to list some factors that led to British rule in India. *(Sample responses: a weakened Mughal empire, economic motivations to profit from colonies, the exploitation of differences among diverse populations in India, and the transfer of power from the East India Company to the British government after the Sepoy Rebellion)* Remind students that a general cause of the Sepoy Rebellion was a lack of respect among the British for Hindu and Muslim traditions. Have students identify some effects of the Sepoy Rebellion. *(Sample responses: a legacy of fear, hatred, and mistrust between the British and Indians; changes in British policy, especially Parliament's taking control of India; more troops were sent to India, and Indians were taxed to pay for troops; some easing of rules that had angered and offended Hindus and Muslims)*

>> The Writers Building in Calcutta, India, was designed in 1777 by the British. Many extensions were added over the years. It was an important administrative office for the British East India Company.

>> **Infer** Indian sepoys were soldiers employed by the British East India Company in the mid-1800s. What item or items in the image reflect India's culture, and which show a British influence?

By the early 1800s, British officials introduced Western education and legal procedures. Missionaries tried to convert Indians to Christianity, which they felt was superior to Indian religions. The British also pressed for social change. They worked to end slavery and the caste system and to improve the position of women within the family. One law banned **sati** (SUH tee), a Hindu custom practiced mainly by the upper classes. It called for a widow to join her husband in death by throwing herself on his funeral pyre.

Increasing Discontent In the 1850s, the East India Company made several unpopular moves. First, it required **sepoys** (SEE poyz), or Indian soldiers in its service, to serve anywhere, either in India or overseas. For high-caste Hindus, however, overseas travel was an offense against their religion. Second, the East India Company passed a law that allowed Hindu widows to remarry. Hindus viewed both moves as a Christian conspiracy to undermine their beliefs.

Then, in 1857, the British issued new rifles to the sepoys. Troops were told to bite off the tips of cartridges before loading them into the rifles. The cartridges, however, were greased with animal fat—either from cows, which Hindus considered sacred, or from pigs, which were forbidden to Muslims. When the troops refused the order to "load rifles," they were imprisoned.

The Sepoy Rebellion Angry sepoys rose up against their British officers. The Sepoy Rebellion swept across northern and central India. Several sepoy regiments marched off to Delhi, the old Mughal capital. There, they hailed the last Mughal ruler as their leader.

In some places, the sepoys brutally massacred British men, women, and children. But the British soon rallied and crushed the revolt. They then took terrible revenge for their earlier losses, torching villages and slaughtering thousands of unarmed Indians.

The Sepoy Rebellion left a bitter legacy of fear, hatred, and mistrust on both sides. It also brought major changes in British policy. In 1858, Parliament ended the rule of the East India Company and put India directly under the British crown. It sent more troops to India, taxing Indians to pay the cost of these occupying forces. While it slowed the "reforms" that had angered Hindus and Muslims, it continued to develop India for Britain's own economic benefit.

 **IDENTIFY CAUSE AND EFFECT** What was the primary cause of the Sepoy Rebellion?

History Background

British East India Company Founded in the 1600s, the British East India Company was the predecessor of the transnational corporation. Until 1858 the company did largely as it pleased, enforcing its will with a private army. Its officers profited personally amid widespread corruption. Because of its monopoly, it could drive down prices, causing destitution among India's weavers, and sell high in Britain. It had many critics; even economist Adam Smith criticized its oppressive policies. Horace Walpole accused the company of having "murdered, deposed, plundered, usurped," and caused "famine in Bengal, in which millions perished" while the company hoarded rice for price gouging. Jawaharlal Nehru noted that it was not accidental that the Hindustani word *loot* was absorbed into the English language. Edmund Burke pointed out that "every rupee of profit made by an Englishman is lost for ever to India."

Answers

Infer *Answers will vary, but students might recognize the headgear as reflecting Indian culture, and the rifle as a British object. The sword could come from either culture, while the uniform looks British.*

Identify Cause and Effect *British officials started policies that violated Hindu beliefs: requiring sepoys to travel, bite off greased cartridge tips, and allow widows to remarry.*

India Under British Rule

After 1858, Parliament set up a system of colonial rule in India called the British Raj. A British **viceroy** in India governed in the name of the queen, and British officials held the top positions in the civil service and army. Indians filled most other jobs. With their cooperation, the British made India the "brightest jewel" in the crown of their empire.

British policies were designed to incorporate India into the overall British economy. At the same time, British officials felt they were helping India to modernize. In their terms, modernizing meant adopting not only Western technology but also Western culture.

An Unequal Partnership Britain saw India both as a market and as a source of raw materials. To this end, the British built roads and an impressive railroad network. Improved transportation let the British sell their factory-made goods across the subcontinent and carry Indian cotton, jute, and coal to coastal ports for transport to factories in England.

New methods of communication, such as the telegraph, also gave Britain better control of India. After the Suez Canal opened in 1869, British trade with India soared. But it remained an unequal partnership, favoring the British. The British flooded India with inexpensive, machine-made textiles, ruining India's once-prosperous hand-weaving industry.

Britain also transformed Indian agriculture. It encouraged nomadic herders to settle into farming and pushed farmers to grow cash crops, such as cotton and jute, that could be sold on the world market. Clearing new farmlands led to massive **deforestation,** or cutting of trees.

The Strain of Population Growth The British introduced medical improvements and new farming methods. Better healthcare and increased food production led to rapid population growth. The rising numbers, however, put a strain on the food supply, especially as farmland was turned over to growing cash crops instead of food. In the late 1800s, terrible famines swept India.

Benefits of British Colonial Rule On the positive side, British rule brought some degree of peace and order to the countryside. The British revised the legal system to promote justice for Indians regardless of class or caste. Railroads helped Indians move around the country, while the telegraph and postal system improved communication. Greater contact helped bridge regional differences and develop a sense of national unity.

>> During the Sepoy Rebellion, the British battled Indian forces around Delhi, a city that was alternately controlled by both the British and the sepoys.

Interactive Gallery

>> This railway station was built in India in 1878 during the British Raj. British architects incorporated traditional Indian architectural features into the design.

Analyze Images

Have students look at the image of the Sepoy Rebellion and try to identify which fighters were British and which were sepoys. Point out that the British forces (in the lower part of the image, with the cannon) included Indians—not all Indian soldiers took part in the rebellion.

India Under British Rule

Tell students that British rule brought some modernizations to India, such as improved methods of agriculture, new railways and communications systems, and better healthcare. Most of these changes served British interests. For example, the conversion to cash crops increased profits, and railways carried Indian raw materials and British goods across India more efficiently.

Online Project the **Interactive Image: The Imperial Durbar, 1877**, and click through the hotspots with students.

ACTIVE CLASSROOM

Use the Conversation With History strategy with the Interactive Image. Have each student write out a dialogue they might have with one of the people in the picture, including a question or two they would like to ask as well as the person's reply.

Guided Reading and Discussion

Remind students that British policies had both positive and negative effects on the Indian people. Discuss how British rule affected lower-caste Indians and upper-class Indians. *(Lower castes benefited from a nondiscriminatory British justice system, but they also suffered from famines. Upper classes took advantage of British education, civil service, and military opportunities. Landowners and princes grew rich from exporting cash crops.)*

Key Terms

Call students' attention to the term **viceroy** (in bold) in the text. Explain that the word part *vice* means "in place of," as in the term *vice president*, and *roy* means "king," or in the case of the British Raj, "queen." Thus the viceroy served in place of the British queen.

Diverse Views on Culture

Under British rule, some Indians (usually from the upper classes) adopted Western education and culture. Others maintained their Hindu or Muslim culture. Most British people dismissed Indian culture as inferior.

Guided Reading and Discussion

What were Ram Mohun Roy's views about Western culture and Indian culture? *(He saw value in both cultures. He introduced Western education in India but wanted Indians to take pride in their own culture; he started a type of Indian nationalism. He also wanted to reform the caste system.)*

The Growth of Indian Nationalism

Tell students that Indians who received a Western-style education came to value ideals such as democracy and equality and wished to end imperial rule. An Indian National Congress was formed in 1885 to advocate for Indian self-rule.

Guided Reading and Discussion

Ask students to explain how the Indian National Congress can be considered an effect of British rule. *(The British set up an education system that promoted democracy and equality—and, by implication, self-rule.)*

The upper classes, especially, benefited from some British policies. They sent their sons to British schools, where they were trained for posts in the civil service and military. Indian landowners and princes, who still ruled their own territories, grew rich from exporting cash crops.

IDENTIFY CAUSE AND EFFECT What were some impacts of British colonial rule on agriculture in India?

ELPS **ELPS 4.F.5** Use images in *India Under British Rule* to activate your prior knowledge on farming.

Diverse Views on Culture

Some educated Indians were impressed by British power and technology and urged India to follow a Western model of progress. These mostly upper-class Indians learned English and adopted Western ways. Other Indians felt that the answer to change lay with their own Hindu or Muslim cultures.

Indian Attitudes In the early 1800s, **Ram Mohun Roy** combined both views. A great scholar, he knew Sanskrit, Persian, and Arabic classics, as well as English, Greek, and Latin works. Roy felt that India could learn from the West. He was a founder of Hindu College in Calcutta, which provided an English-style education to Indians. Many of its graduates went on to establish English schools all over the region. While Roy saw the value of Western education, he also wanted to reform traditional Indian culture.

Roy condemned some traditions, such as rigid caste distinctions, child marriage, sati, and **purdah** (PUR duh), the isolation of women in separate quarters. But he also set up educational societies that helped revive pride in Indian culture. Because of his influence on later leaders, he is often hailed today as the founder of Indian nationalism.

Westerner Attitudes The British disagreed among themselves about India. A few admired Indian theology and philosophy. As Western scholars translated Indian classics, they acquired respect for India's ancient heritage. Western writers and philosophers borrowed ideas from Hinduism and Buddhism.

However, most British people knew little about Indian achievements and dismissed Indian culture with contempt. In an essay on whether Indians should be taught in English or their own languages, British historian Thomas Macaulay arrogantly wrote that "a

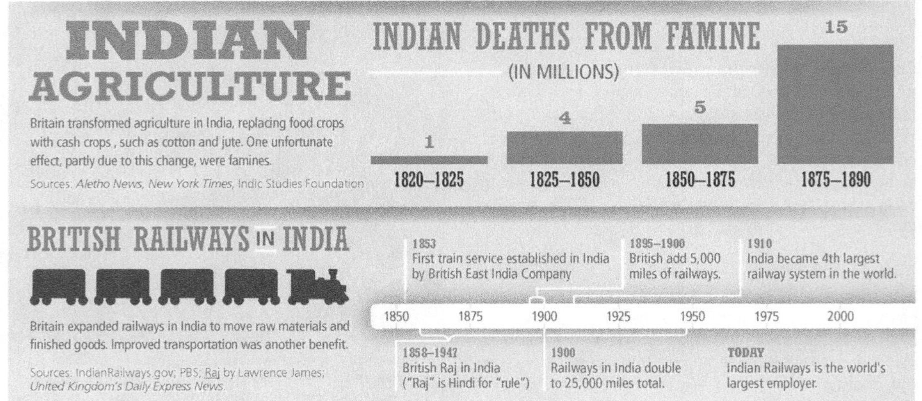
SOME EFFECTS OF THE BRITISH RAJ
INDIAN AGRICULTURE
Britain transformed agriculture in India, replacing food crops with cash crops, such as cotton and jute. One unfortunate effect, partly due to this change, were famines.
Sources: Aletho News, New York Times, Indic Studies Foundation
INDIAN DEATHS FROM FAMINE
(IN MILLIONS)
1
1820–1825
4
1825–1850
5
1850–1875
15
1875–1890
BRITISH RAILWAYS IN INDIA
Britain expanded railways in India to move raw materials and finished goods. Improved transportation was another benefit.
Sources: IndianRailways.gov; PBS; Raj by Lawrence James; United Kingdom's Daily Express News
1853
First train service established in India by British East India Company
1895–1900
British add 5,000 miles of railways.
1910
India became 4th largest railway system in the world.
1850
1875
1900
1925
1950
1975
2000
1858–1947
British Raj in India ("Raj" is Hindi for "rule")
1900
Railways in India double to 25,000 miles total.
TODAY
Indian Railways is the world's largest employer.

>> **Support a Point of View with Evidence** The graph and timeline show some effects of the British Raj. All things considered, was British rule a benefit or a drawback for India? Why?

Interactive Illustration

D Differentiate Challenge/Gifted British society in the 1800s placed many restrictions on women, as did Indian culture. Some Indian cultural practices, such as sati, child marriage, and purdah, were even harsher for women, although Indian leaders such as Ram Mohun Roy were working to end those practices. Have students research for more information about sati and purdah as practiced in 1800s India and write a short summary to share with the class.

Answers

Identify Cause and Effect *The British encouraged more farming of cash crops for global markets; clearing land for new farms led to deforestation. They introduced methods to increase food production, which led to population growth and eventual famine.*

Support a Point of View with Evidence *Answers will vary but could quote information on famine to support the drawback argument or railway growth to support the benefit argument.*

single shelf of a good European library is worth the whole native literature of India and Arabia."

COMPARE AND CONTRAST What were some differing views among British people about the culture of India?

The Growth of Indian Nationalism

During the years of British rule, a class of Western-educated Indians emerged. In the view of Macaulay and others, this elite class would bolster British power. As it turned out, exposure to European ideas had the opposite effect. By the late 1800s, Western-educated Indians were spearheading a nationalist movement. Schooled in Western ideals such as democracy, equality, and human rights, they dreamed of ending imperial rule.

Indian National Congress In 1885, nationalist leaders organized the Indian National Congress, which became known as the Congress party. Its members believed in peaceful protest to gain their ends. They called for greater democracy, which they felt would bring more power to Indians like themselves. The Indian National Congress looked forward to eventual self-rule but supported Western-style modernization.

Formation of the Muslim League At first, Muslims and Hindus worked together for self-rule. In time, however, Muslims grew to resent Hindu domination of the Congress party. They also worried that a Hindu-run government would oppress Muslims. In 1906, Muslims formed the Muslim League to pursue their own goals. Soon, they were talking of a separate Muslim state.

IDENTIFY CAUSE AND EFFECT What was one cause of the Indian nationalist movement?

>> A. C. Mazumdar served as president of the Indian National Congress, which pushed for self-rule for India.

ASSESSMENT

1. **Analyze Information** Why did the Sepoy Rebellion leave "a bitter legacy of fear, hatred, and mistrust on both sides"?
2. **Analyze Information** What was one specific rule put in place by the East India Company that angered and offended sepoys?
3. **Analyze Information** What were the positive and negative effects of British rule on Indians?
4. **Infer** How did Ram Mohun Roy view the British?
5. **Analyze Information** How did British rule contribute to the development of Indian nationalism?

SYNTHESIZE

Online Project the **Digital Activity: Positives and Negatives for India**. Have students identify negative and positive impacts of British rule. *(It was always an unequal partnership between the two countries, with Britain extracting profits and causing problems such as destruction of cottage industries, deforestation, and famine. Some benefits included building roads, railways, irrigation systems, schools, and communication systems.)*

DEMONSTRATE

Online Assign the **Digital Lesson Quiz** for this lesson if you haven't already done so. Students will be offered automatic remediation or enrichment based on their score.

Pose this question to the class on the Discussion Board:

In "India Becomes a British Colony," you read about how a British company gained control of India. After a rebellion against the company by Indian sepoys, the British government took over ruling India. British rule had some advantages but also many disadvantages, and India pursued self-rule.

Analyze Information How did the rules of the East India Company help unify Indian Hindus and Muslims? *(Hindus and Muslims both opposed the rules for religious reasons. These two groups of sepoy soldiers joined forces against the British during the Sepoy Rebellion.)*

Topic Inquiry

Have students continue their investigations for the Topic Inquiry.

Answers

Compare and Contrast *Some admired the history, philosophy, and ancient heritage of India. Others disparaged India's culture.*

Identify Cause and Effect *Indians who received Western-style education applied Western ideals such as democracy and equality to the cause of self-rule for India.*

Assessment

1. The sepoys killed many British men, women, and children during their revolt. The British took revenge, killing thousands of unarmed Indians. The rebellion showed that the British did not understand sensitive issues in Indian culture.
2. Answers should include the rules requiring sepoys to travel anywhere, including overseas; allowing widows to remarry; or requiring sepoys to ingest animal fat when loading rifles. All were offensive to Hindu religious practices.
3. Positive: improved transportation, communication, medical care, farming methods, order, justice, and education; Negative: exploitation, destruction of local industry, deforestation, and famine
4. Roy felt India could learn from the West. He established Western-style schools throughout India; he also wanted to reform traditional Indian culture and did not want to adopt Western ways in their entirety.
5. Western-educated Indians learned Western ideas such as democracy and equality, as well as the effect of British policies against Hindu traditions.

Topic 15 Lesson 5

China and the West

CONNECT

Preview Have students preview the **Lesson Objectives** and the list of **Key Terms**.

Students can also preview all the **Key Terms** and **Academic Vocabulary** using the **Interactive Reading Notepad** on the digital course or preview a summary of the lesson in the **Reading and Note Taking Study Guide**.

Online Use the **Editable Presentation** found on the digital course to present the main ideas for this lesson.

Start Up Activity

Have students answer this question as they get settled: When a product is illegal to use in one country, should traders from that country be allowed to sell the product in another country? Briefly discuss this issue in general terms, and then discuss it in relation to Britain's export of the addictive drug opium to China in return for tea, starting in the late 1700s.

Online You can also project the **Start Up Activity** from the course.

INVESTIGATE

Have students read the lesson using the **Reading and Note Taking Study Guide** to help them take notes and understand the text as they read.

Economic Interest in China

Remind students that China had long resisted trade with the outside world. Because of the country's size and resources, it had managed to be self-sufficient. European countries had economic motivations to gain control of China's resources, goods, and transportation routes.

>> The antiquated Chinese fleet was outmatched by larger, more technologically advanced British warships during the Opium War.

Interactive Flipped Video

15.5 For centuries, Chinese regulations had ensured that China had a favorable balance of trade with other nations. A nation's balance of trade refers to the difference between how much a country imports and how much it exports. By the 1800s, however, Western nations were using their growing power to tilt the balance of trade with East Asia in their favor.

TEKS
1.E, 28.B

>> Objectives

Describe how Westerners tried to gain trade rights in China.

Explain how reformers tried to strengthen China.

Understand why the Qing dynasty fell.

>> Key Terms

balance of trade
trade surplus
trade deficit
indemnity
extraterritoriality
Taiping Rebellion
Sino-Japanese War
Open Door Policy
Guang Xu
Boxer Uprising
Sun Yixian
Opium War

China and the West

Economic Interest in China

Prior to the 1800s, Chinese rulers placed strict limits on foreign traders. European merchants were restricted to a small area in southern China. China sold them silk, porcelain, and tea in exchange for gold and silver. Under this arrangement, China enjoyed a **trade surplus,** or exported more than it imported. Westerners, on the other hand, had a **trade deficit** with China, buying more from the Chinese than they sold to them.

By the late 1700s, two developments were underway that would lead the advance of European imperialism into China. First, China entered a period of decline.

Second, the Industrial Revolution created a need for expanded markets for European goods. At the same time, it gave the West superior military power.

The Opium Trade Leads to War During the late 1700s, British merchants began making huge profits by trading opium grown in India for Chinese tea. Soon, many Chinese had become addicted to the drug. Silver flowed out of China in payment for the drug, disrupting the economy.

The Chinese government outlawed opium and executed Chinese drug dealers. They called on Britain to stop the trade. The British refused, insisting on the right of free trade. In 1839, Chinese warships

 www.PearsonTexas.com Access your Digital Lesson.

668

Aa Vocabulary Builder

1. Have students pronounce the following academic vocabulary terms in this lesson and clarify the part of speech. For difficult or polysyllabic words, break them into syllables and pronounce them with the students.
2. Explain what the word means in common "student-friendly" language using synonyms and antonyms when possible. Provide concrete examples to clarify the meaning, and rephrase the definition.

stipulate: to specifically demand something in an agreement

emphasis: particular attention

principle: value or belief

clashed with British merchants, triggering the **Opium War.** British gunboats, equipped with the latest in firepower, bombarded Chinese coastal and river ports. With outdated weapons and fighting methods, the Chinese were easily defeated.

Unequal Treaties In 1842, Britain made China accept the Treaty of Nanjing (NAHN jing). Britain received a huge **indemnity,** or payment for losses in the war. The British also gained the island of Hong Kong. China had to open five ports to foreign trade and grant British citizens in China **extraterritoriality,** the right to live under their own laws and be tried in their own courts.

The treaty was the first of a series of "unequal treaties" that forced China to make concessions to Western powers. A second war, lasting from 1856 to 1858, ended with France, Russia, and the United States pressuring China to sign treaties stipulating the opening of more ports to foreign trade and letting Christian missionaries preach in China.

DESCRIBE Describe how British trade with China triggered the Opium Wars.

ELPS **ELPS 4.F.6** Ask for peer support when reading *Economic Interest in China.*

The Taiping Rebellion and a Weakened China

By the 1800s, the Qing dynasty was in decline. Irrigation systems and canals were poorly maintained, leading to massive flooding of the Huang valley. The population explosion that had begun a century earlier created hardship for China's peasants. An extravagant imperial court, tax evasion by the rich, and widespread official corruption added to the peasants' burden. As poverty and misery increased, peasants rebelled.

The **Taiping Rebellion** (TY ping), which lasted from 1850 to 1864, was probably the most devastating peasant revolt in history. The leader, Hong Xiuquan (hong shyoo CHWAHN), called for an end to the hated Qing dynasty.

The Taiping rebels won control of large parts of China and held out for 14 years. However, with the help of loyal regional governors and generals, the government crushed the rebellion.

The Taiping Rebellion almost toppled the Qing dynasty. It is estimated to have caused the deaths of between 20 million and 30 million Chinese. The Qing government survived, but it had to share power with regional commanders. During the rebellion, Europeans kept up pressure on China, and Russia seized lands in the north.

EXPLAIN How did the Taiping Rebellion and other internal problems weaken the Qing dynasty?

Reform Efforts in China

By the mid-1800s, educated Chinese were divided over the need to adopt Western ways. Most saw no reason for new industries because China's wealth and taxes came from land. Although Chinese merchants were allowed to do business, they were not seen as a source of prosperity.

Scholar-officials also disapproved of the ideas of Western missionaries, whose emphasis on individual choice challenged the Confucian order. They saw Western technology as dangerous, too, because it threatened Confucian ways that had served China successfully for so long.

By the late 1800s, the empress Ci Xi (tsih shih) had gained power. A strong-willed ruler, she surrounded herself with advisors who were deeply committed to Confucian traditions.

Self-Strengthening Movement In the 1860s, reformers launched the "self-strengthening movement."

>> Troops from the Qing dynasty clash with peasant rebels during the Taiping Rebellion.

Topic 15 Lesson 5

Online Project the **Interactive Map: Imperialist Spheres of Influence in China**, and click through the maps with students.

ACTIVE CLASSROOM

Project the Interactive Map and use a whiteboard tool to divide the base layer map of China into four quadrants. Assign quadrants to groups of students. Have them research their regions of China to find the resources that might have been attractive to imperialist powers, and design a piece of Wallpaper about their region. Students can then take a gallery walk to note what others have created.

Guided Reading and Discussion

Tell students that by the early 1800s, two developments led to the advance of European imperialism into China—a declining China and the Industrial Revolution. Ask students to explain how these factors led to the Opium War and China's defeat. *(The Industrial Revolution created a need for expanded markets for European goods and gave the West superior military power. In the Opium War, technologically advanced British gunboats easily defeated the Chinese.)*

The Taiping Rebellion and a Weakened China

Reform Efforts in China

Point out that Confucian ideals had shaped Chinese government for approximately 2,000 years. In the nineteenth century, reformers started to place pressure on Chinese society to modernize by adopting Western technology, philosophies, and practices.

English Language Proficiency Standards

Reading 4.F.6 Read "Economic Interest in China" aloud. Have students complete one of the following activities.

Beginning Reread the text aloud. Encourage students to raise their hands with questions as you read, and pause to allow questions. Encourage other students to answer the questions before you do.

Intermediate Repeat the Beginning activity, but have small groups of students reread the text aloud.

Advanced Repeat the Beginning activity, but have pairs of students reread the text aloud, pause to ask one another questions, and attempt to answer the questions before asking for teacher support.

Advanced High Follow the instructions for the Advanced activity, but tell students to make a list of both specific and general questions about the topic. Instruct pairs to use classroom resources to find answers to their questions. Encourage partners to share their questions and answers with their classmates.

Answers

Describe *The British introduced opium; when the Chinese tried to stop the opium trade, the British responded with gunboats.*

Explain *Years of turmoil, as well as power given to regional leaders, weakened the Qing dynasty and made China vulnerable to European encroachment.*

Guided Reading and Discussion

Ask students how interior conflicts such as the Taiping Rebellion can make one country vulnerable to another. *(Sample answer: The government's military forces are unavailable to defend against outside attacks, officials are occupied handling discord, resources and funds are used to fix disputes, and destruction and loss of life weaken and divide a population.)*

Key Terms

Call students' attention to the term **Open Door Policy** (in bold) in the text. Explain that the United States promoted this policy to ensure that American companies had as much access to China's goods and markets as Europeans did. Unlike modern "free trade" policies, however, the "open door" was a one-way opening into a weakened China.

They imported Western technology, setting up factories to make modern weapons.

They developed shipyards, railroads, mining, and light industry. The Chinese translated Western works on science, government, and the economy. However, the movement made limited progress because the government did not rally behind it.

The Sino-Japanese War Meanwhile, the Western powers and nearby Japan moved rapidly ahead. Japan began to modernize after 1868. It then joined the Western imperialists in the competition for a global empire.

In 1894, Japanese pressure on China led to the **Sino-Japanese War.** It ended in disaster for China, with Japan gaining the island of Taiwan.

Western Spheres of Influence The crushing defeat revealed China's weakness. Western powers moved swiftly to carve out spheres of influence along the Chinese coast. The British took the Chang River valley. The French acquired the territory near their colony of Indochina. Germany and Russia gained territory in northern China.

The United States, a longtime trader with the Chinese, did not take part in the carving up of China. It feared that European powers might shut out American merchants. A few years later, in 1899, it called for a policy to keep Chinese trade open to everyone on an equal basis. The imperial powers accepted the idea of an **Open Door Policy,** as it came to be called. No one, however, consulted the Chinese.

Hundred Days of Reform Defeated by Japan and humiliated by Westerners, Chinese reformers blamed conservative officials for not modernizing China. They urged conservative leaders to stop looking back at China's past and to modernize as Japan had.

In 1898, a young emperor, **Guang Xu** (gwahng shoo), launched the Hundred Days of Reform. New laws set out to modernize the civil service exams, streamline government, and encourage new industries. Reforms affected schools, the military, and the bureaucracy. Conservatives soon rallied against the reform effort. The emperor was imprisoned, and the aging empress Ci Xi reasserted control. Reformers fled for their lives.

IDENTIFY Identify reformers' solutions for China's internal problems.

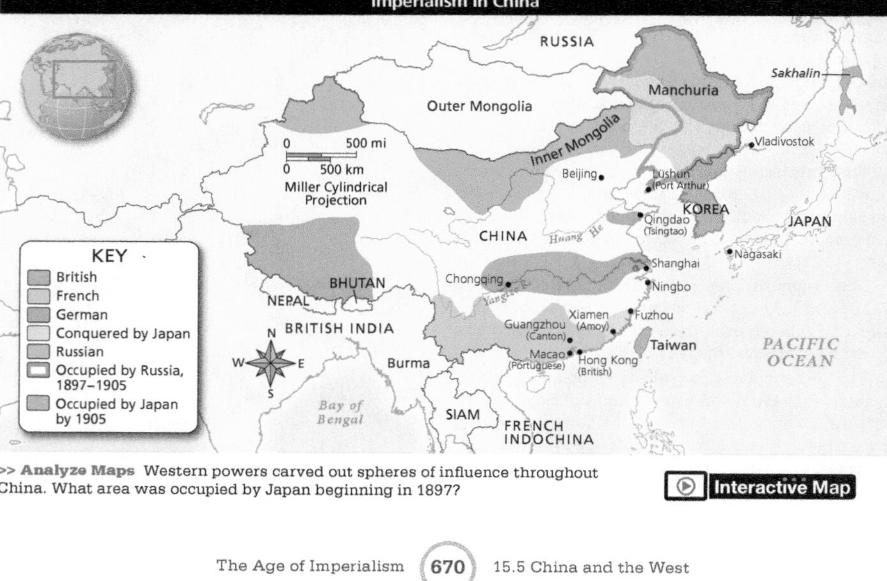

>> **Analyze Maps** Western powers carved out spheres of influence throughout China. What area was occupied by Japan beginning in 1897?

Interactive Map

D Differentiate Extra Support Organize students into pairs and ask them to create a timeline of the events in China covered in "The Taiping Rebellion and a Weakened China" and "Reform Efforts in China." They should scan headings for major events and identify dates. After students assemble their timelines, have them discuss possible cause-and-effect connections between the events.

Answers

Identify *Reformers tried to modernize, incorporate Western technology, build industry, and streamline government.*

Analyze Maps *Manchuria*

The Fall of the Qing Dynasty

As the century ended, China was in turmoil. Anger grew against Christian missionaries who threatened traditional Chinese Confucianism. The presence of foreign troops was another source of discontent. Protected by extraterritoriality, foreigners ignored Chinese laws and lived in their own communities.

The Boxer Uprising Anti-foreign feeling finally exploded in the **Boxer Uprising.** In 1899, a group of Chinese had formed a secret society, the Righteous Harmonious Fists. Westerners watching them train in the martial arts dubbed them Boxers. Their goal was to drive out the "foreign devils" who were polluting the land with their un-Chinese ways, strange buildings, machines, and telegraph lines.

In 1900, the Boxers attacked foreigners across China. In response, the Western powers and Japan organized a multinational force. This force crushed the Boxers and rescued foreigners besieged in Beijing. The empress Ci Xi had at first supported the Boxers but reversed her policy as they retreated.

Consequences of the Uprising China once again had to make concessions to foreigners. The defeat, however, forced even Chinese conservatives to support Westernization. In a rush of reforms, China admitted women to schools and stressed science and mathematics in place of Confucian thought. More students were sent abroad to study.

China also expanded economically. Mining, shipping, railroads, banking, and exports of cash crops grew. Small-scale Chinese industry developed with the help of foreign capital. A Chinese business class emerged, and a new urban working class began to press for rights.

Growth of Chinese Nationalism Although the Boxer Uprising failed, the flames of Chinese nationalism spread. Reformers wanted to strengthen China's government. By the early 1900s, they had introduced a constitutional monarchy. Some reformers called for a republic.

A passionate spokesman for a Chinese republic was **Sun Yixian** (soon yee SHYAHN), also known as Sun Yat-sen. In the early 1900s, he organized the Revolutionary Alliance to rebuild China on "Three Principles of the People." The first principle was nationalism, or freeing China from foreign domination. The second was democracy, or representative government. The third was livelihood, or economic security for all Chinese.

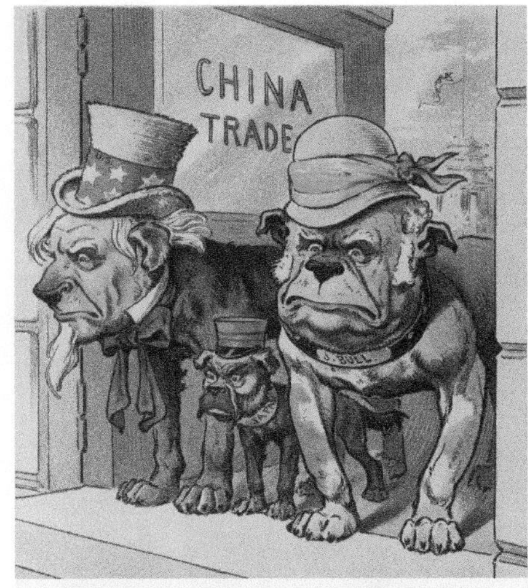

>> **Analyze Political Cartoons** The dogs represent the United States, Japan, and Britain. They guard an open door that says "China Trade." Which country opened the door?

>> Known as the Father of Modern China, Sun Yixian founded the Chinese Nationalist Party and became the first president of China after the fall of the Qing dynasty.

Analyze Images

Focus students' attention on the political cartoon showing guard dogs. Ask them to identify the figure on the left *(Uncle Sam)*; tell them that Japan is in the middle and Britain on the right. Ask what the artist thought were the intentions of these countries toward China. *(Sample response: They valued Chinese trade so much that they made themselves guardians of its trade policies. Like guard dogs, they made sure the door to China would stay open to their countries' interests.)*

The Fall of the Qing Dynasty

Review with students the events that had already weakened China. Explain that the Boxer Rebellion was an uprising against foreign presence and influence in China. It was the result of many years of European intervention and control.

Online Project the **Interactive Gallery: The Boxer Rebellion**, and click through the images with students.

ACTIVE CLASSROOM

Have students choose an image from the gallery and use the Make Headlines strategy to capture the most important aspect of the picture. Have them share the headlines they write with a partner.

Guided Reading and Discussion

Ask students to explain how European imperialism led to the Boxer Rebellion. *(The Boxers rebelled against the effects of European imperialism, including opium addiction, the influence of missionaries, extraterritoriality, foreign control of economic life, and the presence of foreign troops.)*

History Background

Lin Zexu and the Opium Tea Party

Although China outlawed opium in 1729 and again in 1796, the British East India Company used its monopoly on opium growing in India to make enormous profits in China, where opium had ruinous effects. In 1838, Lin Zexu, a humane and just administrator, tried to stop the opium trade. Lin confined 350 foreign merchants in their trading houses until they signed an agreement not to import opium. They refused to sign but were released when they turned over twenty thousand chests of opium. Lin dumped some 3 million pounds of opium into the sea and wrote a letter to Queen Victoria. The British, outraged, sent gunships, which quickly overwhelmed China's antiquated defenses. Lin was blamed at first but was later revered with monuments across China.

Answers

Analyze Political Cartoons *the United States*

Topic 15 Lesson 5

SYNTHESIZE

Online Project the **Digital Activity: The Decline of the Qing Dynasty**. Help students complete the chart. *(Sample causes: the Opium War, the Taiping Rebellion, the Sino-Japanese War, Westernization, nationalism)* Then discuss the role European powers played in the change from Qing China to a Chinese republic. *(Sample response: European powers provoked the Boxer Rebellion, which led to Westernization, nationalism, and reforms—including the establishment of a republic.)*

DEMONSTRATE

Online Assign the **Digital Lesson Quiz** for this lesson if you haven't already done so. Students will be offered automatic remediation or enrichment based on their score.

In "China and the West," you read about the impact of Western imperialism on China and the internal conflicts that led to the fall of the Qing dynasty.

Pose this question to the class on the Discussion Board:

Identify Cause and Effect How did European imperialism indirectly cause the fall of the Qing dynasty? *(Sample response: Pressure from wars and foreign control of land weakened the Qing government. The presence of foreigners raised nationalist sympathies among the Chinese, helping to strengthen support for a republic.)*

Topic Inquiry

Have students continue their investigations for the Topic Inquiry.

A Republic Is Born When Ci Xi died in 1908 and a two-year-old boy inherited the throne, China slipped into chaos. In 1911, uprisings in the provinces swiftly spread. Peasants, students, local warlords, and even court politicians helped topple the Qing dynasty. In December 1911, Sun Yixian was named president of the new Chinese republic. The republic faced overwhelming problems and was almost constantly at war with itself or foreign invaders.

? IDENTIFY CAUSE AND EFFECT What caused the Qing dynasty to fall?

ASSESSMENT

1. **Sequence Events** Describe the sequence of conflicts and their consequences that weakened Qing China.
2. **Generate Explanations** How did Western powers gain greater trading rights in China?
3. **Summarize** What internal problems threatened the Qing dynasty?
4. **Summarize** What were the goals of Chinese reformers?
5. **Synthesize** Describe how a republic replaced the Qing dynasty.

Answers

Identify Cause and Effect *The Boxer Rebellion led to greater Westernization, which led to nationalism, which combined with discontent and a weak emperor (a two-year-old) to topple the dynasty.*

Assessment

1. First, the Opium War led to a large payment to Britain and extraterritoriality to its citizens. The Taiping Rebellion caused massive loss of life and decreased the power of the Qing government. China lost Taiwan during the Sino-Japanese War, and Western nations carved out spheres of influence. Finally, the Boxer Rebellion tilted popular opinion toward Westernization and away from the Qing government.
2. Western powers gained greater trading rights by using or threatening to use force.
3. poor administration, overpopulation, imperial extravagance and corruption, and tax evasion by the rich
4. Chinese reformers sought to modernize and Westernize the economy and government.
5. The rise of nationalism and widespread discontent led to the overthrow of the Qing dynasty and the creation of a republic.

15.6 In 1853, the United States displayed its new military might, sending a naval force to make Japan open its ports to trade. Japanese leaders debated how to respond. While some resisted giving up their 215-year-old policy of seclusion, others felt that it would be wiser for Japan to learn from the foreigners.

>> **Generate Explanations** Emperor Mutsuhito took the name "Meiji," or "enlightened rule," when he came to power. What made his rule "enlightened"?

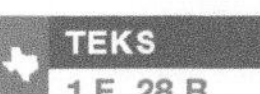

Interactive Flipped Video

The Modernization of Japan

TEKS
1.E, 28.B

>> Objectives

Identify the problems faced by Tokugawa Japan.

Explain how the United States opened Japan to the outside world.

Analyze the causes and effects of the Meiji Restoration.

Describe how Japan began to build an empire.

>> Key Terms

Matthew Perry
Mutsuhito
Tokyo
Meiji Restoration
Diet
zaibatsu
homogeneous society
First Sino-Japanese War
Russo-Japanese War

Unrest in Tokugawa Japan

In the end, Japan chose to abandon its centuries of isolation. The country swiftly transformed itself into a modern industrial power and then set out on its own imperialist path.

In the early 1600s, Japan was still ruled by shoguns, or supreme military dictators. Although emperors still lived in the ceremonial capital of Kyoto, the shoguns held the real power in Edo. Daimyo, or landholding warrior lords, helped the shoguns control Japan. In 1603, a new family, the Tokugawas, seized power.

The Tokugawa shoguns reimposed centralized feudalism, closed Japan to foreigners, and forbade Japanese people to travel overseas. The nation's only window on the world was through Nagasaki, where the Dutch were allowed very limited trade.

For more than 200 years, Japan developed in isolation. Internal commerce expanded, agricultural production grew, and bustling cities sprang up. However, these economic changes strained Japanese society. Many daimyo suffered financial hardship. They needed money in a commercial economy, but a daimyo's wealth was in land rather than cash.

PEARSON realize. www.PearsonTexas.com Access your Digital Lesson.

Topic 15 Lesson 6

The Modernization of Japan

CONNECT

Preview Have students preview the **Lesson Objectives** and the list of **Key Terms**.

Students can also preview all the **Key Terms** and **Academic Vocabulary** using the **Interactive Reading Notepad** on the digital course or preview a summary of the lesson in the **Reading and Note Taking Study Guide**.

Online Use the **Editable Presentation** found on the digital course to present the main ideas for this lesson.

Start Up Activity

Tell students that by the mid-1800s, Japan had a long history of isolation from the outside world. Ask them to predict what level of Westernization Japan would be willing to tolerate in order to modernize.

Online You can also project the **Start Up Activity** from the course.

INVESTIGATE

Have students read the lesson using the **Reading and Note Taking Study Guide** to help them take notes and understand the text as they read.

Unrest in Tokugawa Japan

In the early 1600s, Japan was still ruled by shoguns. In 1603, the Tokugawas took power, brought back centralized feudalism, and closed Japan to foreigners. No foreign travel was allowed. For more than 200 years, Japan developed in isolation. Unrest grew among many Japanese as they suffered from financial hardship, no political power, and heavy taxes. The government tried to revive old ways, emphasizing farming over commerce. The shoguns were no longer strong leaders, corruption was common, and the people of Japan were discontented.

Aa Vocabulary Builder

1. Have students pronounce the following academic vocabulary terms in this lesson and clarify the part of speech. For difficult or polysyllabic words, break them into syllables and pronounce them with the students.
2. Explain what the word means in common "student-friendly" language using synonyms and antonyms when possible. Provide concrete examples to clarify the meaning, and rephrase the definition.

emphasizing: stressing

thereby: by that means; because of that

Answers

Generate Explanations *Emperor Mutsuhito transformed feudal Japan into an industrialized nation with a constitutional government and a more educated population by adapting Western systems to Japan's needs.*

Topic 15 Lesson 6

Guided Reading and Discussion

Ask students to identify the pressures faced by the different levels of society in Tokugawa Japan. *(financial hardships of daimyo and lesser samurai; merchants had no political power; peasants were heavily taxed; failure of reform efforts, weakening of shoguns' power)* Discuss how these conditions made Japan a likely target for Western imperialists. *(Sample response: Such widespread unrest made the Japanese less resistant to outside pressures.)*

The Opening of Japan

Tell students that in 1853, a fleet of well-armed U.S. ships led by Commodore Matthew Perry arrived in Japan, demanding that Japan open its ports. Unable to defend itself, Japan was forced to sign treaties giving the United States trading and other rights. Humiliated, discontented daimyo and samurai led a revolt that replaced the shoguns with an emperor, who began a long reign known as the Meiji Restoration, during which Japan modernized.

Online Project the **Interactive Image: Commodore Perry's Expedition to Japan**, and click through the hotspots with students.

ACTIVE CLASSROOM

Have pairs of students assume the roles of Commodore Perry and a Meiji leader and conduct a Conversation With History between the two. Tell them to record the details of their conversation, which should be based on information from the Interactive Image.

Lesser samurai were unhappy, too, because they lacked the money to live as well as urban merchants. Merchants in turn resented their place at the bottom of the social ladder. No matter how rich they were, they had no political power. Peasants, meanwhile, suffered under heavy taxes.

The government responded by trying to revive old ways, emphasizing farming over commerce and praising traditional values. These efforts had scant success. By the 1800s, shoguns were no longer strong leaders, and corruption was common. Discontent simmered throughout Japan.

IDENTIFY CAUSE AND EFFECT By the mid-1800s, why did so many groups of people in Japan feel discontented?

The Opening of Japan

While the shoguns faced troubles at home, disturbing news of the British victory over China in the Opium War and the way in which imperialists had forced China to sign unequal treaties reached Japan. Surely, Japanese officials reasoned, it would not be long before Western powers turned toward Japan.

>> In this Japanese woodblock print, Japanese boats go out to meet one of Commodore Matthew Perry's ships in Tokyo Bay.

Interactive Illustration

External Pressure Leads to Internal Revolt The officials' fears were correct. In July 1853, a fleet of well-armed American ships commanded by Commodore **Matthew Perry** sailed into lower Tokyo Bay. Perry carried a letter from Millard Fillmore, the president of the United States. The letter demanded that Japan open its ports to diplomatic and commercial exchange.

The shogun's advisors debated what to do. Japan did not have the ability to defend itself against the powerful United States Navy. In the Treaty of Kanagawa in 1854, the shogun Iesada agreed to open two Japanese ports to American ships, though not for trade.

The United States soon won trading and other rights, including extraterritoriality and low taxes on American imports. European nations demanded their own similar rights. Like the Chinese, the Japanese felt humiliated by the terms of these unequal treaties. Some bitterly criticized the shogun for not taking a strong stand against the foreigners.

Foreign pressure deepened the social and economic unrest. In 1867, discontented daimyo and samurai led a revolt that unseated the shogun and "restored" the 15-year-old emperor **Mutsuhito** to power. When he was crowned emperor, Mutsuhito took the name Meiji (MAY jee), which means "enlightened rule." He moved from the old imperial capital in Kyoto to the shogun's palace in Edo, which was renamed **Tokyo,** or "eastern capital."

The Meiji Restoration The young emperor began a long reign known as the **Meiji Restoration.** This period, which lasted from 1868 to 1912, was a major turning point in Japanese history.

The Meiji reformers, who ruled in the emperor's name, were determined to strengthen Japan. Their goal was summarized in their motto, "A rich country, a strong military." The emperor supported and embodied the reforms.

The new leaders set out to study Western ways, adapt them to Japanese needs, and thereby keep Japan from having to give in to Western demands. In 1871, members of the government traveled overseas to learn about Western governments, economies, technology, and customs. The government brought experts from Western countries to Japan and sent young samurai to study abroad, furthering Japan's knowledge of Western industrial techniques.

SUMMARIZE How did Japan react when it was forced to accept unequal treaties?

ELPS 4.F.7 Use peer and teacher support when discussing *The Opening of Japan.*

English Language Proficiency Standards

Reading 4.F.7 Read "The Opening of Japan" aloud. Have students complete one of these activities.

Beginning As you read, pause to retell the content. Ask questions to allow students to show their understanding, and show them how to ask each other questions about the text. Allow students to ask questions, and encourage answers from other students

Intermediate Use the Beginning activity, but have small groups of students reread the text and retell the content. Instruct students to pause while reading to allow questions. Work with students to find answers.

Advanced Have pairs of students reread the text and ask questions. Have partners try to answer the questions and then share their most difficult questions with the group.

Advanced High Have pairs of students read and retell the text, elaborating on the content with their partners. Tell pairs to ask each other questions. Have them share their questions and answers with the class.

Answers

Identify Cause and Effect *The economy changed, but the social structure remained the same, and the shoguns were no longer strong leaders.*

Summarize *Discontented samurai and daimyo restored the emperor to power and set about reforming Japan to allow it to compete more effectively with Western powers.*

Transformation during the Meiji Period

The Meiji reformers faced an enormous task. They were committed to replacing the rigid feudal order with a completely new political and social system and to building a modern industrial economy. Change did not come easily. In the end, however, Japan adapted foreign ideas with great speed and success.

Modernizing Government The reformers wanted to create a strong central government, equal to those of Western powers. After studying various European governments, they adapted the German model. In 1889, the emperor issued the Meiji constitution. It set forth the principle that all citizens were equal before the law. Like the German system, however, it gave the emperor autocratic, or absolute, power. A legislature, or **Diet,** was formed, made up of one elected house and one house appointed by the emperor. Additionally, voting rights were sharply limited.

Japan then established a Western-style bureaucracy with separate departments to supervise finance, the army, the navy, and education. To strengthen the military, it turned to Western technology and ended the special privileges of samurai. In the past, samurai alone were warriors. In modern Japan, as in the West, all men were subject to military service.

>> In 1871, Japanese statesman Iwakura Tomomi led a "learning mission" to the United States to study Western systems of education, administration, finance, and law. After his return, Iwakura became the most powerful man in the Meiji government.

Rapid Industrialization Meiji leaders made the economy a major priority. They encouraged Japan's businesses to adopt Western methods. They set up a modern banking system, built railroads, improved ports, and organized a telegraph and postal system. To get industries started, the government typically built factories and then sold them to wealthy business families who developed them further.

With such support, business dynasties like the Kawasaki family soon ruled over industrial empires. These powerful banking and industrial families were known as **zaibatsu** (zy baht soo).

By the 1890s, industry was booming. With modern machines, silk manufacturing soared. Shipyards, copper and coal mining, and steel making also helped make Japan an industrial powerhouse. As in other industrial countries, the population grew rapidly, and many peasants flocked to the growing cities for work.

Social Changes The constitution ended legal distinctions between classes, thus allowing more people to become involved in nation building. The government set up schools and a university. It hired Westerners to teach the new generation how to use modern technology.

>> This woodblock print shows the announcement of the new Meiji constitution in 1889, which created a European-style government in Japan. **Analyze Images** What other European influences do you see in the print?

Interactive Gallery

Guided Reading and Discussion

Ask students to explain what caused Japan to end more than 200 years of seclusion. *(a request to open their country to trade, backed up by a display of military power by the United States, along with unrest in the country)*

Transformation during the Meiji Period

Tell students that Meiji reformers set out to create a new political and social system and build a modern industrial economy. A legislature was formed, and by the 1890s, industry was booming and modernization was well under way.

Online Project the **Interactive Gallery: The Meiji Restoration, 1868–1912**, and click through the images with students.

ACTIVE CLASSROOM

Use the Quick Write strategy with students after they view the Interactive Gallery. Give them 1 minute to share what they now know about the Meiji Restoration. Challenge them to keep their responses to 140 characters.

Guided Reading and Discussion

Have students identify some of the Western methods adopted by Japan's businesses during the Meiji period. *(created a modern banking system, built railroads, improved ports, created telegraph and postal systems)*

Key Terms

Call students' attention to the term **zaibatsu** (in bold) in the text. Explain that these banking and industrial firms continued to grow through World War II, but after the war, in 1946, the Allies insisted that the zaibatsu be disbanded.

Answers

Analyze Images *Sample response: The people are dressed in European-style clothing.*

Topic 15 Lesson 6

Japan Builds an Empire

Remind students that as a small island nation, Japan lacked many resources essential for industry. The need for natural resources and a strong ambition to equal Western imperial nations spurred Japan to build an empire. In 1876, Japan forced Korea to open its ports to Japanese trade. In 1894, competition between Japan and China in Korea led to the First Sino-Japanese War, which Japan easily won. Japan gained ports in China, won control of Taiwan, and joined the West in the race for an empire. Ten years later, Japan defeated Russia in the Russo-Japanese War. By the early 1900s, Japan was the strongest power in Asia.

Guided Reading and Discussion

Ask students why Japan sought greater influence in Korea. *(Japan wanted to create an empire equal to those of Western powers and to gain natural resources.)* How did Japan assert its power in the region? *(through armed warfare, defeating its rivals in the Sino-Japanese War and the Russo-Japanese War)*

Analyze Images

Direct students' attention to the political cartoon. Explain that the hat, hairstyle, and clothing of the man on the right indicate that he is Chinese. Ask students who the man on the far left might represent. *(Russia)* The man on the ground represents Korea. Ask: What was the artist's point of view about Japan? Which details support your conclusion? *(Sample response: The artist disapproved of Japan's actions, as shown by the depiction of Japan as stepping on Korea with a harsh expression while Korea looks shocked.)*

Despite the reforms, class distinctions survived in Japan as they did in the West. Also, although literacy increased and some women gained an education, women in general were still assigned a secondary role in society. The reform of the Japanese family system, and women's position in it, became the topic of major debates in the 1870s. Although the government agreed to some increases in education for women, it dealt harshly with other attempts at change. After 1898, Japanese women were forbidden any political participation and legally were lumped together with minors.

An Amazing Success Japan modernized with amazing speed during the Meiji period. Its success was due to a number of causes. Japan had a strong sense of identity, partly because it had a **homogeneous society**—that is, its people shared a common culture and language. Economic growth during Tokugawa times had set Japan on the road to development. Japan also had experience in learning and adapting ideas from foreign nations, such as China.

The Japanese were determined to resist foreign rule. By the 1890s, Japan was strong enough to force Western powers to revise the unequal treaties. By then, it was already acquiring its own overseas empire.

>> **Analyze Political Cartoons** Japan began its imperialist agenda in Korea. Based on the cartoon, who else had imperialist ambitions in Korea?

SUMMARIZE What changes did the reforms of the Meiji Restoration bring about in Japan?

Japan Builds an Empire

As in Western industrial nations, Japan's economic needs fed its imperialist desires. As a small island nation, Japan lacked many basic resources that were essential for industrial growth. It depended on other countries to obtain raw materials. Spurred by this dependency and a strong ambition to equal the West, Japan sought to build an empire. With its modern army and navy, it maneuvered for power in East Asia.

Korea Imperialist rivalries put the spotlight on Korea. Located at a crossroads of East Asia, the Korean peninsula was a focus of competition among Russia, China, and Japan. Korea had been a tributary state to China for many years. A tributary state is a state that is independent but acknowledges the supremacy of a stronger state. Although influenced by China, Korea had its own traditions and government.

Korea had also shut its doors to foreigners. It did, however, maintain relations with China and sometimes with Japan.

By the 1800s, Korea faced pressure from outsiders. As Chinese power declined, Russia expanded into East Asia. Then, as Japan industrialized, it, too, eyed Korea. In 1876, Japan used its superior power to force Korea to open its ports to Japanese trade. Faced with similar demands from Western powers, Korea had to accept unequal treaties.

Japan Expands As Japan extended its influence in Korea, it came into conflict with China. In 1894, competition between Japan and China in Korea led to the **First Sino-Japanese War.** ("Sino" means "Chinese.") Although China had greater resources, Japan had benefited from modernization. To the surprise of China and the West, Japan won easily. It used its victory to gain treaty ports in China and control over the island of Taiwan, thus joining the West in the race for empire.

Ten years later, Japan successfully challenged Russia, its other rival for power in Korea and Manchuria. During the **Russo-Japanese War,** Japan's armies defeated Russian troops in Manchuria, and its navy destroyed almost an entire Russian fleet. For the first time in modern history, an Asian power humbled a European nation. In the 1905 Treaty of Portsmouth,

Answers

Summarize *The Meiji Restoration brought about rapid industrialization, modernization, and changes in government and society in Japan.*

Analyze Political Cartoons *Russia and China*

English Language Proficiency Standards

Reading 4.J.1 Read aloud "Transformation During the Meiji Period." Have students complete one activity.

Beginning Display subheads from the text, and model using them to make predictions. Write and display student predictions, and have students copy them into their notebooks. Read the text aloud. Pause to assess whether or not predictions were correct.

Intermediate Have students identify subheads. Display them and ask students to copy them into their notebooks. Discuss how to use subheads to predict content. Display student predictions and have students copy them into their notebooks. Read the text aloud, pausing so students can assess whether predictions were correct.

Advanced Follow the instructions in the Intermediate activity, but ask small groups of students to carry out the process.

Advanced High Follow the instructions in the Intermediate activity, but ask pairs of students to carry out the process.

Japan gained control of Korea as well as rights in parts of Manchuria.

Controlling Korea Japan made Korea a protectorate. In 1910, it annexed Korea outright, absorbing the kingdom into the Japanese empire. Japan ruled Korea for 35 years. Like Western imperialists, the Japanese set out to modernize their newly acquired territory. They built factories, railroads, and communications systems. Development, however, generally benefited Japan. Under Japanese rule, Koreans produced more rice than ever before, but most of it went to Japan.

The Japanese were as unpopular in Korea as Western imperialists were elsewhere. They imposed harsh rule on their colony and deliberately set out to erase the Korean language and identity. Repression bred resentment. And resentment, in turn, nourished a Korean nationalist movement.

Nine years after annexation, a nonviolent protest against the Japanese began on March 1, 1919, and soon spread throughout Korea. The Japanese crushed the uprising and massacred many Koreans. The violence did not discourage people who worked to end Japanese rule. Instead, the March First Movement became a rallying symbol for Korean nationalists.

The Koreans would have to wait many years for freedom. Japan continued to expand in East Asia during the years that followed, seeking natural resources and territory. By the early 1900s, Japan was the strongest power in Asia.

GENERATE EXPLANATIONS How did industrialization help start Japan on an imperialist course?

>> Japan's victory in the Russo-Japanese War forced Russia to abandon its imperialist policies in East Asia.

ASSESSMENT

1. **Cite Evidence** What was one cause of discontent in Tokugawa, Japan?
2. **Identify Main Ideas** What demand did the United States make on Japan in 1853?
3. **Make Generalizations** What was the goal of the Meiji reformers?
4. **Identify Cause and Effect** What was the main reason Japan become an imperialist power?
5. **Summarize** Why was the Russo-Japanese War significant?

SYNTHESIZE

Online Project the **Digital Activity: The Meiji Restoration**. Have students fill in the graphic organizer to show the causes, events, and effects of the Meiji Restoration. *(Causes: social and economic unrest, foreign pressure, daimyo and samurai revolt; Meiji Restoration: strong central government, Western business methods, industrialization, nation building; Effects: builds an empire; influence in Korea, conflict with China, defeats Russia)*

DEMONSTRATE

Online Assign the **Digital Lesson Quiz** for this lesson if you haven't already done so. Students will be offered automatic remediation or enrichment based on their score.

Pose these questions to the class on the Discussion Board:

In "The Modernization of Japan," you read about how Japan became an industrial and imperialist power.

Summarize How did Japan change course in the late 1800s? *(Japan went from isolation and a rigid feudal order to a modern industrial economy and new political and social systems, with a central government and a democratic constitution.)*

Identify Cause and Effect By the 1890s, how had modernized Japan changed its relationship with the West? *(In 1853, the United States forced Japan out of isolation; by the 1890s, Japan was more powerful and started building an empire and revising unequal treaties.)*

Topic Inquiry

Have students continue their investigations for the Topic Inquiry.

Assessment

1. The daimyo suffered financial hardships; merchants had no political power, despite economic gains; the shoguns had reimposed centralized feudalism; and the peasants were burdened by heavy taxes.
2. to open its ports to trade and diplomatic contacts
3. to strengthen Japan through rapid industrialization and modernization
4. to obtain natural resources to support industrialization
5. It was the first time in modern history that a European power lost a war to an Asian nation. It secured Japan's imperialistic goals and ended with Japanese control over Korea and rights to parts of Manchuria.

Answers

Generate Explanations *Japan had few of the natural resources it needed to make industrial products. Expansion increased Japan's access to natural resources and enabled it to build an empire similar to those of the Western powers.*

Topic 15 Lesson 7

Southeast Asia and the Pacific

CONNECT

Preview Have students preview the **Lesson Objectives** and the list of **Key Terms**.

Students can also preview all the **Key Terms** and **Academic Vocabulary** using the **Interactive Reading Notepad** on the digital course or preview a summary of the lesson in the **Reading and Note Taking Study Guide**.

Online Use the **Editable Presentation** found on the digital course to present the main ideas for this lesson.

Start Up Activity

Have students answer this question as they get settled: Based on your knowledge of the effect of European imperialism on other regions, what impact do you think Western imperialists had on Southeast Asia? *(Students should suggest that the imperialists likely exploited Southeast Asia's resources and influenced the region's economic and political systems and its cultures.)*

Online You can also project the **Start Up Activity** from the course.

INVESTIGATE

Have students read the lesson using the **Reading and Note Taking Study Guide** to help them take notes and understand the text as they read.

European Imperialism in Southeast Asia

Military Might and the Philippines

Remind students that imperialism involves economic, political, and cultural control of a region or country by another country. Point out that imperialism is caused by the ruling country's pursuit of economic, political, and/or social gains. The nations of Southeast Asia were especially attractive to European rulers because of their rich natural resources, which were even easier to access after the opening of the Suez Canal in 1860.

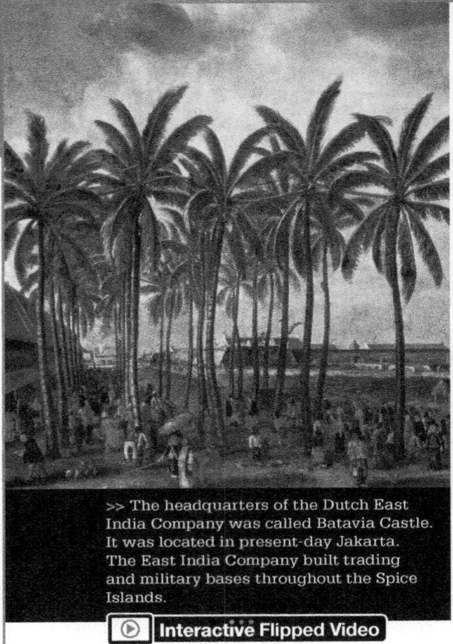

>> The headquarters of the Dutch East India Company was called Batavia Castle. It was located in present-day Jakarta. The East India Company built trading and military bases throughout the Spice Islands.

Interactive Flipped Video

15.7 Leaders throughout Southeast Asia faced the same dilemma as leaders in other parts of the world. As they had in Africa, Western industrial powers divided up the region in search of raw materials, new markets, and Christian converts.

TEKS 1.E, 8.C, 16.B, 28.B

>> Objectives

Describe how Europe and the United States built colonies in Southeast Asia.

Explain how imperialism spread to the islands of the Pacific.

Analyze how Australia and New Zealand achieved self-rule.

>> Key Terms

French Indochina
Mongkut
Spanish-American War
Liliuokalani
indigenous
penal colony
Maori

Southeast Asia and the Pacific

European Imperialism in Southeast Asia

Southeast Asia commands the sea lanes between India and China. The region had been influenced by both civilizations. From the 1500s through the 1700s, European merchants gained footholds in Southeast Asia, but most of the area remained independent. This changed in the 1800s. Westerners—notably the Dutch, British, and French—manipulated local rivalries and used modern armies and technology to colonize much of Southeast Asia.

The Dutch East Indies During the early 1600s, the Dutch East India Company established transportation and trading bases on the island of Java and in the Moluccas, or Spice Islands. From there, the Dutch slowly expanded to dominate the rest of the Dutch East Indies (now Indonesia). The Dutch expected their Southeast Asian colonies to produce profitable crops of coffee, indigo, and spices.

The British in Burma and Malaya In the early 1800s, rulers of Burma (present-day Myanmar) clashed with the British, who were expanding eastward from India. The Burmese suffered disastrous

www.PearsonTexas.com Access your Digital Lesson.

Aa Vocabulary Builder

1. Have students pronounce the following academic vocabulary term in this lesson and clarify the part of speech. Break the word into syllables and pronounce it with the students.
2. Explain what the word means in common "student-friendly" language using synonyms and antonyms when possible. Provide concrete examples to clarify the meaning, and rephrase the definition.

transition: passage from one way to another

defeats in several wars. They continued to resist British rule, however, even after Britain annexed Burma in 1886.

At the same time, the British expanded their influence in Malaya. The busy port of Singapore grew up at the southern tip of the peninsula. Soon, natural resources and profits from Asian trade flowed through Singapore to enrich Britain.

The French in Indochina The French, meanwhile, were building an empire on the Southeast Asian mainland. In the 1500s, Portuguese traders had set up a trading center in what today is Vietnam. Christian missionaries from France and other European countries moved into Vietnam and won some converts. Threatened by growing Western influence, Vietnamese officials tried to suppress Christianity by killing converts and missionary priests. Partly in response, France invaded Vietnam in 1858. The French also wanted more political influence and markets in Southeast Asia.

The Vietnamese fought fiercely but could not withstand superior European firepower. By the early 1860s, France had seized a portion of southern Vietnam. Over the next decades, the French took over the rest of Vietnam and all of Laos and Cambodia. The French and other Westerners referred to these holdings as **French Indochina.** (Mainland Southeast Asia was known during this period as "Indochina.")

Siam Stays Independent The kingdom of Siam (present-day Thailand) lay between British-ruled Burma and French Indochina. The king of Siam, **Mongkut** (mahng KOOT), who ruled from 1851 to 1868, did not underestimate Western power. He studied foreign languages and read widely on modern science and mathematics. He used this knowledge to negotiate with the Western powers and satisfy their goals in Siam by making agreements in unequal treaties. In this way, Siam escaped becoming a European colony.

Mongkut and his son, Chulalongkorn, (CHOO lah lawng kawrn) set Siam on the road to modernization. They reformed the government, modernized the army, and hired Western experts to teach Thais how to use the new technology.

They abolished slavery and gave women some choice in marriage. As Siam modernized, Chulalongkorn bargained to remove the unequal treaties.

Characteristics of Colonial Southeast Asia During this period, many Chinese people migrated to Southeast Asia to take advantage of the economic opportunities there. They left China to escape hardship and turmoil. Despite local resentment, these communities formed vital networks in trade, banking, and other economic activities.

By the 1890s, Europeans controlled most of Southeast Asia. They introduced modern technology and expanded commerce and industry. Europeans directed the mining of tin, the harvesting of rubber, and the building of harbors and railroads. But these changes benefited the European colonizers far more than they did the Southeast Asians.

DESCRIBE How did the Burmese and the Vietnamese respond to colonization attempts?

Military Might and the Philippines

In the 1500s, Spain had seized the Philippines. Catholic missionaries spread Christianity among the Filipinos. As the Catholic Church gained enormous power and wealth, many Filipinos accused the Church of abusing its position. By the late 1800s, their anger fueled strong resistance to Spanish rule.

The opening of the Suez Canal in 1860 helped the economy of the Philippines by making trade with

>> **Draw Conclusions** During the Anglo-Burmese Wars, Britain annexed Burma. Here, a British official addresses Burmese villagers. What does the image communicate about the balance of power during the war?

Online Project the **Interactive Map: Imperialism in Southeast Asia, 1900**, and click through the hotspots with students.

ACTIVE CLASSROOM

Have student pairs do an Audio Tour of the map. Have the first student give the second a verbal "tour" of the map, pointing out the information communicated through the layers. Have the second student give the first an explanation of the map's purpose.

Guided Reading and Discussion

Have students, as a class, list the causes for Western imperialism in Southeast Asia. Then have them classify the causes as political, economic, or social motivations. *(Sample response: Economic: The Dutch profited from coffee, indigo, and spices from the Dutch East Indies; the British benefited from Singapore's port. Social: France supported Catholic missionaries in their work to spread Christianity in French Indochina, as did Spain in the Philippines. Political: The United States took over the Philippines after defeating Spain in the Spanish-American War.)*

Analyze Images

Turn students' attention to the image with the palm trees. Ask them what this picture tells them about the climate of this area. *(It is tropical or subtropical.)* Tell students that nearly all of Southeast Asia lies in the tropics—between the Tropic of Cancer and the Tropic of Capricorn.

D Differentiate Extra Support Students may need further explanation of political, economic, and social motivations, as called for in the Guided Reading. Explain that two countries can clash over reasons that fall into one of the categories. A political conflict could involve the location of a border, for example. An economic conflict could involve trade restrictions one country places on another. A social conflict could refer to religious or ethnic disputes.

Answers

Describe *They fiercely resisted European rule.*

Draw Conclusions *Britain was a more powerful nation with a stronger military. It could come in and demand, or forcefully take, land.*

Strategic Holdings in the Pacific Islands

Explain that the islands of the Pacific, by providing naval bases, allowed for an expanding American military presence. Even islands with few natural resources provided economic motivation for Western control, serving as transportation, whaling, and sealing bases.

Guided Reading and Discussion

Ask students how advanced military and transportation technologies would have helped the United States achieve and maintain imperialist goals in the Pacific. *(Sample response: The small islands of the Pacific did not have the means to resist the American military. They are spread over a vast area, far from other nations, so the United States needed reliable transportation to reach and rule them.)*

Europeans in Australia

New Zealand's Story

Tell students that European colonization of Australia and New Zealand led to the creation of self-ruled nations with strong ties to Britain. The story of Australia and New Zealand differs from that of Southeast Asian countries because they developed into nations with large English-speaking populations. By the time these countries had gained independence from Britain, their indigenous populations were minorities.

European countries easier. Some upper class Filipinos gained access to better education. Leaders such as José Rizal inspired Filipinos to work to gain better treatment from Spain.

The **Spanish-American War** broke out in 1898 between Spain and the United States over Cuba's attempts to win independence from Spain. During the war, American battleships destroyed the Spanish fleet, which was stationed in the Philippines. Encouraged by American naval officers, Filipino rebel leaders declared independence from Spain. Rebel soldiers threw their support into the fight against Spanish troops.

In return for their help, the Filipino rebels expected the Americans to recognize their independence. Instead, in the treaty that ended the war with Spain, the United States agreed to give Spain $20 million in return for control of the Philippines. Within the United States, debate raged over the treaty's ratification. American imperialists wanted to join the European competition for territory. Anti-imperialists wanted the United States to steer clear of foreign entanglements. The United States Senate ratified the treaty by only one vote over the required two-thirds majority.

Bitterly disappointed, Filipino nationalists renewed their struggle. From 1899 to 1901, Filipinos led by Emilio Aguinaldo (ah gee NAHL doh) battled American forces. Thousands of Americans and hundreds of thousands of Filipinos died. In the end, the Americans crushed the rebellion. The United States set out to modernize the Philippines through education, improved health care, and economic reforms.

The United States also built dams, roads, railways, and ports. In addition, the United States promised Filipinos a gradual transition to self-rule some time in the future.

IDENTIFY MAIN IDEAS How did the United States gain control of the Philippines?

>> During the Spanish-American War, the U.S. Navy destroyed Spanish ships in the Battle of Manila Bay in the Philippines.

Strategic Holdings in the Pacific Islands

In the 1800s, the industrialized powers also began to take an interest in the islands of the Pacific. The thousands of islands splashed across the Pacific include the three regions of Melanesia, Micronesia, and Polynesia.

At first, American, French, and British whaling and sealing ships looked for bases to take on supplies in the Pacific. Missionaries, too, moved into the region and opened the way for political involvement.

In 1878, the United States secured an unequal treaty from Samoa, a group of islands in the South Pacific. The United States gained rights such as extraterritoriality and a naval station. Other nations gained similar agreements. As their rivalry increased, the United States, Germany, and Britain agreed to a triple protectorate over Samoa.

Beginning in the mid-1800s, American sugar growers pressed for power in the Hawaiian Islands. When the Hawaiian queen **Liliuokalani** (lih lee uh oh kuh LAH nee) tried to reduce foreign influence, American planters overthrew her in 1893. They then asked the United States to annex Hawaii, which it finally did in 1898. Supporters of annexation argued that if the United States did not take Hawaii, Britain or Japan might do so. By 1900, the United States, Britain, France, and Germany had claimed nearly every island in the Pacific.

RECALL Why did some Americans think the United States should control Hawaii?

Europeans in Australia

The Dutch in the 1600s were the first Europeans to reach Australia. In 1770, Captain James Cook claimed Australia for Britain. For a time, however, Australia remained too distant to attract European settlers.

Answers

Identify Main Ideas *They bought the country from Spain for $20 million and then crushed a Filipino rebellion.*

Recall *If the United States did not take Hawaii, Britain or Japan might.*

Australia's Indigenous People Like most regions claimed by imperialist powers, Australia had long been inhabited by other people. The first settlers had reached Australia perhaps 40,000 years earlier, probably from Southeast Asia, and spread across the continent. These **indigenous,** or original, people were called Aborigines, a word used by Europeans to denote the earliest people to live in a place.

Today, many Australian Aborigines call themselves Kooris. Isolated from the larger world, the Aborigines lived in small hunting and food-gathering bands, much as their Stone Age ancestors had. Aboriginal groups spoke as many as 250 distinct languages. When white settlers arrived in Australia, the indigenous population suffered disastrously.

A Penal Colony During the 1700s, Britain had sent convicts to its North American colonies, especially to Georgia. The American Revolution closed that outlet. Prisons in London and other cities were jammed.

To fill the need for prisons, Britain made Australia into a **penal colony,** or a place where convicted criminals are sent to be punished. The first British ships, carrying about 700 convicts, arrived in Botany Bay, Australia, in 1788. The people who survived the grueling eight-month voyage faced more hardships on shore. Many were city dwellers with no farming skills. Under the brutal discipline of soldiers, work gangs cleared land for settlement.

Emigration to Australia In the early 1800s, Britain encouraged free citizens to emigrate to Australia by offering them land and tools. A prosperous wool industry grew up as settlers found that the land and climate suited sheepherding. In 1851, a gold rush in eastern Australia brought a population boom. Many gold hunters stayed on to become ranchers and farmers.

They pushed into the rugged interior known as the Outback, carving out huge sheep ranches and wheat farms. As the newcomers settled in, they thrust aside or killed the Aborigines.

Self-Rule in Australia Australia was made up of separate colonies scattered around the continent. Britain worried about interference from other European powers. To counter this threat and to boost development, it responded to Australian demands for self-rule. In 1901, Britain helped the colonies unite into the independent Commonwealth of Australia. The new country kept its ties to Britain by recognizing the British monarch as its head of state.

The Australian constitution drew on both British and American models. Unlike Britain and the United States, Australia quickly granted women the right to

>> Queen Liliuokalani reduced benefits to American businesses operating in Hawaii, generating opposition from businessmen like Sanford Dole of the pineapple industry.

>> This Aboriginal art, showing a mythical woman and child with a fish, was found in northern Australia. Aboriginal art often depicts "Dreamtime," the world's origin according to Aboriginal traditions.

Interactive Chart

Online Project the **Interactive Chart: Colonization of Australia and New Zealand**. Drag and drop the characteristics with students.

ACTIVE CLASSROOM

Consider posting the text from the Interactive Chart in different parts of the room to create a Walking Tour of the activity. Partners can visit each country's passage, discussing and summarizing it before investigating another.

Guided Reading and Discussion

Tell students that Britain helped unite Australia under commonwealth status to fend off other European powers. Have students compare the economic motivations for imperialism in Australia and New Zealand with the difficulties of maintaining power over these lands. *(Sample response: Britain benefited from wool, wheat, beef, and other farm products, but because these lands were so far away, it had to pay enormous transportation, military, and administrative costs, and governing would have been a challenge.)*

Key Terms

Call students' attention to the term **penal colony** (in bold) in the text. Explain that distant penal colonies were a means of ridding a country of undesirables—convicts, prisoners of war, political prisoners, or just poor people. They were often forced to provide cheap labor. Tell students that Britain used colonial America as a penal colony, with prisoners often serving as indentured servants, until the American Revolution ended the practice.

English Language Proficiency Standards

Reading 4.F.8 Read "Europeans in Australia" aloud. Have students complete one of the following activities based on their level of English proficiency.

Beginning Reread the text aloud as students read along. Pause to identify challenging words. Encourage students to identify words, too. Display them for students. Then help students use bilingual dictionaries to define no more than five challenging words. Have students write the words and meanings in their notebooks.

Intermediate Follow the instructions in the Beginning activity, but have students identify challenging words independently as you read. Display the words, and have students use dictionaries to define no more than five of them. Have students write the words and meanings in their notebooks.

Advanced Follow the instructions in the Intermediate activity, but have small groups of students read the text aloud and complete the rest of the process.

Advanced High Follow the instructions in the Intermediate activity, but have pairs of students read the text aloud and complete the rest of the process.

Topic 15 Lesson 7

SYNTHESIZE

Online Project the **Digital Activity: The United States and the Philippines**. Have students cite examples from the text to answer the first question. To answer the second question, have students recall the hopes of Filipino rebels after the Spanish-American War.

Discuss Ask: Does McKinley's statement justify American sovereignty over the Philippines? *(Students might suggest that the ideals stated are American and not necessarily Filipino, or that the statement reflects a Social Darwinist attitude—that the Philippines were weak and in need of U.S. leadership.)*

DEMONSTRATE

Online Assign the **Digital Lesson Quiz** for this lesson if you haven't already done so. Students will be offered automatic remediation or enrichment based on their score.

Pose this question to the class on the Discussion Board:

In "Southeast Asia and the Pacific," you have read about European and American imperialism in the nations of Southeast Asia, the Pacific Islands, Australia, and New Zealand.

Generate Explanations Of the countries mentioned in this lesson, only Siam remained independent in this time period. How did Siam resist European imperialism and thrive? *(Instead of rebelling, its king was willing to sign unequal treaties to avoid European control. He also modernized his country, which allowed his government to slowly do away with the unequal treaties.)*

Topic Inquiry

Have students continue their investigations for the Topic Inquiry.

>> Traditional Maori tattooing, which often covers the face, reveals important information about the wearer's family and identity, such as tribal affiliations and social status.

vote. In 1856, it also became the first nation to introduce the secret ballot.

IDENTIFY CAUSE AND EFFECT What effects did colonization have on Australia's indigenous population?

ELPS ELPS 4.F.8 Use peer and teacher support when discussing *Europeans In Australia*.

New Zealand's Story

To the southeast of Australia lies New Zealand. In 1769, Captain Cook claimed its islands for Britain. Missionaries landed there in 1814 to convert the indigenous people, the **Maori** (MAH oh ree), to Christianity.

The Maori Struggle Unlike Australia, where the Aborigines were spread thinly across a large continent, the Maori were concentrated in a smaller area. They were descended from seafaring people who had reached New Zealand from Polynesia in the 1200s. The Maori were settled farmers. They were also determined to defend their land.

White settlers, who were attracted by New Zealand's mild climate and good soil, followed the missionaries. These settlers introduced sheep and cattle and were soon exporting wool, mutton, and beef. In 1840, Britain annexed New Zealand.

As colonists poured in, they took over more and more of the land, leading to fierce wars with the Maori. Many Maori died in the struggle.

Still more perished from disease, alcoholism, and other misfortunes that followed European colonization. By the 1870s, resistance crumbled. The Maori population had fallen drastically, from about 200,000 to fewer than 45,000 in 1896. Only recently has the Maori population started to grow once more.

The Nation of New Zealand Like settlers in Australia, white New Zealanders sought self-rule. In 1907, they won independence, with their own parliament, prime minister, and elected legislature. They, too, preserved close ties to the British empire.

COMPARE AND CONTRAST Compare and contrast the European settlement of Australia and New Zealand.

ASSESSMENT

1. **Identify Supporting Details** How did industrialized powers divide up the various lands of Southeast Asia and the Pacific?
2. **Contrast** How was Siam different from the other nations of Southeast Asia?
3. **Draw Conclusions** Why were Filipino rebels disappointed when the United States took control of the Philippines?
4. **Synthesize** Describe how Hawaii became part of the United States.
5. **Identify Cause and Effect** Why did Britain grant self-rule to Australia and New Zealand?

Answers

Identify Cause and Effect *The Aborigines were killed or pushed out of areas desired by Europeans.*

Compare and Contrast *Both were settled by the British, and the indigenous populations of both were harmed. The Maori in New Zealand, who were farmers, were concentrated in a smaller area than the Aborigines in Australia, who were spread out and who hunted and gathered to support themselves.*

Assessment

1. The Dutch took over the Dutch East Indies; the British took over Burma and Malaysia; the French took over French Indochina; and the United States took over the Philippines and Hawaii.
2. Siam maintained its independence because its leaders reformed the government, modernized the army, and hired Western experts to teach them about new technology. The king also agreed to unequal treaties with the West to preserve independence.
3. The rebels had thought the United States supported their quest for independence.
4. The United States annexed Hawaii after American planters overthrew the queen.
5. Both colonies petitioned for self-government. Because the petitioners were white settlers, Britain believed they were capable of self-government. Britain was also worried about other European powers becoming involved in Australia and wanted to improve economic development in the region.

15.8 Despite bright hopes, democracy failed to take root in most of the newly independent nations of Latin America in the 1800s. Instead, wealth and power remained in the hands of the few. At the same time, new technology such as refrigerated ships helped to intertwine the economies of nations that were thousands of miles apart. Latin American economies became increasingly dependent upon those of more developed countries. Britain, and later the United States, invested heavily in Latin America.

>> Check Understanding The United States helped Cuba fight Spain in the Spanish-American War. The U.S. Navy destroyed a Spanish fleet off Santiago de Cuba in 1898. What did the United States gain after the war?

Interactive Flipped Video

The Americas in the Age of Imperialism

TEKS
1.E, 8.C, 16.B

>> **Objectives**

Identify the political problems faced by new Latin American nations.

Describe Mexico's struggle to achieve stability.

Explain why Latin America entered a cycle of economic dependence.

Analyze the influence of the United States on Latin America, including the opening of the Panama Canal.

Analyze how Canada achieved self-rule.

>> **Key Terms**

regionalism
caudillo
Benito Juárez
La Reforma
peonage
Monroe Doctrine
Panama Canal
confederation
dominion
métis

Political Problems Linger

Simón Bolívar had hoped to create strong ties among the nations of Latin America. But feuds among leaders, geographic barriers, and local nationalism shattered that dream of unity. In the end, 20 separate nations emerged.

These new nations wrote constitutions modeled on that of the United States. They set up republics with elected legislatures. However, true democracy failed to take hold. During the 1800s, many succumbed to revolts, civil war, and dictatorships.

The Legacy of Colonialism Many of the problems in the new nations had their origins in colonial rule. The existing social and political hierarchy barely changed. Creoles simply replaced *peninsulares* as the ruling class. The Roman Catholic Church kept its privileged position and still controlled huge amounts of land.

For most people—mestizos, mulattoes, blacks, and Indians—life did not improve after independence. The new constitutions guaranteed equality before the law, but deep-rooted inequalities remained. Voting rights were limited. Many people felt the effects of racial prejudice. Small groups of people held most of the land. Owners of haciendas

PEARSON realize. www.PearsonTexas.com Access your Digital Lesson.

Topic 15 Lesson 8

The Americas in the Age of Imperialism

CONNECT

Preview Have students preview the **Lesson Objectives** and the list of **Key Terms**.

Students can also preview all the **Key Terms** and **Academic Vocabulary** using the **Interactive Reading Notepad** on the digital course or preview a summary of the lesson in the **Reading and Note Taking Study Guide**.

Online Use the **Editable Presentation** found on the digital course to present the main ideas for this lesson.

Start Up Activity

Have students answer this question as they get settled: Why might the United States have insisted that European powers should stay out of Latin America? *(Sample response: As the strongest nation in the hemisphere, the United States believed that Latin America should be its exclusive sphere of influence.)*

Online You can also project the **Start Up Activity** from the course.

INVESTIGATE

Have students read the lesson using the **Reading and Note Taking Study Guide** to help them take notes and understand the text as they read.

Political Problems Linger

Tell students that many Latin American countries gained independence in the 1800s but had a hard time establishing democratic governments. The legacy of colonialism contributed to lingering political problems; the colonial system favored a wealthy elite over the majority of people. Inequalities remained, voting rights were limited, and there was still some racial prejudice. Dictators arose in some countries, while conservatives and liberals vied for power in other countries.

Aa Vocabulary Builder

1. Have students pronounce the following academic vocabulary terms in this lesson and clarify the part of speech. For difficult or polysyllabic words, break them into syllables and pronounce them with the students.
2. Explain what the word means in common "student-friendly" language using synonyms and antonyms when possible. Provide concrete examples to clarify the meaning, and rephrase the definition.

compile: to put together from several sources

enlightened: educated; informed

tangible: real or concrete

Answers

Check Understanding *The United States forced Cubans to add an amendment to their constitution allowing the United States to establish naval bases in Cuba and giving the U.S. the right to intervene in Cuban affairs.*

Topic 15 Lesson 8

Guided Reading and Discussion

Have students find evidence in the text to support the idea that many of Latin America's problems originated in colonial rule. *(the colonial social and political hierarchy remained the same; the Roman Catholic Church kept a privileged position; inequalities remained; limits on voting rights; racial prejudices; property owned by a privileged few; the peonage system)*

Key Terms

Call students' attention to the term ***caudillos*** (in bold) in the text. Explain that during the fight for independence, *caudillos* were respected for defending their land, but they were later seen as strongmen who wrongfully seized power and ruled in an authoritarian manner. A key characteristic of all *caudillos,* however, was their charisma.

Analyze Information How was regionalism linked to the rise of *caudillos*? *(Regionalism was loyalty to a local area, rather than to a central government.* Caudillos*—locally based strongmen—used their private armies to resist the central government. Sometimes* caudillos *became national dictators themselves.)*

Mexico's Search for Stability

Tell students that Mexico struggled for stability as conservatives and liberals battled for control of the country. The war with the United States over Texas territory increased discord among Mexicans. Liberals tried to reform Mexico, while conservatives extended colonial-type systems such as peonage.

>> Agustín de Iturbide, a Mexican caudillo who became emperor of Mexico in 1822.

>> During the Texas Revolution, defenders of this San Antonio fort were outnumbered by Santa Anna and his Mexican forces. How does this image portray the defenders of the Alamo?

ruled their great estates, and the peasants who worked them, like medieval European lords.

Dictators, Conservatives, and Liberals With few roads and no tradition of unity, **regionalism,** or loyalty to a local area, weakened the new nations. Local strongmen, called ***caudillos*** (kow THEE yohs), assembled private armies to resist the central government. At times, popular caudillos, occasionally former military leaders, gained national power. They looted the treasury and ruled as dictators. Power struggles led to frequent revolts that changed little except the name of the leader. In the long run, power remained in the hands of a privileged few who had no desire to share it.

As in Europe, the ruling elite in Latin America was divided between conservatives and liberals. Conservatives defended the traditional social order, favored press censorship, and strongly supported the Catholic Church. Liberals backed laissez-faire economics, religious toleration, greater access to education, and freedom of the press. Liberals saw themselves as enlightened supporters of progress but often showed little concern for the needs of the majority of the people.

IDENTIFY CAUSE AND EFFECT What political obstacles to democracy were caused by lingering effects of colonial rule in Latin America?

Mexico's Search for Stability

During the 1800s, each Latin American nation followed its own course. Mexico provides an example of the challenges facing many Latin American nations. Large landowners, army leaders, and the Catholic Church dominated Mexican politics. However, bitter battles between conservatives and liberals led to revolts and the rise of dictators. Deep social divisions separated wealthy creoles from mestizos and Indians who lived in poverty.

Santa Anna and War With the United States Between 1833 and 1855, an ambitious and cunning *caudillo,* Antonio López de Santa Anna, gained and lost power many times. At first, he posed as a liberal reformer. Soon, however, he reversed his stand and crushed efforts at reform.

In Mexico's northern territory of Texas, discontent grew. In 1835, settlers who had moved to Texas from the United States and other places revolted. After a brief struggle with Santa Anna's forces, the settlers

Answers

Identify Cause and Effect *Colonial rule left behind a social and political hierarchy that was difficult to change. Voting rights were limited, and racial prejudices lingered. Some rich landowners still had too much power, and regionalism hurt national unity.*

Analyze Images *Defenders of the Alamo are portrayed heroically; they are determined to defend themselves against overwhelming odds.*

gained independence from Mexico. They quickly set up an independent republic.

Then in 1845 the United States annexed Texas. Mexicans saw this act as a declaration of war. In the fighting that followed, the United States invaded and defeated Mexico. In the Treaty of Guadalupe-Hidalgo, which ended the war, Mexico lost almost half its territory. The embarrassing defeat triggered new violence between conservatives and liberals.

La Reforma Brings Changes to Mexico In 1855, **Benito Juárez** (WAHR ez), a liberal reformer of Zapotec Indian heritage, and other liberals gained power and opened an era of reform known as **La Reforma.** Juárez offered hope to the oppressed people of Mexico.

He and his fellow reformers revised the Mexican constitution to strip the military of power and end the special privileges of the Church. They ordered the Church to sell unused lands to peasants.

Conservatives resisted La Reforma and began a civil war. Still, Juárez was elected president in 1861 and he expanded his reforms. His opponents turned to Europe for help. In 1863, Napoleon III sent troops to Mexico and set up Austrian archduke Maximilian as emperor.

For four years, Juárez's forces battled the combined conservative and French forces. When France withdrew its troops, Maximilian was captured and shot. In 1867, Juárez returned to power and tried to renew reform, but opponents resisted. Juárez died in office in 1872, never achieving all the reforms he envisioned. He did, however, help unite Mexico, bring mestizos into politics, and separate church and state.

A Dictator's Order, Progress, and Oppression After Juárez died, General Porfirio Díaz, a hero of the war against the French, staged a military coup and gained power. From 1876 to 1880 and 1884 to 1911, he ruled as a dictator. In the name of "Order and Progress," he strengthened the army, local police, and central government. He crushed opposition.

Under his harsh rule, Mexico made tangible economic advances. Railroads were built, foreign trade increased, some industry developed, and mining expanded. Growth, however, had a high cost. Capital for development came from foreign investors, to whom Díaz granted special rights. He also let wealthy landowners buy up Indian lands.

The rich prospered, but most Mexicans remained poor. Many Indians and mestizos fell into **peonage** to their employers. In the peonage system, hacienda owners would give workers advances on their wages and require them to stay on the hacienda until they had paid back what they owed. Wages remained low, and workers were rarely able to repay the hacienda owner.

>> Benito Juárez, a Mexican lawyer and politician, brought reforms to Mexico and served several terms as president. His reforms helped unite Mexico and bring mestizos into politics.

Many children died in infancy. Other children worked 12-hour days and never learned to read or write.

? **SUMMARIZE** What reforms did Juárez achieve to help Mexico attempt a more stable government and society?

 **ELPS 4.F.9** Use peer and teacher support to identify compound and complex sentence structures in *Mexico's Search for Stability.*

The Economics of Latin America's Dependence

Under colonial rule, mercantilist policies made Latin America economically dependent on Spain and Portugal. Colonies sent raw materials such as cash crops or precious metals to the parent country and had to buy manufactured goods from them. Strict laws kept colonists from trading with other countries and possibly obtaining goods at a lower price. In addition, laws prohibited the building of local industries that would have competed with the parent country. In short, the policies prevented the colonies from developing their own economies.

Guided Reading and Discussion

Ask students to identify the struggles Mexico experienced while trying to achieve stability in the 1800s. *(Sample response: a revolt in Texas; a war with the United States over Texas that led to a huge loss of territory; social and economic inequalities; civil war; war with France; living under the dictatorship of General Díaz)*

Analyze Images

Focus students' attention on the portrait of Benito Juárez. Tell them that Juárez appears to be pointing at something. Ask them what it might be and why the artist would have shown Juárez pointing at it. *(It is likely the constitution, or at least a document suggesting written reforms. Juárez was a reformer who played a key role in revising Mexico's constitution.)*

The Economics of Latin America's Dependence

Explain to students that under colonial rule, Latin American countries generated profits for European countries without much chance to develop their own economies. This pattern of economic dependence did not change greatly after they achieved political independence. Free trade, foreign investment, technological developments, and migration did help Latin American economies make some advances, but only a few elites and a small middle class benefited. A majority of Latin American people remained poor.

Answers

Summarize *Juárez revised the Mexican constitution to strip the military of power and ended the special privileges of the Church, helping separate church and state. He involved mestizos in politics and helped to unify Mexico.*

English Language Proficiency Standards

Reading 4.F.9 Read "Mexico's Search for Stability" aloud. Have students complete one of the following activities based on their level of English proficiency.

Examples of compound sentences from the text:

Still, Juárez was elected president in 1861 and he expanded his reforms.

Wages remained low, and workers were rarely able to repay the hacienda owner.

Beginning Reread the text aloud. Use a compound sentence to demonstrate how to identify independent clauses and connecting words. Repeat the process with a complex sentence from the text. Help students find other examples of both kinds of sentence, and repeat the process.

Intermediate Follow the instructions in the Beginning activity, but encourage students to find compound and complex sentences and identify their elements. Offer help as needed.

Advanced Have small groups of students reread the text aloud and identify one compound and one complex sentence, and then identify the clauses in each sentence. Have students write their sentences in their notebooks and share them with their classmates.

Advanced High Follow the instructions in the Advanced activity, but have pairs of students identify two compound and two complex sentences and their clauses.

Guided Reading and Discussion

Tell students that during the 1800s, the United States stepped up its trade with, and investment in, Latin America, which yielded some benefits for Latin America. Ask them how it also contributed to growing United States imperialism toward Latin America. *(Sample response: Americans thought their investments gave them the right to interfere in Latin American politics to protect those investments.)*

The United States Wields Power and Influence

Tell students that in 1823, U.S. president James Monroe issued a doctrine intended to discourage European powers from establishing colonies in the Americas. The Monroe Doctrine protected Latin America from European colonization, but it also encouraged a more imperialistic attitude toward Latin America in the United States.

Identify Cause and Effect What was a cause of the Monroe Doctrine, and what was an effect? *(Cause: American concern that Europeans would try to recolonize Latin America, jeopardizing British and U.S. trade with Latin America; Effect: helped discourage European interference in Latin America)*

The Cycle of Economic Dependence After independence, this pattern changed very little. The new Latin American republics did adopt free trade, welcoming all comers. Britain and the United States rushed into the new markets, replacing Spain as Latin America's chief trading partners. But the region remained as economically dependent as before.

Foreign Investment and Influence In the 1800s, foreign goods flooded Latin America, creating large profits for foreigners and for a handful of local business people. Foreign investment, which could yield enormous profits, was often accompanied by local interference. Investors from Britain, the United States, and other nations pressured their own governments to take action if political events or reform movements in a Latin American country seemed to threaten their interests.

Some Economic Growth After 1850, some Latin American economies did grow. With foreign capital, they were able to develop mining and agriculture. Chile exported copper and nitrates, and Argentina expanded its livestock and wheat production. Brazil exported the cash crops coffee and sugar, as well as rubber. By the early 1900s, both Venezuela and Mexico were developing important and lucrative oil industries.

Throughout the region, foreigners invested in modern ports and railroads to carry goods from the interior to coastal cities. European immigrants poured into Latin America. The newcomers helped to promote economic activity, and a small middle class emerged.

Thanks to trade, investment, technology, and migration, Latin American nations moved into the world economy. Yet internal development was limited. The tiny elite at the top benefited from the economic upturn, but very little trickled down to the masses of people at the bottom. The poor earned too little to buy consumer goods. Without a strong demand, many industries failed to develop.

IDENTIFY CAUSE AND EFFECT What were some negative effects of foreign investment in Latin America?

The United States Wields Power and Influence

As nations like Mexico tried to build stable governments, a neighboring republic, the United States, expanded across North America. Latin American nations began to feel threatened by the "Colossus of the North," the giant power that cast its shadow over the entire hemisphere.

>> **Analyze Maps** The map shows European and U.S. possessions in Latin America in the early 1900s. Imperialists often acted to protect business interests. What explains the strong U.S. interest in Latin America?

Answers

Analyze Maps *Sample response: The United States is located directly north of Latin America. Latin America had natural resources of interest to the United States, such as bananas, coffee, timber, and sugar. Latin America presented opportunities for American investors.*

Identify Cause and Effect *It was accompanied by foreign interference in Latin American politics and reform movements. It contributed to the cycle of economic dependence for Latin America. It benefited the investors and made some Latin Americans wealthy but did not help economic reform.*

History Background

Monroe Doctrine The Monroe Doctrine reflected the intention of the United States to make Latin America a U.S. sphere of influence. In 1823, when Monroe announced this policy, the United States was not yet a world power. If European nations had challenged the United States' assertion of control over Latin America, U.S. leaders would have had to turn to Britain for help. Over time, as the United States became a more powerful and prosperous nation, its assertion of unilateral authority in the region became more credible, though not more popular.

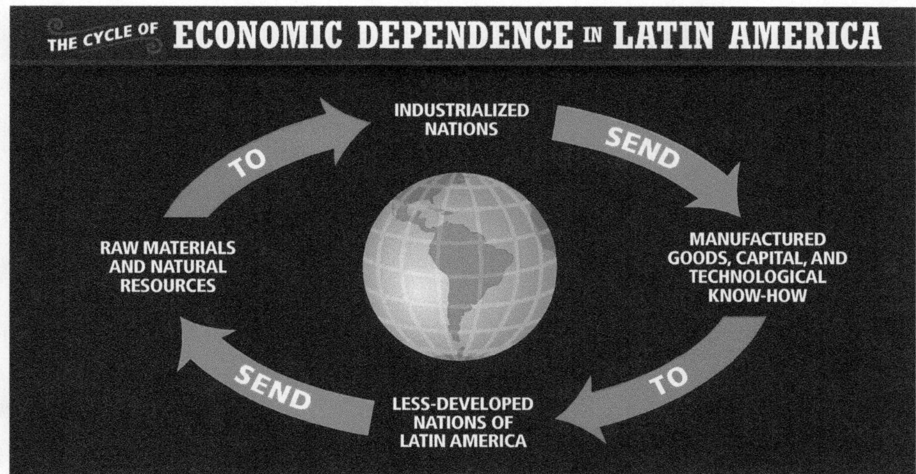

>> **Analyze Charts** This diagram shows the cycle of economic dependence in Latin America. What did developed nations provide to Latin America?

The Monroe Doctrine of 1823 In the 1820s, Spain plotted to recover its American colonies. Britain opposed any move that might close the door to trade with Latin America. British leaders asked American President James Monroe to join them in a statement opposing any new colonization of the Americas.

Monroe, however, wanted to avoid any "entangling alliance" with Britain. Acting alone, he issued the **Monroe Doctrine** in 1823. "The American continents," it declared, "are henceforth not to be considered as subjects for future colonization by any European powers."

The United States lacked the military power to enforce the doctrine. But with the support of Britain's strong navy, the doctrine discouraged European interference. For more than a century, the Monroe Doctrine would be the key to United States policy in the Americas.

The United States Expands Into Latin America and Enters a War As a result of the war with Mexico, in 1848 the United States acquired the thinly populated regions of northern Mexico, gaining all or part of the present-day states of California, Arizona, New Mexico, Nevada, Utah, and Colorado. The victory fed dreams of future expansion. Before the century had ended, the United States controlled much of North America and was becoming involved in overseas conflicts.

For decades, Cuban patriots had battled to free their island from Spanish rule. As they began to make headway, the United States joined their cause, declaring war on Spain in 1898. The brief Spanish-American War ended in a crushing defeat for Spain. At the war's end, Cuba was granted independence.

But in 1901, the United States forced Cubans to add the Platt Amendment to their constitution. The amendment gave the United States naval bases in Cuba and the right to intervene in Cuban affairs.

The Roosevelt Corollary Allows U.S. Interference American investments in Latin America grew in the early 1900s. Citing the need to protect those investments, in 1904 the United States issued the Roosevelt Corollary to the Monroe Doctrine. Under this policy, the United States claimed "international police power" in the Western Hemisphere. When the Dominican Republic failed to pay its foreign debts, the United States sent in troops. Americans collected customs duties, paid off the debts, and remained for years.

Under the Roosevelt Corollary and then President William Howard Taft's policy of Dollar Diplomacy, American companies continued to invest in the countries of Latin America. To protect those investments, the United States sent troops to Cuba, Haiti, Mexico, Honduras, Nicaragua, and other

Online Project the **Interactive Cartoon: Uncle Sam Takes Off—United States Imperialism**, and click through the hotspots with students.

ACTIVE CLASSROOM

Use the If Images Could Talk strategy with the Interactive Cartoon. Have students pick a European power in the cartoon and then write some dialogue for that character. What are the character's motivations? Why does he want to be involved in Latin America? What is the European shouting at Uncle Sam? Also have students write what Uncle Sam might have said in response. Invite students to read their finished dialogues aloud with a partner.

Answers

Analyze Charts *capital, manufactured goods, technological know-how*

Online Project the **Interactive Gallery: The Panama Canal**, and click through the images with students.

ACTIVE CLASSROOM

Use the Quick Write strategy with the Interactive Gallery. Give students up to a minute to answer one of the following questions: How did the desire for a canal influence U.S. imperialism in Latin America? What is the connection between Latin American geography and the building of the Panama Canal?

Guided Reading and Discussion

Ask students to provide an example that supports the idea that the United States acted like an imperialist power in Cuba after the Spanish-American War. *(In 1901, the United States forced Cuba to add the Platt Amendment to the Cuban constitution. The Platt Amendment allowed the United States to set up naval bases in Cuba and gave it the right to intervene in Cuban affairs.)*

Canada Achieves Self-Rule

Canada, a British colony, gained independence and became a **dominion**, or self-governing nation, in 1867. Although Canada had been a colony like the countries of Latin America, there had not been a colonial legacy of racial prejudice or economic injustice to overcome, as there was for Latin American countries. Canada also did not experience imperialism from the United States, as Latin American countries did.

>> **Analyze Information** Two men stand inside one of the Panama Canal lock's enormous gates. The gates allow water to flow in and out, raising or lowering ships to different levels. What does the perspective of the photo indicate about the scale of the project?

Interactive Gallery

>> By the late 1700s, there were still parts of Canada that had not yet been reached by European settlers. By the mid-1800s, the country had begun to grow, and settlements spread to new areas.

countries in Central America and the Caribbean. As a result, like European powers in Africa and Asia, the United States became the target of increasing resentment and rebellion.

The Panama Canal From the late 1800s, the United States had wanted to build a canal across Central America. Panama was a proposed site. However, Panama belonged to Colombia, which refused to sell the United States land for the canal. In 1903, the United States backed a revolt by Panamanians against Colombia. The Panamanians quickly won independence and gave the United States control of the land to build the canal.

Construction began in 1904. Engineers solved many difficult problems in the course of building the canal, including cutting through mountains and excavating about 232 million cubic yards of dirt, rocks, and debris. The **Panama Canal** opened in 1914. The canal cut the distance of a sea journey between such cities as New York and San Francisco by thousands of miles. It was an engineering marvel that boosted trade and shipping worldwide.

To people in Latin America, however, the canal was another example of "Yankee imperialism." Nationalist feeling in the hemisphere was often expressed as anti-Americanism. Panama did not gain complete control over the canal until 2000. It now forms a vital part of the Panamanian economy.

IDENTIFY CAUSE AND EFFECT How did the United States influence the direction of Cuban history?

Canada Achieves Self-Rule

Canada, Australia, and New Zealand won independence faster and more easily than other British colonies in Africa or Asia. The language and cultural roots they shared with Britain helped. Racial attitudes also played a part. Imperialists in nations like Britain felt that whites, unlike nonwhites, were capable of governing themselves.

When France lost Canada to Britain in 1763, thousands of French-speaking Catholic settlers remained. After the American Revolution, about 30,000 British loyalists fled to Canada. They were English-speaking Protestants. In addition, in the 1790s, several groups of Native American peoples still lived in eastern Canada. Others, in the west and the north, had not yet come into contact with European settlers.

Unrest in the Two Canadas To ease ethnic tensions, Britain passed the Constitutional Act of 1791. The act created two provinces: English-speaking Upper

Answers

Analyze Information *Students may notice the enormity of the gates and canal compared to the humans. The photo conveys the magnitude of the Panama Canal construction project.*

Identify Cause and Effect *The United States helped Cubans win their revolt against Spain. In exchange for American help, the U.S. enforced the Platt Amendment: Cuba had to allow United States naval bases in Cuba and give the United States the right to intervene in Cuban affairs.*

History Background

Disease Fighter in Panama Building the Panama Canal required both scientific and engineering expertise. Early efforts by a French company to build the canal had failed, in part because so many workers died of malaria and yellow fever. William Gorgas, an American disease and sanitation expert, solved the problem. Before coming to Panama, Gorgas had overseen sanitation for the U.S. Army in Havana, Cuba. While there, he conducted many experiments to determine how mosquitoes transmit yellow fever. Gorgas realized that by draining swamps and other areas where mosquitoes breed, he could stop the spread of the deadly disease. His work led to the eradication of yellow fever from the Canal Zone.

>> **Analyze Maps** Canada grew throughout the late 1800s. This map shows Canadian provinces from 1867 to 1914 and their natural resources. List the natural resources of Manitoba and Nova Scotia.

Canada (now Ontario) and French-speaking Lower Canada (now Quebec). French traditions and the Catholic Church were protected in Lower Canada. English traditions and laws guided Upper Canada.

During the early 1800s, unrest grew in both colonies. The people of Upper Canada resented the power held by a small group of elites who controlled the government. Lower Canada had similar problems. In 1837, discontent flared into rebellion in both places. Louis Joseph Papineau, the head of the French Canadian Reform party, led the rebellion in Lower Canada. William Lyon Mackenzie led the revolt in Upper Canada, crying, "Put down the villains who oppress and enslave our country!"

Britain's Response The British had learned from the American Revolution. While they hurried to put down the disorder, they sent an able politician, Lord Durham, to compile a report on the causes of the unrest. In 1840, Parliament acted on some of Durham's recommendations by passing the Act of Union.

The act joined the two Canadas into one province. It also gave them an elected legislature that determined some domestic policies. Britain still controlled foreign policy and trade.

The Dominion of Canada In the mid-1800s, thousands of English, Scottish, and Irish people immigrated to Canada. As the country grew, two Canadians, John Macdonald and George-Etienne Cartier, urged **confederation,** or unification, of Britain's North American colonies. These colonies included Nova Scotia, New Brunswick, Prince Edward Island, and British Columbia, as well as the united Upper and Lower Canadas. The two leaders felt that confederation would strengthen the new nation against American ambitions and help its economic development.

Britain finally agreed, passing the British North America Act of 1867. The act created the Dominion of Canada. A **dominion** is a self-governing nation. As a dominion, Canada had its own parliament, modeled on that of Britain.

By 1900, Canada also had some control over its own foreign policy. Still, Canada maintained close ties with Britain.

Canada Expands Like the United States, Canada expanded westward in the 1800s. In 1885, the Canadian Pacific Railway opened, linking eastern and western Canada. Wherever the railroad went, settlers followed. It moved people and products, such as timber and manufactured goods, across the country. In the late 1800s and early 1900s, more immigrants flooded into

Guided Reading and Discussion

Ask students to identify some of the ethnic tensions that Canada experienced. *(They included those between French- and English-speaking settlers and those among European settlers, Native Americans, and métis.)*

Analyze Maps Examine the map of Canada, 1867–1914. What were some natural resources in British Columbia not found in Saskatchewan? *(silver, copper, fish)* Why might British Columbia's resources have partly motivated the building of the Canadian Pacific Railway to reach the far western province? *(Some of its resources could have been sent by rail to the interior provinces.)*

SYNTHESIZE

Online Project the **Digital Activity: Canada and Latin America**. Have students share their answer to the question with a partner.

Discuss Have students identify characteristics of Latin American countries and of Canada that might help explain why Canada did not experience American imperialism in the way Latin America did. *(Canada was a former British colony that had native English speakers, as was the United States. Canada had strong ties to Britain, which would have blocked U.S. imperialism. Latin America had the Isthmus of Panama, which inspired U.S. imperialism for canal building. To keep out European colonizers, the United States involved itself heavily in the region's politics.)*

Answers

Analyze Maps *Nova Scotia: timber, fish, lobster, coal; Manitoba: timber, gold, silver, copper*

DEMONSTRATE

Online Assign the **Digital Lesson Quiz** for this lesson if you haven't already done so. Students will be offered automatic remediation or enrichment based on their score.

Pose this question to the class on the Discussion Board:

In "The Americas in the Age of Imperialism," you read about political problems in Latin American nations after colonization, including Mexico's struggle for stability. Latin American countries entered a cycle of economic dependence with their trading partners, England and the United States, who replaced the previous European colonizers. The United States influenced the development of Latin America, fighting a war against Mexico for territory, and wars against Spain and Colombia to liberate Cuba and Panama. Canada's achievement of self-rule occurred with less imperialist interference and less economic instability.

Compare What are some similarities when comparing Benito Juárez of Mexico with John Macdonald and George-Etienne Cartier of Canada? *(All three men tried to unify and gain self-rule for their countries. Juárez did help unite Mexico. Macdonald and Cartier helped Canada achieve confederation, a type of unification.)*

Topic Inquiry

Have students continue their investigations for the Topic Inquiry.

Canada from Germany, Italy, Poland, Russia, Ukraine, China, and Japan. They enriched Canada's economy and culture.

As in the United States, westward expansion destroyed the way of life of Native Americans in Canada. Most were forced to sign treaties giving up their lands. Some resisted. In central Canada, Louis Riel led a revolt of the **métis,** people of mixed Native American and French Canadian descent, in 1869 and again in 1885. Many métis were French-speaking Catholics who believed that the government was trying to take their land and destroy their language and religion. Government troops put down both uprisings. Riel was executed in 1885.

By 1914, Canada was a flourishing nation. Still, French-speaking Canadians were determined to preserve their separate heritage, making it hard for Canadians to create a single national identity. Also, the cultural and economic influence of the United States threatened to dominate Canada. Both issues continue to affect Canada today.

? ANALYZE INFORMATION What were some reasons that Canada achieved self-rule faster and easier than other British colonies?

ASSESSMENT

1. **Connect** How was Latin America's ruling elite similar to Europe's ruling class, and why was that a political problem?
2. **Identify Cause and Effect** How did dictator General Porfirio Díaz contribute to economic and political instability in Mexico?
3. **Identify Cause and Effect** How did colonial rule contribute to Latin America's continuing economic dependence after colonialism?
4. **Identify Cause and Effect** What effects did the Monroe Doctrine and Roosevelt Corollary have on Latin America?
5. **Summarize** How did the British respond to the Canadians' desire for self-rule?

Answers

Analyze Information *Canadians shared cultural roots with the British, which helped in their self-rule appeals. Racial attitudes also played a part, since British imperialists were more likely to grant self-rule to other whites over nonwhites. In addition, Canadian leaders felt that confederation would strengthen the new nation against American ambitions and help its economic development, and Britain agreed.*

Assessment

1. As in Europe, Latin America's ruling elite was split between conservatives and liberals who did not want to share power, leading to civil wars and feuds.
2. Diaz crushed political opposition, granted advantages to the rich, and kept wages low. Many Indians and mestizos fell into peonage, and most Mexicans were poor.
3. Latin American countries had undeveloped economies. After colonialism, trading partners used trade and investments to exert their influence.
4. The Monroe Doctrine helped protect Latin America from colonialism. The Roosevelt Corollary gave the U.S. "international police power," and the U.S. sent troops to Latin American countries to protect investments.
5. After Britain quelled an armed rebellion, the provinces in Canada were united and allowed to determine domestic policies through an elected legislature. Britain controlled foreign policy and trade until it allowed self-rule.

1. **Identify Influences on Political Revolutions** Identify the influence of ideas such as nationalism on political revolutions. Using the map above and information from the lessons, write a paragraph that describes how the idea of nationalism led to political revolution in the Ottoman empire. Consider the conflict between Muslim beliefs and the beliefs of those living under Ottoman rule, increasing contact with Western Europe, territories controlled by the Ottoman empire, and revolutions in Egypt, Lebanon, and Greece, among other places. 9.D

Ottoman Empire

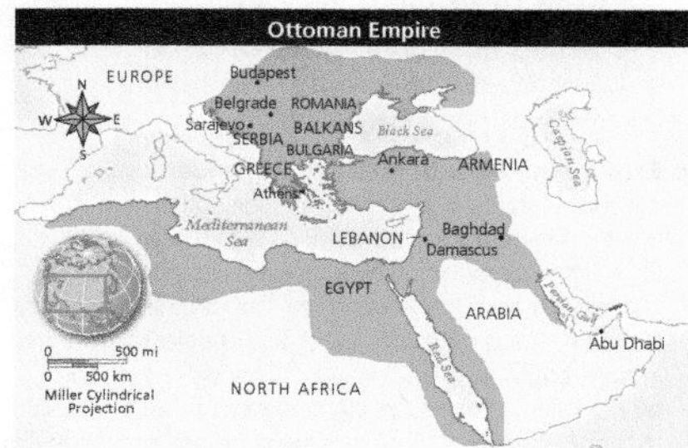

2. **Identify the Influence of Ideas** Identify the influence of ideas, such as human rights on political revolutions. Write a paragraph that describes how the westernization of upper-class Indians led to nationalization and efforts to return India to self-rule. Consider the differing Western attitudes toward Indian culture, policy of educating wealthy Indians in Western-style schools, ideals taught in Western schools, and the Indian National Congress, organized in 1885. 9.D
3. **Identify Causes of European Imperialism** Identify major causes of important turning points in world history from 1750 to 1914, including European imperialism. Write a paragraph that describes how King Leopold of Belgium's actions in the African Congo caused a dramatic increase in European imperialism in Africa. Consider Leopold's public and private motivations for arranging treaties with Africans in the Congo, European need for raw materials and new markets, and the political prestige of owning colonies. 1.E
4. **Describe the Major Effects of European Imperialism** Describe the major effects of important turning points in world history from 1750 to 1914, including European imperialism. Write a paragraph that describes how the actions of the British East India Company led to India being governed directly by the British government. Consider the British East India Company's goals and practices in India, its policies imposed on the sepoys (Indian soldiers) that violated Hindu beliefs, and the results of the Sepoy Rebellion. 1.E
5. **Identify Influences on European Imperialism** Identify the major political motivations that influenced European imperialism. Read the passage below. Then, write a paragraph that describes the factors influencing European imperialism of Africa. Consider the impact of the Industrial Revolution on the West, the impact of Christian missionaries in Africa, European reactions to Belgian exploration of the Congo, and the results of the Berlin Conference of 1884. 8.C

   "The Portuguese carved out large colonies in Angola and Mozambique. Italy reached across the Mediterranean to occupy Libya and then pushed into the 'horn' of Africa, at the southern end of the Red Sea. The newly united German empire took lands in eastern and southwestern Africa, including Cameroon and Togo."

6. **Identify Influences on European Imperialism** Identify the major social motivations that influenced European imperialism. Write a paragraph that describes the role that Christian missionary work played in European imperialism. Consider the Western "paternalistic" view of Africans, Dr. David Livingstone's opposition to the slave trade, and his plan for ending human trafficking. 8.C
7. **Explain Characteristics of European Imperialism** Explain the major characteristics and impact of European imperialism. Write a paragraph that explains how European imperialism affected the African people. Consider the attitude of Westerners toward African culture, spread of Christianity throughout the continent, benefits of westernization, and the rise of nationalism and political unrest in various colonies. 8.D
8. **Explain Major Characteristics** Explain the major characteristics of European imperialism. Write a paragraph to compare the characteristics of the types of rule used by France and Britain in their colonies. Compare the indirect rule and direct rule systems used by the two countries. Which country allowed self-government by local officials? Why would British imperialism be more conducive to building a longer-lasting empire than French imperialism? 8.D
9. **Explain Impact** Explain the impact of European imperialism. Write a paragraph explaining the effects of European imperialism on native peoples. Consider the political, social, and cultural changes in European colonies. How were cultural heritages and native industries at risk when Westerners came into the colonies? 8.D

Answers to TEKS Assessment

1. Students' responses should clearly explain how the Western idea of nationalism led to internal revolts by various ethnic groups who wanted independence from the Ottoman empire. In the Middle East, Muslim reform movements challenged the Ottomans. Nationalism inspired groups of subject peoples in the Ottoman empire to rebel and demand independent states. In the Balkans, Greece, Serbia, Bulgaria, and Romania gained their independence. The Ottomans suppressed uprisings in Arabia, Lebanon, and Armenia. Egypt slipped away from Ottoman control. As the Ottoman empire was weakened by nationalist revolts, Western European powers, eager for new territories, won favorable treaties and intervened in local affairs.

2. Students' responses should clearly explain that providing Western-style education led to the Indians adopting Western ideas such as nationalism, democracy, equality, and human rights. Exposure to Western ideas did not make the Indians more loyal, but it gave them the learning and skills required to establish nationalist movements to free India of colonial rule. Nationalist leaders organized the Indian National Congress in 1885. Its members believed in peaceful protests to achieve their goals and called for greater democracy as a means to help Indians gain power.

3. Student answers will vary but should explain that Leopold's public statement differed from his private goal of conquest and profit. His activities set off a scramble for colonies in Africa by industrialized European nations that needed raw materials such as rubber, petroleum, and palm oil for manufacturing, as well as new markets for their finished goods. European powers acquired new colonies to bolster their national image, believing that a global empire not only increased their economic growth, but also increased their global prestige.

4. Student responses will vary but should explain that the British East India Company's main goal in India was to make money. It pressed for social change, working to end slavery and the caste system. The East India Company required sepoys to serve overseas and passed a law that allowed Hindu widows to remarry. Both violated Hindu religious beliefs. When new weapons were issued, sepoys were required to bite off the tips of rifle cartridges that had been greased with cow or pig fat, which was offensive to both Hindu and Muslim soldiers. When they refused orders, sepoys were imprisoned. The sepoys revolted, massacring British citizens. The British retaliated. After the Sepoy Rebellion, Parliament ended the rule of the East India Company and put India directly under the rule of the British crown.

5. Student answers will vary but should explain that industrialized Western countries needed natural resources to fuel manufacturing, and new markets for finished goods. Christian missionaries introduced Africans to Western culture. King Leopold's activities in the Congo set off a scramble by other nations to acquire African colonies. At the Berlin Conference, European nations set ground rules for claiming African colonies. Nationalism played a role, as European nations grabbed lands to prevent rivals from gaining territory. Countries felt that ruling a global empire increased a nation's prestige.

TEKS ASSESSMENT

10. **Analyze Influence of Human and Geographic Factors on Major Events** Analyze the influence of human and physical geographic factors on major events in world history, including the opening of the Suez Canal. Write a paragraph that explains the political motivation behind the construction of the Suez Canal. Consider the reforms initiated by Muhammad Ali in Egypt, importance of the location of the canal, and the difference in shipping routes before and after the construction. 16.B

11. **Identify Politically Motivated Mass Murders** Identify examples of politically motivated mass murders in Armenia. Write a paragraph that describes the reasons why Turkish nationalists committed genocide against the Armenians. Consider religious differences between the Turks and Armenians, tensions erupting from nationalism, relationship between the Ottoman empire and Russia, and Ottoman policies that lead to the genocide. 22.C

12. **Explain the Roles of Military Technology** Explain the roles of military technology in initiating nineteenth-century imperialism. Write a paragraph supported by evidence that explains how United States military technology affected imperialism in the Pacific. Consider Japan's initial treaties with the United States after Matthew Perry's visit, the influence of Western technology on the growth of Japan's military strength, and its own imperialism in the Pacific region. 28.B

13. **Explain the Roles of Transportation Technology** Explain the roles of transportation technology in advancing nineteenth-century imperialism. Write a paragraph to explain the impact of transportation technology on imperialism. Consider growth of production in colonial lands and newer, more efficient transportation methods. Use the information in the chart to explain the relationship between the amount of cargo shipped by Western powers and new transportation technology. 28.B

14. **Identify Economic Motivations for European Imperialism** Identify the major economic motivations that influenced European imperialism. Refer to the quote below. Write a paragraph that describes Britain's and Belgium's economic motivations for colonizing portions of Africa. Consider the resources in demand after the Industrial Revolution; territories claimed by Belgium and Britain; resources readily found in the Congo, West and East Africa, Egypt, and the Sudan; and diamond mines in South Africa. 8.C

"Publicly, [King] Leopold [of Belgium] spoke of a civilizing mission to carry the light 'that for millions of men still plunged in barbarism will be the dawn of a better era.'"

15. **Explain the Role of Medical Advancements** Explain the role of medical advancements in initiating nineteenth-century imperialism. Write a paragraph about the role of medical technology as it relates to the expansion of imperialism by industrialized nations. Consider the geographic locations of colonial countries in both Latin America and Africa, difficulties faced by nonnative peoples in the climates of these areas, and how medical technology allowed nonnatives to overcome these challenges. 28.B

16. **Explain the Role of Communication Technology** Construct a thesis supported by evidence to explain the role of communication technology in initiating and advancing nineteenth-century imperialism. Write a one-paragraph thesis with supporting evidence about the role of the telegraph in nineteenth-century imperialism. Consider the function of the telegraph, distance between nations and colonies, communication needs of government, and communication needs of trade. How did the telegraph affect the relationship between colonies and parent countries? 28.B, 29.G

17. Reflect on the Essential Question **Write an essay on the Essential Question: Why do people move?** Use evidence from your study of this Topic to support your answer.

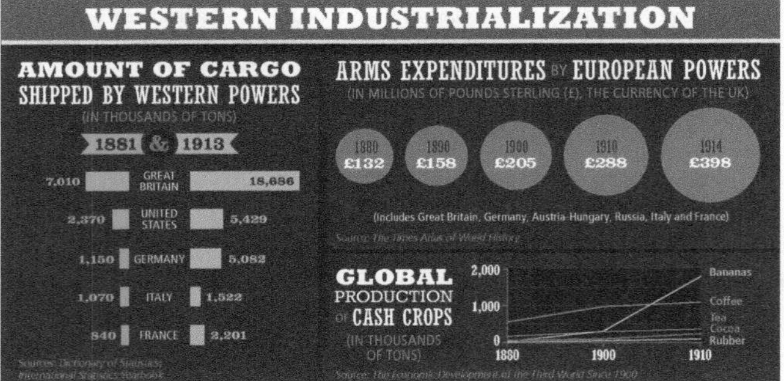

Answers to TEKS Assessment

6. Student answers will vary but should explain that missionaries sought to convert Africans to Christianity. They built churches, schools, and clinics. Missionaries had a paternalistic view of Africans, believing they needed guidance. Missionaries also believed that it was their duty to spread superior Western culture to Africans. Dr. Livingstone was an explorer and missionary who opposed the slave trade. He suggested that opening up the interior of Africa to Christianity and trade could end human trafficking. Other explorers followed Livingstone, including Henry Stanley, who famously found Livingstone in Africa when Livingstone had not been heard from for many years.

7. Students' responses will vary but should explain that Western imperialists viewed native African cultures, languages, and religions as inferior and urged native peoples to adopt Western ways. Many Africans lost their cultural heritage. European countries replaced local governments with imperialist forms of rule. Christian missionaries had a paternalistic view of Africans, believing they were like children who needed guidance. There were some benefits of imperialism for Africans, such as improved transportation and communication systems and improved health care. African efforts to resist imperialism failed because of the West's military and technological advantages. A Western-educated African elite emerged and gradually formed nationalist movements to free themselves from colonial rule.

8. Students' responses should clearly explain the forms of imperial rule that each country used. France used direct rule, and Britain used indirect rule. France sent officials and soldiers to run colonial governments, while Britain used existing local rulers. France imposed French culture on local peoples with the goal of making them French provinces. Britain encouraged the children of the local ruling class to get an education in Britain. In that way, they groomed a new "westernized" generation of leaders to continue indirect imperial rule and spread British civilization. Since Britain's use of indirect rule allowed some self-government involving local officials, there would have been less resentment toward Britain. Western imperialist nations did not hesitate to use military force if their control over a colony was threatened.

9. Students' responses should clearly explain how European imperialism affected native peoples by replacing their political structures with forms of imperial rule. Students should note that Europeans imposed Western culture and religion because they believed that native cultures and religions were degraded. Millions of non-Westerners were robbed of their cultural heritage. Colonization also destroyed native industries such as textiles by bringing in cheaper manufactured goods. Students could juxtapose the benefit of Western-style education for native children with the accompanying negative effects of Western values, language, and religion replacing traditional culture. However, the introduction of Western ideas also led to nationalist movements in the colonies.

10. Students' responses will vary but should explain that Muhammad Ali's economic reforms encouraged the development of local industries and increased farm output. After his death, Egypt came under foreign control. Students should note that a French company was organized to build the Suez Canal. The canal connected the Mediterranean and Red seas, cutting the travel time from London to Bombay, India, by more than 5,000 miles. The Suez Canal gave European imperialists easier access to their colonies, markets, and new territories in Africa and Asia. Britain gained control of the Suez Canal and made Egypt a protectorate.

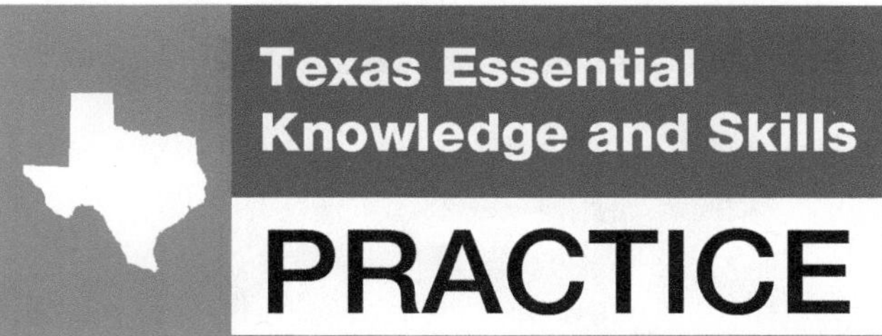

11. Student responses will vary but should explain that the Muslim Ottomans traditionally let minority nationalities practice their own religions. The Armenians were Christians. However, nationalist revolts within the Ottoman empire led to tensions between Turkish nationalists and minority groups like the Armenians, who demanded their own states. Students should note that Muslim Turks accused the Armenians of supporting Russian plans against the Ottoman empire. When the Armenians protested Ottoman policies, the sultan had tens of thousands of Armenians slaughtered, triggering a brutal genocide. An estimated 1.5 million Armenians were killed or died from disease and starvation over the next 25 years.

12. Students' responses will vary but should clearly explain how the display of military power by Commodore Matthew Perry when he first visited Japan forced Japan to agree to unequal treaties with the United States and other Western powers and open up to foreign trade. Japan was humiliated by these unequal treaties. As it modernized, Japan strengthened its military with Western technology. Japan, short of natural resources, then used its modern army and navy to open up Korea for trade with Japan, and eventually annexed Korea. Japan followed the example of imperialist Western nations and acquired its own empire in the Pacific region.

13. Students' responses should clearly explain the relationship between new transportation technologies and the increases in cargo shipped by Western powers during this period of imperialism. The expansion of railroads in colonies allowed for a more rapid delivery of raw materials and finished goods to both parent countries and local markets. New steam-driven ships could carry more cargo and reach destinations more quickly. Ships' travel times were reduced by the Suez and other new canals. Riverboats could penetrate deep into the interiors of previously unreachable regions.

14. Student answers will vary but should explain that Western manufacturers needed resources such as rubber, petroleum, manganese for steel, and palm oil for machinery. Since Africa had these resources, Western European countries colonized the continent. Britain took Egypt, Sudan, South Africa, Rhodesia, and other lands. Belgium got the Congo. The Congo had copper, rubber, and ivory. South Africa was rich in gold and diamonds. All of these resources enriched European countries at the expense of Africans.

15. Students' responses should clearly explain how climate-related tropical diseases in sub-Saharan Africa and Asia prevented exploration, settlement, and colonization by nonnatives. Students should describe how advances in medical technology, such as quinine, allowed nonnatives to survive and overcome deadly tropical diseases such as malaria and yellow fever. With these new medicines, European imperialists could travel to and colonize regions of Asia and Africa that were previously too dangerous.

16. Students' responses will vary but should clearly explain that the telegraph allowed coded messages to be sent over long distances, and this technology strengthened government and economic ties between the parent country and its colonies. New laws, directions, or military orders could be communicated quickly from the ruling nation to leaders in the colonies and between leaders of different colonial regions. The transmission of economic information such as the prices and availability of goods helped businesses. The telegraph kept colonial governments and economies closely connected to the parent country, thus ensuring greater and more efficient control over the colonies.

Topic 15

Answers to TEKS Practice

1. B

2. G

Online To prepare for the End-of-Topic test, have students go online for additional Topic Review and Assessment questions or to review their notes in the **Interactive Reading Notepad** for the lessons in this Topic.

Benchmark Tests

Assign these benchmark tests as you complete the relevant topics to monitor student progress toward mastering the course content and as preparation for the End-of-Course Test.

Benchmark Test 1: Topics 1–5

Benchmark Test 2: Topics 6–10

Benchmark Test 3: Topics 11–15

Benchmark Test 4: Topics 16–21

TEKS PRACTICE

1 Which scenario best illustrates a major political motivation that influenced European imperialism?

A Christian missionaries followed European explorers into central Africa.

B Britain and Germany seized territory in West Africa to prevent France from claiming more land.

C Belgium seized territory in Africa in order to dominate the international rubber and copper trade.

D The Dutch East India Company patrolled the waters of the Indian Ocean with its own fleet to protect its trading vessels.

2

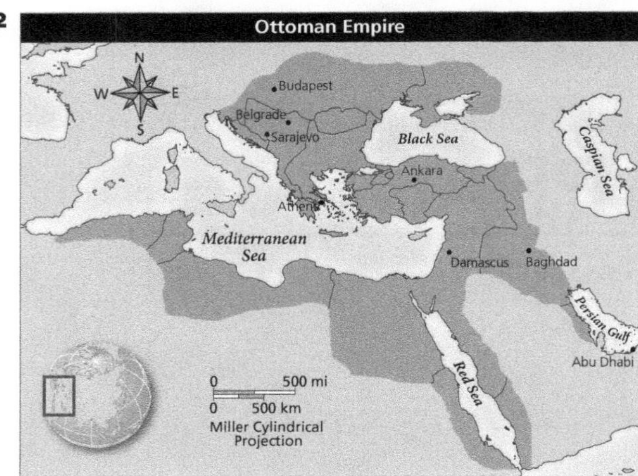

Look at the map of the states that were ruled by the Ottoman Empire. Why did the European idea of nationalism lead to political revolutions within the Ottoman Empire?

F It led the rulers of the empire to reorganize the government, causing conflict between the different Ottoman states.

G It led the different peoples in the empire to desire the ability to govern themselves, causing conflict with the imperial rulers.

H It led the citizens of the empire to want to imitate Western democratic institutions, causing conflict with the conservative Ottoman bureaucracy.

J It led the rulers of the various Ottoman states to push the central government for reforms, causing conflict between religious sects inside the empire.

Test Taking Tips: Tip for Questions With Maps

1. Read the question.
2. Read the map title and look at the map to determine what is shown in the map.
3. Look at the key or legend. What symbols, shades, or patterns are used to show information on the map? Find examples of each symbol, shade, or pattern on the map.
4. Read the question again. What information do you need from the map to answer the question? Use the information in the map title, the key or legend, and on the map itself to find the answer.
5. Answer the question in your own words.
6. Read the answer choices and select the best answer.

3

> *"In April 1884 the Viceroy, Lord Ripon, wrote to Lord Kimberley, the Secretary of State for India, on a question of government policy which was becoming daily more pressing: 'You may rely upon it that there are few Indian questions of greater importance in the present day than those which relate to the mode in which we are to deal with the growing body of natives educated by ourselves in Western learning and Western ideas.'"*

Which statement best explains the concern expressed by Lord Ripon?

A Many Western-educated Indians felt that the ideas of democracy and human rights could best be realized by remaining under British rule.

B Many Western-educated Indians were afraid that the ideas of democracy and human rights would let Muslims dominate an independent India.

C Many Western-educated Indians disagreed with the ideas of democracy and human rights and yearned to reestablish traditional rule in India.

D Many Western-educated Indians were impressed with the ideas of democracy and human rights and wanted to end imperial rule and establish self-rule.

---

4 Toussaint L'Ouverture led a revolt against the French in Hispaniola (Haiti) because he believed in human rights and wanted to end slavery. How can you tell Toussaint was successful in shifting political thought among the people of Hispaniola?

F Toussaint was captured before Hispaniola won independence from France, and he continued to inspire his people by writing to them from prison.

G Toussaint was captured before Hispaniola won independence from France, and he worked with the French government to negotiate a peaceful independence.

H Toussaint was captured and killed before Hispaniola won independence from France; so, the people went back to their lives and continued to be ruled by France.

J Toussaint was captured before Hispaniola won independence from France; yet, the people continued to fight on and eventually abolished slavery and set up an independent nation.

If you have trouble with...				
Question	1	2	3	4
See Lesson	15.1	15.3	15.4	14.2
TEKS	8.C	9.D	9.D	21.C

Topic 15

3. D

4. J

Online Use the **Topic Synthesize** to help students revisit and reflect on the Essential Question for this Topic.

Topic Inquiry

If students have done a Topic Inquiry for this Topic, have them complete the final step of the Inquiry now.

World War I and the Russian Revolution (1914–1924)

TOPIC 16 ORGANIZER	PACING: APPROX. 1 PERIOD, .5 BLOCKS		
	PACING	TEKS	ELPS
Connect	1 period		
MY STORY VIDEO **Wilfred Owen, A Poet in the Trenches**	10 min.		
DIGITAL ESSENTIAL QUESTION ACTIVITY **When is War Justified?**	10 min.		
DIGITAL TIMELINE ACTIVITY **World War I and the Russian Revolution**	10 min.		
TOPIC INQUIRY: PROJECT-BASED LEARNING **Create a Video Docudrama on The Impact of War**	20 min.		
Investigate	2–4 periods		
TOPIC INQUIRY: PROJECT-BASED LEARNING **Create a Video Docudrama on The Impact of War**	Ongoing		
LESSON 1 **World War I Begins**	30–40 min.	1.F, 10.A, 16.A	4.F.10, 5.B.1
LESSON 2 **Fighting the Great War**	30–40 min.	10.B, 22.C, 28.C	5.B.2, 4.G.1
LESSON 3 **World War I Ends**	30–40 min.	1.F, 10.B, 10.C, 10.D, 20.D	4.G.2, 5.C.1
LESSON 4 **Revolution in Russia**	30–40 min.	1.F, 10.D, 18.B, 21.C	4.G.3
Synthesize	1 period		
DIGITAL ESSENTIAL QUESTION ACTIVITY **World War I and the Russian Revolution (1914–1924)**	10 min.		
TOPIC INQUIRY: PROJECT-BASED LEARNING **Create a Video Docudrama on The Impact of War**	20 min.		
Demonstrate	1–2 periods		
DIGITAL TOPIC TEST **World War I and the Russian Revolution**	10 min.		
DIGITAL TEKS MASTERY TEST **TEKS Mastery Test**	10 min.		
TOPIC INQUIRY: PROJECT-BASED LEARNING **Create a Video Docudrama on The Impact of War**	20 min.		

AUTHOR'S NOTE

Total War

The great fact about the war was that it involved national commitment to an extent seldom even approached before. To keep millions of men fed, clothed, armed, and supplied with munitions sufficient for four years of firing at each other over hundreds of miles of front lines required an unparalleled effort by the population involved. World War I thus became the first total war in history.

Total war meant a total national commitment to, and involvement in, the great struggle. Governments took control of national economies as they had never dared do in peacetime. Government boards allocated raw materials, controlled transportation, regulated wages and prices, and rationed food and other essentials. All able-bodied males were liable for conscription into the armed services.

Many women went into the war plants to produce the shells and guns their husbands and sons would use. Almost a million English women worked in munitions factories, and well over half a million French women. Others replaced men drafted for the war in other factories, on farms, as railway conductors, as milk deliverers, and in many other jobs.

New taxes, war loans, and a massive increase in the national debt of the warring countries were additional costs. A continual drain of food, fuel, clothing, and other essentials from the home front also resulted. Russians froze through icy northern winters, Germans went hungry, Austrians starved. Total war thus ravaged European economies even as it strengthened European governments.

This total mobilization of all the resources of great modern states was in its way as striking a feature of the Great War as the raking machinegun fire and billowing clouds of mustard gas that turned European battlefields into no-man's-lands. And it would leave as long a legacy in battered European economies and in governments with newfound powers.
"World War I," one historian of the great debacle has written, "was really a vast global enterprise—Europe became an enormous cauldron into which men and resources from Asia, Africa, and America were poured."

—Anthony Eisler, *The Human Venture,* (Upper Saddle River, New Jersey: Pearson Education 2004), pp. 605–606

TOPIC INQUIRY: PROJECT-BASED LEARNING

Create a Video Docudrama on The Impact of War

In this Topic Inquiry, students work in teams to create video docudramas telling the story of how World War I impacted the lives of civilians, soldiers, and leaders. Learning how war affects the lives of people will contribute to students' understanding of the Topic Essential Question: When is war justified?

STEP 1: CONNECT

Develop Questions and Plan the Investigation

Launch the Project and Generate Questions

Display the Entry Event, which is a fictional assignment from a movie studio. Direct students to the key points in the invitation. Now, display the *Video Docudrama Rubric,* and use it to discuss the essential elements of a docudrama. Finally, tell students that in this project, they will learn about civilians, soldiers, and leaders during World War I, and each team will create a docudrama video to capture and convey how the war impacted one of these groups. Answer any questions students might have.

Plan the Investigation

Divide students into teams and assign each team one of the three groups: civilians, soldiers, or leaders. Have them learn or review the essentials of working as a team by taking a tutorial and signing the *Project Contract*. Display the *Project Roles* document and review with students. Guide students as they complete the *Need-to-Know Questions* for their assigned World War I group.

Suggestion: To control the length of this project, set parameters for how long you want student videos to run and how many days you will allow for video production. To reduce the length of the project, you can also decide to focus students on specific *Need-to-Know Questions* of your choosing.

Resources

- Project Launch
- Project Contract
- Need-to-Know Questions
- Student Instructions
- Video Docudrama Rubric

PROFESSIONAL DEVELOPMENT

Project-Based Learning

Be sure to view the Project-Based Learning Professional Development resources in the online course.

STEP 2: INVESTIGATE

Apply Disciplinary Concepts and Tools

Conduct Research

Assign team member roles or allow teams time to assign roles. To control the length of this project, you may wish to have all students conduct research.

Remind students to focus their research on the *Need-to-Know Questions.* Guide research by directing students to helpful sections of the digital text. You may wish to recommend specific books or specific Web sites such as PBS, the Library of Congress, or the Imperial War Museum. Help students begin to fill out the *Information Organizer.*

Suggestion: If your class has limited access to online resources, here are some books that they might find helpful: *The First World War* by John Keegan; *A World Undone: The Story of the Great War, 1914 to 1918,* by G. J. Meyer; and *World War I,* by H. P. Willmott.

Write and Edit Docudrama

Guide students as they develop their video docudrama's story, characters, script, and images. Remind students to refer to the various project roles and to keep their script focused on the *Need-to-Know Questions* about their group of people in World War I. Encourage students to mix dramatic reenactment and dialogue with historical images and firsthand accounts.

Resources

- Project Roles
- Project Tracker
- Information Organizer

STEP 3: SYNTHESIZE

Evaluate Sources and Use Evidence to Formulate Conclusions

Create Your Video Docudrama

Now, allow students time to put together their video docudrama. Students may use software or a Web site of their or your choosing. Remind them to refer to the *Project Launch* and *Video Docudrama Rubric* as a reminder of the desired elements and qualities of an instructional video docudrama.

Suggestion: Before students get into these final stages, you may wish to show them some finished videos created by your students of previous years. You could also refer them to World War I videos or other student-generated videos on the Internet.

Add an Informative Conclusion to Your Video

Teams should be sure that they have a powerful conclusion that makes a clear statement on the impact of World War I on their assigned group of participants. Tell students that they might even go beyond this to make a comment about the continuing impact of wars today.

Review and Edit Your Video

Ask teams to review and do final edits on their docudrama. They should be sure that they have satisfied the requirements in the project launch documents. Stress that their goal is to excel in each area of the project rubric: Purpose, Content Accuracy, Artistic Creativity, Technology, and Delivery.

Resources

- Project Rubric
- Software or Web site for creating docudrama

STEP 4: DEMONSTRATE

Communicate Conclusions and Take Informed Action

Present Your Video Docudrama

You may wish students to refer to 21st Century Skill Tutorials: *Give an Effective Presentation.* Have students present their video docudramas to the class or a larger audience. Allow time for comments, questions, and answers after each presentation.

Reflect on the Project

After students have finished creating and presenting their docudramas, provide your assessment, and help them go over what worked well and what did not work well so they they can improve their results on the next project.

Suggestion: As an extension activity, invite students to find a recent news video clip reporting on the human impact of an international conflict, civil war, or terrorist attack. Have them present it to the class and draw comparisons between World War I and the news story.

Resources

- Video Docudrama Rubric
- 21st Century Skill Tutorials: *Give an Effective Presentation*
- Self-Assessment

World War I Begins

Objectives

Objective 1: Describe how imperialism, nationalism, and militarism pushed Europe closer to war.

Objective 2: Identify the key event that sparked World War I.

Objective 3: Trace how the alliance system drew nations into the war.

LESSON 1 ORGANIZER	PACING: APPROX. 1 PERIOD, .5 BLOCKS					
	OBJECTIVES	PACING	RESOURCES: Print	RESOURCES: Online	TEKS	ELPS
Connect						
DIGITAL START UP ACTIVITY **The Balkan Powder Keg**		5 min.		●	1.F, 10.A, 16.A	
Investigate						
READ **European Powers Form Alliances**	Objective 3	10 min.	●	●	1.F, 10.A	4.F.10
INTERACTIVE CHART **Alliances and World War I**		10 min.		●	1.F, 10.A	
READ **Major Causes of World War I**	Objective 1	10 min.	●	●	1.F, 10.A	5.B.1
INTERACTIVE CARTOON **Nationalist Struggles in the Balkans**		10 min.		●	1.E, 1.F, 10.A	
READ **The Balkan Powder Keg Explodes**	Objective 2	10 min.	●	●	1.F, 10.A	
READ **The Alliance System Leads to War**		10 min.	●	●	1.F, 10.A, 16.A	
Synthesize						
DIGITAL ACTIVITY **Causes of World War I**		5 min.		●	1.E, 1.F, 10.A	
Demonstrate						
DIGITAL QUIZ **Lesson Quiz and Class Discussion Board**		10 min.		●	1.E, 1.F, 10.A	

NOTES

Fighting the Great War

Objectives

Objective 1: Understand how trench warfare led to a stalemate on the Western Front.

Objective 2: Identify and describe the impact of modern military technology on the fighting.

Objective 3: Outline the course of the war on multiple European fronts.

Objective 4: Explain how World War I was a global conflict.

LESSON 2 ORGANIZER — **PACING: APPROX. 1 PERIOD, .5 BLOCKS**

	OBJECTIVES	PACING	RESOURCES Print	RESOURCES Online	TEKS	ELPS
Connect						
DIGITAL START UP ACTIVITY **In Flanders Fields**		5 min.		●	10.B	
Investigate						
READ **A New Kind of War**	Objective 1	10 min.	●	●	10.B	
INTERACTIVE MAP **Europe in World War I, 1914–1918**				●	10.B	
READ **Trench Warfare**				●	10.B	
READ **Modern Military Technology**	Objective 2	10 min.	●	●	10.B, 28.C	5.B.2
INTERACTIVE GALLERY **Military Technology in World War I**				●	10.B, 28.C	
READ **Other European Fronts**	Objective 3	10 min.	●	●	10.B	
READ **A Global Conflict**	Objective 4	10 min.	●	●	1.F, 22.C	4.G.1
Synthesize						
DIGITAL ACTIVITY **Defining Characteristics**		5 min.		●	1.F, 10.B, 28.C	
Demonstrate						
DIGITAL QUIZ **Lesson Quiz and Class Discussion Board**		10 min.		●	1.F, 10.B, 22.C, 28.A	

PEARSON realize™ www.PearsonTexas.com Access your Digital Lesson

Focus on Texas Standards

Texas Essential Knowledge and Skills

10.B identify major characteristics of World War I, including total war, trench warfare, modern military technology, and high casualty rates

22.C identify examples of politically motivated mass murders in Cambodia, China, Latin America, the Soviet Union, and Armenia

28.C explain the effects of major new military technologies on World War I, World War II, and the Cold War

NOTES

World War I Ends

Objectives

Objective 1: Describe how World War I became a total war.

Objective 2: Explain how U.S. entry into the war led to an Allied victory.

Objective 3: List the effects of World War I in terms of financial costs, high casualty rates, and political impact.

Objective 4: Describe the issues at the Paris Peace Conference and the impact of Woodrow Wilson's Fourteen Points.

Objective 5: Summarize the terms and impact of the Treaty of Versailles.

LESSON 3 ORGANIZER — **PACING: APPROX. 1 PERIOD, .5 BLOCKS**

	OBJECTIVES	PACING	RESOURCES Print	RESOURCES Online	TEKS	ELPS
Connect						
DIGITAL START UP ACTIVITY **An Uneasy Peace?**		5 min.		●	20.D	
Investigate						
READ **Governments Direct Total War**	Objective 1	10 min.	●	●	1.F, 10.B, 21.A	
READ **Morale Breaks Down**	Objective 1	10 min.	●	●	1.F, 10.D, 21.A	
INTERACTIVE GALLERY **World War I Propaganda Posters**	Objective 1	10 min.		●	1.F, 10.B	
READ **The United States Enters the War**	Objective 2	10 min.	●	●	1.F, 10.C	4.G.2
READ **The Great War Ends**	Objective 3	10 min.	●	●	1.F, 10.B	5.C.1
READ **Making the Peace**	Objectives 4, 5	10 min.	●	●	10.C, 20.D	
READ **Effects of the Peace Settlements**	Objectives 4, 5	10 min.	●	●	10.C, 20.D	
INTERACTIVE MAP **Europe in 1914 and 1920**	Objectives 4, 5	10 min.		●	10.C, 15.A	
Synthesize						
DIGITAL ACTIVITY **The Treaty of Versailles**		5 min.		●	10.C	
Demonstrate						
DIGITAL QUIZ **Lesson Quiz and Class Discussion Board**		10 min.		●	1.F, 10.B, 10.C	

PEARSON realize™ www.PearsonTexas.com Access your Digital Lesson

Focus on Texas Standards

Texas Essential Knowledge and Skills

1.F identify major causes and describe the major effects of the following important turning points in world history from 1914 to the present: the world wars and their impact on political, economic, and social systems; communist revolutions and their impact on the Cold War; independence movements; and globalization

10.B identify major characteristics of World War I, including total war, trench warfare, modern military technology, and high casualty rates

10.C explain the political impact of Woodrow Wilson's Fourteen Points and the political and economic impact of the Treaty of Versailles, including changes in boundaries and the mandate system

10.D identify the causes of the February (March) and October revolutions of 1917 in Russia, their effects on the outcome of World War I, and the Bolshevik establishment of the Union of Soviet Socialist Republics

20.D explain the significance of the League of Nations and the United Nations

NOTES

Revolution in Russia

Objectives

Objective 1: Explain the causes of the February (March) Revolution.

Objective 2: Describe the goals of Lenin and the Bolsheviks in the October Revolution.

Objective 3: Summarize the outcome of the civil war in Russia.

Objective 4: Analyze how Lenin built a Communist state in the Soviet Union.

LESSON 4 ORGANIZER — **PACING: APPROX. 1 PERIOD, .5 BLOCKS**

	OBJECTIVES	PACING	RESOURCES: Print	RESOURCES: Online	TEKS	ELPS
Connect						
DIGITAL START UP ACTIVITY **"End the War and Its Bloodshed"**		5 min.		●	10.D	
Investigate						
READ **Causes of the February Revolution**	Objective 1	10 min.	●	●	1.F, 10.B, 10.D	
READ **Lenin Leads the Bolsheviks**	Objective 2	10 min.	●	●	1.F, 10.D, 18.B, 18.C, 21.A, 21.C	4.G.3
READ **Revolution Brings the Bolsheviks to Power**		10 min.	●	●	1.F, 10.D, 21.A, 21.C	
INTERACTIVE CHART **1917—Revolutions in Russia**		10 min.		●	1.F, 10.D 18.B, 21.A, 21.C	
READ **Civil War Erupts in Russia**	Objective 3	10 min.	●	●	1.F, 10.D, 21.A	
READ **The Communist Soviet Union Emerges**	Objective 4	10 min.	●	●	10.D, 18.B, 18.C, 21.C	
INTERACTIVE MAP **From Russian Empire to Soviet Union, 1914–1923**		10 min.		●	10.D, 15.B	
Synthesize						
DIGITAL ACTIVITY **End the War and Its Bloodshed**		5 min.		●	1.F, 10.D	
Demonstrate						
DIGITAL QUIZ **Lesson Quiz and Class Discussion Board**		10 min.		●	1.F, 10.D, 18.B, 21.A, 21.C	

Focus on Texas Standards

Texas Essential Knowledge and Skills

1.F identify major causes and describe the major effects of the following important turning points in world history from 1914 to the present: the world wars and their impact on political, economic, and social systems; communist revolutions and their impact on the Cold War; independence movements; and globalization

10.D identify the causes of the February (March) and October revolutions of 1917 in Russia, their effects on the outcome of World War I, and the Bolshevik establishment of the Union of Soviet Socialist Republics

18.B identify the historical origins and characteristics of communism, including the influences of Karl Marx

21.C identify examples of key persons who were successful in shifting political thought, including William Wilberforce

NOTES

TOPIC 16 TEKS Mastery

World War I and the Russian Revolution (1914–1924)

In this Topic, you will learn about World War I and the Russian Revolution. You will also find lots of interesting ways to master the TEKS associated with this Topic.

Your study will help you master these TEKS:

TEKS

1.E, 1.F, 10.A, 10.B, 10.C, 10.D, 16.A, 18.B, 18.C, 20.D, 21.A, 21.C, 22.C, 28.C, 30.C

LESSON OUTLINE

Connect

Connect with this Topic by watching a video about a fascinating person related to this Topic. You can think about how the Topic connects to your own life. And you'll encounter an intriguing Essential Question: When is war justified?

Begin your study by trying the following:

NBC LEARN **Watch My Story Video:**

Wilfred Owen, A Poet in the Trenches

Launch your Project:

Create a Video Docudrama on the Impact of the War

Investigate

Then you will investigate the Topic through a group of lessons. The story of World War I and the Russian Revolution will come to life as you read and interact with key content. You will get a chance to read about what happened and why. And you'll be able to interact with a lot of fascinating online materials.

You'll also keep working on your Project as you build further mastery of the Topic.

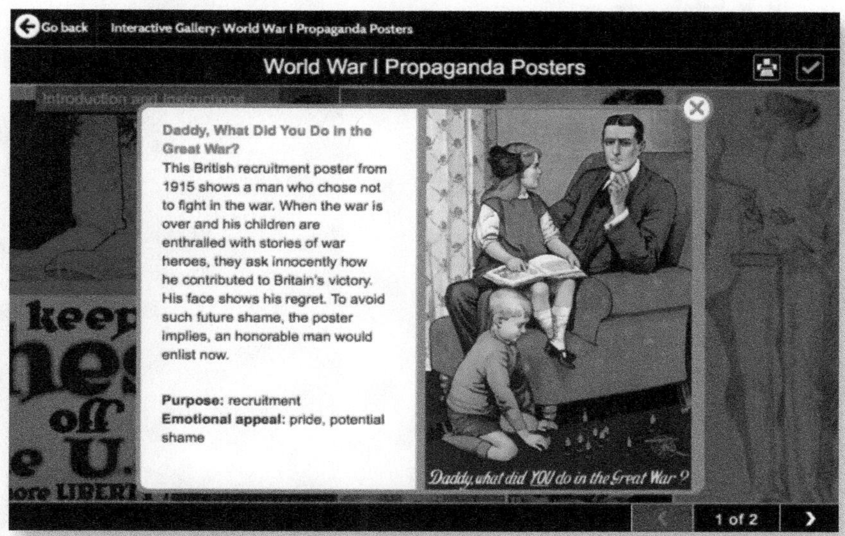

>> Digital interactivity from the online course

Synthesize

You will get a chance to pull together everything you have learned by thinking again about the Essential Question. Consider how you would answer the question now: When is war justified?

Demonstrate

Now you will get to show what you know. You will get a chance to complete the TEKS Review and Assessment pages, answering questions about every TEKS for this Topic. Or you can write an essay, take part in a discussion, or share your Project. No matter which you do, it will be a real-world demonstration of the things you now understand about World War I and the Russian Revolution.

TEKS in Topic 16	Topic Review and Assessment Questions
1.E	2
1.F	1, 3
10.A	4, 9
10.B	5, 8
10.C	7
10.D	12, 13
16.A	9
18.B	16
18.C	14
20.D	10
21.A	6
21.C	15
22.C	11
28.C	8

Topic 16

World War I and the Russian Revolution (1914–1924)

Introduction

In the early 1900s, powerful forces were pushing Europe toward war. These forces included nationalism, militarism, imperialism, and alliance systems. Meanwhile, in Russia, discontent with tsarist rule, peasant unrest, and economic challenges set the stage for revolution. The results were World War I and the Russian Revolution. These upheavals would leave Europe in turmoil and give rise to the Communist Soviet Union.

ESSENTIAL QUESTION

Ask students to think about the Essential Question for this Topic: When is war justified?

Either project the Essential Question activity from the course or share the following with students:

Do you think there are valid reasons for a nation to go to war? The reasons below were applicable to World War I. Which are good and valid reasons to go to war? Which are not? Why?

- To protect your homeland from invasion
- To defend people in a peaceful, neutral country
- To fulfill obligations arising from alliances
- To make your country militarily or economically stronger
- To gain power and territory in other parts of the world
- To secure natural resources vital to your nation's economy
- To help end a war and prevent future wars

Poll students on whether they think each of these causes was a valid reason for going to war. Ask them to give reasons for their opinions.

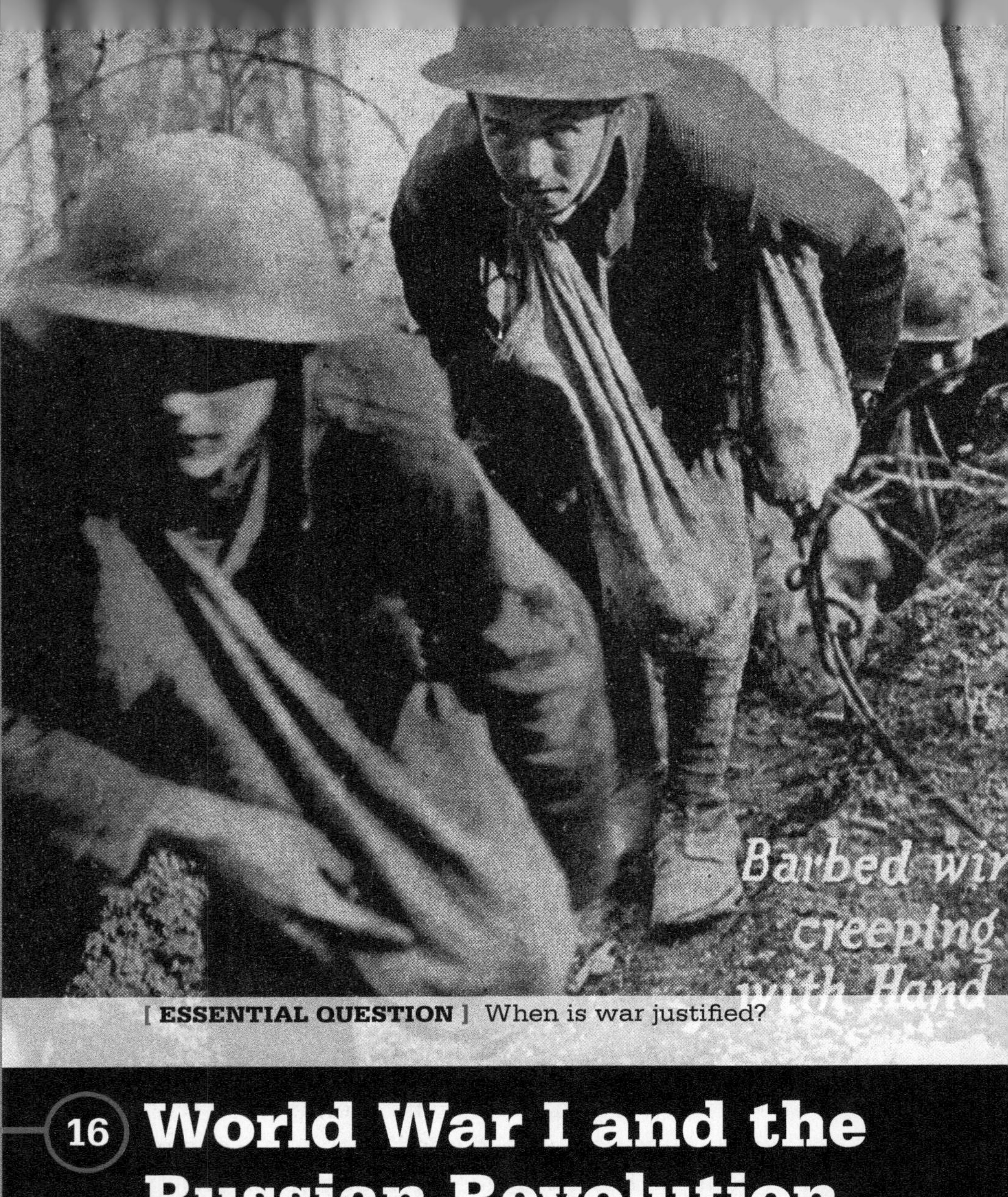

[**ESSENTIAL QUESTION**] When is war justified?

16 World War I and the Russian Revolution (1914–1924)

Analyze Images

Ask students to examine the soldiers shown in this photo. Explain to students why historians call World War I the first total war. Have students discuss the expression on the face of the second soldier. Ask students to describe what the soldiers might be doing and where they might be going.

>> American soldiers in World War I

Enduring Understandings

- Imperial rivalries, militarism, extreme nationalism, and a system of competing alliances contributed to the outbreak of World War I.
- Trench warfare and modern military technology led to a long stalemate and high casualty rates.
- U.S. entry into the war led to an Allied victory.
- Woodrow Wilson tried to build a lasting peace based on his Fourteen Points, but the Treaty of Versailles punished Germany harshly.
- In Russia, wartime hardships sparked the March Revolution, forcing the tsar to abdicate.
- Lenin and the Bolsheviks seized power in the November Revolution and began to build a communist state in Russia.

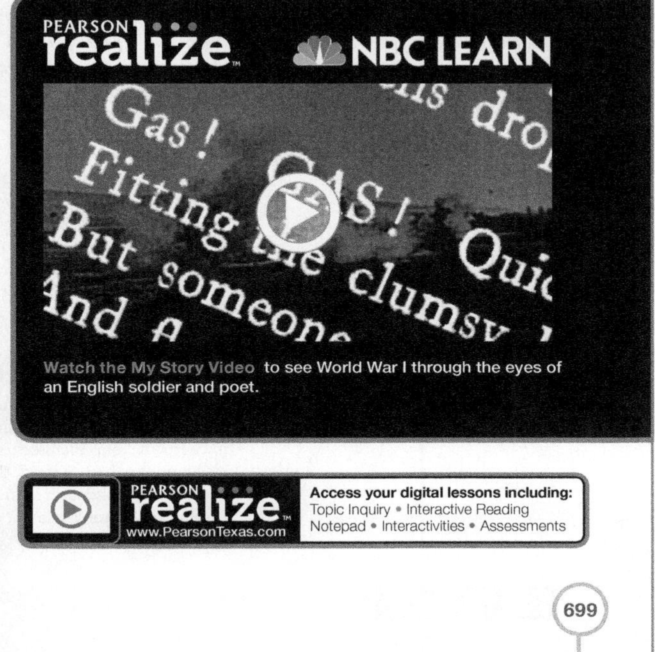

Watch the My Story Video to see World War I through the eyes of an English soldier and poet.

PEARSON realize www.PearsonTexas.com Access your digital lessons including: Topic Inquiry • Interactive Reading Notepad • Interactivities • Assessments

699

Topic Inquiry

If you choose to assign the Topic Inquiry, launch the project with students after introducing the Topic.

D Differentiate Extra Support Ask students which events pertain mostly to the Russian Revolution rather than to World War I.

NBC LEARN MY STORY VIDEO

Project the My Story Video that introduces students to a soldier and poet of World War I.

Online My Story Video: **Wilfred Owen, A Poet in the Trenches**.

Check Understanding What accounts for Wilfred Owen's change of opinion about fighting in World War I? *(His enthusiasm for the war changed after he witnessed firsthand the horrors of modern combat.)*

Determine Author's Purpose What did Wilfred Owen hope to convey through his poetry? *(He wanted to describe the grim reality of combat and the disillusionment he felt about war.)*

OVERVIEW ACTIVITY

Online Project the **Timeline: World War I and the Russian Revolution** showing some key events of World War I and the Russian Revolution. During this Topic, students will learn about all of these events and many more, but this timeline will provide a framework into which they can place the events they learn about.

Check Understanding How long did World War I last? *(a little more than four years, from August 1914 to November 1918)*

Topic 16 Lesson 1

World War I Begins

CONNECT

Preview Have students preview the **Lesson Objectives** and the list of **Key Terms**.

They can preview **Key Terms** and **Academic Vocabulary** using the **Reading and Note Taking Study Guide** or the **Interactive Reading Notepad** on the digital course.

Online Use the **Editable Presentation** found on the digital course to present the main ideas for this lesson.

Start Up Activity

Ask students what they remember about the Balkans from Topic 14. Discuss the meaning of nationalism and ask them to explain why the Balkan region was known as a powder keg.

Discuss Is there a current or recent political issue that has tensions similar to the Balkans? What impact might it have on other nations? How do conflicts in one region or country sometimes lead to larger conflicts?

Online You can also project the **Start Up Activity** from the course.

INVESTIGATE

Have students read the section using the **Reading and Note Taking Study Guide** to help them take notes and understand the text as they read.

European Powers Form Alliances

The alliance system was a major cause of World War I. Increased tensions and suspicions led nations to form alliances, agreeing to defend each other in case of attack. In August and September 1914, Europe went to war. One by one, the countries of Europe honored their alliances and declared war on each other.

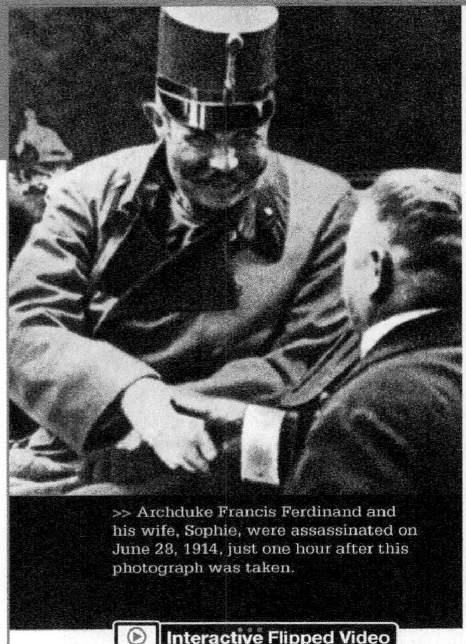

>> Archduke Francis Ferdinand and his wife, Sophie, were assassinated on June 28, 1914, just one hour after this photograph was taken.

Interactive Flipped Video

16.1 By 1914, Europe had enjoyed a century of relative peace. Idealists hoped for a permanent end to the scourge of war. International events, such as the first modern Olympic games in 1896 and the First Universal Peace Conference in 1899, were steps toward keeping the peace. "The future belongs to peace," said French economist Frédéric Passy (pa SEE).

TEKS
1.F, 10.A, 16.A

>> Objectives

Describe how imperialism, nationalism, and militarism pushed Europe closer to war.

Identify the key event that sparked World War I.

Trace how the alliance system drew nations into the war.

>> Key Terms

entente
militarism
Alsace and Lorraine
ultimatum
mobilize
neutrality

World War I Begins

European Powers Form Alliances

Not everyone was so hopeful. "I shall not live to see the Great War," warned German Chancellor Otto von Bismarck, "but you will see it, and it will start in the east." It was Bismarck's prediction, rather than Passy's, that came true.

Nations Form Alliances Despite efforts to ensure peace, the late 1800s saw growing rivalries among the great powers of Europe, including Britain, France, Germany, Austria-Hungary, Italy, and Russia. In an atmosphere of fear and distrust, the great powers set out to protect themselves by forming alliances. Nations signed treaties pledging to defend each other. These alliances were intended to create powerful combinations that no one would dare attack. Gradually, two rival alliances evolved.

The Triple Alliance The first major alliance had its origins in Bismarck's day. He knew that France longed to avenge its defeat in the Franco-Prussian War. Sure that France would not attack Germany without help, Bismarck signed treaties with other powers. By 1882, Germany had formed the Triple Alliance with Italy and Austria-Hungary. Although Bismarck had previously signed an alliance with Russia, Kaiser William II did not preserve that alliance, leaving Russia free to seek other allies.

PEARSON realize. www.PearsonTexas.com Access your Digital Lesson.

700

Aa Vocabulary Builder

1. Have students pronounce the following academic vocabulary terms in this lesson and clarify the part of speech. Break the words into syllables and pronounce them with the students.
2. Explain what the word means in common "student-friendly" language using synonyms and antonyms when possible. Provide concrete examples to clarify the meaning, and rephrase the definition.

status: high standing, rank, or prestige
overseas: across the sea; foreign

In 1914, when war did erupt, Germany and Austria-Hungary fought on the same side. They became known as the Central Powers.

The Triple Entente A rival bloc took shape in 1893, when France and Russia signed a secret treaty. France was eager to end its isolation and balance the growing power of Germany. In 1904, France and Britain signed an **entente** (ahn TAHNT), a nonbinding agreement to follow common policies. Though not as formal as a treaty, the entente led to close military and diplomatic ties. Britain later signed a similar agreement with Russia, creating the Triple Entente. When war began, these powers became known as the Allies.

Britain and France had been rivals for hundreds of years, and France had invaded Russia during the Napoleonic Wars. Still, these three powers joined together in the Triple Entente because they feared Germany wanted to dominate Europe.

Other Alliances Other states were drawn into alliances. Germany signed a treaty with the Ottoman empire. As early as 1867, Britain had signed a treaty to protect Belgium's right to remain neutral in any European conflict. Italy had a secret treaty with France not to attack it. And Russia had agreed to protect Serbia. Britain forged ties with Japan.

Rather than easing tensions, the growth of rival alliance systems made governments increasingly nervous. A local conflict could mushroom into a general war. In 1914, that threat became a reality.

ANALYZE INFORMATION Why did the European nations form opposing alliances?

ELPS ELPS 4.F.10 Use your own experiences and relationships to understand the alliances that led many nations of Europe to war.

Major Causes of World War I

During the late 1800s and early 1900s, tensions were increasing among the great powers of Europe. Aggressive nationalism, economic competition, imperialism, militarism, and an arms race all helped fuel an atmosphere of suspicion and distrust.

Economic and Imperial Rivalry Economic rivalries helped sour the international atmosphere. Germany, the newest of the great powers, was growing into an economic and military powerhouse. Britain felt threatened by Germany's rapid growth. Germany, in

>> Germany, led by Kaiser William II (left), and Austria-Hungary, led by Emperor Francis Joseph (right), became close allies in the years before World War I.

>> A Parisian newspaper presented this view of imperialism. The caption says "France freely gives Morocco civilization, peace, and wealth." **Hypothesize** Who might have opposed this viewpoint? Why?

Guided Reading and Discussion

Ask students to note the importance of the alliance system in causing World War I and involving many countries in the war.

Analyze Information

How did the alliances created at the end of the nineteenth century (Triple Alliance and Triple Entente) relate to the alliances that formed during World War I? *(Sample response: The alliances created in the nineteenth century were the basis for the alliances during World War I. The Triple Alliance became the Central Powers and the Triple Entente became the Allies.)*

Key Terms

Draw students' attention to the key term **entente** (in bold) in the text. Explain that an entente is a type of alliance. Ask students to brainstorm why countries might form alliances.

Major Causes of World War I

Imperialism, militarism, and nationalism were all major causes of World War I, a cataclysm that would mark an historical turning point. Imperialism in the form of rivalries and disputes over colonial territories increased tensions between nations. Militarism made countries more prepared for and more willing to go to war. Nationalism threatened old empires and fed desires to redress perceived wrongs.

English Language Proficiency Standards

Learning Strategies 4.F.10 Read aloud "European Powers Form Alliances." Then have students complete the following activities according to their English proficiency.

Beginning Ask a volunteer to list names of friends and place them in a web with the volunteer's name in the center. Draw lines from the volunteer's name to each friend. Ask the volunteer which friends are friends with each other, and draw lines between those names. Point out that if two friends had a disagreement, the balance of these relationships could change. Model making the connection between this friendship web and the alliance system of World War I. Create a second web to show relationships among European nations and how they took sides in the war.

Intermediate Help students create friendship webs with their own circle of friends. Have them discuss with a partner what might happen if two friends had a disagreement. Ask pairs to consider how their webs resemble relationships among European nations around WWI. Help students create a web to show relationships among the nations of Europe and how they eventually took sides in the war.

Answers

Analyze Information *They wanted to protect themselves from their enemies, and the alliances made them stronger both militarily and economically.*

Hypothesize *Moroccans, because they wanted independence. Germany, because it wanted to exert its own influence in Morocco*

Topic 16 Lesson 1

Online Project the **Interactive Cartoon: Nationalist Struggles in the Balkans**. As a class, discuss the situation in the Balkans in the early twentieth century. Click through the hotspots on the screen, discussing the pop-up text and what it tells students about the cartoon.

ACTIVE CLASSROOM

Before going through the cartoon with the class, use the Closer Look strategy to have pairs of students closely examine the static cartoon and interpret the visual elements in their sections. Ask students to present their conclusions to the class.

Analyze Images Why did the cartoonist represent the Balkans in this way? *(Answers will vary. Students should show a clear understanding that the metaphor of the boiling cauldron represents nationalist desires and conflicts that built pressure and tension in the region.)*

D Differentiate Extra Support Help students understand the concepts of the political cartoon by explicitly explaining the central metaphor of the cartoon, the bubbling cauldron. Tell students to think about what happens when water simmers or boils on the stove. Point out to students that in this case, the cauldron could be said to represent the term *simmering tensions*.

Answers

Analyze Data *Germany had the most soldiers. Britain had the largest navy.*

turn, thought the other great powers did not give it enough respect. It also worried about future economic competition from Russia, which had a huge population and vast natural resources.

Imperialism also divided European nations. In 1905 and again in 1911, competition for colonies brought France and Germany to the brink of war in Morocco, then under France's influence. Although diplomats kept the peace, Germany did gain some territory in central Africa. As a result of the two Moroccan crises, Britain and France strengthened their ties against Germany.

Militarism and the Arms Race The late 1800s saw a rise in **militarism,** or the glorification of the military. Under militarism, the armed forces and readiness for war came to dominate national policy. Militarists painted war in romantic colors. Young men dreamed of blaring trumpets and dashing cavalry charges—not at all the sort of conflict they would soon face.

With international tensions on the rise, the great powers began to build up their armies and navies. The fiercest competition was the naval rivalry between Britain and Germany. To protect its vast overseas empire, Britain had built the world's most respected navy. As Germany began acquiring overseas colonies, it began to build up its own navy. Suspicious of Germany's motives, Britain in turn increased naval spending. Newspapers dramatized the arms race and stirred national public opinion against rival countries.

The arms race helped military leaders gain influence. On matters of peace and war, civilian governments turned to military leaders for advice. Germany generals and British admirals enjoyed great respect and got more funds to build up their forces. As militarism and the arms race fed each other, tensions grew.

Nationalism Aggressive nationalism also caused tension. Nationalism was strong in both Germany and France. Germans were proud of their new empire's military power and industrial leadership. The French were bitter about their 1871 defeat in the Franco-Prussian War and yearned to recover the lost border province of **Alsace and Lorraine.**

In Eastern Europe, Russia sponsored a powerful form of nationalism called Pan-Slavism. It held that all Slavic peoples shared a common nationality. As the largest Slavic country, Russia felt that it had a duty to lead and defend all Slavs. By 1914, it stood ready to support Serbia, a proud young Slavic nation, against any threat.

Two old multinational empires particularly feared rising nationalism. Austria-Hungary worried that nationalism might foster rebellion among the many minority populations within its empire. Ottoman Turkey felt threatened by nearby new nations, such as

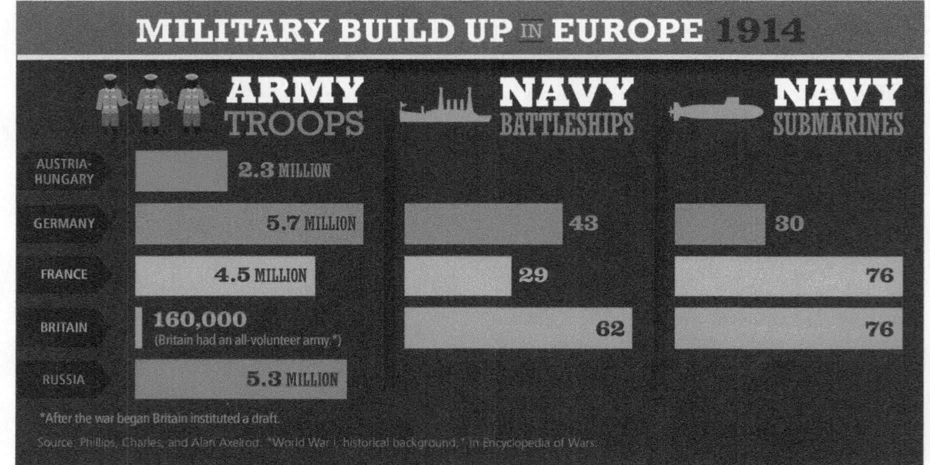

>> **Analyze Data** According to this infographic, which country had the most soldiers? Which country had the largest navy?

English Language Proficiency Standards

Advanced Have students work with a partner to create a friendship web and talk about what could happen if two friends in their webs had a disagreement. Ask pairs to consider how their friendship webs resemble the relationships among European nations around WWI. Facilitate a discussion in which students work together as a class to create another web showing the relationships among the nations of Europe and how they eventually took sides in the war.

Advanced High Have students create a friendship web and consider what could happen if two of those in the web had a disagreement. After students write down their ideas, have them create a web to show alliances among European nations and consider how the two webs resemble each other. Have students participate in a Think-Pair-Share to share their ideas from the first part of the activity and connections to the alliances that led Europe to war.

Serbia. If realized, Serbia's dream of a South Slav state could take territory away from both Austria-Hungary and Turkey.

In 1912, several Balkan states—Serbia, Greece, Bulgaria and Montenegro—attacked Turkey and succeeded in taking a large area of land away from Turkish control. The next year, they fought among themselves over the spoils of war. These brief but bloody Balkan wars raised tensions to a fever pitch. By 1914, the Balkans were called the "powder keg of Europe"—a barrel of gunpowder that a tiny spark might cause to explode.

IDENTIFY CAUSE AND EFFECT How did imperialism heighten tensions in Europe?

The Balkan Powder Keg Explodes

As Bismarck had predicted, the Great War began in Eastern Europe. A regional conflict between tiny Serbia and the huge empire of Austria-Hungary grew rapidly into a general war that would mark one of history's significant turning points.

Archduke Francis Ferdinand Is Assassinated The crisis began when Archduke Francis Ferdinand of Austria-Hungary announced that he would visit Sarajevo (sa ruh YAY voh), the capital of Bosnia. Francis Ferdinand was the nephew and heir of the aging Austrian emperor, Francis Joseph. At the time of his visit, Bosnia was under the rule of Austria-Hungary. But it was also the home of many Serbs and other Slavs.

News of the royal visit angered many Serbian nationalists. They viewed the Austrians as foreign oppressors. Some members of Unity or Death, a Serbian terrorist group commonly known as the Black Hand, vowed to take action.

The archduke ignored warnings of anti-Austrian unrest in Sarajevo. On June 28, 1914, he and his wife, Sophie, rode through Sarajevo in an open car. As the car passed by, a conspirator named Gavrilo Princip (GAV ree loh PREEN tseep) seized his chance and fired twice into the car. Moments later, the archduke and his wife were dead.

Austria Declares War on Serbia When news of the assassination of Francis Ferdinand reached Vienna, the government of Emperor Francis Joseph blamed Serbia. Austria-Hungary believed that Serbia would stop at nothing to achieve its goal of a South Slav empire. Austria decided its only course was to punish Serbia.

>> This political cartoon was published in 1912 in the British magazine *Punch*. **Analyze Political Cartoons** What view of the Balkans does this cartoon present?

 Interactive Cartoon

In Berlin, Kaiser William II was horrified at the assassination. He wrote to Francis Joseph, advising him to take a firm stand toward Serbia. Instead of urging restraint, Germany gave Austria a "blank check," or permission to undertake whatever action it chose.

For weeks, diplomats shuttled notes among the great powers, trying to head off a conflict. Backed by Germany, however, Austria-Hungary sent Serbia a harsh **ultimatum,** or final set of demands. To avoid war, said the ultimatum, Serbia must end all anti-Austrian agitation and punish any Serbian official involved in the murder plot. It must even let Austria join in the investigation. Austria-Hungary gave Serbia 48 hours to reply.

Serbia agreed to most, but not all, of the terms of Austria's ultimatum. This partial refusal gave Austria the opportunity it was seeking. On July 28, 1914, Austria declared war on Serbia.

INTEGRATE INFORMATION How did Austria's alliance system influence Austria's decision to send Serbia an ultimatum?

The Balkan Powder Keg Explodes

Identify Cause and Effect Explain why a global conflict developed after the assassination, and describe the sequence of events. *(Because of the alliance system; Russia threatened Austria and then mobilized troops because Serbia was its ally; Germany declared war on Russia because it had risen up against Austria; Russia appealed to its ally France, and so Germany declared war on France. When German troops marched through Belgium to attack France, Britain (which had guaranteed Belgian neutrality and was a French ally) declared war on Germany.)*

Guided Reading and Discussion

Discuss with students how imperialism, militarism, and nationalism were all major causes of World War I.

Compare and Contrast examples of European nationalism. *(Answers may vary. Sample response: Germany's desire to show its economic and military dominance, France's desire to get back Alsace and Lorraine, Russia's pan-Slavism, and Serbia's desire for a South Slav state)*

Synthesize How were economic rivalries connected to imperialism in Europe before World War I? *(Sample response: European countries gained economically from the resources provided by their colonies. As a result, the country with the most colonies would have access to the most resources. This created a rivalry for colonies and increased tensions.)*

English Language Proficiency Standards

Learning Strategies 5.B.1 Read "Major Causes of World War I" aloud and have students complete one of these activities.

Beginning Help students complete these sentence frames. Define each word choice to improve understanding of the vocabulary words.

- France and Germany were competing for _____ in Morocco. (control, gold, resources)
- Austria-Hungary and Ottoman Turkey were afraid of the _____ of nationalism. (pride, growth, decline)

Intermediate Have students complete the sentence frames in the Beginning activity. Have them define each word choice to improve their understanding of the vocabulary words.

Advanced Have pairs of students write three sentences about the causes of World War I. Provide bilingual dictionaries and other resources for extra support.

Advanced High Have students write five sentences about the causes of World War I. Provide bilingual dictionaries and other resources for extra support.

Answers

Identify Cause and Effect *Countries with overseas empires needed a strong military to protect their colonies from other imperial powers. So, they increased the size of their navies and armies. This arms race made countries more tense and nervous.*

Analyze Political Cartoons *The perspective of this cartoon is that the Balkans is a dangerous place that the larger European powers cannot control.*

Integrate Information *Kaiser William advised his ally Austria to take a firm stand. He said that Germany would support Austria in a war no matter what the cost.*

Topic 16 Lesson 1

The Alliance System Leads to War

Guided Reading and Discussion

Help students understand the connection between the assassination of Francis Ferdinand, nationalism, and alliances as causes of World War I.

Nationalism wasn't just one of many causes of World War I; it was also the immediate cause, the spark that exploded the powder keg. Then, the carefully planned alliances that had developed in the decades before the assassination plunged the world into deeper conflict, as members of each side leaned on their allies for support.

Online Project the **Interactive Chart: Alliances and World War I**. Work as a class to drag each reason for going to war to the appropriate country.

ACTIVE CLASSROOM

Use the Take a Stand strategy to engage students. Have them take a stand on the following statement: Did the alliance system make World War I inevitable? Yes or no? Have a class debate where students on either side of the issue defend their positions.

SYNTHESIZE

Online Project the **Digital Activity: Causes of World War I**. Help students complete the graphic organizer and remind them to include specific examples from the text. Remind students of the Topic Essential Question: When is war justified? Engage them in a discussion about whether they believe World War I was justified and why.

>> To aid its ally Serbia, Russia mobilized its army, including these Cossacks. As World War I began, European armies still sent cavalry units into battle.

>> In August 1914, Germany invaded neutral Belgium to reach France. Here, the German infantry advances across a Belgian field filled with flowers.

The Alliance System Leads to War

The war between Austria and Serbia might have been another "summer war," like most European wars of the previous century. However, the carefully planned alliances soon drew the great powers into the conflict.

Russia and France Support Serbia After receiving Austria's ultimatum, Serbia turned to its ally, Russia. From St. Petersburg, Nicholas II telegraphed William II. The tsar asked the kaiser to urge Austria to soften its demands. When this plea failed, Russia began to **mobilize,** or prepare its military forces for war. On August 1, Germany responded by declaring war on Russia.

Russia, in turn, appealed to its ally France. In Paris, nationalists saw a chance to avenge France's defeat in the Franco-Prussian War. Though French leaders had some doubts, they gave Russia the same kind of backing Germany offered to Austria. When Germany demanded that France keep out of the conflict, France refused. Germany then declared war on France.

Germany Marches Through Belgium By early August, the battle lines were hardening. Italy and Britain still remained uncommitted. Italy chose to stay neutral for the time being. **Neutrality** is a policy of supporting neither side in a war. Britain had to decide quickly whether or not to support its ally France. Then, Germany's war plans suddenly made the decision for Britain.

Germany's worst fear was a war on two fronts, with France attacking from the west and Russia from the east. Years earlier, General Alfred Schlieffen (SHLEE fun) had developed a strategy to avoid a two-front war. Schlieffen reasoned that Russia's lumbering military would be slow to mobilize. Under the Schlieffen Plan, Germany first had to defeat France quickly. Then it would concentrate its forces against Russia.

To ensure a swift victory in the west, the Schlieffen Plan required German armies to march through neutral Belgium and then swing south behind French lines. The goal was to encircle and crush France's army. The Germans embarked on the plan by invading Belgium on August 3.

However, Germany had signed a treaty with Britain and France guaranteeing Belgian neutrality. Outraged by the invasion of Belgium, Britain declared war on Germany on August 4.

Once the machinery of war was set in motion, it seemed impossible to stop. Military leaders insisted that they must mobilize their forces immediately to accomplish their military goals. These military

Answers

Analyze Maps *The map shows the alliances in place in Europe, which caused additional countries to become involved in the war that began with a dispute between Austria-Hungary and Serbia.*

Identify Central Issues *Belgium was a neutral country that did not want to be involved in war. Britain had signed a treaty guaranteeing Belgian neutrality. After Germany violated Belgium's neutrality, Britain declared war on Germany.*

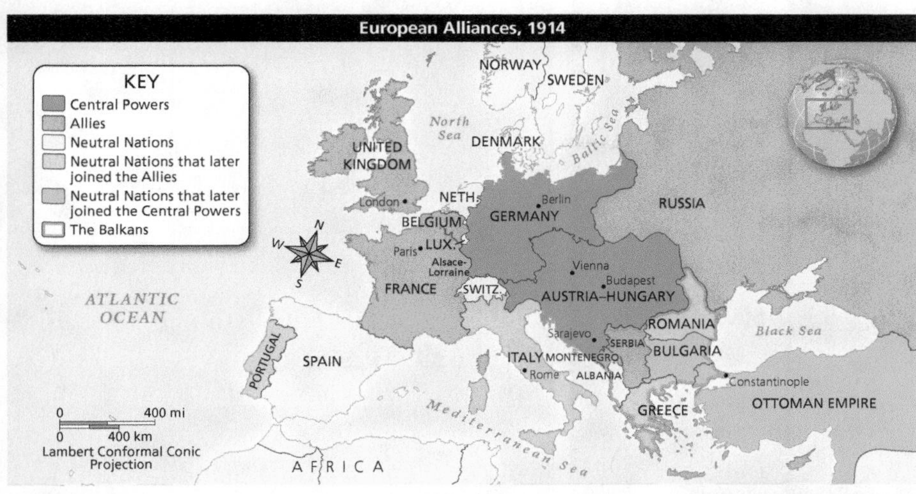

>> **Analyze Maps** How does this map help explain the expansion of World War I from a localized to a global war?

timetables made it impossible for political leaders to negotiate instead of fight.

Whose Fault? How did an assassination lead to all-out war in just a few weeks? During the war, each side blamed the other. Afterward, the victorious Allies blamed Germany. Today, most historians agree that all parties must share blame for a catastrophe nobody wanted.

Each great power believed its cause was just. Austria wanted to punish Serbia for encouraging terrorism. Germany felt that it must stand by its one dependable ally, Austria. Russia saw the Austrian ultimatum to Serbia as an effort to oppress Slavic peoples.

France feared that if it did not support Russia, it would have to face Germany alone later. Britain felt committed to protect Belgium, but also feared the growing power of Germany.

Once the machinery of war was set in motion with the Austrian ultimatum and mobilization of troops, political leaders could no longer save the peace. Although government leaders made the decisions, most people on both sides were committed to military action. Young men rushed to enlist, cheered on by women and their elders. Now that war had come at last, it seemed an exciting adventure.

British diplomat Edward Grey was less optimistic. As armies began to move, he predicted, "The lamps are going out all over Europe. We shall not see them lit again in our lifetime."

 **IDENTIFY CENTRAL ISSUES** How did Germany's invasion of Belgium bring Britain into the war ?

ASSESSMENT

1. **Generate Explanations**How were economic competition and imperialism causes of World War I?
2. **Identify Cause and Effect**Was nationalism a cause of World War I? Why or why not? Give examples.
3. **Identify Central Issues**What is militarism, and how did it influence the nations of Europe prior to World War I?
4. **Integrate Information** How did a single event start a chain reaction that sparked World War I ?
5. **Draw Conclusions** How did the alliance system spread the original conflict between Austria-Hungary and Serbia into a general war involving many countries?

Topic 16 Lesson 1

DEMONSTRATE

Online Assign the **Digital Lesson Quiz** for this lesson if you haven't already done so. Students will be offered automatic remediation or enrichment based on their score.

Pose these questions to the class on the Discussion Board:

Alliances created at the end of the nineteenth century as well as increasing nationalism, imperialism, and militarism among rival countries in Europe all set the stage for one act to trigger a war that changed the world forever.

Evaluate Arguments Was Austria-Hungary justified in going to war against Serbia? Why or why not? *(Answers may vary. Some students might respond that the act of terrorism was enough to warrant declaring war. Others might respond that Serbia gave in to most of Austria-Hungary's demands and therefore Austria-Hungary was not justified.)*

Connect How does nationalism still threaten peace in the world today? *(Answers may vary. Students may consider nationalities seeking fully independent countries of their own such as Palestinians or Kurds, or Muslim groups in Russia. They might think of international rivalries, such as between Israel and Iran, or between North Korea and South Korea.)*

Topic Inquiry

Have students continue their investigations for the Topic Inquiry.

Assessment

1. Economic competition and imperialism contributed to the start of World War I because the European nations competed to increase their economic power at home and to extend their colonies overseas. This increased tensions and caused military build-ups and even some minor wars.
2. Yes, nationalism was a cause of World War I. Nationalism made Europeans more willing to go to war. French nationalism prompted the desire for the return of Alsace and Lorraine. Nationalism made Germans want to protect their growing power. The Austro-Hungarian Empire was threatened by pan-Slavic and Serbian nationalism.
3. Militarism is an emphasis on and glorification of the military. The rise in militarism in Europe fed the arms race, which in turn increased tensions. Militarism also made war seem romantic, which made young men eager to go to war.
4. The assassination of Archduke Ferdinand caused a chain event that escalated out of control because countries were driven by the alliance system, militarism, and nationalism.
5. In the alliance system, countries had a commitment to come to each other's aid in time of war. This meant that as soon as Austria-Hungary and Serbia went to war, all the countries with which they were allied became involved in the conflict. Russia, Germany, France, and Britain entered the war because of alliances and agreements that they had with other countries.

Topic 16 Lesson 2

Fighting the Great War

CONNECT

Preview Have students preview the **Lesson Objectives** and the list of **Key Terms**.

Students can also preview all the **Key Terms** and **Academic Vocabulary** using the **Interactive Reading Notepad** on the digital course or preview a summary of the lesson in the **Reading and Note Taking Study Guide**.

Online Use the **Editable Presentation** found on the digital course to present the main ideas for this lesson.

Start Up Activity

Share the following lines of the poem, "In Flanders Fields." "In Flanders fields the poppies blow/Between the crosses, row on row/That mark our place; and in the sky/The larks, still bravely singing, fly/Scarce heard amid the guns below/ We are the Dead. Short days ago/We lived, felt dawn, saw sunsets glow,/Loved and were loved, and now we lie/In Flanders fields."

Ask students to describe what the poem is about and to think about what they read in the previous lesson about the patriotic excitement people felt as the war began. Does this poem reflect those views and feelings? Why or why not? *(Students should show an understanding that the reality of war as expressed in the poem is different from the romantic view of war described in the previous lesson.)*

Online You can also project the **Start Up Activity** from the course.

INVESTIGATE

Have students read the section using the **Reading and Note Taking Study Guide** to help them take notes and understand the text as they read.

A New Kind of War

During World War I, the war on the Western Front was characterized by trench warfare and a stalemate with neither side able to make significant advances. The stalemate, coupled with deadly new weapons, contributed to high casualty rates as each side launched massive offensives in an attempt to break the stalemate.

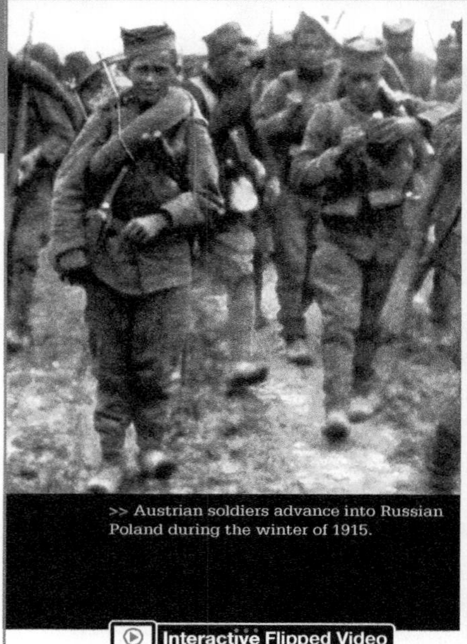

>> Austrian soldiers advance into Russian Poland during the winter of 1915.

Interactive Flipped Video

16.2 **World War I—known at the time as the "Great War"—was the largest conflict in history up to that time. The French mobilized almost 8.5 million men, the British nearly 9 million, the Russians 12 million, and the Germans 11 million. For those who fought, the statistics were more personal. "One out of every four men who went out to the World War did not come back again," recalled a survivor, "and of those who came back, many are maimed and blind and some are mad."**

TEKS
10.B, 22.C, 28.C

>> Objectives

Understand how trench warfare led to a stalemate on the Western Front.

Identify and describe the impact of modern military technology on the fighting.

Outline the course of the war on multiple European fronts.

Explain how World War I was a global conflict.

>> Key Terms

stalemate
zeppelin
U-boat
convoy
Dardanelles
T. E. Lawrence

Fighting the Great War

A New Kind of War

The early enthusiasm for the war soon faded. There were no stirring cavalry charges, no quick and glorious victories. This was a new kind of war, far deadlier than any before.

Stalemate on the Western Front As the war began, German forces fought their way through Belgium toward Paris, following the Schlieffen Plan. The Belgians resisted more than German generals had expected, but the German forces prevailed. However, Germany's plans for a quick defeat of France soon faltered.

The Schlieffen Plan failed for several reasons. First, Russia mobilized more quickly than expected. After Russian forces won a few small victories in eastern Prussia, German generals hastily shifted some troops to the east. This move weakened their forces in the west. Then, in September 1914, British and French troops pushed back the German drive along the Marne River. The first battle of the Marne ended Germany's hopes for a quick victory on the Western Front.

Both sides then began to dig deep trenches to protect their armies from fierce enemy fire. They did not know that the conflict would turn into a long, deadly **stalemate,** a deadlock in which neither side is able

PEARSON realize. www.PearsonTexas.com Access your Digital Lesson.

706

Aa Vocabulary Builder

1. Have students pronounce the following academic vocabulary terms in this lesson and clarify the part of speech. For difficult or polysyllabic words, break them into syllables and pronounce them with the students.
2. Explain what the word means in common "student-friendly" language using synonyms and antonyms when possible. Provide concrete examples to clarify the meaning, and rephrase the definition.

utilized: put to practical use

confronted: faced in opposition

to defeat the other. Battle lines in France would remain almost unchanged for four years.

Trench Warfare On the Western Front, the warring armies burrowed into a vast system of trenches, stretching from the Swiss frontier to the English Channel. An underground network linked bunkers, communications trenches, and gun emplacements.

There, millions of soldiers roasted under the broiling summer sun or froze through long bitter winters. They shared their food with rats and their beds with lice.

Between the opposing trench lines lay "no man's land," an empty tract, pocketed with shell holes. Through coils of barbed wire, soldiers peered over the edge of their trenches, watching for the next enemy attack. They themselves would have to charge into this man-made desert when officers gave the order.

Sooner or later, soldiers obeyed the order to go "over the top." With no protection but their rifles and helmets, they charged across no man's land toward the enemy lines. With luck, they might overrun a few trenches. In time, the enemy would launch a counterattack, with similar results. Each side then rushed in reinforcements to replace the dead and wounded. The struggle continued, back and forth, over a few hundred yards of territory.

High Casualty Rates To break the stalemate on the Western Front, both the Allies and the Central Powers launched massive offensives in 1916. German forces tried to overwhelm the French at Verdun (vur DUN). The French defenders held firm, sending up the battle cry "They shall not pass." The 11-month struggle cost more than a half a million casualties, or soldiers killed, wounded, or missing, on both sides.

An Allied offensive at the Somme River (sum) was even more costly. In a single grisly day, nearly 60,000 British soldiers were killed or wounded. In the five-month battle, more than one million soldiers were killed, without either side winning an advantage.

Some soldiers wrote about their experiences on the front lines:

> The blue French cloth mingled with the German grey upon the ground, and in some places the bodies were piled so high that one could take cover from shell-fire behind them. The noise was so terrific that orders had to be shouted by each man into the ear of the next. And whenever there was a momentary lull in the tumult of battle and the groans of the wounded, one

>> **Analyze Maps** Who do you think was in a better strategic position at the start of the war, the Allies or the Central Powers? Why?

Interactive Map

Online Project the **Interactive Map: Europe in World War I, 1914–1918**. Click through the key to show how the war progressed on the Western Front each year. Help students see that the front lines moved very little from year to year.

ACTIVE CLASSROOM

Have students use the Make Headlines strategies to write headlines that capture the changes depicted by the Interactive Map. Ask: If you were to write a headline capturing the most important main idea that should be remembered, what would that headline be? Exchange your headline with a partner and try to edit and improve each other's headline.

Key Terms

Ask students to find the term **stalemate** (in bold) in the text and explain its meaning. Tell them that the Allies and Central Powers fought to a stalemate in France. Ask them to predict why a stalemate will present problems.

D Differentiate Gifted/Challenge Have students research other quotes, poems, or songs that were written during or about World War I. As a class, discuss the content and point of view of each.

Answers

Analyze Maps *Answers may vary. Most students will answer that the Allies were in a better position because they effectively surrounded the Central Powers. However, other students might point out that Russia was weak, and the Central Powers controlled a great deal of territory at the start of the war.*

Topic 16 Lesson 2

Guided Reading and Discussion

The introduction of deadly machine guns and artillery required much stronger and better defensive positions, like the trench. Sophisticated weapons and better defenses did not prevent high rates of death and injury, however.

Identify Cause and Effect Ask students to explain why the German Schlieffen Plan failed, and what happened as a result. *(Russia armed more quickly than the Germans expected, and German troops had to be reassigned to the east. As a result, in the west the two sides became bogged down in trench warfare. This contributed to high casualty rates.)*

Compare and Contrast Discuss the poem "In Flanders Field" from the **Start Up Activity** and the quote by Schmieder from the text. Have students compare and contrast the two pieces. *(Answers will vary. Students might point out that both texts contrast death with bird songs, both texts represent war in a negative light, or that the texts have similar perspectives even though they were written by people from opposing sides.)*

Modern Military Technology

Modern military technology was a major characteristic of World War I. Discuss with students the effects of new military technologies on the war.

Online Project the **Interactive 3-D Model: Trench Warfare** and click on the red circles to reveal information about the experience of soldiers in World War I trenches. Discuss each aspect of the trench experience.

ACTIVE CLASSROOM

Ask students to have a Conversation with a World War I soldier. Direct each student to write down a question he or she would like to ask a soldier, a response the soldier might make, and then a response the student might offer in return.

Answers

Identify Cause and Effect *The failure of the Schlieffen Plan meant the Germans had to fight the war on both the Western and Eastern Fronts. The opposing armies began to dig defensive trenches, and the war bogged down into a long, deadly stalemate.*

>> This German soldier was one of the many casualties of the fighting during World War I. Massive offenses and new military technology combined to produce extremely high casualty rates.

Interactive 3-D Model

>> Poison gas and machine guns are two examples of the military technology that killed and wounded so many. These British machine gunners wear gas masks during the Battle of the Somme, in July 1916.

Interactive Gallery

heard, high up in the blue sky, the joyful song of birds! Birds singing just as they do at home in spring-time! It was enough to tear the heart out of one's body!

—German soldier Richard Schmieder, writing from the trenches in France

IDENTIFY CAUSE AND EFFECT How did the failure of Germany's Schlieffen Plan to quickly defeat France affect the future course of the war?

Modern Military Technology

The enormous casualties suffered on the Western Front were due in part to the destructive power of modern weapons. Two significant weapons were the rapid-fire machine gun and the long-range artillery gun. Machine guns mowed down waves of soldiers. Artillery allowed troops to shell the enemy from more than 10 miles away. The shrapnel, or flying debris from artillery shells, killed or wounded even more soldiers than the guns.

Poison Gas Efforts to overcome the stalemate of trench warfare led to the use of poison gas. Early on, the French used tear gas grenades, but by 1915, the Germans began employing poison gas on a large scale. Even though the Allies condemned the use of poison gas, both sides developed and used different kinds of poison gases. Poison gas blinded or choked its victims or caused agonizing burns and blisters. It could be fatal. Though soldiers were eventually given gas masks, poison gas remained one of the most dreaded hazards of the war.

One British soldier recalled the effects of being gassed:

> I suppose I resembled a kind of fish with my mouth open gasping for air. It seemed as if my lungs were gradually shutting down and my heart pounded away in my ears like the beat of a drum. . . . To get air into my lungs was real agony.
>
> —William Pressey, quoted in *People at War 1914–1918*

Poison gas was an uncertain weapon. Shifting winds could blow the gas back on the soldiers who launched it. As both sides invented masks to protect

English Language Proficiency Standards

Learning Strategies 5.B.2 Read "Modern Military Technology" aloud to the class. For each activity, make sure the following words are included on the word wall: *military*, *technology*, *weapons*, *casualties*, *shrapnel*, *artillery*, *poison gas*, *tanks*, *submarines*, *zeppelins*, *U-boats*, and *convoys*.

Beginning Create a word wall with students that includes the content-based vocabulary from this section. Distribute sheets of paper among students and review the text together. When you encounter a content-based vocabulary word, pause and ask one student to write that word. Then provide the student with a definition. After the word wall is complete, help students write one sentence about the text using content-area vocabulary correctly.

Intermediate Create a word wall with students that includes the content-based vocabulary from this section. Distribute sheets of paper among students and assign each student one of the vocabulary words listed below. Then review the text together. When you encounter a content-based vocabulary word, pause and ask the student assigned to that word to write it down.

against gas attacks, it became less useful. After the war, disgust and horror with the use of poison gas led to its ban in 1925, which is still in effect today.

Tanks, Airplanes, and Submarines During World War I, advances in technology, such as the gasoline-powered engine, led the opposing forces to use tanks, airplanes, and submarines against each other. In 1916, Britain introduced the first armored tank. Mounted with machine guns, the tanks were designed to move across no man's land. Still, the first tanks broke down often. They failed to break the stalemate.

Both sides also used aircraft. At first, planes were utilized simply to observe enemy troop movements. In 1915, Germany used **zeppelins** (ZEP uh linz), large gas-filled balloons, to bomb the English coast. Later, both sides equipped airplanes with machine guns. Pilots known as "flying aces" confronted each other in the skies. These "dogfights" were spectacular, but had little effect on the course of the war on the ground.

Submarines proved much more important. German **U-boats,** nicknamed from the German word for submarine, *Unterseeboot,*did tremendous damage to the Allied side, sinking merchant ships carrying vital supplies to Britain. To defend against the submarines, the Allies organized **convoys,** or groups of merchant ships protected by warships.

INFER How did U-boat attacks affect the fighting on land?

>> On the Italian front, soldiers trekked through the Alps using snowshoes and skis. At times, they even engaged in battle while wearing their skis. **Analyze Visuals** Based on this image, what else besides deadly weapons caused high casualty rates?

Other European Fronts

From the outset of World War I, Germany and Austria-Hungary battled Russia on the Eastern Front. There, battle lines shifted back and forth, sometimes over large areas. Even though the armies were not mired in trench warfare, casualties rose even higher than on the Western Front. The results were just as indecisive.

Mounting Russian Losses in the East In August 1914, Russian armies pushed into eastern Germany. Then, the Russians suffered a disastrous defeat at Tannenberg. Reeling from the disaster, the Russians retreated. After Tannenberg, the warring armies in the east fought on Russian soil.

As the least industrialized of the great powers, Russia was poorly equipped to fight a modern war. Although Russian factories geared up to produce rifles and other machinery for war, Russia lacked the roads and railroads to carry goods to the front. As the war raged on, some troops even lacked rifles. Still, Russian commanders continued to send masses of peasant soldiers into combat.

War in Southern Europe Southeastern Europe was another battleground. In 1915, Bulgaria joined the Central Powers and helped defeat its old rival Serbia. Romania, hoping to gain some land in Hungary, joined the Allies in 1916, only to be crushed by the Central Powers.

Also in 1915, Italy declared war on Austria-Hungary and later on Germany. The Allies had agreed in a secret treaty to give Italy some Austrian-ruled lands on its northern border. Over the next two years,the Italians and Austrians fought numerous battles, with few major breakthroughs. In October 1917, Italy suffered a major setback during the battle of Caporetto, but French and British forces stepped in to stop the Central Powers from advancing into Italy. Still, Caporetto proved as disastrous for Italy as Tannenberg had been for Russia.

CONTRAST How was the Eastern Front different from the Western Front?

Guided Reading and Discussion

Compare and Contrast Have small groups of students choose two technologies (try to ensure that groups compare different technologies from each other) and compare and contrast their effect on the war, particularly trench warfare and high casualty rates.

Other European Fronts

Introduce students to the other European fronts of World War I. Explain that high casualty rates were a characteristic of the Eastern Front as well as the Western Front.

Online Project the **Interactive Gallery: Military Technology in World War I**. Click through the images and discuss how each technology affected the war.

ACTIVE CLASSROOM

Use the Ranking strategy to have students go through the technologies in the gallery and rank which ones they believe had the greatest impact on Word War I. Poll the class to see if there is agreement on the rankings. Discuss the results of the poll.

Draw Conclusions What effect did major new military technologies have on the Eastern Front? *(The Germans had a greater amount of modern military technology than the Russians. As a result, the German army penetrated far into Russia as the Russian army retreated and suffered very high casualties.)*

D Differentiate On Level Extend the activity by having students rank the World War I technology that has the greatest impact on warfare today. Be prepared to help students link the older technology shown here to current equivalents.

D Differentiate Special Needs Provide students with a simple two-column chart that already has two very different technologies at the head of each column. Ask students to go through the text and write down characteristics of each type of technology.

Then help that student look up and write the definition. After the word wall is complete, instruct students to write two sentences about the text using content-area vocabulary correctly. Circulate among students to offer support as needed.

Advanced Have students work in small groups to create a word wall for the content-based vocabulary from this section. Distribute sheets of paper among groups and have students review the text together. Instruct groups to pause when they encounter a content-based vocabulary word, write it down, and look up the definition in a dictionary or glossary. After the word wall is complete, instruct groups to work together to write a paragraph summarizing the text, using content-area vocabulary correctly.

Advanced High Have students read and review "Modern Military Technology" to make a list of content-based vocabulary words. Instruct students to create a glossary for the terms they find, using classroom resources and context clues to develop their definitions. Then have students write a paragraph to summarize the text using the content-based vocabulary that they found in their writing.

Answers

Infer *U-boats attacked ships carrying supplies to support the war effort to Britain. Loss of supplies affected Britain's abililty to fight on land.*

Contrast *The Eastern Front did not involve trench warfare. Battle lines shifted over large areas. Armies on the Eastern Front suffered higher casualties than those on the Western Front.*

Analyze Visuals *Harsh weather conditions also caused many deaths.*

A Global Conflict

Remind students that World War I was a truly global war fought in Europe, the Middle East, Africa, and Asia. Use the map of the Ottoman Empire to discuss the importance of the battle at Gallipoli and the Arab revolt against Ottoman rule. Use the photo of Armenian refugees to introduce the topic of politically motivated mass murders in Armenia. Use the photo of colonial soldiers to introduce the impact of the war on Europe's colonies.

Summarize What was the status of the Armenians in the Ottoman empire? *(Sample response: The Armenians were a minority people without equal rights in the Ottoman empire. During World War I, the Ottoman government considered them a threat. The Ottoman government deported Armenians from their land. During the deportation, more than a million Armenians died as a result of mass murder, mistreatment, and starvation. Many of the survivors fled to other countries.)*

Online Ask students to explain the role of the Ottoman empire, Arabs, Armenians, and European colonies in World War I.

Guided Reading and Instruction

Draw Inferences Project the map of the Ottoman empire during World War I. Why did Arabs fight against the Ottoman empire during World War I? *(Sample response: Arabs, driven by a spirit of nationalism, wanted to rule their own lands and be free from Ottoman rule.)*

Identify Cause and Effect What were the expectations of some colonial peoples as a result of their involvement in the war? *(Sample response: Some colonial peoples hoped that their efforts in World War I would be rewarded by citizenship or independence.)*

A Global Conflict

Though most of the fighting took place in Europe, World War I was a global conflict. In 1914, Japan joined the Allies by declaring war on Germany. Japan used the war as an excuse to seize German outposts in China and islands in the Pacific. Japan's advances in East Asia and the Pacific would have far-reaching consequences in the years ahead as ambitious Japanese leaders set out to expand their footholds in China.

The Ottoman Empire Joins the War Because of its strategic location, the Ottoman empire was a desirable ally. If the Ottoman Turks had joined the Allies, the Central Powers would have been almost completely encircled. However, the Turks joined the Central Powers in late October 1914. The Turks then cut off crucial Allied supply lines to Russia through the **Dardanelles,** a vital strait connecting the Black Sea and the Mediterranean.

In 1915, the Allies sent a massive force of British, Indian, Australian, and New Zealander troops to attempt to open up the strait. At the battle of Gallipoli (guh LIP uh lee), Ottoman troops trapped the Allies on the beaches of the Gallipoli peninsula. In January 1916, after 10 months and more than 200,000 casualties, the Allies finally withdrew from the Dardanelles.

Despite their victory at Gallipoli, the war did not go well for the Ottomans on a second front, the Middle East. The Ottoman empire included vast areas of Arab land. In 1916, Arab nationalists led by Husayn ibn Ali declared a revolt against Ottoman rule. The British government sent Colonel **T. E. Lawrence**—later known as Lawrence of Arabia—to support the Arab revolt. Lawrence led guerrilla raids against the Ottomans, dynamiting bridges and supply trains. Eventually, the Ottoman empire lost a great deal of territory to the Arabs, including the key city of Baghdad.

Deportation and Mass Murder of Armenians Meanwhile, the Ottoman empire was fighting Russia on a third front in the Caucasus Mountains. This region was home to ethnic Armenians, some of whom lived under Ottoman rule and some of whom lived under Russian rule. As Christians, the Armenians were a minority in the Ottoman empire and did not have the same rights as Muslims. Still, they prospered—much to the resentment of their neighbors.

Starting in 1915, the Ottoman government embarked on a brutal campaign against the Armenians, some of whom had joined the Russian forces. Claiming Armenians were traitors, the government ordered the deportation of the entire Armenian population from the war zone. During barbarous forced marches, between 600,000 and 1.5 million Armenians were killed or died from hunger or thirst. A later wave of atrocities forced most of the remaining Armenians from Turkey. Many

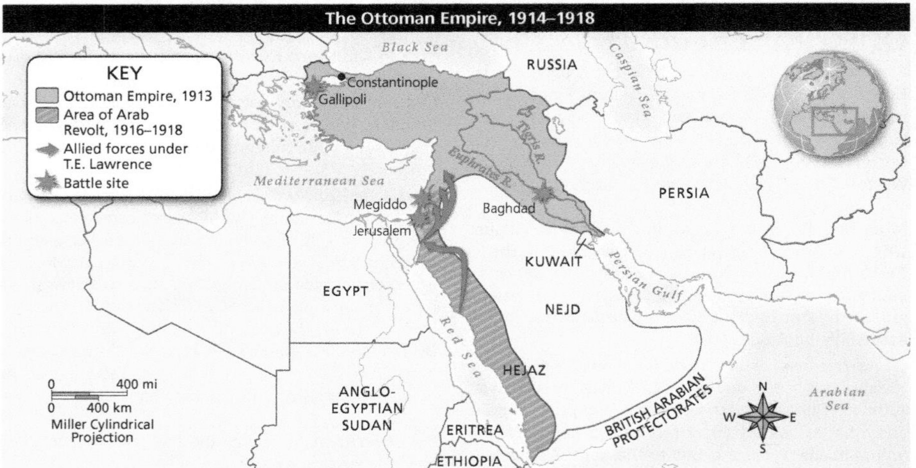

>> **Analyze Maps** How did the Arab revolt against the Ottoman empire affect the Allied cause?

English Language Proficiency Standards

Learning Strategies 4.G.1 Remind students that active reading—pausing to ask questions, rephrasing information, and thinking aloud while reading—can make understanding the information in the text easier.

Beginning Reread "A Global Conflict" aloud to students. Model pausing to retell the content in everyday language. Explain new or challenging vocabulary to students, using context clues from the text when possible. After reading, model confirming comprehension by giving students a brief summary of the text.

Intermediate Reread "A Global Conflict" aloud to students. After reading the first two sentences, pause to model retelling the content in everyday language. Continue reading but ask students to take turns retelling the content after you pause. Help students understand new or challenging vocabulary by using context clues from the text when possible.

Advanced Have students take turns rereading "A Global Conflict" aloud to the group, pausing to retell the information in their own words.

Answers

Analyze Maps *It helped the Allies because Turkish troops were removed from other fronts to fight the revolt. Also, it helped the Allies gain control of the Red Sea.*

Summarize *The Middle East was the Ottoman empire's third front. Aided by the British, Arab nationalists revolted against Ottoman rule and waged a guerrilla war. The Ottoman empire lost a great deal of territory to the Arabs.*

Armenians fled to other countries, including the United States.

European Colonies and the War European colonies were also drawn into the struggle. The Allies overran scattered German colonies in Africa and Asia. They also turned to their own colonies and dominions for troops, laborers, and supplies. Colonial recruits from British India and French West Africa fought on European battlefields. Canada, Australia, and New Zealand sent troops to Britain's aid.

People in the colonies had mixed feelings about serving. Some were reluctant to serve rulers who did not treat them fairly. Other colonial troops volunteered eagerly. They expected that their service would be a step toward citizenship or independence. Such hopes would be dashed after the war.

 **SUMMARIZE** What were the major features and immediate effects of the war in the Middle East?

>> Troops from Europe's colonies fought in World War I. These soldiers in a dugout near Verdun in 1915 are from French Africa.

ASSESSMENT

1. **Identify Central Issues** What is a stalemate, and why did one develop on the Western Front?
2. **Identify Cause and Effect** What were the effects of major new military technologies on World War I?
3. **Draw Conclusions** How did the Ottoman empire's entry into the war on the side of the Central Powers have a negative impact on Russia?
4. **Support Ideas with Evidence** How did the war contribute to the mass murder of the Armenian people? Include details from the text.
5. **Synthesize** How did imperialism influence the war?

Topic 16 Lesson 2

SYNTHESIZE

Online Project the **Digital Activity: Defining Characteristics** and discuss how World War I was a global war. Ask: Do we fight global wars today? *(Answers may vary. Some students may be aware of the international nature of the wars in Afghanistan and Iraq, while others might not.)*

DEMONSTRATE

Online Assign the **Digital Lesson Quiz** for this lesson if you haven't already done so. Students will be offered automatic remediation or enrichment based on their score.

Pose these questions to the class on the Discussion Board:

In this lesson, you have read about how World War I was fought and how modern technology and trench warfare resulted in high casualty rates.

Generate Explanations World War I was also called the Great War. Why do you think it was called that? *(Answers will vary but might include the wide geographic scope of the war and/or its high casualty rate. It was the largest war the world had seen up to that time.)*

Predict Consequences How do you think the nature of World War I affected international politics after the war? *(Sample responses: Countries will want revenge and remain militaristic, or countries will want to avoid war and become pacifists; countries will avoid alliances, or countries will make new alliances; European colonies will want independence.)*

Topic Inquiry

Have students continue their investigations for the Topic Inquiry.

Challenge students to define any difficult words by using context clues as a guide.

Advanced High Have students take turns rereading "A Global Conflict" aloud to a partner, pausing to retell the information in their own words. Challenge students to define any difficult words by using context clues as a guide. Ask students to explain how shared reading helped them understand the text better.

Assessment

1. A stalemate is a deadlock in which neither side can defeat the other. A stalemate developed on the Western Front because both sides were dug into trenches.
2. New military technologies, such as rapid-fire machine guns, long-range artillery, and poison gas, increased the number of casualties and made it difficult for soldiers to advance, which led to a four-year stalemate.
3. The Turks cut off supply lines to Russia through the Dardanelles. As a result, the Russians were less able to withstand the Germans on the Eastern Front.
4. The Ottoman government forcibly removed the Armenians from their ancestral homeland. During the deportation, hundreds of thousands of Armenians died, either from starvation or in planned massacres.
5. Imperialism made the war a global conflict, as battles were fought in the colonies. The colonies gave the European powers access to additional supplies and manpower.

Topic 16 Lesson 3

World War I Ends

CONNECT

Preview Have students preview the **Lesson Objectives** and the list of **Key Terms**.

They can preview **Key Terms** and **Academic Vocabulary** using the **Reading and Note Taking Study Guide** or the **Interactive Reading Notepad** on the digital course.

Online Use the **Editable Presentation** found on the digital course to present the main ideas for this lesson.

Start Up Activity

Ask students to look at the cartoon on page 718 and make three predictions about the peace negotiations following the war. *(Students may say Wilson believes that something called the League of Nations will bring or keep the peace, but his peace proposals will fail because they are too cumbersome or difficult to implement.)*

Online You can also project the **Start Up Activity** from the course.

INVESTIGATE

Have students read the section using the **Reading and Note Taking Study Guide** to help them take notes and understand the text as they read.

Governments Direct Total War

Morale Breaks Down

World War I became a total war as nations directed all resources to the war effort. Governments exerted more control over people's lives by requiring military service, rationing food and other necessities, raising money through taxes and bonds, and controlling information, media, and public opinion. As the economic impact and casualty rates dramatically increased, morale sank. In Russia, revolution erupted.

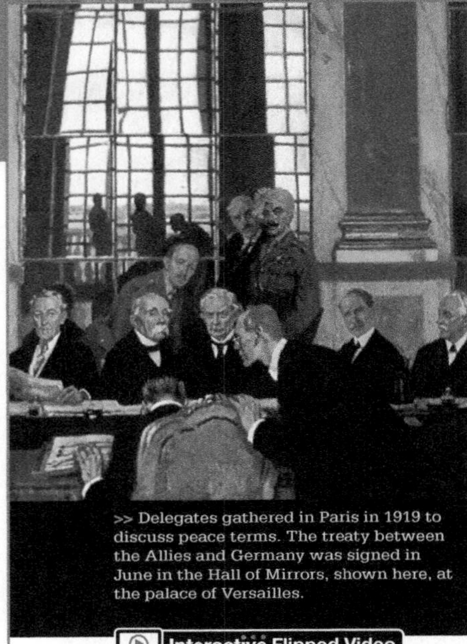

>> Delegates gathered in Paris in 1919 to discuss peace terms. The treaty between the Allies and Germany was signed in June in the Hall of Mirrors, shown here, at the palace of Versailles.

Interactive Flipped Video

16.3 By 1917, European societies were cracking under the strain of war. Casualties on the fronts and shortages at home sapped morale. The stalemate dragged on, seemingly without end. Soon, however, the departure of one country from the war and the entry of another would tip the balance and end the stalemate.

TEKS
1.F, 10.B, 10.C, 10.D, 20.D

>> Objectives

Describe how World War I became a total war.

Explain how U.S. entry into the war led to an Allied victory.

List the effects of World War I in terms of financial costs, high casualty rates, and political impact.

Describe the issues at the Paris Peace Conference and the impact of Woodrow Wilson's Fourteen Points.

Summarize the terms and impact of the Treaty of Versailles.

>> Key Terms

total war
conscription
contraband
Lusitania
propaganda
atrocity
Fourteen Points
self-determination
armistice
pandemic
reparation
radical
collective security
mandate

 www.PearsonTexas.com Access your Digital Lesson.

World War I Ends

Governments Direct Total War

As the struggle wore on, nations realized that a modern, mechanized war required the channeling of a nation's entire resources into the war effort, or **total war.** To achieve total war, governments began to take a stronger role in directing the economic and cultural lives of their people.

Recruiting and Supplying Huge Armies Early on, both sides set up systems to recruit, arm, transport, and supply armies that numbered in the millions. All of the warring nations except Britain immediately imposed universal military **conscription,** or "the draft," which required all young men to be ready for military or other service. Britain, too, instituted conscription in 1916. Germany set up a system of forced civilian labor as well.

Governments raised taxes and borrowed huge amounts of money to pay the costs of war. They rationed food and other products, from boots to gasoline. In addition, they introduced other economic controls, such as setting prices and forbidding strikes.

Blockades and Submarines Impact Economies At the start of the war, Britain's navy formed a blockade in the North Sea to keep ships from carrying supplies into and out of Germany. International law allowed wartime blockades to confiscate **contraband,** or military

712

Aa Vocabulary Builder

1. Have students pronounce the following academic vocabulary terms in this lesson and clarify the part of speech. Break the words into syllables and pronounce them with the students.
2. Explain what the word means in common "student-friendly" language using synonyms and antonyms when possible. Provide concrete examples to clarify the meaning, and rephrase the definition.

eroded: ate into or wore away

widespread: occurring in many places

supplies and raw materials needed to make military supplies. Items such as food and clothing were exempt. Still, the British blockade stopped both types of goods from reaching Germany. As the war progressed, it became harder and harder to feed the German and Austrian people. In Germany, the winter of 1916 and 1917 was remembered as "the turnip winter," because the potato crop failed and people ate turnips instead.

To retaliate, Germany used U-boats to create its own blockade. In 1915, Germany declared that it would sink all ships carrying goods to Britain. In May 1915, a German submarine torpedoed the British liner ***Lusitania***off the coast of Ireland. Almost 1,200 passengers were killed, including 128 Americans. Germany justified the attack, arguing that the *Lusitania*was carrying weapons.

When American President Woodrow Wilson threatened to cut off diplomatic relations with Germany, Germany agreed to restrict its submarine campaign. Before attacking any ship, U-boats would surface and give warning, allowing neutral passengers to escape to lifeboats. Unrestricted submarine warfare stopped—for the moment.

>> This painting portrays the sinking of the *Lusitania* by a German submarine. Unrestricted submarine warfare worsened American public opinion of Germany.

The Propaganda War Total war also meant controlling public opinion. Even in democratic countries, special boards censored the press. Their aim was to keep complete casualty figures and other discouraging news from reaching the public. Government censors also restricted popular literature, historical writings, motion pictures, and the arts.

Both sides waged a propaganda war. **Propaganda** is the spreading of ideas to promote a cause or to damage an opposing cause. Allied propaganda played up the brutality of Germany's invasion of Belgium.

The British and French press circulated tales of **atrocities,** horrible acts committed against innocent people. Although some atrocities did occur, often the stories were distorted by exaggerations or completely made up.

Governments also used propaganda to motivate military mobilization, especially in Britain before conscription started in 1916. In France and Germany, propaganda urged civilians to loan money to the government.

Daddy, what did YOU do in the Great War?

>> Posters such as this British one helped to stoke patriotic emotions. **Determine Author's Purpose** What did the creators of this poster hope that men would do after viewing this image?

Interactive Gallery

Women Contribute to the War Effort Women played a critical role in total war. As millions of men left to fight, women took over their jobs and kept national economies going. Many women worked in war industries, manufacturing weapons and supplies. Others joined women's branches of the armed forces. When food shortages threatened Britain, volunteers

Online Project the **Interactive Gallery: World War I Propaganda Posters**, and remind students that during World War I, there was no Internet or television. Explain that posters hanging in public areas were a common and effective way to convey information and influence public opinion. Make sure students understand the meaning of the word *propaganda* and that government propaganda was one aspect of total war.

ACTIVE CLASSROOM

Break students into six teams, one for each propaganda poster in the Interactive Gallery. Have each team use the Act It Out strategy to present its propaganda poster as if it were a TV commercial. Ask students to "bring the poster to life." Their commercial should clearly represent the message of their propaganda poster.

Key Terms

Ask students to find the key term **propaganda** (in bold) in the text and explain its meaning. Point out that during World War I, governments used propaganda to raise morale and mobilize their citizens. Have students speculate on other ways that a government can try to control or influence public opinion.

Answers

Determine Author's Purpose *support the war effort by enlisting*

Topic 16 Lesson 3

Guided Reading and Discussion

Ask students to explain the concept of total war *(channeling of a nation's entire resources into a war effort)*. Discuss how economic warfare and women's contributions to the war effort were both examples of total war.

Identify Cause and Effect How did total war cause morale of soldiers and civilians to collapse? *(Sample response: Morale collapsed because of food shortages, economic decline, high taxes, and the high number of solders killed, wounded, or captured.)* What were some effects of the decline in morale? *(Sample response: calls for leaders to end the war, antiwar literature, soldiers mutinying and deserting, revolution in Russia)* What impact did the February and October revolutions in Russia have on the war? *(Sample response: The February revolution encouraged the Allies to hope Russia would become a democratic ally, but the October revolution led to Russia's withdrawal from the war, and allowed the Central Powers to focus on the Western Front.)*

Draw Inferences Why might citizens of a nation at war be willing to give up some individual freedoms and accept a more limited standard of living? *(Sample response: They might fear the future if their country does not win the war; they might want to do what is necessary to help the troops and not want to feel guilty about not actively supporting their country.)*

in the Women's Land Army went to the fields to grow their nation's food.

Nurses shared the dangers of the men whose wounds they tended. At aid stations close to the front lines, nurses often worked around the clock, especially after a big "push" brought a flood of casualties. In her diary, English nurse Vera Brittain describes sweating through 90-degree days in France, "stopping hemorrhages, replacing intestines, and draining and reinserting innumerable rubber tubes" with "gruesome human remnants heaped on the floor."

War work gave women a new sense of pride and confidence. After the war, most women had to give up their jobs to men returning home. Still, they had challenged the idea that women could not handle demanding and dangerous jobs. In many countries, including Britain, Germany, and the United States, women's support for the war effort helped them finally win the right to vote, after decades of struggle.

DRAW CONCLUSIONS How can total war increase the power of government and have a lasting political impact?

>> Women worked as nurses at the front in difficult and dangerous conditions. Here, a French general honors a nurse who took part in the battle of Verdun in 1916.

Morale Breaks Down

Despite inspiring propaganda, by 1917 the morale of troops and civilians had plunged. Germany was sending 15-year-old recruits to the front, and Britain was on the brink of bankruptcy.

War-Weary Civilians and Soldiers Long casualty lists, food shortages, and the failure of generals to win promised victories led to calls for peace. Instead of praising the glorious deeds of heroes, war poets like British soldier Siegfried Sassoon began denouncing the leaders whose errors wasted so many lives.

> You smug-faced crowds with kindling eye
>
> Who cheer when soldier lads march by,
>
> Sneak home and pray you'll never know
>
> The hell where youth and laughter go.
>
> —Siegfried Sassoon, "Suicide in the Trenches"

As morale collapsed, troops in some French units mutinied. In Italy, many soldiers deserted during the retreat at Caporetto. In Russia, soldiers left the front to join in a full-scale revolution back home.

Revolution in Russia Three years of war had hit Russia especially hard. Stories of incompetent generals and corruption eroded public confidence. In March 1917, bread riots in St. Petersburg erupted into a revolution that brought down the Russian monarchy. (You'll learn more about the causes and effects of the Russian Revolution in another lesson.) The new Russian government continued the war effort.

At first, the Allies welcomed the overthrow of the tsar. They hoped Russia would institute a democratic government and become a stronger ally. But in October of that year, a second revolution brought V. I. Lenin to power. Lenin had promised to pull Russian troops out of the war. Early in 1918, Lenin signed the Treaty of Brest-Litovsk (brest lih TAWFSK) with Germany. The treaty ended Russian participation in World War I.

Russia's withdrawal had an immediate impact on the war. With Russia out of the struggle, Germany could concentrate its forces on the Western Front. In the spring of 1918, the Central Powers stood ready to achieve the great breakthrough they had sought for so

English Language Proficiency Standards

Reading 4.G.2 Remind students that retelling what they have read in their own words is a good way to make sure they understand the content. Read "The United States Enters the War" aloud to students. Then have students participate in the activities below based on their English proficiency level.

Beginning Reread "Wilson's Fourteen Points" aloud to students. Define challenging terms in the text. Then demonstrate how to summarize by focusing on the first paragraph in that section. Help students retell the details of the second paragraph by asking them to point to three important details that they would include in a summary. Then assist them in combining those details into one or two sentences that summarize the paragraph.

Intermediate Reread "Wilson's Fourteen Points" aloud to students. Help students identify and define challenging terms in the text. Then demonstrate how to summarize by focusing on the first paragraph in that section. Ask students to summarize the second paragraph by telling them to identify three important details. Have students write a sentence that includes those details and summarizes the paragraph.

Answers

Draw Conclusions *To achieve total war, governments take a stronger role in directing the economic and cultural lives of their people. They may raise taxes, increase borrowing, regulate the economy, and more. After the war ends, governments may keep some of those powers.*

long. But by then, Germany faced a new opponent. The United States had been dragged into the war.

CITE EVIDENCE What evidence shows that soldiers' morale declined and negatively affected the war effort?

The United States Enters the War

Soon after the Russian Revolution began, another event altered the balance of forces. The United States declared war on Germany. Many factors contributed to the decision of the United States to exchange neutrality for war in 1917.

Unrestricted Submarine Warfare A major reason for the U.S. entry into the war was German submarine attacks. After the sinking of the Lusitania and under pressure from President Wilson, Germany had agreed to restrict its submarine campaign. By early 1917, however, Germany was desperate to break the stalemate in the war. On February 1, the German government announced that it would resume unrestricted submarine warfare. Wilson angrily denounced Germany.

Anti-German Sentiment Grows Many Americans supported the Allies because of cultural ties. The United States shared a cultural history and language with Britain and sympathized with France as another democracy. On the other hand, some German Americans favored the Central Powers. So did many Irish Americans, who resented British rule of Ireland, and Russian Jewish immigrants, who did not want to be allied with the tsar. The resumption of unrestricted submarine warfare, however, increased anger toward Germany and spurred support for the Allies.

Another German move also angered Americans. In early 1917, the British intercepted a message from the German foreign minister, Arthur Zimmermann, to his ambassador in Mexico. In the note, Zimmerman wrote that if Mexico joined Germany in the event of war with the United States, Germany would help Mexico "to reconquer the lost territory in New Mexico, Texas, and Arizona." Britain revealed the Zimmermann note to the American government. When the note became public, anti-German feeling intensified in the United States.

Wilson Asks for a "War to End War" In April 1917, Wilson asked Congress to declare war on Germany. "We have no selfish ends to serve," he stated. Instead, he painted the conflict idealistically as a war "to make

>> Soldiers ate, slept, fought and died in the trenches. As the war dragged on and casualties mounted, morale was severely tested.

>> Germany resumed unrestricted submarine warfare in 1917. Here, President Wilson reads a German message and ponders what to do. **Analyze Political Cartoons** What does the overflowing waste basket suggest?

Topic 16 Lesson 3

The United States Enters the War

The United States remained neutral during the war's early years. But after Germany's resumption of unrestricted submarine warfare and the release of the Zimmermann note, the United States declared war on Germany in 1917. The entry of the United States into the war brought fresh troops, money, and vigor to the Allies' cause, and ultimately led to Allied victory. President Wilson began to work for a just and lasting peace.

Guided Reading and Discussion

Make Generalizations Tell students that Wilson's Fourteen Points were welcomed by some but criticized by others. Who, in general, would probably support Wilson's Fourteen Points? *(Sample response: those who favored international cooperation and peace, nationalists who wanted independent countries, colonial people who wanted rights and freedoms)* Who, in general, would oppose the Fourteen Points? *(Sample response: militarists, imperialists, rulers of empires)*

Advanced Have student pairs silently reread "Wilson's Fourteen Points." Pairs should then identify and define challenging terms in the text. Ask one student in each pair to summarize the first paragraph in that section and the second student to summarize the second paragraph. Then have two pairs join together to share their summaries and receive feedback on their work.

Advanced High Have students silently reread "Wilson's Fourteen Points." Then have students work independently to write a short summary of the paragraph. Circulate among students to provide support as needed.

Answers

Cite Evidence *Soldiers were disobeying their officers and leaving the fighting. For example, French troops mutinied, Italian soldiers deserted, and Russian soldiers left the front to join the revolution against their government.*

Analyze Political Cartoons *Germany sent many messages in 1917 but did not change its policy.*

Topic 16 Lesson 3

Analyze Visuals Point out the chart "Woodrow Wilson's Fourteen Points," and read through the summaries of Wilson's ideas. To help students understand the political impact of the Fourteen Points, ask them to explain how the Fourteen Points would lead to the creation of new independent countries and the breakup of empires. *(Points 10 through 13 call for various nationalities to have autonomy or independence. Carrying out these ideas would lead to the breakup of empires and the creation of new independent countries.)*

The Great War Ends

The war finally ended, leaving Europe in shambles. More than 8.5 million soldiers had died in battle. Millions of civilians also lost their lives. The economic impact was staggering, with the war costing countries billions of dollars. The governments of several empires collapsed. In other countries, political radicals pushed for extreme change.

D Differentiate **Extra Support** Ask students to work in small groups to identify key terms in the Fourteen Points that they do not fully understand. Have them use a dictionary to define those terms. Then invite them to explain the terms' importance in the Fourteen Points.

Answers

Infer *Possible answer: He thought the war was so horrible that nations would never go to war again.*

Analyze Information *Points 2, 3, 11, 12, 13: Wilson knew that countries' economic prosperity depended on access to international trade.*

the world safe for democracy" and later as a "war to end war."

The United States needed months to recruit, train, supply, and transport a modern army across the Atlantic. But by 1918, about two million American soldiers had joined the war-weary Allied troops fighting on the Western Front. Although relatively few American troops engaged in combat, their arrival gave Allied troops a much-needed morale boost. Just as important to the debt-ridden Allies was American financial aid.

Wilson's Fourteen Points Though he had failed to maintain American neutrality, Wilson still hoped to be a peacemaker. In January 1918, he issued the **Fourteen Points,** a list of his terms for resolving both this war and future wars. He called for freedom of the seas, free trade, large-scale reductions of arms, and an end to secret treaties. For Eastern Europe, Wilson favored **self-determination,** the right of people to choose their own form of government. Finally, Wilson urged the creation of a "general association of nations" to keep the peace in the future.

? INFER Why did President Woodrow Wilson think that World War I was "the war to end wars"?

ELPS **ELPS 4.G.2** Read and summarize *The United States Enters the War.*

The Great War Ends

A final showdown on the Western Front began in early 1918. The Germans badly wanted to achieve a major victory before eager American troops arrived in Europe.

Final Offensives In March 1918, the Germans launched a huge offensive on the Western Front with troops newly freed from fighting in Russia. By July, the spring offensive had driven the Allies back 40 miles, the biggest German breakthrough in three years. The rapid push exhausted the German forces and cost heavy casualties.

By then, fresh American troops were pouring into the Western Front. The Allies launched a counter-offensive, slowly driving German forces back through France and Belgium. In September, German generals told the Kaiser that the war could not be won.

Germany Asks for Peace Uprisings exploded among hungry city dwellers across Germany. German commanders advised the kaiser to step down. William

WOODROW WILSON'S FOURTEEN POINTS	
1. No secret treaties	10. Peoples of Austria-Hungary should have freest opportunity for autonomous development.
2. Freedom of the seas	
3. Free trade	
4. Large-scale reduction of arms	11. Occupation forces to be evacuated from Romania, Serbia and Montenegro; Serbia should have free and secure access to the sea
5. Impartial adjustment of colonial claims based on interests of governments and native populations.	
6. Evacuation of all Russian territory; providing Russia the best opportunity for self-determination	12. Autonomous development for the non-Turkish peoples of the Ottoman Empire; free passage for all ships through the Dardanelles
7. Evacuation and restoration of Belgium as a sovereign nation	13. Independence for Poland, with free and secure access to the sea
8. Liberation of France; return of the region of Alsace-Lorraine to France	14. Formation of a general association of nations to guarantee to its members political independence and territorial integrity (the League of Nations)
9. Readjustment of Italy's frontiers based on recognizable lines of nationality	

>> **Analyze Information** Which of Wilson's Fourteen Points deal with countries having free access to international commerce? Why did Wilson consider this so important?

English Language Proficiency Standards

Writing 5.C.1 Read "The Great War Ends" aloud to the class. After students listen to the text, have them complete one of the following activities depending on their level of English proficiency.

Beginning Develop a list of commonly misspelled words that appear in the text and explain the spelling of each word to students. Have the students either repeat the correct spelling aloud or write each word five times. Choose three words on which to focus and continue practicing spelling those words until students consistently spell them correctly.

Intermediate Develop a list of commonly misspelled words that appear in the text and explain the spelling of each word to students. Have the students either repeat the correct spelling aloud or write each word five times. Then give students a simple spelling test to gauge their understanding of how to spell the words.

Advanced Have students skim the text to develop a list of commonly misspelled words. Discuss the spelling of each word to students. Have the students study the list of words with a partner. Then give students a simple spelling test to gauge their understanding of how to spell the words. Circulate among students to offer support as needed.

Advanced High Have students skim the text to develop a list of commonly misspelled words. Ask students to look up each word to confirm the correct spelling, definition, and part of speech. Then have the students study the list of words with a partner. Ask partners to quiz each other to make sure they know the spelling of each word. Circulate among students to offer support as needed.

The Costs of World War I

COUNTRY	ALLIES				CENTRAL POWERS	
	RUSSIA	BRITISH EMPIRE	FRANCE	UNITED STATES	GERMANY	AUSTRIA-HUNGARY
MOBILIZED FORCES	12,000,000	8,904,467	8,410,000	4,355,000	11,000,000	7,800,000
KILLED	1,700,000	908,371	1,357,800	116,516	1,773,700	1,200,000
WOUNDED	4,950,000	2,090,212	4,266,000	204,002	4,216,058	3,620,000
PRISONERS AND MISSING	2,500,000	191,652	537,000	4,500	1,152,800	2,200,000
TOTAL CASUALTIES	9,150,000	3,190,235	6,160,800	323,018	7,142,558	7,020,000
CASUALTY RATE	76%	36%	73%	7%	65%	90%
FINANCIAL COSTS	$25 billion	$55 billion	$48 billion	$32 billion	$60 billion	$22 billion

SOURCE: *The Harper Encyclopedia of Military*, History, R. Ernest Dupuy and Trevor N. Dupuy; *The Great War*, www.pbs.org.

>> World War I ended in 1918, but its human and economic costs would be felt for decades. Many nations had thrown all their resources into the fight, and their losses were staggering.

II did so in early November, fleeing into exile in the Netherlands.

By autumn, Austria-Hungary was also reeling toward collapse. As the government in Vienna tottered, the subject nationalities revolted, splintering the empire of the Hapsburgs. Bulgaria and the Ottoman empire also asked for peace.

The new German government sought an **armistice,** or agreement to end fighting, with the Allies. At 11 A.M. on November 11, 1918, the Great War at last came to an end.

The Human Toll The human and material costs of the war were staggering. More than 8.5 million men had died in battle. More than twice that number had been wounded, many of them disabled for life. Historians estimate that at least 6 million civilians also lost their lives as a result of the war.

The devastation was made even worse in 1918 by a deadly **pandemic** of influenza. A pandemic is the spread of a disease across a large area—in this case, the whole world. In just a few months, the flu killed more than 20 million people worldwide.

The Economic Toll In battle zones from France to Russia, homes, farms, factories, roads, and churches had been shelled into rubble. People had fled these areas as refugees. Now they had to return and start to rebuild. The costs of reconstruction and paying off huge war debts would burden an already battered world.

Shaken and disillusioned, people everywhere felt bitter about the war. The Allies blamed the conflict on their defeated foes and insisted that the losers make **reparations,** or payments for war damage. The stunned Central Powers, who had viewed the armistice as a cease-fire rather than a surrender, looked for scapegoats on whom they could blame their defeat.

The Political Toll Under the stress of war, governments had collapsed in Russia, Germany, Austria-Hungary, and the Ottoman empire. Political **radicals,** or people who wanted to make extreme changes, dreamed of building a new social order from the chaos. Conservatives warned against the spread of Bolshevism, or communism, as it was soon called.

Unrest also swept through Europe's colonial empires. African and Asian soldiers had discovered that the imperial powers were not as invincible as they seemed. Colonial troops returned home with a more cynical view of Europeans and renewed hopes for independence.

? GENERATE EXPLANATIONS Why might the war cause an economic recession or depression in Europe?

Guided Reading and Discussion

Ask students how the destruction of World War I led to political turmoil and uncertainty.

Compare Points of View After the war, there was disagreement on the issue of reparations. Ask students to identify and compare two different viewpoints that leaders had. Have them express their own opinions on whether reparations were useful and fair. *(Sample response: Many Allied leaders favored reparations so that the defeated countries could pay for the war damages. Many leaders of the Central Powers felt that the costs of war should be shared by all participating countries, not just the defeated ones. Students' opinions should be supported by sound reasoning.)*

Analyze Visuals Point out the chart detailing the costs of World War I. Ask students to spend three minutes jotting down their responses to these two questions on sticky notes: "Which two countries suffered the greatest losses in World War I?" "In what ways?" Ask students to pair up or turn to an assigned partner and share their responses. Poll the class to see if there is general agreement. Discuss the results.

D Differentiate Extra Support Make sure students understand the difference between numbers and percentages, both of which are presented in the graphic. Also point out to students the precise difference between millions and billions.

Answers

Generate Explanations *Sample answer: Total war can leave a nation's economy broken and bankrupt. Citizens may go without many necessities, including food. The cost of reconstruction, reparations, and paying off war debts will leave European economies very fragile, increasing the likelihood of a recession or depression.*

Topic 16 Lesson 3

Making the Peace, Effects of the Peace Settlements

After compromising on conflicting goals, the leaders at the Paris Peace Conference drew up the Treaty of Versailles. It violated several of the Fourteen Points and imposed harsh terms on Germany. As a result of it and other peace settlements, political boundaries changed. Empires broke up, and new nations were created. The mandate system granted Britain and France control over former German colonies and Ottoman territories. The system provided economic benefits to Britain and France but denied self-determination to the people living in the mandates.

Online Project the map activity **Interactive Map: Europe in 1914 and 1920**. Move the slider to compare the two maps of Europe and read the text aloud, or ask a student to do so. Have students answer the questions in the activity.

ACTIVE CLASSROOM

How did the Treaty of Versailles impact the lives of people in Europe? Pair students. Have the first student give the second an Audio Tour of the map, explaining what it shows. Have the second student give the first an explanation of what it means. How did the boundary changes benefit some, but not others? *(Some new nations were created in Europe, but many colonies remained under foreign control.)*

Guided Reading and Discussion

Summarize Ask students to summarize the main goals and weaknesses of the League of Nations. *(Goals: international cooperation for negotiation of disputes, collective security and preservation of peace; Weaknesses: Not all countries were members, the powerful United States did not join, the League could not enforce its will on nonmember states)*

Identify Central Ideas Britain and France treated their new mandates in the Middle East and elsewhere like colonies. What was the political and economic impact of the mandate system on Britain, France, and the mandates? *(Answers will vary. Sample response: Britain and France used the mandates as markets for their goods and sources of raw materials. The mandates were denied self-government and remained under the political and economic control of European powers; they felt betrayed.)*

Making the Peace

Just weeks after the war ended, President Wilson boarded a steamship bound for France. He had decided to go in person to Paris, where Allied leaders would make the peace. Wilson was certain that he could bring a "just peace" to the world. "Tell me what is right," Wilson urged his advisors, "and I'll fight for it."

To a weary, angry world, Wilson seemed a symbol of hope. His talk of democracy and self-determination raised expectations for a just and lasting peace—even in defeated Germany. Sadly, it would not be that easy. Europe was a shattered continent. Its problems, and those of the world, would not be solved for many years afterward.

Allies Have Conflicting Goals The victorious Allies met at the Paris Peace Conference to discuss the fate of Europe, the former Ottoman empire, and various colonies around the world. The Central Powers and Russia, under its new communist government, were not allowed to take part in the negotiations.

Wilson was one of three strong leaders who dominated the Paris Peace Conference. He was a dedicated reformer and at times was so stubbornly convinced that he was right that he could be hard to work with. Wilson urged for "peace without victory" based on the Fourteen Points.

>> In this cartoon, President Wilson says to the dove, "Here's your olive branch. Now get busy." **Analyze Political Cartoons** Does the cartoonist think Wilson's solution will work?

Two other Allied leaders at the peace conference had different aims. British Prime Minister David Lloyd George had promised to build a postwar Britain "fit for heroes"—a goal that would cost money. The chief goal of the French leader, Georges Clemenceau (KLEM un soh), was to weaken Germany so that it could never again threaten France. "Mr. Wilson bores me with his Fourteen Points," complained Clemenceau. "Why, God Almighty has only ten!"

Obstacles to Settlement Crowds of other representatives circled around the "Big Three" with their own demands. Among the most difficult issues were the secret agreements made by the Allies during the war. Italy had signed one such treaty. The Italian prime minister, Vittorio Orlando (awr LAN doh), insisted that the Allies honor their secret treaty to give former Austro-Hungarian lands to Italy. Such agreements often violated the idea of self-determination.

Self-determination posed other problems. Many people who had been ruled by Russia, Austria-Hungary, or the Ottoman empire now demanded national states of their own. The territories claimed by these peoples often overlapped, so it was impossible to satisfy them all. Some ethnic groups became unwanted minorities in newly created states.

Wilson had to compromise on his Fourteen Points. However, he stood firm on his goal of creating an international League of Nations. The League would be based on the idea of **collective security,** a system in which a group of nations acts as one to preserve the peace of all. Wilson felt sure that the League could correct any mistakes made in Paris.

The Treaty of Versailles In June 1919, the Allies ordered representatives of the new German Republic to sign the treaty they had drawn up at the palace of Versailles (vur SY) outside Paris. The German delegates were horrified. The Treaty of Versailles forced Germany to assume full blame for causing the war.

It also imposed huge reparations that would burden an already damaged German economy. The reparations covered not only the destruction caused by the war, but also pensions for millions of Allied soldiers or their widows and families. The total cost of German reparations would come to over $400 billion in today's money.

Other parts of the treaty were aimed at weakening Germany. The treaty severely limited the size of the once-feared German military. It returned Alsace and Lorraine to France, removed hundreds of square miles of territory from western and eastern Germany, and

Answers

Analyze Political Cartoons *The cartoonist does not think that the solution will work. The branch is too large and heavy for the dove to carry.*

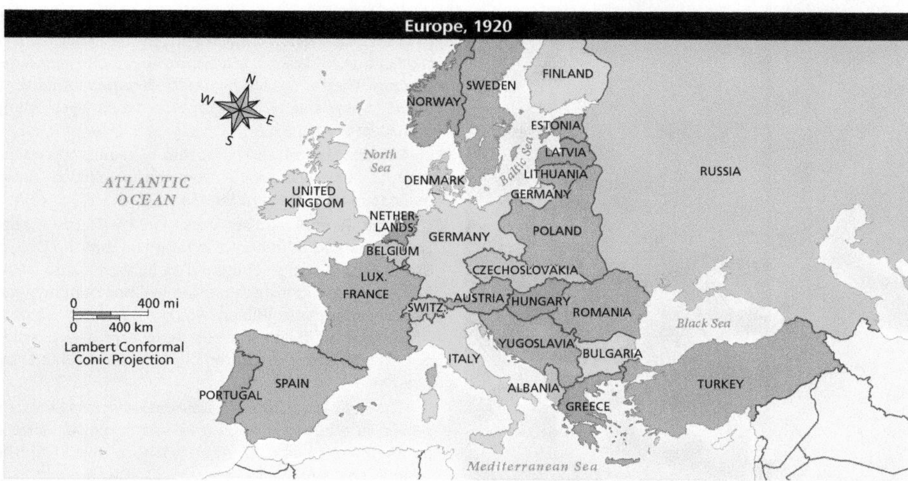

>> **Analyze Maps** Based on this map and the text, why were many Germans unhappy with the territorial changes that occurred after World War I?

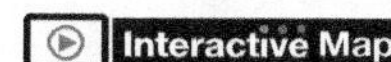

stripped Germany of its overseas colonies. The treaty compelled many Germans to leave the homes they had made in Russia, Poland, Alsace-Lorraine, and the German colonies to return to Germany or Austria.

The Germans signed because they had no choice. However, German resentment of the Treaty of Versailles would poison the international climate for 20 years. It would help spark an even deadlier world war in the years to come.

 **COMPARE POINTS OF VIEW** How did the goals of the Big Three Leaders—Wilson, Lloyd George, and Clemenceau—conflict?

Effects of the Peace Settlements

The Allies drew up separate treaties with the other Central Powers. These treaties redrew the map of Eastern Europe and affected colonial peoples around the globe. Like the Treaty of Versailles, these treaties left widespread dissatisfaction.

New Nations in Europe A key principle of Wilson's Fourteen Points was self-determination. This goal helped a band of new nations emerge in Eastern Europe where the German, Austrian, and Russian empires had once ruled.

Poland became an independent nation after more than 100 years of foreign rule. The Baltic states of Latvia, Lithuania, and Estonia fought for and achieved independence. Three new republics—Czechoslovakia, Austria, and Hungary—rose in the old Hapsburg heartland. In the Balkans, the peacemakers created a new South Slav state, Yugoslavia, dominated by Serbia.

Despite the settlement, Eastern Europe remained a center of political conflict and unrest. The new nations were also relatively poor, with agricultural economies and little capital for industry.

The Mandate System European colonies in Africa, Asia, and the Pacific had looked to the Paris Peace Conference with high hopes. Nationalist leaders in these regions expected that the peace would bring new respect and an end to imperial rule. They took up Wilson's call for self-determination.

However, the leaders at Paris applied self-determination only to parts of Europe. Outside Europe, the victorious Allies added to their overseas empires.

The treaties created a system of **mandates,** territories administered by Western powers. Britain and France gained mandates over German colonies in Africa. Japan and Australia were given mandates over some Pacific islands. The treaties handled lands that

SYNTHESIZE

Online Project the **Digital Activity: The Treaty of Versailles**. Have students use the Think-Pair-Share strategy to answer the questions: What is the German newspaper's opinion of the Treaty of Versailles? *(It opposes the treaty and urges the German people to seek revenge on the Allies who forced Germany to accept it.)* Do you agree or disagree with this newspaper's viewpoint? *(Some students may say the treaty was unjustly harsh on Germany and violated Wilson's Fourteen Points. Others may say Germany was largely responsible for the war, had lost, and should suffer the consequences.)*

Discuss Have pairs think about the following question: Do you think most Germans after World War I would favor pacifism or militarism? Why? Have pairs share their answers with the class. *(Sample responses: pacifism, because most Germans will not want to experience terrible losses again; or militarism, because most Germans will want revenge on the Allies who forced the Treaty of Versailles on them)*

Solve Problems Ask students: If you were at the Paris Peace Conference, what are two ideas you would have supported and two ideas you would have opposed? Why? *(Answers will vary but should be supported by facts and sound reasoning. Students may mention that if the treaty had been less punitive, then there might have been less resentment.)*

Answers

Analyze Maps *Germany lost territory to France, Poland, and other countries. A portion of eastern Germany was cut off from the rest of Germany*

Compare Points of View *Wilson wanted peace without revenge. Lloyd George wanted to reward the heroic British people by punishing Germany and using reparation money for rebuilding projects at home. Clemenceau wanted to weaken Germany so it could never threaten France again.*

Topic 16 Lesson 3

DEMONSTRATE

Online Assign the **Digital Lesson Quiz** for this lesson if you haven't already done so. Students will be offered automatic remediation or enrichment based on their score.

In "World War I Ends," students learned about total war, the war's high human and economic costs, and the effects of the war's peace treaties. Pose these questions to the class on the Discussion Board:

Hypothesize Do you think the world is better off because of international organizations like the League of Nations and the United Nations? Why? *(Sample response: Yes, the world is better off because such an organization requires greater accountability and responsibility for all nations.)*

Predict Consequences How might World War I and its peace settlements have future consequences for the world as a whole? *(Answers will vary; some students may know that hostility regarding the peace settlements would eventually contribute to the outbreak of another world war.)*

Topic Inquiry

Have students continue their investigations for the Topic Inquiry.

>> Delegates attend the first meeting of the League of Nations on December 4, 1920, in the Hall of Reformation in Geneva, Switzerland.

used to be part of the Ottoman empire as if they were colonies, too.

In theory, mandates were to be held until they were able to stand alone. In practice, they became colonies, remaining under the political and economic control of the Allied powers. From Africa to the Middle East and across Asia, people living in the mandates felt betrayed by the peacemakers.

Widespread Discontent Germans and colonial peoples were not the only groups dissatisfied by the peace. Italy was angry because it did not get all the lands promised in its secret treaty with the Allies. Japan protested the refusal of the Western powers to recognize its claims in China. At the same time, China was forced to accept Japanese control over some former German holdings. Russia, excluded from the peace talks, resented the reestablishment of a Polish nation and three independent Baltic states on lands that had been part of the Russian empire.

All of these discontented nations bided their time. They waited for a chance to revise the peace settlements in their favor.

The League of Nations The Paris Peace Conference did offer one beacon of hope with the establishment of the League of Nations. More than 40 nations joined the League. They agreed to negotiate disputes rather than resort to war and to take common action against any aggressor state.

Wilson's dream had become a reality, or so he thought. On his return from Paris, Wilson faced resistance from his own Senate.

Some Republican senators, led by Henry Cabot Lodge, wanted to restrict the treaty so that the United States would not be obligated to fight in future wars. Lodge's reservations echoed the feelings of many war-weary Americans. Wilson would not accept Lodge's compromises. In the end, the Senate refused to ratify the treaty, and the United States never joined the League.

The loss of the United States weakened the League's power. In addition, the League had no power outside of its member states. As time soon revealed, the League could not prevent war. Still, it was a first step toward something genuinely new—an international organization dedicated to maintaining peace and advancing the interests of all peoples.

DRAW CONCLUSIONS How did the refusal of the United States to join the League of Nations weaken the League's power?

ASSESSMENT

1. **Identify Cause and Effect** How did World War I affect the role of women in society?
2. **Analyze Context** Why did it take so long for the United States to enter World War I?
3. **Make Generalizations** How does a long war with a high number of casualties generally affect civilians' and soldiers' opinions of their government?
4. **Compare and Contrast** After World War I, why were conditions ripe for social and political change in Russia, but not in the United States?
5. **Predict Consequences** How might the harsh provisions of the Treaty of Versailles affect conditions in Germany?

Answers

Draw Conclusions *By entering World War I and significantly affecting its outcome, the United States proved itself to be an international power. The League of Nations could not easily implement policies and enforce decisions if one of the most powerful countries of the world was not a participating member.*

Assessment

1. Women played a role in the total war effort by joining various branches of the armed forces or by taking jobs vacated by men who went off to war. During and after the war, women had new strength and confidence, which encouraged efforts to win the vote and gain social equality.
2. Many Americans did not feel it was in America's interest to enter the war, and Americans had different loyalties to European nations, depending on their own backgrounds. For example, many German Americans favored Germany and many Irish Americans opposed Britain.
3. War-weary civilians and soldiers may lose respect for their government and might take democratic or nondemocratic measures to replace leaders, protest their government, or even engage in rebellion.
4. Russia suffered more than the United States in both human casualties and economic collapse. The Eastern Front, on Russian territory, was devastated. The Russian government was weakened, and the people were hungry and demoralized. The United States, on the other hand, entered the war late and suffered relatively few casualties.
5. By leaving Germany in a weakened state, saddling it with reparations payments to all the Allied nations, and not allowing it to participate in the peace negotiations, the treaty would leave Germans embittered, angry, impoverished, and defensive.

16.4 The year 1913 marked the 300th anniversary of the Romanov dynasty. Everywhere, Russians honored the tsar and his family. Tsarina Alexandra felt confident that the people loved Nicholas too much to ever threaten him. "They are constantly frightening the emperor with threats of revolution," she told a friend, "and here,—you see it yourself—we need merely to show ourselves and at once their hearts are ours."

>> Vladimir Ilyich Lenin took his revolutionary ideas directly to the people, addressing crowds in the streets.

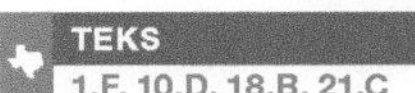

Interactive Flipped Video

Revolution in Russia

TEKS
1.F, 10.D, 18.B, 21.C

>> Objectives

Explain the causes of the February (March) Revolution.

Describe the goals of Lenin and the Bolsheviks in the October Revolution.

Summarize the outcome of the civil war in Russia.

Analyze how Lenin built a Communist state in the Soviet Union.

>> Key Terms

proletariat
soviet
Cheka
commissar

Causes of the February Revolution

Appearances were deceiving. In March 1917, the first of two revolutions would topple the Romanov dynasty and pave the way for even more radical changes. These revolutions are known to Russians as the February and October Revolutions, and to many westerners as the March and November Revolutions.

In 1917, Russia still used an old calendar, which was 13 days behind the one used in Western Europe. Russia did not adopt the Western calendar until 1918.

Roots of Discontent In 1914, the huge Russian empire stretched from Eastern Europe east to the Pacific Ocean. Unlike Western Europe, Russia was slow to industrialize despite its huge potential. Landowning nobles, priests, and an autocratic tsar controlled the government and economy. Much of the majority peasant population endured stark poverty. As Russia began to industrialize, a small middle class and an urban working class emerged.

After the Revolution of 1905, Nicholas had failed to solve Russia's basic political, economic, and social problems. The elected Duma set up after the revolution had no real power. Moderates pressed for a constitution and social change. But Nicholas II, a weak and ineffective

PEARSON realize. www.PearsonTexas.com Access your Digital Lesson.

Aa Vocabulary Builder

1. Have students pronounce the following academic vocabulary terms in this lesson and clarify the part of speech. For difficult or polysyllabic words, break them into syllables and pronounce them with the students.
2. Explain what the word means in common "student-friendly" language using synonyms and antonyms when possible. Provide concrete examples to clarify the meaning, and rephrase the definition.

crucial: of vital importance
withdrawal: the act of leaving

Topic 16 Lesson 4

Revolution in Russia

CONNECT

Preview Have students preview the **Lesson Objectives** and the list of **Key Terms**.

Students can also preview all the **Key Terms** and **Academic Vocabulary** using the **Interactive Reading Notepad** on the digital course or preview a summary of the lesson in the **Reading and Note Taking Study Guide**.

Online Use the **Editable Presentation** found on the digital course to present the main ideas for this lesson.

Start Up Activity

Read the following text. Tell students that it is an excerpt of a letter from a Russian solider, fighting on the Eastern Front of World War I in 1917, to the head of the Russian government.

"Mr. War Minster! We, soldiers from various regiments,... ask you to end the war and its bloodshed at any cost.... If this is not done, then ... we will take our weapons and head out for our own hearths to save our fathers, mothers, wives, and children from death by starvation (which is nigh). And if we cannot save them, then we'd rather die with them in our native lands than be killed, poisoned, or frozen to death somewhere and be cast into the earth like a dog."

Discuss Ask students to recall the long discontent in Russia, the Russian Revolution of 1905, and the German advance into Russia during World War I. Discuss whether students think the soldiers were justified in feeling this way.

Online You can also project the **Start Up Activity** from the course.

INVESTIGATE

Have students read the section using the **Reading and Note Taking Study Guide** to help them take notes and understand the text as they read.

Causes of the February Revolution

As World War I was raging in 1917, Russia suffered from social inequality and economic problems. Tsar Nicholas II continued to use force to limit representative government. The Russian army suffered massive defeats and millions of casualties. At home, food and fuel shortages added to the misery.

Topic 16 Lesson 4

Guided Reading and Discussion

Discuss with students how World War I and the actions of the tsar and tsarina were causes of revolution in Russia.

Solve Problems Divide students into groups. Ask each group to recall the problems that led to the February Revolution and then work together to devise a plan of action that might have solved the problems and delayed or prevented revolution. *(Answers will vary. Sample responses: withdraw from World War I, give the Duma more democratic power, provide land to the peasants and food to the needy, urge the tsar to reduce his power and rule as a constitutional monarch)*

Key Terms

Ask students to find the term **proletariat** (in bold) in the text. Explain that this term was used to describe industrial wage earners whose only possession of substantial economic value was their ability to work.

leader, blocked attempts to limit his authority. Like past tsars, he relied on his secret police and other enforcers to impose his will. A corrupt bureaucracy and an overburdened court system added to the government's problems.

Revolutionaries hatched radical plots. Some hoped to lead discontented peasants to overthrow the tsarist regime. Marxists tried to ignite revolution among the **proletariat**—the growing class of factory and railroad workers, miners, and urban wage earners. A revolution, they believed, would occur when the time was ripe.

World War I Intensifies Discontent The outbreak of war in 1914 fueled national pride and united Russians. Armies dashed to battle with enthusiasm. But like the Crimean and Russo-Japanese wars, World War I quickly strained Russian resources. Factories could not turn out enough supplies. The transportation system broke down, delivering only a trickle of crucial materials to the front. By 1915, many soldiers had no rifles and no ammunition. Badly equipped and poorly led, they died in staggering numbers. In 1915 alone, Russian casualties reached two million.

In a patriotic gesture, Nicholas II went to the front to take personal charge. The decision proved a disastrous blunder. The tsar was no more competent than many of his generals. Worse, he left domestic affairs to the tsarina, Alexandra.

>> Gregory Rasputin's followers, including the tsarina Alexandra, considered him a mystic and a faith healer. His opponents called him the "mad monk."

In Nicholas's absence, Alexandra relied on the advice of Gregory Rasputin, an illiterate peasant and self-proclaimed "holy man." The tsarina came to believe that Rasputin had miraculous powers after he helped her son, who suffered from hemophilia, a disorder in which any injury can result in uncontrollable bleeding.

By 1916, Rasputin's influence over Alexandra had reached new heights and weakened confidence in the government. Fearing for the monarchy, a group of Russian nobles killed Rasputin on December 29, 1916.

Tsar Nicholas II Steps Down By March 1917, disasters on the battlefield, combined with food and fuel shortages on the home front, brought the monarchy to collapse. In St. Petersburg (renamed Petrograd during the war), workers were going on strike. Marchers, mostly women, surged through the streets, shouting, "Bread! Bread!" Troops refused to fire on the demonstrators, leaving the government helpless. Finally, on the advice of military and political leaders, the tsar abdicated.

Duma politicians then set up a provisional, or temporary, government. Middle-class liberals in the government began preparing a constitution for a new Russian republic. At the same time, they continued the war against Germany.

?

1. **IDENTIFY CAUSE AND EFFECT** What were the causes of the Russian Revolution of March 1917?

Lenin Leads the Bolsheviks

Outside the provisional government, revolutionary socialists plotted their own course. In Petrograd and other cities, they set up **soviets,** or councils of workers and soldiers. At first, the soviets worked democratically within the government. Before long, though, the Bolsheviks, a radical socialist group, took charge. The leader of the Bolsheviks was a determined revolutionary, V. I. Lenin.

The Making of a Revolutionary **V. I. Lenin** was born Vladimir Ilyich Ulyanov(ool YAHN uf) in 1870 to a middle-class family. He adopted the name Lenin when he became a revolutionary.

When he was 17, his older brother was arrested and hanged for plotting to kill the tsar. The execution branded his family as a threat to the state and made the young Vladimir hate the tsarist government. As

D Differentiate Challenge/Gifted Ask students to do research to learn more about the influence of the monk Gregory Rasputin over the tsar's family and how that contributed to the February Revolution. Have them write a brief, three-paragraph report on their findings.

Answers

Identify Cause and Effect *The elected Duma had no real power. Moderates pressed for a constitution and social change. But Nicholas II blocked reforms. He relied on his secret police and other enforcers to impose his will. The hardships of World War I worsened conditions for peasants, proletarians, and soldiers, many of whom were attracted to radical socialism. Rasputin's influence over the royal family weakened confidence in the government.*

a young man, Lenin read the works of Karl Marx and participated in student demonstrations. He spread Marxist ideas among factory workers along with other socialists, including Nadezhda Krupskaya (nah DYEZ duh kroop SKY uh), the daughter of a poor noble family.

In 1895, Lenin and Krupskaya were arrested and sent to Siberia. During their imprisonment, they were married. After their release, they went into exile in Switzerland. There, they worked tirelessly to spread revolutionary ideas that would eventually succeed in shifting political thought in Russia and other nations.

Lenin Adapts Marxism Lenin adapted Marxist ideas to fit Russian conditions. Marx had predicted that the industrial working class would rise spontaneously to overthrow capitalism. But Russia did not have a large urban proletariat. Instead, Lenin called for an elite group to lead the revolution and set up a "dictatorship of the proletariat." Though this elite revolutionary party represented a small percentage of socialists, Lenin gave them the name Bolsheviks, meaning "majority."

In Western Europe, many leading socialists had come to think that socialism could be achieved through gradual and moderate reforms such as higher wages, increased suffrage, and social welfare programs.

A group of socialists in Russia, the Mensheviks, favored this approach. The Bolsheviks rejected it. To Lenin, reforms of this nature were merely capitalist tricks to repress the masses. Only revolution, he said, could bring about needed changes.

In March 1917, Lenin was still in exile. As Russia stumbled into revolution, Germany saw a chance to weaken its enemy by helping Lenin return home. Lenin rushed across Germany to the Russian frontier in a special train. He greeted a crowd of fellow exiles and activists with this cry: "Long live the worldwide Socialist revolution!"

EXPLAIN Explain how Lenin adapted Marxist ideas to Russian society and government.

ELPS ELPS 4.G.3 Read and answer questions about *Lenin Leads the Bolsheviks.*

The October Revolution Brings the Bolsheviks to Power

Lenin threw himself into the work of furthering the revolution. Another dynamic Marxist revolutionary, Leon Trotsky, helped lead the fight. To the hungry, war-weary Russian people, Lenin and the Bolsheviks promised "Peace, Land, and Bread."

>> In this 1920 painting, "Bolshevik," by Boris Kustodiev, a giant carries a red banner through a Russian city. **Analyze Art** Who or what does the giant symbolize?

Interactive Chart

Causes of the October Revolution Meanwhile, the provisional government, led by Alexander Kerensky, continued the war effort and failed to deal with land reform. Those decisions proved fatal. Most Russians were tired of war. Troops at the front were deserting in droves. Peasants wanted land, while city workers demanded an end to the desperate shortages.

In July 1917, the government launched the disastrous Kerensky Offensive against Germany. By November, according to one official report, the army was "a huge crowd of tired, poorly clad, poorly fed, embittered men." Growing numbers of troops mutinied. Peasants seized land and drove off fearful landlords.

The Bolsheviks Seize Power Conditions were ripe for the Bolsheviks to make their move. In November 1917, squads of Red Guards—armed factory workers—joined mutinous sailors from the Russian fleet in attacking the provisional government. In just a matter of days, Lenin's forces overthrew the provisional government.

The Bolsheviks quickly seized power in other cities. In Moscow, it took a week of fighting to blast the local government out of the walled Kremlin, the former tsarist

Lenin Leads the Bolsheviks

The October Revolution Brings the Bolsheviks to Power

Following the February Revolution, Russia's provisional government implemented few reforms and continued the war effort. Vladimir Lenin adapted Marx's ideas to fit conditions in Russia. With promises of "Peace, Land, and Bread," Lenin's Bolsheviks led workers and soldiers in the October Revolution that overthrew the provisional government. Lenin then distributed land to peasants, gave workers control of the factories, and established a socialist state.

Online Project the **Interactive Chart: 1917—Revolutions in Russia** and explain to students that they will decide if each item was a cause of the February Revolution, the October Revolution, or both revolutions.

ACTIVE CLASSROOM

Use the Act It Out strategy to have students stage a TV round-table news show. One student acts as the moderator/interviewer. Other students assume various roles such as Tsar Nicholas II, Kerensky, Lenin, a soldier, a peasant, and a factory worker. The focus of the discussion should be whether or not revolution is necessary, and why or why not. Students may wish to record their show and present it as an online video.

Answers

Explain *Because Russia did not have a large urban proletariat, Lenin called for a "dictatorship of the proletariat," an elite revolutionary party that represented a small percentage of socialists, which he called "Bolsheviks."*

Analyze Art *The giant represents the combined strength of the proletariat—the multitude of tiny people in the streets; the giant symbolizes Bolshevism, the power of the new Communist system.*

Guided Reading and Discussion

Discuss with students how the ideas of Karl Marx and Vladimir Lenin shifted political thought and brought about a communist revolution in Russia.

Compare and Contrast Ask: How did Lenin's ideas differ from those of Karl Marx and those of moderate socialists like the Mensheviks? *(Marx predicted the proletariat would revolt and overthrow capitalism. But Russia lacked a large proletariat, so Lenin used a small elite group to lead revolution. Moderate socialists favored gradual moderate reforms.)*

Civil War Erupts in Russia

From 1918 to 1921, civil war raged in Russia with Lenin's Communist "Reds" fighting the counterrevolutionary "Whites." The Whites consisted of Mensheviks, democrats, non-Russian nationalists, and others opposed to the Communists. The Red Army, under the command of the brilliant strategist Leon Trotsky, was triumphant.

Draw Conclusions Ask: Why were the Reds able to defeat the Whites? *(Sample response: The Reds won popular support by appealing to Russian nationalism. They had excellent leadership and training and used terror against their own people and against the Whites.)*

Guided Reading and Discussion

Sequence Events Have students work in groups to create a graphic organizer, such as a flowchart, to show the sequence of the major events during the Russian Civil War.

center of government. Moscow became the Bolsheviks' capital, and the Kremlin their headquarters.

"We shall now occupy ourselves in Russia in building up a proletarian socialist state," declared Lenin.

The Bolsheviks ended private ownership of land and distributed land to peasants. Workers were given control of the factories and mines. A new red flag with an entwined hammer and sickle symbolized union between workers and peasants. Throughout the land, millions thought they had at last gained control over their own lives. In fact, the Bolsheviks—renamed Communists—would soon become their new masters.

DESCRIBE Describe the reasons for the fall of Kerensky's government.

Civil War Erupts in Russia

After the Bolshevik Revolution, Lenin quickly sought peace with Germany. Russia signed the Treaty of Brest-Litovsk in March 1918, giving up a huge chunk of its territory and its population. The cost of peace was extremely high, but the Communist leaders knew that they needed all their energy to defeat a collection of enemies at home. Russia's withdrawal affected the hopes of both the Allies and the Central Powers.

>> A crusading white knight slays the red dragon in this Russian civil war propaganda poster. Its title is "For a United Russia." **Draw Conclusions** Which side in the Russian civil war made this poster? Why?

The Opposing Forces For three years, civil war raged between the "Reds," as the Communists were known, and the counterrevolutionary "Whites." The "White" armies were made up of tsarist imperial officers, Mensheviks, democrats, and others, all of whom were united only by their desire to defeat the Bolsheviks. Nationalist groups from many of the former empire's non-Russian regions joined them in their fight. Poland, Estonia, Latvia, and Lithuania broke free, but nationalists in Ukraine, the Caucasus, and central Asia were eventually subdued.

The Allies intervened in the civil war. They hoped that the Whites might overthrow the Communists and support the fight against Germany. Britain, France, and the United States sent forces to help the Whites. Japan seized land in East Asia that tsarist Russia had once claimed. The Allied presence, however, did little to help the Whites. The Reds appealed to nationalism and urged Russians to drive out the foreigners. In the long run, the Allied invasion fed Communist distrust of the West.

Brutality was common in the civil war. Counterrevolutionary forces slaughtered Communist prisoners and tried to assassinate Lenin. The Communists shot the former tsar and tsarina and their five children in July 1918 to keep them from becoming a rallying symbol for counterrevolutionary forces.

Terror and War Communism The Communists used terror not only against the Whites, but also to control their own people. They organized the **Cheka,** a secret police force much like the tsar's. The Cheka executed ordinary citizens, even if they were only suspected of taking action against the revolution. The Communists also set up a network of forced labor camps in 1919—which grew under Stalin into the dreaded Gulag.

The Communists adopted a policy known as "war communism." They took over banks, mines, factories, and railroads. Peasants in the countryside were forced to deliver almost all of their crops to feed the army and hungry people in the cities. Peasant laborers were drafted into the military or forced to work in factories.

Meanwhile, Trotsky turned the Red Army into an effective fighting force. He used former tsarist officers under the close watch of **commissars,**Communist party officials assigned to the army to teach party principles and ensure party loyalty. Trotsky's passionate speeches roused soldiers to fight. So did the order to shoot every tenth man if a unit performed poorly.

The Reds' position in the center of Russia gave them a strategic advantage. The White armies were

Answers

Describe *The war was badly managed, and troops were deserting in large numbers. Russian peasants were demanding land reform. Urban workers protested serious shortages of goods.*

Draw Conclusions *The Whites made it, portraying themselves as a heroic knight and the Reds as an evil dragon. They hoped the poster would gain support for the Whites.*

English Language Proficiency Standards

Reading 4.G.3 Read "Lenin Leads the Bolsheviks" aloud to students. Then have students answer the questions below based on their English proficiency level.

Beginning Ask students the following questions. Students may answer by pointing to or reciting specific information in the text.

- Who influenced Lenin the most? [Karl Marx]
- What does the name *Bolsheviks* mean? [majority]

Intermediate Ask students to answer the following questions using complete sentences. Allow students to refer to the text for support as needed.

- How did Lenin and Krupskaya influence political thought in Russia?
- How did Lenin adjust Marxist ideas to encourage a political revolution in Russia?

Advanced Ask students to answer the following questions using complete sentences. Allow students to refer to the text for support as needed.

>> **Analyze Maps** Russia was by far the largest of the various republics that made up the Soviet Union. How do you think nationalism affected the Soviet Union?

Interactive Map

forced to attack separately from all sides. They were never able to cooperate effectively with one another. By 1921, the Communists had managed to defeat their scattered foes.

 **INTEGRATE INFORMATION** How did Lenin and Trotsky use brutality and terror to win the Russian Civil War?

The Communist Soviet Union Emerges

Russia was in chaos. Millions of people had died since the beginning of World War I. Millions more perished from famine and disease. Lenin faced the enormous problem of rebuilding a shattered state and economy.

New Government, Old Problems In 1922, Lenin's Communist government united much of the old Russian empire into the Union of Soviet Socialist Republics (USSR), or Soviet Union. The Communists produced a constitution that seemed both democratic and socialist. It set up an elected legislature, later called the Supreme Soviet, and gave all citizens over 18 the right to vote. All political power, resources, and means of production would belong to workers and peasants. The Soviet Union was a multinational state made up of European and Asian peoples. In theory, all the member republics shared certain equal rights.

Reality, however, differed greatly from theory. The Communist party, not the people, reigned supreme. Just as the Russian tsars had, the party used the army and secret police to enforce its will. Russia, which was the largest republic, dominated the other republics.

Lenin Abandons War Communism On the economic front, Lenin retreated from his policy of "war communism," which had brought the economy to near collapse. Under party control, factory and mine output had fallen. Peasants stopped producing grain, knowing the government would only seize it.

In 1921, Lenin adopted the New Economic Policy, or NEP. It allowed some capitalist ventures. Although the state kept control of banks, foreign trade, and large industries, small businesses were allowed to reopen for private profit. The government also stopped squeezing peasants for grain. Under the NEP, peasants held on to small plots of land and freely sold their surplus crops.

Lenin's compromise with capitalism helped the Soviet economy recover and ended armed resistance to the new government. By 1928, food and industrial production climbed back to prewar levels. The standard of living improved, too. But Lenin always saw the NEP

The Communist Soviet Union Emerges

Lenin's Communists won the civil war and established the Union of Soviet Socialist Republics, also called the Soviet Union. Russia, the largest republic, controlled the other republics in this multinational state. The Communist party, not the people, reigned supreme and used the military to enforce its will. But to spur economic improvement, Lenin's New Economic Policy retreated from war communism and allowed some limited capitalism.

Online Project the **Interactive Map: From Russian Empire to Soviet Union, 1914–1923** and click through the layers with students.

ACTIVE CLASSROOM

Have students Write Headlines, one for each layer of the map. Each headline should capture one of the main ideas of the map layer. Ask: If you were to write a headline for this map that conveyed the most important change to be remembered, what would that headline be? Pass your headline to a partner for him or her to review and to improve, if he or she can.

Guided Reading and Discussion

Make sure students understand how Lenin's Communists established the Soviet Union and what the structure and policies of the new government were like.

Identify Cause and Effect Ask: Why did Lenin allow some capitalism in his New Economic Plan? *(Lenin allowed small businesses to operate for private profit.)*

Summarize Ask students to summarize the struggle for power that occurred after Lenin's death.

- How did the death of Lenin's older brother influence his future political career?
- Do you think the creation of the Bolsheviks is a true reflection of Marxist ideals? Why or why not?

Advanced High Ask students to use the questions for the Advanced proficiency level to begin a discussion of the revolution in Russia. Allow students to refer to the text for support as needed.

Answers

Analyze Maps *In a state made up of so many different ethnic groups, nationalism might threaten the unity of the Soviet Union.*

Integrate Information *Communists murdered the tsar and his family. The secret police force executed citizens who were suspected of opposing the Revolution.*

Topic 16 Lesson 4

SYNTHESIZE

Online Project the **Synthesize: "End the War and Its Bloodshed."** Ask students to reconsider their previous answers to the questions in light of what they have learned in this lesson. Then have them respond to the questions about whether or not the Russian revolutions, and violent revolutions in general, are justifiable.

Support a Point of View With Evidence Once students have shared their answers to the Essential Question, divide them into teams of like-minded peers. Conduct a debate. Select any undecided students to act as judges. After the debate, ask students if their peers' arguments have caused them to change their own opinions, and if so, why?

DEMONSTRATE

Online Assign the **Digital Lesson Quiz** for this lesson if you haven't already done so. Students will be offered automatic remediation or enrichment based on their score.

Pose this question to the class on the Discussion Board:

Identify Supporting Ideas In general, do you think the people of Russia will end up better or worse following the revolutions? Why? *(Some might say that any government would be better than the tsarist government; others may say that the Soviet government was just as dictatorial.)*

Topic Inquiry

Have students continue their investigations for the Topic Inquiry.

>> Lenin (left) and Stalin (right) appear together here. But British art historian David King claims that Stalin's image was airbrushed into the photo. **Hypothesize** Why would Stalin want photos of him appearing with Lenin?

as just a temporary retreat from communism. His successor would soon return the Soviet Union to "pure" communism.

Stalin Comes to Power Lenin died in 1924 at the age of 54. His death set off a power struggle among Communist leaders. The chief contenders were Trotsky and Joseph Stalin. Trotsky was a brilliant Marxist thinker, a skillful speaker, and an architect of the Bolshevik Revolution. Stalin, by contrast, was neither a scholar nor an orator. He was, however, a shrewd political operator and behind-the-scenes organizer. Trotsky and Stalin differed on the future of communism. Trotsky urged support for a worldwide revolution against capitalism. Stalin, who was more cautious, wanted to concentrate on building socialism at home first.

Eventually, Stalin isolated Trotsky within the party and stripped him of party membership. Trotsky fled the country in 1929, but continued to criticize Stalin. In 1940, a Stalinist agent murdered Trotsky in Mexico.

In 1922, Lenin had expressed grave doubts about Stalin's ambitious nature: "Comrade Stalin . . . has concentrated an enormous power in his hands; and I am not sure that he always knows how to use that power with sufficient caution." Just as Lenin had warned, in the years that followed, Stalin used ruthless measures to win dictatorial power.

DESCRIBE What capitalist measures did Lenin incorporate into his New Economic Policy?

ASSESSMENT

1. **Identify Cause and Effect** How did the actions of Tsar Nicholas II and his wife lead to revolution in Russia?
2. **Draw Conclusions** How did World War I help to pave the way for the Russian Revolution?
3. **Compare and Contrast** Compare and contrast Lenin's idealistic vision of a socialist state with the reality of communism in the new Soviet Union.
4. **Distinguish** Differentiate between the February Revolution and the October Revolution. What were the outcomes of each?
5. **Hypothesize** If World War I had not taken place, do you think the Russian Revolution would have happened? Support your argument with facts.

Answers

Hypothesize *To convince the Russian people that he should become Lenin's successor*

Describe *He allowed for limited private profit for some small-business owners and peasant farmers.*

Assessment

1. Nicholas II opposed efforts to limit his power. His government led Russia into a disastrous war. The tsarina undermined public confidence in the royal family.
2. The war greatly weakened Russia, which was already troubled by the great inequities. The war pushed the feeble economy to collapse, causing widespread hunger. The number of casualties and losses at the front caused further distress.
3. Ideally, all would work for the good of the whole, with land distributed to the peasants, and factories run by the workers. In the communist reality, the Party used secret police to enforce its will. Factory and mine output dropped, and peasants lost the motivation to grow crops.
4. The February Revolution resulted in the abdication of Tsar Nicholas II. A provisional government was installed. The October Revolution overthrew a failed provisional government, brought the Bolsheviks to power, and a civil war resulted. Lenin's Communists won and established the Soviet Union.
5. Answers will vary. Students arguing yes will point to the weakness and excesses of the tsar, the poverty of the peasants, and the fact that Marx's writings were inspiring young revolutionaries. Students arguing no will point out that without the extreme pressures of World War I, Russia would not have been so terribly weakened.

MILITARY BUILD UP IN EUROPE 1914

	ARMY TROOPS	NAVY BATTLESHIPS	NAVY SUBMARINES
AUSTRIA-HUNGARY	2.3 MILLION		
GERMANY	5.7 MILLION	43	30
FRANCE	4.5 MILLION	29	76
BRITAIN	160,000 (Britain had an all-volunteer army.*)	62	76
RUSSIA	5.3 MILLION		

1. **Identify Major Causes** Identify major causes of the following important turning points in world history from 1914 to the present: World War I. Write a brief explanation identifying the major causes of World War I, including militarism. Consider the impact of imperialism, role of nationalism, and why alliances were formed. Based on the chart, in building up their armies and which countries led the way their naval forces? 1.F
2. **Identify Major Causes** Identify major causes of the following important turning points in world history from 1750 to 1914: European imperialism. Write a paragraph identifying the importance of imperialism in causing World War I. Consider why European nations competed for overseas colonies, the impact colonies had on the economies of European nations, and how imperialist rivalries affected Europe. 1.E
3. **Identify Major Effects** Describe the major effects of the following important turning points in world history from 1914 to the present: World War I, including its impact on social, political, and economic systems. Write a paragraph describing the major effects of World War I on Germany after the war, including the impact on its social, political, and economic systems. Consider the status of Germany under the Treaty of Versailles, economic reparations, status of its military, and territorial changes. 1.F
4. **Identify Importance** Identify the importance of nationalism in causing World War I. Write a paragraph identifying the importance of nationalism in causing World War I. Include specific examples of at least three cases of nationalism among European nations: Germany and France, Russia and Pan-Slavism, Austria-Hungarian minority populations, and conflicts in the Balkan states. 10.A
5. **Identify Major Characteristics** Identify major characteristics of World War I, including trench warfare and high casualty rates. Write a paragraph about how trench warfare and high casualty rates characterized World War I. Consider the extent of the war, mobilization, how trench warfare was related to the stalemate, and causes of high casualty rates. 10.B
6. **Describe Participation** Describe how people have participated in supporting and changing their governments. Write a paragraph describing how women supported and changed their governments during and after World War I. Consider women in industry, in the armed forces, and in medicine. What happened to women after the war? Did the governments of the United States and other nations recognize women's war efforts? 21.A
7. **Explain Impact** Explain the political and economic impact of the Treaty of Versailles, including the mandate system. Write a paragraph explaining the political and economic impact of the mandate system under the Treaty of Versailles. Consider which areas outside of Europe were affected and under what conditions mandate countries could be free from control. How did mandates affect the domestic economies of the Allies? 10.C
8. **Identify Major Characteristics and Effects** Identify major characteristics of World War I, including modern technology and its effects. Write a paragraph about the effects of modern technology on World War I. On the chart above, add in the major types of military technology and other examples as needed. Why were submarines like German U-boats especially effective during the war? 10.B, 28.C

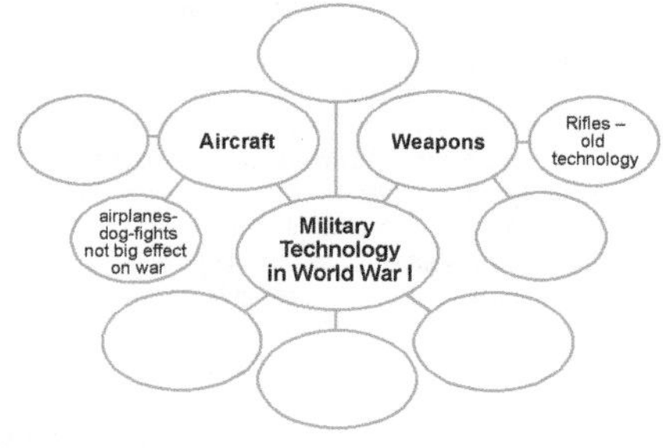

Answers to TEKS Assessment

1. Student answers will vary but should include information on specific reasons that were largely responsible for causing WWI. *Imperialism* sparked global competition among the European nations. Increasing *nationalism* created hostilities between nations and also within multinational empires such as Austria-Hungary, which led to conflicts in the Balkans. Most of the major powers in Europe formed *alliances*, pledging to defend each other if attacked; the Allies included Great Britain, France, and Russia, and the Central Powers included Germany, Austria-Hungary, and Turkey. Many countries, like Britain and Germany, showed *militarism* by competing in building up military force, particularly their naval forces, including submarines.

2. Student answers will vary but should include information on how increasing populations in Europe demanded more resources; overseas colonies were the key to European nations' economic growth and expansion. In the early 1900s before WWI, competition for the colonies often led competing countries to the brink of war; for example, there were tensions between France and Germany in Morocco. These tensions fed into the need for alliances, which also became a cause of WWI.

3. Student answers will vary but should include information on how most of the decisions made by Allied leaders after WWI focused on punishing Germany. The Treaty of Versailles had Germany assume full blame for the war and imposed huge fines (reparations) of $30 billion that would burden its economy. It also limited the German military, returned Alsace and Lorraine to France, reduced Germany's western and eastern lands, and seized its overseas colonies. German resentment of these was severe.

4. Student answers will vary but should include information on how nationalism played a strong part in causing WWI. Germans were proud of their new military and industrial power; the French wanted to recover Alsace and Lorraine. Russia supported Pan-Slavism and backed Serbia against Austria-Hungary. Austria-Hungary had many minority populations within its empire who sought their own nations. In 1912 several Balkan states (Serbia, Greece, Bulgaria, and Montenegro) attacked Turkey and succeeded in taking a large area of land away from Turkish control. The next year, Serbia, Greece, and Romania fought Bulgaria over territory.

5. Student answers will vary but should include information on how World War I had startlingly high casualty rates, especially during major offensives. For example, a stalemate that endured at the Western Front between France and Germany for four or so years (from the failed Schlieffen Plan) was characterized by trench warfare with little advancing or retreating on either side. Allied and Central Powers turned to massive offensives in 1916. The Battle of Verdun resulted in more than half a million casualties in less than a year. A major battle at the Somme River killed or wounded almost 60,000 British soldiers in a single day; one million or so from both sides were killed in the five-month battle.

6. Student answers will vary but should include information on how women kept the national economies going when the men went off to war. They worked in manufacturing industries, joined the women's branches of the military, worked in agricultural endeavors to grow food, and often worked as nurses, even at the front lines. Although many men returned to their jobs after the war, women's accomplishments during the war helped them win the right to vote in the United States, Britain, and other countries.

Topic 16

Answers to TEKS Assessment

7. Student answers will vary but should include information on how the Treaty of Versailles did not apply self-determination to the overseas colonies. Britain and France received control over German colonies in Africa. Japan and Australia were given territories in the Pacific Islands. Other countries received lands that used to be part of the Ottoman empire. Mandate countries were supposed to be held until they could "stand alone." The countries that controlled mandates would have an economic advantage.

8. Student answers will vary but they should add submarines, armored tanks, and poison gas as other major military technologies. New weapons used included rapid-fire machine guns and long-range artillery guns. Aircraft included zeppelins that were large, gas-filled balloons used as bombers. Submarines like German U-boats were particularly effective in damaging Allied merchant ships that carried supplies.

9. Student answers will vary but should include information on how the European nations signed alliances to defend one another, thinking that no one would attack several powers together. However, the alliance system actually contributed to the growth of the war. The Allies, particularly France, Britain, and Russia, surrounded the Central Power nations. Bulgaria and the Ottoman empire in particular were in a strategic location; when they joined the Central Powers, they created a gateway to the southeast.

10. Student answers will vary but should include information on how establishing the League of Nations was one of President Wilson's Fourteen Points. Established after WWI at the Paris Peace Conference, the League hoped to avoid future war by taking common action against aggressor states; however, it had no power outside of the member states. The United States ultimately did not join because senators did not want the United States to be fighting in future wars. This weakened the League. Historically, the League was the first attempt at a cooperative organization of states for the purposes of peace.

11. Student answers will vary but should include information on the massacre of ethnic Armenians who were Christian minorities living in Turkey's northern border region; some lived under Ottoman rule, and others lived under Russian rule. During the Russian advance in 1914, some Turkish Armenians joined the Russians against the Turks. The Ottoman government deported the entire Armenian population south to Syria and Mesopotamia, resulting in 600,000 to 1.5 million deaths from massacres or starvation.

12. Student answers will vary but should include information on how Russia lagged behind Western European nations in industrialization; it still had landowning nobles, priests, and a weak tsar. Peasants lived in poverty, and the country had political, economic, and social instability. World War I temporarily united the country, but Russia could not meet the demands of military support for its soldiers, especially with a dysfunctional transportation system. The February-March 1917 bread riots and strikes resulted in toppling of the Russian monarchy. The Kerensky government continued the war effort. Later in October 1917, the Bolsheviks seized power and withdrew from the war. When Russia left the war, it hurt the Allies because it freed Germany from fighting on two fronts.

13. Student answers will vary but should include information on how Russia had starving people, millions of war deaths, and an economy in disarray. By 1922, the Russian empire was united into the USSR under Lenin with a constitution, an elected legislature, and political power in the hands

TEKS ASSESSMENT

9. **Identify Importance and Locate Places and Regions** Identify the importance of the alliance system in causing World War I, and locate places and regions of historical significance directly related to turning points and major eras. Write a paragraph identifying the reasons for the alliance system that helped cause World War I, and locate the major allies on the map. Describe a feature of the physical location of the Allied nations and the Central Powers. What geographic advantage did the Central Powers gain when Bulgaria and the Ottoman empire joined them? **10.A, 16.A**

10. **Explain Significance** Explain the significance of the League of Nations. Write a paragraph explaining the importance of the League of Nations. Consider its origins after World War I, its weaknesses, and its historical significance. What decision did the United States make regarding membership? **20.D**

11. **Identify Examples** Identify examples of politically motivated mass murders in Armenia. Write a paragraph identifying and describing the politically motivated mass murders in Armenia during the war years. Consider the status of ethnic Armenians and where they lived, role of Turkish Armenians during the Russian advance in 1914, and Ottoman actions against the Armenians. **22.C**

12. **Identify Causes** Identify the causes of the February (March) and October revolutions of 1917 in Russia and their effect on the outcome of World War I. Write a paragraph identifying the causes of the revolutions of 1917 in Russia and their effect on World War I. Consider the economic and social conditions and problems under Tsar Nicholas. What was the impact of the October 1917 revolution on Russia's allies in the war? **10.D**

13. **Identify the Establishment** Identify the Bolshevik establishment of the Union of Soviet Socialist Republics (USSR). Write a paragraph about how the establishment of the Bolsheviks helped the Russian people. Consider the Russian economy prior to 1922; the constitution and legislature under the USSR in 1922; and the power of the Communist Party. **10.D**

14. **Identify Characteristics** Identify the characteristics of socialism. Write a paragraph identifying the characteristics of socialism as practiced in the Union of Soviet Socialist Republics (USSR) under the New Economic Policy (NEP) in the 1920s. Consider the extent of state control over businesses, status of peasants and their surplus crops, and economic recovery. **18.C**

15. **Identify Examples** Identify examples of key persons who were successful in shifting political thought. Write a paragraph about Lenin and how he was successful in adapting Marxism to Russian conditions. What ideas influenced his early life, and what was the political and economic situation in Russia that allowed Lenin and the Bolsheviks to achieve their goal? **21.C**

16. **Identify Origins, Characteristics, and Influences** Identify the historical origins and characteristics of communism and the influences of Karl Marx. Write a paragraph identifying the origins and characteristics of communism and the influences of Karl Marx in Russia as adapted by Lenin. Consider the ideas of Karl Marx, the peasant working class in Russia, the elite group of socialists called the Bolsheviks, and hopes for revolutionary change. **18.B**

17. **Reflect on the Essential Question Write an essay on the Essential Question: When is war justified?** Use evidence from your study of this Topic to support your answer.

Instead, he formed an elite group, the Bolsheviks, and called for revolutionary change and a "dictatorship of the proletariat." In November 1917, the Bolsheviks overthrew the provisional government, which was politically and economically weakened by WWI. Peasants received land, and workers took control of factories.

16. Student answers will vary but should include information on how Karl Marx advocated the revolutionary idea that the industrial working class would rise and overthrow capitalism. Since Russia did not have a large urban proletariat (it was primarily an agricultural society), Lenin adapted Marxist ideas to fit Russian conditions. He created an elite group of socialists to lead the revolution under the name "Bolsheviks." They believed that enacting reforms on a gradual, moderate basis would be ineffective; instead, they advocated a revolution to bring about changes.

17. Student essays will vary.

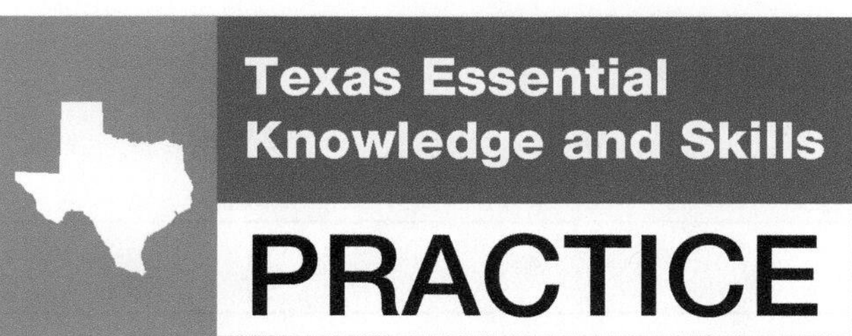

of the workers and peasants. In practice, the Communist Party controlled everything with secret police, just like the tsars.

14. Student answers will vary but should include information on how the USSR abandoned its policy of all-out "war communism" that nearly destroyed the economy. Instead, under the NEP, the state implemented a modified communist policy with control of banks, foreign trade, and large industries. However, it allowed some limited capitalism, with small businesses earning a profit and peasants able to sell surplus crops. These policies helped gain economic stability.

15. Student answers will vary but should include information on how Lenin as a young man learned about Marxist ideas, which he spread among factory workers and during his exile overseas in Switzerland. Lenin adapted Marxist ideas to accommodate Russian conditions, as Russia did not have a large urban proletariat. Lenin did not want gradual and modern reforms to achieve socialism.

Topic 16

Answers to TEKS Practice

1. D
2. G

Online To prepare for the End-of-Topic test, have students go online for additional Topic Review and Assessment questions or to review their notes in the **Interactive Reading Notepad** for the lessons in this Topic.

Benchmark Tests

Assign these benchmark tests as you complete the relevant topics to monitor student progress toward mastering the course content and as preparation for the End-of-Course Test.

Benchmark Test 1: Topics 1–5

Benchmark Test 2: Topics 6–10

Benchmark Test 3: Topics 11–15

Benchmark Test 4: Topics 16–21

TEKS PRACTICE

1

German pride in military power and industrial leadership	French wanted to recover lost border province of Alsace and Lorraine	Russian defense and aid to Pan-Slavism
Minority populations within Austria-Hungary empire	Military tensions in Balkan states over territory	

According to the chart, which of these reasons helped cause World War I?

A Forming a system of alliances

B Economic and political rivalries

C Build-up of military forces

D Extreme nationalism

2

> *"Once war was declared, the army attempted to mobilize the troops very quickly. The fatigued British and French troops, who had been fighting since August 1914, sorely needed the relief offered by the American forces."*

Based on an analysis of the excerpt, why was there a need for American forces?

F American forces contradicted propaganda that the Allies were weaker than others.

G American forces helped break the stalemate that had resulted in prolonged trench warfare.

H American forces showed support for the nations that were bombed most heavily.

J American forces allayed concerns that food rationing was occurring on the front lines.

Test Taking Tips: Tip for Multiple-Choice Tests

1. Read the question carefully. Make sure you understand the question.
2. Read all four answer choices. Even if you think you know the correct answer, check your choice.
3. If you do not understand the question, read it again. If you are still unsure of the answer, use the process of elimination. Begin by rejecting any answer choice that you know is wrong.
4. Look for answer choices that do not relate to the question. (Remember that some answer statements are true, but do not relate to the question.)
5. Look for clue words in the answer choices. Words such as *all, everyone, only,* or *completely* can be wrong because they are too general. A correct answer might use words such as *often, generally,* or *at times.*

3 What conditions in the Soviet Union brought the Bolsheviks to power in October-November 1917?

A The provisional government kicked out the former tsar.
B Powerful landlords financially supported Lenin and the Bolsheviks.
C Hungry peasants revolted against economic shortages and inequality.
D Allied intervention upset nationalists who hated foreigners.

4 How did the Revolution of 1848 in France influence ideas on political revolutions and nationalism across Europe?

F Workers and the middle class revolted to gain basic rights and political power.
G Economic decline caused food shortages that led to extreme nationalism.
H Labor unions won universal suffrage and equal pay for women.
J Nations built up military forces to spread imperialism overseas.

If you have trouble with...				
Question	1	2	3	4
See Lesson	16.1	16.3	16.4	14.1
TEKS	10.A	10.B	10.D	9.D

3. C
4. F

Online Use the **Topic Synthesize** to help students revisit and reflect on the Essential Question for this Topic.

The World Between the Wars (1910–1939)

TOPIC 17 ORGANIZER	PACING: APPROX. 1 PERIOD, .5 BLOCKS		
	PACING	TEKS	ELPS
Connect	1 period		
MY STORY VIDEO **Mohandas Gandhi, The Power of Nonviolence**	10 min.		
DIGITAL ESSENTIAL QUESTION ACTIVITY **What Should Governments Do?**	10 min.	12.A	
DIGITAL TIMELINE ACTIVITY **The World Between the Wars**	10 min.	9.D, 12.A, 12.B, 12.C, 21.A, 22.E	
TOPIC INQUIRY: CIVIC DISCUSSION **Lenin and Stalin**	20 min.		
Investigate	4–8 periods		
TOPIC INQUIRY: CIVIC DISCUSSION **Lenin and Stalin**	Ongoing		
LESSON 1 **Revolution and Nationalism in Latin America**	30–40 min.	9.D, 26.B	4.G.4
LESSON 2 **Nationalist Movements in Africa and the Middle East**	30–40 min.	1.F, 10.C, 15.A, 16.C, 21.A, 23.A, 26.B, 26.C	
LESSON 3 **India Seeks Self-Rule**	30–40 min.	1.F, 21.A, 21.C, 22.E	4.H.2
LESSON 4 **New Forces in China and Japan**	30–40 min.	1.F, 12.C, 13.B	4.I.1
LESSON 5 **The West After World War I**	30–40 min.	1.F, 11.A, 11.B, 12.B, 20.D, 26.B, 26.C, 28.E	5.E
LESSON 6 **Fascism Emerges in Italy**	30–40 min.	1.F, 12.A, 12.B, 18.D, 19.B, 21.A, 21.C	5.F.1
LESSON 7 **The Soviet Union Under Stalin**	30–40 min.	1.F, 11.B, 12.A, 12.B, 19.B, 22.C	4.K, 5.F.2
LESSON 8 **The Rise of Nazi Germany**	30–40 min.	1.F, 11.B, 12.A, 12.B, 21.C, 26.B	3.F.2
Synthesize	1 period		
DIGITAL ACTIVITY **The World Between the Wars (1910–1939)**	10 min.	12.A	
TOPIC INQUIRY: CIVIC DISCUSSION **Lenin and Stalin**	20 min.		
Demonstrate	1–2 periods		
DIGITAL TOPIC TEST **The World Between the Wars**	10 min.		
TOPIC INQUIRY: CIVIC DISCUSSION **Lenin and Stalin**	20 min.		

Access your Digital Lesson

AUTHOR'S NOTE

A Great Authoritarian Tide

Ideologically based dictatorships . . . rose in many lands in these dark years [after World War I]. The most powerful of these governments are often described as totalitarian, vesting total power in a single highly ideological party and appealing to the total commitment of party members to the cause, the movement, and its leader.

Stalin brought Communist party power to a climax in Russia in the 1930s. The new regime built on the tsarist tradition of authoritarian rule but developed the bureaucracy, the army, and the secret police far beyond tsarist models. Communist repression cost the lives of millions of Russians—officially classified as enemies of the working class in Stalinist work camps and prisons, or in the famines of the early 1930s.

Hitler's Nazi party rose to power in 1933, capitalizing on German resentment of the Versailles peace, disillusionment with democracy, and economic collapse. Once in power, Hitler suppressed rival parties, free elections, and free enterprise as he remilitarized his country. He bailed the nation out of the Depression with his public works and rearmament programs, and he unilaterally abrogated the Versailles Treaty. He also introduced Gestapo secret-police terror and SS death camps, massacring six million Jews and millions of others deemed biologically inferior to the "master race."

Mussolini's Fascists seized power in Italy in the early 1920s. In Japan, resentment of an unaggressive parliamentary regime and of *zaivatsu* big business allowed the militarists to dominate affairs in the 1930s. Through assassinations and the threat of a military coup, Japanese generals and admirals cowed civilian authorities into accepting increasingly nationalistic, imperialistic, and reactionary policies.

A great authoritarian wave seemed to be sweeping over the world. One-party rule, military dictatorship, and other forms of autocratic government rose to power in many East European, South American, and Middle Eastern nations. Under the pressure of great economic and political problems, people seemed to be turning their backs on democracy.

—Anthony Esler, *The Human Venture: From Prehistory to the Present* (Upper Saddle River, New Jersey: Pearson Education, 2004), p. 650

TOPIC INQUIRY: CIVIC DISCUSSION

Lenin and Stalin

TEKS 10.D, 12.A, 12.B, 29.C, 29.D, 29.E, 29.F, 29.G, 29.H, 30.A, 30.C

In this Topic Inquiry, students work in teams to examine different perspectives on this issue by analyzing several sources, arguing both sides of a Yes/No question, then developing and discussing their own point of view on the question: **Did Lenin sow the seeds of Stalinism?**

STEP 1: CONNECT

Develop Questions and Plan the Investigation

Launch the Civic Discussion

Divide the class into groups of four students. Students can access the materials they'll need in the online course or you can distribute copies to each student. Read the main question and introduction with the students.

Have students complete Step 1 by reading the Discussion Launch and filling in Step 1 of the Information Organizer. The Discussion Launch provides YES and NO arguments on the main question. Students should extract and paraphrase the arguments from the reading in Step 1 of their Information Organizers.

Next, students share within their groups the arguments and evidence they found to support the YES and NO positions. The group needs to agree on the major YES and NO points and each student should note those points in their Information Organizer.

Resources

- Student Instructions
- Information Organizer
- Discussion Launch

PROFESSIONAL DEVELOPMENT

Civic Discussion

Be sure to view the Civic Discussion Professional Development resources in the online course.

STEP 2: INVESTIGATE

Apply Disciplinary Concepts and Tools

Examine Sources and Perspectives

Students will examine sources with the goal of extracting information and perspectives on the main question. They analyze each source and describe the author's perspective on the main question and key evidence the author provides to support that viewpoint in Information Organizer Step 2.

Ask students to keep in mind:

- **Author/Creator:** Who created the source? An individual? Group? Government agency?
- **Audience:** For whom was the source created?
- **Date/Place:** Is there any information that reveals where and when the source was created?
- **Purpose:** Why was the source created? Discuss with students the importance of this question in identifying bias.
- **Relevance:** How does the source support one argument or another?

Suggestion: Reading the source documents and filling in Step 2 of the Information Organizer could be assigned as homework.

Resources

- Student Instructions
- Information Organizer
- Source documents

STEP 3: SYNTHESIZE

Use Evidence to Formulate Conclusions

Formulate Compelling Arguments With Evidence

Now students will apply perspectives and evidence they extracted from the sources to think more deeply about the main question by first arguing one side of the issue, then the other. In this way students become more prepared to formulate an evidence-based conclusion on their own.

Within each student group, assign half of the students to take the position of YES on the main question and the others to take the position of NO. Students will work with their partners to identify the strongest arguments and evidence to support their assigned YES or NO position.

Present Yes/No Positions

Within each group, those assigned the YES position share arguments and evidence first. As the YES students speak, those assigned NO should listen carefully, take notes to fill in the rest of the Compelling Arguments Chart (Step 3 in Information Organizer), and ask clarifying questions.

When the YES side is finished, students assigned the NO position present while those assigned YES should listen, take notes, and ask clarifying questions. Examples of clarifying questions are:

- I think you just said [x]. Am I understanding you correctly?
- Can you tell me more about [x]?
- Can you repeat [x]? I am not sure I understand, yet.

Suggestion: You may want to set a 5-minute time limit for each side to present. Provide a 2-minute warning so that students make their most compelling arguments within the time frame.

Switch Sides

The students will switch sides to argue the opposite point of view. To prepare to present the other position, partners who first argued YES will use the notes they took during the NO side's presentation, plus add any additional arguments and evidence from the reading and sources. The same goes for students who first argued the NO position.

STEP 4: DEMONSTRATE

Communicate Conclusions and Take Informed Action

Individual Points of View

Now the students will have the opportunity to discuss the main question from their own points of view. To help students prepare for this discussion, have them reflect on the YES/NO discussions they have participated in thus far and fill in Step 4 of their Information Organizers.

After all of the students have shared their points of view, each group should list points of agreement, filling in the last portion of Step 4 on their Information Organizers.

Reflect on the Discussion

Ask students to reflect on the civic discussion, thinking about:

- The value of having to argue both the YES and NO positions.
- Whether their individual views changed over the course of the discussion and why.
- What they learned from participating in the discussion.

Resources

- Student Instructions
- Information Organizer

Revolution and Nationalism in Latin America

Objectives

Objective 1: Identify causes and effects of the Mexican Revolution.

Objective 2: Analyze the effects of economic and political nationalism on Latin America.

Objective 3: Trace the changing relationship between Latin America and the United States.

LESSON 1 ORGANIZER	PACING: APPROX. 1 PERIOD, .5 BLOCKS					
	OBJECTIVES	PACING	RESOURCES: Print	RESOURCES: Online	TEKS	ELPS
Connect						
DIGITAL START UP ACTIVITY **Comparing Experiences of the Mexican Revolution**		5 min.		●	21.A	
Investigate						
READ **The Mexican Revolution**	Objective 1	10 min.	●	●	9.D, 21.A	
INTERACTIVE GALLERY **The Mexican Revolution**	Objective 1	10 min.		●	21.A	
READ **Economic and Social Reforms**	Objective 2	10 min.	●	●	21.A	
READ **Nationalism Spreads in Latin America**	Objective 3	10 min.	●	●	11.A	4.G.4
INTERACTIVE GALLERY **Revolutionary Art**	Objective 3	10 min.		●	26.B	
Synthesize						
DIGITAL ACTIVITY **Mexico's Revolutionary Leaders**		5 min.		●	21.A	
Demonstrate						
DIGITAL LESSON QUIZ **Lesson Quiz and Class Discussion Board**		10 min.		●	21.A, 26.B	

PEARSON realize™ www.PearsonTexas.com Access your Digital Lesson

Focus on Texas Standards

Texas Essential Knowledge and Skills

9.D identify the influence of ideas such as separation of powers, checks and balances, liberty, equality, democracy, popular sovereignty, human rights, constitutionalism, and nationalism on political revolutions	**26.B** analyze examples of how art, architecture, literature, music, and drama reflect the history of the cultures in which they are produced

NOTES

Nationalist Movements in Africa and the Middle East

Objectives

Objective 1: Explain how Africans resisted colonial rule.

Objective 2: Describe the rise of nationalism in Africa.

Objective 3: Describe how Turkey and Persia modernized.

Objective 4: Understand how the mandate system contributed to Arab nationalism and to conflict between Jews and Arabs.

LESSON 2 ORGANIZER	PACING: APPROX. 1 PERIOD, .5 BLOCKS					
			RESOURCES			
	OBJECTIVES	PACING	Print	Online	TEKS	ELPS
Connect						
DIGITAL START UP ACTIVITY **Impact of World War I**		5 min.		●	1.F, 10.C	
Investigate						
READ **Africans Protest Colonial Rule**	Objective 1	10 min.	●	●	1.F, 21.A	
INTERACTIVE MAP **African Resistance to Colonial Rule**	Objective 1	10 min.		●	1.F, 21.A	
READ **A Rising Tide of African Nationalism**	Objective 2	10 min.	●	●	1.F, 21.A, 26.B, 26.C	
INTERACTIVE GALLERY **Writers of the Négritude Movement**	Objective 2	10 min.		●	26.B, 26.C	
READ **Modernization of Turkey and Persia**	Objective 3	10 min.	●	●	1.F, 21.A	
READ **Nationalism and Conflict in the Middle East**	Objective 4	10 min.	●	●	1.F, 10.C, 21.A, 23.A	
Synthesize						
DIGITAL ACTIVITY **Nationalist Movements in Africa and the Middle East**		5 min.		●	21.A	
Demonstrate						
DIGITAL LESSON QUIZ **Lesson Quiz and Class Discussion Board**		10 min.		●	1.F, 21.A	

Focus on Texas Standards

Texas Essential Knowledge and Skills

1.F identify major causes and describe the major effects of the following important turning points in world history from 1914 to the present: the world wars and their impact on political, economic, and social systems; communist revolutions and their impact on the Cold War; independence movements; and globalization

10.C explain the political impact of Woodrow Wilson's Fourteen Points and the political and economic impact of the Treaty of Versailles, including changes in boundaries and the mandate system

15.A create and interpret thematic maps, graphs, and charts to demonstrate the relationship between geography and the historical development of a region or nation

16.C interpret maps, charts, and graphs to explain how geography has influenced people and events in the past

21.A describe how people have participated in supporting or changing their governments

23.A describe the historical origins, central ideas, and spread of major religious and philosophical traditions, including Buddhism, Christianity, Confucianism, Hinduism, Islam, Judaism, Sikhism, and the development of monotheism

26.B analyze examples of how art, architecture, literature, music, and drama reflect the history of the cultures in which they are produced

26.C identify examples of art, music, and literature that transcend the cultures in which they were created and convey universal themes

NOTES

India Seeks Self-Rule

Objectives

Objective 1: Explain the impact of World War I and the Amritsar massacre on Indian nationalism.

Objective 2: Evaluate the ideas of Mohandas Gandhi.

Objective 3: Analyze how Gandhi led resistance to political oppression in India.

LESSON 3 ORGANIZER	PACING: APPROX. 1 PERIOD, .5 BLOCKS					
			RESOURCES			
	OBJECTIVES	PACING	Print	Online	TEKS	ELPS
Connect						
DIGITAL START UP ACTIVITY **Gandhi Pushes for Independence**		5 min.		●	21.C, 22.E	
Investigate						
READ **India's Struggle for Independence Begins**	Objective 1	10 min.	●	●	1.F, 21.A	
READ **Gandhi's Philosophy of Civil Disobedience**	Objective 2	10 min.	●	●	21.C	4.H.2
INTERACTIVE GALLERY **Influences of Gandhi**		10 min.		●	21.C, 22.E	
READ **Gandhi Takes a Stand**	Objective 3	10 min.	●	●	21.A, 21.C, 22.E	
Synthesize						
INTERACTIVE GRAPHIC ORGANIZER **Causes and Effects of Events in the Indian Independence Movement**		5 min.		●	1.F, 21.A, 21.C, 22.E	
Demonstrate						
DIGITAL LESSON QUIZ **Lesson Quiz and Class Discussion Board**		10 min.		●	1.F, 21.A, 21.C, 22.E	

Focus on Texas Standards

Texas Essential Knowledge and Skills

1.F identify major causes and describe the major effects of the following important turning points in world history from 1914 to the present: the world wars and their impact on political, economic, and social systems; communist revolutions and their impact on the Cold War; independence movements; and globalization

21.A describe how people have participated in supporting or changing their governments

21.C identify examples of key persons who were successful in shifting political thought, including William Wilberforce

22.E identify examples of individuals who led resistance to political oppression such as Nelson Mandela, Mohandas Gandhi, Oscar Romero, Natan Sharansky, Las Madres de la Plaza de Mayo, and Chinese student protestors in Tiananmen Square

NOTES

Topic 17 Lesson 4

New Forces in China and Japan

Objectives

Objective 1: Explain the key challenges faced by the Chinese republic in the early 1900s.

Objective 2: Analyze the struggle between nationalists and Communists in China.

Objective 3: Summarize the effects of liberal changes in Japan in the 1920s.

Objective 4: Describe the rise of extreme nationalism and militarism in Japan.

Objective 5: Describe the impact of the Japanese invasion of China.

LESSON 4 ORGANIZER	PACING: APPROX. 1 PERIOD, .5 BLOCKS					
			RESOURCES			
	OBJECTIVES	PACING	Print	Online	TEKS	ELPS
Connect						
DIGITAL START UP ACTIVITY **China Resists Japan's Expanding Empire**		5 min.		●	1.F, 12.C	
Investigate						
READ **Trouble in the Chinese Republic**	Objective 1	10 min.	●	●	13.B	
READ **Nationalists and Communists**	Objective 2	10 min.	●	●	13.B	
INTERACTIVE CHART **Communism vs. Guomindang**		10 min.		●	13.B	
READ **China Faces Japanese Imperialism**	Objectives 2, 5	10 min.	●	●	1.F, 12.C	4.I.1
READ **Conflicting Forces in Japan**	Objective 3	10 min.	●	●	1.F, 12.C	
READ **The Ultranationalist Reaction**	Objective 4	10 min.	●	●	12.C	
READ **Militarists Gain Power**	Objectives 4, 5	10 min.	●	●	1.F, 12.C	
INTERACTIVE GALLERY **Revival of Japanese Glory**		10 min.		●	1.F, 12.C	
Synthesize						
DIGITAL ACTIVITY **Nationalism in China and Japan**		5 min.		●	12.C, 13.B	
Demonstrate						
DIGITAL LESSON QUIZ **Lesson Quiz and Class Discussion Board**		10 min.		●	1.F, 12.C, 13.B	

Focus on Texas Standards

Texas Essential Knowledge and Skills

1.F identify major causes and describe the major effects of the following important turning points in world history from 1914 to the present: the world wars and their impact on political, economic, and social systems; communist revolutions and their impact on the Cold War; independence movements; and globalization

12.C explain the major causes and events of World War II, including the German invasions of Poland and the Soviet Union, the Holocaust, Japanese imperialism, the attack on Pearl Harbor, the Normandy landings, and the dropping of the atomic bombs

13.B summarize the factors that contributed to communism in China, including Mao Zedong's role in its rise, and how it differed from Soviet communism

NOTES

Topic 17 Lesson 5

The West After World War I

Objectives

Objective 1: Analyze how Western society and culture changed after World War I.

Objective 2: Identify the contributions of modern scientists such as Marie Curie and Albert Einstein.

Objective 3: Summarize the domestic and foreign policy issues that the Western democracies faced after World War I.

Objective 4: Describe how the global depression began and spread.

Objective 5: Explain the responses of Britain, France, and the United States to the Great Depression.

LESSON 5 ORGANIZER	PACING: APPROX. 1 PERIOD, .5 BLOCKS					
			RESOURCES			
	OBJECTIVES	PACING	Print	Online	TEKS	ELPS
Connect						
DIGITAL START UP ACTIVITY **Life During the Great Depression**		5 min.		●	11.B	
Investigate						
READ **Social Change After World War I**	Objective 1	10 min.	●	●	1.F, 26.B, 26.C	
READ **Scientific Discoveries**	Objective 2	10 min.	●	●	28.E	5.E
READ **Literature Reflects New Perspectives**	Objective 1	10 min.	●	●	26.B	
READ **Modern Art and Architecture**		10 min.	●	●	26.B	
INTERACTIVE GALLERY **Modern Art Develops**		10 min.		●	26.B	
READ **Postwar Politics in the West**	Objective 3	10 min.	●	●	1.F	
READ **International Relations**		10 min.	●	●	1.F, 20.D	
INTERACTIVE GALLERY **League of Nations Fails to Stop Aggression**		10 min.		●	1.F, 20.D	
READ **Economics in the Postwar Era**		10 min.	●	●	1.F	
READ **The Great Depression**	Objective 4	10 min.	●	●	1.F, 11.A, 12.B, 20.D	
READ **Western Democracies React to the Depression**	Objective 5	10 min.	●	●	1.F, 11.A	
Synthesize						
DIGITAL ACTIVITY **Worldwide Economic Crisis**		5 min.		●	11.B, 12.B	

PEARSON realize™ www.PearsonTexas.com Access your Digital Lesson

LESSON 5 ORGANIZER	PACING: APPROX. 1 PERIOD, .5 BLOCKS					
			RESOURCES			
	OBJECTIVES	PACING	Print	Online	TEKS	ELPS
Demonstrate						
DIGITAL LESSON QUIZ **Lesson Quiz and Class Discussion Board**		10 min.		●	1.F, 11.A, 12.B, 20.D, 26.B	

Focus on Texas Standards

Texas Essential Knowledge and Skills

1.F identify major causes and describe the major effects of the following important turning points in world history from 1914 to the present: the world wars and their impact on political, economic, and social systems; communist revolutions and their impact on the Cold War; independence movements; and globalization

11.A summarize the international, political, and economic causes of the global depression

11.B explain the responses of governments in the United States, Germany, and the Soviet Union to the global depression

12.B explain the roles of various world leaders, including Benito Mussolini, Adolf Hitler, Hideki Tojo, Joseph Stalin, Franklin D. Roosevelt, and Winston Churchill, prior to and during World War II

20.D explain the significance of the League of Nations and the United Nations

26.B analyze examples of how art, architecture, literature, music, and drama reflect the history of the cultures in which they are produced

26.C identify examples of art, music, and literature that transcend the cultures in which they were created and convey universal themes

28.E identify the contributions of significant scientists and inventors such as Marie Curie, Thomas Edison, Albert Einstein, Louis Pasteur, and James Watt

NOTES

Topic 17 Lesson 6

Fascism Emerges in Italy

Objectives

Objective 1: Describe the rise of Mussolini.

Objective 2: Summarize Mussolini's policies as leader of Italy.

Objective 3: Identify the characteristics of totalitarianism and fascism.

LESSON 6 ORGANIZER	PACING: APPROX. 1 PERIOD, .5 BLOCKS					
	OBJECTIVES	PACING	RESOURCES Print	RESOURCES Online	TEKS	ELPS
Connect						
DIGITAL START UP ACTIVITY **Children and Totalitarianism**		5 min.		●		
Investigate						
READ **The Rise of Mussolini**	Objective 1	10 min.	●	●	1.F, 12.A, 12.B, 18.D, 21.A	
READ **Mussolini's Totalitarian Rule**	Objectives 2, 3	10 min.	●	●	12.A, 12.B, 18.D, 19.B	
INTERACTIVE GALLERY **The Makings of an Italian Totalitarian State**		10 min.		●	12.A, 19.B, 21.C	
READ **Characteristics of Fascism**	Objective 3	10 min.	●	●	1.F, 12.A, 12.B, 12.C, 18.D, 19.B, 21.C	5.F.1
INTERACTIVE CHART **Communism vs. Fascism**		10 min.		●	1.F, 12.A, 18.D	
Synthesize						
DIGITAL ACTIVITY **The Economics of Totalitarian Governments**		5 min.		●	1.F, 12.A, 18.D, 19.B	
Demonstrate						
DIGITAL LESSON QUIZ **Lesson Quiz and Class Discussion Board**		10 min.		●	1.F, 12.A, 12.B, 12.C, 18.D, 19.B, 21.C	

Focus on Texas Standards

Texas Essential Knowledge and Skills

1.F identify major causes and describe the major effects of the following important turning points in world history from 1914 to the present: the world wars and their impact on political, economic, and social systems; communist revolutions and their impact on the Cold War; independence movements; and globalization

12.A describe the emergence and characteristics of totalitarianism

12.B explain the roles of various world leaders, including Benito Mussolini, Adolf Hitler, Hideki Tojo, Joseph Stalin, Franklin D. Roosevelt, and Winston Churchill, prior to and during World War II

18.D identify the historical origins and characteristics of fascism

19.B identify the characteristics of the following political systems: theocracy, absolute monarchy, democracy, republic, oligarchy, limited monarchy, and totalitarianism

21.A describe how people have participated in supporting or changing their governments

21.C identify examples of key persons who were successful in shifting political thought, including William Wilberforce

NOTES

The Soviet Union Under Stalin

Objectives

Objective 1: Explain how Stalin built a command economy in the Soviet Union.

Objective 2: Describe how Stalin used terror to build a totalitarian state.

Objective 3: Analyze Stalin's use of propaganda to control thought and the arts.

Objective 4: Summarize the characteristics of Soviet society under Stalin.

Objective 5: Understand the goals of Soviet foreign policy.

LESSON 7 ORGANIZER	PACING: APPROX. 1 PERIOD, .5 BLOCKS					
			RESOURCES			
	OBJECTIVES	PACING	Print	Online	TEKS	ELPS
Connect						
DIGITAL START UP ACTIVITY **Stalin Leads the Soviet Union**		5 min.		●		
Investigate						
READ **Stalin Builds a Command Economy**	Objectives 1, 2	10 min.	●	●	11.B, 12.A, 12.B, 19.B	
READ **Control Through Terror**	Objective 2	10 min.	●	●	12.A, 12.B, 19.B, 22.C	
READ **Stalin Builds a Totalitarian State**	Objectives 2, 3	10 min.	●	●	12.A, 12.B, 19.B, 26.B	4.K
INTERACTIVE GALLERY **Art as Propaganda**		10 min.		●	12.A, 12.B, 19.B, 26.B	
READ **Soviet Society Under Stalin**	Objective 4	10 min.	●	●	12.A, 12.B, 19.B	
READ **Soviet Foreign Policy**	Objective 5	10 min.	●	●	12.B, 12.C	5.F.2
INTERACTIVE GRAPHIC ORGANIZER **Characteristics of Stalin's Rule**		10 min.		●	12.A, 12.B, 19.B, 26.B	
Synthesize						
DIGITAL ACTIVITY **Stalin's Soviet Union**		5 min.		●	1.F, 11.B, 12.A, 12.B, 12.C, 19.B, 26.B	
Demonstrate						
DIGITAL LESSON QUIZ **Lesson Quiz and Class Discussion Board**		10 min.		●	11.B, 12.A, 12.B, 12.C, 19.B, 26.B	

Focus on Texas Standards

Texas Essential Knowledge and Skills

1.F identify major causes and describe the major effects of the following important turning points in world history from 1914 to the present: the world wars and their impact on political, economic, and social systems; communist revolutions and their impact on the Cold War; independence movements; and globalization

11.B explain the responses of governments in the United States, Germany, and the Soviet Union to the global depression

12.A describe the emergence and characteristics of totalitarianism

12.B explain the roles of various world leaders, including Benito Mussolini, Adolf Hitler, Hideki Tojo, Joseph Stalin, Franklin D. Roosevelt, and Winston Churchill, prior to and during World War II

19.B identify the characteristics of the following political systems: theocracy, absolute monarchy, democracy, republic, oligarchy, limited monarchy, and totalitarianism

22.C identify examples of politically motivated mass murders in Cambodia, China, Latin America, the Soviet Union, and Armenia

NOTES

Topic 17 Lesson 8

The Rise of Nazi Germany

Objectives

Objective 1: Summarize the political and economic problems faced by the Weimar Republic.

Objective 2: Analyze Hitler's rise to power.

Objective 3: Describe the political, social, economic, and cultural policies of Nazi Germany.

Objective 4: Explain why Eastern Europe turned to authoritarian rule.

LESSON 8 ORGANIZER — **PACING: APPROX. 1 PERIOD, .5 BLOCKS**

	OBJECTIVES	PACING	RESOURCES: Print	RESOURCES: Online	TEKS	ELPS
Connect						
DIGITAL START UP ACTIVITY **Hitler's Rise to Power**		5 min.		●	12.B	
Investigate						
READ **The Weimar Republic**	Objective 1	10 min.	●	●	1.F, 26.B	
READ **Hitler Leads the Nazi Party**	Objective 2	10 min.	●	●	1.F, 11.B, 12.B	3.F.2
INTERACTIVE TIMELINE **The Rise and Fall of the Weimar Republic**		10 min.		●	1.F, 12.A, 12.B, 12.C, 21.C	
READ **The Third Reich**	Objective 3	10 min.	●	●	12.A, 12.B, 21.C	
INTERACTIVE GALLERY **Growing Up in Nazi Germany**		10 min.		●		
READ **Authoritarian Rule in Eastern Europe**	Objective 4	10 min.	●	●	1.F, 12.A, 21	
Synthesize						
DIGITAL ACTIVITY **Nazi Propaganda**		5 min.		●	1.F, 12.B, 21.C	
Demonstrate						
DIGITAL LESSON QUIZ **Lesson Quiz and Class Discussion Board**		10 min.		●	1.F, 12.A, 12.B	

PEARSON realize™ www.PearsonTexas.com Access your Digital Lesson

Focus on Texas Standards

Texas Essential Knowledge and Skills

1.F identify major causes and describe the major effects of the following important turning points in world history from 1914 to the present: the world wars and their impact on political, economic, and social systems; communist revolutions and their impact on the Cold War; independence movements; and globalization

11.B explain the responses of governments in the United States, Germany, and the Soviet Union to the global depression

12.A describe the emergence and characteristics of totalitarianism

12.B explain the roles of various world leaders, including Benito Mussolini, Adolf Hitler, Hideki Tojo, Joseph Stalin, Franklin D. Roosevelt, and Winston Churchill, prior to and during World War II

21.C identify examples of key persons who were successful in shifting political thought, including William Wilberforce

26.B analyze examples of how art, architecture, literature, music, and drama reflect the history of the cultures in which they are produced

NOTES

The World Between the Wars (1910–1939)

In this Topic, you will learn about people and events between World War I and World War II. You will also find lots of interesting ways to master the TEKS associated with this Topic.

Your study will help you master these TEKS:

TEKS

1.F, 9.D, 10.C, 11.A, 11.B, 12.A, 12.B, 12.C, 13.B, 15.A, 16.C, 18.D, 19.B, 20.D, 21.A, 21.C, 22.C, 22.E, 23.A, 26.B, 26.C, 28.E, 29.F, 31.B

LESSON OUTLINE

17.1: Revolution and Nationalism in Latin America **9.D, 26.B**

17.2: Nationalist Movements in Africa and the Middle East **1.F, 10.C, 15.A, 16.C, 21.A, 23.A, 26.B, 26.C**

17.3: India Seeks Self-Rule **1.F, 21.A, 21.C, 22.E**

17.5: The West After World War I **1.F, 11.A, 11.B, 12.B, 20.D, 26.B, 26.C, 28.E**

17.6: Fascism Emerges in Italy **1.F, 12.A, 12.B, 18.D, 19.B, 21.A, 21.C**

17.7: The Soviet Union Under Stalin **1.F, 11.B, 12.A, 12.B, 19.B, 22.C**

17.8: The Rise of Nazi Germany **1.F, 11.B, 12.A, 12.B, 21.C, 26.B**

Connect

Connect with this Topic by watching a video about a fascinating person related to this Topic. You can think about how this Topic connects to your own life. And you'll encounter an intriguing Essential Question: What should governments do?

Begin your study by trying the following:

NBC LEARN **Watch My Story Video:**

Mohandas Gandhi, The Power of Nonviolence

Launch your Civic Discussion:

Lenin and Stalin

Investigate

A group of lessons will help you investigate the Topic further. Each lesson has interesting text readings and fascinating interactivities. Together, they will bring the world between the wars alive and help you master the TEKS for this Topic.

And keep working on your Civic Discussion. You're almost ready to show what you have accomplished by expressing your position on Lenin and Stalin using the evidence you have gathered.

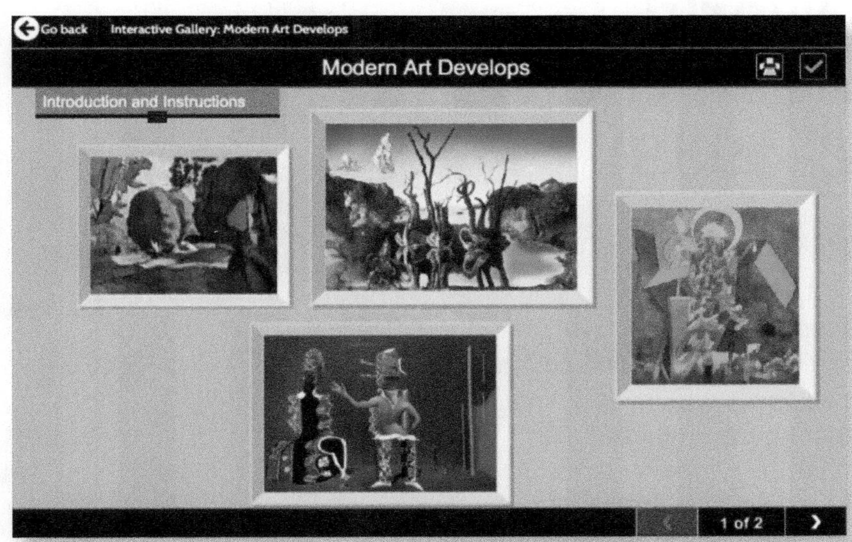

>> Digital interactivity from the online course

Synthesize

You will get a chance to pull together everything you have learned by thinking again about the Essential Question. Consider how you would answer the question now: What should governments do?

Demonstrate

Completing this Topic is like practicing all your soccer skills or rehearsing the scenes in a play. Now you get a chance to pull it all together for the final game or the live performance. You can do this on the Topic Review and Assessment pages. Or you can complete your work your Civic Discussion, Lenin and Stalin.

TEKS in Topic 17	Topic Review and Assessment Questions
1.F	**8, 11, 12, 14, 19**
9.D	**9**
10.C	**1**
11.A	**6**
11.B	**4, 7**
12.A	**5, 12**
12.B	**15, 16**
12.C	**8**
13.B	**20**
18.D	**11**
19.B	**12**
20.D	**17**
21.A	**10, 19**
21.C	**16**
22.C	**13**
22.E	**18**
23.A	**2**
26.B	**21**
26.C	**22**
28.E	**3**
29.F	**7**
31.B	**10**

Topic 17

The World Between the Wars (1910–1939)

Introduction

In the wake of World War I, people around the world questioned their old assumptions. Some protested colonial rule, while others led revolutions against their governments. The Great Depression began in the United States and spread hardship to other lands. In many nations, people looked to strong, authoritarian governments to solve their problems.

[**ESSENTIAL QUESTION**] What should governments do?

17 The World Between the Wars (1910–1939)

ESSENTIAL QUESTION

Ask students to think about the Essential Question for this Topic: What should governments do? Government actions can influence a large number of people both inside and outside a country's borders. What do students believe are the duties of government?

Categorize What types of government actions do you think are generally positive? What types of actions are negative? *(Answers will vary. Many students will say that defending the nation and keeping order are generally positive. Some will have a negative view of taxation, while others may explain that taxes are necessary to pay for services. Students may take a similarly divided view of regulation.)*

Compare Points of View What is an example of a government action that might be viewed negatively by one group and positively by a different group? *(Sample response: Environmentalists would view stricter pollution controls as a positive action, while factory owners might view them as a negative action.)*

Hypothesize Under what circumstances might a head of government pursue a course of action that runs contrary to the accepted role of government? *(Sample response: A head of government might seize more power than is considered acceptable if he or she decides to become a dictator. Governments may assume greater powers during a war or other emergency.)*

Analyze Images

Ask students to examine the illustration of women attending the opera in 1920s Paris. Explain to students that after World War I, a new and more "radical" permissive culture permeated Western society. Ask students to hypothesize why the war's aftermath created this new culture. Ask: How does this image illustrate the emancipation of women after the war?

Texas Essential Knowledge and Skills

1.F, 9.D, 10.C, 11.A, 11.B, 12.A, 12.B, 12.C, 13.B, 15.A, 16.C, 18.D, 19.B, 20.D, 21.A, 21.C, 22.C, 22.E, 23.A, 26.B, 26.C, 28.E, 29.F, 31.B

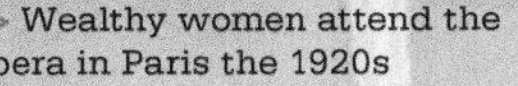

>> Wealthy women attend the opera in Paris the 1920s

Enduring Understandings

- Economic and political inequalities led to the Mexican Revolution.
- Examples of resistance to imperialism included Pan-Africanism, Pan-Arabism, and Gandhi's civil disobedience campaign in India.
- In China, the nationalists under Jiang Jieshi and the communists under Mao Zedong competed for power.
- Postwar disillusion and new mass media reshaped western culture.
- A global economic depression caused widespread misery and threatened the stability of democratic governments.
- Authoritarian and totalitarian states such as Japan, the Soviet Union, Italy, and Germany placed loyalty to the state above individual rights.

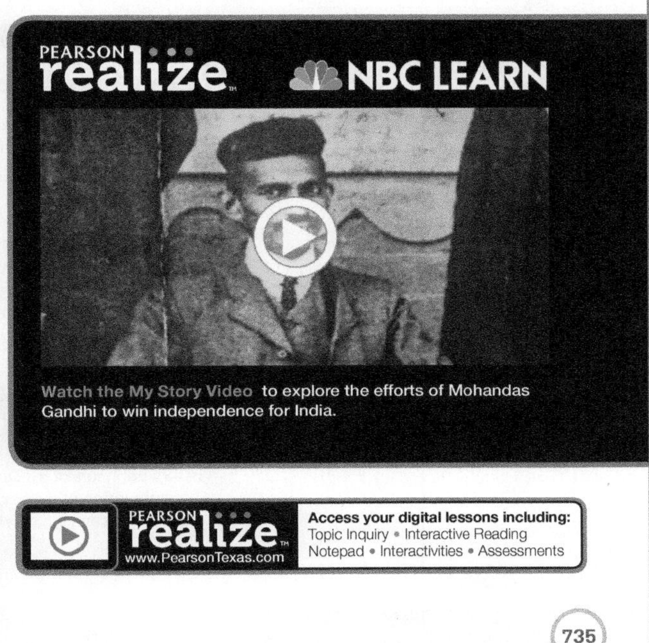

Watch the My Story Video to explore the efforts of Mohandas Gandhi to win independence for India.

PEARSON realize www.PearsonTexas.com **Access your digital lessons including:** Topic Inquiry • Interactive Reading Notepad • Interactivities • Assessments

NBC LEARN MY STORY VIDEO

Project the My Story Video that introduces students to Mohandas Gandhi, who led India to independence.

Online My Story Video: **Mohandas Gandhi, The Power of Nonviolence**

After viewing, ask students to respond to the following questions.

Check Understanding What was Gandhi's concept of satyagraha? *(an approach for winning rights through nonviolent means)*

Identify Patterns How was Gandhi able to influence the civil rights movement in the United States? *(American civil rights leaders recognized the moral power of using nonviolent protests to gain rights and employed many of the same tactics that Gandhi had used in winning independence from Great Britain.)*

OVERVIEW ACTIVITY

Online Project the **1910–1939: Introduction Timeline** showing the major events that occurred between the two world wars. During this Topic, students will learn about all of these events and many more, but this timeline will provide a framework into which they can place the events they learn about.

Check Understanding Which event deals with the overthrow of a government? *(Mexican Revolution)*

Predict What areas do you think Stalin was trying to improve by implementing a five-year plan? *(Sample responses: economic growth; military strength)*

Topic Inquiry

If you choose to assign the Topic Inquiry, launch the discussion after introducing the Topic.

D Differentiate Extra Support While viewing the timeline, explain to students that this Topic covers many different regions around the world. Ask them to name the different regions or countries they see listed on the timeline. Alert students to the need to pay close attention to which region is being discussed at all times.

Topic 17 Lesson 1

Revolution and Nationalism in Latin America

CONNECT

Preview Have students preview the **Lesson Objectives** and the list of **Key Terms**.

Students can also preview all the **Key Terms** and **Academic Vocabulary** using the **Interactive Reading Notepad** on the digital course or preview a summary of the lesson in the **Reading and Note Taking Study Guide**.

Online Use the **Editable Presentation** found on the digital course to present the main ideas for this lesson.

Start Up Activity

Present students with the perspectives of two peasants—one a fictional character—who fought in the Mexican Revolution.

"I am glad to have fought in some cause with Zapata . . . and so many of my dear revolutionary friends who were left behind in the hills, their bones eaten by animals. . . . It's a beautiful thing to fight to realize an ideal."

". . . Am I disappointed [in the revolution]? Perhaps! . . . I hoped to find a meadow at the end of the road. I found a swamp. Facts are bitter; so are men. That bitterness eats your heart out; it is poison, dry rot."

From the quotations, what do you predict you will learn about the Mexican Revolution? *(People had different viewpoints about fighting and that the results were not necessarily what people had hoped for.)*

Online You can also project the **Start Up Activity** from the course.

INVESTIGATE

Have students read the section using the **Reading and Note Taking Study Guide** to help them take notes and understand the text as they read.

The Mexican Revolution

People from every social class opposed Mexican President Porfirio Díaz's dictatorship and supported a political revolution. However, each class generally had different reasons for that support. The peasants wanted social reform and better wages. The middle class wanted democracy, and the elite wanted to take back control of the economy from foreign companies. In 1910, the unrest boiled over into a revolution that lasted for more than a decade.

>> Peasants joined the Mexican revolution in the hopes of improving their lives. Most were untrained and had few supplies, but they continued to fight for social, political, and economic change.

Interactive Flipped Video

17.1 By 1910, the dictator Porfirio Díaz had ruled Mexico for almost 35 years, winning re-election as president again and again. On the surface, Mexico enjoyed peace and economic growth. Díaz welcomed foreign investors who developed mines, built railroads, and drilled for oil.

TEKS
9.D, 26.B

>> Objectives

Identify causes and effects of the Mexican Revolution.

Analyze the effects of economic and political nationalism on Latin America.

Trace the changing relationship between Latin America and the United States.

>> Key Terms

Porfirio Díaz
hacienda
Emiliano Zapata
Venustiano Carranza
nationalization
Lázaro Cárdenas
economic nationalism
cultural nationalism
Good Neighbor Policy

Revolution and Nationalism in Latin America

The Mexican Revolution

Seeds of Discontent However, underneath the surface, discontent rippled through Mexico. The country's prosperity benefited only a small group. The majority of Mexicans were mestizos or Indian peasants who lived in desperate poverty. Most of these peasants worked on **haciendas,** or large plantations, controlled by the landowning elite.

Some peasants moved to cities, where they found jobs in factories, or worked in mines. Everywhere, they earned meager wages. In Mexican cities, middle-class liberals, who embraced the ideals of democracy, opposed the Díaz dictatorship.

The unrest boiled over in 1910 when Francisco Madero, a liberal reformer from an elite family, demanded free elections. After being imprisoned by Diaz, he hoisted the flag of revolution. Soon, revolutionaries all across Mexico joined Madero's cause. Faced with rebellion in several parts of the country, Díaz resigned in 1911.

PEARSON realize. www.PearsonTexas.com Access your Digital Lesson.

736

Aa Vocabulary Builder

1. Have students pronounce the following academic vocabulary terms in this lesson and clarify the part of speech. For difficult or polysyllabic words, break them into syllables and pronounce them with the students.
2. Explain what the word means in common "student-friendly" language using synonyms and antonyms when possible. Provide concrete examples to clarify the meaning, and rephrase the example.

assets: things of value

intervening: coming between two arguing factions

A Complex Struggle Madero became president of Mexico, but he turned out to be too liberal for conservatives and not radical enough for the revolutionaries. In 1913, he was murdered by one of his generals, Victoriano Huerta. Huerta ruled as a military dictator, but was quickly faced with rebellion.

During a long, complex power struggle, several radical leaders emerged. They sometimes joined forces but then fought each other. In southern Mexico, **Emiliano Zapata** led a peasant revolt. Zapata, an Indian peasant farmer, understood the misery of peasant villagers. The battle cry of the Zapatistas, as these rebels were called, was "Tierra y libertad!" which means "land and freedom."

Francisco "Pancho" Villa, a hard-riding rebel from the north, fought mostly for personal power but won the intense loyalty of his peasant followers. Villa and Zapata formed an uneasy coaltion with **Venustiano Carranza,** a rich landowner who wanted political reform but opposed social change.

Fighting flared across Mexico for a decade, killing as many as a million Mexicans. Peasants, small farmers, ranchers, and urban workers were drawn into the violent struggle. Soldaderas, women soldiers, cooked, tended the wounded, and even fought alongside men.

During the revolution, President Woodrow Wilson of the United States twice sent troops to Mexico. In 1914, U.S. forces helped depose, or remove, Huerta. In 1916, they tried to hunt down Pancho Villa, whose raid into New Mexico had killed 16 Americans. After the overthrow of Huerta, Carranza turned on Villa and Zapata and defeated them. In 1917, Carranza was elected president of Mexico. That year, he reluctantly signed a new constitution.

SEQUENCE EVENTS Explain the events of the Mexican Revolution in order.

Economic and Social Reforms

Venustiano Carranza had called for a new constitution during the Mexican Revolution. But he did not like the one he had reluctantly signed in 1917 and did not institute its reforms. In 1920, rival revolutionaries arranged for his assassination. The constitution, however, survived. With some revisions, it is still in effect today.

The Constitution of 1917 The Constitution of 1917 addressed three major issues: land, religion, and labor. The constitution strengthened government control over the economy. It permitted the breakup of large estates, placed restrictions on foreigners owning land, and allowed **nationalization,** or government takeover, of natural resources. Church land was made "the property of the nation." The constitution set a minimum wage and protected the workers' right to strike.

Although the constitution gave suffrage only to men, it did give women some rights. Women doing the same job as men were entitled to the same pay. In response to women activists' efforts to change the Mexican government, Carranza also passed laws allowing married women to draw up contracts, take part in legal suits, and have equal authority with men in spending family funds.

The PRI Takes Control In 1929, the government organized what later became the Institutional Revolutionary Party (PRI). The PRI made political choices to accommodate many groups in Mexican society, including business and military leaders, peasants, and workers. Its leaders backed social reform, even while it kept power in its own hands and suppressed political opposition. It also boosted Mexican industry. Over time, the PRI brought stability to Mexico and carried out many desired reforms. The PRI dominated Mexican politics until 2000.

Madero at the head of his forces

>> Francisco Madero served as president for less than two years before he was overthrown. Though he accomplished little, he remained an inspiration to revolutionaries.

Interactive Gallery

Topic 17 Lesson 1

Online Project the **Interactive Gallery: The Mexican Revolution**. Review the timeline of major events during the Mexican Revolution. Then look at each image individually. Ask students how the images and the information help them understand the complex nature of the revolution. Students should know that different groups were fighting for different beliefs and that many leaders were overthrown or assassinated during this long war.

ACTIVE CLASSROOM

Use the Ranking strategy to have students go through the timeline and images and rank which events seemed to advance the revolution and which seemed to be setbacks. Have students explain the reasons for their choices.

Guided Reading and Discussion

Be sure students understand the causes that led to the Mexican Revolution and the differing motives of each group. For example, Venustiano Carranza wanted political reforms, but opposed the redistribution of land.

Infer Several revolutionary leaders were overthrown or assassinated by other leaders. Why do you think the leaders turned on each other? *(Some of the leaders, who didn't trust each other, had different goals and beliefs.)*

Economic and Social Reforms

Although the Constitution of 1917 addressed land, religion, and labor reform, Carranza was slow to make changes. Three years after signing the constitution, Carranza was overthrown.

In 1929, the government organized the Institutional Revolutionary Party (PRI). The party made some changes, but it kept the real power. The PRI dominated politics until 2000.

History Background

Mexico's Revolutionary Leaders
Differences among Mexico's revolutionary leaders reflected sharp divisions in Mexican society. Zapata was an Indian from southern Mexico. Villa was a mestizo peasant from the north. Madero and Carranza were from upper-class, landowning families. While Madero and Carranza supported democratic political reform, Villa and Zapata pushed for sweeping economic and social changes.

One thing the leaders did have in common, however, was a violent end. Huerta ordered Madero's death, only to die three years later after being released from an American jail. Zapata and Villa were both assassinated, Zapata by agents of Carranza. Carranza himself was murdered as he fled after being overthrown. Only Porfirio Díaz died peacefully in exile.

Answers

Sequence Events *Díaz stepped down as a leader, and Madero was elected president. He was overthrown and assassinated by Huerta, who set up a dictatorship. Carranza, Villa, and Zapata defeated Huerta, then Carranza defeated Villa and Zapata. Carranza became president in 1917 and signed a new constitution.*

Topic 17 Lesson 1

Key Terms

Ask students to find the key term **Lázaro Cárdenas** (in bold) in the text. Explain that he joined the revolutionary forces when he was 18 and later became a general in the Mexican army. After the revolution, he served as governor of Michoacán and then as president of the PNR. In 1934, he was elected president of Mexico, where he established the social and economic reforms the revolutionaries had fought for.

Analyze Images

Direct students' attention to the chart "Land Distributed in Mexico by President, 1915–1940." Explain that one of the goals of the Constitution of 1917 was the redistribution of land. Ask the following questions: What does this map tell you about the Mexican presidents and the government during these years? *(Even though the constitution addressed land reform and redistribution, Carranza and many of the following presidents did not pass reforms.)* Why do you think Carranza distributed only 1 percent of the millions of acres? *(Carranza was a wealthy landowner and probably did not want to give up his land or force his supporters to give up their lands.)* How does it help you understand why fighting continued throughout the 1920s? *(The revolutionaries were not ready to give up. They wanted the government to take the actions that were promised in the constitution.)*

Guided Reading and Discussion

Express Problems Clearly Organize students to debate whether PRI control was good or bad for Mexico. Have them consider the goals of the revolution, the importance of stability, and the location of power.

Nationalism Spreads in Latin America

The end of World War I and the Great Depression affected Latin American economies. Mexico's growing spirit of economic, political, and cultural nationalism spread throughout Latin America.

Social and Economic Reforms At first, the Constitution of 1917 was just a set of goals to be achieved in the future. But in the 1920s and 1930s, as the government finally restored order, it began to carry out reforms.

In the 1920s, the government helped some Indian communities regain lands that had been taken from them. In the 1930s, President **Lázaro Cárdenas** made the decision to redistribute millions of acres of land to peasants under a communal land program. The government supported labor unions and launched a massive effort to combat illiteracy. Schools and libraries were set up. For the first time, Mexicans in rural areas who grew up speaking various Indian languages learned Spanish.

Dedicated teachers, often young women, worked for low pay. While they taught basic skills, they also spread ideas of nationalism that began to bridge the gulf between the regions and the central government. As the revolutionary era ended, Mexico became the first Latin American nation to pursue real social and economic reforms for the majority of its people.

Under the PRI, the government also took a strong role in directing the economy. In 1938, labor disputes broke out between Mexican workers and the management of some foreign-owned petroleum companies. In response, President Cárdenas nationalized Mexico's oil resources. American and British oil companies resisted Cárdenas's decision, but eventually accepted compensation for their losses. Mexicans felt that they were at last gaining economic independence from foreign influence.

IDENTIFY CENTRAL IDEAS How did the PRI accommodate many groups in Mexican society while keeping power for itself?

Nationalism Spreads in Latin America

The issues facing Mexico were echoed in other Latin American nations. In the early 1900s, Latin America's economy was booming because of exports. Latin Americans sold their plentiful natural resources and cash crops to industrialized countries. In return, they bought products made in those countries.

Stable governments helped to keep the region's economy on good footing. Some Latin American nations, such as Argentina and Uruguay, had democratic constitutions. However, military dictators or small groups of wealthy landowners held the real power. The tiny ruling class kept the economic benefits of the booming economy for themselves. The growing middle class and the lower classes—workers and peasants—had no say in their own governments.

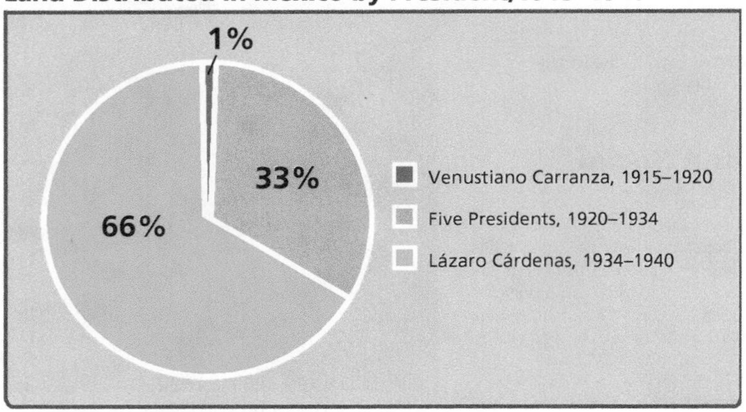

>> **Analyze Graphs** Between 1915 and 1940, nearly 75 million acres of land were distributed to Mexico's people, fulfilling one goal of the constitution. Which president redistributed the most land?

D Differentiate Extra Support Help students understand the pie chart. Remind them that a pie chart is a visual representation of statistics. Have students work in pairs to interpret the pie chart. Then create another graphic that represents the same information, such as a table or bar graph. Have pairs present their graphics. Discuss which is the most helpful. Creating different types of graphics will help them understand the different ways they can present statistics or information.

Answers

Identify Central Ideas *The PRI adopted some of each group's key goals but did not bring about total reform, which allowed party members to keep control. It also suppressed opposition.*

Analyze Graphs *Lázaro Cárdenas*

Economic Nationalism During the 1920s and 1930s, world events affected Latin American economies. After World War I, trade with Europe fell off. The Great Depression that struck the United States in 1929 spread around the world in the 1930s. Prices for Latin American exports plunged as demand dried up. At the same time, the cost of imported consumer goods rose. Latin American economies, dependent on export trade, declined rapidly.

A tide of **economic nationalism,** or emphasis on home control of the economy, swept Latin American countries. It was directed largely at ending economic dependence on the industrial powers, especially the United States and Britain. Since consumers could no longer afford costly imports, local entrepreneurs set up factories to produce goods at home. They urged their governments to raise tariffs, or taxes on imports, to protect these new industries. Following Mexico's lead, some nations nationalized resources or took over foreign-owned industries.

The drive to create domestic industries had limited success. In Mexico, Argentina, Brazil, and a few other countries, some areas of manufacturing grew. Mexico and Venezuela also benefited from a growing demand for their oil. But most Latin American nations lacked the resources to build large industries. As in the past, the unequal distribution of wealth hurt efforts at economic development. Only a few in the wealthy ruling class benefited from economic growth.

Political Nationalism The Great Depression also triggered political changes in Latin America. The economic crisis caused people to lose faith in the ruling oligarchies and the ideas of liberal government. Liberalism, a belief in the individual and in limited government, was a European theory. People began to feel that it did not work in Latin America.

In the midst of economic crisis, authoritarian governments with strong nationalist goals gained power in many countries. Authoritarian rulers imposed stability and supported economic nationalism, but suppressed opposition political parties and silenced critics.

Cultural Nationalism By the 1920s, an upsurge of national feeling led Latin American writers, artists, and thinkers to reject European influences. Instead, they took pride in their own culture, with its blend of Western and Native American traditions.

In Mexico, **cultural nationalism,** or pride in one's own national culture, was reflected in the revival of mural painting, a major art form of the Aztecs and Maya. Diego Rivera, José Clemente Orozco (oh ROHS koh), and other muralists created magnificent works that reflected Mexican culture and history. On the walls of public buildings, they portrayed the struggles of the Mexican people for liberty. The murals have been a great source of national pride ever since.

>> Artist Diego Rivera portrayed the history of Mexico in this mural. The bottom represents Aztec civilization. The top half focuses on the Mexican Revolution and the future of Mexico.

Interactive Gallery

Relations with the United States Nationalism affected how Latin American nations saw the United States. During and after World War I, investments by the United States in Latin America soared, while British influence declined. The United States continued to play the role of international policeman, intervening to restore order when it felt its interests were threatened.

During the Mexican Revolution, the United States stepped in with military force to support the leaders who favored American interests. This interference stirred up anti-American feelings, which increased throughout Latin America during the 1920s. For example, in Nicaragua, Augusto César Sandino led a guerrilla movement against United States forces occupying his country.

The Good Neighbor Policy In the 1930s, President Franklin Roosevelt took a new approach to Latin America. He pledged to follow "the policy of the good neighbor."

Topic 17 Lesson 1

Online Project the **Interactive Gallery: Revolutionary Art**. Work through the image with students. Point out that the entire mural—some of which is shown here—shows the history of Mexico, beginning with the Aztecs through the Mexican Revolution and to the present. Ask students what they find most interesting about the mural and why they think Rivera included so much of Mexico's history. What was he trying to achieve? *(Sample response: Rivera wanted to provide perspective for the revolution and also give Mexicans a sense of pride in their history.)*

ACTIVE CLASSROOM

Have students plan and create a Graffiti Concepts that represents their culture. They should consider what traditions and aspects of their culture they think are the most important to include and how best to illustrate them. Allow students time to find or draw images. Ask students to post their "graffiti" on the board and to look at the various responses. Discuss some of the "graffiti" and why students chose to include certain things.

Guided Reading and Discussion

Discuss the various aspects of nationalism. Ask: How did Latin Americans express nationalism economically? *(by trying to grow domestic industry and by nationalizing existing foreign industry)* How did political and cultural nationalism grow in Latin America? *(Latin Americans began to reject European political ideas and European cultural influences, in favor of more indigenous Latin American ideas.)* Did the Good Neighbor Policy support or undermine nationalism in Latin America? *(It supported it.)*

English Language Proficiency Standards

Reading 4.G.4 Read "Nationalism Spreads in Latin America" aloud to students. Then have students complete the activities below based on their English proficiency level.

Beginning Read "Economic Nationalism" aloud. Model taking notes on the content by stopping whenever you need to write down a key idea or word. Write and display the notes for students to see.

Intermediate Reread "Economic Nationalism" and "Political Nationalism" aloud to students. Then have students work together in small groups to take notes on these two subsections and debate which pieces of information are important enough to be included in the groups' notes. Circulate among students and offer help as needed.

Advanced Have students work with a partner to take notes on "Nationalism Spreads in Latin America." When partners are finished taking notes, have them review their notes and make corrections.

Advanced High Have students take notes on "Nationalism Spreads in Latin America." Have them review their notes and make corrections. Then have students turn to a partner and share and compare their notes on the text.

Topic 17 Lesson 1

SYNTHESIZE

Online Project the **Digital Activity: Mexico's Revolutionary Leaders**. Have students take 5 minutes to sketch out and complete the graphic organizer on their own paper. Then divide the class into small groups, and have each group discuss members' responses. Remind students to consider what they read in the digital texts and what they learned in the interactive activities. Instruct students to record any details they missed on their individual graphic organizers. Fill in the projected graphic organizer as a class.

DEMONSTRATE

Online Assign the **Digital Lesson Quiz** for this lesson if you haven't already done so. Students will be offered automatic remediation or enrichment based on their score.

Post the following to the class on the Discussion Board:

Identify Cause and Effect Have students make a two-column chart labeled *Causes* and *Effects*. Ask: What were the causes and effects of economic nationalism in Latin America? *(Cause: Prices of exports decreased while prices of imports increased as a result of World War I and the Great Depression, leading to economic decline in Latin America. Effect: Wealth was unequally distributed, holding back economic development.)*

Identify Main Ideas How did the relationship between Latin America and the United States change during the first three decades of the twentieth century? What were the effects of these changes? *(In the 1910s and 1920s, the United States regularly interfered in Latin American affairs. The relationship between Latin American countries and the United States deteriorated. In the 1930s, President Franklin Roosevelt decided to improve relations by passing the Good Neighbor Policy.)*

Topic Inquiry

Have students continue their investigations for the Topic Inquiry.

Under the **Good Neighbor Policy,** the United States agreed to stop interfering in the affairs of Latin American nations. The United States withdrew troops stationed in Haiti and Nicaragua and lifted the Platt Amendment, which had limited Cuban independence.

When Mexico nationalized its oil industry in 1938, Roosevelt resisted demands by some Americans to intervene. The Good Neighbor policy survived until 1945 when global tensions led the United States to intervene once again in the region.

? SYNTHESIZE How did political and cultural nationalism grow in Latin America?

ELPS **ELPS 4.G.4** Read and take notes on *Nationalism Spreads in Latin America.*

ASSESSMENT

1. **Identify Central Ideas** How did Mexican artists express cultural nationalism?
2. **Identify Cause and Effect** What caused many Mexicans to struggle for change in the early 1900s?
3. **Identify Central Issues** How did nationalism affect Latin America?
4. **Assess Credibility** How did the PRI fulfill some goals of the Mexican Revolution but not others?
5. **Cite Evidence** What role did the United States play after World War I and during the Mexican Revolution? Cite evidence to support your response.

The World Between the Wars  740 17.1 Revolution and Nationalism in Latin America

Assessment

1. They painted murals that reflected their culture and history and portrayed the struggles of the Mexican people.
2. The middle and lower classes, along with some elites, started a revolution to fundamentally change their government.
3. It led to the development of domestic industry, the nationalization of foreign-owned business, rejection of liberalism, authoritarian regimes, and a resurgence of cultural pride.
4. The PRI distributed some land more fairly, supported labor, and nationalized natural resources. It did not support democracy.
5. The United States continued to act as the international policeman and intervened to restore order when it felt its interests were threatened. For example, in 1916, the U.S. army invaded Mexico after Pancho Villa killed Americans in New Mexico.

Answers

Synthesize *Latin Americans began to reject European political ideas and European cultural influences in favor of more indigenous Latin American ideas.*

17.2 During the early 1900s, more and more Africans felt the impact of colonial rule. European nations exploited, or took advantage, of their colonies to produce profits for the parent country. Although the peoples of Africa had long tried to resist foreign imperialism, calls for change spread, fueling new nationalist movements.

>> Throughout Africa, Europeans operated mines and paid Africans low wages to work in them. Here, South Africans are working in a diamond mine owned by a Dutch company.

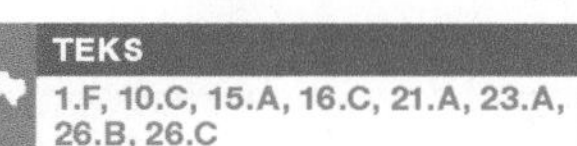

Interactive Flipped Video

Topic 17 Lesson 2

Nationalist Movements in Africa and the Middle East

Nationalist Movements in Africa and the Middle East

TEKS
1.F, 10.C, 15.A, 16.C, 21.A, 23.A, 26.B, 26.C

>> Objectives

Explain how Africans resisted colonial rule.

Describe the rise of nationalism in Africa.

Describe how Turkey and Persia modernized.

Understand how the mandate system contributed to Arab nationalism and to conflict between Jews and Arabs.

>> Key Terms

apartheid
Pan-Africanism
Marcus Garvey
négritude movement
Asia Minor
Atatürk
Reza Khan
Pan-Arabism
Balfour Declaration

Africans Protest Colonial Rule

Exploitation of African Colonies European governments expected their colonies to be profitable. To do so, they exploited the mineral resources of Africa, sending raw materials to feed European factories. In Kenya and Rhodesia, white settlers forced Africans off the best land. Also in Kenya, the British made all Africans carry identification cards, pay a tax, and live or travel only in certain areas.

Everywhere, farmers were forced to work on European-run plantations or in mines to earn money to pay taxes. Those farmers who kept their own land had to grow cash crops, like cotton, for the benefit of the colonizers instead of food. This led to famines in some regions. Increasingly, African people lost their self-sufficiency and became dependent on European goods.

Protesting Imperialism During World War I, more than one million Africans had fought on behalf of their colonial rulers. Many had hoped that their service would lead to more rights and opportunities. Instead,

www.PearsonTexas.com Access your Digital Lesson.

Aa Vocabulary Builder

1. Have students pronounce the following academic vocabulary terms in this lesson and clarify the part of speech. For difficult or polysyllabic words, break them into syllables and pronounce them with the students.
2. Explain what the word means in common "student-friendly" language using synonyms and antonyms when possible. Provide concrete examples to clarify the meaning, and rephrase the example.

assert: maintain or defend

advocated: supported or favored

CONNECT

Preview Have students preview the **Lesson Objectives** and the list of **Key Terms**.

Students can also preview all the **Key Terms** and **Academic Vocabulary** using the **Interactive Reading Notepad** on the digital course or preview a summary of the lesson in the **Reading and Note Taking Study Guide**.

Online Use the **Editable Presentation** found on the digital course to present the main ideas for this lesson.

Start Up Activity

On June 28, 1919, the Treaty of Versailles that ended World War I was signed. Germany and other defeated nations had no say in the peace treaty that, among other things, forced them to surrender their lands in Africa and the Middle East. However, those lands were not granted independence as the people there had hoped. Instead, they were placed under the control of Allied nations.

Remember what you learned about World War I. Then write one prediction based on these questions: How will the people who thought they would gain independence react to foreign control? What future problems might result from these actions? *(Sample responses: They will fight to rule themselves. Conflicts between the people who fought for independence may result after they have won their freedom from foreign rulers because rival groups may claim the same lands.)*

Online You can also project the **Start Up Activity** from the course.

INVESTIGATE

Have students read the section using the **Reading and Note Taking Study Guide** to help them take notes and understand the text as they read.

Africans Protest Colonial Rule

More than one million Africans fought in World War I. When the Axis powers lost the war, people in the African colonies thought that their service in the war would lead to their gaining more rights. This did not happen. Many Africans began protesting colonial rule and fighting to gain independence.

Topic 17 Lesson 2

Online Project the **Interactive Map: African Resistance to Colonial Rule**. First, point out the key and have students identify German colonies that were given to other European powers. Then, look at each colony separately. Have students identify the different ways people resisted colonial rule. *(squatting on land, holding protests, forming labor unions, developing political organizations)*

ACTIVE CLASSROOM

Ask students to use the Rank It strategy to rank the examples of resistance in the order of their effectiveness. Have students provide a justification for the decisions they made. Then have students discuss their ideas with a partner. Finally, take a poll to see if there are any disagreements about the ranking.

Guided Reading and Discussion

Ask students to describe the conditions in colonial Africa during the early 1900s. Record their ideas. *(Sample response: The conditions for black Africans were extremely bad. They lived on the worst land and held the lowest-paying jobs. They were segregated from whites and had no economic or political control.)* Then have them review the list and describe ways that Africans responded to these conditions. Ask: How did colonial abuses and African resistance play out in South Africa? *(Sample response: Whites instituted a repressive system of segregation called apartheid. Black South Africans resisted by forming a political party to protest apartheid by legal means.)*

>> Opposition to imperialism grew among Africans in the 1920s and 1930s. In 1929, Ibo market women in Nigeria demanded a voice in decisions that affected their markets. The "Women's War" soon became a full-fledged revolt.

Interactive Map

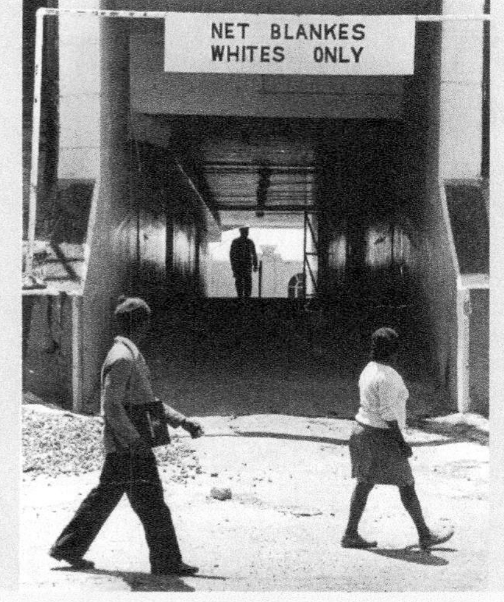

>> Beginning in 1931, laws were passed barring black South Africans from living, working, or owning land in areas designated for whites. Whites eventually controlled more than 80 percent of the land.

the situation after World War I remained mostly the same or even worsened.

Many Western-educated Africans criticized the injustice of imperial rule. Although they had trained for professional careers, the best jobs went to Europeans.

Inspired by President Woodrow Wilson's call for self-determination, Africans condemned the colonial system that excluded them from controlling their own lands. During the 1920s and 1930s, a new generation of leaders proud of their unique heritage struggled to restore Africa for Africans. Protests and opposition to imperialism multiplied. Some of this new generation turned to socialism or the writings of Marx and Lenin.

While large-scale revolts were rare, protests were common. In Kenya, the Kikuyu people protested the loss of their land to white settlers and denounced forced labor and heavy taxes. In the 1920s, Ibo women in Niberia revolted against British policies that threatened their rights. The British eventually ended the "Women's War" with gunfire.

A Policy of Segregation in South Africa Between 1910 and 1940, whites strengthened their grip on South Africa. They imposed a system of racial segregation to ensure white economic, political, and social supremacy. New laws, for example, restricted better-paying jobs in mines to whites only.

Blacks were pushed into low-paid, less-skilled work. South African blacks had to carry passes at all times. They were evicted from the best land and forced to live on crowded "reserves," which were located in dry, infertile areas.

Other laws chipped away at the rights of blacks. In one South African province, educated blacks who owned property had been allowed to vote in local elections. In 1936, the government abolished that right. The system of segregation would become even stricter after 1948, when **apartheid**(uh PAHR tayt), a policy of rigid racial segregation, became law.

Yet South Africa was also home to a vital nationalist movement. African Christian churches and African-run newspapers demanded rights for black South Africans. In 1912, they formed a political party, later called the African National Congress (ANC), to protest unfair laws and demand a change to South Africa's white government. Their efforts had no immediate effect, but the ANC did build a framework for political action in later years.

IDENTIFY CAUSE AND EFFECT How did Africans think that fighting on behalf of their colonial rulers during World War I would impact their lives?

D Differentiate Challenge/Gifted Have students further research one of the events or people featured in the interactive map and write a short newspaper article or blog post about their topic. Have students share their articles or posts.

Answers

Identify Cause and Effect *They thought they would be granted more rights and opportunities as a reward for their service.*

A Rising Tide of African Nationalism

In the 1920s, a movement known as Pan-Africanism began to nourish the nationalist spirit and strengthen resistance. **Pan-Africanism** emphasized the unity of Africans and the people of African descent worldwide. Among its most inspiring leaders was Jamaica-born **Marcus Garvey.** He preached a forceful, appealing message of "Africa for Africans" and demanded an end to colonial rule. Garvey's ideas influenced a new generation of African and African American leaders.

The Pan-African Congress African American scholar and activist W.E.B. DuBois (doo BOYS) organized the first Pan-African Congress in 1919. It met in Paris, where the Allies were holding their peace conference.

Delegates from African colonies, the West Indies, and the United States called on the Paris peacemakers to approve a charter of rights for Africans and an end to colonialism. Although the Western powers ignored their demands, the Pan-African Congress established cooperation among African and African American leaders.

Writers Celebrate African Culture A literary movement further awakened nationalism and self-confidence among Africans. French-speaking writers from West Africa and the Caribbean who were living in Paris founded the **négritude movement.** Writers of the négritude movement expressed pride in their African roots and culture and protested colonial rule. Their work often transcended their time and place to convey universal themes, such as the human desire for freedom and dignity.

The best known writer of the négritude movement was the Senegalese poet Léopold Senghor. Senghor celebrated Africa's rich cultural heritage. He fostered African pride by rejecting the negative views of Africa spread by colonial rulers. Later, Senghor would take an active role in Senegal's drive to independence, and he would serve as its first president in 1960.

Independence for Egypt African nationalism brought little political change, except to Egypt. During World War I, Egyptians had been forced to provided food and workers to help Britain. Simmering resistance to British rule flared as the war ended. Western-educated officials, peasants, landowners, Christians, and Muslims united behind the Wafd (WAHFT) party, which launched strikes and protests.

In 1922 Britain finally agreed to Egyptian independence. In fact, British troops stayed in Egypt to guard the Suez Canal and to back up the Egyptian

>> Jamaican Marcus Garvey traveled to New York City to spread his message designed to inspire pride in African culture. Here, he rides through the Harlem streets in a parade after meeting with delegates from 25 countries.

>> Léopold Senghor inspired many writers of the négritude movement, including Birago Diop and Mongo Beti. He was admired throughout the world as a writer and statesman.

Interactive Gallery

The Rising Tide of African Nationalism

In the 1920s, Pan-Africanism strengthened the nationalist movement and resistance to colonial rule. Leaders like Marcus Garvey and W. E. B. DuBois led movements to improve the rights of Africans.

Online Project the **Interactive Gallery: Writers of the Négritude Movement**. Discuss the négritude movement. The movement developed during the 1930s and continued into the 1950s. Writers protested the mistreatment of Africa and Africans by colonial powers. The writers' work inspired a sense of pride and self-confidence in Africans and strengthened nationalist movements. Their writings transcended their time, however. Long after the end of colonialism, they continue to inspire pride in African cultural achievements and convey universal themes such as the desire of all people for freedom and respect.

ACTIVE CLASSROOM

Ask students to reflect on the négritude movement and design a piece of "Wallpaper" that encapsulates key learnings about the movement. Wallpaper should be posted in the classroom so students can take a gallery/"wisdom" walk and note what others have written/illustrated. Suggest that they jot down ideas that occur to them.

Key Terms

Ask students to find the key term **Pan-Africanism** in the text and explain its meaning. Ask students to predict how Marcus Garvey's idea of an "Africa for Africans" would strengthen the spirit of nationalism within Africa.

Guided Reading and Discussion

Compare Remind students that Egyptians held protests, strikes, and riots after World War I. They finally won independence from Britain in 1922. How did Egyptian nationalists' tactics compare to those of nationalists in South Africa? *(Many young Egyptian nationalists joined the Muslim Brotherhood. In South Africa, the ANC tried to fight injustice using protest and the political system.)*

D Differentiate On-Level Obtain copies of the poem "Prayer to the Masks" by Leopold Senghor. To help students better understand how the négritude movement inspired pride in African accomplishments, pass out the poem. Divide the class into small groups and assign a section of the poem to each one. Have groups discuss their selection, particularly focusing on how Africans might have felt about it. Then have them present their ideas to the class.

Modernization of Turkey and Persia

After World War I, Arab lands were divided among Allied nations. Led by Mustafa Kemal—who later called himself Atatürk—the Turks resisted Western control and fought to build a modern nation. Persian nationalists resented the British and Russians. Inspired by Atatürk's success, they fought to change their government and finally overthrew the shah and began to modernize the nation.

Guided Reading and Discussion

Treaty of Sèvres Remind students that the Ottoman sultan signed the Treaty of Sèvres in 1920. Ask: What were the terms of the treaty, and why did the sultan sign it? What was the significance of this treaty? *(The Ottoman empire was near collapse. The treaty forced the sultan to give up some land in Asia Minor to a number of Allied countries, including Greece.)*

Identify Cause and Effect What were some long-term results of the treaty? *(Greek forces landed in Smyrna to claim their land. Turk nationalists fought to remove foreign influences and change their government. They overthrew the sultan and defeated the Greeks. Then a new treaty was signed that called for more than a million Greeks to leave Turkey. Nearly 400,000 Turks left Greece.)*

Discuss the reforms made by Atatürk. Ask students what possible effects they had, why he might have made these reforms, and what his reforms are modeled on. Ask students what arguments people might have made against some of these reforms.

monarch, King Faud. Displeased with this state of affairs, during the 1930s many young Egyptians joined an organization called the Muslim Brotherhood. This group fostered a broad Islamic nationalism that rejected Western culture and denounced corruption in the Egyptian government.

? SYNTHESIZE How did the négritude movement reflect the history of African culture, and how did this affect Africans?

Modernization of Turkey and Persia

Nationalist movements greatly affected the Middle East in the aftermath of World War I. The defeated Ottoman empire was near collapse in 1918. Its Arab lands were divided between Britain and France. However, in **Asia Minor,** a peninsula in western Asia between the Black Sea and the Mediterranean Sea, ethnic Turks resisted Western control and fought to build a modern nation.

Atatürk Takes Power In 1920, the Ottoman sultan reluctantly signed the Treaty of Sèvres, in which the empire lost its Arab and North African lands. The sultan also had to give up some land in Asia Minor to a number of Allied countries, including Greece. A Greek force landed in the city of Smyrna (now Izmir) to assert Greece's claims.

>> Atatürk stands before a crowd, pointing to letters of the Roman alphabet. He introduced the western alphabet to Turkey as one of his many modernizing reforms.

Turkish nationalists, led by the determined and energetic Mustafa Kemal, overthrew the sultan, defeated the Greeks, and declared Turkey a republic. Kemal later took the name **Atatürk** (ah tah TURK), meaning "father of the Turks." He negotiated a new treaty. Among other provisions, the treaty called for about 1.3 million Greeks to leave Turkey, while some 400,000 Turks left Greece.

Westernization of Turkey Between 1923 and his death in 1938, Atatürk forced through an ambitious program of radical reforms. His goals were to modernize Turkey along Western lines and to separate religion from government.

To achieve these goals, Atatürk mandated that Islamic traditions in several fields be replaced with Western alternatives. For example, he replaced Islamic law with laws based on a European model, replaced the Arabic alphabet with the Latin alphabet, and forced people to wear Western-style clothing. Under Atatürk, state schools replaced religious schools.

Atatürk's government encouraged industrial expansion. The government built railroads, set up factories, and hired westerners to advise on how to make Turkey economically independent.

To achieve his reforms, Atatürk ruled with an iron hand. To many Turks, he was a hero who was transforming Turkey into a strong, modern power. Some Turkish Muslims, however, rejected Atatürk's dictatorial powers and his formation of a secular government. To them, the Quran and Islamic customs provided all the guidance needed.

Persian Nationalism and Reform The success of Atatürk's reforms inspired nationalists in neighboring Persia (present-day Iran). Persian nationalists greatly resented the British and Russians, who had won spheres of influence over Persia in 1907. In 1925, an ambitious army officer, **Reza Khan,** overthrew the shah. He set up his own dynasty, with himself as shah.

Like Atatürk, Reza Khan rushed to modernize Persia and make it fully independent. He built factories, roads, and railroads and strengthened the army. He forced Persians to wear Western clothing and set up modern, secular schools. In addition, he moved to replace Islamic law with secular law and encouraged women to take part in public life. The shah had the support of wealthy urban Persians. However, Muslim religious leaders fiercely condemned his efforts to introduce Western ways.

The World Between the Wars 744 17.2NationalistMovementsinAfricaandtheMiddleEast

Answers

Synthesize *Through their works, négritude writers and artists expressed pride in their African roots and protested colonial rule. This awakened self-confidence in many Africans and inspired some to take an active role in the drive toward independence.*

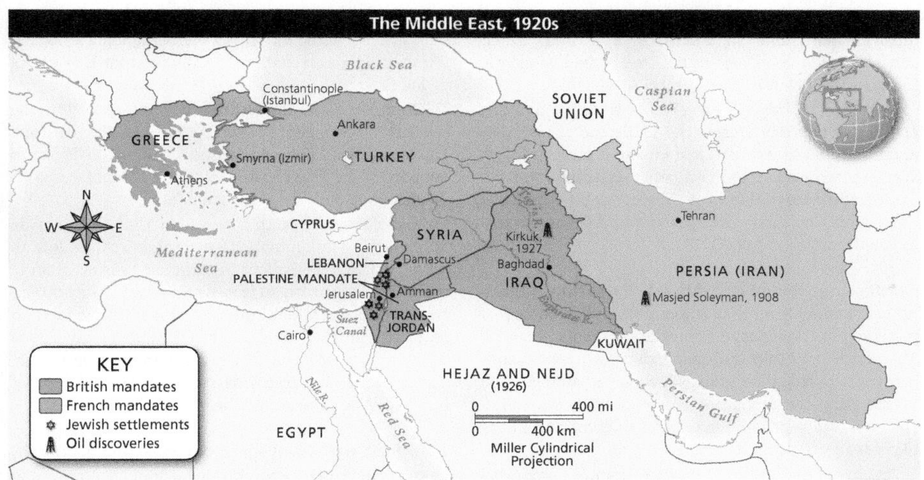

>> **Analyze Maps** Population movement, the Treaty of Versailles, and foreign influences changed the Middle East after World War I. How did foreign influences affect the Middle East?

Reza Khan also persuaded the British company that controlled Persia's oil industry to give Persia a larger share of the profits and insisted that Persian workers be hired at all levels of the company. In the decades ahead, oil would become a major factor in Persia's economy and foreign policy.

INFER Why did Muslim religious leaders disapprove of Reza Khan's reforms?

Nationalism and Conflict in the Middle East

After World War I, the vast Ottoman empire was partitioned into Turkey and several new nations that would make up the modern Arab world. Several Arab lands sat above large oil reserves, giving them global importance in a world that was increasingly dependent on gasoline-powered engines. Instead of granting independence to the Arab states carved out of the Ottoman empire, European powers turned them into mandates under their control.

The Rise of Pan-Arabism Partly in response to foreign influence, Arab nationalism grew after World War I. One form of Arab nationalism was **Pan-Arabism.** This nationalist movement was built on the shared heritage of Arabs who lived in lands from the Arabian Peninsula to North Africa.

Today, this area includes Syria, Jordan, Iraq, Egypt, Algeria, and Morocco. Pan-Arabism emphasized the common history and language of Arabs and recalled the golden age of Arab civilization. The movement sought to free Arabs from foreign domination and unite them in their own state.

The Pan-Arab movement however, faced obstacles. Arabs generally were not united. They tended to identify with their particular tribe, sect, religion, or region rather than with a single, unified nation-state.

European-Controlled Mandates During World War I, some Arab leaders had helped the Allies against the Ottoman empire. These leaders expected to create their own kingdoms after the war. Even before the revolt, however, France and Britain had secretly agreed that they would take over the Arab lands within the Ottoman empire.

The Treaty of Versailles gave control of German and Ottoman colonies to various Allied nations in the form of mandates.The mandates were authorized by the League of Nations.

The former Ottoman territories in the Middle East were put under the control of two Allies. France was

Nationalism and Conflict in the Middle East

The Middle East underwent many changes after World War I. Two of the biggest changes were the discovery of large oil fields and the creation of European-controlled mandates in Syria, Lebanon, Palestine, and Iraq by the Treaty of Versailles. These foreign influences helped give rise to a nationalistic movement called Pan-Arabism and caused long-standing conflicts between the Arabs and Jews in the Palestine Mandate.

Analyze Images

Direct students' attention to the map The Middle East, 1920s. Ask students what this map shows. *(It shows the land that was mandated to Britain and France; the location of Jewish settlements; the population movement of Greeks and Turks; oil discoveries.)* How does this map help you understand the conditions in the Middle East in the 1920s? *(The map shows the many changes the area underwent—different groups were migrating, Britain and France took control of Arab lands, oil was discovered. All of these changes caused instability and tension.)* Where are the Jewish settlements located? Why do you think there are so many Jewish settlements? *(The settlements are located in the Palestine Mandate. The Jews believed the land they called Zion was their ancestral homeland. They wanted to return to it and also escape anti-Semitism in Europe.)*

D Differentiate Challenge/Gifted Have students find news articles about current conflicts or problems in the Middle East. Ask them to consider whether any of these problems stem from events that occurred after World War I. Have them write a short essay expressing their opinion. Allow students time to share their findings with the class.

Answers

Analyze Maps *Britain and France were given mandates in the Middle East to control. Oil was discovered in Iraq and the Palestine Mandate, which was controlled by the British.*

Infer *He forced Persians to wear Western clothing and set up modern, secular schools. In addition, he moved to replace Islamic law with secular law and encouraged women to take part in public life. His changes reduced the influence of Islam and Muslim leaders in Persian life.*

Topic 17 Lesson 2

Guided Reading and Discussion

Discuss the goals of Pan-Arabism. *(to unite Arabs in their own state)* Then ask: How did the Paris Peace Conference affect Arabs? *(Instead of Arabs gaining the independence they had been promised, some of their lands were made mandates of European powers.)* How did the Balfour Declaration further undermine Pan-Arabism? *(The Balfour Declaration encouraged Jewish settlement in Palestine, which was a part of the Arab homeland. The subsequent settlement further weakened Pan-Arab goals, and touched off a conflict that still rages today.)*

given mandates in Syria and Lebanon, and Britain received mandates in Palestine and Iraq. Later, Britain gave a large part of the Palestinian Mandate, TransJordan, to an Arab ally, King Abdullah.

Arabs felt betrayed by the West—a feeling that has endured to this day. During the 1920s and 1930s, their anger erupted in frequent protests and revolts against Western imperialism. A major center of turmoil was the British Mandate of Palestine. There, Arab nationalists increasingly clashed with Jewish nationalists, known as Zionists.

Conflicting Promises About Palestine Since Roman times, Jews in the diaspora had dreamed of returning to their ancient homeland of Israel. In 1897, Theodor Herzl (HURT sul) responded to growing anti-Semitism, or prejudice against Jewish people, in Europe by founding the modern Zionist political movement. His goal was to reestablish a Jewish homeland in the region called Palestine.

In tsarist Russia, brutal pogroms prompted thousands of Jews to migrate to Palestine. They joined the small Jewish community that had lived there since biblical times.

During World War I, the Allies made two vague and conflicting sets of promises that greatly impacted Arab and Jewish nationalists. First, they allowed Arabs to believe they would have their own kingdoms in former Ottoman lands, including in the area that Europeans called Palestine.

Then, in 1917, the British attempted to win the support of European Jews by issuing the **Balfour Declaration.** The declaration affirmed Britain's support for the idea of establishing "a national home for Jewish people" in the Palestine Mandate.

Many Jews took this to mean that Britain was announcing its intention to establish a Jewish homeland, but the Balfour Declaration stopped short of making this promise. In fact, it also noted that "nothing shall be done which may prejudice the civil and religious rights of existing non-Jewish communities in Palestine." Most of those communities were Arab. These conflicting promises set the stage for conflict between Arab and Jewish nationalists.

A Bitter Struggle Begins From 1919 to 1940, tens of thousands of Arabs and Jews immigrated to the Palestine Mandate. Both the Zionist movement and the effects of anti-Semitism in Europe encouraged Jewish immigration. Despite great hardships, Jewish settlers set up factories, built new towns, and established farming communities. At the same time, the Arab population almost doubled. Some were immigrants from nearby lands. As a result, the population of the Palestine Mandate included a changing mix of settlers. The Jewish population, which was less than 60,000 in 1919, grew to about 400,000 in 1936, while the Muslim population increased from about 568,000 in 1919 to about 1 million in 1940.

At first, some Arabs welcomed the money and modern technical skills that the newcomers brought with them. But as more Jews moved to Palestine Mandate, tensions between the two groups developed.

Jewish organizations tried to purchase as much land as they could, while many Arabs sought to slow down or stop Jewish immigration. Arabs attacked Jewish settlements, hoping to discourage settlers. The Jewish settlers established their own military defense force. For the rest of the century and beyond, Arabs and Jews fought over the land.

>> This photograph shows Jewish immigrants arriving in Haifa in Palestine Mandate. Tens of thousands of Jews immigrated to Palestine Mandate in the hopes of building a Jewish homeland.

IDENTIFY CAUSE AND EFFECT Why did the Palestine Mandate become a center of conflict after World War I?

History Background

Kibbutzim During the early 1900s, many Jewish settlers in Palestine wanted to develop a new way of life. They organized collective farms, called *kibbutzim*. Members shared belongings, labor, and proceeds. The settlements were communal, with cooking done in a central dining hall. Children were raised in a home, separate from their parents, so that women could join the kibbutzim workforce. Together, these settlers, called *kibbutzniks*, introduced new techniques of drainage and irrigation. They grew grain, fruit trees, and vegetables, and raised chickens and cows for meat. They planted cypress and palm trees to provide shade from the desert sun. Their efforts later helped the nation of Israel become a world leader in agricultural production.

Answers

Identify Cause and Effect *The Allies gave conflicting promises. The Balfour Declaration supported the idea of a national home for Jews. Some people saw this as Britain planning to enforce this. The Arabs were promised self-rule and believed they would be given the land they called Palestine. As more Jews moved to the Palestine Mandate, tensions grew.*

ASSESSMENT

1. **Synthesize** What significance does the phrase "Africa for Africans" have?
2. **Draw Conclusions** How did nationalism contribute to changes in Africa and the Middle East following World War I?
3. **Identify Central Ideas** How did Africans resist colonial rule?
4. **Compare and Contrast** What are the similarities in the way Atatürk and Reza Khan modernized Turkey and Persia and changed their governments?
5. **Identify Cause and Effect** How did the mandate system affect the Middle East?

SYNTHESIZE

Online Project the **Digital Activity: Nationalist Movements in Africa and the Middle East**. Have students use the Think-Pair-Share strategy to answer the questions in the activity. Ask them to take 5 minutes to write down some brief answers to the questions. Then discuss their responses as a class.

Quick Write Have students read the quotation again and think of a question they would like to ask Jomo Kenyatta or one of the other nationalists they read about. Have them think about what they learned about why people wanted to change their government. Then have students write how they think the person would respond. Discuss their questions and answers as a class.

DEMONSTRATE

Online Assign the **Digital Lesson Quiz** for this lesson if you haven't already done so. Students will be offered automatic remediation or enrichment based on their score.

Post the following to the class on the Discussion Board:

Identify Main Ideas Describe the rise of nationalism in Africa and the Middle East. In what ways did people fight to change their governments?

Identify Cause and Effect How did World War I affect Africa and the Middle East? How did the effects contribute to nationalism and conflict?

Topic Inquiry

Have students continue their investigations for the Topic Inquiry.

Assessment

1. It was used to encourage nationalism and an end to colonial rule, and it united Africans in their desire for independence.
2. It strengthened people's will to resist colonial rule in Africa. It helped Africans take pride in African culture. It also led to Egypt's independence, modernization in Turkey and Persia, and conflict in the Palestine Mandate.
3. They squatted on European plantations and formed labor unions and other organizations to protest colonial rule.
4. Both Atatürk and Reza Khan encouraged industrial expansion, forced people to wear Western clothing, replaced Islamic laws with more secular, Western laws, and set up modern schools. In Persia, Reza Khan also strengthened the army.
5. The mandate system gave control of Ottoman land to European powers. France was given mandates in Syria and Lebanon; Britain was given mandates in Palestine and Iraq. The Palestine Mandate contributed to Arab nationalism and to conflict between Jews and Arabs.

Topic 17 Lesson 3

India Seeks Self-Rule

CONNECT

Preview Have students preview the **Lesson Objectives** and the list of **Key Terms**.

Students can also preview all the **Key Terms** and **Academic Vocabulary** using the **Interactive Reading Notepad** on the digital course or preview a summary of the lesson in the **Reading and Note Taking Study Guide**.

Online Use the **Editable Presentation** found on the digital course to present the main ideas for this lesson.

Start Up Activity

Present this quote from Mohandas Gandhi. "Passive resistance . . . is matchless. It is superior to the force of arms. How, then, can it be considered only a weapon of the weak? Physical force men are strangers to the courage that is requisite in a passive resister. Do you believe that a coward can ever disobey a law that he dislikes?"

Why does Gandhi say that passive resistance requires more courage than violence? *(It is harder to believe in yourself and maintain control when faced with violence or imprisonment. It is human nature, or basic instinct, to fight back when attacked.)*

How can passive resistance be a weapon to fight for independence? *(The other person may feel ashamed of using violence against someone who does not resist. It makes the other person think about his or her actions and recognize that force is not always the answer or necessary.)*

Online You can also project the **Start Up Activity** from the course.

INVESTIGATE

Have students read the section using the **Reading and Note Taking Study Guide** to help them take notes and understand the text as they read.

India's Struggle for Independence Begins

The National Congress party began pressing for self-rule after 1885. However, after World War I and the 1919 Amritsar massacre, the Congress party and other Indians were finally convinced that they needed full independence.

>> The Salt March, shown here, began at Gandhi's ashram in Sabermati. When Gandhi reached the shore, he picked up a handful of salt and claimed he was shaking the British empire's foundation.

Interactive Flipped Video

17.3 **Indians had long struggled to end British control. Since 1885, the Indian National Congress party, called the Congress party, had pressed for self-rule within the British empire but had not yet called for full independence.**

TEKS
1.F, 21.A, 21.C, 22.E

>> Objectives

Explain the impact of World War I and the Amritsar massacre on Indian nationalism.

Evaluate the ideas of Mohandas Gandhi.

Analyze how Gandhi led resistance to political oppression in India.

>> Key Terms

Mohandas Gandhi
Amritsar massacre
ahimsa
civil disobedience
untouchable
boycott
Muhammad Ali Jinnah

India Seeks Self-Rule

India's Struggle for Independence Begins

During World War I, more than a million Indians had served overseas. Under pressure from Indian nationalists, the British promised Indians greater self-government in return for their service.

However, when the fighting ended, Britain proposed only a few minor reforms. The reforms did little to change the system of bureaucratic rule. The British continued to have little regard for Indian beliefs and customs. Indian frustrations continued to mount, and many began calling for independence from British rule.

A New Leader Emerges Congress party members were mostly middle-class, Western-educated elite who had little in common with the masses of Indian peasants. Then a new leader named **Mohandas Gandhi** emerged and was able to unite Indians across class lines. Admiring Indians came to call him Mahatma, or "Great Soul."

Gandhi came from a middle-class Hindu family. At age 19, he went to England to study law. Then, like many Indians, Gandhi went to South Africa. For 20 years, Gandhi fought laws that discriminated against Indians in South Africa. In his struggle against injustice, he began to develop a tactic of nonviolent, or passive, resistance. He called it satyagraha, or "soul force."

PEARSON realize. www.PearsonTexas.com Access your Digital Lesson.

748

Aa Vocabulary Builder

1. Have students pronounce the following academic vocabulary term in this lesson and clarify the part of speech. For difficult or polysyllabic words, break them into syllables and pronounce them with the students.
2. Explain what the word means in common "student-friendly" language using synonyms and antonyms when possible. Provide concrete examples to clarify the meaning, and rephrase the example.

discriminate: to treat differently because of prejudice

In 1915, Gandhi returned to India and was hailed as a national hero for his work in Africa. Gandhi joined the Congress party, and began to campaign for the rights of Indian workers. He was not, however, calling for Indian independence. His views changed thanks to a tragic event in 1919.

The Muslim League Other leaders also worked for Indian independence. **Muhammad Ali Jinnah** was one of the most influential leaders of India's large Muslim population. He was a leader of the Muslim League, which was founded in 1906 to protect Muslim interests. Jinnah and others feared that the Congress Party was only looking out for Hindu interests. The Indian Congress Party, while made up primarily of Hindus, also had Muslim members.

In the early decades of the century, the Congress party and the Muslim League cooperated in working to achieve an independent India. As time passed, however, the two organizations began to diverge.

The Amritsar Massacre In 1919, the British passed the Rowlatt Acts, which allowed British officials to arrest and imprison any Indian citizen suspected of sedition, or urging people to disobey the government. These political prisoners could then be tried without a jury.

Gandhi opposed the act, which also threatened freedom of the press, and helped organize protests. When violence threatened, he called for an end to the protest campaign.

On April 13, 1919, a large but peaceful crowd of Indian protestors jammed into an enclosed field in Amritsar, a city in northern India. The British commander, General Reginald Dyer, had banned public meetings, but many in the crowd were unaware of the order. As Indian leaders spoke, Dyer ordered his troops to open fire on the unarmed crowd, killing nearly 400 people and wounding more than 1,100.

The **Amritsar massacre** was a turning point for many Indians, including Gandhi. Up to that point, Gandhi had hoped to win partial self-rule for India. After Amritsar, he was convinced that India must seek full independence.

IDENTIFY CAUSE AND EFFECT What motivated the Indian independence movement after World War I?

>> **Analyze Images** Because the Jallian wala Bagh in Amritsar had only one entrance, demonstrators could not escape the gunfire. How does this painting help you understand the public's reaction to the massacre?

Interactive Chart

>> In 1913, Muhammad Ali Jinnah joined the Muslim League. Although he and Gandhi disagreed on many things, both believed that a political union between Muslims and Hindus was necessary for Indian independence.

Analyze Images

Direct students' attention to the painting of the Amritsar massacre from the text, "India's Struggle for Independence Begins." Explain that it began as a peaceful protest against the Rowlatt Acts. The massacre was a turning point for many people. What does this image show? How does it help you understand the event and why it caused many Indians to want full independence? *(It shows British soldiers shooting into a crowd. Hundreds of people lie on the ground. The massacre convinced many Indians that the British didn't care about their rights or their lives and gave them more incentive to want the British gone.)*

Guided Reading and Discussion

Recall What were the Rowlatt Acts? *(laws passed by the British government that allowed British officials to arrest and imprison any Indian citizen suspected of sedition)*

Draw Conclusions Why might these acts have been passed? *(Events after World War I sparked discontent and many protests. The British were probably trying to gain more control and stop Indians from protesting.)*

Identify Supporting Details Why did British Commander General Reginald Dyer order 50 soldiers to fire into the crowd at the Amritsar protest? *(He had banned public meetings. The crowd ignored this order. He ordered his soldiers to fire to disband the crowd.)*

Answers

Analyze Images *The painting shows the line of soldiers shooting into an unarmed group of protesters. The people are desperately trying to flee and are not fighting back. This would help convince people that the attack was unjust.*

Identify Cause and Effect *Many Indians had fought for Britain in World War I with the promise that they would be granted more self-government. After the war, however, Britain proposed only a few minor changes. This led many to believe that India needed to gain total independence.*

Gandhi's Philosophy of Civil Disobedience

Gandhi Takes a Stand

Gandhi became the leader of the Congress party in 1920. His words, actions, and ideas inspired people of all religions and backgrounds, and they helped to shift political thought.

Online Interactive Gallery: Influences of Gandhi Project the image gallery and explain that Gandhi's beliefs were inspired by different people and traditions. His actions and ideas influenced independence and civil rights leaders around the world. Ask: Are you familiar with any of these people and their work? Which of these people or traditions surprise you the most? Why?

ACTIVE CLASSROOM

Ask students to conduct a Conversation With History. Tell them to write down a question they would like to ask one of the people whom Gandhi influenced. Then ask students to write down how they think the person they chose would reply. Ask students to explain how they would respond in turn. Then tell them to share their questions and answers with a partner.

Key Terms

Ask students to find the key term **boycott** (in bold) in the text. Ask students to explain how boycotts worked during the struggle for civil rights in the United States during the 1950s and 1960s.

Guided Reading and Discussion

Draw Conclusions Have students work in groups to write a paragraph evaluating Gandhi's ideas and the ways he was able to shift political thought. Discuss their responses as a class.

Answers

Identify Central Ideas *He proposed using the power of love and nonviolent protest to change the hearts of the British. He based his ideas on the ancient Hindu belief of ahimsa, Christian teachings, Western democratic and nationalistic ideas, and the writings of Henry David Thoreau.*

Gandhi's Philosophy of Civil Disobedience

In 1921, Gandhi was elected president of the Congress party. He remained the dominant figure in Indian politics for more than twenty years. His words, actions, and ideas inspired Indians of all religious and ethnic backgrounds.

Nonviolent Protest Gandhi was horrified by the violence at Amritsar, but he also condemned Indian acts of violence in response to the massacre. Instead, he preached a philosophy of nonviolent protest that he had first begun to develop during his years in South Africa. His philosophy was based on the ancient Hindu and Jain doctrine of **ahimsa**(uh HIM sah), or nonviolence and reverence for all life. By using the power of love, Gandhi believed, people could convert even the worst wrongdoer to the right course of action. To fight against injustice, he advocated the use of nonviolent resistance. Hindu tradition also informed Gandhi's belief that all Indians regardless of religion had a common spiritual character and common interests.

Gandhi's philosophy reflected Western as well as Indian influences. He admired Christian teachings about love. He believed in the American philosopher Henry David Thoreau's ideas about **civil disobedience,** the refusal to obey unjust laws. Gandhi also embraced Western ideas of democracy and nationalism.

>> Gandhi taught his ways to people throughout India. Here, he speaks to harijan workers at his ashram, or spiritual retreat, in the village of Sevagram.

Interactive Gallery

Inspired by both Indian and Western ideas, Gandhi rejected the inequalities of the Indian caste system and fought hard to end the harsh treatment of **untouchables,** the lowest caste of Indian society. He called these outcasts Harijans, or "children of God." Gandhi also urged equal rights for all Indians, women as well as men.

Restoring National Pride Over the next two decades, Gandhi initiated a series of nonviolent actions against British rule. He called for Indians to **boycott,** or refuse to buy, British goods, especially cotton textiles. The move was designed to boost local Indian industries and help restore Indian pride. For centuries, India had produced fine textiles, which had declined under British rule. Gandhi wanted to rebuild such traditional industries.

He made the spinning wheel the symbol of the nationalist movement. In a symbolic move, he abandoned Western-style clothing for the *dhota,* the simple white garments traditionally worn by village Indians.

Through his own example, Gandhi inspired Indians to "get rid of our helplessness." When protests led to violent riots, Gandhi would fast, pray, and call on patriotic Indians to practice self control. His campaigns of civil disobedience attracted wide support, and his nonviolent protests caught the attention of the British government and the world.

IDENTIFY CENTRAL IDEAS What force did Gandhi propose using to free India from British colonial rule, and what was the basis for his ideas?

Gandhi Takes a Stand

To mobilize mass support, Gandhi decided to take a stand against the British salt monopoly, which he saw as a symbol of British oppression. Natural salt was available along the shore, and people had traditionally gotten their salt supplies by boiling seawater. But under colonial rule, the British claimed the sole right to produce and sell salt. By taxing those sales, they collected money to maintain their government in India.

The Salt March Early in 1930, Gandhi wrote to the British viceroy in India. He stated his intention to break the hated salt laws and condemned British rule as "a curse."

On March 12, 1930, Gandhi set out with 78 followers on a 240-mile march to the sea. As the tiny

English Language Proficiency Standards

ELPS 4.H.2 Read "Gandhi's Philosophy of Civil Disobedience" aloud. Have students complete one of the activities below based on their English proficiency level.

Beginning Have students draw what is read in the first paragraph. Retell what was read. Provide a glossary of challenging words as they read the next paragraph. Ask simple questions about the reading. If necessary, retell the text.

Intermediate Instruct students to read and visualize the section. Allow the use of bilingual dictionaries or other language supports. After each paragraph, help students retell what they read. Display important information.

Advanced Have students read and visualize the section. Have pairs explain what they read using bilingual dictionaries.

Advanced High Have students read and visualize the section. Have pairs share visualizations and write a summary to share with the class.

band passed through villages, crowds responded to Gandhi's message. By the time they reached the sea, the marchers numbered in the thousands.

On April 6, Gandhi waded into the surf and picked up a lump of sea salt by the edge of the water. He was soon arrested and jailed.

Still, Indians followed his lead. Coastal villagers started collecting salt and evaporating seawater to make it. Indians sold salt on city streets—and went to jail. As Gandhi's campaign gained force, tens of thousands of Indians were imprisoned.

World Opinion Shifts All around the world, newspapers criticized Britain's harsh reaction to the protests. Stories revealed how police brutally clubbed peaceful marchers who tried to occupy a government saltworks. "Not one of the marchers even raised an arm to fend off the blows," wrote an outraged American newspaper.

The Salt March embarrassed Britain, which prided itself on its democratic traditiions. Slowly, Gandhi's campaign forced Britain to hand over some power to Indians. Britain also agreed to meet other demands of the Congress party.

The Future of India In 1939, a new world war exploded. Britain outraged Indian leaders by postponing independence and bringing Indians into the war without consulting them. Angry nationalists launched a campaign of noncooperation and were jailed. Millions of Indians, however, did help Britain during World War II.

When the war ended in 1945, India's independence could no longer be delayed. As it neared, Muslim fears of the Hindu majority increased. Conflict between Hindus and Muslims would trouble the new nation in the years to come.

? ANALYZE INFORMATION How did the Salt March force Britain to respond to Indian demands?

ASSESSMENT

1. **Identify Cause and Effect** What impact did the Amritsar massacre have on the Indian independence movement?
2. **Draw Conclusions** Why was Gandhi able to unite Indians and shift political thought when earlier attempts had not succeeded?
3. **Identify Cause and Effect** How did Gandhi and the National Congress party work for independence in India?
4. **Analyze Information** What were Gandhi's key ideas? How did Gandhi implement these ideas in his fight against political oppression?
5. **Infer** How might fighting discrimination in South Africa have influenced Gandhi when he returned to India?

Topic 17 Lesson 3

SYNTHESIZE

Online Project the **Digital Activity: Causes and Effects of Events in the Indian Independence Movement**. Have students take 5 minutes to complete the organizer with the causes and effects of each event listed in the organizer. Then divide the class into small groups, and have each group discuss member responses. During this discussion, students should add any details they left out.

DEMONSTRATE

Online Assign the **Digital Lesson Quiz** for this lesson if you haven't already done so. Students will be offered automatic remediation or enrichment based on their score.

Post these questions to the class on the Discussion Board:

Identify Main Ideas Explain how Gandhi led the nationalist movement and the effect he had on people of many religions and beliefs. *(Gandhi led boycotts and nonviolent protests and resistance. His beliefs in love and reverence for all life inspired people around the world. Because his values embraced both Christian and Hindu traditions and ideas, he appealed to a variety of people.)*

Express Ideas Clearly Which of Gandhi's ideas and actions do you think were most effective, and why? *(His belief in civil disobedience and the Salt March were the most effective. The Salt March received international attention, which eventually forced Britain to grant some reforms.)*

Topic Inquiry

Have students continue their investigations for the Topic Inquiry.

Answers

Analyze Information *It attracted worldwide attention to Gandhi and India's cause. Many leaders and citizens were appalled by the violent way the British responded, which forced Britain to give Indians more rights.*

Assessment

1. The Amritsar massacre was a turning point that convinced many Indians that they must gain independence, not just a greater degree of self-rule. It also helped motivate Gandhi to get more involved.
2. Gandhi was able to gain support because of his personal character, the appeal of his beliefs, and his emphasis on equality.
3. Under Gandhi's leadership, Indians staged nonviolent protests, boycotts, and the Salt March. At first, Britain only made some concessions, but eventually it granted India independence.
4. He believed in ahimsa, or nonviolence; civil disobedience, the refusal to obey unjust laws; and democracy, or equal rights for all people. He called for Indians to boycott British goods; encouraged nonviolent civil disobedience; and led symbolic protests, including one against the salt monopoly.
5. Gandhi saw firsthand how black Africans and Indians were discriminated against. He saw how they fought for their rights. He most likely brought his experiences and ideas with him to India and was able to put them into practice to fight for independence from Britain.

Topic 17 Lesson 4

New Forces in China and Japan

CONNECT

Preview Have students preview the **Lesson Objectives** and the list of **Key Terms**.

Students can also preview all the **Key Terms** and **Academic Vocabulary** using the **Interactive Reading Notepad** on the digital course or preview a summary of the lesson in the **Reading and Note Taking Study Guide**.

Online Use the **Editable Presentation** found on the digital course to present the main ideas for this lesson.

Start Up Activity

Have students look at the map Japan's Expanding Empire on page 757. Ask students to review the map and answer these questions: Where is Manchuria (Manzhouguo) in relation to Japan? Where is Manchuria in relation to China? *(It is west of Japan, and in the northeast part of China.)* What natural resources might Japan gain by invading mainland Asia? *(Sample response: Japan could gain access to coal, petroleum, iron, copper, bauxite, and gold.)*

Discuss Why might the Japanese people have pushed for territorial expansion? *(Sample response: pressures from the Great Depression)* What natural resources did Japan lack? *(coal, petroleum, iron, copper, bauxite, and gold)*

Online You can also project the **Start Up Activity** from the course.

INVESTIGATE

Have students read the lesson using the **Reading and Note Taking Study Guide** to help them take notes and understand the text as they read.

Trouble in the Chinese Republic

The Republic of China was founded after the Qing dynasty fell in 1911. Nationalists like Sun Yixian wanted to rebuild China and make it a world power. China faced two challenges, however: internal conflict and foreign influence.

>> Mao was introduced to communist ideas while he was working at Peking University as a librarian's assistant. He later became the leader of the Chinese Communist Party.

Interactive Flipped Video

17.4 A new Chinese republic took shape after the fall of the Qing dynasty in 1911. Nationalists like Sun Yixian set the goal of "catching up and surpassing the powers, east and west." But that goal would remain a distant dream as China suffered the turmoil of civil war and foreign invasion.

TEKS
1.F, 12.C, 13.B

>> Objectives

Explain the key challenges faced by the Chinese republic in the early 1900s.

Analyze the struggle between nationalists and Communists in China.

Summarize the effects of liberal changes in Japan in the 1920s.

Describe the rise of extreme nationalism and militarism in Japan.

Describe the impact of the Japanese invasion of China.

>> Key Terms

Twenty-One Demands
May Fourth Movement
vanguard
Guomindang
Jiang Jieshi
Mao Zedong
Long March
ultranationalist
Manchuria
Hirohito

PEARSON realize www.PearsonTexas.com Access your Digital Lesson.

New Forces in China and Japan

Trouble in the Chinese Republic

Struggles for Power Sun Yixian, the "father of modern China," hoped to rebuild China on the Three Principles of the People—nationalism, democracy, and economic security for everyone. But he made little progress. One problem, he noted, was that the Chinese people felt more loyalty to families and clans than to the nation.

> Therefore, even though we have four hundred million people gathered together in one China, in reality they are just a heap of loose sand. Today we are the poorest and weakest nation in the world and occupy the lowest position in international affairs. Other men are the carving knife and serving dish, we are the fish and the meat.
>
> —Sun Yixian

752

Aa Vocabulary Builder

1. Have students pronounce the following academic vocabulary terms in this lesson and clarify the part of speech. For difficult or polysyllabic words, break them into syllables and pronounce them with the students.
2. Explain what the word means in common "student-friendly" language using synonyms and antonyms when possible. Provide concrete examples to clarify the meaning, and rephrase the example.

intellectual: involving the ability to reason or think clearly

faction: a group within a larger group

manipulated: influenced skillfully, often unfairly

In 1912, Sun Yixian stepped down as president in favor of Yuan Shikai (yoo AHN shih KY), a powerful general. Sun hoped that Yuan would create a strong central government. Instead, the ambitious general tried to set up a new dynasty. The military, however, did not support Yuan, and opposition divided the nation. When Yuan died in 1916, China plunged into still greater disorder.

In the provinces, local warlords seized power. As rival armies battled for control, the economy collapsed and millions of peasants suffered terrible hardships. Famine and attacks by bandits added to their misery.

Foreign Imperialism During this period of upheaval, foreign powers increased their influence over Chinese affairs. They dominated Chinese port cities and extended their influence inland. During World War I, Japanese officials presented Yuan Shikai with the **Twenty-One Demands,** a list of demands that sought to make China a Japanese protectorate.

With China too weak to resist, Yuan gave in to some of the demands. Then, at the Paris Peace Conference in 1919, the Allies gave Japan control over some former German possessions in China. That news infuriated Chinese Nationalists.

The May Fourth Movement Seeks Reform In response, student protests erupted in Beijing on May 4, 1919, and later spread to cities across China. "China's territory may be conquered," they declared, "but it cannot be given away!" The students organized boycotts of Japanese goods and businesses.

The protests set off a cultural and intellectual ferment known as the **May Fourth Movement.** Western-educated leaders blamed the imperialists' success on China's own weakness. As in Meiji Japan, Chinese reformers wanted to learn from the West and use that knowledge to end foreign domination. Most reformers rejected Confucian traditions in favor of Western science and ideas such as democracy and nationalism.

Women played a key role in the May Fourth Movement. They campaigned to end traditional practices, such as footbinding and the seclusion of women within the home. Their work helped open doors for women in education and the economy.

Chinese Communism Is Born Some Chinese turned to the revolutionary ideas of Marx and Lenin. The Russian Revolution seemed to offer a model of how a strong, well-organized party could transform a nation.

The Soviet Union trained Chinese students and military officers to become the **vanguard,** or elite leaders, of a communist revolution. By the 1920s, a

>> Sun Yixian fought to end the Qing dynasty and China's 2,000-year system of feudal monarchy. He then served as the first provisional president of the Republic of China in 1912.

>> Yuan Shikai, a leading Qing general, brought the end of the Qing dynasty by forcing the abdication of the child emperor, Puyi. He later became president of the republic.

Topic 17 Lesson 4

Explain that the May Fourth Movement and the birth of the Chinese Communist Party were both reactions to the internal problems and foreign aggression that China faced. Students should also understand that both movements shared the goal of "catching up" to the West.

Guided Reading and Discussion

Be sure students understand how the Twenty-One Demands and the Paris Peace Conference affected Chinese interests. Ask students what common effect they had on China. *(Sample response: Both led to a loss of Chinese control over its own affairs and/or territory.)*

Infer Why would women have been interested in the May Fourth Movement? Cite evidence to support your answer. *(Sample response: In traditional Chinese society, women held a subservient role. Women may have believed that the Western ideas that influenced the movement would help them gain more freedom. This can be seen in their effort to overthrow traditions like foot binding.)*

Contrast In what ways were the goals of the May Fourth Movement and Chinese Communists in conflict? *(Sample response: The May Fourth Movement wanted to adopt Western ways. The goal of Communists was a revolution that would overthrow some of the very institutions—like democratic government—that the May Fourth Movement wanted to establish in China.)*

Key Terms

Ask students to find the key term **Twenty-One Demands** (in bold) in the text. Explain that the phrase describes a list of demands Japan gave China in 1915 that attempted to make China a protectorate of Japan. Ask: Why did China accept some of these demands?

History Background

Mao Zedong Unlike Marx and Lenin, who came from wealthy families, Mao was born a peasant farmer. He loved learning and managed to pursue an education. At 18, he walked for days to join in Sun Yixian's revolution, but was disillusioned when warlords took over. In college, Mao and other student radicals watched and were influenced by Russia's 1918 revolution. However, Marxism was based on the rise of the proletariat, or industrial working class. China had only a small urban working class but an enormous peasant class. Mao believed the peasants could be the heart of China's revolution. Unlike Gandhi, Mao was willing to use ruthless measures to achieve his ideas of justice and equality. His struggle to gain control of China continued until 1949.

Nationalists and Communists

After Sun Yixian's death, Jiang Jieshi took over the Nationalist party, or Guomindang. Jiang cooperated with the Communists in the Northern Expedition to conquer warlords and capture Beijing. Then Jiang turned against the Communists and sent troops to slaughter them. The Communists, led by Mao Zedong, retreated during the Long March. The Communists won peasant support by redistributing land and by showing courage.

Guided Reading and Discussion

Review the violent tactics used by the Guomindang to rid China of Communists and how these policies led to the Long March.

Sequence Events Briefly list the changes in the relationship between the Guomindang and the Communists from 1926 to 1935, in order. *(Sample response: In 1926, they combined forces to defeat the local warlords. In 1927, civil war began between the two groups, and between 1934–1935, the Communists retreated during the Long March*

Point out the Route of the Long March on the map Civil War in China, 1927–1936. Explain that Mao's Communist forces faced nearly daily attacks, forcing them to flee from the Guomindang across the nation. Review the movement of the Communists and the natural features of the land that caused difficulties along their journey.

small group of Chinese Communists had formed their own political party.

IDENTIFY CAUSE AND EFFECT How did warlord uprisings and foreign imperialism lead to the May Fourth movement?

Nationalists and Communists

In 1921, Sun Yixian and his **Guomindang** (gwoh meen DAWNG) or Nationalist party, established a government in south China. Sun planned to raise an army to defeat the warlords and unite China. When Western democracies refused to help, Sun accepted aid from the Soviet Union and joined forces with the small group of Chinese Communists to defeat the warlords. However, he still believed that China's future should be based on his Three Principles of the People.

The Nationalists and Jiang Jieshi After Sun's death in 1925, an energetic young army officer, **Jiang Jieshi** (jahng jeh shur), took over the Guomindang. Jiang Jieshi was determined to smash the power of the warlords and reunite China, but he had little interest in either democracy or communism.

>> Jiang Jieshi led the Guomindang after Sun's death in 1925. He headed the Guomindang government in China from 1928 to 1949.

In 1926, Jiang Jieshi began the Northern Expedition in order to crush or win over local warlords as he advanced on Beijing. In mid-campaign, Jiang turned on his sometime ally the Chinese Communists, who he saw as a threat to his power. The Communists were winning converts among the small working class in cities like Shanghai.

Early in 1927, on orders from Jiang, Guomindang troops slaughtered Communist Party members and the workers who supported them. In Shanghai and elsewhere, thousands of people were killed. This massacre marked the beginning of a bitter civil war between the Communists and the Guomindang that lasted for 22 years.

Communism and Mao Zedong Among the Communists who escaped Jiang's attack was a young revolutionary of peasant origins, **Mao Zedong** (mow dzuh doong). Unlike earlier Chinese Communists, Mao believed that the Communists should seek support not among the small urban working class but among the large peasant masses.

Although the Communists were pursued at every turn by Guomindang forces, Mao was optimistic about eventual success. In southeastern China, Mao and the Communists redistributed land to peasants and offered them schooling and health care.

The Long March Jiang Jieshi, however, was determined to destroy the "Red bandits," as he called the Communists. He led the Guomindang in a series of "extermination campaigns" against them. Mao and about 100,000 of his followers fled the Guomindang in an epic retreat known as the **Long March.** From 1934 to 1935, they trekked more than 6,000 miles, facing daily attacks as they crossed rugged mountains and raging rivers. Mao's forces used guerrilla, or irregular hit-and-run, tactics to fight back. Only about 20,000 of the marchers survived the ordeal.

During the march, the Communists enforced strict discipline. Soldiers were told to treat peasants politely, pay for goods they wanted, and avoid damaging crops. Such behavior made Mao's forces welcome among peasants, many of whom had suffered greatly at the hands of the Guomindang.

For decades, the Long March stood as a symbol of communist heroism and inspired new recruits to follow Mao. At the end of the Long March, the Communists set up a new base in a remote region of northern China.

Answers

Identify Cause and Effect *The warlord uprisings weakened China, allowing countries such as Japan to encroach upon China's possessions. Anger at China's inability to halt foreign imperialism led to the May Fourth Movement.*

English Language Proficiency Standards

ELPS 4.I.1 Read "China Faces Japanese Imperialism" aloud. Then have students complete one of the activities below based on their English proficiency level.

Beginning Reread "China Faces Japanese Imperialism" aloud. Pause after each paragraph to retell the content in accessible language for English language learners. Then help students determine the main idea of the text by underlining the main idea of each paragraph. Help students take those three main ideas and use them to determine the main idea of the whole text.

Intermediate Reread "China Faces Japanese Imperialism" aloud. Pause after each paragraph to help students retell the content in everyday language. Then ask students to underline the main idea of each paragraph. Guide students to take those three main ideas and use them to determine the main idea of the whole text.

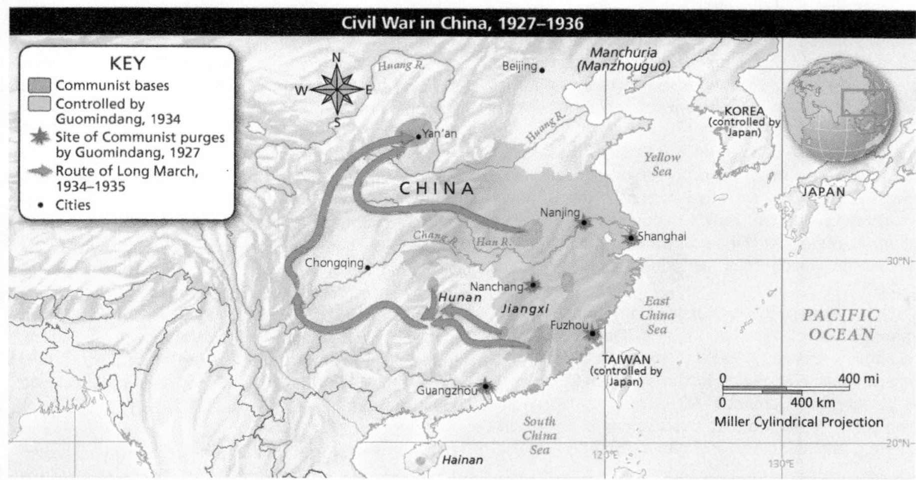

>> **Analyze Maps** The Guomindang and the Communists waged a long and bitter war for control of China. What natural features made the Long March difficult?

Interactive Chart

There, Mao rebuilt his forces and plotted new strategies for fighting the Guomindang.

IDENTIFY SUPPORTING DETAILS How did the communists manage to survive Jiang's "extermination campaigns"?

China Faces Japanese Imperialism

While Jiang was pursuing the Communists across China, the country faced another danger. In 1931, Japan invaded Manchuria in northeastern China, adding it to the growing Japanese empire. As Japanese aggression increased, some of Jiang's generals pushed him to form a united front with the Communists against Japan.

In 1937, the Japanese struck again, starting what became the Second Sino-Japanese War. Airplanes bombed Chinese cities, and Japanese troops overran eastern China, including Beijing and Guangzhou. Jiang Jieshi and his government retreated to the interior and set up a new capital at Chongqing (chawng CHING).

After a lengthy siege, Japanese troops marched into the city of Nanjing (nahn jing) on December 13. Nanjing was an important cultural center and had been the Guomindang capital before Chongqing. After the city's surrender, the Japanese killed hundreds of thousands of soldiers and civilians and brutalized still more. The cruelty and destruction became known as the "Rape of Nanjing."

The invasion suspended China's civil war as the Guomindang and Communists formed a temporary, uneasy alliance. Jiang's army battled Japanese troops, while Communists engaged in guerrilla attacks against the invaders. The Soviet Union sent advisors and equipment to help. Great Britain, France, and the United States gave economic aid.

EXPLAIN Why did the Japanese invasion help unify the Chinese temporarily?

Conflicting Forces in Japan

The Japanese invasions of China were part of a rising tide of Japanese imperialism. Like China, Japan sought to become a major world power, equal to Western nations. However, Japan lacked the resources needed to fuel its industrial achievements. The small nation looked to the West as an example, attempting to conquer lands to form a huge empire. As you will see, the invasion of China takes on new meaning when viewed from the Japanese perspective.

Advanced Have students reread "China Faces Japanese Imperialism." Then lead a class discussion and ask students to retell the content in their own words and highlight the main idea of each paragraph. Have students use the three main ideas to determine the main idea of the whole text. Have students write the main idea and share it with the rest of the class. As a group, refine and clarify the main idea of the text and have students write it in their notes.

Advanced High Have students reread "China Faces Japanese Imperialism." Then ask students to retell the content in their own words to a partner. Pairs should then highlight the main idea of each paragraph. Have pairs use the three main ideas to determine and write down the main idea of the whole text. Pairs should share their work with another pair to refine and clarify the main idea of the text.

Online Project the **Interactive Chart: Communism vs. Guomindang**. Review the tiles and ask students to place them into one of three categories: Guomindang, Communists, or Shared Characteristics. *(Guomindang: Sun Yixian; Jiang Jieshi; Three Principles; Campaign to exterminate rivals. Communists: Mao Zedong; Supported by masses; The Long March; Advocated Karl Marx. Shared: Worked to oppose Japanese invasion; Established totalitarian government; Northern Expedition victory.)*

Compare and Contrast Summarize how Communists were different from the Guomindang.

ACTIVE CLASSROOM

Ask students to break into groups to answer the following: "Which group was more 'revolutionary' in the sense that it would bring broad changes?" Have students conduct a Circle Write in which each student writes as much as they can for 1 minute, then passes the paper to the person on their right. The next person continues writing for another minute where the other person left off. Continue to pass the paper around until it comes back to the first person. The group then decides on the best response and shares it with the larger group.

China Faces Japanese Imperialism

Explain that as the Guomindang chased the Communists across China, Japanese forces invaded and captured the city of Nanjing and committed countless atrocities.

Conflicting Forces in Japan

Explain that the Japanese economy grew enormously during World War I. After the war, the nation cut back on expansionist policies to focus on business relationships with the West and moved toward more widespread democracy at home.

Answers

Analyze Maps *the rivers and mountains the Communists had to cross*

Identify Supporting Details *On the Long March, the Communists retreated from Jiang's forces to a remote region in northern China and used guerrilla tactics to fight back as they marched.*

Explain *The Japanese threatened all Chinese, whether they were Communist or not.*

Topic 17 Lesson 4

Guided Reading and Discussion

Discuss what students know about Japan from the text so far. Be sure students understand that Japan's economy boomed during World War I, and it was based primarily upon production of goods that were exported to the West. Japan reined in imperialist goals following the war and focused on developing business relationships with the West.

Remind students that Japan also faced serious issues following World War I. Despite government moves toward more widespread democracy, the zaibatsu remained very powerful domestically. Military leaders accused government officials of corruption and condemned the rejection of traditional ideals for Western modernity.

Summarize Describe the tensions between the military and the government of Japan during the 1920s. *(The military blasted government corruption and condemned Western influences on Japanese culture.)*

Determine Point of View Why did conservatives resent Western influences? *(They believed Western influences were undermining basic Japanese values of obedience and respect for authority.)*

Unlike China in the 1920s, which was shaken by conflict and economic turmoil, Japan was a powerful, united country with a growing industrial economy. Beneath the surface, however, conflicts brewed that would undermine its moves toward democratic reforms.

Expansion and Economic Growth During World War I, the Japanese economy enjoyed remarkable growth. Its exports to Allied nations soared. Heavy industrial production grew, making Japan a true industrial power. At the same time, it sought to win international recognition as equal to the Western powers.

While Western powers battled in Europe, Japan expanded its influence throughout East Asia. Japan had already annexed Korea as a colony in 1910. During the war, Japan also sought further rights in China with the Twenty-One Demands. After the war, Japan was given some former German possessions in East Asia, including the Shandong province in China.

Liberal Reforms of the 1920s During the 1920s, Japan moved toward more widespread democracy. Political parties grew stronger. Elected members of the Diet—the Japanese parliament—exercised their power. In 1925, all adult men, regardless of class, won the right to vote. Western ideas about women's rights brought some changes.

>> During the Russo-Japanese War in 1904–1905, Japan used Korea as a base for its military operations against Russia. Japanese leaders later annexed Korea.

Overall, however, the status of Japanese women remained below that of men. They would not win suffrage until 1945.

Despite greater democracy, powerful business leaders, called the zaibatsu (**zy baht soo**), strongly influenced the government through donations to political parties. They pushed for policies that favored international trade and their own interests.

Japan's aggressive expansion threatened its economic relationship with the Western powers. To improve relations, moderate Japanese politicians decided to slow down foreign expansion. In 1922, Japan signed an agreement with the United States, Britain, Italy, and France to limit the size of its navy. It also agreed to leave Shandong. The government reduced military spending.

Lurking Problems Behind its seeming well-being, Japan faced some grave problems. The economy grew more slowly in the 1920s than at any time since the country had modernized. Rural peasants did not share in the nation's prosperity. In the cities, factory workers earning low wages were attracted to the ideas of Marx and Lenin.

In the cities, members of the younger generation were also in revolt against tradition. They adopted Western fads and fashions. Also, they rejected family authority for the Western ideal of individual freedom, shocking their elders.

During the 1920s, tensions between the government and the military simmered not far below the surface. Conservatives, especially military officers, blasted government corruption, including payoffs by powerful zaibatsu. They also condemned Western influences for undermining basic Japanese values of obedience and respect for authority.

A devastating earthquake, one of the most destructive quakes in history, struck the Tokyo area in 1923. The earthquake and the widespread fires it caused resulted in the deaths of over 100,000 people and damaged more than 650,000 buildings. Almost half of surviving workers lost their jobs because so many businesses were destroyed. With help from the government, the Tokyo area gradually recovered—just as Japan faced a worldwide economic crisis.

SUMMARIZE How did democratic participation in Japan both grow in the 1920s? How was it limited?

D Differentiate Extra Support To help visual learners, ask students to work in pairs and create a timeline of the events in the 1920s. Have students categorize each event as positive or negative and make a mark above the timeline for a positive event, below the timeline for a negative event. Then have them connect the dots and describe the pattern. Make sure that students understand that Japan's behavior zigzagged between two opposite extremes during this period.

Answers

Summarize *All men were allowed to vote in 1925. However, women did not receive the vote for two decades, and rich zaibatsu had an undue influence on party politicians.*

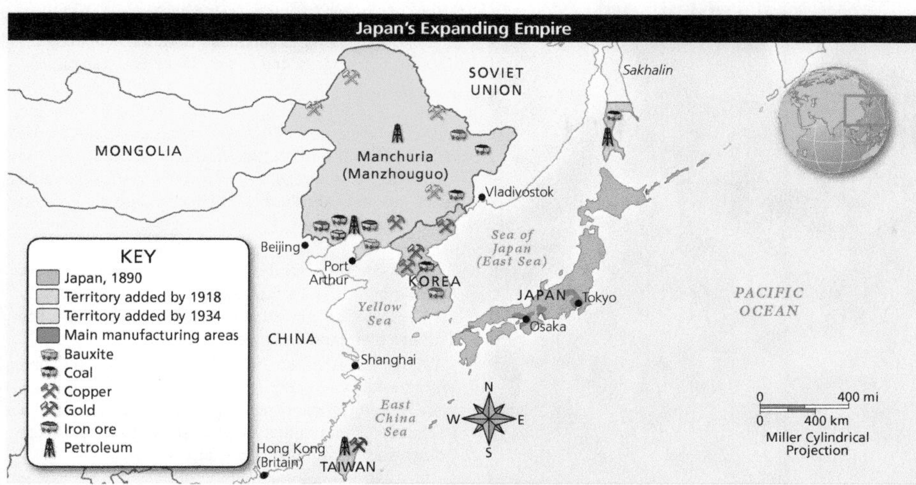

>> **Analyze Maps** Japan expanded its territory in Asia between 1918 and 1934. From the conquered lands, the Japanese acquired natural resources to fuel industry. Where were Japan's main manufacturing areas located?

The Ultranationalist Reaction

In 1929, the Great Depression rippled across the Pacific, striking Japan with devastating force. Trade suffered as foreign buyers could no longer afford to purchase Japanese silks and other exports. Unemployment in the cities soared, while rural peasants were only a mouthful from starvation.

Increasing Unrest Economic disaster fed the discontent of the leading military officials and extreme nationalists, or **ultranationalists.** They condemned politicians for agreeing to Western demands to stop overseas expansion. Western industrial powers, they pointed out, had long ago grabbed huge empires. By comparison, Japan's empire was tiny.

Japanese nationalists were further outraged by racial policies in the United States, Canada, and Australia that shut out Japanese immigrants. The Japanese took great pride in their industrial achievements. They bitterly resented being treated as second-class citizens in other parts of the world.

As the economic crisis worsened, nationalists demanded renewed expansion. An empire in Asia, they argued, would provide much-needed raw materials as well as an outlet for Japan's rapidly growing population. They set their sights on the northern Chinese province of **Manchuria.** This region was rich in natural resources, and Japanese businesses had already invested heavily there.

The Manchurian Incident In 1931, a group of Japanese army officers provoked an incident that provided an excuse to seize Manchuria. They set explosives and blew up tracks on a Japanese-owned railroad line. Then they claimed that the Chinese had committed the act. Claiming self-defense, the army attacked Chinese forces.

Without consulting their own government, the Japanese military forces conquered all of Manchuria and set up a puppet state there that they called Manzhouguo (man choo KWOO). They brought in Puyi, the last Chinese emperor, to head the puppet state.

Politicians in Tokyo objected to the army's highhanded actions, but public opinion sided with the military. When the League of Nations condemned Japanese aggression against China, Japan simply withdrew from the League. The League's member states failed to take military action against Japanese

Analyze Images

Discuss the map Japan's Expanding Empire. High unemployment in the 1930s fed Japanese discontent with the government. Many people in Japan saw aggressive imperialism as a solution to domestic problems. Japan built up its territory and military despite objections. Ask: Which territories did Japan add by 1918? *(Taiwan, Korea, and part of the island directly to the north)*

The Ultranationalist Reaction

Explain that militarists came into power due to high public support. The Great Depression devastated the Japanese economy and led to political instability. Foreign conquests appeared to be a solution to the problems Japan faced.

Identify Cause and Effect Explain how the Great Depression affected Japan. *(Foreign buyers could not buy Japanese exports, causing job loss in cities and near starvation in rural areas.)*

Militarists Gain Power

Japan's military expected to complete its conquest of China within a few years. As World War II broke out in Europe, the conflict quickly spread to Asia, with Japan joining the Axis powers of Germany and Italy.

Online Project the **Interactive Gallery: Revival of Japanese Glory**. Review each image and discuss where it falls on the timeline. Examine the timeline as a whole, and ask students to discuss the relationships between events on the timeline.

ACTIVE CLASSROOM

Have students bring the images in the Interactive Gallery to life with the Act It Out strategy. After reviewing the images, ask students what happens next in the image and what happened before. Students can act out a scene from the images, bringing to life what those people are thinking. Or, choose one image and ask students to write a conversation that could have occurred between the people in that image.

Answers

Analyze Maps *near Tokyo, Osaka, and areas to the south*

Topic 17 Lesson 4

SYNTHESIZE

Online Project **Digital Activity: Nationalism in China and Japan**. Ask students to use the graphic organizer to compare the goals of nationalism in each country and how those goals were expressed. *(Sample response: China—Goals of Nationalism: To lessen foreign domination of China. Effects of Nationalism: Resistance to Japanese invasions; attempts to strengthen China; new intellectual movements and political parties to address perceived problems. Japan—Goals of Nationalism: to build a Japanese empire in Asia. Effects of Nationalism: issuing the Twenty-One Demands; repeated invasions of China; ultranationalists and militarists invoke symbols to inspire service and obedience to the emperor and the state. Both—Goals of Nationalism: to be treated as equals and with respect by Western nations. Effects of Nationalism: created a sense of unity and national identity in each country)*

DEMONSTRATE

Online Assign the **Digital Lesson Quiz** for this lesson if you haven't already done so. Students will be offered automatic remediation or enrichment based on their score.

Pose these questions to the class on the Discussion Board:

Cite Evidence How did China respond to the challenges of internal division and foreign imperialism during the early 1900s? *(The Guomindang and the Communists united against local warlord uprisings, but the Guomindang soon turned against the Communists and civil war ensued for years.)*

Identify Central Issues Why did Japan draw back from its imperialist goals during the 1920s? Why did Japan return to aggressive territorial expansion in the 1930s? *(Japan drew back to strengthen its trade relationships with foreign countries. The Great Depression drove the Japanese to invade other countries for their natural resources.)*

Topic Inquiry

Have students continue their investigations for the Topic Inquiry.

>> Japanese soldiers occupied Beijing in 1937. Japan took control of large parts of China during the Second Sino-Japanese War, from 1937 to 1945.

Interactive Gallery

aggression. Japan also nullified its naval disarmament agreements with the Western powers.

IDENTIFY CAUSE AND EFFECT How did the Great Depression lead to calls for renewed expansion?

Militarists Gain Power

In the early 1930s, ultranationalists were winning support from the people for renewing foreign conquests and taking a tough stand against the Western powers. Members of extreme nationalist societies assassinated a number of politicians and business leaders who opposed expansion. Military leaders plotted to overthrow the government and, in 1936, briefly occupied the center of Tokyo.

Revival of Traditional Values Civilian government survived, but by 1937, the unrest forced the government to accept military domination. To please the ultranationalists, the government cracked down on socialists and suppressed most democratic freedoms. It revived ancient warrior values and built a cult around Emperor **Hirohito,** who had ascended to the throne in 1926. According to Japanese tradition, the emperor was descended from the sun goddess and was himself a living god.

In theory, Hirohito was the nation's supreme authority. In practice, however, he merely approved the policies that his ministries formulated. To spread its nationalist message, the government used schools to teach students absolute obedience to the emperor and service to the state.

Expansion into China Japan took advantage of China's civil war to increase its influence there. By 1937, as you have read, its armies had invaded the Chinese mainland and overran eastern China.

Japan expected to complete its conquest of China within a few years. But in 1939, while the two nations were locked in deadly combat, World War II broke out in Europe. That conflict swiftly spread to Asia, where France and Britain had large empires.

In 1936, Japan had allied with two aggressive European powers, Germany and Italy. These three powers signed the Tripartite Pact in September 1940, cementing the alliance known as the Axis Powers. That alliance, combined with renewed Japanese conquests, would turn World War II into a brutal, wide-ranging conflict waged not only across the continent of Europe but across Asia and the islands of the Pacific as well.

 **IDENTIFY CAUSE AND EFFECT** How did Japanese militarists rise to power in the 1930s?

ASSESSMENT

1. **Summarize** What political and economic changes occurred in Japan during the 1920s?
2. **Identify Cause and Effect** Why did the new republic of China fall into chaos after 1912?
3. **Integrate Information** Why did the Communists and the Guomindang cooperate during the Northern Expedition in 1926? How did the expedition affect their long-term relationship?
4. **Infer** Judging from the example of Japan, why might a nation turn to military leaders and extreme nationalists during a crisis? Cite details from the text.
5. **Identify Central Ideas** How did the Japanese invasion affect the civil war in China?

Answers

Identify Cause and Effect *The export industry suffered, and nationalists argued that expansion could provide new resources.*

Identify Cause and Effect *Public opinion supported foreign conquest. Unrest, caused by assassinations and plots by extremist groups, pushed the civilian government to bow to military control.*

Assessment

1. Democracy expanded as political parties grew stronger and exerted their power in the Diet, extending rights. The economy grew during the 1920s, but it experienced many highs and lows.
2. After Yuan died, warlords battled for control, famine spread, and foreign powers increased their interference in China.
3. They sought to smash the power of the warlords. They wrestled control from local landlords and captured Beijing. Jiang Jieshi turned on the Communists, ending their mutual cooperation until Japan invaded.
4. Military leaders and nationalists help soothe citizens' fears of losing their place in the world and promise a solution and return to prominence. Japanese military leaders promised security, military power, and cultural greatness.
5. The Guomindang and the Communists temporarily ceased fighting each other and united against Japan, their common enemy.

17.5 The catastrophe of World War I shattered the sense of optimism that had grown in the West since the Enlightenment. Despair gripped survivors on both sides as they added up the staggering costs of the war. Europeans mourned a generation of young men who had been lost on the battlefields.

>> Duke Ellington was a composer, pianist, and bandleader. He referred to his music as "American Music" rather than "jazz." His career spanned the 1920s to the 1970s.

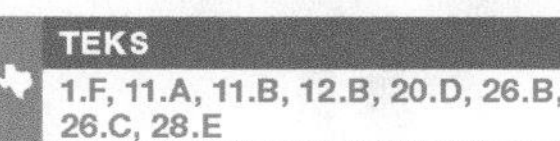

The West After World War I

TEKS 1.F, 11.A, 11.B, 12.B, 20.D, 26.B, 26.C, 28.E

Social Change After World War I

Many people talked about a "return to normalcy," to life as it had been before 1914. But rebellious young people rejected the moral values and rules of the Victorian Age and chased after excitement. Gertrude Stein, an American writer living in Paris, called them the "lost generation." Others saw them as immoral pleasure-seekers.

The Roaring Twenties During the 1920s, new technologies helped create a mass culture shared by millions in the world's developed countries. Affordable cars, improved telephones, and new forms of media such as motion pictures and radio brought people around the world closer together than ever before.

In the 1920s, many radios tuned into the new sounds of jazz. In fact, the decade in the West is often called the Jazz Age. African American musicians combined Western harmonies with African rhythms to create jazz. Jazz musicians, like trumpeter Louis Armstrong and pianist Duke Ellington, took simple melodies and improvised endless subtle variations in rhythm and beat.

Throughout the 1920s, the popularity of jazz moved from the United States to Europe. Europeans embraced American popular culture,

>> Objectives

Analyze how Western society and culture changed after World War I.

Identify the contributions of modern scientists such as Marie Curie and Albert Einstein.

Summarize the domestic and foreign policy issues that the Western democracies faced after World War I.

Describe how the global depression began and spread.

Explain the responses of Britain, France, and the United States to the Great Depression.

>> Key Terms

flapper
Miriam Ferguson
Prohibition
Marie Curie
Albert Einstein
psychoanalysis
Harlem Renaissance
abstract art
dada
surrealism
Maginot Line
Kellogg-Briand Pact
disarmament
general strike
overproduction
finance
Federal Reserve
Great Depression
Franklin D. Roosevelt
New Deal

www.PearsonTexas.com Access your Digital Lesson.

Topic 17 Lesson 5

The West After World War I

CONNECT

Preview Have students preview the **Lesson Objectives** and the list of **Key Terms**.

Students can also preview all the **Key Terms** and **Academic Vocabulary** using the **Interactive Reading Notepad** on the digital course or preview a summary of the lesson in the **Reading and Note Taking Study Guide**.

Online Use the **Editable Presentation** found on the digital course to present the main ideas for this lesson.

Start Up Activity

Ask: What might be some of the problems people faced in their everyday lives during the Great Depression? *(People struggled to find work and feed their families.)* What are some actions governments could take to respond to such an economic crisis? *(The government could institute employment programs, establish soup kitchens, and set controls on the financial market.)*

Discuss The Great Depression threw thousands of people out of work and into lives of poverty. Most governments offered little relief for unemployed workers, desperate farmers, and hungry families. What do you think were some of the possible resources available to those in need of financial assistance during the early 1930s? *(neighbors, family members, churches, charitable organizations)*

Online You can also project the **Start Up Activity** from the course.

INVESTIGATE

Have students read the section using the **Reading and Note Taking Study Guide** to help them take notes and understand the text as they read.

Social Change After World War I

During the 1920s, Western nations were recovering from the world war. Many in those countries threw off the constraints of the past and embraced a popular culture that celebrated freedom and experimentation. This booming era in the United States was known as the Jazz Age.

Aa Vocabulary Builder

1. Have students pronounce the following academic vocabulary terms in this lesson and clarify the part of speech. For difficult or polysyllabic words, break them into syllables and pronounce them with the students.
2. Explain what the word means in common "student-friendly" language using synonyms and antonyms when possible. Provide concrete examples to clarify the meaning, and rephrase the example.

emancipation: freedom from restrictions

spontaneously: caused by inner forces, self-generated

suppressed: put down by force, subdued

affluent: rich, wealthy

Guided Reading and Discussion

Technology and society changed rapidly after World War I. Innovations in mass communication allowed a mass culture to develop. Ask students to discuss a definition for the term *mass culture*. *(Sample response: shared interest in music, fashion, movies, television, online videos, celebrities, etc. Students should also note that these interests are constantly changing.)* How do people learn about the latest fashion trends, celebrity romances, musicians, artists, etc., today? *(Sample response: Web sites, fashion shows, blogs, video Web sites, television, friends, etc.)*

Explain that during the Jazz Age, Victorian morals that had underlain prewar Western culture no longer seemed relevant. Describe the characteristics of the Jazz Age and how flappers embodied society's rejection of Victorian ideals. Be sure students understand that not everyone embraced the new jazz culture. Some joined a strong Christian fundamentalist movement and helped enact Prohibition in the United States.

Identify Cause and Effect How did new technologies affect American society in the 1920s? *(Sample response: They helped spread popular American culture. Labor-saving devices became more common in middle-class homes, enabling more women to work outside the home.)*

Scientific Discoveries

New scientific findings challenged long-held beliefs and reinforced the sense that the old world was falling apart. Scientists such as Marie Curie and Albert Einstein impacted society beyond their fields of study.

Guided Reading and Discussion

Trace the discoveries of Marie Curie and discuss Einstein's theories of relativity. Ask why his theories challenged traditional perspectives. *(Einstein questioned Newtonian science, which described the universe as a predictable machine. As a result, people began to feel that old certainties were falling apart.)*

> "The Flapper awoke from her lethargy (tiredness) ... bobbed her hair, put on her choicest pair of earrings and a great deal of audacity (boldness) and rouge and went into battle. She flirted because it was fun to flirt and ... refused to be bored chiefly because she wasn't boring ... Mothers disapproved of their sons taking the Flapper to dances, to teas, to swim, and most of all to heart.
>
> —Zelda Fitzgerald, flapper and wife of author F. Scott Fitzgerald

>> New fashions, including shorter hairstyles and hemlines, were popularized by the flappers in the 1920s.

with its greater freedom and willingness to experiment. The nightclub and jazz were symbols of that freedom. Jazz came to embody the universal themes of creativity and self-expression.

Much of today's popular music has been influenced by jazz. It has transcended the "Roaring Twenties" American culture to become an international musical language.

After the war, rebellious young people, disillusioned by the war, rejected the moral values and rules of the Victorian Age and chased after excitement. During the Jazz Age, this rebellion was exemplified by a new type of liberated young woman called the **flapper.** The first flappers were American, but their European sisters soon adopted the fashion. Flappers rejected old ways in favor of new, exciting freedoms.

The Flapper awoke from her lethargy (tiredness) ... bobbed her hair, put on her choicest pair of earrings and a great deal of audacity (boldness) and rouge and went into battle. She flirted because it was fun to flirt and ... refused to be bored chiefly because she wasn't boring ... Mothers disapproved of their sons taking the Flapper to dances, to teas, to swim, and most of all to heart.

—Zelda Fitzgerald, flapper and wife of author F. Scott Fitzgerald

Women's Progress Flappers were highly visible, but they were a small minority. Most women saw mixed progress in the postwar period. During the war, women had held a wide range of jobs. Although most women left those jobs when the war ended, their war work helped them win the vote in many Western countries, such as Britain, Germany, the Netherlands, and the United States. A few women were elected to public office, such as Texas governor **Miriam Ferguson** or Lady Nancy Astor, the first woman to serve in the British Parliament.

By the 1920s, labor-saving devices had become common in middle class homes. Washing machines, vacuum cleaners, and canned foods lightened the burden

History Background

Notable Records In the 1920s, records and phonograph players were not new. Yet during this decade, record sales soared. Record companies adopted the small disc format for recordings, making record production easy and records themselves convenient for consumers. Doubled-sided records offered music fans a relatively inexpensive way to hear many of their favorite bands. In 1927 alone, Americans bought over 100 million jazz records. Recordings by acts such as Louis Armstrong's Hot Five brought jazz to remote areas that rarely saw live bands. These phonographic records made the rapid spread of jazz music possible, and for the first time turned music and music production into a major industry.

of household chores. Some women then sought work outside the home or did volunteer work to help the less fortunate.

In the new atmosphere of emancipation, women sought higher education and pursued careers in many areas—from sports to the arts. Women golfers, tennis players, swimmers, and pilots set new records.

Women worked as newspaper reporters, published bestselling novels, and won recognition as artists. Most professions, though, were still dominated by men. Women doing the same work as men earned much less.

Diverse Reactions to the Jazz Age Not everyone approved of the freewheeling lifestyle of the Jazz Age. In 1920, the Eighteenth Amendment to the Constitution of the United States ushered in **Prohibition,** which banned the manufacture and sale of alcoholic beverages. Temperance reformers had long sought the amendment to stop alcohol abuse. It was later repealed in part because it had spurred the growth of organized crime, which supplied illegal alcohol to speakeasies, or illegal bars.

In the United States in the early 1900s, a Christian fundamentalist movement swept rural areas. Fundamentalists support traditional Christian beliefs. Popular fundamentalist preachers traveled around the country holding inspirational revival meetings. Some used the new technology of radio to spread their message.

SOLVE PROBLEMS What problem was Prohibition intended to solve? How well did it succeed?

Scientific Discoveries

Even before World War I, new ideas and scientific discoveries were challenging long-held ideas about the nature of the world and even of people. Like the war, science helped feed a sense of uncertainty that flowed through Western culture.

Curie Experiments with Radioactivity The ancient Greeks were the first to propose that all matter is composed of tiny, indivisible atoms. Over the centuries, most scientists came to accept this idea. But discoveries made in the early 1900s showed that the atom was more complex than anyone suspected.

The Polish-born French scientist **Marie Curie** and others experimented with an atomic process called radioactivity. They found that the atoms of certain elements, such as radium and uranium, spontaneously release charged particles. As scientists studied radioactivity further, they discovered that it can change atoms of one element into atoms of another. Such findings proved that atoms are not solid and indivisible.

>> Albert Einstein received the 1921 Nobel Prize in Physics and is well known for his mass-energy formula. Einstein fled Germany and became an American citizen in 1940.

Einstein Proposes the Theory of Relativity In 1905 and 1916, the German-born physicist **Albert Einstein** introduced his theories of relativity. Einstein argued that measurements of space and time are not absolute but are determined by many factors, including the relative position of the observer. Einstein's ideas raised questions about Newtonian science, which compared the universe to a machine operating according to absolute laws.

In the postwar years, many scientists came to accept the theories of relativity. To the general public, however, Einstein's ideas were difficult to understand. They seemed to further reinforce the unsettling sense of a universe whirling beyond the understanding of human reason.

In 1934, building on Curie's and Einstein's theories, Italian physicist Enrico Fermi and other scientists around the world discovered atomic fission, or the splitting of the nuclei of atoms in two. This splitting produces a huge burst of energy. In the 1940s, Fermi (now an American), along with fellow American physicists J. Robert Oppenheimer and Edward Teller,

Identify Patterns How did Einstein's theories embody the feelings of uncertainty for the future and distrust of tradition that many felt during the postwar period? *(Einstein proposed that the universe did not behave according to absolute laws, but that measurements of space and time were determined by the relative position of the observer.)*

Discuss how Sigmund Freud also challenged people's faith in reason. Ask students to define *subconscious mind*. *(The subconscious is the part of the mind that influences actions that we are not consciously aware of.)* Explain that Freud's theories influenced popular culture. Authors and artists explored the subconscious mind, creating new works that are considered masterpieces today.

Generate Explanations Why were Marie Curie's achievements unique for her time? *(Pursuing a career in science and making groundbreaking discoveries were not traditional expectations for a woman of that period.)*

Answers

Solve Problems *Some people, disillusioned by the war, embraced rebelliousness and experimentation. Many who disapproved of the new freewheeling lifestyle proposed outlawing the manufacture and sale of liquor. Prohibition did not solve the problem it was intended to solve because drinking just went underground, and illegal liquor trade flourished.*

Topic 17 Lesson 5

Literature Reflects New Perspectives

Many authors were reacting to the atrocities experienced during the war and the lingering effects after the fighting ended. Some writers explored new styles of writing to express themselves.

Analyze Images

Point out the picture of the cover of *The Great Gatsby.* Explain that much of the literature of this time was bleak and pessimistic. Ask: How did the war impact many postwar writers' work? *(Their work reflected a lack of connection with the modern world.)* How does the cover of *The Great Gatsby* reflect the pessimism of the times? *(the colors are dark; the eyes look sad; the light at the bottom looks like a fire or an explosion)*

Guided Reading and Discussion

Explain to students that many authors and thinkers expressed disgust with modern warfare and the futility of war.

Remind students of Freud's theories about the subconscious mind, and tell them that they influenced Virginia Woolf and James Joyce, who explored the subconscious in their works. Discuss *nihilism*, a movement represented by Friedrich Nietzsche that held that traditional values were unfounded and human existence was meaningless. Explain that Nietzsche's work expressed the pessimism of the postwar years.

Key Terms

Ask students to find the key term **psychoanalysis** (in bold) in the text. Explain that the word describes a method of treating mental disorders.

>> Austrian neurologist Sigmund Freud founded the field of psychoanalysis. In his later years, Freud used psychoanalysis to interpret religion and culture.

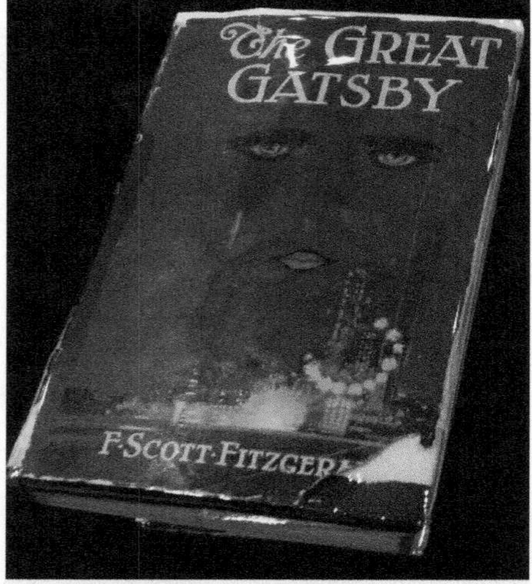

>> F. Scott Fitzerald's 1925 novel *The Great Gatsby* is a portrait of the Jazz Age and Roaring Twenties. It emphasizes the glittering but empty life of parties and excess.

would use this discovery to create the devastating atomic bomb.

Fleming Discovers Penicillin In 1928, the Scottish scientist Alexander Fleming made a different type of scientific discovery. One day, he picked up a discarded laboratory dish that he had used to grow bacteria. The dish had grown some mold, which had killed the bacteria. Fleming called this nontoxic mold "penicillin." Fleming's penicillin was the first antibiotic, or medicine used to kill micro-organisms such as bacteria. Later scientists developed a wide range of antibiotics.

Freud Analyzes the Mind The Austrian physician Sigmund Freud **(froyd)** also challenged faith in reason. He suggested that the subconscious mind drives much of human behavior. Freud said that learned social values such as morality and reason help people to repress, or check, powerful urges. But an individual feels constant tension between repressed drives and social training. This tension, argued Freud, may cause psychological or physical illness.

Freud pioneered **psychoanalysis,** a method of studying how the mind works and treating mental disorders. Although many of his theories have been discredited, Freud's ideas have had an extraordinary impact far beyond medicine. They strongly influenced the art and literature of the postwar West.

IDENTIFY PATTERNS How did scientific discoveries in the 1920s change people's views of the world?

Literature Reflects New Perspectives

In the 1920s, war novels, poetry, plays, and memoirs flowed off the presses. Novels such as *All Quiet on the Western Front* by German author Erich Remarque exposed the grim horrors faced by soldiers in World War I. Other writers heaped scorn on the leaders who took them into war. Their realistic works stripped away any romantic notions about the glories of warfare and reflected a powerful disgust with war that influenced an entire generation.

The Lost Generation To many postwar writers, the war symbolized the moral breakdown of Western civilization. In 1922, the English poet T. S. Eliot published *The Waste Land.* This long poem portrays the modern world as spiritually empty and barren.

In *The Sun Also Rises,* the American novelist Ernest Hemingway shows the rootless wanderings of young people who lack deep convictions. "I did not care

English Language Proficiency Standards

ELPS 5.E Read "Scientific Discoveries" aloud. Have students complete the activities according to their English proficiency.

Beginning Remind students that possessive case shows ownership. Reread "Scientific Discoveries," pointing out each possessive noun. Ask students what Freud, Einstein, Curie, and Fermi "possessed" or owned. Explain that ownership applies not only to physical items but also to ideas.

Intermediate Ask students to explain the possessive case. Reread "Scientific Discoveries" aloud. Ask students to identify each possessive noun and ask what Freud, Einstein, Curie, and Fermi "owned." Explain that ownership applies not only to physical items but also to ideas.

Answers

Identify Patterns *Atomic research changed the Newtonian view of science and led to the development of atomic weapons; the discovery of penicillin paved the way for antibiotics; and Freud's ideas revolutionized psychology.*

what it was all about," says the narrator. "All I wanted to know was how to live in it." In *The Great Gatsby,* American novelist F. Scott Fitzgerald exposed the emptiness of the 1920s world of flappers and parties.

American poet Gertrude Stein considered herself, her writer friends, and young people part of a "lost generation." They had become adults during or right after World War I and were disillusioned by the upheaval of the war and its aftermath.

Literature Explores the Inner Mind As Freud's ideas became popular, many writers began to explore the inner workings of the mind. Some experimented with stream of consciousness. In this technique, a writer appears to present a character's random thoughts and feelings without imposing any logic or order. In the novel *Mrs. Dalloway,* British novelist Virginia Woolf used stream of consciousness to explore the thoughts of people going through the ordinary actions of their everyday lives. In *Finnegans Wake,* the Irish novelist James Joyce explored the inner mind of a hero who remains sound asleep throughout the novel.

>> Irish novelist James Joyce was well known for his experimental literary forms and explorations of inner life. One of his most highly acclaimed works is the novel *Ulysses,* published in 1922.

The Harlem Renaissance A more optimistic literary movement arose in the United States during the 1920s. The **Harlem Renaissance** was an African American cultural awakening. It began in Harlem, a neighborhood in New York City that was home to many African Americans. African American writers and artists expressed their pride in their unique culture.

Among its best known figures was the poet and playwright Langston Hughes. In his poem, "The Negro Speaks of Rivers," Hughes reflects on the rivers associated with the African and African-American experience from the Euphrates, Congo, and Nile to the Mississippi. Novelist and anthropologist Zora Neale Hurston studied African American folklore and traditions.

COMPARE POINTS OF VIEW How did postwar authors show disillusionment with prewar institutions?

Modern Art and Architecture

In the early 1900s, many Western artists rejected traditional styles. Instead of trying to reproduce the real world, they explored other dimensions of color, line, and shape. Painters like Henri Matisse (ma TEES) utilized bold, wild strokes of color and odd distortions to produce works of strong emotion. He and fellow artists outraged the public and were dubbed *fauves*(fohv), or wild beasts, by critics.

>> Henri Matisse's expressive use of color and his frequent focus on domestic subjects can be seen in *The Goldfish Bowl,* painted in the winter of 1921–1922.

Tell students that another movement during the 1920s was the Harlem Renaissance. In this literary and artistic movement, African Americans expressed pride in their unique culture.

Make Generalizations Describe the literature of the postwar period. *(Sample response: Many works of literature reflected a sense of uncertainty, of civilization falling apart. Works of the Harlem Renaissance reflected pride in African American culture.)*

Contrast In what way were the authors of the Harlem Renaissance different from many other writers of the postwar period? *(Sample response: Instead of portraying the horrors of war, Harlem Renaissance writers explored aspects of African American culture and the African American experience.)*

Modern Art and Architecture

Explain to students that many visual artists, like musicians and writers, rejected traditional values and styles after World War I. Some created art to shock the viewer; others rejected representation and explored line, shape, and color; and still others used art to interpret some of the new scientific theories.

Advanced Ask students to explain the possessive case to a partner. Then have pairs take turns rereading "Scientific Discoveries" aloud. Have students underline each possessive noun. Then have pairs discuss what Freud, Einstein, Curie, and Fermi "owned." Have each pair team up with another pair to share the main points of their discussion. As a class, guide students to the understanding that ownership applies not only to physical items but also to intangible things, like ideas and feelings.

Advanced High Have students reread "Scientific Discoveries" and underline each possessive noun. Then instruct students to write a few notes about what Freud, Einstein, Curie, and Fermi "owned." Have each student join a small group of three or four students to share and discuss their ideas. Finally, have groups share their ideas and consider the concept that ownership applies not only to physical items but also to intangible things, like ideas and feelings.

Answers

Compare Points of View *by writing about the horrors of modern warfare and moral emptiness, and by experimenting with new styles of writing*

Online Project the **Interactive Gallery: Modern Art Develops**. Look at each image and discuss how each style reflected a modern perspective. Clarify that, in this context, the word *modern* refers to art that broke from the traditions of the past, rather than meaning "contemporary" as it often does in daily speech.

ACTIVE CLASSROOM

Post images from the Interactive Gallery on individual pages around the room. Ask the students to break into groups to tour the room and Make Headlines for each image. Ask each group to present its summary to the class.

Make Generalizations How would you define "modern art" to someone who has never seen an example before? *(Sample response: It encompasses a variety of styles and techniques used to present artistic expression in a nontraditional way.)*

Guided Reading and Discussion

Explain that these works rejected traditional styles and Victorian values. Have students study the image of the painting by Dali. Discuss how Dali and other artists were influenced by stream-of-consciousness literature and Freud's exploration of the subconscious mind. Ensure students understand that many artists chose to reject realistic representations of their world. Explain that through artistic techniques such as cubism, these artists rejected traditional ways of representing objects in a natural or realistic way.

Categorize Give an example of modern art or architecture that emphasized the importance of technology in the twentieth century. *(Sample response: The Bauhaus school in Germany blended science and technology with design. Bauhaus buildings feature glass, steel, and concrete but have little ornamentation.)*

Draw Conclusions How did cubism reflect some artists' feelings about what was happening to their culture and society after the war? *(Artists portrayed their subjects as fragmented pieces with sharp angles and planes instead of as solid objects. This reflected the belief that the war had shattered old certainties and values.)*

>> Pablo Picasso, one of the most important artists of the 20th century, co-developed the movement known as Cubism. He painted *Woman Sitting in an Armchair* in 1920.

Interactive Gallery

>> Fallingwater, a Pennsylvania home designed by architect Frank Lloyd Wright, incorporates nature into its design. It appears to hover over a tranquil waterfall.

Painters Embrace Revolutionary Trends Before World War I, the Spanish artist Pablo Picasso and the French artist Georges Braque (brak) created a revolutionary new style called cubism. Cubists painted three-dimensional objects as complex patterns of angles and planes. By redefining objects into separate shapes, they offered a new view of reality.

Later, the Russian Vasily Kandinsky and the Swiss Paul Klee moved even further away from representing reality. They created a new style of **abstract art,** composed only of lines, colors, and shapes, sometimes with no recognizable subject matter at all.

During and after the war, the dada movement burst onto the Paris art world. **Dada** was a European art movement that rejected traditional artistic values by producing works that seemed like absurd nonsense. Dada was a revolt against civilization. Paintings and sculptures by Jean Arp and Max Ernst were intended to shock and disturb viewers. Some Dadaists created works made of objects they found abandoned or thrown away.

Cubism and dada both helped to inspire **surrealism,** a movement that attempted to portray the workings of the unconscious mind. Surrealism rejected rational thought, which had produced the horrors of World War I, in favor of irrational or unconscious ideas. The Spanish surrealist Salvador Dali used images of melting clocks and burning giraffes to suggest the chaotic dream state described by Freud.

Architecture Reflects a New World Architects, too, rejected classical traditions and developed new styles to match a new urban, industrialized world. The famous Bauhaus school in Germany influenced architecture by blending science and technology with design. Bauhaus buildings used glass, steel, and concrete but very little ornamentation.

The American architect Frank Lloyd Wright reflected the Bauhaus belief that the function of a building should determine its form. He used materials and forms that fit a building's environment. He believed that "a building should grace its environment rather than disgrace it." One of Wright's most famous designs is Fallingwater, a house in Pennsylvania built on a waterfall. The structure works in harmony with the surrounding environment, as Wright intended.

IDENTIFY CAUSE AND EFFECT What effect did World War I have on artistic movements in the 1920s?

Answers

Identify Cause and Effect *Artists rejected traditional representations and began to look for new and modern ways of expression.*

Postwar Politics in the West

As nations recovered from the war, people began to feel hope rising out of their disillusionment. But soon, the "lost generation" would face a new crisis that would revive many old problems and spark new conflicts.

In 1919, the three Western democracies—Britain, France, and the United States—appeared powerful. They had ruled the Paris Peace Conference and boosted hopes for democracy among the new nations of Eastern Europe. Beneath the surface, however, postwar Europe faced grave problems. To make matters worse, many members of the younger generation who might have become the next great leaders had been killed in the war.

At first, the most pressing issues were finding jobs for returning veterans and rebuilding war-ravaged lands like France and Belgium. Economic problems fed social unrest and made radical ideas more popular. The Russian Revolution unleashed fears of the spread of communism. Some people saw socialism as the answer to economic hardships. Others embraced nationalist political movements.

>> The major outcomes of the Paris Peace Conference were five peace treaties ending World War I, including the Treaty of Versailles with Germany, and the creation of the League of Nations.

Political Parties Clash in Britain In Britain during the 1920s, the Labour party surpassed the Liberal party in strength. The Labour party gained support among workers by promoting a gradual move toward socialism. The Liberal party passed some social legislation, but it traditionally represented middle-class business interests. As the Liberal party faltered, the middle class began to back the Conservative party, joining the upper class, professionals, and farmers. With this support, the Conservative party held power during much of 1920s. After a massive strike of over three million workers in 1926, Conservatives passed legislation limiting the power of workers to strike.

Irish Independence at Last Britain still faced the "Irish question." In 1914, Parliament passed a home-rule bill that was shelved when the war began. Militant Irish nationalists, however, were unwilling to wait any longer. On Easter 1916, a small group launched a revolt against British rule. Although the Easter Rising was quickly suppressed, it stirred wider support for the Irish cause.

When Parliament again failed to grant home rule in 1919, members of the Irish Republican Army (IRA) began a guerrilla war against British forces and their supporters. In 1922, moderates in Ireland and Britain reached an agreement. Most of Ireland became the independent Irish Free State. The largely Protestant northern counties remained under British rule. The settlement ended the worst violence, but the IRA and others never accepted the division of Ireland. In years to come, Catholics in the north faced discrimination, creating new tensions and conflict.

Peacetime Troubles in France Like Britain, France emerged from World War I both a victor and a loser. Fighting on the Western front had destroyed much of northern France. The French had suffered huge casualties. Survivors felt battered and insecure.

After the war, political divisions and financial scandals continued to plague the Third Republic. Several parties—from conservatives to communists—competed for power. During the postwar years, France was again ruled by a series of coalition governments that created temporary alliances among rival political parties.

Postwar Fears in the United States In contrast, the United States emerged from World War I in good shape. A late entrant into the war, it had suffered relatively few casualties and little loss of property. However, the United States did experience some domestic unrest. Fear of radicals and the Bolshevik Revolution in Russia set off a "Red Scare" in 1919 and 1920. Police rounded

Postwar Politics in the West

Western democracies emerged victorious from World War I and appeared powerful. However, both Britain and France faced political unrest as rival parties—some conservative, some socialist or even communist—competed for power. Britain also had to answer Irish calls for independence. The United States faced its own political unrest, particularly a fear of immigrants and radicals.

Summarize How did the British and Irish compromise to achieve Irish independence? *(Sample response: Most of Ireland became the self-governing Irish Free State, while the largely Protestant counties in the north remained under British rule.)*

Guided Reading and Discussion

After the brutal fighting of World War I, people hoped for peaceful democratic solutions rather than violent revolution. However, economic problems fed social unrest during the postwar period, and many began to search for radical solutions to society's problems.

Compare the limitations on workers' rights in Britain with the limitations on immigration in the United States. Point out how both are examples of balancing national needs with civil liberties. Tell students that the United States tried to balance national security with limitations on civil liberties during the "Red Scare" of the 1920s. Ask students to offer examples of this struggle today. *(Sample responses: limitations on strikes for public safety officers; video surveillance in public places; airport screenings; government surveillance of cell phone calls)*

Topic 17 Lesson 5

International Relations

Once World War I's brutal fighting ended, Western nations focused on global peace. However, each nation wanted to ensure domestic security also. This led to the pursuit of contradictory policies such as disarmament on one hand but building up fortifications like the Maginot Line on the other.

Guided Reading and Discussion

Remind students of the lives lost and high economic cost of the war. Politicians and diplomats sought a lasting global peace to ensure such a global conflict would never happen again. Ask students to speculate on policies that might guarantee lasting peace. *(Sample response: international treaties; global military force instead of national ones; disarmament)*

Discuss the international efforts toward peace during the 1920s, using the treaties of Locarno and the Kellogg-Briand Pact as examples. Explain that international treaties had to balance global peace with each nation's interest in its own national security. Remind students that the United States did not join the League of Nations, limiting the power of the organization. Tell them the League was further limited by the unwillingness of member nations to stand up to aggressors during the 1930s, such as Germany, Italy, and Japan.

Identify Central Issues How did the League of Nations respond when Japan invaded Manchuria in 1931? *(It condemned Japan's actions but did nothing to stop it.)*

Make Generalizations Why were the Locarno treaties important? *(The treaties settled the disputed borders of Germany. They symbolized a new era of global peace.)*

up suspected foreign-born radicals, and a number were expelled from the United States.

The "Red Scare" fed growing demands to limit immigration. Millions of immigrants from southern and eastern Europe had poured into the United States between 1890 and 1914. Some native-born Americans sought to exclude these newcomers, whose cultures differed from those of earlier settlers from northern Europe. In response, Congress passed laws limiting immigration from Europe. Earlier laws had already excluded or limited Chinese and Japanese immigration.

? IDENTIFY CENTRAL ISSUES What political issues did France face after World War I?

International Relations

In addition to problems at home, the three democracies faced a difficult international situation. The peace settlements that ended World War I caused friction, especially in Germany and among some ethnic groups in Eastern Europe.

Allies Disagree Over Direction France's chief concern after the war was securing its borders against Germany. The French remembered the German invasions of 1870 and 1914. To prevent a third invasion, France built massive fortifications called the **Maginot Line**(ma zhee NOH) along its border with Germany. The Maginot Line offered a sense of security—a false one. The line would be of little use when Germany invaded again in 1940.

In its quest for security, France also strengthened its military and sought alliances with other countries, including the Soviet Union. It insisted on strict enforcement of the Versailles treaty and complete payment of reparations. France's goal was to keep the German economy weak.

Britain was more interested in protecting its overseas empire and rebuilding trade than in punishing Germany. British leaders strongly supported the limits on German naval power. Still, during the postwar period, many British leaders began to think that the Treaty of Versailles had been too harsh on Germany, and they called for easing its terms. They feared that if Germany became too weak, the Soviet Union and France would become too powerful.

>> **Analyze Political Cartoons** This political cartoon's original caption was "Communism. A Destructive Worm." What message is the cartoonist conveying in this cartoon?

Searching for Peace During the 1920s and 1930s, many people worked for peace. Hopes soared in 1925 when representatives from seven European nations signed a series of treaties at Locarno, Switzerland. These treaties settled Germany's disputed borders with France, Belgium, Czechoslovakia, and Poland.

The Locarno treaties became the symbol of a new era of peace. "France and Germany Ban War Forever," trumpeted a *New York Times* headline.

The hopeful "spirit of Locarno" was echoed in **Kellogg-Briand Pact,** signed in 1928. Almost every independent nation signed this agreement, promising to "renounce war as an instrument of national policy." Although the Kellogg-Briand Pact outlawed war, it provided no way of enforcing the ban.

In the same optimistic spirit, the great powers also pursued **disarmament,** the reduction of armed forces and weapons. The United States, Britain, France, Japan, and other nations signed treaties to reduce the size of their navies. However, they failed to agree on limiting the size of their armies.

The League of Nations Despite grumblings about the Versailles treaty, people around the world put their hope in the League of Nations. From its headquarters in Geneva, Switzerland, the League encouraged cooperation and tried to get members to make a commitment to stop aggression. At first, the League did have some successes. Although the United States never joined, the League grew in the 1920s. In 1926,

Answers

Identify Central Issues *France was plagued by political divisions, financial scandals, and a series of quickly changing coalition governments.*

Analyze Political Cartoons *Communism will eventually destroy law, order, talent, and industry and take away individual rights if it is not stopped.*

after signing the Locarno agreements, Germany joined the League. Later, the Soviet Union was also admitted.

Despite its lofty aims, the League of Nations was powerless to stop aggression. In 1931, the League vigorously condemned Japan's invasion of Manchuria, but it had no military means to stop it. Ambitious dictators in Europe noted the League's weakness. They began to rearm and pursue aggressive foreign policies.

COMPARE POINTS OF VIEW Why did Britain and France disagree over how to enforce the Treaty of Versailles?

Economics in the Postwar Era

The war affected economies all over the world, hurting some and helping others. Britain and France both owed huge war debts to the United States. Both relied on reparation payments from Germany to pay back their loans. Meanwhile, the crushing reparations and other conditions hurt Germany's economy.

Britain and France Recover Britain faced serious economic problems in the 1920s. It was deeply in debt, and its factories were out of date. Unemployment was severe. Wages remained low, leading to worker unrest and frequent strikes. In 1926, a **general strike,** or strike by workers in many different industries at the same time, lasted nine days and involved some three million workers.

In comparison, the French economy recovered fairly rapidly. Financial reparations and territories gained from Germany helped. Still, economic swings did occur, adding to an unstable political scene.

Despite these problems, Europe made a shaky recovery during the 1920s. Economies returned to peacetime manufacturing and trade. Veterans gradually found jobs, although unemployment never ceased to be a problem. Middle-class families enjoyed a rising standard of living.

The American Economy Booms In contrast, the United States emerged from the war as the world's leading economic power. In the affluent 1920s, middle-class Americans enjoyed the benefits of capitalism. American loans and investments backed the recovery in Europe. As long as the American economy prospered, the global economy remained stable.

IDENTIFY CAUSE AND EFFECT How did World War I and its peace treaties affect the international economy?

>> **Analyze Political Cartoons** This political cartoon, called "The Doormat," makes a statement about the world's reaction to Japan's rising militarism. Who is the doormat in the cartoon, and why might this be the case?

Interactive Cartoon

The Great Depression

During the 1920s, European nations made a shaky recovery from World War I, helped in part by American loans and investments. As long as the American economy was healthy, the global economy remained relatively prosperous. Then, at the end of the decade, an economic crisis began in the United States and spread to the rest of the world. This global economic slump, called the **Great Depression,** was the longest, most severe economic downturn to strike the industrialized Western world.

Overproduction and a Drop in Demand Both the American and the world economy had weak points. In the industrial world, a major problem was **overproduction,** meaning that factories and farms produced more goods than were being sold. In other words, supply outpaced demand.

By the 1920s, improved technology and farming methods had led to higher output. When demand for goods slowed, prices fell. Consumers benefited from the lower prices, but farmers, miners, and other suppliers of raw materials did not. Overproduction created a backlog of unsold goods, leading businesses to cut back on output and lay off workers. Unemployed

Online Project the **Interactive Cartoon: League of Nations Fails to Stop Aggression**. Click through the hot spots and discuss the political climate of the postwar period.

ACTIVE CLASSROOM

Arrange students in pairs. Ask one student to give the second a verbal Audio Tour of the cartoon, describing what it shows. Have the second explain what the cartoon means.

Economics in the Postwar Era

World War I was economically devastating for Europe. Following the war, much of Europe relied upon loans and investments from the United States.

Guided Reading and Discussion

Explain that the U.S. was prosperous during the Jazz Age. Although the economies of Britain and France started to recover and stabilize, the global economy relied upon the wealth of the United States.

Ask students to predict the repercussions of a financial crisis in the United States. *(The United States would no longer purchase many of the goods produced in foreign countries and the European economies would suffer.)*

The Great Depression

The Great Depression began in the United States and spread around the world.

Guided Reading and Discussion

Identify developments that led to the Great Depression: overproduction, the stock market crash, and policies of the Federal Reserve. People stopped buying products, creating a surplus of supply, which caused companies to lay off workers, who then reduced purchases.

Answers

Compare Points of View *France wanted strict enforcement to keep Germany weak; Britain wanted loose enforcement to strengthen Germany against the threat of a strong Soviet Union.*

Analyze Political Cartoons *The League of Nations is the doormat, and the members of the League are doing nothing to stop Japan but instead are applying face-saving powder.*

Identify Cause and Effect *Britain and France had huge war debts to the United States and relied on German reparations; Germany's economy was weak due to the burden of reparations and other conditions.*

Have students identify three effects of the Great Depression. *(unemployment; inability to afford food; loss of faith in capitalism and democracy)*

The U.S. economy was central to the international network of trade and finance. When it faltered, it set off a downward spiral of motion that encompassed much of the world. Production in the United States plummeted. Americans had little or no money to invest abroad. Without this money, Europeans could no longer afford American goods and they were unable to pay back loans from the United States.

Sequence Events Describe how the Great Depression began in the United States. *(The price of raw materials and agricultural products fell. Lower prices meant workers were paid less. They could not afford to buy products, reducing demand. The reduced demand and new technology led to overproduction, causing workers to lose their jobs. A stock market crash aggravated the decline.)*

Identify Cause and Effect Why did the Great Depression spread from the United States, eventually affecting world markets? *(The U.S. economy was part of an international network of trade and finance; as its economy faltered, the economies that relied on it faltered, too.)*

workers had no money to spend on buying goods, which slowed demand further and brought more layoffs. This cycle then had a ripple effect throughout the economy.

Crash Leads to Collapse Meanwhile, a crisis in **finance**—the management of money matters, including the circulation of money, loans, investments, and banking—was brewing. Few saw the danger. Prices on the New York Stock Exchange were at an all-time high. Eager investors acquired stocks through risky methods. To slow the run on the stock market, the **Federal Reserve,** the central banking system of the United States, raised interest rates in 1928 and again in 1929.

In the autumn of 1929, jitters about the economy caused brokers to call in the loans made to investors. When investors were unable to repay, financial panic set in. Stock prices crashed in October, wiping out the fortunes of many investors. The stock market crash worsened the economic decline. The Great Depression had begun.

Over the next few years, consumer spending and investment fell, causing still more businesses and factories to close. Millions of people lost their jobs. The cycle spiraled steadily downward. By 1933, between 13 to 15 million Americans were jobless and almost half the banks had closed. The jobless could not afford to buy goods, so more factories had to close, which in turn increased unemployment. People slept on park benches and lined up to eat in soup kitchens.

The Depression Spreads Around the World The economic problems quickly spread around the world. American banks stopped investing or making loans abroad and demanded repayment of foreign loans. Without new investments, European prosperity slowed. Hardest hit were countries, like Britain and Germany, that owed the most to the United States.

In Germany, unemployment rose steeply, leaving one in four workers jobless. Britain was less badly hurt, but its industries and trade were depressed.

Desperate governments tried to protect their economies from foreign competition. The United States imposed the highest tariffs in its history. The policy backfired when other nations retaliated by raising their tariffs. In the end, all countries lost access to the global markets as world trade continued to shrink. The collapse of world trade spread the misery of the Great Depression beyond the industrial world to Latin America, Africa, and Asia.

GENERATE EXPLANATIONS What were three root causes of the Great Depression?

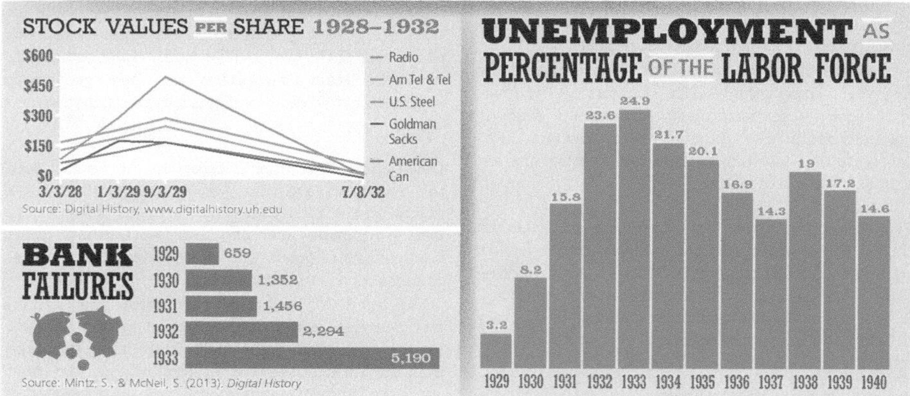

>> **Analyze Information** In what year did unemployment and bank failures peak in the United States?

Answers

Generate Explanations *overproduction by factories, a crisis in finance, and risky speculation in the stock market*

Analyze Information *1933*

Western Democracies React to the Depression

The Great Depression led to changes in government economic policies. For more than a century, Western governments had backed laissez-faire capitalism, the policy that calls for little or no government interference in the economy. During the 1930s, governments in Britain, France, the United States, and elsewhere stepped in to ease the impact of the Great Depression. None of their methods provided a quick fix, but they did alleviate some of the suffering.

>> Striking workers walk down a boulevard in Paris in June 1936.

Britain and France Search for Solutions In response to the Depression, Britain set up a coalition government made up of leaders from all three of its major political parties. The government provided some unemployment benefits. It kept tariffs low throughout the British Empire to boost trade but raised tariffs against the United States and other countries. By the mid-1930s, Britain was slowly recovering from the worst of the Great Depression. Still, unemployment remained high, and the recovery was uneven.

The Great Depression took longer to hurt France than some other countries. However, by the mid-1930s, France was feeling the pinch of decreased production and unemployment. In response, several leftist parties united behind the socialist leader Leon Blum. His Popular Front government tried to solve labor problems and passed some social legislation. But it could not satisfy more radical leftists. Strikes soon brought down Blum's government. Democracy survived, but the country lacked strong leadership able to respond to the clamor for change.

Roosevelt's New Deal Meanwhile, in the United States, President Herbert Hoover firmly believed that the government should not intervene in private business matters. Even so, he did try a variety of limited measures to solve the crisis. Nothing seemed to work.

In 1932, Americans elected a new President, **Franklin D. Roosevelt,** or FDR. Roosevelt argued that the government had to take an active role in combating the Great Depression. He introduced the **New Deal,** a massive package of economic and social programs.

Under the New Deal, the federal government took a more active role in managing the economy than ever before. New laws regulated the stock market and protected bank deposits. Government programs created jobs and gave aid to farmers. A new Social Security system provided pensions for the elderly and other benefits.

As the New Deal programs were being put into effect, a natural disaster in 1934 hit several central states. After years of drought and overfarming, huge winds blew across the plains. The winds picked up and carried away the topsoil exposed by erosion, creating the Dust Bowl. The storms destroyed crops, land, and equipment. Thousands of farmers lost their land. Many migrated to the cities of the West Coast in search of work and a new life.

The New Deal failed to end the Great Depression, although it did ease the suffering for many. Still, some critics fiercely condemned FDR's expansion of the role of government. The debate about the size and role of the U.S. federal government continues to this day.

Loss of Faith in Democracy As the Depression dragged on, many people lost faith in the ability of democratic governments to solve the problems of the modern world. Misery and hopelessness created fertile ground for extremists who promised radical solutions. Communists gloated over what they called the failure of capitalism. Right-wing extremists played on themes of intense nationalism, the failure of democracy, the virtues of authoritarian rule, and the need to rearm. By the late 1930s, aggressive rulers once again threatened the peace.

? EXPLAIN How did the U.S. government react to the Great Depression?

Western Democracies React to the Depression

Britain and France were hit hard by the Great Depression. Both countries instituted policies to provide relief, but their governments hesitated to make radical changes. The U.S. government also took limited measures until Franklin Delano Roosevelt became President.

Guided Reading and Discussion

Remind students how the Great Depression spread from the United States to Europe. Trace the developments and policies each of the Western powers adopted in an effort to lift the Depression. Tell students that the governments of Britain and France lacked strong, decisive action.

The Dust Bowl was an ecological disaster that exacerbated the financial crisis in the United States. Ask students to speculate on how the Dust Bowl affected the entire country. *(Farmers could not produce food; there was massive migration to unaffected states, most notably California.)*

Explain that the massive package of economic and social programs implemented by President Roosevelt, known as the New Deal, greatly expanded the government's role in the daily lives of Americans.

Summarize Summarize Western countries' attempts to end the Great Depression. *(They put into place programs that lessened suffering but did not solve the problems.)*

Identify Patterns As the world struggled to react to the global depression, what unifying political force was lacking in both Britain and France? *(strong leadership capable of taking decisive action)*

D Differentiate Challenge Remind students how FDR's New Deal programs expanded the role of government in the daily lives of Americans. Explain that many Americans disliked this trend, and it remains a central debate in American politics. Ask students to break into groups and stage a classroom debate on this question. Have one side defend the New Deal and the other argue against it.

Answers

Explain *At first, it responded by providing only minimal assistance, but under Roosevelt's New Deal, jobs were created, farmers received aid, Social Security was introduced, and the stock market was regulated.*

Topic 17 Lesson 5

SYNTHESIZE

Online Project the **Digital Activity: Worldwide Economic Crisis**. Explain that the effects of the Great Depression lasted for many years. Ask students to review the readings to identify examples of those effects. *(Economic Effects: vast unemployment and misery; protective tariffs imposed; countries abandon gold standard. Political Effects: governments set up some relief programs; loss of faith in capitalism and democracy; authoritarian leaders emerge. Social Effects: soup kitchens; migration away from the Dust Bowl)*

Draw Conclusions Do you think the Great Depression still has effects today? Explain. *(Yes. Social Security is an example of a policy implemented during the Great Depression that is a standard feature of life today.)*

DEMONSTRATE

Online Assign the **Digital Lesson Quiz** for this lesson if you haven't already done so. Students will be offered automatic remediation or enrichment based on their score.

Post these questions on the Discussion Board:

Draw Conclusions Why did the United States become a leading world economic power during the 1920s? *(Much of Europe had suffered devastating damage during the war. Both Britain and France were heavily in debt to the United States after the war. Also, the United States made significant investments in the recovery and rebuilding that were needed in Europe after World War I.)*

Identify Central Issues How did the Great Depression lay the foundation for the rise of radical extremists? *(It created misery and hopelessness. Governments failed to take decisive action. People were desperate for change.)*

Topic Inquiry

Have students continue their investigations for the Topic Inquiry.

ASSESSMENT

1. **Identify Central Ideas** What cultural changes did Western society experience after World War I?
2. **Make Generalizations** How did the ideas of Einstein and Curie contribute to a sense of uncertainty?
3. **Synthesize** How did Britain and France emerge from World War I as both victors and losers?
4. **Summarize** What were three causes of the Great Depression?
5. **Identify Cause and Effect** How did the Great Depression change government in the United States?

The World Between the Wars  17.5 The West After World War I

Assessment

1. Disillusioned by WWI, the younger generation rebelled against Victorian values. Writers expressed a loss of faith, and artists revolted against traditional styles and created new ways of viewing the world. Advances in science revolutionized scientific thought.
2. Both offered theories that were difficult to understand and questioned many ideas that people previously held as absolute truths.
3. Britain and France, with American help, defeated Germany. Both, however, faced serious political divisions and economic fragility after the war.
4. Three causes of the Great Depression were less demand for raw materials, overproduction of manufactured goods, and the crash of the stock market in 1929.
5. Under the New Deal, the federal government became more directly involved in the lives of Americans than ever before.

17.6 "I hated politics and politicians," said Italo Balbo. Like many Italian veterans of World War I, he had come home to a land of economic chaos and political corruption. Italy's constitutional government, he felt, "had betrayed the hopes of soldiers, reducing Italy to a shameful peace." Disgusted and angry, Balbo rallied behind a fiercely nationalist leader, Benito Mussolini. Mussolini's rise to power in the 1920s served as a model for ambitious strongmen elsewhere in Europe.

>> Mussolini and the National Fascist Party led the March on Rome in October 1922. Fewer than 30,000 men participated in the march, but the king feared a civil war and asked Mussolini to form a cabinet.

Interactive Flipped Video

Fascism Emerges in Italy

TEKS
1.F, 12.A, 12.B, 18.D, 19.B, 21.A, 21.C

>> Objectives

Describe the rise of Mussolini.

Summarize Mussolini's policies as leader of Italy.

Identify the characteristics of totalitarianism and fascism.

>> Key Terms

Benito Mussolini
Black Shirt
March on Rome
totalitarian state
fascism

The Rise of Mussolini

Postwar Discontent When Italy agreed to join the Allies in 1915, France and Britain secretly promised to give Italy certain Austro-Hungarian territories that had large Italian populations. When the Allies won, Italy received some of the promised territories, but others became part of the new Yugoslavia. The broken promises outraged Italian nationalists.

In the postwar years, disorders within Italy multiplied. Inspired in part by the Russian Revolution, peasants seized land, and workers went on strike or seized factories. Their actions frightened landowners and industrialists who had traditionally held power.

Amid the chaos, returning veterans faced unemployment. Trade declined and taxes rose. The government, split into feuding factions, seemed powerless to end the crisis.

Mussolini and the Fascist Party Into this turmoil stepped Benito Mussolini. The son of a socialist blacksmith and a teacher, Mussolini had been a socialist in his youth. During the war, however, he rejected socialism for intense nationalism. In 1919, he organized veterans

771

PEARSON realize. www.PearsonTexas.com Access your Digital Lesson.

Topic 17 Lesson 6

Fascism Emerges in Italy

CONNECT

Preview Have students preview the **Lesson Objectives** and the list of **Key Terms**.

Students can also preview all the **Key Terms** and **Academic Vocabulary** using the **Interactive Reading Notepad** on the digital course or preview a summary of the lesson in the **Reading and Note Taking Study Guide**.

Online Use the **Editable Presentation** found on the digital course to present the main ideas for this lesson.

Start Up Activity

Ask students to look at the image on page 774 of Italian children marching in uniform. Think about why totalitarian governments, which want to limit individual freedoms and demand absolute loyalty from their citizens, would want to win the loyalty of young people. Ask students to answer these questions: Why might young people be attracted to, and be supportive of, totalitarian governments? *(because they did not know any different forms of government, and because totalitarian governments offer a simple view of the world)* How might a totalitarian government recruit children? *(by incorporating totalitarian views into school curricula and through youth groups)*

Online You can also project the **Start Up Activity** from the course.

INVESTIGATE

Have students read the section using the **Reading and Note Taking Study Guide** to help them take notes and understand the text as they read.

The Rise of Mussolini

Explain that Italy was in a state of turmoil after World War I. Many Italians felt cheated by the broken promises made by the Allies. In addition, veterans returned home to economic chaos. When Italians felt they had no strong political leadership to turn to, Benito Mussolini offered hope and stability to Italy.

Aa Vocabulary Builder

1. Have students pronounce the following academic vocabulary terms in this lesson and clarify the part of speech. For difficult or polysyllabic words, break them into syllables and pronounce them with the students.
2. Explain what the word means in common "student-friendly" language using synonyms and antonyms when possible. Provide concrete examples to clarify the meaning, and rephrase the example.

proclaimed: announced officially

ideology: a system of ideas that guides an individual, movement, or political program

Guided Reading and Discussion

Remind students that Mussolini promised to restore the glory of the Roman empire to Italy. Have students identify and define the key term *Black Shirts* from the text. Ask students to list the ways Mussolini and the fascists drew upon the history of ancient Rome. *(Sample response: Fascists took their name from the fasces, which was a symbol of authority in ancient Rome; Mussolini promised to turn the Mediterranean into a "Roman lake.")*

Summarize Summarize the situation in Italy following World War I that led people to support Mussolini. *(Italy had massive unemployment and strikes, rising taxes, and declining trade. The country lacked political unity. Italians desired a new, more effective government and nationalists resented broken promises made by the Allies. Mussolini made big promises but used terror and intimidation to gain political power.)*

> [Only joy at finding such a leader] can explain the enthusiasm [Mussolini] evoked at gathering after gathering, where his mere presence drew the people from all sides to greet him with frenzied acclamations. Even the men who first came out of mere curiosity and with indifference or even hostile feelings gradually felt themselves fired by his personal magnetic influence. . .
>
> —Margherita G. Sarfhatti, *The Life of Benito Mussolini* (tr. Frederic Whyte)

>> In the early 1920s, Benito Mussolini rose to power in Italy. The Italian people were inspired by Mussolini's promises to bring stability and glory to Italy.

and other discontented Italians into the Fascist party. They took the name from the Latin *fasces,*a bundle of sticks wrapped around an ax. In ancient Rome, the fasces symbolized unity and authority.

Mussolini was a fiery and charismatic speaker. He promised to end corruption and replace turmoil with order. He also spoke of reviving Roman greatness, pledging to turn the Mediterranean into a "Roman lake" once again. He held a great deal of power over crowds when he gave his rousing speeches.

> [Only joy at finding such a leader] can explain the enthusiasm [Mussolini] evoked at gathering after gathering, where his mere presence drew the people from all sides to greet him with frenzied acclamations. Even the men who first came out of mere curiosity and with indifference or even hostile feelings gradually felt themselves fired by his personal magnetic influence. . .
>
> —Margherita G. Sarfhatti, *The Life of Benito Mussolini* (tr. Frederic Whyte)

Control by Terror Mussolini organized his supporters into "combat squads." The squads wore black shirts to emulate an earlier nationalist revolt. These **Black Shirts,** or party militants, rejected the democratic process in favor of violent action. They broke up socialist rallies, smashed leftist presses, and attacked farmers' cooperatives. Fascist gangs used intimidation and terror to oust elected officials in northern Italy. Hundreds were killed as new gangs of Black Shirts sprang up all over Italy. Many Italians accepted these actions because they, too, had lost faith in constitutional government.

In 1922, the Fascists made a bid for power. At a rally in Naples, they announced their intention to go to Rome to demand that the government make changes. In the **March on Rome,** tens of thousands of Fascists swarmed toward the capital. Fearing civil war, King Victor Emmanuel III asked Mussolini to form a government as prime minister. Mussolini entered the city triumphantly on October 30, 1922. Without firing a shot, Mussolini

D Differentiate Extra Support To help students practice previewing, ask them to skim headings, images, and boldface key terms before they read the section. Tell them that the subject of the section shifts from a specific topic (Mussolini's rule in Italy) to a broader concept (the nature of fascism) partway through. Based on their previewing, ask them to pinpoint when this shift occurs.

thus obtained a legal appointment from the king to lead Italy.

? DRAW CONCLUSIONS How did postwar disillusionment contribute to Mussolini's rise?

Mussolini's Totalitarian Rule

At first, Fascists held only a few cabinet posts in the new government. By 1925, though, Mussolini had assumed more power and taken the title Il Duce (eel DOO chay), "The Leader." He suppressed rival parties, muzzled the press, rigged elections, and replaced elected officials with Fascist supporters. In 1929, Mussolini received recognition from Pope Pius XI in return for recognizing Vatican City as an independent state, although the pope continued to disagree with some of Mussolini's goals.

In theory, Italy remained a parliamentary monarchy. In fact, it was a dictatorship upheld by terror. Critics were thrown into prison, forced into exile, or murdered. Secret police and propaganda bolstered the regime.

>> The fasces, a bundle of sticks wrapped around an ax, was an ancient Roman symbol of unity and authority. Fascists adopted the name and symbol for their party.

The State Controls the Economy To spur economic growth and end conflicts between owners and workers, Mussolini brought the economy under state control. However, he preserved capitalism.

Under Mussolini's corporate state, representatives of business, labor, government, and the Fascist party controlled industry, agriculture, and trade. This policy did help business, and production increased. This success came at the expense of workers. They were forbidden to strike, and their wages were kept low.

Loyalty to the State To the Fascists, the individual was unimportant except as a member of the state. Men, women, and children were bombarded with slogans glorifying the state and Mussolini. "Believe! Obey! Fight!" loudspeakers blared and posters proclaimed. Men were urged to be ruthless, selfless warriors fighting for the glory of Italy. Women were pushed out of paying jobs. Instead, Mussolini called on women to "win the battle of motherhood." Those who bore more than 14 children were given a medal by Il Duce himself.

Shaping the young was a major Fascist goal. Fascist youth groups toughened children and taught them to obey strict military discipline. Boys and girls learned about the glories of ancient Rome.

Young Fascists marched in torchlight parades, singing patriotic hymns and chanting, "Mussolini is always right." By the 1930s, a generation of young

>> Mussolini viewed propaganda as a key means to win support from the Italian people. The poster here has the Italian words for "to us" written at the bottom, promoting a unified and strong Italy.

Mussolini's Totalitarian Rule

Mussolini's Italy was a dictatorship upheld by terror. Mussolini held absolute power and controlled Italian society, economics, and politics.

Guided Reading and Discussion

Discuss the ways in which Mussolini gained his power. Ask students to speculate as to why it was important for Mussolini to have the support of the pope. *(because many Italians were Roman Catholic and looked to the pope's leadership)*

Explain that Mussolini brought the economy under the control of the state, but he preserved capitalism. Point out that this is a significant difference between communism and fascism. Ensure students understand that the priority of fascism was the success and glory of the state over the interests of the individual. Ask students to think about why people would be willing to relinquish their individual rights. *(Sample response: They did so because people had lost faith in constitutional government in the chaos following World War I.)*

Make Generalizations Briefly summarize the characteristics of a totalitarian state. *(Some basic characteristics of a totalitarian state include a single-party dictatorship; state-controlled economy; use of terror, secret police, and spies; government-sponsored propaganda and strict censorship of the media; use of schools to spread their message.)*

Compare and Contrast Did the lives of women improve under Mussolini's rule? Explain. *(No. Women were pushed out of paying jobs and pressured to stay home to raise children.)*

History Background

All in the Family One of Mussolini's most prominent supporters and assistants was his son-in-law, Galeazzo Ciano. Ciano married Mussolini's favorite daughter, Edda, in 1930. He then served as a diplomat in China before leading a bomber squadron in the Ethiopian war. When Ciano returned to Italy, he climbed high in the Fascist hierarchy, eventually becoming foreign minister in 1936. Many thought that Ciano was Mussolini's natural successor. However, as Italy's position in World War II worsened, Ciano joined with others on the Fascist Grand Council to call on Mussolini to resign. Caught by Mussolini's government in northern Italy, Ciano was tried for treason and executed by a shot in the back in January 1944—despite his close relationship with Mussolini. Ciano's secret diaries, published in 1946, provided a window into behind-the-scenes maneuvering in Fascist Italy.

Answers

Draw Conclusions *It united many Italians in their desire for a new, more effective government, however aggressive.*

Topic 17 Lesson 6

Online Project the **Interactive Gallery: The Makings of an Italian Totalitarian State**. Review each image. Ask: What does each image suggest about how Mussolini used his own image to promote his message? *(Mussolini wanted citizens to be aware of his power and his desire to return Italy to greatness.)*

ACTIVE CLASSROOM

Ask students to review what they have learned using the Wallpaper strategy. Have each student design a piece of Wallpaper that encapsulates key learnings about characteristics of Mussolini's totalitarian state. Post the Wallpaper around the room. Ask students to tour the room and note what others have written or illustrated.

Characteristics of Fascism

Explain that fascism was only one type of totalitarian government. Both fascists and communists established totalitarian governments in which a centralized state controlled all aspects of society.

Online Project the **Interactive Chart: Communism vs. Fascism**. Ask students to place the tiles into the appropriate area: Communism, Fascism, or Both.

ACTIVE CLASSROOM

Have students perform a Write 1–Get 3 activity to answer the question: "What are four key characteristics of fascism?" Have them fold a piece of paper in quarters, write one response in the first box, then move around the classroom asking for other responses. Have them evaluate whether responses are correct and add a correct response until all four boxes are filled. Have students to share their filled pages with the class.

Key Terms

Ask students to find the key term **fascism** (in bold) in the text. The word describes any centralized, authoritarian government system that is not communist and whose policies glorify the state over the individual.

Answers

Identify Main Ideas *Fascist rule changed Italy's government to a dictatorship upheld by terror, brought the economy under state control, and altered domestic life.*

Compare Points of View *Both were characterized by intense loyalty to government or a leader; use of terror; promotion of social change.*

>> Mussolini viewed children as the Fascists of the future and took great interest in education and the youth program. Boys were taught to be strong soldiers and girls were taught to be strong, nurturing mothers.

Interactive Gallery

>> Italians gather at the Palazzio Venezia to hear Mussolini speak at a celebration of the seventh anniversary of Fascist Italy.

soldiers stood ready to back Il Duce's drive to expand Italian power.

Building a Totalitarian State Mussolini and the Fascist Party built the first modern **totalitarian state.** In this form of government, a one-party dictatorship regulates every aspect of the lives of its citizens. Fascist Italy served as a model for fascist rule in other European nations. Still, Fascist rule in Italy was never as absolute as those imposed by the communists in the Soviet Union or the Nazis in Germany.

Mussolini's rule was fascist in nature, as was Hitler's. However, totalitarian governments rise under other kinds of ideology as well, such as communism in Stalin's Soviet Union.

All of these totalitarian governments shared common features. They were single-party dictatorships in which the state controlled the economy. The party was led by a dictator, who used police spies and terrorism to control the people and demanded unquestioning obedience. The government controlled the media and enforced strict censorship. It used every means possible to indoctrinate, or mold, its citizens' ideas and thoughts.

 **IDENTIFY MAIN IDEAS** How did the Fascist party transform Italy's government and economy?

Characteristics of Fascism

Historians still debate the real nature of Mussolini's fascist ideology. Mussolini coined the term, but fascists had no unifying theory as Marxists did. Today, we generally use the term **fascism** to describe any centralized, authoritarian government that is not communist whose policies glorify the state over the individual and are destructive to basic human rights. In the 1920s and 1930s, though, fascism meant different things in different countries.

Features of Fascism All forms of fascism, however, shared some basic features. They were rooted in extreme nationalism. Fascists glorified action, violence, discipline, and, above all, blind loyalty to the state.

Fascists also pursued aggressive foreign expansion. Echoing the idea of "survival of the fittest," Fascist leaders glorified warfare as a noble struggle for survival. "War alone," declared Mussolini, "brings to its highest tension all human energy and puts the stamp of nobility upon peoples who have the courage to face it."

Fascists were also antidemocratic. They rejected the Enlightenment emphasis on reason and the concepts of equality and liberty. To them, democracy led to

English Language Proficiency Standards

ELPS Learning Strategies 5.F.1 Read "Characteristics of Fascism" aloud. Explain that sentence variety makes writing more interesting to read.

Beginning Reread the text. Ask students to name features of fascism. Help students write two simple sentences about fascism. Combine them into a single compound sentence.

Intermediate Repeat the Beginning activity but have students write the two simple sentences themselves. Assist them in combining the two sentences into a single compound sentence.

Advanced Have students reread the text and then work with a partner to list features of fascism and write four simple sentences to describe it. Have them combine the four simple sentences into two compound sentences and share with the class.

Advanced High Have students reread the text, write four to six simple sentences to describe fascism, and then combine them into two or three compound sentences. Have students share sentences with a partner.

corruption and weakness. They claimed democracy put individual or class interests above national goals and destroyed feelings of community. Instead, fascists emphasized emotion and the need for individuals to serve the state.

The Appeal of Fascism Given its restrictions on individual freedom, why did fascism appeal to many Italians? First, it promised a strong, stable government and an end to the political feuding that had paralyzed democracy in Italy. Mussolini projected a sense of power and confidence at a time of disorder and despair. His intense nationalism also revived national pride, which helped further the shift of political thought throughout Italy.

At first, Il Duce received good press outside Italy. Newspapers in Britain, France, and North America applauded the discipline and order of Mussolini's government. "He got the trains running on time," admirers said. Only later, when Mussolini embarked on a course of foreign conquest, did Western democracies protest.

Fascism and Communism Compared Three systems of government competed for influence in postwar Europe. Democracy endured in Britain and France but faced an uphill struggle in hard times. In Italy, fascism offered a different option. As the Great Depression spread, other nations—most notably Germany—looked to fascist leaders. Communism emerged in Russia and won support elsewhere.

Fascists were the sworn enemies of socialists and communists. While communists called for a worldwide revolution of the working class, fascists pursued nationalist goals. Fascists supported a society with defined classes. They found allies among business leaders, wealthy landowners, and the lower middle class. Communists touted a classless society. They won support among both urban and agricultural workers.

Despite basic differences, in practice these two ideologies had much in common. Both flourished during economic hard times by promoting extreme programs of social change. In both communist Russia and fascist Italy, dictators imposed totalitarian governments in order to bring about their revolutions. Both encouraged blind devotion to the state or a charismatic leader. Both used terror to guard their power. In both, a party elite claimed to rule in the name of the national interest.

? COMPARE POINTS OF VIEW Describe the similarities between fascism and communism.

>> This poster depicts Mussolini working alongside Italian builders. Like much Fascist propaganda, it was designed to convey a sense of purpose and strength.

Interactive Chart

ASSESSMENT

1. **Identify Cause and Effect** What problems did Italy face after World War I, and how did these problems help Mussolini win power?
2. **Summarize** Describe one of Mussolini's economic or social goals, and explain the actions he took to achieve it.
3. **Compare and Contrast** List two similarities and two differences between fascism and communism.
4. **Explain** Why is control of the media important in a totalitarian state?
5. **Contrast** How did fascist values differ from democratic principles and goals?

SYNTHESIZE

Online Project the **Digital Activity: The Economics of Totalitarian Governments**. Ask students to answer these questions: Summarize the economic policies of fascism and communism. *(Fascism: brought the economy under state control but preserved capitalism; supported by business leaders, wealthy landowners, and the lower-middle class; Communism: advocated a classless society and complete state control over the economy; supported by urban and agricultural workers)* Why do you think totalitarian governments gained power during economic hard times? *(Because people were tired of economic instability and the social unrest it caused; democracies move slowly and tend to offer incremental changes; however, people had been suffering for many years and wanted immediate and drastic action to be taken for improving the economic situation.)*

DEMONSTRATE

Online Assign the **Digital Lesson Quiz** for this lesson if you haven't already done so. Students will be offered automatic remediation or enrichment based on their score.

Post these questions to the class on the Discussion Board:

Draw Conclusions How and why did fascism rise in Italy? *(Led by Mussolini, fascists took advantage of Italy's postwar turmoil to seize control.)*

Predict Consequences During the 1930s, nations such as Japan and Germany adopt increasingly aggressive foreign policies. How do you think Mussolini will react? *(He could make alliances and join forces with Germany.)*

Topic Inquiry

Have students continue their investigations for the Topic Inquiry.

Assessment

1. The country experienced anger at the loss of promised territories; unemployment, labor disorder, and weak governments; Mussolini exploited these problems in order to unite Italians.
2. Sample response: He wanted economic growth and an end to workplace conflicts. He brought the economy under state control and made strikes illegal.
3. Similarities: Both promoted social change, imposed totalitarian governments, and claimed to rule in the people's interest. Differences: Communists sought world revolution and a classless society, while fascists pursued nationalism and a society with defined classes.
4. It enables the state to censor information and spread propaganda to control the people better.
5. Unlike democracy, fascism rejected the concepts of equality and liberty, placed national goals above individual interests, and emphasized the role of emotion over reason.

Topic 17 Lesson 7

The Soviet Union Under Stalin

CONNECT

Preview Have students preview the **Lesson Objectives** and the list of **Key Terms**.

Students can also preview all the **Key Terms** and **Academic Vocabulary** using the **Interactive Reading Notepad** on the digital course or preview a summary of the lesson in the **Reading and Note Taking Study Guide**.

Online Use the **Editable Presentation** found on the digital course to present the main ideas for this lesson.

Start Up Activity

Through shrewd political maneuvering, Joseph Stalin became leader of the Soviet Union, and his chief rival, Leon Trotsky, fled the country. Stalin eventually ordered Trotsky's murder in 1940. Have students answer this question: Based on Stalin's relationship with Trotsky, what kind of national leader do you think Stalin will be? *(Stalin might be ruthless and cunning, pursuing and silencing critics and potential rivals.)*

Online You can also project the **Start Up Activity** from the course.

INVESTIGATE

Have students read the section using the **Reading and Note Taking Study Guide** to help them take notes and understand the text as they read.

Stalin Builds a Command Economy

Lenin and the Communists were faced with the enormous task of rebuilding Russian society after World War I. Lenin's policy of "war communism" outraged the people and brought the Russian economy to the brink of collapse. After Lenin died in 1924, Stalin took power and instituted a "command economy" in which the government decided what would be produced, how it would be produced, and to whom products and services would be distributed.

>> One million Russians attended Lenin's funeral march in Red Square. His death set off a power struggle within the Soviet Union.

17.7 By 1921, Lenin and the Communists had won the civil war that followed the Russian Revolution. They were then faced with the enormous task of rebuilding Russian society. Millions of Russians had died since the outbreak of World War I, from fighting and from famine, and Russia was in a state of chaos. Lenin's policy of "war communism" outraged the people and brought the Russian economy to the brink of collapse.

TEKS
1.F, 11.B, 12.A, 12.B, 19.B, 22.C

>> Objectives

Explain how Stalin built a command economy in the Soviet Union.

Describe how Stalin used terror to build a totalitarian state.

Analyze Stalin's use of propaganda to control thought and the arts.

Summarize the characteristics of Soviet society under Stalin.

Understand the goals of Soviet foreign policy.

>> Key Terms

command economy
collective
kulak
Gulag
socialist realism
Osip Mandelstam
Boris Pasternak
russification
atheism
Comintern

The Soviet Union Under Stalin

Stalin Builds a Command Economy

That year, Lenin introduced his New Economic Policy, which allowed limited capitalism. This brief compromise with capitalism helped the Soviet economy recover and ended the armed resistance to Lenin's government.

Stalin Takes Charge Lenin died in January 1924. Tens of thousands of people lined up in Moscow's historic Red Square to view his body. Lenin's widow, Nadezhda Krupskaya, had wanted to bury him simply next to his mother. But Joseph Stalin wanted to preserve Lenin's body and put it on permanent display. In the end, Lenin's body was displayed in Red Square for more than 65 years. By preserving Lenin's body, Stalin wanted to show that he would carry on the goals of the revolution.

In fact, Stalin moved the Soviet Union in directions Karl Marx had never foreseen. Marx had predicted that under communism the state would eventually wither away. Instead, Stalin turned the Soviet Union into a totalitarian state controlled by a powerful and complex

www.PearsonTexas.com Access your Digital Lesson.

776

Aa Vocabulary Builder

1. Have students pronounce the following academic vocabulary terms in this lesson and clarify the part of speech. For difficult or polysyllabic words, break them into syllables and pronounce them with the students.
2. Explain what the word means in common "student-friendly" language using synonyms and antonyms when possible. Provide concrete examples to clarify the meaning, and rephrase the example.

conform: to obey a set of standards
access: the ability to get and use

bureaucracy. For almost 30 years, Stalin held more power than any other leader in history.

Stalin's Five-Year Plans Once in power, Stalin set out to make the Soviet Union a modern industrial power. In the past, said Stalin, Russia had suffered because of its economic backwardness. In 1928, he proposed the first of several "five-year plans" aimed at building heavy industry, improving transportation, and increasing farm output.

To achieve his goals, Stalin brought all economic activity under government control. The government owned all businesses and distributed all resources. The Soviet Union developed a **command economy,** in which government officials made all basic economic decisions. By contrast, in a capitalist system, the free market determines most economic decisions. Privately owned businesses compete to win the consumer's choice. This competition regulates the price and quality of goods.

Stalin's five-year plans set high production goals, especially for heavy industry and transportation. The government pushed workers and managers to meet these goals by giving bonuses to those who succeeded—and by punishing those who did not. Between 1928 and 1939, large factories, hydroelectric power stations, and huge industrial complexes rose across the Soviet Union. Oil, coal, and steel production grew. Mining expanded, and new railroads were built.

Industrial Policy Yields Mixed Results During this time, the West was in the grip of the Great Depression. The Soviet Union had little international trade, so it was insulated from many of the harshest effects of the global economic crisis. Some people in Europe and North American pointed to the industrial growth of the Soviet Union as proof that Stalin's economic policies were successful—ignoring the fact that this success came at a staggering human cost.

Despite impressive progress in some areas, Soviet workers had little to show for their efforts. Some former peasants did become skilled factory workers or managers. Overall, though, the standard of living remained low. Wages were low, workers were forbidden to strike, and consumer goods were scarce. Central planning was often inefficient, causing shortages of some goods and surpluses of others. Many managers, concerned only with meeting production quotas, turned out large quantities of low-quality goods.

During and after the Stalin era, the Soviet Union continued to produce well in heavy industry, such as the manufacture of farm machinery. But its planned economy failed to match the capitalist world in making consumer goods, such as clothing and cars.

Forced Collectivization in Agriculture Causes Misery Stalin also brought agriculture under government control, but at a horrendous cost. The government wanted farmers to produce more grain to

EFFECTS OF STALIN'S FIVE-YEAR PLANS

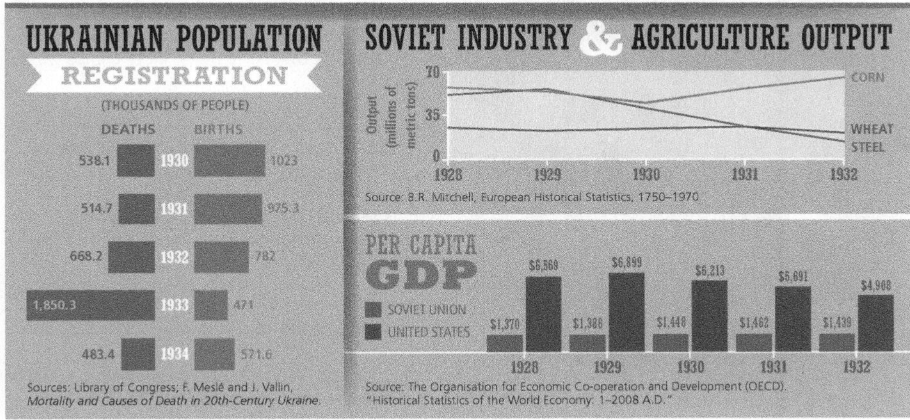

>> **Analyze Information** Describe the effect of the Five-Year Plans on steel and corn production.

Guided Reading and Discussion

Have students explain why many Westerners suffering the effects of the Great Depression might point to the industrial growth of the Soviet Union during this period as proof that Stalin's economic policies were successful.

Generate Explanations Why did Stalin believe peasant-owned farms were a threat to state power? *(Sample response: The state could not control the production of peasant-owned farms. Stalin wanted to ensure that the state controlled all production and strictly controlled access to resources.)*

Answers

Analyze Information *The output for corn went up after 1930, and the output for steel went down after 1929.*

Topic 17 Lesson 7

Control Through Terror

Gulags were forced labor camps. Stalin used the threat of labor camps to control life in the Soviet Union. Stalin also used secret police, torture, and violent purges to ensure absolute obedience. The police monitored private communications, and the government controlled the press.

Guided Reading and Discussion

Discuss the Great Purge that began in 1934 and Stalin's staged "show trials." Ask, "If Stalin had absolute control, why do you think he would bother with a public display of justice?" *(Sample response: to give the public the perception that the trials were legitimate and to display the consequences for disloyalty)* Explain that the Soviet Union lost many of its top experts, writers, thinkers, and military leaders during the Great Purge.

Synthesize Why did Stalin target Old Bolsheviks during the Great Purge? *(Sample response: They were possible rivals for power.)*

feed workers in the cities. It also hoped to sell grain abroad to earn money.

Under Lenin's New Economic Plan (NEP), peasants had held on to small plots of land. Many had prospered. Stalin saw that system as being inefficient and a threat to state power. Stalin wanted all peasants to farm on either state-owned farms or **collectives,** large farms owned and operated by peasants as a group.

On collectives, the government provided tractors, fertilizers, and better seed, and peasants learned modern farm methods. Peasants were permitted to keep their houses and personal belongings, but all farm animals and implements had to be turned over to the collective. The state set all prices and controlled access to farm supplies.

Many peasants resisted collectivization by killing farm animals, destroying tools, and burning crops. The government responded with brutal force. Stalin targeted **kulaks,** or wealthy farmers.

In 1929, Stalin declared his intention to "liquidate the kulaks as a class." To this end, the government confiscated kulaks' land and sent them to slave labor camps, where thousands were executed or died from overwork.

Despite the repression, angry peasants continued to resist by growing just enough to feed themselves.

>> The Gulag was the system of Soviet forced-labor camps. It housed political prisoners as well as actual criminals and became a symbol of political repression in the Soviet Union.

In response, the government seized all of their grain for the cities, purposely leaving the peasants to starve. In 1932, this ruthless policy, combined with poor harvests, led to a terrible famine. Later called the Terror Famine, it caused between five and eight million people to die of starvation in the Ukraine alone. Millions more died in other parts of the Soviet Union.

Although collectivization increased Stalin's control of the peasantry, it did not improve farm output. During the 1930s, grain production inched upward, but meat, vegetables, and fruits remained in short supply. Feeding the population would remain a major problem in the Soviet Union.

? EXPLAIN How did Stalin take control of the Soviet Union's economic life?

Control Through Terror

In addition to tactics like the Terror Famine, Stalin's totalitarian state used secret police, torture, and violent purges to ensure obedience. Stalin tightened his grasp on every aspect of Soviet life, stamping out any signs of dissent even within the Communist elite.

Terror as a Weapon Stalin ruthlessly used terror as a weapon against his own people. He perpetrated crimes against humanity, carried out politically motivated mass murders, and systematically violated his people's individual rights. Police spies did not hesitate to open private letters or plant listening devices. A vast network of internal spies reported on groups or individuals. Nothing appeared in print without official approval. There was no free press, and no safe method of voicing protest. Grumblers or critics were rounded up and sent to the **Gulag,** a system of brutal labor camps, where many died.

Stalin's Great Purge Even though Stalin's power was absolute, he had obsessive fears that rival party leaders were plotting against him. In 1934, he launched the Great Purge. During this reign of terror, Stalin and his secret police cracked down especially on Old Bolsheviks, or party activists from the early days of the revolution. His net soon widened to target army heroes, industrial managers, writers, and ordinary citizens. They were charged with a wide range of crimes, from counter-revolutionary plots to failure to meet production quotas.

Between 1936 and 1938, Stalin staged a series of spectacular public "show trials" in Moscow. Former Communist leaders confessed to all kinds of crimes after officials tortured them or threatened their families or friends.

English Language Proficiency Standards

ELPS 4.K Read "Stalin Builds a Totalitarian State" aloud. Ask students think about their opinions of how Stalin attempted to control the ideas and feelings of Soviet citizens.

Beginning Reread and retell "Propaganda and the 'Cult of Personality.'" Explain that it is important to form opinions about historical events by evaluating the actions of a historical figure. Evaluate Stalin's actions by summarizing the subsection. Offer simple sentences that show a judgment of Stalin's actions and reasons to support that judgment. Ask open-ended questions that guide students to an evaluation of Stalin's actions and goals. Apply this to "Censoring the Arts."

Intermediate Complete the Beginning activity, but have students paraphrase the reading.

Advanced Complete the Intermediate activity, but have students lead the discussion and ask each other questions. If time allows, continue to evaluate Stalin's actions and goals as they are described in the rest of the text. Offer support as needed.

Answers

Explain *Stalin's government took control of all businesses, distributed all resources, and made all basic economic decisions. He also insisted on the collectivization of agriculture.*

Many of the purged party members were never tried but were sent straight to the Gulag. Secret police files reveal that at least four million people were purged during the Stalin years. Some historians estimate the toll to be much greater.

Impact of the Great Purge The purges increased Stalin's power. The purges destroyed the older generation of revolutionaries, replacing them with younger party members who owed absolute loyalty to Stalin. The program of terror increased Stalin's power by impressing on the Soviet people the dangers of disloyalty.

However, the Soviet Union paid a heavy price. Among the victims of the purges were experts in industry, economics, and engineering, and many of the Soviet Union's most talented writers and thinkers. The purged also included most of the nation's military leaders and about half of its military officers. The loss of so many military leaders would come back to haunt Stalin in 1941, when Germany invaded the Soviet Union.

IDENTIFY CAUSE AND EFFECT In what ways did Stalin's terror tactics harm the Soviet Union?

>> Stalin used propaganda to win the hearts and minds of Soviet citizens. This poster reads, "Thanks to dear Stalin for a happy childhood."

 Interactive Gallery

Stalin Builds a Totalitarian State

The use of terror and intimidation was one of the major characteristics of Stalin's totalitarian stage. Like other totalitarian rulers, Stalin sought to control the hearts and minds of Soviet citizens. He tried to do this by tirelessly distributing propaganda, censoring opposing ideas, imposing Russian culture on minorities, and replacing religion with communist ideology.

Propaganda and the "Cult of Personality" Stalin tried to boost morale and faith in the communist system by making himself a godlike figure. He used propaganda as a tool to build up a "cult of personality" around himself.

Using modern technology, the party bombarded the public with relentless propaganda. Radios and loudspeakers blared into factories and villages. In movies, theaters, and schools, citizens heard about communist successes and the evils of capitalism.

Billboards and posters urged workers to meet or exceed production quotas. Headlines in the Communist party newspaper *Pravda*,or "Truth," linked enemies at home to foreign agents seeking to overthrow the Communist regime.

Censoring the Arts At first, the Bolshevik Revolution had meant greater freedom for Soviet artists and writers. Under Stalin, however, the heavy hand of state control also gripped the arts. The government controlled what books were published, what music was heard, and which works of art were displayed. Stalin required artists and writers to follow a style called **socialist realism.** Its goal was to show Soviet life in a positive light. Artists and writers could criticize the bourgeois past, but their overall message had to promote hope in the socialist future. Popular themes for socialist realist artists were peasants, workers, and heroes of the revolution—and, of course, Stalin.

Artists who ignored socialist realism guidelines could not get materials, work space, or jobs. Writers, artists, and composers also faced government persecution. The Jewish poet **Osip Mandelstam,** for example, was imprisoned, tortured, and exiled for composing a satirical verse about Stalin. Out of fear for his wife's safety, Mandelstam finally submitted to threats and wrote an "Ode to Stalin." **Boris Pasternak,** who would later win fame for his novel *Doctor Zhivago,* was afraid to publish anything at all during the Stalin years. Rather than write in the favored style of socialist realism, he translated foreign literary works instead.

Topic 17 Lesson 7

Stalin Builds a Totalitarian State

Under Stalin, the Communists controlled the press, arts, and media. The Communists tried to control every aspect of the people's daily lives. Stalin attempted to remove religious institutions and replace them with communist ideology.

Guided Reading and Discussion

Discuss the all-encompassing nature of Stalin's propaganda. Explain that the Soviet people were unable to escape the barrage of loudspeakers, billboards, films, music, and posters. Authors, musicians, and artists faced dire consequences if they failed to conform to and meet Stalin's expectations. Fear for their own safety and that of their loved ones motivated artists to produce works to please Stalin.

Compare and Contrast Do you think the constant communist propaganda in the Soviet Union is similar to advertising in America today? Explain. *(No. People can ignore advertisements without fear of physical harm.)*

Online Project the **Interactive Gallery: Art as Propaganda**. As students go through the images, explain that art, music, literature, film, and the news media were used to craft an image of a caring, protective, all-powerful leader of the Soviet Union. Point out that Stalin's use of propaganda and strict censorship of the media are key features of a totalitarian state.

ACTIVE CLASSROOM

Have students review the Interactive Gallery. Ask students to Take a Stand on the following question: Is propaganda an effective tool for public persuasion? Divide into two groups based on whether they answer yes or no. Have each group discuss the reason for their answer. Ask a representative from each side to present and defend the group's point of view.

Advanced High Complete the Advanced activity, but have groups of four or five evaluate the use of propaganda and ask each other questions to refine their logic and identify the best sources of factual support.

Answers

Identify Cause and Effect *The country lost many of its intellectual and military leaders.*

Topic 17 Lesson 7

Generate Explanations Briefly explain Stalin's policy of russification. *(Russification was an attempt to unify the diverse peoples of the Soviet Union by imposing Russian culture on all of them. Russia was only one republic in the Soviet Union, but it was the most powerful. Stalin wanted to replace regional identities with a universal Russian identity.)*

Key Terms

Ask students to find the key term **atheism** (in bold) in the text. The word describes the belief that there is no god. What did the Communists do to try to replace the Russian Orthodox Church with atheism?

Analyze Images

Have students look at the map The Soviet Union, 1928–1941. Point out the different republics and the regions of forced labor camps. What does the number of labor camps in the Soviet Union indicate about Stalin's rule? *(There were many labor camps because Stalin needed the threat of imprisonment to guarantee his dominance.)*

Despite restrictions, some Soviet writers produced magnificent works whose themes reflected the history and culture of Stalinist Russia. Yevgeny Zamyatin's classic anti-Utopian novel *We* became well known outside of the Soviet Union, but was not published in his home country until 1989. The novel depicts a nightmare future in which people go by numbers, not names, and the "One State" controls people's thoughts.

And Quiet Flows the Don, by Mikhail Sholokhov, passed the censor. The novel tells the story of a man who spends years fighting in World War I, the Russian Revolution, and the civil war. Sholokhov later won the Nobel Prize for literature.

Russification of the Republics Yet another way Stalin controlled the cultural life of the Soviet Union was by promoting a policy of **russification,** or imposing Russian culture on the diverse Soviet empire. During the Soviet era, the U.S.S.R. came to include 15 separate republics. Russia, or the Russian Soviet Federated Socialist Republic, was the largest and dominant republic. The others, such as Uzbek and the Ukraine, had their own languages, historical traditions, and cultures.

At first, Stalin encouraged the autonomy, or independence, of these cultures. However, in the late 1920s, Stalin turned this policy on its head and systematically tried to promote Russian culture. He appointed Russians to high-ranking positions in non-Russian SSRs and required the Russian language to be used in schools and businesses. Many Russian citizens were sent to settle in the other republics, furthering the spread of Russian customs and culture.

Communists Wage War on Religion In accordance with the ideas of Marx, **atheism,** or the belief that there is no god, became the official Soviet state policy. Early on, the Communists targeted the Russian Orthodox Church, which had strongly supported the tsars. The party seized most religious property, converting many churches into offices and museums. Many priests and other religious leaders were killed in the purges or sent to die in prison camps.

Other religions were persecuted as well. At one show trial, 15 Roman Catholic priests were charged with teaching religion to the young, a counter-revolutionary activity. The state seized Jewish synagogues and banned the use of Hebrew. Islam was also officially discouraged.

The Communists tried to replace religion with their own ideology. Like a religion, communist ideology had its own "sacred" texts—the writings of Marx and Lenin—and its own shrines, such as the tomb of Lenin. Portraits of Stalin replaced religious icons in Russian

>> **Analyze Maps** Stalin used terror and labor camps to control the huge, multinational Soviet Union. In which part of the Soviet Union was the heaviest concentration of Gulag labor camps?

English Language Proficiency Standards

ELPS 5.F.2 Review sentence patterns. Read "Soviet Society Under Stalin" aloud. Have students complete the activities below according to their level of English proficiency.

Beginning Reread the section and retell the content as students follow along. Explain that they will be writing a simple sentence with a noun and a verb about what they learned from this section. Model writing simple sentences.

Intermediate Complete the Beginning activity, but have students retell the content and write two sentences with a noun, verb, and object. Have volunteers share aloud. Display the shared sentences.

Advanced Have students reread the section. Have pairs write three sentences with a subject, verb, indirect object, and direct object or a subject, verb, and complement. Have pairs

Answers

Analyze Maps *in the northwest*

homes. However, millions of Soviets continued to worship, in private and sometimes in public, in defiance of government prohibitions.

IDENTIFY CENTRAL IDEAS How did Stalin use censorship and propaganda to support his rule?

Soviet Society Under Stalin

The terror and cultural coercion of Stalin's rule made a mockery of the original theories and promises of communism. The lives of most Russians did change. But, while the changes had some benefits, they were often outweighed by continuous shortages and restricted freedoms.

The Soviet Elite Takes Control The Communists destroyed the old social order of landowning nobles at the top and peasants at the bottom. But instead of creating the classless society that Marx had predicted, they created a society where a few elite groups emerged as a new ruling class. At the top of society were members of the Communist party. Only a small fraction of Soviet citizens could join the party. Many who did so were motivated by a desire to get ahead, rather than a belief in communism. The Soviet elite also included industrial managers, military leaders, scientists, and some artists and writers.

The elite enjoyed benefits denied to most people. They lived in the best apartments in the cities and rested at the best vacation homes in the country. They could shop at special stores for scarce consumer goods. On the other hand, Stalin's purges often targeted the elite.

Limited Benefits Although excluded from party membership, most people did enjoy several new benefits. The party required all children to attend free Communist-built schools. The state supported technical schools and universities as well.

Schools served many important goals. Educated workers were needed to build a modern industrial state. The Communist party also set up programs for students outside school. These programs included sports, cultural activities, and political classes to train teenagers for party membership. However, in addition to important basic skills, schools also taught communist values, such as atheism, the glory of collective farming, and love of Stalin.

The state also provided free medical care, day care for children, inexpensive housing, and public recreation. While these benefits were real, many people

>> To weaken the power of the Russian Orthodox Church, the party seized church property and converted churches into offices and museums. Here, Red Army soldiers carry off religious relics from a church.

Interactive Chart

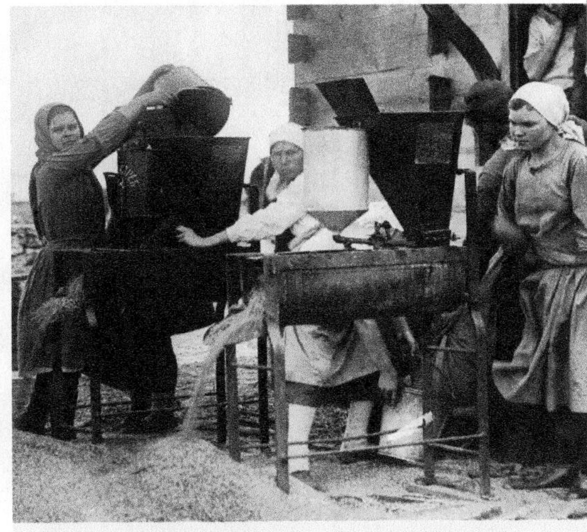

>> The majority of citizens in the Soviet Union were peasants. Here, Soviet women on a collective farm using machinery to clean grain.

Soviet Society Under Stalin

The Communists created a society where a few elite groups had complete government control. Those able to join the party usually did so to gain power and access to special treatment, such as the best housing and finest foods. The majority of the population gained few benefits and lacked adequate housing and many basic foods.

Online Project the **Interactive Graphic Organizer: Characteristics of Stalin's Rule**. Ask students to use the graphic organizer to list characteristics under *Political, Economic,* and *Social* headings. Be sure students understand there is no "right answer" for many characteristics and some can be categorized under more than one heading. *(Row 1: "What were Stalin's goals in this area?" Political: Totalitarian state; Economic: Collectivization and state control of agriculture; Social: Absolute control of cultural expression and thought. Row 2: "What policies did Stalin implement in this area?" Political: Gulags, secret police, and purges; Economic: Command economy, Five-year plans; Social: Propaganda and censorship. Row 3: "What was the impact on Soviet life?" Political: New elite in control of governmental power; Economic: Poor agricultural output led to famine; Social: Women gain equal rights, Low standard of living)*

ACTIVE CLASSROOM

Have students list the characteristics of Stalin's rule, and write their suggestions on the board. Ask students to use the Rank It strategy to rank the characteristics from most significant to least significant. Students should find evidence from the text to support their decisions.

share sentences and choose two sentences to share aloud.

Advanced High Have students reread the section and write four or five sentences about Soviet society. Each should include a subject, verb, indirect object, and direct object or a subject, verb, object, and complement. Have students share their work aloud.

Answers

Identify Central Ideas *Stalin used propaganda to glorify himself, to spread communist ideology, and to malign opponents. He used censorship to stifle those who did not agree with him.*

Guided Reading and Discussion

Discuss the benefits and drawbacks of living under Stalin. Explain that the state provided free medical care, day care, subsidized housing, and public recreation. However, adequate housing and food supply were limited.

Explain that women gained equality under the law and worked alongside men as equals in factories, in construction, on collectives, in engineering, and in the sciences.

Compare Did the lives of women improve under the Communists? Explain. *(Sample response: No. Both women and men were paid low wages under the Communists, were forced to work in harsh conditions, and lacked adequate housing or readily available food.)*

Draw Conclusions Which of Stalin's policies do you think was most effective in maintaining control over the Soviet Union? Why? *(Sample response: The policy of using secret police to spy on people and then send dissenters to the Gulag was probably the most effective because anyone who opposed Stalin risked losing everything.)*

Soviet Foreign Policy

The Soviet Union encouraged worldwide revolution, but also wanted the support of other countries to ensure the security and power of the Soviet Union. Stalin feared a growing threat from Nazi Germany and suggested that Russia, France, and Britain form an alliance. Then, Stalin turned around and signed an alliance with Nazi Germany.

>> Soviet ideology stressed gender equality in labor and education. Many Soviet women held jobs and earned advanced degrees.

>> Lenin founded the Comintern to inspire revolution around the world. Here, he is giving a speech to the delegates of the third congress of the Comintern in 1921.

still lacked vital necessities. Although the state built massive apartment complexes, housing was scarce. Entire families might be packed into a single room. Bread was plentiful, but meat, fresh fruit, and other foods remained in short supply.

Women Win Greater Equality Long before 1917, women such as Lenin's wife, Nadezhda Krupskaya, worked for the revolution, spreading radical ideas among peasants and workers. In 1905, Alexandra Kollontai noted "how little our party concerned itself with the fate of working class women." After becoming the only high-ranking woman in Lenin's government, she continued her campaign for women's rights.

Under the Communists, women won equality under the law. They gained access to education and a wide range of jobs.

By the 1930s, many Soviet women were working in medicine, engineering, or the sciences. By their labor, women contributed to Soviet economic growth. They worked in factories, in construction, and on collectives. Within the family, their wages were needed because men and women earned the same low salaries.

GENERATE EXPLANATIONS How did Communist schools benefit the state and Communist party?

Soviet Foreign Policy

Between 1917 and 1939, the Soviet Union pursued two very different goals in foreign policy. As communists, both Lenin and Stalin wanted to bring about the worldwide revolution that Marx had predicted. But as Soviets, they wanted to guarantee their nation's security by winning the support of other countries. The result was a contradictory and generally unsuccessful foreign policy.

Promoting Communist Revolution In 1919, Lenin formed the Communist International, or **Comintern.** Its purpose was to encourage worldwide revolution. To this end, it aided revolutionary groups around the world and urged colonial peoples to rise up against imperialist powers.

The Comintern's support of revolutionary groups outside the Soviet Union and its loud propaganda against capitalism made Western powers suspicious of the Soviet Union.

In the United States, fear of Bolshevik plots led to the "Red Scare" in the early 1920s. Britain temporarily broke off relations with the Soviet Union when evidence revealed Soviet schemes to turn the 1926 general strike into a revolution.

Answers

Generate Explanations *Schools taught communist values, such as atheism, the glory of collective farming, and love of Stalin, which benefited the Communist party. Schools benefited the state by training workers in the skills needed for an industrial economy, and they provided students with opportunities for higher education and extracurricular activities.*

Seeking Recognition Even while the Comintern supported the global communist struggle, the Soviet Union sought international recognition and trade with capitalist countries, especially the United States and Britain. In 1933, the United States and Soviet Union finally set up diplomatic relations, and the following year, the Soviets joined the League of Nations. However, mistrust still poisoned relations, especially after the Great Purge.

In the early years of Stalin's rule, the Soviet Union remained, for the most part, isolated from the West. By the late 1930s, however, Stalin feared a growing threat from Nazi Germany. In April 1939, he suggested that Russia, France, and Britain form an alliance against Germany. Western suspicions of Soviet intentions made an agreement impossible. Within months, Stalin made an about-face and signed an alliance with Nazi Germany.

ANALYZE INFORMATION How did the Soviet Union's foreign policy goals contradict one another?

ASSESSMENT

1. **Identify Cause and Effect** What were the goals and results of Stalin's five-year plans?
2. **Contrast** For those not in the elite party, how did life change under Soviet rule?
3. **Explain** How did Stalin attempt to control thought in the Soviet Union?
4. **Summarize** What methods did Stalin use to create a totalitarian state?
5. **Compare** What foreign policy goals did both Lenin and Stalin pursue?

Topic 17 Lesson 7

SYNTHESIZE

Online Project the **Digital Activity: Stalin's Soviet Union**. Review the main headings from the lesson. Explain that each heading details an important aspect or characteristic of the Soviet Union during this time period. Ask students to use the graphic organizer to list the main ideas under each heading, and have them reflect on the Topic Essential Question: What should governments do? Have them respond to the question based on what they have learned about the Soviet Union. *(Sample response: Students may point out that governments should benefit their citizens, offer a certain level of personal freedom, and not force citizens to live in constant fear of punishment.)*

Explain How did the Communists try to control the lives of children? *(Sample response: Soviet schools taught students to worship Stalin, to believe in falsely reported benefits of collectivization, and to obey the state blindly.)*

DEMONSTRATE

Online Assign the **Digital Lesson Quiz** for this lesson if you haven't already done so. Students will be offered automatic remediation or enrichment based on their score.

Post these questions to the class on the Discussion Board:

Summarize Briefly summarize the goals and the outcomes of Stalin's five-year plans. *(Sample response: The goal was to build up heavy industry, improve transportation, and increase agricultural output. The outcome was mixed. Industry saw some growth, but there were tremendous shortages in agriculture.)*

Recall Describe Stalin's "show trials." Whom did he target for elimination? *(Sample response: Stalin orchestrated public trials to intimidate the Soviet population while under the guise of a legitimate trial. Stalin targeted anyone he saw as a threat to his power.)*

Topic Inquiry

Have students continue their investigations for the Topic Inquiry.

Assessment

1. The five-year plans were aimed at improving industry and agriculture. The plans resulted in progress in industry but failed to increase agricultural output.
2. People gained access to free schooling, free medical care, and inexpensive housing. However, they also lacked many basic necessities.
3. He distributed state-sponsored propaganda; he censored authors and artists; he forcibly promoted russification; and he destroyed the religious establishment.
4. He tightened control of the economy, setting five-year plans for industry and forcing the collectivization of agriculture. He used secret police, torture, and violent purges to ensure obedience. Stalin tightened his grasp on every aspect of Soviet life, stamping out any signs of dissent within the Communist elites.
5. Both sought to bring about a worldwide revolution and to win the support of other countries.

Answers

Analyze Information *Soviet leaders wanted to increase their country's security by winning the recognition of other countries. However, by aiding revolutionary groups in other countries and urging colonial people to rise up against imperialist powers, the Soviet Union also undermined that goal.*

Topic 17 Lesson 8

The Rise of Nazi Germany

CONNECT

Preview Have students preview the **Lesson Objectives** and the list of **Key Terms**.

Students can also preview all the **Key Terms** and **Academic Vocabulary** using the **Interactive Reading Notepad** on the digital course or preview a summary of the lesson in the **Reading and Note Taking Study Guide**.

Online Use the **Editable Presentation** found on the digital course to present the main ideas for this lesson.

Start Up Activity

As students enter and get settled, read or display this excerpt from Hitler's book *Mein Kampf:*

"Propaganda tries to force a doctrine on the whole people. . . . Propaganda works on the general public from the standpoint of an idea and makes them ripe for the victory of this idea."

Ask: How do you think Hitler viewed propaganda? *(as a tool to allow him to rise to power)*

Online You can also project the **Start Up Activity** from the course.

INVESTIGATE

Have students read the section using the **Reading and Note Taking Study Guide** to help them take notes and understand the text as they read.

The Weimar Republic

The Treaty of Versailles in 1919 officially ended World War I. However, the treaty brought about new problems for Germany. As a result, Germany's new government, the Weimar Republic, suffered from economic hardships.

>> The Nazi Party was active between 1920 and 1945. Hitler served as the party's leader starting in 1921. Initially, the Nazis focused on anti-big business and anti-capitalist rhetoric.

Interactive Flipped Video

17.8 **As World War I drew to a close, Germany tottered on the brink of chaos. Under the threat of a socialist revolution, Kaiser William II abdicated. Moderate leaders signed the armistice and later, under protest, the Treaty of Versailles.**

TEKS 1.F, 11.B, 12.A, 12.B, 21.C, 26.B

>> Objectives

Summarize the political and economic problems faced by the Weimar Republic.

Analyze Hitler's rise to power.

Describe the political, social, economic, and cultural policies of Nazi Germany.

Explain why Eastern Europe turned to authoritarian rule.

>> Key Terms

chancellor
Ruhr Valley
hyperinflation
Adolf Hitler
Third Reich
Gestapo
Nuremberg Laws

www.PearsonTexas.com
Access your Digital Lesson.

The Rise of Nazi Germany

The Weimar Republic

In 1919, German leaders drafted a constitution in the city of Weimar (VY mahr). It created a democratic government known as the Weimar Republic. The constitution set up a parliamentary system led by a **chancellor,** or prime minister. It gave women the right to vote and included a bill of rights. However, the Weimar Republic faced numerous problems, including political extremists, extreme inflation, and the Great Depression, all of which led to the Republic's eventual fall.

Political Turmoil The republic faced severe problems from the start. Politically, it was weak because Germany, like France, had many small parties. The chancellor had to form coalitions that easily fell apart.

The government, led by moderates, came under constant fire from both the left and right. Communists demanded radical changes like those Lenin had brought to Russia. Conservatives—including the old Junker nobility, military officers, and wealthy bourgeoisie—attacked the government as too liberal and weak. They longed for another strong leader like Bismarck.

Germans of all classes blamed the Weimar Republic for the hated Versailles treaty, with its war guilt clause and heavy reparations. Bitter,

784

Aa Vocabulary Builder

1. Have students pronounce the following academic vocabulary terms in this lesson and clarify the part of speech. For difficult or polysyllabic words, break them into syllables and pronounce them with the students.
2. Explain what the word means in common "student-friendly" language using synonyms and antonyms when possible. Provide concrete examples to clarify the meaning, and rephrase the example.

passive: not active

regime: a government in power

they looked for scapegoats. Many blamed Marxists or German Jews for Germany's economic and political problems.

Economic Hardship Economic disaster fed unrest. In 1923, when Germany fell behind in reparations payments, France occupied the coal-rich **Ruhr Valley,** (roor) taking over its iron, coal, and steel industries. German workers in the Ruhr protested using passive resistance and refused to work. To pay the workers, the German government printed huge quantities of paper money.

Inflation soon spiraled out of control, spreading misery and despair. The German mark became almost worthless. An item that cost 100 marks in July 1922 might have cost 944,000 marks by August 1923. Such an extremely rapid and sharp increase in prices is known as **hyperinflation.** Salaries rose by billions of marks, but they still could not keep up with skyrocketing prices. Many middle-class families saw their savings wiped out.

Recovery and Depression With help from the Western powers, the government did bring inflation under control. In 1924, the United States gained British and French approval for a plan to reduce German reparations payments. Under the Dawes Plan, France withdrew its forces from the Ruhr, and American loans helped the German economy recover.

Germany began to prosper. Then the Great Depression hit, reviving memories of the miseries of 1923. Germans turned to an energetic leader, Adolf Hitler, who promised to solve the economic crisis and restore Germany's former greatness.

Culture in the Weimar Republic Despite political and economic turmoil, culture flourished in the Weimar Republic. The tumultuous times helped to stimulate new cultural movements, such as dadaist art and Bauhaus architecture. Berlin attracted writers and artists from around the world, just as Paris did. The German playwright Bertolt Brecht sharply criticized middle-class values with *The Three-Penny Opera*. The artist George Grosz, through scathing drawings and paintings, blasted the failings of the Weimar Republic.

Most of the art and music produced during the Weimar Republic reflected the culture of that time. However, many believed that this modern culture and the Weimar Republic itself were not in keeping with Germany's illustrious past. They condemned the new culture as immoral and rejected American influences, such as jazz.

SUPPORT IDEAS WITH EXAMPLES Describe the problems of the Weimar Republic.

Hitler Leads the Nazi Party

The Great Depression sent the German economy into a downward spiral. As discontent rose, Germans began to listen to the ideas of **Adolf Hitler**, who had operated on the fringe of German politics for a decade.

Early Years Hitler was born in Austria in 1889. When he was 18, he went to Vienna, then the capital of the multinational Hapsburg empire. German Austrians made up just one of many ethnic groups in Vienna. Yet they felt superior to Jews, Serbs, Poles, and other groups. While living in Vienna, Hitler developed the fanatical anti-Semitism, or prejudice against Jewish people, that would later play a major role in his rise to power.

Hitler went to Germany and fought in the German army during World War I. In 1919, he joined a small

>> **Analyze Political Cartoons** The terms of the Treaty of Versailles resulted in Germany losing large amounts of territory as well as its overseas colonies. What do you think the turkey in this cartoon represents?

Interactive Timeline

Online Project the **Interactive Timeline: The Rise and Fall of the Weimar Republic**. Click on each hotspot to discuss the events that contributed to Hitler's rise to power.

ACTIVE CLASSROOM

Ask students to Make Headlines for one of the events from the timeline. Once they make their headline, have them share it with a partner to review and revise if necessary. Allow students to share a few with the class.

Guided Reading and Discussion

The Weimar Republic faced political and economic hardships from its creation. Many Germans blamed the delegates for the hated Versailles Treaty and rejected the government from the start.

Identify Cause and Effect How did the onset of the Great Depression affect the Weimar Republic? *(The Great Depression raised fears of the hyperinflation of 1924. Political parties were divided, and the government had little support.)*

Music and the arts depicted Germany's struggles during the Weimar Republic.

Hypothesize How might works critical of the government affect some Germans? *(Some might view their government with distrust.)*

Hitler Leads the Nazi Party

The instability of the postwar years created an opportunity for Adolf Hitler. Hitler blamed the Weimar government, Jews, and Marxists for Germany's problems and promised that a strong leader could restore Germany to greatness.

Answers

Analyze Political Cartoons *Germany*

Support Ideas With Examples *The Weimar Republic was torn apart by competing extreme parties, and its coalition governments were unstable. It faced conflict with France over the Versailles Treaty. Economically, the republic was troubled by hyperinflation in the 1920s. In the 1930s, the Weimar Republic had to cope with the Great Depression as well as continued political turmoil.*

Topic 17 Lesson 8

Guided Reading and Discussion

Discuss how the Great Depression was a contributing factor in Hitler's rise to power. *(Sample response: Because of the economic hardship, people began to lose faith in their government and turn toward extremist parties, such as the Nazi Party.)*

Ask students to predict how someone like Hitler might take advantage of the weaknesses of the Weimar Republic to rise to power. *(Hitler might strongly criticize the government's weaknesses to encourage people to turn against it even more, and he might promise to be the strong leader they desired.)*

Draw Inferences What impact did the German political system have on the rise of the Nazi Party? *(Sample response: The German government was paralyzed by political divisions, which helped the rise of the Nazi Party. The president of the Weimar Republic made Hitler chancellor to check Communist influence and to gain more control over the Reichstag. That position gave the Nazi Party an opportunity to take full control.)*

The Third Reich

After Hitler was appointed chancellor, he quickly destroyed the Weimar Republic and established the Third Reich. Hitler created a totalitarian state and passed anti-Semitic laws. The Nazis indoctrinated children to help change political thought in Germany.

Answers

Check Understanding *Hitler and the Nazi Party's ideology was based on anti-Semitism, pride in Germany's past, and revenge for the Treaty of Versailles. Hitler planned to defy the Versailles Treaty, create jobs, and bring Germany back to greatness.*

group of right-wing extremists. Like many ex-soldiers, he despised the Weimar government, which he saw as weak. Within a year, he was the unquestioned leader of the National Socialist German Workers, or Nazi, party. Like Mussolini, Hitler organized his supporters into fighting squads. Nazi "storm troopers" fought in the streets against their political enemies.

Hitler's Ideological Manifesto In November 1923, Hitler tried to follow Mussolini's example by staging a small-scale coup known as the Beer Hall Putsch in Munich. The coup failed, and Hitler was soon behind bars. While in prison, Hitler wrote *Mein Kampf ("My Struggle")*.It would later become the basic book of Nazi goals and ideology.

Mein Kampf reflected Hitler's obsessions—extreme nationalism, racism, and anti-Semitism. Germans, he said, belonged to a superior "master race" of Aryans, or light-skinned Europeans, whose greatest enemies were the Jews.

Hitler's ideas were rooted in a long tradition of European anti-Semitism, dating back to the persecutions of the Middle Ages. The rise of nationalism in the 1800s caused people to identify Jews as ethnic outsiders. Hitler viewed Jews not as members of a religion but as a separate race. (He defined a Jew as anyone with one Jewish grandparent.) Echoing a familiar right-wing theme, he blamed Germany's defeat in World War I on a conspiracy of Marxists, Jews, corrupt politicians, and business leaders.

In his recipe for revival, Hitler urged Germans everywhere to unite into one great nation. Germany must expand, he said, to gain *Lebensraum* (LAY buns rowm), or living space, for its people. Slavs and other inferior races must bow to Aryan needs. To achieve its greatness, Germany needed a strong leader, or Führer (FYOO rur). Hitler was determined to become that leader.

Hitler Comes to Power After less than a year, Hitler was released from prison. He soon renewed his table-thumping speeches. The Great Depression played into Hitler's hands. As unemployment rose, Nazi membership grew to almost a million. Hitler's program appealed to veterans, workers, the lower middle classes, small-town Germans, and business people alike. He promised to end reparations, create jobs, and defy the Versailles treaty by rearming Germany.

With the government paralyzed by divisions, both Nazis and Communists won more seats in the Reichstag, or lower house of the legislature. Fearing the growth of communist political power, conservative politicians turned to Hitler. Although they despised him, they believed they could control him. Thus, with conservative support, Hitler was appointed chancellor in 1933 through legal means under the Weimar constitution.

Within a year, Hitler was dictator of Germany. He and his supporters suspended civil rights, destroyed the Communists, and disbanded other political parties. Germany became a one-party, totalitarian state. Like Stalin in Russia, Hitler purged his own party, brutally executing Nazis he felt were disloyal. Nazis learned that Hitler demanded unquestioning obedience.

Hitler's rise to power raises disturbing questions that we still debate today. Why did Germany turn from democracy to totalitarianism? How could a ruthless, hate-filled dictator gain the enthusiastic support of many Germans?

CHECK UNDERSTANDING Describe the ideology of Hitler and the Nazi Party.

ELPS **ELPS 3.F.2** Identify concrete vocabulary in *Hitler Leads the Nazi Party.*

The Third Reich

Once in power, Hitler and the Nazis moved to build a new Germany. Like Mussolini, Hitler appealed to nationalism by recalling past glories. Germany's First Reich, or empire, was the medieval Holy Roman Empire, which had lasted more than 800 years. The Second Reich was the empire forged by Bismarck in 1871. Under Hitler's new **Third Reich,** he boasted, the German master race would dominate Europe for a thousand years. His aggressive goals would eventually lead Germany—and the world—into another war.

To combat the Great Depression, Hitler launched large public works programs (as did Britain and the United States). Tens of thousands of people were put to work building highways and housing or replanting forests. Hitler also repudiated, or rejected, the Versailles treaty. He launched a crash program to rearm Germany and schemed to unite Germany and Austria.

Like Mussolini, Hitler preserved capitalism but brought big business and labor under government control. Few objected to this loss of freedom because their standard of living rose. Nazi propaganda highlighted the improvements.

A Totalitarian State Emerges To achieve his goals, Hitler organized an efficient but brutal system of terror, repression, and totalitarian rule. Nazis controlled all areas of German life—from government to religion to education. Elite, black-uniformed troops, called the SS, enforced the Führer's will. His secret police, the **Gestapo**(guh STAH poh), rooted out opposition.

English Language Proficiency Standards

Speaking 3.F.2 Provide students with a select list of content-related words from "Hitler Leads the Nazi Party."

Beginning Select and display up to seven content-related words on the board. Have students repeat after you as you read each aloud. Discuss their meanings using visuals as support. Use the words to ask questions and provide sentence stems for students to use in their response.

Intermediate Select and display up to seven content-related words on the board. Have students repeat after you as you read each aloud. Discuss their meanings using visuals as support. Use the words to ask questions that require a response that uses the words in phrases or short sentences.

Advanced Select and display up to ten content-related words on the board. Discuss their meanings with the group. Guide the student in writing two questions using the words or that require the words in their answers. Have pairs ask and answer each other's questions.

Advanced High Select and display up to ten content-related words on the board. Have students look up the definitions of the words in a dictionary. The ask students to write a short paragraph using the words. Have students read their paragraphs to the group.

At first, many Germans welcomed Hitler, who took forceful action to ease the effects of the Great Depression and promised to revive German greatness. Any people who criticized Hitler became victims of terror or were cowed into silence in fear for their own safety.

Anti-Semitism Campaign Begins In his fanatical anti-Semitism, Hitler set out to drive Jews from Germany. In 1935, the Nazis passed the **Nuremberg Laws,** which deprived Jews of German citizenship and placed severe restrictions on them. They were prohibited from marrying non-Jews, attending or teaching at German schools or universities, holding government jobs, practicing law or medicine, or publishing books. Nazis beat and robbed Jews and roused mobs to do the same. Many German Jews fled, seeking refuge in other countries.

On November 7, 1938, a young German Jew whose parents had been deported to their native Poland shot and wounded a German diplomat in Paris. Hitler used the incident as an excuse to stage an attack on all Jews. The incident became known as *Kristallnacht*(krih STAHL nahkt), or the "Night of Broken Glass." On the night of November 9 and into the following day, Nazi mobs in Germany, Austria, and Czechoslovakia smashed the windows of Jewish homes and businesses. The experience was terrifying for Jews.

> They broke our windowpanes, and the house became very cold.". . . We were standing there, outside in the cold, still in our night clothes, with only a coat thrown over...Then they made everyone lie face down on the ground. . .'Now, they will shoot us,' we thought. We were very afraid."
>
> —Sophie Nussbaum, quoted in *48 Hours of Kristallnacht*

Kristallnacht reflected so badly on Germany that it was not repeated. Yet Hitler made the Jewish victims of the attacks pay for the damage. Before long, Hitler and his henchmen were making even more sinister plans for what they called the "Final Solution"—the extermination of all Jews.

"They broke our windowpanes, and the house became very cold.". . . We were standing there, outside in the cold, still in our night clothes, with only a coat thrown over...Then they made everyone lie face down on the ground. . .'Now, they will shoot us,' we thought. We were very afraid."

—Sophie Nussbaum, quoted in *48 Hours of Kristallnacht*

>> On the night of November 9, 1938, German mobs smashed the windows of Jewish homes and businesses, looted Jewish shops, and burned synagogues like this one in Baden-Baden. After the Night of Broken Glass, the Nazi government made Jewish victims pay for the damages.

Guided Reading and Discussion

Be sure students understand the emergence and characteristics of totalitarianism, including the role Hitler played in ensuring that only people with similar ideologies held positions of power. Discuss how Hitler's totalitarian state and propaganda were tools to help the Nazis shift political thought and spread anti-Semitic beliefs.

Identify Steps in a Process Explain the steps that the Nazis took to spread their anti-Semitic beliefs and make them official. *(Sample response: Hitler blamed the Jewish people for Germany's problems and then started propaganda campaigns to depict Jews as an inferior race. The Nazis implemented laws against Jews, and eventually the anti-Semitism escalated into violent acts.)*

Key Terms

Ask students to find the key term **Nuremberg Laws** (in bold) in the text. Explain that the laws, approved by the Nazi Party in 1935, deprived Jews of German citizenship and placed severe restrictions on their rights. Ask students to describe the rights Jews lost under these laws.

Authoritarian Rule in Eastern Europe

The new Eastern European states that arose after World War I were marked by racial tension and social and economic inequality. Old rivalries prevented economic cooperation, and it was easier for dictators to rise to power.

Guided Reading and Discussion

Be sure that students understand the impact of World War I on Eastern Europe. Discuss how weak governments made the region ripe for the rise of authoritarian rule.

Identify Cause and Effect How did economics affect the political situation in Eastern Europe? *(Most Eastern European countries lacked capital to industrialize. Poverty and the lack of economic progress contributed to the political instability.)*

Online Project the **Interactive Gallery: Growing Up in Nazi Germany**. Look at each image and discuss the pressures children must have felt growing up in Nazi Germany. Point out the picture of the Jewish boy, and compare it to the girls lining up to march. Explain that indoctrination into racist ideals began at a very early age.

ACTIVE CLASSROOM

Ask students to spend three minutes jotting down a response to the following question: What do these images tell you about life for children in Nazi Germany? *(Sample response: The images of children show the importance of loyalty and physical fitness in Hitler's totalitarian state. They show that youth had many responsibilities and were expected to contribute to society. German Jewish children, on the other hand, were isolated and singled out.)*

Analyze Images

Have students look at the photograph of Hitler Youth on the next page. Ask: Why would Nazi Germany create posters with young, Aryan children on them? *(Sample response: The Nazis wanted to promote their view of the master race, and pictures of blond, blue-eyed children helped spread Nazi ideology.)*

Nazi Social Policies Like Italian Fascists and Soviet Communists, the Nazis indoctrinated young people with their ideology. In passionate speeches, the Führer spewed his message of racism.

He urged young Germans to destroy their so-called enemies without mercy. On hikes and in camps, the "Hitler Youth" pledged absolute loyalty to Germany and undertook physical fitness programs to prepare for war. School courses and textbooks were rewritten to reflect Nazi racial views.

Like Mussolini's Fascists, Nazis sought to limit women's roles. Women were dismissed from upper-level jobs and turned away from universities. To raise the birthrate, Nazis offered "pure-blooded Aryan" women rewards for having more children. Still, Hitler's goal to keep women in the home and out of the workforce applied mainly to the privileged. As German industry expanded, women factory workers were needed.

Purifying German Culture The Nazis used education and the arts as propaganda tools to purge, or purify, German culture. At huge public bonfires, Nazis burned books of which they disapproved. They denounced modern art, saying that it was corrupted by Jewish influences. They condemned jazz because of its African roots. Instead, the Nazis glorified old German myths such as those re-created in the operas of Richard Wagner (VAHG nur).

Hitler despised Christianity as "weak" and "flabby." He sought to replace religion with his racial creed. To control the churches, the Nazis combined all Protestant sects into a single state church. They closed Catholic schools and muzzled the Catholic clergy. Although many clergy either supported the new regime or remained silent, some courageously spoke out against Hitler.

DESCRIBE How did the Nazi Party maintain its control of Germany?

Authoritarian Rule in Eastern Europe

Like Germany, most new nations in Eastern Europe slid from democratic to authoritarian rule in the postwar era. In 1919, a dozen countries were carved out of the old Russian, Austro-Hungarian, Ottoman, and German empires. Although they differed from one another in important ways, they faced some common problems. They were small countries whose rural agricultural economies lacked capital to develop industry. Social and economic inequalities separated poor peasants from wealthy landlords. None had much experience with the democratic process.

>> **Analyze Maps** According to the map, which eastern European nation was the first to have an authoritarian government?

Answers

Describe *The Nazi Party maintained power by keeping some of Hitler's promises and brutally cracking down on dissent.*

Analyze Maps *Bulgaria*

Further complicating the situation, rivalries left over from World War I hindered economic cooperation between countries. Each country in the region tried to be independent of its neighbors, which hurt all of them. The region was hit hard by the Great Depression.

Ethnic Rivalries Old rivalries between ethnic and religious groups created severe tensions. In Czechoslovakia, Czechs and Slovaks were unwilling partners. More than three million Germans lived in northern Czechoslovakia, and some of them wanted to join Hitler's Nazi Germany.

Serbs dominated the new state of Yugoslavia, but restless Slovenes and Croats living there pressed for independence. In Poland, Hungary, and Romania, conflict flared among various ethnic minorities.

Dictators Replace Democracy Economic problems and ethnic tensions contributed to instability, which in turn helped fascist rulers gain power. In Hungary, military strongman Nicholas Horthy (HAWR tay) overthrew a Communist-led government in 1919. By 1926, the military hero Joseph Pilsudski (peel SOOT skee) had taken control of Poland. Eventually, right-wing dictators emerged in every Eastern European country except Czechoslovakia and Finland.

Like Hitler, these dictators promised order and won the support of the military and wealthy. They also turned to anti-Semitism, using Jewish people as scapegoats for many national problems. Meanwhile, strong, aggressive neighbors eyed these small, weak states of Eastern Europe as tempting targets. Before long, Eastern Europe would fall into the orbit of Hitler's Germany and then of Stalin's Soviet Union.

 **IDENTIFY CENTRAL ISSUES** How did World War I impact the growth of authoritarian states in Eastern Europe?

>> The Hitler Youth program emphasized activism, physical training, and Nazi ideology, as well as absolute obedience to Hitler and the Nazi Party.

Interactive Gallery

ASSESSMENT

1. **Describe** Describe the weaknesses of the Weimar Republic.
2. **Support Ideas with Examples** How was Hitler able to shift political thought in Germany in order to establish and maintain a totalitarian state?
3. **Identify Cause and Effect** Describe the effects of Eastern Europe's economic problems and ethnic and religious tensions.
4. **Describe** Describe Hitler's fanatical anti-Semitism and how he tried to drive Jewish people from Germany.
5. Why did the Nazi Party glorify old German myths and denounce modern art?

SYNTHESIZE

Online Project **the Digital Activity: Nazi Propaganda.** Ask students to think of reasons why the German people might have been susceptible to Nazi propaganda during the 1930s. Tell them to take one minute to quickly write about this topic. Have them exchange papers with a classmate to compare ideas.

Ask if they think Hitler would have had as many followers if he hadn't used propaganda in the early 1930s. *(Possible answers: Yes; because Hitler had a forceful personality; No; because the propaganda enabled Hitler to promote his views.)*

DEMONSTRATE

Online Assign the **Digital Lesson Quiz** for this lesson if you haven't already done so. Students will be offered automatic remediation or enrichment based on their score.

Post these questions to the class on the Discussion Board:

In "The Rise of Nazi Germany," you read about the rise and fall of the Weimar Republic resulting in the rise of Hitler and the Nazi Party. Economic hardships and political strife allowed Hitler to take control of the government and implement a totalitarian state. Other Eastern European countries also fell into the hands of authoritarian rule.

Synthesize Ask: How do you think the Treaty of Versailles impacted the rise of authoritarian rule in Eastern Europe?

Topic Inquiry

Have students continue their investigations for the Topic Inquiry.

Answers

Identify Central Ideas *After World War I, many new nations faced economic problems, ethnic tensions, and inexperience in democracy. These issues fostered the rise of authoritarian states in Eastern Europe.*

Assessment

1. The Weimar Republic faced difficulty forming a strong government as many blamed it for the hated Versailles Treaty. The Weimar Republic also faced interference from France after it fell short in reparations payments.
2. Hitler promised to solve Germany's problems and restore it to greatness. His book *Mein Kampf* spread his beliefs. He maintained power by disbanding other political parties and using a system of terror to control all aspects of German life.
3. People lost faith in democracy. New dictators promised order and blamed economic problems on Jewish people.
4. Hitler's anti-Semitism was rooted in the Middle Ages. He used Jewish people as a scapegoat and blamed Germany's destruction on them. He issued the Nuremberg Laws and promoted violent campaigns.
5. The Nazi Party wanted to revive the image of a strong Germany to promote nationalism and German pride; therefore, it glorified old myths. The Nazis wanted to purify German culture and claimed that modern art was corrupted by Jewish influence; therefore, they denounced it.

Answers to TEKS Assessment

1. Lands controlled by Germany and the Ottoman empire were given to Allied nations. Former Ottoman land was given to France (Syria and Lebanon) and Britain (Palestine and Iraq). Britain gave part of the Palestine Mandate to an Arab ally. Arabs were angered that they were not given an independent state. Arab nationalists clashed with Jewish Zionists, and tensions worsened as both Jews and Arabs migrated to Palestine.

2. The ancient Jewish diaspora had led to Jewish migration from the Middle East across Europe. Many Jews wished to return to Israel. In 1897 Theodor Herzl formed a Zionist political movement as a response to anti-Semitism. Many European Jews, including those persecuted in Russia, sought to return to the historic Jewish homeland. Conflicts arose from conflicting promises: The Allies promised Arabs an independent nation, while the Balfour Declaration supported a Jewish homeland in the same territory.

3. Curie, a Polish-born French scientist, found that atoms in radium and uranium release charged particles. Her pioneering work helped subsequent researchers find that atoms are not solid and indivisible and increased understanding of radioactivity.

4. Stalin wanted the Soviet Union to industrialize rapidly. The Soviet Union was insulated from the impact of the Great Depression because it had little international trade. Many outsiders pointed to Russian growth as a success. Still, the standard of living remained low. Central planning was inefficient, consumer goods were scarce, and wages were low.

5. Hitler organized a brutal totalitarian rule enforced by the Gestapo, the secret police. While ending unemployment and reviving German power, Hitler controlled every aspect of German life, from government to religion and education. Hitler instituted an anti-Semitism campaign to drive Jews out of Germany by depriving them of citizenship (Nuremberg Laws), terrorizing them, and preparing to exterminate them. The Nazis also recruited youth to pledge loyalty to Nazi ideology, limited women's roles, and sought to purify German culture.

6. Student answers will vary but should include information on wealth inequities between rural and industrial areas in the United States. Falling demand for raw materials and other items caused prices to fall after the war. Those making less bought less. Factory overproduction led to unemployment. Risky investments and interest rate hikes led to the stock market crash. U.S. banks then stopped overseas lending and demanded repayment, a difficult matter for Germany, France, and Britain. Countries then enacted protective tariffs on imports, which crippled international trade.

TEKS ASSESSMENT

The Middle East, 1920s

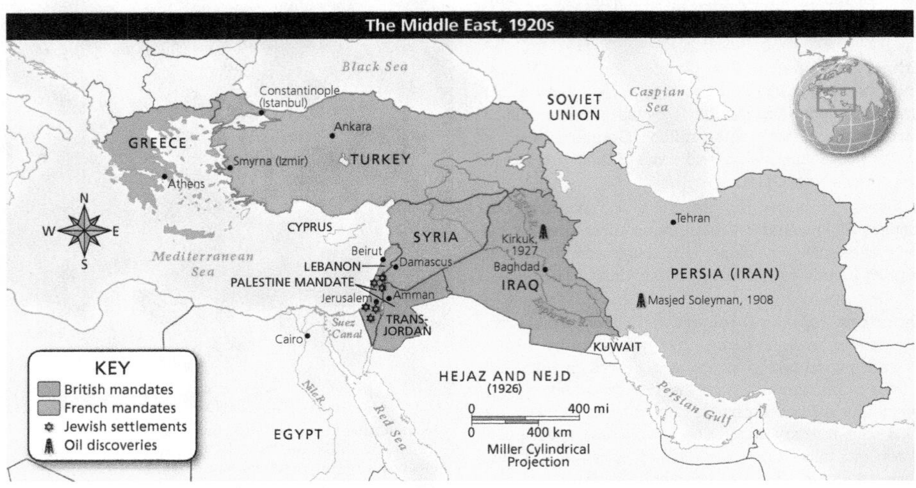

1. **Explain the Impact** Explain the political impact of the Treaty of Versailles, including the mandate system. Write a paragraph explaining the political impact of the mandate system under the Treaty of Versailles. On the above map, locate the British and French mandates created from former German colonies and Ottoman territory. How did the mandates contribute to tensions between Jewish and Arab settlers? 10.C

2. **Describe the Spread** Describe the spread of major religious and philosophical traditions, including Judaism. Write a paragraph describing the spread of Judaism in the migration to the Palestine Mandate. Consider the impact of the Jewish diaspora, role of Theodor Herzl in Zionist movement, conflicts between Jewish and Arab residents in Palestine Mandate, and the British Balfour Declaration. 23.A

3. **Identify Contributions** Identify the contributions of significant scientists: Marie Curie. Write a paragraph about how Marie Curie contributed to scientific study of radioactivity. Describe Marie Curie's work with radium and uranium. 28.E

4. **Explain the Responses** Explain the responses of government in the Soviet Union to the global depression. Write a paragraph explaining the impact, if any, of the global depression on the Soviet Union. Consider Stalin's push for industrialization, why these economic policies backfired, and the results of inefficient central planning. 11.B

5. **Describe the Emergence** Describe the emergence of totalitarianism. Write a paragraph describing the emergence of totalitarianism in Germany under Hitler. Consider the Third Reich, role of the Gestapo, anti-Semitism and the Nuremberg Laws, and the indoctrination of youth in Germany. 12.A

6. **Summarize Causes** Summarize the international, political, and economic causes of global depression. Write a paragraph summarizing the causes of global depression that began in the United States. Consider the distribution of wealth in the United States, factory overproduction, risky investments and the stock market crash, U.S. banks demanding repayment of overseas loans, and the impact of protective tariffs. 11.A

THE GREAT DEPRESSION IN THE UNITED STATES

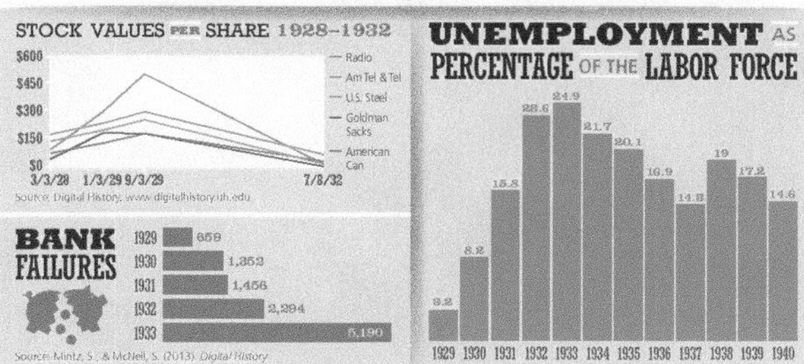

7. **Explain the Responses and Analyze Information** Explain the responses of government in the United States to the global depression, and analyze information by making generalizations and predictions. Write a paragraph explaining the U.S. government's response to the global depression, including generalizations and predictions about its impact. How did President Roosevelt's New Deal programs address bank failures and unemployment? Explain some other New Deal programs, and generalize about their short and long-term effects. **11.B, 29.F**

8. **Identify and Explain the Major Causes and Effects** Identify and explain the major causes and effects of World War II, including Japanese imperialism. Write a paragraph explaining the roots and effects of Japanese imperialism. Consider Japan's growing population, China's weakened political situation, and the effect of the Great Depression. Based on the below map, how did Japan's status as an island nation encourage imperialism? **1.F, 12.C**

9. **Identify Influence** Identify the influence of ideas on political revolutions: liberty, equality, and democracy. Write a paragraph identifying the influence of these ideas on the Mexican Revolution. Consider the rule under Porfirio Díaz in the early 1900s, the status of Mexico's peasants and growing middle class, the results of the Mexican Revolution in 1917, and provisions of the new constitution. **9.D**

10. **Describe People's Participation and Use Decision-Making Process** Describe how people have participated in supporting their government. Use a decision-making process to predict consequences. Write a paragraph describing how Latin Americans developed local industries after the Great Depression, and use a decision-making process to predict consequences. Consider economic nationalism and how governments protected domestic industries. Can you predict what other effects of nationalism occurred in the country? **21.A, 31.B**

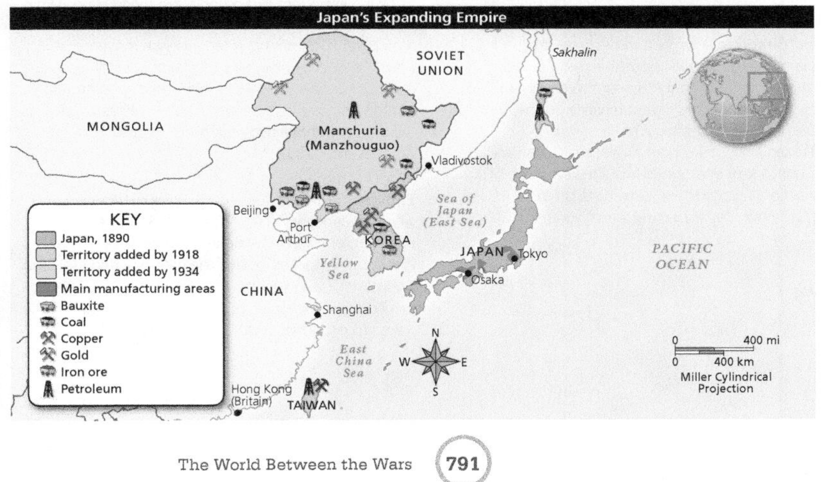

7. Franklin Roosevelt instituted a more active response to the global depression and expanded the role of government. He instituted New Deal programs to spur government spending on large public works projects to help alleviate unemployment and a slow economy. Laws regulated stock market and bank deposits, aid was given to farmers, and a Social Security system provided benefits and a retirement pension. Students may predict how the expanded role of the federal government might have positive or negative long-term effects.

8. Japan needed raw materials to develop as a power and support its growing population. Its aggression against China included the invasion of Manchuria and the Rape of Nanjing. China had been weakened by civil wars. The Great Depression and ensuing economic instability led nationalists to seek further expansion.

9. Mexico's prosperity by 1910 under dictator Porfirio Díaz benefited only a small minority. The majority of Mexicans were poor mestizos or Indian peasants who worked on haciendas or in factories and mines, earning little and desiring land reform and equality. The growing middle class wanted democracy and free elections. Emiliano Zapata, Pancho Villa, and Venustiano Carranza fought against the government. Later, Carranza was elected president in 1917 and signed a new constitution that included setting a minimum wage, allowing worker strikes, and providing male suffrage and equal pay for women.

10. Many Latin American countries in the 1920s, in the spirit of nationalism, started developing local industries (economic nationalism) after the Great Depression to avoid dependence on imports. In turn, governments supported their entrepreneurial efforts by raising tariffs on imports to protect domestic industries. People also felt that government should be less liberal (limited government) and worked for having stronger authoritarian governments to protect their economies. Students should evaluate the successes and failures of these efforts and predict the long-term consequences based on evidence.

Topic 17

Answers to TEKS Assessment

11. Broken promises from the Allies about receiving promised territories after WWI angered Italian nationalists. Economic instabilities led to chaos. The Fascist party under Mussolini arose by promising social change during economic hard times. Many Italians wanted a strong, stable government to end the paralyzed democracy. Fascism is a centralized, authoritarian government that glorifies the state over the individual. Its characteristics include extreme nationalism, violence, discipline, and glorified warfare. Fascists focused on the supremacy of the state over individual liberties.

12. Italy's political and social turmoil after WWI helped bring about the rise of the totalitarian state in Italy. The state regulated all aspects of people's lives, and loyalty to the state was key over individual goals. Mussolini suppressed rivals and the press, rigged elections, controlled the economy, and forbade worker strikes. Fascists constantly bombarded citizens with propaganda regarding the glorification of the state and Mussolini and fighting selflessly for the state. Youth were targeted to toughen them up and impose military discipline that served Mussolini well in the 1930s when he wanted to expand his power.

13. Stalin ruled the Soviet Union with absolute terror, using the secret police in all areas of life and sending any critics of the government to the Gulags, forced labor camps. During his Great Purge, he rounded up Old Bolsheviks and other activists, charged them with bogus crimes, and sent about 4 million people to the Gulag, where they could be tortured or killed. Kulaks, wealthy farmers, were targeted for death or prison camps when they were thought to be behind the failure of collectivization policies in agriculture. Religious persecution against the Russian Orthodox Church resulted in more deaths.

14. By the 1900s most of Africa was colonized, particularly by France and Britain, two European superpowers. Exploitation involved white settlers keeping the best land, suppression of growing profitable crops for those Africans who kept their land, suppression of Africans growing food for themselves, and having wages paid to the government for taxes. Educated professionals condemned colonialism that excluded local land ownership.

15. Upon President Franklin D. Roosevelt's (FDR) election in 1932, he already faced a great crisis, the Great Depression. He believed the government should take an active role. He introduced the New Deal program of economic and social programs that spurred spending in the economy. He instituted stock market and banking regulations, helped farmers, and started the Social Security system. His efforts helped mitigate the worst effects of the depression, but also increased the scope of the federal government.

TEKS ASSESSMENT

European Colonies in Africa After World War I

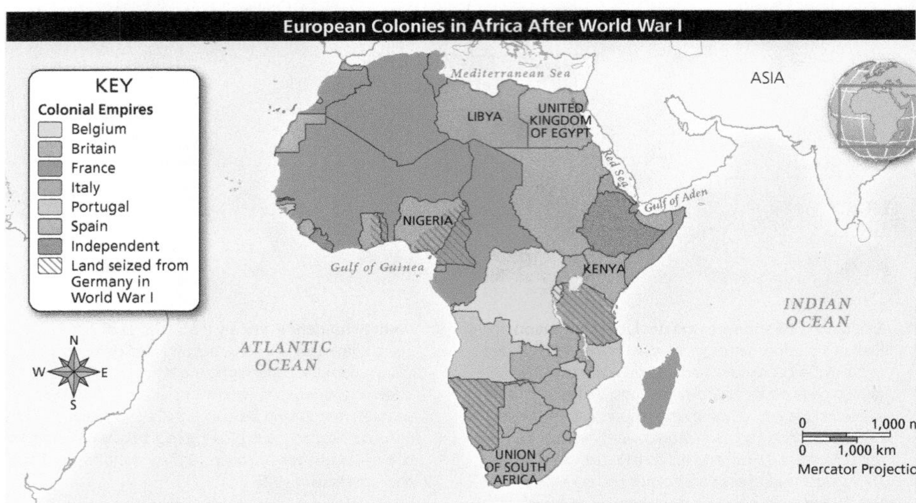

11. Identify Major Causes Identify major causes of the following important turning points in world history from 1914 to the present: World War I's impact on political systems, including the historical origins and characteristics of fascism. Write a paragraph identifying how World War I impacted the rise of fascism in Italy. Include the broken promises from the Allies; characteristics of an authoritarian government; extreme nationalism, and emphasis on supremacy of the state. **1.F, 18.D**

12. Identify and Describe Identify and describe the major effects of the following important turning points in world history from 1914 to the present: World War I, including the emergence and characteristics of political systems such as totalitarianism. Write a paragraph about totalitarianism in Italy under Mussolini. Consider how conditions in Italy after World War I fueled some of Mussolini's actions. How did Italy's fascists promote its values, and why did they especially target youth? **1.F, 12.A, 19.B**

13. Identify Examples Identify examples of politically motivated mass murders in the Soviet Union. Write a paragraph about Stalin's use of the Gulags to suppress critics in the Soviet Union. Consider the approximate number of deaths in the Gulags, the Great Purge and campaign against the Kulaks (wealthy farmers), and religious persecution. **22.C**

14. Identify Major Causes Identify major causes of the following important turning points in world history from 1914 to the present: independence movements. Write a paragraph identifying independence movements in Africa caused by colonial exploitation. On the above map, describe the extent of African colonialism and which two nations dominated by the 1900s. What was the status of those two nations in Europe? How were Africans exploited? **1.F**

15. Explain the Roles Explain the roles of various world leaders, including Franklin D. Roosevelt, prior to World War II. Write a paragraph about how President Roosevelt helped the nation during the Great Depression. Consider his philosophy of government's role and give examples of his policies that returned the nation to economic and social stability. **12.B**

16. **Explain the Roles and Identify** Explain the roles of various world leaders, including Adolf Hitler, prior to World War II, and identify how he was successful in shifting political thought. Write a paragraph explaining how Adolf Hitler used his extremist views to become Germany's dictator. Consider his establishment of a totalitarian state and what happened to civil rights and the opposition. What did Hitler's book, *Mein Kampf*, reveal about his anti-Semitic and other extreme views? **12.B, 21.C**

17. **Explain the Signifiance** Explain the significance of the League of Nations. Write a paragraph explaining President Woodrow Willson's goals for the League of Nations. What were some of its weaknesses? What was significant about its establishment? **20.D**

18. **Identify Examples** Identify examples of individuals who led resistance to political oppression and were successful in shifting political thought: Mohandas Gandhi. Write a paragraph describing how Gandhi led India toward independence by resisting political oppression. Consider his Congress party role in independence efforts, concept of civil disobedience, and the Salt March. **22.E**

19. **Describe Major Causes and Effects** Describe the major causes and effects of the following important turning points in world history from 1914 to the present: independence movements, including how people have participated in changing their governments. Write a paragraph describing how Indians participated in their independence movement from Britain. Consider how India took the first step toward self-rule, the British reaction to the independence movement, and how Mohandas Gandhi united Indians. **1.F, 21.A**

20. **Summarize the Factors** Summarize the factors that contributed to communism in China, including Mao Zedong's role. Write a paragraph summarizing Mao Zedong's role under communism in China. Consider how a weakened China helped contribute to foreign imperialism, the Guomindang (Nationalists) attempts to take over China, Mao Zedong's goals for the peasants under the Communist Party, and the route and significance of the Long March. **13.B**

21. **Analyze Examples** Analyze examples of how art reflected the history of the cultures in which it was produced. Write a paragraph analyzing examples of how Mexican art in the 1920s reflected cultural nationalism. Consider mural paintings by Diego Rivera and José Clemente Orozco, portrayal of Mexican culture and history, and art as a source of national pride. **26.B**

22. **Identify and Analyze Examples** Identify and analyze examples of how literature reflected the history of the cultures in which it was produced, transcended the cultures in which it was created, and conveyed universal themes. Write a paragraph about the négritude movement led by French-speaking writers in West Africa. How did works by writers like poet Léopold Senghor help to reject negative perceptions of Africa? How did Senghor put into practice his beliefs? **26.C**

23. **Reflect on the Essential Question Write an essay on the Essential Question: What should governments do?** Use evidence from your study of this Topic to support your answer.

16. Hitler used his extremist views to take advantage of a weak Weimar Republic after WWI. His anti-Semitism and promises to end reparations and create jobs appealed to many people who were disheartened by a weak government. As Germany's dictator, he established a totalitarian state that threw out civil rights and opposition socialists and communists. He used his forceful personality and nationalistic views to inspire people to join the Nazi Party. Hitler's book detailed his extremism, racism, and anti-Semitism. Hitler shifted political thought in Germany away from belief in democracy toward extreme authoritarian and totalitarian rule.

17. President Woodrow Wilson's Fourteen Points had suggested that an organization be formed to foster international cooperation among nations. To that end, the League of Nations was formed to stop post–World War I aggressions. Although the United States did not join, other nations, including Germany and the Soviet Union, became members. The League became powerless to enforce aggressions by nations, for example, Japan's invasion of Manchuria. The League was significant as a first step toward international peace.

18. Student answers will vary but should include information on the Amritsar massacre. Mohandas Gandhi then became leader of the Congress party, uniting Indians to protest British rule. He preached a philosophy of nonviolence (ahimsa). His use of civil disobedience such as boycotting British textiles and leading the Salt March led Indian efforts toward independence.

19. Since 1885 the Indian National Congress party had wanted self-rule. Indian nationalists expected to be rewarded for their service during WWI. The British reneged and used violence in the Amritsar massacre. Mohandas Gandhi's use of civil disobedience united Indians to shake off British rule and brought worldwide attention to the struggle.

20. Internal chaos, civil wars, and foreign imperialism all contributed to the rise of communism. Foreign merchants, missionaries, and soldiers inhabited Chinese port cities; after WWI, Japan took control over former German possessions in China. The Nationalists, or Guomindang, occupied most of China in the struggle for power but were unable to create a strong central government as warlords took over and peasants suffered hardships. Mao Zedong believed that the Communist Party should focus on peasant masses to have a large role in reform. He led followers through the Long March from 1934 to 1935, fleeing from the opposition who massacred party members. The strict discipline and model behavior of the Communists during the ordeal became a symbol of communist heroism.

21. In the 1920s cultural nationalism reflected a blend of Western and native traditions instead of European influences. Mexican artists like Diego Rivera and José Clemente Orozco painted murals, an art form used by Native American Aztecs and Mayas. The murals can be seen in public buildings and show the struggle for liberty as well as Mexican culture and history.

22. The négritude movement by French-speaking writers instilled pride in their African roots and culture while protesting colonialism. Their work reflected universal themes, such as human desire for freedom and dignity that transcended their time. Léopold Senghor not only instilled African pride in his work, but he also became Senegal's first president in 1960 after working for independence.

Topic 17

Answers to TEKS Practice

1. D

2. H

Online To prepare for the End-of-Topic test, have students go online for additional Topic Review and Assessment questions or to review their notes in the **Interactive Reading Notepad** for the lessons in this Topic.

Benchmark Tests

Assign these benchmark tests as you complete the relevant topics to monitor student progress toward mastering the course content and as preparation for the End-of-Course Test.

Benchmark Test 1: Topics 1–5

Benchmark Test 2: Topics 6–10

Benchmark Test 3: Topics 11–15

Benchmark Test 4: Topics 16–21

TEKS PRACTICE

1 Which of these effectively helped the independence movement in Africa in the 1900s?

A The Muslim Brotherhood helped Egyptians gain independence from Britain.

B African American leaders encouraged revolutionary changes through the négritude movement.

C The Pan-African Congress held in Paris at the time of the peace conference put an end to colonialism.

D Pan-Africanism movements emphasized the unity of Africans for eventual self-rule.

2

Britain	• Most of Ireland breaks away to be self-govening • Fears that Soviet Union and France would become too powerful if Germany was weakened
France	• Insistence that Germany pay war reparations • Security is key goal; strengthened military and alliances
United States	• Political efforts to restrict growing immigration from Europe • Signed disarmament treaty but did not join League of Nations

Look at the chart. How did World War I impact the political, economic, and social systems in the three countries?

F Britain and France both wanted to strengthen its borders from future attacks.

G The United States wanted to restrict immigration by declining to join the League of Nations.

H All three nations wanted peace but were fearful of future war influences.

J The French disagreed with British and U.S. disarmament policies.

Test Taking Tips: Tip for Multiple-Choice Tests

1. Read the question carefully. Make sure you understand the question.
2. Read all four answer choices. Even if you think you know the correct answer, check your choice.
3. If you do not understand the question, read it again. If you are still unsure of the answer, use the process of elimination. Begin by rejecting any answer choice that you know is wrong.
4. Look for answer choices that do not relate to the question. (Remember that some answer statements are true, but do not relate to the question.)
5. Look for clue words in the answer choices. Words such as *all*, *everyone*, *only*, or *completely* can be wrong because they are too general. A correct answer might use words such as *often*, *generally*, or *at times*.

3

> *"More than 57 years after the death of Soviet dictator Joseph Stalin, scholars continue to uncover long-hidden truths about his rise to absolute power and the reign of 'Great Terror' that took more than a million lives and exiled many millions more."*

According to the excerpt, what is the legacy of Joseph Stalin?

A His five-year plans for agricultural projects were brilliant but were defeated by wealthy farmers.

B He effectively built an economic giant but, because of poor product quality, failed to compete globally.

C He built the Soviet Union into a powerful totalitarian state using the secret police, Gulag, torture, and death.

D His autocratic rule failed in every political, economic, and social aspect of life for the Soviets.

---

4 How did imperialism help cause World War I?

F Alliances were often made with nations that could strengthen ties with overseas colonies.

G Competition for gaining overseas colonies often led to conflicts among European nations.

H Overseas colonies were key to European nations' economic growth and power.

J Foreign expansion required little regulation or interference with an international organization.

If you have trouble with...				
Question	1	2	3	4
See Lesson	17.2	17.5	17.7	16.1
TEKS	1.F	1.F	12.B	10.A

3. C
4. G

Online Use the **Topic Synthesize** to help students revisit and reflect on the Essential Question for this Topic.

Topic Inquiry

If students have done a Topic Inquiry for this Topic, have them complete the final step of the Inquiry now.

World War II (1930–1945)

TOPIC 18 ORGANIZER	PACING: APPROX. 1 PERIOD, .5 BLOCKS		
	PACING	TEKS	ELPS
Connect	1 period		
MY STORY VIDEO **Ron Allen, Remembering the Battle of Britain**	10 min.		
DIGITAL ESSENTIAL QUESTION ACTIVITY **When Is War Justified?**	10 min.	1.F, 29.F, 29.G	
DIGITAL TIMELINE ACTIVITY **Events of World War II**	10 min.	13.A, 16.A, 16.C, 20.D, 22.D, 29.C, 29.F, 29.G	
TOPIC INQUIRY: PROJECT-BASED LEARNING **Create a Tribute to World War II Participants**	20 min.		
Investigate	2–5 periods		
TOPIC INQUIRY: PROJECT-BASED LEARNING **Create a Tribute to World War II Participants**	Ongoing		
LESSON 1 **Aggression, Appeasement, and War**	30–40 min.	12.B, 12.C, 16.A, 20.D	5.A
LESSON 2 **Axis Powers Advance**	30–40 min.	12.B, 12.C, 16.A, 28.C	5.G.1
LESSON 3 **The Holocaust**	30–40 min.	12.B, 12.C, 22.D	5.B.2, 5.G.2
LESSON 4 **The Allies Turn the Tide**	30–40 min.	1.F, 12.B, 12.C	5.G.3
LESSON 5 **Victory for the Allies**	30–40 min.	1.F, 12.B, 12.C, 20.D, 28.C	1.A.1
Synthesize	1 period		
DIGITAL ACTIVITY **Reflect on the Essential Question and Topic**	10 min.	1.F, 29.F, 29.G	
TOPIC INQUIRY: PROJECT-BASED LEARNING **Create a Tribute to World War II Participants**	20 min.		
Demonstrate	1–2 periods		
DIGITAL TOPIC TEST **World War II**	10 min.		
TOPIC INQUIRY: PROJECT-BASED LEARNING **Create a Tribute to World War II Participants**	20 min.		

AUTHOR'S NOTE

Causes of World War II

Given what has been said about the nature of totalitarian governments, it is easy to see World War II as a splendid illustration of the "devil theory" of history—aggressive dictators on one side, democracies on the other. Certainly, Germany, Italy, and Japan were aggressive, militaristic, and expansionist in the 1930s. On the other hand, Stalin's Russia was as totalitarian as Hitler's Germany, and "Uncle Joe" at least finished the war on the Allied side. . . .

A related approach having much appeal because it seems to carry a message for our time is to see the cause of the war as Allied appeasement of Axis aggression. Again, there is much truth in this view, as will be apparent when we follow the grim sequence of crises down the thirties to the final confrontation over Poland in 1939. Yet this approach also is incomplete, for it does little to explain why the Axis powers were aggressive and expansionist in the first place.

Deeper, long-range causes for the Second World War include the World Depression, the Versailles peace after World War I, and perhaps, some deeply disturbing features of the global political order.

The Great Depression certainly accounted in significant part for Hitler's rise to power and for the decline of party government in Japan. Military expenditures were also a good way for Hitler and other totalitarian leaders to put people back to work in a hurry. Perhaps most important, however, the Depression left the Western democracies badly weakened in the 1930s. Preoccupied by domestic problems . . . democratic leaders found appeasement and the avoidance of the confrontation as natural as aggressive rhetoric was to the heads of militarized totalitarian states. . . .

Though they didn't know it then, revisionist dictators demanding justice and defenders of the international status quo pointing to the sanctity of treaties, militarists and appeasers, aggressive politicians, and peoples who were simply too busy with the Depression to care about the international situation all in their different ways contributed to the coming of the biggest war in history.

—Anthony Esler, *The Human Venture: From Prehistory to the Present* (Upper Saddle River, New Jersey: Pearson Education, 2004), pp. 654–655

TOPIC INQUIRY: PROJECT-BASED LEARNING

Create a Tribute to World War II Participants

TEKS 1.F, 12, 13.A, 16.A, 16.C, 20.D, 22.D, 29.C, 29.F, 29.G, 30, 31

In this Topic Inquiry, students work in teams to research and create a multimedia tribute to those who fought in or experienced World War II and to their friends and relatives. Learning how war impacts people will contribute to students' understanding of the Topic Essential Question: When Is War Justified?

STEP 1: CONNECT

Develop Questions and Plan the Investigation

Launch the Project, Generate Questions, and Examine Existing War Memorials and Tributes

Display the Project Launch letter from a committee formed to create a tribute for local participants in World War II. Have students work with a team partner to make a list of things to include in a memorial or tribute. Have them refer to the list as they discuss memorials and other tributes with the team. Have them review the *Rubric for a World War II Tribute* to establish expectations.

Then turn to the bulleted list about what makes a tribute effective:

- Its subject must be clear.
- It must present information in a stimulating, memorable way.
- Its design should encourage people to think about the person, event, or experience.
- It should communicate important ideas about the person, event, or experience.
- It can appeal to different senses, such as sight, sound, or touch.

Plan the Investigation

Help the class decide what form its tribute will take. Form students into teams. Have students sign the *Project Contract*, and assign team roles using the *Project Tracker*. Give students more examples of how to break down the Driving Question to begin the *Need-to-Know Questions*.

Suggestion: You can control the length of the project by limiting the complexity and number of different media used in the tribute.

Resources

- Project Launch
- Project Contract
- Need-to-Know Questions
- Student Instructions
- Project Tracker
- Tribute Rubric

STEP 2: INVESTIGATE

Apply Disciplinary Concepts and Tools

Examine Your Contribution

Before students begin their investigation, have them review the Skills Tutorial, *Work in Teams*.

Teams will learn how to assign tasks and monitor their work with the *Project Tracker*. They will brainstorm how to approach their segment of the tribute, keeping in mind the Driving Question: How can we create something that will help people remember the contributions of World War II participants?

To guide their research, teams will create a list of *Need-to-Know Questions* about their segment of the tribute. Help students begin to fill out the *Information Organizer*.

Conduct Research

The many possible components of the research phase of this inquiry may call for careful monitoring. Check to see that each team has allocated research tasks fairly and efficiently. If necessary, remind teams that mastering the technology needed to create the tribute may need as much attention as gathering the information to present.

Write, Edit, and Assemble Your Tribute

The teams should plan how to present the information they have gathered. Next, students should write their presentation and create any visual, sound, or kinetic elements, as well as live performances. When students do peer review of their work, remind them to offer detailed, constructive criticism.

Resources

- Student Instructions
- Project Tracker
- Information Organizer
- Need-to-Know Questions

STEP 3: SYNTHESIZE

Evaluate Sources and Use Evidence to Formulate Conclusions

Create Your Part of the World War II Tribute

Now have students get together to create their presentation. If students are having trouble sharing the work on this part of the project, remind them to review their *Roles for a Group Presentation* in the *Project Tracker*. Review the teams' progress on their presentations to make sure they are on track.

Suggestion: For a less technology-dependent end product, have students restrict media to printed text, photos and other illustrations, and live kinetic elements.

Review Your Part of the World War II Tribute

Have students review each other's work and offer suggestions and edits to improve the text, visuals, and other media of the tribute. Be prepared to offer advice on how to improve the teams' products.

State Conclusions About the Driving Question

Have students write a conclusion about the Driving Question based on their work on the tribute. To help teams start, ask them to think about how social studies ideas can be communicated using visuals and text in a multimedia format. Have each team member write down his or her answer and share those answers with the team.

Resources

- Model Tribute
- Project Tracker

PROFESSIONAL DEVELOPMENT

Project-Based Learning

Be sure to view the Project-Based Learning Professional Development resources in the online course.

STEP 4: DEMONSTRATE

Communicate Conclusions and Take Informed Action

Combine Portions to Create the Class Tribute

Have teams merge their tribute elements, then set up the tribute. Depending on the audience you have chosen to view the tribute, you may need to make arrangements for visitors to your classroom or to transport the tribute.

Present Your World War II Tribute

Have presenters work through the Give an Effective Presentation Skills Tutorial and plan how best to present the tribute. Make sure teams have practiced presenting the combined elements of the complete tribute so that they fit together smoothly and efficiently. After practicing the complete tribute, remind students to think of ways to improve the presentation.

After the presentation, invite the audience to examine the visual elements of the tribute. Have team members make themselves available to answer questions and explain their findings and conclusions.

Reflect on the Project

After students have finished their Team Assessments, help them go over what they thought went well and what did not, so they can be even more effective in the future.

Suggestion: As an extension activity, have students contact and interview a current member of the military or his or her family to learn how the experiences of military families today are similar to and different from the people they have learned about in researching this tribute.

Resources

- Tribute Rubric
- Self-Assessment

Aggression, Appeasement, and War

Objectives

Objective 1: Describe how the Western democracies responded to aggression.

Objective 2: Explain the significance of the Spanish Civil War.

Objective 3: Understand how German aggression led Europe into World War II.

LESSON 1 ORGANIZER — **PACING: APPROX. 1 PERIOD, .5 BLOCKS**

	OBJECTIVES	PACING	RESOURCES Print	RESOURCES Online	TEKS	ELPS
Connect						
DIGITAL START UP ACTIVITY **Aggression Leads to War**		5 min.		●	12.A, 12.B	
Investigate						
READ **A Pattern of Aggression**	Objective 1	10 min.	●	●	12.B, 12.C, 20.D	
INTERACTIVE CARTOON **Hitler's March to European Domination**		10 min.		●	12.B, 12.C, 20.D	
READ **The Spanish Civil War**	Objective 2	10 min.	●	●	12.B	5.A
READ **German Aggression Continues**	Objective 3	10 min.	●	●	12.B, 12.C	
READ **World War II Begins**		10 min.	●	●		
INTERACTIVE GALLERY **Axis Aggression**		10 min.		●	12.B	
Synthesize						
DIGITAL ACTIVITY **Aggression Leads to War**		5 min.		●	TEKS 12.B	
Demonstrate						
DIGITAL QUIZ **Lesson Quiz and Class Discussion Board**		10 min.		●		

Focus on Texas Standards

Texas Essential Knowledge and Skills

12.B explain the roles of various world leaders, including Benito Mussolini, Adolf Hitler, Hideki Tojo, Joseph Stalin, Franklin D. Roosevelt, and Winston Churchill, prior to and during World War II

12.C explain the major causes and events of World War II, including the German invasions of Poland and the Soviet Union, the Holocaust, Japanese imperialism, the attack on Pearl Harbor, the Normandy landings, and the dropping of the atomic bombs

16.A locate places and regions of historical significance directly related to major eras and turning points in world history

20.D explain the significance of the League of Nations and the United Nations

NOTES

Axis Powers Advance

Objectives

Objective 1: Trace the course of German aggression and British resistance in Europe.

Objective 2: Describe the Nazi invasion of the Soviet Union.

Objective 3: Explain how Japanese imperialism and the attack on Pearl Harbor brought the United States into the war.

LESSON 2 ORGANIZER	PACING: APPROX. 1 PERIOD, .5 BLOCKS					
	OBJECTIVES	PACING	RESOURCES Print	RESOURCES Online	TEKS	ELPS
Connect						
DIGITAL START UP ACTIVITY **Axis Powers Advance**		5 min.		●	12.C	
Investigate						
READ **Axis Domination of Europe**	Objective 1	10 min.	●	●	12.B, 12.C, 28.C	
INTERACTIVE GALLERY **London Blitz**	Objective 1	10 min.		●	12.B, 28.C	
READ **Nazis Attack the Soviet Union**	Objective 2	10 min.	●	●	12.B, 12.C	5.G.1
INTERACTIVE MAP **Axis Aggression**	Objective 2	10 min.		●	12.B, 12.C	
READ **U.S Involvement in the War**	Objective 3	10 min.	●	●	12.B, 12.C	
Synthesize						
DIGITAL ACTIVITY **Axis Powers Advance**		5 min.		●	12.C	
Demonstrate						
DIGITAL QUIZ **Lesson Quiz and Class Discussion Board**		10 min.		●		

PEARSON realize™ www.PearsonTexas.com Access your Digital Lesson

Focus on Texas Standards

Texas Essential Knowledge and Skills

12.B explain the roles of various world leaders, including Benito Mussolini, Adolf Hitler, Hideki Tojo, Joseph Stalin, Franklin D. Roosevelt, and Winston Churchill, prior to and during World War II

12.C explain the major causes and events of World War II, including the German invasions of Poland and the Soviet Union, the Holocaust, Japanese imperialism, the attack on Pearl Harbor, the Normandy landings, and the dropping of the atomic bombs

16.A locate places and regions of historical significance directly related to major eras and turning points in world history

28.C explain the effects of major new military technologies on World War I, World War II, and the Cold War

NOTES

The Holocaust

Objectives

Objective 1: Identify the roots of Nazi persecution of the Jews.

Objective 2: Describe how the Nazis carried out a program of genocide.

Objective 3: Describe the various acts of Jewish resistance.

Objective 4: Summarize the response of the Allies to the Holocaust.

LESSON 3 ORGANIZER	PACING: APPROX. 1 PERIOD, .5 BLOCKS					
			RESOURCES			
	OBJECTIVES	PACING	Print	Online	TEKS	ELPS
Connect						
DIGITAL START UP ACTIVITY **The Holocaust**		5 min.		●	12.C, 22.D	
Investigate						
READ **The Nazi Campaign Against the Jews**	Objectives 1, 2	10 min.	●	●	12.B, 12.C, 22.D	5.B.2
INTERACTIVE MAP **Life in the Concentration Camps**		10 min.		●	12.C, 22.D	
READ **Jewish Resistance**	Objective 3	10 min.	●	●	12.C	5.G.2
READ **The Allies Respond to the Holocaust**	Objective 4	10 min.	●	●	12.C, 22.D	
INTERACTIVE GALLERY **Remembering the Holocaust**		10 min.		●	12.C, 22.D	
Synthesize						
DIGITAL ACTIVITY **Speaking Up**		5 min.		●	12.C, 22.D	
Demonstrate						
DIGITAL QUIZ **Lesson Quiz and Class Discussion Board**		10 min.		●	12.B, 12.C, 22.D	

Focus on Texas Standards

Texas Essential Knowledge and Skills

12.B explain the roles of various world leaders, including Benito Mussolini, Adolf Hitler, Hideki Tojo, Joseph Stalin, Franklin D. Roosevelt, and Winston Churchill, prior to and during World War II

12.C explain the major causes and events of World War II, including the German invasions of Poland and the Soviet Union, the Holocaust, Japanese imperialism, the attack on Pearl Harbor, the Normandy landings, and the dropping of the atomic bombs

22.D identify examples of genocide, including the Holocaust and genocide in the Balkans, Rwanda, and Darfur

NOTES

The Allies Turn the Tide

Objectives

Objective 1: Understand how nations committed all of their resources to fighting World War II.

Objective 2: Explain how the Allies began to push back the Axis powers in Europe and the Pacific.

Objective 3: Describe the Normandy landings and the Allied advance toward Germany.

LESSON 4 ORGANIZER	PACING: APPROX. 1 PERIOD, .5 BLOCKS					
			RESOURCES			
	OBJECTIVES	PACING	Print	Online	TEKS	ELPS
Connect						
DIGITAL START UP ACTIVITY **Exit the Axis**		5 min.		●	12.B	
Investigate						
READ **A Commitment to Total War**	Objective 1	10 min.	●	●	1.F, 21.A	
READ **Progress on Three Fronts**	Objective 2	10 min.	●	●	12.B, 12.C	5.G.3
INTERACTIVE CHART **European Turning Points in World War II—Causes and Effects**		10 min.		●	12.B, 12.C	
READ **A Second Front in Europe**	Objective 3	10 min.	●	●	12.B, 12.C	
INTERACTIVE MAP **World War II in Europe, 1942–1945**		10 min.		●	12.C	
3-D MODEL **The B-24 Liberator**		10 min.		●	28.C	
Synthesize						
DIGITAL ACTIVITY **Factors: Turning the Tide**		5 min.		●	1.F	
Demonstrate						
DIGITAL QUIZ **Lesson Quiz and Class Discussion Board**		10 min.		●	1.F, 12.B, 12.C	

Focus on Texas Standards

Texas Essential Knowledge and Skills

1.F identify major causes and describe the major effects of the following important turning points in world history from 1914 to the present: the world wars and their impact on political, economic, and social systems; communist revolutions and their impact on the Cold War; independence movements; and globalization

12.B explain the roles of various world leaders, including Benito Mussolini, Adolf Hitler, Hideki Tojo, Joseph Stalin, Franklin D. Roosevelt, and Winston Churchill, prior to and during World War II

12.C explain the major causes and events of World War II, including the German invasions of Poland and the Soviet Union, the Holocaust, Japanese imperialism, the attack on Pearl Harbor, the Normandy landings, and the dropping of the atomic bombs

NOTES

Victory for the Allies

Objectives

Objective 1: Understand the reasons for the final defeat of the Nazis.

Objective 2: Describe how the Allies began to push back the Japanese in the Pacific.

Objective 3: Explain how the dropping of the atomic bombs ended the war.

Objective 4: Describe the aftermath of World War II and the founding of the United Nations.

LESSON 5 ORGANIZER — **PACING: APPROX. 1 PERIOD, .5 BLOCKS**

	OBJECTIVES	PACING	RESOURCES: Print	RESOURCES: Online	TEKS	ELPS
Connect						
DIGITAL START UP ACTIVITY **Hitler's Vision**		5 min.		●	12.B	
Investigate						
READ **End of the War in Europe**	Objective 1	10 min.	●	●	12.B	
READ **Battles in the Pacific**	Objective 2	10 min.	●	●	12.C, 28.C	
INTERACTIVE MAP **World War II in the Pacific, 1942–1945**	Objective 2	10 min.		●		
READ **End of the War in the Pacific**	Objective 3	10 min.	●	●	12.C, 28.C	1.A.1
READ **Aftermath of the War**	Objective 4	10 min.	●	●	1.F, 12.B, 12.C, 20.D	
READ **The United Nations Is Formed**	Objective 4	10 min.	●	●		
INTERACTIVE TIMELINE **Key Events of World War II in Europe and the Pacific**	Objective 4	10 min.		●	28.C	
Synthesize						
DIGITAL ACTIVITY **Victory in the Pacific**		5 min.		●	1.F, 20.D	
Demonstrate						
DIGITAL QUIZ **Lesson Quiz and Class Discussion Board**		10 min.		●	1.F, 12.B, 12.C, 20.D, 28.C	

PEARSON realize™ www.PearsonTexas.com Access your Digital Lesson

Focus on Texas Standards

Texas Essential Knowledge and Skills

1.F identify major causes and describe the major effects of the following important turning points in world history from 1914 to the present: the world wars and their impact on political, economic, and social systems; communist revolutions and their impact on the Cold War; independence movements; and globalization

12.B explain the roles of various world leaders, including Benito Mussolini, Adolf Hitler, Hideki Tojo, Joseph Stalin, Franklin D. Roosevelt, and Winston Churchill, prior to and during World War II

12.C explain the major causes and events of World War II, including the German invasions of Poland and the Soviet Union, the Holocaust, Japanese imperialism, the attack on Pearl Harbor, the Normandy landings, and the dropping of the atomic bombs

20.D explain the significance of the League of Nations and the United Nations

28.C explain the effects of major new military technologies on World War I, World War II, and the Cold War

NOTES

TOPIC 18 TEKS Mastery

World War II (1930–1945)

In this Topic, you will learn about World War II. You will also find lots of ways to investigate the ideas of this Topic and to master the TEKS.

Your study will help you master these TEKS:

TEKS

1.F, 12.B, 12.C, 16.A, 20.D, 21.A, 22.D, 28.C

LESSON OUTLINE

18.1: Aggression, Appeasement, and War 12.B, 12.C, 16.A, 20.D

18.2: Axis Powers Advance 12.B, 12.C, 16.A, 28.C

18.3: The Holocaust 12.B, 12.C, 22.D

18.4: The Allies Turn the Tide 1.F, 12.B, 12.C

18.5: Victory for the Allies 1.F, 12.B, 12.C, 20.D, 28.C

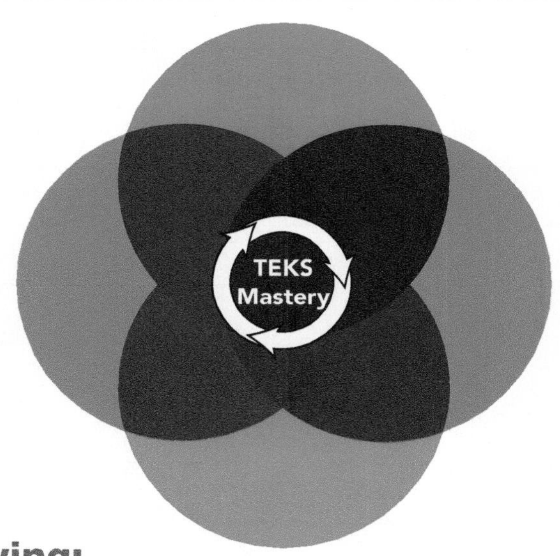

Connect

You will start by connecting with the Topic through a video that tells a personal story about World War II. You will start to think about how the Topic connects with your own experience or to what you have already learned. And you'll get a chance to think about a really big question, or Essential Question: When is war justified?

Begin your study by trying the following:

NBC LEARN **Watch My Story Video:**

Ron Allen, Remembering the Battle of Britain

Launch your Project:

Create a Tribute to World War II Participants

Investigate

The Lesson Outline lists all the lessons you will investigate in this Topic. As you read and interact with key content, the story of World War II will come to life. Read the texts; try the interactivities. Investigate the fascinating story of the challenges and heroes of the war.

And keep working on your Project to help build your mastery of the Topic TEKS.

>> Digital interactivity from the online course

Synthesize

Next you will pull it all together by reflecting on the Essential Question. This will give you a chance to be the storyteller, to show how you would answer this big question: When is war justified?

Demonstrate

Now you will get to show what you know. You will get a chance to complete the TEKS Review and Assessment pages, answering questions about every TEKS for this Topic. Or you can write an essay, take part in a discussion, or complete your Project. No matter which you do, it will be a real-world demonstration of the things you now understand about World War II.

TEKS in Topic 18	Topic Review and Assessment Questions
1.F	**4, 11, 13, 14**
12.B	**3, 6, 9, 16**
12.C	**1, 5, 7, 8, 9, 10, 14**
16.A	**12**
20.D	**15**
21.A	**13**
22.D	**9**
28.C	**2**

Topic 18

World War II (1930–1945)

Introduction

After World War I, many nations suffered from heavy debt, destruction, loss of life, and other consequences of war. Dictators, whom dissatisfied citizens looked to for change, gained power and territory. This aggression sparked World War II. In the war's early years, Germany and Japan overran most of Europe and the Pacific. Neutral at first, the United States eventually entered the war. After more than six years of war, destruction, and unspeakable horror, the dictators were defeated. What kind of world would the war's survivors inherit?

ESSENTIAL QUESTION

Ask students to think about the Essential Question for this Topic: When is war justified? Going to war is always a serious matter with far-reaching consequences for all involved. What circumstances justify the decision to go to war?

Read this list of justifications for war, and ask students to decide which they feel are valid.

- To defend territory and people
- To protect an ally from invasion
- To gain territory or resources
- To stand up for an idea
- To defend human rights and punish wrongdoing
- There are never any valid reasons for going to war.

Support a Point of View With Evidence Choose one of the justifications you feel is valid. What are the reasons you feel this way? What are the reasons you rejected one of the justifications?

Identify Central Issues For what ideas might a country be willing to fight? *(Possible response: human rights, democracy, freedom, religion)*

Identify Cause and Effect For what resources might a country fight? Why? *(Possible response: water, fertile soil, oil, coal; to increase its wealth, gain a source of energy to fuel its factories, improve its economy, feed its people)*

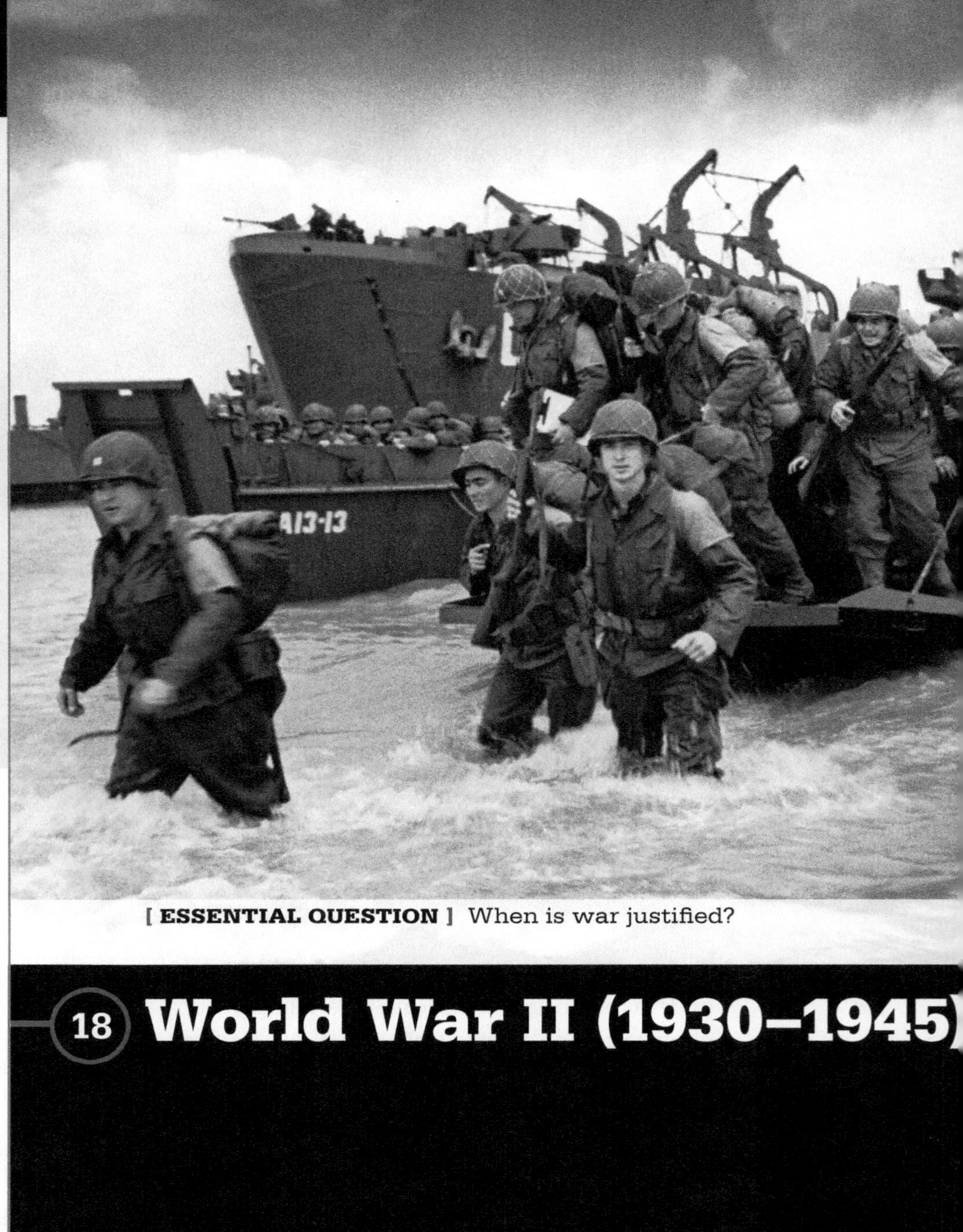

[**ESSENTIAL QUESTION**] When is war justified?

18 World War II (1930–1945)

Analyze Images

Tell students to examine the photograph of the Allied troops landing at Normandy. Ask them if they already know anything about the Normandy invasion. Then tell them that this Allied invasion of German-held France, known as D-Day, involved 3,000 landing craft (a few of which are shown here); 3,000 other ships; more than 13,000 aircraft; and some 160,000 Allied troops. Have students predict what the commanders of the Allied troops were anticipating, given this image and information. Then have students predict what the outcome of D-Day will be.

>> Allied troops landing at the beach at Normandy, France

Enduring Understandings

- Western democracies responded to Axis aggression with appeasement until the Nazi invasion of Poland.
- Early in World War II, Axis forces overran most of Europe and the Pacific, then the tide began to turn in favor of the Allies.
- Neutral at first, the United States joined the Allies after the Japanese bombing of Pearl Harbor.
- The Nazis carried out a plan to exterminate European Jews, now known as the Holocaust.
- After the failed Nazi siege of Stalingrad and the D-Day landings at Normandy, Allied troops closed in on Germany.
- The dropping of atomic bombs on Japan ended the war, but the decision was controversial.

PEARSON realize. NBC LEARN

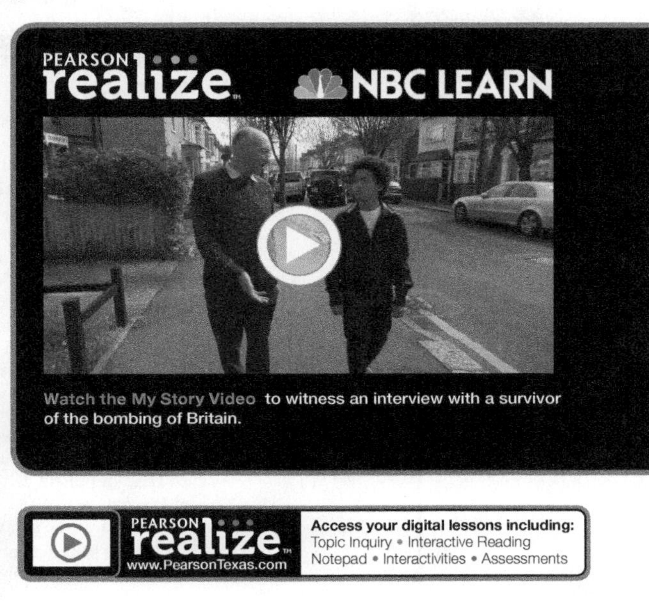

Watch the My Story Video to witness an interview with a survivor of the bombing of Britain.

PEARSON realize. www.PearsonTexas.com **Access your digital lessons including:** Topic Inquiry • Interactive Reading Notepad • Interactivities • Assessments

799

NBC LEARN MY STORY VIDEO

Project the My Story Video about Ron Allen, a survivor of the London blitz.

Online My Story Video: **Ron Allen, Remembering the Battle of Britain**

After viewing, ask students to respond to the following questions.

Check Understanding What was the Battle of Britain? *(the German attack on Britain during World War II)*

Hypothesize Why was the effort to break the will of the British people so ineffective? *(The Germans attacked cities in Britain by dropping bombs during the Blitz and, later, by launching V2 rockets. Despite the damage caused and the lives lost, the will of the British people was not broken. Students may hypothesize that people adjust to the horrors of warfare and remain strong in their determination to carry on their daily lives. They may also mention Britain's need to continue the fight against Nazism and to resist any German threat of invasion.)*

OVERVIEW ACTIVITY

Online Project the **World War II: Introduction Timeline** showing the major events leading up to and during World War II. In this Topic, students will learn about all of these events and many more, but this timeline will provide a framework into which they can place the events they learn about.

Analyze Timelines In which years was the United States at war during World War II? *(1941 through 1945)* How many years had the war been going on before the United States entered the fighting? *(2; the war began in 1939; the United States entered the war in 1941)*

Topic Inquiry

If you choose to assign the Topic Inquiry, launch the project with students after introducing the Topic.

D Differentiate Extra Support For the Overview Activity, ask students how many years passed between Adolf Hitler taking power in Germany and the start of the war. *(6; Hitler took power in 1933; war began in September 1939.)*

Topic 18 Lesson 1

Aggression, Appeasement, and War

CONNECT

Preview Have students preview the **Lesson Objectives** and the list of **Key Terms**.

Students can also preview all the **Key Terms** and **Academic Vocabulary** using the **Interactive Reading Notepad** on the digital course or preview a summary of the lesson in the **Reading and Note Taking Study Guide**.

Online Use the **Editable Presentation** found on the digital course to present the main ideas for this lesson.

Start Up Activity

Explain that Western democracies tried to avoid war despite aggressive actions from Germany, Italy, and Japan in the 1930s. Eventually, these acts would lead to the start of World War II. Have students put the events below in chronological order and write a sentence or two explaining how they may have influenced German aggression in the 1930s.

- Germany suffers from hyperinflation.
- Hitler comes to power.
- The Great Depression begins.
- World War I ends.
- The Weimar Republic is created.

Predict Consequences Consider why Germans detested the Versailles Treaty. Predict the aggressive actions Germany might take as a response. *(Sample response: rebuild the military, recapture lost territory, instill a sense of nationalism and German pride)*

Online You can also project the **Start Up Activity** from the course.

INVESTIGATE

Have students read the section using the **Reading and Note Taking Study Guide** to help them take notes and understand the text as they read.

A Pattern of Aggression

Discuss how the policy of appeasement contributed to the outbreak of World War II. Explain that aggressive actions of dictators were met with only verbal protest from democracies in the 1930s. Democratic leaders hoped to prevent another war. Militaristic dictators viewed the desire for peace as a weakness.

>> Germany rebuilt its military during the 1930s in defiance of the Treaty of Versailles. Here, troops stand at attention during a Nazi rally in Nuremberg, Germany.

Interactive Flipped Video

18.1 Throughout the 1930s, the rulers of Germany, Italy, and Japan were preparing to build new empires. After the horrors of World War I, the leaders of Britain, France, and the United States tried to avoid conflict through diplomacy. During the 1930s, the two sides tested each other's commitment and will.

TEKS
12.B, 12.C, 16.A, 20.D

>> Objectives

Describe how the Western democracies responded to aggression.

Explain the significance of the Spanish Civil War.

Understand how German aggression led Europe into World War II.

>> Key Terms

appeasement
pacifism
Neutrality Acts
Axis powers
Francisco Franco
Anschluss
Sudetenland
Nazi-Soviet Pact

Aggression, Appeasement, and War

A Pattern of Aggression

Challenges to peace followed a pattern. Dictators took aggressive action but met only verbal protests and pleas for peace from the democracies. Mussolini, Hitler, and Japanese militarists viewed that desire for peace as weakness and responded with new acts of aggression. With hindsight, we can see the shortcomings of the policies followed by the democracies. These policies, however, were the product of long and careful deliberation. At the time, many people believed they would prevent war.

Japanese Imperialism Grows One of the earliest tests had been posed by Japan. Japanese military leaders and ultranationalists thought that Japan should have an empire equal to those of the Western powers. In pursuit of this goal, Japan seized the Chinese province of Manchuria in 1931. When the League of Nations condemned the aggression, Japan simply withdrew from the organization.

Japan's easy success strengthened the militarist faction in Japan. In 1937, Japanese armies overran much of eastern China, starting

www.PearsonTexas.com
Access your Digital Lesson.

Aa Vocabulary Builder

1. Have students pronounce the following academic vocabulary terms in this lesson and clarify the part of speech. For difficult or polysyllabic words, break them into syllables and pronounce them with the students.
2. Explain what the word means in common "student-friendly" language using synonyms and antonyms when possible. Provide concrete examples to clarify the meaning, and rephrase the definition.

sanctions: penalty

technology: scientific advances applied to practical purposes the Second Sino-Japanese War. Once again, Western protests did not stop Japan's acts of imperialism.

Italy Invades Ethiopia In Italy, Mussolini decided to act on his own imperialist ambitions. Italy's defeat by the Ethiopians at the battle of Adowa in 1896 still rankled after almost 40 years. In 1935, Italy invaded Ethiopia, located in northeastern Africa. Although the Ethiopians resisted bravely, their outdated weapons were no match for Mussolini's tanks, machine guns, poison gas, and airplanes.

The Ethiopian king Haile Selassie (HY luh suh lah SEE) appealed to the League of Nations for help. The League voted sanctions against Italy for violating international law. League members agreed to stop selling weapons or other war materials to Italy. But the sanctions did not extend to petroleum, which fueled modern warfare. In addition, the League had no power to enforce the sanctions. By early 1936, Italy had conquered Ethiopia.

Hitler Violates the Treaty of Versailles Hitler had also tested the will of the Western democracies, as well as of the League of Nations, and found it weak. First, he built up the German military in defiance of the Treaty of Versailles. Then, in 1936, he sent troops into the "demilitarized" Rhineland bordering France—another treaty violation. Germans hated the Versailles treaty, and Hitler's successful challenge made him more popular at home.

The Western democracies denounced his moves but took no real action. Instead, they adopted a policy of **appeasement,** or giving in to the demands of an aggressor in order to keep the peace.

Reasons for Appeasement The Western policy of appeasement developed for a number of reasons. France was demoralized, suffering from political divisions at home. It could not take on Hitler without British support. The British, however, had no desire to confront the German dictator. Some even thought that Hitler's actions constituted a justifiable response to the terms of the Treaty of Versailles, which they believed had been too harsh on Germany.

In both Britain and France, many saw Hitler and fascism as a defense against a worse evil—the spread of Soviet communism. Additionally, the Great Depression sapped the energies of the Western democracies. Finally, widespread **pacifism,** or opposition to all war, and disgust with the destruction from the previous war pushed many governments to seek peace at any price.

The United States Remains Neutral As war clouds gathered in Europe in the mid-1930s, the United States

>> **Analyze Political Cartoons** British cartoonist David Low was known for speaking out against the policy of appeasement. How does this cartoon reflect his message?

 Interactive Cartoon

>> Here, Japanese cavalry have successfully occupied the northern section of Manchuria. The freezing weather did not stop Japanese imperialism.

Topic 18 Lesson 1

Online Project the **Interactive Political Cartoon: Hitler's March to European Domination** and click on the hotspots to analyze the cartoonist's attitudes about appeasement.

ACTIVE CLASSROOM

Ask students to create a My Simile activity based on the content of the political cartoon. Give them the following prompt to complete: This cartoon shows that _______ is like ______ because _______.

Analyze Images

Ask students to look at the punctuation on the backs of the figures in the cartoon. What do they see? *(question marks, then exclamation points)* Tell them that the exclamation points show that the artist believed Hitler's acts would become increasingly aggressive and alarming. Ask: Why do you think the last figure is labeled "Boss of the Universe"? *(The implication is that one day Hitler will take over the world—and beyond.)*

Guided Reading and Discussion

Direct students to the timeline (on the next page) that identifies acts of aggression committed by Italy, Germany, and Japan, including the invasion and conquering of Ethiopia, the movement of troops into the "demilitarized" Rhineland, and the seizure of Manchuria. Be sure students understand that these acts of aggression were an effect of the policy of appeasement. Discuss why the Western powers chose this policy.

Synthesize Explain the significance of the League of Nations to the Axis powers in the 1930s. *(Sample response: The League of Nations was insignificant because it didn't follow through with consequences. Japan dropped out of the League and continued its invasion of China after the League spoke out against Japanese imperialism.)*

D Differentiate Extra Support After asking students to think of a simile, allow students five minutes to brainstorm different things to which they can compare the term *appeasement* or the name *Chamberlain.* Tell them to use their comparisons to help form a simile. Then continue with the group activity.

Answers

Analyze Political Cartoons *It shows Hitler—with his thumb to his nose—goose-stepping over the spineless leaders of democracy. The cartoon shows Low's view that Hitler was humiliating his appeasers.*

Topic 18 Lesson 1

The Spanish Civil War

The Spanish Civil War was another step in the march toward world war. The civil war was fought between the Republicans, loyal to the established Spanish Republic, and the Nationalists, led by Francisco Franco. The Spanish Civil War is known for the political division it created throughout Europe. Both Hitler and Mussolini were supporters of the Nationalists. The Germans used the war as a way to showcase their advanced military weaponry and as a way to warn the rest of the world of Germany's new power.

Guided Reading and Discussion

Tell students that Hitler and Mussolini saw supporting Franco and the Nationalists during the Spanish Civil War as a way to spread Nazi and fascist ideology. Ask students to think of German advantages in assisting the Nationalists during the Spanish Civil War. *(Sample response: Franco was a fascist and anticommunist, and it would benefit Hitler and Mussolini to have another political ally in Europe. Hitler was also able to test his new military equipment and techniques.)*

Congress passed a series of **Neutrality Acts.** One law forbade the sale of arms to any nation at war. Others outlawed loans to warring nations and prohibited Americans from traveling on ships of warring powers. The fundamental goal of American policy, however, was to avoid involvement in a European war, not to prevent such a conflict.

Formation of the Axis Powers Germany, Italy, and Japan were encouraged by the apparent weakness of the western democracies. The three aggressor nations formed what became known as the **Axis powers,** or the Rome-Berlin-Tokyo Axis. The Axis powers agreed to fight Soviet communism. They also agreed not to interfere with one another's plans for territorial expansion. The agreement cleared the way for these anti-democratic, aggressor powers to take even bolder steps.

? RECALL Describe the early acts of aggression of Germany, Italy, and Japan.

The Spanish Civil War

In 1936, Spain was plunged into civil war. Although the Spanish civil war was a local struggle, it soon drew other European powers into the fighting.

From Monarchy to Republic In the early 1900s, Spain was a monarchy dominated by a landowning upper class. Most Spaniards were poor peasants or urban workers. In 1931, popular unrest against the old order forced the king to leave Spain. A republic was set up with a new, more liberal constitution.

The republican government passed a series of controversial reforms. It took over some Church lands, redistributed some land to peasants, and ended some privileges of the old ruling class. These moves split the country. Communists and others on the left demanded more radical reforms. Conservatives and the military rejected the changes.

In 1936, a conservative general named **Francisco Franco** led a revolt that touched off a bloody civil war. Franco's forces, called Nationalists, rallied conservatives to their side. Supporters of the republic, known as Loyalists, included communists, socialists, and supporters of democracy.

Other Countries Get Involved People from other nations soon jumped in to support both sides. Hitler and Mussolini sent arms and forces to help Franco. The Soviet Union sent soldiers to fight against fascism alongside the Spanish Loyalists. Although the governments of Britain, France, and the United States remained neutral, individuals from those countries, as well as other countries, also fought with the Loyalists. Anti-Nazi Germans and anti-Fascist Italians joined the Loyalist cause as well.

A Bloody War Both sides committed horrible atrocities. The ruinous struggle took more than 500,000 lives.

One of the worst horrors was a German air raid on Guernica, a small Spanish market town, in April 1937. Germans timed their attack for an afternoon on a

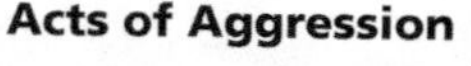
Acts of Aggression

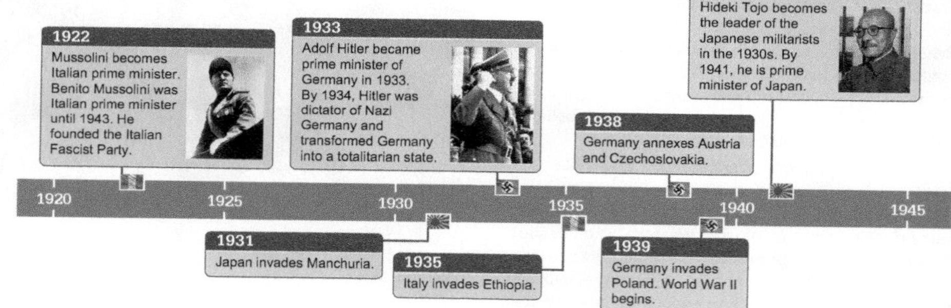
1922
Mussolini becomes Italian prime minister. Benito Mussolini was Italian prime minister until 1943. He founded the Italian Fascist Party.
1933
Adolf Hitler became prime minister of Germany in 1933. By 1934, Hitler was dictator of Nazi Germany and transformed Germany into a totalitarian state.
1941
Hideki Tojo becomes the leader of the Japanese militarists in the 1930s. By 1941, he is prime minister of Japan.
1938
Germany annexes Austria and Czechoslovakia.
1920
1925
1930
1935
1940
1945
1931
Japan invades Manchuria.
1935
Italy invades Ethiopia.
1939
Germany invades Poland. World War II begins.

>> Italy, Germany, and Japan formed an alliance and continued their aggressive actions. **Analyze Information** Why was it important for these three nations to form an alliance?

Answers

Recall *Japan seized Manchuria in 1931 and invaded eastern China in 1937. Italy invaded Ethiopia in 1935 and conquered it the following year. Hitler built up the German military and sent troops into the Rhineland.*

Analyze Information *Possible answers: They wanted to have strong mutual support in case of a larger conflict; they also wanted to make sure they did not interfere with one another's expansion plans.*

History Background

Picasso's *Guernica* In 1937, the Spanish republican government commissioned Pablo Picasso to paint a memorial to the destruction of Guernica. His painting, titled simply *Guernica,* is filled with fragmented structures and broken human bodies. In a scene of overwhelming anguish and suffering, a wailing mother holds her dead child; a distraught woman rushes from a building; and other people appear with arms and heads extended in the pain of death. Picasso also made extensive use of symbolism in this work. The horse may stand for Spain under attack; a bull, familiar from Spanish bullfighting and folk tales, could represent human irrationality. An electric light may symbolize the destructive power of modern technology, while an oil lamp might show humanity's resistance to war's atrocities. In Guernica, Picasso shows how war's destructive power and irrational nature can unleash terror and torment on humankind.

market day with thousands of people in town. German planes dropped their load of bombs, and then swooped low to machine-gun anyone who had survived the bombs. Nearly 1,000 innocent civilians were killed.

To Nazi leaders, the attack on Guernica was an experiment to identify what their new planes could do. To the rest of the world, it was a grim warning of the destructive power of modern warfare. Later, commentators viewed the Spanish Civil War as a "dress rehearsal" for World War II because it had allowed new tactics and weapons to be tested, which would soon be used in a new global war.

By 1939, Franco had triumphed. Once in power, he created a fascist dictatorship similar to the dictatorships of Hitler and Mussolini. He rolled back earlier reforms, killed or jailed enemies, and used terror to promote order.

RECALL Explain how other countries got involved in the Spanish Civil War.

>> Robert Capa's famous photograph, *The Fallen Soldier*, shows the death of a Loyalist militiaman during the Spanish Civil War. The Loyalists were supported by most urban workers and peasants, along with much of the educated middle class, which preferred a liberal democracy.

German Aggression Continues

In the meantime, Hitler pursued his goal of bringing all German-speaking people into the Third Reich. He also took steps to gain "living space" for Germans in Eastern Europe. Hitler, who believed in the superiority of the German people, thought that Germany had a right to conquer the Slavs to the east. Hitler claimed, "I have the right to remove millions of an inferior race that breeds like vermin."

Hitler also had economic and military reasons for expanding eastward. He wanted access to the natural resources of Eastern Europe, which would help boost production of military equipment. New lands would also provide additional markets for German products.

Germany Annexes Austria From the outset, Nazi propaganda had found fertile ground in Austria. By March, 1938, Hitler was ready to engineer the **Anschluss**(AHN shloos), or union of Austria and Germany.

When Austria's chancellor refused to agree to Hitler's demands, Hitler sent in the German army to "preserve order." To indicate his new role as ruler of Austria, Hitler made a speech from the Hofburg Palace, the former residence of the Hapsburg emperors.

The Anschluss violated the Versailles treaty and created a brief war scare. Hitler quickly silenced any Austrians who opposed annexation. And since the Western democracies took no action, Hitler easily had his way.

>> On March 15, 1938, Hitler gave a speech at the Hofburg Palace in Vienna announcing annexation of Austria by Nazi Germany.

German Aggression Continues

World War II Begins

Axis aggression refers to the violent attacks and invasions by Germany, Italy, and Japan prior to and during World War II. Hitler's aggressive acts broke several terms in the Versailles treaty by the time he annexed Austria and claimed the Sudetenland. Western powers decided to meet with the German leader. British Prime Minster Chamberlain thought he was bringing "peace to our time" by forging an agreement to let Hitler have a section of Czechoslovakia. But Hitler shattered hopes for peace with the invasion of Poland. This invasion marked a turning point in history and the beginning of World War II. Discuss with students why the invasion of Poland was a major cause of World War II. *(The invasion proved the failure of appeasement. Britain and France finally realized they had to take a stand against German aggression and declared war on Germany.)*

Key Terms

Direct students' attention to the key term **Anschluss** (in bold). Have them use the phonetic guide to practice the pronunciation. Then ask: Name a few other political unifications that have involved Germany. *(Sample response: the unification of different German states in 1871; the unification of East and West Germany after the Cold War)*

English Language Proficiency Standards

ELPS 5.A Read "The Spanish Civil War" aloud. Have students complete one of the following activities according to their English proficiency.

Beginning Reread the first paragraph of "The Spanish Civil War" aloud. Then write and display the letter *p*. Make the sound of the letter *p* and have students repeat it. Review the text, word by word, looking for words that begin with the *p* sound. Underline and review the pronunciation of each word. Have students repeat each word; then call on volunteers to pronounce the words. Keep practicing until students seem comfortable with pronouncing the words. If time allows, continue the activity with words that begin with the letter *c*.

Intermediate Reread "The Spanish Civil War" aloud. Ask students to find and underline words with *con-*. Write and disply the words; practice pronouncing them with students. Then have small groups write two sentences about the topic that contain a word with *con-* from the text.

Answers

Recall *Hitler and Mussolini sent arms and forces to help the fascists and Franco; Stalin sent troops to fight against Franco; people from other countries who opposed fascism volunteered to fight on the side of the Loyalists.*

Topic 18 Lesson 1

Online Project the **Interactive Gallery: Axis Aggression** and click through the images showing examples of the Axis powers forcefully taking over smaller, independent nations in order to expand their own empires. Notice the roles of the Axis powers leaders, specifically Hitler and Mussolini, as they led aggressive acts against other countries in order to expand territory for their countries.

ACTIVE CLASSROOM

Ask students to select an image from the Interactive Gallery and use the Cartoon It strategy. Instruct them to create a quick drawing of one compelling image from the Interactive Gallery. Then tell students to turn their drawings into political cartoons that illustrate either appeasement or aggression.

Guided Reading and Discussion

Review the acts of German aggression with students, and discuss the role of Adolf Hitler prior to the start of World War II.

Compare and Contrast After the Munich Agreement, Churchill gave a speech to the House of Commons. Contrast Chamberlain's views on appeasement with Churchill's. *(Sample response: Chamberlain believed by giving Hitler the Sudetenland he was bringing "peace to our time," but Churchill thought it was the beginning of the road to war; he felt Hitler wouldn't stop until he was forced to stop.)*

Hypothesize What do you think will happen to the Nazi-Soviet Pact during the war? *(Possible response: Neither side is particularly trustworthy at this point, because each is hoping to gain more territory in Eastern Europe. Their agreement probably won't last.)*

>> British prime minister Neville Chamberlain believed he had delivered peace to Europeans. After the Munich Pact, he assured a jubilant crowd in London that they could sleep soundly, as he returned from Germany bringing peace with honor.

>> German troops ride in a convoy through the streets of Prague during the occupation of Czechoslovakia in March 1939. Czech citizens lined the streets and watched silently in the rain and sleet.

Interactive Timeline

The Czech Crisis Germany turned next to Czechoslovakia. At first, Hitler insisted that the three million Germans in the **Sudetenland** (soo DAY tun land)—a region of western Czechoslovakia—be given autonomy. Czechoslovakia was one of only two remaining democracies in Eastern Europe. (Finland was the other.) Still, Britain and France were not willing to go to war to save it. As British and French leaders searched for a peaceful solution, Hitler increased his demands. The Sudetenland, he said, must be annexed to Germany.

At the Munich Conference in September 1938, British and French leaders again chose appeasement. They caved in to Hitler's demands and then persuaded the Czechs to surrender the Sudetenland without a fight. In exchange, Hitler assured Britain and France that he had no further plans to expand his territory.

The Munich Pact Returning from Munich, British Prime Minister Neville Chamberlain told cheering crowds that he had achieved "peace for our time." He told Parliament that the Munich Pact had "saved Czechoslovakia from destruction and Europe from Armageddon." French leader Edouard Daladier (dah lahd yay) reacted differently to the joyous crowds that greeted him in Paris. "The fools, why are they cheering?" he asked.

British politician Winston Churchill, who had long warned of the Nazi threat, judged the diplomats harshly: "They had to choose between war and dishonor. They chose dishonor; they will have war." Churchill vocalized his strong opposition to appeasement and the Munich Pact in a speech he gave in the House of Commons. He warned:

> "And do not suppose that this is the end. This is only the beginning of the reckoning. This is only the first sip, the first foretaste of a bitter cup which will be proffered to us year by year unless by a supreme recovery of moral health and martial vigour, we arise again and take our stand for freedom as in the olden time."
>
> —Winston Churchill, October 5, 1938

Churchill's warning was largely ignored amid the celebration of the Munich Pact. However, he would very soon play a dominant role in the war he had predicted.

CHECK UNDERSTANDING How did Hitler justify taking over Austria and the Sudetenland?

English Language Proficiency Standards

Advanced Have partners take turns rereading paragraphs of "The Spanish Civil War" aloud, supporting each other as they pronounce challenging words. Instruct pairs to list the words that were difficult to pronounce and share them with the class. Review these words with all the students. Ask volunteers to offer the correct pronunciation. Provide pronunciation support for challenging words.

Advanced High Have students reread "The Spanish Civil War" to themselves. Instruct them to list words that are difficult to pronounce, share the words with a partner, and then practice pronouncing the words with their partner. Provide pronunciation support as needed.

Answers

Check Understanding *He wanted to bring all German-speaking people into the Third Reich. He thought Germans were superior to other races and deserved to have expanded "living space."*

World War II Begins

Just as Churchill predicted, Europe plunged rapidly toward war. In March 1939, Hitler broke his promises and gobbled up the rest of Czechoslovakia. The democracies finally accepted the fact that appeasement had failed. At last, thoroughly alarmed, they promised to protect Poland, most likely the next target of Hitler's expansion.

Nazi-Soviet Pact In August 1939, Hitler stunned the world by announcing a nonaggression pact with his great enemy—Joseph Stalin, the Soviet dictator. Publicly, the **Nazi-Soviet Pact** bound Hitler and Stalin to peaceful relations. Secretly, the two agreed not to fight if the other went to war and to divide up Poland and other parts of Eastern Europe between them.

The pact was based not on friendship or respect but on mutual need. Hitler feared communism as Stalin feared fascism.

But Hitler wanted a free hand in Poland. Also, he did not want to fight a war with the Western democracies and the Soviet Union at the same time. For his part, Stalin had sought allies among the Western democracies against the Nazi menace. Mutual suspicions, however, kept them apart. By joining with Hitler, Stalin tried to protect the Soviet Union from the threat of war with Germany and grabbed a chance to gain land in Eastern Europe.

Germany Invades Poland On September 1, 1939, a week after the Nazi-Soviet Pact, German forces invaded Poland. Two days later, Britain and France declared war on Germany. World War II had begun. History had again arrived at one of its great turning points.

The devastation of World War I and the awareness of the destructive power of modern technology made the idea of more fighting unbearable. Unfortunately, the war proved to be even more horrendous than anyone had imagined.

 **IDENTIFY CENTRAL IDEAS** Why did Britain and France end their policy of appeasement?

WONDER HOW LONG THE HONEYMOON WILL LAST?

>> The cartoon portrays the two long-time enemies, Hitler and Stalin, uniting in marriage, representing the nonaggression pact they signed. **Analyze Political Cartoons** Why would the cartoonist caption this cartoon "Wonder how long the honeymoon will last?"

ASSESSMENT

1. **Identify Central Issues** Why did the western powers follow a policy of appeasement even though it seemed to encourage more aggression?
2. **Synthesize** Why did Germany and Italy become involved in the Spanish Civil War?
3. **Infer** Why did Churchill believe the Munich Pact was the "beginning of the reckoning"?
4. **Describe** How did the Nazi-Soviet Pact contribute to the start of World War II?
5. **Identify Central Ideas** What reaction did Britain have to Germany's invasion of Poland in 1939?

SYNTHESIZE

Online Project the **Digital Activity: Aggression Leads to War**. Ask students to recall the Topic Essential Question, "When is war justified?" Have them use the Think-Pair-Share strategy to write a short dialogue that could have occurred between the two British politicians discussing the policy of appeasement and the Munich Pact. *(Sample response: Churchill should speak out against the Munich Pact and the policy of appeasement. Chamberlain should support appeasement because he thought it would stop aggressive actions without a war.)*

Ask: Do you think Churchill was justified in speaking out against the policy of appeasement to the House of Commons? *(Answers will vary, but many students may agree, in light of the war that followed.)*

DEMONSTRATE

Online Assign the **Digital Lesson Quiz** for this lesson if you haven't already done so. Students will be offered automatic remediation or enrichment based on their scores.

Pose the following question to the class on the Discussion Board:

Summarize List three main causes that led to World War II. *(Sample response: Germany's aggressive actions, appeasement, Nazi-Soviet Pact)*

Evaluate Data Considering what you have learned in this lesson, do you think World War II could have been avoided if the leaders and nations involved had made different decisions? Why or why not? *(Answers will vary. Students who believe World War II could have been avoided will discuss more aggressive responses from the Allied Powers and the League of Nations once Germany began violating the terms of the Versailles treaty. Students who believe World War II could not have been avoided will discuss the unfair terms in the Versailles treaty and the control Hitler and other dictators had over their citizens.)*

Topic Inquiry

Have students continue their investigations for the Topic Inquiry.

Assessment

1. They were trying to keep the peace and prevent the horrors of war.
2. Italy was a fascist state and showed support of Franco. Germany supported Franco and his right-wing political ideas. Both wanted to oppose the Loyalists.
3. Churchill predicted Hitler would continue invading other countries until he was stopped with military force.
4. By signing the Nazi-Soviet Pact, Hitler was assured that the Soviet Union wouldn't counter-attack after Germany invaded Poland. Therefore, Hitler felt able to break the terms of the Munich Pact and invade Poland, starting World War II.
5. Britain and France realized their policy of appeasement was not stopping Hitler, so they declared war on Germany after Germany attacked Poland. Britain did very little in terms of helping Poland.

Answers

Analyze Political Cartoons *Sample response: The cartoonist wrote the question because Hitler broke several other agreements in the 1930s and because the Nazi and Soviet worldviews were so different.*

Identify Central Ideas *When Hitler broke his promise and seized the rest of Czechoslovakia, Britain and France realized he would keep trying to take more territory.*

Topic 18 Lesson 2

Axis Powers Advance

CONNECT

Preview Have students preview the **Lesson Objectives** and the list of **Key Terms**.

Students can also preview all the **Key Terms** and **Academic Vocabulary** using the **Interactive Reading Notepad** on the digital course or preview a summary of the lesson in the **Reading and Note Taking Study Guide**.

Online Use the **Editable Presentation** found on the digital course to present the main ideas for this lesson.

Start Up Activity

Explain that World War II broke out in 1939 and unleashed a wave of destruction in Europe. Read about the experience of Janina Sulkowska, a witness to the German blitzkrieg in Poland.

"It was 10:30 in the morning and I was helping my mother and a servant girl with bags and baskets as they set out for the market. . . . Suddenly the high-pitch scream of diving planes caused everyone to freeze . . . Countless explosions shook our house followed by the *rat-tat-tat* of strafing machine guns. . . . Later reports would confirm that several German Stukas had screamed out of a blue sky and . . . dropped several bombs along the main street—and then returned to strafe the market. The carnage was terrible."

How do you predict airplanes might be used in World War II? *(Sample answer: for bombing, transportation, and reconnaissance)*

Tell students that in this lesson they will be reading about the beginning of World War II and the dominance of the Axis powers.

Online You can also project the **Start Up Activity** from the course.

INVESTIGATE

Have students read the section in the **Reading and Note Taking Study Guide** to help them take notes and understand the text as they read.

Axis Domination of Europe

Tell students that the ruthless efficiency of Germany's "lightning war" surprised many countries, and most of Europe fell under the control of the Axis powers before 1941. However, Germany was unable to subdue Great Britain.

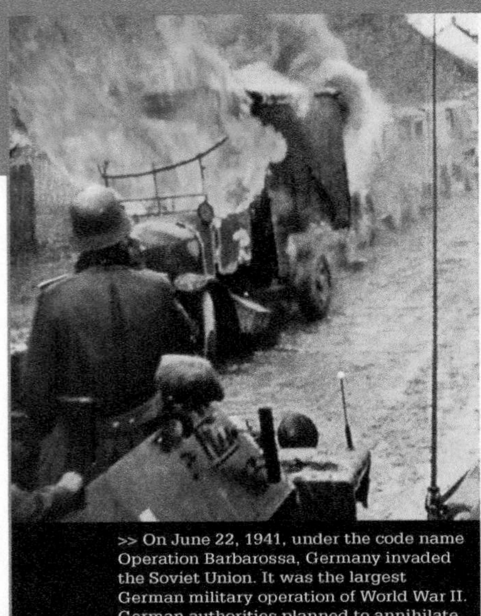

>> On June 22, 1941, under the code name Operation Barbarossa, Germany invaded the Soviet Union. It was the largest German military operation of World War II. German authorities planned to annihilate the Communist nation.

Interactive Flipped Video

18.2 World War II lasted from 1939 to 1945. It pitted the Axis powers against the Allies, which eventually included Britain, France, the Soviet Union, China, the United States, and 43 other nations. Unlike World War I, with its defensive trenches, the new global conflict was a war of aggressive movement. In the early years, things went badly for the Allies as Axis forces swept across Europe, North Africa, and Asia.

TEKS
12.B, 12.C, 16.A, 28.C

>> Objectives

Trace the course of German aggression and British resistance in Europe.

Describe the Nazi invasion of the Soviet Union.

Explain how Japanese imperialism and the attack on Pearl Harbor brought the United States into the war.

>> Key Terms

blitzkrieg
Luftwaffe
Dunkirk
Vichy
Erwin Rommel
Erwin Rommel (1891–1944) was a career military officer and one of Hitler's most successful generals. He took his own life after a failed attempt to assassinate Hitler.
Lend-Lease Act
Atlantic Charter
Hideki Tojo

www.PearsonTexas.com
Access your Digital Lesson.

Axis Powers Advance

Axis Domination of Europe

Germany's "Lightning War" The Nazi invasion of Poland revealed the power of Hitler's **blitzkrieg,** or "lightning war." The blitzkrieg used tank and air power technology to strike a devastating blow against the enemy.

First, the **Luftwaffe,** or German air force, bombed airfields, factories, towns, and cities. Screaming dive bombers attacked troops and civilians. Then fast-moving tanks and troop transports pushed their way into the defending Polish army, encircling whole divisions and forcing them to surrender.

As Germany attacked from the west, Stalin's forces invaded from the east, grabbing lands promised to them under the Nazi-Soviet Pact. Within a month, Poland ceased to exist as an independent nation. Because of Poland's location and the speed of the attacks, Britain and France could do nothing beyond declaring war on Germany.

Hitler passed the winter without much further action. Stalin's armies, however, forced the Baltic states of Estonia, Latvia, and Lithuania to host bases for the Soviet military. Soviet forces also seized part of Finland, which put up stiff but unsuccessful resistance.

In April 1940, Hitler launched a blitzkrieg against Norway and Denmark, both of which soon fell. Next, his forces slammed into the Netherlands and Belgium.

806

Aa Vocabulary Builder

1. Have students pronounce the following academic vocabulary terms in this lesson and clarify the part of speech. For difficult or polysyllabic words, break them into syllables and pronounce them with the students.
2. Explain what the word means in common "student-friendly" language using synonyms and antonyms when possible. Provide concrete examples to clarify the meaning, and rephrase the definition.

available: ready for use; at hand

nullified: made invalid

The Rescue at Dunkirk During that first winter, the French hunkered down behind the Maginot Line, a border created by the French in the 1930s to protect from German invasion. Britain sent troops to wait with them. Some reporters referred to this quiet time as the "phony war."

In May 1940, German forces surprised the French and British by attacking through the Ardennes Forest in Belgium, an area that was considered invasion proof. Bypassing the Maginot Line, German troops poured into France. Retreating British forces were soon trapped between the Nazi army and the English Channel.

In a desperate gamble, the British sent all available naval vessels, merchant ships, and even fishing and pleasure boats across the channel to pluck stranded troops off the beach of **Dunkirk.** Despite German air attacks, the improvised armada ferried more than 300,000 troops to safety in Britain. This heroic rescue raised British morale.

France Surrenders Meanwhile, German forces were heading south toward Paris. In June, Mussolini had declared war on France and Britain. He sent Italian troops to attack France from the south.

Overrun and demoralized, France surrendered. On June 22, 1940, Hitler forced the French to sign the surrender documents in the same railroad car in which Germany had signed the armistice ending World War I. Following the surrender, Germany occupied northern France. In the south, the Germans set up a "puppet state," with its capital at **Vichy** (VEE shee).

Some French officers escaped to England and set up a government-in-exile. Led by Charles de Gaulle, these "free French" worked to liberate their homeland. Within France, resistance fighters used guerrilla tactics against German forces.

Operation Sea Lion With the fall of France, Britain stood alone in Western Europe. Hitler was sure that the British would sue for peace. But Winston Churchill, who had replaced Neville Chamberlain as prime minister, had other plans. Churchill's defiance gave voice to the determination of the British.

> "We shall defend our island, whatever the cost may be, we shall fight on the beaches, we shall fight on the landing grounds, we shall fight in the fields and in the streets, we shall fight in the hills; we shall never surrender."
>
> Winston Churchill, June 4, 1940

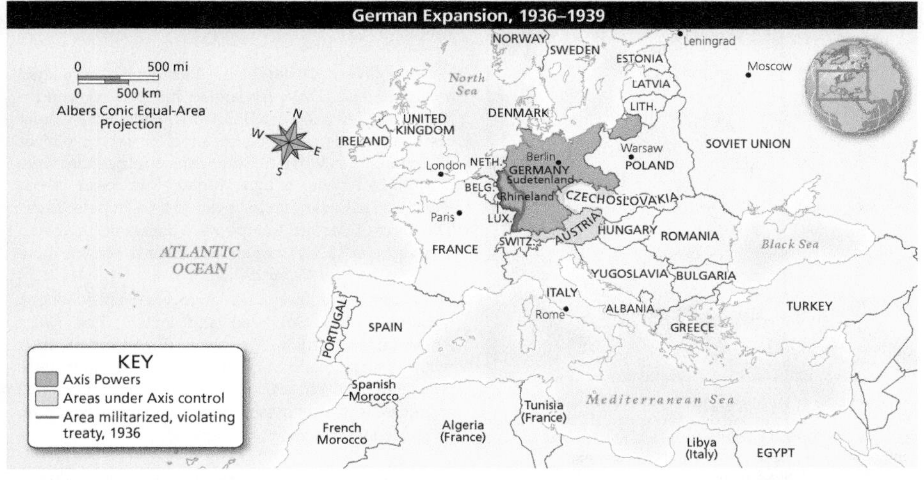

>> Germany advanced aggressively from 1936 to 1939, until its invasion of Poland sparked another world war. **Analyze Maps** How did Germany violate the Treaty of Versailles?

Interactive Map

Analyze Images

Ask students to examine the map "German Expansion, 1936–1939," and trace the Axis advance at the beginning of the war. Ask: How did the Axis powers achieve victories in 1939 and 1940? *(by striking fast, using the awesome power of modern technology, and never giving the enemy time to prepare or defend itself)*

Sequence The Axis powers were able to take control of most of Europe before 1941. Which country was the first to fall to Axis aggression in September 1939? *(Poland)*

Online Project the **Interactive Gallery: London Blitz** and click through the images in the gallery. Introduce the gallery by telling students that for eight consecutive months, the German air force bombed London and other major industrial British cities every night. The British persevered despite the gains the Axis powers had made throughout Europe.

ACTIVE CLASSROOM

Have students use the See-Think-Wonder strategy with a partner. Ask students to select one image from the gallery. Then ask: *What do you see? What does that make you think? What are you wondering about now that you've seen this?* Give students time to discuss with a partner and then share their insights with the class.

History Background

The Trick of the Hitler Two-Step After the surrender of France, the Western Allies saw news reels and photographs that seemingly showed a delighted Hitler doing a victory dance on the very spot where Germany had surrendered at the close of World War I. This humiliating image was continually shown in movie theaters and newspapers across Britain, the United States, and Canada. It enraged viewers. However, the footage was really a clever editing trick by propagandist John Grierson, then the managing director of Canada's Wartime Information Board. When he received footage of Hitler stamping his foot once, he edited the frames and looped them to show Hitler doing a dance. The Allies then continuously aired the fake footage to rally the public to join the war effort.

Answers

Analyze Maps *Sample response: Germany wasn't supposed to rebuild its military or have forces in the Rhineland, but it violated the treaty by rebuilding its military to annex Czechoslovakia and Austria and reoccupying the Rhineland.*

D Differentiate Challenge Ask students to do additional research on the London Blitz and present their findings. During the Blitz, the British persevered and kept their spirits high in order to support the war effort. Churchill gave many speeches and used propaganda effectively to keep the British morale as high as possible throughout the war.

Discuss Examine the importance of high morale for people on the home front during wartime. Ask: What might happen if morale drops? *(Answers will vary, but students might say that enlistment and fundraising for the war effort might also drop, which would hurt success.)*

Guided Reading and Discussion

Italy also acted aggressively, with Mussolini sending troops to support the invasion of France and ordering invasions of Greece and Egypt.

Predict Which side do you think was winning at the end of 1942? *(the Axis, because they controlled most of Europe and had won important victories in Africa)*

>> In his first speech in Parliament, Prime Minister Winston Churchill vowed, "I have nothing to offer but blood, toil, tears and sweat." He ended with the words, "Come then, let us go forward together with our united strength."

>> The Battle of Britain started in July 1940, but by September, Hitler decided on a new tactic. Hitler believed the British would surrender if he targeted civilians, so he began a daily bombing campaign. London was Hitler's first target.

 Interactive Gallery

Faced with this defiance, Hitler made plans for Operation Sea Lion—the invasion of Britain. In preparation for the invasion, he launched massive air strikes against the island nation.

Beginning in August 1940, German bombers began a daily bombardment of England's southern coast. For a month, Britain's Royal Air Force valiantly battled the Luftwaffe. Then the Germans changed their tactics. Instead of bombing military targets in the south, they began to bomb London and other cities.

England Survives the Blitz German bombers first appeared over London late on September 7, 1940. All through the night, relays of aircraft showered high explosives and firebombs on the sprawling capital. The bombing continued for 57 nights in a row and then sporadically until the next May. These bombing attacks are known as "the Blitz." Much of London was destroyed, and thousands of people lost their lives.

London did not break under the Blitz. Defiantly, Parliament continued to meet. Citizens carried on their daily lives, seeking protection in shelters and then emerging to resume their routines when the all-clear sounded. Even Churchill and the British king and queen chose to support Londoners by joining them in bomb shelters rather than fleeing to the countryside.

German planes continued to bomb London and other cities off and on until May 1941. But contrary to Hitler's hopes, the Luftwaffe could not gain air superiority over Britain, and British morale was not destroyed. In fact, the bombing only made the British more determined to turn back the enemy. Operation Sea Lion was a failure.

Hitler's "New Order" As Nazi forces rampaged across Europe, Hitler expanded his plan to build a "new order" in the occupied lands. Hitler's new order grew out of his racial obsessions. He set up puppet governments in Western European countries that were peopled by Aryans, or light-skinned Europeans, whom Hitler and his followers believed to be a "master race." The Slavs of Eastern Europe were considered to be an inferior "race." They were shoved aside to provide more "living space" for Germans.

To the Nazis, occupied lands were an economic resource to be plundered and looted. The Nazis systematically stripped conquered nations of their works of art, factories, and other resources. To counter resistance movements that emerged in occupied countries, the Nazis took savage revenge, shooting hostages and torturing prisoners.

War in North Africa and the Balkans Axis armies also pushed into North Africa and the Balkans. In September 1940, Mussolini ordered forces from Italy's

History Background

Aryan or Not? Nineteenth-century Europeans believed that in around 1500 B.C., a group called Aryans had swept into South Asia, conquered the people already living there, and imposed their culture upon them. The Aryans were thought to have been behind civilization's most brilliant advances. One theory held the Aryans were descended from northern Europeans, and that Germanic or Nordic peoples were the purest and most advanced of all the Aryans, and therefore superior to people of other origins. In recent years, most scholars have rejected the ideas that the Aryans originated in Europe or invaded South Asia. Instead they believe that the group known as Aryans developed in South Asia and drew heavily on the existing culture of that region. Thus, the theories that Hitler based his government upon were not only morally wrong, but untrue as well.

North African colony of Libya into Egypt. When the British army repulsed these invaders, Hitler sent one of his most brilliant commanders, General **Erwin Rommel,** to North Africa. The "Desert Fox," as he was called, chalked up a string of successes in 1941 and 1942. He pushed the British back across the desert toward Cairo, Egypt.

In October 1940, Italian forces invaded Greece. They encountered stiff resistance, and in 1941 German troops once again provided reinforcements. Both Greece and Yugoslavia were added to the growing Axis empire. Even after the Axis triumph, however, Greek and Yugoslav guerrillas plagued the occupying forces. Meanwhile, both Bulgaria and Hungary had joined the Axis alliance. By 1941, the Axis powers or their allies controlled most of Europe.

DESCRIBE Describe how the Axis powers gained control of most of Europe in 1941.

>> Erwin Rommel led the military operation in Libya. Rommel was sent to North Africa to help the Italian forces fight the British. Rommel was an expert at tank warfare.

Nazis Attack the Soviet Union

After the failure in Britain, Hitler turned his military might to a new target—the Soviet Union. The decision to invade the Soviet Union took pressure off Britain. It also proved to be one of Hitler's costliest mistakes.

In June 1941, Hitler broke the Nazi-Soviet Pact by invading the Soviet Union in Operation Barbarossa, a plan which took its name from the medieval Germanic leader, Frederick Barbarossa. Hitler made his motives clear. He wanted to gain "living space" for Germans and to win control of regions rich in resources."If I had the Ural Mountains with their incalculable store of treasures in raw materials," he declared, "Siberia with its vast forests, and the Ukraine with its tremendous wheat fields, Germany under National Socialist leadership would swim in plenty." He also wanted to crush communism in Europe and defeat his powerful rival, Stalin.

A Rapid Advance Hitler unleashed a new blitzkrieg in the Soviet Union. About three million German soldiers invaded. The Germans caught Stalin unprepared. His army was still suffering from the purges that had wiped out many of its top officers.

The Soviets lost two and a half million soldiers trying to fend off the invaders. As they were forced back, Soviet troops destroyed factories and farm equipment and burned crops to keep them out of enemy hands. But they could not stop the German war machine. By autumn, the Nazis had smashed deep into the Soviet Union and were poised to take Moscow and Leningrad (present-day St. Petersburg).

Winter Halts the Blitzkrieg There, however, the German advance stalled. Like Napoleon's Grand Army in 1812, Hitler's forces were not prepared for the fury of "General Winter." By early December, temperatures plunged to 0°F (-18°C).

Cold was a killer. German troops had set out in summer and had no warm winter uniforms. Fuel froze in tanks, and much of the Germans' mechanized equipment was useless. Thousands of German soldiers starved or froze to death.

Siege of Leningrad The Soviets, meanwhile, suffered appalling hardships. In September 1941, the two-and-a-half-year siege of Leningrad began. Food was rationed to two pieces of bread a day. Desperate Leningraders ate almost anything. For example, they boiled wallpaper scraped off walls because its paste was said to contain potato flour.

Although more than a million Leningraders died during the siege, the city did not fall to the Germans. Hoping to gain some relief for his exhausted people, Stalin urged Britain to open a second front in Western

Nazis Attack the Soviet Union

Before the invasion of Poland, Hitler and Stalin agreed to the Nazi-Soviet Pact, as they agreed to support and not oppose each other as they expanded their territory in Eastern Europe. Hitler broke the terms of the Nazi-Soviet Pact when he invaded the Soviet Union. His goals were to stop the spread of communism and gain control of the Soviet Union's natural resources.

Online Project the **Interactive Map: Axis Aggression** and click through the multiple layers of the map to see the spread of Axis conquests between 1936 and 1941.

ACTIVE CLASSROOM

Have students form an Opinion Line to answer the following question: Was Hitler's decision to invade the Soviet Union successful? *Yes* or *No? (Sample responses: Yes; it allowed Germany to weaken an enemy to the east and take control of useful resources. No; it created another enemy on the eastern border of Germany.)*

Guided Reading and Discussion

Tell students that the German army successfully advanced into the Soviet Union until winter arrived, when it became unable to continue its offensive. Discuss why the German invasion of the Soviet Union was a major turning point of World War II. *(Sample response: Germany broke an agreement when it invaded the Soviet Union, which led the Soviet Union to form an alliance with the Allied powers.)*

D Differentiate Extra Support After asking students to take a stand in the Active Classroom activity, allow them five minutes to think about the question individually. Tell them to write down their response (*yes* or *no*) and two reasons why they answered that way. Then continue with the group activity.

English Language Proficiency Standards

ELPS 5.G.1 Read "Nazis Attack the Soviet Union" aloud.

Beginning Retell the information in "Winter Halts the Blitzkrieg." Have students draw pictures to show how Germany invaded the Soviet Union and why Nazi troops stopped their advance.

Intermediate Follow the instructions for the Beginning activity but have students retell the information in their own words before they draw pictures. Tell students to write captions for their pictures.

Advanced Have students reread "Winter Halts the Blitzkrieg," then write a paragraph to tell how Germany invaded the Soviet Union and why Nazi troops stopped their advance. Students may enhance their writing with pictures and share their work with a partner.

Advanced High Follow instructions for the Advanced activity, but have students write their paragraphs from the perspective of a German soldier, a Russian soldier, or an observer. Have students share their work with the rest of the class.

Answers

Describe *Germany invaded Poland in 1939, starting the war. Then Hitler launched a blitzkrieg and captured Norway, Denmark, the Netherlands, and Belgium. Germany invaded France at the same time Italy declared war on France and attacked from the south resulting in the fall of France. Germany and Italy were successful in taking parts of the regions of North Africa, Greece, and Yugoslavia. In addition, Bulgaria and Hungary joined the Axis.*

U.S. Involvement in the War

The United States sought to avoid direct involvement in the war but continued to support the Allies. Roosevelt and Churchill discussed the Atlantic Charter, a statement of common goals for the war. Roosevelt pushed Congress to adopt the Lend-Lease Act and banned the sale of war materials to Japan. As a result, Japan bombed Pearl Harbor, Hawaii. Ask: Why was Roosevelt concerned about the actions of militarists such as Hideki Tojo prior to war? *(Tojo had supported the invasion of China and the formation of the Axis alliance.)* Do you think Roosevelt was justified in calling for a declaration of war after the attack on Pearl Harbor? *(Some may say that Roosevelt was justified because the United States was attacked, and it was important to protect American assets and lives.)*

Key Terms

Direct students' attention to the key term **Lend-Lease Act** (in bold). Tell them that though around 60 percent of the total wartime aid was given to Great Britain, by the end of the war more than 40 countries had received aid. The total value of aid given under the act was more than $49 billion.

Guided Reading and Discussion

Explain that President Roosevelt believed supporting the Allies was important for protecting democracy. Ask students how the bombing of Pearl Harbor shifted American thought about entering World War II and how this helped the Allies. *(Americans were outraged and the country entered the war, increasing the strength of the Allies.)*

Europe. Although Churchill could not offer much real help, the two powers did agree to work together.

? IDENTIFY SUPPORTING DETAILS Why did Hitler nullify the Nazi-Soviet Pact by invading the Soviet Union?

U.S. Involvement in the War

When the war began in 1939, the United States declared its neutrality. Although isolationist feeling remained strong, many Americans, including President Franklin Delano Roosevelt, sympathized with those who battled the Axis powers. In time, Roosevelt found ways around the Neutrality Acts to provide aid, including for Britain, as it stood alone against Hitler.

Roosevelt Supports the Allies In March 1941, FDR persuaded Congress to pass the **Lend-Lease Act.** It allowed him to sell or lend war materials to "any country whose defense the President deems vital to the defense of the United States." The United States, said Roosevelt, would not be drawn into the war, but it would become "the arsenal of democracy," supplying arms to those who were fighting for freedom.

To show further support, Roosevelt met secretly with Churchill on a warship in the Atlantic in August 1941. The two leaders issued the **Atlantic Charter,** which set goals for the war—"the final destruction of the Nazi tyranny"—and for the postwar world. They pledged to support "the right of all peoples to choose the form of government under which they will live" and called for a "permanent system of general security."

Growing Tensions with Japan Although Roosevelt viewed Hitler as the greatest menace to world peace, it was tensions with Japan that finally brought the United States into the war. The United States held several possessions in the Pacific, including the Philippines and Hawaii.

When war broke out in Europe in 1939, the Japanese saw a chance to grab European possessions in Southeast Asia. Japanese forces took control across Asia and the Pacific. Japan claimed that its mission was to help Asians escape Western colonial rule. In fact, the real goal was a Japanese empire in Asia. The rich resources of the region, including oil, rubber, and tin, would be of immense value in fighting Japan's war against the Chinese.

In 1940, with Europeans distracted by war, Japan advanced into French Indochina and the Dutch East Indies. In response, the United States banned the sale of war materials, such as iron, steel, and oil, to Japan.

>> The Soviet Union joined the Allies after Germany's invasion. **Analyze Maps** How might this new enemy affect Germany's war effort in geographic terms?

Answers

Identify Supporting Details *Hitler wanted access to the plentiful raw materials and to crush communism and Stalin.*

Analyze Maps *Sample response: Germany was located between two enemies: Britain and the Soviet Union.*

Identify Central Issues *The United States banned the sale of war materials to Japan. This hampered Japanese expansion efforts and threatened their economy.*

Japanese leaders saw this move as a threat to Japan's economy and its Asian sphere of influence.

Japan and the United States held talks to ease the growing tension. But extreme militarists were gaining power in Japan, including General **Hideki Tojo** who became prime minister in 1941. Prior to the war, Tojo had strongly supported the invasion of China and the formation of the alliance with Germany and Italy. Tojo and other militarists hoped to seize more lands in Asia and the Pacific and believed the United States was interfering with their plans.

The Attack on Pearl Harbor With talks at a standstill, General Tojo ordered a surprise attack. Early on December 7, 1941, Japanese airplanes bombed the American fleet at Pearl Harbor in Hawaii. The attack took the lives of about 2,400 people and destroyed battleships and aircraft.

The next day, a grim-faced President Roosevelt told the nation that December 7 was "a date which will live in infamy." He asked Congress to declare war on Japan. On December 11, Germany and Italy, as Japan's allies, declared war on the United States.

Japanese Victories in the Pacific In the long run, the Japanese attack on Pearl Harbor would be as serious a mistake as Hitler's invasion of the Soviet Union. But in the months immediately after Pearl Harbor, European and American possessions in the Pacific fell one by one to the Japanese.

The Japanese captured the Philippines and other islands held by the United States. They overran the British colonies of Hong Kong, Burma, and Malaya, advanced deeper into the Dutch East Indies, and completed the takeover of French Indochina. By 1942, the Japanese empire stretched from Southeast Asia to the western Pacific Ocean.

The Japanese invaders treated the Chinese, Filipinos, Malaysians, and other conquered people with great brutality. In China, the Philippines, Malaysia, and elsewhere, they killed and tortured civilians. They seized food crops, destroyed cities and towns, and made local people into slave laborers. Whatever welcome the Japanese had first met as "liberators" soon turned to hatred. In the Philippines, Indochina, and elsewhere, resistance forces organized to wage guerrilla warfare against the Japanese invaders.

>> On Sunday morning, December 7, 1941, the U.S. naval base at Pearl Harbor, Hawaii, was jolted awake by a surprise air attack. Japanese planes dropped bombs and torpedoes, stunning Americans.

 **IDENTIFY CENTRAL ISSUES** Why did Japanese leaders view the United States as an enemy?

ASSESSMENT

1. **Integrate Information** How were people of occupied territories treated by the Axis powers?
2. **Describe** Explain why Hitler's blitzkrieg tactics were successful at the beginning of the war.
3. **Synthesize** What was the role of Winston Churchill during World War II?
4. **Describe** Explain the purpose of Hitler's "new order."
5. **Synthesize** What role did Japanese imperialism play in igniting World War II?

Topic 18 Lesson 2

SYNTHESIZE

Online Project the **Digital Activity: Axis Powers Advance**. Ask students to recall the Topic Essential Question, "When is war justified?" Have students sequence the events from 1939 to 1941 into a flowchart. *(Sept. 1939: Germany invades Western Poland, and Soviets invade Eastern Poland; Winter 1939: Soviets invade Estonia, Latvia, Lithuania, and parts of Finland; April 1940: Germany invades Norway, Denmark, Netherlands, and Belgium; June 1940: France surrenders to Germany; August 1940: Battle of Britain; Sept. 1940: Germany begins the Blitz, and Italy and Germany invade North Africa and Balkans; Oct. 1940: Italy and Germany invade Greece and Yugoslavia; Fall 1940: Germany takes over Bulgaria and Hungary, and Japan invades French Indochina and Dutch East Indies; June 1941: Germany invades Soviet Union; 1941; Japan takes over Hong Kong, Burma, and Malaya; Dec. 1941: Japan attacks the United States.)*

Discuss What roles did world leaders Roosevelt, Hitler, Churchill, Stalin, and Tojo play during World War II? How might history be different if these leaders had acted differently?

DEMONSTRATE

Online Assign the **Digital Lesson Quiz** for this lesson if you haven't already done so. Students will be offered automatic remediation or enrichment based on their scores.

Pose the following question to the class on the Discussion Board:

Draw Conclusions Although the United States remained officially neutral before the bombing of Pearl Harbor in December 1941, how did the Lend-Lease Act show the true sympathies of the Roosevelt administration? *(Sample response: Roosevelt's true sympathies lay against the fascist powers, and with the Lend-Lease Act he found a way to aid Britain while still remaining neutral.)*

Topic Inquiry

Have students continue working on their assignments for the Topic Inquiry.

Assessment

1. Both Germany and Japan treated the civilians they encountered with brutality.
2. Hitler used advanced technology to overwhelm enemy forces. First, airplanes bombed a region; then fast-moving ground troops moved in to surround enemy forces. In the beginning, the attacks happened before enemy forces could counteract.
3. Winston Churchill was stoic and kept the British morale high with his powerful stance and speeches during the Blitz and throughout the remainder of the war.
4. Hitler's "new order" was designed to rid Europe of what he believed to be inferior races. He wanted to create more living space for the "master race."
5. Japan wanted to expand its empire by taking over most of Asia and countries in the Pacific. Japanese leaders felt threatened by the United States after it banned the sale of war materials to Japan. Japan attacked the United States in order to stop American interference.

Topic 18 Lesson 3

The Holocaust

CONNECT

Preview Have students preview the **Lesson Objectives** and the list of **Key Terms**.

Students can also preview all the **Key Terms** and **Academic Vocabulary** using the **Interactive Reading Notepad** on the digital course or preview a summary of the lesson in the **Reading and Note Taking Study Guide**.

Online Use the **Editable Presentation** found on the digital course to present the main ideas for this lesson.

Start Up Activity

Explain that during World War II, the Nazis put in place a program of genocide, which became known as the Holocaust, to eliminate Europe's Jewish population. Direct students' attention to the photograph of Jewish families being led off by Nazi soldiers at the top of this page. Discuss the emotions shown on people's faces. Ask students to predict what this photograph reveals about how the Nazis treated the civilians they conquered.

Tell students that in this lesson they will be learning about how the Nazis committed genocide and brought about the horrors of life during the Holocaust.

Online You can also project the **Start Up Activity** from the course.

INVESTIGATE

Have students read the section using the **Reading and Note Taking Study Guide** to help them take notes and understand the text as they read.

The Nazi Campaign Against the Jews

Explain that Hitler originally implemented the concentration camp system for political prisoners or for people who spoke out against the Nazi Party. Eventually, Hitler developed the "Final Solution" as a way to rid the world of cultures the Nazis considered racially inferior and established extermination camps for the purpose of killing. Over 6 million Jews were killed in Nazi concentration camps and extermination camps as a result of anti-Semitism in Nazi Germany.

>> The Warsaw Uprising ended on October 2, 1944. The entire civilian population of the Warsaw ghetto was expelled; most were sent to labor and death camps.

 Interactive Flipped Video

18.3 **Hitler came to power in the midst of the Great Depression, promising to end reparations, create jobs, and defy the hated Versailles treaty by rearming Germany. Hitler also played on anti-Semitism, which had existed for centuries in Europe. Hitler saw Jews as a separate, inferior race whom he blamed for Germany's defeat in World War I. He launched a campaign against the Jews, which began with persecution and escalated to mass murder.**

TEKS
12.B, 12.C, 22.D

>> Objectives

Identify the roots of Nazi persecution of the Jews.

Describe how the Nazis carried out a program of genocide.

Describe the various acts of Jewish resistance.

Summarize the response of the Allies to the Holocaust.

>> Key Terms

concentration camp
crematorium
Holocaust
Auschwitz

The Holocaust

The Nazi Campaign Against the Jews

Early Persecution The Nuremberg Laws of 1935 put Nazi racist ideology into practice. They removed citizenship from German Jews and banned marriage between Jews and Germans. Before long, the Nazis imposed other restrictions that forced Jews from their jobs and homes and embarked on escalating violence and terror against Jews. Schools and the Hitler Youth Movement taught children that Jews were "polluting" German society and culture.

Anti-Semitic propaganda triggered one of the most violent early attacks on Jews. In November 1938, Nazi-led mobs smashed windows, looted, and destroyed Jewish homes, businesses, and places of worship. This wave of violence became known as Kristallnacht, or Night of Broken Glass.

Nazi Concentration Camps After gaining power in 1933, the Nazis began rounding up political opponents and placing them in **concentration camps,** detention centers for civilians who were considered enemies of the state. Before long, they were sending Jews, communists, and others they despised to these camps. By 1934,

 www.PearsonTexas.com Access your Digital Lesson.

812

Aa Vocabulary Builder

1. Have students pronounce the following academic vocabulary terms in this lesson and clarify the part of speech. For difficult or polysyllabic words, break them into syllables and pronounce them with the students.
2. Explain what the word means in common "student-friendly" language using synonyms and antonyms when possible. Provide concrete examples to clarify the meaning, and rephrase the definition.

genocide: the deliberate killing of people who belong to a particular racial, political, or social group

liberated: set free

Hitler had given Heinrich Himmler the power to take full control of the concentration camps throughout Germany.

After World War II began, the Nazis built many more camps to house Jews from Poland and other parts of Eastern Europe as well as resistance fighters, Roma (Gypsies), Slavs, and other "racially undesirable elements." The physically and mentally disabled, homosexuals, and ordinary criminals were also sent to the camps. So, too, were political and religious leaders who spoke out against the Nazis.

During the war, Nazis used prisoners in the camps as forced laborers. Prisoners had to produce weapons and other goods for the German war effort. They faced brutal mistreatment, hunger, disease, and execution. Hundreds of thousands of prisoners died.

> "I was 9 weeks in Majdanek, 9 weeks, you see, 9 weeks! And I never washed my face the whole 9 weeks because then in the barracks there was no water. We had to go out, you know, in a shed, washing the face, or needing to go to the toilet ... When I left Majdanek for Auschwitz, I just take off the clothes in 9 weeks and throw away and take the first shower. And they cut off my hair and everything. And I got a clean shirt and I say to myself there, 'God is still with me.'"
>
> —Solomon Radasky, a Holocaust Survivor

Brutal Medical Experiments In some camps, Nazi doctors conducted painful and deadly medical experiments on prisoners. They tested dangerous new drugs on prisoners and tried out treatments designed to help Axis forces survive injuries. They also ran experiments to prove Nazi racial ideas. Josef Mengele, a physician at the notorious Auschwitz concentration camp, conducted experiments to see how different ethnic groups responded to contagious diseases such as malaria or yellow fever. Still other experiments were linked to the Nazi goal of sterilizing people they claimed were "inferior races."

Hitler's "Final Solution" As Nazi troops advanced into Eastern Europe, they forced Jews in Poland and elsewhere to live in ghettos, or restricted areas where they were sealed off from the surrounding city. By 1941, however, Hitler and other Nazi had devised what they called the "Final Solution to the Jewish question." Their goal was the extermination of all European Jews.

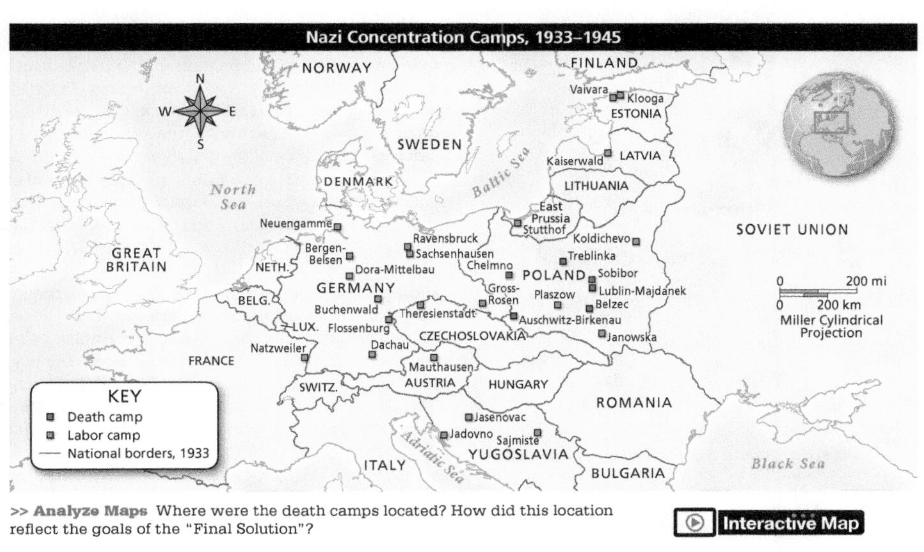

>> **Analyze Maps** Where were the death camps located? How did this location reflect the goals of the "Final Solution"?

Interactive Map

Online Project the **Interactive Map: Concentration Camps** and click through the hotspots on the map.

ACTIVE CLASSROOM

Have students use the Sticky Notes strategy. Ask them to jot down questions, comments, or observations about what they noticed or thought while looking at the images of the concentration camps. Have them post the notes on the classroom wall. Sort and discuss questions as a group.

Guided Reading and Discussion

Be sure that students understand that the Holocaust was an act of genocide, stemming from Hitler's ideology that Jews were an inferior race. Hitler's anti-Semitism grew into a systematic policy of genocide as he devised the "Final Solution of the Jewish question," a plan to exterminate European Jews. Discuss how anti-Semitism grew into genocide during World War II.

Synthesize Explain the roots of Hitler's anti-Semitism. *(Sample response: Hitler believed that Jews were the reason Germany lost World War I. He also believed in the idea of a master race, and Jews, Slavs, Roma, and other ethnic groups were seen as inferior compared to Hitler's own "Aryan" race.)*

Answers

Analyze Maps *Sample response: The death camps were located in Poland, near the work camps. This shows that all detainees might eventually be moved from work camps to death camps. This reveals the Nazis' ruthless policies toward Slavs and Central European Jews.*

English Language Proficiency Standards

ELPS 5.B.2 Read "The Nazi Campaign Against the Jews" aloud. Then have students complete one of these activities.

Beginning Help students create a list of vocabulary words from the text, including *genocide, concentration camps, anti-Semitism, Holocaust,* and *crematorium.* Using context clues and bilingual dictionaries, help students write definitions for each word. Then model writing a sentence for each word that relates to the text.

Intermediate Using the list of vocabulary words in the Beginning activity, show students how to skim the text and underline each word. Help students develop definitions for each word by using context clues and bilingual dictionaries. Then have students write a sentence for each word that relates to the text, and share their sentences with the class.

Advanced Ask pairs to list vocabulary terms from the text, making sure to include all bolded terms. Have pairs use context clues to develop a definition for each word and then compare their definitions to dictionary definitions. Have students write a sentence for each vocabulary word and share them with their partners.

Advanced High Repeat the Advanced activity, but have students work individually to list terms, develop definitions, and write sentences. Have students share their sentences with the class.

Jewish Resistance

Tell students that although 6 million Jews died during the Holocaust, many Jews resisted against Hitler and the Nazis.

Synthesize How did other countries react to Hitler's persecution of the Jews in the 1930s and 1940s? *(Sample response: Many countries didn't provide aid or help to the Jews and blocked immigration, and some even became Nazi collaborators.)*

Guided Reading and Discussion

Remind students that although many resistance movements were unsuccessful, they offered hope to the people suffering from persecution. There were some instances of armed revolts, such as the Warsaw Ghetto uprising. Jews also engaged in spiritual resistance by preserving their culture and traditions.

Key Terms

Point out the key term **Auschwitz** (in bold) to students. Tell them that Auschwitz was the largest of the camps, at a railroad junction with 44 parallel tracks, and it was a main part of the Final Solution. Ask: Why would a railroad junction with many tracks be important to the Nazis? *(because they were shipping Jews and other prisoners by rail from around occupied Europe)*

This campaign of genocide eventually became known as the **Holocaust.**

To accomplish his Final Solution, Hitler had six special "death camps" built in Poland. There, the Nazis shipped Jews and others marked for extermination from all over occupied Europe. Nazi engineers designed efficient means of killing millions of men, women, and children.

As the prisoners reached the camps, they were stripped of their clothes and valuables. Their heads were shaved. Guards separated men from women, and children from their parents. The young, elderly, and sick were targeted for immediate killing. Within a few days, they were herded into "shower rooms" and gassed. Then their bodies were burned in specially designed **crematoriums.** The Nazis worked younger, healthier prisoners to death or used them for their inhumane "medical" experiments.

By June 1945, the Nazis had massacred more than six million Jews. Almost as many other "undesirable" people were killed as well.

? SYNTHESIZE Describe the escalation of Hitler's campaign against the Jews.

>> Anne Frank was one of over a million Jewish children who died during the Holocaust. She and her family lived in hiding in Amsterdam for over two years until they were found and sent to concentration camps. Anne's diary remains a key document of the Holocaust.

Jewish Resistance

Jewish people resisted the Nazis even though they knew their efforts could not succeed. In the early 1940s, Jews in the ghettos of Eastern Europe at times took up arms. The largest uprising occurred in the Warsaw ghetto in occupied Poland.

The Warsaw Ghetto Uprising In July 1942, the Nazis began sending Polish Jews from the Warsaw ghetto to the Treblinka death camp and to slave labor camps. As the mass deportations continued, Jewish groups organized an underground resistance movement.

By the spring of 1943, the German plan to liquidate the Warsaw ghetto was clear, and resistance groups planned a full-scale revolt. Armed with smuggled weapons and homemade bombs, the Jews took over the ghetto and prepared to fight to the end.

After holding out for a month, the resistance forces were crushed. The ghetto was in ruins, and thousands were killed in the fighting. Any survivors were sent to death camps or forced labor camps. Although the uprising was doomed, the courage of the resistance inspired uprisings elsewhere

Continuing Resistance A few Jews escaped the Warsaw ghetto and from ghettos elsewhere in Eastern Europe. They joined resistance groups waging guerrilla warfare against the Nazis. Some joined Soviet units or formed their own Jewish units. In Western Europe, Jews were active in the French and Belgian resistance movements.

Jewish resistance took different forms. In addition to armed uprisings and fighting with guerrilla forces, a few Jews challenged Nazi death camps. Uprisings occurred at Treblinka and Sobibor. In October 1944, a group of Jews in **Auschwitz,** the largest Nazi death camp, destroyed one of the gas chambers.

Jews also resisted by hiding or sending their children into hiding. And despite Nazi persecution, they preserved their culture and traditions as best they could.

Hiding Jews In some parts of Europe, friends, neighbors, or even strangers protected Jews. When Mussolini undertook a vicious campaign against Italian Jews, peasants hid Jews in their villages. Denmark and Bulgaria saved almost all their Jewish populations. The Danish resistance movement, assisted by many common citizens, coordinated the flight of over 7,000 Jews to safety in nearby Sweden.

Many individuals who were not Jewish took great risks to save Jewish lives. One of the best-known stories of the Holocaust is about Anne Frank and her tale of

History Background

Resisting Nazi Rule Across Europe, ordinary citizens resisted Nazi rule by hiding Jewish people or helping them escape to find safety. In Denmark, where few German troops were stationed, the Danish people smuggled almost all of the country's Jews to the safety of Sweden. Another pocket of resistance was Le Chambon, in France, where villagers provided a safe haven for 5,000 Jews.

Even in the death camps themselves, some Jews fought back. In October 1944, for example, a group of Jews in the Auschwitz death camp destroyed one of the death chambers. The rebels were all killed. One woman, Rosa Robota, was tortured for days before she was hanged. Camp inmates were forced to watch her execution.

Answers

Synthesize *Hitler issued the Nuremberg Laws and launched campaigns of persecution such as the Night of Broken Glass. He eventually escalated his plans with the construction of the concentration camp system and the "Final Solution," where he established death camps designed to slaughter millions of Jews in what is known today as the Holocaust.*

silent resistance. Anne and her family hid for just over two years in her father's Amsterdam office building, while eight people from the office worked together to secretly feed and care for the family in hiding. There are many similar stories of courageous citizens who helped to hide and protect Jewish friends, neighbors, and strangers.

Many people, however, closed their eyes to what was happening. Some collaborators, or people who cooperated with the Nazis, informed on Jews in hiding. In France, the Vichy government helped ship thousands of Jewish people to their deaths. Strict immigration policies in many Western countries as well as conscious efforts to block Jewish immigration prevented many Jews from gaining refuge elsewhere.

INFER Explain why the Jews in the Warsaw Ghetto decided to fight back.

The Allies Respond to the Holocaust

Even before the war started, some people outside Germany expressed concern about the Nazi persecution of the Jews. Still, the response was limited. The United States and other countries could have accepted many more Jewish refugees from Germany and Austria.

>> Passengers on the refugee ship *St. Louis* were turned away from Cuba and the U.S. In June 1939, the ship was forced to return to Europe and an uncertain fate.

The Question of Jewish Refugees In the summer of 1938, delegates from 32 countries met in France to discuss the "refugee problem." During the nine-day meeting, delegates expressed sympathy for the refugees, but most countries, including the United States and Britain, offered excuses for not accepting more refugees. In the midst of the Great Depression, many Americans worried that refugees would take jobs away from them and overburden social welfare programs. Widespread racial prejudices among the Allies, including anti-Semitic attitudes, also played a role in the failure to admit more Jewish refugees.

In 1939, the United States refused asylum to Jewish refugees on board the ship the *St. Louis*. The passengers were forced to return to Germany.

On the eve of World War II, Britain briefly lifted some restrictions and accepted almost 10,000 mostly Jewish children from Nazi Europe. Their parents were not allowed to accompany the children, and many children never saw their parents again.

The Allies Take Limited Action After the war began, the Allies were mostly concerned with military strategy. Throughout 1940 and 1941, Britain was fighting the war against the Nazis alone. Even when reliable reports concerning the murder of the Jews started to surface, the Allies were slow to respond. Despite urgent calls from resistance groups in occupied Europe, the Allies did not undertake any military operations.

By 1942, the Allies knew that Jews were being taken to death camps in Poland, but often kept this information classified. They refused to release early photographs taken of the camps. Over the next two years, both Britain and the United States considered the idea of bombing Auschwitz, but neither country took action, focusing instead on their ultimate war aim to defeat the Nazis. The only way to rescue Jews, argued some U.S. officials, was to win the war as fast as possible.

President Roosevelt began to respond to reports of Jewish genocide in 1944. He established the War Refugee Board, a government agency that worked with the Red Cross to save thousands of Eastern European Jews. Its greatest success was due to the brave actions of Raoul Wallenberg, a Swedish diplomat, in Hungary. Wallenberg issued thousands of Swedish passports to Hungarian Jews, which saved them from being deported to Auschwitz. Overall, the War Refugee Board is credited with saving as many as 200,000 Jews.

The Allies Respond to the Holocaust

Tell students that the Allies did little to stop the Holocaust. Most countries would not accept additional Jewish refugees, and even after learning about the death camps, the Allies were focused on winning the war. The enormity of the Holocaust was not known until the Allies liberated the camps late in the war.

Analyze Images

Ask students to look at the photograph of the refugees on the *St. Louis*. Tell them that most of the ship's 938 passengers were Jewish refugees from Germany. After being denied landing in Cuba, the ship sailed so close to the United States that passengers could see city lights. Some even sent word from the ship to President Roosevelt, but never received a response. Ask students what might have happened to the children in the photograph once they returned to Europe.

Answers

Infer *The Jews from the Warsaw Ghetto were being shipped to death camps, so they knew they were facing an inevitable death. They hoped to destroy as many Nazi forces as they could.*

English Language Proficiency Standards

5.G.2 Read "Jewish Resistance" aloud. Have students complete the activities below.

Beginning Reread "Jewish Resistance" to students. Retell the content in accessible language for Beginning English speakers. Then ask students to think about the ways that Jews resisted persecution during WWII. Instruct students to participate in a group writing activity in which they brainstorm details to include in a sentence that describes one way that Jews resisted the Nazis.

Intermediate Reread "Jewish Resistance" to students. Help students retell the content in the text in their own words. Then ask students to think about the ways that Jews resisted persecution during WWII. Instruct students to work in pairs to write two sentences that describe one way that Jews resisted the Nazis.

Advanced Have students reread "Jewish Resistance." Ask students to think about the ways that Jews resisted persecution during WWII. Instruct students to work in pairs to write a brief paragraph that describes two ways that Jews resisted the Nazis.

Advanced High Have students reread "Jewish Resistance." Ask students to think about the ways that Jews resisted persecution and the ways that others assisted the Jews during WWII. Instruct students to write a well-developed paragraph that describes how the Jews resisted the Nazis and how other Europeans assisted the Jews during WWII.

Topic 18 Lesson 3

Online Project the **Interactive Gallery: Remembering the Holocaust** and click through the museum exhibits that showcase life inside the concentration camps. Point out that, while numbers and statistics are often used to describe the Holocaust, it is important to look at individual stories of survivors and victims and remember the people who lived through the Holocaust. These images help remind us that Holocaust victims were more than just numbers. Look again at the image of the toy exhibit from the Yad Vashem Museum and reread how the Bucci sisters recounted their days in Auschwitz. Discuss the importance of imagination, especially for children, in order to survive the everyday horrors of the concentration camps.

ACTIVE CLASSROOM

Have students form a Word Wall. Ask them to choose one of the vocabulary terms for the lesson and make a visual image with a definition. Allow 3–5 minutes. Ask students to post their words and images on the board and then discuss similarities and differences in the responses as a group.

Guided Reading and Discussion

Discuss how people from the liberating countries may have felt after learning the extent of the Holocaust, knowing that their countries may have supported policies to turn away Jewish refugees. Ask: Do you think other countries could have done more to stop Nazi genocide before it was too late? *(Answers will vary, but most will say that countries should have done more.)*

Discuss the responsibility of countries to protect basic human rights around the world. Ask: What obligation do other nations have to protect people in another country from genocide? *(Sample response: If a country's leaders know that another country's leaders have engaged in the systematic elimination of an entire race of people, then they have a moral obligation to try to stop it.)*

"The initial shock was experienced even before entering the camp. The first evidence of the horror to come was a string of about forty railway cars on a siding near the camp entrance. Each car was loaded with emaciated human corpses ... A row of small cement structures near the prison entrance contained a coal-fired crematorium, a gas chamber, and rooms piled high with naked and emaciated human corpses ... I saw a large number of dead inmates lying where they had fallen in the last few hours or days before our arrival."

—Lieutenant Colonel Felix Sparks, commander of the U.S. 45th Infantry Division

>> On April 30, 1945, prisoners at Dachau cheered as American forces liberated the camp. American troops found more than 30 railroad cars filled with bodies that had been brought to Dachau for cremation.

The Liberation of the Concentration Camps The enormity of the Nazi genocide program became real only toward the end of the war, as Soviet and American troops began liberating the camps. These liberators, hardened by war, were not prepared to see the piles of dead bodies, the warehouses full of human hair and jewelry, the ashes from the crematoriums, or the half-dead, emaciated survivors.

Soviet forces were the first to liberate a major Nazi camp in Majdanek, Poland. The Nazis had been surprised by the rapid Soviet advance and attempted to destroy the evidence of mass murders by demolishing the camp. In the summer of 1944, the Soviets also liberated the Belzec, Sobibor, and Treblinka killing centers. By January 1945, the Soviets had liberated Auschwitz.

American and British forces also liberated many camps in Germany. On April 11, 1945, U.S. forces freed more than 20,000 prisoners at Buchenwald. British forces liberated concentration camps in northern Germany, and in mid-April 1945 freed more than 60,000 prisoners from the Bergen-Belsen concentration camp.

Most of the prisoners they released were in critical condition because of a typhus epidemic. More than 10,000 prisoners died within a few weeks of liberation from the effects of malnutrition.

Impact of the Holocaust By 1945, the Nazis had massacred some six million Jews in the Holocaust. Nearly five million other people were killed as well. The scale and savagery of the Holocaust are unequaled in history. The Nazis deliberately set out to destroy the Jews for no reason other than their religious and ethnic heritage. Today, the record of that slaughter is a vivid reminder of the monstrous results of racism and intolerance.

Survivors of the Holocaust often had nowhere to go in Europe. Their homes, villages, and communities had been destroyed. Many ended up in refugee camps in Allied-occupied Germany, waiting to find new homes in other countries. They still faced discrimination, however, and many countries refused to accept them.

D Differentiate Extra Support After asking students to choose a vocabulary word in the Active Classroom activity, allow students 5 minutes to think about synonyms for the word or make a list of adjectives to describe the word. Tell them to use the synonyms and adjectives to help make a visual image for the word. Then continue with the group activity.

Answers

Draw Conclusions *Germany was nearing defeat, and the Allies were advancing on German territory.*

As the horrors of the Holocaust were revealed, worldwide support for an independent Jewish homeland increased. On May 14, 1948, Jewish leader David Ben-Gurion proclaimed the establishment of the state of Israel in Palestine, site of the ancient Jewish kingdom of Israel. Many displaced Holocaust survivors emigrated to Israel to make a new start.

Today, people in the United States and around the world are working to make sure the Holocaust is not forgotten. Holocaust museums can be found in many states and countries. Some of the concentration camps, such as Auschwitz, have been preserved and stand as authentic memorials to preserve the memory of those who suffered.

DRAW CONCLUSIONS Why were Soviet and American forces finally able to liberate many concentration camp victims?

>> Holocaust museums around the world attract millions of visitors each year. Their goal is to remind the world of the horrors of genocide.

Interactive Gallery

ASSESSMENT

1. **Synthesize** In what was Hitler's campaign against German Jews rooted?
2. **Compare and Contrast** Describe the difference between Hitler's "Final Solution" and the Nazis' earlier persecution of the Jews.
3. **Recall** In what ways did Jews resist Nazi persecution?
4. **Infer** Why did the Allied Powers refuse admittance to Jewish refugees before Hitler's launch of the "Final Solution"?
5. **Synthesize** Why are people from around the world making sure the Holocaust is not forgotten?

World War II 817 18.3 The Holocaust

Topic 18 Lesson 3

SYNTHESIZE

Online Project the **Digital Activity: Speaking Up**. Ask students to recall the Topic Essential Question, "When is War Justified?" Reread and discuss with students the meaning behind Niemöller's quotation. Discuss how the statement was aimed at all people for allowing such a terrible event to happen. Next, discuss the importance of memorials and museums for honoring victims and survivors and for educating the world about the horrors of genocide.

Ask: Do you think the delegates from 32 countries that met in the summer of 1938 in France to discuss the Jewish refugee problem share some guilt for the Holocaust? Why or why not? Have pairs share their answers with the class. *(Answers will vary. Some students might think that the countries were not aware of the mistreatment and were only looking out for the people of their own country. Others will think that the countries were aware of the laws against the Jews and the escalation of mistreatment and they should be held responsible for not defending the human rights of others.)*

DEMONSTRATE

Online Assign the **Digital Lesson Quiz** for this lesson if you haven't already done so. Students will be offered automatic remediation or enrichment based on their scores.

Pose this question to the class on the Discussion Board:

Identify Cause and Effect How did the creation of Israel result from the Holocaust? *(Sample response: As the horrors of the Holocaust became evident, many believed the Jewish people deserved a homeland and that creating one might prevent or mitigate future manifestations of anti-Semitism.)*

Topic Inquiry

Have students continue their investigations for the Topic Inquiry.

Assessment

1. Hitler's campaign against German Jews was rooted in his belief in racial purity. He believed in an "Aryan" race and tried to purge Germany of "inferior" groups of people.
2. Hitler's early forms of persecution were aimed at removing Jews from Germany through legal means and terror. As time went on, Hitler escalated to the "Final Solution," which was the extermination of Jews in death camps.
3. Some led armed resistance, while others continued to conduct spiritual meetings and keep Jewish culture alive.
4. Although the Allied Powers expressed sympathy, they did not allow Jewish refugees into their countries because they were preoccupied with the Great Depression and the war, and many had racial prejudices as well.
5. Answers will vary, but may mention to preserve the memory of those who suffered, remind people of the horrid results of racism and intolerance, and to prevent future genocide.

The Allies Turn the Tide

CONNECT

Preview Have students preview the **Lesson Objectives** and the list of **Key Terms**.

Students can also preview all the **Key Terms** and **Academic Vocabulary** using the **Interactive Reading Notepad** on the digital course or preview a summary of the lesson in the **Reading and Note Taking Study Guide**.

Online Use the **Editable Presentation** found on the digital course to present the main ideas for this lesson.

Start Up Activity

Ask students to answer these questions: Who are the Axis Powers? *(Germany, Italy, and Japan)* Who are the Axis country leaders? *(Adolf Hitler, Benito Mussolini, Hideki Tojo)* Then discuss how they know the answers to these questions. *(from classroom discussions and the text)*

Discuss If you were in high school during the war, how would have gotten information about the war? *(Students might mention newspaper articles, newsreels, radio broadcasts, or political cartoons.)*

Online You can also project the **Start Up Activity** from the course.

INVESTIGATE

Have students read the section using the **Reading and Note Taking Study Guide** to help them take notes and understand the text as they read.

A Commitment to Total War

The Allies were on the defensive in early 1942. Japan was attacking the Allies in the Pacific, and Germany was bombing Britain and gaining ground in the Soviet Union. The Allies needed to manufacture enough military equipment to outproduce the Axis and wage total war. The war created millions of new jobs in the United States. Unemployment, which had remained high during the Great Depression, was almost wiped out.

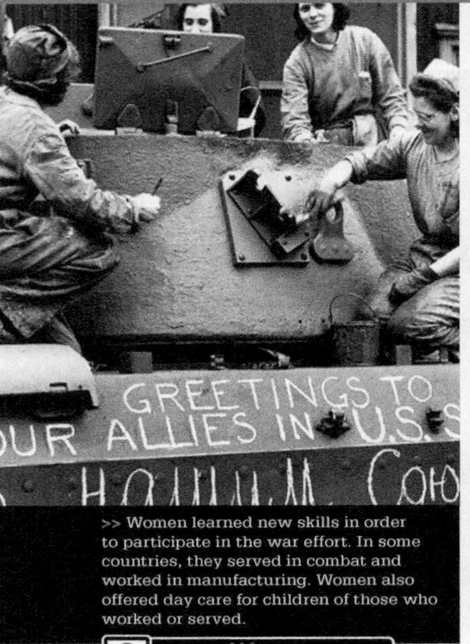

>> Women learned new skills in order to participate in the war effort. In some countries, they served in combat and worked in manufacturing. Women also offered day care for children of those who worked or served.

Interactive Flipped Video

18.4 As 1942 began, the Allies were in trouble. German bombers flew unrelenting raids over Britain, and the German army advanced deep into the Soviet Union. In the Pacific, the Japanese onslaught seemed unstoppable. But helped by extraordinary efforts on the home front and a series of military victories, the tide was about to turn.

TEKS
1.F, 12.B, 12.C

>> **Objectives**

Understand how nations committed all of their resources to fighting World War II.

Explain how the Allies began to push back the Axis powers in Europe and the Pacific.

Describe the Normandy landings and the Allied advance toward Germany.

>> **Key Terms**

Franklin Delano Roosevelt
Winston Churchill
Joseph Stalin
internment
Rosie the Riveter
aircraft carrier
Dwight Eisenhower
Stalingrad
D-Day
Yalta Conference
Dwight Eisenhower

The Allies Turn the Tide

A Commitment to Total War

Like the Axis powers they were fighting, the Allies committed themselves to total war. In total war, nations devote all of their resources to the war effort.

Governments Redirect Resources To achieve maximum war production, democratic governments in the United States and Great Britain increased their economic and political power. They directed economic resources into the war effort, ordering factories to stop making cars or refrigerators and to turn out airplanes or tanks instead.

They raised money by holding war bond drives. By buying bonds, citizens lent their government certain sums of money that would be returned with interest later.

Wartime economic policies placed limits on individual economic freedoms. Governments implemented programs to ration, or control, the amount of certain vital goods consumers could buy. Rationed items included rubber, tin, gasoline, and certain food items. Prices and wages were also regulated. In the United States, the war stimulated the economy by creating millions of new jobs. Unemployment, which

PEARSON realize. www.PearsonTexas.com Access your Digital Lesson.

818

Aa Vocabulary Builder

1. Have students pronounce the following academic vocabulary terms in this lesson and clarify the part of speech. For difficult or polysyllabic words, break them into syllables and pronounce them with the students.
2. Explain what the word means in common "student-friendly" language using synonyms and antonyms when possible. Provide concrete examples to clarify the meaning, and rephrase the definition.

incessant: uninterrupted; ceaseless

inevitable: unavoidable; inescapable

had remained high during the Great Depression, was almost wiped out.

Limits on Individual Rights Under the pressures of war, even democratic governments limited the rights of citizens. They censored the press and used propaganda to win public support for the war. In the United States and Canada, racial prejudice and concerns about security led to the **internment,** or confinement during wartime, of citizens of Japanese descent. Japanese Americans on the West Coast and Japanese Canadians were forced to move to camps inland, where conditions were very poor.

In Britain, Germans, Austrians, and Italians were subjected to internment, although some of them, including Jewish refugees from Nazi Germany, were released. Some 40 years later, both the United States and Canada provided former internees with reparations, or payment for damages. For most, the compensation came too late.

Women Help Win the War As men joined the military, millions of women around the world replaced them in essential war industry jobs. Women, symbolized by the character **"Rosie the Riveter"** in the United States, built ships and planes and produced munitions.

British and American women served in the armed forces in many auxiliary roles—driving ambulances, delivering airplanes, and decoding messages. In occupied Europe, women fought in the resistance. Marie Fourcade, a French woman, helped downed Allied pilots escape to safety. Soviet women served in combat roles. Soviet pilot Lily Litvak, for example, shot down 12 German planes before she herself was killed.

? IDENTIFY CENTRAL ISSUES What changes did the Allies make at home to ensure that they had sufficient resources for fighting World War II?

Progress on Three Fronts

During 1942 and 1943, the Allies won several victories that would turn the tide of battle. They fought on three main fronts— in North Africa and Italy, in the Soviet Union, and in the Pacific.

Japan Suffers Setbacks In the Pacific, the Japanese suffered their first serious setback at the Battle of the Coral Sea. The battle lasted for five days in May 1942. For the first time in naval history, ships engaged in a battle in which they never even saw each other. Attacks were carried out by planes launched from **aircraft carriers,** or ships that transport aircraft and accommodate the

WWII GDP COMPARED TO AIRCRAFT AND TANK PRODUCTION 1939–1945

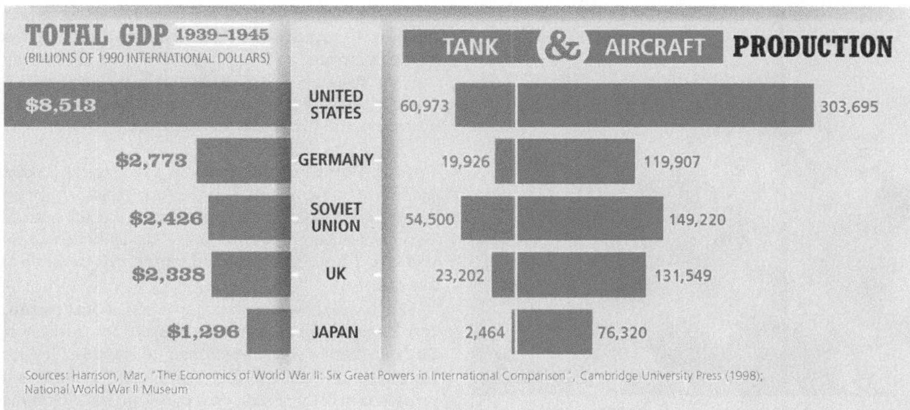

>> The Allies' commitment to all-out war meant a shift in manufacturing from commercial to military goods and equipment. Producing for the war effort also helped keep Americans employed. **Analyze Charts** What generalization can you make about GDP and war production based on the data in the chart?

Analyze Images

Discuss the image of the women putting finishing touches on a British tank. Ask students how the world political situation has changed since the photograph was taken.

Guided Reading and Discussion

Summarize Why did U.S. and Canadian citizens of Japanese descent lose their jobs, have their property seized, and then get sent to internment camps? *(They were thought to be a security risk because of their ethnicity.)*

D Differentiate Challenge/Gifted After answering the Summarize question, have students do further research on the restrictions of civil liberties imposed by the Allied governments. Have them write a brief essay describing their findings and whether or not they believe these restrictions were justified.

Progress on Three Fronts

Explain that more than one front, which included many battles, was necessary to win World War II, and the Allies engaged the Axis in both Europe and the Pacific. After several years with few notable successes, the years from 1942 to 1943 saw the tide beginning to turn for the Allies. Successes on three different fronts—in North Africa and Italy, in the Soviet Union, and in the Pacific—gave the Allies cause for cautious hope.

Key Terms

Have students find the key term **aircraft carriers** (in bold) in the text. Point out that Japan was more than 3,000 miles from some of its conquests in Southeast Asia. Why do you think aircraft carriers were important? *(Large fleets were needed to move airplanes, troops, and supplies around the vast area of the Pacific.)*

History Background

Social Impact of War To meet the needs of total war, Americans of all backgrounds joined the armed forces. Filipino and Korean Americans were especially eager to fight, not only to aid the Allied effort, but also to liberate their homelands from Japanese conquest. African Americans were initially limited to support roles, but they soon were given the opportunity to fight in combat. African American soldiers went on to win nearly 800 medals.

The war also provided new opportunities at home. At first, defense industries did not want to hire African Americans. In 1942, President Roosevelt issued Executive Order 8802, which banned discrimination in job training programs and in defense industries. He also set up the Fair Employment Practices Committee, to review charges of job discrimination. By the end of the war, nearly two million African Americans worked in defense factories.

Answers

Identify Central Issues *The United States and Britain changed from manufacturing commercial products to producing planes and tanks. They rationed food and other goods and sold war bonds.*

Analyze Charts *Sample response: In most cases, the larger the GDP, the greater the war production.*

Topic 18 Lesson 4

Online Project the **Interactive Chart: European Turning Points in World War II: Causes and Effects** and show students how to drag the tiles into their proper position on the chart.

ACTIVE CLASSROOM

Introduce students to the Act It Out strategy by dividing the room into three groups: Great Britain, the Soviet Union, and the United States. Ask students to portray the leaders of these countries—Churchill, Stalin, and Roosevelt—and their advisors. Tell students they will be in an Allied situation room strategizing their campaigns in Europe against the Axis countries. Ask students to include the battles in the North African desert and in the Soviet Union. *(Possible dialogues: Germany is in the middle of Europe. The best offensive is to move in toward Germany from every direction. If troops enter North Africa, they can defeat the German army there and invade Europe through the boot of Italy. At the same time, the Allies could overthrow Mussolini, liberate Italy, and gain more resources. The Soviets will hold their own against the Germans entering into the Soviet Union unless they ask for Allied help. Their goal will be to push the Germans west and back into Germany.)*

Guided Reading and Discussion

Draw Conclusions Why was it important for the Allies to continue constant aerial bombings on Germany when the ground troops were already making progress from all directions? *(Sample response: The aerial attacks were meant to demoralize the Germans and prevent them from manufacturing military products.)*

Discuss Historians have studied World War II for more than 50 years and some still disagree on important issues. Ask students how impressions they had before they began studying the war have changed. *(Responses will vary, but should reflect their knowledge of the facts about the war included in these lessons.)*

take-off and landing of airplanes. The Allies prevented Japan from seizing several important islands. More importantly, the Americans sank one Japanese aircraft carrier and several cruisers and destroyers.

This Allied victory was followed by an even more impressive win at the Battle of Midway in June 1942, which was also fought entirely from the air. The Americans destroyed four Japanese carriers and more than 250 planes. The battle was a devastating blow to the Japanese. After Midway, Japan was unable to launch any more offensive operations.

The loss was a setback to Japanese prime minister Hideki Tojo. Tojo, who also served as war minister, had been popular during Japan's string of victories. After Midway, he faced increasing opposition at home.

"Big Three" Strategize After the United States entered the war, the Allied leaders met periodically to hammer out their strategy. In 1942, the "Big Three"—**Franklin Delano Roosevelt, Winston Churchill,** and **Joseph Stalin**—agreed to focus on finishing the war in Europe before trying to end the war in Asia.

From the outset, the Allies distrusted one another. Churchill and Roosevelt feared that Stalin wanted to dominate Europe. Stalin believed the West wanted to destroy communism. None of the new Allies wanted to risk a breakdown in their alliance, however. At a conference in Tehran, Iran, in late 1943, Churchill and Roosevelt yielded to Stalin by agreeing to let the borders outlined in the Nazi-Soviet Pact stand, against the wishes of Poland's government-in-exile.

Stalin also wanted Roosevelt and Churchill to open a second front against Germany in Western Europe to relieve the pressure on the Soviet Union. Roosevelt and Churchill replied that they did not yet have the resources. Stalin saw the delay as a deliberate policy to weaken the Soviet Union.

>> The Tehran conference was the first meeting of the Allied leaders. Roosevelt and Churchill sought to ensure Soviet cooperation with Allied war policies. Stalin agreed, but the Allies had to make concessions to the Soviet leader.

Victory in North Africa In North Africa, British forces led by General Bernard Montgomery fought Rommel. After the fierce Battle of El Alamein in November 1942, the Allies finally halted the Desert Fox's advance. Allied tanks drove the Axis back across Libya into Tunisia.

Later in 1942, American General **Dwight Eisenhower** took command of a joint British and American force in Morocco and Algeria. Advancing on Tunisia from the west, the Allies trapped Rommel's army, which surrendered in May 1943.

Allied Invasion of Italy With North Africa under their control, the Allies were able to cross the Mediterranean into Italy. In July 1943, a combined British and American army landed first in Sicily and then in southern Italy. They defeated the Italian forces there in about a month.

After the defeats, the Italians overthrew Mussolini and signed an armistice, but fighting did not end. Hitler sent German troops to rescue Mussolini and stiffen the will of Italians fighting in the north. For the next 18 months, the Allies pushed slowly up the Italian peninsula, suffering heavy losses against strong German resistance. Still, the Italian invasion was a decisive event for the Allies because it weakened Hitler by forcing him to fight on another front.

Turning Point in Stalingrad A major turning point occurred in the Soviet Union. After their lightning advance in 1941, the Germans were stalled outside Moscow and Leningrad. In 1942, Hitler launched a new offensive. This time, he aimed for the rich oil fields of the south.

His troops, however, got only as far as **Stalingrad.** The Battle of Stalingrad was one of the costliest of the war. Hitler was determined to capture Stalin's namesake city, and Stalin was equally determined to defend it. The battle began when the Germans surrounded the city.

As winter closed in, a bitter street-by-street, house-by-house struggle raged. A German officer wrote that soldiers fought for two weeks for a single building.

English Language Proficiency Standards

ELPS 5.G.3 Read "Progress on Three Fronts" aloud to the class. Have students complete the activities below according to their level of English proficiency.

Beginning Reread "'Big Three' Strategize" to students. Tell them that explaining a topic requires communicating information in a way that makes it easier to understand. Describe how to compare and contrast something. Then retell the content in everyday language, focusing on the similarities and differences among the "Big Three" leaders. Model comparing and contrasting by explaining, then writing, how Churchill's and Roosevelt's goals for Europe were both the same and different from Stalin's.

Intermediate Reread "'Big Three' Strategize" to students. Tell them to review the information in the text with a partner to determine how Churchill and Roosevelt shared goals and had differences of opinion during WWII. Remind students how to compare and contrast information. Then ask pairs to write several sentences comparing and contrasting Churchill's and Roosevelt's goals for Europe with Stalin's.

Advanced Instruct pairs of students to reread "'Big Three' Strategize" aloud to each other. Tell them to take notes on how Churchill and Roosevelt shared goals and had differences of opinion during WWII. Remind students how to compare and contrast information. Then ask pairs to write several sentences comparing and contrasting Churchill's and Roosevelt's goals for Europe with Stalin's.

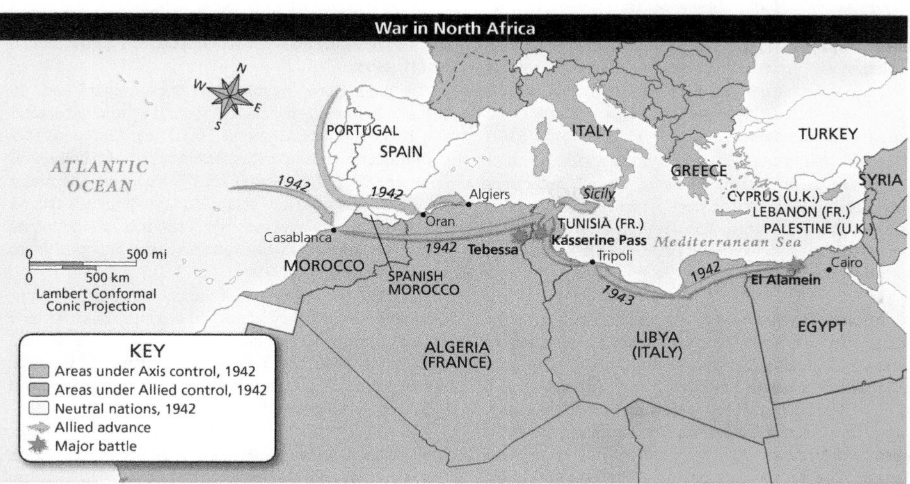

>> The Allies had tremendous challenges to overcome in order to regain control of western Europe and Africa from the Axis. **Analyze Maps** By what two routes did the Allies meet in Tunisia? What do you think was their reason for meeting at this location?

Interactive 3-D Model

Corpses "are strewn in the cellars, on the landings and the staircases," he said. In November, the Soviets encircled their attackers. Trapped, without food or ammunition and with no hope of rescue, the German commander finally surrendered in January 1943.

After the Battle of Stalingrad, the Red Army took the offensive and drove the invaders out of the Soviet Union entirely. Hitler's forces suffered irreplaceable losses of both troops and equipment. By early 1944, Soviet troops were advancing into Eastern Europe.

DRAW CONCLUSIONS What was the impact of the Battles of Coral Sea and Midway?

A Second Front in Europe

By 1944, the Western Allies were at last ready to open a second front in Europe by invading France. General Dwight Eisenhower was made the supreme Allied commander. He and other Allied leaders faced the enormous task of planning the operation and assembling troops and supplies.

To prepare the way for the invasion, Allied bombers flew constant missions over Germany. They targeted factories and destroyed aircraft that might be used against the invasion force. They also destroyed many German cities and bombed railroads and bridges in France that could carry German troops and supplies to the front.

The Normandy Landings The Allies chose June 6, 1944—known as **D-Day**—for the invasion of France. Just before midnight on June 5, Allied planes dropped paratroopers behind enemy lines. Then, at dawn, thousands of ships ferried 156,000 Allied troops across the English Channel. The troops fought their way to shore amid underwater mines and raking machine-gun fire, and the casualties mounted as they reached the shore.

> It all seemed unreal, a sort of dreaming while awake, men were screaming and dying all around me. . . I honestly could have walked the full length of the beach without touching the ground, they were that thickly strewn about.
>
> —Melvin B. Farrell, *War Memories*

A Second Front in Europe

Combined military fronts enabled the Allies to turn the tide on the Axis. From the west, the British, Canadians, and Americans landed at Normandy and advanced toward Germany. Allied forces battled in North Africa, aiming for Europe through southern Italy. Stalin engaged the Germans on Soviet soil and then pushed the Germans west, back to Germany. Tell students that the location of Germany was a weakness that Hitler could not overcome. As the war progressed, Nazi Germany found itself surrounded.

Online Project the **Interactive Map: World War II in Europe, 1942–1945**, and click on each of the layers. There are four layers, one for each of the years from 1942 to 1945. The single layers show the status of the Allies and the Axis for a particular year. As the years progressed, the Allies switched from defensive to offensive positions. What specific events changed the course of the war in Europe?

ACTIVE CLASSROOM

Employ the Make Headlines strategy and have students write a headline that describes the content of the Interactive Map. Ask students this question: If you were to write a headline for this topic right now that captured the map's most important aspect, what would that headline be? *(Answers will vary, but may include "Allies Land at Omaha Beach," "Allies Liberate France," "Desert Fox Loses at El Alamein," "Mussolini Overthrown," "Germans Retreat from Soviet Union.")* Pass your headline to a partner for him or her to review.

Advanced High Instruct students to reread "'Big Three' Strategize" aloud to each other. Tell them to take notes on how Churchill and Roosevelt shared goals and had differences of opinion during WWII. Then ask students to write a paragraph to compare and contrast Churchill's and Roosevelt's goals for Europe with Stalin's.

Answers

Analyze Maps *Sample responses: From the west by way of Morocco and Algeria and from the east by way of Egypt and Libya; It would be their starting point for the invasion of southern Europe by way of Sicily and Italy.*

Draw Conclusions *The massive destruction of the Japanese navy meant that Japan would no longer be able to mount offensives in the Pacific.*

Online Project the **3-D Model: The B-24 Liberator** and explore the parts of the bomber. It was faster than previous American bombers and able to carry a heavy load of bombs on long missions. How do you think this affected the outcome of the war? How do you think it affected Europe in terms of lives lost and rebuilding after the war?

ACTIVE CLASSROOM

Conduct a Thumbs Up When Ready activity. Ask students to think about this statement: "True or false: By the end of 1943, the Allies were poised for final victory in World War II." Ask students to put their thumbs up to indicate that they have finished their thinking. Have them share their thoughts in pairs or small groups.

Analyze Images

Have students compare the map of "World War II in Europe, 1942–1945" with the map of the "War in North Africa" on the previous page. Ask: In which direction did Allied forces move after the battles in North Africa? *(north, through Italy)* By what year had they advanced through Italy to the German border? *(1944)*

Guided Reading and Discussion

Predict Consequences Do you think that if Hitler had kept his aggression to a one-country-at-a-time strategy, he would have been successful in dominating Europe? *(Yes, If the United States and Soviet Union had not joined the war, because Hitler made gains with Austria, Czechoslovakia, Poland, and France. No; while Hitler formed some alliances with European countries, they were not under German control and may have eventually fought against him.)*

Evaluate Impact What was the French Resistance? Why was it so important to the French people and the Allies?

Discuss Some historians who have studied World War II still disagree on important issues. Ask students how impressions they had before they began studying the war have changed.

The Liberation of France Despite heavy losses, the Allied troops clawed their way inland from the beaches of Normandy. In early August, a massive armored division under American General George S. Patton helped the joint British and American forces break through German defenses and advance toward Paris.

Meanwhile, other Allied forces sailed from Italy to land in southern France. In Paris, French resistance forces rose up against the occupying Germans. Under pressure from all sides, the Germans retreated. On August 25, the Allies entered Paris. Within a month, all of France was free.

Advancing Toward Germany After freeing France, Allied forces battled toward Germany. As their armies advanced into Belgium in December 1944, Germany launched a massive counterattack. At the bloody Battle of the Bulge, which lasted more than a month, both sides took terrible losses. The Germans drove the Allies back in several places, but were unable to break through. The battle delayed the Allied advance from the west, but only for six weeks. The Battle of the Bulge was Germany's last major offensive attack.

By this time, Germany was reeling under round-the-clock bombing. For two years, Allied bombers had hammered military bases, factories, railroads, oil depots, and cities. The goal of the bombing was to cripple Germany's industries and destroy the morale of its civilians.

By 1945, Germany could no longer defend itself in the air. In one 10-day period, bombing almost erased the huge industrial city of Hamburg, killing 40,000 civilians and forcing one million to flee their homes. In February 1945, Allied raids on Dresden killed as many as 135,000 people. The attack on Dresden later stirred controversy because the city was not an industrial center and had long been seen as one of Europe's most beautiful cities.

Meanwhile, the Soviet army battled through Germany and advanced on Berlin from the east. Hitler's support within Germany was declining, and he had already survived one assassination attempt by senior officers in the German military. By early 1945, the defeat of Germany seemed inevitable.

The Yalta Conference As the Allies advanced on Germany, the Big Three met in the Soviet city of Yalta. At the **Yalta Conference** in February 1945, Roosevelt, Churchill, and Stalin planned for the final stages of the war and for post-war Europe. The meeting took place in an atmosphere of distrust. Stalin insisted that the Soviet Union needed to maintain control of Eastern Europe to be able to protect itself from future aggression.

>> After the Allies had encircled Germany, they continued to bomb German industrial and military centers. German defenses were eliminated, and the European war came to an end. **Analyze Maps** From which direction did the Allies come when they launched the D-Day invasion?

Interactive Map

Answers

Analyze Maps *from the north*

Topic 18 Lesson 4

Churchill and Roosevelt favored self-determination for Eastern Europe, which would give people the right to choose their own form of government. Although Stalin agreed to hold free elections in the newly liberated nations of Eastern Europe, he soon showed he had no intention of upholding that promise.

The three leaders also outlined a plan for postwar Germany. It would be temporarily divided into four zones, to be governed by American, French, British, and Soviet forces.

Although the war in Europe was almost over, the Allies were less certain of the outcome in the Pacific. Roosevelt and Churchill were eager to get the Russians to declare war on Japan. Stalin agreed that the Soviet Union would enter the war against Japan within three months of Germany's surrender. In return, Churchill and Roosevelt promised Stalin that the Soviets would take possession of southern Sakhalin Island, the Kuril Islands, and an occupation zone in Korea.

EXPLAIN How did the Allied advance toward Germany limit that country's ability to wage war?

>> The Allies launched a massive invasion on the fortified beaches of Normandy, France. By the end of D-Day, they had a foothold in Nazi-occupied France and had taken a major step toward its liberation.

Interactive Chart

ASSESSMENT

1. **Draw Conclusions** What actions did democratic governments take during the war that many citizens would probably reject in peace time?
2. **Summarize** Describe the strategy involved in the invasion of Normandy on D-Day.
3. **Identify Cause and Effect** How did the total war effort in the United States affect the nation's economy?
4. **Identify Main Ideas** What was the significance of Hitler's offensive in the southern Soviet Union?
5. **Interpret** How did Allied nations limits the individual rights of certain people during World War II? Why did this happen?

Assessment

1. limited some citizens' rights, imprisoned people without trials, censored the press, and used propaganda to win public support
2. It was the second front of the War. France was occupied by Germany. Paratroopers were dropped behind military lines, and Allied troops were ferried to the French coast. From there, troops fought their way inland.
3. The increase in production ended the unemployment and economic hardship of the Great Depression.
4. It led to the costly Battle of Stalingrad. Casualties on both sides were high. When the battle was over, the Soviets had won and were able to begin pushing the Germans back.
5. They limited citizens' rights and censored the press. In the United States and Canada, many citizens of Japanese descent lost jobs, property, and civil rights and were interned in camps. The British took similar action against German refugees.

SYNTHESIZE

Online Project the **Digital Activity: Factors: Turning the Tide**. Have students use the Think-Pair-Share activity to answer the question: Which factors do you think played the most important role in turning the tide against Germany, Japan, and Italy? *(Many students will cite the U.S. forces being fully engaged in winning the war as important, along with the fact that Hitler could not defeat U.S. forces. Others may argue that Germany's geographical position doomed it once the Soviet Union opened the Eastern Front.)*

Then ask: What significance do you think the French Resistance had in liberating France? What did many members of this organization do once their country was no longer under the control of the Nazis?

Discuss Have students describe what they believe the post-liberation French government did to assist in ending the war in Europe.

DEMONSTRATE

Online Assign the **Digital Lesson Quiz** if you have not already done so. Students will be offered automatic remediation or enrichment based on their scores.

Pose these questions to the class on the Discussion Board:

Recognize Cause and Effect How did the Allied victories in the European front affect the economic systems of these countries? *(The war destroyed factories, communities, industries, and infrastructure. The rebuilding put people to work and created jobs.)*

Draw Conclusions What do you think would have happened if the Soviets had lost the Battle of Stalingrad? *(Sample response: The Allies wanted to encircle Germany, pushing in from the west through Britain, across the channel through France; from the south from North Africa up through Italy; and from the east from the Soviet Union. Without winning the Battle of Stalingrad, there was the possibility that the Germans could have taken control of the Soviet Union.)*

Topic Inquiry

Have students continue their investigations for the Topic Inquiry.

Answers

Explain *Bombings of German military bases, factories, railroads, oil depots, and cities destroyed industry and demoralized civilians.*

Topic 18 Lesson 5

Victory for the Allies

CONNECT

Preview Have students preview the **Lesson Objectives** and the list of **Key Terms**.

Students can also preview all the **Key Terms** and **Academic Vocabulary** using the **Interactive Reading Notepad** on the digital course or preview a summary of the lesson in the **Reading and Note Taking Study Guide**.

Online Use the **Editable Presentation** found on the digital course to present the main ideas for this lesson.

Start Up Activity

Explain that both before and during World War II, thousands of people emigrated from Europe to escape the brutal persecution of the fascist states. This massive migration included gifted artists, scholars, and scientists, many of whom were Jewish. Hitler showed little concern for the negative impact that the departure of scientists would have on German science. He once said, "If the dismissal of Jewish scientists means the annihilation of contemporary German science, we shall do without science for a few years."

Ask: How do you think Hitler's way of thinking may have contributed to the defeat of Germany in World War II?

Discuss If you had taken part in the fighting against Germany, how would you have felt about your contribution to the Allied victory? *(Answers will vary, but should include a sense of accomplishment and pride in contributing to the defeat of fascism.)*

Online You can also project the **Start Up Activity** from the course.

INVESTIGATE

Have students read the section using the **Reading and Note Taking Study Guide** to help them take notes and understand the text as they read.

End of the War in Europe

Direct students' attention to the image of U.S. and Soviet soldiers shaking hands at the Elbe River. Remind students that the Soviet and U.S. troops were both on the side of the Allies. Explain to students that May 8, 1945 was the day that World War II officially ended in Europe.

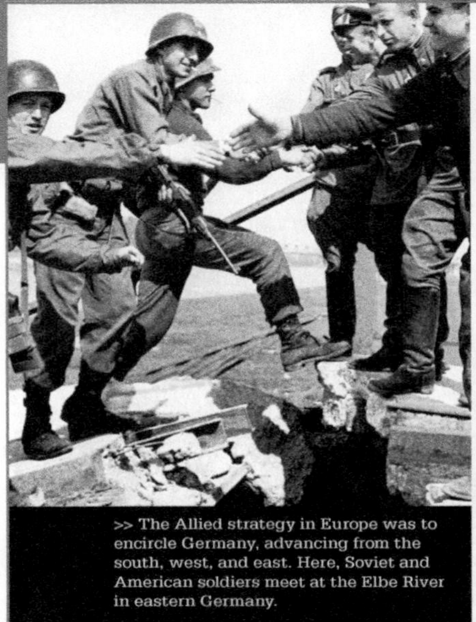

>> The Allied strategy in Europe was to encircle Germany, advancing from the south, west, and east. Here, Soviet and American soldiers meet at the Elbe River in eastern Germany.

Interactive Flipped Video

18.5 **By early spring 1945, the war in Europe was nearing its end. That April, the Allies lost a key leader, Franklin Roosevelt. Though he did not live to see the final victory, he knew the defeat of the Nazis was inevitable.**

TEKS
1.F, 12.B, 12.C, 20.D, 28.C

>> Objectives

Understand the reasons for the final defeat of the Nazis.

Describe how the Allies began to push back the Japanese in the Pacific.

Explain how the dropping of the atomic bombs ended the war.

Describe the aftermath of World War II and the founding of the United Nations.

>> Key Terms

Douglas MacArthur
kamikaze
Hiroshima
Nagasaki
Nuremberg Trials
United Nations (UN)
Bataan Death March
"island-hopping"
Manhattan Project
Harry Truman
V-E Day

Victory for the Allies

End of the War in Europe

Germany Is Defeated By March 1945, the Allies had crossed the Rhine into western Germany. From the east, Soviet troops closed in on Berlin. In late April, American and Soviet soldiers met and shook hands at the Elbe River. All over Europe, Axis armies began to surrender.

In Italy, guerrillas captured and executed Mussolini. As Soviet troops fought their way into Berlin, Hitler committed suicide in his underground bunker. After just 12 years, Hitler's "thousand-year Reich" was bomb-ravaged and in ruins. On May 7, Germany surrendered.

Officially, the war in Europe ended the next day, May 8, 1945, which was proclaimed **V-E Day** (Victory in Europe).

Reasons for Victory in Europe The Allies were able to defeat the Axis powers in Europe for a number of reasons. By 1942, Germany and its allies had to fight on several fronts simultaneously. Hitler insisted on making major military decisions himself and some proved disastrous, especially the invasion of the Soviet Union. He underestimated the ability of the Soviet Union to fight in defense of their land.

The enormous productive capacity of the United States was another factor. By 1944, the United States was producing twice as much as all of the Axis powers combined. Meanwhile, Allied bombing hindered German production. Oil became so scarce because of bombing that

Pearson realize. www.PearsonTexas.com Access your Digital Lesson.

824

Aa Vocabulary Builder

1. Have students pronounce the following academic vocabulary terms in this lesson and clarify the part of speech. For difficult or polysyllabic words, break them into syllables and pronounce them with the students.
2. Explain what the word means in common "student-friendly" language using synonyms and antonyms when possible. Provide concrete examples to clarify the meaning, and rephrase the definition.

objective: something worked toward; a goal

convened: met; assembled

the Luftwaffe was almost grounded by the time of the D-Day invasion.

With victory in Europe achieved, the Allies could focus all their attention on defeating Japan in the Pacific. There, they still faced stiff opposition.

INFER Why were the Allies able to defeat the Axis in Europe?

Battles in the Pacific

During the war in the Pacific, the Japanese at first won a string of victories. They also controlled much of China and Southeast Asia. Despite the early Japanese advances, the Allies slowly turned the tide.

Bataan Death March Just hours after Pearl Harbor, the Japanese bombed the Philippines, which the United States had controlled since 1898. By May 1942, the Japanese had gained control of the islands. After the U.S. and Filipino defenders of Bataan surrendered, the Japanese forced their prisoners to march more than 60 miles in incredible heat with almost no water or food. The cruel **Bataan Death March** resulted in the death of as many as 10,000 prisoners.

One survivor described the ordeal as "a macabre litany of heat, dust, starvation, thirst, flies, filth, stench, murder, torture, corpses, and wholesale brutality that numbs the memory." Many Filipino civilians risked—and sometimes lost—their lives to give food and water to captives on the march.

Americans Take the Offensive After the battle of Midway, the United States took the offensive. That summer, United States Marines landed at Guadalcanal in the Solomon Islands. Victory at Guadalcanal marked the beginning of an **"island-hopping"** campaign. The goal of the campaign was to recapture some Japanese-held islands while bypassing others. Each captured island served as a stepping stone to the next objective. As a result, American forces, led by General **Douglas MacArthur,** gradually moved north towards Japan.

On the captured islands, the Americans built air bases to enable them to carry the war closer to Japan. By 1944, the United States Navy, commanded by Admiral Chester Nimitz, was blockading Japan, and American bombers pounded Japanese cities and industries. In October 1944, MacArthur began the fight to retake the Philippines. The British, meanwhile, were pushing Japanese forces back into the jungles of Burma and Malaya. Despite such setbacks, the militarists

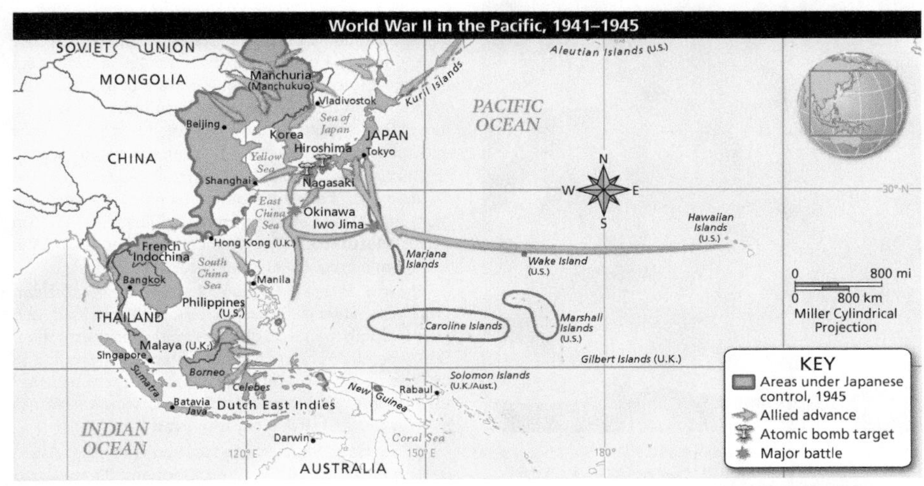

>> After winning the war in Europe, the Allies poured all their resources into victory in the Pacific theater. **Analyze Maps** Based on the map, how would you describe the Allied strategy to defeat Japan?

 **Interactive Map**

Guided Reading and Discussion

Ask students to think about the causes and effects of the decisions by Roosevelt, Stalin, Churchill, and Hitler that led to the end of the war in Europe.

Analyze Images

What symbolic message does the photograph of the American and Soviet troops shaking hands at the Elbe River on the previous page communicate? *(Sample response: The strategies of Roosevelt, Stalin, and Churchill were to surround Germany and push Hitler's troops into retreat from the west and east. This photo shows how that goal was met, with the Soviets advancing from the east and the Americans from the west.)*

Draw Conclusions Why did the Allies believe it important that Germany sign an unconditional surrender? *(Sample response: It was important to each of the Allied countries that they stand united and that Germany be unable to reach different surrender agreements with the Allied countries.)*

Battles in the Pacific

Explain that the Allies were fighting not only on the European front but also in the Pacific. Once the Allies won on the European front, their focus turned to the Pacific theater until Japan was defeated.

History Background

"I Shall Return" A defeated General Douglas MacArthur left the Philippines in 1942. He pledged his determination to free the islands with the words, "I shall return," during a brief statement to the press in Australia, where he had been ordered to command an offensive in the Southwest Pacific Theater. Operations began in 1942, and by 1944 MacArthur and his troops had seized several strategic locations, including the Admiralty Islands and several points in New Guinea. In October 1944, MacArthur's pledge to return to the Philippines became reality when he landed on the island of Leyte. After a series of large and costly operations, MacArthur succeeded in his goals of retaking the Philippines and Borneo. He became commander of all U.S. Pacific forces in early 1945 and oversaw the Japanese surrender in Tokyo Bay in September of that year.

Answers

Infer *Hitler's army had to fight on multiple fronts; he underestimated the Soviet army's fighting ability; he made poor decisions as a military leader; the United States outproduced Germany in war production.*

Analyze Maps *Sample response: The Allies captured specific islands as stepping stones toward Japan and created a sea blockade of Japan. Meanwhile, their planes dropped bombs on Japan.*

Topic 18 Lesson 5

Online Project the **Interactive Map: World War II in the Pacific**. Click through the various layers of the map showing the activity that occurred in the Pacific by year from 1942 to 1945. The last layer will reveal all Allied military activity in one map for those same years.

ACTIVE CLASSROOM

Use the Quick Draw strategy and pair students. Give students a short period of time to share what they know about World War II in the Pacific. Have one student tell her partner what she is going to draw or depict with symbols. Have the second student create the symbols or drawings. Use a document camera or scanner, if available, to scan drawings to add to the class blog.

Guided Reading and Discussion

Refer to the map "World War II in the Pacific, 1941–1945." Be sure that students understand the geography and what types of military weapons were necessary to win the battles in the Pacific. Ask students to list two Allied offensive locations and the type of battles and weapons used to secure these locations in the advancement toward Japan.

End of the War in the Pacific

Draw students' attention to the image of the aftermath of the atomic bomb. Explain that the dropping of the two atomic bombs finally ended the war. Explain that by mid-1945, even though most of the Japanese navy and air force had been destroyed, Japan still had an army of two million men, and the road to victory was predicted to be long and costly. Review how President Truman decided that using atomic weapons would shorten the war and save lives. Finally, discuss the results of the attacks on Hiroshima and Nagasaki.

Key Terms

Ask students to locate the key term **kamikaze** (in bold) in the text. Tell them that the word, which means "divine wind," refers to a typhoon that stopped a Mongol fleet from invading Japan in the 1281.

>> Kamikaze attacks were a desperate attempt to ward off American advances. Japanese pilots crashed into Allied aircraft carriers and other ships, killing American sailors along with themselves.

>> President Harry S. Truman and U.S. Secretary of State James Byrne examine a map of Europe aboard the U.S.S. *Augusta* on their way to the "big three" conference in Potsdam in the summer of 1945.

who dominated the Japanese government rejected any suggestions of surrender.

INFER Why might a naval blockade prove to be an effective war strategy?

End of the War in the Pacific

With war won in Europe, the Allies poured their resources into defeating Japan. By mid-1945, most of the Japanese navy and air force had been destroyed. Yet the Japanese still had an army of two million men. The road to victory, it appeared, would be long and costly.

Japanese Resistance As American forces closed in on Japan, the Japanese put up fierce resistance. By 1944, young Japanese **kamikaze** (kah muh KAH zee) pilots were undertaking suicide missions, crashing their explosive-laden airplanes into American warships.

The next year, in bloody battles on the islands of Iwo Jima from February to March 1945 and Okinawa from April to July 1945, Japanese forces showed that they would fight to the death rather than surrender. Some American officials estimated that an invasion of Japan would cost a million or more casualties.

A Powerful New Weapon While Allied military leaders planned for invasion, scientists offered another way to end the war. Since the early 1900s, scientists had understood that matter, made up of atoms, could be converted into pure energy. In military terms, this meant that by splitting the atom, scientists could create an explosion far more powerful than any yet known.

During the war, Allied scientists—some of them German and Italian refugees—raced to harness the atom before the Germans could. In July 1945, the top secret **Manhattan Project,** successfully tested the first atomic bomb at Alamogordo, New Mexico.

News of this test was brought to the new American president, **Harry Truman.** He realized that the atomic bomb was a terrible new force for destruction. Still, after consulting with his advisors, he decided to use the new weapon against Japan. Truman believed that dropping the atomic bomb would bring the war to a faster end and save American lives.

At the time, Truman was meeting with other Allied leaders in the city of Potsdam, Germany. They issued a warning to Japan to surrender or face "complete destruction" and "utter devastation." When the

Differentiate Challenge/Gifted While viewing the Interactive Map, point out that Allied offensives in the Pacific theater extended beyond the island-hopping of the Philippines. Ask students to list two areas of the Pacific front named on the map where Allied troops won battles and moved toward Japan from those positions. *(Manchuria, Burma)*

Answers

Infer *Blockading an island nation would prevent much-needed food, energy, and other materials from reaching the people of the blockaded nation. As civilian suffering increased, it would put pressure on leaders to end the war.*

Japanese ignored the warning, the United States took action.

Dropping of the Atomic Bombs On August 6, 1945, an American plane dropped an atomic bomb over the city of **Hiroshima.** The bomb flattened four square miles and instantly killed more than 70,000 people. In the months that followed, many more would die from radiation sickness, a deadly aftereffect of exposure to radioactive materials.

Truman warned the Japanese that if they did not surrender, they could expect "a rain of ruin from the air, the like of which has never been seen on this Earth." And on August 8, the Soviet Union declared war on Japan and invaded Manchuria. Again, Japanese leaders did not respond. The next day, the United States dropped a second atomic bomb, this time on the city of **Nagasaki.** More than 40,000 people were killed in this second explosion.

Some members of the Japanese cabinet wanted to fight on. Other leaders disagreed. Finally, on August 10, Emperor Hirohito intervened, an action unheard of for a Japanese emperor. He forced his government to surrender. On September 2, 1945, the formal peace treaty was signed on board the American battleship *Missouri,*anchored in Tokyo Bay. After more than five years of fighting, World War II was over.

An Ongoing Controversy Using the atomic bomb against Japan brought a quick end to World War II. It also unleashed terrifying destruction. Ever since, people have debated whether or not the United States should have used the bomb.

For President Truman, using the bomb was a difficult decision. He later explained that he made his decision based only on military considerations. He was concerned that Japan would not surrender without an invasion, and that would cost an enormous loss of lives. After all, the Japanese still had a home army of 2 million.

Critics of Truman's decision argued that Japan was almost defeated at that point and the bomb was not needed. They also claim that by using the atomic bomb, the United States unleashed a dangerous arms race that grew over the next decades.

Growing differences between the United States and the Soviet Union may also have influenced Truman's decision. Truman may have hoped the bomb would impress the Soviets with American power. The debate over Truman's decision has continued to the present.

INTERPRET What was the purpose of the declaration issued by the Allies at Potsdam?

>> After Japan failed to accept Allied surrender terms, Truman ordered the atomic bombings of Hiroshima and Nagasaki. The destruction was unlike anything the world had seen.

Interactive Timeline

ELPS 1.A.1 Think about what you already know about the atomic bomb. Use this prior knowledge as you read *End of the War in the Pacific* to understand why the atomic bomb was used.

Aftermath of the War

Even as the Allies celebrated victory, the appalling costs of the war began to emerge. The war had killed as many as 50 million people around the world. In Europe alone, over 30 million people had lost their lives, more than half of them civilians. The Soviet Union suffered the worst casualties, with over 20 million dead.

Europe in Ruins "Give me ten years and you will not be able to recognize Germany," Hitler had predicted in 1933. Indeed, Germany in 1945 was an unrecognizable ruin. Parts of Poland, the Soviet Union, Japan, China, and other countries also lay in ruins. Total war had gutted cities, factories, harbors, bridges, railroads, farms, and homes.

Over 20 million refugees wandered Europe. Amid the devastation, hunger, disease, and mental illness took their toll for years after the fighting ended. As

Guided Reading and Discussion

Ask students to think about the causes and effects that led to the decision to use an atomic bomb on Nagasaki and Hiroshima.

Make Predictions If the atomic bombs had not been not dropped, what might have happened on the Pacific front? *(Most students will say that the war would have continued, and many more lives would have been lost.)*

Analyze Context President Truman may have been thinking about postwar relations with the Soviet Union when he made the decision to drop the atomic bombs on Japan. What about the relationship of the United States and the Soviet Union might have concerned Truman? *(Possible response: He probably foresaw future conflicts.)* What message may he have been trying to communicate to Stalin and other Soviet leaders? *(Possible response: that the United States possessed a powerful new weapon it was prepared to use to defend its interests against an enemy)*

Answers

Interpret *The Allies warned Japan to surrender or suffer the consequences.*

English Language Proficiency Standards

Learning Strategies 1.A.1 Explain to students that using what they already know can help them make connections with new information.

Beginning Display the term *atomic bomb* for students. Ask them what comes to mind when they hear this term. Capture these ideas. If students are having trouble, use gestures and movement to illustrate the term. Then read the text "End of the War in the Pacific" to students. Have student complete the sentence frame: The atomic bomb was used because ___________.

Intermediate Have students brainstorm about the term. As a group, write a few sentences summarizing what students know about the atomic bomb. Then read the text aloud to students. Have the group select the sentence on the board that best connects with why the atomic bomb was used.

Advanced Have small groups perform the Intermediate activity. Then have each group read the text aloud. Ask groups to make one connection between the information that they brainstormed and the text.

Advanced High Have students work individually to perform the first step of the Intermediate activity, then have them work with a partner to write their sentences. Have them read the text independently. Ask partners to discuss two connections between the information that they brainstormed and the text.

Topic 18 Lesson 5

Aftermath of the War

The United Nations Is Formed

Explain that the war killed as many as 50 million people, and entire countries lay in ruins. Once the war ended, delegates from 50 nations came together to establish an organization—the United Nations—to prevent such costly conflicts.

Online Project the **Interactive Timeline: Key Events of World War II in Europe and the Pacific**. Ask students to match the tiles with their correct place in history on the timeline.

ACTIVE CLASSROOM

Have students us the Wallpaper strategy to review the information they have learned. Each student should design a piece of "wallpaper" that encapsulates key learnings. The wallpaper is posted. Students then take a gallery walk and note what others have written or illustrated. Students can jot down ideas as they occur to them. A video can be made of the gallery walk and posted on a video-sharing site.

>> Representatives of the four major Allies sat in judgment of Nazi war criminals. It was the first time that war criminals were punished for "crimes against humanity" during war.

>> Prime Minister Tojo did not have the same totalitarian powers as Hitler and Mussolini. Still, he was tried and executed for war crimes committed by Japan during the war.

they had after World War I, the Allies faced difficult decisions about the future.

The Holocaust Is Revealed Numbers alone did not tell the story of the Nazi nightmare in Europe or the Japanese brutality in Asia. During the war, the Allies were aware of the existence of Nazi concentration camps and death camps. But only at war's end did they learn the full extent of the inhumanity of the Holocaust. American General Dwight Eisenhower, who visited the camps, was stunned to come "face to face with indisputable evidence of Nazi brutality and ruthless disregard of every sense of decency."

War Crimes Trials At wartime meetings, the Allies had agreed that Axis leaders should be tried for "crimes against humanity." In Germany, the Allies held the **Nuremberg Trials** in the city where Hitler had staged mass rallies in the 1930s. Nearly 200 Germans and Austrians were tried for war crimes. Most were found guilty. A handful of top Nazis received death sentences. Others were imprisoned.

Similar war crimes trials were held in Italy and Japan. Among those found guilty and executed was Japanese prime minister Tojo. Many of those accused of war crimes were never captured or brought to trial. However, the trials showed that political and military leaders could be held accountable for actions in wartime.

The war crimes trials served another purpose. By exposing the savagery of the Axis regimes, they further discredited the totalitarian and militarist ideologies that had led to the war. Yet disturbing questions remained. Why had ordinary people in Germany, Poland, France, and elsewhere accepted—and even collaborated in—Hitler's "Final Solution"? How could the world prevent dictators from again terrorizing Europe or Asia?

The Allies tried to address those issues when they occupied Germany and Japan. The United States felt that strengthening democracy would ensure tolerance and peace. The Western Allies built new governments in occupied Germany and Japan with democratic constitutions to protect the rights of all citizens. In German schools, for example, Nazi textbooks and courses were replaced with a new curriculum that taught democratic principles. In Japan, the occupying forces under General MacArthur helped Japanese politicians to create a new constitution that gave

History Background

Genocide Defined The Nuremberg Trials marked the first time in history that individuals were put on trial for genocide. After the trials, the new United Nations approved a convention that defined genocide as actions taken to kill, injure, or harm a particular group of people or to prevent them from having or rearing children. Such actions are considered an international crime whether they take place in a period of war or peace, and are punishable even if they are directed by a country's government against its own citizens. In recent years, international courts have tried people, including leaders, from Serbia and Rwanda for their role in organizing and carrying out genocide.

UNITED NATIONS STRUCTURE

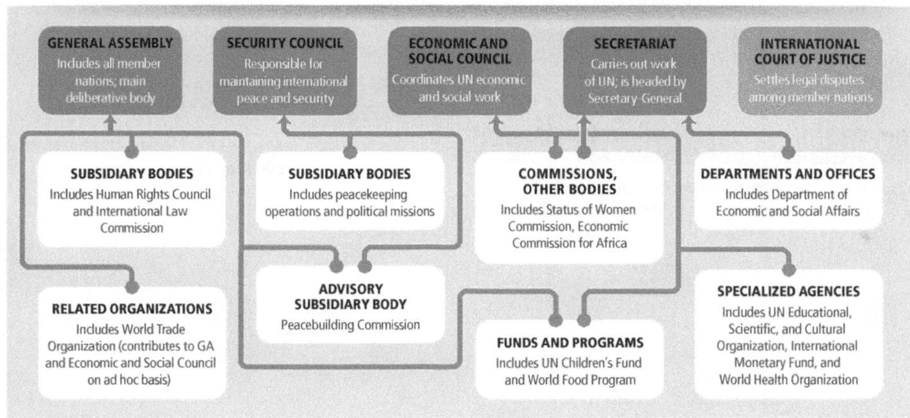

>> The United Nations' originating mission included maintaining international peace and security and solving economic, social, cultural, and humanitarian problems. **Analyze Charts** Under which of the five departments is the World Health Organization?

power to the Japanese people, rather than the emperor and military elite.

ANALYZE INFORMATION What were the main goals of the Allies' post-war policies toward the defeated Axis countries?

The United Nations Is Formed

In April 1945, delegates from 50 nations convened in San Francisco to draft a charter for the **United Nations (UN).** They hoped that, unlike the ineffective League of Nations, the UN would be able to keep peace among nations by providing a forum where differences could be resolved peacefully. In the years to follow, the UN would play a greater role in world affairs than its predecessor did.

Structure of the United Nations Under the UN Charter, each of the member nations has one vote in the General Assembly. A much smaller body called the Security Council has greater power. Each of its five permanent members—the United States, the Soviet Union (today Russia), Britain, France, and China—has the right to veto any council decision. The goal was to give these great powers the authority to ensure the peace.

The Security Council has the power to apply economic sanctions or send a peace-keeping military force to try to resolve disputes. Still, differences between the United States and Russia have continued to hamper Security Council decisions. Since the fall of the Soviet Union in 1991, more peacekeeping delegations have been approved.

UN Activities Over time, the work of the UN would go far beyond peacekeeping. It has taken on many issues from human rights and economic development to health and education. UN agencies have worked to end diseases such as smallpox and set up vaccination programs around the world. It has set up refugee camps and organized resettlement programs for refugees from war zones. It has worked with national governments to reduce poverty and protect the environment.

From the first, the UN has faced critics. Some have argued that the UN is ineffective in preventing or resolving conflicts. Others claimed that UN resolutions interfered with national governments. Differences have also risen between rich industrial nations and the poorer nations of the world. And some smaller nations

Guided Reading and Discussion

Analyze Information Why was the United Nations established? How do the original mission of the United Nations and its mission today differ? *(Sample response: The original purpose of the United Nations in 1945 was to maintain peace. As the number of members increased, the UN's mission expanded to include preventing the outbreak of disease, improving education, protecting refugees, and helping nations manage their new independence and develop economically.)*

Synthesize Why are there only five permanent member countries on the United Nations Security Council? Why were these nations chosen? Would these same five nations be chosen today? Why or why not? *(The United States, Soviet Union (now Russia), Britain, France, and China were the victors in World War II. Some students will note that Britain and France are no longer as powerful as they were following the war and could be replaced by Japan and Germany or by other large developing countries, such as Brazil or India.)*

Answers

Analyze Charts *Economic and Social Council*

Analyze Information *They wanted to encourage the creation of democratic governments, encourage tolerance and peace, protect the basic rights of citizens, and punish war criminals.*

SYNTHESIZE

Online Project the **Digital Activity: Victory in the Pacific**. Have students form small groups to discuss the question in the activity. Then ask them to take five minutes to write down brief answers to the following questions: Do you think the creation of the United Nations will contribute to a more stable world? What approach do you think war-ravaged countries will take to rebuild their social, economic, and political structures? Have the groups present their answers to the class.

Discuss Have students describe what they believe governments can do to promote peace among nations. *(Answers may vary, but students may say that governments need good government officials to be role models, to address people's needs, and to establish policies that promote peace.)*

DEMONSTRATE

Online Assign the **Digital Lesson Quiz** for this lesson if you have not already done so. Students will be offered automatic remediation or enrichment based on their scores.

Pose the question below to the class on the Discussion Board:

Predict Consequences Consider what you have read about World War II. Do you believe that after the war's end, the Allies will continue to be allies? Or will differences in values and goals cause them to break apart? Give reasons for your answer. *(Answers will vary, but most students will be aware that significant social, political, and economic differences between the United States and the Soviet Union led to the Cold War.)*

Topic Inquiry

Have students continue their investigations for the Topic Inquiry.

have criticized the veto power of the five permanent members of the Security Council.

? CONTRAST What is the difference between the United Nations General Assembly and the Security Council?

ASSESSMENT

1. **Draw Conclusions** How did wartime production of resources play a role in Hitler's final defeat?
2. **Distinguish** Which military campaign did the victory at Guadalcanal initiate?
3. **Infer** Why did Japanese emperor Hirohito call for Japan to surrender?
4. **Cite Evidence** How costly was World War II in terms of European and Soviet casualties?
5. **Summarize** How were the Nazis' "crimes against humanity" dealt with at the Nuremberg trials?

Answers

Contrast *The General Assembly is made up of country members at large. Each member has one vote. The smaller Security Council includes the United States, the Soviet Union (today Russia), Britain, France, and China. Each can veto any of the General Assembly's decisions.*

Assessment

1. U.S. wartime production almost doubled Axis wartime production, and U.S. planes bombed German factories and supply lines so that they could no longer produce resources.
2. the island-hopping campaign, in which the Allies would recapture some islands and use them as stepping stones until they arrived at their ultimate destination—Japan
3. Most of the Japanese navy and air force had been destroyed, and now 110,000 civilians had been killed by the atomic bombs.
4. Fifty million people around the world lost their lives; 30 million of those were in Europe and the other 20 million were in the Soviet Union.
5. Nazi leaders were indicted, brought before the court, tried, and, if found guilty, imprisoned or sentenced to death.

1. **Explain the Major Causes of World War II** Explain the major causes of World War II, including the German invasion of Poland. Use the above map and lesson information to write a paragraph describing the German invasion of Poland in 1939. Consider the agreement between Germany and the Soviet Union, how both countries benefited, and the reaction of the Western democracies to the invasion of Poland. 12.C
2. **Explain the Effects of Military Technologies** Explain the effects of major new military technologies on World War II. Write a paragraph explaining how new military technologies affected the events of World War II. Consider the effect on civilians, effect on industry, and number of casualties. 28.C
3. **Explain Roles of World Leaders** Explain the roles of various world leaders, including Hideki Tojo, during World War II. Write a paragraph explaining how Prime Minister Hideki Tojo impacted U.S. involvement in World War II. Consider Japanese economic and political goals in East Asia, American foreign policy prior to the attack on Pearl Harbor, and Tojo's military policy. 12.B
4. **Identify Causes of Turning Points in World War II** Identify major causes of important turning points in world history from 1914 to the present, including World War II and its impact on political systems. Write a paragraph that describes how the Allies tried to prevent further dictatorships from emerging in Europe and Asia after World War II. Consider the Allied postwar policies toward Germany and Japan, Allied belief in democracy, and assistance in developing new constitutions. 1.F
5. **Explain the Major Causes of World War II** Explain the major causes of World War II, including the German invasion of Poland, the German invasion of the Soviet Union, and the attack on Pearl Harbor. Discuss the major causes of World War II by completing the chart with the result(s) of each event. Consider how the event impacted the countries involved, the war participants, and the war's oautcome. 12.C

EVENT	RESULTS
Fall 1939, Invasion of Poland	
May 1940, Invasion of France	
June 22, 1941 Invasion of the Soviet Union	
December 7, 1941, Attack on Pearl Harbor	

6. **Explain Roles of World Leaders** Explain the roles of various world leaders, including Franklin D. Roosevelt, during World War II. Write a paragraph that explains Roosevelt's impact on the Allied war effort. Consider the foreign policy of the United States, Roosevelt's support for Britain and the Allies, and U.S. entry into war. 12.B
7. **Explain Major Events of World War II** Explain the major events of World War II, including the Normandy landings. Review the below map. Write a paragraph explaining the significance of the Allied invasion of Normandy. Consider the objective of the Normandy landings, the geography of France, and the duration of the battle. What were some challenges the Allied forces faced? 12.C

Answers to TEKS Assessment

1. Student responses should clearly explain how Germany and the Soviet Union agreed not to interfere with one another's claims on Poland, and how each country benefited from the agreement. Students should demonstrate understanding of both German and Soviet motives for forming the alliance, as well as how France and Britain responded by finally declaring war on Germany.
2. Student responses should clearly explain how new military technology impacted World War II, including the high number of casualties—both soldier and civilian—and the damage caused by bomber planes, machine guns, tanks, aircraft carriers, and atomic weapons.
3. Student responses should explain how Japan's imperialist policies and actions, such as the attacks on Pearl Harbor and other Pacific territories of the United States, caused the United States to get involved in the war and fight to protect U.S. territory. Students should demonstrate understanding that Tojo became prime minister in 1941 and supported a militaristic policy of aggression that led to the attack on Pearl Harbor. The United States had remained neutral before the attack but joined the Allies afterward.
4. Student responses should clearly explain that the Allies believed strengthening democracy in Axis countries like Germany and Japan would prevent dictators and fascist governments from rebuilding. Students should demonstrate understanding of the methods used by the Allies to change these countries from dictatorships to democracies. Students may mention that the Allies removed Nazi books from German schools and that the Allies helped both Japan and Germany develop new constitutions based on democratic principles.
5. Student responses should clearly explain one or more consequences of each event listed in the chart, such as that the invasion of Poland caused Britain and France to declare war on Germany and officially started World War II; the invasion of France led to France's surrender and left Britain as the lone opponent to the Axis powers; the invasion of the Soviet Union led to the end of the German-Soviet nonaggression pact, drained the German army of troops, and caused Stalin to join the Allies; and the attack on Pearl Harbor led to America's involvement in the war with the addition of troops, equipment, and finances.
6. Student responses should describe the Neutrality Acts of the 1930s and how Roosevelt instituted policies to support Britain, such as the Lend-Lease Act of 1941. Students should also understand Roosevelt's opposition to Japanese expansion in the Pacific, his request for a declaration of war after Pearl Harbor, and his role in developing a two-front war with Churchill.
7. Student responses should clearly explain that the objective of the Normandy invasion was to open a second front in Europe, reach the Seine River, and ultimately liberate Paris. Students should explain the challenges faced by the Allied forces, such as high casualties and strong German resistance, including underwater mines, machine gun fire, and mortars.
8. Student responses should clearly explain that the decision to invade the Soviet Union had disastrous consequences for the Germans because it brought the Soviet Union into the war on the Allied side and forced Germany to fight on two fronts. Students should demonstrate understanding of how this decision gave the Allies time to regroup. Students may also explain how the Germans were not prepared for winter in the Soviet Union, and how the prolonged invasion drained manpower from German forces in other areas.

Topic 18

TEKS ASSESSMENT

8. **Explain the Major Causes of World War II** Explain the major causes of World War II, including the German invasion of the Soviet Union. Write a paragraph that explains how the German invasion of the Soviet Union in 1941 changed the course of the war. Consider Germany's decision to invade the Soviet Union, the benefit to Britain and her allies, and how the decision affected Germany. 12.C

9. **Explain Roles and Identify Examples** Explain the roles of various world leaders, including Adolf Hitler, and identify examples of genocide, including the Holocaust, during World War II. Write a paragraph explaining the role of Adolf Hitler and the Nazis in orchestrating the Holocaust during World War II. Consider the outcome of the Holocaust, how the death camps were operated, Hitler's goal concerning all Jewish people, and differences between concentration camps and death camps. 12. B, 12.C, 22.D

10. **Explain the Major Causes of World War II** Explain the major causes of World War II, including Japanese imperialism. Write a paragraph explaining how the Japanese seizure of Manchuria contributed to the start of World War II. Consider the motivations of Japanese military leaders and ultranationalists, the Western response to Japanese aggression, and Japan's reaction to the West. 12.C

11. **Identify Causes of Turning Points in World War II** Identify major causes of important turning points in world history from 1914 to the present, including World War II's impact on economic systems. Write a paragraph that describes the impact of World War II on Germany's economy. Consider the country's pre- and post–World War II economy and government. 1.F

12. **Locate Regions and Places** Locate regions and places of historical significance directly related to major eras and turning points in world history. Complete the graphic organizer with the locations and dates of examples of Axis aggression, including the significance of the events to the start of World War II. Consider the places involved, the timeline of events, and the responses of other countries. 16.A

Acts of Aggression	
Japan	
Italy	
Germany	

13. **Identify and Describe World War II's Impact and Describe People's Participation** Identify and describe World War II's impact on economic systems, and describe how people have participated in supporting their governments. Write a paragraph identifying and describing the impact of World War II on the U.S. economy and the role of U.S. citizens in the change. Consider the war economy and changing workforce. 1.F, 21.A

14. **Describe Effects of Atomic Bombs in World War II** Describe and explain the major effects of important turning points in world history from 1914 to the present, including the dropping of atomic bombs during World War II. Write a paragraph that describes how the dropping of atomic bombs in World War II affected the outcome of the war. Consider the destruction caused by the bombs, the global "arms race" following World War II, and the historic action of the Japanese emperor (August 10, 1945). 1.F, 12.C

15. **Explain the Significance of the United Nations** Explain the significance of the United Nations. Write a paragraph that describes how the events of World War II influenced the purpose and powers of the United Nations. Consider its purpose, powers held by the UN Security Council, the countries with permanent positions on the UN Security Council, and comparison with the League of Nations. 20.D

16. **Explain Roles of World Leaders** Explain the roles of various world leaders, including Winston Churchill, prior to World War II. Write a paragraph that describes Churchill's attitude toward appeasement and the Munich Pact. Consider the results of appeasement of Germany, Winston Churchill's speech (excerpt below) to the House of Commons in 1938, and the results of Hitler's violation of the Munich Pact in March 1939. 12.B

"This is only the beginning of the reckoning. This is only the first sip, the first foretaste of a bitter cup which will be proffered to us year by year unless by a supreme recovery of moral health and martial vigour, we arise again and take our stand for freedom as in the olden time."
—*Winston Churchill, October 5, 1938*

17. Reflect on the Essential Question **Write an essay on the Essential Question: When is war justified?** Use evidence from your study of this Topic to support your answer.

Answers to TEKS Assessment

9. Student answers should clearly explain that Hitler's goal, called the Final Solution, was the extermination of the Jewish population. Hitler sent Jews to death camps in Poland, where prisoners were executed instead of being put to work as they were in concentration camps. The elderly, the sick, and the young were immediately executed in special gas chambers and their bodies cremated. Other prisoners were worked to death or used for brutal and often deadly "medical" experiments. In all, about 6 million Jews and 5 million other "undesirables" were murdered in the Holocaust.

10. Student responses should clearly show an understanding of how the need for resources and glory led Japan to invade China. Students should explain that this act of aggression was met with only verbal protests, not punitive action. Students should demonstrate understanding of how the lack of action by the League of Nations and other groups encouraged Japan to continue its conquest of Asia.

11. Student responses should clearly explain that World War II had a devastating impact on the economy of Germany. The country was all but destroyed by the war. Students may mention that Germany was so low on resources like fuel by the end of the war that its air force was nearly grounded. Germany also suffered heavy damage from bombing, which destroyed key government structures. Students should demonstrate understanding of the difference in economic strength between prewar Germany and what remained of the country at the end of the war.

12. Student responses should correctly identify the locations and dates of one or more acts of aggression for each Axis power, such as the invasion of Ethiopia (Italy), the repudiation of the Versailles Treaty (or the occupation of the Sudetenland) (Germany), or the Marco Polo Bridge incident (Japan). Students should demonstrate understanding of why these events were significant to the start of World War II.

13. Student responses should correctly identify and clearly describe the ways that U.S. citizens supported their government's war economy, such as by working in factories to produce war equipment, cooperating with rationing, and purchasing war bonds. They should also discuss the addition of large numbers of women to the workforce and the service of women in auxiliary positions.

14. Student responses should clearly explain that the bombing of Japan brought a quick end to World War II. Students may mention the controversy following the dropping of the bombs, as well as the effects of the destruction. Students should demonstrate understanding that the dropping of atomic bombs in World War II led to the global arms race.

15. Student responses should clearly explain that the United Nations has the purpose and power to act (both economically and militarily) to preserve international peace. Students should demonstrate understanding of the UN's ability to respond with force to any international conflict, unlike the policy of appeasement in place during the League of Nations (prior to World War II). Students may also mention that the permanent members of the Security Council are all Allied countries.

16. Student responses should clearly explain that appeasement encouraged Hitler rather than stopping him, that Churchill recognized this, and that the strength of Churchill's beliefs made him speak out against popular opinion. Hitler's invasion of Poland proved Churchill correct.

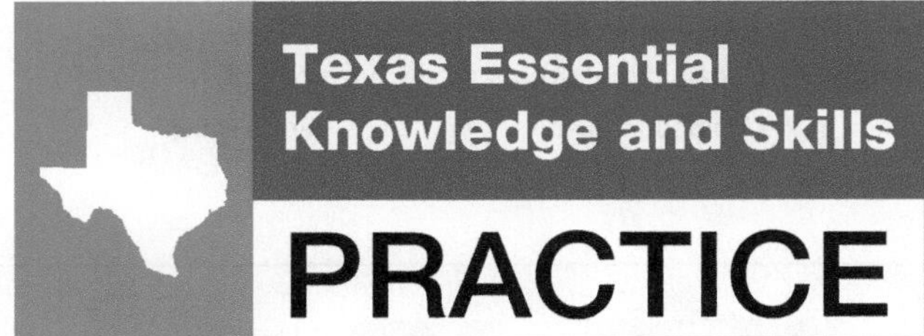
Texas Essential
Knowledge and Skills
PRACTICE

Topic 18

Answers to TEKS Practice

1. D
2. G

Online To prepare for the End-of-Topic test, have students go online for additional Topic Review and Assessment questions or to review their notes in the **Interactive Reading Notepad** for the lessons in this Topic.

Benchmark Tests

Assign these benchmark tests as you complete the relevant topics to monitor student progress toward mastering the course content and as preparation for the End-of-Course Test.

Benchmark Test 1: Topics 1–5

Benchmark Test 2: Topics 6–10

Benchmark Test 3: Topics 11–15

Benchmark Test 4: Topics 16–21

TEKS PRACTICE

1

Why would Benito Mussolini be criticized for the actions depicted in the cartoon prior to World War II?

A He invaded Ethiopia to conduct a religious war against Islam.

B He organized protests against the ruling socialist government.

C He participated in the Holocaust by providing poison gas to Hitler.

D He used modern weapons to defeat poorly equipped armies.

2

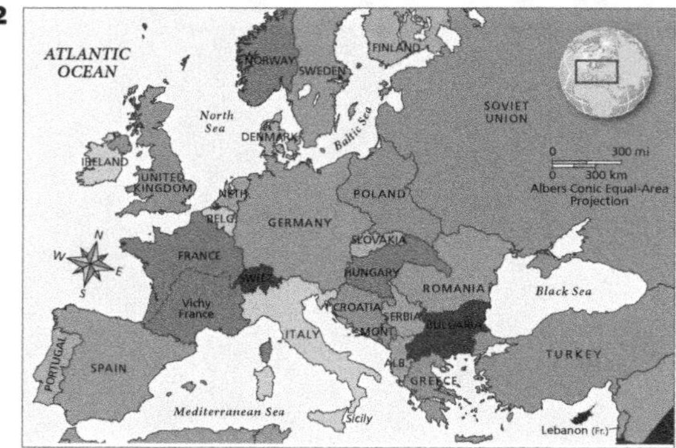

Which location on the map was the site of a major historical turning point in 1939?

F Poland, because the USSR invaded it to attack Nazi Germany

G Poland, because Germany invaded it to take the Polish Corridor

H France, because the USSR invaded it to defeat German troops stationed in Paris

J France, because Germany invaded it to knock the French out of the war before attacking Poland

Test Taking Tips: Tip for Questions With Reading Passages

1. Read the question.
2. Read the title of the passage if it is provided.
3. Determine when the passage or quotation was written or spoken and by whom.
4. Carefully read the entire passage or quotation.
5. Read the question again to be sure you understand what is being asked. Identify details or ideas in the passage or quotation that you will use to answer the question.
6. Answer the question in your own words.
7. Read the answer choices and select the best answer.

www.PearsonTexas.com
Access additional practice questions

3 How is the role of German leader Adolf Hitler during World War II best explained?

A He was responsible for sending German troops to fight against the Italians in 1941.

B He was responsible for the surrender of Britain in 1940 when he sent German planes to bomb London, destroying the city.

C He was responsible for the involvement of the United States in the war by attacking their naval base in Pearl Harbor in 1941.

D He was responsible for the outbreak of the war in 1939 when Germany successfully invaded Poland in a "blitzkrieg" operation.

4

> *"Certain communities formerly belonging to the Turkish Empire have reached a stage of development where their existence as independent nations can be provisionally recognized, subject to the rendering of administrative advice and assistance by a mandatary until such time as they are able to stand alone."*
>
> *Article XXII of the Covenant of the League of Nations, accepted as a condition of the Treaty of Versailles.*

How did this provision affect the regions of Palestine, Lebanon, Syria, and Iraq?

F It gave these countries to the Persian empire.

G It allowed countries to remain in the Ottoman empire.

H It made these countries become colonial subjects.

J It changed these countries into democratic republics.

If you have trouble with...				
Question	1	2	3	4
See Lesson	18.1	18.1	18.2	17.2
TEKS	12.B	16.A	12.B	10.C

3. D
4. H

Online Use the **Topic Synthesize** to help students revisit and reflect on the Essential Question for this Topic.

Topic Inquiry

If students have done a Topic Inquiry for this Topic, have them complete the final step of the Inquiry now.

The Cold War Era (1945–1991)

TOPIC 19 ORGANIZER	PACING: APPROX. 1 PERIOD, .5 BLOCKS		
	PACING	TEKS	ELPS
Connect	1 period		
MY STORY VIDEO **Gabriele Hayes, Remembering the Cold War**	10 min.		
DIGITAL ESSENTIAL QUESTION ACTIVITY **How Should We Handle Conflict?**	10 min.	21.A	
DIGITAL TIMELINE ACTIVITY **The Cold War Era**	10 min.	1.F, 13.A, 13.B, 13.C, 13.D, 18.E, 18.F, 21.A	
TOPIC INQUIRY: CIVIC DISCUSSION **The Cold War**	20 min.		
Investigate	2–5 periods		
TOPIC INQUIRY: CIVIC DISCUSSION **The Cold War**	Ongoing		
LESSON 1 **A New Global Conflict**	30–40 min.	1.F, 13.A, 13.C, 18.A, 18.F, 22.E, 28.C	1.A.2, 5.C.3
LESSON 2 **The Western Democracies and Japan**	30–40 min.	1.F	1.B.1, 5.D.1
LESSON 3 **Communism in East Asia**	30–40 min.	1.F, 13.B, 13.C, 18.B, 22.C	1.B.2
LESSON 4 **War in Southeast Asia**	30–40 min.	1.F, 13.C, 22.C	5.D.3, 1.C.1
LESSON 5 **The Cold War Ends**	30–40 min.	13.D, 18.E, 18.F, 21.A	5.E.1, 1.D.1
Synthesize	1 period		
DIGITAL ESSENTIAL QUESTION ACTIVITY **The Cold War Era**	10 min.	1.F, 13.A, 13.C, 21.A, 28.C	
TOPIC INQUIRY: CIVIC DISCUSSION **The Cold War**	20 min.		
Demonstrate	1–2 periods		
DIGITAL TOPIC TEST **The Cold War Era**	10 min.		
TOPIC INQUIRY: CIVIC DISCUSSION **The Cold War**	20 min.		

AUTHOR'S NOTE

Coexistence and Détente

Over four decades, the Cold War brought the world rebellions, revolutions, wars, and confrontation between the superpowers. The Cold War also, however, turned out to be much more subtle and complicated than a survey of these open clashes might suggest. And in the end, the conflict terminated—dramatically enough, but without the final showdown many had feared.

There was, however, a wide range of nonmilitary contention between the United States and the Soviet Union. There were propaganda broadsides aimed at their own people and at "world opinion." There was espionage of all sorts, from the most sophisticated electronic gear to old-fashioned spying. There was intense technological and economic competition, ranging from the battle to see who could produce the most tungsten or toothbrushes to the race to the moon. And there was, of course, the unending arms race.

Accompanying these varied forms of competition, however, were repeated attempts to improve relations between America and the Soviet Union. Under such rubrics as "coexistence" or *détente*, these efforts provided a counterpoint of hope that the world could avoid a third global war in the twentieth century.

A number of summit meetings occurred between the two states as well as consultations between the foreign ministers, ambassadors, and other lesser officials of the two governments. Direct electronic communications between the White House and the Kremlin were set up for easy and quick discussions when problems arose. Trade relations, while fluctuating with other aspects of the relationship, repeatedly provided a splendid opportunity for America to market its habitual agricultural overproduction and for the Soviet Union to import lifesaving quantities of grain. . . .

And in fact a number of agreements were negotiated limiting arms development in the two super-states—though this proved in the long run perhaps the most difficult problem of all for the two armed camps.

—Anthony Esler, *The Human Venture: From Prehistory to the Present* (Upper Saddle River, New Jersey: Pearson Education, 2004), p. 690

TOPIC INQUIRY: CIVIC DISCUSSION

The Cold War

1.F, 13.A, 13.C, 13.D, 28.C, 29.C, 29.D, 29.E, 29.F, 29.G, 29.H, 30.A, 30.C

In this Topic Inquiry, students work in teams to examine different perspectives on this issue by analyzing several sources, arguing both sides of a Yes/No question, and then developing and discussing their own point of view on the question: Did the end of the Cold War make the world safer?

STEP 1: CONNECT

Develop Questions and Plan the Investigation

Launch the Civic Discussion

Divide the class into groups of four students. Students can access the materials they'll need in the online course, or you can distribute copies to each student. Read the main question and introduction with the students.

Have students complete Step 1 by reading the Discussion Launch and filling in Step 1 of the Information Organizer. The Discussion Launch provides YES and NO arguments on the main question. Students should extract and paraphrase the arguments from the reading in Step 1 of their Information Organizers.

Next, students share within their groups the arguments and evidence they found to support the YES and NO positions. The group needs to agree on the major YES and NO points, and each student should note those points in his or her Information Organizer.

Resources

- Student Instructions
- Information Organizer
- Discussion Launch

PROFESSIONAL DEVELOPMENT

Civic Discussion

Be sure to view the Civic Discussion Professional Development resources in the online course.

STEP 2: INVESTIGATE

Apply Disciplinary Concepts and Tools

Examine Sources and Perspectives

Students will examine sources with the goal of extracting information and perspectives on the main question. They analyze each source and describe the author's perspective on the main question and key evidence the author provides to support that viewpoint in Information Organizer Step 2.

Ask students to keep in mind:

- **Author/Creator:** Who created the source? An individual? Group? Government agency?
- **Audience:** For whom was the source created?
- **Date/Place:** Is there any information that reveals where and when the source was created?
- **Purpose:** Why was the source created? Discuss with students the importance of this question in identifying bias.
- **Relevance:** How does the source support one argument or another?

Suggestion: Reading the source documents and filling in Step 2 of the Information Organizer could be assigned as homework.

Resources

- Student Instructions
- Information Organizer
- Source documents

STEP 3: SYNTHESIZE

Use Evidence to Formulate Conclusions

Formulate Compelling Arguments With Evidence

Now students will apply perspectives and evidence they extracted from the sources to think more deeply about the main question by first arguing one side of the issue and then the other. In this way students become more prepared to formulate an evidence-based conclusion on their own.

Within each student group, assign half of the students to take the position of YES on the main question and the others to take the position of NO. Students will work with their partners to identify the strongest arguments and evidence to support their assigned YES or NO position.

Present Yes/No Positions

Within each group, those assigned the YES position share arguments and evidence first. As the YES students speak, those assigned NO should listen carefully, take notes to fill in the rest of the Compelling Arguments Chart (Step 3 in Information Organizer), and ask clarifying questions.

When the YES side is finished, students assigned the NO position should present while those assigned YES listen, take notes, and ask clarifying questions. Examples of clarifying questions are:

- I think you just said [x]. Am I understanding you correctly?
- Can you tell me more about [x]?
- Can you repeat [x]? I am not sure I understand yet.

Suggestion: You may want to set a 5 minute time limit for each side to present. Provide a two-minute warning so that students make their most compelling arguments within the time frame.

Switch Sides

The students will switch sides to argue the opposite point of view. To prepare to present the other position, partners who first argued YES will use the notes they took during the NO side's presentation, plus add any additional arguments and evidence from the reading and sources. The same for students who first argued the NO position.

STEP 4: DEMONSTRATE

Communicate Conclusions and Take Informed Action

Individual Points of View

Now the students will have the opportunity to discuss the main question from their own points of view. To help students prepare for this discussion, have them reflect on the YES/NO discussions they have participated in thus far and fill in Step 4 of their Information Organizers.

After all of the students have shared their points of view, each group should list points of agreement, filling the last portion of Step 4 on their Information Organizers.

Reflect on the Discussion

Ask students to reflect on the civic discussion, thinking about:

- the value of having to argue both the YES and NO positions.
- if their individual views changed over the course of the discussion, and why.
- what they learned from participating in the discussion.

Resources

- Student Instructions
- Information Organizer

Topic 19 Lesson 1

A New Global Conflict

Objectives

Objective 1: Summarize how the outcome of World War II contributed to the development of the Cold War.

Objective 2: Identify continuing Cold War conflicts in Germany and Eastern Europe.

Objective 3: Explain the growth of the nuclear arms race.

Objective 4: Analyze how the Cold War became a global conflict.

Objective 5: Compare the United States and the Soviet Union in the Cold War.

LESSON 1 ORGANIZER	PACING: APPROX. 1 PERIOD, .5 BLOCKS					
	OBJECTIVES	PACING	RESOURCES: Print	RESOURCES: Online	TEKS	ELPS
Connect						
DIGITAL START UP ACTIVITY **The Berlin Wall**		5 min.		●	13.A	
Investigate						
READ **Wartime Alliance Breaks Apart**	Objective 1	10 min.	●	●	1.F, 12.B, 13.A	1.A.2
READ **Soviet Aggression Grows**	Objective 2	10 min.	●	●	1.F, 12.B, 13.A, 18.F	
READ **Two Opposing Sides in Europe**		10 min.	●	●	13.A, 18.F	5.C.3
READ **The Nuclear Arms Race**	Objective 3	10 min.	●	●	1.F, 13.A, 13.C	
INTERACTIVE GALLERY **Cold War Technologies**		10 min.		●	13.C, 28.C	
READ **The Cold War Around the World**	Objective 4	10 min.	●	●	1.F, 13.A	
INTERACTIVE GALLERY **The Cuban Missile Crisis**		10 min.		●	13.C, 16.C	
READ **The Soviet Union During the Cold War**	Objective 5	10 min.	●	●	18.F, 22.E	
READ **The United States in the Cold War**		10 min.	●	●	18.A	
Synthesize						
DIGITAL ACTIVITY **Actions and Consequences of the Cold War**		5 min.		●	13.A	
Demonstrate						
DIGITAL QUIZ **Lesson Quiz and Class Discussion Board**		10 min.		●		

Focus on Texas Standards

Texas Essential Knowledge and Skills

1.F identify major causes and describe the major effects of the following important turning points in world history from 1914 to the present: the world wars and their impact on political, economic, and social systems; communist revolutions and their impact on the Cold War; independence movements; and globalization

13.A summarize how the outcome of World War II contributed to the development of the Cold War

13.C identify the following major events of the Cold War, including the Korean War, the Vietnam War, and the arms race

18.A identify the historical origins and characteristics of the free enterprise system, including the contributions of Adam Smith, especially the influence of his ideas found in The Wealth of Nations

18.F formulate generalizations on how economic freedom improved the human condition, based on students' knowledge of the benefits of free enterprise in Europe's Commercial Revolution, the Industrial Revolution, and 20th-century free market economies, compared to communist command communities

22.E identify examples of individuals who led resistance to political oppression such as Nelson Mandela, Mohandas Gandhi, Oscar Romero, Natan Sharansky, Las Madres de la Plaza de Mayo, and Chinese student protestors in Tiananmen Square

28.C explain the effects of major new military technologies on World War I, World War II, and the Cold War

NOTES

Topic 19 Lesson 2

The Western Democracies and Japan

Objectives

Objective 1: Analyze the postwar American economy.

Objective 2: Identify developments in American society and government.

Objective 3: Explain how Western Europe rebuilt and moved toward greater unity.

Objective 4: Describe how Japan changed after World War II.

LESSON 2 ORGANIZER	PACING: APPROX. 1 PERIOD, .5 BLOCKS					
			RESOURCES			
	OBJECTIVES	PACING	Print	Online	TEKS	ELPS
Connect						
DIGITAL START UP ACTIVITY **Historical Connections**		5 min.		●	1.F	
Investigate						
READ **Postwar Prosperity in the United States**	Objective 1	10 min.	●	●	1.F, 18.A, 18.B	1.B.1
INTERACTIVE GALLERY **Suburbanization in Postwar America**	Objective 1	10 min.		●	1.F	
READ **The United States Responds to New Challenges**	Objective 2	10 min.	●	●	13.A, 18.A, 21.A	5.D.1
READ **Rebuilding Western Europe**	Objective 3	10 min.	●	●	18.A, 18.B, 18.F, 24.B	
INTERACTIVE CHART **Free Market Economy v. Command Economy**	Objective 3	10 min.		●		
READ **Japan Is Transformed**	Objective 4	10 min.	●	●	18.A, 18.B	
Synthesize						
DIGITAL ACTIVITY **Rebuilding West Germany and Japan**		5 min.		●	13.A, 18.A, 18.B, 18.F	
Demonstrate						
DIGITAL QUIZ **Lesson Quiz and Class Discussion Board**		10 min.		●	1.F, 13.A, 18.B, 18.F, 21.A	

Focus on Texas Standards

Texas Essential Knowledge and Skills

1.F identify major causes and describe the major effects of the following important turning points in world history from 1914 to the present: the world wars and their impact on political, economic, and social systems; communist revolutions and their impact on the Cold War; independence movements; and globalization

NOTES

Topic 19 Lesson 3

Communism in East Asia

Objectives

Objective 1: Analyze how Mao Zedong turned China into a communist state.

Objective 2: Describe China's role in the Cold War.

Objective 3: Explain the causes and impact of the Korean War.

LESSON 3 ORGANIZER	PACING: APPROX. 1 PERIOD, .5 BLOCKS					
			RESOURCES			
	OBJECTIVES	PACING	Print	Online	TEKS	ELPS
Connect						
DIGITAL START UP ACTIVITY **Defining Governments**		5 min.		●	1.F, 13.B, 18.B	
Investigate						
READ **The Chinese Communist Victory**	Objective 1	10 min.	●	●	1.F, 13.A, 13.B, 18.B, 22.C	
INTERACTIVE GALLERY **Communism in China**		10 min.		●	1.F, 13.A, 13.B, 18.B, 22.C	
READ **China and the Cold War**	Objective 2	10 min.	●	●	13.A, 13.B	
READ **The Two Koreas**	Objective 3	10 min.	●	●	13.A, 13.C	1.B.2
INTERACTIVE MAP **The Korean War**		10 min.		●	13.C, 16.C	
Synthesize						
DIGITAL ACTIVITY **Who Benefits from a People's Republic?**		5 min.		●	13.B	
Demonstrate						
DIGITAL QUIZ **Lesson Quiz and Class Discussion Board**		10 min.		●		

PEARSON realize
www.PearsonTexas.com
Access your Digital Lesson

Focus on Texas Standards

Texas Essential Knowledge and Skills

1.F identify major causes and describe the major effects of the following important turning points in world history from 1914 to the present: the world wars and their impact on political, economic, and social systems; communist revolutions and their impact on the Cold War; independence movements; and globalization

13.B summarize the factors that contributed to communism in China, including Mao Zedong's role in its rise, and how it differed from Soviet communism

13.C identify the following major events of the Cold War, including the Korean War, the Vietnam War, and the arms race

18.B identify the historical origins and characteristics of communism, including the influences of Karl Marx

22.C identify examples of politically motivated mass murders in Cambodia, China, Latin America, the Soviet Union, and Armenia

NOTES

Topic 19 Lesson 4

War in Southeast Asia

Objectives

Objective 1: Describe events in Indochina after World War II.

Objective 2: Explain how the United States became involved in the Vietnam War.

Objective 3: Explore the end of the Vietnam War.

Objective 4: Summarize the impact of the war on Vietnam and Cambodia.

LESSON 4 ORGANIZER — **PACING: APPROX. 1 PERIOD, .5 BLOCKS**

	OBJECTIVES	PACING	RESOURCES Print	RESOURCES Online	TEKS	ELPS
Connect						
DIGITAL START UP ACTIVITY **Fighting Communism in Vietnam**		5 min.		●	13.C	
Investigate						
READ **The Road to War in Southeast Asia**	Objective 1	10 min.	●	●	1.F	5.D.3
READ **The United States Enters the War**	Objective 2	10 min.	●	●	13.A, 13.C	1.C.1
INTERACTIVE TIMELINE **Vietnam, 1945–1965—From Independence Struggle to Cold War Battleground**		10 min.		●	1.F, 13.A, 13.C	
READ **The Vietnam War Ends**	Objective 3	10 min.	●	●	13.A, 13.C, 22.C	
INTERACTIVE GALLERY **Fighting a Different War**		10 min.		●	13.C, 28.C	
Synthesize						
DIGITAL ACTIVITY **President Johnson's 1965 Defense of Involvement**		5 min.		●	13.C	
Demonstrate						
DIGITAL QUIZ **Lesson Quiz and Class Discussion Board**		10 min.		●	1.F, 13.A, 13.C, 22.C, 28.C	

Focus on Texas Standards

Texas Essential Knowledge and Skills

1.F identify major causes and describe the major effects of the following important turning points in world history from 1914 to the present: the world wars and their impact on political, economic, and social systems; communist revolutions and their impact on the Cold War; independence movements; and globalization

13.C identify the following major events of the Cold War, including the Korean War, the Vietnam War, and the arms race

22.C identify examples of politically motivated mass murders in Cambodia, China, Latin America, the Soviet Union, and Armenia

NOTES

Topic 19 Lesson 5

The Cold War Ends

Objectives

Objective 1: Understand why the Soviet Union declined.

Objective 2: Identify the reforms introduced by Mikhail Gorbachev.

Objective 3: Describe the collapse of communism in Eastern Europe and the Soviet Union.

Objective 4: Evaluate how the end of the Cold War affected the remaining communist nations and the United States.

LESSON 5 ORGANIZER	PACING: APPROX. 1 PERIOD, .5 BLOCKS					
			RESOURCES			
	OBJECTIVES	PACING	Print	Online	TEKS	ELPS
Connect						
DIGITAL START UP ACTIVITY **The Decline of the Soviet Union**		5 min.		●	18.D	
Investigate						
READ **The Soviet Union Declines**	Objective 1	10 min.	●	●	13.D, 18.E, 18.F	5.E.1
INTERACTIVE MAP **The Fall of the Soviet Union**	Objective 1	10 min.		●	16.C	
READ **The Soviet Union Collapses**	Objective 2	10 min.	●	●	13.D, 22.E	
READ **Eastern Europe Transformed**	Objective 3	10 min.	●	●	13.D, 18.E, 18.F	1.D.1
INTERACTIVE TIMELINE **Fall of Communism in Soviet Bloc**	Objective 3	10 min.		●	13.D, 21.A	
READ **Communism Declines Around the World**	Objective 4	10 min.	●	●	18.E, 18.F	
READ **The Post-Cold War World**	Objective 4	10 min.	●	●		
Synthesize						
DIGITAL ACTIVITY **Pro-Reform and Anti-Reform Leaders**		5 min.		●		
Demonstrate						
DIGITAL QUIZ **Lesson Quiz and Class Discussion Board**		10 min.		●	13.D, 18.E, 21.A	

PEARSON realize™ www.PearsonTexas.com Access your Digital Lesson

Focus on Texas Standards

Texas Essential Knowledge and Skills

13.D explain the roles of modern world leaders, including Ronald Reagan, Mikhail Gorbachev, Lech Walesa, and Pope John Paul II, in the collapse of communism in Eastern Europe and the Soviet Union

18.E explain why communist command economies collapsed in competition with free market economies at the end of the 20th century

18.F formulate generalizations on how economic freedom improved the human condition, based on students' knowledge of the benefits of free enterprise in Europe's Commercial Revolution, the Industrial Revolution, and 20th-century free market economies, compared to communist command communities

21.A describe how people have participated in supporting or changing their governments

NOTES

The Cold War Era (1945–1991)

In this Topic, you will learn about the Cold War. You will also find lots of ways to investigate the ideas of this Topic and to master the TEKS.

Your study will help you master these TEKS:

TEKS

1.F, 13.A, 13.B, 13.C, 13.D, 16.C, 18.A, 18.B, 18.E, 18.F, 21.A, 22.C, 22.E, 24.B, 28.C

LESSON OUTLINE

Connect

You will start by connecting with the Topic through a video that tells a personal story about the times. You will start to think about how the Topic connects with your own experience or to what you already know. And you'll get a chance to think about a really big question, or Essential Question: How should we handle conflict?

Begin your study by trying the following:

NBC LEARN Watch My Story Video:

Gabriele Hayes, Remembering the Cold War

Launch your Civic Discussion:

The Cold War

Investigate

Then you will investigate the Topic through a group of lessons. The story of the Cold War will come to life as you read and interact with key content. You will get a chance to read about what happened and why. And you'll be able to interact with a lot of fascinating online materials

You'll also keep working on your Civic Discussion as you build further mastery of the Topic TEKS.

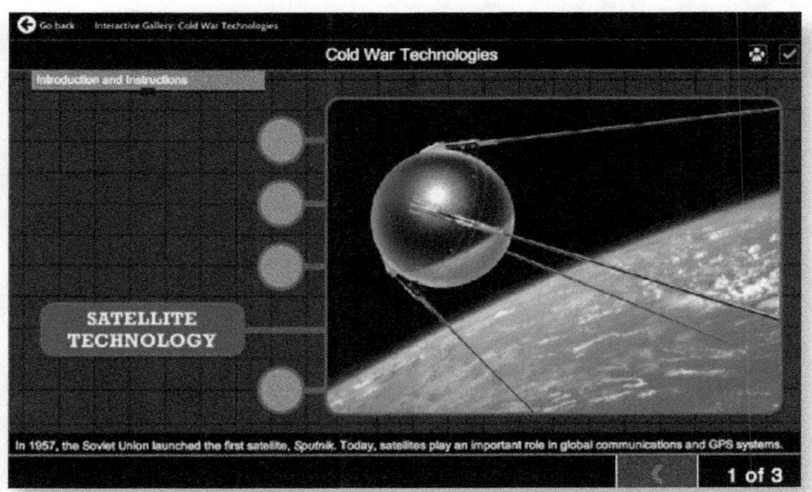
Go back
Interactive Gallery: Cold War Technologies
Cold War Technologies
Introduction and Instructions
SATELLITE TECHNOLOGY
In 1957, the Soviet Union launched the first satellite, Sputnik. Today, satellites play an important role in global communications and GPS systems.
1 of 3

>> Digital interactivity from the online course

Synthesize

Next you will pull it all together by reflecting on the Essential Question. This will give you a chance to be the storyteller, to show how you would answer this big question: How should we handle conflict?

Demonstrate

Finally, you can show what you know. You can write an essay, hold a discussion, or make a presentation. You can answer questions about every TEKS on the Topic Review and Assessment pages. Or you can take part in the Civic Discussion about the Cold War.

TEKS in Topic 19	Topic Review and Assessment Questions
1.F	**2, 3, 13**
13.A	**4, 13, 16**
13.B	**5**
13.C	**8**
13.D	**9, 10**
18.A	**13**
18.E	**1**
18.F	**11**
21. A	**7**
22.C	**6**
22.E	**7, 15**
24.B	**12**
28.C	**14**

Topic 19

The Cold War Era (1945–1991)

Introduction

Following World War II, conflicts quickly increased among some of the Allies. Rivalry between the United States and the Soviet Union turned into a "cold war" in which the two superpowers and their allies competed for global influence. Communism and political oppression spread, nuclear arsenals grew, and "hot" wars broke out, notably in Korea and Vietnam. All of these events played a role in raising tensions. This Cold War, however, finally ended in 1989 with the collapse of the Soviet Union and the breakup of its empire.

ESSENTIAL QUESTION

Ask students to think about the Essential Question for this Topic: How should we handle conflict? Have students develop a five-step process for responding to conflict that could be used by individuals, groups, and even nations. Then have volunteers read their steps. Discuss the results as a class.

Compare and Contrast Have students exchange their processes with a partner. Ask: Would a conflict likely be resolved in the same way using these two processes, or would a different result be probable? *(Pairs may find that some steps are similar but others are different; it is possible that students will find that similar outcomes will result from different five-step processes.)*

Support Ideas With Evidence How would you test the effectiveness of your five-step process for resolving conflict? *(Suggestions will vary; most students will offer a testing scenario involving individuals or local groups.)*

[ESSENTIAL QUESTION] How Should We Handle Conflict?

19 The Cold War Era (1945–1991)

Analyze Images

Ask students to study the photograph of the Berlin Wall, which for much of the Cold War divided communist East Berlin from western-controlled West Berlin. Ask students what this image tells them about why the Cold War ended. *(Answers will vary. Students should note the word* Freedom *written on the wall. They should realize that so many protestors being able to climb on—and over—the Berlin Wall means that the wall is no longer a barrier to freedom. Some students might infer from the photo that young people were the driving force in toppling the Berlin Wall and ending the Cold War.)*

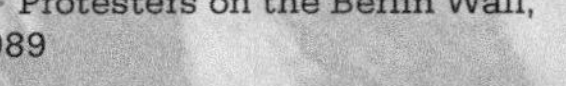

> Protesters on the Berlin Wall, 1989

Texas Essential Knowledge and Skills

1.F, 13.A, 13.B, 13.C, 13.D, 16.C, 18.A, 18.B, 18.E, 18.F, 21.A, 22.C, 22.E, 24.B, 28.C

Enduring Understandings

- Conflicts over Eastern Europe and Germany quickly eroded the wartime alliance between the United States and the Soviet Union.
- In the Cold War, the two superpowers did not confront one another directly, but competed for influence around the world.
- Communism spread to China and Cuba, while Japan became a prosperous democracy.
- The nuclear arms race and the wars in Korea and Vietnam increased Cold War tensions.
- Political oppression and the failures of the command economy led to growing discontent in the Soviet Union and Eastern Europe.
- The Cold War ended with the breakup of the Soviet Union.

Watch the My Story Video to hear a former resident of East Germany describe life behind the iron curtain during the Cold War.

PEARSON realize www.PearsonTexas.com | **Access your digital lessons including:** Topic Inquiry • Interactive Reading Notepad • Interactivities • Assessments

839

NBC LEARN MY STORY VIDEO

Project the My Story Video that introduces students to Gabriele Hayes, who grew up in communist East Berlin. Hayes explains what life was like for residents of East Berlin, living behind the Berlin Wall.

Online My Story Video: **Gabriele Hayes, Remembering the Cold War**

After viewing, ask students to respond to the following questions.

Check Understanding What is the goal of the museum where Gabriele Hayes works? *(The museum is dedicated to the study of the Cold War.)*

Apply Concepts What was the symbolic importance of the destruction of the Berlin Wall? *(The Berlin Wall had symbolized the divide between the communist East and the democratic West during the Cold War. Its destruction signaled the end of the Cold War.)*

OVERVIEW ACTIVITY

Online Project the **Timeline: The Cold War Era**, which shows the major events of the Cold War. In this Topic, students will learn about all of these events and many more, but this timeline will provide a framework into which they can place the events they learn about.

Check Understanding How many years passed between the end of the Korean War and the start of the Vietnam War? *(11 years)*

Topic Inquiry

If you choose to assign the Topic Inquiry, launch the discussion after introducing the Topic.

D Differentiate Extra Support Ask a volunteer to point out the time intervals on the timeline and the overall range of time covered. *(1945–1989; 44 years)* Ask: How many years are there between when John Paul II became pope and the fall of communism? *(11 years)*

Topic 19 Lesson 1

A New Global Conflict

CONNECT

Preview Have students preview the **Lesson Objectives** and the list of **Key Terms**.

Students can also preview all the **Key Terms** and **Academic Vocabulary** using the **Interactive Reading Notepad** on the digital course or preview a summary of the lesson in the **Reading and Note Taking Study Guide**.

Online Use the **Editable Presentation** found on the digital course to present the main ideas for this lesson.

Start Up Activity

Remind students that the Berlin Wall divided the city of Berlin, and it kept residents of communist East Berlin from escaping to West Berlin, which was under the control of the United States, France, and Great Britain. Ask: What do you think it would be like to live in a city that was suddenly split in two by minefields, barbed wire, concrete walls, and guard posts? *(Sample response: It would be difficult. It could cut you off from friends and relatives; it would feel like living in a war zone.)* Have students share their ideas with another student, either in class or through a chat or blog space.

Online You can also project the **Start Up Activity** from the course.

INVESTIGATE

Have students read the lesson using the **Reading and Note Taking Study Guide** to help them take notes and understand the text as they read.

Wartime Alliance Breaks Apart

Ask students: What do you recall about the Soviet Union's government? *(communist dictatorship)* How did it differ from the governments of the other Allies? *(It allowed almost no personal or political freedom.)* Have students explain what united the Allies during World War II. *(unity against the Nazis)* Call out the map of the Warsaw Pact and NATO alliances on page 843. Ask students to list NATO and Warsaw Pact countries.

>> Churchill, Truman, and Stalin shake hands at the Potsdam Conference, held in Germany in July, 1945. Still at war with Japan, the leaders of the wartime alliance hid the growing tensions among them.

Interactive Flipped Video

19.1 Amid the rubble of war, a new power structure emerged. In Europe, Germany was defeated. France and Britain were exhausted. Two other powers, the United States and the Soviet Union, emerged as superpowers, nations with the economic resources and military might to dominate the globe. The United States abandoned its traditional policy of isolationism to counter what President Truman saw as the communist threat.

TEKS
1.F, 13.A, 13.C, 18.A, 18.F, 22.E, 28.C

>> Objectives

Summarize how the outcome of World War II contributed to the development of the Cold War.

Identify continuing Cold War conflicts in Germany and Eastern Europe.

Explain the growth of the nuclear arms race.

Analyze how the Cold War became a global conflict.

Compare the United States and the Soviet Union in the Cold War.

>> Key Terms

superpower
Cold War
Truman Doctrine
containment
Marshall Plan
North Atlantic Treaty Organization (NATO)
Warsaw Pact
détente
Fidel Castro
John F. Kennedy
ideology
Nikita Khrushchev
Leonid Brezhnev

PEARSON realize. www.PearsonTexas.com Access your Digital Lesson.

A New Global Conflict

Wartime Alliance Breaks Apart

Tensions Grow Among the Allies During the war, the Soviet Union and the nations of the West had cooperated to defeat Nazi Germany. By 1945, however, the wartime alliance was crumbling. Conflicting ideologies and mutual distrust soon led to the conflict known as the Cold War.

The **Cold War** was a state of tension and hostility between nations aligned with the United States on one side, and the Soviet Union on the other side. There was no armed conflict between the United States and the Soviet Union, the major rivals during the Cold War.

At wartime conferences and postwar discussions, the Allies had forged a united front. At the Yalta Conference, Churchill and Roosevelt accepted some of Stalin's demands regarding Eastern Europe. They also agreed to the Allied occupation of Germany and the principle of reparations. Despite these agreements, tensions among the Allies deepened once the war ended, helping to create a divided world during the Cold War.

840

Aa Vocabulary Builder

1. Have students pronounce the following academic vocabulary terms in this lesson and clarify the part of speech. For difficult or polysyllabic words, break them into syllables and pronounce them with the students.
2. Explain what the word means in common "student-friendly" language using synonyms and antonyms when possible. Provide concrete examples to clarify the meaning, and rephrase the definition.

invoked: resorted to; called upon

comprised: was made up of

Topic 19 Lesson 1

The Cold War Begins At first, the focus of the Cold War was Eastern Europe. Stalin had two main goals in Eastern Europe. First, he wanted to spread communism into the area. Second, he wanted to create a buffer zone of friendly governments as a defense against Germany, which had invaded Russia during World War I and again in 1941.

As the Red Army pushed German forces out of Eastern Europe, it left behind occupying forces. The Soviet dictator pointed out that the United States was not consulting the Soviet Union about peace terms for Italy or Japan, both of which were defeated and occupied by American and British troops. In the same way, the Soviet Union would determine the fate of the Eastern European lands that it occupied.

Roosevelt and Churchill rejected Stalin's view, making him promise "free elections" in Eastern Europe. Stalin ignored that pledge. Most Eastern European countries had existing Communist parties, many of which had actively resisted the Nazis during the war. Backed by the Red Army, these local Communists in Poland, Czechoslovakia, and elsewhere destroyed rival political parties and even assassinated democratic leaders. By 1948, pro-Soviet communist governments were in place throughout Eastern Europe.

GENERATE EXPLANATIONS What postwar issues caused the Western Allies and the Soviet Union to disagree?

 **ELPS 1.A.2** Reflect on your personal experiences with friendships. As you read *Wartime Alliance Breaks Apart,* use your experiences to better understand why the relationships between world leaders changed.

Soviet Aggression Grows

Stalin soon showed his aggressive intentions outside of Eastern Europe. In Greece, Stalin backed communist rebels who were fighting to overturn a right-wing monarchy supported by Britain. By 1947, however, Britain could no longer afford to defend Greece. Stalin was also menacing Turkey and the vital shipping lane through the Dardanelles.

The Iron Curtain In 1946, Winston Churchill, former prime minister of Britain, spoke of how the Soviet Union was sealing off the countries in Eastern Europe that its armies had occupied at the end of World War II.

> [A]n 'iron curtain' has descended across the Continent. Behind that line lie all of the capitals of the ancient states of Central and Eastern Europe . . . all these famous cities . . . lie in what I must call the Soviet sphere, and are all subject . . . to a very high . . . measure of control from Moscow.
>
> —Winston Churchill

In the West, the "iron curtain" became a symbol of the Cold War fear of communism. It described the division of Europe into an "eastern" and a "western" bloc. In the East were the Soviet-dominated, communist countries of Eastern Europe. In the West were the Western democracies led by the United States.

The Truman Doctrine President Truman saw communism as an evil force threatening countries around the world. To deal with the growing communist threat in Greece and Turkey, he took action. On March 12, 1947, Truman outlined a new policy to Congress: "I believe that it must be the policy of the United States to support free peoples who are resisting attempted subjugation by armed minorities or by outside pressures."

This policy, known as the **Truman Doctrine,** was rooted in the idea of **containment,** limiting

>> The Red Army entered Berlin in April 1945. The Soviets installed communist governments in East Germany and throughout Eastern Europe in the postwar years.

Guided Reading and Discussion

Ask students to explain how Stalin made sure that Eastern Europe came under Soviet influence. *(by leaving Soviet armies in Eastern European countries after the war)* Then have small groups discuss this question: Did Stalin's approach with Eastern European nations fit with his earlier policies? *(Students should mention his purges, treatment of peasants, imprisonment of opponents, and other repressive actions.)* Have the groups share their conclusions with the class.

Soviet Aggression Grows

Two Opposing Sides in Europe

Refer to the map of NATO and Warsaw Pact countries on page 843. Ask students why they think Winston Churchill called the division of Europe the "Iron Curtain," and what the symbolism of each of those words might be. *(iron for force; curtain for dividing; Eastern Europe was now shut off from the rest of the world.)* Ask students how the Soviets took control of the countries behind the Iron Curtain. *(by force)* Then ask: How do you think the Soviets will continue to control these countries? *(by force)*

Answers

Generate Explanations *reparations from Germany and the nature of postwar governments in Eastern Europe*

English Language Proficiency Standards

Learning Strategies 1.A.2 Have students use prior experiences to understand how relationships among world leaders changed following World War II.

Beginning Ask students to recall a time when their relationship with someone changed. Explain that when world leaders disagree, their relationships change. Then read aloud "Wartime Alliance Breaks Apart." Ask students to complete the following: Similar to _______, my relationship changed because of _______.

Intermediate Ask students to recall a time when their relationship with someone changed and to share their experience with a small group. Ask them to speculate about the types of relationships that world leaders have with one another. Read the text aloud, and have students follow along. Ask students to cite similarities between their own experiences and those of Stalin, Churchill, and Roosevelt.

Advanced Follow the instructions in the Intermediate activity, but ask students to work with a partner to read the text and complete the activity.

Advanced High Follow the instructions in the Intermediate activity, but have students recall experiences and make speculations in writing. Have them read the text and discuss why relating to historical figures can improve their understanding of historical events.

Topic 19 Lesson 1

Key Terms

Call students' attention to the term **Marshall Plan** (in bold) in the text. Explain that this program aimed at rebuilding Europe was named after George C. Marshall, the U.S. secretary of state. In a speech in June 1947, he warned that the people of weak and war-torn European nations might be receptive to communist propaganda promising a brighter future.

Analyze Images

Have students look at the image of the airplane and the people awaiting aid, and read the caption. Invite students to choose one word to describe the feelings of the people shown in the photograph. *(Sample responses: hopeful; thankful)*

Guided Reading and Discussion

Ask students to list the key events related to the Berlin Airlift. *(Sample response: The Soviet Union cut off all roads and railroads through East Germany to West Berlin. This isolated the residents of West Berlin. The United States and its allies responded by airlifting supplies to West Berlin. The Soviets ended the blockade after a year.)*

communism to the areas already under Soviet control. Stalin, however, saw containment as "encirclement" by the capitalist world that wanted to isolate the Soviet Union.

The Truman Doctrine would guide the United States for decades. It made clear that Americans would resist Soviet expansion in Europe or elsewhere in the world. Truman soon sent military and economic aid and advisers to Greece and Turkey so that they could withstand the communist threat.

Marshall Plan Aids Europe Postwar hunger and poverty made Western European lands fertile ground for communist ideas. To strengthen democratic governments, the United States offered a massive aid package called the **Marshall Plan.** Under it, the United States funneled food and economic assistance to Europe to help countries rebuild. Billions of dollars in American aid helped war-shattered Europe recover rapidly and reduced communist influence there.

President Truman also offered aid to the Soviet Union and its satellites, or dependent states, in Eastern Europe. However, Stalin declined and forbade Eastern European countries to accept American aid. Instead, he promised help from the Soviet Union in its place.

>> An airplane brings food and other supplies to Berlin as part of the Berlin Airlift. **Cite Evidence** Based on this image, how much progress has been made in the rebuilding of Berlin? Provide evidence.

A Divided Germany Defeated Germany became another focus of the growing tensions between the Soviet Union and the United States. The Soviets took reparations for their massive war losses by dismantling and moving factories and other resources from its occupation zone to help rebuild the Soviet Union. Above all, the Soviets feared the danger of a restored Germany.

The Western powers also took some reparations, but they wanted to create a stable, democratic Germany. Therefore, they united their zones of occupation and encouraged Germans to rebuild industries with Marshall Plan aid. The Soviets were furious at this move and strengthened their hold on Eastern Germany.

Germany became a divided nation. In West Germany, the Western democracies let the people write a constitution and regain self-government. In East Germany, the Soviets installed a socialist dictatorship tied to Moscow.

The Berlin Airlift Stalin's resentment at Western moves to rebuild Germany triggered a crisis over Berlin. Even though it lay deep within the Soviet zone, the former German capital was occupied by all four victorious Allies. In June 1948, Stalin tried to force the Western Allies out of Berlin by sealing off every railroad and highway into the Western sectors of the city. The Western powers responded to the blockade by mounting a round-the-clock airlift. For more than a year, cargo planes supplied West Berliners with food and fuel. Their success forced the Soviets to end the blockade. Although the West had won a victory in the Cold War, the crisis deepened the hostility between the two camps.

New Alliances Tensions continued to grow. In 1949, the United States, Canada, and ten other countries formed a new military alliance called the **North Atlantic Treaty Organization (NATO).** Members pledged to help one another if any one of them were attacked.

In 1955, the Soviet Union responded by forming its own military alliance, the **Warsaw Pact.** It included the Soviet Union and seven satellites in Eastern Europe. Unlike NATO, however, the Warsaw Pact was often invoked by the Soviets to keep its satellites in order.

The Propaganda War Both sides participated in a propaganda war. The United States spoke of defending capitalism and democracy against communism and totalitarianism. The Soviet Union claimed the moral high ground in the struggle against Western

History Background

The Berlin Airlift The planes of the Berlin Airlift, or "Operation Vittles," carried more than 2.3 million tons of food, coal, and supplies into Berlin. Planes landed all day, every day. A new plane touched down every 3 minutes, was unloaded in 17 minutes, and then took off to receive another load. The operation was so large that Berlin's two airfields could not handle all the traffic. American soldiers and German civilians—about 17,000 of them—had to build a third airfield to handle the traffic. Lieutenant Gail Halvorsen came up with the idea for a part of the airlift called "Operation Little Vittles." Soldiers formed tiny parachutes out of handkerchiefs, which were used to drop fruit, candy, and gum to Berlin's children.

Answers

Cite Evidence *Sample response: Not much has been done; people are standing on rubble, and in the left of the photo there is a ruined building.*

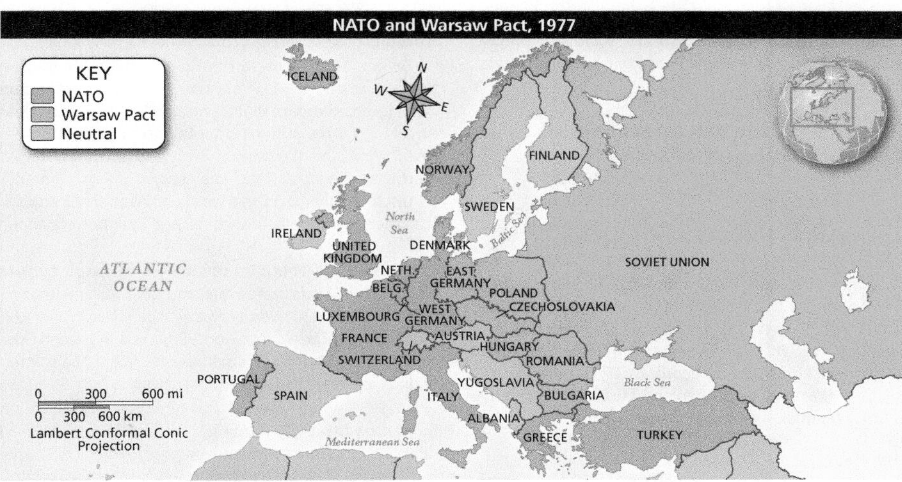

>> Though some countries remained neutral, in general, Western European nations were part of NATO, while Eastern European nations joined the Warsaw Pact. **Analyze Maps** Which Warsaw Pact countries bordered NATO nations?

imperialism. Yet, linked to those stands, both sides sought world power.

 **IDENTIFY MAIN IDEAS** Why did the United States establish the NATO alliance? What was the Soviet Union's response?

Two Opposing Sides in Europe

As the Cold War deepened, the superpowers—the United States and the Soviet Union—faced off against each other in Europe and around the world. For more than 40 years, the Cold War loomed over Europe. In general, the superpowers avoided direct confrontation. Yet several incidents brought Europe to the brink of war.

The Berlin Wall Berlin was a key focus of Cold War tensions. The city was divided into democratic West Berlin and communist East Berlin. In the 1950s, West Berlin became a showcase for West German prosperity. Unhappy with communism, many low-paid East Germans fled into West Berlin.

To stop the flight, the East German government built a wall in 1961 that separated the two sectors of the city. When completed, the Berlin Wall was a massive concrete barrier, topped with barbed wire and patrolled by guards. The wall showed that workers, far from enjoying a communist paradise, had to be forcibly kept from fleeing.

Revolts in Eastern Europe During the Cold War, the Soviet Union had more than 30 divisions of troops stationed across the region. Yet, in East Germany, Poland, Hungary, and elsewhere, unrest simmered. In 1953, about 50,000 workers confronted the Soviet army in the streets of the German capital. The uprising spread to other East German cities, but the protesters could not withstand Soviet tanks.

In 1956, economic woes in Poland touched off riots and strikes. To end the turmoil, the Polish government made some reforms, but dissatisfaction with communism remained. That year, Imre Nagy (nahj), a communist reformer and strong nationalist, gained power in Hungary. He ended one-party rule, ejected Soviet troops, and withdrew from the Warsaw Pact. In response, the Soviet Union invaded Hungary and ended the reforms. Nagy was later executed.

In early 1968, Czechoslovakian leader Alexander Dubcek introduced greater freedom of expression and limited democracy. This movement of freedom became known as the "Prague Spring." Soviet leaders feared

Analyze Information Remind students that East Germany (in 1953), Hungary (in 1956), and Czechoslovakia (in 1968) acted in defiance of Soviet rule. Have them describe the form each action took and how the Soviet Union responded. *(East Germany: Workers confronted the Soviet Army with street demonstrations; Soviet response: Soviet tanks restored order. Hungary: Imre Nagy ended Communist one-party rule, ejected Soviet troops, and withdrew from the Warsaw Pact; Soviet response: military invasion and execution of Nagy. Czechoslovakia: Alexander Dubcek introduced limited democracy; Soviet response: military assault.)*

Infer Ask students to answer the following question: Why do you think the Eastern Europeans continued to resist Communist rule? *(Answers will vary; most students will conclude that Eastern Europeans wanted more freedom, both economic and political, and didn't want to be ruled by another country.)*

Answers

Analyze Maps *Sample response: East Germany, Czechoslovakia, Romania*

Identify Main Ideas *to provide defense of its allies in Western Europe; The Soviet Union responded by creating the Warsaw Pact.*

English Language Proficiency Standards

Writing 5.C.3 Tell students that knowing spelling rules can help them prevent errors in their writing. Read aloud "Two Opposing Sides in Europe." Have students complete the activities below according to their level of English proficiency.

Beginning Explain spelling rules for adding a suffix to a base word. Show that in some cases, the base word remains unchanged, as in *power-ful* and *prosper-ity*. In other cases the spelling of the base word must change when a suffix is added, as in *early* + *-est* = *earliest*. Explain that the *y* had to be changed to an *i* before the suffix was added. Help students come up with other words that exemplify this rule, such as *beautiful* and *merriest*.

Intermediate Follow the initial instructions in the Beginning activity. Display the word *earliest,* and ask students to underline the base word and circle the suffix. Then display: *early* + *-est* = *earliest*. Help students see how the word changed.

Advanced Ask pairs of students to scan the text for words with suffixes, list them, and separate them into their base words and suffixes. Have them write a set of rules for adding suffixes to words, share their rules with the class, and work with other pairs to create a single set of rules for adding suffixes.

Advanced High Follow the instructions in the Advanced activity, but have students work individually.

Topic 19 Lesson 1

The Nuclear Arms Race

Tell students that the competition between the two superpowers during the Cold War resulted in many advances in technology, including military technology. Explain that many of these changes still affect our daily lives.

Online Project the **Interactive Gallery: Cold War Technologies**, and click through the images with students.

ACTIVE CLASSROOM

Review the gallery images, and then have students study the chart "Nuclear Arms Race." Form students into groups, and provide each with a key question based on information in the chart. Have students use the Circle Write strategy to write as much as they can for one minute, and then switch with the person on their right. The next person tries to improve or elaborate on the response where the other person left off. Continue to switch until the paper comes back to the first person. The group then decides which is the best composition (or response) and shares that with the larger group.

Guided Reading and Discussion

Ask students which of the inventions in the Interactive Gallery they believe had the greatest impact, and have them explain why. Group students by which invention they thought was most influential. Have students meet in their groups to write a group statement, combining the ideas of each student. Tell them to select one student to present their statement to the class. After all presentations, discuss the inventions as a class.

that democracy would threaten communist power and Soviet domination. Once again, the Soviets responded with force, sending Warsaw Pact troops to oust Dubcek and end the reforms.

IDENTIFY CAUSE AND EFFECT How was Europe divided following the end of World War II?

The Nuclear Arms Race

One of the most frightening aspects of the Cold War was the arms race. Each side wanted to be able to withstand an attack by the other. At first, the United States, which had the atomic bomb, was the only nuclear power. By 1949, however, the Soviet Union had also developed an atomic bomb. By 1953, both sides in the Cold War had developed the far more destructive military technology—the hydrogen bomb.

The Balance of Terror The United States and the Soviet Union spent vast sums to develop new, more deadly nuclear and conventional weapons. They invested still more to improve "delivery systems"—the bombers, missiles, and submarines to launch these terrifying weapons of mass destruction.

Critics of the arms race argued that a nuclear war would destroy both sides. Yet each superpower wanted to be able to deter the other from launching its nuclear weapons.

By the 1960s, the terrifying possibility of nuclear war led to the idea of mutually assured destruction (MAD), which meant that if one side launched a nuclear attack, the other side would retaliate in kind, and both sides would be destroyed. Even though MAD might discourage nuclear war, the fear of such a conflict haunted the world. In the words of Winston Churchill, the balance of power had become a "balance of terror."

Disarmament Talks To reduce the threat of nuclear war, the two sides met at disarmament talks. Although mutual distrust slowed progress, the rival powers did reach some agreements. In 1963, they agreed to the Nuclear Test Ban Treaty, which prohibited the testing of nuclear weapons in the atmosphere.

In 1969, the United States and the Soviet Union began the Strategic Arms Limitation Talks (SALT) to limit the number of nuclear weapons held by each side. In 1972 and 1979, both sides signed agreements setting these limits.

In 1991, the United States and Russia negotiated a Strategic Arms Reduction Treaty (START), which has been renewed in recent years. These START agreements led to the removal of a large number of nuclear weapons.

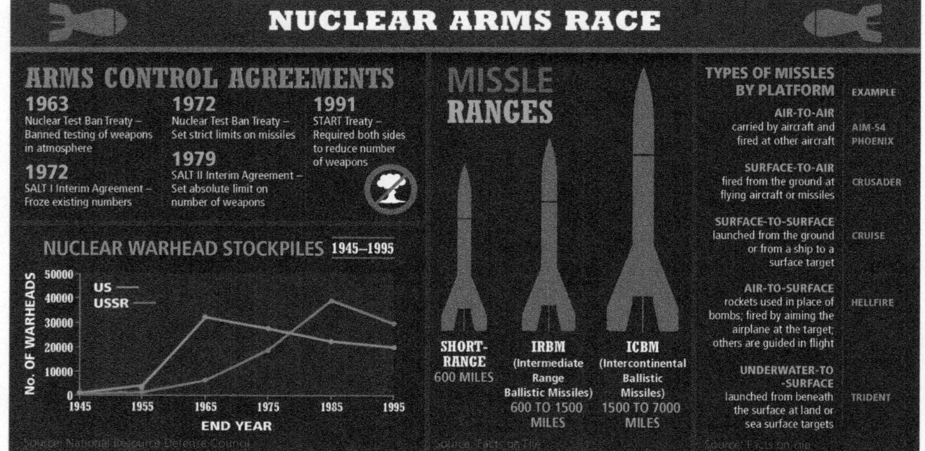

>> **Analyze Charts** Compare the Nuclear Test Ban Treaty of 1963, the SALT II Treaty of 1972, and the START Treaty of 1991. How did each of the later treaties advance beyond the treaty that came before it?

Interactive Gallery

Answers

Identify Cause and Effect *Europe was divided into a democratic region in the west and a communist region in the east.*

Analyze Charts *The Nuclear Test Ban Treaty banned only atmospheric testing; SALT II went on to limit the numbers of weapons; START required actual weapons reductions.*

An Era of Détente During the 1970s, American and Soviet leaders promoted an era of **détente** (day TAHNT), or relaxation of tensions. Détente brought new agreements to reduce nuclear stockpiles as both sides turned to diplomacy to resolve issues. The era of détente ended in 1979, when the Soviet Union invaded Afghanistan.

Limiting the Spread of Nuclear Weapons By the late 1960s, Britain, France, and China had developed their own nuclear weapons. By then, many world leaders were eager to stop the spread of nuclear weapons. In 1968, dozens of nations signed the Nuclear Non-Proliferation Treaty (NPT). They agreed not to develop nuclear weapons and cooperate in the peaceful use of nuclear energy.

INTEGRATE INFORMATION What factors discouraged the use of nuclear weapons in the Cold War?

"She Might Have Invaded Russia"

>> The Soviets responded to Czechoslovakia's "Prague Spring" with brute force. **Analyze Political Cartoons** According to the cartoon, why did the Soviet Union invade Czechoslovakia?

The Cold War Around the World

The superpowers waged the Cold War not only in Europe, but also around the world. By the end of World War II, the Soviets were helping communist forces in China, Korea, and elsewhere. The United States took action to respond to the global threat of communism.

Establishing Alliances and Bases To stop the spread of communism, the United States sought regional alliances with friendly powers. In Europe, it backed NATO. In Asia, the United States promoted another regional alliance, the Southeast-Asia Treaty Organization (SEATO). It included the United States, Britain, France, Australia, Pakistan, Thailand, New Zealand, and the Philippines.

The United States also formed military alliances with individual nations, such as Japan and South Korea. Often, these agreements included the right to set up American military bases. As a result, American bases circled the globe from North America to Europe, Asia, and the islands of the Pacific.

Meanwhile, the Soviet Union formed its own alliances. In addition to the Warsaw Pact in Europe, the Soviet Union formed alliances with newly independent nations in Africa and Asia. However, the Soviet Union had few bases overseas.

Where the Cold War Got Hot Because both superpowers had a global reach, local conflicts in many places played into the Cold War. Often, the United States and its allies supported one side, and the Soviet bloc supported the other. Through such struggles, the superpowers could confront each other indirectly, rather than head to head.

Political shifts around the world added to Cold War tensions. When communist forces won control of mainland China in 1949, the United States feared that a tide of communism would sweep around the world. During this period, European colonies in Africa and Asia battled for independence. Liberation leaders and guerrillas frequently sought help from one or the other Cold War power.

On occasion, the Cold War erupted into "shooting wars," especially in Asia. Both Korea and Vietnam were torn by brutal conflicts in which the United States, the Soviet Union, and China played crucial roles. More commonly, however, the superpowers provided weapons, training, or other aid to opposing forces in Asia, Africa, or Latin America.

The United States and Latin America The United States was especially concerned about the threat of communism in the Western Hemisphere. Seeing reform movements in Latin American countries as communist threats, it backed right-wing, anti-communist dictators and helped topple elected socialist leaders. In 1962,

Topic 19 Lesson 1

The Cold War Around the World

Ask students to define the term *Cold War*. *(a state of tension and hostility between the United States and the Soviet Union, which engaged in armed conflict only indirectly)* Tell them that they will be studying times when the Cold War got "hot" later in the Topic, but that the two superpowers came closest to direct conflict with each other during the Cuban missile crisis.

Online Project the **Interactive Gallery: The Cuban Missile Crisis**, and click through the images with students.

ACTIVE CLASSROOM

Have groups of students use the Graffiti Concepts strategy. Ask them to reflect on the meaning of the Cuban missile crisis and create a visual image and/or phrase that represents that event. Allow up to 5 minutes. Have students post their "graffiti" on the board or on chart paper, and ask them to look at the various responses. Then discuss similarities and differences in the responses as a group.

D Differentiate Challenge/Gifted Ask students to write a series of diary entries of a character they create who was living in the United States, Europe, or Cuba during the Cuban missile crisis. Tell them to use the events in the Interactive Gallery and think about how the character they create would have reacted to these events.

Answers

Integrate Information *Neither side wanted to start a nuclear war that would end in mutually assured destruction. Both sides eventually signed treaties to limit nuclear weapons.*

Analyze Political Cartoons *to prevent the idea of freedom from spreading to the Soviet people*

Topic 19 Lesson 1

Guided Reading and Discussion

Have students identify the various places where the Cold War got hot. Then ask them why the Cold War went global. *(Sample response: The two superpowers were competing with each other; if one superpower gained influence, the other wanted to counter that influence.)*

Cuba, a small island nation just 90 miles from Florida, became the chief focus of United States concern.

The Communist Revolution in Cuba In the 1950s, a young lawyer, **Fidel Castro,** organized an armed rebellion against the corrupt dictator who then ruled Cuba. By 1959, Castro had led his tiny guerrilla army to victory and set about transforming the country into a communist state.

During the Cuban Revolution, Castro nationalized, or took over, foreign-owned businesses. He put most land under government control and distributed the rest to peasant farmers. While Castro imposed harsh authoritarian rule, he did at first improve conditions for the poor. But Castro's revolution angered many Cubans, especially from the middle class. Critics were jailed or silenced. Hundreds of thousands of Cubans fled to the United States.

The United States, alarmed as Castro turned to the Soviet Union for support, attempted to bring down the communist regime next door. In 1961, President **John F. Kennedy** backed a plan by anti-Castro exiles to invade Cuba and lead an uprising against Castro.

The poorly planned plot was a disaster. An invasion force landed at the Bay of Pigs in Cuba, but was quickly crushed. News of the plot helped Castro rally Cuban popular opinion against foreign interference, and the bungled invasion hurt the reputation of the United States.

The Cuban Missile Crisis In 1962, the United States imposed a trade embargo on Cuba. Castro, seeking closer ties with the Soviet Union, let the Soviets build nuclear missile bases in Cuba. The threat of Soviet nuclear bases in its backyard outraged the United States and touched off a dangerous crisis.

In October 1962, President Kennedy imposed a naval blockade on Cuba. Kennedy demanded that the Soviet Union remove its nuclear missiles from Cuba, and for a few tense days, the world faced the risk of nuclear war. Finally, however, Soviet Premier Nikita Khrushchev backed down. He agreed to remove the Soviet missiles, but won a secret pledge from Kennedy to not invade Cuba.

MAKE GENERALIZATIONS How did the United States and the Soviet Union confront each other around the world during the Cold War?

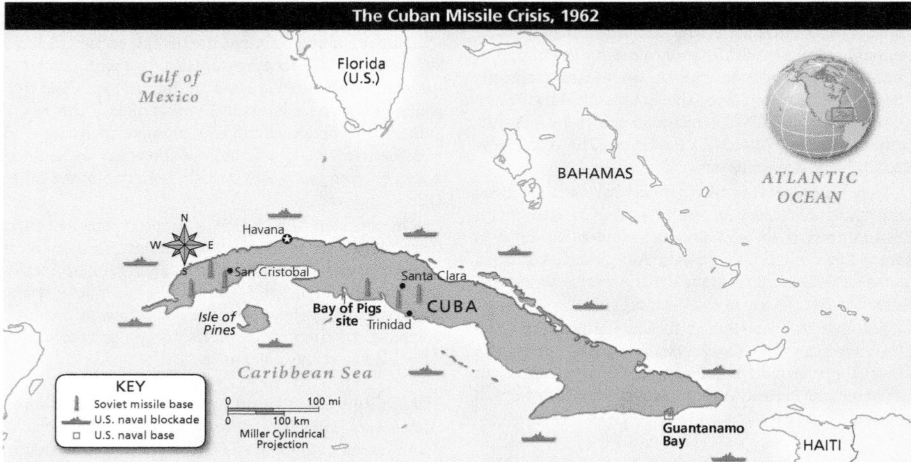

>> **Analyze Maps** Missiles launched from Cuba could strike many areas of the eastern United States in minutes. Where is the U.S. naval base in Cuba located?

Interactive Gallery

Answers

Analyze Maps *Guantánamo Bay*

Make Generalizations *The two nations confronted each other militarily by supporting opposing sides in local conflicts, and politically by assembling opposing alliances.*

The Soviet Union During the Cold War

Victory in World War II brought few rewards to the Soviet people. Stalin continued his ruthless policies. He filled labor camps with "enemies of the state" and seemed ready to launch new purges when he died in 1953.

Soviet Communism In the Soviet Union, the government controlled most aspects of public life. Communists valued obedience, discipline, and economic security. They sought to spread their communist **ideology,** or value systems and beliefs, around the globe.

The Soviet Union also aimed to spread its command economy to other countries. In a command economy, the government makes most economic decisions. A huge bureaucracy, rather than supply and demand, decided what to produce, how much, and for whom. Government planners in Moscow often had little knowledge of local conditions. The government owned most of the property.

Collectivized agriculture remained so unproductive that the Soviet Union often had to import grain to feed its people. Nor could Russia's command economy match the free-market economies of the West in producing consumer goods. Since workers had lifetime job security, they had little incentive, or reason, to produce better-quality goods.

Stalin's Successors After Stalin's death in 1953, **Nikita Khrushchev** (KROOSH chawf) emerged as the new Soviet leader. In 1956, he shocked top Communist Party members when he publicly denounced Stalin's abuse of power. Khrushchev maintained the Communist Party's tight political control, but he closed prison camps and eased censorship. He called for a "peaceful coexistence" with the West.

Khrushchev's successor, **Leonid Brezhnev** (BREZH nef), held power from the mid-1960s until he died in 1982. Under Brezhnev, dissidents, or people who criticized the government, faced arrest and imprisonment.

Dissidents Resist Despite the risk of harsh punishment, some courageous people dared to criticize the government. Andrei Sakharov (SAH kuh rawf), a brilliant physicist, spoke out against human rights abuses. He was exiled to a remote Soviet city.

Another critic, Aleksandr Solzhenitsyn (sohl zhuh NEET sin), wrote a letter to a friend criticizing Stalin. He was sent to a prison camp. Under Khrushchev, he was released and wrote fictional works that drew on his experiences in Soviet prison camps. His writings

>> The Soviet Union celebrated the anniversary of the Bolshevik Revolution with this military parade in Moscow in 1969.

were banned in the Soviet Union, and in 1974, he was deported to West Germany. Despite the government's actions, Sakharov and Solzhenitsyn inspired others to resist communist repression and demand greater freedom.

CHECK UNDERSTANDING How did the Soviet Union handle critics of its policies?

The United States in the Cold War

The Cold War was not just a military rivalry. It was also a competition between two contrasting economic and political value systems. Unlike the communist countries, the democratic, capitalist countries, led by the United States, gave citizens the freedom to make economic and political choices. These nations valued freedom and prosperity. They held that economic freedom and free market principles helped improve the human condition—especially compared to the command economies of the communist world.

Free Markets While communist countries had command economies, capitalist countries had market economies. In market economies, producers and

The Soviet Union During the Cold War

The United States in the Cold War

Turn students' attention to the image of a military parade in Moscow. Ask them to recall how the Soviets gained power in Eastern Europe *(by force)* and how they kept the members of the Warsaw Pact loyal. *(through force, threats of force, and intimidation)* Explain to students that the difference in how the Soviets and Americans treated their allies and their citizens had much to do with their differing political and economic value systems. Ask students to formulate generalizations about how economic freedom improved the human condition. *(Sample responses: It allowed people choice and provided opportunity in both the economic and political realms. It promoted prosperity and growth. It rewarded effort and success.)*

Guided Reading and Discussion

Have students explain how the actions of the United States and the Soviet Union during the Cold War were similar and how they were different. *(Similarities: Both spied on one another, sent disloyal people to prison, stockpiled nuclear weapons, sought allies all over the world, and countered the other's gains. Differences: The Soviet Union didn't allow people to speak freely and imprisoned people for years for speaking out; it also repressed any revolt against communist governments. The United States allowed far greater freedoms and supported its allies with economic aid.)*

Answers

Check Understanding *The Soviet government arrested and imprisoned critics of its policies.*

Topic 19 Lesson 1

SYNTHESIZE

Online Project the **Digital Activity: Actions and Consequences of the Cold War**. Ask students to create and fill in a four-column graphic organizer on Cold War actions and consequences by the United States, Western Europe, Eastern Europe, and the Soviet Union. Time constraints will limit the number of answers students can list. *(Answers will vary.)*

Interpret Ask students to answer this question, using evidence from the graphic organizer: Who benefited most from the events of the Cold War? Why? *(Answers will vary, but students should support their answers with evidence from the text.)*

DEMONSTRATE

Online Assign the **Digital Lesson Quiz** for this lesson if you haven't already done so. Students will be offered automatic remediation or enrichment based on their score.

Pose the following to the class on the Discussion Board:

In "A New Global Conflict," you read about the tensions that drove the World War II allies apart and led to the beginning of the Cold War. The Cold War was rooted in the competing value systems and worldviews of the United States and the Soviet Union and their allies.

Support a Point of View With Evidence Was the United States right to try to contain communism during the Cold War? Why or why not?

Analyze Information Were arms control agreements necessary? Were they successful in meeting their goals?

Topic Inquiry

Have students continue their investigations for the Topic Inquiry.

Answers

Distinguish *The United States sought to remove communist influences at home and followed a policy of containment to check Soviet power around the world.*

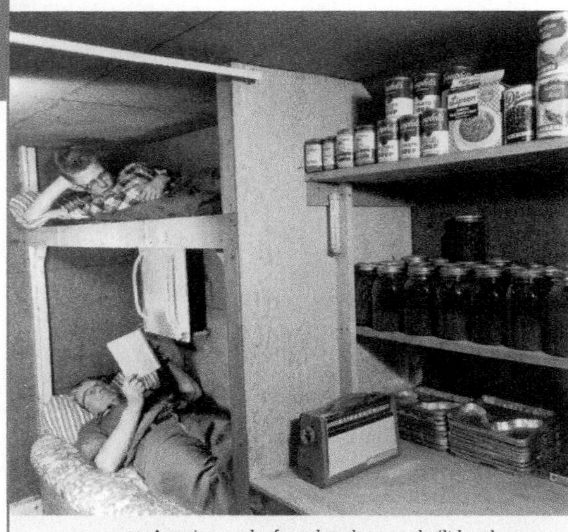

>> Americans who feared nuclear war built bomb shelters in their backyards and stocked them with canned goods and other supplies.

consumers make economic decisions. Prices are based on supply and demand in a free market. Property is privately owned. Producers compete to offer the best products for the lowest prices. By deciding what to buy, consumers ultimately decide which products are produced. In a free enterprise system, producers who win consumers' business make profits and grow.

The United States economy is basically a market economy. However, the United States and Western Europe have what can be called mixed economies, because their governments have an economic role.

The Cold War at Home Early in the Cold War, fierce anti-communists in the United States warned that Soviet agents were operating everywhere within the country. The House Un-American Activities Committee (HUAC) led a campaign to identify supposed communist sympathizers. In the early 1950s, Senator Joseph McCarthy charged many innocent citizens with harboring communist sympathies. Government probes produced little evidence of subversion. Eventually, the Senate condemned McCarthy's reckless behavior, but not before his charges and the investigations of the HUAC had ruined the careers of thousands of Americans.

The fear of a nuclear war also affected Americans. Some families built fallout shelters, where they could hide in the event of a nuclear bomb. Schools conducted air-raid drills in which children were taught to duck under their desks. Although these measures would not have protected children in a nuclear attack, the drills reflected the widespread fear of nuclear war.

? DISTINGUISH How did the United States respond to the threat of communism at home and around the world?

ASSESSMENT

1. **Identify Central Ideas** What foreign policy did the United States establish with the Truman Doctrine?
2. **Make Generalizations** What kinds of conflicts resulted from the global confrontation between the two superpowers?
3. **Infer** How did the buildup of nuclear weapons discourage their actual use?
4. **Cite Evidence** List three occasions when the Soviet Union put down revolts in Eastern Europe during the Cold War.
5. **Compare and Contrast** How were the United States and the Soviet Union alike during the Cold War? How were they different?

Assessment

1. a policy of containment: intervention in foreign conflicts to support allies and limit the spread of communism
2. Tense struggles for influence developed in many parts of the world; a few of these flared into actual military conflicts.
3. It made each side in the Cold War resist using nuclear weapons for fear of unleashing a devastating nuclear attack.
4. East Germany, 1953; Hungary, 1956; Czechoslovakia, 1968
5. The United States and the Soviet Union both feared each other and tried to influence other nations. They built up their nuclear arsenals but then worked to limit them through treaties. Both established alliances for protection, and each supported opposing sides in global conflicts between communism and democracy. The United States had a capitalist economy and political freedoms. The Soviet Union had a command economy and very few political freedoms.

19.2 Despite the tensions of the Cold War, the United States enjoyed a period of great prosperity and growth in the postwar decades. Its booming economy became a symbol of the power of capitalism and democratic freedoms in the ongoing propaganda war against communism.

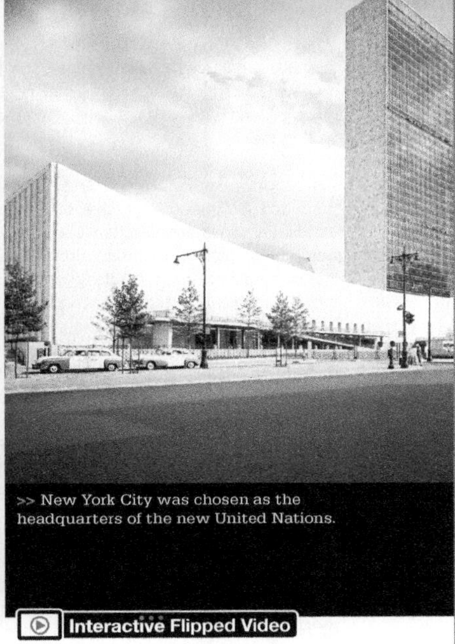

>> New York City was chosen as the headquarters of the new United Nations.

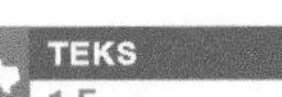 Interactive Flipped Video

The Western Democracies and Japan

TEKS
1.F

>> **Objectives**

Analyze the postwar American economy.

Identify developments in American society and government.

Explain how Western Europe rebuilt and moved toward greater unity.

Describe how Japan changed after World War II.

>> **Key Terms**

suburbanization
interdependence
recession
segregation
discrimination
Dr. Martin Luther King, Jr.
Konrad Adenauer
welfare state
Margaret Thatcher
European Union
gross domestic product (GDP)

Postwar Prosperity in the United States

In the postwar decades, the American economic system flourished. American businesses expanded into markets around the globe. The dollar was the world's strongest currency. Foreigners flocked to invest in American industry and to buy U.S. government bonds. America's wealth was a model for other democracies and a challenge to the stagnant economies of the communist world.

America in a Central Role During the Cold War, the United States was a global political leader. The headquarters of the League of Nations had been symbolically located in neutral Switzerland. The headquarters of the newly formed United Nations was built in New York City.

The United States also played a leading economic role. America had emerged untouched from the horrendous destruction of the Second World War. Other nations needed American goods and

PEARSON realize. www.PearsonTexas.com Access your Digital Lesson.

Aa Vocabulary Builder

1. Have students pronounce the following academic vocabulary term in this lesson and clarify the part of speech. Break the term into syllables and pronounce it with the students.
2. Explain what the word means in common "student-friendly" language using synonyms and antonyms when possible. Provide concrete examples to clarify the meaning, and rephrase the definition.

prospered: succeeded, thrived, did well

Topic 19 Lesson 2

The Western Democracies and Japan

CONNECT

Preview Have students preview the **Lesson Objectives** and the list of **Key Terms**.

Students can also preview all the **Key Terms** and **Academic Vocabulary** using the **Interactive Reading Notepad** on the digital course or preview a summary of the lesson in the **Reading and Note Taking Study Guide**.

Online Use the **Editable Presentation** found on the digital course to present the main ideas for this lesson.

Start Up Activity

Tell students that bombs destroyed large parts of many European cities during World War II. Ask: What challenges would residents of a city face after such heavy destruction? Discuss whether the United States should play a role in Germany's rebuilding.

Online You can also project the **Start Up Activity** from the course.

INVESTIGATE

Have students read the lesson using the **Reading and Note Taking Study Guide** to help them take notes and understand the text as they read.

Postwar Prosperity in the United States

Tell students that in the decades following World War II, the economy of the United States—which had avoided physical destruction during the war—boomed. Americans bought new homes, cars, and appliances. Many moved to the suburbs. The United States established itself as a global economic, political, and military leader.

Topic 19 Lesson 2

Online Project the **Interactive Gallery: Suburbanization in Postwar America**, and click through the images with students.

ACTIVE CLASSROOM

Use the Take a Stand strategy. Ask students to take a stand on the following statement: American society was changed for the better during the 1950s. Have students divide into two groups based on their position and move to separate areas of the classroom. Tell them to talk with each other to compare their reasons for their position. Ask a representative from each side to present and defend the group's point of view.

Key Terms

Ask students to find the key term **suburbanization** (in bold) in the text. Explain that the word *suburban* comes from the Latin words *sub* ("near") and *urbs* ("city"). The ending *-ization* ("process") is the final clue to the word's meaning: "the process of building up areas near a city."

Guided Reading and Discussion

Ask students to explain how the postwar economic boom affected social systems in the United States. *(For the first time, large numbers of Americans could afford to buy cars and homes, and they moved to the suburbs. Many also moved to the Sunbelt, where jobs were becoming more plentiful.)*

services, and foreign trade helped the United States achieve a long postwar boom. The long postwar peace among democratic nations helped to spread this boom worldwide.

An Economic Boom In 1945, the United States produced 50 percent of the world's manufactured goods. Factories soon shifted from making tanks and bombers to peacetime production. With the Cold War looming, government military spending increased, creating many jobs in defense industries.

During the 1950s and 1960s, the American economy was booming. At home, a growing population demanded homes, cars, refrigerators, and thousands of other products. Overseas, American businesses were investing in Europe's recovery and expanding into new markets. American cultural influences spread, and people around the globe enjoyed American movies, television programs, and music—especially jazz and rock and roll.

America's postwar economic strength impacted social systems in the United States. Although segments of the population were left behind, many Americans grew more affluent and moved from the cities to the suburbs. The movement to communities outside an urban core is known as **suburbanization.**

>> In the postwar boom, Americans moved out of the cities and into the suburbs, where they could own a home with a yard. **Connect** What role did the car play in the suburbanization of America?

Interactive Gallery

Suburbanites typically lived in single-family houses with lawns and access to good schools. Suburban highways allowed residents to commute to work by car.

During the postwar decades, many Americans also moved to the Sunbelt, or the states in the South and Southwest of the United States. Jobs in these states were becoming more plentiful than in the industrialized North. The warmer climate was an added bonus. The availability of air conditioning and water for irrigation helped make the movement to the Sunbelt possible.

A Wider Role for Government In the postwar decades, the government's role in the economy grew. Under President Truman, Congress created generous benefits that helped veterans attend college or buy homes. Other Truman programs expanded FDR's New Deal, providing greater security for the elderly and poor.

Truman's successor, Dwight Eisenhower, tried to reduce the government's role in the economy. At the same time, he approved government funding to build a vast interstate highway system. This program spurred the growth of the auto, trucking, and related industries. Highways and home building changed the face of the nation. Suburbanization led to the decay of many inner-city neighborhoods.

The United States and the Global Economy In the postwar decades, the United States profited from the growing global economy. But **interdependence**—mutual dependence of countries on goods, resources, and knowledge from other parts of the world—brought problems, too. In the 1970s, a political crisis in the Middle East led to a global oil shortage and soaring oil prices. In the United States, people waited in long lines for costly gasoline, which made Americans aware of how much they relied on imported oil.

The oil crisis and other economic issues brought periods of **recession,** or economic downturn. For the most part, recessions were fairly mild.

Other economic issues, however, such as competition from nations in Asia and elsewhere posed challenges for the United States. During the 1980s, the United States lost manufacturing jobs to Asia and Latin America. Some American corporations even moved their operations overseas to take advantage of lower wages.

Still, the United States remained a rich nation and a magnet for immigrants. These newcomers came largely from Latin America and Asia. By the 1980s, some Americans were calling for stricter laws to halt illegal immigration.

? How was the U.S. economy linked to the broader global economy during the Cold War?

English Language Proficiency Standards

Learning Strategies 1.B.1 Help students practice self-correcting techniques to improve their speaking skills. Read or have students read "Postwar Prosperity in the United States" aloud.

Beginning Create a concept web on the American postwar economy. Ask students to use the information on the web to complete this sentence frame: The American economy prospered after World War II because ________. Repeat their answers, and correct errors.

Intermediate Complete the Beginning activity, but have students use the web to explain why the United States became an economic leader after World War II. Repeat their answers, and correct errors.

Advanced Complete the Intermediate activity in pairs. Have pairs repeat answers back to each other, correcting any speaking or grammatical errors.

Advanced High Complete the Intermediate activity, but with small groups.

Answers

Connect *People were able to commute by car from their suburban homes, and highways, shopping centers, and parking lots were built to accommodate cars and their drivers.*

Identify Cause and Effect *The U.S. economy relied on sales in overseas markets. It also needed oil produced overseas, so it suffered when oil prices rose in the 1970s.*

ELPS **ELPS 1.B.1** Take turns reading the sections of *Postwar Prosperity in the United States* aloud with a partner. After each turn, discuss how your reading relates to America's postwar economy. Correct any speaking errors made during your discussion.

The United States Responds to New Challenges

The 1950s seemed a peaceful time within the United States. Yet changes were underway that would reshape American society. Among the most far-reaching was the Civil Rights Movement, which sought to ensure the promise of equal opportunity for all Americans.

The Civil Rights Movement Although African Americans had won freedom nearly a century before, many states, especially in the South, denied them equality. **Segregation,** or forced separation, was legal in education and housing. African Americans also faced **discrimination,** or unequal treatment and barriers, in jobs and voting. The Civil Rights Movement of the 1950s and 1960s renewed earlier efforts to end racial injustice.

In 1954, the Supreme Court issued a landmark ruling in *Brown* v. *Board of Education of Topeka*. It declared that segregated schools were unconstitutional. President Eisenhower and his successors used federal power to uphold the order to desegregate public schools.

Martin Luther King, Jr. By 1956, a gifted preacher, **Dr. Martin Luther King, Jr.,** had emerged as a leader of the Civil Rights Movement. Inspired by Gandhi's campaign of civil disobedience in India, King organized boycotts and led peaceful marches to end segregation in the United States. Many Americans of all races joined the Civil Rights Movement. Their courage in the face of sometimes brutal attacks stirred the nation's conscience.

In 1963, at a huge civil rights rally, King made a stirring speech. "I have a dream," he proclaimed, "that one day this nation will rise up and live out the true meaning of its creed: 'We hold these truths to be self-evident, that all men are created equal.'"

Progress and Problems In time, Congress responded. It outlawed segregation in public accommodations, protected the rights of black voters, and required equal access to housing and jobs. Despite these victories, racial prejudice survived, and African Americans faced many economic obstacles. Poverty and unemployment

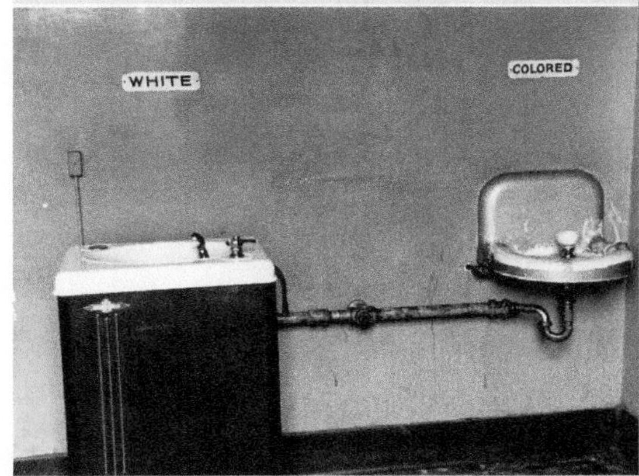

>> Segregated drinking fountains were a common sight in the southern states.

>> People from all over the country came to the March on Washington, held on August 28, 1963. Martin Luther King Jr. was a keynote speaker. **Analyze Information** How do the demands on the signs represent the civil rights movement?

The United States Responds to New Challenges

Tell students that in the 1950s, the civil rights movement grew in numbers and influence. Members of the movement sought equal opportunity for African Americans and an end to racial injustice, especially in the form of segregation. Their work brought some progress. A Supreme Court ruling in 1954 declared segregated schools unconstitutional. Congress later enacted laws protecting voting rights and guaranteeing equal access to housing and jobs.

Analyze Images

Have students look at the image of the drinking fountains. Ask them what else the photograph suggests about the quality of the water in these segregated drinking fountains. *(Students might speculate that the large base of the "White" fountain means that the water in that fountain has been cooled and filtered.)*

D Differentiate **Challenge/Gifted** Have students read the "Letter from Birmingham Jail," the "I Have a Dream" speech, and the biography of Dr. Martin Luther King, Jr. Ask them to write a question they would have liked to ask King. As part of a class discussion, have the class answer the questions written by the students.

Answers

Analyze Information *They show several of the movement's goals: integrated schools, jobs, and equal rights.*

English Language Proficiency Standards

Writing 5.D.1 Read "The United States Responds to New Challenges" aloud. For the following activities, use the following sentences: (1) By 1956, a gifted preacher, Dr. Martin Luther King, Jr., had/have emerged as a leader of the civil rights movement. (2) However, some was/were elected to political office or gained top jobs in business or the military.

Beginning Review the subject-verb agreement rule, and explain that it applies to sentences written in the past tense that also use helping verbs. Highlight examples 1 and 2 from the text, given above. Underline the subject and verb in each sentence. Then help students circle the helping verb. Explain how it agrees with the subject.

Intermediate Follow the instructions in the Beginning activity, but have students underline the subject and verb in each sentence and circle the correct helping verb.

Advanced Follow the instructions in the Intermediate activity, but have pairs of students locate examples in the text and write them out. Pairs should underline the subject and verb in each sentence and explain how the verb agrees with the subject.

Advanced High Have students work individually to follow the instructions in the Advanced activity.

Guided Reading and Discussion

Ask students what the difference is between segregation and discrimination. *(Segregation is a form of legal discrimination involving separation of the races, such as in education or housing. Discrimination on its own is unfair or unequal treatment, or barriers.)* Form students into small groups. Ask each group to brainstorm about other groups that experienced discrimination. *(Latinos, Asians, people with disabilities, Native Americans)* Ask groups to come up with two different ways in which people could protest against discrimination today, besides protest marches. *(Sample responses: through product or service boycotts; through social media)*

Rebuilding Western Europe

Tell students that by the 1950s, thanks in part to the Marshall Plan, Western Europe's economies were growing. West Germany was a special case. Although its people suffered greatly for several years after the war, West Germany rebuilt its cities and developed a robust industrial economy. Britain and other nations of Western Europe also recovered quickly and, through economic cooperation, laid the groundwork for future prosperity and peace.

plagued African American communities in urban areas.

Still, the Civil Rights Movement provided wider opportunities. Many African Americans won elected offices or gained top jobs in business and the military.

Other Groups Demand Equality The Civil Rights Movement inspired other groups, such as Native Americans and Latinos, to campaign for equality. Women, too, renewed their efforts to gain equal rights. New civil rights laws banned discrimination based on gender as well as race in hiring and promotion. More women won political office, and some made progress into high positions in business.

The Great Society During the 1960s, the government further expanded social programs to help the poor and disadvantaged. President Lyndon Johnson created a program that he called the Great Society. It funded Medicare, which ensured health care for the elderly, job training and low-cost housing for the poor, and support for education. Many Americans came to rely on these programs in the next decades.

The Conservative Response In the 1980s, conservatives challenged costly social programs and the growth of government. President Ronald Reagan called for cutbacks in government spending on social programs. Congress ended some welfare programs, reduced government regulation of the economy, and cut taxes. At the same time, military spending increased.

Government spending and tax cuts greatly increased the national deficit, the gap between what a government spends and what it takes in through taxes and other sources. As the deficit grew, conservatives crusaded for deeper cuts in social and economic programs. Debate raged about how far to cut spending on programs ranging from education and welfare to environmental protection.

CITE EXAMPLES Over time, how did the U.S. government expand opportunities for individuals? Give examples.

Rebuilding Western Europe

The impact of—and recovery from—World War II on the political and economic systems of Europe was profound. With Marshall Plan aid from the United States, Western European countries recovered from World War II. They rebuilt industries, farms, and transportation networks destroyed during the war. In the 1950s, economies in Western Europe boomed. Standards of living rose

U.S. Military Spending, 1960-1980

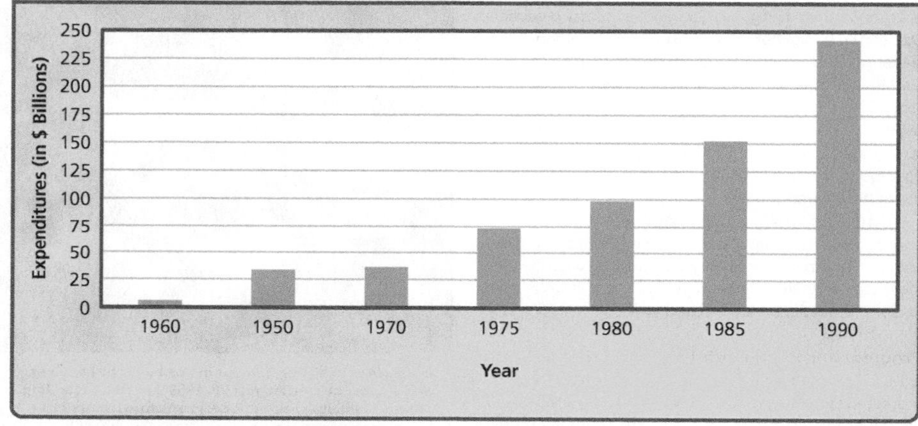

>> **Analyze Charts** U.S. military spending increased dramatically during the Cold War years. In which five-year period did military spending increase the most?

History Background

The Vision of Lyndon B. Johnson The tall Texan dreamed of ridding the United States of poverty and inequality. When Lyndon B. Johnson became president, he oversaw sweeping social reforms. First, he helped get President John F. Kennedy's pending legislation passed. The Civil Rights Act of 1964 outlawed discrimination. The Voting Rights Act of 1965 and the Twenty-Fourth Amendment to the Constitution expanded the right to vote. Johnson added his own vision, the Great Society, and declared a war on poverty. The first piece of legislation in this effort, the Economic Opportunity Act of 1964, introduced Medicare and Medicaid. Yet Johnson's programs did not do enough to mend the fractured society. The culture would continue to break apart over politics, the war in Vietnam, racism, and other issues.

Answers

Analyze Charts *1985–1990*

Cite Examples *The U.S. government stepped in to end segregation and discrimination; to improve life for veterans, the elderly, and the poor; and to expand transportation and housing opportunities.*

EAST AND WEST GERMANY IN 1968 AN ECONOMIC COMPARISON

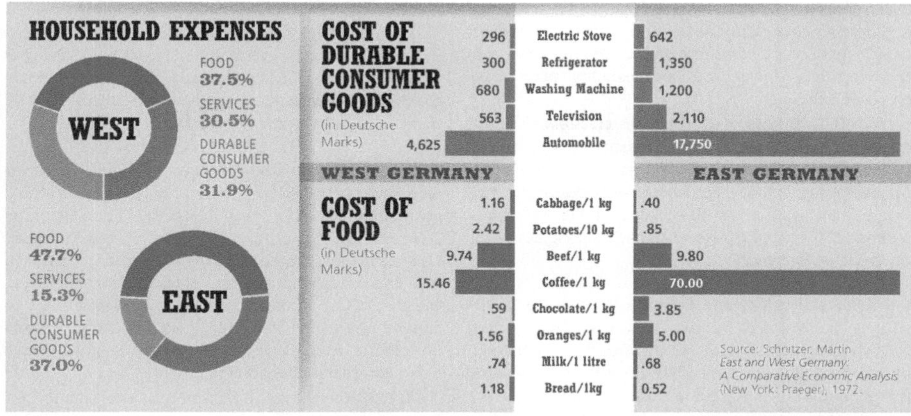

>> **Analyze Charts** What types of goods were expensive in East Germany in 1968? What types of goods were inexpensive?

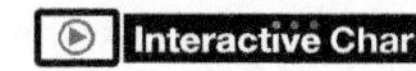

dramatically, and people began to enjoy comforts unheard of in earlier times.

West Germany's Economic Miracle The early postwar years were a desperate time for Germany. People were starving amid a landscape of destruction. The Cold War left Germany divided. West Germany was a member of the Western alliance. East Germany lay in the Soviet orbit. Over the next decades, differences between the two Germanys widened.

Early on, the United States rushed aid to West Germany in order to strengthen it against the communist tide sweeping Eastern Europe. From 1949 to 1963, a strong-minded chancellor, **Konrad Adenauer** (AD eh now er), led West Germans as they rebuilt cities, factories, and trade.

Despite high taxes to pay for the recovery, West Germany created a booming industrial economy. This "economic miracle" raised European fears of a German revival. But West German leaders worked closely with France and the United States in NATO and other international organizations.

While West Germany remained a capitalist country, some later chancellors belonged to the Socialist party. They expanded the **welfare state.** Under this political system, a government keeps most features of a capitalist economy but takes much responsibility for the social and economic needs of its people. In the welfare state, a government provides national health care, unemployment insurance, old-age pensions, and support for qualified students to attend college.

Germany Reunites The postwar decades brought no economic miracle to East Germany. Under communist rule, its economy stagnated. The Soviet Union exploited East German workers and industry for its own benefit. Still, unemployment was low, and East German workers had some basic benefits such as health care and free education.

By 1989, communism was declining in the Soviet Union. Without Soviet power to back them, East Germany's communist leaders were forced out of office. The Berlin Wall was torn down, and in 1990, Germany was reunited.

While Germans welcomed unity, the change brought new challenges. Prosperous West Germans had to pay higher taxes to finance the rebuilding of the east. At the same time, East Germans faced a difficult transition to a market economy.

Britain Recovers World War II left Britain physically battered and economically drained. After the war, Britain could no longer afford its overseas colonies, which demanded independence. Britain gave up global leadership to its close ally, the United States.

The war also impacted the British political system. After the war, British voters elected a Labour Party

Online Project the **Interactive Chart: Free Market Economy vs. Command Economy**, and drag and drop the labels with students.

ACTIVE CLASSROOM

Use the Circle Write strategy. Have groups of four students sit in a circle. One student will respond to this prompt: America's rebuilding after World War II differed from Western Europe's rebuilding because ______________. Have students write as much as they can for one minute and then switch papers with the person on their right. The next person tries to improve or elaborate on the response where the other person left off. Continue to switch until the paper comes back to the first person. The group can then decide which is the best composition (or response) and share it with the larger group.

Guided Reading and Discussion

Remind students that after the war, Britain's Labour Party began building a welfare state. Later, the Conservative party, led by Margaret Thatcher, set out to roll back the welfare state. Ask students to write a paragraph summarizing the positive and negative aspects of the welfare state. *(Paragraphs will vary but may mention free or low-cost housing, education, and services and high tax rates.)*

Answers

Analyze Charts *Sample response: expensive—automobiles, coffee; inexpensive—potatoes, milk*

Topic 19 Lesson 2

Japan Is Transformed

Point out the image of Japanese factory workers on page 855 of the text. Ask: How did World War II end in Asia? *(with the dropping of atomic bombs on Hiroshima and Nagasaki)* Explain that the United States then helped rebuild Japan during the occupation and helped set up a democratic political system and a free enterprise economic system. Then ask students what Japan manufactures today. *(Sample responses: cars and motorcycles; televisions; electronics)*

government, which began building a welfare state. The government nationalized industries and expanded social welfare benefits. It built housing for the poor and opened new state-funded universities. A national health service extended free or low-cost medical care to all citizens. To pay for these benefits, taxes rose tremendously.

By 1979, Britain and the rest of Europe faced economic hard times. Britain's Conservative party, led by **Margaret Thatcher,** won power and set out to roll back the welfare state. Thatcher privatized government-run industries, curbed the power of labor unions, reduced the size of the government bureaucracy, and cut back welfare services.

Other Western Nations Achieve Prosperity Other nations in Western Europe, including France, the Netherlands, and Belgium, rebuilt after the war, helped by Marshall Plan aid. Like Britain, these Europeans powers had to give up their overseas colonial empires. France faced bloody conflicts in Vietnam and Algeria, which it tried to hold on to in the face of nationalist demands for independence.

The Scandinavian countries of Norway, Sweden, and Denmark created extensive socialist welfare programs. By the 1990s, rising costs revived debate about how much people were willing to pay for the welfare state. Yet many peoples saw these social programs as essential to a democratic society.

Postwar Italy faced many challenges, including a multiparty political system that led to frequent changes of government. Corruption and financial scandals shook the government. Despite these problems, Italy made impressive economic gains.

Building the European Union Europe's postwar recovery was helped by economic cooperation. In 1952, six nations—West Germany, the Netherlands, Belgium, Luxembourg, France, and Italy—set up the European Coal and Steel Community. It eased barriers to trade in coal and steel, which spurred economic growth. Later, these nations formed the European Community to expand free trade. Over time, it ended tariffs, or taxes on imports, and allowed workers and capital to move freely across national borders.

In 1993, the European Community was renamed the **European Union** (EU). Since then, it has expanded to include 28 nations, including Britain, Ireland, Denmark, and other European countries. The EU set up a common currency, the euro, which is used by 17 European nations. The EU became a powerful economic force and promoted regional trade and peace by replacing destructive competition with an amazing degree of cooperation.

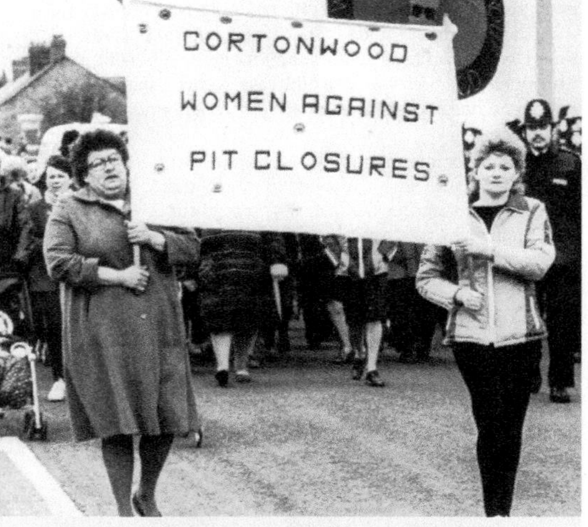

>> British miners protest the closure of a government-operated coal mine. Many British industries were once again privatized under Prime Minister Margaret Thatcher.

COMPARE What are some advantages and disadvantages of the welfare state in Europe?

Japan Is Transformed

In 1945, Japan, like Germany, lay in ruins. It had suffered perhaps the most devastating damage of any nation involved in World War II. Tens of thousands of Japanese were homeless and hungry.

Occupation Bring Changes The war had a deep impact on the political system of Japan. Under General Douglas MacArthur, the American military government set two main goals for the occupation of Japan: to destroy militarism and to ensure democratic government. Japan's armed forces were disbanded. War crime trials were held to punish those responsible for wartime atrocities.

In 1946, Japan adopted a new constitution, which set up a parliamentary democracy. Although the Japanese emperor lost all political power, he remained the symbolic head of the nation. Japan renounced war and banned any military forces, except for its own defense.

Answers

Compare *Advantages included expanded social benefits such as old-age pensions and unemployment insurance. Disadvantages included higher taxes and greater governmental regulation, or control of industry.*

To build Japanese democracy, American occupying forces backed changes to the economic and social systems. They opened the education system to all people and emphasized legal equality for women. A land-reform program bought out large landowners and gave land to tenant farmers, erasing lingering traces of feudalism in Japan. Other reforms protected the rights of workers.

Japan and the Cold War By 1950, Japan was on the road to recovery. At the same time, the Cold War was making the United States eager to end the occupation. As the Cold War erupted into armed conflict in nearby Korea, the United States and Japan signed a peace treaty, and in 1952, the occupation ended.

Japan and the United States had close ties during the Cold War. The American military operated out of bases that they had set up in Japan, while Japan enjoyed the protection of the American "nuclear umbrella." The two nations were trading partners, and in time, competitors for global markets.

>> The American occupation of Japan lasted about seven years and resulted in a firm friendship between the former enemies.

The Japanese Economic Miracle Between 1950 and 1975, Japan produced its own economic miracle, even more spectacular than Germany's. It chalked up huge jumps in **gross domestic product (GDP).** GDP is the total value of all goods and services produced by a nation in a particular year.

Japan's success was built on producing goods for export. At first, it manufactured textiles. Later, it shifted to selling steel and machinery. By the 1970s, Japanese cars, cameras, and televisions found eager buyers on the world market. Soon, a wide range of Japanese electronic goods were competing with Western, and especially American, products.

Japan's economic miracle was due in part to its new modern factories built after the war. Because Japan spent little on its military, it could invest more in its economy. It benefited from an educated and skilled workforce and imposed tariffs and regulations that limited imports and helped Japanese manufacturers at home.

By the 1980s, Japan was seen as an economic superpower. Its vast trade network reached around the world and resulted in a trade surplus for Japan. United States manufacturers claimed that the competition was unfair. Japan's stunning economic growth ended in the 1990s. However, it continued as a major world economic power.

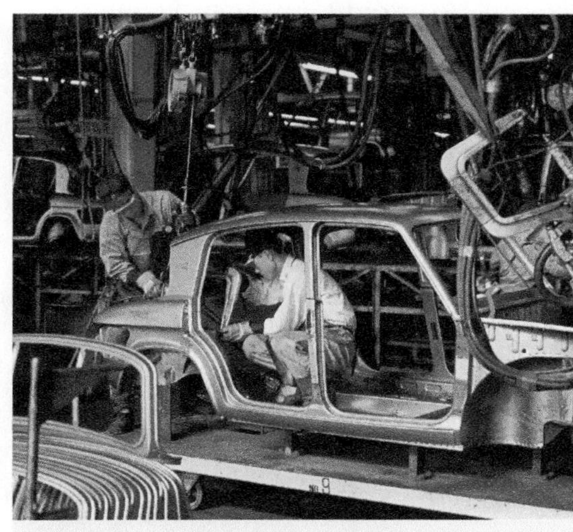

>> Japan became an export powerhouse by building cars, electronics, and other products.

IDENTIFY What factors explain Japan's economic success in the decades after World War II?

Guided Reading and Discussion

Have students work with a partner. Ask one student in each pair to cite benefits to the Japanese of the economic, political, and societal rebuilding after World War II. *(Sample response: new factories, democratic systems, rights for women)* Ask the other to cite benefits of the continuing relationship with the United States. *(military protection, markets for their products)* Ask each pair to answer the following question: How did Japan change after the war? Discuss the question as a class.

Answers

Identify *Japan's economic success was due to U.S. military protection and economic assistance, the opportunity to build modern industries after wartime destruction, an educated and skilled workforce, and government regulation of industry and imports.*

SYNTHESIZE

Online Project the **Digital Activity: Rebuilding West Germany and Japan**. Have students fill out a two-column chart with details of how West Germany and Japan overcame the devastation resulting from World War II.

Discuss Ask students: What were the benefits to the United States of helping West Germany and Japan rebuild? What were some disadvantages? *(benefits: creating new markets for U.S. goods, securing strong allies, promoting democracy; disadvantages: creating formidable trade rivals, taking on the cost of helping defend allies)*

DEMONSTRATE

Online Assign the **Digital Lesson Quiz** for this lesson if you haven't already done so. Students will be offered automatic remediation or enrichment based on their score.

Pose these questions to the class on the Discussion Board:

In "The Western Democracies and Japan," you read about U.S. postwar prosperity and how the civil rights movement expanded. You also learned how the Marshall Plan helped rebuild Europe and how Germany and Japan's restorations were considered economic miracles.

Synthesize What are the strengths and weaknesses of the welfare state?

Evaluate Is Japan right to keep high tariffs on imported goods?

Topic Inquiry

Have students continue their investigations for the Topic Inquiry.

ASSESSMENT

1. **Compare Points of View** How did Democrats and Republicans differ on the best ways to improve opportunity for Americans?
2. **Identify Cause and Effect** What challenges did American democracy face during the 1950s and 1960s? How did Americans respond to these challenges?
3. **Compare** During the Cold War, how was economic development in Western Europe similar to, or different from, that of Japan?
4. **Infer** How would Europe benefit economically from greater unity?
5. **Make Generalizations** How was trade important to the economic development of Western Europe, the United States, and Japan during the postwar decades?

Assessment

1. Democrats believed in expanding social programs, while Republicans believed in reducing the size of government and encouraging free market practices.
2. African Americans, women, and other minorities were denied equal rights in education, housing, employment, and other areas. Economic opportunities were limited. Many Americans responded by protesting for equal rights, both within and outside the government. The government moved to support needy Americans.
3. Japan and much of Western Europe gained prosperity by building modern industries after wartime destruction. While Japan focused on producing goods for export, Western Europe developed strong social benefit programs for its citizens.
4. Economic unions led to lower tariffs, increased trade, and freer movement of workers and capital over national borders. Economic freedoms increased.
5. Because of international trade, all of their economies grew.

19.3 Civil war raged across China during the late 1940s as Mao Zedong (mow dzuh doong) and his Communist forces fought to overthrow Jiang Jieshi's Nationalists. In 1949, Mao's forces triumphed. The defeated Jiang and his supporters fled to the island of Taiwan. After decades of struggle, China was finally united, with the Chinese Communists in control. They renamed the country the People's Republic of China.

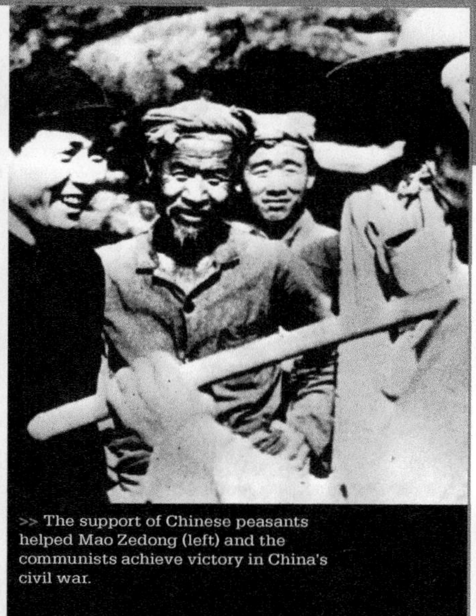

>> The support of Chinese peasants helped Mao Zedong (left) and the communists achieve victory in China's civil war.

Communism in East Asia

TEKS
1.F, 13.B, 13.C, 18.B, 22.C

>> Objectives

Analyze how Mao Zedong turned China into a communist state.

Describe China's role in the Cold War.

Explain the causes and impact of the Korean War.

>> Key Terms

Mao Zedong
collectivization
Great Leap Forward
Cultural Revolution
38th parallel
Kim Il Sung
Syngman Rhee
Pusan Perimeter
demilitarized zone

The Chinese Communist Victory

Soon afterward, the Communists conquered Tibet, claiming it was part of China. In 1959, as the Chinese cracked down, Tibet's revered religious leader, the Dalai Lama, was forced to flee to India.

How the Communists Won Mao's victory in China was due to several causes. Mao had won the support of China's huge peasant population. Peasants had long suffered from brutal landlords and crushing taxes. The Communists promised to redistribute land to peasants and end oppression by landlords. Many women backed the Communists, who rejected the old inequalities of Chinese society. Finally, Mao's army outfought Jiang's armies with guerrilla tactics they had perfected fighting the Japanese.

Jiang and the Nationalists who ruled China had failed to end widespread economic hardship. Many Chinese resented corruption in Jiang's government and his reliance on support from Western powers that had long dominated China. Many educated Chinese were drawn to the Communists' vision of a new China free from foreign domination.

www.PearsonTexas.com
Access your Digital Lesson.

Topic 19 Lesson 3

Communism in East Asia

CONNECT

Preview Have students preview the **Lesson Objectives** and the list of **Key Terms**.

Students can also preview all the **Key Terms** and **Academic Vocabulary** using the **Interactive Reading Notepad** on the digital course or preview a summary of the lesson in the **Reading and Note Taking Study Guide**.

Online Use the **Editable Presentation** found on the digital course to present the main ideas for this lesson.

Start Up Activity

Read or display the following quote from Mao Zedong, China's first Communist leader: "We have closed our ranks and defeated both domestic and foreign oppressors through the People's War of Liberation and the great people's revolution, and now we are proclaiming the founding of the People's Republic of China."

Have students recall what they've learned about communism in the Soviet Union. Then, as a class, discuss the following: What do you think a "People's Republic" would be? Will China be a true people's republic? *(A people's republic would be one run by the people; as a communist country, China is likely to be run by the Communist Party.)*

Online You can also project the **Start Up Activity** from the course.

INVESTIGATE

Have students read the lesson using the **Reading and Note Taking Study Guide** to help them take notes and understand the text as they read.

The Chinese Communist Victory

Explain that Mao Zedong led his Communist army to victory over Nationalist forces led by Jiang Jieshi. In 1949, he proclaimed the People's Republic of China. Communist attempts to industrialize, increase food production, and alter the culture had negative effects, including mass starvation.

Aa Vocabulary Builder

1. Have students pronounce the following academic vocabulary term in this lesson and clarify the part of speech. Break the term into syllables and pronounce it with the students.
2. Explain what the word means in common "student-friendly" language using synonyms and antonyms when possible. Provide concrete examples to clarify the meaning, and rephrase the definition.

communes: commonly owned and operated farms or communities

Topic 19 Lesson 3

Online Project the **Interactive Gallery: Communism in China**, and click through the images with students.

ACTIVE CLASSROOM

Use the Make Headlines strategy. Have students write a headline that captures the main idea of one of the two posters in the Interactive Gallery. Have students write a headline that captures the one aspect of this topic that should be remembered. Have pairs review each other's headlines.

Analyze Images

Focus students' attention on the image with the tractors. Ask them which of Mao's economic strategies are evident in this photograph. *(The tractors suggest industrialization and the modernization of agriculture; the large group of farmers suggests collectivization.)*

Key Terms

Call students' attention to the term **Cultural Revolution** (in bold) in the text. Ask them what was revolutionary about this program. *(Sample response: It asked the Chinese not to make progress, but rather to move backward; it closed schools and factories.)* Be sure students understand that "bourgeois tendencies" refers to a desire for material wealth.

Guided Reading and Discussion

Ask students to explain how the Chinese Communists dealt with opponents. *(They were persecuted, accused of being "counter-revolutionary," sent to labor camps, and often killed.)* Ask them to recall what happened to opponents of the Communist Party in the Soviet Union. Then discuss what this shows about communist states in general.

Remaking Chinese Life Once in power, the Communists set out to turn China from a backward peasant society into a modern industrial nation. Communist ideology guided the government's efforts to reshape the economy and society that China had inherited from the dynastic period. To build socialism, China nationalized all businesses and tried to increase coal and steel output and develop heavy industry. With help from the Soviet Union, the Chinese built hydroelectric plants, dams, and railroads.

To boost agriculture, Mao at first distributed land to peasants. Before long, the government imposed **collectivization,** or the forced pooling of peasant land and labor to increase productivity.

To increase literacy, reformers simplified Chinese characters, making it easier to learn to read and write. Schools were opened for young and old. The Communists sent health-care workers to remote rural areas. Although many had little training, they did help reduce disease and teach better hygiene.

Under China's new constitution, women won equality under the law. Although Chinese woman made real progress, they did not enjoy full equality. Often paid less than men for the same work, women toiled in fields and factories while still maintaining the home.

>> The government forced collectivization on Chinese farmers in order to increase productivity. During the Great Leap Forward, tractors arrive at a farmer's cooperative.

Communism Takes a Huge Toll Like Lenin in the Soviet Union, Mao Zedong built a one-party, Communist totalitarian state. Communist ideology replaced Confucian beliefs and traditional religions. Buddhists, Christians, and others faced persecution and death. The government attacked crime and corruption. It did away with the old landlord and business classes. In their place, peasant and workers were honored as the builders of the new China.

These revolutionary changes came at an enormous human cost. Communist leaders committed politically motivated mass murder, as hundreds of thousands of landlords, middle class property owners, and others suffered persecution, torture, and death. Many more were sent to forced labor camps, where they died under brutal conditions.

Great Leap Forward Fails From 1958 to 1960, Mao pursued a policy known as the **Great Leap Forward,** which was designed to increase farm and industrial output. To make agriculture more efficient, he created communes. The communes were composed of several villages, thousands of acres of land, and up to 25,000 people.

Rural communes set up "backyard" industries to produce steel and other products. The Great Leap Forward was a disastrous failure. Backyard industries turned out useless goods. The commune system slowed food output. Bad weather added to the problems and led to a terrible famine. Between 1959 and 1961, as many as 55 million Chinese are thought to have starved to death.

The Cultural Revolution In 1966, Mao launched a new program known as the **Cultural Revolution.** Its goal was to purge China of "bourgeois" (non revolutionary) tendencies. He urged young Chinese to experience revolution firsthand, as his generation had.

During the Cultural Revolution, bands of teenaged Red Guards, waving copies of the "Little Red Book," *Quotations From Chairman Mao Tse-tung,* attacked people they considered bourgeois. The accused were publicly humiliated, beaten, and sometimes murdered. Skilled workers and managers were forced out of their jobs and sent to work on rural farms or put into forced labor camps. Schools and factories closed. As the economy stalled and unrest rose, Mao finally had the army restore order.

COMPARE What were the main successes and failures of the Chinese Communist Revolution?

D Differentiate Extra Support Help students better understand the definition of the academic vocabulary term *commune*: a commonly owned and operated farm or community. Display the definition, and have students find the two words in it that resemble *commune*. (commonly *and* community*)* Tell them that in this context, *commonly* means "by all members of a group." Then have them rephrase the definition, substituting that meaning. *(a farm or community owned and operated by all members of a group)*

Answers

Compare *main successes: improved public infrastructure and somewhat improved public hygiene; main failures: purges of intellectuals, failure of the Great Leap Forward, and inadequate progress in improving productivity*

China and the Cold War

The Communist victory in China dominated the Cold War in the years after 1949. The United States had supported Jiang Jieshi in the civil war. After Jiang fled to Taiwan, the United States continued to support the Nationalist government there, providing military and economic aid as it faced shelling from the mainland. For decades, the United States refused to recognize the People's Republic of China, or, as many Americans called it, "Red China."

An Uneasy Alliance with the Soviet Union Despite a treaty of friendship between China and the Soviet Union, the two communist giants were uneasy allies. In fact, Chinese communism differed from Soviet communism. In the 1950s, Stalin sent economic and technical experts to help China modernize. But he and Mao disagreed on many issues, especially on Marxist ideology. A key difference was the role of the peasantry. Mao believed that peasants were the major force behind communist revolution, while Soviets trusted in a "revolutionary elite" of urban intellectuals and workers.

By 1959, border clashes and disputes over ideology led the Soviets to withdraw all aid and advisors from China and end their alliance. Western powers welcomed the split, which eased fears of the global threat posed by communism.

China and the United States The rift between the United States and China deepened when they supported opposing sides in the Korean War. For years, the United States tried to isolate China, which it saw as an aggressive communist power seeking to expand across Asia.

As the Cold War dragged on, however, the United States reassessed its policy towards China. There were strategic advantages to improving relations with China after its split with the Soviet Union. By "playing the China card," the United States might isolate the Soviets between NATO in the west and a hostile China in the east.

In 1971, China won admission to the United Nations. A year later, American President Richard Nixon visited Mao in Beijing, opening the door to improved relations. Formal diplomatic relations finally came in 1979.

The Nationalists in Taiwan During the Cold War, Jiang Jieshi (Chiang Kai-shek) exercised authoritarian rule over Taiwan, hoping one day to regain control of China. By the early 1990s, however, Taiwan had made the transition to democratic government.

On the mainland, Mao and his successors saw Taiwan as a breakaway province and insisted that

>> Mao Zedong's "Little Red Book" of quotations became required reading for all Chinese. Here, peasants take a break from their work in the fields to read it. **Infer** Why do you think the picture of Mao is displayed?

Interactive Gallery

>> **Analyze Political Cartoons** The Soviet Union and China, both communist, had a tense relationship. In 1978, China rejected a Soviet proposal to improve relations. Who does the bear represent? Who has the upper hand in this cartoon?

China and the Cold War

Tell students that China's victory over the U.S.-backed Nationalist Chinese meant that the United States would have to deal with another huge Communist state during the Cold War. China had a complex relationship with the Soviet Union—the Soviets offered technical aid to China, but ancient territorial disputes and certain ideological differences eventually turned the countries against each other. China and the United States fought on opposite sides in the Korean War, but in the 1970s, U.S. policy toward China softened.

Guided Reading and Discussion

Review the postwar position that the United States took on the spread of communism. *(The Truman Doctrine said that the United States should oppose communism and support anticommunist movements around the world; the United States supported NATO governments economically to resist communism in Western Europe, and it opposed the communist revolution in Cuba.)* Ask students why they think the United States eventually decided to engage with communist China. Remind them of the saying "My enemy's enemy is my friend." Then explain that in the 1970s, the United States backed China in its disputes with the Soviet Union, because U.S. leaders believed that the Soviets were a greater threat.

History Background

Ping-Pong Diplomacy The warming in relations between the United States and China was a gradual process. The first tentative communications were sent via Yahya Khan, the president of Pakistan, who was friendly with both governments. In the first public sign of improved relations, Mao's regime invited the U.S. Ping-Pong team to visit China. The team toured the Great Wall and the Summer Palace and played exhibition games against their host. The trip became known as Ping-Pong Diplomacy. Soon after, presidential advisor Henry Kissinger secretly traveled to China to meet Premier Zhou Enlai, paving the way for Nixon's historic visit.

Answers

Infer *Sample response: To remind peasants of their love for their leader, Mao; he's treated like a god.*

Analyze Political Cartoons *the Soviet Union; China*

Topic 19 Lesson 3

The Two Koreas

Tell students that the division of Korea along the 38th parallel after World War II became a seemingly permanent split during the Cold War. In June 1950, communist North Korea invaded noncommunist South Korea, starting the Korean War. American and South Korean forces, under UN authority, opposed the North Koreans. The fighting ended in 1953 with an armistice.

Online Project the **Interactive Map: The Korean War**, and click through the layers with students.

ACTIVE CLASSROOM

Use the Make Headlines strategy. Have students examine the nighttime satellite image of the two Koreas and write a headline that captures the most important aspect of this image that should be remembered. Have them present their headlines to the class. As a class, discuss what the image represents about the differences between the communist/command and democratic/capitalist systems.

Guided Reading and Discussion

Ask students to explain why UN forces were taking a big risk by invading North Korea in 1950. *(There was a chance that communist China would invade if UN forces got too close to the Yalu River, the Korean border with China; the Chinese did invade, supporting the North Koreans and prolonging the war.)*

it must someday be reunited with China. Tensions between Taiwan and the mainland continued throughout the Cold War, but in recent years, trade and other links between the two have grown. Although few countries recognized Taiwan, it became an economic powerhouse in Asia and a center of computer technology.

SUMMARIZE How did China's relationships with the Soviet Union and the United States change during the Cold War?

The Two Koreas

In 1950, the Cold War erupted into a "shooting war" in Korea, a peninsula on the northeastern edge of Asia. The Korean War pitted UN forces, largely from the Western democracies, against communist North Korea, which was supported by the Soviet Union and China. It was a key event of the Cold War.

A Nation Divided Korea was an independent kingdom until Japan annexed the country in 1910 and imposed a harsh regime. After Japan's defeat in World War II, Soviet and American forces agreed to divide Korea temporarily along the **38th parallel** of latitude. American forces occupied the south, while the Soviets held the north.

During the Cold War, Korea's division—like Germany's—seemed to become permanent. North Korea, ruled by the dictator **Kim Il Sung,** became a communist ally of the Soviet Union.

In South Korea, the United States backed an authoritarian—but noncommunist—leader, **Syngman Rhee.** Each leader wanted to reunite the country—under his own rule.

The Korean War Begins In June 1950, North Korean forces invaded South Korea and soon overran most of the peninsula. Backed by the UN, which condemned the invasion, the United States organized an international force to help South Korea.

UN forces, mostly Americans and South Koreans under the command of General Douglas MacArthur, fell back in the face of the North Korean advance. They took up a defensive line known as the **Pusan Perimeter,** holding their ground against repeated North Korean attacks. MacArthur then landed troops at Inch'on, behind enemy lines, and drove the invaders back across the 38th parallel. He continued to push northward toward the Yalu River on the border of China.

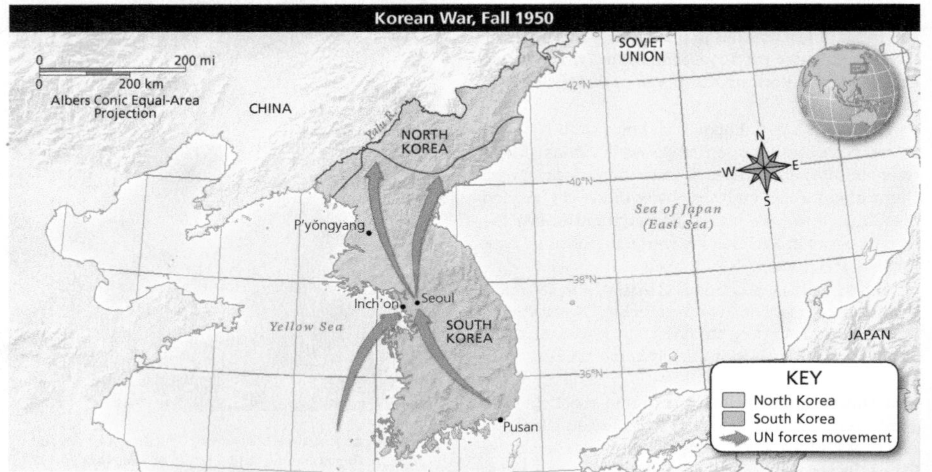

>> **Analyze Maps** War broke out in Korea in 1950. Communist North Korea invaded South Korea in an effort to reunite Korea. In the fall of 1950, who controlled most of the Korean Peninsula?

Interactive Map

Answers

Summarize *China's relationship with the Soviet Union deteriorated because of rivalries over ideology and borders. China's relationship with the United States improved as the Cold War progressed, because the United States saw China as a useful partner in its conflict with the Soviet Union.*

Analyze Maps *UN forces*

Explain *China got involved in the Korean War when it felt threatened by UN forces near its border. China wanted to help its ally, communist North Korea.*

English Language Proficiency Standards

Learning Strategies 1.B.2 Read aloud "The Two Koreas." Then display and explain the five-step writing process.

Beginning Retell "The Two Koreas" in accessible language. Ask students to brainstorm ideas for writing about the relationship between North and South Korea. Ask students to identify which stage of the process comes next. Help them write an introductory sentence.

Intermediate Reread "The Two Koreas." Have groups brainstorm how to write about the relationship between North and South Korea, and then choose a topic and write a paragraph. Have them trade drafts with another group for review, and then revise.

Advanced Have pairs brainstorm, draft, revise, edit and proofread, and publish a paragraph on the relationship between North and South Korea. Tell pairs to keep a record of each stage of the writing process.

Advanced High Have students work individually to complete the Advanced activity.

China Responds MacArthur's success alarmed China, which feared an American invasion. Mao Zedong sent Chinese troops to help the North Koreans. In tough winter fighting, the Chinese and North Koreans pushed the UN forces back across the 38th parallel. The Korean War then turned into a long, deadly stalemate.

Korea Remains Divided Fighting continued until 1953, when both sides signed an armistice to end the fighting. Almost two million North Korean and South Korean troops dug in on either side of the **demilitarized zone (DMZ),** an area with no military forces, near the 38th parallel. American forces, too, remained in South Korea to guarantee the peace. The ceasefire has held for more than 60 years, but no peace treaty has ever been negotiated.

After the war, the two Koreas slowly rebuilt their economies which were destroyed by the fighting and by the Japanese occupation. Korea itself remained a focus of Cold War rivalry. The United States funneled aid to South Korea, while the Soviets helped communist North Korea.

South Korea Prospers For decades, a dictatorial government backed by the military ruled South Korea. By 1987, however, growing prosperity and fierce student protests forced the government to ease controls and hold direct elections. The country also faced new social pressures as more people moved to the cities, undermining traditional rural ways of life.

North Korea Isolates Itself Under Kim Il Sung, North Korea recovered from the war, but by the late 1960s, growth stalled. Kim emphasized self-reliance and kept North Korea isolated from much of the world. When its old partners, the Soviet Union and China, tried out economic reforms in the 1980s, North Korea clung to hardline communism and its command economy in which the government controlled economic decisions.

In North Korea, a barrage of propaganda glorified Kim as the "Great Leader." Kim's successors, his son and grandson, continued to isolate the country and impose ruthless totalitarian control over all aspects of life.

For years, North Koreans lived on the edge of starvation as the country suffered from food shortages, natural disasters, and economic mismanagement. North Korea, meanwhile, poured resources into developing nuclear weapons in spite of international condemnation.

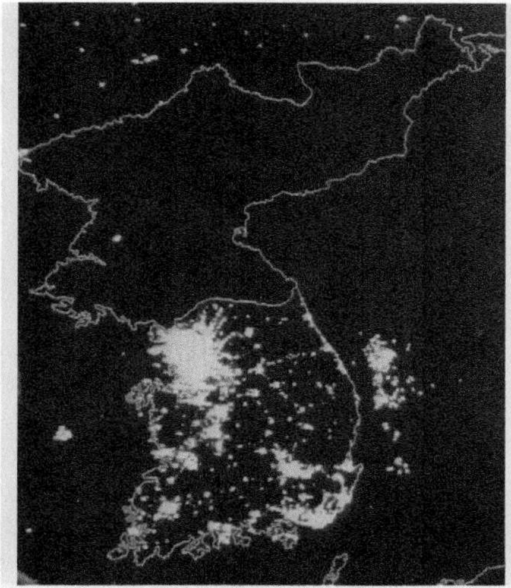

>> South Korea has a modern economy and infrastructure, while North Korea's infrastructure is limited. This 2006 nighttime satellite image shows an eerily dark North Korea and a brightly lit South Korea.

EXPLAIN Explain why China became involved in the Korean War.

ASSESSMENT

1. **Contrast** How did Chinese communism differ from Soviet communism?
2. **Infer** How did the United States use the changing relationship between China and the Soviet Union to its own advantage?
3. **Predict** How might Korea be different if UN forces had not stepped in to oppose the North Korean invasion in 1950?
4. **Summarize** Why was the Great Leap Forward a failure?
5. **Recall** How did North Korea's economic performance compare with South Korea's?

SYNTHESIZE

Online Project the **Digital Activity: Who Benefits from a People's Republic?** Have students fill out a table that identifies and explains (1) who benefited and (2) who was hurt as a result of China's policies in land reform, collectivization, the Great Leap Forward, and the Cultural Revolution.

Explain Who benefited from the policies in North Korea? Who was hurt? *(The leaders benefited; the people were hurt.)*

Make Generalizations Based on this example, who benefits most from communism? *(the party and the leaders, not the people)*

DEMONSTRATE

Online Assign the **Digital Lesson Quiz** for this lesson if you haven't already done so. Students will be offered automatic remediation or enrichment based on their score.

Pose the following to the class on the Discussion Board:

In "Communism in East Asia," you read about the Chinese Communist Revolution and China's role in the Cold War. You also learned how UN and South Korean forces battled Chinese and North Korean forces in the Korean War.

Make Generalizations Were Mao Zedong's initial goals of the communist revolution in China fulfilled? *(Students may say yes, because Mao won the support of the large peasant population by redistributing land and ending oppression by landlords.)*

Cite Evidence Was the United Nations' intervention in Korea worthwhile? Support your answer with information from the text. *(Sample responses: No, because North Korea is still communist and poses a threat to the United States today. Yes, because the UN intervention kept communism out of South Korea.)*

Topic Inquiry

Have students continue their investigations for the Topic Inquiry.

Assessment

1. Mao believed that a communist state could be achieved by organizing the peasants, so he did not initially stress industrialization or depend on an urban revolutionary vanguard. In addition, Mao did not enforce collectivization as ruthlessly as Stalin had in the Soviet Union. Also, China did not promote the spread of communism or control satellite states the way the USSR did.
2. The United States played the China card in order to isolate the Soviet Union.
3. Without UN involvement, communist aggression might have succeeded in Korea and the nation would be united today, but communist.
4. It failed because its programs produced inferior industrial products and cut food output by reducing agricultural incentives for individual farmers. Millions died of starvation in the resulting famine.
5. North Korea's economic performance was poor compared with the prosperity experienced in South Korea.

Topic 19 Lesson 4

War in Southeast Asia

CONNECT

Preview Have students preview the **Lesson Objectives** and the list of **Key Terms**.

Students can also preview all the **Key Terms** and **Academic Vocabulary** using the **Interactive Reading Notepad** on the digital course or preview a summary of the lesson in the **Reading and Note Taking Study Guide**.

Online Use the **Editable Presentation** found on the digital course to present the main ideas for this lesson.

Start Up Activity

Tell students that during the Cold War the United States was sometimes willing to give aid to governments that may not have had democratic systems or treated their people very well. Encourage class discussion about why the United States was willing to do this. Ask: What was the overriding concern of the United States during the Cold War? *(stopping the spread of communism)*

Online You can also project the **Start Up Activity** from the course.

INVESTIGATE

Have students read the lesson using the **Reading and Note Taking Study Guide** to help them take notes and understand the text as they read.

The Road to War in Southeast Asia

Ask students to identify the motivations behind the communist revolutions in Russia, China, and Cuba. *(land, better living conditions, more responsive government, less power to a small elite)* Explain that the origins of the Vietnamese struggle were very different. The Vietnamese worked to force their French colonial rulers to leave Vietnam; they wanted to establish an independent nation.

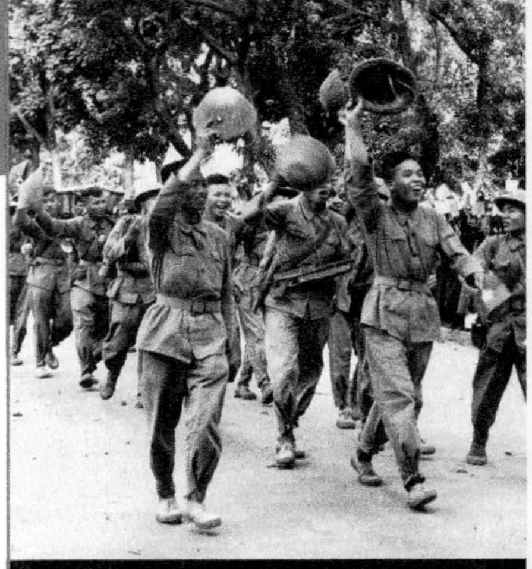

>> Vietnam became the focus of Cold War tensions when communist guerrillas fighters fought against French rule. Here, Viet Minh troops enter Hanoi on October 14, 1954.

Interactive Flipped Video

19.4 **During World War II, Japan seized much of Southeast Asia from the European colonial powers that ruled the region. After Japan's defeat, local nationalists rejected European efforts to reclaim their colonial empires. Some Southeast Asian nations won freedom without much violence. Others, like Vietnam, faced long wars of liberation.**

TEKS
1.F, 13.C, 22.C

>> Objectives

Describe events in Indochina after World War II.

Explain how the United States became involved in the Vietnam War.

Explore the end of the Vietnam War.

Summarize the impact of the war on Vietnam and Cambodia.

>> Key Terms

guerrilla
Ho Chi Minh
Dien Bien Phu
domino theory
Viet Cong
Tet Offensive
Khmer Rouge
Pol Pot

War in Southeast Asia

The Road to War in Southeast Asia

Cold War tensions complicated the drive for freedom. The United States supported independence for colonial people in principle. But the West was anxious to stop the spread of communism. As a result, the United States helped anti-communist leaders win power, even if they had little popular support.

The Long War Begins In mainland Southeast Asia, an agonizing liberation struggle tore apart the region once known as French Indochina. It affected the emerging nations of Vietnam, Cambodia, and Laos. The 30-year conflict was a key event of the Cold War and had two major phases: the battle against the French from 1946 to 1954, and the Cold War conflict that involved the United States and lasted from 1955 to 1975.

In 1946, the French set out to reestablish their authority over Indochina. In Vietnam, the French faced opposition forces led by **Ho Chi Minh** (hoh chee min). Ho, a nationalist and a communist, had waged warfare against Japanese occupying forces using **guerrillas,** or small groups of loosely organized soldiers making surprise raids.

PEARSON realize. www.PearsonTexas.com Access your Digital Lesson.

862

Aa Vocabulary Builder

1. Have students pronounce the following academic vocabulary term in this lesson and clarify the part of speech. Break the term into syllables and pronounce it with the students.
2. Explain what the word means in common "student-friendly" language using synonyms and antonyms when possible. Provide concrete examples to clarify the meaning, and rephrase the definition.

terminate: finish; bring to an end

In 1954, Ho Chi Minh's guerilla forces decisively defeated French troops at the battle of **Dien Bien Phu** (dyen byen foo). The defeat forced France to end its efforts to reclaim Indochina. Cambodia, and Laos meanwhile, had won independence separately.

Vietnam Is Divided By 1954, the struggle in Vietnam had become part of the Cold War. At an international conference that year, Western and communist powers agreed to a temporary division of Vietnam.

Ho and the communists ruled North Vietnam. A fierce anti-communist government, led by Ngo Dinh Diem (ngoh dee EM) and supported by the United States, ruled South Vietnam.

The agreement called for elections to be held to reunite Vietnam within a year. The elections never took place, however, largely because the Americans and Diem feared the communists might win.

Although prodded by the United States, Diem refused to undertake needed reforms, and his increasingly dictatorial rule and corrupt government alienated many South Vietnamese. By 1959, South Vietnam was facing a growing challenge from both communist guerrillas and rising discontent with Diem.

IDENTIFY CENTRAL IDEAS Why did Vietnamese guerrillas fight the French in Indochina?

The United States Enters the War

American officials believed in the **domino theory,** which held that a communist victory in South Vietnam would cause noncommunist governments across Southeast Asia to fall to communism—like a row of dominoes. To prevent such a disaster, the United States stepped in to shore up the Diem government.

However, there were limits to what American power could achieve in Vietnam. President John F. Kennedy realized that the United States alone could not prop up the unpopular Diem government in South Vietnam. In an interview, he noted:

> I don't think that unless a greater effort is made by the Government to win popular support that the war can be won out there. . . . We can help them, we can give them equipment, we can send our men out there as advisors, but they have to win it, the people of Vietnam, against the Communists.
>
> —President John F. Kennedy

Diem was overthrown and killed in early November 1963 by South Vietnamese military leaders. After Diem's death, the United States became more deeply involved in Vietnam, working with the ruling generals against the growing threat from communist rebels.

American Involvement In North Vietnam, Ho Chi Minh was determined to reunite the country under communist rule. He helped the **Viet Cong,** the communist rebels trying to defeat South Vietnam's government. At first, the United States sent only supplies and military advisers to South Vietnam. But as the Viet Cong won control of more areas, the United States was dragged into the fighting, turning a local struggle into a major Cold War conflict.

In August 1964, the *Maddox,* an American warship in the Gulf of Tonkin, reported attacks by North Vietnamese torpedo boats in retaliation for South Vietnamese commando raids nearby. Without mentioning the commando raids, President Lyndon Johnson used the attacks to win congressional approval for the Gulf of Tonkin Resolution. It authorized

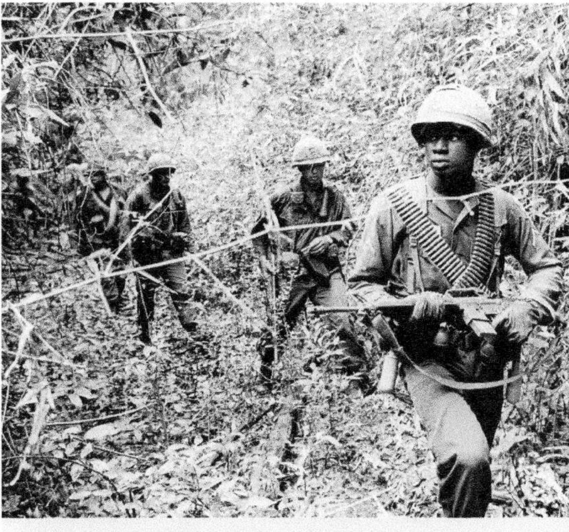

>> U.S. soldiers search for Viet Cong hideouts in the jungle northeast of Saigon.

Interactive Gallery

Guided Reading and Discussion

Remind students that the Vietnam War started as a struggle for independence against French colonialists. Ask them how that conflict resembled earlier African or Latin American independence struggles or even the American Revolution. *(Similarities include the length of the war, the involvement of other nations, the rebels' lack of resources, and guerrilla tactics.)*

The United States Enters the War

Tell students that as the threat of a communist takeover of Vietnam grew, the United States increased its aid. At first it sent only supplies and military advisers to South Vietnam; then it began bombing North Vietnam; soon thousands upon thousands of American troops were pouring into the country.

Online Project the **Interactive Timeline: Vietnam, 1945–1965—From Independence Struggle to Cold War Battleground**, and click through the images with students.

ACTIVE CLASSROOM

Ask students to Take a Stand on the following question: Should the United States get involved in the Vietnam War? Organize them into two groups based on their answer, and have them move to separate areas of the classroom. Ask students to talk with each other to compare the reasons for their answers. Ask a representative from each side to defend the group's point of view.

English Language Proficiency Standards

Writing 5.D.3 Read "The Road to War in Southeast Asia" aloud.

Beginning Explain that verb tenses indicate whether an action occurred in the past, present, or future and must agree within a sentence. Help students choose a verb for these sentences: (1) The French (conquered/conquer/will conquer) Indochina in the 1800s. (2) Southeast Asia (played/plays/will play) a key role in the Cold War.

Intermediate Use the explanation about tenses from the Beginning activity, and help groups write two sentences about the text in the past tense.

Advanced Ask students to identify the verb tense used most in the text *(past)*. Have pairs write three sentences about the text in the past tense.

Advanced High Ask students to explain the purpose of using different verb tenses. Have them identify the verb tense used most in the text, and then write a short paragraph about the text in the past tense.

Answers

Identify Central Ideas *Vietnamese guerrillas fought the French in an effort to win independence.*

Key Terms

Call students' attention to the term **Tet Offensive** (in bold) in the text. Tell them that this 1968 offensive gained the Viet Cong little ground and severely depleted their forces. Nevertheless, it turned the American public against the war. Soon after, President Johnson refused to send more troops to Vietnam, ceased bombing Hanoi, began peace talks, and chose not to run for reelection.

Guided Reading and Discussion

Ask students to identify events that led to U.S. involvement in Vietnam. *(U.S. leaders supported the unpopular but anticommunist Diem; believing in the domino theory, they sent military aid to help South Vietnam; after North Vietnam reportedly attacked a U.S. ship in the Gulf of Tonkin, the United States began bombing and sent ground troops to Vietnam.)* Ask students to select the one event they think did the most to move the United States toward involvement in Vietnam. Discuss their selections as a class.

Answers

Analyze Maps *Laos, Cambodia*

Apply Concepts *U.S. leaders hoped to stop a communist victory in South Vietnam that they believed would cause communism to spread across Southeast Asia, one country after another, like falling dominoes.*

the president to take all necessary measures to prevent further aggression.

The United States soon began bombing targets in North Vietnam, although no war was ever declared. When air strikes failed to force Ho to abandon the war, the United States committed more and more troops to the conflict. By 1969, more than 500,000 American troops were serving in Vietnam. Meantime, the Soviet Union and China sent aid—but no troops—to help North Vietnam.

Guerrilla Warfare Like the French before them, American forces faced a guerrilla war. Many rebels in South Vietnam were local peasants who knew the countryside. They often found safe haven among villagers who resented the foreign troops and bombings that destroyed their homes and crops. American forces were hard put to tell whether villagers were rebels or innocent civilians.

Supplies for the guerrillas came from North Vietnam, along a series of trails, known as the Ho Chi Minh Trail. These trails wound through the rainforests of neighboring Laos and Cambodia. In an effort to stop the flow of supplies, the United States sent bombers and ground troops across the border into these nations, widening the war in Southeast Asia.

The Tet Offensive Even with massive American help, South Vietnam could not defeat the Viet Cong and their North Vietnamese allies. In January 1968, communist forces launched the **Tet Offensive,** a series of attacks by the Viet Cong on cities across the south. North Vietnamese forces assaulted an American marine base. The attacks were unexpected because they took place during Tet, the Vietnamese New Year.

During bloody fighting, the communists lost many troops and were unable to hold any cities against the American counterattacks. Still, the Tet Offensive marked a turning point in American public opinion. Up to then, Americans believed that the war was winnable. Tet shook public confidence in the war and its leaders.

APPLY CONCEPTS How did the domino theory lead the United States to send troops to Vietnam?

ELPS ELPS 1.C.1 When you have completed reading *The United States Enters the War*, create a concept map of America's involvement in Vietnam.

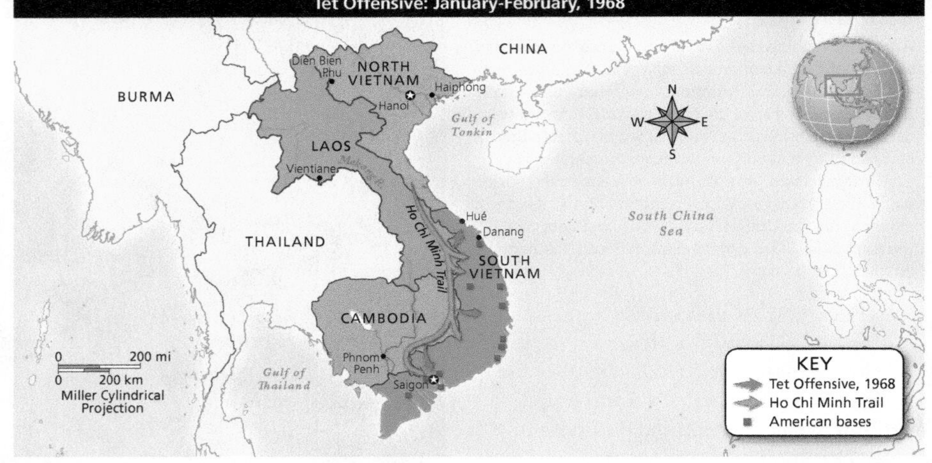

>> **Analyze Maps** The Tet Offensive was a series of attacks by communist guerrillas on South Vietnamese cities. Through which countries did the Ho Chi Minh Trail pass on the way to South Vietnam?

Interactive Timeline

English Language Proficiency Standards

Learning Strategies 1.C.1 Read aloud "The United States Enters the War." Then have students learn how to use a strategic learning technique by creating a concept map of U.S. involvement in Vietnam.

Beginning Display a concept map with "U.S. involvement in the Vietnam War" in the center circle. Then reread the text aloud and model how to identify important details. Add these details and connect them to the main circle with lines. Then have students provide additional details for the map as you continue reading.

Intermediate Follow the instructions in the Beginning activity, but as you reread the text aloud, have students identify the important details. Add these details to the concept map.

Advanced Have students work with a partner to develop a concept map of U.S. involvement in the Vietnam War. Instruct them to write "U.S. involvement in the Vietnam War" in the center circle of their concept map. Have pairs reread the text and identify important details to include in their maps. When student pairs have completed the maps, have them share them with the group.

Advanced High Have students work individually to follow the instructions in the Advanced activity, and then review its details with a partner.

The Vietnam War Ends

In the United States, the bombing of North Vietnam and increasing American casualties helped inflame anti-war opinion. Growing numbers of American troops were prisoners of war (POWs) or missing in action (MIAs). Many opponents called the Vietnam War a quagmire, or swamp, in which the United States was trapped without the possibility of victory.

American Opposition to the War Grows As the United States committed more troops and poured vast sums into the war, the nation grew increasingly divided. At first, the majority of Americans backed the war effort to stop the spread of communism. By the mid-1960s, a growing number of Americans were calling for an end to the war. They questioned why the United States was sending its troops to fight in a local conflict in Southeast Asia.

By 1967, the anti-war movement was spreading. Television news programs relayed vivid pictures of American casualties and the burning ruins of Vietnamese villages. On college campuses, students rallied against the war, especially as more young men faced the draft, or compulsory military service.

Prominent leaders from all walks of life joined the protests in cities across the nation. Many Americans had mixed feelings. "I want to get out," said one woman, "but I don't want to give up."

A Negotiated Peace Faced with mounting protests at home, President Johnson, who had greatly widened the war, decided not to run for a second term in 1968. His successor, President Richard Nixon, eventually arranged a cease-fire agreement in 1973. Under the agreement, the United States began to withdraw troops from South Vietnam. North Vietnam agreed it would not send any more troops to the south. The accord left South Vietnam to determine its own future.

Vietnam Is Reunited Two years after American troops withdrew, the North Vietnamese captured Saigon, capital of South Vietnam. In 1976, they renamed the city Ho Chi Minh City, in honor of their liberation leader. Hanoi, the capital of North Vietnam, became the capital of the reunited nation.

The communist victors imposed harsh rule on the south. Tens of thousands of Vietnamese fled in small boats. Many of these "boat people" drowned. Survivors ended up in refugee camps in nearby countries. Eventually, some were accepted into the United States or other countries.

Vietnam had to rebuild a land mangled by decades of war. Recovery was slow due partly to government inefficiency and partly to an American-led boycott of

>> People gathered on the Mall in Washington, D.C., on November 15, 1969, to protest the Vietnam War. The Peace Moratorium was estimated to be the largest demonstration in U.S. history.

>> Between the 1973 ceasefire and the final American pullout in 1975, refugees flooded seaports in Vietnam to escape. This Vietnamese navy ship carried more than 7,000 refugees.

The Vietnam War Ends

Tell students that as the Vietnam War dragged on and American casualties mounted, the antiwar movement gained more and more followers. Lengthy negotiations finally led to a cease-fire agreement in 1973, and American troops withdrew. Two years later, North Vietnam captured Saigon, South Vietnam's capital. Vietnam became a communist country, as did its neighbor, Cambodia.

Online Project the **Interactive Gallery: Fighting a Different War**, and click through the images with students.

ACTIVE CLASSROOM

Use the Speaking With History strategy. Ask students to imagine they are having a conversation with one of the people in the images or the text in this lesson. Have them first write down a question they'd like to ask, then how that person would answer, and finally what students would say in response.

Analyze Images

Focus students' attention on the image of the protestors. Ask students what the photograph tells them about this protest. *(It was massive.)* Ask: How might such a large protest in the nation's capital affect Congress? How might it affect public opinion?

Guided Reading and Discussion

Ask students why opposition to the Vietnam War increased in the late 1960s and early 1970s. *(Sample response: the Tet Offensive; heavy American casualties)* Discuss whether the United States made the right decision when it pulled out of Vietnam.

D Differentiate Extra Support Ask: What does the word *terminate* mean in this sentence: *Johnson's successor, President Nixon, came under increasing pressure to terminate American involvement*? Note that the word is a verb. Ask students what actions President Nixon was being pressured to take. Use this strategy to help students figure out what *terminate* means.

Answers

Summarize *The United States withdrew because it wasn't winning and faced tremendous domestic pressure from citizens who opposed American involvement in the war.*

Topic 19 Lesson 4

SYNTHESIZE

Online Project the **Digital Activity: Peace Without Conquest**. Give students a few minutes to answer the questions.

Discuss What pressures for and against continued involvement did President Johnson face? *(Sample responses: against—domestic factors such as the rising death toll, media coverage of casualties, war protests, and increasing doubts about the justness of the war; for—loyalty to allies, fear of appearing weak toward communists, and domestic political concerns)*

DEMONSTRATE

Online Assign the **Digital Lesson Quiz** for this lesson if you haven't already done so. Students will be offered automatic remediation or enrichment based on their score.

Pose the following to the class on the Discussion Board:

In "War in Southeast Asia," you read about how the Vietnam War began, how the United States got involved in the war, and how the war finally ended.

Generate Explanations What did the United States gain or lose through its involvement in the Vietnam War? *(Sample response: The U.S. gained little, because it did not achieve its objective; it lost many soldiers and the support of people within the country and beyond.)*

Evaluate Arguments Should the United States have intervened when the Khmer Rouge gained power in Cambodia? *(Some may argue that the United States needed to end its involvement in Southeast Asia. Others might say that the Khmer Rouge should have been stopped for moral reasons.)*

Topic Inquiry

Have students continue their investigations for the Topic Inquiry.

>> The Khmer Rouge used children as soldiers in its five-year-long civil war to establish a communist government in Cambodia.

Vietnam. For years, the country was mired in poverty. By the 1990s, however, a new generation of Vietnamese leaders opened the door to investors by introducing free-market reforms. After the Cold War ended, the United States and Vietnam edged toward better relations.

Politically Motivated Mass Murder in Cambodia During the Vietnam War, fighting spilled over into neighboring Cambodia. The North Vietnamese sent supplies through Cambodia to guerrilla forces in South Vietnam. In 1969, the United States bombed those routes and then briefly invaded Cambodia.

After the Americans left, Cambodian communist guerrillas, the **Khmer Rouge** (kuh MEHR roozh), gained ground and overthrew the government in 1975. Led by the brutal dictator **Pol Pot,** the Khmer Rouge unleashed a reign of terror. To destroy all Western influences, they drove people from the cities and forced them to work in the fields. They slaughtered, starved, or worked to death more than one million Cambodians, about a third of the population.

In 1979, Vietnam invaded and occupied Cambodia, ending the genocide. Pol Pot and his forces retreated to remote areas. In 1993, UN peacekeepers supervised elections. Despite guerrillas who still terrorized parts of the country, a new government began to rebuild Cambodia.

? SUMMARIZE Why did the United States withdraw its troops from Vietnam?

ASSESSMENT

1. **Draw Conclusions** Why did the French withdraw from Indochina in the 1950s?
2. **Apply Concepts** How was American involvement in Vietnam an extension of the Truman Doctrine?
3. **Compare Points of View** What different opinions did Americans have about U.S. involvement in the Vietnam War?
4. **Synthesize** When the text states that "dominoes fell" after the Vietnam War, what does this mean?
5. **Summarize** How did the local struggle in Vietnam reflect the larger Cold War conflict?

Assessment

1. They were losing the battle against guerrilla forces led by Ho Chi Minh.
2. The Truman Doctrine stated that the United States should intervene to prevent, or contain, the spread of communism. The United States entered the Vietnam War to prevent communism from spreading in Southeast Asia.
3. Many Americans felt it was a quagmire and that America should withdraw. Others felt America needed to stay in Southeast Asia to prevent the spread of communism.
4. Some nations in Southeast Asia fell under communist rule.
5. The United States entered the war on South Vietnam's side to stop the spread of communism, while the Soviet Union and China supported communist North Vietnam.

19.5 During the Cold War, relations between the Soviet Union and the United States swung back and forth between confrontation and détente. The superpowers confronted each other over issues such as the Berlin Wall, Soviet intervention in Eastern Europe, and Cuba. However, in the 1970s, Soviet leader Leonid Brezhnev pursued détente and disarmament with the United States.

>> Missiles are paraded in Red Square in Moscow. The heavy military commitments of the Soviet Union was one of the factors that led to its decline.

The Cold War Ends

TEKS
13.D, 18.E, 18.F, 21.A

The Soviet Union Declines

Détente came to an abrupt end in 1979, after the Soviet Union invaded Afghanistan to ensure its influence in that neighboring nation. Like the Vietnam War in the United States, the Afghan War drained the Soviet economy and provoked a crisis at home.

The Soviets in Afghanistan The Soviet Union invaded Afghanistan in late 1979 to support an Afghan communist government that had seized power a year earlier. The new government's efforts to introduce social reforms and redistribute land roused bitter resentment among the anti-communist, devoutly Muslim Afghan people. As insurgencies, or uprisings, threatened the government, the Soviet Union stepped in.

For ten years, Soviet forces battled widely scattered groups of **mujahedin** (moo jah heh DEEN), or Muslim guerrilla fighters. Despite 100,000 troops, the Soviets controlled only the cities, not the countryside. When the Soviets turned to bombing rural areas, millions of Afghan refugees fled into neighboring Pakistan. The United States funneled weapons and other military supplies to help the insurgents battle Soviet troops.

By the late 1980s, the Afghan War had become a quagmire for the Soviet Union. It was draining badly needed resources and costing many casualties. In 1989, the Soviets withdrew from Afghanistan to focus on troubling issues at home.

>> Objectives

Understand why the Soviet Union declined.

Identify the reforms introduced by Mikhail Gorbachev.

Describe the collapse of communism in Eastern Europe and the Soviet Union.

Evaluate how the end of the Cold War affected the remaining communist nations and the United States.

>> Key Terms

mujahedin
Mikhail Gorbachev
glasnost
perestroika
Lech Walesa
Solidarity
Václav Havel
Nicolae Ceausescu

www.PearsonTexas.com
Access your Digital Lesson.

Topic 19 Lesson 5

The Cold War Ends

CONNECT

Preview Have students preview the **Lesson Objectives** and the list of **Key Terms**.

Students can also preview all the **Key Terms** and **Academic Vocabulary** using the **Interactive Reading Notepad** on the digital course or preview a summary of the lesson in the **Reading and Note Taking Study Guide**.

Online Use the **Editable Presentation** found on the digital course to present the main ideas for this lesson.

Start Up Activity

Have students discuss their answers to this question as they get settled: What do you think would happen to the Union of Soviet Socialist Republics (Soviet Union) if a number of its republics decided they wanted to leave the union? *(Sample responses: The Soviet Union might descend into civil war; if the republics succeeded, the union might be broken apart.)*

Online You can also project the **Start Up Activity** from the course.

INVESTIGATE

Have students read the lesson using the **Reading and Note Taking Study Guide** to help them take notes and understand the text as they read.

The Soviet Union Declines

Tell students that a war in Afghanistan (1979–1989) severely strained the Soviet Union's economy, as did the nuclear arms race. Its command economic system, with its inefficiencies and waste, could not fund these efforts and still keep the economy strong. In the 1980s, Soviet leader Mikhail Gorbachev instituted economic and governmental reforms, along with a policy of increased political and social openness.

Aa Vocabulary Builder

1. Have students pronounce the following academic vocabulary term in this lesson and clarify the part of speech. Break the term into syllables and pronounce it with the students.
2. Explain what the word means in common "student-friendly" language using synonyms and antonyms when possible. Provide concrete examples to clarify the meaning, and rephrase the definition.

incentive: something that encourages a person to take action or work harder

Topic 19 Lesson 5

Key Terms

Ask students to find the key term **glasnost** (in bold) in the text. Explain that Gorbachev thought this "openness" would support perestroika by encouraging public discussion of the country's problems. An unforeseen consequence of glasnost was that journalists began exposing government corruption and undermining public respect for the state.

Analyze Images

Point out the image of Gorbachev and President Reagan. Ask students what this image suggests about how the Cold War was going. *(Sample response: The friendly handshake and smiles suggest a reduction in the animosity that had characterized much of the Cold War.)*

Guided Reading and Discussion

Explain that the Soviet Union's command economy could not keep up with the West's free market systems. Ask students how the arms race put pressure on the Soviet economy. *(The inefficient Soviet economy had stagnated, and the Soviets, already involved in a costly war in Afghanistan, were unable to produce the weaponry needed to keep up with the United States.)*

The Soviet Union Collapses

Gorbachev's restructuring sent the economy into a tailspin, leading to shortages, higher prices, and unemployment. Meanwhile, glasnost opened the communist system to criticism and undermined the government's strict control over the Soviet empire. One by one, Soviet republics broke away and declared their independence. The Soviet Union officially dissolved in December 1991.

The Command Economy Stagnates The Soviet economy faced severe problems. Unlike the economies of Western Europe and the United States, which experienced booms during the Cold War, the communist economies of Eastern Europe and the Soviet Union stagnated. Central economic planning led to inefficiency and waste. In competition with free market economies of the West, the Soviet command economy began to collapse. It could not match the West in production of quality consumer goods. People saw little improvement in their lives and envied their western neighbors.

The arms race put an additional strain on the Soviet economy. By the 1980s, both superpowers were spending massive sums on costly weapons systems. U.S. President Ronald Reagan began a massive military buildup, partly because he believed that the Soviet Union could not afford to spend as much on defense as the United States. When Reagan launched a new round of missile development, it was clear that the Soviet economy could not afford to match it.

Gorbachev Tries Reform In 1985, an energetic new leader, **Mikhail Gorbachev** (GAWR buh chawf), came to power in the Soviet Union. In foreign policy, Gorbachev sought to end Cold War tensions. To ease tensions, Gorbachev renounced the Brezhnev Doctrine, which had asserted the Soviet Union had a right to intervene militarily in any Warsaw Pact nation.

He signed arms control treaties with the United States and eventually pulled Soviet troops out of Afghanistan.

At home, Gorbachev launched a two-pronged effort at reform. First, he called for **glasnost,** or openness. He ended censorship and encouraged people to talk openly about the country's problems.

Second, he urged **perestroika** (pehr uh STROY kuh), or the restructuring of government and the economy. Gorbachev's reforms also included a lessening of restraints on emigration. Natan Sharansky, a Soviet scientist and human rights activist, had been imprisoned for ten years for treason. Long denied permission to emigrate, he was released in exchange for a Soviet spy in 1986 and settled in Israel.

Streamlining government and reducing the size of the bureaucracy, he hoped, would boost efficiency and output. He backed some free-market ideas, including limited private enterprise. But he still wanted to keep the essence of communism.

Corrupt or inefficient officials were dismissed. To produce more and higher-quality goods, factory managers, instead of central planners, were made responsible for decisions. To increase food supplies, farmers were allowed more land on which to grow food to sell on the free market.

>> Gorbachev struggled at home, but the United States welcomed Soviet reforms. President Ronald Reagan and Mikhail Gorbachev shake hands before a summit near Geneva in 1985. In a 1987 speech near the Berlin Wall, Reagan urged Gorbachev to "tear down this wall!"

IDENTIFY SUPPORTING DETAILS What economic problems did the Soviets face in the 1970s and 1980s?

The Soviet Union Collapses

Gorbachev faced a host of problems. His policies brought rapid change that led to economic turmoil. Shortages grew worse, and prices soared. Factories that could not survive without government help closed, throwing thousands out of work. Old-line Communists and bureaucrats whose careers were at stake denounced the reforms. At the same time, other critics demanded even more changes.

The Soviet Empire Crumbles Glasnost encouraged unrest in the multinational Soviet empire. The Baltic republics of Estonia, Latvia, and Lithuania, which had been seized by the Soviet Union in 1940, broke away in 1990, declaring independence soon after. In Eastern Europe, countries from Poland to Bulgaria broke out of

Answers

Identify Supporting Details *The Soviets had an inefficient command economy that produced inferior consumer goods and led to inefficiency and waste. Heavy military spending further strained the Soviet economy.*

English Language Proficiency Standards

Writing 5.E.1 Read "The Soviet Union Declines" aloud, and use it for the following.

Beginning Explain to students that there are more verb tenses than just past, present, and future. For example, the past progressive tense lets a reader know that an action that occurred in the past was in progress over a period of time. Use the following two sentences to demonstrate the difference between the simple past tense and the past progressive tense. Underline the verbs in both sentences and explain the difference between the two verb forms. (1) The arms race put an additional strain on the Soviet economy. (2) By the 1980s, both superpowers were spending massive sums on costly weapons systems.

Intermediate Complete the Beginning activity, but have students underline the verbs in both sentences. Help them identify and explain the difference between the two verb forms.

Advanced Explain the past progressive tense. Have small groups of students find sentences in the text with verbs in the past progressive tense.

>> **Analyze Maps** The Soviet Union officially dissolved in 1991, and many former republics gained independence. Which of the former Soviet republics is the largest?

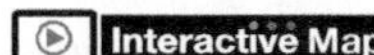

the Soviet orbit, beginning in 1989. Russia's postwar empire seemed to be collapsing.

In mid-1991, Soviet hardliners tried to overthrow Gorbachev and restore the old order. Their attempted coup failed, but it further weakened Gorbachev. By year's end, as other Soviet republics declared independence, Gorbachev resigned.

End of the Soviet Union In December 1991, the Union of Soviet Socialist Republics was officially dissolved after almost 70 years. Its 15 republics became separate independent nations. Russia, the largest republic, had dominated the Soviet Union.

After the breakup, Russia and its new president, Boris Yeltsin, faced a difficult future. They struggled to build a market economy and prevent violent conflict between pro-democracy and pro-communist groups. Like Russia, the other former Soviet republics like Ukraine and Kazakhstan faced hard times. They wanted to build stable governments and improve their standards of living. But ethnic violence and economic troubles proved obstacles. Some republics had stores of nuclear weapons, which they agreed to give up in exchange for aid and investment from the West.

 **SUMMARIZE** How did Gorbachev's reforms lead to a new map of Europe and Asia?

Eastern Europe Transformed

During the Cold War, Eastern Europe lay in the Soviet orbit. Efforts to resist Soviet domination were met with harsh repression. Despite the Soviet threat, some nations in Eastern Europe slowly made reforms. After Mikhail Gorbachev announced that the Soviet Union would no longer intervene in Eastern Europe, a "democracy movement" swept the region, and the nations of Eastern Europe were remarkably transformed.

Poland Struggles Toward Democracy Poland was the Soviet Union's most troublesome satellite. In 1956, protests had led to some reforms, but dissatisfaction with communism remained strong. The Roman Catholic Church, which often faced persecution, became a rallying symbol for Poles who opposed the communist regime.

In 1980, economic hardships ignited strikes of shipyard workers. Led by **Lech Walesa** (lek vah WEN suh), they organized an independent labor union, called **Solidarity.** It soon claimed millions of members, who pressed for political change.

Under pressure from the Soviet Union, the Polish government outlawed Solidarity and arrested its leaders, including Walesa. Still, unrest simmered.

Online Project the **Interactive Map: The Fall of the Soviet Union**, and observe the changes that occur when the slider is moved.

ACTIVE CLASSROOM

Use the Rank It strategy. Put four pieces of chart paper on the wall that list key reasons the Soviet Union declined and collapsed (Afghanistan, Stagnation of command economy, Arms race, Glasnost). Form small groups. Assign each group one reason, and have them come up with an explanation of why it contributed to the Soviet decline and collapse. Have a representative from each group write their explanation on their reason's chart paper. Discuss as a class.

D Differentiate Challenge/Gifted Have a group of students research and present to the class a "You Are There" news report about the fall of communism in Eastern Europe and the Soviet Union. If available, use audiovisual equipment to record the presentation or incorporate video into it.

Guided Reading and Discussion

Remind students that in the Soviet command economy, workers were guaranteed employment and health care. Have students explain why Gorbachev's restructuring caused economic turmoil. *(shortages; factories closed; unemployment soared; disagreement over whether reforms were going too fast or too slow)*

Have them write these sentences in their notes and underline the verb forms in each one. Then have each group write two sentences of their own about the weaknesses of the Soviet Union, using the past progressive tense.

Advanced High Have students work in pairs to follow the instructions in the Advanced activity.

Answers

Analyze Maps *Kazakhstan*

Summarize *Gorbachev's policies led to the weakening of centralized communist power. As a result, countries under Soviet domination broke free, and the republics of the Soviet Union separated into 15 independent nations.*

Eastern Europe Transformed

Explain that the satellite states of the Soviet Union, such as Hungary, Czechoslovakia, and Romania, moved from communism to democracy following its collapse. In the 1980s, Polish workers organized an independent labor union and fought for economic and political reforms.

Online Project the **Interactive Timeline: The Fall of Communism in Eastern Europe**, and sort the tiles with students.

ACTIVE CLASSROOM

Use the If Photos Could Talk strategy. Have students form small groups. Ask each group to create a question to ask one of the people pictured in photographs in this text. Then, ask them to trade questions with another group and answer the question they receive.

Guided Reading and Discussion

Remind students that the Soviet Union responded to Eastern European resistance in the 1950s and 1960s with repression and violence. Ask them to explain why Eastern European reforms were allowed to happen in the late 1980s. *(Sample responses: because Gorbachev had renounced the Brezhnev Doctrine, which had asserted that the Soviet Union had a right to intervene militarily in any Warsaw Pact nation; because Gorbachev himself was pushing for political reforms—though not democratization)*

>> Lech Walesa traveled to Italy in 1981 to meet Pope John Paul II, the first Polish pope. The pope was a great supporter of the Solidarity movement.

Interactive Timeline

>> Residents of East and West Berlin walk atop the Berlin Wall in front of the Brandenburg Gate on November 11, 1989. The wall was torn down shortly after.

Walesa became a national hero and the Polish government eventually released him from prison.

Pressure from the world community further strained Poland's communist government and helped hasten its collapse. Pope John Paul II visited Poland, met with Solidarity leaders, and criticized communist policies. The pope was the former Karol Wojtyla, archbishop of the Polish city of Cracow.

In the late 1980s, Poland—like the Soviet Union—began to introduce radical economic reforms. It legalized Solidarity and in 1989 sponsored the first free elections in 50 years. Lech Walesa was soon elected president of Poland. The new government began a difficult but peaceful transition from socialism to a market economy. It helped mark the start of the collapse of Soviet domination and communism in Eastern Europe.

Revolution and Freedom By 1989, the "democracy movement" in Eastern Europe was sweeping out old governments and ushering in new ones. People took to the streets, demanding reform.

In the 1970s and 1980s, Hungary had quietly introduced some modest economic reforms. Later, in the spirit of glasnost, Hungarians began to criticize their government more openly. Under growing pressure, the communist government allowed other political parties and opened its border with Austria.

That move allowed thousands of East Germans to escape into Hungary, and from there, to the West. Within a few months, Germans tore down the Berlin Wall, a move that would soon lead to the reunification of Germany.

One by one, communist governments fell across Eastern Europe. In Czechoslovakia, **Vaclav Havel** (VAHTS lahv HAH vul), a dissident writer and human rights activist, was elected president. Most changes came peacefully, but when **Nicolae Ceausescu** (chow SHES koo), Romania's long time dictator, refused to step down, he was overthrown and executed.

For the first time since 1945, Eastern European countries were free to settle their own affairs. They withdrew from the Warsaw Pact and requested that Soviet troops leave. By then, Soviet power itself was crumbling.

Ethnic Tensions in Eastern Europe Centuries of migrations and conquest left most Eastern European nations with ethnically diverse populations. Most countries had a majority population with one or more ethnic minorities that asserted their own identities. Nationalism helped unite some countries such as Poland and Hungary, but it was also a divisive force.

English Language Proficiency Standards

Learning Strategies 1.D.1 Read aloud "Eastern Europe Transformed." Have students identify unfamiliar words, and use synonyms to help them understand how Eastern Europe changed in the late 20th century.

Beginning Reread the first paragraph of the text aloud. Have students identify words they do not know by completing the following: I'm not sure what ________ means. Use gestures or movements to illustrate the word so that students can come up with a synonym. Have students replace the unfamiliar word with the synonym to see if they now understand the meaning of the word.

Intermediate Reread the first paragraph of the text aloud. Have students identify words they do not know, and list them. Have groups use dictionaries, thesauruses, or other resources to find synonyms for each word. Ask them to replace each target word with any of its synonyms, and discuss whether the meaning of the sentence remains the same.

Advanced Have pairs read the text to identify words they do not know, and then follow the instructions in the Intermediate activity.

Advanced High Have students work individually to read the text and identify words they do not know, and then follow the instructions in the Intermediate activity. Have students share and compare their lists of synonyms with a partner.

Faced with ethnic tensions, Czechoslovakia peacefully split into two countries, the Czech Republic and Slovakia. In 1991, however, ethnic conflict tore apart the Balkan nation of Yugoslavia.

The Breakup of Yugoslavia During World War II, a skilled guerrilla leader, Josip Tito, had battled Germany occupying forces. Later, Tito set up a communist government in Yugoslavia, but he pursued a path independent of Moscow. He refused to join the Warsaw Pact and claimed to be neutral in the Cold War.

After Tito's death and the fall of communism, a wave of nationalism tore Yugoslavia apart. The country consisted of six republics, including Bosnia-Herzegovina, Croatia, Macedonia, Montenegro, Serbia, and Slovenia. In 1992, Slovenia and Croatia broke away after a bitter conflict with Serbia. That year, another conflict erupted in Bosnia, which declared independence.

Most Bosnians were Muslims, but many Serbs and Croats lived there. Bosnian Serbs rejected independence, and with money and arms from Serbia, they seized much of Bosnia. In a brutal war, Serbs practiced "ethnic cleansing," forcibly removing other ethnic groups from the areas they controlled. Hundreds of thousands of Bosnians became refugees. Others were tortured or killed. Sarajevo, the capital of Bosnia, came under a deadly siege by Bosnian Serb forces.

Restoring Peace Bosnia became a test case for the role of the United States and the Western powers in the post Cold-War world. For three years, the UN tried unsuccessfully to bring about peace. As Bosnian Serbs advanced, the United States and its NATO allies debated whether or not to intervene militarily or whether to arm the Bosnian Muslims and Croats.

In 1995, the United States helped broker a peace agreement, known as the Dayton Accords, which ended the war in Bosnia. NATO peacekeepers enforced the agreements in the troubled Balkan region, and the various new nations set out to recover from the brutal ethnic conflict.

 **IDENTIFY CAUSE AND EFFECT** How did glasnost in the Soviet Union contribute to the end of communist rule in Eastern Europe?

ELPS **ELPS 1.D.1** Create a list of words in the text that you do not understand. Ask a partner or your teacher to help you find synonyms for each unfamiliar word.

>> At a 1992 peace demonstration in Sarajevo, the capital of Bosnia, protesters crouch to avoid fire from Serbian snipers on a hotel roof. The Bosnian special forces soldier returns fire.

Communism Declines Around the World

The collapse of communism in the Soviet Union and Eastern Europe affected other communist nations. Cuba, which had long depended on Soviet aid and support, faced severe difficulties. Its economy suffered, too, from sanctions imposed by the United States decades earlier.

In 2006, Raul Castro, brother of the ailing leader, Fidel Castro, took over the Cuban government. He allowed some market reforms and sought investment from countries in Europe, Asia, and Latin America. Despite some economic easing, Castro kept tight political control over the island nation.

Other Communist Nations Adopt Market Reforms China began to introduce limited market reforms, such as allowing some private enterprise and foreign investment, in the early 1980s. The reforms brought increased prosperity for some Chinese. By the early 2000s, China's economy was booming, and its many new factories were turning out manufactured goods for a growing global market.

In China, as in Cuba, economic change did not bring political reform. The Chinese Communist party kept its

Communism Declines Around the World

The Post–Cold War World

Remind students that during the Cold War, the Soviet Union and countries such as China, Vietnam, North Korea, and Cuba had communist dictatorships and command economies. Explain that since the fall of the Soviet Union, communism has declined. Cuba and North Korea are the only communist countries that still have command economies. China and Vietnam, though still politically repressive, have embraced aspects of capitalism. Explain also that the United States is the sole remaining superpower.

Guided Reading and Discussion

Tell students that in China, state ownership of industry has decreased markedly since the 1980s, and gross domestic product (GDP) has soared. Discuss how these two economic trends are related. *(Students should understand that China's introduction of market reforms, however limited, has helped spur the economy.)* Tell students that one thing is unchanged—the complete political control of the Communist Party, which means that the state still has a great influence on China's economy.

History Background

The Writer's Life While campaigning for democracy in Czechoslovakia, Václav Havel was arrested many times. His offenses included organizing dissidents and writing plays and essays that implied that the Czech government was absurd, demoralizing, and corrupt. (In his best-known play, *The Memorandum,* office workers are forced to speak a nonsensical language under the assumption that it will make them communicate with each other more effectively.) Once in power, Havel was criticized for being too soft and too thoughtful an administrator, and he often admitted that he felt personally unsuited to be president. However, his policies brought civil liberties and rights to his country.

Answers

Identify Cause and Effect *Glasnost led to a loosening of Soviet control in Eastern Europe and to a greater ability for Eastern European nations to resist Soviet rule.*

SYNTHESIZE

Online **Project the Digital Activity: Cold War Leaders.** Give students a few minutes to construct their graphic organizers, in which they categorize leaders as either pro-reform or anti-reform. Have them share their categorizations with the class.

Discuss Why do you think North Korea and Cuba have remained repressive communist states with command economies? *(Sample response: The people are afraid that pressuring the government to change would bring greater repression.)*

DEMONSTRATE

Online Assign the **Digital Lesson Quiz** for this lesson if you haven't already done so. Students will be offered automatic remediation or enrichment based on their score.

Pose the following to the class on the Discussion Board:

In "The Cold War Ends," you read about why the Soviet Union declined and ultimately collapsed and how a democratization movement swept Soviet-dominated Eastern Europe. You also learned how the end of the Cold War affected other communist nations and the United States.

Hypothesize Was the fall of communism inevitable? Support your answer with evidence.

Identify Central Issues Will the United States continue to be the world's sole superpower? Why or why not?

Topic Inquiry

Have students continue their investigations for the Topic Inquiry.

monopoly on power, and the government cracked down on any signs of discontent.

China's government undertook no major political reforms. However, as the global economic crisis that began in 2008 led to factory closings, protests by unemployed workers increased. China's government responded with a $600 billion stimulus package to retrain workers and improve productivity.

Different Paths for Vietnam and North Korea Two other communist nations in Asia, Vietnam and North Korea, took different paths. Vietnam allowed some market reforms and won increased foreign investment. North Korea, however, clung to its old ideology, continuing its strict isolation from the world.

COMPARE How did other communist countries react to the collapse of the Soviet bloc?

The Post-Cold War World

When the Cold War ended in the early 1990s, Americans hoped for a more peaceful world. But as the sole superpower, the United States played a leading role in trying to resolve world conflicts. The United States led coalition forces in several missions around the world.

The United States and its European allies were also eager to help the new nations of Eastern Europe to make the difficult transition to democracy and capitalism. They provided advice and loans, but also required far-reaching economic reforms.

The Move Toward Market Economies In the aftermath of the Cold War, the nations of Eastern Europe—as well as Russia and the former Soviet republics—set out to build stable democratic governments and replace their old command economies with free-market economies. Although the experiences of each nation differed, all faced similar challenges.

To attract badly needed foreign investment, governments had to push radical economic reforms. They privatized industries and stopped keeping prices for basic goods and services low. They ended many benefits from the old days such as free tuition at universities. At first, the changes brought hardships such as high unemployment, soaring prices, and crime. Consumer goods were more plentiful, but few people could afford them.

A further stumbling block to progress was the global economic recession that started in 2008. Economic hard times brought a rise of anti-foreign sentiment along with anti-Semitic and anti-Roma (Gypsy) hate speech from extremist groups. Despite these challenges, the governments of Eastern Europe remained democratic.

SUMMARIZE What steps did former Communist nations have to take to transition to market economies?

ASSESSMENT

1. **Draw Conclusions** Why was the Soviet Union unable to keep up with the market economies of the West?
2. **Summarize** How did Gorbachev's reforms lead to the breakup of the Soviet empire?
3. **Identify Cause and Effect** Why were Eastern Europeans able to break free of communist governments and Soviet domination in the late 1980s?
4. **Infer** How did the collapse of the Soviet Union affect the United States?
5. **Infer** Why might some communist nations have adopted market principles after the fall of the Soviet Union?

The Cold War Era  872 19.5 The Cold War Ends

Answers

Compare *Cuba and North Korea remained committed to communism and command economies. Vietnam and China moved toward market economies, though they did not loosen political oppression.*

Summarize *They privatized industries and stopped fixing prices for basic goods and services. They also ended many benefits.*

Assessment

1. Central control was cumbersome and inefficient. Workers lacked incentive.
2. Gorbachev instituted reforms that allowed for criticism of the government and an increase in private enterprise. Reforms encouraged opposition to the Soviet system and a new market economy.
3. In the late 1980s, Gorbachev said that the Soviet Union would not interfere with reforms in Eastern Europe. Without Soviet backing, the communist governments of Eastern Europe fell.
4. America emerged as the world's sole superpower.
5. They were suffering from economic stagnation and were probably hoping to benefit economically from increased trade and greater interaction with the West.

EAST AND WEST GERMANY IN 1968 AN ECONOMIC COMPARISON

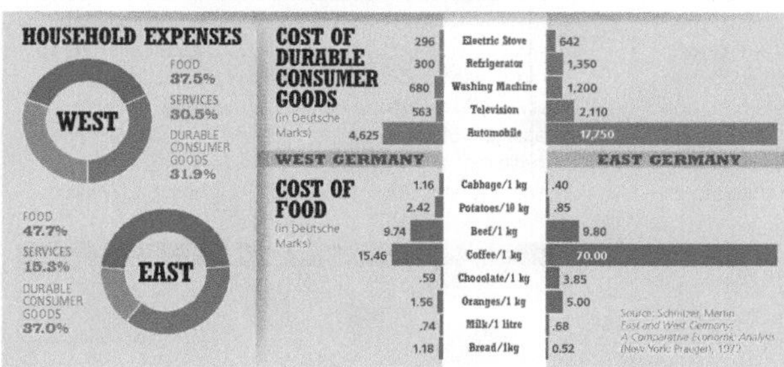

1. **Explain Economic Collapse** Explain why communist command economies collapsed in competition with free market economies at the end of the twentieth century. Look at the above chart. Write a paragraph that explains why communist command economies could not compete with free market economies in the two Germanys. Consider the cost of durable consumer goods, cost of food, West Germany's economy, and East Germany's economy. **18.E**
2. **Describe Effects** Describe the major effects of World War II's impact on social and political systems. Write one or two paragraphs describing how the fear of the spread of communism impacted U.S. social and political systems after World War II. Consider Senator Joseph McCarthy and the House Un-American Activities Committee, anti-communist propaganda, and creation of fallout shelters and air-raid drills. **1.F**
3. **Describe Effects** Describe the major effects of World War II's impact on political and economic systems. Read the quote below. Write one or two paragraphs describing how the "iron curtain" influenced political and economic systems after World War II. Consider the Truman Doctrine, Marshall Plan, NATO, and Warsaw Pact. **1.F**

   "An 'iron curtain' has descended across the Continent. Behind that line all of the capitals of the ancient states of Central and Eastern Europe . . . all these famous cities . . . lie in what I must call the Soviet sphere, and are subject . . . to a great measure of control from Moscow."

   —Winston Churchill
4. **Summarize Outcome and Identify Major Events** Summarize how the outcome of World War II contributed to the development of the Cold War, and identify the following major events of the Cold War, including the arms race. Write one or two paragraphs about how the outcome of World War II lead to the Cold War and the arms race. Consider the joint occupation of Germany, opposing U.S. and Soviet goals to support Eastern Europe, increased threat during the nuclear arms race, and Western actions in occupying Japan and Italy. **13.A**
5. **Summarize Role and Differences** Summarize Mao Zedong's role in the rise of communism in China and how communism in China differed from Soviet communism. Write a paragraph about how communism implemented by Mao Zedong in China differed from Soviet communism. Consider the roles of the Chinese peasantry, the industrial and agricultural goals of Mao's Great Leap Forward, and the Cultural Revolution. **13.B**
6. **Identify Examples** Identify examples of politically motivated mass murders in China. Write a paragraph that explains how the Chinese Communist Party used violence and murder for political means. Consider which groups the government viewed as a threat, how religious groups were treated, the Cultural Revolution, and why Mao wanted the threat of violence to be publicized. **22.C**
7. **Identify and Describe** Identify examples of individuals who led resistance to political oppression: Natan Sharansky, and describe how people have participated in changing their governments. Write a paragraph that identifies Natan Sharansky and other activists who worked for citizen-led political change during the Cold War era. Consider why Sharansky was imprisoned and the circumstances of other leaders who fought for workers' rights and human rights. **21.A, 22.E**
8. **Identify Events** Identify the following major events of the Cold War, including the Vietnam War. Write a paragraph about how the Vietnam War became a major event of the Cold War. Consider attempts to conquer Vietnam during World War II, the split between North Vietnam and South Vietnam, and why the United States chose to get involved. **13.C**

Answers to TEKS Assessment

1. Students should explain that in communist command economies, the government makes all economic decisions, while in free market economies, producers and consumers make the economic decisions. Students should identify West Germany as a free market economy and East Germany as a command economy. Students should note that inefficient command economies could not meet consumer needs during the Cold War and produced inferior goods. Students should also cite the higher food and durable goods costs in East Germany as one reason for the collapse of communist command economies and the transition to free market economies.

2. Students should describe how the threat of communism and fear of nuclear war led Americans to build fallout shelters in case of nuclear attack. Students should explain how fear and anti-communist propaganda led to a "Red Scare" in which Americans were targeted for alleged communist sympathies. Senator McCarthy led a hunt for suspected American communists in the United States government and became notorious for his unproven charges. Students should also explain how the House Un-American Activities Committee sought to identify suspected communists in Hollywood's high-profile movie industry.

3. Students should describe that the "iron curtain" resulted from the Soviet Union's imposition of its political and economic systems on the countries of Eastern Europe that it occupied after World War II. Students should explain how the "iron curtain" separated the communist East from the democratic West. The "iron curtain" led to military, political, and economic alliances in the West, such as NATO, and the Warsaw Pact in the East. These alliances directly opposed one another. Students should use specific details to describe how the United States, per the Truman Doctrine, wanted to contain the spread of communism as the Soviet Union looked to expand its influence.

4. Students should explain how the alliance between the United States and the Soviet Union dissolved over the issues of reparations from Germany and the Soviet Union's refusal to allow free elections in the Eastern European countries it occupied after the war. The Soviets pointed out that the United States was not consulting them about peace terms for Italy or Japan. Students should understand that the Cold War was escalated by advancements in military technology and the nuclear arms race, as each superpower developed new weapons to deter the other from launching its nuclear arsenal.

5. Students should explain that Mao's version of communism differed from Soviet communism because it placed more power in the hands of the peasantry, identifying them as the major force behind the communist revolution. The Soviets trusted in a revolutionary elite of urban intellectuals and workers. Also, a cult of personality developed around Mao that was not matched by any Cold War leader in the Soviet Union. The student should also understand that Mao implemented the Great Leap Forward to increase industrial output and farm production. The failure of this program led to terrible famines and millions of deaths. Students should note that Mao also began the Cultural Revolution to purge China of "bourgeois" tendencies, with the accused publicly beaten, humiliated, sent to labor camps, or even killed. These programs differed from Soviet communism.

6. Students should explain how mass murder was used after China's communist revolution as a means of eliminating landowners and other middle-class or wealthy citizens who were viewed as counterrevolutionary and oppressive to the peasant classes. The student should also understand that religion was viewed as being against communist

Answers to TEKS Assessment

ideology and that open practice of religion could result in death. The student should also understand that the goal of the Cultural Revolution was to purge China of "bourgeois" or nonrevolutionary tendencies so the younger generation could experience revolution firsthand. Students may suggest that Mao probably wanted the threat of violence to be publicized to instill fear and maintain order.

7. Students should explain that Natan Sharansky was a Soviet scientist and human rights activist who tried to emigrate to Israel. He was convicted of treason and imprisoned for ten years before he was finally allowed to emigrate. Students should also discuss other important leaders in Eastern Europe, such as Lech Walesa, who led Solidarity, the Polish labor union, and was imprisoned for his activities. He was later elected president of Poland. Václav Havel of Czechoslovakia was a dissident writer and human rights activist who was elected president of Czechoslovakia.

8. Students should explain that Vietnam was a French colony in the 1800s and that Japan controlled Vietnam during World War II. France attempted to reclaim Vietnam in 1946 but was defeated by communist Vietnamese forces led by Ho Chi Minh. In 1954, after the French defeat, Vietnam was divided into communist North Vietnam and South Vietnam, which was headed by a pro-West dictator. Students should note that the United States sent advisers to South Vietnam when communist guerrillas tried to overthrow South Vietnam's government. The United States applied the domino theory to prevent more countries from falling to communist forces. As more U.S. troops were sent, a regional struggle became a Cold War conflict.

9. Students should explain that Gorbachev's economic reform policies resulted in turmoil and hardship in the Soviet Union. Shortages grew worse and prices soared. Factories closed, leading to high unemployment. Gorbachev's policies also led to unrest in Eastern Europe, as countries in the Soviet orbit broke away. This caused hardline Soviet communist leaders to try to overthrow Gorbachev. Although they failed, these problems weakened Gorbachev's government, led to his resignation, and promoted the fall of communism.

10. Students should explain that Lech Walesa became a national hero for his leadership of the Polish Solidarity movement, which demanded political and economic change. Walesa was jailed when the Polish government outlawed the union. Pope John Paul II, who was from Poland, visited Poland and met with Walesa and other Solidarity leaders to show his support. The pope also criticized communist policies. This added to the international pressure on Poland's communist government to make reforms. Other Eastern European communist governments also began to feel both domestic and international pressure for reforms.

11. Students should explain that under communist command economies, the government made all economic decisions. Command economies did not produce adequate consumer goods, so their citizens had poor "quality of life" compared with the West. Students should discuss how the shift to free enterprise systems in Eastern Europe and Poland provided choices and opportunities for private and public investment that build wealth and improve the quality of life and the human condition. Free market economies also provide consumer goods that improve the human condition. Students should draw conclusions based on evidence and statistics comparing the quality of life under command economies to that of free market economies.

TEKS ASSESSMENT

9. **Explain Roles** Explain the roles of modern world leaders, including Mikhail Gorbachev, in the collapse of communism in Eastern Europe and the Soviet Union. Write a paragraph explaining how Gorbachev's policies lead to the collapse of communism in Eastern Europe and the Soviet Union. Consider the problems caused by his efforts at reform, how these policies created opposition, and how these tensions contributed to the fall of the Soviet Union. 13.D

10. **Explain Roles** Explain the roles of modern world leaders, including Lech Walesa and Pope John Paul II, in the collapse of communism in Eastern Europe and the Soviet Union. Write a paragraph explaining the roles of Lech Walesa and Pope John Paul II in the fall of communism in Poland. Consider Walesa's role in the Polish Solidarity movement and the Pope's criticism of communism. How did this lead to pressure for reforms by other communist countries? 13.D

11. **Formulate Generalizations** Formulate generalizations on how economic freedom improved the human condition based on the benefits of free enterprise in twentieth-century free market economies compared to communist command communities. Write a paragraph that explains the benefits of free enterprise and democracy for the Polish people. Consider economic reforms in Poland, choices that build wealth and improve the quality of life, and the issues with communist command industries. 18.F

12. **Describe Influences** Describe the major influences of women during major eras of world history: Margaret Thatcher. Write a paragraph describing how Prime Minister Margaret Thatcher influenced policies in social spending and private industry. Consider the effect of the welfare state and changes made in social spending levels, privatization of certain industries, and curbing the power of the labor unions. 24.B

Welfare Collected in United Kingdom

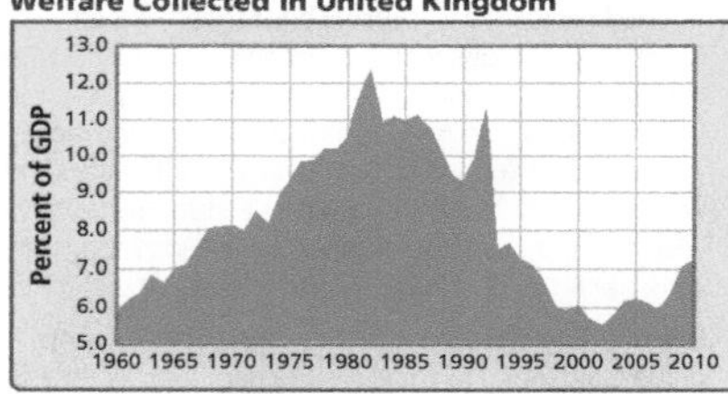

13. **Describe Major Effects, Summarize Outcome, and Identify Characteristics** Describe the major effects of communist revolutions and their impact on the Cold War, summarize how the outcome of World War II contributed to the development of the Cold War, and identify characteristics of the free enterprise system. Write a paragraph about how U.S. support after World War II was used to prevent communist revolutions in several European countries. Consider the geographic locations of countries that received American aid and those that did not, the goal of postwar international aid programs, and how U.S. aid supported a Western market economy. 1.F, 13.A, 18.A

NATO and Warsaw Pact, 1977

14. **Explain Effects** Explain the effects of major new military technologies on the Cold War. Write a paragraph that describes how the new forms of military technology impacted the Cold War. Consider anti-ballistic missiles, the Cuban Missile Crisis, nuclear arms, and the space race and satellite technology. 28.C

15. **Identify Individuals** Identify examples of individuals who led resistance to political oppression. Write a paragraph that describes how Andrei Sakharov, Natan Sharansky, and Aleksandr Solzhenitsyn resisted political oppression in the Soviet Union. Consider their complaints against the Soviet government, their punishments, and the reasons for publicizing their cases. 22.E

16. **Summarize Outcome** Summarize how the outcome of World War II contributed to the development of the Cold War. Write a paragraph that describes how post-World War II decisions led to regional conflicts that contributed to the Cold War. Consider opposing ideologies of the two superpowers, the use of occupying forces by both sides in East Asia, Soviet support for communist China, and the events that led to the start of the Korean War. 13.A

17. **Reflect on the Essential Question Write an essay on the Essential Question: How should we handle conflict?** Use evidence from your study of this Topic to support your answer.

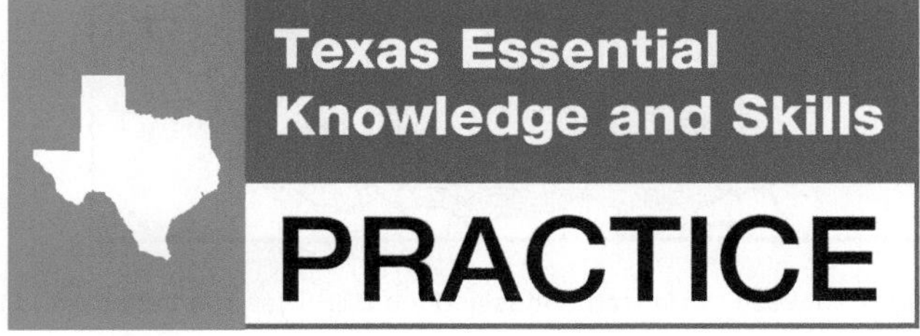

12. Students should explain that British conservatives denounced the welfare state as being too inefficient and expensive, with high taxes, too much regulation of private industry, and government takeovers of basic industries. Students should also understand that Margaret Thatcher's Conservative administration responded by reducing spending on social welfare programs, privatizing government-run industries, curbing the power of labor unions, and reducing the size of government. Her policies led to protests in Great Britain, but other European countries soon limited their social welfare benefits and privatized industries.

13. Students should explain that post–World War II Europe was in ruins. Seeing that this would prove fertile ground for communist revolutions, the United States implemented the Marshall Plan to provide food and economic assistance to strengthen democratic Western European nations. They rebuilt quickly. Stalin forbade U.S. aid to Eastern Europe. Students should note that the Truman Doctrine called for the containment of communism. The United States provided military and economic aid to help Greece and Turkey withstand communist threats. Students should understand that the United States had and supported a free enterprise system in which prices are based on supply and demand, property is privately owned, and producers and consumers decide what goods are produced.

14. Students should identify several new forms of military technology from the period and how these weapons contributed to the escalation of the arms race and the Cold War. Anti-ballistic missiles (ABMs) could defend against missile attacks and led to fears that the protected side would attack. The placement of Soviet nuclear missiles in Cuba, close to the United States, led to an international crisis. Students should explain how the threat of more precise and destructive nuclear weapons and advanced launch systems cultivated a sense of fear throughout the world.

15. Students should explain how Soviet dissidents like Andrei Sakharov and Natan Sharansky challenged the Soviet government by pointing out human rights abuses. Sakharov was exiled to a remote city. Sharansky was convicted of treason and imprisoned in a Siberian labor camp. Another dissident, Aleksandr Solzhenitsyn, was sent to a labor camp after he criticized Stalin in a letter to a friend. His writing was banned, and he was eventually exiled. These men became symbols of resistance to Soviet communism and inspired others. The publicizing of their cases demonstrated the abuses of the Soviet government and the communist system.

16. Students should explain that after World War II, the world was dominated by two superpowers, the United States and the Soviet Union. These countries had conflicting political and economic ideologies. The Soviet Union spread communism to the Eastern European countries it occupied after the war and supported the new communist government in China. The United States wanted to contain communism and provided support to countries resisting communist forces. After World War II, the United States and the Soviet Union agreed to temporarily divide Korea. North Korea had a pro-Soviet communist dictator, and South Korea had a dictator backed by the United States. When North Korean troops invaded South Korea to "unite" Korea, it triggered the Korean War. The war in Vietnam began in a similar way. The Cold War was characterized by an uneasy strategy of maintaining military, economic, and strategic balance between the two superpowers, both in East Asia and globally.

Topic 19

Answers to TEKS Practice

1. B
2. J

Online To prepare for the End-of-Topic test, have students go online for additional Topic Review and Assessment questions or to review their notes in the **Interactive Reading Notepad** for the lessons in this Topic.

Benchmark Tests

Assign these benchmark tests as you complete the relevant topics to monitor student progress toward mastering the course content and as preparation for the End-of-Course Test.

Benchmark Test 1: Topics 1–5

Benchmark Test 2: Topics 6–10

Benchmark Test 3: Topics 11–15

Benchmark Test 4: Topics 16–21

TEKS PRACTICE

1

Why did relations between the United States and the USSR fall apart after World War II?

A Stalin wanted to continue the war until he owned France.

B Stalin wanted to create a buffer zone of satellite states to prevent invasion.

C Stalin demanded to annex all of the land once owned by Germany.

D Stalin wanted to be paid for all of the damage that Germany had committed in the USSR.

---

2 How did World War II impact social systems?

F Discrimination against Jews ended in all parts of the world.

G U.S. aid to Europe through the Marshall Plan helped to increase the standard of living in many European nations.

H The Great Depression ended, and fewer people were unemployed.

J Many women who had joined the workforce wanted to remain working outside of the home.

The Cold War Era 876

Test Taking Tips: Tip for Questions With Maps

1. Read the question.
2. Read the map title and look at the map to determine what is shown in the map.
3. Look at the key or legend. What symbols, shades, or patterns are used to show information on the map? Find examples of each symbol, shade, or pattern on the map.
4. Read the question again. What information do you need from the map to answer the question? Use the information in the map title, the key or legend, and on the map itself to find the answer.
5. Answer the question in your own words.
6. Read the answer choices and select the best answer.

3 How did the Communist revolution in Vietnam impact the Cold War?

A It weakened relations between the Soviet Union and China as they disagreed about tactics and which side to support.

B The United States and the Soviet Union continued to funnel aid and military supplies to their allied regions, escalating the conflict.

C It caused the Soviet Union to demand a withdrawal of U.S. forces from all of Asia to protect the actions of South Vietnam.

D Ho Chi Minh broke a peace treaty signed by Western and Communist powers that called for the reunification of North and South Vietnam, causing the Vietnam War.

4

Americans!
SHARE THE MEAT
as a wartime necessity
To meet the needs of our armed forces and fighting allies, a Government order limits the amount of meat delivered to stores and restaurants.
To share the supply fairly, all civilians are asked to limit their consumption of beef, veal, lamb, mutton and pork to 2½ lbs. per person per week.
YOUR FAIR WEEKLY SHARE
Men, women and children over 12 yrs. old 2½
Children 6 to 12 yrs. old 1½
Children under 6 yrs. old .... ¾
You can add these foods to your share: liver, sweetbreads, kidneys, brains and other variety meats; also poultry and fish.
HELP WIN THE WAR!
Keep within your share

How did rationing change the wartime economy?

F Citizens were expected to share instead of relying on supply and demand.

G Prices soared, and most people could no longer afford to purchase food.

H Some people were forced to give up canned food and sugar for the rest of the war.

J Poor people were forced to go to food pantries and share products with their neighbors.

If you have trouble with...				
Question	1	2	3	4
See Lesson	19.1	19.2	19.4	18.4
TEKS	13.A	1.F	1.F	1.F

3. B
4. F

Online Use the **Topic Synthesize** to help students revisit and reflect on the Essential Question for this Topic.

Topic Inquiry

If students have done a Topic Inquiry for this Topic, have them complete the final step of the Inquiry now.

New Nations Emerge (1945–Present)

TOPIC 20 ORGANIZER	PACING: APPROX. 1 PERIOD, .5 BLOCKS		
	PACING	TEKS	ELPS
Connect	1 period		
MY STORY VIDEO **Aung San Suu Kyi, Struggle for Democracy**	10 min.		
DIGITAL ESSENTIAL QUESTION ACTIVITY **What Should Governments Do?**	10 min.	21.A, 21.B	
DIGITAL TIMELINE ACTIVITY **New Nations Emerge**	10 min.	1.F, 13.E, 13.F, 14.A, 22.D	
TOPIC INQUIRY: PROJECT-BASED QUESTION **How Should Nations Respond to Genocide?**	20 min.		
Investigate	2–4 periods		
TOPIC INQUIRY: DOCUMENT-BASED QUESTION **How Should Nations Respond to Genocide?**	Ongoing		
LESSON 1 **New Nations in South Asia and Southeast Asia**	30–40 min.	1.F, 13.E, 15.A, 24.B	1.E.1, 5.F.1
LESSON 2 **African Nations Win Independence**	30–40 min.	1.F, 13.E, 22.D	1.E.2
LESSON 3 **The Modern Middle East Takes Shape**	30–40 min.	10.C, 13.E, 13.F, 15.A, 16.A, 16.C, 25.D	1.E.3, 5.F.3
LESSON 4 **Conflicts in the Middle East**	30–40 min.	13.E, 13.F, 14.A, 16.A	5.G.1
Synthesize	1 period		
DIGITAL ESSENTIAL QUESTION ACTIVITY **New Nations Emerge**	10 min.	1.F, 13.E, 13.F, 14.A, 21.A, 21.B, 22.D	
TOPIC INQUIRY: DOCUMENT-BASED QUESTION **How Should Nations Respond to Genocide?**	20 min.		
Demonstrate	1–2 periods		
DIGITAL TOPIC TEST **New Nations Emerge**	10 min.		
TOPIC INQUIRY: DOCUMENT-BASED QUESTION **How Should Nations Respond to Genocide?**	20 min.		

AUTHOR'S NOTE

The Liberation Struggle

The great liberation [of Africa from European colonialism] dramatically transformed the global political picture. A total of ninety new countries emerged between the mid-1940s and the 1990s. Well over a billion people—a third of the earth's population—gained their independence of foreign rule. . . .

The liberation struggles were a complex, confusing business, but some general patterns can be detected.

The leaders of the various movements for colonial emancipation tended to be both Westernized and charismatic. As Western-educated people, they could deal effectively with their European rulers. The internationally known poet Léopold Senghor of French West Africa of the British Gold Coast colony (today's Ghana), educated in France and in Britain and the United States, had no trouble dealing effectively with Westerners. As charismatic figures, flamboyant personalities such as Sukarno of the Dutch East Indies (Indonesia) and saintly ones such as Mahatma Gandhi in India could move their own people to action.

The strength of many colonial revolts also resided in powerful independence parties put together by the new colonial leadership. These intensely nationalistic organizations were strongly centralized on the person of the leader. They helped to overcome regional, religious, tribal, or other differences within the colony, to articulate common demands, and to mobilize mass support for challenges to colonial authority. After independence was achieved, however, these parties tended to become a stronger focus for loyalty than the new nation itself. In some places, they became the core of one-part governments.

In some of the emerging nations, as we shall see, bitter and sometimes long-drawn-out revolutions were fought before independence was achieved. In general, however, a relatively low level of violence—by comparison, say, with the long revolutions of the first half of the century—accompanied the great liberation.

—Anthony Esler, *The Human Venture: From Prehistory to the Present* (Upper Saddle River, New Jersey: Pearson Education, 2004), pp. 695–696

TOPIC INQUIRY: DOCUMENT-BASED QUESTION

How Should Nations Respond to Genocide?

TEKS 22.D, 29.C, 29.F, 29.G, 30.C, 30.D

In this Topic Inquiry, students work individually to analyze six documents that address in different ways the problem of genocide and how nations should respond to it. The documents include a first-person narrative, a photograph, a cartoon, and three essay excerpts from articles. Students will answer questions about each document, reflect on the ideas, draw their own conclusions, and then write an essay on the following question: How should nations respond to genocide? Learning how nations might choose to respond to genocide will contribute to students' understanding of the Topic Essential Question: What should governments do?

STEP 1: CONNECT

Develop Questions and Plan the Investigation

Launch the DBQ Writing Activity

Begin this activity by reminding students that genocide is defined as "a deliberate attempt to destroy an entire religious or ethnic group." Then ask students to work with a partner to discuss and write a list of five principles the world community should follow to decide if it should intervene to prevent or stop genocide. Have a volunteer read the examples. Suggest that they keep this list handy as they read the documents, answer the questions, and write their essays.

Suggestion: Have volunteers read their lists, and ask the rest of the class to discuss them. Ask: What are some risks a nation might face in intervening in another country's genocide?

Generate Questions

Divide the class into small groups and have them record their questions about whether nations should intervene to prevent or stop genocide.

Suggestion: Help students generate questions by asking them to think of genocides they have read about, such as the Holocaust. Ask them to consider what the United States or other nations did, did not do, or could have done to prevent or stop this genocide.

Resources

- Student Instructions
- Need-to-Know Questions

STEP 2: INVESTIGATE

Apply Disciplinary Concepts and Tools

Analyze the Documents

Have students analyze the six documents to see how they relate to the question: How should nations respond to genocide? Then, have them write an essay expressing their own opinions about this difficult question. Document A is the story of a survivor of the genocide in Rwanda, told on the CBS news program *60 Minutes*. Document B is a photograph of a moment in the lives of refugees at a refugee camp in South Sudan. In Documents C and D, two commentators debate in the *Chicago Tribune* whether the United States should intervene in the Bosnian genocide of the 1990s. Document E is a political cartoon addressing world inaction in cases of genocide. Document F is an excerpt from an article about a soldier who led the United Nations intervention in Bosnia and how the assignment affected him.

Suggestion: You can control the length of the DBQ by having students read just the two documents that focus on Bosnia (C and D) and the cartoon (E), or the three that focus on African problems (A, B, and F) and the cartoon (E).

Check Understanding

After students finish reading each individual document, have them answer the multiple-choice and short-answer questions attached to each document. Review the questions and discuss the answers after students have answered the questions for all the documents.

Resources

- Information Organizer

STEP 3: SYNTHESIZE

Evaluate Sources and Use Evidence to Formulate Conclusions

Write Your Essay

Have students consider all of the evidence and viewpoints and draw their own conclusions. Using the documents and their knowledge of history, have them write an essay on the following topic: **How should nations respond to genocide?**

Remind students that their essays should have the following characteristics: a topic sentence that states their views; evidence from at least *three* of the documents, clearly identified; relevant facts; an explanation and rebuttal of at least one opposing viewpoint; logical organization, including an introduction and a conclusion; and correct spelling, grammar, and punctuation.

Suggestion: Remind students that they need to anticipate disagreements readers may have with the points they make. Anticipating readers' objections will help them strengthen their own arguments and evidence.

Edit Your Essay

Remind students that they should revise their first draft and create a final draft of their essay before turning it in. You may want to suggest that they ask a classmate to peer edit their essay.

Resources

- Writing Rubric

STEP 4: DEMONSTRATE

Communicate Conclusions and Take Informed Action

Present Your Essay

Have students make a neat, clean copy of their essays. Then ask volunteers to read their essays aloud to the class.

Suggestion: As an alternative, have students publish their essays on a class Web site, bulletin board, or other online vehicle.

Reflect on the Project

Have students briefly discuss what they found challenging in their essays and what they feel they did well. Encourage them to use the lessons they learned writing this essay so they can write even more effectively in future writing projects.

Suggestion: As an extension activity, have students research a specific genocide situation, either one studied in this activity or one they have read about. Ask them to write a three-paragraph essay in which they describe how different countries actually responded to the situation. Have students share their descriptions with the class.

PROFESSIONAL DEVELOPMENT

Document-Based Question

Be sure to view the Document-Based Question Professional Development resources in the online course.

Topic 20 Lesson 1

New Nations in South Asia and Southeast Asia

Objectives

Objective 1: Explain how independence led to the partition of India.

Objective 2: Describe the national development of India, Pakistan, and Bangladesh.

Objective 3: Define the role of South Asia in the Cold War.

Objective 4: Explain the impact of independence on nations of Southeast Asia.

LESSON 1 ORGANIZER — **PACING: APPROX. 1 PERIOD, .5 BLOCKS**

	OBJECTIVES	PACING	RESOURCES Print	RESOURCES Online	TEKS	ELPS
Connect						
DIGITAL START UP ACTIVITY **The Struggle for Unity**		5 min.		●	1.F	
Investigate						
READ **Independence and Partition in South Asia**	Objective 1	10 min.	●	●	1.F, 13.E	
INTERACTIVE GALLERY **Indian Independence and Partition**	Objective 1	10 min.		●	1.F, 13.E	
READ **Challenges to Modern India**	Objective 2	10 min.	●	●	1.F, 13.E, 24.B	1.E.1
READ **Pakistan and Bangladesh Separate**	Objective 2	10 min.	●	●		
INTERACTIVE MAP **South Asian Borders**	Objective 2	10 min.		●	1.F, 16.A	
READ **South Asia in the Cold War**	Objective 3	10 min.	●	●	1.F	
READ **Independent Nations in Southeast Asia**	Objective 4	10 min.	●	●	1.F	
READ **Populous Indonesia Faces Challenges**	Objective 4	10 min.	●	●		
READ **Struggle for Democracy in the Philippines**	Objective 4	10 min.	●	●	1.F	5.F.1
Synthesize						
DIGITAL ACTIVITY **Independence in Southeast Asia**		5 min.		●	1.F	
Demonstrate						
DIGITAL QUIZ **Lesson Quiz and Class Discussion Board**		10 min.		●	1.F	

Focus on Texas Standards

Texas Essential Knowledge and Skills

1.F identify major causes and describe the major effects of the following important turning points in world history from 1914 to the present: the world wars and their impact on political, economic, and social systems; communist revolutions and their impact on the Cold War; independence movements; and globalization

13.E summarize the rise of independence movements in Africa, the Middle East, and South Asia and reasons for ongoing conflicts

15.A create and interpret thematic maps, graphs, and charts to demonstrate the relationship between geography and the historical development of a region or nation

24.B describe the major influences of women such as Elizabeth I, Queen Victoria, Mother Teresa, Indira Gandhi, Margaret Thatcher, and Golda Meir during major eras of world history

NOTES

African Nations Win Independence

Objectives

Objective 1: Summarize how African nations won independence.

Objective 2: Analyze the issues facing new African nations and the different paths they took.

Objective 3: Identify examples of and summarize the reasons for ethnic conflict and genocide in African nations.

LESSON 2 ORGANIZER — **PACING: APPROX. 1 PERIOD, .5 BLOCKS**

	OBJECTIVES	PACING	RESOURCES: Print	RESOURCES: Online	TEKS	ELPS
Connect						
DIGITAL START UP ACTIVITY **Challenges of Independence**		5 min.		●	1.F, 13.E	
Investigate						
READ **The New Nations of Africa**	Objective 1	10 min.	●	●	1.F, 13.E	1.E.2
READ **A Variety of New Governments**	Objective 2	10 min.	●	●	13.E	
INTERACTIVE MAP **Imperialism and Independence in Africa**		10 min.		●	1.F, 13.E, 16.A	
READ **Case Studies: Five African Nations**	Objective 2	10 min.	●	●	13.E	
INTERACTIVE GALLERY **Independence in Congo**		10 min.		●	13.E	
READ **The Wars of Southern Africa**	Objective 3	10 min.	●	●	22.D	
READ **Ethnic Conflict and Genocide**		10 min.	●	●	22.D	
Synthesize						
DIGITAL ACTIVITY **Addressing the Challenges of Independence**		5 min.		●	1.F, 13.E	
Demonstrate						
DIGITAL QUIZ **Lesson Quiz and Class Discussion Board**		10 min.		●	1.F, 13.E, 22.D	

Focus on Texas Standards

Texas Essential Knowledge and Skills

1.F identify major causes and describe the major effects of the following important turning points in world history from 1914 to the present: the world wars and their impact on political, economic, and social systems; communist revolutions and their impact on the Cold War; independence movements; and globalization

13.E summarize the rise of independence movements in Africa, the Middle East, and South Asia and reasons for ongoing conflicts

22.D identify examples of genocide, including the Holocaust and genocide in the Balkans, Rwanda, and Darfur

NOTES

The Modern Middle East Takes Shape

Objectives

Objective 1: Analyze the development of modern nations in the Middle East.

Objective 2: Describe the founding of Israel and the impact of the Arab rejection of Israel.

Objective 3: Understand how oil has affected nations of the Middle East.

Objective 4: Examine the impact of Islam on government, law, and the lives of women.

Objective 5: Define the "Arab Spring."

LESSON 3 ORGANIZER — **PACING: APPROX. 1 PERIOD, .5 BLOCKS**

	OBJECTIVES	PACING	RESOURCES Print	RESOURCES Online	TEKS	ELPS
Connect						
DIGITAL START UP ACTIVITY **Ties to the Land**		5 min.		●	13.E	
Investigate						
READ **The Challenges of Diversity**	Objective 1	10 min.	●	●	10.C, 13.E	
INTERACTIVE MAP **Religious Diversity in the Middle East**		10 min.		●	13.E, 16.A	
READ **The Founding of Israel**	Objective 2	10 min.	●	●	13.E, 13.F, 24.B	1.E.3
INTERACTIVE CHART **Birth of Israel**		10 min.		●	13.E, 13.F	
READ **New Nations in the Middle East**	Objectives 1, 5	10 min.	●	●	10.C, 13.E, 16.A, 21.A	5.F.3
READ **The Importance of Oil in the Middle East**	Objective 3	10 min.	●	●	13.E, 16.A	
READ **Islam and the Modern World**	Objective 4	10 min.	●	●	13.E, 14.A, 25.D	
Synthesize						
DIGITAL ACTIVITY **The Changing Middle East**		5 min.		●	13.E, 13.F, 25.D	
Demonstrate						
DIGITAL QUIZ **Lesson Quiz and Class Discussion Board**		10 min.		●	10.C, 13.E, 13.F, 21.A, 25.D	

PEARSON realize

www.PearsonTexas.com
Access your Digital Lesson

Focus on Texas Standards

Texas Essential Knowledge and Skills

10.C explain the political impact of Woodrow Wilson's Fourteen Points and the political and economic impact of the Treaty of Versailles, including changes in boundaries and the mandate system

13.E summarize the rise of independence movements in Africa, the Middle East, and South Asia and reasons for ongoing conflicts

13.F explain how Arab rejection of the State of Israel has led to ongoing conflict

15.A create and interpret thematic maps, graphs, and charts to demonstrate the relationship between geography and the historical development of a region or nation

16.A locate places and regions of historical significance directly related to major eras and turning points in world history

16.C interpret maps, charts, and graphs to explain how geography has influenced people and events in the past

25.D explain how Islam influences law and government in the Muslim world

NOTES

Conflicts in the Middle East

Objectives

Objective 1: Explain the ongoing Israeli-Palestinian conflict and the obstacles to peace.

Objective 2: Explain the causes and effects of conflicts in Lebanon and Syria.

Objective 3: Understand why Iraq became a battleground.

LESSON 4 ORGANIZER			PACING: APPROX. 1 PERIOD, .5 BLOCKS			
			RESOURCES			
	OBJECTIVES	PACING	Print	Online	TEKS	ELPS
Connect						
DIGITAL START UP ACTIVITY **Independence and Violence**		5 min.		●	13.E	
Investigate						
READ **Israel and Palestine**	Objective 1	10 min.	●	●	13.E, 13.F, 24.B	5.G.1
READ **The Difficult Road to Peace**		10 min.	●	●		
INTERACTIVE MAP **Changing Boundaries of the State of Israel**		10 min.		●	13.E, 13.F, 16.A	
READ **Conflict in Lebanon and Syria**	Objective 2	10 min.	●	●	13.E, 14.A	
READ **Warfare in Iraq**	Objective 3	10 min.	●	●	13.E, 25.D	
INTERACTIVE TIMELINE **Conflicts in the Middle East**		10 min.		●		
Synthesize						
DIGITAL ACTIVITY **Independence and Unrest**		5 min.		●	13.E, 13.F	
Demonstrate						
DIGITAL QUIZ **Lesson Quiz and Class Discussion Board**		10 min.		●	13.E, 13.F, 14.A	

PEARSON realize™ www.PearsonTexas.com Access your Digital Lesson

Focus on Texas Standards

Texas Essential Knowledge and Skills

13.E summarize the rise of independence movements in Africa, the Middle East, and South Asia and reasons for ongoing conflicts

13.F explain how Arab rejection of the State of Israel has led to ongoing conflict

14.A summarize the development and impact of radical Islamic fundamentalism on events in the second half of the 20th century, including Palestinian terrorism and the growth of al Qaeda

16.A locate places and regions of historical significance directly related to major eras and turning points in world history

NOTES

New Nations Emerge (1945–Present)

In this Topic, you will learn about new nations that emerged in the late twentieth and early twenty-first centuries. You will also find lots of ways to investigate the ideas of this Topic and to master the TEKS.

Your study will help you master these TEKS:

TEKS

1.F, 10.C, 13.E, 13.F, 14.A, 15.A, 16.A, 16.C, 22.D, 24.B, 25.D, 31.B

LESSON OUTLINE

20.1: New Nations in South Asia and Southeast Asia 1.F, 13.E, 15.A, 24.B

20.2: African Nations Win Independence 1.F, 13.E, 22.D

20.3: The Modern Middle East Takes Shape 10.C, 13.E, 13.F, 15.A, 16.A, 16.C, 25.D

20.4: Conflicts in the Middle East 13.E, 13.F, 14.A, 15.A, 16.A

Connect

My Story Video and Topic Essential Question—see how they connect to your past experience or to what you have already learned. The Essential Question for this Topic is: What should governments do?

Begin your study by trying the following:

NBC LEARN **Watch My Story Video:**

Aung San Suu Kyi, Struggle for Democracy

Launch your Document-Based Question:

How Should Nations Respond to Genocide?

Investigate

The Lesson Outline lists all the lessons you will investigate In this Topic,. As you read and interact with key content, the story of emerging nations will come to life. Read the texts; try the interactivities. Investigate the fascinating story of modern nations and the challenges they face.

And keep working on your Document-Based Question. You're almost ready to show what you have accomplished by expressing your opinion using the evidence you have gathered.

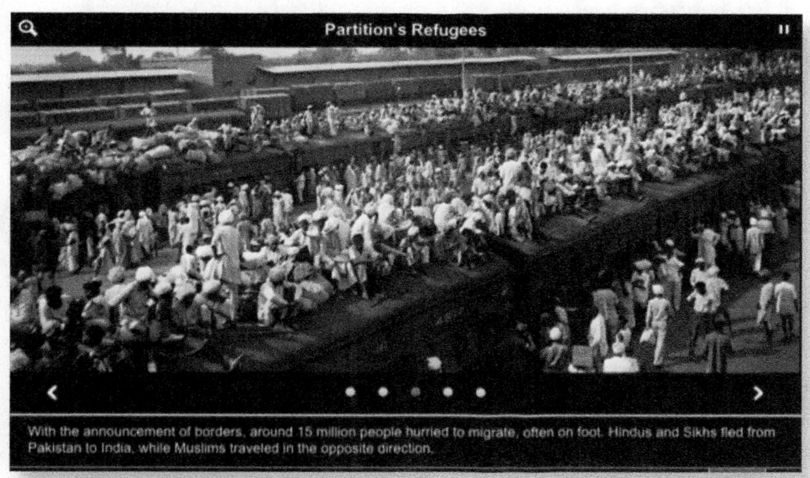

Partition's Refugees
With the announcement of borders, around 15 million people hurried to migrate, often on foot. Hindus and Sikhs fled from Pakistan to India, while Muslims traveled in the opposite direction.

>> Digital interactivity from the online course

Synthesize

You will get a chance to pull together everything you have learned by thinking again about the Essential Question. Consider how you would answer the question now: What should governments do?

Demonstrate

Completing this Topic is like practicing all your soccer skills or rehearsing the scenes in a play. Now you get a chance to pull it all together for the final game or the live performance. You can do this on the Topic Review and Assessment pages. Or you can complete your work your essay for the Document-Based Question, How Should Nations Respond to Genocide?

TEKS in Topic 20	Topic Review and Assessment Questions
1.F	**6, 8**
13.E	**1, 2, 3, 6, 7, 8, 9, 13, 16**
13.F	**14**
14.A	**15**
15.A	**10**
16.A	**1, 13, 15**
22.D	**4, 5**
24.B	**11, 12**
25.D	**10**
31.B	**2**

Topic 20

New Nations Emerge (1945–Present)

Introduction

As European imperial powers declined after World War II, colonies in Africa and Asia gained independence. Some nations achieved independence peacefully, while others had to fight for their freedom. The legacy of colonialism had serious effects even many years after independence, as ethnic and religious conflict plagued many parts of the world, including the Middle East, South Asia, Rwanda, Darfur, and Sri Lanka.

ESSENTIAL QUESTION

Ask students to think about the Essential Question for this Topic: What should governments do? Share the following with students:

After reflecting on what you have learned about governments throughout history, work with a partner to list three rules for deciding what governments should do. Your rules must apply to all levels of government in all countries. Here is a possible rule to get you started in thinking about how we should decide the legitimate roles of government:

"Government should take on no role that can be done better by private individuals or companies."

Support a Point of View With Evidence Ask: Why did you choose these three rules? Explain your answer. *(Students should be able to offer valid reasons for their choices; evidence may include philosophical or moral reasons, evidence of what governments did in the past, and references to current government roles.)*

Make a Prediction Do you think governments will do more, less, or about the same in the future? Why? *(Some students will predict greater government activity in the future as problems become too large for the private sector to address, while others may point to growing antigovernment feeling, which may reduce the role of government.)*

[**ESSENTIAL QUESTION**] What should governments do?

20 **New Nations Emerge (1945–Present)**

Analyze Images

The women in the photograph are celebrating Kenyan independence, which was won in 1963. Point out the symbol on the flag, which shows spears and a shield. Ask students to reflect on the importance of new national symbols for countries that gain independence. Ask them what meanings could be behind the Kenyan flag image.

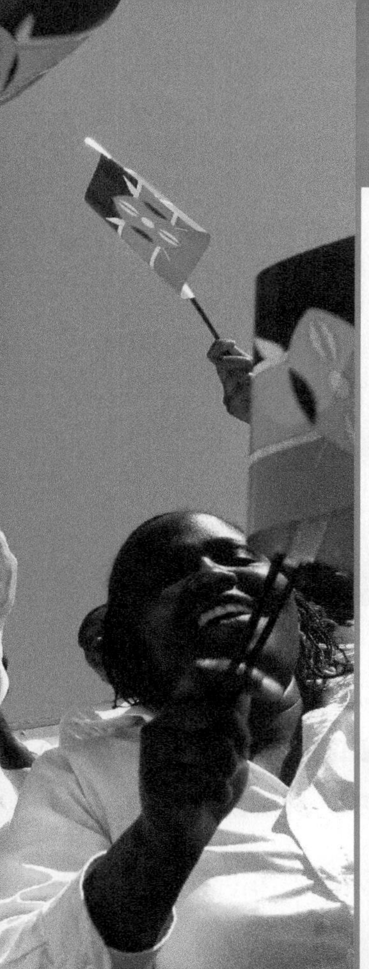

>> Women in Kenya celebrating the anniversary of winning independence

Texas Essential Knowledge and Skills

1.F, 10.C, 13.E, 13.F, 14.A, 15.A, 16.A, 16.C, 22.D, 24.B, 25.D, 31.B

Enduring Understandings

- As European imperial powers declined after World War II, colonies in Africa and Asia gained independence.
- South Asia was partitioned into Hindu-dominated India and Muslim-dominated Pakistan, setting the stage for decades of conflict.
- Some African nations achieve independence peacefully, while others had to fight for their freedom.
- In the Middle East, the new Jewish State of Israel faced immediate opposition from its Arab neighbors.
- Factors shaping the modern Middle East include Islam, oil, and religious and ethnic diversity.

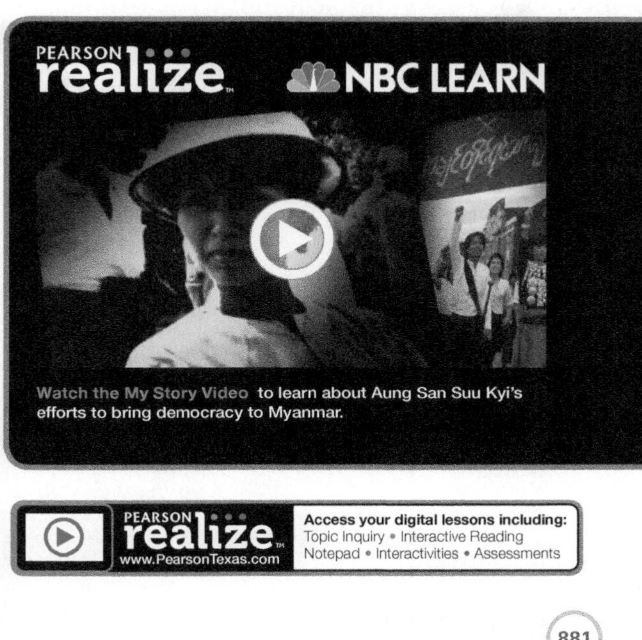

Watch the My Story Video to learn about Aung San Suu Kyi's efforts to bring democracy to Myanmar.

PEARSON realize www.PearsonTexas.com **Access your digital lessons including:** Topic Inquiry • Interactive Reading Notepad • Interactivities • Assessments

881

NBC LEARN MY STORY VIDEO

Project the My Story Video that tells about Aung San Suu Kyi's efforts to bring democracy to her homeland of Myanmar.

Online My Story Video: **Aung San Suu Kyi, Struggle for Democracy**

After viewing, ask students to respond to the following questions.

Check Understanding What price did Aung San Suu Kyi pay in her struggle for human rights? *(She was placed under house arrest for 15 years.)*

Determine Point of View What does Aung San Suu Kyi mean when she says she made a choice and not a sacrifice in her life? *(She chose to fight for human rights and suffer the consequences, but her family—from whom she was separated—had to sacrifice.)*

OVERVIEW ACTIVITY

Online Display the timeline showing the major events concerning new nations in the second half of the twentieth century. During the Topic, students will learn about all of these events and many more, but this timeline will provide a framework into which they can place the events they learn about.

Check Understanding About how many years after the founding of Israel was a partial agreement signed between Israelis and Palestinians? *(45)*

Topic Inquiry

If you choose to assign the Topic Inquiry, launch the project with students after introducing the Topic.

D Differentiate Challenge/Gifted
Suggest that students copy the timeline onto their own paper and add entries to it as they read the chapter. Have them make a final, clean copy after they read all four lessons, and discuss the new entries as a class.

Topic 20 Lesson 1

New Nations in South Asia and Southeast Asia

CONNECT

Preview Have students preview the **Lesson Objectives** and the list of **Key Terms**.

Students can also preview all the **Key Terms** and **Academic Vocabulary** using the **Interactive Reading Notepad** on the digital course or preview a summary of the lesson in the **Reading and Note Taking Study Guide**.

Online Use the **Editable Presentation** found on the digital course to present the main ideas for this lesson.

Start Up Activity

Tell students that after World War II, a global independence movement began. Read or display the following from Sukarno, leader of one of these newly independent nations:

"[W]e are establishing an Indonesian state which all of us must support. All for all. Not the Christians for Indonesia, not the Islamic group for Indonesia . . . but the Indonesians for Indonesia—all for all!"

Discuss Besides religious differences, what factors might hinder national unity? *(Possible answers: differences in language, ethnicity, race, political opinions, wealth, use of land and resources)*

Online You can also project the **Start Up Activity** from the course.

INVESTIGATE

Have students read the section using the **Reading and Note Taking Study Guide** to help them take notes and understand the text as they read.

Independence and Partition in South Asia

Explain that the European colonial powers had been weakened by World War II. Nationalists in the colonies were ready to fight for their freedom, and many Europeans had no desire for further conflict. Among the first new nations to win independence were the former British colonies of South Asia.

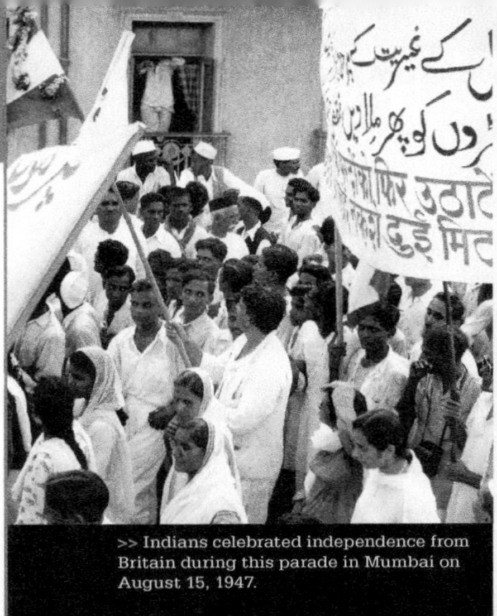

>> Indians celebrated independence from Britain during this parade in Mumbai on August 15, 1947.

Interactive Flipped Video

20.1 At the same time that the Cold War was unfolding, a global independence movement was reshaping the world. The European colonial powers, especially Britain and France, had been weakened by World War II. Their military and financial resources were exhausted, and so was their will. While nationalists in the colonies were ready to fight for their freedom, many war-weary Europeans had no desire for further conflict.

TEKS
1.F, 13.E, 15.A, 24.B

>> Objectives

Explain how independence led to the partition of India.

Describe the national development of India, Pakistan, and Bangladesh.

Define the role of South Asia in the Cold War.

Explain the impact of independence on nations of Southeast Asia.

>> Key Terms

partition
Sikh
Kashmir
Jawaharlal Nehru
dalits
Indira Gandhi
Punjab
Golden Temple
Bangladesh
nonalignment
autocratic
Aung San Suu Kyi
Sukarno
Suharto
East Timor
Ferdinand Marcos
Benigno Aquino
Corazon Aquino

www.PearsonTexas.com
Access your Digital Lesson.

New Nations in South Asia and Southeast Asia

Independence and Partition in South Asia

Among the first new nations to win independence were the former British colonies of South Asia, or the Indian subcontinent. Nationalists in British-ruled India had demanded self-rule since the late 1800s. As independence neared, however, a long-simmering issue surfaced. What would happen to the Muslim minority in a Hindu-dominated India?

The Formation of India and Pakistan Like Mohandas Gandhi, most of the leaders and members of the Congress Party were Hindus. However, the party wanted a unified India that would include both Muslims and Hindus.

The Muslim League, led by Muhammad Ali Jinnah, had a different view of liberation. Although they had cooperated with the Congress Party in the drive for independence, they feared discrimination against the Muslim minority in a unified India. Therefore, the Muslim

Aa Vocabulary Builder

1. Have students pronounce the following academic vocabulary terms in this lesson and clarify the part of speech. For difficult or polysyllabic words, break them into syllables and pronounce them with the students.
2. Explain what the word means in common "student-friendly" language using synonyms and antonyms when possible. Provide concrete examples to clarify the meaning, and rephrase the definition.

compelled: made to or forced

predominant: most common or numerous

League demanded the creation of a separate nation, called Pakistan, that would include the parts of British India where Muslims formed a majority. In the 1940s, tensions between Muslims and the Hindu majority in British India led to increasing violence.

After World War II, the British government decided that it could no longer afford to resist Indian demands for independence. As independence approached, violence between Hindus and Muslims accelerated.

In response, Britain decided to accept the idea of **partition,** or dividing the subcontinent into two nations. Hindu-dominated India and Pakistan, which had a Muslim majority, both won independence on August 13, 1947.

Partition Leads to Violence However, Hindus and Muslims still lived side by side in many cities and rural areas. As soon as the new borders became known, a mass migration began. On the Pakistani side of the borders, millions of Hindus and **Sikhs** (SIK khs), members of a South Asian religious minority, packed their belongings and fled to the new India. At the same time, millions of Muslims fled from India into newly created Pakistan. An estimated 10 million people left their homes, most of them on foot.

Muslims fleeing along the crowded roads into Pakistan were slaughtered by Hindus and Sikhs. Muslims massacred Hindu and Sikh neighbors. Around one million people died in these massacres. Others died of starvation and exposure on the road.

The Battle for Kashmir Since independence, India and Pakistan have fought a series of wars over **Kashmir,** a state in the Himalayas. In 1947, Kashmir's Hindu ruler tried to join India. However, Kashmir's Muslim majority wanted to be part of Pakistan.

For decades, Kashmiri separatists, often supported by Pakistani militants, have fought Indian troops. Indian and Pakistani forces have also battled along Kashmir's mountainous border. Today, Kashmir remains a flashpoint in the tense relations between India and Pakistan.

A Nuclear Arms Race In the 1970s, first India and then Pakistan developed nuclear weapons programs. By 1998, both nations had successfully tested nuclear weapons. The emergence of these two nuclear powers alarmed neighbors in South Asia and the world, in part because of the ongoing hostility between India and Pakistan. Another concern was the danger that extremists might get access to nuclear technology or even nuclear weapons.

Ongoing Conflict in Sri Lanka The island of Ceylon won freedom from Britain in 1948. Later, it took the name Sri (sree) Lanka. Most Sri Lankans are Buddhists who speak Sinhalese. However, a large Tamil-speaking Hindu minority lives in the north and east. The Sri Lankan government favored the Sinhalese majority, which angered many Tamils.

In the late 1970s, Tamil rebels battled to set up their own separate nation. For three decades, terrorism and brutality fed a deadly conflict between government forces and Tamil rebels. By 2009, the government had regained control of Tamil-held towns and started to resettle those displaced by the conflict, but peace was by no means assured.

IDENTIFY MAIN IDEAS Why is Kashmir a source of conflict between India and Pakistan?

Challenges to Modern India

Upon achieving independence, India established a parliamentary democracy. Although India remains the world's largest democracy, it has faced many challenges. Ethnic and religious tensions threatened

>> Indian refugees crowd onto trains after India and Pakistan are separated into two independent states. Muslims fled to Pakistan and Hindus fled to India in one of the largest transfers of population in history.

Interactive Gallery

Topic 20 Lesson 1

Review British colonial rule of India and the independence movement led by Mohandas Gandhi. Explain that the British granted India self-rule in 1947, but the region was partitioned into Hindu-dominated India and Muslim-dominated East and West Pakistan.

Online Project the **Interactive Gallery: Indian Independence and Partition**, and click through the images.

ACTIVE CLASSROOM

Ask students to create a quick copy of an image from the gallery on a piece of paper. Have them Cartoon It into a political cartoon that illustrates a key concept or main idea from the reading "Independence and Partition in South Asia."

Key Terms

Ask students to find the key term **partition** (in bold) in the text and explain its meaning. Have students predict the problems that might arise when an entire nation is partitioned.

Guided Reading and Discussion

Discuss the causes and effects of South Asian partition. Make sure students understand that the Muslim minority in South Asia wanted its own nation, which was carved from the northeast and northwest of India. As Hindus and Muslims moved over the borders, violence erupted.

Sequence Events Name major events that led from British rule over India to armed conflict in Kashmir. *(The independence movement in India led to Britain granting the country self-rule. One condition of self-rule was the partition between India and East and West Pakistan. The region of Kashmir had a Hindu ruler but a Muslim majority, and both nations wanted to claim it. The region is still under dispute.)*

History Background

Muhammad Ali Jinnah Muhammad Ali Jinnah, the architect of Pakistani independence, studied law in London. Over 6 feet tall and weighing less than 120 pounds, Jinnah had a striking presence. Although Jinnah at first favored Muslim-Hindu unity, he later advocated partition as the only solution to guarantee the rights of Muslims. Jinnah became Pakistan's first governor-general. Although he had advocated partition, he was horrified by the bloodshed that occurred as a result.

Answers

Identify Main Ideas *Each country wants to control this region, which is home to both Muslims and Hindus.*

Topic 20 Lesson 1

Challenges to Modern India

Pakistan and Bangladesh Separate

Explain that a series of strong prime ministers, including Jawaharlal Nehru, his daughter Indira Gandhi, and her son Rajiv Gandhi, contributed significantly to developing a modern India. Indira Gandhi also had significant influence in her role as one of the world's few female leaders. Religious conflicts are still an ongoing problem, however. Ethnic and economic differences between West and East Pakistan caused the rise of an independence movement in East Pakistan, leading to the formation of Bangladesh.

Online Project the **Interactive Map: South Asian Borders**, and click through the sequence, pointing out the differences in national borders through time. Students should notice that borders between the 1947 and present-day maps do not change, but East and West Pakistan became the nations of Bangladesh and Pakistan, while Ceylon became the nation of Sri Lanka.

>> Indira Gandhi served as India's prime minister for almost 15 years, though not consecutively. She lost her election in 1977 due to unpopular policies, but won back the seat in 1980.

>> In 2011, 25,000 Sikhs marched in London to mark the 1984 attack on the Golden Temple in India. Indira Gandhi had ordered the military to open fire on the holy site.

its unity. Its people speak over 100 languages and many dialects. Hundreds of millions of Indians lived in desperate poverty. Despite unrest and diversity, India has emerged as a major world power.

Strong Prime Ministers Set Goals During its early decades, India benefited from strong leadership. The Congress Party, which had spearheaded the independence movement, worked to turn India into a modern nation. From 1947 to 1964, **Jawaharlal Nehru** (juh WAH huhr lahl NAY roo), leader of the Congress Party, was India's prime minister. He promoted economic growth and social change. Under Nehru, food output rose, but so did India's population. The government encouraged family planning to reduce the birthrate, but with limited success.

Although India's 1947 constitution banned discrimination against **dalits,** or people in the lowest castes, discrimination based on caste continued. Nehru's government set aside jobs and places in universities for dalits and other lower-caste Indians. Still, higher-caste Hindus generally got better schooling and jobs.

Later, Nehru's daughter, **Indira Gandhi,** served as prime minister for most of the years between 1966 and 1984. She had a global influence and challenged traditional discrimination against women.

Religious Conflicts Persist India was a land of many religions. A majority of Indians were Hindu, but millions were Muslim, Sikh, Christian, or Buddhist. At times, religious divisions led to violence.

Some Sikhs wanted greater autonomy for **Punjab,** a prosperous, largely Sikh state in northern India. Sikh dissidents engaged in nonviolent protests against government policies. These protests were organized from the **Golden Temple,** the most prominent Sikh house of worship. Indira Gandhi planned an attack on the Golden Temple.

As news of this planned attack leaked, Sikh activists fortified the Golden Temple with arms and weapons. Over a thousand Sikhs were killed and many religious artifacts were destroyed. Soon after, Gandhi was assassinated by two of her Sikh bodyguards. In the violence that followed, thousands more Sikhs were killed.

In the late 1980s, the Hindu nationalist party, Bharatiya Janata Party (BJP), challenged the secular, or nonreligious, Congress Party. The BJP wanted a government based on Hindu traditions and sometimes encouraged violence against Muslims.

SUMMARIZE How did the Indian government try to improve conditions for lower castes?

New Nations Emerge 884 20.1 New Nations in South Asia and Southeast Asia

Answers

Summarize *It reserved jobs and spots at universities for them.*

English Language Proficiency Standards

1.E.1 Read "Challenges to Modern India" aloud to students. Then instruct students to complete one of the following activities based on their level of English proficiency.

Beginning Write and display the words *think, read,* and *discuss* for students. Read the words aloud and have students repeat them. Begin by using each word in a basic sentence to demonstrate how these words are used daily. Then guide students to use the information in "Challenges to Modern India" to compose short phrases or sentences using these words. Have students write the words and phrases in their notebooks.

Intermediate Write and display the words *think, read,* and *discuss* for students. Read the words aloud and have students repeat them. Help students develop basic sentences for each word to demonstrate how these words are used daily. Then support students as they use the information in "Challenges to Modern India" to compose short phrases or sentences using these words. Have students write the words and phrases in their notebooks.

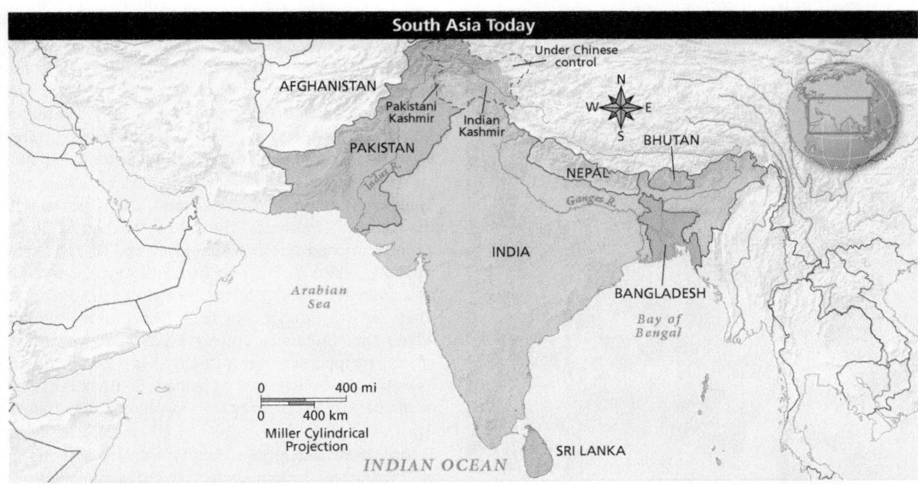

>> **Analyze Maps** This map shows South Asia today. West Pakistan is now called Pakistan. East Pakistan is now called Bangladesh. Ceylon is now called Sri Lanka. What geographic reason made it difficult for Pakistan to retain control of Bangladesh?

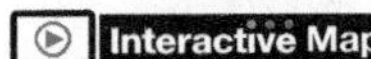

Pakistan and Bangladesh Separate

Pakistan gained independence in 1947, at the same time as India. Geographically, it was a divided country, with West Pakistan and East Pakistan located on either side of India. A thousand miles of Indian territory separated the two regions, and India made trade and travel between the two Pakistans difficult.

Bangladesh Declares Independence From the start, West Pakistan dominated the government even though East Pakistan had a larger population. The government concentrated most economic development programs in West Pakistan, while East Pakistan remained deep in poverty. Most people in East Pakistan were Bengalis, while West Pakistan was home to other ethnic groups. Many Bengalis resented governmental neglect of East Pakistan.

In 1971, Bengalis in East Pakistan declared independence. They named their country **Bangladesh,** or "Bengali nation." When the Pakistani army tried to crush the rebellion, India sent forces to help Bangladesh. Pakistan was then compelled to recognize the new country.

Pakistan's Unstable Government After independence, Pakistan struggled to build a stable government. Power shifted back and forth between elected civilian leaders and military rulers. Tensions among the country's diverse ethnic groups posed problems. The fiercely independent people in the northwestern "tribal areas" were left largely on their own and resisted government control.

The activities of Islamic fundamentalists created tension. The fundamentalists wanted a government that followed strict Islamic principles, while other Pakistanis wanted greater separation between religion and state.

Militants in Pakistan In 2008, after nine years in power, General Pervez Musharraf allowed elections. Before the election, Islamic extremists assassinated one of the candidates, Benazir Bhutto, a popular former prime minister. Pakistan's new civilian government faced tough challenges, including the global economic recession that began that year.

Meanwhile, support for Islamic fundamentalist groups based in Pakistan grew, especially in the northwest. In November 2008, Islamic militants from Pakistan launched terror attacks on hotels and tourists

ACTIVE CLASSROOM

Distribute sticky notes to use for the Sticky Notes strategy. Give students three minutes to write their comments or observations about the changes in South Asian nations from 1947 to today. Have them consider positive and negative aspects of those changes. Then ask students to post their sticky notes on the board, and have them look at the various responses. Discuss similarities and differences in the responses.

Guided Reading and Discussion

Ask questions to encourage discussion of Bangladeshi independence and ongoing conflicts in South Asia.

Summarize Ask: What economic and geographic factors led to the creation of Bangladesh? Use evidence from the text to support your answer. *(West Pakistan dominated the government and concentrated most economic advancement on West Pakistan. The residents of faraway East Pakistan, mostly Bengalis, grew tired of living in poverty and governmental neglect, and declared independence in 1971.)*

Advanced Write and display the words *leadership* and *modern*. Use these words in a group discussion about some aspect of daily life. Use informal assessment to make sure all students understand the meanings of the two words. Then have students work with a partner to create sentences about the information in "Challenges to Modern India" for each word. Pairs should write their sentences in their notebooks and then share them with the class.

Advanced High Write and display the words *leadership* and *modern*. Have students talk to a partner about some aspect of daily life, using these words in their conversation. Then have students create sentences about the information in "Challenges to Modern India" for each word. Students should write their sentences in their notebooks and then share them with the class.

Answers

Analyze Maps *East and West Pakistan were separated by India.*

Summarize Have students describe the ongoing South Asian conflicts and issues mentioned in the text. *(Sample response: India and Pakistan dispute ownership of the Kashmir region. Tamil rebels in Sri Lanka call for independence. India's many different religious groups sometimes come into conflict. Pakistan's government is often unstable because of the conflicts between different ethnic groups, military and civilian leaders, and Islamic fundamentalists. Additionally, Taliban supporters have been hiding in Pakistan. Bangladesh faces crippling poverty and recurring natural disasters.)*

South Asia in the Cold War

Review the goals of the United States and the Soviet Union during the Cold War. Explain that emerging nations such as India and Pakistan were wary of picking sides in the global conflict. In 1955, India and Pakistan helped organize a conference of new nations, marking the start of the nonaligned movement. The group's conferences, which still occur, consist of leaders from countries that achieved independence in the twentieth century.

>> Afghan children, refugees in Pakistan, are transported by truck. Since the 1970s, millions of Afghan refugees have fled into Pakistan.

>> A woman walks through flooded streets in Dhaka, the capital of Bangladesh.

in Mumbai, India, fueling tensions between the hostile neighbors.

Islamic traditions were strong in the rugged border area between Pakistan and Afghanistan. When the Soviet Union invaded Afghanistan in 1979, one million Afghan refugees fled into Pakistan. There, many joined Islamic fundamentalist groups to battle the invaders.

After Russia withdrew from Afghanistan, the Taliban, an extreme Islamist group, seized power with the support of Pakistan. The Taliban backed Al Qaeda, which launched terrorist attacks on the United States in 2001. When U.S. forces invaded Afghanistan and overthrew the Taliban, its supporters fled into Pakistan. They set up strongholds in northwestern Pakistan, where their influence spread. Pakistan's government officially supported the United States. However, many Pakistanis were angered by American missile attacks on suspected terrorists within the country's borders.

Bangladesh Struggles Bangladesh ranks among the world's poorest, most crowded countries. Its population, more than half as large as that of the United States, lives in an area the size of Alabama. The flat Ganges Delta, just a few feet above sea level, covers much of the country. Bangladesh has suffered repeatedly from devastating tropical storms and floods. Explosive population growth has strained resources further. More than 50 million people live below the poverty level.

During its early years, Bangladesh was ruled by authoritarian military governments that controlled the economy. In the 1990s, the nation moved from military to democratic rule. The new civilian government encouraged foreign investment. Foreign companies took advantage of cheap labor costs to make clothes in Bangladesh. However, human rights group protested the widespread use of child labor and other harsh conditions.

One hopeful program came from the Grameen Bank, founded by Bangladeshi economist Muhammad Yunus. It gave tiny loans, or "microcredit," to poor people so they could open small businesses. Although microcredit helped only a few, it offered a model to poor nations around the world. In 2006, Yunus was awarded the Nobel Peace Prize for his efforts.

SUMMARIZE How does geography pose challenges for Bangladesh?

South Asia in the Cold War

India and Pakistan were among the first of more than 90 new nations to emerge after World War II. By the 1930s, nationalist movements had taken root in European

D Differentiate Challenge/Gifted The Nonaligned Movement summit still exists. Have students research the organization today and find out how its goals have changed since the end of the Cold War. Ask students to share their findings about what changes have occurred in the movement now that its original reason for existing, the Cold War, has ended.

Answers

Summarize *Bangladesh lies just a few feet above sea level at the mouth of the Ganges River. As a result, it experiences frequent floods and tropical storms. In addition, it is densely populated.*

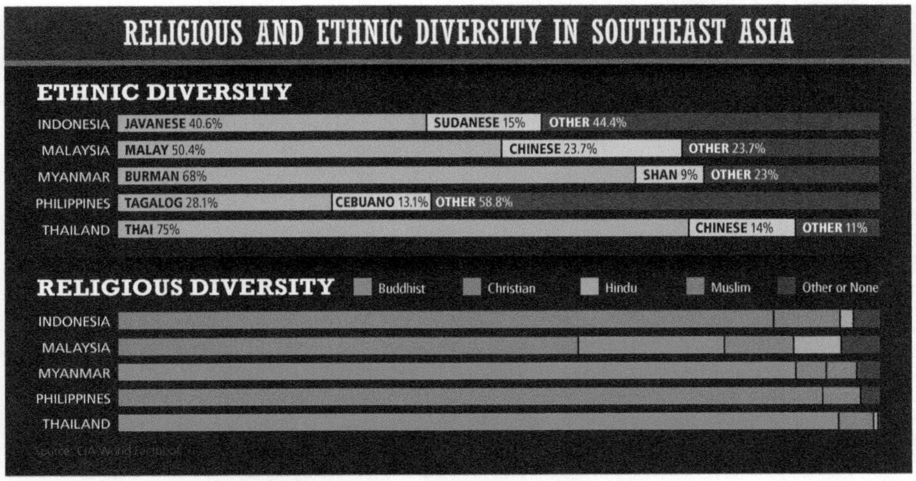

RELIGIOUS AND ETHNIC DIVERSITY IN SOUTHEAST ASIA

>> **Analyze Charts** Southeast Asian countries are ethnically and religiously diverse. What are the predominant religions in Indonesia and Thailand?

colonies across Africa, Asia, and the Middle East. After India and Pakistan gained independence, nationalist leaders in other regions demanded the same for their countries.

India, Pakistan, and other new nations condemned colonialism. They also rejected Cold War expansion and the divisions between the West and the Soviet Union. In response, they sought **nonalignment,** or political and diplomatic independence from the Cold War superpowers. In 1955, India and Pakistan helped organize a conference of newly independent nations in Bandung, Indonesia, which marked the birth of the nonaligned movement.

The nonaligned movement had its first formal meeting in 1961 in Yugoslavia. India was a leader of the nonaligned movement, which came to include more than 100 nations, mainly in Asia, Africa, and Latin America. Because they rejected both the Western allies, or the First World, and the Soviet alliance, or the Second World, the Nonaligned Movement was seen as the voice of a "Third World" of countries.

IDENTIFY MAIN IDEAS What important global role did India and Pakistan play after independence?

Independent Nations in Southeast Asia

Southeast Asia includes part of the Asian mainland and thousands of islands that stretch from the Indian Ocean to the South China Sea. In 1939, most of the region was under colonial rule by European nations or the United States. During World War II, Japan seized the region. After the war, nationalist groups demanded independence and resisted reoccupation by European nations.

Mainland Southeast Asia is a region of contrasts. Thailand and Malaysia have mostly prospered as market economies, although they have been affected by global financial crises. However, nearby Myanmar has suffered under a brutal **autocratic,** or repressive, government with unlimited power.

Malaysia Prospers British colonies on the Malay Peninsula and the island of Borneo gained independence in the 1950s and joined to form the nation of Malaysia. The oil-rich monarchy of Brunei, on Borneo, and the prosperous city-state of Singapore gained independence as separate nations.

Malaysia has a very diverse population. People of Chinese and Indian descent have long dominated business. They have made the nation a Southeast Asian leader in profitable industries such as rubber

Guided Reading and Discussion

Work with students to fill in a cause-and-effect organizer to record the causes and effects of the nonaligned movement. *(Causes: By 1930, independence was on the rise in colonies in Africa, Asia, and the Middle East; Post–World War II, leaders like Gandhi and Nehru emerged; India and Pakistan gained independence; Independent nations rejected Cold War practices of the Soviet Union and the West. Effects: 100 nations joined to maintain independence from the Cold War superpowers; India became the leader of the movement; The nonaligned movement became the voice of the "Third World" countries.)*

Analyze Images

Use the bar graph on religious diversity to make a table listing the major religions of Southeast Asia at the top of four columns and listing the countries in which each is practiced in rows beneath the columns.

Independent Nations in Southeast Asia

Populous Indonesia Faces Challenges

Struggle for Democracy in the Philippines

Have students recall the role of imperialism in Southeast Asia. Explain that after South Asian nations achieved independence, the nations of Southeast Asia followed. As in South Asia, some of the new countries faced challenges relating to national identity and unity among diverse groups. Relatively equal distribution of wealth and peace among ethnic groups has helped Malaysia reach prosperity, but Myanmar, Indonesia, and the Philippines have all struggled with internal conflict.

History Background

History of Diversity Indonesia is a diverse nation made up of thousands of islands and hundreds of different ethnic groups. Before independence, Indonesia was a Dutch colony. Before Dutch rule, however, Indonesia was made up of hundreds of independent sultanates and chiefdoms. Some parts of Indonesia, such as the provinces of Aceh and Papua, resisted Dutch rule right into the 1900s and have continued to resist Indonesian rule to this day. While a majority of Indonesians live on the crowded island of Java, even Java has three main ethnic groups, not including its sizable ethnic Chinese minority. A majority of Indonesians are Muslims, but more ethnic Chinese are Buddhists, and substantial Christian minorities exist on several islands. The island of Bali is noted for its ancient Hindu culture, brought by travelers from India more than a thousand years ago.

Answers

Analyze Charts *Indonesia: Islam; Thailand: Buddhism*

Identify Main Ideas *They helped organize the international nonalignment movement.*

Guided Reading and Discussion

Use these questions to spark class discussion about Southeast Asia after independence.

Analyze Information How do autocratic rulers stunt the growth of nations in Southeast Asia and elsewhere? *(Autocratic rulers in countries such as Myanmar, Indonesia, and the Philippines have hurt their countries through limitations in foreign trade, the silencing or murder of dissenters, and economic policies that benefited only them and their supporters.)*

Cite Evidence What have been the main causes of violence in Indonesia? Cite evidence from the text to support your answer. *(Sample response: Violence in Indonesia has been caused by religious and ethnic conflicts. In the Moluccas, fighting broke out between Christians and Muslims, killing thousands. Attacks have occurred throughout the country against people of Chinese descent. Muslim separatists and those living in Papua have all sought independence through violence.)*

and electronics. The government, however, has tried to include the Malay majority in the country's prosperity. The result has been a more equal distribution of wealth in Malaysia than in most countries in the region.

Suffering and Oppression in Myanmar Burma won independence from Britain in 1948 and took the name Myanmar in 1989. Ethnic tensions and a repressive government have plagued the country. The Burmese majority dominated other ethnic groups. The harsh military government limited foreign trade, and living standards remained low.

Under mounting pressure, the military held elections in 1990. When an opposition party won the election, the military rejected the results. It put the opposition leader, **Aung San Suu Kyi,** (awn sahn soo chee) under house arrest, and jailed, killed, or exiled many opponents. In 1991, Suu Kyi won the Nobel Peace Prize for her "nonviolent struggle for democracy and human rights."

For twenty years, the military silenced demands for new elections and crushed peaceful demonstrations by Buddhist monks. It even prevented humanitarian aid from reaching areas of Myanmar that were devastated by a cyclone in 2008. In 2010, Myanmar held Parliamentary elections, and former prime minister Thein Sein was chosen as the country's president.

Though Thein Sein continued the practice of appointing military figures to national office, the politically moderate leader worked on substantial reforms, including releasing many political prisoners and enacting laws to protect human rights and freedom of information. Under this government, Aung San Suu Kyi has regained political office as a member of Parliament.

>> Aung San Suu Kyi attends a Burmese cultural event in London. Since her release from house arrest, she has reentered politics and works to improve Myanmar.

COMPARE How did Malaysia's approach to ethnic diversity differ from Myanmar's?

Populous Indonesia Faces Challenges

After the Japanese were defeated in World War II, the Netherlands attempted to regain power in Indonesia, formerly the Dutch East Indies. The Dutch, however, were forced to give up their possessions when the Indonesian government declared independence in 1949.

Geography and diversity posed an obstacle to unity in Indonesia and has in some cases led to conflict. Indonesia includes more than 13,000 islands, many very small but some as large as European nations. Javanese make up almost half of the population, but there are hundreds of other ethnic groups. About 90 percent of Indonesians are Muslims, but the population includes substantial Christian, Buddhist, and Hindu minorities.

Search for Stability Upon achieving independence, Indonesia formed a parliamentary government under its first president, **Sukarno.** But Sukarno shifted from democracy to authoritarian rule. In 1967, an army general, **Suharto,** seized power.

Suharto claimed that communists were responsible for an earlier attempt by military officers to overthrow the government and ordered the slaughter of hundreds of thousands of communists and suspected communists. For decades, Suharto imposed his will on Indonesia. A financial crisis finally forced Suharto to resign from power in 1998.

Since then, elected governments have worked to build democracy, strengthen the economy, and fight corruption. Indonesia is home to the world's largest Muslim population. But Islamic extremists have challenged Indonesia's long tradition of religious tolerance. Terrorist groups in Indonesia have targeted foreigners and non-Muslims and threatened the stability of the government.

Answers

Compare *Malaysia sought to ensure the welfare of all ethnicities, while Myanmar gave preference to those of Burmese ethnicity.*

English Language Proficiency Standards

5.F.1 Read "Struggle for Democracy in the Philippines" aloud to the class.

Beginning Write and display several simple sentences about the progression of democracy in the Philippines. Show students how to add descriptive words to the sentences. Finally, provide students with cloze sentences and instruct them to add a descriptive word to improve each sentence. For example: A growing population is a strain on _____ resources.

Intermediate Write and display several simple sentences about the progression of democracy in the Philippines. Use one or two of the example sentences to show students how to add descriptive words to lengthen their sentences and make them more interesting. Then ask student volunteers to contribute descriptive words to the remaining example sentences. Rewrite the sentences with the additional descriptive words. Read them aloud and have students repeat them.

The Independence Movement in East Timor Indonesia seized **East Timor** in 1975, just after it had been granted independence by Portugal. However, most East Timorese wanted independence. For years, the government battled the mostly Catholic East Timorese.

East Timor finally won independence from Indonesia in 2002. This very poor new nation struggled to meet its people's need for jobs and decent living standards.

Ethnic Conflicts and Natural Disasters Religious and ethnic conflicts fueled violence in parts of Indonesia. In the Moluccas, a group of eastern islands, fighting between Muslims and Christians killed thousands. Discrimination against Chinese people led to vicious attacks. Rebels in Papua, on the island of New Guinea, sought independence, as did Muslim separatists in Aceh (AH chay) in the northwest.

Natural disasters have added to Indonesia's troubles. In 2004, a tsunami (tsoo NAH mee), or giant wave, devastated the coast of Aceh and killed more than 100,000 people. The tsunami also ravaged Thailand, Sri Lanka, and other lands around the Indian Ocean. Following the disaster, rebels in Aceh and the Indonesian government signed a peace accord. Helped by international aid donors, they worked together to rebuild Aceh.

IDENTIFY MAIN IDEAS How has diversity posed challenges to Indonesia?

Struggle for Democracy in the Philippines

Like Indonesia, the Philippines include thousands of islands with diverse ethnic and religious groups. Catholics are predominant, but many Muslims live in the south. In 1946, the Philippines gained independence after almost 50 years of American rule. American influence remained strong through military and economic aid.

Marcos Becomes a Dictator Although the Filipino constitution set up a democratic government, a wealthy elite controlled politics and the economy. The peasant majority was poor. For years, the government battled Huks (hooks), local communists with strong peasant support. **Ferdinand Marcos,** elected president in 1965, abandoned democracy. He became a dictator and cracked down on basic freedoms. He even had **Benigno Aquino** (beh NEE nyoh ah KEE noh), a popular rival, murdered.

>> Ferdinand Marcos and his wife, Imelda, meet with the press at their palace. The pair was accused of embezzling government money to fund their lavish lifestyle.

A Demand for Democracy When Marcos finally held elections in 1986, voters chose **Corazon Aquino** (kawr ah SOHN), the widow of the slain Benigno. Marcos tried to deny the results, but massive protests forced him to resign during the "people power" revolution. Under Aquino and her successors, this fragile democracy survived, despite many political scandals. Economic growth was limited, and poverty remained widespread. With the highest birth rate in Asia, the population continues to rise rapidly, straining already limited resources.

Clashes with Rebels For decades, various rebel groups have waged guerrilla wars across the Philippines. Some rebels were communists. Others were Muslim separatists. Some Muslim rebels have links to international terrorist groups such as Al Qaeda. In the early 2000s, the Filipino government accepted aid from its ally, the United States, to fight rebels and pursue President George W. Bush's "war on terror." Even so, terrorist groups with separatist agendas continue to operate throughout the islands.

 **IDENTIFY CAUSE AND EFFECT** Why has the Philippines had trouble preserving its democracy?

Draw Inferences Why has economic growth in the Philippines been limited? Consider the factors that have been discussed in the text. *(Sample response: The government was set up as a democracy but was actually controlled by a wealthy elite. The majority of the country was poor, and Ferdinand Marcos ruled as a dictator. Marcos eventually lost power to his successor, who worked to keep the country a democracy. However, the economy continues to be fragile. Contributing to all of this is the fact that the country has the highest birth rate in Asia, taxing the country's resources even more.)*

Compare and Contrast Choose two of the independent nations discussed in this lesson (India, Pakistan, Sri Lanka, Bangladesh, Malaysia, Myanmar, Indonesia, and the Philippines). Compare and contrast the road to independence between the two nations. What led to each nation's desire for independence, how did they gain their independence, and what effect did independence have on the growth and development of each nation? *(Answers will vary. Students should choose two of the listed nations and compare and contrast how they came to independence. Students should discuss all of the items listed in the prompt, reflecting accurately information in the text. Examples might mention the violence that accompanied the independence process.)*

Advanced Instruct students to work in pairs to write several sentences about the development of democracy in the Philippines. Remind students to use descriptive clauses and phrases to make their writing more interesting and accurate. Then have two pairs of students come together to create a group of four. Instruct small groups to share their sentences and give one another feedback on their writing.

Advanced High Instruct students to write several sentences about the development of democracy in the Philippines. Remind students to use descriptive clauses and phrases to make their writing more interesting and accurate. Then have students turn to a partner to share sentences and give each other feedback on their writing.

Answers

Identify Main Ideas *Guerrilla of religious, ethnic, and political groups has led to conflict and violence.*

Identify Cause and Effect *Guerrilla rebels, poverty, a high birth rate, and a lack of economic growth have held the Philippines back.*

Topic 20 Lesson 1

SYNTHESIZE

Online Project the **Digital Activity: Independence in Southeast Asia**. Help students complete the graphic organizer. Remind students that the diverse nature of nations in South and Southeast Asia often causes marginalized groups to develop independence or separatist movements.

Identify Patterns Some South and Southeast Asian nations had similar struggles with building new nations. Name some common problems that occurred across the region. *(Sample responses: minority groups' desire for independence, power struggles between military and civilians, religious fundamentalism, dictators, natural disasters)*

DEMONSTRATE

Online Assign the online **Digital Lesson Quiz** for this lesson if you haven't already done so. Students will be offered automatic remediation or enrichment based on their score.

Pose the following to the class on the Discussion Board:

In this lesson, you learned about independence movements in South and Southeast Asia. Nations across the region gained independence, with varying results.

Generate Explanations How has geography had a similar impact on the development of Indonesia and the Philippines as nations? *(Sample response: Both countries include large groups of islands. The distance between the islands and the differences among the populations make national unity difficult. Isolation of some islands might also complicate government business.)*

Topic Inquiry

Have students continue their investigations for the Topic Inquiry.

ASSESSMENT

1. **Identify Cause and Effect** Why did the partition of British India cause a refugee crisis?
2. **Summarize** Why did Bangladesh separate from Pakistan?
3. **Draw Conclusions** How did a policy of nonalignment influence the relations of India and Pakistan with the Cold War superpowers?
4. **Compare** Why did policies toward ethnic diversity lead to prosperity in Malaysia but to conflict in other parts of Southeast Asia?
5. **Synthesize** How have religious and ethnic diversity affected the recent history of Indonesia?

Assessment

1. Religious violence between Muslims and Hindus drove people to flee areas where their religion was in the minority.
2. The people of East Pakistan broke away to form Bangladesh because of ethnic differences and the belief that West Pakistanis dominated the government.
3. Both Pakistan and India sought to avoid control by either superpower, in accordance with nonalignment.
4. Malaysia's policies to aid disadvantaged ethnic groups brought internal peace and economic prosperity. In other countries, such as Indonesia and Myanmar, ethnic discrimination led to violence.
5. It has brought deadly violence and discrimination and has led to independence struggles in Papua New Guinea and Aceh.

20.2 After World War II, European colonial powers could no longer afford to hold on to their colonies. As nationalist demands forced Britain to withdraw from India, African leaders, too, pressed for independence. One by one, European colonies in Africa won independence. In the new nations, crowds celebrated their freedom, while bands played new national anthems. However, even as independence celebrations took place, African nations faced tough challenges.

>> Kwame Nkrumah and others wave to a crowd during independence celebrations. **Analyze Visuals** How are the men in this image dressed? What does this reveal about their attitude toward their culture?

Interactive Flipped Video

African Nations Win Independence

TEKS
1.F, 13.E, 22.D

>> Objectives

Summarize how African nations won independence.

Analyze the issues facing new African nations and the different paths they took.

Identify examples of and summarize the reasons for ethnic conflict and genocide in African nations.

>> Key Terms

savanna
Kwame Nkrumah
Jomo Kenyatta
coup d'état
Mobutu Sese Seko
Islamist
Katanga
Biafra
Hutus
Tutsis
Darfur

The New Nations of Africa

A Geographically Diverse Continent Africa is the world's second-largest continent, more than three times the size of the United States. Tropical rain forests cover central Africa's Congo Basin and coastal West Africa.

Vast **savannas,** or grasslands with scattered trees, make up interior West Africa, East Africa, and much of central and southern Africa. Africa has the world's largest desert—the Sahara—in the north and the smaller Kalahari Desert in the south, as well as fertile coastal strips in North and South Africa.

Africa's people are concentrated in the most fertile areas, such as the savanna and forest regions of Nigeria and the moist highlands of East Africa. These regions produce enough food to support large populations. Like people in other parts of the world, however, millions of Africans are migrating, or moving, from rural areas to cities.

Africa has rich deposits of minerals such as gold ore, copper ore, and diamonds. Some African nations produce valuable cash crops, including coffee and cacao—used to make chocolate. Some regions

Aa Vocabulary Builder

1. Have students pronounce the following academic vocabulary terms in this lesson and clarify the part of speech. For difficult or polysyllabic words, break them into syllables and pronounce them with the students.
2. Explain what the word means in common "student-friendly" language using synonyms and antonyms when possible. Provide concrete examples to clarify the meaning, and rephrase the definition.

export: goods sent to another country

resources: important assets

strategic: related to purposeful planning for an event

African Nations Win Independence

CONNECT

Preview Have students preview the **Lesson Objectives** and the list of **Key Terms**.

Students can also preview all the **Key Terms** and **Academic Vocabulary** using the **Interactive Reading Notepad** on the digital course or preview a summary of the lesson in the **Reading and Note Taking Study Guide**.

Online Use the **Editable Presentation** found on the digital course to present the main ideas for this lesson.

Start Up Activity

After students enter and get settled, have students recall the independence movements of the post–World War II era. Have them form pairs to come up with a list of responses to the following question: What are the three biggest challenges a new nation might face? To help guide discussions, have students consider what new institutions would need to be created, how new rulers would be chosen and trained, and what social, economic, and political differences would have to be bridged. Instruct students to keep their lists as they learn about the new nations of Africa.

Online You can also project the **Start Up Activity** from the course.

INVESTIGATE

Have students read the section using the **Reading and Note Taking Study Guide** to help them take notes and understand the text as they read.

The New Nations of Africa

Explain that just as nationalist demands forced Britain to withdraw from India, African leaders, too, pressed for independence. One by one, European colonies in Africa won independence. Remind students that the nations of Africa won independence over a long period, but that most gained independence after World War II, during the 1950s and 1960s.

Answers

Analyze Visuals *Sample response: The men are dressed in traditional African clothing rather than Western suits. This indicates their pride in their cultural traditions.*

Topic 20 Lesson 2

Online Project the **Interactive Map: Imperialism and Independence in Africa**, and focus students' attention on the second layer that shows the dates of African independence.

ACTIVE CLASSROOM

Have students engage in the My Metaphor strategy by completing the following sentence: This map shows that _________ is like _________ because ___________________.

Guided Reading and Discussion

Review the information in the text about the geography of Africa. Remind students of the impact of the independence movements of Africa and help students summarize the rise of those movements. Explain that some movements were violent, while others were relatively peaceful.

Generalize Ask: What effect did World War II have on the independence of African nations, and why? *(Sample response: World War II depleted European energies and resources, giving independence movements in Africa the opportunity to grow and achieve success.)*

A Variety of New Governments

After independence, African nations followed many different paths but also faced many challenges and ongoing conflicts.

also have large oil reserves. European powers had established colonies in Africa to tap into these natural resources.

Nationalism Leads to Freedom By the 1950s, nationalist movements in Africa had grown stronger. Skilled organizers such as **Kwame Nkrumah**(KWAH may un KROO muh) in Gold Coast (later Ghana), **Jomo Kenyatta** in Kenya, and Léopold Senghor (sahn GAWR) in Senegal led independence movements in their own countries.

Most African nations won independence through largely peaceful means. Drained by World War II, European powers had few resources to resist the pressure to give up their colonial empires. The struggle for freedom turned violent, however, in a few colonies where large numbers of Europeans had settled, such as Kenya and Algeria. Later, you will examine five of these nations in detail.

IDENTIFY CAUSE AND EFFECT How did World War II affect African independence efforts?

A Variety of New Governments

Some new nations enjoyed peace and had democratic governments. Others were plunged into crisis by civil war, military rule, or corrupt dictators. In recent decades, a number of African nations have taken steps toward democracy.

Old Boundaries, New Problems The new nations of Africa faced many difficulties, including the need to unify their people. European colonial powers had drawn boundaries around their colonies without regard to the many rival ethnic groups living in a particular region. Upon achieving independence, most African nations included a patchwork of peoples with different languages, religions, and traditions. The colonial boundaries were, and have continued to be, maintained by the new African nations.

Within these new nations, people often felt their first loyalty was to their own ethnic group, not to a distant national government. As a result, ongoing conflict between different ethnic groups has plagued many African nations.

The Rise of Dictators Many leaders of the new nations were heroes of the liberation struggle. Some

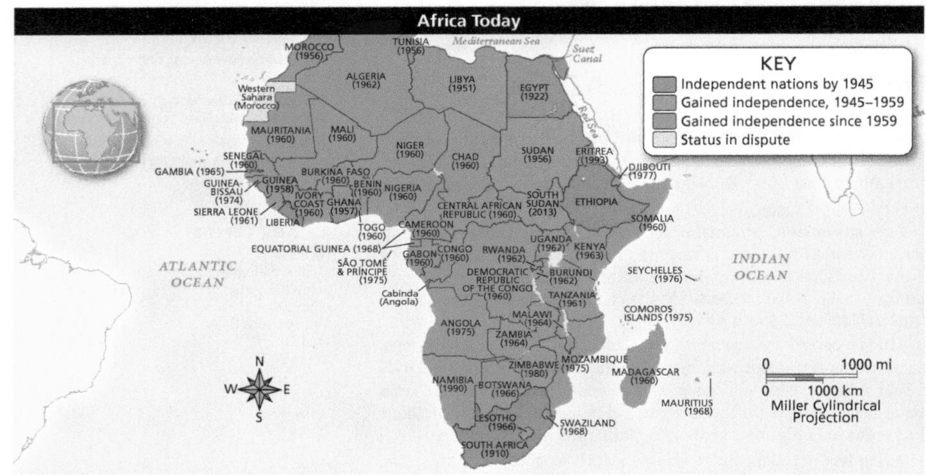

>> Over the course of many years, African nations gained their independence from European powers. **Analyze Maps** What do the dates on this map tell you about when nations gained independence?

Interactive Map

English Language Proficiency Standards

ELPS 1.E.2 Read "The New Nations of Africa" aloud. Display the words *continent, forest, coastal,* and *desert*.

Beginning Read the words aloud and have students repeat them. Use each word in a sentence. Guide students to use the words in short phrases or sentences about the information in the text.

Intermediate Help students develop basic sentences for each word. Then support students as they use the information in the text to write short phrases or sentences using these words.

Advanced Have students use the words in a group discussion about geography. Informally assess student understanding of the words. Then have student pairs write sentences about the text for each word.

Advanced High Have student pairs use the words in a discussion about geography. Then have students write sentences about the text for each word.

Answers

Identify Cause and Effect *Much of Europe was destroyed by the war and most colonial powers did not have the resources to fight against the desire among Africans for independence.*

Analyze Maps *Sample response: Most countries in Africa won their independence after 1959.*

chose to build one-party states. These leaders claimed that multiparty systems encouraged disunity. In time, these one-party governments became repressive, and some liberation leaders became dictators. Dictators often used their positions to enrich themselves and their supporters at the expense of the nation.

In many nations, when unsuccessful policies or corrupt governments led to civil unrest, the military seized power. More than half of all African nations suffered military coups (kooz) at one time or another.

A coup, or **coup d'état**(koo day TAH) is the forcible overthrow of a government. Some military rulers were brutal tyrants. Others tried to end corruption and improve conditions. Military leaders usually promised to restore civilian rule. But in many cases, they only surrendered power when they were toppled by another coup.

Democracies Emerge By the 1990s, some African nations were moving away from strongman rule. Western governments and lenders, such as the World Bank, demanded political reforms before granting loans. In response, some governments allowed opposition parties to emerge and expanded freedom of expression. In nations such as Nigeria, Tanzania, and Benin, multiparty elections were held, removing long-ruling leaders from office.

Outside Influences on African Nations Even after African nations won independence, colonial powers and foreign companies often retained control of businesses and resources in these former colonies. Many new nations remained dependent on their former colonial rulers for aid, trade, and investment.

The new nations were also buffeted by the Cold War. Both the United States and the Soviet Union competed for military and strategic advantage through alliances with several African countries. The United States, for example, backed **Mobutu Sese Seko,** the dictator of Zaire (now called the Democratic Republic of Congo). It wanted to counter Soviet influence in nearby Angola. During the 1970s, the United States backed Somalia, while the Soviet Union supported neighboring Ethiopia. Both African countries were important because they controlled access to the Red Sea, a vital world shipping route.

INFER Why did one-party rule often lead to repression and tyranny?

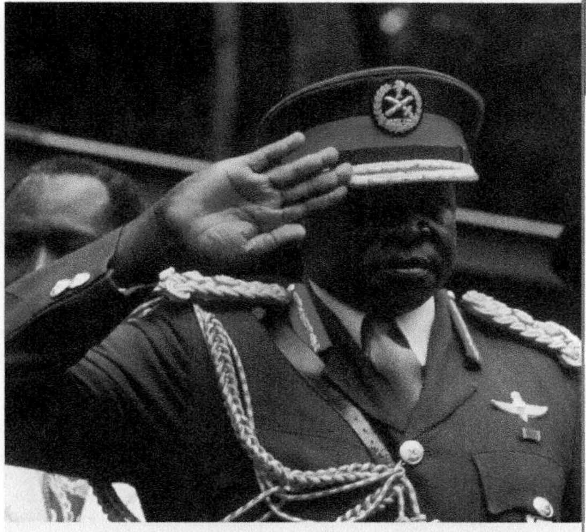

>> Idi Amin gained power in Uganda through a military coup in 1971. A particularly brutal dictator, he was driven out of the country in 1979.

Case Studies: Five African Nations

While the new nations of Africa faced many of the same challenges, each nation had a unique history. To gain a better understanding of the process of nation-building in Africa, we will examine the histories of five important nations.

Ghana In 1957, Ghana was the first African nation south of the Sahara to win independence. Britain had called this colony Gold Coast, for its rich mineral resources. Under independence leader Kwame Nkrumah, it took the name Ghana, after the ancient West African kingdom.

As president, Nkrumah supported socialism and government ownership of major industries. He backed the building of a huge dam to provide electric power, but the project left Ghana with massive debts. Nkrumah's government became increasingly corrupt and dictatorial. In 1966, Nkrumah was toppled by the first of several military coups.

This pattern repeated itself in many new African nations. Large costly projects, often poorly planned, left many countries in debt to foreign lenders. Coups and dictators became common.

Discuss Note that most newly independent nations kept the same boundaries that were established by European colonial powers. Ask: What effects might this have had? *(Possible response: It might have allowed some stability and continuity; or, it might have introduced problems, as old borders might not have reflected the territories and loyalties of different groups.)*

Key Terms

Ask students to find the key term **coup d'etat** (in bold) in the text and explain its meaning. Point out that more than half of Africa's new nations suffered military coups. Ask students to predict why there were so many changes of power and struggles for control in the emerging nations.

Guided Reading and Discussion

Ask questions to start a discussion about the new governments that arose among the newly independent African nations.

Summarize What do you think are the main reasons for ongoing ethnic conflicts in Africa? *(Sample response: Loyalty to tribe or ethnic group before country; in some countries, several ethnic groups are competing for power and resources.)*

Discuss Have a class discussion about the effect of one-party governments on various states in Africa. What was frequently the reason for the one-party state? *(Sample response: Leaders argued that multiple parties would lead to disunity.)* Does this reason have any merit? *(Some students might argue that the leaders only wanted power. Others might point out that leaders had a legitimate concern about possible conflict and civil war.)* What was the result? *(The one-party system often led to dictatorships and military coups.)*

History Background

Kwame Nkrumah When Kwame Nkrumah helped design Ghana's new national flag, he chose the Pan-African colors and a black star symbolizing his hope that Ghana would be a beacon of independence for all of Africa. Nkrumah built modern roads, schools, and universities, the Volta Dam for hydroelectric power, and an aluminum industry. He also spent lavishly on his goal of liberating and uniting all of Africa. However, as other countries gained freedom, they resisted unification. Meanwhile, once-thriving Ghana became mired in foreign debt, and Nkrumah resorted to more and more repressive tactics to maintain control. In 1966 the army overthrew Nkrumah. The rejoicing populace destroyed his statues and renamed the roads and buildings that had been named for him.

Answers

Infer *Without multiple parties there was no opposition. A leader of the one-party state became too powerful, which led to abuse of power and corruption.*

Case Studies: Five African Nations

Remind students of the five African nations profiled: Ghana, Kenya, Algeria, Democratic Republic of Congo, and Nigeria.

Online Project the **Interactive Gallery: Independence in Congo**, and click through each image. Discuss the story that is revealed from viewing all the images.

ACTIVE CLASSROOM

Use the See-Think-Wonder strategy with this map. Pair students with partners. Ask: What story is revealed through this gallery of images? Why do you think that? How does this compare to the other African nations you have learned about? Share insights with the class.

Guided Reading and Discussion

Help students identify and summarize the reasons for ongoing conflicts in Africa.

Compare and Contrast Work with students to compare and contrast the five nations profiled. Create a table with five columns, one for each nation. The table should have three rows. The first row should be labeled "Independence," where major points about the countries' independence can be recorded. The second row might be labeled "Country Details" for details about whether the countries had a large variety of ethnic groups, whether they had access to valuable resources, and so forth. The third row should be labeled "Post-Independence," where major points about what happened after independence can be recorded. Points might include the type of government established, whether countries suffered a civil war, and whether dictatorships developed or military coups occurred.

In the 1980s, Jerry Rawlings, a military officer, took power in a coup. He strengthened the economy and moved Ghana toward democracy. In 1992, Rawlings allowed multiparty elections and was chosen president. Other elections followed. Although the economy suffered from falling prices for cocoa and gold, its main exports, Ghana made progress toward improving life for its people. The recent discovery of offshore oil raised hopes for more economic growth.

Kenya While Ghana made a peaceful transition to freedom, Kenya faced an armed struggle. A large number of white settlers had built successful plantations on the fertile highlands once occupied by the Kikuyu (kee KOO yoo), Kenya's largest ethnic group. White Kenyans had passed laws to ensure their domination over the black majority. Nationalist leader and Kikuyu spokesman Jomo Kenyatta had long sought justice for the black majority and called for nonviolent means to end oppressive laws.

In the 1950s, some black Kenyans turned to guerrilla warfare, attacking and killing white settlers. The British called them Mau Mau. Claiming that he was a secret leader of the Mau Mau, the British imprisoned Kenyatta. Both sides committed terrible atrocities during this period, and thousands of Kikuyu were killed. In 1963, the British finally withdrew, and Kenyatta became the first leader of an independent Kenya.

Kenyatta and his successor dominated the country for decades. They limited freedom of expression and resisted free elections. Since the 1990s, Kenya has held multiparty elections, but corruption has remained widespread.

In 2007, a disputed election sparked violence and ethnic unrest. The conflict hurt tourism—one of Kenya's largest industries. In 2013 the country held tense but largely peaceful elections.

Algeria Like Kenya, the French colony of Algeria had a large population of European settlers. Over one million French people called Algeria home and were determined to remain part of France. The French government, which had recently lost its Asian colony, Vietnam, also wanted to hold on to Algeria, especially after deposits of oil and natural gas were discovered there. As a result, the struggle for independence turned violent in the 1950s.

Algerian nationalists set up the National Liberation Front, which turned to guerrilla warfare to win freedom. From 1954 to 1962, more than one million Algerians were killed in this bloody conflict. When public opinion in France finally turned against the war, Algeria won independence.

Algeria's oil and gas resources have helped it economically. Politically, it has suffered through periods of military rule and internal conflict. During the 1970s, the government nationalized, or took over, foreign-owned companies and created a command economy. Since the 1980s, Algeria has been moving toward a market economy.

By the 1990s, a growing struggle had erupted between the military and **Islamists,** people who want a government based on Islamic law and beliefs. In 1992, the Algerian government allowed free elections. When an Islamist party won, the military rejected the results. For seven years, civil war raged between Islamist militants and the military, leaving as many as 150,000 dead. The violence slowed after 1999, but tensions remained.

Democratic Republic of Congo The Democratic Republic of Congo (or Congo), a former Belgian colony, covers a vast region of central Africa. It includes a million square miles of rain forest and savanna centered on the Congo River basin.

The Belgians were eager to keep control of Congo's rich resources, such as the copper and diamonds of the **Katanga** province. In 1960, therefore, it rushed to declare the colony independent, though the Congolese were not prepared for self-government. This allowed

>> Patrice Lumumba was newly independent Congo's first prime minister. Here, Lumumba waves to a crowd after receiving a 41–2 vote of confidence from the Congolese senate in September 1960.

Interactive Gallery

D Differentiate Extra Support Help students complete the table by having groups review the text and highlight portions they think might be relevant. Then have groups share and compare their findings with the rest of the class. Finally, complete the table as a class.

Belgian mining companies, working with politicians in Katanga, to control the province.

Katanga rebelled against Congo shortly after independence. The country's first prime minister, Patrice Lumumba, appealed for Soviet help to fight the rebels. Seeing the appeal to the Soviets as a Cold War challenge, the United States backed Lumumba's rival, Colonel Joseph Mobutu, later known as Mobutu Sese Seko. Mobutu captured Lumumba, who was executed soon afterward. The United Nations ended the Katanga rebellion in 1963.

For 32 years, Mobutu's harsh, corrupt rule brought poverty and unrest to Congo. Rebels finally forced Mobutu from power in 1997. But civil war again raged as rival military leaders battled to control Congo's mineral riches.

The country's first free elections in 41 years brought Joseph Kabila to power in 2006. As on and off violence continued in the eastern region, Kabila had to reduce corruption, calm ethnic tensions, protect Congo's mineral resources, and heal the scars caused by decades of war.

>> By the year 2009, when this photo was taken, Robert Mugabe was being forced to share power, but Zimbabwe still faced terrible inflation, food shortages, and disease epidemics.

Nigeria Nigeria, on the coast of West Africa, includes diverse people and climates. Nigeria's huge population is the largest in Africa. Its people belong to more than 250 ethnic groups, speak many languages, and practice different religions. The dominant groups are the mainly Christian Ibo (EE boh) and Yoruba (YOH roo buh) in the south, and the Muslim Hausa (HOW suh) in the north.

Nigeria won independence peacefully from Britain in 1960. The next year, oil was discovered, raising hopes for the country's economic future. Instead, the country faced military coups, corruption, and economic crises.

In 1966, the Ibo people in the oil-rich south rebelled and set up the independent Republic of **Biafra.** A brutal civil war led to famine and the death of an estimated half a million people. After three years, Nigeria defeated the rebels and ended Biafra's independence.

Between 1996 and 1999, the military was in and out of power in Nigeria. Military leaders ruled with an iron hand but failed to improve Nigeria's government or its economy. In 1999, Nigeria again held elections. A new civilian government introduced reforms to strengthen the economy and restore political freedom.

Because Nigeria relied heavily on oil exports, it was affected by the rise and fall of oil prices. Nigeria also faced ethnic and religious violence. In the north, Islamists wanted strict Sharia law. In the oil-producing Niger Delta region, local people were bitter about the environmental damage caused by oil drilling and the huge profits going to foreign companies. Armed groups attacked pipelines and held foreign oil workers for ransom.

IDENTIFY CENTRAL ISSUES How did the conflicts in Katanga and Biafra reflect the challenges that new African nations faced after independence?

The Wars of Southern Africa

Most African nations achieved independence through peaceful means during the 1950s and 1960s. In southern Africa, however, the road to freedom was marked by some long, violent struggles.

Zimbabwe As African nations won independence, whites in Southern Rhodesia refused to share power with the black majority. Conservative whites, led by Ian Smith, declared independence in 1965. For years, black guerrilla groups fought for majority rule. In 1980, after a ceasefire and elections, the country gained independence and was renamed Zimbabwe.

Robert Mugabe, a liberation leader, was elected president. Although popular at first, Mugabe grew

Topic 20 Lesson 2

The Wars of Southern Africa

Ethnic Conflict and Genocide

Ethnic tensions and power struggles led to genocide in the nations of Rwanda and Sudan. Work with students to review the material.

Guided Reading and Discussion

Review how the Cold War rivalry between the United States and the Soviet Union led to ongoing conflict in the southern African nations of Zimbabwe, Angola, and Mozambique. Help students understand why the events in Darfur and Rwanda are examples of genocide.

Cite Evidence Display for students a definition of *genocide*. Then have students review the text to find evidence that shows that the events in Rwanda and Darfur are examples of genocide and explain why. *(Answers may vary but should show an understanding that people in Rwanda and Darfur were killed solely because of their political affiliation or their ethnic group.)*

History Background

A History of Repression Colonialism in Algeria left a bitter legacy. Under French rule, Muslims faced discrimination. French settlers owned and operated large farms, businesses, and industries while Algerian Muslims labored on tiny farms or in menial jobs. Muslims were prevented from taking an active role in government. In the 1950s, resentment erupted into guerrilla war. The French moved two million Algerians to internment camps in the desert, where thousands perished. Algerians responded with terrorist attacks. Nearly a million Algerians and 10,000 French soldiers died overall. Since independence, Algeria has experienced cycles of repression and violence. In the 1990s, attacks by government and opposition forces killed up to 150,000 civilians.

Answers

Identify Central Issues *Answers should reflect an understanding that many African nations faced serious problems as a result of internal ethnic divisions.*

Analyze Images

Point out the photograph of the victims of genocide. Explore with students what the image shows and read the caption. Discuss whether or how it illustrates the effects of ethnic violence and genocide. Ask: Is this an effective memorial? Why or why not? *(Some students may feel that showing photographs of victims does not effectively convey the violence done to them, while others might feel that the images of the victims make the genocide more "real.")*

SYNTHESIZE

Online Project the **Digital Activity: Addressing the Challenges of Independence**.

Remind students that at the beginning of this lesson, they made lists of three challenges a newly independent nation might face. Using what they have learned, have them add to their lists. Discuss as a class how different countries addressed these challenges and how successful they were.

Compare Points of View Ask: Has your point of view about African nations changed based on what you have learned about the challenges of independence? Challenge students to use details from the lesson to support their views.

>> The Kigali Memorial Centre in Kigali, Rwanda, displays photographs of people killed in the genocide. **Analyze Image** How could these photographs affect a person's understanding of the genocide?

>> Angolan soldiers learn how to use a bazooka in 1964 during the war of independence.

increasingly dictatorial. He cracked down on opponents and was accused of electoral fraud. Despite international pressure and an economic crisis, the aging Mugabe held on to power.

Angola and Mozambique While Britain and France gave up their African possessions, Portugal clung fiercely to its colonies of Angola and Mozambique. In response, nationalist groups waged a long guerrilla war. In 1975, after Portugal finally agreed to withdraw, Angola and Mozambique celebrated independence.

Both countries then faced brutal civil wars fueled by Cold War rivalries. Some liberation leaders had ties to the Soviet Union or to the African National Congress, a group opposed to the racial policies of South Africa. As a result, the United States and the government of South Africa aided a rebel group in Angola. South Africa also supported a rebel group in Mozambique. The fighting continued until 1992 in Mozambique and 2002 in Angola. Decades of war had ravaged both countries, which slowly began to rebuild.

 **DRAW CONCLUSIONS** Why did fighting continue after Angola and Mozambique achieved independence?

Ethnic Conflict and Genocide

After independence, ethnic conflicts plagued several African nations. The causes were complex. Historic resentments divided ethnically diverse nations. Unjust governments and regional rivalries fed ethnic violence.

Rwanda and Burundi Power struggles between ethnic groups led to a deadly genocide in Rwanda, a small central African nation. The country was home to two main ethnic groups. **Hutus** were the majority group, but **Tutsis** had long dominated Rwanda. Both groups speak the same language and share a culture. Before independence, the Tutsis controlled the government. After obtaining independence, the majority Hutu came into power and violence against Tutsis increased. Over the next 30 years, many Tutsis fled to neighboring countries.

In 1990, a Tutsi-led rebel army, the Rwandan Patriotic Front, began to attack Rwanda. By early 1994, the president of Rwanda had reached a power-sharing agreement with the rebels. But then he and the president of neighboring Burundi were killed in a suspicious plane crash. Immediately after this crash, the genocide against the Tutsis began. Extremist Hutu officials urged civilians to turn on their Tutsi neighbors. At least 800,000 Tutsis and moderate Hutus were

Answers

Analyze Image *Sample response: They bring reality to the concept of genocide by showing the victims' faces. The people in the photographs are of all ages, and you can tell from this photograph that there are many victims.*

Draw Conclusions *Answers should reflect an understanding that because of the Cold War, the United States and the Soviet Union funded rebel groups, which led to ongoing civil wars.*

slaughtered. Millions of Rwandans lost their homes to destructive mobs. Even as the death toll rose, the world community was slow to act to stop the genocide.

In July 1994, a Tutsi exile army conquered Rwanda and set up a unity government. Those accused of genocide faced trials in an international court.

Nearby Burundi faced similar ethnic tensions between Hutus and Tutsis. In 1993, Tutsi military officers killed Burundi's Hutu president in a failed coup attempt. Violence erupted, but did not lead to genocide as in Rwanda. In 2005, voters approved a new constitution that guaranteed both groups' participation in the government and military.

Rebellion and Civil War in Sudan Genocide also took place in oil-rich Sudan. Since independence, Sudan's Arab Muslim north has dominated the non-Muslim, non-Arab south. Sudan's Muslim government even tried to impose Islamic law in non-Muslim areas. For decades, rebel groups in the south battled northern political domination. The fighting also spilled into neighboring Chad. Sudan's north-south conflict killed millions and displaced many more.

In 2005, the Sudanese government and rebels in the south agreed to a peace accord. In 2011, the south of the country gained its freedom and became the new nation of South Sudan.

A different fight occurred in the Muslim but non-Arab western region of **Darfur.** In 2003, rebels began to fight against Sudan's Arab-dominated government. With government backing, Arab militias conducted widespread killings of non-Arab civilians in Darfur. They burned homes and drove farmers off the land.

The United States and other countries sent humanitarian aid to the refugees. Sudan allowed UN peacekeepers into the region, but they were unable to end the violence. In 2009 and 2010, the International Criminal Court (ICC) charged Sudan's president, Omar al-Bashir, with crimes against humanity and genocide and issued an arrest warrant for him. However, the ICC is not recognized in Sudan, and no arrest was ever made. In 2010, al-Bashir won reelection, though many believe those elections were not fair or free.

? **DESCRIBE** Why was there conflict between northern and southern Sudan?

>> Children celebrate with a Republic of South Sudan flag cake during Sudanese independence celebrations in 2011.

ASSESSMENT

1. **Analyze Information** Where did struggles for independence in Africa turn violent and why?
2. **Compare and Contrast** What were the issues facing the Democratic Republic of Congo and Kenya as they achieved independence and what paths did those countries take?
3. **Synthesize** Why did many new nations in Africa have difficulty building democratic governments?
4. **Summarize** How did the ethnic conflict in Rwanda become a genocide?
5. **Compare** How was the conflict in Darfur similar to the conflict in Rwanda?

Topic 20 Lesson 2

DEMONSTRATE

Online Assign the online **Digital Lesson Quiz** for this lesson if you haven't already done so. Students will be offered automatic remediation or enrichment based on their score.

Pose the following to the class on the Discussion Board:

In this lesson, you have read about how the nations of Africa gained independence, and the challenges they faced and the successes they achieved post-independence.

Generate Explanations What were the most important reasons that new African nations faced struggles after independence? *(Possible responses: impact of Cold War rivalries, ethnic tensions, struggles over resources, corrupt governments, poverty)*

Topic Inquiry

Have students continue their investigations for the Topic Inquiry.

Answers

Describe *Sample response: The northern Muslim Arab area wanted to politically and culturally dominate the southern non-Muslim non-Arab area.*

Assessment

1. Students may point to Algeria, Kenya, Zimbabwe, Angola, or Mozambique, but answers should reflect understanding that most countries where the independence struggle became violent had large European populations.
2. Sample response: Kenya and Congo achieved independence differently. Kenya's came through violence, while the Congo won independence peacefully. While both countries have histories of corruption and limits to freedom, Kenya never had a civil war or a military coup. Congo was immediately involved in a civil war and then was led by a dictator who was removed 32 years later during another civil war.
3. Answers should reflect understanding that ethnic divisions (created by old colonial boundaries), Cold War competition for influence, and many leaders' resistance to multiparty states contributed to the difficulties in building democratic societies.
4. Extremist Hutu officials and civilians took advantage of a power vacuum and encouraged the killing of Tutsis and moderate Hutus.
5. In both conflicts, government targeted a minority group in an effort to eradicate it.

Topic 20 Lesson 3

The Modern Middle East Takes Shape

CONNECT

Preview Have students preview the **Lesson Objectives** and the list of **Key Terms**.

Students can also preview all the **Key Terms** and **Academic Vocabulary** using the **Interactive Reading Notepad** on the digital course or preview a summary of the lesson in the **Reading and Note Taking Study Guide**.

Online Use the **Editable Presentation** found on the digital course to present the main ideas for this lesson.

Start Up Activity

Explain to students that different religious groups have used their faiths and sacred writings as justification for claim to the same land in the Middle East. Ask: How might a religious conflict over land impact a region? *(Possible response: Religion might make settlement difficult because it often involves belief in divine authority and may transcend questions of life and death.)*

Online You can also project the **Start Up Activity** from the course.

INVESTIGATE

Have students read the section using the **Reading and Note Taking Study Guide** to help them take notes and understand the text as they read.

The Challenges of Diversity

Recall that most borders in the Middle East were drawn by European powers after World War I without regard for ethnic or religious divisions. Recall the difficulties African leaders faced because national borders did not match ethnic divisions. Ask students to predict how such borders might lead to difficulties in the Middle East.

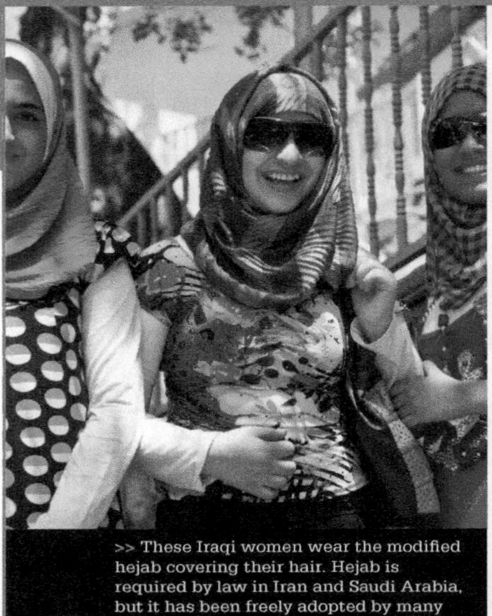

>> These Iraqi women wear the modified hejab covering their hair. Hejab is required by law in Iran and Saudi Arabia, but it has been freely adopted by many Muslim women worldwide as a sign of their faith.

Interactive Flipped Video

20.3 The Middle East, as we use the term in this lesson, is the region stretching from Egypt in the west to Iran in the east and from Turkey in the north to the Arabian Peninsula in the south. Although the majority of people in the region today are Muslims, there are also Christian communities and the mostly Jewish nation of Israel.

TEKS
10.C, 13.E, 13.F, 15.A, 16.A, 16.C, 25.D

>> Objectives

Analyze the development of modern nations in the Middle East.

Describe the founding of Israel and the impact of the Arab rejection of Israel.

Understand how oil has affected nations of the Middle East.

Examine the impact of Islam on government, law, and the lives of women.

Define the "Arab Spring."

>> Key Terms

kibbutz
Golda Meir
Suez Canal
Gamal Abdel Nasser
Anwar Sadat
Ruhollah Khomeini
theocracy
secular
hejab

The Modern Middle East Takes Shape

The Challenges of Diversity

As a world crossroads since ancient times, the Middle East is home to many ethnic groups. Arabs are a majority in some countries, such as Egypt, Saudi Arabia, and Syria. In other countries, the majority populations are non-Arab Muslims, such as the Turks of Turkey and the Persians of Iran.

Mandates Gain Independence At the end of World War I, the Treaty of Versailles and other agreements parceled out many of the lands once dominated by the defeated Central Powers. Britain and France were given mandates over large parts of the Middle East.

Under the mandate system in the Middle East, territories taken from the defeated Ottoman empire were administered, or run, by Europeans. Britain, for example, controlled the Palestine mandate and three provinces of the old Ottoman empire that were joined together into modern-day Iraq. The stated goal of the mandate system was to move the mandates gradually toward independence.

From the outset, Arabs resisted the mandates. In British-ruled Palestine, tensions also grew between Arab and Jewish residents. In the Balfour Declaration, Britain had supported a Jewish national

www.PearsonTexas.com Access your Digital Lesson.

Aa Vocabulary Builder

1. Have students pronounce the following academic vocabulary terms in this lesson and clarify the part of speech. For difficult or polysyllabic words, break them into syllables and pronounce them with the students.
2. Explain what the word means in common "student-friendly" language using synonyms and antonyms when possible. Provide concrete examples to clarify the meaning, and rephrase the definition.

diverse: showing variety; very different

domination: complete control over someone or something

intervened: came between two events or people

home in part of the Palestine mandate, while Arabs in the region demanded self-rule. During the 1930s, independence movements and nationalist calls for an end to European control grew. Following World War II, the former mandates became the independent countries of Iraq, Syria, and Jordan. The Palestine mandate was partitioned into Arab areas and Israel.

Religious and Ethnic Divisions The borders of the new nations were artificially drawn and lumped together diverse ethnic and religious communities. Some ethnic minorities demanded self-rule, or even independence.

Different religious sects, or groups loyal to their own set of beliefs, further divided the new nations. Many countries were home to both Shiite and Sunni Muslims, along with Alawites, Druze, different Christian sects, and Jews. In Iraq and Bahrain, for example, the Shiite majority was ruled by the Sunni minority. Sectarian violence, or conflict based on religious loyalties, posed challenges to unity. Many nations like Syria and Lebanon had diverse groups, including Muslim and Christian Arabs, Assyrians, Greeks, Armenians, and Kurds.

Kurdish Nationalism The Kurds are an ethnic group with their own language and culture. They form important minorities in Turkey, Iran, and Iraq. Kurdish nationalists have long called for an independent homeland. In Turkey, Kurdish rebels resisted government efforts to suppress their culture. In Iraq, a Kurdish uprising in 1991 was brutally suppressed. Today, Kurds in Iraq have much autonomy, but many Kurds still want their own state.

EXPRESS PROBLEMS CLEARLY What is the main cause of ethnic and sectarian violence in the Middle East?

The Founding of Israel

As early as the 1880s, Jews had begun actively organizing and advocating for the re-establishment of a home in their ancient homeland. The horrors of the Holocaust created strong worldwide support for a Jewish state. Many Jews, including Holocaust survivors, migrated to the Palestine mandate after World War II. In 1947, the UN drew up a plan to meet the competing demands of Arab and Jewish nationalists. The UN General Assembly voted to adopt the plan. While the Jews accepted partition, Arabs rejected the partition plan.

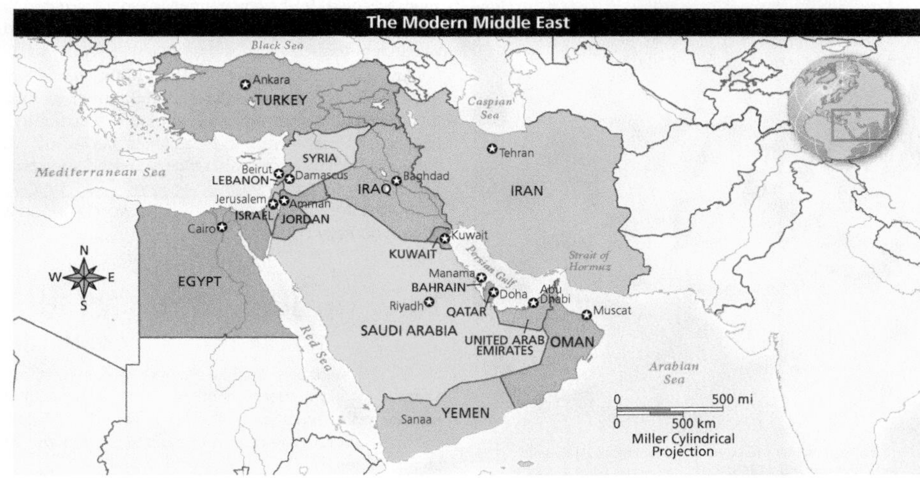

>> **Analyze Maps** This map shows the countries of the modern Middle East. Saudi Arabia, Kuwait, and Iran are three of the world's largest oil-producing countries. Why might control of the Straits of Hormuz be important?

Interactive Map

Online Project the **Interactive Map: Religious Diversity in the Middle East**, and click through the layers.

ACTIVE CLASSROOM

Have student pairs work on a See-Think-Wonder strategy. Project the layers of the map. Allow students to look at the map quietly for two minutes. Ask them: What do you see? What does that make you think? What are you wondering about now that you've seen this? Repeat with each layer. Have students share their insights with their partner, and then with the class.

Guided Reading and Discussion

Remind students that much of the Middle East was once part of the Ottoman empire. After World War I, these areas became part of the mandate system under British and French control as a result of the Treaty of Versailles and other agreements. People who lived in these areas resisted these developments and sought independence.

Connect Ask: How did the mandate system contribute to violence in the Middle East? *(The mandates increased tension between Arabs and Jews, who both wanted to establish independent nations. The mandates were divided into Iraq, Syria, Lebanon, Jordan, and Israel. However, new borders grouped together diverse ethnic and religious communities.)*

The Founding of Israel

Explain that the State of Israel was created as a safe haven for the Jews after World War II. In 1947, the UN drew plans to divide the Palestine Mandate into a Palestinian state and a Jewish state. Israelis accepted the plan; Palestinian Arabs rejected it. In 1948, the State of Israel was declared.

D Differentiate Extra Support What do you think the word *mandates* means? Based on this meaning, what does it mean when the text states: "Britain and France were given mandates over large parts of the Middle East"? *(Sample response: In this example, the word* mandate *means "a territory given to a European country to administer following World War I." The mandates were given to Britain and France to administer territories that were taken from the defeated Ottoman empire and transferred to Europeans to run.)*

Answers

Analyze Maps *Sample response: Much of the world's oil supply would pass through this sea lane.*

Express Problems Clearly *The region is home to many religious and ethnic groups with differing goals and values.*

Topic 20 Lesson 3

Online Project the **Interactive Chart: Birth of Israel**, and have students complete the Interactive Chart.

Express Problems Clearly How has Arab rejection of Israel led to continued conflict? *(Arab states immediately declared war on the new State of Israel. Many Palestinians who fled Israel lived in refugee camps for decades. Radical Palestinian groups have employed terrorism, and most Arab states refused to recognize the existence of Israel.)*

ACTIVE CLASSROOM

Use the If Photos Could Talk strategy. Use the image of Palestinian refugees on p. 900. Ask each student to pick one figure from the photo. Have them imagine the 30 minutes before this photo was taken and the 30 minutes after. (Some questions to pose: Where are they coming from? Where are they headed? Who or what have they left behind?) Ask students to write down a description of both before and after. Students can then meet together with others who selected the same figure and compare notes.

Guided Reading and Discussion

Note that Israel has become a multiparty democracy, one of the only democratic countries in the Middle East.

Explain How did Golda Meir contribute to the founding of Israel? *(She grew up in the United States and emigrated to Palestine in the 1920s. She worked for Israeli independence and became one of the nation's prime ministers.)*

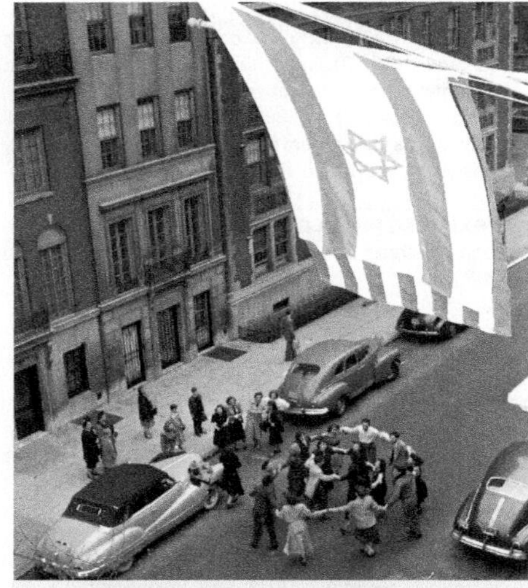

>> Israeli flags fly in New York City to celebrate the birth of Israel, which became an independent state on May 14, 1948. **Explain** Why was an Arab state not established as well?

Interactive Gallery

>> Palestinian women and children flee to Arab-held territories in June 1948. Refugee camps were set up to accept those who could not find shelter. **Recall** How long did some Palestinian refugees live in the refugee camps?

Arabs and Israelis in Conflict In 1948, when Britain withdrew from the Palestine mandate, Jews proclaimed the independent State of Israel. Neighboring Arab nations launched the first of several wars against Israel, but were defeated. As a result of these wars, Israel gained control of more territory. After the 1948 war, Jordan took control of the West Bank and East Jerusalem, while Egypt took the Gaza Strip. Today, Palestinian Arabs do not have an independent state, but a series of negotiations over the years has resulted in peace treaties between Israel and Egypt and the creation of an autonomous Palestinian authority within Israeli-controlled territories.

The 1948 Arab-Israeli war created a huge refugee problem. Hundreds of thousands of Palestinian Arabs fled their homes in Israeli territory. The UN housed them in temporary camps in nearby countries, where they remained for decades. At the same time, hundreds of thousands of Jewish refugees expelled from Arab lands fled to Israel.

The Growth of Israel After the 1948 war, Israel developed rapidly. A skilled workforce set up businesses. Kibbutzim produced crops for export. A **kibbutz** (kih BOOTS) is a collective farm. In 1950, Israel passed a law called the right of return, granting every Jew the right to live in Israel and become an Israeli citizen. This was a response to the Holocaust when countries closed their doors to Jews fleeing the Nazis. This law established Israel as a safe haven for the Jewish people. Jews from around the world migrated to Israel. They joined native Israelis who had struggled to win independence.

An early leader was **Golda Meir,** who had emigrated from Russia to the United States as a child. In the 1920s, she moved to a kibbutz in Palestine and later joined the Jewish independence movement. In 1969, she became Israel's first woman prime minister.

 **INFER** Why did people around the world support a Jewish homeland in Palestine?

New Nations in the Middle East

After independence, Middle Eastern nations set out to build strong modern economies. Only a handful of nations in the region had rich oil reserves. Most Middle Eastern nations were poor, and each faced its own set of challenges.

In some countries, nationalist military leaders seized power. They wanted to promote economic growth and end foreign influence, but they were also authoritarian

English Language Proficiency Standards

1.E.3 Read "The Founding of Israel" aloud to students.

Beginning Write and display the word *kibbutz* for students. Read *kibbutz* aloud and have students repeat the word. Give students a simple definition, and display a visual, if available. Guide students in a discussion of the implications of Jews returning to Israel to work on kibbutzim.

Intermediate Write and display the word *kibbutz* for students. Read *kibbutz* aloud and have students repeat the word. Give students a simple definition, and display a visual, if available. Ask students to work in small groups to discuss the implications of Jews returning to Israel to work on kibbutzim. Circulate among students to offer support as needed.

Advanced Write and display the word *kibbutz* for students. Read *kibbutz* aloud and have students repeat the word. Show students a visual of a kibbutz and instruct students to develop a definition for the term using the visual and the text. Ask students to work in pairs to discuss

Answers

Explain *Arabs rejected the initial proposal for a Jewish and an Arab state.*

Recall *for decades*

Infer *People supported a Jewish homeland because centuries of persecution and genocide had threatened Jewish survival.*

rulers who suppressed critics, often brutally. Some countries, such as Jordan and Saudi Arabia, had hereditary monarchs. Only Israel and Turkey had stable multiparty systems.

Egypt's Leadership in the Arab World Egypt is the most populous nation in the Arab world. Since most of Egypt is desert, its population is crammed into the narrow Nile River valley.

Egypt controls the **Suez Canal,** the vital waterway that provides the shortest sea route between Europe and Asia. Egypt also shares a border with Israel.

In 1952, **Gamal Abdel Nasser** seized power in Egypt. Determined to modernize Egypt and end Western domination, Nasser soon nationalized the Suez Canal, ending British and French control. Nasser's Arab nationalism made him popular in the Arab world. He led two unsuccessful wars against Israel. Egypt relied on Soviet aid during the Cold War.

In 1979, Nasser's successor, **Anwar Sadat,** reduced ties with the Soviet Union and sought aid from the United States. He also became the first Arab leader to make peace with Israel. In exchange for peace, Israel returned the Sinai Peninsula to Egypt. Sadat was assassinated by Islamist extremists in 1981. Hosni Mubarak took over and cracked down hard on extremists, jailing even moderate critics.

The Arab Spring and Its Impact In 2011, popular unrest swept across the Middle East, launching pro-democracy movements, known as the Arab Spring. Frustration with corrupt and dictatorial governments, along with high unemployment, fed demands for change. The Arab Spring, which started in Tunisia, spread to Egypt and other nations. During the Arab Spring, massive street protests forced Egypt's Hosni Mubarak to step down after 30 years in office.

The "Arab Spring" took different paths in different nations. Some governments suppressed the protests. Other countries, such as Egypt, held elections. Egyptians went to the polls with great hopes in 2012. An Islamist leader, Mohammed Morsi, was elected president. Within a year, however, he was ousted by the Egyptian military after mass protests erupted against his government. New elections are scheduled for 2014.

The results of the Arab Spring also varied from country to country. In Tunisia, Islamist and **secular,** or nonreligious, parties formed a coalition to work together for democratic reform. Hopes for democratic reforms, however, faced an uncertain future in other nations. In Egypt, any new leader will face severe social and economic problems as well the deep divide and ongoing conflict between Islamists and secularists.

>> This photograph shows members of the royal family of Saudi Arabia, one of the most oil-rich nations on Earth. Most power remains with the king and royal family, but tribal sheikhs also have influence. **Recall** Which other Middle Eastern state has a hereditary monarchy? Which two states have multiparty systems?

>> Women played an important role in the Arab Spring movement. This massive demonstration took place in Cairo on July 8, 2011. **Hypothesize** What motivated women to participate in the Arab Spring movement?

Topic 20 Lesson 3

New Nations in the Middle East

Remind students that many nations of the Middle East had been part of European empires and, later, the mandate system set up after World War I. After independence, some of these nations set up military governments. Others had hereditary monarchies or set up multiparty democracies.

Tell students that one of the countries that had a hereditary monarchy was Iran. The shah, or king, of Iran was allied during the Cold War with the United States. He westernized and modernized Iran. Islamic fundamentalists overturned the shah in 1979 and established the Islamic Republic of Iran, a theocracy led by the Ayatollah Khomeini until his death in 1989.

Guided Reading and Discussion

Many of the countries in this lesson have gone through major changes since the end of World War II. Iran has gone from being an ally of the United States to being one of its most vocal critics. Egypt was once allied with the Soviet Union. Saudi Arabia's oil wealth has made it important on the world stage.

Compare and Contrast How were the Islamic Revolution and the Arab Spring alike? *(In both, the people changed their government because they thought it was corrupt.)* How were they different? *(The Arab Spring was a pro-democracy movement in which people wanted a greater say in their government; the Islamic Revolution's goal was to set up an Islamic state run by Muslim clerics according to Sharia law.)*

Key Terms

Ask students to find the key term **secular** (in bold) in the text. Point out that in many Middle Eastern nations, those advocating secular government and law struggle for control with those advocating traditions. Ask how each of these approaches might appeal to citizens of the Middle East.

the implications of Jews from around the world returning to Israel to work on kibbutzim. Circulate among students to offer support as needed.

Advanced High Have students reread "The Founding of Israel" and focus on key academic terms in the subsection "The Growth of Israel." Instruct students to develop definitions for the key term using appropriate visuals and the text. Ask students to work in small groups to discuss the implications of Jews from around the world returning to Israel after 1950. Circulate among students to offer support as needed.

Answers

Recall *Jordan is the other monarchy; Israel and Turkey have multiparty systems.*

Hypothesize *discontent with high unemployment and unresponsive governments, as well as a desire for more rights and freedoms*

The Importance of Oil in the Middle East

Explain that OPEC (Organization of Petroleum Exporting Countries) was set up in 1960 to end the power of Western nations to set oil prices.

Guided Reading and Discussion

Review with students that even though some of the oil-producing nations are not in the Middle East, many of the largest producers are. Therefore, the oil economy has a great impact on the region, and the region has a great impact on the oil economy.

Infer Read the information about the Organization of Petroleum Exporting Countries (OPEC). Based on what you've read, what is the effect of OPEC's production quotas on the global economy? *(Since OPEC controls much of the world's oil resources, OPEC production quotas have a major impact on the global economy. If OPEC lowers production quotas, supply drops and the cost of oil goes up. If OPEC raises production quotas, or keeps them steady, the cost of oil should remain steady or go down. Fluctuating oil prices have a large effect on the buying power of the global economy.)*

Analyze Images

Use the map on the facing page. Have students list the five countries with the greatest oil reserves. *(Saudi Arabia, Oman, Kuwait, Iraq, Iran)*

Elsewhere, similar political, religious, and other divisions posed challenges. In Syria, pro-democracy protests pitched Syria into a horrendous civil war. Many people grew disillusioned with the "Arab Spring," which had not brought promised changes. Others argued that change would take time.

An Islamic Revolution in Iran Because of its vast oil fields, Iran was a focus of Cold War rivalries. Its ruler, Shah Mohammad Reza Pahlavi, favored the West but faced nationalist critics at home, led by Mohammad Mosaddeq (MAW sah dek). After Mosaddeq was elected prime minister in 1951, he nationalized the foreign-owned oil industry. The shah, with U.S. help, ousted Mosaddeq and retuned the oil industry to Western control. This move outraged many Iranians.

Although the shah modernized industry, redistributed land to peasants, and gave new rights to women, opposition to his rule grew, especially among the Islamic clergy. In response, the government brutally silenced critics.

The shah's foes rallied behind Ayatollah **Ruhollah Khomeini** (ROO hoh lah koh MAY nee). The Ayatollah, a religious leader, condemned Western influences and accused the shah of violating Islamic law. In 1979, massive protests drove the shah from power. Khomeini and his supporters proclaimed the Islamic Republic of Iran.

The new government was a **theocracy,** or government by religious leaders. The Iranian Revolution introduced strict Islamic law. Like the shah, the new leaders silenced critics. In 1979, Islamists seized the American embassy in the capital and held 52 hostages for more than a year.

The new Islamic republic soon faced a long, bloody war with its neighbor Iraq, and tense relations with the West. The United States accused Iran of backing terrorists. Along with its allies, the United States imposed harsh economic sanctions to keep Iran from developing nuclear weapons. In 2013, Iranians elected a self-proclaimed moderate, Hassan Rouhani, as president.

Hopes rose for an easing of tensions between Iran and the West. At home, however, Rouhani faced an economy hurt by years of economic sanctions and deep political divisions between hardliners and reformists.

>> Ayatollah Khomeini was Iran's ultimate political and religious authority for 10 years after the Iranian Revolution. Khomeini, who died in 1989, is still revered in Iran. This mural is in Tehran.

Modern Turkey Once the heart of the Ottoman empire, Turkey became a republic in the 1920s under Ataturk. It has the third-largest population in the Middle East after Egypt and Iran. Although it is a Muslim country, most of its people are Turks, not Arabs. Turkey commands a strategic location, straddling Europe and Asia, and has served as a link between Europe and the Middle East. Turkey applied to join the European Union, but some EU members demanded that it make economic and other reforms. Turkey also sought closer ties with its Middle Eastern neighbors.

Although the military intervened in the past, today Turkey is a multiparty democracy with a market economy. Clashes erupted in 2013, however, that pitted the moderate Islamist government against protesters who opposed the growing authoritarianism of the government. The clashes reflected a divide between supporters of the older secularist ideology of Ataturk and those supporting the more Islamist-oriented policies of the government.

 **CATEGORIZE** What types of governments are most common in the Middle East?

The Importance of Oil in the Middle East

Parts of the Middle East have huge oil resources, giving the region global importance. A handful of oil-producing nations prospered. They included Saudi Arabia, Iran, Iraq, Kuwait, and several small states along the Persian Gulf. The oil-producing nations also border

English Language Proficiency Standards

5.F.3 Explain that all sentences must include an independent clause, which includes a subject + verb. Demonstrate how to use connecting words and punctuation to create compound and complex sentences from simple sentences and phrases.

Beginning Work together with students to use connecting words like *but, and,* and *or* to write compound sentences of their own in their notebooks about content in "New Nations in the Middle East."

Intermediate Then guide students to use connecting words like *but, and,* and *or* to write compound sentences of their own in their notebooks.

Advanced Then instruct student to work with a partner to write one complex and two compound sentences of their own in their notebooks.

Advanced High Have students work independently to write a brief paragraph using a variety of compound and complex sentences about "New Nations in the Middle East."

Answers

Categorize *Most Middle Eastern countries have authoritarian rulers and a strong military; only Israel and Turkey have stable multiparty systems.*

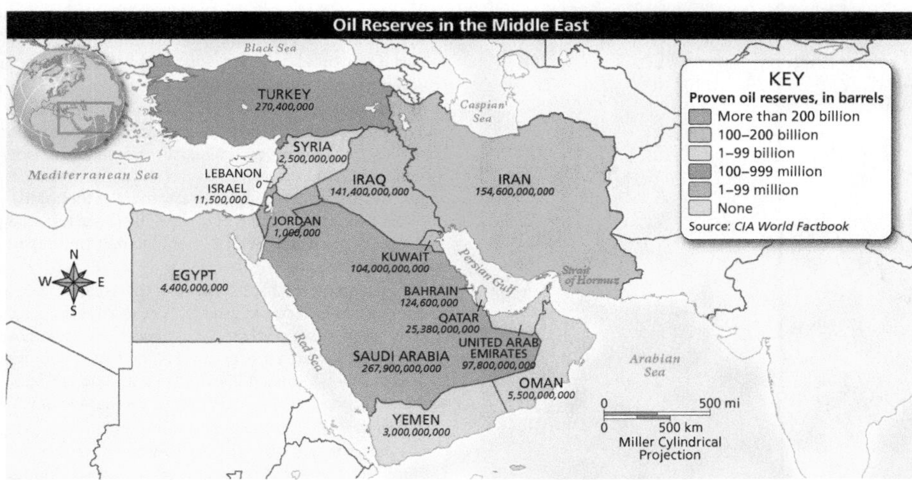

>> **Analyze Maps** This map shows the known oil reserves of Middle Eastern countries. On what body of water do the nations with the largest oil reserves lie?

vital shipping lanes that carry oil from the region to the world. Even though these oil-rich countries provide aid to their neighbors, most Middle Eastern nations lack oil and have struggled economically.

OPEC In 1960, the oil-producing nations of the Middle East, along with Venezuela, set up the Organization of Petroleum Exporting Countries (OPEC). OPEC wanted to end the power of Western oil companies and set its own oil production quotas and prices.

In 1973, Middle Eastern members of OPEC used oil as a political weapon. They stopped oil shipments to the United States and other countries that had supported Israel in a recent Arab-Israeli war. This oil embargo triggered a global recession and led other countries to try to develop other sources of oil. Since then, OPEC has focused on setting production quotas and has added new members.

Saudi Arabia Saudi Arabia has one of the world's largest oil reserves. It exports vast amounts of oil to the West. In return, it has received military aid from the United States. Its ruling family is committed to Wahhabism, a strict sect within Sunni Islam. Oil wealth allowed Saudi Arabia to modernize its infrastructure, such as transportation and communication systems. At the same time, the government has suppressed opposition.

? **INFER** How can OPEC influence global events?

Islam and the Modern World

After independence, some Middle Eastern countries adopted Western-style secular governments. Leaders in Egypt and Syria, for example, saw secular government as a means to modernization. In time, however, many secular leaders became authoritarian rulers. At the same time, Western cultural influences, introduced during the age of imperialism, spread. In cities, people bought goods imported from the West. They wore Western fashions and watched American television shows and movies.

Islamic Revival Some Muslims claimed that Western culture and capitalism were undermining Islamic society. They called for a return to Sharia, or Islamic law based on the Quran, and to traditional customs and values. These conservative reformers, known as Islamists or Islamic fundamentalists, blamed social and economic ill on the West. Only a renewed commitment

Islam and the Modern World

Tell students that many people of the Middle East saw Western secularism as a threat to their Islamic identity. These Islamists (or Islamic fundamentalists) called for a return to Sharia law, based on the Quran. In Iran, they overthrew the shah and established an Islamic republic, a theocracy. Tell students that in some countries of the region women have full rights, but in other, more conservative countries, their activities are restricted.

Guided Reading and Discussion

Remind students that one important belief of Islamic fundamentalism is that Sharia law, the law based on the Quran, should be the law of the land in Muslim countries.

Cite Evidence Based on the text, what is the relationship between the Islamic religion and the various governments in the Middle East? Cite evidence from the text to support your answer. *(In response to the influence of Western culture, Islamic fundamentalists began to blame social and economic ills in the Middle East on the influence of the West. This led to a renewed commitment to the tenets of Islam among some. These fundamentalists have worked to overthrow many of the westernized secular governments. Conflict between those who believe in more moderate Islam and fundamentalists has led to violence.)*

SYNTHESIZE

Online Project the **Digital Activity: The Changing Middle East**. Have students fill out the graphic organizer itemizing changes in the last 65 years to Israel, Egypt, Iran, and Turkey.

Support Ideas With Examples Cite examples from Israel, Egypt, Iran, and Turkey in which religion played an important role in events. *(Sample answer: Israel: desire to create a safe haven for Jews; Egypt: election of Muhammed Morsi; Iran: Islamic Revolution; Turkey: clashes between Islamists and supporters of individual freedoms)*

History Background

Shiites and Sunnis The split between Sunni and Shiite Muslims dates back to the middle 600s A.D., just a few decades after Islam first appeared. Muhammad's son-in-law, named Ali, was the fourth caliph, or spiritual and temporal ruler, of Islam after Muhammad. He died in a struggle between his followers and others. The Shiites believe that only Ali and his descendants are the legitimate leaders of the Islamic world. Shiites number between 60 and 80 million people, which is about one in every ten Muslims. They are a majority in Iran and Iraq, though there are sizable Shiite communities in other nations. Shiites have rarely had political power outside of modern Iran. Shiite religious leaders have guided Iran's government since the Islamic Revolution of 1979.

Answers

Analyze Maps *Persian Gulf*

Infer *OPEC can reduce or increase the supply of oil to the world, and as a result, the cost of oil will rise or fall. This can have a large impact on the global economy.*

Topic 20 Lesson 3

DEMONSTRATE

Online Assign the online **Digital Lesson Quiz** for this lesson if you haven't already done so. Students will be offered automatic remediation or enrichment based on their score.

Pose the following to the class on the Discussion Board:

Discuss Ask: How do religious and ethnic differences affect the Middle East? *(Different ethnic and religious groups are often in conflict with each other over land and self-determination.)*

Identify Cause and Effect What were some of the causes of the declaration of the State of Israel? *(the exodus of Jews from Europe following the Holocaust; the Balfour Declaration; the breakup of the mandate system; the UN partition plan)* What were some of the effects? *(Arab rejection of the State of Israel; creation of Jewish and Palestinian refugees; the 1948 Arab-Israeli War)*

Topic Inquiry

Have students continue their investigations for the Topic Inquiry.

Answers

Explain *Islamists feel that secular government has led to social and economic ills. They believe that returning to Islamic principles will solve these problems.*

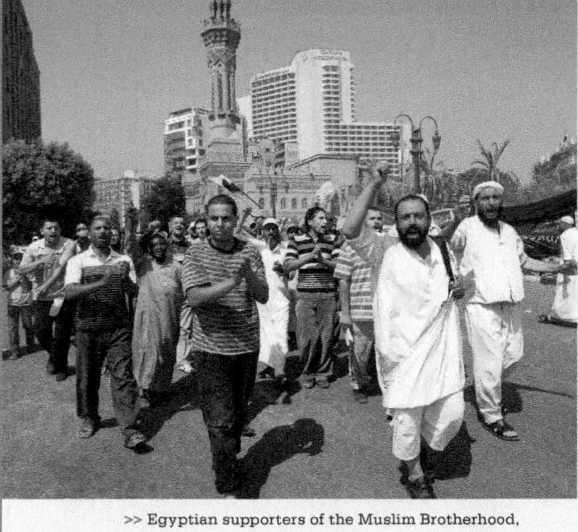

>> Egyptian supporters of the Muslim Brotherhood, an Islamist organization, celebrate the election of Muhammed Morsi. Morsi, who won the first election held in Egypt after the "Arab Spring," was overthrown by the military in 2013.

to Islam, they declared, could improve conditions for Muslims around the world.

Many Muslims welcomed the Islamic movement as a way to cope with rapid social and economic changes. Moderate Islamists wanted to work toward democratic reforms within Islam. Radical Islamists, or fundamentalist extremists, however, advocated violence to achieve their goal.

Radical Islam Radical Islamic fundamentalist groups in Egypt, Saudi Arabia, and elsewhere sought to overthrow governments that they saw as too closely allied to the West. They also targeted Israel, which had defeated Arabs in several wars, and the United States. Although many governments cracked down on radical Islamic fundamentalists, these groups survived. In 1979, Islamic fundamentalists welcomed Iran's revolution. Iran became the first modern nation to topple a secular government and replace it with a government based on Sharia.

Islam and the Lives of Women Conditions for women vary greatly across the Muslim Middle East. In most countries, women won equality before the law, but women still faced legal and social hurdles, especially to jobs. Over time, however, educated women entered professions such as law and medicine.

In Turkey, Egypt, and Syria, many urban women had given up wearing the **hejab,** or traditional Muslim headscarf, or loose, ankle-length garments meant to conceal. With the Islamic revival, many educated women returned to the hejab as a symbol of their faith. In religiously conservative countries like Saudi Arabia and Iran, women must follow local Islamic traditions, such as wearing the hejab.

Women stood on the front lines of the "Arab Spring" to demand democratic reforms and equal opportunity. "I grew up in a world where we believed we could not do anything," noted a young woman and online activist in Jordan. "Generations believed we could do nothing, and now, in a matter of weeks, we know that we can."

Some women's rights advocates pointed out that their goals were not based on Western values but on the traditions of early Islam that improved the status of women. Women's rights movements faced serious challenges, however. While access to education has improved for women, girls are often less likely to attend school than boys because of the tradition that girls do not need a formal education for their expected roles as wives and mothers. Although governments recognized the productive value of women in the workforce, local cultural restrictions often kept women from holding jobs outside the home.

? RUN-IN HEAD Why do Islamists oppose secular government and culture in the Muslim world?

ASSESSMENT

1. **Identify** What are two events that have powerfully influenced the development of the modern nations of the Middle East?
2. **Express Problems Clearly** How do religious and ethnic differences affect the Middle East?
3. **Identify Cause and Effect** What effect did the Arab rejection of the State of Israel have on today's Palestinians?
4. **Describe** What are some ways oil wealth has affected the nations of the Middle East?
5. **Cite Evidence** What influence has Islam had on the government of Iran since the overthrow of the Shah?

Assessment

1. Peace agreements following World War I, establishment of the State of Israel, the Islamic Revolution in Iran, and the Arab Spring have had great impacts on the Middle East.
2. Ethnic and religious groups are often in conflict over land and self-determination.
3. When the Arabs rejected the UN plan in 1947, most Palestinians left the Palestine mandate, soon to become Israel. They remain without a state and continue to live as refugees in other countries or in the West Bank and Gaza.
4. Nations belonging to OPEC have power to influence the rest of the world. Oil-rich monarchies have become extremely wealthy, and foreign workers outnumber native-born citizens. All of the oil-rich nations must plan for a future after their oil resources are exhausted.
5. Islamic activists united behind the Ayatollah Khomeini and launched the Islamic Revolution in 1979. This brought to power a theocracy, which rules Iran according to Islamic law.

20.4 **Modern Israel was established in 1948 under the United Nations Partition Plan. Palestinian Arabs and nearby Arab nations rejected the UN plan as illegal, even though it offered Palestinians territory for their own state. Instead, they called for the destruction of Israel.**

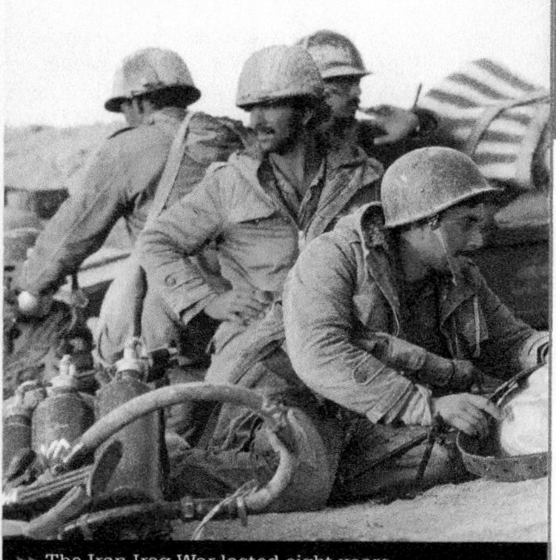

>> The Iran-Iraq War lasted eight years and took an enormous toll on both countries. These Iraqi soldiers were photographed near Basra, Iraq, in 1984.

Interactive Flipped Video

Conflicts in the Middle East

TEKS
13.E, 13.F, 14.A, 16.A

>> Objectives

Explain the ongoing Israeli-Palestinian conflict and the obstacles to peace.

Explain the causes and effects of conflicts in Lebanon and Syria.

Understand why Iraq became a battleground.

>> Key Terms

Yasir Arafat
intifada
Yitzhak Rabin
Jerusalem
militia
Saddam Hussein
no-fly zone
weapon of mass destruction (WMD)
insurgent

Israel and Palestine

Arab rejection of the State of Israel has led to ongoing conflict. In 1948, five Arab nations invaded the newly independent Israel and were defeated. Israel and its Arab neighbors fought three more wars, in 1956, 1967, and 1973. In these wars, Israel fought for its existence, and in the process of turning back attacking Arab forces gained more land. Between and since these wars, Israel has faced many terrorist attacks within its borders, and ongoing rocket attacks from Gaza and Lebanon. The United States and other nations worked to find a solution to the long-standing conflict.

The West Bank, Gaza, and the Golan Heights In the 1967 war, in response to ongoing hostility by its Arab neighbors, Israel took control of the West Bank and East Jerusalem from Jordan along with the Gaza Strip and Sinai Peninsula from Egypt. Israel also took the Golan Heights from Syria. Hindering the possibility of peace, several months after the Six Day War ended, Arab countries held a summit at Khartoum and issued the "Three NOs": no recognition of Israel, no negotiations with Israel, and no peace with Israel.

905

PEARSON realize. www.PearsonTexas.com Access your Digital Lesson.

Topic 20 Lesson 4

Conflicts in the Middle East

CONNECT

Preview Have students preview the **Lesson Objectives** and the list of **Key Terms**.

Students can also preview all the **Key Terms** and **Academic Vocabulary** using the **Interactive Reading Notepad** on the digital course or preview a summary of the lesson in the **Reading and Note Taking Study Guide**.

Online Use the **Editable Presentation** found on the digital course to present the main ideas for this lesson.

Start Up Activity

Have students recall what they have learned about the recent history of the Middle East. Ask students to write a brief paragraph that summarizes the general challenges to peace facing the region.

Online You can also project the **Start Up Activity** from the course.

INVESTIGATE

Have students read the section using the **Reading and Note Taking Study Guide** to help them take notes and understand the text as they read.

Israel and Palestine

The Difficult Road to Peace

Modern Israel was established in 1948 under the United Nations Partition Plan. Palestinian Arabs and Arab nations rejected the plan as illegal, even though it offered territory for a Palestinian state. In 1948, Arab nations attacked the newly independent Israel and were defeated. The two sides fought again in 1956, 1967, and 1973. Israel has continued to face terrorist attacks from Palestinians and radical fundamentalist Islamists.

Aa Vocabulary Builder

1. Have students pronounce the following academic vocabulary terms in this lesson and clarify the part of speech. For difficult or polysyllabic words, break them into syllables and pronounce them with the students.
2. Explain what the word means in common "student-friendly" language using synonyms and antonyms when possible. Provide concrete examples to clarify the meaning, and rephrase the definition.

established: set up or created

immigrated: came to live in a foreign country

radical: referring to an extreme faction of a political party

Topic 20 Lesson 4

Online Project the **Interactive Map: Changing Boundaries of the State of Israel**, and click through the map layers to show the changes in Israel's borders over time.

ACTIVE CLASSROOM

Use the Make Headlines strategy to have students write a headline that captures the action in one layer of the Interactive Map. Students should strive to capture the most important aspect of the time represented. Have students pass their headline to a partner for review.

Guided Reading and Discussion

As a class, complete a graphic organizer summarizing causes and effects of the conflict between Israelis and Palestinians. *(Causes—United Nations Partition Plan; Arab nations invade Israel between 1948 and 1973; 1967 war; 1973 Yom Kippur War; Effects—establishes Israel as a state; Israel takes control of the West Bank, East Jerusalem, Gaza Strip, Golan Heights, and Sinai Peninsula; Arabs fail to regain occupied territories)*

Explain: In the wars of 1967 and 1973, Israel took the West Bank, East Jerusalem, the Gaza Strip, the Sinai Peninsula, and the Golan Heights. Palestinians refer to these as the occupied territories. The Palestine Liberation Organization, led by Yasir Arafat, sought to destroy Israel and establish a Palestinian state.

Many attempts at forging peace have been made. Still, conflicts continue. The most recent peace talks occurred in the aftermath of the Arab Spring. Little progress was made.

Answers

Identify Central Ideas *Arab nations rejected Israel. They immediately attacked Israel and engaged in three later wars.*

Analyze Maps *Israel is surrounded by Arab nations, which were hostile to its existence.*

In 1973, these Arab nations attacked Israel on Yom Kippur, the holiest day of the Jewish calendar. In the Yom Kippur War, Arabs failed to regain the lands that they had lost to Israel in 1967. Arabs referred to these lands as the "occupied territories." Later, Israel annexed East Jerusalem and the Golan Heights. Israel then allowed Jewish settlers to build homes in some of these territories, which increased bitterness among the Palestinians.

The PLO and Intifada The number of Palestinians in refugee camps grew in the decades after 1948. Many supported the Palestinian Liberation Organization (PLO), which led the struggle against Israel. Led by **Yasir Arafat,** the PLO called for the destruction of Israel and waged guerrilla war against Israelis at home and abroad. The PLO gained world attention with airplane hijackings and the killing of Israeli athletes at the 1972 Olympic Games.

In 1987, Palestinians in the West Bank and Gaza started to resist Israel with **intifadas,** or uprisings. Young Palestinians demanded an end to Israeli control and hurled rocks at or fired on Israeli soldiers. Suicide bombers blew up buses, stores, and clubs in Israel. Israel responded by sealing off and raiding Palestinian towns and targeting terrorist leaders. The violence killed many civilians on both sides.

IDENTIFY CENTRAL IDEAS How did Arab nations respond to the creation of Israel?

The Difficult Road to Peace

In the early 1970s, the United States, the UN, and other nations kept pushing for peace between Israel and the Arab world. At the time, Golda Meir was the prime minister of Israel. A founder of the state of Israel, she had immigrated to the Palestine mandate in 1921 and served in many posts in the Israeli government before becoming Israel's first female head of state. Meir was planning peace talks when Arab nations attacked in 1973.

The 1973 Yom Kippur War was the last full-scale war fought by Arab nations against Israel. Eventually, Egyptian leader Anwar Sadat agreed to peace talks. The two nations signed a peace accord in 1979 in which Egypt became the first Arab nation to officially recognize and normalize relations with Israel, and Israel returned the Sinai Peninsula to Egypt. In 1994, Jordan's King Hussein made peace with Israel. However, talks between Syria and Israel failed over various issues, including control of the Golan Heights.

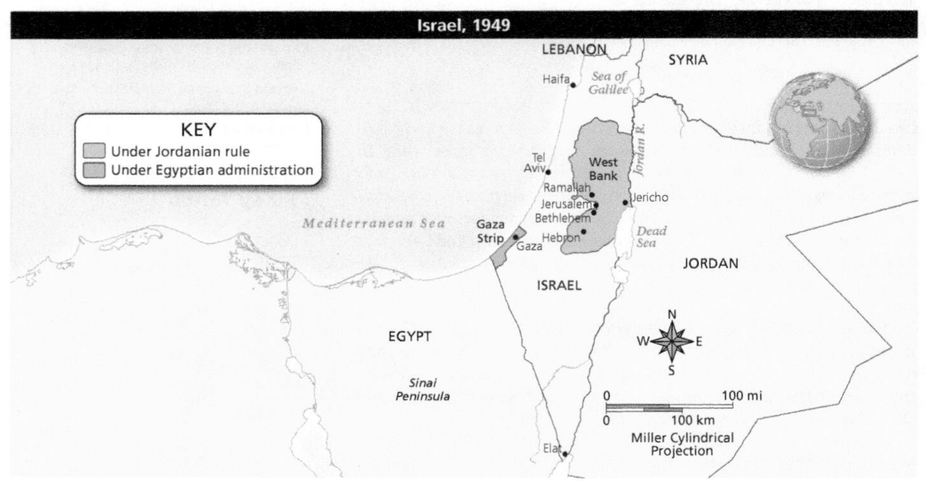

>> **Analyze Maps** This map shows the boundaries of the State of Israel in 1949. How does the map illustrate one challenge to achieving Mideast peace?

Interactive Map

English Language Proficiency Standards

5.G.1 Read "Israel and Palestine" aloud to the class. Have students complete one activity according to their level of English proficiency.

Beginning Retell the content of "Israel and Palestine" in accessible language. Tell students that they will be working together to develop a narrative about the life of Palestinian leader Yasir Arafat. Use information from the text and glossary to develop a narrative about Arafat's political life.

Intermediate Reread "Israel and Palestine" aloud and ask them to follow along in their texts. Then tell students they will be working in small groups to develop a narrative about the life of Palestinian leader Yasir Arafat. Use information from the text and glossary to develop a basic narrative about Arafat's political life.

Advanced Instruct students to reread "Israel and Palestine." Then tell students they will be working with a partner to develop a narrative

The Oslo Accords In 1993, Yasir Arafat and Israeli Prime Minister **Yitzhak Rabin**(rah BEEN) agreed to the Oslo Accords. This plan gave Palestinians in Gaza and the West Bank limited self-rule under a Palestinian Authority. The PLO recognized Israel's right to exist and pledged to stop terrorist attacks on Israel. Arafat led the Palestinian Authority until his death in 2004.

Violence Continues Although Arafat's successor, Mahmoud Abbas (ah BAHS), pledged to stop Palestinian attacks on Israel, violence continued. Fierce divisions split the Palestinian Authority between Fatah, the party of Arafat and his successors, and Hamas, a radical Islamist group. Hamas was funded by Iran and rejected Israel's right to exist. In 2007, Hamas seized control of Gaza, ousting Fatah supporters. From Gaza, Hamas launched rocket attacks on Israel. The Israeli military responded with air strikes and a short-lived invasion. As of 2014, Hamas continued to launch rocket attacks from Gaza on civilian areas of Israel.

Obstacles to Peace Decades of conflict and mistrust have made peace hard to achieve. The two sides differ on a number of issues. One obstacle to peace concerns the Palestinian refugees who fled or were forced off their lands in earlier wars. They and their descendants want the "right of return," or the right to resettle on their land in Israel proper. Israelis oppose this demand, which could overwhelm the only Jewish state with large numbers of Palestinians. Israelis view this demand as an attempt to destroy Israel.

A second obstacle is **Jerusalem,** a city sacred to Jews, Christians, and Muslims. Jordan controlled East Jerusalem and the Old City from 1948 to 1967 and did not allow Jewish access to holy sites. Israel gained control in 1967 and later added it to the capital of Israel, reuniting the city of Jerusalem. Muslims and Christians control their holy sites within the city. Palestinians, however, want East Jerusalem to be the capital of a future Palestinian state.

A third stumbling block is the issue of Jewish settlements in East Jerusalem and the West Bank, areas claimed by Palestinians. Israel voluntarily withdrew all of its settlements in the Sinai and in Gaza but has not withdrawn from the West Bank and East Jerusalem. Disagreements about final borders affect negotiations over the future of the West Bank.

Another issue is security. Israel fears that if extremists gained control over a Palestinian state, they could attack Israel as Hamas has done since Israel withdrew from Gaza. Israel therefore wants to limit the military capacity of any Palestinian state and control security in the area. Palestinians argue that security will improve when Palestinians have their own state.

>> In 1977, Egyptian president Anwar Sadat became the first Arab leader to visit and recognize Israel. Here, he exchanges gifts with former Israeli prime minister Golda Meir.

>> The growth of new Jewish communities in the West Bank and East Jerusalem evokes different reactions in Israeli society. Here, some Israelis protest the building of housing units in East Jerusalem, which they see as an obstacle to peace between Israelis and Palestinians.

Have students identify the three main obstacles to peace between Israel and Palestine and identify why each is an issue. *(1. Land claims—Palestinians want to reclaim their lands taken by Israel. 2. Jewish settlements in the West Bank—Palestinians want Jewish settlers to leave the West Bank as they have left Gaza. 3. Jerusalem—Palestinians want East Jerusalem as the capital of any Palestinian state.)*

Tell students that Israel's first female prime minister, Golda Meir, was elected in March 1969 and was planning peace talks in 1973 when Arab nations attacked Israel. She resigned as prime minister in 1974 following the Yom Kippur War. She was succeeded by Yitzhak Rabin.

Predict Consequences Christians, Jews, and Muslims all have strong feelings about the holy city of Jerusalem. How might these feelings affect the conflict over the area? *(Possible answer: Because people care deeply about their religion, they may be less likely to compromise on any issues related to key religious sites.)*

D Differentiate Challenge/Gifted To challenge students to solve historical problems, have them use the Internet to research Palestinian claims to land within Israel and Israeli claims to land within the disputed areas. Have them create a list of arguments both for and against Palestinian claims to a right of return. Then have them write a letter to the editor on this issue. Their letters should propose a solution and use arguments based on their research. Letters can be posted to the class Web site.

about the life of Palestinian leader Yasir Arafat. Instruct students to use information from the text, glossary, and other classroom resources to develop a narrative about Arafat's political life. Invite partners to share their narratives with the class.

Advanced High Instruct students to reread "Israel and Palestine." Then tell students they will be developing a narrative about the life of Palestinian leader Yasir Arafat. Instruct students to use information from the text, glossary, and other classroom resources to develop a narrative about Arafat's political life. Invite students to share their narratives with the class.

Topic 20 Lesson 4

Conflict in Lebanon and Syria

Tell students that Lebanon is home to diverse ethnic and religious groups. There is a delicate balance among Arab Christians, Sunni Muslims, Shiite Muslims, and Druze. In 1975, civil war broke out, and eventually Israel and Syria were drawn into the fighting. In 2006, a radical group backed by Iran and Syria, called Hezbollah, launched attacks against Israel from Lebanon. In response, Israel invaded Lebanon. In 2012, a civil war in Syria caused a huge number of refugees to flee to Lebanon, straining the small country's resources.

Guided Reading and Discussion

Be sure students understand that the Israeli-Palestinian conflict has consequences for other countries in the area. Palestinians moved to Lebanon, disrupting the Muslim-Christian balance. Muslims outnumbered Christians. Attacks on Israel from Lebanon brought counterattacks from Israel. Israel attacked bases in Lebanon that it saw as a threat.

Predict Consequences Why would one conflict in a region with diverse groups living in close contact fuel other conflicts so easily? *(Sample response: People with strong beliefs have a hard time separating one issue from another. One area of conflict can easily be tied to another.)*

Identify Patterns How is the Lebanese civil war similar to civil wars in other countries you have read about? *(People of different ethnicities and religions fought over access to power.)*

Analyze Images

Look at the image of the refugee camp on the next page. What details in the photograph provide information about conditions in the camp? *(Possible answer: Bare ground makes it appear a barren place where it is difficult to grow things; blowing clothes make it look windy; tent indicates that people are living in makeshift shelters.)*

Over time, the Israeli-Palestinian conflict has fueled the anger of fundamentalist, radical Islamist groups such as Hamas in Gaza and Hezbollah in Lebanon. These radical groups reject Israel's right to exist. They condemn its ally, the United States, along with any Arab government involved in the peace process. Ongoing violence and threats from these groups increases Israel's security concerns and impedes the peace process.

Another important issue is how to allocate and protect water resources. The distribution of water resources impacts negotiations between Israel and the Palestinians concerning the control of the water supply, water consumption, and the costs of investments in water management. The rights to water resources are also major issues between countries in the region.

A Two-State Solution For years, peace talks have revolved around the idea of a two-state solution, with peaceful coexistence between Israel and a stable, democratic Palestinian state. To achieve this, peacemakers drew up the "road map" to peace, calling for an end to violence and terrorism. Some Israeli and Palestinian leaders accepted the two-state plan. Iran and radical Islamist groups rejected it.

>> A woman is helped by the military after a bombing in Beirut, Lebanon, in 1986. **Analyze Visuals** What does this image tell you about the way that the Lebanese civil war was fought?

Interactive Timeline

The most recent peace talks opened in the aftermath of the "Arab Spring." The uprisings did little to improve the outlook for peace between Israelis and Palestinians. Islamists won power in some elections, while turmoil engulfed Egypt and Syria.

INTEGRATE INFORMATION Why is Jerusalem so important to both Israelis and Palestinians?

Conflict in Lebanon and Syria

Internal divisions and the ongoing Israeli-Palestinian conflict impacted neighboring Lebanon and Syria. Both nations gained independence in the 1940s. Both are home to diverse religious and ethnic groups.

The Lebanese Civil War Historically, Lebanon was a thriving center of commerce. After gaining independence from France in 1943, its government depended on a delicate balance among diverse Arab Christian sects, such as the Maronites, Sunni and Shiite Muslims, and Druze, people with a religion related to Islam. Palestinian immigration after the 1948 and 1967 wars increased the Muslim population. By the 1970s, Muslims outnumbered Christians. In 1971, PLO fighters were expelled from Jordan after attempting to overthrow its government. The enlarged PLO presence in Lebanon and the intensification of fighting on the Israeli-Lebanese border added to the internal unrest in Lebanon.

Tensions among the diverse groups erupted into civil war that lasted from 1975 to 1990. Christian and Muslim **militias,** or armed groups of citizen soldiers, battled each other. Syria invaded Lebanon and Syrian troops remained for 29 years. Israel briefly invaded Lebanon to stop cross-border attacks first by PLO guerrillas and later by Hezbollah fighters, the militant group backed by Iran and Syria.

Sectarian divisions remained even after a fragile peace was restored. By 2012, the civil war in neighboring Syria threatened renewed violence among rival militias in Lebanon. In addition, a huge number of refugees fled the civil war in Syria, straining Lebanon's resources.

The Syrian Civil War Syria's diverse population includes Armenians, Assyrians, Christians, Druze, Kurds, Alawite Shiites, and Arab Sunnis. For decades, Hafez al-Assad and later his son, Bashir al-Assad, ruled the country and its diverse population with an iron hand. The Assads opposed peace with Israel

Answers

Integrate Information *Sample response: Jerusalem is important because it is sacred to both Jews and Muslims, as well as to Christians.*

Analyze Visuals *Answers may vary, but students should recognize that the war was fought on the streets and that civilians were affected by it as well as the military.*

and supported militant groups such as Hezbollah and Hamas.

During the "Arab Spring," the Syrian government met pro-democracy protests with brutal force, plunging the country into civil war. Rebel groups were deeply divided between moderates and extremist groups. Hezbollah and Iran supported the Assad regime. Western countries, however, hesitated to support the rebels, fearful that weapons could fall into the hands of radical groups. After Assad was accused of using chemical weapons, global condemnation forced Syria to agree to give up its chemical arms stockpiles.

As the death toll mounted above 100,000, millions more Syrians were displaced by the fighting. Refugees flooded into nearby countries and raised fears that the Syrian civil war could destabilize the region. International efforts to negotiate peace were complicated by disunity among rebel groups and Assad's continued grip on power.

RECALL What is Hezbollah, and why is it signficant?

>> Huge refugee camps have been established in countries bordering Syria. These women and girls were photographed in 2013 at the Atma refugee camp on the Turkish-Syrian border.

Warfare in Iraq

The modern nation of Iraq was carved out of the Ottoman empire after World War I. Its population included Sunni and Shiite Arabs, as well as Kurds who lived in the north. Although Shiites were the majority population, Sunnis controlled the government. Kurds distrusted the government and wanted self-rule.

Divisions among these groups fed tensions in Iraq. During the Cold War, the United States and the Soviet Union competed for influence in Iraq, which had vast oil resources and was strategically located on the Persian Gulf.

The Iran-Iraq War In 1980, Iraq's neighbor Iran was engulfed in its Islamic Revolution. Iraqi dictator, **Saddam Hussein,** took advantage of the turmoil to seize a disputed border region. His action sparked the long, costly Iran-Iraq War. After both sides attacked foreign oil tankers in the Persian Gulf, the United States sent naval forces to protect shipping lanes. The war ended in a stalemate in 1988, but with huge human and economic costs for both Iran and Iraq.

During the war, Saddam Hussein brutally suppressed a Kurdish revolt, using chemical weapons on civilians. His actions sparked international outrage and charges of genocide.

The 1991 Gulf War In 1990, Iraq invaded its oil-rich neighbor, Kuwait. Saddam Hussein wanted Kuwait's vast oil fields and greater access to the Persian Gulf. The United States saw the invasion as a threat to its ally, Saudi Arabia, and to the vital oil resources of the region.

In 1991, a U.S.-led coalition of international forces under the UN banner drove Saddam's forces out of Kuwait. Despite this defeat, Saddam remained in power. He brutally crushed revolts by Shiite Iraqis and Kurds. To protect the Shiites and Kurds, the UN set up **no-fly zones,** or areas where Iraqi aircraft were banned.

The Iraq War The 2001 terrorist attacks on the U.S. led to new moves against Saddam Hussein. The United States organized a new international coalition to remove Saddam from power. The U.S. claimed that the Iraqi dictator supported terrorists. The country also charged that Iraq was stockpiling **weapons of mass destruction (WMDs),** or nuclear, biological, and chemical weapons. In 2003, coalition forces quickly toppled Saddam. However, no weapons of mass destruction were ever found.

Saddam Hussein was later tried for war crimes by an elected Iraqi government. He was executed in 2006.

Iraq Continues to Struggle After Saddam's overthrow, Iraq became a bloody battleground as

Warfare in Iraq

In 1979, Saddam Hussein took power as dictator of Iraq. In the 1980s, he fought with Iran, and in 1990, Iraq invaded Kuwait. In response, the United States led a coalition that liberated Kuwait and crushed Iraqi forces in 1991. This conflict was known as the Gulf War. In 2003, the United States led a coalition that invaded Iraq again and overthrew Saddam Hussein. Hussein was later tried for war crimes by an elected Iraqi government. He was found guilty and executed in 2006.

Online Project the **Interactive Timeline: Conflicts in the Middle East**. Challenge students to correctly match the events to the conflicts in the Middle East.

Key Terms

Ask students to find the key term **weapons of mass destruction** (in bold) in the text and read its meaning. Ask students to recall past uses of weapons of mass destruction through history.

Guided Reading and Discussion

Be sure students understand that ethnic and religious differences in Iraq are a major cause of the fighting in Iraq. Differences between the Shiites and Sunnis continue to cause conflict.

Cite Evidence Identify several of the negative consequences of continued internal conflict in Iraq. *(The economy has been hurt due to the destruction of its oil fields, and corruption and sabotage have also slowed oil exports. Millions of Iraqis fled the country and are not willing to return until safety and stability are established.)*

Answers

Recall *Hezbollah is a militant group supported by Iran and Syria that attacked Israel from Lebanon and supports Syria's Assad regime. It is significant because it participates in and adds to the conflicts in the Middle East.*

Topic 20 Lesson 4

SYNTHESIZE

Online Project the **Digital Activity: Independence and Unrest**. Ask students to review the opinions they formulated at the beginning of the lesson. Ask: Have your opinions changed at all after completing the lesson? Use events from the lesson to support your opinion.

Ask students to recall the past two lessons and describe how earlier events led to current conditions in the Middle East. *(Borders drawn under the mandate system did not consider ethnic and religious divisions; the founding of Israel is still not acknowledged by many; nationalist leaders who seized power misruled their countries, leading to recent pro-democracy movements; dissatisfaction with the shah of Iran led to a revolution; the Cold War and the Islamic Revolution facilitated Saddam Hussein's rise to power.)*

DEMONSTRATE

Online Assign the online **Digital Lesson Quiz** for this lesson if you haven't already done so. Students will be offered automatic remediation or enrichment based on their score.

Pose the following to the class on the Discussion Board:

Draw Conclusions Why has the Arab-Israeli conflict been difficult to solve? *(Both sides claim land. Use of violence and terror has made resolution challenging.)*

Generate Explanations What were the causes of Lebanon's civil war? *(An influx of Muslim Palestinian refugees upset Lebanon's ethnic and religious balance.)*

Topic Inquiry

Have students continue their investigations for the Topic Inquiry.

Answers

Draw Conclusions *Sunnis were a minority in Iraq, and they did not share power with the majority Shiites. Also, the Kurds did not trust the Sunnis and wanted self-rule.*

rival factions fought for power. **Insurgents,** or rebels, from Shiite and Sunni groups targeted civilians and government workers along with coalition forces. The death toll grew to over 162,000 Iraqis. The United States sent more troops in a "surge" to end the fighting. The United States also worked to convince moderate Sunnis, who had prospered under Saddam, to back the newly elected Iraqi government.

It also tried to improve Iraqi security forces. In 2011, the last American troops withdrew, leaving a Shiite-led government in control.

Iraq still faced steep hurdles. Car bombings, suicide attacks, and assassinations continued to plague the country. The main political parties, representing Shiites, Sunnis, and Kurds, were often deadlocked over key issues.

The ongoing violence hurt efforts to rebuild Iraq's once-prosperous economy. Although Iraq has the world's third-largest oil reserves, decades of conflict had left much of the country, and its oil fields, in ruins. In addition, corruption and sabotage slowed oil exports.

During the fighting, millions of Iraqis fled the country. Many more were displaced within Iraq. Some refugees returned, but others were unwilling to risk moving back until security and stability were assured.

? DRAW CONCLUSIONS Why did Sunni control of government in Iraq create tension in that country?

ASSESSMENT

1. **Identify Central Issues** How did the Israeli-Palestinian conflict begin?
2. **Compare Points of View** Why has peace between Israel and the Palestinians been so difficult to achieve? Include issues from both perspectives.
3. **Identify Cause and Effect** How did the Israeli-Palestinian conflict affect Lebanon and why?
4. **Draw Conclusions** How has the growth of radical Islamic fundamentalism affected conflicts in the Middle East?
5. **Cite Evidence** Why did the removal of Saddam Hussein's regime fail to bring peace to Iraq? Use details from the text in your answer.

Assessment

1. Sample response: The United Nations established the state of Israel in 1948. Palestinian Arabs, as well as other Arabs, rejected this and called for the destruction of Israel.
2. Answers may vary, but should include mutual distrust caused by Palestinian terrorism and removal of Palestinians from their lands, as well as the conflict over Jerusalem and settlements in the occupied territories.
3. Answers may vary, but students should include that Lebanon has had several civil wars and long periods of unrest in part because of the effect of Palestinian refugees on the balance of power in the country, as well as invasions by Israel.
4. Answers may vary, but students should understand that radical fundamentalism has increased divisions and conflict in the region.
5. Sample response: After the fall of Saddam Hussein, Iraq was divided by rival factions that wanted power and did not trust one another. Saddam was a Sunni who had kept the majority Shiites out of power. Kurds in Iraq wanted self-rule, and their uprising had been brutally put down by Saddam.

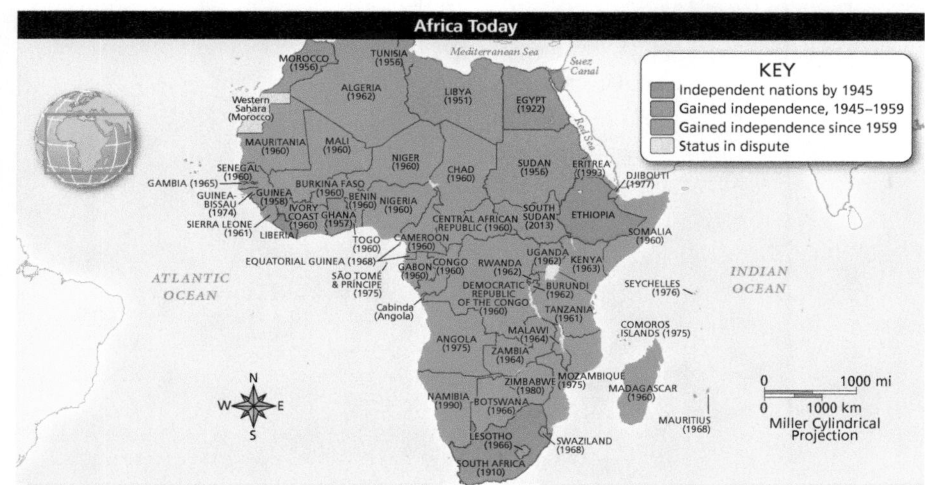

1. **Summarize and Locate Places** Summarize the rise of independence movements in Africa, and locate places and regions of historical significance directly related to major eras and turning points in world history. Review the above map. Write a paragraph summarizing the rise of independence movements in Africa and when most countries gained independence. Describe the rise of the independence movement in one African country. Locate that country on the map, and describe how it achieved independence and the challenges it faced. 13.E, 16.A
2. **Summarize Reasons and Use a Decision-Making Process** Summarize the reasons for Africa's ongoing conflicts, and use a decision-making process to gather information, identify options, predict consequences, and take action to implement a decision. Write a paragraph summarizing the reasons for ongoing conflicts in many African nations. Then, describe how the international community could use a decision-making process to provide assistance reducing poverty, for example. Consider the size of the African continent, the number of languages spoken, and issues regarding colonial boundaries and newly independent nations. 13.E, 31.B
3. **Summarize** Summarize the rise of independence movements in Africa. Write a paragraph summarizing the tensions under new governments after African nations achieved independence. Consider the type of governments established for new African nations, how retention of colonial boundaries after independence increased conflicts, and why the military often seized control. 13.E
4. **Identify Examples** Identify examples of genocide, including genocide in Darfur. Write a paragraph identifying and describing the actions of the Arab Muslim and non-Arab Muslim population that caused genocide in Darfur. Consider the rebellion in 2003 against Sudan's Arab-dominated government, widespread killings of non-Arab civilians, and reaction of the international community. Discuss if the attempt to try Sudan's president for genocide was effective? 22.D
5. **Identify Examples** Identify examples of genocide, including genocide in Rwanda. Write a paragraph about how the conflicts between the Hutus and Tutsis resulted in genocide. Consider the causes for ethnic violence after independence, reaction to the death of the Rwandan president, and whether any group was held accountable for committing genocide. 22.D
6. **Identify Major Causes** Identify major causes of the following important turning points in world history from 1914 to the present: independence movements. Write a paragraph identifying the major causes for the decision to partition South Asia into India and Pakistan. Consider Britain's attitude toward independence after World War II and the tensions between the Hindus and Muslims toward self-rule. 1.F, 13.E

Answers to TEKS Assessment

1. Students' answers will vary but should include information on how the independence movements in Africa, whether peaceful or violent, resulted in a number of other problems that caused military intervention, ethnic tensions, and conflicts with foreign nations.

2. *Gather information that represents reasons for conflicts:* second-largest continent, over 2,000 languages spoken, many ethnicities and religious groups, ties with former colonialists, one-party governments, dictatorships, poverty

   Identify options: Languages, ethnicities, and religion are beyond control. Types of governments may be difficult to influence. Poverty and health issues are nonpolitical issues that international communities can help with.

   Predict consequences: By working on poverty and health issues, countries may help to stabilize funding for social services and help to prevent radical groups from gaining control.

   Take action to implement a decision: Tap into the international community to offer education and health care services.

3. Students' answers will vary but should include information on how different governments were established as African nations gained independence and tried to aim for democracy. One issue was that colonial boundaries were retained without regard to various ethnic groups living in different areas. If civil unrest ensued, the military would often seize power.

4. Students' answers will vary but should include information on how Sudan's Arab Muslim population in the north dominates the country, while the western area of Darfur had a largely non-Arab Muslim population. Rebels in 2003 fought against the Arab-dominated government. The government retaliated by committing genocide against non-Arabs in Darfur.

5. Students' answers will vary but should include information on how the two main ethnic groups in Rwanda, the Hutus and Tutsis, were in conflict. Before independence, Tutsis controlled the government; afterward, the Hutus were in power, and violence ensued.

6. Students' answers will vary but should include information on how after World War II Britain's military and financial resources were drained, and they did not want to face more conflicts. India's Congress Party wanted a unified nation to include both groups; however, the Muslim League wanted a separate state called Pakistan.

Answers to TEKS Assessment

7. Students' answers will vary but should include information on how the creation of Pakistan in 1947 was determined by the location of Muslim majorities in two separate areas. West Pakistan dominated the government, and most economic programs benefited the western region. East Pakistan had more people and was severely impoverished; it resented governmental neglect in its area.

8. Students' answers will vary but should include information on how Britain partitioned its former colony into two nations, India and Pakistan, both of which became independent in 1947. After independence, partition led to escalating violence.

9. Students' answers will vary but should include information on how Pakistan's many ethnicities and the power struggles within the government have caused great instability.

10. Students' answers will vary but should include information on how some Muslims believe that Western culture and capitalism are negative influences on Islamic society. Regarding the Palestinians, after Arabs failed to regain land lost to Israel in previous wars, Jewish settlers built homes in those territories, causing more bitterness.

11. Students' answers will vary but should include information on how Indira Gandhi served from the 1960s to the 1980s as the third prime minister since independence. She tried to improve women's rights and dealt with poverty and ethnic and religious tensions.

TEKS ASSESSMENT

South Asia Today

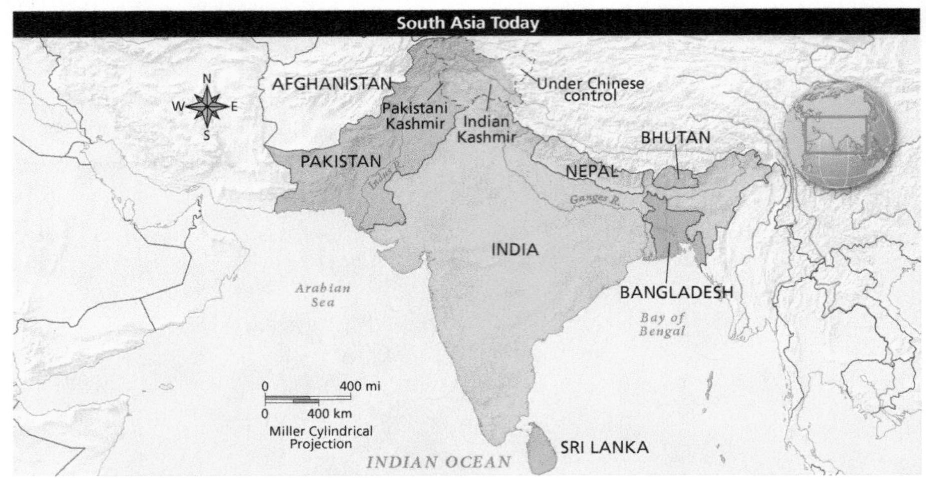

7. **Summarize** Summarize the rise of independence movements in South Asia. Write a paragraph summarizing the rise of independence movements in Pakistan and Bangladesh in South Asia. Locate Pakistan and Bangladesh on the above map. How did geographic location affect the formation of Pakistan when it achieved independence in 1947? Why did people in East Pakistan revolt to gain their own independence? **13.E**

8. **Identify Effects** Identify effects of the following important turning points in world history from 1914 to the present: independence movements. Write a paragraph identifying the migration of Hindu and Muslim minorities after India and Pakistan became independent in 1947. Why did each minority group flee to the other country? Explain why the migrations turned violent. **1.F, 13.E**

9. **Summarize Reasons** Summarize the reasons for South Asia's ongoing conflicts. Write a paragraph summarizing the reasons for ongoing conflicts within Pakistan and Bangladesh in South Asia. Consider the various ethnicities in Pakistan and how its proximity to Afghanistan helped the cause of Islamic fundamentalists. What is the primary issue in Bangladesh, and why is foreign investment an issue for its people? **13.E**

10. **Summarize Development and Explain Influences** Summarize the development of radical Islamic fundamentalism, including Palestinian terrorism, and explain how Islam influences law and government in the Muslim world. Write a paragraph about radical Islamic fundamentalism, including Palestinian terrorism, and explain Islam's influences in Muslim law and government. Why is the West blamed for social and economic problems? What would a return to Sharia accomplish? Why do the Palestinians not have an independent state, and what tensions have arisen from this? **15.A, 25.D**

11. **Describe Major Influences** Describe the major influences of women during major eras of world history: Indira Gandhi. Write a paragraph describing the major influence of Indira Gandhi on India. Consider some of her accomplishments and the challenges she faced. How did she respond to the Golden Temple Incident in 1984? How accurate do you think Gandhi's statement was in the following excerpt? **24.B**

"A New York Times obituary paraphrased those from India who stated that Indira Gandhi had no program and no worldview and that she largely reacted to events instead of shaping them. This is her response to a journalist in 1974:

Ms. Gandhi said, 'This is one of the countries in the world where the economy, although under severe strain, is not collapsing. Do you think it is easy to keep a country like India united? You say promises are not kept. I assert with all authority: Who in the world has kept more promises?'"

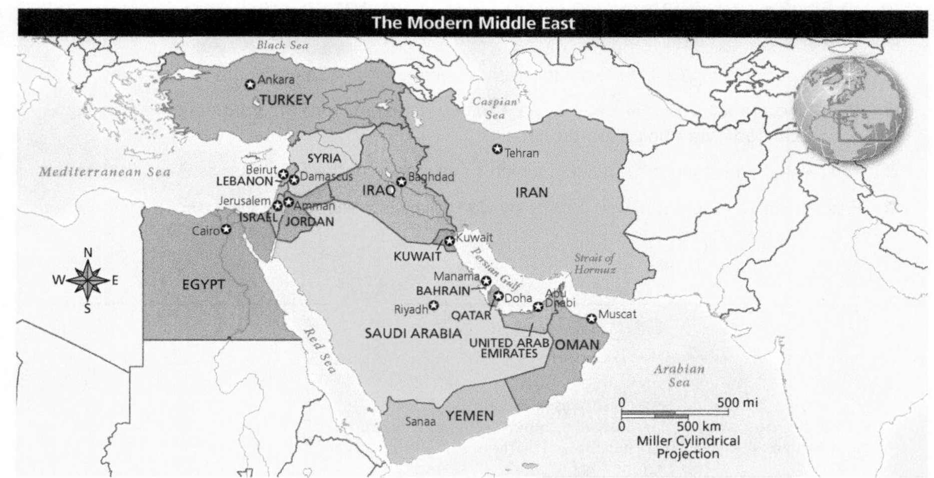

12. **Describe Major Influences** Describe the major influences of women during major eras of world history: Golda Meir. Write a paragraph describing the major influences of Golda Meir. Consider her role in Israel's independence movement and her accomplishments. **24.B**

13. **Summarize and Locate Places** Summarize the rise of independence movements in the Middle East, and locate places and regions of historical significance directly related to major eras. Review the map above. Write a paragraph summarizing the significance of post-World War I mandates in the Middle East. Consider how the mandates were divided into independent nations, and identify and locate these countries on the above map. How were the borders of the new nations drawn up, and why did this cause tensions? What role did Gamal Abdel Nasser play in Arab nationalism? **13.E, 16.A**

14. **Explain** Explain how Arab rejection of the State of Israel has led to ongoing conflict. Write a paragraph explaining how Arab rejection of the State of Israel has led to ongoing conflict. Consider the 1947 United Nations plan for division of Palestine into Arab and Jewish states, who accepted the plan and who rejected it, Israeli independence and Arab reaction, and the status of Palestinians after Israel won independence. Why does the Arab-Israeli conflict continue today? **13.F**

15. **Summarize Impact** Summarize the impact of radical Islamic fundamentalism on events in the second half of the 20th century. Write a paragraph summarizing the impact of Palestinian terrorism in the Arab-Israeli conflict. Consider the impact of the peace talks in 1993 Oslo Accords between the Palestinians and Israelis; how radical Islamists, like Hamas, affect the peace process; and some of the obstacles to peace concerning Palestinian and Jewish claims to the same territory. What has happened to nations who try to intervene? **14.A, 16.A**

16. **Summarize the Reasons** Summarize the reasons for the Middle East's ongoing conflicts. Write a paragraph about the political, religious, and ethnic divisions in the conflicts of the Middle East. Consider poverty in the Middle East and power seized by military leaders, and conflicts between Islamists and secularists. How did the Arab Spring pro-democracy movements in 2011 affect Egypt and other countries? Based on the quotation below, what do women hope to gain from these movements? **13.E**

"I grew up in a world where we believed we could not do anything . . . Generations believed we could do nothing, and now, in a matter of weeks, we know that we can."

17. **Reflect on the Essential Question** **Write an essay on the Essential Question: What should governments do?** Use evidence from your study of this Topic to support your answer.

12. Students' answers will vary but should include information on how Golda Meir was one of the founders of the State of Israel and later rose to become prime minister after serving in many government posts. She became Israel's first female prime minister in 1969.

13. Students' answers will vary but should include information on how post–World War I mandates in the Middle East were territories taken from the defeated Ottoman empire and run by European nations. The mandates were divided up artificially into Iraq, Syria, Lebanon, Jordan, and Israel without regard for diverse ethnic and religious communities.

14. Students' answers will vary but should include information on how a United Nations plan in 1947 proposed to divide Palestine into an Arab and a Jewish state. One reason the Arab-Israeli conflict continues today is that many Arabs continue to reject the state of Israel.

15. Students' answers will vary but should include information on the status of the Arab-Israeli peace agreement and continuing issues. A two-state solution has been presented with little progress; radical Islamist groups not only reject Israel's right to exist but also have launched terrorist activities.

16. Students' answers will vary but should include information on how political, religious, and ethnic divisions plague the Middle East. The Arab Spring pro-democracy movement erupted in 2011 from frustration with corrupt and authoritarian governments along with economic instability.

Answers to TEKS Practice

1. D
2. G

Online To prepare for the End-of-Topic test, have students go online for additional Topic Review and Assessment questions or to review their notes in the **Interactive Reading Notepad** for the lessons in this Topic.

Benchmark Tests

Assign these benchmark tests as you complete the relevant topics to monitor student progress toward mastering the course content and as preparation for the End-of-Course Test.

Benchmark Test 1: Topics 1–5

Benchmark Test 2: Topics 6–10

Benchmark Test 3: Topics 11–15

Benchmark Test 4: Topics 16–21

TEKS PRACTICE

1 Why did East Pakistan want to become independent from West Pakistan and become Bangladesh?

A India's support of West Pakistan for trade benefits shrunk East Pakistan's economy.

B In addition to a 1,000-mile separation, the two Pakistans had different majority languages, which caused communication problems.

C East Pakistan was mostly Muslim, which conflicted with the Hinduism of West Pakistan.

D East Pakistan was populated mostly by Bengalis who resented government neglect by West Pakistan rulers.

2

Some Middle Eastern countries adopted secular, or nonreligious, governments after independence as a way to modernize. Western culture influenced them as it influenced many countries globally.

An Islamic revival occurred, condemning Western culture and capitalism that were blamed for undermining Islamic society. Some conservative reformers, called Islamic fundamentalists, wanted a return to traditional Muslim values. They wanted a return to Sharia, Islamic law based on the Quran, to cope with rapid social and economic changes.

Radical Islamists, sometimes called fundamentalist extremists, wanted to achieve the same goals through violent means. They not only wanted to overthrow governments associated with the West, but they also targeted Israel and the United States. They welcomed the religious government established in Iran, a theocracy, after it overthrew the secular government.

Read the chart. How does Islam influence law and government in the Muslim world?

F Radical Islamists use Sharia law to justify overthrow of Western nations allied with Israel.

G Some Muslims want to return to Sharia and traditional values to cope with modernization.

H Islamists want theocracies for Muslim nations achieved through peaceful means.

J Many Muslims believe that Western culture and capitalism are responsible for all of mankind's problems.

Test Taking Tips: Tip for Questions With Reading Passages

1. Read the question.
2. Read the title of the passage if it is provided.
3. Determine when the passage or quotation was written or spoken and by whom.
4. Carefully read the entire passage or quotation.
5. Read the question again to be sure you understand what is being asked. Identify details or ideas in the passage or quotation that you will use to answer the question.
6. Answer the question in your own words.
7. Read the answer choices and select the best answer.

3 Which of these is the general underlying reason for the genocide that occurred in Darfur?

A This is an example of different factions wanting to seize control of oil and gas reserves.

B This is an example of how tensions of ethnic differences over government rule resulted in crimes against humanity.

C This is an example of resentment toward foreign investors who control key economic resources, aided by a minority group.

D This is an example of how Cold War tensions can spill over into civil wars with critical financing.

4

> *"In the mid-1980s, through glasnost—openness and freedom—and perestroika—economic restructuring—Gorbachev had demonstrated willingness to loosen government strangleholds in the Soviet Union and Eastern Europe, including East Germany."*

How did Gorbachev's policies described in the excerpt lead to the collapse of communism in the Soviet Union?

F He took advantage of a weakened government to overthrow military hardliners who had ruined the economy.

G He thought that limited capitalism under glasnost would be better than a command economy.

H His open policies and reforms worsened the Soviet economy, which encouraged unrest there and in Eastern Europe.

J His perestroika (restructuring) plans caused ethnic violence directed toward centralized government planning.

If you have trouble with...				
Question	1	2	3	4
See Lesson	20.1	20.2	20.3	19.5
TEKS	13.E	22.D	25.D	13.D

3. B
4. H

Online Use the **Topic Synthesize** to help students revisit and reflect on the Essential Question for this Topic.

End-of-Course Tests

Assign End-of-Course Test 1 or 2 to measure students' progress in mastering the course content.

The World Today (1980–Present)

TOPIC 21 ORGANIZER	PACING: APPROX. 1 PERIOD, .5 BLOCKS		
	PACING	TEKS	ELPS
Connect	1 period		
MY STORY VIDEO **Jennifer Correiro, Taking IT Global**	10 min.		
DIGITAL ESSENTIAL QUESTION ACTIVITY **What Are the Benefits and Risks of Interdependence?**	10 min.	17.C	
DIGITAL MAP ACTIVITY **The World Today**	10 min.	15.A, 17.C	
TOPIC INQUIRY: DOCUMENT-BASED QUESTION **How Do Developed and Developing Countries Differ?**	20 min.		
Investigate	4–9 periods		
TOPIC INQUIRY: DOCUMENT-BASED QUESTION **How Do Developed and Developing Countries Differ?**	Ongoing		
LESSON 1 **Challenges of Development**	30–40 min.	15.A, 15.B, 24.A	1.F.1
LESSON 2 **Challenges for African Nations**	30–40 min.	13.E, 18.C, 21.C, 22.E	
LESSON 3 **Rapid Development in China and India**	30–40 min.	18.F	1.A.1
LESSON 4 **Latin American Nations Move Toward Democracy**	30–40 min.	22.C, 22.E	1.A.2
LESSON 5 **The Industrialized World**	30–40 min.	18.E, 18.F, 22.D	1.B.1
LESSON 6 **Globalization and Trade**	30–40 min.	1.F, 15.B, 17.C, 20.D, 28.D	1.B.1
LESSON 7 **Social and Environmental Issues**	30–40 min.	17.C, 20.D, 24.A	2.B.1, 1.C.1
LESSON 8 **Terrorism and International Security**	30–40 min.	13.E, 13.F, 14.A, 14.B, 25.D	2.C.1, 1.D.1
LESSON 9 **Advances in Science and Technology**	30–40 min.	28.D	2.C.2
Synthesize	1 period		
DIGITAL ESSENTIAL QUESTION ACTIVITY **The World Today**	10 min.	17.C	
TOPIC INQUIRY: DOCUMENT-BASED QUESTION **How Do Developed and Developing Countries Differ?**	20 min.		

TOPIC 21 ORGANIZER	PACING: APPROX. 1 PERIOD, .5 BLOCKS		
	PACING	TEKS	ELPS
Demonstrate	1–2 periods		
DIGITAL TOPIC TEST **The World Today**	10 min.		
TOPIC INQUIRY: DOCUMENT-BASED QUESTION **How Do Developed and Developing Countries Differ?**	20 min.		

AUTHOR'S NOTE

The Ties That Globalize

A striking embodiment of the evolving international order around 2000 was a growing number of what we might call *global people*, true citizens of the world whose lives and labors were helping to weld the world's many communities into one. . . .

A major globalizing structure was the web of *technological links* which brought the peoples of the planet closer together. . . . In the twentieth century, the automobile and the airplane, the super-tanker and the high-speed train had further revolutionized transport, while the telephone, radio, television, computer, and World Wide Web had transformed communications. . . .

Closely related to these technological links were the growing *economic ties* that bound the nations of the world more closely with every passing decade. When the European empires crumbled after World War II, the economic relationships between the western nations and their former colonies forged in earlier centuries survived. Raw materials and industrial products, investment capital and labor in search of employment flowed with increasing freedom around the globe. Critics stressed the exploitative dimension of these ties, dubbing them "economic imperialism." But the growing global economy bound both parties. A third-world country that negotiated a development loan incurred an immense debt which it would find desperately hard to repay. But default on a loan large enough to help a whole nation could put the biggest western bank in jeopardy.

—Anthony Esler, *The Human Venture: From Prehistory to the Present* (Upper Saddle River, New Jersey: Pearson Education, 2004), pp. 770–771

TOPIC INQUIRY: DOCUMENT-BASED QUESTION

How Do Developed and Developing Countries Differ?

TEKS 15.B, 17.C, 18.A, 18.F, 29.F, 29.H, 30.C

In this Topic Inquiry, students work individually to analyze five documents that address in different ways the differences between developed and developing countries. The documents are in the form of charts, graphs, maps, and models, all compiled from raw data from various international sources. Students will answer questions about each document, analyze and compare geographic patterns and distributions, draw their own conclusions, and then write an essay on the following question: What are the differences between developed and developing countries?

STEP 1: CONNECT

Develop Questions and Plan the Investigation

Launch the DBQ Writing Activity

Have students make their lists of the characteristics of developed nations and developing nations. If necessary, remind students that developed countries are those with highly developed industrial and service economies, high standards of living, and high per capita gross domestic products. Developing countries are those that are working toward higher levels of development. Suggest they keep these definitions in mind as they read the documents, answer the questions, and write their essays.

Suggestion: Have volunteers read their lists and have the rest of the class discuss them. Ask: What are some countries that fit each of your definitions? Why do you categorize them in this way?

Generate Questions

Divide the class into small groups and have them record their questions about the differences between developed nations and developing nations.

Professional Development

Document-Based Questions

Be sure to view the Document-Based Questions resources in the online course.

Resources

- Student Instructions
- Need-to-Know Questions

STEP 2: INVESTIGATE

Apply Disciplinary Concepts and Tools

Analyze the Documents

Have students analyze the five documents to see how they relate to the question "What are the differences between developed and developing countries?" Then, ask them to write an essay and express their own opinions about what these differences are.

Ask students what current events, media, or personal experiences have made them aware of the differences between developed and developing countries. How have these sources of information shaped their understanding of the differences between developed and developing countries? Point out that these documents tell the same story using charts, graphs, maps, and models.

Suggestion: You can control the length of the DBQ by having students examine only documents A and E, which focus on demographic changes, or only those that focus on economic changes, B, C, and D.

Check Understanding

After students finish reading each individual document, have them answer the multiple-choice and short-answer questions attached to each document. Review the questions and discuss the answers after students have answered the questions for all the documents.

Resources

- Information Organizer

STEP 3: SYNTHESIZE

Evaluate Sources and
Use Evidence to Formulate Conclusions

Write Your Essay

Have students consider all of the evidence and draw their own conclusions, and then write their essays to express their own opinion about the question: What are the differences between developed and developing countries?

Remind students that their essays should have the following: a topic sentence; evidence from at least *three* of the documents, clearly identified; relevant facts; an explanation and rebuttal of at least one opposing viewpoint; logical organization, including an introduction and a conclusion; and correct spelling, grammar, and punctuation.

Suggestion: If students struggle with content, ask pairs to take turns explaining to each other what each document shows.

Edit Your Essay

Have students read over their first drafts. Suggest they ask themselves these questions: Does it state what I think is the main idea about the differences between developed and developing countries? Does it need more details to support the main idea? Is my point of view clear? What can I do to make it clearer? Then have students proofread and edit their essays, revising as needed, and create a final draft of their essay before turning it in. You may want to suggest that they ask a classmate to peer edit their essay.

Resources

- Writing Rubric

STEP 4: DEMONSTRATE

Communicate Conclusions
and Take Informed Action

Present Your Essay

Have students make a neat, clean copy of their essays. Then ask volunteers to read their essays aloud to the class.

Suggestion: As an alternative, have students publish their essays on a class Web site, bulletin board, or other online vehicle.

Reflect on the Project

Have students briefly discuss what they found challenging in their essays and what they feel they did well. Encourage them to use the lessons they learned writing this essay so they can write even more effectively in future writing projects.

Suggestion: As an extension activity, have students present their essays to the class using presentation software, with illustrations added.

PROFESSIONAL DEVELOPMENT

Document-Based Question

Be sure to view the Document-Based Question Professional Development resources in the online course.

Topic 21 Lesson 1

Challenges of Development

Objectives

Objective 1: Understand how nations in the developing world have tried to build strong economies.

Objective 2: Describe obstacles to development in the global South.

Objective 3: Explain how development is changing patterns of life in the developing world.

LESSON 1 ORGANIZER	PACING: APPROX. 1 PERIOD, .5 BLOCKS					
			RESOURCES			
	OBJECTIVES	PACING	Print	Online	TEKS	ELPS
Connect						
DIGITAL START UP ACTIVITY **The Developing World**		5 min.		●		
Investigate						
READ **Working Toward Development**	Objective 1	10 min.	●	●	18.E	1.F.1
READ **Challenges to Development**	Objective 2	10 min.	●	●		
INTERACTIVE MAP **Global Population Growth**		10 min.		●		
READ **Development Brings Social Change**	Objective 3	10 min.	●	●	24.A	
INTERACTIVE GALLERY **Children of the Developing World**		10 min.		●	24.A	
Synthesize						
DIGITAL ACTIVITY **The Risks and Benefits of Global Development**		5 min.		●		
Demonstrate						
DIGITAL QUIZ **Lesson Quiz and Class Discussion Board**		10 min.		●	17.C, 18.E, 24.A	

PEARSON realize
www.PearsonTexas.com
Access your Digital Lesson

Focus on Texas Standards

Texas Essential Knowledge and Skills

15.A create and interpret thematic maps, graphs, and charts to demonstrate the relationship between geography and the historical development of a region or nation

15.B analyze and compare geographic distributions and patterns in world history shown on maps, graphs, charts, and models

24.A describe the changing roles of women, children, and families during major eras of world history

NOTES

Challenges for African Nations

Objectives

Objective 1: Summarize the struggle for equality in South Africa, and identify how Nelson Mandela led resistance efforts.

Objective 2: Describe choices African nations had to make as they developed their economies.

Objective 3: Understand the challenges African nations face.

LESSON 2 ORGANIZER	PACING: APPROX. 1 PERIOD, .5 BLOCKS					
			RESOURCES			
	OBJECTIVES	PACING	Print	Online	TEKS	ELPS
Connect						
DIGITAL START UP ACTIVITY **Nelson Mandela**		5 min.		●	21.C, 22.E	
Investigate						
READ **The Struggle for Equality in South Africa**	Objective 1	10 min.	●	●	21.C, 22.E	
INTERACTIVE TIMELINE **The Struggle Against Apartheid**	Objective 1	10 min.		●	21.C, 22.E	
READ **African Nations Face Economic Choices**	Objective 2	10 min.	●	●	18.C	
READ **Continuing Challenges to Development**	Objective 3	10 min.	●	●	13.E	
INTERACTIVE GALLERY **Environmental Challenges in Africa**	Objective 3	10 min.		●	13.E	
Synthesize						
DIGITAL ACTIVITY **Glory and Hope**		5 min.		●	13.E, 21.C, 22.E	
Demonstrate						
DIGITAL QUIZ **Lesson Quiz and Class Discussion Board**		10 min.		●	13.E, 18.C, 21.C, 22.E	

PEARSON realize www.PearsonTexas.com Access your Digital Lesson

Focus on Texas Standards

Texas Essential Knowledge and Skills

13.E summarize the rise of independence movements in Africa, the Middle East, and South Asia and reasons for ongoing conflicts

18.C identify the historical origins and characteristics of socialism

21.C identify examples of key persons who were successful in shifting political thought, including William Wilberforce

22.E identify examples of individuals who led resistance to political oppression such as Nelson Mandela, Mohandas Gandhi, Oscar Romero, Natan Sharansky, Las Madres de la Plaza de Mayo, and Chinese student protestors in Tiananmen Square

NOTES

Topic 21 Lesson 3

Rapid Development in China and India

Objectives

Objective 1: Describe how China has moved toward a free market economy without allowing democratic reform.

Objective 2: Identify continuing challenges that China faces.

Objective 3: Explain how India has built its economy.

Objective 4: Summarize social reforms in modern India.

LESSON 3 ORGANIZER	PACING: APPROX. 1 PERIOD, .5 BLOCKS					
			RESOURCES			
	OBJECTIVES	PACING	Print	Online	TEKS	ELPS
Connect						
DIGITAL START UP ACTIVITY **"Made in China"**		5 min.		●	18.F	
Investigate						
READ **Reform and Repression in China**	Objective 1	10 min.	●	●	18.F, 22.E	
INTERACTIVE GALLERY **Protests in Tiananmen Square**	Objective 1	10 min.		●	22.E	
READ **Reforms Bring Growth and Challenges**	Objective 2	10 min.	●	●	18.F	1.A.1
READ **India Builds a Modern Economy**	Objective 3	10 min.	●	●	18.F, 24.A, 24.B	
READ **Social Reform in India**	Objective 4	10 min.	●	●	18.F, 24.A	
INTERACTIVE GALLERY **India on the Rise**	Objective 4	10 min.		●	17.C	
Synthesize						
DIGITAL ACTIVITY **The Economies of China and India**		5 min.		●	18.F	
Demonstrate						
DIGITAL QUIZ **Lesson Quiz and Class Discussion Board**		10 min.		●	17.C, 18.F, 24.A	

PEARSON realize™ www.PearsonTexas.com Access your Digital Lesson

Focus on Texas Standards

Texas Essential Knowledge and Skills

18.F formulate generalizations on how economic freedom improved the human condition, based on students' knowledge of the benefits of free enterprise in Europe's Commercial Revolution, the Industrial Revolution, and 20th-century free market economies, compared to communist command communities

NOTES

Topic 21 Lesson 4

Latin American Nations Move Toward Democracy

Objectives

Objective 1: Analyze how Latin America has grappled with poverty.

Objective 2: Describe the struggles of Latin American nations to build democratic governments.

Objective 3: Explain the struggle between repression and freedom in Argentina.

LESSON 4 ORGANIZER	PACING: APPROX. 1 PERIOD, .5 BLOCKS		RESOURCES			
	OBJECTIVES	PACING	Print	Online	TEKS	ELPS
Connect						
DIGITAL START UP ACTIVITY **Fighting Poverty**		5 min.		●		
Investigate						
READ **Poverty Challenges Latin America**	Objective 1	10 min.	●	●		1.A.2
INTERACTIVE MAP **Economic Activities in Latin America**		10 min.		●		
READ **Dictatorships and Civil War**	Objective 2	10 min.	●	●	22.C, 22.E	
READ **U.S.–Latin American Relations**		10 min.	●	●		
READ **The Long Road to Democracy in Argentina**	Objective 3	10 min.	●	●	22.C, 22.E	
INTERACTIVE GALLERY **Argentina's Long Road to Democracy**		10 min.		●	22.C, 22.E	
Synthesize						
DIGITAL ACTIVITY **The Poor in Latin America**		5 min.		●		
Demonstrate						
DIGITAL QUIZ **Lesson Quiz and Class Discussion Board**		10 min.		●	1.F, 17.C, 22.C, 23.B	

Focus on Texas Standards

Texas Essential Knowledge and Skills

22.C identify examples of politically motivated mass murders in Cambodia, China, Latin America, the Soviet Union, and Armenia	**22.E** identify examples of individuals who led resistance to political oppression such as Nelson Mandela, Mohandas Gandhi, Oscar Romero, Natan Sharansky, Las Madres de la Plaza de Mayo, and Chinese student protestors in Tiananmen Square

NOTES

Topic 21 Lesson 5

The Industrialized World

Objectives

Objective 1: Examine social, political, and economic trends in Europe since the Cold War.

Objective 2: Describe how the breakup of Yugoslavia led to war and genocide.

Objective 3: Analyze the challenges facing Russia since the end of the Soviet Union.

Objective 4: Summarize economic developments in Asia.

LESSON 5 ORGANIZER — **PACING: APPROX. 1 PERIOD, .5 BLOCKS**

	OBJECTIVES	PACING	RESOURCES Print	RESOURCES Online	TEKS	ELPS
Connect						
DIGITAL START UP ACTIVITY **Russia's GDP**		5 min.		●		
Investigate						
READ **A New Europe**	Objective 1	10 min.	●	●	17.C, 18.E	1.B.1
INTERACTIVE MAP **Evolution of the European Union**	Objective 1	10 min.		●	18.E	
READ **Shifts in Global Power**	Objective 3	10 min.	●	●	18.E	
READ **The Former Soviet Republics**	Objective 3	10 min.	●	●		
READ **War in Yugoslavia**	Objective 2	10 min.	●	●	22.D	
INTERACTIVE TIMELINE **War in Bosnia**	Objective 2	10 min.		●	22.D	
READ **A New Role for Asia**	Objective 4	10 min.	●	●	18.F	
Synthesize						
DIGITAL ACTIVITY **Post–Cold War World**		5 min.		●	17.C, 18.E, 18.F	
Demonstrate						
DIGITAL QUIZ **Lesson Quiz and Class Discussion Board**		10 min.		●	18.E, 18.F, 22.D	

Focus on Texas Standards

Texas Essential Knowledge and Skills

18.E explain why communist command economies collapsed in competition with free market economies at the end of the 20th century

18.F formulate generalizations on how economic freedom improved the human condition, based on students' knowledge of the benefits of free enterprise in Europe's Commercial Revolution, the Industrial Revolution, and 20th-century free market economies, compared to communist command communities

22.D identify examples of genocide, including the Holocaust and genocide in the Balkans, Rwanda, and Darfur

NOTES

Topic 21 Lesson 6

Globalization and Trade

Objectives

Objective 1: Summarize the impact of globalization on the modern world.

Objective 2: Describe the role of international organizations and treaties in expanding trade.

Objective 3: Analyze the costs and benefits of globalization.

LESSON 6 ORGANIZER	PACING: APPROX. 1 PERIOD, .5 BLOCKS					
			RESOURCES			
	OBJECTIVES	PACING	Print	Online	TEKS	ELPS
Connect						
DIGITAL START UP ACTIVITY **The Beginnings of Globalization**		5 min.		●	1.E, 1.F, 17.C	
Investigate						
READ **Global Interdependence**	Objective 1	10 min.	●	●	1.F, 17.C, 28.D	
INTERACTIVE GALLERY **Aspects of Globalization**	Objective 1	10 min.		●	1.F, 17.C, 28.D	
READ **Global Organizations and Trade Agreements**	Objective 2	10 min.	●	●	1.F, 17.C, 20.D	
READ **Benefits and Costs of Globalization**	Objective 3	10 min.	●	●	1.F, 17.C	1.B.1
INTERACTIVE GALLERY **Smart Phones—American-Made?**	Objective 3	10 min.		●	1.F, 17.C, 28.D	
Synthesize						
DIGITAL ACTIVITY **Globalization**		5 min.		●	1.F, 17.C	
Demonstrate						
DIGITAL QUIZ **Lesson Quiz and Class Discussion Board**		10 min.		●	17.C	

PEARSON realize™ www.PearsonTexas.com Access your Digital Lesson

Focus on Texas Standards

Texas Essential Knowledge and Skills

1.F identify major causes and describe the major effects of the following important turning points in world history from 1914 to the present: the world wars and their impact on political, economic, and social systems; communist revolutions and their impact on the Cold War; independence movements; and globalization

15.B analyze and compare geographic distributions and patterns in world history shown on maps, graphs, charts, and models

17.C summarize the economic and social impact of 20th century globalization

20.D explain the significance of the League of Nations and the United Nations

28.D explain the role of telecommunication technology, computer technology, transportation technology, and medical advancements in developing the modern global economy and society

NOTES

Social and Environmental Issues

Objectives

Objective 1: Explain the impact of poverty, disasters, and disease on nations around the world.

Objective 2: Describe global efforts to protect human rights.

Objective 3: Evaluate the environmental challenges facing the world.

LESSON 7 ORGANIZER — **PACING: APPROX. 1 PERIOD, .5 BLOCKS**

	OBJECTIVES	PACING	RESOURCES Print	RESOURCES Online	TEKS	ELPS
Connect						
DIGITAL START UP ACTIVITY **Global Challenges**		5 min.		●	17.C, 20.D	
Investigate						
READ **Global Challenges**	Objective 1	10 min.	●	●	17.C, 17	2.B.1
READ **Human Rights**	Objective 2	10 min.	●	●	17.C, 20.D, 24.A	
INTERACTIVE GALLERY **Women's Lives in the 21st Century**		10 min.		●	20.D, 24.A	
READ **Development and the Environment**	Objective 3	10 min.	●	●	17.C	1.C.1
INTERACTIVE MAP **Global Environmental Challenges**		10 min.		●		
Synthesize						
DIGITAL ACTIVITY **"The Same Boat"**		5 min.		●	17.C	
Demonstrate						
DIGITAL QUIZ **Lesson Quiz and Class Discussion Board**		10 min.		●	17.C, 20.D, 24.A	

PEARSON realize™ www.PearsonTexas.com Access your Digital Lesson

Focus on Texas Standards

Texas Essential Knowledge and Skills

17.C summarize the economic and social impact of 20th century globalization

20.D explain the significance of the League of Nations and the United Nations

24.A describe the changing roles of women, children, and families during major eras of world history

NOTES

Terrorism and International Security

Objectives

Objective 1: Explain how nuclear, biological, and chemical weapons threaten international security.

Objective 2: Analyze the growth of terrorist groups such as al Qaeda.

Objective 3: Explain how the United States and other nations have responded to terrorism from September 11, 2001, to the present.

LESSON 8 ORGANIZER	PACING: APPROX. 1 PERIOD, .5 BLOCKS					
			RESOURCES			
	OBJECTIVES	PACING	Print	Online	TEKS	ELPS
Connect						
DIGITAL START UP ACTIVITY **Looking Back—September 11, 2001**		5 min.		●	14.A, 14.B	
Investigate						
READ **The Threat of New Weapons**	Objective 1	10 min.	●	●	13.C, 28.C	
READ **The Growing Threat of Terrorism**	Objective 2	10 min.	●	●	13.E, 14, 14.A, 14.B, 25.D	2.C.1
INTERACTIVE MAP **Terrorism Around the World**		10 min.		●	13.E	
READ **The U.S. Response to Terrorism**	Objective 3	10 min.	●	●	14.B, 25.D	1.D.1
INTERACTIVE GALLERY **September 11, 2001**		10 min.		●	14.B	
Synthesize						
DIGITAL ACTIVITY **Taken by Surprise**		5 min.		●	14.A, 14.B	
Demonstrate						
DIGITAL QUIZ **Lesson Quiz and Class Discussion Board**		10 min.		●	14.A, 14.B	

PEARSON realize™ www.PearsonTexas.com Access your Digital Lesson

Focus on Texas Standards

Texas Essential Knowledge and Skills

13.E summarize the rise of independence movements in Africa, the Middle East, and South Asia and reasons for ongoing conflicts

13.F explain how Arab rejection of the State of Israel has led to ongoing conflict

14.A summarize the development and impact of radical Islamic fundamentalism on events in the second half of the 20th century, including Palestinian terrorism and the growth of al Qaeda

14.B explain the U.S. response to terrorism from September 11, 2001, to the present

25.D explain how Islam influences law and government in the Muslim world

NOTES

Advances in Science and Technology

Objectives

Objective 1: Describe the exploration of space and the innovations that have resulted.

Objective 2: Analyze the development and impact of computer technology and telecommunications.

Objective 3: Summarize key advancements in medicine and biotechnology.

LESSON 9 ORGANIZER	PACING: APPROX. 1 PERIOD, .5 BLOCKS					
			RESOURCES			
	OBJECTIVES	PACING	Print	Online	TEKS	ELPS
Connect						
DIGITAL START UP ACTIVITY **Instant Communication**		5 min.		●	28.D	
Investigate						
READ **Space Exploration**	Objective 1	10 min.	●	●	28.D	2.C.2
INTERACTIVE TIMELINE **The Age of Space Exploration**	Objective 1	10 min.		●	28.D	
READ **The Computer Revolution**	Objective 2	10 min.	●	●	28.D	
READ **Breakthroughs in Medicine and Biotechnology**	Objective 3	10 min.	●	●	28.D	
INTERACTIVE TIMELINE **Medical Milestones**	Objective 3	10 min.		●	28.D	
Synthesize						
DIGITAL ACTIVITY **Advances in Science and Technology**		5 min.		●	28.D	
Demonstrate						
DIGITAL QUIZ **Lesson Quiz and Class Discussion Board**		10 min.		●	28.D	

PEARSON realize™ www.PearsonTexas.com Access your Digital Lesson

Focus on Texas Standards

Texas Essential Knowledge and Skills

28.D explain the role of telecommunication technology, computer technology, transportation technology, and medical advancements in developing the modern global economy and society

NOTES

The World Today (1980–Present)

In this Topic, you will learn about the world today. You will also find lots of ways to investigate the ideas of this Topic and to master the TEKS.

Your study will help you master these TEKS:

TEKS

1.F, 13.E, 13.F, 14.A, 14.B, 15.A, 15.B, 17.C, 18.C, 18.E, 18.F, 20.D, 21.C, 22.C, 22.D, 22.E, 24.A, 24.B, 25.D, 28.D, 31.A

LESSON OUTLINE

Connect

Connect with this Topic by watching a video about a fascinating person related to the world today. You can think about how this Topic connects to your own life. And you'll encounter an intriguing Essential Question: What are the benefits and risks of interdependence?

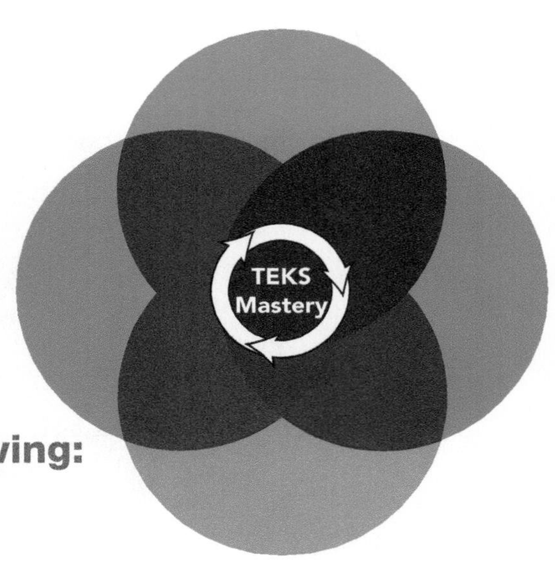

Begin your study by trying the following:

NBC LEARN Watch My Story Video:

Jennifer Corriero, Taking IT Global

Launch your Document-Based Question:

Differences Between Developed and Developing Countries

Investigate

The Lesson Outline lists all the lessons you will investigate in this Topic. As you read and interact with key content, the story the world today will come to life. Read the texts; try the interactivities. Investigate the fascinating story of modern day nations and the ways in which they interact.

And keep working on your Document-Based Question to help build your mastery of the Topic TEKS.

>> Digital interactivity from the online course

TEKS in Topic 21	Topic Review and Assessment Questions
1.F	3
13.E	7
13.F	14
14.A	14, 15
14.B	19
15.B	1
17.C	2, 16
18.C	5
18.E	11
18.F	9
20.D	6
21.C	20
22.C	12
22.D	17
22.E	10, 20
24.A	1, 18
24.B	8
25.D	13
28.D	4
31.A	16

Synthesize

Next you will pull it all together by reflecting on the Essential Question. This will give you a chance to be the storyteller, to show how you would answer this big question: What are the benefits and risks of interdependence?

Demonstrate

Finally, you can show what you know. You can write an essay, hold a discussion, or make a presentation. You can answer questions about every TEKS on the Topic Review and Assessment pages. Or you can complete your essay on developed and developing countries.

Topic 21

The World Today (1980–Present)

Introduction

In the world today, great differences exist in the economic, political, social, and religious spheres, with the starkest gaps existing between the mostly developed global North and the mostly less-developed global South. Globalization, created by modern technology, free trade agreements, and international organizations, has changed the balance in some ways. Many challenges remain, however, including fighting poverty, protecting human rights, protecting the environment, and defeating terrorism. Will the nations of the world be able to work together to address these daunting problems?

ESSENTIAL QUESTION

Ask students to think about the Essential Question for this Topic: What are the benefits and risks of interdependence? Share the following with students:

Identify Main Ideas Do you think interdependence can help the world address such problems as the struggle for human rights, destruction of the environment, and terrorism? Why or why not? *(Some students may say that these problems are so challenging that only international cooperation can overcome them, while others may argue that many countries are unreliable allies.)*

Predict Consequences What do you think might happen if the divide between rich and poor countries continues to grow? Explain. *(Many students will predict more conflict, famine, and other social and economic distress.)*

Connect How do you think increasing interdependence will affect your life? Explain. *(Some students will forecast positive changes, such as growing cooperation to address problems, while others may be more pessimistic and predict greater social, economic, and environmental problems.)*

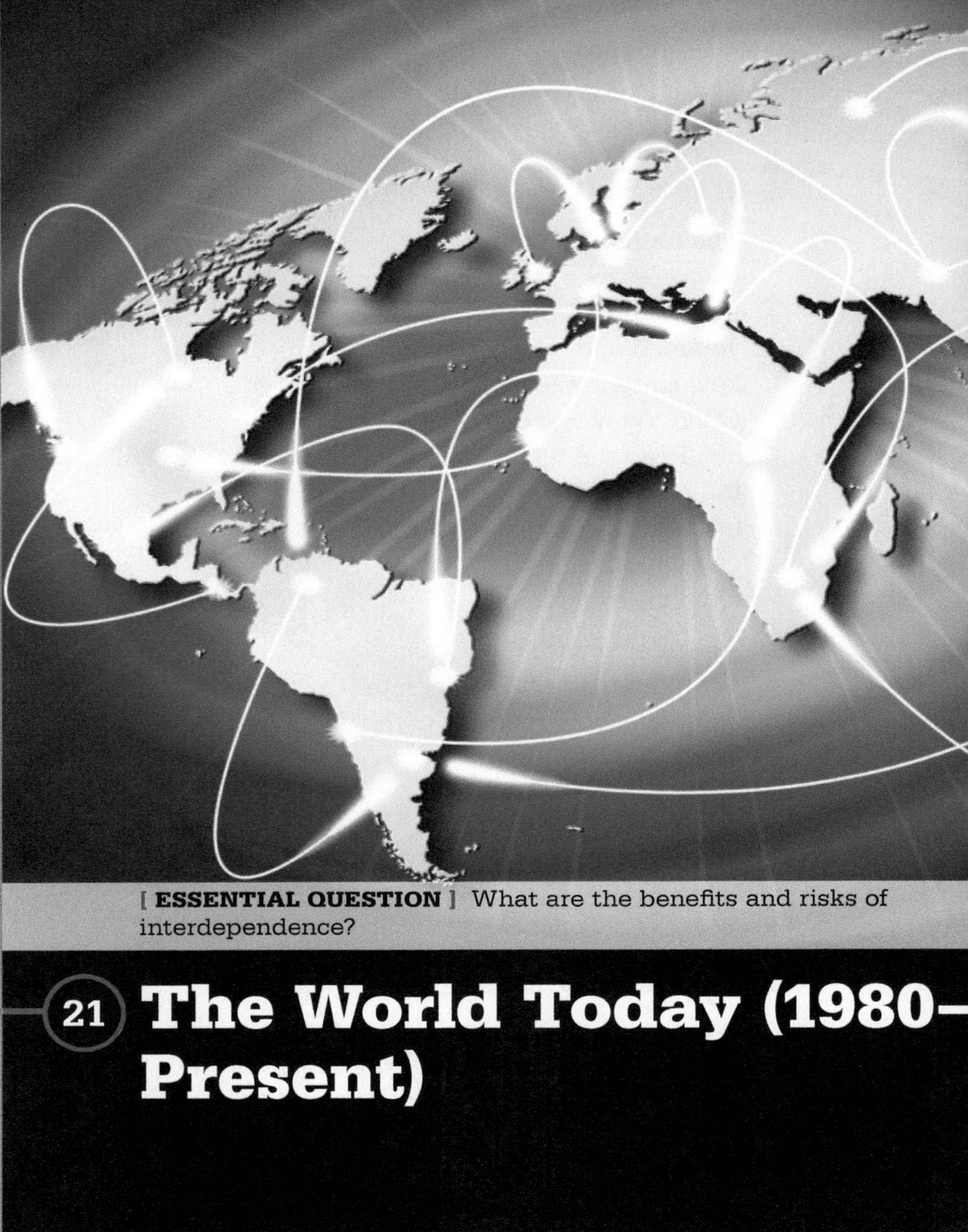

[**ESSENTIAL QUESTION**] What are the benefits and risks of interdependence?

21 The World Today (1980–Present)

Analyze Images

Ask students to examine the artist's rendition of an interdependent world. Tell them that there are many ways in which the modern world is interdependent. Ask them to brainstorm on what these ways are. *(Students may give examples of technological, economic, or political interdependence.)*

Texas Essential Knowledge and Skills

1.F, 13.E, 13.F, 14.A, 14.B, 15.A, 15.B, 17.C, 18.C, 18.E, 18.F, 20.D, 21.C, 22.C, 22.D, 22.E, 24.A, 24.B, 25.D, 28.D, 31.A

Enduring Understandings

- The industrialized world and the developing world are interdependent economically and politically.
- Developing nations in Africa and Latin America have worked to build stable economies and governments.
- In South Africa, the African majority won a long battle against the apartheid system of white minority rule.
- China and India have developed into economic superpowers.
- Technology, free trade, and international organizations have contributed to globalization.
- Issues of global concern include poverty, human rights, and the environment.
- Terrorism has become a growing concern, especially since September 11, 2001.

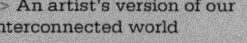

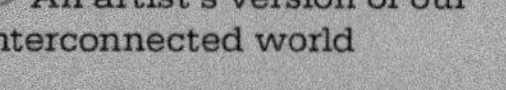
>> An artist's version of our interconnected world

Watch the My Story Video to learn how young people created a technology-based organization to deal with world issues.

Access your digital lessons including:
Topic Inquiry • Interactive Reading Notepad • Interactivities • Assessments

919

NBC LEARN MY STORY VIDEO

Project the video about Jennifer Correiro's new technology-based organization.

Online My Story Video: **Jennifer Correiro, Taking IT Global**

After viewing, have students respond to the following questions.

Check Understanding What is the goal of Taking IT Global? *(to empower young people around the world, through technology, to connect and take action on social issues)*

Compare and Contrast How has technology changed the way people around the world can communicate today, as opposed to 50 years ago? *(Today communication can be instantaneous, as compared to the recent past, when people communicated by mail or telephone or had to travel long distances for face-to-face contact.)*

OVERVIEW ACTIVITY

Online Project the **Map: The World Today** showing sites of important events and places of today. During this Topic, students will learn about all of these events and places, but this map will provide a framework into which they can place what they learn. Ask students to use the map to point out ways the countries and people of the world have become more closely connected.

Analyze Maps Have students look at the map. Tell them to think about what they already know about the world today, and to point out to a partner ways the countries and people of the world have become more closely connected and interdependent in the 21st century. *(Students may point out that Russia, since the end of the Cold War and the fall of communism, has made some efforts to join the world community, or that China and India have become economic superpowers.)*

Topic Inquiry

If you choose to assign the Topic Inquiry, launch the DBQ Activity with students after introducing the Topic.

D Differentiate Extra Support For the Overview Activity, ask: What advantage does Mexico possess over India and China in trading with the United States? *(It is much closer.)*

Topic 21 Lesson 1

Challenges of Development

CONNECT

Preview Have students preview the **Lesson Objectives** and the list of **Key Terms**.

Students can also preview all the **Key Terms** and **Academic Vocabulary** using the **Interactive Reading Notepad** on the digital course or preview a summary of the lesson in the **Reading and Note Taking Study Guide**.

Online Use the **Editable Presentation** found on the digital course to present the main ideas for this lesson.

Start Up Activity

Ask students to brainstorm some ideas on how they would define the term *developing world*. Then, ask them what it might mean to live in a country in the developing world. *(Students may note differences in living conditions, opportunities, education, and lifestyle.)*

Tell students that in this lesson they will learn about the developing world—nations that are working toward creating a more advanced economy and higher living standards.

Online You can also project the **Start Up Activity** from the course.

INVESTIGATE

Have students read the section using the **Reading and Note Taking Study Guide** to help them take notes and understand the text as they read.

Key Terms

Call students' attention to the term **development** in the lesson introduction text. Explain that here the word is used to describe the process of making a society wealthier. Ask students to predict the challenges that might occur in trying to develop an entire nation.

Working Toward Development

Tell students that many new nations emerged in Africa and Latin America after World War II. These nations focused on development—the building of stable governments, improving agriculture and industry, and raising the standard of living. These areas are sometimes known as the global South because the areas are mostly south of the Tropic of Cancer.

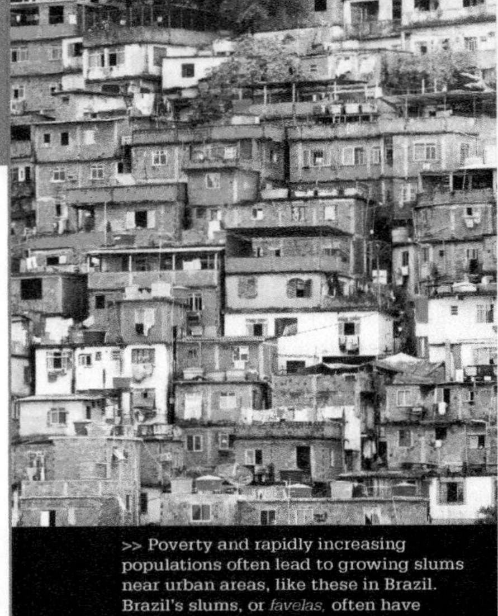

>> Poverty and rapidly increasing populations often lead to growing slums near urban areas, like these in Brazil. Brazil's slums, or *favelas*, often have serious problems with crime, gangs, and drugs.

21.1 **Many new nations emerged in Africa and Asia in the decades after World War II. These new nations, along with countries in Latin America, focused on development. Development is the process of building stable governments, improving agriculture and industry, and raising standards of living.**

TEKS
15.A, 15.B, 24.A

>> Objectives

Understand how nations in the developing world have tried to build strong economies.

Describe obstacles to development in the global South.

Explain how development is changing patterns of life in the developing world.

>> Key Terms

development
literacy
developing world
traditional economy
Green Revolution
fundamentalist
shantytown

Challenges of Development

Working Toward Development

The countries wrote constitutions that set up representative governments and protected the rights of citizens. Their leaders also pushed to build strong modern economies. Since a modern economy needs well-trained workers, developing nations built schools to increase **literacy,** or the ability to read and write.

The Global South The nations working toward development in Africa, Asia, and Latin America are known collectively as the **developing world.** The developing world is sometimes called the global South because it is located mostly south of the Tropic of Cancer.

The global South holds 75 percent of the world's people and much of its natural resources. It is poor, however, compared to the global North, the rich industrial nations located mostly north of the Tropic of Cancer. From the beginning, nations in the developing world faced many challenges.

Traditional Economies Despite these goals, much of the developing world still lived and worked in traditional economies. **Traditional economies** are economic systems that rely on custom and tradition,

PEARSON realize. www.PearsonTexas.com Access your Digital Lesson.

Aa Vocabulary Builder

1. Have students pronounce the following academic vocabulary term in this lesson and clarify the part of speech. Break the term into syllables and pronounce it with the students.
2. Explain what the word means in common "student-friendly" language using synonyms and antonyms when possible. Provide concrete examples to clarify the meaning, and rephrase the definition.

procure: make an effort to get

and tend not to change over time. In traditional economies, most people are farmers or craftspeople who use simple tools and methods of production passed down from earlier generations. They make or grow enough to meet their own needs, and trade any surplus, or extra, for goods they cannot make themselves. Property is often owned in common by a family or tribe.

Moving Toward Modernization Leaders of new nations in the developing world set ambitious economic goals. They wanted to increase food output; develop industry; construct roads, airports, and railroads; and build power plants.

Developing nations needed vast amounts of capital to finance projects to modernize their economies. After independence, some political leaders tried to speed development by replacing traditional and market economies with government-led command economies. This meant that governments owned most businesses and controlled farming.

Many countries that adopted command economies suffered. When their governments seized land and businesses, they destroyed the economic base of the upper class. Land redistribution programs gave land to more people, but in many cases did not increase productivity.

In Ethiopia, for example, farmers were limited to small plots and had little financial incentive to produce high yields, because prices were limited by the government to below market value. Low productivity, combined with drought, led to a severe famine in Ethiopia in the 1980s.

In addition, many developing nations fell into heavy debt. To pay for development, they procured large loans from banks and governments in the global North. When poor economic conditions made it difficult for these countries to repay their loans, lenders insisted that developing countries sell government businesses, hold free elections, and establish market economies. Lenders required these changes so developing countries could pay off debts and be eligible for new loans.

After developing countries shifted to market economies, companies and individuals from the global North invested in industries in these countries. Investors put money into businesses that produced profits for them and consumer goods for the industrialized world. Some critics have argued that these economic decisions benefited foreign investors more than the developing nation's economy.

The Green Revolution During the 1950s and 1960s, new high-yield seeds, fertilizers, and pesticides, along

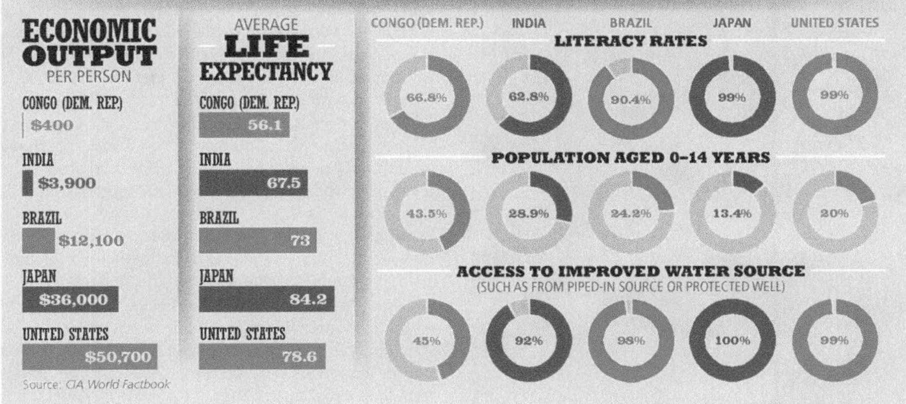

>> This chart compares developed and developing nations on a number of measures. **Analyze Charts** What generalization can you make about the age distribution in developed and developing countries, based on the data in this chart?

Interactive Map

Topic 21 Lesson 1

Analyze Images

Ask students to look at the image of the slum on the previous page. Ask: What does the photo suggest about life in the global South? *(Some people live in poverty.)* What does it suggest about the choice between city life and rural life facing those in the developing world? *(For many, city life involves poverty and hardship. Since so many people still choose city life, conditions are probably even worse in rural areas.)*

Guided Reading and Discussion

Discuss how the Green Revolution increased farm output but hurt smaller farmers. *(As production increased, prices for crops dropped. Only big landowners who could afford the new tools and methods could survive the drop in crop prices.)*

Ask: What are the main features of a traditional economy? *(property owned by families or ethnic groups; economic activity and consumer choice limited by custom; production limited to fulfilling the needs of the group)* Review the definition of *market economy. (an economic system in which decisions on production and consumption are based on voluntary exchanges in markets according to the laws of supply and demand)*

Be sure students understand how countries that adopted a command economy suffered. Governments seized land and businesses. Land redistribution gave people land, but there was little incentive to expand crop and livestock production.

Identify Cause and Effect Explain that during the Green Revolution, many small farmers had to sell their farms and move to cities. Ask: What hardships might they have faced in the city? *(lack of housing; not trained for available jobs)*

History Background

The People Behind the Green Revolution American scientist Norman Borlaug helped start the Green Revolution. He created a new kind of wheat that helped Mexico triple its grain production. This news reached Chidambaram Subramaniam, who was in charge of India's agriculture. Worried about his country's chronic food shortages, Subramaniam flew thousands of tons of Borlaug's seeds to India and brought Borlaug to teach farmers how to grow them. Wheat production in India soared by 60 percent. For his work, Borlaug won the 1970 Nobel Peace Prize.

Critics have said that the use of fertilizer and pesticide along with grain hurts the environment. Borlaug responded that by producing higher yields, his approach helped prevent deforestation that would result from the need to clear more land for farming.

Answers

Analyze Charts *Developing countries have younger populations than developed countries.*

Challenges to Development

Online Project the **Interactive Map: Global Population Growth**, and click on the layers of the map.

ACTIVE CLASSROOM

Have students Make Headlines about population growth based on what they learned in the Interactive Map. Ask: If you were to write a headline about predicted population growth right now, what would that headline be? Tell them to pass their headlines to a partner for them to review.

Guided Reading and Discussion

Summarize Ask students to explain the issues surrounding expanding populations in developing countries. Tell them to trade their papers with a partner and then read the summaries aloud to one another. *(Sample response: The growing population needs food, housing, education, jobs, and health care. Lack of money and resources leads to a cycle of poverty.)*

Make Generalizations Explain that some developing countries have a one-crop economy. Ask students how this can hinder the economic stability of the country. What could be done to create a more stable economy for the country? *(Sample response: The country must reduce its dependence on one crop. By diversifying the products it produces, the country can weather fluctuations in global demand.)*

D Differentiate Extra Support Have students write one cause-and-effect statement for each heading in the reading. Discuss with students how, if at all, each cause could be modified to improve the outcome or effect.

with mechanical equipment such as tractors, were introduced in many parts of the developing world. These new products, along with new methods of farming, are known as the **Green Revolution.**

The Green Revolution raised farm output in developing countries. But it had unforeseen consequences. Only big landowners could afford these new tools and methods. Because they farmed more land, they could grow crops more cheaply than farmers with small plots. As a result, prices for crops dropped below what smaller farmers needed to make to earn a living. Many were forced to sell their farms to big landowners. They became farm workers or moved to cities.

? DESCRIBE By what means did leaders of developing nations first try to modernize their economies?

ELPS ELPS 1.F.1 To learn new words about economic development, create a graphic organizer of each key term that includes the term's actual definition and one you write in your own words.

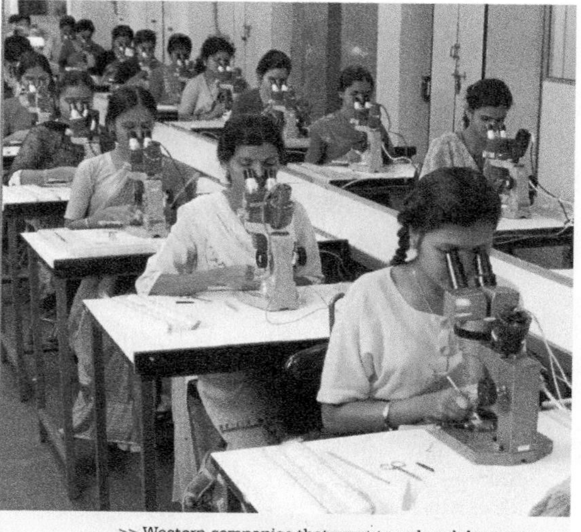

>> Western companies that want to reduce labor costs find a large, available workforce in developing nations. In this factory in India, women create computer parts for a rapidly growing electronics industry.

Challenges to Development

Despite ambitious goals, many new nations made little progress toward development. The reasons varied, but many countries shared similar problems. Poverty, rapidly rising populations, economic dependence, and unstable governments all posed challenges to development.

Populations Skyrocket In developing countries, improved healthcare and greater food supplies lowered death rates and led to explosive population growth. But with a booming population comes new challenges. All of these people need food, housing, education, jobs, and healthcare. Meeting these needs puts a huge burden on governments already strapped for funding.

Although the governments of many developing nations have tried to slow population growth, their efforts have met with limited success. In many cultures with traditional economies, children are valued as a source of labor and a support for parents in old age. Religious traditions also encourage large families.

Across the developing world, millions are trapped in a cycle of poverty. Many people, especially children, die each year from starvation, disease, and other effects of poverty. Because of malnutrition and the lack of good schools, millions are prone to disease and unable to earn a living wage. They and their children are unable to escape this tragic cycle.

Economic Dependence Despite their efforts to build industry, many developing nations remain economically dependent on their former colonial rulers. Western nations had used their colonies as sources of raw materials. They used the raw materials to produce manufactured goods that they sold to their colonies.

This pattern continued after colonies won their independence. Industrialized countries purchase agricultural goods and raw materials from the developing world. In turn, the industrial nations provide technology, investment, and manufactured goods to developing countries. However, in recent years, lower labor costs have led Western companies to relocate their manufacturing operations to the global South.

Some developing nations produce only a single export crop or commodity, such as sugar or cocoa. Their economies depend on global demand for the cash crop or commodity. If demand weakens and prices drop, their economies suffer.

Unstable Governments Civil wars and other conflicts hinder development in some countries. Poor leadership and corrupt governments also prevent

English Language Proficiency Standards

Learning Strategies 1.F.1 Review the key terms in "Working Toward Development." Guide students to use accessible words to learn these new terms by completing graphic organizers.

Beginning Using visuals where possible as support, discuss the meaning of each of the key terms in "Working Toward Development." Provide a short definition for each word. Then, as a group, create a graphic organizer for each key term by completing it with its actual definition and a definition created by students with accessible words.

Intermediate Using visuals where possible, discuss the meaning of each key term in "Working Toward Development." Have small groups create a graphic organizer for the key terms, including the actual definition and their own definition using accessible words. Have each group share their work.

Advanced Have partners look up the key terms in "Working Toward Development" in the glossary or a dictionary. Using these definitions, have them write their own definitions using accessible words

Answers

Describe *by establishing government control of the economy and borrowing large sums to finance new projects*

growth. Dictators spend resources on weapons instead of on education or healthcare. Corrupt leaders loot their nations' treasuries and allow a culture of bribery to thrive.

SUMMARIZE How did dependence on colonial rulers affect economic progress in the developing world?

Development Brings Social Change

Economic development has unleashed great changes across the developing world. Just as the Industrial Revolution disrupted traditional ways of life in Europe and North America, economic development is now transforming life in the global South.

Opportunity Increases for Women In the developing world, the move away from traditional ways of life has brought new opportunities for women. New constitutions granted equality to women, at least on paper. In some countries, such as India, Argentina, and Liberia, women have served as heads of state. Although women still have less access to education than men, the gap has narrowed. Women are joining the work force in growing numbers and contributing their skills to their nations' wealth.

Child Labor In traditional economies, children worked alongside parents, farming or herding to meet the family's needs. When development forces people off their farms, they often move to cities and take low-paying manufacturing jobs. Because these jobs do not pay enough to cover basic needs, parents depend on the low wages that children earn in factory jobs to survive. In India, around 44 million children work for pay. In Pakistan, children make up 10 percent of the workforce.

Religious Fundamentalism In recent decades, religious revivals have swept many developing nations. Some religious leaders are called **fundamentalists,** because they call for a return to what they see as the fundamental, or basic, values of their faiths. Many seek political power to oppose changes that undermine their valued religious traditions.

Rapid Growth of Cities Across the developing world, people have flooded into cities to escape rural poverty and find jobs. Besides economic opportunities, cities offer attractions such as entertainment and sports.

>> In 2006, Ellen Johnson Sirleaf became president of Liberia. She is the first elected female head of state in Africa. At a conference in Canada, she spoke of her determination to build democracy in her nation.

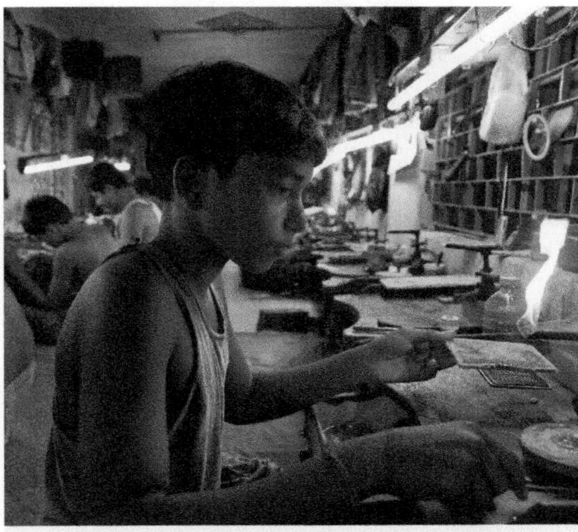

>> In Kolkata, India, a young boy works along with adults in a factory that produces gold jewelry. Many of the hundreds of goldsmiths in Kolkata employ children, who work 14 to 18 hours a day.

 Interactive Gallery

Topic 21 Lesson 1

Development Brings Social Change

Economic development is changing life in the global South. New constitutions have granted equality to women, and in some countries women have served as heads of state. Women are joining the workforce in growing numbers. Many children work in factories for low wages to help families survive.

Online Project the **Interactive Gallery: Children of the Developing World**, and click through the images of the gallery.

ACTIVE CLASSROOM

Ask students to use the Graffiti Concepts strategy to reflect on life for children in the developing world and then to create a phrase that represents that concept. Allow approximately 3–5 minutes, and then ask students to post their "graffiti" on the board or on chart paper. Have them look at the various responses and then discuss similarities and differences in the responses as a group.

Guided Reading and Discussion

Ask students to explain the effects of economic development. Discuss how repressive governments place economic development over the rights of citizens. Many developing nations also face religious fundamentalists trying to take power.

Identify Cause and Effect In many developing countries, children have to work to help support their families. Ask: What effects might countries with high child labor rates experience in the future? *(If children work and do not get an education, the country may face a shortage of educated workers in the future.)*

and then complete a graphic organizer with their own definitions and those from the glossary or dictionary. Have them share their definitions with the group.

Advanced High Have students work independently to complete the Advanced activity.

Answers

Summarize *The old pattern of reliance on the colonial power as a market for resources continued, and in some cases, countries have become reliant on only one export to support their economies.*

SYNTHESIZE

Online Project the **Digital Activity: The Risks and Benefits of Global Development**. Ask students to recall the Topic Essential Question, "What are the benefits and risks of interdependence?" How does this relate to the dependence of the developing world on the developed world? Have students write down some brief answers to these questions and then share them with a talking partner. *(Students should think about the attempts of developing nations to remove themselves from their former colonial rulers. Students should also consider how effective these attempts have been in light of the interdependence between the labor force and industrialization in the developed and developing world.)*

DEMONSTRATE

Online Assign the **Digital Lesson Quiz** for this lesson if you haven't already done so. Students will be offered automatic remediation or enrichment based on their score.

Pose these questions to the class on the Discussion Board:

Predict Consequences How do you think increased social and economic roles for women and better educational prospects for children will affect developing countries? *(Possible response: Living standards will rise as women assume greater roles in the economy and children are able to receive more education.)*

Identify Central Issues How has rapid population growth affected developing nations? *(It has put pressure on local and national governments to try to provide public services and has led to poverty and high unemployment.)*

Topic Inquiry

Have students continue their investigations for the Topic Inquiry.

Answers

Explain *Women have somewhat greater equality and opportunity for education and employment.*

With no money and few jobs, most newcomers settle in **shantytowns,** crowded, dangerous slums on the edges of cities. These crime-ridden slums lack basic services such as running water, electricity, or sewer systems.

EXPLAIN In what ways have women's lives changed due to economic development in the developing world?

ASSESSMENT

1. **Express Ideas Clearly** Describe how economic policy in developing nations has changed in the years since independence.
2. **Summarize** What are the main obstacles to economic and political progress in developing nations?
3. **Recall** What are four ways that development has changed life in the developing world?
4. **Contrast** Describe the differences between the global South and the global North.
5. **Explain** What is the Green Revolution, and how did it affect the developing world?

Assessment

1. First, leaders established government control over businesses and borrowed heavily. Then, when the nations were in debt, the leaders switched to market economies.
2. high population growth, economic dependence on former colonial rulers, reliance on export, and government conflicts
3. greater opportunities for women, more children working in factories, increased fundamentalism, and explosive growth of cities
4. The global South is located south of the Tropic of Cancer, holds 75 percent of the world's people, contains much of Earth's natural resources, and is mostly poor. The global North is north of the Tropic of Cancer and holds most of the industrialized nations.
5. The Green Revolution was the spread of high-yield seeds, fertilizers, and pesticides, along with mechanical equipment, to the developing world. It raised farm output but also forced small farmers off their lands.

21.2 In the 1950s and 1960s, dozens of new African nations won independence from colonial rule. In South Africa, however, the struggle for freedom was different. South Africa had achieved self-rule from Britain as early as 1910. Freedom, however, was limited to white settlers. The black majority was denied the right to vote. Whites made up less than 20 percent of the population but controlled the government and the economy. The white-minority government passed racial laws that severely restricted the black majority.

>> Nelson Mandela and F. W. de Klerk won the Nobel Peace Prize in 1994 for their work to end apartheid.

 Interactive Flipped Video

Challenges for African Nations

TEKS 13.E, 18.C, 21.C, 22.E

>> Objectives

Summarize the struggle for equality in South Africa and identify how Nelson Mandela led resistance efforts.

Describe choices African nations had to make as they developed their economies.

Understand the challenges African nations face.

>> Key Terms

apartheid
African National Congress (ANC)
Sharpeville
Nelson Mandela
Desmond Tutu
F.W. de Klerk
socialism
desertification
urbanization
endangered species
Wangari Maathai
sustainable development

The Struggle for Equality in South Africa

Apartheid Is Established In 1948, the government expanded the existing system of racial segregation, and created the policy known as **apartheid,** or the separation of the races. Under apartheid, all South Africans were registered by race: Black, White, Colored (people of mixed ancestry), Asian. Supporters of apartheid claimed it would allow each race to protect its culture. In fact, the policy was designed to keep white control over South Africa.

Under apartheid, nonwhites faced many restrictions. Increasingly, blacks were treated like foreigners in their own land. Laws were passed that stipulated segregated restaurants, beaches, and schools. Other laws restricted where people could live and banned marriages between the races. Among the most hated were the Pass Laws enacted in 1952, which required all blacks to carry pass books at all times, wherever they went. Black workers were paid less than whites for the same job. Blacks could not own land in most areas. Low wages and inferior schooling condemned most blacks to poverty.

 www.PearsonTexas.com Access your Digital Lesson.

Aa Vocabulary Builder

1. Have students pronounce the following academic vocabulary terms in this lesson and clarify the part of speech. For difficult or polysyllabic words, break them into syllables and pronounce them with the students.
2. Explain what the word means in common "student-friendly" language using synonyms and antonyms when possible. Provide concrete examples to clarify the meaning, and rephrase the definition.

stipulated: required; specified

subsidize: support with government spending

Challenges for African Nations

CONNECT

Preview Have students preview the **Lesson Objectives** and the list of **Key Terms**.

Students can also preview all the **Key Terms** and **Academic Vocabulary** using the **Interactive Reading Notepad** on the digital course or preview a summary of the lesson in the **Reading and Note Taking Study Guide**.

Online Use the **Editable Presentation** found on the digital course to present the main ideas for this lesson.

Start Up Activity

Have students examine the photograph of Nelson Mandela and F. W. de Klerk. Ask: What do you know about Mandela and his influence on Africa and the world? *(Possible answer: Mandela worked to end apartheid. He was elected president in the first multiracial election. He worked with former opponents to bring peace and racial equality to South Africa.)*

Discuss Engage the class in a discussion about people who have helped change the world. How did they make an impact? *(Students might mention local leaders or famous leaders such as Mohandas Gandhi or Martin Luther King, Jr.)*

Online You can also project the **Start Up Activity** from the course.

INVESTIGATE

Have students read the section using the **Reading and Note Taking Study Guide** to help them take notes and understand the text as they read.

The Struggle for Equality in South Africa

Discuss with students the features of apartheid and what effect it had on the people of South Africa. Ask students: What effect did Sharpeville have on Nelson Mandela, and why? *(The Sharpeville massacre radicalized Mandela, and he shifted from a policy of nonviolence to believing that armed struggle was necessary.)*

Online Project the **Interactive Timeline: The Struggle Against Apartheid**, and work with students to correctly position each event. Encourage students to use the text to find any information they need.

ACTIVE CLASSROOM

Have students use the Make Headlines strategy to write headlines that capture the conditions depicted by the timeline. Ask: If you were to write a headline capturing the most important idea of the struggle against apartheid, what would the headline be? Exchange your headline with a partner and try to edit and improve each other's headlines.

Key Terms

Draw students' attention to the key term **F. W. de Klerk** (in bold) in the text. Tell them that after freeing political prisoners and lifting the ban on the ANC, de Klerk's government passed legislation repealing South Africa's discriminatory laws. A vote in 1992 indicated that more than 69 percent of white South Africans supported the government's reforms.

Guided reading and Discussion

Discuss how people in South Africa struggled for equality and how Nelson Mandela serves as an example of individuals who led resistance to political oppression.

Help students understand how apartheid became a more restrictive and violent system.

Draw Conclusions How did Nelson Mandela shift political thought in his own country and around the world? *(Sample response: Through his example, he convinced people that blacks in South Africa deserved justice. He also served as an example for others struggling against injustice.)*

>> More than 5,000 people attended the funerals of some of the people killed at Sharpeville. **Analyze Visuals** How does this image convey the impact of the Sharpeville massacre?

Interactive Timeline

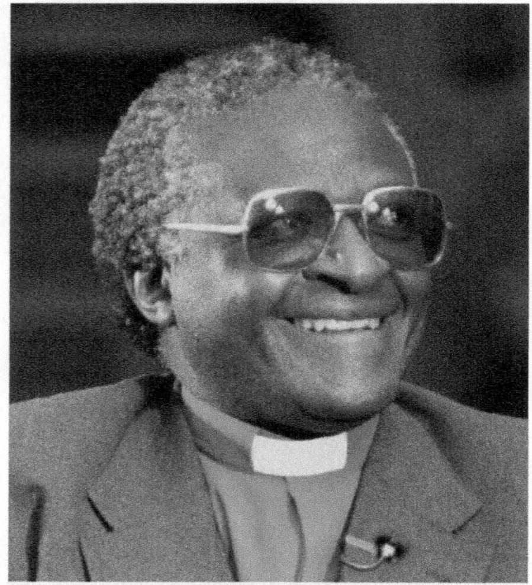

>> Archbishop Desmond Tutu has inspired the world with his unflinching opposition not only to apartheid in South Africa but to injustice everywhere.

Resistance Against Apartheid Black South Africans resisted apartheid. The **African National Congress (ANC)** emerged as the main party opposed to apartheid and led the struggle for majority rule. In the 1950s, the government imposed strict new rules to separate the races. The ANC organized marches, boycotts, and strikes.

In 1960, police gunned down 69 men, women, and children during a peaceful protest in **Sharpeville,** a black township. The government then outlawed the ANC and cracked down on other groups that opposed apartheid. The Sharpeville massacre led some ANC activists to shift from nonviolent protest to armed struggle.

Some leaders, like **Nelson Mandela,** went underground. As an ANC leader, Mandela had first mobilized young South Africans to peacefully resist apartheid laws. As government oppression grew, Mandela joined ANC militants and helped form a military wing within the ANC. Mandela was arrested, tried, and, in 1964, condemned to life in prison for treason. Even in prison, he remained a powerful symbol of the struggle for freedom and resistance against political oppression.

In 1976, as a shocked world looked on, almost 600 people were killed in protests that began in the township of Soweto and international pressure against the regime began to grow. In the 1980s, demands for an end to apartheid and for Mandela's release began to have an effect. Many countries imposed economic sanctions on South Africa, including the United States, which began to impose sanctions in 1986. In 1984, black South African bishop **Desmond Tutu** won the Nobel Peace Prize for his nonviolent opposition to apartheid.

Majority Rule Is Established Outside pressure and protests at home finally convinced South African president **F. W. de Klerk** to end apartheid. In 1990, he lifted the ban on the ANC and freed Mandela. In 1993, Mandela and de Klerk jointly won the Nobel Peace Prize for their efforts in ending apartheid.

Finally in 1994, South Africans of every race were allowed to vote for the first time. Voters chose Nelson Mandela as president in South Africa's first multiracial election. Mandela worked to heal the country's wounds. "Let us build together," he declared. He welcomed old foes into his government, including whites who had supported apartheid. Through his powerful example, he helped shift the political climate in South Africa.

Since 1994, South Africa has faced huge challenges. With majority rule, black South Africans expected a better life. Although South Africa was a rich, industrial country, it had limited resources to spend on housing,

Answers

Analyze Visuals *The row of coffins shows that many people were killed. The large number of mourners shows that people were strongly affected by the deaths.*

education, and other programs. The income and education gap between blacks and whites remained large. Poverty and unemployment were high among blacks. The AIDS epidemic hit South Africa severely. As South Africa's government struggled with these problems, the global economic slowdown created new challenges.

? SUMMARIZE What factors finally brought about the end of apartheid?

African Nations Face Economic Choices

The African nations that achieved independence after World War II are part of the developing world. As they set out to build stable governments and modern economies, they faced serious challenges.

The Challenges of Development In Africa, as elsewhere, development meant building productive economies and raising standards of living. To achieve these goals, African nations had to establish industries, build transportation systems, increase literacy, and reduce poverty. Many countries had little capital to invest in such projects.

Each nation had to make difficult choices about how to achieve their goals. To obtain the capital necessary to develop their economies, many African countries maintained close ties with their former colonial rulers. The European countries provided the new African nations with strong trade relationships, direct investment, and loans.

Socialism or Capitalism? Many newly independent nations were attracted to **socialism,** a system in which the people as a whole own all property and operate all businesses. Through socialism, the new nations hoped to reduce dependence on their former colonial rulers and end the inequalities between rich and poor. To regulate the economy, socialism relied on large, generally inefficient bureaucracies.

Socialism is different than communism, and in some African countries a specific brand of socialism developed. "African socialism" was based on village traditions of cooperation and shared responsibility. While many countries in Africa have had socialist governments, no country in Africa has ever been strictly communist.

Some nations chose capitalism, or market economies with private ownership of property, as a path to development. To get the huge sums needed for development, they turned to foreign lenders to invest capital in new industries. These countries often had more efficient economies, but foreign lenders took more profits out of the country.

>> Many industries flourish throughout Africa. In Nigeria, for example, the oil industry is dominant. These men are working on an oil rig in Nigeria's River State.

Still, by the 2010s, many African nations were making major strides toward economic development. The African nations with the fastest growing economies in 2013 included Malawi, Mozambique, Angola, Ethiopia, and Zambia.

Cash Crops or Food? Governments tried to raise development funds by raising cash crops for export, such as coffee or cotton, or exporting a commodity, such as copper or oil. However, dependence on a single crop or commodity is risky because it puts economies at the mercy of sudden price changes in the market.

Because land used for cash crops could not be used to produce food, some countries had to buy costly imported food. To prevent unrest among the urban poor, many governments kept food prices artificially low. However, low prices discouraged local farmers from growing food crops. Governments then had to subsidize part of the cost of importing food.

? GENERATE EXPLANATIONS Why did some African governments promote cash crops? What problems did this create?

African Nations Face Economic Choices

After independence, African nations developed different economic systems. Some chose socialism, and others chose capitalism. A key economic issue was reliance on a single cash crop. Help students identify the characteristics of socialism in Africa.

Identify Steps in a Process Ask: How could the reliance on cash crops lead to an economic deficit? What would have to happen for the cash crop to be an economic benefit? *(Cash crops mean less land for growing food, which leads to the need to import food, which leads to money spent on food rather than on development. The government would have to make more from the crop than it spent on importing food.)*

Guided Reading and Discussion

Discuss how African nations developed economically. Make sure students understand the difference between socialism and communism. Also point out that some African nations were making important strides toward prosperity.

Compare Points of View Ask: Why did some leaders believe socialism was the best economic choice? *(They thought it would help reduce inequality.)* Why did others hope capitalism was the best choice? *(They thought it would promote foreign lending and more development.)*

Analyze Context Ask: How might the history of the continent have influenced some leaders' decisions? *(Students should show an understanding that some leaders might have felt anger toward their former rulers and wanted to distance their countries from them.)*

D Differentiate Challenge/Gifted Have students learn more about African socialism. Who were its proponents? Why was it developed? Did it succeed? Why or why not? How was it different from other forms of socialism around the world?

Answers

Summarize *armed struggle, internal protests, strikes and boycotts, external sanctions and pressure*

Generate Explanations *Governments needed the money for development projects, but this meant that they were not growing enough food.*

Topic 21 Lesson 2

Continuing Challenges to Development

Online Project the **Interactive Gallery: Environmental Challenges in Africa**, and take students through the items in it. Help students recognize how deforestation and desertification are linked.

ACTIVE CLASSROOM

Ask students to Take a Stand on the following question: Do the economic needs of Africa outweigh the risks and drawbacks of development? Ask students to divide into two groups based on their answer and move to separate areas of the classroom. Ask students to talk with each other to compare their reasons for answering *yes* or *no*. Ask a representative from each side to present and defend the group's point of view.

Analyze Images

Call students' attention to the infographic showing the growth of Lagos, Nigeria. Ask: By how much is Lagos's population expected to grow during the period 2015–2025? *(by more than 10 million people)*

Guided Reading and Discussion

Help students summarize how Africa's challenges are among the reasons there are ongoing conflicts there. Ask: Is the urbanization of Africa similar to industrialization in Europe and North America? Why or why not?

D Differentiate Special Needs Help students understand how deforestation leads to desertification. In two trays, plant seedlings. Once the seedlings are growing, cut all the seedlings in one tray. Then lower the amount of watering. Note that the soil with the growing seedlings stays moist longer than the tray with the exposed soil.

Continuing Challenges to Development

Developing African nations face numerous problems. The challenges include famine, rapid population growth, epidemics, and damage to the environment and wildlife.

Desertification and Famine From time to time, droughts struck parts of Africa, killing livestock and crops. The Sahel, a semidesert region just south of the Sahara, was especially hard hit in the late 1960s. The drought, which lasted for decades, led to famine. Overgrazing and farming in this fragile area removed topsoil and led to **desertification,** or a change of semidry land into desert. International relief efforts eased the famine, but wars that raged in several countries in the Sahel added to the suffering.

The AIDS Epidemic Since the 1980s, the deadly disease AIDS (Acquired Immune Deficiency Syndrome), has spread across Africa. AIDS is caused by HIV, a virus that damages the body's ability to fight infections. In South Africa and Botswana, up to one third of adults were infected with HIV. More than 11 million children in Africa have been orphaned by the AIDS epidemic.

The loss of so many skilled and productive workers hurt the economies of African countries. A global effort to combat AIDS led to the development of drugs to treat people infected with HIV. African nations set up treatment programs and worked hard to stop the spread of AIDS.

Migration from Villages to Cities African nations experienced rapid **urbanization,** or the movement of people from rural areas to cities. The newcomers hoped to find a better life. Instead, millions faced unemployment, terrible living conditions, and crime. However, in much of West Africa, the growth of cities has provided increased opportunities for women, who have historically dominated urban markets as traders.

Urbanization also brought people from different ethnic groups together and helped replace ethnic loyalties with a larger national identity. But modern urban lifestyles weakened traditional cultures and undermined ethnic and kinship ties. Despite rapid urbanization, most people in Africa still lived in villages.

Environmental Concerns In Africa, as elsewhere, urbanization, population growth, farming, and logging led to the destruction of Africa's animal habitats. As habitats were destroyed, some animals became **endangered species,** or species threatened with

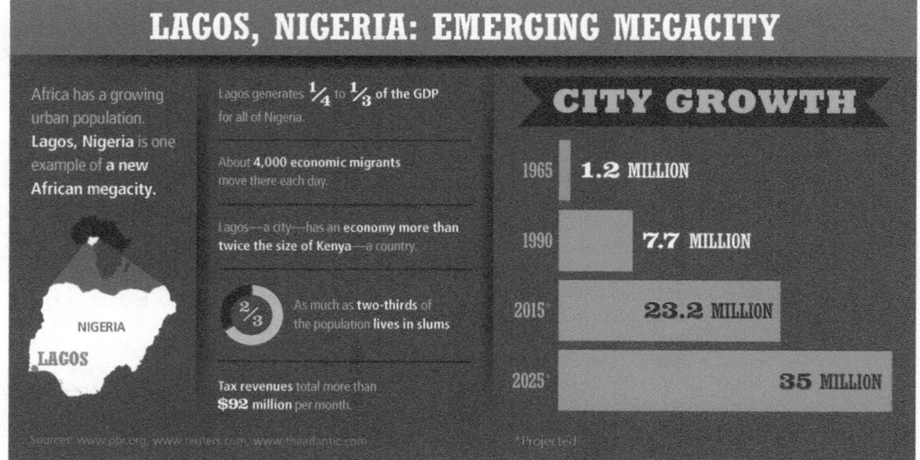

>> Lagos, Nigeria, is growing rapidly and is one of the biggest cities in Africa. **Analyze Data** What does the data shown here tell you about the benefits and drawbacks of rapid urban growth?

History Background

The threats to Africa's endangered species include a loss of habitats and poaching, or illegal hunting. Elephants, for example, have been killed for their valuable tusks. Leopards have been killed to meet foreign demand for their skins. In addition, most of Africa's forests have been disturbed or cut down. However, Africans are now taking steps to save their rich wildlife, in part because it draws foreign tourists. These tourists provide a steady income to local guides and tour operators, which gives Africans a stake in preventing poaching. Many African nations have set aside preserves to protect endangered species, such as mountain gorillas in Rwanda.

Answers

Analyze Data *Rapid urban growth can create huge revenues for a city but can also lead to poverty and urban blight.*

extinction. Foreign demand for elephant tusks to make ivory, or for rare pelts or furs, has encouraged impoverished Africans to kill endangered animals, even when it is illegal.

In Kenya, **Wangari Maathai** (mah THY), an environmental activist, started the Green Belt Movement. She was inspired to plant trees with women to help them meet basic needs, such as energy, clean drinking water, and nutritious food. Maathai wanted to heal the land, empower women, and promote **sustainable development,** or development that meets the needs of the present without compromising the ability of future generations to meet their own needs.

IDENTIFY CAUSE AND EFFECT Why has the AIDS epidemic so profoundly affected the economies of Africa?

>> Drought is a problem in many areas of Africa. This woman in Kenya digs for water at the bottom of a dry riverbed.

Interactive Gallery

>> Wangari Maathai of Kenya won the Nobel Peace Prize in 2004 for her work in promoting sustainable development.

ASSESSMENT

1. **Summarize** How did Nelson Mandela help shift political thought in South Africa?
2. **Describe** Describe the apartheid regime and the struggle for equality in South Africa.
3. **Infer** Why did some African leaders believe that "African socialism" would work better than a European model? What problems arose?
4. **Identify Central Issues** What do you think is the greatest challenge facing developing African countries today? Give reasons for your answer.
5. **Make Predictions** What effect will urbanization have on Africa? Will it be positive or negative?

Topic 21 Lesson 2

SYNTHESIZE

Online Project the **Digital Activity: Glory and Hope**. Remind students of the main issues connected to the lesson and the challenges faced by Africa as it moves to modernize. Project the Synthesize screen, and have students read the excerpt and answer the questions.

Discuss Ask: What does Mandela mean by "the healing of the wounds"? What does he mean by "there is no easy road to freedom"? Why does he talk of "national reconciliation"?

DEMONSTRATE

Assign the **Digital Lesson Quiz** for this lesson if you haven't already done so. Students will be offered automatic remediation or enrichment based on their score.

Pose this question to the class on the Discussion Board:

Predict Consequences What do you think will happen in Africa in the next 50 years, and why? *(Answers will vary. Some students may believe that the problems facing the nations of Africa will lead to a bleak future for the continent. Other students may point to positive shifts in African economics and politics.)*

Topic Inquiry

Have students continue their investigations for the Topic Inquiry.

Assessment

1. He fought for the rights of his people and went to jail for his beliefs; he also negotiated with his enemies and included them in his government.
2. Answers should mention pass laws, lack of voting rights, and segregation. Strikes, boycotts, protests, and armed struggle should be included in the opponents' response.
3. African leaders thought that socialism based on traditional beliefs and political systems would be better for their people and more effective. However, corruption and large, inefficient bureaucracies were problems.
4. Possible responses: AIDS epidemic, environmental damage, poverty, corruption, or war
5. Some students might argue that urbanization will lead to increased poverty and a loss of traditional values, while others might point to the growth of a middle class spurred by industrialization and a decrease in ethnic violence.

Answers

Identify Cause and Effect *AIDS robbed Africa of its most productive generations and left millions of orphans who require care, placing economic and social pressure on the countries affected.*

Topic 21 Lesson 3

Rapid Development in China and India

CONNECT

Preview Have students preview the **Lesson Objectives** and the list of **Key Terms**.

Students can also preview all the **Key Terms** and **Academic Vocabulary** using the **Interactive Reading Notepad** on the digital course or preview a summary of the lesson in the **Reading and Note Taking Study Guide**.

Online Use the **Editable Presentation** found on the digital course to present the main ideas for this lesson.

Start Up Activity

Ask students if they have ever seen the phrase "Made in China" on anything they own. Is there anything in the classroom that was made in China? Tell students that many of the things that people buy all around the world are made in China. Economic reforms made in the 1980s more than quadrupled China's economic output by the early 2000s. Then have students predict how China's transformation into an economic powerhouse has impacted the world economy.

Online You can also project the **Start Up Activity** from the course.

INVESTIGATE

Have students read the section using the **Reading and Note Taking Study Guide** to help them take notes and understand the text as they read.

Reform and Repression in China

China is a leading Asian and global power. Mao Zedong, China's first communist leader, died in 1976 and was replaced by a more moderate leader, Deng Xiaoping. Deng's main interest was in improving the economy in China. Collectively owned farms were dismantled. Deng welcomed foreign capital, technology, and investment.

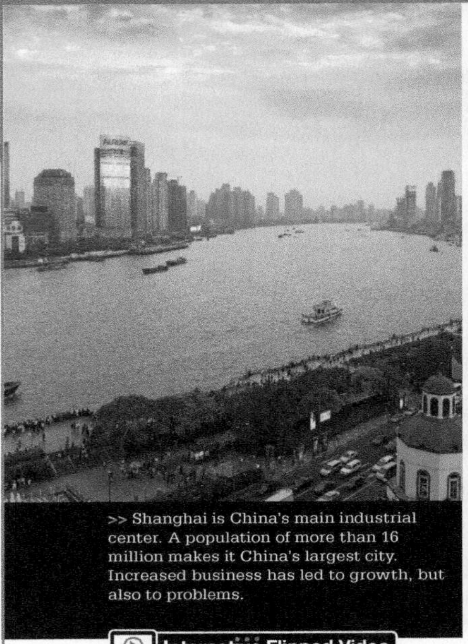

>> Shanghai is China's main industrial center. A population of more than 16 million makes it China's largest city. Increased business has led to growth, but also to problems.

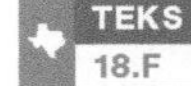 Interactive Flipped Video

21.3 China and India dominate much of Asia. Together, they are home to about two fifths of the world's population. China is a major industrial nation. Although India's economy is smaller, like China, it is a leading Asian and global power. Over the last 60 years, China and India have taken different paths toward development.

TEKS
18.F

>> Objectives

Describe how China has moved toward a free market economy without allowing democratic reform.

Identify continuing challenges that China faces.

Explain how India has built its economy.

Summarize social reforms in modern India.

>> Key Terms

Deng Xiaoping
Tiananmen Square
one-child policy
Kolkata
Mumbai
Mother Teresa
dalit

Rapid Development in China and India

Reform and Repression in China

A New Approach to the Chinese Economy Mao Zedong, China's communist revolutionary leader, died in 1976. After Mao's death, more moderate leaders took control of China. By 1981, **Deng Xiaoping** (dung show ping), had taken a new approach to China's economy. Deng was a practical reformer, more interested in improving economic output than in political purity. "I don't care if a cat is black or white," he declared, "as long as it catches mice."

Deng's program, the Four Modernizations, emphasized agriculture, industry, science, and defense. The plan allowed some features of a free market, such as some private ownership of property. Communes, or collectively owned farms, were dismantled, and peasant families were allotted plots of farmland in what was called the "responsibility system." Farmers still did not own the land, and the government took a share of their crops. However, farmers could sell any surplus produce and keep their profits.

Chinese entrepreneurs were allowed to set up businesses. Managers of state-run factories were given more freedom, but they had to make their plants more efficient. Deng also welcomed foreign

 www.PearsonTexas.com Access your Digital Lesson.

930

Aa Vocabulary Builder

1. Have students pronounce the following academic vocabulary terms in this lesson and clarify the part of speech. For difficult or polysyllabic words, break them into syllables and pronounce them with the students.
2. Explain what the word means in common "student-friendly" language using synonyms and antonyms when possible. Provide concrete examples to clarify the meaning, and rephrase the definition.

disperse: break up and scatter

stimulus: something that causes something else to happen

impose: to use authority to make someone do something

capital and technology. Investors from Japan, Hong Kong, Taiwan, and Western nations invested heavily in Chinese firms.

Economic reforms brought a surge of growth. In coastal cities, foreign investment created an economic boom. Some Chinese enjoyed an improved standard of living. They bought refrigerators, televisions, and cars. On the other hand, crime and corruption increased and a growing economic and regional gap developed between poor rural farmers and wealthy city dwellers.

Protest in Tiananmen Square Economic reforms and increased contact with the West led some Chinese to demand greater political freedom. In the late 1980s, students, workers, and others created a democracy movement similar to those sweeping across Eastern Europe. However, Deng and other Chinese leaders refused to allow democratic reforms.

In 1989, thousands of protesters, many of them students, occupied **Tiananmen (*TYEN* ahn mun) Square,** a huge public plaza in Beijing. They raised banners calling for democracy. The government ordered the protesters to disperse. When they refused, the government sent in troops and tanks. Thousands of demonstrators were killed or wounded in the Tiananmen Square Massacre. Many others were imprisoned and tortured. The crackdown showed that the communist government was determined to keep control.

? DRAW CONCLUSIONS What unintended consequences did the Chinese government's reforms during the 1980s have on the Chinese population?

Reforms Bring Growth and Challenges

Economic reforms had more than quadrupled China's economic output by the early 2000s. China's industrial power made it a growing rival of the United States. China's achievements—symbolized by the newly built Beijing National Stadium—were displayed to the world when it hosted the 2008 summer Olympic games. But the country still faced serious internal challenges.

Rapid Industrialization Boom times led to rapid urbanization as millions of rural workers flooded into China's cities. Urban newcomers worked for low wages in manufacturing jobs. Although these workers lived in poverty, their needs strained local resources. Rapid development brought other problems. Industrial production led to dangerously polluted air and water. One scientific study attributed pollution as the cause of premature death for some 1.2 million Chinese in 2010. Increased travel and trade helped spread AIDS and other diseases across China.

The global economic recession that began in 2008 took its toll. Chinese factories closed as overseas orders fell. As the economy slowed and unemployment rose, many workers returned to family homes in rural areas. Protests by unemployed urban workers increased. To prevent social unrest, the government announced an economic stimulus package to improve productivity and retrain workers. In 2013, some economists declared that the Chinese economy might be headed into a recession, as manufacturing slowed, retail sales dipped, and the number of jobs created did not keep pace with previous levels of expansion.

Human Rights Abuses Despite the global outcry after the Tiananmen Square Massacre, China continued to jail critics and limit freedom. Human rights activists inside and outside China protested abuses such as lack of free speech and the use of prison labor to produce cheap goods for export.

Many protests have focused on Tibet, a region that has been under Chinese control since the 1950s. The Chinese government has suppressed Tibet's ancient Buddhist culture.

>> The day after the massacre in Tiananmen Square, a lone protestor stepped in front of a line of tanks. The "Tank Man" became a worldwide symbol of individuals standing against government oppression.

Interactive Gallery

Online Project the **Interactive Gallery: Protests in Tiananmen Square**, and review each image.

ACTIVE CLASSROOM

Use the See-Think-Wonder strategy with students as they review the gallery of the protest in Tiananmen Square. Ask them to talk about the following questions: What do you see? What does that make you think? What are you wondering about now that you've seen this? Have groups discuss their answers with others in the class. *(Possible response: The images show anger, passion, and fear. Students may wonder what the protesters' lives are like without the freedoms offered in other countries.)*

Key Terms

Direct students' attention to the key term **Tiananmen Square** (in bold) in the text. Tell them that this wasn't the only protest for democracy happening in China at the time. Protests took place in hundreds of cities, including Shanghai.

Guided Reading and Discussion

Be sure students understand that while Chinese leaders wanted economic expansion, they did not want an expansion in personal freedoms.

Predict Consequences Ask: Do you think that China can continue to develop economically without making political reforms? Explain. *(Possible response: No; a lack of democratic rights will lead to political unrest that will hurt economic development.)*

D Differentiate Challenge/Gifted Have students find out more about the history of Tiananmen Square and create an infographic, using charts and/or a timeline to present the information.

History Background

Three Gorges Dam China recently completed construction of the world's largest dam. Located on the Chang (Yangtze) River, Three Gorges Dam is 607 feet high and around 1.4 miles long. It created a huge reservoir that allows ships to travel some 1,400 miles inland. Its turbines are capable of producing 22,500 megawatts of electricity. Still, the dam—thought to have cost as much as $75 billion to build—has sparked controversy. Officials say it protects millions from floods, generates electric power for one of the country's most underdeveloped regions, and improves navigation along the river. Critics point out that the new lake flooded 13 cities and 140 towns, forcing some 1.5 million people to relocate. In addition, the lake destroyed more than 1,000 important archaeological sites. Many people feared that pollution from industrial areas would run off into the reservoir and pollute it.

Answers

Draw Conclusions *They led to a greater desire for political freedom and a push for democracy, which in turn led to the massacre at Tiananmen Square.*

Reforms Bring Growth and Challenges

Economic reforms quadrupled China's economic output by the early 2000s. This growth led to rapid urbanization and industrialization. Pollution and disease spread across China, and human rights abuses continued.

Analyze Images

Direct students' attention to the mural of parents and a baby. Tell students that the one-child policy slowed population growth but also resulted in a population in which the elderly make up a large percentage. Ask: What emotions do you think this mural is trying to convey? *(Sample response: that parents should embrace the idea of one child and be happy)*

Guided Reading and Discussion

Tell students that in 2013, some political and social reforms were enacted, including a new policy allowing parents to have a second child. Ask students: Why did China's government want to limit population growth? *(Leaders believed that population growth could damage economic development.)* Have students think about how limiting population size too much could have negative consequences.

Predict Consequences Air and water pollution remains a problem in China. Ask: What are possible consequences if pollution is not controlled? *(Possible answer: continued premature deaths, more illness, less productivity, and a slowing of the economy)*

India Builds a Modern Economy

After independence in 1947, India adopted a socialist model but was pushed to a market economy in the 1980s. In the 1990s, Indian textiles, technology, and some other industries began to expand, and by 2000, India was a leader in information technology.

>> China imposed a strict one-child policy in the 1980s. This mural encourages parents to be satisfied with a single child.

>> Representatives meet in the Parliament Building in New Delhi, India. As a democracy, India has a constitution and elected leaders, including a president, chosen by an electoral college, and a parliament, elected by the voters.

China's trading partners called for an end to human rights abuses. Party leaders said that outsiders had no right to try to impose "Western-style" ideas of human rights on China. However, China's cabinet issued the country's first human rights action plan in 2009. It included the right to question government policies.

Limited Reform on Human Rights Issues In November 2013, the Chinese government took more tentative steps toward economic, social, and political reform when it announced new policies on some of China's most notorious human rights issues. These reforms included an easing of the government's family-planning policy and an end to labor camps, which had long been used to punish political dissidents.

In the 1980s, the government had imposed a **one-child policy** that limited urban families to a single child, and rural families to two children. The goal was to keep population growth from hurting economic development. China's population, at more than 1.3 billion, is the largest in the world. The government enforced the policy with fines and other penalties.

Although the one-child policy was harshly condemned, it did slow population growth. In 2013, the government announced a new policy that allows couples to have a second child if one of the parents is an only child.

Other reforms announced by the Chinese government included greater freedom for farmers to sell land for financial benefit, and an improved judicial system. However, many critics still pointed to the fact that no real political reforms were announced. The government still holds a tight rein on individual rights and freedoms.

IDENTIFY CAUSE AND EFFECT How did the global economic recession affect China?

ELPS 1.A.1 Think about what you already know about industrialization. As you read *Reforms Bring Growth and Challenges,* identify connections between your prior knowledge and the effects of industrialization in China.

India Builds a Modern Economy

Like China, India is a big country with a large, diverse population and widespread poverty. After gaining independence in 1947, India set up a democratic government and planned to develop a modern economy.

Developing a Market Economy Like other developing nations, India was determined to use

English Language Proficiency Standards

Learning Strategies 1.A.1 Have students use prior knowledge to create a concept web on industrialization. Read "Rapid Industrialization" aloud and help students identify connections between what they already know and what they just learned.

Beginning Display the word *industrialization.* Guide students in a brainstorming activity in which they use their prior knowledge to describe what comes to mind when they think about industrialization. Create a word web for student responses. Then reread "Rapid Industrialization" aloud and pause whenever the text connects with information in the word web.

Intermediate Guide students in a brainstorming activity in which they use their prior knowledge to describe what comes to mind when they think about *industrialization.* Have students create a word web for their responses. Then reread "Rapid Industrialization" aloud and invite students to identify connections between the text and the information in the concept web.

Advanced Have small groups work together to create a word web that describes what

Answers

Identify Cause and Effect *Factories closed, and unemployment rose. Workers returned to rural family homes. The government passed a stimulus package to improve productivity and retrain workers.*

modern technology to expand agriculture and industry. The government at first followed a socialist model, using five-year plans to set economic goals and manage resources. Development, however, was uneven. India built some industries, but it lacked oil and natural gas, key resources for economic growth. Instead, it had to rely on costly imported oil.

India benefited from the Green Revolution. High-yield crops, chemical fertilizers, and better irrigation systems increased output. Still, most farmers used traditional methods and relied on seasonal rains for water. They produced enough to survive, but little surplus.

By the 1980s, an economic slowdown and outside pressure pushed India toward a market economy. Some industries were privatized and limits on foreign investment were eased. During the 1990s, Indian textiles, technology, and other industries saw rapid expansion. By 2000, India was a leader in information technology, providing computer software services to the world.

India's booming economy slowed after 2008 as a result of the global recession. By 2013, India was still Asia's third-largest economy, but growth occurred at a much slower pace. Job creation was unable to keep pace with the ever-increasing workforce. In addition, the value of the rupee, Indian's unit of currency, had dropped significantly, and prices were climbing. Many economists worried that India's period of skyrocketing economic growth had come to an end. Policymakers debated how best to deal with the economic slowdown.

Impact of Rapid Population Growth In India, as in China, rapid population growth hurt efforts to improve living conditions. As food output rose, so did demand. More than one third of Indians lived in poverty, unable to meet basic needs for food, clothing, and shelter. The growing population put added pressure on India's healthcare system, which faced additional challenges after 1990 from the spread of AIDS.

The population boom and the labor-saving methods of the Green Revolution led millions of rural families to migrate to cities. But overcrowded cities like **Kolkata** (or Calcutta) and **Mumbai** (or Bombay) could not provide jobs for everyone or even basic services, such as water or sewage systems. To help the urban poor, **Mother Teresa,** a Roman Catholic nun, founded the Missionaries of Charity in Calcutta. This group provides food and medical care to thousands. Still, millions more remained in desperate need.

The Indian government supported family planning but did not adopt the harsh policies that were used in China. Efforts to slow population growth had limited success. Poor families, especially in rural areas, saw

>> As India's economy grows, so does demand for cars. India is now the world's sixth-largest carmaker. Traffic in the narrow streets of crowded cities is a growing problem, as is air pollution.

Interactive Gallery

>> This photograph shows Mother Teresa at her mission in Kolkata, surrounded by some of the many poor children she helped in her lifetime.

they know about *industrialization.* Have each group reread "Rapid Industrialization" and identify connections between the text and the information in their concept web. Have students take notes and share them with the entire group.

Advanced High Have partners work together to create a word web to describe what they know about *industrialization.* Instruct pairs to reread "Rapid Industrialization" and identify connections between the text and the information in their concept web. Have partners take notes and share them with the group.

Guided Reading and Discussion

Tell students that India's rapid population growth hurt efforts to improve living conditions. Many Indians migrated to cities, where many lived in poverty.

Cite Evidence How did the booming technology industry in India lead to social change? *(Possible response: It led to increased education and mobility, which led to a change in traditional ways of life for many.)*

Social Reform in India

Online Project the **Interactive Gallery: India on the Rise**, and click on the images and charts one at a time.

ACTIVE CLASSROOM

Using the Sticky Notes strategy, have students spend 3 minutes jotting down their response to this question on sticky notes: What do these graphs tell you about the economy of India? Have students turn to a partner and share their responses. *(The services area of the GNP is growing, while agriculture and industry are staying relatively the same.)*

Guided Reading and Discussion

Tell students that Mother Teresa's mission helped fight poverty but did not end it. What did government do to end poverty in India? *(Possible answer: banned the caste system and discrimination against people of the lowest class; provided jobs and education to the poorest groups)*

SYNTHESIZE

Online Project the **Digital Activity: The Economies of China and India**.

Ask students to reflect on the cartoon's meaning based on what they have read. Ask: What are the reasons for China's economic successes? India's? *(Both moved toward free market economies.)* Describe the path each country took to become a major factor in the global economy. *(China allowed privatization of businesses and land. Foreign investment was encouraged. Economic reforms brought growth. India followed a socialist model, and then switched to a market economy. Industries were privatized, and foreign investment was broadened. Some industries, like information technology, saw rapid expansion.)*

Topic 21 Lesson 3

DEMONSTRATE

Online Assign the **Digital Lesson Quiz** for this lesson if you haven't already done so. Students will be offered automatic remediation or enrichment based on their scores.

Pose these questions to the class on the Discussion Board:

Draw Conclusions Which problem facing India or China do you think is the most significant? Explain your answer. *(Possible answers include: poverty, population growth, debt, human rights, economic and political reform, or environmental damage. Answers should be well reasoned and supported with facts.)*

Make Generalizations How has rapid population growth affected India and China? *(It has put pressure on governments to try to provide public services and has led to poverty and high unemployment.)*

Topic Inquiry

Have students continue their investigations for the Topic Inquiry.

>> This woman is a dalit, a member of the lowest caste. She has one of the jobs traditionally assigned to dalits: she is a "scavenger," which means she empties latrines.

children as an economic resource to work the land and care for parents in old age.

IDENTIFY CAUSE AND EFFECT How did market reforms affect India's economy in the 1990s?

Social Reform in India

In India, as elsewhere, urbanization, education, and the growth of a modern economy undermined traditional ways of life. These changes benefited India's lowest social castes and women. In the cities, many people adopted western-style clothing and bought modern consumer goods. Yet most Indians still lived in villages and followed traditional ways.

Dalits India's constitution banned discrimination against **dalits,** or people of the lowest caste. To improve conditions, the government set aside jobs and places in universities for members of these groups. However, discrimination based on caste continued. Higher-caste Hindus generally receive better education and jobs.

Women Work to Improve Their Lives India's constitution granted equal rights to women. In the cities, girls from well-to-do families were educated. Women entered many professions. Some, like Indira Gandhi, won political office. Girls from poor families, however, received little or no education. Although women in rural areas worked the land or contributed to household industries, few received wages. Across India, women organized self-help groups to start small businesses and improve their lives.

EXPLAIN How did the Indian government try to improve the status of dalits?

ASSESSMENT

1. **Describe** How did China move toward economic reform without allowing for political reform?
2. **Identify Central Issues** What challenges does the Chinese government continue to face?
3. **Generate Explanations** How has India built a modern economy?
4. **Express Problems Clearly** What social reforms has the Indian government made over the last few decades, and why?
5. **Identify Cause and Effect** How does a rapidly expanding population affect life in India?

Answers

Identify Cause and Effect *India's textile and technology industries grew rapidly.*

Explain *by setting aside jobs and university spots for them*

Assessment

1. The Chinese government allowed some private ownership of property and businesses, and allowed foreign investment. Exposure to the West created a demand for political freedom, but the government refused to allow democratic reforms.
2. rapid urbanization; strained resources; increased tension among urban and rural Chinese; pollution; the spread of diseases; continued human rights issues
3. by moving toward a market economy, privatizing some industry, allowing increased foreign investment, and rapidly expanding in certain areas
4. Women and dalits have gained more rights to education and employment because of increased education, urbanization, and economic expansion.
5. It has outpaced food production, job availability, and the provision of basic services. At least one-third of Indians cannot meet basic needs. The rising population is also straining India's health care system.

21.4 Latin America comprises Mexico, Central America, the Caribbean, and South America. It includes 33 independent nations, ranging from small islands, such as Grenada, to giant Brazil. For decades, Latin American nations have faced political, economic, and social challenges similar to those of other developing nations—rapid population growth, poverty, illiteracy, political instability, and authoritarian governments.

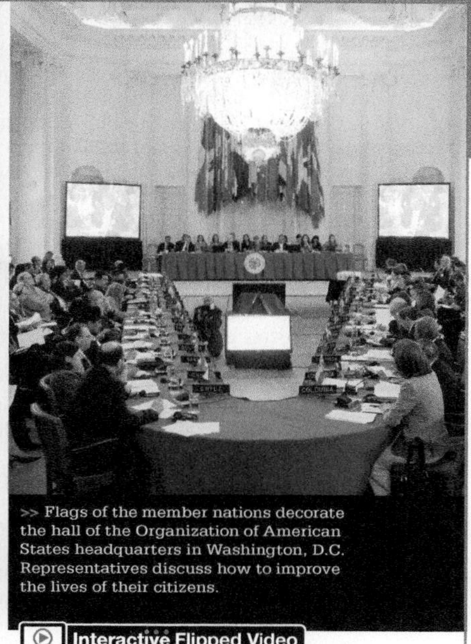

>> Flags of the member nations decorate the hall of the Organization of American States headquarters in Washington, D.C. Representatives discuss how to improve the lives of their citizens.

Interactive Flipped Video

Latin American Nations Move Toward Democracy

TEKS 22.C, 22.E

>> Objectives

Analyze how Latin America has grappled with poverty.

Describe the struggles of Latin American nations to build democratic governments.

Explain the struggle between repression and freedom in Argentina.

>> Key Terms

import substitution
agribusiness
liberation theology
indigenous
Sandinista
contra
Organization of American States (OAS)
Juan Perón
Mothers of the Plaza de Mayo
Oscar Romero

Poverty Challenges Latin America

From the 1950s to the 1980s, economic development failed to change deep-rooted inequalities in many Latin American countries. Due to inequality and growing populations, most countries saw little improvement in living standards.

Promoting Industry and Agriculture In Latin America, as in other developing regions, nations often relied heavily on a single cash crop or commodity to earn money for needed imports. If harvests failed or if world demand fell, their economies were hard hit.

To reduce their dependence on imported goods, many Latin American governments adopted a policy of **import substitution,** or manufacturing goods locally to replace imports. This policy, pursued mainly in the 1950s and 1960s, was a mixed success. Many of the new industries needed government help or foreign capital to survive.

In time, Latin American governments moved away from import substitution because of its high cost. Instead, they have tried to generate income by promoting exports. Specifically, they have focused

935

PEARSON realize. www.PearsonTexas.com Access your Digital Lesson.

Topic 21 Lesson 4

Latin American Nations Move Toward Democracy

CONNECT

Preview Have students preview the **Lesson Objectives** and the list of **Key Terms**.

Students can also preview all the **Key Terms** and **Academic Vocabulary** using the **Interactive Reading Notepad** on the digital course or preview a summary of the lesson in the **Reading and Note Taking Study Guide**.

Online Use the **Editable Presentation** found on the digital course to present the main ideas for this lesson.

Start Up Activity

Read or display this quote from Carolina Maria de Jesus, a Brazilian who moved to São Paulo, hoping to improve her life.

"July 16 . . . I went to Senhor Manuel, carrying some cans to sell . . . He gave me 13 [coins]. I kept thinking that I had to buy bread, soap, and milk . . . The 13 [coins] wouldn't make it. I returned . . . to my shack, feeling nervous and exhausted. I thought of the worrisome life that I led. Carrying paper, washing clothes for children, staying in the street all day long."

—*Child of the Dark*

Ask students: What challenges do you think Latin American nations have faced in their struggle toward development?

Tell students that in this lesson they will be learning about Latin America's road to democracy.

Online You can also project the **Start Up Activity** from the course.

INVESTIGATE

Have students read the section using the **Reading and Note Taking Study Guide** to help them take notes and understand the text as they read.

Poverty Challenges Latin America

For decades, Latin American nations have faced rapid population growth, poverty, illiteracy, political instability, and authoritarian governments. Many Latin American nations have also depended on a single cash crop.

Aa Vocabulary Builder

1. Have students pronounce the following academic vocabulary terms in this lesson and clarify the part of speech. For difficult or polysyllabic words, break them into syllables and pronounce them with the students.
2. Explain what the word means in common "student-friendly" language using synonyms and antonyms when possible. Provide concrete examples to clarify the meaning, and rephrase the definition.

allege: assert, charge, claim

comprise: to be made up of something

Topic 21 Lesson 4

Online Project the **Interactive Map: Economic Activities in Latin America**, and click through all of the layers.

ACTIVE CLASSROOM

Pair students. Have the first student give the second an Audio Tour of the map. What does the map show? What different economic activities are prominent in Latin America? Have the second student give the first an explanation of what it means.

Key Terms

Draw students' attention to the key term **agribusinesses** (in bold) in the text. Point out that much of the best farmland in Latin America belongs to these giant commercial farms. Discuss how this might affect individual farmers.

Guided Reading and Discussion

Ask students to provide details about the population explosion in Latin America and how it has contributed to poverty. *(Possible response: Supporting Detail 1: More people made life hard for rural peasant farmers. Supporting Detail 2: Millions of people moved to cities. Supporting Detail 3: Shanty towns are huge.)*

Summarize Ask: Why has the gap between rich and poor grown in Latin America? What steps could be taken to change this inequality? *(Sample response: Most benefits of economic growth went to the wealthy elite. The government could step in to create policies to support the smaller farmers and business owners.)*

D Differentiate Challenge/Gifted Have students choose a Latin American country and investigate the ethnic makeup of its people and the impact of that ethnic makeup on the country. Ask them to create an infographic, including a graph showing the different ethnic backgrounds in the population, a timeline of important events in ethnic relations, and other visuals showing the role ethnic differences play in the country.

Answers

Analyze Graphs *Sample response: It has nearly quadrupled.*

on developing a variety of cash crops and encouraging industries that they hope will produce goods for export.

Governments also backed efforts to open more land to farming through irrigation and the clearing of forests. Much of the best farmland belongs to **agribusinesses,** or giant commercial farms owned by multinational corporations. In Central America and Brazil, developers continue to clear tropical rain forests for use as farmland. This practice has had serious environmental costs.

The Income Gap One major obstacle to progress in Latin America is the uneven distribution of wealth. In many countries, a tiny elite controls the land, businesses, and factories. These powerful groups oppose changes that might undermine their position. As a result, the gap between the rich and the poor has widened, fueling discontent.

Population Growth Contributes to Poverty Latin American nations, like the rest of the developing world, experienced a population explosion that contributed to poverty. Although population growth rates slowed somewhat in the 1990s, economies were hard-pressed to keep pace with growing populations. Overall, the population of Latin America was more than 580 million in 2012.

In rural areas, population pressures made life more difficult for peasant farmers. Even though a family might own a small plot to grow its own food, most farmers worked on the estates of large landowners for low wages. Their wages pay for needed essentials like clothing, tools, and the food they cannot grow themselves.

Harsh conditions and limited land drove millions of peasants to the cities. Today, more than half of all people in Latin America live in cities. Some newcomers found jobs in factories, offices, and stores. Many more, like Carolina de Jesus, survive by working odd jobs. They fill the shantytowns on the edges of Latin American cities such as Mexico City and Sao Paulo. The shantytowns in these cities are among the largest in the world.

The Role of Religion in Latin America The Catholic Church remained a powerful force across Latin America. Although it was often tied to the ruling class, some church leaders spoke up for the poor. During the 1960s and 1970s, many priests, nuns, and church workers crusaded for social justice and an end to poverty. This movement, known as **liberation theology,** urged the church to become a force for reform. Meanwhile, evangelical Protestant groups won converts among the poor in many countries.

In 2013, Argentine archbishop and cardinal Jorge Mario Bergoglio became the first person from the Western Hemisphere to be chosen as pope, the leader

>> **Analyze Graphs** What has happened to Brazil's per capita GDP over the last quarter-century?

Interactive Map

English Language Proficiency Standards

Learning Strategies 1.A.2 Read "Poverty Challenges Latin America" aloud to students. Then have students use their personal experiences to help them enhance their understanding of the term and concept of poverty.

Beginning Reread "Poverty Challenges Latin America" aloud to students. Write and display the word *poverty*. Use simple cloze sentences to help them connect prior experiences with the concept of poverty, such as:

- When populations __________, poverty increases. (grow quickly/stay the same)
- When the economy suffers, there are ________ jobs; this can cause an increase in poverty. (fewer/more)

Intermediate Reread the section, and display the word *poverty*. Ask students questions to help them connect prior experiences with the concept of poverty. Questions can tap into students' of the Roman Catholic Church. Bergoglio selected the name of Francis, in honor of Saint Francis of Assisi, who lived a life of service to the poor. Pope Francis was well known for his own advocacy for the poor during his life in Argentina and continued to address the issue as pope.

DRAW CONCLUSIONS What problems did the gap between the rich and the poor cause in Latin America?

ELPS 1.A.2 Use your prior experiences both in and out of class to improve your understanding of poverty.

> Let us always remember this: only when we are able to share do we become truly rich... The measure of the greatness of a society is found in the way it treats those most in need, those who have nothing apart from their poverty!
>
> —Pope Francis, address on World Youth Day, July 2013

>> Thousands of Catholics crowd into St. Peter's Square in Rome to see and hear Pope Francis on Easter Day 2013. Pope Francis, who is from Argentina, is the first pope from the Americas.

Dictatorships and Civil War

Democracy was difficult to achieve in Latin American nations plagued by poverty and inequality. From the 1950s on, many groups pressed for reforms. They included liberals, socialists, urban workers, peasants, and Catholic priests and nuns. Although they differed over how to achieve their goals, all wanted to improve conditions for the poor. Conservatives, however, resisted reforms. Conflict between conservatives and reformers contributed to political unrest in many nations.

Military Leaders Seize Power Between the 1950s and 1970s, as social unrest grew, military leaders in Argentina, Brazil, Chile, and other nations seized power. Claiming the need for order, they imposed harsh, autocratic regimes that in some cases carried out politically motivated mass murder. These military rulers outlawed political parties, censored the press, and closed universities. They also imprisoned and executed thousands.

"Death squads" linked to the government murdered many more. Latin American writers, such as Pablo Neruda of Chile and Gabriel García Márquez of Colombia, went into exile after speaking out against repressive governments or social inequality.

Revolutions Break Out Beginning in the 1950s, leftist guerrillas battled repressive

Dictatorships and Civil War

Democracy was difficult for Latin American nations plagued by poverty and inequality. Many pushed to improve conditions for the poor, while conservatives resisted reforms. Between the 1950s and 1970s, as social unrest grew, military leaders in several nations seized power. Leftist guerrillas battled repressive governments and pushed socialism.

Civil wars shook parts of Central America. In Guatemala, the military targeted the indigenous populations. Archbishop Oscar Romero was assassinated in El Salvador for preaching liberation theology. When socialist rebels, called Sandinistas, came to power in Nicaragua, the United States supported the Contras, guerrillas who fought the Sandinistas. By the 1990s, democratic reforms led to free elections in many countries.

Guided Reading and Discussion

Remind students that military leaders enforced strict rules restricting rights, outlawed political parties, censored the press, closed universities, and imprisoned or murdered thousands of political opponents. One example of a person killed for speaking out against military rule was Archbishop Oscar Romero in El Salvador. He was shot while saying mass in 1980.

Draw Conclusions Ask: Why would a military regime close universities? *(Sample response: Authoritarian leaders have more power over uneducated people. They also did not want groups of young people meeting and discussing ideas.)*

Summarize Ask: What countries in Central America were torn by civil wars? Why did these wars start? *(Guatemala, El Salvador, and Nicaragua were three. These wars started when revolutionaries fought against authoritarian, military governments.)*

experiences of observing poverty in their communities and the issues related to poverty they have previously learned about in class.

Advanced Instruct small groups to reread "Poverty Challenges Latin America" aloud together. Instruct the groups to discuss the connections between their prior experiences with the concept of poverty. Students can discuss their experiences of observing poverty and issues related to poverty they have previously learned about in class.

Advanced High Instruct pairs of students to reread "Poverty Challenges Latin America" aloud together. Have partners discuss the connections between prior experiences with the concept of poverty. Students can discuss personal experiences of observing poverty and the issues of poverty they have learned about in class.

Answers

Draw Conclusions *Political unrest grew as attempts at reform were defeated by the wealthy elite.*

Topic 21 Lesson 4

U.S.–Latin American Relations

The United States has had a powerful influence on Latin America. It has dominated the Organization of American States (OAS). During the Cold War, the United States backed dictators who were anticommunist. The United States has also pressed Latin American governments to help stop the drug trade. Many Latin Americans alleged that the problem was not in Latin America but rather in the United States, where the demand for drugs was high.

Guided Reading and Discussion

Discuss the power struggle that has raged in much of Latin America. Have students identify the different participants, and explain their views. Then ask: How did Latin America's political struggles evolve in the 1990s and early 2000s? *(Several nations, such as El Salvador, have moved toward greater democracy.)* Why does the United States have such strong views about events in Latin America? *(These nations are just to the south of the United States, so events there can affect citizens here.)*

Identify Cause and Effect How did the Cold War affect U.S. relations with Latin American nations? *(In order to prevent the Soviet Union from gaining allies in Latin America, the United States intervened when it believed that revolutions might bring socialist governments into power or when it wanted to help topple socialist leaders.)*

governments across much of Latin America. They believed that only socialism could end inequalities. Others were nationalists who opposed economic and cultural domination by the United States.

Cold War fears about the spread of Marxism complicated moderate reform efforts. Many Latin American conservatives saw any call for reform as a communist threat. These groups were often supported by the United States.

Civil War in Central America Several Central American nations were torn by civil wars as revolutionaries battled authoritarian governments. In 1954, the United States helped the Guatemalan military overthrow an elected, leftist government. Leftists and others fought the military regime, which responded savagely.

The military targeted Guatemala's **indigenous,** or native, people, slaughtering tens of thousands. The fighting ended in the 1990s, after the government finally held elections and signed a peace accord with leftist guerillas.

In the 1970s and 1980s, reformers and revolutionaries challenged El Salvador's landowning and military elite. One reformer, Archbishop **Oscar Romero,** preached liberation theology until he was assassinated while celebrating mass in 1980. A brutal civil war shook El Salvador until the rebels and the military agreed to a UN-backed peace plan in 1991.

>> Archbishop Oscar Romero of El Salvador became widely known for defending the poor and oppressed. His sharp criticism of the government gained him a large following, but also many enemies.

In 1979, the **Sandinistas,** socialist rebels in Nicaragua, toppled the ruling Somoza family. The Sandinistas introduced land reform and tried to redistribute wealth to the country's poor.

Claiming that Nicaragua could become "another Cuba," United States President Ronald Reagan financed the **contras,** guerrillas who fought the Sandinistas. Fighting raged until a 1990 compromise brought peace and multiparty elections.

Movement Toward Democracy By the 1990s, pressure from democracy activists and foreign lenders led military rulers to restore civilian rule. Argentina, Brazil, Chile, and other countries held elections. In some countries, such as Brazil, Venezuela, and Bolivia, leftist leaders won office. These new leaders challenged U.S. economic and political dominance over the region.

In Mexico, which had escaped military rule, demands for reform grew. There, a single party–the Institutional Revolutionary Party (PRI)–had controlled the government for 70 years. It claimed to represent all groups in Mexican society. But in reality, PRI bosses moved forcefully against any serious opposition.

Under pressure, the PRI made some reforms in the 1990s. In 2000, Vicente Fox became the first candidate from an opposition party to be elected president. Fox and his successor, conservative Felipe Calderón, faced tough challenges, ranging from desperate rural poverty to crime, corruption, and violent drug gangs. PRI candidate Enrique Peña Nieto was elected in 2012 amid accusations of election fraud. Nieto's election was confirmed after a recount, and his administration pledged numerous reforms and promises to improve the economy and fight organized crime.

IDENTIFY CAUSE AND EFFECT What social and political conditions led to civil wars in many Latin American countries?

U.S.–Latin American Relations

Politically, a fact of life for Latin Americans has been the looming presence of the United States. An economic and military giant, the United States has dominated the **Organization of American States (OAS),** a group formed in 1948 to promote democracy, economic cooperation, and peace in the Americas. Today, Latin America and the United States are still closely linked.

Answers

Identify Cause and Effect *Poverty and inequality led to social unrest and demands for reform and caused conflict between different political groups. All of these factors contributed to the outbreak of civil wars.*

The United States is the region's most important investor and trading partner.

Despite these links, the United States and Latin American nations view each other very differently. The United States sees itself as the defender of democracy and capitalism in the region. It also provides much-needed aid.

While many Latin Americans admire the wealth of the United States, they resent what they see as its political, economic, and cultural domination. However, in 2000, when the United States honored its 1977 treaty and turned control of the Panama Canal over to Panama, many Latin American nations welcomed it as a sign of respect for Panama's independence.

U.S. Intervention During the Cold War, the United States backed anti-communist dictators in Latin America. On several occasions, it intervened militarily to stop the spread of communism. As you have read, in 1954, the United States helped overthrow Guatemala's leftist government. In 1961, President John F. Kennedy supported the Bay of Pigs invasion of Castro's Cuba. Since that failed invasion, the United States has imposed economic sanctions on Cuba. In 1973, the United States secretly backed the military coup that toppled Chile's democratically elected socialist president, Salvador Allende (ah YEN day), putting military dictator, Augusto Pinochet (pee noh SHAY), in power.

In 1994, a UN force led by the United States stepped into Haiti to restore its elected leader three years after a military coup. In 2004, the United States withdrew, leaving UN peacekeepers the job of restoring democracy to poverty-stricken, hurricane-ravaged Haiti.

The War on Drugs In the 1980s, illegal drug use grew in the United States, leading the U.S. government to declare a "war on drugs." The United States tried to stop illegal drugs from being smuggled into the country from Colombia, Peru, Bolivia, and elsewhere. It pressed Latin American governments to destroy drug crops and crush the drug cartels, or criminal gangs that ran the drug trade.

Governments cooperated, but critics in Latin America alleged that the main problem was growing demand for illegal drugs in the United States. Efforts to stop the drug trade led drug gangs to bribe government officials and hire assassins to kill judges, journalists, and others who worked against them. In 1989, U.S. forces invaded Panama and arrested its president, Manuel Noriega (noh ree AY guh), for drug trafficking. He was later tried and convicted.

>> American soldiers joined UN forces to keep the peace after the coup in Haiti. Peacekeepers also did practical work, such as building, supplying food, and spreading cement to repair roads.

Migration Poverty and unrest led many people to flee their homes in Latin America for the United States. Many entered the country legally. A large number were illegal immigrants. Their remittances, or the earnings they sent home, helped raise the standard of living for their families in Latin America. As the economic slowdown worsened after 2008, many newcomers lost their jobs and returned to their homelands. The number of illegal immigrants coming to the United States leveled off after 2009, but in 2013 some experts predicted that the numbers might be on the rise once again.

DRAW CONCLUSIONS Why do people in Latin America have mixed opinions of the United States?

The Long Road to Democracy in Argentina

Once the most prosperous country in Latin America, Argentina enjoyed a robust economy based on exports of beef and grain. It attracted millions of immigrants. But since the Great Depression of the 1930s, Argentina has experienced more than 60 years of political and economic upheavals.

The Long Road to Democracy in Argentina

Online Project the **Interactive Gallery: Argentina's Long Road to Democracy**, and click through the gallery images.

ACTIVE CLASSROOM

Have students use the Act It Out strategy on one of the Interactive Gallery images. Have students make the picture come to life. Tell them to explain what happens next in the image, and what happened before. Tell them to imitate the characters in the image and become a living tapestry, using a script that they have written.

Analyze Images

Point out the photo of the Mothers of the Plaza de Mayo on the next page. Ask: Why do you think the mothers are carrying signs with photos? *(Using photos brings human faces to the issue; they want to ensure that no one forgets their missing children.)*

Guided Reading and Discussion

Explain that the mothers of the "disappeared" in Argentina marched each week as tens of thousands of people disappeared during the "dirty war."

Identify Central Issues How are the words *military* and *oppression* connected in Latin American politics? *(Military leadership often involves oppression.)*

Draw Conclusions How might military control have limited Argentina's economic development? *(Accompanying violence and unrest make it hard to do business.)*

Answers

Draw Conclusions *They admire the wealth of the United States but resent its interference in their governments; its claims that Latin America is responsible for the illegal drug trade; and its political, economic, and cultural domination.*

SYNTHESIZE

Online Project the **Digital Activity: The Poor in Latin America.**

Have students reread the quote from Carolina Maria de Jesus. Discuss the details that illustrate life in poverty. *(selling cans, not having enough coins to buy basic items, living in a shack)* Ask: How have uneven wealth distribution, population growth, and poverty affected development of democracy in Latin America? *(Uneven wealth distribution and poverty have caused political unrest. The population explosion contributed to poverty. This led to social unrest and propelled military dictators into power. Many countries suffered through civil wars.)*

DEMONSTRATE

Online Assign the **Digital Lesson Quiz** for this lesson if you haven't already done so. Students will be offered automatic remediation or enrichment based on their score.

Pose this question to the class on the Discussion Board:

Predict Consequences Many developing nations are ruled by dictators or one party. What do you think could be the consequences of this type of rule on the economy of the country? *(Possible response: Political dissatisfaction can cause unrest and hurt economic growth. Too many limits can be placed on individuals by an unchallenged government.)*

Topic Inquiry

Have students continue their investigations for the Topic Inquiry.

Answers

Explain *Failed policies and its loss to Britain in the war over the Falkland Islands forced the military to restore civilian rule.*

>> The Mothers of the Plaza de Mayo gathered weekly in Argentina's capital, carrying photos of their "disappeared" children, who had been kidnapped and probably killed by the government.

 Interactive Gallery

The Military Takes Control From 1946 to 1955, nationalist president **Juan Perón** enjoyed great support from workers. He increased the government's economic role, boosted wages, and backed labor unions. He also suppressed opposition.

When Perón's policies led to an economic crisis, he was ousted in a 1955 military coup. Although Perón was reelected in 1973, the military was in and out of power for two decades. In 1976, as a wave of political unrest swept Argentina, the military again seized control.

As the military battled leftist guerrillas, it waged a "dirty war" of torture and murder against its own citizens. As many as 20,000 people were kidnapped by the government and disappeared. Every week, women, known as the **Mothers of the Plaza de Mayo,** marched in Buenos Aires, the capital of Argentina. They demanded to know what had happened to their missing sons and daughters.

Restoration of Democracy By 1983, failed policies and a lost war with Britain over the Falkland Islands forced the military to restore civilian rule and allow elections. A financial crisis in 2001 devastated Argentina's economy and brought widespread poverty. Argentina's democracy survived the economic crisis and its economy recovered after 2003. However, like other Latin American nations, Argentina's economic progress was undermined by the 2008 global recession. By the end of 2013, the nation still struggled with high inflation and other economic woes.

? EXPLAIN Why did the military restore democratic rule in Argentina?

ASSESSMENT

1. **Describe** What changes did Latin American nations make to economic policy to try to cope with poverty and economic hardship?
2. **Identify Cause and Effect** Why did Latin American nations find it difficult to establish democratic governments?
3. **Identify Central Ideas** How have repeated U.S. interventions in Latin America affected Latin American attitudes toward the United States?
4. **Draw Conclusions** Why do you think many of the repressive dictatorships in Latin America were led by the military?
5. **Sequence Events** Describe the changes Argentina's government went through after the 1930s. List significant events in the order in which they occurred.

Assessment

1. Many established import substitution at first. Once this was deemed too expensive, they moved to a policy of promoting exports, both industrial and agricultural, to try to develop the economy.
2. Poverty and inequality plagued Latin American nations, and disagreement arose about how best to deal with the problems. Civil war broke out as repressive regimes took over.
3. Many Latin Americans view U.S. intervention as political and economic domination.
4. Students may say that the military had strength in both force and numbers and could more easily fight its way to power.
5. Students' lists might contain the following: Perón's initially successful rule, 1946–1955, which ended with economic hardship and a military coup in 1955; Perón was reelected in 1973, but the military seized power again in 1976 and held control until 1983, when it allowed elections and restored civilian rule.

21.5 The end of the Cold War created favorable conditions for the spread of democracy. It also marked the beginning of a new global economy. Growing economic ties and increased international trade would become a driving force shaping the world in the new millennium.

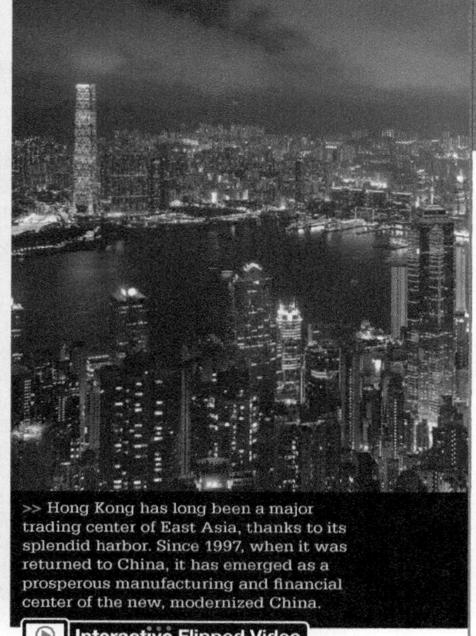

>> Hong Kong has long been a major trading center of East Asia, thanks to its splendid harbor. Since 1997, when it was returned to China, it has emerged as a prosperous manufacturing and financial center of the new, modernized China.

Interactive Flipped Video

The Industrialized World

TEKS
18.E, 18.F, 22.D

>> Objectives

Examine social, political, and economic trends in Europe since the Cold War.

Describe how the breakup of Yugoslavia led to war and genocide.

Analyze the challenges facing Russia since the end of the Soviet Union.

Summarize economic developments in Asia.

>> Key Terms

European Union (EU)
euro
default
Vladimir Putin
surplus
deficit
Pacific Rim
Northern Ireland
Good Friday Agreement
Chechnya
multiethnic
Slobodan Milosevic
ethnic cleansing

A New Europe

The collapse of communism ended decades of division between communist Eastern Europe and democratic Western Europe. Trade, business, travel, and communications across the continent became easier. At the same time, many European nations had to deal with issues such as large-scale immigration from the developing world, growing discrimination against foreigners, and rising unemployment.

A Reunited Germany After more than 45 years of division, East and West Germany were reunited in 1990. Germans welcomed reunification, but they also faced new challenges. East Germany's economy and infrastructure were weak and had to be modernized.

Unemployment rose in the former East Germany when inefficient communist-era factories were closed. West Germans paid higher taxes to finance the rebuilding of the eastern part of the country.

Reunification brought social problems as well. Racist groups, such as neo-Nazis, a hate group modeled on the Nazi party, blamed immigrants for the country's problems and viciously attacked foreign workers. The vast majority of Germans condemned such actions.

941

PEARSON realize. www.PearsonTexas.com Access your Digital Lesson.

The Industrialized World

CONNECT

Preview Have students preview the **Lesson Objectives** and the list of **Key Terms**.

Students can also preview all the **Key Terms** and **Academic Vocabulary** using the **Interactive Reading Notepad** on the digital course or preview a summary of the lesson in the **Reading and Note Taking Study Guide**.

Online Use the **Editable Presentation** found on the digital course to present the main ideas for this lesson.

Start Up Activity

Tell students that a nation's GDP (gross domestic product) is the total value of all goods and services produced in that nation during a particular year. Then explain that between 1990 and 1999, the value of Russia's economy fell. The GDP dipped from over $500 billion to about $200 billion. Ask: Why do you think this happened? *(Sample response: This might have happened because the country was struggling to develop a market economy after the breakup of the Soviet Union and the collapse of the command economy.)*

Online You can also project the **Start Up Activity** from the course.

INVESTIGATE

Have students read the section using the **Reading and Note Taking Study Guide** to help them take notes and understand the text as they read.

A New Europe

Ask students to remember what was happening in Europe, the United States, and the Soviet Union in the 1950s. *(the Cold War, rebellions from Warsaw Pact countries, Western Europe is rebuilding from destruction of World War II)* Then tell them that the collapse of communism ended decades of division between Eastern and Western Europe and improved trade, business, travel, and communication across Europe

Aa Vocabulary Builder

1. Have students pronounce the following academic vocabulary term in this lesson and clarify the part of speech. Break the term into syllables and pronounce them with the students.
2. Explain what the word means in common "student-friendly" language using synonyms and antonyms when possible. Provide concrete examples to clarify the meaning, and rephrase the definition.

inflation: a rise in prices linked to an increase in the amount of money available

Topic 21 Lesson 5

Online Project the **Interactive Map: Evolution of the European Union** and go through the layers.

Hypothesize Ask students: Why do you think it took until 2004 for most of the former Warsaw Pact countries to join the EU? *(Possible answer: It took several years to make the transition from a command economy to a free market economy.)*

ACTIVE CLASSROOM

Have students Write Headlines that capture the action in the maps of the growing European Union. If you were to write a headline or a slogan that captured the most important aspect that should be remembered, what would that headline be? Ask them to pass their headline to a partner to review. Then, ask them to share their headlines with the class.

Guided Reading and Discussion

Review with students the changes to NATO membership. *(NATO extended, like the EU, to include many former Warsaw Pact countries and has always included Turkey.)* Review the challenges to German reunification. *(It was difficult economically, because the East German economy was inefficient, and socially, because there was a resurgence in neo-Nazi activity.)*

Infer What enabled Germany to successfully reunite in spite of the difficult challenges? *(Sample response: Germans were able to reunite because the German people welcomed the idea.)*

Cite Evidence Why is Turkey's membership in the European Union controversial? *(Sample response: Some people think Turkey should have full membership in the EU because it is a part of NATO. Others think that Turkey should not be admitted because they believe it has a poor record on human rights and may not share European traditions and values.)*

Twenty years after reunification, Germany remains an economic giant and a strong European leader.

Changes in NATO The collapse of the Soviet Union ended the Warsaw Pact. Many of the nations of Eastern Europe wanted to join NATO. Poland, Hungary, and the Czech Republic joined in 1999, soon followed by other countries. Russia disliked NATO's eastward expansion, but agreed to a NATO-Russia Council to consult on issues of common interest.

Europe was changing and NATO had to reassess its purpose. Many NATO officials believed that NATO's primary goal should become that of peacekeeper and protector of human rights. Following terrorist attacks in the United States, Europe, and elsewhere, the fight against terrorism has become a priority for the alliance with NATO troops joining the U.S. in Afghanistan.

Growth of the European Union The end of the Cold War also changed trade relations in Europe. In 1993, the European Economic Community became the **European Union (EU),** a bloc of European nations that work together to promote a freer flow of capital, labor, services, and goods. Members also cooperate on security matters. Like NATO, the Europe Union has expanded over the years to add nations from Eastern Europe.

In 2002, the **euro** became the common currency for most of Western Europe. By then, EU passports had replaced national passports. Today, the expanded EU has the world's largest economy and competes with economic superpowers like the United States and Japan.

Some European leaders supported even greater economic and political unity for the region. However, many ordinary citizens felt greater loyalty to their own nations than to the EU. Also, the economies of Eastern Europe were weaker than those in the West, causing worries about the EU's overall economic outlook.

Turkey, long a member of NATO, has sought full membership in the EU. But Turkey's application faced opposition because of its poor record on human rights and other issues. Also, some Europeans are concerned about admitting Eastern European countries with large Muslim populations into the EU. They worry that if the EU changes too quickly, it will be less stable.

Conflict in Northern Ireland The modern era saw the end of one long-standing European conflict. When Ireland won independence in 1922, Britain kept control of **Northern Ireland,** the six northern counties that had a Protestant majority. Faced with discrimination, minority Catholics demanded civil rights and unification with the rest of Ireland. Protestants wanted Northern Ireland to remain part of Britain.

>> This map shows the European Union in 2013. **Analyze Maps** Which EU members border the Black Sea?

 Interactive Map

English Language Proficiency Standards

Learning Strategies 1.B.1 Read aloud or have students read "A Reunited Germany." Remind students that listening to their own speech can help them hear and correct their own mistakes.

Beginning Reread the text aloud. As a group, create a cause-and-effect chart. Have students use the chart to answer questions about reunification. Repeat what they say and correct any mistakes.

Intermediate Have students complete the Beginning activity but ask them leading questions to help them correct their mistakes.

Advanced Have students reread the text independently. Ask them to work in small groups, asking one another questions about Germany's reunification to practice speaking in English about the content. Have them help each other identify and correct mistakes.

Advanced High Have students complete the Advanced activity, working with a partner to pose questions and identify mistakes.

Answers

Analyze Maps *Romania and Bulgaria*

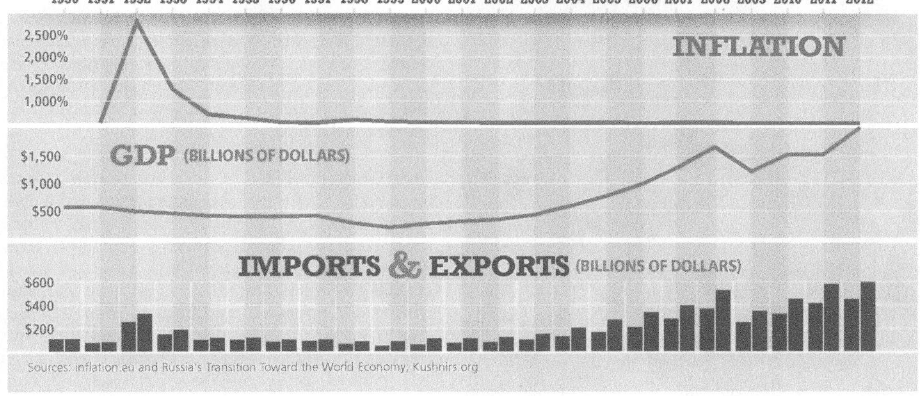

>> **Analyze Graphs** After the fall of the Soviet Union, Russia's economy took time to adapt to a free market economy. In what year did inflation start to drop in Russia?

In the 1960s, extremists on both sides turned to violence and terrorism. The mostly Catholic Irish Republican Army (IRA) attacked Protestants, while armed Protestant groups targeted Catholics. The violence, known as "the Troubles," raged for three decades. Finally, in 1998, both sides signed a peace accord, known as the **Good Friday Agreement.** Protestants and Catholics set up a power-sharing government in 2007. Although there have been isolated acts of violence, most people expect that peace will last.

CITE EVIDENCE What challenges did Germany face after reunification?

ELPS **ELPS 1.B.1** Read "A Reunited Germany" and summarize what you have read aloud. Listen to your own speech and try to identify any mistakes. Then practice correcting those mistakes.

Shifts in Global Power

After the Cold War ended, the balance of global power shifted. The United States became the world's sole superpower. Recently, though, Russia has reemerged as a powerful force.

Russia Rebuilds Russia faced hard times after the breakup of the Soviet Union. In an effort to shift to a market economy, Russia's president, Boris Yeltsin, privatized many state-run industries and collective farms. This change brought great hardships to many Russians as unemployment and prices soared.

In 1998, Russia barely avoided financial collapse. It **defaulted,** or failed to make payments, on much of its foreign debt. High inflation and the collapse of the ruble, Russia's currency, forced many banks and businesses to close. People lost their savings and jobs, although some Russians did prosper in the new economy.

In 2000, **Vladimir Putin** was elected president in Russia's second free election. Putin helped rebuild Russia's economy. However, his government was plagued by corruption and Putin came under fire for increasing the power of the central government at the expense of people's civil liberties. In 2008, Putin stepped down as president, but in 2012 he was elected to another six-year term. Economically, Russia has benefited from rising prices for its oil and gas exports. While the 2008 global economic slowdown posed challenges, oil prices have since recovered and so has Russia's economy. In 2011, Russia joined the World Trade Organization, the international body that supervises world trade.

History Background

EU Candidates There are several nations listed by the European Union as official candidate countries "on the road to EU membership." These include Albania, Iceland, Montenegro, Serbia, the former Yugoslav republic of Macedonia, and Turkey. For all but Iceland, the EU has required that certain measures be put in place before membership status will be granted. Some of the countries have made progress toward those goals. Iceland applied but then put its application "on hold" in 2013 after conservative leaders took over the Icelandic government. Many Icelanders are opposed to EU membership, primarily because of disputes over EU fishing regulations and quotas. The country still enjoys many of the benefits of EU membership, however, such as free trade.

Shifts in Global Power

The Former Soviet Republics

Ask students to describe the relationship between the United States and the Soviet Union during the Cold War. *(Sample response: They were enemies who divided the world into two different influence areas.)* Draw students' attention to the picture of Vladimir Putin and Barack Obama. Explain to students that as the Cold War ended and the Soviet Union shrank to become just Russia, the relationship between the two countries changed. Russia experienced hard times economically in the 1990s and has lost much of its territory, but it is still important. It is a large oil producer, a member of the UN Security Council, and one of the largest economies in the world.

Identify Steps in a Process What early steps in shifting to a market economy did Boris Yeltsin take? What was the effect? *(Sample response: Boris Yeltsin privatized state-run industries and collective farms in an effort to shift to a market economy. The change brought hardships to many Russians because unemployment and prices soared.)*

Answers

Analyze Graphs *1993*

Cite Evidence *Germany faced economic challenges such as integrating East Germany's weak economy and social challenges such as racist groups within the nation.*

Topic 21 Lesson 5

Summarize How did Vladimir Putin help Russia? What do his critics think of his leadership? *(Sample response: Vladimir Putin helped Russia by rebuilding the economy. His critics think that he is corrupt and that under his control the central government took too much power at the expense of civil liberties.)*

Guided Reading and Discussion

Remind students that as the world's only superpower, the United States has a great deal of military and political influence. After terrorist attacks on the United States in September 2001, President George W. Bush declared a "war on terror." In 2002, the United States sent forces first to Afghanistan and the next year to Iraq. American involvement in Iraq ended in August 2010. In May 2011, American forces killed Osama bin Laden, the architect of the September 2001 attack. Ask: Why might some Americans believe a strong show of force is necessary to fight terrorism? *(Sample response: They believe that the United States has to be willing to stand up to acts of terror and show that it has the strength and the willingness to fight back.)*

>> Russian president Vladimir Putin and American president Barack Obama confer at the G20 Summit in Mexico in June 2012. The United States and Russia are powerful forces in the United Nations and other international organizations.

>> This street scene in Moscow suggests some of the ways that Russia has changed since the fall of communism. **Identify Central Ideas** What changes in the Russian economy are reflected in this image?

As Russia rebounded, it defended its interests, which sometimes caused tensions with the West. Despite UN sanctions against Iran, Russia assisted Iran with its nuclear energy program.

In 2013, Russia similarly opposed military action against Syria, who had reportedly used chemical weapons against its own citizens during its civil war. Ultimately, the United States, Russia, and Syria agreed that Syria's chemical weapons would be placed under international control.

New Challenges for the United States As the world's only superpower, the United States has a great deal of military and political influence. After terrorist attacks on the United States in September 2001, President George W. Bush declared a "war on terror." In 2002, the United States sent forces to Afghanistan, where the terrorist plot had been hatched. The next year, U.S. forces invaded Iraq and toppled its dictator Saddam Hussein. When Barack Obama, the nation's first African American President, took office in January 2009, U.S. forces still occupied Afghanistan and Iraq. Obama ended American involvement in Iraq in August 2010. In May 2011, American forces killed Osama bin Laden, the architect of the September 2001 attack. Shortly after, President Obama set an accelerated timetable for the withdrawal of troops from Afghanistan.

The United States weathered economic ups and downs. An economic boom in the 1990s produced a budget **surplus,**or money left over after expenditures. During George W. Bush's presidency, slower growth, massive military spending, and tax cuts led to a huge budget **deficit,** or gap between what the government spends and what it takes in through taxes and other measures.

In 2008, a financial crisis shook the American economy, sparking a global recession. The U.S. GDP contracted 8.9% in the last 3 months of 2008. Millions of Americans lost their jobs as businesses cut back or closed. President Obama responded with a multi-billion dollar economic stimulus package that called for increased federal spending and tax cuts to revive the economy. In addition, the federal government provided financial support for banks and car manufacturers. By 2013, the stock market had recovered, but unemployment remained high.

CHECK UNDERSTANDING What troubles did Russia face after the collapse of the Soviet Union?

Answers

Identify Central Ideas *The presence of McDonald's, a major American corporation, as well Minnie Mouse show that American companies and cultural influences have taken root in Russia.*

Check Understanding *Russia defaulted on its foreign debt. High inflation and the collapse of the ruble forced banks and businesses to close. Unemployment rose and corruption plagued the government.*

>> This map shows the Russian Caucasus region, which had been part of the Soviet Union. Three former Soviet republics (Georgia, Armenia, and Azerbaijan) gained independence. There has been ethnic tension in the territories that remain within Russia. **Analyze Maps** Which part of Azerbaijan is separated by Armenia from the main part of the country?

The Former Soviet Republics

The end of the Cold War did not mean peace in the former Soviet Union. Ethnic and religious tensions fueled conflict in Russia and in several former Soviet republics.

Trouble in Chechnya In 1994, separatists in **Chechnya** tried to break away from Russian rule. Chechnya was home to diverse ethnic and religious groups, including Muslim Chechens.

Russia crushed the Chechen revolt, killing many civilians. During two wars and nearly ten years of fighting, both sides committed atrocities. In the early 2000s, Chechen rebels launched terrorist attacks on Moscow, and killed school children in the city of Beslan. Since 2009, the conflict in Chechyna has subsided, but sporadic violence by Chechen separatists has continued, including a terrorist attack in a Moscow subway.

Azerbaijan, Armenia, and Georgia In the oil-rich former Soviet republic of Azerbaijan, Azeris are the majority. In the region of Nagorno-Karabakh, however, ethnic Armenians outnumbered Azeris. When Armenians declared independence, fierce fighting raged. The Armenians gained control of the region, creating one million Azeri refugees.

In Georgia, another former Soviet republic, two provinces, South Ossetia and Abkhazia, wanted to break away. Russia backed the separatists. In 2008, after Georgia attacked separatists in South Ossetia, fighting erupted between Russian and Georgian troops. International pressure soon ended the conflict, and Georgia has resolved most of the problems through the political process.

IDENTIFY CAUSE AND EFFECT What were the causes of the conflicts that erupted in the former Soviet Union?

War in Yugoslavia

Ethnic, nationalist, and religious tensions tore Yugoslavia apart during the 1990s. Before 1991, Yugoslavia was **multiethnic,** or made up of several ethnic groups. These groups included Serbs, Montenegrins, and Macedonians, who were Orthodox Christians; Croats and Slovenes, who were Roman Catholics; and the mostly Muslim Bosniaks and

Analyze Images

Draw students' attention to the map of the South Caucasus region. Remind them of the developments in the former Soviet Union in the early 1990s. *(Sample response: Many of the former Soviet Republics were breaking away and declaring independence; by 1991, many of the more populous and wealthy former republics were independent.)* Why would Russia want to hold on to Chechnya? *(Answers will vary. Chechnya may have oil wealth like Azerbaijan; Russia might be afraid that the example of a breakaway Chechnya would encourage other parts of Russia to seek independence.)*

War in Yugoslavia

Review the issues surrounding the disintegration of Yugoslavia in the 1990s. Tell students that ethnic, nationalist, and religious tensions had developed between people who had been forced to live with each other in a state assembled without taking into account their differences.

Online Project the **Interactive Timeline: War in Bosnia**. Go through the events, and have students read the captions. Ask students to answer the question at the end.

ACTIVE CLASSROOM

Use the Rank It strategy. List the following events on the whiteboard: Independence of Slovenia/Croatia; Beginning of Ethnic Cleansing; Beginning of Siege of Sarajevo; Srebrenica Massacre; NATO Bombing; Second Market Bombing. Ask students to rank them from most to least influential. Ask students to provide a justification for the ranking decisions they made. Then ask students to work in pairs to share their rankings and justifications. Poll the class to see if there is agreement on the ranking.

D Differentiate Extra Support Have students look up *genocide* in the glossary. *(deliberate attempt to destroy an entire religious or ethnic group)* Ask them for an example of genocide. *(Examples include the Armenian genocide, the Holocaust, Cambodia under Pol Pot, and Rwanda.)* Ask them if they think that ethnic cleansing in Yugoslavia should be considered genocide. *(Responses will vary, but it fits the definition because it targeted a specific ethnic group.)*

Answers

Analyze Maps *Nakhchivan*

Identify Cause and Effect *Ethnic and religious divisions and nationalism led to conflicts.*

Topic 21 Lesson 5

Key Terms

Draw students' attention to the key term **ethnic cleansing** (in bold) in the text, and have them explain its meaning. Remind them of another key term they have learned: *genocide* (the systematic elimination of an entire group of people based on race, religion, or ethnicity). Tell them that while some scholars use the terms interchangeably, others draw a distinction based on purpose: The goal of ethnic cleansing is to establish ethnically homogeneous areas, which is sometimes accomplished through genocide but also through forcing groups to leave an area.

Guided Reading and Discussion

Tell students that ethnic, nationalist, and religious tensions were the root of the problems in Yugoslavia during the 1990s. The multiethnic country had people of different religions who identified more closely with their own regional or ethnic group than with their national government.

Analyze Interactions Why do you think Serbs wanted to create areas that were purely Serbian and drive people of other ethnicities away? *(Sample response: Serbs wanted to create purely Serbian areas to focus their control. If people of other ethnicities did not live there, the Serbs could live as they wanted.)*

Integrate Information Read the second paragraph of "War in Kosovo." What does the text convey about the people on both sides of the war? *(Sample response: Serbs were oppressing Kosovo Albanians, so a small guerrilla force of Albanians emerged to fight the Serbs. People on both sides of the war were fighting for their own ethnic group.)*

Albanians. A majority of Yugoslavians—including the Serbs, Montenegrins, Croats, and Bosniaks—all spoke the same language, Serbo-Croatian, but these groups had different religions. Albanians, Slovenes, and Macedonians spoke minority languages.

Yugoslavia was made up of six republics, similar to states in the United States. These were Slovenia, Croatia, Serbia, Bosnia and Herzegovina (often known as Bosnia for short), Montenegro, and Macedonia. Each republic had a dominant ethnic group but also was home to ethnic minorities.

Serbs formed the majority in Serbia but were an important ethnic minority in several of the other republics. Serbs dominated Yugoslavia, which was held together and controlled by its Communist Party.

Republics Break Away The fall of communism fed nationalist unrest throughout Yugoslavia. The Serbian-dominated government tried to preserve the country. In 1991, however, Slovenia and Croatia declared independence. This move triggered fighting between Croats and the Serbian minority within Croatia. Macedonia and Bosnia soon broke away from Yugoslavia as well, leaving only Serbia and Montenegro. In 2006, Montenegro also went its own way, separate from Serbia.

Civil War in Bosnia When Bosnia declared independence in 1992, civil war erupted among Bosniaks, Serbs, and Croats. Bosnian Serbs wanted to set up their own government. They received money and arms from Serbian president **Slobodan Milosevic** (mih LOH shuh vich), an extreme Serb nationalist.

The largest group in Bosnia, the Muslim Bosniaks, lived scattered across Bosnia. They did not want the country divided into ethnic regions.

During the war, all sides committed atrocities. Some observers made charges of genocide. Bosnian Serbs conducted a vicious campaign of **ethnic cleansing.** This meant killing people from other ethnic groups or forcibly removing them from their homes to create ethnically "pure" areas, in this case for Serbs. Tens of thousands of Bosniaks and Croats were brutalized or killed, sometimes in mass executions. Croat and Bosnian fighters took revenge. Croats launched an ethnic cleansing campaign to drive ethnic Serbs from parts of Croatia.

Many observers, in the United States and elsewhere, argued that ethnic cleansing was a form of genocide and that intervention was necessary. Finally, NATO air strikes against the Bosnian Serb military forced the warring parties to the peace table. Guided by the United States, the rival groups signed the Dayton

>> In 1990, Yugoslavia was the dominant country in southeastern Europe. By 2003, it no longer existed, replaced by seven independent nations. **Analyze Maps** Which new nation does not share a border with Serbia?

Interactive Gallery

Answers

Analyze Maps *Slovenia*

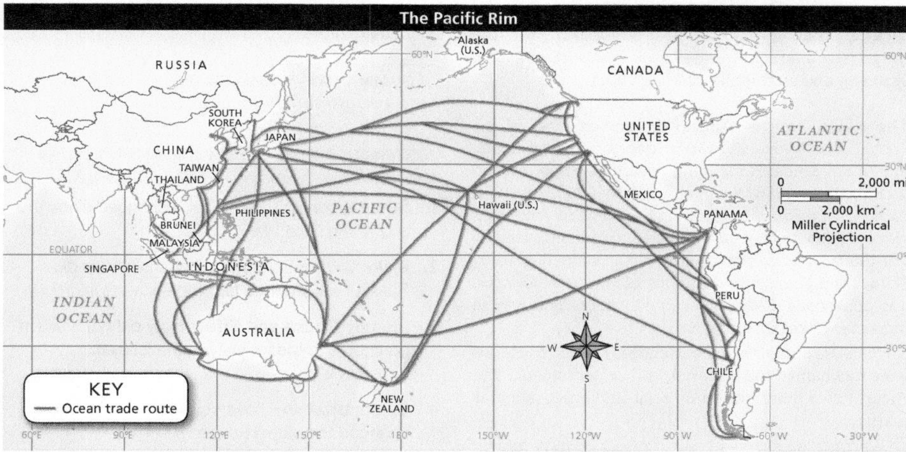

>> The countries of the Pacific Rim have geographic, cultural, and economic ties. The region is a major center of ocean trade routes. **Analyze Maps** According to the map, with which Asian country does the United States trade most?

Accords, ending the war in 1995. An international force helped maintain a fragile peace in Bosnia.

War in Kosovo As Bosnia reached a tense peace, a crisis broke out in the Serbian province of Kosovo. Over the centuries, many Albanians, mostly Muslim, had settled in Kosovo. By the 1990s, they made up about 90 percent of Kosovo's population. The rest of the population was mostly Serb.

In 1989, Serbian leader Slobodan Milosevic began oppressing Kosovo Albanians. By the mid-1990s, a small guerrilla force of Kosovo Albanians had emerged. It attacked Serbian targets. Milosevic rejected international peace efforts and stepped up a campaign of ethnic cleansing against Kosovo Albanians. In response, NATO launched air attacks against Serbia in 1999.

The air strikes forced Milosevic to withdraw Serbian forces from Kosovo. UN and NATO forces then supervised a tense peace. After years of negotiation, Kosovo declared independence in 2008. While Kosovo Albanians celebrated, Serbs angrily protested. For them, Kosovo was a historic part of Serbia. A small NATO force remained in Kosovo to keep the peace between the majority Albanians and the minority Serbs.

IDENTIFY CAUSE AND EFFECT How did the breakup of Yugoslavia lead to ethnic cleansing in Bosnia-Herzegovina?

A New Role for Asia

Much of Asia today remains part of the developing world. However, several Asian nations are fully industrialized, developed nations. As such, they have experienced the successes and downturns of being key players in the global economy.

Strength in the Pacific Rim A major force in the global economy is the **Pacific Rim,** the many Asian nations that border the Pacific Ocean. The Pacific Ocean first became a highway for world trade in the 1500s. By the mid-1900s, links across the Pacific had grown dramatically. By the 1990s, the volume of trade across the Pacific was greater than that across the Atlantic. Some analysts predict that the 2000s will increasingly become the "Pacific century" because of this region's potential for further growth.

For decades, Japan dominated the Asian Pacific Rim. But in the 1990s, as Japan suffered a long economic downturn, China's economy boomed. In 2010, China

A New Role for Asia

Draw students' attention to the map of the Pacific Rim. Have them name the most economically important countries (the ones with the most trade routes) on the map. *(United States, Australia, Japan, Singapore, China)*

Infer Why might the twenty-first century be called the "Pacific Century"? *(Sample response: because of the region's economic dominance and potential for growth)*

Guided Reading and Discussion

Ask students if they know the term *Asian Tigers.* Explain that the Asian Tigers are four Asian countries—Taiwan, Hong Kong, Singapore, and South Korea—with very strong economies that are growing rapidly due to low wages, long hours, and other worker sacrifices. Each stresses education as a way to increase worker productivity. These countries have export-driven economies and dominate the electronics and other industries.

Cite Evidence Why are nations in the Pacific well poised to take a leading role in trade? Cite evidence from the text to support your answer. *(Sample response: Nations in the Pacific are well poised to take a leading role in trade because the Pacific Ocean is the "highway" for world trade. The volume of trade across the Pacific is greater than that of the Atlantic. The area has enormous potential for future growth.)*

Answers

Analyze Maps *Japan*

Identify Cause and Effect *Serbs, who had dominated Yugoslavia, feared a loss of power in Bosnia, where they were a minority. Serbs killed non-Serbs or drove them out of parts of Bosnia so that they could create and control "ethnically cleansed" areas.*

Topic 21 Lesson 5

SYNTHESIZE

Online Project the **Digital Activity: The Industrialized World**. Ask students to reflect on the lesson and answer the following question: How did the end of the Cold War and of communism affect Germany, Russia, the United States, Yugoslavia, and Asia? *(Germany: brought about reunification; Russia: struggled to forge a market economy; United States: became the world's only superpower; Yugoslavia: was torn apart by ethnic, nationalist, and religious tensions; Asia: experienced successes and downturns of global economy)*

DEMONSTRATE

Online Assign the **Digital Lesson Quiz** for this lesson if you haven't already done so. Students will be offered automatic remediation or enrichment based on their score.

Pose the following to the class on the Discussion Board:

Predict Consequences Who will dominate the global economy in the coming years? Explain. *(Sample response: I think the United States will dominate the global economy in the coming years. The recession seems to be nearing an end, and we do not face some of the challenges of India and China. Germany and the Asian Tigers will also play leading roles. They are strong countries that are industrialized and have productive workers.)*

Topic Inquiry

Have students continue their investigations for the Topic Inquiry.

overtook Japan as the world's second largest economy. Japan's economy suffered a severe shock from the global recession and was set back even further by the Tsunami and earthquake of March 2011.

The Asian Tigers Among the powerhouses of the Pacific Rim were Taiwan, Hong Kong, Singapore, and South Korea. Hong Kong, which had been leased to Britain in 1898, was returned to China in 1997. Although these Asian dynamos differed in important ways, all had quickly modernized and industrialized by the 1980s. All four were influenced to some degree by China, and Confucian traditions of loyalty, hard work, and consensus. Each stressed education as a way to increase worker productivity.

Because of their economic success, these countries were nicknamed the "Asian tigers" or "four tigers." The Asian tigers first focused on light industries, such as textiles.

As their economies grew, they shifted to higher-priced exports, such as electronics. Their stunning growth was due in part to low wages, long hours, and other worker sacrifices. Like other export-driven economies, the Asian tigers were hurt by the 2008 global economic slowdown, but all have recovered and continue to grow.

SUMMARIZE Why did the Asian tigers enjoy strong economic growth?

ASSESSMENT

1. **Summarize** How has Europe changed since the end of the Cold War?
2. **Make Generalizations** What challenges did Russia face after the fall of the Soviet Union?
3. **Identify Cause and Effect** How did nationalism contribute to the violence in the former Yugoslavia?
4. **Summarize** How have developments in Asia changed the global economy?
5. **Compare** What are two similarities between the breakup of the former Yugoslavia and the breakup of the Soviet Union?

Answers

Summarize *Worker sacrifices, such as long hours and low wages, and a shift to higher-priced electronics exports led to strong economic growth.*

Assessment

1. The EU and NATO have grown and Germany is now a strong, unified country.
2. Its command economy fell apart and it was difficult to change its command economy to a market economy. Ethnic divisions led to former republics breaking away.
3. Nationalism encouraged the Serbians to pass laws that drove the Slovenes, Croatians, and Bosnians to declare their independence; it also drove the Serbians in Bosnia to engage in ethnic cleansing.
4. New Asian nations (South Korea, Taiwan, Singapore, and Hong Kong) are joining China and Japan to play a leading role in the world economy.
5. Ethnic identity encouraged people to break off and form their own countries after the end of communist rule; there were some violent conflicts.

Topic 21 Lesson 6

21.6 **Globalization defines the world of the post-Cold War and represents a major historical turning point. Globalization is the process by which national economies, politics, cultures, and societies become integrated with those of other nations around the world. Globalization began on a small scale 500 years ago, with the European Age of Exploration. By the 2000s, globalization was occurring at a dramatic, unprecedented pace.**

>> This textile plant in India represents one of the many industries that have migrated from European and North American countries to the developing world.

Interactive Flipped Video

Globalization and Trade

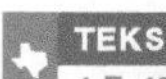

TEKS
1.F, 15.B, 17.C, 20.D, 28.D

>> Objectives

Summarize the impact of globalization on the modern world.

Describe the role of international organizations and treaties in expanding trade.

Analyze the costs and benefits of globalization.

>> Key Terms

globalization
interdependence
outsourcing
multinational corporation
World Trade Organization (WTO)
protectionism
bloc
sustainability,

Global Interdependence

One major effect of globalization is economic interdependence. **Interdependence** is the dependence of countries on each other for goods, resources, knowledge, and labor from other parts of the world. Recent improvements in transportation and the ability to communicate over long distances—telecommunications—have been dramatic. In addition, the spread of democratic systems and the rise of free trade—the buying and selling of goods by private individuals and corporations in a free market—have made the world increasingly interdependent.

The spread of goods and ideas has even led to the development of a global culture. All of these links, from economic to cultural, have created both challenges and opportunities.

Working in the Global Economy The world's rich and poor nations are linked. The nations of the developed world control much of the world's capital, trade, and technology. Yet they increasingly depend on largely low-paid workers in developing countries to produce manufactured goods cheaply. Companies in industrial nations also choose to outsource jobs. **Outsourcing** is the practice of sending

949

PEARSON realize. www.PearsonTexas.com Access your Digital Lesson.

Globalization and Trade

CONNECT

Preview Have students preview the **Lesson Objectives** and the list of **Key Terms**.

Students can also preview all the **Key Terms** and **Academic Vocabulary** using the **Interactive Reading Notepad** on the digital course or preview a summary of the lesson in the **Reading and Note Taking Study Guide**.

Online Use the **Editable Presentation** found on the digital course to present the main ideas for this lesson.

Start Up Activity

Explain that globalization is the integration of economies, politics, cultures, and societies of nations around the world. Globalization began with the European Age of Exploration. Ask: What might you expect to see in an early trading center or port city? *(Possible answer: ships, many people, flags from other countries, goods being loaded)* Ask: What might you see in a port city today? *(similar things, though with larger ships and more advanced technology)*

Tell students that in this lesson they will be learning about globalization in the modern world.

Online You can also project the **Start Up Activity** from the course.

INVESTIGATE

Have students read the section using the **Reading and Note Taking Study Guide** to help them take notes and understand the text as they read.

Global Interdependence

Explain that improvements in transportation and communication, the spread of democracy, and the rise of free trade have made the world increasingly interdependent. The spread of goods and ideas has led to development of a global culture. The rapid pace and impact of these developments make globalization a historical turning point.

Aa Vocabulary Builder

1. Have students pronounce the following academic vocabulary terms in this lesson and clarify the part of speech. For difficult or polysyllabic words, break them into syllables and pronounce them with the students.
2. Explain what the word means in common "student-friendly" language using synonyms and antonyms when possible. Provide concrete examples to clarify the meaning, and rephrase the definition.

asset: any property that has exchange value

integrate: to combine two or more things to make one thing

Topic 21 Lesson 6

Online Project the **Interactive Gallery: Aspects of Globalization**, and click through the images. Explain that globalization, the integration of national economies, politics, and cultures, defines the post–Cold War world.

ACTIVE CLASSROOM

Have students form groups. Ask them to explain the importance of global communication to the world economy. Have students write as much as they can for one minute, then switch with the person to their right. The next person tries to improve or elaborate on the response where the other person left off. Continue to switch until the paper comes back to the first person. The group then decides which is the best response and shares with the larger group.

Key Terms

Ask students to find the key term **interdependence** (in bold) in the text on the previous page and explain its meaning. Ask them to identify ways that nations can be interdependent. Write their answers on the board.

Guided Reading and Discussion

Ask students to identify the causes and effects of the global economic downturn in the 2000s and review them as a class.

Summarize How has debt harmed the developing world? *(Developing countries borrowed heavily to modernize. When the demand for their goods fell, they had difficulty repaying the loans, stalling development.)*

Identify Central Issues Describe the role of energy resources in the global economy. Why could a change in the global oil supply have a global impact? *(Energy in the form of oil is critical for transportation and industry. Limiting supplies or raising prices can hurt economies around the world.)*

work to the developing world in order to save money or increase efficiency. For example, many companies in the developed world have outsourced technological jobs to India, Russia, China, and the Philippines.

Growth of Multinational Corporations Globalization has led to the growth of huge, powerful, multinational corporations. **Multinational corporations** have assets in many countries and sell their goods and services worldwide.

These corporations have invested heavily in the developing world. They brought new technology to industries, built factories, improved transportation networks, and provided much-needed jobs to people in developing nations. Critics, however, have blasted multinational corporations for taking large profits out of developing countries, causing environmental damage, and paying low wages.

Global Economic Crises Globalization led to financial interdependence in the world's markets. As a result, an economic crisis in one country or region can have a global impact. In 1997, a financial crisis struck Thailand and quickly spread across Asia.

In 2007, American homeowners began defaulting on mortgages that they could no longer afford. During the 1990s, regulations on borrowing had been relaxed, enabling banks to make high-risk loans. Many Americans borrowed too much and could no longer pay their high bank notes. A banking crisis unfolded. Banks became unwilling to loan money to buyers, which contributed to a real estate crash. The resulting 2008 banking crisis in the United States and Europe set off the worst economic decline since the Great Depression.

World stock markets plunged. While the severity differed, nearly every nation around the world felt the impact. For example, Iceland saw the collapse of international investment banks, its stock market plummeted, and many feared "national bankruptcy." Other European countries, such as Spain, Ireland, and Greece, saw their economies plunge to near-depression levels, with high unemployment, falling GDPs, and social unrest.

Other nations fared better. Canada's strictly regulated banking system helped to protect the nation better than many others. Wealthy nations shored up their economies with economic stimulus packages and costly bailout plans for banks and other troubled industries. While these efforts provided limited relief, most nations are still struggling to recover to pre-crisis economic levels. Developing countries have also felt the impact as prices for their goods fell and international aid has decreased.

KEY EVENTS OF THE GLOBAL ECONOMIC DOWNTURN 2005–2012

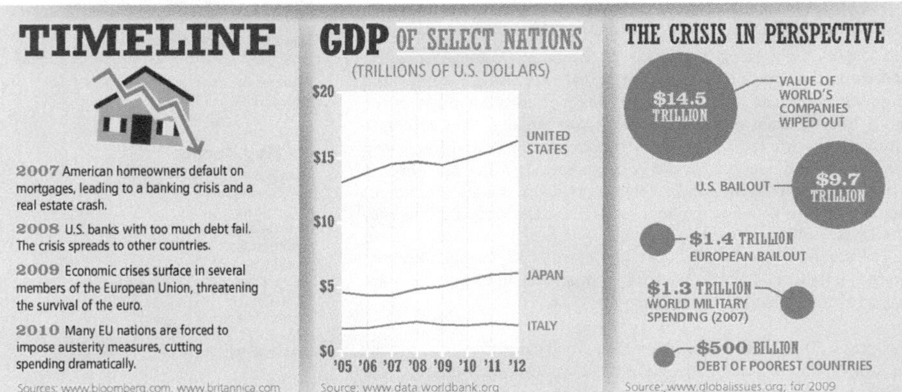

TIMELINE
2007 American homeowners default on mortgages, leading to a banking crisis and a real estate crash.
2008 U.S. banks with too much debt fail. The crisis spreads to other countries.
2009 Economic crises surface in several members of the European Union, threatening the survival of the euro.
2010 Many EU nations are forced to impose austerity measures, cutting spending dramatically.
Sources: www.bloomberg.com, www.britannica.com
GDP OF SELECT NATIONS
(TRILLIONS OF U.S. DOLLARS)
$20
$15
$10
$5
$0
UNITED STATES
JAPAN
ITALY
'05 '06 '07 '08 '09 '10 '11 '12
Source: www.data.worldbank.org
THE CRISIS IN PERSPECTIVE
$14.5 TRILLION
VALUE OF WORLD'S COMPANIES WIPED OUT
U.S. BAILOUT
$9.7 TRILLION
$1.4 TRILLION EUROPEAN BAILOUT
$1.3 TRILLION WORLD MILITARY SPENDING (2007)
$500 BILLION DEBT OF POOREST COUNTRIES
Source: www.globalissues.org; for 2009

>> **Analyze Charts** Which year of the downturn was the low point for the U.S. GDP? For Japan? For Italy? Based on information in the infographic, what is a likely reason why Italy's low point was different from that of the U.S. and Japan?

Interactive Gallery

D Differentiate Extra Support Have students work in pairs to define *interdependence*. Ask them how nations that are oil consumers and nations with oil reserves are interdependent. Have them discuss the advantages and disadvantages of interdependence as it relates to oil.

Answers

Analyze Charts *2009, 2009, 2010; According to the timeline on the left, European nations began austerity measures in 2010, which reduced economic activity.*

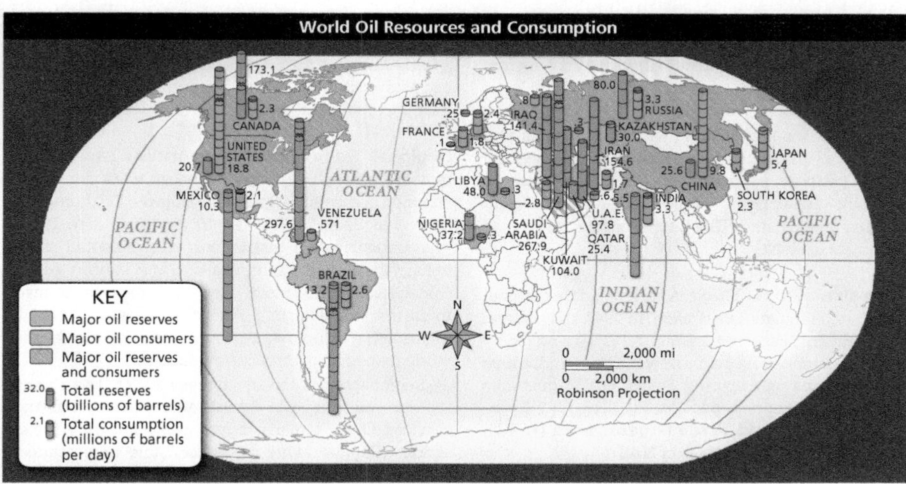

>> This map shows world oil reserves and consumption by country. **Analyze Data** Which nations contain both major oil reserves and are major oil consumers?

Changing Oil Prices Energy resources play a huge role in the global economy. All nations, for example, need oil for transportation and to manufacture products ranging from plastics to fertilizers. Any change in the global oil supply can have a huge impact worldwide.

In 1973, OPEC limited oil exports and raised prices, creating shortages and hurting economies throughout the world. Since then, whenever oil prices have risen sharply, people have faced economic uncertainties. In 2008, oil prices shot up, partly because the growing economies in China, India, and elsewhere led to increased demand. When the global economic crisis slowed demand, prices fell. This sudden, rapid change in oil prices has led to renewed calls to develop alternative energy sources. Still, the world has remained largely dependent on oil.

Debt and the Developing World Developing nations borrowed heavily in order to modernize. In the 1980s, bank interest rates rose as the world economy slowed. As demand for their goods fell, poor nations could not repay their debts or even interest on their loans. Their economies stalled as they spent much of their export incomes on payments to foreign creditors.

The debt crisis hurt rich nations, too. Banks were stuck with billions of dollars of bad debts. To ease the crisis, lenders made agreements with debtor nations to lower interest rates or allow more time to repay their loans. Some debts were canceled. In return, debtor nations had to accept market reforms to help improve their economies. Debt has remained a major issue throughout the developing world.

? IDENTIFY CAUSE AND EFFECT How do changes in the supply of oil affect economies around the world?

Global Organizations and Trade Agreements

Many international organizations and treaties connect people and nations around the world. These organizations have various goals, such as supporting development, settling economic issues, and promoting free trade.

International Organizations The United Nations is an international organization whose membership has grown from 50 nations in 1945 to 193 in 2014. As a result, its global role has expanded. The UN has sent peacekeepers to many trouble spots, including Cambodia, Congo, and the Balkans. In addition, the UN deals with economic and social development, human rights, humanitarian aid, and international law.

Other organizations deal with economic issues. The World Bank, for example, offers loans and technical

Topic 21 Lesson 6

Compare Points of View Why do multinational corporations typically invest heavily in the developing world? Why are some people critical of multinational corporations? *(Sample response: The corporations want to make a greater profit. Critics say they pay low wages and cause environmental damage.)*

Global Organizations and Trade Agreements

Many international organizations and treaties make global trade possible. The United Nations deals with a broad range of issues. The World Bank gives loans and advice to developing nations. The International Monetary Fund promotes global economic growth. The World Trade Organization (WTO) tries to ensure that trade flows smoothly and freely. It opposes protectionism—the use of tariffs to protect a country's industries from competition. Regional trade blocs, such as the EU in Europe, NAFTA in North America, and APEC in Asia, promote trade within regions.

Analyze Images

Draw students' attention to the map "World Oil Resources and Consumption." Have them compare the amounts of reserves in different countries. Ask them if there is anything that surprised them about these numbers. Which country has the largest oil reserves in the world? *(Venezuela)*

Guided Reading and Discussion

Using the Numbered Heads strategy, have students list each global organization or treaty on the board or on chart paper. For each, have students describe the organization or treaty, its impact on globalization, and its goals. Discuss the goals of each as well as any problems that have resulted. Ask students how their reading confirmed or caused them to revise their prediction about the goals and problems of trade organizations.

History Background

Outsourcing Improved communications technologies and the removal of barriers to trade have made it easier for companies in the developed world to move jobs to developing countries, where the pay is lower. This process, known as outsourcing or offshoring, allows companies to cut labor costs. During the 1980s and 1990s, outsourcing mainly affected manufacturing jobs, but since 2000, more service jobs have moved to developing countries. Critics of outsourcing say that these moves threaten the strength of the U.S. economy, which depends on such jobs. Advocates respond that outsourcing helps the American economy by allowing companies to sell products and services to consumers at lower prices and by improving companies' profits.

Answers

Analyze Data *China, Canada, Russia*

Identify Cause and Effect *higher energy prices and higher manufacturing and transportation costs worldwide*

Compare and Contrast How does the work of the World Bank differ from the World Trade Organization? *(Sample response: The World Bank offers loans and technical advice to developing nations. The World Trade Organization monitors trade and opposes tariffs and other restrictions.)*

Benefits and Costs of Globalization

Global trade has many social and economic benefits and costs. It brings consumers a variety of goods and services. It generally keeps prices lower. It also exposes people to new ideas and technology. However, some people oppose globalization of trade. They claim that rich countries exploit poor countries and that the emphasis on profits encourages too-rapid development.

Online Project the **Interactive Gallery: Smart Phones—American-Made?** and click through the hotspots.

ACTIVE CLASSROOM

Have students write a headline that captures the key point of the Interactive Gallery. Ask: If you were to write a headline for this topic right now that captured the most important aspect that should be remembered, what would that headline be?

Guided Reading and Discussion

Create two columns on the board, labeled *Costs* and *Benefits*. Have students list the costs or benefits of globalization in the appropriate column. Discuss how, if at all, each item differs for developed and developing nations.

Answers

Summarize *The IMF lends money to countries in crisis and helps developing nations solve economic problems.*

advice to developing nations. The International Monetary Fund (IMF) encourages global economic growth, promotes international monetary cooperation, and helps developing nations solve economic problems. It also lends to countries in crisis.

Organizations not affiliated with governments also provide aid. These nongovernmental organizations (NGOs) perform a variety of functions, such as monitoring human rights, supplying disaster relief, and providing medical care. The International Red Cross is an example of an NGO.

Treaties and Global Trade A variety of international treaties help regulate world trade. In 1947, the General Agreement on Tariffs and Trade (GATT) was signed by 23 nations. Its goal was to expand world trade and reduce tariffs, or taxes on imported goods. GATT gradually expanded over the next decades. In 1995, GATT was replaced by the **World Trade Organization (WTO),** which included 159 nations as of 2013.

Its goal was to set global rules to ensure that trade flows as smoothly and as freely as possible. The WTO opposes **protectionism,** or the use of tariffs and other restrictions that protect a country's home industries against international competition.

>> Officials of the African Union meet with European representatives in Addis Ababa, Ethiopia, in 2013. The AU is one of many regional organizations that engages in peacekeeping, emergency relief, and other operations.

The Group of Eight (G-8) is an organization of industrialized nations that meets annually to discuss a wide range of economic and other issues. The G-8 consists of Canada, France, Germany, Great Britain, Italy, Japan, Russia, and the United States.

Regional Trade Blocs Many nations have formed regional **blocs,** or groups, to boost trade and meet common needs. Among the largest is the EU (European Union.) In 1994, NAFTA (North American Free Trade Association) eased restrictions and promoted trade among the United States, Canada, and Mexico. APEC (Asian-Pacific Economic Cooperation) was formed to further trade among Pacific Rim nations. OPEC, representing oil-producing countries, regulates the production of oil to stabilize the market.

Regional trade groups like these work to lower trade barriers and encourage the free exchange of goods and services. Often, regional organizations like the African Union (AU) deal with both economic and political issues.

SUMMARIZE How does the IMF help developing nations?

Benefits and Costs of Globalization

With advanced communications and increased economic ties, globalization is expected to increase in the years ahead. Yet the debate about the impact of globalization on people and nations around the world continues.

Benefits Globalization brings many economic and social benefits. Global trade provides consumers with a greater variety of goods and services. And because many companies around the world compete to provide these goods and services, prices are generally lower. People in the industrial world, especially, have benefited from these changes.

Millions of people worldwide moved from rural areas to cities. There, they often had better access to education and health care. Globalization introduced people to new ideas, technologies, and communications. The money that developing nations earn from trade can be used to improve infrastructure, raise standards of living, and provide better services. Nations that practice free trade often become more democratic.

Costs Critics point to the social and economic costs of free trade and globalization. Generally, the anti-globalization movement focuses on poverty. They

English Language Proficiency Standards

Listening Strategies 1.B.1 Read "Benefits and Costs of Globalization" aloud to students.

Beginning With students, develop a two-column chart of the benefits and costs of globalization. Point out challenging words, and show how to spell them. Write two sentences, one in each column of the chart. Demonstrate how to make revisions and edits.

Intermediate Have students develop a two-column chart on the benefits and costs of globalization. Point out challenging words and explain how to spell them. Have groups write sentences to complete the chart. Review the sentences to demonstrate how to make revisions.

Advanced Instruct pairs to develop a two-column chart on the benefits and costs of globalization, completing the chart with full sentences. Review and demonstrate how to make revisions.

Advanced High Have individuals create and complete the two-column chart, and then have a partner review and suggest any revisions.

claim that rich nations exploit, or take advantage of, poor countries by raising their debt and lowering their standard of living. Many anti-globalizers target the World Bank and the IMF. Although these organizations provide aid to ease economic problems, they also require developing nations to make tough reforms and cut costly social programs. Anti-globalizers also criticize the United States, which they view as a driving force behind economic globalization.

Environmentalists have also criticized globalization. They claim that industries eager for profits encourage too-rapid development, endangering **sustainability,** or development that balances people's needs today with the need to preserve the environment for future generations.

SUPPORT IDEAS WITH EVIDENCE How has globalization improved the lives of many people around the world?

>> The Pantip Plaza shopping center in Bangkok, Thailand, offers a dizzying array of electronics from around the world. Globalization has greatly enabled the quicker and easier worldwide movement of consumer and other goods.

Interactive Gallery

ASSESSMENT

1. **Compare and Contrast** How does globalization affect economies around the world?
2. **Compare** In what ways are developed and developing countries affected differently by economic interdependence? Explain.
3. **Make Generalizations** How do international organizations work to expand trade?
4. **Apply Concepts** Do you think that increased globalization is inevitable? Explain.
5. **Compare Points of View** Describe one of the criticisms against multinational corporations.

>> Some people believe that globalization negatively impacts society. The World Trade Organization has sometimes met with stormy opposition to its role in increasing globalization.

Topic 21 Lesson 6

SYNTHESIZE

Online Project the **Digital Activity: Globalization**. Ask students to study the Venn diagram on globalization and then write a paragraph comparing and contrasting the effects of globalization on developed and developing nations. *(Paragraphs could include the following: Developing nations produce goods and services cheaply for consumers in developed countries. Developed countries may lose jobs to outsourcing. Developing nations may borrow from developed nations, losing some measure of control. Rapid development can cause challenges for developing countries. Globalization spreads technology and ideas around the globe, but the economies of countries become tied together.)*

DEMONSTRATE

Online Assign the **Digital Lesson Quiz** for this lesson if you haven't already done so. Students will be offered remediation or enrichment based on their score.

Pose these questions to the class on the Discussion Board:

Identify Cause and Effect How does outsourcing jobs affect both the home country and the country where the jobs are outsourced? *(Sample response: Outsourcing creates jobs in the country where the jobs are outsourced and eliminates some jobs in the home country.)*

Summarize Summarize the benefits and costs of globalization. *(Sample response: Globalization has exposed people to new ideas and technologies. However, it may allow rich nations to exploit poorer nations, and it could lead to increased economic imbalances.)*

Topic Inquiry

Have students continue their investigations for the Topic Inquiry.

Assessment

1. Globalization makes economies and societies more connected. It has both positive and negative impacts, which may vary from region to region.
2. Developed nations benefit from low-cost workers and imports. However, they are vulnerable to problems that arise in developing nations, such as excessive debt. Developing nations benefit from improvements in communication and technology, but they may suffer from exploitation of their labor and resources.
3. They work to lower trade barriers and encourage the free exchange of goods and services.
4. Yes, because technology has created ties among nations. No, because people can always reestablish old barriers.
5. Critics accuse multinational corporations of taking large profits and paying workers low wages.

Answers

Support Ideas With Evidence *Sample response: Global trade brings a variety of goods to consumers, generally at low prices. It improves technology and communications.*

Topic 21 Lesson 7

Social and Environmental Issues

CONNECT

Preview Have students preview the **Lesson Objectives** and the list of **Key Terms**.

Students can also preview all the **Key Terms** and **Academic Vocabulary** using the **Interactive Reading Notepad** on the digital course or preview a summary of the lesson in the **Reading and Note Taking Study Guide**.

Online Use the **Editable Presentation** found on the digital course to present the main ideas for this lesson.

Start Up Activity

Ask students to brainstorm some of the world's environmental problems. *(Sample responses: loss of rain forests, species extinction, overpopulation, global warming, fossil fuel dependency, pollution)* How might these problems affect not only a country or a region but also the entire world? *(Sample response: Problems like these impact Earth as a whole. Pollution can spread through the air, plants, animals, or water to places other than where it was originally created.)* Have students share their responses with other students, either in class or through a chat or blog space.

Online You can also project the **Start Up Activity** from the course.

INVESTIGATE

Have students read the section using the **Reading and Note Taking Study Guide** to help them take notes and understand the text as they read.

Global Challenges

Explain that poverty, disasters, and disease have always been part of the human experience. The difference is that today's world is interconnected in unprecedented ways. Today, these problems have a far-reaching social and economic impact.

>> A homeless child in Katmandu, Nepal, sleeps on the sidewalk. Half of the world's people live in extreme poverty.

21.7 Globalization involves much more than economic links and the spread of technology. It has brought all kinds of issues to the world's attention. Half of the world's population, or almost 3 billion people, live on less than $2 a day. Almost 1 billion people cannot read or write. About 790 million people in the developing world suffer from hunger—many from extreme hunger. Millions suffer from life-threatening diseases. Although such problems mainly affect the developing world, they have global dimensions that often require global solutions.

Interactive Flipped Video

TEKS
17.C, 20.D, 24.A

>> Objectives

Explain the impact of poverty, disasters, and disease on nations around the world.

Describe global efforts to protect human rights.

Evaluate the environmental challenges facing the world.

>> Key Terms

tsunami
epidemic
famine
refugee
acid rain
deforestation
erosion
global warming
indigenous peoples

Social and Environmental Issues

Global Challenges

Worldwide Poverty Experts cannot agree on the exact number of people living in poverty worldwide, in part because there are many ways to measure poverty. Experts do agree about some trends, however. First, the gap between rich and poor nations is huge and growing. Second, some progress has been made toward reducing poverty, but it has been uneven. India and China, for example, have enjoyed economic growth, which has meant fewer people overall living in poverty there, but extreme poverty still persists.

Poverty is a complex issue with many causes. Many poor nations owe billions in debt and have no extra money to spend to improve living conditions. Political upheavals, civil war, corruption, and poor planning also inhibit efforts to reduce poverty worldwide. Rapid population growth—especially in India, China, and the nations of Africa and Latin America—has made it harder for countries to provide basic services.

 www.PearsonTexas.com Access your Digital Lesson.

Aa Vocabulary Builder

1. Have students pronounce the following academic vocabulary terms in this lesson and clarify the part of speech. For difficult or polysyllabic words, break them into syllables and pronounce them with the students.
2. Explain what the word means in common "student-friendly" language using synonyms and antonyms when possible. Provide concrete examples to clarify the meaning, and rephrase the definition.

inhibit: to hold back or keep from some action

fluctuation: swing; the rising and falling of something

Organizations like the World Bank believe that erasing poverty is essential to global security and peace. In this spirit, they call on poor nations to limit population growth. They also encourage rich nations to forgive the debt of poor nations, making more funds available for education, healthcare, and other services.

Natural Disasters Natural disasters range from earthquakes, floods, and avalanches to droughts, fires, hurricanes, and volcanic eruptions. They strike all over the world all the time. They cause death, destruction, and unsanitary conditions that often lead to disease. Although such events may strike anywhere, they often hit developing nations especially hard due to such factors as heavy population concentrations and inadequate building construction.

In 2004, a huge underwater earthquake in the Indian Ocean triggered a massive tidal wave, or **tsunami** (tsoo NAH mee). It swept over islands and the coasts of 11 countries ringing the Indian Ocean. More than 160,000 people were killed, mainly in Indonesia, Thailand, Sri Lanka, and India. Millions were left homeless or lost their livelihood. The following year, 2005, Hurricane Katrina struck the gulf coastal regions of Louisianna and Mississippi. The 30-foot storm surge and high winds washed out parts of the earthen levees and floodwalls surrounding New Orleans, resulting in massive flooding and some 1,800 fatalities. The Federal Emergency Management Agency (FEMA) calls Katrina "the single most catastrophic natural disaster and costliest hurricane in U.S. history."

Even a local disaster can disrupt the economy of an entire country and have a ripple effect on the global economy. For example, a recent typhoon destroyed Myanmar's rice producing region, leading to the threat of famine in that country. One benefit of globalization is that news of natural disasters spreads instantly and triggers a quick aid response.

Global Diseases With millions of people on the move daily, diseases can spread rapidly. Still, health experts, working together, can often identify and limit outbreaks of many diseases. In the early 2000s, air travelers spread SARS (severe acute respiratory syndrome), a respiratory disease, from China to more than two dozen countries. Health officials took quick action to stop the SARS outbreak.

Other diseases, including the avian flu (bird flu), mad cow disease, West Nile virus, swine flu (H1N1), and influenza have raised concerns about the global spread of disease. Diseases often spread before health officials know they exist. Globalization has meant that health experts around the world cooperate to quickly identify and contain outbreaks of disease.

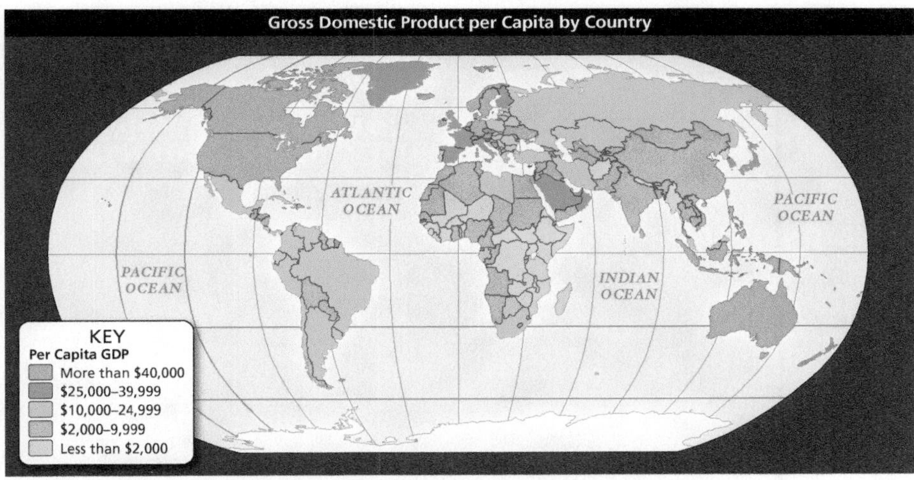

>> **Analyze Maps** This map shows the relative wealth and poverty of nations as determined by the gross domestic product (GDP) per capita. What areas of the world have the highest GDP?

Topic 21 Lesson 7

Discuss Ask students to use their prior knowledge to identify some of the world's wealthiest nations *(United States, Canada, Australia, Norway, Sweden)* and poorest nations *(Afghanistan, Ethiopia, Somalia, Myanmar, Zimbabwe)*. Have them identify patterns of wealth and poverty according to continents or other geographical areas. Ask how other global challenges might relate to this distribution of wealth and poverty: environmental problems, hunger and famine, natural disasters, education, and human rights.

Analyze Images

Draw students' attention to the world map. Explain that it shows the relative wealth and poverty of nations according to their GDP per capita. Briefly explain gross domestic product. It is an economic term that measures a country's output, or production—that is, the total value of the goods and services it produces in a certain time period, usually a year. Ask: Which continent has the largest number of countries with a per capita GDP of less than $2,000? *(Africa)* Tell students that *per capita* is a Latin phrase that means "per head," or "per person." GDP per capita is GDP divided by the number of people in the country. It is not a measure of individual income. Rather, it is a formula for measuring a nation's average standard of living.

D Differentiate Challenge/Gifted Have students do additional research on the complex interaction between globalization and human mobility. Ask them to answer the question, How and why does the United States both encourage and discourage immigration? *(Certain industries, such as agriculture, depend on the low-cost labor provided by unskilled migrants, while other industries are in need of highly educated, skilled workers from abroad. Factors that discourage immigration include U.S. immigration laws and the fears of some that immigrants will take jobs, drive down wages, be dependent on costly government services, and alter the cultural and political identity of the American people.)*

Answers

Analyze Maps *North America, Australia, Northern European countries*

Key Terms

Draw students' attention to the key term **refugees** (in bold) in the text. Tell them that as of 2013, there were more than 10 million refugees around the world, and around 75 percent were in Africa and Asia.

Guided Reading and Discussion

Ask students to locate the infographic about global migration on this page. Point out the various reasons why people leave their homeland and migrate to other countries. Call attention to the Top Five lists of countries that people leave (Countries of Origin) and countries they move to (Destination Countries). Notice which country is on both lists. Ask: Why might this be the case? *(The people migrating to a certain country are not the same ones who are leaving it, and the two groups may have different reasons for migrating—mostly economic in one case, and mostly political in another, for example.)*

Draw Inferences Ask: How does international migration influence globalization? *(As people move from one country to another, they bring their language and customs with them, which adds diversity to the population of the host country. Those migrants often send money home to family members left behind, which adds to the economy in the home country.)* Alternatively, how does globalization influence migration? *(Advances in global communication and technology make it easier than ever for people to share information, transfer money, and travel from one place to another. Multinational corporations need workers from a wide variety of national backgrounds.)*

Some diseases have proved hard to contain. When a disease spreads rapidly, it is called an **epidemic.** HIV/AIDS is an epidemic that began in the 1980s. HIV/AIDS has taken a staggering human and economic toll worldwide, especially in southern Africa and Southeast Asia. As of 2011, an estimated 35 million people had died from HIV/AIDS and as many as 70 million were infected with HIV.

The treatment and prevention of AIDS had been a global priority for more than a decade. In some nations, education about how to prevent the transmission of AIDS had lowered infection rates. Despite progress, HIV/AIDS continues to spread, especially in Africa, Asia, and Eastern Europe.

Hunger and Famine For tens of millions of people, hunger poses a daily threat. A major problem is that food does not get distributed to the people who need it most—especially in countries racked by poverty and civil strife. Hunger escalates into **famine** when large numbers of people in a region or country face death by starvation.

Natural disasters can cause famine. Human activity can also cause famine. War disrupts food distribution. During the 1970s and 1980s, civil wars raging in Ethiopia and Sudan intensified the effects of drought, leading to famine. Each side in the conflict tried to keep relief supplies from reaching the other. In many instances, only the efforts of international aid groups have saved millions of people from starvation. Ongoing hostilities in those nations have kept the crises going into the 21st century.

People Search for a Better Life Globalization has led to a vast movement of people around the world. Although some people choose to migrate to find jobs or reunite with their families, millions more are **refugees,** people who are forced to move because of poverty, war, persecution, natural disasters, or other crises.

Many migrants find jobs and homes and create better lives in their new countries. But others face hostility and discrimination. Many people in developed countries resent immigrants, who they claim take away jobs and services from natural-born citizens. Millions of migrants, both legal and illegal, head to Europe, Asia, and North America. Each year, the United States alone receives about one million legal immigrants and 300,000 or more illegal immigrants. Since World War II, Germany has welcomed large numbers of Turkish, Italian, and Russian immigrants to make up for the part of the labor force that was lost in two world wars.

As migration has grown, so has the smuggling of human beings across borders. Many illegal immigrants pay smugglers large sums to help them reach their

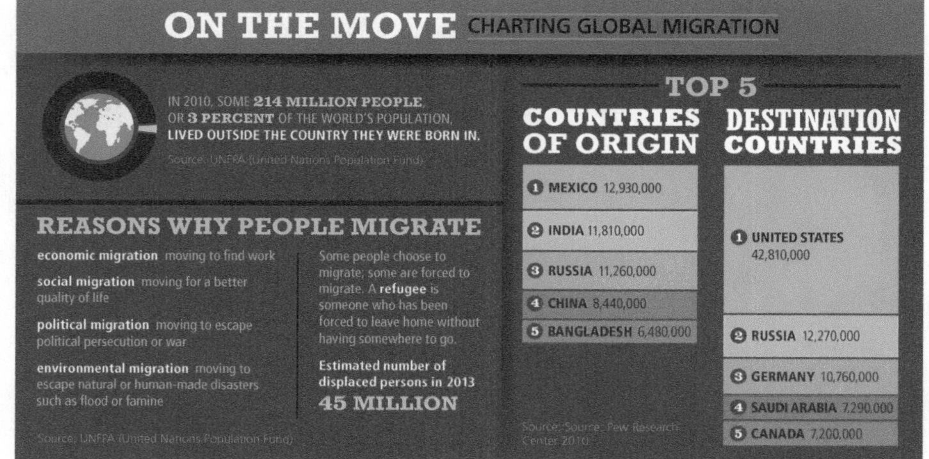

ON THE MOVE
CHARTING GLOBAL MIGRATION
IN 2010, SOME 214 MILLION PEOPLE, OR 3 PERCENT OF THE WORLD'S POPULATION, LIVED OUTSIDE THE COUNTRY THEY WERE BORN IN.
Source: UNFPA (United Nations Population Fund)
REASONS WHY PEOPLE MIGRATE
economic migration moving to find work
social migration moving for a better quality of life
political migration moving to escape political persecution or war
environmental migration moving to escape natural or human-made disasters such as flood or famine
Some people choose to migrate; some are forced to migrate. A refugee is someone who has been forced to leave home without having somewhere to go.
Estimated number of displaced persons in 2013
45 MILLION
Source: UNFPA (United Nations Population Fund)
TOP 5
COUNTRIES OF ORIGIN
1 MEXICO 12,930,000
2 INDIA 11,810,000
3 RUSSIA 11,260,000
4 CHINA 8,440,000
5 BANGLADESH 6,480,000
DESTINATION COUNTRIES
1 UNITED STATES 42,810,000
2 RUSSIA 12,270,000
3 GERMANY 10,760,000
4 SAUDI ARABIA 7,290,000
5 CANADA 7,200,000
Source: Source: Pew Research Center 2010

>> **Analyze Graphs** The United States has more than three times the number of international migrants than any other country. What is the second-highest-ranked country in terms of destination?

English Language Proficiency Standards

Listening 2.B.1 Read "Global Challenges" aloud to students.

Beginning Explain long and short vowel sounds for each of the six vowels (*a, e, i, o, u,* and *y*). Find example words for each vowel sound in the text. Have students repeat the words after they hear them spoken.

Intermediate Review long and short vowel sounds for the six vowels in the alphabet (*a, e, i, o, u,* and *y*). Find example words for each vowel sound in the text. Display the words, read them aloud, and underline the vowel in each word. Repeat on other examples students find in the text.

Advanced Have pairs of students scan "Global Challenges" for three examples of each short vowel and each long vowel. Then have pairs share their lists.

Advanced High Have individuals scan "Global Challenges" for three examples of each short vowel and each long vowel. Ask students to share their lists.

Answers

Analyze Graphs *Russia*

destinations. In 2006, the United Nations estimated that human smuggling was a $10-billion-a-year global industry.

CONTRAST Explain both the negative and positive effects of globalization on the spread of disease.

Human Rights

In 1948, UN members approved the Universal Declaration of Human Rights. It stated that all people are entitled to basic rights, which include: "life, liberty and security of person"; freedom from slavery, torture, or discrimination; "freedom of thought, conscience and religion"; the right to work and to rest and leisure; the right to an education; and the right to "a standard of living adequate for the health and well-being of himself and of his family."

In 1975, nations signing the Helsinki Accords guaranteed such basic rights as freedom of speech, religion, and the press as well as the rights to a fair trial, to earn a living, and to live in safety. Despite such agreements, human rights abuses—ranging from arbitrary arrest to torture and slavery—occur daily around the world.

>> In 1946, former First Lady Eleanor Roosevelt became head of the UN Commission on Human Rights, and the only woman to help draft the Universal Declaration of Human Rights.

World Community Confronts Abuses Human rights abuses are not new, but globalization has brought them to the attention of the world in a new way. And the spread of democracy has forced people to question how human rights abuses can still happen in a modern world. In response, the world community has pressed countries to end abuses. In the 1980s, for example, economic pressure was used against South Africa to end apartheid, its system of legalized segregation.

Sometimes there is no stable government to pressure, or direct pressure does not work. Still, the UN, the United States, and human rights groups monitor and report on human rights violations, from Afghanistan to Bosnia to Congo. They even monitor human rights in nations that are part of the developed world, such as Russia.

The Struggle for Women's Rights For decades, a global women's movement has focused attention on the needs of women worldwide. The UN Charter supported "equal rights for men and women."

By 1950, women had won the right to vote in most European nations, as well as in Japan, China, Brazil, and other countries. In most African nations, both women and men won the vote when their countries gained independence. Women have headed elected governments in many nations, including Britain, Germany, Israel, India, Pakistan, and the Philippines.

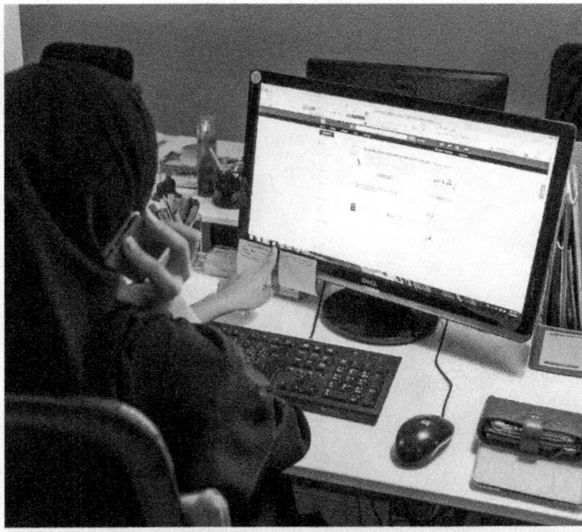

>> In Saudi Arabia, many women are highly educated but struggle to find jobs. By law, men and women may not work together. Women must have separate offices, entrances, and security guards.

Topic 21 Lesson 7

Human Rights

Students may be familiar with the phrase from the Declaration of Independence: "We hold these truths to be self-evident, that all men are created equal, that they are endowed by their Creator with certain unalienable Rights, that among these are Life, Liberty and the pursuit of Happiness." Explain that other nations hold both similar and dissimilar views of the "unalienable rights" of human beings. In 1948, the United Nations set out to list and define those rights to which all people are entitled. Legal and cultural discrimination has been aimed at women, children, and indigenous people, as well as people of certain races, religions, and other categories.

Online Project the **Interactive Gallery: Women's Lives in the 21st Century**, and review the images. Focus on the third image in the gallery, showing a billboard in China. What is the intent of that billboard? *(to solicit support for China's one-child policy)*

ACTIVE CLASSROOM

Using the Cartoon It activity, have each student draw a quick copy of one compelling image from this lesson. The image can be from the Interactive Gallery: Women's Lives in the 21st Century, or the section "Human Rights." Then have students turn their drawings into political cartoons that illustrate a key concept or main idea.

History Background

Changing U.S. Immigration Policies Until the early twentieth century, the United States placed few restrictions on immigration from Europe, though immigrants from Asia faced obstacles. Beginning in the 1920s, the United States sharply limited immigration. In the 1960s, the United States again opened the way for expanded immigration, though regulations still limited the number of legal immigrants. To get around limits, many immigrants crossed the border between Mexico and the United States illegally. Latin American immigrants became an important part of the workforce in some states. When President George W. Bush took office in 2001, he had hoped to make it easier for Latin Americans to work in the United States legally. However, terrorist attacks in 2001 created great concern about the safety of the U.S. borders, and immigration continues to be a source of extensive political debate.

Answers

Contrast *Negative: Globalization has led to increased movement of people around the world, which spreads disease farther and more rapidly than before. Positive: Globalization enables health experts to track the spread of disease and deliver aid and disease-prevention education to people in need.*

Topic 21 Lesson 7

Guided Reading and Discussion

Remind students that the human rights of women and children are often connected. Why is that? Countries that value individual human rights are usually the same countries that value women's rights and those of children. Nevertheless, discrimination against various groups exists in most countries.

Explain What is the basis for discrimination, and why does discrimination exist in the twenty-first century? *(The basis of discrimination is the idea that people are not equal, but that some people, by virtue of their gender, social position, religion, ethnicity, race, or other characteristics, are better than others. Discrimination exists because it benefits the people in power, who enjoy privileges at the expense of those who are discriminated against.)*

Evaluate Impact Break students into six teams. Assign each team five consecutive articles of the Universal Declaration of Human Rights. Have the teams investigate their assigned rights and report back to the class in the following manner: Briefly explain the meaning of each article, state whether everyone on the team agrees with its content, and give an illustration of how a particular country either recognizes or fails to recognize that universal right.

>> Even in wealthy nations, women are more likely to live in poverty than men. This homeless woman in Miami Beach, Florida, pushes her belongings in a shopping cart.

>> Two Hmong women work in a field in Laos. Globally, most women who work outside the home work in agriculture.

Interactive Gallery

Still, a report to the UN noted that while women represent half of the world's people, "they perform nearly two-thirds of all working hours, receive only one-tenth of the world's income, and own less than one percent of world property." The UN and other groups thus carefully monitor the human rights of women. They also condemn violence and discrimination against women. More than 165 countries have ratified a new women's human rights treaty.

Changing Roles for Women In the developed world, more and more women now work outside their homes. They have gained high-profile jobs as business owners and executives, scientists, and technicians.

Yet women often receive less pay for the same job than men do, and many must balance demanding jobs with childrearing and housework. Still, many women do not have the option of staying at home, because many families need two incomes to provide the necessities of life.

The education gap has been narrowing in developing nations, and women from the middle and elite classes have entered the workforce in growing numbers. Still, women often shoulder a heavy burden of work. In rural areas, especially in Africa where many men have migrated to cities to work, women do much of the farm work in addition to household tasks. In other regions, such as Southeast Asia, young women often leave home in search of work to support the family or to pay for their brothers' education. In many places, cultural traditions still confine women to the home or segregate men and women in the workplace.

The Rights and Protection of Children Worldwide, children suffer terrible abuses. A 2005 UN report showed that half of the world's children suffer the effects of extreme poverty, armed conflict, and AIDS.

Children are also the targets of human rights violations. In some nations, children are forced to serve as soldiers or even slaves. The resulting abuses not only damage children but also hurt a country's hope for the future.

In 1989, the UN General Assembly approved the Convention on the Rights of the Child. This human rights treaty sets standards for basic rights for children, including the right to life, liberty, education, and healthcare. But ensuring these rights has proved difficult or even impossible.

In developing countries, tens of millions of children between the ages of 5 and 14 do not attend school. Instead, they work full time. Often, these child laborers work long hours in dangerous, unhealthy conditions for little pay. Many are physically abused by their employers and live in conditions of near slavery. Still, their families need the income the children earn. In some cases, children must work to pay off a family's debt. Human rights groups, the UN, and developed nations have focused a spotlight on child labor in order to end such practices.

Threats to Indigenous Peoples **Indigenous peoples** are generally those considered to be the descendants of the earliest inhabitants of a region. They include such ethnic and cultural groups as Native Americans, the Aborigines of Australia, and the Maoris of New Zealand. Indigenous peoples in many areas face discrimination and other abuses. Often, their lands have been forcibly taken.

In South America, developers have pushed into once-isolated areas, threatening the ways of life of indigenous peoples. Many Indians have died of diseases carried by the newcomers. During Guatemala's long civil war, the government targeted Mayan villagers, killing tens of thousands. The UN has worked to set standards to protect the rights of indigenous peoples.

CATEGORIZE What common characteristics are found in countries that deny human rights to women?

>> Decades of armed conflict in Colombia have forced some 41,000 indigenous people from their ancestral lands. Here, displaced families struggle to survive in makeshift huts.

Development and the Environment

Since earliest times, people have taken what they wanted from the environment. In the past, damage was limited because the world's population was small and technology was simple. Industrialization and the world population explosion have increased the damage done to the environment.

As you have read, development improves lives and strengthens economies—but at a price. One of the great challenges of the twenty-first century is how to achieve necessary development without causing permanent damage to the environment.

Threats to the Environment Since the 1970s, environmentalists have warned about threats to the environment. Strip mining provides ores for industry but destroys land.

Chemical pesticides and fertilizers produce larger food crops but harm the soil and water and may cause certain cancers. Oil spills pollute waterways and kill marine life. Gases from power plants and factories produce **acid rain,** a form of pollution in which toxic chemicals in the air fall back to Earth as rain, snow, or hail. Acid rain has damaged forests, lakes, and farmland.

>> Fire boats battle an explosion on the offshore oil rig Deepwater Horizon in 2010. The disaster in the Gulf of Mexico, off the coast of Louisiana, caused the worst oil spill in U.S. history.

Topic 21 Lesson 7

Development and the Environment

Globalization has contributed to environmental problems around the world. Ask students to list different types of environmental concerns. *(air, water, and soil pollution and the varieties of pollution: radiation, chemical, toxic waste, litter; habitat encroachment and species extinctions; climate and land use concerns: deforestation, desertification, climate change/global warming)*

Identify Cause and Effect Break students into teams, and have each team choose one of the environmental concerns listed above. Have each team identify the causes of the problem and its effects on the environment.

Online Project the **Interactive Map: Global Environmental Challenges**, and view each hotspot while a student reads the text aloud. Have the students write their answer to the follow-up question.

ACTIVE CLASSROOM

Use the Ranking strategy with the Interactive Map. Have students rank the environmental challenges shown on the map according to how critical it is to solve immediately.

Answers

Categorize *Countries that deny rights to women may share similar cultural traditions that grant men a higher status than women. Discrimination against women is, therefore, embedded in the culture. Undeveloped countries are characterized by widespread poverty, which often forces women to live and work in abusive conditions.*

Topic 21 Lesson 7

Drawing Conclusions In the course of doing the Active Classroom activity, students might conclude that it is not possible or realistic to rank the environmental challenges, as all are interconnected and all are critical. However, the act of ranking will force students to consider which challenges have the most widespread or influential effects on human lives.

Guided Reading and Discussion

Have students debate the pros and cons of the Kyoto Protocol. Assemble two teams, one in favor of the protocol and one opposed. In addition, choose a team of judges. Have each team choose three students who will be the debaters, while the remaining team members contribute research. All students should research the topic in order to develop informed opinions. The students chosen as judges should review the rules of debate. Finally, hold the debate in class and have the judges decide a winner.

Answers

Identify Supporting Details *Possible answer: Acid rain and air pollution—toxic chemicals released into the air in one place can fall back to Earth many miles away as acid rain.*

Pollution from nuclear plants is another concern. In 1986, an accident at the Chernobyl nuclear power plant in the Soviet Union exposed people, crops, and animals to deadly radiation over a wide area. Another nuclear accident occurred in 2011, after a tsunami off the coast of Japan devastated the country's northeastern coast, killing more than 19,000 people. The tsunami severely damaged the Fukushima nuclear power plant there, causinga partial meltdown in the reactor core that released radioactive materials into the environment. Such accidents have prompted citizens to call on industries and governments to develop better safety measures.

Changes to Deserts and Forests As you have read, desertification is a major problem, especially in the Sahel region of Africa. Another threat—especially in Africa, Latin America, and Asia—is **deforestation,** or the cutting of trees without replacing them. In many developing countries, people see economic growth as their highest priority, and the forests are resources that provide needed jobs and increased wealth. People cut trees for firewood or shelter, or to sell in markets abroad. Some burn down forests to make way for farms and cattle ranches, or for industry. In the Amazon basin region of Brazil, the world's largest rain forest, forests are also cleared in order to tap into rich mineral resources.

However, once forests are cleared, rains wash nutrients from the soil, destroying its fertility. Deforestation also causes **erosion,** or the wearing away of land, which encourages flooding.

The deforestation of rain forests is particularly worrisome. Rain forests like the Amazon play a key role in absorbing poisonous carbon dioxide from the air and releasing essential oxygen. They are also home to millions of animal and plant species, many of which have become extinct because of deforestation.

>> A soy plantation in the Amazon rain forest in Brazil shows how acres of forest are cleared for agricultural purposes.

Interactive Map

The Debate Over Climate Change Another environmental challenge—one that is hotly debated—is **global warming.** Global warming refers to the increase in Earth's average surface temperature over time. A rise in Earth's temperature could bring about changes such as the following: a rise in sea level, changes in weather patterns, increased desertification in some areas, and an increase in precipitation in others. Because climates in some areas could become colder, many scientists prefer to call the trend "climate change."

Scientists agree that Earth's temperature has risen slightly over the past century. Many scientists think that this warming comes from gases released into the atmosphere by human activity such as the burning of fossil fuels. These "greenhouse" gases trap warmth in Earth's atmosphere.

Some scientists, however, and many policymakers, argue that global warming is due to natural fluctuations in Earth's climate.

The debate over a treaty called the Kyoto Protocol points to a central challenge facing world leaders: Does economic development have to conflict with protecting the environment? The treaty, signed by 140 countries, with the major exceptions of the United States and Australia, went into effect in 2005. Its purpose is to lower the emissions of carbon dioxide and other "greenhouse" gases that contribute to global warming. Many developing nations refuse to sign because they say they must exploit their resources in order to develop fully. The United States has not signed the Kyoto Protocol because it believes the treaty could strain economic growth. Nations that have signed the treaty, however, argue that developed nations must lead the way in slowing emissions.

IDENTIFY SUPPORTING DETAILS Describe how a regional environmental problem can affect other parts of the world.

English Language Proficiency Standards

Learning Strategies 1.C.1 Retell or have students reread "Development and the Environment." Have students select one of the environmental threats described and illustrate the threat and its effects in a drawing or diagram, including captions or labeling as appropriate.

Beginning Retell the text using accessible language. Then work with students to create a drawing or diagram that illustrates one of the environmental threats, such as acid rain or deforestation, described in the text. As a group, assist them in writing a caption explaining the diagram. Make sure they use specific terms, such as *environment* or *pollution*, in the caption.

Intermediate Complete the Beginning activity, but have students create a drawing or diagram with captions independently.

Advanced Have students complete the Intermediate activity independently, including labels for different parts of their illustration. Then have students show and explain their diagrams to a partner.

Advanced High Have students read the text and create a labeled diagram. Ask students to write a paragraph to explain their work.

ELPS **ELPS 1.C.1** Choose one of the environmental threats described in *Development and the Environment* and create a drawing or diagram illustrating the threat and its effects.

ASSESSMENT

1. **Infer** Why might the elimination of poverty be considered essential to global security and peace?
2. **Identify Patterns** What are some of the causes of migration? What characteristics might a migrant look for in a new country?
3. **Identify Central Ideas** How are the human rights of children around the world violated?
4. **Explain** Explain the significance of the United Nations in relation to human rights.
5. **Compare and Contrast** Give three examples of how development can conflict with the preservation of a clean environment.

SYNTHESIZE

Online Project the **Digital Activity: "The Same Boat."** Ask students to write their answers to the questions. Have students pair with a partner and share their answers. Have partners compare and contrast the two quotes—how are they the same, and how are they different? Ask: What did Kennedy mean when he said, "Things are different now"? Different from when? Different how?

Discuss Ask students to recall the Topic Essential Question, "What are the benefits and risks of interdependence?" How do the two quotes above relate to the question?

DEMONSTRATE

Online Assign the **Digital Lesson Quiz** for this lesson if you haven't already done so. Students will be offered automatic remediation or enrichment based on their score.

Pose these questions to the class on the Discussion Board: What are the benefits of globalization? What are the drawbacks? Explain why some aspects of globalization can fall into both categories.

Topic Inquiry

Have students continue their investigations for the Topic Inquiry.

Assessment

1. Poverty often causes political instability and civil unrest, which can lead to wars and terrorism.
2. Poverty, famine, discrimination, natural disasters, or war; a migrant would be attracted to economic and educational opportunities, freedom from war and persecution, and, possibly, communities of fellow immigrants.
3. In some countries, children are forced to serve as soldiers or to work as slaves. They are denied education and forced to work at young ages in unsafe and unhealthy conditions.
4. The UN set the standard for defining human rights in its Universal Declaration of Human Rights. It monitors human rights violations in nations around the world, and condemns and publicizes those violations.
5. Possible answer: Deforestation supplies timber for development but is impacting Earth's critical rain forests; strip mining produces necessary ores but destroys land and pollutes the surrounding environment; oil provides necessary energy, but burning it pollutes the air, and transporting it can result in oil spills that pollute the water, land, and wildlife.

Terrorism and International Security

CONNECT

Preview Have students preview the **Lesson Objectives** and the list of **Key Terms**.

Students can also preview all the **Key Terms** and **Academic Vocabulary** using the **Interactive Reading Notepad** on the digital course or preview a summary of the lesson in the **Reading and Note Taking Study Guide**.

Online Use the **Editable Presentation** found on the digital course to present the main ideas for this lesson.

Start Up Activity

Explain that the terrorist attacks of September 11, 2001, were a major turning point in U.S. history. Since those attacks, the United States has waged two wars and undertaken many security measures domestically that affect people's everyday lives. Ask: In what other ways do you think the events of September 11, 2001, have affected the United States in the years since the attacks? *(Sample response: September 11 destroyed many people's sense of safety, and now national security measures often come at the price of personal freedom and privacy.)*

Online You can also project the **Start Up Activity** from the course.

INVESTIGATE

Have students read the section using the **Reading and Note Taking Study Guide** to help them take notes and understand the text as they read.

The Threat of New Weapons

In the 1900s, nations developed weaponry capable of quickly killing masses of people. The creation of these weapons brought a new urgency to international negotiations. Nuclear, biological, and chemical weapons work in different ways, but all have the same goal. Controlling access to them, preventing the spread and use of them, and even eliminating them has become a focus of twenty-first century diplomacy.

>> A soldier takes cover during a 2008 bombing in Mumbai, India. A group of Pakistani terrorists stormed various sites in the city, killing more than 160 people.

Interactive Flipped Video

21.8 During the Cold War, the United States and the Soviet Union challenged one another around the world and built huge arsenals of nuclear weapons. The end of the Cold War seemed to promise an end to global conflict and the threat of nuclear war. However, since the fall of the Soviet Union, new and unpredictable threats continue to haunt the world. The weapons developed during the Cold War still exist. Keeping nuclear, chemical, and biological weapons out of the hands of dangerous groups has become an important issue.

TEKS 13.E, 13.F, 14.A, 14.B, 25.D

>> Objectives

Explain how nuclear, biological, and chemical weapons threaten international security.

Analyze the growth of terrorist groups such as al Qaeda.

Explain how the United States and other nations have responded to terrorism from September 11, 2001, to the present.

>> Key Terms

proliferate
terrorism
al Qaeda
Afghanistan
Taliban

Terrorism and International Security

The Threat of New Weapons

The Nuclear Nonproliferation Treaty In 1968, during a thaw in the Cold War, the United States, the Soviet Union, and 60 other nations signed the Nuclear Nonproliferation Treaty (NPT). The purpose of the treaty was to ensure that nuclear weapons did not **proliferate,** or rapidly spread, to nations that had no nuclear weapons. The NPT recognizes the United States, Britain, Russia, France, and China as nuclear weapons states. Since then, the treaty has been renewed, with 190 nations agreeing not to develop or possess nuclear weapons. The International Atomic Energy Agency (IAEA) monitors nations regularly to check that they comply with the treaty.

Four nations have not signed the NPT: India, Pakistan, Israel, and South Sudan. India and Pakistan tested nuclear weapons in 1998, raising fears of a nuclear arms race in Asia. North Korea has also openly tested nuclear weapons. A few signers of the NPT, such as Iran, have tried to sidestep the treaty by acquiring nuclear technology

www.PearsonTexas.com
Access your Digital Lesson.

962

Aa Vocabulary Builder

1. Have students pronounce the following academic vocabulary terms in this lesson and clarify the part of speech. For difficult or polysyllabic words, break them into syllables and pronounce them with the students.
2. Explain what the word means in common "student-friendly" language using synonyms and antonyms when possible. Provide concrete examples to clarify the meaning, and rephrase the definition.

priority: something deemed more important than other things

monitor: to watch closely

acquire: to gain or come to have something

that they claim is being used to develop nuclear power as an energy source.

Nuclear Weapons in Russia After the collapse of the Soviet Union, stockpiles of nuclear weapons and materials were scattered across former Soviet territory, especially Russia. During the 1990s, the United States and Russia agreed to reduce their nuclear arsenals. With aid from the United States and Europe, Russia dismantled, or took apart, some nuclear weapons. Despite the agreements, however, both the United States and Russia held on to their nuclear stockpiles. In recent years, Russian support for nuclear power programs in Iran have led to renewed tensions between Russia and the United States.

Weapons of Mass Destruction As you have read, weapons of mass destruction (WMDs) include nuclear, biological, and chemical weapons. Nuclear weapons include the atomic bomb. Biological weapons refer mainly to germs that can be released into the air or into water supplies. Chemical weapons are toxins, such as nerve gas and mustard gas.

Recently, the danger from WMDs has grown, as terrorist groups and "rogue states"— nations that ignore international law and threaten other nations— try to acquire them. One concern is that terrorists will seize nuclear weapons during transport. Another fear is that terrorists, or those who sympathize with their causes, will gain access to nuclear weapons programs in countries with unstable governments, such as Pakistan.

COMPARE AND CONTRAST How are rogue nations similar to terrorist organizations? How are they different?

The Growing Threat of Terrorism

Since the 1990s, the world has witnessed a growing threat from terrorism. **Terrorism** is the use of violence, especially against civilians, by groups of extremists to achieve political goals. Terrorists' goals range from getting political prisoners released to gaining territory or autonomy for a particular ethnic group. Terrorists have bombed buildings, slaughtered civilians, police, and soldiers, and assassinated political leaders. Although terrorists have seldom achieved their larger goals, they have inflicted terrible damage and generated widespread fear.

Terrorists use headline-grabbing tactics to draw attention to their demands. They have attacked hotels and tourists in Mumbai, bombed commuter trains in Madrid, and blown themselves up as "suicide bombers" to kill Israeli or Iraqi civilians. The spread of terrorism has led to greater international cooperation between governments in an effort to prevent further attacks.

Regional Terrorist Groups Regional terrorist groups have operated in the developed world for decades. A Serbian terrorist group played a key role in the outbreak of World War I. From the 1960s to the 1990s, the Irish Republican Army (IRA) used terrorist tactics to force Britain out of Northern Ireland. Protestant paramilitary groups loyal to Great Britain responded with the same tactics. During the Cold War, the communist Red Brigade in Italy used violence in an attempt to gain power. The ETA, a Basque terrorist group, wants the Spanish government to grant independence to the Basque region in northern Spain.

In South America, leftist groups like the Shining Path in Peru and FARC in Colombia use kidnappings, murder, and bombings to overthrow national governments. They finance their operations with the sale of illegal drugs.

In Asia, terrorist activities were linked to the long conflict between India and Pakistan over Kashmir. The Tamil Tigers, a separatist group in Sri Lanka, pioneered the use of suicide bombings as a terrorist weapon and

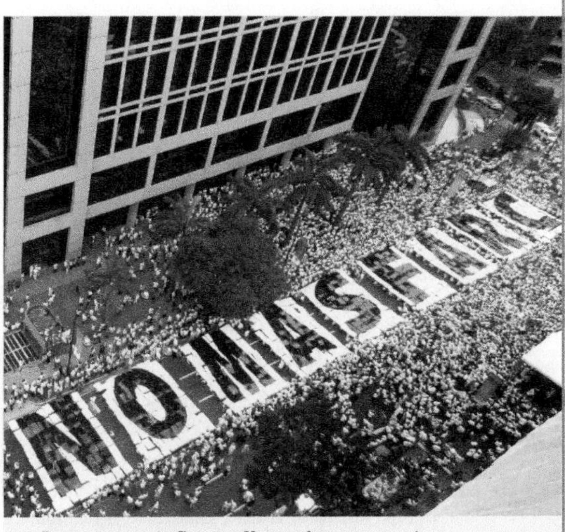

>> Demonstrators in Caracas, Venezuela, protest against the Revolutionary Armed Forces of Colombia, or FARC, in 2008.

Interactive Map

Key Terms

Ask students to find the key term **proliferate** (in bold) on the previous page, and explain its meaning. Point out that a major worry in the twenty-first century is that weapons of mass destruction will proliferate around the world. Ask students to brainstorm problems that might result from this. What steps might nations take to control the spread of weapons?

Guided Reading and Discussion

Remind students that the Nuclear Nonproliferation Treaty (NPT), signed in 1968, allows for five countries to have nuclear weapons—the United States, Russia, the United Kingdom, France, and China. Countries without nuclear weapons agree not to acquire them but can develop nuclear programs for peaceful domestic uses. To date, 190 countries have signed. Three countries that have not signed—India, Pakistan, and Israel—have all developed nuclear weapons. North Korea originally signed but has withdrawn and now has a nuclear program.

Support a Point of View With Evidence Is it fair for the five nuclear states to forbid other countries from developing such weapons?

The Growing Threat of Terrorism

Remind students that terrorism has existed for centuries. However, it has taken on new dimensions in recent decades. The growth of international terrorist groups with the strength, scope, and financial backing of al Qaeda is a relatively new phenomenon. Such groups often recruit members from the dissatisfied youth of impoverished or war-torn nations and seem to offer them a sense of purpose.

Answers

Compare and Contrast *Both ignore the rule of international law and attempt to realize their political goals without regard for other nations. A rogue nation differs from a terrorist group in that it has identifiable borders and a self-contained population.*

Topic 21 Lesson 8

Online Project the **Interactive Map: Terrorism Around the World**, and point out that terror is (or has been) practiced by various groups around the world and is not unique to any particular culture.

ACTIVE CLASSROOM

Introduce the Write 1 Get 3 activity. Ask: "What are four key characteristics of terrorism?" Have students write down one response and then go around the room asking for three other responses. They should write down responses they think are correct, and they should keep asking and writing until they have three more responses. Have students share and discuss responses with the class. *(Possible responses include using the element of surprise, political goals, use of violence to achieve goals, targeting of civilians, destruction of life and property, creation of fear and panic, secret networks, and desire for media attention.)*

Guided Reading and Discussion

Tell students that by the 1980s, Islamic fundamentalism—often referred to as Islamism—was on the rise. This conservative reform movement wanted to revive its view of proper Islamic values and install governments that strictly followed Islamic law, or Sharia. The movement was partly a response to the rise of secular governments in many Muslim nations and the impact of Western culture. It was also a backlash against foreign support for Israel and the presence of foreign powers in the Middle East. Not all Islamists support terrorism, but in many places, the movement has fed the growth of terrorism.

The Islamist terrorist group al Qaeda, founded by Osama bin Laden, has struck numerous times, but the major blow came when al Qaeda attacked the United States on September 11, 2001. Nearly 3,000 people died in the attacks. The swift U.S. response to the terror attacks would have far-reaching consequences in the United States and overseas.

carried out the assassinations of the president of Sri Lanka and Prime Minister Rajiv Gandhi of India.

Growth of Terrorism in the Middle East Increasingly, the Middle East has become a training ground and source for terrorism. Much of this activity has stemmed from Arab rejection of the state of Israel and the continuing Israeli-Palestinian conflict. In 1964, a group of Arabs founded the Palestine Liberation Organization (PLO), with the goal of creating an independent Palestinian state and destroying Israel. In its early years, the PLO used terrorist methods, such as the kidnapping and killing of Israeli athletes at the 1972 Olympic games.

The PLO officially renounced terrorism in 1988. But other terrorist groups have emerged and continue their calls for the establishment of a Palestinian state and the destruction of Israel. The Al-Aqsa Martyrs Brigade, Hamas, Hezbollah, and Islamic Jihad are among the groups that practice terror to achieve their goals.

They found support in poverty-stricken Palestinian refugee camps in Gaza and trained suicide bombers to attack Israeli civilian targets.

Islamic Fundamentalism By the 1980s, Islamic fundamentalism—often referred to as Islamism—was on the rise. This conservative reform movement wanted to revive Islamic values and install governments that strictly followed Islamic law, or Sharia. The Islamist movement was partly a response to the rise of secular governments in many Muslim nations and the impact of Western culture. It was also a backlash against foreign support for Israel and the presence of foreign powers in the Middle East. Islamic fundamentalists made Israel or Western nations scapegoats for their problems.

The 1979 Iranian revolution brought an Islamist government to power. Later, an Islamist group called the Taliban gained power in Afghanistan. Fundamentalist movements have also emerged in countries from Algeria to Indonesia.

Not all Islamists support terrorism, but in many places, the movement has fed the growth of terrorism. Iran and Saudi Arabia have both provided financial support for terrorist organizations. For some, terrorism is connected to the concept of *jihad,* an Arabic word meaning "struggle." The word is most frequently used to describe an inner struggle in God's service. However, some extremist groups, such as Islamic Jihad, have interpreted the word to mean a violent holy war to defend or spread Islam.

>> The Taliban is an Islamist group that took control of Afghanistan in 1996 and was removed from power in 2001. Here, Taliban members are preparing to surrender their weapons to anti-Taliban forces in Afghanistan.

Al Qaeda and the September 11 Attacks The most widely known Islamist terrorist organization is **al Qaeda** (ahl KY duh), which means "the Base" in Arabic. The founder and leader of al Qaeda was Osama bin Laden, a wealthy Saudi businessman.

In the 1980s, bin Laden joined Muslim fighters battling Soviet forces in Afghanistan. Later, he broadened his goals to include the overthrow of governments considered "un-Islamic" and the expulsion of non-Muslims from Muslim countries. In the 1990s, bin Laden mobilized al Qaeda to expel U.S. interests and military power from Saudi Arabia.

Al Qaeda built a global network to train and finance terrorist activities. In 1998, al Qaeda terrorists bombed the American embassies in Kenya and Tanzania. But the major blow came when al Qaeda struck inside the United States.

On September 11, 2001, the Al Qaeda Islamic terrorist group hijacked four commercial passenger airplanes and crashed two of them into the World Trade Center in New York City and one into the Pentagon in northern Virginia. A fourth plane, aimed at the White House, crashed into a Pennsylvania field after passengers rushed the hijackers in the cockpit. Nearly 3,000 people died in the attacks. President George W. Bush described the events as "evil despicable acts of terror." The swift U.S. response to the terror attacks

History Background

Civil Liberties and War on Terrorism Two months after the September 11 attacks in 2001, Congress passed the Patriot Act. Congress's action reflected an urgent desire to protect the nation, even at the cost of certain freedoms. Among the act's most hotly debated provisions were new laws allowing the federal government easier access to private records, including personal financial, library, travel, phone, and medical records that previously had been off-limits to the government without a court-issued warrant. It also became easier for the government to conduct phone taps and other surveillance. Civil liberties advocates argued that fighting terrorism did not justify eroding the rights of American citizens. Proponents of the law countered that the government needed expanded powers to protect the nation.

would have far-reaching consequences in the United States and overseas.

MAKE GENERALIZATIONS What characteristics do global and regional terrorist groups share, regardless of their various goals?

ELPS ELPS 2.C.1 Working with a partner, take turns reading short phrases or entire sentences from *The Growing Threat of Terrorism* to each other. After each turn, the listener should categorize what was read as either a fragment or complete sentence.

The U.S. Response to Terrorism

Al Qaeda's attack on the United States triggered a startling global shake-up. Governments around the world questioned their ability to keep their citizens safe. U.S. President George W. Bush declared a "war on terror" in general, and against al Qaeda in particular.

New Security Measures Introduced After the 2001 attacks, the United States made national security a top priority. To this end, the government strengthened and reorganized its intelligence services and passed new counterterrorism laws. In the United States and elsewhere, more rigorous security measures were put in place at airports and public buildings.

A longterm effort was launched to find out how terrorist groups were funded, with the goal of cutting off terrorists' money supply and limiting their activities. The United States worked with other countries to coordinate intelligence about terrorist groups.

These measures were costly. In addition, some believed the federal government was using the threat of terrorism to increase its power and violate the constitutional rights and freedoms of its citizens. For example, the National Security Agency (NSA) was given broader powers to monitor telephone and Internet communications, raising concerns about invasion of privacy. But many felt that the threat was serious enough to justify extreme measures.

War in Afghanistan As part of its "war on terror," the United States made it a priority to find and punish the organizers of the 2001 attacks. Osama bin Laden was based in **Afghanistan.** The government of Afghanistan, an extreme Islamic fundamentalist group called the **Taliban,** refused U.S. demands to surrender the terrorists. The United States then formed a coalition of nations to invade Afghanistan.

>> Smoke billowed from the twin towers of the World Trade Center in New York City after Islamist terrorists piloted planes into each building. Shortly afterward, the towers collapsed.

 Interactive Gallery

>> Following the 9/11 attacks, the Transportation Security Administration implemented new screening measures at American airports. Passengers were required to remove their shoes and empty their pockets for security personnel.

Topic 21 Lesson 8

Hypothesize How might Americans' confidence in their own safety on American soil have been shaken by the terrorist attacks of September 11, 2001? *(Sample response: No attack of this scale had ever taken place on American soil. Many Americans became very fearful that the next attack was just around the corner.)*

The U.S. Response to Terrorism

To help students understand the significance of September 11, 2001, set the stage. On September 10 of that year, the United States was at peace. Terrorism was not something Americans worried about very much. There had been terrorist strikes before in the United States, but they seemed to be the acts of a few isolated individuals. The September 11 strikes were the kind of attacks no one had imagined.

Analyze Images

Ask: Based on the photograph of screening procedures at airports, how would you describe the impact of the September 11, 2001, attacks on daily life for average Americans?

Answers

Make Generalizations *All terrorist groups have a political goal that they have determined cannot be achieved through legal or nonviolent means, and are willing to inflict random death and destruction on innocent people in order to spread fear, uncertainty, and instability in pursuit of that goal.*

English Language Proficiency Standards

Listening 2.C.1 Use content from "The Growing Threat of Terrorism" to help students hear the difference between a fragment and a complete sentence.

Beginning Display: *greater international cooperation between governments*. Say the phrase aloud and have students repeat it. Model how to create a complete sentence using this phrase and details in the text, and read the phrase and complete sentence aloud. Then read another phrase, have students determine whether it is a fragment or a sentence, and then help them create a complete sentence with it.

Intermediate Display: *greater international cooperation between governments*. Complete the rest of the Beginning activity, but have the group work together to make the phrase a complete sentence.

Advanced Have pairs of students write three complete sentences and three fragments about the text. Ask pairs to read their work aloud to the group, and have the group categorize each as either a sentence or a fragment.

Advanced High Have student write three complete sentences and three fragments about the text. Ask students to read their work aloud to a partner, who should categorize each as either a sentence or a fragment and explain the reasoning behind each categorization.

Topic 21 Lesson 8

Online Project the **Interactive Gallery: September 11, 2001**, and have students view the images and respond to the question.

ACTIVE CLASSROOM

Break students into groups and introduce the Circle Write activity. Remind students of the images they just viewed. Provide a writing prompt of your choice, or use this one: "September 11, 2001, began as a beautiful day with bright blue skies. No one expected it would become one of the most important days in American history. But then . . ."

Guided Reading and Discussion

Days after the Sept. 11 attacks, President Bush announced a "war on terror." He said, "Our war on terror begins with al Qaeda, but it does not end there. It will not end until every terrorist group of global reach has been found, stopped, and defeated."

Compare and Contrast Ask: How is America's war on terror similar to a conventional war? How is it different?

In 2002, with the help of Afghan warlords, American and allied forces overthrew the Taliban and drove al Qaeda into hiding or flight.

Bin Laden and many Taliban leaders escaped capture for many years. Finally, in May 2011, U.S. military and C.I.A. operatives located bin Laden's compound in Pakistan and stormed it in the middle of the night. Bin Laden was killed in the process.

Coalition forces helped Afghanistan hold elections for a new government. The new government lifted many harsh Taliban laws, such as those that forbid girls and women from getting an education. From hideouts along the Pakistan border, Taliban fighters resisted the new government and its Western allies. The war soon spilled into neighboring Pakistan, where Taliban and al Qaeda fighters took refuge. Many Pakistanis, including some in official positions, supported and protected these fighters. Since the United States and Pakistan are allies, this caused problems between the two countries.

War in Iraq In 2003, President Bush urged Congress to agree to an invasion of Iraq, citing intelligence reports that said Iraq was secretly producing WMDs. The Bush administration also suggested that Iraq was involved in the 2001 terrorist attacks against the United States. The war was bitterly debated among Americans and around the world, because no WMDs were found after the U.S. invasion. Many critics also argued that U.S. forces should have remained focused on the war in Afghanistan, which had proven ties to Al Qaeda.

BREAKING NEWS
OSAMA BIN LADEN IS DEAD
President Obama : Justice has been done
BBC NEWS 09:02 AD" • THERE ARE REPORTS

>> Almost 10 years after the September 11 attacks, U.S. forces found and killed Osama bin Laden in Pakistan.

While running for President in 2008, Barack Obama vowed to end the Iraq war. In 2011, President Obama announced the final troop withdrawal from combat mission in Iraq, officially ending nine years of war in that country. At that point, U.S. military focus had shifted back to Afghanistan, where troops remained through 2014.

Iran, Syria, and North Korea Pose Threats When Iran announced a plan to develop nuclear power plants in the early 2000s, the United States and other nations feared that Iran truly intended to develop nuclear weapons. Although Iran insisted its nuclear energy program was for peaceful purposes, the UN Security Council imposed some sanctions on Iran. After years of negotiations with world leaders, Iran agreed in 2013 to some preliminary agreements designed to temporarily suspend its nuclear program while efforts proceed to try to obtain a permanent agreement. World and regional leaders are especially concerned about Iran's nuclear program because Iran already possesses advanced long-range missile technology that may threaten neighboring nations.

Although Syria signed the Nuclear Nonproliferation Treaty (NPT), it has been subject to international scrutiny of its nuclear program. Its adversarial relationship with Israel was largely behind the suspicion that it may have had ambitions to develop nuclear weapons. In 2012, as Syria erupted into civil war, the world's attention turned to Syria's chemical weapons. In 2013, chemical weapons killed 300 civilians in Damascus, and the government and rebels each blamed the other. Although responsibility for the attack remained unclear, President Bashar al-Assad agreed, in a U.S.-Russia brokered deal, to allow international inspectors to dismantle and destroy Syria's chemical weapons cache.

For years, North Korea violated its agreement under the NPT and worked on developing nuclear weapons. Tensions grew as the United States tried to pressure North Korea to stop its nuclear weapons program. In 2003, North Korea withdrew from the NPT. In 2006, it tested a small nuclear bomb, and by 2013 it had conducted three such tests.

Many people feared that if Iran, Syria, or North Korea developed nuclear weapons, nuclear technology could be passed on to terrorist groups. Those nations,

English Language Proficiency Standards

Learning Strategies 1.D.1 Have students use "The U.S. Response to Terrorism" to see how synonyms can help them understand content.

Beginning Make a list of words from the text, define them, and have students suggest drawings for each. Then provide and define synonyms for each word, and include drawings. Help students match each word to its synonym.

Intermediate Display and define the word list and the synonyms. Have students work together to match each word to its synonym, and then reread the text using the synonyms.

Advanced Display the word list and have students define each. Next, present and define the synonyms. Have pairs match the words and synonyms, and then reread the text using the synonyms.

Advanced High Have students define the words and find synonyms. Have pairs discuss the meanings of each word and the synonyms, and then reread the text using the synonyms.

if armed with nuclear weapons, might also pose threats to their regions and to world peace.

CONNECT How was the war in Afghanistan related to the terrorist attacks of September 11, 2001?

ELPS **ELPS 1.D.1** Create a list of words in *The U.S. Response to Terrorism* that you do not understand. Ask a partner or your teacher to help you find the definition and synonyms for each unfamiliar word.

>> North Korean leader Kim Jong Un uses binoculars to view South Korean territory from a military post near the border. North Korea has been criticized for its nuclear weapons testing.

ASSESSMENT

1. **Check Understanding** How do nuclear, biological, and chemical weapons threaten international security?
2. **Identify Cause and Effect** How has Arab rejection of the state of Israel led to ongoing conflict?
3. **Draw Conclusions** How does Islam influence government and law in fundamentalist Muslim nations?
4. **Generate Explanations** Why did President George W. Bush declare a "war on terror" following September 11, 2001?
5. **Draw Conclusions** What are the reasons for the growth of terrorist groups such as al Qaeda over the past two decades?

SYNTHESIZE

Online Project the **Digital Activity: Taken by Surprise**. Ask students to recall their responses to the question from the Start Up activity. Next, project the quote from journalist George Packer, which is a response to the same question. After reading Packer's thoughts, ask: In what ways do you think fighting terrorism is difficult? How did the events of September 11, 2001, change the United States and the world?

DEMONSTRATE

Online Assign the **Digital Lesson Quiz** for this lesson if you haven't already done so. Students will be offered automatic remediation or enrichment based on their score.

Pose these questions to the class on the Discussion Board:

Identify Central Issues What is the relationship between Islamists and terrorism? *(Sample response: Not all Islamists support terrorism, but some Islamists and Islamist governments have supported it.)*

Draw Conclusions Why might a "war on terror" sometimes be controversial? *(Sample response: Identifying actual terrorist threats is not easy. The quest to uncover threats may lead governments to take measures that challenge concepts of civil liberties and freedom.)*

Topic Inquiry

Have students continue their investigations for the Topic Inquiry.

Answers

Connect *Al Qaeda was based in Afghanistan. Unhappy with the Afghan government's lack of cooperation in dealing with the terrorists, a coalition of U.S. and other national forces invaded Afghanistan.*

Assessment

1. They are weapons of mass destruction and threaten international security because they can be used against vast numbers of innocent people.
2. Arab countries see Israel as a theft of Palestinian lands. Countries that support Israel have established a presence in the Muslim Middle East. Islamic fundamentalism has grown in response to Israel and to secular Western interests.
3. There is little or no separation of church and state. Islamic laws and values influence or determine the national government and laws.
4. The attack was conducted by terrorists, so Bush declared war on terror, not a war on a nation.
5. They have succeeded in inflicting terrible damage and generating widespread fear, which call attention to their goals. Also, the fundamentalist Islamic jihadist movement provides a religious justification for violence in the minds of some followers.

Topic 21 Lesson 9

Advances in Science and Technology

CONNECT

Preview Have students preview the **Lesson Objectives** and the list of **Key Terms**.

Students can also preview all the **Key Terms** and **Academic Vocabulary** using the **Interactive Reading Notepad** on the digital course or preview a summary of the lesson in the **Reading and Note Taking Study Guide**.

Online Use the **Editable Presentation** found on the digital course to present the main ideas for this lesson.

Start Up Activity

Explain that in 2000, about 6 percent of the world's population could access the Internet. Today, more than one third of the world's population has Internet access. Eighty percent of these people access social media regularly, and Internet users spend an average of 28 hours every week online.

Ask: What do these data say about the role of technology in our world? What are the benefits and drawbacks of instant access to communications? Explain.

Tell students that in this lesson they will be learning about major technological advancements of recent decades.

Online You can also project the **Start Up Activity** from the course.

INVESTIGATE

Have students read the section using the **Reading and Note Taking Study Guide** to help them take notes and understand the text as they read.

Space Exploration

Since 1945, scientific and technological developments have transformed human existence. One example is the exploration of space. Driven by the Cold War, the United States and Soviet Union explored military uses of space and sent spy satellites to orbit Earth. By 1969, the United States had landed a human on the moon. Since the end of the Cold War, nations have worked in space together.

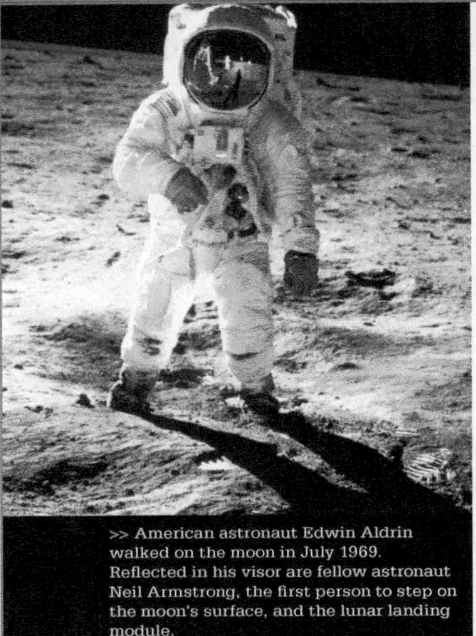

>> American astronaut Edwin Aldrin walked on the moon in July 1969. Reflected in his visor are fellow astronaut Neil Armstrong, the first person to step on the moon's surface, and the lunar landing module.

Interactive Flipped Video

21.9 Since 1945, scientific research and technological development have had a transforming effect on human history. Startling new inventions, the computer revolution, and advances in the life sciences have redefined the world we live in and the lives we lead. One of the most dramatic advances was the exploration of space.

TEKS 28.D

>> Objectives

Describe the exploration of space and the innovations that have resulted.

Analyze the development and impact of computer technology and telecommunications.

Summarize key advancements in medicine and biotechnology.

>> Key Terms

artificial satellite
International Space Station (ISS)
Internet
biotechnology
laser
genetics
genetic engineering

Advances in Science and Technology

Space Exploration

By the second half of the twentieth century, there were few places on Earth that people had not begun to explore. Space was seen as the "final frontier"—an unknown world filled with opportunity. Within a few short decades, people had developed the transportation technology to capture this opportunity. Humans had traveled to this frontier and had used its resources to help develop practical applications that transformed their lives.

The Space Race Rockets are projectiles or vehicles propelled by the ejection of burning gasses from the rear of the rocket. In the early twentieth century, pioneers in rocketry like the American physicist Robert Goddard probed the potential of liquid-fueled rockets.

From the beginning, Goddard believed that a rocket could carry people to the moon. At first people met his ideas with disbelief. Increasingly, German scientists took interest in Goddard's work, prompting him to work with great secrecy. Nevertheless, during World War II German scientists, led by Wernher von Braun, developed Germany's "secret weapon," the V-2 rockets that flew across the English Channel to rain down on London.

PEARSON realize. www.PearsonTexas.com Access your Digital Lesson.

968

Aa Vocabulary Builder

1. Have students pronounce the following academic vocabulary terms in this lesson and clarify the part of speech. For difficult or polysyllabic words, break them into syllables and pronounce them with the students.
2. Explain what the word means in common "student-friendly" language using synonyms and antonyms when possible. Provide concrete examples to clarify the meaning, and rephrase the definition.

manipulation: the skillful handling of something with the purpose of achieving a specific result

conduct: to manage or direct something

applications: the ways things are used

During the Cold War, the United States and the Soviet Union competed with each other to build both rocket-propelled weapons and rocketry for the purpose of space exploration. Von Braun, who moved to the United States after World War II, became a leader in the American missiles and space program.

In 1957, the space age began when the Soviet Union launched into orbit *Sputnik*, the first **artificial satellite,** or manmade object that orbits a larger body in space. In 1969, the United States Apollo program landed the first man on the moon. Both superpowers also explored the military uses of space and sent spy satellites to orbit Earth. Since the end of the Cold War, the United States and Russia have cooperated in joint space ventures.

Science in Space In the decades since *Sputnik* and *Apollo*, rockets have been launched to other planets and beyond. Robotic space vehicles have penetrated the mists of Venus and the rings of Saturn, landed on Mars, and circled the moons of Jupiter. Rocket missions have various goals. They can take scientific measurements, release permanent satellites or telescopes, and if they are manned, conduct medical or biological experiments. They can also provide information about the composition and formation of the universe itself.

Increasingly, nations have worked together to explore space. For example, Russia, the United States, Canada, Japan, and several countries in Europe are developing the **International Space Station (ISS).**

Construction on the ISS began in 1998. Since its completion in 2010, it has served as a space laboratory, allowing scientists from many different countries to observe space, conduct research, and develop new space-related technologies.

In the 21st century, space travel and exploration is no longer the business of only governments. Several private companies now launch rockets into space. One California company founded in 2002, SpaceX, has the goal of enabling people to live on other planets.

Artificial Satellites The thousands of artificial satellites that orbit Earth have a number of very specific applications. These applications can be divided into three groups—communications, observation, and navigation.

Communications satellites relay information that is used in advanced telecommunications—that is, communication over a long distance. Examples include television, telephone, and high-speed data transmission. This capability is critical to the smooth function of today's global economy. Observation satellites observe Earth, providing data to scientists, weather forecasters, and military planners. Navigation satellites beam precise locations to ship captains and others who need to navigate Earth's surface. These satellites also make possible portable global positioning system (GPS) devices, which provide information about location and give directions.

By 2000, artificial satellites had revolutionized global communications and transformed global society. Maintaining stationary orbits over specific points on Earth's surface, artificial satellites can transmit phone messages or television pictures anywhere on Earth. Linked to cell phones or computers, they allow people, separated by thousands of miles, to communicate instantly.

INTERPRET What is the International Space Station and what is its significance?

ELPS **ELPS 2.C.2** With a partner, take turns reading the second paragraph of *Space Exploration* aloud. Listen for the expression "the final frontier" and try to determine its meaning.

>> An Italian astronaut takes photographs on board the International Space Station in June 2013. Scientists at the station must deal with the long-term effects of weightlessness while they conduct research and develop new technologies.

Interactive Timeline

Topic 21 Lesson 9

Online Project the **Interactive Timeline: The Age of Space Exploration**, and have students consider the space race. Ask: Why have nations throughout history found it important to explore new frontiers? *(access to new resources and new areas of influence)*

ACTIVE CLASSROOM

Use the Conversation With History strategy. Have students imagine they are having a conversation with one of the people mentioned in the reading about space exploration. They could choose Neil Armstrong, Robert Goddard, or another famous astronaut or scientist from the early space program. Have them write down a question, then a possible response from the person. Tell them to share their dialogues with a partner.

Guided Reading and Discussion

Review the different ways nations have explored space. Write the term *space race* on the board, and ask students to define and describe it. Then discuss how interaction between nations about the use of space has changed since the end of the Cold War.

Summarize Considering the history of the Cold War, explain why the United States and Russia competed against each other to achieve dominance in the space race. *(Each nation felt that winning the space race would show the superiority of its political system. In addition, domination in space could play a role in the arms race.)*

Make Predictions How do you think the International Space Station will help advance science? *(Possible answer: Scientists from many different countries sharing ideas can develop new technologies faster.)*

English Language Proficiency Standards

Listening 2.C.2 Have students listen for the use of the phrase *the final frontier* as you read "Space Exploration" aloud. Guide students as they determine and discuss the expression's meaning.

Beginning Display the phrase *the final frontier*. Say it aloud and have students repeat it. Tell students to listen for it as you read the second paragraph of the text aloud. Help students understand its meaning using gestures, examples, and the text.

Intermediate Display the phrase, read it aloud, and have students repeat it. Have students listen for it as you read the second paragraph of the text. Help students understand its meaning, then repeat the activity with the expression *secret weapon*.

Advanced Have students complete the Intermediate activity in small groups.

Advanced High Have pairs of students complete the Intermediate activity. Invite pairs to share the main points of their discussions.

Answers

Interpret *It is a multinational research center and space laboratory, allowing scientists from many different countries to observe space, conduct research, and develop new space-related technologies.*

Topic 21 Lesson 9

The Computer Revolution

The invention of the computer has led to the "Information Age." Computers have replaced typewriters and account books. Factories use computerized robots, and computers remotely control satellites. The Internet links computers worldwide and allows instant communication and access to vast storehouses of information. Computers are now an essential part of the modern global economy and society.

Analyze Images

Draw students' attention to the illustration "Social Networking." Point out the fact, "Internet users spend 28 hours each week writing emails and searching for information." Have them speculate on what activities people might have given up to spend this time on the computer. *(Sample responses: writing letters, reading books, making phone calls, watching TV)*

Guided Reading and Discussion

Summarize Ask: How has life changed since the invention of personal computers? *(Personal computers enable people to access information, create documents, and perform complex tasks rapidly and easily.)*

Make Predictions Predict the future of the Internet. What advantages and disadvantages come with this technology? *(The Internet will continue to grow. Advantages: accessibility of information; fast, easy communication; e-commerce; entertainment. Disadvantages: personal information theft; lack of privacy; plagiarism; spam; inappropriate content; isolation; lack of physical exercise)*

The Computer Revolution

The invention of the computer in the twentieth century caused an unprecedented information revolution. It has helped spur development of the modern global economy and society. Few, if any, aspects of modern life remain untouched by computers. Computers run businesses and power plants, help scientists conduct advanced research, and when connected to satellites, make global communications possible. The development of computer technology has given rise to the term "Information Age."

The Birth of Computers Although most people use computers every day, not everyone can define exactly what a computer is. On the most basic level, a computer is a device for making mathematical calculations and for storing, processing, and rapidly manipulating data. Computers have made it possible to preserve vast amounts of data. And when linked up in a vast network, they allow people to communicate instantaneously over enormous distances.

The first electronic computers, built in the 1940s, were huge, slow machines. Later, thanks to inventions like the silicon chip, the computer was reduced in size. Personal computers became widely available in the 1970s for individual users, both at work and at home. By inserting basic programs into the machine, the user could perform complex and difficult tasks quickly and easily.

Over the next few decades, personal computers replaced typewriters and account books in homes and businesses worldwide. At the same time, computer technology spread into many different fields. Computerized robots operate in factories. Computers remotely control satellites and probes in space, and students use them in school classrooms. And computers increasingly aid scientists and architects in developing models to predict disasters, understand environmental changes, and plan urban development.

The Internet In the 1970s, various branches of the U.S. government along with groups in several American universities led efforts to link computer systems together via cables and satellites. In 1989, British computer scientist Tim Berners-Lee proposed a system of linked documents that could be reached through a computer network. His proposal quickly developed into the World Wide Web, or Internet. Using the **Internet,** a person can instantly communicate with other users around the world. The same person can also instantly access vast storehouses of information of all sorts.

By 2000, the Internet had grown to a gigantic network, linking individuals, governments, and businesses around the world. E-commerce, or buying

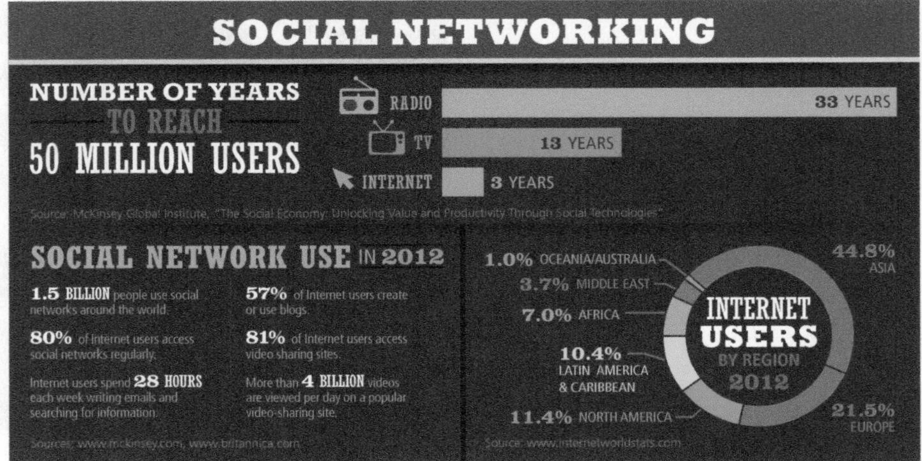
SOCIAL NETWORKING
NUMBER OF YEARS TO REACH 50 MILLION USERS
RADIO
33 YEARS
TV
13 YEARS
INTERNET
3 YEARS
Source: McKinsey Global Institute, "The Social Economy: Unlocking Value and Productivity Through Social Technologies"
SOCIAL NETWORK USE IN 2012
1.5 BILLION people use social networks around the world.
57% of Internet users create or use blogs.
80% of Internet users access social networks regularly.
81% of Internet users access video sharing sites.
Internet users spend 28 HOURS each week writing emails and searching for information.
More than 4 BILLION videos are viewed per day on a popular video-sharing site.
Sources: www.mckinsey.com, www.britannica.com
INTERNET USERS BY REGION 2012
1.0% OCEANIA/AUSTRALIA
3.7% MIDDLE EAST
7.0% AFRICA
10.4% LATIN AMERICA & CARIBBEAN
11.4% NORTH AMERICA
44.8% ASIA
21.5% EUROPE
Source: www.internetworldstats.com

>> **Analyze Graphs** More than 1 billion people around the world use social networking sites. Which region of the world has the highest percentage of Internet users?

History Background

The Internet Brings Change When the Internet was first invented, pundits announced that it would change the way we live. In the United States, the Internet has changed people's ways of getting information and news, ways of shopping, and even ways of meeting socially. In many foreign countries, computers and the Internet have also brought significant changes. For instance, in Peru, farmers have been able to increase their profits by selling their products online—some farmers report earning five times their former profit. In Africa, the Internet has helped farmers prepare for droughts and fend off potential famine. In China, Internet outrage after a prisoner died in police custody led the government to change laws on how it detains prisoners.

Answers

Analyze Graphs *Asia*

and selling on the Internet, contributed to economic growth. The Internet also began to shape life in developing nations.

At the beginning of the twenty-first century, about 6 percent of the world's population could access the Internet. This percentage is growing rapidly. In 2012, an estimated 35 percent of the world's population had access to the Internet— connecting them to a new world of ideas and information.

SUMMARIZE What impact have personal computers had on people's lives?

Breakthroughs in Medicine and Biotechnology

Science and technology have revolutionized our understanding and our control of both human life and other forms of life on this planet. Developments in medicine and **biotechnology,** the application of biological research to industry, engineering, and technology, have resulted in new ways to combat and prevent disease.

Medical Advances In the postwar era, pioneers in the life sciences such as Dr. Jonas Salk became household names. Before the 1950s, the paralyzing disease polio had crippled thousands of children and adults—including President Franklin D. Roosevelt. Salk developed the first vaccine to prevent polio, which has since been almost wiped out. Other medical researchers developed vaccines to help prevent the spread of smallpox and other diseases.

Breakthroughs in surgery also transformed the field of medicine. In the 1970s, surgeons learned to transplant organs, including the human heart, to save lives. **Lasers** made many types of surgery safer and more precise. Lasers are high-energy light beams that surgeons use to cut or repair tissues and organs. Scientists have also had success in treating some cancers, a disease that affects the global population. In recent decades, computers and other technologies have become partners with doctors in diagnosing and treating disease. They have also made it easier for people to share information, thus making diseases easier to treat.

The Rise of Biotechnology and Genetic Engineering In the past couple of decades, the field of biotechnology has exploded. Biotechnology companies make products including vaccinations, medicines, and industrial bacteria that can be used to treat waste or clean up toxic spills.

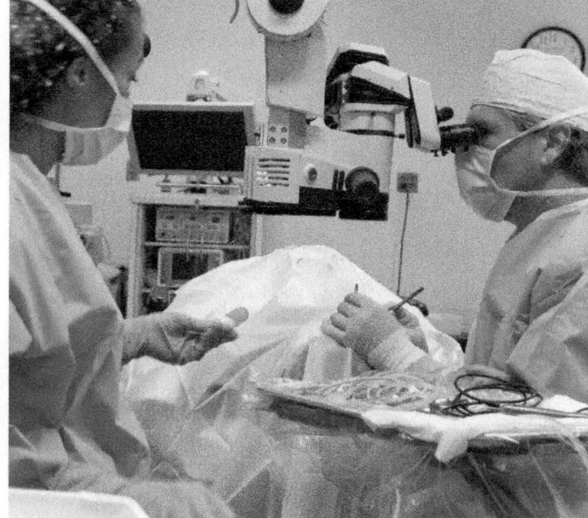

>> An ophthalmologist uses a laser to perform cataract surgery on a patient. The use of lasers has revolutionized many types of surgery.

Interactive Timeline

Biotechnology is closely related to the fields of genetics and genetic engineering, which have also made dramatic advances in recent years. **Genetics** is the study of genes and heredity, while **genetic engineering** is the manipulation of genetic material to produce specific results. Beginning in the 1950s, genetic researchers, spearheaded by John Watson, Francis Crick, and Rosalind Franklin, examined the chemical code carried by all living things. Their research established the central role of DNA— deoxyribonucleic acid—in the chromosomes that determine human heredity. Their work revealed the "double helix," spiral-shaped DNA that carries hereditary traits from parents to children.

Ongoing genetic research has produced new drug therapies to fight human diseases. Research has also created new strains of fruits and vegetables that are intended to resist disease or thrive in conditions that usually inhibit growth. Genetic cloning, or the process of creating identical organisms from the cell of a host organism, has many practical applications in raising livestock and in biological research.

Biotechnology and genetic engineering have brought benefits, but also debate. Some people believe that genetically modified foods are unnatural and potentially dangerous. The possibility of cloning genetically identical mammals—including human

Breakthroughs in Medicine and Biotechnology

Important developments have occurred in medicine and biotechnology. Vaccines help prevent the spread of diseases. Surgeons now transplant human organs. Lasers have made many types of surgery safer and more precise. Computers and other technologies aid in diagnosis and treatment.

Online Project the **Interactive Timeline: Medical Milestones**, and review the medical advancements made over the years.

ACTIVE CLASSROOM

Have students write a headline that captures one key concept in this section of the lesson. Ask: If you were to write a headline for this topic or issue right now that captured the most important aspect that should be remembered, what would the headline be? Have students trade headlines with a partner to review and discuss.

Key Terms

Ask students to notice the key term **biotechnology** (in bold) in the text. Clarify that *bio* means "life." Discuss other types of technology that students have read about. Ask students to suggest ways that technology could affect life. Have them read to find out whether their ideas on biotechnology are accurate.

Guided Reading and Discussion

Tell students that although biotechnology has provided many benefits, some fear it will change food in unsafe ways and that it could give people dangerous power to create or change life.

Make Generalizations Ask: How have scientific advances affected people's standard of living? What challenges are brought about by these advances?

Answers

Summarize *They enable people to access information, create documents, and perform complex and elaborate tasks rapidly and easily.*

Topic 21 Lesson 9

SYNTHESIZE

Online Project the **Digital Activity: Advances in Science and Technology**.

Have students write one or two paragraphs comparing and contrasting various impacts of science and technology in our world. Student responses should discuss the following questions:

- How have advances in space impacted our world?
- What is the continuing impact of computers on our world?
- How has biotechnology changed the world we live in?

DEMONSTRATE

Online Assign the **Digital Lesson Quiz** for this lesson if you haven't done so already. Students will be offered automatic remediation or enrichment based on their scores.

Pose these questions to the class on the Discussion Board:

Identify Cause and Effect What impact has the computer had on globalization? *(It has brought nations into closer contact and allowed individuals access to global information, communication, and trade.)*

Summarize Summarize the impact of science and technology on modern life. *(Space exploration has led to new knowledge and advances in communications technology. Computers link people to each other and to information, speeding up many business processes.)*

Topic Inquiry

Have students continue their investigations for the Topic Inquiry.

Answers

Analyze Political Cartoons *Possible answer: Instead of food, the tomatoes contain only DNA.*

Make Generalizations *They have increased agricultural output and reduced the impact of disease.*

>> **Analyze Political Cartoons** Below the tomato plant in this cartoon lies a double helix, which is the structural arrangement of DNA. DNA is the genetic information contained in plant or animal cells. What is the cartoonist trying to portray in this cartoon?

beings—has also raised ethical questions about the role of science in creating and changing life.

Standards of Living Rise As you have read, science and technology have often had a direct and powerful impact on human life. Advances in diagnosing and treating disease and increased agricultural output have raised life expectancies worldwide, as well as standards of living. Yet great challenges still remain, from overpopulation to disasters to war.

In the decades ahead, people will look for ways to solve global problems. Technology and information sharing will be one set of tools to use in building the future. But to use that information properly, we must continue to understand and learn from the past.

 **MAKE GENERALIZATIONS** How have scientific advances affected people's standard of living?

ASSESSMENT

1. **Generate Explanations** How have advances in biotechnology and genetic engineering been built on past discoveries?
2. **Synthesize** Why did the United States and the USSR compete against each other to achieve dominance in the space race?
3. **Identify Cause and Effect** What impact has the computer revolution had on globalization?
4. **Summarize** Biotechnology has provided many benefits, but many people worry about its long-term effects. Explain why this is so.
5. **Run-in head** What impact do artificial satellites have on modern life?

Assessment

1. Biotechnology and genetic engineering are based on the work in the 1950s of Watson, Crick, and Franklin, who discovered DNA, by which genetic information is passed to offspring.
2. Each nation felt that winning the space race would show the superiority of its political system. In addition, domination in space could play a role in the arms race.
3. It has brought nations into closer contact and allowed individuals access to global information and the ability to communicate and trade globally.
4. Some people fear that biotechnology will change food in unsafe ways; some also fear that it could give people dangerous power to create or change life.
5. They are used for communications, including television, phones, and high-speed data transmission. They provide data for scientific observations, weather forecasts, and military purposes. They also are used in navigation applications.

TEKS ASSESSMENT

Under-five Mortality Rate by Region, 1970–2011

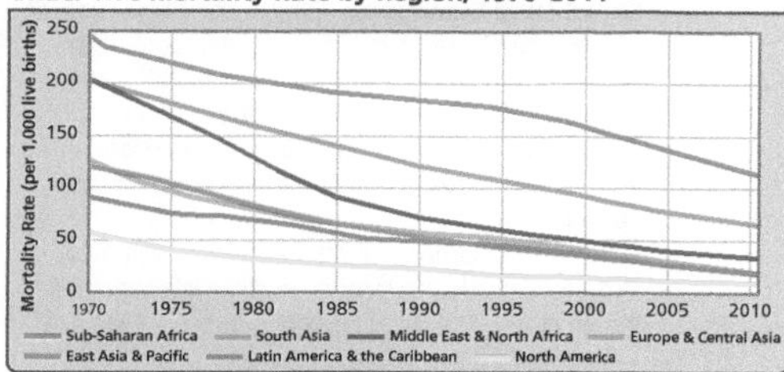

1. **Describe Changing Roles and Compare Geographic Distributions and Patterns** Describe the changing roles of children during major eras of world history; also, compare geographic distributions and patterns in world history shown on graphs. Write a paragraph describing children's issues, including mortality rate. Consider children's continuing role as a labor source in developing countries and some of the hardships they have suffered. Which geographic areas shown on the chart have the highest mortality rate for children under age five? What is one trend or pattern that is consistent for all geographic regions between 1970 and 2010? **15.B, 24.A**
2. **Summarize Impact** Summarize the social impact of 20th century globalization. Write a paragraph summarizing the social impact of 20th century globalization. Consider the social benefits and costs of globalization in the twentieth century: urbanization, foreign investment, and industrial development. Would factors such as the spread of ideas and technology help to improve society? **17.C**
3. **Identify Major Causes** Identify major causes of the following important turning points in world history from 1914 to the present: globalization. Write a paragraph about how globalization has led to increased world interdependence. Consider transportation and communication improvements, spread of democratic systems, and the rise of free trade and the spread of goods and ideas. **1.F**
4. **Explain the Role** Explain the role of transportation technology in developing the modern global economy and society. Write a paragraph explaining the advances in space exploration. Consider competition between the United States and the Soviet Union to build rocket-propelled weapons and rocketry, joint efforts to develop the International Space Station, and the role of private companies in space exploration. **28.D**
5. **Identify Characteristics** Identify the characteristics of socialism. Write a paragraph identifying the characteristics of socialism in newly independent African nations. Consider the appeal of socialism, how countries expected that socialism would affect relations with former colonial rulers, and the focus of the African brand of socialism. **18.C**
6. **Explain the Significance** Explain the significance of the United Nations. Write a paragraph explaining the significance of the United Nations as a global organization. How has it increased in importance since the days of its predecessor, the League of Nations? What type of activities does it engage in around the world? **20.D**
7. **Summarize Reasons** Summarize the reasons for South Asia's ongoing conflicts. Write a paragraph about ongoing conflicts between India and Pakistan that have affected the international community. Consider possible Pakistani support of terrorist groups, relationship between Pakistan and the United States, and nuclear capabilities of India and Pakistan. **13.E**
8. **Describe Major Influences** Describe the major influences of women during major eras of world history: Mother Teresa. Write a paragraph describing Mother Teresa's accomplishments in India. What impact did improved agricultural technology and urbanization in India have on the poor and needy? **24.B**
9. **Formulate Generalizations** Formulate generalizations on how economic freedom improved the human condition, based on what you have learned about the benefits of free enterprise in twentieth-century free market economies, compared to communist command communities. Read the passage below. Write a paragraph about the effects of China's economic reforms under Deng Xiaoping. Consider how his approach differed from his predecessors, the benefits to farmers and entrepreneurs, the role of foreign capital and technology, and the impact on economic growth. **18.F**

Deng Xiaoping was a more moderate communist leader in China who took a new approach to China's economy in the 1980s. He was more interested in improving economic output than in communist purity. "I don't care if a cat is black or white," he declared, "as long as it catches mice."

Answers to TEKS Assessment

1. Students' answers should include how children still suffer from poverty, wars, AIDS, and human rights violations. In many developing countries, children between ages 5 and 14 work full time in poor working conditions with little pay. The highest mortality rates for children under age five are in sub-Saharan Africa, in South Asia, and in the Middle East and North Africa. However, between 1970 and 2010, the mortality rate for this age group has decreased in all regions.
2. Students' answers will vary but might mention benefits such as better educational opportunities and access to health care. In urban areas, people are exposed to new ideas, technologies, and communications. Social costs, however, may be high, especially if foreign investment is involved. The standard of living may decrease, and industrial development may hurt the environment.
3. Students' answers should include information on how globalization leads to the integration of national economies, politics, cultures, and societies. It has accelerated as a result of the interdependence of countries for faster movement of products, knowledge, and labor. Transportation and communication improvements, the spread of democratic systems, and the rise of free trade have increased interdependence and promoted the spread of goods and ideas, leading to the development of a global culture.
4. During the Cold War, the United States and the Soviet Union built rocket-propelled weapons and rocketry for space exploration. Rocket missions provide valuable scientific information on the universe and for medical or biological experiments. The United States, Russia, Canada, Japan, and other nations jointly developed the International Space Station (ISS) for research. Private companies are also launching rockets into space.
5. Responses should include information on how socialism appealed to newly independent African countries because the people as a whole owned all property and businesses. Some thought this would help to reduce dependence on former colonial rulers. African socialism was based on village traditions of cooperation and shared responsibility.
6. Students' answers will vary but should include information on how the role of the United Nations has increased since the days of the League of Nations. The United Nations has grown from 50 nations in 1945 to a membership of 193 nations in 2014. The UN promotes international peace and security. It also works on economic and social development, human rights, humanitarian aid, and international law.
7. Students' answers should include information on tensions between India and Pakistan and their relationship with the international community. After the Taliban was overthrown in Afghanistan in 2002, many Taliban and al Qaeda members went into hiding in Pakistan, supported by some Pakistanis. The official alliance between Pakistan and the United States is strained. In 2008, Pakistani terrorists attacked Mumbai, India, and killed more than 160 people. Also, India and Pakistan tested nuclear weapons in 1998, and neither has signed the Nuclear Nonproliferation Treaty.
8. Students' answers should include information on how Mother Teresa, a Roman Catholic nun, founded the Missionaries of Charity in Calcutta. Her group provided food and medical care to thousands. Better agricultural technology, like the Green Revolution, required fewer farmers, which resulted in migration to cities. Rapid urbanization led to overcrowded cities with inadequate water and sewage systems. Unemployment resulted, and people were unable to provide for basic needs and health care.

Answers to TEKS Assessment

9. Students' answers should mention that under Deng Xiaoping, China took a more moderate approach to the economy, called the Four Modernizations. The country would still be politically communist but could change its economic framework to include some aspects of free enterprise. Farmers did not own the land but could keep a share in their crops, sell surplus produce, and keep their profits. Entrepreneurs could establish businesses; foreign capital and technology were welcomed. With greater economic freedom, economic growth increased and raised the standard of living.

10. Students' answers should mention how economic reforms and increased contact with the West starting in the 1980s led some Chinese to demand greater political freedom. Students at Tiananmen Square took up this democracy movement. After protesters refused to stop protesting, the government killed or wounded many; others were tortured and imprisoned. The government rejected any talk of democratic reforms.

11. Students' answers will vary but should include information on how command economies suffered for several reasons. Government ownership of land destroyed the economic base of the upper class. Land redistribution programs do not necessarily increase productivity, since the government sets prices. When developing nations borrowed to pay for development, sometimes their poor economic conditions did not allow for repayment. Lenders then made other conditions to pay off debts and be eligible for new loans. Shifting to market economies produced profits for investors as better consumer goods were produced.

12. Students' answers will vary but should mention that, from the 1950s to the 1970s, many Latin American nations suffered from poverty, inequality, and political and economic instability. Military leaders in Argentina, Brazil, and Chile seized power. They outlawed opposition parties, censored the media, and closed universities. Autocratic rule sometimes led to imprisonment or mass murder of critics.

13. Students' answers will vary but should mention that Islamism is a conservative reform movement wanting to revive Islamic values and follow Sharia. Islamists oppose secular governments in Muslim nations and the influences of Western culture. Terrorism is sometimes connected to jihad, which some extremist groups use to justify violence in defense of Islam. Islamists took power in countries like Iran and Afghanistan, and Islamist terrorist groups have grown in countries from Algeria to Indonesia.

14. Students' answers will vary but should include information on how the continuing Israeli-Palestinian conflict stems from Arab rejection of Israel. In 1964, the Palestinian Liberation Organization (PLO) was founded to create an independent Palestine and destroy Israel. Although the PLO renounced terrorism in 1988 under Yasser Arafat, a surge of Islamic fundamentalism has given rise to other militant terrorist groups.

15. Students' answers will vary but should mention al Qaeda as the most widely known terrorist organization. Its goal is to overthrow governments considered enemies to Islam and to expel non-Muslims from Muslim countries. It built a global terrorist network that resulted in several key terrorist attacks. In 1998, American embassies in Kenya and Tanzania were bombed. In 2001, the al Qaeda Islamist terrorist group hijacked four commercial airplanes and crashed two into the World Trade Center in New York City and one into the Pentagon in northern Virginia. The fourth airplane, aimed at the White House, crashed into a Pennsylvania field after passengers rushed the hijackers in the cockpit. Events like these have led to more cooperation between nations to combat terrorist attacks.

TEKS ASSESSMENT

10. **Identify Examples** Identify examples of individuals who led resistance to political oppression: Chinese student protestors in Tiananmen Square. Write a paragraph describing how Chinese student protestors demanded greater political freedom. Consider how China's economic reforms affected the political climate, why students were emboldened to take action, and how the government reacted to the student protests. **22.E**

11. **Explain the Collapse** Explain why communist command economies collapsed in competition with free market economies at the end of the 20th century. Write a paragraph explaining why many developing nations turned to free market economies at the end of the 20th century. Consider the disadvantages of command economies, productivity under land distribution programs, bank repayment terms for poorly performing economies, and advantages of market economies for investors and consumers. **18.E**

12. **Identify Examples** Identify examples of politically motivated mass murders in Latin America. Write a paragraph identifying examples of politically motivated mass murders in Latin America between the 1950s and 1970s. Consider the economic and social status in many Latin American nations; the goals of military rulers in countries like Argentina, Brazil, and Chile; and the development of autocratic rule. **22.C**

13. **Explain Influences** Explain how Islam influences law and government in the Muslim world. Write a paragraph explaining how Islamic fundamentalism influences law and government in the Muslim world. Consider its core values, how radical Islamists try to carry out their goals, and how terrorism is connected to the concept of jihad. How has Islam influenced the governments in Iran and Afghanistan and the growth of terrorist groups elsewhere? **25.D**

14. **Explain and Summarize** Explain how Arab rejection of the state of Israel has led to ongoing conflict, and summarize the development and impact of radical Islamic fundamentalism events in the second half of the 20th century, including Palestinian terrorism. Write a paragraph explaining how the continuing Israeli-Palestinian conflict stems from Arab rejection of Israel. Consider the founding of the Palestinian Liberation Organization, its status today regarding terrorism, and the emergence of other terrorist groups. **13.F, 14.A**

15. **Summarize the Development** Summarize the development and impact of radical Islamic fundamentalism on events in the second half of the 20th century, including the growth of al Qaeda. Write a paragraph summarizing the development of al Qaeda and its status and goals today. Consider its global training and financing, attacks it has carried out, and how the international community has addressed terrorist events. **14.A**

16. **Summarize Impact and Use a Problem-Solving Process** Summarize the economic impact of 20th century globalization. Use a problem-solving process to identify a problem, gather information, consider advantages and disadvantages, choose and implement a solution, and evaluate the effectiveness of the solution. First, interpret the information on the chart below for developing countries and developed countries in the areas of economic output, literacy rate, and life expectancy. What are the benefits and costs of globalization? Write a paragraph using a problem-solving process for solutions to improve literacy rates in developing countries that may help with economic output. **17.C, 31.A**

SELECTED DEVELOPED & DEVELOPING NATIONS

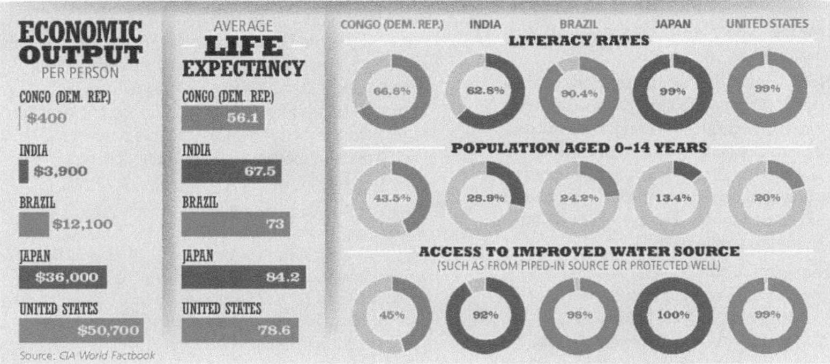

17. **Identify Examples** Identify examples of genocide, including genocide in the Balkans. Write a paragraph identifying genocide in the Balkans. On the above map, locate the seven new nations of the former Yugoslavia. How did ethnic, religious, and nationalist tensions in Yugoslavia after the fall of communism result in civil war in 1992? Why did fighting among the Bosniaks, Serbs, and Croats all result in atrocities? How did the international community intervene to end the war? 22.D

18. **Describe Changing Roles** Describe the changing roles of women during major eras of world history. Write a paragraph describing the struggle for women's rights. Consider the 1950s status of women's suffrage in European, Asian, and African countries; women in elected government positions in many countries; changes for working women in developed and developing countries; and the income gap with men and status of education. Given these changes, have women's lives met the basic rights, as stated below, stated in the UN declaration of human rights? 24.A

In 1948, the United Nations approved the Universal Declaration of Human Rights. It stated that all people are entitled to basic rights that include "life, liberty and security of person"; freedom from slavery, torture, or discrimination; "freedom of thought, conscience and religion"; the right to work and to rest and leisure; the right to an education; and the right to "a standard of living adequate for the health and well-being of himself and of his family."

19. **Explain** Explain the U.S. response to terrorism from September 11, 2001 to the present. Write a paragraph explaining the U.S. response to terrorism from September 11, 2001 to the present. Consider the efforts to prioritize national security, strengthening and reorganizing intelligence services, passing new counterterrorism laws, attempts to stop terrorist funding, and U.S. military action in Afghanistan. 14.B

20. **Identify Examples** Identify examples of individuals who led resistance to political oppression and were successful in shifting political thought: Nelson Mandela. On the chart, what percentages do whites and blacks have in the total South African population? How is this related to the apartheid policy in the second half of the twentieth century? Write a paragraph describing how Nelson Mandela led resistance to political oppression and changed apartheid laws. Consider Mandela's role in the African National Congress, why he was jailed, the international community's role, and the actions of President F.W. de Klerk. 21.C, 22.E

South Africa's Population by Race

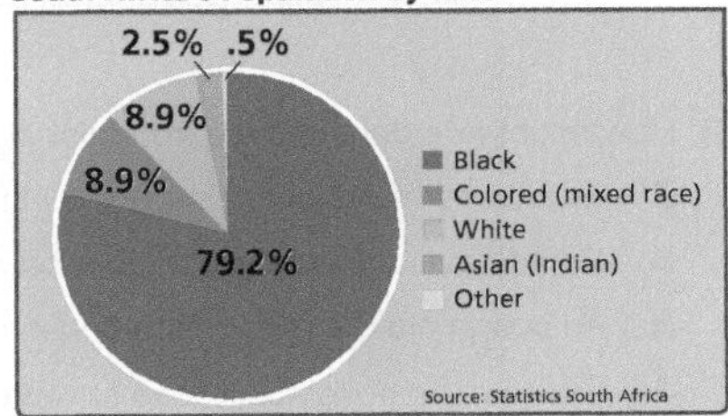

21. **Reflect on the Essential Question** **Write an essay on the Essential Question: What are the benefits and risks of interdependence?** Use evidence from your study of this Topic to support your answer.

16. Students' answers will vary but should interpret the information on the chart as showing lower economic output, literacy rate, and life expectancy for several sample developing countries (Democratic Republic of the Congo and India) versus developed countries (Japan and the United States). Benefits of globalization generally include more variety of goods and services, lower prices, and better access to education and health care. Costs may include exploitation of poor nations by richer nations for low labor costs that might lower developing nations' standard of living.

17. Students' answers will vary but should include information on how nationalistic, ethnic, and religious tensions in Yugoslavia after the fall of communism erupted into conflicts. Most of the six nations broke off from Yugoslavia in the early 1990s. Civil war erupted in Bosnia after it declared independence in 1992. Fighting among Bosniaks, Serbs, and Croats included committing atrocities. Bosnian Serbs conducted ethnic cleansing against Bosniaks and Croats, many in mass executions. Croats retaliated by conducting ethnic cleansing against the Serbs. NATO air strikes forced rival groups to sign the Dayton Accords for peace in 1995.

18. Students' answers will vary but should include information on the struggle for women's rights, which the UN supported in its charter. In the 1950s, women had suffrage in most European countries, Japan, China, Brazil, and other countries. African women generally gained the right to vote when their countries gained independence. Women have had elected government positions in many countries (Britain, Germany, Israel, India, Pakistan, Philippines). In developed countries, more women have professional jobs, but the income gap with men still exists. In developing nations, the education gap is narrowing; women have entered the workforce. Although women have made strides in equality, right to work, and an adequate standard of living, this has mostly been in the developed countries. Women in developing countries generally still lag in work opportunities, education, and standard of living; they may be more subject to human rights abuses.

19. Student answers will vary but should include information on how al Qaeda's attack on the United States in 2001 placed an urgent focus on national security. The United States, like other countries, strengthened and reorganized intelligence services and passed new counterterrorism laws, including more rigorous security measures at airports and in public buildings and attempts to cut off terrorist funding. The United States invaded Afghanistan, where the ruling Taliban supported al Qaeda. Al Qaeda members fled, many to neighboring Pakistan. Osama bin Laden was found and killed there in 2011.

20. Students' answers will vary but should include information on how the apartheid policy, starting in 1948, kept white minority control over South Africa. Nelson Mandela worked his entire life to oppose apartheid and lead the struggle for majority rule. Mandela was one of the African National Congress (ANC) leaders. He first led peaceful resistance against apartheid laws; he then joined ANC militants and was jailed in 1964, becoming a powerful symbol of the struggle for freedom. In the 1980s, countries imposed economic sanctions to stop apartheid and demanded that Mandela be released. In 1990, South African president F.W. de Klerk ended apartheid and freed Mandela; in 1994, Mandela was elected president. His actions and example shifted political thought away from minority rule toward greater democracy and cooperation among ethnic groups.

Topic 21

Answers to TEKS Practice

1. B
2. H

Online To prepare for the End-of-Topic test, have students go online for additional Topic Review and Assessment questions or to review their notes in the **Interactive Reading Notepad** for the lessons in this Topic.

Benchmark Tests

Assign these benchmark tests as you complete the relevant topics to monitor student progress toward mastering the course content and as preparation for the End-of-Course Test.

Benchmark Test 1: Topics 1–5

Benchmark Test 2: Topics 6–10

Benchmark Test 3: Topics 11–15

Benchmark Test 4: Topics 16–21

TEKS PRACTICE

1 Estimates of Land Area Belonging to Vulnerability Classes and Corresponding Number of Impacted Population

VULNERABILITY CLASS	AREA SUBJECT TO DESERTIFICATION		POPULATION AFFECTED	
	SQUARE KILOMETERS	PERCENTAGE	MILLIONS	PERCENTAGE OF AFRICAN POPULATION
Low	4,225,000	14.2	154.5	19.9
Moderate	4,741,000	15.9	196.1	25.3
High	3,213,000	10.8	134.8	17.4
Very High	1,466,000	4.9	22.4	2.9

SOURCE: U.S. Department of Agriculture

Using the chart and information from the lessons, which of these represents the problem of desertification in Africa?

A A shortage of basic food supplies is predicted for almost the entire African continent.

B About one fifth of the affected population is in the two worst classes of vulnerability, showing a dangerous level.

C Close to 30 percent of African land is subject to drying out and thus killing livestock and crops.

D People in the lowest vulnerability classes can hardly survive on their own lands without international aid.

2 How might interdependence from globalization negatively affect developing countries?

F Standards of living can improve only with foreign investment in agriculture and industry.

G Rapid development can bring in new technology to combat environmental dangers.

H An economic depression starting in one country can have a global impact.

J Global aid can ironically lead to more poverty and hunger in cities.

Test Taking Tips: Tip for Questions With Reading Passages

1. Read the question.
2. Read the title of the passage if it is provided.
3. Determine when the passage or quotation was written or spoken and by whom.
4. Carefully read the entire passage or quotation.
5. Read the question again to be sure you understand what is being asked. Identify details or ideas in the passage or quotation that you will use to answer the question.
6. Answer the question in your own words.
7. Read the answer choices and select the best answer.

www.PearsonTexas.com
Access additional practice questions

3 How does the U.S. response to terrorism from September 11, 2001, sometimes cause mixed reactions in the United States and other countries?

A Increased efforts to strengthen and coordinate intelligence services to address terrorism may intrude on constitutional rights.

B Security measures at airports mean invasive questions about checked luggage and travel forms.

C Public buildings have tighter security that means less accessibility by government workers.

D More scrutiny of personal and business phone calls creates public distrust of government interference.

4

> *"There is a longstanding history of tension between the Tutsi and Hutu ethnic groups in Rwanda, even though they speak the same language, follow similar traditions and live side by side."*

What is one cause of the underlying tension between the Tutsis and Hutus that led to the genocide in 1994?

F Close ties with neighboring African nations that benefited the Hutus economically caused the Tutsis to rebel.

G During colonial rule, the Belgians favored the minority Tutsis, which led to resentment amongst the Hutu majority.

H When the Hutus came to power, they wanted to rid the country of groups that spoke different languages.

J Both groups blamed the United Nations for failing to provide basic humanitarian goods to the country.

If you have trouble with...				
Question	1	2	3	4
See Lesson	21.2, 21.7	21.6	21.8	20.2
TEKS	17.C	1.F	14.B	22.D

Topic 21

3. A
4. G

Online Use the **Topic Synthesize** to help students revisit and reflect on the Essential Question for this Topic.

Topic Inquiry

If students have done a Topic Inquiry for this Topic, have them complete the final step of the Inquiry now.

End-of-Course Tests

Assign End-Of-Course Test 1 or 2 to measure students' progress in mastering the course content.

Stock Connection Blue/Alamy

Constitution Quick Study Guide

978

Amendments

1st Amendment:	**Freedom of Religion, Speech, Press, Assembly, and Petition**
2nd Amendment:	**Right to Keep, Bear Arms**
3rd Amendment:	**Lodging Troops in Private Homes**
4th Amendment:	**Search, Seizures, Proper Warrants**
5th Amendment:	**Criminal Proceedings, Due Process, Eminent Domain**
6th Amendment:	**Criminal Proceedings**
7th Amendment:	**Jury Trials in Civil Cases**
8th Amendment:	**Bail; Cruel, Unusual Punishment**
9th Amendment:	**Unenumerated Rights**
10th Amendment:	**Powers Reserved to the States**
11th Amendment:	**Suits Against the States**
12th Amendment:	**Election of President and Vice President**
13th Amendment:	**Slavery and Involuntary Servitude**
Section 1.	Slavery and Involuntary Servitude Prohibited
Section 2.	Power of Congress
14th Amendment:	**Rights of Citizens**
Section 1.	Citizenship; Privileges and Immunities; Due Process; Equal Protection
Section 2.	Apportionment of Representation
Section 3.	Disqualification of Officers
Section 4.	Public Debt
Section 5.	Powers of Congress
15th Amendment:	**Right to Vote—Race, Color, Servitude**
Section 1.	Suffrage Not to Be Abridged
Section 2.	Power of Congress
16th Amendment:	**Income Tax**
17th Amendment:	**Popular Election of Senators**
Section 1.	Popular Election of Senators
Section 2.	Senate Vacancies
Section 3.	Inapplicable to Senators Previously Chosen
18th Amendment:	**Prohibition of Intoxicating Liquors**
Section 1.	Intoxicating Liquors Prohibited
Section 2.	Concurrent Power to Enforce
Section 3.	Time Limit on Ratification
19th Amendment:	**Equal Suffrage—Sex**
Section 1.	Suffrage Not to Be Abridged
Section 2.	Power of Congress
20th Amendment:	**Commencement of Terms; Sessions of Congress; Death or Disqualification of President-Elect**
Section 1.	Terms of President, Vice President, members of Congress
Section 2.	Sessions of Congress
Section 3.	Death or Disqualification of President-Elect
Section 4.	Congress to Provide for Certain Successors
Section 5.	Effective Date
Section 6.	Time Limit on Ratification
21st Amendment:	**Repeal of 18th Amendment**
Section 1.	Repeal of Prohibition
Section 2.	Transportation, Importation of Intoxicating Liquors
Section 3.	Time Limit on Ratification
22nd Amendment:	**Presidential Tenure**
Section 1.	Restriction on Number of Terms
Section 2.	Time Limit on Ratification
23rd Amendment:	**Inclusion of District of Columbia in Presidential Election Systems**
Section 1.	Presidential Electors for District
Section 2.	Power of Congress
24th Amendment:	**Right to Vote in Federal Elections—Tax Payment**
Section 1.	Suffrage Not to Be Abridged
Section 2.	Power of Congress
25th Amendment:	**Presidential Succession; Vice Presidential Vacancy; Presidential Inability**
Section 1.	Presidential Succession
Section 2.	Vice Presidential Vacancy
Section 3.	Presidential Inability
26th Amendment:	**Right to Vote—Age**
Section 1.	Suffrage Not to Be Abridged
Section 2.	Power of Congress
27th Amendment:	**Congressional Pay**

The Preamble states the broad purposes the Constitution is intended to serve—to establish a government that provides for greater cooperation among the States, ensures justice and peace, provides for defense against foreign enemies, promotes the general well-being of the people, and secures liberty now and in the future. The phrase We the People emphasizes the twin concepts of popular sovereignty and of representative government.

PREAMBLE

We the People of the United States, in Order to form a more perfect Union, establish Justice, insure domestic Tranquility, provide for the common defence, promote the general Welfare, and secure the Blessings of Liberty to ourselves and our Posterity, do ordain and establish this Constitution for the United States of America.

Legislative Department

Section 1. Legislative power; Congress

Congress, the nation's lawmaking body, is bicameral in form; that is, it is composed of two houses: the Senate and the House of Representatives. The Framers of the Constitution purposely separated the lawmaking power from the power to enforce the laws (Article II, the Executive Branch) and the power to interpret them (Article III, the Judicial Branch). This system of separation of powers is supplemented by a system of checks and balances; that is, in several provisions the Constitution gives to each of the three branches various powers with which it may restrain the actions of the other two branches.

Article I.

Section 1.

All legislative Powers herein granted shall be vested in a Congress of the United States, which shall consist of a Senate and House of Representatives.

Section 2. House of Representatives

▶ Clause 1. **Election** Electors means voters. Members of the House of Representatives are elected every two years. Each State must permit the same persons to vote for United States representatives as it permits to vote for the members of the larger house of its own legislature. The 17th Amendment (1913) extends this requirement to the qualification of voters for United States senators.

▶ Clause 2. **Qualifications** A member of the House of Representatives must be at least 25 years old, an American citizen for seven years, and a resident of the State he or she represents. In addition, political custom requires that a representative also reside in the district from which he or she is elected.

▶ Clause 3. **Apportionment** The number of representatives each State is entitled to is based on its population, which is counted every 10 years in the census. Congress reapportions the seats among the States after each census. In the Reapportionment Act of 1929, Congress fixed the permanent size of the House at 435 members with each State having at least one representative. Today there is one House seat for approximately every 700,000 persons in the population.

The words "three-fifths of all other persons" referred to slaves and reflected the Three-Fifths Compromise reached by the Framers at Philadelphia in 1787; the phrase was made obsolete, was in effect repealed, by the 13th Amendment in 1865.

* The gray words indicate portions of the Constitution altered by subsequent amendments to the document.

▶ Clause 4. **Vacancies** The executive authority refers to the governor of a State. If a member leaves office or dies before the expiration of his or her term, the governor is to call a special election to fill the vacancy.

Section 2.

▶ 1. The House of Representatives shall be composed of Members chosen every second Year by the People of the several States, and the Electors in each State shall have the Qualifications requisite for Electors of the most numerous Branch of the State Legislature.

▶ 2. No Person shall be a Representative who shall not have attained to the age of twenty-five Years, and been seven Years a Citizen of the United States, and who shall not, when elected, be an Inhabitant of that State in which he shall be chosen.

▶ 3. Representatives and direct Taxes* shall be apportioned among the several States which may be included within this Union, according to their respective Numbers, which shall be determined by adding to the whole Number of free Persons, including those bound to Service for a Term of Years and excluding Indians not taxed, three fifths of all other Persons. The actual Enumeration shall be made within three Years after the first Meeting of the Congress of the United States, and within every subsequent term of ten Years, in such Manner as they shall by Law direct. The Number of Representatives shall not exceed one for every thirty Thousand, but each State shall have at Least one Representative; and, until such enumeration shall be made, the State of New Hampshire shall be entitled to choose three, Massachusetts eight, Rhode Island and Providence Plantations one, Connecticut five, New York six, New Jersey four, Pennsylvania eight, Delaware one, Maryland six, Virginia ten, North Carolina five, South Carolina five, and Georgia three.

▶ 4. When vacancies happen in the Representation from any State, the Executive Authority thereof shall issue Writs of Election to fill such Vacancies.

▶5. The House of Representatives shall choose their Speaker and other Officers; and shall have the sole Power of Impeachment.

▶**Clause 5. Officers; impeachment** The House elects a Speaker, customarily chosen from the majority party in the House. Impeachment means accusation. The House has the exclusive power to impeach, or accuse, civil officers; the Senate (Article I, Section 3, Clause 6) has the exclusive power to try those impeached by the House.

Section 3.

▶1. The Senate of the United States shall be composed of two Senators from each State chosen by the Legislature thereof for six Years; and each Senator shall have one Vote.

▶2. Immediately after they shall be assembled in Consequences of the first Election, they shall be divided, as equally as may be, into three Classes. The Seats of the Senators of the first Class shall be vacated at the Expiration of the second Year; of the second Class, at the Expiration of the fourth Year; and of the third Class, at the Expiration of the sixth Year; so that one-third may be chosen every second Year; and if Vacancies happen by Resignation, or otherwise, during the Recess of the Legislature of any State, the Executive thereof may make temporary Appointments until the next Meeting of the Legislature, which shall then fill such Vacancies.

▶3. No Person shall be a Senator who shall not have attained to the Age of thirty Years, and been nine Years a Citizen of the United States, and who shall not, when elected, be an Inhabitant of that State for which he shall be chosen.

▶4. The Vice President of the United States shall be President of the Senate but shall have no Vote, unless they be equally divided.

▶5. The Senate shall choose their other Officers, and also a President pro tempore, in the Absence of the Vice President, or when he shall exercise the Office of President of the United States.

▶6. The Senate shall have the sole Power to try all Impeachments. When sitting for that Purpose, they shall be on Oath or Affirmation. When the President of the United States is tried, the Chief Justice shall preside: And no Person shall be convicted without the Concurrence of two thirds of the Members present.

▶7. Judgment in Cases of Impeachment shall not extend further than to removal from Office, and disqualification to hold and enjoy any Office of honor, Trust, or Profit under the United States: but the Party convicted shall nevertheless be liable and subject to Indictment, Trial, Judgment and Punishment, according to Law.

Section 3. Senate

▶ **Clause 1. Composition, election, term** Each State has two senators. Each serves for six years and has one vote. Originally, senators were not elected directly by the people, but by each State's legislature. The 17th Amendment, added in 1913, provides for the popular election of senators.

▶ **Clause 2. Classification** The senators elected in 1788 were divided into three groups so that the Senate could become a "continuing body." One-third of the Senate's seats are up for election every two years.

The 17th Amendment provides that a Senate vacancy is to be filled at a special election called by the governor; State law may also permit the governor to appoint a successor to serve until that election is held.

▶ **Clause 3. Qualifications** A senator must be at least 30 years old, a citizen for at least nine years, and must live in the State from which elected.

▶ **Clause 4. Presiding officer** The Vice President presides over the Senate, but may vote only to break a tie.

▶ **Clause 5. Other officers** The Senate chooses its own officers, including a president pro tempore to preside when the Vice President is not there.

▶ **Clause 6. Impeachment trials** The Senate conducts the trials of those officials impeached by the House. The Vice President presides unless the President is on trial, in which case the Chief Justice of the United States does so. A conviction requires the votes of two-thirds of the senators present.

No President has ever been convicted. In 1868 the House voted eleven articles of impeachment against President Andrew Johnson, but the Senate fell one vote short of convicting him. In 1974 President Richard M. Nixon resigned the presidency in the face of almost certain impeachment by the House. The House brought two articles of impeachment against President Bill Clinton in late 1998. Neither charge was supported by even a simple majority vote in the Senate, on February 12, 1999.

▶ **Clause 7. Penalty on conviction** The punishment of an official convicted in an impeachment case has always been removal from office. The Senate can also bar a convicted person from ever holding any federal office, but it is not required to do so. A convicted person can also be tried and punished in a regular court for any crime involved in the impeachment case.

981

Section 4. Elections and Meetings

▶ Clause 1. **Election In 1842** Congress required that representatives be elected from districts within each State with more than one seat in the House. The districts in each State are drawn by that State's legislature. Seven States now have only one seat in the House: Alaska, Delaware, Montana, North Dakota, South Dakota, Vermont, and Wyoming. The 1842 law also directed that representatives be elected in each State on the same day: the Tuesday after the first Monday in November of every even-numbered year. In 1914 Congress also set that same date for the election of senators.

▶ Clause 2. **Sessions** Congress must meet at least once a year. The 20th Amendment (1933) changed the opening date to January 3.

Section 5. Legislative Proceedings

▶ Clause 1. **Admission of members; quorum** In 1969 the Supreme Court held that the House cannot exclude any member-elect who satisfies the qualifications set out in Article I, Section 2, Clause 2.

A majority in the House (218 members) or Senate (51) constitutes a quorum. In practice, both houses often proceed with less than a quorum present. However, any member may raise a point of order (demand a "quorum call"). If a roll call then reveals less than a majority of the members present, that chamber must either adjourn or the sergeant at arms must be ordered to round up absent members.

▶ Clause 2. **Rules** Each house has adopted detailed rules to guide its proceedings. Each house may discipline members for unacceptable conduct; expulsion requires a two-thirds vote.

▶ Clause 3. **Record** Each house must keep and publish a record of its meetings. The Congressional Record is published for every day that either house of Congress is in session, and provides a written record of all that is said and done on the floor of each house each session.

▶ Clause 4. **Adjournment** Once in session, neither house may suspend (recess) its work for more than three days without the approval of the other house. Both houses must always meet in the same location.

Section 4.

▶1. The Times, Places and Manner of holding Elections for Senators and Representatives, shall be prescribed in each State by the Legislature thereof; but the Congress may at any time by law make or alter such Regulations, except as to the Places of choosing Senators.

▶2. The Congress shall assemble at least once in every Year, and such Meeting shall be on the first Monday in December, unless they shall by Law appoint a different Day.

Section 5.

▶1. Each House shall be the Judge of the Elections, Returns and Qualifications of its own Members, and a Majority of each shall constitute a Quorum to do Business; but a smaller Number may adjourn from day to day, and may be authorized to compel the Attendance of absent Members, in such Manner, and under such Penalties, as each House may provide.

▶2. Each House may determine the Rules of its Proceedings, punish its Members for disorderly Behavior, and, with the Concurrence of two thirds, expel a Member.

▶3. Each House shall keep a Journal of its Proceedings, and from time to time publish the same, excepting such Parts as may in their Judgment require Secrecy; and the Yeas and Nays of the Members of either House on any question shall, at the Desire of one fifth of those Present, be entered on the Journal.

▶4. Neither House, during the Session of Congress, shall, without the Consent of the other, adjourn for more than three days, nor to any other Place than that in which the two Houses shall be sitting.

982

Section 6.

▶1. The Senators and Representatives shall receive a Compensation for their Services, to be ascertained by Law, and paid out of the Treasury of the United States. They shall in all Cases, except Treason, Felony, and Breach of the Peace, be privileged from Arrest during their Attendance at the Session of their respective Houses, and in going to and returning from the same; and for any Speech or Debate in either House, they shall not be questioned in any other Place.

▶2. No Senator or Representative shall, during the Time for which he was elected, be appointed to any civil Office under the Authority of the United States, which shall have been created, or the Emoluments whereof shall have been increased during such time; and no Person holding any Office under the United States, shall be a Member of either House during his Continuance in Office.

Section 7.

▶1. All Bills for raising Revenue shall originate in the House of Representatives; but the Senate may propose or concur with amendments as on other Bills.

▶2. Every Bill which shall have passed the House of Representatives and the Senate, shall, before it become a law, be presented to the President of the United States: If he approve, he shall sign it, but if not he shall return it, with his Objections to that House in which it shall have originated, who shall enter the Objections at large on their Journal, and proceed to reconsider it. If after such Reconsideration two thirds of the House shall agree to pass the Bill, it shall be sent, together with the Objections, to the other House, by which it shall likewise be reconsidered, and if approved by two thirds of that House, it shall become a Law. But in all such Cases the Votes of both Houses shall be determined by Yeas and Nays, and the Names of the Persons voting for and against the Bill shall be entered on the Journal of each House respectively. If any Bill shall not be returned by the President within ten Days (Sunday excepted) after it shall have been presented to him, the Same shall be a law, in like Manner as if he had signed it, unless the Congress by their Adjournment, prevent its Return, in which Case it shall not be a Law.

▶3. Every Order, Resolution, or Vote to which the Concurrence of the Senate and House of Representatives may be necessary (except on a question of adjournment) shall be presented to the President of the United States; and before the Same shall take Effect, shall be approved by him, or, being disapproved by him, shall be repassed by two thirds of the Senate and House of Representatives, according to the Rules and Limitations prescribed in the Case of a Bill.

Section 6. Compensation, Immunities, and Disabilities of Members

▶ Clause 1. **Salaries; immunities** Each house sets its members' salaries, paid by the United States; the 27th Amendment (1992) modified this pay-setting power. This provision establishes "legislative immunity." The purpose of this immunity is to allow members to speak and debate freely in Congress itself. Treason is strictly defined in Article III, Section 3. A felony is any serious crime. A breach of the peace is any indictable offense less than treason or a felony; this exemption from arrest is of little real importance today.

▶ Clause 2. **Restrictions on office holding** No sitting member of either house may be appointed to an office in the executive or in the judicial branch if that position was created or its salary was increased during that member's current elected term. The second part of this clause—forbidding any person serving in either the executive or the judicial branch from also serving in Congress—reinforces the principle of separation of powers.

Section 7. Revenue Bills, President's Veto

▶ Clause 1. **Revenue bills** All bills that raise money must originate in the House. However, the Senate has the power to amend any revenue bill sent to it from the lower house.

▶ Clause 2. **Enactment of laws; veto** Once both houses have passed a bill, it must be sent to the President. The President may (1) sign the bill, thus making it law; (2) veto the bill, whereupon it must be returned to the house in which it originated; or (3) allow the bill to become law without signature, by not acting upon it within 10 days of its receipt from Congress, not counting Sundays. The President has a fourth option at the end of a congressional session: If he does not act on a measure within 10 days, and Congress adjourns during that period, the bill dies; the "pocket veto" has been applied to it. A presidential veto may be overridden by a two-thirds vote in each house.

▶ Clause 3. **Other measures** This clause refers to joint resolutions, measures Congress often passes to deal with unusual, temporary, or ceremonial matters. A joint resolution passed by Congress and signed by the President has the force of law, just as a bill does. As a matter of custom, a joint resolution proposing an amendment to the Constitution is not submitted to the President for signature or veto. Concurrent and simple resolutions do not have the force of law and, therefore, are not submitted to the President.

Section 8. Powers of Congress

▶ **Clause 1.** The 18 separate clauses in this section set out 27 of the many expressed powers the Constitution grants to Congress. In this clause Congress is given the power to levy and provide for the collection of various kinds of taxes, in order to finance the operations of the government. All federal taxes must be levied at the same rates throughout the country.

▶ **Clause 2.** Congress has power to borrow money to help finance the government. Federal borrowing is most often done through the sale of bonds on which interest is paid. The Constitution does not limit the amount the government may borrow.

▶ **Clause 3.** This clause, the Commerce Clause, gives Congress the power to regulate both foreign and interstate trade. Much of what Congress does, it does on the basis of its commerce power.

▶ **Clause 4.** Congress has the exclusive power to determine how aliens may become citizens of the United States. Congress may also pass laws relating to bankruptcy.

▶ **Clause 5.** has the power to establish and require the use of uniform gauges of time, distance, weight, volume, area, and the like.

▶ **Clause 6.** Congress has the power to make it a federal crime to falsify the coins, paper money, bonds, stamps, and the like of the United States.

▶ **Clause 7.** Congress has the power to provide for and regulate the transportation and delivery of mail; "post offices" are those buildings and other places where mail is deposited for dispatch; "post roads" include all routes over or upon which mail is carried.

▶ **Clause 8.** Congress has the power to provide for copyrights and patents. A copyright gives an author or composer the exclusive right to control the reproduction, publication, and sale of literary, musical, or other creative work. A patent gives a person the exclusive right to control the manufacture or sale of his or her invention.

▶ **Clause 9.** Congress has the power to create the lower federal courts, all of the several federal courts that function beneath the Supreme Court.

▶ **Clause 10.** Congress has the power to prohibit, as a federal crime: (1) certain acts committed outside the territorial jurisdiction of the United States, and (2) the commission within the United States of any wrong against any nation with which we are at peace.

Section 8.

The Congress shall have Power

▶1. To lay and collect Taxes, Duties, Imposts and Excises to pay the Debts and provide for the common Defence and general Welfare of the United States; but all Duties, Imposts and Excises, shall be uniform throughout the United States;

▶2. To borrow Money on the credit of the United States;

▶3. To regulate Commerce with foreign Nations, and among the several States, and with the Indian Tribes;

▶4. To establish an uniform Rule of Naturalization, and uniform Laws on the subject of Bankruptcies throughout the United States;

▶5. To coin Money, regulate the Value thereof, and of foreign Coin, and fix the Standard of Weights and Measures;

▶6. To provide for the Punishment of counterfeiting the Securities and current Coin of the United States;

▶7. To establish Post Offices and post Roads;

▶8. To promote the Progress of Science and useful Arts, by securing, for limited Times to Authors and Inventors the exclusive Right to their respective Writings and Discoveries;

▶9. To constitute Tribunals inferior to the supreme Court;

▶10. To define and punish Piracies and Felonies committed on the high Seas, and Offences against the Law of nations;

984

11. To declare War, grant Letters of Marque and Reprisal, and make Rules concerning Captures on Land and Water;

Clause 11. Only Congress can declare war. However, the President, as commander in chief of the armed forces (Article II, Section 2, Clause 1), can make war without such a formal declaration. Letters of marque and reprisal are commissions authorizing private persons to outfit vessels (privateers) to capture and destroy enemy ships in time of war; they were forbidden in international law by the Declaration of Paris of 1856, and the United States has honored the ban since the Civil War.

12. To raise and support Armies; but no Appropriation of Money to that Use shall be for a longer Term than two Years;

13. To provide and maintain a Navy;

Clauses 12 and 13. Congress has the power to provide for and maintain the nation's armed forces. It established the air force as an independent element of the armed forces in 1947, an exercise of its inherent powers in foreign relations and national defense. The two-year limit on spending for the army insures civilian control of the military.

14. To make Rules for the Government and Regulation of the land and naval Forces;

Clause 14. Today these rules are set out in three principle statutes: the Uniform Code of Military Justice, passed by Congress in 1950, and the Military Justice Acts of 1958 and 1983.

15. To provide for calling forth the Militia to execute the Laws of the Union, suppress Insurrections and repel Invasions;

16. To provide for organizing, arming, and disciplining the Militia, and for governing such Part of them as may be employed in the Service of the United States, reserving to the States respectively the Appointment of the Officers, and the Authority of training the Militia according to the discipline prescribed by Congress;

Clauses 15 and 16. In the National Defense Act of 1916, Congress made each State's militia (volunteer army) a part of the National Guard. Today, Congress and the States cooperate in its maintenance. Ordinarily, each State's National Guard is under the command of that State's governor; but Congress has given the President the power to call any or all of those units into federal service when necessary.

17. To exercise exclusive Legislation in all Cases whatsoever, over such District (not exceeding ten Miles square) as may, by Cession of Particular States, and the Acceptance of Congress, become the Seat of the Government of the United States, and to exercise like Authority over all Places purchased by the Consent of the Legislature of the State in which the Same shall be, for the Erection of Forts, Magazines, Arsenals, Dockyards and other needful Buildings;—And

Clause 17. In 1791 Congress accepted land grants from Maryland and Virginia and established the District of Columbia for the nation's capital. Assuming Virginia's grant would never be needed, Congress returned it in 1846. Today, the elected government of the District's 69 square miles operates under the authority of Congress. Congress also has the power to acquire other lands from the States for various federal purposes.

18. To make all Laws which shall be necessary and proper for carrying into Execution the foregoing Powers and all other Powers vested by this Constitution in the Government of the United States, or in any Department or Officer thereof.

Clause 18. This is the Necessary and Proper Clause, also often called the Elastic Clause. It is the constitutional basis for the many and far-reaching implied powers of the Federal Government.

Section 9.

1. The Migration or Importation of such Persons as any of the States now existing shall think proper to admit, shall not be prohibited by the Congress prior to the Year one thousand eight hundred and eight, but a Tax or duty may be imposed on such Importation, not exceeding ten dollars for each Person.

Section 9. Powers Denied to Congress

Clause 1. The phrase "such persons" referred to slaves. This provision was part of the Commerce Compromise, one of the bargains struck in the writing of the Constitution. Congress outlawed the slave trade in 1808.

▶ **Clause 2.** A writ of habeas corpus, the "great writ of liberty," is a court order directing a sheriff, warden, or other public officer, or a private person, who is detaining another to "produce the body" of the one being held in order that the legality of the detention may be determined by the court.

▶2. The Privilege of the Writ of Habeas Corpus shall not be suspended, unless when in Cases of Rebellion or Invasion the public safety may require it.

▶ **Clause 3.** A bill of attainder is a legislative act that inflicts punishment without a judicial trial. See Article I, Section 10, and Article III, Section 3, Clause 2. An ex post facto law is any criminal law that operates retroactively to the disadvantage of the accused. See Article I, Section 10.

▶3. No Bill of Attainder or ex post facto Law shall be passed.

▶ **Clause 4.** A capitation tax is literally a "head tax," a tax levied on each person in the population. A direct tax is one paid directly to the government by the taxpayer—for example, an income or a property tax; an indirect tax is one paid to another private party who then pays it to the government—for example, a sales tax. This provision was modified by the 16th Amendment (1913), giving Congress the power to levy "taxes on incomes, from whatever source derived."

▶4. No Capitation, or other direct, Tax shall be laid, unless in Proportion to the Census of Enumeration hereinbefore directed to be taken.

▶ **Clause 5.** This provision was a part of the Commerce Compromise made by the Framers in 1787. Congress has the power to tax imported goods, however.

▶5. No Tax or Duty shall be laid on Articles exported from any State.

▶ **Clause 6.** All ports within the United States must be treated alike by Congress as it exercises its taxing and commerce powers. Congress cannot tax goods sent by water from one State to another, nor may it give the ports of one State any legal advantage over those of another.

▶6. No Preference shall be given by any Regulation of Commerce or Revenue to the Ports of one State over those of another: nor shall Vessels bound to, or from, one State, be obliged to enter, clear or pay Duties in another.

▶ **Clause 7.** This clause gives Congress its vastly important "power of the purse," a major check on presidential power. Federal money can be spent only in those amounts and for those purposes expressly authorized by an act of Congress. All federal income and spending must be accounted for, regularly and publicly.

▶7. No Money shall be drawn from the Treasury, but in Consequence of Appropriations made by Law; and a regular Statement and Account of the Receipts and Expenditures of all public Money shall be published from time to time.

▶ **Clause 8.** This provision, preventing the establishment of a nobility, reflects the principle that "all men are created equal." It was also intended to discourage foreign attempts to bribe or otherwise corrupt officers of the government.

▶8. No Title of Nobility shall be granted by the United States: And no Person holding any Office of Profit or Trust under them, shall, without the Consent of the Congress, accept of any present, Emolument, Office, or Title, of any kind whatever, from any King, Prince, or foreign State.

Section 10. Powers Denied to the States

▶ **Clause 1.** The States are not sovereign governments and so cannot make agreements or otherwise negotiate with foreign states; the power to conduct foreign relations is an exclusive power of the National Government. The power to coin money is also an exclusive power of the National Government. Several powers forbidden to the National Government are here also forbidden to the States.

▶ **Clause 2.** This provision relates to foreign, not interstate, commerce. Only Congress, not the States, can tax imports; and the States are, like Congress, forbidden the power to tax exports.

Section 10.

▶1. No State shall enter into any Treaty, Alliance, or Confederation; grant Letters of Marque and Reprisal; coin Money; emit Bills of Credit; make any Thing but gold and silver Coin a Tender in Payment of Debts; pass any Bill of Attainder, ex post facto Law, or Law impairing the Obligation of Contracts, or grant any Title of Nobility.

▶2. No State shall, without the Consent of the Congress, lay any Imposts or Duties on Imports or Exports, except what may be absolutely necessary for executing its inspection Laws; and the net Produce of all Duties and Imposts, laid by any State on Imports or Exports, shall be for the Use of the Treasury of the United States; and all such Laws shall be subject to the Revision and Control of the Congress.

986

▶3. No State shall, without the Consent of Congress, lay any Duty of Tonnage, keep Troops, or Ships of War in time of Peace, enter into any Agreement or Compact with another State, or with a foreign Power, or engage in War, unless actually invaded, or in such imminent Danger as will not admit of delay.

▶ **Clause 3.** A duty of tonnage is a tax laid on ships according to their cargo capacity. Each State has a constitutional right to provide for and maintain a militia; but no State may keep a standing army or navy. The several restrictions here prevent the States from assuming powers that the Constitution elsewhere grants to the National Government.

Article II

Section 1.

▶1. The executive Power shall be vested in a President of the United States of America. He shall hold his Office during the Term of four Years, and, together with the Vice President, chosen for the same Term, be elected as follows:

▶2. Each State shall appoint, in such Manner as the Legislature thereof may direct, a Number of Electors, equal to the whole Number of Senators and Representatives to which the State may be entitled in the Congress: but no Senator or Representative, or Person holding an Office of Trust or Profit, under the United States, shall be appointed an Elector.

▶3. The Electors shall meet in their respective States, and vote by Ballot for two Persons, of whom one at least shall not be an Inhabitant of the same State with themselves. And they shall make a List of all the Persons voted for, and of the Number of Votes for each; which List they shall sign and certify, and transmit sealed to the Seat of the Government of the United States, directed to the President of the Senate. The President of the Senate shall, in the Presence of the Senate and House of Representatives, open all the Certificates, and the Votes shall then be counted. The Person having the greatest Number of Votes shall be the President, if such Number be a majority of the whole Number of Electors appointed; and if there be more than one who have such Majority, and have an equal Number of Votes, then, the House of Representatives shall immediately choose by Ballot one of them for President; and if no Person have a Majority, then from the five highest on the List the said House shall in like Manner choose the President. But in choosing the President, the Votes shall be taken by States, the Representatives from each State having one Vote; a quorum for this Purpose shall consist of a Member or Members from two thirds of the States, and a Majority of all the States shall be necessary to a Choice. In every Case, after the Choice of the President, the Person having the greatest Number of Votes of the Electors shall be the Vice President. But if there should remain two or more who have equal Votes, the Senate shall choose from them by Ballot the Vice President.

Executive Department

Section 1. President and Vice President

▶ **Clause 1. Executive power, term** This clause gives to the President the very broad "executive power," the power to enforce the laws and otherwise administer the public policies of the United States. It also sets the length of the presidential (and vice-presidential) term of office; see the 22nd Amendment (1951), which places a limit on presidential (but not vice-presidential) tenure.

▶ **Clause 2. Electoral college** This clause establishes the "electoral college," although the Constitution does not use that term. It is a body of presidential electors chosen in each State, and it selects the President and Vice President every four years. The number of electors chosen in each State equals the number of senators and representatives that State has in Congress.

▶ **Clause 3. Election of President and Vice President** This clause was replaced by the 12th Amendment in 1804.

987

▶ Clause 4. **Date** Congress has set the date for the choosing of electors as the Tuesday after the first Monday in November every fourth year, and for the casting of electoral votes as the Monday after the second Wednesday in December of that year.

▶4. The Congress may determine the Time of choosing the Electors, and the Day on which they shall give their Votes; which Day shall be the same throughout the United States.

▶ Clause 5. **Qualifications** The President must have been born a citizen of the United States, be at least 35 years old, and have been a resident of the United States for at least 14 years.

▶5. No Person except a natural born Citizen, or a Citizen of the United States, at the time of the Adoption of this Constitution, shall be eligible to the Office of President; neither shall any person be eligible to that Office who shall not have attained to the Age of thirty-five Years, and been fourteen Years a Resident within the United States.

▶ Clause 6. **Vacancy** This clause was modified by the 25th Amendment (1967), which provides expressly for the succession of the Vice President, for the filling of a vacancy in the Vice Presidency, and for the determination of presidential inability.

▶6. In Case of the Removal of the President from Office, or of his Death, Resignation, or Inability to discharge the Powers and Duties of the said Office, the Same shall devolve on the Vice President, and the Congress may by Law provide for the Case of Removal, Death, Resignation or Inability, both of the President and Vice President, declaring what Officer shall then act as President, and such Officer shall act accordingly, until the Disability be removed, or a President shall be elected.

▶ Clause 7. **Compensation** The President now receives a salary of $400,000 and a taxable expense account of $50,000 a year. Those amounts cannot be changed during a presidential term; thus, Congress cannot use the President's compensation as a bargaining tool to influence executive decisions. The phrase "any other emolument" means, in effect, any valuable gift; it does not mean that the President cannot be provided with such benefits of office as the White House, extensive staff assistance, and much else.

▶7. The President shall, at stated Times, receive for his Services, a Compensation, which shall neither be increased nor diminished during the Period for which he shall have been elected, and he shall not receive within that Period any other Emolument from the United States, or any of them.

▶ Clause 8. **Oath of office** The Chief Justice of the United States regularly administers this oath or affirmation, but any judicial officer may do so. Thus, Calvin Coolidge was sworn into office in 1923 by his father, a justice of the peace in Vermont.

▶8. Before he enter on the Execution of his Office, he shall take the following Oath or Affirmation:
"I do solemnly swear (or affirm) that I will faithfully execute the Office of President of the United States, and will to the best of my Ability, preserve, protect and defend the Constitution of the United States."

Section 2. President's Powers and Duties

▶ Clause 1. **Military, civil powers** The President, a civilian, heads the nation's armed forces, a key element in the Constitution's insistence on civilian control of the military. The President's power to "require the opinion, in writing" provides the constitutional basis for the Cabinet. The President's power to grant reprieves and pardons, the power of clemency, extends only to federal cases.

Section 2.

▶1. The President shall be Commander in Chief of the Army and Navy of the United States, and of the Militia of the several States, when called into the actual Service of the United States; he may require the Opinion, in writing, of the principal Officer in each of the executive Departments, upon any Subject relating to the Duties of their respective Offices, and he shall have Power to Grant Reprieves and Pardons for Offences against the United States, except in Cases of Impeachment.

988

2. He shall have Power, by and with the Advice and Consent of the Senate, to make Treaties, provided two thirds of the Senators present concur; and he shall nominate, and by and with the Advice and Consent of the Senate, shall appoint Ambassadors, other public Ministers and Consuls, Judges of the supreme Court, and all other Officers of the United States, whose Appointments are not herein otherwise provided for, and which shall be established by Law: but the Congress may by Law vest the Appointment of such inferior Officers, as they think proper, in the President alone, in the Courts of Law, or in the Heads of Departments.

Clause 2. **Treaties, appointments** The President has the sole power to make treaties; to become effective, a treaty must be approved by a two-thirds vote in the Senate. In practice, the President can also make executive agreements with foreign governments; these pacts, which are frequently made and usually deal with routine matters, do not require Senate consent. The President appoints the principal officers of the executive branch and all federal judges; the "inferior officers" are those who hold lesser posts.

3. The President shall have Power to fill up all Vacancies that may happen during the Recess of the Senate, by granting Commissions which shall expire at the End of their next Session.

Clause 3. **Recess appointments** When the Senate is not in session, appointments that require Senate consent can be made by the President on a temporary basis, as "recess appointments." Recess appointments are valid only to the end of the congressional term in which they are made.

Section 3.

He shall from time to time give to the Congress Information of the State of the Union, and recommend to their Consideration such Measures as he shall judge necessary and expedient; he may, on extraordinary Occasions, convene both Houses, or either of them, and in Case of Disagreement between them, with Respect to the Time of Adjournment, he may adjourn them to such Time as he shall think proper; he shall receive Ambassadors and other public Ministers; he shall take Care that the Laws be faithfully executed, and shall Commission all the Officers of the United States.

Section 3. President's Powers and Duties

The President delivers a State of the Union Message to Congress soon after that body convenes each year. That message is delivered to the nation's lawmakers and, importantly, to the American people, as well. It is shortly followed by the proposed federal budget and an economic report; and the President may send special messages to Congress at any time. In all of these communications, Congress is urged to take those actions the Chief Executive finds to be in the national interest. The President also has the power: to call special sessions of Congress; to adjourn Congress if its two houses cannot agree for that purpose; to receive the diplomatic representatives of other governments; to insure the proper execution of all federal laws; and to empower federal officers to hold their posts and perform their duties.

Section 4.

The President, Vice President and all Civil Officers of the United States, shall be removed from Office on Impeachment for and Conviction of, Treason, Bribery, or other high Crimes and Misdemeanors.

Section 4. Impeachment

The Constitution outlines the impeachment process in Article I, Section 2, Clause 5 and in Section 3, Clauses 6 and 7.

Article III

Section 1.

The judicial Power of the United States, shall be vested in one supreme Court, and in such inferior Courts as the Congress may from time to time ordain and establish. The Judges, both of the supreme and inferior Courts, shall hold their Offices during good Behaviour, and shall, at stated Times, receive for their Services, a Compensation, which shall not be diminished during their Continuance in Office.

Judicial Department

Section 1. Judicial Power, Courts, Terms of Office

The judicial power conferred here is the power of federal courts to hear and decide cases, disputes between the government and individuals and between private persons (parties). The Constitution creates only the Supreme Court of the United States; it gives to Congress the power to establish other, lower federal courts (Article I, Section 8, Clause 9) and to fix the size of the Supreme Court. The words "during good Behaviour" mean, in effect, for life.

989

Section 2. Jurisdiction

▶ Clause 1. **Cases to be heard** This clause sets out the jurisdiction of the federal courts; that is, it identifies those cases that may be tried in those courts. The federal courts can hear and decide—have jurisdiction over—a case depending on either the subject matter or the parties involved in that case. The jurisdiction of the federal courts in cases involving States was substantially restricted by the 11th Amendment in 1795.

▶ Clause 2. **Supreme Court jurisdiction** Original jurisdiction refers to the power of a court to hear a case in the first instance, not on appeal from a lower court. Appellate jurisdiction refers to a court's power to hear a case on appeal from a lower court, from the court in which the case was originally tried. This clause gives the Supreme Court both original and appellate jurisdiction. However, nearly all of the cases the High Court hears are brought to it on appeal from the lower federal courts and the highest State courts.

▶ Clause 3. **Jury trial in criminal cases** A person accused of a federal crime is guaranteed the right to trial by jury in a federal court in the State where the crime was committed; see the 5th and 6th amendments. The right to trial by jury in serious criminal cases in the State courts is guaranteed by the 6th and 14th amendments.

Section 2.

▶1. The judicial Power shall extend to all Cases, in Law and Equity, arising under this Constitution, the Laws of the United States, and Treaties made, or which shall be made, under their Authority;— to all Cases affecting Ambassadors, other public ministers, and Consuls;— to all Cases of Admiralty and maritime Jurisdiction;— to Controversies to which the United States shall be a Party;— to Controversies between two or more States;— between a State and Citizens of another State;— between Citizens of different States;— between Citizens of the same State claiming Lands under Grants of different States, and between a State, or the Citizens thereof, and foreign States, Citizens, or Subjects.

▶2. In all Cases affecting Ambassadors, other public Ministers and Consuls, and those in which a State shall be a Party, the supreme Court shall have original Jurisdiction. In all the other Cases before mentioned, the supreme Court shall have appellate Jurisdiction, both as to Law and Fact, with such Exceptions, and under such Regulations as the Congress shall make.

▶3. The trial of all Crimes, except in Cases of Impeachment, shall be by Jury; and such Trial shall be held in the State where the said Crimes shall have been committed; but when not committed within any State, the Trial shall be at such Place or Places as the Congress may by Law have directed.

Section 3. Treason

▶ Clause 1. **Definition** Treason is the only crime defined in the Constitution. The Framers intended the very specific definition here to prevent the loose use of the charge of treason—for example, against persons who criticize the government. Treason can be committed only in time of war and only by a citizen or a resident alien.

▶ Clause 2. **Punishment** Congress has provided that the punishment that a federal court may impose on a convicted traitor may range from a minimum of five years in prison and/or a $10,000 fine to a maximum of death; no person convicted of treason has ever been executed by the United States. No legal punishment can be imposed on the family or descendants of a convicted traitor. Congress has also made it a crime for any person (in either peace or wartime) to commit espionage or sabotage, to attempt to overthrow the government by force, or to conspire to do any of these things.

Section 3.

▶1. Treason against the United States shall consist only in levying War against them, or in adhering to their Enemies, giving them Aid and Comfort. No Person shall be convicted of Treason unless on the Testimony of two Witnesses to the same overt Act, or on Confession in open Court.

▶2. The Congress shall have Power to declare the Punishment of Treason, but no Attainder of Treason shall work Corruption of Blood, or Forfeiture except during the Life of the Person attainted.

990

Article IV

Section 1.

Full Faith and Credit shall be given in each State to the public Acts, Records, and judicial Proceedings of every other State. And the Congress may by general Laws prescribe the Manner in which such Acts, Records and Proceedings shall be proved, and the Effect thereof.

Section 2.

▶1. The Citizens of each State shall be entitled to all Privileges and Immunities of Citizens in the several States.

▶2. A Person charged in any State with Treason, Felony, or other Crime, who shall flee from justice, and be found in another State, shall on Demand of the executive Authority of the State from which he fled, be delivered up, to be removed to the State having Jurisdiction of the Crime.

▶3. No Person held to Service or Labor in one State, under the Laws thereof, escaping into another, shall, in Consequence of any Law or Regulation therein, be discharged from Service or Labor, but shall be delivered up on Claim of the Party to whom such Service or Labor may be due.

Section 3.

▶1. New States may be admitted by the Congress into this Union; but no new State shall be formed or erected within the Jurisdiction of any other State; nor any State be formed by the Junction of two or more States, or Parts of States, without the Consent of the Legislatures of the States concerned as well as of the Congress.

▶2. The Congress shall have Power to dispose of and make all needful Rules and Regulations respecting the Territory or other Property belonging to the United States; and nothing in this Constitution shall be so construed as to Prejudice any Claims of the United States, or of any particular State.

Section 4.

The United States shall guarantee to every State in this Union a Republican Form of Government, and shall protect each of them against Invasion; and on Application of the Legislature, or of the Executive (when the Legislature cannot be convened) against domestic Violence.

Relations Among States

Section 1. Full Faith and Credit

Each State must recognize the validity of the laws, public records, and court decisions of every other State.

Section 2. Privileges and Immunities of Citizens

▶ **Clause 1. Residents of other States** In effect, this clause means that no State may discriminate against the residents of other States; that is, a State's laws cannot draw unreasonable distinctions between its own residents and those of any of the other States. See Section 1 of the 14th Amendment.

▶ **Clause 2. Extradition** The process of returning a fugitive to another State is known as "interstate rendition" or, more commonly, "extradition." Usually, that process works routinely; some extradition requests are contested however—especially in cases with racial or political overtones. A governor may refuse to extradite a fugitive; but the federal courts can compel an unwilling governor to obey this constitutional command.

▶ **Clause 3. Fugitive slaves** This clause was nullified by the 13th Amendment, which abolished slavery in 1865.

Section 3. New States; Territories

▶ **Clause 1. New States** Only Congress can admit new States to the Union. A new State may not be created by taking territory from an existing State without the consent of that State's legislature. Congress has admitted 37 States since the original 13 formed the Union. Five States—Vermont, Kentucky, Tennessee, Maine, and West Virginia—were created from parts of existing States. Texas was an independent republic before admission. California was admitted after being ceded to the United States by Mexico. Each of the other 30 States entered the Union only after a period of time as an organized territory of the United States.

▶ **Clause 2. Territory, property** Congress has the power to make laws concerning the territories, other public lands, and all other property of the United States.

Section 4. Protection Afforded to States by the Nation

The Constitution does not define "a republican form of government," but the phrase is generally understood to mean a representative government. The Federal Government must also defend each State against attacks from outside its border and, at the request of a State's legislature or its governor, aid its efforts to put down internal disorders.

991

Provisions for Amendment

This section provides for the methods by which formal changes can be made in the Constitution. An amendment may be proposed in one of two ways: by a two-thirds vote in each house of Congress, or by a national convention called by Congress at the request of two-thirds of the State legislatures. A proposed amendment may be ratified in one of two ways: by three-fourths of the State legislatures, or by three-fourths of the States in conventions called for that purpose. Congress has the power to determine the method by which a proposed amendment may be ratified. The amendment process cannot be used to deny any State its equal representation in the United States Senate. To this point, 27 amendments have been adopted. To date, all of the amendments except the 21st Amendment were proposed by Congress and ratified by the State legislatures. Only the 21st Amendment was ratified by the convention method.

National Debts, Supremacy of National Law, Oath

Section 1. Validity of Debts

Congress had borrowed large sums of money during the Revolution and later during the Critical Period of the 1780s. This provision, a pledge that the new government would honor those debts, did much to create confidence in that government.

Section 2. Supremacy of National Law

This section sets out the Supremacy Clause, a specific declaration of the supremacy of federal law over any and all forms of State law. No State, including its local governments, may make or enforce any law that conflicts with any provision in the Constitution, an act of Congress, a treaty, or an order, rule, or regulation properly issued by the President or his subordinates in the executive branch.

Section 3. Oaths of Office

This provision reinforces the Supremacy Clause; all public officers, at every level in the United States, owe their first allegiance to the Constitution of the United States. No religious qualification can be imposed as a condition for holding any public office.

Ratification of Constitution

The proposed Constitution was signed by George Washington and 37 of his fellow Framers on September 17, 1787. (George Read of Delaware signed for himself and also for his absent colleague, John Dickinson.)

Article V

The Congress, whenever two thirds of both Houses shall deem it necessary, shall propose Amendments to this Constitution, or, on the Application of the Legislatures of two thirds of the several States, shall call a Convention for proposing Amendments, which, in either Case, shall be valid to all Intents and Purposes, as Part of this Constitution, when ratified by the Legislatures of three fourths of the several States, or by Conventions in three fourths thereof, as the one or the other Mode of Ratification may be proposed by the Congress; Provided that no Amendment which may be made prior to the Year One thousand eight hundred and eight shall in any Manner affect the first and fourth Clauses in the Ninth section of the first Article; and that no State, without its Consent, shall be deprived of its equal Suffrage in the Senate.

Article VI

Section 1.

All Debts contracted and Engagements entered into, before the Adoption of this Constitution, shall be as valid against the United States under this Constitution, as under the Confederation.

Section 2.

This Constitution, and the Laws of the United States which shall be made in Pursuance thereof; and all Treaties made, or which shall be made, under the Authority of the United States, shall be the supreme Law of the Land; and the Judges in every State shall be bound thereby, anything in the constitution or Laws of any State to the Contrary notwithstanding.

Section 3.

The Senators and Representatives before mentioned, and the Members of the several State legislatures, and all executive and judicial Officers, both of the United States and of the several States, shall be bound by Oath or Affirmation, to support this Constitution; but no religious Test shall ever be required as a Qualification to any Office or public Trust under the United States.

Article VII

The ratification of the Conventions of nine States, shall be sufficient for the Establishment of this Constitution between the States so ratifying the same.

992

Done in Convention by the Unanimous Consent of the States present the Seventeenth Day of September in the Year of our Lord one thousand seven hundred and Eighty-seven and of the Independence of the United States of America the twelfth. In witness whereof We have hereunto subscribed our Names.

Attest:
William Jackson,
Secretary
George Washington,
President and Deputy from Virginia

New Hampshire
John Langdon
Nicholas Gilman

Massachusetts
Nathaniel Gorham
Rufus King

Connecticut
William Samuel Johnson
Roger Sherman

New York
Alexander Hamilton

New Jersey
William Livingston
David Brearley
William Paterson
Jonathan Dayton

Pennsylvania
Benjamin Franklin
Thomas Mifflin
Robert Morris
George Clymer
Thomas Fitzsimons
Jared Ingersoll
James Wilson
Gouverneur Morris

Delaware
George Read
Gunning Bedford, Jr.
John Dickinson
Richard Bassett
Jacob Broom

Maryland
James McHenry
Dan of St. Thomas Jenifer
Daniel Carroll

Virginia
John Blair
James Madison, Jr.

North Carolina
William Blount
Richard Dobbs Spaight
Hugh Williamson

South Carolina
John Rutledge
Charles Cotesworth Pinckney
Charles Pinckney
Pierce Butler

Georgia
William Few
Abraham Baldwin

993

The United States Constitution

Amendments

The first 10 amendments, the Bill of Rights, were each proposed by Congress on September 25, 1789, and ratified by the necessary three-fourths of the States on December 15, 1791. These amendments were originally intended to restrict the National Government—not the States. However, the Supreme Court has several times held that most of their provisions also apply to the States, through the 14th Amendment's Due Process Clause.

1st Amendment. Freedom of Religion, Speech, Press, Assembly, and Petition

The 1st Amendment sets out five basic liberties: The guarantee of freedom of religion is both a protection of religious thought and practice and a command of separation of church and state. The guarantees of freedom of speech and press assure to all persons a right to speak, publish, and otherwise express their views. The guarantees of the rights of assembly and petition protect the right to join with others in public meetings, political parties, interest groups, and other associations to discuss public affairs and influence public policy. None of these rights is guaranteed in absolute terms, however; like all other civil rights guarantees, each of them may be exercised only with regard to the rights of all other persons.

1st Amendment

Congress shall make no law respecting an establishment of religion, or prohibiting the free exercise thereof, or abridging the freedom of speech, or of the press; or the right of the people peaceably to assemble, and to petition the Government for a redress of grievances.

2nd Amendment. Bearing Arms

The right of the people to keep and bear arms was insured by the 2nd Amendment.

2nd Amendment

A well-regulated Militia being necessary to the security of a free State, the right of the people to keep and bear Arms, shall not be infringed.

3rd Amendment. Quartering of Troops

This amendment was intended to prevent what had been common British practice in the colonial period; see the Declaration of Independence. This provision is of virtually no importance today.

3rd Amendment.

No Soldier shall, in time of peace be quartered in any house, without the consent of the Owner, nor, in time of war, but in a manner to be prescribed by law.

4th Amendment. Searches and Seizures

The basic rule laid down by the 4th Amendment is this: Police officers have no general right to search for or seize evidence or seize (arrest) persons. Except in particular circumstances, they must have a proper warrant (a court order) obtained with probable cause (on reasonable grounds). This guarantee is reinforced by the exclusionary rule, developed by the Supreme Court: Evidence gained as the result of an unlawful search or seizure cannot be used at the court trial of the person from whom it was seized.

4th Amendment.

The right of the people to be secure in their persons, houses, papers, and effects, against unreasonable searches and seizures, shall not be violated, and no Warrants shall issue, but upon probable cause, supported by Oath or affirmation, and particularly describing the place to be searched, and the persons or things to be seized.

5th Amendment. Criminal Proceedings; Due Process; Eminent Domain

A person can be tried for a serious federal crime only if he or she has been indicted (charged, accused of that crime) by a grand jury. No one may be subjected to double jeopardy—that is, tried twice for the same crime. All persons are protected against self-incrimination; no person can be legally compelled to answer any question in any governmental proceeding if that answer could lead to that person's prosecution. The 5th Amendment's Due Process Clause prohibits unfair, arbitrary actions by the Federal Government; a like prohibition is set out against the States in the 14th Amendment. Government may take private property for a legitimate public purpose; but when it exercises that power of eminent domain, it must pay a fair price for the property seized.

5th Amendment.

No person shall be held to answer for a capital, or otherwise infamous crime, unless on a presentment or indictment of a Grand Jury, except in cases arising in the land or naval forces, or in the Militia, when in actual service in time of War, or public danger; nor shall any person be subject for the same offence to be twice put in jeopardy of life or limb; nor shall be compelled in any criminal case to be a witness against himself, nor be deprived of life, liberty, or property, without due process of law; nor shall private property be taken for public use, without just compensation.

6th Amendment

In all criminal prosecutions, the accused shall enjoy the right to a speedy and public trial, by an impartial jury of the State and district wherein the crime shall have been committed, which district shall have been previously ascertained by law, and to be informed of the nature and cause of the accusation; to be confronted with the witnesses against him; to have compulsory process for obtaining witnesses in his favor, and to have the Assistance of Counsel for his defence.

6th Amendment. Criminal Proceedings

A person accused of crime has the right to be tried in court without undue delay and by an impartial jury; see Article III, Section 2, Clause 3. The defendant must be informed of the charge upon which he or she is to be tried, has the right to cross-examine hostile witnesses, and has the right to require the testimony of favorable witnesses. The defendant also has the right to be represented by an attorney at every stage in the criminal process.

7th Amendment

In Suits at common law, where the value in controversy shall exceed twenty dollars, the right of trial by jury shall be preserved, and no fact tried by a jury, shall be otherwise re-examined in any Court of the United States, than according to the rules of the common law.

7th Amendment. Civil Trials

This amendment applies only to civil cases heard in federal courts. A civil case does not involve criminal matters; it is a dispute between private parties or between the government and a private party. The right to trial by jury is guaranteed in any civil case in a federal court if the amount of money involved in that case exceeds $20 (most cases today involve a much larger sum); that right may be waived (relinquished, put aside) if both parties agree to a bench trial (a trial by a judge, without a jury).

8th Amendment

Excessive bail shall not be required, nor excessive fines imposed, nor cruel and unusual punishment inflicted.

8th Amendment. Punishment for Crimes

Bail is the sum of money that a person accused of crime may be required to post (deposit with the court) as a guarantee that he or she will appear in court at the proper time. The amount of bail required and/or a fine imposed as punishment must bear a reasonable relationship to the seriousness of the crime involved in the case. The prohibition of cruel and unusual punishment forbids any punishment judged to be too harsh, too severe for the crime for which it is imposed.

9th Amendment

The enumeration in the Constitution, of certain rights, shall not be construed to deny or disparage others retained by the people.

9th Amendment. Unenumerated Rights

The fact that the Constitution sets out many civil rights guarantees, expressly provides for many protections against government, does not mean that there are not other rights also held by the people.

10th Amendment

The powers not delegated to the United States by the Constitution, nor prohibited by it to the States, are reserved to the States respectively, or to the people.

10th Amendment. Powers Reserved to the States

This amendment identifies the area of power that may be exercised by the States. All of those powers the Constitution does not grant to the National Government, and at the same time does not forbid to the States, belong to each of the States, or to the people of each State.

995

11th Amendment. Suits Against States

Proposed by Congress March 4, 1794; ratified February 7, 1795, but official announcement of the ratification was delayed until January 8, 1798. This amendment repealed part of Article III, Section 2, Clause 1. No State may be sued in a federal court by a resident of another State or of a foreign country; the Supreme Court has long held that this provision also means that a State cannot be sued in a federal court by a foreign country or, more importantly, even by one of its own residents.

11th Amendment

The Judicial power of the United States shall not be construed to extend to any suit in law or equity, commenced or prosecuted against one of the United States by Citizens of another State, or by Citizens or Subjects of any Foreign State.

12th Amendment. Election of President and Vice President

Proposed by Congress December 9, 1803; ratified June 15, 1804. This amendment replaced Article II, Section 1, Clause 3. Originally, each elector cast two ballots, each for a different person for President. The person with the largest number of electoral votes, provided that number was a majority of the electors, was to become President; the person with the second highest number was to become Vice President. This arrangement produced an electoral vote tie between Thomas Jefferson and Aaron Burr in 1800; the House finally chose Jefferson as President in 1801. The 12th Amendment separated the balloting for President and Vice President; each elector now casts one ballot for someone as President and a second ballot for another person as Vice President. Note that the 20th Amendment changed the date set here (March 4) to January 20, and that the 23rd Amendment (1961) provides for electors from the District of Columbia. This amendment also provides that the Vice President must meet the same qualifications as those set out for the President in Article II, Section 1, Clause 5.

12th Amendment

The Electors shall meet in their respective States and vote by ballot for President and Vice President, one of whom, at least, shall not be an inhabitant of the same State with themselves; they shall name in their ballots the person voted for as President, and in distinct ballots the person voted for as Vice President, and they shall make distinct lists of all persons voted for as President, and of all persons voted for as Vice President, and of the number of votes for each, which lists they shall sign and certify, and transmit sealed to the seat of the government of the United States, directed to the President of the Senate;— The President of the Senate shall, in the presence of the Senate and the House of Representatives, open all the certificates and the votes shall then be counted;— the person having the greatest Number of votes for President shall be the President, if such number be a majority of the whole number of Electors appointed; and if no person have such a majority, then, from the persons having the highest numbers not exceeding three on the list of those voted for as President, the House of Representatives shall choose immediately, by ballot, the President. But in choosing the President, the votes shall be taken by States, the representation from each State having one vote; a quorum for this purpose shall consist of a member or members from two thirds of the States, and a majority of all the States shall be necessary to a choice. And if the House of Representatives shall not choose a President whenever the right of choice shall devolve upon them, before the fourth day of March next following, then the Vice President shall act as President, as in case of death or other constitutional disability of the President. The person having the greatest number of votes as Vice President, shall be the Vice President, if such number be a majority of the whole number of Electors appointed, and if no person have a majority, then from the two highest numbers on the list, the Senate shall choose the Vice President; a quorum for the purpose shall consist of two thirds of the whole number of Senators, a majority of the whole number shall be necessary to a choice. But no person constitutionally ineligible to the office of President shall be eligible to that of Vice-President of the United States.

13th Amendment. Slavery and Involuntary Servitude

Proposed by Congress January 31, 1865; ratified December 6, 1865. This amendment forbids slavery in the United States and in any area under its control. It also forbids other forms of forced labor, except punishments for crime; but some forms of compulsory service are not prohibited—for example, service on juries or in the armed forces. Section 2 gives to Congress the power to carry out the provisions of Section 1 of this amendment.

13th Amendment

Section 1. Neither slavery nor involuntary servitude, except as a punishment for crime whereof the party shall have been duly convicted, shall exist within the United States, or any place subject to their jurisdiction.

Section 2. Congress shall have power to enforce this article by appropriate legislation.

14th Amendment

Section 1. All persons born or naturalized in the United States and subject to the jurisdiction thereof, are citizens of the United States and of the State wherein they reside. No State shall make or enforce any law which shall abridge the privileges or immunities of citizens of the United States; nor shall any State deprive any person of life, liberty, or property, without due process of law; nor deny to any person within its jurisdiction the equal protection of the laws.

14th Amendment. Rights of Citizens

Proposed by Congress June 13, 1866; ratified July 9, 1868. Section 1 defines citizenship. It provides for the acquisition of United States citizenship by birth or by naturalization. Citizenship at birth is determined according to the principle of jus soli—"the law of the soil," where born; naturalization is the legal process by which one acquires a new citizenship at some time after birth. Under certain circumstances, citizenship can also be gained at birth abroad, according to the principle of jus sanguinis—"the law of the blood," to whom born. This section also contains two major civil rights provisions: the Due Process Clause forbids a State (and its local governments) to act in any unfair or arbitrary way; the Equal Protection Clause forbids a State (and its local governments) to discriminate against, draw unreasonable distinctions between, persons.

Most of the rights set out against the National Government in the first eight amendments have been extended against the States (and their local governments) through Supreme Court decisions involving the 14th Amendment's Due Process Clause.

Section 2. Representatives shall be apportioned among the several States according to their respective numbers, counting the whole number of persons in each State, excluding Indians not taxed. But when the right to vote at any election for the choice of electors for President and Vice President of the United States, Representatives in Congress, the Executive and Judicial officers of a State, or the members of the Legislature thereof, is denied to any of the male inhabitants of such State, being twenty-one years of age and citizens of the United States, or in any way abridged, except for participation in rebellion, or other crime, the basis of representation therein shall be reduced in the proportion which the number of such male citizens shall bear to the whole number of male citizens twenty-one years of age in such State.

The first sentence here replaced Article I, Section 2, Clause 3, the Three-Fifths Compromise provision. Essentially, all persons in the United States are counted in each decennial census, the basis for the distribution of House seats. The balance of this section has never been enforced and is generally thought to be obsolete.

Section 3. No person shall be a Senator or Representative in Congress, or elector of President and Vice President, or hold any office, civil or military, under the United States, or under any State, who, having previously taken an oath, as a member of Congress, or as an officer of the United States, or as a member of any State legislature, or as an executive or judicial officer of any State, to support the Constitution of the United States, shall have engaged in insurrection or rebellion against the same, or given aid or comfort to the enemies thereof. But Congress may, by a vote of two thirds of each House, remove such disability.

This section limited the President's power to pardon those persons who had led the Confederacy during the Civil War. Congress finally removed this disability in 1898.

Section 4. The validity of the public debt of the United States, authorized by law, including debts incurred for payment of pensions and bounties for services in suppressing insurrection or rebellion, shall not be questioned. But neither the United States nor any State shall assume or pay any debt or obligation incurred in aid of insurrection or rebellion against the United States, or any claim for the loss or emancipation of any slave; but all such debts, obligations and claims shall be held illegal and void.

Section 4 also dealt with matters directly related to the Civil War. It reaffirmed the public debt of the United States; but it invalidated, prohibited payment of, any debt contracted by the Confederate States and also prohibited any compensation of former slave owners.

Section 5. The Congress shall have power to enforce, by appropriate legislation, the provisions of this article.

997

15th Amendment. Right to Vote—Race, Color, Servitude

Proposed by Congress February 26, 1869; ratified February 3, 1870. The phrase "previous condition of servitude" refers to slavery. Note that this amendment does not guarantee the right to vote to African Americans, or to anyone else. Instead, it forbids the States from discriminating against any person on the grounds of his "race, color, or previous condition of servitude" in the setting of suffrage qualifications.

15th Amendment

Section 1. The right of citizens of the United States to vote shall not be denied or abridged by the United States or by any State on account of race, color, or previous condition of servitude.

Section 2. The Congress shall have power to enforce this article by appropriate legislation.

16th Amendment. Income Tax

Proposed by Congress July 12, 1909; ratified February 3, 1913. This amendment modified two provisions in Article I, Section 2, Clause 3, and Section 9, Clause 4. It gives to Congress the power to levy an income tax, a direct tax, without regard to the populations of any of the States.

16th Amendment

The Congress shall have power to lay and collect taxes on incomes, from whatever source derived, without apportionment among the several States, and without regard to any census or enumeration.

17th Amendment. Popular Election of Senators

Proposed by Congress May 13, 1912; ratified April 8, 1913. This amendment repealed those portions of Article I, Section 3, Clauses 1 and 2 relating to the election of senators. Senators are now elected by the voters in each State. If a vacancy occurs, the governor of the State involved must call an election to fill the seat; the governor may appoint a senator to serve until the next election, if the State's legislature has authorized that step.

17th Amendment

The Senate of the United States shall be composed of two Senators from each State, elected by the people thereof, for six years; and each Senator shall have one vote. The electors in each State shall have the qualifications requisite for electors of the most numerous branch of the State legislatures.

When vacancies happen in the representation of any State in the Senate, the executive authority of such State shall issue writs of election to fill such vacancies: Provided, That the legislature of any State may empower the executive thereof to make temporary appointments until the people fill the vacancies by election as the legislature may direct.

This amendment shall not be so construed as to affect the election or term of any Senator chosen before it becomes valid as part of the Constitution

18th Amendment. Prohibition of Intoxicating Liquors

Proposed by Congress December 18, 1917; ratified January 16, 1919. This amendment outlawed the making, selling, transporting, importing, or exporting of alcoholic beverages in the United States. It was repealed in its entirety by the 21st Amendment in 1933.

18th Amendment.

Section 1. After one year from the ratification of this article the manufacture, sale, or transportation of intoxicating liquors within, the importation thereof into, or the exportation thereof from the United States and all territory subject to the jurisdiction thereof for beverage purposes is hereby prohibited.

Section 2. The Congress and the several States shall have concurrent power to enforce this article by appropriate legislation.

Section 3. This article shall be inoperative unless it shall have been ratified as an amendment to the Constitution by the legislatures of the several States, as provided in the Constitution, within seven years of the date of the submission hereof to the States by Congress.

19th Amendment. Equal Suffrage—Sex

Proposed by Congress June 4, 1919; ratified August 18, 1920. No person can be denied the right to vote in any election in the United States on account of his or her sex.

19th Amendment

The right of citizens of the United States to vote shall not be denied or abridged by the United States or by any State on account of sex.

Congress shall have power to enforce this article by appropriate legislation.

20th Amendment

Section 1. The terms of the President and Vice President shall end at noon on the 20th day of January, and the terms of Senators and Representatives at noon on the 3d day of January, of the years in which such terms would have ended if this article had not been ratified; and the terms of their successors shall then begin.

Section 2. The Congress shall assemble at least once in every year, and such meeting shall begin at noon on the 3d day of January, unless they shall by law appoint a different day.

Section 3. If, at the time fixed for the beginning of the term of the President, the President elect shall have died, the Vice President elect shall become President. If a President shall not have been chosen before the time fixed for the beginning of his term, or if the President-elect shall have failed to qualify, then the Vice President elect shall act as President until a President shall have qualified; and the Congress may by law provide for the case wherein neither a President elect nor a Vice President elect shall have qualified, declaring who shall then act as President, or the manner in which one who is to act shall be selected, and such person shall act accordingly until a President or Vice President shall have qualified.

Section 4. The Congress may by law provide for the case of the death of any of the persons from whom the House of Representatives may choose a President whenever the right of choice shall have devolved upon them, and for the case of the death of any of the persons from whom the Senate may choose a Vice President whenever the right of choice shall have devolved upon them.

Section 5. Sections 1 and 2 shall take effect on the 15th day of October following the ratification of this article.

Section 6. This article shall be inoperative unless it shall have been ratified as an amendment to the Constitution by the legislatures of three fourths of the several States within seven years from the date of its submission.

20th Amendment. Commencement of Terms; Sessions of Congress; Death or Disqualification of President-Elect

Proposed by Congress March 2, 1932; ratified January 23, 1933. The provisions of Sections 1 and 2 relating to Congress modified Article I, Section 4, Clause 2, and those provisions relating to the President, the 12th Amendment. The date on which the President and Vice President now take office was moved from March 4 to January 20. Similarly, the members of Congress now begin their terms on January 3. The 20th Amendment is sometimes called the "Lame Duck Amendment" because it shortened the period of time a member of Congress who was defeated for reelection (a "lame duck") remains in office.

This section deals with certain possibilities that were not covered by the presidential selection provisions of either Article II or the 12th Amendment. To this point, none of these situations has occurred. Note that there is neither a President-elect nor a Vice President-elect until the electoral votes have been counted by Congress, or, if the electoral college cannot decide the matter, the House has chosen a President or the Senate has chosen a Vice President.

Congress has not in fact ever passed such a law. See Section 2 of the 25th Amendment, regarding a vacancy in the vice presidency; that provision could some day have an impact here.

Section 5 set the date on which this amendment came into force.

Section 6 placed a time limit on the ratification process; note that a similar provision was written into the 18th, 21st, and 22nd amendments.

21st Amendment

Section 1. The eighteenth article of amendment to the Constitution of the United States is hereby repealed.

Section 2. The transportation or importation into any State, Territory, or possession of the United States for delivery or use therein of intoxicating liquors, in violation of the laws thereof, is hereby prohibited.

Section 3. This article shall be inoperative unless it shall have been ratified as an amendment to the Constitution by conventions in the several States, as provided in the Constitution, within seven years from the date of the submission hereof to the States by the Congress.

21st Amendment. Repeal of 18th Amendment

Proposed by Congress February 20, 1933; ratified December 5, 1933. This amendment repealed all of the 18th Amendment. Section 2 modifies the scope of the Federal Government's commerce power set out in Article I, Section 8, Clause 3; it gives to each State the power to regulate the transportation or importation and the distribution or use of intoxicating liquors in ways that would be unconstitutional in the case of any other commodity. The 21st Amendment is the only amendment Congress has thus far submitted to the States for ratification by conventions.

999

22nd Amendment. Presidential Tenure

Proposed by Congress March 21, 1947; ratified February 27, 1951. This amendment modified Article II, Section I, Clause 1. It stipulates that no President may serve more than two elected terms. But a President who has succeeded to the office beyond the midpoint in a term to which another President was originally elected may serve for more than eight years. In any case, however, a President may not serve more than 10 years. Prior to Franklin Roosevelt, who was elected to four terms, no President had served more than two full terms in office.

22nd Amendment

Section 1. No person shall be elected to the office of the President more than twice, and no person who has held the office of President, or acted as President, for more than two years of a term to which some other person was elected President shall be elected to the office of the President more than once. But this Article shall not apply to any person holding the office of President, when this Article was proposed by the Congress, and shall not prevent any person who may be holding the office of President, or acting as President, during the term within which this Article becomes operative from holding the office of President or acting as President during the remainder of such term.

Section 2. This article shall be inoperative unless it shall have been ratified as an amendment to the Constitution by the legislatures of three fourths of the several states within seven years from the date of its submission to the States by the Congress.

23rd Amendment. Presidential Electors for the District of Columbia

Proposed by Congress June 16, 1960; ratified March 29, 1961. This amendment modified Article II, Section I, Clause 2 and the 12th Amendment. It included the voters of the District of Columbia in the presidential electorate; and provides that the District is to have the same number of electors as the least populous State—three electors—but no more than that number.

23rd Amendment.

Section 1. The District constituting the seat of Government of the United States shall appoint in such manner as the Congress may direct:

A number of electors of President and Vice President equal to the whole number of Senators and Representatives in Congress to which the District would be entitled if it were a State, but in no event more than the least populous State; they shall be in addition to those appointed by the States, they shall be considered, for the purposes of the election of President and Vice President, to be electors appointed by a State; and they shall meet in the District and perform such duties as provided by the twelfth article of amendment.

24th Amendment. Right to Vote in Federal Elections—Tax Payment

Proposed by Congress August 27, 1962; ratified January 23, 1964. This amendment outlawed the payment of any tax as a condition for taking part in the nomination or election of any federal officeholder.

24th Amendment.

Section 1. The right of citizens of the United States to vote in any primary or other election for President or Vice President, for electors for President or Vice President, or for Senator or Representative in Congress, shall not be denied or abridged by the United States or any State by reason of failure to pay any poll tax or other tax.

Section 2. The Congress shall have power to enforce this article by appropriate legislation.

25th Amendment. Presidential Succession, Vice Presidential Vacancy, Presidential Inability

Proposed by Congress July 6, 1965; ratified February 10, 1967. Section 1 revised the imprecise provision on presidential succession in Article II, Section 1, Clause 6. It affirmed the precedent set by Vice President John Tyler, who became President on the death of William Henry Harrison in 1841. Section 2 provides for the filling of a vacancy in the office of Vice President. The office had been vacant on 16 occasions and remained unfilled for the rest of each term involved. When Spiro Agnew resigned the office in 1973, President Nixon selected Gerald Ford per this provision; and, when President Nixon resigned in 1974, Gerald Ford became President and chose Nelson Rockefeller as Vice President.

25th Amendment.

Section 1. In case of the removal of the President from office or of his death or resignation, the Vice President shall become President.

Section 2. Whenever there is a vacancy in the office of the Vice President, the President shall nominate a Vice President who shall take office upon confirmation by a majority vote of both Houses of Congress.

1000

Section 3. Whenever the President transmits to the President pro tempore of the Senate and the Speaker of the House of Representatives his written declaration that he is unable to discharge the powers and duties of his office, and until he transmits to them a written declaration to the contrary, such powers and duties shall be discharged by the Vice President as Acting President.

This section created a procedure for determining if a President is so incapacitated that he cannot perform the powers and duties of his office.

Section 4. Whenever the Vice President and a majority of either the principal officers of the executive departments or of such other body as Congress may by law provide, transmit to the President pro tempore of the Senate and the Speaker of the House of Representatives their written declaration that the President is unable to discharge the powers and duties of his office, the Vice President shall immediately assume the powers and duties of the office as Acting President.

Thereafter, when the President transmits to the President pro tempore of the Senate and the Speaker of the House of Representatives his written declaration that no inability exists, he shall resume the powers and duties of his office unless the Vice President and a majority of either the principal officers of the executive department or of such other body as Congress may by law provide, transmit within four days to the President pro tempore of the Senate and the Speaker of the House of Representatives their written declaration that the President is unable to discharge the powers and duties of his office. Thereupon Congress shall decide the issue, assembling within forty-eight hours for that purpose if not in session. If the Congress, within twenty-one days after receipt of the latter written declaration, or, if Congress is not in session, within twenty-one days after Congress is required to assemble, determines by two-thirds vote of both Houses that the President is unable to discharge the powers and duties of his office, the Vice President shall continue to discharge the same as Acting President; otherwise, the President shall resume the powers and duties of his office.

Section 4 deals with the circumstance in which a President will not be able to determine the fact of incapacity. To this point, Congress has not established the "such other body" referred to here. This section contains the only typographical error in the Constitution; in its second paragraph, the word "department" should in fact read "departments."

26th Amendment.

Section 1. The right of citizens of the United States, who are eighteen years of age or older, to vote shall not be denied or abridged by the United States or by any State on account of age.

Section 2. The Congress shall have the power to enforce this article by appropriate legislation.

26th Amendment. Right to Vote—Age

Proposed by Congress March 23, 1971; ratified July 1, 1971. This amendment provides that the minimum age for voting in any election in the United States cannot be more than 18 years. (A State may set a minimum voting age of less than 18, however.)

27th Amendment.

No law varying the compensation for the services of the Senators and Representatives, shall take effect, until an election of Representatives shall have intervened.

27th Amendment. Congressional Pay

Proposed by Congress September 25, 1789; ratified May 7, 1992. This amendment modified Article I, Section 6, Clause 1. It limits Congress's power to fix the salaries of its members—by delaying the effectiveness of any increase in that pay until after the next regular congressional election.

[Declaration of Independence]

Introduction

By signing the Declaration of Independence, members of the Continental Congress sent a clear message to Britain that the American colonies were free and independent states. Starting with its preamble, the document spells out all the reasons the people of the United States have the right to break away from Britain.

Primary Source

The Unanimous Declaration of the Thirteen United States of America

When in the Course of human events, it becomes necessary for one people to dissolve the political bands which have connected them with another, and to assume among the powers of the earth, the separate and equal station to which the Laws of Nature and of Nature's God entitle them, a decent respect to the opinions of mankind requires that they should declare the causes which impel [force] them to the separation. We hold these truths to be self-evident, that all men are created equal, that they are endowed [gifted] by their Creator with certain unalienable [cannot be taken away] Rights, that among these are Life, Liberty and the pursuit of Happiness. That to secure these rights, Governments are instituted among Men, deriving their just powers from the consent of the governed. That whenever any Form of Government becomes destructive of these ends, it is the Right of the People to alter or to abolish it, and to institute new Government, laying its foundation on such principles and organizing its powers in such form, as to them shall seem most likely to effect their Safety and Happiness. Prudence [cautiousness], indeed, will dictate that Governments long established should not be changed for light and transient causes; and accordingly all experience hath shown that mankind are more disposed to suffer, while evils are sufferable, than to right themselves by abolishing the forms to which they are accustomed. But when a long train of abuses and usurpations [unjust uses of power], pursuing invariably the same Object evinces a design to reduce them under absolute Despotism [rule of absolute power], it is their right, it is their duty, to throw off such Government, and to provide new Guards for their future security.

Such has been the patient sufferance of these Colonies; and such is now the necessity which constrains them to alter their former Systems of Government. The history of the present King of Great Britain is a history of repeated injuries and usurpations, all having in direct object the establishment of an absolute Tyranny over these States. To prove this, let Facts be submitted to a candid world.

He has refused his Assent to Laws, the most wholesome and necessary for the public good.

He has forbidden his Governors to pass Laws of immediate and pressing importance, unless suspended in their operation till his Assent should be obtained; and when so suspended, he has utterly neglected to attend to them.

He has refused to pass other Laws for the accommodation of large districts of people, unless those people would relinquish [give up] the right of Representation in the Legislature, a right inestimable [priceless] to them and formidable to tyrants only.

He has called together legislative bodies at places unusual, uncomfortable, and distant from the depository of their public Records, for the sole purpose of fatiguing them into compliance with his measures.

He has dissolved Representative Houses repeatedly, for opposing with manly firmness his invasions on the rights of the people.

He has refused for a long time, after such dissolutions [closing down], to cause others to be elected; whereby the Legislative powers, incapable of Annihilation, have returned to the People at large for their exercise; the State remaining in the mean time exposed to all the dangers of invasion from without, and convulsions [riots] within.

He has endeavoured to prevent the population of these States; for that purpose obstructing the Laws for Naturalization of Foreigners; refusing to pass others to encourage their migrations hither, and raising the conditions of new Appropriations of Lands.

He has obstructed the Administration of Justice by refusing his Assent to Laws for establishing Judiciary powers.

He has made Judges dependent on his Will alone, for the tenure [term] of their offices, and the amount and payment of their salaries.

He has erected a multitude of New Offices, and sent hither swarms of Officers to harass our people, and eat out their substance.

He has kept among us, in times of peace, Standing Armies without the Consent of our legislatures.

He has affected to render the Military independent of and superior to the Civil power.

He has combined with others to subject us to a jurisdiction foreign to our constitution, and unacknowledged by our laws; giving his Assent to their Acts of pretended Legislation:

For quartering [lodging] large bodies of armed troops among us:

For protecting them, by a mock Trial, from punishment for any Murders which they should commit on the Inhabitants of these States:

For cutting off our Trade with all parts of the world:

For imposing Taxes on us without our Consent:

For depriving us in many cases, of the benefits of Trial by Jury: For transporting us beyond Seas to be tried for pretended offences:

For abolishing the free System of English Laws in a neighbouring Province, establishing therein an Arbitrary government, and enlarging its Boundaries so as to render it at once an example and fit instrument for introducing the same absolute rule into these Colonies:

For taking away our Charters, abolishing our most valuable Laws, and altering fundamentally the Forms of our Governments:

For suspending our own Legislatures, and declaring themselves invested with power to legislate for us in all cases whatsoever.

He has abdicated Government here, by declaring us out of his Protection and waging War against us.

He has plundered our seas, ravaged our Coasts, burnt our towns, and destroyed the lives of our people.

He is at this time transporting large Armies of foreign Mercenaries [soldiers] to complete the works of death, desolation, and tyranny, already begun with circumstances of Cruelty and perfidy [dishonesty] scarcely paralleled in the most barbarous ages, and totally unworthy the Head of a civilized nation.

He has constrained our fellow Citizens taken Captive on the high Seas to bear Arms against their Country, to become the executioners of their friends and Brethren, or to fall themselves by their Hands.

He has excited domestic insurrections amongst us, and has endeavoured to bring on the inhabitants of our frontiers, the merciless Indian Savages whose known rule of warfare, is an undistinguished destruction of all ages, sexes and conditions.

In every stage of these Oppressions We have Petitioned for Redress [correction of wrongs] in the most humble terms: Our repeated Petitions have been answered only by repeated injury. A Prince, whose character is thus marked by every act which may define a Tyrant, is unfit to be the ruler of a free people.

Nor have We been wanting in attentions to our British brethren. We have warned them from time to time of attempts by their legislature to extend an unwarrantable jurisdiction over us. We have reminded them of the circumstances of our emigration and settlement here. We have appealed to their native justice and magnanimity [generosity], and we have conjured [begged] them by the ties of our common kindred, to disavow these usurpations, which would inevitably interrupt our connections and correspondence. They too have been deaf to the voice of justice and of consanguinity [relation by blood]. We must, therefore, acquiesce in the necessity, which denounces our Separation, and hold them, as we hold the rest of mankind, Enemies in War, in Peace Friends.

We, therefore, the Representatives of the United States of America, in General Congress, Assembled, appealing to the Supreme Judge of the world for the rectitude [justness] of our intentions, do, in the Name, and by Authority of the good People of these Colonies, solemnly publish and declare, That these United Colonies are, and of Right ought to be Free and Independent States; that they are Absolved from all Allegiance to the British Crown, and that all political connection between them and the State of Great Britain, is and ought to be totally dissolved; and that as Free and Independent States, they have full Power to levy War, conclude Peace, contract Alliances, establish Commerce, and to do all other Acts and Things which Independent States may of right do. And for the support of this Declaration, with a firm reliance on the protection of Divine Providence, we mutually pledge to each other our Lives, our Fortunes and our sacred Honor.

ASSESSMENT

1. **Identify Cause and Effect** How might the ideas about equality expressed in the Declaration of Independence have influenced later historical movements, such as the abolitionist movement and the women's suffrage movement?
2. **Identify Key Steps in a Process** Why was the Declaration of Independence a necessary document for the founding of the new nation?
3. **Draw Inferences** English philosopher John Locke wrote that government should protect "life, liberty, and estate." How do you think Locke's writing influenced ideas about government put forth in the Declaration of Independence?
4. **Analyze Structure** How does the Declaration organize its key points from beginning to end?

Answers

1. The Declaration of Independence famously asserts that all men are created equal. However, at the time of writing, many people were not seen as equal in the eyes of the law, including women and African Americans. These groups would later draw on the Declaration to argue that the principle of equality put forth in this document should extend to all people in the country, not just white men.

2. In order to separate from Britain, the states first had to declare their intentions to do so. The Declaration let the king know in official terms that the states would no longer be his colonies. The Declaration also helped the thirteen states unite as a new nation.

3. The Declaration of Independence states that people have the right to life, liberty, and the pursuit of happiness. This language sounds as if it is taken from Locke, replacing estate, or property, with happiness. The framers accepted Locke's idea that government should protect these key aspects of its citizens' lives. Because in their eyes the British government was not protecting these rights, they had the right to form a new government that would.

4. The document first lists the reasons for writing the Declaration. Then it explains under what circumstances a people must reject their government and create another. Next, it lists the grievances against the king. Finally, it ends by formally declaring independence.

Answers

1. Writing down the laws ensured that everyone knew what they were and they could go back to the laws to read them if they were uncertain or if they were challenged. Organizing the laws and writing them down also made it more likely that they would be applied consistently and uniformly. Moreover, by writing down these laws, Hammurabi created a lasting system and a legacy that would survive even after he no longer ruled.

2. Having written laws could have ensured that people received equal treatment under the law. People might also have been more reluctant to commit crimes if they knew what the punishments would be. Having consistent laws regulating commerce, property, inheritance, and debt likely helped financial interactions run more smoothly, and so there may have been fewer private feuds and problems.

3. The *Code of Hammurabi* was one of the first models for writing and codifying laws. Other written laws likely built on this model, establishing codes of conduct and putting legal, judicial, and financial regulations in place. The idea that governments have written laws that create consistent rules for everyone to follow would have come from earlier codes such as this.

[Code of Hammurabi]

Introduction

Hammurabi ruled Babylon for over forty years. The "Code of Hammurabi," believed to date back to at least 1750 B.C., is a series of laws Hammurabi decreed when the ancient city was at the peak of its power. The Code consisted of 300 laws with sections on civil, criminal, and family laws and punishments. It was inscribed on stone columns more than 7 feet high so the public could read and know each law. The Code is considered one of the earliest examples of laws put in place to control the government.

Primary Source

If a man practice [robbery] and be captured, that man shall be put to death. . . .

If a man has come forward in a lawsuit for the witnessing of false things, and has not proved the thing that he said, if that lawsuit is a capital case [punishable by death], that man shall be put to death. If he came forward for witnessing about corn or silver, he shall bear the penalty [punishment] [which applies to] that case.

If a man has concealed in his house a lost slave or slave-girl belonging to the Palace or to a subject, and has not brought him [or her] out at the proclamation [public announcement] of the Crier, the owner of the house shall be put to death.

If a fire has broken out in a man's house, and a man who has gone to extinguish it has cast his eye on the property of the owner of the house and has taken the property of the owner of the house, that man shall be thrown into the fire.

If a man is subject to a debt bearing interest, and Adad [the Weather- god] has saturated his field or a high flood has carried [its crop] away, or because of lack of water he has not produced corn in that field, in that year he shall not return any corn to [his] creditor. He shall . . . not pay interest for that year.

If a man has donated field, orchard or house to his favourite [favorite] heir and has written a sealed document for him [confirming this], after the father has gone to his doom, when the brothers share he [the favorite heir] shall take the gift that his father gave him, and apart from that they shall share equally in the property of the paternal [relating to a father] estate.

If an artisan has taken a child for bringing up, and has taught him his manual skill, [the child] shall not be [re]claimed. If he has not taught him his manual skill, that pupil may return to his father's house.

If a man aid a male or female slave . . . to escape from the city gates, he shall be put to death. . . .

If a man be in debt and sell his wife, son, or daughter, or bind them over to service, for three years they shall work in the house of the purchaser or master; in the fourth year they shall be given their freedom. . . .

If a builder has made a house for a man but has not made his work strong, so that the house he made falls down and causes the death of the owner of the house, that builder shall be put to death. If it causes the death of the son of the owner of the house, they shall kill the son of the builder.

If a man would put away [divorce] his wife who has not borne him children, he shall give her money to the amount of her marriage settlement and he shall make good to her the dowry [money brought by a bride to her husband] which she brought from her father's house and then he may put her away.

If a son has struck his father, they shall cut off his hand.

If a man has destroyed the eye of a man of the "gentleman" class, they shall destroy his eye. If he has broken a gentleman's bone, they shall break his bone. If he has destroyed the eye of a commoner or broken a bone of a commoner, he shall pay one mina [about $300] of silver. If he has destroyed the eye of a gentleman's slave, he shall pay half the slave's price.

If a gentleman's slave strikes the cheek of a man of the "gentleman" class, they shall cut off [the slave's] ear.

If a gentleman strikes a gentleman in a free fight and inflicts an injury on him, that man shall swear "I did not strike him deliberately," and he shall pay the surgeon.

ASSESSMENT

1. **Determine Author's Purpose** Why do you suppose these laws were written down and codified?
2. **Cause and Effect** What do you think were the effects of Hammurabi's Code on ancient Babylonian society?
3. **Identify Cause and Effect** How do you think the "Code of Hammurabi" might have paved the way for later codes of law, like government constitutions?

[Psalm 23]

Introduction

The Psalms are a collection of 150 religious hymns. These songs reflect the Israelites' belief in God as the powerful savior of Israel. Many of the psalms praise the faithfulness of God to each of his people. In Psalm 23, the speaker describes his faith in God's protection and celebrates the Israelites' sense of a special relationship with a loving God.

Primary Source

The LORD is my shepherd,
I shall not want;

he makes me lie down in green pastures.
He leads me beside still waters;

he restores [return to a former condition] my soul.
He leads me in paths of righteousness for his name's sake.

Even though I walk through the valley of the shadow of death,
I fear no evil;
for thou art with me;
thy rod and thy staff [walking stick],
they comfort me.

Thou preparest a table before me in the presence of my enemies;
thou anointest [rub into a part of the body as part of a religious ceremony] my head with oil, my cup overflows.

Surely goodness and mercy shall follow me all the days of my life;
and I shall dwell in the house of the LORD for ever.

ASSESSMENT

1. **Analyze Style and Rhetoric** How would you describe the tone of this psalm? How does this tone reflect the relationship the Israelites had with God?
2. **Determine Central Ideas** How does this psalm reflect the Israelites' belief that God is a powerful savior?
3. **Determine Author's Purpose** Why do you think this psalm uses so many instances of metaphor? What might the speaker hope to convey?

[*The Republic*, Plato]

Introduction

Plato was an ancient Greek teacher and philosopher. In *The Republic*, he examines the question: Is it always a good thing to be just? The book takes the form of a long conversation between Socrates (Plato's teacher) and several of his friends. Before deciding whether it is always good for a person to be just, Socrates suggests discussing what makes a city-state just. For much of the book, the characters work out their plan for a perfect city-state.

In this translation, Socrates is the narrator.

Primary Source

"Yes," I said, "I too would have good judges and good physicians. But do you know whom I think good?"

"Will you tell me?"

"I will, if I can. Let me however note that in the same question you join two things which are not the same."

"How so?" he asked.

"Why," I said, "you join physicians and judges. Now the most skilful physicians are those who, from their youth upwards, have combined with the knowledge of their art the greatest experience of disease; they had better not be robust [strong] in health, and should have had all manner [kinds; sorts] of diseases in their own persons. For the body, as I conceive [see it], is not the instrument with which they cure the body; in that case we could not allow them ever to be or to have been sickly; but they cure the body with the mind, and the mind which has become and is sick can cure nothing."

"That is very true," he said.

"But with the judge it is otherwise; since he governs mind by mind; he ought not therefore to have been trained among vicious minds, and to have associated with them from youth upwards, and to have gone through the whole calendar of crime, only in order that he may quickly infer the crimes of others as he might

Answers

1. The tone is peaceful and calm. This emphasizes the great appreciation the speaker has for God and all that God provides. The speaker also sounds strong and empowered, emphasizing his unwavering faith and commitment.

2. The psalm shows God providing for and leading the Israelites. In this way, the psalm shows God to be a savior who will watch over the Israelites and keep them from harm.

3. Possible answer: The use of metaphor makes the psalm stronger and more compelling than it might be if the ideas were stated directly. For example, the psalm compares God to a shepherd and compares life to a valley of the shadow of death. These examples help the reader picture the guidance God provides through dark times. The metaphors indicate what kind of figure God is and characterize the relationship he has with the Israelites.

1. Sample answer: He believes that physicians should have been exposed to the things they will deal with—diseases and cures—from an early age so that they will know more about them. But judges should not have been exposed to the things they will deal with—criminals and evil—as a child because it would corrupt them.

2. Sample answer: No. I believe it's possible that someone can be exposed to criminals as a child and still grow up to be an honest person.

3. Sample answer: Reasoned judgment. I believe it's reasonable to assume that a person who is sick a lot as a child will grow up to be a good doctor because they will know what it's like to be sick and so sympathize with their patients more.

4. Opinion. Sample answer: It can't be a fact because you'd have to prove that every single person who grew up around dishonest people became a dishonest adult, and I don't think that's true. I don't think it's reasoned judgment because I believe there must be plenty of examples of people who knew dishonest people while they were growing up but became honest adults.

Answers

1. Aristotle's account of democracy is an opinion. It reflects his personal view that democracy is not a good form of government. Aristotle includes supporting evidence, as when he declares that democracy only takes into account the interests of the needy. However, this is not a factual statement, as it is not completely true and could be argued against. His account of democracy would require more factual evidence to be considered a reasoned judgment rather than an opinion.

their bodily diseases from his own self-consciousness; the honourable mind which is to form a healthy judgment should have had no experience or contamination of evil habits when young. And this is the reason why in youth good men often appear to be simple, and are easily practised upon [deceived] by the dishonest, because they have no examples of what evil is in their own souls."

"Yes," he said, "they are far too apt to be deceived."

"Therefore," I said, "the judge should not be young; he should have learned to know evil, not from his own soul, but from late and long observation of the nature of evil in others: knowledge should be his guide, not personal experience."

"Yes," he said, "that is the ideal [model of perfection] of a judge."

ASSESSMENT

1. **Explain an Argument** Why does Socrates suggest that physicians and judges should have such different childhoods?
2. **Assess an Argument** Do you agree with the argument you described above? Why or why not?
3. **Distinguish Among Fact, Opinion, and Reasoned Judgment** Is Socrates's statement about the effect a sickly childhood will have on a future physician fact, opinion, or reasoned judgment? Explain your answer.
4. **Distinguish Among Fact, Opinion, and Reasoned Judgment** Is Socrates's statement about the effect a childhood spent among dishonest people will have on a future judge fact, opinion, or reasoned judgment? Explain your answer.

[*Politics*, Aristotle]

Introduction

The Greek philosopher Aristotle (384–322 B.C.) was suspicious of democracy, which he thought could lead to mob rule. Instead, Aristotle favored rule by a single strong and virtuous leader. In this excerpt from *Politics*, Aristotle outlines the forms of government and discusses the strengths and weaknesses of each type. Besides describing the ideal state, Aristotle also writes about practical matters relating to the preservation and improvement of government.

Primary Source

First, let us consider what is the purpose of a state, and how many forms of government there are by which human society is regulated. We have already said, in the first part of this treatise [written agreement] . . . that man is by nature a political animal. And therefore, men, even when they do not require one another's help, desire to live together . . . and are also brought together by their common interests . . . well-being . . . is certainly the chief end, both of individuals and of states. . . .

The conclusion is evident: that governments which have a regard to the common interest are constituted [made or composed of] in accordance with strict principles of justice, and are therefore true forms; but those which regard only the interest of the rulers are all defective and perverted forms, for they are despotic [characteristic of a tyrant or absolute ruler], whereas a state is a community of freemen. . . .

Of forms of government in which one rules, we call that which regards the common interests kingship or royalty; that in which more than one, but not many, rule, aristocracy; and it is so called, either because the rulers are the best men, or because they have at heart the best interests of the state and of the citizens. But when the citizens at large administer the state for the common interest, the government is called by the generic [general] name—a constitution. . . .

Of the above-mentioned forms, the perversions are as follows: of royalty, tyranny; of aristocracy, oligarchy; of constitutional government, democracy. For tyranny is a kind of monarchy which has in view the interest of the monarch only; oligarchy has in view the interest of the wealthy; democracy, of the needy; none of them the common good of all.

ASSESSMENT

1. **Distinguish Among Fact, Opinion, and Reasoned Judgment** Is Aristotle's account of democracy a fact, opinion, or reasoned judgment, and how do you know?
2. **Determine Central Ideas** Based on this excerpt, what qualities is Aristotle looking for in an ideal

government? What kind of government do you think he might advocate for?

3. **Draw Conclusions** Do you think Aristotle's view of democracy is accurate? Why or why not?

[*Edicts,* Asoka]

Introduction

During his rule of India under the Maurya Empire, Asoka converted to Buddhism, rejected violence, and resolved to rule by moral example. He published messages on stone pillars all across the lands of his empire to pronounce moral edicts, or commands, and describe the just actions of his government. The following are excerpts from several of the pillars.

Primary Source

All men are my children. Just as I seek the welfare and happiness of my own children in this world and the next, I seek the same things for all men.

It is difficult to achieve happiness, either in this world or in the next, except by intense love of Dharma [teaching of the Buddha], intense self-examination, intense obedience, intense fear [of sin], and intense enthusiasm. Yet as a result of my instruction, regard for Dharma and love of Dharma have increased day by day and will continue to increase. . . . For these are the rules: to govern according to Dharma, to administer justice according to Dharma, to advance the people's happiness according to Dharma, and to protect them according to Dharma.

The faiths of others all deserve to be honored for one reason or another. By honoring them, one exalts [raises up] one's own faith and at the same time performs a service to the faith of others. By acting otherwise, one injures one's own faith and also does disservice to that of others. . . . Therefore concord [friendly relations or peace] alone is commendable.

Whatever good deeds I have done the people have imitated, and they have followed them as a model. In doing so, they have progressed and will progress in obedience to parents and teachers, in respect for elders, in courtesy to priests and ascetics [people who choose a life of self-denial], to the poor and distressed, and even to slaves and servants.

There is no gift that can equal the gift of Dharma. . . . If one acts in this way, one achieves . . . happiness in this world and infinite merit [worth] in the world to come.

I have commanded this edict on Dharma to be inscribed so that it may last forever and so that my descendants may conform to it.

ASSESSMENT

1. **Determine Central Ideas** What are the major themes expressed in the Edicts?
2. **Identify Cause and Effect** What effect do you think Asoka's edicts may have had on the peace and prosperity of the Maurya Empire?

[*Analects,* Confucius]

Introduction

The *Analects* of Confucius (551–479 B.C.) is a collection of teachings by the great Chinese philosopher published in China around the year 1190. Divided into 20 "books," the *Analects* features Confucius dialoguing with his students about numerous moral and ethical matters. Among the topics are how to respect one's elders, how to comport oneself in society, and how to maintain a government that is honest and principled.

Primary Source

BOOK I

. . . CHAP. III. The Master said, "Fine words and an insinuating [subtle, crafty] appearance are seldom associated with true virtue." CHAP. IV. The philosopher Tsang said, "I daily examine myself on three points:— whether, in transacting business for others, I may have been not faithful;— whether, in intercourse [conversation] with friends, I may have been not sincere;— whether I may have not mastered and practiced the instructions of my teacher." . . . CHAP. VI. The Master said, "A youth, when at home, should be filial [respectful of one's parents], and, abroad, respectful to his elders. He should be earnest and truthful. He should overflow in love to all, and cultivate the friendship of the good. When he has time and opportunity, after the performance of

Answers

2. Aristotle seeks a form of government that will foster the well-being of the citizens. He fears that monarchy, oligarchy, and democracy do not represent the best interests of the state or its people. Based on this excerpt, it seems his ideal government could consist of a few people specially chosen for their skills, or perhaps a rotating group of representatives.

3. Sample answer: I disagree with Aristotle's view of democracy. His characterization of democracy seems particularly negative and inaccurate. It doesn't reflect the principles of liberty and freedom that are typically associated with contemporary democratic governments. It doesn't seem as if he gives enough credit to the ordinary citizens to be able to make their own decisions.

Answers

1. The edicts emphasize how to live well and how to treat others. They focus on peace and well-being, in accordance with the teachings of the Buddha. Asoka addresses moral behavior, right governance, and the importance of the Dharma.

2. Asoka's Edicts instruct people to follow the Buddha's teachings and to care for others. Given this emphasis on tolerance, respect for others, and well-being, Asoka's rule most likely led to a period of peace in the Maurya empire. This harmony would have brought prosperity to the empire.

these things, he should employ them in polite studies." CHAP. VII. Tsze-hsia said, "If a man withdraws his mind from the love of beauty, and applies it as sincerely to the love of the virtuous; if, in serving his parents, he can exert his utmost strength; if, in serving his prince, he can devote his life; if, in his intercourse with his friends, his words are sincere:— although men say that he has not learned, I will certainly say that he has."

BOOK II.

CHAP. I. The Master said, "He who exercises government by means of his virtue may be compared to the north polar star, which keeps its place and all the stars turn towards it." CHAP. II. The Master said, "In the Book of Poetry [a very old collection of Chinese poetry, collected by Confucius] are three hundred pieces, but the design of them all may be embraced in one sentence— 'Having no depraved [very evil] thoughts.'" CHAP. III. 1. The Master said, "If the people be led by laws, and uniformity sought to be given them by punishments, they will try to avoid the punishment, but have no sense of shame. 2. "If they be led by virtue, and uniformity sought to be given them by the rules of propriety [morally correct behavior], they will have the sense of shame, and moreover will become good."

BOOK XV

CHAP. XVII. The Master said, "The superior man in everything considers righteousness to be essential. He performs it according to the rules of propriety. He brings it forth in humility. He completes it with sincerity. This is indeed a superior man." CHAP. XVIII. The Master said, "The superior man is distressed by his want [lack] of ability. He is not distressed by men's not knowing him." . . . CHAP. XX. The Master said, "What the superior man seeks, is in himself. What the mean man seeks, is in others." CHAP. XXI. The Master said, "The superior man is dignified, but does not wrangle [quarrel, bicker]. He is sociable, but not a partizan [a very strong supporter of a particular idea or person]." CHAP. XXII. The Master said, "The superior man does not promote a man simply on account of his words, nor does he put aside good words because of the man." CHAP. XXIII. Tsze-kung asked, saying, "Is there one word which may serve as a rule of practice for all one's life?" The Master said, "Is not RECIPROCITY such a word?"

ASSESSMENT

1. **Summarize** What does Confucius say will happen if people are led by virtue rather than laws?
2. **Determine Central Ideas** What are the qualities of a "superior man," in Confucius' view? Cite examples from the text.
3. **Analyze Style and Rhetoric** The *Analects* is structured as a dialogue. Is the structure effective for Confucius' teachings? Cite examples from the text.
4. **Analyze Interactions** How might Confucius' teachings about the "superior man" relate to his teachings about honest government? Cite details from the text to support your answer.

[*First Letter to the Corinthians*, Paul]

Introduction

Around A.D. 51, Paul founded a Christian community in the thriving commercial city of Corinth. After his departure, he wrote two letters to the newly converted Christians to encourage and guide them in their faith. In this excerpt from Paul's First Letter to the Corinthians, Paul declares that, for a Christian, love is more important than any other quality.

Primary Source

If I speak in the tongues of men and of angels, but have not love, I am a noisy gong or a clanging cymbal [musical instrument]. And if I have prophetic [able to predict events] powers and understand all mysteries and all knowledge, and if I have all faith, so as to remove mountains, but have no love, I am nothing. If I give away all I have, and if I deliver my body to be burned, but have not love, I gain nothing.

Love is patient and kind; love is not jealous or boastful; it is not arrogant or rude. Love does not insist on its own way; it is not irritable or resentful; it does not rejoice at wrong, but rejoices in the right. Love bears all things, believes all things, hopes all things, endures [suffers] all things.

Answers

1. People will learn to have a sense of shame and desire to become good; in other words, they will develop their own sense of good and bad, rather than having it imposed on them from the outside in the form of laws and punishments.

2. A superior man is one who is humble, loving, and sincere. He is respectful of his parents and his elders. He is kind, honorable, and fair. He is also committed to bettering himself through education; as Confucius says, the superior man is distressed by any "want of ability."

3. The structure of the text makes Confucius' teachings more lucid and applicable for his students. For example, in Book I, Chapter VI, Confucius mentions being "respectful to his elders." His student Tsze-hsia follows in the next chapter by saying that a virtuous man should, "in serving his parents . . . exert his utmost strength."

4. Confucius stresses the importance of a government leader having "virtue" and leading by it. This connects to his descriptions of the "superior man," who possesses, according to Confucius, "righteousness," "humility," and "sincerity." If a government leader strove to be a "superior man," then he or she would certainly be virtuous as well.

Love never ends; as for prophecies, they will pass away; as for tongues, they will cease; as for knowledge, it will pass away. For our knowledge is imperfect and our prophecy is imperfect; but when the perfect comes, the imperfect will pass away. When I was a child, I spoke like a child, I thought like a child, I reasoned like a child; when I became a man, I gave up childish ways. For now we see in a mirror dimly, but then face to face. Now I know in part; then I shall understand fully, even as I have been fully understood. So faith, hope, love abide [remain], these three; but the greatest of these is love.

ASSESSMENT

1. **Determine Central Ideas** What does Paul think will happen to people when they have love?
2. **Analyze Style and Rhetoric** Paul uses repetition of words and phrases throughout this letter. What purpose does this serve?
3. **Determine Author's Purpose** What do you think Paul wanted to teach the people of Corinth with this letter?

[The Quran]

Introduction

The Quran, the holy scriptures of Islam, contains 114 *suras*, or chapters, which are divided into verses. Muslims believe that the Quran is the word of God as revealed to Muhammad. They also believe that God instructed Muhammad to arrange the chapters into the order in which they appear. The following excerpts from the Quran tell Muslims how to be righteous and faithful. They also encourage believers to fast and observe the holy month of Ramadan.

Primary Source

Righteousness is not whether you turn your face towards East or West; but the righteousness is to believe in Allah, the Last Day, the Angels, the Books [Scriptures] and Prophets, and to spend wealth out of love for Him on relatives, orphans, helpless, needy travelers, those who ask for and on the redemption [freedom by payment of ransom] of captives; and to establish Salah (prayers), to pay Zakah (alms) [charity given freely to the poor], to fulfill promises when made, to be steadfast in distress, in adversity [misfortune], and at the time of war. These people are the truthful and these are the pious.*

—The Quran 2:177

O, believers! Fasting is prescribed [ordered] for you as it was prescribed for those before you so that you may learn self-restraint.* Fast the prescribed number of days; except if any of you is ill or on a journey, then fast a similar number of days later. For those who can not endure it for medical reasons, there is a ransom [act of devotion]: the feeding of one poor person for each missed day. Whoever does more good than this voluntarily, it is better for him. However, if you truly understand the rationale of fasting, it is better for you to fast.*

It is the month of Ramadhãn in which the Qur'an was revealed, a guidance for mankind with clear teachings showing the Right Way and a criterion of truth and falsehood. Therefore, anyone of you who witnesses that month should fast therein, and whoever is ill or upon a journey shall fast a similar number of days later on. Allah intends your well-being and does not want to put you to hardship. He wants you to complete the prescribed period so that you should glorify His Greatness and render [give] thanks to Him for giving you guidance.*

—The Quran 2:183–185

ASSESSMENT

1. **Determine Central Ideas** Why is Ramadan considered an important and holy month?
2. **Identify Supporting Details** Islam has Five Pillars, or primary obligations: profession of faith, prayer, almsgiving, fasting during Ramadan, and pilgrimage to Mecca. How does this excerpt from the Quran support the Five Pillars?
3. **Identify Cause and Effect** How do you think the revelation of the Quran to Muhammad has affected the lives of Muslims?

[The Magna Carta]

Introduction

King John ruled England from 1199 to 1216. During his troubled reign, he found himself

Answers

1. Paul suggests that people will live better if they have love. They will be kinder and more patient, and will get along well with others. He also says that love will enable people to develop greater understanding, and to be better understood.

2. Paul uses repetition to highlight his main points. By repeating "love," he makes clear that this is his central idea or topic. Such emphasis helps make his letter more persuasive. The repetition of sentence structures also helps the letter flow smoothly. Rather than sounding like a list of harsh commands, Paul creates a softer style that matches his content—the loving relationship Christians maintain with God.

3. When Paul left Corinth, the people had recently converted to Christianity. He therefore wanted to teach them how to be good Christians. He teaches them that love is the most important quality for Christians to possess. He reminds them to have a loving relationship with God, even if that relationship is tested at times.

Answers

1. Ramadan is an important and holy month because it is the month in which the Quran was revealed to Muhammad.

2. This passage details how Muslims can fulfill several of these pillars. It emphasizes the importance of almsgiving and instructs Muslims to give wealth to others. It also explains the importance of Ramadan, charging the devout to fast during this month.

3. The Quran issues guidelines for how Muslims can be righteous. As a result, Muslims have a clear sense of distinguishing right from wrong and of what they need to do to be faithful and devout.

Answers

1. The barons wrote the Magna Carta to uphold their rights against the power of the king. This served to protect their interests while limiting the king's authority and reach. In detailing their rights, the barons also list things that the king cannot do, such as tax them excessively, take private property, or imprison others without just cause. The Magna Carta ensured that the king was following certain rules, rather than imposing his will on others.

2. Sample answer: The most important right is the right to have a credible witness because it is the basis for many of the other rights detailed here. The idea that there must be believable evidence to charge someone with a crime ensures that accusations are based on facts and not the arbitrary will of those in power. From this principle is derived the idea of the trial, in which the evidence is weighed and evaluated by a jury or judge. It is therefore foundational to other rights in the Magna Carta, as well as rights that we enjoy in the United States.

3. The Magna Carta laid the foundation for later constitutional democracies. It established the principle that people have rights and liberties the government cannot take away. In outlining the rights of the barons, it suggests that laws cannot reflect the arbitrary will of the king. Instead, they must be reasonable and clear, and protect citizens' rights. These principles are foundational to a constitutional democracy. A constitution spells out the government's authority, including its limitations, in order to ensure the protection of citizens' rights.

in conflict with England's feudal barons. The nobles especially resented John's attempts to tax them heavily. In 1215, the barons forced John to sign the Magna Carta, or Great Charter. Most of this document was intended to protect the rights of the barons. However, over time, the document came to guarantee some basic rights of English citizens. When English colonists came to North America, they brought these ideas with them. Eight of the 63 clauses of the Magna Carta are printed here.

Primary Source

12. No [tax] nor aid shall be imposed on our kingdom, unless by common counsel [consent] of our kingdom, except for ransoming our person, for making our eldest son a knight, and for once marrying our eldest daughter; and for these there shall not be levied more than a reasonable aid. . . .

30. No sheriff or bailiff [tax collector] of ours, or other person, shall take the horses or carts of any freeman for transport duty, against the will of the said freeman.

31. Neither we nor our bailiffs shall take, for our castles or for any other work of ours, wood which is not ours, against the will of the owner of that wood. . . .

38. No bailiff for the future shall, upon his own unsupported complaint, put any one to his "law," without credible [believable] witnesses brought for this purpose.

39. No freeman shall be taken or imprisoned . . . or exiled or in any way destroyed, nor will we go upon him nor send upon him, except by the lawful judgment of his peers [people of equal rank] or by the law of the land.

40. To no one will we sell, to no one will we refuse or delay, right or justice. . . .

45. We will appoint as justices, constables, sheriffs, or bailiffs only such as know the law of the realm [kingdom] and mean to observe it well. . . .

63. Wherefore it is our will, and we firmly enjoin [order], that the English Church be free, and that the men in our kingdom have and hold all the aforesaid liberties, rights, and concessions, well and peaceably, freely and quietly, fully and wholly, for themselves and their heirs, of us and our heirs, in all respects and in all places for ever, as is aforesaid.

ASSESSMENT

1. **Determine Author's Purpose** Why did the barons write the Magna Carta, and how did it affect the power of the king?
2. **Determine Central Ideas** What do you think is the most important right that this excerpt from the Magna Carta protects? Explain your answer.
3. **Identify Steps in a Process** How was the Magna Carta an important first step in the development of constitutional democracy?

[*Travels*, Ibn Battuta]

Introduction

Moroccan *qadi*, or judge, Ibn Battuta (1304–c.1368) was born in Tangier to a Berber family of the Muslim faith. After he completed his education at the age of 21, Battuta decided to make the hajj, or Muslim pilgrimage to Mecca. What started as a reasonably challenging trek for the period became one of the great journeys of medieval times. During nearly 30 years of travel, Battuta visited much of Southwest Asia, West Africa, southern Russia, India, and China. Along the way he gained fame and wealth and met kings, sheiks, and holy men—including the Byzantine emperor and the sultan of Delhi—as well as ordinary people. In this excerpt from his book, the *Rihlah*, or *Travels*, Battuta describes the unique trading tradition of Mogadishu.

Primary Source

On leaving Zayla we sailed for fifteen days and came to Maqdashaw [Mogadishu], which is an enormous town. Its inhabitants are merchants and have many camels, of which they slaughter hundreds every day [for food]. When a vessel [ship] reaches the port, it is met by sumbuqs, which are small boats, in each of which are a number of young men, each carrying a covered dish containing food. He presents this to one of the merchants on the ship saying "This is my guest," and all the others do the same.

Each merchant on disembarking [leaving] goes only to the house of the young man who is his host, except those who have made frequent journeys to the town and know its people well; these live where they please. The host then sells his goods for him and buys for him, and if anyone buys anything from him at too low a price, or sells to him in the absence of his host, the sale is regarded by them as invalid [not legally recognized]. This practice is of great advantage to them. . . . We stayed there three days, food being brought to us three times a day, and on the fourth, a Friday, the qadi [judge] and one of the wazirs [Arab official] brought me a set of garments. We then went to the mosque and prayed...

ASSESSMENT

1. **Identify Supporting Details** What details in the text reveal to you that Battuta and other travelers were treated well by the people of Mogadishu?
2. **Determine Author's Purpose** Why do you think Battuta recorded this description of Mogadishu in his travels?
3. **Analyze Interactions** How did Battuta's faith affect his travels and his interactions with other Muslims?

[*The Destruction of the Indies*, Bartolomé de Las Casas]

Introduction

Bartolomé de Las Casas was a Roman Catholic priest born in Seville, Spain, in 1484. In his youth, he met Christopher Columbus and traveled to the West Indies. There, he observed the conquest of the Americas and was horrified by the treatment of Native Americans by the conquistadors.

Las Casas dedicated his long life to protecting Native Americans from Spanish abuse. On several occasions, he returned to Spain to plead their case before the Spanish throne. His writings and discussions shocked Spanish leaders who attempted to pass laws to protect the Native Americans. The conquistadors' friends at court, however, often had the policies reversed. Below is an excerpt from a 1542 work detailing the abusive policies of the Spanish.

Primary Source

There are two main ways in which those who have traveled to this part of the world pretending to be Christians have uprooted these pitiful peoples and wiped them from the face of the earth. First, they have waged war on them: unjust, cruel, bloody and tyrannical [using power unjustly] war. Second, they have murdered anyone and everyone who has shown the slightest sign of resistance. . . . This latter policy has been instrumental [an important tool] in suppressing the native leaders, and, indeed, given that the Spaniards normally spare only women and children, it has led to the annihilation [complete destruction] of all adult males. . . .

The reason the [Spanish] have murdered on such a vast scale and killed anyone and everyone in their way is purely and simply greed. They have set out to line their pockets with gold. . . . The Spaniards have shown not the slightest consideration for these people, treating them (and I speak from first-hand experience, having been there from the outset) not as brute animals—indeed, I would to God they had done and had shown them the consideration they afford their animals—so much as piles of dung in the middle of the road. They have had as little concern for their souls as for their bodies, all the millions that have perished having gone to their deaths with no knowledge of God and without the benefit of the Sacraments [sacred right of the Christian church]. . . .

The indigenous [native to a region or country] peoples never did the Europeans any harm whatever; on the contrary, they believed them to have descended from the heavens, at least until they or their fellow-citizens had tasted, at the hands of these oppressors, a diet of robbery, murder, violence, and all other manner of trials and tribulations [great sorrows].

ASSESSMENT

1. **Determine Central Ideas** How did Las Casas view the conquest of the Americas?
2. **Determine Author's Purpose** Why do you think Las Casas wrote this detailed account about the treatment of Native Americans by the Spanish?

Answers

1. Battuta explains that merchants become guests in the homes of their hosts, who also help them make fair sales in the marketplace, and that he was brought to stay in Mogadishu for several days with people who provided food and clothes. Leaders in the community came to see him and pray with him.

2. Battuta may have wanted to remind himself of his experience and to share the details with others. In an age when few people traveled as widely as he did and information about other parts of the world was more limited, Battuta's description would have been of interest to many who were curious about what life was like for others around the world.

3. Battuta's Muslim faith played a role in where he visited, as he began his travels on a religious pilgrimage to Mecca. Although he did not travel solely to Muslim regions, he did go to a number of places, such as Mogadishu, where he met other Muslims. While there, he joined with other Muslim leaders who brought him to the mosque to pray together.

Answers

1. Las Casas viewed it as a tragedy. He lamented the cruel way in which the Native Americans were treated and the unnecessary loss of life. He wished for the spread of Christianity among indigenous people, rather than the death and destruction he witnessed.

2. Las Casas wanted others to know how the conquistadors were treating Native Americans and wrote this record to show the Spanish leaders. He hoped for condemnation of this treatment and limits on the actions of the conquistadors in the Americas.

Answers

3. Spanish leaders may have been horrified to hear of how the conquistadors were treating the Native Americans. Some, however, may have been more interested in the acquired gold and sided with the conquistadors.

Answers

1. Possible answer: Both documents lay out reasons why the documents' writers are unhappy. In the Declaration of Independence, Thomas Jefferson lists the grievances the colonists have with King George III. In the English Bill of Rights, Parliament lists its issues with King James II.

2. Possible answer: The English Bill of Rights introduces the idea of checks and balances. For example, the executive of the country—in England's case, the king; in the United States, the President—cannot execute laws that have not been approved—or passed—by the legislative body. In England, that meant Parliament; in the United States, that meant Congress.

3. Possible answer: Common people benefited from the English Bill of Rights in legal matters. For example, bail should not be unnecessarily expensive, nor should legal fines. The bill outlaws cruel and unusual punishments. Also, people serving on juries should not be forced into service for excessively long periods of time.

4. Many of the rights laid out by the document concern the granting of powers to Parliament, especially those that previously the monarch held exclusively. For example, the monarch was required to obtain parliamentary consent before taxing people, raising an army during times of peace, and enacting any law.

3. **Draw Inferences** How might Spanish leaders have responded to Las Casas's description of the conquistadors?

[English Bill of Rights]

Introduction

When the Catholic king, James II, was forced from the English throne in 1688, Parliament offered the crown to his Protestant daughter Mary and her husband, William of Orange. Parliament, however, insisted that William and Mary submit to a bill of rights. This document sums up the powers that Parliament had been seeking since the Petition of Right in 1628.

Primary Source

Whereas, the late King James II . . . did endeavor to subvert and exirpate [eliminate] the Protestant religion and the laws and liberties of this kingdom . . . and whereas the said late king James II having abdicated the government, and the throne being vacant. . . . The said Lords [Parliament] . . . being now assembled in a full and free representative [body] of this nation . . . do in the first place . . . declare

That the pretended [untruthfully claimed] power of suspending the laws or the execution of laws by regal authority without consent of Parliament is illegal;

That the pretended power of dispensing with laws or the execution of laws by regal authority, as it hath been assumed and exercised of late, is illegal; . . .

That levying [collecting] money for or to the use of the Crown by pretence of prerogative [a right exclusive to a king or queen], without grant of Parliament, for longer time, or in other manner than the same is or shall be granted, is illegal;

That it is the right of the subjects to petition [make a request of] the king, and all commitments and prosecutions for such petitioning are illegal;

That the raising or keeping a standing army within the kingdom in time of peace, unless it be with consent of Parliament, is against law;

That the subjects which are Protestants may have arms for their defence suitable to their conditions and as allowed by law;

That election of members of Parliament ought to be free;

That the freedom of speech and debates or proceedings in Parliament ought not to be impeached [discredited] or questioned in any court or place out of Parliament;

That excessive bail ought not to be required, nor excessive fines imposed, nor cruel and unusual punishments inflicted;

That jurors ought to be duly [done at a proper time] impaneled [registered on a panel of jurors] and returned [released from service], and jurors which pass upon men in trials for high treason ought to be freeholders [property owners with unconditional rights];

That all grants and promises of fines and forfeitures of particular persons before conviction are illegal and void;

And that for redress [correction] of all grievances, and for the amending, strengthening and preserving of the laws, Parliaments ought to be held frequently.

ASSESSMENT

1. **Analyze Interactions** Review the American Declaration of Independence. What similarities do you notice between the two documents?
2. **Determine Central Ideas** Which ideas in the English Bill of Rights influenced the formation of the United States government?
3. **Cite Evidence** How did the English Bill of Rights expand the rights of common Englishmen? Cite specific examples from the text to support your answer.
4. **Determine Central Ideas** How did the English Bill of Rights make Parliament more powerful? Provide specific examples from the text in your response.

[*Two Treatises of Government*, John Locke]

Introduction

English philosopher John Locke (1632–1704) published *Two Treatises of Government* in 1690. Locke believed that all people had the same natural rights of life, liberty, and property. In this essay, Locke states that the primary purpose of government is to protect these natural rights. He also states that governments hold their power only with the consent of the people. Locke's ideas greatly influenced revolutions in America and France.

Primary Source

But though men, when they enter into society give up the equality, liberty, and executive power they had in the state of Nature into the hands of society . . . the power of the society or legislative constituted by them can never be supposed to extend farther than the common good. . . . Whoever has the legislative or supreme power of any commonwealth, is bound to govern by established standing laws, promulgated [published or made known] and known to the people, and not by extemporary [without any preparation] decrees, by indifferent and upright judges, who are to decide controversies by those laws; and to employ the force of the community at home only in the execution of such laws, or abroad to prevent or redress foreign injuries and secure the community from inroads [advances at the expense of someone] and invasion. And all this to be directed to no other end but the peace, safety, and public good of the people. . . .

The reason why men enter into society is the preservation of their property; and the end while they choose and authorize a legislative is that there may be laws made, and rules set, as guards and fences to the properties of all the society, . . .

Whensoever, therefore, the legislative [power] shall transgress [go beyond; break] this fundamental rule of society, and either by ambition, fear, folly, or corruption, endeavor to grasp themselves, or put into the hands of any other, an absolute power over the lives, liberties, and estates of the people, by this breach of trust they forfeit the power the people had put into their hands for quite contrary ends, and it devolves [passes] to the people; who have a right to resume their original liberty, and by the establishment of a new legislative (such as they shall think fit), provide for their own safety and security. . .

ASSESSMENT

1. **Summarize** What does Locke say is the duty of government?
2. **Cite Evidence** What evidence is there in the text to support Locke's belief that a land should only be governed with the consent of the governed?
3. **Identify Cause and Effect** Based on what you already know, what aspects of Locke's *Treatises* likely affected the events leading to the founding of America? Cite evidence from the text to support your response.

[*The Spirit of the Laws,* Baron de Montesquieu]

Introduction

In 1748, the French aristocrat Baron de Montesquieu (1689–1755) wrote *The Spirit of the Laws*, in which he concluded that the separation of the executive, legislative, and judicial powers was in the best interests of the people. Both the French revolutionary thinkers and the Framers of the United States Constitution were influenced by Montesquieu's ideas.

Primary Source

The principle of democracy is corrupted not only when the spirit of equality is extinct, but likewise when they fall into a spirit of extreme equality, and when each citizen would fain be [be satisfied] upon a level with those whom he has chosen to command him. Then the people, incapable of bearing the very power they have delegated, want to manage everything themselves, to debate for the senate, to execute for the magistrate [judicial officer of limited authority], and to decide for the judges.

When this is the case, virtue can no longer subsist [survive] in the republic. The people are desirous of exercising the functions of the magistrates, who cease to be revered. . . .

Democracy has, therefore, two excesses to avoid—the spirit of inequality, which leads to aristocracy or monarchy, and the spirit of extreme equality, which leads to despotic [authoritarian; tyrannical] power, as the latter is completed by conquest. . . .

In the state of nature, indeed, all men are born equal, but they cannot continue in this equality. Society makes them lose it, and they recover it only by the protection of the laws.

Such is the difference between a well-regulated democracy and one that is not so, that in the former men are equal only as citizens, but in the latter they

Answers

1. Locke feels that a government's job is to protect the rights of its people to equality, liberty, safety, and peace. Put more generally, a government should provide for—and protect—the common good.

2. Locke says explicitly that the people who govern the land should never extend beyond the laws that are in place—laws that are known by the people. Further, while he admits that people do give up some freedoms when they choose to enter an organized society of laws, the "common good" of the people should never be violated. If it were, the people—the governed—could take the power back.

3. Possible answer: The American Revolution was born out of the colonists' frustration with the oppressive policies of England's government. This connects to Locke's ideas in the *Treatises* in that he says that when a government transgresses its role as protector of society, then the people may take the power back. Additionally, this idea may have contributed to the parts of the U.S. Constitution that provide for the impeachment of judges and elected officials. This is another way that the people—through their representatives—can take power back.

Answers

1. Montesquieu argues that a functional democracy is one in which the separate parts of the government act as a check on the power of the other parts. If this separation is not attained (and maintained), then one part may become more powerful than the others, resulting in a loss of liberty.

2. The U.S. Constitution subscribes to the principle of separation of powers, as evidenced in the fact that the Founders established separate executive, legislative, and judicial branches, each with its own powers.

3. Liberty refers to personal freedom, but excessive freedom, says Montesquieu, has no place in a functioning democracy. Democracy requires citizens to obey the laws set down by the government, which, in turn, is run by elected representatives. If the government is not separated into different bodies, each with its own powers, then liberty cannot subsist.

are equal also as magistrates, as senators, as judges, as fathers, as husbands, or as masters.

The natural place of virtue is near to liberty; but it is not nearer to excessive liberty than to servitude. . . .

Democratic and aristocratic states are not in their own nature free. Political liberty is to be found only in moderate governments; and even in these it is not always found. It is there only when there is no abuse of power. . . .

To prevent this abuse, it is necessary from the very nature of things that power should be a check to power. A government may be so constituted, as no man shall be compelled to do things to which the law does not oblige him, nor forced to abstain from things which the law permits. . . .

When the legislative and executive powers are united in the same person, or in the same body of magistrates, there can be no liberty; because apprehensions may arise, lest the same monarch or senate should enact tyrannical laws, to execute them in a tyrannical manner. . . .

Again, there is no liberty, if the judiciary power be not separated from the legislative and executive. Were it joined with the legislative, the life and liberty of the subject would be exposed to arbitrary control; for the judge would be then the legislator. Were it joined to the executive power, the judge might behave with violence and oppression.

There would be an end of everything, were the same man or the same body, whether of the nobles or of the people, to exercise those three powers, that of enacting laws, that of executing the public resolutions, and of trying the causes of individuals.

ASSESSMENT

1. **Determine Author's Purpose** For what reasons does Montesquieu promote the separation of powers?
2. **Analyze Interactions** How is the influence of Montesquieu's ideas revealed in the United States Constitution?
3. **Determine Meaning** Explain the distinction Montesquieu makes between democracy and liberty (or equality).

[*The Social Contract,* Jean-Jacques Rousseau]

Introduction

Jean-Jacques Rousseau (1712–1778) was one of the leaders of the intellectual movement known as the Enlightenment. Enlightenment philosophers, inspired by the scientific advances made by Isaac Newton and others, tried to explain various aspects of human existence based on logic and reason.

In *The Social Contract* (1762), Rousseau states that early people living in a state of nature were free, in the sense that they could do whatever they wanted. Of course, they were also at the mercy of other people who were doing whatever they wanted.

In forming or joining a society, Rousseau says, each person enters into an implicit contract. A social contract exists between each person and the group of all people. The individual gives up some of his or her freedom in exchange for the protection and benefits offered by the group.

Rousseau referred to this group of people, acting as one for the benefit of all, as the "body politic," or the "Sovereign." It is this Sovereign that establishes the government.

Primary Source

What we have just said confirms . . . that the depositaries of [people who are entrusted with] the executive power are not the people's masters, but its officers; that it can set them up and pull them down when it likes; that for them there is no question of contract, but of obedience and that in taking charge of the functions the State imposes on them they are doing no more than fulfilling their duty as citizens, without having the remotest right to argue about the conditions. . . .

It is true that . . . the established government should never be touched except when it comes to be incompatible with the public good; but the circumspection [careful thought and judgment] this involves is a maxim [general truth or rule of conduct] of policy and not a rule of right, and the State is no more bound to leave civil authority in the hands of its rulers than military authority in the hands of its generals. . . .

The periodical assemblies of which I have already spoken are designed to prevent or postpone this calamity, above all when they need no formal summoning; for in that case, the prince cannot stop them without openly declaring himself a law-breaker and an enemy of the State.

The opening of these assemblies, whose sole object is the maintenance of the social treaty, should always take the form of putting two propositions that may not be suppressed, which should be voted on separately.

The first is: "Does it please the Sovereign to preserve the present form of government?"

The second is: "Does it please the people to leave its administration in the hands of those who are actually [currently] in charge of it?"

ASSESSMENT

1. **Determine Meaning** What does the underlined pronoun refer to in this excerpt, and what effect does this usage have on Rousseau's message? "What we have just said confirms . . . that the depositaries of [people who are entrusted with] the executive power are not the people's masters, but its officers; that it can set them up and pull them down when it likes . . . ."
2. **Determine Author's Purpose** In Paragraph 3 of the excerpt, what does the phrase "this calamity" refer to, and how does it affect Rousseau's overall purpose?
3. **Compare and Contrast** According to Rousseau, how is the government like the military?
4. **Assess an Argument** The assemblies Rousseau mentions are periodic meetings of all the citizens of a State in which various matters are voted upon. Do you think this is a good idea? Explain your reasoning.

[*The Interesting Narrative of the Life of Olaudah Equiano,* Olaudah Equiano]

Introduction

In the first several chapters of his narrative, Olaudah Equiano describes how slave traders kidnapped him and his sister from their home in West Africa and transported them to the African coast. During this six- or seven-month journey, Equiano was separated from his sister and held at a series of way stations. After reaching the coast, Equiano was shipped with other slaves to North America. The following account describes this horrifying journey.

Primary Source

At last when the ship we were in, had got in all her cargo, they made ready with many fearful noises, and we were all put under deck, so that we could not see how they managed the vessel. But this disappointment was the least of my sorrow. The stench of the hold [the cargo area of a ship, often below deck] while we were on the coast was so intolerably loathsome, that it was dangerous to remain there for any time, and some of us had been permitted to stay on the deck for the fresh air; but now that the whole ship's cargo were confined together, it became absolutely pestilential [deadly; disease-ridden]. The closeness of the place, and the heat of the climate, added to the number in the ship, which was so crowded that each had scarcely room to turn himself, almost suffocated us.

This produced copious [plentiful; abundant] perspirations, so that the air soon became unfit for respiration, from a variety of loathsome smells, and brought on a sickness among the slaves, of which many died—thus falling victims to the improvident [reckless, rash] avarice [greediness], as I may call it, of their purchasers. This wretched [deeply distressing; miserable] situation was again aggravated by the galling [chafing] of the chains, now become insupportable, and the filth of the necessary tubs, into which the children often fell, and were almost suffocated. The shrieks of the women, and the groans of the dying, rendered the whole a scene of horror almost inconceivable. Happily perhaps, for myself, I was soon reduced so low here that it was thought necessary to keep me almost always on deck; and from my extreme youth I was not put in fetters [chains]. In this situation I expected

Answers

1. The underlined pronoun refers to "the people," in other words, the body politic or the sovereign. It shows that the power lies with the people, not the executive.

2. The phrase "this calamity" refers to the government becoming incompatible with the public good. Rousseau asserts that the government must exist for the good of the community as a whole and that there should be limited government control.

3. Both are ultimately run by the people. The people appoint rulers and generals to carry out their will, but they, not the rulers or generals, are the ones in charge.

4. Sample answer: Yes. I think our country would be better off if everyone of voting age voted. The assembly would have to be virtual, because there are too many Americans of voting age to fit in one place. People could debate, discuss, and vote over the Internet or using social media.

every hour to share the fate of my companions, some of whom were almost daily brought upon deck at the point of death, which I began to hope would soon put an end to my miseries. Often did I think many of the inhabitants of the deep much more happy than myself.

ASSESSMENT

1. **Analyze Style and Rhetoric** What sensory details does Olaudah Equiano use to tell his story? How effective are they in making the story come alive? Cite specific examples from the text in your answer.
2. **Analyze Interactions** *The Interesting Narrative of the Life of Olaudah Equiano* was published in 1789. How might it have been used by abolitionists?
3. **Determine Author's Purpose** Why do you think Olaudah Equiano wrote this slave narrative? Explain your reasoning.

[*The Federalist* No. 51]

Introduction

Federalist No. 51 was first published on February 8, 1788, and was probably written by James Madison. It argues that the federal system and the separation of powers proposed in the Constitution provide a system of checks and balances that will protect the rights of the people.

Primary Source

TO WHAT expedient [resource], then, shall we finally resort, for maintaining in practice the necessary partition of power among the several departments, as laid down in the Constitution? The only answer that can be given is, that as all these exterior provisions are found to be inadequate, the defect must be supplied, by so contriving the interior structure of the government as that its several constituent parts may, by their mutual relations, be the means of keeping each other in their proper places. Without presuming to undertake a full development of this important idea, I will hazard a few general observations, which may perhaps place it in a clearer light, and enable us to form a more correct judgment of the principles and structure of the government planned by the convention.

In order to lay a due foundation for that separate and distinct exercise of the different powers of government, which to a certain extent is admitted on all hands to be essential to the preservation of liberty, it is evident that each department should have a will of its own; and consequently should be so constituted that the members of each should have as little agency as possible in the appointment of the members of the others. Were this principle rigorously adhered to, it would require that all the appointments for the supreme executive, legislative, and judiciary magistracies should be drawn from the same fountain of authority, the people, through channels having no communication whatever with one another. Perhaps such a plan of constructing the several departments would be less difficult in practice than it may in contemplation appear. Some difficulties, however, and some additional expense would attend the execution of it. Some deviations, therefore, from the principle must be admitted. In the constitution of the judiciary department in particular, it might be inexpedient to insist rigorously on the principle: first, because peculiar qualifications being essential in the members, the primary consideration ought to be to select that mode of choice which best secures these qualifications; secondly, because the permanent tenure by which the appointments are held in that department, must soon destroy all sense of dependence on the authority conferring them.

It is equally evident, that the members of each department should be as little dependent as possible on those of the others, for the emoluments [monetary payments] annexed to their offices. Were the executive magistrate, or the judges, not independent of the legislature in this particular, their independence in every other would be merely nominal.

But the great security against a gradual concentration of the several powers in the same department, consists in giving to those who administer each department the necessary constitutional means and personal motives to resist encroachments [intrusions; unwanted advances] of the others. The provision for defense must in this, as in all other cases, be made commensurate to the danger of attack. Ambition must be made to counteract ambition. The interest of the man must be connected with the constitutional rights of the place. It may be a reflection on human nature, that such devices should be necessary to control the abuses of government. But what is government itself, but the greatest of all reflections on human nature? If men were angels, no government would be necessary. If angels were to govern men, neither external nor internal controls on

Answers

1. Equiano describes sounds ("fearful noises"), smells ("loathsome smells"), feelings ("the closeness of the place"), and sights ("we could not see how they managed the vessel") as part of his overall description. These details are extremely effective in painting a picture of utter horror.

2. Possible answer: Equiano's descriptions of the slave trade are horrific. Further, he puts his own face and name on the experience; this would have certainly shocked many people and perhaps persuaded them to join the abolitionist cause to oppose slavery in America.

3. Possible answer: I think Equiano wanted to bring to the attention of the public the horrible way in which enslaved persons were treated, and in particular, how terrible the journey was from Africa to the Americas (or England).

government would be necessary. In framing a government which is to be administered by men over men, the great difficulty lies in this: you must first enable the government to control the governed; and in the next place oblige it to control itself. A dependence on the people is, no doubt, the primary control on the government; but experience has taught mankind the necessity of auxiliary precautions.

This policy of supplying, by opposite and rival interests, the defect of better motives, might be traced through the whole system of human affairs, private as well as public. We see it particularly displayed in all the subordinate distributions of power, where the constant aim is to divide and arrange the several offices in such a manner as that each may be a check on the other—that the private interest of every individual may be a sentinel over the public rights. These inventions of prudence cannot be less requisite in the distribution of the supreme powers of the State.

But it is not possible to give to each department an equal power of self-defense. In republican government, the legislative authority necessarily predominates. The remedy for this inconveniency is to divide the legislature into different branches; and to render them, by different modes of election and different principles of action, as little connected with each other as the nature of their common functions and their common dependence on the society will admit. It may even be necessary to guard against dangerous encroachments by still further precautions. As the weight of the legislative authority requires that it should be thus divided, the weakness of the executive may require, on the other hand, that it should be fortified. An absolute negative on the legislature appears, at first view, to be the natural defense with which the executive magistrate should be armed. But perhaps it would be neither altogether safe nor alone sufficient. On ordinary occasions it might not be exerted with the requisite firmness, and on extraordinary occasions it might be perfidiously [traitorously; treachorously] abused. May not this defect of an absolute negative be supplied by some qualified connection between this weaker department and the weaker branch of the stronger department, by which the latter may be led to support the constitutional rights of the former, without being too much detached from the rights of its own department?

If the principles on which these observations are founded be just, as I persuade myself they are, and they be applied as a criterion to the several State constitutions, and to the federal Constitution it will be found that if the latter does not perfectly correspond with them, the former are infinitely less able to bear such a test.

There are, moreover, two considerations particularly applicable to the federal system of America, which place that system in a very interesting point of view.

First. In a single republic, all the power surrendered by the people is submitted to the administration of a single government; and the usurpations [illegal seizures of power] are guarded against by a division of the government into distinct and separate departments. In the compound republic of America, the power surrendered by the people is first divided between two distinct governments, and then the portion allotted to each subdivided among distinct and separate departments. Hence a double security arises to the rights of the people. The different governments will control each other, at the same time that each will be controlled by itself.

Second. It is of great importance in a republic not only to guard the society against the oppression of its rulers, but to guard one part of the society against the injustice of the other part. Different interests necessarily exist in different classes of citizens. If a majority be united by a common interest, the rights of the minority will be insecure. There are but two methods of providing against this evil: the one by creating a will in the community independent of the majority—that is, of the society itself; the other, by comprehending in the society so many separate descriptions of citizens as will render an unjust combination of a majority of the whole very improbable, if not impracticable. The first method prevails in all governments possessing an hereditary or self-appointed authority. This, at best, is but a precarious security; because a power independent of the society may as well espouse the unjust views of the major, as the rightful interests of the minor party, and may possibly be turned against both parties. The second method will be exemplified in the federal republic of the United States. Whilst all authority in it will be derived from and dependent on the society, the society itself will be broken into so many parts, interests, and classes of citizens, that the rights of individuals, or of the minority, will be in little danger from interested combinations of the majority.

In a free government the security for civil rights must be the same as that for religious rights. It consists in the one case in the multiplicity of interests, and in the other in the multiplicity of sects. The degree of security in both cases will depend on the number of interests and sects; and this may be presumed to depend on the extent of country and number of people comprehended under the same government. This view of the subject must particularly recommend a proper federal system to all the sincere and considerate friends of republican government, since it shows that in exact proportion as the territory of the Union may be formed into more circumscribed Confederacies, or States oppressive combinations of a majority will be facilitated: the best security, under the republican forms, for the rights of every class of citizens, will be diminished: and consequently the stability and independence of some member of the government, the only other security, must be proportionately increased. Justice is the end of government. It is the end of civil society. It ever has been and ever will be pursued until it be obtained, or until liberty be lost in the pursuit. In a society under the forms of which the stronger faction can readily unite and oppress the weaker, anarchy may as truly be said to reign as in a state of nature, where the weaker individual is not secured against the violence of the stronger; and as, in the latter state, even the stronger individuals are prompted, by the uncertainty of their condition, to submit to a government which may protect the weak as well as themselves; so, in the former state, will the more powerful factions or parties be gradually induced, by a like motive, to wish for a government which will protect all parties, the weaker as well as the more powerful. It can be little doubted that if the State of Rhode Island was separated from the Confederacy and left to itself, the insecurity of rights under the popular form of government within such narrow limits would be displayed by such reiterated oppressions of factious majorities that some power altogether independent of the people would soon be called for by the voice of the very factions whose misrule had proved the necessity of it.

In the extended republic of the United States, and among the great variety of interests, parties, and sects which it embraces, a coalition of a majority of the whole society could seldom take place on any other principles than those of justice and the general good; whilst there being thus less danger to a minor from the will of a major party, there must be less pretext, also, to provide for the security of the former, by introducing into the government a will not dependent on the latter, or, in other words, a will independent of the society itself. It is no less certain than it is important, notwithstanding the contrary opinions which have been entertained, that the larger the society, provided it lie within a practical sphere, the more duly capable it will be of self-government. And happily for the REPUBLICAN CAUSE, the practicable sphere may be carried to a very great extent, by a judicious modification and mixture of the FEDERAL PRINCIPLE.

ASSESSMENT

1. **Assess an Argument** Do you agree with Madison that, "In a free government the security for civil rights must be the same as that for religious rights"? Considering the history of the United States on the issue of civil rights for both women and racial minorities, in what way is Madison's remark ironic?
2. **Analyze Interactions** What effect did *Federalist* No. 51 have on the final U.S. Constitution?
3. **Explain an Argument** Why does Madison think it is important that the new government exercise a separation of powers?

[Declaration of the Rights of Man and the Citizen]

Introduction

The National Assembly issued this document in 1789 after having overthrown the established government in the early stages of the French Revolution. The document was modeled in part on the English Bill of Rights and on the American Declaration of Independence. The basic principles of the French declaration were those that inspired the revolution, such as the freedom and equality of all male citizens before the law. The Articles below identify additional principles.

Primary Source

Therefore the National Assembly recognizes and proclaims, in the presence and under the auspices [approval and support] of the Supreme Being, the following rights of man and of the citizen:

1. Men are born and remain free and equal in rights. Social distinctions may be founded only upon the general good.

2. The aim of all political association is the preservation of the natural and imprescriptible [that which

Answers

1. Possible answer: I agree that civil rights are as important as religious rights, but the Founders did not include women and African Americans in their vision for an equal and civil society. It is ironic, as it reveals the attitudes of the times in which Madison lived and could write such a phrase—not to mention the sections on protecting "minorities"—yet exclude so many groups of Americans.

2. The U.S. Constitution does indeed have a separation of powers; there are three separate branches of government, and each is subject to a system of checks and balances.

3. Madison feels that it is important that the branches of government be separate so that one does not take on too much power over the others. He also sees separation of powers as an essential tool for fighting against factions that might rise up and oppress minority groups.

cannot be rightfully taken away] rights of man. These rights are liberty, property, security, and resistance to oppression. . . .

4. Liberty consists in the freedom to do everything which injures no one else. . . .
5. Law can only prohibit such actions as are hurtful to society. . . .
6. Law is the expression of the general will. Every citizen has a right to participate personally, or through his representative, in its formation. It must be the same for all, whether it protects or punishes. All citizens, being equal in the eyes of the law, are equally eligible to all dignities and to all public positions and occupations, according to their abilities, and without distinction except that of their virtues and talents.
7. No person shall be accused, arrested, or imprisoned except in the cases and according to the forms prescribed by law. . . .
11. The free communication of ideas and opinions is one of the most precious of the rights of man. Every citizen may, accordingly, speak, write, and print with freedom. . . .
13. A common contribution is essential for the maintenance of the public [military] forces and for the cost of administration. This should be equitably distributed among all the citizens in proportion to their means.

ASSESSMENT

1. **Analyze Interactions** How does the fourth principle, concerning liberty, connect to the idea that certain guaranteed freedoms in American life are limited in some ways?
2. **Draw Conclusions** Many of the Declaration's principles are broad and idealistic. Choose one to analyze, addressing the potential problems that could arise when it becomes implemented as a law.
3. **Paraphrase** Tell in your own words what the Declaration says about law and fairness. Pay particular attention to Article 6 as you formulate your answer.
4. **Summarize** Explain how the Declaration protects individual liberties. Cite details in the text to support your response.

[*Democracy in America*, Alexis de Tocqueville]

Introduction

Alexis de Tocqueville, a young French writer, visited the United States in 1831. During his travels, he observed firsthand the impact of Jacksonian democracy. After returning to France, Tocqueville began writing *Democracy in America*, a detailed look at American politics, society, economics, religion, and law. The first volume was published in 1835. The book is still studied and quoted by historians and politicians today. In these excerpts from *Democracy in America*, Tocqueville discusses the role of the American people in their government and gives his view of the American character.

Primary Source

The general principles which are the groundwork of modern constitutions–principles which were imperfectly known in Europe, and not completely triumphant even in Great Britain, in the seventeenth century–were all recognized and determined by the laws of New England: the intervention of the people in public affairs, the free voting of taxes, the responsibility of authorities, personal liberty, and trial by jury, were all positively established without discussion. From these fruitful principles consequences have been derived and applications have been made such as no nation in Europe has yet ventured to attempt.

. . . it is at least true that in the United States the county and the township are always based upon the same principle, namely, that everyone is the best judge of what concerns himself alone, and the most proper person to supply his private wants.

In America the people name those who make the law and those who execute it; they themselves form the jury that punishes infractions [violations] of the law. Not only are the institutions democratic in their principle, but also in all their developments; thus the people name their representatives directly and generally choose them every year in order to keep them more completely under their dependence. It is therefore really the people who direct. . . . This majority is composed principally of peaceful citizens who, either by taste or by interest, sincerely desire the good of the country. Around them parties constantly agitate. . . .

Answers

1. The fourth principle defines liberty as the right to do anything that does not harm anyone else; this is similar to the idea that while freedom of speech is guaranteed in the U.S. Bill of Rights, the government has passed laws limiting speech in instances in which someone might be harmed. For example, a person cannot yell "fire" in a crowded movie theater. Another example would be those laws that protect people against libel.

2. Sample answer: The fifth principle of the Declaration states, "Law can only prohibit such actions as are hurtful to society." However, this principle does not address who and what will determine what qualifies as "hurtful to society." The question becomes, what happens when not everyone agrees on what is hurtful?

3. Possible answer: Law is created out of what most people in society want in order to maintain a general peace and the common good. In order for laws to be effective, they must be the same for all people, and they must be created by the people or their representatives.

4. Possible answer: The Declaration explicitly states those individual freedoms that should be proclaimed and respected. For example, article 11 allows for freedom of individual expression. The Declaration also expresses that people are free *from* certain things as well; article 7 protects people from unlawful imprisonment.

Answers

1. People in America participate in their democracy by electing judges, representatives, and the President. They elect and reelect their representatives as a way of keeping them accountable. People also participate in a democracy by sitting on juries.

2. Tocqueville was clearly struck with the success of American democracy; he marveled at the ideas behind it and the participation. He also was impressed with the general American character, which was marked by a sincere desire to improve the "good of the country," as well as a passionate spirit of adventure and innovation.

3. Reading how impressed Tocqueville was with the level of participation by Americans in the early 1800s might motivate citizens today to be more active in their government. For elected officials, Tocqueville's books serve as a reminder that the power of the American government rests in the hands of the people, not the powerful.

Answers

1. Readers probably would have been shocked by the squalid state of the building, how many children were living there, and the deaths Riis describes. Muckrakers like Riis wanted their writing to lead to reform. By shocking readers with details about how tenement children were living, Riis could convince his audience that conditions needed to change.

2. The "Other Half" refers to the millions who live in tenements. The description suggests that Riis's readers are wealthier Americans and emphasizes the divide between them and the "others." Riis's title suggests that his book is going to reveal what life is like in tenements to unaware readers.

The American taken randomly [chosen without a plan] will therefore be a man ardent [intense] in his desires, enterprising [full of energy; willing to take on new projects], adventurous—above all, an innovator [a person who creates a new way of doing something]. This spirit is in fact found in all his works; he introduces it into his political laws, his religious doctrines, his theories of social economy, his private industry; he brings it with him everywhere, into the depths of the woods as into the heart of towns.

To evade the bondageof system and habit, of family maxims, class- opinions, and in some degree, of national prejudices; to accept tradition only as a means of information, and existing facts only as a lesson used in doing otherwise and doing better; to seek the reason of things for oneself, and in oneself alone; to tend to results without being bound to means, and to aim at the substance through the form;—such are the principle characteristics of what I shall call the philosophical method of the Americans. But if I go further, and if I seek among those characteristics the principle one which includes almost all the rest, I discover that, in most operations of the mind, each American appeals only to the individual effort of his own understanding.

ASSESSMENT

1. **Determine Central Ideas** In what way do the people "direct" the American democracy, according to Tocqueville?
2. **Summarize** What impressed Tocqueville during his time in America? Cite examples to support your answer.
3. **Draw Conclusions** In what way could Tocqueville's book be relevant today?

[*How the Other Half Lives*, Jacob Riis]

Introduction

Jacob Riis immigrated to the United States from Denmark in 1870. After living for several years in extreme poverty, he found a job as a police reporter for the *New York Tribune*. He became one of the leading muckrakers of the Progressive Era. Riis's writing and photographs helped expose the harsh living conditions in the crowded tenements of New York City. This excerpt is from Riis's 1890 book, *How the Other Half Lives*.

Primary Source

The problem of the children becomes, in these swarms, to the last degree perplexing. Their very number make one stand aghast [horrified]. I have already given instances of the packing of the child population in East Side tenements. They might be continued indefinitely until the array [orderly arrangement] would be enough to startle any community. For, be it remembered, these children with the training they receive— or do not receive— with the instincts they inherit and absorb in their growing up, are to be our future rulers, if our theory of government is worth anything. More than a working majority of our voters now register from the tenements.

I counted the other day the little ones, up to ten years or so, in a Bayard Street tenement that for a yard has a triangular space in the center with sides fourteen or fifteen feet long, just room enough for a row of ill-smelling closets [toilets] at the base of the triangle and a hydrant at the apex [highest point]. There was about as much light in this "yard" as in the average cellar. I gave up my self-imposed task in despair when I had counted one hundred and twenty-eight in forty families. . . .

Bodies of drowned children turn up in the rivers right along since summer whom no one seems to know anything about. When last spring some workmen, while moving a pile of lumber on a North River pier, found under the last plank the body of a little lad crushed to death, no one had missed a boy, though his parents afterward turned up. The truant [a pupil who misses school without permission] officer assuredly does not know, though he spends his life trying to find out, somewhat illogically, perhaps, since the department that employs him admits that thousands of poor children are crowded out of the schools year by year for want of room.

ASSESSMENT

1. **Identify Supporting Details** What details in this excerpt may have shocked readers of the time period? Why do you think muckrakers sought to shock their audience?

2. **Determine Meaning** To whom does the "Other Half" in the title refer? Why do you think Riis uses this phrase?
3. **Identify Cause and Effect** How do you think Riis's account might have contributed to social reforms for tenement housing?

[*Hind Swaraj,* Mohandas Gandhi]

Introduction

Mohandas Gandhi led a successful, peaceful revolution in India against British rule. In the following excerpt from his book *Hind Swaraj* (*Indian Home Rule*), Gandhi explains the ideas behind his nonviolent method of passive resistance in the form of an imaginary conversation between an editor and a reader. *Hind Swaraj* was first published in 1909 in South Africa, but was banned in India.

Primary Source

Editor: Passive [accepting or allowing] resistance is a method of securing rights by personal suffering; it is the reverse of resistance by arms. When I refuse to do a thing that is repugnant [offensive] to my conscience, I use soul-force. For instance, the government of the day has passed a law which is applicable to me. I do not like it. If by using violence, I force the government to repeal the law, I am employing what may be termed body-force. If I do not obey the law, and accept the penalty for its breach [act of breaking a law], I use soul-force. It involves sacrifice of self.

Everybody admits that sacrifice of self is infinitely superior to sacrifice of others. Moreover, if this kind of force is used in a cause that is unjust, only the person using it suffers. He does not make others suffer for his mistakes. Men have before now done many things which were subsequently found to have been wrong. No man can claim that he is absolutely in the right, or that a particular thing is wrong, because he thinks so, but it is wrong for him so long as that is his deliberate judgment. It is therefore meet [proper] that he should not do that which he knows to be wrong, and suffer the consequence whatever it may be. This is the key to the use of soul-force.

Reader: You would then disregard laws—this is rank [complete and utter] disloyalty. We have always been considered a law-abiding nation. You seem to be going even beyond the extremists. They say that we must obey the laws that have been passed, but that, if the laws be bad, we must drive out the lawgivers even by force.

Editor: Whether I go beyond them or whether I do not is a matter of no consequence to either of us. We simply want to find out what is right, and to act accordingly. The real meaning of the statement that we are a law-abiding nation is that we are passive resisters. When we do not like certain laws, we do not break the heads of law-givers, but we suffer and do not submit to the laws.

ASSESSMENT

1. **Draw Inferences** Why does Gandhi advocate suffering and self- sacrifice?
2. **Analyze Style and Rhetoric** Why do you think Gandhi chooses to structure his book as a conversation between an editor and a reader? How does this help him to get his point across?
3. **Draw Conclusions** Gandhi helped bring about Indian independence from British rule. Why do you think his approach was effective in enacting social and political change?

[*The Fourteen Points,* Woodrow Wilson]

Introduction

In a speech to Congress on January 8, 1918, President Wilson laid out America's war aims and his vision for peace after the war. His speech included fourteen key points upon which he believed the peace following the war must be based. However, not all of Wilson's ideas were adopted at the Paris Peace Conference.

Primary Source

. . . What we demand in this war, therefore, is nothing peculiar [unique] to ourselves. It is that the world be made fit and safe to live in; and particularly that it be

Answers

3. Riis's account probably brought greater social awareness to wealthier Americans about the terrible conditions in which many people, mainly immigrants, were living. This might have inspired people to try to improve these living conditions. For example, social reforms could improve tenement houses and provide better educational opportunities.

Answers

1. Gandhi believes that suffering and self-sacrifice are the best ways to bring about political change. Passive resistance requires self-sacrifice. A person may suffer and be punished for breaking the law. However, others will not be hurt through violence, and that sacrifice may ultimately cause the law to change.

2. Gandhi structures the book as though a reader is asking him, the editor, questions about his nonviolent philosophy. Through these questions, his audience learns about his views. This structure allows Gandhi to raise objections, opinions, and common misconceptions through the voice of the reader, and then address them as the editor.

3. Possible answer: Gandhi's nonviolent approach probably put pressure on Britain to change its rule. If enough people followed Gandhi and refused to obey British laws, it might have become hard for Britain to continue enforcing these rules. Refusing to obey unjust laws would have called attention to the injustices Indians faced. Other governments might have begun looking unfavorably at Britain if it continued to enforce these policies.

made safe for every peace-loving nation which, like our own, wishes to live its own life, [and] determine its own institutions [choose its own government]. . . . The program of the world's peace, therefore, is our only program; and that program, the only possible program as we see it, is this:

1. Open covenants [formal agreements] of peace, openly arrived at, after which there shall be no private international understandings of any kind but [instead] diplomacy shall proceed always frankly [openly and honestly] and in the public view.

2. Absolute freedom of navigation upon the seas, outside territorial waters, alike in peace and in war, except as the seas may be closed in whole or in part by international action for the enforcement of international covenants.

3. The removal, so far as possible, of all economic barriers and the establishment of an equality of trade conditions among all the nations consenting to the peace and associating themselves for its maintenance.

4. Adequate guarantees given and taken that national armaments will be reduced to the lowest point consistent with domestic safety.

5. A free, open-minded, and absolutely impartial adjustment of all colonial claims, based upon a strict observance of the principle that in determining all such questions of sovereignty the interests of the populations concerned must have equal weight with the equitable claims of the government whose title is to be determined....

14. A general association [organization] of nations must be formed under specific covenants for the purpose of affording mutual guarantees of political independence and territorial integrity to great and small states alike.

ASSESSMENT

1. **Compare and Contrast** Points 6–13 deal with specific territorial issues, such as breaking up the Ottoman and Austro-Hungarian Empires and restoring sovereignty to Belgium and Poland. To an American in 1918, how would those points be different from the ones excerpted here?
2. **Draw Conclusions** Preventing war seems like an admirable goal. Why might a country reject some or all of Wilson's points?
3. **Integrate Information From Diverse Sources** Why might isolationists oppose some or all of Wilson's Fourteen Points?
4. **Draw Inferences** What political impact do you think Wilson's Fourteen Points had?

[*Anne Frank: The Diary of a Young Girl*, Anne Frank]

Introduction

In 1933, Adolf Hitler was elected Chancellor of Germany. During World War II, his Nazi Party rounded up European Jews, many of whom were transported to death camps. Anne Frank was a young Jewish girl who hid with her family in small concealed rooms in her father's office. Frank kept a diary from June 12, 1942 to August 1, 1944, when her family's hiding place was discovered. She died in a concentration camp in 1945. Frank's father survived and published her diary to share Anne's story with the world.

Primary Source

Saturday, June 20, 1942

My father was thirty-six when he married my mother, who was then twenty-five. My sister Margot was born in 1926 in Frankfort-on-Main. I followed on June 12, 1929, and, as we are Jewish, we emigrated to Holland in 1933, where my father was appointed Managing Director of Travies N.V. This firm is in close relationship with the firm of Kolen & Co. in the same building, of which my father is a partner.

The rest of our family, however, felt the full impact of Hitler's anti-Jewish laws, so life was filled with anxiety. In 1938 after the pogroms [organized killing and other persecution of Jews], my two uncles (my mother's brothers) escaped to the U.S.A. My old grandmother came to us, she was then seventy-three. After May 1940 good times rapidly fled: first the war, then the capitulation [surrender], followed by the arrival of the Germans, which is when the sufferings of us Jews really began.

Anti-Jewish decrees followed each other in quick succession. Jews must wear a yellow star. Jews must

Answers

1. Those points do not affect the United States directly; the points excerpted here limit what the United States can and cannot do.

2. Sample answer: Some countries might not like having other nations put limits on what they can do.

3. Sample answer: Isolationists opposed entering the war. They did not want the United States to become involved in Europe. Some of Wilson's points, especially the formation of the League of Nations, required that.

4. Sample answer: It promoted the idea for an international organization to promote peace and guarantee political independence to all. It laid the groundwork for the United Nations.

1022

hand in their bicycles. Jews are banned from trains and are forbidden to drive. Jews are only allowed to do their shopping between three and five o'clock and then only in shops which bear the placard [sign] "Jewish shop." Jews must be indoors by eight o'clock and cannot even sit in their own gardens after that hour. Jews are forbidden to visit theaters, cinemas, and other places of entertainment. Jews my not take part in public sports. Swimming baths, tennis courts, hockey fields, and other sports grounds are all prohibited to them. Jews may not visit Christians. Jews must go to Jewish schools, and many more restrictions of a similar kind.

So we could not do this and were forbidden to do that. But life went on in spite of it all. Jopie [Jacqueline van Mearsen, Anne's best friend] used to say to me, "You're scared to do anything, because it may be forbidden." Our freedom was strictly limited. Yet things were still bearable.

Thursday, November 19, 1942

Countless friends and acquaintances have gone to a terrible fate. Evening after evening the green and gray army lorries [trucks] trundle [roll] past. The Germans ring at every front door to inquire if there are any Jews living in the house. If there are, then the whole family has to go at once. If they don't find any, they go on to the next house. No one has a chance of evading [avoiding] them unless one goes into hiding. Often they go around us with lists, and only ring when they know they can get a good haul. Sometimes they let them off for cash—so much per head, it seems like the slave hunts of olden times. But it's certainly no joke; it's much too tragic for that. In the evenings when it's dark, I often see rows of good, innocent people accompanied by crying children, walking on and on, in charge of a couple of these chaps, bullied and knocked about until they almost drop. No one is spared—old people, babies, expectant mothers, the sick—each and all join in the march of death.

How fortunate we are here, so well cared for and undisturbed. We wouldn't have to worry about all this misery were it not that we are so anxious about all those dear to us whom we can no longer help.

I feel wicked sleeping in a warm bed, while my dearest friends have been knocked down or have fallen into a gutter somewhere out in the cold night. I get frightened when I think of close friends who have now been delivered into the hands of the cruelest brutes that walk the earth. And all because they are Jews!

Wednesday, May 3, 1944

Why all this destruction? The question is very understandable, but no one has found a satisfactory answer to it so far. Yes, why do they make still more gigantic planes, still heavier bombs and, at the same time, prefabricated [mass-produced] houses for reconstruction? Why should millions be spent daily on the war and yet there's not a penny available for medical services, artists, or for poor people?

Why do some people have to starve, while there are surpluses [extra amounts] rotting in other parts of the world? Oh, why are people so crazy?

Saturday, July 15, 1944

In spite of everything I still believe that people are really good at heart. I simply can't build up my hopes on a foundation consisting of confusion, misery, and death. I see the world gradually being turned into a wilderness, I hear the ever approaching thunder, which will destroy us too, I can feel the sufferings of millions and yet, if I look up into the heavens, I think that it will all come right, that this cruelty too will end, and that peace and tranquility [calm] will return again.

ASSESSMENT

1. **Draw Inferences** What was the purpose of the restrictions the Nazis imposed on Jews? What were the effects of these laws?
2. **Analyze Style and Rhetoric** How would you describe the tone of Frank's diary? How does she relate to her subject matter?
3. **Determine Central Ideas** How does reading Frank's diary differ from reading a secondary source about the Holocaust? What might her diary teach readers today that other sources cannot?

[Charter of the United Nations]

Introduction

After World War I, more than 50 countries joined together to form the League of Nations. The League was supposed to prevent future wars by providing a forum for the peaceful settlement of international disputes. The United States never joined the League.

The idea of an international peacekeeping organization was revisited after World War II.

Answers

1. The restrictions served to identify Jews and separate them from the rest of society. They limited what Jews could do and where they could go, preventing Jews from living their normal lives. The effect was to make Jews isolated and afraid. The laws also probably encouraged others to view Jews as different and as outsiders. This made it easier to round up Jews and take them away.

2. Much of the diary is matter-of-fact in tone. Frank comes across as a close observer who provides a detailed and informative account of events. Later entries show her questioning the world, as when she wonders why there is so much destruction and offers hope for the future.

3. The diary provides a first-hand account of what it was like to be a Jew who was being persecuted during World War II. It makes the events feel vivid and immediate. A secondary source might be more removed from these events. It might not show as directly what people did, thought, and felt at this time.

In 1944, representatives from the United States, the Soviet Union, China, and the United Kingdom met for several months to work out the framework for the United Nations.

In 1945, representatives of 50 countries met in San Francisco to sign the United Nations charter, bringing the organization into being.

Here are the preamble and first two articles of that charter.

Primary Source

WE THE PEOPLES OF THE UNITED NATIONS DETERMINED

to save succeeding [later] generations from the scourge of war, which twice in our lifetime has brought untold sorrow to mankind, and

to reaffirm faith in fundamental human rights, in the dignity and worth of the human person, in the equal rights of men and women and of nations large and small, and

to establish conditions under which justice and respect for the obligations arising from treaties and other sources of international law can be maintained, and

to promote social progress and better standards of life in larger freedom,

AND FOR THESE ENDS

to practice tolerance and live together in peace with one another as good neighbours, and

to unite our strength to maintain international peace and security, and

to ensure, by the acceptance of principles and the institution of methods, that armed force shall not be used, save in the common interest, and

to employ international machinery for the promotion of the economic and social advancement of all peoples,

HAVE RESOLVED TO COMBINE OUR EFFORTS TO ACCOMPLISH THESE AIMS

Accordingly, our respective Governments, through representatives assembled in the city of San Francisco, who have exhibited their full powers found to be in good and due form, have agreed to the present Charter of the United Nations and do hereby establish an international organization to be known as the United Nations.

CHAPTER I: PURPOSES AND PRINCIPLES

Article 1

The Purposes of the United Nations are:

1. To maintain international peace and security, and to that end: to take effective collective measures for the prevention and removal of threats to the peace, and for the suppression of acts of aggression or other breaches of the peace, and to bring about by peaceful means, and in conformity with the principles of justice and international law, adjustment or settlement of international disputes or situations which might lead to a breach of the peace;
2. To develop friendly relations among nations based on respect for the principle of equal rights and self-determination of peoples, and to take other appropriate measures to strengthen universal peace;
3. To achieve international co-operation in solving international problems of an economic, social, cultural, or humanitarian character, and in promoting and encouraging respect for human rights and for fundamental freedoms for all without distinction as to race, sex, language, or religion; and
4. To be a centre for harmonizing the actions of nations in the attainment of these common ends.

Article 2

The Organization and its Members, in pursuit of the Purposes stated in Article 1, shall act in accordance with the following Principles.

1. The Organization is based on the principle of the sovereign equality of all its Members.
2. All Members, in order to ensure to all of them the rights and benefits resulting from membership, shall fulfill in good faith the obligations assumed by them in accordance with the present Charter.
3. All Members shall settle their international disputes by peaceful means in such a manner that international peace and security, and justice, are not endangered.
4. All Members shall refrain in their international relations from the threat or use of force against the territorial integrity or political independence of any state, or in any other manner inconsistent with the Purposes of the United Nations.

1024

5. All Members shall give the United Nations every assistance in any action it takes in accordance with the present Charter, and shall refrain from giving assistance to any state against which the United Nations is taking preventive or enforcement action.

6. The Organization shall ensure that states which are not Members of the United Nations act in accordance with these Principles so far as may be necessary for the maintenance of international peace and security.

7. Nothing contained in the present Charter shall authorize the United Nations to intervene in matters which are essentially within the domestic jurisdiction of any state or shall require the Members to submit such matters to settlement under the present Charter; but this principle shall not prejudice the application of enforcement measures under Chapter VII.

ASSESSMENT

1. **Cite Evidence** The government of a country is inflicting terrible human rights abuses on members of the opposition party. Based on the excerpt, can the United Nations intervene? Cite the part(s) of the charter that support your opinion.
2. **Explain an Argument** Several years of drought in western Asia have led to widespread famine. The UN arranges to bring convoys of food to starving people. One country, a member of the UN, does not want to let relief workers come inside its borders. Does any part of the charter cited here support or rebut the country's position? Explain your answer.
3. **Draw Conclusions** Has the United Nations been successful in its mission "to save succeeding generations from the scourge of war"? Explain your answer.

[Universal Declaration of Human Rights]

Introduction

The General Assembly of the United Nations adopted this declaration on December 10, 1948. The document sets forth the basic liberties and freedoms to which all people are entitled.

Primary Source

Article 1 All human beings are born free and equal in dignity [worthiness] and rights. They are endowed with reason and conscience and should act toward one another in a spirit of brotherhood.

Article 2 Everyone is entitled to all the rights and freedoms set forth in this Declaration, without distinction [difference] of any kind, such as race, colour, sex, language, religion, political or other opinion, national or social origin, property, birth or other status. . . .

Article 3 Everyone has the right to life, liberty and security of person.

Article 4 No one shall be held in slavery or servitude. . . .

Article 5 No one shall be subjected [forced to undergo] to torture or to cruel, inhuman or degrading [humiliating] treatment or punishment.

Article 9 No one shall be subjected to arbitrary arrest, detention or exile.

Article 13 Everyone has the right to freedom of movement. . . .

Article 18 Everyone has the right to freedom of thought, conscience and religion. . . Article 19 Everyone has the right to freedom of opinion and expression. . . .

Article 20 Everyone has the right to freedom of peaceful assembly and association. . . .

Article 23 Everyone has the right to work, to free choice of employment, to just and favourable conditions of work and to protection against unemployment . . .

Article 25 Everyone has the right to a standard of living adequate [satisfactory] for the health and well-being of himself and of his family, including food, clothing, housing and medical care and necessary social services, and the right to security in the event of unemployment, sickness, disability, widowhood, old age or other lack of livelihood in circumstances beyond his control.

Article 26 Everyone has the right to education. Education shall be free, at least in the elementary and fundamental stages. . . .

ASSESSMENT

1. **Analyze Interactions** How do you think the U.S. Bill of Rights might have influenced this declaration?

Answers

1. Sample answer: Article 2, Principle 7 says that the UN will not interfere in purely domestic matters. What is happening in that country is terrible, but it does not affect other countries, so the UN cannot intervene.

2. Sample answer: Article 1, Purpose 3 says, "To achieve international co-operation in solving international problems of an economic, social, cultural, or humanitarian character." This is clearly an international humanitarian problem, so the nation must cooperate.

3. No; Sample answer: There are still wars being fought in countries around the world. War has not been prevented.

Answers

1. The U.S. Bill of Rights lists rights that Americans have by virtue of being U.S. citizens. It may have promoted the idea of listing rights in a public document to make sure those rights are known. It may also have helped establish certain rights as necessary, such as the rights to freedom of religion and peaceful assembly.

Answers

2. The United Nations wrote this declaration to establish universal rights for people around the world, regardless of the government they have. It may have hoped that articulating these liberties would inspire governments to work to protect human rights and better ensure that people have the protection and opportunities they need. The declaration may also have given hope to people living under an oppressive regime that they were entitled to these universal human rights.

3. Human rights are unalienable rights that all people have. They include the right to freedom, work, education, and to the services people need to lead healthy and productive lives. Human rights cannot be taken away.

Answers

1. He says colonies are backwards in education, in science, in agriculture, and in industry. The people who live there are not treated on the same level as peoples of independent countries, and often there are disturbances and political tension.

2. They must make up for being centuries behind more established nations in their economic development.

3. Sample answer: Not always. There are countries in the world that are independent but have constant conflicts and political strife. I would rather live in a colony that is governed.

2. **Determine Author's Purpose** Why do you think the members of the United Nations wrote this declaration, and what did they hope it would accomplish?
3. **Determine Central Ideas** Based on this passage, how would you define the term "human rights"?

[*Autobiography,* Kwame Nkrumah]

Introduction

Kwame Nkrumah led the people of the Gold Coast in their quest for independence from Britain. After succeeding in 1957, Nkrumah became the first prime minister and renamed the country Ghana. In this excerpt from his Autobiography, Nkrumah speaks of the need to establish economic independence as a means of maintaining political independence. Nkrumah describes the difficult work of building an independent economy.

Primary Source

. . . Independence for the Gold Coast was my aim. It was a colony, and I have always regarded colonialism as the policy by which a foreign power binds territories to herself by political ties with the primary object of promoting her own economic advantage. No one need be surprised if this system has led to disturbances and political tension in many territories. There are few people who would not rid themselves of such domination if they could. . . .

I saw that the whole solution to [our] problem lay in political freedom for our people, for it is only when a people are politically free that other races can give them the respect that is due to them. It is impossible to talk of equality of races in any other terms. No people without a government of their own can expect to be treated on the same level as peoples of independent sovereign [self-governing] states. It is far better to be free to govern or misgovern yourself than to be governed by anybody else. . . .

Once this freedom is gained, a greater task comes into view. All dependent [subject to the rule of another country] territories are backward in education, in science, in agriculture, and in industry. The economic independence that should follow and maintain political independence demands every effort from the people, a total mobilization of brain and manpower resources. What other countries have taken three hundred years or more to achieve, a once dependent territory must try to accomplish in a generation if it is to survive. . . .

ASSESSMENT

1. **Summarize** How does Nkrumah characterize life in a colony?
2. **Summarize** Based on Nkrumah's remarks, what makes economic independence difficult for newly independent nations to achieve?
3. **Assess an Argument** Do you agree with Nkrumah that it is "far better to be free to govern or misgovern yourself than to be governed by anybody else"? Why or why not?

["*Tear Down This Wall,*" Ronald Reagan]

Introduction

On June 12, 1987, President Reagan spoke in West Berlin, near the Berlin Wall, not far from where the Brandenburg Gate stood in the eastern sector. His speech acknowledged the new Soviet leader Mikhail Gorbachev's efforts at reform in the Soviet Union. However, Reagan was not satisfied with Gorbachev's limited measures. He challenged the Soviet leader to show a real commitment to reform by tearing down the Berlin Wall that had stood between East and West Berlin since 1961. This wall symbolized the division between communism and democracy.

Primary Source

In the 1950s, Khrushchev predicted: "We will bury you." But in the West today, we see a free world that has achieved a level of prosperity and well-being unprecedented [never having happened or existed before] in all human history. In the Communist world, we see failure, technological backwardness, declining standards of health, even want of the most basic kind—too little food. Even today, the Soviet Union still cannot feed itself. After these four decades, then, there stands before the entire world one great and inescapable conclusion: Freedom leads to prosperity. Freedom replaces the ancient hatreds among the nations with comity [courtesy] and peace. Freedom is the victor [winner].

And now the Soviets themselves may, in a limited way, be coming to understand the importance of freedom. We hear much from Moscow about a new policy of reform and openness. Some political prisoners have been released. Certain foreign news broadcasts are no longer being jammed. Some economic enterprises have been permitted to operate with greater freedom from state control.

Are these the beginnings of profound changes in the Soviet state? Or are they token gestures, intended to raise false hopes in the West, or to strengthen the Soviet system without changing it? We welcome change and openness; for we believe that freedom and security go together, that the advance of human liberty can only strengthen the cause of world peace. There is one sign the Soviets can make that would be unmistakable, that would advance dramatically the cause of freedom and peace.

General Secretary Gorbachev, if you seek peace, if you seek prosperity for the Soviet Union and Eastern Europe, if you seek liberalization: Come here to this gate! Mr. Gorbachev, open this gate! Mr. Gorbachev, tear down this wall!

ASSESSMENT

1. **Distinguish Among Fact, Opinion, and Reasoned Judgment** When Reagan says, "freedom is the victor," is that a fact, an opinion, or a reasoned judgment? Cite evidence from the speech to support your answer.

[*"Freedom from Fear,"* Aung San Suu Kyi]

Introduction

Aung San Suu Kyi, leader of the National League for Democracy in Myanmar (Burma) and winner of the Nobel Peace Prize, has worked courageously for human rights and democracy in her country. Because of her opposition to Myanmar's ruling military junta, she was held under house arrest from 1989 to 1995 and severely restricted until 2010. In this essay, Aung San Suu Kyi describes the need for courage when living under an oppressive government.

Primary Source

Fearlessness may be a gift but perhaps more precious is the courage acquired through endeavor, courage that comes from cultivating the habit of refusing to let fear dictate one's actions, courage that could be described as 'grace under pressure'—grace which is renewed repeatedly in the face of harsh, unremitting [not letting up] pressure.

Within a system which denies the existence of basic human rights, fear tends to be the order of the day. Fear of imprisonment, fear of torture, fear of death, fear of losing friends, family, property or means of livelihood, fear of poverty, fear of isolation, fear of failure. A most insidious [meant to harm] form of fear is that which masquerades as common sense or even wisdom, condemning as foolish, reckless, insignificant or futile the small, daily acts of courage which help to preserve man's self-respect and inherent [part of one's basic nature] human dignity. It is not easy for a people conditioned by fear under the iron rule of the principle that might is right to free t hemselves from the enervating [weakening] miasma [harmful atmosphere] of fear. Yet even under the most crushing state machinery courage rises up again and again, for fear is not the natural state of civilized man.

The wellspring [source] of courage and endurance in the face of unbridled power is generally a firm belief in the sanctity of ethical principles combined with a historical sense that despite all setbacks the condition of man is set on an ultimate course for both spiritual and material advancement. . . . It is man's vision of a world fit for rational, civilized humanity which leads him to dare and to suffer to build societies free from want and fear. Concepts such as truth, justice and compassion cannot be dismissed as trite [overused and uninteresting] when these are often the only bulwarks [defenses] which stand against ruthless power.

Answers

1. Sample answer: It wasn't a fact yet, because Communism still existed. I think it was a reasoned judgment. As Reagan pointed out, the free world was wealthier, healthier, and more technologically advanced than the communist world. And then the fact that Gorbachev was moving the USSR toward freedom could be considered evidence that freedom was going to win.

Answers

1. In this essay, Suu Kyi speaks out against the fear imposed by Myanmar's military junta. It is probably very risky for her to state her opposition to the government. However, she refuses to let fear of the government keep her from writing this piece. In encouraging her audience to develop the courage necessary to resist those in power, she is also demonstrating that courage herself.

2. Essays like "Freedom from Fear" can remind people that resistance is possible. In showing that there are people like Suu Kyi resisting military rule and working to bring about a better society, others can feel hopeful and inspired to work for change as well. Audiences may feel encouraged to find even small, everyday ways of resisting the government. When people in other countries read passages like this, they may feel inspired to help bring about change, too.

ASSESSMENT

1. **Assess an Argument** How is this excerpt from Suu Kyi's essay an example of the courage she advocates?
2. **Draw Conclusions** How do you think essays like "Freedom from Fear" can help bring about political change in places such as Myanmar?
3. **Determine Author's Purpose** President Franklin D. Roosevelt used "freedom from fear" in his 1941 State of the Union, and the phrase is also included in the United Nation's Universal Declaration of Human Rights. Why do you think Suu Kyi chose this phrase for the title of her essay?

Answers

3. The title supports Suu Kyi's main idea that individuals must live courageously, rather than in fear. It also emphasizes the need for freedom, both for individuals currently living in fear and for Myanmar. Suu Kyi might have drawn on the words of Roosevelt and the UN to connect the struggles for freedom in Myanmar with a larger history of twentieth-century struggles for human rights. This helps give her argument more weight and might have helped audiences take seriously the political situation in her country.

["*Glory and Hope*," Nelson Mandela]

Introduction

Nelson Mandela delivered this speech after having been elected president in South Africa's first multiracial election in 1994. Knowing that the injustices of apartheid would be hard to overcome, Mandela asked the people to work together for peace and justice.

Primary Source

Today, all of us do, by our presence here, and by our celebrations . . . confer [give] glory and hope to newborn liberty.

Out of the experience of an extraordinary human disaster that lasted too long must be born a society of which all humanity will be proud.

Our daily deeds as ordinary South Africans must produce an actual South African reality that will reinforce humanity' s belief in justice, strengthen its confidence in the nobility of the human soul and sustain all our hopes for a glorious life for all. . . .

The time for the healing of the wounds has come . . . .

The time to build is upon us.

We have, at last, achieved our political emancipation [freedom from bondage or control by others]. We pledge ourselves to liberate all our people from the continuing bondage [slavery] of poverty, deprivation [lack of materials necessary for survival], suffering, gender and other discrimination. . . .

We have triumphed in the effort to implant [insert] hope in the breasts of the millions of our people. We enter into a covenant [binding agreement] that we shall build the society in which all South Africans, both black and white, will be able to walk tall, without any fear in their hearts, assured of their inalienable right to human dignity—a rainbow nation at peace with itself and the world. . . .

We understand it still that there is no easy road to freedom.

We know it well that none of us acting alone can achieve success.

We must therefore act together as a united people, for national reconciliation [a settling of differences that results in harmony], for nation building, for the birth of a new world.

Let there be justice for all. Let there be peace for all. Let there be work, bread, water, and salt for all. . . . The sun shall never set on so glorious a human achievement!

ASSESSMENT

1. **Explain an Argument** When apartheid ended, there was a danger of a backlash by blacks against whites who supported apartheid. How does Mandela's speech respond to that danger?
2. **Determine Author's Point of View** How would you describe the tone of Mandela's speech? How does this tone reflect Mandela's view of his country and its future?
3. **Determine Author's Purpose** Why do you think Mandela talks about building a new world, not just a new South Africa?

Answers

1. Mandela's speech emphasizes unity and working together. In this way, he reassures whites that there will not be a divisive backlash against those who supported apartheid. Mandela does not talk about retribution or the ills of apartheid. He emphasizes moving forward, rather than dwelling on the past. This approach probably eased concerns about backlash as well.

2. Mandela's speech is very positive and inspiring. It emphasizes hope and suggests that there is a better future awaiting South Africa. The tone suggests that Mandela has an optimistic view of his country and the future. Although he mentions that there will be challenges, he sounds confident that they will be overcome.

3. Possible answer: Mandela probably knew that many people were listening to his speech, not just South Africans. Mandela's vision of a new future probably could not happen only in one country, but would require a worldwide effort to bring justice, freedom, and dignity to all people.

Sequence TEKS 29.F

Sequence means "order," and placing things in the correct order is very important. What would happen if you tried to put toppings on a pizza before you put down the dough for the crust? When studying history, you need to analyze the information by sequencing significant events, individuals, and time periods in order to understand them. Practice this skill by using the reading below. Which words indicate sequence?

> **The Persian Empire** Before modern times, Iran was called Persia. Ancient Persia was influenced by Mesopotamian civilization, in modern-day Iraq. Around 550 b.c., the Persian king Cyrus the Great conquered the Babylonian empire, in Mesopotamia, and many other lands. He created the Persian empire.
>
> Cyrus and the rulers who followed him spread Persian control from modern Pakistan and Afghanistan in the east to modern Turkey, Cyprus, and Egypt in the west. This empire lasted about two hundred years. A Persian ruler was called the King of Kings, or the Great King.

[1.] Identify the topic and the main events that relate to the topic. Quickly skim titles and headings to determine the topic of the passage. As you read the passage, write a list of significant events, individuals, or time periods related to the topic.

[2.] Note any dates and time words such as "before" and "after" that indicate the chronological order of events. Look through your list of events, individuals, or time periods and write down the date for each. This will give you information to apply absolute chronology by sequencing the events, individuals, or time periods. Remember that some events may have taken place over a number of months or years. Is your date the time when the event started or ended? Make sure to note enough details that you can remember the importance of the information. If no date is given, look for words such as "before" or "after" that can tell you where to place this event, time period, or individual compared to others on your list. This will allow you to apply relative chronology by sequencing the events, individuals, or time periods.

[3.] Determine the time range of the events. Place the events in chronological order on a timeline. Look for the earliest and latest events, individuals, or time periods on your list. The span of time between the first and last entries gives you the time range. To apply absolute chronology, sequence the entries by writing the date of the first event on the left side of a piece of paper and the date of the last event on the right side. Draw a line connecting the two events. This will be your timeline. Once you have drawn your timeline, put the events in order by date along the line. Label their dates. To apply relative chronology, sequence the significant individuals, events, or time periods on an undated timeline, in the order that they happened. You now have a clear image of the important events related to this topic. You can organize and interpret information from visuals by analyzing the information and applying absolute or relative chronology to the events. This will help you understand the topic better when you can see how events caused or led to other events. You will also be able to analyze information by developing connections between historical events over time.

1029

Categorize TEKS 29.F

When you analyze information by categorizing, you create a system that helps you sort items into categories, or groups with shared characteristics, so that you can understand the information. Categorizing helps you see what groups of items have in common. What categories are shown on the chart below? Name at least one challenge you would list under each category. Then create your own chart following the steps below.

Foreign Policy Challenge	Economic Challenge

[1.] Identify similarities and differences among items you need to understand. You need to pay careful attention and sometimes do research to find the similarities and differences among the facts, topics, or objects that you need to understand. Scientists find groups, or categories, of related animals by analyzing the details of the animals' bodies. For example, insects with similar wings, legs, and mouthparts probably belong in the same category. Gather similar information about all the things you need to understand. For example, if you know the location of one thing, try to find the locations of all the things you are studying. If you have different types of information about your topics, you will not be able to group them easily.

[2.] Create a system to group items with common characteristics. Once you have gathered similar kinds of information on the items you need to understand, look for items that share characteristics or features. Create categories based on a feature shared by all of the facts, topics, or objects you need to understand. For example, if you have gathered information on the population and political systems of several countries, you could categorize them by the size of their population or their type of political system.

1030

[3.] Form the groupings. Put each of the items that you are studying into one of the categories that you have created. If some items do not fit, you may need to make a new category or modify your categories. Label each category for the characteristic shared by its members. Examples of labels for categories might include "Countries with more than 100 million people," "Countries with fewer than 1 million people," "Democracies," or "Dictatorships."

Analyze Cause and Effect TEKS 29.F

When you analyze information by identifying cause-and-effect relationships, you find how one event leads to the next. It is important to find evidence that one event caused another. If one event happened earlier than another, it did not necessarily cause the later event. Understanding causes and effects can help you solve problems. Practice this skill as you read the text below. What words in the text indicate the causes of the end of communism in the Soviet Union and the eastern bloc? Which indicate effects?

> Economic stagnation, external pressure from the West, and internal dissent eroded the Soviet bloc. In the 1980s, the reformist Soviet leader Mikhail Gorbachev pushed both *perestroika*, a wide-ranging restructuring of political and economic life, and *glasnost*, a policy of openness where the Soviet government increased its tolerance of dissent and freedom of expression. The hunger for openness spread to the central European Soviet bloc countries. In 1989, the Polish reform party Solidarity competed in parliamentary elections, Hungarians enjoyed the freedom to visit Austria, and pro-democratic protests in East Germany led Communist governments to fold throughout the region.

[1.] Choose a starting point of observation. When trying to understand a historical event, choose the time of that event. If you are trying to understand a current event, you can work backward from a starting point in the present.

[2.] Consider earlier events to try to find connections to your starting point, including any language that signals causes. Put the evidence together to identify true causes. When reading, look for events that come before your starting point. Analyze whether these earlier events caused later events. Identify words that signal cause, such as "reason," "because," and "led to." Analyze the information by developing connections between historical events. Make sure that there is evidence showing that the earlier events caused the later events and did not just happen earlier.

[3.] Consider later events to try to find connections to your starting point, including any language that signals effects. Put the evidence together to determine true effects. Look for events that come after your starting point. Analyze the information in order to determine whether these later events are effects of earlier events. Identify words that signal effect, such as "led to," "so," and "therefore." Make sure that there is evidence showing that these later events were caused by earlier events and did not just happen later.

1031

[4.] Summarize the cause-and-effect relationship and draw conclusions. Once you have identified the cause-and-effect relationships between different events, describe these relationships. Draw a diagram that develops the connections between the two historical events. Draw conclusions about any relationships that you see.

Compare and Contrast TEKS 29.F

When you analyze information by comparing and contrasting two or more things, you look for similarities and differences between them. This skill helps you understand the things that you are comparing and contrasting. It is also a skill that you can use in making choices. Practice this skill as you study the Venn diagram comparing socialism and communism. What words would you use to compare and contrast the two economic systems?

COMPARING AND CONTRASTING SOCIALISM AND COMMUNISM

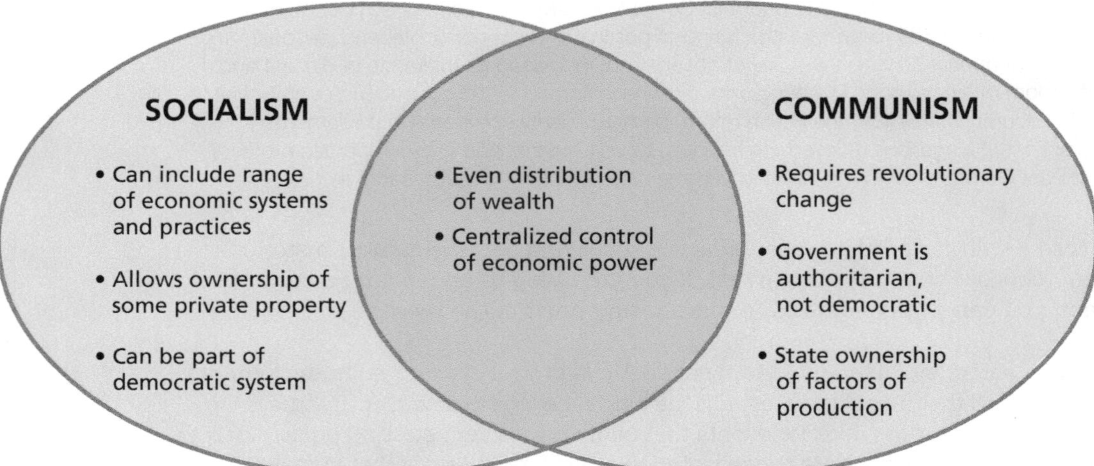
SOCIALISM
• Can include range of economic systems and practices
• Allows ownership of some private property
• Can be part of democratic system
• Even distribution of wealth
• Centralized control of economic power
COMMUNISM
• Requires revolutionary change
• Government is authoritarian, not democratic
• State ownership of factors of production

[1.] Look for related topics and characteristics that describe them. When you are looking for similarities and differences between two things, it can help to start by identifying relationships between them. What do the two things have in common? If two things have nothing in common, such as a dog and a piece of pie, it will be difficult to find similarities or differences. On the other hand, you can compare and contrast two countries or political systems. Look through the information you have on the things or topics you want to compare and contrast, and identify the characteristics, or features, that describe those things or topics.

[2.] Look for words that signal comparison ("both," "similar to," "also") or contrast ("unlike," "different," "instead"). Look for words that show comparison, or similarity, and those that show contrast, or difference. Take notes on these similarities and differences. This will make it possible to analyze information more quickly.

[**3.**] Identify similarities and differences in the topics, and draw conclusions about them. Look through your notes and analyze the ways in which your topics are similar and different. Usually, topics have both similarities and differences. Try to find patterns in these similarities and differences. For example, all the similarities between two countries might be related to climate, and all the differences might be related to economics. Draw conclusions based on these patterns. In this example, you might conclude that a country's economy does not depend on its climate. Identifying similarities and differences by comparing and contrasting two topics lets you draw conclusions that help you analyze both topics as well as other topics like them.

Identify Main Ideas and Details TEKS 29.F

You can analyze information in a selection by finding the main idea. A main idea is the most important point in a selection. Identifying the main idea will help you remember details, such as names, dates, and events, which should support the main idea. Practice this skill by reading the paragraph on this page. Find the main idea of this paragraph and the supporting details.

> During his first hundred days in office, which became known as the Hundred Days, Roosevelt proposed and Congress passed 15 major bills. These measures had three goals: relief, recovery, and reform. Roosevelt wanted to provide relief from the immediate hardships of the depression and achieve a long-term economic recovery. He also instituted reforms to prevent future depressions.

[**1.**] Scan titles, headings, and visuals before reading to see what the selection is about. Often, important ideas are included in titles, headings, and other special text. Special text may be primary sources, words that are highlighted, or ideas listed with bullet points. Also, take a look at visuals and captions. By analyzing these parts of the text, you should quickly get a sense of the main idea of the article.

[**2.**] Read the selection and then identify the main point of the selection, the point that the rest of the selection supports: this is the main idea. Read through the selection to identify the main idea. Sometimes, the main idea will be the first or second sentence of one of the first few paragraphs. Sometimes, it will be the last sentence of the first paragraph. Other times, no single sentence will tell you the main idea. You will have to come up with your own sentence answering the question, "What is the main point of this selection?"

[**3.**] Find details or statements within the selection that support or build on the main idea. Once you have identified the main idea, look for details that support the main idea. Many or most of the details should be related to the main idea. If you find that many of the details are not related to what you think is the main idea, you may not have identified the main idea correctly. Identify the main idea that the details in the selection support. Analyze the information in the text by finding the main idea and supporting details.

1033

Summarize TEKS 29.F

When you analyze information by summarizing, you restate the main points of a passage in your own words. Using your own words helps you understand the information. Summarizing will help you understand a text and prepare for tests or assignments based on the text. Practice this skill by follow the steps to summarize the excerpt below.

> One of the most terrifying aspects of the Cold War was the arms race that began right after World War II. At first, the United States was the only nuclear power. By 1949, however, the Soviet Union had also developed nuclear weapons.
>
> Critics argued that a nuclear war would destroy both sides. Yet each superpower wanted to be able to deter the other from launching its nuclear weapons. Both sides engaged in a race to match each other's new weapons. The result was a "balance of terror." Mutually assured destruction—in which each side knew that the other side would itself be destroyed if it launched its weapons—discouraged nuclear war. Still, people around the world lived in constant fear of nuclear doom.

[1.] Identify and write down the main point of each paragraph in your own words. You may identify the main idea right at the beginning of each paragraph. In other cases, you will have to figure out the main idea. As you read each paragraph, ask yourself, "What is the point this paragraph makes?" The point the paragraph makes is the main idea. Write this idea down in your own words.

[2.] Use these main points to write a general statement of the overall main idea of the passage in your own words. Once you have written down the main idea for each paragraph, write down the main idea of the passage. Write the main idea in your own words. If you have trouble identifying the main idea of the passage, review the titles and headings in the passage. Often, titles and headings relate to the main idea. Also, the writer may state the main idea in the first paragraph of the passage. The main idea of a passage should answer the question, "What is the point this passage makes?"

[3.] Use this general statement as a topic sentence for your summary. Then, write a paragraph tying together the main points of the passage. Leave out unimportant details. Analyze the information in the passage by summarizing. Use the main idea of the passage as a topic sentence for your summary paragraph. Use the main ideas that you identified for each paragraph of the passage to write sentences supporting the main idea of the passage. Leave out details that are not needed to understand the main idea of the passage. Your summary should be in your own words, and it should be much shorter than the original passage. Once your summary is written, review it to make sure that it contains all the main points of the passage. If any are missing, revise your summary to include them. If the summary includes unimportant details, remove them.

Generalize TEKS 29.F

One good way to analyze materials about a particular subject is to make generalizations and predictions. What are the patterns and connections that link the different materials? What can you say about the different materials that is true of all them? Practice this skill by reading the following statements. What generalization can you make about how new thought and inventions change the economy and society?

- Beginning in the 1500s, profound changes took place in the sciences. These new understandings about the physical world became part of what is now called the Scientific Revolution. These startling discoveries radically changed the way Europeans viewed the physical world.
- The Industrial Revolution brought radical change to people's lives. Before industrialization, people lived in villages and farmed. The economy was based on farming and craftwork. By the late 1800s, the economy had shifted. Manufacturing by machine in factories and urbanization became commonplace.
- The invention of the computer in the twentieth century caused an unprecedented information revolution. It has helped spur development of the modern global economy and society. Few, if any, aspects of modern life remain untouched by computers.

[1.] Make a list. Listing all of the specific details and facts about a subject will help you find patterns and connections.

[2.] Generate a statement. From your list of facts and specific details, decide what most of the items listed have in common. Analyze your information by making generalizations and predictions.

[3.] Ensure your generalization is logical and well supported by facts. Generalizations can be valid or invalid. A generalization that is not logical or supported by facts is invalid.

Make Predictions TEKS 29.F

You can analyze information by making generalizations and predictions. Predictions are educated guesses about the future, based on clues you find in written material and information you already have. When you analyze information by making generalizations and predictions, you are thinking critically about the material you read. Practice this skill by analyzing the passage below and predicting the impact this epidemic might have on society and the economy.

> In the mid 1300s, a disease moved throughout Europe and North Africa. The bubonic plague, or Black Death, spread quickly. Boils erupted all over the body—a sign that the plague would likely claim more victims because the disease spread through contact. The plague brought terror and bewilderment, as people had no way to stop the disease. Entire villages were wiped out. It ravaged Europe: one in three people died.

[**1.**] Review the content. Read your material carefully and research any terms or concepts that are new to you. It's important to understand the material before analyzing the information to make a prediction.

[**2.**] Look for clues. Gathering evidence is an important part of making predictions. Look for important words, statements, and evidence that seem to support the writer's point of view. Ask questions about what you are reading, including who, what, where, when, why, and how. Look for and analyze clues to help you generalize and predict.

[**3.**] Consider what you already know. Use related prior knowledge and/or connect to your own experiences to help you make an informed prediction. If you have experience with the subject matter, you have a much better chance of making an accurate prediction.

[**4.**] Generate a list of predictions. After studying the content, list the clues you've found. Then use these clues, plus your prior knowledge, to form your predictions. List as many possible outcomes as you can based on clues in the material and the questions you have considered.

Draw Inferences TEKS 29.F

What is the author trying to tell you? To make a determination about the author's message, you analyze information by drawing inferences and conclusions. You consider details and descriptions included in the text, compare and contrast the text to prior knowledge you have about the subject, and then form a conclusion about the author's intent. Practice this skill by analyzing the primary source report below to infer the feelings of the crew towards Magellan.

> . . . Talking began amongst the crews about the old eternal hatred between the Portuguese and the Spaniards, and about Magellan's being a Portuguese. He, they said, could do nothing more glorious for his own country than to cast away this fleet, with so many men. Nor was it credible [believable] that he should wish to discover the Moluccas [a group of spice islands]. . . . Nor even had their course begun to turn towards those happy Moluccas, but rather to distant snow and ice, and to perpetual storms.
>
> Magellan, very much enraged by these sayings, punished the men, but rather more harshly than was proper for a foreigner, especially when commanding in a distant country.
>
> –Maximillianus Transylvanus, report to King Charles I of Spain

[**1.**] Study the image or text. Consider all of the details and descriptions included. What is the author trying to tell you? Look for context clues that hint at the topic and subject matter.

[**2.**] Make a connection. Use related prior knowledge to connect to the text or image. Analyze information by asking questions such as who, what, where, when, and how. Look for cause-and-effect relationships; compare and contrast. This strategy will help you think beyond the available surface details to understand what the author is suggesting or implying.

[3.] Form a conclusion. When you draw an inference, you combine your own ideas with evidence and details you found within the text or image to form a new conclusion. This action leads you to a new understanding of the material.

Draw Conclusions TEKS 29.F

When you analyze information by drawing inferences and conclusions, you connect the ideas in a text with what you already know in order to understand a topic better. Using this skill, you can "fill in the blanks" to see the implications or larger meaning of the information in a text. Practice this skill by reading the excerpt of text below. What conclusions can you draw based on the information in the passage?

> Indian merchants and Hindu priests filtered into Southeast Asia, slowly spreading their culture. Later, Buddhist monks and scholars introduced Theravada beliefs. Following the path of trade and religion came the influence of writing, law, government, art, architecture, and farming.
>
> In time, local Indian families exercised considerable power in Southeast Asia. Also, people from Southeast Asia visited India as pilgrims or students. As these contacts increased, Indian beliefs and ideas won widespread acceptance. Indian influence reached its peak between 500 and 1000.
>
> Long after Hinduism and Buddhism took root in Southeast Asia, Indians carried a third religion, Islam, into the region. By the 1200s, Muslims ruled northern India. From there, traders spread Islamic beliefs and Muslim culture throughout the islands of Indonesia and as far east as the Philippines. Today, Indonesia has the largest Muslim population of any nation in the world.

[1.] Identify the topic, main idea, and supporting details. Before reading, look at the titles and headings within a reading. This should give you a good idea of the topic, or the general subject, of a text. After reading, identify the main idea. The main idea falls within the topic and answers the question, "What is the main point of this text?" Find the details that the author presents to support the main idea.

[2.] Use what you know to make a judgment about the information. Think about what you know about this topic or a similar topic. For example, you may read that the English settlers of Jamestown suffered from starvation because many of them were not farmers and did not know how to grow food. Analyzing the information about their situation and what you know about people, you could draw the conclusion that these settlers must have had little idea, or the wrong idea, about the conditions that they would find in America.

www.PearsonTexas.com
View Video Tutorials and other 21st Century Skills

[3.] Check and adjust your judgment until you can draw a well-supported conclusion. Look for details within the reading that support your judgment. Reading a little further, you find that these settlers thought that they would become rich after discovering gold or silver, or through trading with Native Americans for furs. You can use this information to support your conclusion that the settlers were mistaken about the con ditions that they would find in America. By analyzing the information further, you might infer that the settlers had inaccurate information about America. To support your conclusions, you could look for reliable sources on what these settlers knew before they left England.

Interpret Sources TEKS 29.B, 29.D, 29.H

Outlines and reports are good sources of information. In order to interpret these sources, though, you'll need to identify the type of document you're reading, identify the main idea, organize the details of information, and evaluate the source for point of view and bias. Practice this skill by finding a newspaper or online report on a recent meeting between the President or Secretary of State and a foreign leader. What steps will you take to interpret this report?

[1.] Identify the type of document. Is the document a primary or secondary source? Determine when, where, and why it was written.

[2.] Examine the source to identify the main idea. After identifying the main idea, identify details or sections of text that support the main idea. If the source is an outline or report, identify the topic and subtopics; review the supporting details under each subtopic. Organize the information from the outline or report and think about how it connects back to the overall topic listed at the top of the outline or report.

[3.] Evaluate the source for point of view and bias. Primary sources often have a strong point of view or bias; it is important to analyze primary sources critically to determine their validity. Evaluating each source will help you interpret the information they contain.

Create Databases TEKS 30.C

Databases are organized collections of information which can be analyzed and interpreted. You decide on a topic, organize data, use a spreadsheet, and then pose questions which will help you to analyze and interpret your data. Practice this skill by creating a database of population statistics for five countries in the Middle East. Show information for each country for each decade from 1910 to 2010, then compare the statistics. What conclusions can you draw from your data?

[1.] Decide on a topic. Identify the information that you will convert into a table. This information may come from various sources, including textbooks, reference works, and Internet sites.

[2.] Organize the data. Study the information and decide what to include in your table. Only include data that is pertinent and available. Based on the data you choose, organize your information. Identify how many columns there will be and what the column headings will be. Decide the order in which you are going to list the data in the rows.

[3.] Use a spreadsheet. A spreadsheet is a computer software tool that allows you to organize data so that it can be analyzed. Spreadsheets allow you to make calculations as well as input data. Use a spreadsheet to help you create summaries of your data. For instance, you can compute the sum, average, minimum, and maximum values of the data. Use the graphing features of your spreadsheet program to show the data visually.

[4.] Analyze the data. Once all of your data is entered and you have made any calculations you need, you are ready to pose questions to analyze and interpret your data. Organize the information from the database and use it to form conclusions. Be sure to draw conclusions that can be supported by the data available.

Analyze Data and Models TEKS 29.H

Data and models can provide useful information about geographic distributions and patterns. To make sense of that information, though, you need to pose and answer questions about data and models. What does the data say? What does it mean? What patterns can you find? Practice this skill as you study the data below.

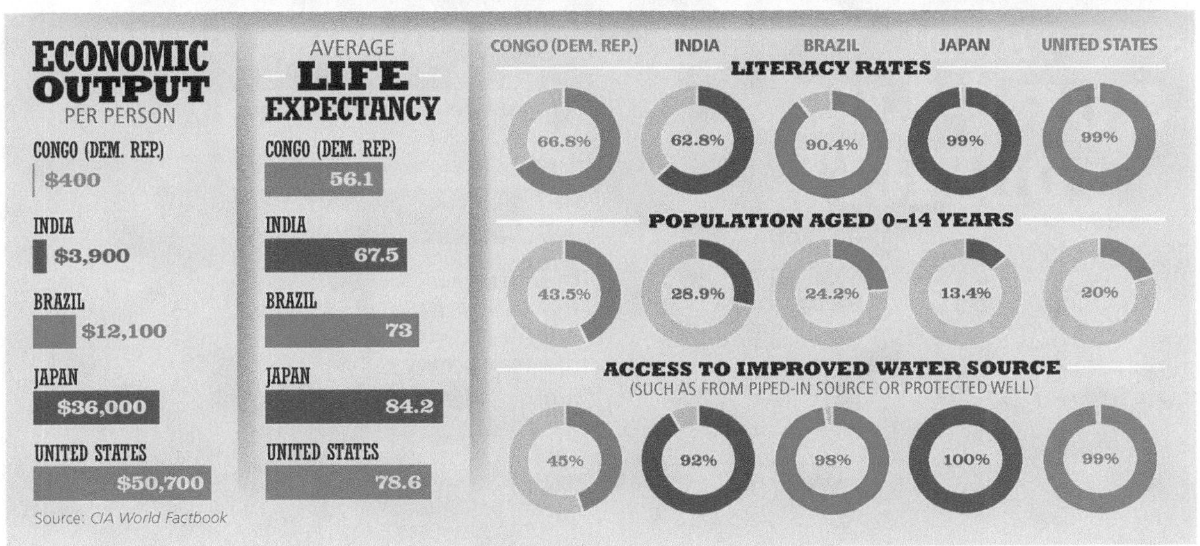

Source: *CIA World Factbook*

[1.] Read the title to learn the geographic distributions represented by the data set, graph, or model.

[2.] Read the data given. When reviewing a graph, read the labels and the key to help you comprehend the data provided. Pose and answer questions to further understand the material. For example, you might ask "Who could use this data?" or "How could this data be used?" or even "Why is this data presented in this particular format?" Thinking critically about the data presented will help you make predictions and comprehend the data.

[3.] Study the numbers, lines, and/or colors to find out what the graphs or data represent. Next, find similarities and differences between multiple models of the same data. Do any additional research to find out more about why the information in the models differs.

[4.] Interpret the graph, data set, or model. Look for interesting geographic distributions and patterns in the data. Look at changes over time or compare information from different categories. Draw conclusions.

Read Charts, Graphs, and Tables TEKS 29.H

If you pose and answer questions about charts, graphs, or tables you find in books or online, you can find out all sorts of information, such as how many calories are in your favorite foods or what the value of a used car is. Analyzing and interpreting the information you find in thematic charts, graphs, and tables can help you make decisions in your life. Practice this skill as you study the inforgraphic below.

TRADE SURPLUS & DEFICIT
TRADE SURPLUS
occurs when a country exports more than it imports
TRADE DEFICIT
occurs when a country imports more than it exports
TRADE BETWEEN BRITAIN & CHINA 1830
EXPORTS FROM BRITAIN TO CHINA
£13,244,702
(mainly woolen and mechanical goods)
EXPORTS FROM CHINA TO BRITAIN
£72,680,541
(mainly tea, silk, porcelain)
£ = British Pound sterling, the basic unit of British currency
Britain had a substantial trade deficit with China, mostly due to Britons' love of tea. Britain started importing tea from China in the 16th century. By 1800, annual per capita tea consumption was over two pounds, or about two cups a day.
Sources: British Trade and the Opening of China 1800–1842 by Michael Greenberg; The Cambridge Economic History of Modern Britain edited by Roderick Floud and Paul Johnson

[**1.**] Identify the title and labels of a chart, graph, or table, and read the key, if there is one, to understand the information presented. The title often tells you the topic of the chart, graph, or table, or the type of information you will find. Make sure you understand how the graph shows information. A key or legend often appears in a small box near the edge of the graph or chart. The key will tell you the meaning of lines, colors, or symbols used on the chart or graph. Notice also the column and row headings, and use your reading skills to figure out the meanings of any words you don't know.

[**2.**] Determine consistencies and inconsistencies, to see whether there is a trend in a graph, chart, or table. Organize information from visuals such as charts and graphs and decide whether or not there is a trend or pattern in the information that you see. Evaluate the data and determine whether the trend is consistent, or steady. Remember that there could be some inconsistencies, or exceptions to the pattern. Try not to miss the overall pattern because of a couple of exceptions.

[**3.**] Draw conclusions about the data in a chart, graph, or table. Once you understand the information, try to analyze and interpret the information and draw conclusions. If you see a pattern, does the pattern help you to understand the topic or predict future events?

[**4.**] Create a chart or graph to make the data more understandable or to view the data in a different way. Does the data in the chart or graph help you answer questions you have about the topic or see any causes or effects? For example, you could use your mathematical skills to create circle graphs or bar graphs that visually organize the data in a different way that allows you to interpret the data differently.

[**5.**] Use the data or information in charts and graphs to understand an issue or make decisions. Use your social studies skills to make inferences, draw conclusions, and take a stand on the issue.

Create Charts and Maps TEKS 30.C

Thematic charts, graphs, and maps are visual tools for representing information. When you create a thematic chart, graph, or map you will start by selecting the type of data you want to represent. Then you will find appropriate data to include, organize your data, and then create symbols and a key to help others understand your chart, graph, or map. Practice this skill by creating a map of Asia showing which countries have a democratic government. Use computer software to generate the map, color the democratic countries, and create the key.

[**1.**] To create a chart or map, first select a region or set of data. Use a map to represent data pertaining to a specific region or location; use a chart to represent trends reflected in a set of data.

[2.] Research and find the data you would like to present in the chart or map. Your choice of data will be based on the theme you wish to explore. For example, a chart or map that explores the theme of changing demographics in Texas might include data about the location of different ethnic groups in Texas in the nineteenth, twentieth, and twenty-first centuries.

[3.] Organize the data according to the specific format of your chart or map.

[4.] Create symbols, a key (as needed), and a title. Create symbols to represent each piece of data you would like to highlight. Keep each symbol simple and easy to understand. After you have created the symbols, place them in a key. Add a title to your map or chart that summarizes the information presented. Your symbols and key will make it easier for others to interpret your charts and maps.

Analyze Political Cartoons TEKS 29.C

Political cartoons are visual commentaries about events or people. As you learn to analyze political cartoons, you will learn to identify bias in cartoons and interpret their meaning. You can start by carefully examining the cartoon and considering its possible meanings. Then you can draw conclusions based on your analysis. Practice this skill as you study the political cartoon below.

1042

[1.] Fully examine the cartoon. Identify any symbols in the cartoon, read the text and title, and identify the main character or characters. Analyze the cartoon to identify bias and determine what each image or symbol represents. Conduct research if you need more information to decipher the cartoon.

[2.] Consider the meaning. Think about how the cartoonist uses the images and symbols in the cartoon to express his or her opinion about a subject. Try to interpret the artist's purpose in creating the image.

[3.] Draw conclusions. Use what you have gleaned from the image itself, plus any prior knowledge or research, to analyze, interpret, and form a conclusion about the artist's intentions.

Read Physical Maps TEKS 29.H

What mountain range is closest to where you live? What major rivers are closest to you? To find out, you would look at a physical map. You can use appropriate reading skills to interpret social studies information such as that found on different kinds of maps. Physical maps show physical features, such as elevation, mountains, valleys, oceans, rivers, deserts, and plains. Practice this skill as you study the map below.

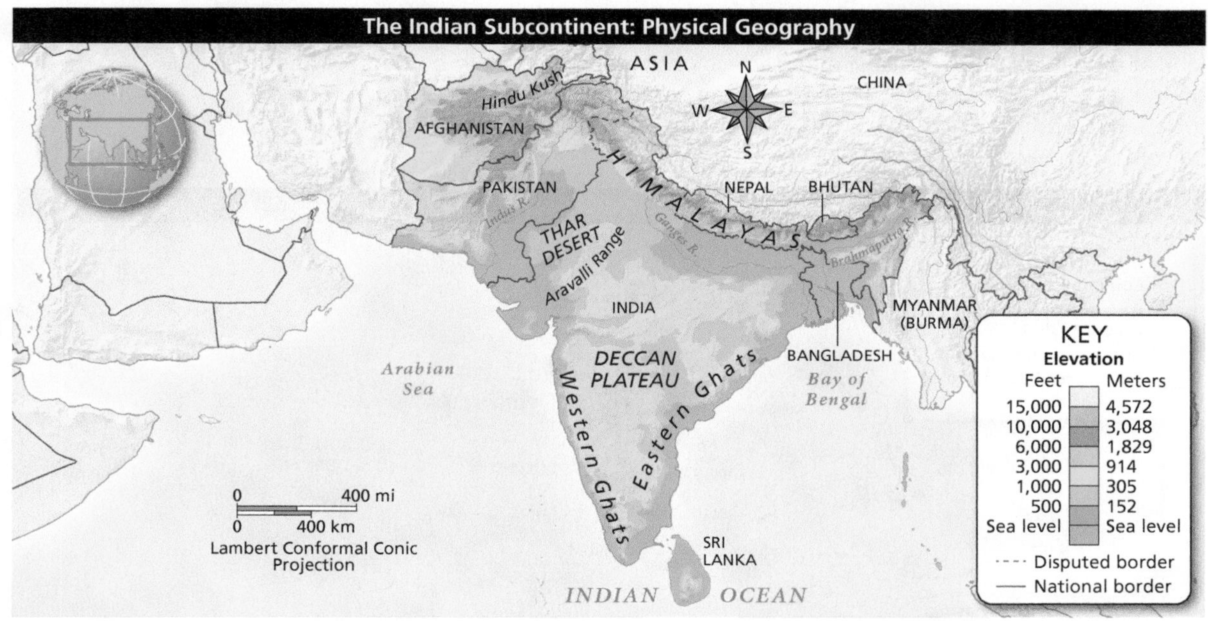

[1.] Identify the title and region shown on a map. A map's title can help you to identify the region covered by the map. The title may also tell you the type of information you will find on the map. If the map has no title, you can identify the region by reading the labels on the map.

[2.] Use the map key to interpret symbols and colors on a map. A key or legend often appears in a small box near the edge of the map. The legend will tell you the meaning of colors, symbols, or other patterns on the map. On a physical map, colors from the key often show elevation, or height above sea level, on the map.

[3.] Identify physical features, such as mountains, valleys, oceans, and rivers. Using labels on the map and colors and symbols from the key, identify the physical features on the map. The information in the key allows you to interpret the information from visuals such as a map. Rivers, oceans, lakes, and other bodies of water are usually colored blue. Colors from the key may indicate higher and lower elevation, or there may be shading on the map that shows mountains.

[4.] Draw conclusions about the region based on natural resources and physical features. Once you understand all the symbols and colors on the map, try to interpret the information from the map. Is it very mountainous or mostly flat? Does it have a coastline? Does the region have lots of lakes and rivers that suggest a good water supply? Pose and answer questions about geographic distributions and patterns shown on the map. Physical maps can give you an idea of lifestyle and economic activities of people in the region.

Read Political Maps TEKS 29.H

What is the capital of your state? What countries border China? To find out, you could look at a political map. Political maps are colorful maps that show borders, or lines dividing states or countries. They also show capitals and sometimes major cities. Practice reading political maps by studying the map below.

[**1.**] Identify the title of the political map and the region shown. A map's title can help you identify the region covered by the map. The title may also tell you the type of information you will find on the map. If the map has no title, you can identify the region by reading the labels on the map.

[**2.**] Use the map key to interpret symbols and colors on the map. A key or legend often appears in a small box near the edge of the map. The key will help you interpret information from visuals, including maps, by telling you the meaning of colors, symbols, or other patterns on the visual.

[**3.**] Identify boundaries between nations or states. Evaluate government data, such as borders, using the map. It is often easy to see borders, because each state or country will be a different color. If you cannot find the borders, check the key to find the lines used to mark borders on the map.

[**4.**] Locate capital cities. Look at the key to see how capital cities are shown on the map. They are often marked with a special symbol, such as a star.

[**5.**] Draw conclusions about the region based on the map. Once you understand all the symbols and colors on the map, use appropriate reading and mathematical skills to interpret social studies information, such as that shown on the map, in order to draw conclusions about the region. For example, are some countries very large with many cities? These countries are likely to be powerful and influential.

Read Special-Purpose Maps TEKS 29.H

Some maps show specific kinds of information. These special- purpose maps may show features such as climate zones, ancient trade routes, economic and government data, geographic patterns, or population. Locating and interpreting information from visuals, including special-purpose maps, is an important research skill. Practice this skill as you study this map.

www.PearsonTexas.com
View Video Tutorials and other 21st Century Skills

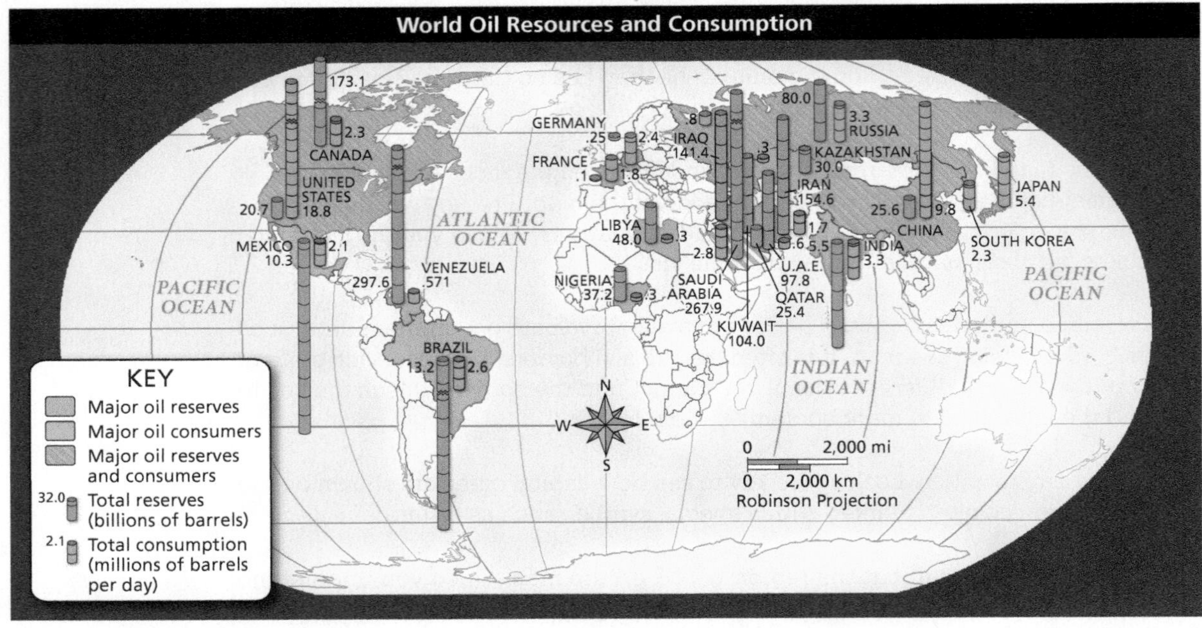

[1.] Identify the title and determine the purpose of a map. A map's title can help you identify the region covered by the map. The title may also tell you the purpose of the map. If the map has no title, see what information the map shows to determine its purpose.

[2.] Use the map key to make sense of symbols and colors on a map. A key or legend often appears in a small box near the edge of the map. The key will tell you the meaning of colors, symbols, or other patterns on the map. Special-purpose maps use these colors and symbols to present information.

[3.] Draw conclusions about the region shown on a map. Once you understand all the symbols and colors on the map, you can use appropriate skills, including reading and mathematical skills, to analyze and interpret social studies information such as maps. You can pose and answer questions about geographic patterns and distributions that are shown on maps. For example, a precipitation or climate map will show you which areas get lots of rainfall and which are very dry. You can evaluate government and economic data using maps. For example, a population map will show you which regions have lots of people and which have small, scattered populations. A historical map will show you the locations of ancient empires or trade routes. Thematic maps focus on a single theme or topic about a region. For example, you can interpret information from a thematic map representing various aspects of Texas during the nineteenth or twentieth century by studying the Great Military Map, which shows forts established in Texas during the nineteenth century, or by studying a map covering Texas during the Great Depression and World War II. By mapping this kind of detailed information, special-purpose maps can help you understand a region's history or geography.

Use Parts of a Map TEKS 29.H

If you understand how to organize and interpret information from visuals, including maps, you will be able to find the information you are looking for. Understanding how to use the parts of a map will help you find locations of specific places and estimate distances between different places. Practice this skill as you study the map below.

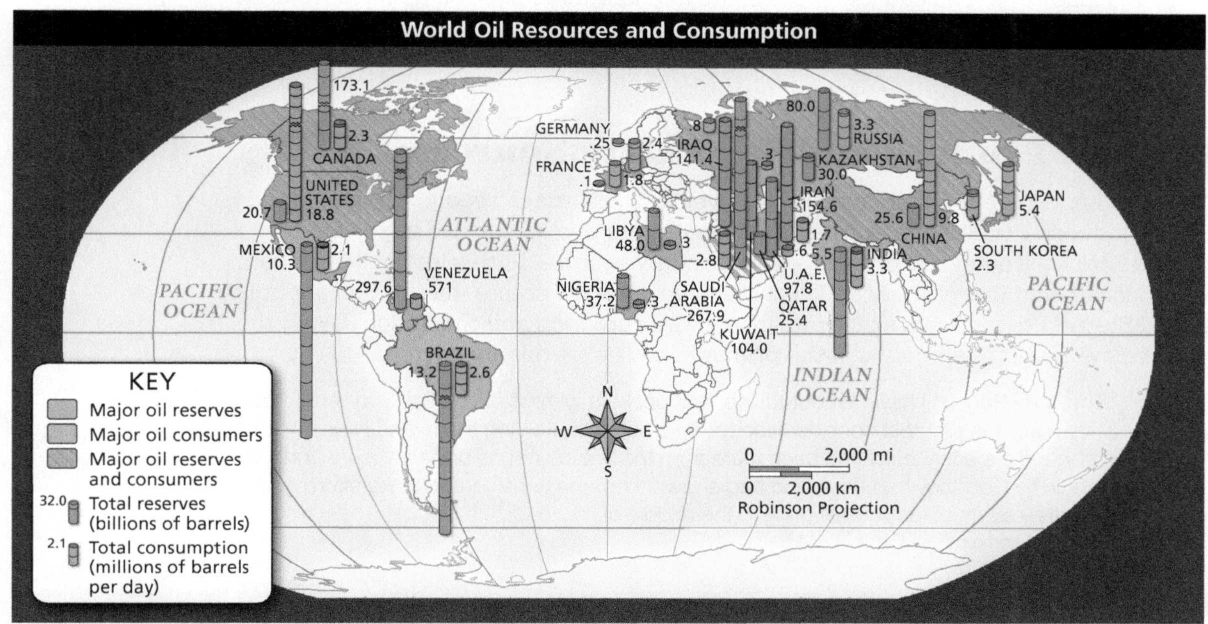

[1.] Identify the title and region of a map. Use appropriate reading skills to interpret social studies information such as map labels. A map's title can help you to identify the region covered by the map. The title may also tell you the type of information you will find on the map. If the map has no title, you can identify the region by reading the labels on the map.

[2.] Use the compass rose to determine direction. Although on most maps north is at the top of the map, you should always double check the compass rose. Often, on the compass rose, the first letter of each direction represents that direction. For example, "N" represents the direction "north." Some compass roses are as simple as an arrow pointing north.

[3.] Use the scale to estimate the distance between places. Use appropriate mathematical skills to interpret social studies information such as a map scale. The scale on a map shows how a measurement on the map compares to the distance on the ground. For example, if one inch on the map represents a mile, the number of inches between two places on the map is the distance in miles.

1047

[4.] Use the key or legend on a map to find information about colors or symbols on a map. A key or legend often appears in a small box near the edge of the map. The legend will tell you the meaning of colors, symbols, or other patterns on the map.

[5.] Use the latitude and longitude grid to determine absolute locations. An absolute location is an exact description of a location on Earth's surface based on latitude and longitude. You can use the latitude and longitude lines on a map to find the absolute location of a place.

Analyze Primary and Secondary Sources TEKS 29.C

Primary sources are firsthand accounts of events. By contrast, secondary sources are secondhand accounts of events. Both sources are useful, but it is important to differentiate between valid primary and secondary sources. In this lesson, you'll learn how to locate and use primary and secondary sources to acquire information about the United States. Practice this skill by analyzing the quotation and the image. Using the steps below, distinguish between the primary and the secondary source.

> "They [the Spanish] have set out to line their pockets with gold. . . . The Spaniards have shown not the slightest consideration for these people, treating them (and I speak from first-hand experience, having been there from the outset) not as brute animals—indeed, I would to God they had done and had shown them the consideration they afford their animals—so much as piles of dung in the middle of the road."
>
> –Bartolomé de Las Casas, 1542

www.PearsonTexas.com
View Video Tutorials and other 21st Century Skills

[1.] Determine who created the source as well as when and why it was created. Determine whether it is a primary or secondary source. Identify the author of the document. Next, look for the date the document was written or the date when the document was first published. Most primary sources are written close to the date of the events described. Secondary sources are often written well after the events described. Firsthand observers or participants in an event create primary sources. People who did not witness an event create secondary sources. Primary sources record an event. Secondary sources analyze or draw conclusions about events. Secondary sources rely on both primary and secondary sources. Good research requires you to analyze and evaluate the validity of information, arguments, and counterarguments from a primary or secondary source for frame of reference.

[2.] Identify the main idea and supporting details, and determine whether they are facts or opinions. Read the text carefully and ask yourself, "What point is this text making?" This point is the main idea. Then reread the text and list details that support this main idea. Decide whether these details are facts or opinions. If the details are facts, it should be possible to confirm them in other sources. If the author uses emotional language that shows feelings, the supporting details are probably opinions. Carefully analyze and evaluate the validity of information, arguments, and counterarguments from primary and secondary sources for point of view.

[3.] Decide whether the source's information is biased or if it is accurate and credible. Check statements in the text against reliable sources, such as encyclopedias or books written by experts on the topic. If reliable sources agree with the text, it is probably fairly accurate. If most of the text seems to be opinions rather than facts, it is not an accurate source of information. Still, these opinions can teach you about the author's world. A writer who observed an exciting or scary event may use emotional language to describe the event, but the source may still be a reliable account. An important part of research is analyzing and evaluating the validity of the information, arguments, and counterarguments from primary and secondary sources for bias or propaganda.

Compare Viewpoints TEKS 29.B, 29.C

When people disagree about a topic, they have different viewpoints. Knowing how to analyze and evaluate the validity of information, arguments, and counterarguments from both primary and secondary sources for point of view can help you to learn more about a topic. Practice this skill by reading the following quotes and comparing the viewpoints.

> "Dictatorship...involves costs which the American people will never pay: The cost of having our children brought up, not as free and dignified human beings, but as pawns...
>
> –Franklin Roosevelt, State of the Union Address, January 4, 1939

> "The [Nazi Party] has laid down the directive...we must insist that all organs of education... have to [fulfill]their duty towards the community...
>
> –Adolf Hitler, Speech delivered in German Reichstag on January 30, 1937

1049

[**1.**] Identify the authors of texts presenting different points of view and identify each author's frame of reference. Frame of reference is a term that describes the experiences, values, and ideas that influence a person's opinions and actions. It can also be referred to as *point of view*. First, identify the group or individual that wrote each text. Determine if the source is primary or secondary. As you read, take note of any information about the author's experiences or background. Also, look for any signs of what the author thinks is important. These types of statements can help you analyze and evaluate the validity of information, arguments, and counterarguments from both primary and secondary sources for point of view.

[**2.**] Recognize any similarities and differences between the authors' frames of reference and identify the opinion of each author. Pay attention to any similarities and differences between the two authors' experiences, values, and ideas. Read carefully to identify the opinion of each author. In an article about a rock band, an author who played guitar in a band for ten years argues that Band A is the best band today because of its great guitarist. In a second article, another author who sang for many years argues that Band B is the best because of its lead singer. Notice how authors' arguments and counterarguments are shaped by their frame of reference, or point of view.

[**3.**] Draw conclusions about similarities and differences between authors' points of view. With some information about the point of view of each author, you can understand why they have different opinions. This helps you to analyze and evaluate the validity of the information, arguments, and counterarguments. In the example of the two authors writing about rock bands, each author stresses his or her own areas of expertise. You might decide to listen to the band recommended by the singer if you share an interest in vocals. If you are more interested in instrumentals, you might choose the band recommended by the guitarist.

Identify Bias TEKS 29.E

Being able to analyze and evaluate the validity of information, arguments, and counterarguments for bias helps you to determine whether primary or secondary sources you find online, in books, or in the media are reliable. When you are able to identify bias in written, oral, and visual material, you can see when someone is presenting only one side of an issue or basing an argument on emotion instead of facts. Use the Internet to locate an English-language newspaper in a foreign country. Practice identifying bias as you read an editorial or a political cartoon.

[**1.**] Identify the author of a source and the author's purpose. First, identify the author of the source. The author may be a group or an organization rather than a single person. The author may state his or her purpose very clearly in the source. If not, the type of source may give you an idea of the purpose. For example, the writer of an encyclopedia aims to summarize information about a subject. The author of a political Web site may want you to vote for a candidate.

[**2.**] Identify the main idea, and check whether the main idea is supported with facts or opinions. Read the document carefully and ask yourself, "What is the main point of this selection?" Your answer to this question is the main idea. Reread the document and list details that support this main idea. Decide whether these details are facts or opinions. To find out whether they are facts, check whether other reliable sources include the same information. If your source uses statements that shows feelings, those statements are probably opinions.

[**3.**] Look for the use of emotional language or one-sided opinions. Look for words that can show opinions such as "good" and "bad." Be aware of statements that make you feel angry, scared, or excited. Also, watch out for statements that only express one side of an issue. These are all signs of bias.

[**4.**] Draw conclusions about the author's bias, if any. Is the author using mostly emotional language with few facts to support his or her ideas? Are there insults or other very negative language in the source? If so, the source is probably biased. Similarly, if you notice that the author is presenting only one side of an issue, the source is probably not reliable. It is important to analyze and evaluate the information, arguments, and counterarguments in both primary and secondary sources for bias.

Evaluate Existing Arguments TEKS 29.B, 29.C, 29.E

When you evaluate existing arguments, you must evaluate and analyze the point of view and biases of your sources and their authors. Who is the author and what is he or she trying to accomplish? How valid are the arguments in your primary and secondary sources? If you master these skills, you will be able to analyze and interpret social studies information such as speeches. Practice this skill as you read and evaluate the excerpt below.

> There are two main ways in which those who have traveled to this part of the world pretending to be Christians have uprooted these pitiful peoples and wiped them from the face of the earth. First, they have waged war on them: unjust, cruel, bloody and tyrannical [using power unjustly] war. Second, they have murdered anyone and everyone who has shown the slightest sign of resistance. . . .
>
> The reason the [Spanish] have murdered on such a vast scale and killed anyone and everyone in their way is purely and simply greed. They have set out to line their pockets with gold. . . . The Spaniards have shown not the slightest consideration for these people, treating them (and I speak from first-hand experience, having been there from the outset) not as brute animals—indeed, I would to God they had done and had shown them the consideration they afford their animals—so much as piles of dung in the middle of the road. They have had as little concern for their souls as for their bodies. . . .
>
> —Bartolomé de Las Casas, *The Destruction of the Indies*, 1542

[**1.**] Identify the claim or thesis. What is the author or source claiming? The claim or thesis is usually found in the introduction and/or conclusion of a written or spoken argument.

[2.] Identify the reasons (claims to truth or facts) the author offers in support of his or her claim. What evidence does the author or source provide to support their claims? Make a list of the evidence provided to support each claim.

[3.] Evaluate the argument. Analyze and evaluate the validity of the evidence presented to support each claim. Use the appropriate skills to analyze and interpret social studies information, such as speeches. Research each claim to be sure that the author's statements are accurate. Carefully check for evidence of bias or propaganda. Be sure you understand the author's point of view and his or her frame of reference. Finally, check to be sure that the author's conclusions follow logically from the evidence presented. If the evidence is accurate, the author is free from bias, and conclusions follow logically from the evidence, the claims are probably valid.

Consider and Counter Opposing Arguments TEKS 29.B, 29.C, 29.E

Before you can effectively counter opposing arguments, you'll need to analyze possible counterarguments for frame of reference, bias, point of view, and propaganda. You'll plan your response ahead of time, collecting research and data. Then, you'll make a point of acknowledging the opposing view before presenting your counterarguments. To practice this skill, suppose you are preparing for a debate about whether the United States should take a more active role in promoting human rights in other parts of the world. Choose a side of the debate to support. What arguments will you use to support your side of the debate? What counterarguments will you anticipate the other side using? Why is it useful to anticipate the other side's arguments?

[1.] Fully understand your argument and the potential counter points. Do research as needed to find out more about other opposing views. Analyze and evaluate the validity of possible counterarguments from primary and secondary sources for frame of reference, bias, point of view, and propaganda.

[2.] Make predictions and outline a response to several of the opposing views. Continue researching as needed. Researching, analyzing, and evaluating the validity of opposing arguments will help you support and strengthen your own. Opposing arguments can consist of any reasons, conclusions, or claims that oppose yours. Outline your response to each opposing reason, conclusion, or claim.

[3.] To counter an opposing argument, first acknowledge the opposing view. This strategy shows that you have heard the opposing argument and are responding accordingly. Consider using statements such as "I understand your point, but you should also consider the following..." You can also respond by refuting facts, logic, etc. Be sure to respond to each opposing argument. Ignoring or dismissing a counterargument shows that your response is weak and unsupported.

Participate in a Discussion or Debate TEKS 29.G, 30.C

When you participate in a discussion or debate, your goal is to explain, analyze, and defend a point of view–often related to a current political or economic issue. To be a successful debater, you'll do your research, present your position, and defend your point of view in a courteous manner. Use the steps below to prepare for a discussion on this question: Do you think the United States should act as a "global policeman?" Why or why not?

[**1.**] Research. Before participating in a discussion or debate, do research to gain knowledge of your subject so that you may be an informed and prepared participant. Take notes as needed to help you prepare. Jot down main points and any questions you may have. As you research, decide where you might stand on the issue. Be sure to gather research and sources that will allow you to explain, analyze, and defend your point of view.

[**2.**] Present your position. After you have organized your thoughts and decided where you stand, explain and defend your point of view. Be sure to stay focused on the topic and your line of argument. Ask questions that challenge the accuracy, logic, or relevance of opposing views.

[**3.**] During the discussion or debate, be patient and courteous. Listen attentively, be respectful and supportive of peers, and speak only when instructed to do so by the moderator. Be sure to allow others to express their views; do not monopolize the debate or discussion. Speak clearly and slowly.

Give an Effective Presentation

When you create a written, visual, and oral presentation, you teach, convince, or share information with an audience. Effective presentations use both words and visuals to engage audiences. Delivery is also important. For example, you can use the way you move, speak, and look at the audience to keep people interested. Use the steps below to prepare and deliver a presentation on the Silk Road.

[**1.**] Identify the purpose of your presentation and your audience. Think about the purpose of your written, visual, and oral presentation. If this is a research report, you will need facts and data to support your points. If you are trying to persuade your audience, look for powerful photos. Keep your audience in mind. Consider their interests and present your topic in a way that will engage them.

[**2.**] Write the text and find visual aids for your presentation. Look online and in books and magazines for information and images for your presentation. Organize the information and write it up carefully so that it is easy for your audience to understand. Diagrams can show complicated information in a clear way. Visuals also get people interested in the presentation. So choose large, colorful images that people in the back of the audience will be able to see.

[3.] Practice and work to improve your presentation. Keep practicing your oral presentation until you know the material well. Then, practice some more, focusing on improving your delivery.

[4.] Use body language, tone of voice, and eye contact to deliver an effective presentation. Answer questions if the audience has them. At the beginning of your oral presentation, take a breath, smile, and stand up tall. Speak more loudly and more clearly than you would in normal conversation. Also, try not to rush through the presentation. Glance at your notes but speak naturally, rather than reading. Look at people in the audience. If people are confused, pause to clarify. Finally, leave time for people in the audience to ask questions.

Write an Essay TEKS 30.A, 30.B, 30.C

There are four steps to writing an essay. You'll start by selecting a topic and research sources, then you'll write an outline and develop a thesis or point of view. After drafting your essay, you'll carefully proofread it to be sure you've used standard grammar, spelling, sentence structure, and punctuation. Finally, you'll revise and polish your work. To practice this skill, select a topic that interests you about the early history of Africa and develop a thesis. Then explain to a partner the steps you will take to write your essay.

[1.] Choose your topic and research sources. Check which types of sources you will need. Gather different types of reliable sources that support the argument you will be making.

[2.] Write an outline and generate a thesis. First write your topic at the top of the page then list all the points or arguments you want to make about the topic; also list the facts and examples that support these points. Your thesis statement will inform the reader of the point you are making and what question you will be answering about the topic. When writing your thesis, be as specific as possible and address one main idea.

[3.] Draft your essay. After finishing your research and outline, begin writing the body of your essay; start with the introduction then write a paragraph for each of your supporting points, followed by a conclusion. As you write, do your best to use standard grammar, spelling, sentence structure, and punctuation. Be sure any terminology is used correctly.

[4.] Revise. An important part of the writing process involves checking for areas in which information should be added, removed, or rewritten. Try to imagine that this paper belongs to someone else. Does the paper have a clear thesis? Do all of the ideas relate back to the thesis? Read your paper out loud and listen for awkward pauses and unclear ideas. Lastly, check for mistakes in standard grammar, spelling, sentence structure, punctuation, and usage.

Avoid Plagiarism TEKS 30.C

When you don't attribute ideas and information to source materials and authors, you are plagiarizing. Plagiarizing–claiming others' ideas and information as your own–is considered unethical. You can avoid plagiarizing by carefully noting down which authors and sources you'll be using, citing those authors and sources in your paper, and listing them in a bibliography. To practice this skill, suppose you have been assigned to write a research paper on the development of river valley civilizations. Name three types of sources you might use to help you gather information. Explain how you will avoid plagiarism when you use these sources.

[1.] Keep a careful log of your notes. As you read sources to gain background information on your topic, keep track of ideas and information and the sources and authors they come from. Write down the name of each source next to your notes from that particular source so you can remember to cite it later on. Create a separate section in your notes where you keep your own thoughts and ideas so you know which ideas are your own. Using someone else's words or paraphrasing their ideas does not make them yours.

[2] Cite sources in your paper. You must identify the source materials and authors you use to support your ideas. Whenever you use statistics, facts, direct quotations, or paraphrases of others' views, you need to attribute them to your source. Cite your sources within the body of your paper. Check your assignment to find out how they should be formatted.

[3.] List your sources in a bibliography at the end of your paper. List your source materials and authors cited in alphabetical order by author, using accepted formats. As you work, be sure to check your list of sources from your notes so that none are left out of the bibliography.

Solve Problems TEKS 31.A

Problem solving is a skill that you use every day. It is a process that requires an open mind, clear thinking, and action. Consider the fact that many of natural resources are in high demand around the world, and that some may be in danger of being depleted. Consider one source of power, such as natural gas, oil, or electricity, and use the steps below to solve the problem of conserving energy.

[1.] Understand the problem. Before trying to solve a problem, make sure that you gather as much information as possible in order to identify the problem. What are the causes and effects of the problem? Who is involved? You will want to make sure that you understand different perspectives on the problem. Try not to jump to conclusions or make assumptions. You might end up misunderstanding the problem.

[**2.**] Consider possible solutions and choose the best one. Once you have identified the problem and gathered some information, list and consider a number of possible options. Right away, one solution might seem like the right one, but try to think of other solutions. Be sure to consider carefully the advantages and disadvantages of each option. It can help to take notes listing benefits and drawbacks. Look for the solution whose benefits outweigh its drawbacks. After considering each option, choose the solution you think is best.

[**3.**] Make and implement a plan. Choose and implement a solution. Make a detailed, step-by-step plan to implement the solution that you choose. Write your plan down and assign yourself a deadline for each step. That will help you to stay on track toward completing your plan. Try to think of any problems that might come up and what you will do to address those problems. Of course, there are many things that you cannot predict. Stay flexible. Evaluate the effectiveness of the solution and adjust your plan as necessary.

Make Decisions TEKS 31.B

Everyone makes decisions. The trick is to learn how to make good decisions. How can you make good decisions? First, identify a situation that requires a decision and gather information. Then, identify possible options and predict the consequences of each option. Finally, choose the best option and take action to implement a decision. You know there are many issues in the world that affect children who are just like you. Some children face hunger, poverty, lack of schools or medical facilities, poor water supplies, or other challenges. What could you do to help? Practice this skill by following these steps to decide which issue you can best support and how you can help.

[**1.**] Determine the options between which you must decide. In some cases, like ordering from a menu at a restaurant, your options may be clear. In other cases, you will need to identify a situation that requires a decision, gather information, and identify the options that are available to you. Spend some time thinking about the situation and brainstorm a number of options. If necessary, do a little research to find more options. Make a list of options that you might choose.

[**2.**] Review the costs and benefits of each option. Carefully predict the consequences of each option. You may want to make a cost-benefit list for each option. To do this, write down the option and then draw two columns underneath it. One column will be the "pro" or benefit list. The other column will be the "con" or cost list. Note the pros and cons for each of your options. Try not to rush through this process. For a very important decision, you may even want to show your list to someone you trust. This person can help you think of costs and benefits that you had not considered.

[**3.**] Determine the best option and act on it. Look through your cost-benefit lists. Note any especially serious costs. If an option has the possibility of an extremely negative consequence, you might want to cross it off your list right away. Look closely at the options with the most benefits and the fewest costs, and choose the one that you think is best. Once you have made a choice, take action to implement a decision. If necessary, make a detailed plan with clear steps. Set a deadline to complete the steps to keep yourself moving toward your goal.

Being an Informed Citizen TEKS 21.B

Informed citizens understand the responsibilities, duties, and obligations of citizenship. They are well informed about civic affairs, involved with their communities, and politically active. When it comes to issues they personally care about, they take a stand and reach out to others.

[**1.**] Learn the issues. A great way to begin to understand the responsibilities of citizenship is to first find topics of interest to you. Next, become well informed about civic affairs in your town, city, or country. Read newspapers, magazines, and articles you find online about events happening in your area or around the world. Analyze the information you read to come to your own conclusions. Radio programs, podcasts, and social media are also great ways to keep up with current events and interact with others about issues.

[**2.**] Get involved. Attend community events to speak with others who know the issues. Become well informed about how policies are made and changed. Find out who to speak to if you would like to take part in civic affairs and policy creation. There are government websites that can help direct you to the right person. These websites will also provide his or her contact details.

[**3.**] Take a stand and reach out. Write, call, or meet with your elected officials to become a better informed, more responsible citizen. Do research about candidates who are running for office to be an informed voter. Start your own blog or website to explore issues, interact with others, and be part of the community or national dialogue.

www.PearsonTexas.com
View Video Tutorials and other 21st Century Skills

1057

Political Participation TEKS 21.B

Political participation starts with an understanding of the responsibilities, duties and obligations of citizenship, such as serving the public good. When you understand your role as a political participant, you can get involved through volunteering for a political campaign, running for office, or interacting with others in person or online.

[1.] Volunteer for a political campaign. Political campaigns offer a wide variety of opportunities to help you become involved in the political process and become a responsible citizen by serving the public good. As a political campaign volunteer you may have the opportunity to attend events, make calls to voters, and explore your community while getting to know how other voters think about the responsibilities, duties, and obligations of citizenship.

[2.] Run for office in your school or community. A good way to become involved in your school or community is to run for office. Student council or community positions offer a great opportunity for you to become familiar with the campaign and election process.

[3.] Reach out to others. Start or join an interest group. Interest groups enable people to work together on common goals related to the political process. Write a letter or email to a public official. By contacting an elected official from your area, you can either support or oppose laws or policies. You can also ask for help or support regarding certain issues.

[4.] Interact online. Social networking sites and blogs offer a great way for people of all ages to interact and write about political issues. As you connect with others, you'll become more confident in your role as a citizen working for the public good.

Voting TEKS 21.B

Voting is not only a right. It is also one of the primary responsibilities, duties, and obligations of citizenship. Before you can legally vote, however, you must understand the voter registration process and the criteria for voting in elections. You should also understand the issues and know where different candidates stand on those issues.

[1.] Check eligibility and residency requirements. In order to vote in the United States, you must be a United States citizen who is 18 years or older, and you must be a resident of the place where you plan to vote.

[**2.**] Register to vote. You cannot vote until you understand the voter registration process. You can register at city or town election offices, or when you get a driver's license. You can also register by mail or online. You may also have the option of registering at the polls on Election Day, but this does not apply in all states. Make sure to find out what you need to do to register in your state, as well as the deadline for registering. You may have the option of declaring a political party when registering.

[**3.**] Learn the issues. As the election approaches, research the candidates and issues in order to be an informed voter. Watch televised debates, if there are any. You can also review the candidates' websites. By doing these things and thinking critically about what you learn, you will be prepared to exercise your responsibility, duty and obligation as a United States citizen.

[**4.**] Vote. Make sure to arrive at the correct polling place on Election Day to cast your ballot. Research to find out when the polls will be open. Advance voting, absentee voting, and voting by mail are also options in certain states for those who qualify.

Serving on a Jury TEKS 21.B

As an American, you need to understand the duties, obligations and responsibilities of citizenship; among these is the expectation that you may be required to serve on a jury. You will receive a written notice when you are summoned to jury duty and you'll receive instruction on the special duties and obligations of a juror. You'll follow the American code of justice which assumes that a person is innocent until proven guilty, and you'll follow instructions about keeping trial information confidential.

[**1.**] Wait to receive notification. If you are summoned to serve as a juror, you will be first notified by mail. If you are chosen to move on to the jury selection phase, lawyers from both sides will ask you questions as they select the final jury members. It is an honor to serve as a juror, as it is a responsibility offered only to American citizens.

[**2.**] Follow the law and remain impartial. Your job is to determine whether or not someone broke the law. You may also be asked to sit on the jury for civil cases (as opposed to criminal cases); these cases involve lawsuits filed against individuals or businesses for any perceived wrong doing (such as broken contracts, trespassing, discrimination, etc.). Be sure to follow the law as it is explained to you, regardless of whether you approve of the law or not. Your decision about the trial should not be influenced by any personal bias or views you may have.

[**3.**] Remember that the defendant is presumed innocent. In a criminal trial, the defendant must be proven guilty "beyond a reasonable doubt" for the verdict to be guilty. If the trial team fails to prove the defendant to be guilty beyond a reasonable doubt, the jury verdict must be "not guilty."

[**4.**] During the trial, respect the court's right to privacy. As a juror, you have specific duties, obligations, and responsibilities under the law. Do not permit anyone to talk about the case with you or in your presence, except with the court's permission. Avoid media coverage once the trial has begun so as to prevent bias. Keep an open mind and do not form or state any opinions about the case until you have heard all of the evidence, the closing arguments from the lawyers, and the judge's instructions on the applicable law.

Paying Taxes TEKS 21.B

Paying taxes is one of the responsibilities of citizenship. How do you go about figuring out how much you've already paid in taxes and how much you still owe? It's your duty and obligation to find out, by determining how much has been deducted from your pay and filing your tax return.

[**1.**] Find out how taxes are deducted from your pay. In the United States, payroll taxes are imposed on employers and employees, and they are collected and paid by the employers. Check your pay stub to find out how much money was deducted for taxes. Be sure to also save the W-2 tax form your employer sends to you. You will need this form later on when filing your tax paperwork. Also save any interest income statements. All this information will help you fulfill your obligation as an American taxpayer.

[2.] Check the sales taxes in your state. All but five states impose sales and use taxes on retail sale, lease, and rental of many goods, as well as some services. Sales tax is calculated as the purchase price times the appropriate tax rate. Tax rates vary widely from less than one percent to over ten percent. Sales tax is collected by the seller at the time of sale.

[3.] File your tax return. Filing your tax return is more than an obligation: it's also a duty and responsility of citizenship. You may receive tax forms in the mail, or pick them up at the local Post Office or library. Fill the forms in and then mail or electronically send completed tax forms and any necessary payments to the Internal Revenue Service (IRS) and your state's department of revenue. The IRS provides free resources to help people prepare and electronically file their tax returns; go to IRS.gov to learn more. Note: certain things such as charitable donations and business expenses are tax deductible.

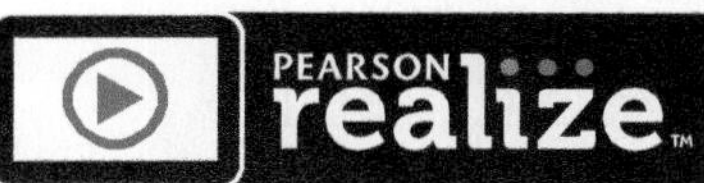

www.PearsonTexas.com
View Video Tutorials and other 21st Century Skills

The United States: Political

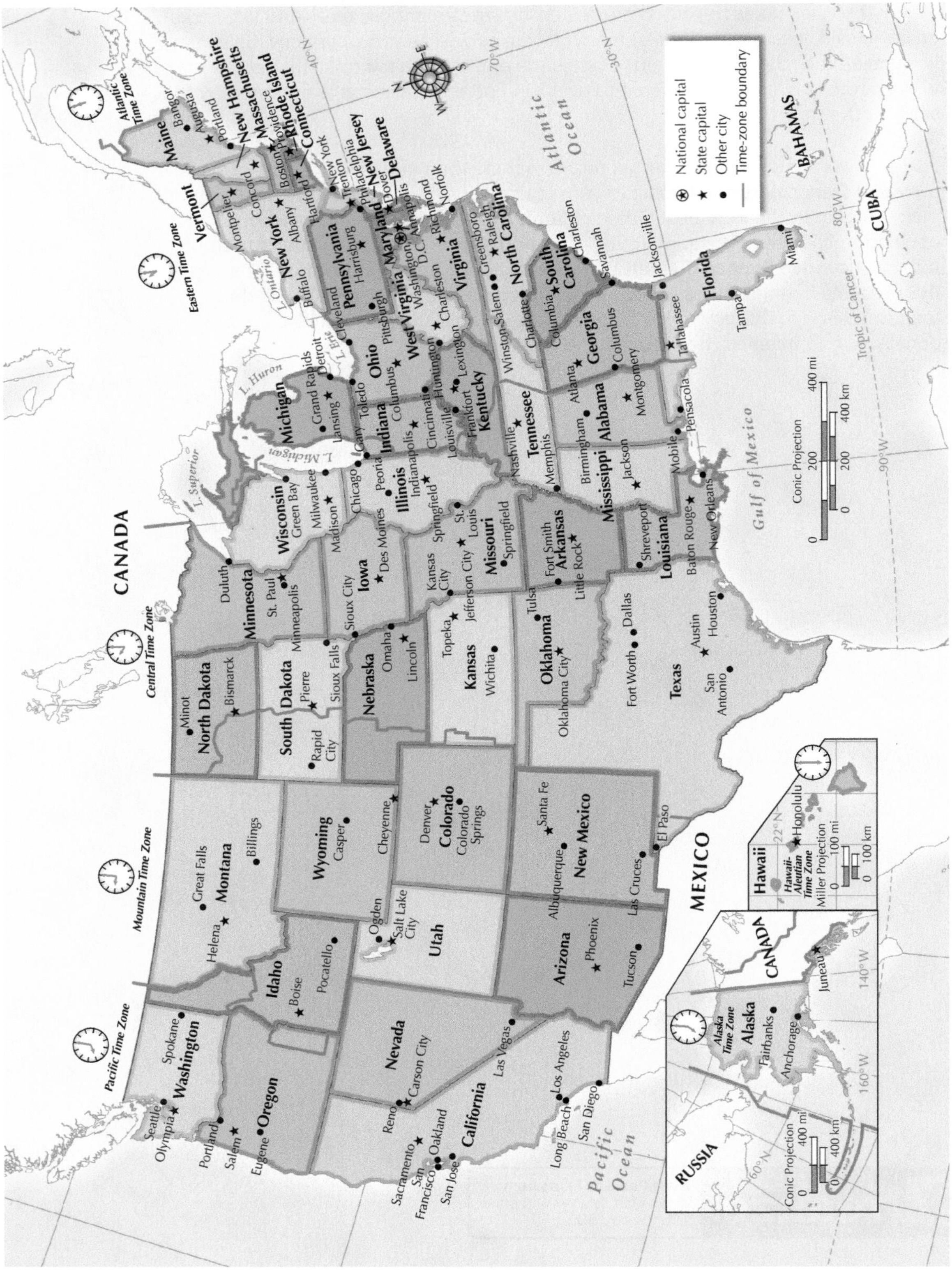

1062

The United States: Physical

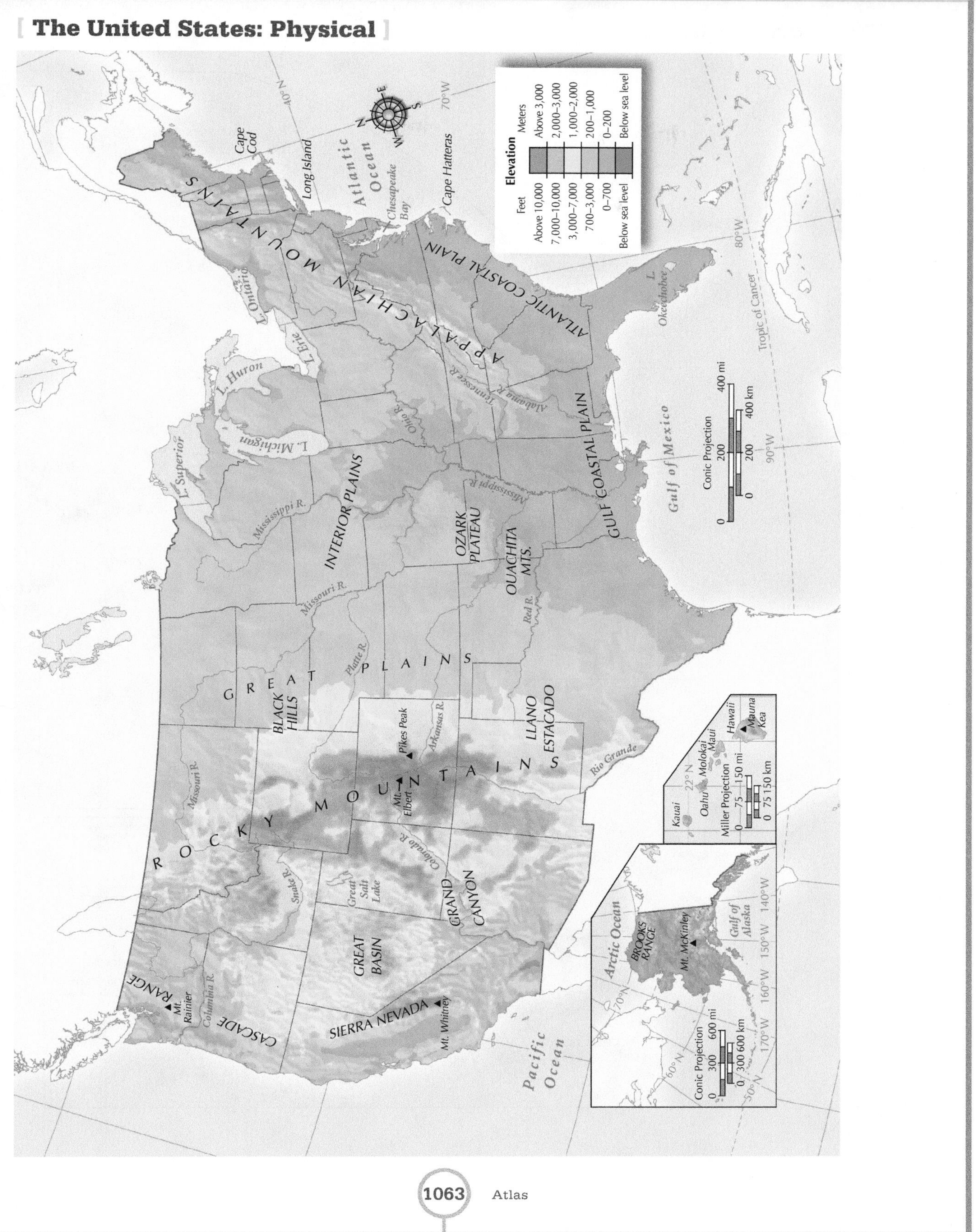

Elevation
Feet
Meters
Above 10,000
Above 3,000
7,000–10,000
2,000–3,000
3,000–7,000
1,000–2,000
700–3,000
200–1,000
0–700
0–200
Below sea level
Below sea level
Cape Cod
Long Island
Atlantic Ocean
Chesapeake Bay
Cape Hatteras
APPALACHIAN MOUNTAINS
ATLANTIC COASTAL PLAIN
L. Ontario
L. Erie
L. Huron
L. Michigan
L. Superior
L. Okeechobee
Tropic of Cancer
Tennessee R.
Alabama R.
Ohio R.
Mississippi R.
Missouri R.
Platte R.
Arkansas R.
Red R.
Rio Grande
Colorado R.
Snake R.
Columbia R.
INTERIOR PLAINS
OZARK PLATEAU
OUACHITA MTS.
GULF COASTAL PLAIN
Gulf of Mexico
GREAT PLAINS
BLACK HILLS
LLANO ESTACADO
Pikes Peak
Mt. Elbert
ROCKY MOUNTAINS
Great Salt Lake
GRAND CANYON
GREAT BASIN
SIERRA NEVADA
Mt. Whitney
CASCADE RANGE
Mt. Rainier
Pacific Ocean
Conic Projection
0 200 400 mi
0 200 400 km
Kauai
Oahu
Molokai
Maui
Hawaii
Mauna Kea
Miller Projection
0 75 150 mi
0 75 150 km
Arctic Ocean
BROOKS RANGE
Mt. McKinley
Gulf of Alaska
Conic Projection
0 300 600 mi
0 300 600 km
40° N
70° W
80° W
90° W
22° N
140° W
150° W
160° W
170° W
70° N
60° N
50° N

The World: Political

Arctic Ocean
Arctic Circle
ICELAND
see inset below
EUROPE
RUSSIA
ASIA
KAZAKHSTAN
MONGOLIA
GEORGIA
AZER.
ARMENIA
UZBEK.
TURKMEN.
KYRGYZSTAN
TAJIKISTAN
Tehran
Beijing
NORTH KOREA
SOUTH KOREA
Seoul
JAPAN
Tokyo
CHINA
Shanghai
MOROCCO
ALGERIA
LIBYA
ISRAEL
IRAQ
IRAN
AFGHAN.
JORDAN
KUWAIT
BAHRAIN
QATAR
PAKISTAN
NEPAL
BHUTAN
New Delhi
Cairo
EGYPT
SAUDI ARABIA
U.A.E.
Karachi
OMAN
INDIA
MYANMAR (BURMA)
BANGLADESH
LAOS
Hong Kong
TAIWAN (Claimed by China)
Pacific Ocean
Mumbai
AFRICA
CHAD
SUDAN
ERITREA
YEMEN
DJIBOUTI
Addis Ababa
ETHIOPIA
SOMALIA
THAILAND
Bangkok
VIETNAM
CAMBODIA
PHILIPPINES
MARSHALL ISLANDS
SRI LANKA
CEN. AFR. REP.
SOUTH SUDAN
CAMEROON
DEM. REP. OF THE CONGO
UGANDA
KENYA
RWANDA
BURUNDI
TANZANIA
GABON
CONGO
SÃO TOMÉ AND PRÍNCIPE
see inset below
MALDIVES
BRUNEI
MALAYSIA
SINGAPORE
FEDERATED STATES OF MICRONESIA
KIRIBATI
NAURU
INDONESIA
Jakarta
TIMOR-LESTE
PAPUA NEW GUINEA
SOLOMON ISLANDS
TUVALU
SEYCHELLES
COMOROS
Indian Ocean
ANGOLA
MALAWI
ZAMBIA
MOZAMBIQUE
MADAGASCAR
OCEANIA
FIJI ISLANDS
VANUATU
Atlantic Ocean
ZIMBABWE
BOTSWANA
MAURITIUS
NAMIBIA
AUSTRALIA
New Caledonia (France)
SWAZILAND
SOUTH AFRICA
LESOTHO
Cape Town
Sydney
NEW ZEALAND
Robinson Projection
0 1,000 2,000 mi
0 1,000 2,000 km
Southern Ocean
ANTARCTICA
Western Sahara (Morocco)
ALGERIA
MAURITANIA
MALI
NIGER
SENEGAL
GAMBIA
GUINEA-BISSAU
GUINEA
BURKINA FASO
BENIN
TOGO
SIERRA LEONE
CÔTE D'IVOIRE
GHANA
NIGERIA
LIBERIA
Lagos
Atlantic Ocean
Azimuthal Equidistant Projection
0 200 400 mi
0 200 400 km
Gulf of Guinea
EQUATORIAL GUINEA
Barents Sea
SWEDEN
FINLAND
NORWAY
Conic Projection
0 200 400 mi
0 200 400 km
ESTONIA
LATVIA
LITHUANIA
RUSSIA
Moscow
North Sea
IRELAND
UNITED KINGDOM
DENMARK
Baltic Sea
NETHERLANDS
London
Berlin
BELARUS
GERMANY
POLAND
BELGIUM
LUX.
Kiev
UKRAINE
Atlantic Ocean
Paris
CZECH REP.
SLOVAKIA
LIECH.
Bay of Biscay
FRANCE
SWITZ.
AUSTRIA
HUNGARY
MOLDOVA
SLOVENIA
CROATIA
ROMANIA
ANDORRA
MONACO
ITALY
BOS. AND HERZ.
SERBIA AND MONT.
PORTUGAL
Madrid
SPAIN
Corsica (France)
SAN MARINO
Rome
BULGARIA
Black Sea
Istanbul
Sardinia (Italy)
VATICAN CITY
ALBANIA
MAC.
Gibraltar (U.K.)
Ceuta (Spain)
Melilla (Spain)
Balearic Islands (Spain)
Sicily (Italy)
GREECE
TURKEY
MOROCCO
ALGERIA
TUNISIA
MALTA
Mediterranean Sea
Crete (Greece)
CYPRUS
LEBANON
SYRIA

1065

Africa: Political

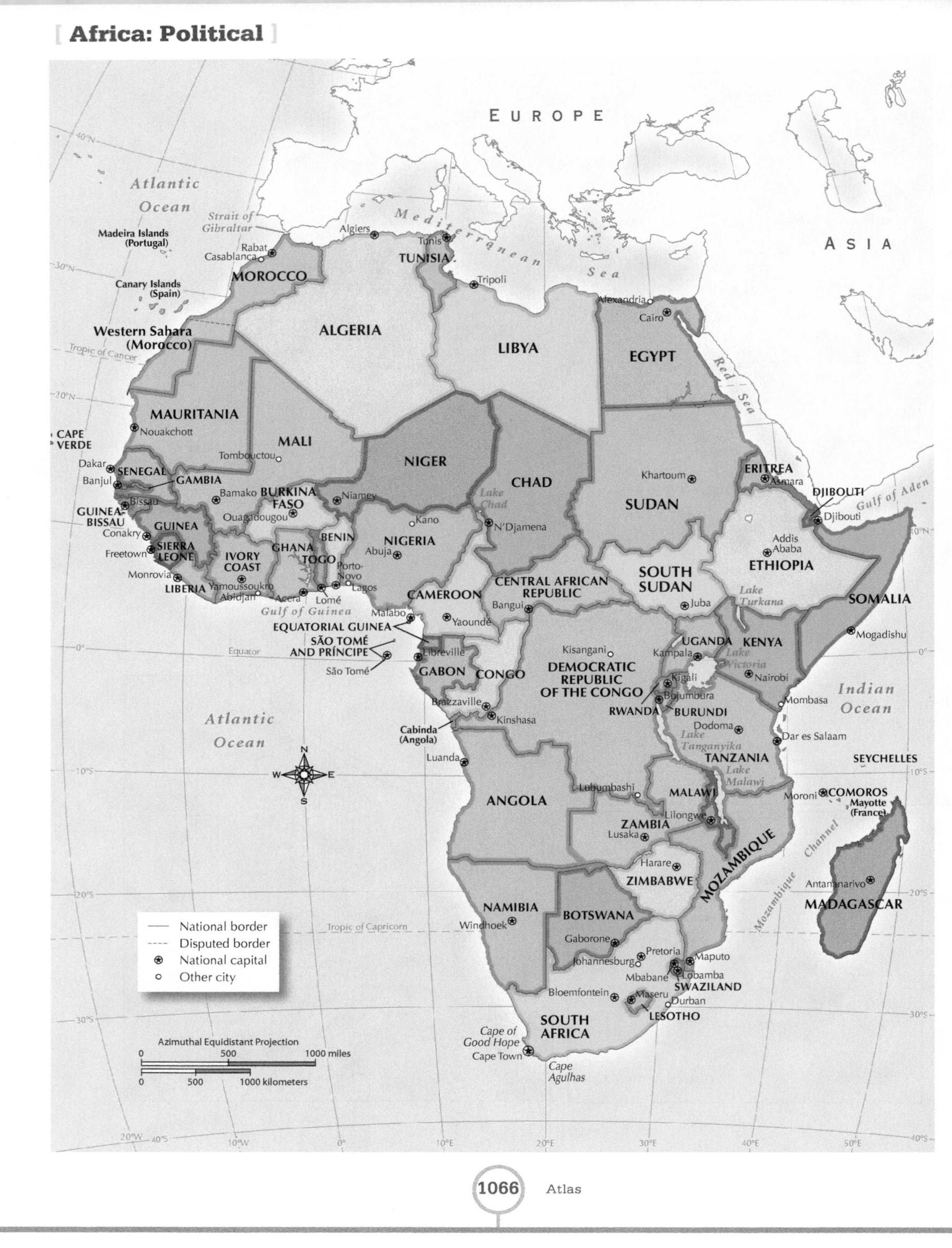

Africa: Physical

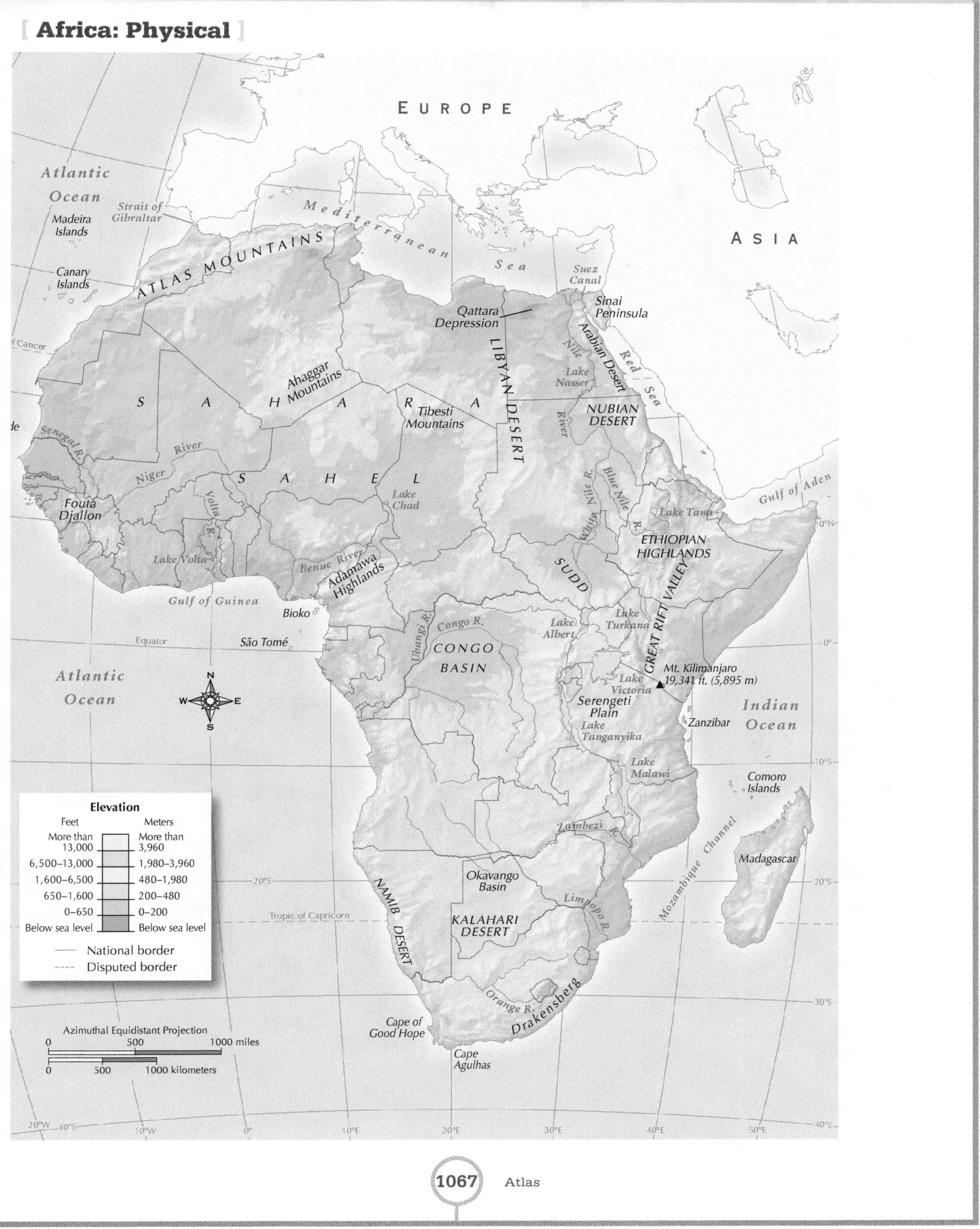

EUROPE
ASIA
Atlantic Ocean
Madeira Islands
Strait of Gibraltar
Canary Islands
Mediterranean Sea
ATLAS MOUNTAINS
Suez Canal
Sinai Peninsula
Qattara Depression
LIBYAN DESERT
Arabian Desert
Nile
Lake Nasser
Red Sea
Ahaggar Mountains
S A H A R A
Tibesti Mountains
NUBIAN DESERT
River
Senegal R.
Niger River
S A H E L
Lake Chad
Blue Nile R.
White Nile R.
Lake Tana
Gulf of Aden
Fouta Djallon
Volta R.
Lake Volta
ETHIOPIAN HIGHLANDS
Benue River
Adamawa Highlands
SUDD
GREAT RIFT VALLEY
Gulf of Guinea
Bioko
Lake Turkana
Lake Albert
Congo R.
Ubangi R.
Equator
São Tomé
CONGO BASIN
Mt. Kilimanjaro 19,341 ft. (5,895 m)
Atlantic Ocean
Lake Victoria
Serengeti Plain
Indian Ocean
Zanzibar
Lake Tanganyika
Lake Malawi
Comoro Islands
Zambezi R.
Mozambique Channel
Madagascar
Okavango Basin
NAMIB DESERT
KALAHARI DESERT
Limpopo R.
Tropic of Capricorn
Orange R.
Drakensberg
Cape of Good Hope
Cape Agulhas
Elevation
Feet
Meters
More than 13,000
More than 3,960
6,500–13,000
1,980–3,960
1,600–6,500
480–1,980
650–1,600
200–480
0–650
0–200
Below sea level
Below sea level
National border
Disputed border
Azimuthal Equidistant Projection
0 500 1000 miles
0 500 1000 kilometers
N
S
E
W
10°N
0°
10°S
20°S
30°S
40°S
20°W
10°W
0°
10°E
20°E
30°E
40°E
50°E

Asia: Political

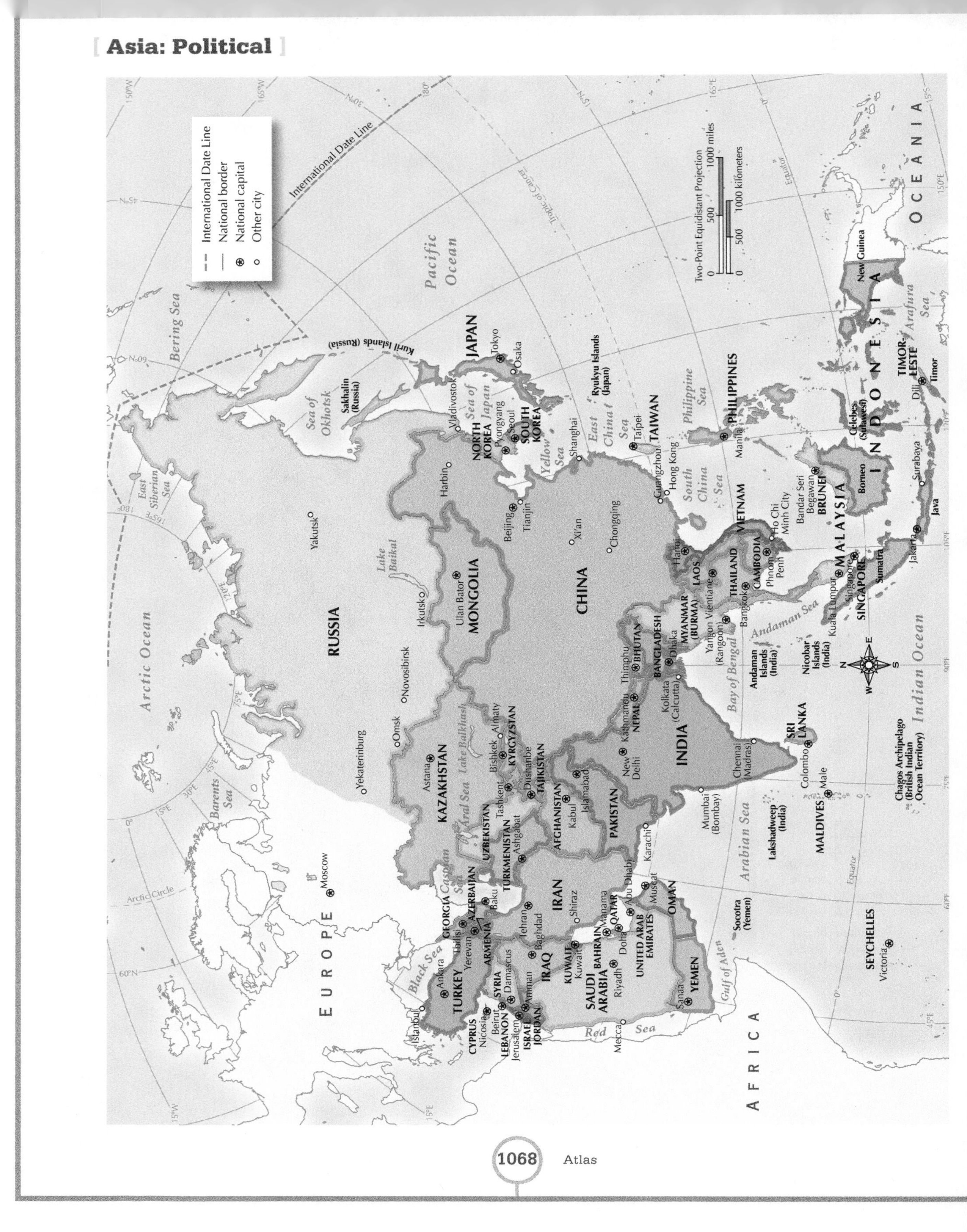

1068

Asia: Physical

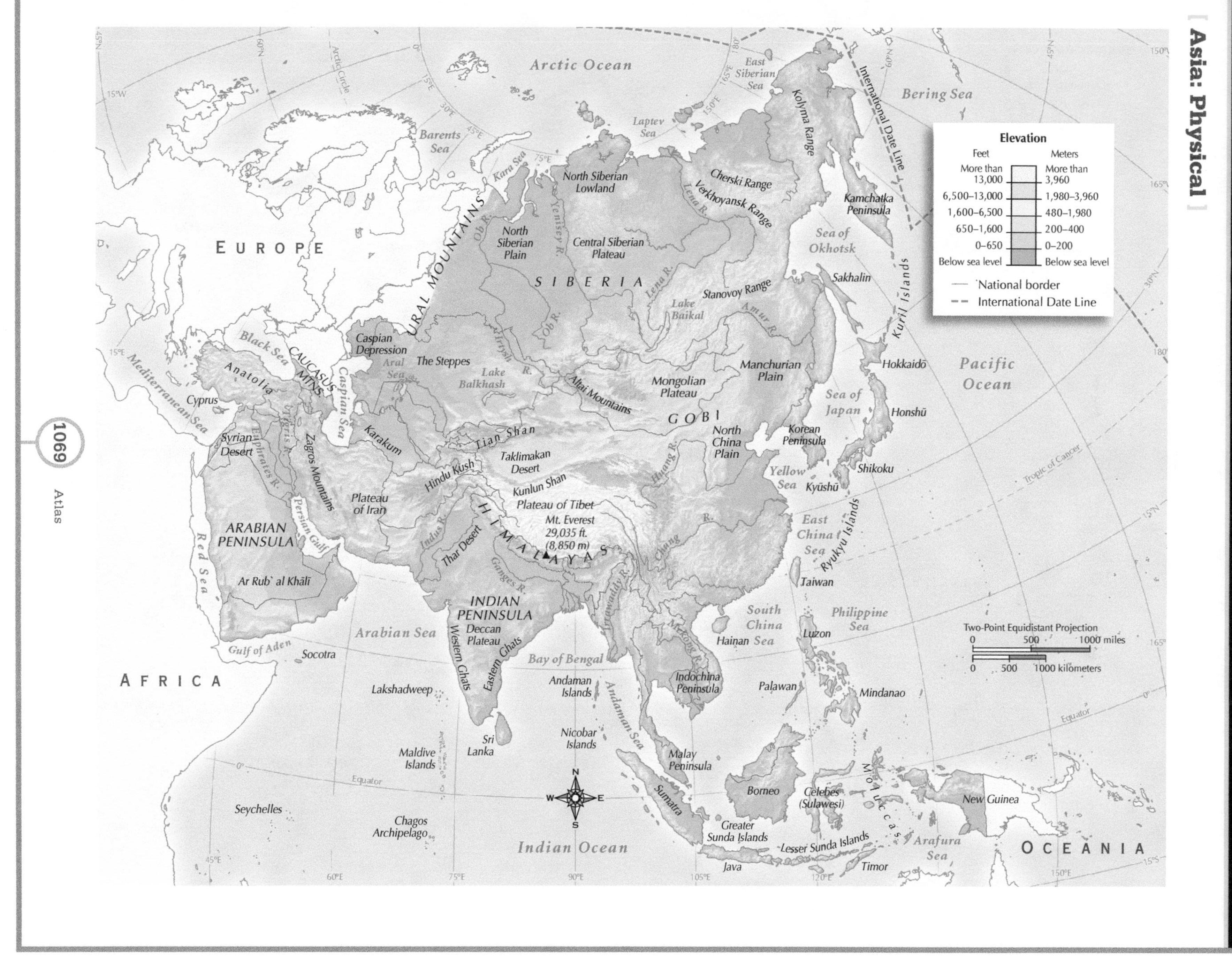

Europe: Political

1070

Europe: Physical

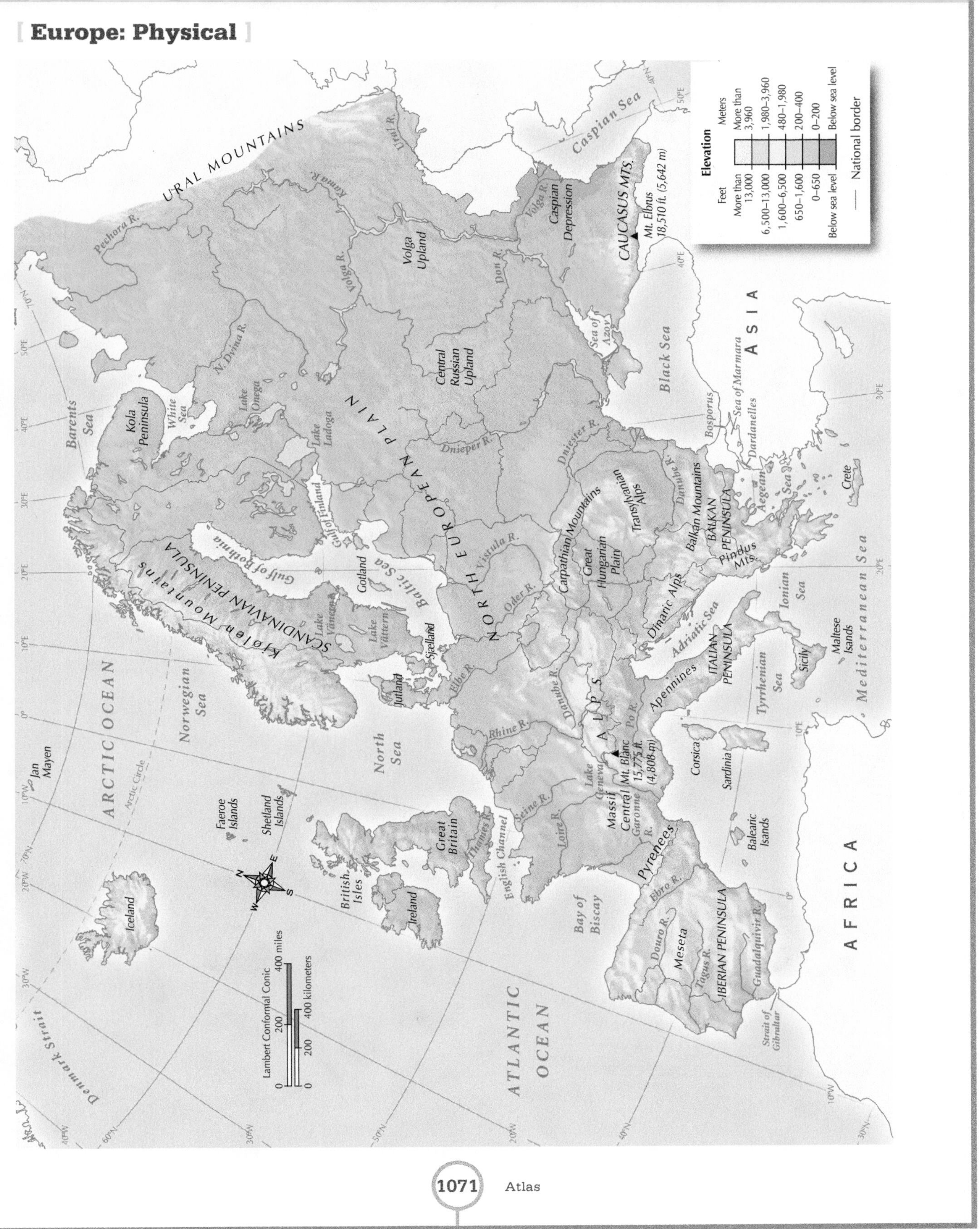

URAL MOUNTAINS
Pechora R.
Kama R.
Ural R.
Caspian Sea
Volga R.
Caspian Depression
CAUCASUS MTS.
Mt. Elbrus 18,510 ft. (5,642 m)
Volga Upland
Don R.
Sea of Azov
Black Sea
Central Russian Upland
N. Dvina R.
Lake Onega
White Sea
Kola Peninsula
Barents Sea
Lake Ladoga
NORTH EUROPEAN PLAIN
Dnieper R.
Dniester R.
Bosporus
Sea of Marmara
Dardanelles
ASIA
Aegean Sea
Crete
Danube R.
Transylvanian Alps
Balkan Mountains
BALKAN PENINSULA
Pindus Mts.
Carpathian Mountains
Great Hungarian Plain
Vistula R.
Gulf of Finland
Gulf of Bothnia
Gotland
Baltic Sea
SCANDINAVIAN PENINSULA
Kjølen Mountains
Lake Vänern
Lake Vättern
Sjælland
Oder R.
Dinaric Alps
Adriatic Sea
Ionian Sea
ITALIAN PENINSULA
Maltese Isands
Sicily
Mediterranean Sea
Tyrrhenian Sea
Apennines
Jutland
Elbe R.
Danube R.
ALPS
Po R.
Rhine R.
Mt. Blanc 15,775 ft. (4,808 m)
Lake Geneva
Corsica
Sardinia
Balearic Isands
Massif Central
Garonne R.
Seine R.
Loire R.
Pyrenees
Ebro R.
Bay of Biscay
IBERIAN PENINSULA
Meseta
Douro R.
Tagus R.
Guadalquivir R.
Strait of Gibraltar
AFRICA
ATLANTIC OCEAN
English Channel
Thames R.
Great Britain
British Isles
Ireland
North Sea
Norwegian Sea
Shetland Islands
Faeroe Islands
ARCTIC OCEAN
Arctic Circle
Jan Mayen
Iceland
Denmark Strait
Lambert Conformal Conic
0 200 400 miles
0 200 400 kilometers
Elevation
Feet
Meters
More than 13,000
More than 3,960
6,500–13,000
1,980–3,960
1,600–6,500
480–1,980
650–1,600
200–480
0–650
0–200
Below sea level
Below sea level
National border

1071

North and South America: Political

National border
International Date Line
National capital
Other city

Lambert Azimuthal Equal-Area Projection

0 1000 2000 miles
0 1000 2000 kilometers

North and South America: Physical

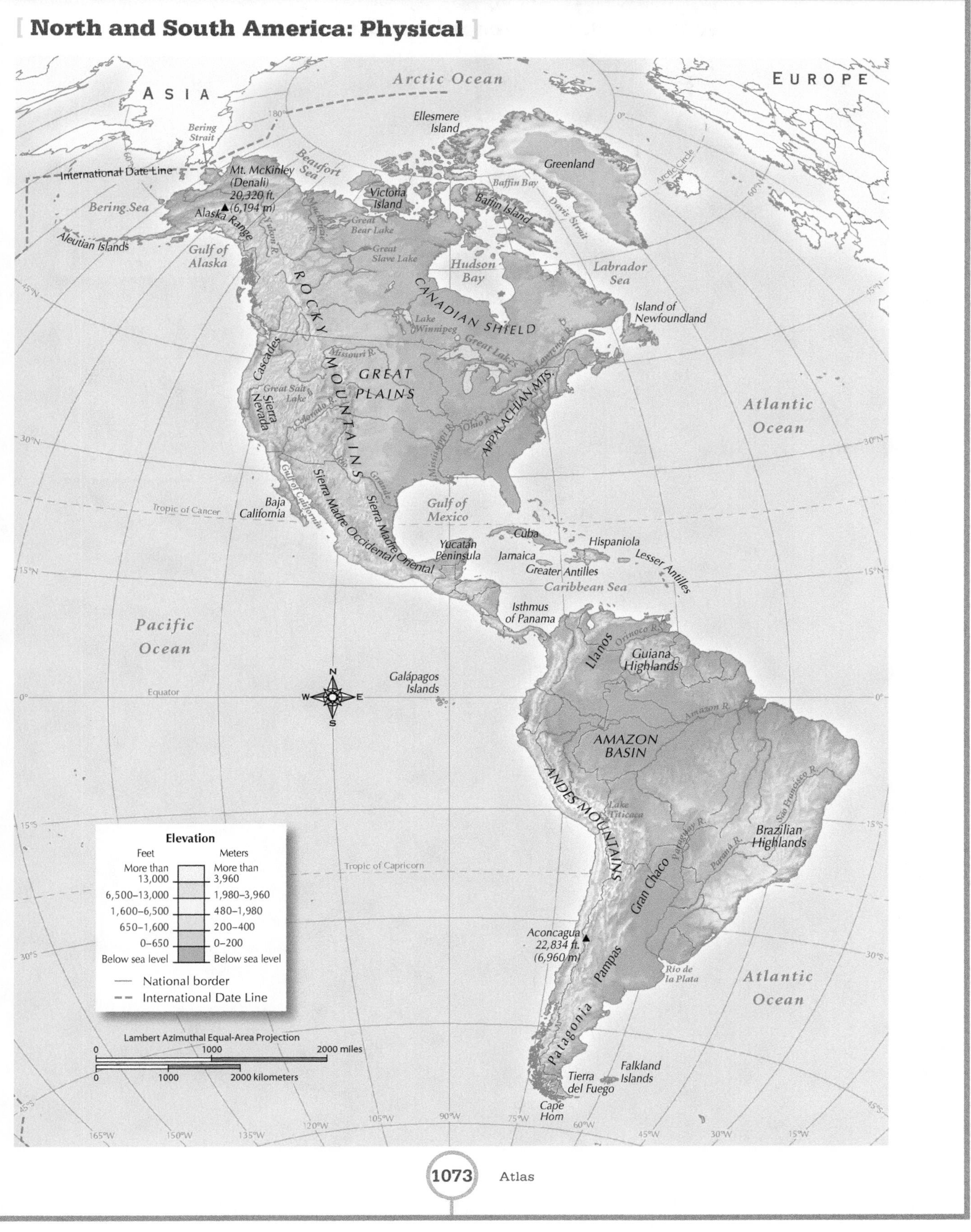
Arctic Ocean
ASIA
EUROPE
Bering Strait
Ellesmere Island
Greenland
Beaufort Sea
International Date Line
Mt. McKinley (Denali) 20,320 ft. (6,194 m)
Victoria Island
Baffin Bay
Baffin Island
Davis Strait
Bering Sea
Alaska Range
Great Bear Lake
Aleutian Islands
Gulf of Alaska
Great Slave Lake
Hudson Bay
Labrador Sea
ROCKY MOUNTAINS
CANADIAN SHIELD
Island of Newfoundland
Lake Winnipeg
Great Lakes
Missouri R.
St. Lawrence R.
Cascades
GREAT PLAINS
Great Salt Lake
Sierra Nevada
Colorado R.
APPALACHIAN MTS.
Ohio R.
Mississippi R.
Atlantic Ocean
Rio Grande
Gulf of California
Sierra Madre Occidental
Sierra Madre Oriental
Tropic of Cancer
Baja California
Gulf of Mexico
Cuba
Hispaniola
Yucatán Peninsula
Jamaica
Lesser Antilles
Greater Antilles
Caribbean Sea
Isthmus of Panama
Pacific Ocean
Llanos
Orinoco R.
Guiana Highlands
Galápagos Islands
Equator
Amazon R.
AMAZON BASIN
ANDES MOUNTAINS
São Francisco R.
Lake Titicaca
Brazilian Highlands
Paraguay R.
Paraná R.
Tropic of Capricorn
Gran Chaco
Aconcagua 22,834 ft. (6,960 m)
Pampas
Río de la Plata
Atlantic Ocean
Patagonia
Falkland Islands
Tierra del Fuego
Cape Horn
Elevation
Feet
Meters
More than 13,000
More than 3,960
6,500–13,000
1,980–3,960
1,600–6,500
480–1,980
650–1,600
200–480
0–650
0–200
Below sea level
Below sea level
National border
International Date Line
Lambert Azimuthal Equal-Area Projection
0
1000
2000 miles
0
1000
2000 kilometers
165°W
150°W
135°W
120°W
105°W
90°W
75°W
60°W
45°W
30°W
15°W
45°N
30°N
15°N
0°
15°S
30°S
45°S
180°
0°

Australia, New Zealand, and Oceania: Political-Physical

International Date Line
National border
State border
Reef
National capital
State capital
Other city

Elevation

Feet	Meters
More than 13,000	More than 3,960
6,500–13,000	1,980–3,960
1,600–6,500	480–1,980
650–1,600	200–480
0–650	0–200
Below sea level	Below sea level

Mercator Projection

The Arctic: Physical

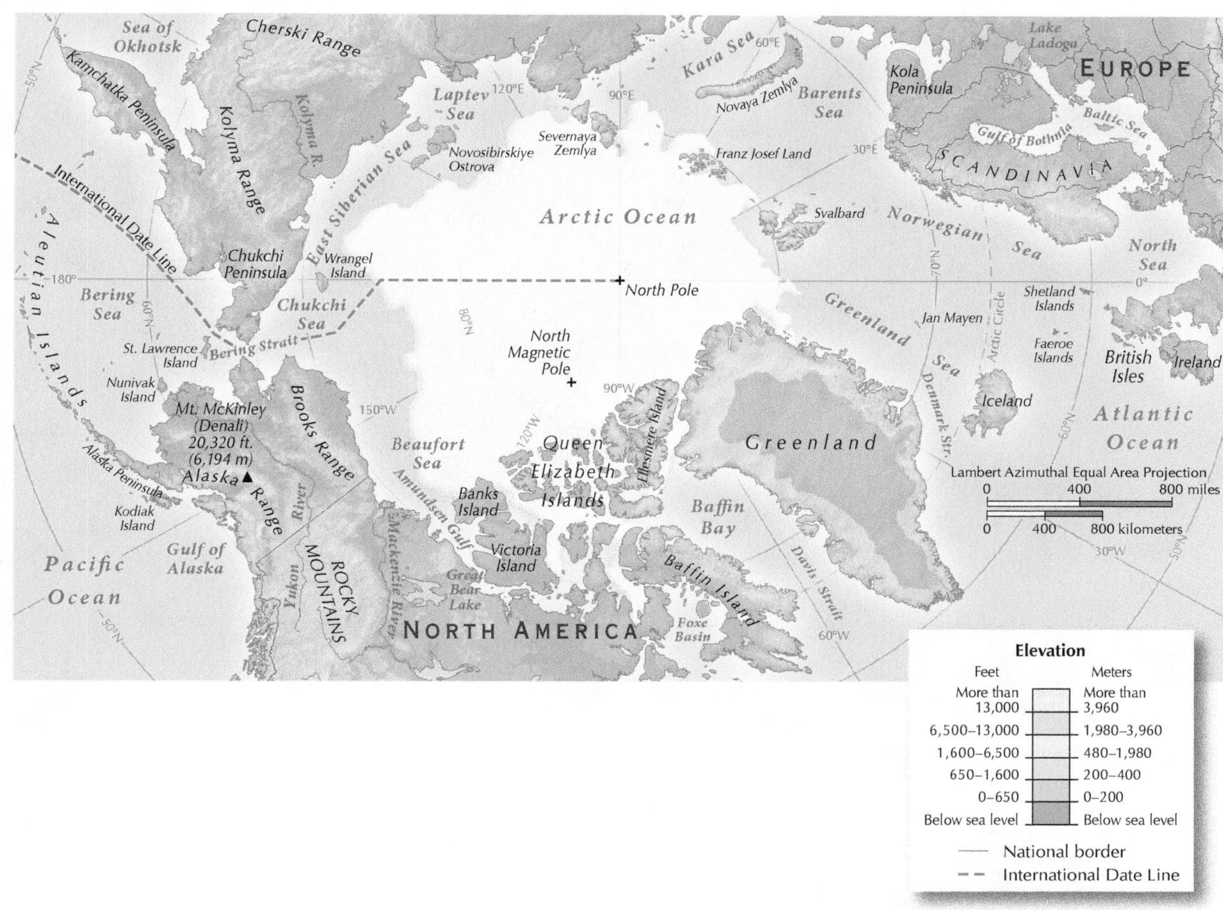

1075

Antarctica: Physical

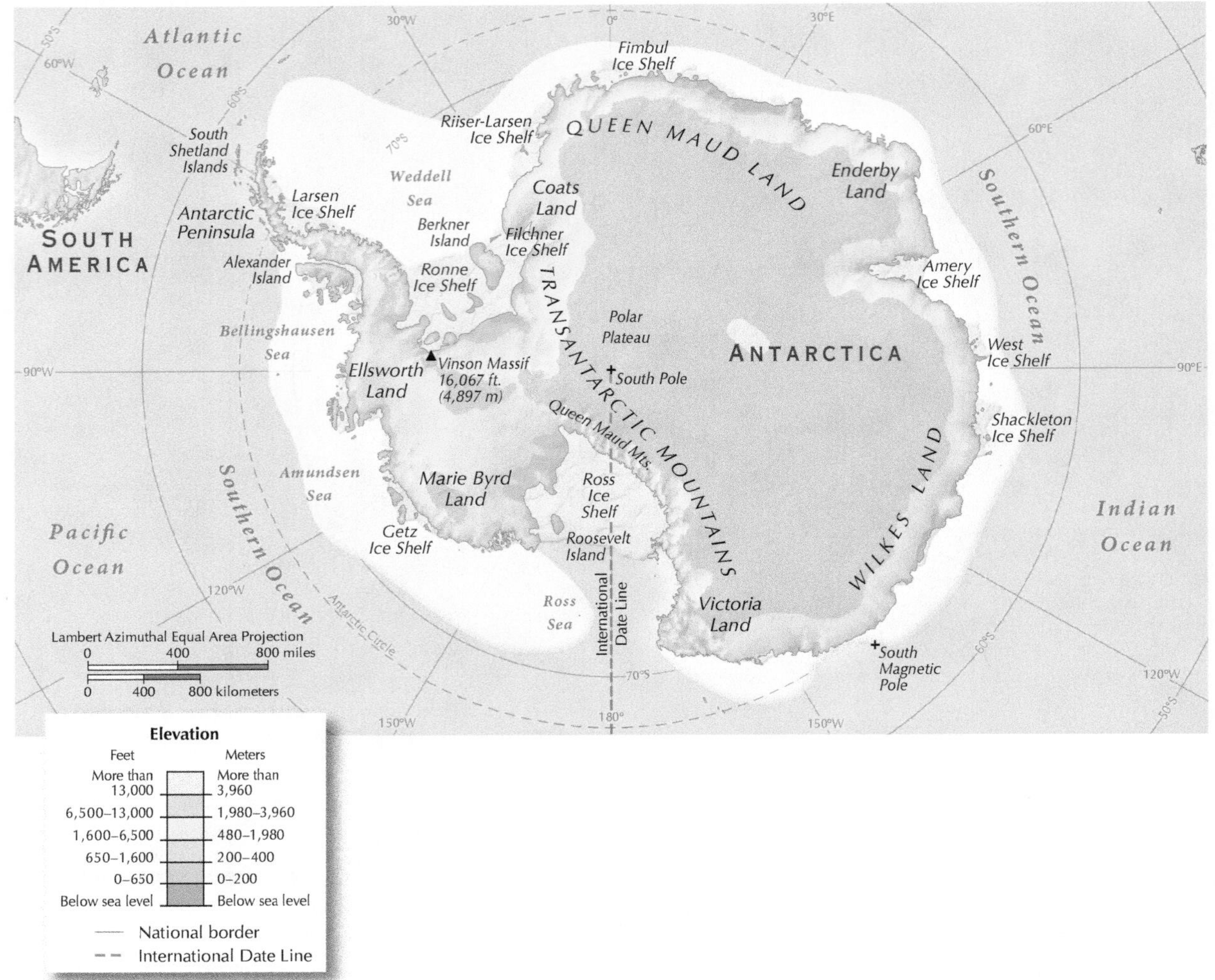

A

Abbasids dynasty that ruled in Bagdad from 750–1258
Abbasids dinastía que gobernó Bagdad durante los años 750–1258

abdicate to give up or step down from power
abdicar renunciar de un puesto de poder

abolition movement the campaign against slavery and the slave trade
movimiento por la abolición campaña contra la esclavitud y contra el tráfico de esclavos

absentee landlord one who owns a large estate but does not live there
dueño ausente dueño de una gran propiedad que no vive en ella

absolute monarch ruler with complete authority over the government and lives of the people he or she governs
monarca absoluto gobernante que tiene autoridad absoluta sobre la administración y la vida de los que están bajo su mando

abstract style of art composed of lines, colors, and shapes, sometimes with no recognizable subject matter at all
abstracto estilo de arte compuesto de líneas, colores y formas, y que a veces no tiene un tema reconocible

acculturation the blending of two or more cultures
aculturación mezcla de dos o más culturas

acid rain a form of pollution in which toxic chemicals in the air come back to Earth in the form of rain, snow, or hail
lluvia ácida forma de polución en la que los productos químicos tóxicos que se encuentran en el aire vuelven a la tierra en la lluvia, nieve o granizo

acropolis highest and most fortified point within a Greek city-state
acrópolis el punto más alto y fortificado de una ciudad-estado griega

acupuncture medical treatment, originated in ancient China, in which needles are inserted into the skin at specific points to relieve pain or treat various illnesses
acupuntura tratamiento médico, originario de China, por el que se introducen agujas en la piel en puntos específicos para aliviar el dolor o como tratamiento de diversas enfermedades

adobe a mixture of clay and plant fibers that becomes hard as it dries in the sun and that can be used for building
adobe mezcla de arcilla y fibras vegetales que se endurece al secarse al sol y se puede usar en la construcción

Adulis strategic trading port of the kingdom of Axum
Adulis puerto comercial estratégico del reino de Axum

Afghanistan an Islamic country in Central Asia; invaded by the Soviet Union in 1979; later home to the radical Islamist Taliban and the terrorist al Qaeda
Afganistán país islámico en Asia Central; invadido por la Unión Soviética en 1979; más tarde hogar de los radicales islamistas Talibán y de los terroristas de al Qaeda

African National Congress the main organization that opposed apartheid and pushed for majority rule in South Africa; later a political party
Congreso Nacional Africano principal organización que se opuso al apartheid y que abogó por el gobierno de la mayoría de Sudáfrica; posteriormente, partido político

agribusinesses giant commercial farms, often owned by multinational corporations
industria agropecuaria inmensas granjas comerciales, generalmente administradas por corporaciones multinacionales

ahimsa Hindu belief in nonviolence and reverence for all life
ahimsa creencia hindú en la no violencia y en el respeto a todas las formas de vida

aircraft carriers ships that accommodate the taking off and landing of airplanes, and transport aircraft
portaaviones buque dotado de las instalaciones necesarias para el transporte, despegue y aterrizaje de aparatos de aviación

al Qaeda a fundamentalist Islamic terrorist organization led by Saudi Arabian Osama bin Laden
al Qaeda organización fundamentalista islámica terrorista liderada por el saudí Osama bin Laden

Alexandria an ancient Hellenistic city in Egypt
Alejandría antigua ciudad helenista en Egipto

alliance formal agreement between two or more nations or powers to cooperate and come to one another's defense
alianza acuerdo formal de cooperación y defensa mutua entre dos o más naciones o potencias

alphabet writing system in which each symbol represents a single basic sound
alfabeto sistema de escritura en el que cada símbolo representa un único sonido

Alsace and Lorraine provinces on the border of Germany and France, lost by France to Germany in 1871; regained by France after WWI
Alsacia y Lorena provincias en la frontera entre Alemania y Francia, que Alemania arrebató a Francia en 1871, y que Francia recuperó después de la Primera Guerra Mundial

Amritsar massacre an incident in 1919 in which British troops fired on an unarmed crowd of Indians
masacre de Amritsar incidente en 1919 en el que las tropas británicas dispararon contra un grupo de indios indefensos

anarchist someone who wants to abolish all government
anarquista persona que quiere abolir toda forma de gobierno

ancien régime old order; system of government in pre-revolution France
ancien regime antiguo orden; sistema de gobierno en la Francia prerevolucionaria

anesthetic drug that prevents pain during surgery
anestesia fármaco que suprime el dolor durante la cirugía

animism the belief that spirits and forces live within animals, objects, or dreams
animismo creencia de que los espíritus y fuerzas pueden vivir en animales, objetos o sueños

annex add a territory to an existing state or country
anexar agregar un territorio a un estado o país existente

Anschluss union of Austria and Germany
Anschluss unión de Austria y Alemania

anthropology the study of the origins and development of people and their societies
antropología estudio del origen y desarrollo de los pueblos y sus sociedades

anti-ballistic missiles missiles that can shoot down other missiles
misiles anti-balísticos misiles que pueden derribar otros misiles

anti-Semitism prejudice against Jews
antisemitismo prejuicio contra los judíos

apartheid a policy of rigid segregation of nonwhite people in the Republic of South Africa
apartheid política de estricta separación racial en Sudáfrica que fue abolida en 1989

apostle leader or teacher of a new faith or movement
apóstol líder o maestro de una nueva fe o movimiento
appeasement policy of giving in to an aggressor's demands in order to keep the peace
contemporización política de aceptación de las exigencias de un agresor para mantener la paz
apprentice a young person learning a trade from a master
aprendiz persona joven que aprendía un oficio de un maestro
aqueduct in ancient Rome, underground or bridgelike stone structure that carried water from the hills into the cities
acueducto en la antigua Roma, estructura parecida a un puente que llevaba agua desde las colinas hasta las ciudades
archaeology the study of people and cultures through their material remains
arqueología estudio de pueblos y culturas antiguas por medio de sus restos materiales
archipelago chain of islands
archipiélago cadena de islas
aristocracy government headed by a privileged minority or upper class
aristocracia gobierno encabezado por una minoría privilegiada o de clase alta
armada fleet of ships
armada flota de barcos
armistice agreement to end fighting in a war
armisticio acuerdo para dejar de luchar en una guerra
artifact an object made by human beings
artefacto objeto hecho por seres humanos
artificial satellite man-made object that orbits a larger body in space
satélite artificial objeto artificial que gira en el espacio alrededor de un cuerpo más grande
artisan a skilled craftsperson
artesano trabajador cualificado que hace objetos a mano
Asante kingdom kingdom that emerged in the 1700s in present-day Ghana and was active in the slave trade
reino Asante reino que surgió en el siglo XVIII en el actual Ghana y que tenía comercio de esclavos
Asia Minor the Turkish peninsula between the Black Sea and the Mediterranean Sea
Asia Menor la península turca entre el Mar Negro y el Mar Mediterráneo
assassination murder of a public figure, usually for political reasons
asesinato acto de dar muerte a una figura pública, generalmente por razones políticas
assembly line production method that breaks down a complex job into a series of smaller tasks
cadena de montaje método de producción que divide un trabajo complejo en una serie de tareas menores
assimilate absorb or adopt another culture
asimilar absorber o adoptar otra cultura
atheism belief that there is no god
ateísmo creencia de que no existen dioses
Athens a city-state in ancient Greece
Atenas ciudad-estado en la antigua Grecia
atman in Hindu belief, a person's essential self
atman según la creencia hindú, el ser esencial de una persona
atrocity horrible act committed against innocent people
atrocidad acto brutal cometido en contra de inocentes
autocrat ruler who has complete authority
autócrata gobernante que tiene autoridad total
autocratic having unlimited power
autocrático que tiene poder ilimitado
autonomy self-rule
autonomía autogobierno
Axis powers group of countries led by Germany, Italy, and Japan that fought the Allies in World War II
Potencias del Eje grupo de países liderado por Alemania, Italia y Japón que luchó contra los Aliados durante la Segunda Guerra Mundial
Axum trading center, and powerful ancient kingdom in northern present-day Ethiopia
Axum ciudad capital, centro de comercio y poderoso antiguo reino del norte de la presente Etiopía
ayllu in the Inca empire, a close-knit village
ayllu en el imperio Inca, aldea muy unida

B

Baghdad capital city of present-day Iraq; capital of the Muslim empire during Islam's golden age
Baghdad capital del actual Iraq; capital del imperio musulmán durante la época dorada del islam
balance of power distribution of military and economic power that prevents any one nation from becoming too strong
equilibrio de poder distribución del poder military y económico que evita que una nación se vuelva demasiado fuerte
balance of trade difference between how much a country imports and how much it exports
balance commercial diferencia entre lo que importa y exporta un país
Balfour Declaration statement issued by the British government in 1917 supporting the establishment of a homeland for Jews in Palestine
Declaración Balfour declaración hecha por el gobierno británico en 1917 en la que apoyaba la constitución de un estado judío en Palestina
Balkan Peninsula triangular arm of land that juts from southeastern Europe into the Mediterranean
Península Balcánica extensión triangular de tierra que sobresale del sudeste de Europa hasta el Mediterráneo
Bangladesh nation east of India that was formerly part of Pakistan
Bangladesh país al este de India que antiguamente formaba parte de Pakistán
Bantu root language of West Africa on which some early African migration patterns are based
Bantú lengua madre del África occidental en la que están basados algunos patrones migratorios africanos
baroque ornate style of art and architecture popular in the 1600s and 1700s
barroco estilo artístico y arquitectónico elaborado que se dio en los siglos XVII y XVIII
barter economy economic system in which one set of goods or services is exchanged for another
economía de trueque sistema económico en el que se utiliza el intercambio de mercancías o servicios
Bastille fortress in Paris used as a prison; French Revolution began when Parisians stormed it in 1789
Bastilla fortificación en París usada como prisión; la Revolución Francesa empezó cuando los parisinos la asaltaron en 1789

1078

Bataan Death March during World War II, the forced march of Filipino and American prisoners of war under brutal conditions by the Japanese military
Jornada de la Muerte desde Baatan episodio acaecido durante la Segunda Guerra Mundial, en el que prisioneros de guerra filipinos y estadounidenses fueron obligado a marchar bajo condiciones brutales por parte de militares japoneses

Battle of Tours battle in 732 in which the Christian Franks led by Charles Martel defeated Muslim armies and stopped the Muslim advance into Europe
Batalla de Tours batalla en 732 en la que los francos cristianos liderados por Charles Martel derrotaron al ejército musulmán y detuvieron el avance árabe en Europa

Bedouin a desert-dwelling Arab nomad
Beduino nómada árabe que vive en el desierto

Benedictine Rule rules drawn up in 530 by Benedict, a monk, regulating monastic life. The Rule emphasizes obedience, poverty, and chastity and divides the day into periods of worship, work, and study.
Regla Benedictina en 530, reglas establecidas por Benedicto, un monje, para regular la vida monástica. La Regla enfatizaba la obediencia, pobreza y castidad, y divide el día en períodos de adoración, trabajo y estudio.

Biafra region of southeastern Nigeria that launched a failed bid for independence from Nigeria in 1966, launching a bloody war
Biafra región del sudeste de Nigeria que lanzó un fallido intento de independizarse de Nigeria en 1966, y por el que se desató una cruenta guerra

biotechnology the application of biological research to industry, engineering, and technology
biotecnología la aplicación de investigaciones biológicas en la industria, la ingeniería y la tecnología

bishop high-ranking Church official with authority over a local area, or diocese
Obispo funcionario eclesiástico de alto nivel con autoridad sobre un área local o diócesis

Black Death an epidemic of the bubonic plague that ravaged Europe in the 1300s
Peste Negra epidemia de la peste bubónica que arrasó Europa en el siglo XIV

Black Shirt any member of the militant combat squads of Italian Fascists set up under Mussolini
Camisa Negra cualquier miembro de las escuadras militantes de combate de los fascistas italianos que estableció Mussolini

blitzkrieg lightning war
blitzkrieg guerra relámpago o guerra intensa y muy breve

bloc a group of nations acting together in support of one another
bloque grupo de naciones que actúan conjuntamente en apoyo mutuo

Boer War a war in which Great Britain defeated the Boers of South Africa
Guerra Boer guerra en la que Gran Bretaña venció a los Boer de Sudáfrica

Boers Dutch people who settled in Cape Town, Africa, and eventually migrated inland
Boers holandeses establecidos en Ciudad del Cabo, África, que con el tiempo emigraron hacia el interior

bourgeoisie the middle class
burguesía clase media

Boxer Uprising anti-foreign movement in China from 1898–1900
Rebelión Bóxer movimiento en contra de los extranjeros ocurrido en China de 1898 a 1900

boyar landowning noble in Russia under the tsars
boyar noble ruso que poseía tierras en la época de los zares

boycott refuse to buy
boicot negarse a comprar

brahman in the belief system established in Aryan India, the single spiritual power that resides in all things
brahman en el sistema de creencias establecido en la India aria, el único poder espiritual que reside en todas las cosas

bureaucracy system of government that includes different job functions and levels of authority
burocracia sistema de gobierno que incluye diferentes trabajos y niveles de autoridad

bushido code of conduct for samurai during the feudal period in Japan
bushido código de conducta de los samuráis durante el período feudal japonés

C

cabinet parliamentary advisors to the king who originally met in a small room, or "cabinet"
gabinete miembros del parlamento consejeros del rey que originalmente se reunían en un pequeño cuarto o "gabinete"

cahier notebook used during the French Revolution to record grievances
memorándum cuaderno usado durante la Revolución Francesa para anotar los agravios

Cahokia in Illinois, the largest earthwork of the Mississippian culture, c. A.D. 700
Cahokia en Illinois, el mayor terraplén de la cultura de los mississippianos, construido alrededor del 700 D.C.

calculus a branch of mathematics in which calculations are made using special symbolic notations; developed by Isaac Newton
cálculo rama de las matemáticas en la que los cálculos se hacen con notaciones simbólicas especiales; fue desarrollado por Isaac Newton

caliph successor to Muhammad as political and religious leader of the Muslims
califa sucesor de Mahoma como líder religiosoy político de los musulmanes

calligraphy the art of producing beautiful handwriting
caligrafía arte de producir una bella escritura a mano

canon law body of laws of a church
ley canónica serie de leyes de una iglesia

canonize recognize a person as a saint
canonizar reconocer a una persona como santo

Cape Town seaport city and legislative capital of South Africa; first Dutch colony in Africa
Ciudad del Cabo ciudad portuaria y capital legislativa de Sudáfrica; fue la primera colonia holandesa en África

capital money or wealth used to invest in business or enterprise
capital dinero o bienes que se usan para invertir en negocios o empresas

capital offense crime punishable by death
ofensa capital crimen que puede castigarse con la muerte

1079

capitalism economic system in which the means of production are privately owned and operated for profit
capitalismo sistemo económico por el que los medios de producción son propiedad privada y se administran para obtener beneficios

cartel a group of companies that join together to control the production and price of a product
cartel asociación de grandes corporaciones formada para controlar la producción y el precio de un producto

cartographer mapmaker
cartógrafo persona que hace mapas

caste in traditional Indian society, an unchangeable social group into which a person is born
casta grupo social en la sociedad tradicional de India, en el que una persona nace y del que no se puede cambiar

Çatalhüyük one of the world's first villages, established in modern-day Turkey around 7000 B.C.
Çatalhüyük una de las primeras aldeas del mundo establecida en la Turquía actual alrededor del 7000 A.C.

cataract waterfall
catarata cascada, caída de agua

caudillo military dictator in Latin America
caudillo dictador militar en América Latina

celadon porcelain made in Korea with an unusual blue-green glaze
celadon porcelana hecha en Korea con brillo azulverdoso poco común

censorship restriction on access to ideas and information
censura restricción en el acceso a ideas o información

census population count
censo recuento de la población

chancellor the highest official of a monarch, prime minister
canciller oficial con más rango dentro de una monarquía, primer ministro

character written symbol in writing systems such as that of the Chinese
carácter símbolo escrito en los sistemas de escritura como en el chino

charter in the Middle Ages, a written document that set out the rights and privileges of a town
fuero en la Edad Media, documento escrito que establecía los derechos y privilegios de un pueblo

Chavín a culture that thrived in the Andean region from about 900 B.C. to 200 B.C.
chavín cultura que tuvo su apogeo en la región andina, desde alrededor de 900 A.C. a 200 A.C.

Chechnya a republic within Russia where rebels have fought for independence
Chechenia república dentro del territorio ruso en la que grupos rebeldes luchan por su independencia

Cheka early Soviet secret police force
Cheka una de las primeras fuerzas policiales secretas soviética

chinampas in the Aztec empire, artificial islands used to cultivate crops and made of mud piled atop reed mats that were anchored to the lakebed with willow trees
chinampas en el imperio azteca, islas artificiales que se usaban para la agricultura y que estaban hechas de barro apilado sobre esteras de junco ancladas al fondo del lago con ramas de sauce

chivalry code of conduct for knights during the Middle Ages
caballería código de conducta para los caballeros durante la Edad Media

Choson dynasty Korean dynasty that ruled from 1392 to 1910, the longest-lived of Korea's three dynasties
dinastía Choson dinastía coreana que gobernó desde 1392 a 1910, la que más duró de las tres dinastías coreanas

circumnavigate to travel completely around the world
circunnavegar viajar alrededor del mundo

citizen a native or resident of a town or city
ciudadano nativo o residente de un pueblo o ciudad

city-state a political unit that includes a city and its surrounding lands and villages
ciudad estado unidad polítca compuesta por una diudad y las tierras que la rodean

civil disobedience the refusal to obey unjust laws
desobediencia civil negarse a obedecer leyes injustas

civil law branch of law that deals with private rights and matters
derecho civil cuerpo legal que trata de los derechos y asuntos privados de los individuos

civil servant government official
funcionario público oficial del gobierno

civil war war fought between two groups of people in the same nation
guerra civil guerra en la que luchan dos grupos de personas de una misma nación

civilization a complex, highly organized social order
civilización orden social complejo y altamente organizado

clan group of families with a common ancestor
clan grupo de familias con un antepasado en común

clergy the body of people who conduct Christian services
clero grupo de gente que oficia en los servicios religiosos cristianos

coalition temporary alliance of various political parties
coalición alianza temporal de varios partidos políticos

codify to arrange or set down in writing
codificar organizar o establecer por escrito

Cold War state of tension and hostility between nations aligned with the United States on one side and the Soviet Union on the other that rarely led to direct armed conflict
Guerra Fría estado de tensión y hostilidad entre las naciones alineadas con Estados Unidos, por una parte, y con la Unión Soviética, por la otra, que salvo raras excepciones desembocó en un conflicto armado

collective large farm owned and operated by peasants as a group
granja colectiva granja grande que pertenece a campesinos que la administran en grupo

collective security system in which a group of nations acts as one to preserve the peace of all
seguridad colectiva sistema por el que un grupo de naciones actúa como una para preservar la paz común

collectivization the forced joining together of workers and property into collectives, such as rural collectives that absorb peasants and their land
colectivización unión forzada de trabajadores y propiedad en colectivos, como colectivos rurales que absorben a campesinos y sus tierras

1080

colony territory settled and ruled by people from another land
colonia territorio poblado y gobernado por personas de otro lugar

colossus giant
coloso gigante

Columbian Exchange the global exchange of goods, ideas, plants and animals, and disease that began with Columbus' exploration of the Americas
Intercambio colombino intercambio global de bienes, ideas, plantas, animales y enfermedades que comenzaron con la exploración de las Américas por parte de Colón

comedy in ancient Greece, play that mocked people or social customs
comedia en la antigua Grecia, obra de teatro donde se hacía burla de personas o costumbres

Comintern Communist International, international association of communist parties led by the Soviet Union for the purpose of encouraging worldwide communist revolution
Comintern Internacional Comunista, asociación internacional de partidos comunistas liderada por la Unión Soviética con el propósito de extender por el mundo una revolución comunista

command economy system in which government officials make all basic economic decisions
economía controlada sistema en el que los funcionarios del gobierno toman todas las decisiones económicas básicas

commissar Communist party officials assigned to the army to teach party principles and ensure party loyalty during the Russian Revolution
comisario funcionario del partido comunista asignado al ejército para enseñar los principios del partido y para asegurar la lealtad al mismo durante la revolución rusa

commodity valuable product
mercancía producto valioso

common law a legal system based on custom and court rulings
derecho consuetudinario sistema legal basado en la costumbre y en las sentencias de los tribunales

communism form of socialism advocated by Karl Marx; according to Marx, class struggle was inevitable and would lead to the creation of a classless society in which all wealth and property would be owned by the community as a whole
comunismo forma de socialismo defendido por Karl Marx; según Marx, la lucha de clases era inevitable y llevaría a la creación de una sociedad sin clases en la que toda la riqueza y la propiedad pertenecería a la comunidad como un todo

compact an agreement among people
pacto acuerdo

compromise an agreement in which each side makes concessions; an acceptable middle ground
compromiso acuerdo en el que cada parte hace concesiones; un término medio aceptable

concentration camp detention center for civilians considered enemies of the state
campo de concentración centro de detención de los civiles que se considera enemigos del estado

Concert of Europe a system in which Austria, Russia, Prussia, and Great Britain met periodically to discuss any problems affecting the peace in Europe; resulted from the post-Napoleon era Quadruple Alliance
Concierto de Europa sistema por el cual Austria, Rusia, Prusia y Gran Bretaña se reunían periódicamente para discutir cualquier problema que afectara a la paz en Europa; resultado de la Cuádruple Alianza de la era postnapoleónica

concession special economic rights given to a foreign power
concesión derechos económicos especiales que se dan a un poder extranjero

confederation unification
confederación unificación

Congress of Vienna assembly of European leaders that met after the Napoleonic era to piece Europe back together; met from September 1814 to June 1815
Congreso de Viena asamblea de líderes europeos que se reunió después de la era napoleónica para reconstruir Europa; se reunieron desde septiembre de 1814 a junio de 1815

conquistador Spanish explorers who claimed lands in the Americas for Spain in the 1500s and 1600s
conquistador los exploradores españoles que apropiaron tierras en América para España en los siglos XVI y XVII

conscription "the draft," which required all young men to be ready for military or other service
conscripción llamado a filas que exigía que todos los hombres jóvenes estuvieran listos para el servicio militar u otro servicio

consensus general agreement
consenso acuerdo general

Constantinople the capital of the eastern Roman empire; capital of the Byzantine and Ottoman empires, now called Istanbul
Constantinopla capital del Imperio Romano Oriental; capital de los imperios bizantino y otomano, en la actualidad llamada Estambul

constitutional government government whose power is defined and limited by law
gobierno constitucional gobierno cuyo poder está definido y limitado por las leyes

consul in ancient Rome, official from the patrician class who supervised the government and commanded the armies
cónsul funcionario de la clase patricia que en la Roma antigua supervisaba el gobierno y dirigía los ejércitos

containment the U.S. strategy of keeping communism within its existing boundaries and preventing its further expansion
contención estrategia de Estados Unidos de mantener el comunismo dentro de sus fronteras existentes y de prevenir su expansión

Continental System blockade designed by Napoleon to hurt Britain economically by closing European ports to British goods; ultimately unsuccessful
sistema continental bloqueo diseñado por Napoleón para dañar a Gran Bretaña económicamente que consistía en cerrar los puertos europeos a los productos británicos; con el tiempo no tuvo éxito

contraband during wartime, military supplies and raw materials needed to make military supplies that may legally be confiscated by any belligerent
contrabando durante el tiempo de guerra, provisiones militares y materias primas necesarios para fabricar artículos militares, y que pueden ser confiscados legalmente por cualquiera de las partes beligerantes

contras guerrillas who fought the Sandinistas in Nicaragua
contras grupo guerrillero que luchó contra los sandinistas en Nicaragua

convoy group of merchant ships protected by warships
convoy grupo de barcos mercantes protegidos por barcos de guerra

corporation business owned by many investors who buy shares of stock and risk only the amount of their investment
corporación empresa propiedad de muchos inversores que compran acciones y que sólo arriesgan el monto de su inversión

Council of Trent a group of Catholic leaders that met between 1545 and 1563 to respond to Protestant challenges and direct the future of the Catholic Church
Concilio de Trento grupo de líderes católicos que se reunieron entre 1545 y 1563 para tratar los retos protestantes y liderar el futuro de la Iglesia Católica

coup d'état the forcible overthrow of a government
golpe de estado derrocamiento por la fuerza de un gobierno

covenant a binding agreement; specifically, in the Jewish tradition, the binding agreement God made with Abraham
convenio acuerdo vinculante; específicamente, en la tradición judía, el acuerdo vinculante hecho entre Dios y Abraham

creole person in Spain's colonies in the Americas who was an American-born descendent of Spanish settlers
criollo descendiente de colonos españolas nacido en las colonias españolas de América

Crimean War war fought mainly on the Crimean Peninsula between the Russians and the British, French, and Turks from 1853–1856
Guerra de Crimea guerra librada principalmente en la península de Crimea entre los rusos y los británicos, franceses y turcos entre 1853 y 1856

criminal law branch of law that deals with offenses against others
derecho penal rama de la ley que se ocupa de los delitos contra otros

Crusades a series of wars from the 1000s through 1200s in which European Christians tried to win control of the Holy Land from Muslims
Cruzadas serie de guerras entre el siglo XI y el siglo XIII en las que los cristianos europeos intentaron ganar el control sobre los musulmanes de la Tierra Santa

cult of domesticity idealization of women and the home
culto a lo doméstico idealización de las mujeres y del hogar

cultural diffusion the spread of ideas, customs, and technologies from one people to another
difusión cultural divulgación de ideas, costumbres y tecnología de un pueblo a otro

cultural nationalism pride in the culture of one's country
nacionalismo cultural orgullo de la cultura del país propio

Cultural Revolution a Chinese Communist program in the late 1960s to purge China of nonrevolutionary tendencies that caused economic and social damage
Revolución Cultural programa de la China comunista a finales de la década de 1960 que pretendía eliminar de China todas las tendencias no revolucionarias y que causó daños económicos y sociales

culture the way of life of a society, which is handed down from one generation to the next by learning and experience
cultura forma de vida de una sociedad que se pasa de una generación a la siguiente mediante el aprendizaje y la experiencia

cuneiform in the ancient Middle East, a system of writing that used wedge-shaped marks
cuneiforme en el antiguo Oriente Medio, sistema de escritura cuyos caracteres tenían forma de cuña

Cuzco capital city of the Inca empire
Cuzco capital del imperio Inca

Cyrillic relating to the Slavic alphabet derived from the Greek and traditionally attributed to St. Cyril; in modified form still used in modern Slavic languages
cirílico relativo al alfabeto eslavo, derivado del griego y tradicionalmente atribuido a San Cirilo; todavía en uso, de forma modificada, en las lenguas eslavas modernas

D

dada artistic movement in which artists rejected tradition and produced works that often shocked their viewers
dadaísmo movimiento artístico en el que los artistas rechazaban la tradición y producían obras que a menudo sorprendían a su público

dalits outcastes or members of India's lowest caste
dalits los marginados o miembros de las castas más bajas de India

Dardanelles vital strait connecting the Black Sea and the Mediterranean Sea in present-day Turkey
Dardanelos estrecho de vital importancia que conecta el Mar Negro y el Mar Mediterráneo en la actual Turquía

Darfur a region in western Sudan where ethnic conflict threatened to lead to genocide
Darfur región occidental de Sudán donde un conflicto étnico amenaza con provocar un genocidio

D-Day code name for June 6, 1944, the day that Allied forces invaded France during WWII
Día D nombre en clave del día en que las fuerzas aliadas invadieron Francia durante la Segunda Guerra Mundial

decimal system system of numbers based on 10
sistema de decimal sistema numérico basado en el número 10

decipher to figure out the meaning of
descrifrar descubrir el significado de algo

default fail to make payments
cese de pagos imposibilidad de realizar pagos

deficit gap between what a government spends and what it takes in through taxes and other sources
déficit diferencia entre los gastos de un gobierno y las recaudaciones por impuestos y otras fuentes de ingresos

deficit spending situation in which a government spends more money than it takes in
gasto deficitario situación en la que un gobierno gasta más de lo que recauda

deforestation the destruction of forest land
deforestación destrucción de tierras forestales

Delhi the third-largest city in India; capital of medieval India
Delhi tercera ciudad más grande de India; capital de la India medieval

delta triangular area of marshland formed by deposits of silt at the mouth of some rivers
delta área triangular de tierra pantanosa que se forma con los depósitos de limo en la desembocadura de algunos ríos

demilitarized zone a thin band of territory across the Korean peninsula separating North Korean forces from South Korean forces; established by the armistice of 1953
zona desmilitarizada estrecha franja de tierra que cruza la península de Corea y que separa las fuerzas de Corea del Norte y las fuerzas de Corea del Sur; establecida por el armisticio de 1953

democracy government in which the people hold ruling power
democracia forma de gobierno en el que la soberanía reside en el pueblo

1082

depopulation reduction in the number of people in an area
despoblación reducción del número de la población en una zona

desertification process by which fertile or semidesert land becomes desert
desertización proceso por el que la tierra fértil o semifértil se convierte en desierto

détente the relaxation of Cold War tensions during the 1970s
distensión relajamiento de las tensiones de la Guerra Fría en los años 70

developing world nations working toward development in Africa, Asia, and Latin America
mundo en desarrollo países en vías de desarrollo de á frica, Asia y Latinoamérica

development the process of building stable governments, improving agriculture and industry, and raising the standard of living
desarrollo proceso de establecer gobiernos estables, mejorar la agricultura, la industria y las condiciones de vida

dharma in Hindu belief, a person's religious and moral duties
dharma según la creencia hindú, las obligaciones morales y religiosas de un individuo

Diaspora the spreading of the Jews beyond their historic homeland
Diáspora diseminación de los judíos más allá de su patria histórica

dictator ruler who has complete control over a government; in ancient Rome, a leader appointed to rule for six months in times of emergency
dictador dirigente con control absolute sobre el gobierno; en la antigua Roma, líder designado para gobernar durante seis meses en casos de emergencia

Dienbienphu small town and former French army base in northern Vietnam; site of the battle that ended in a Vietnamese victory, the French withdrawal from Vietnam, and the securing of North Vietnam's independence
Dienbienphu pequeño pueblo y antigua base del ejército francés en el norte de Vietnam; lugar de la batalla que terminó con la victoria vietnamita, la expulsión de los franceses de Vietnam y la obtención de la independencia de Vietnam del Norte

diet assembly or legislature
dieta asamblea o cuerpo legislativo

direct democracy system of government in which citizens participate directly in the day-today affairs of government rather than through elected representatives
democracia directa sistema de gobierno en el que los ciudadanos participan directamente en lugar de hacerlo a través de representantes electos en los asuntos diarios del gobierno

disarmament reduction of armed forces and weapons
desarme reducción del ejército y del armamento

discrimination unequal treatment or barriers
discriminación tratamiento desigual o barreras

dissent ideas that oppose those of the government
disentir ideas que se oponen a las del gobierno

dissenter Protestant whose views and opinions differed from those of the Church of England
disidente protestante cuyos puntos de vista y opiniones diferían de los de la Iglesia de Inglaterra

divine right belief that a ruler's authority comes directly from God
derecho divino creencia de que la autoridad de un gobernante proviene directamente de Dios

domesticate to tame animals and adapt crops so they are best suited to use by humans
domesticar domar animales y adaptar plantas con el propósito de adecuarlos para el uso humano

dominion self-governing nation
dominio nación que se gobierna a sí misma

domino theory the belief that a communist victory in South Vietnam would cause noncommunist governments across Southeast Asia to fall to communism, like a row of dominoes
teoría del dominó creencia de que una victoria comunista en Vietnam del Sur podría causar que los gobiernos no comunistas del sudeste de Asia cayeran bajo dominio del comunismo, como una fila de fichas de dominó

dowry in some societies, payment a bride's family makes to the bridegroom and his family; payment a woman brings to a marriage
dote en algunas sociedades, pago de la familia de la novia al novio y a su familia; pago que una mujer proporciona a sumatrimonio

Dreyfus affair a political scandal that caused deep divisions in France between Royalists and liberals and republicans; centered on the 1894 wrongful conviction of Alfred Dreyfus, a Jewish officer in the French army
Caso Dreyfus escándalo político que causó divisiones profundas en Francia entre los realistas, liberales y republicanos; basado en la in justa condena en 1894 de Alfred Dreyfus, un oficial judío del ejérci to francés

Dual Monarchy the monarchy of Austria-Hungary
monarquía dual monarquía de Austria-Hungría

due process of law the requirement that the government act fairly and in accordance with established rules in all that it does
garantías procesales debidas requisito para que el gobierno actúe justamente y en concordancia con las normas establecidas en todo lo que hace

Duma elected national legislature in Russia
Duma en Rusia, asamblea legislative nacional electa

Dunkirk port in France from which 300,000 Allied troops were evacuated when their retreat by land was cut off by the German advance in 1940
Dunkirk puerto de Francia desde donde fueron evacuadas 300,000 tropas aliadas en 1940 al ser bloqueada su retirada terrestre por el avance del ejército alemán

Dutch East India Company a trading company established by the Netherlands in 1602 to protect and expand its trade in Asia
Compañía Holandesa de las Indias Orientales compañía de comercio establecida por Holanda en 1602 para proteger y aumentar su comercio con Asia

dynamo a machine used to generate electricity
dínamo máquina que se usa para generar electricidad

dynastic cycle rise and fall of Chinese dynasties according to the Mandate of Heaven
ciclo dínastico florecimiento y caída de las dinastías chinas de acuerdo con el Mandato del Cielo

dynasty ruling family
dinastía familia gobernante

E

earthwork an embankment or other construction made of earth
terraplén muro de contención u otra construcción hecha de tierra

East Timor a former Portuguese colony, seized by Indonesia, that gained independence in 2002
Timor Oriental antigua colonia portuguesa, ocupada por Indonesia, que obtuvo su independencia en 2002

economic nationalism an emphasis on domestic control and protection of the economy
nacionalismo económico énfasis en el control nacional y en la protección de la economía

Edict of Nantes law issued by French king Henry IV in 1598 giving more religious freedom to French Protestants
Edicto de Nantes ley promulgada por el rey francés Enrique IV en 1598 por la que se concedía mayor libertad religiosa a los protestantes frances

Eightfold Path as taught by the Buddha, the path one must follow to achieve nirvana
Óctuple Sendero como enseñó Buda, el camino que debe seguir todo individuo para conseguir el nirvana

elector one of seven German princes who would choose the Holy Roman emperor
elector uno de los siete príncipes germanos que elegían al emperador del Sacro Romano

electorate body of people allowed to vote
electorado conjunto de personas a quienes se permite votar

elite upper class
élite clase alta

emancipation granting of freedom to serfs or slaves
emancipación concesión de libertad a esclavos o siervos

emigration movement away from one's homeland
emigración trasladarse de su propio país a otro

émigré person who flees his or her country for political reasons
exiliado persona que deja su país por razones políticas

empire a group of states or territories controlled by one ruler
imperio grupo de estados o territorios controlados por un gobernante

enclosure the process of taking over and consolidating land formerly shared by peasant farmers
cercamiento proceso de consolidar y apropiarse de una tierra que anteriormente compartían campesinos

encomienda right the Spanish government granted to its American colonists to demand labor or tribute from Native Americans
encomienda derecho a exigir tributo o trabajo a los natives americanos, que el gobierno español otorgó a sus colonos en América

endangered species species threatened with extinction
especies en vías de extinción especies amenazadas de extinción, es decir, de desaparición

engineering application of science and mathematics to develop useful structures and machines
ingeniería aplicación de las ciencias y matemáticas al desarrollo do máquinas y estructuras útiles

English Bill of Rights series of acts passed by the English Parliament in 1689 that limited the rights of the monarchy and ensured the superiority of Parliament
Declaración de derechos de los ingleses serie de leyes aprobadas por el parlamento inglés en 1689 que limitaba los derechos de la monarquía y establecía la primacía del parlamento

engraving art form in which an artist etches a design on a metal plate with acid and then uses the plate to make multiple prints
grabado forma de arte en la que un artista graba un diseño con ácido en una placa de metal y después la usa para producir múltiples impresiones

enlightened despot absolute ruler who used his or her power to bring about political and social change
déspota ilustrado gobernante absoluto que usa su poder para precipitar cambios políticos y sociales

entente nonbinding agreement to follow common policies
entendimiento acuerdo no vinculante de seguir normas comunes

enterprise a business organization in such areas as shipping, mining, railroads, or factories
empresa entidad empresarial en áreas como transportes, minería, ferrocariles o fábricas

entrepreneur person who assumes financial risk in the hope of making a profit
empresario persona que asume riesgos financieros con la esperanza de obtener beneficios

Epic of Gilgamesh Mesopotamian narrative poem that was first told in Sumer
El poema de Gilgamesh poema narrativo de Mesopotamia que se contó por primera vez en Sumeria

epidemic outbreak of a rapidly spreading disease
epidemia brote de una enfermedad que se extiende rápidamente

erosion the wearing away of land
erosión el desgaste paulatino de la tierra

estate social class
estado clase social

Estates-General legislative body made up of representatives of the three estates in prerevolutionary France
Estados Generales cuerpo legislativo formado por representantes de los tres estados en la Francia prerevolucionaria

ethics moral standards of behavior
ética estándar moral de conducta

Ethiopia ancient Greek term for Axumite kingdom; present-day country in East Africa
Etiopía antiguo término griego para el reino de Axumite; también es un país actual del este de África

ethnic cleansing the killing or forcible removal of people of different ethnicities from an area by aggressors so that only the ethnic group of the aggressors remains
limpieza étnica la matanza o expulsión forzosa de personas de diferentes grupos étnicos de una zona, llevadas a cabo por agresores para que su grupo étnico tenga permanencia exclusiva

ethnic group large group of people who share the same language and cultural heritage
étnico grupo grande de personas que comparten el idioma y la herencia cultural

Etruscans a people who inhabited early Italy
estrucos pueblo que habitaba principalmente al norte the Roma

euro common currency used by member nations of the European Union
euro moneda común usada por las naciones que pertenecen a la Unión Europea

European Community an international organization dedicated to establishing free trade among its European member nations
Comunidad Europea organización internacional dedicada a establecer un comercio libre entre sus naciones europeas miembros de todos los productos

European Union an international organization made up of over two dozen European nations, with a common currency and common policies and laws
Unión Europea organización internacional compuesta por más de dos docenas de países, con una misma moneda, y políticas y leyes en común

excommunication exclusion from the Roman Catholic Church as a penalty for refusing to obey Church law
excomunión exclusión de la Iglesia Católica Romana como castigo por rehusar obedecer la ley de la Iglesia

expansionism policy of increasing the amount of territory a government holds
expansionismo política de aumentar el territorio que posee un gobierno

extraterritoriality right of foreigners to be protected by the laws of their own nation
extraterritorialidad derecho de los extranjeros a recibir protección de las leyes de su propio país

F

faction dissenting group of people
facción grupo de disidentes

famine a severe shortage of food in which large numbers of people starve
hambruna escasez severa de alimentos por la que perece gran número de personas

fascism any centralized, authoritarian government system that is not communist whose policies glorify the state over the individual and are destructive to basic human rights
fascismo cualquier sistema de gobierno autoritario centralizado no comunista cuya política glorifica al estado por encima del individuo y que destruye los derecho humanos fundamentales

federal republic government in which power is divided between the national, or federal, government and the states
república federal gobierno en el que el poder se divide entre el gobierno nacional o federal y los estados

Federal Reserve central banking system of the United States, which regulates banks
Reserva Federal sistema central de banca de Estados Unidos que regula los bancos

Fertile Crescent region of the Middle East in which civilizations first arose
Medialuna Fértil región de Oriente Medio en la cual surgieron las primeras civilizaciones

feudal contract exchange of pledges between lords and vassals
contrato feudal intercambio de garantías entre los señores y los vasallos

feudalism loosely organized system of government in which local lords governed their own lands but owed military service and other support to a greater lord
feudalismo sistema de gobierno poco organizado en el que los señores goberna ban sus propias tierras, pero debían servicio militar y otras formas de apoyo a un superior

fief in medieval Europe, an estate granted by a lord to a vassal in exchange for service and loyalty
estado feudal durante la Edad Media, terreno que un señor cedía a un vasallo a cambio de servicio y lealtad

filial piety respect for parents
piedad filial respeto hacia los padres

finance the management of money matters including the circulation of money, loans, investments, and banking
finanzas o gestión de los asuntos monetarios incluyendo la circulación de dinero, préstamos, inversiones y banca

First Sino-Japanese War conflict between China and Japan in 1894–1895 over control of Korea
Primera guerra sino-japonesa conflicto entre China y Japón de 1894 a 1895 por el control de Corea

Flanders a region that included parts of presentday northern France, Belgium, and the Netherlands; was an important industrial and financial center of northern Europe during the Middle Ages and Renaissance
Flandes región que incluye partes de los actuales norte de Francia, Bélgica y Holanda; fue un importante centro industrial y financiero del norte de Europa durante la Edad Media y el Renacimiento

flapper in the United States and Europe in the 1920s, a rebellious young woman
flapper mujer joven y rebelde en los años 20 en Estados Unidos y Europa

Florence a city in the Tuscany region of northern Italy that was the center of the Italian Renaissance
Florencia ciudad de la región de Toscana en el norte de Italia que fue el centro del Renacimiento italiano

flying buttresses stone supports on the outside of a building that allowed builders to construct higher, thinner walls that contained large stained-glass windows
contrafuertes flotantes soportes de piedra en la parte exterior de un edificio que permitía a los constructores construir paredes más finas y más altas que contenían ventanas con vidrieras

Four Noble Truths as taught by the Buddha, the four basic beliefs that form the foundation of Buddhism
Cuatro Verdades Nobles como enseñó Buda, las cuatro creencias básicas que forman la base del budismo

Fourteen Points list of terms for resolving WWI and future wars outlined by American President Woodrow Wilson in January 1918
Catorce puntos lista de condiciones para resolver la Primera Guerra Mundial y futuras guerras, esbozada por el presidente estadounidense Woodrow Wilson en enero de 1918

Franks a Germanic tribe that conquered presentday France and neighboring lands in the 400s
francos tribu germánica que conquistó la actual Francia y las tierras colindantes en el siglo V

free trade trade between countries without quotas, tariffs, or other restrictions
libre comercio comercio entre países, sin cuotas, tasas u otras restricciones

French and Indian War war between Britain and France in the Americas that happened from 1754 to 1763; it was part of a global war called the Seven Years' War
Guerra franco-india guerra entre Gran Bretaña y Francia en América, que duró desde 1754 a 1763; fue parte de una guerra global que se conoció como la Guerra de los Siete Años

1085

French Indochina Western name for the colonial holdings of France on mainland Southeast Asia; present-day Vietnam, Laos, and Cambodia
Indochina francesa nombre occidental para las colonias de Francia en el sudeste asiático continental

fresco colorful painting completed on wet plaster
fresco pintura colorida realizada sobre una pared de yeso húmedo

friar a medieval European monk who traveled from place to place preaching to the poor
fraile monje de la Europa medieval que viajaba de un lugar a otro predicando a los pobres

fundamentalists religious leaders who call for a return to what they see as the fundamental, or basic, values of their faiths
fundamentalistas líderes religiosos que abogan por el retorno de lo que consideran ser los valores fundamentales, o básicos, de sus creencias

G

general strike strike by workers in many different industries at the same time
huelga general huelga de trabajadores de muchas industrias diferentes al mismo tiempo

genetic engineering manipulation of living organisms' chemical code in order to produce specific results
ingeniería genética alteración del código genético que portan todas las formas de vida con el fin de producir resultados específicos

genetics a branch of biology dealing with heredity and variations among plants and animals
genética rama de la biología que trata sobre la herencia y las variaciones entre sí de los animales y las plantas

Geneva Swiss city-state which became a Calvinist theocracy in the 1500s; today a major city in Switzerland
Ginebra ciudad estado suiza que se convirtió en una teocracia calvinista en el siglo XVI; en la actualidad es una de las principales ciudades de Suiza

genocide deliberate attempt to destroy an entire religious or ethnic group
genocidio intento deliberado de destruir la totalidad de un grupo religioso o étnico

gentry wealthy, landowning class
alta burguesía clase social rica, dueña de tierras

germ theory the theory that infectious diseases are caused by certain microbes
teoría de los gérmenes teoría de que las enfermedades infecciosas son causadas por ciertos microbios

Gestapo secret police in Nazi Germany
Gestapo policía secreta de la Alemania nazi

Ghana early West African trading kingdom located in parts of present-day Mauritania and Mali
Ghana antiguo reino comerciante de África occidental ubicado en partes de la actual Mauritania y Mali

ghetto separate section of a city where members of a minority group are forced to live
gueto área separada de una ciudad donde se fuerza a vivir a los miembros de una minoría

glasnost "openness" in Russian; a Soviet policy of greater freedom of expression introduced by Mikhail Gorbachev in the late 1980s
glasnost "apertura" en ruso; política soviética de mayor libertad de expresión introducida por Mikhail Gorbachev a finales de la década de 1980

global warming the rise of Earth's surface temperature over time
calentamiento global el aumento de la temperatura de la superficie terrestre a través del tiempo

globalization the process by which national economies, politics, cultures, and societies become integrated with those of other nations around the world
globalización proceso mediante el cual las economías nacionales, la política, la cultura y la sociedades se integran con las de otros países del mundo

Goa a state in western India; formerly a coastal city that was made the base of Portugal's Indian trade
Goa estado en el oeste de India; antiguamente una ciudad costera que se convirtió en la base del comercio en la India de Portugal

golden age period of great cultural achievement
edad de oro período de grandes logros culturales

Golden Bull of 1222 charter that strictly limited royal power in Hungary
Bula de Oro de 1222 carta constitucional que limitaba rigurosamente el poder de la realeza en Hungría

Golden Horde the Mongol armies that invaded Europe in 1237 and ruled Russia for over two centuries
Horda Dorada los ejércitos mongoles que invadieron Europa en 1237 y que gobernaron Rusia durante más de dos siglos

Golden Temple the Sikh religion's holiest shrine
Templo Dorado santuario de mayor peso sagrado de la religión sikh

Good Friday Agreement an agreement to end the conflict in Northern Ireland signed in 1998 by Protestants and Catholics
Acuerdo del Viernes Santo acuerdo firmado por protestantes y católicos en 1998 para poner fin al conflicto en Irlanda del Norte

Good Neighbor Policy policy in which American President Franklin Roosevelt promised that the United States would interfere less in Latin American affairs
Política del Buen Vecino politica con la que el presidente estadounidense Franklin Roosevelt prometio que Estados Unidos interferiria menos en los asuntos de America Latina

Gothic style type of European architecture that developed in the Middle Ages, characterized by flying buttresses, ribbed vaulting, thin walls, and high roofs
estilo gótico tipo de arquitectura europea que se desarrolló en la Edad Media caracterizada por contrafuertes flotantes, bóvedas estriadas, paredes finas y techos altos

gravity force that pulls objects in Earth's sphere to the center of Earth
gravedad fuerza que atrae los objetos dentro de la esfera terrestre al centro de la Tierra

Great Depression a painful time of global economic collapse, starting in 1929 and lasting until about 1939
Gran Depresión período nefasto de colapso de la economía mundial que empezó en 1929 y duró hasta 1939

Great Leap Forward a Chinese Communist program from 1958 to 1960 to boost farm and industrial output that failed miserably
Gran Salto hacia Adelante programa de la China comunista de 1958 a 1960 para aumentar la producción agrícola e industrial que fracasó miserablemente

Great Schism the official split between the Roman Catholic and Byzantine churches that occurred in 1054
Gran Cisma división oficial entre las iglesias católica romana y bizantina ocurrida en 1054

Great Zimbabwe powerful East African medieval trade center and city-state located in southeastern present-day Zimbabwe
Gran Zimbabwe poderoso centro de comercio medieval de África oriental y ciudad estado ubicada en el sureste del actual Zimbabwe

Green Revolution the improved seeds, pesticides, mechanical equipment, and farming methods introduced in the developing world beginning in the 1950s
revolución verde la introducción, en los países en vías de desarrollo durante la década de 1950, de semillas, pesticidas, equipo mecánico y métodos de agricultura perfeccionados

griot professional storyteller in early West Africa
griot antiguo narrador de historias profesional en África occidental

gross domestic product the total value of all goods and services produced in a nation within a particular year
producto interior bruto valor total de todos los productos y servicios producidos en una nación en un determinado año

Guangzhou a coastal city in southeastern China, also known as Canton
Guangzhou ciudad costera del sudeste de China, también conocida como Cantón

guerrilla a soldier in a loosely organized force making surprise raids
guerrilla pequeños grupos de soldados pertenecientes a una fuerza poco organizada que despliega ataques por sorpresa

guerrilla warfare fighting carried on through hit-and-run raids
guerra de guerrillas lucha que se caracteriza por rápidos ataques y retiradas

guild in the Middle Ages, an association of merchants or artisans who cooperated to uphold standards of their trade and to protect their economic interests
gremio en la Edad Media, asociación de mercaderes o artesanos que cooperaban para mantener los valores de sus oficios y para proteger sus intereses económicos

guillotine device used during the Reign of Terror to execute thousands by beheading
guillotina aparato usado durante el Reinado del Terror para decapitar a miles de personas

Gulag in the Soviet Union, a system of forced labor camps in which millions of criminals and political prisoners were held under Stalin
Gulag en la Unión Soviética, un sistema de campos de trabajo forzado donde millones de criminales y prisioneros políticos fueron detenidos durante el gobierno de Stalin

Guomindang Nationalist party; active in China 1912 to 1949
Guomindang partido nacionalista, activo en China entre 1912 y 1949

H

habeas corpus principle that a person cannot be held in prison without first being charged with a specific crime
habeus corpus principio por el que no puede encarcelarse a una persona sin haber sido antes acusada formalmente de un delito específico

hacienda a large plantation
hacienda plantación grande

hajj one of the Five Pillars of Islam, the pilgrimage to Mecca that all Muslims are expected to make at least once in their lifetime
hayyi uno de los Cinco Pilares del Islam, la peregrinación a la Meca que se espera hagan todos los musulmanes por lo menos una vez en la vida

hangul alphabet that uses symbols to represent the sounds of spoken Korean
hangul alfabeto que usa símbolos para representar gráficamente los sonidos del idioma coreano

Hapsburg empire Central European empire that lasted from the 1400s to the 1900s and at its height included the lands of the Holy Roman Empire and the Netherlands
Imperio Habsburgo imperio centroeuropeo que duró desde el siglo XV hasta el siglo XX, y que en su plenitud abarcó los territorios del Sacro Imperio Romano y Holanda

Harappa large ancient city of the Indus civilization, located in present-day Pakistan
Harappa antigua gran ciudad de la civilización del Indo, ubicada en el presente Pakistán

Harlem Renaissance an African American cultural movement in the 1920s and 1930s, centered in Harlem
Renacimiento de Harlem movimiento cultural afroamericano durante las décadas de 1920 y 1930, que estaba centrado en Harlem

hejab headscarves and loose-fitting, ankle-length garments meant to conceal the body
hejab velos, pañuelos y prendas de vestir amplias y hasta los tobillos cuya finalidad es ocultar el cuerpo

heliocentric based on the belief that the sun is the center of the universe
heliocéntrico sistema basado en la creencia de que el Sol es el centro del universo

heresy religious belief that is contrary to the official teachings of a church
herejía creencia religiosa contraria a las enseñanzas oficiales de la iglesia

hierarchy system of ranking groups
jerarquía sistema que clasifica a las personas de una sociedad

hieroglyphics system of writing in which pictures called hieroglyphs represent objects, concepts, or sounds
jeroglíficos sistema de escritura cuyos dibujos, llamados jeroglíficos, representan objetos, conceptos o sonidos

hijra Muhammad's journey from Mecca to Medina in 622
héjira trayecto de Mahoma de la Meca a Medina en el año 622

Hiroshima city in Japan where the first atomic bomb was dropped in August 1945
Hiroshima ciudad de Japón donde fue lanzada la primera bomba atómica en agosto de 1945

historian a person who studies how people lived in the past
historiador persona que estudia el modo de vida de la gente en el pasado

Holocaust the systematic genocide of about six million European Jews by the Nazis during World War II
Holocausto el genocidio sistemático por parte de los nazis de alrededor de seis millones de judíos europeos durante la Segunda Guerra Mundial

Holy Land Jerusalem and other places in Palestine where Christians believe Jesus had lived and preached
Tierra Santa Jerusalem y otros lugares en Palestina donde los cristianos creen que Jesús vivió y predicó

1087

Holy Roman Empire empire of west central Europe from 962 to 1806, comprising present-day Germany and neighboring lands
Sacro Imperio Romano imperio de la Europa central occidental desde 962 a 1806, que comprendía la actual Alemania y las tierras aledañas

home rule local self-government
autogobierno autogobierno local

homogeneous society society that has a common culture and language
sociedad homogénea sociedad que tiene un lenguaje y una cultura común

Huari a culture that thrived in the Andean region from about A.D. 600–A.D. 1000
huari cultura que tuvo su apogeo en la región andina desde alrededor de 600 D.C. a 1000 D.C.

Huguenots French Protestants of the 1500s and 1600s
Hugonotes protestantes franceses de los siglos XVI y XVII

humanism an intellectual movement at the heart of the Renaissance that focused on education and the classics
humanismo movimiento intelectual durante el auge del Renacimiento que se centraba en la educación y los clásicos

humanities study of subjects such as grammar, rhetoric, poetry, and history, that were taught in ancient Greece and Rome
humanidades estudio de asignaturas como la gramática, la retórica, poesía e historia que se enseñaban en las antiguas Grecia y Roma

Huns a nomadic people of central Asia
hunos pueblo nómada del centro de Asia

Hutus the group that forms the majority in Rwanda and Burundi
Hutus grupo mayoritario de Ruanda y Burundi

hypothesis an unproved theory accepted for the purposes of explaining certain facts or to provide a basis for further investigation
hipótesis teoría sin probar aceptada con el propósito de explicar determinados hechos o de proveer una base para una investigación posterior más profunda

I

icon holy image of Christ, Mary, or a saint venerated in the Eastern Orthodox Church
ícono imagen sagrada de Cristo, María o de un santo venerado por la iglesia ortodoxa oriental

ideology system of thought and belief
ideología sistema de pensamiento y creencias

illumination the artistic decoration of books and manuscripts
iluminación decoración artística de libros y manuscritos

immunity natural protection, resistance
inmunidad protección natural, resistencia

imperialism domination by one country of the political, economic, or cultural life of another country or region
imperialismo dominio por parte de un país de la vida política, económica o cultural de otro país o región

import substitution manufacturing goods locally to replace imports
sustitución de importaciones la producción local de bienes para reemplazar su importación

impressionism school of painting of the late 1800s and early 1900s that tried to capture fleeting visual impressions
impresionismo escuela de pintura de finales del siglo XIX y principios del siglo XX que trataba de captar impresiones visuales fugaces

indemnity payment for losses in war
indemnización compensación como pago por pérdidas de guerra

indigenous original or native to a country or region
indígena originario o nativo de un país o región

indulgence in the Roman Catholic Church, pardon for sins committed during a person's lifetime
indulgencia perdón por los pecados cometidos en vida concedido por la Iglesia Católica Romana

inflation economic cycle that involves a rapid rise in prices linked to a sharp increase in the amount of money available
inflación ciclo económico caracterizado por un rápida subida de los precios ligada a un aumento rápido del dinero disponible

Inquisition a Church court set up to try people accused of heresy
Inquisición tribunal de la Iglesia establecido para juzgar a la gente acusada de herejía

insurgents rebel forces
insurgentes fuerzas rebeldes

intendant official appointed by French king Louis XIV to govern the provinces, collect taxes, and recruit soldiers
intendente oficial publico nombrado por el rey francés Luis XIV para gobernar las provincias, recaudar impuestos y reclutar soldados

interchangeable parts identical components that can be used in place of one another in manufacturing
repuestos intercambiables componentes idénticos que pueden usarse unos en lugar de otros en el proceso de producción

interdependence mutual dependence of countries on goods, resources, labor, and knowledge from other parts of the world
interdependencia dependencia mutua de los países con los de otras partes del mundo en cuanto a productos, recursos, mano de obra y conocimientos

interdict in the Roman Catholic Church, excommunication of an entire region, town, or kingdom
interdicto en la Iglesia Católica Romana, excomunión de una región, pueblo o reino

International Space Station an artificial structure built and maintained by a coalition of nations with the purpose of research
Estación Espacial Internacional estructura artificial construida y mantenida por una coalición de naciones con el fin de llevar a cabo investigaciones

Internet a huge international computer network linking millions of users around the world
Internet inmensa red internacional de computadoras que une a millones de ususarios en todo el mundo

Inti the Inca sun god
Inti dios sol inca

intifada Palestinian Arab uprisings against the Israeli occupation
intifadas levantamientos de árabes palestinos en contra de la ocupación israelí

Iroquois League political alliance of five Iroquois groups, known as the Five Nations, in the late 1500s
Liga de los iroqueses alianza política de cinco grupos iroqueses, conocida como las Cinco Naciones, de finales del siglo XVI

Isfahan capital of Safavid empire during the 1600s; located in present-day Iran
Isfahan capital del imperio safavid durante el siglo XVII, situada en actual Irán

1088

Islamist a person who wants government policies to be based on the teachings of Islam
islamista persona que desea que las políticas del gobierno tengan su fundamento en las enseñanzas del Islam

island-hopping during World War II, Allied strategy of recapturing some Japanese-held islands while bypassing others
salto entre islas estrategia aliada durante la Segunda Guerra Mundial de retomar algunas de las islas ocupadas por los japoneses e ignorar y pasar de largo de otras

Istanbul capital of the Ottoman empire; located in the northwest of present-day Turkey; formerly Constantinople
Estambul capital del imperio otomano; situada en el noroeste de la actual Turquía; anteriormente llamada Constantinopla

J

Jacobin member of a radical political club during the French Revolution
jacobino miembro de un club político radical durante la Revolución Francesa

janizary elite force of the Ottoman army
jenízaro fuerza de élitedel ejército otomano

Jericho the world's first village, established in the modern-day West Bank between 10,000 and 9000 B.C.
Jericó la primera aldea del mundo establecidas en la actual Cisjordania entre alrededor del año 10,000 y 9000 A.C.

Jerusalem capital of the Jewish state of Judea in ancient times and capital of the modern State of Israel; city sacred to Jews, Muslims, and Christians
Jerusalén capital del estado judío de Judea en la antigüedad, y capital del actual estado de Israel; ciudad sagrada para los judíos, musulmanes y cristianos

jihad in Islam, an effort in God's service
yihad en el Islam, un esfuerzo al servicio de Dios

joint family family organization in which several generations share a common dwelling
familia extendida organización familiar en la que varias generaciones comparten una vivienda

journeyman a salaried worker employed by a guild master
oficial trabajador asalariado empleado por el maestro del gremio

jury legal group of people sworn to make a decision in a legal case
jurado grupo de personas que han prestado juramento para tomar una decisión en un caso legal

Justinian's Code collection of Roman laws organized by the Byzantine emperor Justinian and later serving as a model for the Catholic Church and medieval monarchs
Código Justiniano recopilación de leyes romanas organizada por el emperador bizantino Justiniano y que luego sirvió como modelo para la iglesia católica y los monarcas medievales

K

Kaaba the most sacred temple of Islam, located at Mecca
Kaaba el templo más sagrado del islam, ubicado en La Meca

kaiser emperor of Germany
kaiser emperador de Alemania

kamikaze Japanese pilot who undertook a suicide mission
kamikaze piloto japonés que emprendía una misión suicida

kana in the Japanese writing system, phonetic symbols representing syllables
kana en el sistema japonés de escritura, símbolos fonéticos que representan sílabas

karma in Hindu belief, all the actions that affect a person's fate in the next life
karma según la creencia hindú, todas las acciones que afectan el destino de una persona en su próxima vida

Kashmir a former princely state in the Himalayas, claimed by both India and Pakistan, which have fought wars over its control
Cachemira antiguo estado principesco de los Himalayas, reclamado tanto por India como Pakistán, y por cuyo control han librado varias guerras

Katanga a province of the Democratic Republic of the Congo with rich copper and diamond deposits that tried to gain independence from Congo in 1960
Katanga provincia de la República Democrática del Congo con ricos depósitos de cobre y diamantes, que intentó independizarse del Congo en 1960

Kellogg-Briand Pact an international agreement, signed by almost every nation in 1928, to stop using war as a method of national policy
Pacto de Kellogg-Briand acuerdo internacional firmado por casi todas las naciones en 1928 para erradicar el uso de la guerra como un metodo de politica nacional

Khmer Rouge a political movement and a force of Cambodian communist guerrillas that gained power in Cambodia in 1975
Khmer Rouge movimiento político y fuerza guerrillera comunista de Camboya que llegó al poder en ese país en 1975

kibbutz a collective farm in Israel
kibbutz en Israel, granja comunitaria

Kiev capital of medieval Russia and of presentday Ukraine
Kiev capital de la Rusia medieval y de la actual Ucrania

kiva large underground chamber that the Anasazi used for religious ceremonies and political meetings
kiva gran sala subterránea que usaban los anazasi para ceremonias religiosas y reuniones políticas

knight a European noble who served as a mounted warrior
caballero noble europeo que servía como guerrero montado

Knossos an ancient Minoan city on the island of Crete
Cnosos antigua ciudad minoica en la isla de Creta

Kolkata a large city in India, also known as Calcutta
Kolkata ciudad grande de India, conocida también como Calcuta

Koryo dynasty Korean dynasty that ruled from 935 to 1392
dinastía Koryo dinastía coreana que gobernó desde 935 a 1392

Kosovo a province of Serbia with an Albanian ethnic majority that was the site of an ethnic conflict during the 1990s
Kosovo provincia de Serbia de mayoría étnica albanesa que sufrió un conflicto étnico durante la década de 1990

kulak wealthy peasant in the Soviet Union in the 1930s
campesino adinerado de la Unión Soviética en la década de 1930

Kulturkampf Bismarck's "battle for civilization," intended to make Catholics put loyalty to the state above their allegiance to the Church
Kulturkampf "batalla por civilización" de Bismarck, cuyo objetivo era que los católicos pusieran la lealtod al estado por encima de la lealtad a la Iglesia

1089

L

La Reforma an era of liberal reform in Mexico from 1855 to 1876
La Reforma era de reforma liberal en México desde 1855 a 1876

labor union workers' organization
sindicato organización de trabajadores

laissez faire policy allowing business to operate with little or no government interference
laissez faire política que permite a los negocios y empresas operar con poca o ninguna interferencia del gobierno

land reform breakup of large agricultural holdings for redistribution among peasants
reforma agraria división de grandes propiedades dedicadas a la agricultura para distribuirlas entre los campesinos

laser a high-energy light beam that can be used for many purposes including surgery, engineering, and scientific research
láser haz luminoso de alta energía que puede ser usado para muchos fines, entre ellos la cirugía, la ingeniería y la investigación científica

latifundia huge estates bought up by newly wealthy Roman citizens
latifundios grandes propiedades adquiridas por los ciudadanos romanos que se habían vuelto ricos recientemente

lay investiture appointment of bishops by anyone who is not a member of the clergy
investidura nombramiento de obispos por cualquiera que no sea miembro del clero

legion basic unit of the ancient Roman army, made up of about 5,000 soldiers
legión unidad básica del ejército de la antigua Roma, que consistía de unos 5,000 soldados

legislature lawmaking body
asamblea legislativa cuerpo encargado de promover y promulgar las leyes

legitimacy principle by which monarchies that had been unseated by the French Revolution or Napoleon were restored
legitimidad principio por el que las monarquías que habían sido derrocadas por la Revolución Francesa o por Napoleón fueron restituidas

Lend-Lease Act act passed by the U. S. Congress in 1941 that allowed the president to sell or lend war supplies to any country whose defense was considered vital to the United States
Ley de Préstamo y Arriendo decreto aprobado por el Congreso de Estados Unidos en 1941 que permitió al presidente vender o arrendar materiales de guerra a cualquier país cuya defensa fuese considerada de vital importancia para Estados Unidos

levée morning ritual during which nobles would wait upon French king Louis XIV
recepción matutina ritual de la mañana en el que los nobles atendían al rey Luis XIV

libel knowing publication of false and damaging statements
libelo publicación intencional de declaraciones falsas que perjudican a alguien

liberation theology movement within the Catholic Church that urged the church to become a force for reform, social justice, and put an end to poverty
teología de la liberación movimiento dentro de la Iglesia Católica que urgía a la iglesia a liderar un llamamiento por la reforma, la justicia social el fin de la pobreza

limited monarchy government in which a constitution or legislative body limits the monarch's powers
monarquía limitada gobierno en el que la constitución o el cuerpo legislativo limitan los poderes de la monarquía

Line of Demarcation line set by the Treaty of Tordesillas dividing the non-European world into two zones, one controlled by Spain and the other by Portugal
Línea de demarcación línea establecida por el Tratado de Tordesillas que dividía el mundo fuera de Europa en dos zonas: una controlada por España y otra por Portugal

lineage group claiming a common ancestor
linaje grupo que reivindica un antepasado en común

literacy the ability to read and write
alfabetismo capacidad de leer y escribir

literacy rate percentage of people who can read and write
tasa de alfabetización porcentaje de personas que pueden leer y escribir

Liverpool city and one of the largest ports in England; first major rail line linked Liverpool to Manchester in 1830
Liverpool ciudad y uno de los puertos más grandes de Inglaterra; línea importante de ferrocarril unió Liverpool con Manchester en 1830

loess fine windblown yellow soil
loes tierra fina y amarilla que se llava el viento

logic rational thinking
lógica pensamiento racional

Long March epic march in which a group of Chinese Communists retreated from Guomindang forces by marching over 6,000 miles
Gran Marcha marcha épica en la que un grupo de comunistas chinos marcharon en retirada de las fuerzas del Guomindang por más de 6,000 millas

longbow six-foot-long bow that could rapidly fire arrows with enough force to pierce most armor
arco largo arco de seis pies de largo que podía disparar rápidamente flechas con suficiente fuerza como para agujerear una armadura

Louisiana Purchase territory purchased by Thomas Jefferson from France in 1803
Compra de Luisiana territorio que Thomas Jefferson compró a Francia en 1803

Luftwaffe German air force
Luftwaffe fuerza aérea alemana

Lusitania British liner torpedoed by a German submarine in May 1915
Lusitania crucero británico torpedeado por un submarino alemán en mayo de 1915

M

Macao region of southeastern China made up of a peninsula and two islands, a Portuguese territory from the mid-1800s to 1999
Macao región al sudeste de China formada por una península y dos islas; fue territorio portugués desde mediados del siglo XIX a 1999

1090

Maginot Line massive fortifications built by the French along their border with Germany in the 1930s to protect against invasion
Línea Maginot fortificaciones masivas construídas por los franceses a lo largo de la frontera france sa con Alemania en la década de 1930 para protegerse contra invasiones futuras

Magna Carta the Great Charter approved by King John of England in 1215; it limited royal power and established certain rights of English freemen
Carta Magna carta constitucional aprobada por el Rey Juan de Inglaterra en 1215; limitaba el poder real y establecía ciertos derechos de los ingleses libres

Magyars an ethnic group centered in present-day Hungary
magiar grupo étnico establecido en la actual Hungría

Mahdi a Muslim savior of the faith
Mahdi salvador musulmán de la fe

maize corn
maíz elote

Malacca a state and coastal city in SW Malaysia, was an early center of the spice trade
Malacca estado y ciudad costera en el sudoeste de Malasia; fue uno de los primeros centros del comercio de especias

Mali medieval West African trading empire located in present-day Mali
Mali imperio comerciante de África occidental medieval ubicado en el actual Mali

Malindi a coastal town in SE Kenya
Malindi pueblo costero al sudeste de Kenia

Manchester city in England; one of the leading industrial areas; example of an Industrial Revolution city; first major rail line linked Manchester to Liverpool in 1830
Manchester ciudad de Inglaterra; una de las principales áreas industriales; ejemplo de ciudad de la Revolución Industrial; la primera línea importante de ferrocarril unió Manchester con Liverpool en 1830

Manchuria historic province in northeastern China; rich in natural resources
Manchuria provincia histórica en el noreste de China; rica en recursos naturales

Manchus people originally from Manchuria, north of China, who conquered the Ming dynasty and ruled China as the Qing dynasty from the mid-1600s to the early 1900s
manchus personas originalmente de Manchuria, al norte de China, que derrotaron a la dinastía Ming y gobernaron como la dinastía Chin desde mediados del siglo XVII a principios del siglo XX

mandate after World War I, a territory administered by a Western power
mandato territorio administrado por un poder occidental después de la Primera Guerra Mundial

Manhattan Project code name for the project to build the first atomic bomb during WWII
Proyecto Manhattan nombre en clave del proyecto para la fabricación de la primera bomba atómica durante la Segunda Guerra Mundial

Manifest Destiny American idea that the United States should stretch across the entire North American continent
Destino Manifiesto idea estadounidense de que Estados Unidos debería extenderse hasta ocupar todo el continente norteamericano

manor during the Middle Ages in Europe, a lord's estate which included one or more villages and the surrounding lands
señorío durante la Edad Media en Europa, propiedad de un señor que incluía uno o más pueblos y sus terrenos adyacentes

Maori indigenous people of New Zealand
maorie pueblo indígena de Nueva Zelanda

March on Rome planned march of thousands of Fascist supporters to take control of Rome; in response Mussolini was given the legal right to control Italy
Marcha sobre Roma marcha planeada de miles de simpatizantes fascistas sobre Roma para tomar su control; en respuesta a ella a Mussolini se le concedió el derecho legal del control de Italia

Marseilles French port city; troops marched to a patriotic song as they marched from this city, the song eventually became the French national anthem
Marsella ciudad portuaria francesa; las tropas que marcharon al ritmo de una canción patriótica desde esta ciudad inspiraron el himno nacional francés

Marshall Plan massive aid package offered by the U. S. to Europe to help countries rebuild after WWII
Plan Marshall paquete de ayuda a gran escala ofrecido por Estados Unidos a Europa para apoyar la reconstrucción de los países después de la Segunda Guerra Mundial

martyr person who suffers or dies for his or her beliefs
mártir persona que sufre o muere por sus creencias

matrilineal term for a family organization in which kinship ties are traced through the mother
matrilineal organización familiar en la que los lazos de parentesco se siguen a través de la madre

May Fourth Movement cultural movement in China that sought to reform China and make it stronger
Movimiento del Cuatro de Mayo movimiento cultural de China que se centró en reformar China y hacerla más fuerte

means of production farms, factories, railways, and other large businesses that produce and distribute goods
medios de producción granjas, fábricas, ferrocarriles y otros grandes negocios que producen y distribuyen mercancías

Mecca a city in western Saudi Arabia; birthplace of Islam's prophet Muhammad and most holy city for Islamic people
Meca ciudad en el oeste de Arabia Saudita; lugar de nacimiento del profeta Mahoma y ciudad sagrada para los creyentes islámicos

medieval referring to the Middle Ages in Europe or the period of history between ancient and modern times
medieval se refiere a la Edad Media en Europa, es decir, el período de la historia entre la edad antigua y la edad moderna

Medina a city in western Saudi Arabia; a city where Muhammad preached
Medina ciudad en el oeste de Arabia Saudita; ciudad donde predicó Mahoma

Meiji Restoration in Japan, the reign of emperor Meiji from 1868 to 1912 which was marked by rapid modernization and industrialization
restauración de Meiji en Japón, reino del emperador Meiji desde 1868 a 1912 que fue marcado por la rápida modernización e industrialización

mercantilism policy by which a nation sought to export more than it imported in order to build its supply of gold and silver
mercantilismo política por la que una nación trataba de exportar más de lo que importaba para aumentar sus reservas de o ro y plata

mercenary soldier serving in a foreign army for pay
mercenario soldado que sirve en un ejército extranjero a cambio de dinero
Meroë capital of the ancient kingdom of Nubia
Meroë capital del antiguo reino de Nubia
Mesa Verde the largest complex of Anasazi cliffdwellings in the United States Southwest, built between about A.D. 1150 and A.D. 1300
Mesa Verde el mayor complejo de viviendas anazasi construidas en acantilados en el sudoeste de Estados Unidos, entre alrededor de 1150 D.C. y 1300 D.C.
Mesoamerica region of North America, including Mexico and Central America, in which civilizations with common cultural features developed before Europeans entered the continent
Mesoamérica región de América del Norte, que incluye a México y América Central, en la cual se desarrollaron, antes de la llegada de los europeos al continente, civilizaciones con características culturales similares
Mesopotamia region within the Fertile Crescent that lies between the Tigris and Euphrates rivers
Mesopotamia región del Creciente Fértil que se encuentra entre los ríos Tigris y Éufrates
messiah savior sent by God
mésias salvador enviado por Dios
mestizo person in Spain's colonies in the Americas who was of Native American and European descent
mestizo persona de las colonias españolas de América descendiente de nativos y europeos
métis people of mixed Native American and French Canadian descent
métis pueblo de descendientes con mezcla de indígenas americanos y franceses canadienses
middle class a group of people, including merchants, traders, and artisans, whose rank was between nobles and peasants
clase media grupo de personas, incluyendo mercaderes, comerciantes y artesanos, cuyo rango estaba entre los nobles y los campesinos
Middle Passage the leg of the triangular trade route on which slaves were transported from Africa to the Americas
Travesía Intermedia parte de la ruta del comercio triangular en la que los esclavos eran transportados desde África a las Américas
militarism glorification of the military
militarismo glorificación de las fuerzas armadas
militias armed groups of citizen soldiers
milicias grupos armados de soldados-ciudadanos
minaret slender tower of a mosque, from which Muslims are called to prayer
minarete torre esbelta de una mezquita desde la que se convoca a los musulmanes a la oración
Ming dynasty Chinese dynasty in which Chinese rule was restored; held power from 1368 to 1644
dinastía Ming dinastía china en la que se restauro el gobierno chino; se mantuvo en el poder desde a 1644
missionary someone sent to promote religious conversion in a territory or foreign country
misioneros personas enviadas para hacer trabajos religiosos en un territorio u otro país
mobilize prepare military forces for war
mobilizar preparar las fuerzas militares para la guerra
Moche a culture that thrived in the Andean region from about 400 B.C. to A.D. 600
moche cultura preincaica que tuvo su apogeo en la región andina, desde alrededor de 400 A.C. a 600 D.C.
Mohenjo-Daro ancient city of the Indus civilization, located in present-day Pakistan
Mohenjo-Daro antigua ciudad de la civilización del Indo, ubicada en el presente Pakistán
moksha in Hindu belief, the ultimate goal of existence, which is to achieve union with brahman
moksha según la creencia hindú, el objetivo final de la existencia, que es llegar a la unión con el brahman
Moluccas a group of islands in eastern Indonesia; was the center of the spice trade in the 1500s and 1600s
Molucas grupo de islas en el este de Indonesia; fue el centro del comercio de especias en los siglos XVI y XVII
Mombasa a city in southeastern Kenya, located on a small coastal island
Mombasa ciudad al sudeste de Kenia, localizada en una pequeña isla costera
monarchy government in which a king or queen exercises central power
monarquía gobierno en el que el poder reside en el rey o la reina
money economy economic system in which goods or services are paid for through the exchange of a token of an agreed value
economía de dinero sistema económico en el que las mercancías y los servicios se pagan mediante el intercambio de una moneda con un valor establecido
monopoly complete control of a product or business by one person or group
monopolio control total de un producto o negocio por una persona o grupo
monotheistic believing in one God
monoteísta creencia en un solo Dios
Monroe Doctrine American policy of discouraging European intervention in the Western Hemisphere
Doctrina Monroe política estadounidense de rechazo a la intervención europea en el hemisferio occidental
monsoon seasonal wind that regularly blows from a certain direction for part of the year
monzón viento estacional que regularmente sopla desde una dirección específica durante una parte del año
mosaic picture made from chips of colored stone or glass
mosaico imagen hecha con pedazos de piedras o vidrios de colores
mosque Muslim house of worship;
mezquita templo musulmán
Mothers of the Plaza de Mayo a movement of women who protested weekly in a central plaza in the capital of Argentina against the disappearance or killing of relatives
Madres de la Plaza de Mayo asociación de mujeres que se reunían semanalmente en una céntrica plaza de la capital de Argentina para protest por la desaparición o asesinato de sus familiares
Mughal Muslim dynasty that ruled much of present-day India from 1526 to 1857
Mughal dinastía musulmana que gobernó gran parte de la India actual de 1526 a 1857
Mughal empire Muslim empire that ruled most of northern India from the mid-1500s to the mid-1700s; also known as the Mogul or Mongol empire
imperio Mughal imperio musulmán que gobernó la mayor parte del norte de India desde mediados del siglo XVI a mediados del siglo XVIII; también se conoce como imperio Mogul o Mongol

1092

mujahedin Muslim religious warriors
mujaedin guerreros religiosos musulmanes
mulatto in Spain's colonies in the Americas, person who was of African and European descent
mulato en las colonias españolas de América descendiente de africanos y europeos
multiethnic made up of several ethnic groups
multiétnico compuesto de varios grupos étnicos
multinational corporation company with branches in many countries
corporación multinacional empresa con sucursales en muchos países
Mumbai a large city in India, also known as Bombay
Mumbai ciudad grande de India, conocida también como Bombay
mummification the preservation of dead bodies by embalming and wrapping them in cloth
momificación práctica de preservar los cuerpos de los muertos embalsamándolos y envolviéndolos en vendas
mutiny revolt, especially of soldiers or sailors against their officers
motín revuelta, especialmente de soldados y marineros contra sus oficiales
mutual-aid societies self-help groups to aid sick or injured workers
sociedades de ayuda mutua grupos de apoyo establecidos para ayudar a los trabajadores enfermos o heridos en accidentes laborales
mystic person who devotes his or her life to seeking direct communion with divine forces
místico persona que dedica su vida a buscar la comunión directa con las fuerzas divinas

N

Nagasaki a coastal city in southern Japan on the island of Kyushu; city in Japan where the second atomic bomb was dropped in August, 1945
Nagasaki ciudad costera en el sur de Japón en la isla de Kyushu; ciudad de Japón donde fue lanzada la segunda bomba atómica en agosto de 1945
Napoleonic Code body of French civil laws introduced in 1804; served as model for many nations' civil codes
Código Napoleónico cuerpo de las leyes civiles francesas presentadas en 1804, que sirvieron como modelo para los códigos civiles de muchos países
nationalism a strong feeling of pride in and devotion to one's country
nacionalismo fuerte sentimiento de orgullo y devoción hacia el país propio
nationalization takeover of property or resources by the government
nacionalización apropiación de propiedades o recursos por parte del gobierno
natural law rules of conduct discoverable by reason
leyes naturales normas de conducta que se pueden descubrir mediante la razón
natural right right that belongs to all humans from birth, such as life, liberty, and property
derecho natural derecho que pertenece a todos los humanos desde el nacimiento: vida, libertad y propiedad
Nazca a culture that thrived in the Andean region from about 200 B.C. to A.D. 600
Nazca cultura que tuvo su apogeo en la región andina desde alrededor de 200 A.C. a 600 D.C.
Nazi-Soviet Pact agreement between Germany and the Soviet Union in 1939 in which the two nations promised not to fight each other and to divide up land in Eastern Europe
Pacto nazi-soviético acuerdo en 1939 entre Alemania y la Unión Soviética mediante el cual las dos naciones prometen no atacarse mutuamente y dividirse entre sí territorio de Europa del Este
négritude movement movement in which writers and artists of African descent expressed pride in their African heritage
movimiento de la negritud movimiento en el que los escritores y artistas descendientes de africanos expresabansu orgullo por la herencia africana
Neolithic Period the final era of prehistory, which began about 9000 B.C.; also called the New Stone Age
período Neolítico era final de la prehistoria que empezó hacia el 9000 A.C.; también llamado Nueva Edad de Piedra
Neolithic Revolution the period of time during which the introduction of agriculture led people to transition from nomadic to settled life
revolución neolítica período durante el cual el comienzo de la agricultura llevó a la gente a la transición de la vida nómada a la vida sedentaria
neutrality policy of supporting neither side in a war
neutralidad política de mantenerse al margen en una guerra
Neutrality Acts a series of acts passed by the U.S. Congress from 1935 to 1939 that aimed to keep the U. S. from becoming involved in WWII
Leyes de Neutralidad serie de decretos aprobados por el Congreso de Estados Unidos de 1935 a 1939 con el fin de evitar la implicación del país en la Segunda Guerra Mundial
New Deal a massive package of economic and social programs established by FDR to help Americans during the Great Depression
Nuevo Tratado paquete masivo de programas económicos y sociales establecidos por FDR para ayudar a los estadounidenses durante la Gran Depresión
New France French possessions in present-day Canada from the 1500s to 1763
Nueva Francia posesiones francesas en el actual Canadá desde el siglo XVI a 1763
New Stone Age the final era of prehistory, which began about 9000 B.C.; also called the Neolithic Period
Nueva Edad de Piedra era final de la prehistoria que empezó aproximadamente hacia el 9000 A.C.; también llamado período Neolítico
nirvana in Buddhist belief, union with the universe and release from the cycle of rebirth
nirvana en el budismo, unión con el universo y liberación del ciclo de la reencarnación
no-fly zones in Iraq, areas where the United States and its allies banned flights by Iraqi aircraft after the 1991 Gulf War
zonas de exclusión del espacio aéreo zonas de Iraq en las que Estados Unidos y sus aliados prohibieron el vuelo a la aviación iraquí después de la Guerra del Golfo en 1991
nomad a person who moves from place to place in search of food
nómada persona que se traslada de un lugar a otro en busca de alimentos

1093

nonalignment political and diplomatic independence from both Cold War powers
no alineación independencia política y diplomática de ambas potencias de la guerra fría

North Atlantic Treaty Organization a military alliance between several North Atlantic states to safeguard them from the presumed threat of the Soviet Union's communist bloc; countries from other regions later joined the alliance
Organización del Tratado del Atlántico Norte alianza militar entre varios estados del Atlántico norte para salvaguardarlos de la supuesta ameneza del bloque comunista liderado por la Unión Soviética; más tarde se incorporarían a la alianza países de otras regiones

Northern Ireland the northern portion of the island of Ireland, a part of the United Kingdom that has had a long religious conflict
Irlanda del Norte parte norte de la isla de Irlanda y territorio del Reino Unido, que ha sufrido un conflicto religioso durante mucho tiempo

Nubia ancient kingdom in northeastern Africa, also called Kush
Nubia antiguo reino del noreste africano, también llamado Kush

nuclear family family unit consisting of parents and children
familia nuclear unidad familiar que consta de los padres y sus hijos

Nuremberg Germany city where Hitler staged Nazi rallies in the 1930s, and where Nazi war crimes trials were held after WWII
Nuremberg ciudad del sur de Alemania donde Hitler escenificó manifestaciones nazis durante la década de 1930, y donde se celebraron los juicios por crímenes de guerra nazis después de la Segunda Guerra Mundial

Nuremberg Laws laws approved by the Nazi Party in 1935, depriving Jews of German citizenship and taking some rights away from them
Leyes de Nuremberg leyes aprobadas por el partido nazi en 1935, que eliminaba algunos de los derechos de los judíos en Alemania

O

occupied territories areas controlled by a nation that are part of another entity; Palestinians use this term for certain lands Israel gained after the 1967 war.
territorios ocupados zonas controladas por una nación que forman parte de otra entidad. Los palestinos usan esta palabra para referirse a los territorios ocupados por Israel después de la guerra de 1967

Old Stone Age the era of prehistory that lasted from 2 million B.C. to about 9000 B.C.
Antigua Edad de Piedra era de la prehistoria que duró desde aproximadamente 2 millones de años A.C. hasta el 9000 A.C.; también llamado período Paleolítico

Olduvai Gorge a gorge in Tanzania in which many hominid remains have been found
desfiladero Olduvai desfiladero en Tanzania donde se han encontrado muchos restos de homínidos

oligarchy government in which ruling power belongs to a few people
oligarquía gobierno en el que el poder está en manos de unas pocas personas

Olmecs the earliest American civilization, located along the Gulf Coast of Mexico from about 1500 B.C. to 400 B.C.
olmecas la primera civilización americana, ubicada a lo largo de la costa del Golfo de México, desde alrededor de 1500 A.C. a 400 A.C.

one-child policy a Chinese government policy limiting urban families to a single
child política de un sólo hijo medida del gobierno chino que limita a las familias urbanas a tener únicamente un hijo

Open Door Policy American approach to China around 1900, favoring open trade relations between China and other nations
Política de puertas abiertas política estadounidense con respecto a China a principios del siglo XX, que abogaba por las libres relaciones comerciales entre China y otras naciones

Opium War war between Great Britain and China over restrictions to foreign trade
Guerra del opio guerra librada entre Gran Bretaña y China por las restricciones sobre el comercio exterior

oracle bone in Shang China, animal bone or turtle shell used by priests to predict the future
hueso de oráculo en la China Shang, hueso de animal o caparazón de tortuga usado por los sacerdotes para predecir el futuro

Organization of American States a group formed in 1948 to promote democracy, economic cooperation, and human rights in the Americas
Organización de los Estados Americanos grupo formado en 1948 con el fin de promover la democracia, la cooperación económica y los derechos humanos en las Américas

ostracism practice used in ancient Greece to banish or send away a public figure who threatened democracy
ostracismo en la antigua Grecia, el acto de desterrar o enviar lejos a una figura pública que amenazaba la democracia

Ottomans Turkish-speaking nomadic people who migrated from Central Asia into northwestern Asia Minor
otomanos grupo nómada de habla turca que emigró de Asia Central al noroeste de Asia Menor

outpost a distant military station or a remote settlement
fuerte fronterizo estación militar distante o asentamiento lejano

outsourcing the practice of sending work to companies in the developing world in order to save money or increase efficiency
subcontratación práctica empresarial de enviar trabajo a compañías de países en vías de desarrollo con el fin de ahorrar dinero o aumentar el rendimiento

overproduction condition in which production of goods exceeds the demand for them
superproducción condición en la que la producción de mercancías excede la demanda

Oyo empire Yoruba empire that arose in the 1600s in present-day Nigeria and dominated its neighbors for a hundred years
imperio Oyo el imperio Yoruba que surgió en el siglo XVII en la actual Nigeria y dominó a sus vecinos durante cien años

P

Pacific Rim vast region of nations, including countries in Southeast Asia, East Asia, and the Americas, that border the Pacific Ocean
Cuenca del Pacífico vasta región de naciones, que incluye los países del sureste y este asiático y de las Américas, que limitan con el océano Pacífico
pacifism opposition to all war
pacifismo oposición a las guerras
paddy rice field
arrozal campo de arroz
pagoda multistoried Buddhist temple with eaves that curve up at the corners
pagoda templo budista de varios pisos con aleros que se curvan en las esquinas
Paleolithic Period the era of prehistory that lasted from at least 2 million B.C. to about 9000 B.C.; also called the Old Stone Age
período Paleolítico era de la prehistoria que duró desde aproximadamente 2 millones de años A.C. hasta el 9000 A.C.; también llamado la Antigua Edad de Piedra
Pan-Africanism movement which began in the 1920s that emphasized the unity and strength of Africans and people of African descent around the world
Panafricanismo movimiento que empezó en la década de 1920 que se centraba en la unidad y fuerza de los africanos y personas con ascendencia africana en todo el mundo
Panama Canal man-made waterway connecting the Atlantic and Pacific oceans
Canal de Panamá canal artificial que conecta los océanos Atlántico y Pacífico
Pan-Arabism movement in which Arabs sought to unite all Arabs into one state
Panarabismo movimiento en el que los árabes pretendían unir a todos los árabes en un sólo estado
pandemic spread of a disease across a large area, country, continent, or the entire world
pandemia propagación de una enfermedad a una gran área, país, continente o al mundo entero
papal supremacy the claim of medieval popes that they had authority over all secular rulers
supremacía papal demanda de los papas medievales de que ellos tenían autoridad sobre todos los gobernantes laicos
Parthenon the chief temple of the Greek goddess Athena on the Acropolis in Athens, Greece
Partenón el principal templo de la diosa griega Atena, situado en la Acrópolis de Atenas en Grecia
papyrus plant used to make a paper-like writing material in ancient Egypt
papiro planta usada por los antiguos egipcios para hacer un material de escritura parecido al papel
Parliament the legislature of England, and later of Great Britain
Parlamento asamblea legislativa de Inglaterra, y más tarde de Gran Bretaña
parliamentary democracy a form of government in which the executive leaders are chosen by and responsible to the legislature , are also members of it
democracia parlamentaria forma de gobierno en la que la dirección ejecutiva es elegida por la asamblea legislativa y controlada por la misma, además de formar parte de ella
partition a division into pieces
partición división en partes
partnership a group of merchants who joined together to finance a large-scale venture that would have been too costly for any individual trader
asociación grupo de mercaderes que se unen para financiar una empresa más grande que hubiera sido demasiado costosa para un solo comerciante
pasha provincial ruler in the Ottoman empire
bajá gobernante provincial del imperio otomano
paternalistic the system of governing a country as a father would a child
paternalista sistema de gobernar un país como un padre lo hace con su hijo
patriarch in the Roman and Byzantine empires, highest church official in a major city
patriarca en el Imperio Romano y imperio bizantino, el funcionario de rango más alto en la iglesia de una ciudad importante
patriarchal relating to a society in which men hold the greatest legal and moral authority
patriarcal relacionado con una sociedad en la que los hombres tienen la autoridad legal y moral
patrician in ancient Rome, member of the landholding upper class
patricio miembro de la clase alta terrateniente en la antigua Roma
patrilineal term for a family organization in which kinship ties are traced through the father
patrilineal organización familiar en la que los lazos de parentesco se siguen a través del padre
patron a person who provides financial support for the arts
mecenas persona que proporciona apoyo financiero a la cultura y las artes
Peace of Westphalia series of treaties that ended the Thirty Years' War
Paz de Westfalia serie de tratados por los que se puso fin a la Guerra de los Treinta Años
penal colony place where people convicted of crimes are sent
colonia penal lugar al que se manda a los condenados por crímenes
peninsulare member of the highest class in Spain's colonies in the Americas
peninsular miembro de la clase más alta en las colonias españolas de América
peon worker forced to labor for a landlord in order to pay off a debt
peón trabajador forzado a trabajar para un terrateniente para pagar una deuda
peonage system by which workers owe labor to pay their debts
peonaje sistema en el que los trabajadores deben trabajo como pago por sus deudas
perestroika a Soviet policy of democratic and free-market reforms introduced by Mikhail Gorbachev in the late 1980s
perestroika "reestructuración" en ruso; política soviética de reformas democráticas y de libre mercado que introdujo Mikhail Gorbachev a finales de la década de 1980
personal computer a small computer meant to be used by individuals or small businesses
computadora personal pequeña computadora diseñada para uso individual o por parte de pequeñas empresas

1095

perspective artistic technique used to give paintings and drawings a three-dimensional effect
perspectiva técnica artística usada para lograr el efecto de tercera dimensión en dibujos y pinturas
phalanx in ancient Greece, a massive tactical formation of heavily armed foot soldiers
falange en la antigua Grecia, sólida formación táctica de soldados a pie fuertemente armados
pharaoh title of the rulers of ancient Egypt
faraón título de los gobernantes del antiguo Egipto
Philippines a country in southeastern Asia made up of several thousand islands
Filipinas país al sudeste de Asia formado por varios miles de islas
philosophe French for "philosopher"; French thinker who desired reform in society during the Enlightenment
philosophe palabra francesa que significa "filósofo"; pensador francés que abogaba por reformas en la sociedad durante la Ilustración
philosopher someone who seeks to understand and explain life; a person who studies philosophy
filósofo persona que trata de comprender y explicar la vida; persona que estudia la filosofía
philosophy system of ideas
filosofía sistema de ideas
pictograph a simple drawing that looks like the object it represents
pictografía dibujo sencillo que se parece al objeto que representa
Pilgrims English Protestants who rejected the Church of England
peregrinos protestantes ingleses que rechazaron la Iglesia de Inglaterra
plantation large estate run by an owner or overseer and worked by laborers who live there
plantación gran propiedad administrada por un dueño o capataz y cultivada por trabajadores que viven en ella
plateau raised area of level land
meseta área elevada de tierra plana
plebeian in ancient Rome, member of the lower class, including farmers, merchants, artisans, and traders
plebeyo en la antigua Roma, miembro de clase baja, que incluía granjeros, mercaderes, artesanos y comerciantes
plebiscite ballot in which voters have a direct say on an issue
plebiscito votación en la que los votantes expresan su opinión sobre un tema en particular
pogrom violent attack on a Jewish community
pogrom ataque violento de una multitud hacia una comunidad judía
polis city-state in ancient Greece
polis ciudad-estado de la antigua Grecia
polytheistic believing in many gods
politeísta creencia en muchos dioses
pope head of the Roman Catholic Church; in ancient Rome, bishop of Rome who claimed authority over all other bishops
papa cabeza de la iglesia Católica Romana; obispo de Roma que afirmaba tener autoridad sobre los otros obispos
popular sovereignty basic principle of the American system of government which asserts that the people are the source of any and all governmental power, and government can exist only with the consent of the governed
soberanía popular principio básico del sistema de gobierno estadounidense en el que se determina que el pueblo es la fuente de todo poder gubernamental, y que el gobierno sólo puede existir con el consentimiento de los gobernados
potlatch among Native American groups of the Northwest Coast, ceremonial gift-giving by people of high rank and wealth
potlatch entre los grupos indígenas de la costa noroeste, ceremonia en que la gente de alto rango o riqueza hacía regalos
predestination Calvinist belief that God long ago determined who would gain salvation
predestinación creencia calvinista de que Dios decidió hace mucho tiempo quién conseguiría la salvación
prehistory the period of time before writing was invented
prehistoria período anterior a la invención de los sistemas de escritura
premier prime minister
premier primer ministro
price revolution period in European history when inflation rose rapidly
revolución del precio período en la historia de Europa en que la inflación aumentó rápidamente
privateer privately owned ship commissioned by a government to attack and capture enemy ships, especially merchant's ships
corsario barco privado comisionado por un gobierno para atacar y capturar barcos enemigos, especialmentelos barcos mercantes
Prohibition a ban on the manufacture and sale of alcohol in the U. S. from 1920 to 1933
Prohibición restricción de la fabricación y venta de bebidas alcohólicas en Estados Unidos desde 1920 a 1933
proletariat working class
proletariado clase trabajadora
proliferate to multiply rapidly
proliferar multiplicarse rápidamente
propaganda spreading of ideas to promote a cause or to damage an opposing cause
propaganda divulgación de ideas para promover cierta causa o para perjudicar una causa opuesta
prophet spiritual leader who interprets God's will
profeta líder espiritual a quien se le atribuye la interpretación de la voluntad de Dios
protectionism the use of tariffs and other restrictions to protect a country's home industries against competition
proteccionismo el uso de aranceles y otras medidas restrictivas para proteger a las empresas de un país de la competencia
protectorate country with its own government but under the control of an outside power
protectorado país con su propio gobierno pero que está bajo el control de una potencia exterior
provisional temporary
provisional temporal
Prussia a strong military state in central Europe that emerged in the late 1600s
Prusia estado centroeuropeo militarmente poderoso que emergió a finales del siglo XVII
psychoanalysis a method of studying how the mind works and treating mental disorders
psicoanálisis método que estudia el funcionamiento de la mente y trata los trastornos mentales
pueblo Native American village of the United States Southwest
pueblo poblado indígena del sudoeste de Estados Unidos

Pueblo Bonito the largest Anasazi pueblo, built in New Mexico in the A.D. 900s
Pueblo Bonito el mayor poblado anazasi, construido en Nuevo México en el siglo X D.C.

Punjab state in northwestern India with a largely Sikh population
Punjab estado del noroeste de India de población mayoritariamente sikh

purdah isolation of women in separate quarters
purdah aislamiento de las mujeres en recintos separadas

Puritans members of an English Protestant group who wanted to "purify" the Church of England by making it more simple and more morally strict
puritanos miembros de un grupo de protestantes ingleses que querían "purificar" la Iglesia de Inglaterra, haciéndola más sencilla y moralmente más estricta

Pusan Perimeter a defensive line around the city of Pusan, in the southeast corner of Korea, held by South Korean and United Nations forces in 1950 during the Korean War; marks the farthest advance of North Korean forces
Perímetro de Pusan línea defensiva alrededor de la ciudad de Pusan, en el sudeste de Corea, custodiada por Corea del Sur y las fuerzas de las Naciones Unidas en 1950 durante la Guerra de Corea; marca el mayor avance de las fuerzas de Corea del Norte

putting-out system a system developed in the 18th century in which tasks were distributed to individuals who completed the work in their own homes; also known as cottage industry
sistema de trabajo a domicilio sistema desarrolla do en el siglo XVIII en el que las tareas se distribúan a individuos quienes completaban el trabajo en sus hogares; tambien se conoce como industria familiar

Q

Qajars members of the dynasty that ruled present-day Iran from the late 1700s until 1925
Qajars miembros de la dinastía que gobernó la zona del actual Irán desde fines del siglo XVIII hasta 1925

Qing dynasty dynasty established by the Manchus in the mid 1600s and lasted until the early 1900s; China's last dynasty
dinastía Chin dinastía establecida por los manchus a mediados del siglo XVII que duró hasta principios del siglo XX; fue la última dinastía china

Quran the holy book of Islam
Corán el libro sagrado del islam

quipu knotted strings used by Inca officials for record-keeping
quipu cuerdas con nudos que usaban los incas como llevar registros

R

racism belief that one racial group is superior to another
racismo creencia de que un grupo racial es superior a otro

radicals those who favor extreme changes
radicales persona que quiere hacer cambios extremos

rajah in ancient India, the elected warrior chief of an Aryan tribe
rajah jefe guerrero electo de una tribu aria en la antigua India

realism 19th-century artistic movement whose aim was to represent the world as it is
realismo movimiento artístico del siglo XIX cuyo objetivo era representar el mundo tal como es

Realpolitik realistic politics based on the needs of the state
Realpolitik política realista basada en las necesidades del estado

recession period of reduced economic activity
recesión periodo de reducción de la actividad económica

Reconquista during the 1400s, the campaign by European Christians to drive the Muslims from present-day Spain
Reconquista durante el siglo XV, campaña por parte de cristianos europeos para expulsar a los musulmanes de la actual España

refugee a person who flees from home or country to seek refuge elsewhere, often because of political upheaval or famine
refugiado persona que abandona su hogar o país en busca de refugio en otro lugar, a menudo como consecuencia de inestabilidad política o hambruna

regionalism loyalty to a local area
regionalismo lealtad a un área local

Reich German empire
Reich imperio alemán

Reign of Terror time period during the French Revolution from September 1793 to July 1794 when people in France were arrested for not supporting the revolution and many were executed
Reinado del terror período durante la Revolución Francesa desde septiembre de 1793 a julio de 1794, en el que la gente en Francia era arresta da por no apoyar la revolución; mucha gente fue ejecutada

reincarnation in Hindu belief, the rebirth of the soul in another bodily form
reencarnación según la creencia hindú, renacimiento del alma en otra forma corporal

reparation payment for war damage, or damage caused by imprisonment
indemnización pago por daños causados por guerra o encarcelamiento

repeal cancel
revocar cancelar

republic system of government in which officials are chosen by the people
república sistema de gobierno en el que los gobernantes son elegidos por el pueblo

revenue money taken in through taxes
rentas públicas dinero que se recauda por impuestos

rhetoric art of skillful speaking
retórica arte de hablar con habilidad

rococo personal, elegant style of art and architecture made popular during the mid-1700s that featured designs with the shapes of leaves, shells, and flowers
rococó estilo de arte y arquitectura elegante y personal que se hizo popular a mediados del siglo XVIII y que incluía diseños con formas de hojas, conchas y flores

romanticism 19th-century artistic movement that appealed to emotion rather than reason
romanticismo movimiento artístico del siglo XIX que apelaba a la emoción más que a la razón

1097

Rosetta Stone stone monument that includes the same passage carved in hieroglyphics, demotic script, and Greek and that was used to decipher the meanings of many hieroglyphs
piedra de Rosetta piedra arquitectónica que incluye el mismo pasaje esculpido con caracteres jeroglíficos, demóticos y en escritura griega que se usó para descifrar el significado de muchos jeroglíficos
Rosie the Riveter popular name for women who worked in war industries during WWII
Rosita la Remachadora nombre popularmente dado a las mujeres que trabajaban en las fábricas de armamento durante la Segunda Guerra Mundial
rotten borough rural town in England that sent members to Parliament despite having few or no voters
"distrito podrido" en Inglaterra, ciudad rural que enviaba miembros al parlamento a pesar de no tener o tener pocos votantes
Ruhr Valley coal-rich industrial region of Germany
Valle del Ruhr región industrial alemana rica en carbón
russification making a nationality's culture more ethnically Russian
rusificación hacer la cultura nacionalista más étnicamente rusa
Russo-Japanese War conflict between Russia and Japan in 1904–1905 over control of Korea and Manchuria
Guerra ruso-japonesa conflicto entre Rusia y Japón de 1904 a 1905 por el control de Corea y Manchuria

S

Sabbath a holy day for rest and worship
sabbat día sagrado para descansar y rendir culto
sacrament sacred ritual of the Roman Catholic Church
sacramento ritual sagrado de la Iglesia Católica Romana
Safavid Shiite Muslim empire that ruled much of present-day Iran from the 1500s into the 1700s
Safávida imperio musulmán chiíta que gobernó la mayor parte del actual Irán desde el siglo XVI hasta el siglo XVIII
Sahara largest desert in the world, covering almost all of North Africa
Sahara desierto más grande del mundo que cubre casi todo el norte de África
salon informal social gathering at which writers, artists, *philosophes*, and others exchanged ideas
salón reuniones sociales informales en las que escritores, artistas, filósofos y otros intercambiaban ideas
samurai member of the warrior class in Japanese feudal society
samurai miembro de la clase guerrera en la sociedad japonesa feudal
Sandinistas a socialist political movement and party that held power in Nicaragua during the 1980s
sandinistas partido y movimiento político socialista que gobernó Nicaragua durante la década de 1980
sans-culotte working-class man or woman who made the French Revolution more radical; called such because he or she wore long trousers instead of the fancy knee breeches that the upper class wore
sans-culotte hombre o mujer de la clase obrera que hicieron la Revolución Francesa más radical; llamados así porque llevaban pantalones largos a la rodilla como los que llevaba en vez de los pantalones ajustados la clase altas a la rodilla como los que llevaba la clase alta
Sapa Inca the title of the Inca emperor
Sapa Inca título del emperador inca
sati Hindu custom that called for a widow to join her husband in death by throwing herself on his funeral pyre
sati costumbre hindú que requería que la esposa se uniera a su marido en la muerte arrojándose a su pira funeraria
satirize make fun of
satirizar burlarse de algo
savanna grassy plain with irregular patterns of rainfall
sabana planicie con pastizales cuyo régimen de lluvias es irregular
schism permanent division in a church
cisma división permanente de una iglesia
scholasticism in medieval Europe, the school of thought that used logic and reason to support Christian belief
escolástica en la Edad Media europea, escuela de pensamiento que usaba la lógica y el razonamiento para apoyar las creencias cristianas
scientific method careful, step-by-step process used to confirm findings and to prove or disprove a hypothesis
método científico proceso cuidadoso y de varios pasos que se usa para confirmar descubrimientos y para aprobar o desaprobar una hipótesis
scorched-earth policy military tactic in which soldiers destroy everything in their path to hurt the enemy
política de tierra quemada táctica militar en la que los soldados destruyen todo lo que tienen a su paso para perjudicar al enemigo
scribe in ancient civilizations, a person specially trained to read, write, and keep records
escriba en las civilizaciones antiguas, persona especialmente educada para leer, escribir y mantener registros
secede withdraw
separar retirarse
secret ballot votes cast without announcing them publicly
voto secreto votos que se dan sin hacerlos públicos
sect a subgroup of a major religious group
secta subgrupo de un grupo religioso importante
secular having to do with worldly, rather than religious, matters; nonreligious
secular que tiene que ver más con asuntos mundanos que religiosos; no religioso
segregation forced separation by race, sex, religion, or ethnicity
segregación separación forzada por razón de raza, sexo, religión o etnia
selective borrowing adopting or adapting some cultural traits but discarding others
préstamo selectivo adoptar o adaptar algunos rasgos culturales y descartar otros
self-determination right of people to choose their own form of government
autodeterminación derecho de los pueblos a elegir su propia forma de gobierno
sepoy Indian soldier who served in an army set up by the French or English trading companies
sepoy soldado indio que sirvió en un ejército establecido por las compañías de comercio francesas o inglesas
serf in medieval Europe, a peasant bound to the lord's land
siervo en la Europa medieval, campesino vinculado a las tierras del señor
shah king
sha rey

1098

shantytowns slums of flimsy shacks
barrio de chabolas barrios muy pobres de casuchas endebles

Sharia body of Islamic law that includes interpretation of the Quran and applies Islamic principles to everyday life
Sharía ley canónica del islam que incluye la interpretación del Corán y que aplica los principios islámicos a la vida diaria

Sharpeville a black township in South Africa where the government killed anti-apartheid demonstrators in 1960
Sharpeville municipio sudafricano habitado por personas de raza negra donde el gobierno mató a decenas de manifestantes antiapartheid en 1960

Shiite a member of one of the two major Muslim sects; believe that the descendents of Muhammad's daughter and son-in-law, Ali, are the true Muslim leaders
chiíta miembro de una de las dos sectas musulmanas principales; creedor de que los descendientes de la hija y el yerno de Mahoma, Alí, son los verdaderos líderes musulmanes

Shinto principal religion in Japan that emphasizes the worship of nature
Shinto principal religión de Japón que enfatiza la adoración a la naturaleza

shogun in Japanese feudal society, supreme military commander, who held more power than the emperor
shogún en la sociedad feudal japonesa, jefe military supremo con más poder que el emperador

shrine altar, chapel, or other sacred place
santuario altar, capilla u otro lugar sagrado

Sikhism religion founded by Nanak that blended Islamic and Hindu beliefs
sikhismo religión fundada por Nanak que incorpora creencias islámicas e hindúes

Sikhs members of an Indian religious minority
sikhs miembros de una minoría religiosa de India

Silla dynasty Korean dynasty that ruled from 668 to 935
dinastía Silla dinastía coreana que gobernó desde 668 a 935

Sino-Japanese War war between China and Japan in which Japan gained Taiwan
Guerra Sinojaponesa guerra entre China y Japón por la que Japón obtuvo el control de Taiwán

smelt melt in order to get the pure metal away from its waste matter
refinar fundir mineral para separar el mineral puro de las impurezas

social contract an agreement by which people gave up their freedom to a powerful government in order to avoid chaos
contrato social acuerdo mediante el cual el pueblo cede sus libertades a un gobierno poderoso para evitar el caos

social democracy political ideology in which there is a gradual transition from capitalism to socialism instead of a sudden violent overthrow of the system
democracia social ideología política en la que hay una transición gradual del capitalismo al socialismo en vez de un derrocamiento violento del sistema

social gospel movement of the 1800s that urged Christians to do social service
evangelio social movimiento del siglo XIX que urgía a los cristianos a que hicieran servicios sociales

social mobility the ability to move in social class
movilidad social la capacidad de cambiar de clase social

social welfare programs to help certain groups of people
bienestar social programas para ayudar a ciertos grupos de personas

socialism system in which the people as a whole rather than private individuals own all property and operate all businesses
socialismo sistema en el que el pueblo como un todo, en vez de los individuos, son dueños de todas la propiedades y manejan todos los negocios

socialist realism artistic style whose goal was to promote socialism by showing Soviet life in a positive light
realismo socialista estilo artistico cuyo objetivo era promover el socialismo mostrando la vida en la Union Sovietica desde un perspectiva postiva

Solidarity a Polish labor union and democracy movement
Solidaridad sindicato laboral y movimiento democrático polaco

Song dynasty Chinese dynasty from 960 to 1279; known for its artistic achievements
dinastía Song dinastía china desde 960 a 1279; conocida por sus grandes logros artísticos

Songhai medieval West African kingdom located in present-day Mali, Niger and Nigeria
Songhai reino medieval de África occidental ubicado en el presente Mali, Níger y Nigeria

sovereign having full, independent power
soberano tener poder pleno e independiente

soviet council of workers and soldiers set up by Russian revolutionaries in 1917
soviet consejo de trabajadores y soldados establecido por los revolucionarios rusos en 1917

Spanish-American War conflict between the United States and Spain in 1898 over Cuban independence
Guerra entre Estados Unidos y España conflicto entre Estados Unidos y España en 1898 por la independencia de Cuba

Sparta city-state in ancient Greece
Esparta antigua ciudad-estado en Grecia

speakeasies illegal bars
speakeasies bares ilegales

sphere of influence area in which an outside power claims exclusive investment or trading privileges
esfera de influencia área sobre la que un poder exterior se reserva privilegios comerciales o la exclusividad de realizar inversiones

St. Petersburg capital city and major port that Peter the Great established in 1703
San Petersburgo ciudad y capital con un puerto importante, establecida en 1703 por Pedro el Grande

stalemate deadlock in which neither side is able to defeat the other
estancamiento punto muerto en una confrontación, en el que ninguna de las partes puede vencer a la otra

Stalingrad now Volgograd, a city in SW Russia that was the site of a fierce battle during WWII
Stalingrado actual Volgogrado; ciudad del sudoeste de Rusia donde se libró una encarnizada batalla durante la Segunda Guerra Mundial

Stamp Act law passed in 1765 by the British Parliament that imposed taxes on items such as newspapers and pamphlets in the American colonies; repealed in 1766
Ley del Timbre ley promulgada en 1765 por el Parlamento Británico que imponía gravá menes a artículos como diarios y panfletos en las colonias americanas; revocada en 1766

standard of living measures the quality and availability of necessities and comforts in a society
estándar de vida medida de la calidad y disponibilidad de las necesidades básicas y de los lujos en una sociedad

stela in the ancient world, a tall, commemorative monument that was often decorated
estela en el mundo antiguo, gran monumento monolítico conmemorativo que comúnmente estaba decorado

steppe sparse, dry, treeless grassland
estepa tierra de pastos escasos y secos sin árboles

stipend a fixed salary given to public office holders
estipendio salario fijo de los funcionarios públicos

stock shares in a company
acciones títulos o valores de una compañía

strait narrow water passage
estrecho paso angosto de agua

stupa large domelike Buddhist shrine
stupa gran altar budista en forma de cúpula

subcontinent large landmass that juts out from a continent
subcontinente gran masa de tierra que sobresale de un continente

suburbanization the movement to built-up areas outside of central cities
suburbanización proceso de construcción en áreas fuera del centro de la ciudad

Sudetenland a region of western Czechoslovakia
Sudetenland región occidental de la antigua Checoslovaqui

Suez Canal a canal linking the Red Sea and Indian Ocean to the Mediterranean Sea, which also links Europe to Asia and East Africa
Canal de Suez canal que une el Mar Rojo y el Océano Índico con el Mar Mediterráneo, que a la vez une Europa con Asia y África Oriental

suffrage right to vote
sufragio derecho al voto

Sufis Muslim mystics who seek communion with God through meditation, fasting, and other rituals
sufis místicos musulmanes que buscan la comunión con dios mediante la meditación, el ayuno y otros rituals

sultan Muslim ruler
sultán gobernante musulmán

Sumer site of the world's first civilization, located in southeastern Mesopotamia
Sumeria lugar de la primera civilización del mundo, ubicada en el sureste de Mesopotamia

Sunni a member of one of the largest Muslim sects; Sunnis believe that inspiration came from the example of Muhammad as recorded by his early followers
sunita miembro de una de las dos sectas musulmanas principales; los sunitas creen que la inspiración proviene del ejemplo de Mahoma según fue registrada por sus primeros seguidores

superpower a nation stronger than other powerful nations
superpotencia nación suficientemente poderosa para influir en los actos y políticas de otras naciones poderosas

surplus an amount that is more than needed, excess
excedente cantidad de algo superior a lo que se necesita; exceso

surrealism artistic movement that attempts to portray the workings of the unconscious mind
surrealismo movimiento artístico que trata de mostrar el funcionamiento del inconsciente

sustainability the ability to meet the needs of the present without compromising the needs of future generations
sostenibilidad capacidad de satisfacer las necesidades actuales sin poner en peligro las necesidades de generaciones futuras

sustainable development development that meets the needs of the present without compromising the ability of future generations to meet their own needs
desarrollo sostenible desarrollo que cubre las necesidades del presente sin perjudicar la capacidad de las generaciones futuras de cubrir sus necesidades

Swahili an East African culture that emerged about 1000 A.D.; also a Bantu-based language, blending Arabic words and written in Arabic script
swahili cultura del este de África que emergió alrededor del año 1000 D.C.; también un idioma basado en el Bantú, que mezcla palabras árabes y usa la escritura árabe

T

Taiping Rebellion peasant revolt in China
Rebelión Taiping revuelta campesina en China

Taliban Islamic fundamentalist faction that ruled Afghanistan for nearly ten years until ousted by the United States in 2002
Talibán facción islámica fundamentalista que gobernó Afganistán durante casi diez años hasta que fue expulsada por Estados Unidos en 2002

Taj Mahal a tomb built by Shah Jahan for his wife
Taj Mahal tumba construida por Shah Jahan para su esposa; considerado como uno de los monumentos más importantes del imperio mughal

Tang dynasty Chinese dynasty from 618 to 907
dinastía Tang dinastía china desde 618 a 907

tariff tax on imported goods
tasa impuesto a mercancías importadas

technology the skills and tools people use to meet their basic needs
tecnología herramientas y destrezas que usan las personas para satisfacer sus necesidades básicas

Tehran capital of the Qajar dynasty and presentday Iran
Teherán capital de la dinastía Qajar y del actual Irán

temperance movement campaign to limit or ban the use of alcoholic beverages
campaña de moderación campaña para limitar o prohibir el uso de bebidas alcohólicas

tenant farmer someone who would pay rent to a lord to farm part of the lord's land
agricultor arrendatario alguien que paga un alquiler a un señor para poder cultivar la tierra de éste

tenement multistory building divided into crowded apartments
apartamento de vecindad edificio de varios pisos dividido en apartamentos donde vive mucha gente

1100

Tennis Court Oath famous oath made on a tennis court by members of the Third Estate in France
Juramento del juego de pelota famoso juramento hecho en una cancha de frontón por los miembros del Tercer Estado en Francia

Tenochtitlán capital city of the Aztec empire, on which modern-day Mexico City was built
Tenochtitlán capital del imperio azteca, sobre la cual se construyó la actual Ciudad de México

Teotihuacán city that dominated the Valley of Mexico from about A.D. 200 to A.D. 750 and that influenced the culture of later Mesoamerican peoples
Teotihuacán ciudad que dominó el Valle de México desde alrededor de 200 D.C. a 750 D.C., y que influyó en la cultura de los pueblos mesoamericanos posteriores

terrorism deliberate use of random violence, especially against civilians, to achieve political goals
terrorismo uso deliberado de la violencia indiscriminada, especialmente en contra de civiles, para lograr fines políticos

Tet Offensive a massive and bloody offensive by communist guerrillas against South Vietnamese and American forces on Tet, the Vietnamese New Year, 1968; helped turn American public opinion against military involvement in Vietnam
Ofensiva Tet ofensiva masiva y sangrienta de las guerrillas comunistas contra los sudvietnamitas y las fuerzas estadounidenses durante el Tet, el Nuevo Año vietnamita, en 1968; ayudó a que la opinión pública estadouniden se se volviera en contra de la ocupación militar en Vietnam

theocracy government run by religious leaders
teocracia gobierno administrado por líderes religiosos

Third Reich official name of the Nazi party for its regime in Germany; held power from 1933 to 1945
Tercer Reich nombre oficial del partido nazi durante su mandato en Alemania; mantuvo el poder desde 1933 a 1945

38th parallel an imaginary line marking 38 degrees of latitude, particularly the line across the Korean Peninsula, dividing Soviet forces to the north and American forces to the south after WWII
paralelo 38 línea imaginaria que marca los 38 grados de latitud, en particular la línea a 38 grados de latitud norte que cruza la península coreana, que dividía las fuerzas soviéticas al norte y las fuerzas estadounindenses al sur después de la Segunda Guerra Mundial

Tiahuanaco a culture that thrived in the Andean region from about A.D. 200–A.D. 1000
tiahuanaco cultura preincaica que tuvo su apogeo en la región andina desde alrededor de 200 D.C. a 1000 D.C.

Tiananmen Square a huge public plaza at the center of China's capital, Beijing
Plaza de Tiananmen inmensa plaza pública en el centro de Beijing, la capital de China

Tokyo capital of Japan
Tokio capital de Japón

Torah the most sacred text of the Hebrew Bible, including its first five books
Tora el texto más sagrado de la Biblia judía que incluye sus cinco primeros libros

total war channeling of a nation's entire resources into a war effort
estado de guerra canalización de todos los recursos de una nación hacia la guerra

totalitarian state government in which a oneparty dictatorship regulates every aspect of citizens' lives
estado totalitario gobierno en el que una dictadura de partido único regula todos los aspectos de la vida de los ciudadanos

tournament a mock battle in which knights would compete against one another to display their fighting skills
torneo batalla simulada en la que los caballeros competían entre ellos para lucir sus destrezas de lucha

trade deficit situation in which a country imports more than it exports
déficit comercial situación en la que un país importa más de lo que exporta

trade surplus situation in which a country exports more than it imports
excedente commercial situación en la que un país exporta más de lo que importa

traditional economies economies that rely on habit, custom, or ritual and tend not to change over time
economía de subsistencia economía basada en hábitos, costumbres o rituales y que no suele cambiar con el paso del tiempo

traditional economy undeveloped economic systems that rely on custom and tradition
economía tradicional sistemas económicos sin desarrollar dependen de costumbres y tradiciones

tragedy in ancient Greece, a play about human suffering often ending in disaster
tragedia en la antigua Grecia, obra teatral que trataba del sufrimiento humano y que a menudo terminaba con un desastre

Treaty of Paris treaty of 1763 that ended the Seven Years' War and resulted in British dominance of the Americas
Tratado de París en 1763, tratado que terminó con la Guerra de los Siete Años y resultó en el dominio británico de las Américas

Treaty of Paris peace treaty made final in 1783 that ended the American Revolution
Tratado de París tratado de paz de 1783 que dio final a la Revolución Americana

Treaty of Tordesillas treaty signed between Spain and Portugal in 1494 which divided the non-European world between them
Tratado de Tordesillas tratado firmado por España y Portugal en 1494 por el que se dividían entre ellos el mundo fuera de Europa

triangular trade colonial trade routes among Europe and its colonies, the West Indies, and Africa in which goods were exchanged for slaves
comercio triangular ruta colonial de comercio entre Europa y sus colonias en las Indias Occidentales y África, en donde las mercancías se cambiaban por esclavos

tribunes in ancient Rome, official who was elected by the plebeians to protect their interests
tribuno en la antigua Roma, funcionario elegido por los plebeyos para proteger sus intereses

tributary state independent state that has to acknowledge the supremacy of another state and pay tribute to its ruler
estado tributario estado independiente que debe reconocer la supremacía de otro estado y pagar tributo a su gobernante

tribute payment that conquered peoples may be forced to pay their conquerors
tributo pago que los conquistadores podían obligar a pagar a los pueblos conquistados
Trojan War in Greek epic poems and myths, a ten-year war between Mycenae and the city of Troy in Asia Minor
Guerra de Troya en los mitos y poemas griegos, guerra de diez años de duración entre Micenas y la ciudad de Troya situada en Asia Menor
troubadour a wandering poet or singer of medieval Europe
trovador poeta o cantante itinerante de la Europa medieval
Truman Doctrine United States policy, established in 1947, of trying to contain the spread of communism
Doctrina Truman estrategia política establecida en 1947 con el propósito de contener la expansión del comunismo
tsar title of the ruler of the Russian empire
zar título del regente del imperio ruso
tsunami very large, damaging wave caused by an earthquake or very strong wind
tsunami ola enorme y destructiva causada por un terremoto o vientos muy fuertes
turnpike private road built by entrepreneurs who charged a toll to travelers who used it
autopista de peaje carretera construida con capital privado; el dueño de la carretera cobra una tarifa a los viajeros por usarla
Tutsis the main minority group in Rwanda and Burundi
Tutsis principal minoría de Ruanda y Burundi
Twenty-One Demands list of demands given to China by Japan in 1915 that would have made China a protectorate of Japan
Veintiuna Exigencias lista de exigencias dadas por Japón a China en 1915 por las que, si hubiera estado de acuerdo, China se habría convertido en un protectorado de Japón
tyrant in ancient Greece, ruler who gained power by force
tirano en la antigua Grecia, gobernante que llegó al poder por medio de la fuerza

U

U-boat German submarine
U-Boat submarino alemán
ultimatum final set of demands
ultimátum serie final de exigencias
ultranationalist extreme nationalist
ultranacionalista nacionalista radical
Umayyads members of the Sunni dynasty of caliphs that ruled a Muslim empire from 661 to 750
omeyas miembros de la dinastía Sunita de califas que gobernó un imperio musulmán de 661 a 750
United Nations international organization established after World War II with the goal of maintaining peace and cooperation in the international community
Naciones Unidas organización internacional establecida después de la Segunda Guerra Mundial con el propósito de preservar la paz y la cooperación en la comunidad internacional
universal manhood suffrage right of all adult men to vote
sufragio universal masculino derecho de todos los hombres adultos a votar
untouchable in India, a member of the lowest caste
intocable en India, miembro de la casta más baja
urban renewal the process of fixing up the poor areas of a city
renovación urbana reconstrucción de las áreas pobres de una ciudad
urbanization movement of people from rural areas to cities
urbanización movimiento de personas de las áreas rurales a las ciudades
utilitarianism idea that the goal of society should be to bring about the greatest happiness for the greatest number of people
utilitarismo idea de que el objetivo de la sociedad debería ser lograr la mayor felicidad para el mayor número de personas
utopian idealistic or visionary, usually used to describe a perfect society
utópico idealista o visionario, normalmente se usa para describir una sociedad perfecta

V

V-E Day Victory in Europe Day, May 8, 1945, the day the Allies won WWII in Europe
Día de la Victoria en Europa día en que los aliados vencieron en Europa durante la Segunda Guerra Mundial
Valley of Mexico valley in Mexico in which the numerous Mesoamerican civilizations, including the Aztecs, arose
Valle de México valle en México en el cual se desarrollaron numerosas civilizaciones mesoamericanas, incluyendo los aztecas
vanguard group of elite leaders
vanguardia grupo de líderes de la élite
vassal in medieval Europe, a lord who was granted land in exchange for service and loyalty to a greater lord
vasallo durante la Edad Media, señor a quien se le cedía un terreno a cambio de servicio y lealtad al señor más importante
Vedas a collection of prayers, hymns, and other religious teachings developed in ancient India beginning around 1500 B.C.
Vedas con onjunto de oraciones, himnos y otras enseñanzas religiosas desarrolladas en la antigua India a partir de alrededor del siglo XVI a. de C.
veneration special regard
veneración estima especial
vernacular everyday language of ordinary people
vernáculo lenguaje diario de la gente corriente
Versailles royal French residence and seat of government established by King Louis XIV
Versalles residencia de la realeza francesa y sede de gobierno establecidos por el rey Luis XIV
veto block a government action
veto bloquear una acción del gobierno
viceroy representative who ruled one of Spain's provinces in the Americas in the king's name; one who governed in India in the name of the British monarch
virrey representante que regía una de las provincias de España en las Américas en nombre del rey; quien gobernaba en India en nombre del monarca británico

1102

Vichy city in central France where a puppet state governed unoccupied France and the French colonies
Vichy ciudad en el centro de Francia desde donde un gobierno títere dirigió la Francia no ocupada y las colonias francesas
Viet Cong communist rebels in South Vietnam who sought to overthrow South Vietnam's government; received assistance from North Vietnam
Vietcong rebeldes comunistas en Vietnam del Sur que buscaban derrotar el gobierno de Vietnam del Sur; recibieron ayuda de Vietnam del Norte
Vikings Scandinavian peoples whose sailors raided Europe from the 700s through the 1100s
vikingo pueblo escandinavo cuyos marineros asaltaron Europa durante los siglos VIII al XII
vizier chief minister who supervised the business of government in ancient Egypt
visir ministro principal que supervisaba los asuntos de gobierno en el antiguo Egipto

W

War of the Austrian Succession series of wars in which various European nations competed for power in Central Europe after the death of Hapsburg emperor Charles VI
Guerra de Sucesión Austriaca serie de guerras en las que diversos países europeos lucharon por la hegemonía en centroeuropa después de la muerte de Carlos IV, emperador Habsburgo
warlord local military ruler
jefe militar cabeza de un ejército local
warm-water port port that is free of ice yearround
puerto de aguas templadas puerto en el que sus aguas nunca se congelan a lo largo del año
Warsaw Pact mutual-defense alliance between the Soviet Union and seven satellites in Eastern Europe set up in 1955
Pacto de Varsovia alianza de defensa mutua establecida en 1955 entre la Unión Soviética y siete países de Europa del Este pertenecientes a su esfera de influencia
weapons of mass destruction biological, nuclear, or chemical weapons
armas de destrucción masiva armas biológicas, nucleares o químicas
welfare state a country with a market economy but with increased government responsibility for the social and economic needs of its people
estado de bienestar país con una economía de Mercado, pero con un gobierno con mayor responsabilidad sobre las nece sidades económicas de su pueblo
westernization adoption of western ideas, technology, and culture
occidentalización adopción de ideas, tecnología y cultura occidentales
Wittenberg a city in northern Germany, where Luther drew up his 95 theses
Wittenberg ciudad al norte de Alemania donde Lutero redactó sus 95 tesis
women's suffrage right of women to vote
sufragio femenino derecho de las mujeres a votar
World Trade Organization international organization set up to facilitate global trade
Organización Mundial del Comercio organización internacional constituida para facilitar el comercio en el ámbito mundial

Y

Yalta Conference meeting between Churchill, Roosevelt, and Stalin in February 1945 where the three leaders made agreements regarding the end of World War II
Conferencia de Yalta reunión mantenida en febrero de 1945 entre Churchill, Roosevelt y Stalin en la que los tres mandatarios alcanzaron un acuerdo con respecto a la finalización de la Segunda Guerra Mundial
Yathrib final destination of Muhammad's hijra and the home of the first community of Muslims; later renamed Medina; located in the northwest of present-day Saudi Arabia
Yathrib destino final de la hégira de Mahoma y hogar de la primera comunidad de musulmanes; posteriormente rebautizada como Medina; ubicada en el noroeste de la actual Arabia Saudita
Yorktown, Virginia location where the British army surrendered in the American Revolution
Yorktown, Virginia lugar donde el ejército británico se rindió en la Revolución Americana
Yuan dynasty Chinese dynasty ruled by the Mongols from 1279 to 1368; best known ruler was Kublai Khan
dinastía Yuan dinastía china gobernada por los mongoles desde 1279 a 1368; su gobernante más conocido fue Kublai Khan

Z

zaibatsu since the late 1800s, powerful banking and industrial families in Japan
zaibatsu familias japonesas de banqueros e industriales poderosos desde finales del siglo XIX
zemstvos local elected assembly set up in Russia under Alexander II
zemstvos asambla local electa que se estableció en Rusia en la época de Alejandro II
Zen the practice of meditation; a school of Buddhism in Japan
zen práctica de meditación; escuela del budismo en Japón
zeppelin large gas-filled balloon
zepelín dirigible, globo grande lleno de gas
ziggurat in ancient Mesopotamia, a large, stepped platform thought to have been topped by a temple dedicated to a city's chief god or goddess
zigurat templo piramidal de la antigua Mesopotamia dedicado al dios o diosa principal de una ciudad
Zionism a movement devoted to rebuilding a Jewish state in Palestine
zionismo movimiento dedicado a la reconstrucción del estado judío en Palestina

1103

A

1105

B

1106

1107

1108

1109

D

1110

1111

F

1112

G

1113

1114

H

1116

J

K

L

M

1121

N

O

1123

1124

Q

R

1125

S

1127

1128

1129

T

U

1131

V

W

1132

X

Y

1133

Z

1134

[Maps]

XNR Productions, Inc.

[Photography]

Cover, GlowImages/Alamy; **Page iv,** Dfikar/Fotolia; **v,** Goodluz/Shutterstock; **vii,** Fuse/Getty Images; **xlviii,** Zimmytws/Fotolia; **001,** Bettmann/Corbis; **004, 005,** Melba Photo Agency/Alamy; **006,** Kenneth Garrett/Getty Images; **007,** Peter Horree/Alamy; **008B,** Sabena Jane Blackbird/Alamy; **008T,** James Quine/Alamy; **011,** The Art Archive/SuperStock; **012B,** Chris Howes/Wild Places Photography/Alamy; **012T,** National Geographic Image Collection/Alamy; **013B,** Image Asset Management Ltd./SuperStock; **013T,** Eddie Gerald/Alamy; **016,** Egyptian/Getty Images; **018,** Robert Harding World Imagery/Corbis; **020,** Julian Money-Kyrle/Alamy; **024,** PhotoStock-Israel/Alamy; **025,** Luca Tettoni/Bridgeman Images; **030,** Larry Lilac/Alamy; **032,** Mary Evans Picture Library/Alamy; **036,** Heritage Image Partnership Ltd./Alamy; **037,** Dea/M. CARRIERI/De Agostini/Getty Images; **039B,** Interfoto/Alamy; **039T,** Interfoto/Alamy; **044,** ArtPix/Alamy; **046B,** Eddie Gerald/Alamy; **046T,** Jozef sedmak/Alamy; **050,** Heritage Image Partnership Ltd/Alamy; **054,** SuperStock/Alamy; **055, 055B,** Jose Ignacio Soto/Shutterstock; **057,** 300dpi/Shutterstock; **058,** Pius Lee/Shutterstock; **061L,** Incamerastock/Alamy; **068,** Ke Wang/Shutterstock; **070,** Dea/A DAGLI ORTI; **072,** Dea/G NIMATALLAH; **073,** Dea Picture Library; **075,** Dinodia Photos/Alamy; **076,** Visvamitra visits Vasishtha's hermitage, Kulu, Punjab Hills, 1700 (w/c & gold on paper), Indian School, (18th century)/ University of East Anglia, Norfolk, UK/Robert and Lisa Sainsbury Collection/The Bridgeman Art Library; **077,** Pitchaya Thammasamisorn/Alamy; **078,** Gianni Dagli Orti/The Art Archive at Art Resource, NY; **079,** Ivan Nesterov/Alamy; **081,** Borromeo/Art Resource, NY; **082B,** Ephotocorp/Alamy; **082T,** Mary Evans Picture Library/Alamy; **084,** A Brahmin doctor taking a pulse,1827–35 (colour litho), Burnouf, M.E. (fl.1827–35)/Private Collection/The Stapleton Collection/The Bridgeman Art Library; **085,** Dinodia/The Image Works; **086,** SCPhotos/Alamy; **087,** The Metropolitan Museum of Art. Image source/Art Resource, NY; **088,** V&A Images, London/Art Resource, NY; **090,** SSPL/The Image Works; **091,** RMN-Grand Palais/Art Resource, NY; **092,** DoctorKan/Shutterstock; **093,** Bibliotheque Municipale, Poitiers, France/Giraudon/The Bridgeman Art Library; **093T,** The Art Archive at Art Resource, NY; **094,** Lcm Nw/Alamy; **095,** BL/Robana; **096B,** Building the Great Wall of China (gouache on paper), McBride, Angus (1931–2007)/Private Collection/Look and Learn/The Bridgeman Art Library; **096T,** Erich Lessing/Art Resource, NY; **097B,** Snark/Art Resource, NY; **097T,** Lapas77/Fotolia; **099B,** Asian Art & Archaeology, Inc/Corbis; **099T,** A Confucian Classroom (Sodang) (colour print), Hong-Do, Kim (18th; century)/National Museum, Seoul, Korea/The Bridgeman Art Library; **100B,** Danita Delimont/Alamy; **100T,** SSPL/The Image Works; **101,** Dk/Alamy; **110,** Afterdan/ Fotolia; **112,** Dea Picture Library/Art Resource, NY; **114B,** Danita Delimont/Alamy; **114T,** Zbiq/ Shutterstock; **116B,** Richard Maschmeyer/Robert Harding Picture Library/SuperStock; **116T,** Jess Kraft/Shutterstock; **119B,** Gianni Dagli Orti/The Art Archive at Art Resource, NY; **119T,** Akg-images/ The Image Works; **120,** Gianni Dagli Orti/The Art Archive at Art Resource, NY; **121,** Mark Green/ Alamy; **122,** Lordprice Collection/Alamy; **123,** Kelsey Green/Shutterstock; **126,** Robert Shantz/Alamy; **128B,** Richard A. Cooke/Corbis; **128T,** Ira Block/National Geographic/SuperStock; **138,** Drimi/Fotolia; **140,** Imagebroker/Alamy; **141,** Leonid Serebrennikov/Alamy; **142B,** VPC Travel Photo/Alamy; **142T,** De Agostini Picture L/Age Fotostock; **144,** Peter Phipp/Travelshots.com/Alamy; **146,** Ancient Art & Architecture Collection Ltd/Alamy; **147B,** De Agostini Picture Library/L. Pedicini/The Bridgeman Art Library; **147T,** Lescourret, Jean-Pierre/SuperStock/Alamy; **149B,** Bpk, Berlin/Art Resource, NY; **149T,** The Museum of Fine Arts, Boston; **150,** Steve Vidler/SuperStock; **152,** Erin Babnik/Alamy; **153B,** Johannes Laurentius/Art Resource, NY; **153T,** Erich Lessing/Art Resource, NY; **154,** Vanni Archiv/Art Resource, NY; **156B,** Vidler/Age Fotostock; **156T,** Alinari/Art Resource, NY; **157B,** Erich Lessing/Art Resource, NY; **157T,** Museumslandschaft Hessen Kassel/Ute Brunzel/The Bridgeman Art Library; **158,** Eric VANDEVILLE/Gamma-Rapho via Getty Images; **159,** Nimatallah/Art Resource, NY; **160,** Prisma Archivo/Alamy; **162,** Album/Art Resource, NY; **163B,** Image Asset Management Ltd./Alamy; **163T,** De Agostini Picture Library/G. Costa/The Bridgeman Art Library; **165,** Gianni Dagli Orti/The Art Archive at Art Resource, NY; **172,** Fazon/Fotolia.com; **177B,** AGE Fotostock; **177T,** Prisma Archivo/Alamy; **180,** RMN-Grand Palais/Art Resource, NY; **181,** Time & Life Pictures/Getty Images; **182B,** Caesar Dictating his Commentaries (oil on canvas), Palagi, Pelagio (1775–1860)/Palazzo del Quirinale, Rome, Italy/The Bridgeman Art Library; **182T,** RMN-Grand Palais/Art Resource, NY; **188B,** North Wind Picture Archives/Alamy; **188T,** Erich Lessing/Art Resource, NY; **190,** Adam Eastland Art + Architecture/Alamy; **191B,** Horatius Cocles, from the Sala dell'Udienza, 1496–1500(fresco), Perugino, Pietro(c.1445–1523)/Collegio del Cambio, Perugia, Italy/Giraudon/The; Bridgeman Art Library; **191T,** Lacma/Alamy; **192,** Erich Lessing/Art Resource, NY; **193B,** Erich Lessing/Art Resource, NY; **193T,** Alan Williams/Dorling Kindersley; **194,** Ivy Close Images/Alamy; **195,** Martin Froyda/Shutterstock; **196,** Alfredo Dagli Orti/The Art Archive at Art Resource, NY; **197,** Hemis/ Alamy; **199B,** Richard Goodrich/Alamy; **199T,** Scala/Art Resource, NY; **201,** Gianni Dagli Orti/The Art Archive at Art Resource, NY; **208,** Claudio Giovanni Colombo/Shutterstock; **210,** Chronicle/ Alamy; **214,** North Wind Picture Archives/Alamy; **217,** Pantheon/SuperStock; **218,** Index/Bridgeman Art Library; **220,** North Wind Picture Archives/Alamy; **223,** North Wind Picture Archives/Alamy; **224,** Gianni Dagli Orti/Corbis; **226,** Stefano Bianchetti/Corbis; **228,** Florilegius/Alamy; **231,** North Wind Picture Archives/The Image Works; **234B,** Ms 297/1338 f.122v Usury, from the Book of Good Morals, by Jacques le; Grant (1360–1415) (vellum), French School, (15th century)/Musee Conde, Chantilly, France/Giraudon/The Bridgeman Art Library; **234T,** Bettmann/Corbis; **235B,** North Wind Picture Archives/Alamy; **235T,** Italian School/The Bridgeman Art Library; **236,** French School/The Bridgeman Art Library/Getty Images; **238,** Mary Evans Picture Library/The Image Works; **240,** 19th era 2/Alamy; **241,** UIG/Getty Images; **242,** GL Archive/Alamy; **243B,** 19th era/Alamy; **243T,** The Art Gallery Collection/Alamy; **244,** De Agostini/Getty Images; **246,** British Library Board/Robana/Art Resource, NY; **248B,** Image Asset Management Ltd./Alamy; **248T,** Ivy Close Images/Alamy; **251,** De Agostini Picture Library/Getty Images; **253,** Chronicle/Alamy; **254,** Peter Anderson/DK Images; **255B,** Italian School/The Bridgeman Art Library/Getty Images; **255T,** Tarker/Corbis; **256B,** Ben Ramos/Alamy; **256T,** Mary Evans Picture Library/Alamy; **257B,** Topham/The Image Works; **257T,** S.Borisov/ Shutterstock; **258,** Dmitry Kalinovsky/Shutterstock; **259,** Corbis; **260,** Prisma Archivo/Alamy; **264,** Erich Lessing/Art Resource, NY; **265B,** Ivan Vdovin/Alamy; **265T,** AlxYago/Shutterstock; **266,** Interfoto/Alamy; **269B,** Album/Oronoz/Album/SuperStock; **269T,** Heritage Image Partnership Ltd/ Alamy; **280,** Tupungato/Shutterstock; **282,** Universal Images Group/Art Resource, NY; **283B,** EPA european pressphoto agency b.v./Alamy; **283T,** Historical image collection by Bildagentur-online/ Alamy; **284B,** Gfc Collection/Alamy; **284T,** MidoSemsem/Shutterstock; **285B,** Robert Harding Picture Library Ltd/Alamy; **285T,** Roland and Sabrina Michaud/Akg-images; **287,** Monasterio de El Escorial, El Escorial, Spain/Index/The Bridgeman Art Library; **288B,** Atif Saeed/Alamy; **288T,** Robert Harding World Imagery/Alamy; **290,** The Trustees of the British Museum/Art Resource, NY; **291,** Sheila Terry/ Science Source; **294,** Werner Forman/TopFoto/The Image Works; **296,** World Religions Photo Library/ Alamy; **297,** Prisma Archivo/Alamy; **298,** SPL/Science Source; **299,** The Art Gallery Collection/Alamy; **300,** Juan Francisco Jiménez Martín/Alamy; **301,** Interfoto/Alamy; **302B,** Chronicle/Alamy; **302T,** Bora/Alamy; **304,** AC Manley/Alamy; **305,** Photo Mere Travel 3/Alamy; **306,** John Warburton Lee/ SuperStock; **307,** Jon Bower-art and museums/Alamy; **310,** Akg-images; **315,** Heritage Image Partnership Ltd/Alamy; **316,** Stefan Auth/imagebroker/Alamy; **319B,** John Warburton Lee/ SuperStock; **319T,** Gavin Hellier/Robert Harding Picture Library Ltd/Alamy; **321,** Robert Holmes/ Corbis; **322,** Robert Harding Picture Library Ltd/Alamy; **323B,** Imagebroker/Alamy; **323T,** Ceremonial wine bowl/Werner Forman Archive/The Bridgeman Art Library; **324,** The Art Archive/Alamy; **325,** Age fotostock/Alamy; **334,** Jorg Hackemann/Shutterstock; **336,** Mughal School/Getty Images; **338,** Dinodia Photos/Alamy; **339B,** David Grossman/Alamy; **339T,** Art Directors & TRIP/Alamy; **340,** Charpentier/Getty Images; **341,** Peter Cook/DK Images; **342,** British Library/Robana via Getty Images; **343B,** Art Archive, The/SuperStock; **343T,** Image Asset Management Ltd./Alamy; **344B,** Werner Forman/Art Resource, NY; **344T,** Carlos Amarillo/Shutterstock; **345,** The Art Gallery Collection/ Alamy; **346,** Werner Forman/Art Resource, NY; **348,** Art Archive, The/SuperStock; **349,** Art Resource, NY; **351B,** Ancient Art & Architecture Collection Ltd/Alamy; **351T,** North Wind Picture Archives/ Alamy; **352,** GL Archive/Alamy; **353B,** Interfoto/Alamy; **353T,** Kharbine-Tapabor/The Art Archive at Art Resource, NY; **354,** Rob Walls/Alamy; **356,** Travel Pictures/Alamy; **358,** Rick Browne/Photo Researchers, Inc.; **361,** Peter Horree/Alamy; **362,** Niday Picture Library/Alamy; **363,** Japanese School, (17th century)/Detroit Institute of Arts, USA/The Bridgeman Art Library; **364,** Werner Forman/Art Resource, NY; **365,** Nichiren summoning the divine Shinpu wind to destroy the Mongol-Chinese; fleet attacking Japan in 13th century (engraving), Kuniyoshi, Utagawa (1798–1861)/Private Collection/ Ancient Art and Architecture Collection Ltd./The Bridgeman Art Library; **366B,** Japanese School, (17th century)/Brooklyn Museum of Art, New York, USA/Gift of W. W. Hoffman/The Bridgeman Art Library; **366T,** Culver Pictures, Inc./SuperStock; **368,** Chris Willson/Alamy; **369,** Cristiano Burmester/ Alamy; **370,** Ivan Trizlic/Fotolia; **372,** Olga Lipatova/Shutterstock; **373,** Wolfgang Kaehler/SuperStock; **380,** Dennis Hallinan/Alamy; **382,** Gianni Dagli Orti/The Art Archive/Alamy; **383B,** Georgios Kollidas/ Alamy; **383T,** Look and Learn/The Bridgeman Art Library; **385B,** WorldPhotos/Alamy; **385T,** SuperStock/SuperStock; **386B,** A Traverler/Alamy; **386T,** SuperStock/Alamy; **387B,** Image Asset Management Ltd./Alamy; **387T,** Interfoto/Alamy; **388,** The Print Collector/Alamy; **389,** Antiquarian Images/Alamy; **390T,** SuperStock/SuperStock; **391B,** GL Archive/Alamy; **391T,** Photos 12/Alamy; **394,** Akg images; **395,** Akg-images/The Image Works; **396,** North Wind Picture Archives/Alamy; **397B,** Prisma Archivo/Alamy; **397T,** bpk, Berlin/Art Resource, NY; **400,** Ntpl/e. Witty/The Image Works; **401,** Tom Taylor/Alamy; **402B,** Visual & Written/SuperStock; **402T,** World History Archive/ Image Asset Management Ltd./Alamy; **403B,** Album/Prisma/Album/SuperStock; **403T,** Collection Dagli Orti/The Art Archive/Alamy; **405,** 2d Alan King/Alamy; **406,** Image Asset Management Ltd./ SuperStock; **407,** Huens, Jean-Leon (1921–82)/National Geographic Creative/The Bridgeman; Art Library; **409B,** Everett Collection Historical/Alamy; **409T,** Glasgow University Library, Scotland/The Bridgeman Art Library; **410,** North Wind Picture Archives/Alamy; **418,** Exactostock/SuperStock; **420,** Mary Evans Picture Library/Alamy; **422,** Historic Map Works LLC and Osher Map Library; **425,** Pictorial Press Ltd/Alamy; **426,** Universal Images Group/SuperStock; **427,** North Wind Picture Archives/Alamy; **428B,** Heritage Image Partnership Ltd/Alamy; **428T,** The Trustees of the British Museum/Art Resource, NY; **429B,** Matteo Ricci, c.1850 (w/c on paper), Weld, Charles (fl.1850)/By permission of the Governors of Stonyhurst College/The Bridgeman Art Library; **429T,** Dea/G. DAGLI ORTI/Getty Images; **431B,** Fine Art Images/SuperStock; **431T,** Image Asset Management Ltd./Alamy; **432,** Gianni Dagli Orti/The Art Archive at Art Resource, NY; **433,** Album/Art Resource, NY; **434B,** North Wind Picture Archives/Alamy; **434T,** Album/Art Resource, NY; **436B,** North Wind Picture Archives/Alamy; **436T,** bpk, Berlin/Ethnologisches Museum/Staatliche Museen/Art Resource, NY; **439,** Scala/Art Resource, NY; **440,** Age fotostock/Alamy; **442,** Deagostini/SuperStock; **447,** ClassicStock/Alamy; **448B,** North Wind Picture Archives/Alamy; **450,** 2d Alan King/Alamy; **453,** Theodore de Bry/Getty Images; **456B,** Dea Picture Library/Getty Images; **456T,** UIG via Getty Images; **457,** Customs House, from 'A Book of the Prospects of the Remarkable Places in and about the City of London', c.1700 (engraving), Morden, Robert (fl.1682–1703)/O'Shea Gallery, London, UK/The Bridgeman Art Library; **464,** Scala/Art Resource, NY; **466,** Erich Lessing/Art Resource, NY; **467,** Lebrecht Music and Arts Photo Library/Alamy; **468,** Paul M.R. Maeyaert/Akg images; **470B,** Erich Lessing/Art Resource, NY; **470T,** Peter Horree/Alamy; **471B,** Akg Images; **471T,** Adoc-photos/Art Resource, NY; **472B,** Forget Patrick/Sagaphoto.Com/Alamy; **472T,** Gianni Dagli Orti/The Art Archive at Art Resource, NY; **474B,** North Wind Picture Archives/Alamy; **475,** De Agostini/Getty Images; **476,** De Agostini/Getty Images; **478,** Akg Images/De Agostini Pict.Lib.; **479,** Akg Images; **480,** Fine Art Images/SuperStock; **481B,** The Art Gallery Collection/Alamy; **481T,** UIG/Getty Images; **482,** Neveshkin Nikolay/Shutterstock; **484,** Akg Images; **485,** Akg Images; **486B,** Lebrecht Music and Arts Photo Library/Alamy; **486T,** Glasshouse Images/Alamy; **487,** John Singleton (1738–1815)/Boston Public Library, Boston, Massachusetts, USA/The Bridgeman Art Library; **488B,** GeorgiosArt/iStockphoto; **488T,** Akg Images; **490,** Getty Images; **492,** Balthasar Nebot/Getty Images; **493,** Jean-Leon Huens/National Geographic Image Collection/Alamy; **494,** Stefano Bianchetti/Corbis; **496B,** Tate, London/Art Resource, NY; **496T,** Erich Lessing/Art Resource, NY; **497,** Guildhall Library & A/Heritage Image/AGE fotostock; **498,** SuperStock/SuperStock; **499B,** Pictorial Press Ltd/Alamy; **499T,** Lebrecht Music and Arts Photo Library/Alamy; **500,** Fine Art Images/AGE fotostock; **502,** North Wind Picture Archives/Alamy; **504,** Akg Images; **505,** Everett Collection/Alamy; **506B,** Onur ERSIN/Shutterstock; **506T,** Getty Images; **508,** Mary Evans Picture Library/Alamy; **509B,** Thomas Naudet/Getty Images; **509T,** RMN-Grand Palais/Art Resource, NY; **511,** Stefano Bianchetti/Corbis; **512,** Gianni Dagli Orti/The Art Archive/Art Resource, NY; **513,** Hulton Archive/Getty Images; **514B,** Akg-images; **514T,** The Gallery Collection/Corbis; **516,** Akg-images; **517,** Mary Evans Picture Library/AGE Fotostock; **519,** The Art Gallery Collection/Alamy; **520,** French School/The Bridgeman Art Library/Getty Images; **521,** Everett Collection Historical/Alamy; **523,** Nick Hanna/Alamy; **524,** Laurent Lecat/Akg-images; **525B,** Jean-Leon Gerome/Christie's Images/Corbis; **525T,** The Print Collector/Alamy; **528B,** SuperStock/Alamy; **528T,** Prisma Archivo/Alamy; **529,** The Print Collector/Alamy; **530,** North Wind Picture Archives/Alamy; **540,** Image Asset Management Ltd/Alamy; **542,** Everett Collection/SuperStock; **543,** 19th century/Private Collection/Ancient Art and Architecture Collection Ltd/Bridgeman Images; **544,** North Wind Picture Archives/Alamy; **546,** Lebrecht Music and Arts Photo Library/Alamy; **547B,** ClassicStock.com/SuperStock; **547T,** C.L.Doughty, (1913–85)/Private Collection/Look and Learn/Bridgeman Images; **549B,** Glasshouse Images/Alamy; **549T,** H-D Falkenstein/ima/imagebroker.net/SuperStock; **551,** Pantheon/SuperStock; **553B,** Niday Picture Library/Alamy; **553T,** Akg-images; **554,** Corbis; **555,** Album/Art Resource, NY; **556,** Everett Collection Inc/Alamy; **557,** The Print Collector/Alamy; **558,** Austrian Archives/Corbis; **560,** Everett Collection Inc/Alamy; **562B,** Hulton Archive/Stringer/Getty Images; **562T,** Archive Pics/Alamy; **564B,** Chronicle/Alamy; **564T,** The Art Archive/Alamy; **566B,** Hulton-Deutsch Collection/Corbis; **566T,** Pictorial Press Ltd/Alamy; **567B,** Images.com/Alamy; **567T,** Akg-images/The Image Works; **568,** Keystone-France/Getty Images; **569,** Library of Congress/Photri Images/Alamy; **570,** Oote Boe 1/Alamy; **571,** Archive Pics/Alamy; **572,** Science and Society/SuperStock; **573B,** Eileen Tweedy/The Art Archive/Art Resource, NY; **573T,** The Print Collector/Alamy; **574,** Underwood & Underwood/Corbis; **575B,** Lebrecht Music and Arts Photo Library/Alamy; **575T,** The Art Gallery Collection/Alamy; **576B,** Peter Horree/Alamy; **576T,** V&A Images/Alamy; **577B,** Michael Freeman/Alamy; **577T,** Akg-images; **578,** Album/Art Resource, NY; **586, 587,** Stuart Forster/Alamy; **588,** Image Asset Management Ltd./Alamy; **589,** Prisma/SuperStock; **591,** Gianni Dagli Orti/The Art Archive/Alamy; **592,** Defence of a Barricade, 29th July 1830 (colour litho), French School, (19th century)/Musee de la Ville de Paris, Musee Carnavalet, Paris, France/Giraudon/Bridgeman Images; **594,** Art Resource, NY; **597,** Oronoz/SuperStock; **598,** Mary Evans Picture Library/The Image Works; **599,** The Unfinished Revolution. Father Hidalgo and the Mexican Revolution, Embleton, Ron (1930–88)/Private Collection/Look and Learn/Bridgeman Images; **600B,** Iberfoto/SuperStock; **600T,** Gianni Dagli Orti/The Art Archive/Art Resource, NY; **602,** SuperStock/SuperStock; **604,** Niday Picture Library/Alamy; **605,** Interfoto/Alamy; **606B,** Image Asset Management Ltd./Alamy; **606T,** Interfoto/Alamy; **607B,** Niday Picture Library/Alamy; **607T,** Akg-images; **608,** Interfoto/Alamy; **609,** Intaerfoto/Personalities/Alamy; **610B,** De Agostini Picture Lib./A. De Gregorio/Akg-images; **610T,** Interfoto/Personalities/Alamy; **611,** The Cartoon Collector/Print Collector/Getty Images; **612,** Collection Dagli Orti/The Art Archive/Alamy; **613,** The Art Archive/Alamy; **614,** London Metropolitan Archives, City of London/Bridgeman Images; **615B,** Scala/White Images/Art Resource, NY; **615T,** GL Archive/Alamy; **616,** North Wind Picture Archives/Alamy; **617B,** North Wind Picture Archives/Alamy; **617T,** Image Asset Management Ltd./Alamy; **619B,** 19th era/Alamy; **619T,** Everett Collection Historical/Alamy; **621,** Tarker/Corbis; **622,** Gianni Dagli Orti/The Art Archive/Alamy; **623B,** Interfoto/Personalities/Alamy; **623T,** Akg-images; **624,** Akg-images; **625,** (20th century)/Musee National de l'Education, Rouen, France/Archives Charmet/Bridgeman Images; **626,** Library of Congress; **628B,** Kurz and Allison (fl.1880–98)/Collection of the New-York Historical Society, USA/Bridgeman Images; **628T,** Glasshouse Images/Alamy; **630,** North Wind Picture Archives/Alamy; **631,** Alfredo Dagli Orti/The Art Archive/Art Resource, NY; **632,** World History Archive/Image Asset Management Ltd./Alamy; **634,** Deagostini/SuperStock; **635,** Pantheon/SuperStock; **636B,** Akg-images/The Image Works; **636T,** HIP/Art Resource, NY; **637,** Snark/Art Resource, NY; **646, 647,** Derek Bayes/Lebrecht Music & A/Lebrecht Music & Arts/Corbis; **648,** RMN-Grand Palais/Art Resource, NY; **649,** Isaac Holden & Sons' Alston, Bradford, United Kingdom/Universal History Archive/UIG/The Bridgeman Art Library; **650B,** The French in Algeria, engraved by P. Louis (19th century), from 'The History of France', by Emile de Bonnechose, published by Ward, Lock and Co, London (engraving), Schuler, Jules Theophile (1821–78) (after)/Private Collection/The Bridgeman Art Library; **650T,** PhotoQuest/Contributor/Archive Photos/Getty Images; **651B,** Carol practice in a French mission in China, early twentieth century (b/w photo),./Bibliotheque des Arts Decoratifs, Paris, France/Archives Charmet/Bridgeman Images; **651T,** Chinese School/The Bridgeman Art Library/Getty Images; **653,** Dea Picture Library/Getty Images; **654,** Bojan Brecelj/Corbis; **655,** Freetown, Sierra Leone (engraving), English School, (19th century)/Private; Collection/The Bridgeman Art Library; **656,** Prisma Archivo/Alamy; **657,** Popperfoto/Getty Images; **658,** The Art Gallery Collection/Alamy; **660B,** Everett Collection/Newscom; **660T,** Thomas Nast/CartoonStock; **661B,** British Artillery Men with Gun, c. 1882-3 (b/w photo), English Photographer, (19th century)/Private Collection/The Bridgeman Images; **661T,** Apic/Contributor/Hulton Fine Art Collection/Getty Images; **663,** The Print Collector/Alamy; **664B,** Pictorial Press Ltd/Alamy; **664T,** Stuart Forster/Alamy; **665B,** The British Raj Great Indian Peninsular Terminus (w/c on paper), Haig, Axel; (1835–1921)/British Library, London, UK/Bridgeman Images; **665T,** British Library/Robana/Hulton Fine Art Collection/Getty Images; **667,** Hulton-Deutsch Collection/Corbis; **668,** British ships destroying an enemy fleet in Canton, 1841. First Opium War, China, 19th century./De Agostini Picture Library/The Bridgeman Images; **669,** The Art Archive/Art Resource, NY; **671B,** Everett Collection Inc/Alamy; **671T,** Everett Collection Historical/Alamy; **673,** Popperfoto/Getty Images; **674,** Glasshouse Images/Alamy; **675B,** Toyohara Chikanobu; **675T,** Japan's first foreign mission, headed by Prince Iwakura, Ambassador Extraordinary and Plenipotentiary leaving Yokohama for the United States, 1871 (print)/Private Collection/The Bridgeman Images; **676,** Rykoff Collection/Corbis; **677,** Apic/Contributor/Hulton Archive/Getty Images; **678,** The Castle of Batavia, as Seen from Kali Besar West, c.1656 (oil on canvas), Beeckman, Andries (fl.1651)/Rijksmuseum, Amsterdam, The Netherlands/Bridgeman Images; **679,** Hulton Archive/Stringer/Getty Images; **680,** Naval Battle, (oil on canvas), Tyler, James Gale (1855–1931)/Private; Collection/Photo (c) Christie's Images/The Bridgeman Images; **681B,** Penny Tweedie/Alamy; **681T,** Akg-images/Newscom; **682,** Alinari/Getty Images; **683,** Interim Archives/Contributor/Archive Photos/Getty Images; **684B,** The Last Stand at the Alamo, 6th March 1836 (colour litho), Wyeth, Newell; Convers (1882–1945)/Private Collection/The Bridgeman Images; **684T,** Gianni Dagli Orti/The Art Archive/Art Resource, NY; **685,** Image Asset Management Ltd./Alamy; **688B,** Settler's Log House, 1856 (oil on canvas), Krieghoff, Cornelius (1815–72)/Art Gallery of Ontario, Toronto, Canada/The Bridgeman Images; **688T,** H.N. Rudd/Historical/Corbis; **698, 699,** Susan Law Cain/Shutterstock; **700,** Bettmann/Corbis; **701B,** Mary Evans Picture Library/Alamy; **701T,** DIZ Muenchen GmbH, Sueddeutsche Zeitung Photo/Alamy; **703,** Bettmann/Corbis; **704B,** General Photographic Agency/Getty Images; **704T,** S&M/ANSA/UIG/Getty Images; **706,** Akg-images/Alamy; **708B,** Hulton-Deutsch Collection/Corbis; **708T,** Hulton-Deutsch Collection/Corbis; **709,** Comando Supremo, Italian Army/National Geographic Society/Corbis; **711,** Akg-images/Alamy; **712,** Imperial War Museum/The Art Archive/Art Resource, NY; **713B,** Pictorial Press Ltd/Alamy; **713T,** Akg-images/The Image Works; **714,** Photos 12/Alamy; **715B,** Robert Hunt Library/Mary Evans/The Image Works; **715T,** Akg-images/Alamy; **718,** WW/Alamy; **720,** Bettmann/Corbis; **721,** Hulton Archive/Getty Images; **722,** Fine Art Images/Heritage Images/The Image Works; **723,** Image Asset Management Ltd./Alamy; **724,** Fine Art Images/Agefotostock; **726,** Everett Collection Historical/Alamy; **734, 735,** Chronicle/Alamy; **736,** Corbis; **737,** PF-(bygone)/Alamy; **739,** Emiliano Rodriguez/Alamy; **741,** FPG/Staff/Archive PhotosGetty Images; **742B,** Gallo Images/Alamy; **742T,** Pearson Education; **743B,** Sophie Bassouls/Sygma/Corbis; **743T,** Everett Collection Inc/Alamy; **744,** DIZ Muenchen GmbH, Sueddeutsche Zeitung Photo/Alamy; **746,** Josef Schweig/Fox Photos/Getty Images; **748,** Dinodia/AGE Fotostock; **749B,** GandhiServe/Archiv Peter Rhe/Akg Images; **749T,** Yvan Travert/Akg Images; **750,** Dinodia/AGE Fotostock; **752,** Hulton Archive/Getty Images; **753B,** Everett Collection Historical/Alamy; **753T,** Interfoto/Alamy; **754,** Kevin O'Hara/AGE fotostock/Alamy; **756,** Pictorial Press Ltd/Alamy; **758,** Interfoto/Alamy; **759,** Bettmann/Corbis; **760,** Lordprice Collection/Alamy; **761,** Keystone Pictures USA/Alamy; **762B,** Dennis Van Tine/LFI/Photoshot/Newscom; **762T,** Everett Collection Historical/Alamy; **763B,** Peter Horree/Alamy; **763T,** Lebrecht Music and Arts Photo Library/Alamy; **764B,** Mark Burnett/Alamy; **764T,** Painting/Alamy; **765,** Hulton Archive/Getty Images; **766,** Bettmann/Corbis; **767,** 'The Doormat' (i.e. the League of Nations), published in the London Evening Standard in 1932 depicting Japan's rising militarism (litho), Low, Sir David (1891–1963)/Private Collection/Peter Newark Military Pictures/The Bridgeman Art Library; **769,** Interfoto/Alamy; **771,** Hulton-Deutsch Collection/Corbis; **772,** Image Asset Management Ltd./SuperStock; **773B,** De Agostini/Getty Images; **773T,** UIG/Getty Images; **774B,** Getty Images; **774T,** Hulton-Deutsch Collection/Corbis; **775,** Stefano Bianchetti/Corbis; **776,** Hulton-Deutsch Collection/Corbis; **778,** Akg-images; **779,** Heritage Image Partnership Ltd/Alamy; **781B,** Bettmann/Corbis; **781T,** Heritage Image Partnership Ltd/Alamy; **782B,** Getty Images; **782T,** SSPL/Getty Images; **784,** Mary Evans Picture Library/Alamy; **785,** SSPL/The Image Works; **787,** SZ Photo/The Image Works; **789,** Interfoto/Alamy; **798,** Bettmann/Corbis; **800,** FPG/Getty Images; **801B,** Bettmann/Corbis; **801T,** David Low, Evening Standard, 08 July 1936, British Cartoon Archive, University of Kent/Solo Syndication; **803B,** AP Images; **803T,** Robert Capa International Center of Photography/Magnum Photos; **804B,** AP Images; **804T,** Akg-images/Interfoto; **805,** United Kingdom, Great Britain, Cartoon depicting Adolf Hitler and Joseph Stalin/De Agostini Picture Library/The Bridgeman Art Library; **806,** IBL Collections/Mary Evans/Everett Collection (10426968); **808B,** Courtesy Everett Collection; **808T,** The National Archives/SSPL/Getty Images; **809,** Berliner Verlag/Archiv/picture-alliance/dpa/AP Images; **811,** Interfoto/Alamy; **812,** US National Archives/Alamy; **814,** Anne Frank Fonds/Anne Frank House/Getty Images; **815,** Akg-images; **816,** UIG/Getty Images; **817,** Jim Hollander/Epa/Corbis; **818,** Hulton-Deutsch Collection/Corbis; **820,** AP Images; **823,** Lightroom Photos/Alamy; **824,** AP Images; **826B,** Bettmann/Corbis; **826T,** Interfoto/Alamy; **827,** Roger Viollet/Getty Images; **828B,** Pictorial Press Ltd./Alamy; **828T,** Corbis; **838,** Robert Maass/Corbis; **840,** AP Images; **841,** Hulton-Deutsch Collection/Corbis; **842,** Walter Sanders/Life Magazine/Time & Life Pictures/Getty Images; **845,** A 1968 Herblock Cartoon, The Herb Block Foundation; **847,** Sovfoto/UIG via Getty Images; **848,** Universal Images Group Limited/Alamy; **849,** Bert Morgan/Getty Images; **850,** Bettmann/Corbis; **851B,** AP Images; **851T,** Elliott Erwitt/Magnum Photos; **854,** AP Images; **855B,** Jerry Cooke/Corbis; **855T,** John Florea//Time Life Pictures/Getty Images; **857,** Keystone/Getty Images; **858,** Keystone-France/Gamma-Keystone via Getty Images; **859B,** Library of Congress, Prints & Photographs Division, drawing by Edmund S. Valtman, LC-DIG-ppmsc-07964; **859T,** AFP/Getty Images; **861,** Jason Reed/Reuters/Corbis; **862,** AP Images; **863,** Horst Faas/AP Images; **865B,** Staff/Afp/Gettyimages; **865T,** JP Laffont/Sygma/Corbis; **866,** Bettmann/Corbis; **867,** Sovfoto/UIG/Getty Images;

868, Scott Stewart/AP Images; **870B,** AP Images; **870T,** Fabian Cevallos/Sygma/Corbis; **871,** MIKE PERSSON/AFP/Getty Images; **880,** Daniel Irungu/Epa/Newscom; **882,** Dinodia Photos/Alamy; **883,** Bettmann/Corbis; **884B,** Janine Wiedel Photolibrary/Alamy; **884T,** RIA Novosti/Alamy; **886B,** Mike Goldwater/Alamy; **886T,** David Edwards/National Geographic Society/Corbis; **888,** Homer W Sykes/ Alamy; **889,** Bettmann/Corbis; **891,** Bettmann/Corbis; **893,** Allstar Picture Library/Alamy; **894,** Bettmann/Corbis; **895,** Gallo Images/Alamy; **896B,** Bettmann/Corbis; **896T,** Stuart Forster/Alamy; **897,** Eddie Gerald/Alamy; **898,** dbimages/Alamy; **900B,** Bettmann/Corbis; **900T,** Bettmann/Corbis; **901B,** Claudia Wiens/Alamy; **901T,** Art Directors & TRIP/Alamy; **902,** Stefano Politi Markovina/ Alamy; **904,** Claudia Wiens/Alamy; **905,** peter jordan/Alamy; **907B,** Gali Tibbon/Getty Images; **907T,** AFP/Getty Images; **908,** Bernard Bisson/Sygma/Corbis; **909,** Kaiser/Caro/Alamy; **918, 919,** massimo_g/Fotolia; **920,** thakala/Fotolia; **922,** Dinodia Photos/Alamy; **923B,** National Geographic Image Collection/Alamy; **923T,** CHRIS WATTIE/Reuters/Corbis; **925,** Greg Marinovich/Africa Media Online/The Image Works; **926B,** Bettmann/Corbis; **926T,** Baileys Archive/africanpictures/The Image Works; **927,** Eye Ubiquitous/Alamy; **929B,** Micheline Pelletier/Corbis; **929T,** Eye Ubiquitous/Alamy; **930,** Jane Sweeney/info@awl-images.com/JAI/Corbis; **931,** Reuters/Corbis; **932B,** B Mathur/Reuters/ Corbis; **932T,** jeremy sutton-hibbert/Alamy; **933B,** Tim Graham/Alamy; **933T,** dbimages/Alamy; **934,** Friedrich Stark/Alamy; **935,** epa european pressphoto agency b.v./Alamy; **937,** Stephen Bisgrove/ Alamy; **938,** Alain Keler/Sygma/Corbis; **939,** Peter Turnley/Corbis; **940,** Micheline Pelletier/Sygma/ Corbis; **941,** leeyiutung/Fotolia; **944B,** Caro/Alamy; **944T,** epa european pressphoto agency b.v./ Alamy; **949,** Dinodia Photos/Alamy; **952,** Dereje Belachew/Alamy; **953B,** David Hoffman Photo Library/Alamy; **953T,** Greg Balfour Evans/Alamy; **954,** Francois Werli/Alamy; **957B,** Bryan Denton/ Corbis; **957T,** FPG/Staff/Getty Images; **958B,** Joerg Boethling/Alamy; **958T,** Jeff Greenberg 5 of 6/ Alamy; **959B,** US Coast Guard Photo/Alamy; **959T,** imagebroker.net/SuperStock; **960,** BrazilPhotos. com/Alamy; **962,** AP Photo/David Guttenfelde; **963,** Howard Yanes/AP Images; **964,** Patrick Robert/ Corbis; **965B,** Universal Images Group/SuperStock; **965T,** Beth Dixson/Alamy; **966,** dacology/Alamy; **967,** AP Images; **968,** Interfoto/Alamy; **969,** NASA Photo/Alamy; **971,** Disability Images/Alamy; **972,** dieKleinert/Alamy; **978,** Stock Connection Blue/Alamy

[Text Acknowledgments]

Topic 1, Source: http://www.britannica.com/EBchecked/topic/304498/Donald-C-Johanson. Reprinted with permission from Encyclopædia Britannica, © 2014 by Encyclopædia Britannica, Inc; **Topic 1,** Source: http://www.britannica.com/EBchecked/topic/99072/Catalhuyuk. Reprinted with permission from Encyclopædia Britannica, © 2014 by Encyclopædia Britannica, Inc; **Topic 1,** Source: http:// www.britannica.com/EBchecked/topic/99072/Catalhuyuk. Reprinted with permission from Encyclopædia Britannica, © 2014 by Encyclopædia Britannica, Inc; **Topic 1,** Source: http://www. britannica.com/EBchecked/topic/427425/Olduvai-Gorge. Reprinted with permission from Encyclopædia Britannica, © 2014 by Encyclopædia Britannica, Inc; **Topic 1,** Source: http://www. britannica.com/EBchecked/topic/333892/Mary-Douglas-Leakey. Reprinted with permission from Encyclopædia Britannica, © 2014 by Encyclopædia Britannica, Inc; **Topic 1,** Source: http://www. britannica.com/EBchecked/topic/281363/Iceman. Reprinted with permission from Encyclopædia Britannica, © 2014 by Encyclopædia Britannica, Inc; **Topic 1,** Source: http://www.britannica.com/ EBchecked/topic/302707/Jericho; **Topic 2,** Letters to a Law Student: A Guide to Studying Law at University by Nicolas McBride. Copyright (c) Pearson. Used by permission; **Topic 2,** Holy Bible: King James Version, 1611 Edition. Copyright (c) 2006 by Hendrickson Publishers; **Topic 2,** The Code of Hammurabi by King, L. W. Copyright (c) 1999 by NuVision Publications; **Topic 2,** Letters to a Law Student by Nicholas J McBride. Copyright (c) 2012 by Pearson Education; **Topic 4,** Source: http:// www.britannica.com/EBchecked/topic/88408/Cahokia. Reprinted with permission from Encyclopædia Britannica, © 2014 by Encyclopædia Britannica, Inc; **Topic 4,** Sacredness of Teotihuacan, Mexico Christopher L.C.E. Witcombe. Source: http://witcombe.sbc.edu/sacredplaces/teotihuacan.html; **Topic 4,** Source: http://yaleglobal.yale.edu/about/zero.jsp; **Topic 4,** Source: Life in Ancient South America by Hazel Richardson Copyright (c) 2005 by the Crabtree Publishing; **Topic 4,** Source: http:// www.britannica.com/EBchecked/topic/284568/Inca-religion; **Topic 5, Source A,** Everyday Life in Ancient Greece by C.E. Robinson. Copyright (c) Oxford University Press; **Topic 5, Source C,** Life in Ancient Athens: The Social and Public Life of a Classical Athenian from Day to Day by T.G. Tucker. Copyright (c) Macmillan Press, Ltd.; **Topic 5, Source E,** Everyday Life in Ancient Greece by C.E. Robinson. Copyright (c) Oxford University Press; **Topic 6, Lesson 3,** "Livy, The History of Rome" from The Classical Roman Reader: New Encounters with Ancient Rome by Kenneth J. Atchity (ed.). Copyright (c) 1998 Oxford University Press; **Topic 6, Lesson 4,** Matthew 5:5-9 from The Holy Bible with the Apocrypha. Copyright (c) 1994 National Council of the Churches of Christ; **Topic 6, Lesson 10,** C. Suetonius Tranquillus. 2008. Lives of the Caesars. Catharine Edwards (trans). Oxford University Press; **Topic 6, Lesson 3,** Natural History by Pliny the Elder and D.E. Eicholz (trans.). Copyright (c) 1967 Harvard University Press; **Topic 6** University of Pennsylvania. Dept. of History: Translations and Reprints from the Original Sources of European history, (Philadelphia, University of Pennsylvania Press [1897?–1907?]), Vol 4:, 1, pp. 28–30. This text is in the public domain; **Topic 6** "Marcus Tullius" by Cicero from Cicero: De re Publica (On the Republic), Clinton W. Keyes (trans.). Copyright (c) 1928 Harvard University Press; **Topic 6** Peter Brown Interview, Princeton University. // HIS.PRINCETON.EDU/PEOPLE/E56/PETER_BROWN_INTERVIE.HTML; **Topic 6** Source: http://www. poetryintranslation.com/PITBR/Latin/VirgilAeneidI.htm#_Toc535054289; **Topic 6** Source: http://www. pbs.org/wgbh/pages/frontline/shows/religion/maps/primary/josephusmasada.html; **Topic 6** Source: http://penelope.uchicago.edu/Thayer/E/Roman/Texts/Plutarch/Lives/Tiberius_Gracchus*.html; **Topic 7, Lesson 4,** "Apprenticeship in the Weaving Industry" from A Source Book for Medieval Economic History by Roy C. Cave and Herbert H. Coulson. Copyright (c) 1965 The Bruce Publishing Company; **Topic 7, Lesson 4,** Fulcher of Chartres. Chronicle of the First Crusade by Martha Evelyn translated by McGinty. Copyright (c) 1941 University of Pennsylvania Press; **Topic 7, Lesson 6,** "Reading and Keeping the Books" by Boncompagno de Signa from Books, Banks, Buttons: And Other Inventions from the Middle Ages by Chiara Frugoni and William McCuaig (trans). Copyright (c) 2005 Columbia University Press; **Topic 7, Lesson 6,** Christine de Pisan from Sources of the West, Volume 1: From the Beginning to 1715 by Mark Kishlansky and Daniel Gordon (trans.). Copyright (c) 2011 Pearson; **Topic 7, Lesson 8,** God's Playground: A History of Poland, Vol. 1: The Origins to 1795 by Norman Davies. Copyright 2005 Columbia University Press; **Topic 7, Lesson 8,** 48 Hours of Kristallnact: Night of Destruction/Dawn of the Holocaust by Michael Goeffrey Bard. Copyright (c) 2008 Globe Pequot; **Topic 7,** History of the Christian Church by Phillip Schaff. Copyright (c) 2005 Christian Classics Ethereal Library; **Topic 7,** William the Conqueror by David Bates. Copyright (c) 2001 Tempus Pub Limited; **Topic 7,** Philotheos, quoted in "Tsar and People: Studies in Russian Myths" by Michael Cherniavsky. Copyright (c) 2011 Yale University Press; **Topic 7,** Source: http://www.fordham.edu/ halsall/source/domesday1.asp; **Topic 8, Source A,** The Fifteen Decisive Battles of the World: From Marathon to Waterloo. Edward S Creasy Dover Military History, Weapons, Armor.© 2008 Dover Publications; **Topic 8,** CORPUS OF EARLY AFRICAN SOURCES FOR WEST AFRICAN HISTORY. edited by N. Levtzion, edited and translated by J. F. P. Hopkins. Copyright © 1981 University of Ghana, International Academic Union and Cambridge University Press. Reprinted with the permission of Cambridge University Press; **Topic 8, Lesson 7,** Ibn Battuta: Travels in Asia and Africa 1325–1354 by Ibn Battua and H.A.R Gibb (trans.). Copyright (c) 1986 Routledge; **Topic 8, Source D,** Excerpt from History of the Arabs: From the Earliest Times to the Present by Philip K Hitti. Copyright (c) Macmillan; **Topic 8, Source E,** "Part II: The Ascendancy of Islam, 711-1031" from A History of Medieval Spain by Joseph F. Callaghan. Copyright (c) Cornell University Press; **Topic 8, Source B,** "Introduction" from Islam and the West by Bernard Lewis. Copyright (c) Oxford University Press; **Topic 8,** Source: Sundiata: An Epic Of Old Mali by D.T. Niane and Pickett (trans). Copyright © 1995 Demco Media; **Topic 8,** Source: Kishwar Rizvi, The Suggestive Portrait of Shah 'Abbas: Prayer and Likeness in a Safavid Shahnama. http://arthistory.yale.edu/faculty/faculty/RizviShah.pdf; **Topic 9, Source B,** "The Era Of His Ways" from The Washington Post; 12/31/1995 ©1995 copying, redistribution, or retransmission of this Content without express written permission is prohibited; **Topic 9, Source D,** Genghis Khan: Founder of the Mongol Empire. David W Del Testa ed. Government Leaders, Military Rulers and Political Activists; **Topic 9, Lesson 1,** "The Fall of Constantinople" from The Age of Feudalism by Geoffrey Villehardouin and Timothy L. Biel (ed.). Copyright (c) 1994 Lucent Books; **Topic 9, Lesson 3,** The True Dates of the Chinese Maritime Expeditions in the Early Fifthteenth Century by Jan Julius Lodewijk Duyvendak. Copyright (c) 1959 Brill Academic Publishers; **Topic 9, Source A,** Genghis Khan: The Emperor of All Men by Harold Lamb. Copyright (c) Amereon Limited; **Topic 9, Source C,** The Secret History of the Mongols: The Life and Times of Chinggis Khan by Urgunge Onon. Copyright (c) Taylor and Francis; **Topic 9, Source E,** Excerpts from Chapter 19 of The Great Armies of Antiquity by Richard A Gabriel. Copyright (c) Praeger Publishers; **Topic 9,** Source: The Tale of Genji by Murasaki Shikibu. Copyright (c) 2006 by Tuttle Publishing, 2006; **Topic 9,** Source: http://www.shsu.edu/~his_ncp/Polo.html; **Topic 9,** Source: http://www.britannica.com/EBchecked/topic/607892/tsunami; **Topic 9,** Source: Traditional Japanese Literature: An Anthology, Beginnings to 1600 by Haruo Shirane. Copyright (c) 2008 by Columbia University Press; **Topic 9,** Source: http://www-maths.mcs.st-andrews.ac.uk/ homepages/joc.html; **Topic 9,** Source: http://www-maths.mcs.st-andrews.ac.uk/homepages/efr.html; **Topic 9,** Source: http://www.ncbi.nlm.nih.gov/pmc/articles/PMC1381134/; **Topic 9,** Source: Tea in Japan: Essays on the History of Chanoyu by H. Paul Varley, Isao Kumakura. Copyright (c) 1989 by University of Hawaii Press; **Topic 9,** Source: The Truth of Nanak and the Sikhs Part One by Anthony John Monaco. Copyright (c) 2004 by AuthorHouse; **Topic 10, Lesson 1,** Age of Revolution 1789–1848 by Eric Hobsbawm?. Copyright (c) 2010 by Orion Publishing Group Ltd; **Topic 10, Lesson 3,** "The Growing Challenge" by Martin Luther from The Reformation by Sarah Flowers. Copyright (c) 1995 Lucent Books; **Topic 11,** Source: http://www.britannica.com/EBchecked/topic/381398/Middle-Passage. Reprinted with permission from Encyclopædia Britannica, © 2014 by Encyclopædia Britannica, Inc; **Topic 11,** Source: http://www.britannica.com/EBchecked/topic/353691/George-Macartney-Earl-Macartney-Viscount-Macartney-of-Dervock-baron-of-Lissanoure-Baron-Macartney-of-Parkhurst-and-of-Auchinleck-Lord-Macartney. Reprinted with permission from Encyclopædia Britannica, © 2014 by Encyclopædia Britannica, Inc; **Topic 11, Lesson 1,** The Discoverers by Daniel J. Boorstein. Copyright (c) 1983 Vintage Books; **Topic 11, Lesson 1,** The Discoverers by Daniel J. Boorstin. Copyright (c) 1985 by Vintage Books; **Topic 11, Lesson 4,** Arms for Empire by Edward Douglas Leach. Copyright (c) 1973 Macmillan; **Topic 11, Lesson 4,** The French and Indian War. by Walter R. Borneman. Copyright (c) 2007 Harper Collins; **Topic 11, Lesson 4,** Arms for Empire by Douglas Edward Leach. Copyright (c) 1973 by MacMillan Publishers; **Topic 11, Lesson 4,** The French and Indian War by Borneman, Walter R. Copyright (c) 2007 by HarperCollins; **Topic 11, Lesson 5,** Life on an African Slave Ship by Joseph Kleinman & Eileen Kurtis-Kleinman. Copyright (c) 2000 Lucent Books; **Topic 11,** Source: A Pillar of Fire to Follow: American Indian Dramas, 1808–1859 by Priscilla Sears. Copyright © 1982 by Popular Press; **Topic 11,** Source: http://www.britannica.com/ EBchecked/topic/502216/Matteo-Ricci; **Topic 11,** Source: http://www.britannica.com/EBchecked/ topic/719243/Chinese-painting/283421/Qing-dynasty-1644-191112; **Topic 12, Lesson 2,** "The Making of Peace" from The Thirty Years War by Geoffrey Parker. Copyright (c) 1997 Military Heritage Press; **Topic 12, Lesson 4,** To Come; **Topic 12, Lesson 6,** "Political Authority" by Denis Diderot from Diderot's Selected Writings by Lester G. Crocker (Ed.) and Derek Coltman (Trans.). Copyright (c) 1966 Macmillan; **Topic 12, Lesson 10,** A Source Book for Russian History, Vol. 2. 1972. G. Vernadsky (trans.) New Haven: Yale University Press; **Topic 12, Lesson 10,** "Catherine the Great, Decree on

Serfs" from A Source Book for Russian History translated by G. Vernadsky. Copyright (c) 1972 by the Yale University Press; **Topic 12,** The Age of Napoleon by J. Christopher Herold (ed.). Copyright (c) 2002 American Heritage; **Topic 12,** Power and Faction in Louis XIV's France by R. Mettam. Copyright (c) 1988 Oxford: Basil Blackwell; **Topic 12,** The Massacre of Saint Bartholomew. by Henri Nogueres. Copyright (c) 1962. Allen & Unwin; **Topic 12,** Source: http://www.brainyquote.com/quotes/quotes/l/ludwigvonm402346.html; **Topic 13,** Source: http://www.britannica.com/EBchecked/topic/445964/Louis-Pasteur/281418/Implications-of-Pasteurs-work. Reprinted with permission from Encyclopædia Britannica, © 2014 by Encyclopædia Britannica, Inc; **Topic 13, Lesson 2,** Locke, John. 2005. The Wealth of Nations. Pennsylvania State University; **Topic 13, Lesson 4,** "The Solitude of Self," January 18, 1892 by Elizabeth Cady Stanton from The Elizabeth Cady Stanton-Susan B. Anthony Reader: Correspondence, Writings, Speeches by Ellen Carol DuBois and Gerda Lerner. Copyright (c) 1987 Schocken Books; **Topic 13,** Source: Germinal: Easyread Comfort Edition by Emile Zola. Copyright (c) 2006 by ReadHowYouWant.com; **Topic 13,** Source: Max Domarus. _The Complete Hitler: A Digital Desktop Reference to His Speeches and Proclamations 1932–1945_. 4 vols. Wauconda: Bolchazy-Carducci, 2007; **Topic 14, Source E,** John Newsinger The Great Irish Famine: A Crime of Free Market Economics. Monthly Review: Vol 47, Issue 11, April 1996; **Topic 14, Source C,** God and the English made the Irish famine-by Brendan Graham-The Indy. www.independent.co.uk.; **Topic 14, Source D,** Monoculture and the Irish Potato Famine: Cases of Missing Genetic Variation. Understanding Evolution. University of California Museum of Paleontology. http://evolution.berkeley.edu/evolibrary/article/agriculture_02; **Topic 14, Source F,** No need to apologise for the potato famine-by Ruth Dudley Edwards-The Indy. www.independent.co.uk.; **Topic 14,** Source: http://www.britannica.com/EBchecked/topic/466210/pogrom. Reprinted with permission from Encyclopædia Britannica, © 2014 by Encyclopædia Britannica, Inc; **Topic 14, Lesson 1,** Dialectics and Revolution, Volume 2 by DeGrood, David H Copyright (c) 1978 by John Benjamins Publishing; **Topic 14, Lesson 1,** Dialectics and Revolution, Volume 2 by DeGrood, David H Copyright (c) 1978 by John Benjamins Publishing; **Topic 14, Lesson 6,** Clemenceau and the Third Republic by J. Hampden Jackson. Copyright (c) 1979 Macmillan; **Topic 14, Lesson 6,** "I ACCUSE…!" Open Letter to the President of the French Republic by Emile Zola and Shelley Temchin and Jean-Max Guieu (trans.). Copyright (c) 2011 Shelley Temchin and Jean-Max Guieu, Georgetown University; **Topic 14, Lesson 8,** "Bulgarian Statesman interviewed by Leon Trotsky" from The Balkans, 1804–1999 by Marsha Glinny (ed.). Copyright (c) 2001 Penguin; **Topic 14, Source B,** A History of Ireland: From Earliest Times to 1922 by Edmund Curtis. Copyright (c) Routledge; **Topic 14, Source A,** A History of Ireland by Mike Cronin. Copyright (c) Palgrave Macmillan; **Topic 14, Source G,** Ireland: Contested Ideas of Nationalism and History by Hugh F Kearney. Copyright (c) New York University Press; **Topic 14,** "How Masha Secured Her Freedom" in Memoirs of a Revolutionist by Peter Kropotkin and Georg Brandes. Copyright (c) 2009 Houghton Mifflin Harcourt; **Topic 14,** "Secret Memorandum to Tsar Alexander I, 1820" by Clemens von Metternich in Western Civilization: Sources, Images, Interpretations, from the Renaissance to the Present by Dennis Sherman (ed.). Copyright (c) 2003 McGraw-Hill; **Topic 14,** Source: http://people.hofstra.edu/alan_j_singer/CoursePacks/ToussaintLOuvertureandtheHaitianRevolution.pdf; **Topic 14,** Source: http://www.princeton.edu/~achaney/tmve/wiki100k/docs/Realpolitik.html; **Topic 14,** Source: 50 Political Ideas You Really Need to Know by Ben Dupre. Copyright (c) 2011 by Quercus; **Topic 14,** Source: http://www.tamu.edu/faculty/ccbn/dewitt/adp/archives/documents/hidalgo.html; **Topic 15,** Class Structure and Economic Growth: India & Pakistan since the Moghuls by Angus Maddison. Copyright (c) 1971 George Allen & Unwin Limited; **Topic 15,** "Chapter 3: The Economic and Social Impact of Colonial Rule in India" by Angus Maddison from Class Structure and Economic Growth: India & Pakistan Since the Moghuls. Copyright (c) Routledge, Ltd.; **Topic 16, Lesson 3,** Copyright Siegfried Sassoon by kind permission of the Estate of George Sassoon; **Topic 16, Lesson 2,** "Democracy and Dictatorship: The Western World in Crisis, German War Letter: 'One Blood-Soaked, Corpse-Strewn Field'" from Aspects of World Civilization: Problems and Sources in History, Volume 2 by Perry M. Rogers. Copyright (c) 2002 Prentice Hall; **Topic 16, Lesson 2,** William Pressey quoted in People at War 1914–1918 by Michael Moynihan (ed.). Copyright (c) 1988 David & Charles; **Topic 16,** Source: Conspiracy Encyclopedia by Thom Burnett. Copyright (c) 2006 by Franz Steiner Verlag; **Topic 16,** Source: http://www.archive.india.gov.in/knowindia/culture_heritage.php?id=44; **Topic 16,** Source: http://www.princeton.edu/~achaney/tmve/wiki100k/docs/Pan-Slavism.html; **Topic 16,** Source: Apostles and Agitators: Italy's Marxist Revolutionary Tradition by Richard Drake. Copyright (c) 2009 by Harvard University Press; **Topic 16,** Source: Memoirs of a Revolutionary by Victor Serge. Copyright (c) 2002 by University of Iowa Press; **Topic 17, Source B,** Lenin: A New Biography, Author Dwight D Murphey, in The Journal of Social, Political and Economic Studies, Vol 23, No 3 Fall 1998. www.jspes.org; **Topic 17,** India Home Rule by Mohandas Gandhi. Copyright (c) Navajivan Trust; **Topic 17, Source F,** Review: Lenin: A Biography", Author: Yuri Maltsev, in Ideas of Liberty: Vol 52, Issue 3, March 2002; **Topic 17, Lesson 2,** A History of the African People, Fifth edition by Jomo Kenyatta. Copyright (c) n.d. George Spindler; **Topic 17, Source A,** Chapter 6: Building Communism: 1921-1953 from The History of Russia by Charles E. Ziegler. Copyright (c) Greenwood Press; **Topic 17, Source D,** Rethinking the Soviet Experience: Politics and History Since 1917 by Stephen F. Cohen. Copyright (c) Oxford University Press; **Topic 17, Source E,** Lenin's Testament 1922 by Vladimir Lenin from Lenin, Collected Works, Vol. 36. Copyright (c) Progress Publishers; **Topic 17, Source G,** "Like Talking the Napoleon Chapters Out of "War and Peace" by Simon Karlinsky from The New York Times, April 25, 1976. Copyright (c) The New York Times; **Topic 17,** Adapted from Western Pennsylvania Conservancy; **Topic 17,** Source: http://public.wsu.edu/~brians/world_civ/worldcivreader/world_civ_reader_2/mao.html; **Topic 17,** Source: http://www.shsu.edu/~his_ncp/MarRom.html; **Topic 17,** Source: http://www.skeptically.org/links/id4.html; **Topic 17,** Source: http://www.britannica.com/EBchecked/topic/96883/Venustiano-Carranza; **Topic 17,** Source: "Adana Çiftçileriyle Konusma" (16 March 1923); English translation as delivered in an address by Talat S. Halman (10 November 1995), quoted in The Turkish Times (1 December 1995); **Topic 17,** Source: Freedom Fighters of India (in Four Volumes) by M G Agrawal. Copyright (c) 2008 by Gyan Publishing House; **Topic 17,** Source: All Quiet on the Western Front by Erich Maria Remarque. Copyright (c) 2010 by Random House; **Topic 18,** Source: http://www.britannica.com/EBchecked/topic/55717/Bataan-Death-March. Reprinted with permission from Encyclopædia Britannica, © 2014 by Encyclopædia Britannica, Inc; **Topic 18,** Source: http://www.britannica.com/EBchecked/topic/397522/Munich-Agreement. Reprinted with permission from Encyclopædia Britannica, © 2014 by Encyclopædia Britannica, Inc; **Topic 18,** Source: http://www.britannica.com/EBchecked/topic/104904/Neville-Chamberlain. Reprinted with permission from Encyclopædia Britannica, © 2014 by Encyclopædia Britannica, Inc; **Topic 18,** Source: http://www.britannica.com/EBchecked/topic/55717/Bataan-Death-March. Reprinted with permission from Encyclopædia Britannica, © 2014 by Encyclopædia Britannica, Inc; **Topic 18,** Source: http://www.britannica.com/EBchecked/topic/401619/Nagasaki. Reprinted with permission from Encyclopædia Britannica, © 2014 by Encyclopædia Britannica, Inc; **Topic 18, Lesson 2,** "Address to the House of Commons, June 4, 1940" from Wartime Speeches by Winston Churchill. Copyright (c) n.d. The Churchill Society; **Topic 18,** Source: http://europa.eu/about-eu/eu-history/founding-fathers/pdf/winston_churchill_en.pdf; **Topic 18,** "Source: http://www.britannica.com/EBchecked/topic/562617/Joseph-Stalin"; **Topic 18,** Source: http://www.britannica.com/EBchecked/topic/269548/Holocaust; **Topic 18,** Source: http://www.britannica.com/EBchecked/topic/16380/Allied-Powers; **Topic 19, Source B,** Mikhail Gorbachev. Is the World Really Safer Without the Soviet Union? The Nation, January 6-19, 2012; **Topic 19, Source A,** Peace in the Post-Cold War World, Author: Michael Cohen, in The Atlantic, December 15,2011, http://www.theatlantic.com/international/archive/2011/12/peace-in-the-post-cold-war-world/249863/; **Topic 19, Lesson 3,** "The Chinese People Have Stoop Up, September 21, 1949" from Selected Works of Mao Tse-Tung by Mao Tse-Tung. Copyright (c) 1965 Foreign Languages Press; **Topic 19, Source C,** Overview of the Human Security Report 2009/2010: The Cause of Peace and the Shrinking Costs of War. Copyright (c) The Human Security Research Group; **Topic 19,** Source: Quotable Quotes by Saraswathy. Copyright (c) by D C Books; **Topic 19,** Source: As quoted in The Memoirs of Stalin's Former Secretary (1992) by Boris Bazhanov; **Topic 19,** Source: U.S. Foreign Policy: A Documentary and Reference Guide by Akis Kalaitzidis, Gregory W. Streich. Copyright © 2011 by ABC-CLIO, 2011; **Topic 19,** Source: http://novaonline.nvcc.edu/eli/evans/his242/notes/dominos.html; **Topic 19,** Source: US History, Volume II: 1865—present, (Boundless 2013); **Topic 19,** Source: Mao's Great Famine: The History of China's Most Devastating Catastrophe, 1958-62 by Frank Dikötter. Copyright © 2010 by Bloomsbury; **Topic 19,** Source: The Pentagon Papers, Gravel Edition, Vol. 1 (Boston: Beacon Press, 1971), p. 597–8 https://www.mtholyoke.edu/acad/intrel/pentagon/ps11.htm; **Topic 19,** Source: http://www.britannica.com/EBchecked/topic/553374/Solidarity